R 328.73 CON 1998
Congressional quarterly almanac.

WITHDRAWN

STAFFORD LIBRARY
COLUMBIA COLLEGE
1001 ROGERS STREET
COLUMBIA, MO 65216

CONGRESSIONAL QUARTERLY

1998

ALMANAC®

105TH CONGRESS
2ND SESSION

VOLUME LIV

STAFFORD LIBRARY
COLUMBIA COLLEGE
1001 ROGERS STREET
COLUMBIA, MO 65216

Congressional Quarterly Inc.

1414 22nd Street N.W.
Washington, D.C. 20037

CONGRESSIONAL QUARTERLY 1998 ALMANAC

Editor Jan Austin
Production Editor Melinda W. Nahmias

President & Publisher Robert W. Merry
Executive Editor, Sr. V.P. David Rapp

CQ WEEKLY

Managing Editor Sara Fritz
Assistant Managing Editors Paul Anderson, Colette Fraley
Senior Editor Stephen Gettinger

News Editors
Susan Benkelman, Mike Christensen,
David Hawkings, Judi Hasson, Cathy Shaw

Copy Desk Chief Ron Brodmann
Design Editor Marileen C. Maher

Senior Writers
Carroll J. Doherty, Jackie Koszczuk,
Pat Towell

Reporters
Mary Agnes Carey, Dan Carney, Karen Foerstel,
Alan Greenblatt, Jeffrey L. Katz, Sue Kirchhoff,
Chuck McCutcheon, Lori Nitschke, Alan K. Ota,
Daniel J. Parks, Miles A. Pomper,
Charles Pope, Andrew Taylor

Contributing Reporters
Rebecca Adams, Andrew D. Beadle,
Sumana Chatterjee, Emily Church, Russ Freyman,
Bob Gravely, Lara Hearnburg, Julie R. Hirshfeld,
Peter H. King, Pherabe Kolb, Elizabeth A. Palmer,
Emily Pierce, Matthew Tully

Copy Editors
Margaret Bowen, Patricia Joy, Maura Mahoney,
Jody Rupprecht, Kelli L. Rush, Charles Southwell
Yolie Dawson (Design Editor/Production)

Graphic Artist
Marilyn Gates-Davis

News Research
Nell Benton, Vanita Gowda,
Mark Hankerson, Adam S. Marlin

Indexer
M. Jessie Barczak

Editorial Assistants
Sandra Basu, Lantie Ferguson, Micaele Sparacino

Office Manager
Joy Rodman

HOUSE ACTION REPORTS
Managing Editor Kerry Jones

CQ DAILY MONITOR
Editor Kinsey Wilson

CQ.COM ONCONGRESS
Editors George Codrea, Susan Dillingham, Dan Gainor, Amy Stern

CQ RESEARCHER
Editor Sandra Stencel

BUSINESS OFFICES

Marketing and Sales, Assoc. Publisher, Sr. V.P. Patrick Rockelli
Advertising/Communications C. Robert Kincaid
Strategic Planning Bob Shew
Circulation Sales Director Jim Gale
Chief Financial Officer Gordon Taylor
Operations Director, V.P. Michael K. Connelly
Customer Service Bethany Braley
Books, Reference Publishing, General Manager, V.P. John A. Jenkins

Published by
CONGRESSIONAL QUARTERLY INC.
Chairman Andrew Barnes
Vice Chairman Andrew P. Corty
Founder Nelson Poynter
(1903-1978)

Congressional Quarterly Inc.

Congressional Quarterly Inc. is a publishing and information services company and the recognized national leader in political journalism. For more than half a century, CQ has served clients in the fields of business, government, news and education with complete, timely and nonpartisan information on Congress, politics and national issues.

The flagship publication is CQ Weekly, a news magazine on Congress and its legislative activities. The award-winning reporters and editors of CQ Weekly are widely considered top experts in their subject specialities. They track the inner workings of legislation as it is created in subcommittee, committee, floor, House-Senate conferences and leadership offices, providing detail and analysis unavailable anywhere else.

The CQ Daily Monitor is a morning news report on Congress and the scheduled hearings and markups of congressional committees. It provides a comprehensive breaking news report of everything that just happened or is about to happen on Capitol Hill. The news and schedules are updated continuously on CQ NewsAlert, a password-protected site on the World Wide Web.

CQ now offers the most comprehensive, detailed and up-to-the-minute legislative tracking information on the Internet. CQ.com OnCongress is a web-based service with immediate access to exclusive CQ coverage of bill action, votes, schedules and member profiles, with direct links to relevant texts of bills, committee reports, testimony and verbatim transcripts.

CQ also publishes specialized publications on campaign politics and trends: CQ OnPolitics is a weekly newsletter of campaign developments in the 50 states and 435 congressional districts; Campaigns & Elections magazine is a monthly trade journal for candidates and campaign consultants; and Campaign Insider is a weekly fax newsletter for political professionals.

CQ serves the academic and education markets with a special weekly publication — the CQ Researcher — which focuses each week on a single topic of widespread interest.

CQ Press also publishes a variety of books, including political science textbooks, to keep journalists, scholars and the public abreast of developing issues and events. This includes a line of print and web-based directories, including the Congressional Staff Directory, plus reference books on the federal government, national elections and politics.

The Congressional Quarterly Almanac®, published annually, provides a legislative history for each session of Congress. Congress and the Nation, published every four years, provides a record of government for a presidential term.

Copyright 1999, Congressional Quarterly Inc. (CQ).

CQ reserves all copyright and other rights herein, except as previously specified in writing. No part of this publication may be reproduced, electronically or otherwise, without CQ's prior written consent.
To obtain additional copies, call 800-432-2250, ext. 279.

Library of Congress Catalog Number 47-41081
ISBN: 1-56802-269-7   ISSN: 0095-6007

CONGRESSIONAL QUARTERLY OFFERS A COMPLETE LINE OF PUBLICATIONS AND RESEARCH SERVICES.

The New CQ Almanac

"The story of Congress is the sum of the work of these members on the floor, in the lobbies, in committees in Washington and on the road, and home and abroad, in session and during recess."

A little more than 50 years ago, CQ founders Henrietta and Nelson Poynter prefaced the 1946 edition of the CQ Almanac with those words. They had only recently initiated the unprecedented task of compiling the only complete reference work on the actions of each session of Congress.

A half century later, Congressional Quarterly Inc. is proud to maintain the Poynter legacy and Poynter mission. This 1998 edition of the CQ Almanac, edited by CQ Weekly News Editor Jan Austin and Production Editor Melinda Nahmias, covers the actions, votes and other deeds of the second session of the 105th Congress. It provides a permanent collection of articles from CQ Weekly, our award-winning, flagship news magazine, with articles tracking some 80 pieces of legislation that received action at the full committee, floor or conference level.

In addition, the new CQ Almanac also contains extensive coverage of the impeachment of President Clinton, from the time the Monica Lewinsky scandal became public in January 1998, through the release of the report by Independent Counsel Kenneth W. Starr, to the House impeachment votes in December.

The Almanac also pulls together all the recorded votes in the House and Senate, important presidential statements and responses from members of Congress, and public laws. And the CQ Vote Studies provide exclusive statistical analyses of presidential support, party unity and voting attendance.

The bills — selected as the most significant of the year by Congressional Quarterly's editors — range from the huge, omnibus appropriations package cleared at the end of the session, to narrowly targeted bills on such issues as Internet gambling and aid to charter schools. Most reached the floor of at least one chamber.

The volume also covers the 13 regular appropriations bills, the budget resolution, the fate of the line-item veto, authorization bills for the Defense and State departments, attempts to overhaul the financial services industry, the $218 billion surface transportation bill, and measures on patients' rights and parental consent for abortion.

Most sections begin with a brief introduction, followed by articles from the CQ Weekly arranged in chronological order and marked with the date of the magazine in which they appeared.

In the back, you will find a number of appendixes, including:

● **Congress and Its Members:** A 11-page glossary of terms that arise in discussing Congress and legislation and a list of members of the House and Senate in the second session.

● **Vote studies.** CQ's popular study of the roll call votes cast in Congress during the year. Separate studies analyze the level of presidential support, party unity and member participation during the year, as well as tracing the demise of the "conservative coalition."

● **Key votes.** An account of the votes chosen by the CQ editors as most critical in determining the outcome of congressional action on major issues during the year.

● **Texts.** Presidential statements, Republican responses and a variety of materials related to the impeachment proceedings against Clinton.

● **Public laws.** A detailed list of all the bills enacted into law during the year.

● **Roll call votes.** A complete set of roll call vote charts for both chambers.

CQ produces the Almanac for public policy specialists, scholars, journalists and all interested citizens and students of the U.S. legislative system. As the Poynters wrote at the very beginning: "Congressional Quarterly presents the facts in as complete, concise and unbiased form as we know how. The editorial comment on the acts and votes of Congress, we leave to our subscribers."

David Rapp
Executive Editor

CQ "By providing a link between the local newspaper and Capitol Hill we hope Congressional Quarterly can help to make public opinion the only effective pressure group in the country. Since many citizens other than editors are also interested in Congress, we hope that they too will find Congressional Quarterly an aid to a better understanding of their government.

Foreword, Congressional Quarterly, Vol. I, 1945
Henrietta Poynter, 1901-1968
Nelson Poynter, 1903-1978

SUMMARY TABLE OF CONTENTS

CHAPTER 1 – INSIDE CONGRESS	1-3
CHAPTER 2 – APPROPRIATIONS	2-3
CHAPTER 3 – ABORTION	3-3
CHAPTER 4 – AGRICULTURE	4-3
CHAPTER 5 – BANKING & FINANCE	5-3
CHAPTER 6 – BUDGET	6-3
CHAPTER 7 – CONGRESSIONAL AFFAIRS	7-3
CHAPTER 8 – DEFENSE	8-3
CHAPTER 9 – EDUCATION	9-3
CHAPTER 10 – EMPLOYMENT & LABOR	10-3
CHAPTER 11 – ENVIRONMENT	11-3
CHAPTER 12 – EXECUTIVE BRANCH	12-3
CHAPTER 13 – GOVERNMENT	13-3
CHAPTER 14 – HEALTH	14-3
CHAPTER 15 – INDUSTRY & REGULATION	15-3
CHAPTER 16 – INTERNATIONAL AFFAIRS	16-3
CHAPTER 17 – LAW & JUDICIARY	17-3
CHAPTER 18 – POLITICS & ELECTIONS	18-3
CHAPTER 19 – SCIENCE	19-3
CHAPTER 20 – SOCIAL POLICY	20-3
CHAPTER 21 – TAXES	21-3
CHAPTER 22 – TECHNOLOGY & COMMUNICATION	22-3
CHAPTER 23 – TRADE	23-3
CHAPTER 24 – TRANSPORTATION & INFRASTRUCTURE	24-3

APPENDIXES

Congress and Its Members	A-3
Vote Studies	B-3
Key Votes	C-3
Texts	D-3
Public Laws	E-3
Roll Call Votes	
House	H-4
Senate	S-4
General Index	I-3

Table of Contents

Chapter 1 – Inside Congress

Session Overview 1-3
   Cloture Votes 1-4
   Presidential Vetoes 1-5

Session Overview *(cont'd)*
   Session's Highlights 1-6

Chapter 2 – Appropriations

Fiscal 1999
  Agriculture 2-3
   Chart 2-10
  Commerce-Justice-State 2-12
   Chart 2-19
  Defense 2-20
   Chart 2-29
   Supplemental Defense Bill 2-30
  District of Columbia 2-32
   Chart 2-35
  Energy-Water 2-36
   Chart 2-42
  Foreign Operations 2-45
   The IMF in Brief 2-46
   Chart 2-55
  Interior 2-57
   Chart 2-62
  Labor-HHS-Education 2-64
   Chart 2-73
  Legislative Branch 2-75
   Chart 2-79

  Military Construction 2-80
   Projects Restored to FY98 Bill 2-82
   Chart 2-83
  Transportation 2-84
   Chart 2-89
  Treasury-Postal Service 2-91
   Clinton Gives Up FY98 Line-Item Veto Suit 2-93
   Chart 2-99
  VA-HUD 2-101
   Chart 2-109
  Omnibus Spending Bill 2-112
  FY99 Supplemental Bill 2-117
   'Emergency' Spending 2-117
   Extra Money for the Drug War 2-119

Fiscal 1998
  FY98 Supplemental Bill 2-121
   Bills Compared 2-128
   Final Provisions 2-129

Fiscal 1999 Appropriations Mileposts 2-131

Chapter 3 – Abortion

Parental Consent 3-3

'Partial Birth' Ban 3-7

Chapter 4 – Agriculture

Agriculture Research 4-3

Chapter 5 – Banking & Finance

Financial Services Overhaul 5-3
  Highlights of House Bill 5-4
Bankruptcy Overhaul 5-15
  Highlights of Senate Bill 5-21

Credit Union Expansion 5-25
Class-Action Securities Lawsuits 5-30

Chapter 6 – Budget

Budget Resolution 6-3
    Kasich's Troubles 6-13
    Budget Surplus 6-16

Line-Item Veto 6-17
    Excerpts of District Court Ruling 6-18
    Excerpts of Supreme Court Ruling 6-22
    Clinton Gives Up 6-23

Chapter 7 – Congressional Affairs

Ethics
    New Rules for House Ethics Committee 7-3
Leadership
    Gingrich Resignation 7-4
    New House Chairmen for 106th 7-6

Leadership *(cont'd)*
    New Republican Leadership 7-7
        Leadership Votes 7-9

Chapter 8 – Defense

Defense
    Defense Authorization 8-3
        Sex-Integrated Training Retained 8-9
        Pentagon Officials Seek Budget Increase 8-14
    Anti-Missile Defenses 8-17

Defense *(cont'd)*
    Chemical Weapons Treaty 8-20
    NATO Expansion 8-21
Intelligence
    Intelligence Authorization 8-25

Chapter 9 – Education

Higher Education Act 9-3
Education Savings Accounts 9-14
Head Start 9-19
District of Columbia Student Vouchers 9-24

Bilingual Education 9-25
National Testing 9-28
Charter Schools 9-29

Chapter 10 – Employment & Labor

Job Training 10-3
Union 'Salting' 10-5
Comp Time, Overtime Pay 10-7

Minimum Wage 10-7
Worker Safety 10-8

Chapter 11 – Environment

Nevada Nuclear Waste Site 11-3
Superfund Overhaul 11-5
National Parks 11-6

Forest Recovery 11-7
Grazing on Federal Land 11-8

Chapter 12 – Executive Branch

Clinton Impeachment 12-3
   Chronology of Starr Investigation 12-4
   Ideological Leanings of House Judiciary Panel ... 12-11
   Perjury Charge 12-16
   Points of Contention 12-18
   History of Independent Counsel Law 12-21

Clinton Impeachment *(cont'd)*
   House Launches Inquiry 12-24
   Democrats Offer Censure Resolution 12-41
   Text of Impeachment Resolution 12-42
   Articles of Impeachment 12-46
   Those Who Voted Against Party Lines 12-48

Chapter 13 – Government

Year 2000 Census 13-3
Puerto Rico Plebiscite 13-6

Ronald Reagan National Airport 13-7

Chapter 14 – Health

Managed Care 14-3
   Republican Plan 14-7
   Side-by-Side Comparison of Bills 14-10

Home Health Care 14-16

Chapter 15 – Industry & Regulation

Tobacco Settlement 15-3
   Settlement, Senate Bill Compared 15-4
   Senate Bill Highlights 15-8
Electricity Deregulation 15-16
Product Liability Overhaul 15-18

Regulatory Overhaul 15-20
   Overhaul Provisions 15-22
Property Rights 15-23
Baseball's Antitrust Exemption 15-25

Chapter 16 – International Affairs

State Department Authorization 16-3
   Conference Report Highlights 16-6
Religious Persecution 16-9
Iran Sanctions 16-16
   Iran Sanctions History 16-17
   Current U.S. Global Sanctions 16-20
   House Targets Nuclear Power 16-23

Relations With China 16-23
   Satellite Scandal 16-24
      Top Campaign Donor 16-25
      Sanctions History 16-28
   Trade Status 16-34
   Clinton Trip 16-34
   Human Rights 16-37
International Monetary Fund 16-38

Chapter 17 – Law & Judiciary

Skilled Worker Visas 17-3
Immigration Initiatives 17-8
Prayer Amendment 17-9
Flag Desecration Amendment 17-11

Judicial Powers 17-12
   Justice Department Authorization 17-14
Juvenile Crime 17-15
Identity Theft 17-16
Assisted Suicide 17-18

Chapter 18 – Politics & Elections

Campaign Finance 18-3
   Sanchez Probe Ends 18-4
   Bills Compared 18-8

Campaign Finance *(cont'd)*
   House Bill Highlights 18-15

Chapter 19 – Science

Human Cloning 19-3

NASA Authorization 19-4
   Private Space Shuttles 19-9

Chapter 20 – Social Policy

WIC Reauthorization 20-3
Child Support 20-6
Public Housing Overhaul 20-7
   Major Provisions 20-12

Mortgage Insurance 20-9
Government Help for Home Buyers 20-11
Benefits for Immigrants 20-16

Chapter 21 – Taxes

Internal Revenue Service Overhaul 21-3
   House, Senate Bills Compared 21-5
   Overhaul Provisions 21-9

Tax Credit Extensions 21-14
   Highlights of House Bill 21-16
Internet Tax Moratorium 21-19

Chapter 22 – Technology & Communication

Digital Copyrights 22-3
   Internet Gambling 22-7
On-Line Pornography 22-10
Satellite Fees/Cable TV Rates 22-14

Encryption Exports 22-19
Year 2000 Computer Glitch 22-21
Cellular Phone Fraud 22-23
'Slamming,' 'Spamming' Restrictions 22-24

Chapter 23 — Trade

Fast-Track Trade Authority 23-3
   Main Provisions of Trade Bill 23-5

Relations With Vietnam 23-9
Africa Trade, Investment 23-10

Chapter 24 — Transportation

Surface Transportation 24-3
   House, Senate Bills Compared 24-5
   Ethanol Proposal 24-18
   Highlights of Conference Report 24-22

Surface Transportation *(cont'd)*
   Bill Provisions 24-27
FAA Reauthorization 24-34

Appendixes

Congress and Its Members
Glossary of Congressional Terms A-3
List of Members, 105th Congress, 2nd Session . A-14

Vote Studies
Voting Analyses
  Presidential Support B-3
    History, Definition B-4
    Leading Scorers B-5
  Party Unity B-6
    Definition B-6
    History, ... B-7
    Leading Scorers B-8
  Conservative Coalition B-9
    History, Definition B-9
    Leading Scorers B-10
  Voting Participation B-11
    History, Definition B-11
  Guide to Voting Analyses B-12
Background Material
  Presidential Support
    Definitions and Data B-13
    List of Votes B-14
    Individual House Members' Scores B-16
    Individual Senators' Scores B-18
  Party Unity
    Definitions and Data B-19
    List of Votes B-20
    Individual Senators' Scores B-21
    Individual House Members' Scores B-22
  Conservative Coalition
    Definitions and Data B-24
    List of Votes B-25
    Individual House Members' Scores B-26
    Individual Senators' Scores B-28
  Voting Participation
    Individual Senators' Scores B-29
    Individual House Members' Scores B-30

Key Votes
Key Senate Votes C-3
Key House Votes C-9
Individual Members' Votes
  Senate C-16
  House C-18

Texts
State of the Union Address D-3
  Republican Response D-8
Agriculture Appropriations Veto Message D-11
State Dept. Authorization Veto Message D-12
Clinton Impeachment
  Presidential Address D-13
    Senators Respond D-13
    Gingrich Calls for Decorum D-14
  Independent Counsel's Report D-15
    White House Response D-22
  Clinton's Grand Jury Testimony D-23
  Judiciary Committee's Opening Statements D-29
  Judiciary Committee Counsels' Statements D-34
  Hyde, Conyers, Starr Statements D-37
  Articles of Impeachment D-40
  Judiciary Committee's Report D-42
  Democratic Reaction to Impeachment Vote D-46

Public Laws E-3

Roll Call Votes
House
  Bill Number Index H-3
  Roll Call Votes H-4
  Subject Index H-158
Senate
  Bill Number Index S-3
  Roll Call Votes S-4
  Subject Index S-49

General Index I-3

Chapter 1
INSIDE CONGRESS

Session Overview 1-3
  Cloture Votes 1-4
  Presidential Vetoes 1-5

Session Overview *(cont'd)*
  Session's Highlights 1-6

Inside Congress

Members Made the Deals, But Scandal Made the News

Sidetracked by Clinton impeachment, Congress compiled a modest record

The House took 547 roll call votes in 1998 and the Senate took 314, but history is likely to take note of just two: the House votes Dec. 19 to impeach President Clinton.

SUMMARY

Those votes closed out a year in which the president's affair with former White House intern Monica Lewinsky and his denial under oath of a sexual relationship cast a long shadow over Washington. From the time the titillating details of the relationship began to emerge in January, the scandal was never far in the background for the administration or for Congress.

Sometimes it took center stage, such as when Clinton went to Capitol Hill on Jan. 27 to deliver his State of the Union address, six days after the first reports of the Lewinsky affair. Though many pundits and members of Congress predicted that Clinton had finally used up his nine political lives, the president ignored the embarrassing reports and steadily delivered his legislative agenda. *(Text, p. D-3)*

Other times, the scandal seemed to take a back seat to initiatives facing floor votes or other pivotal decisions. But even then, Republicans and Democrats, the powerful and the obscure, found themselves asked time and again for their opinion on the president's conduct and possible punishments, not about legislative details.

Congress had a hand in creating much of the quagmire that ensued, especially when the House voted Sept. 11 to release the salacious details of Independent Counsel Kenneth W. Starr's report on Clinton's behavior and Starr's conclusion that 11 counts of impeachable offenses could be upheld. That action, which came before anyone in Congress had read the report, significantly added to the frenzy that consumed much of Congress' energy.

Splits Slow GOP Agenda

Many Republican leaders believed that voter support for Clinton would eventually wane as it became clear that he had at least misled the public and at worst had lied to a grand jury, and they thought Republicans would reap the benefits at election time.

As a result, they did not push a legislative agenda as strongly as they had in previous years. In any case, recurrent divisions within the party would have made it difficult to push a coherent agenda, even if leaders had tried.

The GOP split its votes on issues that ranged from transportation funding, to a ban on cloning, to military training for men and women in the same units. Democrats also faced some divisive votes, splitting on an education savings account plan in the Senate and on the resolution to release the Starr report in the House.

The distractions and fractures, particularly among House Republicans, created a political vacuum that allowed the president and a few congressional lone wolves, such as House Transportation Committee Chairman Bud Shuster, R-Pa., and Rep. Nita M. Lowey, D-N.Y., a family planning and abortion rights proponent, to step in and win passage of legislation that would have likely met with defeat in the earlier, headier days of the Republican revolution.

The second session of the 105th Congress also was notable for what it did not do, including the failure to pass a budget resolution or a major tax cut bill.

As 1998 began, perhaps the most important domestic issue on Congress' plate was the groundbreaking $368.5 billion agreement between tobacco companies and state attorneys general to combat teenage smoking.

The failure of legislation to implement the tobacco settlement — which expanded well beyond the parameters of the original deal — served as an apt metaphor for the entire year. That bill died in the Senate when GOP conservatives objected to its sharply higher cigarette taxes and new bureaucracies. In other words, it was simply too big.

Congress did clear consequential measures on foreign policy, immigration, housing and other matters. In April, the Senate voted overwhelmingly to expand NATO's borders to include three former Warsaw Pact nations. With concerns over the budget deficit quickly fading, Congress passed a $217.9 billion transportation bill that boosts spending on highways and mass transit by 40 percent.

Yet those achievements were largely predictable and had all the political difficulty of a three-foot putt. None of Congress' accomplishments approached

'Cloture' Was the Senate's Byword

In the second session of the 105th Congress, the Senate voted 11 times in 29 attempts to invoke cloture, thereby limiting debate and providing for an up-or-down vote on a particular piece of legislation. Cloture requires a 60-vote majority to succeed.

The result was a 38 percent success rate for Majority Leader Trent Lott, R-Miss. In the first session, cloture was invoked seven times in 24 attempts, a 29 percent rate.

As the chart below shows, when the Senate invoked cloture this year, it always did so by a wide margin. The closest successful cloture vote was 71-24, 11 more votes than necessary.

On successful cloture motions, the majority averaged 88 votes. In most instances, Lott sought cloture votes in order to restrict the use of a piece of legislation as a vehicle for extraneous amendments.

But two other times, Lott came within just one vote of winning cloture on one of his top priorities for the year. On May 13 and Sept. 9, 59-41 tallies kept the Senate from taking up legislation (S 1873) to make it U.S. policy to deploy an anti-missile defense system.

Those were not the only "do overs" on this year's cloture list. Sometimes a series of votes were held — even when failure was a certainty — so that sponsors could drive home their view that an obstinate minority was holding up action. It took four votes against invoking cloture on the sweeping tobacco legislation (S 1415) before the measure was shelved. And the Senate voted three times against invoking cloture on similar forms of campaign finance legislation.

Technically, invoking cloture allows the leaders to break off filibusters. But true filibusters — in which opponents hold the floor for hours on end to stymie supporters of a bill — have become rare. Now, simply the threat of a filibuster prompts leaders to file a cloture motion to gauge support for a measure.

The number of cloture votes also speaks to the continued level of partisanship in the Senate. Democrats spent all year assailing Republicans for minimal accomplishments, and Republicans spent the year declaring that was because the Democrats were thwarting the popular will. "How can the president accuse us of doing little when his own party is blocking bill after bill," Lott said toward the end of the session.

"The minority has rights in the Senate, and we intend to exercise them," replied Minority Leader Tom Daschle, D-S.D., who often pressed his troops to vote against cloture in an effort to make bills available as vehicles for top Democratic priorities — proposals that he knew would never be brought to the floor for debate any other way.

DATE	BILL	VOTE	DESCRIPTION	VOTE
Feb. 10		8	**To confirm David Satcher to be surgeon general**	**75-23**
Feb. 11	S 1601	10	To ban human cloning research	42-54
Feb. 26	S 1663	16	To add campaign finance bill (S 25) to bill to restrict political use of union dues	51-48
Feb. 26	S 1663	17	To restrict political use of union dues	45-54
March 11	**S 1173**	**28**	**To reauthorize highway and mass transit programs**	**96-3**
March 17	**HR 2646**	**34**	**Motion to proceed to bill to expand benefits of education savings accounts**	**74-24**
March 19	HR 2646	38	To expand benefits of education savings accounts	55-44
March 26	HR 2646	46	To expand benefits of education savings accounts	58-42
May 13	S 1873	131	Motion to procede to a bill to make it U.S. policy to deploy an anti-missile defense	59-41
June 2	HR 1270	148	To create interim facility near Yucca Mountain, Nev., to store nuclear waste	56-39
June 9	S 1415	150	To set an array of federal policies to curb smoking	42-56
June 10	S 1415	153	To set an array of federal policies to curb smoking	43-55
June 11	S 1415	156	To set an array of federal policies to curb smoking	43-56
June 17	S 1415	161	To set an array of federal policies to curb smoking	57-42
July 7	**S 648**	**184**	**Motion to proceed to bill to limit punitive damages in product liability suits**	**71-24**
July 9	S 648	188	To limit punitive damages in product liability lawsuits	51-47
July 13	S 2271	197	Motion to proceed to bill to allow federal court challenges of local zoning decisions	52-42
July 21	**HR 4112**	**213**	**To make fiscal 1999 legislative branch appropriations**	**83-16**
Sept. 9	S 1873	262	Motion to procede to a bill to make it U.S. policy to deploy an anti-missile defense	59-41
Sept. 9	**S 1301**	**263**	**Motion to proceed to a bill to overhaul consumer bankruptcy laws**	**99-1**
Sept. 10	S 2237	264	To add campaign finance bill (S 25) to fiscal 1999 Interior appropriations bill	52-48
Sept. 11	**S 1645**	**265**	**Motion to proceed to bill to punish evasion of abortion parental consent laws**	**97-0**
Sept. 14	S 1981	266	Motion to proceed to a bill to place curbs on union organizing	52-42
Sept. 22	S 1645	282	To punish evasion of abortion parental consent laws	54-45
Sept. 24	**S 2176**	**285**	**Motion to proceed to bill to limit presidential appointment powers**	**96-1**
Sept. 28	S 2176	289	To limit presidential appointment powers	53-38
Sept. 29	**S 442**	**292**	**Motion to proceed to bill to ban taxes on sales over the Internet for two years**	**89-6**
Oct. 5	**HR 10**	**297**	**To overhaul laws separating banking, brokerage and insurance**	**93-0**
Oct. 7	**S 442**	**302**	**To ban taxes on sales over the Internet for two years**	**94-4**

Note: Instances when cloture was invoked are in **bold**.

Session Overview

the magnitude of last year's budget agreement, which helped wipe away the deficit and provided the first tax cut since Ronald Reagan's first term as president.

Busting the Budget

This year, just completing the routine business of governing proved to be a formidable challenge. For the first time since the modern budget process was established in 1974, Congress did not produce a fiscal budget resolution. House and Senate Republicans were simply unable to agree on a spending plan.

That slowed the appropriations process to a crawl, eventually forcing GOP leaders to cobble together a $500 billion, budget-busting omnibus spending bill that wrapped in eight individual appropriations measures and served as the vehicle for much of this year's limited legislative output.

The huge catchall bill, defended as a practical necessity by departing House Speaker Newt Gingrich, R-Ga., was roundly denounced by GOP conservatives and moderates alike as a cave-in to Clinton. Just as galling to Republican activists was watching their hopes for a sizable tax cut go up in smoke without even a Senate vote.

Despite Republicans' early hopes for a tax cut of about $100 billion over five years, their leadership gave up because party members in the House and Senate could not reach agreement on the numbers. In addition, Clinton scared many Republicans by calling on Congress to "save Social Security first" and not to use any budget surplus for major tax breaks.

Clinton took advantage of the protracted budget negotiations to shift the focus, at least temporarily, from his own troubles to the Democrats' agenda of 100,000 new teachers and tighter curbs on managed care.

While Democrats were surprisingly effective in communicating their election-year message, they were frustrated in the legislative arena. The demise of the tobacco bill was especially disappointing to them, because Clinton and the Democrats were counting on money from new cigarette taxes to expand aid for child care and other programs.

Democrats managed to pick up a modest amount of GOP backing for initiatives to impose new restrictions on managed care health plans and tough rules on political fundraising. But while the House shocked nearly everyone by approving a campaign finance bill, that measure met a predictable demise in the Senate.

The House also approved a GOP-backed bill on managed care. But the Senate never addressed the issue as Republicans and Democrats squabbled over parameters of the debate.

Democrats did score some important victories in the budget deal, including a $1.1 billion down payment on Clinton's new teacher program. In a bitter defeat for social conservatives, the final version of that bill included a provision requiring federal employee health plans to cover contraceptives if they cover other prescription drugs.

Achievements Subdued

While the two parties spent most of the year locked in conflict, they came together on some important issues. With little fanfare, Congress enacted a major reauthorization of the Head Start program. Lawmakers also agreed on a badly needed overhaul of federal public housing programs.

The high-tech community had considerable success, reflecting its growing political muscle. Congress passed measures to impose a three-year moratorium on taxes on Internet commerce and to expand copyright protection for digitally produced works.

And after a bitter battle, lawmakers provided $17.9 billion in new credits for the International Monetary Fund (IMF), in return for modest reforms by the global lender.

But even when Democrats and Republicans could agree, it was seldom a cause for celebration. Clinton never had a public signing ceremony for the Head Start bill — an extraordinary act by a Democratic president — because he did not want to hand Republicans a victory on education.

The omnibus budget bill included generous funding for a host of GOP priorities, including $1 billion for an anti-missile defense program. But Gingrich's attempt to highlight those provisions was drowned by a cacophony of conservative criticism of the bill.

Clinton's 1998 Vetoes

President Clinton vetoed five bills in 1998, bringing the total for the 105th Congress to eight. Lawmakers did not attempt to override any of the 1998 vetoes. The five bills would have:

- Expanded the tax benefits of education savings accounts (HR 2646). Vetoed July 21.
- Created school vouchers in the District of Columbia (S 1502). Vetoed May 20.
- Punished countries, especially Russia, that offered technical assistance to Iran's missile program (HR 2709). Vetoed June 23.
- Appropriated less for agriculture and nutrition programs than the president wanted (HR 4101). Vetoed Oct. 7.
- Reauthorized and reorganized the State Department (HR 1757). Vetoed Oct. 21.

However, lawmakers did succeed in overriding one of the three 1997 vetoes, salvaging a bill (HR 2631) that restored $287 million in military construction spending. Clinton had tried to block the spending with his short-lived line-item veto. The measure became law without the president's signature (PL 105-159) on Feb. 25.

An attempt to override a second 1997 veto — of a bill (HR 1122) to ban what sponsors describe as "partial birth" abortions — failed in the Senate Sept. 18.

The outgoing Speaker accurately summarized the session in his last regular speech on the House floor, when he defended the budget agreement. In a divided government, he said, some compromises are necessary: "If we don't work together on the big issues, nothing gets done." Certainly, that was true in 1998.

Following is a summary of what Congress did and did not accomplish this year. ◆

Inside Congress

Session's Highlights

Congress did:

• Bust its own balanced-budget caps, set in 1997, to reach compromises on spending for fiscal 1999.
• Pass a six-year, $217.9 billion authorization bill for highway and mass transit projects.
• Overhaul federal public housing policy.
• Impose a three-year moratorium on state taxes on Internet commerce.
• Overhaul the Internal Revenue Service to make it more "customer friendly."
• Expand Head Start, move to increase aid for hiring new teachers and reauthorize college student loans.
• Make it a crime to transport a minor across state lines to get an abortion, thereby circumventing her home state's parental-consent law.
• Block U.S. implementation of the Kyoto treaty on global warming.
• Partially reorganize the foreign affairs bureaucracy to consolidate functions in the State Department.
• Increase funding for the International Monetary Fund by $18 billion.
• Launch an impeachment inquiry based on allegations that President Clinton lied about an illicit affair.
• Rename Washington National Airport in honor of former President Ronald Reagan.

Congress did not:

• Act to restrict advertising of cigarettes or sales of tobacco products to minors.
• Revise campaign finance laws despite spotlighting bipartisan abuses in the 1996 election cycle.
• Address rising rates of juvenile crime.
• Increase protections for patients in managed care health plans.
• Override Clinton's veto of a bill that would have banned an abortion procedure that opponents call "partial birth" abortion.
• Update Depression-era banking laws to meet the needs of today's financial-services industry, or update personal bankruptcy rules.
• Increase the minimum wage.
• Complete work on an overhaul of the superfund hazardous waste cleanup program.
• Deregulate the electric power industry.
• Pass a significant tax cut despite an unexpected budget surplus.
• Extend "fast track" trade negotiating authority for the president.
• Resolve a partisan dispute over the way the 2000 census will be conducted.
• Pass a constitutional amendment to ban desecration of the American flag.

SECOND SESSION BY THE NUMBERS

The second session of the 105th Congress closed at 2:36 p.m. on Dec. 19, 1998, when the House adjourned *sine die*. The Senate had adjourned sine die at 2:33 p.m. on Oct. 21. Both chambers started the year Jan. 27.

Here is a statistical portrait of the session compared with the past 10 years:

		1998	1997	1996	1995	1994	1993	1992	1991	1990	1989
Days in Session	Senate	143	153	132	211	138	153	129	158	138	136
	House	119	132	122	168	123	142	123	154	134	147
Time in Session	Senate	1,095	1,093	1,037	1,839	1,244	1,270	1,091	1,201	1,250	1,003
(hours)	House	999	1,004	919	1,525	905	982	857	939	939	749
Avg. Length Daily	Senate	7.7	7.1	7.9	8.7	9.0	8.3	8.5	7.6	9.1	7.4
Session (hours)	House	8.4	7.6	7.5	9.1	7.4	6.9	7.0	6.1	7.0	5.1
Public Laws Enacted		241	153	245	88	255	210	347	243	410	240
Bills/Resolutions	Senate	1,321	1,839	860	1,801	999	2,178	1,544	2,701	1,636	2,548
Introduced	House	2,253	3,662	1,899	3,430	2,104	4,543	2,714	5,057	2,769	4,842
	Total	3,574	5,501	2,759	5,231	3,103	6,721	4,258	7,758	4,405	7,390
Recorded Votes	Senate	314	298	306	613	329	395	270	280	326	312
	House[1]	547	640	455	885	507	615	488	444	536	379
	Total	861	938	761	1,498	836	1,010	758	724	862	691
Vetoes		5	3[2]	6	11	0	0	21[3]	4[3]	11[3]	10[3]

[1] includes quorum calls; [2] does not include line-item vetoes; [3] includes pocket vetoes

Chapter 2
APPROPRIATIONS

Fiscal 1999
  Agriculture 2-3
    Chart 2-10
  Commerce-Justice-State 2-12
    Chart 2-19
  Defense 2-20
    Chart 2-29
    Supplemental Defense Bill 2-30
  District of Columbia 2-32
    Chart 2-35
  Energy-Water 2-36
    Chart 2-42
  Foreign Operations 2-45
    The IMF in Brief 2-46
    Chart 2-55
  Interior 2-57
    Chart 2-62
  Labor-HHS-Education 2-64
    Chart 2-73
  Legislative Branch 2-75
    Chart 2-79

  Military Construction 2-80
    Projects Restored to FY98 Bill 2-82
    Chart 2-83
  Transportation 2-84
    Chart 2-89
  Treasury-Postal Service 2-91
    Clinton Gives Up FY98 Line-Item Veto Suit 2-93
    Chart 2-99
  VA-HUD 2-101
    Chart 2-109
  Omnibus Spending Bill 2-112
  FY99 Supplemental Bill 2-117
    'Emergency' Spending 2-117
    Extra Money for the Drug War 2-119

Fiscal 1998
  FY98 Supplemental Bill 2-121
    Bills Compared 2-128
    Final Provisions 2-129

Fiscal 1999 Appropriations Mileposts 2-131

Farm Aid Rift Prompts Veto, Forces Agriculture Bill Into Year-End Spending Package

Box Score

- **Bill:** HR 4328 — PL 105-277.
- **House action:** The House adopted the conference report (H Rept 105-825) on HR 4328, 333-95, on Oct. 20. It adopted the conference report (H Rept 105-763) on HR 4101, 333-53, on Oct. 2. The House first passed HR 4101, 373-48, on June 24.
- **Senate action:** The Senate cleared the bill, 65-29, on Oct. 21. It cleared HR 4101, 55-43, on Oct. 6. It passed HR 4101, 97-2, on July 16.
- **Presidential action:** Clinton signed the bill Oct. 21. He vetoed HR 4101 on Oct. 7.

SUMMARY

Bucking tradition, controversy enveloped consideration of the $55.9 billion agriculture spending measure and forced it into the session-ending omnibus spending bill. Contentious House-passed abortion language first complicated the bill's trip through conference, but settling on a level of financial aid to help an ailing farm economy proved even more difficult. President Clinton vetoed the original bill (HR 4101) on Oct. 7, calling its farm relief spending inadequate.

Forced by the veto to find more money than they had intended, Republicans in Congress agreed to provide more funds in exchange for tax cuts. Roughly $1 billion in tax cuts over five years were included as part of the "emergency" package for farmers and ranchers, which also contained $5.9 billion in increased spending.

Clinton argued that the original agriculture package did not go far enough to help producers devastated by regional weather problems and disasters, overproduction and declining exports. The vetoed measure contained $4.2 billion worth of farm relief, but Clinton favored a Senate Democratic plan that was $3 billion richer.

Republicans objected not just to the dollar amount of the Democratic plan but to its proposal to lift caps on marketing loan rates imposed by the so-called Freedom to Farm law (PL 104-127) of 1996, one of the major deregulatory triumphs of the Republican congressional majority. That proposal was not in the final package.

The tax portion of the final bill allows 100 percent deductibility of health insurance premiums paid by the self-employed by 2003, instead of 2007 as previously specified; permits income averaging for farmers and ranchers, and includes a five-year "carry back" provision, which allows farmers who suffer an operating loss in one year to receive a refund against taxes paid in an earlier, profitable year.

The remainder of the emergency agriculture spending includes $3.1 billion in one-time payments to farmers and ranchers to adjust to the loss of export markets, $2.4 billion to compensate for disaster losses, $200 million in emergency livestock feed assistance, and $3 million in indemnity payments to compensate some dairy farmers for losses.

Controversial House-passed, abortion-related provisions were dropped during House-Senate negotiations on the original measure. The provisions would have barred the Food and Drug Administration (FDA) from using federal funds to test or approve abortion-inducing drugs such as RU-486, a prescription drug developed in France.

The final measure appropriated $75 million for the administration's food safety initiative, which includes projects of the Department of Agriculture and the FDA to increase surveillance, research and education concerning food-borne illnesses.

The measure, however, blocked two other programs favored by the administration — the Fund for Rural America and a competitive research grant program authorized by the agriculture research measure (PL 105-185) that was enacted in June.

The bulk of the $55.9 billion agriculture spending goes toward nutrition programs, such as food stamps and school lunches, as well as to pay the bills at the Agriculture Department and FDA.

Committees Give Quick Approval

JUNE 13 — The agriculture appropriations bill got off to its usual quick start the week of June 8, winning approval from three spending panels in as many days.

"It should be an easy bill this year," said Senate Appropriations Chairman Ted Stevens, R-Alaska.

Despite overwhelming approval from committees in both the House and Senate, the bill is home to annual floor fights over sugar and peanut subsidies and will face a battle over milk pricing as well. Committee action also pointed to possible policy disputes that may remove a bit of the glow of good feeling from the bill.

On June 10, the House Appropriations Subcommittee on Agriculture, Rural Development, FDA and Related Agencies approved, 11-1, a draft bill that would provide $56.1 billion in new budget authority for fiscal 1999 for agriculture, rural development and food and nutrition programs, including $13.6 billion in discretionary spending.

The full committee will mark up the bill June 16.

The lone opponent was David R. Obey of Wisconsin, the ranking Democrat on the Appropriations Committee, who objected to the bill's provisions on milk pricing and international sanctions.

Senate Action

On June 11, the Senate Appropriations Committee unanimously approved its version (S 2159 — S Rept

Appropriations

105-212), which would provide $56.8 billion in new budget authority, including $13.7 billion in discretionary spending. The bill was approved, 27-0, en bloc with two other spending packages.

The Senate Subcommittee on Agriculture, Rural Development and Related Agencies had approved the measure by voice vote two days earlier.

Both the House and the Senate versions provide about $7 billion more than was allocated for fiscal 1998, with most of the difference attributable to mandatory payments to the Commodity Credit Corporation, which extends subsidy payments to farmers.

Some commodities, such as wheat and barley, are experiencing low prices this year. Sales to Asian markets are dwindling due to the region's economic woes. And some farmers are battling crop disease, notably a fungus in the upper Plains called "scab."

The Clinton administration had requested $57.8 billion in new spending, including $13.7 billion for discretionary accounts.

The House on June 5 rejected, 0-421, a bill (HR 3989) that contained various user fees, including $573 million in agriculture inspection fees, proposed by the administration's fiscal 1999 budget. *(Vote 207, p. H-60)*

The appropriations committees in both chambers adopted amendments to exempt food products from sanctions imposed on India and Pakistan for exploding nuclear bombs. Members from wheat-growing states argued that the sanctions served mainly to hurt U.S. farmers as other nations encroach on those markets. The administration supports the move.

New Milk Rules

The Senate package contains no legislative language, but the House bill would continue to block the Agriculture Department (USDA) from implementing new rules on milk marketing orders for an additional six months, until October 1999.

Obey argued that extending the status quo would put dairy farmers in the upper Midwest at a competitive disadvantage.

But defenders of the language said it represented a compromise, since it was included in place of other proposed initiatives that would have extended a regional dairy compact in the Northeast and created a new compact in the South.

"I don't like compromising on this because, frankly, I think we have the votes" to prevail, said Republican James T. Walsh of N.Y.

Obey's amendment to strike the dairy language was defeated, 3-9.

Unlike the Senate bill, the House measure contains funding for USDA to litigate charges of racial discrimination. Black farmers claim numerous instances of USDA discrimination, notably a May 27 conference call in which a department lawyer allegedly used a racial slur.

In Senate action, Robert F. Bennett, R-Utah, agreed to withhold until floor debate a controversial amendment to remove the Commodity Futures Trading Commission's jurisdiction over a portion of the derivatives market known as swaps.

Both versions of the bill would zero out funding for the Fund for Rural America, a grants and infrastructure program for research and education that was created by the 1996 farm law (PL 104-127).

Democrats have vowed to find funding for the program, as well as increased funding for food safety inspections.

House Panel OKs Bill Despite Dairy Policy Dispute

JUNE 20 — Offering a preview of fights likely to be revisited on the floor, the House Appropriations Committee on June 16 approved a $55.9 billion agriculture spending bill for fiscal 1999.

The bill (HR 4101 — H Rept 105-588), which includes $13.6 billion in new discretionary spending authority, was approved by voice vote. It is scheduled to reach the House floor June 24.

David R. Obey of Wisconsin, the ranking Democrat on House Appropriations, offered a series of amendments to allow administrative changes to dairy policy. He readily conceded that he did not have the votes to prevail in committee but wanted to set the stage for floor debate.

Jose E. Serrano, D-N.Y., withheld an amendment until floor action that would allow minority farmers who allege racial discrimination, including an alleged racial slur in a May 27 conference call, in Agriculture Department (USDA) business to seek redress, although the statute of limitations has passed in some instances.

Also certain to be fought out on the House floor are perennial disputes to kill funding for peanut and sugar subsidies.

Dairy Fights

Obey sought unsuccessfully to strike language from the bill that would push back the date that USDA could implement new rules to consolidate milk marketing orders, a complex system of regional price supports designed to ensure that all regions have access to highly perishable dairy products, from April 4, 1999, to Oct. 1, 1999.

Obey contended that extending the status quo would keep dairy farmers in the upper Midwest at a competitive disadvantage. The Depression-era subsidy law requires that farmers be paid more for fluid milk the farther they are from Eau Claire, Wis.

He also said the provision is an attempt to keep Agriculture Secretary Dan Glickman from altering the milk marketing system, saying the intent of the six-month delay is to guarantee that Congress would be in session and able to overturn any change proposed by Glickman.

House Appropriations Chairman Robert L. Livingston, R-La., conceded that the intent is to give Congress a chance to weigh in on the issue.

"Let the legislative process take a look at the [USDA] work product," Livingston said, arguing further that the six-month delay represents a compromise, fending off other proposals that sought an advantage in pricing for certain regions, such as the Northeast and Southeast.

Obey's amendment was rejected by voice vote, as was his amendment to guarantee that the USDA terminate a dairy compact among six Northeastern states on April 4, 1999.

Other Amendments

Both the Senate and House measures include language to exempt food products from sanctions being imposed on India and Pakistan for their tests of nuclear bombs.

The House Agriculture Committee on June 18 approved a bill (HR 3654) that would, in effect, discourage the inclusion of agricultural products in wide embargoes.

Since George Nethercutt, R-Wash., inserted the exemption at the subcommittee level June 10, the Congressional Budget Office (CBO) has estimated its cost at $35 million.

"To me, that's nonsensical," Nethercutt said. "CBO is basically saying if you impose sanctions and then remove them, there's a cost." He offered an amendment to treat the cost as "emergency" spending so it would not eat into funds for other programs.

Republican Mark W. Neumann of Wisconsin argued that such an approach would cut against the grain of budgetary frugality.

"We are now designating things in our bills as emergency spending," Neumann said. "It is going to artificially increase the [spending] caps."

But despite an expression of fear from Livingston, who said the Nethercutt amendment would set a dangerous precedent that could prompt other members to seek emergency funds as a way of skirting spending limits, it was adopted by voice vote.

Nita M. Lowey, D-N.Y., offered an amendment that would have granted the USDA the authority to impose fines against plants and slaughterhouses that violate food safety regulations. Currently, USDA can pursue criminal but not civil remedies in such cases.

Predicting that authorizers would raise a point of order against legislating on a spending bill, Tom Latham, R-Iowa, added that many food-borne diseases are caused by transportation and handling of food, not by processing.

Lowey's amendment was rejected, 19-25.

Anti-Abortion Amendment Rides On Agriculture Bill

JUNE 27 — House opponents of abortion found a new avenue of attack June 24, offering the first-ever anti-abortion amendment to an agriculture spending bill.

"Obviously it raises another dynamic we haven't really considered on agriculture before," said Appropriations Chairman Robert L. Livingston, R-La.

On a largely party-line vote, the House approved, 223-202, an amendment to the fiscal 1999 agriculture appropriations bill (HR 4101 — H Rept 105-588) that would prevent the Food and Drug Administration (FDA) from approving abortion-inducing drugs, such as RU - 486, the so-called French abortion pill. (*Vote 260, p. H-76*)

The $55.9 billion agriculture spending bill funds the Agriculture Department (USDA) and the FDA, and pays for nutrition programs such as food stamps.

HR 4101 would spend $6.4 billion more than fiscal 1998 levels because of increased mandatory payments to farmers through the Commodity Credit Corporation. The bill's discretionary accounts have shrunk by about $130 million in the fiscal 1999 package, to $13.6 billion in new budget authority.

HR 4101 passed overwhelmingly, 373-48, on June 24, in part because supporters and opponents do not believe the abortion provision will survive a conference with the Senate. (*Vote 264, p. H-76*)

"The Senate looks at things differently than we do. It might cause them some problems," said James T. Walsh, R-N.Y., a senior member of the Agriculture Appropriations Subcommittee.

The $56.8 billion Senate version of the bill (S 2159 — S Rept 105-212) has been held up on the floor since June 18, when Democrats tried to attach unrelated tobacco legislation to it. The Senate is expected to take up S 2159 after the July Fourth recess.

If the abortion fight seemed like a replay to members who have debated the issue on other bills, so did the controversies over peanut and sugar price supports.

As an often-revisited argument about dairy policy raged on, retiring Agriculture Committee Chairman Bob Smith, R-Ore., said, "Thank God, I will not be here to have to enlist in this argument again."

Abortion Vote

The abortion vote, which came on the second day of floor debate on HR 4101, was largely symbolic. Democrats threatened that President Clinton would veto the bill if it contained the FDA restriction.

Even Republican Tom Coburn of Oklahoma, an obstetrician and the amendment's sponsor, conceded that his language would be removed when the bill reached the president's desk.

The Coburn amendment would prohibit the FDA from spending money to test, develop or approve any drug for the "chemical inducement of abortion." Because that phrase does not have a defined medical meaning, Coburn said, his amendment would have no effect unless drug manufacturers used those words on applications.

The amendment's opponents, however, charged that the language not only represented meddling in affairs best left to FDA scientists, but was so broad as to threaten approval of drugs designed to treat everything from ulcers to cancer that have side effects harmful during pregnancy.

"If we pass this amendment, the development of new life-saving drugs would be blocked," warned Rosa DeLauro, D-Conn., who has battled ovarian cancer.

But little of the debate focused on the scientific merits of such abortion-inducing drugs as RU-486, which has not received final approval from the FDA for use in the United States. Instead, members expressed more general and heated feelings about the question of abortion rights.

Abortion opponents complained that the federal government had no reason to subsidize abortion, in this case by testing new drugs.

"RU - 486 is just the newest form of baby pesticide, a drug that has no benefit for the baby, that kills the baby," said Christopher H. Smith, R-N.J.

Still, most of the amendment's opponents voted for HR 4101 on final passage.

"It mattered a lot," Lynn Woolsey, D-Calif., said of the abortion language. "But not enough to undermine a basically good bill."

Milk Marketing Orders

David R. Obey of Wisconsin, the ranking Democrat on the Appropriations Committee, tried to strike language in the bill that would push back — from April 4, 1999, to Oct. 1, 1999 — the date that USDA could implement new rules to consolidate

Appropriations

milk marketing orders, a complex system of regional price supports designed to ensure that all sections of the country have access to highly perishable dairy products.

A Depression-era subsidy law requires that farmers be paid more for fluid milk the farther they are from Eau Claire, Wis.

Obey maintained that the delay was designed as a warning to Agriculture Secretary Dan Glickman not to bother making any changes in dairy policy because Congress would "hammer you down legislatively."

Lawmakers representing other dairy regions made no secret that such was their intent. "It ensures that the damaging USDA proposal cannot be implemented while Congress is out of town and cannot respond to a rule that levies heavy costs on producers around the country to the clear benefit of one region," said Rules Committee Chairman Gerald B.H. Solomon, R-N.Y.

Arguing that his side had the votes to maintain the status quo as long as he desired, Solomon said the six-month moratorium represented a compromise.

Obey's amendment to prevent the extension failed on a voice vote. A related amendment, to terminate a dairy compact among six New England states on April 4, 1999, was blocked on a point of order.

Much of the dairy debate centered on the questions of whether the federal role in determining prices hurt consumers and represented "corporate welfare" for giant agribusinesses, or whether the government helped protect small farmers against being squeezed by large processors.

"I think if it does cost a few cents more for a gallon of milk, the American people understand how important it is to preserve the family farm," said Bernard Sanders, I-Vt.

Notably, similar rhetorical points were scored during the annual arguments about the peanut and sugar price-support programs. Producers of these crops were less affected by the 1996 farm law (PL 104-127) than producers of such commodities as wheat and soybeans. Supporters of the programs argued that their current outlines should be maintained out of fairness to farmers until the farm law expires in 2002. (*1996 Almanac, p. 3-15*)

Mark W. Neumann, R-Wis., offered an amendment to limit the peanut price-support loan rate to $550 per ton. The 1996 law guarantees a minimum rate of $610 per ton.

Neumann said the program is archaic and hits consumers unfairly in the pocketbook.

Supporters of the peanut loan program countered that it helps farmers stay competitive against foreign growers.

The Neumann amendment failed, 181-244. (*Vote 258, p. H-74*)

Analogous debate points, pro and con, were scored on an amendment to lower the loan rates that USDA provides to sugar cane processors from 18 cents to 17 cents per pound, and to sugar beet processors from 22.9 cents to 21.9 cents per pound. It failed, 167-258. (*Vote 261, p. H-76*)

Ed Royce, R-Calif., offered an amendment to delete HR 4101's $90 million in funding for the Market Access Program, which helps farmers and food processors advertise their products in foreign markets. Royce termed the program "a relic from our former government-heavy agricultural system."

But the program's supporters noted that other countries subsidize their farmers and said the program returns far more dollars to American coffers than it costs.

The Royce amendment failed, 118-307. (*Vote 262, p. H-76*)

Other Provisions

The House rejected, by voice vote, an amendment to transfer $49.3 million from earmarked grants for agriculture research to pay for programs authorized by a newly enacted agriculture research law (PL 105-185).

HR 4101 also would lift sanctions on food products being imposed on India and Pakistan in the wake of their testing of nuclear bombs.

Sponsors of that language, led by George Nethercutt, R-Wash., argued that the sanctions are hurting American farmers because India and Pakistan are turning to other countries to buy wheat and other commodities since the sanctions were imposed unilaterally by the United States.

A Nethercutt amendment offered during committee consideration of the bill would have designated the cost of lifting the food sanctions as "emergency" spending. In order to avoid such above-budget spending and offset the cost of lifting the sanctions, the rule (H Res 482) governing floor debate instead reduced by $20 million the USDA's long-term account for building repair and for grain inspection.

International Relations Chairman Benjamin A. Gilman, R-N.Y., expressed some reservations about lifting the food sanctions, particularly on an appropriations bill, but conceded that he did not have the votes to stop the move.

Also as part of H Res 482, the House, by voice vote, approved an amendment that would allow farmers who allegedly suffered racial discrimination between 1983 and 1996 in official business with USDA to pursue legal remedies if the statute of limitations has passed through no fault of their own. Some farmers missed their court filing deadlines waiting for administrative action on their complaints.

Senate Considers Possible Solutions To Farmers' Woes

JULY 18 — Faced with a set of regional farm crises, the Senate contemplated a wide range of possible governmental responses during debate on the fiscal 1999 agriculture spending bill.

The $57.3 billion bill (HR 4101) was passed, 97-2, on July 16 after three days of debate. (*Vote 209, p. S-33*)

Republicans blamed the poor prices farmers are receiving this year for many commodities, including wheat, barley and pork, on weather and an export market softened by the Asian economic crisis.

Democrats, on the other hand, blamed Republicans for the mess, claiming that rural economic woes are being exacerbated by the 1996 farm law (PL 104-127), which left farmers more exposed to the whims of the free market. (*1996 Almanac, p. 3-15*)

Democrats succeeded in adding legislative language for disaster relief to the appropriations bill, which will now have to survive conference with the House. The House passed its version of HR 4101 on June 24.

Floor action on the Senate bill had been delayed for a month because of an unrelated tobacco amendment, leaving appropriators in both cham-

Agriculture

bers skeptical about the prospects for a conference before the August recess.

"Hopefully we'll have this thing back before September," said Dale Bumpers, D-Ark., the ranking Democrat on the Senate Appropriations Subcommittee on Agriculture, Rural Development and Related Agencies.

"The last thing we want is a CR [continuing resolution]."

The agriculture spending bill is typically one of the least controversial spending packages. It funds the Agriculture Department (USDA), Food and Drug Administration (FDA) and nutrition programs such as food stamps and the Women, Infants and Children (WIC) program.

House and Senate conferees will have to pull off a fiscal juggling act as they attempt to reconcile their bills. The Senate bill provides about $1 billion more in total spending than the House version. The Senate bill would provide more money for research, the source of most of the difference.

For instance, the House disallows funding for mandatory research programs contained in a recent agriculture law (PL 105-185) for which the Senate provides $120 million.

But the House allocates more than the Senate in all but a handful of the bill's 300-odd accounts, according to a House Appropriations aide.

And the House approved language that would block the FDA from testing or approving drugs that induce abortion. President Clinton opposes the language. The Senate bill contains no such block.

Farm Woes

Many Republicans think that farmers can find their way out of the present fix through increased exports. Toward that end, Senate Republicans offered an amendment that would have made it more difficult for the United States to impose unilateral economic sanctions, preventing farmers from losing access to some foreign markets.

But the amendment was tabled (killed), 53-46. (Vote 201, p. S-32)

Republicans were able to add a non-binding resolution outlining a 10-point agenda of trade proposals they would like to see voted on before the end of the session. Highlighted issues included offering so-called fast track trade negotiating authority to the president, extending normal trade relations with China, and fully funding the International Monetary Fund.

Despite the opposition of many senators to one individual aspect of the wish list or another, the amendment passed easily, 71-28. (Vote 206, p. S-33)

At a July 17 news conference, House Speaker Newt Gingrich, R-Ga., and House Agriculture Chairman Bob Smith, R-Ore., outlined a farm agenda similar in many particulars to the Senate resolution.

Although most Senate Democrats echoed the GOP calls for stepped-up trade, they argued that farmers' problems demanded quicker solutions.

Democrats repeatedly described the farm outlook in the Midwest, where wheat is selling for about $3 a bushel, as a "crisis," a 50 percent drop from $4.55 a bushel in 1995-96.

Tom Harkin of Iowa, the ranking Democrat on the Senate Agriculture Committee, argued that "the 1996 farm bill is not the Ten Commandments. It was not written in stone for all time."

Democrats sought to begin the process of reopening the farm law with an amendment that would have lifted its caps on marketing loan rates, which were capped at 1995 rates, at a cost of $1.6 billion.

The amendment also would have extended the period in which farmers could repay marketing loans from nine months to 15 months. Democrats argued that these changes would allow farmers to hold their crops in storage until prices rose.

But Agriculture Committee Chairman Richard G. Lugar, R-Ind, a chief architect of the 1996 law, countered that the amendment would further lower prices by increasing supplies over the long haul.

"This is not even a good quick fix," Lugar said. "It is a prescription for enormous difficulty."

The loan amendment was tabled, 56-43. (Vote 200, p. S-32)

But Democrats were successful with a number of amendments, notably a proposal by Kent Conrad of North Dakota to provide $500 million in emergency assistance to farmers suffering because of shrinking income, bad weather, or crop disease such as "scab," which is plaguing wheat crops in the high plains.

Although it was approved by voice vote and has Clinton's endorsement, the proposal faces a cloudy future in conference. The $500 million was declared "emergency," or off-budget, spending, and the House has shown itself wary of such maneuvers around discretionary spending caps.

"It's not that we're opposed to dealing with disasters, but it's hard to know before a fiscal year begins what the needs are going to be," said Agriculture Appropriations Chairman Thad Cochran, R-Miss.

He suggested that conferees might add more strings in terms of eligibility requirements to the language, which currently leaves payments largely to the discretion of the USDA.

Food Safety and Smoking

Harkin offered an amendment to increase spending for Clinton's food safety initiative to $69 million. The House bill provides only $17 million.

Harkin had hoped to fully fund Clinton's $101 million request but could find only $66 million worth of offsets, including cuts to USDA computer and buildings and facilities accounts.

The amendment also would eliminate federal payments to the tobacco price-support program, which is largely funded by growers and tobacco companies.

Cochran argued that the bill already provided more than $600 million to various food safety programs. He nevertheless agreed to accept Harkin's amendment, as he had several other proposals, in the spirit of moving the sometimes sluggish debate toward its conclusion.

But Harkin demanded a recorded vote, and his amendment was adopted, 66-33. (Vote 207, p. S-33)

Harkin was less successful with an attempt to boost the FDA's teen smoking prevention accounts from $34 million to $134 million. His amendment would have raised additional funds by assessing fees to tobacco companies in proportion to their share of the market.

"The money we approve today is a bargain compared with what we'd spend in medical costs," said Frank R. Lautenberg, D-N.J.

But Wendell H. Ford, D-Ky., argued

Appropriations

that the fees on companies amounted to a new tax that had no place on an appropriations bill.

Majority Leader Trent Lott, R-Miss., had a look of concern on his face as a cast of characters familiar from the nearly four-week Senate debate on a tobacco bill (S 1415 — S Rept 105-180) gathered on the floor.

Lott requested a short time agreement, and Harkin, recognizing he would not have the 60 votes necessary to waive a budget point of order against his amendment, consented. The amendment violated budget rules because the assessment fees did not properly offset the $100 million spending increase.

The amendment was taken down, 49-50. (Vote 208, p. S-33)

Earlier, the Senate had voted 43-55 against waiving budget rules in respect to a tobacco amendment, based on a version of S 1415, that had been offered on June 18. (Vote 198, p. S-32)

Minority Farmers

Among the dozens of amendments the Senate agreed to by voice vote was a proposal to waive the statute of limitations for claims by black and Hispanic farmers that they suffered racial discrimination between 1981 and 1996 in official business with the USDA. The House bill contains similar language.

At a NAACP convention July 15, Agriculture Secretary Dan Glickman repeated his apologies for instances of past USDA discrimination.

The Senate gave voice vote approval to amendments that would require produce and beef and lamb products to be labeled by their country of origin.

"It has never made sense to me that the American consumer knows where shoes and auto parts come from, but doesn't know where meat comes from," said Tim Johnson, D-S.D.

Although the meat-labeling amendment had the support of ranchers and packers, another amendment that would create a three-year pilot program to require slaughterhouses and other large meat purchasers to report the prices they pay livestock producers was more controversial.

It was adopted by voice vote after a motion to table it failed, 49-49. (Vote 205, p. S-33)

Struggle To Aid Distressed Farmers Endangers Bill

SEPTEMBER 26 — The annual agriculture spending package is typically one of the easiest appropriations bills to pass. But widespread price problems in farm country are putting the fiscal 1999 version of the package in jeopardy.

A conference on the agriculture spending bill (HR 4101) scheduled for Sept. 25 was postponed as appropriators struggled to present relief to farmers in a form that could be enacted. Democrats found it too stingy and some Republicans wanted its cost to be offset.

The bill faces a veto threat. The Clinton administration on Sept. 24 declared HR 4101's $3.9 billion in emergency aid inadequate, and raised objections to an anti-abortion provision.

Aside from Democratic resistance, Republicans are concerned about losing votes within their own caucus. GOP budget hawks are resisting the idea of the disaster funding, because it would be deemed "emergency" spending and not counted against budget limits.

"We're in a bad situation here," conceded House Agriculture Chairman Bob Smith, R-Ore.

Farm and livestock producers are suffering severe losses this year due to regional weather problems and prices depressed by overproduction and falling exports. The Senate version of HR 4101 contains disaster indemnification assistance worth about $500 million.

But with farm problems worsening over the summer, Republican agriculture appropriators and authorizers crafted a relief package worth nearly $4 billion. The package includes:

- $2.35 billion in direct payments to farmers, including those who have suffered multi-year losses; and
- $1.6 billion for farmers experiencing market losses this year.

But Senate Democrats contend the package is not nearly enough for the farmer who has suffered through floods or droughts, not to mention hurricanes and tornados this year, and the White House shares their point of view.

Market Loans

The Clinton administration warned that the president would veto any relief package that did not lift a freeze on marketing loan rates.

Marketing loans allow farmers to borrow money against anticipated crop sales, allowing farmers to withhold crops from market until prices rise.

Senate Democrats on Sept. 21 unveiled a $7.1 billion relief package which would lift marketing loan rates at a cost of $5 billion.

The loan rates were frozen at 1995 levels by the 1996 farm law (PL 104-127), the so-called Freedom to Farm law, which was designed to wean farmers from government assistance in exchange for giving them more control about planting decisions. (1996 Almanac, p. 3-15)

Republicans are willing to help farmers in a crisis, but are reluctant to begin unraveling the law, one of their major deregulatory triumphs.

The conference on HR 4101, rescheduled for Sept. 28, will be the scene of several policy fights.

Senate appropriators are expected to accept a House provision that would block the Food and Drug Administration from approving any drug that chemically induces abortions.

The Senate is also expected to accept House language that will prevent the Agriculture Department from implementing changes to milk marketing orders for six months, from April 4, 1999, to Oct. 1, 1999.

The Senate version of the bill contains language requiring beef packers to label the country of origin of their meat, but the final bill will likely call instead for a study of international meat labeling. Other controversial provisions, such as an effort to divorce food products from international sanctions, may be dropped.

House Passage Sets Stage For Confrontation

OCTOBER 3 — The House voted 333-53 on Oct. 2 to approve a $55.9 billion fiscal 1999 agriculture spending bill, setting the stage for a possible showdown with the Clinton administration over disaster relief for farmers.

Senate Minority Leader Tom Daschle, D-S.D., said he believed the White House might follow through with a threat to veto the bill (HR 4101 — conference report: H Rept 105–763). He said he agreed with the administration that the bill's $4.2 billion disaster relief package was not enough.

Daschle and other Democrats were expected to oppose the bill on the Senate floor the week of Oct. 5.

In the House, Republican leaders cleared the way for passage by agreeing to delete a House provision to bar the Food and Drug Administration from using federal funds to test or approve abortion-inducing drugs such as RU-486, a prescription drug developed in France. The drug was declared safe and effective by the FDA in 1996 but is limited to use in clinical trials.

House Agriculture Appropriations Subcommittee Chairman Joe Skeen, R-N.M., said he doubted the administration would veto the bill after the removal of the RU-486 ban.

"Shutting down agriculture . . . would be insanity," Skeen said.

The RU-486 battle went down to the wire. On Sept. 28, two Republicans, Arlen Specter of Pennsylvania, and Slade Gorton of Washington, joined six Democratic Senate negotiators in voting against the RU-486 ban in conference committee.

After three days of wrangling, the ban's sponsor, Rep. Tom Coburn, R-Okla., finally withdrew the provision on the eve of the House vote.

He said he had failed to persuade Specter and Gorton that the charter for the FDA did not allow it to approve the sale of "drugs that kill people."

The drug, also known as mifepristone, interferes with the attachment of an embryo to the uterus. Researchers have studied the drug for its impact on brain tumors.

Rep. Rosa DeLauro, D-Conn., recalled her own bout with ovarian cancer, and she argued the ban on RU-486 could lead to efforts to block other cancer drugs on grounds they can cause miscarriages. "It is science, not politics, that should determine whether or not a drug is safe," DeLauro said.

Disaster Relief Dispute

Meanwhile, lawmakers traded partisan shots over the size of the Republican disaster relief plan contained in the bill for farmers.

At the heart of the dispute was the amount and form of aid for producers of commodity crops such as wheat and soybeans, which have been hit by natural disasters and poor export sales.

Republicans argued for a $4 billion plan and defended provisions of the 1996 "Freedom to Farm" law (PL 104-127). That law provided transition payments to farmers as part of a plan to eliminate government controls on commodity prices and production.

Democrats attacked the 1996 farm law, but failed in a last-ditch effort to recommit the agreement to conference with instructions to increase disaster relief. The vote was 156-236. *(Farm Act, 1996 Almanac, p. 3-15)*

Bruce L. Gardner, an agriculture economist at the University of Maryland, said Democrats were responding to discontent in the Farm Belt over sagging prices and exports to Asia, which have affected their profits.

"After the price declines over the summer, some farmers are wondering now whether they would have gotten more money under the old system," Gardner said.

David R. Obey of Wisconsin, ranking Democrat on the Appropriations Committee, called the 1996 law "a colossal failure" and said it should be dubbed the "Freedom to Farm and Lose Your Shirt Act."

Leading Democrats and the administration endorsed a $7.5 billion emergency relief package. It included a $5 billion waiver of marketing loan caps established in the 1996 law, effectively tying loans to a formula based on historical market prices. Senate conferees rejected the Democratic plan, voting 6-7 on party lines, on Sept. 28.

Regional Pull

Apart from the partisan split on loan caps, the debate was marked by regional differences. The Democratic plan targeted a larger share of disaster relief than the Republican plan. That would have meant more money for farmers in the Midwest who have suffered repeated problems with crop disease and flooding. The Republican plan focused more money on crop losses in 1998, such as those caused by the recent drought in the Southeast.

Daschle attacked the smaller Republican disaster relief plan as "no solution at all." But a farm lobbyist predicted that Daschle and other "prairie populists" would be defeated by a coalition of Republicans and Democrats outside the Midwest. Rep. Marcy Kaptur, D-Ohio, said she hoped more disaster relief could be provided in a supplemental spending bill.

The Republican disaster relief plan called for $1.5 billion in payments to farmers for crop losses from natural disasters, $1.65 billion for losses in export sales, $675 million to provide for multi-year losses, $175 million for livestock feed assistance and $200 million for other emergency-related aid.

The bill included $50 million to assist Alaskan Natives, hurt by poor salmon runs over the last two years, and $27 million in aid aimed at specific products and groups of farmers, including loan programs for producers of mohair and honey, and a matching program to provide aid to a group of cotton farmers in Georgia.

It also included a provision to extend the deadline from 2001 to 2005 for phasing out the use of methyl bromide to fight fungus on fruit crops.

Clinton Vetoes Legislation Over Farm Aid Rift

OCTOBER 10 — President Clinton and congressional Republicans share a goal of sending financial help to an ailing farm economy. But differences over the amount of aid and the method of delivery sent the fiscal 1999 agriculture appropriations bill into limbo.

The Senate on Oct. 6 cleared, 55-43, the $55.9 billion package (HR 4101), but Clinton vetoed the measure the next day. *(Vote 298, p. S-46)*

In an Oct. 8 statement, Clinton said he was "disappointed that the Congress has reacted to this agriculture emergency situation by sending me a bill that fails to provide an adequate safety net for our farmers."

With the session drawing to a close, agriculture spending was expected to be rolled into a larger omnibus appropriations package.

Republicans were careful not to predict that they would have to boost

Appropriations

Agriculture Spending

Agriculure portion of the fiscal 1999 omnibus spending law (HR 4328 — PL 105-277) signed by the president Oct. 21. *(Budget authority, in thousands of dollars.)*

	Fiscal 1998 Appropriation	Fiscal 1999 Clinton Request	House Bill	Senate Bill	Conference Agreement
Agriculture Programs					
Crop insurance	$ 1,584,135	$ 1,504,036	$ 1,504,036	$ 1,504,036	$ 1,504,036
Agricultural Research Service	744,382	776,828	755,816	768,221	781,950
Commodity Credit Corporation	783,507	8,439,000	8,439,000	8,439,000	8,439,000
Farm Service Agency	702,129	727,928	726,949	713,292	716,949
Food safety and inspection	588,761	149,566	609,250	605,149	605,250
Cooperative State Research					
Extension Service	423,376	418,651	416,789	432,181	434,122
Research and education	431,410	412,589	431,125	432,982	481,216
Buildings and facilities	80,630	35,900	61,380	31,930	56,436
Animal and plant inspection	430,132	422,952	429,700	423,673	433,503
Other	1,172,313	1,028,842	970,840	946,457	965,368
Loan authorizations	*2,400,693*	*2,991,034*	*2,627,031*	*2,365,027*	*2,284,958*
Subtotal	**$ 6,940,775**	**$ 13,916,292**	**$ 14,344,885**	**$ 14,296,921**	**$ 14,417,830**
Conservation Programs					
Conservation operations	632,853	742,231	641,243	638,664	641,243
Watershed and flood prevention	101,036	49,000	97,850	101,036	99,443
Other	52,585	35,096	45,264	52,585	52,386
Subtotal	**$ 786,474**	**$ 826,327**	**$ 784,357**	**$ 792,285**	**$ 793,072**
Rural Economic and Community Development Programs					
Rural Housing Service	1,122,324	1,154,369	1,125,037	1,151,783	1,141,467
Rural Utilities Service	118,407	123,040	124,119	125,556	126,155
Other	846,491	942,709	924,625	897,465	907,612
Loan authorizations	*6,024,527*	*5,797,116*	*6,172,101*	*6,141,898*	*6,168,726*
Subtotal	**$ 2,087,222**	**$ 2,220,118**	**$ 2,173,781**	**$ 2,174,804**	**$ 2,175,234**
Domestic Food Programs					
Food stamp program	25,140,479	24,701,806	22,591,806	23,781,806	22,585,106
Child nutrition programs	7,767,816	9,229,897	9,218,647	9,219,897	9,176,897
Women, Infants and Children	3,924,000	4,081,000	3,924,000	3,948,000	3,924,000
Other	390,224	429,502	380,392	391,704	381,196
Subtotal	**$ 37,222,519**	**$ 38,442,205**	**$ 36,124,845**	**$ 37,341,407**	**$ 36,067,199**
Foreign Assistance and Related Programs					
PL 480 — Food for Progress	1,063,054	967,000	1,037,239	1,063,054	1,056,695
Program level	*1,111,508*	*978,558*	*1,059,514*	*1,088,083*	*1,081,724*
CCC export loan program	411,450	257,085	256,320	3,820	3,820
Loan guarantees	*5,500*	*4,615,000*	*4,615,000*	*0*	*0*
Foreign Agricultural Service	131,295	141,087	131,295	131,795	136,203
Subtotal	**$ 1,605,799**	**$ 1,365,172**	**$ 1,424,854**	**$ 1,198,669**	**$ 1,196,718**
Related Agencies					
Food and Drug Administration					
Appropriation	925,145	970,100	965,715	952,717	977,217
New proposed user fees	*0*	*0*	*0*	*0*	*0*
Other	65,829	65,925	64,705	63,565	63,565
Subtotal	**$ 990,974**	**$ 1,036,025**	**$ 1,030,420**	**$ 1,016,282**	**$ 1,040,782**
Emergency Appropriations					
Subtotal	**$ 159,800**	**$ 1,761,405**	**0**	**0**	**$ 4,258,405**
Scorekeeping Adjustments	−243,408	−1,505,188	3,717	354,217	−4,052,188
GRAND TOTAL	**$ 49,550,155**	**$ 58,062,356**	**$ 55,886,859**	**$ 57,174,585**	**$ 55,897,052**
Loan authorizations	*$ 8,430,720*	*$ 13,403,150*	*$ 13,414,132*	*$ 8,510,148*	*$ 8,453,684*

SOURCE: House and Senate Appropriations committees

Agriculture

their relief package for farmers, suffering from low prices caused by bumper crops, regional weather problems and disasters, and declining exports, from its present $4.2 billion total.

"If it [HR 4101] gets vetoed, it will be in the omnibus," House Appropriations Chairman Robert L. Livingston, R-La., said hours before the veto.

Livingston said the question of adding more money for farmers "would be a leadership matter, something for the Speaker, the [Senate] majority leader and [White House Chief of Staff] Erskine Bowles to determine."

Other Republicans accused Clinton of holding up a bill that funds the Agriculture Department and Food and Drug Administration, as well as such programs as food stamps, the Women, Infants and Children (WIC) nutrition program, and school lunches.

"We believe the president is delaying this aid for American farmers strictly for political purposes," said House GOP Conference Chairman John A. Boehner of Ohio at an Oct. 7 news conference attended by farm-state Republicans urging Clinton's signature.

Clinton backs a $7.3 billion plan, promoted by Democratic senators from the Midwest led by Minority Leader Tom Daschle of South Dakota and Tom Harkin of Iowa, that would lift a cap on marketing loan rates.

Marketing loans allow farmers to borrow against anticipated crop sales, giving them flexibility to withhold crops from the market until prices rise. The rates farmers can receive were capped at 1995 levels by the 1996 farm law (PL 104-127), known as the "Freedom to Farm" Act. (*1996 Almanac, p. 3-15*)

Loan Rates

Republicans maintained that removing the marketing loan rate cap would prove counterproductive by driving up supply and further lowering prices. They added that farmers in areas such as Texas, where some have lost their entire crops due to drought, would receive no benefit because they have no crops to use as collateral.

The proposal to "increase loan rates for one year will depress market prices next year, and beyond," said House Agriculture Appropriations Chairman Joe Skeen, R-N.M.

The Republican disaster-relief package, added to HR 4101 during its House-Senate conference, calls for $1.5 billion in payments to farmers for crop losses from natural disasters; $1.65 billion for losses in export sales; $675 million to provide for multi-year losses; $175 million for livestock feed assistance; and $200 million for other emergency-related aid.

Sen. Pat Roberts, R-Kan., said he did not object to helping farmers caught in a short-term pinch. But he said he opposed lifting the marketing loan caps because such a move would start to unravel the market-oriented 1996 farm law.

"Let's not turn on the fire hose and let it get away and destroy a policy that makes sense over the long term," Roberts said.

Even many House Democrats were willing to accept the GOP proposal.

"Given budget realities . . . most of our farmers and ranchers would have been satisfied," said Charles W. Stenholm of Texas, ranking Democrat on the House Agriculture Committee.

But White House and Senate Democratic opposition to the GOP plan was sufficient to sink the bill.

Sen. Kent Conrad, D-N.D., said the $4.2 billion package is "totally inadequate. . . . It is not going to prevent literally thousands of family farmers from being forced off the land."

The most likely post-veto scenario appears to be an increase in the dollar amount of the disaster package, but with a method other than boosting the marketing loan rates, so that Republicans could save face and maintain that they had preserved the structure of the Freedom to Farm law.

Republicans Add Tax Breaks To Farm Aid Bill

OCTOBER 17 — Forced by a presidential veto to pony up more money for agriculture than they had intended, Republicans in Congress swallowed the pill with the help of their favorite sweetener — tax cuts.

The session-ending omnibus spending bill (HR 4328) would offer just over $1 billion in tax breaks over five years.

The tax cuts were not offset and will eat into the projected budget surplus. They were included as part of an "emergency" aid package to farmers, which also contains $5.94 billion worth of increased aid to farmers and ranchers.

House Agriculture Chairman Bob Smith, R-Ore., who had been highly critical of President Clinton's Oct. 7 veto of the fiscal 1999 agriculture appropriations bill (HR 4101), praised the revised package that the veto provoked: "I think it's better because of the tax cuts."

Clinton had argued that the original agriculture package did not contain sufficient aid for farmers and ranchers devastated by weather and falling prices and exports. HR 4101 contained $4.2 billion worth of farm relief, but Clinton favored a Senate Democratic plan that was $3 billion richer.

"The amount of disaster assistance, and the way to distribute it, was the only real point of contention," said Tom Latham, R-Iowa, a member of the House Agriculture Appropriations Subcommittee.

Republicans objected not just to the dollar amount of the Democratic plan but to its method of lifting caps on marketing loan rates. Such a move would have led to an unraveling of the so-called Freedom to Farm law (PL 104-127) of 1996, one of the major deregulatory triumphs of the Republican regime. (*1996 Almanac, p. 3-15*)

"We recognized that Freedom to Farm might need some slight adjustment, but it was a sound policy that needed to be kept intact," said Sen. Larry E. Craig, R-Idaho.

The revised agriculture spending package would allow 100 percent deductibility of health insurance for independently owned businesses and the self-employed by 2003, up from 45 percent in 1998, at a cost of $880 million over five years.

The package also would allow farmers and ranchers to average out their incomes over five-year periods for tax purposes, at a cost of $45 million over five years.

The bill further includes a "carry-back" provision, which would allow farmers who suffer an operating loss in one year to receive a refund against taxes paid in an earlier, profitable year, at a cost of $81 million over five years.

Appropriations

Farmers and ranchers would be offered $3.1 billion in direct payments. An additional $875 million would be available to farmers, especially in the Upper Plains, who have suffered multi-year losses.

Ranchers requiring livestock feed assistance would find a pot of $200 million available, and the bill offers $3 million in indemnity payments to compensate some dairy farmers for losses.

Ranchers won an additional victory with a one-year pilot program that would require meat packers to post their prices, creating greater transparency in meat markets. Cattlemen have complained that packers unfairly withhold price information in order to lowball them, but packers deny this.

Most of HR 4101 went unchanged in the latest round of negotiations. The bulk of agriculture spending goes toward nutrition programs such as food stamps and school lunches, as well as paying the bills at the Agriculture Department (USDA) and Food and Drug Administration.

Like HR 4101, the omnibus spending package would lift sanctions imposed on India and Pakistan for exploding nuclear devices.

Two tobacco-related amendments floated by Republicans during the budget wrap-up did not make it into the final bill.

One would have lifted a 5-year-old ban against USDA funds paying for the promotion of tobacco products overseas. The other would have required the federal Health Care Financing Administration to get permission from states before taking a share of money the states receive from legal settlements with tobacco companies. ◆

Census Dispute Jeopardizes Full-Year Funding For Commerce-Justice-State

Conflicts over how to conduct the 2000 census led to the adoption of a partial-year appropriation for the departments of Commerce, Justice and State, and the federal judiciary.

SUMMARY

The measure cuts off funding — a total of $33.7 billion — on June 15, 1999, unless Congress and the president agree before then on a separate authorization bill that specifies whether statistical sampling may be used to augment the traditional headcount during the 2000 census.

The White House and House Republicans faced off early on the issue, which had been a bone of contention for fiscal 1998 as well. Republicans generally oppose statistical sampling, insisting that the Constitution requires an "actual enumeration." The GOP also contends that the administration's proposal would open the census to political manipulation and error that could lead to congressional district alignments more favorable to Democrats.

Most Democrats and academicians favor statistical sampling as a way to adjust for the acknowledged census undercount of those who do not speak English, the poor and the homeless.

Senate consideration of its version of its original CJS bill (S 2260) focused on almost everything but the funding. As the bill was debated, it began to look more like a telecommunications bill, with immigration and a handful of other issues thrown in for good measure. Eventually, it became the vehicle for many policy issues that had stalled as free-standing legislation.

The House version of the the bill (HR 4276) carried a number of controversial riders, including a requirement that federal prosecutors abide by state ethics guidelines, a provision that remained in the final bill. Negotiators dropped more sweeping curbs on federal prosecutors, however.

The final bill also retained a provision that prohibits the FBI from charging gun dealers a fee for its National Instant Check System, which will screen would-be gun purchasers to determine whether they are disqualified from owning a firearm. It also delays, until March 30, 2001, an automated border entry-exit check that critics said would result in traffic jams along the U.S.-Canada border. And it bars use of the Internet to transmit material harmful to minors.

The bill includes $475 million for payments to the United Nations for back U.S. dues, but that was contingent on enactment of separate legislation (HR 1157) that Clinton vetoed.

Box Score

- **Bill:** HR 4328 — PL 105-277.
- **House action:** The House adopted the conference report (H Rept 105-825) on HR 4328, 333-95, on Oct. 20. It passed HR 4276 (H Rept 105-636), 225-203, on Aug. 6.
- **Senate action:** The Senate cleared the bill, 65-29, on Oct. 21. It passed S 2260 (S Rept 105-235), 99-0, on July 23.
- **Presidential action:** Clinton signed the bill Oct. 21.

Clinton Raises Stakes in Battle Over Census-Taking

JUNE 27 — The White House and House Republicans are on another collision course over the 2000 census, as demonstrated by the early squabbling over the fiscal 1999 bill that would fund the count.

This time it is the White House that is taking the toughest stance, insisting on language that would shut down three government departments next March if a deal cannot be struck on how the census would be conducted.

House and Senate lawmakers the week of June 22 unveiled their respective versions of the $33 billion bills funding the departments of Commerce, Justice and State and the judiciary. The Senate bill was reported out of subcommittee on June 23 and full committee on June 25, while the House bill made it through subcommittee on June 24.

The Senate bill is not totally without controversy: A provision affecting fishing in the North Pacific threatens to hold up the bill until the Washington state and Alaska delegations can resolve a major dispute over foreign vessels.

The House bill, meanwhile, has a second controversy over spending for the Legal Services Corporation, which provides legal counsel to the poor. The House bill would halve funding for the agency to $141 million.

But the largest front in this year's funding battle appears to be over the method the Census Bureau will employ in its decennial head count — specifically whether it will use a process known as statistical sampling. The bill stops funding for the bureau March 31, 1999, if Congress and the president do not agree on a separate authorization bill deciding once and for all whether this process will be allowed.

In an ironic twist, the Clinton administration does not argue directly against the language, having long since resigned itself to restrictions. Rather, it argues the entire bill's funding — not just the Census Bureau's — should be contingent on an agreement on the census method by next March.

Administration officials argue that just holding up the census funding would not put enough pressure on lawmakers and the president to come to an agreement. They also argue that this broad restriction of funds was part of a deal reached last fall between the White House and House Speaker Newt Gingrich, R-Ga.

"Whether you think that is a sensible agreement or not, that was the agreement that was made," said Rep. Alan B. Mollohan of West Virginia, ranking Democrat on the House subcommittee.

The sampling process is designed to approximate the number of people who, for reasons ranging from poor English to lack of a permanent residence, are missed by census-takers. It is also designed to weed out some of those who are counted twice, usually because they have a second home.

The process is favored by most professional demographers, and by Democrats, who are believed to represent most of the people missed by a traditional count. It is opposed by many Republicans, who argue it amounts to mathematical hocus-pocus.

The bureau is currently conducting "dress rehearsals" for the census, using sampling in some communities and not in others.

Senatorial Non-Census

The Senate, meanwhile, seems uninterested in the census debate.

"We represent the same amount of people, no matter how they count them," observed Senate subcommittee Chairman Judd Gregg, R-N.H., pointing out one of the salient features of the census: It affects congressional districts but not state lines.

The major sticking point in the Senate bill is a narrow but bitter contest of wills between two states. The battle erupted when Committee Chairman Ted Stevens, R-Alaska, added language to the bill restricting foreign-owned vessels fishing in Alaskan waters after 2000. He took his first step in subcommittee, then modified his original language in full committee.

Stevens argued the U.S. Coast Guard has misinterpreted federal policy to allow a number of foreign factory trawlers to fish the North Pacific, flying a United States flag. His language would require such ships to be at least 75 percent U.S.-owned.

That language, said Slade Gorton, R-Wash., would put out of business 10 large ships based in Seattle and employing crews from that area. The ships, owned by Norwegian and Korean companies, he argued, were well within the law, and were being targeted by Stevens in an effort to steer business to smaller Alaska-based trawlers that bring their catch into Alaskan ports for processing.

Normally this type of dispute would be a footnote to such a major bill. Gregg summed up the position of most senators when he said: "I don't have a fish in this fight."

But an irate Gorton threatened to wreak havoc on the entire bill, filibustering it at every stage when it reaches the Senate floor, starting with a motion to proceed.

Gorton admitted this type of aggressive approach to a must-pass spending bill is frowned upon. But Stevens' language, he said, gave him no alternative. Stevens, for his part, vowed to fight back and not to be intimidated.

"We're going to do eight cloture votes if we have to," he said. "I'm not going to accept that threat."

COLA Controversies

Other controversies in the bills include a provision in the Senate version giving federal judges a 3.1 percent cost of living increase. A number of lawmakers argue judges should get pay raises only when members of Congress vote raises for themselves.

The biggest portion of both bills ($17.9 billion in the Senate version and $18.3 billion in the House) goes to the Justice Department, mostly for fighting crime and policing borders.

The funding includes a major new initiative — $129 million in the House and $194 million in the Senate — for a program to help cities prepare for a terrorist attack using biological or chemical weapons.

The Justice funding also includes full funding in both bills ($1.4 billion) for President Clinton's Community Oriented Policing Service (COPS), a program established in the 1994 crime bill (PL 103-322) that is designed to put 100,000 police officers on the streets. (1994 Almanac, p. 273)

The Senate bill would designate $175 million for policing schools. The administration has in the past fiercely opposed setting aside money in the COPS program for specific purposes. But in light of the recent school shootings, senators from both parties said they doubt the administration will come out against this one.

Other provisions include:
- $1.7 billion in both bills for the State Department. Both measures also provide $475 million in new funds (another $100 million is left over from last year) to pay United Nations' past dues, but holds them until passage of an authorization bill stalled over abortion.
- $4.8 billion in the House bill and $4.9 billion in the Senate for the Commerce Department. Both provide $1.1 billion for the Census Bureau, including over $900 million for the upcoming count.
- $2.5 billion for the Immigration and Naturalization Service in the

Appropriations

House bill, and $2.3 billion in the Senate. Neither bill includes language favored by Rep. Harold Rogers, R-Ky., dividing the agency into three parts.

House Committee Provides Glimpse Of Battle Ahead

JULY 18 — The House Appropriations Committee on July 15 approved only partial funding for the upcoming census, continuing the collision course Republicans have set with the Clinton White House.

Drafted in subcommittee, the census language is the most problematic issue in the $33 billion bill funding the departments of Commerce, Justice and State for fiscal 1999. President Clinton threatens to veto the bill because of it.

The bill would also continue the annual fight over the Legal Services Corporation, which provides legal counsel to the poor, by cutting its budget by half, to $141 million. A new, controversial element was added in committee in the form of an amendment by Joseph M. McDade, R-Pa., that would subject federal prosecutors to strict new ethical standards.

The bill now goes to the floor, and ultimately to conference committee, where it will be melded with the Senate bill (S 2260). That bill does not contain any problematic census language. But it is laden with minor controversies.

The census language in the House bill would provide $956 million for the upcoming count. But it would prevent half of that from being spent unless Congress and Clinton pass a separate authorization bill by March 31 outlining how to conduct the count.

Underlying the dispute is the question of whether to use a method known as statistical sampling. Professional demographers and statisticians, along with most Democrats, support it on the grounds it will yield the most accurate count. Most Republicans argue it amounts to a kind of numerical hocus-pocus.

The Census Bureau needs to know in the next 12 months or so whether it will use sampling. If a decision is to be made on the CJS spending bill, it would have to be made by Oct. 1, the beginning of fiscal 1999.

The language contained in the bill attempts to buy another six months after Oct. 1 by punting the final decision to a separate piece of legislation due next March.

This adds a new element of complexity to an intensely partisan fight. By threatening to veto the spending measure, Clinton is signaling he wants the sampling issue resolved this fall, and is willing, even eager, to play a game of brinksmanship to accomplish that. He is counting on the implicit threat of a partial shutdown of three major departments to bring the requisite pressure to get a deal on the census.

Clinton may be willing to put off a final decision until next March, but only if that same pressure can be brought to bear then. In other words, he would sign what amounts to a six-month CJS spending bill, with the second six months contingent on a census deal. But he is not willing to sign a bill that cuts off only the census funding after six months. Republicans, he reasons, will not feel much pressure if only census funding is at stake.

If the dispute seems almost Byzantine in its nuances, it is. Rather than try to resolve their differences, the two sides are determined to fight a pitched battle to the end. And now they are fighting over the timing of the battle and the weapons to be used.

Whether or not sampling is used will affect the total count of Americans, as well as the counts in individual communities. This, in turn, will affect the distribution of federal funds and the allocation of congressional and state legislative districts.

The use of sampling will likely result in more funding and better representation in areas where people are often missed by a traditional count: inner cities, non-English speaking neighborhoods and remote rural areas. Politically, Democrats have the most to gain by sampling.

Hoping to avoid a showdown, Alan B. Mollohan, D-W.Va., offered an amendment that would provide full funding for the census, allowing the Census Bureau to prepare for a count that uses sampling as well as one that uses a traditional head count. His amendment was rejected by a party-line, 22-31 vote.

Limiting Prosecutors' Powers

The bill's other controversy relates to the 1996 acquittal of McDade on bribery charges after an eight-year prosecution that cost him $950,000. (1996 *Almanac*, p. 1-35)

Incensed by what they consider the misplaced zeal of the federal prosecutors in the case, McDade and John P. Murtha, D-Pa., have made a cause out of limiting powers of federal prosecutors.

During discussion of the fiscal 1998 bill, the two pushed an amendment to reimburse the legal fees of members and staffers who are the subject of federal cases that do not result in conviction. It was later expanded to include ordinary citizens, as long as the Justice Department could not show it had "substantial justification" for bringing the suit. The provision died in conference committee.

This year, the two have taken a different approach. Their language would make federal prosecutors subject to new restrictions and new ethical guidelines.

They would have to abide by a new federal code of ethics barring certain activities, such as sitting on evidence that would exonerate a person or indicting without probable cause. They would also be subject to any similar codes promulgated by the states in which they operate.

Complaints against federal prosecutors could be filed with the attorney general. If he or she takes no action against the prosecutor, the case would automatically be referred to an outside panel on prosecutorial misconduct. The panel would consist of seven people, three appointed by the president, and four by Congress.

Punishments for the errant prosecutors would range from suspension and demotion to being prosecuted themselves.

The provision is sure to be controversial among members who take a hawkish view on crime fighting. It may be perceived as contradictory in tone to the trend over the past decade of stepping up the federal presence in crime fighting and prosecution.

"I'm concerned it would allow legitimate prosecutions to be tied down with Lilliputian strings," said Harold Rogers, R-Ky., chairman of the subcommittee that drafted the CJS legislation.

Rather than have a vote on the amendment, Rogers accepted it with the proviso that an amendment to strike it would be allowed on the floor.

Other amendments considered during the July 15 markup included one by David E. Skaggs, D-Colo., to terminate TV Marti, a broadcast to Cuba that has been effectively jammed by the Castro regime since its inception in 1990. Skaggs withdrew his amendment.

A proposal by Jay Dickey, R-Ark., to shave $2 million from a proposed increase for the Equal Opportunity Employment Commission was rejected, 11-37.

Senate Measure Attracts Swarm Of Amendments

AUGUST 8 — S 2260 is a bill to fund the departments of Commerce, Justice and State for fiscal 1999. But as it was debated and passed by the Senate the week of July 20, it began to look more like a telecommunications bill, with immigration and a handful of other issues thrown in for good measure.

Before being passed, 99-0, on July 23, the $33 billion spending bill became the vehicle for many policy issues that have stalled as free-standing legislation. It was amended scores of times over three days of debate. (Passage, Vote 234, p. S-37)

"I've never seen this many amendments move in such a short time," said Ernest F. Hollings, D-S.C., who has been in the Senate for 32 years.

So overwhelming was the crush of amendments that the Senate mistakenly approved by voice vote a controversial provision that would have increased the number of "H-1b" visas for highly skilled immigrants. It had meant to approve a non-controversial amendment dealing with United Nations arrearages. The visa language was later stripped from the bill.

Among those immigration issues that were purposely added to the bill was a provision that would increase the number of farm workers brought in to harvest seasonal crops.

In the realm of telecommunications, the bill would ban Internet gambling, with some exceptions. Disseminating X-rated material to minors would be subject to new federal penalties. Internet service providers would be required to offer software that can block access to adult sites. And the same would be required of schools and libraries that want to receive federal grants to enhance their telecommunications services.

The bill also ventures into the area of gun ownership and gun restrictions. The Senate approved a proposal that would bar the FBI from collecting taxes on gun purchases to finance its new criminal background database, created by the 1993 Brady Act (PL 103-159). It rejected two Democratic amendments, one that would require that trigger locks be sold with handguns, and another to hold owners liable if their guns are used in the commission of a crime. (Brady Act, 1993 Almanac, p. 300)

None of the major amendments dealt with funding levels. Rather, they were the types of legislative fixes that some lawmakers insist should not be attached to appropriations bills.

The measure now has to be melded with the House version (HR 4276), which is expected to be on the floor the week of July 27. House debate likely will center on funding for the upcoming census, and a proposed amendment by Rep. Joel Hefley, R-Colo., to block funding for President Clinton's recent executive order extending federal work force affirmative action guidelines to gays.

Platform for Debates

Overall, the Senate bill would provide $33.2 billion, a $1.1 billion increase over fiscal 1998 and a $3.6 billion decrease from Clinton's request.

As always, the lion's share of the money, $17.8 billion, would go to the Justice Department, whose mission of fighting crime, prosecuting criminals and policing the borders is highly popular with lawmakers.

The biggest increase in the bill would go to the Census Bureau, whose budget would almost double, to $1.1 billion, to gear up for the 2000 census.

But with none of these spending issues prompting serious opposition, the bill became a platform for other debates, chief among them the Internet gambling ban.

Offered by Jon Kyl, R-Ariz., and Richard H. Bryan, D-Nev., it passed overwhelmingly, 90-10. The measure would make Internet gambling a crime punishable by up to four years in prison and $20,000 in fines or the total amount of gambling proceeds. (Vote 229, p. S-36)

The proposal divided gambling interests. Bryan took the position that the Internet could cut into casino profits. But many casino operators are interested in moving to the Internet.

The ban would offer a number of exceptions, including allowing states to create their own "closed loop" computer gambling networks that do not extend to any machines out of state.

Larry E. Craig, R-Idaho, tried to modify the amendment to exempt Indian tribes. But his amendment failed, 18-82. (Vote 228, p. S-36)

Bryan argued that a nationwide ban was necessary because Internet gambling is hard to police and essentially circumvents state gambling laws. Exempting tribal sites, he said, would defeat the entire purpose of the amendment.

"What logic is it that a child in Utah, which is prohibited from all forms of gaming, would be able to surf the Web, access the Indian gaming site in Idaho?" Bryan said.

Craig responded that screening software, not a nationwide ban, was the proper way of preventing children from gambling on the Internet.

Screening software was presented as the answer in two other amendments, both approved by voice vote. The first, offered by Christopher J. Dodd, D-Conn., would require any Internet service provider to offer a way to block access to objectionable sites.

The second, offered by Commerce Committee Chairman John McCain, R-Ariz., would make the same requirement of schools and libraries that hope to receive grants to enhance their computer capabilities.

The latter amendment angered library groups and Conrad Burns, R-Mont., who argued that the amendment would mandate blocking software that may be quickly obsolete.

Burns said he was personally offended by the amendment and vowed to alter it in conference. He favors language that does not mandate specific technologies but requires schools and

Appropriations

libraries to stipulate they have policies designed to prevent students and users from accessing pornographic sites.

Burns, who had been working with McCain on alternative language, said "I'm deeply disappointed that the chairman of the Commerce Committee chose not to compromise on this very important issue."

An amendment by Daniel R. Coats, R-Ind., adopted by voice vote, would create a federal crime punishable by up to six months' incarceration and a fine of $50,000 for using the World Wide Web to disseminate inappropriate material to minors.

The measure is an attempt to achieve some of the results of the communications decency portion of the 1996 Telecommunications Act (PL 104-104). That provision, which made it a crime if indecent material posted or mailed on the Internet was accessed by a minor, was struck down the following year by the Supreme Court. (*1997 Almanac, p. 5-25*)

The new measure would make it a crime only if the distributor of the material failed to take certain actions designed to limit access by minors. These would include requiring a credit card number or a debit account number, or complying with another procedure to be authorized by the Federal Communications Commission. Such actions would not necessarily prevent all minors from accessing the material. But they would be considered a good-faith attempt on the part of the distributor to screen out minors.

The definition of the material covered would be narrower as well. It would only cover material that is "harmful to minors," which is defined as appealing to prurient interests, graphically depicting or describing patently offensive material and lacking serious literary, artistic, political or scientific value.

The 1996 act also covered "indecent" material, which can include profanity.

Farm Labor Amendment

On the immigration front, the measure included an amendment offered by Gordon H. Smith, R-Ore., that would create a new national registry of farm laborers and require the attorney general to admit into the country more foreign workers when labor shortages occur. The amendment was approved, 68-31. (*Vote 233, p. S-37*)

Democrats vehemently objected to the amendment, saying it would drive down wages for low-skilled workers and encourage more illegal immigration.

"If the growers can't find the workers they need, [they should] pay better wages, provide better conditions," said Paul Wellstone, D-Minn.

Supporters of the amendment argued that they were the ones who were on the side of the workers. Whatever Congress does, illegal immigrants will come to pick fruits and vegetables in American fields, said Slade Gorton, R-Wash. By making them legal, they would be afforded more rights and a stronger bargaining position.

"Do we want the labor that is there, and will be there tomorrow, to be legal or illegal?" Gorton asked.

In the end, the Democrats were able to alter the amendment somewhat with provisions added by Dianne Feinstein, D-Calif., and Edward M. Kennedy, D-Mass.

The Feinstein provision would allow the secretary of the Department of Labor to set a cap on the number of new immigrants admitted. The Kennedy provision would allow the president to suspend the program for a variety of reasons, including if he determined that it was detrimental to the working conditions of farm workers. Both were agreed to by voice votes.

Crime and Gun Issues

Gun issues were a big part of the debate as well. Democrats used the bill to test support for two new gun restrictions that would have been the first since Republicans took control of Congress in 1995. They came up short on both.

By a vote of 61-39, the Senate tabled (killed) an amendment offered by Barbara Boxer, D-Calif, and Herb Kohl, D-Wis., that would have required gun locks to be sold with each new handgun. (*Vote 216, p. S-34*)

Initially, the amendment had been targeted for a pending juvenile crime bill (S 10). But that bill has been bottled up since last summer, when it was approved by the Judiciary Committee. (*1997 Almanac, p. 5-6*)

Democrats had seen it as a potential winner and hoped to convince moderate Republicans to peel off and support it. But, even in light of a number of recent school shootings, the issue of gun locks never resonated with the public.

A second amendment, offered by Richard J. Durbin, D-Ill., would have held gun owners responsible if their guns were used in the commission of a crime by a juvenile. It was tabled, 69-31. (*Vote 224, p. S-35*)

As if to drive home how gun rights activists still hold the upper hand, the Senate adopted by voice vote an amendment by Robert C. Smith, R-N.H., that would prevent the FBI from financing its new, instant-check, criminal-records database by imposing a tax on gun purchases. The database is scheduled to be up and running by Dec. 1.

Smith's measure would also bar the FBI from keeping any records in its system pertaining to people who passed the background check and did not have any criminal records preventing them from purchasing a weapon.

Other changes to the bill included:

● **North Pacific Fishing.** Language on fishing trawlers that sparked a fight between Alaska and Washington state lawmakers was deleted by voice vote.

● **Lawyers' fees.** An amendment to prevent court-appointed attorneys in death-penalty cases from being paid more than the U.S. attorney prosecuting the case was approved, 53-47. (*Vote 230, p. S-36*)

House Passes Tough Rules For Prosecutors

AUGUST 8 — In a surprising rebuke to accepted orthodoxy on crime, prosecution and the Justice Department, the House voted Aug. 6 to place new restrictions on federal prosecutors, including independent counsels such as Kenneth W. Starr.

The action came on the $33 billion bill (HR 4276) funding the departments of Commerce, Justice and State, which was passed 225-203. The bill generated several controversies, including the debate over counting methods to be used in the 2000 census and whether a 1969 executive order addressing race and gender discrimination in the federal workplace should be extended to include sexual orientation. (*Vote 402, p. H-114*)

But for sheer drama and indication of changing sentiment, nothing matched the the debate on the Justice Department. Voting 82-345, the House rejected an effort to remove from the bill standards for federal prosecutors. The rules would require federal prosecutors to abide by state ethics guidelines wherever they operate, create a new set of federal ethical guidelines and establish a special panel to review charges of prosecutorial misconduct. (*Vote 397, p. H-112*)

Not only did the House accept these guidelines for conventional prosecutors, it voted 249-182 to adopt an amendment that would apply them to independent counsels named to investigate allegations against high-level officials. (*Vote 396, p. H-112*)

The debate was rife with emotional appeals. At times the authors of the guidelines seemed themselves surprised at the support they gathered along the way.

"Sometimes we in the House forget watersheds that come our way and the moments of history that arrive," said Joseph M. McDade, R-Pa., author of the new guidelines and himself the subject of a Justice Department probe that resulted in a 1996 acquittal. "[This] involves the liberty of every citizen of this country." (*McDade, 1996 Almanac, p. 1-35*)

McDade's guidelines were in the underlying bill as it came to the floor. They were added by the Appropriations Committee without debate or a recorded vote. Opponents reasoned they had little chance of victory in committee, where there is considerable sympathy for longtime member McDade after the ordeal he went through.

But if opponents thought they would prevail on the floor, they were sorely mistaken. As the effort gathered momentum, conservative and liberal lawmakers cheered each other on as they shared stories of overzealous federal prosecutors. McDade's allies talked of the bribery probe he endured for six years. Harold E. Ford Jr., D-Tenn., spoke of his father, Harold E. Ford Sr., D-Tenn. (1975-97), who was the target of an unsuccessful bank-fraud, mail-fraud and conspiracy prosecution brought by legendary prosecutor Hickman Ewing Jr., now a deputy to Starr. (*1993 Almanac, p. 71*)

Several Republicans recalled the experience of Iran-contra figure Elliot Abrams, who, under extraordinary scrutiny by independent counsel Lawrence E. Walsh, pleaded guilty to four misdemeanor charges before being pardoned by President George Bush. Democrats spoke of the dozens of Arkansans and White House aides who have had to spend millions of dollars on lawyers' fees connected with Starr's probe of President Clinton. (*1992 Almanac, p. 572*)

In the end, the vote was a rout that stunned many of McDade's opponents.

"It is very dangerous, what we did today," said Asa Hutchinson, R-Ark., sponsor of the failed amendment to remove the McDade proposal. "This will give defendants, defense attorneys and the cartels another weapon to use."

Hutchinson said his side was overcome by anecdotes and emotion, coupled with sympathy for McDade.

In an indication of some lawmakers' weariness of federally prosecuted scandals, the guidelines were expanded to include independent counsels as well as conventional prosecutors. That decision was made in an amendment offered by John Conyers Jr., D-Mich. Forty-eight Republicans joined the vast majority of Democrats in the vote.

That vote ran contrary to the accepted wisdom among many in the Republican Party that — no matter what one's general views on independent counsels — taking any action now is inadvisable because it would be seen as a personal attack on Starr.

Witnessing the events of the evening, particularly the rejection of the Hutchinson amendment, Charles T. Canady, R-Fla., was at a near-total loss for an explanation. Asked what he thought was behind the vote, he shrugged and said: "Pent-up frustration with law enforcement. That's all I can think of."

An Uphill Battle

Despite its popularity in the House, however, the McDade proposal, with or without the addition by Conyers, faces an uphill battle at best. A majority of Senate Judiciary Committee members signed a letter opposing it. And the Senate, which has already passed its version of the appropriations bill without the guidelines, is likely to resist the change in conference committee.

The Justice Department opposes it with great vehemence as well, and would probably prevail on Clinton to veto the bill in the event it reached his desk with the McDade language intact. Clinton has already threatened to veto the bill because of objections to the census language.

Nevertheless, the popularity of the McDade and Conyers initiatives indicates a substantial change in accepted wisdom about crime and prosecution at the federal level. Until very recently, such a broad attack on the Justice Department's prosecutorial functions would have been unheard of.

Charged with the popular function of fighting drugs, crime and terrorism, as well as policing the borders, the department has seen its budget doubled in the Clinton years alone, as numerous federal crimes have been created through the 1994 crime bill (PL 103-322) and other laws. (*Crime bill, 1994 Almanac, p. 273*)

"From the day the Founding Fathers met, they warned us about a national police force," McDade said. "We're heading in that direction, and I find that very worrisome."

The new federal guidelines would consist of 10 prohibitions on practices such as bringing indictments without probable cause or sitting on evidence that could exonerate a defendant. As obvious as these types of prohibitions seem, McDade said they were all things that at least one federal prosecutor had done in recent years.

To enforce these strictures, McDade's guidelines would create a new board on prosecutorial misconduct to review complaints brought by targets of prosecution. The board's members would be appointed by Congress and the president.

The Justice Department particularly opposes portions of the bill dealing with state guidelines and establishing the misconduct board.

Requiring federal prosecutors to follow state guidelines would seriously hamper the department's efforts in interstate prosecutions, Associate Attorney General Ray Fisher said in a briefing with reporters.

"It might prevent federal prosecutors from bringing some of our most important multistate cases, such as those involving large-scale drug conspiracies, telemarketing fraud, child

Appropriations

sexual exploitation on the Internet and terrorist attacks," said Fisher.

The misconduct board, he said, would have access to critical department evidence. And a savvy defense attorney could get copies of it by filing a complaint.

A Reflection on Starr

Adding independent counsels to the language was something of a coup for Conyers, who was able to deftly take advantage of the open rule under which the bill was debated. By offering the amendment, he put McDade's Republican backers in a quandary. They could follow the advice of senior Republicans and defer until next year any effort to review the work of Starr and other independent counsels.

But by doing so they would be taking an inconsistent position: It is hard to make a case against prosecutors run amok and exempt the most powerful and unrestricted of them all.

The Conyers amendment gave Democrats a chance to vent their anger at Starr, who is investigating Clinton for possible perjury and obstruction of justice in connection with an alleged affair with former White House intern Monica S. Lewinsky. Maxine Waters, D-Calif., called Starr "the poster boy for unethical prosecutors."

The vote also may have been an early indication of what could be in store for the independent counsel statute (PL 103-270) when it comes up for reauthorization next year. Some members want to abolish it entirely, while others think it should be — in fact, must be — maintained, but in some restricted form.

Other Controversies

In addition to the prosecutorial language, the bill contained several other controversies.

By a vote of 201-227, the House rejected an amendment by Alan B. Mollohan, D-W.Va., striking language restricting the funding for the upcoming census. The vote was along party lines, and the divisions closely mirrored those that appeared last year and in committee earlier this year. (Vote 388, p. H-110)

Clinton and congressional Democrats want to allow the Census Bureau to use a counting technique known as statistical sampling. Republicans want to block this.

Many lawmakers believe a resolution of this issue is more likely to come in direct negotiations between the White House and House leaders than by floor debate.

The House also rejected an effort by Joel Hefley, R-Colo., to block funding for a recent presidential executive order extending federal workplace anti-discrimination language to include homosexuals.

A group of 63 Republicans, largely moderates, broke ranks to help defeat the measure, 176-252. Opponents of the language said that, whatever one's views on homosexuality, it is wrong to discriminate against people in the workplace. (Vote 398, p.H-112)

Proponents argued that Clinton's order was an expansion of affirmative action and a bid to legislate from the White House.

In other actions, the House:

- Accepted by a vote of 255-170 an amendment increasing funding for the Legal Services Corporation from $141 million to $250 million. (Vote 381, p. H-108)
- Accepted by voice vote an amendment striking language that would have extended the state waters of Alabama, Mississippi and Louisiana nine miles into the Gulf of Mexico.

Census Dispute Could Prompt Funds Suspension

OCTOBER 17 — Because of continued disagreement over the method to be used to conduct the 2000 census, spending for the departments of Commerce, Justice, and State and the federal judiciary could come to a screeching halt June 15. The fiscal 1999 omnibus spending bill (HR 4328) contains language shutting off the funding spigot on that date unless Congress passes a separate bill determining how the census will be conducted.

The highly unusual move serves two purposes: By delaying determination of how the census will be conducted, lawmakers will give the Supreme Court a chance to rule on the constitutionality of a method known as statistical sampling, which is favored by most Democrats. By putting $33 billion and three Cabinet departments on the line, the two sides are giving themselves ample incentive to resolve the census matter by June.

Lawmakers have for years been arguing over whether sampling should be used in the decennial count. The method uses statistical estimations to count people often missed by a traditional count: non-English speakers, the homeless, the rural poor and others who might not be comfortable dealing with a census taker.

Most Democrats, as well as professional statisticians, say sampling will yield a more accurate count than a traditional door-to-door survey. Republicans argue it is unconstitutional because the Constitution calls for an "actual enumeration."

Sampling is likely to yield a higher count of people in inner cities, which, in turn, would mean more federal dollars for these areas. It would also likely translate into a gain in the number of congressional seats held by Democrats.

Republicans had wanted to hold up funding for the Census Bureau only if the two sides could not agree by June. The administration argued that this approach would not provide enough incentive to reach agreement. In the end, it won, much to the chagrin of many Republicans.

"I think it's insane," said Harold Rogers, R-Ky., chairman of the House Appropriations subcommittee in charge of the bill. "It's unfair to hold hostage to this dispute all these other areas, particularly the third branch of government."

Beyond the Census

This year Internet issues also became a stumbling block. One of the last items to be resolved was the inclusion of a provision in the Senate bill prohibiting Internet sites from disseminating material that is "harmful to minors."

Another key stumbling block was payment of approximately $1 billion in back dues owed by the United States to the United Nations. Social conservatives linked the payment to language restricting family planning programs. The issue was resolved only by denying both sides what they wanted. The conservatives did not get their language. And President Clinton did not get the money.

Commerce-Justice-State Spending

Commerce-Justice-State portion of the fiscal 1999 omnibus spending law (HR 4328 — PL 105-277) signed by the president on Oct. 21. *(Budget authority, in thousands of dollars.)*

	Fiscal 1998 Appropriation	Fiscal 1999 Clinton Request	House Committee	Senate Committee	Final Bill
Department of Justice					
State and local law enforcement	$ 2,891,400	$ 2,369,400	$ 2,927,150	$ 2,676,650	$ 2,921,950
Other Office of Justice programs	1,908,775	2,077,970	1,963,759	1,966,557	1,927,057
Legal activities	2,509,673	2,931,282	2,629,029	2,638,245	2,637,541
Organized-crime drug enforcement	294,967	304,014	304,014	294,967	304,014
Federal Bureau of Investigation	2,974,548	3,032,470	2,977,258	2,956,461	2,971,448
Drug Enforcement Administration	1,135,378	1,178,260	1,209,290	1,217,054	1,213,780
Immigration and Naturalization Service	3,797,389	4,188,939	4,137,588	3,940,543	3,860,373
Offsetting fees	−1,455,338	−1,465,416	−1,570,014	−1,560,308	−1,306,046
Federal prison system	3,404,910	3,357,050	3,302,850	3,298,712	3,299,850
Other	302,758	537,896	349,261	371,236	383,983
TOTAL, Justice Department	**$ 17,764,460**	**$ 18,511,865**	**$ 18,230,185**	**$ 17,800,117**	**$ 18,213,950**
Related Agencies					
EEOC	242,000	279,000	260,500	253,580	279,000
Legal Services Corporation	283,000	340,000	250,000	300,000	300,000
The Judiciary					
Supreme Court	32,645	36,966	36,495	36,930	36,459
Courts of Appeals, district courts	3,286,031	3,619,418	3,492,896	3,417,577	3,467,761
Administrative Office of the U.S. Courts	52,000	56,156	54,500	54,682	54,500
Other	92,959	94,320	92,865	98,397	92,408
TOTAL, Judiciary	**$ 3,463,635**	**$ 3,806,860**	**$ 3,676,756**	**$ 3,607,586**	**$ 3,651,128**
Department of Commerce					
National Institute of Standards and Technology	677,852	830,041	624,184	646,308	647,150
National Oceanic and Atmospheric Admin.	2,002,139	4,908,271	2,009,861	2,201,167	2,166,001
Census Bureau	693,091	1,187,886	1,252,034	1,139,885	1,323,049
Telecommunications and Information Admin.	57,550	47,940	47,940	51,776	49,940
International Trade Administration	283,066	286,452	281,523	303,314	284,664
Patent and Trademark Office (offsetting fees)	*(716,000)*	*(785,052)*	*(785,526)*	*(785,523)*	*(785,526)*
Economic Development Administration	361,028	397,969	393,379	301,695	392,379
Other	240,679	217,725	273,553	247,979	257,011
TOTAL, Commerce Department	**$ 4,315,405**	**$ 7,876,284**	**$ 4,882,474**	**$ 4,892,124**	**$ 5,120,194**
Related Agencies					
Federal Communications Commission (net)	23,991	40,454	8,991	25,398	19,477
Federal Trade Commission	18,500	101,167	3,990	3,167	10,179
Maritime Administration	138,825	178,203	174,975	177,468	168,678
Securities and Exchange Commission	33,477	341,098	324,000	–	324,000
Small Business Administration	716,132	724,424	708,140	613,616	718,959
Department of State					
Administration of Foreign Affairs	2,773,743	3,014,943	2,693,625	2,897,825	2,676,756
International organizations and conferences	1,211,515	1,637,996	1,609,000	1,562,811	1,628,000
Other	51,992	61,720	53,720	43,992	54,022
TOTAL, State Department	**$ 4,037,250**	**$ 4,714,659**	**$ 4,356,345**	**$ 4,504,628**	**$ 4,358,778**
Related Agencies					
Arms Control and Disarmament Agency	41,500	43,400	41,500	43,400	41,500
U.S. Information Agency	1,105,858	1,119,300	1,089,411	1,051,801	1,101,576
Other, rescissions	−$60,126	−$5,246	−$30,046	−$34,095	−107,715
GRAND TOTAL	**$ 32,123,907**	**$ 38,071,468**	**$ 33,977,221**	**$ 33,238,790**	**$ 34,199,704**
Crime trust fund	$ 5,225,000	$ 5,513,977	$ 5,511,940	$ 5,511,700	5,509,700

SOURCE: House and Senate Appropriations committees

Appropriations

Some of the most important policy decisions in the final days of negotiating the spending measure dealt with immigration. The final package has a number of key additions and omissions.

It does not include a provision in the Senate bill that would have increased the number of temporary agriculture workers allowed into the United States. It also does not include a Rogers proposal to divide the Immigration and Naturalization Service into three parts.

It does include language delaying for 30 months implementation of a registry of all entries and exits over U.S. land borders. The registry, created in the 1996 immigration bill (104-208), is opposed by business interests, who say it would cause excessive delays. (*1996 Almanac*, p. 5-3)

The bill includes two major immigration policy changes that did not originate in the bill. One increases the number of visas for highly skilled immigrants. The other grants permanent residency status to approximately 49,700 Haitian refugees.

The final bill includes $690 million for drug interdiction efforts, an item touted by Republicans. Part of this is funded through the departments of Justice and State.

It also includes a provision, pushed by gun owners' rights groups, prohibiting the FBI from funding its new national gun registry by fees collected from gun purchasers. ◆

Defense Bill Clears Minus 'Readiness' Funds; Clinton Looks to Supplemental

The $250.5 billion defense appropriations bill for fiscal 1999 provided $488 million less than President Clinton had requested. But there was no significant congressional debate this year over the total size of the defense budget.

SUMMARY

The long-range budget plan in the 1997 balanced-budget law (PL 105-33) limited the total defense budget for fiscal 1999 to $271.5 billion. Clinton's overall defense request — including the Pentagon, defense-related nuclear programs conducted by the Energy Department and small amounts for miscellaneous other agencies — totaled $270.6 billion.

Although defense-minded members contended that the services' combat readiness was eroding because Clinton's budget was too tight, there was no serious effort to add money to his request until September, by which time work on the defense appropriations measure was all but wrapped up.

For the most part, the $488 million reduction in the final version of the bill reflected congressional action moving funds out of the defense bill and into the separate military construction appropriations bill (HR 4059 — PL 105-237).

By the time House-Senate conferees finished work on the defense bill, Clinton had requested a $1 billion supplemental appropriation for spare parts, equipment overhauls and other readiness-related purposes. Anticipating that Congress would approve the request, appropriations conferees left out of their agreement (H Rept 105-746) at least $400 million for spare parts and repairs, using the money instead to fund other priorities.

The defense bill did not include $1.87 billion needed to pay for U.S. peacekeeping forces in Bosnia through the fiscal year. The Senate version (S 2132 — S Rept 105-200) had included the money, as Clinton asked, but the House bill (H Rept 105-591) did not, since deficit-minded members balked at Clinton's request that the money be declared emergency funds and, thus, exempt from the budget caps. The Bosnia funds were included in the omnibus spending bill (PL 105-277) as emergency spending.

The final measure made no dramatic changes in the amount Clinton requested for major weapons programs. But, as usual, Congress directed a couple of billion dollars to members' pet projects, including $400 million for C-130 cargo planes built next door to the district of House Speaker Newt Gingrich, R-Ga. Most of the congressional initiatives added to the bill involved far smaller sums, such as the $10 million designated to convert an unused National Guard armory in Chicago into a public military high school.

These congressional additions were paid for, in effect, by across-the-board cuts that the conferees said reflected changing economic conditions. For example, the bill cut more than $400 million because of lower than anticipated inflation and more than $500 million because of the declining price of fuel oil.

The bill provided $3.45 billion of the $3.59 billion requested for anti-missile defenses. The largest reduction was $376 million — nearly half the $822 million requested — for the Army's Theater High-Altitude Area Defense (THAAD) system, intended to protect U.S. forces deployed overseas. All five THAAD flight tests have failed.

The bill added $202 million to the budget request to pay for the 3.6 percent military pay raise approved by the companion defense authorization bill

Box Score

- **Bill:** HR 4103 — PL 105-262
- **House action:** The House adopted the conference report (H Rept 105-746) on HR 4103, 369-43, on Sept. 28. It passed HR 4103 (H Rept 105-591), 358-61, on June 24.
- **Senate action:** The Senate cleared the conference report on HR 4103, 94-2, on Sept. 29. It passed HR 4103 on July 30, 97-2, after substituting the text of S 2132 as amended on the Senate floor.
- **Presidential action:** Clinton signed HR 4103 on Oct. 17.

(HR 3616 — PL 105-261) instead of the 3.1 percent raise Clinton had requested. But the appropriations bill also included a provision requiring the Pentagon to report to Congress early next year on the adequacy of the whole military compensation package, including pay, pensions and medical care.

Dropped from the bill was a House provision, sponsored by David E. Skaggs, D-Colo., that would have required the president to obtain congressional authorization before sending U.S. forces on an offensive military operation. The provision was aimed at a prospective deployment of U.S. forces in Kosovo, a province of Serbia wracked by ethnic violence pitting the region's Albanian majority against forces of the Serb-dominated government. The administration had threatened to veto the bill if it included Skaggs' provision.

Also dropped was a Senate provision, sponsored by Tim Hutchinson, R-Ark., that would have denied U.S. visas to Chinese officials associated with policies of compulsory abortion and religious persecution.

The bill did include a Senate provision by Pat Roberts, R-Kan., that would bar the deployment of U.S. forces in Yugoslavia, Albania or Macedonia — other than the small observation force currently in Macedonia — unless the president sent Congress a report outlining the expected scope, duration and cost of the mission. However, the president could waive the reporting requirement in an emergency.

Committees Flout Clinton's Plea For Bosnia Funds

JUNE 6 — Neither the Senate Appropriations Committee nor the House National Security Appropriations Subcommittee included in their respective fiscal 1999 bills $1.9 billion President Clinton requested to keep U.S. troops in Bosnia as part of a NATO-led peacekeeping force. Clinton had asked that the money be designated "emergency" spending, exempt from balanced-budget limits.

Senior Pentagon officials and top-ranking military brass have warned that if they must absorb the Bosnia expenses within the $271 billion defense budget limit, they will have to make draconian cuts in training and maintenance operations.

While acknowledging those warnings, Senate Appropriations Committee Chairman Ted Stevens, R-Alaska, has balked at the White House request.

A decision by the appropriations panels on how to fund the Bosnia deployment likely will await the results of a Senate floor debate on Clinton's Bosnia policy when lawmakers consider the fiscal 1999 defense authorization bill (S 2057 — S Rept 105-189).

Action on the authorization bill awaits disposition of tobacco legislation (S 1415) that has tied up the Senate since late May.

On the Same Track

The House and Senate defense appropriations bills so far are similar to one another and to Clinton's $251 billion request. Combined with defense-related funds that will be included in other appropriations bills, the Senate and House measures would use up nearly the entire $271 billion allowed for national defense under the 1997 balanced budget law (PL 105-33).

The defense spending bill approved 27-0 on June 4 by the Senate Appropriations Committee (S 2132) would provide $250.3 billion — $481 million less than Clinton requested — for all Pentagon military programs except the construction of facilities, which is funded by a separate military construction bill.

The counterpart bill approved the same day by the House National Security Appropriations Subcommittee, by voice vote, would provide $250.5 billion, about $270 million less than Clinton's request. The House panel also included in its bill $1.6 billion in "emergency" funding — exempt from the budget ceiling — to help the Pentagon improve the security of its computer systems and solve the year 2000 problem.

Subcommittee Chairman C.W. Bill Young, R-Fla., said the full Appropriations Committee would review the House bill June 17, with floor action tentatively scheduled the week of June 22.

Stevens said he hoped the Senate would take up its version during the week of June 8, but that depends on clearing away both the tobacco bill and the defense authorization measure.

Anti-Missile Programs

The most significant change either bill made to any major weapons program involved anti-missile defenses.

Both bills approved the $950 million Clinton requested to continue developing a system to protect U.S. territory from a limited number of attacking missiles.

Each bill sliced funds from the amount requested for the Army's Theater High-Altitude Area Defense (THAAD) missile. All five THAAD test flights have failed, the latest one in May. The Pentagon insists the program is fundamentally sound, saying that the failures have been caused by minor and unrelated technical glitches. But since the program has been slowed down, the House subcommittee cut $406 million from the $822 million requested for the program; the Senate committee cut $324 million.

The Senate committee also cut $150.5 million from the $343 million requested for production of the Army's PAC-3 short-range anti-missile system, an upgrade of the Patriot, noting that key flight tests for that weapon had been delayed.

On the other hand, both bills would increase funding for the Navy Theater Wide anti-missile system, a long-range shipborne counterpart of THAAD, which also has had test failures. The House bill would provide $340 million for the program — $150 million more than was requested — while the Senate bill would provide $295 million.

Raise in Pay

Both bills would approve the budget request for a 3.1 percent military pay raise. The House panel thus disregarded the provision of the House-passed defense authorization bill (HR 3616 — H Rept 105-532) calling for a 3.6 percent pay increase.

Both would approve the $746 million requested to pay for deployments to the Persian Gulf region. In addition, the Senate committee bill would provide $50 million for unspecified initiatives to boost morale and reenlistments for some personnel who might

Appropriations

be reluctant to stay in the service because of frequent overseas missions.

For the so-called Nunn-Lugar program to help former Soviet republics dispose of their nuclear, chemical and biological weapons, the House subcommittee's bill would provide the $417 million authorized by HR 3616. The Senate bill would provide $440 million — $2 million less than was requested. However, the Senate bill earmarks $35 million of that total to dispose of old nuclear-powered submarines moldering in Russian ports on the Pacific.

The submarine provision is one of several reflecting the interest in the Pacific Rim by Stevens and senior Democrat Daniel K. Inouye of Hawaii.

Weapons Programs

For most major weapons programs, both bills would approve the amounts requested, including:

- $313 million to develop the Army's Crusader mobile artillery piece.
- $2.6 billion for 13 C-17 wide-body cargo jets.

On the other hand, there are some funding differences over major programs.

To buy three Navy destroyers equipped with the Aegis anti-aircraft system, the Senate committee approved $2.67 billion while the House panel approved $2.62 billion.

The Senate committee approved $665 million, as requested, to buy seven V-22 Ospreys — hybrid airplane/helicopters that the Marines will use to haul troops — plus components for future production. The House panel approved $696 million for eight aircraft plus components.

To continue developing the Army's Comanche missile-armed helicopter, the administration requested $368 million, the House panel recommended $392 million and the Senate committee $349 million.

To buy two F-22 fighters plus components that would be used in future production, the Senate bill would provide $785 million, as requested. The House subcommittee recommended $715 million.

Like the Senate version of the companion defense authorization bill, the Senate Appropriations measure would add to the budget $50 million as a down payment on a $1.4 billion helicopter carrier that would be built by Litton Industries in Pascagoula, Miss., hometown of Majority Leader Trent Lott, R-Miss., and home to constituents of Senate Defense Subcommittee member Thad Cochran, R-Miss.

The Senate committee's bill also would reject all funds requested to buy passenger vehicles — sedans, buses, pickup trucks, ambulances and the like — requiring the Pentagon to lease such vehicles rather than buy them.

In all, the panel eliminated from the budget $38.6 million requested to buy commercial vehicles and replaced it with $6.7 million earmarked for vehicle leases.

For its part, the House subcommittee, following the lead of the authorization bill, incorporated some initiatives dealing with major aircraft programs:

- It added $86 million to upgrade the Air Force's fleet of 21 B-2 "stealth" bombers.
- Besides approving the $463 million requested for two Joint STARS radar command planes, it added $72 million for components that could be used if the Pentagon decides to buy more than the 13 Joint STARS already funded.

House Panel Strips Funds For Computers From Defense Bill

JUNE 20 — Under pressure from budget conservatives, House Republican leaders said they would retract $1.6 billion in emergency spending approved by the Appropriations Committee for Pentagon computer problems.

The extra money was part of a $252 billion defense appropriations bill approved June 17 by the committee. The additional funds, nearly all to help the Pentagon solve its Year 2000 computer problem, were designated as emergency spending and would be exempt from limits in the balanced-budget law (PL 105-33).

The bill also would provide $250.7 billion in regular funding for the Pentagon. Combined with defense-related appropriations in other bills, this would use up practically all the budget authority allowed by the balanced-budget law.

The committee rejected by voice vote an amendment by Republican Mark W. Neumann of Wisconsin that would have deleted the emergency computer funds.

"This is not about the computer problem," Neumann insisted. "It's about integrity in keeping the budget caps."

The committee later included similar emergency spending in the Treasury-Postal Service Appropriations bill to help other federal agencies solve their Year 2000 computer problem.

But Neumann and his allies objected to House leaders who announced, after a June 19 meeting, that the emergency funding would be removed from both bills. The money may be considered in separate legislation that might include offsetting budget cuts.

Bosnia Breakdown

The committee's defense bill does not include $1.9 billion in emergency spending that President Clinton requested to keep U.S. forces in Bosnia as part of a NATO-led peacekeeping force through fiscal 1999.

Pentagon officials repeatedly have warned that unless the additional funds for the Bosnia operation are provided, over and above the defense total allowed by the budget deal, spending could be cut for training, maintenance and modernization.

Many members of Congress are frustrated that Clinton, having sent troops into Bosnia without congressional approval, has twice ignored his own deadline for withdrawing them and now refuses to set a date at all. Neither chamber is likely to approve funding for Bosnia until congressional skeptics and the administration work out a compromise, probably as an amendment to the annual defense authorization bill (HR 3616 — H Rept 105-532; S 2057 — S Rept 105-189).

In addition to exempting the computer funding from the budget ceilings, the House appropriations bill would use $637 million from the sale of surplus Navy ships to other countries to cover part of the cost of the bill.

The budget law's cap on defense outlays would have required a reduction of at least $2.6 billion in the amount provided by the bill. But Republican leaders prevented that by ordering the Congressional Budget

Office to reduce its estimate of the bill's cost.

Branding the committee's bill a "budget buster," senior Appropriations Committee Democrat David R. Obey of Wisconsin said that it included nearly $4.7 billion more than the budget agreement would have allowed, "if you had honest accounting numbers."

War Powers

The Appropriations Committee adopted, 30-25, an amendment by David E. Skaggs, D-Colo., prohibiting the use of funds for "offensive military operations" unless they are authorized by Congress. In March, the committee added a similar Skaggs amendment to this year's supplemental spending bill (PL 105-174). The provision was dropped from the supplemental in conference.

Skaggs argued that his amendment would acknowledge the authority of Congress to decide when U.S. forces should go to war. But senior National Security Subcommittee Democrat John P. Murtha of Pennsylvania warned that the amendment might inhibit NATO's ability to pressure Serbia against using force in the secession-minded province of Kosovo.

The committee also rejected by voice vote an Obey amendment that would have shifted $199 million the committee added to the bill to buy C-130 cargo planes built by Lockheed Martin in Marietta, Ga., near the district of Speaker Newt Gingrich, R-Ga., and used it instead to buy three F/A-18 "E" and "F" model jet fighters, built in St. Louis by Boeing near the district of Minority Leader Richard A. Gephardt, D-Mo.

House Funds Projects in Key Members' Districts

JUNE 27 — The defense appropriations bill passed by the House June 24 is $2.2 billion smaller than President Clinton asked and includes $3 billion for programs and projects the House liked better than his.

One of the costliest examples: $422 million for seven additional C-130 cargo planes built by Lockheed Martin in Marietta, Ga., the hometown of House Speaker Newt Gingrich, R-Ga.

Clinton had asked for one.

The $251 billion bill (HR 4103), which passed 358-61 with minimal debate, achieved most of its net savings by omitting $1.9 billion Clinton requested for the continued deployment of U.S. troops in Bosnia. (*Vote 266, p. H-76*)

The money that the House redirected includes dozens of weapons programs that would bring work to the districts of particular members, though most are more modest than the Lockheed purchase.

For instance, Ohio Republican David L. Hobson, a member of the National Security Appropriations Subcommittee, secured $18 million for three research projects at Wright-Patterson Air Force Base in his district. Hobson also announced that a high school in his district is one of three in the country that will start up new Marine Corps Junior ROTC units with $1 million the House bill would add to the budget.

A large portion of the money spent on congressional initiatives — $1.4 billion — would go to beef up maintenance of facilities and equipment rather than to buy products.

The cost of those added programs would be more than offset by cuts in other parts of the defense budget request, including such major weapons systems as:

• $406 million from the $822 million requested for the Theater High-Altitude Area Defense (THAAD), an anti-missile program that has failed in several tests.

• $220 million from the $2.8 billion requested for F/A-18 "E" and "F" model Navy fighter jets.

Most savings in the bill would come from price reductions since the budget was drafted and from several efficiency measures that the committee insisted would have no negative impact on Pentagon operations.

Combined with the military construction appropriations bill (HR 4059 — H Rept 105-578) passed June 22 and defense-related appropriations in other spending bills, HR 4103 would bring defense-related funding for fiscal 1999 to roughly $271 billion, the ceiling set by last year's balanced-budget law (PL 105-33).

Floor Action

When the House turned to the defense bill June 24, it first adopted by a near-party line vote of 221-201 the rule governing debate on the measure. The rule stripped from the bill $1.6 billion that the Appropriations committee had added to help the Pentagon solve its Year 2000 computer problem and to beef up computer network security. (*Vote 265, p. H-76*)

Since those computer funds were designated as emergency spending, they were exempt from the budget limit on defense spending. After some Republicans objected to what they considered a circumvention of the budget agreement, GOP leaders decided to remove the $1.6 billion from the defense bill and to combine it, in a separate bill, with $2.25 billion that had been added to the fiscal 1999 Treasury, Postal Service appropriations bill (HR 4104 — H Rept 105-592) to fix the Year 2000 problem in non-defense agencies.

Before passing the defense bill, the House adopted two amendments by voice vote.

One, by Bernard Sanders, I-Vt., would bar the Defense Department from buying anything from companies owned by the Chinese government or its People's Liberation Army. Sanders said Chinese Army-owned companies were supplying bearings used in the B-2 stealth bomber and other front-line combat planes.

The other amendment, by Democrat Ken Bentsen of Texas, would prohibit the Defense Department from bringing toxic PCBs purchased overseas to the United States for disposal. They mainly are used as electrical insulators.

There was no debate on a provision in the bill, sponsored by David E. Skaggs, D-Colo., that would bar the use of funds for U.S. forces to conduct offensive military operations unless authorized by Congress pursuant to its constitutional authority to declare war. Administration officials have said that Clinton would veto the bill if Skaggs' provision were included in the final version.

Skaggs added a similar provision last spring to the House version of the supplemental appropriations bill (PL 105-174), but it was dropped in conference with the Senate.

Appropriations

Senate Passes Bill, Backing Troop Levels In Balkans

AUGUST 1 — Decisively rejecting a challenge to President Clinton's deployment of U.S. troops in Bosnia, the Senate passed a $252 billion defense appropriations bill July 30 that includes $1.9 billion Clinton requested to continue the peacekeeping mission.

By a vote of 68-31, the Senate tabled (killed) an amendment by Republican Kay Bailey Hutchison of Texas that would have required the Pentagon to reduce the roughly 6,700-member U.S. force currently in Bosnia to 5,000 troops by Oct. 1, 1999. (*Vote 249, p. S-39*)

Despite warnings that Clinton might soon send additional troops to keep the peace in Kosovo, a restive province of Serbia, the Senate overwhelmingly rejected an amendment that would have barred the use of U.S. forces for offensive military operations unless authorized by Congress. The amendment by Richard J. Durbin, D-Ill., was rejected, 84-15. (*Vote 251, p. S-39*)

The Senate's action bespoke grudging acquiescence in Clinton's use of military force in the Balkans rather than enthusiastic support. But it was a clear defeat for opponents of the Bosnia mission, who have been gearing up for months to try to force Clinton to start reducing the U.S. role in the NATO-led peacekeeping operation.

"Where the rubber meets the road, [senators] are going to respect the commander in chief's power to decide," said Connecticut Democrat Joseph I. Lieberman.

But Lieberman, who strongly supports the Bosnia mission, also contended that the Senate's action reflected a belief, even among skeptics, that the peacekeeping process in Bosnia was showing results. "People realize that it's working, and they don't want to upset it," he said.

Keep It Moving

The debate over the use of military forces highlighted the Senate's fast-paced action on the annual defense bill (HR 4103), which was completed in a single day. Sporting an "Incredible Hulk" necktie, Appropriations Committee Chairman Ted Stevens, R-Alaska, drove the legislative locomotive, alternately wheedling and bullying his colleagues to expedite action on the bill.

As the debate wore on into Thursday afternoon, and senators chafed to begin their four-week-long August recess, the combative Stevens threatened to keep them in session through the weekend, if necessary, to conclude work on the measure. "My plane doesn't leave until Monday," he said.

After adopting dozens of non-controversial amendments by voice vote and dealing with a handful of others by roll calls, the Senate substituted the text of its own bill for the text of the House-passed version and then passed the latter by a vote of 97-2. (*Vote 252, p. S-39*)

Liberal Democrats Russell D. Feingold of Wisconsin and Paul Wellstone of Minnesota cast the two "nay" votes.

The Senate-passed bill closely tracks both Clinton's budget request and the House-passed version. One provision that sets the Senate bill apart is its approval of a 3.6 percent military pay raise, instead of the 3.1 percent that Clinton requested and the House approved. The Senate approved the higher figure by voice vote.

Stevens predicted that a House-Senate conference report on the funding bill could be completed by mid-September.

The Senate's rejection of Hutchison's Bosnia amendment apparently closes an effort by congressional critics to limit the U.S. mission, barring trouble in the Balkan state.

These critics began gearing up last December when, for the second time, Clinton brushed aside a self-imposed deadline for ending the mission. Declaring that such deadlines were self-defeating, he announced that, while the number of U.S. troops in Bosnia would be reduced, they would remain as part of the international peacekeeping force. Most of the other countries participating in the mission have said they would withdraw their forces if U.S. troops were pulled out.

In his fiscal 1999 budget request, Clinton had asked that the $1.9 billion needed to pay for the Bosnia mission be designated as emergency funding and exempt from the limits on defense spending set out in last year's balanced-budget agreement (PL 105-33). (*1997 Almanac, p. 2-47*)

But early in the year, Hutchison, one of the most prominent critics of the Bosnia deployment, and senior Appropriations Committee Democrat Robert C. Byrd of West Virginia began floating legislative proposals designed to ratchet down the number of U.S. personnel in Bosnia.

When the Appropriations panel approved the defense bill on June 4, Stevens omitted the Bosnia funds, pending a test of Senate sentiment on the issue.

But shortly after the Senate took up the bill on July 30, it adopted, by voice vote, an amendment by Stevens that added the $1.9 billion requested for Bosnia and designated it emergency funding.

Hutchison then offered her amendment to pare the size of the U.S. force, arguing that the Bosnia mission was sapping morale and combat readiness out of proportion to its significance to U.S. national security.

Noting that the mission has cost nearly $9 billion to date, she argued: "If you look at all the responsibilities America has around the world, we are spending too much on Bosnia."

She and Byrd insisted they wanted only to pressure U.S. allies in Europe into carrying a greater share of the burden. "The United States cannot continue to pick up the largest share of every NATO military mission," Byrd contended.

But Defense Secretary William S. Cohen and Joint Chiefs of Staff Chairman Gen. Henry H. Shelton weighed in with a letter strongly opposing the amendment, insisting that military commanders needed the ability to determine how many troops they needed for the mission.

They warned that a mandate from Congress to cut the number of troops in Bosnia "would invite heightened intransigence and extremism" from those in Bosnia opposed to the U.S.-sponsored peace process.

Since the troops are already deployed, Congress should not second-guess the commanders on the details, argued Armed Services Committee Republicans Daniel R. Coats of Indiana and John McCain of Arizona. That argument appeared to carry the day.

"When military leaders say, 'You endanger our troops when you set artificial [manpower] levels,' the Senate responds," McCain said later.

War Powers

The Senate also rejected Durbin's amendment that would have required congressional authorization of offensive actions before troops were sent overseas, a move parallel to the 1973 War Powers Resolution (PL 93-148), which no president has acknowledged and no Congress has enforced.

Joseph R. Biden Jr. of Delaware, the ranking Democrat on the Foreign Relations Committee, backed Durbin's proposal. The argument for unfettered presidential authority to send troops overseas had been justified by the urgency of the Cold War, he said. "It is time that Congress, with the changed world, reassert its rightful role in [decisions about] the use of force."

Hutchison, Arlen Specter, R-Pa., and 13 Democrats opposed a motion to table the amendment. "Members of the Senate are not prepared to accept the responsibility," Durbin lamented after the vote. "They had a chance to take a share of that responsibility and they turned it down."

The Senate approved by voice vote two amendments with a bearing on Balkan operations.

One, by Hutchison, would require a Pentagon report on the combat readiness of U.S. forces, with specific attention to the impact of the Bosnia deployment. The other amendment, by Pat Roberts, R-Kan., would require the president to report certain information to Congress if he deployed U.S. troops elsewhere in the former Yugoslavia or in neighboring Albania or Macedonia.

Persecution Sanctions

The Senate adopted, by voice vote, an amendment by Tim Hutchinson, R-Ark., that would deny U.S. visas to officials of foreign governments directly involved in implementing policies of religious persecution, forced abortion or sterilization, or female genital mutilation.

As originally offered, the amendment was aimed at Chinese officials involved in religious persecution or forced population control. A motion to table the proposal was rejected, 29-70. But by a vote of 99-0, Hutchinson's amendment then was modified to add genital mutilation to a list of activities that would draw sanctions, making the bill applicable to officials of any government, and restricting its application to officials directly involved in those policies. *(Votes 248, 250, p. S-39)*

The only amendment specifically aimed at a major weapons system was an effort by Feingold to cut $220 million from the $2.79 billion requested for 30 F/A-18 E and F model jet fighters. The amendment was tabled, 80-19. *(Vote 247, p. S-39)*

Among the dozens of other amendments adopted by voice vote without debate were relatively minor land transfers, funding allocations of up to several million dollars and some policy initiatives, such as the following:

● By Pete V. Domenici, R-N.M., and Tom Harkin, D-Iowa, requiring the Pentagon to report on the number of military families who receive food stamps, a number estimated to reach 12,000. The amendment would also require the Pentagon to propose options to reduce the number of soldiers on food stamps.

● By Patrick J. Leahy, D-Vt., to bar U.S. forces from training with security forces of other countries, if those foreign units have committed human rights violations.

● By Phil Gramm, R-Texas, barring states from dropping military personnel from their voting rolls because of absences due to military orders.

● By Harkin, requiring the Pentagon to provide service members and dependents with smoking cessation therapy, such as nicotine replacement gum or patches.

Lawmakers Push Pet Projects, Head For Conference

AUGUST 22 — The Pentagon is showing the strain of balancing smaller armed forces, a busier agenda, modernization plans and a flat budget, but House and Senate negotiators are unlikely to pick up any extra money as they fashion a compromise version of the defense appropriations bill next month.

At most, the conference report on the measure (HR 4103) would likely provide about $252 billion for fiscal 1999, just what the Senate passed in July and about $500 million less than President Clinton requested.

Both the House and Senate cut a few billion dollars from Clinton's request — for such things as price changes and production delays — and put some of the savings into maintenance and other accounts likely to boost combat readiness.

But even while they publicly worried over the declining defense budget, lawmakers found enough money — $4 billion in the Senate bill, by one estimate — for their own pet projects, such as cleaning up a garbage dump in Alaska, building a telemedicine network based in Hawaii and repairing a bridge to the former Philadelphia Naval Shipyard.

Though most of these special projects are modest in terms of the overall budget, a few stand out, such as a $50 million downpayment on a $1.3 billion helicopter carrier to be built in the hometown of Senate Majority Leader Trent Lott, R-Miss., and $254 million to $398 million for cargo planes built next door to Republican House Speaker Newt Gingrich's district in Georgia.

The Pentagon did not ask for the ship or the planes.

Bosnia Debate

A $252 billion bill may be a hard sell in the House, since it would include $1.86 billion Clinton requested and the Senate approved to keep U.S. troops in Bosnia as part of a NATO-led peacekeeping force. Designated emergency spending, the money would be exempt from the long-term defense budget ceiling set by the 1997 balanced-budget legislation (PL 105-33). *(1997 Almanac, p. 2-47)*

Pentagon civilians and military leaders insist the services' readiness budgets will be devastated if they have to absorb the Bosnia costs within the budget ceiling. Nevertheless, the $251 billion House version of the bill omitted the Bosnia funds.

Though efforts in the Senate to end the Bosnia operation have collapsed, the House has taken a tougher stand

Appropriations

against the mission. Moreover, many House Republicans vehemently oppose exempting any appropriations from the limits set last year.

The Bosnia deployment is one of the few major issues in the defense bill on which the House and Senate disagree. Thus, a conference report could be wrapped up by mid-September.

But GOP leaders may put off final action on the defense conference report so it can be used as a vehicle for appropriations that otherwise might face delaying tactics in the closing days of the session.

Citing flagging re-enlistment rates and anecdotal evidence of combat units short of personnel, equipment and training, Gingrich and Lott have lined up with senior members of the defense committees for higher defense budgets.

Defense Secretary William S. Cohen and other top Pentagon officials insist that U.S. forces could still win two nearly simultaneous regional wars — a central article of defense policy for decades. But they concede that some units not currently overseas show signs of losing their edge.

Joint Chiefs of Staff Chairman Gen. Henry H. Shelton estimates that it would take longer than had been assumed to wrap up the second of two regional wars, something that would raise casualties.

However, budget politics apparently rule out giving the Pentagon any more money than last year's agreement allows and Clinton has requested for fiscal 1999.

Congress is debating what to do with federal budget surpluses projected to total $1.6 trillion over the next 10 years, but the talk focuses on tax cuts and changes in the Social Security system, rather than military spending.

"We clearly have to raise the [defense spending] caps," Senate Appropriations Chairman Ted Stevens, R-Alaska, said in mid-July, "but I'm not sure we have the time in this Congress to get the attention of Congress and the administration."

Following are highlights of the House and Senate versions of the defense spending measure:

Personnel Issues

Nearly as important to many military leaders as money for the Bosnia operation is a Senate provision that would give military personnel a 3.6 percent pay raise rather than the 3.1 percent requested by Clinton.

Military pay raises lag behind those in the private sector because, by law, government pay raises are a half-percent less than an index of private-sector pay increases. Proponents of the 3.6 percent raise contend that erasing that differential might shore up sagging morale.

But a 3.6 percent pay raise for military personnel would cost about $200 million more than Clinton's budget for military pay. If Congress insists on giving civilian Pentagon employees the same raise, that would nearly double the cost.

Both versions of the bill would cut $301 million from the military payroll request because of a technical change in budget procedures. Both have made large additional cuts in the military and civilian payroll request — $435 million in the House version and $734 million in the Senate bill — because the Pentagon's work force is shrinking faster than the budget request assumed.

However, those funds have been used to pay for congressional initiatives in the bills.

Operations and Maintenance

Both bills would add hundreds of millions of dollars to various maintenance accounts intended to bolster combat readiness:

• For spare parts to keep Navy and Air Force planes flying, the House would add $214.5 million, the Senate $154 million.

• To maintain and repair facilities, the House would add $850 million, the Senate $264 million.

• For routine upkeep costs often short-changed in the budget request, the House would add $500 million and the Senate $270 million.

Because those increases would be spread throughout the military, they may have a tough time competing against narrowly targeted congressional additions to the budget that would benefit a particular contractor or base.

Both the House and Senate found other savings. Citing lower than projected fuel prices, the House cut $295 million and the Senate $454 million.

The House bill would cut an additional $215 million and the Senate version $137 million on the argument that the dollar's strength against foreign currencies would result in lower than expected operating costs for U.S. forces abroad.

The House bill would also add $300 million to the amount requested for overhauls of ships, planes and other equipment. The Senate bill adds only $16 million.

The House bill would add $60 million to the Army's operations budget for transporting combat units from their bases to a national training center at Fort Irwin, Calif. The Army planned to make units absorb these costs within their regular training budgets, but the House Appropriations Committee objected.

Also included in the House bill is $2 million to continue the Army's lease of facilities at the former George Air Force Base in Victorville, Calif., about 60 miles from Fort Irwin. Though the airbase was closed in 1992, the city began operating it as a civilian airport in 1994, and is trying to attract cargo flights. At the instigation of House Appropriations Committee member Republican Jerry Lewis of California, who represents the area, the fiscal 1996 defense appropriations bill (PL 104-61) required the Army to fly troops bound for Fort Irwin into Victorville, rather than Las Vegas, which is farther from the training center.

Ground Combat

The Army plans to pay for developing a radically new generation of lightweight tanks and other combat equipment by cutting back the amount it spends upgrading M-1 tanks and other gear currently in service.

But in its report accompanying HR 4103 (H Rept 105-591), the House Appropriations Committee contended that the plan would saddle some of the Army's first-line units with second-rate weaponry for years to come. It ordered the services to accelerate modernization of M-1 tanks, and it cut $5 million the administration requested to begin designing a new light tank.

The Senate bill approved the more austere tank upgrades the Army proposed.

Both bills approved the $313 million requested to develop a mobile artillery piece called Crusader. The House National Security and Senate Armed Services committees, which drafted the companion defense authorization bill (HR 3616), have criticized the cannon as too heavy to fit into the lightweight forces the Army hopes to field by 2025.

To continue developing the Comanche scout helicopter, the House version of the appropriations bill includes $392 million, $24 million more than Clinton requested. The Senate bill would trim $19 million from the Comanche request because of delays in the program.

Because of testing problems, the Army has deferred its plan to begin buying Land Warrior sets — computer-equipped backpacks and other high-tech gear connecting individual soldiers to a digital communications web for combat units of the future. Accordingly, both bills drop the $51 million for Land Warrior procurement that was included in the budget. The House bill would add $20 million to continue developing the system.

Both bills reject the Army's request for $25 million to begin upgrading some of its "Humvee" utility trucks. Instead, the House bill would add $46 million and the Senate bill $66 million to continue purchasing new Humvees.

Air Combat

The Senate bill approves the $2.8 billion the administration requested to buy 30 of the Navy's F/A-18 E and F model fighters. The House bill would cut three planes ($205 million) from that request, which the Navy opposes.

Both bills would approve the $1.6 billion requested to continue developing the Air Force's F-22 fighter. The Senate version would approve the $595 million requested to buy the first two production-line copies of the plane, while the House bill would trim $70 million from that amount.

For the third major jet fighter program on the Pentagon's agenda, the House bill approves the $920 million requested to develop the Joint Strike Fighter, intended to be built in three versions that would replace several 1970s-vintage Navy, Air Force and Marine Corps jets. The Senate bill would add to that amount $15 million to develop an alternative jet engine for the new plane.

The House bill would add $60 million for two F-16 fighter-bombers that were not requested.

The Air Force requested $190 million for specialized equipment to support the 21 B-2 bombers previously funded. The House bill added $86 million for several upgrades that were recommended last year by a congressionally mandated advisory panel. The Senate version cut $30 million from the $190 million request.

Both bills would include the $463 million requested for two Joint STARS radar planes designed to find ground targets far behind enemy lines. The House bill would add $72 million for components that could be used if the Pentagon decided to buy additional planes.

Naval Forces

Both bills would approve the major elements of the Navy's request for building new warships:
- $2.7 billion for three destroyers equipped with the Aegis anti-aircraft system.
- $1.5 billion for a nuclear-powered submarine plus $505 million for components to be used in future subs.
- $275 million to refuel and modernize a nuclear-powered carrier.
- $125 million for components that would be used in a new carrier. Most of the $4.6 billion total cost would be in the fiscal 2001 budget.

The Senate bill would approve the $85 million requested to design a new class of destroyer — the DD-21 — better equipped than current ships to attack distant land targets. But the House bill would approve only $16 million.

Air and Sea Transport

The Senate bill would add $50 million for components to be used in a new helicopter carrier — about the size of a World War II aircraft carrier — designed to carry nearly 2,000 Marines and as many as 30 helicopters.

The Navy has seven of these ships in service or under construction, the newest of which cost $1.3 billion. It also has five older versions which, like the new vessels, were built by Litton Industries in Lott's hometown of Pascagoula, Miss.

The Navy plans to begin overhauling the older helicopter carriers to extend their service life — work that might be done at any of several shipyards. But if new ships were built instead — as the Senate bill would require — the work would go to Pascagoula.

Both bills approve the budget's two major sealift projects:
- $639 million for an LPD-17-class transport ship designed to carry Marine combat units and the landing vessels to haul them ashore.
- $251 million for a large cargo ship intended to haul tanks and other heavy combat equipment from U.S. ports to distant trouble spots.

The Senate bill includes $611 million, as the administration requested, for seven V-22 Osprey aircraft — hybrid airplane/helicopters the Marines will use to carry troops ashore faster and farther than conventional helicopters. The House bill would add $78 million for an eighth aircraft.

The $2.6 billion requested to buy 13 additional C-17 long-range cargo planes is included in both bills.

Other Provisions

Both bills would add money for research and treatment of several diseases. Among them are breast cancer, for which the House includes $160 million and the Senate $135 million, and prostate cancer, for which the House provides $10 million and the Senate $40 million.

As it has done for years, the House bill would add funds — $34 million this time — for a program that registers military personnel willing to donate bone marrow to treat leukemia victims. The project is sponsored by House National Security Appropriations Subcommittee Chairman C.W. Bill Young, R-Fla.

To reduce the amount of new budget authority the Pentagon would need in fiscal 1999, both bills credit the Defense Department with $637 million that foreign governments are expected to buy ships the Navy has retired from service.

Each bill would further offset some of its cost by rescinding, or canceling, Pentagon appropriations made in prior years and use the money instead to cover fiscal 1999 costs. The House bill includes $268 million in rescissions, the Senate bill $70 million.

Appropriations

Conferees Leave Funding Shortfalls For Supplemental

OCTOBER 3 — The $250.5 billion defense appropriations bill that Congress cleared Sept. 29 largely conformed to President Clinton's fiscal 1999 defense budget request. But House-Senate conferees left out as much as $400 million for spare parts and repairs after Clinton announced that he would ask for at least $1 billion in supplemental spending for just such things in the name of combat readiness. The conferees found other uses for their money.

The House adopted the conference report to HR 4103 on Sept. 28 by a vote of 369-43. The Senate adopted the report Sept. 29 by a vote of 94-2, thus clearing the bill for the president. (*House vote 471, p. H-134; Senate vote 291, p. S-45*)

On Oct. 1, the companion defense authorization bill (HR 3616) was cleared for the president's signature when the Senate adopted the conference report on that measure by a vote of 96-2. (*Vote 293, p. S-45*)

The defense appropriations bill, combined with defense-related funding in other appropriations measures, would spend practically the entire amount allocated for defense in fiscal 1999 under the 1997 balanced-budget law (PL 105-33). (*1997 Almanac, p. 2-47*)

Clinton plans to send Congress a supplemental budget request including $1.9 billion for military operations in Bosnia and at least $1 billion for additional spare parts and training to beef up combat readiness.

Clinton wants Congress to designate the Bosnia money as emergency funding exempt from the spending caps. He said he would pay for his proposed increases with cuts in other parts of the defense budget.

Some deficit-minded House Republicans are demanding that any additional defense appropriations be offset with spending reductions to stay within the spending caps.

Key Pentagon allies on Capitol Hill insist that the Defense Department needs a larger infusion of readiness funds — at least $2 billion to $3 billion — and that the added money must be over and above the limit set by the budget legislation. This would set the stage for a large defense budget increase in fiscal 2000 that would shred the defense budget ceilings.

The Joint Chiefs of Staff recommended such an increase at a hearing Sept. 29. Several of the service chiefs said that without a clear political commitment in the form of stepped up defense spending, the military could deteriorate within five years into the ineffectual "hollow force" of the late 1970s.

The chiefs said they need about $20 billion more in fiscal 2000 than the $270 billion budget that Clinton had planned to send Capitol Hill next February. The increase would have to be sustained in subsequent budgets, they said, to reverse a decline in combat readiness caused by trying to do too much with not enough money.

They said they would use any additional appropriations to increase pay and pensions, reduce the backlog of maintenance on weapons, facilities and housing, and accelerate the purchase of new equipment to replace overaged gear that costs too much and takes too much work to keep in service.

Several members of the Armed Services Committee, who had tried in vain for several years to increase military spending above Clinton's requests, welcomed the chiefs' public support, but bitterly complained that it had been too long in coming.

Budget Gamesmanship

Anticipating Clinton's supplemental budget request, House-Senate conferees on the defense appropriations bill left out some funds that both the House and Senate had planned to add to Clinton's February budget request.

For instance, after the Pentagon acknowledged that it had not budgeted enough money for aircraft spare parts, the House version of the bill added $215 million to the administration's request, and the Senate version added $154 million. The conference report includes no additional funding for aircraft spares.

Similarly, the conference report added only $101 million to the amount requested for the overhaul of ships, planes and other equipment, much less than Congress typically supplements. The House version of the appropriations bill would have added $300 million to the maintenance request.

"Without the supplemental [request], this bill will not be adequate," said John P. Murtha of Pennsylvania, the ranking Democrat on the House National Security Appropriations Subcommittee.

And the conferees found a way to pay for some of those projects with across-the-board cuts in the budget request, which, they said, reflected changing economic conditions.

For instance, they cut $401 million because of lower-than-anticipated inflation, $502 million because fuel prices are lower than the budget assumed, and $194 million because the dollar's strength against foreign currencies would reduce the cost of goods and services purchased by U.S. forces stationed overseas.

As usual, conferees found a couple of billion dollars for members' pet projects, including $400 million for six C-130 cargo planes built next to the district of House Speaker Newt Gingrich, R-Ga.

Policy Differences

The conferees dropped from the final bill a House provision, sponsored by David E. Skaggs, D-Colo., that would have required the president to obtain congressional authorization before sending U.S. forces on an offensive military operation. The Clinton administration had threatened to veto the bill because of the Skaggs provision.

Also dropped was a Senate provision, sponsored by Tim Hutchinson, R-Ark., that would have denied U.S. visas to Chinese officials associated with policies of compulsory abortion and religious persecution. The provision was one of several anti-China bills that have had mixed success in Congress. (*Background, 1997 Almanac, p. 8-38*)

The conference report included, in modified form, a Senate provision, sponsored by Pat Roberts, R-Kan., that would bar the deployment of U.S. forces to Yugoslavia, Albania or Macedonia — other than the small observation force currently in Macedonia — unless the president sends Congress a report outlining the anticipated scope, duration and cost of the mission. The provision allows the president to waive the reporting requirement in an emergency.

Defense Spending

Conference agreement on HR 4103 — H Rept 105-746, as cleared by the Senate on Sept. 29 and signed by the president Oct. 17 (PL 105-262). *(Budget authority, in thousands of dollars.)*

	Fiscal 1998 Appropriation	Fiscal 1999 Clinton Request	House Bill	Senate Bill	Conference Report
Personnel					
Army	$ 20,452,057	$ 21,002,051	$ 20,908,851	$ 20,822,051	$ 20,841,687
Navy	16,493,518	16,613,053	16,560,253	16,532,153	16,570,754
Marines	6,137,899	6,272,089	6,241,189	6,253,189	6,263,387
Air Force	17,102,120	17,311,683	17,201,583	17,205,660	17,211,987
National Guard and reserves	9,284,911	9,578,210	9,639,935	9,673,210	9,719,751
Subtotal	$ 69,470,505	$ 70,777,086	$ 70,551,811	$ 70,486,263	$ 70,607,566
Operations and Maintenance					
Army	16,754,306	17,223,063	16,936,503	17,212,463	17,185,623
Navy	21,617,766	21,877,202	21,638,999	21,813,315	21,872,399
Marines	2,372,635	2,523,703	2,585,118	2,576,190	2,578,718
Air Force	18,492,883	19,127,004	19,024,233	19,064,941	19,021,045
Defense agencies	10,369,740	10,750,601	10,804,542	10,259,231	10,914,076
National Guard and reserves	9,310,912	9,521,298	9,650,898	9,766,298	9,810,398
Environmental restoration	1,296,937	1,259,431	1,224,431	1,265,431	1,268,431
Humanitarian assistance	47,130	63,311	56,111	50,000	50,000
Former Soviet threat reduction	382,200	442,400	417,400	440,400	440,400
Overseas contingencies	1,884,000	746,900	746,900	746,900	439,400
Barracks improvements	360,000	0	850,000	0	455,000
Other	6,952	7,324	7,324	337,144	7,324
Subtotal	$ 82,895,461	$ 83,542,237	$ 83,942,459	$ 83,532,313	$ 84,042,814
By transfer	(150,000)	(150,000)	(150,000)	(−129,820)	(150,000)
Procurement					
Army	7,123,765	8,172,985	8,254,786	8,475,830	8,568,384
Navy	19,414,980	19,414,227	19,228,995	19,240,134	19,345,745
Marines	482,398	745,858	812,618	954,177	874,216
Air Force	15,866,628	17,474,826	17,999,404	17,474,647	17,505,242
National Guard and reserves	653,000	0	120,000	500,000	352,000
Defense agencies	2,106,444	2,041,650	2,055,432	1,932,250	1,944,833
Subtotal	$ 45,647,215	$ 47,849,546	$ 48,471,235	$ 48,577,038	$ 48,590,420
Research, development and testing					
Army	5,156,507	4,780,545	4,967,446	4,891,640	5,031,788
Navy	8,115,686	8,108,923	8,297,986	8,215,519	8,636,649
Air Force	14,507,804	13,598,093	13,577,441	13,693,153	13,758,811
Defense agencies	10,111,327	9,591,016	9,075,169	9,307,259	9,329,402
Subtotal	$ 37,891,324	$ 36,078,577	$ 35,918,042	$ 36,107,571	$ 36,756,650
Other programs					
General provisions	−2,418,900	71,000	−1,100,320	−1,305,400	−2,446,059
Revolving and management funds	2,046,900	549,666	767,866	764,066	802,866
Chemical agents destruction	600,700	855,100	796,100	780,150	780,150
Drug interdiction	712,882	727,582	764,595	742,582	735,582
Inspector general	138,380	132,064	132,064	132,064	132,064
Defense health program	10,369,075	10,055,822	10,127,622	10,337,322	10,149,872
Subtotal	$ 11,449,037	$ 12,391,234	$ 11,487,927	$ 11,450,784	$ 10,154,475
Related agencies					
CIA retirement, disability	196,900	201,500	201,500	201,500	201,500
Intelligence community management	121,080	138,623	136,123	134,623	129,123
Other	37,000	20,000	18,000	28,000	28,000
Subtotal	$ 354,980	$ 360,123	$ 355,623	$ 364,123	$ 358,623
Emergency funds		*1,858,600**		*1,858,600**	
GRAND TOTAL	$ 247,708,522	$ 252,857,403	$ 250,727,097	$ 252,376,692	$ 250,510,548

* *For Bosnia mission*

SOURCE: House and Senate Appropriations committees

Appropriations

Supplemental Defense Bill Includes Boosts For Anti-Missile Systems, Intelligence

OCTOBER 17 — Less than three weeks after sending President Clinton a $251 billion defense appropriations bill for fiscal 1999, Congress has agreed with the White House on about $9 billion in supplemental spending for defense-related items, including up to $1 billion for anti-missile defense and up to $2 billion for intelligence operations.

The added spending is roughly double the supplemental defense funds Clinton asked for.

Details of the mammoth bill (HR 4328) were sketchy a day after Clinton and congressional leaders announced the package, and some spending was only vaguely related to the Defense Department, including money for U.S. embassy security and for drug interdiction by police agencies.

However, the bill marked the first time since 1985 that the Pentagon would receive an inflation-adjusted budget increase.

GOP leaders cited the additional funding to buttress their argument that Clinton has undermined national security by reducing the size of the military too much, sending it overseas too often and cutting its budget too much.

Most of Clinton's roughly $4.5 billion supplemental request was incorporated into the bill, including $1.9 billion to cover the cost of keeping U.S. forces in Bosnia as part of a NATO-led peacekeeping operation and $1.1 billion to fix the Year 2000 problem in Pentagon computers.

Also reportedly included in the bill, as Clinton requested, was about $254 million to repair flood-damaged U.S. bases in Korea.

To relieve strains on combat-readiness and morale outlined to Congress late last month by the Joint Chiefs of Staff, the bill includes the $1 billion Clinton requested for spare parts, equipment overhauls, facility repairs, recruiting and routine base operations.

In addition to the anti-missile defense increase, pushed by Senate Appropriations Committee Chairman Ted Stevens, R-Alaska, and the extra money for intelligence, demanded by House Speaker Newt Gingrich, R-Ga., the bill reportedly includes two other initiatives promoted by Republican leaders:
- $210 million for the Coast Guard, at Stevens' behest.
- $200 million for repairs to bases in Mississippi and other states damaged by Hurricane Georges, a request by Senate Majority Leader Trent Lott, R-Miss.

The final version of the bill did not include a provision proposed by John P. Murtha of Pennsylvania, the senior Democrat on the House National Security Appropriations Subcommittee, that would have partly reversed a 1986 change in the military retirement system that is a major source of discontent among military personnel.

While those who joined the service before 1986 will collect 50 percent of their basic pay if they retire after 20 years, those who joined in 1986 and since will receive only 40 percent of basic pay and will receive less generous cost-of-living adjustments.

Although members of the Joint Chiefs of Staff urged that the disparity be eliminated, members of the Senate Armed Services Committee objected to so radical a change in policy on such short notice and without hearings.

Anti-Missile Defenses

House National Security Appropriations Chairman C.W. Bill Young, R-Fla., said Oct. 15 that he favored giving the Pentagon considerable flexibility in allocating the money the bill would add to the fiscal 1999 budget for anti-missile programs.

As much as $150 million of that total might be allocated to the national missile defense program, which is intended to develop a system that could protect U.S. territory against a small number of attacking missiles.

Personnel and Readiness

The conference report added $202 million to the budget request for a 3.6 percent military pay raise, instead of the 3.1 percent pay increase in the budget request. The administration now supports the larger raise.

The conferees warned that the dissatisfaction many in the military feel with their pay and quality of life includes a perception that key fringe benefits, such as pensions and medical care, are being eroded by the budget squeeze. So they included in the conference report a provision, sponsored by C.W. Bill Young, R-Fla., chairman of the House Appropriations National Security subcommittee, requiring the Pentagon to review the adequacy of overall military compensation and include any recommendations for change in the fiscal 2000 budget request to be sent to Congress early next year.

To reduce the backlog of buildings overdue for maintenance and repair, the conferees added $455 million to the bill, all but $5 million of which was specified for quality-of-life projects such as improvements to barracks.

They also added $300 million to the bill for operating costs of military bases, a budget account that routinely is shortchanged in budget requests.

The conferees expressed "significant concern" over the impact on military readiness of Defense Secretary William S. Cohen's plan to save $6 billion a year by allowing private contractors to bid on jobs at military bases currently performed by 150,000 civilian federal employees. They ordered a report detailing the criteria that would be used to decide which jobs could be contracted out.

In some cases, the conferees' skepticism went further: They demanded three months' notice before the Penta-

Defense

However, the money would be used to hedge against possible problems in the development program, not to speed up deployment.

Under the current plan, four flight tests of the system are scheduled between the summer of 1999 and the summer of 2000. If a decision to deploy the nationwide defense is made in mid-2000, the plan is to field the system by 2003.

Senior Pentagon officials, including Air Force Lt. Gen. Lester Lyles, who heads the anti-missile effort, insisted to the Senate Armed Services Committee Oct. 2 that it would be impossible to accelerate the nationwide defense program which, they said, already is on a very ambitious schedule.

But additional funds could be used to schedule additional ground tests of key components of the system.

Other potential uses of the extra anti-missile money include:
- $135 million for the Navy's "theater-wide" system, a ship-based defense against long-range missiles.
- $132 million for the Army's long-range THAAD (Theater High-Altitude Area Defense) and associated radar.
- $78 million for the short-range PAC-3, a modification of the Patriot air defense system used by U.S. forces during the 1991 war with Iraq.

Anti-Terrorism and Intelligence

The omnibus spending bill would fully fund President Clinton's $1.8 billion request for rebuilding U.S. embassies in Kenya and Tanzania as well as upgrading the security of others worldwide.

The request called for spending $200 million to re-establish U.S. diplomatic operations in temporary quarters and to begin building new embassies in Dar-es-Salaam, Tanzania, and Nairobi, Kenya, both hit by bombs Aug. 7.

The package also includes $1.2 billion to improve security at diplomatic facilities around the world, adding more guards, as well as video cameras and other equipment.

The remaining money would cover the Pentagon's cost of responding to the two embassy attacks and for other security-related efforts as well as to increase security training, provide disaster-related assistance to Kenya and Tanzania and expand the FBI's roster of anti-terrorism response teams.

The administration originally planned to concentrate funding on foreign outposts it considered most vulnerable. But Harold Rogers of Kentucky, chairman of the House Appropriations Commerce-Justice-State Subcommittee, objected along with other Republicans, saying a wider range of facilities needed to be upgraded.

The omnibus bill also includes up to $2 billion sought by Gingrich, which lawmakers of both parties said was for the Central Intelligence Agency and other intelligence agencies. The money would be given out over several years.

"I'm very satisfied this bill does an extraordinary job of meeting their needs. . . . This basically culminates several debates that we've been having," said House Intelligence Chairman Porter J. Goss, R-Fla., in an Oct. 15 interview.

Although spending levels are classified, the fiscal 1999 intelligence authorization conference report (HR 3694 — H Rept 105-780) that cleared Congress this month is believed to call for spending at a level slightly higher than the $26.7 billion level enacted for fiscal 1998.

Sources said the omnibus spending bill includes money to address recent recommendations from two independent panels that examined national security matters. The first panel, chaired by retired Adm. David Jeremiah, looked into the CIA's failure to predict nuclear tests by India in May.

The Jeremiah panel identified a series of structural weaknesses, including a lack of trained and skilled analysts to sift through intelligence data, a shortage of human agents on the ground and a lack of coordination between different agencies.

The other panel, led by former Defense Secretary Donald H. Rumsfeld, warned in July that foreign governments are becoming increasingly adept at concealing nuclear missiles and nuclear, biological and chemical weapons programs from satellites and other intelligence gathering.

---

gon takes steps to privatize jobs at three Army arsenals in Arkansas, Illinois and New York.

They also added $21 million to the budget request to forestall a planned reduction in civilian jobs at a Marine Corps maintenance depot in Barstow, Calif., a city represented by House Appropriations Committee member Jerry Lewis, R-Ca.

Anti-Missile Defense

The conferees approved $3.45 billion of the $3.59 billion requested for the Pentagon's anti-missile defense program. The biggest cut was $376 million — almost half the $822 million Clinton requested — from the Army's THAAD system, intended to protect U.S. troops and allies overseas against long-range missiles. All five THAAD flight tests have failed.

The conferees also approved:
- $951 million, as requested, to continue developing a system that would protect U.S. territory against a small number of attacking missiles;
- $338 million, $148 million more than requested, to continue developing a long-range, Navy anti-missile system.
- $74 million more than requested to accelerate development of a satellite armed with an anti-missile laser.

Outside the anti-missile program's budget, the conferees approved $267 million of the $292 million requested for an Air Force effort to mount an anti-missile laser in the nose of a Boeing 747 cargo jet.

Ground and Air Combat

The conferees kept on track the Army's top two weapons priorities, approving $368 million, as requested, to continue developing the Comanche stealth helicopter and $317 million for the Crusader mobile cannon.

The conference report makes only

Appropriations

minor changes in funding requests for the Pentagon's three major combat airplane programs, approving:

• $581 million — $14 million less than requested — for the first two production-line versions of the Air Force's F-22 fighter.

• $2.8 billion for 30 F/A-18 E and F model Navy fighters, a reduction of $15 million from the budget request.

• $927 million to continue developing the Joint Strike Fighter, intended to be built in three versions to replace 1970s-vintage planes currently used by the Navy, Air Force and Marine Corps. This is an increase of almost $8 million above the request.

The conference report also halved what the House bill included for several aircraft programs: $30 million for a single Air Force F-16 fighter instead of two for $60 million; $50 million of the $86 million the House added for upgrading B-2 stealth bombers and $36 million for components in case the Pentagon decides to buy another Joint STARS radar plane. The House wanted $72 million for components of two planes.

Naval Forces

The conference report included $2.67 billion for three Navy destroyers equipped with the Aegis anti-aircraft system, $5 million less than was requested.

Both chambers had approved the other major shipbuilding requests:

• $1.5 billion for a new nuclear-powered submarine, plus $505 million for the nuclear reactor and other components to be used in another sub slated for funding in fiscal 2001.

• $275 million to refuel one of the nuclear-powered carriers currently in service plus $125 million for components to be used in a new carrier — the 10th ship of the *Nimitz* class. Most of the $4.6 billion cost would be included in the fiscal 2001 budget.

The conference report includes only $105 million of the roughly $180 million requested to design a new aircraft carrier — cheaper to operate than the *Nimitz* class — the first of which would enter service in 2013.

On the other hand, the conferees approved the $85 million requested to design a new destroyer.

They approved $278 million instead of the $179 million requested to continue developing and installing in warships a "cooperative engagement capability" — a digital communications network over which all the ships and planes in a force could exchange data about the location of enemy units.

Air and Sea Transport

A seemingly minor addition of $45 million to the administration's budget request lays the groundwork for a major additional cost in some future budget.

The funds in the fiscal 1999 conference report are for components that would be used by Litton Industries to build a new helicopter carrier in Pascagoula, Miss., the hometown of Senate Majority Leader Trent Lott, R-Miss. The Navy has seven of these ships, the newest of which cost $1.3 billion.

The planned carrier would replace an older ship the Navy had planned to refurbish at the cost of about $1 billion.

Both the House and Senate had approved the amount requested ($639 million) for a transport ship to carry a Marine Corps landing force and a cargo ship to carry the tanks and other equipment of a U.S.-based Army unit.

Both also had approved the $2.6 billion requested for 13 C-17 widebody cargo jets.

The conference report approved $611 million for seven C-22 Osprey tiltrotor aircraft to be used by the Marines as troop carriers. The House bill had added $86 million for an eighth. ◆

Mixed Bag of Amendments Gives District of Columbia 'Lemons ... With the Sweets'

The enactment of the fiscal 1999 omnibus appropriations bill (HR 4328) ended another year of divisiveness over spending for the District of Columbia.

SUMMARY

Appropriators folded the provisions — a federal payment to the city of $494.6 million, and a separate $125 million payment to fund the city's revitalization plan — into the omnibus package after action on the separate fiscal 1999 D.C. measure (HR 4380) stalled.

The D.C. bill had moved smoothly out of the House and Senate Appropriations committees, but it ran into trouble on the House floor. There, Republicans pushed through a number of legislative riders that were blasted by Democrats. The House passed the bill, 214-206, largely along partisan lines, but Senate leaders, wary of the controversy surrounding the measure, never brought it to the floor.

Among the amendments attached by House Republicans were three that the Clinton administration had previously stated would spark a veto. The amendments sought to bar unmarried couples from adopting children, to establish a school voucher program, and to prohibit the city

Box Score

• **Bill:** HR 4328 — PL 105-277.

• **House action:** The House adopted the conference report (H Rept 105-825) on HR 4328, 333-95, on Oct. 20. It passed HR 4380 (H Rept 105-670) on Aug. 7 by a vote of 214-206.

• **Senate action:** The Senate cleared the bill, 65-29, on Oct. 21. It did not act on the committee-approved version of S 2333 (S Rept 105-254).

• **Presidential action:** Clinton signed the bill Oct. 21.

from supporting groups that conducted needle exchange programs, in which clean hypodermic needles are given to people, often drug addicts,

District of Columbia

to prevent needle sharing and stem the spread of AIDS.

The first two provisions were dropped in the omnibus bill, but the needle-exchange restrictions survived. That led the sole operation that conducts a needle-exchange program in the city — the Whitman-Walker Clinic — to turn its program over to a newly formed corporation to protect the funding the AIDS clinic receives from the city.

In addition to the partisan disputes, city officials unsuccessfully fought language that repeals a city ordinance requiring most new city government workers to live in D.C. Members from the Virginia and Maryland suburbs insisted that the ordinance be repealed.

Still, city officials praised a number of other parts of the bill, including $25 million for "management reforms," $3.24 million for raises for city firefighters, and $25 million for a subway station to serve a proposed convention center.

Chambers Differ Over Economic Development, Transportation

JULY 25 — So far, the road appears unusually smooth for the fiscal 1999 spending bills for the District of Columbia, despite clear differences between the House and Senate bills over funding levels for infrastructure improvements and other projects.

The Senate measure (S 2333) was approved quickly and with near unanimity by the Senate Appropriations Committee July 21. The panel voted 27-1 to approve a $6.8 billion spending plan for the nation's capital, and to make a federal contribution of slightly less than $482 million in lieu of property taxes the city cannot collect on federal property. Patrick J. Leahy, D-Vt., was the dissenter.

The $6.8 billion House bill, which includes a $430 million federal contribution, was approved 6-4 along party lines on July 24 by the House Appropriations District of Columbia subcommittee.

The House panel's top Democrat, James P. Moran of Virginia, criticized the measure for what he said was lack of funding for foster care and anti-drug initiatives. At Moran's insistence, however, the panel agreed by voice vote to increase by $20.4 million funding for the District's public schools.

"I'm glad that we made a little progress, but it was insufficient progress," Moran said after the meeting. "It is still a bad bill."

The House bill would fund a number of projects — including $3 million to improve the Washington Marina, $8.5 million for a U.S. Park Service helicopter and $3.3 million to boost salaries of the city's firefighters.

The Senate bill includes some choice projects for the District, but appropriators also took steps to make clear they play a significant, actually determinant, role in running the city.

Unlike the House bill, the Senate measure includes $75 million to improve the city's roads and bridges, and would allow the city to use $25 million of that to expand a Washington Metropolitan Area Transit Authority station to serve a proposed convention center.

House Subcommittee Chairman Charles H. Taylor, R-N.C., included in his bill only $1 million in funding for the Metro subway project.

Senate D.C. Appropriations Subcommittee Chairman Lauch Faircloth, R-N.C., included $7.1 million to expand Boys Town USA facilities in the city. The money would be used to build, and operate for one year, an emergency short-term housing center for girls and four long-term homes. The House bill includes $4 million for Boys Town facilities, though $3 million in matching funds would be required.

Much of the debate so far has surrounded the city's Economic Development Corporation. Faircloth declined to include $50 million for the corporation, choosing instead to place in the bill $500,000 to study the issue and $25 million to fund continued overhauls of city management.

"That is a reasonable way to create momentum," Faircloth said of the study. The House bill has no such funds.

Administration Objections

Moran criticized House Republicans for not including funds for the development agency, and the Clinton administration said in a July 21 policy statement that the corporation "is essential in order to ensure effective management coordination and oversight of the projects in the District."

The administration also opposed a provision, which is in both bills, to prohibit the city from using federal or local funds to cover the cost of abortion procedures for employees.

Meanwhile, Eleanor Holmes Norton, the city's non-voting congressional delegate, spoke out against a provision in the Senate bill to repeal a D.C. law requiring new city employees to be D.C. residents. "The entirely reasonable residency law passed by the council would have no effect on the current work force and contains broad waiver language ensuring that the District can select the best employees," she said in a statement.

Still, Democrats praised Republicans for avoiding issues, such as changes to wage requirements on some public projects, that in recent years have bogged down the bill.

The debate over District spending is heating up as the city experiences a tremendous economic spurt. The city is expected to finish this year with a $254 million surplus, according to Senate Appropriations Committee documents. Faircloth said "a financial recovery is under way" in a city that "had spun into a chaotic condition."

Norton said the economic good times should bode well for the city.

"The committee and Congress want to avoid the impression that no matter how well or poorly the District does, it will get the same response from Congress," she said.

School Voucher Fight Likely As Bill Heads For House Floor

AUGUST 1 — Aside from minor skirmishes, the debate over the fiscal 1999 appropriations bill for the District of Columbia, normally a magnet for controversy, has been relatively mild so far this year.

The House Appropriations Committee on July 30 approved a $486 mil-

Appropriations

lion fiscal 1999 D.C. spending bill by voice vote. The committee even accepted a number of provisions requested by congressional Democrats and the Clinton administration. Moreover, a mixture of members from both parties defeated or watered down the most divisive amendments that were offered.

The harmony may end the week of Aug. 3, as the bill heads to the House floor, where some Republicans are expected to push a controversial amendment to provide school vouchers to District residents.

The vouchers, which sent the fiscal 1998 spending bill spiraling into partisanship, could be used by District residents to send their children to any private or public schools. That provision was dropped at the end of last year's legislative session, smoothing the path to enactment. *(1997 Almanac, p. 9-27)*

Since taking control of the Congress in 1995, Republicans have made vouchers a main element of their education platform. Republicans argue that vouchers would give parents, especially low-income parents, more control over their children's education. They point to the problem-plagued Washington, D.C., schools as a prime example of a system that could benefit from competition. Democrats counter that vouchers would rob resources, and the best students, from public schools.

Beyond Vouchers

There are other warning signs that fighting over the D.C. appropriations bill will intensify. City advocates are criticizing the committee's refusal to allow money to be spent on the city's 37 advisory neighborhood commissions. They also oppose inclusion of a provision in the bill that would mandate a study of the city's medical malpractice laws.

The spending bill would cover the costs of the District's courts and prisons, as well as a host of other initiatives. The committee increased total spending in the bill by $56 million during its four-hour meeting — thanks to an amendment by Charles H. Taylor, R-N.C., the chairman of the D.C. Appropriations Subcommittee, that would provide funding for a number of Democratic priorities.

Taylor's amendment added $24 million for a Washington Metropolitan Area Transit Authority station to serve a proposed convention center, and $21 million to repair and maintain the city's streets and bridges. It would provide $7 million for environmental studies and cleanup at the Lorton Correctional Complex in Virginia, and $4 million to fund drug testing and other programs for parolees and people on probation.

Democrats spent no time debating the amendment, helping to pass it by voice vote as quickly as Taylor could explain it. And though it was the most substantial of seven amendments offered, the panel spent much more time on most of the others.

The longest debate was over an amendment by Steny H. Hoyer, D-Md., to repeal a D.C. law requiring most new city government workers to live in the city.

Eleanor Holmes Norton, the Democrat who serves as the District's nonvoting delegate, defended the residency requirement in a letter to committee Chairman Robert L. Livingston, R-La., arguing that the city should not be forced to employ people who contribute little to its economy. Hoyer dismissed the law as divisive and said it does not take into account high housing costs in the District. The panel adopted the amendment, 24-20.

The debate, however, showcased a philosophical flip-flop, as some committee Republicans criticized Hoyer for seeking to interfere with the city's "home rule." That is the same argument Democrats often use when GOP members seek to mandate social policies in the city.

"You will take any argument and turn it into what you want to say," said Julian C. Dixon, D-Calif.

The committee defeated, by voice vote, Kansas Republican Todd Tiahrt's amendment to prohibit couples that are not married or related by blood from adopting children in the city. While some Democrats said the amendment was aimed at homosexual couples, Chet Edwards, D-Texas, pointed out it would prevent a pair of nuns from adopting.

Tiahrt then offered an amendment to prohibit the city from using federal or local funds on needle exchange programs. Moran successfully narrowed the scope of the amendment, convincing the committee to vote, by a 24-15 tally, to remove restrictions on local funds before passing it by voice vote.

It was one sign that committee members may want to avoid a repeat of last year's showdown.

"The District of Columbia appropriations bill is never easy to enact; it always seems to be the most contentious," said James P. Moran of Virginia, the top Democrat on the subcommittee that handles the bill. "This year may be different."

Vouchers, Other Issues Push Parties Into Confrontation

AUGUST 8 — The weeks of good will and collegiality over the fiscal 1999 spending bill (HR 4380) for the District of Columbia came to a screeching halt Aug. 6 as social ideologies burst back into the debate, bringing end-of-session tensions to the surface and clouding the measure's future.

After an almost 10-hour debate that included angry outbursts and party-line votes on Republican amendments — including one to add school vouchers — the House voted 214-206 to pass the bill at nearly 1 a.m. on Aug. 7. *(Vote 416, p. H-118)*

Action on the $491 million spending bill sets the stage for a veto showdown with President Clinton if the most controversial provisions remain in the bill through House-Senate conference committee. The Senate has not yet acted on its bill (S 2333), which does not include many of the divisive provisions now in the House bill.

The breakdown was no surprise, as House conservatives had long signaled they planned to resurrect a number of social policy priorities. But the intensity of the debate seemed overblown to some who said Congress should be able to quickly dispose of the smallest of its 13 appropriations bills.

"Why go through this bruising battle of attaching these amendments only to remove them later?" Tony P. Hall, D-Ohio, asked, describing a process that has plagued D.C. bills in previous years.

The debate was capped by an aggressive exchange of finger-pointing between House Speaker Newt Gingrich, R-Ga., and Eleanor Holmes Norton, the city's Democratic, nonvoting delegate, over school vouchers.

Just before midnight, Gingrich appeared on the floor to defend a Republican amendment to provide school vouchers to about 2,000 D.C. children. Parents could use the vouchers to send their children to the private or public schools of their choice.

The amendment, one of three that had drawn veto threats from the Clinton administration earlier in the week, was approved 214-208. *(Vote 411, p. H-116)*

Republicans have made vouchers a core point of their education platform, arguing that they would give educational opportunities to children of all income classes. Critics say vouchers would steal students and funding from struggling public schools. After debating the merits and drawbacks of vouchers, lawmakers got personal.

"You're denying the children of this District money," Gingrich said, pointing his finger straight at Norton. "They are desperate to leave the schools you have trapped them in."

Gingrich accused Norton and other Democrats of bowing to teachers' unions, which oppose vouchers, and left the podium to a standing ovation from dozens of Republicans who had gathered to watch his angry, rousing two-and-a-half-minute speech.

Norton rushed to the podium to respond, speaking slowly and sharply as she argued for local control.

"This member got 90 percent of the vote in the District of Columbia and does not have to answer to unions anymore than she has to answer to you," she said, staring at Gingrich.

Other Amendments

The confrontation ended a debate that included consideration of more than a dozen amendments to a bill that would fund the city's courts and jails and provide money for a number of other initiatives that have drawn praise from those representing the city.

It would allow the city to spend up to $25 million for a train station to serve a proposed convention center, increase the salaries of D.C. firefighters and make $21 million in street and bridge repairs.

Before it arrived on the floor, the bill also included a number of contro-

D.C. Spending

District of Columbia portion of the fiscal 1999 omnibus spending law (HR 4328 — PL 105-277) signed by the president on Oct. 21. (Budget authority, in thousands of dollars.)

	Fiscal 1998 Appropriation	Fiscal 1999 Clinton Request	House Bill	Senate Bill	Final Bill
Total Federal Funds	$533,000	$486,200	$491,181	$481,800	$494,590
Total D.C. Budget	$4,962,967	$6,767,680	$6,794,938	$6,767,680	$6,790,169

SOURCE: House Appropriations Committee

versial provisions. It would prevent the city from using funds on abortion services in most cases or on a lawsuit to give the city's congressional representatives the right to vote on bills on the floor, and it would repeal a city law requiring most new city employees to live in the district.

When it hit the floor, the GOP led efforts to shoot down requests by Norton to remove some spending restrictions in the bill, then offered their own amendments. The House voted 250-169 to prevent city funding of needle-exchange programs, adding to a provision prohibiting the use of federal funds for such purposes. *(Vote 412, p. H-116)*

Steve Largent, R-Okla., pushed through, 227-192, an amendment to bar unrelated, unmarried couples from adopting children. *(Vote 414, p. H-118)*

While Democrats argued the GOP amendments would lead Clinton to veto the bill, Republicans said they were fulfilling their duty to oversee the city.

"Sometimes you have to come to a point where tough love is the message you send," said Todd Tiahrt, R-Kan.

D.C. Funding Rolled Into Omnibus Package

OCTOBER 24 — Advocates for the District of Columbia had mixed reactions to the final fiscal 1999 appropriations for the city, as increased spending for a number of programs was countered by complaints that Congress has once again hampered the city's ability to make its own decisions.

The bill, which was rolled into the omnibus spending measure (HR 4328) signed by President Clinton on Oct. 21, calls for a $494.6 million federal payment to the city. The funding represented a $360 million decrease from last year, but that was because payments to the city's correctional facilities are now included in the spending bill for the departments of Commerce, Justice and State, and a $125 million appropriation to fund the city's revitalization plan was included elsewhere in the catchall bill.

The city's representatives had little complaint about funding levels. But "serious violations of home rule remain in the bill," said Eleanor Holmes Norton, a Democrat who serves as the city's non-voting House delegate. She characterized the bill as having "lemons in there with the sweets."

In recent years the District spending bill has been used by conservatives in the House to promote their social policy agenda on issues from school choice to abortion. This year was no different, as the House, after 10 hours of debate, included a wide range of amendments that had nothing to do with funding the nation's capital. By the time the House voted on Aug. 7, largely along party lines, to approve the bill, it included a trio of GOP-sponsored policy riders that Clinton said would provoke a veto and several other provisions that city officials had blasted.

Two of the items that Clinton said would cause a veto — a provision to bar

Appropriations

unmarried couples from adopting children and another to establish a school voucher program to allow residents to attend the public or private schools of their choice — were removed in the last stages of negotiations over the omnibus bill. A provision to prevent the city from using its funds to support needle-exchange programs, or to give money to groups that conduct such programs, was kept in the bill.

Republican supporters of that provision said there is no proof that such programs reduce the rates of disease transmission, and argued they condone illegal drug use. The provision forced the Whitman-Walker Clinic, a nonprofit AIDS treatment center, to privatize its needle-exchange program.

The bill blocks $573,000 in funding for the city's Advisory Neighborhood Commissions that appropriators initially included, but city officials were pleased that the funding could be available if steps are taken to prevent abuses.

City representatives were not able to win battles over a number of other provisions in the bill, including:

● A repeal of a city ordinance requiring most new District government workers to live in the city. With no commuter tax on workers who live in the Maryland or Virginia suburbs, city officials say the ordinance is a matter of fairness. But House members from the two states pushed through an amendment to repeal the ordinance.

● A prohibition on using any federal or city funds to pay for abortion services, unless a woman's life is in danger, or in cases of rape and incest. Norton fought unsuccessfully for compromise language to allow the city to fund abortions for low-income women in certain cases.

● Language preventing the city from using its funds to support an ongoing lawsuit to win voting representation in the House, and prohibiting the city from entering into a contingency fee agreement with private lawyers to sue tobacco companies. Many states have sued the industry to recover Medicaid and other health care costs. The bill also blocks the use of city funds to hold a ballot initiative on the legalization of marijuana.

"What kind of dictatorship is this?" asked Paul Strauss, one of the city's non-voting, elected representatives in the Senate. ". . . The omnibus process really stole what little power we have to change things."

Despite the policy riders, city officials were pleased with a number of other aspects of the bill. It includes $25 million for "management reforms," such as new communications equipment and additional emergency medical staff; $3.24 million for raises for city firefighters; $25 million for an expanded Metro train station to serve a proposed convention center at Mount Vernon Square; and $7 million for environmental studies at the Lorton Correctional Complex. It also includes millions for an array of projects — including $700,000 to establish an American music museum and $1 million for improvements at the Georgetown Waterfront Park.

Norton and others have criticized an $8.5 million appropriation for a helicopter for the U.S. Park Police, arguing that it is a regional benefit that should come out of the larger Interior Department budget.

A separate $125 million appropriation for the revitalization plan in the omnibus bill was a welcome sight to the city officials. Among other things, that money would fund $50 million in road and bridge repairs and $20 million to help ensure the city's computers are ready for the year 2000.

The D.C. bill came quietly out of the Senate Appropriations Committee in July, but stalled in that chamber after the House included the controversial provisions. With the threat of a veto and Democrats promising to offer a long list of their own initiatives, it became clear by early September that the bill would not be able to succeed on its own. ◆

Energy-Water Spending Bill Not Last Word in Dispute Over TVA Funding

Two weeks after President Clinton signed into law a $20.9 billion energy and water development package, Congress was back for a second big gulp of funds, adding $800 million more to such programs in the omnibus appropriations bill (HR 4328).

That two weeks meant all the difference for the federal subsidy for non-power activities of the Tennessee Valley Authority (TVA). The $50 million was zeroed out in HR 4060, as demanded by the House, but promptly restored in HR 4328.

House conferees, at least initially, had prevailed in negotiations over the TVA subsidy, even though the Senate-passed bill (S 2138) provided $70 million and the administration had requested $77 million for such agency activities as flood control, navigation, dam maintenance and environmental initiatives. In the end, however, TVA advocates in the Senate — including appropriators Mitch McConnell, R-Ky., Richard C. Shelby, R-Ala., and Tennessee Republicans Fred Thompson and Bill Frist — prevailed.

The omnibus appropriations measure also included provisions to permit TVA to refinance its $3 billion debt to the Federal Financing Bank, and $7 million for continued TVA management of the Land Between the Lakes Recreation Area — 170,000 acres along the Kentucky-Tennessee border.

The energy and water appropriations bill provided $388 million less in total funding than had been requested by the president for Energy Depart-

Energy-Water

ment programs, dams, beach repair and navigation projects of the Army Corps of Engineers and regulatory agencies such as the Nuclear Regulatory Commission. The final funding level was just $34 million less than the Senate had provided but $255 million more than the House level.

In spite of tight budget caps from the 1997 balanced-budget agreement (PL 105-33), lawmakers still found a way to allocate money to their favorite programs — water projects popular in the House, as well as nuclear weapons programs dear to the Senate.

The measure provided a 77 percent increase over Clinton's request for Army Corps of Engineers construction projects, for a total of $1.4 billion. Among other water projects, the measure also provided $75 million for revitalization of the San Francisco Bay and Sacramento-San Joaquin River Delta in California.

Atomic energy defense programs of the Energy Department, meanwhile, received appropriations of $11.9 billion — nearly 60 percent of the bill's total funding. About $5.6 billion of that was for defense-related environmental management.

The bill provided a total of $727 million for energy supply programs, including solar and renewable energy, nuclear energy, fusion energy, and environment, safety and health programs. The measure also appropriated $2.7 billion for Energy Department research programs, $212 million more than requested.

The omnibus bill provided funding for other energy and water development programs, much of it "emergency" spending to help Russia. It included $200 million to dispose of 50 tons of Russian nuclear weapons-derived plutonium and $325 million to buy Russian nuclear weapons-derived uranium.

It provided $60 million for renewable energy programs of the Energy Department, an extra $35 million for the Corps of Engineers for salmon habitat projects along the Columbia River, and $15 million for the administration's Next Generation Internet project.

The omnibus carried the pet projects of several lawmakers. It included $750,000 to repair the Archusa Dam in the home state of Senate Majority Leader Trent Lott, R-Miss., and $340,000 for flood mitigation in Pierre, S.D., home state of Senate Minority Leader Tom Daschle.

Senate Panel Boosts Spending For Water Projects

JUNE 6 — Senate appropriators defied the Clinton administration on two fronts the week of June 1, issuing stinging criticism of the Nuclear Regulatory Commission (NRC) and including millions of dollars in water projects despite White House opposition.

The full Appropriations Committee endorsed both positions June 4 when it approved, 27-0, a $21.3 billion fiscal 1999 spending bill for energy and water development.

Overall, the draft bill — which funds Energy Department programs, the Tennessee Valley Authority and other agencies — would provide $87 million more than the fiscal 1998 appropriations and $376 million less than the president's budget request.

On the NRC, which regulates the nation's 104 domestic nuclear power plants, the Energy and Water Development Appropriations Subcommittee initially approved a draft report June 2 that called for a nearly 25 percent reduction in agency staff.

The rebuke of the NRC as an overzealous, bloated bureaucracy drew a pointed response from the administration, which said that if carried out, the subcommittee's recommendations would undermine safety.

"A reduction of this magnitude would severely impair the NRC's ability to independently identify and resolve safety challenges at the nation's 104 nuclear power plants," Shirley Ann Jackson, the NRC chairman, said in a statement released in response to the subcommittee action.

Appropriators responded in full committee, agreeing by voice vote to drop the staff reductions. However, the panel retained a long section in the report devoted to the shortcomings of the agency. "It is a commission that desperately needs some oversight," said Pete V. Domenici, R-N.M., chairman of the subcommittee.

Box Score

- **Bills:** HR 4060 — PL 105-245; HR 4328 — PL 105-277
- **House action:** The House adopted the conference report (H Rept 105-749) on HR 4060, 389-25, on Sept. 28. It passed HR 4060 by 405-4 on June 22.
  The House adopted the conference report (H Rept 105-825) on HR 4328, 333-95, on Oct. 20.
- **Senate action:** The Senate cleared the conference report on HR 4060 by voice vote on Sept. 29. It passed S 2138, 98-1, on June 18.
  The Senate cleared the conference report on HR 4328, 65-29, on Oct. 21.
- **Presidential action:** Clinton signed HR 4060 on Oct. 7. He signed HR 4328 on Oct. 21.

Jackson acknowledged the criticism, saying the commission was already familiar with most of the charges.

"Without question, there is room for improvement in the NRC regulatory program," she said. "The commission will examine the criticisms in the Committee report in a constructive effort to see what more needs to be done."

On water project funding, the committee sent an unequivocal message to the administration that it will fight for millions of dollars worth of dams, beach erosion repairs and flood control projects prized by senators.

In its fiscal 1999 budget request, the administration proposed a sharp cut from current year funding in construction for the Army Corps of Engineers, which dredges rivers, builds dams and repairs storm-ravaged beaches.

Domenici said the administration had shortchanged water projects. But he said funding was so tight that the best he could do was hold the line on appropriations for projects to levels closer to those in the current year.

The bill would appropriate $1.2 billion for the Corps' construction budget, a 15 percent reduction from fiscal 1998 funding. In contrast, the Clinton budget request was $784 million, a

Appropriations

47 percent cut from the current year.

"While not at the optimum level, it is significantly better than the program proposed by the administration and will allow contractors to move forward with the expectation of being paid for their completed work," said Domenici.

The tussle in the energy and water bill is a classic example of how Congress and the administration push different priorities when it comes to doling out money for public works.

Administration officials say Congress has committed the nation to funding billions of dollars in new water projects that are draining resources from other initiatives high on the administration's priority list, such as alternative energy research.

In fiscal 1998 alone, appropriators included funding for 62 new construction starts, only 12 of which were requested by the administration. And officials estimate that just to finish projects now under way would cost about $16 billion and take 16 years.

"This administration has not placed a particularly high priority on water projects," said David Kenyon, chief of the program, formulation and evaluation branch at the Army Corps of Engineers, who works on budget issues.

Water Wars

Appropriators recognize that senators and House members look to the energy and water bill for projects that win points with constituents.

Water projects are a small part of the overall bill. For example, the Corps of Engineers would receive $3.5 billion, but the Energy Department would receive $16.5 billion.

Such projects, however, have attracted bipartisan support for the bill in the past and are the source of power for appropriators who control the public works purse strings.

At the same time, Domenici contends that federal funding is an essential element in maintaining the nation's infrastructure. In drawing up the bill, Domenici said he faced some difficult tradeoffs, particularly when it came to protecting the Corps' account for major construction projects.

To help ward off further cuts, he said, he chose to include no construction starts, although he acknowledged that the House, where support for water projects is even stronger, is likely to push for new projects.

But he said he also had to keep funding flat for other programs to protect Corps construction, and he acknowledged that he aimed to hit programs the administration supported.

For example, the Clinton administration strongly favors research on solar and renewable energy to develop technologies to help replace oil, gas and other fossil fuels implicated by scientists in global warming.

The bill would include $345 million for solar and renewable research, about equal to the $346 million in current year funding, but $92 million less than the Clinton request of $437 million.

"We are going to hear from some people that we didn't put enough into solar and renewable," said Domenici.

Among the projects included in the bill are three in Mississippi that were not requested by the administration, including $10 million for dredging Pascagoula Harbor, a project that will benefit the hometown of Senate Majority Leader Trent Lott.

Kenyon said the administration could not justify putting the project in its budget given overall funding constraints. "There was no prejudice against that project," he said.

The administration, with support from environmental groups, favors limiting federal funding for water projects and allowing local and state governments to pick up more of the cost.

"There are hundreds of projects like the Pascagoula dredging project that don't serve the national interest and should be funded by local interests," said Scott Faber, director of flood plain programs for American Rivers, an environmental group.

The committee also included $651 million, or $43 million less than current year funding, for the Bureau of Reclamation, which builds dams and manages flood control projects in 17 western states.

Nuclear Politics

In previous years, the NRC has been a relative footnote in the report, but this year it came under intense criticism from appropriators.

The full committee contended in its report that the agency has stepped up its scrutiny of the nation's nuclear plants, despite substantial improvements in their safety records.

For example, cases of radiation exposure have decreased 35 percent since 1991 and the number of "significant events," such as breakdowns in safety equipment, have decreased by 70 percent, according to the committee.

In spite of that record, the number of civil penalties for significant safety violations, such as lapses in plant security or poor accident prevention procedures, have increased from 25 in 1995 to 71 in 1997.

"The increased issuance of fines and violations is not a reflection on the safety of the nuclear utility industry," the committee report said. "It is the result of a change in regulatory culture at the NRC that defies the achieved improvement in safety."

The report approved by the subcommittee recommended that the agency trim its staff from the current 2,934 positions to 2,210 by fiscal 2000.

The agency responded that improved safety records are a result of effective enforcement and that staff reductions would compromise safety.

At full committee, appropriators agreed to an amendment dropping the staff reductions and including a slight funding increase. As it stands, the agency would receive $466 million, almost equal to the $468 million in current year funding.

The number was a significant increase for the agency over the $460 million included in the subcommittee version, because $20 million of that appropriation was to pay costs related to the proposed staff reductions.

While the overall critique of the agency was softened somewhat in the full committee report, appropriators retained language supporting a revamp of agency regulations, such as outdated paperwork requirements and overly prescriptive rules.

The agency is scheduled to be the subject of hearings this year before the Senate Environment and Public Works Committee. The debate is unfolding as the nuclear industry faces intense economic pressure because of the push to deregulate the utility industry and allow greater competition. In the new era of competition, utilities have an incentive to cut costs and reduce bureaucratic red tape in order to produce electricity at competitive prices.

"As the industry goes through a period of change and restructuring, the

Energy-Water

NRC has to adjust to recognize the expertise we've gained over 40 years and the safety improvements we've made," said Steve Unglesbee, a spokesman for the Nuclear Energy Institute, which represents the domestic nuclear utility industry. "It is time for the NRC to undertake a discriminating self-examination determining the right number of employees and the right focus to ensure public safety."

The committee also took steps on safeguarding the world's supply of weapons-grade plutonium. The report asserted funds for turning U.S. plutonium stockpiles into a non-weapons form should be tied to Russian pledges to convert the same amount of excess weapons-grade plutonium.

"We have to ensure that Russia destroys at least as much weapons plutonium as we do because they have many times as much as we do," said Domenici.

House Cuts TVA Funding; Senate Solidifies Stance

JUNE 13 — House appropriators are gunning for a fight in their drive to eliminate the federal subsidy for the Tennessee Valley Authority, the once sacrosanct New Deal power agency, but they face formidable opposition in the Senate.

The House Appropriations Subcommittee on Energy and Water Development on June 10 approved by voice vote a $21.1 billion draft spending bill for energy and water programs that deleted funding for the authority, which provides power to southeastern states, and oversees navigation, recreation and other "non-power" services along the Tennessee River.

The overall bill, which funds Energy Department programs, dams, beach restoration and navigation projects through the Army Corps of Engineers, and regulatory agencies such as the Nuclear Regulatory Commission, would provide $184 million less than the fiscal 1998 appropriation and $648 million less than the administration's budget request.

Proponents of TVA privatization, including Joseph M. McDade, R-Pa., chairman of the Appropriations subcommittee, contended that in an era of increasing competition among utilities, the government should no longer subsidize the authority.

McDade said he was making good on a compromise written into the fiscal 1998 energy and water conference report (PL 105-62; H Rept 105-271) to eliminate funding for the agency in fiscal 1999.

"There is no justification for taxpayer dollars to go to the TVA," he said. "TVA is a multibillion-dollar operation and should be treated like a private utility."

But Senate appropriators disagree. The Senate Appropriations Committee approved its own version of the energy and water development bill (S 2138) June 4 that included $70 million for the agency, slightly below the $77 million requested by the administration.

Senators from southeastern states — including appropriators Mitch McConnell, R-Ky., and Richard C. Shelby, R-Ala., and Tennessee Republicans Fred Thompson and Bill Frist — vigorously defended the agency's programs, such as flood control, as necessary government services.

The authority, created in 1933 under President Franklin D. Roosevelt, has come under fire in recent years from fiscal conservatives who say the government should not fund an agency that competes with investor-owned utilities.

The TVA is one of the largest power producers in the nation. According to the General Accounting Office, the agency had operating revenues of about $5.6 billion in fiscal year 1997. Its 80,000 square mile service area includes most of Tennessee and parts of Alabama, Georgia, Kentucky, Mississippi, North Carolina and Virginia.

The agency is required to approve all structures along the Tennessee River that may hinder navigation or flood control. That is in addition to overseeing more than 479,000 acres of reservoirs, 11,000 miles of shoreline and 435,000 acres of public land.

In the Senate report, appropriators argued that it would be unfair for the federal government to stop paying for basic services, such as flood control and navigation, in the Tennessee Valley that it pays for in other areas of the country.

Many of those services are now funded elsewhere through the Army Corps of Engineers, and proponents of the agency said withdrawing federal funding for the agency would force TVA ratepayers to assume the cost.

"It is not fair to suggest that Tennessee ratepayers should pick up the tab for these federal responsibilities by paying more for their electricity," said Thompson. "That singles us out for an unfair tax that no one else has to pay."

Proponents of privatizing the authority say some of its non-power duties could be transferred to the Corps of Engineers.

Many of the agency's Republican supporters in the House also represent districts that depend on the TVA and are facing tough re-election fights.

By not protecting the agency, the House Republican leadership could hurt re-election prospects of some of its most vulnerable members. A case in point is freshman Robert B. Aderholt, R-Ala., who is being challenged by Democratic lawyer Don Bevill, who has made delivering federal projects for the district a theme in his campaign.

Bevill is the son of former 15-term Rep. Tom Bevill, D-Ala. (1967-96), who championed the agency as the longtime chairman of the Energy and Water Development Appropriations Subcommittee.

Water Projects

One area where House appropriators appear to be more in agreement with their Senate counterparts is funding for dams, beach restoration, flood control and other water projects.

Following the lead of Senate appropriators, McDade said he rejected the big cuts in water projects called for in President Clinton's budget request.

Water projects are prized by House members, and they have helped members win votes for the bill. According to numbers released by the committee, the Corps would receive $3.96 billion, an increase of $741 million over Clinton's request, but $206 million below fiscal 1998 funding.

McDade said the bill includes no new construction starts. Pointedly, the committee opted against including any money for a new Clinton administration flood control initiative.

Under the administration proposal, known as Challenge 21, the Corps would refocus some of its efforts away from "structural" flood control efforts, such as levees, and instead help to re-

Appropriations

store wetlands that absorb flood waters before damage occurs or buy up property in flood-prone areas. The administration requested $25 million for the program in its fiscal 1999 budget.

Appropriators are in no mood to grant concessions to the administration, given the large cuts in its budget.

"We got a budget that is the most disingenuous budget since I've been here," said McDade, echoing a sentiment expressed by McDade's Senate counterpart, Energy and Water Appropriations Subcommittee Chairman Pete V. Domenici, R-N.M.

The House bill tracks funding included in the Senate bill for the Nuclear Regulatory Commission, which regulates the nation's nuclear plants.

Larry E. Craig, R-Idaho, said he is considering a floor amendment that would bar the Energy Department from using an account financed by the nuclear power industry to pay for department legal fees.

The account is supposed to be used for disposing of waste from nuclear power plants. Utilities are suing the government, contending that it has reneged on its responsibility to dispose of the waste produced by their plants.

A major fight is likely on the Senate floor over an amendment expected to be offered by James M. Jeffords, R-Vt., and William V. Roth Jr., R-Del., that would increase by $80 million the account for solar and renewable energy research.

While the actual line item for the solar and renewable account is listed as $345 million, almost equal to the amount for current year spending, elsewhere in the bill the committee subtracted $48 million for science research and $50 million in an outright cut, according to Jeffords' staff.

Renewable Energy A Winner, as Senate Passes Bill

JUNE 20 — Senate supporters of funding for solar and renewable energy research won a partial victory the week of June 15, easily pushing through an amendment to restore millions of dollars in research money to the fiscal 1999 spending bill for energy and water development.

After little debate on the floor, the Senate on June 18 passed, 98-1, the $21.4 billion energy and water bill (S 2138) after approving a major amendment that would increase by $70 million, to $327 million, funding for solar and renewable energy research. (Vote 165, p. S-27)

While the overall account is still well below the administration's request of $372 million, the amendment was seen as a major victory for the administration and its allies in the Senate, who say research is essential to breaking the nation's dependence on fossil fuels.

The House, where the Appropriations Committee approved its own version of the bill (HR 4060) two days before Senate passage, is set to act on June 22. The outlook there is bright, and no single sticking point is expected to hold up the bill in conference.

Still, there are some issues to be resolved by House and Senate negotiators, including big differences over funding for levees, dams and other water projects. Overall, the Senate bill is $294 million more than the $21.1 billion House bill.

The Clinton administration is also pushing to protect funding for energy research, and opposes the House committee's decision to cut science funding, including zero funding for the Department of Energy's work on the Next Generation Internet, a faster, more efficient version of the existing worldwide computer network.

Also high on the administration's list is funding for the California Bay-Delta program, a project that is repairing environmental damage in Northern California. The Senate bill included $65 million for the project, the House level was $75 million, and both figures were well below the president's budget request of $143 million.

"This is a very tough bill to present," said Vic Fazio of California, ranking Democrat on the House Energy and Water Appropriations Subcommittee. "There are a lot of members . . . who have every reason to complain" because they did not get the projects they wanted.

Solar Power

In drawing up the Senate bill, Pete V. Domenici, R-N.M., chairman of the Senate Energy and Water Appropriations Subcommittee, faced a balancing act. He sought to protect funding for the Army Corps of Engineers, which builds dams, conducts navigation projects and restores eroded beaches.

Water projects are a priority for senators and House members, who relish bringing home federal dollars to local communities for everything from harbor dredging to levee repair.

But to safeguard the Corps' budget, Domenici had to take money from other domestic accounts, and he specifically targeted funding for solar and renewable energy. Domenici chose his priorities carefully. The administration supports deep cuts in the Corps' budget, but wants more funding for solar and renewable energy research.

Alternative energy research is a cornerstone of the administration's effort to reduce the effects of global warming. Many scientists contend that an increasing buildup of carbon dioxide and other greenhouse gases in the atmosphere is causing the earth to warm. Greenhouse gases are produced by fossil fuels such as oil, gas and coal. The development of alternative power sources, such as solar and wind, could help slow their production, according to the administration.

In a June 18 statement, the administration highlighted its opposition to funding reductions.

"These changes would seriously undercut the Department of Energy's ability to continue some of the most promising research now underway, eliminate accelerated introduction of clean power sources, and restrict our ability to lower greenhouse gas emission levels," it said.

In the Senate, cutting renewable energy research was opposed by a coalition led by James M. Jeffords, R-Vt., who contended that energy research is crucial to developing alternatives to fossil fuels and breaking the nation's dependence on foreign oil.

According to Department of Energy figures, the bill included an appropriation of $257 million for the solar and renewable energy account, well below the $372 million requested by the administration.

Jeffords proposed an amendment that would increase the appropriation by $70 million, for a grand total of $327 million. The Senate adopted the amendment by voice vote.

Conference Outlook

No matter what course the House takes, the conference committee will have to reconcile the two bills' overall spending levels while maintaining funding for water projects.

For example, the House bill included $1.46 billion for the Corps construction account, while the Senate number is $1.25 billion, a $208 million gap. Both levels are well above the $784 million requested in the Clinton budget.

Neither Domenici nor Republican Joseph M. McDade of Pennsylvania, Domenici's House counterpart, have indicated they intend to do anything in conference to erode funding for water projects, and they have leveled harsh criticism at the Clinton administration for proposing deep cuts.

In fact, the House report took aim at Clinton administration proposals to shift the Corps away from traditional flood control and navigation projects toward environmental restoration of wetlands and flood plains.

"The committee is wary of further efforts to sap the nation of its water infrastructure expertise in order to feed the unrestrained growth of a federal environmental bureaucracy," the report said.

Another issue to be resolved in conference is funding for the Department of Energy's stockpile stewardship program, which is responsible for maintaining and refurbishing the nation's nuclear arsenal. Funding is a priority for Domenici because national laboratories in New Mexico play a big part in the program.

The Senate bill included $4.4 billion for the weapons activities account, which includes stockpile stewardship, an increase of $299 million above current year funding, including as much as $50 million in unspent revenue from previous years that Energy Department officials say will probably be available in fiscal 1999.

The House bill included $4.1 billion. But Energy Department officials note that the figure included $305 million in unspent revenue from previous years, and they say that most of that money is not available.

Both the House and Senate included funding to begin construction on a $1.3 billion neutron source at the Oak Ridge National Laboratory in Tennessee.

The machine, which is expected to take seven years to complete, would be used to produce neutrons so that scientists can peer into materials such as plastics to better understand how they are made and to eventually produce new and better products. The House included $100 million for the project, while the Senate level is much higher at $157 million, equal to the president's budget request.

Recreation Area At Center Of TVA Fight

JUNE 27 — The fiscal 1999 energy and water development spending bill breezed through the Senate and House with little controversy, but a tough behind-the-scenes battle is brewing over the future of the Tennessee Valley Authority.

Central to the fight is future management of a 170,000-acre recreation area along the Kentucky-Tennessee border prized as much for its educational programs on the environment and history as its bison and elk.

The battle over the Land Between the Lakes National Recreation Area is part of a broader struggle over funding for the TVA, which manages the property, that will be hashed out in the upcoming House-Senate conference on the funding bill.

After relatively little debate, the House voted 405-4 on June 22 to pass its $21.1 billion version of the energy and water development bill (HR 4060), which eliminated funding for TVA. *(Vote 253, p. H-74)*

The House vote came less than a week after the Senate passed its own $21.4 billion bill (S 2138) on June 18, including $70 million for the authority.

There is broad agreement that the recreation area, established in 1963 under the administration of President John F. Kennedy, should remain under federal control. The issue for conferees is which federal agency is best equipped to manage it.

That question could have long-range implications for the quality of services provided in the recreation area, 90 miles northwest of Nashville, and the $600 million-a-year tourist industry that depends on it.

Proponents of eliminating funding for the TVA, one of the largest power producers in the nation, contend that in an era of increasing competition among electric utilities, the government should not be providing the authority with a subsidy. They say the government subsidy would give TVA the ability to offer cheaper rates to outbid private utilities.

The House report clearly seeks to finesse the future management of Land Between the Lakes. On the one hand, it calls on TVA to keep funding the recreational area, while on the other it acknowledges proposals to transfer it to "another federal resource agency," such as the U.S. Forest Service.

The House and Senate versions of the fiscal 1999 Interior Appropriations bill contain provisions that would transfer management of Land Between the Lakes to the Forest Service, if the energy and water bill does not provide sufficient funds for its operations.

In contrast to the House, Senate appropriators provided $70 million, or $6.8 million below President Clinton's budget request, for the authority, including $6.9 million for operation and management of the recreation area.

Senators from Southeastern states, including appropriators such as Mitch McConnell, R-Ky., who is on the conference committee, say that the authority does an effective job of managing its non-power projects and that taxpayers would be ill-served if those functions were transferred out.

Rep. John Tanner, D-Tenn., agreed. He said the authority provides effective management of the area, pays special attention to it and is worried that the property would not receive adequate attention from another agency.

Tanner noted that the Forest Service is already burdened by a major backlog in maintenance projects, and that Land Between the Lakes could get swallowed up in the bureaucracy.

"There is no doubt in my mind that there will be disruptions in services and activities," said Tanner.

Possible Compromise

McConnell said that while his preference is to maintain funding for Land Between the Lakes and TVA's other non-power programs, he and other proponents of the agency are hedging

Appropriations

Energy-Water Development Spending

Energy and water appropriations (HR 4060 — PL 105-245) signed by the president Oct. 7.
(Budget authority in thousands of dollars.)

	Fiscal 1998 Appropriation	Fiscal 1999 Clinton Request	Senate Bill	House Bill	Conference Report
Army Corps of Engineers (Defense Department)					
General construction	$ 1,473,373	$ 806,000	$ 1,248,068	$ 1,456,529	$ 1,429,885
Operation and maintenance	1,845,210	1,603,000	1,667,572	1,637,719	1,653,252
Mississippi River flood control	296,212	280,000	313,234	312,077	321,149
Flood control and coastal emergencies	4,000	—	—	—	—
Other	550,804	555,000	559,390	560,823	555,747
TOTAL, Defense Department	**$ 4,169,599**	**$ 3,244,000**	**$ 3,788,264**	**$ 3,967,148**	**$ 3,960,033**
Interior Department					
Bureau of Reclamation					
Water and related resources	698,868*	640,124	671,869	596,254	617,045
California Bay-Delta ecosystem restoration	85,000	143,300	65,000	75,000	75,000
Central Valley project restoration fund	33,130	49,500	39,500	33,130	33,130
Other	57,983	60,425	60,425	58,425	55,421
Subtotal, Bureau of Reclamation	**$ 874,981**	**$ 893,349**	**$ 836,794**	**$ 762,809**	**$ 780,596**
Central Utah project completion	41,153	40,948	44,948	40,948	42,500
TOTAL, Interior Department	**$ 916,134**	**$ 934,297**	**$ 881,742**	**$ 803,757**	**$ 823,096**
Energy Department					
Energy supply, research and development	906,807	1,129,042	786,854	882,834	727,091
Atomic energy defense					
Weapons activities	4,146,692	4,500,000	4,445,700	4,142,100	4,400,000
Defense environmental cleanup	4,429,438	4,259,903	4,293,403	4,358,554	4,310,227
Defense nuclear waste disposal	190,000	190,000	185,000	190,000	189,000
Defense environmental privatization	200,000	516,857	241,857	286,857	228,357
Defense facilities closure projects	890,800	1,006,240	1,048,240	1,038,240	1,038,240
Other defense activities	1,666,008	1,667,160	1,658,160	1,761,260	1,696,676
Subtotal, atomic energy defense	**$ 11,522,938**	**$ 12,140,160**	**$ 11,872,360**	**$ 11,777,011**	**$ 11,862,500**
Decontamination and decommissioning	220,200	272,000	196,827	225,000	220,200
General science and other research	2,235,708	2,470,460	2,634,207	2,399,500	2,682,860
Civilian nuclear waste disposal	160,000	190,000	190,000	160,000	169,000
Departmental administration	87,417	109,258	98,225	38,835	63,945
Power Marketing Administrations	240,945	250,945	252,528	239,180	237,510
Other	524,559	481,500	445,754	481,200	460,200
TOTAL, Energy Department	**$ 15,898,574**	**$ 17,043,365**	**$ 16,476,755**	**$ 16,203,560**	**$ 16,423,306**
Independent Agencies					
Appalachian Regional Commission	170,000	67,000	67,000	65,900	66,400
Nuclear Regulatory Commission	468,000	486,891	466,000	462,700	465,000
Revenues	−450,000	−152,341	−416,000	−444,700	−444,800
Tennessee Valley Authority	70,000	76,800	70,000	—	—
Other	19,600	20,450	40,100	19,100	39,100
TOTAL, Independent Agencies	**$ 277,600**	**$ 498,800**	**$ 227,100**	**$ 103,000**	**$ 125,700**
Net Total	**$ 21,261,907**	**$ 21,720,462**	**$ 21,373,861**	**$ 21,077,465**	**$ 21,332,135**
Scorekeeping adjustments	*−529,705*	*−424,000*	*−432,000*	*−424,000*	*−424,000*
GRAND TOTAL	**$ 20,732,202**	**$ 21,296,482**	**$ 20,941,861**	**$ 20,653,465**	**$ 20,908,135**

*Includes emergency appropriations in PL 105-174.

SOURCE: House and Senate Appropriations committees

their bets with the Interior provisions.

"We don't know how it is going to play out," said McConnell.

Rep. Edward Whitfield, R-Ky., a proponent of the agency, said the Interior provisions are intended to bring some long-term stability to the management of Land Between the Lakes.

"The problem I have with TVA appropriations is that every year we have this big battle," said Whitfield. "In some ways, it would lend stability to the property if it were transferred to the Forest Service."

Rep. Zach Wamp, R-Tenn., a proponent of TVA and an appropriator, said supporters of the agency are trying to ease its transition into a deregulated marketplace. "Our problem right now is building a bridge from now until deregulation," said Wamp, adding that it is important to "establish a process to make sure Land Between the Lakes is not left out in the cold."

Conferees Eliminate TVA Support

SEPTEMBER 26 — After a flurry of last-minute activity, House and Senate conferees hammered out a $20.9 billion package for energy and water spending for fiscal 1999, accepting a controversial House-passed proposal to eliminate funding for non-power programs run by the Tennessee Valley Authority (TVA).

The bill (HR 4060) calls for spending of $388 million less than President Clinton's budget request. The measure, which in the past has been well-greased with pet projects, may face unusual scrutiny this year because of the TVA cuts.

If the controversy over TVA funding is resolved, the bill would likely fly through both chambers. Under caps from last year's balanced-budget agreement (PL 105-33), lawmakers did not have much latitude to allocate money to favorite projects. (*Budget agreement, 1997 Almanac, p. 2-27*)

Nonetheless, lawmakers were able to find $1.59 billion for Army Corps of Engineer general investigations and construction projects, $635 million more than Clinton requested.

Unlike last year, lawmakers will not have to fear a presidential line-item veto of these projects. The Supreme Court struck down the veto June 25. Last year, the president used the veto to strike eight projects totaling $19.3 million.

To pay for the increase in Army Corps of Engineers spending, lawmakers shifted funds from the Energy Department's non-defense environmental cleanup costs and science programs, including Oak Ridge National Laboratory, said Senate Subcommittee Chairman Pete V. Domenici, R-N.M.

The draft report also includes:
- $708 million for energy supplies, including nuclear, solar and renewable energy programs, which is $421 million less than requested and nearly $200 million less than fiscal 1998.
- $425.5 million for non-defense environmental management, $26.5 million less than requested and $71.5 million less than the fiscal 1998 amount.
- $4.2 billion, close to the requested amount, for defense environment and waste management;
- More than $1 billion for defense facility closures, close to the amount requested; and
- $189 million in defense nuclear waste disposal, virtually the same as the administration's request.

TVA Controversy

On TVA, the draft conference report released Sept. 25 calls for the elimination of the authority's non-power projects, which include flood control, navigation, dam maintenance and environmental programs.

The White House indicated that it was not pleased. "The conference committee's action in zeroing out TVA is completely misguided, unjustified, unfair, and it seriously undermines TVA's important role in enhancing the Tennessee Valley," Tennesee native Vice President Al Gore said in a statement.

Cuts in the TVA, however, were not unexpected. This year's fight mirrored the fiscal 1998 TVA battle in which the House eliminated funding for non-power projects while the Senate funded them.

However, last year the Senate prevailed in conference and the money was restored in the final law (PL 105-62). House lawmakers, however, were able to insert language into the conference report that set the stage for this year's action. (*1997 Almanac, p. 9-31*)

The TVA was created in 1933 as a public works program to generate electricity for the southeastern region while also providing for the "economic and social well-being of the people."

The agency controls the Tennessee River to prevent floods, regulates navigation, encourages reforestation and soil conservation and provides other services.

"It's been an uphill battle," lamented Sen. Jeff Sessions, R-Ala., who last year joined Republican senators Richard C. Shelby of Alabama and Bill Frist and Fred Thompson of Tennessee in calling on Clinton to veto the fiscal 1998 bill if lawmakers eliminated the funds.

Appropriations for TVA's non-power programs have dwindled from $288 million in fiscal 1981 to the $70 million provided in fiscal 1998. (*1980 Almanac, p. 161*)

Without the non-power funding, TVA's management of the Land Between the Lakes National Recreation Area, a 170,000-acre area along the Kentucky-Tennessee border, would likely be jeopardized, said Sen. Mitch McConnell, R-Ky. The recreational area is prized as much for its educational programs on the environment and history as its bison and elk.

Preparing for the action, the Interior Appropriations bills (S 2237, HR 4193) call on the U.S. Forest Service to manage the land if the TVA lacks funding. Another idea being discussed is allowing the TVA to refinance its assets to raise funding.

Final Measure Ends Decades Of TVA Funding

OCTOBER 3 — It came down to a test of wills. Bucking their Senate counterparts, House appropriators for weeks refused to budge in their determination to eliminate funding for the Tennessee Valley Authority (TVA).

In the end, the House negotiators prevailed. The fiscal 1999 energy and water appropriations conference report (HR 4060) cleared the Senate Sept. 29 by voice vote, a day after the House voted 389-25 to adopt it. (*House vote 472, p. H-134*)

Appropriations

The $20.9 billion measure would eliminate federal funding for the TVA, which provides power to Southeastern states and oversees navigation, recreation and other non-power services along the Tennessee River. It also funds Energy Department programs, dams, beach repair and navigation projects through the Army Corps of Engineers and regulatory agencies such as the Nuclear Regulatory Commission (NRC). The conferees agreed to overall spending of $33.7 million less than the Senate-passed measure and $254.7 million more than the House bill.

While the House-passed version included no funding for TVA, the Senate bill would have provided $70 million, slightly below the $77 million requested by the administration. House appropriators said they were holding fast to language in the fiscal 1998 bill (PL 105-62) that called for eliminating federal funding for TVA in fiscal 1999. *(1997 Almanac, p. 9-31)*

The action came despite some powerful advocates in the Senate — including appropriators Mitch McConnell, R-Ky., Richard C. Shelby, R-Ala., and Tennessee Republicans Fred Thompson and Bill Frist. Vice President Al Gore also opposed the cuts. President Clinton, however, is expected to sign the bill.

Agency defenders argued vigorously that TVA's non-power services, such as navigation and recreation, are federal services that should be funded by taxpayers. Without federal funding, they say, TVA ratepayers will have to foot the bill. They note that elsewhere such services are provided by federal agencies such as the Army Corps of Engineers.

"The federal government has decided to duck its obligation to provide funding for TVA," Frist said. "The committee's actions will force TVA to fund its non-power programs through its power accounts, resulting in an unprecedented unfunded mandate."

But TVA's defenders faced strong opposition from Republican House appropriators from the Northeast, including Energy and Water Appropriations Subcommittee Chairman Joseph M. McDade of Pennsylvania and fellow subcommittee member Rodney Frelinghuysen of New Jersey.

They held fast to their position that the federal government had no business offering financial support to an electricity producer. In an era of increasing competition among utilities, they said, federal funding provided TVA with a competitive advantage over investor-owned utilities. They said it was unfair for taxpayers in their districts to subsidize power rates for consumers of electricity in the Tennessee Valley.

"New Jersey consumers have shouldered regular increases in their electricity rates over the past 10 years," said Frelinghuysen. "What is more astonishing is that while New Jersey consumers pay more for electricity with their rate dollars, they are subsidizing the TVA with their income tax dollars."

End of an Era

The decision to eliminate funding for the agency marked the end of an era and set off a round of finger-pointing among lawmakers over who would be held responsible for the cuts.

The authority, created in 1933 under Democratic President Franklin D. Roosevelt, has been a target of fiscal conservatives and investor-owned utilities, which have long argued that federal subsidies allow TVA to offer cheaper rates to consumers.

But the TVA's fortunes began to change with the GOP's takeover of Congress in 1995 and the empowerment of fiscal conservatives such as Frelinghuysen, who wanted to shrink the federal government.

While many of the agency's staunchest defenders are Republicans, such as Frist and Thompson, TVA's clout with appropriators has declined.

The last Democratic subcommittee chairman, former Rep. Tom Bevill of Alabama (1967-97), was an ardent defender of the agency, which provided flood control and other services to his north-central Alabama district.

But TVA also did its part to fuel the fire of the opposition. TVA Board Chairman Craven Crowell floated a plan last year to eliminate the federal appropriations, but he later backed off amid strong opposition from the agency's backers in Congress. *(1997 Almanac, p. 4-24)*

Supporters of the agency, such as Bob Clement, D-Tenn., also point to the political clout of investor-owned utilities, which are concerned that the federal subsidy provides TVA with a competitive advantage because the authority is able to sell electricity at cheaper rates.

With operating revenues of $5.6 billion in fiscal 1997, the authority is not about to go belly-up. But its supporters say they are concerned that TVA will eventually have to raise electric rates to pay for services now funded by taxpayers.

Eliminating TVA money has already emerged as a hot campaign issue in the region. In Tennessee, Democrat Jerry Cooper, who is challenging Republican Rep. Van Hilleary, has blamed Hilleary for the cuts.

In Alabama, Republican Rep. Robert B. Aderholt is being challenged by Democratic lawyer Don Bevill (son of the former congressman), who has made delivering federal projects a theme in his campaign.

"This is a reckless decision by the enemies of the TVA," said Aderholt.

The agency's proponents held out some hope that funding could be restored in a catch-all appropriations bill, but they consider a turnaround unlikely.

Water Projects

The showdown over TVA was the biggest controversy during the conferees' deliberations. Negotiations in other areas, notably funding for dams, beach restoration, flood control and other water projects, were easy by comparison.

Both House and Senate appropriators strongly rejected big cuts in water projects proposed by the Clinton administration. The conference report included $3.96 billion for the Army Corps of Engineers. That was $7.1 million below the House-enacted version, $172 million above the Senate bill and $716 million above the president's budget request.

"If the [conference] committee had accepted the administration's proposal — which represented the lowest budget in the history of the civil works program — then scores of ongoing construction projects would be terminated, dozens more would be placed on fragile life support . . . and contractor shutdowns would be legion," said McDade.

The Energy Department, by far the biggest account in the bill, would receive $16.4 billion, $525 million above fiscal 1998 funding but $620 million below the $17 billion budget request. ◆

Foreign Operations

Clinton Wins Backing For IMF Funds, Loses Effort To Repay U.N. Debts

Box Score

- **Bill:** HR 4328 — PL 105-277.
- **House action:** The House adopted the conference report (H Rept 105-825) on HR 4328, 333-95, on Oct. 20. The House passed HR 4569, 255-161, on Sept. 17.
- **Senate action:** The Senate cleared the bill, 65-29, on Oct. 21. It passed S 2334, 90-3, on Sept. 2.
- **Presidential action:** Clinton signed the bill Oct. 21.

After more than a year of wrangling on foreign policy priorities, GOP leaders in Congress agreed to President Clinton's demands for $17.9 billion in credit for the International Monetary Fund (IMF) and stepped-up aid to Russia and other former Soviet republics, while at the same time dropping abortion-related restrictions on international family planning funds.

SUMMARY

The deals were made in October as the House and Senate versions of the fiscal 1999 foreign operations appropriations bill (HR 4569, S 2334) were folded into the omnibus spending bill (HR 4328).

Abortion has become an annual battleground for foreign aid legislation. A House-passed provision sponsored by Rep. Christopher H. Smith, R-N.J., would have banned funds for international family planning organizations that perform or advocate abortions, even if they use their own money. These so-called Mexico City restrictions faced strong opposition in the Senate, and the administration warned that President Clinton would veto any bill that included them.

As in 1997, Republican leaders finally agreed to fund family planning groups at the current level of $385 million, with no more than 8.3 percent of the total to be spent each month.

GOP leaders retained the Mexico City anti-abortion language in the fiscal 1998-99 State Department authorization bill (HR 1757 — Conference Report 105-432) where it was linked to the U.S. payment of back dues to the United Nations. Clinton vetoed that bill Oct. 21, although some key provisions, including foreign affairs reorganization, were included in the omnibus bill.

No funds were provided for the U.N. Population Fund, because of that organization's involvement with China and its sometimes coercive efforts to limit families to one child.

The omnibus package appropriates $12.8 billion for foreign aid and export assistance, $750 million less than the president's request. The legislation provides assistance for foreign governments and non-governmental organizations, contributions to multilateral financial institutions, dues for international organizations and export assistance for U.S. firms.

While the omnibus measure grants the president's request for credit for the IMF to replenish its coffers depleted by financial crises in Asia, Russia and elsewhere, the release of the funds is contingent on the IMF instituting a series of internal and external changes demanded by critics in Congress angered by the fund's handling of the global financial crisis. The House-passed bill had provided only $3.4 billion for the IMF.

The measure also provides $3 billion in aid for Israel and $2.1 billion for Egypt. However, for the first time since the signing of the Camp David accords between Israel and Egypt in March 1979, it cuts economic assistance to the two countries as a part of a 10-year phaseout in U.S. economic aid. It also provides $847 million for the republics of the former Soviet Union, including $46 million in "emergency" supplemental funds, and $35 million for the Korean Peninsula Energy Development Organization, money that would be available only after March 1999 and only if the president certifies that North Korea is making progress toward ending its nuclear and ballistic missile programs.

The measure maintains the current law imposing military and economic sanctions against Azerbaijan, codifies sanctions against Serbia and provides aid to Bosnia. For the first time in 20 years, it provides no military financing assistance to either Greece or Turkey.

The measure appropriates $657 million for export assistance programs and provides $193 million for the Global Environment Facility, a controversial program administered by the World Bank that the House had cut.

House Panel Trims President's IMF Request

JULY 18 — Supporters of the International Monetary Fund are gaining ground in their campaign to step up U.S. contributions to the lending institution.

For almost a year, Republican lawmakers led by House Majority Leader Dick Armey of Texas, have stymied the Clinton administration's bid for an additional $18 billion in credit for the IMF, which critics say only helps countries avoid making the tough economic choices they need to attract private funds.

Armey, Majority Whip Tom DeLay, R-Texas, and Joint Economic Committee Chairman H. James Saxton, R-N.J., have repeatedly argued that even if the aid is granted, it should be tied to a list of reforms they say would make the IMF more accountable and transparent.

But Republicans have come under pressure to grant the credit, because bolstering faltering economies in Asia and Russia would increase demand for U.S. farm products. House Speaker Newt Gingrich, R-Ga., last month promised a renewed effort for the IMF funds.

Appropriations

The IMF in Brief

JANUARY 10 — The International Monetary Fund is a cooperative organization of 182 nations intended to stabilize the exchange of currencies and the world economy. It has a staff of about 2,600 in 110 countries, and is administered by a 24-member executive board chaired by Managing Director Michel Camdessus of France. Each member nation has a voice on the Board of Governors.

The fund was established after World War II to prevent another international economic collapse on the scale of the Great Depression. Final negotiations for creating the IMF took place at an international conference held in Bretton Woods, N.H., in July 1944. The organization began operations with 39 member nations. The IMF's primary role is overseeing the international monetary system, but it is best known to the public for lending money to countries in financial crisis. During the international debt crisis of 1983 and 1984, it lent $28 billion to member countries that owed money to other members. In 1995, it extended more than $17 billion in credit to Mexico and $6.2 billion to Russia. All past loans, however, are dwarfed by the more than $100 billion it is extending to East Asia nations.

Upon joining the IMF, each member contributes a certain sum of money called a quota subscription, which is a kind of membership fee. Quotas form a pool of money from which the IMF can draw to lend to members in financial difficulty. They also form a basis for determining how much the contributing member can borrow from the IMF, and for the member's clout in a complicated voting system. The United States, which contributes 18 percent of total quotas, has about 265,000 votes, while the Marshall Islands has 275.

The IMF currently has the equivalent of $196 billion in quotas. In December, the executive board proposed a 45 percent increase in quotas, to about $287 billion, partly in response to the crisis in East Asia. The U.S. quota would increase by about $14.5 billion. If lawmakers approve the one-time appropriation, the money would not all necessarily leave the Treasury, but would be available to the IMF as needed. (The United States would also make available $3.5 billion for a new $25 billion IMF program, the New Arrangements to Borrow, which would supplement other loan programs.)

The largest contributors to the IMF quotas are the United States, Germany, Japan, France and the United Kingdom, with percentages as follows:

U.S.A.	18.25 percent
Germany	5.67 percent
Japan	5.67 percent
France	5.1 percent
United Kingdom	5.1 percent

The House Appropriations Foreign Operations Subcommittee took a first step July 15, approving $3.4 billion in credit to the IMF as part of its fiscal 1999 foreign aid spending bill. The money would fund the "new arrangements to borrow," a credit line for developing countries.

It would carry a series of restrictions on IMF practices, including directing the organization to press recipient countries to comply with international trade agreements, end subsidized government loans or grants to favored industries, and give foreign creditors equal status with domestic lenders in bankruptcies.

The measure also would call for the IMF to release edited versions of its board minutes and major documents and end subsidized interest rates for regular borrowers.

Working on Compromise

Subcommittee members beat back an attempt by ranking Democrat Nancy Pelosi of California to chip in another $14.5 billion to the IMF's regular lending pool, as President Clinton asked.

Appropriations Committee Chairman Robert L. Livingston, R-La., urged panel members to hold off voting for the additional funds until GOP leaders can work out a compromise. He pledged that the issue would be taken up at a later stage in the legislative process — most likely at a full committee markup the week of July 20. In the meantime, lawmakers said GOP leaders will try to agree on how to deal with anti-abortion restrictions on family planning aid that have dogged previous foreign aid bills.

In a July 15 speech to the U.S. Chamber of Commerce, Armey conceded he was losing his battle against the IMF funds.

"In the end, I suppose they will pretty much get as much money as they are looking for with as little accountability as they desire," Armey said.

Funding for the IMF is a highlight of a foreign aid bill that cuts Clinton's budget request by so much that Secretary of State Madeleine K. Albright and a top House Democrat are threatening to try to scuttle the measure.

The panel approved spending $12.5 billion on new and continuing programs, $316 million below current spending and $1.1 billion under the amount that Clinton requested.

The subcommittee also approved only $352 million of the half-billion dollars Clinton requested to repay debts to international financial institutions such as regional development banks and the Global Environmental Facility.

Subcommittee Chairman Sonny Callahan, R-Ala., said that in a telephone conversation on July 14, Albright told him she would recommend that Clinton veto the bill because of the low funding levels.

But Callahan said the administration could not expect appropriators to grant more money than last year. "The allocation we have is the allocation we have to live with," Callahan said.

Threatening Interests

The reduced spending prompted David R. Obey of Wisconsin, ranking Democrat on the Appropriations Committee, to say that he would vote against the bill. "This is more threatening to American interests than in defense of them," Obey said.

With Russia facing a financial crisis, Obey criticized the bill for cutting funding to Russia and the other successor states of the Soviet Union to $590 million, $335 million below Clinton's request and $180 million below current spending.

Not only was the funding too low, Obey said, but what remained was boxed in by far too many restrictions.

"The funding for the former Soviet Union is probably worse than providing no funding at all," said Obey. "It's so tied up, there are so many earmarks, that we have no ability to influence policy."

The measure renews a restriction in recent spending bills tying half of Russia's aid to ending Moscow's nuclear and missile cooperation with Iran, although this sanction could be waived by the president.

The bill also would prevent any individual former Soviet republic from obtaining more than $147.5 million in aid. The administration had requested about $225 million each for Russia and Ukraine.

And the bill would reserve $195 million of the aid for the Southern Caucasus region, including $78 million set aside to encourage Armenia and neighboring Azerbaijan to resolve their longstanding conflict.

Democrats quarreled with Callahan's decision to slash money for the Global Environmental Facility, a relatively new organization that lends money for environmental and energy projects in developing countries.

The administration had requested nearly $300 million for the facility — $107.5 million in new funding and $192.5 million to pay off U.S. debts. Callahan followed the recent GOP practice of slashing funds for the organization, providing only $43 million in current funds.

Pelosi sought to add $50 million toward U.S. debts to the organization, arguing that without the extra money, the facility could run dry by next spring. But Joe Knollenberg, R-Mich., argued that the money was a back-door way to implement the Kyoto protocol on global warming and other environmental pacts pushed by the administration and not endorsed by the Senate.

Pelosi's amendment was defeated largely along party lines, 8-7.

Korean Energy

Callahan's bill also takes a crack at another international organization favored by the Clinton administration — the Korean Peninsula Energy Development Organization.

The organization was set up under the 1994 agreement between the United States and North Korea that sought to freeze and dismantle Pyongyang's budding nuclear weapons program and the graphite-moderated nuclear reactors that fed it.

The development organization directs money from international donors toward the construction of two light-water nuclear reactors and deliveries of heavy fuel oil to meet North Korea's energy needs.

But at a hearing of the Senate Foreign Relations Subcommittee on East Asian and Pacific Affairs July 14, administration officials acknowledged that the organization has plunged $38 million into debt, slowing the oil deliveries, because contributions from foreign donors, particularly Japan and South Korea, have been well below expectations.

Administration officials said they would ask Congress for an additional $15 million this year, beyond the $35 million already requested, and would request extra money in the future to pay off the debts, arguing that the expense was justified by the program's success in halting Pyongyang's nuclear program.

The claims were undercut by a July 7 General Accounting Office report that North Korea has refused full access to its nuclear sites, making it difficult to determine if the country has hidden enough plutonium to build nuclear bombs.

The report is likely to fuel the skepticism of Republican lawmakers who have long seen the program as nuclear blackmail. Callahan's bill calls for $30 million in funds for the deal, $5 million below Clinton's request.

To obtain the funds, Clinton would have to certify that North Korea has terminated its nuclear weapons program and stopped transferring ballistic missile technology to terrorist states such as Iran.

The cuts in the program passed without debate at the July 15 markup.

Israel and Egypt

But panel members vigorously debated a historic change: a multi-year phaseout of economic assistance to Israel and Egypt that would save about $100 million in fiscal 1999.

Following an Israeli pledge to wean itself from $1.2 billion in annual U.S. economic assistance over 10 years, the panel agreed to cut Israel's economic aid to slightly below $1.1 billion next year. At the same time, it agreed to raise Israel's military assistance from $1.8 billion to $1.86 billion.

Egypt, which is usually given about two-thirds as much aid as Israel, escaped a similar reduction. The subcommittee approved by voice vote an amendment by Knollenberg and Nita M. Lowey, D-N.Y., leaving Egypt's military assistance at $1.3 billion, but cutting its economic assistance by $40 million instead of $80 million. Lowey said that Egypt needed economic assistance more than military aid.

Obey voted for the measure, but expressed his reluctance to grant Israel additional military funds, noting that the Israeli government has yet to make good on its commitment last year to transfer some of its aid to Jordan.

House Markup Delayed; Senate Panel Avoids Controversy

JULY 25 — Two House Republican leaders with broader political ambitions are sparring over an $18 billion credit package for the International Monetary Fund (IMF), endangering funds the Clinton administration says are essential to the stability of economies from Russia to Brazil to East Asia.

Faced with opposition to the package by Majority Leader Dick Armey, R-Texas, House Speaker Newt Gingrich, R-Ga., stepped in July 21 and told Appropriations Committee Chairman Robert L. Livingston, R-

Appropriations

La., to delay the next day's scheduled markup of the fiscal 1999 foreign operations spending bill that was to include the IMF credit.

Armey, who had all but conceded defeat on July 15, telling a business audience that the IMF had enough congressional support to get anything it wanted, did an about-face after a torrent of criticism from conservative commentators who accused him of "betraying" his long-time opposition to the credit package.

At a July 20 news conference, Armey said he had reassessed the strength of the coalition opposed to granting the full $18 billion.

Armey has long argued that the IMF aid only encourages countries to think that they will be bailed out after making poor economic decisions and that it violates free-market principles.

He and Joint Economic Committee Chairman H. James Saxton, R-N.J., have argued that the IMF already has a substantial pool of money it can tap as well as the ability to float bonds on the private market.

In his July 20 remarks, Armey said he would only support providing $3.4 billion for a new IMF fund aimed at stemming currency crises in developing countries. The Foreign Operations Appropriations Subcommittee approved those funds July 15 as part of the draft foreign aid bill.

Armey warned the full Appropriations Committee not to chip in an additional $14.5 billion in credit that the administration has requested as part of the regular replenishment of the IMF. Administration officials have said that after lending tens of billions of dollars to Korea, Russia, Indonesia and other nations, the IMF's credit pool is drying up.

"If they bring the bill to the House floor with more than the $3.4 [billion], they should expect a very big fight on the floor, and I have to say, in all candor, they should not expect to win that," Armey said.

Armey's remarks directly challenged Livingston, who has supported funding all of Clinton's IMF request. The two have a personal stake in the debate: Livingston has said that he will vie with Armey for the Speaker's chair if Gingrich steps down to run for president after the 1998 elections.

Livingston said it would be both imprudent and politically unwise for Republicans not to increase funds to the IMF, because the increase is backed by two key GOP constituencies — agriculture and business.

Faced with these divisions, Gingrich, who has pledged his support for the IMF funding, told appropriators to hold off on marking up the foreign aid bill until September to see if GOP leaders could work out their differences.

"We have some differences in opinion across the board," Livingston said. "We thought it was important not to put [committee members] on the spot one way or another."

Foreign Operations Subcommittee Chairman Sonny Callahan, R-Ala., snapped that Armey should submit "constructive, realistic conditions" for the IMF. "I don't think he [Armey] has the ability to kill whatever he wants just because he is the leader," Callahan said. "Maybe I'm wrong, but I don't think so."

Treasury Secretary Robert E. Rubin on July 22 called on the House to stop delaying. "I think there will be sufficient votes" once a bill is brought to the floor, he told reporters.

Federal Reserve Chairman Alan Greenspan also urged lawmakers to approve the funds to avoid further Asian turmoil.

"When your house is potentially burning down and . . . the sparks are going in your direction, your concern is to make sure that the fire does not spread," Greenspan told the House Banking Committee July 22.

Ties to the Economy

IMF funding faces a much smoother path in the Senate, where on July 21 the Appropriations Committee approved its foreign aid bill (S 2334), including all of the $18 billion in credit for the IMF, by a vote of 26-1.

The Senate approved the IMF package earlier this year as part of the fiscal 1998 supplemental spending bill (PL 105-174), but the funds later were stripped out in a House-Senate conference.

During the July 21 markup, Senate Budget Committee Chairman Pete V. Domenici, R-N.M., warned that "the failure of this Congress to approve these funds could cause the American economy to go down."

While the Senate panel avoided the IMF controversy, committee members tackled some issues of their own.

Arlen Specter, R-Pa., offered an amendment, approved without objection, that would allow funding for preparatory meetings on the Comprehensive Nuclear Test Ban Treaty (Treaty Doc 105-28).

But Specter held off introducing an amendment that would have called for setting aside $29 million that President Clinton requested to lay the groundwork for implementing the pact. Mitch McConnell, R-Ky., chairman of the Foreign Operations Subcommittee, promised Specter they could work out a compromise on the issue before the bill comes to the Senate floor.

Specter and Joseph R. Biden Jr., D-Del., have been gathering co-sponsors on a proposed resolution calling for the Senate to consider the treaty, which is strongly supported by the White House. Specter said recent nuclear tests by India and Pakistan only "emphasize the importance of stopping nuclear tests worldwide."

But Republicans, led by Foreign Relations Committee Chairman Jesse Helms, R-N.C., have blocked consideration of the treaty, saying the accord could not be verified or enforced.

McConnell also pledged to work with committee chairman Ted Stevens, R-Alaska, Slade Gorton, R-Wash., and Patty Murray, D-Wash., to correct a provision he included in the bill that other lawmakers complained could affect billions of dollars in U.S. exports.

The provision would ban the Export-Import Bank from providing loans or loan guarantees for exports to state-owned enterprises in the former Soviet Union, as part of a $102 million increase in funds for the export development agency.

Stevens said the provision could hurt the participation of U.S. companies in oil exploration off Russia's Sahkalin Island. Murray said it could halt the sale of 10 Boeing aircraft to Russia.

Still, the Senate bill is more generous to the former Soviet Union than the draft House bill, providing $740 million instead of $590 million.

However, the Senate bill would set aside much of the additional money for Ukraine ($210 million), Georgia ($95 million) and Armenia ($90 million).

The House subcommittee's bill

would prohibit any former Soviet republic from receiving more than one-quarter of the total aid pool: $147.5 million.

The House bill also would reserve $195 million for the Southern Caucasus, which includes Armenia, Georgia and Azerbaijan. Of that, $78 million would be set aside as a peace dividend to encourage Armenia and Azerbaijan to resolve their longstanding conflict.

The Senate measure would renew benefits that Congress first granted Azerbaijan in the fiscal 1998 foreign operations spending bill (PL 105-118). *(1997 Almanac, p. 9-37)*

That measure allowed the oil-rich state to receive loans and investment insurance and help in feasibility studies from the Export-Import Bank, the Overseas Private Investment Corporation, and the Trade and Development Agency.

In the current spending bill, the Senate Appropriations Committee's ranking Democrat, Robert C. Byrd of West Virginia, included report language encouraging these agencies to assist efforts to build an oil pipeline from Azerbaijan to a port on Turkey's Mediterranean coast.

Under pressure from the United States, Azerbaijan recently announced it would support such a pipeline, even though it is more expensive than alternative routes through Russia and Iran.

Some lawmakers, including Livingston and Sen. Sam Brownback, R-Kan., have urged the United States to reciprocate by lifting a 6-year-old ban on direct aid to Azerbaijan.

But several House members continue to insist that Azerbaijan first lift its blockade of Armenia, an embargo instituted by the predominantly Muslim state to win back the disputed enclave of Nagorno-Karabakh from control by Armenia, which is mostly Orthodox.

These House Republicans included report language in their bill that funds could only be released, before an accord, to countries that are willing to engage in "direct or proximity peace talks without preconditions."

Armenia has pushed for direct talks that would include Armenian leaders in Nagorno-Karabakh, while Azerbaijan has preferred negotiations through mediators, including Russia, France and the United States.

In another break from the House bill, the Senate measure would set aside $100 million in aid for Indonesia, which has suffered from the economic crisis in Asia and from a political crisis that led to the departure of its dictator, Suharto.

McConnell also inserted a provision in the Senate bill that would hold off $800 million in aid to the World Bank pending a General Accounting Office audit of the international institution. Bank President James Wolfensohn has ordered an extensive investigation of allegations of widespread internal corruption.

Russia, IMF Aid Lead Debate As Senate OKs Bill

SEPTEMBER 5 — As financial markets tumble from Moscow to Caracas, lawmakers and Clinton administration officials are finding it difficult to reach a consensus on how to deal with the global financial crisis.

The Senate took a first step Sept. 2, passing, 90-3, a fiscal 1999 foreign aid spending bill (S 2334) that includes $17.9 billion in additional credit for the International Monetary Fund (IMF). The fund's coffers have been depleted by $40 billion in bailouts for several Asian nations and Russia. *(Vote 259, p. S-40)*

The House appears likely to take a more cautious approach. The House Appropriations Committee is set to mark up its version of the foreign aid bill Sept. 10. That bill now includes only $3.4 billion for the IMF to fund a special line of credit for developing countries.

House Appropriations Committee Chairman Robert L. Livingston, R-La., originally hoped his panel would chip in an additional $14.5 billion that the administration has requested to replenish the IMF's coffers.

But in an Aug. 31 interview, Livingston said, "My inclination is to report out the bill as is."

Livingston said the near collapse of the Russian economy had made him "sit up and notice" the possible "waste of the taxpayers' dollars" in the proposed $22.6 billion IMF bailout package for Russia.

"I am having second thoughts about that support," Livingston said, further dampening prospects for aid that is already opposed by key Republican leaders such as House Majority Leader Dick Armey of Texas.

White House Strategy

In the face of congressional resistance, the administration continues to press hard for the money. Treasury Secretary Robert E. Rubin wrote to lawmakers Sept. 1 urging them to act with the "utmost dispatch."

But during a two-day summit meeting with Russian President Boris Yeltsin in Moscow, President Clinton said that until Russia undertakes significant reforms, it should not look to the U.S. government to bail it out of its financial crisis.

"How long it will take to get better depends a lot more on you and what happens here than anything else we outsiders can do," Clinton told a Russian reporter at a press conference. "Although, if there is a clear movement towards reform, I'll do everything I can to accelerate outside support of all kinds."

Some lawmakers said the administration was being too cautious in reacting to events in Russia.

Sens. Daniel Patrick Moynihan, D-N.Y., and Gordon H. Smith, R-Ore., chairman of the Foreign Relations Committee's European Affairs Subcommittee, said the United States should eventually support a massive aid program for its former Cold War adversary akin to the post-World War II Marshall Plan for Western Europe.

"It is in our interest to take an active approach," Smith said. "This is not a project for a few years, this is a project for several decades."

But Sen. Mitch McConnell, R-Ky., who plays a key role as chairman of the Appropriations Committee's Foreign Operations Subcommittee, said Russia was already too dependent on Western aid.

McConnell said previous loans had not been invested to generate jobs and economic growth but had merely fueled current consumption.

"Russia's addiction to international loans is not healthy — for their economy or our interests," McConnell said. "The administration must follow through and use our aid for programs which will sustain the needed tax and commercial reforms, or the current crisis

Appropriations

will only get worse, if that is possible."

Despite his skepticism, McConnell led efforts to win full funding for the IMF.

"While I was less concerned in the spring about the IMF's financial standing, I now believe the time has come for the Congress to complete our commitment," McConnell said. "I think the fund's solid financial footing avoids further U.S. bilateral commitment of funds and is key to the recovery of our Pacific trading partners which, I expect, in turn, will help stave off a slow-down of our economy."

Conditional Payments

McConnell helped beat back an attempt by GOP Sen. Jon Kyl of Arizona to revive restrictions on IMF money the Appropriations Committee added to an early version (S 1769 — S Rept 105-169) of the fiscal 1998 supplemental spending bill (PL 105-174). The IMF payment was removed from the final supplemental bill.

Kyl proposed that the IMF receive the additional funds only if it agreed to require all borrowing countries to abide by international trade agreements, to stop directing loans or subsidies to favored companies or institutions, and to ensure that U.S. creditors receive the same treatment in bankruptcy proceedings as their own creditors.

The bill as passed urges the IMF to adopt such requirements but does not compel it to do so. Kyl said such requirements were needed to "assure that the money will not be wasted" on bailing out corrupt and inefficient economies.

"That is the difference — do you try to pursue it or do you guarantee it before you give this taxpayer money?" Kyl asked.

But Joseph R. Biden Jr. of Delaware, ranking Democrat on the Foreign Relations Committee, said that by requiring the United States to win support from other IMF members, Kyl's amendment would guarantee an indefinite delay in giving the IMF funds at a time when world markets need a "shot of confidence."

Senate Appropriations Committee Chairman Ted Stevens, R-Alaska, and other members agreed, and Kyl's amendment was tabled (killed), 74-19. (Vote 256, p. S-40)

Though the bill includes Secretary of State Madeleine K. Albright's top objective — IMF funding — she has recommended that Clinton veto the measure because it falls about $1 billion short of his budget request.

The bill calls for spending $12.6 billion, aside from money allocated for debts to the IMF and other international organizations.

For example, the bill would cut U.S. aid to the states of the former Soviet Union and steer most of it to countries other than Russia.

It would set aside most of the $740 million in aid for Ukraine ($210 million), Georgia ($95 million) and Armenia ($90 million), following a pattern in which Ukraine has become the third-largest recipient of U.S. aid in recent years, after Israel and Egypt.

Still, the bill's total for the former Soviet states is well above the $590 million total called for in the draft House bill. Both measures fall short of the $925 million requested by the Clinton administration.

Prodded by Stevens, senators also agreed to drop a provision that would have prohibited the Export-Import Bank from providing loans or loan guarantees for exports to state-owned enterprises in the former Soviet Union, as part of a $102 million increase in funds for the agency, whose purpose is to develop U.S. exports.

Stevens and some other senators had feared that the restrictions could cost billions of dollars in exports.

Powerful Lobby

The White House lost its effort to lift the six-year-old restrictions on U.S. aid to Azerbaijan, an oil-rich country beside the Caspian Sea in Central Asia. Azerbaijan and neighboring Armenia are locked in a struggle over the enclave of Nagorno-Karabakh.

Sen. Sam Brownback, R-Kan., chairman of the Foreign Relations Subcommittee on Near Eastern and South Asian Affairs, had planned to add a provision to the bill abolishing the restrictions. Brownback changed his mind, however, and said he lacked enough votes to pass the measure, with members reluctant to take on the formidable Armenian-American lobby in an election year.

Korean Provocations

The White House also fell short on two key votes on the foreign aid bill.

Senators reacted sharply to North Korea's Aug. 31 test launch of a medium-range missile that passed over northern Japan, as well as to recent revelations that Pyongyang may be building a nuclear reactor in violation of a 1994 agreement with the United States.

Sen. John McCain, R-Ariz., said the tests formed part of "an extraordinarily consistent North Korean pattern of alternating minor and manipulative gestures of good will with acts of terror and provocation toward its South Korean neighbors. To that list, we can now add new provocations toward Japan and the United States."

Those provocations, McCain said, should lead the United States to follow Japan's lead and cut off funding to an international organization — the Korean Peninsula Energy Development Organization, set up under the 1994 agreement.

In that accord, North Korea agreed to freeze and dismantle its nascent nuclear weapons program and the graphite-moderated nuclear reactors that fed it. In return, the United States, Japan, South Korea and other Western nations set up the energy organization to funnel money from international donors into the construction of two light-water nuclear reactors in North Korea and into deliveries of heavy fuel oil to meet North Korea's needs.

The Senate fell short of a complete end to funds for the energy organization, instead adopting an amendment by McCain that would condition the $35 million allocated to the international organization on a presidential certification that North Korea has halted its nuclear program, or a waiver by the president on national security grounds. The Senate failed to table McCain's amendment, 11-80. (Vote 257, p. S-40)

Under pressure from the administration, McCain backed off plans to condition North Korean aid to an end to Pyongyang's exports of missile technology to such countries as Pakistan and Iran.

Daniel R. Coats, R-Ind., withdrew an amendment that would have shifted funds from the Korean energy organization to counterterrorism activities. Coats did succeed in adding a provision that would require the administration to share its intelligence on North Korea's nuclear program with six congressional committees.

The Senate action on the Korean energy organization marked the end of administration plans to win increased funds to compensate for lower than expected contributions from other nations.

"If U.S. funding for [the energy pact] is the pillar of our non-proliferation policy and the key to burden sharing, I think it is time we start building a new foundation for our policy," McConnell said. "Secret nuclear facilities, flight testing, ballistic missiles and who knows what other activities are not a non-proliferation policy, they are simply a non-policy."

Test Ban Test Vote

The White House also suffered a setback to its counter-proliferation policy when a test vote indicated less than overwhelming support for the Comprehensive Nuclear Test Ban Treaty (Treaty Doc 105-28).

For months, the administration has pressed the Senate to approve the treaty, arguing that the accord was more necessary after India and Pakistan conducted nuclear tests earlier this year.

But Foreign Relation Committee Chairman Jesse Helms, R-N.C., backed by Majority Leader Trent Lott, R-Miss., has blocked consideration of the treaty, saying it cannot be verified or enforced. Helms also said he first wants to consider treaties the administration has yet to submit, such as the 1997 Kyoto Treaty on global warming. *(1997 Almanac, p. 4-13)*

Hoping to break the logjam, Arlen Specter, R-Pa., sought to demonstrate enough Senate support for the test ban treaty that Helms would be forced to allow his panel to consider the accord.

As a test vote, Specter introduced an amendment that would authorize $29 million to fund an international commission laying the groundwork and installing technical equipment to monitor compliance with the treaty.

The Senate approved the amendment, 49-44, far short of the two-thirds majority needed to pass the treaty itself. *(Vote 254, p. S-40)*

Nearly all Republicans opposed the amendment, with Lott urging them to vote against it. Lott noted his continuing opposition to the treaty but also claimed that any funds appropriated now would likely be wasted because the treaty was unlikely to enter into force in the near future.

Serbian Sanctions

Taking on another controversial issue, the Senate adopted, by voice vote, an amendment by Gordon Smith that would write into law sanctions the administration imposed on Serbia and Montenegro, initially to punish Serbian aggression in Bosnia.

Under the sanctions, the United States opposes aid to Serbia by international financial institutions and opposes Serbia's designation as the legitimate successor to the former Yugoslavia before Jan. 1, 2000, unless it meets certain conditions.

Serbia must contribute to the peace process in Bosnia, turn over suspected war criminals to international authorities and make progress on a settlement with ethnic Albanian rebels in the Serbian province of Kosovo.

The amendment comes as the Serbs are driving Kosovo's Albanians from their homes, provoking concern among Western countries.

NATO officials have devised options for military action. But so far, allied leaders have held off sending in military forces.

"What we are asking for is responsible behavior," Smith said. "Before lifting the outer wall of sanctions, which in effect is a reward for Serbia, we should expect nothing less."

Shifting Middle East

Lawmakers sought to bolster opposition to Saddam Hussein's government in Iraq by including $10 million to help form a coalition against him and build the case for indicting him as a war criminal.

The measure also included some significant changes in the pattern of U.S. foreign aid.

In a historic change, Israel and Egypt saw their aid cut. Economic assistance to Israel would fall from $1.2 billion to $1.08 billion, while military aid would rise to $1.86 billion from $1.8 billion.

Aid to Egypt, which has customarily been set at two-thirds of Israeli aid, would be cut proportionately, with military aid holding steady at $1.3 billion and economic aid falling $40 million to $775 million.

The bill would end military aid to NATO allies Greece and Turkey.

At the same time, some countries have now become significant recipients of U.S. largess.

Tunisia, one of the few Arab states seeking to establish friendly relations with Israel, was rewarded with $7 million and promises of future support.

Lawmakers agreed to set aside $100 million for Indonesia, which is under massive political and economic strain in the Asian financial crisis. They also approved an amendment by Dianne Feinstein, D-Calif., urging increased humanitarian aid to Indonesia.

The Senate bill would cut off aid to Congo (formerly Zaire), currently engaged in a civil war.

And senators adopted, by voice vote, an amendment by Mike DeWine, R-Ohio, that would require the United States to distribute much of its aid to Haiti through non-governmental organizations until the Haitian government overcomes political paralysis and meets a set of legislative conditions.

House Panel Approves Its Bill Despite Veto Threat

SEPTEMBER 12 — The House Appropriations Committee approved a fiscal 1999 foreign aid bill Sept. 10 that includes anti-abortion language President Clinton has threatened to veto but not $14.5 billion in credit for the International Monetary Fund (IMF) that he has sought.

The $12.5 billion foreign operations bill was approved by voice vote.

Even before the committee met, Secretary of State Madeleine K. Albright urged Clinton to veto the bill because it would fall about $1 billion short of his budget request, excluding the repayment of U.S. debts to international organizations and the IMF.

A Senate bill (S 2334 — S Rept 105-255) passed Sept. 2 includes roughly the same amount of spending on bilateral foreign aid activities. But the Senate included the administration's full request for funds for the IMF and left out the anti-abortion provision.

Appropriations

The House bill includes $3.4 billion for a special IMF credit line aimed at developing countries. But Appropriations Committee Chairman Robert L. Livingston, R-La., urged members to hold off approving the additional $14.5 billion in credit the Clinton administration has sought to replenish the IMF's coffers, depleted by financial crises in emerging markets in Asia, Eastern Europe and Latin America.

Livingston said he wanted Treasury Secretary Robert E. Rubin first to agree to a requirement that the IMF conduct its operations with greater openness and accountability. He noted that Russia's chief negotiator with the IMF has recently boasted that he had "conned" the fund out of billions of dollars in loans by lying about the extent of his country's financial problems.

"The question is, do we give them the money and not have any conditions? Or do we work out the conditions? Or maybe if we don't work out the conditions — not give them the money?" Livingston asked.

Committee members supported Livingston's position by defeating, 22-30, an amendment by Nancy Pelosi of California, the ranking Democrat on the Foreign Operations Subcommittee, which would have added the $14.5 billion for the IMF.

Pelosi said the money was needed to restore confidence in sagging world financial markets and to prevent the crisis from spreading.

"This is not a free vote," Pelosi said. "Contagion trumps all other concerns. We cannot have a Congress that says to the world, 'Stop, we want to get off.' "

But House Majority Whip Tom DeLay, R-Texas, argued that the increase was unnecessary. "The IMF is an anachronism in today's modern global economy," DeLay said. "We ought to be talking in terms of phasing out the IMF."

Foreign Operations Subcommittee Chairman Sonny Callahan, R-Ala., who considers himself an IMF supporter, reassured panel members that they could wait until the issue was resolved in a House-Senate conference committee.

"There's plenty of time to add an increase," Callahan said.

The committee also defeated, 24-28, another Pelosi amendment that would have called on the IMF to consider labor rights and environmental protection in making loans. The bill already includes some conditions.

Family Planning Redux

The administration also suffered a setback when the committee approved, by voice vote, an amendment by Roger Wicker, R-Miss., adding antiabortion restrictions to international family planning aid.

The abortion debate has held up the foreign operations spending bill each year since 1995, sometimes for weeks, sometimes for months.

The Wicker amendment is identical to restrictions in a State Department authorization bill (HR 1757) cleared by Congress in April but not yet sent to Clinton, who has threatened to veto it.

The provision would reinstate a policy of the Reagan and Bush administrations banning aid to international family planning groups that perform, lobby for or otherwise advocate abortion, even if they use their own money.

In a relaxation of the Reagan/Bush standard, the president would be allowed to waive the section of the bill related to groups that perform abortions. But if he did, spending on family planning programs would be limited to $356 million a year, $29 million below current spending.

The amendment passed the committee with little debate, but Pelosi said she will challenge the provision when the bill reaches the House floor.

Democrats were more vigorous but no more successful in trying to block Republican attempts to cut off funds to the Korean Peninsula Energy Development Organization.

Republicans have long criticized the organization, a consortium formed primarily by the United States, Japan and South Korea to supply North Korea's energy needs as part of a 1994 agreement to curb North Korea's nascent nuclear weapons program.

Oil for Peace?

Republicans have described the agreement as blackmail and have said North Korea continues to develop nuclear weapons in secret. The accusations gained new force after Pyongyang's recent test of a medium-range ballistic missile and revelations that it may be building a nuclear reactor in secret.

In its bill, the Senate voted to condition the $35 million it appropriated to the energy organization on a presidential certification that North Korea has halted its nuclear program.

House appropriators went a step further, approving by voice vote a Livingston amendment that follows Japan's lead by cutting off all aid to the organization.

Pelosi sought to counter Livingston by offering a substitute amendment that would have added a condition to the bill's previous restrictions requiring the United States to be able to have access to North Korean facilities in order to "assure their compliance with the framework agreement." Pelosi's amendment was defeated, 16-29, largely along party lines.

The committee action came as the State Department announced a resumption in talks with North Korea on its missile and nuclear programs and pledged to send several hundred thousand tons of fuel oil to Pyongyang. U.S. officials reportedly also are considering stepped-up food aid.

In the talks with North Korea, U.S. negotiators are seeking access to possible nuclear or weapons facilities.

Republicans also defeated Democratic attempts to add funds for the Global Environmental Facility, an international organization formed along the lines of the World Bank that provides grants to developing countries for environmental initiatives.

In his budget request, Clinton had asked for $300 million for the Global Environmental Facility — $107.5 million for fiscal 1999 spending and $192.5 million for back payments. But House appropriators only granted $42.5 million.

Pelosi sought to add another $50 million to pay debts, saying the organization was running out of funds.

But DeLay repeated Republican contentions that the funds would effectively implement the Kyoto protocol on climate change even though the Clinton administration has not sent the Senate the treaty, which is opposed by many lawmakers.

"Call me crazy, but I have a problem providing funding in support of treaties that the Congress has not even ratified yet," DeLay said.

Pelosi disputed that the funds would implement the Kyoto treaty.

"This is not a manifestation of a sinister international plot to restrict U.S. industrial growth," she said. Her amendment was defeated, 19-27.

Caspian Policy

Livingston also succeeded with amendments that would revamp U.S. policy toward Armenia and Azerbaijan.

Committee members endorsed, by voice vote, his proposal to lift a six-year-old ban on direct aid to Azerbaijan, an oil-rich, former Soviet republic on the Caspian Sea in Central Asia. They also approved report language encouraging the Overseas Private Investment Corporation to increase the amount of risk insurance and investment finance it would be willing to provide toward construction of oil and gas pipelines in the region. *(1992 Almanac, p. 523)*

Since the breakup of the Soviet Union, Armenia and Azerbaijan have been locked in a fight over the largely Armenian enclave of Nagorno-Karabagh.

Although Armenian troops have occupied the enclave for several years, U.S. and Azeri officials say it is legally part of Azerbaijan. A cease-fire has held since 1994, but attempts by the United States, France and Russia to broker a settlement have fallen through.

Albright and other Clinton administration officials argue that the aid restrictions have hurt the ability of the United States to act as an honest broker in the dispute. They and other supporters of lifting the restrictions, particularly U.S. oil companies, have argued that the ban hinders U.S. efforts to persuade Azerbaijan and other Caspian Sea countries to ship their oil through a Western-oriented pipeline to Turkey rather than through Iran or Russia.

The restrictions, Livingston said, "endanger our national interest by impeding our Caspian energy diplomacy efforts."

But longtime supporters of Armenia and Armenian-American interests said that the change would reward a government in Azerbaijan that is corrupt and has engaged in ethnic cleansing.

They said that the 1992 law (PL 102-511) had taken the appropriate stance by cutting off direct aid to the Azerbaijan government unless it stopped blockading Armenia.

Rep. John Edward Porter, R-Ill., said the ban "can end tomorrow. We don't need to do anything in Congress. Azerbaijan simply needs to say that the blockade is over."

Negotiations Continue Over IMF Credit Line

OCTOBER 10 — As congressional Republicans and the White House continued to haggle over the outlines of a catchall spending bill, some of the thorniest issues were in the foreign policy arena.

The most important dispute was over $14.5 billion in credit that President Clinton requested to bolster reserves of the International Monetary Fund (IMF).

The Senate included the funds in its version of the foreign operations appropriations bill (S 2334 — S Rept 105-255) passed Sept. 2. But the House did not include the money in its bill (HR 4569 — H Rept 105-719) approved on Sept. 17. Both measures did include $3.4 billion in credit for a special fund aimed at stemming currency crises in developing countries.

As the IMF bailed out battered economies from South Korea to Brazil during the past year, President Clinton repeatedly pleaded with Congress to approve the credit, saying it was needed to restore confidence in the world economy.

Republicans, particularly House Majority Leader Dick Armey, R-Texas, have resisted those appeals, saying IMF loans only encourage creditors to lend money to poorly managed countries, knowing that they will be bailed out by the fund if borrowers have difficulty repaying the loans.

For most of the year, Clinton and Treasury Secretary Robert E. Rubin have said the United States needed to pay its share of the IMF increase before asking for major reforms of the international financial institution.

As Clinton told the world's finance ministers at the annual meeting of World Bank and IMF officials Oct. 6, "I have told Congress — we can debate how to reform the operations of the fire department, but there is no excuse for refusing to supply the fire department with water while the fire is burning."

Still, at the meetings, Clinton moved in Armey's direction, with a series of proposals designed, in part, to respond to GOP criticisms of the IMF.

These included efforts to make more information about the IMF and its agreements with borrowing countries available to the public, to press countries to adhere to international banking and accounting standards, and to make private lenders bear more of the cost of bad loans to debtor countries.

Clinton also proposed a new IMF credit line to help countries that had sound economic policies but whose currency had come under financial pressure from speculators.

Attaching Conditions

At an Oct. 6 press briefing, Armey told reporters that he was "gratified" by Clinton's recent policy statements and more inclined to support the full credit for the IMF.

"I think everybody now understands that the IMF has got to be made workable, if it is going to have resources to use in international financial circles," he said.

Yet, Armey, Clinton and congressional Democrats continue to differ about precisely what conditions should be attached to the new IMF funding.

Meeting with Rubin and White House Chief of Staff Erskine Bowles Oct. 8, Republicans added four conditions to those already in the bills approved by the House and Senate.

Under the GOP proposal, money would only be disbursed if Rubin and Federal Reserve Chairman Alan Greenspan certify that the world's major economic powers have agreed to:

- Require recipient countries to liberalize trade restrictions, eliminate government-subsidized loans to favored companies and give foreign lenders the same treatment as domestic creditors in bankruptcy proceedings;
- Require the IMF to make more of its information publicly available;
- Lend money at market rates, rather than subsidized rates;
- Limit loans to one year at a time.

Congressional aides said that in the end, it was likely that the call for one-year loan maturities and an end to below-market loans would be watered

Appropriations

down or eliminated, since the White House believes that gaining agreement from other countries would be impossible at this point.

Meanwhile, the White House faced opposition from congressional Democrats to the provision calling for liberalized trade and investment regimes.

"If they want to force the administration to take these conditions right now . . . I'm very concerned about that," Senate Minority Leader Tom Daschle, D-S.D., said Oct. 9.

House Appropriations Committee Chairman Robert L. Livingston of Louisiana was more upbeat.

"We've made great progress," Livingston said of the IMF negotiations. "It's 80 percent to 90 percent complete."

State Department Authorization

IMF funds are not the only foreign policy issue that negotiators were trying to resolve in the omnibus bill.

Daschle and Senate Foreign Relations Committee Chairman Jesse Helms, R-N.C., were trying to insert provisions of a State Department authorization bill (HR 1757) that would repay $1 billion in U.S. payments to the United Nations and reorganize the foreign affairs bureaucracy, without anti-abortion restrictions demanded by House Republicans. Because Clinton threatened to veto the bill over those restrictions, Helms and Senate Majority Leader Trent Lott, R-Miss., have not sent it to the president, even though it cleared April 28.

But Livingston said he would oppose any effort to add the U.N. funds to the catchall bill. "They could have sent that to the president six months ago. It doesn't have to be in our bill."

Disagreements also had to be resolved over funding for the United Nations Fund for Population Activities and the Korean Peninsula Energy Development Organization.

Catchall Measure Includes Clinton's IMF Request

OCTOBER 17, 24 — The Clinton administration won congressional backing for some of its key foreign policy priorities in the fiscal 1999 omnibus spending bill (HR 4328), including nearly $18 billion in credit for the International Monetary Fund (IMF) and close to $1 billion for countries of the former Soviet Union.

But a longstanding partisan dispute over abortion derailed another of President Clinton's top goals: getting Congress to support paying off nearly $1 billion in debts to the United Nations.

The mixed results highlighted continued Republican reluctance to participate in multilateral organizations, and the key role business groups and religious conservatives play in determining how the GOP approaches foreign policy issues.

For more than a year, the administration has been seeking to extend additional credit to the IMF, which depleted its reserves bailing out tottering economies from South Korea to Russia to Brazil.

Some Republicans, led by House Majority Leader Dick Armey of Texas, have resisted, saying IMF loans only encourage creditors to lend money to poorly managed countries, knowing that they would be bailed out.

However, GOP resistance has been worn down over the last several months as influential business and farm groups pressed Republican leaders to approve the credits, saying they were essential to reviving American farm and other exports to economies damaged by the global financial crisis.

Illusory Triumph

Armey and other Republicans still held firm against another $14.5 billion the administration sought to replenish the IMF's reserves. GOP leaders insisted that the IMF would not get the money unless it took several steps to make the fund more open and less likely to rescue risky investors.

Announcing the budget deal Oct. 15, Armey claimed victory on the issue, saying the U.S. contribution would be conditioned on major developing countries approving a series of changes in the IMF.

Because of Congress, Armey said at a press conference, "The IMF will no longer work in secret. The IMF will no longer be able to engage in transactions as they've done that have been harmful — harmful to the people in the nations while too attentive to the high rollers in international finance."

Diplomats, IMF officials and congressional aides said Armey's triumph was somewhat illusory, as most of the "conditions" require the IMF to do things it is already doing.

"From what I have seen, these are constructive suggestions that will help us pursue reforms that we have already started," said IMF Managing Director Michel Camdessus.

For instance, the bill would create special conditions on loans to countries facing a run on their currencies because of balance-of-payments problems and a loss of market confidence. But those conditions were established by the IMF when it set up the Supplemental Reserve Facility in December 1997.

Both the IMF and the bill would require that those borrowers be offered only short-term loans that would have to be repaid within one to two-and-a-half years at a rate 3 percent above the average market rates in five major industrialized countries.

The conditions would not apply to run-of-the-mill IMF loans, some of which are offered at below-market rates for periods as long as 10 years.

Other conditions on the IMF credit include:

- Liberalized trade restrictions by countries that receive loans, particularly South Korea. They would have to eliminate subsidized loans and treat foreign lenders on a par with domestic creditors.
- More public information about the IMF's loans and operations.
- A temporary bipartisan advisory commission to examine the future role and responsibilities of international financial institutions — the IMF, the World Trade Organization and the Bank for International Settlements.
- A recommendation that the IMF create a permanent international advisory committee of elected members of national legislatures.

The bill would also enact a series of changes previously approved by the House Banking Committee and calls for a new fund focus on worker rights and the environment.

Eastern Bloc Grant

The administration won more money for countries of the former Soviet Union, particularly Russia. Clinton had sought $925 million for the former Soviet republics earlier this year, but

Foreign Aid Spending

Foreign aid portion of the fiscal 1999 omnibus spending law (HR 4328 — PL 105-277) signed by the president on Oct. 21. *(Budget authority, in thousands of dollars.)*

	Fiscal 1998 Appropriation	Fiscal 1999 Clinton Request	House Bill	Senate Bill	Conference Report
Multilateral Aid					
World Bank					
Global Environment Facility	$ 47,500	$ 300,000	$ 42,500	$ 47,500	$ 192,500
International Development Association	1,034,503	800,000	800,000	800,000	800,000
Inter-American Development Bank	46,446	46,763	46,763	46,763	46,763
Limitation on callable capital	*(1,503,719)*	*(1,503,719)*	*(1,503,719)*	*(1,503,719)*	*(1,503,719)*
Enterprise for the Americas	30,000	50,000	50,000	50,000	50,000
North American Development Bank	56,500	—	—	—	—
Asian Development Bank	163,222	263,222	223,222	200,222	223,222
African Development Fund	45,000	155,000	128,000	5,000	128,000
European Development Bank	35,779	35,779	35,779	35,779	35,779
International Monetary Fund	—	17,861,000	3,361,000	17,861,000	17,861,000
Other	191,999	321,000	157,249	169,999	186,999
TOTAL, Multilateral aid	**$ 1,650,949**	**$ 19,832,764**	**$ 4,844,513**	**$ 19,216,263**	**$ 19,524,263**
Bilateral Aid					
Agency for International Development (AID)					
Development assistance	1,210,000	1,265,798	1,174,000	1,904,000	1,225,000
Child and disease programs	650,000	502,836	650,000	—	650,000
International disaster aid	190,000	205,000	150,000	200,000	200,000
AID operating expenses	473,000	483,858	460,000	475,000	479,950
Debt restructuring	27,000	72,000	36,000	25,000	33,000
Economic Support Fund	2,400,000	2,513,600	2,326,000	2,305,600	2,367,000
Assistance for Eastern Europe	485,000	464,500	450,000	432,500	430,000
Assistance for ex-Soviet states	770,000	925,000	590,000	740,000	801,000
International fund for Ireland	19,600	—	19,600	—	19,600
Other	84,255	133,605	83,552	86,552	95,302
Subtotal, AID	**$ 6,308,855**	**$ 6,566,197**	**$ 5,939,152**	**$ 6,168,652**	**$ 6,300,852**
State Department					
International narcotics control	230,000	275,000	275,000	222,000	261,000
Migration and refugee aid	705,000	670,000	670,000	670,000	670,000
Non-proliferation, de-mining and anti-terrorism assistance	133,000	215,900	152,000	170,000	198,000
Subtotal, State Department	**$ 1,068,000**	**$ 1,160,900**	**$ 1,097,000**	**$ 1,062,000**	**$ 1,129,000**
Peace Corps	222,000	270,335	230,000	221,000	240,000
Other	—	36,000	33,840	3,000	—
TOTAL, Bilateral aid	**$ 7,598,855**	**$ 8,033,432**	**$ 7,299,992**	**$ 7,451,652**	**$ 7,669,852**
Bilateral Military Aid (appropriated to the president)					
Foreign military financing (grants)	3,296,550	3,275,910	3,335,910	3,322,910	3,330,000
Foreign military loans	*(657,000)*	*(167,000)*	*(167,000)*	*(167,000)*	*(167,000)*
Loan subsidy	60,000	20,000	20,000	20,000	20,000
International military education and training	50,000	50,000	50,000	50,000	50,000
Special defense acquisition fund (offsetting collections)	– 106,000	– 19,000	– 19,000	– 19,000	– 19,000
Peacekeeping operations	77,500	83,000	62,250	75,000	76,500
TOTAL, Military aid	**$ 3,378,050**	**$ 3,409,910**	**$ 3,449,160**	**$ 3,448,910**	**$ 3,457,500**
Export Assistance					
Export-Import Bank	680,614	834,940	770,777	809,000	790,000
Trade and Development Agency	41,500	50,000	41,500	43,000	44,000
Overseas Private Investment Corporation (loan levels)	*(1,933,000)*	*(2,800,000)*	*(2,800,000)*	*(2,800,000)*	*(2,800,000)*
Subsidy/offsets	– 159,000	– 176,000	– 177,000	– 178,000	– 177,500
TOTAL, Export assistance	**$ 563,114**	**$ 708,940**	**$ 635,277**	**$ 674,000**	**$ 656,500**
GRAND TOTAL	**$ 13,190,968**	**$ 31,985,045**	**$ 16,228,942**	**$ 30,790,825**	**$ 31,308,115**

SOURCE: House and Senate Appropriations committees

Appropriations

the figure dropped as low as $590 million in the version of the foreign operations appropriations bill (HR 4569 — H Rept 105-719) that passed the House on Sept. 17.

But with White House officials worried about the state of the Russian economy and the political survival of Russian President Boris Yeltsin, the administration persuaded Congress to allocate $847 million to the region, including $46 million in emergency supplemental funds.

The money included:

• $195 million for Ukraine. Half will be withheld and released after four months if Albright certifies that Kiev has undertaken economic reforms, including progress on complaints by U.S. investors about corruption, red tape and other impediments. Last year's foreign aid bill (PL 105-118) included a similar provision, and Albright ultimately let the aid go forward.

• $228 million for the southern Caucasus, including at least $84 million for Georgia and $80 million for Armenia. Another $40 million was set aside as an initial peace dividend if Armenia and Azerbaijan are able to settle their longstanding conflict over Nagorno-Karabakh.

• $10 million for Turkmenistan, largely to develop a pipeline to carry natural gas across the Caspian Sea rather than through neighboring Iran.

New NATO members Poland, Hungary and the Czech Republic will receive $30 million in military aid to help integrate them into the alliance. And the Baltic states of Latvia, Lithuania and Estonia, formerly under the control of the Soviet Union, will receive $15 million to make their militaries more compatible with those of NATO, in hopes of joining the alliance in the future.

Other Foreign Aid

The bill cuts off money for the United Nations Population Fund because of that group's involvement with China and its sometimes coercive efforts to limit families to one child.

The bill also begins a 10-year phaseout of economic assistance to Israel, by cutting such aid from $1.2 billion in fiscal 1998 to less than $1.1 billion in fiscal 1999. During the same period, aid to Egypt is also set to be cut in half from about $800 million. Israel, however, will receive increased military aid.

Meanwhile, Jordan will receive $150 million in U.S. aid, and Tunisia, $7 million, both for supporting the Middle East peace process.

Other major recipients include Indonesia ($75 million) and Northern Ireland (almost $20 million).

Republicans remain skeptical of aid to Haiti and brushed aside administration attempts to set aside $140 million for that Caribbean nation. In another slap at Haiti, the bill limits spending on any one country in the Western Hemisphere to no more than 17 percent of total funds.

Republicans also are wary of giving money to the Korean Peninsula Energy Development Organization. The organization was formed after a 1994 agreement between the United States and North Korea to meet North Korea's energy needs as long as it curbed its nuclear program.

But this year, Republicans threatened to cut off funds for the organization, accusing Pyongyang of cheating on the agreement. They ultimately allowed $35 million, as long as certain conditions are met. But the measure also requires the appointment of a senior presidential envoy to review U.S. policy toward North Korea. Among the favorites for the job, aides said, is former Defense Secretary William J. Perry.

Abortion Restrictions Dropped

In agreeing to the IMF credits, Republican leaders agreed to cut the link between the IMF funds and a GOP attempt to reimpose Reagan and Bush administration abortion restrictions on international family planning aid that had prompted Clinton to threaten to veto the House-passed foreign operations appropriations bill.

The omnibus bill retains provisions from the fiscal 1998 bill (PL 105-118) that allow the administration to spend $385 million per year on international family planning aid without the Reagan/Bush restrictions. *(1997 Almanac, p. 9-37)*

In a related development, however, House GOP leaders continued to condition payment of U.S. debts to the United Nations on adoption of the anti-abortion restrictions, despite administration and Senate opposition.

Senate Republicans broke ranks, with Foreign Relations Committee Chairman Jesse Helms, R-N.C., joining Joseph R. Biden Jr. of Delaware, the committee's ranking Democrat, and Senate Minority Leader Tom Daschle, D-S.D., in pushing to drop the abortion restrictions and include in the omnibus bill $200 million in U.N. dues, along with proposed reforms of the international organization and the foreign affairs reorganization.

Administration officials said that amount of money was needed to ensure that the United States would retain its seat in the United Nations General Assembly, a claim dismissed by Republicans as an empty threat.

The Senate's efforts were supported in the House by David R. Obey of Wisconsin, ranking Democrat on the Appropriations Committee, who pushed for even more money for the United Nations. But the effort was resisted by anti-abortion House Republicans led by Christopher H. Smith of New Jersey.

Some Democrats said Clinton should threaten to veto the entire omnibus spending bill and force a government shutdown if the U.N. funds were not included.

But Secretary of State Madeleine K. Albright told Democratic leaders that Clinton would not issue such a threat as long as the omnibus bill incorporated the other portions of the State Department authorization bill (which Clinton vetoed over the abortion restrictions), including the reorganization of the foreign affairs agencies, and as long as Helms agreed to have the Senate approve several diplomatic nominations he had held up.

"Albright caved," a Democratic aide said. "In the end, they didn't care that much."

Yet, Democrats said it might be more difficult to address the U.N. funding issue next year, especially if, as many political observers expect, Republicans pick up additional seats in November's congressional elections.

And Obey warned that "every year this goes on, it becomes more difficult. Both sides have their mailing list and they use this to raise money, so both sides dig the hole even deeper and their positions get hardened." ◆

Interior

Funding Increased, Host of GOP Riders Fall In $14.1 Billion Interior Bill

Box Score

- **Bill:** HR 4328 — PL 105-277.
- **House action:** The House adopted the conference report (H Rept 105-825) on HR 4328, 333-95, on Oct. 20. The House passed its Interior bill (HR 4193 — H Rept 105-609) on July 23, 245-181.
- **Senate action:** The Senate cleared the conference report, 65-29, on Oct. 21. The Senate's stand-alone bill (S 2237 — S Rept 105-227) was pulled from the floor Sept. 16.
- **Presidential action:** Clinton signed the bill Oct. 21.

SUMMARY

The familiar battle lines over the Interior Department spending bill formed once again as lawmakers cobbled together a $14.1 billion fiscal 1999 measure that angered environmentalists along with some Western Republicans. The final version was cleared as part of the fiscal 1999 omnibus appropriations bill (HR 4328).

The House passed a stand-alone Interior appropriations bill (HR 4193) in July, settling several tough issues, including a decision to fund the National Endowment for the Arts (NEA), before the measure reached the floor. However, the House bill drew a veto threat centered on what the administration said was inadequate funding for priority programs and on a number of environmental riders.

The Senate never completed action on its version of the bill. Majority Leader Trent Lott, R-Miss., pulled the measure from the floor after two weeks of debate in September because it was mired in non-germane amendments. With time running out, the only avenue left was the omnibus bill.

The final $14.1 billion package contained numerous compromises. It provided $2.8 billion for the Forest Service and $1.3 billion for the National Park Service — more than in either the House or Senate bills — and $98 million for the embattled NEA.

White House negotiators were able to pry loose $1.7 billion for the president's Clean Water Action Plan, a five-year initiative to address problems caused by agricultural and storm water runoff; $328 million for the Land and Water Conservation Fund, the government's primary tool for acquiring land that is ecologically important and threatened; and $1 billion for climate change initiatives, with most of the money going to research into energy efficiency and renewable energy. The latter provision was controversial because it was linked to the Kyoto treaty on global warming, which is highly unpopular in Congress.

The White House said most of the environmental riders that had drawn strong administration objections had been removed or largely defanged.

The administration was able to persuade Sen. Slade Gorton, R-Wash., to withdraw language that would have dismantled the Columbia Basin Ecosystem Management Plan, a novel, seven-state agreement to protect endangered salmon while allowing property owners more use of their land.

To the relief of environmentalists, negotiators also deleted riders that would have allowed construction of a single-lane gravel road through Alaska's Izembek National Wildlife Refuge, and allowed additional logging in the Tongass National Forest. A rider that would have allowed American Indians to build a road through the Chugach National Forest in Alaska was also dropped.

Republican Sens. Ted Stevens and Frank H. Murkowski of Alaska had fought hard for the Izembek Road. Under the compromise, the road project was abandoned in return for $37.5 million to improve an all-weather airport in Cold Bay, to fund a new road along a different route and dock facilities in the town, and to beef up the medical clinic.

House lawmakers also agreed to eliminate a $50 million annual subsidy to timber companies logging on federal land. The purchaser road credit program has long been a target of environmentalists because it allows timber companies to cut more trees to offset the cost of roads those companies build on public land.

But the bill still contained an array of items that left environmental groups disappointed, including provisions to allow additional logging in three national forests in California; delay a new formula for determining royalties oil companies must pay for extracting oil from public lands for eight months; and allow automatic renewal of grazing leases on some public lands.

House Panel Zips Through Interior Measure

JUNE 20 — Hemmed in by budget caps and a desire to douse its most incendiary issue, a House subcommittee June 18 effortlessly approved a $13.4 billion Interior appropriations bill.

The action on the fiscal 1999 spending plan came in quick order as all but one of a handful of amendments were turned back, and the toughest question of all — funding for the National Endowment for the Arts (NEA) — was left for the House to decide.

Under an agreement with the House leadership, Interior Appropriations Subcommittee Chairman Ralph Regula, R-Ohio, deleted all funding for the NEA but said a separate vote on the House floor will be held to decide whether $98 million in the fiscal 1999 budget should be restored.

The issue has become so polarizing, Regula said, that it is best addressed by the full House. "Let the members decide," Regula said. "That's democracy."

Appropriations

An aide to Regula said the chairman decided on the new approach after the 1997 fight when the committee tried to zero out funding for the agency that offers grants to artists in every state. The money was restored by the Senate.

With virtually all controversial items left out, and with no spare money to be found, the committee wrapped up its work in less than two hours.

Unlike previous years, the road ahead is most noticeable for the aggressive approach in avoiding flashpoints. The bill would end the controversial timber purchase road credit program, which critics said was a $50 million subsidy for loggers to cut trees in public forests. It provided no money for contested road projects in Alaska's Izembek National Wildlife Refuge. It would:

● Extend recreational fee programs for two more years under which national parks, forests and other public lands keep 100 percent of fees collected;

● Provide $80 million for restoration of water flow in the Florida Everglades; and

● Include a $10 million increase for law enforcement on tribal lands and $41 million for construction of hospitals and health clinics for American Indians.

But environmentalists and other critics were angered that only $139 million was allocated for the land and water conservation fund, a federal program that buys and preserves threatened areas. That figure compares with the $699 million in the fiscal 1998 appropriation.

The package for 1999, $800 million less than the administration's request and $700 million less than fiscal 1998, is focused on shoring up "operational shortfalls" and backlogged maintenance for the Department of Interior and its agencies, including the Bureau of Land Management and Indian programs, as well as the U.S. Forest Service.

Nuclear Waste Dump

Only a handful of minor amendments were offered, and the only one to pass involved a proposal by the Skull Valley Band of Goshutes, an Indian tribe in Utah, to build a nuclear waste dump. The amendment stripped out language in the bill that would stop development of the facility for at least a year. The waste site, which will have to gain all federal and state permits, is intended to hold intensely radioactive spent fuel from commercial power plants until the government opens a permanent site in Nevada which is waiting for congressional approval.

The success of the amendment came as a surprise because Utah's governor, Republican Michael O. Leavitt and the state's congressional representatives oppose the project and supported the one year delay. The Goshutes, however, saw the project as an opportunity to improve the local economy.

In the end, the Goshutes won when the amendment to remove the moratorium was approved 6-5. The amendment was offered by David R. Obey, D-Wis.

Cutbacks

Elsewhere, the budget would provide $1.3 billion for operating the National Park System but sharply scales back the Park Services engineering and architectural center in Denver. The budget calls for the work force in Denver to fall from 500 to 250. The action was taken after a management study found the center does not watch costs.

Two days before the subcommittee addressed the bill, Vice President Al Gore warned Congress to avoid riders.

"We will not tolerate stealth tactics that do unacceptable harm to our environment or threaten public health," Gore said. "In the past, such actions have led to vetoes. . . . Congress should remember these precedents before trying to rob the American people of our precious environmental protections in the dead of night."

With easy passage through the subcommittee, the road will start getting more treacherous next week when it reaches the full committee. It will become even more arduous in the Senate, where the bill often becomes a magnet for controversial riders.

Interior Bill Includes Funding For Arts Agency

JULY 18 — The House Appropriations Committee staged a familiar dance June 25 over funding for the arts. But this year, the music proved to be out of key for conservative Republicans.

In a surprising vote that set the stage for a showdown on the House floor, the committee voted 31-27 to restore $98 million in funding for the National Endowment for the Arts (NEA), the much-maligned agency that some House Republicans have been trying to dismantle for a number of years.

The money was included in the fiscal 1999 Interior appropriations bill, a $13.4 billion package to fund the Department of Interior and its agencies, including the Bureau of Land Management, Indian programs, the National Park Service and the Agriculture Department's Forest Service.

But unlike previous years, when fights broke out on several fronts, only arts funding drew sustained attention from House appropriators, who were hemmed in by tight budget caps and a desire to avoid controversy.

With the exception of the arts line item, "the bill itself is quite a good bill," said ranking member Sidney R. Yates, D-Ill.

Only hours after the House committee resolved its arts dispute, the Senate Appropriations Committee approved its own version of the fiscal 1999 Interior appropriations bill, 27-0. As in previous years, the Senate included money for the NEA. The 1999 budget calls for the agency to get $100 million.

Other Issues

Before approving its bill, Senate appropriators agreed to language not included in the House version that would delay a new formula for determining royalties from oil and gas leases on federal property.

Another major difference between the two bills is a Senate provision providing for an easement for a road through the Izembek National Wildlife Refuge and Wilderness Area in Alaska. The plan is opposed by environmental groups, but it has become a passion for committee Chairman Ted Stevens, R-Alaska, who insists that the road is needed so sick and injured people have access to the only airport in the area.

Both bills are likely to be the focus of attention because they would provide roughly $800 million less overall than the Clinton administration wanted.

Even so, if the arts funding holds, that will defuse the most incendiary of all issues.

Interior

David R. Obey of Wisconsin, the House committee's ranking Democrat, promised a presidential veto if Congress passed a bill without arts funding. "This will be funded or there will be no presidential signature," Obey said.

That message struck a chord with five moderate Republicans — Michael P. Forbes of New York, Rodney Frelinghuysen of New Jersey, Jim Kolbe of Arizona, John Edward Porter of Illinois and James T. Walsh of New York — who sided with Democrats to carry the vote. The result shattered a delicate Republican plan to sidestep an issue that has caused the party political pain.

Obey, who sponsored the amendment to restore the funding before the final vote, scolded the committee, saying it was trying to shirk its responsibility by passing the decision to the full House.

"This committee has an obligation to speak out whether we support the arts or not," Obey said, adding that he was not confident that a vote would come to the floor. "I do not trust promises made by this institution because I've seen promises welshed on too many times."

Interior Subcommittee Chairman Ralph Regula, R-Ohio, came up with the strategy himself to delete the funding and allow the question to be decided by the full House.

NEA Funding

The question was decided sooner than Regula expected. But critics vowed an all-out effort to kill the agency when the bill comes to the floor.

Meanwhile, the Supreme Court on June 25 upheld a controversial 1990 law that required the National Endowment for the Arts to consider decency standards when deciding which artists should get grant money.

With the question of the arts decided, the committee moved quickly to finish work on the bill. It moved from the committee by voice vote.

In the House package is $700 million less than fiscal 1998. The priority for fiscal 1999, Regula said, is to chip away at billions of dollars of backlogged maintenance and to shore up "operational shortfalls."

The bill moved easier than in past years because of tight budget caps, which allow for no new programs. The bill also avoided traditional sticking points by deleting such controversial items as the $50 million subsidy for loggers to cut trees in public forests.

Compromise Goes A Long Way In House Debate

JULY 25 — The House on July 23 passed a $13.4 billion Interior appropriations bill for fiscal 1999 that was notable for taming two unruly issues and for the Republicans' ability to stick to a tightly choreographed plan.

The bill (HR 4193), approved 245-181, avoided the venomous debate that had been the bill's signature in past years. Hemmed in by budget caps and mindful of approaching elections, Republicans eliminated most of the mischief by crafting two agreements that could be embraced by moderates in their own party as well as some Democrats. (Vote 331, p. H-94; caps, 1997 Almanac, 2-18)

The most closely watched deal provided $98 million for the National Endowment for the Arts (NEA).

The second, though less prominent, could have a more profound result by reshaping debate over forest policy. That agreement eliminated a $50 million annual subsidy to timber companies logging on federal land. The purchaser road credit program has long been a target of environmentalists because it allows timber companies to cut more trees to offset the cost of roads those companies build on public land. Like the NEA, the road credit has been a source of intense debate.

"This has been a 10-year fight," Michael A. Francis, director of forest programs for The Wilderness Society, said of the road program. "We've accomplished a major goal."

Despite those agreements, the bill is studded with contentious provisions, several of which the White House warned could trigger a veto. Among the biggest concerns:

• Lack of funding for climate change initiatives. Republicans said the administration's funding request was a backdoor attempt to implement portions of the Kyoto treaty on global warming. That treaty has yet to be ratified. (1997 Almanac, p. 4-13)

• Elimination of an eco-management program in the Pacific Northwest.

• Money for a road easement in Alaska's Chugach National Forest, backed by Don Young, R-Alaska, and other members of the delegation. Efforts to deny the road, Young said in one of the sharpest debates, "is evil because you're going against the will" of Alaskans.

Despite the NEA vote, Interior Secretary Bruce Babbitt denounced the bill and riders that are "slashing funding for our environment and our natural heritage across the board."

Public Lands

Another concern is a significant cut in funding for programs to buy public lands, from $270 million to $139 million. In all, the bill was less than the administration's request for global warming programs and public land purchases by more than $300 million.

The administration warned that the bill would be vetoed unless those provisions were changed.

Despite those threats, the bill moved largely intact, with the House turning back efforts to prohibit new roads from being built in the Tongass National Forest in Alaska and a challenge to extending for two more years a program to charge entrance fees at national parks and forests.

The bill, which provides funding to the Department of the Interior and its agencies, including the Bureau of Land Management and Indian programs as well as the U.S. Forest Service, the National Park Service and cultural institutions such as the Smithsonian Institution, is $680 million less than the fiscal 1998 appropriation and $839 million less than the administration requested.

The House version, which is similar in many respects to its Senate counterpart (S 2237), places a priority on chipping away billions of dollars in backlogged maintenance at national parks and forests, said Ralph Regula, R-Ohio, chairman of the Appropriations Interior Subcommittee.

In the end, only the NEA objection was fully addressed. Republicans narrowed the difference over funding energy efficiency programs by adding $45 million, leaving the account about $133 million short of the administra-

Appropriations

tion's goal of $808 million.

Democrats and the administration were angered by a provision that dismantles the Columbia Basin Ecosystem Management Plan, the program in the Pacific Northwest hailed as a novel approach to protecting endangered habitat and species.

An amendment by Jim McDermott, D-Wash., to save the initiative failed, 202-221, even though Clinton said he would veto the bill unless it was protected. Republicans, however, echoing complaints from local officials and residents in the region, called it a heavy-handed effort that denied property owners full use of their land. (*Vote 327, p. H-94*)

One of the loudest critics was Republican George Nethercutt of Washington who called the plan a "monstrosity" because it would limit what people could do with their property in the name of protecting endangered species.

Richard "Doc" Hastings, R-Wash., chided supporters of the plan as outsiders. "What we have heard so far are opinions of people who don't live in the area," he said.

Throughout three days of debate, Regula said he understood requests for additional money but said the bill was a fair balance.

Among the achievements, Regula said, is a $147.4 million increase in funding for the Indian Health Service, to $2.2 billion; $1.3 billion for national parks, an increase of $99.3 million over fiscal 1998; and $246 million for national wildlife refuges, an $18 million increase.

NEA Battle Ends

In adding money to the bill, the House included funding for the NEA. That action virtually guarantees the existence of the agency because the Senate has pledged $100 million for fiscal 1999.

The battle over the NEA was the most conspicuous subplot during three days of floor debate. Mindful of negative publicity that accompanied efforts to kill the NEA in past years, Regula structured a deal approved by Republican leaders in which the rule that would allow funding for the agency would be deleted on a point of order and then immediately restored.

Despite complaints by Democrats such as David R. Obey of Wisconsin, who criticized the rule as "a Mickey Mouse procedure," the plan unfolded as intended: $98 million in funding for the agency was deleted on a technical point of order. The entire amount was then restored by an amendment offered by Nancy L. Johnson, R-Conn. The amendment passed, 253-173, a stunningly comfortable margin. (*Vote 312, p. H-90*)

The NEA, created in 1965, provides grants to arts organizations in every state. The agency has long been a target of conservatives who say it supports objectionable and obscene projects. But supporters pointed out that only 40 out of 100,000 grants since the NEA's inception have drawn criticism. Some concerns about the NEA were softened by steps taken this year to provide closer congressional oversight and more equitable distribution of grants.

The victory was significant for NEA defenders, who have had to fight in recent years to save the agency from extinction.

"The old debate over the existence of the NEA finally has given way to a more thoughtful dialogue about the appropriate level of federal arts funding in America," the endowment's chairman, William J. Ivey, said in a July 21 statement.

Timber Battles

With the NEA's future decided, the second, and more significant, subplot came into view, according to some observers.

Under that arrangement orchestrated by John Edward Porter, a moderate Republican from Illinois, the $50 million road credit would be abolished in return for promises from Porter's allies that they would not pursue additional cuts in timber programs this year.

The deal evolved over three months of talks between moderates such as Porter and Western Republicans, such as Helen Chenoweth, R-Idaho, a strong ally of the timber industry.

"The catalyst was reasonable people sat down together and decided that there were areas we could agree on and not have to get down on the floor and fight it out," Chenoweth said. "I was very pleased with it."

Chenoweth praised the agreement, saying it was worth giving up the road credits to protect more important programs. But according to Porter, timber interests were drawn to the negotiations by an erosion of their position on the floor. Votes on key timber issues have been close. In 1997, for example, an amendment to save the road credit program passed, 211-209. (*1997 Almanac, p. 9-47*)

"Simply put, the Westerners were worried we had the votes," Porter said, adding that members decided to deal "rather than make this a contentious, bloody fight on the floor."

The Republican leadership, interested in cooling an issue that has divided the party, also signed off on the plan because "a nasty floor fight can leave bitter feelings that can spill over into other areas," Porter said.

The strength of the agreement was displayed when Elizabeth Furse, D-Ore., withdrew an amendment backed by environmental groups that would have reduced funding for the Forest Service's timber program by $81 million in fiscal 1999.

"I decided to withdraw my amendment today in exchange for the commitment that funding for the purchaser road credit program will be eliminated," she said. "Eliminating the . . . program is a step in the right direction."

The agreement came into play at least twice more, when amendments by Maurice D. Hinchey, D-N.Y., to strip language allowing for the road easement in Alaska's Chugach National Forest was defeated, 176-249. It also contributed to the defeat, 186-237, of an amendment by George Miller, D-Calif., to prohibit new road construction in Tongass National Forest. (*Votes 328, 329, p. H-94*)

Riders Prompt Hot Debate and Veto Threat

SEPTEMBER 12 — After being distracted for two days by an attempted campaign finance overhaul and the investigation of President Clinton, the Senate found refuge Sept. 10 in the always partisan and volatile Interior appropriations bill.

That comfort, however, did not translate into progress. Senate leaders had hoped to finish — or at least make a serious dent in the $13.4 billion spending plan for fiscal 1999 for the Department of the Interior and related agencies, including a portion of the Forest Service's budget and the National Park Service. By week's end, however, the Senate voted only twice on the bill on a series of technical changes and a campaign finance amendment.

Senators will try again the week of Sept. 14, but the lifting will be just as heavy. The bill, S 2237, is studded with two dozen objectionable riders and an assortment of controversial items dealing with logging, roads in wilderness areas, grazing and mining royalties. The administration has threatened to veto the bill if any one of several items remains, and environmental groups are vowing an all-out attack to strip out language. Marty Hayden, director of policy and legislation for the Washington, D.C.- based Earthjustice Legal Defense Fund, formerly the Sierra Club Legal Defense Fund, called the bill a "crime against nature."

Fights are certain to break out on many fronts, ranging from traditionally fractious issues such as logging on federal lands to grazing and new roads in wilderness areas.

Road to King Cove

One of the fiercest battles will be over whether to build the Izembek Road, a 30-mile, one-lane gravel road connecting the remote Alaska town of King Cove to Cold Bay, which has an all-weather airport. Supporters, most notably Appropriations Committee Chairman Sen. Ted Stevens, R-Alaska, argue the road is a medical necessity because the airport at Cold Bay offers the fastest service to Anchorage for medical care. Otherwise, the injured and ill are forced to take a marine ambulance or a helicopter to Cold Bay, which is often impossible because of stormy weather blowing inland from the Bering Sea.

Environmentalists, the Clinton administration and Interior Secretary Bruce Babbitt all oppose the road because it would be the first time permission has been granted to slice a road through a federal wilderness area.

Conservation groups insist the road, which is projected to cost between $10 million and $29 million, would result in irreparable damage to wildlife and provide a dangerous precedent of building roads through other wild habitats.

Stevens scoffs at such arguments, and the force of his will leads many to believe the language will remain, just as it did in the House's version of the Interior bill (HR 4193).

"I have never, in all my years in the Senate, seen anything more stupid than the opposition we are getting now," Stevens said in June. "These groups [opposing the road] make it sound like this is a pristine wilderness area that has never been touched. We are only calling for 10 miles of unpaved road [through the refuge] to help people who need serious medical attention. Once again, our state is severely under attack by outside environmental groups who do not understand the circumstances in which Alaskans live."

With such an array of issues and competing interests, the Interior bill is traditionally a polarizing force.

Those extremes will come into sharp focus when Democrat Max Baucus of Montana offers an amendment to strip out seven of the most objectionable riders, including the proposed Izembek Road.

"These are riders, they've got to come off. They're riders, people don't like riders, the country doesn't like riders. They shouldn't be on appropriations bills so we're going to do what we can to get them off. The administration supports our efforts strongly," Baucus said in a Sept. 10 interview.

Both environmentalists and industrial interests expect the vote on Baucus' amendment to be close, and they agree it is likely to influence the outcome of the entire bill.

While the Baucus vote will be perhaps the most closely watched and contested, the bill will provide other flashpoints.

"As always, putting this bill together has been a great challenge," Slade Gorton, R-Wash., chairman of the Interior subcommittee and the bill's floor manager, said Sept. 8. "The subcommittee received more than 2,000 individual requests from senators regarding particular projects."

In keeping with the sharp rhetoric that usually accompanies the bill, Gorton wasted little time defending the riders, turning instead to an attack on the Clinton administration.

"But perhaps the single most common reason that legislative provisions and limitations on the use of funds are included in this bill is the overzealous use of regulatory powers by the executive branch without adequate involvement of Congress or the public," Gorton said.

The Clinton administration chimed in on the same day, issuing a threat to veto the bill because it falls short of funding levels for priority programs and because it contains at least 24 objectionable riders.

Most distressing to the administration and environmentalists was language to terminate the Interior Columbia Basin Ecosystem Management Project in six Northwestern states that has been praised by some as a model for protecting endangered salmon while allowing logging and other activities.

Another rider that will provoke strenuous debate — and a veto threat — would require a 50 percent increase in timber that can be harvested from the Tongass National Forest, one of Alaska's most pristine forests. Another rider would block the government from increasing royalties for offshore oil.

Sen. Dale Bumpers, D-Ark., has also vowed to fight a rider that would impose a 27-month moratorium on proposed regulations for updating environmental standards for hardrock mining on public lands.

"We don't need another study to determine whether we need to protect the environment," Bumpers said. "Hardrock mining, which occurs mostly in the West . . . continues to damage the environment."

Aside from individual policies and programs, environmentalists maintain that the Senate's handling of the Interior bill will determine the 105th Congress' place in environmental history.

"If these measures become law, they will seriously undercut national forest protections, retard the cleanup of toxic waste and weaken our effort to save endangered species," said Rodger Schlickeisen, president of Defenders of Wildlife, a Washington-based environmental lobbying group.

Appropriations

Interior Spending

Interior portion of the fiscal 1999 omnibus spending law (HR 4328 — PL 105-277) signed by the president on Oct. 21. *(Budget authority, in thousands of dollars.)*

	Fiscal 1998 Appropriation	Fiscal 1999 Clinton Request	Senate Bill	House Bill	Final Bill
Interior Department					
Bureau of Land Management					
Management of lands & resources	$ 582,082	$ 660,310	$ 633,058	$ 596,425	$ 619,311
Wildland fire management	280,103	298,353	288,975	286,895	286,895
Payments in lieu of taxes	120,000	120,000	125,000	140,000	125,000
Other	153,816	154,996	153,664	152,237	159,489
Subtotal	**$ 1,136,001**	**$ 1,233,659**	**$ 1,200,697**	**$ 1,175,557**	**$ 1,190,695**
Fish and Wildlife Service					
Resource management	594,592	675,828	624,019	607,106	661,136
Construction	76,636	37,000	48,734	66,100	50,453
Land acquisition	62,632	60,500	62,120	30,000	48,024
Other	38,679	44,900	62,479	41,679	42,579
Subtotal	**$ 772,539**	**$ 818,228**	**$ 797,352**	**$ 744,885**	**$ 802,192**
National Park Service					
Operations	1,234,004	1,320,828	1,288,903	1,333,328	1,285,604
Construction	222,769	175,000	210,116	149,000	226,058
Land acquisition, state aid	143,290	138,087	88,100	69,000	147,925
Other	55,071	119,187	74,412	54,751	88,637
Subtotal	**$ 1,655,134**	**$ 1,753,102**	**$ 1,661,531**	**$ 1,606,079**	**$ 1,748,224**
Bureau of Indian Affairs					
Indian programs	1,529,638	1,638,681	1,544,695	1,558,425	1,584,124
Construction	125,279	152,054	123,421	121,695	123,421
Claim settlements, payments to Indians	43,352	38,396	28,882	28,396	28,882
Other	5,000	15,005	5,001	5,001	10,001
Subtotal	**$ 1,703,269**	**$ 1,844,136**	**$ 1,701,999**	**$ 1,713,517**	**$ 1,746,428**
Department offices	250,073	260,679	252,549	248,800	266,052
Geological Survey	760,358	806,883	772,115	774,838	797,896
Minerals Management Service	150,314	128,520	123,393	122,520	124,020
Surface Mining Reclamation	273,061	276,956	275,966	278,765	278,769
TOTAL, Interior Department	**$ 6,700,749**	**$ 7,122,163**	**$ 6,785,602**	**$ 6,664,961**	**$ 6,954,276**
Forest Service (Agriculture Department)					
National Forest System	1,357,744	1,417,708	1,129,098	1,231,421	1,298,570
Wildland fire management	586,559	554,437	587,885	631,737	560,176
Forest and rangeland research	187,796	198,122	212,927	197,444	197,444
Reconstruction and construction	166,015	160,914	353,840	271,444	297,352
State and private forestry	209,178	162,900	165,091	156,167	170,722
Other	58,258	162,728	173,693	34,671	2,275,589
TOTAL, Forest Service	**$ 2,565,550**	**$ 2,656,809**	**$ 2,622,534**	**$ 2,522,884**	**$ 2,751,853**
Energy Department					
Energy conservation	611,723	808,500	677,701	675,250	691,701
Fossil energy research and development	362,403	383,408	376,431	315,558	384,056
Naval Petroleum and Oil Shale Reserve	107,000	22,500	14,056	14,000	14,000
Clean-coal technology (rescissions/deferrals)	−101,000	−40,000	−40,000	0	−40,000
Other	275,525	267,121	223,621	228,621	267,121
TOTAL, Energy Department	**$ 1,255,651**	**$ 1,441,529**	**$ 1,251,809**	**$ 1,233,429**	**$ 1,316,878**
Other Related Agencies					
Indian Health Service	2,098,712	2,118,349	2,152,118	2,246,128	2,239,787
Indian education	—	—	—	—	—
Smithsonian Institution	402,258	419,800	404,554	397,449	407,554
National Endowment for the Humanities	110,700	136,000	110,700	110,700	110,700
National Endowment for the Arts	98,000	136,000	100,060	98,000	98,000
Other agencies	178,873	237,607	230,329	155,953	226,603
Priority land acquisitions	699,000	—	—	—	—
GRAND TOTAL	**$ 14,109,493**	**$ 14,268,257**	**$ 13,657,706**	**$ 13,429,504**	**$ 14,105,651**

SOURCE: Senate and House Appropriations committees

Clinton Prevails On Clean Water, Climate Initiatives

OCTOBER 24 — When details began oozing out about the environmental pieces of the omnibus spending bill for fiscal 1999, the reaction in most quarters was more resignation than celebration.

The $14.1 billion package that finances the Interior Department and related agencies was brimming with compromises that allowed negotiators to declare victory while avoiding some supercharged debates that often accompany the bill.

The bill, HR 4328, includes $98 million in funding for the embattled National Endowment for the Arts and $328 million for the Land and Water Conservation Fund, the government's principal tool for buying threatened but sensitive land.

It also provides $1.3 billion for the cash-strapped National Park Service, a $99 million increase over this year's level. And it provides $2.8 billion for the Forest Service, $229 million more than the House approved.

The park service budget included $3.6 million to build a satellite parking lot for Zion National Park in Utah to reduce the number of cars entering the park, as well as $14 million for a water system at Everglades National Park. By any measure, Everglades was a big winner. In all, $140 million was tucked into the budget for an array of Everglades projects.

The administration was particularly proud of the $1.7 billion for the president's Clean Water Action Plan, a five-year initiative to keep runoff from farms and urban areas from polluting water sources.

The administration also prevailed by getting $1 billion for climate change initiatives, with most of the money going to research into energy efficiency and renewable energy. That was controversial because it was linked to the Kyoto treaty on global warming, which is highly unpopular in Congress. Nonetheless, the final agreement is $117 million more than the amount approved by the House, although less than the $1.29 billion requested by the White House.

To the relief of environmentalists, negotiators deleted riders that would have allowed a single-lane gravel road to be built through Alaska's Izembek National Wildlife Refuge and another provision that would have allowed additional logging in the Tongass National Forest. A third Alaska rider, to grant American Indians an easement to build a road through the Chugach National Forest, was also deleted, as well as language that would have prevented the park service from limited commercial fishing in Glacier Bay National Park. To appease Western Republicans and ranchers, a provision called for automatically renewing grazing leases in New Mexico.

For oil and gas interests, the legislation postponed for eight months imposition of a new, higher royalty formula for crude oil taken from federal lands. For mining interests, it delayed for a year tougher environmental regulations.

But even with the changes, the language left plenty of people feeling raw.

Road to Civilization

Chief among them were Sens. Ted Stevens and Frank H. Murkowski, Republicans from Alaska who pushed hard for the Izembek Road.

Under the compromise, the road project was abandoned in return for $37.5 million to improve an all-weather airport in Cold Bay, to fund a new road along a different route and dock facilities in the town, and to beef up the medical clinic.

Most disappointed were environmental groups, which mounted an aggressive, but unsuccessful, campaign to shear off more than three dozen riders as the Interior bill approached the Senate floor. While some of their top targets were kept off the omnibus bill, many remained.

What enthusiasm there was for the bill waned as they learned about the fine print.

"We recognize the bill is improved; a number of attacks on the environment have been erased or removed. But . . . we took several short steps backward rather than some large steps," said Greg Wetstone, legislative director for the Natural Resources Defense Council, an environmental group.

While environmental groups lauded White House negotiators for stripping some objectionable riders from the bill, they said more should have been removed.

"It's like somebody coming to rob you and asking if you want $200 stolen or $100," said Lexi Shultz, an attorney for the U.S. Public Interest Research Group. ◆

Appropriatons

Medical Research, Education Are Big Winners In Labor-HHS Spending Bill

SUMMARY

Disputes on the fiscal 1999 funding bill for the departments of Labor, Health and Human Services, and Education were so numerous — and the underlying policy disagreements so fundamental — that neither the House nor the Senate was able to pass its version of the legislation (HR 4274, S 2440).

At the end of the session, House and Senate appropriators met informally to work out a compromise version of the bill, and then congressional leaders met with White House negotiators to reach a final deal. It became the most expensive title in the omnibus spending package (PL 105-277).

In the end, what started off in the House as a bill that ignored President Clinton's priorities was the centerpiece of a package that fulfilled many of his wishes for the year.

Bowing to instructions from the leadership, the House Appropriations Committee had reported a bill (HR 4274) that tilted heavily to conservative views on both funding and policy. The measure was laden with controversial provisions — such as requiring parental notification or a court order before a minor could obtain Title X family planning services. And it eliminated funding for some administration priorities, such as the Low-Income Home Energy Assistance Program (LIHEAP) and the summer youth job program, while sharply cutting appropriations for others — the Goals 2000 education reform program, for example. According to the Office of Management and Budget, that House bill also would have provided $2 billion less for education than the administration requested.

The bill stalled for more than two months, in large measure because Republican moderates and conservatives could not agree on how the rule for floor debate would structure amendments on the family planning language. Not until the very end of the session — after House and Senate appropriators had already begun to negotiate a final Labor-HHS deal to be included in the omnibus measure — did the GOP factions strike a deal on how the family planning amendments should be handled.

On Oct. 8, the House considered the bill and reaffirmed the language on parental notification. The measure was then pulled from further House consideration.

The Senate Appropriations Committee approved a bill (S 2440) was much closer to the administration's requests, including $1.1 billion for LIHEAP and $871 million for summer jobs. But knowing that the bill would be a magnet for amendments, Senate Majority Leader Trent Lott, R-Miss., made clear he had no plans to put it on the floor.

With no floor action in either chamber, Republicans were in a weak bargaining position during negotiations over the omnibus bill. The administration won numerous victories as a result. One of the most significant was an appropriation not included in either of the original House or Senate bills — $1.2 billion as a first installment on the administration's proposal to hire 100,000 new teachers in the next seven years to reduce the class sizes in grades one, two and three. The deal also reinstated funding for the summer jobs program at the fiscal 1998 level of $871 million as requested by the president, and provided $1.1 billion for LIHEAP.

Other agencies that won large funding increases included the National Institutes of Health, which got a nearly $2 billion (15 percent) increase, and the Ryan White AIDS programs, which received a $262 million (24 percent) increase.

The final bill does not include the controversial Title X parental notification language. Conservatives were

Box Score

- **Bill:** HR 4328 — PL 105-277.
- **House action:** The House adopted the conference report (H Rept 105-825) on HR 4328, 333-95, on Oct. 20. The House Appropriations Committee approved HR 4274 (H Rept 105-635), 32-23, on July 14.
- **Senate action:** The Senate cleared the conference report on HR 4328, 65-29, on Oct. 21. The Senate Appropriations Committee approved S 2440 (S Rept 105-300), 28-0, on Sept. 3.
- **Presidential action:** Clinton signed the bill Oct. 21.

pleased, however, that the bill bans federal funding for needle exchanges, and prohibits federal funding of a special Teamsters election.

The measure also bans the use of federal education funds to develop, plan or administer any national test, unless explicitly authorized in statute. And it includes a modified version of the Hyde abortion limitation language (named for House Judiciary Chairman Henry J. Hyde, R-Ill.), which bans the use of funds in the bill to pay for abortions except in cases of rape or incest or if the life of the woman was endangered. It expands this prohibition to apply to trust funds, in order to clarify that it covers younger women who receive Medicare benefits because they are disabled.

House Panel Rejects Agenda Set by Clinton

JUNE 27 — House Republicans made it clear on June 23 that they plan to use annual spending bills as a main stage for playing to their party's conservative flank, whose support is crucial in November's midterm elections.

The House Appropriations Subcommittee on Labor, Health and Human Services, Education and Related Agencies approved, 8-7, a fiscal 1999 spending measure that would eliminate Low-Income Home Energy Assistance Program (LIHEAP) and summer jobs for poor youth, ignore President Clinton's education agenda, and make it more difficult for the Labor Department to enforce some workplace regulations.

Zeroing out LIHEAP and summer jobs would help finance a $1.2 billion increase in the budget of the National Institutes of Health (NIH), a favorite of both parties.

If Republicans were itching for a confrontation with the White House, they quickly got it.

"I'm going to keep fighting to advance education," President Clinton said June 24 after the committee action. "If they [Republicans] continue to fight against all these things it will, I expect, be the major conflict of the coming months."

The bill, the largest and traditionally most contentious annual domestic spending measure, would provide $81.9 billion in fiscal 1999 discretionary funds and $214.5 billion for mandatory programs such as Medicare.

No Democrats supported the bill. Jay Dickey, R-Ark., voted against it after his amendment to reduce funding for the National Labor Relations Board by 15 percent from the level in the measure was defeated.

Subcommittee Chairman John Edward Porter, R-Ill., maintained that the cuts were necessary because the 1997 balanced-budget law (PL 105-33) set binding caps on discretionary spending. While the deal increased domestic programs in fiscal 1998, it did not allow as generous an increase this year and provides even less flexibility in the future — a policy that is beginning to chafe.

"We must choose priorities. It's our job to choose which programs work for people and which don't," Porter said.

David R. Obey, D-Wis., said Republicans took the money from the "weakest and most vulnerable," adding the bill "aimed more at solving the political problems of the majority party . . . than the health and education problems of Americans."

Moderates Restive

Obey said the cuts were deeper than needed because Senate Republicans had killed comprehensive tobacco legislation.

The tobacco bill (S 1415) would have raised $516 billion over 25 years, revenues the White House wanted to tap into for research facilities such as NIH and pay for new education programs, such as Clinton's plan to hire 100,000 new teachers and reduce class sizes in early grades. Congress has not authorized Clinton's class size plan.

The bill is a sharp departure from the fiscal 1998 measure (PL 105-78), which provided a 10.5 percent increase for the Education Department and a 7 percent jump for the Department of Health and Human Services (HHS).

The subcommittee bill pleased conservatives, but some House Republican moderates said they would not support the measure, raising doubts about whether GOP leaders would be able to come up with enough votes for passage.

Furthermore, the Senate Labor and Human Resources Committee on June 24 approved, 18-0, legislation (S 2206) that would reauthorize LIHEAP for five years. The program provides aid to 4.3 million low-income households for heating and cooling bills.

Republican senators, including James M. Jeffords of Vermont, sharply criticized the House subcommittee's action. House Republicans said that with energy costs at near-record lows, the program had outlived its usefulness.

Livingston Turns Active

House Appropriations Committee Chairman Robert L. Livingston, R-La., who in the past has decried the practice of attaching controversial policy riders to spending bills, attached several of his own to this one.

The bill includes a Livingston provision that would rewrite federal bilingual education programs in an effort to move students more rapidly into English. It would limit students to two years of dual-language classes and give states more flexibility to use federal funds for alternative instruction, such as English immersion. Bilingual and immigrant aid would receive $354 million, the same as in fiscal 1998.

The plan is similar to a measure (HR 3892) approved by the House Education and the Workforce Committee on June 4.

Livingston also attached language that would help schools remove from classrooms disabled students who are violent and keep them out of the classroom longer, though still guaranteeing them access to a public education. Democrats said the move violated a compromise that resulted in 1997 legislation to overhaul the Individuals with Disabilities Education Act (IDEA).

A Livingston aide said he made the move after meeting with Louisiana school officials. The bill would provide $5 billion for education of the disabled, $503 million above Clinton's request.

Livingston has begun campaigning for Speaker on the assumption that Newt Gingrich, R-Ga., will run for president in 2000. House Republican leaders and conservative groups, including the Christian Coalition and Family Research Council, held a summit last month to air disagreements. Lobbyists for some of those groups complain that Porter is too moderate, particularly on abortion. They said Livingston this year has shown more willingness to work with them.

Education Ups and Downs

The measure would provide $30.6 billion in budget authority for the Education Department, down from Clinton's $31.2 billion request but up $1.1 billion from last year.

Funding for Clinton's controversial Goals 2000 program to improve education quality would be cut in half from fiscal 1998, to $246 million. The bill would cut Eisenhower Grants for teacher training to $285 million, a $50 million decrease from fiscal 1998. Further, the measure would let states roll remaining Goals 2000 and Eisenhower funds into an existing elementary and secondary block grants, which the administration had wanted to eliminate. Voting 6-8, the subcommittee rejected an amendment by Steny H. Hoyer, D-Md., to eliminate the block grant plan.

As with last year's bill, the measure would bar Clinton from implementing voluntary national math and reading tests until Congress passed authorizing legislation or until fiscal 2000.

It did not include the administration's request for $60 million to replenish a federal revolving fund for

Appropriations

Perkins Loans. The low-interest loans aid 788,000 needy college students annually. Education Department officials said the move could reduce loan volume.

The subcommittee maintained level funding for Title I aid to disadvantaged elementary and secondary students at $7.5 billion, $422 million below Clinton's request. It increased the maximum Pell Grant for low-income college students by $150 to $3,150 — higher than the administration request. It also increased grants to help disadvantaged students enter college.

Edward Kealy, executive director of the Committee for Education Funding, a coalition of education groups, said while the committee increased some funding, the bill "falls far short of what we think is necessary." He warned education could fare worse in the Senate if lawmakers try to restore aid for LIHEAP and summer jobs.

The subcommittee voted 15-0 for an amendment by Rep. Ernest Istook, R-Okla., to require schools to put filtering software on computers bought or operated with federal funds in order to prevent students from viewing pornography on the Internet.

Health Spending Riders

The bill would provide $34.13 billion for HHS, below Clinton's request but up $1.3 billion from 1998. NIH would receive $14.9 billion, a $1.2 billion increase. The Centers for Disease Control and Prevention would get $2.5 billion, a $207 million boost.

Although Clinton complained on June 24 that the bill would cut funding for Head Start, it provides a $153 million increase to $4.5 billion and implements a White House request to increase funding for services to infants and toddlers. Clinton sought a $313 million increase.

The bill increases aid for services to AIDS patients, community health centers, and breast and cervical cancer screening, among others.

"I'm overwhelmed by the generosity of the subcommittee in helping the poor and disabled communities I've championed for many years," said Rep. Henry Bonilla, R-Texas.

The bill would bar HHS from implementing pending rules in fiscal 1999 to transform the way organs are distributed for transplantation, from a system based regionally to one based on medical need.

It also would prohibit HHS from implementing rules that would require hospitals to inform local organ procurement organizations of all deaths in their facilities.

For the second year in a row, HHS would not be allowed to use federal funds for needle exchange programs that are designed to reduce the risk of spreading disease among illegal drug users. HHS announced April 20 that scientific evidence found such programs were effective. But the administration said it would not use federal funds for them.

As in past years, the bill includes the so-called Hyde language barring use of federal funds for abortions except in the case of rape, incest or danger to the life of the mother. This year, however, the language would be expanded to cover the Medicare trust fund to resolve confusion about whether the prohibition would apply to younger, disabled Medicare recipients.

Swipes at Labor

The bill would reduce the Labor Department budget to $9.6 billion, from $10.7 billion in fiscal 1998. It would eliminate $871 million for summer jobs. Because the program is funded a year in advance, the move would not affect this summer's participants. The bill includes the full amount requested by Clinton for the Job Corps and Youth Job Training.

In a nod to the business community, the bill takes several swipes at the Occupational Safety and Health Administration (OSHA), which regulates workplace safety.

The bill would require peer review of new OSHA health and safety standards. It would reduce by $5.6 million funding for inspections and other actions to enforce workplace laws, instead spending that money on education and other compliance efforts.

The bill would allocate $890,000 for a study of the scientific literature on ergonomics, but does not include language barring OSHA from issuing new ergonomics standards for workplaces. Democrats said they expected the Senate to include a ban. The agency came out with a draft ergonomics plan in 1995 but said it is nowhere near ready to release a final plan.

The bill provides the same level of funding for the National Labor Relations Board as in fiscal 1998. Porter said that because the board would have to use part of its funding on computer needs, the funding level would force a cut in personnel.

House Measure Is Loaded With Hot-Button Issues

JULY 18 — As congressional Republicans and the White House head toward a another fall showdown over federal spending, the fiscal 1999 Labor, Health and Human Services, and Education appropriations bill is shaping up as a political flashpoint.

The House Appropriations Committee approved its version of the measure, 32-23, on July 14, after adding amendments that would overturn a Clinton administration directive requiring states to cover the impotence drug Viagra under Medicaid; give women in managed-care plans easier access to gynecologists; and require clinics receiving federal family planning funds to notify parents before providing contraceptives to minors.

Democrats spent much of the markup session railing against provisions in the Republican-drafted bill that would eliminate summer jobs for poor youths, end the Low-Income Home Energy Assistance Program (LIHEAP) and reduce spending for President Clinton's education priorities.

Clinton himself stepped up the rhetoric, announcing in a strongly worded statement on July 14 that he would veto the bill — which would provide $81.9 billion in discretionary spending and $214.5 billion in mandatory funds — because it would deny education and training opportunities to students across the country.

"By turning their backs on America's young in this bill, the House Republicans are taking a step backward," Clinton said in a statement.

The White House Office of Management and Budget sent the committee a nine-page letter outlining specific objections, ranging from the measure's two-year time limit on federal bilingual education aid to provisions that it said would weaken federal labor law.

Despite the tough talk, however, Democrats made few moves to restore education and social service spending cuts during the more than four-hour committee session.

The truth is that Democrats face the same constraints that, in part, forced Republicans to make the cuts: tight spending caps imposed under the 1997 balanced-budget law (PL 105-33).

To get around the caps and increase education and health programs, Clinton's fiscal 1999 budget relied on expected revenues from comprehensive tobacco legislation (S 1415) that would have raised $516 billion over 25 years. The bill was killed by Senate Republicans.

Without additional tobacco revenues, Democrats must find offsetting spending cuts in order to increase aid for White House priorities.

"The Democrats' argument is not with us, their argument is with what their own leadership and the president of the United States agreed to last year," said Appropriations Committee Chairman Robert L. Livingston, R-La.

"What they really want is more money. If you're going to follow last year's balanced-budget act, there isn't any more," he said.

While some House Republican moderates have threatened to oppose the bill, Livingston said he believed it would pass. The legislation is tentatively scheduled for House floor debate before the end of the month.

A Senate Appropriations Committee aide said that chamber's panel might not mark up a companion bill until September.

Viagra for the Poor

Instead of focusing on provisions in the underlying bill, lawmakers spent most of the markup debating a series of policy riders.

Panel members, like the rest of American society, had sharp opinions about Viagra, the anti-impotence drug approved by the Food and Drug Administration earlier this year.

The administration on July 2 announced that state-run Medicaid programs, which provide health coverage for the poor, elderly and disabled, would cover Viagra when medically necessary. The directive was in keeping with overall policy requiring state Medicaid programs to cover FDA-approved medicines.

State governors, who jointly fund the Medicaid program, objected to the decision, citing lack of medical consensus on the need for the drug and the high cost, as much as $10 per dose.

David R. Obey, D-Wis., offered an amendment, approved by voice vote, that would bar use of federal funds to reimburse states for providing Viagra. The savings the amendment would generate — as much as $100 million — would instead be spent on mental health services to youth at risk of violent behavior.

"Given the mixed results so far with the drug in question, and given the fact that there are so many other health maladies that are not covered, there is no need at this time to use scarce Medicaid dollars for Viagra," Obey said.

The committee by voice vote later adopted an amendment by Mark W. Neumann, R-Wis., drafted with the aid of the National Governors' Association, that would bar use of federal funds to punish states that chose not to offer Viagra. States could still use their own funds to provide the drug.

Finally, the panel approved a third amendment by Randy "Duke" Cunningham, R-Calif., that would allow federal funds for Viagra in post-surgical treatment, such as in cases of prostate cancer.

Managed Care

By a 29-25 vote, the committee approved an amendment by Nita M. Lowey, D-N.Y., that would allow women to designate obstetrician-gynecologists as their primary care physicians in both private and federal managed care plans. It would also ensure that women who did not choose their gynecologist as their main doctor would have direct access to routine ob-gyn services without first having to get authorization.

Approval of Lowey's amendment reflected the sensitivity of both parties to voter concerns about the quality of care in managed-care plans, which is emerging as a top political issue. Both Republicans and Democrats have introduced broader proposals to expand patients' rights that include provisions similar to Lowey's.

"If we can't deliver on a patients' bill of rights, let's simply deliver on this," Lowey said.

By voice vote, the committee adopted an amendment by Carrie P. Meek, D-Fla., to add a new label to cigarettes warning of the particular health risks of smoking for African-Americans. Two studies released this month found that African-Americans absorb more nicotine than other smokers, which may be one reason they are more likely to develop lung cancer.

The Meek amendment would add a fifth warning label to the four warning labels that now rotate on cigarette packages. It would read, "Surgeon General's Warning: African-Americans suffer the highest death rates from several diseases caused by smoking."

The committee approved, 32-24, an amendment by Ernest Istook, R-Okla., that would require clinics receiving Title X family planning funds to notify parents in writing at least five business days before dispensing contraceptives to minors. A second provision, adopted 56-0, would require clinics to comply with state laws requiring notification of sexual abuse, rape, incest or other crimes.

On a 26-26 vote, the committee defeated an effort by Todd Tiahrt, R-Kan., that would have required family planning groups receiving Title X funds to physically separate abortion and family planning activities.

The Istook and Tiahrt amendments were supported by Christian conservatives, who have criticized the House Republican leadership for paying too little attention to their core issues. House Majority Whip Tom DeLay, R-Texas, a member of the committee who was absent for most of the proceedings, showed up for the family planning votes.

Mine Safety

The committee defeated, 19-33, an amendment by Rosa DeLauro, D-Conn., that would have eliminated a rider that has been attached to the bill every year since 1979 barring the Labor Department's Office of Mine Safety and Health Administration from enforcing training requirements in sand and gravel pits.

The ban was originally based on concern that safety standards developed for coal mines were not applicable to open-pit quarries. But DeLauro said that 600 workers have died in

Appropriations

quarries since the safety agency was first barred from enforcing training rules. "It is time to take the preventive measure of eliminating this rider," DeLauro said.

Labor-HHS Subcommittee Chairman John Edward Porter, R-Ill., and Anne M. Northup, R-Ky., argued against removing the rider, saying the industry and administration were meeting to try to reach a compromise. They said that if the rider was removed, there would be no incentive for the two sides to reach an agreement.

"We all want the same thing, and that is to have safety in the workplace," Northup argued.

In one of the few efforts to alter the spending priorities in the underlying bill, Steny H. Hoyer, D-Md., offered an amendment to eliminate a provision that would allow states to roll Clinton's Goals 2000 education improvement program, as well as the Eisenhower grants program for teacher training, into an existing block grant and use the funding for other purposes. It failed, 24-29.

Spending Reductions

The bill would eliminate the $1.1 billion LIHEAP program and would not include any funds for summer jobs for low-income youths in fiscal 1999, a savings of $871 million. Those reductions would help pay for a $1.2 billion increase for the National Institutes of Health.

Republicans included no funding for Clinton's proposal to hire 100,000 new teachers and reduce average class size in early grades, which was to be funded partly through tobacco revenues.

The bill would bar the administration from implementing voluntary national math and reading tests, limit student participation in federally funded bilingual education programs to two years and deny federal funds to schools unless they install software on their computers to block students from accessing pornography on the Internet.

It would bar the Health and Human Services Department from implementing pending rules to transform the way organs are distributed for transplantation, from a system based regionally to one based on medical need.

However, the bill would increase funding for some education programs, including aid to disabled students. It raises the maximum Pell Grant for disadvantaged college students by $150 to $3,150 per year, above the administration request.

The bill also would increase funding for the Centers for Disease Control and Prevention, the Head Start preschool program, and breast and cervical cancer screening, among other programs.

OMB said that, overall, the bill was $2 billion below Clinton's request for education spending. Acting OMB Director Jacob J. Lew said the administration was willing to work with Republicans to find either spending offsets or user fees to increase funding. Democrats have offered few proposals.

"Your side has had an opportunity for the last four hours to shape the bill in a different way. . . . The difficulty is that you can't bring yourselves to say 'no' to anything," said Porter.

He added that the Democrats' lack of spending restraint was a big reason that Republicans now control Congress.

Senate Spurns Cuts Made By House In Interior Bill

SEPTEMBER 5 — Rejecting a slew of House proposals to cut job training and education programs, the Senate Appropriations Committee on Sept. 3 approved a $287.6 billion fiscal 1999 spending bill for the departments of Labor, Health and Human Services and Education. The more moderate approach won cautious support from the White House.

The bipartisan measure, moved by a vote of 28-0, includes $1.1 billion for the Low Income Home Energy Assistance Program (LIHEAP) and $871 million for summer jobs for low-income youth — two programs that would be zeroed out in the House measure (HR 4274).

Using accounting sleight of hand to increase available funding, senators made it clear that they wanted to avoid sharp cuts in domestic spending in an election year. House Republicans, playing instead to party conservatives as they shaped their competing bill, took a more confrontational tack.

"This bill, while not perfect, takes a more responsible approach" than the House, said Tom Harkin, D-Iowa, the ranking Democrat on the Senate Appropriations Subcommittee on Labor, Health and Human Services and Education.

President Clinton has threatened to veto the House bill, which is awaiting floor action, because of its proposed spending cuts and a host of legislative riders on issues, ranging from requiring parental notification before minors could receive birth control at federally funded clinics to delaying proposed federal rules governing organ donations.

In a Sept. 1 statement from Moscow, where he was holding a summit meeting with Russian President Boris Yeltsin, Clinton said he was "pleased that a bipartisan group of senators voted to reject parts of the extreme House Republican education and training budget."

Clinton added, however, that the Senate bill was still short of his budget proposals for social services spending. He termed the Senate measure "a good first step" but added, "There is still more work to do."

The Senate committee's action will put pressure on the House to modify its strategy of relying on Republican votes to pass a Labor-HHS bill. There were signs that plan was already in trouble before the August recess, when controversy over family planning stymied agreement on a rule for debating the measure. Further, House committee leaders have already indicated they plan to partially restore funding for LIHEAP and summer jobs.

The Senate bill would increase spending for education programs cut by the House and boost funding for the National Institutes of Health (NIH) by nearly $2 billion from fiscal 1998 levels, to $15.6 billion. The House bill includes a smaller NIH increase but would allocate more generous funding for the Centers for Disease Control (CDC) and other health programs.

Senate Appropriations Committee Chairman Ted Stevens, R-Alaska, and Senate Budget Committee Chairman Pete V. Domenici, R-N.M., said they were also trying to find ways to provide additional funding for the bill.

One possible avenue for getting

more cash would be for the Budget Committee to move away from Congressional Budget Office (CBO) estimates governing the bill and instead allow more optimistic Office of Management and Budget (OMB) projections of fiscal 1999 spending for aid to disabled students.

The OMB has forecast less in spending for that program than the CBO because its analysis takes into account some recently approved policy changes. Switching to OMB figures could free up about $200 million for the bill without breaching discretionary spending caps in the 1997 balanced-budget law. The bill includes $4.8 billion in state grants for the disabled.

Similar budget re-estimates were used earlier this year to increase defense and highway outlays.

"I believe there will be a later opportunity to deal with additional funding," Stevens told the committee.

A move to boost spending could result from expected negotiations with the White House on a final Labor-HHS bill or a catchall spending measure that would be needed to fund federal programs in fiscal 1999 if freestanding appropriations bills have not been signed into law. Congress has cleared just one of the 13 annual bills even though the current fiscal year ends Sept. 30.

The Senate Labor-HHS measure already relies on several accounting maneuvers to increase discretionary spending on social programs without breaking the fiscal 1999 budget caps. The legislation defers about $4 billion in spending for Head Start, Title I aid to the disadvantaged and AIDS programs to fiscal 2000. It contains emergency funding for LIHEAP and a new, $158.8 million initiative to fight bioterrorism.

The Senate committee, unlike the House, freed up funds by cutting the Social Services Block Grant to $1.9 billion from $2.3 billion in fiscal 1998. Overall, the Senate bill is about $4 billion closer to Clinton's budget than the House, administration aides said.

Tough Road Ahead

The Senate bill includes $82.7 billion in budget authority for discretionary spending. The bulk of the $287.6 billion bill is devoted to mandatory funds for the Medicare and Medicaid health insurance programs and other required spending.

Despite the bipartisan cooperation in the Senate committee, the prospects for getting a final bill are still dicey. The bill is the largest of the spending measures, and usually one of the most troublesome to pass because it is such an inviting target for controversial policy riders.

The committee by voice vote adopted a few amendments, including a proposal by Kay Bailey Hutchison, R-Texas, to prevent HHS from creating a national health care identity number without congressional approval, and a plan by Christopher S. Bond, R-Mo., to increase funding for community health centers by $75 million. But lawmakers made it clear there would be vigorous debate when the bill reached the full Senate the week of Sept. 7.

Among the issues deferred to the Senate floor were: a proposal to rework a provision of the 1997 balanced-budget act (PL 105-33) cutting Medicare reimbursement to home health agencies; a plan to turn categorical elementary and secondary education programs into block grants; a requirement that private health plans cover government-approved prescription birth control pills or devices if they covered other prescription drugs; and allowing senior citizens in Medicare to see doctors outside the system, at their own expense, a practice known as private contracting.

"This is the last train out of the station," said Sen. Larry E. Craig, R-Idaho, noting that Labor-HHS was the final bill reported out of the committee.

Stevens, who pushed members to defer riders, responded that the committee was "just the staging area for the train; it goes through the Senate."

Account by Account

The Senate bill includes $34.4 billion for the Department of Education, including $7.68 billion for Title I education grants to states for disadvantaged youth, a slightly more than $300 million increase from fiscal 1998.

Grants to the states for education of the disabled would be increased to $4.8 billion, about $300 million above fiscal 1998 and the White House request. The Senate bill does not include a House rider opposed by the Clinton administration that would make is easier for schools to discipline disabled students who are violent.

The bill includes $354 million for bilingual and immigrant education, the same amount as last year. The Senate did not include House language that would limit students to two years in federally supported bilingual programs.

Likewise, the Senate bill includes $496 million for Clinton's Goals 2000 program of grants to improve quality of education, more than double the House amount. The House bill would also allow states to roll Goals 2000 and a separate teacher training program into block grants for other education uses.

The Senate bill would increase by $100 to $3,100 per year the maximum amount for Pell Grants, which are need-based grants for college. It also would provide $75 million to improve teacher training, $100 million for school construction and renovation and $151 million for a new program to combat school violence through mental health counseling and other services. The bill would provide $4.66 billion for Head Start, the level desired by the White House.

The legislation would include $15.6 billion for NIH, a $2 billion increase over fiscal 1998. The House bill would provide $14.9 billion. The NIH has been one of the fastest growing areas of federal spending, and some lawmakers worry it is being monitored too loosely.

"I do wonder who's been doing the overseeing on NIH," said Domenici. "That is a very big program and growing extremely fast."

The CDC would receive $2.32 billion, a slight reduction from 1998, while AIDS funding would grow by about $218 million, to $1.4 billion.

The bill would specify that health plans contracting with Medicare would not be required to provide abortion services, although those services would have to be available to beneficiaries outside the plan.

Department of Labor

The bill would provide $9.16 billion for the Department of Labor.

The Senate bill would allocate $1.3 billion for the Job Corps, a $54 million increase from 1998, and fund the Occupational Safety and Health Administration at $349 million, up $12 mil-

Appropriations

lion from the current fiscal year.

The bill includes $184.5 million for the National Labor Relations Board, slightly more than fiscal 1998.

House Approves Rule, Sends Bill To House Floor

OCTOBER 3 — After months of wrangling, the House on Oct. 2 voted 216-200 to approve a rule for the fiscal 1999 Labor, Health and Human Services and Education spending bill (HR 4274). The measure may come to the floor the week of Oct 5.

Democrats who voted against the rule called the action a hollow gesture, charging that the bill was months late and billions of dollars short of President Clinton's request.

Rep. David R. Obey of Wisconsin, the ranking Democrat on the Appropriations Committee, said House and Senate negotiators had already been in preliminary discussions on a compromise Labor-HHS package that would be folded into an omnibus spending bill. He said any final plan would likely be billions of dollars above the proposed House measure.

"This is a sham bill," Obey said.

John Edward Porter, R-Ill., chairman of the Labor-HHS subcommittee, conceded that floor consideration of the bill was late, but said it was important to debate the measure.

Rather than reaching out to moderates as in the past, this bill was drafted with an eye to conservatives. Even when it became apparent the measure was short of votes, conservatives kept fighting to bring it up — fearful that if they could not get a vote, House leaders next year would once again write a more liberal bill.

The measure would require that parents be notified before minors could receive contraceptives from federally funded family planning clinics.

Conservatives initially wanted only an up-or-down vote on striking that language. The rule lets moderates offer a substitute amendment calling on clinics to involve parents in decisions on contraceptives. Conservatives could then offer a second amendment to put parental notification back in.

Stalled Measure Likely To Migrate To Omnibus Bill

OCTOBER 10 — According to the script drafted earlier this year by House Republican leaders, the fiscal 1999 Labor, Health and Human Services (HHS) and Education appropriations bill was to be an austere document reflecting a tighter budget and conservative priorities.

Instead, congressional leaders and the White House spent the week of Oct. 5 trying to figure out how to increase funding for health and education programs and shake off a list of controversial policy riders dear to the right flank of the Republican Party.

Short of time and votes, appropriators have not brought the approximately $285 billion committee-passed Labor-HHS measures (HR 4274, S 2440) to either the House or the Senate floors. Instead, Republicans are working with the Clinton administration to devise an agreement that would fund social programs as part of a fiscal 1999 omnibus spending bill.

With public opinion polls showing that improving the quality of schools was a top issue for voters, Republicans were especially sensitive to President Clinton's repeated charges that their bills, especially the House-drafted version, had given short shrift to his agenda.

After an Oct. 9 White House meeting with Democrats on the budget, Clinton warned lawmakers that he could keep Congress in session until he got what he wanted.

"This budget is purely and simply a test of whether after nine months of doing nothing, we are going to do the right thing about our children's future," Clinton said. "Members of Congress should not go home until they pass a budget that will strengthen our public schools for the 21st century."

Lawmakers were eager to blunt the criticism, with Republicans holding a news conference Oct. 9 to profess their support for education. Aides said congressional and White House negotiators had reached tentative agreements to restore $1.1 billion in funding for the Low-Income Energy Assistance Program and $871 million for summer jobs for low-income youth. Both programs had been zeroed out in the original House Labor-HHS bill but funded in the Senate committee version (S 2440).

Further, negotiators appeared ready to embrace a $2 billion increase in the National Institutes of Health budget, bringing it in line with the $15.6 billion in the Senate bill.

House and Senate Republican leaders were also poised to increase funding for a host of education programs that had been cut in the House bill, and were debating the addition of about $1 billion to reduce class size, aides said.

The money, sought by the White House, would be a down payment on Clinton's State of the Union proposal to hire 100,000 new teachers and reduce average class size to 18 in the early grades.

Lawmakers and aides cautioned, however, that a host of prickly policy riders remained on the House bill, including proposals to bar Clinton's plan for national voluntary math and reading tests, limit federally funded bilingual education to two years, make it easier under federal law to discipline violent disabled children, and bar HHS from proceeding with a proposed change in the national policy governing organ donations.

Spending bill talks were spilling over into other legislation. House Republican aides warned that lawmakers might delay final action on a literacy bill (HR 2614) Clinton wanted until they received assurances that the ban on national testing would be in any omnibus bill.

On the Floor, Off the Floor

As a concession to conservatives, Republican leaders brought the House bill to the floor Oct. 8 under a rule that limited votes to a policy rider that would require parents to be notified before minors received contraceptives from a federally funded clinic.

The move brought lawmakers to the floor for a series of votes, interrupting negotiations on the omnibus bill. Asked if the votes were a waste of time, John Edward Porter, R-Ill., chairman of the Labor-HHS Appropriations Subcommittee replied, "complete, utter."

"What in God's name are we doing?" said David R. Obey, D-Wis. "This debate does nothing but satisfy political problems in the majority."

Tom Coburn, R-Okla., said conservatives hope to use the vote in political campaigns. The House voted 224-200 to retain the family planning rider, while adding language that would provide counseling to minors seeking contraceptives and require training for counselors. (Vote 504, p. H-142)

Billions Allocated For Schools, Medical Research

OCTOBER 17 — Lawmakers went on a social services spending spree the week of Oct. 12, with the White House and Republican negotiators agreeing to fiscal 1999 Labor, Health and Human Services, and Education spending that would provide billions of dollars in new funding for public schools and medical research.

The roughly $290 billion proposal, which was expected to clear Congress as part of the omnibus spending bill (HR 4328), was estimated by the Clinton administration to be more than $3 billion above fiscal 1998 spending on education alone, though final numbers were being tallied.

The bill includes $1.2 billion sought by President Clinton as a down payment on a longer-term initiative to hire 100,000 new teachers and reduce average class size to 18 in grades 1-3.

The deal would also fund a $26 million literacy initiative and an increase in college grants for low-income students.

The legislation would give $15.6 billion to the National Institutes of Health, a nearly $2 billion, or 14 percent, increase over fiscal 1998. Under the measure, the Centers for Disease Control would get $2.6 billion while $1.4 billion would be allocated for AIDS assistance.

Republicans also increased discretionary spending for the Department of Labor by about 3 percent from last year, the administration said, including Clinton's request for more funding for the National Labor Relations Board — a favorite target of Republicans.

The extra funding would be offset, in part, by deferring billions of dollars in education spending until fiscal 2000 and cutting programs such as the Social Services Block Grant. Some funds would also be designated as emergency spending and therefore not subject to caps on discretionary spending in the 1997 balanced-budget act (PL 105-33).

"By standing together, we were able to achieve historic victories for the American people," Clinton said at a White House budget event Oct. 16.

"We fought for and won vital new investments, especially for our children," he said.

Conservatives were furious about the spending increases in the overall spending deal.

"This is a bad bill for the American people," Rep. David M. McIntosh, R-Ind., said Oct. 15. He called the agreement a return to the Great Society big government era.

Conservatives did win some victories, however. For the second year in a row, the measure prevents Clinton from proceeding with voluntary national tests to assess fourth graders in reading and eighth graders in math, unless authorized by Congress.

The bill would impose a one-year moratorium on a proposal by the Department of Health and Human Services (HHS) to set up a new national system for allocating organs for donation. During that time, the Institute of Medicine, which is part of National Academy of Sciences, would conduct a study of the issue.

Under the proposed HHS rule, potential organ recipients would have been prioritized nationally, with available organs then going to those at the top of the list. Legislators from states with their own longstanding systems were skittish about the change.

"The regulations proposed by HHS would have forced the smaller transplant centers that serve the uninsured and underinsured to close, as the vast majority of organs went to the handful of the nation's largest transplant centers," Sen. Robert G. Torricelli, D-N.J., said in a statement.

The HHS maintained that the revisions were necessary to make the organ donor system work more effectively.

For the second year in a row, HHS would not be allowed to use federal funds for needle exchange programs designed to cut the risk of transmitting disease among illegal drug users.

Riders Dropped

During talks with the White House, congressional negotiators dropped or modified a long series of other legislative riders that had been attached to the House bill.

The final measure did not include a House provision that would have required parents to be notified before minors received birth control from a federally funded clinic.

A plan to limit students to two years of federally supported bilingual instruction was replaced with a study on the effectiveness of bilingual programs. Also eliminated was a provision that would have made it easier for schools to discipline violent disabled students.

A provision of the House bill that would have allowed women in managed care plans to designate their obstetrician-gynecologist as their primary care provider was deleted.

Early on, White House and congressional negotiators decided to restore $1.1 billion for the Low-Income Home Energy Assistance Program and $871 million for summer jobs for poor youth. The House Appropriations Committee had voted to eliminate both programs.

One of the biggest bones of contention was Clinton's class size plan — which, if enacted, would become one of the largest federal elementary and secondary education spending programs.

Republicans, who said the plan constituted unwarranted federal interference in local schools, refused to comply with an administration request to underwrite special bonds for school construction. They agreed to go along with the class-size plan only after the White House agreed to modify it.

The final plan is a grant to states and local school districts, although funding levels for each district will depend on the number of poor students it serves. Republicans groused that despite the win on local control, most of the money could go to urban districts represented by Democrats.

Up to 15 percent of the funds could be used for teacher training. The Education Department said it expected 30,000 teachers to be hired under the plan next year.

The National School Boards Association supported the plan, but cautioned that because the bill would provide just a one-year appropriation,

Appropriations

with no long-term authorization or guaranteed funding, schools could face some difficult budget choices.

"It's very tough on a school district to say, 'Go hire 100,000 new teachers this year.' Then what do we do with them next year?" said Anne Bryant, NSBA executive director.

Democrats were confident Congress would approve additional funding in fiscal 2000. "Do you think you're going to be able to kill that program when it starts?" asked a House Democratic leadership aide.

Written by Committee

To a greater extent than other measures folded into the omnibus spending package, the Labor-HHS measure was written by a small committee of lawmakers and administration aides. While the House and Senate Appropriations Committees approved separate versions of the bill, it did not come to the floor of either chamber.

The original House bill was more than $2 billion under the White House request for education. The Senate bill, which relied on budget sleight-of-hand such as spending deferrals and forward funding, was far closer.

The lower funding in the House bill was due partly to the fact that the White House had relied on revenues from a proposed tobacco settlement, which did not clear Congress, to fund its agenda. But House Republican leaders made a calculated decision to write a bill this year that would appeal to conservatives. In the end, that strategy went by the wayside.

On education, the bill includes an increase in the maximum college Pell grant to low-income students to $3,125 from the current $3,000 and $260 million for the first year of a two-year literacy program. The bill folds in another measure (HR 2614) authorizing the literacy program.

The initiative is designed to improve teacher training in reading, upgrade instructional materials and enhance state and local coordination of reading efforts to reach as many students — and parents — as possible.

The legislation would provide $870 million for college work study and $120 million for a new program to help more low-income middle school students prepare for college, authorized in the Higher Education Act, which was signed into law by President Clinton on Oct. 7 (PL 105-244).

Clinton won a $160 million increase for after-school assistance and $4.6 billion overall for the Head Start preschool program. The White House also won increased funding for educational technology programs.

The deal dropped a House policy rider that would have required peer review of new Occupational Health and Safety Administration (OSHA) health and safety standards.

It would allocate funding for a study of the scientific literature on ergonomics, but does not extend language that was in the 1998 bill barring OSHA from proceeding with new rules to combat repetitive motion injuries in the workplace. Furthermore, lawmakers are expected to make it clear in a letter that the study is not to be used to force a delay in work on possible rules.

The agreement allows funds for a new youth opportunity work initiative authorized as part of a rewrite of job training programs (HR 1853). It fully funds the White House request for the Job Corps and other youth training programs.

Final Bill Includes NIH Increase

OCTOBER 24 — Congress splurged on federal medical spending for fiscal 1999, approving unprecedented increases in funding to accelerate research into the cure and prevention of cancer, AIDS and other serious diseases.

The omnibus spending bill (HR 4328) signed by President Clinton on Oct. 21 dedicated $15.6 billion to the National Institutes of Health. That is a 15-percent increase from fiscal 1998 and the beginning of a five-year push to greatly expand the agency's budget.

"The $2 billion increase for NIH is simply breathtaking. It's extraordinary — the single largest dollar increase in NIH history," Health and Human Services Secretary Donna E. Shalala said in an Oct. 21 statement.

The NIH provisions are part of the Labor, Health and Human Services and Education section of the fiscal 1999 omnibus spending bill, which funds programs from the nationally prominent to the narrowly parochial.

The fiscal 1999 bill, more than past years, is also loaded with a long list of spending designations, including $65 million to renovate existing hospitals and medical facilities. It includes $6 million for the Robert J. Dole Institute for Public Service and Public Policy at the University of Kansas campus in Lawrence, and $1 million for the Oregon Institute of Public Service and Constitutional Studies at the Mark O. Hatfield School of Government at Portland State University.

Overall, the bill provides about $290 billion in spending for health, education and labor programs. The majority of spending is for mandatory programs.

Discretionary spending will grow to $83.2 billion, from $81.1 billion. The Education Department budget increased by nearly $3.5 billion, including $1.2 billion for a White House initiative designed to eventually hire 100,000 new public school teachers. The education funding exceeded Clinton's budget request.

Medical Funding

The White House has called for a 50 percent increase in NIH funding over five years. Some academic and medical groups want to double it. In line with its priorities, the Clinton administration proposed a 9 percent boost for fiscal 1999. That was quickly trumped by Congress.

"I have been fighting for years to double NIH funding, and we're on that path," said Sen. Tom Harkin, D-Iowa.

Medical groups such as the Association of American Medical Colleges also praised the increase. "These funds will allow us to conquer disease and provide healthier and more productive lives for all Americans," said group President Dr. Jordan J. Cohen.

The rise in funds has been accompanied by increased pressure to dedicate some of the NIH budget to research specific diseases. Rep. John Edward Porter, R-Ill., chairman of the House Labor-HHS Appropriations Subcommittee, has fought efforts to earmark NIH funding, believing as did his predecessor, William Natcher, D-Ky. (1953-94), that those decisions should be left to experts.

Due in part to Porter's opposition, lawmakers drafting the conference report dropped a proposal by Senate Ap-

Labor-HHS-Education Spending

Labor-HHS-Education portion of the fiscal 1999 omnibus spending law (HR 4328 — PL 105-277) signed by the president on Oct. 21. *(Budget authority, in thousands of dollars.)*

	Fiscal 1998 Appropriation	Clinton Request	House Committee	Senate Committee	Final Bill
Labor Department					
Training and employment services	$ 5,232,737	$ 5,323,373	$ 3,750,873	$ 5,159,375	$5,022,324
Trade adjustment, allowances	349,000	360,700	360,700	360,700	360,700
Unemployment insurance (advance)	392,000	357,000	357,000	357,000	357,000
Trust fund	*3,273,621*	*3,206,076*	*3,122,476*	*3,077,476*	*3,132,076*
Black lung disability	1,007,000	1,021,000	1,021,000	1,021,000	1,021,000
Occupational Safety & Health	336,678	355,045	336,678	348,983	353,000
Other, including rescissions	2,026,543	2,074,483	2,016,079	1,917,351	1,931,356
Total, Labor Department	**$ 9,343,958**	**$ 9,491,601**	**$ 7,842,330**	**$ 9,164,409**	**$ 9,045,380**
Health and Human Services					
Public Health					
Health resources and services	3,661,720	3,826,256	3,947,810	4,045,188	4,267,328
Ryan White AIDS program	*1,149,512*	*1,312,982*	*1,330,600*	*1,367,800*	*1,411,300*
Disease control	2,332,638	2,454,459	2,540,433	2,315,644	2,558,520
National Institutes of Health	13,622,386	14,763,313	14,862,023	15,582,386	15,612,386
Substance abuse/mental health	2,147,156	2,274,643	2,458,005	2,151,643	2,488,005
Health care financing					
Medicaid grants to states	100,959,559	107,916,644	107,916,644	107,916,644	107,916,644
Medicare and other Medicaid	60,904,000	62,953,000	62,953,000	62,953,000	62,953,000
Public Welfare					
Low-income home energy assistance	1,000,000	1,100,000	0	1,100,000	1,100,000
Refugee assistance	415,000	415,000	415,165	415,000	415,000
Community services block grants	489,685	489,100	500,000	490,600	500,000
Child care block grant	1,002,672	1,176,672	1,000,000	1,000,000	1,000,000
Social Services block grants	2,299,000	1,909,000	2,299,000	1,909,000	1,909,000
Head Start	4,347,433	4,660,000	4,500,000	3,295,000	4,660,000
Programs for the aging	871,020	871,050	861,020	876,050	882,020
Foster care, adoption assistance	4,311,000	5,141,500	4,921,500	5,121,500	4,921,500
Other, including rescissions	–4,477,906	347,364	53,064	1,683,339	402,392
Total, HHS	**$ 193,885,363**	**$ 210,298,001**	**$ 209,227,664**	**$ 210,854,994**	**$ 211,585,795**
Education Department					
Elementary and Secondary Education					
Goals 2000	491,000	501,000	245,500	496,000	491,000
Compensatory education (Title 1)	8,021,827	8,495,892	8,056,132	8,334,781	8,370,520
Impact aid	808,000	696,000	848,000	810,000	864,000
School improvement	1,541,188	1,475,800	1,542,334	1,655,188	2,811,134
Bilingual, immigrant education	354,000	387,000	354,000	354,000	380,000
Special education	4,531,685	4,554,685	5,034,685	5,043,985	5,054,685
Higher Education					
Pell grants, student financial aid	7,344,934	7,594,000	8,178,654	8,527,551	7,704,000
Guaranteed student loans	46,482	48,482	48,482	46,482	46,482
Higher education grants	943,738	1,288,405	944,198	1,138,944	1,307,846
Vocational, adult education	1,147,147	1,150,147	1,154,247	1,146,650	1,154,247
Rehabilitation services	2,591,195	2,645,266	2,646,640	2,645,266	2,652,584
Education research	431,438	689,367	447,667	479,338	664,867
Other, including rescissions	3,897,082	4,064,524	2,889,518	3,689,466	4,059,727
Total, Education Department	**$ 32,149,716**	**$ 33,590,568**	**$ 32,930,057**	**$ 34,367,651**	**$ 35,561,092**
Domestic Volunteer Service Programs	256,604	278,422	251,369	275,039	276,039
Corporation for Public Broadcasting	300,000	340,000	340,000	340,000	340,000
Supplemental Security Income	16,370,000	21,797,000	21,747,000	21,840,000	21,804,000
Other related agencies	9,951,776	10,811,247	10,751,172	10,750,379	10,794,797
GRAND TOTAL	**$ 262,257,417**	**$ 286,606,839**	**$ 283,089,592**	**$ 287,592,472**	**$ 289,407,103**
Trust Funds	*$ 9,663,495*	*$ 9,678,172*	*$ 9,576,963*	*$ 9,270,995*	*$ 9,591,766*

SOURCE: House and Senate Appropriations committees

Appropriations

propriations Committee Chairman Ted Stevens, R-Alaska, a prostate cancer survivor, to dedicate $175 million to research on that disease. However, the report urges NIH to make prostate cancer research a top priority.

The Juvenile Diabetes Foundation publicly thanked House Speaker Newt Gingrich, R-Ga., for helping to secure $30 million for research into autoimmune diseases, which could include juvenile-onset diabetes, lupus and other related illnesses.

Gingrich, whose mother-in-law is diabetic, has actively worked to secure more research funding as well as expand Medicare coverage of the treatments for the disease.

Not everyone was happy. Some lobbyists and staff aides admitted it was an open question whether NIH could efficiently absorb the additional funding and whether Congress is able to oversee such highly technical work.

Others said the campaign for steady increases in funding, while well-intentioned, could crowd out spending for other programs. "All of a sudden, you get to the end [of the budget process] and you don't have money for what you need to do," said Martha Phillips, executive director of the Concord Coalition, a budget watchdog group.

One such program is the Social Services Block Grant, reduced by $390 million. Funding for these grants, which states and localities use to operate Meals on Wheels, child care and other programs, was also reduced as part of the 1996 welfare law (PL 104-193).

"Cuts to the Social Services Block Grant over the past three years clearly have had a negative impact on communities," advocacy groups for the poor and disabled, including the Children's Defense Fund, said in a letter to lawmakers.

Other Health Programs

The conference report includes $216 million for an administration initiative to combat bioterrorism and infectious diseases. The entire amount would be designated emergency funding, meaning that it is not subject to discretionary spending caps in the 1997 balanced-budget law (PL 105-33).

The Health Care Financing Administration, which oversees Medicare and Medicaid, would receive a budget increase, as would the Centers for Disease Control and programs for AIDS research and assistance to those suffering from that disease.

The bill would elevate the Office of Alternative Medicine, part of NIH, to a more prominent Center for Complementary and Alternative Medicine. That will direct more money and staff to work on unconventional therapies such as acupuncture, nutrition supplements and herbal remedies.

Under the conference report, states will be required to provide the anti-impotence drug Viagra, when medically necessary, in their Medicaid programs. The House would have overturned a Clinton administration directive that mandated the Medicaid coverage.

The administration in July announced that state-run Medicaid programs, which insure the poor, elderly and disabled, would prescribe Viagra when medically necessary. Noting concerns about the "clinical and financial abuse" of such drugs, the conference report called for rigorous oversight.

The bill would extend the longstanding ban on most federal coverage of abortion to disabled individuals in the Medicare program. Managed care plans contracting with the government under the Medicare+Choice program of expanded health care options would not be required to provide abortion services, though such services would have to be available to private beneficiaries.

It would also bar the Clinton administration from proposing rules for a national health identifier, sort of like a Social Security number.

The $65 million to build and renovate hospitals and health care facilities would be allocated to a host of institutions, including the University of Pennsylvania School of Dental Medicine, Magee-Womens Hospital of Pittsburgh, Philadelphia College of Osteopathic Medicine, Fulton County Medical Center in Pennsylvania and Mercy Health System of Philadelphia. Other states that won projects include New York, North Carolina, Mississippi, Alaska and Washington, D.C.

In a nod to Sen. Alfonse M. D'Amato, R-N.Y., who is locked in a nasty election battle against Democratic Rep. Charles E. Schumer, the bill includes language pushed by the senator to require health insurers to cover breast reconstruction after mastectomies.

Education Aid Goes Up

While Clinton did not get the tax breaks for school construction he sought from Congress, the administration was a big winner when it came to funding for education.

The White House secured $1.2 billion as the down payment on a long-term plan to hire 100,000 new teachers; $260 million for a new literacy initiative and $120 million for a program to persuade more low-income children to attend college. There were complaints that in order to fund some of the spending increases, lawmakers as part of the broader omnibus bill dipped into the District of Columbia pension trust fund.

The bill includes a $160 million increase in aid, to $200 million, sought by the White House for after-school programs. Lawmakers designated a healthy chunk of that funding including: $500,000 for a three-year after-school program in Chippewa Falls, Wis.; $300,000 for the Bay Shore Community Learning Wellness and Fitness Center for Drug Free Lifestyles in Bay Shore, N.Y.; and $2.5 million for an after-school anti-drug program in Chicago public schools.

The bill also includes $87 million for three new education technology programs: $75 million for teacher training; $10 million for computer learning centers in low-income areas and $2 million for national activities.

Longstanding programs saw significant increases in funding, including aid to the disabled, a Republican priority. State grants for educating the disabled rose to $5.1 billion, a $523 million increase; grants for education of disadvantaged children rose to $7.8 billion, an increase of $301 million.

To finance the increased spending, aides performed a series of accounting contortions — including deferring more than $6 billion in education funding into fiscal 2000.

The conference report drops a House provision that would have required schools or libraries receiving federal funds to install software to screen out pornographic Internet material.

It includes a slight increase in discretionary funding for the Labor Department, $4 million for a child care apprenticeship initiative and $5 million for seasonal farmworker activities. ◆

Legislative Branch

Allotment For Capitol Police Increased as Congress Clears Second of 13 Spending Bills

> **Box Score**
>
> ● **Bill:** HR 4112 — PL 105-275
>
> ● **House action:** The House adopted the conference report (H Rept 105-734) on HR 4112, 356-65, on Sept. 24. It passed HR 4112 (H Rept 105-595) on June 25, 235-179.
>
> ● **Senate action:** The Senate cleared the conference report on HR 4112 on Sept. 25 by voice vote. It passed HR 4112 (S Rept 105-204) on July 21 by a vote of 90-9.
>
> ● **Presidential action:** Clinton signed HR 4112 on Oct. 21.

SUMMARY

The deaths of two officers in a July 24 shootout in the Capitol sparked heightened interest in security matters in the fiscal 1999 legislative branch appropriations bill.

The bill provided $83 million for the Capitol Police, a 12 percent increase over fiscal 1998 spending. It allowed, for the first time, overtime pay for officers who work nights and on holidays and Sundays.

Overall, the legislative spending bill provided $2.35 billion for the House, Senate and various congressional agencies and offices, such as the Library of Congress, General Accounting Office (GAO) and Congressional Budget Office (CBO). That amounted to a 2.7 percent increase. The House received $734 million, a 3.5 percent increase. The Senate got $470 million, a 1.7 percent increase.

The bill included extra funds to allow the GAO to hire 50 new employees to help it assess the progress of federal agencies in fixing the so-called Year 2000 computer problem.

The measure had $1 million for repairs at the Congressional Cemetery, where 92 members of Congress and other dignitaries are buried. Matching private funds will be added for the cemetery, which has fallen into disrepair.

Both chambers used the bill to take aim at the CBO. In the House, Republicans criticized CBO's consistent underestimates of a federal surplus, prompting Democrats to charge that the GOP was trying to pressure the agency to project a larger surplus to accommodate larger tax cut proposals. In the Senate, a pair of Democrats complained that CBO failed to note that the surplus comes from including "off budget" Social Security trust fund balances.

An additional $207 million for Capitol security improvements, including the construction of a visitors' center, was added as "emergency" spending in the omnibus appropriations bill (HR 4328 — PL 105-277).

Senate Panel Easily Approves Funds for Legislative Branch

JUNE 6 — Senate appropriators on June 4 approved $1.6 billion in fiscal 1999 funding for the legislative branch, exclusive of items funded by the House.

The total was $51.5 million above the fiscal 1998 level but $74.6 million below President Clinton's request.

The Senate Appropriations Committee approved the legislation (S 2137) 27-0 at a markup that also moved the defense and energy-water appropriations bills.

The measure provoked little discussion among Senate appropriators. "I don't see anything particularly controversial about this [bill]," said Sen. Robert F. Bennett, R-Utah, chairman of the Senate Legislative Branch Appropriations Subcommittee. "We've tried to be good stewards and hold the line appropriately, but at the same time take care of the needs."

The bill funds members' personal offices, Capitol buildings and adjacent office complexes, as well as several legislative branch operations, including the Library of Congress, the Congressional Budget Office, the Government Printing Office, the Capitol Police and the Architect of the Capitol.

Traditionally, the two chambers have maintained a mutual hands-off policy when it comes to members' offices, with the House approving its own spending and the Senate doing likewise. The two chambers then agree on the level of spending for each of the agencies they jointly fund and on a total number.

Bennett said the panel's most significant challenge was to properly maintain the Capitol building and provide for its security. "The Capitol, of course, is a tremendous magnet for people who would like to create mischief for us," he said.

The bill would increase appropriations for the Capitol Police by $6.3 million, to $80.4 million. That includes an additional $1.2 million for security equipment.

Also, funds for the Architect of the Capitol included $475,000 to develop a master plan for several projects for the Capitol Police, such as a communication, command and control facility, a training facility, and an explosive storage facility. An additional $1 million would be provided for design funds.

The new measure includes $469.4 million in Senate expenses, $8.3 million more than the year before. That is largely due to a $10.6 million increase in the account for salaries, legislative assistance and office expenses, which would rise to $239.2 million. Each Senate office would receive an additional $50,000 for administrative and clerical assistance.

On another matter, Sen. Byron L. Dorgan, D-N.D., expressed frustration that the General Accounting Office has lacked a permanent comptroller general since Charles A. Bowsher retired on Sept. 30, 1996.

Dorgan said he was "deeply disap-

Appropriations

pointed" that the congressional leadership has not agreed with Clinton on a replacement. James F. Hinchman is serving as acting comptroller general.

CBO, Consultants, Cemetery Enliven House Panel Debate

JUNE 13 — The Senate Appropriations Committee on June 4 approved a bill that included $469.4 million for Senate expenses, $8.3 million more than in fiscal 1998, an increase of about 1.8 percent.

Overall, the House subcommittee approved $1.8 billion in fiscal 1999 funding for the legislative branch, not including the Senate's internal budget. That amount was $27.7 million above the fiscal 1998 level, an increase of about 1.6 percent. The broader funding level includes money for agencies that the House and Senate fund jointly, such as the Library of Congress, the Congressional Budget Office (CBO), the Government Printing Office, the Capitol Police and the Architect of the Capitol.

The House measure would provide an overall 3.1 percent cost of living adjustment for most of the employees in agencies funded under the bill. At the same time, it would reduce the full-time equivalent employment level by 546 jobs.

CBO Controversy

While the overall spending engendered little controversy during the hourlong markup, members tangled briefly over three items.

In an ominous sign of displeasure with the CBO, the measure directs the agency to explain why some of its forecasts have been so far off the mark. The order was provoked by a June 9 letter to subcommittee Chairman James T. Walsh, R-N.Y., by House Speaker Newt Gingrich, R-Ga., and other GOP leaders that sharply criticized CBO's projections and suggested that the agency's funding be cut if it could not improve.

Republicans have long complained that CBO underestimates revenues that could provide room for larger GOP-backed tax cuts. In the letter, Gingrich noted that CBO changed its fiscal 1998 budget estimate from a $222 billion deficit in May 1996 to a $53 billion surplus in May 1998.

Noting that the agency has "not been very accurate of late," Walsh said he wants to have CBO "explain the methodology and give us their best analysis of what went wrong and how they're going to fix it."

Minority Leader Richard A. Gephardt, D-Mo., issued a statement that accused Republican leaders of pressuring the agency "to issue higher budget surplus forecasts to justify larger tax breaks for the wealthy."

CBO Director June E. O'Neill said in an interview that she welcomed the opportunity to explain how the agency makes its forecasts and why the latest estimates have been off.

She attributed the discrepancies to factors that caught most economists by surprise, including the much better than expected economy and related surges in the stock market, real estate and upper-income tax revenues.

Consultants for Leaders?

On another matter, the bill would allow the Speaker, the majority leader and the minority leader each to use leadership funds to hire a consultant.

Walsh said the leaders would have wide latitude in how they used their consultants but could pay them no more than the highest-paid congressional staff member, about $134,000.

Zach Wamp, R-Tenn., said initially that he would try to kill the provision in full committee markup. He said having the leaders hire outside consultants "seems to me a poor precedent to set."

But after hearing more about the plan from aides to the Speaker, Wamp signaled that he would probably drop his opposition. He said he was assured that the leaders would have to use existing funds and could not hire pollsters or political consultants. The three leaders now receive about $1.6 million each from their leadership accounts.

In a move that sparked minor controversy, the bill included a one-time appropriation of $1 million to help form an endowment for the Congressional Cemetery. Walsh said that the money, which would be matched by private donations, would improve upkeep of the Washington, D.C., cemetery, which has fallen into disrepair.

Among those buried there are former FBI Director J. Edgar Hoover and composer John Philip Sousa.

However, Randy "Duke" Cunningham, R-Calif., expressed reservations, saying it was indicative of Congress' spendthrift ways. "We spend too much money in this place," he said.

Vote of Confidence For CBO; Bill Sent to House Floor

JUNE 20 — House appropriators publicly reaffirmed their commitment to the independence of the Congressional Budget Office (CBO) even as they continued to pressure the agency to better account for its economic forecasts.

Democrats sought the reaffirmation as a rhetorical counterweight to recent Republican criticism of CBO's forecasts and apparent GOP pressure on the agency to provide more latitude for tax cuts.

The issue is playing out on the fiscal 1999 legislative branch appropriations bill. The House Appropriations Committee gave voice vote approval June 18 to the unnumbered measure, which provides $1.8 billion for internal House operations and agencies funded jointly by the House and the Senate, such as the CBO, the Library of Congress, the Government Printing Office, the Capitol Police and the Architect of the Capitol.

The bill, which excludes funds for internal Senate operations, is $29.8 million above the 1998 level, an increase of about 1.7 percent. The House provided a 3.5 percent increase for its own internal spending, which would rise to $734.1 million.

Agency Off the Mark?

The CBO matter has been the closest thing to a sustained controversy on the bill, whose funding provisions have generated little dissent so far among appropriators.

Republicans have complained that some of CBO's deficit forecasts in particular have been wildly off the mark. House Speaker Newt Gingrich, R-Ga., and other Republican leaders sent a letter June 9 to subcommittee Chairman James T. Walsh, R-N.Y., that sharply criticized CBO's projections and suggested that the agency's funding be cut if it could not improve its accuracy.

Although the letter focused on CBO's deficit forecasts, Republicans have long complained that CBO underestimates revenues that could provide room for larger GOP-backed tax cuts.

The committee report directs CBO to describe its track record in estimating the effects of tax cuts over the past 20 years and to explain why its recent estimates of budget deficits or surpluses have been off the mark. The information must be submitted to congressional leaders and key committee chairmen by Aug. 30 or the start of a House-Senate conference on legislative branch spending, whichever comes first.

Ranking Appropriations Democrat David R. Obey of Wisconsin introduced an amendment that states that the committee "unequivocally supports having an impartial, independent" CBO. It says the panel "will utterly reject" any attempt to pressure the CBO to base forecasts on anything other than its best judgment.

Obey said he did not object to the provision requiring CBO to report on its forecasts, but was concerned about the Gingrich letter. He said the Republican campaign against CBO was "meant to put pressure on people who are expected to be objective and neutral."

Walsh said the amendment "really is restating the obvious" and is "sort of a swipe at the Republican leadership."

Appropriations Chairman Robert L. Livingston, R-La., said Republicans were not trying to pressure the agency in a partisan manner, but providing a "motivation for CBO to get their numbers more accurate."

Livingston said that threatening to withhold money from an agency is "a pretty common practice" by the Appropriations Committee. "That is our bludgeon, that is our opportunity to require adequate, competent performance," he said.

Obey's amendment was approved by voice vote. Livingston said later that he did not contest it because "it was innocuous. And it was quite apparent we were going to lose."

In other matters on the bill:

• The committee gave voice vote approval to an amendment by Steny H. Hoyer, D-Md., that would permit employees of the House to be provided with transit subsidies that Hoyer said could be worth up to $21 per month.

• The panel gave voice vote approval to an amendment by Marcy Kaptur, D-Ohio, that says that artwork in the Capitol "severely underrepresents the accomplishments of women in our society" and commends efforts to rectify the situation. Kaptur said that only about 3 percent of Capitol artwork depicts women.

GOP Preserves Special Fund For Future Probes

JUNE 27 — Insisting there was nothing wrong with the practice, House Republicans killed Democratic attempts to inhibit the GOP's use of a special fund to pay for aggressive investigations — many of Democrats and their labor union allies — in the next Congress.

The GOP has used a similar "reserve fund" in the current Congress to pay for committee investigations into such matters as campaign fundraising abuses and the Teamsters Union.

The debate occurred June 25 during House consideration of the fiscal 1999 legislative branch appropriations bill. The House voted 235-179 to pass the bill (HR 4112 — H Rept 105-595). (Vote 272, p. H-78)

The legislation provides $1.8 billion for internal House operations and agencies funded jointly by the House and the Senate, such as the Congressional Budget Office, the Library of Congress, the Government Printing Office and the Capitol Police.

The bill, which excludes funds for internal Senate operations, is $29.8 million above the 1998 level, an increase of about 1.7 percent. As part of the bill, the House increased its own internal funding about 3.5 percent, to $734.1 million.

Democrats complained that Republicans were setting aside about $8.3 million in a reserve fund to bankroll future investigations. David R. Obey of Wisconsin, the Appropriations Committee's ranking Democrat, referred to the reserve as a "slush fund."

Obey accused Republicans of using "back-door shenanigans" to find the money to pay for future investigations.

Subcommittee Chairman James T. Walsh, R-N.Y., said the reserve fund amounts to only about 10 percent of the budget for House committees and "any business worth its salt" sets aside money for contingencies.

Obey's motion to return the spending bill to the Appropriations Committee with instructions to strike the money for the reserve fund was defeated, 192-222. (Vote 271, p. H-78)

Currently, the fund is used by approval of the House Oversight Committee, with recommendations by Speaker Newt Gingrich, R-Ga. "We have seen far too many party witch hunts in this House in the last year-and-half," said Democrat Steny H. Hoyer of Maryland.

But Deborah Pryce, R-Ohio, said the reserve fund represented "sound business practices" and that House Oversight's actions on it were "all very public."

The House use of the reserve fund this year has included:

• $1.8 million for the Government Reform and Oversight Committee to investigate campaign fundraising abuses.

• $1.3 million for the Judiciary Committee to monitor a Department of Justice investigation of campaign fundraising.

• $747,275 for an investigation of the Teamsters by the Education and the Workforce Committee.

The current Congress still has $1.3 million that could be used for further committee activity.

In other action, House Oversight Committee Chairman Bill Thomas, R-Calif., managed to strike a provision that would have let House employees receive transit subsidies. Thomas objected that the provision violated House rules by including authorizing language in an appropriations bill.

Appropriations

Senate Passes 'Straightforward' Spending Bill

JULY 25 — Easily disposing of one of the least contentious of this year's appropriations bills, the Senate July 21 passed legislation providing $1.6 billion in spending for legislative branch operations in fiscal 1999.

The Senate approved the bill (HR 4112) by a 90-9 vote, after some conservatives tried but failed to hijack the bill as a vehicle for their proposal to eliminate the so-called marriage penalty, the higher taxes paid by some married couples. *(Vote 214, p. S-34)*

The legislation will move next to a House-Senate conference committee. As in the past, the Senate set funding levels for its operations in the bill, as the House had in the bill it approved June 25. The two chambers typically defer to each other on that spending. In terms of programs that are common to both bills, the differences appear to be relatively modest.

This is a nuts-and-bolts bill that provides funding for the upkeep of the Capitol and adjacent buildings. It also funds members' offices and a number of legislative branch organizations, including the Architect of the Capitol and the Library of Congress.

"It's a fairly straightforward bill," said Utah Republican Robert F. Bennett, who chairs the Appropriations Subcommittee on the Legislative Branch.

The only controversy arose when conservatives, led by Missouri Republican John Ashcroft, tried to attach a provision to the bill repealing the marriage tax penalty. But Democrats objected, and GOP leaders moved to shut off debate on the legislation.

"If we didn't take that [the marriage penalty proposal] off, we would have been looking at Democratic amendments on managed care and the minimum wage," Bennett said.

The Senate voted 83-16 to shut off debate on the bill. In doing so, the Senate got past the tax-cut imbroglio, but it also prevented a vote on an amendment by Arizona Republican John McCain to require the director of the Congressional Research Service (CRS) to begin posting CRS reports on the Internet.

McCain praised the CRS reports on policy issues as "both factual and unbiased — a rarity in Washington."

But the amendment drew opposition from senior members of the Rules Committee, which has jurisdiction over the CRS. Rules Chairman John W. Warner, R-Va., defended the current practice under which members of Congress authorize the public release of CRS reports. "We are concerned that this proposal would take the member out of the sequence of making this information available to the public," Warner said.

McCain vowed to continue the fight and warned he might try to attach his provision to any continuing resolution Congress approves this fall to stand in for unfinished appropriations bills.

The legislative branch bill offers few surprises. For senators' personnel and office expenses, the bill would provide $239 million, an increase of about $11 million over the fiscal 1998 level.

Unlike the House, the Senate provided no funding for the Congressional Cemetery, where 92 members of Congress are buried. The House included a $1 million appropriation — to be supplemented with matching private funds — as an endowment for the cemetery, which has deteriorated in recent years.

While the bulk of the bill is devoted to fairly routine housekeeping matters, some political and policy-related issues did arise. For instance, the bill includes $2 million to establish a 12-member Trade Deficit Review Commission to study the causes of persistent U.S. trade deficits. The proposal was championed by Sen. Byron L. Dorgan, D-N.D., who has consistently warned against the dangers of trade imbalances.

And, as in the House, members of the Senate took aim at the Congressional Budget Office (CBO), which is funded by the bill. In the House, Republicans criticized CBO's consistent underestimates of the federal surplus, prompting a counterattack from Democrats who accused them of pressuring the agency to create bigger surplus projections to accommodate larger GOP tax cut proposals.

But in the Senate, a pair of Democrats — Dorgan and Sen. Ernest F. Hollings, D-S.C. — wrote CBO Director June E. O'Neill to complain that CBO projections fail to note that the surplus comes from including the "off-budget" Social Security trust fund balances. The senators said the CBO should note that, without the trust funds, the nation is still running a deficit.

In a letter to the two senators, O'Neill acknowledged that the CBO had failed to report the "on-budget deficit." She said in future reports "CBO will provide separate totals for on-budget programs."

Conferees Reach Agreement On Final Version

SEPTEMBER 19 — House and Senate conferees agreed Sept. 18 to a final version of the bill to fund legislative operations with an increase for Capitol security. Even more funds, they said, were necessary, but belonged in a supplemental funding measure.

At approximately $2.3 billion, the final legislative branch appropriations bill (HR 4112), approved by voice vote, represents a minor increase over the $2.28 billion given for fiscal 1998.

The bill includes $76.8 million for salaries for the Capitol police, including additional pay for officers who work Sundays, holidays and nighttime hours. In the wake of the July 24 Capitol shootings that left two officers dead, lawmakers have moved to increase compensation. Overall, the Capitol Police sought $1.5 million more for fiscal 1999. The House had approved $76.4 million and the Senate had approved $80.6 million.

Additional security improvements, including a visitor's center, which have been requested by the police and the Architect of the Capitol, will likely be considered in a supplemental funding bill.

Funding for the so-called Year 2000 computer problem in the General Accounting Office was addressed in a compromise to fund no more than 50 new employees.

Senate Appropriations Committee Chairman Ted Stevens, R-Alaska, made a brief appearance at the conference to press for the funding. Employees would work to solve the problem in which some computers will mistake the year 2000 for 1900 unless computer codes are changed.

House members had suggested funding only 25 employees, with a preference for hiring them on a temporary contractual basis.

"I urge you not to skimp on this," Stevens said. "They need the money and they need it now."

Both Stevens and House Appropriations Legislative Branch Subcommittee Chairman James T. Walsh, R-N.Y., said they expect a supplemental request next year for even more funds to address the glitch.

The Senate agreed to a $1 million House request to fix up the Congressional Cemetery, where 92 members of Congress are buried. Matching private funds would be added for the cemetery, which has fallen into disrepair in recent years.

Conferees denied approval of $2 million for a one-year commission to study and report on the trade deficit. House Ways and Means Committee Chairman Bill Archer, R-Texas, had criticized the proposal of Sen. Byron L. Dorgan, D-N.D, saying that the Ways and Means Trade Subcommittee and the Senate Finance International Trade Subcommittee already provide all necessary information on the trade deficit.

Members also defeated a new request by Rep. Jose E. Serrano, D-N.Y., to allow the trust territories of the Mariana Islands to have a delegate to represent the commonwealth in Congress, similar to the delegates from Puerto Rico, the Virgin Islands and American Samoa. The move was defeated not on its merits but because members said that a last-minute decision by a conference committee would not allow for a full floor debate.

Legislative Branch Spending Bill Sent To President

SEPTEMBER 26 — The Senate on Sept. 25 cleared a conference report on the fiscal 1999 appropriations bill for its own operations (HR 4112) by

Legislative Branch Spending

Conference agreement on HR 4112 — H Rept 105-595 cleared by the Senate Sept. 25 and signed by the president Oct. 21.
(Budget authority, in millions of dollars.)

	Fiscal 1998 Enacted	House Bill	Senate Bill	Final Bill
Congressional Operations				
House of Representatives	$ 709.0	$ 734.1	$ 734.1	$734.1
Senate	461.1	—	469.4	469.4
Joint Items	86.7	89.1	93.2	96.1
Office of Compliance	2.5	2.1	2.3	2.1
Congressional Budget Office	24.8	25.7	25.7	25.7
Architect of the Capitol	192.2	121.4	184.9	184.2
Congressional Research Service	64.6	66.7	67.9	67.1
Government Printing Office (congressional printing and binding)	81.7	74.5	75.5	74.5
Subtotal	**$ 1,622.5**	**$ 1,113.5**	**$ 1,652.7**	**$ 1,653.2**
Related Agencies				
Botanic Garden	$ 3.0	$ 3.0	$ 3.2	$ 3.1
Library of Congress (except CRS)	282.3	291.7	296.1	296.5
Architect of the Capitol (library buildings and grounds)	11.6	12.9	12.6	13.7
Government Printing Office (Superintendent of Documents)	29.1	29.3	29.6	29.3
General Accounting Office	339.5	354.2	363.3	354.3
Subtotal	**$ 665.5**	**$ 691.2**	**$ 706.8**	**$ 696.8**
GRAND TOTAL	**$ 2,288.0**	**$ 1,804.7**	**$ 2,361.5**	**$ 2,349.9**

SOURCE: House Appropriations Committee

voice vote, sending the second of the 13 appropriations bills to President Clinton.

The legislative appropriations bill includes a significant increase for the Capitol Police, in the wake of the deaths of two officers in a July 24 shootout in the Capitol.

The $83 million allotment for the Capitol Police represents a 12 percent increase over current year spending. The bill allows, for the first time, overtime pay for officers who work nights and on holidays and Sundays.

The final bill does not include funding for additional security improvements, including the construction of a visitors' center, that have been requested by the police and congressional leaders. That funding likely will be considered in a supplemental appropriations bill that is expected to move separately.

The House approved the conference report 356-65 on Sept. 24, with no one speaking against it. *(Vote 457, p. H-130)*

House debate mostly consisted of tributes to Rep. Vic Fazio, D-Calif., who was known as the "Mr. Goodwrench of the House" for his stewardship of the bill and of such sensitive matters as pay raises during his chairmanship of the Appropriations Legislative Branch Subcommittee from 1980 to 1994. Fazio, now chairman of the Democratic Caucus, is retiring at the end of the session.

Overall, the conference agreement would provide about $2.35 billion for the House, Senate and various congressional agencies and offices, such as the Library of Congress, General Accounting Office

Appropriations

(GAO) and Congressional Budget Office. The total is 2.7 percent above fiscal 1998 levels.

The total, Appropriations Legislative Branch Subcommittee Chairman James T. Walsh, R-N.Y., noted with pride, is $41 million below the amount appropriated four years earlier.

The agreement includes $734 million for the House, the same amount that was included in the House-passed bill, and 3.5 percent more than current levels.

The $470 million in the bill for the Senate also is identical to the amount in the Senate bill and is 1.7 percent more than current levels.

The bill includes extra funds to allow the GAO to hire 50 new employees to help it assess the progress of all federal agencies in fixing the so-called Year 2000 computer problem.

The measure has $1 million for repairs at the Congressional Cemetery, recently called one of the most endangered historical sites in the country. Private funds will match the total. ◆

Military Construction Is First Spending Bill To Reach the Finish Line

SUMMARY

Military construction spending is usually the least controversial of the 13 annual spending measures, and the fiscal 1999 bill was no exception.

It sailed through the House and Senate with minimal debate and was the only appropriations bill signed into law by the Oct. 1 start of the fiscal year.

The bill provided a total of $8.45 billion for military construction projects, $666 million more than President Clinton requested, but $759 million less than the fiscal 1998 level.

Members of both parties lamented the budget constraints that have limited funds for military construction and family housing.

The bill included $3.5 billion for family housing, $3.3 billion for military construction, and $1.6 billion for activities associated with the last two rounds of base closings and realignments.

While family housing and construction for the active duty military were cut from current levels, spending for the National Guard and reserves was increased. The $142.4 million for the Army National Guard was double what the House passed.

The measure also provided funding for base construction in Bosnia and contained language requiring congressional notification before the Pentagon spent additional funds on projects related to NATO enlargement.

While this year's bill was routine, last year's measure (PL 105-45) was the center of the first battle over the line-item veto law (PL 104-130) when Clinton used the authority to strike 38 military construction projects. Congress then cleared a new bill (HR 2631) overturning the president's line-item vetoes. Clinton vetoed that, but Congress handily overrode his veto in February 1998, enacting the law (PL 105-159).

House Begins Work On Military Construction Bill

JUNE 13 — Military construction spending legislation for fiscal 1999 that began moving through Congress the week of June 8 is expected to escape the line-item veto battle that plagued its predecessor.

Though appropriators in both the House and Senate added hundreds of millions of dollars to President Clinton's $7.8 billion military construction budget request, they stayed well below the $9.2 billion level enacted for fiscal 1998.

The House Military Construction Appropriations Subcommittee on June 10 approved by voice vote an $8.2 billion bill, as yet unnumbered. The Senate Appropriations Committee followed suit on June 11 by approving, 27-0, a version (S 2160) containing $8.5 billion.

Military construction is typically

Box Score

- **Bill:** HR 4059 — PL 105-237
- **House action:** The House adopted the conference report (H Rept 105-647) on HR 4059, 417-1, on July 29. The House passed HR 4059, 396-10 on June 22.
- **Senate action:** The Senate cleared the conference report on HR 4059, 87-3, on Sept. 1. The Senate passed the bill with amendments by voice vote on June 25.
- **Presidential action:** Clinton signed the bill on Sept. 20.

the least controversial of the 13 annual spending bills. But it drew more attention than usual last year when Clinton used the line-item authority enacted in 1996 (PL 104-130) to block funds for 38 projects worth $287 million in the fiscal 1998 bill (PL 105-45). *(1996 Almanac, p. 2-28)*

Clinton later acknowledged he had acted on flawed information, in some cases. The House and Senate restored the money and then overrode Clinton's veto of the restoration legislation (PL 105-159).

Ron Packard, R-Calif., chairman of the House subcommittee, said he would be "very surprised" if Clinton repeats himself.

"He learned a good lesson last year," Packard said in an interview. This year's bill "is so underfunded that for him to line-item veto anything out would be unconscionable."

Conrad Burns, R-Mont., chairman of the Senate Military Construction Appropriations Subcommittee, said all projects in the Senate version

Military Construction

were reviewed to ensure they fit within the Defense Department's spending plans.

The Senate committee said the administration had not adequately addressed the construction backlog.

Both the House and Senate versions added money for new family housing and improvements to existing units. The Senate version includes $3.6 billion for family housing, $98 million above Clinton's request but almost $317 million below the 1998 level. The House version contains $3.5 billion.

Both include about $3 billion for troop barracks, hospitals and medical facilities, and other construction projects. The Senate provided $142 million more than requested for 46 barracks modernization projects for single personnel.

As in the past, Appropriations Committee members took special interest in the military construction needs of their own states.

The Senate version includes $63 million for projects in Alaska, home to Appropriations Chairman Ted Stevens, a Republican. That amount is $39 million above what Clinton requested. It also contains $211 million, or $52 million more than the president sought, for projects in Hawaii, home of Daniel K. Inouye, the Defense Subcommittee's ranking Democrat.

Leaders' States Fare Best In House Panel

JUNE 20 — The House Appropriations Committee followed a well-tested political formula in fleshing out its $8.2 billion military construction bill (HR 4059), approved by voice vote on June 16.

Much of the the $450 million added to President Clinton's budget request was specified for housing, day care and recreation centers and for facilities of the National Guard and reserves.

Although the extra money was widely distributed — 37 states got a piece of the action — states with influential House members did particularly well, including seven of the top nine beneficiaries:

● Texas, the home of Majority Leader Dick Armey, a Republican, got $41 million.

● Virginia, which has three members on the National Security Committee, including Republican Herbert H. Bateman, chairman of the Military Readiness Subcommittee, got $30 million.

● Louisiana, the residence of Republican Robert L. Livingston, chairman of the Appropriations Committee, got $25 million.

● North Carolina, the home of W.G. "Bill" Hefner, the senior Democrat on the Military Construction Subcommittee, got $25 million.

● California, the home state of Republican Ron Packard, chairman of the Military Construction Appropriations Subcommittee, got $23 million.

● Colorado, the home of Republican Joel Hefley, chairman of the House National Security Military Installations Subcommittee, got $23 million.

● Missouri, the home of the House's top Democrat, Minority Leader Richard A. Gephardt, got $23 million.

The bill would provide $3 billion for operational facilities and barracks, $3.5 billion to build, renovate and maintain family housing units, and $1.7 billion for construction and environmental cleanup associated with closing and consolidating military bases.

Typically the least controversial of the 13 appropriations bills, the military construction measure likely will be approved by the House as early as June 22.

The bill includes $12 million requested by the Army as the down payment on an $85 million physical fitness center at West Point. The private National Guard Association has criticized the project, saying the Army is willing to underfund the Guard while spending on luxuries for the active-duty military. Army officials insist that the existing West Point gym is woefully inadequate.

The House committee would add $129 million to Clinton's request for the National Guard and reserves.

The House bill also would add $68 million to Clinton's budget request for barracks for unmarried personnel, $29 million for family housing and $8 million for day care centers.

House Adds $450 Million To Request

JUNE 27 — The House passed an $8.2 billion military construction spending bill for fiscal 1999 on June 22 that adds $450 million to President Clinton's budget request but remains well short of what many members say is needed. The Senate passed an amended version June 25 by voice vote.

Rarely controversial, the legislation (HR 4059) passed the House 396-10 with almost no debate and without amendments. (Vote 254, p. H-74)

Much of the $450 million added to Clinton's request was specified for housing, day care and recreation centers, and for facilities of the National Guard and reserves.

The bill followed a longtime practice by directing most of the additional money to states with influential House members, including seven of the top nine beneficiaries.

Despite the added funding, however, the bill remains well below the $9.2 billion enacted for fiscal 1998. It is also $3 billion below the appropriated level in 1995. "That is a huge hit on a budget which is really in the $10 billion category . . . in the first place," said John W. Olver, D-Mass., a member of the Military Construction Appropriations Subcommittee.

Olver noted that the account for family housing at military installations has dropped by 19 percent in inflation-adjusted dollars since fiscal 1996. The House bill includes $3.5 billion for family housing next year, or about $29 million more than Clinton's request.

"Whereas 40 years ago only about 40 percent of our military personnel had families, now . . . it is over 60 percent," Olver said.

Subcommittee Chairman Ron Packard, R-Calif., said he did the best he could under the constraints of last year's budget agreement (PL 105-33).

"It does not meet the needs, nor the requirements, of military construction, but it is basically all that we have to work with. The numbers were given to us," he said.

Pointing to the recently enacted transportation authorization law (PL

Appropriations

$287 Million in Projects Restored to 1998 Bill

FEBRUARY 28 — Congress on Feb. 25 overturned President Clinton's most sweeping use of his controversial line-item veto authority, when the Senate voted to restore 38 projects worth $287 million to the fiscal 1998 military construction appropriations bill (PL 105-45).

Congress had passed the bill (HR 2631) last fall, but Clinton vetoed it on Nov. 13. The House voted 347-69 to override that veto Feb. 5, setting the stage for the Senate's final 78-20 vote. *(Senate vote 13, p. S-5; House vote 10, p. H-6)*

Both chambers reaffirmed their support for the projects by much larger margins than the two-thirds majority necessary to override Clinton's veto. Hefty majorities of both Senate party caucuses — 46 Republicans and 32 Democrats — voted for the override, only the second of Clinton's administration.

The projects at issue were included in the $9.2 billion military construction bill that Congress passed last fall. Clinton had used the line-item veto authority enacted in 1996 (PL 104-130) to block use of the funds Congress had earmarked for the 38 projects.

The Supreme Court agreed on Feb. 27 to review a Feb. 12 decision by U.S. District Judge Thomas F. Hogan that the line-item veto law is unconstitutional. Hogan called the law "an unauthorized surrender to the president of an inherently legislative function, namely the authority to permanently shape laws and package legislation." The case will be argued before the high court on April 27.

But during the Senate's Feb. 25 debate on the disputed military construction projects, Arizona Republican John S. McCain — a leading proponent of the line-item veto — argued that, by overriding Clinton's use of that authority, Congress was demonstrating that it had not yielded its authority to the president. "So the process works," he declared. "There has not been a huge transfer of power."

Though McCain supported Clinton's veto of the 38 projects, he acknowledged before the vote that his side would lose the fight.

Merits Debated

For years, the line-item veto has been touted by Republicans as a check on "pork-barrel" spending by Congress. Without this authority, proponents insisted, members could force the president to accept items of parochial interest by tucking them deep in major tax or spending bills.

The line-item law allows the president to sign an appropriations measure or a tax bill but then to cancel funding for individual programs — or tax breaks for a very small number of beneficiaries — unless Congress passes a bill to cancel his action.

The president could, of course, veto a cancellation bill. But that veto could be overridden by a two-thirds majority in each chamber.

Proponents of the line-item procedure had assumed that members would be loathe to vote for a handful of congressional add-ons once a president had isolated them and stigmatized them as wasteful projects.

But in developing the list of targets in the military construction bill, the Clinton administration fumbled: It justified the selection of the 38 projects on grounds that, in some cases, turned out to be inaccurate.

For instance, the administration asserted it had taken aim only at projects that were not already included in the Pentagon's long-range budget plan or not far enough along in design for construction to begin in fiscal 1998. Several days after Clinton slashed the 38 projects last October, the Pentagon acknowledged that several of them did not meet the administration's stated criteria for being blocked.

During the Senate's Feb. 25 debate, McCain argued for sustaining Clinton's veto, contending that the disputed projects would absorb scarce funds for which the Pentagon had more urgent requirements.

"The message we will send to our pilots is that, even though they have lost significant training opportunities due to budget cuts, Congress thinks it more important that there's a new $9.5 million facility at the Asian-Pacific Center for Security Studies in Hawaii," McCain said, singling out one of the added projects as an example.

Other projects that Clinton struck from the bill included a $7.7 million ammunition supply and oil facility at Fort Bliss, Texas, and a $6.9 million launch pad renovation at White Sands Missile Range, N.M.

But other senators insisted that the battle was a legitimate disagreement over priorities for defense funding.

Larry E. Craig, R-Idaho, challenged Clinton's motives in trying to block the 38 projects added by lawmakers. "The administration never tried to negotiate or object to any of these projects when they came before Congress for a vote," Craig said. "It seems apparent that these vetoes were either afterthoughts or politically motivated."

All told, Clinton used his line-item veto authority on nine of the 13 regular appropriations bills Congress enacted last year. But after the flap caused by the military construction vetoes, the administration pulled in its horns: In the eight other bills on which the authority was exercised, Clinton blocked a total of less than $200 million worth of funding for 43 projects — about two-thirds the amount he had tried to cut from the military construction bill alone.

No effort is under way in Congress to overturn Clinton's action on any of those projects in the other eight bills.

105-178), Chet Edwards, D-Texas, said, "It seems to me that a Congress that can somehow find $20 billion to $30 billion for increased funding for potholes and highways ... ought not to have to cut day-care centers and housing programs for men and women willing to put their lives on the line for this country."

In addition to family housing, the bill includes $2.8 billion for military construction and $1.7 billion for costs associated with closing and consolidating military bases.

Even before the Supreme Court on June 25 struck down the line-item veto law (PL 104-130), lawmakers had predicted this year's military construction bill would be so underfunded that it would not be subject to any line-item vetoes like its predecessor.

Clinton used the line-item authority last year to block funds for 38 projects worth $287 million in the fiscal 1998 bill.

But after the president acknowledged he had acted on flawed information in some cases, the House and Senate restored the money and then overrode Clinton's veto of the restoration legislation (PL 105-159). (1997 Almanac, p. 9-6)

Conference Report Gets Speedy House Approval

AUGUST 1 — The House on July 29 adopted the conference report on an $8.45 billion military construction bill for fiscal 1999, the first of 13 annual appropriations measures to be put in final form.

With almost no debate, House members voted 417-1 to adopt the conference report on the legislation (HR 4059 — H Rept 105-647). The lone dissenting vote was cast by Ron Paul, R-Texas, a former Libertarian presidential candidate and staunch supporter of cuts in federal spending. (Vote 353, p. H-100)

The Senate is expected to take up the report shortly after returning from the August recess.

The House vote came after negotiators reached swift agreement July 27 on the measure, which adds $666 million to President Clinton's request.

Military Construction Spending

Conference agreement on HR 4059 — H Rept 105-647 cleared by the Senate Sept. 1 and signed by the president Sept. 20.
(Budget authority, in thousands of dollars.)

	FY 99 Clinton Request	House Bill	Senate Bill	Conference Committee
Military Construction				
Army	$790, 876	$780,599	$810,476	$868,726
Navy	468,150	570,643	565,030	604,593
Air Force	454,810	550,475	627,874	615,809
Defense agencies	491,675	611,075	560,485	553,114
Rescission				–5,000
National Guard and Reserves	179,529	309,025	446,565	480,315
NATO infrastructure	185,000	169,000	152,600	154,000
Subtotal	**$2,570,040**	**$2,990,817**	**$3,163,030**	**$3,271,557**
Family Housing				
Army	$1,208,173	$1,180,537	$1,229,223	$1,229,987
Navy	1,196,083	1,045,750	1,201,883	1,207,883
Air Force	1,016,030	993,084	1,092,690	1,064,169
Defense agencies	37,244	37,244	37,244	37,244
Homeowners Assistance Fund	12,800	7,500	12,800	-0-
Housing Improvement Fund	7,000	242,438	7,000	2,000
Subtotal	**$3,477,330**	**$3,506,553**	**$3,580,840**	**$3,541,283**
Base Realignment and Closure				
Part III — 1993 round	$ 433,464	$ 433,464	$ 433,464	$ 427,164
Part IV — 1995 round	1,297,240	1,297,240	1,297,240	1,203,738
Subtotal	$1,730,704	$1,730,704	$1,730,704	$1,630,902
Adjustments	6,000	6,000	6,000	6,000
GRAND TOTAL	**$7,784,074**	**$8,234,074**	**$8,480,574**	**$8,449,742**

SOURCE: House and Senate Appropriations committees

The military construction bill is by tradition the fastest moving and least contentious of the annual spending measures. Members of both parties said they were even more constrained this year by limits in last year's budget agreement (PL 105-33). (1997 Almanac, p. 2-47)

The conference report would provide $216 million more than the House bill but remains $31 million below the Senate version.

Although the total is more than Clinton sought, it is $759 million below fiscal 1998 spending, an 8 percent decline. Members of both parties have lamented the lack of money available to meet the military's construction and family housing needs. "We can only do the best with what we have, and that is exactly what we are doing," said House Military Construction Appropriations Subcommittee Chairman Ron Packard, R-Calif. "We are doing lots with little and hoping it's enough."

Ranking subcommittee Democrat W.G. "Bill" Hefner of North Carolina agreed that the decline in spending in recent years is a cause for concern. "Giving our men and women a decent place to live and work is not just one of the keys to military readiness and retention," he said. "It is also a basic responsibility we all shoulder."

Packard said the quality of housing on military bases is "a near-crisis situation," pointing to a $32 billion backlog of repairs to unsuitable facilities and new housing construction.

Helping Home States

The bill includes $3.5 billion for family housing, $3.3 billion for military construction and $1.6 billion for costs associated with closing military bases.

While family housing and construction for the active duty military were cut from current levels, spending for the National Guard and reserves was increased. The $142.4 million for the Army National Guard was double what the House passed.

Appropriations

Despite the widespread concern from members about the lack of available funds, Sen. John McCain, R-Ariz., has criticized Appropriations Committee members for adding additional money for projects in their states.

McCain, who has become known for combing through bills in search of what he considers wasteful spending, singled out such add-ons as $3.1 million for a vehicle wash facility at Fort Wainwright, Alaska, home of Republican Appropriations Chairman Ted Stevens, and $8.3 million for fencing at Fort Bragg, N.C., home of Republican committee member Lauch Faircloth.

McCain also noted that as training programs suffer personnel and funding cuts, the measure includes $13.5 million for a "regional training institute" at Camp Dawson, W.Va., home state of ranking Appropriations Democrat Robert C. Byrd.

Senate Clears Bill With Little Debate

SEPTEMBER 5 — The Senate on Sept. 1 ensured that at least one spending bill will be sent to President Clinton before the end of the current fiscal year by easily adopting the conference report on an $8.45 billion military construction bill.

With little debate, the Senate voted, 87-3, to adopt the report on the legislation (HR 4059), the first of the 13 annual appropriations measures to be put in final form. (Vote 253, p. S-40)

The House adopted the conference report on July 29 by a 417-1 vote. Clinton is expected to sign the measure.

The conference report would add $666 million to Clinton's budget request, nearly half of it for the National Guard and reserves. It would provide $216 million more in overall spending than the House bill but $31 million less than the Senate version.

Senators of both parties joined their House counterparts in lamenting spending constraints in last year's budget agreement (PL 105-33). Although the report contains more than Clinton sought, it is $759 million below fiscal 1998 spending, an 8 percent decline.

"Given the tight budget confines in which we were operating, there were many worthy projects that we could not fund," said Patty Murray of Washington, the ranking Democrat on the Senate Military Construction Appropriations Subcommittee.

But John McCain, R-Ariz., who has become known for combing through bills in search of what he considers wasteful spending, said he still found "an egregious number" of low-priority military projects added at the request of members. McCain joined fellow Arizona Republican Jon Kyl and Democrat Charles S. Robb, of Virginia in opposing the bill.

McCain submitted a list of what he said were 142 questionable additions requested by members, including $23.5 million for a land purchase for barracks at Fort Schofield, Hawaii, home state of Daniel K. Inouye, the ranking Democrat on the Defense Appropriations Subcommittee. The list also includes $23 million each for a rail-yard expansion at Fort Carson, Colo., and barracks at Fort Leonard Wood, Mo., in the home states of Appropriations Committee Republicans Ben Nighthorse Campbell and Christopher S. Bond, respectively.

McCain also pointed to 45 added projects for the National Guard and reserves, as well as five control towers at Air Force bases that he said currently have operational control towers.

"The fact remains that funds for our national defense are limited," McCain said. "Robbing from readiness to pay for unadulterated construction projects does not contribute to that end."

But Conrad Burns, R-Mont., chairman of the Military Construction Appropriations Subcommittee, praised Congress for adding extra money for the Guard and Reserve.

"For the first time in the history of this country, better than 50 percent of our military forces are found in our National Guard and our Reserves," Burns said. "If we continue to trend that way ... they will need the infrastructure in which to operate." ◆

Popular Transportation Bill Seen as Engine Pulling Omnibus Spending Package

SUMMARY

The $47 billion fiscal 1999 transportation appropriations bill seemed to be sailing toward quick passage. Highway funding was set at guaranteed levels by the six-year surface transportation reauthorization law (PL 105-178). Overall levels of transportation spending were nearly the same in the initial Senate and House versions of the bill, and there were only narrow differences on other issues.

But after the Senate and House finished their versions of the bill in July, long delays began. And at the end of the session, the transportation bill became the vehicle that carried the omnibus appropriations bill. The transportation appropriations subcommittee chairmen, Sen. Richard C. Shelby, R-Ala., and Rep. Frank R. Wolf, R-Va., could only watch while House and Senate leaders loaded their bill with seven other spending bills, a supplemental spending package and assorted other provisions.

The transportation bill provided more than $25.5 billion in highway funding, nearly 20 percent more than fiscal 1998. It included $5.4 billion for mass transit, 11 percent more than fiscal 1998.

The highway and mass transit funding conformed to the levels laid out in the six-year surface transportation law.

But lawmakers increased funding in some areas, including $75 million for President Clinton's welfare-to-work initiative, $25 million more than was authorized, to help low-income workers commute to jobs.

Controversial riders inserted in the bill included a freeze on corporate average fuel economy standards for automobiles and several waivers of environmental reporting requirements for road projects, such as the construction of ramps between two exits on Interstate 495 in New York's Suffolk County. Other riders were jettisoned, including provisions to waive hazardous material sign requirements for fertilizer haulers and to permit direct appeals to the Supreme Court for lawsuits challenging a minority set-aside program.

Wolf lost a battle when negotiators dropped his provision aimed at toughening truck safety inspections by transferring the Federal Highway Administration's Office of Motor Carriers, which regulates long-haul carriers, to the National Highway Traffic Safety Administration.

Appropriators continued a turf war with the House Transportation and Infrastructure Committee and its chairman, Bud Shuster, R-Pa., over provisions in the six-year surface transportation law that guarantee spending and give appropriators little room to fund their own highway projects. Shuster's committee argued that funding levels are guaranteed for specific earmarked projects in the six-year law. But appropriators put a provision in the omnibus spending bill that reinforced the Federal Highway Administration's decision to give states flexibility to decide the priority and timing of projects within state program allocations.

Appropriators produced a long list of earmarks for mass transit, research and projects to deploy innovative signs and road designs to improve safety and relieve traffic congestion. A study by Sen. John McCain, R-Ariz., found that more than $200 million was appropriated for dozens of earmarked bus projects, and it found $137 million for mass transit projects, including $10 million for ferries in Alaska or Hawaii.

Lawmakers agreed to nearly match the funding request of Amtrak, providing $609 million. The funding is supposed to help the national passenger railway move toward self-sufficiency under its newly elected chairman, Republican Wisconsin Gov. Tommy G. Thompson.

Appropriators cut the budget for the Coast Guard by $21 million to $3.9 billion for fiscal 1999, but they offset that cut by providing two big emergency supplemental appropriations, totaling $344 million, mainly for expansion of the drug interdiction fleet and replacement of routine patrol boats and planes.

The bill provided a total of $9.6 billion to the Federal Aviation Administration, including $2 billion for airport grants. The omnibus bill also included a six-month reauthorization of the FAA, that will force debate early in 1999 of controversial proposals by McCain to nurture airline competition by increasing flights at four crowded airports: Ronald Reagan Washington National Airport, O'Hare International Airport in Chicago, and LaGuardia and John F. Kennedy airports in New York.

The short-term FAA reauthorization will also set the stage for Shuster to launch his campaign to increase aviation funding and revamp the Aviation Trust Fund next year.

Amtrak Wins, As Subcommittee OK's $47.5 Billion Bill

JULY 11 — A $47.5 billion transportation spending bill approved by the Senate Appropriations subcommittee for fiscal 1999 will keep Amtrak rolling with federal subsidies for another year.

The bill was approved by voice vote on July 8 after Transportation Appropriations Subcommittee Chairman Richard C. Shelby, R-Ala., agreed to a compromise to provide Amtrak with $555 million for fiscal 1999.

A sharp critic of Amtrak, Shelby backed away from his push to end its federal subsidy after supporters of the passenger railroad won the backing of many senators, including Senate Majority Leader Trent Lott, R-Miss. The bill called for $47.5 billion for the Transportation Department, about 15 percent more than the administration's

Box Score

- **Bill:** HR 4328 — PL 105-277.
- **House action:** The House adopted the conference report (H Rept 105-825) on HR 4328 by a vote of 333-95 on Oct. 20. The House passed its version of the bill (H Rept 105-648) by a vote of 391-25 on July 30.
- **Senate action:** The Senate cleared the conference report, 65-29, on Oct. 21. The Senate passed its version of the bill (S 2307 — S Rept 105-249) by a vote of 90-1 on July 24.
- **Presidential action:** Clinton signed HR 4328 on Oct. 21.

request of $41.3 billion. The proposal included a hefty increase in highway and mass transit funding that was approved as part of the new six-year surface transportation law (PL 105-178).

The spending bill provided the first glimpse of the impact of the new transportation law, which created firewall restrictions that effectively prevented appropriators from reducing authorized levels of highway and mass transit spending. Overall, the new law will increase surface transportation spending 40 percent over six years compared with the prior six-year period.

Shelby said appropriators were "faced with difficulty in trying to adhere to the spending levels" in the transportation law, which prevented shifting funds designated for highways and mass transit. Staff aides said the amount designated for earmarked projects in the new law meant there was less money available for appropriators, noting that no new bus capital projects were inserted, compared with about $400 million in such projects in 1997.

Amtrak Gets Big Increase

After a long impasse on Amtrak, Shelby reached a key agreement with pro-Amtrak senators, led by Frank R. Lautenberg of New Jersey, the ranking Democrat on the subcommittee.

Shelby charged that the railroad was losing "substantial sums of money"

Appropriations

on nearly all of its routes, except those connecting big East Coast cities. He cited a General Accounting Office study showing there is a $47 federal subsidy for every Amtrak ticket sold, regardless of destination.

Extra money was found for Amtrak after negotiations with Lautenberg and the administration, Shelby said.

The bill gave no operating funds to Amtrak, but provided $555 million in capital funding to allow Amtrak to use more of its own revenue for operations.

George D. Warrington, acting president and chief executive officer of Amtrak, said the subcommittee's action would help Amtrak meet its goal to become self-sufficient by 2002. "We hope the House will act quickly by fully funding Amtrak's request," Warrington added. Amtrak is receiving $594 million this year and has requested $621 million for fiscal 1999.

Labor Contract Squabble

While appropriators reached accord on Amtrak, a battle was brewing between Republicans and Democrats over a provision that would effectively skirt executive orders and memorandums of the Clinton administration on labor-related policies. The provision was aimed at labor contracts encouraged by President Clinton as a way to improve efficiency by establishing work rules, wage rates and no-strike agreements. Supporters of the provision said it was meant to deflect executive orders and memorandums on labor practices that favored unions.

The administration was preparing to strongly oppose the provision, arguing that it was written so broadly it would pre-empt a range of rules covering occupational safety and non-labor policies.

Other battles were also brewing for a planned markup in full committee on the week of July 13.

Draft amendments were being prepared that would grant exemptions to carriers of fertilizer from federal requirements for safety placards on hazardous materials. And other amendments were expected to exempt carriers of certain commodities, including sugar beets, from truck weight limits.

Spending Increases

The bill would increase highway spending 15 percent, to $27 billion, and raise transit funding 11 percent, to $5.36 billion. It would slightly raise Coast Guard funding to $4 billion and fully fund the administration's request for $369 million for drug interdiction.

The bill provided $902.8 million in earmarked mass transit projects. Big projects included $70 million for a light-rail project near Bergen, N.J.; $59.7 million for a regional bus plan in Houston; $47 million for a commuter rail project connecting Seattle and Tacoma, Wash.; and $40 million for a Long Island Rail Road tunnel project to Grand Central Station in New York City.

Appropriators elected not to fully fund President Clinton's access-to-jobs program for welfare recipients, providing $50 million of the $100 million he had requested. They directed that $10 million go to rural areas, including $500,000 for South Dakota.

Shelby weighed in on the issue of airline competition with report language urging the Transportation Department to proceed cautiously on proposed guidelines aimed at nurturing competition at regional hub airports. The report suggested that cases of anti-competitive practices be referred to the Justice Department for investigation.

Appropriators Chafe Under Constraints Of New Law

JULY 18 — The Senate Appropriations Committee approved a $47.5 billion transportation spending bill (S 2307) July 14, setting the stage for disputes over Amtrak and other programs under spending constraints of the new transportation law (PL 105-178), signed in June.

The panel approved, 28-0, a spending bill that would give Amtrak $555 million in capital funding for fiscal 1999. But Amtrak supporters pledged to continue a battle for more money.

The House Transportation Appropriations Subcommittee approved by voice vote July 16 an unnumbered $46.9 billion transportation spending bill, which nudged Amtrak funding up to $609 million. Amtrak said that money virtually matched its request.

Both House and Senate versions of the bill matched the funding levels, or firewalls, established by the new transportation law: $25.5 billion for highways and $5.4 billion for mass transit over six years. But there are disparities in other programs, such as Amtrak, which are not covered by guarantees.

There also were problems with other funding. For example, the House bill would provide $9.5 billion to the Federal Aviation Administration (FAA), compared with $9.9 billion in the Senate bill.

Appropriators complained that the new law left little leeway to shift funding from mass transit and highways to other programs, and they warned that some programs would have to to be cut because of the constraints.

Amtrak Battle

Sen. Richard C. Shelby, R-Ala., a critic of Amtrak subsidies, argued in favor of keeping the pressure on the passenger railroad to cut losses. He lost his bid to slash Amtrak funding but succeeded in full committee in preserving language that would require Amtrak to print on each ticket the amount it loses per passenger. The General Accounting Office recently estimated that the average loss is $47 per ticket.

Sen. Kay Bailey Hutchison, R-Texas, argued that the ticket requirement would be misleading because it ignored subsidies for other modes of transportation. She is expected to offer a floor amendment to strike the requirement.

The Amtrak squabble was just one example of lawmakers' struggle to protect pet programs and cut others.

House Transportation Appropriations Subcommittee Chairman Frank R. Wolf, R-Va., said the new law effectively forces him to deny needed funding to the Coast Guard, FAA and traffic safety programs while taking care of Amtrak, highways and mass transit.

He charged that the transportation law had "undermined the flexibility" of appropriators to shift money from program to program and blamed it for the House bill's Coast Guard allotment of $3.9 billion, about $29 million less than fiscal 1998 funding. Wolf increased the Coast Guard's drug interdiction funding by 11 percent, to $406 million.

In a June 15 letter to colleagues, Wolf warned there was not enough money to comply with requests for $2.8 billion in earmarked rail projects and $1.7 billion in bus projects. The House bill had $900 million in rail projects and $200 million in bus projects.

Shelby was cautious in evaluating the law: "It will make it difficult, if not impossible, to spend above the firewall. And the firewalls put pressure on other accounts, forcing us to make choices."

Labor Fight

While Amtrak and the Coast Guard scrambled for funding, the administration opposed a Senate provision that would bar certain mandates on labor agreements for transportation projects.

The Republican-backed provision reopened an issue that flared in 1997 during the confirmation hearing for Labor Secretary Alexis Herman. Under a 1997 compromise, President Clinton agreed to issue a memorandum encouraging the use of agreements with unions to set work conditions and cut costs on big projects. The memorandum is to expire when he leaves office, unlike an executive order, which would remain in effect. But critics are now angered by more administration efforts to encourage agreements, charging they are a political payoff to unions and exclude non-union labor.

Democrats, led by Sen. Frank R. Lautenberg of New Jersey, threatened a floor fight, charging that the Republican provision was too broad in barring contract mandates that are not required by law.

Senate Appropriations Committee Chairman Ted Stevens, R-Alaska, said he liked the labor agreements based on their success in his state, but he said Clinton and Vice President Al Gore went too far in promoting the agreements.

Senate Bill Leaves Room for Dispute In Conference

JULY 25 — The Senate passed a $47.1 billion transportation spending bill (S 2307) on July 24, setting the stage for a conference committee attempt to resolve a dispute over funding for programs not guaranteed in the new transportation law (PL 105-178).

The vote was 90-1, with the lone dissenter, Republican Jon Kyl of Arizona, arguing that the bill would spend too much money and would continue to deny adequate funding to Arizona and other states that receive less than $1 in funding for each $1 of gas taxes they pay.

The final vote came after voice vote approval of several key amendments, including a provision that would ban smoking on all intrastate, interstate and international airline flights.

The House Appropriations Committee approved by voice vote July 22 a $46.9 billion transportation spending bill (HR 4328). House floor debate is expected to begin the week of July 27.

Both bills match funding guarantees set by the transportation authorization law: $25.5 billion for highways and $5.4 billion for mass transit. The law was signed by President Clinton on June 9.

Among the major differences to be resolved in conference are funding levels for other Transportation Department programs, including the Coast Guard, which would face a $29 million cut from current funding, to $3.9 billion in the House bill.

Aftershocks

Lawmakers blamed the funding cut for the Coast Guard on the new transportation law, which guaranteed funding for highways and mass transit and reduced flexibility to shift money to other programs.

House Transportation Appropriations Subcommittee Chairman Frank R. Wolf, R-Va., portrayed the proposed Coast Guard cut as a direct result of the funding guarantees, or firewalls, which prevent the use of highway and mass transit funds for other programs. Wolf said the Coast Guard, the Federal Aviation Administration (FAA) and traffic safety programs all had been denied sufficient funding.

In the Senate, Coast Guard supporters, led by Mike DeWine, R-Ohio, pushed for a $37.5 million increase to support drug interdiction. The offset was a proposed cut in the Transportation Department's administrative budget.

Lawmakers also rallied behind efforts by the FAA to find more funding for weather observation to help prevent accidents. The House Appropriations Committee approved by voice vote an amendment giving the FAA priority to receive funding in conference committee, which was omitted in the House bill for two weather observation systems.

Labor Dispute Resolved

Senators also reached a bipartisan agreement to remove a potential obstacle to their bill, adopting by voice vote an amendment that would deny money for any efforts to "compel, direct or require" use of project labor agreements, which set work rules and no-strike agreements for big construction projects.

The administration had threatened a veto over a deleted provision that would have prevented use of mandates that are not required by law, including rules covering the labor agreements, drug testing and work safety. The compromise language was approved by the administration.

The smoking provision expanded a ban that was enacted in 1989 as part of another spending law (PL 101-164). The earlier ban covered virtually all domestic flights, but it exempted flights lasting longer than six hours, including international flights and flights to Hawaii and Alaska. The new ban would remove all exemptions and include international flights. *(1989 Almanac, p. 749)*

On another key issue, Democratic Sen. Carol Moseley-Braun of Illinois warned that she would strongly oppose a provision to allow a direct appeal to the Supreme Court of any federal district decision involving a constitutional challenge to the disadvantaged business enterprise program, which sets a goal of giving 10 percent of construction contracts to businesses owned by members of minority groups or women. The amendment was adopted by voice vote. The sponsor, Mitch McConnell, R-Ky., lost a previous campaign to eliminate the program in the debate over the new transportation law.

Other key amendments, adopted by voice vote, included:

● A one-year exemption to states that give truck haulers of agricultural materials, such as fertilizer, a waiver from a

Appropriations

federal requirement to carry hazardous material placards.
- A requirement for airline tickets to be printed with details of federal subsidies for aviation.

House Leaves Coast Guard, FAA Funding For Conference

AUGUST 1 — The House passed a $46.9 billion transportation appropriations bill on July 30, setting up a battle in conference committee in September over funding for key programs, including the Coast Guard and the Federal Aviation Administration (FAA).

The House voted 391-25 for HR 4328 after angry negotiations pitting appropriators of both parties against House Transportation and Infrastructure Committee Chairman Bud Shuster, R-Pa., and other senior members of his panel. *(Vote 355, p. H-100)*

Jerrold Nadler, D-N.Y., triggered the dispute with his proposal to kill one of the 1,850 earmarked special road projects contained in the six-year surface transportation law (PL 105-178), signed by President Clinton on June 9. The project would help pay for designing and lowering a highway in New York City, improving the views for a condominium complex developed by real estate tycoon Donald Trump, according to Nadler.

It was the latest in a series of squabbles over the new law, which angered appropriators by reducing their ability to shift funds to pay for special needs.

Like the spending bill (S 2307) approved by the Senate on July 24, the House version would match funding guarantees set by the new transportation law: $25.5 billion for highways and $5.4 billion for mass transit.

The conference committee must resolve issues involving funding levels for other programs, including the FAA and the Coast Guard. The House bill would cut the Coast Guard's budget by $29 million, to $3.9 billion, and deny funding for some aviation initiatives, including two new weather observation systems.

Nadler's Challenge

On the floor, the key battle was set off by Nadler, who sits on Shuster's committee but strongly disagreed with one provision in the new law. The provision authorized $6 million to pay for the relocation of Miller Highway, part of the West Side Highway, in Manhattan.

The relocation would lower the recently rebuilt elevated highway, which runs past the planned Riverside South luxury condominiums, developed by Trump. Nadler called the plan a "boondoggle" designed to benefit Trump and provide better vistas from his posh condominiums overlooking the Hudson River.

Nadler found support from budget hawks and appropriators who have been anxious to challenge provisions in the new law.

Nadler considered testing a provision in the new law that declared out of order any effort to lower the law's funding obligation levels. Shuster and his allies argued that the provision protected all projects in the law. Nadler and the appropriators said projects could be cut if funding was redirected to projects in the same state.

Nadler finally agreed to a compromise amendment, approved by voice vote, to bar the use of any additional funds in the upcoming fiscal year for the $350 million project. That would force supporters to get earmarked federal funding to pay for construction and redesign of the highway passing Trump's development in later years.

Scramble for Money

While both sides claimed victory in the Nadler dispute, lawmakers maneuvered for expected battles in a conference committee that will start after the August recess.

The dispute between appropriators and Shuster is expected to continue. By raising points of order, Shuster and Tom Petri, R-Wis., retained $5 million in unspent funding and deleted limits placed on funding for the Pennsylvania Train Station in New York City.

On another issue, Transportation Appropriations Subcommittee Chairman Frank R. Wolf, R-Va., and Shuster fought to a draw. Wolf agreed to delete a provision that would have transferred $52.5 million for the regulation of motor carriers from the Federal Highway Administration to the National Highway Traffic Safety Administration.

But another provision in the bill blocks the use of funds by the Federal Highway Administration to regulate trucks, effectively forcing that function to be carried out by another arm of the Transportation Department.

Other battles loom in conference, where supporters of the Coast Guard seek to offset a $29 million cut in current funding contained in the bill.

On July 28, the Clinton administration urged more funding for the Coast Guard, air-traffic control upgrades and highway safety programs. It opposed House provisions barring the use of funds for the study of user fees or developing tougher fuel economy standards for automobiles.

Negotiators Try To Wrap Up Transportation Bill

OCTOBER 3 — House and Senate negotiators began meeting Oct. 2 to complete the transportation appropriations bill (HR 4328), focusing on disputes over funding for aviation and the Coast Guard.

During a brief meeting on Oct. 2, negotiators said they hoped the spending measure could be kept out of an omnibus spending bill because they feared it could be ensnared in disputes over unrelated issues.

Frank R. Lautenberg, D-N.J., said he hoped senators would agree to the higher level of funding for Amtrak in the House version of the bill.

The House bill would provide $609 million to Amtrak; the Senate version, $555 million.

Senate negotiators have joined the Clinton administration in opposing a House provision to transfer regulation of commercial trucks from the Federal Highway Administration to the National Highway Traffic Safety Administration.

Senate Appropriations Committee Chairman Ted Stevens, R-Alaska, said he hoped the bill could be passed the week of Oct. 5 because there are no major disagreements to be resolved.

Transportation Spending

Transportation portion of the fiscal 1999 omnibus spending law (HR 4328 — PL 105-277) signed by the president on Oct. 21. *(Budget authority, in thousands of dollars.)*

	Fiscal 1998 Appropriation	Fiscal 1999 Clinton Request	House Bill	Senate Bill	Final Bill
Transportation Department					
Office of the Secretary	$ 78,224	$ 78,406	$ 73,231	$ 76,925	$ 81,256
Coast Guard					
Operating expenses	2,415,400	2,462,705	2,400,000	2,461,603	2,400,000
Acquisition, construction, improvements	388,850	406,773	389,000	426,173	395,465
Retired pay	653,196	684,000	684,000	684,000	684,000
Other	459,000	415,300	414,000	425,461	416,000
Subtotal, Coast Guard	**$ 3,916,446**	**$ 3,968,778**	**$ 3,887,000**	**$ 3,997,237**	**$ 3,895,465**
Federal Aviation Administration					
Operations and offsetting collections	5,301,934	5,588,130	5,532,558	5,538,259	5,562,558
User fees appropriation	0	0	0	0	0
Facilities and equipment	1,900,477	2,130,000	2,000,000	2,044,683	1,900,000
Research, engineering, development	199,183	290,000	145,000,	173,627	150,000
Airport and Airway Trust Fund limit	*1,700,000*	*1,700,000*	*1,800,000*	*2,100,000*	*1,950,000*
Subtotal, FAA	**$ 7,401,594**	**$ 8,008,130**	**$ 7,677,558**	**$ 7,756,569**	**$ 7,612,558**
Federal Highway Administration					
Direct spending	300,000	250,000	0	200,000	0
Highway Trust Fund limit	*21,584,825*	*21,600,000*	*25,511,000*	*25,611,000*	*25,611,000*
Trust fund exempt obligations	*1,597,000*	*1,265,000*	*1,211,614*	*1,207,903*	*1,211,614*
National Highway Traffic Safety Administration					
Direct spending	77,201*	2,300	89,400	89,400	89,400
NHTSA Highway Trust Fund limit	*256,261*	*403,602*	*372,000*	*272,000*	*272,000*
Federal Railroad Administration					
Amtrak grants	543,000	621,476**	609,230	555,000	609,230
Northeast Corridor improvement	250,000	0	0	0	0
Other	143,790	129,883	120,086	154,650	140,561
Subtotal, railroads	**$ 936,790**	**$ 751,359**	**$ 729,316**	**$ 709,650**	**$ 749,791**
Federal Transit Administration					
Formula grants					
Direct spending	240,000	0	570,000	570,000	570,000
Trust Fund grants and limit	*2,260,000*	*0****	*2,280,000*	*2,280,000*	*2,280,000*
Other	343,738	190,342	543,200	543,200	568,200
Subtotal, transit	**$ 583,738**	**$ 190,342**	**$ 1,113,200**	**$ 1,113,200**	**$ 1,138,200**
Emergency and other spending					
Rescissions					
TOTAL, Transportation Department	**$ 12,666,888**	**$ 13,357,124**	**$ 13,681,453**	**$ 13,663,504**	**$ 13,678,569**
Related Agencies, Commissions					
National Transportation Safety Board	54,771	54,200	54,300	54,473	54,473
Other	4,640	47,847	5,147	9,506	9,247
GRAND TOTAL	**$ 12,726,299**	**$ 13,459,171**	**$ 13,740,900**	**$ 13,727,483**	**$ 13,742,289**
Total limitations and exempt obligations	*$ 29,398,086*	*$ 29,553,952*	*$ 33,156,014*	*$ 33,442,703*	*$ 33,307,414*

* Does not include mandatory spending provided by new transportation law (PL 105-178).
** Administration requested capital funding with flexibility for use on expenses related to operations.
*** Administration requested combining formula and discretionary grants.

SOURCE: House and Senate Appropriations committees.

Appropriations

Highway funding was set at levels prescribed in the six-year surface transportation law (PL 105-178).

But there are disputes over funding for other programs.

While the six-year law explicitly targeted funding for a plethora of highway projects, it gave leeway to appropriators to earmark funding for mass transit and research and development projects.

The Clinton administration has criticized 400 designated transit and research projects in the Senate version of the bill, and 300 earmarked mass transit projects in the House version.

Sen. Richard J. Durbin, D-Ill., criticized a Senate provision to ban smoking on international airline flights that take off or land in the United States. The provision has been attacked by the tobacco industry, and Durbin said he was looking for other bills to which it could be attached.

Lautenberg, the senior Democrat on the Transportation Appropriations Subcommittee, said there was still a chance the bill could be put onto a continuing resolution if disputes continue over other appropriations bills.

Controversial Riders Dropped; Senate OK's Bill

OCTOBER 24 — Sen. Frank R. Lautenberg, D-N.J., said the popularity of the fiscal 1999 transportation spending bill made it a prime candidate to be the "choo-choo" to haul the omnibus spending package through the Senate on final passage Oct. 21.

"It's a good bill," Lautenberg said after the Senate voted, 65-29, to approve the package, HR 4328 (PL 105–277). "But I'm not sure anyone has read all of it." *(Vote 314, p. S-48)*

The underlying transportation portion of the legislation provided $47 billion for transportation programs in fiscal 1999, an increase of $4.9 billion over fiscal 1998.

But even appropriators such as Lautenberg were not certain of all the provisions in the package. Shortly after the vote, for example, Sen. Conrad Burns, R-Mont., said he was not sure of the final outcome of his provision to permit a waiver of hazardous material sign requirements for carriers of fertilizer and other agricultural materials.

It was deleted. But Burns' loss was softened by funding inserted in the bill for Montana road projects, including $1 million apiece for two roads in Glacier National Park and Charles M. Russell National Wildlife Refuge.

In the end, the House and Senate leaders decided to pare a host of controversial "riders," such as the Burns provision, and other riders opposed by the Clinton administration. One backed by Sen. Mitch McConnell, R-Ky., permitted direct appeal to the Supreme Court for challenges to a minority set-aside public works program and another would have allowed helicopters in Alaskan wilderness areas.

Truck Regulation Battle

Rep. Frank R. Wolf, R-Va., criticized the deletion of his proposal to move the Federal Highway Administration's Office of Motor Carriers, which regulates long-haul vehicles, to the National Highway Traffic Safety Administration. "The trucking industry lobby applied the pressure, and the brakes were put on the transfer," Wolf said.

The bill included environmental riders, as well. Among them were a freeze on corporate average fuel economy standards for automobiles, and measures to limit or waive environmental reviews to hasten construction of a toll road in Orange and San Diego counties in California, new ramps between exits 57 and 58 on Interstate 495 in Suffolk County, N.Y., and a highway in the East Foley corridor in Alabama.

Special Project Dispute

In a one-sentence provision buried in the bill, appropriators attacked a guarantee for designated funding championed by House Transportation and Infrastructure Committee Chairman Bud Shuster, R-Pa., in the six-year transportation law (PL 105-178). The fight began nearly two months after the law's passage, when appropriators challenged the funding guarantee, which was intended to protect 1,850 road projects in the six-year authorization from cuts in the appropriations process.

The provision inserted by House Appropriations Committee Chairman Robert L. Livingston, R-La., directed that the guarantee would be applied "consistent with past practices of the administering agency permitting states to decide high-priority project funding priorities within state program allocations." The language echoed a Federal Highway Administration decision in June to allow states flexibility on the priority and timing of the road projects.

Several legislative aides said House Speaker Newt Gingrich, R-Ga., was expected to support the funding guarantee for the road projects in the six-year transportation law.

While challenging Shuster, appropriators inserted $20 million for about 20 research projects and $105 million for 62 projects to deploy new designs for roads, signs and other techniques aimed at relieving congestion and increasing safety. A review by Sen. John McCain, R-Ariz., found that more than $200 million was appropriated for dozens of bus projects that had not previously been authorized. His office also found that about two dozen mass transit projects got about $137 million, including $10 million for ferries in Alaska or Hawaii and $1 million for a light-rail feasibility study in Birmingham, Ala.

The omnibus bill also contained a six-month reauthorization of the Federal Aviation Administration.

And Senate Transportation Appropriations Subcommittee Chairman Richard C. Shelby, R-Ala., inserted language to bar the Transportation Department from requiring "peanut-free" zones to protect allergic airplane passengers. ◆

Treasury-Postal Bill Stalls Despite Second Conference; Clears in Year-End Package

SUMMARY

The fiscal 1999 Treasury-Postal Service bill, traditionally one of the more nettlesome of the 13 annual appropriations measures, faced so many obstacles on its way through the legislative process that it had to be rolled into the end-of-session omnibus spending bill (HR 4328).

The problems the bill encountered along the way were due primarily to its legislative provisions rather than its funding levels. The version incorporated into the omnibus bill appropriated $26.8 billion for the Treasury Department, Postal Service, Executive Office and general government functions. It included provisions requiring federal employee health plans that cover prescription drugs to cover a full range of contraceptives, and it permitted about 50,000 Haitian refugees to remain permanently in the United States.

The House was able to pass its version of the bill (HR 4104) only after two attempts.

On June 25, the House overwhelmingly defeated a rule setting the terms of debate for the bill, 125-291. Republicans objected because the rule would have protected the provision on contraceptives from being removed on a point of order. Democrats objected because the rule would have eliminated $2.25 billion in "emergency" appropriations to help federal agencies deal with year 2000 computer problems.

The second rule, which the House adopted 218-201 on July 15, protected only a provision that denied a cost of living adjustment (COLA) to members, federal judges and high executive branch officials. The House responded by striking about 50 provisions, including the emergency spending for the computer problem. Although the contraceptive provision also was eliminated on a point of order, its author, Democrat Nita M. Lowey of New York, reworked the provision as an amendment that was adopted, 224-198.

The Senate began consideration of its version of the bill (S 2312) before the August recess, but halted consideration on July 30, after Democrats threatened to stall the bill over a disputed provision that would have placed term limits on the top two staff officials at the Federal Election Commission (FEC). The Senate returned to the bill after the August recess, and, after weakening the FEC term-limit language, passed the measure, 91-5, on Sept. 3.

Disputes over legislative provisions sank the first conference report on the measure. On Oct. 1, the House defeated the rule for the first conference report, 106-294. Some Republicans objected to the provisions on contraceptives and Haitians. Democrats opposed the provision limiting the terms of the top two FEC officials.

Conferees agreed on a second conference report, which was identical to the first one except that it dropped the provisions on contraceptives, Haitians and the FEC, as well as federal child care subsidies for low-income federal workers.

The House adopted the second conference agreement on Oct. 7, 290-137. However, the agreement stalled in the Senate when Harry Reid, D-Nev., objected to dropping the contraceptive provision — which had been endorsed by voice vote on the Senate floor and by roll call in the House.

In the end, the provision on contraceptives was one of the last issues resolved in top-level negotiations over the omnibus spending bill. The final version specifically exempts five religious health plans from the requirement along with individual doctors who refuse to prescribe contraceptives because such activities would be contrary to their religious beliefs or moral convictions.

Box Score

- **Bill:** HR 4328 — PL 105-277.
- **House action:** The House adopted the conference report (H Rept 105-825) on HR 4328, 333-95, on Oct. 20.

  The House adopted the second conference report (H Rept 105-789) on HR 4104, 290-137, on Oct. 7. It defeated the rule for the first conference report (H Rept 105-760), 106-294, on Oct. 1. The House passed HR 4104, 218-203, on July 16.
- **Senate action:** The Senate cleared the conference report on HR 4328, 65-29, on Oct. 21. The Senate passed its version of the bill (S 2312) on Sept. 3, 91-5.
- **Presidential action:** Clinton signed HR 4328 on Oct. 21.

House Bill Would Defer Hill COLA, Limit FEC Terms

JUNE 13 — Powerful though they are, House appropriators know when they are outmatched.

So rather than wage a losing battle for a congressional pay raise in an election year, they decided to run up the white flag at a June 11 markup by the Treasury, Postal Service and General Government Subcommittee.

Members reluctantly gave voice vote approval to a bipartisan amendment, offered by Chairman Jim Kolbe, R-Ariz., and ranking Democrat Steny H. Hoyer of Maryland, to freeze the automatic cost of living increase for fiscal 1999. Otherwise, Kolbe conceded, rank-and-file members were sure to prevail on a pay-freeze amendment sometime later in the process.

"I'd prefer to do it now and avoid the controversy later," he said.

Members then approved the as-yet-unnumbered bill by voice vote. It is expected to be marked up in full com-

Appropriations

mittee during the week of June 15.

Even though the salary issue has been disposed of, the measure has plenty of provisions certain to spark sharp partisan battles and White House opposition.

With the backing of Appropriations Chairman Robert L. Livingston, R-La., the bill would impose a four-year term limit on the staff director and general counsel of the Federal Election Commission (FEC). Democrats charged that the provision was a back-door attempt to undermine FEC investigations of campaign finance violations and likely to draw a veto threat from President Clinton.

Almost as contentious, the measure would place restrictions on White House spending for overtime costs. It would also fund new office space for the Patent and Trademark Office, even though members conceded that the lease's cost of up to $1.5 billion over 20 years may be unreasonably high.

And it would continue to bar federal employee health insurance plans from covering abortions — a provision sure to spur many Democrats to vote against the bill on the House floor.

All in all, this is shaping up as another rocky year for the Treasury-Postal Service bill. Even though the base funding for the Treasury Department, White House, postal service and a grab bag of agencies attracts little criticism, small-money items such as the congressional pay raise invariably leave the measure open to attack from both the right and the left.

Party-Line Votes

Overall, the bill would provide $26.8 billion in budget authority. That is an increase of $1.4 billion over fiscal 1998, but $237 million less than the administration requested.

In a sign that the budget is comparatively flush, the measure would end a one-year moratorium on appropriating money for the construction of new government buildings. It would spend $527.1 million on courthouses and other buildings — some $483 million more than the administration's request.

Much of the partisan debate at the subcommittee markup erupted over the FEC provision and White House budget.

Hoyer said the proposed FEC term limits would greatly weaken the independent agency, and charged that the real GOP motivation was to punish it for investigating Republican-leaning groups such as the Christian Coalition.

"It appears that the FEC is looking a little too closely at some people," Hoyer said.

Far from disagreeing, Livingston responded that the FEC is "politically biased, in favor of your party and against ours." But he insisted that the provision, rather than being politically motivated, merely builds on language in last year's measure (PL 105-61) that restricts FEC commissioners to serving no more than a single six-year term.

"I don't believe anyone ought to have office in perpetuity," Livingston said.

On a party-line vote, 4-7, the subcommittee rejected a Hoyer amendment to strip out the FEC provision. But Democrats left little doubt that they will continue to hammer at the issue as the bill moves ahead.

On an identical 4-7 vote, the subcommittee rejected another Hoyer amendment that would have given the White House flexibility over spending $630,000 for overtime costs. Instead, the bill would fence off the money until the General Accounting Office finishes a report on White House expenses, including the costs of hosting overnight guests.

Despite Democratic objections, the subcommittee gave voice vote approval to an amendment by Livingston that would prevent agencies from transferring funds to the National Bioethics Advisory Commission, which oversees such controversial issues as human cloning.

Fiscal Hawks Fight Effort To Skirt Budget Caps

JUNE 20 — An effort by the House Appropriations Committee hierarchy to use the fiscal 1999 Treasury-Postal Service appropriations bill to get around tight spending "caps" agreed to under last year's balanced-budget law was quickly quashed by GOP budget hawks.

The unnumbered bill, approved June 17 by voice vote, funds the Treasury Department, Postal Service subsidies, the executive office of the president and several independent agencies.

The usually low-profile measure earned unwelcome controversy for a special $2.25 billion fund for government agencies' efforts to fix so-called Year 2000 glitches in their computers. House Appropriations Chairman Robert L. Livingston, R-La., pushed to designate the money an emergency appropriation, meaning it would not count toward the discretionary spending caps set by last year's balanced-budget agreement. A similar plan is under way in the Senate.

But the proposal immediately came under heavy fire from many in the GOP rank and file, who objected to efforts to breach the caps. Leading the effort was Mark W. Neumann, R-Wis., a zealous budget hawk, and more than 50 members who demanded and won a special GOP Conference meeting June 19 at which it was determined that the emergency computer money would be stripped out and advanced in a separate emergency supplemental bill. Neumann said he would insist that that bill be financed by offsetting cuts in other programs but Livingston raised doubts about whether such offsets could be found.

The spending issues in the annual bill are usually non-controversial, but the bill seems to attract more than its share of controversy on issues such as members' pay and abortion coverage for federal employees. It typically passes the House by a narrow margin.

Removing the controversial computer money would ease the way for the measure, which would otherwise combine $15.6 billion in discretionary spending and emergency computer money with $13.6 billion in mandatory spending in pension and health benefits for certain retired federal employees and their survivors.

Most of the emergency Year 2000 computer money would be spread across agencies not covered by the Treasury-Postal measure. Senior appropriators such as subcommittee Chairman Jim Kolbe, R-Ariz., called fixing the computer glitch a genuine emergency. He said the $2.25 billion is needed to head off a looming crisis.

Neumann said the issue was a matter

Administration Accepts Loss in Suit Over FY98 Line-Item Veto

JANUARY 10 — The Clinton administration, in a tactical retreat, has admitted defeat in one of three lawsuits challenging the constitutionality of the line-item veto. It is still fighting the other two on procedural grounds.

Judge Thomas F. Hogan of the U.S. District Court for the District of Columbia on Jan. 6 approved an agreement between the National Treasury Employees Union and the Justice Department to invalidate the president's line-item veto of legislation to permit some federal employees to switch pension plans. The union and the Justice Department had reached the agreement in December.

The development came as lawyers in the two remaining cases (City of New York v. Clinton and Snake River Potato Growers Inc. v. Rubin) prepare for Jan. 14 oral arguments before Hogan. The cases have been consolidated.

The line-item veto, signed into law in April 1996 (PL 104-130), strengthens the president's power to cancel individual items in enacted appropriations bills as well as certain provisions in tax and spending bills.

In folding its cards in the employees union case, Justice acknowledged that President Clinton did not have the authority to "cancel" the pension language when applying the line-item veto to the fiscal 1998 Treasury-Postal Service spending law (HR 2378 – PL 105-61).

The provision in question, a policy "rider" added in a House-Senate conference, permits about 1.1 million federal workers hired before 1983 to switch from the old Civil Service Retirement System to the Federal Employees Retirement System. Now restored, the provision enables longtime employees to take advantage of tax-deferred savings plans and allows widowed federal employees to receive higher Social Security survivor's benefits.

In his Oct. 16 cancellation of the provision, which would have saved $854 million over five years, Clinton said he was killing a "dollar amount of discretionary budget authority." That is the authority for federal agencies to spend or otherwise obligate money. But as Justice conceded, no budget authority was involved. The veto instead would have effectively reduced federal revenues because workers who switch plans would contribute a smaller portion of their wages into the system.

The question of whether Clinton had the authority to issue the veto in this instance was only half of the union's challenge. The union's suit and the two remaining cases also challenge the underlying law's constitutionality.

Under Article I of the Constitution, all legislative power is vested with Congress; the president can only accept or reject bills. The new veto, the lawsuits argue, gives the president the power to change a law — or amend it — after he has signed it.

To the frustration of the law's opponents, the administration so far has kept the constitutional substance of the case from being brought before the high court. On June 26, the court dismissed a suit by Sen. Robert C. Byrd, D-W.Va., and other lawmakers (Byrd v. Raines) on the grounds that they had not been injured by the law and therefore lacked standing to sue.

The Justice Department did not challenge the union's legal standing to sue, conceding that some of its 150,000 members had been injured by the veto. But Justice argues that the New York City government and the potato growers cooperative lack standing to sue because they have not been injured.

"The [union] case was the best case," said a Senate aide. "We're back to square one. We have to get over the hurdle of standing."

In the New York case, Clinton canceled a provision in last year's budget law (PL 105-33) that would have helped New York finance its Medicaid program. The potato farmers cooperative contends that Clinton's veto of a provision in last year's tax law (PL 105-34) that provided tax incentives for the sale of food processing plants to farmer-owned co-ops ended the Snake River cooperative's ability to close such a deal.

of budgetary principle, and he accused GOP leaders of trying to systematically sneak around the spending caps by giving certain spending an "emergency" designation. The status permits Congress to appropriate the money — which would reduce future budget surpluses by a commensurate amount — without having to cut other spending to fit under discretionary caps set by last year's balanced-budget law (PL 105-33).

The Treasury-Postal add-on came on top of $1.6 billion in emergency money included in the Pentagon appropriations bill to fix Defense Department computers. That money would also be moved in the separate supplemental.

Neumann's attempt to strip the emergency spending in committee was rebuffed, 14-32.

Amendments

The Treasury-Postal bill draws controversy because it funds unpopular agencies such as the Internal Revenue Service and the Bureau of Alcohol, Tobacco and Firearms.

It also features an annual debate over whether federal employees should be able to receive abortions through their taxpayer-subsidized health care plans. The committee rejected, 20-20, an attempt by Democrats to strip language from the bill that blocks such abortion coverage, except in cases of rape, incest and when the life of the woman is endangered. Democrats reversed a decade-

Appropriations

long ban on such abortions after President Clinton took office in 1993, but Republicans reinstated it after they took over Congress in 1995. *(1995 Almanac, p. 11-77)*

In a surprise victory for Democrats, the committee voted 28-26 to require each health plan for federal employees to provide a full range of contraception services.

The committee also approved, 30-20, a bid by Anne M. Northup, R-Ky., to replace the U.S. Postal Service with the Office of the U.S. Trade Representative as the U.S. negotiator in future overseas postal talks on rules regarding international mail.

The decision was a big win for the United Parcel Service of America, which lobbied hard for the change. It argued that the Postal Service negotiates with other countries for access for its Global Package Link express service to the unfair disadvantage of private carriers.

House Members Shoot Holes In Treasury Bill

JULY 18 — The House Treasury, Postal Service and general government spending bill (HR 4104) fell victim to parliamentary warfare before passing July 16, 218-203, on a cliffhanger vote that changed more than half a dozen times as House leaders tried to line up support. *(Vote 293, p. H-84)*

The House Rules Committee issued an invitation to havoc when it crafted a rule for floor debate that shielded only one provision in the bill — language to block an annual cost of living increase for members of Congress. That left unprotected — and vulnerable to deletion — any other provision that violated House rules by, for example, providing funds for unauthorized programs or legislating on a spending bill. Despite rules against such provisions, they often are inserted and lawmakers typically look the other way.

This time, however, lawmakers readily accepted the unusual rule as an invitation to strike about 50 items from the bill.

Leading the charge were Democrats who complained that Republicans were trying to remove controversial provisions favored by Democrats, including money to fix Year 2000 computer problems and language requiring health care plans for federal employees to provide coverage for contraceptives if they also cover other prescription drugs.

"I didn't invent the rule," said David R. Obey of Wisconsin, the top Democrat on the Appropriations Committee, who was responsible for striking most of the items that were removed. "I'm not going to let the Republican leadership decide they can knock out things our people think are important and not see the consequences."

Most of the items removed were policy provisions, not funding items — so most of the bill's funding remained intact. Jim Kolbe, R-Ariz., chairman of the Treasury-Postal Service Appropriations Subcommittee, said he expected many of the deleted provisions to be restored in a House-Senate conference.

Before coming to the floor, the legislation would have provided $29.2 billion in funding for fiscal 1999. After House action, it would provide $26.95 billion, according to committee aides.

In a much less contentious debate July 14, the Senate Appropriations Committee approved a $29.9 billion fiscal 1999 Treasury-Postal Service spending bill (S 2312) by a vote of 28-0.

Bumpy Ride

The House bill's chaotic journey began June 25 when GOP leaders first tried to bring it to the floor. They were caught off guard when conservative Republicans joined with Democrats to reject the original rule, 125-291. *(Vote 268, p. H-78)*

Led by abortion opponent Christopher H. Smith, R-N.J., 155 Republicans voted against the rule because it would have protected the language on contraceptives for federal employees.

In addition, 135 Democrats and Independent Rep. Bernard Sanders of Vermont opposed the rule because it would have removed $2.25 billion in emergency funding to fix a glitch in federal government computers that may cause them to go haywire or shut down on Jan. 1, 2000. Emergency appropriations do not count toward spending caps set in the 1997 budget spending law (PL 105-33).

After a two-week recess, House leaders returned with an even more controversial rule. Rules generally protect language that technically violates House rules but that makes the measure attractive to certain lawmakers. But this rule only protected language that would bar an otherwise automatic cost of living increase for members of Congress.

It aimed to bring conservatives back on board by leaving the contraception language open to deletion, said John Linder, R-Ga., a Rules Committee member. Republicans also tried to bully Democrats into voting for the rule by claiming a vote against it was a vote in support of a congressional pay raise.

"I think it helped pass the rule," said Linder, who heads the National Republican Congressional Committee, the House Republicans' political arm. He put out a news release July 15 warning Democrats that Republicans would try to claim that those voting against the rule were voting for a pay raise.

Despite losing 23 Republicans, the rule passed July 15, 218-201, with the help of 20 Democrats. *(Vote 284, p. H-82)*

The next day, still steamed by GOP efforts to turn debate on the rule into a vote on the pay raise, W.G. "Bill" Hefner, D-N.C., who is retiring at the end of the 105th Congress, offered an amendment to remove the provision to freeze the cost of living increase.

"It was absolutely intellectually dishonest," Hefner said of the GOP's tactics. His amendment, however, was defeated, 79-342. *(Vote 289, p. H-84)*

Democrats were responsible for removing most of the 50 provisions deleted from the bill, but Republicans also used the opportunity to strike items they opposed.

Mark W. Neumann, R-Wis., succeeded in striking the $2.25 billion in emergency funding to fix the Year 2000 computer glitch. Republican leaders said they plan to include the money in a supplemental appropriations bill.

But Senate Appropriations Committee Chairman Ted Stevens, R-Alaska, said he would prefer to keep the money in the Treasury spending bill. The Senate's bill includes $3.25 billion

Treasury-Postal Service

for ensuring that the federal government's computers are fixed. "Clearly it's an emergency," Stevens said.

Abortion Fight

Another major controversy erupted over the language on contraceptives, sponsored by Rep. Nita M. Lowey, D-N.Y., which had been added in committee.

Todd Tiahrt, R-Kan., succeeded in striking the language because it sought to legislate on an appropriations bill. Tiahrt and Christopher H. Smith, R-N.J., one of Congress' most vocal abortion opponents, objected to federal funding for contraceptives because, Smith claimed, some of them can be used to chemically induce abortions.

Democrats, however, outmaneuvered Smith and his allies, scoring a surprising victory when they came to the floor with a slightly reworded version of the Lowey language.

The amendment would bar federal funds from being used to renew contracts with health care plans for federal employees that provide coverage for prescription drugs but do not include coverage for contraceptives. The amendment exempted five health care plans with a religious orientation.

The amendment was in line with House rules, which allow for limitations on how money is spent. The House adopted it, 224-198.

Despite the loss, Smith was not ready to give up. He countered with an amendment seeking to bar the use of contraceptives that chemically induce abortions.

Lowey charged that Smith was trying to outlaw funding for all contraceptives. "The gentleman from New Jersey is saying to every woman who may take a birth control pill or use another one of the five accepted methods of contraception that they are abortionists," she said to applause from many female lawmakers.

Smith, however, said the pill and the diaphragm would be allowed under his amendment. Nonetheless, his amendment was rejected, 198-222. *(Vote 292, p. H-84)*

It was not the only abortion-related issue to emerge.

Rosa DeLauro, D-Conn., offered an amendment to remove a long-standing provision in the bill barring funding for abortions through federal employee health care plans.

Smith led the move to defeat DeLauro's amendment, 183-239. *(Vote 288, p. H-84)*

"Americans should not be forced to underwrite the costs of destroying unborn babies," Smith said.

In protesting the rule, Obey struck exceptions to the abortion ban that allow funding of abortions in cases of rape, incest or to save the life of the woman. He said he supports the exceptions but "wasn't playing favorites."

Other Controversies

Democrats scored a few other victories besides the Lowey amendment.

Carolyn B. Maloney, D-N.Y., struck language that would impose a four-year term limit on the staff director and general counsel of the Federal Election Commission (FEC). Democrats charged that Republicans added the provision in retribution against the FEC for targeting GOP-leaning organizations, such as the Christian Coalition, for investigations of campaign finance violations.

Maloney and Vince Snowbarger, R-Kan., also sponsored an amendment, approved 214-210, that would add $2.8 million to the FEC's budget, bringing its total to $36.5 million. *(Vote 287, p. H-82)*

Appropriations Committee Chairman Robert L. Livingston, R-La., objected to the boost, saying that despite past funding increases, the FEC has failed to do its job effectively or fairly.

The House rejected, 195-226, an amendment offered by Bernard Sanders, I-Vt., to require congressional approval before the president can make any loan or credit to a foreign government or entity of more than $250 million from the Treasury Department's Exchange Stabilization Fund. *(Vote 291, p. H-84)*

Senate Action

The Senate markup was much tamer, and Chairman Stevens moved quickly after the markup to defuse a potential controversy.

Like the House measure, the Senate bill contains language that would freeze the cost of living increase for members of Congress for fiscal 1999.

Herb Kohl of Wisconsin, the top Democrat on the Treasury-Postal Service Appropriations Subcommittee, said he was concerned because the language differed slightly from the House provision, making the item open for debate in a House-Senate conference.

After initially dismissing such concerns, Stevens decided to change the provision to make it identical to the House's language.

The panel approved by voice vote an amendment, offered by Frank R. Lautenberg, D-N.J., that would require the federal government to tap into the frozen assets of nations labeled as terrorist states to pay for judgments rendered by U.S. courts against those countries for acts of terrorism in cases brought by U.S. citizens.

"This sends the strongest possible message to terrorist states," Lautenberg said.

The Treasury Department, however, has objected to the language, saying it would impair the president's ability to use the money as a bargaining chip when dealing with hostile countries, according to a letter sent to Kohl.

Harry Reid, D-Nev., planned to offer an amendment similar to the Lowey contraception language but withdrew it after being told that the Governmental Affairs Committee, which has jurisdiction over the issue, objected to such a move. He said he would offer the amendment when the bill goes to the Senate floor.

Senate Halts Action After Dispute Over Term Limits At FEC

AUGUST 1 — Action on the fiscal 1999 Treasury and general government spending bill came to a halt in the Senate on July 30 after Democrats threatened to stall the measure over a provision to place term limits on two top staff members at the Federal Election Commission (FEC).

Work on the $29.9 billion measure (S 2312), which funds the Treasury Department, Postal Service subsidies, executive office of the president and several independent agencies, was almost complete before Democrats

Appropriations

raised their threat.

When Republican and Democratic leaders could not resolve the dispute, action was put off until after the August recess. Senate leaders said that during the break they will try to hammer out a compromise that would allow the bill to move forward when senators return the week of Aug. 31.

"It can be worked out," said Senate Majority Leader Trent Lott, R-Miss. But he added, "If the Democrats don't want the Treasury Department and White House funded, what do I care?"

The House passed its version of the legislation (HR 4104) on July 16 after a lengthy parliamentary battle in which dozens of legislative provisions were stripped from the bill.

FEC Under Attack

At issue in the Senate was an amendment by Mitch McConnell, R-Ky., to place a four-year term limit on the FEC's general counsel and staff director. The tenures of both could be extended by the vote of four out of six members of the commission, which is made up of three Democrats and three Republicans. The Senate voted 45-54, along party lines, against tabling (killing) McConnell's amendment. (*Vote 246, p. S-39*)

The House bill had a similar provision, but it was stripped out because it violated a House rule that prohibits legislating on an appropriations bill.

Senate Democrats charged that McConnell's amendment was politically motivated and was aimed primarily at the current general counsel, Lawrence Noble. John Glenn, D-Ohio, and Carl Levin, D-Mich., also said it was intended to stifle the FEC's scrutiny of soft money donations, which are largely unregulated contributions to political parties.

"This amendment would have members of Congress deciding whether or not the Federal Election Commission should or should not go after certain practices by using the threat of term limits on their career officials," Levin said.

McConnell, the Senate's leading foe of campaign finance overhaul legislation, said the amendment would have the opposite effect. "The amendment guarantees that the FEC will operate on a bipartisan basis" because it would require the general counsel and staff director to gain the support of both Democratic and Republican commission members to be reappointed, said McConnell, who chairs the National Republican Senatorial Committee.

McConnell denied that the amendment was targeted at Noble, but he did say Noble has not "demonstrated great bipartisanship in the past." He did not provide specifics.

Noble said July 31: "My office has acted in a totally nonpartisan way. . . . It is important to keep in mind that all I do is make recommendations." On the McConnell amendment, he said: "The message it sends to the general counsel and staff director is, if you anger either side, you're going to be in trouble."

After the Senate's vote against tabling McConnell's proposal, Levin threatened to stall action on the bill by adding a steady stream of second-degree amendments to the amendments that were already pending. (*Vote 246, p. S-39*)

Levin said he wanted more time to debate the McConnell amendment than it had been given. When GOP and Democratic leaders agreed July 29 to place time limits on debate on the remaining amendments to S 2312, they set aside only 20 minutes for McConnell's amendment. Levin said he was unaware of the agreement until July 30.

President Clinton sent a letter to Senate Minority Leader Tom Daschle, D-S.D., urging senators to oppose the amendment, saying it was an "indefensible step to weaken our nation's election laws."

When the Senate returns to the bill, it is expected to vote on an amendment by Glenn to add $2.8 million to the FEC's budget. If adopted, it would bring proposed FEC funding up to $36.5 million, the amount requested by Clinton.

Taxes at Issue

Before debate disintegrated, the Senate rejected an amendment by Tim Hutchinson, R-Ark., to scrap the federal tax code by Dec. 31, 2002. The amendment would require Congress to pass a replacement by July 4, 2002.

The tax code "has mutated from its original form into an 800,000-word, 7,500-page monster preying on the American taxpayer," Hutchinson said.

Hutchinson's amendment was effectively defeated, 49-49, on a procedural motion. The motion was to waive budget rules that require offsets to make up for revenue losses in a bill. It would have required 60 votes to pass. (*Vote 241, p. S-38*)

Critics said it would be irresponsible for Congress to vote to get rid of the federal tax system without having an alternative in place.

"To tear down the tax code before Americans know what will replace it is dangerous," said Finance Committee Chairman William V. Roth Jr., R-Del. "We must work to change the current system. . . . But we must do it in an organized and orderly way."

Treasury Secretary Robert E. Rubin warned that he would recommend a veto of the bill if the amendment was added to it.

The House passed a bill (HR 3097) on June 17 to sunset the tax code by the end of 2002.

Many senators who backed Hutchinson's amendment also supported a proposal by Republicans Sam Brownback of Kansas and John Ashcroft of Missouri to eliminate the so-called marriage penalty, which requires some two-income married couples to pay more in taxes than they would pay if they filed separately.

"It is time . . . to return America to a tax policy that does not discriminate against marriage," Ashcroft said. Married couples who face the penalty pay an average of $1,400 a year more than they would if they filed separately, he said.

The amendment would allow those couples to be taxed individually as if they were unmarried. Ashcroft said the provision would cost about $151.3 billion over five years.

Democrats said they support eliminating the penalty, but they criticized the amendment's authors for not providing offsetting spending cuts. Budget rules require lawmakers to specify offsets to pay for a provision, although Ashcroft and others suggested it could be paid for with budget surpluses.

Democrats said that because almost all the projected budget surplus would be made up of surplus Social Security revenues, Ashcroft's proposal would amount to tapping Social Security trust funds to finance the tax cut.

Roth warned that the provision could complicate prospects for passage of the Treasury-Postal Service bill. If the amendment were added, any member of the House could object to the provision because all revenue measures must originate in the House.

After senators defeated, 48-51, a motion by Roth to table the amendment, Brownback agreed to withdraw it because of Roth's concerns. (Vote 242, p. S-38)

Daschle countered with his own marriage penalty amendment that would have allowed couples to deduct 20 percent of the salary of the spouse who earns less if the couple's combined income was below $50,000. It was tabled, 57-42. He proposed offsetting the cost by eliminating some tax breaks for corporations and investors. (Vote 243, p. S-38)

Other Amendments

In other action, the Senate adopted by voice vote an amendment by John W. Warner, R-Va., and John H. Chafee, R-R.I., to shift $14 million from a Transportation Department building account to Capitol security. Warner said the money could be used to help pay for a Capitol Hill visitors' center, which congressional leaders are proposing in the wake of the July 24 shooting deaths of two Capitol police officers.

With no debate, the Senate by voice vote added an amendment that had sparked considerable controversy in the House before it was adopted.

The amendment, by Harry Reid, D-Nev., and Olympia J. Snowe, R-Maine, would require federal employee health plans that cover prescription drugs to also provide coverage for contraceptives. Health plans with a religious orientation would be exempt. Reid said he believed Republicans accepted the proposal without debate because some GOP senators did not want to vote on the issue.

By voice vote, the Senate also adopted an amendment by Republican Mike DeWine of Ohio to ban federal employee health care plans from paying for abortions except in cases of rape or incest or to save the life of the woman.

Ted Stevens, R-Alaska, planned to offer an amendment to give lawmakers and other high-level federal officials an opportunity to increase their pensions, but he withdrew it.

Senate Passes Bill After GOP Avoids FEC Debate

SEPTEMBER 5 — To move fiscal 1999 Treasury-Postal Service spending legislation to passage, Senate Republicans weakened an effort to impose term limits on top staff members at the Federal Election Commission (FEC). But it appeared the issue would remain controversial during an upcoming conference with the House.

Mitch McConnell, R-Ky., altered his amendment to the Treasury spending bill (HR 4104) to make it more acceptable to Democrats who had threatened to stall the bill indefinitely. McConnell's move opened the way for passage, 91-5. (Vote 260, p. S-41)

McConnell's original amendment would have imposed a four-year term limit on the FEC's general counsel and staff director. To be reappointed, both officials would have needed the votes of four members of the six-member commission, which is evenly split between Democrats and Republicans.

GOP Senate leaders were forced to pull the bill from the floor July 30 after Carl Levin, D-Mich., threatened to add a series of lengthy second-degree amendments to the bill in protest over McConnell's amendment.

But while Levin appeared to have won this round, the language could be restored in conference or emerge in another form that Democrats oppose. McConnell, who is not a conferee, said he had not decided whether to further pursue the issue.

A similar provision was included in the House's version of the bill but was stripped on a procedural motion on the floor. The provision was backed by House Appropriations Committee Chairman Robert L. Livingston, R-La.

The Senate measure would provide $29.9 billion for the Treasury Department, executive office of the president, U.S. Postal Service and several independent agencies, including the FEC. The House version, passed July 16, would provide $26.6 billion.

Levin and other Democrats said McConnell's original amendment was aimed at the current general counsel, Lawrence Noble, and the FEC's efforts to crack down on "soft money" — largely unregulated contributions to political parties. They also said it would make FEC officials fearful of losing their jobs if they angered either party.

"It was an obvious effort to influence the actions of the Federal Election Commission," Levin said.

But McConnell and other Republicans said the provision was intended to ensure that the FEC operates in a bipartisan manner by requiring its top officials to gain the support of both Democrats and Republicans.

McConnell, a leading foe of overhauling federal campaign finance laws, said he agreed to change his amendment to move the bill along. "I didn't feel like we ought to allow [the Democrats] to kill the whole" spending bill over the issue, he said.

His revised amendment, adopted by voice vote, would establish six-year terms, beginning Jan. 1, 1999, for the FEC's staff director and general counsel. Their initial appointments would have to be approved by four commission members. But the officials would have to gain the support of only three members to be reappointed.

The amendment would allow Noble to stay in his current job until 2008 without a commission vote on reappointment.

As part of the deal worked out with Levin, Republicans also agreed to accept an amendment by John Glenn, D-Ohio, to increase the FEC's budget by $2.8 million. The increase, approved by voice vote, would bring the agency's funding for fiscal 1999 to $36.5 million, the amount requested by President Clinton.

Year 2000 Problem

In addition to the FEC language, House and Senate negotiators will have several other issues to hammer out in conference.

Among the biggest differences between the measures is $3.25 billion in emergency funding included in the Senate bill to help the federal government fix the Year 2000 computer glitch.

GOP budget hawks in the House opposed the inclusion of $2.25 billion in Year 2000 funding in the House bill because emergency funding measures do not count toward the discretionary

Appropriations

budget caps set in the 1997 budget spending law (PL 105-33). They succeeded in stripping the money from the bill on the House floor.

Clinton submitted a request Sept. 2 for $3.25 billion in supplemental fiscal 1998 funding to fix the problem.

Senate Appropriations Committee Chairman Ted Stevens, R-Alaska, said he was not concerned about which vehicle congressional leaders decide to use to appropriate the money for the problem as long as lawmakers "get it done before the first of October," when the new fiscal year begins.

Conference Report Fails To Reach House Floor

OCTOBER 3 — An unusual alliance of critics opposed to provisions on contraceptives, Haitian immigrants and the Federal Election Commission combined Oct. 1 to defeat an effort to bring the conference report on the fiscal 1999 Treasury-Postal Service spending bill to the House floor, leaving the measure's fate in doubt.

The legislation (HR 4104) would provide about $27 billion for the Treasury Department, U.S. Postal Service subsidies, executive office of the president and several independent agencies. But the provisions that sank the rule for debate on the conference report, by a vote of 106-294, had nothing to do with funding. (*Vote 475, p. H-134*)

All but 17 Democrats voted against the rule governing debate largely because of a provision in the conference report (H Report 105-760) that would place term limits on the top officials of the Federal Election Commission (FEC).

A coalition of conservative Republicans, led by abortion foe Christopher H. Smith, R-N.J., opposed the legislation over a provision that would require health care plans for federal employees to help pay for all prescription contraceptives approved by the Food and Drug Administration (FDA), if the plan covered prescription drugs.

A third issue that galvanized opposition to the rule by lawmakers who favor immigration restrictions would give some Haitians permanent residency in the United States.

Leaders must now decide whether to send the measure back to a House-Senate conference to remove offending provisions, or to add it to a catchall spending bill to be considered at the end of the session. Appropriations leaders were leaning toward the catchall bill.

Contraceptives Raise Ire

Even though both the House and Senate versions of the bill included the provision requiring contraceptive coverage, conservatives tried to remove or modify it during negotiations.

Smith and others opposed the provision because, they said, it would require coverage of some contraceptives that they claim would chemically induce abortions.

Work on the conference report halted Sept. 28 over the contraception issue after lawmakers reached agreement on all other provisions.

In negotiations Oct. 1, conferees settled the dispute by agreeing to adopt the House bill's language and adding language stating that the provision could not be used to require coverage of abortion or abortion-related services. But that did little to appease Smith and other critics.

Rep. Nita M. Lowey, D-N.Y., who wrote the House provision on contraceptives, insisted that it had little to do with abortion and was intended only to ensure that female federal employees had coverage for the right contraceptive. "No abortions will be covered by this amendment," she said. "Women need the full range of options [because] not every women can use one form."

Following the vote, Smith said he would continue to fight to have the item removed from HR 4104 or any omnibus spending measure.

Term Limits at FEC

Meanwhile, appropriators also managed to anger many Democrats by adding language to impose four-year term limits on the FEC's general counsel and staff director. The amendment would require both officials to gain the support of four members of the six-member commission, which is split along party lines, to be appointed and re-appointed. It would go into effect in January 1999.

The provision was originally added to the House bill in committee but was removed on the floor in a procedural move. Republicans were forced to weaken a similar amendment offered in the Senate by Mitch McConnell, R-Ky., after Democrats led by Carl Levin of Michigan threatened to stall the legislation over the issue.

The alternative amendment included in the Senate bill required only three votes for the FEC officials to be reappointed. It also allowed the current general counsel, Lawrence Noble, to stay in his job without having to be reappointed until 2008.

Democrats said the FEC provision accepted by conferees was targeted at Noble because he recommended investigations against GOP-affiliated groups.

Levin said he may filibuster the conference report if it comes before the Senate with the FEC provision included. He and other Democrats charged that the provision added by conferees would keep FEC officials from recommending investigations against either party out of fear of losing their jobs.

It "is an outrageous attempt to intimidate the Federal Election Commission so it turns into nothing but a gutless overseer," said David R. Obey of Wisconsin, the House Appropriations Committee's top Democrat.

But Appropriations Chairman Robert L. Livingston, R-La., said it was aimed at ensuring that the top staff members were unbiased in choosing and carrying out investigations.

Other Provisions

The third poison pill included in the conference report would grant about 40,000 Haitians, according to supporters, permanent residency in the United States. The provision was added in the Senate bill by Sens. Bob Graham, D-Fla., and Connie Mack, R-Fla. It mirrored legislation added to the fiscal 1998 District of Columbia spending bill (PL 105-100) that granted legal status to some Cubans and Nicaraguans. (*1997 Almanac, p. 9-27*)

Graham and others said it was unfair of Congress to allow those groups to stay while denying the same benefit to Haitians who also face difficulties in returning home.

But Rep. Lamar Smith, R-Texas,

Treasury-Postal Service Spending

Treasury-Postal Service portion of the fiscal 1999 omnibus spending law (HR 4328 — PL 105-277) signed by the president on Oct. 21. *(Budget authority, in thousands of dollars.)*

	Fiscal 1998 Appropriation	Fiscal 1999 Clinton Request	House Bill	Senate Bill	Conference Report
Treasury Department					
U.S. Customs Service					
Salaries and expenses	$ 1,516,165	$ 1,638,065	$ 1,638,065	$ 1,630,273	$ 1,642,565
Air and marine interdiction	88,288	98,488	100,688	113,488	113,688
Other	5,406	5,000	5,000	5,000	5,000
Subtotal, Customs	**$ 1,609,859**	**$ 1,741,553**	**$ 1,743,753**	**$ 1,748,761**	**$ 1,761,253**
Internal Revenue Service					
Processing tax returns, assistance	2,925,874	3,162,430	3,025,013	3,077,353	3,086,208
Tax law enforcement	3,142,822	3,169,539	3,164,189	3,164,399	3,164,189
Information systems	1,597,487	1,863,884	1,434,032	1,467,055	1,476,456
Earned-income compliance	138,000	143,000	143,000	143,000	143,000
Rescissions	− 62,330	—	—	—	—
Subtotal, IRS	**$ 7,741,853**	**$ 8,338,853**	**$ 7,766,234**	**$ 7,851,807**	**$ 7,869,853**
Bureau of Alcohol, Tobacco and Firearms	533,956	576,324	530,624	529,489	541,574
U.S. Secret Service	573,147	601,102	601,102	592,970	608,370
Bureau of the Public Debt	169,426	173,100	172,100	172,100	172,100
Financial Management Service	207,790	202,510	198,510	196,490	196,490
Other	542,453	510,485	521,190	526,914	524,102
TOTAL, Treasury Department	**$ 11,378,484**	**$ 12,143,927**	**$ 11,533,513**	**$ 11,539,237**	**$ 11,673,742**
Postal Service					
TOTAL, Postal subsidies	$ 86,274	$ 100,195	$ 71,195	$ 71,195	$ 71,195
Executive Office of the President					
President's compensation	250	250	250	250	250
White House Office	51,199	52,344	52,344	52,344	52,344
Executive residence	8,245	8,691	8,061	8,691	8,691
National Security Council	6,648	6,806	6,806	6,806	6,806
Office of Management and Budget	57,440	60,617	59,017	60,617	60,617
Office of National Drug Control Policy	35,016	36,442	36,442	48,042	48,042
Federal drug control programs	159,007	162,007	162,007	183,977	182,477
Other	251,120	304,094	254,894	3,490,684*	255,394
TOTAL, Executive Office	**$ 568,925**	**$ 631,251**	**$ 579,821**	**$ 3,851,411***	**$ 614,621**
Independent Agencies					
General Services Administration					
Federal Buildings Fund	—	—	479,300	508,752	450,018
Limitation on use of revenues	*(4,835,934)*	*(5,156,833)*	*(5,624,128)*	*(5,648,680)*	*(5,605,018)*
Other	143,565	140,735	142,735	140,735	143,835
Subtotal, GSA	**$ 143,565**	**$ 140,735**	**$ 622,035**	**$ 649,487**	**$ 593,853**
Office of Personnel Management					
Annuitants, health benefits	4,338,000	4,632,000	4,632,000	4,632,000	4,632,000
Annuitants, life insurance	32,000	35,000	35,000	35,000	35,000
Civil Service retirement, disability	8,336,000	8,682,297	8,682,297	8,682,297	8,682,297
Salaries and expenses	85,350	85,350	85,350	85,350	85,350
Subtotal, OPM	**$ 12,792,310**	**$ 13,435,607**	**$ 13,435,607**	**$ 13,435,607**	**$ 13,435,607**
Federal Election Commission	31,650	36,504	36,500	36,500	36,500
National Archives	221,305	242,463	229,191	239,343	241,927
U.S. Tax Court	33,921	34,490	34,490	32,765	32,765
Other, scorekeeping adjustments	69,334	74,317	72,317	68,067	72,317
GRAND TOTAL	**$ 25,325,768**	**$ 26,839,489**	**$ 26,614,669**	**$ 29,923,612**	**$ 26,772,527**

* *Includes $3.25 billion to fix Year 2000 computer problems*

SOURCE: House Appropriations Committee

Appropriations

who generally takes a hard line on immigration issues, said the provision would "set a terrible precedent. All others will line up to seek the same treatment."

During the Sept. 28 conference meeting, Livingston proposed an amendment, rejected by voice vote, that would have required the Haitians to prove on a case-by-case basis that it would be "an extreme hardship" to return to Haiti. But Rep. Carrie P. Meek, D-Fla., argued that many Haitians would be unable to secure the legal help needed for such a process.

Meanwhile, conferees voted to remove $3.25 billion, which was included in the Senate's version of the bill, to help the federal government fix the Year 2000 computer problem, which left uncorrected could cause computer systems to malfunction when the date changes to Jan. 1, 2000. Senate Appropriations leaders said the Year 2000 money would be included in a fiscal 1999 emergency supplemental spending bill.

Conferees also agreed to keep a provision in the Senate bill that would allow U.S. courts to seize the U.S.-held assets of countries found to be responsible for sponsoring terrorist attacks, in order to pay for legal judgments brought against those nations in lawsuits filed by U.S. victims. The provision, however, was modified to allow the president to waive it for national security reasons.

Compromise Bill Adopted In House, Stalls In Senate

OCTOBER 10 — After GOP leaders stripped four controversial riders, the House adopted a revised conference report (H Rept 105-789) on legislation to provide $26.7 billion in fiscal 1999 for the Treasury Department, Postal Service subsidies, executive office of the president and several independent agencies. The vote Oct. 7 was 290-137. (Vote 494, p. H-140)

But the legislation (HR 4104) stalled in the Senate on Oct. 9 as Harry Reid, D-Nev., objected to removal of a rider that would have required federal health plans that cover prescription drugs to also cover contraceptives. The bill then appeared headed for inclusion in a catchall spending bill to be enacted before lawmakers leave Washington for the year.

Even before then, House-Senate conferees had walked a tortuous path, requiring two tries to come up with a conference report acceptable to enough lawmakers.

Much of the controversy centered on four provisions that GOP leaders pulled from the bill after they failed to reach a deal with Democrats that would also mollify Republican critics.

In addition to the measure on contraceptives, the provisions would have:

● Placed four-year term limits on the Federal Election Commission's (FEC) general counsel and staff director and required a vote of four of the agency's six members for them to be re-appointed.

● Allowed about 40,000 Haitians to gain permanent residency in the United States.

● Allowed federal agencies to use some of their funds to help low-income federal workers pay for child care.

The White House and Democratic supporters of the provisions on Haitians and contraceptives said they would try to have them added to the catchall spending bill as well.

Elusive Compromise

Appropriators reopened the conference on the bill Oct. 6 after conservative Republicans and most House Democrats combined Oct. 1 to defeat the rule needed to begin House floor debate on the conference report.

Democrats were protesting the FEC provision, which they said aimed to intimidate the agency and punish the current general counsel for launching investigations against GOP-leaning organizations.

Some Republicans opposed the provisions on Haitians and contraceptives.

When conferees met for the second time, Rep. Jim Kolbe, R-Ariz., chairman of the Treasury-Postal Service Appropriations Subcommittee, suggested that conferees remove the FEC, Haitian and child care provisions and retain the contraceptives measure with language that would exempt religious-based health care plans.

Democrats rejected the offer. They argued that since all but the FEC provision had bipartisan support, only that provision should be dropped.

Republicans would not yield, however, and Kolbe said appropriations leaders were left with little choice but to take out all four provisions. "We could not get this bill to the floor without taking them out," he said.

Republicans who opposed the provisions on contraceptives and on Haitians came back on board when the two measures were deleted.

Contraceptives Draw Fire

But Democrats were upset that the GOP gave in to Republican abortion foes who opposed the contraceptive coverage.

Nita M. Lowey, D-N.Y., who sponsored the provision in the House, noted that it was the only one of the four items stripped from the bill that was included in both chambers' versions of it. "A provision that passed the House and the Senate and was in the conference report . . . that it can be taken out by the leadership is an extraordinary way to run the shop," Lowey said.

House Democrats made a last-ditch effort to force the issue by moving to send the legislation back to conference with instructions to restore the contraceptives measure. It was rejected, 202-226. (Vote 493, p. H-140)

Some moderate Republicans, who strongly supported the contraceptives measure and voted to recommit the bill to conference, blamed Democrats for not supporting the conference report when it first came to the floor Oct. 1 with contraceptive coverage included.

"The Democrats simply decided that contraceptive coverage was expendable" in favor of other items, said Rep. Nancy L. Johnson, R-Conn.

Despite the controversy on the four riders, several Democrats supported the bill on final passage.

Rep. Steny H. Hoyer of Maryland, the top Democrat on the Treasury-Postal Service Appropriations panel, said that while he opposed stripping the provisions on contraceptives, Haitians and day care, he voted for the conference report because it was "99.9 percent pure and good." ◆

Housing Policy Overhaul Gets Ride to Enactment On VA-HUD Spending Bill

Box Score

- **Bill:** HR 4194 — PL 105-276
- **House action:** The House adopted the conference report (H Rept 105-769) on HR 4194, 409-14, on Oct. 6. The House passed the bill, 259-164, on July 29.
- **Senate action:** The Senate cleared the conference report on HR 4194, 96-1, on Oct. 8. The Senate passed HR 4194 on July 30 by voice vote, after substituting the text of S 2168, initially passed on July 17 by voice vote.
- **Presidential action:** Clinton signed the bill on Oct. 21.

SUMMARY

Narrowly avoiding being absorbed into the catchall omnibus appropriations bill, the $93.4 billion spending bill for the departments of Veterans Affairs (VA) and Housing and Urban Development (HUD) and for independent agencies ended up as one of just five separately enacted fiscal 1999 spending measures. It served as a vehicle for the enactment of an overhaul of public housing programs (originally HR 2).

The overwhelming votes on final passage in both chambers (just 14 "nays" in the House and one in the Senate) belied the controversies that had earlier bedeviled the bill.

In the Senate, consideration was delayed for more than a week as Democrats tried to attach unrelated patients' rights legislation. When they finally withdrew the amendment, the Senate quickly passed the bill after tabling, 69-27, an amendment to scale back provisions allowing the Federal Housing Administration (FHA) to insure mortgages on higher-cost homes.

Similar FHA loan provisions were in the House-passed bill (HR 4194), and ultimately in the final agreement. But they were originally left unprotected by the recommended rule for House consideration of the bill. House leaders were forced to take the unusual step of amending the rule on the floor to protect those provisions and garner enough votes to adopt the rule.

The move to add the public housing overhaul to the VA-HUD spending measure touched off a contentious debate on the House floor, but it was agreed to by 230-181. There was also a House debate on provisions and committee report language prohibiting the administration from implementing a global climate treaty it endorsed in Kyoto, Japan, in December 1997 and signed in November 1998, that would require the United States to substantially reduce greenhouse gas emissions. The House adopted, 226-198, an amendment overruling committee report language that suggested the Environmental Protection Agency (EPA) and Council on Environmental Quality refrain from conducting educational seminars or outreach programs on global warming.

The Kyoto provision was a sticking point in conference as well. After intense negotiations, conferees agreed to prohibit the use of EPA funds to "propose or issue rules, regulations, decrees or orders for the purpose of implementation or in preparation of implementation of the Kyoto Protocol." The language made clear it was intended to bar actions "called for solely under the Kyoto Protocol," thereby allowing EPA to carry out activities already authorized in other laws.

There was also controversy over flammability standards for children's sleepwear. The House-passed bill included language prohibiting the Consumer Product Safety Commission from implementing less stringent flammability standards it adopted in 1996, requiring instead that prior standards be reimposed. Conferees agreed instead to require the safety commission to reconsider its 1996 decision, and to have the General Accounting Office study whether more children have been injured or killed in fires since the new standards took effect.

The final agreement did not include controversial House language to prohibit federal funds from being used to implement a San Francisco ordinance that would have required parties doing business with the city to provide health care benefits to the unmarried domestic partners of their employees. That language had been added to the bill through an amendment by Rep. Frank Riggs, R-Calif., that was adopted, 214-212, after a heated House debate.

The final agreement included $24.3 billion for HUD programs and activities, a 14 percent increase over fiscal 1998; $1.5 billion for superfund hazardous waste cleanups, $650 million less than requested by the president; $3.7 billion for National Science Foundation activities, a 7 percent increase; $2.3 billion for NASA's international space station project, as requested; and $426 million for the president's AmeriCorps national service program, equal to prior year funding.

The House bill had included no funds for the AmeriCorps program, a perennial target of House GOP conservatives.

Conservatives Use Bill To Critique Kyoto Treaty

JUNE 13 — Conservative Republicans have long argued that the Kyoto Treaty, a plan to reduce greenhouse gas emissions and combat global warming, would hurt the U.S. economy. And they are hoping to use the fiscal 1999 spending bill (S 2168) for veterans, housing, environment and space programs to make their point.

Appropriations

When the Senate Appropriations Committee approved the $93.3 billion bill, 27-0, on June 11, it adopted by voice vote a proposal by Larry E. Craig, R-Idaho, to require the Environmental Protection Agency (EPA) to provide Congress with detailed plans on how it would implement the treaty, which must be ratified by 1999. A similar provision is likely to be included in a House bill expected to begin moving the week of June 15.

The Clinton administration and the leaders of 167 other countries endorsed the treaty on global warming in December 1997 in Kyoto, Japan. The agreement would require the United States to reduce greenhouse gas emissions by 7 percent below 1990 levels no later than 2012.

The treaty has been actively opposed by conservative Republicans since its inception. Many question whether global warming is actually occurring and say the treaty could cost as many as 3.2 million U.S. jobs because some industries would nearly be eliminated while others would scale back to meet the cost of complying with new regulations.

The amendment did not prompt controversy during the committee markup, but it may raise objections from the Clinton administration and could prompt debate on the Senate floor.

In addition to Craig's proposal, other members signaled that they are likely to bring up other contentious amendments.

Among them: An attempt by Democrat Herb Kohl of Wisconsin and other members to remove a provision that would allow the Federal Housing Administration (FHA) to insure mortgages worth as much as $197,000, and a perennial effort by Democrat Dale Bumpers of Arkansas to kill the International Space Station.

Both will likely provoke lengthy debate and could disrupt the consensus measure that Bond and Barbara A. Mikulski, D-Md., have attempted to put together on the bill, which funds the departments of Veterans Affairs (VA) and Housing and Urban Development (HUD) and independent agencies. Bond is chairman of the VA-HUD Appropriations Subcommittee, and Mikulski is the ranking Democrat.

Bond warned that the FHA provision would prompt attacks from a bipartisan group, not just Kohl, the only one to speak against it in full committee.

"They'll have significantly more firepower when they come to the floor," Bond said. In addition, Bumpers' attempt to kill the space station may draw more attention than usual because it will be the retiring Democrat's swan song on the issue.

Nevertheless, Bond and Mikulski shepherded their measure through the full committee and the subcommittee, which approved it June 9 by voice vote, with little controversy.

And they appear to have sidestepped one controversy. A spokesman for Craig said he is unlikely to offer a plan to require the EPA to receive authorization from local officials before expanding the Bunker Hill Superfund site in Idaho, an amendment that would have prompted a vociferous floor debate.

House Prospects

Similar issues are expected to surface when the House Appropriations Committee moves its version of the bill. The VA-HUD Subcommittee is expected to mark up its measure June 18, with the full committee likely to take it up June 25. The bill is expected on the House floor after the July Fourth recess.

The House measure is less likely than the Senate's to seek an increase in FHA loan limits and as likely to include strong language against the Kyoto Treaty. Subcommittee leaders and staff are still determining how much spending they will set aside for veterans' health care programs.

Their task is made somewhat easier than the Senate's because the House subcommittee has been given $71 billion in discretionary budget authority, compared with the Senate's $70 billion. Both would appropriate $23 billion in mandatory spending for veterans' programs.

Senate Markups

As is customary, the measure drew little heat in the Senate markups. Bond and Mikulski had worked with other members to avoid problems.

The measure that emerged included a $42.5 billion VA budget, $373 million more than the administration requested and $1.55 billion more than it received in fiscal 1998. Though mandatory spending on veterans' benefits would take up the lion's share — $1.37 billion — of that increase, the Veterans Health Administration would get $215.7 million more than in fiscal 1998 and $232 million more than the administration requested.

Mikulski said the extra funding aimed to appease veterans angry that Congress cut medical benefits for smoking-related illnesses not related to military service as a way to pay for the transportation bill (HR 2400 — PL 105-178). She said she hoped the provision would "go a ways in ensuring the quality of health care to veterans and laying to rest that they were short-changed."

It also would appropriate $25.5 billion for HUD, with $1.4 billion of it paid for by cuts to the Section 8 subsidized housing program's fiscal 1998 budget, made in the midyear supplemental spending measure (HR 3579 — PL 105-174).

In addition, the bill would increase the FHA loan limit. Currently, the FHA can ensure mortgages worth $86,000 in most areas and $170,000 in high-cost areas. The bill would increase the limits to $109,000 and $197,000 respectively. The administration had wanted to raise the limits to $227,150, but Bond and Mikulski said they believed that would expand the FHA's authority too broadly.

About $676 million would go to the Section 202 housing program for the elderly. The Clinton administration had proposed cutting the program to $100 million to pay for a new housing voucher initiative for people moving from welfare to work. The bill would set up a $40 million voucher pilot program in eight cities and counties.

The bill would provide $7.4 billion for the EPA, slightly more than in fiscal 1998, and $381 million less than the administration requested. Funding for the superfund program would remain at $1.4 billion. The administration had requested $600 million more.

The bill also would provide $13.6 billion for NASA, including $2.3 billion for the space station. It would create a separate account for the space station so members could more easily track its funding.

Bid To Raise Mortgage Limit Proves Tricky For House Panel

JUNE 20 — The Federal Housing Administration, which has critics on both the left and the right but enthusiastic fans in the middle, is poised to become a major sticking point for the fiscal 1999 spending bill for veterans, housing, space and science programs.

A proposal to raise the FHA home mortgage limit slowed progress June 18 as a House Appropriations subcommittee approved by voice vote its unnumbered $94.2 billion bill for the departments of Veterans Affairs (VA) and Housing and Urban Development (HUD) and independent agencies. The proposed amendment would allow the FHA to insure home mortgages worth as much as $109,000 in most areas and $197,000 in high-cost areas. Its current limits are $86,000 and $170,000, respectively.

Panel Chairman Jerry Lewis, R-Calif., appealed to the amendment's sponsors — Rodney Frelinghuysen, R-N.J., and Mark W. Neumann, R-Wis. — to withhold consideration of the plan until the full committee meets June 25. The two reluctantly agreed, in part to allow GOP leaders time to develop a strategy on the issue.

But it is clear the amendment — which is already in a version of the bill (S 2168) that the Senate Appropriations Committee approved June 11 — will not go away.

Increasing the limits would allow more people to buy homes with a lower down payment through FHA programs, which guarantee the mortgage payment. That would increase the amount of money the FHA brings in by about $80 million in fiscal 1999 and $400 million over the next five years, according to Neumann. But the FHA has a higher default rate than most private lenders; critics say that has created urban blight in cities such as Chicago.

Appropriators appear ready to allow the increase, but authorizers disagree on it. House Banking and Financial Services Committee Chairman Jim Leach, R-Iowa, opposes the increase, while Senate Banking, Housing and Urban Affairs Committee Chairman Alfonse M. D'Amato, R-N.Y., supports it.

And the chairmen of the two panels' housing subcommittees, Rep. Rick A. Lazio, R-N.Y., and Sen. Connie Mack, R-Fla., hope to use the issue as leverage to negotiate on their languishing public housing overhaul bills (HR 2, S 462) with HUD Secretary Andrew M. Cuomo. Cuomo and the Clinton administration want to increase the FHA limit to $227,150 – which most lawmakers who support raising the limit say is too high.

Appropriators' discussions about the limit appeared to have spurred Lazio and Mack into action, nonetheless, as their staffs met with those of congressional Democrats and the administration June 19 to work out differences on their housing measures. The House and Senate passed the legislation in 1997, but it has been stalled ever since in informal House-Senate negotiations.

Members have not yet met, but staff aides have been told authorizers will try to complete their work in time to add the overhaul to the VA-HUD spending bill before it goes to a House-Senate conference, probably in July.

Helping Whom?

At the subcommittee markup, Frelinghuysen and Neumann argued that the FHA limits needed to be increased to keep pace with inflated housing costs and to help more people buy homes. Neumann, who worked in real estate before coming to Congress, said he had observed the value of FHA programs and did not regard the amendment as a "gross expansion of a government program."

But Majority Whip Tom DeLay, R-Texas, challenged Neumann's assertion, saying the amendment was "expanding the role of the federal government into a sector where the private market's thriving."

DeLay was joined in opposition by unusual allies. Democrat Carrie P. Meek of Florida argued that raising the limit would detract from the FHA's mission of helping low-income people. And Marcy Kaptur, D-Ohio, opposed the plan because she said the FHA had a poor management record and a large number of defaults on mortgages. "I don't think the way you get them out of the box is to raise their loan limit," she said.

Another Frelinghuysen amendment proposed to place a moratorium on a VA pharmaceutical list, known as a formulary, that tells VA hospital doctors what drugs they can prescribe for their patients. Frelinghuysen said the drugs generally are limited to one brand-name and one generic drug per illness, even though some veterans might benefit from a different medication. Frelinghuysen said the issue was particularly important for those with mental illnesses. But Lewis read a VA statement that said the formulary had helped reduce medical care costs by $340 million this year and was not a list set in stone.

Frelinghuysen withdrew the amendment after many members said they did not know enough about the issue, but he is likely to bring it up again at the full committee markup.

Neumann and DeLay offered other contentious amendments that were withdrawn until full committee. Neumann's proposal would specify that certain fees charged by mortgage brokersnder the 1974 Real Estate Settlement Procedures Act (PL 93-533) are legal. The fees are currently the subject of dozens of lawsuits. DeLay's amendment would prevent funding of the Triana, a NASA satellite designed to transfer its photos of the Earth directly to the Internet. Vice President Al Gore has expressed support for the satellite.

Funding Levels

The bill would provide $70.9 billion in discretionary spending plus $23.3 billion in mandatory spending on veterans benefits, about $3.5 billion more than fiscal 1998 levels. In a controversial move, it would not fund AmeriCorps, the president's national service program.

The measure includes:
- $19 billion for discretionary veterans programs, $168 million more than President Clinton requested and $66 million more than the programs received in fiscal 1998.
- $26.6 billion for HUD, including $10.2 billion to renew expiring Section 8 subsidized housing contracts. The total is $1.7 billion more than the administration requested and $5.1 billion more than in fiscal 1998.

Appropriations

- $7.4 billion for the Environmental Protection Agency, $59 million more than in fiscal 1998 but $367 million less than the administration requested. The superfund cleanup program would receive $1.5 billion, the same as in fiscal 1998 and $650 million less than Clinton sought. The bill also would prohibit the EPA from creating new programs to implement the Kyoto climate change treaty.
- $13.3 billion for NASA, $137 million less than the administration requested and $373 million less than in fiscal 1998.

Battles Over Treaty May Delay House Action

JUNE 27 — Several Democrats share most Republicans' opposition to the Kyoto climate control treaty, a plan to reduce greenhouse gas emissions and combat global warming.

But when the House Appropriations Committee approved an unnumbered fiscal 1999 spending measure June 25 for veterans, housing, space and science programs, Democratic leaders signaled that they believed the GOP had gone too far in its efforts to tie the White House's hands on issues relating to the agreement.

The spending bill, approved by voice vote, included a provision that might prevent the Environmental Protection Agency (EPA) and the administration not only from issuing regulations on any topic related to the treaty but also from discussing the subject in public.

The provision, crafted by Republican Joe Knollenberg of Michigan, would ensure that no funds appropriated by the bill could be used to "develop, propose or issue rules, regulations, decrees or orders for the purpose of implementation, or in contemplation of implementation of the Kyoto Protocol."

The bill's committee report also included language directing the EPA to "refrain from conducting educational outreach or informational seminars on policies underlying the Kyoto Protocol."

The treaty, endorsed by the United States and 167 other countries in December 1997 in Kyoto, Japan, must be ratified by 1999.

Vic Fazio, D-Calif., charged that the language Knollenberg had written was "in effect a gag rule on those people who differ from him," and Fazio offered an amendment to strike portions of the language. It was defeated 18-27 in a mostly party-line vote, with Democrats Robert E. "Bud" Cramer of Alabama, Alan B. Mollohan of West Virginia and Peter J. Visclosky of Indiana voting against it and Republican John Edward Porter of Illinois voting for it.

Committee Chairman Robert L. Livingston, R-La., and Majority Whip Tom DeLay, R-Texas, defended the provision.

Livingston said he was "concerned that the administration is attempting to achieve through the backdoor that which they can't get through the front door."

The Senate is not expected to ratify the treaty, though such action would be necessary by 1999 for the United States to become a signatory to it. In a 95-0 vote in July 1997, the Senate passed a non-binding resolution (S Res 98) that demanded any agreement on climate change include restrictions on developing nations and that the United States sign no treaties that would hurt its economy.

The treaty would require the United States to reduce greenhouse gas emissions by 7 percent below 1990 levels no later than 2012.

While many Democrats and some Republicans support the attempt to address the reported effects of global warming, others fear the treaty would hurt some parts of the U.S. economy. And some question the existence of global warming altogether.

The issue is expected to surface again when the measure comes to the House floor, possibly July 15, and in a House-Senate conference committee to work out differences between the two chambers' bills. The Senate bill (S 2168) includes a less stringent provision that would require the EPA to provide detailed plans of any attempt to implement the treaty. In addition, the unnumbered spending bill for the Interior Department also includes language to prevent treaty implementation.

Mortgage Lending Increase

Committee members adopted by voice vote with little opposition a housing proposal that was expected to generate controversy.

The amendment, by Rodney Frelinghuysen, R-N.J., and Mark W. Neumann, R-Wis., would increase the value of home mortgages that the Federal Housing Administration (FHA) could insure from $86,317 to $109,032 in most areas and from $170,362 to $197,620 in high-cost areas.

Though some members had expressed opposition to the proposal when the Appropriations Subcommittee for the departments of Veterans Affairs (VA) and Housing and Urban Development (HUD) took up the bill June 18, most members who spoke at the full committee markup supported the proposal or wanted the loan limits further increased.

Most members agreed with Frelinghuysen that "the bottom line is that this proposal would add 85,000 new home buyers over the next five years."

Several Democrats said they would like the limits increased to the Clinton administration's across-the-board proposal of $227,150, because housing costs in their region were escalating.

But other members urged caution.

Martin Olav Sabo, D-Minn., said he did not think a larger increase was warranted for the FHA, which he said was not "this model of efficiency."

And Livingston said he remained "concerned about the extent to which the FHA crowds out the private market."

FHA critics say that poor administration has caused blight in many of the minority and low-income neighborhoods that the FHA aims to help.

Others suggest that private mortgage insurance companies, which came into existence about 20 years after the FHA was created in 1934, and government-sponsored enterprises such as Fannie Mae and Freddie Mac can more efficiently generate homeownership.

But Bill Apgar, recently appointed HUD assistant secretary and FHA commissioner, said the FHA often takes chances on inner-city neighborhoods from which private and government-sponsored lenders shy away, at least initially. "As people begin to look at our loan experience, they realize that there are markets to be had," he said.

Other Provisions

The spending bill would appropriate $71.3 billion in discretionary spending to the VA, HUD and 17 independent agencies, including the EPA, NASA and the National Science Foundation.

It would provide $22.3 billion in mandatory spending for veterans benefits.

The measure would appropriate $3.5 billion more than in fiscal 1998, with HUD the big winner. It would receive $26.6 billion, $5.1 billion more than in fiscal 1998. Much of the increase, though, will go to meet the continuing costs of renewing contracts with private landlords who provide so-called Section 8 federally subsidized housing for those with low incomes.

Among the losers is AmeriCorps, President Clinton's national service program, which would receive no funding under the bill. It received $425.5 million in fiscal 1998. The Senate measure would appropriate that amount again in fiscal 1999, and House Appropriations Committee leaders have said they expect the bill to be enacted with some funding for the program.

Surprise Senate Rider Leaves Bill in Limbo

JULY 11 — During a lull in Senate debate on a spending bill July 7, Minority Leader Tom Daschle, D-S.D., caught colleagues by surprise: He introduced the Democrats' managed care plan as an amendment to the appropriations bill (S 2168) for the departments of Veterans Affairs (VA) and Housing and Urban Development (HUD) and 17 independent agencies.

Democrats had been looking for a legislative vehicle for the health plan (S 1890), but Daschle's move to attach it to a must-pass spending bill seemed to catch nearly everyone off guard — including Edward M. Kennedy, D-Mass., a top sponsor of S 1890, who took to the floor to defend the plan, and Majority Leader Trent Lott, R-Miss., who quickly pulled S 2168 from consideration.

Daschle said his move was necessary because Republicans would not agree to an open debate on health care. Lott's staff said the majority leader had made two offers to bring Kennedy's health care measure to the floor, though not in the way Democrats wanted. Their bill would give consumers more power to fight their health plans' coverage decisions and seek legal recourse over disputes.

Lott, displeased with Daschle's action, quickly moved on to the conference report on a bill (HR 2676) to overhaul the Internal Revenue Service.

"This appropriations bill has been sent to limbo for all intents and purposes," said a Lott staff member.

Left in the lurch were Sens. Christopher S. Bond, R-Mo., and Barbara A. Mikulski, D-Md., and their staffs, who had worked diligently the week of July 6 to iron out most members' concerns about the $93.3 billion spending bill and to ensure that lengthy debate would occur on only two amendments — one to kill the international space station and the other to scale back the bill's proposed increase in Federal Housing Administration (FHA) loan limits. Bond chairs the Senate's VA-HUD Appropriations Subcommittee and Mikulski is the ranking Democrat.

Despite their disappointment at the setback, staff members said they were confident that the pressing need to pass appropriations bills would prompt Lott and Daschle to reach an agreement soon to move S 2168 and other spending measures.

The House plans to bring its VA-HUD measure (HR 4194) to the floor July 15.

Before Daschle introduced the health care amendment, the Senate accepted by voice vote two non-controversial amendments from Bond and Mikulski, and defeated a bid to kill the space station, 33-66. (*Vote 185, p. S-30*)

One amendment would add $8 million to the $9.8 million already in the bill for anti-terrorism initiatives at the Federal Emergency Management Agency. The other would require the Environmental Protection Agency to establish different policies for dealing with animal or vegetable oil spills than for those involving petroleum.

Senate Moves Swiftly; House Gets Caught Up In Housing Debate

JULY 18 — Long-simmering disputes between top Republican housing authorizers and appropriators boiled over the week of July 13 as the House and Senate considered $93.3 billion measures to fund fiscal 1999 housing, veterans, space and science programs.

In the House, appropriators fumed as authorizers successfully attached a voluminous public housing overhaul bill (HR 2) to the spending measure (HR 4194). Appropriators believed inclusion of the languishing and controversial housing legislation would delay enactment of their spending bill.

Meanwhile, Connie Mack, R-Fla., chairman of the Senate Banking Subcommittee on Housing, figured prominently in an unsuccessful effort to scale back a proposal in the Senate bill (S 2168) that would allow the Federal Housing Administration (FHA) to insure mortgages on higher-cost homes. The Senate tabled (killed) the effort July 17. It then passed the spending measure by voice vote.

Both the House and Senate housing efforts resulted from differences, and often a lack of consultation, between authorizers, who set policy, and appropriators, who set funding levels. Though the Senate issue was addressed far more politely, it was clear in both chambers that the crux of the problem was authorizers' inability, after three years of debate, to shepherd a major overhaul of public housing to enactment.

Congress has not reauthorized the Department of Housing and Urban Development (HUD) since 1992, and year after year, appropriators have included in their bills changes to housing programs — policy decisions that are supposed to be left to authorizers.

Since Republicans took control of Congress in 1995, authorizers have attempted to enact a major overhaul of public housing programs, generally aiming to give block grants and more programming leeway to the local officials who run public housing projects.

Appropriations

The House and the Senate passed overhaul bills in 1996 and again in 1997.

But in both cases the House bill has taken a more aggressive stance in seeking to bring the working poor into public housing and in making other changes. Mack and his House counterpart, Housing Subcommittee Chairman Rick A. Lazio, R-N.Y., have never achieved a compromise.

Both have decried what they say is the Clinton administration's lack of interest in working with them to craft a final bill.

With both spending bills including a provision the administration dearly wants — an increase in FHA mortgage loan limits — Lazio and House Banking and Financial Services Committee Chairman Jim Leach, R-Iowa, believed the best chance for enacting their housing measure would be to attach it to a must-pass bill with a provision the administration and HUD Secretary Andrew M. Cuomo could not ignore.

But that effort did not sit well with leaders of the Appropriations Subcommittee for the departments of Veterans Affairs (VA) and HUD. The panel's ranking Democrat, the generally soft-spoken Louis Stokes of Ohio, charged that "virtually every significant housing legislation provision passed during the last three-and-a-half years" has been in an appropriations bill. The Banking Committee has "not been able to do their job," Stokes said. "This year, they seem to be admitting defeat earlier than usual."

Democrats in general opposed attaching the housing overhaul bill, although more than one-third of them had voted for it in May 1997.

In addition, many members opposed the rule (H Res 501) structuring debate on the VA-HUD measure because it would have left the provision increasing the FHA's loan limits subject to a motion to strike it for violating House rules against legislating on a spending bill. After it became clear July 16 that enough members opposed the rule because of housing matters and other issues, House leaders took the unusual step of amending the rule on the floor to protect the FHA loan limits. The rule subsequently passed, 227-195. *(Vote 285, p. H-82)*

The House then began consideration of the VA-HUD measure, but did not finish before adjourning July 17 for the week. The chamber is expected to continue debate July 21.

The Senate resumed consideration of its bill late July 16 and passed the measure the next morning. Action became possible when Minority Leader Tom Daschle, D-S.D., withdrew an amendment that would have attached the Democrats' controversial health care plan (S 1890) to the bill. Daschle had offered it July 7, prompting Majority Leader Trent Lott, R-Miss., to pull the bill from the floor.

On July 16, Daschle said he believed "the prospects are greater than they've been in some time" to reach a separate agreement on health care legislation and he withdrew the amendment, enabling the Senate to quickly move the VA-HUD measure.

Senate Consideration

The Senate spent most of its time debating the amendment pushed by Mack and sponsored by Majority Whip Don Nickles, R-Okla., to scale back a provision that would increase the worth of mortgages the FHA could insure.

The FHA has helped more than 24 million Americans purchase homes since its inception in 1934. It stimulates mortgage lending by guaranteeing loans for those who cannot afford to make the once-customary 20 percent down payment. It charges borrowers fees for that service, then uses those fees — and the proceeds from the resale of foreclosed properties — to insure mortgages. If the fund should run dry, however, the federal Treasury would be responsible for meeting its obligations.

Cuomo has strongly supported increasing the FHA loan limits, saying it will further stimulate home ownership, especially for minorities and others who may not be well served by private lenders. He proposed a $227,150 across-the-country limit, instead of numerous existing limits.

The Senate agreed to increase the limits, but not to the level the administration wanted. The bill would increase the limits from $86,317 to $109,032 in most areas, and from $170,362 to $197,620 in high-cost areas such as parts of New York and California. The House bill was amended by the Appropriations Committee to include the same provision.

But Nickles, Mack, Herb Kohl, D-Wis., and others said the increase, particularly for high-cost areas, was unnecessary and would move the program away from its mission of fostering home ownership for those with low and moderate incomes. Their amendment would have removed the increase for high-cost areas, leaving the FHA loan limits at $170,362 in cities such as Seattle, New York and Los Angeles. It also would have attempted to dissuade private lenders from steering potential homeowners into the FHA program by reducing by 12 basis points (.12 percent) the fees they receive when selling an FHA-guaranteed mortgage to the Government National Mortgage Association (Ginnie Mae).

Nickles said the high-income limit was not needed because "you have to have a pretty good income to be able to afford a $200,000 mortgage" and such buyers could obtain mortgages privately.

Mack argued that the provision should not stand because his Housing Subcommittee had chronicled many cases of mismanagement in the FHA program, information he said appropriators had not taken to heart.

"I am concerned that the Appropriations Committee did not consider the views of the authorizing committee," he said.

But ranking Banking Committee Democrat Paul S. Sarbanes of Maryland said that high housing costs in many areas keep firefighters, teachers and others from buying a home in the communities where they work. And VA-HUD Subcommittee Chairman Republican Christopher S. Bond of Missouri said that "many families would be unable to purchase their homes without the benefit of FHA mortgage insurance."

The Senate voted 69-27 to table (kill) the amendment. *(Vote 211, p. S-34)*

Senators also voted July 17 to table an amendment by Jeff Sessions, R-Ala., that would have shifted funds from the AmeriCorps national service program to NASA programs. The vote was 58-37. *(Vote 212, p. S-34)*

An amendment by Paul Wellstone, D-Minn., to restore medical benefits to veterans affected by smoking-related illnesses was killed when it fell six votes short of the 60 needed to waive a point of order against it. Congress had voted to repeal the medical benefits to pay for a massive transportation measure (PL 105-178).

Public Housing Measure

The House spent most of its time debating the authorizers' bill to overhaul the public housing system.

Lazio and Leach had offered the public housing measure as an amendment to the spending bill to ensure it would not die in another Congress.

Though Democrats and some Republicans, including VA-HUD Subcommittee Chairman Jerry Lewis, R-Calif, charged that attaching such a massive authorizing measure to an appropriations bill made a mockery of House rules, Leach and Lazio said the action was warranted because the House had already fully debated the measure and passed it.

The bill would give local authorities block grants and greater leeway over choosing tenants and setting rents. It also aims to create a greater income mix in public housing by attracting the working poor and others able to pay more rent. The Senate's version of the measure (S 462) would retain more spots in public housing and in housing voucher programs for the very poor.

While Leach and Lazio argued that voting against attaching the amendment would be a vote against the bill, their Democratic counterparts, ranking Banking Committee Democrat John J. LaFalce of New York and ranking Housing Subcommittee Democrat Joseph P. Kennedy II of Massachusetts vociferously opposed attaching the amendment.

Both oppose the income targeting provisions in HR 2. LaFalce said the House should have officially appointed conferees to work out differences on the housing bill instead of attaching it to a spending measure. LaFalce said Leach and Lazio had refused to agree to such a conference to keep House Democrats from joining with both parties in the Senate to adopt the Senate's less strident provisions.

Kennedy charged that the move to attach the bill was simply an attempt to "jam it down the throat of the administration." In a statement, Cuomo called HR 2 "repugnant." LaFalce said President Clinton would be likely to veto the VA-HUD bill should HR 2 remain intact in it.

It is highly unlikely the bill would survive verbatim, however. Leach said GOP leaders intended to convene a "subconference" to work out differences between the two chambers' overhaul bills at the same time conferees work out differences between the VA-HUD spending bills.

The House voted 230-181 to attach HR 2 to the spending measure.

It defeated, 201-215, a Stokes amendment that would have increased by 17,200 the number of housing vouchers available to welfare recipients looking for work.

When the House returns to the bill July 21, it is expected to consider amendments to kill the international space station and to temper the bill's language opposing the Kyoto climate control treaty.

House Restricts Rulemaking On Global Warming

JULY 25 — The Kyoto Treaty on climate change took center stage when the House resumed debate July 23 on the fiscal 1999 spending measure for science, space, housing and veterans programs.

The House left intact provisions in the bill (HR 4194) that would prevent the Clinton administration from implementing the treaty through regulatory actions if the Senate does not ratify it — and the Senate is not expected to do so. Environmentalists cut short their efforts to reverse those provisions.

The treaty, which the Clinton administration and delegates from 167 other countries agreed to in Kyoto, Japan, in December 1997, would require the United States to reduce greenhouse gas emissions by 7 percent below 1990 levels no later than 2012.

The House adopted, 226-198, an amendment by David R. Obey, D-Wis., to overrule language in the bill's report that suggested the Environmental Protection Agency (EPA) and the Council on Environmental Quality refrain from conducting educational seminars or outreach programs on global warming. (Vote 332, p. H-96)

But then James C. Greenwood, R-Pa., and Henry A. Waxman, D-Calif., opted not to offer amendments to turn back a bill provision that they worry could keep the EPA from implementing current laws that might overlap with the treaty.

Greenwood and Waxman conceded that they did not have the votes to pass their amendments, and they wanted to end consideration of the Kyoto issue with the Obey amendment. Both said it is likely that the language that emerges from a House-Senate conference will differ from the House provisions. The Senate bill (S 2168) includes language on Kyoto, but it would only require that the administration provide Congress with details of any plans to implement the treaty.

Besides the Obey amendment, the House spent considerable time on an amendment to overrule several paragraphs in the bill's committee report. Those paragraphs would attempt to delay EPA action on controversial issues such as issuing regulatory standards for mercury emissions and dredging bodies of water and implementing a program designed to reduce regional haze.

Waxman, who offered the amendment after removing Kyoto language from it, said the report was "part of a steady stream of attacks" on the environment since Republicans took control of Congress in 1995.

But Jerry Lewis, R-Calif., chairman of the Appropriations Subcommittee that funds the departments of Veterans Affairs (VA), Housing and Urban Development (HUD) and independent agencies, pointed out that report language is non-binding. "Report language does little damage," Lewis said. "It's just trying to get their attention."

The House defeated the amendment, 176-243. (Vote 334, p. H-96)

The chamber also debated an amendment by Tim Roemer, D-Ind., and Dave Camp, R-Mich., to cut $1.6 billion from the bill's funding of the international space station. The amendment would leave $500 million for close-out costs. The amendment — a perennial that the House has never adopted — is expected to be defeated when the House resumes work on the $93.3 billion measure July 28.

Appropriations

Measure Goes to Conference With Side Issues In Tow

AUGUST 1 — In its first two weeks on the House floor, the fiscal 1999 spending bill for veterans, housing, and science programs was a venue for debate on a public housing overhaul and the Kyoto Treaty on climate change.

In the bill's third and final floor stint before passage the week of July 27, debate was again consumed by ancillary provisions: a San Francisco ordinance requiring companies and organizations that do business with the city to provide benefits to the "domestic partners" of unmarried workers, and proposed regulations on fireproofing furniture upholstery and children's pajamas.

The measure (HR 4194) now goes to a conference committee charged with working out differences between the House and Senate bills. Both measures would provide $93.3 billion in spending, but the money is distributed differently, and the House bill contains a major policy rider: a languishing public housing overhaul bill (HR 2) that will likely be worked out in a separate "subconference" between housing policy authorizers who have been attempting to resolve their differences for three years.

The House tacked on other provisions before voting July 29 to pass the measure, which funds the departments of Veterans Affairs (VA) and Housing and Urban Development (HUD) and 17 independent agencies. The vote was 259-164. (Vote 352, p. H-100)

The most controversial of these add-ons was an amendment by Frank Riggs, R-Calif., to prevent the city of San Francisco from applying its ordinance, known as 2(b), to contracts that involve federal funds. The ordinance, which went into effect in June 1997, requires businesses and organizations with city contracts to offer the same benefits to the domestic partners of unmarried employees, including homosexuals, as they do to married couples. At least one organization — the Salvation Army — has opted not to comply and thus will not provide services for the homeless and others when its contract expires in December.

The issue, Riggs said, was "whether we want to elevate that relationship to the same status as marriage." But Democrats and some Republicans, including VA-HUD Appropriations Subcommittee Chairman Jerry Lewis, R-Calif., said the issue was one of local autonomy.

The provision, said Rep. Nancy Pelosi, D-Calif., who represents San Francisco, would "single out one city, and I ask my colleagues, do you want your city to be singled out next?"

Though the word "gay" was rarely mentioned during debate, Dennis J. Kucinich, D-Ohio, an opponent of the Riggs amendment, said, "There's an undercurrent here that is not worthy of this Congress."

But when Bob Filner, D-Calif., suggested that the amendment was part of a Republican agenda, Lewis signaled that the party does not speak with one voice on such issues. "I would really regret it if we paint an issue like this in partisan terms," he said.

Although few members spoke in favor of the Riggs amendment, it passed 214-212, with 33 Republicans voting against it and 25 Democrats voting for it. (Vote 349, p. H-100)

The House also passed, 231-200, an amendment by Van Hilleary, R-Tenn., to take a $21 million increase for the Housing Opportunities for Persons with AIDS program and transfer it to veterans' medical care. (Vote 347, p. H-98)

Another major topic of debate involved two provisions on flammability standards for upholstery and children's sleepwear.

At the request of Roger Wicker, R-Miss., the bill contained a provision to prevent the Consumer Product Safety Commission from promulgating rules that would lead to increased chemical treatment of upholstery fabrics. Democrats attempted to remove the provision through a motion to send the bill back to committee, which failed, 164-261. (Vote 351, p. H-100)

And after heated debate, the House approved by voice vote an amendment by Rosa DeLauro, D-Conn., that would prevent the commission from spending any funds appropriated by the bill to implement a 1996 regulation that loosened rules requiring children's pajamas size 14 and smaller to be treated to extinguish any small fire to which they were exposed.

The bill originally had required that the commission propose new rules no later than 90 days after bill enactment, but the provision was removed by Henry Bonilla, R-Texas, who objected to including legislative language on an appropriations bill, which is against House rules.

In other action, the House:

- Defeated, 109-323, an amendment by Tim Roemer, D-Ind., and Dave Camp, R-Mich., to cut $1.6 billion from the NASA budget and terminate the international space station. (Vote 345, p. H-98)

- Defeated, 146-285, an amendment by Maurice D. Hinchey, D-N.Y., to prohibit the VA from spending funds to implement a plan that would shift funding from VA hospitals in states with dwindling populations of veterans to those where the numbers are growing, such as Florida and Arizona. (Vote 346, p. H-98)

- Approved, 351-73, an amendment by Tom Coburn, R-Okla., to transfer $304 million from the Federal Housing Administration to veterans' medical programs. (Vote 350, p. H-100)

Conferees Send Compromise To House Floor

OCTOBER 3 — Determined to retain control of their bill and keep it out of a looming catchall spending package, House and Senate conferees for the fiscal 1999 appropriations measure for veterans, housing and science programs put aside numerous disputes Oct. 1 and approved a compromise $93.9 billion bill.

The conference report on the measure (HR 4194), which funds the departments of Veterans Affairs (VA), Housing and Urban Development (HUD) and independent agencies, is expected to come to the House floor the week of Oct. 5. [The Senate adopted the conference report by voice vote Oct. 7; the House cleared the bill Oct. 9 by a vote of 422-1.] (Vote 483, p. H-138)

Attached to it will be another work of compromise — a bill to overhaul the nation's public housing system. In separate negotiations, top Republicans

VA-HUD-Independent Agencies Spending

Conference agreement on HR 4194 — H Rept 105-769 adopted by the House on Oct. 6, cleared by the Senate on Oct. 8, and signed by the president Oct. 21. (*Budget authority, in thousands of dollars.*)

	Fiscal 1998 Appropriation	Fiscal 1999 Clinton Request	House Bill	Senate Bill	Conference Report
Veterans Affairs					
Veterans benefits	$ 22,228,312	$ 23,502,393	$ 23,502,393	$ 23,502,393	$ 23,502,393
Compensation and pensions	*20,482,997*	*21,857,058*	*21,857,058*	*21,857,058*	*21,857,058*
Veterans Health Administration	17,404,256	17,387,975	17,741,396	17,620,000	17,685,000
Construction projects	352,900	238,000	318,000	317,300	317,300
Other	991,331	1,021,369	1,091,369	1,082,667	1,083,667
TOTAL, Veterans Affairs	**$ 40,976,799**	**$ 42,149,737**	**$ 42,653,158**	**$ 42,522,360**	**$ 42,588,360**
Housing and Urban Development					
HOME program	1,500,000	1,883,000	1,600,000	1,550,000	1,600,000
Public housing capital fund	2,500,000	2,550,000	3,000,000	2,550,000	3,000,000
Public housing operating fund	2,900,000	2,818,000	2,818,000	2,818,000	2,818,000
Section 8 subsidized housing	9,373,000	8,981,188	10,240,542	10,013,542	10,326,542
Severely distressed public housing	550,000	550,000	600,000	600,000	625,000
Indian housing block grants	600,000	600,000	620,000	600,000	620,000
Federal Housing Administration	201,305	271,343	−32,657	−32,657	−32,657
Limitation on guaranteed loans	*127,400,000*	*128,100,000*	*128,100,000*	*128,100,000*	*128,100,000*
Ginnie Mae (receipts)	−204,000	−370,000	−370,000	−370,000	−370,000
Limitation on guaranteed loans	*130,000,000*	*150,000,000*	*150,000,000*	*150,000,000*	*150,000,000*
Homeless assistance	823,000	1,150,000	975,000	1,000,000	975,000
Community development grants	4,805,000	4,725,000	4,725,000	4,750,000	4,750,000
Rescissions, other	−1,603,740	1,656,733	1,969,293	615,233	30,293
TOTAL, HUD	**$ 21,444,565**	**$ 24,815,264**	**$ 26,145,178**	**$ 24,094,118**	**$ 24,342,178**
NASA					
Human space flight	5,506,500	5,511,000	5,309,000	—	5,480,000
Science, aeronautics and technology	5,690,000	5,457,400	5,541,600	—	5,653,900
International space station	—	—	—	2,300,000	—
Launch vehicles	—	—	—	3,241,000	—
Science and technology	—	—	—	4,257,400	—
Aeronautics and space transportation	—	—	—	1,305,000	—
Mission support, other	2,451,500	2,496,600	2,477,600	2,511,600	2,531,100
TOTAL, NASA	**$ 13,648,000**	**$ 13,465,000**	**$ 13,328,200**	**$ 13,615,000**	**$ 13,665,000**
Environmental Protection Agency					
Superfund	1,453,359	2,040,307	1,447,763	1,447,563	1,447,763
State and tribal assistance grants	3,213,125	2,902,657	3,233,132	3,255,000	3,386,750
Other	2,696,562	2,847,311	2,741,844	2,710,499	2,725,839
TOTAL, EPA	**$ 7,363,046**	**$ 7,790,275**	**$ 7,422,739**	**$ 7,413,062**	**$ 7,560,352**
Selected Independent Agencies					
Community Devel. Financial Institutions	80,000	125,000	80,000	55,000	80,000
Federal Emergency Management Agency	829,958	843,582	817,282	1,362,195	826,902
Disaster relief	*320,000*	*307,745*	*307,745*	*846,000*	*307,745*
Food and shelter program	*100,000*	*100,000*	*100,000*	*100,000*	*100,000*
National Science Foundation	3,429,000	3,773,000	3,626,700	3,644,150	3,671,200
Research	*2,545,700*	*2,846,800*	*2,745,000*	*2,725,000*	*2,770,000*
Education	*632,500*	*683,000*	*642,500*	*683,000*	*662,000*
Consumer Product Safety Commission	45,000	46,500	46,000	46,500	47,000
Selective Service System	23,413	24,940	24,176	24,940	24,176
Corporation for National Service	428,500	502,316	—	428,500	428,500
GRAND TOTAL	**$ 88,392,163**	**$ 93,688,871**	**$ 94,375,545**	**$ 93,331,942**	**$ 93,390,780**

SOURCE: House Appropriations Committee

Appropriations

and Democrats from both chambers' Banking panels on housing reached agreement with HUD on a bill (HR 2) that would transfer most operational decisions to local authorities, who would receive their federal money in block grants.

Though the chairmen of the House and Senate VA-HUD Appropriations subcommittees had initially opposed including the voluminous housing measure in their bill, it became clear that attaching it to the spending bill was the only way to ensure the housing measure's passage. "We do not want to lose this whole bill," said House VA-HUD Appropriations Subcommittee Chairman Jerry Lewis, R-Calif.

The panel agreed to attach the housing compromise — without ever seeing it — after granting Lewis, his Senate counterpart Christopher S. Bond, R-Mo., and both panel's ranking Democrats — Rep. Louis Stokes of Ohio and Sen. Barbara A. Mikulski of Maryland — the power to make technical changes after examining it.

Though the conference committee avoided a lengthy discussion on public housing by transferring powers to the four panel leaders, it did not escape cumbersome and circular debates on two other contentious issues.

The biggest obstacle to the bill's passage involved an effort to prevent the Environmental Protection Agency (EPA) from attempting to implement the Kyoto Treaty, a climate control agreement the Clinton administration endorsed in December 1997.

After intense negotiations over the meaning of words such as "solely" and "develop," the chief proponent of the more encompassing House language — Joe Knollenberg, R-Mich. — gave in to the more specific language proposed by Senate Appropriations Committee ranking Democrat Robert C. Byrd of West Virginia. Byrd, a well-known wordsmith, convinced Knollenberg with this final parry: "As Mark Twain said, the difference between the right word and the almost right word is the difference between the lightning and the lightning bug."

The language, adopted by conferees by voice vote, would prohibit the use of funds to "propose or issue rules, regulations, decrees or orders for the purpose of implementation or in preparation of implementation of the Kyoto Protocol." Report language explains that the bill aims to prevent the administration from implementing actions "called for solely under the Kyoto Protocol," allowing the EPA to carry out actions already authorized in other laws.

The panel also held an hourlong discussion on flammability standards for children's pajamas, a debate that returned time and again to what members, or their wives, looked for when shopping for children's clothing. The argument stemmed from a 1996 decision by the Consumer Product Safety Commission to revoke a 20-year-old requirement that children's pajamas be flame resistant.

House Democrats and some Republicans argued that Congress should overturn the decision, but Bond and Mikulski said the conference committee was not in a better position to judge the risk to children than the safety commission. To split their differences, the panel adopted by voice vote language that would require the commission to reconsider its decision and the General Accounting Office to study whether more children have been injured or killed in fires since the new standards took effect.

Other Issues

Though panel members reached agreement, ranking House Appropriations Committee Democrat David R. Obey of Wisconsin told the panel that the White House had concerns with at least seven items in the bill.

Most involved funding for programs near to President Clinton's heart, such as the AmeriCorps national service program, or environmental issues, such as superfund waste cleanup.

But Lewis and Bond said they had increased funding for most of the programs on the White House list and hoped that would satisfy the administration. For instance, AmeriCorps would receive $428.5 million under the conference agreement, up from the House's appropriation of zero and the Senate's $425.5 million.

The administration is less likely to be happy with funding for superfund. The conference appropriated $1.5 billion, the same as in fiscal 1998, and $650 million of it would not be available unless the controversial program is reauthorized.

The measure that emerged from the conference committee includes:

• $17.3 billion for veterans' medical care, $29.6 million more than the administration requested.

• $23.5 billion in mandatory spending for veterans' benefits.

• $24.3 billion for HUD, $283 million of which will go to provide 50,000 new housing vouchers, a concession to HUD Secretary Andrew M. Cuomo. The vouchers go to low-income people to subsidize rent in private apartments.

• Senate language that would increase the value of homes that could be insured through the Federal Housing Administration (FHA) from $86,317 to $109,032 in most areas, and from $170,362 to $197,620 in high-cost areas.

• Language added in conference that would require HUD within 90 days to clarify its position on fees charged by mortgage brokers. The amendment, by Rep. Mark W. Neumann, R-Wis., was accepted by voice vote.

• $80 million for Community Development Financial Institutions, which provide grants to local financial institutions that make loans in poor areas.

• $13.7 billion for NASA and a change in policy that would allow the agency to contract with Russian entities other than the government to complete the international space station.

• $7.56 billion for the EPA, including $1.35 billion for Clean Water Act programs.

• $2.77 billion for the National Science Foundation.

The conference did not include in the final measure controversial House language that would have prevented the city of San Francisco from applying its "domestic partners" ordinance when awarding city contracts involving federal funds.

The ordinance, known as 2(b), requires businesses and organizations with city contracts to offer the same benefits to the domestic partners of unmarried employees, including homosexuals, as they do to married couples. The language, sponsored by Frank Riggs, R-Calif., had been added to the bill on the House floor in a 214-212 vote.

The deal on a public housing measure came quietly Oct. 1 as the sponsor of the House measure — Rick A. Lazio, R-N.Y. — and the Senate measure — Connie Mack, R-Fla. — worked out a deal with HUD behind closed doors.

For three years, Lazio and Mack had been meeting to attempt to bridge their differences on overhauling public housing. Both agreed that the best way to fix public housing — and save it from conservatives who wanted to dismantle it — was to loosen the federal government's grip on funding and operational decisions, but they differed on details.

The most stubborn disagreement involved a key component of both chambers' bills: how much public housing to reserve for the very poor welfare recipients who now make up the majority of tenants and how much to make available to the working poor and others with higher incomes.

Lazio and Mack both insisted that a mix of incomes in public housing would solve many problems, providing welfare recipients with working neighbors as role models and helping housing authorities make ends meet through the higher rents working tenants could pay. But Cuomo insisted that public housing be reserved for those who need it most.

Details of the compromise were not announced the week of Sept. 28 because appropriators had yet to review it, but the final income-targeting numbers are likely to be more like those in the Senate's bill than the House's bill.

The Senate bill (S 462) would reserve at least 40 percent of public housing units for the very poor — those making less than 30 percent of an area's median income — and would require that at least 70 percent of units be filled by those making no more than 60 percent. The rest could go to those making 80 percent of the median income. The House bill would have reserved 35 percent for the very poor but the rest could have gone to those making 80 percent, or $45,300 for a family of four in most areas of the United States.

It was expected that conferees dropped a contentious House provision to repeal the 1937 Housing Act, the bedrock of public housing, and reduced to a demonstration project a plan to allow cities to claim some housing funds if their local housing authority was troubled. ◆

Appropriations

Rosy Surplus Numbers Energize Clinton, Congress To Stuff Omnibus Bill

> **Box Score**
>
> ● **Bill:** HR 4328 — PL 105-277.
> ● **House action:** The House adopted the conference report (H Rept 105-825) on HR 4328, 333-95, on Oct. 20.
> ● **Senate action:** The Senate cleared the bill, 65-29, on Oct. 21.
> ● **Presidential action:** Clinton signed the bill Oct. 21.

SUMMARY

After a yearlong confrontation between the White House and House Republicans, election year deadline pressure pushed eight of the 13 appropriations bills for the year into the fiscal 1999 omnibus appropriations bill that broke through budget caps set in 1997.

The measure incorporated the spending bills for Agriculture, Commerce-Justice-State, District of Columbia, foreign operations, Interior, Labor-HHS-Education, Transportation, and Treasury-Postal Service.

The bill also served as a legislative locomotive that pulled many other bills, big and small, into law.

The approximately $500 billion measure cleared after more than a week of negotiations between top GOP and White House officials, led by soon-to-retire Chief of Staff Erskine Bowles. Despite President Clinton's perceived weakness because of the pending impeachment inquiry, the administration extracted numerous spending concessions, ultimately getting more in discretionary spending than he had requested in his February budget submission.

Republicans, eager to obtain the president's signature on the mammoth bill, conceded on one spending demand after another, and dropped many of the conservative policy "riders" that had dotted the bills. For Republicans, the bill contained a boost in defense spending, new anti-drug programs and some riders, such as an extended ban on taxpayer-funded needle-exchange programs and continued curbs on Clinton's national educational testing initiative.

Non-spending bills that caught a ride on the omnibus spending bill included: legislation to extend tax credits, a reorganization of U.S. foreign policy agencies, an increase in the number of visas for high-tech workers, new curbs on minors' access to pornography on the Internet, and a measure to implement the recently ratified Chemical Weapons Convention.

In the end, Clinton obtained his long-sought $18 billion for the International Monetary Fund, though Republicans came away satisfied with conditions they imposed on the much-criticized agency.

The bill's passage capped a turbulent year for appropriations. House GOP leaders, aiming to placate conservatives, insisted that appropriators craft Republican-tilting bills instead of the bipartisan bills passed in the wake of last year's budget deal. The result was a stormy summer and numerous differences — not only between Republicans and the White House, but also among Republicans. The Senate wrote bipartisan bills that used "emergency" spending that does not count against budget caps and other accounting devices to pump more money into the bills. But Democrats politicized debate on several bills, and four measures failed to pass the Senate. The omnibus bill also contained $21 billion in supplemental spending for such items as Bosnia peacekeeping, anti-terrorism efforts and federal computer upgrades.

When Clinton re-entered the fray in October, he pressed for new education money, particularly for his initiative to help local school districts hire 100,000 new teachers. The debate began after the House voted Oct. 8 to start an impeachment inquiry, and Democrats relished an opportunity to change the subject. Negotiations dragged on.

The sometimes chaotic talks produced a bloated bill that conservatives and budget hawks loathed, through a process that no one was willing to defend: decisions made by senior White House aides in a room with a small group of lawmakers. Democrats felt shut out of the process, but they won concessions that they would not have obtained had the 13 bills been negotiated individually and sent separately to the White House.

The sheer weight of the bill outraged many Republicans — some publicly, many privately — who disliked the concessions to Clinton and numerous hometown projects included in the bill. Their leaders responded that the outcome was the inevitable result of a divided federal government.

Spending Binge Seen as Likely To Compound 1999 Headaches

OCTOBER 17 — In agreeing on a mammoth spending bill for fiscal 1999, a Republican Congress that for months had touted its record for fiscal discipline caved in to a weakened president's demands for additional spending — and then added more spending of its own.

President Clinton and congressional Republicans closed out a difficult budget season with a plan that eats up about one-third of the budget surplus, shattering the budget goals they set barely a year ago. Given this year's experience, in which Congress and the White House demonstrated repeatedly that they lack the will to live up to those goals, it is difficult to imagine they can avoid a repeat of this year's election-season surplus-spending spree.

Republicans and the White House capped a week of sometimes difficult negotiations with a torrent of new spending as they patched together an end-of-session appropriations bill that included about $500 billion and also served as the

Omnibus Spending Bill

engine to drive a slew of unrelated legislation into law. The bill (HR 4328) contains eight of the 13 annual spending bills, the most since President Ronald Reagan blasted the "one big bill" practice in 1988.

Republicans were eager to leave town, and they faced a president playing a strong hand. Clinton and his Democratic allies succeeded in changing the subject from a sex scandal involving Clinton's relationship with former White House intern Monica Lewinsky to issues such as education, where public opinion polls give Democrats an edge.

"We have certainly gotten the subject back to the issues, and on the issues we are doing extremely well," said Rep. Vic Fazio, D-Calif. "There has certainly been — for the first time since the Lewinsky affair became a national media obsession — an opportunity for us to talk about what we know our constituents want this Congress to address."

Whether Democrats can blunt GOP electoral gains in the upcoming midterm elections remains to be seen. But as they reaped concession after concession, Democrats earned a slew of campaign-trail talking points and new spending from a Republican majority that negotiated like a pro football team that had racked up a big lead and was seeking to limit Democratic scores to field goals instead of touchdowns.

Along the way, it seemed that virtually every key lawmaker won a pet provision or hometown project.

A blizzard of frantic deal-cutting gave Clinton much of what he wanted on spending and denied Republicans a chance to trumpet conservative gains on social issues.

Despite his weakened political condition, Clinton won such victories as the full $18 billion in new contributions to the International Monetary Fund and a $1.2 billion down payment on a plan to hire 100,000 new teachers — part of a Labor-HHS-Education spending bill (HR 4274) whose funding exceeded his budget request by more than $3 billion. He won many "emergency" spending items, including funding for the Bosnia peacekeeping mission, Year 2000 computer fixes, anti-terrorism efforts and farm relief.

Republicans countered with their own spending demands and won a $690 million anti-drug initiative and $9.2 billion in additional defense spending, including money for operations such as intelligence and missile defense.

But victories on conservative policy "riders" were scarce. When selling the bill to conservatives, House Speaker Newt Gingrich, R-Ga., noted that it contained a ban on taxpayer funding of needle exchange programs in the District of Columbia and blocked Clinton's voluntary nationwide educational testing program — two wins that were merely extensions of current law.

Gingrich at times appeared defensive. Responding to a column by conservative guru Robert Novak that accused Republicans of being adrift, he issued a two-page news release defending the bill and the GOP's accomplishments. At a subsequent news conference he praised as conservative a provision written by liberal New York Democrat Nita M. Lowey that would exempt doctors with moral objections from having to prescribe contraceptives under a new requirement that federal employee health care plans cover a full range of contraceptives.

Republican leaders put on a brave face. "I can tell you Mr. and Mrs. America, for the most part, your surplus is still intact," said House Majority Leader Dick Armey, R-Texas. Hours later, Armey took to the floor to plead with his colleagues to stop beseeching GOP leaders for more add-ons.

Conservatives were appalled and budget hawks dismayed. None of the GOP Budget or Appropriations committee chairmen attended the Oct. 15 news conference — which noticeably lacked the enthusiasm of a competing White House event — in which Republican leaders tried to claim victory.

"What upsets us here at the Budget Committee is not just the new spending but the precedent this sets for allowing people to get around the caps," said Senate Budget Committee spokesman Robert G. Stevenson.

In addition to the unprecedented $20-plus billion "emergency" spending that represents a direct end run around the caps, the bill includes about $7 billion in other new spending above the amounts in the original versions of the bill, only $3 billion of that offset by savings elsewhere in the budget. About another $4 billion was paid for through accounting tricks such as postponing other spending to fiscal 2000, which means budget scorekeepers do not count the new money against the caps. Lawmakers will have an enormous headache next year when they revisit the budget, because everyone will expect the additional spending to continue.

GOP rebels, under heavy pressure from the leadership to keep their deep dismay over the bill from boiling over into open revolt, were grinding their teeth.

"Let me say emphatically, this is a bad bill for the American people," said Rep. David M. McIntosh, R-Ind., chairman of the Conservative Action Team (CAT). "It does not provide any meaningful tax relief for American families. And it busts the budget caps. . . . It spends $20 billion from the surplus that just a few weeks ago, President Clinton said he wanted to set aside for Social Security." At the same time, however, McIntosh heeded a warning from Gingrich not to declare that he would vote against the bill.

Top House Appropriations Committee Democrat David R. Obey of Wisconsin — who spent much of the week accurately knocking down GOP claims that a deal was imminent — retorted that the House conservatives' strategy had backfired. Obey said the conservative-driven decision to make the annual appropriations process more combative and to produce GOP-tilted bills delayed the process and ensured a dominant White House role. While House Democrats objected to being shut out of the process, the White House obtained far greater concessions than congressional Democrats could have won.

"I'd like to thank the CATs for that," Obey said.

Said a House GOP Appropriations aide: "We'd have been better off if we passed the president's Labor-HHS bill on the day after he sent up his budget."

Something for Everyone

Republican leaders also fell over themselves to award goodies to junior or endangered members.

Members from the South came away grinning over treatment of the Tennessee Valley Authority (TVA). They had come under fire from opponents in September when Republicans eliminated the agency's subsidy during final negotiations on the energy and

Appropriations

water spending bill (PL 105-245), so they obtained a provision to refinance the TVA's long-term debt at a higher cost to taxpayers. Then they got back the agency's $50 million subsidy.

"It's a double play for the TVA," said Rep. Zach Wamp, R-Tenn., who came to Congress as part of the firebrand class of '94 but now has shifted his allegiances to the go-along-get-along group that still dominates the Appropriations Committee, on which he sits.

The most audacious items went to top appropriators and GOP leaders. Senate Appropriations Committee Chairman Ted Stevens, R-Alaska, for example, failed in his bid to win approval of a road across an Alaskan wilderness area to provide safer emergency medical transportation for the 700-resident town of King Cove, a precedent that environmentalists were desperate to avoid. Instead, he obtained a $37.5 million earmark (about $54,000 per resident) for a different road, a new ferry, airport improvements and an upgrade of the town clinic.

The negotiations involved virtually any lawmaker with a legislative item that had any life in it. Proposals were floated, shot down and floated again. At one point, tax lobbyists were pessimistic about the fate of a popular measure (HR 4738) to extend expired tax breaks such as the research and development tax credit. But the $9.2 billion measure was inserted at the last minute, even though adding it to the omnibus bill amounted to treading on the well-guarded turf of the tax-writing House Ways and Means and Senate Finance committees.

The epicenter of the talks was Gingrich's office, where, under the watchful eye of the speaker's famed Tyrannosaurus Rex dinosaur head, White House Chief of Staff Erskine Bowles, Office of Management and Budget Director Jacob Lew and other White House team members wrangled for days with Republicans. Shuttling back and forth from the "dinosaur room" to the offices of Senate Minority Leader Tom Daschle, D-S.D., and House Minority Leader Richard A. Gephardt, D-Mo., Bowles attracted swarms of reporters eager for any hint of progress.

Inside the room, hundreds of big and small side deals were cut. In the aftermath, staff aides responsible for drafting precise bill language lamented that in many cases negotiators had not put the deals in writing nor decided who would provide the legislative text. Many deals, such as one on the agriculture portion of the bill, were difficult to keep closed. The result was a huge delay in piecing together the final bill, which members had hoped to vote on Oct. 16. Instead, they were sent home for the weekend and will vote the week of Oct. 19.

The tortuous process required a third, fourth and fifth continuing resolution or "CR" — Washington argot for stopgap funding measures that keep the government running after the fiscal year ends Sept. 30 — to prevent a government shutdown. The fifth CR (H J Res 136) runs through midnight on Oct. 20, by which time Congress expects to get the bill to Clinton.

House Democrats entered final negotiations with a history of sometimes rocky relations with the White House, and they were shut out of the room. But in the wake of the impeachment scandal, they were confident the White House would not cut and run.

It did not. Among the final sticking points were the issues of statistical sampling in the 2000 census and Lowey's proposal to require federal health plans to cover contraceptives. Conservatives objected because they believe some methods of contraception abort fertilized eggs. Both issues were resolved largely to Democrats' satisfaction. "We did okay on census and we did fine on contraception," said senior Gephardt aide George Kundanis.

"Why the Republicans want a debate on contraception three weeks before an election is beyond my comprehension," Fazio said.

Daschle played a major role in talks over agriculture, which produced a $5.9 billion package that exceeded the amount of emergency relief aid in the vetoed agriculture spending bill (HR 4101) by about $1.7 billion. But he failed in a bid to rewrite the 1996 farm law (PL 104-127). "There was enough money for farmers to buy both of the Dakotas," Rep. James P. Moran, D-Va., told The Washington Post.

Playing Defense

In the orgy of additional spending, Republicans were reduced to claiming victory for the new items that they successfully blocked, such as Clinton's $7.9 billion school construction tax initiative, which would have subsidized the interest on state bond issues.

Republicans also thwarted Clinton's much-sought bid to repay the United States' back dues to the United Nations. That proposal will not go forward as long as Clinton kills the attempt by anti-abortion activists to block U.S. family planning aid to overseas groups that lobby on abortion.

Others said that when they stepped back to look at the broader picture, they found that Republicans had largely blocked Clinton's ambitious February budget plans, which called for about $114 billion in additional spending over five years and proposed $24 billion in tax breaks for child care, school construction and environmental initiatives. Much of Clinton's plans depended on revenues from a tobacco bill (S 1415) that died in the Senate.

"If you back off and look at the whole picture, we've kept a guy who wants to spend every dime he can get . . . to about $10-12 billion," said Rep. Richard H. Baker, R-La. "In the scheme of things, we've come out of this very well."

Congress Heads Home on a Trail Of Broken Budget Caps

OCTOBER 24 — After months of talking past each other and trying — mostly in vain — to use the budget to score political points, President Clinton and congressional Republicans came up with a spending plan that failed to settle the key issue dividing them: What to do with the budget surplus.

Lawmakers banked fiscal 1998's $70 billion surplus and spent more than $20 billion of even bigger surpluses that may stretch well into the future. How to handle those surpluses, estimated to total $1.6 trillion over the next 10 years, is the key challenge facing lawmakers and Clinton in 1999.

If both sides stick to their rhetoric — with Republicans promising a smaller government and Clinton blocking any surplus-financed tax cut — expect more

Omnibus Spending Bill

of the same: yearlong gridlock, followed by a last-minute spending spree.

This year's massive spending bill breaks the budget discipline that Clinton and Congress put in place with much fanfare last year. The debate ended with Clinton in a superior but not commanding tactical position on the new battleground of surplus politics. He obtained modest new spending for education and got a budget bump for many existing programs, but the gains represented only a fraction of his ambitious February budget.

The result nonetheless was an end-of-session spending bill (HR 4328) that blew a hole in last year's pact. Set against the backdrop of a $1.7 trillion budget, a still vibrant economy, and lawmakers suddenly confronted with what to do with a steadily growing budget surplus rather than a deficit, the additional spending was hard to avoid.

No Pride in Process

What everyone wants to avoid is a repeat of this autumn's chaotic budget finale, which produced a 16-inch, 40-pound, nearly 4,000-page measure that was far bigger and stuffed with more extraneous provisions than Democrats had ever delivered to Presidents Ronald Reagan or George Bush. The more than $520 billion bill contains many concessions to Clinton, a few GOP victories, and hundreds of hometown pet projects of the sort Republicans railed against when they were in the congressional minority.

To House Speaker Newt Gingrich, R-Ga., the legislative sausage was the price of having government divided between Republicans in Congress and a Democrat in the White House. To many in the no-more-business-as-usual GOP Class of 1994, it was a return to precisely that.

If the bill had been produced by an all-Democratic government, Republicans could have had a field day.

"At a time when we are dealing with a weakened president . . . you would think that our leadership, who professed to be conservatives leading this revolution, could stand tough within that budget cap and stay true to the commitment we came to and came here for in 1994," said conservative Rep. Jon Christensen, R-Neb. "We have failed in this process."

Retorted Gingrich, passionately closing debate on the bill: "The fact is there is a liberal Democrat in the White House. . . . And there are things he wants in order to sign a bill, and that is legitimate and a part of precisely what the Founding Fathers established: a balance of power."

Still, no one took pride in a process that produced a take-it-or-leave-it vote on a tome that virtually no one had read and in which decisions were made by very few people: top GOP leaders, White House officials and the chairmen and ranking Democrats on the Appropriations committees.

"I am not going to defend the process. I hate the process," said House Appropriations Committee Chairman Robert L. Livingston, R-La. Livingston said the inability to pass the annual budget resolution and demands by conservative outside groups stalled too many bills and put Republicans in a disadvantageous negotiating position.

With Republicans eager to win promises of Clinton's signature, the president gained far more in the bill than he would have had Congress shipped him individual appropriations bills. Many bills stalled after veto threats from the White House, House-Senate differences and intra-GOP wrangling. As a result, the omnibus bill encompasses eight of the 13 annual appropriations bills and is laced with legislative riders, large and small. The hastily drafted document contains handwritten provisions scribbled in the margins, unnumbered and misnumbered pages and language killed at the last minute that was crossed out but not deleted.

Among the last decisions was a move by House Ways and Means Committee staff aides to block David Kaczynski from receiving, on a tax-free basis, a $1 million federal reward for turning in his brother, Unabomber Theodore Kaczynski. Instead, David Kaczynski — who has promised to turn the money over to victims' families — will have to pay about $355,000 in taxes before doing so.

"I have never seen a more disgraceful action on the part of anyone in this Congress," thundered top House Appropriations Committee Democrat David R. Obey of Wisconsin. "Yet that is one of the pieces of garbage we had to swallow" to get the bill passed.

The process left lawmakers all over the Capitol expressing shame.

"It does not generate respect for the institution," lamented Rep. Robert L. Ehrlich Jr., R-Md. "It puts people in difficult political positions. It doesn't reflect the true philosophical orientation" of Republicans.

Despite considerable reservations from Republicans uneasy about the new spending and from Democrats squeezed out of the legislative process, Congress easily cleared the bill, closed up shop and went home to campaign.

The House adopted the conference report (H Rept 105-825) on the bill, 333-95, on Oct. 20. The Senate cleared it, 65-29, the next day, and Clinton immediately signed it. (*House vote 538, p. H-152; Senate vote 314, p. S-48*)

The bill had something for everyone to like and dislike.

"Now someone said . . . that making legislation is like making sausage," said Sen. Robert C. Byrd. D-W.Va., the top Democrat on Appropriations. "Don't kid yourself. I have made sausage, and I can tell you that what we did this year is significantly more sloppy." Byrd originally said he would hold his nose and vote for the bill, but the next day he changed his mind: "I made such a good speech last night that I convinced myself to vote against" the bill, which, as usual, was larded with projects for West Virginia.

All told, the measure includes most of the annual appropriations bills, encompassing the bulk of the discretionary budget that Congress has to pass each year. It contains $21 billion in "emergency" spending that does not count against tight spending caps that were such a prominent feature of last year's balanced-budget law (105-33). Such spending allows budget writers to get around the caps, as do accounting tricks and offsetting savings that squeezed another $7 billion to $8 billion into the bills. (*Budget deal, 1997 Almanac, p. 2-3*)

For Democrats eager to change the subject from Clinton's sex scandal and impeachment inquiry, the measure provided many campaign talking points, especially a $1.2 billion appropriation to establish a teacher hiring program aimed at reducing class size in the early grades.

For Republicans, the bill contained a boost in defense spending, drug interdiction programs and some rem-

Appropriations

nants of conservative "riders" that contributed to this year's appropriations stalemate.

The bill is also loaded with non-spending items that are probably of little interest to voters but that represent significant accomplishments for lawmakers who have toiled for years on obscure issues. For example, the measure would reorganize U.S. foreign policy agencies, increase the number of visas for high-tech workers, curb minors' access to pornography on the Internet and implement the recently ratified Chemical Weapons Convention.

The bill also contains dozens of smaller measures that Congress and the White House could not advance under the regular legislative process. To a remarkable degree, authorizing committees looked to the appropriations process to advance their legislative agendas.

Republicans conceded that the process was ugly. Decisions were made, announced, and then undone. The influence of corporate lobbyists was evident, as late battles tended to break in favor of the GOP's business allies, including:

- **Commercial truckers.** In a move that pleased the commercial trucking industry, Republican leaders dropped language that would have transferred industry regulation from the Federal Highway Administration to the National Highway Traffic Safety Administration. The industry feared tighter regulation.
- **Meatpackers.** Meatpacking industry representatives prevailed in final negotiations when lawmakers dropped language requiring price reporting by meat processing and packing companies. Price reporting was strongly supported by Senate Minority Leader Tom Daschle, D-S.D., and Conrad Burns, R-Mont. Cattle ranchers in Western states have complained that the tightly consolidated industry conceals the price paid for cattle, and that ranchers have no way to know the true market value of their cattle.
- **Big airlines.** Larger airlines won a delay in implementation of rules aiming to protect start-up airlines from anti-competitive tactics.

- **Oil companies.** The bill would extend for eight months a ban that has blocked the Minerals Management Service from imposing new regulations on the collection of royalties on oil and gas produced on federal property.

Late add-ons for consumers included the following:

- **Home health care.** In a boost for Medicare patients at risk of losing their home health care, negotiators added a $1.7 billion increase for home health care reimbursements. Providers had protested that the reimbursement formula set in last year's balanced-budget law was driving many out of business and forcing others to deny care.
- **Breast surgery.** A rare defeat for an industry — insurance — was orchestrated by Sen. Alfonse M. D'Amato, R-N.Y., who obtained a provision to require insurers to cover breast reconstruction procedures after mastectomies. D'Amato is in a tough re-election battle against Democratic Rep. Charles E. Schumer. But it was only a partial victory: D'Amato failed to win language to curb so-called drive-by mastectomies. That provision in his original bill (S 249) would have allowed doctors, not insurance companies, to determine how long a patient should stay in the hospital after a mastectomy.

No Guidelines

Neither Clinton nor lawmakers displayed much enthusiasm during the year for debating budget and tax issues. After dropping his poll-tested budget in Congress' lap in February, Clinton and his congressional allies pressed other issues, such as health insurance changes, a campaign finance overhaul and anti-smoking legislation, each of which died.

For all their talk of cutting taxes, Republicans never tried to piece together a realistic tax cut. The House managed to pass an $80 billion tax cut bill (HR 4579), but Senate GOP leaders could not muster a simple majority to pass it, much less reach the 60-vote hurdle needed to overcome Democratic parliamentary maneuvers. They never took it up.

Catching less attention was the regular budget process, especially passage of the annual budget resolution that is supposed to serve as the guideline for subsequent action on spending and taxes. For the first time since passing the 1974 Budget Act (PL 93-344), Congress failed to pass such a resolution. The Senate passed a version (S Con Res 86) that mostly rubber-stamped last year's agreement. But House Budget Committee Chairman John R. Kasich, R-Ohio, who is considering a presidential run in 2000, insisted on crafting a budget- and tax-cutting plan (H Con Res 284) that took months to pass.

His Senate counterpart, Pete V. Domenici, R-N.M., did not try to hide his contempt for Kasich's plan, which relied on unrealistic appropriations cuts and often-rejected cuts in mandatory spending. Domenici refused to negotiate a final accord. At no point did anyone believe Congress would piece together a budget reconciliation bill to build on 1997's deficit-cutting success.

Meanwhile, lawmakers of both parties found opportunities to spend more money. They started with a big transportation bill (HR 2400 — PL 105-178), followed by appropriations bills that took advantage of the emergency spending loophole and accounting tricks. Then lawmakers and Clinton topped it off with a spending binge that appalled budget hawks.

Complicating the task were the ever-growing budget surplus estimates. Clinton's February budget predicted a $10 billion deficit for fiscal 1998 and small surpluses heading into the next century. When he admonished Republicans to "save Social Security first" before cutting taxes, he killed the GOP's tax cut plans.

But by the time summer arrived, surplus projections had surged and, to no one's surprise, lawmakers started making plans to spend some of it.

Said Brookings Institution budget analyst Robert D. Reischauer: "The fact that Congress has abandoned the [budget] discipline to the tune of $10-20 billion should probably be viewed as about as good as one could expect." ◆

FY99 Supplemental

Omnibus Spending Package Provides $20.8 Billion In 'Emergency' Funds

Box Score

- **Bill:** HR 4328 — PL 105-277
- **House action:** The House adopted the conference report (H Rept 105-825) on HR 4328, 333-95, on Oct. 20.
- **Senate action:** The Senate cleared the bill, 65-29, on Oct. 21.
- **Presidential action:** Clinton signed the bill Oct. 21.

Catching a ride on the massive fiscal 1999 catchall spending bill was a $21 billion supplemental spending package that blended elements of President Clinton's priorities with Republicans'.

SUMMARY

To the dismay of budget hawks, the measure was almost entirely financed from the new budget surplus, which Clinton had said should be banked until the Social Security system is overhauled in 1999. That galled Republicans, who watched their tax cut hopes evaporate after Clinton vowed in January to "save Social Security first."

Any supplemental spending request must be designated as "emergency" spending or counted against budget caps set in the 1990 budget deal (PL 101-508) and since extended, most recently in 1997 (PL 105-33). Usually such spending is for genuine emergencies such as natural disaster aid. Until this year, Republicans had paired supplemental bills with other cuts in spending — though the cuts usually were not deep enough to fully offset the new spending.

But with appropriators already struggling to live up to the caps, the level of emergency spending exploded during negotiations over the omnibus spending bill. Both Clinton and Republicans supported funding, often at different levels, for the Bosnia peacekeeping mission ($1.9 billion), year 2000 computer fixes ($3.4 billion), embassy security ($1.8 billion) and farm relief ($5.9 billion).

For Republicans, the measure contained $6.8 billion in new money for the Pentagon, a key demand of House Speaker Newt Gingrich, R-Ga., who wanted to be able to assure his party that every extra dollar for the domestic side of the ledger was matched with one for defense. Gingrich pushed for new intelligence spending ($1.5 billion), while Senate Appropriations Committee Chairman Ted Stevens, R-Alaska, countered with demands for missile defense ($1 billion).

In the run-up to negotiations over the emergency spending, House budget hawks pushed to require at least some offsets. GOP leaders such as Gingrich paid lip service to the demand, but in private they acknowledged that significant cuts were not possible.

In the chaotic finale over the omnibus bill, the price of the supplemental kept shifting. But in the end, with the surplus having surged to about $70 billion for fiscal 1998, the pressure was on to tap it for much more emergency spending than had previously been expected.

'Emergency' Spending

The omnibus appropriations bill (HR 4328) contains $20.8 billion in "emergency" spending, roughly split between domestic and defense items, including the following:

National security and military readiness	$ 6.8 billion
Bosnia peacekeeping	1.9 billion
Missile defense	1 billion
Anti-terrorism efforts	2.4 billion
Embassy security	1.8 billion
Capitol security/ visitors center	207 million
Year 2000 computer problems	3.35 billion
Defense fixes	1.1 billion
Agency fixes	2.25 billion
Hurricane Georges and other disaster relief	1.55 billion
Anti-drug program	690 million
Farm relief	5.9 billion

Clinton Calls On All Nations To Fight Terrorism

SEPTEMBER 26 — President Clinton launched a two-pronged campaign against terrorism Sept. 21, calling on U.N. members to cooperate in a global effort and unveiling a $1.8 billion emergency budget request to rebuild two embassies in Africa destroyed by bombs and make others more safe from attack.

In an address to the U.N. General Assembly, Clinton tried to mobilize the international community to fight terrorism, even those countries whose citizens are not targets.

"Each violent act saps the confidence that is so crucial to peace and prosperity," Clinton said. "People are struggling to build better futures based on bonds of trust connecting them to their fellow citizens and with partners and investors from around the world.

"The question is not only how many lives have been lost in each attack," he said, "but how many futures have been lost in their aftermath."

Clinton denounced as "terribly wrong" the belief in an inevitable clash between Western societies and Islamic cultures. "The only dividing line is between those who practice, support or tolerate terror, and those who understand that it is murder, plain and simple," he said.

Clinton outlined a common agenda all governments should follow to deal with a common adversary:

- Deny support and sanctuary to terrorists and pressure other states to do likewise.

Appropriations

- Expedite the extradition and prosecution of terrorists.
- Sign several treaties intended to fight terrorism and restrict the availability of chemical or biological weapons.
- Increase controls on the manufacture and export of explosives.
- Beef up security at international airports.

Acknowledging that terrorism has roots in economic deprivation, Clinton called on all governments to "combat the conditions that spread violence and despair."

Embassy Renewal

The lion's share of the $1.8 billion anti-terrorism supplemental budget request would be for enhancing the physical security of U.S. missions overseas. The White House is requesting the money as an emergency addition to the fiscal 1998 budget.

The proposal calls for spending $200 million to re-establish U.S. diplomatic operations in temporary quarters and to begin building new embassies in Dar-es-Salaam, Tanzania, and Nairobi, Kenya, both hit by bombs Aug. 7.

The package also includes $1.2 billion to improve security at diplomatic facilities around the world, adding more guards, video cameras and other equipment.

According to congressional aides, the State Department has concluded that 220 of the 260 U.S. embassies and consulates around the globe do not meet current security standards and that many of them need to be moved to new buildings that are set back a considerable distance from public streets.

Administration officials have declined to be specific in identifying particularly vulnerable sites for fear of encouraging terrorists to target them.

"This will not solve all the problems that we have," White House National Security Adviser Samuel R. Berger told reporters Sept. 21, "but we've looked at the most serious problems, and these are the ones that we need to address on an emergency basis."

The State Department would receive $1.4 billion of the $1.8 billion request. The supplemental request also includes:

- $200 million to cover the cost to the Pentagon of its response to the two embassy attacks, and for other security-related efforts.
- $90 million for the Treasury Department to increase training of Secret Services agents who escort senior U.S. officials abroad and for law enforcement training for the police of host nations.
- $70 million for disaster-related assistance to Kenya and Tanzania, where the powerful bombs that destroyed the embassies and killed 12 Americans also killed 250 bystanders, injured 5,500 others and destroyed or severely damaged nearby buildings.
- $22 million for the FBI to expand its roster of anti-terrorism response teams.
- $6 million for the National Park Service to increase security for some areas under its jurisdiction, which include much of the heart of Washington, D.C.

Reading the Fine Print

Most of the lawmakers who will scrutinize the request, such as Sen. Jon Kyl, R-Ariz., and Rep. Harold Rogers, R-Ky., said Sept. 23 that they had not had time to pore over the details and did not want to immediately comment.

But House International Relations Committee Chairman Benjamin A. Gilman, R-N.Y., raised some concerns about the request in a letter to House Appropriations Committee Chairman Robert L. Livingston, R-La.

Gilman said he believed too much of the State Department's request was being dedicated to physical construction at U.S. embassies. He suggested that more funds be used to train officers in preventing terrorist attacks and in using computers to track terrorists.

For example, a Gilman aide said funds could be used to have U.S. Border Patrol agents train their foreign counterparts to better identify terrorists.

The aide said the government's electronic databases need to be overhauled to better account for lost or stolen passports and to combine information on terrorists from different federal agencies.

Inman Commission

Gilman's concern that too much money is being spent on physical security relative to other counterterrorism needs is shared by retired Adm. Bobby R. Inman, who chaired a 1985 commission that called for spending $4 billion to improve security at U.S. embassies and other diplomatic buildings. (1985 Almanac, p. 105)

Inman said the federal government not only did not spend enough money on embassy security but particularly erred in not spending more money on State Department security officers and local guards.

"We said throwing money at the problem will not totally solve it," Inman said in an interview. "You need a program laid out over some years, and you need to beef up the staff. They didn't do either."

The funding shortage, Inman said, was both a reflection and a cause of the lack of emphasis on security in the State Department.

"They disappoint me," Inman said. "One of the things we set out to do was upgrade the competence of internal advice, create a diplomatic security service, recruit much higher quality people, give them better potential. The issue is still, are they listened to?"

And he warned that as soon as the crisis passes, the State Department could return to its old habits.

"My real concern here is that they'll just think about it for a year or two and then forget about it," Inman said.

Last-Minute Spending Signals Shift in Drug War

OCTOBER 24 — In what some lawmakers called a significant salvo in the war on drugs, Congress made room in the final omnibus spending package for $870 million to buy more radar surveillance planes, patrol boats, X-ray devices and other big-ticket items to detect and prevent smuggling.

The last-minute shopping spree pushed the government's anti-drug spending for the year to around $18 billion, equal to the cost of the entire Justice Department.

The spending bill that cleared Congress and was signed into law the week of Oct. 19 (PL 105-277) also contains language authorizing additional spending over the next three fiscal years to continue to combat drug trafficking. Some Republicans say such money is needed to augment the Clinton administration's focus on prevention and education, which they complain has pushed U.S. drug policies out of balance.

"We have a long way to go to restore this balance," Sen. Mike DeWine, R-Ohio, said in an Oct. 21 floor speech. "We will be back next year to continue this war. But make no mistake about it, this bill is a major step towards keeping drugs out of our country."

House Judiciary Crime Subcommittee Chairman Bill McCollum, R-Fla., said the anti-drug money in the omnibus bill "will give us a jump-start" to stem the flow of heroin, cocaine and other illegal narcotics entering the United States.

"There is not a single plane or ship today in the eastern Pacific patrolling the waters and patrolling the air looking for drugs that are coming up from Colombia to Mexico to the United States," McCollum said in an Oct. 15 floor speech. "That is wrong. It is very dangerous."

Some Democrats representing states at the center of the drug fight, such as California and Florida, also expressed satisfaction with the anti-drug portions of the omnibus appropriations bill.

The provisions "will have a direct impact on our efforts to prevent illegal narcotics from being transported over the Southwest border," Sen. Dianne Feinstein, D-Calif., said Oct. 16. "These provisions are good news for California."

War of Many Budgets

Even before it approved the omnibus bill, Congress had added money for fiscal 1999 to beef up drug enforcement at other agencies, such as the Defense Department. Although the White House Office of National Drug Control Policy is still compiling comprehensive figures for fiscal 1999, one agency official said Oct. 23 the total could range between $17.6 billion and $17.9 billion, compared with $16 billion for fiscal 1998.

Congress increased the budget of the Drug Enforcement Administration (DEA) from $1.1 billion in fiscal 1998 to $1.2 billion in fiscal 1999.

In the fiscal 1999 defense appropriations bill (PL 105-262), spending on Pentagon drug interdiction and anti-drug activities rose from $713 million last year to $736 million for fiscal 1999.

The drug policy office's director, retired Gen. Barry McCaffrey, helped work out a compromise over the increased anti-drug spending in this year's omnibus package with a bipartisan group of lawmakers.

McCaffrey said education and prevention programs aimed at school-age children remain critical to the administration's efforts.

"This war isn't going to be won by any army," he said in a Sept. 30 speech at a Naval Institute symposium in Virginia Beach, Va. He added that parents "have to sit down at the dining room table" and talk with children about the dangers of drugs.

Republicans who want a shift in administration strategy toward stopping drug supplies routinely cite statistics showing teenagers' use of heroin and cocaine has risen in recent years. Republicans have accused President Clinton of not taking the problem seriously enough.

But some advocacy groups are deeply skeptical that spending more to fight drug traffickers will solve the problem. They are calling for an end to drug eradication programs and less reliance on economic sanctions against countries that fail to make progress against the cultivation, processing and transportation of illicit drugs.

"It's time to stop throwing good money after bad," the Institute for Policy Studies, a Washington think tank, and the New Mexico-based Interhemispheric Resource Center said in a joint statement Oct. 21 accompanying four reports assailing U.S. drug control initiatives.

McCaffrey told the Senate Judiciary Committee in June that "there are signs [the administration's approach] is working." He noted that drug use by 12- to 17-year-olds living at home dropped from 1995 to 1996, and that marijuana use by teen-agers has stabilized, while alcohol consumption has declined.

Supplemental Spending

The omnibus package includes drug treatment language from a bill (HR 4550) that easily passed the House on Sept. 16 by a 396-9 vote. That measure would authorize money to establish a comprehensive treatment system for state and local prison inmates, as well as to provide grants to non-profit anti-drug organizations and extend drug-free workplace programs to small businesses.

"We have got to get prevention into our prisons, into our jails," said Rep. Rob Portman, R-Ohio, in an Oct. 15 floor speech. "This legislation does that on a model basis, the first time this Congress has really taken a step in this regard."

But the centerpiece of the drug effort in the omnibus bill is a separate measure (HR 4300), also approved Sept. 16, that proponents hope can increase international efforts to find and eradicate drugs at their source in Central and South America, as well as halt their transport by boat and plane. The House passed that bill, 384-39.

That legislation authorizes more than $2 billion through 2001 for a variety of programs. It would enhance monitoring of areas with high drug-trafficking rates and help drug-prevention organizations in Peru, Colombia and Bolivia to buy more equipment,

Extra Money For the Drug War

Congress added $870.2 million in emergency supplemental funds to the budgets for several agencies for anti-drug activities.

(In millions of dollars.)

Defense Dept.	$ 42.0
Transportation Dept.	
Coast Guard	271.7
Agriculture Dept.	
Agriculture Research Service	23.0
Justice Dept.	
Drug Enforcement	
Administration	10.2
Immigration &	
Naturalization Service	10.0
State Dept.	232.6
Treasury Dept.	1.5
U.S. Customs Service	276.0
Office of the President	
Office of National	
Drug Control Policy	1.2
Special Forfeiture Fund	2.0
Total	**$ 870.2**

Appropriations

hire more police and develop programs to get local farmers to replace their illegal crops with legal ones.

"These resources are absolutely essential," McCollum said. "If we provide them and do the right thing that this legislation sets out, we have a very real chance to cut the flow of drugs coming into this country."

As a down payment on such initiatives, the omnibus spending bill includes $184 million to help the three Latin American nations, which McCollum said produce all of the cocaine coming to the United States.

Included in that total are such items as $96 million in State Department funds for six UH-60 "Black Hawk" helicopters, along with $40 million to buy and upgrade 34 other UH-1H/1N helicopters. All of the helicopters will be used by the Colombian Police.

The remaining State Department funds are for such items as purchasing observation planes for Peru and Colombia, supporting those countries' drug-eradication operations and upgrading Colombia's prison security systems.

Another $276 million in the omnibus spending bill will go to the U.S. Customs Service. Much of the Customs money will go to buying six additional P-3B reconnaissance planes used for detecting and tracking aircraft flying over the Caribbean. Another $80 million will be spent on surveillance cameras, upgraded X-ray equipment and other "non-intrusive inspection technology" in areas along the U.S.-Mexico border. The Immigration and Naturalization Service also will get $10 million for extra sensors, motion detectors, remote video surveillance cameras and infrared optics.

Such technologies, McCaffrey said, can assist officials in adapting more quickly to the methods used by drug smugglers, and can be more effective than manual searches of trucks or boats.

The Coast Guard will receive an additional $272 million in the omnibus bill. That amount includes money for new aircraft, eight patrol boats and two cutters as well as electronic sensing and communications systems.

The Defense Department received an extra $42 million for anti-drug activities, including $20 million for the National Guard and $8 million for surveillance and spraying aircraft.

In addition to such new equipment, the spending package includes additional money for the Department of Agriculture's Agricultural Research Service to conduct anti-drug research — $23 million for such programs as herbicide research and development, new crop eradication technology and research into the development of alternative crops.

Another $12 million will be given to the Drug Enforcement Administration, CIA and National Security Agency for intelligence upgrades, including a data-retrieval system for the DEA.

Lawmakers did not stop at putting increased funding in the omnibus spending package in dealing with drug use. The measure also includes language as part of the fiscal 1999 foreign operations bill (HR 4569) that requires the State Department to set up an international law enforcement academy in Roswell, N.M.

The department has resisted putting the academy in New Mexico. But the state delegation's two senior Republicans — Sen. Pete V. Domenici and Rep. Joe Skeen — insisted on adding the language. The academy would train Latin American law enforcement officials in dealing with drug trafficking and other issues. ◆

Careful Veto Dance Ends in Enactment of Unencumbered Supplemental Spending Bill

> **FY98 Supplemental**
>
> ## Box Score
>
> - **Bill:** HR 3579 — PL 105-174
> - **House action:** The House adopted the conference report (H Rept 105-504) on HR 3579, 242-163, on April 30.
> - **Senate action:** The Senate cleared the conference report, 88-11, on April 30.
> - **Presidential action:** Clinton signed the bill May 1.

SUMMARY

Displaying a pragmatic streak not seen when they considered a similar bill in 1997, Republicans sent President Clinton a $6.1 billion supplemental spending bill for fiscal 1998 to fund disaster aid and overseas peacekeeping. He promptly signed it into law.

The measure included $2.6 billion for winter and spring disaster relief and $2.9 billion for the Pentagon, chiefly for the Bosnia peacekeeping mission and U.S. operations in the Middle East.

Unlike their experience in 1997, when Republicans took a political pounding after they sought to use a disaster aid bill as a way to push conservative agenda items past Clinton (who vetoed it), Republicans went out of their way to avoid a partisan clash with the president.

But it took many weeks to make the bill acceptable to both chambers and the president. Republicans had to settle a House-Senate divide over funding for the International Monetary Fund (IMF). The Senate approved such funding by a large majority, but House conservatives resisted. It was dropped.

Next came the question of whether to "pay for" the bill through offsetting spending cuts. House budget hawks demanded such cuts, as had been the practice in prior supplementals (though many of those cuts were cosmetic). They won only a half-victory: GOP leaders offset the disaster aid but not the Pentagon money.

The precedent of using such "emergency" money came back to haunt budget writers in October when Clinton and GOP leaders stuffed the year-end catchall spending bill (HR 4328) with $21 billion in emergency spending not subject to budget caps extended in 1997.

With decisions on IMF funding and offsets made outside the conference room, conferees haggled for days over items such as GOP attempts to block new Clinton regulations on organ transplants and offshore oil royalties. Implementation of both sets of regulations was delayed — then delayed again under the omnibus spending law (PL 105-277).

Rough Going for Supplemental Bill

MARCH 7 — President Clinton's request for a supplemental spending bill to finance U.S. military operations in Bosnia and Iraq and make good on commitments to international organizations is about to start on what promises to be a tortuous path toward enactment.

Clinton sent Congress the remaining pieces of his fiscal 1998 supplemental request March 3, and the chairmen of the House and Senate Appropriations committees plan to start action the week of March 9.

Clinton had already asked for $17.9 billion to replenish International Monetary Fund (IMF) reserves and create a new IMF lending program, as well as $921 million to pay U.S. arrears to the United Nations.

The new request includes $487 million to fund U.S. troop deployments in Bosnia beyond the previous June 30 withdrawal date, $1.4 billion for military operations in the Middle East, and $642 million to repair damage stemming from El Niño-related storms, ice storms in the Northeast and typhoon damage to military bases in Guam.

Clinton also amended his fiscal 1999 budget to add a request for $1.9 billion to finance Bosnia operations. Republicans had criticized the White House for not incorporating Bosnia money in the February budget submission, but they appear poised to provide the money beyond Clinton's $253 billion request for regular Pentagon operations.

Abortion Rider Returns

The supplemental measure should advance quickly through the Appropriations committees, but it faces several challenges in moving further. A major threat comes from anti-abortion forces in the House. Led by Christopher H. Smith, R-N.J., abortion opponents are poised to try to use the measure as a vehicle to carry language to bar U.S. aid to foreign family planning groups that offer abortions or abortion counseling or that lobby other countries on the issue.

The Senate and the White House oppose the anti-abortion language. Smith has tried to attach it to the annual foreign aid spending bill for three years, but he has been forced to settle for cuts in international family planning aid.

One option under consideration is to retain the abortion language in a measure (HR 1757, S 903), now pending in conference, to reauthorize the State Department. That measure would also carry a provision to authorize payment of U.N. dues. Under this scenario, backed by top Republican leaders such as House Speaker Newt Gingrich, R-Ga., the U.N. dues would be held hostage to the abortion rider, but the IMF and Bosnia money would not be.

Another volatile political issue is the plan by GOP leaders to reverse the prior practice of "paying for" supplemental spending bills with offsetting cuts in other appropriations. Republicans will follow the longstanding practice of Democrats, when they controlled Congress, of designating supplemental bills as emergency

Appropriations

spending that does not count against discretionary budget caps. That practice does, however, affect overall spending by increasing the deficit or reducing any surplus.

In reality, previous GOP attempts to finance supplemental bills have been incomplete, and Republicans have always designated supplemental spending as emergency money exempt from budget caps. That was required because the spending cuts attached as offsets involved unused budget authority provided to agencies instead of actual outlays from the Treasury. In some cases, those offsets did not pass muster with Congressional Budget Office scorekeepers because the money was not going to be spent anyway.

This distinction was largely lost on junior Republicans, who generally accepted assurances from GOP leaders such as House Appropriations Chairman Robert L. Livingston, R-La., that supplemental spending bills such as last year's flood relief bill (PL 105-18) were fully paid for.

Supplemental spending for operations in Bosnia and the Middle East have generally been an exception, financed by real cuts in other defense programs. But the Pentagon has made a persuasive case that it cannot find offsetting cuts this time without ravaging readiness and training programs.

Lawmakers and staff aides said the bill is expected to include the following elements of Clinton's request:

• **Defense.** The $487 million for 1998 Bosnia operations will be included. The 1999 money will likely be included in the regular Pentagon spending bill, designated as emergency spending that does not count against budget caps. The $1.4 billion request for Middle East operations is larger than previously expected but should be fully appropriated.

• **IMF.** It is generally accepted that the measure will carry the smaller, $3.4 billion appropriation for a new IMF lending program. The larger $14.5 billion piece, Livingston said, "is a question mark." But it could still be included in the annual foreign operations spending bill.

• **Disaster aid.** The question is whether Congress will increase the $642 million for disaster aid before sending the bill to Clinton.

• **U.N. dues.** This portion of the request faces antipathy from GOP leaders such as Senate Foreign Relations Committee Chairman Jesse Helms, R-N.C., and Senate Majority Leader Trent Lott, R-Miss. Its path into law would be even more problematic if it is stripped from the supplemental bill and included in the State Department authorization measure along with the anti-abortion rider.

GOP Splits Clinton Request

MARCH 14 — Top Republican leaders have decided upon a divide and conquer strategy as they prepare for action on what has become an annual ritual: getting a reluctant GOP caucus to pass President Clinton's spring supplemental spending request.

Instead of advancing Clinton's request for fiscal 1998 emergency money for military operations in Bosnia and Iraq, disaster aid, and U.S. payments to the United Nations and the International Monetary Fund (IMF) as one big bill, GOP leaders announced that they will split the request in two.

One bill would finance the Pentagon and disaster aid requests, while more controversial U.N. and IMF funding requests would travel on their own and remain linked to a bitter battle regarding overseas abortions.

The strategy appears to boost chances for relatively speedy passage of Clinton's request for Bosnia ($487 million), Iraq ($1.36 billion) and disaster aid ($642 million). But prospects for the much larger and more politically challenging request for U.N. arrearages ($921 million) and the IMF ($17.9 billion) appear much shakier. The latter measure is still linked to the fate of efforts by abortion opponents to attach a provision to block U.S. aid to overseas family planning groups that lobby foreign governments on abortion.

The plan to split the request in two was devised March 10 by House and Senate GOP leaders. The rationale is that the need for emergency money for the Pentagon and for El Niño-related disaster aid is more urgent than funding for the IMF and the United Nations.

Senate Majority Leader Trent Lott, R-Miss., said Bosnia, Iraq and disaster aid could be characterized "as true emergencies, whereas you can't on the IMF. It's really just simply a logical decision."

But dividing the request also effectively segregates the two elements least popular with Republicans — U.N. arrearages and replenishing IMF reserves — from the must-pass defense measures. The Pentagon says that without speedy action on its request, money needed for training missions and readiness of non-deployed forces would have to be sacrificed to finance the missions in Bosnia and the Middle East.

Democrats and the administration met the plan to divide the supplemental measure — and the continued political link to divisive abortion issues — with dismay. The administration argues that the time has long passed for the United States to pay its debt to the United Nations, particularly as U.S. officials try to line up international support for potential military action against Iraq. And instability in Asian financial markets has the White House and the business and farm lobbies pushing hard for the IMF money.

"These are big-league issues, and they shouldn't be delayed until the seventh-inning stretch," said top House Appropriations Democrat David R. Obey of Wisconsin.

The Pentagon may get its money relatively quickly, but questions linger over whether Republicans will cut spending in other programs to pay for defense. There is considerable sentiment within the House GOP caucus to produce a bill with such rescissions. Previous GOP-drafted supplemental spending bills have rescinded prior appropriations, but appropriators now say that all easy cuts in discretionary programs have been made. The recent pattern of raiding other defense accounts to pay for overseas missions cannot be repeated this year without causing real pain at the Pentagon, lawmakers said.

House Appropriations Committee Chairman Robert L. Livingston, R-La. — with the support of Speaker Newt Gingrich, R-Ga. — is pushing to advance the measure without offsetting cuts attached. (The IMF and U.N. money were included in last year's budget agreement and do not count toward the "caps" on discretionary

FY98 Supplemental

spending. Deficit hawks are not pressing for corresponding spending cuts for that measure.)

"We've gone as far as we can, and our non-deployed forces are paying heavily to keep our deployed forces going," Livingston said. "The Budget Act envisions true emergencies, and I think at this point we've reached that catastrophe."

But members in both the conservative and moderate wings of the GOP caucus continue to press for offsetting reductions in other spending.

"Once you go beyond the spending caps for one reason, it becomes much easier to do it again for another reason," said Rep. Ernest Istook, R-Okla. "You need to make offsets against non-defense spending."

Republican deficit hawks will offer spending cuts when the emergency spending bill hits the floor. But they acknowledge that a unified bloc of Democrats and a sizable group of Republicans will probably defeat their efforts.

The Senate has no intention of producing a bill that includes corresponding spending cuts. A March 12 Senate Appropriations drafting session was postponed until March 17 because of a scheduling conflict.

House leaders want to pass the measure before the spring recess that begins April 2. Tentative plans call for an Appropriations Committee markup the week of March 23, panel staff aides said.

Spat Over Offsets Highlights Struggle Of House GOP To Govern

MARCH 21 — Imperative for cuts in domestic programs could lead to political fallout and provokes early skirmish in battle for Speaker's job

Appropriations Committee Chairman Robert L. Livingston, R-La., left a meeting with House GOP leaders March 17 and strode purposefully through Statuary Hall, a new weight on his shoulders.

A supplemental spending bill that Livingston had hoped would sail though the House had just gotten a lot heavier. House Speaker Newt Gingrich, R-Ga., and other leaders had ordered Livingston to find cuts in domestic programs to pay for the roughly $2.9 billion in additional spending for domestic disaster aid and for military operations in Bosnia and Iraq.

The political fallout from that decision could be vast. Cutting that much money from already tight budgets for popular domestic programs could give Democrats and even some Republicans a reason to vote no, complicating floor passage.

It could also give President Clinton an opening to veto the bill and criticize Republicans for cutting important domestic programs — a tactic he has deployed with great success in past showdowns with House GOP leaders.

In a similar fight a year ago over flood relief aid (PL 105-18), Clinton used his veto to embarrass Republicans into removing controversial items before he would sign the bill. If Republicans provoked and lost another such confrontation in an election year, the price could be high.

The internal spat over offsets also marked an early skirmish in Livingston's ongoing campaign to succeed Gingrich as Speaker in an election that could come as soon as next year, if Gingrich exits Congress to run for the GOP presidential nomination. In a showdown with his chief rival, House Majority Leader Dick Armey, R-Texas, Livingston had just been forced to back down.

So Livingston chose his words carefully as he walked briskly from Gingrich's office toward his own. "The leadership has decided to offset everything with non-defense discretionary spending," he said. "I intend to follow the dictates of our leadership." Asked about the bill's prospects for success, Livingston repeated his response, word for word.

Just a week earlier, Livingston and Gingrich had agreed that the supplemental spending bill ought to advance without offsetting cuts. The need for cuts seemed less compelling, now that a budget surplus was projected for fiscal 1998. And appropriators figured that moving the bill without offsetting cuts would assure smooth passage of a measure on which Republicans were not looking for trouble.

The Majority's Burden

Forcing Livingston to perform an about-face over the offsets was just the latest chapter in the long-running struggle by House Republicans to deal with the challenges of being the majority party. Tensions continue between making the compromises inherent in governing and sticking to the ideological imperatives that many believe won them the majority in the first place.

Livingston's instinct was to avoid offering up the bill in a potential veto showdown with the president.

Robert D. Reischauer, a senior fellow at the Brookings Institution, considers a veto struggle a realistic possibility. By insisting on offsets, Reischauer said, House Republicans have chosen a path that "raises the stakes, raises the level of political conflict and gives the president an opportunity. And the president is a black belt when it comes to parrying the offensive action of the Republican Party on appropriations bills."

Searching for offsets in domestic spending programs is already causing discomfort among some of the moderate Republicans who insisted on finding the spending cuts in the first place.

And it has set the stage for another showdown between hard-line House Republicans and the more accommodationist Senate, where Budget Committee Chairman Pete V. Domenici, R-N.M., is skeptical about finding acceptable offsets.

As for the personal political repercussions for Livingston, the incident seemed to be a win for Armey, who better reflected the House Republicans' conservative impulses on this issue. The skirmish reinforced the view of some House Republicans that Livingston is too quick to compromise with Democrats. Mark Souder, R-Ind., said Livingston's willingness to abide by the leadership's decision without a fight "was a sign he was listening a tad more than usual" now that he is campaigning for Speaker.

"I will let Mr. Livingston speak for himself," Armey said tersely, when asked about Livingston's position. "I am committed to the offsets."

The decision to find offsets was made in a meeting of GOP leaders who hold elected party posts. According to those who attended, there was wide-

Appropriations

spread support for the idea. When Gingrich asked if moderates would support the position, it was noted that 14 of them had released a letter March 12 urging offsets.

GOP Policy Committee Chairman Christopher Cox, R-Calif., said: "Everybody understands that we can't pass it without the offsets."

Livingston, included in a subsequent and larger meeting of GOP leaders, expressed concern but said he would abide by the group's wishes. While it is clear that Republicans would abandon the bill if it had no offsets, appropriators worry that the measure could have a rough ride if all Democrats vote no and some Republicans waver.

GOP budget hawks hailed the outcome. "That is a monumental change from where we were a week ago," said Mark W. Neumann, R-Wis. Budget Committee Chairman John R. Kasich, R-Ohio, called it a "great victory. I don't care where it's offset from, as long as it's paid for."

But the decision to take all of the offsets from domestic programs has consequences. Traditionally, increases in defense or domestic programs have been offset by reductions in similar programs. However, GOP leaders agreed that raiding other defense accounts to pay for overseas missions could not be repeated this year without seriously impinging on training missions and readiness of non-deployed forces

Some of the GOP moderates who had pushed for offsets later expressed their opposition to cutting domestic programs to pay for additional defense spending. "I have tremendous problems with our failure to realize there's waste, fraud and abuse in defense," said Christopher Shays, R-Conn.

Democrats reacted more strongly. "Again, they're looking for confrontation on an issue where we ought to be looking for cooperation," said David R. Obey of Wisconsin, the Appropriations Committee's ranking Democrat.

Even Charles W. Stenholm of Texas, a leader of conservative Democrats and an outspoken proponent of fiscal responsibility, was unsure about the necessity for finding offsets. "It's going to be tough," he said.

"This would require unacceptable reductions in important domestic programs, potentially resulting in deadlock," said Linda Ricci, a spokesman for the Office of Management and Budget. "It will clearly make reaching bipartisan agreement far more difficult."

It is also likely to pit House GOP appropriators against their Senate brethren. The Senate Appropriations Committee approved its version of the supplemental bill without offsets on the same day House leaders decided to include them.

"I think it's too late in the year, and there's no way to do it," Senate Budget Chairman Domenici said of looking for offsets.

If another showdown with Clinton develops over disaster relief, House Republicans are counting on several significant differences from last year's battle. Among them: This fight would be waged over fiscal responsibility, not unrelated legislative riders; Clinton may have less credibility with the public than he had a year ago, and the need for disaster relief and defense funds may be less urgent than it was for last year's flood relief legislation.

"I don't think the lesson from last year is, don't pay for anything" to offset the costs of disaster relief, said Jim Nussle, R-Iowa. "I think the lesson is, plan ahead."

But House GOP leaders appeared to be taking an incremental approach to moving the first supplemental spending bill, which could be marked up in the House Appropriations Committee March 24 and considered by the full House the following week.

Chambers Go Separate Ways

MARCH 28 — The combatants know that at least part of President Clinton's request for emergency spending must become law. But all sides are justifiably nervous as they ponder how an increasingly balkanized Congress will manage to do it — and get Clinton to approve.

Clinton's request for additional fiscal 1998 funding for disaster aid and military action in Bosnia and Iraq — as well as U.S. commitments to the United Nations and the International Monetary Fund (IMF) — did well in the Senate, which completed work March 26 on the request (S 1768).

But in the House, GOP leaders embarked on a collision course with Clinton, advancing his request through the Appropriations Committee as two separate bills: a must-pass draft measure to finance military operations and disaster aid and a second, more troubled, draft bill to cover U.S. dues to the United Nations and the IMF — and to potentially carry abortion-related language that would prompt a Clinton veto.

Even before the legislation gets to Clinton, Republicans must address deep rifts among themselves. One involves whether to send one bill to the president or to split Clinton's request as House and Senate GOP leaders earlier had agreed to do. The idea was to avoid embarrassing delays by moving the must-do requests for the Pentagon and disaster aid without attaching more controversial measures on the United Nations, IMF or abortion.

But a group of Republican senators who strongly back the $17.9 billion in IMF funding (S 1769) outflanked the leadership and added that money to the smaller, must-pass bill (S 1768). The senators, led by Chuck Hagel of Nebraska and Appropriations Chairman Ted Stevens of Alaska, worked closely with the administration, Federal Reserve Chairman Alan Greenspan and — once they demonstrated that they had the votes to pass the amendment over the objections of Majority Leader Trent Lott, R-Miss. — IMF skeptics such as Phil Gramm, R-Texas. Hagel, Gramm and Mitch McConnell, R-Ky., devised a compromise financing package that moved in the White House's direction to ease IMF restrictions in the committee-approved version. The Senate adopted the compromise March 26 by a sweeping 84-16 vote that lifted the hopes of IMF funding supporters. *(Vote 44, p. S-10)*

Republicans are also battling among themselves over whether to finance the emergency spending with cuts in other programs. House deficit hawks insist that the military and disaster aid bill include offsetting cuts in domestic spending, putting them sharply at odds with their Senate colleagues, who not only produced no offsets but spent almost a week larding their bill with add-ons.

The package of cuts drawn up by House Republicans would gore Clinton priorities such as housing and the AmeriCorps national service program.

Those offsets, which angered some GOP moderates, set the stage for a difficult House floor vote the week of March 30. Republicans will probably have to pass the bill with little or no Democratic support — a difficult task for such a narrow and fractious majority. "It's a hell of a mess by any measure," said a senior GOP House Appropriations Committee staff aide.

Because the House traditionally passes appropriations bills before the Senate, the Senate did not officially pass S 1768 or S 1769. Instead, it agreed to employ a now fairly common parliamentary maneuver under which the measures will be automatically "deemed" passed once the Senate receives the comparable House-passed bill or bills.

Senate Floor

The emergency bill (S 1768) arrived on the Senate floor March 23 with $2.6 billion in new discretionary spending and $550 million in mandatory spending for veterans' pensions and benefits. By the time lawmakers wrapped up work March 26, senators of various stripes had added another $2.6 billion in discretionary items. Some, such as $1.6 billion for the Federal Emergency Management Agency, were for disaster aid. But many were non-emergency and parochial.

When funding to replenish IMF lending reserves — which officially counts as new spending but does not contribute to the deficit — was added on, the bill had swelled to $23.1 billion.

To help House Republicans, who say they cannot move one big bill through the House, Lott had signed off on a House plan to divide Clinton's request in two. That would segregate the emergency disaster and military money from potential language to deny U.S. aid to overseas family-planning groups that lobby on abortion. (The abortion language is expected to be added on the House floor.)

The issue has been an annual sticking point on the foreign aid spending bill, which also carries U.N. and IMF funding. Abortion language was included in the conference report on the State Department reauthorization bill (HR 1757), which has drawn a veto promise from Clinton.

But Lott could not restrain IMF supporters, who were determined to preserve the option of a single-bill strategy linking the IMF money to must-pass Pentagon money. An impassioned Stevens termed the IMF funding critical to stabilizing Asian markets. He criticized the two-bill strategy as potentially creating too much delay.

"I do not want to see games played with the IMF," Stevens said. "The IMF is serious to us. I want to make sure the first bill that goes to the president has IMF on it."

Under new language worked out with the Treasury Department, the $3.4 billion for a new IMF loan program could be released without restrictions; the $14.5 billion to replenish IMF reserves could be released after the Treasury secretary certified that the United States and its major "G-7" industrial partners had agreed to push for several IMF reforms, including requiring borrowing countries to abide by international trade agreements.

In the Senate's most closely matched fight of the week, GOP Whip Don Nickles of Oklahoma struck $16 million from the bill that was to help the Health Care Financing Administration enforce the 1996 health insurance portability law (PL 104-191), aimed at ensuring that workers who change jobs or get sick can retain their health insurance. Nickles' move had strong backing from the insurance industry. An attempt by the law's sponsor, Edward M. Kennedy, D-Mass., to preserve half of the enforcement funds was killed, 51-49. (Vote 45, p. S-10)

As the bill lingered on the floor, it served as a magnet for members' add-ons. Christopher S. Bond, R-Mo., for example, won $272.5 million to buy for the Marines eight F/A-18 aircraft manufactured in his state by McDonnell Douglas Corp. Jon Kyl, R-Ariz., obtained $151 million for research on missile defense systems. A raft of smaller amendments were accepted by voice vote with minimal debate. For example, $11 million was added to repair damaged railroads and $10 million to compensate dairy farmers who could not get their milk to market because of ice storms.

Patrick J. Leahy, D-Vt., soothed the anxiety of Midwestern members by adding an amendment to clarify a provision in a new law (PL 105-160) that had designated Lake Champlain as the sixth Great Lake to make it eligible for National Sea Grant research funds. He rewrote the provision to drop the designation but still qualify for the federal aid.

House Committee

In the House, after a lengthy and contentious markup March 24, the Appropriations Committee approved two draft bills. First the committee approved by voice vote a measure combining $17.9 billion for the IMF, $505 million for U.N. dues, $550 million for veterans benefits and $127 million in other requests.

Under direction from GOP leaders, the committee substantially reworked the bipartisan IMF bill (HR 3114) approved March 5 by the Banking and Financial Services Committee.

The new language imposed several conditions on the release of IMF funds that the Treasury Department promptly deemed unworkable. Dropped were several provisions added by Banking Committee Democrats to press the IMF to pressure borrowers on human rights, labor rights and the environment. An attempt by ranking Democrat David R. Obey of Wisconsin to restore the bipartisan Banking language failed, 25-29.

The panel then turned to a $2.9 billion draft bill for disaster aid and Bosnia and Iraq operations, approving it along party lines. The measure includes $570 million in disaster aid, $487 million for military operations in Bosnia and $1.3 billion for the Middle East.

On that bill, GOP leaders forced Appropriations Committee Chairman Robert L. Livingston, R-La., to work against his instincts, which were to advance Clinton's request in a bipartisan manner that would not require paying for the emergency money with cuts in other programs.

That would have been a departure from prior GOP supplemental bills, in which Bosnia operations were financed by reductions in other Pentagon programs. That well is dry, however, and House Republicans instead opted to raid domestic appropriations — ordinarily protected by so-called firewalls that segregate defense and domestic spending — to finance the Iraq and Bosnia missions.

Appropriations

Republican deficit hawks insisted on following the practice established when Republicans took over Congress: to attach spending cuts to finance emergency spending, at least on paper.

Any such "offsets" would alienate most Democrats, so it was no surprise that Livingston — who is actively campaigning to become Speaker of the House if Newt Gingrich, R-Ga., vacates the position to run for president — produced a roster of offsets that gouged $2.9 billion in Democratic-backed programs. The cuts included $1.9 billion from the Section 8 public housing program, $610 million in airport grants, $250 million from the AmeriCorps program and $75 million for bilingual education. Democrats howled that the list was an open invitation for a veto. "The confrontation artists are calling the shots," said Obey.

In a surprise move, the panel adopted by voice vote an amendment by David E. Skaggs, D-Colo. — over the protests of John P. Murtha, D-Pa. — to block any offensive attack on Iraq until Congress passes a law to permit such operations. Livingston supported Skaggs, and no one called for a roll call vote.

House leaders vow to bring the smaller military and disaster aid bill to the floor the week of March 30 and delay a vote on the IMF measure until after the two-week spring recess.

It is doubtful the competing House and Senate bills can be reconciled before the break. "This is not going to be an easy conference," Stevens said.

Senate Panel OKs Supplemental — With Strings

MARCH 21 — By approving a fiscal 1998 supplemental spending bill (S 1769) to appropriate $17.9 billion for the International Monetary Fund (IMF), the Senate Appropriations Committee on March 17 sent a mixed signal to the Clinton administration:

On one hand, senators are on course to pass the entire amount requested by President Clinton. On the other, they are attaching such contentious conditions to the bill that the 182-member organization may be unable to approve them. For example, they are insisting that the IMF make loans only to countries that honor certain trade agreements.

"I think that the Senate Appropriations Committee took a very important step forward in approving the full $18 billion for the IMF," Treasury Secretary Robert E. Rubin said March 18. But he added that for the IMF, the conditions may be "not doable." Administration officials say IMF funding is needed to stabilize the Asian financial crisis and protect American jobs.

Difficult as the IMF provisions were for the administration, the committee's action on the United Nations was even more problematic. It left out Clinton's request for $921 million in back payments to the United Nations, as Appropriations Chairman Ted Stevens, R-Alaska, said he wanted to wait for authorizing legislation.

Despite such controversies, appropriators approved the bill, 26-2, saving much of the debate for the floor. By the same vote, they approved another supplemental bill (S 1768) that contains $2.5 billion for troop deployments in Iraq and Bosnia, as well as disaster relief across much of the country. The bill does not include spending offsets.

The House Appropriations Committee is expected to mark up both bills March 24. That will provide little more cheer for the administration, as Republicans are pressing to attach IMF conditions that are only somewhat less stringent than the Senate's, and to include only about $500 million of the U.N. funding. House Republicans want to include a provision barring overseas family planning groups that receive U.S. aid from discussing abortions — a proposal that has already drawn a White House veto threat. House leaders also want to offset the $2.5 billion in S 1768 with cuts in domestic discretionary spending.

The Senate panel gave voice vote approval to an amendment by Robert C. Byrd, D-W.Va., that would restrict foreign governments that receive IMF aid, such as South Korea, from subsidizing their steel manufacturers. The amendment was modified by Ernest F. Hollings, D-S.C., to bar subsidies as well to textile and automobile producers.

Such language, as well as a similar provision in the underlying bill restricting subsidies to the semiconductor industry, is a priority for U.S. businesses that compete with Asian firms. Other controversial IMF conditions would mandate that the organization open its books to review by General Accounting Office auditors and lend only to countries that develop internationally acceptable financial and bankruptcy systems.

Logging Divide

Rather than debating national policy issues, senators at the markup focused on more provincial matters. The biggest debate erupted over an amendment by Larry E. Craig, R-Idaho, that would encourage the Forest Service to designate expanded areas for logging that can be reached by existing roads, to offset timber industry losses to be incurred by the administration's moratorium on building forest roads. Otherwise, the Forest Service would have to pay as much as $5 million to local governments to compensate them for lost tax revenues from the timber business.

The amendment drew sharp objections from some Democrats, who said it would lead to considerable environmental damage and the harvesting of as much as 275 million board feet of wood. They urged Craig to come up with another way to compensate local governments. Stevens modified the language to direct Congress to appropriate $2 million of the money for local governments, and the amendment was approved by voice vote with the logging language intact.

In another blow to environmentalists, the committee without discussion approved an amendment by Pete V. Domenici, R-N.M., that would give ownership of land near the Petroglyph National Monument to Albuquerque. The city may use it as a right-of-way to build a highway, which environmentalists say would lead to urban sprawl.

The committee approved by voice vote an amendment by Patrick J. Leahy, D-Vt., steering $4.5 million in aid to maple syrup producers.

At Stevens' request, the committee agreed by voice vote to remove a provision to prohibit the Federal Communications Commission (FCC) from requiring broadcasters to provide free or discounted air time to political candidates. The FCC is crafting proposals that could lead to such a requirement. Senate Commerce Committee Chairman John McCain, R-Ariz., said he urged Stevens to remove the provision because he was concerned that Clinton would "demagogue the issue as he has before and claim we were responsible for not getting aid to disaster victims."

The committee also included language requiring the FCC to develop a plan to restructure programs that provide subsidies for schools, libraries and rural health care facilities to hook up to the Internet. The provision stems from a February GAO report that said the FCC had no authority to create two nonprofit corporations to administer the schools and libraries fund and rural health care fund.

House Bill Heads for Collision With Senate

APRIL 4 — The House ignored a veto threat and embarked on a collision course with the Senate as it passed a $2.9 billion measure to provide emergency disaster aid and to finance military operations in Bosnia and Iraq.

The bill (HR 3579) squeaked through the House on March 31, in a 212-208 vote. Only late in the tally did it become clear that the bill would pass. Seventeen Republicans, including several moderates opposed to the bill's cuts in domestic programs, voted against it. (Vote 88, p. H-28)

As expected, Democrats overwhelmingly opposed the bill because the emergency spending is offset by cuts in domestic programs favored by Democrats: low-income housing subsidies, the AmeriCorps national service program and bilingual education.

The annual ritual over the spring emergency spending bill highlights the Republican leadership's growing pains as it weighs the need to be the governing party — with responsibility to quickly advance must-do legislation — against its desire to adhere to conservative principles such as paying for emergency spending out of existing programs. The need to placate conservatives runs counter to a wish to avoid picking a losing fight with President Clinton, who is especially adroit at winning concessions on spending bills.

The White House promptly vowed to veto the fiscal 1998 measure over the cuts in presidential priorities. "We urge you to avoid actions that would result in gridlock and that will be detrimental to our troops abroad and our citizens at home in a time of need," said an administration statement.

The White House is also scrambling to win passage of its $17.9 billion request for U.S. contributions to the International Monetary Fund and $921 million in overdue payments to the United Nations. The House bill ignores both requests, although a committee-approved bill (HR 3580) that includes IMF funding and some U.N. money may be considered after the spring recess.

Beyond the potential train wreck with Clinton, a difficult conference on HR 3579 awaits with the Senate, which, acting under a previous order, automatically passed a vastly different bill after the House vote. The Senate version of HR 3579 includes the full IMF request but no money for U.N. arrearages and few offsets.

The dueling measures are expected to head to a House-Senate conference when Congress returns from its two-week recess the week of April 20.

Key lawmakers and aides responsible for advancing the measure could offer few insights into how the bill would safely complete its journey into law.

Perhaps the biggest problem for House GOP strategists will be the possible mass defections by conservatives as the measure drifts in Clinton's direction. Meanwhile, House GOP leaders have yet to show any sign that they will permit the types of changes that would satisfy Democrats. Any major concessions promise to cause a revolt within the GOP Conference, a conundrum that has Republican leaders perplexed. "It's going to be tough," said Conference Chairman John A. Boehner, R-Ohio.

Before the bill could advance, GOP leaders had to muscle the measure through the House with minimal Democratic support. Democrats complained bitterly about the measure's $2.9 billion in spending cuts, each coming from a Democratic priority and breaching so-called fire walls that are intended to prevent Congress from raiding domestic programs to pay for defense spending, or vice versa. They blamed Republican leaders — who originally planned to advance the measure without offsets — for caving in to deficit hawks who demanded them.

"It would effectively end the AmeriCorps program and could lead to more than 100,000 of our elderly citizens losing their housing," said Minority Leader Richard A. Gephardt, D-Mo.

The driving force behind the legislation is a need to give the Pentagon $1.8 billion to replenish defense accounts that have been tapped to finance the ongoing peacekeeping mission in Bosnia and the stepped up deployment in the Middle East to place a check on Iraqi President Saddam Hussein. Unless the department gets this money, it will have to curtail training programs, put off maintenance and possibly furlough workers.

Rep. John P. Murtha of Pennsylvania, the top Democrat on the National Security Appropriations Subcommittee, said the House and Senate versions of HR 3579 are so different that the Pentagon cannot assume it will get its money. That raises the possibility that it will have to start cutbacks that would be difficult to reverse once under way.

The House measure also contains new funds for intelligence programs. The figure is classified but The Wall Street Journal reported it at almost $260 million. David R. Obey of Wisconsin, ranking Democrat on the Appropriations Committee, complained that the intelligence budget was raided last year to finance other defense programs and took the unusual step of trying to send the House into closed session to debate the matter. A motion to do so, however, was rejected, 194-227. (Vote 86, p.H-26)

The bill came to the floor under a tightly structured rule that permitted only Republican-sponsored changes, including a sense of Congress amendment by David M. McIntosh, R-Ind., and Mark W. Neumann, R-Wis., that called for fully financing any emergency appropriations. (Despite the offsets, the bill would increase spending by $333 million over five years.) Another amendment, sponsored by Todd Tiahrt, R-Kan., replaced a $244 million cut in airport grants with a matching cut in

Appropriations

Supplemental Bills Compared

The House passed a fiscal 1998 supplemental spending bill (HR 3579) on March 31 to provide $2.9 billion in disaster aid and funding for overseas military operations. The Senate has passed a $23.1 billion bill (HR 3579, formerly S 1768) for disaster relief, military operations and the International Monetary Fund. The measures are now headed for a House-Senate conference. After the spring recess, the House may debate a committee-approved bill (HR 3580) to provide $17.9 billion for the IMF and $505 million in U.N. dues. The Senate has "deemed passed" (once it receives companion House-passed legislation) a separate $17.9 billion bill (S 1769) to fund the IMF.

HR 3579	House	Senate
Proposed spending		
Disaster relief	$ 575 million	$ 2.73 billion
Defense	2.29 billion	2.42 billion
Middle East	(1.3 billion)	(1.3 billion)
Bosnia	(487 million)	(383 million)
Other	(503 million)	(717 million)
IMF	—	17.9 billion
New loan program	—	(3.4 billion)
Replenish reserves	—	(14.5 billion)
U.N. dues	—	No funding
Veterans compensation *	—	550 million
Miscellaneous	—	270 million
Rescissions	—	-263 million
TOTAL (discretionary)	$2.9 billion	$23.1 billion
Proposed offsets	$ 2.9 billion	
Section 8 housing	2.2 billion	
Airport grants in aid	366 million	
AmeriCorps	250 million	
Bilingual education	75 million	

SOURCE: House and Senate Appropriations committees   * Mandatory spending

Section 8 public housing subsidies. The House passed the rule governing debate, 220-199, with the amendments included. (*Vote 85, p. H-26*)

As the bill moves into conference, major House-Senate differences that need to be resolved include:

● **Offsets.** The House bill contains $2.9 billion in cuts in domestic programs, breaching so-called fire walls. The Senate version includes only $263 million in offsets, mostly small rescissions suggested by the administration.

The Senate is not expected to accept all the offsets. A halfway step advocated by House Appropriations Committee Chairman Robert L. Livingston, R-La., is to finance the domestic disaster relief with cuts in domestic programs but to observe the fire walls and not require additional cuts to finance deployments in Bosnia and the Middle East.

The easiest available pot of money is $3.7 billion in reserves for the Section 8 program. They can be tapped now, but would have to be replaced later this year when the fiscal 1999 appropriations bills begin to advance. But under rules governing appropriations, replacing the Section 8 money in 1999 would require equal cuts in other domestic programs — a headache for appropriators. One option is a repeat of last year's shell game, in which Section 8 reserves helped finance the big flood aid bill (PL 105-18) but were restored later in the year through a special exemption from budget caps on discretionary spending. That would be difficult to repeat, given the vigilance of conservatives.

● **IMF.** The Senate voted overwhelmingly to attach Clinton's request for $17.9 billion in new IMF funding to the military operations and disaster aid bill. The lead Senate conferee, Appropriations Committee Chairman Ted Stevens, R-Alaska, strongly backs sending Clinton a single supplemental measure.

House GOP leaders want to advance the Clinton request in two pieces, HR 3579 and the second bill (HR 3580), which combines the IMF request, $505 million to repay U.S. arrearages to the U.N. and other generally routine supplemental spending. Anti-abortion activists have won assurances from House leaders that they will be allowed to offer an amendment to HR 3580 to bar U.S. aid to overseas family planning groups that lobby on abortion. The provision has attracted a veto threat. Complicating matters, Majority Leader Dick Armey, R-Texas, said April 2 that he wants to delay consideration of the IMF money.

● **U.N. dues.** Both the House and Senate have detached U.N. dues from the more popular Pentagon and disaster aid bills. Any money appropriated is subject to authorization, but the conference report on the State Department authorization (HR 1757 — H Rept 105-432) is stalled in the Senate and has attracted a veto promise.

Republicans hope to avoid a repeat of last year, when Clinton won a showdown over the flood aid bill. They say this year's dynamics are different. But since the disastrous 1995-96 government shutdowns, every time Clinton has vetoed a spending bill, he has won key concessions. "We're a little bit in the same game of chicken that has been played over the last three years," said Steny H. Hoyer, D-Md. "It shouldn't be played and it can't be won."

Supplemental Bill Enacted, Stripped of IMF, U.N. Provisions

MAY 2 — Displaying a pragmatic streak not seen last year, Congress cleared a $6.1 billion disaster aid and overseas peacekeeping bill April 30, and President Clinton signed it May 1.

Final passage of the fiscal 1998 supplemental spending bill (HR 3579) rids the GOP leadership of a legislative headache that has been pounding all spring.

Clinton signed the bill, even though it does not contain requested funding for the International Monetary Fund (IMF) or U.S. dues to the United Nations, both of which are top White House priorities.

The administration tipped its hand April 29 with a letter from Office of Management and Budget (OMB) Director Franklin D. Raines that vowed a veto only if the bill denied the IMF and U.N. funding while including a "wide range of extraneous issues." Two objectionable provisions were included, but Republicans dropped or decided not to offer several others.

At an April 30 news conference in which Clinton never mentioned a veto, the president said: "I call on Congress to step up to its responsibility and renew our commitment to the International Monetary Fund and to pay our United Nations dues. I am confident we can do this in a bipartisan fashion."

But the IMF and U.N. funds remain tied in knots over an unrelated dispute between anti-abortion activists and the White House over overseas family planning aid. It is unclear whether the two proposals can advance on their own now that the must-pass spending bill has cleared without them.

House and Senate conferees sealed an agreement the morning of April 30, after spending the previous two days steadily working through their differences. The House adopted the conference report, 242-163, and the Senate immediately cleared it for Clinton's signature, 88-11. (*House vote 121, p. H-36; Senate vote 118, p. S-20*)

This year's end game stood in sharp contrast to the disastrous experience of 1997, when GOP leaders insisted on flouting Clinton veto threats and loaded a major flood relief bill with controversial "riders." After he vetoed that bill (HR 1469), Republicans beat a quick retreat and passed another (PL 105-18) without the riders.

This year, Congress took the veto threats seriously. In the end, the only objectionable provisions were a temporary cut in housing programs and a proposal to permit a road to be built across a corner of Petroglyph National Monument in New Mexico. Clinton agreed to a similar housing cut last year, and the road has the support of New Mexico Democratic Sen. Jeff Bingaman.

The conference featured a few theatrical moments as Chairman Ted Stevens, R-Alaska, who chairs the Senate Appropriations Committee, marched lawmakers through mostly middle-tier issues or decisions that GOP leaders had already made.

Decisions to advance the IMF and U.N. funding in a second bill (HR 3580) and not to require offsets for the $2.9 billion in Pentagon spending were made before the conference convened.

That left conferees to wrangle over issues such as organ transplant policy, offshore oil royalties, exceptions to a newly broadened ban on assault weapon imports, and funding for new dam and levee repair projects.

GOP leaders made the two biggest decisions outside the conference room. On April 29, they abandoned efforts to add provisions from a conference report on a crop insurance bill (S 1150 — H Rept 105-492) that would restore food stamp benefits to the most vulnerable legal immigrants. The White House objected to plans to break up that conference report and leave the administration-backed food stamp provision behind. Seventy-one senators signed a letter urging that the agriculture bill move as a whole on its own.

House Republican leaders were also intent on adding to the bill a provision from a broad education reauthorization measure (HR 6) to subsidize bank participation in the federal guaranteed student loan program. But the inclusion of that provision — the main engine driving HR 6 — drew a White House veto promise April 30. The Senate objected to the loan subsidy because it would have required lowering already tight spending caps on domestic programs by at least $1 billion through 2002.

The White House blasted the student loan provision as a giveaway to the banking industry because it would subsidize interest rates paid to banks by about half a percentage point. Republicans wanted to add it to the bill because of a looming July 1 rules change that would lower interest rates in the program, prompting many banks to drop out. Once it was dropped, the disaster aid bill sped to the floor.

Final Bill

House and Senate conferees reached agreement April 30 on a $6.1 billion fiscal 1998 supplemental spending bill (HR 3579), as follows:

Proposed spending
Disaster relief . . . . $ 2.6 billion
Defense . . . . 2.86 billion
   Middle East . . . . 1.3 billion
   Bosnia . . . . 478.9 million
   Other . . . . 482 million
IMF . . . . None in this bill
U.N. dues . . . . None in this bill
Veterans
   compensation * . . . . 550 million
Miscellaneous . . . . 142 million

TOTAL (discretionary) . . . . . $ 5.6 billion

Offsets . . . . 2.6 billion
   Section 8 housing . . . . 2.3 billion
   Airport grants in aid . . . . 241 million
   Miscellaneous . . . . 142.6 million*

* Mandatory spending

SOURCE: House Appropriations Committee

Annual Ritual

The annual spring supplemental spending bill is driven by a need to finance disaster assistance and replenish Pentagon accounts tapped to finance overseas peacekeeping missions. When the conference opened, Stevens gravely warned that if it did not conclude by May 1, the Pentagon would have to issue furlough notices, cancel training missions and stop maintenance of military facilities.

Republican leaders walked a tightrope to get the bill to this point. Internal GOP disagreements over IMF financing and the fight with Clinton over abortion had prompted a two-bill strategy in which the must-pass portions of the request would be sent to Clinton, but the IMF portion would have to advance on its own, tied to the U.N. funds and the longstanding controversy over abortion.

Little of the conference debate involved the spending items in the bill, which were generally agreed upon ahead of time.

The measure contains $1.8 billion

Appropriations

for peacekeeping missions in Bosnia and the Middle East; $2.6 billion in disaster aid programs, including $1.6 billion for the Federal Emergency Management Agency; $550 million in mandatory spending for veterans benefits; and $142 million in miscellaneous appropriations for projects such as repairing the Capitol dome ($27.5 million) and readying federal computers for the year 2000 ($74.8 million).

At the insistence of House GOP conservatives, the bill contains $2.3 billion in temporary cuts from the Section 8 subsidized housing program that will not be needed or used in fiscal 1998. An even bigger cut was used last year to finance the fiscal 1997 supplemental, but the money was replaced under the budget pact. The housing money will have to be replaced again this year. A central question is whether appropriators will have to find cuts in other domestic programs as they consider the upcoming fiscal 1999 spending bills or whether a bookkeeping mechanism can be found to avoid the cuts.

Conservatives bowed to Stevens' insistence that the bill include no offsets for the Pentagon money.

Instead of debating the appropriated items, lawmakers mostly discussed things that their colleagues tried to slip into the must-pass bill. For example, Sen. Kay Bailey Hutchison, R-Texas, and House Appropriations Committee Chairman Robert L. Livingston, R-La., teamed up to delay until Oct. 1 a new regulation that would increase royalties on oil drilled on federal lands.

Livingston orchestrated another move to delay until Oct. 1 new rules governing the allocation of scarce organs for transplant. The rules would require that the sickest patients receive organs first. The current system favors the closest available recipient. Local hospital centers such as Louisiana State University, which fears it would lose organs to larger nationwide facilities, lobbied for the delay, which will allow Congress to review the new regulations.

Sen. Larry E. Craig, R-Idaho, wanted the bill to carry a provision to provide relief to gun importers who had bought and paid for assault weapons subject to the administration's widened ban on weapons imports. Craig wanted to exempt weapons that were being shipped when the ban was imposed last November, but the administration threatened a veto, and Craig backed down.

The most intense debate occurred over dam and levee projects sought by the Senate. The House resolutely resisted the half-dozen projects because they were not requested by the administration nor approved by the House and Senate authorizing committees. The House would not back down, and Stevens argued at length with Rep. Joseph M. McDade, R-Pa., over the projects, recessing the conference to confer privately in a knot of members and staff aides. Ultimately, Stevens emerged with up to $5 million for flood protection in Elba, Ala., at the request of Sen. Richard C. Shelby, R-Ala. ◆

Appropriations Mileposts

BILL	HOUSE	SENATE	FINAL	PAGE
Agriculture (HR 4328 — PL 105-277)	Adopted conference report 10/20/98	Cleared conference report 10/21/98	President signed 10/21/98	Story, p. 2-3
Commerce, Justice, State, Judiciary (HR 4328 — PL 105-277)	Adopted conference report 10/20/98	Cleared conference report 10/21/98	President signed 10/21/98	Story, p. 2-12
Defense (HR 4103 — PL 105-262)	Adopted conference report 9/28/98	Cleared conference report 9/29/98	President signed 10/17/98	Story, p. 2-20
District of Columbia (HR 4328 — PL 105-277)	Adopted conference report 10/20/98	Cleared conference report 10/21/98	President signed 10/21/98	Story, p. 2-32
Energy and Water Development (HR 4060 — PL 105-245)	Adopted conference report 9/28/98	Cleared conference report 9/29/98	President signed 10/7/98	Story, p. 2-36
Foreign Operations (HR 4328 — PL 105-277)	Adopted conference report 10/20/98	Cleared conference report 10/21/98	President signed 10/21/98	Story, p. 2-45
Interior (HR 4328 — PL 105-277)	Adopted conference report 10/20/98	Cleared conference report 10/21/98	President signed 10/21/98	Story, p. 2-57
Labor, Health and Human Services, Education (HR 4328 — PL 105-277)	Adopted conference report 10/20/98	Cleared conference report 10/21/98	President signed 10/21/98	Story, p. 2-64
Legislative Branch (HR 4112 — PL 105-275)	Adopted conference report 9/24/98	Cleared conference report 9/25/98	President signed 10/21/98	Story, p. 2-75
Military Construction (HR 4059 — PL 105-237)	Adopted conference report 7/29/98	Cleared conference report 9/1/98	President signed 9/20/98	Story, p. 2-80
Transportation (HR 4328 — PL 105-277)	Adopted conference report 10/20/98	Cleared conference report 10/21/98	President signed 10/21/98	Story, p. 2-84
Treasury, Postal Service, General Government (HR 4328 — PL 105-277)	Adopted conference report 10/20/98	Cleared conference report 10/21/98	President signed 10/21/98	Story, p. 2-91
Veterans Affairs, HUD, Independent Agencies (HR 4194 — PL 105-276)	Adopted conference report 10/6/98	Cleared conference report 10/8/98	President signed 10/21/98	Story, p. 2-101
Fiscal 1999 Omnibus Appropriations (HR 4328 — PL 105-277)	Adopted conference report 10/20/98	Cleared conference report 10/21/98	President signed 10/21/98	Story, p. 2-112

Chapter 3
ABORTION

Parental Consent 3-3   **'Partial Birth' Ban** 3-7

Under Veto Threat, Parental Notification Bill Stalls in the Senate

Box Score

- **Bills:** HR 3682; S 1645
- **House action:** The House passed HR 3682 (H Rept 105-605), 276-150, on July 15.
- **Senate action:** The Senate voted 54-45 to invoke cloture on S 1645 (S Rept 105-268) on Sept. 22, six votes short of the 60 required.

SUMMARY

Legislation that would make it a federal crime to take a minor across state lines for an abortion to avoid her state's parental consent or notification laws shot forward in the House this summer, but failed in the Senate.

The bill would have subjected those convicted of the proposed crime to a prison sentence of as long as one year and to civil liability and fines of as much as $100,000. An exception in the bill would allow an out-of-state abortion without parental notification if the pregnancy was life-threatening. Neither the youngster nor her parents could be penalized under the bill, even if both parents did not agree to an abortion.

The issue died after Republican lawmakers rejected changes that the White House said were required in order to win President Clinton's support. The Office of Management and Budget issued a statement before House passage, saying the president would support a "properly crafted" bill, but that the president's advisers would recommend a veto unless modifications were made.

Among the changes the White House wanted was an exemption from criminal and civil liability for grandparents and other close family members. Another amendment the administration sought would have protected from liability individuals who provide information, counseling, referral or medical services.

In the Senate, Democrats opposed invoking cloture — thereby stalling the measure — when they realized that those amendments would not be allowed by the GOP. On Sept. 22, the Senate failed to reach cloture on a 54-45 vote, six short of the 60 votes needed. Three moderate Republicans voted against ending debate, while two Democrats voted for cloture.

Sponsors of the bill said it would enforce state laws and ensure that parents have the opportunity to counsel their children. They also said that leaving parents out of abortion decisions could endanger teenagers' health because parents may know medical information about their children that would be important for doctors to know.

Critics said the bill would endanger teenagers. They said young women would be increasingly likely to travel alone across state lines for abortions once their relatives and friends realized that accompanying them could result in prosecution.

House Bill Bolsters States' Parental Consent Laws

JUNE 13 — A bill that abortion rights opponents believe will give them new power to curb abortions moved easily through a House panel June 11.

The House Judiciary Constitution Subcommittee voted 7-2 along party lines to approve the measure (HR 3682) that would make it a federal crime to take a minor across state lines to evade state laws requiring parental notification before an abortion can be performed. The House Judiciary Committee has scheduled a markup June 17.

While the Senate Judiciary Committee has held hearings on a companion bill (S 1645), sponsored by Spencer Abraham, R-Mich., no markup has been scheduled.

Charles T. Canady, R-Fla., chairman of the House subcommittee, said the legislation would prevent children from being "taken from their families to out-of-state abortion clinics in flagrant disregard of the legal protections the states have provided."

But opponents, such as Robert C. Scott of Virginia, the subcommittee's ranking Democrat, said the legislation "will have the cruel practical effect of encouraging young girls to risk their lives traveling alone across state lines to obtain safe and legal procedures."

Scott and Jerrold Nadler, D-N.Y., made several unsuccessful attempts to amend the bill. One amendment would have prohibited prosecution of ministers, rabbis and other religious leaders, family physicians or relatives such as grandparents, cousins, siblings or aunts and uncles. Another would have prohibited prosecution of an individual who assisted a minor after the abortion — by helping her get home safely, for example. Both failed by voice vote.

The panel approved by voice vote a Canady amendment that broadened the bill's definition of "parent" to include a guardian, legal custodian or "a person standing in loco parentis who has care and control of the minor, and with whom the minor regularly resides."

Emotions Flare As Judiciary Panel Begins Debate

JUNE 20 — The deep-seated emotions that surround the abortion debate surfaced as the House Judiciary Committee on June 17 took up legislation that would make it a federal crime to take a minor across state lines to evade state laws requiring parental notification before an abortion can be performed.

The panel took no final action on

Abortion

the bill (HR 3682). Democrats failed in nearly a dozen attempts to soften provisions of the measure, but succeeded in slowing down the process. Final action is expected when the panel resumes consideration of the bill June 23.

Abortion rights supporters view the measure as an effort to curb a woman's constitutional right to an abortion.

"That is the real motivation, and that is what is driving this bill, not the concern about parental involvement," said Jerrold Nadler, D-N.Y.

He and other opponents said it could make doctors, nurses, even cab drivers who drove a minor home after the procedure, liable for prosecution. In addition, relatives such as grandparents and aunts also could be liable.

"No big government mandate can make minors talk more to their parents than they already do," said Robert C. Scott, D-Va.

Violators would be subject to prison terms of as much as one year and fines of up to $100,000. The minor and her parents, however, could not be prosecuted.

Opponents of abortion rights said the measure was necessary to ensure parents' ability to protect their children.

"In many cases, only a girl's parents know of her prior psychological and medical history, including allergies to medication," said Charles T. Canady, R-Fla., a cosponsor of the bill.

The bill would allow a minor to seek a judge's permission to bypass the law, a provision that Canady said would be useful in special situations — such as incest. Opponents countered that a minor who is reluctant to tell her parents she is pregnant and wants an abortion is not likely to tell a judge.

The debate is likely to be replayed in House and Senate consideration of the measure. In a June 17 letter to ranking House Judiciary Democrat, John Conyers Jr. of Michigan, White House Chief of Staff Erskine Bowles said the administration would not support the legislation unless specific changes — many of which were defeated by the committee — were made.

Numerous Amendments

They include amending the bill to exclude close family members from criminal and civil liability and to ensure that people who provide only information, counseling, referral or medical services to the minor cannot be subject to liability.

The committee defeated:

• An amendment by Sheila Jackson-Lee, D-Texas, to permit a minister, rabbi, pastor, priest or "other religious leaders" to take a minor across state lines to receive an abortion. It failed on a 5-17 vote.

• An amendment by Scott to permit a minor's sibling to take her across state lines. The measure failed, 6-15.

• An amendment by Melvin Watt, D-N.C., to broaden the bill's exception clause to permit a minor to be taken across state lines for an abortion if it were needed to prevent serious illness or disability. His amendment was defeated on an 11-16 vote. The underlying bill allows such abortions if they are needed to save the minor's life.

While the Democrats' amendments failed, Canady prevailed with two amendments that passed by voice votes. One would give the individual transporting the minor responsibility for making sure the parental notification laws of her home state are followed, even if she is taken to another state for an abortion. The second changed the bill to say a parent could not be prosecuted or sued under the law for taking a child across state lines for an abortion, even if both parents did not agree to the procedure. That amendment also provided for an "affirmative defense" to permit an individual who is accused of violating the law to state why he or she thought they were in compliance.

In the Senate, Spencer Abraham, R-Mich., a sponsor of similar legislation (S 1645), said he hoped the Senate Judiciary Committee could mark up his bill before the July Fourth recess.

Committee OKs Out-of-State Abortion Curb

JUNE 27 — Gearing up for a mid-July floor battle, a divided House Judiciary Committee on June 23 approved legislation (HR 3682) that would make it a crime to transport a minor across state lines for an abortion to avoid her state's parental consent or notification laws.

Under the bill, adopted 17-10 along party lines, offenders would face a prison sentence of up to one year, up to $100,000 in fines and civil liability.

In a markup that highlighted the two parties' long-held differences on abortion, Republicans refused to adopt several Democratic amendments, many of which were suggested by the Clinton administration.

Republicans, who are expected to use the issue to appeal to their core conservative constituencies in this fall's campaigns, hope to bring the measure to the floor shortly after the July Fourth recess. A similar bill (S 1645) is pending in the Senate Judiciary Committee.

Republicans, led by cosponosr Charles T. Canady of Florida, argued that the measure would ensure that state abortion laws to involve parents are not circumvented.

Democrats countered that the bill would drive minors to seek abortions alone, particularly if family members could be sued or prosecuted for helping them cross state lines for the procedure. Neither the minor nor her parents could be penalized under the bill, even if both parents did not agree.

Twenty-nine states have parental consent or notification laws in effect.

The bill would allow prosecuted people to defend themselves by saying that they believed the parents had been notified as required by state law. An exception in the bill would allow an out-of-state abortion without parental notification if the abortion was necessary to save the minor's life.

Much of the debate centered on an amendment offered by Sheila Jackson-Lee, D-Texas, at the behest of the White House. The amendment, which failed 8-16 along party lines, would have exempted grandparents from penalties. Her amendments to protect aunts, uncles or first cousins were rejected as a package, 9-16.

"If a grandmother intervenes on the side of compassion and love for her granddaughter, why in the world would we want to subject her to criminal penalties?" said Barney Frank, D-Mass.

Canady argued that people who take a minor across state lines for the procedure are violating her parents' rights and, if they lacked access to her medical records, jeopardizing her health.

Parental Consent

"I would like to point out that we are acting to protect the health and safety of minors," he said.

The committee also defeated by voice vote an administration-suggested amendment by Robert C. Scott, D-Va., to clarify that medical facilities that perform abortions would be exempt from penalties.

Canady said that while the bill does not focus on abortion clinics or doctors, "if providers engage in conspiracy or are otherwise engaged in this activity, they should not get an exemption . . ."

The committee rejected another Democratic amendment that would have required federal prosecutors to certify that each case brought under the law was of a significant federal interest that state laws did not address. Another defeated amendment would have allowed out-of-state abortions to protect the health of the minor.

Senate Panel's Poor Attendance Delays Action On Abortion Bill

JULY 11 — After weeks of delays, the Senate Judiciary Committee on July 9 took up legislation that would make it a federal crime to transport a minor across a state line for the purposes of avoiding a parental consent law pertaining to abortion.

But soon after taking up S 1645, Chairman Orrin G. Hatch, R-Utah, realized he would be hard pressed to maintain a quorum and delayed action until the week of July 13.

The delay has been typical of the committee this summer. At times Hatch has looked less like a committee chairman than a schoolteacher, sternly lecturing his pupils on the importance of attendance. The combination of absent members and a proclivity for extended debate among those who do show up has made the committee's work very difficult of late.

The abortion bill stalled before members could even vote on the first amendment, a proposal by Edward M. Kennedy, D-Mass., that would require a Justice Department certification process. His language would require that before an individual could be prosecuted under the new law, Justice would have to show that no state had plans to prosecute the individual, and that the federal government had an interest in doing so.

Before turning to the specifics of this amendment, committee Democrats expressed broad objections to the bill, sponsored by Spencer Abraham, R-Mich. Dianne Feinstein, D-Calif., said it was "one more step in the long march to making abortion illegal."

But much of the debate centered on whether the measure violated federalist principles. Ranking Democrat Patrick J. Leahy of Vermont argued that it did, saying the federal government would essentially apply the laws of one state to the people in another. Why, he asked, should the federal government do this in the case of abortion laws, when it has not in other areas — such as gun laws?

But Fred Thompson, R-Tenn., argued that no principles of federalism would be violated since the measure was narrowly crafted and applied only to an act of escorting a minor over state lines, not to the broader issue of crossing state lines for the purposes of obtaining an abortion.

GOP Stands Firm On Criminalizing Aid to Minors

JULY 18 — President Clinton will be called upon to veto at least one abortion bill before the November election. The first likely target: A measure that would make it a federal crime to transport a girl across state lines to obtain an abortion in circumvention of parental consent and notification laws in her home state.

The House passed its version of the bill (HR 3682) on July 15 by a vote of 276-150. The Senate Judiciary Committee approved its companion measure (S 1645) the next day, 10-6. The committee approved a substitute that conformed to the House bill. *(House vote 280, p. H-80)*

But in the House and in the Senate committee, GOP lawmakers rejected amendments that the White House says are a condition for President Clinton to sign such a bill.

The House tally fell eight votes short of the two-thirds majority needed to override a veto.

One amendment offered in the Senate committee would have exempted members of a girl's family — such as grandmothers — from prosecution. It was rejected, 7-9. Another, rejected 6-9, would have required the attorney general to certify that a case involved a significant federal public interest before prosecution could occur.

California Sen. Dianne Feinstein and other Democrats said they would have considered voting for the bill had the amendments been adopted. But the lawmakers said they could not support it now, particularly without protection for family members.

"If this is about family values, then this amendment should be accepted without controversy," argued Sen. Richard J. Durbin, D-Ill.

"Federal laws do not create family ties," said ranking Democrat Patrick J. Leahy of Vermont. "Only families can do that."

Republicans countered that girls who fear telling their parents can try to persuade a judge to exempt them from the state law.

"We are only trying to enforce laws that states have," said sponsor Spencer Abraham, R-Mich. "This legislation doesn't attempt to go beyond that, nor do we impose regulations on states that do not have these laws."

Senate Majority Leader Trent Lott, R-Miss., said the bill "is high on our list of must-pass legislation" and will be brought to the floor shortly.

Fines and White House Approval

The bill would subject those convicted of the proposed new crime to a prison sentence of up to one year, as much as $100,000 in fines and civil liability. An exception in the bill would allow an out-of-state abortion without parental notification if the pregnancy is life-threatening.

The Office of Management and Budget issued a statement before the House vote saying the White House would support a "properly crafted" bill, but that the president's advisers would recommend a veto of the bill in its current form.

Among the changes the White House wants is an exemption for grandparents and other close family

Abortion

members from criminal and civil liability. Another change would be to protect from liability individuals who provide information, counseling, referral or medical services.

House Democrats wanted to offer the White House-backed provisions as amendments, but, on a 247-173 vote, the House adopted a rule that prevented those amendments from being offered. *(Vote 278, p. H-80)*

On passage, 14 Republicans voted against the bill, while 67 Democrats voted for it.

During the House debate, the legislation's backers cited the need to ensure parents' rights are protected.

"This bill seeks to reinforce the primacy of parents," said Judiciary Chairman Henry J. Hyde, R-Ill.

Opponents countered that the bill would make it harder to get a legal abortion, and would isolate minors and drive them to seek abortions alone.

"We do not need a bill that isolates teenagers and puts them at risk," said Nita M. Lowey, D-N.Y.

Neither the minor nor her parents could be penalized under the bill, even if both parents did not agree to an abortion.

The bill also would establish a defense to the bill's prohibitions for individuals who can prove that they "reasonably believed" that parental consent was given before they transported the minor across state lines.

'Partial Birth' Override Likely

The next target for anti-abortion Republicans is Clinton's veto of a bill (HR 1122) to ban a controversial procedure that critics call "partial birth" abortion. A House override vote is scheduled for July 23.

Doctors who perform that form of abortion could face jail and fines. Clinton vetoed the bill Oct. 10.

Measure Stalls In the Senate as Cloture Vote Fails

SEPTEMBER 26 — A bill (S 1645) that would make it a federal crime to take a minor across state lines for an abortion to avoid parental consent or notification laws is unlikely to see further congressional action this year.

On Sept. 22, the Senate failed to reach cloture on the bill, voting 54-45, six short of the 60 needed. Three Republicans voted against ending debate: James M. Jeffords of Vermont, John H. Chafee of Rhode Island and Arlen Specter of Pennsylvania. Two Democrats voted for cloture: Harry Reid of Nevada and Ernest F. Hollings of South Carolina. *(Vote 282, p. S-44)*

Spencer Abraham, R-Mich., the chief sponsor of the bill, said that tally plus the crowded Senate calendar made any possible return to the measure "very unlikely" before adjournment.

The House on July 15 passed similar legislation.

The failed cloture vote was the second defeat this month for opponents of abortion rights. On Sept. 18, the Senate failed to override President Clinton's veto of legislation (HR 1122) that would have banned a procedure opponents refer to as "partial birth" abortion. The 64-36 vote fell three short of the two-thirds majority needed for an override.

Clinton made it clear that he also would have vetoed the bill prohibiting the transport of minors across state lines unless it was significantly changed.

A Sept. 9 statement from the Office of Management and Budget said the administration wanted the bill amended to exclude close family members from criminal and civil liability. House and Senate Democrats sought similar changes. Under the bill, grandparents or siblings, for example, could face criminal prosecution. Offenders would face a prison sentence of up to one year and $100,000 in fines and civil liability.

Partisan Split

Although many Democrats joined Republicans in a 97-0 vote on Sept. 11 to pass a motion to proceed to the bill, that bipartisanship was never expected to continue. Democrats blocked cloture when it became clear that some of their amendments would be either blocked or ruled out of order.

Sponsors of the bill said it would help teenagers because parents could offer support or provide additional medical information that a relative or close friend may not know.

"Parents have the right and duty to be involved in the moral and medical decisions that affect their children's welfare," said Sen. Mike DeWine, R-Ohio.

But opponents said the bill would endanger teenagers because they might be forced to travel alone across state lines for an abortion if relatives or friends accompanying them could face possible prosecution. They also said that teenagers may not always be able to discuss pregnancy with a parent.

"If a young woman feels she cannot involve her parents for whatever reason ... she should not be discouraged from seeking the counsel of a trusted adult," said Carl Levin, D-Mich.

Backers of the bill said its judicial bypass option would have allowed teenagers to appeal directly to a judge to exempt them from state law. But opponents said teenagers who fear telling their parents about a pregnancy are unlikely to reveal it to a judge. ◆

Senate Sustains Veto of 'Partial Birth' Abortion Ban For Second Time

> **Box Score**
>
> ● **Bill:** HR 1122
>
> ● **House action:** The House voted 296-132 on July 23 to override the veto.
>
> ● **Senate action:** Senate voted 64-36 on Sept. 18 on veto override, three votes short of necessary two-thirds majority.

The Senate again refused to override President Clinton's veto of legislation that would have outlawed a controversial abortion procedure, although the House voted to do so for the second Congress in a row.

SUMMARY

Clinton vetoed HR 1122 on Oct. 10, 1997, just as he had vetoed a similar measure cleared by the 104th Congress. Both times he criticized the bill's failure to provide exceptions when the health of the woman is in danger.

Both chambers had passed HR 1122 in 1997, but bill sponsors pushed for 1998 votes on overriding the veto, hoping to put more pressure on senators up for re-election.

In the House, override advocates garnered 10 votes more than needed, including that of House Minority Leader Richard A. Gephardt, D-Mo.

However, the Senate on Sept. 18 failed by three votes to override the veto. The 64-36 tally was the same as the vote by which the Senate passed HR 1122 on May 20, 1997. Fifty-one Republicans and 13 Democrats voted in favor of the override, while four Republicans and 32 Democrats voted against it.

The bill would have made the procedure, which obstetricians call "dilation and extraction," a federal crime unless it was necessary to save the woman's life. Medical professionals but not their patients would have been subject to criminal and civil penalties.

The procedure was defined as one in which the person performing the abortion "partially vaginally delivers a living fetus before killing the fetus and completing delivery."

Abortion rights supporters warned that overriding Clinton's veto would be a step toward eroding abortion rights.

A bipartisan group of senators failed to get support for a proposal that would have outlawed the procedure unless it was necessary to prevent "grievous injury" to the woman's physical health. The bipartisan alternative would have required two doctors — including an independent physician who was not treating the woman and would not perform the abortion — to certify that the circumstances met the grievous injury test.

Senate Minority Leader Tom Daschle, D-S.D., proposed a similar measure without the two-physician requirement in 1997, but it was rejected, 36-64.

The issue has become a major rallying point for anti-abortion groups. Led by Sen. Rick Santorum, R-Pa., override advocates call the procedure "infanticide." Although these lawmakers were stymied by Clinton's vetoes, they vowed to renew the battle next year. "This will not be the end of the debate," said Senate Judiciary Committee member John Ashcroft, R-Mo. "We will vote again."

House Vote Sets Up Senate Showdown

JULY 25 — Setting the stage for a pivotal Senate vote on abortion just weeks before the fall elections, the House on July 23 overwhelmingly voted to override President Clinton's veto of legislation to ban a controversial procedure that opponents call "partial birth" abortion.

The 296-132 vote, in which 77 Democrats — including House Minority Leader Richard A. Gephardt, D-Mo. — voted with 219 Republicans, gave supporters of the ban 10 more than the two-thirds needed to override Clinton's Oct. 10 veto. (Vote 325, p. H-94)

Proponents of the ban face an uphill battle in the Senate, however, where an override vote is expected in September. The Senate passed the vetoed bill (HR 1122) in May 1997 by a vote of 64-36, three votes shy of the needed two-thirds.

While no senator has announced a change in position since last year, Senate Minority Leader Tom Daschle, D-S.D., said July 23 that the outcome was "a close call" that could not be predicted. Daschle was one of 13 Senate Democrats to vote for the ban last year.

Clinton rejected the bill in October because, he said, it would not provide exceptions to allow the procedure to protect the woman's health.

Supporters of the ban, however, dismissed that argument as specious, saying the procedure that would be banned would never be needed to protect a woman's health.

"There is never an instance in which a woman would have to have a partial-birth abortion," said Tom Coburn, R-Okla., a doctor who has delivered thousands of babies.

The underlying bill would make the abortion procedure, which obstetricians call "dilation and extraction," a federal crime unless it is necessary to save the life of the pregnant woman. The bill defines the procedure as one in which "the person performing the abortion partially vaginally delivers a living fetus before killing the fetus and completing delivery."

House consideration of the override brought out many of the same emotions that have characterized previous debates over the issue.

House Judiciary Committee Chairman Henry J. Hyde, R-Ill., drew parallels between the procedure and the Holocaust and slavery in having the effect of "dehumanizing people."

"Partial-birth abortion concerns the very nature of man," Hyde said. "Our beloved America is becoming the killing fields," he said later.

Abortion

Political Considerations

Opponents of the legislation, most of whom are Democrats, criticized supporters of the measure for focusing on one procedure rather than all late-term abortions. Many of them charged that the GOP was pushing this particular bill not in the expectation that it would become law, but in the hope that it could turn the political tide this fall against Democrats in tight races.

Democrats argued that a preferable proposal is a measure (HR 1032) sponsored by James C. Greenwood, R-Pa., and Steny H. Hoyer, D-Md., that would ban all types of late-term abortions, with exemptions if the woman's life was in jeopardy or if she faced serious adverse health consequences without the procedure. That measure, they argued, more likely would be signed into law and judged constitutional by the courts.

Supporters of the ban said the Greenwood-Hoyer measure would allow partial-birth abortions to continue because some are performed before the fetus is viable.

Opponents of the ban say it is no coincidence that the House leadership waited until closer to the fall elections to have the vote.

"This bill is not about reducing abortions," said Nita M. Lowey, D-N.Y. "It's about defeating Democrats."

Kate Michelman, president of the National Abortion and Reproductive Rights Action League, said the House leadership had made "a blatant attempt to appease their increasingly restless social conservative base during an election year."

While the League and other abortion rights groups expect the Senate to maintain its opposition to the ban, proponents of the override are expected to use the coming weeks to put pressure on senators who opposed the bill last year.

"It's long past time for 36 senators to stop defending the indefensible, brutal practice of partial-birth abortion," said Douglas Johnson, legislative director for the National Right to Life Committee, an anti-abortion group. "It is appalling that any senator would vote to allow thousands of living babies to be mostly delivered and then stabbed through the head."

The action replayed events of the 104th Congress, when the Republicans took control and anti-abortion forces scored one of their biggest legislative victories in years. Congress cleared a bill to ban the procedure, Clinton quickly vetoed it and then Republicans waited until near the election to attempt the override. The House cleared the override but the Senate was nine votes short. (*1996 Almanac, p. 6-43*)

Senate Narrowly Sustains Veto

SEPTEMBER 19 — As expected, abortion rights opponents failed to override President Clinton's veto of legislation (HR 1122) that would ban a procedure they refer to as "partial birth" abortion.

The 64-36 Senate vote Sept. 18 broke along party lines, with most Republicans voting to override and most Democrats voting to sustain Clinton's veto. The tally fell three short of the two-thirds majority needed to override a presidential veto. Thirteen Democrats and 51 Republicans voted for the override; 32 Democrats and four Republicans voted to sustain the veto.

President Clinton vetoed the bill Oct. 10, 1997, because he said it did not provide exceptions to permit the procedure when necessary to protect a woman's health. The House voted 296-132 on July 23 to override the veto. (*Clinton veto, 1997 Almanac, p. 6-12*)

Under the measure, doctors who performed the abortion procedure could have been sentenced to two years in prison and could have faced fines and lawsuits for civil damages. The measure would have exempted the woman from criminal penalties.

The procedure is defined in the bill as one in which "the person performing the abortion partially vaginally delivers a living fetus before killing the fetus and completing delivery." The procedure is performed in the second and third trimesters of pregnancy; other methods are also used at that time.

The Senate debate was similar to the one in May 1997 when it voted 64-36 to pass the legislation. Many senators did not relish tackling the topic again, especially so close to the November elections.

Rick Santorum, R-Pa., the leader of the override effort, deemed the procedure "infanticide. . . . This is a baby just inches away from being born." Bill Frist, R-Tenn., a heart surgeon, said the procedure is dangerous to women's health and inhumane to the fetus.

Several Democrats, including Barbara Boxer of California, said the bill would "force doctors to make decisions that jeopardize women's health" because they could perform the procedure only if it was necessary to save the mother's life, not to protect her health.

Boxer and others said it was critical that doctors and their patients — not Congress — make any decisions concerning abortion. "No woman wants to visit her doctor and see her senator lurking over her doctor's shoulder," Boxer said.

Carol Moseley-Braun, D-Ill., concurred. "Congress as a body does not have the right to practice medicine," she said.

Abortion rights advocates also warned that allowing Clinton's veto to be overridden would be the first step to eroding abortion rights. "This is just one way they are going to get to their ultimate goal," Boxer said.

Before the Sept. 17 floor debate began, a bipartisan group of senators proposed an alternative they hoped would provide a middle ground on the issue.

The group, including Democrats Richard J. Durbin of Illinois and Robert G. Torricelli of New Jersey and Maine Republicans Olympia J. Snowe and Susan Collins, said its measure would outlaw the procedure to be performed on a viable fetus — one that can live outside the womb — except when necessary to prevent "grievous injury" to the mother's physical health.

Senate Minority Leader Tom Daschle, D-S.D., proposed a similar measure last year, but it was rejected on a vote of 36-64.

The bipartisan alternative, however, would require that two physicians — the woman's doctor plus an independent physician who is not treating the woman and would not perform the abortion — certify that the procedure met the "grievous injury" test. Daschle's proposal did not mandate that two doctors concur on the decision.

Both the bipartisan alternative and the underlying bill (HR 1122) would permit the procedure if it is necessary to save the mother's life.

Durbin said it was "unlikely" that the measure would be considered this year. Douglas Johnson, legislative director for the National Right to Life Committee, said it was just another attempt by abortion rights supporters to gain "political cover" and "diffuse" the troublesome issue.

Even though abortion rights opponents lost their battle to override Clinton's veto, John Ashcroft, R-Mo., said the issue will return.

"This will not be the end of the debate," Ashcroft said. "We will come back, we will vote again."

But the continued debate is not good for the country, said Kate Michelman, president of the National Abortion and Reproductive Rights Action League. "The public long ago decided who should decide" the issue of abortion, she said. "They don't appreciate having this [debate] over and over again." ◆

Chapter 4
AGRICULTURE

Agriculture Research 4-3

Law Funds Crop Insurance, Restores Food Stamps For Legal Immigrants

President Clinton on June 23 signed into law legislation to authorize funding for various Agriculture Department (USDA) research, extension and education programs, and to provide mandatory crop insurance funding for the next five fiscal years.

The measure endured a long and tortured journey to final passage because it carried contentious provisions restoring food stamp benefits to certain legal immigrants who were bumped from the rolls by the 1996 welfare overhaul (PL 104-193).

The bill authorized $818 million over five years to restore food stamp benefits to 250,000 elderly and disabled legal immigrants, as well as children under 18, who were in the country when the welfare law was signed in August 1996.

Conservatives opposed the provisions, furiously resisting rollback of any more of the welfare law. Clinton in 1997 had forced Congress to restore Supplemental Security Income and Medicaid benefits to the legal immigrants, and he threatened to veto this bill unless the food stamp restoration was included. *(1997 Almanac, p. 6-31)*

In the end, agriculture, nutrition and immigrant groups formed a coalition to support the legislation, and the alliance managed to nurse it to final passage. Farm state lawmakers, in particular, pleaded for enactment of the agriculture provisions, especially those providing $1 billion in mandatory funding over five years to pay the commissions of agents who sell federally subsidized crop insurance policies. With federal subsidies in decline and the federal government no longer providing disaster aid, mandatory funding for the federal crop insurance program became a rallying cry for growers.

The legislation also included $600 million in mandatory funding for competitive grants for agriculture research in food safety, crop yields and genetic engineering. It reauthorized the administration's Fund for Rural America; set up a variety of new programs, such as a honey promotion system funded through assessments on honey producers; and directed the USDA to develop new priorities and to solicit public input regarding its research and education programs.

In a rebuke to the administration and final twist to the bill's saga, two of the programs reauthorized by the measure — the mandatory research program and the Fund for Rural America — were specifically denied funding in fiscal 1999 through provisions in the omnibus appropriations bill (HR 4328 — PL 105-277).

Restoring Federal Nutrition Aid Creates Food Fight

JANUARY 10 — Rep. Charles W. Stenholm, D-Texas, has troubles. Tens of thousands of legal immigrants in his state have lost food stamps as a result of the far-reaching 1996 welfare overhaul that severed their monthly nutrition benefits.

But restoring federal nutrition aid, as President Clinton is set to propose in his fiscal 1999 budget, could mean taking money away from farm interests that help form the economic backbone of Stenholm's district and support his power base on the Agriculture Committee.

Nutrition and farm groups, historically linked behind federal food support programs, are now mired in a messy battle over how to spend $1.25 billion in federal savings that could come from a complicated change in allocating food stamp administrative funds to states.

The $1.25 billion appears small in relation to the $37.2 billion that Congress will spend on nutrition programs this year. But the fight over it is emblematic of the politics of food in the 1990s, where tight budgets have forced tradeoffs between nutrition and farm aid.

Budget cuts, along with demographic changes that have strengthened suburban interests at the expense of urban and rural groups, have also frayed the traditional alliance of farm and nutrition advocates that helped create the food stamp program in 1964.

More broadly, the fight is yet another element in the debate over whether the 1996 welfare overhaul (PL 104-193) went too far, especially with regard to legal immigrants. The administration began proposing changes to the law even before the ink was dry, but supporters have resisted most White House efforts to restore the food stamps. *(1996 Almanac, p. 6-3)*

The debate leaves Stenholm torn between two key interest groups. He is trying to foster a deal, or at least a dialogue.

"I'm trying to convince both sides that part of something is better than all of nothing," Stenholm said. "Those savings should be used for purposes of food and nutrition. Both the consumption and production of it."

Box Score

- **Bill:** S 1150 — PL 105-185
- **House action:** The House cleared the conference report (H Rept 105-492) on S 1150, 364-50, on June 4. The House defeated the first recommended rule for consideration of the conference report, 120-289, on May 22. It passed S 1150, with an amendment, by voice vote on Feb. 24. The House passed its initial version of the bill (HR 2534), 291-125, on Nov. 8, 1997.
- **Senate action:** The Senate adopted the conference report on S 1150, 92-8, on May 12. It passed S 1150 by voice vote on Oct. 29, 1997.
- **Presidential action:** Clinton signed the bill June 23.

Agriculture

Immigrant Groups Weigh In

The $1.25 billion at issue represents potential savings included in the Senate bill (S 1150) to reauthorize agriculture research programs. The savings would be achieved through a limit on the amount of money that the federal government pays to states for administering food stamp programs. By capping the reimbursements, the Senate measure, which was passed Oct. 29, would capture the savings and use it to help pay for expanding agriculture research.

In the House, however, immigrant groups have decided to wage a last-minute effort to win some of that money for the 935,000 legal aliens dropped from the food stamp rolls in the 1996 welfare overhaul. The House measure (HR 2543) passed Nov. 8, but did not include the cap on administrative costs.

The White House, meanwhile, is expected to propose reinstating the food stamp program for some legal immigrants, and congressional aides say the administration is eyeing the $1.25 billion to help pay for it.

An Alliance Unraveling

For decades, food and agriculture groups maintained a fruitful, if awkward, marriage of political convenience. Farm-state lawmakers expanded food stamps as part of broad crop subsidy measures. The nutrition aid attracted much-needed urban votes, helping ensure passage of farm bills even as the rural population declined.

In recent years, however, the emphasis on balancing the federal budget has squeezed the amount of money available to the House and Senate Agriculture committees, which oversee both crop and nutrition programs. That has forced direct funding trade-offs between the interests, and the gradual shift from cooperation to competition between the two groups.

"It's quite a little melodrama," said Terry Nipp, president of AESOP Enterprises, a consulting firm representing land grant universities on the research measure. "The [university] community is very sensitive about not getting into a no-win situation between science program activities and feeding legal immigrants. It's a larger social debate."

Farm lobbyists say they are willing to compromise, to a point, to preserve the research bill.

With the White House now engaged on the issue, immigrant and nutrition groups hope to win a couple of billion dollars to restore benefits, including a chunk of the $1.25 billion in the research measure. That would be enough to aid select immigrants such as the elderly, disabled or families with children.

Since the welfare law went into effect, roughly a dozen states, including Texas, New York, Florida and California, either have put programs in place or are creating systems to provide state-funded aid to legal immigrants.

While most of the attention on the welfare law has focused on five-year time limits and work requirements, about half its savings came from food stamps. The law cut $27 billion over six years, the largest dollar reduction in the program's history.

Advocates for the poor say the impact of the changes has been stark. From September 1996 to September 1997, the number of people receiving food stamps fell 3.9 million, to 20.9 million. That compares with a drop of about 1 million in the previous year.

Robert Greenstein, executive director of the Center on Budget and Policy Priorities, a liberal think tank, said the decline appears far larger than can be explained by a strong economy and cutoffs in the welfare law.

He worries that people are not applying because they are scared off by reports that the government is tightening such programs. Other advocates cite reports of increased demand at food banks, including a December report by the U.S. Conference of Mayors, to argue that Congress must restore food stamps, starting with immigrants.

"What we have in the midst of this booming economy, in the midst of people going off welfare . . . we have one sector that is going hungry," said Josh Bernstein, policy analyst at the National Immigration Law Center.

However, Rep. Robert W. Goodlatte, R-Va., chairman of the House Agriculture Subcommittee on Department Operations, Nutrition and Foreign Agriculture, said the data do not point to higher-than-expected demand.

Goodlatte said he will monitor need and ensure that Congress supports food banks. He also plans further hearings to examine whether the federal government is doing enough to crack down on fraud and quality control problems in the food stamp program. Agriculture Department officials have told Congress that such problems could cost as much as $3 billion a year.

"Not providing food stamps to non-citizens is something that's been well established in this country going back a long, long ways. Restoring that principle was part of welfare reform," Goodlatte said. "Now is not the time to go back."

The welfare debate in 1995 and 1996 illustrated both the strength and weakness of the farm-food coalition.

In one indication of the alliance's strength, the House Agriculture Committee successfully fought House leaders and Republican governors who wanted to turn food stamps from an entitlement into a state block grant program. Farm-state senators subsequently blocked a move to let states run school lunch programs.

At the same time, however, farm groups quietly lobbied to make deeper cuts in nutrition programs in order to protect funding for crop and environmental programs.

"The word [from farm groups] was 'look for someplace else [other than crop aid] to make the cuts,' " said a Senate agriculture aide. "In our jurisdiction, farm programs and nutrition are the only two of consequence."

The bulk of food stamp cuts came in the form of accounting changes that limited inflationary adjustments and made other technical changes to the program. The welfare overhaul also changed income deductions, ended benefits to legal immigrants and limited able-bodied adults ages 18 to 50 without dependents to three months of benefits in three years, unless they worked 20 hours a week. Congress relaxed the latter provision in the 1997 budget law (PL 105-33).

Farm Aid

While nutrition groups are seeking to restore food stamp money, farm groups must also adjust to a new world.

In 1996, Congress made fundamental changes in crop subsidy programs in place since the New Deal. The seven-year farm law (PL 104-127) signed in April 1996 freed farmers from rigid federal planting requirements, while providing fixed-support payments. The law boosted subsidies in 1996 and

Agriculture Research

1997 but gradually decreased fixed payments to growers. Aid will fall from $5.8 billion in fiscal 1998 to $4 billion in 2002. *(1996 Almanac, p. 3-15)*

Commodity lobbyists point out the law was one in a series of measures cutting agriculture, including the 1993 budget-reconciliation act (PL 103-66) that reduced farm programs while increasing food stamps. *(1993 Almanac, p. 107)*

Many Democrats opposed the 1996 farm legislation, saying it would help big agri-businesses at the expense of small farmers, and they have vowed to revisit the issue.

After the magnitude of changes in the 1996 farm law, the agriculture community is lobbying for stepped-up research funds, saying that as growers are weaned from federal aid, the government must help develop new markets.

In a nod to the nutrition community, the Senate research bill also had $151 million for child nutrition programs. After fending off other lawmakers who wanted the food stamp money for their own initiatives, the Senate passed the research bill by unanimous consent.

Immigrant groups got involved as the House Agriculture Committee prepared to bring its version to the floor. Among other things, they wanted a commitment that some of the $1.25 billion in the Senate bill would be redirected to legal immigrants. The National Governors' Association opposes limiting food stamp administrative money.

In the end, Rep. David R. Obey, D-Wis., blocked a House-Senate conference on the bill Nov. 8, angry that the Senate bill made research a mandatory spending program while his Appropriations Committee was being forced to find money for other programs such as crop insurance.

Stenholm had hoped to avoid the blowup. He tried to work out an understanding with the Agriculture Committee Republican leadership and brought nutrition, immigration and commodity groups together to exhort them to compromise before the House debate.

"My own assessment of those meetings is they were good positive first steps. Coalition building is not something you do in a 100-yard sprint," Stenholm said.

Democrats also have been working to secure more agriculture funding in the administration's upcoming budget, saying the White House must be careful to avoid a backlash from farm groups, thereby harming its own efforts to restore immigrant aid.

"We are all fighting for limited dollars, but we have to recognize a new dynamic," argues Chandler Keys, vice president of the National Cattlemen's Beef Association. "Rural and urban people are under siege here and we are under siege from the suburbs. The suburbs don't care about agriculture research and they don't care about food stamps."

But David Beckmann, president of Bread for the World, recalls a forum Stenholm set up last spring to try to start a dialogue among all parties.

"His idea was to try to get people who work on agriculture and food issues to work more together. . . . It was sort of an eerie silence from the ag groups," he said. "The ag interests haven't rallied around on these massive food stamp cuts very much."

Congress Plans To Debate Food Stamp Issue

MARCH 28 — In yet another move to relax provisions of the 1996 welfare law (PL 104-193), Congress is set to debate legislation that would restore food stamps to 250,000 legal immigrants who were cut from federal benefit rolls.

Senate proponents hope to take up the measure before the April 2 recess. The outlook for moving the legislation is somewhat dicier in the House, where some key Republicans threatened to vote against it. Democrats said they could likely deliver enough votes to ensure an overall majority. Reinstating the aid is a top White House priority.

The immigrant provisions were part of a broader House-Senate conference agreement reached March 24 on a measure (S 1150) to reauthorize federal agriculture research programs. The compromise bill calls for $600 million in new, mandatory spending over five years to expand food safety, genetic engineering and other education programs; about $1 billion to pay agent commissions under the federal crop insurance program; and $100 million for programs for rural development and research.

Aside from concern over the immigrant aid, some House lawmakers were upset that the measure created a new mandatory spending program for agriculture research at a time when federal funds are scarce. John A. Boehner of Ohio, chairman of the House Republican conference, ruled out speedy action.

"The problem with the conference report is taking agriculture research and putting it into a mandatory spending category. There is growing concern about that," he said.

The new competitive grants for agriculture research are a top priority of farm state lawmakers, particularly as the federal government gradually reduces crop subsidies under a 1996 farm law (PL 104-127). *(1996 Almanac, p. 3-15)*

The new spending in the legislation would be paid for largely by limiting the amount of money the federal government allocates to states for administering the food stamp program. The cap would save about $1.8 billion over five years.

The final measure is a complicated compromise among the Senate, which had originally planned to use nearly all the administrative cost savings for research; the White House and the House Hispanic caucus, which pushed hard to restore food stamps to immigrants; and farm state lawmakers worried about a funding shortfall that threatened the crop insurance program.

Competition From Budget Panel

House and Senate lawmakers had dithered over the measure for months. In recent weeks it became clear that unless they quickly cut a deal, they faced the prospect of ending up without any money at all. That is because other committees were beginning to eye their funding source.

The Senate Budget Committee on March 18 approved a fiscal 1999 budget resolution that would use the food stamp administrative funds as offsets to cover increased spending in other federal programs, including the surface transportation authorization bill.

"There's an urgency to move on this or it . . . will be devoured by ISTEA and that will be the end of the entire

Agriculture

exercise," said Senate Agriculture Committee Chairman Richard G. Lugar, R-Ind. After conferees sealed the deal, aides worked around the clock to file the conference report in an effort to ensure that it would not be overtaken by the budget resolution.

An estimated 935,000 immigrants lost food stamps under the welfare legislation. Congress last year moved to reinstate federal disability benefits to legal immigrants as part of the 1997 budget-reconciliation bill. (PL 105-33)

The agriculture legislation provides more than $800 million that would restore food stamps to elderly and disabled immigrants who were in the United States when the welfare law was signed on Aug. 22, 1996, as well as children under age 18 who were in the country at that time. Refugees and those granted political asylum would be allowed to receive food stamps for seven years, up from the current five.

Agriculture Secretary Dan Glickman threatened to oppose the research measure unless it included immigrant aid. In a March 26 statement, he praised the conference report and said he would urge President Clinton to sign it.

"Immigrants who are in this country legally, paying taxes, contributing to our economy and enriching our society deserve our assistance when they need it," Glickman said.

Clinton's fiscal 1999 budget, released Feb. 2, called for more than $2 billion over five years in aid to immigrants.

The debate put farm state lawmakers, such as Rep. Charles W. Stenholm, D-Texas, in a tough position, forcing them to choose between aid to farm programs and aid to immigrants. Stenholm helped work out the deal.

Advocates for the poor called the measure a good first step, but warned that more would be needed.

But Rep. Robert W. Goodlatte, R-Va., chairman of the House Agriculture Subcommittee on Department Operations, Nutrition, and Foreign Agriculture, said he opposed the plan. He has said that longstanding U.S. policy calls for immigrants to be self-sufficient.

Negotiators also struggled to come up with a way to pay annual subsidies to insurance agents who sell federal crop policies. The policies reimburse farmers affected by bad weather or other natural disasters.

Under a 1994 law, Congress required farmers participating in federal crop subsidy programs to take out insurance. There are about 1.3 million policies now in effect. Appropriators had to scramble last year to come up with $200 million to pay commissions. Some lawmakers worried that the uncertainty over funding could force insurers to drop out of the program. (1994 Almanac, p. 194)

Senate Shifts Funds For Food Aid To Highways

APRIL 4 — Legislation to restore food stamps to legal immigrants, a White House priority, could be the first casualty of Congress' high-speed push to increase road funding.

The Senate adjourned for a two-week recess April 3 without debating the food stamp measure. Instead, it approved a fiscal 1999 budget resolution (S Con Res 86) that would use the more than $1.7 billion earmarked for food stamps and agriculture programs in the bill (S 1150) to pay for increased highway spending.

The developments were a big blow for the Senate and House Agriculture committees, which had rushed the week of March 24 to complete the conference report in an effort to beat the Budget Committee to the floor.

Passage of the budget resolution does not kill the food stamp measure, but makes it politically much more difficult for farm-state lawmakers to claim the needed funds to pay for it. The Agriculture Committee could still capture the money if their bill was signed into law before Congress completed work on a budget resolution, aides said.

The legislation's already precarious position was further weakened April 3, when Senate Majority Leader Trent Lott, R-Miss., who by all accounts had been working with the White House to move the measure, suggested that the bill's funding could be better used to pay for transportation needs. "I think that money should go for the highway bill, personally," Lott said at a news conference just before the recess.

Lott said he would work with the Agriculture Committee to pass a bill that would expand agriculture research and crop insurance, possibly with different funding offsets. He said he opposed the restoration of food stamps.

Food Stamps, Farm Funding

Programs in the agriculture research bill would be paid for largely by limiting the amount of money the federal government allocates to states for administering the food stamp program. The limitation would save more than $1.7 billion over five years.

In addition to setting aside about $800 million over five years to restore food stamps to 250,000 legal immigrants, the legislation included $600 million for a new, mandatory agriculture research program, about $1 billion for crop insurance and $100 million for rural development.

Frustrated supporters of the agriculture bill warned that the week's developments were a portent of troubles to come as Congress pushed ahead with the budget plan to provide $18.5 billion in increased outlays for highways, to be paid for by cutting other mandatory domestic programs.

"Our farmers, our refugees, our asylees, should not be penalized ... because of this odd parliamentary situation we have," said Sen. Tom Harkin, D-Iowa.

Harkin said that hundreds of thousands of farmers had catastrophic crop insurance policies that would soon begin to lapse, and might not be renewed, unless Congress passed the agriculture legislation. That could leave growers who plant in the summer for winter crops without protection.

The impasse was also a classic example of how Senate rules allow lawmakers to stall legislation. Senate Minority Leader Tom Daschle, D-S.D., complained that four senators had placed "holds" on the bill to block it. One was Sen. Phil Gramm, R-Texas.

"I want people to come to America with their sleeves rolled up ready to go to work, not to get food stamps," said Gramm. The senator further wanted to protect needed funding for highway projects.

Earlier in the week, White House Chief of Staff Erskine Bowles called Lott to enlist his help. Aides said that Lott tried to persuade senators to drop their objections, but he found greater opposition to the legislation than he had expected.

Senate Agriculture Committee aides groused that the emphasis on restoring aid to legal immigrants was killing their best hope to expand agriculture research programs. The Senate last year approved a version of the measure that did not include immigrant provisions.

The White House weighed in early this year, with Agriculture Secretary Dan Glickman cautioning that he would not accept any measure that did not include a food stamp restoration.

The impasse could hurt some Republicans. Sen. Alfonse M. D'Amato of New York, who is up for re-election this year, has said he will push to restore food stamps to legal immigrants. Members of the Senate Agriculture Committee had written to Lott urging him to move the bill.

House Outlook Unclear

While things are bollixed up in the Senate, the measure also faces trouble in the House where key Republicans oppose both restoration of food stamps and provisions that would make agriculture research spending mandatory.

The House leadership did not schedule debate on the bill before the recess, though House Agriculture Committee Chairman Bob Smith, R-Ore., urged action, aides said. Tension was evident during House debate April 1 on the transportation measure (HR 2400).

"We are using real bullets in this bill," Rep. Charles W. Stenholm, D-Texas, said on the House floor. "Agriculture has priorities . . . and they are the first casualties of this bill."

An estimated 935,000 legal immigrants lost food stamps under the 1996 welfare law (PL 104-193). The bill would restore food stamps to elderly and disabled immigrants who were in the United States when the law was signed on Aug. 22, 1996, as well as children under age 18 in the country at that time. Refugees and those granted political asylum would be allowed to receive food stamps for seven years, up from the current five.

The bill would also provide about $1 billion to pay annual subsidies to insurance agents who sell federal crop policies, which reimburse farmers affected by weather or other natural disasters.

Under a 1994 law, Congress required farmers participating in federal crop subsidy programs to take out insurance. Appropriators had to scramble last year to come up with $200 million to pay commissions. (1994 Almanac, p. 194)

Senate Adopts Conference Report With Food Stamps Provision Restored

MAY 16 — In a re-emergence of a potent alliance of food and farm groups, the Senate on May 12 voted to restore food stamps to 250,000 legal immigrants as part of a broader measure expanding crop insurance and reauthorizing agriculture research programs.

Despite the 92-8 Senate vote and strong White House support, the conference report (S 1150) may face tough going in the House. Republican leaders have said they do not want to bring the measure to the floor, in part because of opposition to the food stamp restoration. (Vote 129, p. S-22)

House Republican Conference Chairman John A. Boehner of Ohio said aid to legal immigrants is "not high on our priority list."

Some members of the House Appropriations Committee are also concerned about provisions of the bill that would create a five-year, $600 million mandatory agriculture research spending program.

House Republican leaders instead have been discussing the possibility of moving just one segment of the bill, which would provide $200 million a year to fund a shortfall in the federal crop insurance program, through the appropriations process.

"I'm confident we'll deal with crop insurance in a constructive way, and clearly we'd like to do it sooner rather than later," Boehner said.

With segments of the agriculture economy in the doldrums, and farm-state lawmakers anxious about a series of Republican policies ranging from trade to crop subsidies, House leaders could face increasing pressure to bring up the bill.

Further, Republicans are eager to court Hispanic voters in the midterm elections. That process would not be helped by opposing the food stamp restoration, which Hispanic groups have made a priority. Most House Democrats are expected to support the bill, and the Clinton administration has pushed for its passage.

For weeks, it appeared as if the legislation might not come to a vote in the Senate, in part because Phil Gramm, R-Texas, had put a hold on the measure.

But nutrition and farm groups, who have been at loggerheads in recent years as they competed for scarce funds, worked together to round up more than 70 senators' signatures on a letter in support of the bill. And a Boston group, Physicians for Human Rights, released a study early this month that found high levels of hunger among immigrants in three states.

Gramm's Last Stand

During floor debate, Gramm offered a motion to recommit the bill to the conference committee to eliminate provisions that would allow refugees and those seeking asylum in the United States to collect benefits for seven years, up from the current five. The motion failed, 23-77. (Vote 128, p. S-22)

"The biggest problem with the bill is it puts a great big neon sign on the border of the United States of America, and the neon sign says: 'Come to America and get welfare,'" Gramm said.

He argued that lawmakers were too eager to undo the 1996 welfare law (PL 104-193), which ended food stamp eligibility for 935,000 legal immigrants. (1996 Almanac, p. 6-3)

Supporters of the measure said Gramm's effort to send it back to committee would effectively kill it, harming refugees who must prove they are in danger of persecution in order to be admitted to the United States.

"Asylees and refugees are not swarming across our border. . . . They do not have sponsors. They come with the shirts on their backs," said Senate Agriculture, Nutrition and Forestry Committee Chairman Richard G. Lugar, R-Ind.

The legislation would provide $818 million over five years to restore food stamp benefits to elderly and disabled legal immigrants who were in the country when the welfare law was signed Aug. 22, 1996, as well as children under age

Agriculture

18. Refugees and those granted political asylum would be allowed to receive food stamps for seven years, up from the current five. It also would restore benefits to Hmong and Lao refugees.

The welfare law also cut Supplemental Security Income disability benefits and other aid to legal immigrants. In the 1997 balanced-budget law (PL 105-33), Congress restored some of that aid.

Crop Insurance Vital

The legislation would provide $1 billion in mandatory crop insurance funding over five years — $470 million in new funding, and the rest from offsetting cuts elsewhere in the program. The money would be used to pay the commissions of agents who sell federally subsidized crop insurance policies.

Without action, some crop insurance firms have warned they may stop writing policies this July. Many banks require growers to carry crop insurance policies in order to qualify for loans.

"Without full funding for this program, farmers could face cancellation of hundreds of thousands of crop insurance policies," said Sen. Tom Harkin, D-Iowa.

The legislation initially started out as a straightforward measure to expand agriculture research. The food stamp provisions were added in conference committee after threats from Agriculture Secretary Dan Glickman that the White House would not accept any bill that did not include them. House members were also under pressure from the Appropriations Committee, which had been looking for ways to pay for annual crop insurance shortfalls.

The final bill includes $600 million for a program of competitive grants for agriculture research into areas such as food safety and crop yields. Land grant colleges and universities say the bill would provide a much-needed infusion of funds to ensure that U.S. research retains its pre-eminent position.

The research dollars take on particular importance to farm state lawmakers as their growers try to adapt to the 1996 farm law (PL 104-127), which freed them from rigid planting requirements but also gradually reduced federal subsidies. (1996 Almanac, p. 3-15)

The aid is seen as a way to develop new markets for farm products as government supports are reduced.

The bill would also provide $100 million for the federal Fund for Rural America, which funds economic development programs in rural areas.

Should the bill pass, it could pose budget problems down the line.

The bulk of the legislation would be funded by capping the amount of money the federal government pays to states to administer the federal food stamp program. The change would save about $1.7 billion over five years.

The Senate budget resolution (S Con Res 86), which passed April 2, calls for using the food stamp administrative funds to help pay for a new highway bill (HR 2400).

House Budget Committee Chairman John R. Kasich, R-Ohio, in a draft budget released this week, wants to use the money to help finance complete or partial repeal of the so-called marriage penalty, whereby some married couples must pay higher taxes than they would have to filing as unmarried individuals.

House Republicans Suffer Blow as Rule Is Defeated

MAY 23 — House Republican leaders suffered a major defeat on May 22, when members of their own party rebelled against an effort to strip provisions that would restore food stamps to 250,000 legal immigrants from a compromise bill (S 1150) to expand agriculture research and fund crop insurance.

After an emotional debate on the House floor, lawmakers defeated, 120-289, a rule for floor debate that would have allowed a point of order automatically stripping the immigrant aid. The conference report passed the Senate, 92-8, on May 12.

Republicans defected en masse on the rule out of concern both for the immigrants and a desire to preserve the new agriculture money. There were 98 Republican "no" votes, and Agriculture Committee Chairman Bob Smith, R-Ore., voted "present."

Failure of the rule meant farm-state lawmakers went home for the Memorial Day recess without needed funding for crop insurance. Some crop insurers have warned that they will stop writing policies in July unless Congress makes up a funding shortfall. The impasse was also a setback to Republican efforts to reach out to Hispanic voters.

"The Statue of Liberty must be weeping," said Tony P. Hall, D-Ohio.

The defeat was clearly a blow for House GOP leaders who, after weeks of internal debate, decided to move forward with the legislation. But Joe L. Barton, R-Texas, told the leadership on May 21 he would object to bringing up the bill by unanimous consent, forcing them to draft a rule. Barton was joined by other conservatives demanding a vote on the immigrant provisions.

The rule approved by the Rules Committee near midnight May 21 spurred a revolt by both Republicans and Democrats on the House floor. The original rule would have allowed lawmakers to raise a point of order to strip the funding source for most of the legislation, as well as the point of order on immigrant food stamps.

The bill would be paid for by capping federal payments to states to administer the food stamp program. The change would save $1.7 billion over five years.

An angry Charles W. Stenholm, D-Texas, called for the House to adjourn, a move that brought Speaker Newt Gingrich, R-Ga., and Majority Leader Dick Armey, R-Texas, to the floor for a long huddle with Smith and others.

The result was a compromise rule that protected most of the $1.7 billion in funding, but still allowed a motion to strike the immigrant provisions.

It is unclear what will happen next. House Rules Chairman Gerald B.H. Solomon, R-N.Y., said he would not write a rule for the bill as long as it included the provisions for food stamps to legal immigrants.

He argued that lawmakers were too eager to undo the 1996 welfare law (PL 104-193), which ended food stamp eligibility for 935,000 legal immigrants. (1996 Almanac, p. 6-3)

But opponents warned that eliminating aid to immigrants would kill the bill. President Clinton has threatened to veto it if the food stamp restoration is not included. Democrats called the effort a mean-spirited move that would send the measure back to the Senate, where it would be bottled up.

They also charged that Republicans

were undermining family farmers. GOP leaders said they had gone out of their way to accommodate new funding for crop insurance and agriculture research — but could not go along with immigrant aid.

"If you want a scapegoat in the matter, you're not going to find one here," Armey said. He asserted that lawmakers were willing to sacrifice funding for crop insurance to protect immigrants.

That brought a sharp rebuke from Stenholm, who charged that Republican leaders had promised to open export markets to make up for declining federal crop subsidies in a 1996 farm law (PL 104-127) but then blocked vital trade initiatives. (*1996 Almanac, p. 3-15*)

"This is another backdoor [effort] to gut agriculture," Stenholm said.

Provisions

The legislation would provide $818 million over five years to restore food stamp benefits to elderly and disabled legal immigrants who were in the country when the welfare law was signed Aug. 22, 1996, as well as children under age 18. Refugees and those granted political asylum would be allowed to receive food stamps for seven years, up from the current five. The legislation also would provide $1 billion in mandatory crop insurance funding over five years. The money would be used to pay the commissions of agents who sell federally subsidized crop insurance policies.

The bill includes $600 million for competitive grants for agriculture research into areas such as food safety and crop yields.

House Clears Bill, With Food Stamp Benefits Restored

JUNE 6 — In a swift political turnabout, the House on June 4 passed and sent to the White House legislation to restore food stamps to 250,000 legal immigrants, expand agriculture research and make up a $1 billion shortfall in the federal crop insurance program.

The overwhelming, 364-50 House vote for the bill (S 1150) gave little indication of its tortured journey to final passage. Until June 3, it was unclear that Republican leaders — torn between conservatives who opposed the food stamp provisions and farm-state lawmakers pleading for crop insurance funding — would even allow it to come to the floor. (*Vote 204, p. H-60*)

Less than two weeks earlier, before leaving for a weeklong Memorial Day recess on May 22, Republican leaders tried to consider the bill under a rule that would have automatically stripped the immigrant provisions. Nearly 100 Republicans voted against the proposal, which went down 120-289, handing their leaders an embarrassing defeat.

At the time, House Majority Leader Dick Armey, R-Texas, was one of the chief opponents of restoring food stamps to immigrants, arguing that Congress was too eager to undo provisions of the 1996 welfare law (PL 104-193). The law eliminated food stamps to 935,000 legal immigrants. (*1996 Almanac, p. 6-3*)

In the end, Armey reversed position — not only allowing the bill to come to the floor under a procedure protecting the immigrant provisions, but voting for final passage.

After the May 22 rule defeat, House leaders came under sharp criticism from rural lawmakers, who were worried that crop insurance agents would stop underwriting policies at the end of the month unless Congress acted to make up a $200 million annual shortfall in the program.

"We certainly made the point that this is a political issue. Time is running out. We need crop insurance," said House Agriculture Committee Chairman Bob Smith, R-Ore.

Further, farm prices are falling even as federal support is beginning to decline under the 1996 "Freedom to Farm" legislation (PL 104-127), which gradually decreases crop subsidies through 2002. (*1996 Almanac, p. 3-15*)

Agriculture groups told House leaders that they had agreed to the law only after receiving assurances that Congress would expand trade and research programs.

"The condition of the farm economy rivals what we saw during the farm recession of the mid-1980s," said David Minge, D-Minn.

President Clinton had threatened to veto the bill unless the food stamp aid was included. The White House wants a broader restoration of food stamp benefits but called the legislation a crucial first step. After passage, a White House spokesman said Clinton would sign the bill.

"This should have been a no-brainer but, once again, the House leadership decided to attack the most vulnerable in our society," said Democrat Sam Farr of California.

Approval was a victory for Democrat Charles W. Stenholm of Texas, who helped to unite agriculture, nutrition and immigrant groups behind the bill.

Rebuilding a Coalition

Commodity and nutrition groups, which have historically worked together, in recent years have been battling each other for scarce funds.

The bill would provide $818 million over five years to restore food stamp benefits to elderly and disabled legal immigrants who were in the country when the welfare law was signed Aug. 22, 1996, as well as children under 18.

Refugees and those granted political asylum would be allowed to receive food stamps for seven years, up from the current five.

The bill would also provide $1 billion in mandatory crop insurance funding over five years. About half of the spending would be offset by cuts elsewhere in the crop insurance program. The money is needed to pay the commissions of agents who sell federally subsidized crop insurance policies.

With federal subsidies in decline and the federal government no longer providing disaster aid, crop insurance has added importance for growers.

The legislation includes $600 million in mandatory funding for competitive grants for agriculture research into areas such as food safety, crop yields and genetic engineering. It also sets up new programs, such as a honey promotion system funded through assessments on honey producers.

Before final voting, the House defeated, 324-91, a point of order by Rules Committee Chairman Gerald B.H. Solomon, R-N.Y., to strike $1.7 billion in spending offsets. The bill would be paid for by reducing federal payments to states to administer the food stamp program. Solomon said the change would impose an unfunded mandate on the states. (*Vote 203, p. H-60*) ◆

Chapter 5

BANKING & FINANCE

Financial Services Overhaul 5-3
  Highlights of House Bill 5-4
Bankruptcy Overhaul 5-15
  Highlights of Senate Bill 5-21

Credit Union Expansion 5-25
Class-Action Securities Lawsuits 5-30

Banking & Finance

Financial Services Overhaul Dies in Senate, A Victim of Friendly Fire

Box Score

- **Bill:** HR 10
- **House action:** The House passed HR 10, 214-213, on May 13.
- **Senate action:** The measure was briefly considered on the Senate floor during October.

SUMMARY

Despite an unprecedented agreement between the banking and insurance industries, Congress was once again unable to clear legislation to overhaul the financial services industry. The bill would have revised the 1933 Glass-Steagall Act and other laws that separate banking, securities and insurance.

As passed by the House and approved by the Senate Banking, Housing and Urban Affairs Committee, the measure would have removed restrictions on affiliations between the banking, insurance and securities industries, allowing the creation of financial holding companies through which banks could underwrite and sell insurance and securities, and insurance companies and brokerage houses could acquire banks.

The legislation received a major push in early March when House GOP leaders, determined to enact modernization legislation, announced a compromise between competing committees' bills approved the previous year.

Strongly supported by securities and insurance groups, the House legislation was largely opposed by banks that were already offering many securities and insurance services under court and regulatory decisions.

The bill passed the House in mid-May by just a single vote (after being pulled from the floor in late March because members objected to combining it with a popular credit union bill, HR 1151 — PL 105-219). Speaker Newt Gingrich, R-Ga., had to pressure a half-dozen members to vote "aye."

It passed despite a veto threat over the bill's regulatory structure. The administration favored allowing securities and insurance activities to be conducted in bank operating subsidiaries, regulated by the Treasury Department. The bill required those activities to be conducted in separate affiliates, with the Federal Reserve acting as an umbrella regulator.

Senate consideration of the bill quickly bogged down as Phil Gramm, R-Texas, and Richard C. Shelby, R-Ala., fought the bill's Community Reinvestment Act requirements. The Senate Banking Committee eliminated reinvestment requirements for securities firms and insurance companies, but Gramm and Shelby vowed floor amendments to eliminate existing reinvestment requirements on banks.

The bill received an unexpected boost in the closing days of Congress when banks and insurance agents reached an agreement over rules for state regulation of bank insurance products, which virtually eliminated the agents' opposition to the measure. However, with little time remaining, and no agreements on community reinvestment or operating subsidiaries, Senate Majority Leader Trent Lott, R-Miss., killed the bill.

House Leaders Unveil Plans To Overhaul Glass-Steagall Act

MARCH 14 — As financial panic spread far and wide in the Depression years, Sen. Carter Glass, D-Va. (1920-46), and Rep. Henry Steagall, D-Ala. (1915-43), shepherded through Congress a measure to prevent the three legs of the country's financial services sector — banking, securities and insurance — from mixing their assets and setting themselves up for a bigger financial fall.

But as the Depression and war years gave way to economic prosperity, the industries pressured federal regulators and Congress to reinstate the freedoms they had before 1933. Regulators and courts have provided some relief to banks, but Congress has never come close to demolishing what remains of Glass-Steagall's walls.

House Republican leaders announced a deal the week of March 9 that they believe offers the best chance in decades.

But the failures of the past were not far from their minds. The powerful banking industry signaled displeasure with several portions of the bill. Rank-and-file Republicans expressed little faith in the bill's ability to move past the House floor. Democrats howled that they had not been included in writing the deal and therefore would not support it. And the troublesome matter of whether to attach a fix for the nation's credit unions remained unresolved. The Supreme Court ruled Feb. 25 that credit unions had overstepped their bounds in seeking new members, and many lawmakers want to reverse the ruling.

"We've never made any bones about the fact that it's a very delicate issue," said Rep. Michael G. Oxley, R-Ohio, chairman of the Commerce subcommittee that oversees securities. "It's a 'Perils of Pauline' sort of thing. We still may end up strapped to that railroad track."

Nonetheless, Speaker Newt Gingrich, R-Ga., Majority Leader Dick Armey, R-Texas, and GOP Conference Chairman John A. Boehner of Ohio, the deal's chief negotiator, all insisted the bill would be on the floor by the end of March. Boehner said he believed it would get "broad bipartisan support."

That is what it needs if it is to have a chance for Senate consideration, said that chamber's Banking, Housing and Urban Affairs Committee chairman, Alfonse M. D'Amato, R-N.Y. D'Ama-

Banking & Finance

Highlights of House Banking Bill

March 14 — The new version of HR 10 that Republican leaders unveiled the week of March 9, like previous measures approved in 1997 by the House Banking and Commerce committees, would demolish what remains of the crumbling walls Congress erected in 1933 between the banking, securities and insurance industries. In major provisions, the revised bill would:

● **Financial holding companies.** Remove restrictions on affiliations among the bank, securities and insurance industries. It would create "financial holding companies" that would enable banks to acquire securities and insurance firms, and securities and insurance firms to acquire banks. The companies would also be allowed to acquire a limited number of commercial businesses not related to financial services. Financial holding companies affiliated with banks could engage in commercial activity as long as the activity did not exceed $500 million or 5 percent of the holding company's consolidated annual gross revenue, whichever was lower. A holding company could not acquire any company with assets of $750 million or more. Financial holding companies affiliated with securities or insurance firms could retain all the investments they held or the activities they engaged in as of Sept. 30, 1997, as long as the activities did not constitute more than 15 percent of the company's annual gross revenues before the company acquired a bank. The financial holding companies would have broader powers than traditional bank holding companies, which Congress created in 1956 to allow banks to offer limited securities and other services. Those holding companies also would continue to exist, though they would be likely to affiliate with the new, broad-powered financial holding companies. These provisions reflect HR 10 as approved in 1997 by the House Commerce Committee.

● **State law and insurance sales.** Generally pre-empt state laws regulating affiliations between insurance companies and banks. It lays out specific guidelines for insurance products that banks and other financial institutions could offer. States would be barred from "preventing" or "significantly interfering" with the institution's ability to sell insurance. This would codify the Supreme Court's 1996 decision in Barnett Bank of Marion County v. Nelson, which paved the way for national banks to sell insurance from small-town branches. The bill does not lay out exactly what constitutes prevention or significant interference, but it gives states some guidance on how they could regulate insurance sold by national banks. As long as state regulations were no more stringent than those in Illinois, they would be allowed. Illinois reached a compromise between the banking and insurance sectors in 1997, and its statute defines what banks can do. This provision combines and adds to measures from the Banking and Commerce bills.

● **Other insurance regulation.** Allow bank federal holding companies to underwrite insurance policies. If a national bank or its subsidiary was not providing insurance in a state at the time of bill enactment, it could begin to do so only by acquiring a company that had been licensed to provide insurance in that state for at least two years. Within one year of enactment, federal banking regulators would have to issue consumer protection regulations that would govern the sale of insurance by national banks or affiliates. These provisions were in the Commerce version of the bill.

● **Securities activities.** Amend the Securities Exchange Act of 1934 to allow the sale of securities and investment advice by banks to be regulated by the Securities and Exchange Commission (SEC). However, many "traditional" bank activities, such as sale of government securities, would be exempt from SEC regulation and would remain under the control of the Office of the Comptroller of the Currency (OCC). Banks that made fewer than 500 securities transactions a year would be exempt from SEC regulation regardless of the nature of the sales. The new bill would exempt more activities from SEC regulation than the Commerce version but less than the Banking version. It also adds language to allow the SEC to determine if a new product offered by a bank is a security, and thus subject to SEC regulation.

● **Thrift charters.** Stop the granting of federal unitary thrift charters after Sept. 16, 1997, but allow existing thrifts to continue operating. Thrifts are savings institutions originally created to offer home loans. In recent years, insurance companies and other corporations have applied to open one savings bank, or a "unitary thrift." Multiple thrift holding companies could continue and would be regulated by the Office of Thrift Supervision until Jan. 1, 2000, when the office would be merged with the OCC. Existing thrifts would then be regulated by the Federal Reserve. The bill would merge the Bank Insurance Fund and the Savings Association Insurance Fund, as Congress laid out in an omnibus 1996 law (PL 104-208), and would require thrifts to retain 10 percent of their assets in home mortgages. The provision combines the Banking and Commerce versions. *(1996 Almanac, p. 2-43)*

to, who faces a rigorous re-election race this year, has never been thought likely to push a measure that would force him to choose among bankers, brokers and insurance executives.

Garnering broad support for a bill that aims for a "fair playing field" for the three main lines of business in the financial services system has never been easy, as GOP leaders realized when they jump started efforts to pass a bill by giving the Banking and Commerce committees until March 4 to resolve their differences over a measure (HR 10) that stalled last year.

The bill presupposes that something is wrong with the current financial system, even though many are profiting from it at record levels. Congress and a broad cross section of the financial services industry agree that the 1933 law created inefficiencies because institutions cannot offer all the services their customers want.

But the current system does benefit some. Banks, whose federal regulators tend to be sympathetic, for the most part have profited from rules and court decisions that have allowed them to offer some securities and insurance services through bank holding companies, which Congress allowed in the 1950s.

The version of HR 10 that emerged the week of March 9 would allow banks, securities firms and insurance companies to own one another, with some limitations. This was especially important to securities and insurance firms, which are now not allowed to own banks. The bill would allow nationally chartered banks to sell insurance, although states would retain most of their traditional jurisdiction over such sales.

In addition, financial holding companies set up by banks or insurance companies could sell securities, which would be regulated by the Securities and Exchange Commission. The deal would also phase out the unitary thrift charter, which has allowed commercial companies to open savings banks.

While securities and insurance groups generally support the deal, the banking industry was deliberately quiet most of the week. The American Bankers Association (ABA), a dominant industry group, privately floated a letter early in the week preparing for a public clash with Republicans on the bill.

Banks and savings institutions have the most to lose if the bill goes forward. Most banking industry associations said they were studying the bill and would not comment until their boards of directors considered it. A day after the new version of the bill was released, the ABA issued a diplomatically worded statement outlining provisions the group liked and provisions it did not. "ABA plans to continue to work to seek improvements," group President William T. McConnell said in a written statement.

Bankers may have been hedging their statements as they waited to see how Republican leaders would address the credit union situation. Some lobbyists have speculated that the GOP would temper a credit union fix if bankers agreed to go along with the broader financial services bill.

Democrats were not shy about their distaste for the deal. Rep. John D. Dingell of Michigan, ranking Democrat on the Commerce Committee, called it "a compromise between supporters. It's not an honest compromise between all points of view."

GOP leaders were pleased that they had managed to bring the bill this far, but the failure of past congresses could not be ignored. "This is a very complex, very difficult area with very powerful interests who all jealously guard their own turf," Gingrich said before meeting with Republicans on March 11 to plot a strategy for the bill.

Republicans Tout 'One-Stop Shopping' As Bill's Key Benefit

MARCH 21 — Republicans charged with rewriting the nation's outdated financial services laws have not lacked for outside help. The banking, securities and insurance industries have been more than willing to offer their advice in remaking the laws — particularly the 1933 Glass-Steagall Act — that govern how they interact.

But when Republican leaders announced earlier this month that they had reached a tentative deal on a Glass-Steagall rewrite, many of the benefits they touted were directed at a fourth, and largely silent, group — the consumers who write the checks, invest in mutual funds and buy insurance.

"These historic reforms will mean far greater security and freedom for every American consumer," the bill's chief architect, Rep. John A. Boehner, R-Ohio, said March 10 while unveiling the new version of a financial services overhaul bill (HR 10) that stalled last year. "We are unshackling the American economy and the American people to confront the challenges ahead."

Boehner's focus on consumers notwithstanding, the changes he proposed were initiated by industry groups, not by the man in the teller line or the woman using her ATM card. As a Congressional Research Service report pointed out in 1997,

"The momentum . . . is largely industry-driven. Few customers are actively petitioning Congress to allow one-stop financial shopping."

Republicans tout such shopping as one of the main consumer benefits of HR 10. Breaking down the walls that 1930s-era legislation erected among the banking, securities and insurance industries will allow consumers to visit just one institution, probably their bank, to apply for a loan, purchase stock and buy an insurance policy. Such consolidated service will help consumers monitor their overall financial plans and will likely lead to reductions in fees as bigger institutions provide more efficient services to more people, Republicans say. Federal regulators have tended to agree with them, with the Treasury Department estimating that consumers could save as much as $15 billion a year through reduced fees and other lower rates.

Representatives for the industries involved, even those who strongly support HR 10, say such "shops" are nearing reality now and will continue to evolve even if Congress does not pass an overhaul bill. Federal regulators, particularly the Office of the Comptroller of the Currency and the Federal Reserve, have consistently allowed banks to offer more and more financial services through affiliates known as holding companies. The courts have generally upheld those decisions.

Industry officials say an overhaul bill could bring quicker, more efficient consolidation. It would lift many of the regulatory barriers the industries now face, but which they evade through cumbersome labor or technological procedures that add to consumer fees.

A securities industry lobbyist described the changes consumers will see as: "No. 1, there should be efficiencies in delivery. No. 2, people should find it more convenient. And No. 3, because of the competition, they'll get a better buy for their money."

But consumer advocates doubt that financial institutions, particularly banks — which have increased ATM fees in recent years despite some public opposition — will feel compelled to lower consumer costs. In Canada, deregulation has resulted in higher fees.

"If it was done right, it could mean more competition," said Mary Griffin,

Banking & Finance

insurance counsel for Consumers Union, "but we're afraid of it just being another opportunity to bilk consumers out of more money for fees."

More Buyouts Ahead

Industry and consumer advocates are united on one front: All believe that the overhaul bill would result in a host of acquisitions between banks, securities firms and insurance companies.

News of financial business mergers now occurs almost daily — often between huge companies. The week of March 16, for example, the country's largest savings and loan company, Washington Mutual Inc. of Seattle, announced that it would buy the second-largest, H.F. Ahmanson & Co. of Irwindale, Calif., to create a company large enough to compete with commercial banking giants. Other recent banking buyouts include First Union's plan to acquire CoreStates and NationsBank's purchase of Barnett Banks. Among brokerage firms, Morgan Stanley and Dean Witter have merged, as have Travelers and Salomon Brothers.

But the 1933 law largely prevents mergers between industries, and analysts of all stripes predict that lifting the barriers will prompt a new barrage of buyouts. Some observers question how much competition will be fostered by consolidation, and thus how much consumer fees will be reduced.

"If there are more mergers . . . it's hard to argue that it's going to reduce fees," said Martin Mayer, a guest economics scholar with the Brookings Institution and the author of several books on banking.

Others argue that competition will grow because more companies will be fighting to offer the type of banking, securities, and insurance plans that consumers want.

"If you have six gas stations within a six-block area, you're not going to find one charging $1.25 [per gallon] when everyone else is at $1.02," said the securities lobbyist, who requested anonymity. "If you have six financial services companies offering their wares within a short distance, you're sure that they're going to be very competitive in pricing because you could walk across the street."

Mayer said he believes fees for electronic banking, such as banking via personal computer and possibly ATM transactions, will decrease because they do not cost banks as much to provide as traditional, labor-intensive services. He also believes consumers will see a dramatic reduction in their insurance costs, particularly for car and life insurance policies, as they purchase more policies from banks instead of insurance agents, who charge higher fees.

Some observers say the bill will help consumers by allowing them to create a customized financial plan and to track all their financial products on the same monthly statement.

"What's out there now is like a 375-channel cable TV," said David Pratt, senior vice president for federal affairs at the American Insurance Association. "There's not enough products that are easily understandable and easily accessible."

Consumer Advocates Worry

Griffin, one of the main consumer advocates on the issue, does not dispute that the leadership's proposed bill is better than it could have been.

"Modernizing the financial services law isn't a bad goal, as long as consumer laws are modernized to make sure that consumers are protected in this new world," she said.

Griffin and others worry that that will not happen, and they do not believe the consumer protections in the new law are firm enough.

Both Griffin and Mayer said legislators and regulators must ensure that financial institutions will not misuse their broad powers by "tying" services together — for instance, by requiring prospective homebuyers to buy their home insurance with the same institution if they want their mortgage approved.

"That's a perfect example of the coercion they'll be able to do," Griffin said. Her group wants the issue addressed in the financial services bill.

Mayer termed such practices "bad news," but said federal regulators, not lawmakers, should keep an eye on them and clamp down if necessary. Mayer said he favors leeway because some customers may want to take advantage of "tied" offers, which might include better rates.

The bill would require federal banking regulators within one year of enactment to devise regulations that would prevent most lenders from leading a customer to believe that the extension of credit will be based on the purchase of an insurance product from the company or its affiliates.

Another major concern of Griffin's is that consumers may think that their securities investments or insurance policies are backed by the Federal Deposit Insurance Corporation (FDIC), or other federal insurance funds, because they are bought at a bank in which deposits are insured by the FDIC. The bill does require institutions to disclose in writing that certain products are uninsured, but it would allow states to enact their own laws.

Griffin worries that "banks are going to use their status as taxpayer-backed, federally insured institutions" to say they are "safe and sound" regardless of what products are offered. If disclosures are tough and mandatory, "people [will] know they're not necessarily going to get a better deal at banks. Then they're going to shop, and banks have to compete."

The Cost of Inaction

Consumer advocates and others worry about the effect on consumers, but they are also concerned about what will happen if Congress does not address the constantly changing financial services sector.

Some are worried about how House Republicans, who continued the week of March 16 to negotiate a final version of the bill before markups begin, will deal with commercial, non-banking companies, such as General Electric or Archer Daniels Midland, an agricultural conglomerate, that want to own banks. Both companies have applied for a thrift charter. That would allow them to operate a savings bank, which has broader leeway to offer securities and insurance products.

Griffin is concerned that if such "merchant banking" were allowed on a broad scale, banks could begin to limit credit only to those companies in which they owned a stake, limiting the growth of competitors if the number of financial institutions dwindled significantly. Most of the world's developed countries have such merchant banking systems.

The bill would generally keep large commercial conglomerates out of the banking business. It would allow firms to establish financial holding companies to acquire banks, but only 15 percent of the companies' annual gross revenues could come from commercial holdings. That provision is expected to allow securities and insurance firms to buy banks. Banks could establish holding companies to buy securities and insurance firms, but their commercial activity could not surpass 5 percent of the holding company's consolidated annual gross revenue.

In addition, the bill would shut down the unitary thrift charter as of Sept. 16, 1997. The charter has allowed commercial companies to acquire a single savings institution.

If Congress does not deal with the thrift charter, it will effectively be allowing merchant banking "by omission," said Edward Yingling, executive director of government relations for the American Bankers Association. "There is nothing to prevent GE . . . from buying one of the largest regional banks and running it as a thrift," Yingling said.

Yingling's association, which represents large banks, is withholding judgment on the overall package until reviewing a final version.

But Yingling downplayed the effects such a bill would have on consumers, regardless of final details.

The trends consumers see now, such as banks selling more and more securities and insurance products, will continue, he said, in part because they are consumer driven. "You're just going to see more and more of that," he said. "The old distinctions between products just don't work any more. People go to their bank to talk about savings and investments and transactions, and many of them now are insurance or securities or hybrids."

Bankers' Group Deems Legislation 'Badly Flawed'

MARCH 28 — The long-expected opposition of the leading banking industry group to a broad financial services overhaul measure surfaced the week of March 23, as the powerful American Bankers Association announced its opposition to the bill.

Although Republican leaders knew that the association, the largest of many industry groups, disliked several sections of the measure, the association's public announcement, and the opposition of several other industry groups, called into question how the bill (HR 10) would fare if reached the House floor the week of March 30, as leaders had pledged.

At a meeting with Federal Reserve Board Chairman Alan Greenspan, one of the bill's high-profile supporters, House Speaker Newt Gingrich, R-Ga., reiterated the hope that "this bill will pass before we leave next week."

With supporting and opposing sides digging trenches for warfare, GOP leaders dickered throughout the week about how best to move the bill and a separate measure (HR 1151) that would allow but limit the growth of credit unions. The credit union bill may be attached to HR 10.

The securities and insurance industries, which strongly support HR 10, bought several full-page ads in Hill newspapers and launched an effort to drum up support in Congress, especially from conservative and moderate Democrats. Several large banks, including Banc One and NationsBank, also support the measure.

The bankers association opposed the bill, but leaders said the group would continue to work with Congress. Others were not so diplomatic. America's Community Bankers, which represents savings institutions, termed the bill "so badly flawed it cannot be fixed." The bill would eliminate the unitary thrift charter, which allows corporations to open a single savings bank.

Republican Leaders Withdraw Measure From House Floor

APRIL 4 — House Republican leaders, thwarted in their efforts to bring a historic overhaul of Depression Era financial services laws to the floor, began to pick up the pieces March 31 and search for a new formula to enact the measure.

They had long known that passing the bill (HR 10) would be difficult, but their failure to gather enough support to even bring it up for consideration was a major disappointment.

Leaders had spent the early part of the week attempting to patch together support for the bill. They agreed to give some members a chance to amend it. They tinkered with the thrift provisions to appease savings and loans. They added a popular credit union bill (HR 1151) in an attempt to transfer some of its support to the broader measure.

But when leaders finally tried to bring HR 10 to the floor, they awkwardly found themselves without their customary partners, the bankers, and with a phalanx of opposition from Republicans and Democrats alike, who objected to the deals that leaders had accepted to get things moving. Lawmakers objected on many grounds, from technical concerns to fears the bill would lead to too much or too little industry consolidation.

With time running out in debate over the rule to govern floor consideration, Rules Committee Chairman Gerald B.H. Solomon, R-N.Y., abruptly withdrew the bill from the floor, declaring that Capitol phones were "ringing off the hook" as bankers called to lobby against the bill. It was an effort the likes of which, he said, "I've never seen in my life."

At a news conference shortly after Solomon's statement, Republican Conference Chairman John A. Boehner of Ohio, the bill's main architect, attributed the GOP's retreat not to the bankers but to the leadership's underestimating members' opposition to combining HR 10 and the credit union bill. "I think what we learned was the opposite of what we thought," Boehner said. "Putting the two issues together put members in a very uncomfortable position."

That was mostly because members wanted to vote for the credit union bill and not for the financial services measure. But Boehner said he felt "pretty good about the potential passage of HR 10" and pledged that the House would consider it the week of May 4. The bill would tear down the walls that 1930s laws built between the banking, securities and insurance industries and would allow the three industries to enter each others' lines of business.

Banking & Finance

But other members were not as optimistic. During floor debate, Commerce Committee Chairman Thomas J. Bliley Jr., R-Va., urged members to support the bill, saying, "If we stop it tonight, as we can do if we vote against this rule, there will be no bill this year."

The GOP's retreat on the issue was part of the House's long history of rejecting or refusing to consider measures that would substantially alter the 1933 Glass-Steagall Act and other Depression-era laws that prevent banks, securities firms and insurance companies from affiliating. Such a measure has never passed the House. *(1996 Almanac, p. 2-51)*

House leaders allowed the credit union bill, once considered the engine to carry HR 10 to passage, to come to the floor as a stand-alone measure April 1. It garnered quick, bipartisan support. The bill would allow credit unions to continue to expand, within limits, despite a recent Supreme Court ruling that said they had overstepped legal bounds in seeking new members.

Making Enemies of Friends

The banking community had long been expected to oppose HR 10. The major banking organizations and most of their members came out against the bill, saying that many of its provisions represented a step backward instead of toward the modernization leaders touted. For banks, which for decades had gained powers under the watch of sympathetic federal regulators, the bill represented a loss of competitive advantage over the securities and insurance industries. A few of the largest banks, including BancOne and NationsBank, supported the measure because they believed it would improve their ability to compete with foreign banks.

With most of the banking community already lined up against the measure, Republicans made matters worse when the Rules Committee met March 30 and agreed to scale back plans to eliminate the unitary thrift charter, one of the few provisions banks had favored. The thrift charter allows commercial companies and other businesses to open savings institutions, which often compete with banks.

"There's nothing in this bill" for the banking community, said Edward Yingling, executive director of government relations for the American Bankers Association, the leading industry group.

Three key Republicans agreed with the banks and sent a letter to lawmakers March 30 urging them to oppose the bill. "As members who support true financial modernization ... the Financial Services Competition Act raises many issues that give us pause," wrote Bill McCollum of Florida, Richard H. Baker of Louisiana and David Dreier of California.

Some members said the letter was effective in swaying Republicans who had doubts or knew little about the bill.

Democrats were also given an extra incentive to oppose the measure when the Clinton administration sent a statement to the House saying the president would veto the bill.

But many members doubted that the bill would ever make its way down Pennsylvania Avenue, even if the House passed it. The Senate had been lukewarm about taking it up, and Senate Banking, Housing and Urban Affairs Committee Chairman Alfonse M. D'Amato, R-N.Y., had repeatedly said he would take it up only if it received a broad bipartisan vote in the House. The House was far from achieving that by March 31.

Some bill supporters estimated that they were almost a dozen votes short of passing the rule to bring HR 10 to the floor. Democrats said the margin may have been greater. They expected at least 30 and perhaps as many as 60 Republicans to join nearly all Democrats in voting against the rule.

Piecing Together a Majority

With the credit union bill removed as a potential engine, Republican leaders began to look for other ways to forge a consensus to pass HR 10. Banking Chairman Jim Leach, R-Iowa, pointed to two issues that were likely to be intensely debated because they could sway lawmakers, Clinton and industry groups.

One was how much leeway to give operating subsidiaries of banks to engage in activities not allowed for the parent bank. Banks and the Treasury Department are pushing for unlimited powers for operating subsidiaries, but Congress and the Federal Reserve have been hesitant about such broad leeway. Leach said he thinks Republicans may return to an earlier version of HR 10, approved last year by the Banking Committee, that would give federal regulators some leeway to expand the powers of operating subsidiaries, but would prevent them from underwriting insurance or real estate development.

Another issue that could bring additional support to the bill involves the 1977 Community Reinvestment Act (PL 95-128). Democrats are pushing to broadly expand it. A proposed Democratic amendment to HR 10 would have extended to securities and insurance firms the act's requirement that financial institutions provide lending opportunities to people with low and moderate incomes.

Many Democrats see the reinvestment act as key to improving inner cities, although Republicans see it as a prime example of government intervention in the free market. Some Republicans are moving to scale back the reinvestment act, especially as it applies to small banks.

Changes aimed at operating subsidiaries or community reinvestment could make the bill more attractive to Clinton and banks but could also alienate some Republicans and the securities and insurance industries. Despite the complications, congressional leaders said they believed some version of HR 10 could again emerge. "I think we can revisit financial modernization," LaFalce said. "There's always a new day."

Huge Merger Increases Pressure On Lawmakers

APRIL 11 — In the financial houses of New York, the Travelers Group's proposal to marry Citicorp in a $70 billion, record-breaking merger was greeted with admiration. As the two companies' stocks surged April 6, business leaders praised the attempt to create Citigroup Inc., a banking, securities and insurance conglomerate that would tear down what little remained of the aged laws separating the industries.

In Washington, the reaction was

markedly different. The proposed merger — the largest attempted stock swap in history, based on the price of Traveler's stock just before the deal was announced — showed once again how the nation's fast-moving financial services sector seeks to stretch the limits of its own regulations, putting federal officials in the uncomfortable position of following their lead or rejecting a proposal that would increase U.S. dominance in the world financial market. The merger must be approved by the Federal Reserve, which, if it follows current law, would require the company to divest certain insurance sales and underwriting activities.

Coming the week after House Republicans failed to win enough support to bring to the floor a bill (HR 10) to establish a looser legal framework for financial services mergers, the proposed birth of Citigroup also seemed like an attempt to poke Congress in the eye.

Supporters and opponents of HR 10 (H Rept 105-164, Parts 1-4) predicted that the proposed merger would increase lobbying pressure on Congress to pass the financial services bill, but few were certain that such pressure would push the bill to enactment this year.

"The question is, will it be enough to ignite Congress to reassert its leadership role or will Congress be content to watch the parade pass them by again?" said Paul A. Equale, executive vice president of public affairs at the Independent Insurance Agents of America, which supports the bill. "They should not sit by and watch two captains of industry basically redefine the financial landscape. They are not here as spectators."

Republican staff members reiterated that their bosses, gone for the two-week spring recess, intended to bring up HR 10 again the week of May 4. Democratic staff aides said they were ready to negotiate any time.

In a statement released April 6, House Banking and Financial Services Committee Chairman Jim Leach, R-Iowa, a consistent supporter of overhauling the nation's financial services laws, said the merger "underscores the need for prompt congressional action."

Senate Banking, Housing and Urban Affairs Committee Chairman Alfonse M. D'Amato, R-N.Y., who has not shown great enthusiasm for taking up HR 10, praised the merger as one that would "help keep New York the premier financial center of the world." D'Amato also said that the merger demonstrated that Congress "should move forward despite the intransigence or opposition of some in the financial services industry to creating a level playing field."

It is unclear how much the merger will change the bill's prospects, but it will win at least one big convert: Citicorp, which spent millions on lobbying campaigns last year, reportedly will switch from opponent to proponent, joining four other large banks — NationsBank, BancOne, Bank of America and J.P. Morgan — in support of HR 10.

Congressional staff and bill supporters said they hoped the merger would draw other banks to the table as part of an effort to compete with the new, mammoth Citigroup, but much of the banking industry is likely to continue to oppose the bill. Industry lobbyists say it would hamper banks' competitiveness instead of producing the flexible, modern system supporters tout.

The American Bankers Association, the largest industry group and a representative of large and small banks, said its position against the bill had not changed. "The things we liked, we still like; and the things we disliked, we still dislike," said Patricia Cinelli, a spokeswoman for the group.

Robert E. Litan, director of economic studies for the Brookings Institution, predicted that the merger "will do as much to invigorate the opponents of financial modernization as it will do to invigorate the proponents. . . . The politicians will basically try to resurrect the dead patient, but I just don't think there's enough time this year. . . . I've watched this battle for almost 20 years and I haven't seen much sign that the logjam is going to break any time soon."

Record-Breaking Deal

When the proposed merger of banking-based Citicorp and securities and insurance giant Travelers Group was announced April 6, the beaming chairmen of the companies, Citicorp's John S. Reed and Travelers' Sanford I. Weill, said they had planned the merger in anticipation of changes in federal laws that would allow them to fully merge.

Under current law, Citigroup would have to sell off Travelers' insurance underwriting function and its casualty and property insurance sales (which make up about half of Traveler's revenues) two to five years after the merger is approved by the Federal Reserve, the Justice Department and state insurance regulators. That is because bank holding companies, which Travelers would become, are not allowed to engage in those activities.

Despite Reed and Weill's statement that they believed the law would "change in the foreseeable future," their merger application will be judged "on the basis of the present law, not something that's being considered in Congress," said Joseph R. Coyne, assistant to the Federal Reserve Board.

But the Federal Reserve and its counterpart in bank oversight, the Office of the Comptroller of the Currency, have tended to accept industry plans. Through regulations, they have revised the 1933 Glass-Steagall Act and other federal laws to give banks, through affiliated umbrella organizations known as holding companies, an opportunity to sell and underwrite securities and to sell some insurance policies.

Even if the Federal Reserve does not approve the merger, Citicorp could achieve it by converting its bank charter to a savings and loan run by Travelers, some business leaders have speculated. Savings and loans, also known as thrifts, are monitored by the Office of Thrift Supervision, not the Federal Reserve, and face fewer restrictions than banks in selling and underwriting insurance and securities products.

Vindication

For lobbyists on all sides, the merger announcement provided a vindication of what they had long been saying.

The securities industry held up the merger as proof that brokers were at a disadvantage in such cases, even though some financial experts say Travelers, which owns securities stalwart Salomon Smith Barney, is technically buying Citicorp. "What it said to me is that without legislation, the securities firms can't go out and be aggressive in structuring their own deal," said Steve Judge, senior vice president

Banking & Finance

of government affairs with the Securities Industry Association. "This deal doesn't happen without Citicorp going and talking to the Fed. You need a bank. For the vast majority of securities firms, they have to wait to be chosen by a bank before they can go out there and do this."

For consumer groups, the merger was an example of what will happen if the walls erected by Glass-Steagall and subsequent laws are torn down. Consumer advocate Ralph Nader said the merger "would be a massive and dangerous concentration of economic resources" and "clearly destructive to the public interest." Nader said that instead of considering HR 10, Congress should modernize antitrust laws and consolidate financial regulators into a single agency with more power to take on big companies. Nader urged the Federal Reserve and Congress to reject the proposed merger, saying, "Left unchecked, the merger will ignite others in a mad and dangerous rush to be big for the sake of being big."

Many financial experts agreed that a Citicorp-Travelers merger would spawn similar merger attempts as companies try to compete with Citigroup, which with assets of nearly $700 billion and more than 100 million customers in 100 countries would be the largest financial services company in the world.

Rumors of such prohibited mergers between banks and securities and insurance firms had circulated on Wall Street for weeks before the Citicorp-Travelers announcement. For instance, word had circulated of a possible merger between Chase Manhattan and securities giant Merrill Lynch. The rumor has not panned out, but such companies clearly would face serious competition from Citigroup. Chase Manhattan had $365 billion in assets in 1997; Merrill Lynch had $446 billion.

Whether other companies follow Citigroup or wait for congressional action, the market for mergers is not likely to cool down as U.S. companies compete for market share with large, diversified foreign banks.

Such high-profile mergers also may draw the public's attention to the state of the industry and to Congress' efforts to change the laws governing it.

"This merger proposal is the kind of thing that is provided for in the pending bill," said David Runkel, spokesman for Republicans on the House Banking Committee. "You might get some actual public interest in this bill for the first time, because here's a dramatic example of what it could do."

House Passes Overhaul Bill By One Vote

MAY 16 — The House reached a milestone May 13 as it finally passed a measure to tear down the barriers that Depression-era laws erected between the banking, securities and insurance sectors.

But the victory, after decades of attempts, was far from jubilant. The bill (HR 10) passed by one vote, 214-213, and only after a half-dozen Republicans voted 'aye' or switched from 'no' to 'aye' at the last moment as Speaker Newt Gingrich pressured members on the floor. (Vote 151, p. H-44)

The slim success prompted many opponents to label it "a hollow victory" because it did not appear to meet the requirement Senate Banking Chairman Alfonse M. D'Amato, R-N.Y., had set for consideration in that chamber: broad bipartisan support. Both parties were fractured by the vote, with Republicans supporting it by a margin of about 2-to-1, and Democrats opposed by about the same margin.

D'Amato buoyed supporters' hopes after the vote, however, when he said he would hold hearings on the issue this year. "What everyone agrees on is the need for financial modernization," he said. "It is the specific direction ... of financial reform that is contentious."

House Banking and Financial Services Committee Chairman Jim Leach, R-Iowa, said he believed there were "decent prospects" that the Senate would "seriously review the issue this year."

But even if the Senate Banking Committee marked up the measure, its many contentious provisions and the Clinton administration's opposition would make passage difficult. While Leach and House GOP Conference Chairman John A. Boehner of Ohio, the bill's main facilitator, insisted that the Senate might move the measure this year, others were not optimistic. The close vote on the bill was "another way of throwing this bill in the trash can," said Rep. Bruce F. Vento, D-Minn., who opposed the measure.

The bill would remove restrictions on affiliations among the banking, insurance and securities sectors, allowing the creation of financial holding companies that would let banks sell insurance and underwrite securities, and insurance companies and brokerage houses acquire banks. The Federal Reserve would regulate the holding companies.

Lobbyists from the securities and insurance sectors, which strongly favor the measure, reiterated their support.

Lobbyists for major banking organizations including the American Bankers Association, who mobilized local bankers in opposition, felt confident they could keep the Senate from considering it. Small- and medium-size banks have more powerful friends in the Senate, and banking lobbyists said they could count on Midwestern and Southern senators to side with local banks. Small banks believe the bill would allow already large financial institutions to expand, threatening the existence of independent institutions.

While Boehner said the bankers' opposition "did not help" GOP leaders pass the bill, he also pointed to apathy as a problem. "Not many people ever believed it was going to happen, so there was no need to look at it closely," he said. Given the House's history of refusing to even bring such bills to the floor, "a one-vote victory looks like a landslide," he said.

A Painstaking Process

The history of financial services legislation has never been placid. The bill would overhaul the 1933 Glass-Steagall Act, which prevented cross-ownership of banks, brokerages and insurance companies. It aimed to put a leash on financial companies that Congress felt had made questionable investment decisions leading to the 1929 stock market crash.

Subsequent Congresses have tried dozens of times to repeal Glass-Steagall. The Senate last tried in 1988, only to find the House in disarray. Many senators then declared that the House would have to go first. The House last tried in 1991. (1991 Almanac, p. 75)

The impetus for passing such legislation has increased recently. Republicans' traditional business allies were rejuvenated by the GOP's rise to power in 1994, and the world financial marketplace has changed dramatically in the era of the mega-merger. Several huge pending mergers, including the $70 billion marriage of Citicorp and Travelers Group, put pressure on Congress to enact a bill.

After the House Banking and Commerce committees approved competing versions of HR 10 last year, the GOP leadership appointed Boehner to put together a bill. He said he met with "thousands" of bankers, brokers and insurance agents. Big banks, brokerages and insurance firms and agents supported the measure because it would allow them to buy banks, and otherwise compete domestically and globally. But small and mid-size banks, which did not see much more for them in the bill than they already had through regulatory changes, opposed it.

With so many groups to appease, leaders went to the floor May 13 with uncertain prospects. They had been forced to pull the bill from the floor March 31 for lack of support. They had won over some high-profile Democrats, such as ranking Commerce Committee member John D. Dingell of Michigan, by adding consumer safeguards to the bill. And prospects brightened when members voted down two amendments that Rules Committee Chairman Gerald B.H. Solomon, R-N.Y., had said would "kill the bill."

The amendments — one by Vento and ranking Banking Committee Democrat John J. LaFalce of New York; the other by Richard H. Baker, R-La. — would have allowed banks to shift certain non-traditional operations to a subsidiary instead of a holding company. Bill sponsors and others considered the amendment to be anti-taxpayer because federal depository insurance could be triggered if financial problems in subsidiaries caused a bank failure.

The House then adopted, 229-193, an amendment by Leach, Doug Bereuter, R-Neb., and Tom Campbell, R-Calif., to prevent financial holding companies from owning commercial businesses. (Vote 146, p. H-44)

"The movement to go beyond the integration of financial services and eliminate the traditional legal barriers between commerce and banking is simply a bridge we should not cross," Leach said. "Would an individual hoping to open a restaurant in a town where the only bank was owned by McDonald's be able to obtain a loan?"

Boehner said the Leach amendment's effect on the final vote was "minimal to none," but others said it complicated the issue. Leach said it created more supporters.

For the final vote, leaders pulled out the big guns. With the bill down more than a dozen votes, Gingrich, R-Ga., paced up and down the aisles methodically seeking out wavering members, as a staff aide crossed them off a list.

More than a half-dozen Republicans changed their votes from 'no' to 'aye' or cast last-minute 'aye' votes after a visit from Gingrich. Among the last to switch were four Florida Republicans — Dan Miller, Michael Bilirakis, Dave Weldon and Cliff Stearns. After Jim Maloney, D-Conn., switched his vote from 'aye' to 'nay' to put the bill one vote short, Education Committee Chairman Bill Goodling, R-Pa., who is in a tight re-election race and had stood for several minutes holding both a red 'nay' card and green 'aye' card, voted 'aye.'

The LaFalce-Vento and Baker amendments were multifaceted proposals that could have cost the bill many supporters.

Both sought to allow banks to continue structuring some of their non-traditional operations, such as securities or insurance sales, as a subsidiary. As such, the activity would still be counted as part of the bank's bottom line. The bill would have required such activities to be part of a financial holding company, an umbrella company that would contain the bank and distinct securities and insurance businesses.

The issue may have seemed arcane, but it was at the heart of a long-standing battle between the Treasury Department and the Federal Reserve. The Treasury's Office of the Comptroller of the Currency regulates bank operating subsidiaries and the Federal Reserve oversees holding companies.

Treasury Secretary Robert E. Rubin said May 12 that he would not characterize the two entities' differences as a stand-off, but members and lobbyists blamed much of the bill's difficulty on a "turf war" between the two. Both are federal agencies, but the Federal Reserve is an independent entity expected to operate outside partisan politics. The Treasury Department is headed by presidential appointees and takes direction from the White House.

The operating subsidiary issue also contained policy implications.

Commerce Committee Chairman Thomas J. Bliley Jr., R-Va., said that by allowing banks to count insurance and securities activities on their ledgers, Congress would be making federal deposit insurance funds, and thus taxpayers, liable for larger dollar amounts in case of bank failures. But Democrat Barney Frank of Massachusetts said the holding company structure "says to small banks . . . that none of these new powers are available to you" because they could not afford to set up a holding company.

The House defeated the LaFalce-Vento proposal to allow banks to conduct activities through operating subsidiaries. It would not have given them the power to develop real estate or underwrite insurance. The vote was 115-306. (Vote 144, p. H-42)

It then defeated, 140-281, the Baker amendment to allow banks to continue establishing operating subsidiaries. The amendment also would have exempted banks with assets of less than $100 million from the 1977 Community Reinvestment Act (PL 95-128), which requires them to lend in low-income or minority neighborhoods. (Vote 145, p. H-42)

Maneuvering By Gramm Delays Bill

SEPTEMBER 5 — Sen. Phil Gramm has a knack for killing or stalling financial services bills, big and small, as Congress nears adjournment. He demonstrated again Sept. 3 why he is every Banking Committee chairman's nightmare.

The Texas Republican prompted panel Chairman Alfonse M. D'Amato, R-N.Y., to call off a vote on a major bill (HR 10) to overhaul the nation's outdated Depression-era fi-

Banking & Finance

nancial services laws.

Gramm, along with Richard C. Shelby, R-Ala., was pushing amendments to strip out a House provision that would require financial companies that stood to benefit from the sweeping new powers bestowed by the bill to earn satisfactory grades from regulators on their community-lending performance. They also supported a less controversial move to kill language to require banks to provide low-cost basic bank accounts to low-income people.

The community-lending controversy promised again to expose an embarrassing rift between D'Amato and his fellow panel Republicans over the Community Reinvestment Act, a 1977 law (PL 95-128) that requires banks to document their efforts to meet the credit needs of their communities. The law has been used successfully by community activists — who can protest applications by banks to merge or otherwise expand their operations — to boost lending in underserved areas.

D'Amato is one of the few GOP supporters of the law. His reasons are pragmatic: Any weakening of it guarantees a filibuster or a presidential veto. D'Amato was positioned to be the sole Republican to vote with committee Democrats to kill Gramm's community reinvestment amendment, an embarrassing but not unprecedented prospect. D'Amato voted with Democrats not to exempt small banks from community reinvestment requirements during an April markup of a bill (HR 1151) on credit union membership.

The controversy Sept. 3 over community reinvestment was the most politically resonant issue holding up the markup, but a few other issues remained unsettled. With the reinvestment issue unresolved, deals were scarce on a few remaining subjects, such as blocking transfers of so-called unitary thrift powers, which have been awarded to a limited number of existing companies to give them the power to mingle commercial and financial operations.

"The committee has made substantial progress in resolving the major issues that have divided the financial services community for years," D'Amato said in a statement to reporters. "We have not been able to resolve all the differences." D'Amato wants to convene the markup the week of Sept. 7.

But given limited time, prospects for the measure are uncertain. The Senate has little time for bills that are controversial, and any determined senator can probably kill the measure.

Stubborn Texan

It was only the latest in a string of end-of-session performances by Gramm. In 1996, he held up passage of a securities bill (PL 104-290) until the final days of the session as he negotiated changes. Two years earlier, he held up action on an interstate banking and branching bill in a standoff with former House Banking Committee Chairman Henry B. Gonzalez, D-Texas, over a home state issue. And in 1992, he singlehandedly killed a widely backed bill to curb abuses that occurred when limited partnerships were reorganized or "rolled up." (*1996 Almanac, p. 2-55; 1994 Almanac, p. 93; 1992 Almanac, p. 131*)

Gramm's opposition to the Community Reinvestment Act language exasperated many of the financial services lobbyists who packed the committee room and hallway outside. To them, the issue is dwarfed in importance by other provisions in the bill. The bill would eliminate decades-old but steadily crumbling prohibitions that have separated the banking, securities and insurance industries. Decisions by regulators and the courts have already stripped away many restrictions, and the three industries can already offer many of the products traditionally reserved for their competitors. Recent and proposed mergers such as the pending one between CitiBank and Travelers Insurance Group have also boosted momentum for the bill.

The bill has significant support from insurance and securities interests, and from some large banks. The American Bankers Association and the Independent Bankers Association of America have said the House bill would inhibit competition, especially in insurance sales. Both groups supported Senate compromises that the Banking Committee was poised to bless.

On the critical issue of insurance sales, the panel was poised to adopt a bank-friendly provision that would, after three years, eliminate state regulators' ability to treat bank sales more stringently than agent sales.

Senate Committee OKs Bill After Industry Nudge

SEPTEMBER 12 — A Senate panel approved a measure Sept. 11 to allow cross-ownership of banks, brokerages and insurance firms, ensuring that the 105th Congress will come closer than any before to tearing down the 1933 Glass-Steagall Act and other legal impediments to integrated financial services companies.

But it is uncertain if the bill (HR 10), approved 16-2 by the Banking, Housing and Urban Affairs Committee, can jump the hurdles in the path to enactment.

Several senators withdrew divisive amendments during the markup and are likely to try to offer them when the bill goes to the floor. But panel Chairman Alfonse M. D'Amato, R-N.Y., said he did not think there would be much time for floor amendments.

Majority Leader Trent Lott, R-Miss., said Sept. 10 that he expected the measure would be considered in a fashion similar to the chamber's speedy July debate on a bill (HR 1151 — PL 105-219) to allow credit unions to continue expanding their membership bases. The Senate considered few amendments to that bill and sent it quickly to the House, which cleared it without a conference.

Lobbyists said senators hope to avoid a conference on HR 10, should it pass the Senate. But a staff member said House leaders have not agreed to that.

The Banking Committee's approval came after a week in which the securities industry stepped up pressure for the bill. David Komansky, chairman and CEO of Merrill Lynch & Co., told the National Press Club that "if we don't reform our banking laws, there will be a price to pay in American economic leadership." Banking groups, which opposed the House version of HR 10, found more to their liking in the Senate version. The bill, said ranking committee Democrat Paul S. Sarbanes of Maryland, is "supported, or at least acquiesced to, by most of the involved groups."

Holding the markup was in itself an accomplishment. The panel

Financial Services Overhaul

planned to take up the bill Sept. 3 but postponed the markup when Phil Gramm, R-Texas, insisted on introducing an amendment to remove provisions that would apply the 1977 Community Reinvestment Act (PL 95-128) to the new financial giants. The act requires federal regulators to take into account a bank's lending record to all segments of its community when determining whether to approve an application for a new branch, merger or other endeavor.

The markup was rescheduled when members reached a compromise — one that Gramm did not support. The compromise was to remove a provision from the House-passed bill that would have allowed regulators to require banks with poor community reinvestment ratings to divest some holdings. And it required that only banks and wholesale financial institutions affiliated with banks meet reinvestment requirements, leaving out securities firms and insurance companies affiliated with banks.

Gramm and Richard C. Shelby, R-Ala., said at the markup that they still opposed reinvestment requirements, and both voted against the bill. Gramm offered an amendment to establish penalties for bankers who pay people who protest the bank's reinvestment record. He said banks occasionally make such payments to keep community groups from challenging a merger, instead of making loans in low-income areas, as the act intends.

He also offered an amendment that would have removed requirements that federal regulators issue a new reinvestment score for institutions when they attempt to merge or open a new branch, allowing the last annual score to suffice. But Gramm withdrew both amendments when it became clear that even ardent reinvestment opponents such as Connie Mack, R-Fla., would vote against them to keep the bill alive.

Jack Reed, D-R.I., withdrew an amendment that may be revived on the floor. It aimed to stem a long-term disagreement between the Federal Reserve and the Treasury Department on the bill's mandate that all new financial giants be organized as bank affiliates under a holding company structure instead of as an operating subsidiary. Reed's amendment would have allowed banks' securities underwriting activities to be organized as operating subsidiaries. Reed withdrew it after several members, including Sarbanes, said it likely would not stem the Treasury Department's opposition to the bill. The department opposes the holding company concept as strongly as the Federal Reserve supports it.

The committee accepted, 10-8, an amendment by Wayne Allard, R-Colo., to remove a provision to require banks to establish low-cost accounts for low-income people. It also approved by voice vote an amendment by D'Amato and Richard H. Bryan, D-Nev., to incorporate a measure (HR 4321) that would make it a federal crime to fraudulently collect private information from financial institutions. The House Banking Committee approved the bill in August.

Senate Floor Fight Lies Ahead Despite Industry Truce

OCTOBER 3 — In a truce akin to the Hatfields and McCoys laying down their arms, bankers and insurance agents have settled a decades-old feud over which insurance products banks can offer. It buoyed hopes that Congress will clear a sweeping rewrite of financial services laws that date back to the Depression.

But Senate leaders moved slowly to bring the bill to the floor after the compromise was announced Sept. 30. The measure (HR 10) is now set to come up Oct. 5, when the Senate is to vote on whether to limit debate, or invoke cloture, on proceeding to the bill. If the Senate invokes cloture, the bill is likely to be on the floor most of the week, where opponents on the left and the right are likely to threaten to block the bill at every turn. If deals cannot be made, the Senate may need a second cloture vote, on the measure itself.

The bill would tear down decades-old prohibitions on mingling the ownership and operations of banks, brokerages and insurance firms. It would likely spawn mergers similar to the Citicorp-Travelers marriage that the Federal Reserve tentatively approved Sept. 23. Consumers would probably find their banks offering more investment and insurance services.

Community Reinvestment

The measure is bringing back longstanding Senate political disputes. Conservatives such as Phil Gramm, R-Texas, and Richard C. Shelby, R-Ala., oppose the bill because it would apply the 1977 Community Reinvestment Act (PL 95-128) to the new financial giants. Gramm has compared that act to "extortion" and says it is often used by organized community groups to force banks to contribute to their causes, instead of providing loans to deserving low-income and minority customers, as he believes the act intended.

But most Democrats say the act is key to ensuring that minority communities have access to financial services. They want more of such legislation. Paul Wellstone, D-Minn., is expected to offer an amendment that would reinstate a House-passed provision requiring banks to provide low-cost services to people with low bank account balances. The provision, known as "life-line banking," was removed during the Senate Banking Committee's markup Sept. 11 and is considered anathema to banks.

The prospect of floor fights is especially trying for bill supporters in the securities, insurance and banking industries because they believe that the bank-insurance deal, coupled with a compromise on securities regulation reached earlier in the week, would allow the House to take up the measure that the Senate passes and clear it without a House-Senate conference.

The bank-insurance deal changed technical language regarding when state insurance regulators can issue different rules for banks and independent insurance agents. The bill specifies 13 areas in which differing rules can exist, including some requirements that banks ensure that consumers are informed when the products they purchase are not federally insured.

The securities deal, reached between Senate Banking Committee Chairman Alfonse M. D'Amato, R-N.Y., and House Commerce Committee Chairman Thomas J. Bliley Jr., R-Va., would allow the Securities and Exchange Commission (SEC) to define when a new product offered by a bank was a security, and thus subject to

Banking & Finance

SEC oversight. But the Federal Reserve could stay enforcement actions taken by the SEC on such matters, and could then take the SEC to court.

Even if the Senate manages to pass HR 10 and the House resists the urge to tinker with it, bill supporters know another, possibly insurmountable, obstacle awaits.

Administration officials have said that if the bill reaches President Clinton's desk without substantial changes requested by Treasury Secretary Robert E. Rubin, the measure will be vetoed. Rubin opposes the way new financial conglomerates would be structured, but most observers believe that he is particularly upset because the Federal Reserve, and not Treasury, would oversee the new giants.

Some supporters believe both chambers could pass the measure with veto-proof majorities, especially if D'Amato can reach a deal with Gramm and Shelby, but Congress is not likely to be in session when a veto arrives. Clinton will have 10 days after receiving the bill to make a decision, and Congress is not likely to send him the measure until the end of the session.

Some bill supporters still harbor hopes that Clinton and Rubin can be persuaded to change their minds.

Sens. Rod Grams, R-Minn., and Jack Reed, D-R.I., want to offer an amendment that they hope would make it harder for Rubin to maintain his hard-line stance. The amendment would allow banks to organize certain operations — such as securities underwriting and merchant banking — as operating subsidiaries, or entities whose bottom line was reflected on the parent bank's financial ledger.

Their approach would give Rubin some, but not all, of what he wants. Rubin says the new financial giants should be able to choose between organizing all of their new entities as operating subsidiaries of the bank or as separate businesses with separate financial ledgers under an umbrella holding company. The bill now requires all financial conglomerates to be organized in the latter fashion, as Federal Reserve Chairman Alan Greenspan has insisted.

The Fed would regulate financial holding companies; the Treasury Department would regulate operating subsidiaries.

If HR 10 clears, Rubin and Clinton will be pressured to change their position, especially if the final bill includes the Grams-Reed amendment.

Senate Roadblocks, Veto Threat Kill Bill's Chances

OCTOBER 10 — In another context, the apparent failure of Federal Reserve Board Chairman Alan Greenspan and the most powerful people on Wall Street to get what they wanted from Congress would have been extraordinary.

But persuading Congress to repeal the 1933 Glass-Steagall Act and allow banks, brokerages and insurance firms to combine operations was always a long shot, even for leaders of the financial world.

Almost since the day Sen. Carter Glass, D-Va. (1920-46), and Rep. Henry Steagall, D-Ala. (1915-43), won passage of a measure to erect barriers between banks and other businesses — to stem Depression-era financial failures — Congress has tried to repeal their handiwork. Dozens of attempts have failed, including the most recent, and perhaps most promising: It appeared to die in the closing days of the 105th Congress despite efforts to revive it by Greenspan, securities brokers, insurance officials and some bankers.

The measure (HR 10) was doomed by friend and foe alike. Senate consideration was stymied by parliamentary roadblocks that kept the bill from moving separately. The last hope was to move it as part of the omnibus spending measure.

Led by Phil Gramm, R-Texas, conservative Republicans who supported most of the bill blocked its progress over a provision that would apply community investment requirements to the new financial giants the bill would allow. But had they not stopped it, that role might have been played by Democrats who do not consider bigger and better synonymous. Byron L. Dorgan, D-N.D., had threatened to make passage difficult.

Even if the measure made it through the Senate and was cleared by the House, Senate leaders knew that President Clinton was likely to ignore their hard work and veto the bill. That contributed to their hesitance to pressure Gramm to drop his opposition. Senate Majority Leader Trent Lott, R-Miss., said Oct. 6: "We don't want to take a chance on having that bill vetoed."

Clinton was expected to veto the measure because Treasury Secretary Robert E. Rubin opposed it. Rubin objected to provisions that would require diversified financial companies to be structured as separate entities under one umbrella holding company. Such companies are regulated by the Federal Reserve. Rubin wanted to allow the conglomerates to operate entities such as a securities or insurance company as subsidiaries of a parent bank, and part of the bank's bottom line. The Treasury Department regulates operating subsidiaries.

Because Rubin backed the operating subsidiary concept as strongly as Greenspan insisted on the holding company structure, most observers had labeled the feud between the otherwise friendly officials as a turf war.

Despite Rubin's intransigence, some bill supporters hoped they could persuade him to sign on if it became clear the measure was going to pass. A handful of members from both chambers offered proposals to allow banks to structure some, but not all, activities as operating subsidiaries. They hoped this would make Clinton less likely to veto the bill, risking the wrath of Greenspan and Wall Street.

Senate and House Action

But preparation for a possible veto did not appear necessary, because the bill seemed unlikely to make it to a final vote in the Senate.

Members voted 93-0 on Oct. 5 to stem debate on proceeding to the bill and 88-11 on Oct. 7 to take up the measure, but Gramm managed to slow Senate debate to a crawl. *(Votes 297 and 301, p. S-46)*

Gramm's major objection was to provisions that would apply the 1977 Community Reinvestment Act (CRA) to the new conglomerates and increase penalties for non-compliance to $1 million a day. The act (PL 95-128) requires federal regulators when ruling on applications for a merger or new branch to take into consideration the bank's lending record to all segments of its community.

Gramm and his partner in the effort, Republican Sen. Richard C. Shelby of Alabama, have long compared the act to legalized extortion, and Gramm laid down his demands plainly Oct. 5. "For those who want the bill now, there is one thing you have to do to get this bill. You will have to do something about the expansive CRA provisions. . . . The clock is running out, and if you are going to fix it, you better do it fast."

While the bill was stalled in the Senate, the House on Oct. 9 passed by voice vote a smaller measure (HR 4364) that would offer banks some relief by allowing the Federal Reserve to pay interest on the funds they must keep on hand. It also would allow banks to pay interest on business checking accounts. ◆

GOP, Administration Fail To Reach Compromise On Bankruptcy Overhaul

Despite its high-ranking position on the business community's wish list, a broad overhaul of consumer bankruptcy laws did not make it through the 105th Congress. Republicans could not find a compromise to which both the Clinton administration and creditors would agree.

Charles E. Grassley, R-Iowa, sponsor of the Senate measure, and some farm-oriented House members salvaged a provision from the bill that reauthorized the Chapter 12 bankruptcy program for family farmers. The provision, which extended Chapter 12 through April 1999, was included in the omnibus spending package (HR 4328 — PL 105-277) that President Clinton signed Oct. 21.

Prospects for the overall bankruptcy measure had looked uncertain from the outset because the main provisions in the Senate and House bills were substantially different. Both bills aimed to stem a record number of personal bankruptcy filings, but they took different approaches. Grassley's bill would have tweaked the existing system to give judges another reason to move a debtor from Chapter 7, which absolves debts after sale of the debtor's assets, to Chapter 13, in which debts are restructured to help the debtor pay off bills in three to five years. Under the bill, a debtor's ability to pay 30 percent or more of unsecured debts, such as credit cards, would constitute a reason to move a case to Chapter 13.

SUMMARY

The House bill, sponsored by George W. Gekas, R-Pa., set up a stricter system for determining who could file for Chapter 7 protection. Under the bill, a person who earned the median income or more — about $51,000 for a family of four — and could pay off at least 20 percent of unsecured debts would be precluded from Chapter 7 protection. Such debtors would have to file under Chapter 13, or work out their debts privately.

Grassley, Gekas and other Republicans reached a compromise that would have required debtors to file under Chapter 13 if they had an above-median income and could pay off at least 25 percent of their unsecured debts over five years.

But Democrats, including Sen. Richard J. Durbin of Illinois, a cosponsor of the original bill, said they had been left out of decisions and opposed the conference report. It died in the Senate without a final vote.

Republicans tried to find a place for the measure in the omnibus spending bill, but the Clinton administration insisted on changes to the means test that creditors said they could not accept.

Senate Panel Approves Tighter Bankruptcy Laws

APRIL 4 — Much-anticipated efforts to overhaul the bankruptcy system met their first test April 2 as a Senate Judiciary subcommittee approved an overhaul measure, giving it a head start over a stricter House bill.

The bill (S 1301), approved 6-1 by the Subcommittee on Administrative Oversight and the Courts, would tighten bankruptcy laws to allow judges to dismiss Chapter 7 cases outright or force filers to repay as many debts as possible, if it were determined that they could repay 20 percent or more of their debts.

Chapter 7, the least restrictive bankruptcy program, allows filers to erase all debts not paid off by the sale of their assets.

The bill is less far-reaching than its main House competitor (HR 3150), which would withhold Chapter 7 protection from debtors who earn more than 75 percent of the median income in their geographic area and could pay off all of their secured debt, such as a home or car, and 20 percent of their unsecured debt, such as credit cards. The House Judiciary Committee is expected to begin moving its bill shortly after the the spring recess.

Although some GOP senators indicated they were willing to include some of the House's tougher provisions in S 1301, bill sponsor and sub-

Box Score

- **Bill:** HR 3150
- **House action:** The House adopted the conference report (H Rept 105-794) on HR 3150, 300-125, on Oct. 9. It passed HR 3150 (H Rept 105-540), 306-118, on June 10.
- **Senate action:** The Senate passed HR 3150, 97-1, on Sept. 23 after substituting the text of its version (S 1301 —

Banking & Finance

committee Chairman Charles E. Grassley, R-Iowa, said a bill with the so-called means testing provision included in the House measure could not pass the Senate, at least not before it was tempered by conference committee negotiations.

The subcommittee markup was a largely congenial affair in which members from both parties agreed to continue to work to iron out differences on some provisions. But Democrats signaled that the bill might have trouble as it progresses.

Ranking subcommittee Democrat Richard J. Durbin of Illinois said that even though he cosponsored the measure, he would vote to send it to the floor "with some reluctance and mounting concern." Durbin said he feared the bill was too weighted against the poor, and he urged Congress to "just try to pass a bill that catches abuses without so contorting the system."

Grassley said the full Judiciary Committee intends to take up the bill in late April or early May, followed by floor action in the summer.

Creditors, particularly credit card companies, have been strongly lobbying Congress to change bankruptcy laws in light of large increases in filings over the past decade. The number of people filing for bankruptcy increased from slightly more than 500,000 in 1986 to 1.4 million in 1997.

The most far-reaching amendment, by Herb Kohl, D-Wis., and Jeff Sessions, R-Ala., would cap at $100,000 the amount that bankruptcy filers could keep from the sale of their home. The subcommittee accepted it 7-0. The provision would affect seven states that allow greater homestead exemptions, including some in which filers are entitled to the total value of their home.

One of those states, Florida, has been home to several high-profile cases in which people on the verge of bankruptcy flee to Florida and buy a house. In spite of such cases, the states involved have traditionally launched spirited defenses of their laws and are expected to do so again.

The subcommittee also adopted by voice vote a Durbin amendment that would prevent Chapter 7 bankruptcy filers who made less than the median family income ($45,300 for a family of four) from being forced into Chapter 13, which requires them to repay as much of their debt as possible over three to five years.

House Democrats Stage Blockade; Senate To Consider Narrower Measure

APRIL 25 — Rep. George W. Gekas, R-Pa., shepherded his bill to substantially overhaul the bankruptcy system through a Judiciary subcommittee unscathed April 23, despite 21 Democratic attempts to change it. But as he savored his measure's voice vote victory, he also cast a cautious eye to the future.

The partisan nature of the Commercial and Administrative Law Subcommittee's markup was "a predictor of what we will see" when the full Judiciary Committee considers the bill (HR 3150) on April 29, Gekas said. The measure is expected on the House floor the week of May 11, about the same time the Senate may take up a companion bill (S 1301) that its Judiciary Subcommittee on Administrative Oversight and the Courts approved April 2.

That measure is less sweeping than Gekas' bill, which seeks to reduce the number of people granted Chapter 7 bankruptcy protection. Such protection absolves filers of their debts, some of which are paid off by a sale of their assets, and allows them to start over.

The Senate bill would allow creditors and bankruptcy court trustees to be more aggressive in determining whether applicants filing for bankruptcy protection can repay all or some of their debts.

The Gekas bill would prevent those who earn more than 75 percent of the median income in their region and can pay off all their secured debt (such as a home) and 20 percent of their unsecured debt (such as credit card bills) from filing for Chapter 7 protection. Those whose resources exceeded the income and repayment test would have to file under Chapter 13, which requires repayment of as many debts as possible over three to five years.

The differences between the bills are likely to cause major conflict in a House-Senate conference that leaders hope to convene in June. Senate bill sponsor Charles E. Grassley, R-Iowa, has expressed doubt that a Gekas bill could pass in the Senate, and Gekas said he did not "see how we could compromise 100 percent on a means-based concept."

But before facing senators, Gekas has to deal with House Democrats.

At the April 23 markup, Democrats offered amendments aimed at holding creditors responsible for increased bankruptcy filings and at keeping some income away from creditors after a person files for bankruptcy. Filings jumped from 500,000 in 1986 to 1.4 million in 1997, most of them under Chapter 7.

All the amendments were either withdrawn or defeated on party-line votes. Most are expected to resurface at the April 29 markup.

Ranking panel Democrat Jerrold Nadler of New York offered an amendment to prevent creditors from seeking repayment of gambling debts if the money was lent in or near a casino, through, for example, an automated teller machine. It was defeated, 2-5, in a party-line vote.

A second Nadler amendment sought to prevent repayment of debt from a credit card that creditors extended even though it would allow the filer's total debts to surpass 40 percent of his income. It was defeated by voice vote.

Democrats withdrew a handful of other amendments that sought to exempt certain types of income from repayment plans after Gekas said he would work with them on amendments that might be accepted by the full committee. Among them were plans by Nadler to allow bankruptcy filers to keep the proceeds from veterans' payments and some court settlements. Gekas also pledged to work with Sheila Jackson-Lee, D-Texas, on an amendment to ensure that bankruptcy filers had enough money to make child support payments.

The panel accepted by voice vote a substitute amendment by Gekas that incorporated a plan from a Nadler bill (HR 3146) to shield payments from Individual Retirement Accounts from creditors. It also adopted a portion of a bill (HR 2604) by Ron Packard, R-Calif., that would prevent courts from recalling religious and charitable donations that a person made before filing for bankruptcy.

The substitute amendment also allowed adjustments to the bill's Chapter 7 income limits for filers with large families.

Martin T. Meehan, D-Mass., said the subcommittee was "short of even a shred of consensus," but Gekas pointed out that his bill was cosponsored by James P. Moran, D-Va., and supported by other Democrats.

But those from the more liberal wing of the Democratic party were not convinced. Gekas said his bill would "create the fiscal disciplines that will ensure our families a brighter future," but Nadler charged that "the underlying assumption of the bill is that millions of Americans are deadbeats."

House Panel OKs Means Test For Chapter 7

MAY 16 — During the three days it took the House Judiciary Committee to send to the floor a bill seeking to rewrite the nation's bankruptcy code, members agreed on the need for wide-scale change but split on specifics. The committee approved the bill (HR 3150), 18-10, in a largely party-line vote.

It should be on the floor before Memorial Day, where it will face another round of criticism from Democrats, consumer advocates and others who say that by seeking to make it more difficult for people to wipe out their debts, the bill is cruel. "By and large, it is tilted way too far in favor of the creditors," said Ken Klee, legislative chairman of the National Bankruptcy Conference, a group of judges, lawyers and academics. "The harm to the public would be substantial."

The legislation, however, has many supporters and significant momentum resulting from a consumer bankruptcy rate that has more than doubled in the past eight years. Last year, despite a booming economy and low unemployment, a record 1.4 million people filed for bankruptcy.

"Bankruptcy has become a financial planning tool for many who could repay their debts," said Rick Boucher, D-Va., one of only two panel Democrats to endorse the bill. The other was Steven R. Rothman of New Jersey.

Sponsor George W. Gekas, R-Pa., said the legislation is based on the idea that Chapter 7 of the bankruptcy code — which allows people to walk away from most unsecured debts, such as credit cards — should be available only to those who truly cannot pay their bills. The legislation relies on "personal responsibility and personal accountability," he said.

The bill would establish a strict "means test" to determine who is eligible for Chapter 7 bankruptcy protection, sending those who do not qualify home or to Chapter 13, which requires a repayment plan.

Gekas said the bill, which also makes less controversial changes in commercial bankruptcy law, would protect those in the most dire straits and make bankruptcy less attractive to others. But his point of view was sharply questioned by many panel Democrats, who said many bankruptcy problems can be traced to lenders who recklessly hand out credit.

The 177-page bill calls for the most sweeping changes to the bankruptcy code in two decades. It would require people to repay most credit card debts incurred during the 90 days before they file for bankruptcy, or incurred without "reasonable expectations" that they could be repaid.

"The ability to pay one's bills should be seen as a badge of honor," said Steve Buyer, R-Ind.

The bill also would require tax returns and paycheck stubs to be included in bankruptcy petitions, and would strengthen the rights of creditors, allowing them to request that a debtor be transferred from Chapter 7 to Chapter 13. Democrats said that would lead to massive litigation, putting further stress on bankruptcy courts. But they made little headway with the GOP.

Means Test

The committee began its markup May 12, with Democrats raising a host of concerns. They said the means test was too stringent and would not consider individual financial circumstances. Over three days, they offered 31 amendments, many of which were rejected.

But on one of the final amendments, offered by panel Chairman Henry J. Hyde, R-Ill., and Sheila Jackson-Lee, D-Texas, bill supporters made their greatest concession.

The amendment sought to raise the income threshold for determining whether a debtor would be eligible for Chapter 7. The bill initially said anyone earning 75 percent of the nation's median income would not be eligible for Chapter 7, if the person could repay all secured debt, such as for a home or car, and at least 20 percent of unsecured debt over five years.

The amendment, approved by voice vote, increased the threshold from 75 percent to 100 percent of the median income. Hyde called it "the humanization of this bill."

Though happy with the change, Jerrold Nadler, D-N.Y., a fierce bill critic, said the test was "still too stringent."

Also by voice vote, the committee accepted a series of amendments aimed at quelling concerns that the bill, by giving high priority to repayment of credit card and other unsecured debt, would make it more difficult to collect child support payments.

One amendment, offered by Hyde, would lower the priority level for repayment of credit card debt, and two others, offered by Boucher, said child support would take priority over unsecured debts, and that judges would retain the flexibility to determine repayment rates for overdue child support.

Despite the overwhelming support both parties gave to these amendments, Democrats said they did not go far enough. "Child support will now compete with credit card companies for restitution," said ranking Democrat John Conyers Jr. of Michigan.

By a 12-13 vote, Republicans shot down a Jackson-Lee amendment that sought to ensure that unsecured debt payments were not ordered to be paid before all past and current child support bills were paid. Amendment critics said child support would continue to be given higher priority than debts not secured by collateral.

Siding often with the GOP, Boucher pushed through by voice vote an amendment to allow necessities bought on credit within 90 days of declaring bankruptcy to be wiped out, as

Banking & Finance

long as the purchases did not exceed $250 per creditor.

The panel also accepted an amendment by Bill Delahunt, D-Mass., that would establish a $100,000 nationwide cap on "homestead exemptions," which vary from state to state and allow people who file for bankruptcy to shield equity in their home from creditors.

As the House committee worked, the Senate Judiciary Committee postponed work on its bankruptcy overhaul legislation (S 1301). The Senate bill, sponsored by Charles E. Grassley, R-Iowa, and Richard J. Durbin, D-Ill., would make it easier for judges to transfer a case out of Chapter 7 into Chapter 13. That bill is expected to be marked up May 20.

Throughout the House markup, Democrats argued that the consumer provisions in the bill were a gift to the credit card industry. Nadler blasted the legislation as "anti-family."

Jackson-Lee was even more critical, urging President Clinton to veto the legislation if it reaches his desk. She said the bill would hurt those people who most need the second chance offered by bankruptcy. "It hurts African-American and Hispanic families who are just emerging into the middle class," she said. "It's a sham; it's a drive-by. It has no business in the legislative process."

Supporters countered the anti-family charges with equally impassioned arguments. Mike McGarry, director of public affairs at Visa USA, said the $40 billion in consumer debt wiped out by bankruptcy last year cost the average American family $400.

Bill McCollum, R-Fla., said supporters are looking out for those who pay their bills on time but face increased costs as consumers and higher interest rates as borrowers. "This bill is not harmful to families," McCollum said. "It is pro-family. You don't think these big credit card companies are absorbing these costs, do you?"

In related action, the panel approved a bill (HR 2604) on May 14, sponsored by Ron Packard, R-Calif., that would protect donations to charity and tithing to churches when a person declares bankruptcy. The bill would prohibit creditors from seizing certain donations to either group. The Senate passed a similar bill (S 1244), 100-0, on May 13. *(Vote 132, p. S-22)*

Bipartisan Support In Committee May Not Hold On Senate Floor

MAY 23 — A measure to make it easier for courts and creditors to require bankrupt debtors to pay some of their bills passed easily through the Senate Judiciary Committee on May 21.

But the bipartisan coalition that supported the bill, approving it 16-2, showed signs of fracture. Several Democrats who voted for the bill (S 1301) said they would offer controversial amendments when it came to the floor. One of the two who voted against the legislation was Edward M. Kennedy, D-Mass., who issued a diatribe against it and will probably try to slow it down when it reaches the floor in mid- to late June. The other opponent was Russell D. Feingold, D-Wis.

Republicans generally held their tongues and did not offer their most controversial amendments as leaders tried to retain Democratic support for the bill, sponsored by Charles E. Grassley, R-Iowa, and Richard J. Durbin, D-Ill. But in the full committee markup May 21 and the Administrative Oversight and the Courts Subcommittee markup April 2, Durbin signaled that he had doubts about the measure. He said he would attempt on the floor to shift some of the burden to credit card companies and other creditors who solicit customers through mass mailings or who operate automated teller machines in places where customers may be vulnerable, such as in casinos.

The bill would tighten bankruptcy laws to allow judges to dismiss certain cases under Chapter 7 of the bankruptcy code, or force filers who could repay at least 20 percent of their debt to repay as many debts as possible. Chapter 7, the least restrictive bankruptcy program, allows filers to erase all debts not paid off by the sale of their assets. Many of the debtors would be forced into Chapter 13, which requires them to pay back most of their debts over three to five years.

The Senate measure is considered less stringent than a proposal (HR 3150) that is expected on the House floor shortly after Congress returns June 2 from its Memorial Day break.

The House bill would withhold Chapter 7 protection from debtors who earned more than the median income in their geographic area — the national median income is a little more than $51,000 a year for a family of four — and could pay off all their secured debt, such as a home or car loan, and 20 percent of their unsecured debt, such as credit cards.

Some conservative Senate Republicans favor the House approach, but they held back from offering it as a substitute in committee and also may refrain from doing so on the floor, according to lobbyists and a high-level Republican aide. Instead, they expect the choice between the Senate plan to tweak the current system or the House proposal to establish an income limit for bankruptcy filings to be made in a House-Senate conference.

Dividing the Pie

Bipartisan support for the Senate bill emerged after the panel accepted by voice vote an amendment to require bankruptcy filers to give priority to paying child support and alimony.

Grassley, Jon Kyl, R-Ariz., and committee Chairman Orrin G. Hatch, R-Utah, offered the amendment to head off Democrats' contention that the bill would take money from debtors' children and give it to credit card companies. The amendment would elevate child support and alimony to the No. 1 repayment responsibility of bankruptcy filers, up from No. 7 in current law, behind such debts as mortgage payments, student loans and legal fees. "Deadbeat dads should be given no chance to manipulate bankruptcy laws," Hatch said.

But Durbin and Kennedy said the amendment would not ensure that former spouses and children get their payments. Because the bill would elevate the importance of repaying almost all debts, Durbin said, "We're creating more competition for limited funds. The important question is how many other people will be in the pool." Added Kennedy: "You're not going to correct it by an amendment here and an amendment there."

That provoked an angry response from Kyl, who said, "I don't know how

Bankruptcy Overhaul

you can do more. . . . I would hope there would be some recognition that we have done something good here." Said Grassley: "I don't think that Republicans can be made to look bad on this issue now."

In a letter to the committee, the Clinton administration expressed support for the amendment, and a top GOP staff aide said after the markup that the administration was "excited" about the provision and seemed more likely to support the overall bill.

The committee also voted, 10-7, for an amendment by Spencer Abraham, R-Mich., that would require Chapter 13 bankruptcy filers to pay off the full cost of items such as cars or televisions that decrease in value shortly after they are purchased. Current law "crams down" the value of the item, requiring debtors to pay back the item's value at the time they file for bankruptcy. The difference between the price they paid and the market value becomes an unsecured debt, which debtors are not required to pay off in full.

The committee also defeated, 9-9, two amendments by Feingold and Arlen Specter, R-Pa. One would have waived fees for people who could not afford the $110 to $175 required to file for bankruptcy. The other aimed to lessen the likelihood that a debtor's attorney would be required to reimburse the court for fees if it was determined that the debtor should have filed under Chapter 13 instead of Chapter 7. The amendment would have required the court to show that the filing had been "frivolous."

House-Passed Bill Demands More From Debtors

JUNE 13 — As debate over the nation's bankruptcy laws heated up this year, supporters of a dramatic system overhaul remained loyal to their key message: People who declare bankruptcy should be forced to pay back at least a portion of their debts, if they can.

It was clear June 10 that the message was out, as the House voted overwhelmingly for a bill that would make it more difficult for people to walk away from their debts.

The House passed the bill (HR 3150) by a vote of 306-118 with no dissenting Republicans and with support from 84 Democrats, some of them brought on board by a bankruptcy rate that hit a record level in 1997. The vote sent a clear signal that wide-scale change to the bankruptcy system is a top House priority. *(Vote 225, p. H-66)*

"We are running out of time, and we can no longer say it is up to the next generation to fix what is broken," said bill sponsor George W. Gekas, R-Pa., chairman of the House Judiciary Subcommittee on Commercial and Administrative Law.

Supporters will now turn to the Senate, where the Judiciary Committee has approved a less stringent measure (S 1301) that the full chamber has yet to act on. Those pushing hardest for a bankruptcy revamp — a coalition of retailers and lenders such as credit card companies, credit unions and banks — are hoping the House vote sends a message to the Senate and President Clinton that changes must be made.

But Democratic opponents and consumer groups are promising to continue their fight against a bill they say lacks compassion for those suffering financially and puts more stock on rigid formulas than on individual circumstances. "People are not just walking away [from their debts]," argued Bill Delahunt, D-Mass. "They are being crushed by debt." The Clinton administration issued a policy statement June 10 calling a key part of the bill "rigid and arbitrary."

The key part is a "means test" that would determine who could file for bankruptcy under Chapter 7 of the bankruptcy code, which allows individuals to liquidate their assets and wipe away many of their unsecured debts, such as credit cards. The bill would transfer into a Chapter 13 repayment plan anyone who earned at least the national median income — about $51,000 for a family of four — and was found able to pay back 20 percent or more of unsecured debts over five years.

The bill also seeks to force those declaring bankruptcy to repay any debt incurred in the 90 days before they file, addressing concerns that some people rack up large debts knowing they can walk away from liability. Seeking to educate debtors, the bill includes requirements that people be informed about alternatives to bankruptcy before they file. It would also create a pilot program on financial management for some who do file.

Small Business

The bill's provisions regarding business bankruptcies have produced little controversy. Some critics say, however, that the legislation would hurt small businesses, which would be subject to new reporting requirements, and would have to submit reorganization plans within 90 days of filing for bankruptcy. Chapter 12 of the bankruptcy code, which gives protection to family farmers, would be extended permanently.

During a seven-hour debate June 10, Republicans turned back Democratic amendments that sought to weaken key aspects of the bill — including the means test — and pushed through several amendments aimed at increasing support for the legislation.

The final vote was convincing, but the debate was often bitter, with members on both sides reiterating the arguments that have taken them this far.

Supporters came armed with statistics showing that a record 1.35 million people — or one in every 70 households — filed for consumer bankruptcy in 1997, up from 1.1 million in 1996. According to figures from the American Bankruptcy Institute, the upward trend has continued this year, with 20,000 more people filing for bankruptcy in the first quarter of 1998 than in the same three-month period in 1997.

The solution, Gekas and others said, is to make bankruptcy less attractive and to establish safeguards to prevent system abuses. With a quick trip to bankruptcy court, they argued, a person can now erase mounds of credit card debt, leaving creditors and other consumers to pick up the tab. "It's the easy street," said Scott McInnis, R-Colo. "It's the easy way out."

Bill supporters argued that the ease and benefits of declaring bankruptcy have worn away the stigma that used to be attached to filing. Even some of those who strongly oppose the bill agree that society is more accepting of bankruptcy.

"It used to be that people would

Banking & Finance

whisper about the guy in the neighborhood who declared bankruptcy, like he had run down Main Street with his clothes off," said Stephen H. Case, a member of the National Bankruptcy Conference, an organization of bankruptcy lawyers, judges and academics. "Yes, the stigma is gone."

But bill critics, including Case, say supporters have ignored some key factors. They say, for example, that many people enter bankruptcy reluctantly, pushed there by illness, job loss or divorce. With its means test, the bill makes too many assumptions without considering the route each individual takes to bankruptcy court.

Opponents also said lenders should be held responsible for aggressive marketing techniques and reckless lending practices. Delahunt produced a copy of a loan offer his daughter received from a credit card company. The offer included a check for $2,875 that could be immediately cashed at the bank. "My daughter is a full-time student with no regular income," Delahunt said.

One of the bill's fiercest opponents, Jerrold Nadler, D-N.Y., called it "one of the worst special interest bills we have considered in years. . . . This is a bill of, by and for the credit card companies."

Amendments

Democrats had planned to offer numerous amendments but were disappointed when the Rules Committee, which sets the parameters of floor debate, decided to allow votes on only a dozen measures. "The American people are being cheated because they will not get an open debate," Nadler said.

The House accepted by voice vote an amendment by Rick Boucher, D-Va., to place child support and alimony as the top priority in Chapter 13 repayment plans. It also accepted by voice vote an amendment by E. Clay Shaw Jr., R-Fla., to allow parents to place liens on credit card payments made by a parent who owes child support.

Both amendments were aimed at quelling criticism that the bill, by giving credit card companies more ability to recover losses from those who declare bankruptcy, would make it harder for people to collect past-due child support and alimony. Some Democrats said the amendments did not go far enough, but supporters disagreed. "It's about as good a protection as we can get in there," Shaw said.

By a 222-204 vote, the House adopted an amendment by Gekas to remove the bill's $100,000 cap on "homestead exemptions." The exemptions vary from state to state, shielding at least a portion of a person's residence from creditors during the bankruptcy process. The cap was blasted by politicians from states that have no such limits. In a letter to Judiciary Chairman Henry J. Hyde, R-Ill., Texas Gov. George W. Bush called the provision "a clear violation of states' rights." *(Vote 221, p. H-64)*

The House defeated,140-288, an amendment by Nadler to eliminate the test to determine who can enter Chapter 7, as well as restrictions to make it more difficult to erase credit card debts. Gekas said the amendment would have struck at the heart of the bill. "Personal responsibility," he said, "has to be returned to our society." *(Vote 223, p. H-66)*

Senate Agreement Improves Chances For Bill's Passage

SEPTEMBER 12 — Proponents of overhauling the consumer bankruptcy system made substantial progress in the Senate as Democrats and Republicans reached agreements likely to pave the way to the bill's passage the week of Sept. 14.

After a late-night negotiating session Sept. 10, bill sponsor Charles E. Grassley, R-Iowa, and Richard J. Durbin, D-Ill., announced that they had come up with a plan to whittle the 42 amendments Democrats had planned to offer to about a dozen, and to give two senators a chance to offer extraneous amendments.

When the Senate resumes debate on the measure (S 1301), probably Sept. 15, Edward M. Kennedy, D-Mass., will offer an amendment to increase the minimum wage by $1 over the next two years. That amendment must be tabled (killed), or the Grassley-Durbin deal is off. Later in the week, Alfonse M. D'Amato, R-N.Y., will offer a plan to prevent banks from charging non-customers to use their automated teller machines (ATMs).

The agreement was key to the bill's survival. Without it, the Senate would have voted on a motion to invoke cloture, or stem debate, on the measure, a vote that bill supporters would likely have lost. Facing such a prospect, Majority Leader Trent Lott, R-Miss., warned Sept. 10 that "if it doesn't pass, we really have to go on" to other bills.

The agreement is likely to allow the Senate to pass the measure, but the bill's prospects are unclear after that. The House passed a more stringent bill (HR 3150) in June, and observers say House-Senate conferees may not have time to work out a compromise. Bankruptcy is under the purview of the House and Senate Judiciary committees, and the House panel is expected to be bogged down with Independent Counsel Kenneth W. Starr's report on his investigation into alleged misdeeds by President Clinton.

Nevertheless, supporters were buoyed Sept. 9 when the Senate voted 99-1 to proceed to the bill, after Kennedy and other Democrats abandoned plans to drag out debate on taking up the bill and shifted their strategy to attaching amendments to it. *(Vote 263, p. S-41)*

The bill would make it harder for people to file for bankruptcy protection-nder Chapter 7, which absolves filers of debts after eligible assets are sold to pay bills. It would require bankruptcy judges to take into account whether someone filing under Chapter 7 could pay off at least 20 percent of credit card bills and other unsecured debt when determining whether to move the filer to Chapter 13, which requires payment of as many bills as possible over three to five years.

Grassley touted the measure as "a bipartisan effort which keeps the best of old law while curbing abuses." And Durbin, a cosponsor, said it was "at its heart a good bill."

But Durbin has often seemed on the verge of pulling his support, and he stressed during debate that the bill should be modified to hold credit card companies responsible for some of the record number of bankruptcies. About 1.35 million consumers filed for bankruptcy in 1997, up from 500,000 in 1986. Credit card companies and other bill supporters say bankruptcy rates are rising because the stigma is gone and people are using bankruptcy as a finan-

How Bankruptcy Code Would Change

SEPTEMBER 26 — The Senate passed a consumer bankruptcy bill (HR 3150) on Sept. 23 that would build on the changes Congress made to the bankruptcy code in 1984. That measure (PL 98-353) allowed judges to dismiss bankruptcy cases or force debtors to file under a different section of the bankruptcy code if their filing clearly constituted "substantial abuse" of the system. (1984 Almanac, p. 263)

The bankruptcy code is divided into several sections, or chapters, two of which are reserved for consumers. Under Chapter 7 — the most heavily used — all debts are dismissed after the debtor sells non-exempt assets to pay creditors. Because state and federal laws exempt key items from sale — including home furnishings, work tools and, in some cases, homes — fewer than 5 percent of those who file under Chapter 7 actually have non-exempt assets to sell.

Under the other consumer category, Chapter 13, debtors must restructure their budgets to pay off as many debts as possible over three to five years. In exchange, they may keep all assets. If they cannot complete the payment plan, they are either transferred to Chapter 7 or their debts are dismissed after three to five years.

The Senate bill would make the following changes:

- **Dismissals and transfers.** Judges, in determining whether a petition for bankruptcy should be dismissed, or whether to move a filer from Chapter 7 to Chapter 13, would be required to consider whether the person could pay at least 30 percent of unsecured debt such as credit cards.

Judges also could dismiss cases in which they found "abuse" by the filer, a lesser legal standard than the "substantial abuse" required by current law.

The bill specifies that creditors could bring a motion alleging a debtor's "abuse" in court and provide evidence to judges of such abuse, unless the debtor's family income was below the national median. Creditors cannot now make such challenges.

- **Reimbursement.** The bill would require a debtor's attorney to reimburse the trustee for reasonable costs associated with a motion to dismiss the case or convert it to Chapter 13, if it was determined that the debtor was not "substantially justified" in filing under Chapter 7. The provision is aimed at "bankruptcy mills" — law firms that represent many of those who file for bankruptcy protection. However, creditors would be required to reimburse debtors' legal costs if a motion to dismiss or transfer a case to Chapter 13 was denied.

- **Credit counseling.** Within 90 days before filing for bankruptcy protection, a debtor would have to make a "good faith attempt" to create a debt repayment plan outside the bankruptcy system through a credit counseling program. The debtor would have to complete a credit counseling course before any debts would be discharged.

- **Debtors' rights.** The bill addresses the controversial issue of reaffirmation agreements — pacts between creditors and debtors in which debtors agree to make payments to a creditor after declaring bankruptcy. Debtors often sign such agreements to keep a product, re-establish a line of credit or appease a pesky creditor. The bill would make creditors subject to damages and debtors' attorney costs if the creditor did not live up to the reaffirmation agreement and the debtor sued.

The bill would bar creditors from contesting the discharge of some of a filer's debt if the debtor had made a good-faith effort to negotiate a reasonable repayment schedule and the creditor "unreasonably" refused. The burden of proof would be on the debtor.

- **Homestead exemption.** The bill would cap the amount of a home's value that the Chapter 7 debtor was entitled to keep at $100,000. In cases where the debtor's home was valued at $100,000 or less, this would allow the debtor to keep the home. In other cases the debtor would receive $100,000 from the sale of the home; the rest of the proceeds would go to creditors.

Current laws in five states (Florida, Kansas, Iowa, South Dakota and Texas) entitle bankruptcy filers to keep the full value of their home, regardless of its worth. According to the Senate Judiciary Committee, most states cap the exemption at $40,000 or less. The differing exemptions have prompted some once-wealthy filers to move to such states as Florida or Texas, buy million-dollar houses and keep them after declaring bankruptcy.

- **Child support, alimony.** The bill would move child support and alimony to the top of the list of items debtors must pay off regardless of their bankruptcy filing. Other such debts include certain taxes, some court settlements and government-guaranteed student loans.

- **Restricting repeat filers.** The measure would limit to 30 days a key benefit of filing for bankruptcy — an automatic stay that gives a filer breathing room by blocking efforts to repossess property or force payments — if the debtor filed for bankruptcy the previous year and the case was dismissed.

- **Cramdowns.** The bill would prevent courts from "cramming down" the amount of debts owed to secured creditors under Chapter 13. Bankruptcy officials often employ the "cramdown" to reduce the amount of money a debtor owes on expensive items, such as a car, purchased with secured loans. In cramdown cases, debtors are required to pay off the amount of money the car is worth at the time of bankruptcy, not the amount they may have agreed to pay for the car.

- **Statistics and audits.** The Administrative Office of the U.S. Courts would be required to publish statistics on consumer and business bankruptcy from districts around the country. The attorney general would set procedures to audit bankruptcy filings for accuracy. At least one of every 500 cases in each of the 12 federal judicial districts would have to be audited.

- **Additional bankruptcy judges.** The bill would authorize 18 temporary bankruptcy judges in 10 states to deal with a spate of bankruptcy filings.

Banking & Finance

cial tool, not as a last resort.

Under the Grassley-Durbin deal, Democrats plan to offer amendments to limit credit card solicitations.

Conferees Face Widely Differing Versions of Bill

SEPTEMBER 26 — Sen. Charles E. Grassley, R-Iowa, has spent much of the last year and almost all of the past two weeks prodding his colleagues to pass a measure aimed at stemming the record number of personal bankruptcies.

He has consistently reiterated his desire to move the bill the way bankruptcy overhaul measures have moved in the past 100 years — with support from the minority party.

Grassley and bill cosponsor Richard J. Durbin, D-Ill., achieved that goal with stunning success Sept. 23 as the Senate voted 97-1 for their bill (HR 3150, formerly S 1301). Only Paul Wellstone, D-Minn., voted against it. *(Vote 284, p. S-44)*

But Grassley and Durbin's determination to keep that bipartisan relationship robust will soon be tested.

Their measure and the House version, sponsored by George W. Gekas, R-Pa., are substantially different. With only two weeks left before the session is supposed to end, the conference committee appointed to work out the variations will have much to do.

Grassley said after the bill passed that a conference was "doable," noting that it would be difficult only "if the House takes the view that their bill is perfect." He said he had not yet spoken to Gekas.

Representatives of business and retail groups pushing the measure also said they thought it was possible to clear the bill before lawmakers leave Washington on Oct. 9.

It has been clear from the start that business groups prefer the House bill, which for the first time would set income limits for those seeking protection under Chapter 7 of the bankruptcy code. Most consumers file for bankruptcy under one of two chapters — Chapter 7, which absolves their debts after non-essential assets are sold to pay off creditors, or Chapter 13, which prevents creditors from repossessing a debtor's property while the debtor tries to pay off bills over three to five years.

Both bills aim to move more of the 1.35 million consumers who filed for bankruptcy protection in 1997 from the heavily used Chapter 7 to Chapter 13, where creditors stand a better chance of recovering some of their money. But the bills differ in approach.

The Senate bill would allow a judge to move Chapter 7 filers to Chapter 13 if the judge determined that they could pay more than 30 percent of their unsecured debts, such as credit cards. The House bill would preclude debtors from filing under Chapter 7 if they earned more than the median income — roughly $51,000 for a family of four — and could pay more than 20 percent of their unsecured debts. They could still file for protection under Chapter 13.

Another major difference is in how the two bills handle homestead exemptions, which vary from state to state. The Senate bill would cap such exemptions — which allow debtors to keep their home or a certain percentage of its value — at $100,000. According to the Senate Judiciary Committee, most states now cap such exemptions at $40,000, but five states have no cap at all. Two of them, Texas and Florida, have reputations as havens for well-heeled debtors who move to the state, buy a mansion and then file for bankruptcy, knowing they are safe in their million-dollar home.

The House bill would not impose a cap, but it aims to prevent debtors from moving to a state with more favorable bankruptcy laws. It would require filers to have lived in a state for one year before the new state's homestead exemption would apply, up from 180 days in current law. If a debtor declared bankruptcy before meeting the residency requirement, the homestead exemption from the former state would still apply.

In addition, the House bill would tighten the code for businesses that file for bankruptcy protection; the Senate bill would not. Grassley has introduced a separate measure (S 1914) on the subject, but it has not been marked up by the Judiciary Committee.

The House and business groups are expected to push for the House version, but Grassley and Durbin have the White House's support. In a statement released Sept. 17, the White House encouraged the passage of S 1301 and said it would only support enactment of a bankruptcy overhaul measure "if the essential reforms incorporated by the Senate . . . are preserved and strengthened and the unbalanced and arbitrary elements of the current House bill are omitted."

Senate Action

During sporadic two-week consideration, the Senate made several changes to its bill, moving closer to what the chamber's Democrats wanted and away from the House bill.

The week of Sept. 14 the chamber gave voice vote approval to a Grassley-Durbin amendment that increased from 20 percent to 30 percent the amount of debt a bankruptcy filer would have to be able to pay off before moving from Chapter 7 to Chapter 13.

It also adopted an amendment by Jack Reed, D-R.I., that would prevent credit card companies from either dropping customers who pay off all their debts each month, or charging them fees. Some companies do that because such customers do not generate income for the company. Reed's amendment was adopted by voice vote after the Senate defeated an attempt to table (kill) it, 47-52. *(Vote 273, p. S-42)*

The latter amendment cut to the heart of one main difference between Republicans and Democrats. Republicans tend to blame increased bankruptcy filings on the declining social stigma; Democrats say aggressive marketing techniques by credit card companies to college students and others with little income are a main cause of record bankruptcy rates.

Also the week of Sept. 14, the Senate voted to table (kill) several Democratic amendments to restrict credit card solicitations, including a 58-40 vote to table a plan by Christopher J. Dodd, D-Conn., that would have made it more difficult for 18- to 21-year-olds to receive credit cards. *(Vote 274, p. S-43)*

It voted 72-26 to table an amendment by Alfonse M. D'Amato, R-N.Y., to prevent banks from charging noncustomers to use their automated teller machines. *(Vote 275, p. S-43)*

However, the Senate defeated 47-52 a motion to table an amendment by Jack Reed, D-R.I., to stop compa-

Bankruptcy Overhaul

nies from either charging customers who pay off their bills each month, or dropping their accounts. After the motion to table failed, the Senate adopted the amendment by voice vote. *(Vote 273, p. S-42)*

The argument over who was to blame for increased bankruptcy filings resurfaced the week of Sept. 21. The Senate adopted by voice vote an amendment by Dianne Feinstein, D-Calif., that would require the Federal Reserve to study the solicitation practices of the consumer credit industry and make public its report within 24 months.

The amendment would also allow the Federal Reserve to issue regulations that would require additional disclosures to consumers or to take any other action consistent with its statutory authority to "ensure responsible industry-wide practices."

The Senate voted, 63-36, to table (kill) a proposal by Reed that would have allowed judges to consider a creditor's record of fair lending practices when ruling on the creditor's request to move a bankruptcy filer from Chapter 7 to Chapter 13 or to dismiss the case. *(Vote 281, p. S-44)*

The Senate tabled, 57-42, an amendment by Russell D. Feingold, D-Wis., that would have made debtors liable for court costs amassed in efforts to move from one chapter to the other. The bill would make debtors' attorneys liable, in an effort to stem "bankruptcy mills," or law firms that specialize in representing bankrupt debtors. *(Vote 279, p. S-43)*

Another Feingold amendment — to waive Chapter 7 filing fees for some low-income debtors — was accepted by voice vote after a motion to table it failed, 47-52. The filing fee is now $175. *(Vote 280, p. S-43)*

House Adopts Conference Report; Senate Democrats Not Convinced

OCTOBER 10 — Efforts to revamp the nation's bankruptcy laws hung in the balance during the session's final days, as Democrats assailed a Republican-fashioned conference report as overly harsh on debtors.

The House adopted the conference report on the bill (HR 3150), 300-125, on Oct. 9, and the Senate passed a procedural hurdle the same day, voting 94-2 to take up the bill. With consumer bankruptcy filings at record highs, supporters in both parties said the measure was needed to stop people with means from walking away from their debts. *(House vote 506, p. H-144; Senate vote 313, p. S-48)*

But Sen. Richard J. Durbin, D-Ill., who had added consumer protection provisions to the Senate version, assailed the conference report for leaving out many of the protections. And the Clinton administration indicated that the president would veto the bill if the Senate cleared it.

"As it is, I don't see how we could support it," White House spokesman Joe Lockhart said Oct. 8.

However, some bill supporters hoped to convince the Clinton administration, during end-of-session bargaining, to include the bill in the omnibus spending measure.

Prior to the Oct. 7 release of the conference report, lawmakers on both sides of the aisle expressed some optimism about clearing a stand-alone bill. But then Republicans left Democrats out of last-minute negotiations, sparking a partisan fight over a measure that had passed both chambers by strong bipartisan majorities.

"This didn't have to happen," Durbin said hours after the conference report was released. "We're still open for business."

Republicans argued there was no reason for Democratic opposition. "The bill protects responsible consumer activity and holds creditors more accountable for irresponsible actions," said Charles E. Grassley of Iowa, the main GOP architect of the Senate bill.

Repayment Requirements

At the core of the conference agreement is a provision that would steer more debtors into Chapter 13 of the bankruptcy code, under which they would have to enter repayment agreements, and away from Chapter 7, which would allow them to discharge their debts.

Debtors would generally have to file under Chapter 13 if they met certain financial criteria: an above-median income and the ability to pay off at least 25 percent of their debts over five years. Under special circumstances, such as a major illness in the family, a judge could permit them to file under Chapter 7.

Supporters of the agreement said it struck a middle ground between more stringent requirements in the House version and the broad discretion given to judges in the Senate version. They said the bill would give creditors reasonable assurance of being repaid without forcing destitute debtors into repayment plans.

"No poor person ever will be denied a right to a fresh start," said Rep. George W. Gekas, R-Pa.

But some Democrats said the bill would give little discretion to judges and instead force uniform treatment of debtors in widely varying circumstances. Some analysts also said the 25 percent requirement could spur borrowers to run up their debts before filing for bankruptcy, since the higher the debt, the less likely that the debtor could pay off 25 percent of it.

Members of the two parties also squared off over consumer protection provisions. The Senate version, at the insistence of Durbin and other Democrats, would have required credit companies to include information on every monthly statement showing how long it would take the borrower to pay off the balance if only the minimum payment was made every month.

But the conference report replaced that with more general language, requiring annual warnings to consumers that minimum payments would result in higher interest penalties. The Federal Reserve Board would also study the issue of disclosure requirements for lenders.

A stunned Durbin said the conference report "stripped out every significant consumer protection."

But creditors said the Senate disclosure requirements would have been impractical, since there is no way to predict how long it will take to repay a debt when interest rates can fluctuate.

Another controversial provision would bar debtors from filing class-action lawsuits over "reaffirmations." These are private repayment agreements that have sometimes drawn fire as being overly harsh on debtors.

Banking & Finance

Consumer advocates and creditors came down sharply on opposing sides of the bill.

Mary Rouleau of the Consumer Federation of America denounced the bill as "totally not acceptable." She said it would severely weaken debtors in court while doing nothing to curb abusive practices by creditors.

On the other side, William P. Binzel of MasterCard International Inc. lauded the measure because it would stop Americans from walking away from their debts. "The principle of the bill is personal responsibility," he said.

House Action

Debate on the House floor Oct. 9 mirrored the chamber's discussions when it passed the original bankruptcy overhaul measure, 306-118, on June 10.

Liberal Democrats, led by Jerrold Nadler of New York, charged that the bill would not address the increase in personal bankruptcy filings because it did nothing to stop credit card companies from soliciting college students and others with little recourse to pay their debts. "It serves only the big banks, against the interest of middle- and low-income Americans," Nadler said.

But moderate Democrats teamed up with Republicans, as they had in the previous debate, to push for an overhaul. Seventy-six Democrats supported the bill.

"What was once the option of last resort is becoming the option of choice," said James P. Moran, D-Va., adding that Congress needed to overhaul the system during prosperous economic times. "We will not have the political resolve to fix it when times are not so good," he said.

Divide Too Wide; Bill's Chances Slip Away

OCTOBER 17 — The last hope for a comprehensive overhaul of consumer bankruptcy laws — a ride on the omnibus spending package — expired as Republicans failed to find a compromise that the Clinton administration and creditors could accept.

President Clinton wanted to weaken a means test that would require judges to consider moving higher-income filers from Chapter 7 of the bankruptcy code, which absolves debts, to Chapter 13, a repayment plan. But that would have cost the bill the support of its main proponents, the credit card industry and other creditors.

The omnibus measure (HR 4328) did include a six-month extension of Chapter 12 for family farmers, which expired Sept. 30. The House also passed a bill (HR 4831) by voice vote Oct. 15 to extend Chapter 12. Its extension was a top priority for Sen. Charles E. Grassley, R-Iowa, sponsor of the Senate bankruptcy bill (HR 3150, formerly S 1301).

In a statement Oct. 14, Grassley said, "I am disappointed our efforts to seal the cracks in the consumer bankruptcy code did not prevail this year. . . . I'll be back next year."

Many parts of the bankruptcy measure were controversial, but extending Chapter 12 had few public detractors. The chapter, considered pro-debtor, focuses on restructuring farmers' budgets so they can pay some of their debts and keep their land.

Without Chapter 12, farmers would have to file under Chapter 11, which is generally for businesses, or Chapter 13, which focuses on repaying debts in three to five years. Proponents of Chapter 12 say neither alternative is structured to help farmers get out of financial difficulties. Chapter 12 may be useful this year in parts of the country where farmers are suffering from record low prices and poor growing conditions. The modern version of Chapter 12 was enacted in 1986 (PL 99-554) and reauthorized in 1993 (PL 103-65). (*1986 Almanac, p. 310*) ◆

Congress Clears Legislation Allowing Credit Unions To Expand Membership

Box Score

- **Bill:** HR 1151— PL 105-219
- **House action:** The House cleared HR 1151 by voice vote Aug. 4.
- **Senate action:** The Senate passed the bill, 92-6, on July 28.
- **Presidential action:** Clinton signed the bill Aug. 7.

SUMMARY

President Clinton on Aug. 7 signed into law a bill to allow credit unions to continue expanding their membership bases, ending a debate that pitted the banking industry against the nation's credit unions.

The bill cleared after the House agreed to the Senate's removal of a provision that in effect would have made credit unions subject to the 1977 Community Reinvestment Act (PL 95-128), which governs neighborhood lending by banks.

The reinvestment act requires federal regulators, when considering a bank's application for a merger, new branch or other activity, to take into account the bank's lending record in low-income and minority neighborhoods.

Action on the credit union bill was spurred by a Feb. 25 Supreme Court ruling that said credit unions had overstepped their legal bounds by accepting members and groups that did not have a "common bond," such as a shared occupation, with the credit union's chartering organization.

Credit unions organized a grass-roots campaign to persuade Congress to overturn the ruling, warning that it would force 20 million people out of credit unions. As enacted, HR 1151 allows credit unions to continue accepting members from an unrelated group, as long as the number of potential members is fewer than 3,000.

The banking industry fought the bill vigorously, insisting it would not try to force credit unions to expel existing members, but arguing that continued expansion was unfair. Credit unions enjoy a nonprofit and tax-exempt status that banking lobbyists say gives them an edge when it comes to interest rates on loans and savings accounts. The banks' arguments essentially fell on deaf ears.

But in an effort to appease the banks somewhat, the House Banking Committee attached requirements for credit unions similar to the reinvestment mandates on banks.

During Senate floor action, Richard C. Shelby, R-Ala., tried to amend HR 1151 to lift the reinvestment requirement on banks with less than $250 million in assets. That drew a veto threat, and the Senate tabled the amendment. However, Phil Gramm, R-Texas, a vehement opponent of the 1977 law, prevailed on an amendment deleting the provision requiring credit unions to meet the community lending standards.

House Responds To Ruling By Supreme Court

MARCH 28 — A much-anticipated fix for credit unions whose expansion was jeopardized by a recent Supreme Court ruling won voice vote approval March 26 from the House Banking and Financial Services Committee, after nearly seven hours of debate and a close vote on a deal-breaking amendment on commercial lending.

Tense moments at the markup notwithstanding, committee Chairman Jim Leach, R-Iowa, said the House may take up the bill (HR 1151) the week of March 30. Alternatively, the bill may be attached to a broader but more controversial financial services overhaul plan (HR 10) that GOP leaders may bring to the floor March 31 or April 1.

Credit union supporters generally want the bill moved separately, because they fear HR 10 may stall.

At a March 26 Senate hearing on credit unions, Banking, Housing and Urban Affairs Committee Chairman Alfonse M. D'Amato, R-N.Y., who has said he will push HR 10 only if it gets a broad, bipartisan vote in the House, showed more enthusiasm for a credit union measure.

D'Amato, who has scheduled another hearing April 2, predicted that Congress "will see to it that the situation that exists today is remedied." He said he did not "believe there's an issue that's been as important or needs the action of Congress as expeditiously" as the Supreme Court's Feb. 25 decision on credit unions.

The court ruled that credit unions and their federal overseer, the National Credit Union Administration, had overstepped legal bounds in seeking new members from groups that did not have a common occupational, employer or geographic bond with the credit union's chartering group. The ruling would affect about 20 million of 70 million credit union members. The nation has 11,500 credit unions.

Committee Action

The measure considered by the House Banking Committee was the product of negotiations between top panel members and credit union officials. Banks, which had contributed suggestions earlier, were not involved.

The bill that emerged offered credit unions less than the original HR 1151, which would have reversed the Supreme Court's ruling outright. But it gave much more than banks had been willing to give credit unions in a measure they proffered. The bill would:

- Allow the 20 million credit union members jeopardized by the court ruling to retain their membership.
- Allow credit unions to accept members from an unrelated group, as long as the number of potential members from that group did not exceed 3,000. Groups that joined would also have to be located within "reasonable proximity" of the credit union.

Banking & Finance

- Require the credit union administration to more specifically define who could join a credit union because of being in a current member's "immediate family or household" or living in a certain geographic area.
- Extend for one year current regulations that allow credit unions to make commercial loans, as long as the loans to any one member or group of members did not exceed $75,000, or 15 percent of a credit union's reserves.
- Require credit unions to serve members of "modest means" and require the credit union administration to set up criteria for periodically reviewing credit unions' lending records to ensure compliance with the provision. It is similar to requirements of the 1977 Community Reinvestment Act, which applies to banks.
- Require the credit union administration to promulgate regulations that would apply capital requirements to credit unions to ensure "safety and soundness." Such requirements, which deal with such items as reserves and collateral, now apply to banks.
- Allow the credit union administration to increase the funds that credit unions must pay into the National Credit Union Share Insurance Fund, a federal fund that insures deposits.
- Require the Federal Reserve to pay interest at least quarterly on the so-called sterile reserves that banks are required to keep.

The bill's three major provisions — on commercial lending, community reinvestment requirements and the scope of membership — prompted the most debate.

Banks vs. Credit Unions

Arguments over the major provisions mirrored differences between what credit unions and banks wanted.

Banks opposed the measure, saying it would benefit nonprofit credit unions at the expense of tax-paying banks. They were inconspicuous at the markup, however, largely because the committee was widely expected to approve the bill. Credit unions brought dozens of members who paced the committee room and wore buttons calling for "consumer choice." They also launched advertising and grass-roots campaigns that reached congressional offices.

The most contentious amendment, by Richard H. Baker, R-La., would have capped the amount of commercial loans a credit union could make at 5 percent of its total assets. It also would have prevented a credit union member or an associated group of members from having more than $1 million in outstanding loans from the credit union at one time.

Baker acknowledged that less than 1 percent of credit unions' business nationwide was in commercial loans, but said he feared that without limits, some credit unions might become entangled in financial troubles reminiscent of the problems savings and loans faced in the 1980s. "While activities are sound, the economy is good, let's prescribe reasonable limits," he said, adding that there is a "very small number" of credit unions "very large in size, who are potentially creating a problem."

But several members charged that Baker's amendment would jeopardize a subset of credit unions organized to provide members of certain credit-poor occupations, such as farmers, truckers and cab drivers, with loans to maintain their businesses. Bruce F. Vento, D-Minn., said about 200 credit unions would be adversely affected.

Paul E. Kanjorski, D-Pa., a sponsor of the original version of HR 1151, called Baker's amendment "a solution without a problem."

In response, the committee agreed by voice vote to a secondary amendment by Marge Roukema, R-N.J., to allow the credit union administration to exempt credit unions from the 5 percent cap if it determined the cap would cause "significant and continuing harm to the achievement of the credit union's purposes."

But even with Roukema's amendment, Kanjorski said, "the agreement that was made on this bill no longer will stand in place."

Credit Union National Association President and former Rep. Daniel A. Mica, D-Fla. (1979-89), confirmed Kanjorski's statement during a break before the panel voted on Baker's amendment. Mica said he would "pull the plug" on the bill if the amendment was accepted. Without the support of credit unions — and the 200 House members who signed onto the original version of HR 1151 — the bill would have died.

When the panel returned, Leach and committee ranking Democrat John J. LaFalce of New York offered a substitute amendment to freeze current credit union administration commercial lending regulations for one year, while the agency puts together a report to Congress on what lending limits should be put in place.

The committee voted 27-25 for the Leach-LaFalce plan over the Baker-Roukema plan.

The panel then moved to a controversial amendment by Bill McCollum, R-Fla., to strike the fair lending requirements from the bill.

McCollum and other Republicans said they opposed extending the ideals of the reinvestment act because its paperwork requirements had proved costly to banks. "Because the banks do it doesn't mean we ought to make the credit unions do it," McCollum said. Spencer Bachus, R-Ala., added that the provision was just "a little sop to bankers" that bill authors had added in an attempt to make the measure more palatable.

But Democrats countered that the reinvestment act had greatly improved banks' and savings institutions' lending rates to minorities and low-income people. "Paperwork is necessary sometimes if you're going to be intent upon eliminating discrimination," said Joseph P. Kennedy II, D-Mass.

The committee defeated McCollum's amendment, 22-32. It also defeated, 18-33, a subsequent attempt by Thomas M. Barrett, D-Wis., to require that evaluations of credit unions' lending records to low- and middle-income people be made public.

The panel also considered an amendment by Baker that would have limited the size of separate groups eligible to join a credit union to 1,000, down from the bill's 3,000 limit. But Baker dropped his amendment when Bernard Sanders, I-Vt., said he would amend it to increase the limit to 7,500.

Bill Cut Loose From Financial Services Overhaul

APRIL 4 — Hours before the House was to adjourn for spring break April 1, members overwhelmingly passed a bill to ease the concerns of many constituents. By a vote of 411-8, the House passed a measure (HR 1151) to allow credit unions to continue to expand and current credit union members to retain their accounts. The bill essentially would overturn a Feb. 25 Supreme Court ruling that said credit unions had overstepped legal bounds in seeking new members who did not have a common employer, organization or geographic tie to the chartering organization. *(Vote 92, p. H-28)*

The quick action became possible when Republican leaders decided March 31 to allow the bill to move on its own, releasing it from a marriage to a broader and more controversial measure (HR 10) to overhaul the financial services industry.

Credit union supporters had strenuously objected to linking the two measures. Rep. John J. LaFalce of New York, the ranking Democrat on the Banking and Financial Services Committee, likened the credit union bill's attachment to HR 10 to "a first-class ticket on the ship Titanic."

Republican leaders were forced to split the two when it became clear they did not have enough votes to move a combined bill. They announced March 31 that they would not try to move HR 10 again until the week of May 4, but they scheduled the credit union bill for consideration under an expedited floor procedure allowing no amendments and requiring a two-thirds majority for passage.

The quick action on HR 1151 was both a sign of the broad-based support it had garnered — more than 200 members had signed on to the original version, including Speaker Newt Gingrich, R-Ga., and Minority Whip David E. Bonior, D-Mich. — and of the grass-roots power of credit unions. With more than 70 million members, 20 million of whom could be affected by the high court's ruling, the credit unions presented a formidable presence on the Hill, both in person and by phone and letter.

After House leaders announced that they would pull HR 10 from the floor, Banking Committee Chairman Jim Leach, R-Iowa, quickly pointed out that the credit union bill would move because "we think it's important that people be relieved of any angst."

The Senate, which held a hearing on the credit union issue April 2, is expected to take up a measure addressing the court ruling when it returns from the break. Senate Banking, Housing and Urban Affairs Committee Chairman Alfonse M. D'Amato, R-N.Y., who has been hesitant to move HR 10, has pledged his support to credit unions. He wants some changes in HR 1151, but said he expects to see legislation enacted this year.

Feeding the Movement

The bill the House passed April 1 would allow credit unions to continue accepting members from groups unrelated to the chartering organization, but those groups could not include more than 3,000 potential members. Such affiliations often occurred when a business with a credit union shut down and left members in limbo.

The limit on the size of new membership groups was a Banking Committee compromise between the 7,500 sought by credit unions and the 1,000 proposed by banks, which opposed the expansion of credit unions. Banks said they, as taxpaying companies, should not have to compete with credit unions, which do not pay taxes. Credit union officials countered that their members pay taxes and that unlike banks, credit unions are run to benefit their members, not investors.

The Banking Committee version of the bill, approved March 26, included a provision to require the Federal Reserve to pay interest on "sterile reserves" that banks are required to keep. But the provision, which aimed to soften the credit union bill's blow to banks, was pulled before House debate because of Clinton administration concerns about its estimated $800 million cost over five years.

Credit Union Bill Survives Scuffles In Senate Banking

MAY 2 — A heavily lobbied bill to allow credit unions to sidestep a Supreme Court ruling and continue expanding their membership won approval from the Senate Banking, Housing and Urban Affairs Committee on April 30, but not without a fight that indicated trouble to come on the Senate floor. The vote was 16-2.

The issue that sparked pointed exchanges was the 1977 Community Reinvestment Act (PL 95-128), which requires a bank to meet the borrowing needs of people in the community it serves, including those in low-income and minority neighborhoods. The regulation, a priority for most Democrats and anathema to most Republicans, also makes the bank's lending records public.

To appease banks, who oppose the credit union measure (HR 1151), House members included a provision that generally would extend many of the reinvestment act's requirements to credit unions. The House easily passed the bill April 1. *(1977 Almanac, p. 126)*

But several Senate Republicans said they found that trade-off "just plain silly," as Connie Mack, R-Fla., put it. Added Lauch Faircloth, R-N.C.: "To me, this is a trainload of new regulations and requirements. We should be lifting it from banks, particularly small banks, not putting it on credit unions."

Phil Gramm, R-Texas, introduced an amendment to remove the reinvestment provisions from the bill, and Richard C. Shelby, R-Ala., attempted to attach a provision that would lift reinvestment requirements from banks with assets of less than $250 million.

But Banking Committee Chairman Alfonse M. D'Amato, R-N.Y., urged his Republican colleagues to "exercise some restraint," saying the attempts were "counterproductive to our effort of dealing with the credit unions up front."

Ranking Democrat Paul S. Sarbanes of Maryland warned that past efforts to repeal the act had prompted veto threats from President Clinton. "We are going to greatly complicate moving this matter toward final passage," Sarbanes said. Shelby said he believed "we would have the votes to override a presidential veto."

After D'Amato voted with Democrats and Shelby's amendment failed, 9-9, Gramm withdrew his amendment. But both Shelby and Gramm said their amendments would be back on the Senate floor. Chuck Hagel, R-Neb., who joined Mack in voting against the bill, said he was preparing an amendment to another controversial provision that would restrict cred-

Banking & Finance

it union business loans to members.

Gramm vowed not to delay the bill, but after the markup Sarbanes lamented that "all of this is just throwing clouds of dust around this legislation."

Compromise on Expansion

The impetus for the credit union bill came Feb. 25, when the Supreme Court ruled that credit unions and their federal overseer, the National Credit Union Administration, had overstepped legal boundaries in seeking members who shared no "common bond" in employment, profession or location to the chartering organization.

Officials at the Credit Union National Association and the National Association of Federal Credit Unions had long expected the ruling and set out immediately to overturn it, mobilizing many of the nation's 70 million credit union members to write letters and make calls. Both House Speaker Newt Gingrich, R-Ga., and Minority Whip David E. Bonior, D-Mich., signed on to the original version of HR 1151, which would have overturned the court's decision outright.

But banks strongly opposed that legislation, saying it created little distinction between credit unions and banks except that credit unions do not pay taxes.

The House Banking and Financial Services Committee tempered the plans, approving a bill that would let credit union members keep their accounts and permit credit unions to join with unrelated groups, as long as the groups would not provide more than 3,000 members. The bill suffered a momentary setback when House GOP leaders combined it with a measure (HR 10) to revamp financial services laws. Allowed to move on its own, the credit union bill passed overwhelmingly.

Credit union backers expected they might have a tougher task in the Senate, where small community banks have more powerful supporters. But GOP and Democratic staff members along with credit union and bank lobbyists worked out deals April 29 that addressed the most controversial amendments, including the commercial lending issue.

The compromise, which the committee accepted as part of the bill, would prevent credit unions from placing more than 1.75 times their net worth in business loans to members. Hagel plans to offer a floor amendment that would further restrict such lending by counting more loans as business loans. Currently, the credit union administration counts any loan of less than $50,000 as a personal loan. Hagel's amendment would remove that threshold.

The compromise included increased "safety and soundness" standards, such as provisions requested by the Treasury Department to strengthen the federal account that insures credit union deposits.

The committee also approved by voice vote a Shelby amendment that would require a majority vote of members for a credit union to convert to a mutual savings bank.

Senate Passes Bill; Differences With House Remain

AUGUST 1 — A measure to allow credit unions to continue expanding their membership bases won easy Senate approval July 28 when it finally reached the floor after months on the shelf. The vote was 92-6. (Vote 239, p. S-38)

Issues that had delayed consideration of the bill (HR 1151) since April, when the Banking, Housing and Urban Affairs Committee approved it, surfaced during floor debate. Although the Senate accepted a controversial amendment, the House may nevertheless swallow the changes and clear the bill the week of Aug. 3 instead of sending the measure to a House-Senate conference committee to resolve differences.

The amendment the Senate adopted by voice vote July 28 removed a provision that would have applied regulations similar to those in the 1977 Community Reinvestment Act (PL 95-128) to credit unions. The act now applies only to banks. It requires federal regulators, when considering a bank's application for a merger, new branch or other endeavor, to take into account whether the bank made loans to all geographic areas within its community — including low-income and minority neighborhoods. (1977 Almanac, p. 126)

The chamber voted 44-50 on July 27 against tabling (killing) the amendment. (Vote 236, p. S-37)

Its sponsor, Phil Gramm, R-Texas, repeatedly described the reinvestment act as "extortion" and contended that it could not logically apply to a cooperative organization such as a credit union. But Democrats defended the 1977 law as a tool that has made commercial banks more responsive to minorities and others who once found it difficult to obtain credit. Some House Democrats say that credit unions also need to be encouraged to loan to lower-income members and to seek out more such members. And, in a statement, the administration said the provision was "particularly important to keeping credit unions focused on their public mission."

Removal of the provision, however, did not prompt a veto threat. Another amendment did. The proposal, by Richard C. Shelby, R-Ala., would have lifted community reinvestment requirements on banks with less than $250 million in assets. The Senate voted 59-39 to table Shelby's amendment. (Vote 238, p. S-37)

It also voted 53-42 to table a controversial amendment by Republican Chuck Hagel of Nebraska to limit the amount of business loans that credit unions could make to members. (Vote 237, p. S-37)

Appeasing Banks and Democrats

The provision that caused the most consternation during Senate debate would allow federal regulators to examine credit unions' lending records to ensure they were providing "affordable" services to people of modest means who were eligible to join the credit union. That is a scaled-down version of reinvestment requirements on banks.

The provision first appeared when the House Banking and Financial Services Committee approved its version of HR 1151 on March 26 and sought to temper bankers' opposition to the bill.

Banks and credit unions have long feuded over who should be allowed to join a credit union, in large part because banks view credit unions as competitors who have the advantage of paying no federal income tax. The fight culminated in February in a Supreme Court ruling that credit unions and their federal overseer, the National Credit Union Administration, had overstepped legal boundaries in seeking members from groups that did not share a "common bond" with the originating group.

Leaders of the two main credit union associations — the Credit Union National Association and the National Association of Federal Credit Unions — had been lobbying Congress, using the credit unions' considerable grass-roots operations, to overturn the decision even before it was announced. According to the groups, about 70 million Americans belong to credit unions and 20 million could have found their memberships jeopardized by the court ruling.

The issue soon became a consumer rights matter. Leaders of both parties were quick to sign on to a measure that would have overturned the court's decision outright.

But banks vociferously opposed the measure and used their considerable financial firepower to lobby against it. To appease the banks somewhat, the House Banking Committee decided to attach requirements similar to the Community Reinvestment Act — which some bankers consider onerous — to the credit union bill.

The addition never appeased bankers enough to prompt them to support the bill, but it made the measure even sweeter for many liberal Democrats.

At the Senate Banking Committee markup in April, many Republicans objected to the reinvestment provision. But Gramm agreed to withhold an amendment to remove it until floor debate. Shelby's amendment to lift reinvestment requirements for small banks was defeated, 9-9, when panel Chairman Alfonse M. D'Amato, R-N.Y., joined all committee Democrats in voting against it.

When the full Senate took up the bill, Shelby again introduced his amendment. "Since HR 1151 increases the competitive advantage credit unions have over banks . . . this amendment is necessary to reduce the inequities in this area," he said.

But Democrats and D'Amato argued that Shelby's amendment would jeopardize the bill's chances for enactment. And John Kerry, D-Mass., challenged Shelby's claim that small banks naturally lend to the entire community. "It's very simple," Kerry said. Before the reinvestment act, "they weren't doing it."

Most Democrats also opposed Gramm's amendment, but D'Amato supported it, saying there was no evidence that credit unions had been "redlining" or otherwise discriminating against minority or low-income people who wanted to take out loans.

The Senate tabled Hagel's amendment to make the bill's caps on business loans made by credit unions more stringent. The proposal would have prevented a credit union from making commercial loans totaling more than 7 percent of its net worth, down from 12.25 percent in the bill.

The amendment also would have overturned regulations that allow credit unions to count any loans under $50,000 as personal loans, even if they might cover business expenses. And it would have required credit unions that made commercial loans to have employees with at least two years of "direct professional experience" in business lending.

Credit unions set up specifically to make loans in traditionally credit-poor industries, such as farming or trucking, would be exempted from commercial lending caps in the bill and in Hagel's amendment.

Hagel and amendment cosponsor Robert F. Bennett, R-Utah, said the proposal was necessary to ensure that credit unions remain financially sound if they intend to make business loans.

But D'Amato and others said it would severely hamper many credit unions' ability to make business loans to their members. D'Amato questioned the need to limit credit unions' business loans when the $40 billion in commercial loans to businesses made by credit unions annually is approximately 3 percent of total loans to businesses.

House Accepts Senate Changes

AUGUST 8 — The House cleared legislation Aug. 4 to allow credit unions to continue expanding their membership bases, as lawmakers swallowed two controversial changes made by the Senate. President Clinton signed the bill Aug. 7.

The measure (HR 1151 — H Rept 105-472, S Rept 105-193) passed by voice vote as numerous members praised it. Banking and Financial Services Committee Chairman Jim Leach, R-Iowa, called credit unions "democracy at work in the marketplace" and said the measure ensured that current credit union members would not lose their accounts because of a February Supreme Court ruling. In that decision, *National Credit Union Administration v. First National Bank & Trust Co.*, the court ruled 5-4 that credit unions and their federal overseer had overstepped legal boundaries in seeking new members who did not share a common occupational, organizational or regional bond with charter members. Credit union activists said the ruling could have affected 20 million members.

But the bill contained more provisions than the clause that would allow members to keep their accounts. And some House Democrats, who had worked hard to attach a provision that would have required credit unions to provide affordable services to people of all incomes, were dismayed by the Senate's decision to remove it.

Joseph P. Kennedy II, D-Mass., denounced the Senate version, saying, "They went into the back room . . . and they knocked out all of the provisions that are supposed to protect the consumer." But ranking Banking Committee Democrat John J. LaFalce of New York said the credit union administration could impose such requirements, and he urged passage. LaFalce said he was more concerned about a Senate provision that would allow credit unions to convert to thrifts without a majority of members voting for the change. ◆

Banking & Finance

Loophole Fix Moves Class-Action Securities Suits From State to Federal Courts

Despite their disagreements over a 1995 law (PL 104-67) to restrict securities fraud lawsuits, Congress and President Clinton came together on a measure to further cut down on class-action lawsuits against companies whose earnings do not meet expectations. The law makes federal courts the sole venue for class action lawsuits involving 50 or more plaintiffs that allege securities fraud by a nationally traded company. Bill proponents said the follow-up measure was necessary because some law firms had begun to file "baseless" lawsuits in state courts after enactment of the 1995 law, which increased the amount of information a plaintiff had to disclose to file in federal court and made it harder to prove fraud.

SUMMARY

Box Score

- **Bill:** S 1260 — PL 105-353
- **House action:** The House cleared the conference report (H Rept 105-803) on S 1260, 319-82, on Oct. 13. It passed S 1260, 340-83, on July 22, after substituting the language of its version (HR 1689 — H Rept 105-640).
- **Senate action:** The Senate adopted the conference report on S 1260 by voice vote Oct. 13. The Senate passed S 1260 (S Rept 105-182), 79-21, on May 13.
- **Presidential action:** Clinton signed S 1260 on Nov. 3.

Senate Panel Aims To Block End Run Around 1995 Law

MAY 2 — In 1995, a measure that aimed to make it harder to sue nationally traded companies for securities fraud took more than nine months to make it through Congress. Some Democrats railed against it; the Securities and Exchange Commission (SEC) endorsed it reluctantly, and President Clinton vetoed it. The bill's bipartisan backers won a major victory, however, when Congress overrode the veto.

Three years later, the bill's supporters are finding it easier to move a follow-up measure that they say would plug a perceived loophole blocking the 1995 law's effectiveness. That loophole, they say, has allowed a handful of sly law firms to bypass the 1995 law's (PL 104-67) higher standards and file their cases in state court.

When the Senate Banking, Housing and Urban Affairs Committee took up the follow-up bill (S 1260) on April 29, its few opponents acknowledged that their objections could not stop it from becoming law.

Opponents became resigned to their loss April 28 when presidential advisers Bruce Lindsey and Gene Sperling sent a letter to committee Chairman Alfonse M. D'Amato, R-N.Y., and bill sponsors Phil Gramm, R-Texas, and Christopher J. Dodd, D-Conn., saying the administration would support the bill if the committee accepted changes that had been worked out with the SEC.

The measure would require securities fraud class-action suits involving more than 50 parties to be filed in federal court, where the tougher standards of the 1995 act would apply.

The SEC changes redefined class action, increasing the limit on the number of parties allowable in state suits from 25 to 50. The changes also would allow shareholders to continue to bring lawsuits in Delaware courts under a state law that holds information corporations give to shareholders to higher standards than that they give to the general public. In addition, senators agreed to include report language that clarified that the 1995 act did not intend to prohibit plaintiffs from filing claims alleging "reckless misconduct" by a nationally traded company.

A day later, the committee accepted those changes and approved the bill, 14-4. Voting against it were three Democrats — ranking member Paul S. Sarbanes of Maryland, Richard H. Bryan of Nevada and Tim Johnson of South Dakota — and one Republican, Richard C. Shelby of Alabama.

The bill is thought to be on a fast track. The House Commerce Committee is expected to move a companion measure (HR 1689) soon, and Senate leaders have pledged to bring the bill to the floor before Congress leaves for its Memorial Day break May 22. However, a Republican House aide said it did not appear the bill would move to the House floor before the recess.

Curbing a Trend

When Congress overrode Clinton's veto in 1995, it aimed to stem the practice of filing lawsuits against companies whose stock had not met company predictions, even though fraud was not involved. (*1995 Almanac, p. 2-90*)

Suits sometimes were filed "within minutes of stock fluctuations," Dodd said, and sometimes triggered by computer programs searching for volatile stocks.

Sponsors believed that by requiring plaintiffs to cite specific facts to back their claims and by creating a "safe harbor" for companies to make predictions about future earnings without being liable for them if they were paired with cautionary statements, they would prompt a free flow of information.

Consumer advocates, trial lawyers and large institutional investors such as government finance officers, however, worried that the changes would hamper access to the courts for those who had been wronged.

Both groups turned out to be wrong, largely because the law did not preclude plaintiffs from moving their cases to state courts, which generally had less stringent rules than the filing standards spelled out in the 1995 law.

According to a February study by

the accounting firm of Price Waterhouse, the number of class-action securities suits similar to cases generally filed in federal courts before 1995 jumped in state court from a total of 12 in 1995 to 71 in 1996 before declining to 39 in 1997. About half of the 1997 cases were filed simultaneously with a related case in federal court.

The number of federal cases also rebounded. According to the SEC, the number of companies sued in federal class-action suits dropped from 158 in 1995 to 105 in 1996, but then increased to 175 in 1997.

Dodd said the numbers showed that investors had not been precluded from filing suits, as opponents had alleged in 1995, and that the number of state suits was increasing. Even if it was not a "flood-tide," Dodd said, "there are clear indications that's where it's going."

But the statistics prompted opponents to question the need for legislation. "No need has been demonstrated to pre-empt state causes of action that may be more favorable to investors," Sarbanes said.

Amendments

Sarbanes, Bryan and Johnson offered three amendments that aimed to prevent the pre-emption of certain state laws or to redefine the bill's provision on what constituted a class-action suit. All three were defeated.

The committee rejected 6-12 two amendments by the three senators that would have allowed plaintiffs required to file in federal court to import laws from their states that gave them longer to file a suit after possible fraud and that allowed them to sue people who "aided or abetted" securities fraud. The senators said 33 states had longer statutes of limitations than the federal law, which requires plaintiffs to file within one year of learning of fraud and within three years of its occurrence. Forty-nine states allow plaintiffs to sue those who "aided and abetted" fraud.

It defeated 5-13 an amendment by Sarbanes and Bryan to remove a portion of the bill that would allow state judges to lump together securities suits against a common defendant and ship the consolidated case to federal court if more than 50 parties were involved.

Bill supporters said they had inserted the language to prevent law firms from finding another loophole to negate the 1995 law, but Sarbanes said he feared that it would hurt individual investors. "The pendulum swings too much in the other direction," he said.

Sarbanes said he worried that the bill was coming at a bad time, when 43 percent of adult Americans have invested in the stock market. "History suggests that at some point, the bull market will end, and when it does, it's reasonable to anticipate that securities fraud will be exposed," he said, adding that investors will then be surprised to find that Congress has limited their options.

But D'Amato said the bill was "an attempt to protect the investor" by making companies' financial information more available. And he called it a "narrow" bill designed only to limit class action suits, not individual suits or the ability of state or federal regulators to pursue cases of fraud.

Senate Passes Bill To Move Suits To Federal Courts

MAY 16 — Legislation aimed at curbing class action lawsuits against companies with volatile stocks passed the Senate on May 13 after lawmakers turned back two Democratic amendments. The bill (S 1260) would make federal courts the sole venue for class action suits alleging securities fraud. The vote was 79-21. *(Vote 135, p. S-23)*

A House panel will mark up a companion measure (HR 1689) after the Memorial Day break, said Rep. Michael G. Oxley, R-Ohio, chairman of the Commerce Subcommittee on Finance and Hazardous Waste. Oxley said he expected his panel, which plans to hold a hearing on its bill May 19, to adapt it to the Senate measure to clear the legislation easily. The measure has the support of the Clinton administration and the Securities and Exchange Commission.

The bills aim to close a loophole in a measure (PL 104-67) that Congress enacted in 1995 over President Clinton's veto. That law, which sought to stem what sponsors believed to be a growing number of baseless lawsuits against publicly traded companies, forced plaintiffs to cite specific facts to back their claims and otherwise changed rules governing federal class action suits. It also aimed to foster a free flow of market information by giving company executives legal cover to predict their stock's performance as long as they included cautionary statements.

But the act applied only to federal courts. Supporters of S 1260 say that has allowed a handful of law firms to move their cases to state courts, which generally have less stringent standards than the 1995 act.

Many of the lawsuits "clearly are a stain on the rightful practice of law," said Alfonse M. D'Amato, R-N.Y., chairman of the Banking, Housing and Urban Affairs Committee. He said the stockholders end up paying for the lawsuits because companies typically settle out of court and pay with proceeds that otherwise would be distributed. "These suits appear like they are intended to protect stockholders, but it is the little guys with the stock that end up paying the bill," D'Amato said.

The bill's sponsors, Phil Gramm, R-Texas, and Christopher J. Dodd, D-Conn., said many of the lawsuits are initiated by lawyers targeting volatile stocks, such as those issued by high-technology companies, not by aggrieved investors.

But the panel's ranking Democrat, Paul S. Sarbanes of Maryland, said that by attempting to stem a few abusive lawsuits, the bill would preclude some investors who had been defrauded from seeking redress. The bill, Sarbanes said, was "swinging the pendulum well beyond the problem. . . . In and of itself, it creates additional problems."

He found little company for those arguments. Only 18 Democrats and two Republicans — John McCain of Arizona and Richard C. Shelby of Alabama — joined him in voting against the bill.

Provisions

The bill would require securities fraud class action suits, defined as those involving more than 50 parties, to be filed in federal court. It would apply only to nationally traded securities. The bill would allow shareholders to continue to bring class action suits against companies in state court in Delaware if they believed the compa-

Banking & Finance

nies had violated a Delaware law that holds information given to shareholders to higher standards than data given to the general public.

The committee report on the bill also includes language clarifying that the 1995 act did not intend to prevent investors from suing firms for "reckless misconduct." Some courts had interpreted the statute that way. Sarbanes said he believed the issue should have been codified in the bill and not just included in report language.

Sarbanes made three efforts to change the bill, succeeding only once.

He offered an amendment that would have allowed plaintiffs who were required to file in federal court to import statute-of-limitation laws from their states that give them longer to file a suit. It was tabled (killed), 69-30. (Vote 133, p. S-22)

Another amendment would have removed a portion of the bill that would allow state judges to lump together securities suits against a common defendant and ship the consolidated case to federal court if more than 50 parties were involved. The Senate tabled it, 72-27. (Vote 134, p. S-23)

The third, approved by voice vote, would make certain that states, other political subdivisions or state pension funds could not be prevented from bringing a class action securities fraud suit in conjunction with other government entities.

House Commerce Subcommittee OKs Measure

JUNE 13 — A bill to cut state courts' jurisdiction over securities class-action lawsuits continued its easy march through Congress on June 10 as a House Commerce subcommittee approved it, 21-4.

The measure (HR 1689) appears to have no obstacles. Both the Securities and Exchange Commission and the White House have issued letters in support of a companion Senate measure (S 1260). And to avoid sending the bill to a House-Senate conference after House passage, the Finance and Hazardous Materials Subcommittee approved by voice vote a substitute amendment that added most features of the Senate bill, which that chamber passed May 13. The House Commerce Committee may debate the measure in the next two weeks.

The bill aims to plug a loophole in a law (PL 104-67) Congress passed in 1995 to stem what sponsors believed to be a growing number of baseless lawsuits against publicly traded companies with volatile stocks. The measure toughened the rules regarding such class-action suits in federal court. But since the law was enacted, some trial lawyers, including Bill Lerach, a San Diego lawyer often mentioned during the subcommittee markup, have shifted their efforts to state courts.

This year's measure would define securities class-action fraud suits as those in which more than 50 parties were allegedly defrauded in transactions involving nationally traded stock. Those suits would have to be filed in federal court. Also, state judges could consolidate cases in which 50 or more individuals had filed separate cases involving similar claims and transfer the consolidated case to federal court.

As in the Senate debate, a small but vocal group of Democrats opposed the measure at the House panel markup.

The four Democrats who voted against the measure — Bart Stupak and John D. Dingell, both of Michigan; Diana DeGette of Colorado; and Edward J. Markey of Massachusetts — said the bill would prevent defrauded investors from seeking redress.

While bill sponsor Rick White, R-Wash., and subcommittee Chairman Michael G. Oxley, R-Ohio, argued that individual investors' right to sue in state courts was protected, Stupak said the provision giving judges discretion would mean that "you get involuntarily placed in these situations." Added Dingell: "You're rigging the market so it favors scam artists."

Markey offered two amendments, both of which he said had been requested by the SEC.

One would have extended the federal statute of limitations — the timeline under which investors must sue — to five years after the fraud occurred or three years after it was discovered. Under current law, investors have three years after the fraud or one year after its discovery to sue. It was defeated, 6-20.

The other would have restored the ability of allegedly defrauded investors to sue accountants, lawyers or others who might have aided a fraud. In a 1994 ruling in *Central Bank of Denver v. First Interstate Bank of Denver*, the Supreme Court eliminated that right. Markey's amendment failed by voice vote.

Full Committee Gives Its Approval To Amended Bill

JUNE 27 — Bipartisan proponents of a bill to make federal courts the sole venue for class action securities fraud lawsuits tried to appease the measure's few remaining detractors, as the House Commerce Committee approved the measure by voice vote June 24.

In a substitute amendment to the bill (HR 1689) that the committee accepted by voice vote, panel Chairman Thomas J. Bliley Jr., R-Va., addressed some Democratic concerns that had surfaced when the Finance and Hazardous Materials Subcommittee approved the measure June 10.

Among the additions: a provision pushed by committee ranking Democrat John D. Dingell of Michigan stipulating that state judges would retain the discretion to determine if 50 or more individual cases share a common bond, such as the same defendant, and should be consolidated into a class action suit and transferred to federal courts.

The bill would require that class action suits involving 50 or more parties be transferred from state to federal courts, which have the stricter standards for plaintiffs prescribed by a 1995 law (PL 104-67) that Congress enacted over President Clinton's veto. (*1995 Almanac, p. 2-90*)

That law aimed to stem what proponents believed was an increasing number of baseless lawsuits filed against companies that happened to have volatile stocks — such as high-technology businesses — but had not committed fraud. Because the law toughened federal rules but did not address state cases, several lawyers who had been filing those cases shifted their efforts to state court, in effect nullifying the law, bill supporters say.

Other additions in Bliley's substitute amendment included a provision pushed by Thomas J. Manton, D-N.Y., to encourage states to respect subpoenas sent by securities regulators from other states seeking information about a potential fraud. The provision also would streamline the subpoena process used by enforcers at the Securities and Exchange Commission (SEC).

Bliley's amendment attached a separate measure (HR 1262) to the bill that would authorize $351.3 million in fiscal 1999 for the SEC. The House passed that non-controversial bill in November, but the Senate never acted on it.

Many of Bliley's actions aimed to assuage some Democrats' opposition to the bill, but a few said they still strongly opposed the measure. Diana DeGette of Colorado said she feared the bill would "substantially hurt state securities laws."

But Anna G. Eshoo, D-Calif., who cosponsored the bill with Rick White, R-Wash., said the 1995 law had been undermined. "As long as the threat of state actions remains, the reforms will never be implemented," she said.

The Senate easily passed its version (S 1260) of the bill May 13. Though Bliley and other House Commerce leaders have attempted to amend the House measure to make it nearly identical to the Senate bill — and thus avoid a House-Senate conference — White said June 24 that he believed a conference would be necessary.

The House and Senate bills differ on the specifics of a provision allowing state and local governments, including state pension plans, to continue to file securities class action suits in state courts.

House Passage Sends Legislation To Conference

JULY 25 — A priority measure for high-technology businesses headed for a House-Senate conference July 22 after the House passed it, 340-83. The bill (HR 1689) would make federal courts, with their tougher standards, the sole venue for most class action lawsuits alleging securities fraud against companies with volatile stocks, such as high-tech firms. *(Vote 318, p. H-92)*

The Senate passed a similar bill (S 1260) on May 13.

Though the two bills were nearly identical when introduced, changes made in House markups and on the Senate floor will need to be resolved.

The major differences include the House's inclusion of a separate measure (HR 1262) to reauthorize the Securities and Exchange Commission (SEC) and varying provisions in both bills specifying when local governments can sue for securities fraud.

The bills would allow state and local governments, including state pension plans, to sue in a class action in state courts. They would generally be exempt from the new law directing suits to federal court, as long as the class action was made up only of government entities.

But the House bill would require that the entities authorize their participation in the case and be named as plaintiffs. They could not benefit from a favorable verdict in a class action suit in which they were not named, even if they were defrauded by the defendant. This would limit the number of entities that could receive awards after winning a case. The Senate bill does not contain those requirements.

In addition, the House Judiciary Committee objects to certain provisions added by the Commerce Committee, which marked up the bill. The Judiciary Committee did not mark up the bill despite having jurisdiction over some provisions, but it objected to language that would streamline the subpoena process used by enforcers at the SEC. The provision was removed from HR 1689 before the House passed it, but Commerce Committee Chairman Thomas J. Bliley Jr., R-Va., assured provision sponsor Thomas J. Manton, D-N.Y., that he would fight to include it in the final version.

The bills aim to close a loophole in a measure (PL 104-67) that Congress enacted in 1995 over President Clinton's veto. That law, which sought to stem what sponsors believed to be a growing number of baseless lawsuits against publicly traded companies, forced plaintiffs to cite specific facts to back their claims and otherwise changed rules governing federal class action suits. *(1995 Almanac, p. 2-90)*

But the act applied only to federal courts. Supporters of the bills, such as House sponsors Rick White, R-Wash., and Anna G. Eshoo, D-Calif., say that a handful of law firms have moved their cases to state courts to avoid the heightened federal standards.

The bills would require that any class action suit involving 50 or more parties be transferred to federal court. It also would allow state court judges to consolidate cases that share a common bond, such as the same plaintiff, and ship them to federal court as one class action suit involving 50 or more parties.

Senate, House Adopt Report, Quickly Clear Bill

OCTOBER 17 — With the stock market in a volatile cycle, Congress cleared a measure Oct. 13 that aims to cut down on class action lawsuits against companies whose earnings do not meet expectations.

The Senate adopted the conference report on the bill (S 1260) by voice vote Oct. 13 and the House cleared it, 319-82, the same day. *(Vote 528, p. H-150)*

President Clinton is expected to sign the bill, even though it would expand a law (PL 104-67) that Congress enacted in 1995 over his veto. The administration's position has changed, in part because Congress addressed some concerns of the Securities and Exchange Commission (SEC) in this year's measure, and in part because of the ease with which Congress overrode the 1995 veto. *(1995 Almanac, p. 2-90)*

The 1995 measure increased the standards for bringing a lawsuit, requiring more specific information before plaintiffs could bring to federal court a class action suit alleging securities fraud. But the act did not address standards in state courts. The result, bill proponents said, was that a handful of law firms that represent most plaintiffs in securities fraud suits moved their efforts to state courts.

This year's measure would move all securities fraud class action suits involving 50 or more parties to federal courts. In addition, 50 or more securities fraud cases filed separately in the same state court and involving "common questions of law" could be consolidated and moved to federal court.

Banking & Finance

Bill proponent Michael G. Oxley, R-Ohio, chairman of the House Commerce Committee's panel on Finance and Hazardous Materials, said such action was necessary because some plaintiffs would attempt to capitalize on the stock market's ups and downs. "If fraud were the only reason that stock prices dropped, then today's volatile markets would suggest that there is not an honest company out there," he said.

But John D. Dingell of Michigan, the Commerce Committee's ranking Democrat, charged that the bill was "shamelessly fleecing investors . . . This conference report nails the state courthouse door shut to little investors," he said.

The most difficult issue to be resolved between the House and Senate bills involved clarifying whether the 1995 act intended to remove "reckless misconduct" by nationally traded companies as a basis for securities fraud suits.

Many senators wanted bill language that would definitively preserve "reckless misconduct" as the basis for suits, but some House Republicans were hesitant to go along. Negotiators agreed to include language in the conference report explaining that Congress did not mean to change the "reckless misconduct" standard when it passed the 1995 bill. Some courts had interpreted the law as removing "reckless misconduct" as a basis for suits.

Democrats were angered Oct. 13 when they found out that the language had been omitted from the conference report that bill managers filed. Republicans said the omission was a mistake, and they attached it to the final version before either chamber adopted it.

The bill would allow state and local governments, including state pension plans, to continue filing securities fraud class action suits in state courts, as long as all the plaintiffs were government entities. It also would authorize $351.3 million in SEC funding in fiscal 1999. ◆

Chapter 6
BUDGET

Budget Resolution 6-3
   Kasich's Troubles 6-13
   Budget Surplus 6-16

Line-Item Veto 6-17
   Excerpts of District Court Ruling 6-18
   Excerpts of Supreme Court Ruling 6-22
   Clinton Gives Up 6-23

Congress Fails To Agree On Budget Resolution For the Coming Fiscal Year

Box Score

- **Bills:** H Con Res 284, S Con Res 86
- **House action:** The House passed H Con Res 284, 216-204, on June 5.
- **Senate action:** The Senate passed S Con Res 86, 57-41, on April 2.

For the first time since the modern congressional budget progress was established in 1974, Congress failed to agree on a budget resolution for the coming fiscal year.

SUMMARY

The House and Senate passed dramatically different versions and never even began formal negotiations to work out the differences, which largely involved the size of a proposed tax cut and the consequent spending cuts needed to offset it.

The Senate Budget Committee's blueprint (S Con Res 86) hewed closely to spending levels called for under last year's budget law (PL 105-33), and would have permitted tax cuts totaling $30 billion over five years, provided they were paid for with either spending cuts in mandatory programs or new revenues. The major difference between the committee proposal and last year's budget agreement was that the panel proposed $18.5 billion more in transportation spending than last year's agreement.

When the Senate committee's plan hit the floor, Republican conservatives contended it did nothing to advance GOP principles: reducing the size of the government and cutting taxes. GOP leaders worked behind the scenes to defuse this opposition and conservatives accepted a promise from Senate Majority Leader Trent Lott, R-Miss., that the final conference agreement would be closer to the conservative position. The Senate passed the resolution by a nearly party-line vote, 57-41.

Much later in the year than usual, the House committee approved a resolution that called for cutting taxes by a total of $101 billion over five years — to be offset by spending cuts of an equal amount.

Republican moderates, appropriators and deficit hawks all opposed the plan. It was only after the House leadership made an all-out effort to obtain the necessary votes that the resolution passed June 5, 216-204.

Senate Republicans made little effort to hide their disdain for the House version, contending it would require deep cuts in appropriations accounts that already had been trimmed to the bone, did not account for the recently enacted highway bill (PL 105-178) and recommended politically untenable cuts in entitlement programs.

GOP May Leave Surplus Alone

MARCH 7 — In the month since President Clinton unveiled his fiscal 1999 budget proposal, the Republican response has been slow to jell.

It looks increasingly like Congress will pass a budget resolution that deviates only slightly from the landmark budget laws (PL 105-33, PL 105-34) enacted last summer, although steadily improving budget surplus figures — including numbers released March 3 that project a surplus this year — raise the potential for more ambitious plans.

Senate Budget Committee Chairman Pete V. Domenici, R-N.M. — with the backing of top Senate leaders — is intent on passing a budget blueprint that would dash the hopes of both Republicans who want a big tax cut and Democrats backing Clinton's new spending plans. Domenici hopes to mark up the resolution March 11.

In the House, top GOP leaders have yet to solve their most difficult problem: how much additional money to devote to highway programs and whether that will come at the expense of other domestic programs. A leadership group led by Speaker Newt Gingrich, R-Ga., has yet to make much progress toward a compromise. "I don't think there's a bigger problem in this budget," said a top House GOP aide. "The meetings are going slowly and painfully."

Plans for a sizable tax cut financed in part by the budget surplus have been replaced by an expectation that a hike in tobacco taxes will help finance a modest tax cut bill.

About the only thing Republicans have agreed on so far is that they will not break "caps" on total discretionary appropriations, which impose a strict ceiling on the one-third of the $1.7 trillion federal budget over which Congress has direct control.

But even as they declare the caps sacrosanct, GOP budget writers are trying to devise ways to get around them while technically staying in compliance. Consensus appears far away. "I just don't think we've come to any conclusions yet," said Sen. Daniel R. Coats, R-Ind. "It's still very fluid."

Added Republican Sen. Connie Mack of Florida: "There are those who want to pay down the [national] debt. There are those who want to reduce taxes. There are those who want to do both. The surplus issue clearly affects the debate, so there's been no conclusion. We need more time to work through this."

With consensus so elusive, it seems the most likely outcome will be to preserve the status quo — which would be fine with Domenici and a growing faction in Congress who believe the budget surplus should be left alone and devoted to paying off a fraction of the national debt. "We should just be rubber-stamping what we did last year," said a top Domenici aide.

Still, conservatives inside Congress and out are pressing for a more ambitious tax cut than envisioned by the leadership or considered acceptable to Clinton. But they acknowledge that

Budget

there are not enough votes to pass one. Moderate Republicans in both chambers are generally not enthusiastic.

"I'm not in favor of any tax cuts," said Sen. John H. Chafee, R-R.I. "I'm in favor of paying down the debt."

Even as progress was slow on resolving differences on taxes and reaching final figures on highway spending, developments came on several fronts the week of March 2:

● **Surplus estimates.** The Congressional Budget Office (CBO) released new budget projections that confirmed what private-sector economists have been saying for months — that the government will run a surplus this year. The estimate predicts a fiscal 1998 surplus of $8 billion and a fiscal 1999 surplus of $9 billion. The surpluses generally rise steadily after the turn of the century, reaching $138 billion in 2008.

At the same time, CBO disputed Clinton's contention that his budget includes sufficient new revenues to fully finance $118 billion in proposed new spending over five years. Even after allowing Clinton to assume $65 billion in tobacco-related revenues, CBO estimates that his plan, if fully implemented, would reduce the surplus by $43 billion over the five years.

● **Highway spending.** The Senate approved an amendment to a huge bill (S 1173) that would increase highway spending over levels assumed in last year's budget by nearly $26 billion over six years. That raises the possibility that other domestic spending programs, already facing a tight squeeze under the discretionary spending caps, will face further cuts. Over the four years (1999-2002) governed by the caps, the compromise amendment would produce $14 billion in outlays counting toward the caps.

One financing scheme offered by Domenici would, in effect, allow appropriators to evade the caps. He wants to allow appropriators to claim savings from a Clinton proposal to deny veterans new health benefits for smoking-related illnesses caused by smoking after they leave the armed services. But the offset — which also has been eyed by tax-cutting committees — would only finance about $6 billion in new spending. Domenici promises to find other offsets to make up the difference.

House leaders have yet to reach agreement on the issue.

● **Social Security.** GOP leaders, particularly House Budget Committee Chairman John R. Kasich of Ohio, sought to trump Clinton's vow to use any surplus to "save Social Security first" by floating a plan to use it to establish government-subsidized Individual Retirement Accounts to supplement Social Security benefits. Meanwhile, Gingrich declared that the surplus must be reserved for Social Security and not used to cut taxes — a reversal of testimony he gave to the Budget Committee last year.

Tobacco Revenue Drives Debate In Senate Panel

MARCH 21 — The first official Republican response to President Clinton's poll-tested plans for new spending is a cautious fiscal 1999 budget blueprint that hews closely to last year's budget accord.

The Senate Budget Committee approved the draft budget resolution March 18 in a 12-10 party-line vote after a two-day debate that focused mostly on a fight over how to spend tobacco-related revenue that may never materialize.

The panel's action did little to clarify the ultimate outcome of this year's budget debate. Congressional Republicans and the administration continue to talk past each other.

And before negotiating with the White House, Republicans must agree among themselves. There is no sign of that. Instead, Republicans remain severely divided over tax cuts and what to do with any new tobacco revenue. Many senior Republicans have floated trial balloons, but no consensus has emerged on which ones will stay aloft.

About the only thing both sides can agree on is that the tight budget "caps" on appropriated spending are sacrosanct. Still, much of the energy of both the White House and Republicans has been directed toward finding ways to spend more than the caps allow. They would do this by using, to an unprecedented degree, savings from mandatory programs to finance more discretionary appropriations.

The Senate Republican plan ignored Clinton priorities such as new spending programs for child care, education and health. In his Feb. 2 budget submission, Clinton proposed financing a raft of initiatives with $66 billion in new revenues that would flow from a settlement of lawsuits between the major tobacco companies and the states.

Republicans moved to parry Clinton's plans to use tobacco money to finance new domestic spending without breaking the appropriations caps. They forged a political link between the tobacco revenue and the popular Medicare program, proposing to deposit any tobacco-related revenues into the Medicare trust fund that pays hospital bills.

GOP Senate leaders cast the maneuver as vital to saving financially troubled Medicare, the federal health insurance program for the elderly. But even some panel Republicans all but acknowledged that the real purpose of the move was to provide a politically potent counter to Clinton's popular spending plans — just as he had stymied Republican plans for tax cuts with his call to "save Social Security first."

Said GOP Sen. Phil Gramm of Texas: "People understood the president when he said 'save Social Security first.' I think they will understand when we say, 'save Medicare first.' "

Sen. Budget Committee Chairman Pete V. Domenici, R-N.M., perhaps resorting to hyperbole, claimed that directing the tobacco money to any purpose besides Medicare "hastens the demise" of the program. But Republicans are split on the issue. House Speaker Newt Gingrich, R-Ga., has said he wants to devote the tobacco money to tax cuts.

Sen. Richard J. Durbin, D-Ill., said: "Sen. Domenici has trumped us politically by saying 'save Medicare first,' just as we trumped Republicans by saying let's save Social Security with the surplus. So we're kind of at a standoff in terms of strategy."

Set against the backdrop of a $1.7 trillion budget, the amount of money provoking the quarrel is relatively modest. The Congressional Budget Office estimates that the Clinton budget would increase spending by $118 billion over five years and break the

1999 budget cap by $12 billion.

But in this election-year climate, the White House is also seeking political gain from the debate. Clinton is spoiling for a fight. On the day that the Budget Committee wrapped up work, Clinton trumpeted his plans for federal grants to help schools reduce class size and his efforts to promote child care and to permit uninsured senior citizens to buy into Medicare. At the same time, he attacked the Republican blueprint.

"These are very important things," Clinton said of his initiatives. "We can afford to do these things. But there are some troubling signals coming out of Washington that the Republican budget may not embody this commitment to education and our future."

The modest blueprint apparently was not a universal hit among Senate Republicans. Junior panel member Rod Grams, R-Minn., sharply criticized the Domenici draft as permitting too much government and not enough in tax cuts. He voted for the plan only reluctantly: "I've got a 'no' vote in my pocket, but I'm not going to use it tonight," he said.

Non-Binding Recommendations

In a year in which the Senate is not planning on a budget reconciliation bill to write new tax and spending policy into law, passing the annual budget resolution is largely a procedural exercise. (The panel measure includes no reconciliation instructions.) Other than the yearly lump sum allocation to the Appropriations committees, which control one-third of the budget, the spending recommendations are non-binding. Domenici's blueprint puts the appropriations totals at levels set by last year's omnibus spending cut bill (PL 105-33). The fiscal 1999 discretionary spending handed out by appropriators would total $561 billion in outlays. Of that, defense would receive $267 billion, $2.6 billion less than in fiscal 1998. Domestic programs would get $295 billion, a $6.2 billion increase.

The other substantive provision in the GOP plan would build room under the budget caps to provide $18.5 billion in additional outlays for highway construction over five years without raiding other discretionary programs to finance the increase. The resolution would permit the Appropriations Committee to use $19 billion in offsets from the mandatory side of the federal ledger to pay for the new highway spending, which is included in the just-passed $214 billion reauthorization (S 1173) of highway and mass transit programs. Such mandatory offsets are often claimed by appropriators to finance discretionary spending, but never to the degree anticipated this year.

The Budget Committee markup did little to signal the outcome of GOP senators' clash with Clinton. If Republicans do not pass a reconciliation bill — the House wants to, the Senate does not — the battle will probably play out over the summer as Congress advances the 13 annual appropriations bills. The bipartisan atmosphere that permeated last year's appropriations cycle is expected to evaporate as Republicans deny funding for many Clinton initiatives. The White House strategy is to extract end-of-session concessions as a condition of signing appropriations bills and allowing Republicans to go home to campaign.

"The absolute fencing of tobacco [revenue] for only one purpose . . . makes it much more difficult to accomplish the ends of the appropriations bills through other means," said top White House lobbyist Lawrence Stein. "It closes down the range of options and in so doing bodes ill for an early departure this year."

Tobacco Battles

Much of the March 17-18 markup involved lengthy and repetitious debate over tobacco issues.

Democrats accused Domenici of virtually killing prospects for legislation to implement the tobacco settlement. They want to claim the revenue for anti-smoking programs and health research. By placing procedural roadblocks in front of any effort to devote tobacco revenue for anything other than Medicare, the budget would remove incentives for those trying to pass legislation, Democrats said. Under the terms of the resolution, any attempt to spend new tobacco-related revenue for non-Medicare-related programs would be subject to a point of order that would require 60 votes to waive.

"Every major tobacco bill introduced in the Congress and the proposed resolution between state attorneys general and the tobacco industry last June included new funding for these initiatives," said Kent Conrad of North Dakota, the Democrats' point man on tobacco legislation. Under the GOP budget resolution, he said, "none of these bills could be brought to the Senate floor without facing a budget point of order. Not one."

Domenici countered with a Columbia University study that estimated that 14 percent of Medicare costs are due to tobacco-related illnesses and said that Medicare should claim the tobacco money instead of new Washington-based social programs.

And Republicans said Democrats were making too much of the 60-vote barrier to devoting tobacco proceeds for purposes other than Medicare. Any tobacco bill that passes will have to be bipartisan enough to garner 60 votes anyway, said Majority Whip Don Nickles, R-Okla. Republicans said it was silly to fight over tobacco-related revenue when the tobacco bill may not be enacted.

"I'm not going to pull up a [tobacco] bill on the floor . . . unless it has pretty strong support and a bunch of Dems. And I don't see it," Nickles said.

The panel approved, on a bipartisan 14-8 vote, a non-binding sense of the Senate amendment offered by top committee Democrat Frank R. Lautenberg of New Jersey that "comprehensive tobacco legislation should increase the price of each pack of cigarettes sold by at least $1.50" within three years.

Nuts and Bolts

The battles over tobacco overshadowed the discussion of Domenici's draft resolution, which, except for additional highway spending, would rubber stamp last year's balanced-budget and tax laws. The budget anticipates:

- **Spending.** A federal budget totaling $1.73 trillion in fiscal 1999, a 3.6 percent increase from fiscal 1998 levels of $1.67 trillion.
- **Surplus.** A surplus of $8 billion in 1999, $1 billion in 2000, $13 billion in 2001, $67 billion in 2002, and $58 billion in 2003. Five year total: $147 billion.
- **Taxes.** No net tax cut, though the plan envisions five-year tax cuts of $30

Budget

billion, offset by new tax revenues or reductions in mandatory spending programs. Senate Majority Leader Trent Lott, R-Miss., said he wants that figure to rise to $45 billion, but finding offsetting spending cuts to finance a larger tax cut will prove difficult.

● **Transportation.** Funding for highways would be increased by $25.9 billion in contract authority over five years and $18.5 billion in outlays above levels anticipated in last year's budget agreement. Mass transit would receive $5 billion in additional budget authority but no actual outlays within the five years.

The additional transportation money would be offset by spending cuts that include: reversing a Department of Veterans Affairs policy that would compensate veterans for all smoking-related illnesses, instead of those caused by smoking during their term of service ($10.5 billion over five years); Medicaid and food stamp administrative cost reforms ($1.9 billion and $1.7 billion, respectively); and cuts in social services block grants ($3.1 billion).

Senate Adopts Domenici's Plan For FY99 Budget

APRIL 4 — The Senate spent a week in campaign-style debate on the fiscal 1999 budget resolution, using the floor as a forum to showcase party-defining issues such as taxes, child care and education.

The underlying blueprint, which deviates only slightly from last year's budget deal, emerged unscathed. Despite sometimes heated rhetoric, senators made no substantive changes to the budget resolution (S Con Res 86) as drafted by Budget Committee Chairman Pete V. Domenici, R-N.M.

After surviving a momentary scare April 1 from conservatives who threatened to sink the measure, it passed April 2 on a nearly party-line vote of 57-41. *(Vote 84, p. S-15)*

The rump group of conservatives, led by John Ashcroft, R-Mo., ultimately agreed to back the resolution after winning assurances that the final version that emerges from a House-Senate conference will permit additional tax cuts, allow consideration of a budget-reconciliation bill to resolve tax and spending policy issues, and try to ease the so-called marriage tax penalty.

The behind-the-scenes skirmishing highlighted divisions within the Republican Conference between members of the old guard such as Domenici and the more junior members who pushed Majority Leader Trent Lott, R-Miss., into the leadership.

"Along with other Republican senators elected in the last few years, I was sent to cut taxes, cut government and cut the debt," Ashcroft said. "The only thing this budget cuts is against the grain of those who elected us."

Lott and Majority Whip Don Nickles, R-Okla., were sympathetic to the renegades' aims. They told the group, however, to settle for promises that the final product would be more pleasing, and that it was too late to change the resolution pending on the floor.

"Those guys are my base; they're my closest allies," Lott said. "I'm with them, and that's part of my argument: 'Do you have a better chance of getting more of this done supporting me or opposing me?' The answer's obvious."

The backstage developments were among the few moments of drama in a week that otherwise featured debate on dozens of non-binding sense of the Senate amendments on issues such as Social Security, tax cuts, "sunsetting" the tax code, and President Clinton's budget initiatives on education, health and child care. Clinton said April 3 the budget blueprint would "squeeze out critical investments in education and children."

Competing Visions

The debate over the budget resolution provides an annual forum for the opposing parties to engage in partisan debate on their competing visions of the size and role of government. But it is an imperfect vehicle at best. The resolution is non-binding, other than determining the amount of discretionary money available to the Appropriations committees for fiscal 1999. It leaves fights over taxes, changes in entitlement programs and trade-offs among discretionary appropriations accounts for subsequent legislation.

The Domenici plan hews closely to last year's twin budget laws (PL 105-33, PL 105-34). The chief difference is that it would allow appropriators to finance $18.5 billion more in transportation spending over five years than anticipated in last year's landmark budget. It would do this by using otherwise impermissible cuts in several mandatory spending programs to finance highway spending. It also would place procedural hurdles in front of any attempt to use new tobacco-related revenues for anything except to shore up the hospital trust fund for Medicare, the federal health insurance program for the elderly and disabled.

It is only subsequent bills that would actually adjust federal spending and cut taxes. While the Senate slogged through its little-watched debate, it was largely overshadowed by other major budget-related developments: House passage of a $218 billion transportation bill (HR 2400); sweeping Senate Commerce Committee approval of a $506 billion bill (S 1415) to implement the settlement of a historic lawsuit between the major tobacco companies and 40 states; and House passage of a $2.9 billion fiscal 1998 emergency spending bill (HR 3579).

The GOP budget plan anticipates a $1.73 trillion federal budget in fiscal 1999, up 3.6 percent from the current year. It foresees a surplus of $8 billion in 1998 and surpluses totaling $147 billion over five years. It calls for no net tax cuts but would permit $30 billion in such cuts over five years, provided they were paid for with spending offsets or new revenues.

As Domenici's modest blueprint hit the floor, it quickly became apparent that members of the Senate's conservative wing were not happy.

In a stinging floor speech March 30, Ashcroft, who is considering a run for president, attacked the plan for doing nothing to advance Republican principles such as cutting government and reducing taxes. Two days later, he held a news conference with Rod Grams, R-Minn., and Robert C. Smith, R-N.H., in which each issued an unequivocal challenge saying he would oppose the measure if it were not significantly changed. Other conservatives, including James M. Inhofe, R-Okla., and Sam Brownback, R-Kan., also were poised to reject the Domenici plan, raising the possibility that it might not pass if Democrats held ranks.

Those developments set off a mini-crisis for GOP leaders. Lott dispatched Larry E. Craig, R-Idaho, to negotiate a solution. By that time, it was too late to force changes to the measure, and to do so would have risked alienating the party's moderate wing.

The conservatives agreed to settle for promises from Lott that the final measure would tilt further in their direction on taxes and that there would most likely be a budget-reconciliation bill to implement a tax cut, with a reduction in the marriage penalty as the top priority. Total repeal of the penalty, under which some married working couples pay higher taxes when filing jointly than they would if they were single, is not under consideration because it would cost almost $30 billion annually. The House is eyeing tax cuts of about $60 billion over five years. Easing the marriage penalty is among the few tax cuts that Republicans think Clinton might sign.

In an indication of conservative dissatisfaction with the Domenici plan, two-thirds of the GOP caucus supported an amendment by Paul Coverdell, R-Ga., to cut taxes by $196 billion over five years, financed largely through cuts in domestic spending. A motion to waive budget rules and adopt the amendment failed, 38-62. (Vote 55, p. S-11)

Divided Over Taxes

But Republicans are not united on the tax front. Even as conservatives won pledges to use budget surpluses to ease the marriage penalty, Republicans sent a contradictory message April 1 in approving a non-binding amendment by Finance Chairman William V. Roth Jr., R-Del., backing the creation of federally subsidized personal retirement accounts, financed by the budget surplus, to supplement Social Security. The amendment was approved, 51-49. (Vote 56, p. S-11)

The idea of these new retirement accounts is also backed by House Speaker Newt Gingrich, R-Ga., and House Budget Committee Chairman John R. Kasich, R-Ohio. Kasich is preparing his budget plan, which will not be marked up until late April at the earliest.

The debate allowed Democrats to highlight their priorities, although every major Democratic plan was easily swatted away. Proposals to establish deficit-neutral "reserve funds" to finance Clinton budget proposals to increase spending on child care, reduce elementary school class size and boost funding for the environment were struck down on near party-line votes.

Republicans needed several Democratic votes to turn back a move by John D. Rockefeller IV, D-W.Va., to strip from the bill a provision to reverse a new Department of Veterans Affairs policy that compensates veterans for all smoking-related illnesses, not just for illnesses caused by smoking during a veteran's term of service. The provision is crucial because it would provide $10.5 billion in savings over five years that would help finance the highway bill. The Senate voted 52-46 to keep the offset. (Vote 76, p. S-14)

The budget resolution would also permit $1.7 billion in administrative savings from the food stamp program to be claimed for new highways. That is one reason a conference report on an agricultural research, crop insurance and food stamp bill (S 1150) — which also claims the savings — has stalled.

The resolution contains non-binding language calling for "sunsetting" the tax code after 2001. Byron L. Dorgan, D-N.D., tried to strip the provision, but Republicans trumped him with a procedural move. The "scrap the code" idea has substantial support among Republicans, but a top GOP leader acknowledged that it could not have survived an up-or-down vote.

A move by Nickles to prohibit future budget resolutions from being used as vehicles for dozens of non-binding sense of the Senate resolutions came within one vote of succeeding. A motion to overturn a point of order against Nickles' proposal came within one vote of the 60 needed to prevail. At one point late in the tally, the vote reached 60, and Judd Gregg, R-N.H., who was presiding, called the vote, ignoring the appeals of Richard J. Durbin, D-Ill., who was seeking recognition to change his "aye" to "nay," making the tally 59-39. Democrats angrily protested — such resolutions are among the ways the minority party can win votes for its agenda — and GOP leaders allowed Durbin to change his vote. (Vote 80, p. S-15)

Kasich Struggles To Line Up Votes; Appropriators Dust Off Plan B

MAY 9 — Reps. Ralph Regula and John R. Kasich are Republican allies from Ohio, but their roles within the House put them sharply at odds.

Kasich, as chairman of the Budget Committee, is visibly struggling to assemble a fiscal 1999 budget blueprint that will draw 218 Republican votes and pass. Regula, as chairman of an Appropriations subcommittee, is getting eager to move his annual bill to finance the Interior Department.

Kasich's call to slash domestic spending to finance a bold agenda of lower taxes and less government does not sit well with appropriators such as Regula, who are charged with getting their bills signed into law.

The tension was typified by a jesting joust between the two just off the House floor on May 7.

Regula, knowing full well that Kasich is having an exhausting time crafting a budget that each GOP faction can endorse: "How's it going, John?"

Kasich: "Great. We're going to pay down debt, save Social Security, cut government and get rid of the marriage [tax] penalty."

Regula: "That sounds like a great platform [should Kasich run for president in 2000, as he is considering]. Hold off until after the 15th, and then we can go ahead without you," referring to the mid-May date at which appropriators can begin to move bills without a budget resolution having passed.

Kasich: "It'll be amazing how you'll get the votes. Call Bernie Sanders. He'll vote with you." The Vermont independent is among the most liberal members of the House.

Kasich and Regula were teasing each other, but as the old saying goes, "Many a truth is said in jest." The exchange went to the very heart of the dilemma facing Republicans as they try to pass the budget resolution and get the 13 annual spending bills signed into law.

Many of those who follow the budget process closely wonder whether

Budget

Kasich will be able to cobble together a budget plan that can win support from both the conservative tax-cutting wing of the GOP and from moderates and pragmatists who are content with last year's budget pact.

With just an 11-seat GOP majority and little if any help expected — or desired — from Democrats, Kasich and his fellow Republican leaders face a difficult task, to say the least. Congress might fail to produce a budget resolution for the first time since the Budget Act (PL 93-344) was enacted in 1974.

"I wouldn't give it more than 50-50 odds in the House," said former Congressional Budget Office (CBO) Director Robert D. Reischauer, now at the Brookings Institution. And if one should pass the House, Reischauer added, "I would think the conference [with the Senate] would be very, very difficult."

Added Rep. Jim Kolbe, R-Ariz.: "I would admit it looks like it's going to be tough to do. . . . It's going to be tough to do alone in the House, much less get the Senate to agree to it."

The Senate passed a budget resolution April 2 that sticks closely to last year's landmark balanced-budget law (PL 105-33).

CAT and the Tuesday Group

Kasich wants to go beyond the budget deal he helped negotiate and polish the reputation of the GOP as the party of smaller government and lower taxes.

Kasich's original plan, which called for a menu of $154 billion in spending cuts over five years, received a decidedly chilly reception from members such as Republican Sherwood Boehlert of New York, a leader of the Tuesday Group, a band of moderates.

"I think his budget proposal is totally unrealistic," Boehlert said. "A massive tax cut is just not appropriate at this time, at a time when we're starving for resources in important areas like education."

After several days of negotiations, the blueprint had shrunk to about $100 billion in spending cuts and was likely to shrink further — fast. Kasich has very tentatively scheduled a markup of the resolution for May 14, a Budget Committee member said.

One of the selling points for the plan will be that it would enable Republicans to ease the so-called marriage tax penalty, a top GOP priority. The penalty causes some married couples to pay more in federal income tax than they would if they filed separately.

Meanwhile, both the Senate and the Clinton administration view Kasich's plan as violating the very terms of the budget agreement he played such a major role in negotiating. The idea of cutting appropriated spending below the budget "caps" set last year is a "direct violation" of the agreement, said Office of Management and Budget Director Franklin D. Raines.

"It calls into question the very agreement we signed last year," Raines said.

"The Senate is right at the caps, and that's a position I'm comfortable with," said Slade Gorton, R-Wash., a member of both the Budget and Appropriations committees.

At the other end of the spectrum is the House's Conservative Action Team (CAT), about 40 members strong, which is pressing hard for a five-year tax cut of $100 billion or more.

It is impossible to make all sides happy.

"If you satisfy the concerns of the CATs, you create problems with the Tuesday lunch bunch. And every time you satisfy the Tuesday lunch bunch, you create problems with the CATs," said Richard May, former Budget Committee chief of staff under Kasich, now an associate at a lobbying firm. "That's the balancing act Kasich is going through."

The competing factions shuttled in and out of meetings with Kasich the week of May 4 to register their concerns and learn of the budget chairman's evolving plans. For example, Kasich's original plan to scuttle the international space station has been shelved. The Energy Department, which he had targeted, will likely survive, but the Commerce Department will remain on the chopping block.

"We dropped a couple of items that became clear to me that we couldn't pass," Kasich said. "And we have a process now where we're going to have to go back and vet some more and drop some things out, no doubt about it."

But as Kasich's budget- and tax-cutting plans become more modest, the GOP's conservative wing will grow restive.

Rallying the Faithful

In pressing for a bold blueprint, Kasich is defying recent history and attempting a steep legislative climb. Congress typically takes a breather in years that follow big deficit-cutting efforts.

But Kasich is also trying to motivate a Republican base that many GOP strategists describe as listless.

"We face the prospect in November of record low turnout and record high straight-ticket voting," said GOP consultant Ed Gillespie. "Bill Clinton has recognized this, and he's put forth a budget that excites liberal Democrats. . . . Republicans should put forth a budget that excites Republicans: lower taxes, less spending, fewer new programs."

Kasich's blueprint is taking shape even as estimates of the budget surplus continue to grow. The CBO, which in March estimated a fiscal 1998 budget surplus of only $8 billion, revised that figure May 6 to between $43 billion and $63 billion, a level private-sector economists had predicted for months.

But Kasich has no plans to devote any of the surplus to tax cuts, heeding President Clinton's admonition to hold off on "spending" any portion of the surplus until the Social Security program is overhauled. House Ways and Means Committee Chairman Bill Archer, R-Texas, however, still has designs to devote part of the surplus to a tax cut, and House Speaker Newt Gingrich, R-Ga., has again switched course to support that idea, given the size of the surplus.

To devote part of the surplus to tax cuts or to cut discretionary appropriations — the roughly one-third of the budget that Congress doles out each year — would violate budget rules Republicans extended only last year. Any attempt would run into procedural hurdles in the Senate that would ultimately require 60 votes to overcome.

The same budget rules would block any attempt in the Senate to cut spending below the caps to finance tax cuts. Not that there is any stomach to do so anyway. Asked about the House idea, Senate Appropriations Committee Chairman Ted Stevens, R-Alaska, said: "My on-the-record comment would be that it indicates that Pete Domenici has the worst job in the U.S. Senate."

Budget Resolution

Added a senior aide to Budget Committee Chairman Domenici, R-N.M.: "I just don't see us reducing discretionary spending below the caps. At some point we have to govern, and we have to be realistic."

For their part, Republicans on the House Appropriations Committee also make no secret of their displeasure at Kasich's drive to cut below the already tight budget caps. "The Appropriations Committee is very concerned that we set something they can't achieve," Kasich acknowledged.

Indeed, there is little real appetite to cut discretionary spending. As they sought to finance the six-year transportation reauthorization bill (HR 2400), lawmakers opted not to force cuts in other domestic appropriations, but instead relied on savings from mandatory spending programs.

Plan B

The budget resolution would set the parameters for any budget-reconciliation bill that would implement tax and spending cuts from mandatory programs. But it also would set the overall allocation of discretionary dollars to the Appropriations committees. Once they get that allocation, appropriators divvy it up among the 13 subcommittees, which can then begin moving their annual bills.

But appropriators are anxious about the delays in producing a budget resolution, and they are beginning to prepare for moving ahead without one. If there is no budget, spending bills can begin moving through the House starting May 15, though appropriators will probably wait until after the Memorial Day recess.

Ordinarily, budget rules do not permit the Senate to move appropriations bills without a budget resolution. But in anticipation of a logjam in the House, the Senate in April passed a measure (S Res 209) that allows the Appropriations Committee to proceed with a temporary allocation of $561 billion in discretionary spending.

"We do have to move forward with the appropriations bills," Majority Leader Trent Lott, R-Miss., said May 4. "If the House has not acted [on a budget resolution] by the end of this month, I have to go to Sen. Stevens and wave him on through. The appropriators have got to go."

Kasich Drops Cuts After Authorizers, Senate Flay Plan

MAY 16 — House Budget Committee Chairman John R. Kasich has toiled over the last few months to produce a budget blueprint to illustrate to voters that the Republican party stands for smaller government and lower taxes. What Kasich, R-Ohio, has ended up illustrating, however, is how difficult it will be to complete another round of spending cuts.

Kasich's specific proposals leaked out May 13, and the next day — nudged by House leaders such as Speaker Newt Gingrich, R-Ga. — he announced plans to scrap them. His $100 billion roster of spending cut proposals alienated many House GOP moderates, drew sarcastic barbs from Democrats and had Senate Republicans rolling their eyes.

Instead, the Budget Committee plans to mark up a budget resolution the week of May 18 that would still recommend $100 billion in cuts, but leave it up to the policy-making committees to produce them — although those panels would not have an easy time either. The budget resolution may be a blueprint for a subsequent reconciliation bill, which would seek to reconcile tax and spending policies with overall budget goals.

The chief purpose of that measure would be an election-year tax cut, most likely a reduction in the so-called marriage penalty. Still undecided is whether to use part of any budget surplus for the tax cut.

Kasich worked for weeks to piece together a list of cuts to polish the GOP's tax- and budget-cutting bona fides. But he produced a list of recommendations that immediately came under heavy fire. Many of his proposals were hardy perennials that had been rejected before. Several — such as killing President Clinton's cherished Americorps national service program or repealing the 1931 Davis-Bacon Act, which requires companies with federal contracts to pay workers "prevailing wages" — could never pass the House, much less clear the Senate or get signed by Clinton.

Stung by the backlash over the details, Kasich has stepped back to focus on a broader theme: Cut just 1.1 percent from the growth of federal spending, bringing it down to the rate of inflation. The savings could ease the marriage penalty, which requires more than 21 million married couples to pay an annual average of $1,400 more in taxes than they would if they filed as single people. "Letting the government grow at the rate of inflation is not a hard proposition for people who live outside the Beltway," Kasich said.

But what Kasich does not mention is that almost 80 percent of the federal budget — Social Security, Medicare and Medicaid benefits, defense and interest payments on the national debt — would be left untouched, leaving already cash-strapped domestic spending accounts to bear much of the pain.

The proposal would cut non-defense discretionary spending by $46 billion over five years, a reduction of 3.5 percent under budget "caps" that appropriators are already trying to breach. Mandatory spending programs would face a $54 billion cut, though many of the most politically viable of those savings have already been gobbled up to pay for a massive bill (HR 2400) to increase federal spending on transportation programs. That bill is now in a House-Senate conference.

The White House and congressional Democrats heaped scorn on Kasich's proposals as a replay of the government shutdown politics of 1995 and an abrogation of last year's budget agreement.

"We are appalled. If you take all of these proposals together, they amount to a rank repudiation of the bipartisan budget agreement we shook hands on one year ago tomorrow," Office of Management and Budget Director Franklin D. Raines said May 14. "This is, quite frankly, a formula for gridlock."

Added Rep. John M. Spratt Jr. of South Carolina, the top Democrat on the Budget Committee: "I have wondered what John Kasich has been doing for the last six weeks. Now I know. He's been in the bone yard digging up bad ideas that were buried a long time ago."

GOP Divisions

The plan was not a universal hit among Republicans. The party remains split over whether to attempt another round of spending cuts or to

Budget

pause and let last year's budget pact take root. "We . . . should not try to disengage from an agreement that was made last year on a five-year basis that's made a lot of sense," said Amo Houghton of New York.

Groups representing the moderate and conservative wings of the party both registered protests of the plan.

"The total amount of mandatory and discretionary spending cuts are still of such a magnitude that they are neither desirable nor attainable," wrote Michael N. Castle of Delaware, Fred Upton of Michigan and Nancy L. Johnson of Connecticut, co-chairs of the Tuesday Group, a band of moderates, in a May 13 letter to Kasich. "We cannot support the proposal in its current form."

On the other side of the spectrum was the Conservative Action Team, which vowed to oppose any budget resolution that does not provide $100 billion in tax cuts over five years — a level the moderates cannot accept. The team also demanded increases in defense spending and a change in budget rules that block lawmakers from using the budget surplus and cuts in appropriations to pay for tax cuts.

"If we fail to make the distinction between Republicans and Democrats on the size and scope of government, our status as the majority party in Congress will be in serious jeopardy in November," wrote conservative David M. McIntosh, R-Ind., in a May 13 letter to Gingrich.

Dead on Arrival

Kasich's plan recycled already rejected Republican proposals to kill the Commerce and Energy departments, sell off power marketing administrations, cut the earned income tax credit and kill the Legal Services Corporation.

If Congress did not follow up on the budget resolution with a reconciliation bill, the only binding effect of the resolution would be to set the amount of money that could be doled out through the 13 annual spending bills that will begin moving through the House in June.

In this area, Kasich's plan is more modest: trimming $2 billion from domestic appropriations for fiscal 1999. But even those cuts are meeting fierce resistance as appropriators come to grips with a serious squeeze on funds. Kasich's plan would reduce domestic discretionary outlays from $289 billion to $287 billion, while calling for significantly greater (and non-binding) cuts in future years.

Members of the House Appropriations Committee privately blasted Kasich's plans to cut their piece of the budget pie, but their public statements tended to be more diplomatic. They could not hide their pleasure at watching Kasich struggle to sell his plan.

"It is helpful to me as an appropriator for the Budget Committee to learn the facts of life as we deal with them every day," said a top House Appropriations Committee staff aide.

For their part, several of the Senate's "Old Bulls" made little effort to hide their disdain for Kasich's efforts.

"I don't know where we're going to get this $45 billion" in discretionary cuts, said Appropriations Committee Chairman Ted Stevens, R-Alaska. "I don't think Congress could function. I think there'd be a stalemate."

Both Stevens and Senate Budget Committee Chairman Pete V. Domenici, R-N.M., vow to block any further cuts in appropriations. Even if the House manages to pass its budget resolution in early June — which is no sure thing — a long and difficult conference would await with the Senate, which passed its resolution (S Con Res 86) on April 2. By that time, appropriations bills would have leapfrogged ahead of the budget resolution.

Both House and Senate appropriators are seeking ways to get around the caps. For example, Stevens plans to finance next year's military deployments in Bosnia and the Middle East by declaring them to be "emergency" budget items that do not count toward the caps. The same would apply to efforts to prepare federal computer systems for problems related to the arrival of 2000.

House Panel Approves Kasich's Moderated Plan

MAY 23 — The small green cards were in front of Budget Committee Republicans as they took their places at the panel dais May 20. They read: "Budget Message: Can we find 1% (or just a penny on the dollar) to shrink the growth of government so we can repeal the marriage penalty?"

That is the budget- and tax-cutting mantra that House Republicans have settled upon as they work to pass their fiscal 1999 draft budget resolution. No longer are Republicans boasting of plans to kill Cabinet departments, terminate President Clinton's AmeriCorps national service program or sell off federal power marketing administrations that provide inexpensive electricity to consumers.

Instead, by a party-line vote of 22-16, the committee approved a budget blueprint designed by Chairman John R. Kasich, R-Ohio, that was shorn of such controversial specifics. Kasich's plan totals $9 trillion over five years and $1.72 trillion in fiscal 1999. It would require $101 billion in savings over five years, but only $4 billion in fiscal 1999.

In a concession to appropriators who complained that earlier drafts were too draconian, Kasich restored $2 billion in domestic discretionary appropriations for fiscal 1999 that he had earlier proposed to cut. That left appropriations at "caps" set by last year's balanced-budget law (PL 105-33). The Kasich proposal calls for $46 billion in future cuts from domestic discretionary programs, but those are non-binding.

The indefatigable Kasich has been struggling for weeks to develop a budget plan that can get enough Republican votes to pass. But he has run up against a GOP caucus that shows little enthusiasm for another budget showdown with Clinton or another round of spending cuts. With the government running a surplus for the first time in three decades, many rank-and-file Republicans see little reason for a reprise of their unsuccessful battles with Clinton.

The difficulty in producing a budget resolution casts a spotlight on the numerous hurdles Republicans will face as they try to cut taxes and spending again. They still face significant intraparty differences, especially between the House and Senate, plus an abbreviated congressional schedule in this election year.

Breaking the Agreement

Congress usually takes a breather and accepts the status quo after a big budget deal such as last year's. But Kasich — to the increasingly public consternation of his Senate counterpart, Budget Committee Chairman Pete V. Domenici, R-N.M. — wants to lead an election-year spending cut drive. The goal is to scrap the marriage tax penalty, which requires many married couples to pay more in taxes than they would if they filed as singles.

Kasich's budget, with its proposed cuts in Clinton-backed domestic spending, breaks with the balanced-budget agreement that he played such a key role in negotiating a year ago. But many Republicans are worried that their core voters are unenthusiastic about the November elections, and Kasich is trying to use the budget to whip up the GOP base.

"Balancing the budget was never really the goal for me," Kasich said. "Balancing the budget was a very effective rallying cry to move the troops to be able to reduce the power of government."

The House is about two months late in producing a budget, and the Republican whip organization still has heavy lifting to do to pass the measure with only a 10-seat majority in the House. Even with the draft proposal stripped of politically unpalatable details, several GOP moderates are unenthusiastic about it, while conservatives fear it may be watered down further.

After the markup, Kasich expressed guarded optimism that the measure will pass when Congress returns from its Memorial Day recess. "I just think this penny on a dollar is a very doable thing, and I would hope we wouldn't have to retreat from it," he said.

Countered top panel Democrat John M. Spratt Jr. of South Carolina: "This budget won't fly. . . . I think in this resolution we've got one that won't go anywhere past this committee."

Even if the House does pass it, the Kasich proposal remains a flop with Senate veterans such as Domenici, who vows to block any further cuts from appropriations. "I'm not going to go to conference in one day and agree to this," Domenici said. "We might not be able to get a budget resolution in conference."

Domenici was mostly silent for weeks as Kasich assembled his budget. But he abandoned his reticence after learning of Kasich's plans to slash already tight appropriated accounts by more than 3 percent below the existing freeze under the caps. Most Republicans vow to stick to the caps, even as they and the White House devise ways to evade them.

For example, conference negotiators on a mammoth transportation funding bill (HR 2400) have been scrambling to find cuts in mandatory programs to finance spending above levels spelled out under last year's budget. And appropriators plan to finance peacekeeping operations in Bosnia and the Middle East as emergency spending that does not count against the caps.

"I'm absolutely certain that over the next five years we cannot live with the freeze that we've got," Domenici said May 19 as he blasted Kasich's budget. "The notion that it's less onerous a [budget] resolution because it doesn't ask you to consider specifics is just not so. . . . Where is it going to come from? What is going to be cut?"

Domenici's reaction increased the possibility that Congress may fail to produce a budget resolution for the first time since it passed the Budget Act in 1974. The annual resolution is a nonbinding road map that illustrates the majority party's fiscal agenda; carrying out that agenda requires subsequent legislation, usually a so-called reconciliation bill, a filibuster-proof measure that fleshes out tax and spending guidelines with precise legislative language.

If House and Senate Republicans cannot agree on a budget resolution, GOP efforts to cut taxes will likely be fruitless. They will be subject to a Senate filibuster and possibly to other procedural challenges. For example, any budget bill that used cuts in discretionary appropriations to finance tax cuts would violate Senate rules that do not permit such offsets. Senate Democrats could raise a point of order against such a bill, and 60 votes would be required to waive it. But only 55 senators are Republicans.

Similarly, so-called pay-as-you-go budget rules — as well as Clinton's State of the Union admonition to "save Social Security first" before spending the surplus — would block any attempt to use the budget surplus to help pay for a tax cut.

The Kasich plan would permit Congress to use the surplus to create federally subsidized individual retirement accounts (IRAs) to supplement Social Security, a priority of both Kasich and House Speaker Newt Gingrich, R-Ga. If that effort failed, the surplus would be dedicated to paying down a portion of the $5.5 trillion national debt. Gingrich has flip-flopped on the question of whether to use the surplus for tax cuts, saying May 21 that he opposes such use.

The plan seeks to yield a fiscal 1999 surplus of $34 billion, down from a projected $55 billion this year. The surplus would peak at $77 billion in 2002 — the year originally predicted to yield the first balanced budget under last year's landmark budget pact.

Democrats Pile On

With Republicans in disarray, White House spokesman Mike McCurry did not address the Kasich plan on its merits when asked about it May 20. "It was already declared dead on arrival by Sen. Domenici . . . [who] has said that [Kasich's] budget is a mockery, because it doesn't deal seriously with the issues," McCurry said. "And so for the moment, we'll leave this to be what it is — a spat among Republicans who can't agree about where they stand on budget issues."

The May 20 markup provided panel Democrats with a forum to try to poke political holes in the GOP plan.

Of the Republicans' penny on a dollar slogan, Spratt said: "That doesn't sound too draconian, but that's true only if you believe that these cuts will come across the board, across the whole budget. But we can't cut interest on the national debt. . . . The chairman doesn't propose cutting Social Security, he doesn't propose cutting national defense."

Democrats said that after such programs are placed off limits, the resulting cuts in discretionary programs are much deeper than 1 percent. According to Democratic calculations, after adjusting for inflation and population growth, the GOP plan would ultimately cut non-defense appropriations 18 percent. And as is typical of both Democratic and Republican budgets, the toughest cuts would fall at the end. Almost two-thirds would come in fiscal 2002 and 2003.

As is usually the case — last year was an exception — the drafting of

Budget

the fiscal 1999 resolution was a majority party-only affair. That left Democrats offering amendments designed to point out flaws and promote Democratic initiatives. But with Republicans in lock step opposition, they easily turned back Democratic amendments to reverse the spending cuts, including proposals:

- **IRAs.** By Earl Pomeroy of North Dakota, to drop language permitting the creation of surplus-financed IRAs to supplement Social Security. It was rejected, 19-20.
- **Child care.** By Lloyd Doggett of Texas, to finance Clinton initiatives to boost funding for child care grants and tax credits. It was rejected, 17-21.
- **Appropriations.** By Alan B. Mollohan of West Virginia, to restore the $46 billion cut in discretionary appropriations by reducing the tax cuts by an equal amount. It was rejected, 17-22.

Just before the end of the markup, Kasich thanked all Republicans for helping him advance the resolution, despite reservations among the rank and file and prior skepticism from House leaders. Clearly relieved, Kasich said after the session, "Three weeks ago you would have said it probably couldn't have been done."

House GOP Musters Votes To Pass Budget

JUNE 6 — House Republican leaders used an all-out whip effort June 5 to pass their long-overdue fiscal 1999 budget resolution.

The House passed the budget blueprint (H Con Res 284) by a vote of 216-204 — a tally that required an all-out drive by GOP leaders, who encountered significant resistance from moderates, appropriators and defense hawks in the days and hours preceding the vote. Ultimately, several Republicans who had earlier declared that they would oppose the measure came back into line.

House passage of the non-binding budget measure represents the high-water mark for Budget Committee Chairman John R. Kasich's drive to cut spending below levels agreed to in last year's balanced-budget pact to finance an election-year tax cut.

A sizable minority of the GOP rank and file was indifferent or hostile to Kasich's effort to cut $101 billion in spending over five years. It was only after an exhaustive effort led by Majority Whip Tom DeLay, R-Texas, that the measure mustered the votes to pass.

Debate on the annual budget lacked the passion of 1995, when Republicans launched their bold deficit-cutting drive over bitter and politically potent objections from Democrats. Nor did it have the historic overtones of last year's bipartisan balanced-budget effort. (*1995 Almanac*, p. 2-3)

Even the most ardent supporters of Kasich's budget acknowledge that little of it is likely to find its way into a subsequent — and binding — reconciliation bill. It appeared that many lawmakers were merely going through the motions. "It's not going anywhere," said a senior GOP lawmaker, who was nonetheless attending strategy meetings and helping line up votes.

In many ways, the Kasich plan has been overtaken by events. The Appropriations committees have already started to advance the fiscal 1999 round of 13 spending bills at levels set under last year's balanced-budget law (PL 105-33) instead of at the slightly more austere figures envisioned by Kasich, R-Ohio. And the issue that is driving the House effort — elimination of the so-called marriage tax penalty — has come alive on tobacco legislation (S 1415) that is advancing slowly through the Senate.

Key senators such as Budget Committee Chairman Pete V. Domenici, R-N.M., have done little to hide their disdain for the Kasich budget, which would require deep cuts from already cash-strapped appropriations accounts, does not account for the recently passed transportation bill (HR 2400) and recommends politically untenable cuts in mandatory spending programs such as welfare and Medicaid. "They're not going to cut Medicare," said a top Domenici aide. "What else is there? You're not going to go back to Medicaid. . . . You're not going to go back to welfare reform. . . . It ain't there."

Domenici's staff took the unusual step of criticizing the House plan in a weekly newsletter. An entry in the Senate Budget Committee's May 26 "Budget Bulletin" was headlined: "House Budget Resolution Ignores Highway Bill, 1999 Caps."

It appears increasingly doubtful that any tax-cutting effort will be financed by another round of sizable spending cuts. Instead, lawmakers are looking at tapping into tobacco-related revenues to pay for easing the marriage penalty. Others, including Rep. Bill Archer, R-Texas, chairman of the tax-writing Ways and Means Committee, want to pay for another tax-cutting round by using part of the budget surplus, which the Office of Management and Budget projects at $54 billion in fiscal 1999.

Kasich publicly pitched his plan as requiring only modest belt-tightening. Federal spending under his budget would total $9 trillion from fiscal 1999 through 2003, only $101 billion less than would be provided under the 1997 budget deal. But most of the budget, including Social Security, defense and interest payments on the national debt, is exempt from cuts. Savings from the leftover domestic programs are difficult to make, a point that was drilled home when Kasich was forced to rewrite his plan to drop $10 billion in proposed savings from the Medicare health insurance program for the elderly and disabled.

Kasich submitted a substitute plan to the House Rules Committee late June 3 that served as the vehicle for floor debate. The Medicare cuts were replaced with proposed cuts from income security programs such as welfare block grants to the states, a development that drew the ire of the nation's governors and key architects of the 1996 welfare overhaul law (PL 104-193) such as E. Clay Shaw Jr., R-Fla.

"Welfare reform is the most successful Republican program that's out there. For us to cut it would be a terrible mistake," Shaw said. "I'm very optimistic that this figure will not hold through conference."

Kasich also dropped from the original resolution language that would have permitted the budget surplus to be used to establish federally subsidized personal retirement accounts to supplement Social Security, a top goal of Kasich and Speaker Newt Gingrich, R-Ga. Congress recently passed a bill (HR 3546) to establish a commission to study ways to shore up the Social Security system, and Clinton and Congress are expected to turn to the issue in 1999.

Before passing the Kasich plan, the

Appropriators Balk at Herculean Task Of Finding Kasich His Savings

JUNE 6 — House GOP leaders finally passed their long-overdue budget plan, but that does not mean the Republican faithful are any closer to delivering an election-year tax cut to the voters.

Next comes a more difficult task: constructing and passing a so-called budget-reconciliation bill to turn House Budget Committee Chairman John R. Kasich's non-binding budget blueprint (H Con Res 284) into law.

Budget reconciliation — the process that implemented last year's budget — requires the authorizing committees, which make policy, to produce savings from mandatory programs that can then be used to cut taxes. Under the terms of the Kasich plan, the authorizing committees would have three weeks to produce $55 billion in five-year savings.

They cannot do it, say senior staff aides. Asked whether the Banking and Financial Services Committee could cut funding for flood insurance, a senior GOP committee aide said: "It's going to be very hard."

How about charging airlines fees on takeoff and landing slots ($2.5 billion) or increasing fees on the federal inland waterway system ($2 billion)? "None of those ideas have ever gone anywhere in the House or Senate," said a House Republican staff aide to the Transportation and Infrastructure Committee.

The problem bedeviling Kasich, R-Ohio, is that almost all the politically viable savings were grabbed by last year's budget bill (PL 105-33). Most of what is left over was claimed by the big highway bill (HR 2400) that is on President Clinton's desk or by an agriculture research and food stamp bill (S 1150) that the House cleared June 4. That takes about $15 billion in savings envisioned by Kasich off the table.

What is left? The big pots of mandatory spending include such politically sensitive programs as Medicare, welfare and Medicaid. They are not going to face cuts in an election year, said a top Senate Budget Committee staff aide. If anything, the pressure is to reverse small parts of the 1996 welfare overhaul law (PL 104-193) by, for example, restoring food stamp benefits to the most vulnerable legal immigrants.

"They're not going to cut Medicare. What else is there?" queries the aide.

With mandatory savings so elusive, Kasich is seeking $46 billion in cuts in discretionary spending — the one-third of the budget doled out by the Appropriations committees each year — to finance tax cuts.

Even if appropriators would accept that, which is unlikely, it is against the rules to use cuts in appropriations to offset tax cuts. It would permit Senate Democrats to kill the reconciliation bill on a point of order.

House defeated substitute plans that would have:

● **Democratic alternative.** Generally hewed to last year's budget deal, while providing for $10 billion in Clinton initiatives over five years to reduce classroom size, permit senior citizens to buy into Medicare and boost child care efforts. Tax cuts of $30 billion would have been financed by closing tax "loopholes." It was rejected, 164-257, June 5.

● **Conservative Action Team.** Cut taxes by $150 billion over five years, increased defense spending by $86 billion over Kasich's plan, and limited growth in federal spending to the rate of inflation (2.6 percent), which would require budget cuts of $145 billion below Kasich's budget. It was rejected, 158-262, on June 5.

House leaders did not permit the so-called Blue Dog Democrats, a group of moderates, to offer their plan, which closely mirrored both the Senate budget resolution (S Con Res 86) and last year's budget pact. Several moderate Republicans expressed an interest in the plan, but GOP leaders feared it might pass.

Conservatives In Senate Back House's Tax Cuts

JUNE 13 — A difficult negotiation lies ahead for House and Senate Republican leaders seeking to reconcile differences over their fiscal 1999 budget plans. Conflicting promises made to opposite wings of the party as they scrambled to pass their competing budgets will be impossible to keep.

To get their ambitious plan (H Con Res 84) to cut spending and taxes by $101 billion over the next five years through the House, Republican leaders assured moderates that the final version would be scaled back.

But that conflicts with promises made by Senate Majority Leader Trent Lott, R-Miss., more than two months ago when he bowed to a band of conservatives who threatened to scuttle the Senate's more moderate plan, which sticks closely to last year's balanced-budget pact. Led by John Ashcroft, R-Mo., the group was quick to remind Lott that he promised the final House-Senate compromise would reflect the House's significantly higher tax cut goal. The Senate-passed budget plan (S Con Res 86) contains no net tax cut, but makes room for $30 billion in cuts with offsets.

"Given your pledge of last April, we expect the Senate delegation to request and accept no less than $101 billion in tax cuts over the next five years," the Senate conservatives wrote

Budget

in a June 9 letter to Lott. The Senate conservatives issued no ultimatums as they left a June 11 meeting with Lott, but the House Conservative Action Team did: "We will oppose any budget conference report that does not contain at least [$101 billion] in tax relief," the group wrote in a June 10 letter to Lott.

But Senate Budget Committee Chairman Pete V. Domenici, R-N.M., has made little effort to hide how much he dislikes the House budget plan, assembled by Budget Committee Chairman John R. Kasich, R-Ohio.

"I am dead set against cuts of that magnitude," Domenici said. He and Senate Appropriations Chairman Ted Stevens, R-Alaska, are adamant that the discretionary appropriations will not be cut below spending "caps" set by last year's budget law (PL 105-33).

Domenici left open the question of whether the House and Senate — for the first time since the Budget Act (PL 93-344) was passed in 1974 — might be unable to agree on a final budget.

Assuming a deal can be reached, an even more difficult task awaits: assembling a budget-reconciliation bill to implement the spending and tax cuts recommended by the non-binding budget resolution. The Republican goal is to ease the so-called marriage tax penalty. An amendment by Sen. Phil Gramm, R-Texas, to alleviate the marriage penalty for couples with incomes under $50,000 per year was added to the Senate tobacco bill (S 1415) on June 10. The Senate's move raises the possibility that the tobacco bill would become the de facto budget vehicle that carries the GOP's tax agenda.

It is plain that the final version of the annual budget resolution will have to end up somewhere between the competing Domenici and Kasich documents. "They couldn't pass theirs without promising the conservatives on tax cuts. We couldn't pass ours without promising the moderates on spending cuts," said House Ways and Means Committee spokesman Ari Fleischer. "If that's not the basis for compromise, what is?"

Lott weighed in June 8 with a call for tax cuts of $60 billion to $70 billion, about the same figures discussed in April when he promised to accept whatever the House passed. "But you also have to deal with getting the votes," Lott said of his moderate wing.

House leaders were able to pass the $101 billion plan only by promising moderates that it would be changed. For example, to obtain the votes of moderates such as Fred Upton, R-Mich., Kasich at the last minute dropped $10 billion in Medicare savings from his budget, replacing them with equal cuts from income security accounts. But those cuts will also have to be scaled back, a promise won by moderates such as E. Clay Shaw Jr., R-Fla.

Moreover, Kasich's budget includes about $15 billion in savings that has already been claimed by other legislation, including the highway law (PL 105-178) signed by President Clinton on June 9.

Budget Forecast Renews GOP Hope for Tax Cuts

JULY 18 — Yet another upward surge in forecasts of a big budget surplus is tempting GOP lawmakers to tap part of it for an election year tax cut.

But the rosy budget picture — surpluses projected to total $520 billion over the next five years — does little to lower the political and logistical hurdles that stand in the way of a Republican tax-cutting drive.

A prerequisite for any serious tax cut effort would be to pass the long-overdue fiscal 1999 budget resolution. But talks between Senate Budget Committee Chairman Pete V. Domenici, R-N.M., and his House counterpart, John R. Kasich, R-Ohio, have yielded little progress.

Domenici and Kasich have a fundamental philosophical difference about the budget. Domenici wants — and the Senate passed — a budget resolution (S Con Res 86) that sticks closely to last year's balanced-budget pact. Kasich, a potential presidential candidate in 2000, is pushing a five-year, $101 billion spending and tax cut plan (H Con Res 284) that would break with last year's budget deal, which promised President Clinton higher domestic spending in exchange for a GOP-driven tax cut.

When Domenici and Kasich met July 14 for the first time since the July Fourth recess, Domenici offered a plan for a modified budget-reconciliation bill that could produce a tax cut as high as $70 billion through 2003. But the plan would ignore most of Kasich's controversial spending cuts and leave it to the Senate Finance and House Ways and Means committees, which share jurisdiction over taxes and entitlement programs such as Medicare and Medicaid, to produce the offsetting spending cuts.

Top GOP leaders have made it plain that they have no appetite for sizable reductions in such programs. And there is equal distaste among Republican moderates for the considerable cuts in discretionary appropriations called for by the House.

Domenici devised his plan to give conservatives who favor cuts and moderates who oppose them a vehicle that both could support. It would avoid committing to cuts of a specific size while paving the way for a budget and tax bill to flesh out the non-binding blueprint set forth by the budget resolution. "It just kicks the can further down the dusty road," said a top Domenici staff aide.

Kasich and Ways and Means Committee Chairman Bill Archer, R-Texas, reacted coolly to Domenici's idea. "We can't end up with any decent tax bill on that basis," Archer said.

CBO Forecasts

The uncertain budget picture was muddied further July 15 when the Congressional Budget Office (CBO) issued its revised surplus forecasts. The scorekeeping agency projects a budget surplus for fiscal 1998 of $63 billion. More significantly, projected surpluses in future years would rise impressively above prior predictions. For fiscal 1999, for example, CBO foresees an $80 billion surplus, rising to $139 billion in fiscal 2002.

The surplus forecast came as welcome news to Republicans frustrated by severe splits in the party over the budget, and it reignited calls to use part of the surplus for a tax cut.

House Speaker Newt Gingrich, R-Ga., who has vacillated over the question of whether to use some of the surplus to finance a tax bill, again shifted course to embrace the idea.

"In light of these new estimates, we hope the administration will work with us to phase out the marriage penalty, cut the capital gains tax and eliminate the [estate] tax altogether," Gingrich said July 15. Easing the so-called marriage penalty, under which about 21 million married couples pay higher taxes than they would if they filed as singles, is at the top of Republicans' election year tax agenda.

Testing the Waters

The difficulty in producing a budget was illustrated by Domenici's recent effort to test the Senate's appetite for cutting spending along the lines envisioned by the House. He and Majority Leader Trent Lott, R-Miss., met with several chairmen of authorizing committees — including Banking, Commerce and Energy — to see whether their panels could contribute savings to a budget-reconciliation bill. Not surprisingly, they received an unenthusiastic response.

Said Banking Chairman Alfonse M. D'Amato, R-N.Y., of Kasich's bid to raise flood insurance premiums: "It will not see the light of day."

Energy Chairman Frank H. Murkowski, R-Alaska, just as breezily dismissed a House proposal to sell several regional power marketing administrations. "Obviously there's not enough support in the committee," Murkowski said.

A top GOP aide said Domenici anticipated those responses and wanted to impress upon Lott the difficulty of moving beyond the Senate's stand-pat budget resolution. Lott has promised conservatives that the final budget resolution will tilt significantly toward the House plan, but it may not be a promise he can deliver.

With two to three weeks remaining before Congress' August recess and about a month left after members return in September, time is running short for Republicans to agree among themselves and negotiate with Clinton. So far there have been no serious talks with Clinton about a deal that could give both sides a victory. Any such effort would be likely to follow the model that worked last year, which allowed Clinton higher domestic spending in exchange for GOP-supported tax cuts.

But Republicans have yet to show interest in dealing with the White House. To the contrary, most of them view sticking with stringent "caps" on appropriations as sacrosanct. House Republicans have rejected efforts by appropriators to get around the caps by designating certain programs — such as fixing the federal government's year 2000 computer woes — as emergency spending not subject to the caps.

At the same time, Clinton is resisting tax cuts and may be poised to extract several billion dollars in the appropriations end game, an outcome that some Republicans privately acknowledge would suit them. "The caps are too tight," said a top Republican aide to the House Appropriations Committee.

Also driving the debate is election year politics. Many Republicans want to appeal to their core voters and view concessions to Clinton as likely to cause consternation among an already restless conservative base.

Clinton's February budget called for an ambitious set of spending initiatives in areas such as child care, education, scientific research and Medicare. But Clinton also proposed financing his budget plans largely with revenues gleaned from tobacco legislation (S 1415), an effort that died in the Senate in June. The Republican-crafted fiscal 1999 spending bills that are moving through the House and Senate reject most of Clinton's initiatives.

The Numbers

CBO has come under fire from Republicans for its conservative surplus and economic forecasts. Only six months ago, CBO forecast a small budget deficit for fiscal 1998. But unexpectedly strong tax revenues in the first nine months of fiscal 1998 have brightened the budget picture beyond lawmakers' dreams when they passed last year's balanced-budget and tax laws (PL 105-33, PL 105-34).

Even more important than the fiscal 1998 surplus are projections for future years — those covered by any potential tax legislation. CBO's predicted surplus of $80 billion for fiscal 1999 is more than double its prediction of only two months ago. Similar figures are forecast for fiscal 2000 and 2001.

By 2002, when 1997's budget agreement was originally expected to achieve balance, the surplus would rise to $139 billion. Total surpluses from fiscal 1998 through 2008 would add up to $1.6 trillion.

Still, until fiscal 2005, the surplus would accumulate because the surplus in the "off-budget" portion of the budget — mainly Social Security revenues in excess of benefits — would run well in excess of $100 billion a year. This is a delicate area for lawmakers. Democrats have made the politically potent argument that any tax cut financed by the Social Security surplus would weaken the system and threaten beneficiaries. Republican budget hawks such as Rep. Mark W. Neumann of Wisconsin agree.

But in fiscal 2006, CBO predicts the government would run an operating surplus of $44 billion, money that Republicans would like to return to voters.

"With a whopping $1.5 trillion surplus over 10 years, we can preserve, protect and strengthen Social Security while also passing significant tax relief for hard-working Americans," Gingrich said.

Chambers Remain Divided Over Budget, Taxes

AUGUST 1 — House and Senate Republicans are heading toward a September showdown as they go separate ways in trying to fashion an election year tax agenda, imperiling prospects for getting any tax legislation to President Clinton's desk.

A philosophical chasm separates the two bodies. The Senate, as it departed Washington for the August recess, was no closer to agreement with the House over budget and tax issues than it was months ago.

"I'm willing to sit down and talk about anything, but we're very, very far apart," Senate Budget Committee Chairman Pete V. Domenici, R-N.M., told reporters July 29. "It seems to me that we are farther apart now than when we began."

At the core of the disagreement is what to do with a budget surplus projected to total $1.6 trillion over the next 10 years. House GOP leaders want to dedicate about half of the surplus to cutting taxes — although they appear more enthusiastic than many in

Budget

$70 Billion Budget Surplus

OCTOBER 31 — What to do with the first budget surplus since 1969 was an issue that tied lawmakers in knots all year. In the end, a $70 billion fiscal 1998 surplus ended up in the bank, taking a nibble out of the $5.5 trillion national debt.

President Clinton announced the official surplus Oct. 28. Only last year, Clinton and GOP lawmakers thought it would take until 2002 for their budget pact (PL 105-33) to produce balance, much less such a large surplus.

But the booming economy produced an impressive surge in tax revenues, which were largely responsible for a surplus that only the most optimistic economists had foreseen. To a lesser extent, reduced spending for "safety net" programs such as welfare and food stamps contributed to the favorable numbers.

The budget picture brightened steadily all year, sometimes leaving Republican leaders, especially in the House, uncertain about what to do with it. When they tried to cut taxes, Clinton easily scuttled their plans with the potent political argument that any tax cuts should wait until Social Security is overhauled, perhaps next year.

Both the White House's Office of Management and Budget and the Congressional Budget Office (CBO) say budget surpluses will grow steadily into the next century. CBO forecasts a fiscal 1999 surplus of $80 billion, with surpluses for 2000 and 2001 about that level, then rising to $139 billion in 2002.

Those estimates were issued in August, before Congress and the White House went on a $21 billion year-end spending spree, passing a surplus-financed emergency package as part of the omnibus fiscal 1999 appropriations bill (HR 4328 — PL 105-277).

Economists caution that an unexpected downturn could reverse the budget picture. In an $8 trillion economy, small changes can produce wild swings in surplus or deficit projections.

the rank and file. Senate Republicans are fashioning a plan that would delay any major tax cut until after the Social Security system is overhauled in 1999.

Social Security is at the center of the debate because almost all of the surplus would be made up of surplus Social Security revenues in the system's trust funds. Democrats are poised to depict any surplus-driven tax cut as a raid on Social Security, although the situation is more subtle than that. Social Security funds are segregated from the rest of the federal budget, but the program's surpluses are part of the government's overall surplus or deficit picture.

Still, sensitive that any tax cut could be seen as undercutting Social Security, Domenici, Phil Gramm, R-Texas, and Majority Leader Trent Lott, R-Miss., among others, are shaping a proposal that would build a sturdier "fire wall" to protect Social Security trust funds. Under the plan, any significant tax bill would await a determination of how much money was needed to shore up Social Security, with anything left over devoted to tax cuts.

In the House, Republican leaders remained united in their intention to advance a tax bill that would provide as much as $167 billion in tax relief over five years and $700 billion over 10 years. The figure was derived from calculations by Budget Committee Chairman John R. Kasich, R-Ohio. Kasich proposes to devote that part of the surplus equal to excess Social Security payroll taxes to the trust funds while reserving an amount equal to Social Security interest revenues for tax cuts.

House leaders say their plan would devote every penny of Social Security taxes to the trust funds, which are made up of more than $650 billion in government bonds. An amount equal to about $44 billion in annual interest income would be devoted to tax cuts, although the interest would still be reinvested in the trust funds as under current law. Any tax cut would be financed by other revenues and by devoting less of the surplus to buying down debt held by the public.

"The tax cut would still come out of revenues generated by the rest of the government other than Social Security," said a top House Budget Committee staff aide.

In the Senate, the still-evolving proposal would invest some or all of Social Security surpluses into private debt instruments as a way to guarantee that the government will not spend the money. Under current policy, the government borrows from the Social Security trust funds to finance its other operations, which critics say amounts to spending the Social Security surplus. Defenders of the system say that there is no more secure investment than government bonds and that it is inconceivable that the government would not redeem the bonds when it has to tap the trust funds to pay Social Security benefits.

GOP Acrimony

House leaders briefed top Senate Republicans on their proposal July 22 at a meeting that quickly turned acrimonious. Moderate and conservative senators attacked the plan as bad politics and bad policy. A common refrain among Senate Republicans was that Social Security must be fixed before tax cuts — as proposed by Clinton in January.

Budget process rules would allow Senate Democrats to kill any attempt to use the surplus to cut taxes, but not before they and Clinton hammer away at Republicans on Social Security.

"Some of this is the realization among the Republicans in the Senate that they are setting themselves up to be clobbered by the president," said former Congressional Budget Office Director Robert D. Reischauer, now a senior fellow with the Brookings Institution.

House Republicans are frustrated because they believe that tax cuts are a winner with voters and that unless taxes are cut, Congress and Clinton will devote the surplus to new spending programs. They were not expecting such raw skepticism from the Senate.

"I don't think they anticipated what we had to say," said Sen. Connie Mack, R-Fla., a conservative who nevertheless preaches caution on surplus-financed tax cuts.

Absent any substantive progress on taxes, two Senate conservatives, John Ashcroft, R-Mo., and Sam Brownback, R-Kan., forced a symbolic vote on the leading GOP tax issue, eliminating the so-called marriage penalty on two-income couples. By a 48-51 vote July 29, the Senate refused to kill an amendment to the fiscal 1999 Treasury-Postal Service appropriations bill (S 2312) to eliminate the marriage penalty. The two senators subsequently withdrew the amendment. *(Vote 242, p. S-38)*

In the House, the specific size and content of any tax bill has yet to take shape. Specifics will not be ready before September, despite some conservatives' wish to pass a bill they can brag about to their constituents over the upcoming recess. Instead, Republicans will try to use the issue to whip up grass-roots support and appeal to their conservative base over the break.

"We're still doing a lot of preliminary thinking about what we want to do on taxes, mainly in terms of the aggregate size of the package," said House Ways and Means Committjee Chairman Bill Archer, R-Texas.

But Republican leaders may be ahead of the rank and file. Moderates such as Reps. Amo Houghton, R-N.Y., and Michael N. Castle, R-Del., support fiscal caution and would almost certainly be unwilling to back a bill as big as envisioned by their leaders. Kasich and others have done little to sell the sketchy plan to the GOP Conference.

Many House Republicans prefer paying down the $5.6 trillion national debt to cutting taxes. And many are hearing the same message from voters.

Moderate Rodney Frelinghuysen, R-N.J., for example, sent his constituents a questionnaire about what they want Congress to do on budget and tax issues. Of those who responded, 48 percent preferred reducing the national debt, 14 percent wanted to replenish Social Security trust funds, and only 13 percent wanted a tax cut, he said.

Alternatives

After the heated meeting, no substantive negotiations between House and Senate Republicans took place the week of July 27. Republicans acknowledge the possibility that Congress may adjourn for the year without passing the annual budget resolution.

Asked whether the House and Senate could come together on the budget, Majority Whip Don Nickles, R-Okla., said: "I'd like to say yes, but I'm not sure that we will."

Other than avoiding the embarrassment of not passing a budget resolution, the only pressing reason for one would be to permit the Senate to consider a budget-reconciliation bill as a vehicle for a tax cut. Such bills are the only Senate measures not subject to a filibuster.

The other option would be to take up a free-standing tax bill subject to a filibuster. "It's still very much my intention to try to see if we can't pass a tax cut this year," Nickles said. "We may do it without reconciliation."

Another option under consideration by the Senate — admittedly a long shot — would be to create surplus-financed retirement savings accounts to supplement Social Security benefits. The idea is also backed by Kasich and House Speaker Newt Gingrich, R-Ga. ◆

Few Lawmakers Grieve As Supreme Court Justices Give Line-Item Veto the Ax

Few in Congress shed any tears when the Supreme Court struck down the 1996 Line Item Veto Act (PL 104-130), which gave the president the power to kill individual items in appropriations bills.

SUMMARY

The court struck down the new law — one of the few "Contract With America" bills that President Clinton had eagerly signed — in a 6-3 decision on June 25, 1998. The ruling capped years of debate over whether Congress could, by statute, transfer such potentially sweeping power over the lawmaking process to the president.

To the delight of Sen. Robert C. Byrd, D-W.Va., and other fervent foes, the court declared the law unconstitutional because it permitted the president to rewrite bills that he had already signed. Under the Constitution, the president must accept or reject bills in their entirety.

Congress is unlikely to try to revive the line-item veto in the new political climate based on a budget surplus, after decades of deficits. To do so, it would either have to pass a constitutional amendment or enact a milder version of the bill. One such version, backed by Senate Budget Committee Chairman Pete V. Domenici, R-N.M., would require Congress to vote on the president's proposed line-item vetoes, which would not take effect automatically, as under the 1996 law.

The court ruling capped a two-year

Box Score

- **Bill:** HR 2631— PL 105-159
- **House action:** The House voted to override Clinton's veto of the disapproval bill (HR 2631), 347-69, on Feb. 5.
- **Senate action:** The Senate voted to override Clinton's veto, 78-20, on Feb. 25.

experiment with the new veto tool, which presidents since Ulysses S. Grant had sought. Supporters of the line-item veto said it would curb the practice of slipping "pork barrel" spending into huge appropriations bills that presidents have little choice but to accept. Opponents said it gave away too much of Congress' power of the purse and handed the executive branch a club with which to beat Congress on other issues.

As used by Clinton, however, the veto did not become a club, nor did it

Key Points of Hogan's Ruling

FEBRUARY 14 — U.S. District Judge Thomas F. Hogan ruled Feb. 12 that the line-item veto law (PL 104-130) is unconstitutional. The following are excerpts from his ruling:

"... the Court finds ... that the Line Item Veto Act violates the procedural requirements ordained in Article I of the United States Constitution and impermissibly upsets the balance of powers so carefully prescribed by its Framers. The Line Item Veto Act therefore is unconstitutional."

On procedural requirements: "The Constitution carefully prescribes certain formal procedures that must be observed in the enactment of laws. The Line Item Veto Act impermissibly attempts to alter these constitutional requirements through mere legislative action. ...

"Article I, section 7 of the Constitution sets forth dual requirements for the enactment of statutes: bicameral passage and presentment to the President. ...

"The Constitution requires that both the amendment and repeal of statutes also conform with these Article I requirements."

"Here, while the initial passage of the Balanced Budget Act and the Taxpayer Relief Act complied with the Article I requirements, the Line Item Veto Act then authorized the President to violate those requirements by producing laws that had not adhered to those requirements. ... The laws that resulted after the President's line-item veto were different from those consented to by both Houses of Congress. There is no way of knowing whether these laws, in their truncated form, would have received the requisite support from both the House and the Senate. Because the laws that emerged after the Line Item Veto are not the same laws that proceeded through the legislative process, as required, the resulting laws are not valid.

"Furthermore, the President violated the requirements of Article I when he unilaterally canceled provisions of duly enacted statutes. Unilateral action by any single participant in the law-making process is precisely what Bicameralism and Presentment Clauses were designed to prevent. Once a bill becomes law, it can only be repealed or amended through another, independent legislative enactment, which itself must conform with the requirements of Article I. Any rescissions must be agreed upon by a majority of both Houses of Congress."

"Congress knew that a simple Line Item Veto, performed prior to the President's signature, would violate Article I's requirement that the president sign or return the bills in toto. ... This limitation on the President has been clear since George Washington's tenure. ... Congress cannot evade this long-accepted requirement by merely changing the timing of the President's cancellation."

On separation of powers: "Furthermore, the Line Item Veto Act is unconstitutional because it impermissibly disrupts the balance of powers among the three branches of government. The separation of powers into three coordinate branches is central to the principles on which this country was founded. ...

"Pursuant to the doctrine of separated powers, certain functions are divided between the legislative and executive branches. Article I, section 1 vests all legislative authority in Congress. ... With regard to lawmaking, the President's function is strictly a negative one: to veto a bill in its entirety.

"... Congress can delegate certain rulemaking authority to other branches. ... Congress may not, however, delegate its inherent lawmaking authority. ...

"The line between permissible delegations of rulemaking authority and impermissible abandonments of lawmaking power is a thin one. ...

"The Line Item Veto Act impermissibly crosses the line between acceptable delegations of rulemaking authority and unauthorized surrender to the President of an inherently legislative function, namely, the authority to permanently shape laws and package legislation. The Act enables the President ... to pick and choose among portions of an enacted law to determine which ones will remain valid. The Constitution, however, dictates that once a bill becomes law, the President's sole duty is to 'take care that the laws be faithfully executed.' His power cannot expand to that of 'co-designer' of the law — that is Congress' domain."

---

curb Congress' appetite for parochial pet projects. He first used it against three obscure provisions in the 1997 balanced-budget and tax laws (PL 105-33, PL 105-34), which generated the successful constitutional challenge.

When the first of the fiscal 1998 spending bills was sent to the White House in the autumn of 1997, Clinton provoked outrage with his vetoes of numerous military construction projects. Later, he used the new tool more delicately, taking care not to alienate powerful allies or enemies and limiting his vetoes to projects that were parochial or even downright silly. He never tried to use veto threats to win votes on unrelated issues. Clinton's desire not to alienate lawmakers weighing a big vote on a "fast track" trade initiative may have prompted him to use the veto with a light touch.

Congress' only challenge to Clinton's line-item vetoes came in response to his military construction vetoes, which totaled 38 projects worth $287 million. Using a mechanism built into the line-item veto law, both chambers passed a subsequent bill to overturn the cuts. After Clinton vetoed that bill (HR 2631) in 1997, both chambers voted in 1998 to override his veto. It was only the second time a Clinton veto had been overridden. (The first was a 1995 law, PL 104-67, to curb securities litigation.)

District Judge Hits Line-Item Veto

FEBRUARY 14 — For the second time in less than a year, a federal judge has tossed out a 1996 law that gave President Clinton the line-item veto.

In a Feb. 12 decision, U.S. District Judge Thomas F. Hogan ruled that the 1996 law was an "unauthorized surrender to the president of an inherently legislative function, namely, the authority to permanently shape laws and package legislation."

If upheld by the Supreme Court, the ruling would rob Clinton of his power to strike individual provisions from tax and spending bills without vetoing the entire bill. The 1996 law (PL 104-130) was one of the landmark accomplishments of the war-torn 104th Congress and one of the few issues upon which Clinton and the new GOP congressional majority could agree. *(1996 Almanac, p. 2-28)*

The White House will appeal the decision directly to the Supreme Court, which will probably decide the case during its current term, ending around June 30. Last June, the high court reversed a similar ruling by U.S. District Judge Thomas Penfield Jackson on a lawsuit filed by six members of Congress, holding that they lacked legal standing to sue because they had not been directly harmed by the line-item veto law.

But the plaintiffs in the two cases before Hogan, *City of New York v. Clinton* and *Snake River Potato Growers Inc. v. Rubin*, stood to benefit from provisions that Clinton struck from last year's twin tax and spending bills (PL 105-34, PL 105-33).

"In the simplest terms, Plaintiffs had a benefit and the President took that benefit away," Hogan wrote of the New York City case. "That is injury."

The constitutionality of the line-item veto law has been in doubt since Congress passed it two years ago. The law permits the president to "cancel" new entitlement programs and special interest tax breaks that meet certain criteria. It also gives him new power to rescind individual items in appropriations bills, and Clinton was active in using that power on fiscal 1998 spending bills.

Under the line-item veto law, presidential actions take effect automatically unless Congress passes a bill to overturn them — and the president can veto that bill.

Core Argument

The core of the argument against the law is that it permits the president to revise a bill after he has already signed it into law. The Constitution permits the president only to accept or reject bills in their entirety, not change them after they arrive at his desk.

"The president cannot single-handedly revise the work of the other two participants [the House and Senate] in the lawmaking process, as he did here when he vetoed certain provisions of these statutes," Hogan wrote.

Hogan's decision mirrors that of Jackson, who ruled last April that "the power to 'make' the laws of the nation is the exclusive, non-delegable power of Congress." It was that ruling that fell when the Supreme Court said the members of Congress who filed the first lawsuit *(Byrd v. Raines)* did not have standing to sue. The line-item veto had not been used at that time.

One Supreme Court justice, John Paul Stevens, said in his dissent in *Byrd v. Raines* that he also would find the law unconstitutional.

The plaintiffs before Hogan have a firmer claim to standing than the previous plaintiffs, and if the high court agrees with Hogan that they have standing, the matter will be finally decided.

Clinton issued a brief statement following Hogan's ruling: "Although I am disappointed with today's ruling, it is my belief that ultimately the line-item veto will be ruled constitutional by the U.S. Supreme Court."

Challengers

The New York suit protested Clinton's cancellation of a provision in the 1997 budget spending law that would have helped New York state finance its Medicaid program through the use of taxes on health care providers. Hogan noted that the state ultimately could be forced to repay the federal government $2.6 billion if Clinton's veto were allowed to stand. And a portion of that total would have been borne by New York City, the lead plaintiff in the suit.

The second challenge was brought by an Idaho potato farmers' cooperative. Clinton vetoed a provision of the 1997 tax-cut law (PL 105-34) that would have deferred capital gains taxes on the sale of food processing plants to farmer-owned cooperatives. The language permits farmer-owned cooperatives equal footing with corporations when purchasing processing facilities. Corporations can structure such deals as stock swaps to avoid capital gains taxes; cooperatives cannot.

The government argued that there was a long history of the president declining to spend money appropriated by Congress. But legal analysts believed that the use of the line-item veto against tax and "direct spending" provisions gave Clinton, in effect, the ability to repeal tax and spending provisions that had already been enacted.

Hogan rejected the government's contention that the president's actions did not amount to a real "veto" of legislative provisions and that they remained on the books, even though they had been rendered to have "no legal force or effect." He cited the famed aphorism used by the late Richard Cardinal Cushing: "When I see a bird that walks like a duck and swims like a duck and quacks like a duck, I call that bird a duck."

The government argued that Congress had the right to delegate to the president the authority to rescind portions of a law.

But the judge disagreed. "Congress may not . . . delegate its inherent lawmaking authority," Hogan wrote.

Clinton's Struggles

While Clinton eagerly sought the veto power, he seemed to struggle over how extensively to wield it. For example, when he issued the line-item vetoes at issue in these cases, he said he found some merit in both provisions.

And Clinton got himself into trouble with many lawmakers when he subsequently used line-item vetoes on nine of last year's appropriations bills. Only last week, the House voted to override Clinton's veto of a bill (HR 2631) to reinstate $287 million for 38

Budget

projects that Clinton struck last year from the fiscal 1998 military construction spending law (PL 105-45).

Bipartisan outrage about those vetoes seemed to prompt Clinton to be more cautious on subsequent spending bills. He was also cautious last fall to avoid alienating members whose votes he was trying to corral to renew his "fast track" trade negotiating authority.

History

Presidents dating to Ulysses S. Grant have asked for the line-item veto, but the idea gained renewed currency when Ronald Reagan and other Republicans sought it as a weapon against wasteful "pork barrel" spending woven into spending bills.

When Republicans took over Congress in 1995, some senators such as Pete V. Domenici, R-N.M., initially resisted the idea, but the determined efforts of line-item veto advocates such as Sens. John McCain, R-Ariz., and Daniel R. Coats, R-Ind., pushed the measure into law.

The law's most vocal opponent, Sen. Robert C. Byrd, D-W.Va., who sat in Hogan's courtroom during oral arguments, was predictably jubilant: "This is a victory for the American people. It is their Constitution, their republic, and their liberties that have been made more secure."

High Court Hears Arguments On Line-Item Veto

MAY 2 — President Clinton did not use his new line-item veto like a machete to lop tons of "pork" out of spending bills. Nor did he successfully use it to bludgeon lawmakers into supporting his agenda.

Soon, he may not be able to use it at all. The Supreme Court may declare the budget-slicing tool unconstitutional, as have two lower court judges.

During oral arguments on the line-item veto case April 27, several justices appeared poised to join Justice John Paul Stevens in voting to overturn the 1996 line-item veto law (PL 104-130). Stevens said last year he believed it was unconstitutional. A decision is expected before the term ends this summer.

The high court threw out an initial challenge to the law in 1997, ruling that Democratic Sen. Robert C. Byrd of West Virginia and other members who brought the case (*Byrd v. Raines*) did not have legal standing to sue because they had not been injured by the law. Stevens was the only justice to express an opinion on the merits of that case.

Standing remains an issue. At the April 27 arguments, Justice Antonin Scalia questioned whether the plaintiffs in the current combined case (*Clinton v. City of New York, Rubin v. Snake River Potato Growers Inc.*) had been directly injured when Clinton vetoed provisions in last year's balanced- budget and tax laws (PL 105-33, PL 105-34).

The line-item veto law, a key accomplishment of the Republican congressional majority, was struck down by a federal judge for the second time Feb. 12. Judge Thomas F. Hogan said the law gives the president too much lawmaking authority. U.S District Judge Thomas P. Jackson reached a similar conclusion in 1997.

Questions about the law's constitutionality have dogged it since 1995. The law does not let the president strike text from bills when he signs them, which lawmakers thought would breach the constitutional requirement that the president accept or reject legislation in its entirety. Instead, the law uses "enhanced rescissions," permitting the president to automatically cancel certain tax and entitlement provisions and rescind appropriated items unless Congress passes a subsequent bill to overturn him.

But Hogan ruled that enhanced rescissions violated the requirement on accepting or rejecting bills in their entirety. "Once a bill becomes law, it can only be repealed or amended through another, independent legislative enactment," Hogan wrote.

Oral Arguments

Charles Cooper, a Reagan-era assistant attorney general who represented New York City, told the high court that Clinton had unilaterally repealed a provision of last year's budget law that would have helped New York finance its share of the Medicaid program.

"A measure that ... effectively repeals a law must follow the same process in Congress that an enactment of a law follows, which is passage by a majority of both houses and presentment to the president for his approval," Cooper said. "That is not what happened to the items that were canceled."

Solicitor General Seth P. Waxman defended the line-item veto, saying that Clinton, rather than repealing a law, was using "a limited discretionary authority to execute the law" in killing the New York Medicaid provision and a tax break aimed at making it easier to sell processing plants to farmer-owned cooperatives, such as the potato growers involved in the Snake River case.

But Waxman drew skeptical questions from several justices, who interrupted him repeatedly.

"That sounds to me like legislating," said Justice Ruth Bader Ginsburg as Waxman defended the use of the line-item veto against the tax provision on farmer-owned cooperatives. It was part of the tax code for several days last August before Clinton canceled it, leaving it with "no legal force or effect," as spelled out in the line-item veto law.

Several justices appeared sympathetic to the plaintiffs' argument that the use of the veto against the Medicaid and farmer cooperative provisions involved a partial repeal of last year's budget and tax laws.

"What is the constitutional distinction between lawmaking and law repealing?" asked Justice David H. Souter.

The questioning seemed to indicate that the justices, if they ruled on the merits, would agree with Hogan that the law was unconstitutional.

But Scalia and others appeared to doubt that New York City and the Idaho-based farmers' cooperative had standing to sue. The state of New York, which pays for Medicaid jointly with the federal government, did not join in claiming injury, and the tax benefit on the farm provision goes to the seller of the plant, not the purchaser, who brought suit.

"I hate to ask this question, but what's it to you?" Scalia asked Louis R. Cohen, attorney for Snake River Potato Growers Inc., which claims the veto of a tax provision to defer capital gains on the sales of processing plants to farm cooperatives blocked its purchase of a potato processing plant last year. "None of these provisions affect your clients at all."

Cohen said Congress clearly intended the law to help farmers.

Outside the courthouse, lawyers for the plaintiffs expressed confidence. "Their questioning of Waxman was much more severe than of the other two counsels," said former Rep. Bill Orton, D-Utah (1991-97), who represents the Snake River cooperative. "I counted six of the justices who raised serious questions."

The veto was aimed chiefly at appropriated spending, but the case before the court deals with its use to "cancel" limited tax benefits and new direct (mandatory) spending. Congress has long given the president discretion in doling out appropriations. Spending bills contain lump sum allocations and accompanying reports that help guide spending decisions, and the president has had the power to impound, or refuse to spend, appropriations – even though that power was scaled back in 1974. The government argues that using the line-item veto against spending bills is part of this tradition.

On tax and spending provisions, however, the president does not have the kind of flexibility that he has on appropriations. Many legal experts say the use of the veto against a tax bill is unconstitutional because it amounts to a unilateral repeal of part of a law.

The balanced-budget laws came to Clinton before the annual round of 13 fiscal 1998 spending bills. Clinton vetoed only two tax breaks from a list of 79, many of which he supported. He voiced support for the farmers' cooperative tax break when he vetoed it, but said it had been poorly drafted.

Sought for Years

Republicans had sought the line-item veto for years when Democrats controlled Congress and the GOP held the White House. Despite reservations among some senior Republican senators, they pushed the legislation even though they might be giving the line-item veto to a Democratic president. It was a key accomplishment of the 104th Congress.

But many Republicans changed their minds when Clinton started using the new power last summer and fall. Lawmakers were so outraged after he killed 38 projects worth $287 million in the military construction spending law (PL 105-56) that they passed legislation to insist on the spending and overrode Clinton when he vetoed that measure (PL 105-159).

After that scalding on the military construction bill, Clinton used the line-item veto with a lighter hand, vetoing 43 additional projects totaling less than $200 million. He appeared uneasy at the prospect of alienating members whose votes he needed for a major fast-track trade negotiating authority bill (HR 2621), which ultimately failed. A higher proportion of his vetoes fell on GOP-sponsored projects.

On the military construction bill, Clinton applied the line-item vetoes according to a formula that disregarded who sponsored the provision. He ended up vetoing many administration-backed projects. Later, on bigger bills with many tempting targets, Clinton worked from lists of projects identified by the Office of Management and Budget. In paring the lists he often spared projects of Democratic allies and powerful Republican leaders.

Supreme Court Strikes Down Line-Item Veto

JUNE 27 — When historians evaluate Congress' uneasy experiment with the line-item veto, they will examine a law that failed to live up to its advance billing. Under President Clinton, the budget-cutting tool was neither the pork-slashing sword envisioned by proponents nor the presidential club opponents feared would beat Congress into following White House orders.

Nor did the law appear to have any effect on Congress' appetite for parochial pet projects.

Even some Republicans who eagerly voted for the law in 1996 breathed a sigh of relief June 25 when the Supreme Court struck it down in a 6-3 ruling.

Others immediately proffered new bills aimed at giving the president some ability to curb congressional spending. They conceded that these bills had poor prospects. Now that the budget deficit is just a memory, Congress appears less likely to volunteer again to give away part of its cherished power of the purse — which means congressional pork-busters will have to police their colleagues, which they have done previously with limited success.

The court, accepting arguments that opponents had voiced from the onset of debate in 1995, said the law (PL 104-130) was unconstitutional because it permitted the president to rewrite bills he had already signed into law.

"If the Line-Item Veto Act were valid, it would authorize the president to create a different law — one whose text was not voted on by either House of Congress or presented to the president," Justice John Paul Stevens wrote for the court. "If there is to be a new procedure in which the president will play a different role in determining the final text of what may 'become a law,' such change must come not by legislation but through . . . amendment."

The law's opponents were jubilant. Sen. Robert C. Byrd, D-W.Va., who rarely holds a news conference, summoned reporters to declare: "This is a great day for the Constitution of the United States of America. . . . The liberties of the American people have been assured. God save this honorable court!"

Byrd and other opponents had fought for years to block the line-item veto, saying it would shift far too much power from Congress to the president, an argument echoed by Justice Anthony M. Kennedy in a concurring opinion: "Separation of powers was designed to implement a fundamental insight: Concentration of power in the hands of a single branch is a threat to liberty."

The court's decision gave Byrd a victory it denied him a year ago when it threw out Byrd's challenge to the law, saying he did not have legal standing to sue because he had not been directly harmed by the law.

But after Clinton used the power to "cancel" from last year's twin tax and budget laws (PL 105-33, PL 105-34) two narrowly targeted tax breaks and a "direct spending" provision to help the state of New York finance its Medicaid program, two other lawsuits (*Clinton v.*

Excerpts From the Opinions

JUNE 27 — The Supreme Court ruled 6-3 on June 25 that the 1996 line-item veto law (PL 104-130) is unconstitutional. The court said it violated Article I, Section 7 of the Constitution, which says, in part, that every bill "which shall have passed the House of Representatives and the Senate, shall, before it becomes a Law, be presented to the President of the United States; If he approves he shall sign it, but if not he shall return it." The following are excerpts from the majority opinion, written by Justice John Paul Stevens, and from the opinion of Justice Antonin Scalia, who dissented:

From Justice Stevens:

"There is no provision in the Constitution that authorizes the President to enact, to amend, or to repeal statutes. Both Article I and Article II assign responsibilities to the President that directly relate to the lawmaking process, but neither addresses the issue presented by these cases." [Article I allows the president to veto a bill; Article II allows the president to recommend legislation.]

"There are important differences between the President's 'return' of a bill pursuant to Article I, Section 7, and the exercise of the President's cancellation authority pursuant to the Line Item Veto Act. The constitutional return takes place *before* the bill becomes law; the statutory cancellation occurs *after* the bill becomes law. The constitutional return is of the entire bill; the statutory cancellation is of only a part. . . . The Constitution . . . is silent on the subject of unilateral Presidential action that either repeals or amends parts of duly enacted statutes.

"There are powerful reasons for construing constitutional silence on this profoundly important issue as equivalent to an express prohibition. . . . Our first President understood the text of the Presentment Clause as requiring that he either 'approve all the parts of a Bill, or reject it in toto.' What has emerged in these cases from the President's exercise of his statutory cancellation powers, however, are truncated versions of two bills that passed both Houses of Congress. They are not the product of the 'finely wrought' procedure that the Framers designed."

"The Line Item Veto Act authorizes the President himself to effect the repeal of laws, for his own policy reasons, without observing the procedures set out in Article I, Section 7. The fact that Congress intended such a result is of no moment. Although Congress presumably anticipated that the President might cancel some of the items in the Balanced Budget Act and in the Taxpayer Relief Act, Congress cannot alter the procedures set out in Article I, Section 7, without amending the Constitution.

"Neither are we persuaded by the Government's contention that the President's authority to cancel new direct spending and tax benefit items is no greater than his traditional authority to decline to spend appropriated funds. . . . The critical difference between this statute and all of its predecessors . . . is that unlike any of them, this Act gives the President the unilateral power to change the text of duly enacted statutes.

"If the Line Item Veto Act were valid, it would authorize the President to create a different law — one whose text was not voted on by either House of Congress or presented to the President for signature."

From Justice Scalia:

" . . . The President's discretion under the Line Item Veto Act is . . . no broader than the discretion traditionally granted the President in his execution of spending laws."

" . . . there is not a dime's worth of difference between Congress's authorizing the President to *cancel* a spending item, and Congress's authorizing money to be spent on a particular item at the President's discretion. And the latter has been done since the Founding of the Nation."

New York and *Snake River Potato Growers Inc. v. Rubin*) were filed by plaintiffs who had been injured by the vetoes. U.S. District Judge Thomas F. Hogan ruled the law unconstitutional in February; his colleague Thomas Penfield Jackson had ruled in Byrd's favor in 1997 before being reversed by the Supreme Court.

In defending the law's constitutionality, the government argued that Congress was delegating to the president additional discretion to enforce laws, not ceding any lawmaking power. And the president has long had the authority to impound or refuse to spend money appropriated by Congress, although such authority was curtailed in 1974 in response to President Richard M. Nixon's provocations. (*1974 Almanac, p. 145*)

Joining Stevens and Kennedy in striking down the law were Chief Justice William H. Rehnquist and Justices David H. Souter, Clarence Thomas and Ruth Bader Ginsburg.

Justices Antonin Scalia, Stephen G. Breyer and Sandra Day O'Connor dissented. Scalia, reading his dissent from the bench, said the veto power was "entirely in accord with the Constitution." He wrote: "There is not a dime's worth of difference between Congress's authorizing the president to *cancel* a spending item and Congress's authorizing money to be spent on a particular item at the president's discretion."

Presidents dating back to Ulysses S. Grant have yearned for the line-item veto, which permits the executive to strike individual items from bills without having to veto the entire measure. Forty-four governors have the power.

The strongest recent call came from Republican President Ronald Reagan, who complained of having to accept wasteful spending in huge appropriations bills that he had to sign. The veto was a dead letter as long as Democrats controlled Congress, but the idea was a key plank in the House GOP's 1994 "Contract With America," and Republicans overcame their qualms about giving it to Clinton. It was among the few contract items on which Clinton and Congress wholly agreed.

"The decision is a defeat for all Americans," Clinton said. "It deprives the president of a valuable tool for eliminating waste in the federal budget and for enlivening the public debate over how to make the best use of public funds."

Enhanced Rescissions

Giving the president a true line-item veto would require amending the Constitution, which proponents believe is not politically viable. Instead, Republicans devised a procedure in which they significantly strengthened the president's power to rescind spending that he has already approved.

Under this "enhanced rescissions" framework, within five days of signing a bill the president sends a list of proposed rescissions of spending items in appropriations bills or cancellations of narrowly focused tax benefits and new entitlement spending. These cuts automatically take effect unless Congress passes a bill to reverse them. The president can veto such a disapproval bill.

That is exactly what happened after Clinton killed 38 projects worth $287 million last year on the fiscal 1998 military construction law (PL 105-45). Congress overturned the vetoes, many of which were based on out-of-date or faulty information from the Pentagon.

After taking a scalding from lawmakers in both parties, Clinton used the new power much more tentatively, vetoing only projects that seemed difficult to defend, such as $1.9 million to dredge a Mississippi lake for a private marina and conference center.

Clinton and his aides also refrained from threatening members' projects to get them to vote for his priorities, such as his failed bid to renew "fast track" trade negotiating authority. "The potential was there" for such threats, said a senior aide to House Minority Leader Richard A. Gephardt, D-Mo., "it just wasn't used."

Nor was there any horse trading on spending decisions. When former Office of Management and Budget Director Franklin D. Raines offered during negotiations on the fiscal 1998 defense spending bill (PL 105-56) to forgo any vetoes in exchange for funding of administration priorities, he was rebuffed.

"We basically kind of dismissed them and said, 'Go ahead, make our day,' " recalled House Appropriations Committee Staff Director James W. Dyer. "This is a law that really did not make a significant contribution to reducing the deficit and was poorly handled to the point it was an embarrassment to the administration and the Hill both."

Although most members were unaffected by the line-item veto, several of those who got hit by the veto were outraged. Even conservatives such as Sen. Larry E. Craig, R-Idaho, did quick about-faces after losing home state projects. Craig also was a sponsor of one of the tax provisions that Clinton killed last August. It aimed to make it easier to sell food processing plants to farmer-owned cooperatives.

Supporters of the line-item veto vowed to rejoin the battle.

"This is a temporary defeat for the American people, for fiscal responsibility," said Sen. Daniel R. Coats, who co-sponsored the law with Sen. John McCain, R-Ariz. "But . . . this is one battle in a war to address the issue of fiscal responsibility and to represent the American taxpayer so that the light of day can be shed on the way in which the Congress spends their money."

McCain and Coats immediately introduced an alternative bill (S 2221) under which Congress would pass appropriations bills as it does now, but the bills would then be unbundled with each item sent to the president as a separate bill to be signed or vetoed. The Senate took this approach in 1995 when it originally passed the line-item veto. *(1995 Almanac, p. 2-40)*

This separate enrollment approach — the version of the veto filibustered to death in 1985 — was revived in 1995 not because line-item veto proponents thought it was a good idea but instead to head off a collision in Senate GOP ranks between McCain and old-timers such as Budget Chairman Pete V. Domenici, R-N.M. At the time, Domenici and Ted Stevens, R-Alaska, supported a milder "expedited rescissions" framework in which Congress would vote on proposed presidential rescissions but be able to reject them by majority vote, instead of the two-thirds required to override a veto. *(1985 Almanac, p. 468)*

Privately, McCain and Coats acknowledge that sending the president hundreds or thousands of separate bills is logistically unworkable, and the Senate quickly ceded that issue to the House during conference talks in 1995-96.

In the House, Budget Chairman John R. Kasich, R-Ohio, said the best response to the court's decision would be a constitutional amendment, but he conceded that it was unlikely to pass. Kasich reintroduced an expedited rescissions bill (HR 4174) similar to bills that passed the House in 1994, 1993 and 1992. But it is unlikely any scaled-back measure could become law this year. Under existing rules, the president can request rescissions, but Congress can ignore him. *(1994 Almanac, p. 87)*

The court decision capped a frustrating period for McCain, a former prisoner of war who was also the chief GOP advocate of the now-dead anti-smoking bill (S 1415). "This has been a wonderful two weeks for me personally," McCain said. "I really haven't had quite so much fun since my last interrogation in Hanoi." ◆

Clinton Gives Up On Veto Power

JULY 18 — President Clinton has officially given up on the line-item veto.

The Office of Management and Budget (OMB) announced July 17 that the 43 line-item vetoes that were not part of a successful challenge to the 1996 Line Item Veto Act (PL 104-130) were rendered void by the Supreme Court's June 25 decision to overturn the law.

The budget agency will now release the funding for projects such as a $900,000 biocontrol and insect-rearing laboratory in Mississippi.

It was widely assumed that money for projects not covered by the Supreme Court case (*Clinton v. New York*) would be restored, but administration lawyers took three weeks to conclude the funds would be released.

Chapter 7

CONGRESSIONAL AFFAIRS

Ethics
   New Rules for House Ethics Committee 7-3

Leadership
   Gingrich Resignation 7-4
   New House Chairmen for 106th 7-6

Leadership *(cont'd)*
   New Republican Leadership 7-7
      Leadership Votes 7-9

Congressional Affairs

House Ethics Committee Reconvenes; Panel To Operate Under New Set of Rules

SUMMARY

The House ethics committee reopened for business in January after being shut down most of 1997 because of the extraordinary bad blood provoked by its investigation of Speaker Newt Gingrich, R-Ga.

The Committee on Standards of Official Conduct, as it is formally known, began the year with a new set of rules developed in late 1997 and new members. The biggest rules change involved imposing a ban on the filing of complaints against House members by anyone other than lawmakers, despite opposition from some lawmakers and congressional watchdog groups. (*1997 Almanac, p. 1-32*)

Hopes for greater comity began with the leadership of Chairman James V. Hansen, R-Utah, and ranking Democrat Howard L. Berman of California. They replaced committee leaders Nancy L. Johnson, R-Conn., and Jim McDermott, D-Wash., whose relationship deteriorated into partisan name-calling during the Gingrich case.

Business, however, was not brisk. It took much of the year to dispense with pending cases; even then, it left a few matters hanging.

- **Gingrich.** The panel did not decide until Oct. 10 to drop the final ethics charges against Gingrich. The decision ended a process in which Gingrich in 1997 became the first sitting Speaker to be sanctioned by his peers for violations of House ethics rules. He was reprimanded by the House and penalized $300,000 for costs related to the ethics committee's difficulties in sorting out misleading statements he gave during the panel's investigation. (*1997 Almanac, p. 1-11*)

Hansen and Berman said Gingrich had repeatedly violated House Rule 45, which prohibits using outside consultants to conduct House duties. But because the violations occurred "so long ago" and because there was no evidence that such violations persisted, the committee dropped the complaint.

It also dropped charges that GOPAC, a political action committee Gingrich once headed, had improperly subsidized his 1990 campaign, and that he had personally benefited from its support.

In a related matter, Gingrich announced Sept. 14 that he would not need a loan from former Senate Majority Leader Bob Dole (House, 1961-69; Senate, 1969-96), R-Kan., to help pay off the $300,000 penalty. The controversial loan had kept Dole from registering as a lobbyist or contacting Gingrich on behalf of any clients.

- **Kim.** On Oct. 9, the committee announced that Jay C. Kim, R-Calif., had violated federal campaign laws and House rules in at least six instances. However, the panel said it would take no action against Kim because he was defeated in the June 2 GOP primary.

The ethics committee found evidence that Kim lied to the panel in regard to a series of complicated financial deals, from loans and campaign contributions to gifts of golf equipment. He and his wife, June, pleaded guilty in federal court in August 1997 to 10 counts stemming from the receipt of more than $230,000 in illegal contributions. He was sentenced to two months of home detention, one year of probation, 200 hours of community service and a $5,000 fine. (*1997 Almanac, p. 1-35*)

- **Shuster.** The committee will decide next year whether to continue its investigation of Transportation and Infrastructure Committee Chairman Bud Shuster, R-Pa. The panel announced June 10 that it was curtail its investigation in order to steer clear of an ongoing Justice Department criminal probe. Shuster reportedly is being investigated for helping two businessmen get better deals for property acquired for Boston's $11 billion "Big Dig" highway project in exchange for their campaign contributions.

A subcommittee of the ethics panel, led by Joel Hefley, R-Colo., and Zoe Lofgren, D-Calif., was formed in November 1997, to investigate allegations that Shuster improperly accepted gratuities. The complaint centers around Shuster's long relationship with Ann Eppard, who was the congressman's chief of staff from 1973 to 1994. She quit the day after the GOP won control of the House to become a lobbyist specializing in matters before Shuster's committee while remaining Shuster's campaign fundraiser. (*1997 Almanac, p. 1-36*)

There has been speculation that both Eppard and Shuster are targets of a federal grand jury investigating corruption connected with the Big Dig project. Eppard was indicted April 9 on charges that she took $230,000 from a lobbyist but did not report it. She also was charged with tax evasion.

- **Brown.** The ethics panel confirmed that it has also asked Corrine Brown, D-Fla., about several ethical questions raised by recent newspaper stories. The fact-finding involves — but apparently is not limited to — a $10,000 check that she received from an embattled Baptist leader and a luxury car worth nearly $50,000 that her daughter received from an aide to a West African businessman whom the lawmaker tried to keep out of prison.

- **McDermott.** Elsewhere, a federal district judge on July 28 dismissed a lawsuit by Rep. John A. Boehner, R-Ohio, against Rep. Jim McDermott, D-Wash., for disclosing a taped cell phone conversation concerning the ethics investigation of Gingrich.

U.S. District Judge Thomas F. Hogan ruled that McDermott's First Amendment rights were paramount in the case. He said McDermott had obtained the tape legally and had a constitutional right to disclose its contents. But the judge chastised the Democrat, noting that McDermott was serving on the House ethics committee at the time. (*1997 Almanac, p. 1-35*) ◆

Congressional Affairs

Shakeup in the House: Disaffected Republicans Force Gingrich Out

NOVEMBER 7 — House Republicans knew their post-election conversations would be consumed with whether certain transgressions merited removal from office.

What surprised them was the subject of those talks. Instead of discussing whether to impeach President Clinton for lying about an affair, they forced Speaker Newt Gingrich, R-Ga., to step down from his leadership post after the party lost a net five House seats in the Nov. 3 election. Other leaders were expected to face serious challenges as well.

Gingrich's Nov. 6 decision to resign came just hours after he drew a challenge from a candidate with the stature and connections to beat him — Appropriations Committee Chairman Robert L. Livingston, R-La. More candidacies were expected to follow.

In the four years since they took the House in a conservative revolution, the Republicans' agenda seemed to run out of steam. Until now, Gingrich has survived periodic rumblings of discontent from rank-and-file members who felt that he had a tendency to become disengaged and was unable to form broad coalitions needed to run the House.

In choosing his successor Nov. 18, Republicans must come to terms with the bitter splits within their ranks, primarily the fissure that divides conservatives and moderates — a division that reflects a broader struggle within the national party.

No matter who wins the leadership posts, it is clear House GOP members wanted a shift in strategy, perhaps to something more pragmatic, but certainly to an agenda they can better articulate to voters.

The decision by Gingrich not to seek another term as Speaker put practically every leadership post up for grabs. It followed days of recriminations among GOP members over who was to blame for the election results, which handed House Republicans the thinnest margin a majority has held in 46 years.

The election "has shown us unequivocally that the American people want more than politicians with good speeches," Livingston said. "They want politicians with ideas — and ideas that work." Too often the party's message "has gotten lost in the haze of high rhetoric and miscast priorities; lost in a management style where process is subordinated to polls and self-initiated crises."

In contrast to Gingrich, whom he repeatedly referred to as a friend, Livingston said he would be more of a "stay at home type" of Speaker, dealing with "day-to-day governing" of the House.

He would also be more pragmatic than Gingrich and less of a visionary. As Speaker, he would likely concentrate more on the nuts and bolts of advancing a legislative agenda than Gingrich, a discipline that would be invaluable in working with such a thin Republican margin.

Other posts are at stake besides the speakership. Steve Largent of Oklahoma announced Nov. 6 that he would challenge Majority Leader Dick Armey of Texas, while George P. Radanovich of California, Rick A. Lazio of New York and Peter Hoekstra of Michigan were possible opponents for House Republican Conference Chairman John A. Boehner of Ohio.

"It's abundantly clear that on Nov. 3 the Republican Party hit an iceberg," Largent said. "And I think the question that's before our conference today is whether we retain the crew of the Titanic or look for some new leadership."

"To paraphrase Raymond Chandler, congressional Republicans are feeling the edge of the carving knife and studying each other's necks," said John J. Pitney Jr., an associate professor of government at Claremont McKenna College in California.

This is only the second time since the Civil War that the party not in control of the White House lost seats in a midterm election, and many Republicans were seriously considering a shakeup as a result. The party is left with 223 seats, compared with 211 Democrats and one Independent.

"All of my political instincts say we've lost two in a row, we need a leadership change," said Republican Mark Souder of Indiana.

No matter who is in charge, managing the assemblage will be even more of a chore. The election sliced the Republicans' scant, hard-to-manage 11-vote majority into an even thinner six-vote edge.

"If you thought the 105th Congress was chaotic, the 106th is going to be even more so," said William F. Connelly Jr., a professor of politics at Washington and Lee University in Virginia.

Republicans could be held hostage on any particular vote not just by a faction, but by a small gathering of disgruntled members. Any huddle of a half-dozen Republicans could be a cabal. Absences brought about by the flu or the weather could tip the balance of power on any given day. "If a plane is late from California, they could lose a vote," said a Democratic leadership aide, with evident glee.

Majority Whip Tom DeLay, R-Texas, has had the difficult job of assembling a majority for every vote. Because of his success in that tough assignment, DeLay seems the most secure of GOP leaders. "There aren't many members saying, 'I want to be the person responsible for getting to 218,' " Souder said.

The Republicans' loss of House seats and the disarray that followed also throws further doubt on their ability to assemble a majority to impeach Clinton. It becomes more likely that lawmakers will ultimately seek an alternative punishment, such as censure.

Indeed, many Republicans blame

the party's obsession with Clinton and his possible impeachment for their electoral setback. Other criticisms, depending on one's ideology, included the leadership's inability to develop and communicate a broad message, its unwillingness to stick to a conservative agenda and the lack of legislative accomplishments.

Hardly anyone seemed to focus, as Gingrich urged, on the fact that Republicans won their third consecutive House election for the first time since the Great Depression.

For the current crop of House Republicans, the Great Depression now refers to their mood — fears that their hard-earned majority status is slipping away.

A Growing Discontent

GOP lawmakers had commented privately throughout the year that their leaders were less cohesive and effective than they had been in the early days of Republican control of the House in 1995.

Then, of course, the party had its "Contract With America" to unite behind. Dissension in the ranks grew after the partial government shutdowns in the winter of 1995-96, and the so-called disaster relief debacle last year, when the party linked unrelated matters to emergency flood relief, delaying the aid. Misgivings about Gingrich crystallized with the aborted coup against him in July 1997, plotted with the consent of some party leaders. *(1997 Almanac, p. 1-11)*

Gingrich survived the overthrow attempt and strengthened his hand this year. But the ill will blossomed again when lawmakers stitched together an unwieldy omnibus fiscal 1999 appropriations bill (PL 105-277) and when GOP leaders made a failed, last-ditch attempt to improve their electoral standing with television commercials that focused on Clinton's affair with former White House intern Monica Lewinsky.

"The last couple of months have been a giant screw up," said E. Clay Shaw Jr., R-Fla.

Even party stalwart Henry J. Hyde, R-Ill., chairman of the Judiciary Committee, commented, "Leadership takes credit when things go right. They ought to take blame when things go wrong."

Ralph Hellman, a former DeLay aide who now lobbies for the National Federation of Independent Business, said, "I think everyone is trying to blame each other when the reality is dealing with an 11-seat majority is just a bear. A six-seat majority is going to be even tougher."

Gingrich, never at a loss for words, sounded stumped when talking to reporters Nov. 4. "I frankly don't understand all the things that happened yesterday," he admitted, "and I'm not sure anyone else in the country does either."

Gingrich acknowledged that Republicans had underestimated how quickly people tired of the Lewinsky scandal, though he said the media was preoccupied with it. But he also said that the GOP should have been more aggressive in telling voters "what we're trying to do is find a way to reform government, cut taxes, save Social Security, win the war on drugs, reform education and strengthen national defense."

With barely two weeks between Election Day and the meeting for members to choose their leadership team, there is little time to gin up a campaign and develop coalitions. That they are scattered across the country and dependent on reaching one another by telephone makes it even more difficult.

And it is difficult for outsiders to assess how a leadership campaign is faring because, more so than on most issues, it is a member-to-member process with little input from staff and less desire than usual to tell all to the press.

Nagging Doubts

Gingrich built a strong following within the party for having led Republicans to control of the House after 40 years in the minority.

But there have been persistent, nagging doubts about his ability to lead Republicans in the majority. He may ultimately be seen as a transitional figure, someone whose divisiveness alienated many mainstream voters and who was unable to build a large and stable coalition.

"Before you can govern Congress as a majority in the House, you have to learn to govern yourself, that is, your own factions," Connelly said. "It's not clear he's successfully made the transition from opposition to governing. The House Republican Party overall is having trouble making that transition."

Added one Republican strategist: "We've got a leadership problem. We've got a followership problem too."

Conservatives were especially bitter about the outcome. "I felt like '94 was a referendum on the President's failed leadership," Largent told the Tulsa World. "I think '98 was a referendum on the Republicans' failed leadership."

Shortly after the election, Gingrich began taking the offensive to save his job, reaching out to members by phone.

"He's very open and receptive and he's listening to members' concerns and trying to learn what can be done better," a leadership aide said Nov. 5.

Christina Martin, Gingrich's press secretary, issued a statement Nov. 6 expressing the Speaker's resolve to run for another term.

Hours later, Gingrich held a conference call with confidants saying that he had a change of heart.

"The Republican conference needs to be unified, and it is time for me to move forward where I believe I still have a signficiant role to play for our country and our party," Gingrich said in a statement released late in the day. "I urge my colleagues to pick leaders who can both reconcile and discipline, who can work together and communicate effectively."

Livingston's Loyalty

Livingston had previously been upfront both about his interest in serving as Speaker and his loyalty to Gingrich. After the election, he seemed more serious about the former than the latter.

He said earlier in the year that he wanted the job. He quickly followed through, rounding up commitments from more than 100 members who said they would support him if Gingrich stepped down during the next two years.

This early spadework could turn out to be enormously valuable for Livingston, who posed his challenge to Gingrich with two weeks' notice and most members ensconced in their districts.

He also comes across reasonably well on television — a talent many rank-and-file members are desperate to see in the leadership team — has an ability to raise money, has shown

Congressional Affairs

New House Chairmen for 106th

NOVEMBER 7 — The most powerful committee job in the House likely will be up for grabs this month with Appropriations Chairman Robert L. Livingston, R-La., running for House Speaker.

Livingston said Nov. 6 he would challenge Speaker Newt Gingrich, R-Ga., who reportedly decided within hours not to run for re-election.

Competition for the Appropriations post could be intense. Gingrich picked Livingston over three more-senior members in 1994, and two of them remain — C.W. Bill Young of Florida and Ralph Regula of Ohio.

Further down the Appropriations roster, the retirement of Joseph M. McDade, R-Pa., opens the way for Joe Knollenberg, R-Mich., to become chairman of the Energy and Water Subcommittee. But if the decision is based on overall committee seniority, the chairmanship would go most likely to Ron Packard of California, a close Livingston ally and now chairman of the Military Construction Subcommittee. In all, Republicans will have three open seats to fill; Democrats will have six.

Other key committee changes:

● **Rules.** David Dreier, R-Calif., will take the helm of the committee that sets floor procedure, succeeding Gerald B.H. Solomon, R-N.Y., who is retiring. Dreier is a little more polished than the more emotional Solomon, but the overall agenda is set by the House leadership.

● **Agriculture.** Larry Combest, R-Texas, will take over as chairman from Bob Smith, R-Ore., who is retiring. Combest has served on the Agriculture Committee his entire House career and has good relations with Agriculture Secretary Dan Glickman.

● **International Relations.** The new ranking Democrat, Sam Gejdenson of Connecticut, could hardly be more different from his predecessor, Lee H. Hamilton of Indiana, who is retiring.

Gejdenson is an emotional firecracker more prone to partisan shouting matches or effusive speeches than the low-key, measured Hamilton. But Gejdenson may be able to work with Chairman Benjamin A. Gilman, R-N.Y. Gejdenson wants to make deals. Gejdenson and Gilman also are among the strongest supporters of Israel in the House.

The committee loses Vince Snowbarger, R-Kan., a major opponent of paying debts to the United Nations. His defeat and the shrinking GOP majority may make it easier to get U.N. funds through the House without abortion restrictions.

● **Ways and Means.** Both the chairman and ranking Democrat are leaving the Social Security Subcommittee, which could play a significant role next year as Congress debates legislation to overhaul the federal retirement system.

Subcommittee Chairman Jim Bunning, R-Ky., was elected to the Senate. His successor is likely to be moderate Amo Houghton, R-N.Y., former Corning Glass Works chief executive officer.

Ranking Democrat Barbara B. Kennelly of Connecticut failed in her gubernatorial bid. She may be replaced by either Benjamin L. Cardin of Maryland or Sander M. Levin of Michigan.

● **Commerce.** Joe L. Barton, R-Texas, is expected to take over as chairman of the Energy and Power Subcommittee, replacing retiring Dan Schaefer, R-Colo.

Possible candidates to replace Barton as chairman of the Oversight Subcommittee: J. Dennis Hastert, R-Ill., and Fred Upton, R-Mich.

● **Education and the Workforce.** Michael N. Castle, R-Del., a moderate, is in line to replace the retiring Frank Riggs, R-Calif., as chairman of the Early Childhood, Youth and Families Subcommittee, which will have a key role in rewriting the Elementary and Secondary Education Act next year. Some education groups are courting Rep. Howard P. "Buck" McKeon, R-Calif.

his leadership abilities as chairman of Appropriations and has allies in different factions.

Challenging Gingrich involved upending the man who handpicked him as Appropriations chairman four years ago and enabled him to bypass three more senior members.

And yet Livingston, in a phone conversation with Gingrich on Nov. 4, broached the subject of Gingrich stepping down.

Livingston could face criticism from some who have seen his red-hot temper. Hard-core conservatives believe he is too quick to compromise with Democrats. Moderates might find him less receptive than Gingrich, who has of late been particularly open to the ideas of more centrist members.

Livingston, according to several people who have spoken to him, was said to be reluctant to form a leadership slate. However, he might need to build a coalition that includes conservatives in order to coerce enough votes from the party's right wing.

Ways and Means Committee Chairman Bill Archer of Texas said Nov. 6 that he was considering running for Speaker. Aides to James M. Talent of Missouri said he was mulling a bid as well.

With Gingrich out as Speaker, much of the rest of his team may have to struggle to stay in place. Armey, Boehner and Conference Vice Chairman Jennifer Dunn of Washington all said they planned to seek re-election to their posts.

Armey has long been seen as the most vulnerable GOP leader. Bill Paxon, R-N.Y., was gearing up to challenge him earlier this year, with DeLay's blessing, before Paxon abruptly announced his retirement.

The name most frequently mentioned as a potential opponent against Armey was Largent, a rock-ribbed conservative from the feisty Class of '94. J.C. Watts of Oklahoma and Hoekstra were also being mentioned for an undetermined leadership slot.

Many Republican lawmakers were calling for making the post of chairman of the National Republican Congressional Committee an elected position instead of one appointed by the Speaker. That would likely mean a replacement for John Linder, R-Ga., who has been widely criticized in the wake of the election. Jim McCrery of Louisiana and Thomas M. Davis III, R-Va., are possible candidates.

And if Livingston ascends into leadership, that would leave an important vacancy at Appropriations. C.W. Bill Young, R-Fla., would be next in line, though there would almost certainly be some jostling for it.

Developing an Agenda

The election amplified the views of Republicans who complained about the lack of an identifiable agenda. "I think that there are a few people spending a disproportionate share of their time trying to kill the messenger when what we should be doing is refining the message," said Sherwood Boehlert, R-N.Y.

The agenda could be a more centrist one. "They need to have an agenda that is sufficiently appealing to their conservative base to galvanize them and yet at the same time they have to be able to broaden their appeal to moderate voters," said Ronald M. Peters Jr., who heads the Carl Albert Congressional Research and Studies Center at the University of Oklahoma.

"Clearly we have to find a more positive, inclusive message and stay on it ... and talk abut issues in a way that the general public understands and relates to," said Lazio, a moderate.

Many conservatives, naturally, were leery of that approach. "We need to give our conservative base some red meat," said Richard H. Baker, R-La. "At least they would see somebody fighting for what they believe in." That could mean an all-out struggle for a large tax cut or education vouchers usable for private schools.

But some conservatives were receptive to a wider appeal. Republicans have to "formulate an agenda out there that will appeal to moderates and conservatives, said Robert L. Ehrlich Jr., R-Md. "And it's not just cutting capital gains."

Moderates and conservatives even spoke to one another about forming a coalition to unseat one or more incumbent leaders, particularly Boehner and Linder.

"Republicans, as always, are fractious," said Pitney, "and they define the problem differently. It will take an enormous amount of skill and discipline to bring them together."

Democrats, meanwhile, said they were eager to step into the breach. They will have two relatively low-key races for leadership positions of their own during the week of Nov. 16, to replace caucus Chairman Vic Fazio of California and Vice Chairman Barbara B. Kennelly of Connecticut, both of whom are retiring.

They are eager to talk about the issues that they believe brought them to the brink of retaking the House. "People don't want deadlock," said Minority Leader Richard A. Gephardt, D-Mo., adding that Democrats will still push for a managed care patients' bill of rights, more money for teachers and classrooms, and saving the surplus for Social Security. ◆

For New Republican Leaders, Watchword Is Realism Not Revolution

NOVEMBER 21 — Four years ago, House Republicans chose leaders who wanted nothing less than to reshape the federal government. But after a long journey from revolution toward realism, Republicans installed a new team Nov. 18 with a more modest mandate: to govern effectively and stop the party's political hemorrhaging.

By the time they return in January, Republicans hope to close ranks behind a legislative agenda and shed the impeachment albatross that seemed to hurt them at the polls. Many Republicans are convinced that problems with their message nearly cost them control of the House on Nov. 3.

But that is easier said than done. Republicans remain deeply divided over key issues, with hard-core conservatives on one side and moderates on other. Their margin of error is narrower than ever; defection of only six Republicans on a party-line vote can spell defeat.

In party leadership elections Nov. 18, Republicans opted to entrust their fragile majority to Robert L. Livingston of Louisiana, who forced out his old friend, Speaker Newt Gingrich of Georgia. Livingston offers a steadier hand than the mercurial Gingrich. Livingston will get a fresh opportunity to build public support when he is formally elected Speaker of the 106th Congress in January.

"We didn't run out of ideas, we simply neglected to run on our ideas," Livingston said in his acceptance speech, explaining the GOP's poor performance at the polls two weeks earlier. "But let's make sure we don't misinterpret a warning for a whipping."

Livingston will be tested in new ways. He has not said how Republicans can bridge ideological differences over tax cuts, social policy, spending limits and environmental policy. Nor has he offered a blueprint for resolving the impeachment inquiry against President Clinton, beyond suggesting that it be finished this year.

Rather than confining his search for votes almost solely to the diminishing pool of Republicans, as Gingrich did, Livingston signaled a willingness to work with Democrats. As Appropriations Committee chairman, he was willing to go after votes wherever they were available, wooing Democrats sometimes even if it meant alienating some Republicans.

In a sentiment rarely expressed by Gingrich, Livingston said, "We're going to be reaching out to Democrats who believe as we do that our principles are sound for the nation."

Congressional Affairs

The scramble for votes is necessary because Republicans have slowly lost their grip on the House for two consecutive elections. Another such setback could toss them back into minority status at a time when they hope to regain the White House.

"The overarching objective in the Senate and the House is to remain harmonious for the biggest battle of all, in 2000," said Marshall Wittmann, director of congressional relations at the conservative Heritage Foundation. In the House, "with a six-seat margin, that is a Herculean task."

Republicans were eager to launch a new era. They applauded Gingrich at the conference meeting for having the vision and moxie that enabled them to seize control of the House four years ago. But many sounded relieved that he had stepped aside and ended his chaotic reign.

"We knew as long as he was around, he was the issue," said Robert L. Ehrlich Jr. of Maryland.

"I really believe that with Newt's departure that we all can breathe a little easier," added Steve Largent of Oklahoma, who sounded optimistic about the GOP despite losing a challenge to Majority Leader Dick Armey of Texas. "We don't start on defense, we can start on offense. It was a heavy load."

Armey bucked the Republicans' desire for change, though it took him three ballots to beat back Largent and Jennifer Dunn of Washington.

The No. 3 House Republican, Tom DeLay of Texas, was unopposed for another term as whip. Members were happy to let him keep coaxing votes out of their thin majority.

But the yearning for a new image cost John A. Boehner of Ohio his leadership post. He was upended by J.C. Watts, a popular speaker and the only black House Republican, for chairmanship of the GOP Conference.

The winds of change also cost John Linder of Georgia his slot as chairman of the National Republican Congressional Committee (NRCC). He lost to Thomas M. Davis III of Virginia.

The New Teamwork

"We are united," Livingston declared at his first public appearance with the other GOP leaders.

That remains to be seen, but indeed, Republicans sounded confident that their new team would give them new energy. Joe Scarborough of Florida, a conservative who backed Largent and Watts, said Republicans were more satisfied now than they were at organizational meetings two years ago, when no major changes were made.

"A lot of people are excited about Bob Livingston running the House in an effective, professional manner over the next two years," he said.

Competence was a recurring theme. "Livingston has the advantage of a fresh start and extraordinarily valuable experience in moving critical pieces of legislation," said Christopher Cox of California, who flirted with running for Speaker himself before settling for another term as GOP Policy Committee chairman.

Livingston mastered the appropriations process, while Gingrich, before and after taking control, was more interested in bold visions than legislative details.

Understandably, few chose to dwell on the party's ideological divisions. But the fallout from Election Day exposed internal tensions that have plagued House Republicans since they took power four years ago. Those tensions stemmed not just from ideology, but from personalities as well.

The teamwork that marked the early days of GOP control steadily eroded. At the nadir of their relationship, Armey, DeLay and Boehner conferred with junior members who plotted to overthrow Gingrich in July 1997.

Afterward, Armey, more than DeLay and Boehner, seemed to have rebuilt his relationship with Gingrich. But his following among the rank and file grew more tenuous. He survived a challenge Nov. 18; now he must solidify his standing with Livingston.

The two have had frequent policy differences. They battled over Armey's insistence in 1997 on linking disaster assistance for Midwest flood victims to unrelated issues. And they tussled again this year when Armey opposed aid to the International Monetary Fund.

John Edward Porter of Illinois said Armey's authority is "going to depend upon the relationship between Livingston and Armey, and that hasn't been particularly good in the past."

But Livingston also is surrounding himself with long-time allies. He is expected to name at least three deputies: Sonny Callahan of Alabama, Michael P. Forbes of New York and Howard P. "Buck" McKeon of California.

That is not intended as a slap at Armey, said Callahan. "It's just a recognition by Livingston that we have a lot to accomplish, and he's going to need some help," he said.

Callahan and Forbes have served with Livingston on the Appropriations Committee. McKeon, who chairs a subcommittee of the Education and the Workforce Committee, has forged bipartisan coalitions on education issues.

The three will have the title of assistant to the Speaker. "They'll be his eyes and ears, and they'll be part of the leadership," said one source.

DeLay and Livingston have had their differences over the years, too, particularly when DeLay pushed for policy-oriented legislative riders on issues such as environmental regulation on appropriations bills.

Their alliance may be tested by the impeachment dilemma. While Livingston urged Judiciary Committee Chairman Henry J. Hyde, R-Ill., to finish the matter by January, DeLay has been a prominent proponent of letting the impeachment process play out. However, DeLay has kept a low profile since the Nov. 3 election.

Conservatives gave several signals that they will close ranks behind Livingston, at least initially.

David M. McIntosh of Indiana, a leader of the party's most right-wing members, the Conservative Action Team (CAT), said, "We realize as CATs we're not going to win every vote. And we can't go out and threaten to hold up the process unless there's something seriously wrong."

On Nov. 19, a day after Livingston was nominated by his GOP colleagues, a group of conservatives led by Tom Coburn of Oklahoma dropped plans — once Livingston formally declared his opposition to them — to try to weaken the power of the leadership and committee chairmen.

"They're cutting Livingston a little slack — until he gets his sea legs," said Ray LaHood of Illinois.

Other leadership challenges among Republicans seem inevitable in the future because there is no clear line of succession. Despite his victory, Armey has long faced questions about his ability to take on the larger and more visible tasks of Speaker, and the outcome of that election did not put those concerns to rest.

DeLay has professed no interest in in ascending to a higher post, and members seem to think he is well-positioned where he is.

How Long a Honeymoon?

That peace prevails among Republicans is significant, given the turmoil of recent years. But it is uncertain how long this harmony will last when Republicans get down to the tough task of developing an agenda.

The new leadership team must first find its way through the impeachment morass. While Hyde and other Republicans on the Judiciary Committee are proceeding full speed ahead with the impeachment investigation, other GOP lawmakers regard the probe as a strategic blunder.

Porter suggested that articles of impeachment drawn on the basis of Clinton's misconduct arising from a sexual affair would garner support from only about half of the House Republicans.

Thus far, Livingston has approached the impeachment issue cautiously. He has expressed full confidence in Hyde's handling of the investigation, but also has said he wants the matter wrapped up before he formally takes over as Speaker.

The party's conservative base is still staunchly in favor of following through with an impeachment vote, even as moderates regard that with trepidation.

The dilemma GOP leaders face is hardly easier on taxes, social issues and the environment.

House Budget Committee Chairman John R. Kasich of Ohio is pressing for deep tax cuts, another priority of the base. Moderates worry that Clinton will once again paint Republicans into a corner with accusations they are bent on raiding Social Security to finance the tax reductions.

Several Republicans expressed confidence that Livingston's emphasis on competence and managerial efficiency will enable Congress to avoid train wrecks in the appropriations process, which has become a yearly embarrassment for Republicans.

To do so, he will have to find his way around substantive policy differences between Republicans and Democrats, and within the GOP.

Still, Wittmann of the Heritage Foundation predicted conservatives will accede to Livingston and resist loading up annual spending bills with policy-related amendments. "That might be the most concrete result of the leadership change," he said.

For now, GOP lawmakers are elated by the new atmosphere in the caucus. Livingston and other leaders have vowed to be more solicitous of the views of committee chairmen, who sometimes were given short shrift in the Gingrich regime.

Moderates and conservatives alike said they expected to have increased access to the top. "The new team might not be any friendlier on my issues," said Sherwood Boehlert, a moderate from New York, a leading advocate of tough environmental measures. "But I know they'll listen and that they're a hell of a lot smarter."

Majority Leader Challenge

Soon after Gingrich announced Nov. 6 that he would resign, attention turned to the majority leader's race.

Armey was challenged from his right, where Largent enjoyed the support of social conservatives. And he drew flak from moderates, some of whom lined up behind Dunn.

In addition, Chief Deputy Minority Whip J. Dennis Hastert of Illinois allowed his name to be placed in nomination.

Hastert had asked Armey on Nov. 9 to release him from a previous commitment to support Armey for majority leader so that he could consider making the race on his own. When Armey turned him down, Hastert said he would not actively run.

Hastert's legislative experience might have made him a formidable candidate with a full-fledged campaign. But the draft effort faltered, and he was dropped after the first ballot.

Armey's other challengers assumed his support would diminish if he was denied a majority on the first ballot. Instead, Armey's and Dunn's totals were largely unchanged in the second ballot and Dunn was forced out.

Largent said he had expected to win as the results were being counted in his

Republican Leadership

Leadership Votes

Voting on Nov. 18 for Republican leadership posts was conducted by secret ballot. Under party rules, if no candidate received a majority, the one with the lowest total was dropped and another vote was conducted.

Majority Leader

First Ballot
Dick Armey 100
Steve Largent 58
Jennifer Dunn 45
Dennis Hastert 18

Second Ballot
Dick Armey 99
Steve Largent 73
Jennifer Dunn 49

Third Ballot
Dick Armey 127
Steve Largent 95

Conference Chairman

J.C. Watts 121
John A. Boehner 93

Conference Vice Chairman

First Ballot
Tillie Fowler 90
Anne M. Northup 43
Peter Hoekstra 39
Sue Myrick 37

Second Ballot
Tillie Fowler 108
Others conceded

National Republican Campaign Committee

Thomas M. Davis III 130
John Linder 77

one-on-one contest with Armey on the third ballot. "We felt he was leaking oil all over the floor," Largent said.

Afterward, even some Armey supporters were measured in their tributes for the gravel-voiced Texan. Boehlert lavishly praised Armey's staff, suggesting that was a decisive factor.

Armey's victory was "hardly a mandate," said Matt Salmon of Arizona, a Largent backer. "He's got to understand, business as usual is not acceptable."

Congressional Affairs

Other Offices

Many Republicans were jubilant over the election of Watts. For a party badly in need of young, telegenic faces, the former University of Oklahoma football star may fill the bill.

"If we're smart, we're going to put him forward whenever we can," Salmon said.

Watts becomes the highest-ranking African-American in Congress and the highest ranking since former Rep. William H. Gray III, D-Pa., served as majority whip in 1989-91.

Watts promised House Republicans would have an easier time selling their message to voters than they had this year. "We had a very bad product as Republicans coming down the stretch," he said. "And whether it was true or not, the perception was the president's problems and Monica Lewinsky became our agenda."

Bob Ney of Ohio, who helped Boehner's bid for another term, said the incumbent took the fall for the party's broader problems. "Boehner got blamed for a lack of an agenda," he said.

Another target was Linder, who was appointed NRCC chairman by Gingrich. Linder said he succeeded in raising cash for the GOP. But his fate seemed sealed after the Republicans' disappointing showing Nov. 3.

Members changed House GOP rules to make the post an elected one, then opted for Davis, who had picked up key support from DeLay.

"The mood in there was for change," Linder said. "I'm a perfect target for them."

Also joining the leadership team was Tillie Fowler of Florida. She agrees with the party's more conservative faction on many issues, from taxes to immigration. She is a defense hawk, but she supports abortion rights.

Cox and GOP House Conference Secretary Deborah Pryce of Ohio ran unopposed for new terms in their posts.

Even as they said goodbye to their former hero Gingrich, members looked forward to Livingston's narrower focus on the Capitol instead of on the world around him.

"Mr. Livingston doesn't get up in the morning saying, 'I want to make history today,' " said Van Hilleary of Tennessee. "He says, 'I want to do a good job in the House.' "

Livingston Pulls Out Of Speaker's Race; Hastert Gets Nod

DECEMBER 22 — Shortly after coming to Congress in 1979, a young Georgia Republican named Newt Gingrich was already dreaming of the way he would one day run the House. "The Congress in the long run can change the country more dramatically than the president," he said. "One of my goals is to make the House the co-equal of the White House."

In the heady days after he engineered the 1994 Republican takeover, it seemed he had done just that. Gingrich created a new speakership for an ascendant House. He compared himself with Henry Clay, the 19th century Speaker who devised a package of sweeping legislative proposals he called the "American System." His colleagues went even further, comparing Gingrich with a prime minister.

The extent to which this vision of the speakership has imploded was evident on Dec. 19 as Speaker-designate Robert L. Livingston, R-La., announced he will not run for Speaker and intends to resign from the House in six months. The move, which followed Gingrich's announced resignation by only 43 days, was brought on by an admission of extramarital affairs.

The man slated to inherit this job is J. Dennis Hastert, an affable and respected Illinois Republican known for his relaxed style and low profile. He is expected to be something of a throwback to the Speakers who preceded Gingrich. He might resemble a more conservative version of former Minority Leader Robert H. Michel, R-Ill. (1957-95). As far as Speakers go, Hastert's style might be compared to that of Thomas P. "Tip" O'Neill Jr., D-Mass. (1953-87), who served as House leader more than as party spokesman, rather than to Gingrich.

If he is lucky, Hastert will not be part of the Speaker-as-victim cycle that has crippled the House since O'Neill, who was the last Speaker to retire voluntarily. Scandal took James C. Wright, D-Texas (1955-89), who was Speaker for two-and-a-half years. Voters ousted Democrat Thomas S. Foley of Washington (1965-95), partly as a result of their displeasure with Clinton and partly because of Foley's own positions. With Gingrich and Livingston, it was a combination of scandal and dissent within party ranks that did them in.

If Hastert turns out to be a Speaker in a distinctly pre-Gingrich mold, it will be ironic. The attack politics that led to his ascension are partly Gingrich's making.

Gingrich brought a new level of partisanship to the job. He rose to power through a confrontational style unknown before his arrival. He sparred frequently with O'Neill, but did not really cut his teeth until he succeeded in forcing Wright to resign. It was Gingrich who publicized Wright's financial improprieties, including a highly dubious plan for selling his autobiography wholesale to Washington interest groups. Gingrich effectively used the media to get the story of scandal out to the public.

Leading a Splintered Group

If Hastert wants to take the speakership and the House back to an earlier era of bipartisanship, he may not find his task easy. His House and the Republican conference are both divided.

Returning to the notion — which now seems almost quaint — that the Speaker presides over the entire House and not just the majority party will be difficult, given Democratic ire over the Clinton impeachment. Hastert must also contend with factions within his own party, and with ongoing frustration over Clinton's political resilience. When the Republicans took control of the House after the 1994 election, they thought they would be able to outmaneuver Clinton legislatively. They failed. Though they achieved some victories, such as the 1996 welfare overhaul (PL 104-193), they also suffered some defeats, most notably the blame they took for the 1995 government shutdown. (*Welfare, 1996 Almanac, p. 6-3; Government shutdown, 1995 Almanac, p. 11-3*)

When Clinton's sexual peccadilloes were exposed, many Republicans assumed he would be humiliated out of his job. When this did not happen, they developed an almost palpable rage that ended in impeachment.

This is the atmosphere in which

Hastert must lead. His job is further complicated by the fact that he must work with a six-seat majority and with an often splintered caucus. He may have to invent a new kind of speakership of low expectations.

A New Beginning

But Hastert has qualities not seen in recent Speakers. Almost universally, his fellow Republicans refer to him as a "healer."

In rallying behind him, Republicans signaled their interest in a new type of leader who would not follow the bomb-throwing style of Gingrich, but instead focus on the behind-the-scenes consensus building. They wanted someone who would represent a new beginning.

"Hastert is the kind of guy we probably need in a healing-type situation," said David L. Hobson, R-Ohio. "He gets along with everyone. Democrats could work with him."

Moderates saw in Hastert someone who would reach out to a diverse array of Republicans and not be held hostage to conservative factions.

"It's important to make sure moderates have access to the floor," said James C. Greenwood, R-Pa., adding that Hastert would allow that to happen.

Conservatives found him attractive as well. Though Livingston's resignation prompted a half-dozen would-be successors to rally their troops, Hastert quickly emerged as the overwhelming favorite. This was due in part to the fact that Majority Whip Tom DeLay of Texas rallied behind him.

DeLay organized Hastert's sudden candidacy for Speaker, returning the favor to the man who championed him for whip in 1994. Bob Barr, R-Ga., one of the most conservative members of the House, signed a letter supporting Hastert as Speaker.

Hastert, who turns 57 on Jan. 2, has a solid conservative voting record. He was intimately involved in pushing major elements of the GOP's "Contract With America" through the House in 1995. In 1996, he scored 100 with the American Conservative Union, and a zero with the liberal Americans for Democratic Action.

He was tapped by Gingrich to draft a managed care bill for the Republican leadership, giving him a taste of what it is like to go head-to-head with the White House on an issue that Clinton has been able to seize. A task force led by Hastert produced a market-based plan that would have imposed fewer government regulations on the health care industry than Democratic plans. On July 24, it passed the House, 216-210, and drew a veto threat from Clinton, who said it would provide too few patient protections.

Hastert also chaired the GOP's anti-drug task force, winning an extra $870 million in the omnibus spending bill (PL 105-277) to provide new radar planes to patrol the Caribbean and Pacific and enhance anti-drug technology at the Mexican border.

A former high school wrestling coach, the burly Hastert is known as a negotiator who can gently twist arms in Congress.

Unlike Gingrich, Hastert is not known to most Americans. As the House Republicans' chief deputy whip for the past four years, he has skillfully counted votes for the GOP but remains almost unknown outside of Congress and his home district.

Hastert's popularity in the House was evident this past November when he garnered 18 votes during the race for House majority leader — even though he refused to run for the post.

And in this era when politicians' personal lives are being examined under a microscope, Hastert is seen as having a clean past. New York Republican Sue W. Kelly — a strong supporter of Hastert — laughed out loud when asked if she feared any dirt could be dug up on him.

"If you knew him, you wouldn't ask that question," she said. "He's just one of the nicest persons I know."

But Hastert's affable demeanor did not assure his victory. Indeed, he was actively pursuing the speakership within minutes of Livingston's announcement at 9:30 in the morning. Within half an hour, Hastert had called his wife and discussed his interest in running for Speaker, said a member who supported Hastert. Within another 45 minutes, 20 members of the whip team led by DeLay had gathered to divide up campaign duties and start making phone calls to build support for Hastert. By midafternoon, Hastert had officially announced his campaign and released a statement outlining his leadership abilities.

"If elected Speaker, I will make a particular effort to build bridges across the aisle, not just to pass legislation, but to ensure that common-sense ideas and principles become law," the statement read.

By the end of the day, Hastert's supporters had shored up the promised votes of 120 Republicans — more than half the conference. A major boost came when he picked up the support of Gingrich. While Gingrich was unable to control all elements of the party, he still held considerable influence because he was revered by many as the man who led the party back to power after 40 years in the minority.

During a closed-door meeting of House Republicans following the impeachment vote, Gingrich stood before weary GOP troops and said Hastert should become their next leader. That endorsement finished off the chances of two other candidates who were actively considering a run for Speaker.

Christopher Cox, R-Calif., and Steve Largent, R-Okla., were testing the waters throughout the afternoon following Livingston's announcement to see what kind of support they had. But neither was seen as having the potential to be a healing force, and both officially dropped their bids by the end of the day.

Under a Cloud

Livingston's stunning announcement to the House came only two days after he confessed he had "on occasion" engaged in adulterous affairs. His confession of the affairs, which were first disclosed in the on-line version of the Capitol Hill newspaper Roll Call, came before an emotional Dec. 17 House GOP caucus.

It came after Livingston learned that Hustler magazine publisher Larry Flynt — who had offered to pay people who could disclose affairs with lawmakers — was preparing a story on Livingston's relationships with several women. Livingston acknowledged the affairs in a statement, but said they had not involved staff and that he had never testified about them under oath.

Republicans initially rallied behind the Speaker-designate after his disclosure. But Bonnie, his wife of 33 years, was devastated by the controversy, said Republican sources, and rumors swept the Capitol that the problems would on-

Congressional Affairs

ly escalate with further revelations about his affairs.

Complicating matters was dissatisfaction among a group of about a dozen conservatives who were grumbling about Livingston's indiscretions and his failure to disclose them before being nominated as Speaker. Others wanted him to to reconsider taking the post.

"With a slim majority, it would have been hard enough to lead Republicans," Livingston told The Washington Post. "But under a cloud, it would have been very difficult indeed."

Added Livingston friend Mike Parker, R-Miss.: "You have got some people on the Republican side who he knows will tear him to shreds. He knows that. They'll never stop."

Only a few of his colleagues, family members, friends and key staff knew of Livingston's decision when he strode to the well of the House on Dec. 19. He had made the decision the night before.

Livingston's speech started plainly. He made the case for and against Clinton, and then told the president, "You sir, may resign your post."

Democrats erupted. Maxine Waters, D-Calif., and a few others shouted: "You resign! You resign!"

"I can only challenge you in such fashion if I am willing to heed my own words," Livingston went on. "I was prepared to lead our narrow majority as Speaker, and I believe I had it in me to do a fine job. But I cannot do that job or be the kind of leader I would like to be under current circumstances. So I must set the example that I hope President Clinton will follow. I will not stand for Speaker of the House."

Livingston, 55, said that he would instead become a "backbencher" and resign his seat in about six months. Former Ku Klux Klansman David Duke announced that he would run for the seat, a prospect sure to make Livingston uneasy.

The stunning developments capped a tumultuous year for Livingston, a 22-year veteran of the House. He was poised to announce his retirement earlier this year and then changed his mind with an eye to a future run for Speaker on the assumption that Gingrich would run for president in 2000.

But after the Republicans' disappointing showing in the midterm elections, Livingston forced his longtime friend Gingrich aside and quickly sealed up the nomination for Speaker. It was Gingrich who had tapped Livingston to head the Appropriations Committee. There, he earned generally good marks, though he frequently clashed with junior conservatives and House leaders.

As Speaker, Livingston promised to restore civility to a chamber where partisan tensions have boiled over. He vowed to make the legislative trains run on time. He was well-liked by Democrats, although he had angered them with his decision to block a Democratic effort to censure Clinton.

Still, it was Democrats who were most adamant that Livingston should reconsider. "Bob Livingston is a worthy and good and honorable man," said Minority Leader Richard A. Gephardt, D-Mo. "I believe his decision to retire is a terrible capitulation to the negative forces that are consuming our political system and our country." ◆

Chapter 8
DEFENSE

Defense
Defense Authorization 8-3
   Sex-Integrated Training Retained 8-9
   Pentagon Officials Seek Budget Increase 8-14
Anti-Missile Defenses 8-17

Defense *(cont'd)*
Chemical Weapons Treaty 8-20
NATO Expansion 8-21

Intelligence
Intelligence Authorization 8-25

Defense Authorization Calls For Reduced Force Size, Trims Anti-Missile Spending

> **Box Score**
>
> ● **Bill:** HR 3616 — PL 105-261
>
> ● **House action:** The House adopted the conference report (H Rept 105-736) on HR 3616, 373-50, on Sept. 24. The House passed HR 3616 (H Rept 105-532), 357-60, on May 21.
>
> ● **Senate action:** The Senate cleared the conference report on HR 3616, 96-2, on Oct. 1. The Senate passed S 2057 (S Rept 105-189), 88-4, on June 25. It then passed the House version (HR 3616) by voice vote after substituting the text of the Senate bill.
>
> ● **Presidential action:** Clinton signed HR 3616 on Oct. 17.

Congress in late September cleared a bill authorizing $271.5 billion, plus $1.9 billion for peacekeeping operations in Bosnia. Although this was $339 million more than President Clinton requested, Congress made only a handful of significant changes in the administration's defense program.

The balanced-budget law passed in 1997 (PL 105-33) pre-empted serious debate over the size of the fiscal 1999 defense budget until after Congress had all but completed work on the annual authorization bill. Clinton in February requested $271 billion for the Defense Department and for defense-related programs conducted by the Department of Energy — essentially, the maximum allowed under a defense budget cap set by the budget law.

At the same time, he requested $1.9 billion to continue the deployment of U.S. troops in Bosnia through fiscal 1999 as part of a NATO-led peacekeeping force. But he asked Congress to approve the Bosnia money as emergency funding, exempt from the budget cap.

By mid-September — shortly before Congress cleared the authorization measure for the White House — it became clear Clinton would send Congress a supplemental fiscal 1999 funding request totaling at least $1 billion in an effort to stem growing problems with military morale and combat readiness. But that prospect had no impact on final negotiations over the authorization bill that the Senate and House had passed earlier in the summer.

The bill was the venue for the year's most contentious defense policy debate on Capitol Hill: an unsuccessful effort by conservative Republicans to make the armed services train male and female recruits in separate units. An outside advisory panel chaired by former Kansas Republican Sen. Nancy Kassebaum Baker (1978-97) recommended late in 1997 that recruits be segregated by sex in their smallest training units, and that they be housed in separate barracks.

This drew strong objections from the armed services, except for the Marine Corps, which already follows the suggested policies. The House version of the defense bill included provisions mandating gender-separate housing and training units. The conference report requires only separate housing, though it includes a non-binding expression by the House that men and women also should train in separate units.

One significant change the authorization bill makes in administration policy is in setting the annual military pay raise at 3.6 percent, instead of the 3.1 percent Clinton proposed. As requested, the bill sets a ceiling of 1.4 million active-duty personnel, a reduction of 36,000 from the fiscal 1998 personnel cap.

On the other hand, it makes relatively few changes in Clinton's funding requests for major weapons programs. In fact, although Republicans have pressed Clinton to accelerate deployment of anti-missile defenses, the bill authorizes $104 million less than the $3.6 billion Clinton requested. The bill approves the $951 million in the budget request to develop a system intended to protect U.S. territory. Most of the net reduction in anti-missile funding reflects a cut from the request for the Army's Theater High-Altitude Area Defense (THAAD) system, which failed five flight tests.

As usual, the bill adds to Clinton's program several projects favored by influential members of Congress, such as $483 million for C-130 cargo planes built by Lockheed Martin in Marietta, Ga., adjacent to the district of House Speaker Newt Gingrich, R-Ga. Congress also added to the bill $50 million for components to be used in a $1.3 billion helicopter carrier to be built by Litton Industries in Pascagoula, Miss., hometown of Senate Majority Leader Trent Lott, R-Miss. The Navy had planned to overhaul an older ship for $1 billion rather than building a new one.

The bill authorizes $177 million, which is $20 million more than was requested, for the Energy Department's effort to develop a new source of tritium, a radioactive form of hydrogen gas used to boost the explosive power of nuclear weapons. Since the gas loses its radioactivity over time, it must be replenished periodically. No tritium has been produced since 1988, and the Clinton administration is in the process of choosing between two methods for future production.

The final bill does not include a House provision that would have forced the administration to build a new tritium production facility at the Energy Department's Savannah River Facility in South Carolina. Instead, the bill delays for at least a year selection of a tritium production plan.

Spurred by allegations that China had improved its long-range missiles with technology gleaned from U.S.-built satellites sent to China for

Defense

launching, Congress added to the bill a provision transferring jurisdiction over satellite export controls from the Commerce Department to the State Department.

House Panel Votes To Separate Recruits by Sex

MAY 2 — In the continuing debate over the role of women in the military, the House National Security Subcommittee on Military Personnel on April 30 approved a provision of the fiscal 1999 defense authorization bill that would require male and female recruits to be housed in separate barracks as soon as possible.

The provision also would require that training platoons and other small units for recruits be segregated by sex.

Both provisions were among several recommended by an outside panel chaired by former Kansas Republican Sen. Nancy Kassebaum Baker (1978-97). The Defense Department, on the recommendations of the Army, Navy and Air Force, rejected those elements of the Kassebaum Baker report.

However, House subcommittee member Republican Roscoe G. Bartlett of Maryland said, "It is time to abandon the politically correct but operationally insane theory of 'gender neutral' basic training."

The subcommittee also included a provision requiring the president and secretary of Defense to meet the same moral and ethical standards that are required of military officers. Subcommittee Chairman Steve Buyer, R-Ind., said the provision was in response to allegations of sexual misconduct against President Clinton, allegations that could result in a court-martial or discharge if they were made against an officer.

Subcommittee Democrats Jane Harman of California and Patrick J. Kennedy of Rhode Island objected that the provision "politicizes our efforts," in Harman's words.

The action came as House defense subcommittees began drafting sections of the defense bill the week of April 27. Resigned to living within a budget they consider too tight, committee members are expected to produce a bill that would provide basically the amount Clinton requested — about $257 billion.

By shifting around funds within the $61.8 billion total allocated for military personnel costs, Buyer's subcommittee came up with $186 million for a 3.6 percent military pay raise instead of the 3.1 percent raise Clinton requested. By the same means, the panel added $100 million to the amount sought for military recruiting and advertising. The panel approved its section of the bill 12-2 on April 30.

The Military Readiness Subcommittee, which approved its portion of the bill April 30 by voice vote, rearranged funds within the $94.8 billion allocated to operations and maintenance to add more than $800 million to programs that would boost combat readiness. The increases included $235 million for overhauls of ships, planes and land vehicles, $200 million to increase aircraft spare parts inventories, $175 million for facilities maintenance, and $125 million for training center improvements.

The Military Installations and Facilities Subcommittee, along with subsidiary panels on Merchant Marine and Morale, Welfare and Recreation, approved sections of the bill by voice vote April 29.

Defense markups will continue the week of May 4 in the House and Senate.

Basic Training, Base Closings May Dominate Defense Debate

MAY 9 — Whether young men and women should go through boot camp together and whether President Clinton is meddling in military base-closings could lead to debate when the fiscal 1999 defense authorization bills reach the House and Senate floors in coming weeks.

Republicans on the defense committees say President Clinton's $271 billion defense budget is too stingy and could hurt military readiness, but last year's budget agreement will keep them from making more than minor adjustments.

During a week of markups on both sides of Capitol Hill, the House National Security Committee decided May 6 that military recruits should be housed and trained separately to prevent sexual harassment and distraction. The Senate Armed Services Committee wants to wait until January for a new report on basic training before suggesting any changes.

In the wake of sex scandals at some Army bases, a commission chaired by former Kansas Republican Sen. Nancy Kassebaum Baker (1978-97) recommended in March that male and female recruits be housed in separate barracks and trained in different platoons.

The chiefs of the military services strongly object to such a course — except for the Marine Corps, which has always used sex-segregated training — and Defense Secretary William S. Cohen has allowed them to continue joint training, as long as men and women live on separate floors of recruit barracks.

The House committee's bill (HR 3616) would require the services to begin training men and women separately and to house them in different barracks starting in April 1999, with the conversion complete by October 2001. The committee even threw in $8 million for new locks and barricades for current barracks.

The committee rejected, 23-30, an amendment by Florida Republican Tillie Fowler that would have eliminated the requirement. Fowler said she would not try again when the bill reached the House floor but was confident the Senate would not accept the House provision.

The Senate Armed Services Committee bill would prohibit any change in current policies until a basic training commission established by the fiscal 1998 defense bill (PL 105-85) issues a report, now due in September. The Senate bill (S 1812) would delay the report until Jan. 31, 1999.

Base Closing Revisited

The administration's request for another round of military base closings, rejected last year, appears headed for the same fate, but not before the Senate chews over the issue.

Defense Authorization

The Senate Armed Services Committee rejected the request for more shutdowns; its House counterpart ignored the issue.

Cohen and top military officers insist that to modernize their forces within stringent budget limits, they need to close facilities no longer needed by an active-duty military that is one third smaller than in the mid-1980s.

Large cutbacks were made between 1988 and 1995 under independent commissions set up by Congress. Political support for that approach collapsed after Clinton promised to save jobs at large Air Force maintenance bases in California and Texas slated for closure in 1995 by turning them over to private contractors. *(1995 Almanac, p. 9-19)*

Although the Pentagon insists that companies using the disputed bases have to compete for maintenance contracts against other companies and the remaining Air Force maintenance depots, critics cited a leaked Pentagon memo as evidence that, as recently as April, the White House was trying to steer work to the California base by prodding Lockheed Martin, a major defense contractor, to bid on work there.

The White House denied doing anything improper, but Cohen subsequently announced that the bidding process would be subject to outside review.

Senate Armed Services rejected, 8-10, an amendment to the defense bill by John McCain, R-Ariz., and Carl Levin, D-Mich., that would have created a commission to select bases for closure and deny the president the right to make any changes. The committee then rejected, 7-10, an amendment by Republican John W. Warner of Virginia that would have created a bipartisan commission to review the previous base-closing process and recommend changes.

Both proposals will be offered as amendments during floor debate. Last year, the Senate rejected further rounds of base closures by a vote of 66-33.

House and Senate leaders hope to move promptly on the defense bills. Senate Majority Leader Trent Lott, R-Miss., said May 7 he hoped the Senate would take up its version of the bill the week of May 11. The House tentatively plans to take up HR 3616 the week of May 18. That would mean the House-Senate conference on the bill could begin early in June.

Since the House and Senate have not reached agreement on a fiscal 1999 budget resolution, the defense committees would authorize slightly different totals: $270.8 billion, as Clinton requested, in the House version and $270.6 billion in the Senate version. Both committees made it clear that the final version of the bill would authorize the maximum allowed by the balanced budget legislation (PL 105-33), which is the amount Clinton requested.

Looking Overseas

Though neither committee has challenged President Clinton's continued commitment of troops to Bosnia — both approved his $1.9 billion budget for the mission over and above the defense bill totals — the Senate panel plans to reconvene and review the issue before its bill reaches the floor. The committee could decide to offer a floor amendment putting conditions on the money.

The House committee bill would repeal a 1996 law imposing stringent limits on the use by U.S. forces of anti-personnel land mines, beginning in 1999. The Senate bill is silent on the issue, but the administration is pushing hard for repeal of the 1996 law.

The House National Security Committee approved by voice vote an amendment by Rep. Lindsey Graham, R-S.C., to repeal the moratorium on land mines in the fiscal 1996 defense authorization bill (PL 104-106). *(1996 Almanac, p. 8-12)*

The legislation was one of several initiatives in a long-running campaign led by Sen. Patrick J. Leahy, D-Vt., and Rep. Lane Evans, D-Ill., to outlaw anti-personnel mines, which have been scattered by the millions in dozens of countries where they kill and maim non-combatants — often children.

But Pentagon officials contend that U.S. land mines do not contribute to that problem, since all of them have battery-powered fuses and either self-destruct within a few days of being deployed or run out of power within several weeks. They insist that such mines are essential to deter North Korean troops poised within artillery range of South Korea's capital. The 1996 legislative ban on anti-personnel mines contains an exemption for mines in the Korean De-Militarized Zone. But Pentagon planners say they need the flexibility to use them outside that four-kilometer-wide strip.

Other Policy Issues

By a vote of 45-4, the House committee adopted an amendment by Republican Duncan Hunter of California that would continue for another year a provision of the fiscal 1998 defense authorization bill barring a Chinese shipping firm from acquiring a U.S. Navy base in Long Beach, Calif., that has been closed.

The House panel rejected 20-29 an amendment by Jane Harman, D-Calif., that would have allowed female service personnel and dependents stationed overseas to obtain abortions in U.S. military hospitals provided they paid for the procedure. The amendment would have repealed a provision enacted in 1995 that banned abortions under those conditions. In 1997, the House upheld the ban by a vote of 196-224. *(1995 Almanac, p. 11-21)*

Members of both committees complained that the Pentagon was short-changing military retirees who had been assured when they enlisted that they and their dependents would be eligible for lifetime medical care in the military medical system. Base closures and reductions in the size of the services' medical staffs have made it more difficult for many retirees and dependents to obtain such care.

The Senate committee added to its bill a provision drafted by Dirk Kempthorne, R-Idaho, and Max Cleland, D-Ga., providing $60 million annually in each of the next three years for three pilot programs intended to test alternative methods of improving health care for military retirees over 65.

The House committee could not find the funds to pay for any pilot programs but told the Pentagon to come up with a plan by next March.

Weapons Programs

At the instigation of Warner, who chairs the Seapower Subcommittee, the Senate panel added $50 million to

Defense

buy components for a helicopter carrier for the Marines. The Navy has seven of these ships currently in service or under construction, the newest of which, funded in fiscal 1996, cost upwards of $1.3 billion.

Five older ships of a similar design are also in service, and the Navy plans to begin major overhauls to extend their service life. All the vessels were built by a Litton Industries shipyard in Pascagoula, Miss., home state of Senate Majority Leader Trent Lott, R-Miss. The Pascagoula yard would certainly build the new ship, if it were funded, but would not necessarily win the contract to refurbish one of the older ships.

For its part, the House committee laid the groundwork to enlarge the planned fleet of JSTARS radar surveillance planes — modified jetliners designed to spot ground targets at distances of more than 100 miles. The Pentagon had planned to buy 19 of the planes, which are built by Northrop Grumman Corp. But last year, the Pentagon reduced its planned purchase to 13, the last two of which Clinton requested — and the two committees approved — in the fiscal 1999 budget.

In a report on long-range Pentagon planning published last December, an outside advisory panel criticized that cutback. The House committee agreed, adding to its bill $72 million for components that would be used in additional JSTARS to be funded in future budgets.

Senators Seek Compromise With White House On Bosnia

MAY 16 — By the time the Senate resumes work on its $271 billion defense authorization bill for fiscal 1999, members of the Armed Services Committee hope to have worked out with the Clinton administration a compromise amendment on the U.S. military's peacekeeping mission in Bosnia.

The Senate took up the defense bill (S 2057) May 13, but set it aside May 14 after considering only a few amendments. Since it likely will spend most of the week of May 18 dealing with the contentious tobacco bill (S 1415), the Senate is not likely to resume work on the defense measure until early June, after the Memorial Day recess.

As approved by the Armed Services Committee on May 7, the bill would authorize the $1.9 billion requested by the Clinton administration to pay for the deployment of U.S. military units in Bosnia as part of a NATO-led peacekeeping force.

But President Clinton's decision late last year to drop any deadline for ending the deployment is strongly opposed by some members of Congress, who insist that European NATO members should provide the combat troops who police the Bosnian cease-fire on a day-to-day basis.

The critics contend that the U.S. role in Bosnia should emphasize intelligence-gathering, communications and transportation missions for which U.S. forces are uniquely equipped, as well as the provision of a combat reserve force stationed outside Bosnia but close enough to be quickly moved into the country should trouble erupt.

The administration counters that the roughly 8,000 U.S. troops in Bosnia constitute about one-fourth of the international force.

Currently, there are at least two Bosnia amendments that might be offered to the Senate defense bill:

● Robert C. Byrd, D-W.Va., and Kay Bailey Hutchison, R-Texas, may offer as an amendment their free-standing bill (S 2036) that would require the administration to reduce the size of the U.S. force in Bosnia to no more than 2,500 by February 2000.

● Carl Levin, D-Mich., is considering an amendment that would allow some number of members of either the Senate or House — perhaps 15 to 20 percent of the membership — to force Congress to vote on whether to cut off Bosnia funds for the last three months of fiscal 1999.

The senior Armed Services members negotiating with the Pentagon hope to avoid a showdown on either of those proposals by working out an amendment that would more carefully define the role of U.S. troops while putting pressure on European forces to do more of the heavy lifting.

The relatively narrow range of disagreement between these critics and the administration may be significant. Byrd, who ramrodded legislation requiring a withdrawal of troops from Somalia in 1993, and Hutchison, one of the most persistent Senate critics of the Bosnia mission, currently seek only to reduce the size of the U.S. combat force in Bosnia, not to eliminate it. *(Somalia, 1993 Almanac, p. 486)*

Floor Amendments

When the Senate took up the defense bill May 13, it adopted by voice vote an amendment by Armed Services Chairman Strom Thurmond, R-S.C., that cut $254 million from the $752 million the panel had approved to continue development of the Army's THAAD anti-missile system. The amendment also cut $21 million from the AMRAAM missile program and added the resulting $275 million savings to the intelligence budget.

The committee had already sliced $70 million from the administration's $822 million request for THAAD, citing delays in the program.

After a THAAD test on May 12 yielded the fifth failure in five tries at intercepting a target missile, the committee decided that the additional reduction would not affect the program, since it would be further delayed.

The committee was on the lookout for such savings because of strong opposition to cuts totaling about $500 million that it had recommended in various secret intelligence programs. In additional views appended to the Armed Services Committee's report on S 2057, John Glenn, D-Ohio, a member of both that panel and the Select Intelligence Committee, blasted Armed Services for taking a "meat axe" approach to the intelligence budget.

The Senate adopted two other amendments on May 14, both sponsored by Tim Hutchinson, R-Ark.

One would require the president to publicly identify companies controlled by the Chinese Army that do business in the United States. After a motion by Rod Grams, R-Minn., to table this amendment was rejected, 24-76, the amendment was adopted by voice vote. *(Vote 136, p. S-23)*

Also adopted by voice vote was a Hutchinson amendment requiring a report on imports produced by prison labor or forced child labor.

Defense Authorization

House Passes Bill, After Vote To Ban Chinese Missiles

MAY 23 — The House voted overwhelmingly to ban U.S. satellite makers from using inexpensive Chinese rockets to launch their products, after a debate in which Republicans accused the companies of undermining national security in their pursuit of profits.

Some senior Democratic defense specialists in the House warned that the amendments to the fiscal 1999 defense authorization bill (HR 3616), approved May 20, would complicate relations with China and handicap U.S. satellite companies in the face of international competition. But most Democrats laid low during the debate and supported the four amendments.

White House officials said 20 lawmakers who voted for the amendments had earlier urged Clinton to waive export restrictions so satellites could be launched on Chinese missiles.

The China amendments were the highlight of two days of debate on the $271 billion defense bill, which the House passed May 21 by a vote of 357-60. (Vote 183, p. H-54)

The bill basically would approve the amount President Clinton requested for the Pentagon and defense-related projects of the Energy Department, which is the maximum allowed by the 1997 balanced-budget law (PL 105-33).

The Senate version of the fiscal 1999 defense authorization bill (S 2057) authorizes $1.9 billion over and above the regular defense budget for U.S. peacekeeping forces in Bosnia, but the House version (HR 3616) does not. The House bill prohibits the Defense Department from spending more than $1.9 billion from its regular authorization for Bosnia operations.

House members had drafted several highly controversial amendments that would have reduced the total authorization by more than $2 billion, ended the Bosnia mission and eliminated a National Security Committee provision requiring separation of men and women in basic training. But, by a vote of 304-108, the House adopted a rule governing floor debate that did not allow any of those three amendments to be offered. (Vote 166, p. H-48)

Most debate centered on the amendments inspired by reports that China has improved its nuclear-armed missiles with technical know-how acquired from launching U.S. commercial satellites. Both types of rockets are essentially the same.

Because China charges less to launch satellites than U.S. or other overseas companies — as little as $25 million a trip — U.S. satellite makers have a powerful incentive to deal with China. But since a civilian communications satellite can cost several hundred million dollars, the companies and insurers have a stake in the reliability of China's launch rocket.

According to the Non-proliferation Policy Education Center, a private think tank opposed to such arrangements, Chinese engineers inevitably acquire technical know-how that has improved their *Long March* satellite launcher in ways that also could improve Chinese missiles' ability to reach U.S. targets with nuclear warheads.

For example, the technology that allows a rocket to place several satellites in different orbits could turn a single warhead missile into a MIRV (multiple independently targeted re-entry vehicle) weapon, which could aim several warheads at different targets.

U.S. government licenses, under which American firms are allowed to send satellites to China for launch, restrict the information that company officials are allowed to pass along to Chinese officials. The licenses also require that Chinese access to the satellites themselves be tightly limited.

The restrictions on satellite technology transfer became less stringent in 1996, when Clinton moved the regulation of launch deals from the State Department to the Commerce Department.

Loral Case

The case at the heart of the congressional furor began in February 1996, when a Chinese rocket crashed while trying to launch an Intelsat satellite built by Loral Space & Communications and destined for use by media mogul Rupert Murdoch's News Corp. and cable TV giant Tele-Communications Inc. (TCI).

Before they would cover future *Long March* launches, the insurance industry insisted that non-Chinese engineers review the Chinese post-mortem of the crash, to check its adequacy.

In a May 19 statement, Loral emphasized that the outside review team, chaired by a senior Loral official, was intended "to obtain information from the Chinese, not to help the Chinese solve their problem." The review team concurred in the Chinese conclusion that the accident probably was due to the failure of a solder joint.

Loral conceded that the review team violated company policy by reporting the team's findings to the Chinese before consulting the appropriate State Department officials. The company insisted that no U.S. law was violated and that U.S. security was not harmed. However, it also said it was cooperating with a Justice Department investigation into whether export control laws were violated.

Some critics argue that even affirming China's own diagnosis of so mundane a problem as a loose electrical connection improves the reliability of China's nuclear missiles as well as its satellite launchers.

"We don't want Chinese missiles to be reliable," said Rep. Duncan Hunter, R-Calif. "When the guillotine is over our head and it's sticking, we don't say, 'I think I see your problem.'"

Senior National Security Committee Democrat Ike Skelton of Missouri warned that the four GOP-sponsored amendments to restrict the transfer of U.S.-built satellites to China would undermine the U.S. effort, dating from the Bush administration, to encourage the Chinese government to promote international stability.

"The effort to coax China along, to help those responsible figures in this government to proceed in a positive direction, will probably suffer if we succeed in bashing China today in an attempt to criticize administration policy," Skelton warned.

The four amendments were:

● By National Security Committee Chairman Floyd D. Spence, R-S.C., and International Relations Committee Chairman Benjamin A. Gilman, R-N.Y., expressing the sense of Congress that business interests must not be placed above national security interests and that, during his visit to China in June, Clinton should not negotiate any of several proposed agree-

Defense

ments that would liberalize current limits on the transfer of satellite or missile technology to China. Agreed to 417-4. (Vote 167, p. H-50)

• By Doug Bereuter, R-Neb., prohibiting any "U.S. person" from participating in any analysis of a failure by a Chinese rocket to launch a U.S.-built satellite. Bereuter speculated that his amendment would discourage U.S. companies from launching their satellites on unreliable Chinese rockets. Agreed to 414-7. (Vote 168, p. H-50)

• By Joel Hefley, R-Colo., prohibiting any export to China of missile equipment or technology. In effect, this amendment would eliminate the president's authority in current law to waive the general prohibition, subject to certain conditions. Agreed to 412-6. (Vote 169, p. H-50)

• By Hunter, prohibiting any transfer to China of satellites, including transfers for the purpose of using Chinese launchers. Agreed to 364-54. (Vote 170, p. H-50)

Other Issues

The House also weighed in on the export of civilian nuclear reactors and related technology. By a vote of 405-9 it adopted a Gilman amendment requiring detailed reports to Congress before the Energy Department approves any proposed nuclear sale to a country other than the major traditional allies. (Vote 181, p. H-54)

Gilman said the provision would put Congress in a better position to try to head off proposed nuclear deals that might foster the spread of nuclear weapons. "I'm thinking, of course, of India," he said.

Some senior National Security Committee Democrats objected that the additional review period would handicap U.S. nuclear energy companies competing for business in developing countries that are expected to invest in reactors to generate electricity.

By 420-0, the House adopted an amendment by Gilman that would exempt U.S. military forces from any restrictions under the Kyoto Treaty on Climate Change, which would set limits on carbon-fuel emissions to preserve the ozone layer. Proponents of the amendment said that, before the treaty was negotiated, the Clinton administration had turned down a Defense Department request for such an exemption. (Vote 172, p. H-50)

Almost a year to the day after Marines patrolling the Rio Grande border with Mexico mistakenly killed a U.S. civilian, the House adopted an amendment by James A. Traficant Jr., D-Ohio, that would authorize the president to deploy military forces in support of Border Patrol and Customs Service personnel. The House adopted Traficant's amendment by a vote of 288-132 after rejecting a substitute by Silvestre Reyes, D-Texas, by a vote of 179-243. (Votes 179, 180, p. H-52)

The amendment would not give the president any authority he does not currently have. During the debate, Reyes and his allies, including several Hispanic members from the Southwest, openly opposed the use of military forces along the border.

In an annual test of strength for opposing sides in the war over abortion rights, the House rejected 190-230 an amendment by Nita M. Lowey that would have repealed the law barring female members of the armed forces or female military dependents overseas from obtaining abortions in U.S. military hospitals abroad, even if the procedure were paid for privately. (Vote 171, p. H-50)

Senate Debate To Focus on Bosnia, Basic Training

JUNE 13 — Major debates over the continued presence of U.S. troops in Bosnia and the separation of men and women in basic training are expected when the Senate resumes work on the fiscal 1999 defense authorization bill (S 2057), possibly as early as the week of June 15.

Aside from those issues, Clinton's defense budget of more than a quarter of a trillion dollars is moving through the Republican-controlled Congress with hardly a ripple.

Clinton requested $271 billion, plus $1.9 billion in emergency spending on the Bosnia mission. The version of the defense authorization bill reported May 11 by the Senate Armed Services Committee is only $280 million below that request. The counterpart measure (HR 3616) reported May 12 by the House National Security Committee and passed by the House May 21 is $395 million less than Clinton asked.

The defense bill's smooth sailing is due partly to public and congressional disinterest in defense and partly to the lack of any alternative defense program that commands widespread GOP support. While defense proponents in both parties complain that Clinton's budget is too stingy, Republican budget-cutters, led by House Budget Committee Chairman John R. Kasich, R-Ohio, stand in the way of any significant increase in Pentagon spending.

In the case of Bosnia, money is only part of an increasingly complex political issue. While many members opposed sending U.S. forces into the wartorn country, others have become frustrated by the fact that Clinton, after twice ignoring his own deadline for ending the mission, now refuses to set a date for withdrawal.

Other lawmakers are less critical of the deployment since peace appears to be taking hold in Bosnia. Senators likely will have to choose among amendments that vary in the degree to which they would force Clinton to limit the Bosnia mission.

Ground Combat

Both bills would underwrite the Army's plan to modernize its current forces with high-tech communications links while developing a new generation of combat gear for a more agile combat force after about 2010.

The Army unveiled June 9 the outlines of its plan for a slimmer Army in the years ahead that would rely more on electronics and updated weapons for greater mobility.

Both defense bills would authorize the $45 million that Clinton requested to continue developing the digital communication system intended to give tank commanders, helicopter pilots and infantry commanders a shared map of friendly and enemy forces. The Senate bill includes an additional $4 million to probe more diligently for vulnerabilities in the digital system that an enemy might exploit.

Both bills would authorize the $676 million the administration requested to continue upgrading M-1 tanks with larger cannon, digital links and improved night-vision gear. Both also would authorize the $286 million requested to upgrade some Bradley armored troop carriers with digital communications and night-vision equipment. The House version would add $75 million for more limited upgrades of additional Bradleys to be allocated to National Guard units.

The $612 million the administration requested to equip missile-armed Apache helicopters with digital links and Longbow target-finding radar would be authorized by the House bill. The Senate version would add $40 million for training equipment and engine modifications.

Both bills would deny the request for $49 million to continue developing a lightweight weapon for airborne units: a guided missile that could be launched from a light truck and steered to a target several miles away by a fiber-optic cable to a TV camera in the missile's nose. Massachusetts-based Raytheon is the contractor.

Pentagon planners believe that U.S. ground troops' ability to operate at night gives them a powerful advantage over most other forces. Accordingly, the administration asked for $77 million for night-vision equipment for the Army and Marines. The Senate bill would add $25 million to that request; the House bill, $9 million.

Both bills would authorize the $51 million requested to begin equipping individual infantry soldiers with digital communications links. Citing Army studies that indicate full-torso body armor could prevent half of all life-threatening wounds, the House bill would add $5 million to buy body armor.

The House bill also would add $15 million to buy Shortstop electronic jammers that would detonate most incoming artillery shells long before they get close enough to be dangerous.

To accelerate the development of "non-lethal" weapons that could immobilize a large crowd of civilians without causing them permanent injury, the Senate bill would add $13 million to the $23 million requested.

Making the Grade

One of the two new Army weapons being developed for the future — a stealthy Comanche helicopter built by Boeing and United Technologies and intended to quarterback a digitally linked force — is strongly supported by both bills. Clinton asked for $368 million. The Senate bill would add $24 million, the House bill $62 million.

The committees complained, however, that the Army's other major new weapons program — the Crusader mobile cannon — may be too cumbersome for the future Army. The gun was intended to have a longer range than the Army's existing cannon and to be more mobile and easier to keep supplied. But technical problems spiked a key element of the design: The use of a liquid propellant instead of gunpowder.

As a result, critics complain, the new gun will not have a dramatically longer range than current weapons. At a projected weight of 60 tons, the Crusader may lack the speed and ease of transport the Army will require.

United Defense, owned by the privately held, Washington, D.C.-based Carlyle Group, and General Dynamics, whose armored vehicle business is based near Detroit, are the lead contractors for the $12 billion program that is slated to produce 824 cannon and the same number of armored supply vehicles, beginning in 2005.

The Senate committee's bill would authorize the $313 million requested to continue developing the program but the committee told the Army to consider radical changes, including buying fewer cannon.

The House bill would cut $60 million from the budget request, and the committee told the Army to consider revising the program to incorporate composite armor and other features that would make the gun lighter and more mobile.

Air Combat

With only minor changes, both versions of the bill would authorize the Pentagon's plan to fund three major jet fighter programs.

Indeed, the House bill goes a step further and would add $60 million to buy two additional F-16s, built in Fort Worth, Texas, by Lockheed Martin. According to the National Security Committee, the planes are needed to make sure that losses due to crashes and wear and tear do not leave the Air Force short of F-16s in 2010.

The bills would authorize the administration's request for $785 million for two Lockheed Martin F-22 fighters (to be built in Marietta, Ga.), $190 million for F-22 components that

Sex-Integrated Training Retained

JUNE 13 — Defense Secretary William S. Cohen announced June 8 that the Army, Navy and Air Force would continue to train men and women together in boot camp and could even house them in the same barracks, so long as their living quarters were separated by a combination of physical barriers and direct supervision.

Basic training will continue to be gender-segregated for Marines and for Army men destined for combat units.

When the Senate resumes work on the fiscal 1999 defense authorization bill (S 2057), Sam Brownback, R-Kan., will try to overturn Cohen's policy and require the separation of all men and women in basic training.

A commission chaired by former Kansas Republican Sen. Nancy Kassebaum Baker (1978-97) in December recommended keeping men and women apart in training and living quarters.

The committee said putting men and women together in training platoons weakens discipline and distracts the recruits. It also called for making training duty more attractive to experienced sergeants and petty officers.)

The services adopted most of the panel's recommendations. But senior officers of the Army, Navy and Air Force balked at separating the sexes in training, insisting that recruits needed to become accustomed to working alongside members of the opposite sex.

The version of the authorization bill passed May 21 by the House (HR 3616) would require that male and female recruits be organized and housed separately. The Senate version would bar any change in current policy until a congressionally mandated outside panel completes its review early next year.

Defense

would be used in planes funded in future budgets and $1.58 billion to continue flight testing the stealthy F-22.

The General Accounting Office has complained that the Pentagon plans to commit to production of the F-22 before the prototypes have flown enough test flights. The Senate bill included a provision that would bar additional production funds until at least 4 percent of the test flight program has been completed.

The Senate bill would authorize the $2.89 billion requested for 30 of the Navy's "E" and "F" model F/A-18s, plus components for additional planes slated for future funding. The House bill would cut $213 million (three planes) from the purchase. The planes — larger variants of the F/A-18s in use by the Navy and Marine Corps — are built in St. Louis by former aerospace giant McDonnell Douglas, now a part of Boeing.

Both versions of the bill would authorize $920 million requested by the administration to develop the Joint Strike Fighter that would be built in three versions in the next decade to replace 1970s-vintage planes used by the Navy, Air Force and Marines. Boeing and Lockheed Martin are competing for the contract.

The House bill would add to the budget $86 million to improve the Air Force's fleet of 21 B-2 stealth bombers.

Both bills would authorize the $463 million requested to buy the last two of 13 Joint STARS surveillance planes, which have radar that can detect enemy tank columns from a distance of 100 miles. Both bills would add to the budget $72 million to buy components that could be used for additional planes.

A request for $114 million to buy 15 additional Predator drone airplanes, like the ones that have carried reconnaissance equipment over Bosnia, would be authorized by both bills.

Both versions would authorize stepped-up production by Teledyne Ryan Aeronautical of the Global Hawk, a drone with airliner-sized wings and a business jet-sized body designed to carry a ton of surveillance gear while flying for 24 hours over a target 3,000 miles from its base. The bills would add $33 million to the $90 million requested for the program.

The long-range surveillance drone DarkStar, developed by Lockheed Martin and Boeing, fared less well. It carries a smaller payload over a shorter range but has a stealthy design that would allow it to orbit heavily defended targets. The first DarkStar prototype crashed in 1996 on its second flight. The House bill would authorize the $41 million requested for the program, but the Senate bill would deny the funds for the program, which Senate Armed Services describes as "an unfortunate case of overreach."

Missiles and Anti-Missiles

Changes that the House and Senate bills make in Clinton's $4 billion request for missile defense programs have less to do with policy differences than technical and budget issues.

Both bills would authorize the $951 million Clinton requested to continue developing a system to protect U.S. territory against a limited number of missiles. Neither bill calls for accelerating a decision to deploy such a system. Democrats have blocked Senate action on a separate bill declaring that such a defense should be deployed "as soon as is technologically possible."

Because Lockheed Martin's THAAD anti-missile system, designed to protect U.S. forces overseas from long-range missiles, had its fifth consecutive test failure in May, the Senate bill would authorize only $498 million of Clinton's $822 million request for the program. The House would authorize the requested amount but would instruct the Pentagon to prepare another contractor to take over the program if there is no improvement.

Both bills would add $120 million to the $190 million requested for the Navy's Theater-Wide system, a shipborne counterpart to THAAD.

The House and Senate committees are frustrated with the administration's refusal to say whether it will stick with the mobile MEADS system intended to protect front-line combat units. The House bill would authorize the $43 million requested but only if Defense Secretary William S. Cohen certifies that his department will continue to seek money for the program. The Senate bill would authorize only $10 million to study an alternative to MEADS.

The budget requests $94 million for work on a space-based anti-missile laser, slated to be launched in 2005. While the House bill would authorize $20 million less than requested, the Senate bill would double the authorization to $188 million, reflecting the program's strong support from Robert C. Smith, R-N.H., who chairs Armed Services' Strategic Forces Subcommittee. To offset the extra money, the Senate bill would cut $97 million from the $292 million requested to continue work on an airborne laser, carried in a Boeing 747, intended to destroy ballistic missiles as they rise from launchers up to 300 miles from the plane.

In its report, the Senate committee said that the plane would be too vulnerable to enemy attack and that atmospheric turbulence would dissipate the laser's lethal power. However Air Force Gen. Richard Hawley, chief of the Air Combat Command, told reporters that his fighters could protect the laser plane just as they now protect other converted airliners used as Joint STARS and AWACS radar planes. Hawley also said that atmospheric data collected by the Air Force indicated the airborne laser could operate effectively.

Both bills would authorize the request for $323 million to buy five additional Trident II, long-range, submarine-launched, nuclear-armed missiles. Both also would add funds to the $91 million requested to upgrade Minuteman nuclear-armed missiles. The Senate bill would add $46 million to accelerate the replacement of out-dated missile guidance systems. The House bill would add $23 million to test the use of Minuteman to attack deeply buried targets with a precision-guided non-nuclear warhead.

Naval Forces

Both House and Senate bills would authorize the $125 million requested for components of a nuclear-powered aircraft carrier designated CVN-77. Most of the ship's $4.6 billion cost is slated for inclusion in the fiscal 2001 budget.

The Navy had planned CVN-77 as an upgraded version of the *Nimitz*-class carriers it has been building for three decades. For its next carrier, designated CVX, it planned to develop a new design that would have a much smaller crew and would be harder for radar to detect. But to avoid the cost of a completely new design, the service has decided to introduce new features piecemeal into the *Nimitz*-class design.

The budget requested $39 million

Defense Authorization

for design work on CVN-77 and an additional $190 million to develop CVX. Both bills would authorize those amounts, but with the proviso that $50 million of the CVX funds be used instead to improve CVN-77.

The bills also would authorize $275 million requested to overhaul and refuel a nuclear-powered carrier.

A nuclear-powered submarine ($1.5 billion) and three destroyers equipped with the Aegis anti-aircraft system ($2.68 billion) would be authorized by the bills with minor changes.

The Senate bill would authorize the $179 million Clinton requested to develop and install the "cooperative engagement capability," a wireless computer network that allows ships and planes in a fleet to exchange targeting data. The House bill would increase that amount by $61 million.

Air and Sea Transport

The $2.9 billion the administration requested for 13 wide-body, C-17 cargo jets plus components for future purchases would be authorized by both bills.

As has been routine for years, both versions of the bill would add several hundred million dollars to buy various versions of the C-130 cargo plane built by Lockheed Martin in Marietta, Ga. The administration requested $64 million for one plane. The Senate bill would authorize $382 million for five, and the House bill would authorize $461 million for eight.

Both bills would authorize the $639 million requested for a ship designed to carry 700 Marines, their equipment and landing craft.

But both also would add to the budget small down payments — $50 million in the Senate bill, $10 million in the House bill — on a $1.4 billion helicopter carrier that would be built by Litton Industries in Pascagoula, Miss.

The shipyard, Mississippi's largest private employer, is located in the hometown of Senate Majority Leader Trent Lott and in the district represented by Gene Taylor, a senior Democrat on House National Security.

The ship, which would carry nearly 2,000 Marines and 30 helicopters, would replace an older helicopter carrier the Navy plans to keep in service after an extensive overhaul.

Both bills would add to the budget $16 million to accelerate the planned overhaul of the air-cushion landing barges used to haul tanks and other heavy gear ashore from amphibious landing ships.

Military Personnel

The Senate bill would authorize an active-duty force of 1,395,778, as Clinton requested. The House bill would increase that level by nearly 11,000.

The House also would authorize a more generous military pay raise: 3.6 percent rather than the 3.1 percent Clinton requested and the Senate committee approved. The larger raise would cost $186 million more. However, the companion defense appropriations bill drafted by a House subcommittee would fund only a 3.1 percent increase.

Both bills include provisions that would allow the services to offer larger recruiting bonuses for key, hard-to-fill jobs. The House bill also would add $100 million to the amounts requested for recruiting and advertising.

For the National Guard and military reserves (including the Coast Guard Reserve), the Senate bill would authorize the requested manpower level of 885,094. The House bill would allow an additional 1,000.

Operations and Maintenance

As usual, each version of the bill shuffles around several hundred million dollars within the $95 billion requested for operations and maintenance and for revolving funds that pay for certain types of maintenance work. Each of the committees added funds to budget accounts they said would boost combat readiness.

The Senate bill would add $55 million and the House bill $236 million to the amounts requested for major overhauls of ships and planes.

The Senate bill would add $75 million and the House bill $200 million to increase stocks of aircraft spare parts.

Each bill would increase funding for maintenance and facility repair — the Senate bill $284 million, the House measure $175 million.

Each of the committees offset some or all of those increases with cuts they said would have no impact on Pentagon operations.

For instance, because fuel prices have dropped since the budget was drafted, the Senate bill would cut $304 million and the House bill $240 million from the fuel budget requests.

Because the Pentagon's civilian payroll is dropping faster than Clinton's budget request assumed, the Senate bill would cut $659 million and the House bill $538 million that had been requested for jobs that are vacant.

Because the dollar is gaining strength against many foreign currencies, U.S. forces stationed abroad who buy goods and services locally will need less money than the budget assumed. The Senate bill would cut $119 million, the House bill $108 million.

For the Nunn-Lugar program intended to help Russia and other former Soviet republics dispose of nuclear, chemical and biological weapons, the Senate bill would authorize $440 million of the $442 million requested. The House bill would cut $25 million from the request.

Democrats Parry GOP Thrusts On China, Bosnia

JUNE 27 — With President Clinton off to China and tensions rising in the Balkans, the Senate spent more time debating foreign policy than military affairs during consideration of the fiscal 1999 defense authorization bill.

The $274 billion measure (S 2057) passed 88-4 June 25. The Senate then passed the House version (H 3616) by voice vote after substituting the text of its bill. *(Vote 181, p. S-29)*

Senate Democrats blocked several Republican amendments they said were designed mainly to undermine Clinton on the eve of his nine-day China visit.

The amendments, offered by Tim Hutchinson, R-Ark., would have condemned Chinese human rights abuses and required a tougher U.S. stance toward Beijing's bids for international stature and financial assistance.

Hutchinson insisted that, by emphasizing the importance of human rights policy, his amendments would have strengthened Clinton's hand in talks with Chinese leaders.

Democrats said Hutchinson threatened to violate the time-honored tradition that Congress close ranks behind a president when he is abroad. "It

Defense

is simply designed to embarrass the president of the United States on the eve of his trip," complained Minority Leader Tom Daschle, D-S.D.

Vowing to prevent any vote that could be interpreted as a Senate reproof of Clinton's China policy, Daschle threatened to bring work on the authorization bill to a standstill unless the China amendments were dropped. After some inconclusive procedural sparring, Hutchinson withdrew the amendments in return for a commitment that the Senate debate later this year a House-passed bill (HR 2358) that incorporated several of his proposals.

The administration's Senate allies also blunted attacks against the deployment of U.S. troops in Bosnia and sustained the administration's decision not to segregate military recruits by gender during their first several weeks of training.

The administration's only major policy defeat was the Senate's approval June 25, by a vote of 48-45, of an amendment by James M. Inhofe, R-Okla., that would tighten the existing limits on the Pentagon's ability to close or scale down military bases without congressional approval. (Vote 174, p. S-28)

The vote was the most recent of several to reflect congressional anger that the White House interfered in the 1995 base-closing process to save jobs in the vote-rich states of California and Texas.

There was little Senate debate on the spending authorized by the bill. The $274 billion covers all Pentagon operations and the defense-related activities of the Energy Department, including $1.9 billion Clinton requested to continue the Bosnia operation through fiscal 1999. The bill would authorize $462 million more than Clinton requested.

The Senate handily rejected two amendments that would have reduced the total authorized for defense programs. These were amendments:

• By Tom Harkin, D-Iowa, that would have transferred $329 million from the Defense Department to the Department of Veterans Affairs. Rejected, 38-55. (Vote 175, p. S-28)

• By Paul Wellstone, D-Minn., that would have dunned all Pentagon budget accounts by enough to add $270 million to the Pentagon's child-care system. Rejected, 18-74 (Vote 173, p. S-28)

On the other hand, it adopted by voice vote an amendment by Conrad Burns, R-Mont., that would authorize $200 million for military construction projects. The Military Construction Appropriations Subcommittee, which Burns chairs, added that amount to its bill (S 2160 — S Rept 105-213), which also passed June 25.

China Skirmish

Hutchinson offered four amendments dealing with U.S. policy toward China. They would have:

• Condemned the Chinese government's use of forced sterilization and forced abortion as population control techniques — a practice which reportedly occurs, despite official disavowals. The provision also would have barred travel to the United States by any official who enforced such a policy.

• Denied a U.S. visa to any Chinese official involved in the repression or harassment of persons because of their religious practices.

• Required the U.S. government to oppose subsidized loans to China by the World Bank.

• Transferred from the Commerce Department to the State Department licensing authority for the shipment of U.S.-built satellites to China.

In an effort to make senators take a stand on the package of amendments, John W. Warner, R-Va. — who supported the amendments — offered a motion to table (kill) the package. But Democrats — many of whom opposed the amendments — countered by voting against the tabling motion, which was rejected 14-82. (Vote 167, p. S-27)

When Hutchinson's amendments were taken up individually, a similar procedural minuet was carried out on the first of the four — the one condemning forced abortions. A motion to table that amendment was rejected, 0-96. (Vote 168, p. S-27)

Bosnia and Basic Training

By a vote of 90-5, the Senate adopted a non-binding amendment by Armed Services Committee Chairman Strom Thurmond, R-S.C., expressing the sense of Congress that U.S. combat troops should be withdrawn from Bosnia "within a reasonable period of time." (Vote 170, p. S-28)

But the Senate tabled (killed), by a vote of 65-31, an amendment by Robert C. Smith, R-N.H., that would have required the Senate to conduct a non-binding vote by March 31 on whether to continue the Bosnia mission. "That just told me that Congress doesn't want to go on record," Smith later said. "They like to talk and do nothing." (Vote 171, p. S-28)

Sam Brownback, R-Kan., offered an amendment that would have required the Pentagon to house male and female recruits in separate barracks during basic training.

That proposal was overridden by a second-degree amendment offered by Olympia J. Snowe, R-Maine, and Max Cleland, D-Ga., reaffirming the provision in the bill that would prohibit any immediate change in the current policy under which Navy and Air Force recruits and Army recruits headed for non-combat units are housed on different floors or in different wings of the same barracks.

The Snowe-Cleland amendment was adopted, 56-37, after which the amended Brownback amendment was adopted by voice vote. (Vote 172, p. S-28)

Subsequently, the Senate rejected, 39-53, an amendment by Robert C. Byrd, D-W.Va., that would have required separate barracks and separate training units for male and female recruits. (Vote 180, p. S-29)

Other Amendments

By a vote of 44-49, the Senate rejected an amendment by Patty Murray, D-Wash., that would have repealed a section of the fiscal 1996 defense authorization bill (PL 104-106) that bars female service members or military dependents stationed overseas from obtaining abortions in U.S. military hospitals abroad, even if the procedure is paid for with private funds. (Vote 176, p. S-29; 1995 Almanac, p. 9-3)

The Senate also adopted by voice vote dozens of non-controversial amendments. One of these, offered jointly by the Republican and Democratic leadership, would name the bill in honor of the 95-year-old Thurmond, who has announced he will step down as chairman at the end of this session.

Among other amendments adopted by voice vote:

• By Thurmond, authorizing a 3.6 percent military pay raise instead of the 3.1 percent increase the administration requested.

Defense Authorization

- By Dianne Feinstein, D-Calif., as amended by Brownback, condemning the Indian and Pakistani governments for conducting nuclear test explosions and supporting the U.S. economic sanctions against the two countries. The amendment also urged the two countries to scale back their nuclear weapons programs and urged the Clinton administration to try to negotiate with them steps that could result in a lifting of the U.S. sanctions.
- By Thurmond, giving the president authority to waive a one-year moratorium on the use of anti-personnel landmines, that is slated to begin in February 1999.
- By Patrick J. Leahy, D-Vt., reserving $17 million to develop alternatives to anti-personnel mines.
- By Thurmond, to trim a total of $422 million from several parts of the bill because of reduced estimates of the cost of inflation. The reduction would be partly offset by the addition of $120 million to the amount allocated to the Army National Guard's budget for operations and maintenance and the addition of $20 million to the Energy Department's authorization for arms control verification technology.
- By Mike DeWine, R-Ohio, and Inhofe, requiring military physicians to have unrestricted licenses to practice medicine. In a Pulitzer Prize-winning story, the Dayton [Ohio] Daily News reported last year that 77 military doctors held "special" licenses for which the testing criteria were less rigorous.
- By Rod Grams, R-Minn., and Alfonse M. D'Amato, R-N.Y., to extend for one year, through Sept. 30, 1999, the Defense Production Act of 1950, which is the legal basis for the government's authority to allocate critical resources in time of emergency.

Conferees Agree; Integration of Sexes To Continue In Basic Training

SEPTEMBER 19 — House and Senate negotiators reached agreement Sept. 17 on a $270.5 billion defense authorization bill (HR 3616) for fiscal 1999 that would keep men and women together in basic training and delay a contentious decision on the production of the nuclear material tritium.

The conference report could come before the full House and Senate the week of Sept. 21. Although it contains provisions the Clinton administration has objected to, a veto is unlikely, partly because of accumulating concern over the military's combat readiness.

The conference agreement would transfer jurisdiction over the licensing of satellite exports from the Commerce Department to the State Department. The State Department had responsibility for satellite controls before Commerce officials argued that technology once judged to have military characteristics was widely available commercially.

Conferees also authorized the purchase of four C-130 cargo planes for the National Guard and reserves and two C-130s for the Marine Corps that the Pentagon had not sought. And they authorized a $50 million down payment on a $1.3 billion helicopter carrier to be built in the hometown of Senate Majority Leader Trent Lott, R-Miss.

Although the administration had planned to decide by the end of the year where to produce tritium, an ingredient in enhancing nuclear weapons explosions, conferees delayed a decision for one year.

They rejected House language that would have ordered the Army, Navy and Air Force to revert to single-sex basic training and to housing male and female recruits in separate barracks.

House Adopts Conference Report; Senate Expected To Follow Suit

SEPTEMBER 26 — Brushing aside objections from some social conservatives, the House Sept. 24 approved, 373-50, the conference report on HR 3616, the fiscal 1999 defense authorization bill. The Senate is expected to follow suit the week of Sept. 28. *(Vote 458, p. H-130)*

House National Security Committee member Roscoe G. Bartlett, R-Md., backed by the Family Research Council, the Christian Coalition and other conservative groups, opposed the compromise version of the bill because it did not include a provision he sponsored in the House version that would have forced the armed services to train male and female recruits separately.

An outside advisory panel chaired by former Kansas Republican Sen. Nancy Kassebaum Baker (1978-97) had recommended in late 1997 that basic training be separated by sex. Senior military leaders objected strongly.

The defense bill conferees included a provision requiring that permanent walls separate male and female recruits in barracks. But the Senate had voted against separate units by a large margin, so the final report included only a non-binding expression by the House that basic training should be separate.

Bartlett was one of only 11 Republicans voting against the conference report.

The bill would authorize more than $272 billion for the departments of Defense and Energy, including $270.5 billion in regular budget authority, which is $406 million less than President Clinton requested.

The remaining $1.86 billion, also requested by Clinton, would pay for U.S. troops in Bosnia for the next year. But because these funds were requested and approved as emergency spending, they are exempt from the defense budget ceiling set by the 1996 balanced-budget law (PL 105-33). *(1997 Almanac, p. 2-47)*

Military Personnel

Members of the armed forces would get a 3.6 percent pay raise in fiscal 1999 rather than the 3.1 percent requested by Clinton. The increase was initiated by the House, agreed to earlier by the Senate and now accepted by the administration.

As requested, the conferees approved an active-duty force of slightly fewer than 1.4 million personnel, a reduction of nearly 36,000 from the fiscal 1998 level. The House bill had made a cut only about two-thirds that large.

For the part-time troops of the National Guard and reserves, the conference report set a manpower ceiling of more than 885,000 — roughly what Clinton requested but nearly 10,000 fewer than last year.

Defense

Pentagon Presses for Budget Increase, Saying Readiness Is Slipping

SEPTEMBER 19— For months, top Pentagon officers have kept a wary eye on signs of strain in the ranks caused by shrinking defense budgets and the increasing pace of overseas operations. But they have been firm in their assurances to Congress that there is enough money, manpower and morale to get the job done.

Now the facade of confidence is slipping, no doubt helped by the prospect of a substantial federal budget surplus next year.

Citing mounting evidence that combat readiness is eroding, Pentagon leaders are asking President Clinton to increase future defense budgets, reportedly by as much as $10 billion to $15 billion a year above the ceiling set by the 1997 balanced-budget legislation (PL 105-33). *(1997 Almanac, p. 2-47)*

The tone of the military chiefs seemed to shift this summer when Joint Chiefs of Staff Chairman Gen. Henry H. Shelton issued an assessment that it would be more difficult now for U.S. forces to meet the longstanding goal of winning two regional wars that broke out nearly simultaneously.

Complaints by service members about pay, fringe benefits, frequent deployments overseas and aging equipment were publicized during Defense Secretary William S. Cohen's visits to several military bases beginning in August — visits Cohen said were intended to help him gauge morale.

On Sept. 14, Air Force Chief of Staff Gen. Michael Ryan told reporters that the decline in readiness previously acknowledged had gone further than the chiefs had anticipated. "We thought it would stabilize, and it hasn't," Ryan said.

By all accounts, Clinton received a correspondingly grim account the following day during a previously scheduled conference with Cohen, the Joint Chiefs and the senior combat commanders in chief at Washington's Fort McNair.

"The way [Shelton] has put it is that in the last year or so, readiness trends have nosed down," Pentagon spokesman Kenneth Bacon told reporters. "We want to pull back on the stick before there's a nose dive."

Bacon insisted that Pentagon leaders did not go into the meeting to present Clinton with a laundry list of expensive new programs. But he said, "The president's a smart man, and he can draw his own conclusions from what he's being told."

Defense advocates in Congress want the chiefs to take the same message to Capitol Hill during Senate Armed Services Committee hearings slated to begin Sept. 29. "Hopefully with the acquiescence of the president, the chiefs are going to outline the need for additional defense spending," said Republican committee member John W. Warner of Virginia.

Question of Priorities

Even though many senior members of the defense committees, along with House Speaker Newt Gingrich, R-Ga., and Senate Majority Leader Trent Lott, R-Miss., have called for higher defense spending, the idea has gained no political traction. Earlier this summer, in fact, Clinton reportedly rejected Lott's proposal for a defense budget increase on grounds that it would reopen the contentious debate settled in 1997 by the balanced-budget deal.

However, a public call for more funds by the military chiefs could radically change the political dynamic.

Even in that event, higher defense spending would meet stiff resistance from many liberal Democrats and some conservative Republicans intent on reducing the deficit and cutting taxes.

On Sept. 17, two days after Clinton's meeting with the military chiefs, the libertarian Cato Institute issued a paper contending that the Pentagon could live

---

To help recruiters in an increasingly difficult market, the conference report would authorize $36 million more than Clinton requested for advertising; $22 million more for bonuses paid to recruits who sign up for critical or hard-to-fill jobs; and $20 million more than was requested for education benefits, a prime recruiting incentive.

The conferees also ordered the Pentagon to test options for improving medical care for military retirees age 65 and older. Because those people are eligible for Medicare, they now receive only limited coverage from the Pentagon's health care system. This has become a very sore point not only with the large population of military retirees but also with active-duty personnel nearing the time when they typically decide whether to make the military a career.

The conference report would authorize:

● A three-year program, conducted in at least six locations, allowing retirees and their families to participate in the relatively generous health insurance program available to civilian federal employees.

● A test program in two locations for using the Pentagon's Tricare dependent medical insurance program to supplement Medicare coverage for retirees, along the lines of commercially available "Medi-gap" supplemental insurance.

Readiness and Facilities

Citing contradictions between the Pentagon's official assessment that military forces remain fully combat

Defense Authorization

with a smaller budget, if the country adopted a less interventionist foreign policy.

But Senate Armed Services Democrat Joseph I. Lieberman of Connecticut, an advocate of higher defense budgets, contends that past resistance to more Pentagon spending may be diminishing as budget deficits give way to surpluses far larger than were anticipated only a year ago.

"We're in the politics of surplus," Lieberman said. "This is the time for those of us who think we've been shortchanging defense to speak up."

People Problems

The military services report growing strains in a variety of activities, including training, maintenance and modernization. But much of the current political focus is on shortfalls in enlistment and re-enlistment — particularly the departure from the service of pilots, who are being recruited by the expanding airline industry, and the exodus of other highly trained specialists with marketable skills.

One problem that carries a clear price tag is the argument by members of the military that their pay and fringe benefits are being eroded.

A broad range of military personnel complain that the purchasing power of basic pay — the lion's share of service members' take-home pay — has dropped nearly 14 percent since 1980, compared with the pay for civilians in similar occupations. This is based on the fact that annual military pay raises are usually a half-percent lower than a government index of comparable private-sector jobs.

In the fiscal 1999 defense authorization bill, Congress has changed the practice, approving a 3.6 percent pay raise for military personnel, rather than the 3.1 percent Clinton requested.

The administration apparently has accepted this change, which will cost about $200 million in fiscal 1999. Moreover, the administration has promised even more generous raises in fiscal 2000, when it plans to request a 4.4 percent pay increase.

For a staff sergeant with 10 years of service whose basic pay in fiscal 1998 was slightly more than $22,000, the combination of a 3.6 percent raise in 1999 and a 4.4 percent increase in 2000 would be worth about $150 per month.

But some congressional defense specialists contend that the perception of a pay gap is less corrosive to morale than the widespread belief among troops that there is an erosion of promised fringe benefits, particularly pensions and medical care for dependents and retirees.

Shifting Pensions

Congress made cost-cutting changes in the military pension system in 1980 and again in 1986, each time applying the changes only to relatively junior service members. Those who had already built up seniority were left in existing pension plans. Thus, while all active-duty personnel can retire after 20 years of service, the amount of their monthly pensions will depend on when they entered the service:

• Members who joined up before Sept. 8, 1980, would get 50 percent of their basic pay at retirement and an annual cost of living increase equal to the consumer price index.

• For those who joined between Sept. 8, 1980, and July 31, 1986, the system would work the same, except that their payment would be the average of their basic pay during the three years it was highest.

• Members who joined after July 31, 1986, would get only 40 percent of their average basic pay during their highest three years. When they reached age 62, their pensions would be increased to what they would have been had they been paid 50 percent of the highest average. But both before and after that one-time adjustment, their cost of living increases would be 1 percent lower than the consumer price index.

A dozen years after the most recent, and much less generous, system took effect in 1986, it has become a focal point for troops' frustration, as the first personnel subject to its provisions approach the mid-career point at which most decide whether to stay in for at least a 20-year career.

Senate Republican leader Lott and Appropriations Committee Chairman Ted Stevens, R-Alaska, have both called for a new retirement system that would be more generous to members who joined the military after 1986.

ready and the growing consensus among top officials that the military is under a heavy strain from budget cuts and workload, the conferees added a provision requiring that a more accurate readiness reporting system be implemented by Jan. 15, 2000.

To shore up readiness in the meantime, they authorized modest increases to several budget accounts. They approved $5.9 billion — $151 million more than Clinton requested — for the routine overhaul of ships, planes and vehicles and their engines and electronic gear. They also approved $3.9 billion, which is $296 million more than requested, for maintenance of barracks and operational facilities.

The conference report added to the budget request $155 million for spare parts to keep Navy and Air Force planes flying, and $178 million for day-to-day operating costs of military bases.

For military facilities and family housing, the conferees approved $8.6 billion, adding $666 million to Clinton's request.

Of the increase, $301 million was specified for reserve and National Guard units.

Anti-Missile Defense

Although Republicans have pressed Clinton to accelerate the deployment of anti-missile defenses, the conference report would authorize $104 million less than the $3.6 billion requested for anti-missile programs.

Among the most controversial projects are these:

• Development of a system to pro-

Defense

tect U.S. territory against a relatively small number of missiles. The bill would authorize Clinton's request for $951 million.

- The Army's Theater High-Altitude Area Defense (THAAD) system, intended to protect troops and allies abroad from long-range missiles. All five flight tests have failed. The conference report would authorize $527 million, $294 million less than Clinton asked. The conferees urged Pentagon managers not to overreact to the test failures but to redouble their efforts to make the program work.
- The Navy's long-range anti-missile system, a counterpart to THAAD. The conferees authorized $310 million, which is $120 million more than requested.
- A laser-armed anti-missile satellite. The conference report would authorize $188 million, double the amount requested.
- The Army's battlefield anti-missile system, called MEADS. The conferees approved only $24 million of the $43 million requested. Moreover, they included in the bill a provision barring the use of those funds until the Defense secretary certifies to Congress that the program will be funded in future Pentagon budgets.

Separately from the anti-missile defense program, the Air Force is developing an anti-missile laser to be carried by a large cargo plane. The conference report approved $235 million of the $292 million requested for this project.

Nuclear Weapons

For defense-related programs of the Energy Department, the conferees approved $12 billion, which is $330 million less than Clinton requested.

That authorization includes:

- $487 million for the stockpile stewardship program, which uses computer simulations and micro-explosions to verify the reliability of the nation's stock of nuclear weapons. That is $30 million less than requested.
- $485 million for facilities associated with stockpile stewardship, $30 million less than was requested.
- $682 million for the Office of Naval Reactors, $16 million more than Clinton asked.
- $177 million for production of tritium, a radioactive form of hydrogen gas used to boost the explosive power of nuclear weapons. Since tritium loses its punch in 12 years and has not been produced since 1988, the administration is trying to decide between two methods for producing more of the gas.

The House version of the defense bill included a provision that, in effect, would have forced the administration to build a new tritium production facility at the Savannah River Site in South Carolina. The conferees dropped that provision, adding one that would defer for at least one year the selection of a tritium production plan.

China Policy

The conference report includes several Senate provisions that had been included because of allegations that China has improved its long-range missiles with technology gleaned from launching U.S.-made satellites.

The most significant of the provisions would transfer authority over satellite export controls from the Commerce Department to the State Department. Clinton had moved the authority to Commerce in 1996 at the urging of satellite manufacturers, who complained that the State Department took too long deciding on transfers.

The conference report also includes a provision that would bar the secretary of the Navy from leasing a former Navy base in Long Beach, Calif., to a Chinese government-owned shipping line.

Major Weapons Programs

Relatively few of the administration's requests for major weapons programs were changed by either the House or Senate. The compromise bill eliminated several changes that only one chamber had approved.

For instance, the conference report would authorize, as Clinton requested, the purchase of 30 F/A-18 E and F model Navy fighter jets, cutting only $14 million from the $2.9 billion request. The House version of the bill had trimmed three planes from the purchase, a cut of $205 million.

On the other hand, the conferees approved $743 million to buy eight V-22 Ospreys, hybrid airplane/helicopters used by the Marine Corps. The budget requested, and the Senate approved, $665 million for seven aircraft, but the House added an additional plane.

One congressional addition that could cast a long shadow in future budgets was $50 million for advance purchases of components to be used in a helicopter carrier that could cost upward of $1.3 billion. The conferees said that the ship, which would be built by Litton Industries in the hometown of Senate Majority Leader Trent Lott, R-Miss., would replace an older helicopter carrier for which the Navy had planned a $1 billion overhaul.

Reserves and National Guard

As usual, Congress is using the bill to provide more equipment to reserve and National Guard units than the Pentagon requested. The conferees approved $745 million for the Guard and reserves, in addition to the $1.36 billion worth of gear that was earmarked for them in Clinton's budget request.

The largest single addition was $306 million for four C-130 cargo planes. The conferees also approved $112 million for two tanker versions of the C-130 for the Marine Corps. In all, the conference report would authorize $483 million for seven C-130s, all of which are built by Lockheed Martin in Marietta, Ga., adjoining the district of House Speaker Newt Gingrich, R-Ga. The administration had requested $64 million for one aircraft.

The conferees dropped a House provision that would have enlarged Arlington National Cemetery, across the Potomac River from Washington. Local officials complained that they had been cut out of the decision to incorporate into the cemetery some adjacent vacant land.

The conference report also included a non-binding provision expressing the sense of the House that the president and secretary of Defense should adhere to the standard of "exemplary conduct" required of military commanders. ◆

Republicans Succeed In Shoring Up Funds For Anti-Missile Defenses

SUMMARY

Three times in 1998 Congress provided funds for the Pentagon's anti-missile defense programs: first in the fiscal 1998 emergency supplemental (HR 3579), then in the fiscal 1999 defense appropriations bill (HR 4103) and finally in the fiscal 1999 omnibus spending package (HR 4328).

Republicans succeeded in adding $1 billion to anti-missile defense programs in the omnibus bill. The fiscal 1999 defense spending bill already provided $3.45 billion for those programs, basically tracking the fiscal 1999 defense authorization bill (HR 3616 — PL 105-261).

The Pentagon has discretion in spending the $1 billion in emergency funding provided in the omnibus bill. It may allocate $150 million to the national anti-missile defense program, which is intended to develop a system to protect U.S. territory from an attack by a limited number of missiles.

Other priorities include the Navy's ship-based defense against long-range missiles; the Army's long-range Theater High-Altitude Area Defense (THAAD) and its associated radar; and the short-range PAC-3, a modification of the Patriot air defense system used in the 1991 Persian Gulf War.

The defense appropriations bill (HR 4103) met President Clinton's full $951 million national anti-missile defense request. The major cut made by that bill — blunted somewhat in the omnibus supplemental — was from the Army's THAAD system. All five THAAD flight tests have failed.

Republicans also tried to bring to the Senate floor legislation (S 1873) that would have repudiated Clinton's plan to wait until 2000 before deciding whether to deploy a national anti-missile defense. Democratic filibusters twice blocked debate on the bill, which would declare it national policy to deploy an anti-missile defense as soon as technologically possible.

The Pentagon is part way through a three-year program to develop a national missile defense by 2000, when the administration will decide, based on the system's performance and the world situation, whether to deploy it by 2003. Delaying the decision, Republican critics contend, creates uncertainty in the minds of government officials and contractors.

Funding for anti-missile defense was also included in the fiscal 1998 supplemental appropriations measure (HR 3579). The bill provides $179 million for several programs intended to boost the ability of existing U.S. and Israeli anti-missile weapons to deal with new Iranian and North Korean missiles.

House Panel Calls For Expedited Missile Defenses

MARCH 21 — The House National Security Committee on March 17 approved a bill that would authorize $147 million to speed the deployment of defenses against new missiles of Iran and North Korea. The vote was 45-0.

Committee Chairman Floyd D. Spence, R-S.C., said he hoped the funding authorized by the bill (HR 2786) would be included in a fiscal 1998 supplemental appropriations measure (S 1768) that the House is expected to take up later this month. However, he conceded that the outlook was uncertain, given the stringent budget.

The bill was drafted last fall by Curt Weldon, R-Pa., after Israeli and U.S. intelligence agencies reported that Iran might, within a year, deploy a ballistic missile called Shahab-3 with a range sufficient to reach targets in Israel, Turkey and Saudi Arabia. The United States also was caught off guard last year when North Korea's No Dong 1 missile was deployed unexpectedly soon after its first test firing.

Since both of these new weapons fly farther than the Iranian and North Korean missiles already in service, they fly much faster. "Our currently deployed missile defense systems were designed against older and slower threats and have only limited capabilities against this new generation of more capable missiles," Spence said.

The funds authorized by the bill would be parceled out for a variety of programs that the Pentagon said could adapt existing defenses against the new threats, pending deployment of more sophisticated anti-missile defenses still under development. Under the bill:

- $41 million would go to enable the current defenses to make more effective use of the data from existing missile detection equipment.
- $15 million would accelerate the use of equipment that would allow deployment of newer, PAC-3 versions of the Patriot missile that can be spread

---

Box Score

- **Bills:** HR 4328 — PL 105-277; HR 4103 — PL 105-262; HR 3579 — PL 105-174
- **House action:** The House adopted the conference report (H Rept 105-825) on HR 4328, 333-95, on Oct. 20. It adopted the conference report (H Rept 105-746) on HR 4103, 369-43, on Sept. 28. The House adopted the conference report (H Rept 105-504) on HR 3579, 242-163, on April 30.
- **Senate action:** The Senate cleared the conference report on HR 4328, 65-29, on Oct. 21. The Senate cleared the conference report on HR 4103, 94-2, on Sept. 29. The Senate cleared the conference report on HR 3579, 88-11, on April 30. Senate failed to invoke cloture on S 1873, 59-41, on May 13 and on Sept. 9.
- **Presidential action:** Clinton signed HR 4328 on Oct. 21, HR 4103 on Oct. 17 and HR 3579 on May 1.

Defense

out to defend a larger area.
- $40 million would be used to test the capability of existing PAC-3 and Navy Standard missiles against high-speed targets that would mimic the new Iranian and North Korean missiles.
- $41 million would be used to expand the PAC-3 production line to increase the maximum production rate.
- $10 million would go to improve the military's ability to electronically link U.S. and Israeli anti-missile defenses.

Democrats led by Owen B. Pickett of Virginia and John M. Spratt Jr. of South Carolina backed the bill after Weldon made changes in the original version, one of which was a reduction of the total cost from $330 million.

House Authorizes Extra $147 Million For Defenses

APRIL 4 — To counter a threat posed by new missiles in Iran and North Korea, the House passed legislation (HR 2786) on March 30, by voice vote, that would authorize an additional $147 million for the Pentagon in fiscal 1998 to speed the deployment of missile defenses.

Despite the tight budget, prospects are good that additional spending for the program this fiscal year, apart from the authorization, will be approved, since it is supported by the Defense Department and by both Democratic and Republican defense specialists on Capitol Hill.

The Senate included $151 million for a similar missile defense package in its version of the emergency supplemental appropriations bill (HR 3579) approved March 31. The House-passed version of the supplemental did not include the funds that HR 2786 would authorize. Appropriations Committee Chairman Robert L. Livingston, R-La., said he would try to include the funds in the compromise final version of the funding bill.

The authorization bill was drafted last fall by Curt Weldon, R-Pa., amid intelligence reports that Iran might deploy within a year the new Shahab-3 ballistic missile, which could strike targets in Israel, Turkey and Saudi Arabia. The United States also was caught off guard last year by reports that North Korea may have deployed a small number of No Dong missiles after only a single test flight.

Because the new missiles fly farther than previous Iranian and North Korean weapons, they approach their targets at a higher speed. U.S. missile defenses now in the field and those nearing deployment are designed to deal with the slower missiles and would have only a limited ability to shoot down the newly emerging threats.

The funds authorized by HR 3579 would go to several programs intended to boost the ability of existing U.S. and Israeli anti-missile weapons to deal with the new Iranian and North Korean weapons pending deployment of more advanced U.S. defenses, currently slated to occur in the middle of the next decade.

The package of programs the House authorized March 30 differed in only one major respect from the package for which the Senate approved appropriations: HR 2786 would authorize $41 million to expand the production line for the Patriot PAC-3 interceptor missile. The Senate's version of the supplemental appropriated $45 million to help Israel enlarge its force of Arrow anti-missile missiles.

Senate Panel Endorses National Missile Policy

APRIL 25 — Legislation that would call for, but not require, a national defense against ballistic missiles was approved by the Senate Armed Services Committee on April 21.

The bill (S 1873), approved by a party-line vote of 10-7, would declare a national policy to deploy "as soon as is technologically possible" a system to protect U.S. territory from a limited number of incoming missiles.

Mississippi Republican Thad Cochran, the bill's sponsor, said it was a way to break the 15-year deadlock between those who want to build an anti-missile shield against an accidental or terrorist attack and those who say that too hasty a deployment could undermine the 1972 treaty limiting anti-ballistic missile (ABM) weapons and could poison relations with Russia.

Cochran and his allies emphasized that the bill makes no reference to the treaty, which allows the type of limited defense the bill calls for.

Senior Armed Services Democrat Carl Levin of Michigan and other critics reject the argument that technical feasibility alone should determine whether to deploy anti-missile defenses. The decision, they say, should consider whether a threat is imminent and whether deployment might lead Russia to renege on agreements to reduce its arsenal of long-range missiles.

In an April 21 letter to Levin, Joint Chiefs of Staff Chairman Gen. Henry H. Shelton cited those and other reasons for opposing Cochran's bill. Instead, Shelton endorsed the Clinton administration's plan to develop a nationwide defense system by 2000 but deploy it only if a threat warrants.

Although S 1873 has 49 cosponsors, only three are Democrats: Hawaiians Daniel K. Inouye and Daniel K. Akaka and Ernest F. Hollings of South Carolina. Armed Services Committee member Joseph I. Lieberman, D-Conn., who earlier said he was considering supporting the bill, abstained from the panel's April 21 vote.

India's Test Fuels Senate Debate; Cloture Vote Fails

MAY 16 — India's test of nuclear weapons did not help Senate Republicans pass legislation May 13 that would encourage the development of a national anti-missile defense system. In fact, lawmakers on both sides of the issue drew arguments from the Indian tests.

Sponsors of the bill (S 1873) came up one vote shy of the 60 needed to begin debate on the legislation that calls for, but does not require, deployment of the defense system as soon as technologically possible.

The nearly party line vote of 59-41 came on a cloture motion that would have blocked a promised Democratic filibuster against a motion to take up the bill. All Republicans voted for cloture, as did four Democrats: Daniel K. Inouye and Daniel K. Akaka of Hawaii, Ernest F. Hollings of South

Anti-Missile Defenses

Carolina and Joseph I. Lieberman of Connecticut. *(Vote 131, p. S-22)*

Republicans want to quickly develop and deploy a system capable of knocking down at least a limited number of incoming ballistic missiles. The Clinton administration wants to develop the system but wait until 2000 before deciding, based on the threat at that time, whether to build it. *(1996 Almanac, p. 8-13)*

Unseen Threats

Proponents of the bill pointed to India's nuclear blasts, along with unforeseen progress by India and other countries in the development of long-range ballistic missiles, as proof that the administration's policy was hopelessly flawed.

"We can't be sure," said Thad Cochran, R-Miss., the bill's chief sponsor. "And if we can't be sure that we can detect the threat, we need to be prepared to defend against that threat."

Opponents of the bill, led by Michigan Democrat Carl Levin, argued that the tests underscored the importance of trying to reduce the risk that nuclear weapons might be acquired by more countries and by terrorist groups. Deep cuts in Russia's nuclear arsenal required by the START I and START II arms control treaties would help reduce that risk, they said. But they warned that Russia would reverse its nuclear drawdown if Congress passed the Cochran bill, which the Russians would see as a step toward nullifying the 1972 treaty limiting anti-ballistic missile (ABM) systems.

"Arms control is giving us missile defense that works, right now," said Byron L. Dorgan, D-N.D., arguing against the bill.

Cochran pointed out that his bill makes no reference to the ABM Treaty, which would allow certain types of very limited anti-missile systems. But Levin insisted that the bill was a Trojan horse: Many of the bill's leading supporters have called for ending the treaty, he said, and the bill itself does not require that the defense shield comply with the treaty. "Those words are missing, and they are not missing inadvertently," he said.

Fifth Failure

Each side read its own meaning into the May 12 failure of the Army's THAAD missile, which missed its target for the fifth time. It is intended to protect U.S. forces in the field against missiles flying a shorter distance than those that would be launched against U.S. territory. As in the earlier incidents, the problem appeared to have been unrelated to the basic design of the weapon.

Jeff Bingaman, D-N.M., warned that the Cochran bill would create political pressure to speed work on a national missile defense, resulting in what a Pentagon advisory panel had called a "rush to failure" that fostered the mistakes bedeviling THAAD.

But Jon Kyl, R-Ariz., said THAAD was a reminder that complex weapons typically take longer to field that anticipated.

Report Buoys Supporters Of Missile System

JULY 18 — Advocates of a national anti-missile system hope to gain political advantage from a warning by a commission of outside arms experts that hostile countries, including North Korea, could have ballistic missiles within five years able to reach U.S. territory, much sooner than the Clinton administration has estimated.

The commission, led by former Defense Secretary Donald H. Rumsfeld, also said the United States might have little or no warning before a potential adversary fielded dangerous missiles.

Governments are becoming more adept at concealing missiles and nuclear, chemical or biological weapons programs from prying satellites and other intelligence gathering, the commission said, and they find it easier to obtain foreign help in developing or acquiring the technologies.

The report, issued July 15, summarized a much longer, classified document the commission delivered to Congress the previous day.

Anti-missile proponents have made many of the same points, but the Clinton administration, backed by most congressional Democrats, has deferred a commitment to deploy an anti-missile system pending evidence that new and potentially threatening missiles are going to be deployed. The administration insists that its development program could yield a missile defense as early as 2003.

The public has shown little or no interest in the debate.

A 1995 intelligence report concluded that no missile threat was likely to arise for 15 years, except from North Korea. A threat from Korea could materialize in 10 years, the report concluded. It did not allow for the possibility that a country might receive outside help in developing missiles.

Among the nine panel members concurring in the report were Barry M. Blechman, deputy director of the Arms Control and Disarmament Agency in the Carter administration; Richard L. Garwin, a leading arms control intellectual, and retired Air Force Gen. Lee Butler, who commanded U.S. strategic nuclear forces in 1992-94 and is a leading advocate of deep reductions in the number of nuclear weapons.

Senate Defeats Second Attempt To Cut Off Debate

SEPTEMBER 12 —Republicans have tried fruitlessly for several years to convince the nation that it needs to develop and deploy a system that could intercept a limited number of incoming ballistic missiles — a more modest legacy of President Ronald Reagan's "star wars" program.

The most recent bill (S 1873), sponsored by Sen. Thad Cochran, R-Miss., calls for, but does not require, an anti-missile defense as soon as technologically possible. The administration wants to develop such a defense but to wait until 2000 before deciding, based on the threat then in view, whether to build it.

A Democrat filibuster stalled the bill by one vote in May.

But Cochran and his allies made another attempt on Sept. 9, looking for help from several recent events, including North Korea's Aug. 31 test of a long-range missile that flew over Japanese territory.

A July 15 report by a congressionally mandated commission of experts,

Defense

chaired by former Defense Secretary Donald H. Rumsfeld, warned that the United States might have little or no warning before hostile countries such as North Korea fielded ballistic missiles able to reach U.S. territory with nuclear, chemical or biological warheads.

The Sept. 9 vote came on a cloture motion to block a threatened Democratic filibuster of the motion to take up Cochran's bill. All 55 Republicans voted for cloture, as did four Democrats: Joseph I. Lieberman of Connecticut, Daniel K. Inouye and Daniel K. Akaka of Hawaii and South Carolina's Ernest F. Hollings.

The remaining Democrats opposed cloture, putting the tally at 59-41 — a majority that was one vote shy of the 60 needed to shut off debate. *(Vote 262, p. S-41)*

But Clinton's policy had been powerfully buttressed by a strong endorsement from the Joint Chiefs of Staff. The military chiefs' view was expressed by their chairman, Gen. Henry H. Shelton, in an April 24 letter to James M. Inhofe, R-Okla. Inhofe, who chairs the Senate Armed Services Committee's Subcommittee on Readiness, had asked the Joint Chiefs in July to comment on the Rumsfeld report.

Writing on behalf of all the chiefs, Shelton endorsed the current plan of developing a defense by late 1999 and deciding in 2000 whether it should be deployed. He acknowledged that there was some risk that an adversary could acquire a long-range missile without being detected, but said the chiefs regarded this as "an unlikely development."

Senate Majority Leader Trent Lott, R-Miss., said further action on S 1873 was unlikely. But the House may vote on a similar bill as early as the week of Sept. 14. The legislation (HR 4402) would declare it national policy to deploy a national missile defense. While it would have no practical effect, the bill would repudiate Clinton's plan to wait until 2000 to decide whether to deploy the system being developed. ◆

Chemical Weapons Bill Wrapped Into Omnibus Spending Package

A year and a half after the Senate ratified a treaty banning chemical weapons, Congress cleared legislation to implement the pact in this country. The measure was a last-minute addition to the omnibus fiscal 1999 spending package (HR 4328 — PL 105-277) that was signed into law Oct. 21.

SUMMARY

The implementing legislation (S 610) puts into domestic law the Chemical Weapons Convention (Treaty Doc 103-21), which outlaws the development, use or stockpiling of chemical weapons and establishes an international agency to conduct inspections and collect data to verify compliance. The new law authorizes the president to issue regulations applying the treaty's prohibitions to anyone in the United States and to U.S. citizens anywhere in the world. It also establishes a legal framework for compliance inspections.

The Senate had passed the bill (S 610) in May 1997, a month after ratifying the treaty. But the measure languished for months in the House, where GOP leaders attached it to a separate bill (HR 2709) aimed at punishing overseas companies and research labs, primarily in Russia, that provide missile technology to Iran. Republicans hoped the move would force President Clinton to agree to economic sanctions he opposed. Instead, in July, Clinton vetoed the Iran sanctions bill, and with it the treaty implementing provisions. *(1997 Almanac, p. 8-13)*

On Sept. 16, a nonpartisan arms control group released a study warning that failure to act on the treaty legislation this year could set off an international crisis. Issued by the Henry L. Stimson Center, the report said major U.S. trading partners, such as China, Germany and Japan, were threatening to prohibit chemical weapons inspections in their countries because no inspections had occurred at U.S. commercial plants.

The report also said that no "challenge inspections" — those demanded by one country against another — had been launched, in part because other nations were waiting to see how the United States confronted and punished those attempting to violate the treaty.

Finally, in the days leading up to adjournment in October, House GOP leaders included the chemical weapons provisions in the omnibus spending bill (HR 4328 — H Rept 105-825).

Though pleased that the measure was enacted, proponents remained troubled by some of the law's provisions. They cited restrictions giving the president the right to block surprise inspections on national security grounds as well as require that no chemical samples leave the United States for testing.

"Passage of the implementing legislation is certainly a positive step, but the exceptions in the legislation will greatly damage the treaty's verification regime and need to be fixed at some point in the near future," said Amy E. Smithson, a senior associate at the Stimson Center. ◆

Box Score

- **Bill:** HR 4328 — PL 105-277
- **House action:** The House passed the conference report (H Rept 105-825) on HR 4328, 333-95, on Oct. 20. The House had agreed to Senate amendments to HR 2709, clearing the bill, June 9.
- **Senate action:** The Senate cleared HR 4328, 65-29, on Oct. 21. The Senate passed HR 2709, 90-4, on May 22.
- **Presidential action:** Clinton signed HR 4328 on Oct. 21. He vetoed HR 2709 on June 23.

Lawmakers Seek To Limit NATO Expansion To Three New Members

Box Score

- **Bill:** Treaty Doc 105-36 (Executive Rept 105-14)
- **Senate action:** The Senate adopted the ratification resolution, 80-19, on April 30.

SUMMARY

The Senate voted in favor of admitting Poland, Hungary and the Czech Republic to NATO, making them the first new members since Spain was accepted in 1982. Once the rest of the 16 current members agree, the three Central European nations will formally join next April 4 at a 50th anniversary meeting of the alliance in Washington.

The Senate vote was 80-19 on April 30.

The bipartisan vote to amend the 1949 North Atlantic Treaty and admit the three countries to the alliance was far larger than the two-thirds majority required. However, several senators who urged approval of this expansion warned against hasty moves to add more former Eastern bloc nations to the alliance.

NATO members, including the United States, are agreeing to defend the former Warsaw Pact nations from attack, just as they have agreed to defend Western Europe.

In February, the Pentagon endorsed a NATO analysis that concluded that the total cost of beefing up alliance-wide communications networks and selected bases, through which the three new members could receive reinforcements if they were under attack, would be $1.5 billion over 10 years. This does not include the much larger amount the three countries will have to spend to modernize their forces and make them operationally compatible with current NATO members.

Critics had warned that admitting the three countries would poison relations with Russia, divert the attention of the three countries from economic reform to military issues and overextend U.S. military commitments.

But the administration had built support for the expansion slowly and carefully. Foreign Relations Chairman Jesse Helms, R-N.C., signed on in late 1997 after Secretary of State Madeleine K. Albright assured him that Russia would gain no significant influence over NATO's deliberations as the result of a consultation arrangement that was established to ease Moscow's concern about the expansion.

Joseph R. Biden Jr. of Delaware, ranking Democrat on the Foreign Relations Committee who helped guide the expansion through the Senate, said lawmakers now want to wait for evidence that Poland, Hungary and the Czech Republic can be integrated successfully before considering admitting any more nations.

An amendment by John W. Warner, R-Va., that would have barred membership invitations to additional countries for three years was rejected, 41-59. But the "ayes" included some strong proponents of admitting the three countries, including Helms, who had held several hearings in 1997 on the subject.

Republicans who opposed the deployment of U.S. forces in Bosnia tried to use the resolution to ensure that a draft overall NATO strategy would not lead to more peacekeeping commitments beyond the territory of NATO members. Their efforts, however, were brushed aside by overwhelming margins.

Nonetheless, underscoring the diverse nature of opposition to NATO expansion, the "nay" votes spanned the ideological gamut from conservative Republican John Ashcroft of Missouri to liberal Democrat Paul Wellstone of Minnesota.

Senate Poised To OK Expansion

MARCH 7 — The Senate is expected to vote on and approve NATO expansion within the next two weeks, after Majority Leader Trent Lott, R-Miss., rejected a request by opponents to put off debate until June.

The Senate Foreign Relations Committee on March 3, by a vote of 16-2, backed the resolution approving NATO membership for Poland, Hungary and the Czech Republic. Committee Chairman Jesse Helms, R-N.C., predicted the Senate would approve the measure by "an overwhelmingly positive vote."

A two-thirds vote of approval is necessary because the Senate is acting on three amendments, or protocols (Treaty Doc 105-36), to the 1949 North Atlantic Treaty.

Underscoring the diverse nature of opposition to NATO expansion, the two "nay" votes in committee were cast by conservative Republican John Ashcroft of Missouri and liberal Democrat Paul Wellstone of Minnesota.

As of March 5, eight Republicans and eight Democrats had signed a letter written by Robert C. Smith, R-N.H., and Tom Harkin, D-Iowa, asking Lott to delay floor action on NATO expansion until after June 1. They argue that too few senators have focused on the issue and that too many questions about the cost and implications were unanswered.

"Enlargement . . . will commit the United States, by law, to the military defense of a vast new expanse of European territory," the letter said. "It would not be wise to enter a treaty commitment that raises more questions than it answers."

Expansion supporters, led by William V. Roth Jr., R-Del., countered with their own letter to Lott, insisting that the Senate move on the issue during March, as planned. Helms noted that his panel had held several hearings last October and November on the proposal.

Lott, who strongly supports NATO expansion, rejected the request for a de-

Defense

lay before it was made, saying March 3 that he planned to bring the resolution before the Senate within a week or two.

Critics are geared up to offer amendments to the resolution that would impose conditions on U.S. ratification of the enlargement.

One anticipated amendment, by Daniel Patrick Moynihan, D-N.Y., would delay NATO membership for the three countries until they are admitted to the European Union. Another, by John W. Warner, R-Va., would bar membership invitations to any other country for three years.

Estonia, Latvia and Lithuania, which the Soviet Union annexed in 1940, are among the countries clamoring for admission to NATO. But Russia, which is reluctantly reconciled to the admission of Poland, Hungary and the Czech Republic, is expected to oppose more vehemently the admission of any former Soviet republic. The United States never recognized the annexation of the three Baltic countries.

The administration strongly opposes any legislated "pause" in the expansion process. But some senators, such as Foreign Relations member John Kerry, D-Mass., who will vote for admission of the first three countries, have indicated they want NATO to move slowly in deciding whether to invite additional members.

All 16 current NATO members must approve the new members. To date, Canada, Denmark and Norway have done so. The three countries invited to join also must ratify the agreement.

Different Worries

NATO expansion is an issue that transcends party and ideology. Wellstone, for instance, said he was concerned that adding the three former Soviet satellites would exacerbate tensions between Moscow and the West.

Ashcroft did not object to NATO's enlargement but argued that the Senate should use the enlargement debate as an opportunity to gain influence over the future evolution of NATO policy. With the end of the Cold War, he said, the organization had taken on a more vaguely defined role of protecting members' interests — an aim that might entangle the United States in Bosnia-like peacekeeping missions around the globe.

Senior committee Democrat Joseph R. Biden Jr. of Delaware responded that, from its beginning, NATO had a broader international role than defending Western Europe from invasion.

The committee included in its resolution of approval a condition requiring that the president consult with the Senate on NATO's revision of its "strategic concept," a process now under way.

Another condition in the resolution would require the president to reaffirm that an agreement negotiated last year between NATO and Russia does not give Moscow a veto over NATO actions.

Still another would require the president to report periodically to the Senate on whether other NATO members are paying a fair share of alliance costs.

In February, the Pentagon endorsed a NATO analysis that concluded that the total cost of beefing up alliance-wide communications networks and selected bases, through which the three new members could receive reinforcements if they were under attack, would be $1.5 billion over 10 years. This does not include the much larger amount the three countries would have to spend to modernize their forces and make them operationally compatible with current NATO members.

An earlier U.S. study estimated that the comparable cost would be about $6 billion. The administration attributes much of the difference to the fact that facilities in the three countries are in better shape than had been assumed.

Senate Suddenly Defers Action On NATO Bill

MARCH 21 — As abruptly as the Senate began debate the week of March 16 on the proposed expansion of NATO, Senate leaders postponed action on the issue, possibly until after the spring recess.

Eventual Senate approval of NATO membership for Poland, Hungary and the Czech Republic appears all but certain. Majority Leader Trent Lott, R-Miss., said, however, that scheduled action on the issue the week of March 23 would have to give way to more urgent business, including a fiscal 1998 supplemental appropriations bill.

When the Senate resumes consideration of NATO expansion, floor debate likely will focus on Virginia Republican John W. Warner's call for a three-year "pause" before NATO could invite additional countries to join.

Warner's amendment is one of several the Senate will debate that would add conditions to the resolution of consent to the proposed expansion. The conditions would address only U.S. policy and would not deny admission to the three nations.

Since admission of the three countries requires amendment of the 1949 North Atlantic Treaty, which created NATO, the resolution of Senate approval requires the same two-thirds majority that the Constitution requires for Senate approval of a treaty. But the resolution can be amended by a simple majority.

Theoretically, it would be easier for opponents of NATO expansion to muster the 34 votes needed to kill the approval resolution outright than the 51 votes needed to amend the measure. Practically speaking, however, admission of the three current applicants appears politically unstoppable.

"I'm confident that, when all is said and done, the Senate will reaffirm the principle that every NATO ally has upheld since 1949 — that our alliance is and always will be open to those European democracies able to contribute to its goals," Secretary of State Madeleine K. Albright said at a White House ceremony March 20.

The Clinton administration has orchestrated support for expansion from a wide array of groups, including ethnic heritage associations, labor unions and veterans' organizations. The opposition has gained little public support and remains a relatively small corps of academic specialists and politicians.

Moreover, President Clinton has so deeply committed U.S. prestige to the admission of these three countries that even some leading critics fear that Senate rejection of the proposal would undermine U.S. diplomatic clout.

Playing for Time

The desultory floor debate on NATO began March 17 during a hia-

NATO Expansion

tus in the consideration of an education bill (S 1133).

Warner argued that his proposed three-year delay in admitting new members would give the alliance time to better assess how long it would take and how much it would cost for Poland, Hungary and the Czech Republic to bring their military forces up to NATO's standard.

Warner also pointed out that the delay would ensure that Clinton's successor would have a role in deciding future membership invitations. "Shouldn't the next president have a say on this?" Warner demanded.

But the Clinton administration and its Senate allies vigorously oppose Warner's resolution. They contend that a pause would demoralize governments in central and eastern Europe for whom the prospect of NATO membership is a powerful incentive toward democratization and free market economic reform.

Sen. Carl Levin, D-Mich., argued that Warner's proposal was superfluous. "Given the deliberative process that was involved in NATO's enlargement decision," Levin said, "it is clear that it will take some time before any new nations will be chosen for accession."

The question of which countries would be invited to join next may be more contentious than when. Pressing hard for inclusion are the Baltic nations of Estonia, Latvia and Lithuania, which the Soviet Union annexed in 1940 — an act the United States never recognized — and may be reluctant to see join NATO.

In addition to Warner's call for a pause in expansion, amendments to the NATO resolution are expected to be offered by the following senators:

• Daniel Patrick Moynihan, D-N.Y., would seek to delay NATO membership for any country until after it has been admitted to the European Union.
• Appropriations Committee Chairman Ted Stevens, R-Alaska, would seek to ensure that the U.S. share of NATO costs does not increase as a result of the alliance's expansion. One proposal Stevens may offer would require NATO to reduce the U.S. share of the alliance's organizational budget.
• Tom Harkin, D-Iowa, would attempt to ensure that all U.S. subsidies to the three invited countries be counted under any limitation the Senate places on the U.S. share of the cost of expansion. Another of several possible Harkin amendments would require that the United States contribute no more than 25 percent of the subsidies that all NATO members grant to any of the three countries to help them gear their military forces to NATO standards.
• Kay Bailey Hutchison, R-Texas, would require that NATO establish a formal mechanism to resolve disputes among members.

Senate Approves Three Nations' Memberships

MAY 2 — Even as the Senate strongly endorsed admitting Poland, Hungary and the Czech Republic to NATO, it sent the alliance a clear signal not to rush into inviting any more former Eastern Bloc nations to join.

"Quick entry of other members will compound all the problems," warned Jack Reed, D-R.I., who supported expanding the alliance this time. "I would be very wary of the integration of other countries into NATO."

The Senate voted 80-19 on April 30 in favor of admitting Poland, Hungary and the Czech Republic, the first new NATO members since Spain was accepted in 1982. Once all 16 current members agree, the three Central European nations would formally join next April 4 at a 50th anniversary meeting of the alliance in Washington. (Vote 117, p. S-20)

Joseph R. Biden Jr. of Delaware, the ranking Democrat on the Foreign Relations Committee who helped guide the expansion agreement through the Senate, said lawmakers now want to wait for evidence that Poland, Hungary and the Czech Republic can be integrated without the adverse effects critics had predicted.

In an interview after the Senate vote, Biden said he had just given that message to President Clinton. "[Senators] are not opposed to expansion beyond this," Biden said he told the president, "but they are in the mode of, 'show me.'"

The sentiment was reflected in the vote on an amendment by John W. Warner, R-Va., that would have barred membership invitations to additional countries for three years. The amendment was rejected 41-59, but the "ayes" included some strong proponents of admitting the three countries, including Foreign Relations Committee Chairman Jesse Helms, R-N.C. (Vote 112, p. S-19)

The bipartisan, pro-expansion vote was far larger than the two-thirds majority required by the Constitution for Senate approval of a treaty or treaty amendment and was evidence of deep groundwork both by the administration and congressional leaders.

As is customary on such solemn occasions, the senators took their seats for the vote and rose in turn to answer the roll call. The only senator not voting was Arizona Republican Jon Kyl, a supporter of expansion. He had already left on an overseas trip.

The vote was to approve President Clinton's ratification of an amendment to the 1949 North Atlantic Treaty (Treaty Doc 1-5-36, Executive Rept 105-14) that would add the three countries to NATO. Four other current members of the alliance — Canada, Denmark, Norway and Germany — have ratified the change.

Alliance members, including the United States, are agreeing to defend the three former Warsaw Pact nations from attack, just as they have agreed to defend Western Europe.

Critics had warned that admitting the three countries would poison relations with Russia, divert the attention of the three countries from economic reform to military issues and over-extend U.S. military commitments overseas.

Republicans who oppose the deployment of U.S. forces in Bosnia tried to use the resolution to ensure that a revised overall NATO strategy now being drafted would not lead to more U.S. peacekeeping commitments beyond the territory of NATO members.

"How many more Bosnias are out there that we are going to be obligated to support as a result of increasing our commitment to NATO?" demanded James M. Inhofe, R-Okla.

The Senate brushed aside a raft of amendments to the resolution that would have delayed admission of Poland, Hungary and the Czech Re-

Defense

public or confined NATO's role to defense of its members' territory.

In a statement, Clinton said the Senate's vote sent a clear message: "American support for NATO is firm, our leadership for security on both sides of the Atlantic is strong, and there is a solid, bipartisan foundation for an active U.S. role in the world."

A Strong Hand

Democratic and Republican leaders have been committed to NATO expansion since 1994. During the 1996 presidential campaign, GOP nominee Bob Dole's only objection to Clinton's handling of the issue was that he was moving too slowly.

Dealt a strong political hand on the issue, the Clinton team played it skillfully. For nearly a year, Jeremy Rosner, a special assistant to the president, has been quarterbacking the administration's lobbying effort, rounding up support for the three invited countries from veterans, labor and ethnic organizations. Secretary of State Madeleine K. Albright and Defense Secretary William S. Cohen, both of whom are steeped in NATO issues, and Clinton himself have pressed the case for admitting the three countries.

Senate support for the proposal began to jell last summer, when Majority Leader Trent Lott, R-Miss., announced his backing for the effort. Helms signed on once Albright assured him last October that Russia would gain no significant influence over NATO's deliberations as the result of a consultation arrangement that was established to ease Moscow's concern over the expansion.

Facing an uphill fight from the beginning, opponents of expansion never gained political momentum. For example, their warning that expansion would undermine relations with Russia was stymied by the Russian government's acquiescence to the first round of invitations.

During the Easter recess and the following week, there was a surge of activity by opponents, including a series of TV and radio ads bought by business executives organized by Ben Cohen, of Ben & Jerry's Ice Cream.

As the Senate buckled down to four final days of debate, beginning April 27, it was evident that opponents had made no significant headway among senators.

Amendments

Besides rejecting the Warner amendment calling for a three-year pause before adding more countries to NATO, the Senate dealt with the following amendments to the resolution:

● By Tom Harkin, D-Iowa, limiting U.S. expenditures on helping the three countries fit into NATO's military structure to no more than 25 percent of the assistance provided by all NATO members. Rejected 24-76. *(Vote 106, p. S-19)*

● By Ted Stevens, R-Alaska, requiring congressional authorization of any U.S. spending related to NATO enlargement. Approved by voice vote.

● By Stevens, urging the president to propose a gradual reduction of the U.S. share of NATO's budget. Agreed to by voice vote.

● By Larry E. Craig, R-Idaho, barring ratification of enlargement until Congress authorizes the current U.S. deployment in Bosnia. Rejected 20-80. *(Vote 110, p. S-19)*

● By Robert C. Smith, R-N.H., barring ratification until Congress votes on the current Bosnia mission. Rejected 16-83. *(Vote 116, p. S-20)*

● By John Ashcroft, R-Mo., requiring that NATO's mission remain focused on the defense of members' territory. Tabled 82-18. *(Vote 114, p. S-20)*

● By Jeff Bingaman, D-N.M., barring ratification until NATO agrees on a new strategy. Rejected, 23-76. *(Vote 115, p. S-20)*

● By Jon Kyl, R-Ariz., expressing the sense of the Senate that NATO retain its strategic priorities, adopted in 1991. Agreed to, 90-9. *(Vote 107, p. S-19)*

● By Kay Bailey Hutchison, R-Texas, delaying ratification until the administration proposes to NATO a formal process to resolve international disputes involving alliance members. Rejected 37-62. *(Vote 109, p. S-19)*

● By Kent Conrad, D-N.D., urging the administration to try to negotiate a reduction in the Russian arsenal of short-range nuclear weapons. Rejected, 16-84. *(Vote 113, p. S-20)*

● By Daniel Patrick Moynihan, D-N.Y., delaying NATO membership for the three countries until they are admitted to the European Union. Rejected 17-83. *(Vote 111, p. S-19)*

● By Smith, requiring the president to certify before ratification that the three countries are cooperating with efforts to resolve the cases of U.S. personnel who are missing-in-action. Agreed 97-0. *(Vote 108, p. S-19)*

The Senate also adopted by voice vote a package of noncontroversial amendments by Helms and Biden, including a requirement for detailed reports on how the three countries were meeting their NATO military obligations. ◆

Intelligence Agencies Receive Small Spending Increase, Expanded Wiretap Authority

Box Score

- **Bill:** HR 3694 — PL 105-272
- **House action:** The House adopted the conference report (H Rept 105-780) on HR 3694, 337-83, on Oct. 7. It passed HR 3694 (H Rept 105-508) by voice vote May 7.
- **Senate action:** The Senate cleared the conference report by voice vote Oct. 8. It passed S 2052 (S Rept 105-185) by voice vote June 26.
- **Presidential action:** Clinton signed HR 3694 on Oct. 20.

SUMMARY

The fiscal 1999 intelligence authorization bill provided more money to intelligence agencies while giving enhanced wiretapping authority to federal law enforcement agencies and protecting employees who use classified data to blow the whistle on problems in federal agencies.

Although spending totals are classified, the measure raised the amount allocated for intelligence activities slightly above the level enacted last year. It restored cuts made to the Senate version that the Clinton administration feared would reduce the level of battlefield intelligence support.

The legislation also named CIA headquarters in Langley, Va., for former President George Bush, the agency's director in 1976 and 1977.

House Committee OKs Authorization For Intelligence

MAY 2 — The House Intelligence Committee on April 29 approved a fiscal 1999 authorization bill (HR 3694) for intelligence activities, including funds for enhanced covert action capabilities, electronic eavesdropping equipment and greater analysis capacity in areas that deserve special attention, according to committee Chairman Porter J. Goss, R-Fla.

The bill, approved by voice vote behind closed doors, includes funding for the Central Intelligence Agency (CIA), the National Reconnaissance Office, the National Security Agency and other intelligence organizations.

Although details of the bill, including funding levels, are classified, the number is slightly above what was requested by the Clinton administration, according to Republican Rep. C.W. Bill Young of Florida.

After the Federation of American Scientists, a private watchdog group, successfully sued the CIA for access to its budget figures under the Freedom of Information Act, the agency revealed that its 1997 budget was $26.6 billion.

In an unusual move last month, Director of Central Intelligence George J. Tenet announced that the fiscal 1998 budget for intelligence and security-related activities is $26.7 billion. Tenet said releasing previously classified information would not harm security but added that the CIA continues to reserve the right to withhold budget numbers and will not release the proposed budget for next year.

Both Chambers Seek To Redefine Intelligence Role

MAY 9 — In an era with no single ominous threat overseas, Congress continues to redefine the role that U.S. intelligence agencies should play.

According to proponents, the intelligence authorization bills for fiscal 1999 are attempting to address "real-world threats" — proliferation of weapons of mass destruction and missile technology among rogue nations, as well as terrorism, narcotics, counter-espionage and even computer hackers.

The House bill (HR 3694), passed May 7 by voice vote, would add funds to modernize telecommunications, computer technology and other tools to overcome adversaries' attempts to foil U.S. interception of communications and signals.

Concerned by the rising cost of the National Reconnaissance Office, despite a shift to smaller satellites, the House Intelligence Committee wrote that it is exploring the possibility of cost limits on the agency's acquisitions.

"Systematic coordinated attacks" by computer hackers on Pentagon computers in February greatly alarmed the House committee. While the individuals appeared to be driven by the challenge rather than malicious intent, their attacks underscored how vulnerable national security is to technology.

"Information technology has become this nation's strength as well as its Achilles heel," said committee Chairman Porter J. Goss, R-Fla., during the floor debate.

Also on May 7, the Senate Intelligence Committee approved its authorization bill (S 2052). [The Senate subsequently passed the bill by voice vote on June 26.]

After years of focusing on the "red menace," the CIA is short of linguists and specialists in areas other than former Cold War enemies, according to a Senate aide knowledgeable on intelligence matters. Measures in both chambers would add funds to critical personnel areas and revitalize clandestine espionage programs.

"We are badly outnumbered . . . in a lot of dangerous places in the world. That is intolerable, unacceptable and unnecessary," said Goss, a former CIA agent.

The House panel concluded that a lack of reliable intelligence from Iraq may have hampered President Clinton's ability to deal with a potential crisis in-

Defense

volving that country earlier this year.

"The failure of the Clinton administration's efforts to contain [Iraqi President] Saddam Hussein may, in part, reflect the inadequacy of our government's analysis of Iraqi internal dynamics, as well as gaps in our understanding of Iraq's policies and economy," said Michael N. Castle, R-Del. "Like other rogue states, Iraq demands a rigorous and aggressive analytical posture on the part of our intelligence community. We must do a better job of analyzing trends within such hard targets."

The House bill would also re-emphasize the need for covert capabilities. Goss was careful to point out that "nobody is calling for covert action. We are calling for more arrows in the quiver in case we do need it to suit the needs of today's world and how to deal with problems we come against."

Both chambers endorsed the importance of countering terrorist organizations, drug cartels and groups involved in weapons proliferation.

The Senate committee added money to the president's request in those specific areas. Said committee Chairman Richard C. Shelby, R-Ala.: "It costs money to keep informed."

Conferees Restore Cuts Approved In Senate Measure

OCTOBER 3 — Conferees reached agreement Oct. 1 on an intelligence authorization bill for fiscal 1999. The conferees restored cuts made to the Senate version of the bill that drew protests from the Clinton administration.

The legislation (HR 3694 — H Rept 105-508; S 2052 — S Rept 105-185) authorizes funding for the Central Intelligence Agency, National Reconnaissance Office and other intelligence-gathering organizations. The House is expected to vote on the conference report as early as Oct. 6.

When the Senate passed its version of the measure in June, senators said they tried to cut only low-priority intelligence programs and activities. But the White House Office of Management and Budget said the proposed cuts in the Senate version "could have severe near- and long-term effects on the ability of the intelligence community to provide battlefield support."

The intelligence authorization conference report also includes legislation designed to protect whistleblowers who use classified information to reveal fraud or other problems in intelligence agencies.

Conferees reached a compromise on the House version of the whistleblower legislation (HR 3829), which the House Intelligence Committee approved in July, and the Senate version (S 1668), which passed in March.

Final Bill Protects Whistleblowers, Expands Wiretap Authority

OCTOBER 10 — Congress has sent President Clinton an intelligence authorization bill for fiscal 1999 that would provide more money to intelligence agencies while giving enhanced wiretapping authority to federal law enforcement agencies and protecting employees who use classified data to blow the whistle on problems in intelligence agencies.

The House voted 337-83 on Oct. 7 to adopt the conference report on the legislation (HR 3694). The Senate adopted the conference report Oct. 8 by voice vote and without debate. (Vote 487, p. H-138)

Clinton is expected to sign the measure, which would raise spending for intelligence activities slightly above the level enacted last year. It would restore cuts made to the Senate version that the Clinton administration feared would reduce the level of battlefield intelligence support.

The bill sets guidelines for intelligence activities of 11 federal agencies, including the Central Intelligence Agency, National Security Agency and FBI. Although the spending total is classified, the authorization is believed to be slightly higher than the $26.7 billion level enacted for fiscal 1998.

House Intelligence Chairman Porter J. Goss, R-Fla., said the measure "incorporates the lessons learned" from recent months. Since House passage of the bill in May, he noted, Pakistan and India each have conducted nuclear tests, two U.S. embassies in Africa were bombed and the United States attacked suspected terrorist sites in Afghanistan and Sudan with cruise missiles.

But one of the biggest controversies over the legislation arose from an issue that has raised hackles for years — the ability of law enforcement officials to conduct roving wiretaps, which follow a person from phone to phone, to combat terrorism.

Under current law, authorities seeking such a wiretap must show that the target is changing phones with a criminal intent to evade a tap, a standard considered difficult to meet. The conference report would remove the need to consider the individual's motive.

The provision drew protests from civil liberties groups as well as from House conservatives led by Bob Barr, R-Ga. Barr has long fought efforts by federal law enforcement officials to expand wiretap authority because of concerns that it tramples on individual civil liberties. (1996 Almanac, p. 5-18)

Republican Bill McCollum of Florida, chairman of the House Judiciary Crime Subcommittee, described the provision as "a very minor change" that continues to protect innocent individuals.

The House defeated Barr's move to send the bill back to conference and strip the wiretap language, 148-267. (Vote 486, p. H-138)

Whistleblower Protection

The conference report also includes language designed to protect whistleblowers who use classified information to reveal fraud or other problems in intelligence agencies.

The agreement largely leaves intact the House version of whistleblower legislation (HR 3829 — H Rept 105-747), that the House Intelligence Committee approved in July. The Senate passed a separate version (S 1668 — S Rept 105-165) in March.

Under the agreement, CIA employees who witness or are informed of a violation will report the complaint to the CIA inspector general, who will be required within 14 days to determine the credibility of the complaint. If the complaint is subsequently referred to the CIA director, the director will have one week to determine its credibility and forward it to the House and Senate intelligence committees.

The conference report also includes funding authority for enhanced covert operations against Iraq. Lawmakers in recent months have stepped up pressure on Clinton to take action against the regime of Iraqi dictator Saddam Hussein.

Lawmakers of both parties said House Speaker Newt Gingrich, Ga., was seeking to put into the omnibus spending bill for fiscal 1999 as much as $1.7 billion for intelligence activities, including covert operations in Iraq.

The Senate on Oct. 7 cleared by voice vote a bill (HR 4655) authorizing up to $97 million for defense services, military education and training for democratic organizations in Iraq. It also authorizes up to $2 million to support radio and television broadcasts to Iraq by those organizations. The House had passed the bill, 360-38, on Oct. 5. *(Vote 482, p. H-136)*

The intelligence bill also would name CIA headquarters in Langley, Va., for former President George Bush, the agency's director from January 1976 to January 1977. ◆

Chapter 9
EDUCATION

Higher Education Act	9-3	**Bilingual Education**	9-25
Education Savings Accounts	9-14	**National Testing**	9-28
Head Start	9-19	**Charter Schools**	9-29
District of Columbia Student Vouchers	9-24		

Higher Education Act Reduces Interest Rates, Increases Grants

SUMMARY

Congress cleared a five-year reauthorization of the Higher Education Act, expanding federal assistance to college students, a sharp reversal from 1995 Republican proposals to cut student loan subsidies.

The measure reduces interest rates on federally backed student loans, creates a $300 million-a-year program of grants for teacher training and recruitment, and includes a White House-sought $200 million program to help low-income middle school students prepare for college. It also creates an organization in the Education Department to oversee performance-based student lending and gradually increases the maximum authorized Pell Grant for low-income students. It forgives up to $5,000 in loans to students who teach for five years in underserved areas and requires loan guaranty agencies to return $250 million in reserves to the government.

Republicans and Democrats worked closely to develop the bill. The biggest hurdle was a threat by commercial bankers to pull out of college lending unless Congress altered a long-planned change in the formula for calculating interest rates on student loans. Bankers contended the formula, set in the 1993 budget-reconciliation act (PL 103-66), would make such lending unprofitable.

The formula, which was to take effect on July 1, 1998, would have for the first time pegged interest rates to long-term treasury bonds, rather than the 91-day short-term notes that had been used. However, unexpected increases in long-term bond yields and decreases in short-term yields over the past five years meant the planned formula would have cut rates more than anticipated.

Determined to avert a disruption in lending, Rep. Howard P. "Buck" McKeon, R-Calif., and Rep. Dale E. Kildee, D-Mich., worked out a compromise based partially on a White House recommendation that kept the formula tied to short-term bonds. Under the new two-tiered rate plan, students would pay 1.7 percent above the rate while in school and 2.3 percent in repayment. Bankers would receive a second, slightly higher rate, which would be 2.2 percent higher than the short-term note while a student was in school and 2.8 percent higher while in repayment. The federal government will provide millions of dollars in subsidies to banks to guarantee that rate of return.

The White House supported the student loan interest rate but complained that the formula was far too generous to banks.

Box Score

- **Bill:** HR 6 — PL 105-244
- **House action:** The House adopted the conference report (H Rept 105-750) on HR 6 by voice vote on Sept. 28. It passed the committee-approved bill (H Rept 105-481) on May 6 by a vote of 414-4.
- **Senate action:** The Senate cleared the conference report on Sept. 29, 96-0. It passed its version of the bill (S 1882 — S Rept 105-181) on July 9 by a vote of 96-1.
- **Presidential action:** Clinton signed HR 6 on Oct. 7.

White House Offers New Plan For Student Loans

FEBRUARY 28 — Seeking to prevent a possible disruption in student lending, the White House on Feb. 25 unveiled a compromise plan that would reduce interest rates on federally backed college loans, but not as much as originally planned.

Bankers have threatened to stop making student loans unless Congress reworks a new formula that would result in lower interest rates beginning July 1. But they said the White House plan did not go far enough to guarantee them enough profit on the loans.

"We are very disappointed and concerned," said Joe Belew, president of the Consumer Bankers Association. Commercial bankers make 70 percent of all student loans.

Congress must decide how to resolve the politically sensitive issue of whether to help students or bankers. Lawmakers have stressed that they want to find a bipartisan solution. The House Education and the Workforce Subcommittee on Postsecondary Education, Training and Life-Long Learning on March 4 will begin work to reauthorize the 1965 Higher Education Act, which governs federal college aid.

At issue is a provision of the 1993 budget-reconciliation law (PL 103-66) that will move the college aid program from the current formula based on the 91-day Treasury bill rate to one based on the 10-year Treasury bond rate.

At a White House briefing, Vice President Al Gore released a Treasury Department analysis concluding that the new formula could force some bankers out of the program.

Commercial bankers complain that because short-term interest rates have risen and long-term rates have fallen since the 1993 law was written, the formula will produce lower returns than originally projected.

Gore outlined an alternative that would continue to base the formula on the 91-day Treasury-bill rate, but reduce the subsidy to lenders the federal government adds above that level. The White House said its plan would produce interest rates of 7 percent, compared with 7.8 percent under current law. That would mean $650 in interest savings over 10 years for a student borrowing $12,000. As part of its fiscal 1999 budget plan, the White House also proposed to reduce the 4 percent origination fee students pay when they take out loans.

Education

Further, the Education Department's direct student lending program, created in the 1993 law, has captured only 30 percent of market share and could not handle the volume of loans if private lenders drop out.

The Treasury Department analysis showed that under the current law, banks are making a pre-tax return on student loans that exceeds what it considers a reasonable range. But it found the 1993 formula would push returns below the acceptable level.

"Such a reduction need not imply an immediate crisis . . . but it could be problematic for lenders in the longer term," the report said.

House Panel Defers Hot Issues To Full Committee

MARCH 7 — A House Education and the Workforce subcommittee approved a stripped-down bill March 4 to reauthorize the Higher Education Act of 1965, but the exercise served more to highlight a host of problems than to solve them.

Lawmakers on the Postsecondary Education, Training and Life-Long Learning Subcommittee decided to defer votes on contentious issues such as teacher training and aid to Hispanic-serving colleges and universities until the full education panel takes up the five-year reauthorization bill (HR 6) later this month.

Further, the skeleton measure, which was approved by voice vote, did not include Title IV federal student loan, grant and work study programs, the guts of the Higher Education Act. That is because lawmakers have been unable to reach a consensus on how to deal with a pending change in the formula for calculating interest rates on student loans, set to take place July 1.

The proposed formula was originally approved as part of a 1993 budget-reconciliation law (PL 103-66) that also created the Education Department's direct student lending program. The formula would tie student loan interest rates to long-term Treasury bonds rather than to the 91-day Treasury bills that are currently used, reducing interest rates at least initially by about a full percentage point. Student groups welcome the change, but bankers say it will make college loans unprofitable.

Commercial banks, which account for 70 percent of the college loan market, say that if Congress does not prevent the new formula from taking effect, they will cut back on lending. The dilemma leaves lawmakers with the unpalatable choice of either scaling back the pending interest rate reduction or risking a disruption in the higher education finance market that could leave students who depend on loans without access to college funds.

After it passed the reauthorization bill, the subcommittee on March 5 held a hearing on the interest rate issue. But while lenders, student groups and Clinton administration officials all agreed there was a problem, they could not agree on a cure. Committee aides said they hoped to reach a bipartisan consensus before March 18, when the full committee is slated to mark up the bill.

"While some may be tempted to play politics with this issue, we simply cannot allow that to happen. The stakes are too high, the consequences too alarming," said Rep. Howard P. "Buck" McKeon, R-Calif., subcommittee chairman.

Reauthorization Debate Begins

The reauthorization bill approved by the subcommittee would simplify the Higher Education Act by eliminating 36 unfunded programs and about a dozen commissions and studies. Programs slated for extinction include a faculty development fellowship and grants for sexual offenses prevention programs.

The measure would create a new "performance-based organization" within the Department of Education, with a chief operating officer to oversee student financial aid programs and simplify the process of applying for federal loans and grants.

During debate, Rep. Rubén Hinojosa, D-Texas, offered but withdrew an amendment that would create a new part under Title III of the 1965 Higher Education Act to govern federal aid to Hispanic-serving colleges and universities. His amendment would also authorize funding for graduate programs.

Title III of the act provides financial support to historically black colleges and universities, and other institutions, to help provide equal educational opportunity and greater financial stability. The law includes a separate reference for Hispanic-serving institutions.

Hinojosa argued that the language needs to be expanded in light of the growing population of Hispanic students and that creating a separate part of the law for Hispanic-serving institutions would help persuade appropriators to increase aid from the $12 million level in fiscal 1998.

As written, HR 6 already increases the authorization for Hispanic-serving schools and makes it easier for Hispanic institutions to qualify for funds. The administration's fiscal 1999 budget calls for a $44 million, or 20 percent, increase in funding for Title III programs, including a more than doubling of support for traditionally Hispanic institutions.

Hinojosa's plan, however, has caused concern among the supporters of historically black colleges and universities, who worry it will increase competition for federal funds.

"It is not my intent to be in competition, but to work together," he said. He said he was optimistic that he could work out a compromise amendment before the full committee meets.

Federal support for state teacher training programs was another issue discussed, but delayed until full committee. Both parties and the White House have put forth plans to help states revamp their processes for teacher instruction and certification.

According to current projections, schools will need to hire 2 million new teachers over the next decade due to expanded enrollment, retirements and efforts to reduce class size.

President Clinton has called for a $12 billion, seven-year program to hire 100,000 new teachers and reduce average class size to 18 through third grade.

Aside from concerns about teacher shortages, particularly in inner cities and underserved rural areas, there is also concern that teachers are not getting sufficiently grounded in the academic areas they will instruct.

Rep. Bill Goodling, R-Pa., chairman of the full committee, offered but withdrew an amendment that would replace 16 teacher-training programs with a federal grant. States would compete for the block grant funds, which could be used to improve certification procedures and overhaul colleges of education to ensure that teachers are proficient in their subject areas.

The money also could be used to develop alternatives to regular certification programs to more easily move qualified individuals into teaching positions, as well as initiatives that would make it easier to remove unqualified or incompetent teachers from schools.

Goodling, who said he would work with other lawmakers on the issue before it goes to full committee, complained that colleges seemed to be able to find money to build new stadiums, but stinted on teacher-training programs, treating them like "Cinderella before she met the prince."

Not everyone saw a need for greater federal involvement, however.

"The solution to the teacher-training problem is for schools to no longer hire untrained teachers," said Rep. Bill Barrett, R-Neb.

Interest in Student Loans

The overriding concern for the subcommittee, however, remains the federally guaranteed student loan program. The current interest rate formula is based on the 91-day rate, plus 2.5 percent when the borrower is in school and 3.1 percent during repayment. The new formula would set rates at the 10-year Treasury bond plus 1 percent.

Banks say aside from being unprofitable, the formula creates unpredictability because they would have to pay higher short-term interest rates to attract capital but would be forced to lend at long-term rates that are often lower. The White House on Feb. 25 unveiled a Treasury Department study that showed the formula would reduce banks' profits to unacceptable levels.

The White House proposed a compromise that would continue to peg interest rates to short-term notes, but provide a lower subsidy to banks, resulting in a 7 percent interest rate, down from 7.8 percent under the existing law.

Lenders and analysts told the subcommittee that the administration proposal was flawed and would not allow banks a sufficient profit margin.

Jonathan Gray, a senior research analyst at Sanford C. Bernstein and Co., a New York brokerage firm, challenged Clinton administration findings that banks had made excess profits on student loans.

"If current law is not changed, there is no question as to whether or not it will curtail availability of loans. I promise you it will," Gray said.

Lawmakers, students and colleges agreed that Congress needed to move back to a short-term funding measure, likely the 91-day T-bill. They floated possible alternatives to the July 1 change, including continuing with the present formula.

Assistant Secretary for Postsecondary Education David A. Longanecker said the direct lending program, which competes with commercial student loans, could pick up only 500 to 1,000 schools quickly if private lenders dropped out.

He said the secretary of Education could compel Sallie Mae, which buys student loans from banks, to act as lender of last resort in a market disruption.

House Committee OKs Compromise On Interest Rates

MARCH 21— Attempting to split the difference between students and banks, lawmakers moved closer to resolving the politically sensitive issue of where to set interest rates on federally backed college loans.

In approving a five-year reauthorization of the Higher Education Act of 1965, the House Committee on Education and the Workforce agreed March 19 to cut interest rates on student loans but also provide hundreds of millions of dollars in special subsidies to commercial banks.

The compromise bill (HR 6) approved 38-3, seeks to respond to threats by commercial lenders, who provide 70 percent of student loans, that they will drop out of the federally guaranteed lending program unless Congress reworks a scheduled July 1 change in the formula for setting interest rates.

Bankers have warned that the pending July formula change would reduce interest rates to the point that student loans would be unprofitable. But student groups and college officials, citing rising tuition costs, have made the interest rate reduction a top priority, putting lawmakers in a tough spot.

The committee bill was an effort to satisfy both sides. It would give students interest rate relief but provide $300 million a year or more in special payments to banks. While it gained broad support with lawmakers and student groups, lenders were unhappy, maintaining it would not provide banks with a high enough return.

Education Secretary Richard W. Riley criticized the legislation, saying the new subsidy to lenders was unwarranted.

Despite the bankers' unease, lawmakers were confident that the measure would easily pass the House, which is expected to consider the measure in late April. The higher education law governs tens of billions of dollars in loans, grants and work-study funds.

"This legislation is one of the most important things Congress will do this year. It will ensure every American has access to a quality postsecondary education at an affordable price," said committee Chairman Bill Goodling, R-Pa.

He exhorted the Senate to begin work quickly on its version of the measure to ensure there is no disruption in college lending.

The Senate Labor and Human Resources Committee may debate the bill before the April recess, though it has not yet set a markup date.

In an effort to respond to concerns about the quality of teachers, as well as a shortage of instructors in low-income urban and rural areas, the House reauthorization measure includes a plan by Goodling to create new, competitive block grants that states could use to beef up teacher certification requirements. The plan is an alternative to Clinton's call to hire 100,000 new teachers.

The legislation would dramatically increase the maximum allowable Pell grant for disadvantaged students from the current $3,000 to $4,500 per student in academic year 1999-2000. The grants would gradually increase to $5,300 in 2003-04. The measure would partially forgive student loans for teachers who agree to work in underserved areas and calls on colleges to take cost-cutting steps.

Education

The bill would create a "performance-based" organization within the Department of Education, with a chief operating officer to oversee student financial aid programs and simplify the process of applying for federal loans and grants.

Interest Rates Key

Committee leaders have been working for months to come up with a bipartisan solution on interest rates, the thorniest issue facing the panel.

The planned July 1 formula change was originally approved as part of a 1993 budget-reconciliation law (PL 103-66) that also created the Education Department's direct student lending program. The formula would tie student loan interest rates to long-term Treasury bonds rather than the three-month Treasury bills that are currently used, reducing interest rates at least initially by about a full percentage point.

The current interest formula is the 91-day Treasury rate, plus 2.5 percent when the borrower is in school and 3.1 percent during repayment. The July formula would set rates at the 10-year Treasury bond plus 1 percent.

Banks say that aside from being unprofitable, the formula creates unpredictability because they would have to pay higher short-term interest rates to attract capital but would be forced to lend at long-term rates that are often lower. The White House on Feb. 25 unveiled a Treasury Department study that said banks made too much under the current formula, but would earn too little under the July 1 change.

Vice President Al Gore proposed a compromise that would continue to peg interest rates to 91-day Treasury bills, but add a smaller 2.3 percent when a loan was in repayment and 1.7 percent while a student was in school. Lenders said that plan was too draconian.

Howard P. "Buck" McKeon, R-Calif., and Dale E. Kildee, D-Mich., decided to split the difference. The committee bill uses the student loan interest rate formula in the White House plan, but also creates a second, slightly higher, interest rate for banks.

Under the committee bill, as with the White House proposal, students in academic year 1998-99 would pay an estimated 7.43 percent interest rate during repayment, down from the current 8.23 percent. Banks would get a 7.93 percent interest rate, slightly higher than students would pay.

The separate bank formula would cost from $1.2 billion to $3.8 billion over five years, depending on what methodology Congress ultimately adopts, according to the Congressional Budget Office.

In a March 17 letter to the committee, a group of lenders including the Consumer Bankers Association and Sallie Mae, which buys student loans from banks, supported the lower interest rate for students, but warned that the new rate for banks would still be too low.

"The result of your proposal would leave students and schools in a vulnerable situation, threatening access to necessary loan funds and reducing high-quality service for students," said the letter.

Some Democrats were skeptical about the deal but did not make a major push to change it.

"Not all of us are convinced the compromise is totally justified," said Robert E. Andrews, D-N.J., who offered an unsuccessful amendment to reduce by 1 percentage point the 4 percent origination fee students pay when taking out loans. The White House plan also included the origination fee cut.

Andrews and the Clinton administration also objected to a provision of HR 6 that would eliminate a requirement in current law that Sallie Mae and other guaranty agencies act as lenders of last resort in case of a breakdown in the commercial market.

McKeon called availability of loans the paramount concern, saying the committee may have gone too far. Adding to the uncertainty, aides conceded that, given the tight budget situation, they did not know where they would find the money to pay for it.

Beyond Student Loans

In other action on student aid, the committee by voice vote adopted an amendment sponsored by Lindsey Graham, R-S.C., and Kildee to partially forgive student loans for teachers who worked for at least three years in high-poverty public and private schools.

It also approved an amendment by Mark Souder, R-Ind., that would bar student aid to anyone convicted of a drug charge. Students could lose eligibility for at least a year, and possibly longer, depending on the severity of the crime.

Democrats, led by Kildee, offered a White House-backed proposal that would have created four new teacher training programs, including partnerships between colleges and local education agencies and a new effort to recruit teachers to work in high-poverty urban and rural areas. The amendment failed, 18-19.

According to current projections, schools will need to hire 2 million new teachers over the next decade because of expanded enrollment, retirements and efforts to reduce class size. Aside from worries about teacher shortages, some lawmakers are concerned that teachers are not sufficiently grounded in their subject areas.

By voice vote, the panel defeated an amendment by Bill Barrett, R-Neb., to eliminate the Goodling teacher training block grant in the bill.

The Goodling plan, which includes some elements developed by committee Democrats, would provide $18.5 million annually in block grants that states could use to toughen certification requirements to ensure that teachers are knowledgeable in their subject areas, revamp college teacher preparation programs, create or expand efforts to provide alternative routes to certification and develop initiatives to more quickly remove incompetent or unqualified teachers from classrooms.

"There is a national education crisis out there. We would be derelict in our duty if we didn't help in some way to get these teachers trained," said Marge Roukema, R-N.J.

Riley said in a statement that he was disappointed the panel had ignored a White House plan to connect low-income school districts with postsecondary teacher education programs.

In a compromise that defused a dispute between the black and Hispanic caucuses, the panel by voice vote approved an amendment to move language governing aid to Hispanic-serving institutions from Title III of the act to a separate part of the law.

Rubén Hinojosa, D-Texas, had wanted to create a new section under Title III, which provides financial sup-

Higher Education Act

port to historically black colleges and universities, to recognize the growing needs of Hispanic students. Members of the black caucus had worried that the change could, among other things, increase competition for federal funds. William L. Clay, D-Mo., offered the compromise amendment.

The committee adopted an amendment by Chaka Fattah, D-Pa., to implement a White House initiative promoting partnerships between colleges and middle and junior high schools in poor areas to provide counseling, tutoring and other services.

Senate Panel Follows House On Loan Issue

APRIL 4 — Following the House's lead, a Senate committee moved to defuse a bitter fight between bankers and student groups that threatens to disrupt this year's college lending market.

The Senate Committee on Labor and Human Resources on April 1 approved a five-year reauthorization of the Higher Education Act of 1965 that would cut interest rates to students while providing hundreds of millions of dollars in special subsidies to commercial banks. The bill (S 1882) was approved 18-0, despite protests by some Democrats that the aid to banks was unwarranted.

Commercial lenders, who make 70 percent of student loans, have threatened to drop out of the federally guaranteed lending program unless Congress revamps a scheduled July 1 change in the formula for setting interest rates that could have cut them even more steeply.

Bankers say the July change would reduce their returns to the point that student loans would be unprofitable. The Treasury Department and Congressional Budget Office (CBO) in separate reports have supported the bankers' claims. Student groups, however, have made lower rates a top priority.

The measure represents an attempt to find a political middle ground by creating a new two-tiered system that would provide one interest rate for students and a second, slightly higher rate for banks. The proposed formula was approved by the House Committee on Education and the Workforce on March 19 as part of HR 6, its version of the bill.

Edward M. Kennedy, D-Mass., offered but withdrew an amendment that would have provided a slightly lower interest rate for banks than the committee's bill. He reiterated White House warnings that the bill exceeded domestic spending caps and could force across-the-board cuts in other programs.

Committee Chairman James M. Jeffords, R-Vt., said the proposal was the best the committee could do. "We've got to get it done before July or the [market] could collapse."

Under the House and Senate bills, students in academic year 1998-99 would pay an estimated 7.43 percent interest rate during repayment, down from the current 8.23 percent. Banks would get a 7.93 percent interest rate.

The bank formula would cost the Treasury about $1.2 billion to $3.8 billion over five years to make up the difference, according to CBO. While student groups support the proposal, bankers oppose it, saying it would reduce profits to unacceptable levels.

Revamping Student Aid

In an effort to respond to concerns about the quality of teachers, as well as a shortage of instructors in low-income urban and rural areas, the Senate reauthorization measure would replace existing programs with $300 million in competitive block grants that states could use to revamp teacher training. Grants could also be made to local partnerships including schools, state education agencies and colleges. President Clinton has called for hiring 100,000 new teachers to meet a possible shortage and reduce class size.

The legislation would increase the maximum allowable Pell grants for disadvantaged students from the current $3,000 to $5,000 in academic year 1999-2000. The maximum would rise by $200 a year thereafter. That is higher than the House bill, which would increase Pell grants to $4,500 in 1999-2000, rising to $5,300 in 2003-2004.

The Senate measure would provide up to $10,000 in loan forgiveness for teachers who promise to work in schools in low-income rural and urban areas. Loan forgiveness would begin to phase in after three years of teaching. Like the House measure, the bill would create a "performance-based" organization within the Department of Education to oversee financial aid programs and simplify the application process.

It would require colleges and universities to report more information on costs and tuition. Under an amendment by Christopher J. Dodd, D-Conn., adopted 10-8, schools not complying could face annual fines of up to $25,000.

The committee also adopted by voice vote an amendment by Judd Gregg, R-N.H., to bar student loans to anyone convicted of a drug charge. Students could lose eligibility for a year, and possibly longer, depending on the severity of the crime. There would be exceptions for students completing rehabilitation.

The panel approved by voice vote a plan by Sen. Tom Harkin, D-Iowa, that would allow reduced interest rates for students who promptly paid off direct college loans.

Jeff Bingaman, D-N.M., offered an amendment, which was approved by voice vote, that would expand language governing aid to Hispanic-serving institutions and tribal institutions, while moving it from Title III of the act to a separate part of the law.

Title III provides financial support to historically black colleges and universities. Members of the black caucus had worried that elevating aid to Hispanic schools could increase competition for funds. The amendment is modeled on a House compromise between the black and Hispanic congressional caucuses.

Interest Rate Deal Falters; President Threatens Veto

MAY 2 — Congressional efforts to prevent a threatened disruption of the federal student loan program got tangled up in White House veto threats and budget wrangling during the week of April 27, leaving all sides in legislative limbo.

Lawmakers are racing to head off a pending July 1 change in the govern-

Education

ment formula for calculating interest rates on federally guaranteed student loans. Commercial lenders, who account for 70 percent of college lending, warn that the planned formula could cut interest rates so sharply they would be forced to drop out of the program.

Increasingly worried that the student loan market could be upended, Republican leaders worked throughout the week to attach bipartisan, compromise language to a must-pass fiscal 1998 supplemental spending bill (HR 3579). The proposed language was an attempt to soften the blow for banks while still reducing interest rates to students.

But lawmakers dropped the plan at the last minute, unable to agree on offsetting spending cuts to pay for it. The White House, which says the proposal is too generous to banks, warned that adding the provisions to the supplemental could have drawn a veto.

The failure puts increased pressure on the House and Senate to move five-year measures (HR 6; S1882) reauthorizing the Higher Education Act.

The House on April 29 opened debate on its bill and planned to finish the week of May 4. The House version contains the interest rate fix and a promise to come up later with all the spending cuts needed to pay for it.

The Senate may also take up its bill, which contains identical interest rate provisions.

Complicating the outlook, however, the White House on April 28 threatened to veto the House authorizing bill because of concerns about the interest rate change and elimination of the National Board for Professional Teaching Standards, which accredits teachers.

The White House also opposes a pending amendment that would alter college affirmative action programs.

Pointing out that the interest rate plan had broad, bipartisan support, Republicans fumed that the White House was not playing fair.

"If we don't fix it by July 1, you're looking at the worst disaster you'll ever want to see. This [impasse] is all over politics," charged Rep. Bill Goodling, R-Pa., chairman of the House Committee on Education and the Workforce.

Goodling and Rep. Howard P. "Buck" McKeon, R-Calif., chairman of the Subcommittee on Postsecondary Education, Training and Life-Long Learning, said the White House was fighting efforts to aid banks in the hopes that a disruption of the commercial market would entice students to turn to the administration's favored direct lending system. The competing program, run by the Education Department, accounts for 30 percent of student loans.

Administration officials called such assertions baseless. They said they believed the plan simply provided too much to banks and would reduce the amount of money available for other education priorities.

Supplemental Sparring

Republican leaders had hoped to quickly move the compromise plan, which would reduce the interest rate on federally backed student loans to about 7.43 percent for students after they leave school and 7.93 percent for banks. That compares with the current rate of 8.23 percent.

The plan would provide bankers a higher rate of return than they would receive if the July 1 formula went into effect.

The administration and the Congressional Budget Office in reports have supported the bankers' contentions that the formula change would make student lending unprofitable.

Student groups and colleges support the loan plan. But commercial lenders had asserted it was still too stingy. They have begun to change their tune, however, concerned that nothing will happen before July 1. Banks wanted to add the plan to the supplemental bill.

Underscoring the importance of the issue to its bottom line, Sallie Mae, which buys student loans from banks, has spent more than $1 million lobbying in the past six months and has given nearly $80,000 in "soft money" and campaign contributions, according to the Center for Responsive Politics.

Ensuring the higher profits to banks would cost anywhere from about $1 billion to $3 billion over five years. Appropriators scrambled to find offsetting cuts, looking at everything from mineral sales to trimming farm programs.

The House debate on the authorizing bill opened amid White House concerns about an amendment by Rep. Frank Riggs, R-Calif., to bar public colleges from providing preferential treatment in admissions based on race, sex or national origin.

The amendment is modeled on California's Proposition 209. It is also part of an overall, though faltering, push by Republicans to revamp federal affirmative action policies.

The House on April 1 defeated an amendment to the transportation reauthorization bill (HR 2400) by Rep. Marge Roukema, R-N.J., to soften current requirements that the Transportation Department contract with female or minority-owned firms for 10 percent of transportation projects.

Riggs said that, unlike the debate on the Roukema proposal, House Republican leaders had agreed to get behind his amendment. In a bid to conservatives worried about federal interference in private schools, he modified it to apply solely to public institutions.

"I think we've got a pretty good shot at almost all the Republican votes" as well as a few Democrats, Riggs said.

McKeon and White House officials said they did not think it would pass.

The reauthorization would gradually increase Pell grants to needy students from the current $3,000 to $5,300 in academic year 2003-2004. It would create block grants for teacher training.

During debate on April 29 the House:

- Adopted by voice vote a plan by George Miller, D-Calif., to allow federal aid to teacher preparation programs only if they met quality standards, to be determined by states.

- Adopted by voice vote an amendment by Goodling to create a new grant program to combat violent crimes against women at college campuses; allow students to consolidate outstanding loans at a capped interest rate of 8.25 percent; and refine bill provisions making it easier for colleges to provide financial packages to encourage early retirement of faculty.

- Adopted by voice vote an amendment by Mark Souder, R-Ind., to modify a provision in the bill denying loans to individuals convicted of drug charges. The plan would let aid resume if students completed rehabilitation programs.

Higher Education Act

House Rejects Affirmative Action, Sets Interest Rates

MAY 9 — After defeating a Republican effort to bar race- or sex-based preferences in public college admissions, the House on May 6 easily approved legislation to reauthorize federal higher education programs.

Lawmakers passed the five-year bill (HR 6) by a lopsided 414-4 vote despite strong White House opposition to a provision that would cut interest rates on federally guaranteed student loans while providing special subsidies to banks. (Vote 135, p. H-40)

The administration contends that the interest rate plan, which would cost from $1 billion to $3 billion over five years, would enable banks to reap excessive profits and force Congress to cut education and other domestic programs to pay for it.

The Senate is set to take up its version of the measure (S 1882), which includes an identical interest rate fix, the week of May 11.

Given the broad support for the bill, lawmakers said they were increasingly confident that President Clinton would not veto it over the interest rate issue alone.

Commercial bankers, who make 70 percent of all student loans, have threatened to pull out of guaranteed lending unless Congress acts to stave off even deeper cuts in interest rates, set to take effect July 1. With that in mind, many lawmakers said they were willing to err on the side of caution in order to ensure the availability of loans to students.

"I wish I were omniscient like the White House seems to be," said Howard P. "Buck" McKeon, chairman of the Education and the Workforce Subcommittee on Postsecondary Education, Training and Life-Long Learning.

The Clinton administration veto threat was based on a number of concerns, including the bill's elimination of the National Board for Professional Teaching Standards and the possibility the House would adopt the anti-affirmative action amendment.

Further, assuming the House and Senate can devise a way to completely pay for the interest rate reduction — something neither body has yet done — the White House now appears to have only limited leverage to push for major changes in conference.

"I don't think that [not having spending offsets] will necessarily mean that we don't bring the bill to the floor," said Senate Labor and Human Resources Committee Chairman James M. Jeffords, R-Vt.

The House bill would increase the maximum authorization for Pell grants to disadvantaged students, currently appropriated at $3,000 a year, to $5,300 for the 2003-2004 school year.

In an effort to respond to concerns about the quality of teachers, as well as a shortage of instructors in low-income urban and rural areas, it would roll existing programs into new, competitive block grants that states could use to beef up certification and training.

The measure would partially forgive student loans for teachers who agree to work in underserved areas. It includes a White House initiative to promote partnerships between colleges and middle and junior high schools in poor areas to provide counseling, tutoring and other services.

The bill would bar student aid to anyone convicted of a drug charge. Students could lose eligibility for a year, and possibly longer, depending on the severity of the crime. Aid could be reinstated if they completed a rehabilitation program.

Preferences Ban Defeated

The House considered dozens of amendments, including a plan by Frank Riggs, R-Calif., to end admissions preferences based on race, sex, ethnicity, color or national origin. The amendment, modeled on California's 1996 Proposition 209, would apply to public colleges and universities that received federal funds under the bill.

While intended to make affirmative action a defining issue between the two parties, the amendment and other Republican proposals instead served to expose internal splits within the GOP.

The House defeated the plan 171-249, despite what Riggs said were pledges from the Republican leadership to help pass it. Fifty-five Republicans voted no, including J.C. Watts of Oklahoma, the lone black Republican in the House. Watts joined John Lewis, D-Ga., a former civil rights leader, on a letter to colleagues urging opposition. (Vote 133, p. H-40)

Marge Roukema, R-N.J., and House Education and the Workforce Committee Chairman Bill Goodling, R-Pa., who both face conservative challengers in upcoming primaries, voted "yea."

"I acknowledge that discrimination continues to exist in our society and that it is morally wrong," Riggs said. "But I believe we will never end discrimination by practicing discrimination. It is time for the U.S. Congress to end preferences, once and for all."

William L. Clay of Missouri, ranking Democrat on the Education Committee, said the Riggs amendment would "return the system of higher education to the bad old days of racial segregation. If we follow that direction, our schools will again become a bastion of white, male, good old boys."

The House on April 1 defeated an amendment to the transportation reauthorization bill (HR 2400) by Roukema to soften current requirements that the Transportation Department contract with female-or minority-owned firms for 10 percent of transportation projects.

The House also grappled with the issue of wrestling, specifically a provision that would have required colleges to report if they expected to drop any sports programs in the next four years.

The provision was championed by Dennis Hastert, R-Ill., a former wrestler and coach frustrated that schools have been dropping less glamorous sports such as wrestling to save money. But the House voted 292-129 to adopt an amendment by Tim Roemer, D-Ind., to delete it. (Vote 130, p. H-38)

The debate brought out the tensions arising from Title IX of the 1972 Education Amendments (PL 92-318) that has required schools to provide women with equal access to sports programs. Critics say the law has forced schools to cut funds for some men's programs. (1972 Almanac, p. 385)

"The people who have gained are the women's sports, and that is great. The sports that have lost are men's sports," Hastert said. He said the notification was essential because many students based decisions about college partly on athletic programs offered.

Education

Constance A. Morella, R-Md., called the requirement to predict which sports might be dropped absurd.

"I am concerned that this reporting requirement will lead colleges and universities to blame reduction in men's non-revenue sports, such as wrestling, on compliance with Title IX," she said.

Interest Rate Debate Ahead

The key issue in coming weeks, however, will be the resolution of the student loan issue — specifically whether lawmakers can find needed spending offsets to completely pay for it, and whether Congress can get a bill enacted prior to a planned July 1 change in interest rates.

The planned formula change was originally approved as part of a 1993 budget-reconciliation bill (PL 103-66) that also created the Education Department's direct lending program. The change would tie student loan interest rates to long-term Treasury bonds, rather than the three-month Treasury bills that are currently used. If allowed to take effect, the formula could reduce rates to both lenders and students by more than a full percentage point.

Both the administration and lawmakers agreed that the July drop would be too steep for bankers. They disagree on just how to solve the problem.

While mindful of the need to help banks, they were also under pressure from student groups and colleges that made lower rates a top priority.

The administration on Feb. 25 proposed a plan to reduce interest rates for both students and banks to 7.43 percent after a student left school, down from the current 8.23 percent. The House and Senate bills adopt the student rate, but provide a second, higher rate to banks of 7.93 percent.

Lawmakers must come up with about $1 billion in offsetting spending cuts, based on Congressional Budget Office projections, to pay for the plan. The Office of Management and Budget (OMB) puts the price tag higher, nearly $3 billion over five years. The administration has warned that unless Congress finds a way to pay for the change, the bill could force across-the-board cuts in other domestic spending.

Projections by the OMB, rather than CBO, are used to trigger across-the-board cuts.

Congress tried unsuccessfully to add the provisions to a supplemental spending bill that passed Congress on April 30 and was signed into law May 1 (PL 105-174). They were stymied by White House veto threats and the offset issue.

The House version of the bill includes more than $600 million in spending cuts, including scaling back guaranty agency funds and giving students more time to get their financial affairs in order before student loans are considered to be in default. The Budget Committee is charged with providing the other offsets.

Lenders do not like the plan, but have moved from trying to alter it to asking Congress to pass it before July 1.

In other action, the House adopted:
- By voice vote an amendment by Mark Foley, R-Fla., allowing schools to disclose disciplinary records of students who commit violent crimes.
- By a vote of 220-187, an amendment by Jim McGovern, D-Mass., to increase Pell grants to students who graduate in the top 10 percent of their high school class. (*Vote 124, p. H-36*)
- By a vote of 393-28 an amendment by George Miller, D-Calif., expressing the sense of Congress that colleges adopt merchandise licensing codes to ensure goods are not made in sweatshops. (*Vote 131, p. H-38*)

Lawmakers Add Interest Rate Fix To Transit Bill

MAY 23 — In a last-ditch effort to prevent a possible disruption of the college loan market, lawmakers added a provision to the surface transportation conference report that would reduce interest rates on federally backed student loans, starting July 1, while providing special bank subsidies.

Commercial lenders, who make 70 percent of all student loans, have threatened to pull out of federally guaranteed lending unless Congress acts to stave off even deeper cuts in interest rates, which are set to take effect July 1.

The House on May 6 passed HR 6, the higher education reauthorization act, which is designed to fix the problem by reducing interest rates to 7.43 percent after a student leaves school, down from the current 8.23 percent. It would provide a second, higher rate to banks of 7.93 percent.

But the Senate has not yet acted on the bill, and lawmakers are worried that a final measure will not be approved before July 1. Further, the White House opposes the interest rate plan as an unwarranted subsidy to banks. Adding to the uncertainty, lawmakers have not been able to come up with the $3 billion the Office of Management and Budget says is needed to pay for a five-year fix.

The transportation bill (HR 2400) would implement the HR 6 interest rate from July 1 through October 1. By that time, Congress is expected to approve a permanent solution.

[The final surface transportation bill included a provision specifying an interest rate subsidy of about one-half of 1 percentage point for student loans made over three months, starting July 1, 1998.]

Senate Passes Bill, Despite Objections To Bank Subsidies

JULY 11 — The Senate on July 9 passed a five-year reauthorization of the Higher Education Act that would reduce interest rates on federally guaranteed loans, create a $300 million system of block grants to help states improve teacher training, and expand Pell grants for low-income students.

The Senate passed the bill (S 1882) 96-1, despite complaints from Education Secretary Richard W. Riley that it provided "arbitrary and excessive subsidies" to banks, which make 70 percent of college loans. The administration opposed enactment of the bill in its current form. (*Vote 195, p. S-31*)

The House approved an identical student loan plan May 6 as part of its version of the bill (HR 6).

Commercial banks had threatened to drop out of the college lending program unless Congress rolled back a long-planned July 1 change in the federal formula for setting interest rates, which would have sharply reduced their expected returns. To avoid any possible market disruption, Congress

Higher Education Act

on May 22 included a provision in the transportation bill (PL 105-178), implementing the proposed interest rate plan from July 1 to October 1.

The temporary plan, which the House and Senate bills would put in place for five years, would create a two-tiered system providing one interest rate for students and a second, slightly higher rate for banks. Though banks would receive millions of dollars in special interest subsidies, the new rates would be lower than under current law.

The rates would be variable, based on short-term Treasury bonds. Sallie Mae, based on July 10 rates, said students in the 1998-99 academic year would receive an estimated 7.46 percent interest rate during repayment. Banks would get an estimated 7.96 percent rate. Earlier this year, both rates were 8.23 percent.

The administration supports the student rate, which is based on a proposal put forward by Vice President Al Gore, but it opposes the bank subsidy.

The Office of Management and Budget estimated the bill would provide $2.4 billion in subsidies to lenders over five years and complained that the cost is not offset by spending reductions elsewhere.

Without changes in a House-Senate conference, OMB warned that the bill would exceed current spending limits and could force across-the-board cuts in other mandatory programs.

Republicans defended the plan. "This bill will make college more accessible for more Americans," said Labor and Human Resources Committee Chairman James M. Jeffords, R-Vt.

The Senate defeated, 39-58, an amendment by Edward M. Kennedy, D-Mass., backed by the administration, that would have created a pilot program to test the feasibility of auctioning off the right to offer student loans. The idea was to have the market, not Congress, set rates. (Vote 192, p. S-31)

Teacher Training, More Grants

In an effort to respond to concerns about the quality of elementary and secondary teachers, as well as a shortage of instructors in low-income areas, the bill would replace existing federal programs with $300 million in block grants to revamp teacher training.

The Senate bill would increase the maximum authorization for Pell grants for disadvantaged students, currently appropriated at $3,000 per student, to $5,000 in academic year 1999-2000. The cap would rise $200 per year thereafter. The House bill would increase the grants to $4,500 in 1999-2000 and $5,300 in 2003-04.

The bill would provide up to $10,000 in loan forgiveness for teachers who work in schools in low-income rural and urban areas, set up a "performance-based organization" in the Education Department to improve student aid delivery, and expand campus-based child care.

During debate the Senate:

• Approved, 56-42, an amendment by Paul Wellstone, D-Minn., that would give states the option of allowing welfare recipients to enroll in vocational or postsecondary education for two years without losing monthly benefits. Current law, which requires states to have 50 percent of welfare caseloads working by fiscal 2002, allows one year of vocational training. (Vote 191, p. S-31)

• Approved by voice vote an amendment by Bob Graham, D-Fla., that would make it easier for veterans who receive veterans' education benefits to qualify for other federal college aid programs. GI benefits are now counted as income when determining eligibility for other programs.

• Defeated, 41-56, an amendment by Tom Harkin, D-Iowa, that would have reduced the 4 percent origination fee on student loans. (Vote 194, p. S-31)

Agreement Near On Rewrite Of Education Act

SEPTEMBER 26 — House and Senate negotiators on Sept. 25 said they had reached agreement on nearly all elements of a five-year rewrite of the Higher Education Act that would cut interest rates on federal college loans to the lowest level in nearly 20 years, expand grants to low-income students and create a new teacher training program.

Lawmakers said they expected to quickly wrap up a few remaining details on the bill (HR 6) and predicted final approval by Congress during the week of Sept. 28. Congress is working against an Oct. 1 deadline to implement the interest rate plan.

At a House news conference, Democrats and Republicans outlined their agreement, even while aides admitted they were still trying to nail down final spending offsets to pay for the interest rate plan. They expected the final agreement to pass with broad support.

"This is one of the most important pieces of legislation we will pass in Congress this session," said House Education and the Workforce Committee Chairman Bill Goodling, R-Pa.

Rep. Dale E. Kildee, D-Mich., and other lawmakers praised the measure as a triumph of bipartisan cooperation. "The federal government does good things in this country. . . . This is a bill that will make a real difference in education."

Education Secretary Richard W. Riley said in a statement he supported the deal despite disappointment that it provided new subsidies to bankers.

Teacher Training

The proposed conference report would create three new grant programs, authorized at a total of $300 million in fiscal 1999, to help states improve teacher training and performance and recruit qualified teachers. The funding could be used for such initiatives as upgrading teacher certification programs or providing merit pay to excellent teachers.

In an effort to address shortages of teachers in rural and low-income urban areas, the measure would forgive up to $5,000 of college loans, and in some instances more, for newly graduated teachers who stay in the profession for at least five years.

Blending suggestions from the White House and House- and Senate-passed measures, the conference report would create a "GEAR UP" program of expanded outreach to low-income youths in middle school. The initiative, authorized at $200 million in fiscal 1999, is designed to increase the number of poor students who attend college.

Pell Grants

The agreement would gradually increase the maximum authorized Pell Grant for low-income college students to $5,800 in academic year 2003-04,

Education

up from the current appropriated level of $3,000. It would expand eligibility of Pell Grants to postgraduate teaching programs and set up a discretionary program of financial awards, equal to a student's Pell Grant, to college freshmen and sophomores who graduated in the top 10 percent of their high school class.

The deal would increase the authorization for college work study to $1 billion in fiscal 1999, up from the fiscal 1998 appropriated level of $830 million.

It would set up a performance-based organization in the Education Department to improve oversight of federal student aid. The federal government provided more than $48 billion in grants, loans and federal work study funding in fiscal 1998.

Responding to violence on some U.S. campuses that have tried to crack down on drinking, the agreement would create a program to combat college alcohol abuse. It would provide grants for child care for low-income students and to combat violent crime against women on college campuses.

Despite the bipartisan glow surrounding the bill, some Republicans groused that the Clinton administration had been of little help during negotiations on the package.

"They want a signing ceremony badly," Rep. Howard P. "Buck" McKeon, R-Calif., chairman of the House Education and the Workforce Subcommittee on Postsecondary Education, Training and Life-Long Learning, said before the deal was finalized. "If you were President Clinton, would you want to sign a higher education bill or talk about Monica Lewinsky?"

Interest Rates Key

As it has been since lawmakers started work on the bill last year, the issue of where to set interest rates on student loans was the major dispute.

Commercial banks earlier this year had threatened to drop out of the college lending program unless Congress rolled back a long-planned July 1 change in the federal formula for setting interest rates, which would have sharply reduced their expected returns. To avoid any possible disruption, Congress on May 22 included a provision in the transportation bill (PL 105-178) that put in place a compromise rate plan from July 1 to Oct 1.

The temporary fix would be extended until 2003 under the conference report. The measure would create a two-tiered system providing one interest rate for students and a second, slightly higher rate for banks. Though banks would receive hundreds of millions of dollars in special interest subsidies, the new rate would be lower than under previous law.

The rates, based on short-term treasury bonds, would vary annually. Based on July 1 data, students in the 1998-99 academic year would receive a 7.46 percent interest rate during repayment. Banks would get an estimated 7.96 percent rate. Earlier this year, those rates were 8.23 percent.

The Clinton administration initially opposed the interest rate formula, arguing that it was too generous to banks.

A big sticking point for lawmakers was finding the hundreds of millions of dollars needed to pay for the bank subsidies. After months of negotiations, the conferees were planning to come up with the cash by preventing students from discharging debt if they declared bankruptcy. They were also hoping to wring some savings out of federal mortgage guarantee programs.

The agreement would require federal student loan guaranty agencies to return $250 million in outstanding reserve funds to the federal government, sets up a federal student loan reserve fund and reduces guaranty agencies' share of collections on loan defaults.

Loan Consolidation

Lawmakers had to deal with an unexpected controversy when the Education Department this summer announced that it would apply the lower student interest rate not only to new college loans, but also to students who consolidated direct and guaranteed loans into one package for easier repayment. In effect, that announcement allowed students to refinance outstanding loans at a lower rate of interest.

Commercial lenders complained the move gave the Education Department, which directly competes with them through its direct loan program, an unfair advantage. The agreement would let the Education Department offer the lower rate on consolidated loans until Feb. 1, 1999.

Conference Report Wins Easily In Both Chambers

OCTOBER 3 — Without a single dissenting vote, Congress on Sept. 29 cleared a five-year reauthorization of the 1965 Higher Education Act that reduces student loan interest rates to their lowest level in nearly two decades, increases grants for needy students and sets up a new teacher training program.

In sharp contrast to the bitter sparring among lawmakers over possible impeachment hearings, a Republican-proposed tax cut, and appropriations bills, the conference report won overwhelming bipartisan support.

"I am sure that some are surprised that this Congress, in this political environment, would be able to produce a conference report of this magnitude," said Howard P. "Buck" McKeon, R-Calif., chairman of the House Education and the Workforce Subcommittee on Postsecondary Education, Training and Life-Long Learning.

The House passed the bill (HR 6) by voice vote Sept 28; the Senate followed with a 96-0 vote Sept. 29. *(Senate vote 290, p. S-45)*

President Clinton, in a statement, praised the measure and urged lawmakers to appropriate the money needed to fund its new initiatives. Eager to claim credit on an issue that is highly popular with Americans, Clinton is expected to sign the bill the week of Oct. 5.

"This bill will make it easier for millions of Americans to get the higher education they need to succeed in the global economy," Clinton said.

The U.S. Student Association, an organization that represents college students, said it was taking a "vocally silent" position on the bill. The group, college associations and the Education Department are unhappy that Congress decided to apply the lower interest rate only through Feb. 1, 1999, to students who consolidate outstanding loans for easier repayment. Students and colleges were also unhappy about a provision making it more difficult for students to discharge student loan debt if they declared bankruptcy.

Higher Education Act

Some Democrats were upset that conferees dropped a provision by Democratic Sen. Paul Wellstone of Minnesota that would have made it easier for welfare recipients to attend college or vocational schools without losing their benefits.

"If you are able to go on and complete two years or four years of higher education, you are going to be in a better position to find a good job and give your children the care you know they need and deserve," Wellstone said.

The Wellstone amendment would have allowed states to count education toward work requirements imposed by Congress in the 1996 welfare law (PL 104-193). The final bill calls for a General Accounting Office study on the role of education in helping welfare recipients become employed.

The bill reduces interest rates to students, at least initially, by nearly a full percentage point. Interest rates in academic year 1999-2000 will be 7.46 percent for students during the standard 10-year repayment period, down from 8.23 percent earlier this year. To help lenders' profitability, the government would provide a subsidy to ensure that banks make 7.96 percent on student loans. The rates are set by a formula based on short-term Treasury notes and vary annually.

Lending Controversy

Earlier this year, some commercial banks threatened to drop out of the college lending program unless Congress rolled back a long-planned July 1 change in the federal formula for setting interest rates, which would have sharply reduced their expected returns.

That rate cut was included in the 1993 budget-reconciliation law (PL 103-66) that also created the Education Department's direct student lending program. The Clinton administration had hoped the lending program would have captured a majority of the student aid market by now. Furthermore, the plan would have pegged student loans to long-term, as opposed to short-term, interest rates. But in the meantime, long-term rates have fallen, making the formula unacceptable to banks.

To avoid a disruption, Congress on May 22 included a provision in the surface transportation reauthorization bill (PL 105-178) that put in place a temporary compromise rate, based on 91-day Treasury bill yields, from July 1 to Oct. 1. Until HR 6 is signed, the Education Department has the power to maintain the status quo.

Under the reauthorization, the temporary fix will be extended until 2003.

While the rates vary from year to year, lawmakers estimated that a student who borrowed $12,000 would save $650 in interest over the 10-year repayment period. The White House complained that the two-tiered rate was too generous to bankers, but lenders asserted that they were still taking a financial hit.

"While this legislation requires significant sacrifices on the part of student loan providers, it ensures that students will continue to have access [to loans]," said Mark R. Cannon, executive director of the Coalition for Student Loan Reform, a group of guarantee agencies.

The bill lets the Education Department apply the lower rate only until Feb. 1, 1999, for students who consolidate outstanding loans. After Congress approved the temporary fix this summer, the department announced it would extend the reduced rate to consolidation loans. That prompted howls from bankers who said it would give the department, which runs a direct lending program in competition with the commercial market, an unfair advantage.

The measure gradually increases the maximum allowable Pell grant for low-income students to $5,800 in academic year 2003-04, up from the current appropriated level of $3,000. Need criteria are relaxed to make it easier for students to work without exceeding income limits for financial aid and help non-traditional students, many with children, to qualify.

The authorization for college work-study programs increases to $1 billion in fiscal 1999, up from the appropriated level of $830 million.

The bill sets up a performance-based organization in the Department of Education to run student aid programs and requires the education secretary to provide information to the public about college tuition increases.

To pay for the interest rate changes, the legislation alters provisions of bankruptcy law to make it more difficult for students to discharge student loan debt. Students will still be able to discharge their payments if they prove severe economic hardship. The bill also increased the Government National Mortgage Association's (Ginnie Mae) guarantee fee to nine basis points, from six basis points, in fiscal 2005-07.

It calls for a study of using market-based mechanisms, such as auctions, to set college loan interest rates.

Training Programs

Responding to reports that more than one-third of teachers of core subjects such as math and science were not trained in their subject area, the bill consolidates more than a dozen programs into block grants to states to improve teacher preparation. It authorizes $300 million for the initiative in fiscal 1999.

States can use the funds to improve certification programs, provide merit pay for excellent teachers and create alternative certification programs, where individuals with expertise in an outside field can quickly be prepared to teach. Further, states are required to identify teacher-training programs that performed poorly.

"This bill will take giant steps in improving teacher preparation," said Senate Labor Committee Chairman James M. Jeffords, R-Vt.

In a second effort to address a shortage of qualified teachers, especially in poor areas, the bill provides up to $5,000 in loan forgiveness for new teachers who work in underserved school areas for five years. Teachers must have a degree in the subject matter they teach.

The bill takes steps to reach out to non-traditional students, such as older individuals or those who take longer than the standard four years to earn an undergraduate degree.

The act provides child care grants to help low-income students attend school. It allows experiments with "distance learning" so that students who live far away from a regular campus can attend via computers and other technology.

"Distance learning can open the doors of higher education to many students who cannot attend classes on college campuses because they live in remote areas or because of their job and family responsibilities," said Sen.

Education

Edward M. Kennedy, D-Mass.

The legislation blends House, Senate and White House suggestions to create a new "GEAR UP" program of outreach to low-income middle school students. The initiative, authorized at $200 million in fiscal 1999, is designed to help low-income students attend college.

The bill eases some federal regulations on vocational schools or career colleges, which in the past have been plagued by high student loan default rates and other problems. Lawmakers said they were satisfied that the schools had improved their performance.

The bill bars federal aid to students convicted on a drug charge. Students lose eligibility for one year after a first conviction, two years after a second and indefinitely after a third. ◆

President Blocks GOP Drive To Give Tax Breaks for Education Savings Accounts

In July, President Clinton vetoed a bill (HR 2646) that would have created tax-preferred savings accounts for elementary and secondary education expenses, including private school tuition.

Clinton had been threatening a veto since House passage near the end of the first session. He sent the bill back to Congress saying it would "weaken public education and shortchange our children."

In an election year when voters had rated education as a top priority, the president contended that Congress had ignored his proposals to reduce average class size and build or repair schools.

Republicans charged that the White House had caved in to pressure from teachers' unions that opposed the bill. The GOP insisted that the measure would have helped middle-class parents by allowing them to set aside $2,000 in special savings accounts and withdraw the principal and interest tax-free for education-related expenses, including private school tuition, tutoring, home computers and transportation costs.

Democrats assailed the bill as slanted toward affluent Americans who can afford to set aside thousands of dollars a year. "This only helps one class of people — upper-income constituents who live in the suburbs and send their children to private schools," said Rep. Martin Frost, D-Texas.

In the Senate, Democrats had blocked action on the House-passed bill in late 1997, but Republicans came back in 1998 with a larger, more comprehensive bill (S 1133) that the Senate passed under threat of a presidential veto. *(1997 Almanac, p. 7-6)*

Savings Accounts Measure Draws Early Veto Threats

FEBRUARY 14 — Reopening a battle with the White House, the Senate Finance Committee Feb. 10 approved legislation to let taxpayers shelter up to $2,000 a year in education savings accounts for elementary and secondary school tuition and other expenses, as well as college costs.

The bill (S 1133) expands on a provision in the 1997 tax law (PL 105-34) that allows contributions of up to $500 a year for college. In a nod to Democrats, the overall measure would also expand tax breaks for employer-paid education assistance to cover graduate level courses and provide tax-free treatment of state prepaid college tuition plans.

"This legislation helps to provide to the American people much-needed tools to afford a quality education," said William V. Roth Jr., R-Del., the committee chairman.

The plan was approved 11-8 largely along party lines after unsuccessful efforts by Roth to broker a wider bipartisan compromise. However, Sens. John B. Breaux, D-La., and Bob Graham, D-Fla., who opposed a similar bill on the floor last year, voted for the measure.

Box Score

- **Bill:** HR 2646
- **House action:** The House adopted the conference report (H Rept 105-577) on HR 2646, 225-197, on June 18. The House initially passed the bill, 230-198, on Oct. 23, 1997.
- **Senate action:** The Senate cleared HR 2646, 59-36, on June 24. It passed the bill, after substituting the text of S 1133 (S Rept 105-164), 56-43, April 23.
- **Presidential action:** Clinton vetoed the bill July 21.

Roth had hoped to pick up more support from Democrats on the panel by offering to include tax credits to holders of bonds issued by state and local governments for school construction, costing the federal government more than $1 billion over 10 years.

Neither party was willing to embrace the specific proposal during a closed-door caucus. Roth said he will try to work out a deal before a floor vote.

Adding to the difficulty for the bill, a key element of the Senate GOP's agenda, Education Secretary Richard W. Riley and Treasury Secretary Robert E. Rubin in a Feb. 9 letter renewed White House veto threats. They said the accounts would mainly benefit affluent taxpayers, while diverting funding from public schools.

The elementary and secondary savings accounts, named "A-plus accounts" by sponsor Sen. Paul Coverdell, R-Ga., were part of the 1997 tax legislation, but were deleted after protests from the White House. The House passed a similar, free-standing bill (HR 2646) in October. Democrats twice blocked efforts to invoke cloture on a separate Senate measure.

Education Savings Accounts

Sen. Edward M. Kennedy, D-Mass., said he will fight the legislation again this year.

The Finance Committee package would let families deposit up to $2,000 per child into the accounts annually from 1999 through 2002. The savings and the tax-free earnings they generated could be used for private school tuition, fees, tutoring, transportation and other public or private education expenses.

Families, relatives, businesses or tax-exempt foundations could contribute. The accounts would begin to phase out for individuals with annual adjusted gross incomes of $95,000 ($150,000 for couples) and would be eliminated for those at $110,000 a year ($160,000 for couples).

Cloture Votes Fail As Daschle, Lott Bicker Over Rules

MARCH 21 — Proponents of legislation (HR 2646) to expand tax-deferred college savings accounts to cover elementary and secondary school expenses hoped to complete work on the measure during the week of March 23, but movement was contingent on a deal between Republican and Democratic leaders on the terms of engagement.

Both parties want to use the measure, introduced by Sen. Paul Coverdell, R-Ga., and cosponsored by Sen. Robert G. Torricelli, D-N.J., as the vehicle for a wide-ranging, election-year showdown over the federal role in education. The bill's prospects appeared favorable on March 17 when the Senate voted 74-24 to proceed with debate. (Vote 34, p. S-8)

Later in the week, Senate Majority Leader Trent Lott, R-Miss., and Senate Minority Leader Tom Daschle, D-S.D., were unable to agree on how many amendments Democrats should be allowed to offer, including White House-backed proposals for billions of dollars in school construction and expanded after-school care. On March 19, another cloture motion was defeated, 55-44, as all Democrats voted no. Sixty votes are needed for cloture. (Vote 38, p. S-9)

Lott and Daschle hoped to work out an acceptable list of amendments that would allow for relatively speedy action. Another cloture vote was set for March 24. Democratic opponents concede that Coverdell may have enough votes to eventually pass the legislation, but are bolstered by White House threats to veto the bill. The House passed a similar version of the bill last year.

The legislation is an effort by Republicans to appeal to middle-class voters and to move beyond the party's more narrow emphasis on federally funded vouchers for private school education. The broader focus, and sweeteners added in committee, have helped Coverdell attract the support of a growing number of Democrats.

After the March 19 cloture vote, Coverdell accused Democrats of playing politics to protect teachers' unions, which oppose the bill. "The minority leader is doing the bidding of the White House" and teachers' unions, he said.

Daschle retorted that the tax breaks in the bill would be of minimal benefit to average families and to children in public school. "This is about $7 worth of help for public schools," Daschle said, saying it was enough for "some Elmer's glue, a couple of pencils."

The measure would allow family members, charitable groups or private donors to contribute up to $2,000 a year per child in special accounts for private school tuition, tutoring, transportation costs, home computers or other education expenses. Contributions could generally be made until a student turned 18. Interest on the accounts would accrue tax-free, and any unused savings could be rolled over into the next year and eventually be used for college expenses.

The accounts would begin to phase out for individuals with annual adjusted gross incomes of $95,000 ($150,000 for couples) and would be eliminated for those at $110,000 a year ($160,000 for couples). The measure builds on a provision in the 1997 tax law (PL 104-34) that allows families to set aside $500 a year solely for college.

In an attempt to attract Democratic votes, Republicans added provisions during Finance Committee consideration that would make pre-paid college tuition plans completely tax deductible and extend a tax deduction for employee education.

Senate Leaders Agree on Rules For Debate

MARCH 28 — Senate leaders have put off until April 20 a showdown over an education savings account bill that gives both parties their only good shot to highlight the issue in an election year.

After nearly two weeks of bickering, Senate Majority Leader Trent Lott, R-Miss., and Senate Minority Leader Tom Daschle, D-S.D., on March 27 settled on ground rules for debating legislation (S 1133) to create tax-preferred savings accounts for elementary and secondary school expenses.

Under the agreement, 12 Democratic and five Republican amendments, all education related, could be offered.

The deal, which still had to be run past one absent senator, came only after Republicans on March 26 failed to muster enough support to invoke cloture and begin consideration of the bill. The cloture vote was 58-42, and 60 votes are needed. The measure, sponsored by Sen. Paul Coverdell, R-Ga., would allow individuals to set aside up to $2,000 a year for elementary and secondary private school tuition, tutoring, home computers and other expenses. (Vote 46, p. S-10)

Three Democrats — John B. Breaux of Louisiana, Joseph I. Lieberman of Connecticut and Robert G. Torricelli of New Jersey, a main cosponsor — supported cloture after voting against it on March 19.

The defections gave Republicans hope that they would eventually prevail, and Lott had set another cloture vote for March 30. "We're almost there. I'm now confident that this filibuster will be ended and we'll get on to the main debate," said Coverdell.

Daschle was equally adamant that Democrats would hang tough unless Lott made concessions. "He'd be mistaken if he thought he was winning. He lost again today," Daschle said.

In the end, Republicans agreed to a deal that calls for them to offer more amendments than they had originally

Education

planned. Democrats want to use the debate to highlight White House proposals, including school construction and after-school care.

Democrats concede that Coverdell's bill may eventually pass. President Clinton has threatened to veto the measure, which the administration calls a tax cut for the wealthy.

The legislation builds on a provision in the 1997 tax law (PL 105-34) that allows families to set aside $500 a year for college. Interest on the accounts would accrue tax-free, and any unused savings could be rolled over into the next year and eventually used for college.

Both the current and expanded accounts would begin to phase out for individuals with annual adjusted gross incomes of $95,000 ($150,000 for couples) and would be eliminated for those at $110,000 a year ($160,000 for couples). To attract Democratic votes, Republicans added provisions in Finance Committee debate to make prepaid college tuition plans completely tax-deductible and extend a tax break for employee education.

President Calls Senate Measure 'Bad Policy'

APRIL 25 — Moving to fundamentally reshape the federal role in education, the Senate April 23 approved legislation (HR 2646) that would turn more than half the Education Department's elementary and secondary schools budget into block grants, allow tax breaks for private and public schools and bar President Clinton's planned national tests.

Before voting 56-43 on final passage, senators defeated White House-backed initiatives to train 100,000 new teachers and allow local governments to issue $22 billion dollars in bonds to finance school construction and renovation. (Vote 102, p. S-18)

The debate gave voters, who list education as one of their top issues, a clear election-year choice: a Republican agenda providing states greater control over federal education spending vs. Democratic efforts to increase assistance from Washington.

While the legislation provided fodder for November campaigns, there was virtually no chance it would become law without major changes in a House-Senate conference.

The president vowed to veto the bill, calling it bad education and bad tax policy.

"The Republicans have a 'one ideology fits all.' They want to privatize Social Security. They want to privatize Medicare. And they want to privatize education in this country," said Edward M. Kennedy, D-Mass.

But Republicans argued that it was Democrats who were the enemies of public schools, defenders of an education bureaucracy that had produced falling test scores and rising public dissatisfaction.

Paul Coverdell, R-Ga., the chief sponsor of the measure, warned the president to reconsider before he "cast his lot with the status quo and becomes another obstructionist."

Clinton had long threatened to veto the underlying bill, which would establish tax-preferred savings accounts to help families pay for private school tuition, tutoring, home computers and other education expenses.

The House in October passed a similar measure allowing $2,500 savings accounts.

The Senate's legislation would allow family members, charitable groups or private donors to contribute up to $2,000 a year per child to the special accounts. Contributions could generally be made until a child turned 18. Interest would accrue tax free and any unused savings could be rolled over into the next year and eventually used for college.

The plan builds on a provision in the 1997 tax law (PL 105-34) that allows families to set aside $500 a year solely for college.

As the Senate debated the bill, Clinton, Minority Leader Tom Daschle, D-S.D., and other Democratic opponents said the savings account plan would divert money from public schools. They cited numbers from the Joint Committee on Taxation showing that 52 percent of the tax benefits would go to about 7 percent of taxpayers — families with children in private schools. At the same time, they argued the tax breaks were too paltry to do anyone much good — about $7 to $37 a year, according to the committee.

Democratic Support

Still, five Democrats voted for the measure and Robert G. Torricelli of New Jersey was a main cosponsor. Supporters said it would spur much-needed savings. They argued that unlike previous Republican proposals for private education federal vouchers, the bill would also aid children in public schools.

Early in the week, lobbyists and lawmakers predicted the measure could pass with more than 60 votes. That changed after April 22 when the Senate, on a largely party-line vote of 50-49, approved an amendment by Slade Gorton, R-Wash, that could turn $10.3 billion in annual elementary and secondary programs, including aid to the disadvantaged and bilingual education, into broad block grants. (Vote 91, p. S-16)

The Senate also approved 52-47 an amendment by John Ashcroft, R-Mo., to bar the Clinton administration from proceeding with plans for voluntary national exams to assess fourth graders in reading and eighth-graders in math, unless specifically authorized by Congress. (Vote 94, p. S-17)

"We've gone from doing little to doing real damage," Daschle said.

After the amendments passed, some Democrats who had planned to vote for the bill changed their minds, including Joseph R. Biden Jr. of Delaware. He contended the value of the savings accounts paled when compared with the changes under Gorton's amendment. "The horse won't carry that sleigh," he said.

Torricelli and other Democrats who voted "aye" also sent a letter to Senate Majority Leader Trent Lott, R-Miss., warning that unless the Gorton and Ashcroft amendments were dropped in conference, "unfortunately our support and bipartisan cooperation . . . cannot be counted on."

Republican aides said the Gorton language could fail in conference, but the test ban would likely remain.

Though Lott and Coverdell supported the two contentious amendments, they also made a series of efforts to attract Democratic support.

During markup Feb. 10, the Senate Finance Committee had added several

Education Savings Accounts

Democratic initiatives, including tax-free treatment of state pre-paid college tuition plans and extension of tax breaks for employer-paid tuition assistance to cover graduate education.

Finance Committee Chairman William V. Roth Jr., R-Del., sponsored a floor amendment that would add $58 million in tax credits over five years to leverage up to $3 billion in school construction bonds. Some Republicans complained most of the provisions in the underlying bill were put in at the behest of Democrats.

While the Republicans worked to find a middle ground on savings accounts, their efforts to win bipartisan support went only so far. Their list of amendments was designed, like the Democrats', to showcase their broader education agenda. The Gorton block grant amendment was a key example.

The Senate approved a similar plan last year as part of the fiscal 1998 appropriations bill funding the departments of Labor, Health and Human Services, and Education, but dropped it in conference.

Programs covered by the amendment include Title I aid to disadvantaged students, bilingual education, Clinton's Goals 2000 education improvement program, technology grants and aid to drug-free schools.

States could continue funding under current rules, create state-wide block grants or channel aid directly to local school districts.

"What my bill does is prefer children to bureaucrats," Gorton said. "This is a way to target more dollars to the classroom."

Democrats said the amendment would gut the Education Department and weaken current law, which bars states from using federal funds to supplant state dollars.

The Ashcroft amendment, which would bar the Clinton administration from moving forward with its proposal to test fourth graders in reading and eighth graders in math, showed that Clinton has virtually no chance of moving forward on national testing. It reversed an 87-13 vote last year for a compromise plan to allow testing.

The House on Feb. 5 passed HR 2846, sponsored by Rep. Bill Goodling, R-Pa., chairman of the Committee on Education and the Workforce to bar the tests.

Amendments

The Senate also:

● Approved, 74-26, an amendment by Jeff Bingaman, D-N.M, to create a national program to try to reduce the high school dropout rate. The plan includes an initial authorization of $150 million for teacher training, curriculum improvement and other changes. (*Vote 101, p. S-18*)

● Voted 56-41 to table, or kill, a substitute by Kennedy that would replace the savings account provisions with a plan to provide federal student loan forgiveness to teachers who served in schools with a high number of poor students. The amendment was designed to fulfill Clinton's pledge to hire 100,000 new teachers. (*Vote 86, p. S-16*)

● Tabled, or killed, by a 56-42 vote, a substitute by Carol Moseley-Braun, D-Ill., that would have provided tax credits to leverage $22 billion in local bonds for school construction and renovation. This was also a White House priority. (*Vote 90, p. S-16*)

● Approved by a 63-35 vote an amendment by Connie Mack, R-Fla., and Alfonse M. D'Amato, R-N.Y., to provide incentive payments to states that carried out teacher testing and merit pay. (*Vote 88, p. S-16*)

● Defeated, 46-54, an amendment by Daniel R. Coats, R-Ind., that would have provided a 110 percent tax deduction for donations to scholarship programs for low-income children. The cost would have been offset by eliminating the federal deductibility of gambling losses. The gaming industry lobbied against the plan. (*Vote 95, p. S-17*)

● Passed, 69-29, an amendment by Kay Bailey Hutchison, R-Texas, to allow use of federal funds for same-sex classrooms or schools. (*Vote 89, p. S-16*)

Bill Passes House; Votes Lacking For Veto Override

JUNE 20 — Even as it passed a bill to create tax-preferred savings accounts for private school tuition, the House sounded the death knell June 18 for the bill by falling short of the two-thirds majority needed to override a promised presidential veto.

Lawmakers approved the conference report on HR 2646 by a 225-197 vote, sending it to the Senate. (*Vote 243, p. H-70*)

President Clinton opposes the measure, which Republicans have made a key plank of their election-year education platform.

The bill would let families set aside $2,000 in tax-preferred savings accounts annually for education-related expenses, including private school tuition, tutoring, home computers and transportation expenses.

Minority Leader Richard A. Gephardt, D-Mo., called the bill a "frivolous, unserious, ridiculous piece of legislation." It represents a "missed opportunity" to improve public schools, he said.

Republicans said the savings accounts were not the whole answer to the problems bedeviling public schools, but called them an important first step toward giving parents more control over their children's education.

"It's not a big tax break; it's a very important principle that we're beginning to enshrine in law," said Republican Phil English of Pennsylvania.

At a June 17 news conference with House Democrats, Education Secretary Richard W. Riley cited a study that concluded that the bill would provide, on average, a benefit of $7 per year to parents of children in public schools and only $37 for those in private schools.

Twelve Democrats voted for the measure, while 10 Republicans voted against it. Sponsors hope to pick up support from about one-fourth of Democratic senators when the Senate takes up the bill, possibly June 23.

Before final passage, the House defeated, 196-225, a motion by Democrat Charles B. Rangel of New York to send the bill back to a House-Senate conference committee and replace it with a Democratic proposal to create tax-free bonds for public school construction and renovation. (*Vote 242, p. H-70*)

Republicans charged that Clinton was set to veto the bill largely under pressure from teachers' unions, which have provided generous campaign contributions to Democrats.

Majority Leader Dick Armey, R-Texas, said lawmakers are "not here to defend the public schools. . . . We're here to improve the public schools."

Education

Building on Tax Law

The bill, originally introduced by Sen. Paul Coverdell, R-Ga., would allow families, charitable groups or private donors to contribute a combined total of $2,000 a year to the savings accounts. The contributions would be in after-tax dollars. Earnings would accrue tax-free as long as they were spent on approved uses.

The legislation builds on a provision in the 1997 tax law (PL 105-34) that allows families to set aside $500 per year for college. Any unused balance of the expanded accounts could be rolled over for college.

Individuals with annual adjusted gross incomes of up to $95,000 ($150,000 for couples) could contribute the full $2,000. Contributions would be gradually phased out for individuals with incomes up to $110,000 ($160,000 for couples).

The legislation also would create a program to train teachers in reading instruction methods, including use of phonics. The 1997 budget deal included $210 million for a literacy program.

It would expand the current $5,250 tax exclusion for employer-paid tuition assistance from June 1, 2000, through Dec. 31, 2002. The measure would expand existing law to make state prepaid college tuition plans completely tax free and, starting in 2006, allow private colleges to offer prepaid tuition plans.

The bill is likely to be the main piece of legislation targeted at elementary and secondary education, to pass Congress this year.

While both parties have said that education is an election-year priority, they have been unable to bridge differences on the issue. Advocacy groups warn that caps on discretionary spending, approved as part of the 1997 budget deal, could force the appropriations committees to cut some federal education programs in coming weeks.

That is not the appropriators' only challenge. During the conference on the savings account legislation, lawmakers dropped a Senate-passed provision that would have barred Clinton from implementing his proposed voluntary national math and reading tests.

House and Senate GOP leaders promised, however, to include the ban in the fiscal 1999 Labor, Health and Human Services appropriations bill.

Senate Clears Bill, Offers No Hope For Blocking Veto

JUNE 27 — The Senate on June 24 cleared legislation (HR 2646) that would let families set aside $2,000 per child annually in tax-preferred savings accounts for private school tuition, tutoring and other education expenses, sending it to President Clinton for a long-promised veto.

The bill, a GOP priority, passed 59-36, well short of the two-thirds majority needed for an override. Eight Democrats supported it while two Republicans voted nay. *(Vote 169, p. S-28)*

Despite the gloomy outlook, congressional Republican leaders, along with Sen. Robert G. Torricelli, D-N.J., a prime sponsor, held a public ceremony to formally enroll the bill and launch its expected round trip on Pennsylvania Avenue.

"If President Clinton vetoes this bill, he will have to answer to a nation crying for help," said Sen. Paul Coverdell, R-Ga., the bill's sponsor.

The measure is designed to appeal to the middle class and move the GOP beyond its traditional emphasis on federally funded vouchers for private school tuition.

Republicans have made it a centerpiece of their education agenda, responding to public opinion polls that show voters are concerned about the quality of American schools.

Democratic leaders called the legislation a squandered opportunity, noting that the GOP defeated a host of amendments that would have implemented Clinton's plan to hire 100,000 new teachers and renovate aging public schools.

Senate Minority Leader Tom Daschle, D-S.D., termed the measure an "exercise in total futility."

The bill would let families set aside $2,000 in tax-preferred savings accounts for education-related expenses, including private school tuition, tutoring, home computers and transportation expenses.

Contributions would be in after-tax dollars. Earnings would accrue tax-free as long as they were spent on approved uses. The Joint Committee on Taxation has estimated that the bill would provide, on average, a benefit of $7 per year to parents of children in public schools and $37 for those in private schools.

Republican Leaders Decry Veto

JULY 25 — House Republican leaders protested President Clinton's July 21 veto of legislation that would have created tax-preferred savings accounts for elementary and secondary education expenses, including private school tuition. But they did not plan to attempt an override.

After months of promising to veto the measure, Clinton sent the bill (HR 2646) back to Congress, saying it would "weaken public education and shortchange our children."

In an election year when voters have rated education as a top priority, the president complained that Congress had ignored his proposals to reduce average class size and build or repair schools.

Republicans charged that the White House had caved in to pressure from teachers' unions that opposed the bill.

"There is only one reason the president vetoed this immensely popular, bipartisan bill: to pay back the big labor unions for their millions of dollars in campaign contributions," said House Speaker Newt Gingrich, R-Ga.

The Senate passed the bill, 59-36, on June 24; the House adopted the conference report, 225-197, on June 18. Neither chamber was near the two-thirds margin needed to override a veto.

A spokeswoman for Sen. Paul Coverdell, R-Ga., the main sponsor of the measure, said there would be no override effort in the Senate. Instead there might be a move to attach parts of the legislation to other must-pass bills or try again next year.

The bill would have let families set aside $2,000 in tax-preferred savings accounts for education-related expenses, including private school tuition, tutoring, home computers and transportation costs.

Contributions would be in after-tax dollars. Earnings would accrue tax-free as long as they were spent on approved uses. Under the 1997 tax law (PL 105-34), families can now set aside $500 per year for college. ◆

Compromise Head Start Bill Sidesteps Controversy, Focuses on Program Quality

SUMMARY

Congress approved a five-year reauthorization of the 1965 Head Start preschool program for low-income children, designed to both improve quality and expand full-day, full-year child care services for women moving from welfare to work. The act also extended the Low-Income Home Energy Assistance Program (LIHEAP) and Community Services Block Grant.

The Senate version (S 2206) was approved by the Labor Committee by voice vote after debate over a provision allowing for-profit centers to be named primary Head Start providers. The road was rockier in the House.

During markup of the House bills (HR 4241 and HR 4271) the Education and the Workforce Committee approved amendments that would have ended the requirement that the government comply with Davis-Bacon prevailing wage laws on Head Start projects; required low-income mothers to cooperate in establishing the paternity of their children as a condition for aid; and allowed limited use of vouchers for private child care.

Democrats voted against the bill, and the Clinton administration condemned it. Committee Chairman Bill Goodling, R-Pa., resolved the dispute by bringing a substitute to the floor that did not include the disputed provisions. It passed easily.

The final act requires that by 2003 a majority of Head Start instructors have an associate or bachelor's degree in early childhood education or a related field. It dedicates 60 percent of new funds in fiscal 1999 for quality improvements, such as better training. Under previous law, three-quarters of new funds went to expand enrollment and one-fourth to quality.

The ratio would revert to 75-25 by 2003. It doubles funding for Early Head Start, which serves infants and toddlers to age 3, to 10 percent of the overall program, and would allow for-profit child care agencies to be designated as primary Head Start providers.

LIHEAP was extended for five years. Funding was unspecified for 2000-01 and capped at $2 billion in 2002-04. The Community Services Block Grant was extended for five years, with new authorization for family literacy, community policing and youth development activities, as well as parenting and gang prevention programs.

Faith-based organizations would be allowed to receive grant funding.

The legislation includes a five-year pilot program of savings accounts where contributions by low-income individuals would be matched with private or public funds. The accounts could be used to begin a business, pay for school or buy a house. Funding would be capped at $25 million a year.

Senate Panel Approves Five-Year Reauthorization

JUNE 27 — A sign at the Head Start center on the outskirts of Washington, D.C. spells "math and science" in six languages, reflecting the mosaic of nationalities hard at play in its sunny classrooms. Though divided by culture, the chattering preschoolers are united by a common bond: They come from needy families who rely on the full-day, full-year education, health and social services provided at the Gum Springs Head Start Children's Center through a complex patchwork of state, county and federal funds.

As Congress begins writing legislation to reauthorize Head Start, Gum Springs is an example of the direction in which many lawmakers and the Clinton administration want to move the 33-year-old federal program, designed to give disadvantaged children an extra boost as they prepare for school.

Head Start now typically operates only part-time, serving primarily 4-year-olds. As more women enter the labor force — a process accelerated by tougher welfare laws — there is a push under way to pair Head Start with other programs to provide full-time care. With new research showing the importance of early brain development, policy-makers also want to expand services to infants and toddlers.

"Head Start is going to change as more and more women are working. The mechanics are going to change. The philosophy, the respect [for families] is not," said Judith Rosen, director of the Fairfax County, Va., Office for Children, which oversees the Gum Springs center.

The idea sounds simple, but making it work could be tough. Pairing Head Start with other social programs would require cutting through layers of bureaucracy to integrate longstanding practices and policies that were not designed to mesh.

The Senate Labor and Human Resources Committee on June 24 approved a five-year reauthorization

Box Score

- **Bill:** S 2206 — PL 105-285
- **House action:** The House cleared the conference report (H Rept 105-788) on S 2206 by voice vote on Oct. 9. It approved S 2206, 346-20, on Sept. 14. The House Education and the Workforce Committee approved two bills, HR 4241 and HR 4271 (H Rept 105-686), to extend the programs on July 29. The House approved a substitute for the two bills under S 2206 on Sept. 14.
- **Senate action:** The Senate adopted the conference report by voice vote on Oct. 8. It passed S 2206 (S Rept 105-256) by voice vote July 27.
- **Presidential action:** Clinton signed S 2206 on Oct. 27.

Education

bill (S 2206) that would boost funding for Early Head Start, which covers children up to age 3, and would give centers incentives to follow Gum Springs' lead in offering comprehensive services. The House Committee on Education and the Workforce will consider its version after the July Fourth recess.

The emphasis on full-time care is just one component of a wider plan to improve Head Start, one of the most popular achievements of President Lyndon B. Johnson's "war on poverty." An equally important effort is improving the program's educational basis.

Despite tougher standards imposed by a 1994 reauthorization (PL 103-252) — including improved education and social services — and a push by the Department of Health and Human Services (HHS) to eliminate sub-par programs, there is concern that the quality of services is far too uneven across the country. (*Reauthorization, 1994 Almanac, p. 369*)

There are also charges that Head Start, which costs about $5,000 annually per student, is too expensive compared with private preschools. Bill Goodling, R-Pa., chairman of the House education panel, wants to aim the bulk of future funding increases at quality improvements such as better training for Head Start instructors — only half of whom have college degrees — rather than at program expansion.

Over the past several years, Congress and the White House have increased the program's funding, from $2.2 billion in fiscal 1992 to $4.4 billion in fiscal 1998. President Clinton's goal is to enroll 1 million children in Head Start by 2002 and double the Early Head Start program, which serves infants and toddlers, to 80,000.

The Senate bill includes Clinton's plan to expand Early Head Start funding, but House Republicans are skeptical. It would build on the 1994 reauthorization by requiring new standards to ensure children are ready for school; improve literacy training, and teaching and access for the disabled; and require assessments of individual programs. It also steps up efforts to help children make the transition to kindergarten to minimize a fade-out effect, in which educational gains diminish after two or three years in elementary school.

"Conservatives, liberals, Democrats, Republicans and everyone in between . . . can say this is something we can unite on," said Sen. Daniel R. Coats, R-Ind., chief author of the bill, adopted 18-0 by the Labor Committee. Sponsors expect a full Senate vote soon after the Fourth of July recess.

Mimicking a provision in the 1996 welfare overhaul, House Republicans may require mothers to cooperate in establishing paternity for their children before receiving aid.

Demographics and Destiny

Head Start is based on the premise that early intervention with disadvantaged children and their parents will improve their chances for academic success and family self-sufficiency. The program offers more than day care or most other preschool programs do. It includes social services such as dental screening and mental health referrals, an education program, and it requires considerable parental involvement.

When Head Start began in 1965, about 40 percent of American women were in the labor force. Because many states did not even have kindergarten programs, it stood alone on the frontier of early childhood development.

Times have changed. There has long been a recognition that Head Start, which is usually run as a half-day program that closes down in the summer, needed to become more responsive to a growing number of families in which both parents work, as well as to single-parent households.

That does not mean lawmakers want to turn the program into glorified day care or even use Head Start funds for full-time services. Rather, the push is to combine Head Start with existing child care and a growing host of state programs for families who work, and allow coordination of the expanding universe of early childhood efforts.

The push to provide comprehensive care has taken on new urgency in light of state and federal welfare laws that move people quickly into jobs.

The 1996 welfare law (PL 104-193) requires states to have 50 percent of welfare recipients working by 2002. Nationwide last year, nearly half the children in Head Start came from families on welfare. (*1996 Almanac, p. 6-3*)

"Both welfare reform and the trend to mothers working have increased the need for full-day services," said Olivia Golden, principal deputy assistant secretary for children and families at HHS. Head Start has always focused on helping parents as well as children.

"What matters to children is that their parents succeed," she said.

HHS last year focused millions of dollars on collaboration projects in which Head Start centers worked with state and local governments to provide expanded care. Of the roughly 37,000 additional children who entered the program in 1997, 30,000 received full-time care. Overall, about 10 percent of Head Start programs are full-time, though studies show about 40 percent of its families need full-time care.

Quality vs. Quantity

The 1994 reauthorization focused squarely on quality. HHS Secretary Donna E. Shalala appointed a 47-member commission to recommend long-term changes. The findings were incorporated into the law in the form of the performance standards.

Yale University psychology professor Edward Zigler, who helped create the original program and was a member of Shalala's 1994 group, told the House education panel earlier this month that Head Start was improving but more must be done. He suggested boosting teacher salaries, which average $17,000 a year compared with $28,000 for elementary school teachers, and said policy-makers should experiment with a national curriculum.

Others also say that the program, which is run by 1,500 local organizations, does not have a clear enough instructional mandate.

"Head Start has lost interest in educational results," argues Diane Ravitch, an education expert with New York University and the Brookings Institution. "It's a kind of bizarre situation of a federal program that responds to local control to the nth degree."

In one sign of a greater emphasis on quality, more than 80 Head Start programs have lost funding or left the program in the past five years.

Another question is whether Head Start is worth the average $5,000 per pupil. Rep. Frank Riggs, R-Calif., drafting the House reauthorization, had been promoting a pilot program to provide federal vouchers for low-income children to attend private preschools.

"I'm not sure that would survive, but it's important we clearly indicate what the Republican version of Head Start ideally might be," he said.

Childhood Emphasis

Head Start may still be setting the pace, but it is no longer alone. Governors, many of whom have the luxury of comfortable budget surpluses, are pumping billions of dollars into their own early childhood programs, spurred by recent research showing the importance of brain development from birth to age 3.

Last year, 21 states increased aid for pre-kindergarten or Head Start, the Children's Defense Fund said.

GOP Gov. George V. Voinovich of Ohio will spend about $80 million this year on that state's Head Start program. As chairman of the National Governors' Association, Voinovich, along with vice chair Gov. Thomas R. Carper, a Delaware Democrat, has asked Congress to give states a voice in running Head Start.

In a June 12 letter to Congress, they said that with states taking greater responsibility for welfare, child care and other formerly federal programs, Head Start cannot afford to be a "separate and isolated" system. The Senate bill would include some of the governors' suggestions, including more input into grants.

Bill Moves To House Floor, Despite Protests

AUGUST 1 — The popular Head Start program has united lawmakers across party lines since its founding in 1965. This year, its bipartisan coalition appears to be splintering.

The House Committee on Education and the Workforce on July 29 approved, on a mostly party-line vote of 23-18, a bill (HR 4241) to reauthorize the preschool program for low-income children through 2003.

Approval came after the committee accepted controversial Republican amendments. One would disqualify children from Head Start if their mothers did not cooperate in establishing paternity. Another would create a limited number of government-funded "parental certificates," or vouchers, for alternative child care.

Angry about the amendments and a provision that would eliminate use of the federal prevailing wage law on Head Start construction, Democrats said they were forced into the unusual position of opposing legislation to extend and expand one of President Lyndon B. Johnson's war on poverty programs.

"I am sad . . . about a day when we face a [Head Start] reauthorization that fails to be bipartisan in every way," said Matthew G. Martinez, D-Calif.

The bickering contrasted with action in the Senate, which passed its bipartisan version of the measure (S 2206) by voice vote July 27. The Senate bill does not include the contentious provisions.

Even before the House committee voted, Health and Human Services (HHS) Secretary Donna E. Shalala warned Chairman Bill Goodling, R-Pa., in a letter that the administration would "strongly oppose" the measure.

Shalala said the bill did not quickly enough increase funding for Early Head Start, which serves babies and toddlers to age 3, and would limit expansion of the core program, which serves mainly 4-year-olds. President Clinton's goal is to have 1 million children in Head Start by 2002. About 830,000 children are now enrolled.

Goodling defended the bill, which would focus the bulk of new funding during the first two years of the five-year reauthorization on quality improvements, such as teacher training, rather than enrolling more children.

"If you want a partisan issue, it will be a partisan issue," Goodling told Democrats. "I will stand here and fight until the end of time. . . . The quality issue is one that I will not back off of."

The committee-passed bill would make it easier for states to provide full-day, full-year care to meet the needs of working women and those moving off welfare. It would require half the Head Start teachers to have a degree in early childhood education by 2003, set new education standards to ensure that children are ready to learn reading when they leave the program, mandate studies of effectiveness and set aside funds for family literacy programs.

While Goodling disagreed with the White House on how fast to expand the program, he had been willing to compromise on other issues. The markup was delayed for a week in an effort to negotiate with Democrats.

Goodling offered a substitute bill that did not include the paternity establishment or voucher provisions, both of which were in a draft developed by Frank Riggs, R-Calif., chairman of the Subcommittee on Early Childhood, Youth and Families. Goodling's substitute also eliminated a Riggs provision that would have allowed private, for-profit groups to compete for Head Start grants.

Davis-Bacon a Key Issue

But the wheels came off during the markup, in part due to Democratic anger over a provision that would eliminate the requirement that Head Start comply with the 1931 Davis-Bacon Act, which requires federal construction contractors to pay workers the local prevailing wage.

Donald M. Payne, D-N.J., offered an amendment, which was defeated 16-21, to continue applying Davis-Bacon to Head Start projects.

"It is truly objectionable that the majority party has decided to use Head Start now as another [vehicle] to push their anti-labor agenda," Payne said.

Republicans countered that Democratic dependence on campaign contributions from organized labor forced them to fight for an outdated law that inflated wages.

"This is an opportunity to prevent money from being taken away from children," said Cass Ballenger, R-N.C.

The fight over Davis-Bacon poisoned the atmosphere, prompting Republicans to push other controversial proposals.

Voting 22-17, the committee approved Riggs' plan for government-funded certificates that could be used to pay for alternative child care. The certificates could be used in cases where Head Start centers had been closed and a replacement had not been named. HHS said the provision was unneeded because it routinely names interim providers in such cases.

"A lot of us believe it would be a

Education

good thing to infuse competition and choice into Head Start," Riggs said.

Democrats worried it was a step toward broader vouchers for the program.

By 20-19, the panel approved a Riggs amendment, which mimics a provision of the 1996 welfare law (PL 104-193) that would require women to cooperate in establishing the paternity of their children. About half the Head Start children come from welfare families. (*1996 Almanac, p. 6-3*)

"Imagine punishing a 3-year-old for being born into a family where the parent is absent," said Democrat Lynn Woolsey of California.

The House and Senate Head Start bills move in the same general direction, though there are some major differences. Both bills would gradually increase funding for Early Head Start to 10 percent of program funds. The Senate bill places more emphasis on increased enrollment and would allow private, for-profit groups to receive direct grants. To help welfare recipients who move into the work force, the House bill would increase to 25 percent, from 10 percent, the number of children in the program whose family income exceeds the poverty line.

Heating and Community Services

The House committee by voice vote also approved a bill (HR 4271) to reauthorize the Community Services Block Grant Act, which aids social service programs, for five years. It extended the Low-Income Home Energy Assistance Program (LIHEAP) for two years. The Senate put Head Start, the block grants and the energy program into one bill.

The committee defeated, 17-22, an amendment by Ron Kind, D-Wis., to extend LIHEAP for five years, in line with the Senate. The House Appropriations Committee on July 14 approved a fiscal 1999 Labor, Health and Human Services, and Education spending measure (HR 4274) that would eliminate the program.

The committee by voice vote approved an amendment by Mark Souder, R-Ind., to create a four-year, $100 million pilot program of special savings accounts for low-income individuals. The accounts could be used to buy a home, start a business or pay for education. Sen. Daniel R. Coats, R-Ind., included a similar plan in the Senate's bill.

Measure Heads For Conference Without Voucher, Paternity Provisions

SEPTEMBER 19 — Avoiding a potentially bitter battle with the Clinton administration and the Senate, the House on Sept. 14 passed a stripped-down bill (S 2206) to extend the Head Start program for low-income preschoolers.

Lawmakers by a 346-20 vote passed substitute legislation by Education and the Workforce Committee Chairman Bill Goodling, R-Pa., that did not include three controversial amendments approved by his panel during a July 29 markup. (*Vote 426, p. H-120*)

The substitute dropped provisions that would have required single mothers to help establish paternity as a condition for enrolling their children in Head Start, allowed limited use of vouchers for private preschools and ended a requirement that the government comply with Davis-Bacon prevailing wage laws on Head Start construction projects.

"This is neither the time nor the bill to debate these controversial issues," Goodling said, explaining his decision to override fellow committee Republicans. "We have only a few short weeks before the end of session. Time dictates that the House pass a bipartisan Head Start bill."

Democrats who had voted against the measure when it was reported out of committee — a highly unusual move given the bipartisan support the program has had since its creation in 1965 — backed the leaner version on the floor. (*1965 Almanac, p. 270*)

"The chairman interceded in some of the really, really difficult issues that we had not resolved, and we do have a bipartisan bill," said Matthew G. Martinez, D-Calif.

The House-passed bill would set more rigorous education standards for Head Start and require a majority of instructors to have college degrees; gradually increase Early Head Start, which serves infants and toddlers to age 3, to 10 percent of program funding; and create incentives for providers to offer full-day care for children of mothers on welfare who move to work.

The bill would reauthorize the Community Services Block Grant program for five years and extend the Low-Income Home Energy Assistance Program (LIHEAP) for two years at the fiscal 1998 appropriated level of $1.1 billion. It would create a four-year, $100 million pilot program of special savings accounts where contributions by low-income individuals would be matched with public or private funds. The savings could be used to start a business, buy a home or pay for education. (*LIHEAP, 1997 Almanac, p. 9-56*)

House-Senate Differences

Frank Riggs, R-Calif., sponsor of the contentious amendments dropped by Goodling, had angrily opposed efforts to change the committee bill. He was not present for the floor vote due to illness.

The Senate passed its version by voice vote July 27. House and Senate aides expect a conference report in a couple of weeks.

Though the House and Senate bills move in the same general direction, conferees must address some key differences. The Senate measure, in line with White House priorities, directs most of the additional funding for Head Start toward increasing enrollment. President Clinton wants Head Start enrollment to reach 1 million children by 2002, up from about 830,000 now.

Current policy, which would be continued under the Senate bill, is to use 75 percent of any new funding to increase enrollment. The House bill would set aside 65 percent of new funds for quality improvements in fiscal 1999 and 2000, a number that would decrease gradually through 2003, when 25 percent would be directed to improving the quality of instruction.

Head Start now targets the poorest of the poor, or children from families with incomes at or below the federal poverty line. As parents move from welfare to work under more stringent state and federal laws, however, Head Start providers have been concerned that children will lose services.

To provide continuity, the House bill would allow providers to have up to 25 percent of total enrollment over the poverty level. The Senate bill continues the current 10 percent exemption.

Both bills include incentives to providers to offer full-day, full-year services. The Senate bill would let for-profit child care facilities be designated as primary Head Start grantees. The House would not. The Senate bill reauthorizes LIHEAP for five years, while the House's has a two-year expansion.

Sarah M. Greene, chief executive officer of the National Head Start Association, a group of providers, said her organization wanted conferees to drop both the Senate's for-profit designation as well as a provision in the House bill establishing a pilot literacy program she called redundant. On the issue of whether to direct new funding to quality improvement or program expansion, she said the group could live with either approach.

Lawmakers Send Compromise Bill To President

OCTOBER 10 — With bipartisan support, Congress on Oct. 9 cleared a five-year reauthorization (S 2206) of the popular Head Start program that would set tougher quality standards, give incentives for providers to offer full-day, full-year care, and expand the Early Head Start program, which serves infants and toddlers to age 3.

The Senate adopted the conference report by voice vote Oct. 8, with the House following suit on Oct. 9, voting to clear the bill and send it to President Clinton, who is expected to sign it.

The measure also would extend the Community Services Block Grant and Low-Income Home Energy Assistance Program (LIHEAP) for five years. It would also set up a new program of savings accounts, developed by Republican Sen. Daniel R. Coats of Indiana, that could be used by low-income individuals for purposes including starting a business.

Coats called Head Start, created in 1965 by President Lyndon B. Johnson, one of the nation's most successful programs for children. "These programs are a true measure of our compassion as a nation," he said.

The administration was generally pleased with the measure, though disappointed that Congress chose to focus the bulk of new funding in the initial years of the reauthorization on qualitative improvements, such as teacher training, rather than expansion.

The White House has set a goal of increasing enrollment to 1 million by 2002, up from the present 830,000.

"At a time when we have enormous prosperity, it is important that we look at the needs of the children, and particularly poor children," said Sen. Edward M. Kennedy, D-Mass.

Insistence on Quality

The compromise was a victory for House Education and the Workforce Committee Chairman Bill Goodling, R-Pa., who persuaded senators to accept his argument that Congress should emphasize quality over quantity.

Under current law, three-quarters of new funds are spent on expanding programs and one-fourth on qualitative improvements. The compromise would require that 60 percent of new funds in fiscal 1999 be used for qualitative improvements such as higher salaries and better training. The ratio would gradually return to 75-25 by 2003.

Responding to recent research on the importance of early brain development, the bill would gradually increase the amount of money allocated to the Early Head Start program to 10 percent from the current level of 5 percent.

The final bill includes a requirement to set aside at least $3 million for technical aid to Head Start providers that offer family literacy programs, which aim to improve parents' reading skills.

It would allow for-profit agencies to be designated as primary Head Start providers. In response to an increasing number of mothers in the labor force, especially as work requirements of the 1996 welfare law (PL 104-193) take effect, the bill provides incentives for Head Start to provide full-day, full-year services. *(1996 Almanac, p. 6-3)*

The bill would require the Department of Health and Human Services to develop tougher performance standards in 1999.

Beyond Head Start

The legislation extends LIHEAP for five years. Funding for fiscal 2000 and 2001 would be unspecified. The program would be capped at $2 billion annually from 2002-04.

House appropriators had recommended eliminating funding for the program, but an omnibus spending measure for fiscal 1999 is expected to include about $1.1 billion in aid.

House conservatives had sought to eliminate the LIHEAP program, but were rebuffed by the White House and Senate moderates who said the aid is vital to keep millions of poor Americans from losing heat in the winter and air conditioning in the summer.

The measure expands the Community Services Block Grant program for five years for unspecified amounts, while allowing grants for family literacy, youth development, community policing and fatherhood initiatives, as well as adding permission for parenting and gang prevention programs.

Finally, the bill allows a pilot program of special savings accounts where contributions by low-income individuals would be matched with public or private funds. The savings could be used to start a business, buy a home or pay for education.

The conference report authorizes the demonstration program of savings accounts for five years, with a ceiling of $25 million per year. ◆

Education

Clinton Vetoes Voucher Measure For D.C. Schoolchildren

Box Score

- **Bill:** S 1502
- **House action:** The House passed S 1502, 214-206, on April 30, 1998.
- **Senate action:** The Senate had passed the bill by voice vote Nov. 9, 1997.
- **Presidential action:** Clinton vetoed the bill May 20.

SUMMARY

In late spring, when presented with the legislation, President Clinton followed through on his threat to veto the measure that would have provided vouchers of up to $3,200 a year to help up to 2,000 low-income District of Columbia children attend private schools or public schools of their choice.

House passage of the bill in April was symbolic and designed to set up a showdown with the White House. As one of its final acts in the last hours of the first session of the 105th Congress, the Senate spun off the measure from the fiscal 1998 District of Columbia appropriations bill (PL 105-100). Clinton had threatened to veto the spending bill because of the school voucher provision. (*1997 Almanac, p. 9-27*)

The GOP leadership's decision to remove vouchers from the D.C. bill marked its second capitulation to the White House on the issue in two Congresses. It took five months for Republicans to relent in 1995, but only a few weeks in 1997.

Republicans made private school vouchers a major plank of their education platform, arguing that too many low-income children are trapped in substandard schools. GOP leaders from Speaker Newt Gingrich, R-Ga., on down, attempted to use the issue to reach out to minority voters. They pointed to polls showing rising support for vouchers among African-American voters.

As the House neared passage of the measure, Education Secretary Richard W. Riley complained that the bill would provide eight times as much federal money to students attending private schools as is now spent, on average, for those in public schools. Riley also protested that schools receiving the vouchers would not have to comply with federal civil rights laws.

Eleanor Holmes Norton, the District's Democratic delegate, said the problems in D.C. schools are like those in large cities across the nation, and warned Congress not to treat the city system like "colonial schools."

Republicans Send D.C. Voucher Bill To Certain Veto

MAY 2 — In a symbolic vote setting up a showdown with the White House, the House on April 30 cleared Republican legislation (S 1502) that would provide vouchers of up to $3,200 a year to help low-income District of Columbia children attend private schools.

The measure, a priority of House Majority Leader Dick Armey, R-Texas, passed 214-206. The Senate approved the bill by voice vote on Nov. 9, 1997. (*House vote 119, p. H-36*)

Because the House and Senate versions are identical, the bill goes directly to President Clinton. The administration has promised a veto on the grounds that federal aid should be targeted at public school students.

Republicans have made private school vouchers a major plank of their education platform, arguing that too many low-income children are trapped in substandard public schools.

GOP leaders, from House Speaker Newt Gingrich, R-Ga., on down, have attempted to use the issue to reach out to minority voters. They point to polls showing rising support for vouchers among African-American voters.

"To all my friends on the left, I don't understand how you can walk the streets, look the children in the eye and cheat them," Gingrich said.

In an April 30 letter to Gingrich, Education Secretary Richard W. Riley complained that the bill would provide eight times as much federal money to students who attended private schools as is now spent, on average, for those in U.S. public schools. He also said schools receiving the vouchers would not have to comply with key federal civil rights law.

Most of the Washington government, including its schools, is now being run by a federally created oversight board. District schools have been plagued by problems from lack of maintenance — which delayed their opening for weeks last fall — to high dropout rates and low test scores.

An angry Eleanor Holmes Norton, the District's Democratic delegate, said that the problems were endemic of large cities across the nation and warned Congress not to treat the city system like "colonial schools."

"The real needs of children in my district are too serious to engage in a political exercise," Norton said.

The legislation would create a private, nonprofit corporation to oversee federally funded vouchers for low-income students. It would provide $7 million in fiscal 1998, $8 million in fiscal 1999 and $10 million annually from fiscal 2000 to 2002.

An estimated 2,000 children per year would be eligible for vouchers to help pay for private school tuition as well as suburban public schools. Students would have to come from families with incomes of less than 185 percent of the federal poverty line, or less than $30,000 for a family of four. The bill would provide 2,000 tutoring scholarships of as much as $500 for students in public schools.

Lawmakers attempted to pass a similar measure last year as part of the fiscal 1998 D.C. appropriations bill. House Republican leaders dropped the plan because of veto threats.

Veto Message Calls For Strengthening Public Schools

MAY 23 — President Clinton vetoed a bill May 20 that would have provided vouchers to help some poor children in Washington, D.C., attend private schools.

"If we are to prepare our children for the 21st century by providing them with the best education in the world, we must strengthen our public schools, not abandon them," Clinton said in his veto message.

House Speaker Newt Gingrich of Georgia said children in the district's public schools are "being destroyed by bureaucracies that refuse to reform."

The measure (S 1502), a priority of House Majority Leader Dick Armey, R-Texas, was passed by the House on April 30 by a vote of 216-206. The Senate approved the bill by voice vote in November, 1997.

The bill would have provided vouchers worth as much as $3,200 each for 2,000 children to use at religious or other private schools or suburban public schools. ◆

House Passes Bill To Convert Bilingual Education Aid Into Block Grants to States

Box Score

- **Bill:** HR 3892
- **House action:** The House passed HR 3892, by 221-189, Sept. 10. The bill (H Rept 105-587) was reported out of committee June 19.
- **Senate action:** None.

SUMMARY

A push by House conservatives to revamp federally supported bilingual education was first weakened and then dropped for the year.

The House Republicans' hope of restyling education for non-English-speaking children shrank under sharp criticism from the Clinton administration and a shrug of the shoulders from Senate Republicans.

Funding for federal bilingual education would have been shifted to states in block grant packages under legislation (HR 3892) passed by the House.

Faced with such opposition, House Republicans mounted a late-session effort to have a limited demonstration project authorized as one of myriad riders to the omnibus appropriations measure (HR 4328 — PL 105-277). When that idea was blocked by the White House, conservatives first considered requiring a study of the efficacy of existing language-transition programs. When administration officials balked again, Republicans removed the issue from the bill.

Despite the departure of Frank Riggs, R-Calif., retiring chairman of the House Education and the Workforce Subcommittee on Early Childhood, Youth and Families, conservatives vowed to revive the controversial issue in 1999.

A temporary victory for conservatives came on Sept. 10, when the House voted by 221-189 to pass the measure. All but 10 Republicans voted for the bill, but they were joined by only 14 Democrats.

The bill, sponsored by Riggs, would have turned over the funding authority for bilingual and immigrant education programs to the states. Supporters wanted to allow states and localities more latitude to try alternatives such as English immersion. Children would have been limited to no more than three years of participating in federally funded bilingual programs. The bill would have required that 90 percent of bilingual education grants be used for English-language programs.

Critics said the measure would handicap the efforts of children who are trying to learn English.

House Bill Reflects Movement Against Bilingual Education

JUNE 6 — Responding to a growing backlash against bilingual education, the House Committee on Education and the Workforce on June 4 approved a bill that would turn federal bilingual and immigrant education programs into block grants, giving states and localities more latitude to try alternatives such as English immersion.

The committee passed the Republican-drafted measure (HR 3892) on a straight party-line vote of 22-17, with Democrats opposed. The Clinton administration has strong objections to the bill.

The move came on the heels of voter approval June 2 of California's Proposition 227, which will dismantle that state's 30-year-old bilingual education program and replace it with a system that favors English-only instruction. The initiative, which won more than 60 percent of the vote, would move students into mainstream classrooms after one year of intensive language instruction.

While early polling suggested a majority of Hispanic voters supported Proposition 227, exit polls showed about 60 percent voted against the initiative.

Some other states and school districts are beginning to move away from bilingual education, in which teachers instruct students in both their native language and English. The goal of bilingual education is to help students who are not proficient in English learn the language while at the same time keeping pace with their peers in other subjects.

Critics charge that bilingual instruction has instead held too many students back and prevented them from becoming fluent in English. As

Education

the number of immigrant children in American schools increases — more than 3 million children across the country have limited English skills — the issue has become more heated.

The emerging debate has the potential to pit Republicans in Congress against Hispanics, a growing voting bloc that GOP leaders have repeatedly said they want to court.

"This is not xenophobia," said Marge Roukema, R-N.J., who voted for the bill. She charged that some lawmakers may "like ethnic enclaves for political purposes, but that is not what is right."

Others said the legislation went too far and too fast in dismantling federal programs and that it represented little more than minority bashing.

"Do we forget our constitutional polar star, which is equality, and sail instead in the dark, driven by political winds which are always changing? Or do we remember where we came from: a nation of immigrants," said Dennis J. Kucinich, D-Ohio.

Ambivalence was evident during committee debate. Republican Frank Riggs of California, the main sponsor of the legislation, volunteered that he considered his state's ballot measure "draconian" and pointed out that state Attorney General Dan Lungren, the GOP nominee for governor, opposed it.

"We shouldn't be driven to reform bilingual programs by a millionaire Californian's initiatives," said Tim Roemer, D-Ind., referring to Silicon Valley businessman Ronald Unz, who wrote Proposition 227.

President Clinton and Education Secretary Richard W. Riley both publicly opposed the California initiative and called for a series of changes to improve bilingual instruction. The administration wants states to move children out of bilingual programs in three years and to double the funding to train teachers in bilingual and other English instruction.

A Broad Measure

The House measure would turn existing federal bilingual and immigrant education programs into block grants to states, with money allocated under a national formula. Under existing law, bilingual aid is distributed on a competitive basis.

The federal government in fiscal 1998 will provide $354 million for bilingual and immigrant education, including program development and grants to expand existing instruction.

Under the bill, parents would have to sign permission forms before their children could be placed in English instruction programs, and schools would be required to let parents remove their children from bilingual programs.

The bill would require that programs receiving federal funding be designed so that within two years students would move to a classroom where instruction was not tailored to those learning English.

None of the funds could be used to teach a child who had been in a bilingual program for three years. The measure would void compliance agreements between the federal government and local school districts or states that have required development of special bilingual programs.

Riggs and other supporters contend that the federal government coerced the agreements in an effort to expand bilingual instruction. Opponents call such charges baseless.

The measure would change the name of the Education Department's Office of Bilingual Education and Minority Languages Affairs to the Office of English Language Acquisition.

In a June 4 letter to the committee, Riley said the provisions voiding compliance agreements were an effort to stop federal enforcement of the Civil Rights Act (PL 88-352) as it applied to educating language minority children.

Riley further said the bill set "artificial and arbitrary deadlines" for moving children out of bilingual instruction and into regular classrooms.

During debate, the committee made few changes to the measure. It approved a modified amendment by Carlos Romero-Barceló, Puerto Rico's Democratic delegate, to soften language that originally said it was "imperative" for every person in the United States to learn English.

The federal government has helped fund bilingual education programs since 1968. The Supreme Court, ruling in the 1974 case *Lau v. Nichols*, ordered states to provide assistance to students who did not speak English.

A rapidly growing immigrant population has put increasing stress on school districts nationwide. There are now 3.2 million students who are not proficient in English. Nearly 73 percent are Hispanic, followed by Vietnamese, Hmong, Cantonese and Cambodian. The vast majority of students with limited English attend schools in low-income areas.

The Department of Education said that 1.3 million students are in state and local bilingual programs. California has about half of all students whose first language is not English. Of those, only 30 percent are in bilingual education programs, in large part because of a shortage of qualified instructors.

A High Dropout Rate

Opponents of bilingual education often link such programs to the stubbornly high Hispanic dropout rate. Nearly one-third of Hispanics drop out of school, a higher rate than any other segment of the U.S. population.

Matthew G. Martinez, D-Calif., said at the markup that it was unfair to draw a direct connection between the two, since most students in his state did not receive such instruction.

He said opposition to bilingual education was based in part on "emotion and the unwillingness of most Americans to pay for instruction in two languages."

Other committee members said that instead of rapidly moving students into regular classes, bilingual education instead trapped too many for years in separate programs. They pointed to the academic success of many Vietnamese immigrants to make the case that Spanish-speaking students could make rapid gains without bilingual programs.

"We're refusing to give these people an opportunity," said Cass Ballenger, R-N.C., who voted for the bill. He said employers in his region of the country had difficulty hiring Hispanics for good, higher-wage jobs because too few spoke English.

Studies of the effectiveness of bilingual programs have not provided conclusive findings.

Hispanic Voters

Committee aides have held preliminary discussions with the House Republican leadership about the timing for bringing the measure to the floor, though no decision has yet been made.

House Majority Whip Tom DeLay, R-Texas, has introduced a similar bill (HR 3720) that would eliminate the Education Department's office of bilingual education and void agreements between states or school districts and the federal government on using bilingual education to serve immigrant students.

At the same time, House Republican leaders have stressed that they want to reach out to Hispanic voters, many of whom were alienated by 1996 legislation (PL 104-208) that clamped down on illegal immigration and in some cases restricted legal immigration. *(1996 Almanac, p. 5-3)*

The 1996 welfare overhaul (PL 104-193) also denied disability and food stamps to legal immigrants. Congress restored disability aid in the 1997 balanced-budget law (PL 105-33). And, after a long battle, the House on June 4 approved legislation to reinstate food stamps to about 250,000 of the nearly 1 million legal immigrants cut off the federal rolls.

House Speaker Newt Gingrich, R-Ga., on May 5 met with Raul Yzaguirre, president of the National Council of La Raza, an Hispanic advocacy group, who has been sharply critical of many Republican initiatives. Gingrich endorsed a bill (HR 2538) sponsored by Rep. Bill Redmond, R-N.M., that would let the descendants of former Mexican citizens file claims on land seized in 1848 at the end of the U.S.-Mexican War.

The Riggs bill is not the first time Congress has waded into the issue of language instruction. Lawmakers have proposed making English the official language of the United States.

The Senate has passed legislation, sponsored by Sen. Slade Gorton, R-Wash., to turn a host of federal education programs, including bilingual education, into broad block grants. It is now attached to an education savings account bill (HR 2646) awaiting action by a House-Senate conference committee.

House Appropriations Committee Chairman Robert L. Livingston, R-La., earlier this year proposed cutting bilingual education funding to offset spending in a fiscal 1998 supplemental spending bill, but later dropped the plan.

Full House Passes Controversial Bill In Partisan Vote

SEPTEMBER 12 — Despite heavy opposition from the White House, the Congressional Hispanic Caucus and several major education groups, the House on Sept. 10 passed a measure (HR 3892) backers say will help immigrant children learn English faster. Opponents charged the measure would cripple ongoing bilingual education and hinder the efforts of children who are trying to become English proficient.

The bill, which passed 221-189, along mostly party lines, would turn federal bilingual and immigrant education programs into block grants, which sponsors say will give states and localities more latitude to try alternatives such as English immersion. *(Vote 424, p. H-120)*

Programs receiving federal funding would be required to move students within two years into a classroom where instruction is not tailored to students who lack proficiency in English.

Sponsor Frank Riggs, R-Calif., said the bill would provide for an additional year of bilingual instruction if necessary. None of the bill's funds could be used to teach children who have been in federally funded bilingual programs for more than three years.

The measure, however, would not affect state and local funding for bilingual education, nor would it interfere with bilingual education under Title I, a federal program for impoverished schools, Riggs said.

Prospects for Senate action are uncertain. While there is no companion bill to Riggs' measure, it could be enacted as an appropriations rider to the fiscal 1999 spending bill (HR 4274) for the departments of Labor, Health and Human Services, and Education.

Strong Opposition

Several lawmakers said Riggs' bill would turn back the clock on bilingual education.

Congressional Hispanic Caucus Chairman Xavier Becerra, D-Calif., said the bill would "severely hurt Latino and other children who are on their way to learning English."

Democrat Esteban E. Torres of California said the bill demonstrated "an anti-immigrant movement in this body."

Opponents said that the measure ignores the fact that children's ability to learn English varies, and that some may need additional time to master the language beyond the period allotted in Riggs' bill.

But Republican Bill Goodling of Pennsylvania, chairman of the House Committee on Education and the Workforce, said opponents were reluctant to admit that the current approach to bilingual education was not working and that it was time for new ideas.

In an Aug. 6 statement, the White House said the bill would force school districts to arbitrarily cut off services to students who need them and deny funds to school districts if they fail to make such cuts.

Amendments

Rep. Matthew G. Martinez, D-Calif., tried unsuccessfully to defeat a Riggs amendment that would withhold federal funds from school districts not in compliance with state laws governing bilingual education. Martinez offered his own amendment stating that compliance with federal law should take prominence, even if it is different from state law. His effort failed on a 205-208 vote. *(Vote 422, p. H-120)*

Riggs' amendment won by a vote of 230-184. *(Vote 423, p. H-120)*

The chamber also approved several amendments by voice vote, including:

- An amendment by Nick Smith, R-Mich., to permit the use of bill funds for family literacy programs.
- An amendment by Henry Bonilla, R-Texas, eliminating a provision requiring states to conduct standardized tests only in English for students who have resided in and have been educated in the same school district for three years.
- A Riggs amendment to add tutoring programs to the bill's list of approved activities for children with limited proficiency in English and immigrant children. Such programs provide early intervention services to prevent such children from dropping out of school.

In addition, Riggs also offered an

Education

amendment that guarantees for the first five years after the bill's enactment, each state would receive at least 100 percent of the amount the state and all school districts within the state receive in fiscal 1998 under current law. It was accepted on voice vote.

Riggs also broadened the criteria by which students' academic progress would be judged. It would be determined by both the number and percentage of children who have mastered English at the end of the school year and outline the design for measures to evaluate the English language skills of students based on their grade level. His amendment was accepted by voice vote. ◆

Administration Fails Again In Its Quest To Establish Voluntary National Testing

SUMMARY

After more than a year of debate, the White House again lost its fight to promote voluntary national testing of fourth-graders in reading and eighth-graders in math.

For the second straight year, Republicans won a ban on testing; this year's version was one of the hundreds of policy "riders" attached to the fiscal 1999 omnibus appropriations bill (HR 4328). *(1997 Almanac, p. 9-50)*

The provision bars use of federal funds for pilot testing, field testing or distribution of national tests, unless Congress enacts an authorization beforehand.

Also the independent National Assessment Governing Board and the National Academy of Sciences are ordered to report to Congress on certain testing issues.

By Sept. 30, 1999, the board must describe the purpose and intended uses of any federally sponsored national tests, define "voluntary" as it applies to administration of any test, and describe achievement levels and reporting methods to be used in grading any national test.

The governing board must react to an academy report that suggests there are flaws in the achievement levels for the current National Assessment of Educational Progress tests, on which the proposed national tests are to be based. By Sept. 30, the academy is required to report on the technical feasibility and reliability of including test items from the national assessment tests or other existing tests in state and district assessments for the purpose of providing a common measuring stick.

The congressional response to President Clinton's persistent calls for such tests began in the House. On Feb. 5, the House passed a bill (HR 2846) to bar the administration from developing or implementing national math and reading tests until specifically authorized by Congress. The vote was 242-174. *(Vote 9, p. H-6)*

Rep. Bill Goodling, R-Pa., chairman of the Committee on Education and the Workforce, said the legislation was necessary because the Clinton administration, by planning field testing when the fiscal year ends Sept. 30, was not living up to the spirit of a 1997 deal barring trial testing of the exams. The agreement was included in the fiscal 1998 Labor, Health and Human Services appropriations bill (PL 105-78).

House Republicans argued that the tests could lead to a national curriculum. "Once again Congress has spoken on federal testing and said there should be no new federal tests unless authorized," Goodling said.

The Senate did not act on the House bill. But in April, Republican Sen. John Ashcroft of Missouri added an anti-testing amendment to legislation (HR 2646) that would have expanded tax-sheltered educational savings accounts created under the 1997 tax-cut law (PL 105-34). His amendment was adopted, 52-47, but ultimately it was dropped in conference. *(Vote 94, p. S-17)* ◆

Lawmakers Authorize $100 Million in Aid To Charter Schools

SUMMARY

In a bipartisan move to encourage innovation in public schools, President Clinton on Oct. 22 signed legislation to expand federal aid to so-called charter schools, authorizing up to $100 million for fiscal year 1999, with unspecified sums allowed through 2003.

Charter schools are publicly funded but operate free from many state regulations if school officials meet certain performance criteria. Parents, community activists, teachers or private companies may set up schools under a special charter, depending on state law.

Both Clinton and congressional Republicans support the experimental schools, viewing them as a way to test innovative teaching and organizational plans and to offer families a broader choice within the context of public education. Clinton set a goal of 3,000 charter schools to be operating by 2002, up from 1,000 in 1998.

Some educators criticize the schools, however, warning that they are not a panacea for the problems besetting education and that they are sometimes poorly run.

The House originally passed the bill in 1997. The Senate passed an amended version by voice vote Oct. 8. The House cleared the bill Oct. 10 by a vote of 369-50. (*Vote 519, p. H-148; 1997 Almanac, p. 7-9*)

The newly enacted law HR 2616 — PL 105-278) targets extra funds to states that improve regulation and encourage the creation of charter schools. For fiscal 2001, apropriations in excess of $51 million will be directed first to states that give charter schools broad autonomy and that measure whether each school is meeting the terms of its charter and the academic performance mandated by state law.

For fiscal 2002 and 2003, the Department of Education must distribute all appropriations, not just funds in excess of $51 million, to states meeting those criteria.

The department is required to reserve up to $8 million a year for administrative purposes and for studies to gauge the effectiveness of charter schools. The dollars set aside would be used to inform charter schools about the availability of federal funds and programs. The department would also use the money to complete a four-year study of charter schools that began in 1995 and to underwrite other evaluations of the impact of charter schools, including an analysis of student attendance reported on the basis of race, age, disability, gender, limited English proficiency and previous enrollment in public school. ◆

Box Score

- **Bill:** HR 2616 — PL 105-278
- **House action:** The House cleared the bill Oct. 10, 369-50. The House originally passed the bill (H Rept 105-321) on Nov. 7, 1997.
- **Senate action:** The Senate passed an amended version of the bill by voice vote Oct. 8.
- **Presidential action:** Clinton signed the bill Oct. 22.

Chapter 10
EMPLOYMENT & LABOR

Job Training 10-3	Minimum Wage 10-7
Union 'Salting' 10-5	Worker Safety 10-8
Comp Time, Overtime Pay 10-7	

Employment & Labor

Congress Clears Legislation To Consolidate More Than 60 Job Training Programs

Box Score

- **Bill:** HR 1385 — PL 105-220
- **House action:** The House cleared the conference report (H Rept 105-659) on HR 1385 by voice vote July 31. It initially passed HR 1385 (H Rept 105-93), 343-60, on May 16, 1997.
- **Senate action:** The Senate adopted the conference report on HR 1385 by unanimous consent July 30. It passed HR 1385, 91-7, on May 5, after substituting the text of S 1186 (S Rept 105-109).
- **Presidential action:** Clinton signed the bill Aug. 7.

SUMMARY

In response to criticism that federal job training and placement programs were antiquated and redundant, Congress approved an overhaul that gives individuals and states new power to design systems tailored to their specific needs.

The legislation consolidates more than 60 federal programs into block grants that states will administer. Individuals will receive vouchers they can use to purchase training services. The legislation makes major changes to the longstanding Job Corps residential education and training program for disadvantaged youth and reauthorizes vocational rehabilitation and adult literacy programs.

The original Senate bill (S 1186), drafted by Mike DeWine, R-Ohio, included federal secondary and postsecondary vocational education programs as well. The House opted to pass separate bills on job training (HR 1385) and vocational education (HR 1853).

Conservative groups, such as the Eagle Forum, worried that including vocational programs in an overall job training rewrite could have the effect of directing young people toward the workplace rather than college. Vocational education groups also wanted their own bill. Due to the pressures, the final training package did not include vocational education, though Congress later approved and sent to the White House the free-standing vocational bill (PL 105-332).

Under the job training act, adults who seek training will use individual accounts, or vouchers, to purchase services. One-stop service centers will provide information about labor market opportunities and available aid. Nearly 1,000 such centers are already in operation nationwide.

State and local job training boards and providers will have to meet tougher performance standards. For example, providers will have to publicly report graduation and job retention rates and average earnings of graduates.

The job training measure links local business more closely to the Job Corps program, extends follow-up counseling to participants for 12 months, sets detailed performance standards for centers and tries to ensure that training programs relate to job opportunities in surrounding areas.

It extends vocational rehabilitation and adult literacy programs. More than 1.25 million disabled Americans were served by rehabilitation programs in 1995.

Vocational Programs Present Hurdle For Conferees

MAY 9 — Legislation to reorganize a patchwork of federal job training and education programs breezed through the Senate on May 5, but the measure faces a potential fight in the House-Senate conference over the role of vocational education.

Critics on both sides of the aisle have long contended that the current maze of job training and education programs duplicates services and lacks coordination, making the system so confusing that it alienates the very people it is designed to help.

The bill (HR 1385), which passed the Senate 91-7, seeks to correct this problem by creating a streamlined system for job training, adult education and training for the disabled, and reorganizing about 70 job training and education programs. (*Vote 119, p. S-20*)

Under the measure, some existing programs would be consolidated. All of the programs would be funded under four types of block grants to states, including vocational education, adult education, training and vocational rehabilitation.

There is strong support in both the House and Senate for remaking the system. The House passed its version of HR 1385 in May 1997 by a vote of 343-60. (*1997 Almanac, p. 7-18*)

While the House and Senate versions are quite similar, negotiators differ on whether to include a section on vocational education in the broader job training bill, and that disagreement threatens to hold up conference talks.

The Senate version, originally S 1186, includes a section aimed at ensuring students get both academic and vocational training, expanding the use of technology in education and giving states flexibility to tailor programs to local needs.

Labor Committee Chairman James M. Jeffords, R-Vt., the chief sponsor of the Senate bill, wanted to include the section to ensure that vocational programs prepare students to compete in the job market. Vocational programs have often been criticized for teaching students outdated skills and for paying little regard to the needs of employers.

"What we need to make sure we do is make sure our young people are trained for jobs that are needed," said Jeffords.

The House opted to pass a separate vocational education bill (HR 1853) last summer. That bill is similar to the Senate job training mea-

Employment & Labor

sure, although it would change existing funding formulas to reach more people between the ages of 15 and 24, the general target for such programs. The Senate retains current formulas, which allocate money to the states for secondary and postsecondary vocational education.

House Education and the Workforce Chairman Bill Goodling, R-Pa., said he favors keeping the two issues separate largely because of political opposition from pro-family groups, such as Phyllis Schlafly's Eagle Forum and the Family Research Council. These groups oppose the single-bill approach because they say it will lead to a government system that wrongly segregates students into training for menial work while sacrificing academic achievement.

Goodling noted that the family groups helped torpedo similar job legislation in the 104th Congress, and he is trying to avoid another showdown. (*1996 Almanac, p. 7-11*)

"I think it invites all sorts of problems we don't need," said Goodling.

Need for Consolidation

There is broad agreement that the current federal job training system is in need of major changes. A 1995 study by the General Accounting Office found that the federal government funds 163 different programs scattered across 15 separate agencies.

The current conglomeration of programs is largely the making of Congress, which has, over the past three decades, gradually added new programs, often with little regard to how the system works as a whole.

A big goal of the bill's sponsors is to foster greater cooperation between job programs and local employers. Critics contend that training programs too often train participants for jobs that are in short supply or do not exist.

Under the bill, federal job corps centers, residential facilities that help young people advance their educations and acquire job training, would be required to have an "industry council" made up of local business leaders.

The councils would evaluate the local job market and make recommendations on vocational training that should be offered at the center.

Mike DeWine, R-Ohio, chairman of the Senate Labor Subcommittee on Employment and Training, noted that the bill would build more accountability into the system by requiring that programs be evaluated by factors such as graduation rates and job placement.

DeWine said the bill would "make the federally funded job training program more accountable, better coordinated with the business community and therefore better able to serve the customer."

House Sends Job Training Bill To White House

AUGUST 1 — The House on July 31 cleared and sent to the White House legislation (HR 1385) that would consolidate more than 60 federal job training programs into three block grants to states, while providing individuals with vouchers to purchase training services.

The House passed the conference report by voice vote. The Senate approved the bill by unanimous consent July 30. The measure would create block grants for adult education, adult training and training for disadvantaged youth. Vocational education programs, which were in the original Senate bill, were dropped in conference.

Some conservative groups, such as the Eagle Forum, had objected to including vocational aid in the overall bill, saying that young people would be directed into narrow training programs.

Democrats and Republicans agreed on the need to consolidate training services. A 1995 General Accounting Office study found that the federal government funds 163 different job programs scattered across 15 separate agencies. ◆

Senate Fight, Veto Threat Stymie GOP Effort To Ban Union 'Salting'

SUMMARY

Legislation that would have permitted employers to refuse to hire "salts" — union organizers or supporters who seek a job with a non-union employer in order to organize the workers from within — faced tough going in the 105th Congress. The House barely passed its bill, and the Senate was unable to muster the 60 votes to break a Democratic filibuster.

The measure, strongly opposed by organized labor, also faced a veto threat from the White House.

On March 26, with 17 Democrats absent (some were traveling with President Clinton in Africa), the House passed HR 3246, 202-200. The bill would have banned the tactic of salting and made other changes to labor law that were opposed by unions.

On Sept. 14, Senate Democrats defeated a Republican attempt to cut off debate on a motion to take up a similar bill (S 1981). The vote was 52-42, short of the 60 votes needed. Only one Republican, Ben Nighthorse Campbell of Colorado, joined all the Senate Democrats in voting against cloture.

House Committee Targets Unions' Organizing Practice

MARCH 14 — A controversial bill (HR 3246) that would give employers new clout to keep out union organizers won the approval March 11 of the House Education and the Workforce Committee.

Unions have long engaged in a practice known as "salting," in which organizers apply for jobs at non-union plants hoping to work from the inside to push fellow workers to sign union cards.

Labor leaders say the practice is legal and defensible. They point to a 1995 Supreme Court ruling, *National Labor Relations Board v. Town & Country Electric Inc.*, in which the court said that a worker may be considered an "employee" under federal labor laws even if he or she is being paid by the union to organize fellow workers.

But businesses and their Republican allies in Congress have long been irked by the practice. They argue that job applicants should be willing to work for the employer, and that their purpose in signing up for a job should not be to organize a union.

HR 3246, approved 23-18 on a party-line vote, would attempt to end salting by saying that employers would not have to hire a job applicant whose "primary purpose" was not to work at a company.

Republican supporters of the bill, including committee Chairman Bill Goodling of Pennsylvania, said it would protect the legal rights of workers while protecting employers from having to hire applicants who have little interest in working for the company.

"Salting tactics are often a deliberate attempt to run non-union contractors out of business," said Goodling. "[This provision] protects the employer by making it clear that an employer is not required to hire someone who is not a 'bona fide' applicant."

But Democrats contended that if the bill were enacted, employers would use its anti-salting provisions to intimidate prospective job applicants with union ties. "It would permit employers to discriminate against workers on the basis of the workers' union support," said William L. Clay of Missouri, the ranking Democrat on the panel.

The bill would also require the National Labor Relations Board to conduct hearings to determine what group of unionized employees can negotiate a contract with a company. While this practice is in place today, Republicans

Box Score

- **Bills:** HR 3246; S 1981
- **House action:** The House passed HR 3246 (H Rept 105-453), 202-200, on March 26.
- **Senate action:** The Senate failed, 52-42, on Sept. 14 to invoke cloture on a motion to take up S 1981.

wanted to put it in law to pre-empt any attempts by the administration to change the rules in a way that could limit businesses' flexibility.

HR 3246 appears to face an uphill fight. Labor Secretary Alexis M. Herman in a March 11 letter to Goodling said she would recommend a veto of the measure. The bill also faces strong opposition from labor groups, who are likely to play a big role in Democratic re-election efforts.

Proponents Win Close House Vote On 'Salting' Ban

MARCH 28 — Few issues highlight the divisions between Democrats and Republicans like a debate over union clout. And true to form, House consideration of labor legislation touched off a brutally partisan battle over the rights of unions to organize workers.

The focus of the debate was Republican-sponsored legislation (HR 3246), passed 202-200 by the House on March 26, that would provide employers with a new legal tool to keep out union organizers. *(Vote 78, p. H-24)*

It also included a provision on workplace elections that labor unions fear would provide employers additional clout to block union organizing, a point that business groups dispute.

The fight played out in a political atmosphere that is likely to become more highly charged as the November elections draw closer. Republicans are still boiling over the money organized labor spent to help Democrats in the 1996 elections.

On HR 3246, House Republican

Employment & Labor

vote counters worked furiously to build support for the bill until the very last minute, and were able to squeak out victory partly because 17 Democrats were absent.

'Salting' Provisions

Much of the debate centered on a legal practice known as "salting," in which a union loyalist applies for a job at a non-union business and then works from the inside to organize fellow workers.

Republican proponents of the anti-salting bill argued on the floor that the practice is unfair to employers, who should have the right to hire employees who are "bona fide" applicants and not moles for the union.

Sam Johnson, R-Texas, likened the practice to a form of economic warfare that is used "to sabotage the company and drive them out of business. . . . Either way it's criminal, and it's not the American way."

To give employers new powers to keep out such organizers, the measure would provide that a company would not have to hire a job applicant if his "primary purpose" was not to work for the company.

But Democrats shot back that the measure was a thinly veiled attempt to undermine organized labor. They noted that salting was perfectly legal, and that the Supreme Court affirmed the practice in a 1995 case, *National Labor Relations Board v. Town & Country Electric Inc.*

They said the bill would open the door for employers to discriminate against workers, make intrusive inquiries into job applicants' backgrounds and lead to the blacklisting of job applicants who are union sympathizers.

"It opens up an Orwellian can of worms whereby the employer has all kinds of rights to ask what the motivation of the employee is," said Robert E. Andrews, D-N.J.

By most accounts, the measure's proponents face an uphill battle. There is still no companion legislation in the Senate. The Clinton administration is threatening a veto and is likely to go to the mat for organized labor in an election year.

Despite efforts by the bill's sponsors to amend the bill to win more support, William L. Clay of Missouri, the ranking Democrat on the House Education and the Workforce Committee, argued that the bill was fatally flawed. "You can't fix this piece of trash," he said.

Warring Strategy

Throughout the debate, the Republican proponents stressed the argument that the measure was aimed at building greater fairness into the workplace. They said they wanted to protect small businesses from union intimidation.

"The issue [with] salting [is that] you go into a small business and try and destroy it," said Randy "Duke" Cuningham, R-Calif. "You go in and tie them up before the board and actually force them out of business."

But many Democrats rejected this argument. They said unions are on the decline, often face a hostile reception by most employers and organizing workers is more difficult than ever.

"One of the most precious freedoms of working men and women in this country is their right to organize," said Clay. "The bill Republicans have brought to the floor today would have a devastating effect on the labor movement in this country."

Peggy Taylor, legislative director for the AFL-CIO, said the anti-salting bill was part of a Republican strategy to push through incremental legislation that would undermine labor.

She said Republicans are focusing on smaller issues because they do not have the votes for sweeping legislation, such as an overhaul of the Occupational Safety and Health Administration, which enforces workplace safety laws.

"Rather than the frontal attack, what they're doing is coming at things under the radar screen," she said.

A case in point, she said, is a provision in the anti-salting bill that would require the NLRB to use certain criteria in determining whether workers of a company with multiple outlets can organize and hold elections at individual locations. Labor groups oppose the measure, saying it would allow employers to delay organizing drives by filing lengthy appeals of agency decisions on single or multiple-site workplace representation.

Business groups counter that the provision would ensure a fair hearing in cases where it makes sense to have multi-site organizing.

Senate Democrats Block Cloture On 'Salting' Bill

SEPTEMBER 19 — Senate Democrats on Sept. 14 blocked a Republican effort to take up legislation, sought by some businesses, that would prevent a practice known as "salting" in which a union loyalist applies for a job at a non-union business and then works from the inside to organize the workplace.

The vote on invoking cloture, which requires 60 votes, was 52-42. The only GOP member to break ranks was Ben Nighthorse Campbell, of Colorado, who voted with Democrats opposing cloture. *(Vote 266, p. S-41)*

The measure (S 1981) would allow employers to refuse to hire union organizers who are seeking employment with the intent of promoting unionization of a company's workers.

President Clinton has pledged to veto the bill. A Sept. 11 statement from the White House said the measure would "seriously erode fundamental . . . protections of workers' rights to organize by allowing businesses" to refuse to hire union organizers. ◆

Senate Democrats Halt GOP Efforts To Pass Comp Time Bill

SUMMARY

Republicans were unable to get a key item on their labor agenda — flexibility for employers to offer workers a choice between compensatory time off and overtime pay — through the Senate. Democrats in that chamber managed to block a comp time bill in June 1997, convinced that it would force employees to take compensatory time off instead of receiving overtime pay.

Some thought the issue would resurface in 1998, but it never saw the light of day in the Senate. *(1997 Almanac, p. 7-22)*

Republicans argued that the nation's labor laws were outdated and should be amended to provide maximum flexibility in the workplace. The legislation would have amended the 1938 Fair Labor Standards Act so employees could choose compensatory time off or overtime pay, as a means of giving working parents more time to attend to family matters or emergencies.

Democrats argued that the proposals contained inadequate safeguards to assure that the employee's choice of comp time as an alternative to cash compensation for overtime would be truly voluntary.

Along with the Clinton administration, they favored expanding the 1993 Family and Medical Leave Act (PL 103-3) to give workers an additional 24 hours of unpaid leave each year for parents to attend their children's school activities or attend to routine needs like doctor and dentist appointments.

The House bill (HR 1), which passed in March 1997, would have permitted private-sector employers to give their employees the option of being paid at one-and-a-half times their hourly rate for hours worked beyond the 40-hour week, or taking time off at the rate of one and-a-half hours off for each hour of overtime.

The Senate bill (S 4) would have permitted biweekly work schedules under which employees could agree to work 80 hours over a two-week period without being paid overtime. For example, an employee could work one 50-hour week and one 30-hour week and not receive any overtime pay.

President Clinton threatened to veto both measures. ◆

Democrats' Attempt To Raise Minimum Wage Fizzles In Senate

SUMMARY

Splitting largely along party lines, the Senate voted Sept. 22 to table (kill) an amendment to the consumer bankruptcy bill (S 1301) that would have raised the federal minimum wage by $1 over the next two years, to $6.15 per hour. The vote was 55-44. *(Vote 278, p. S-43)*

House Minority Whip David E. Bonior, Mich., introduced similar legislation (HR 3510), but no action occurred in the House.

Two Republican senators voted with Democrats against the motion to table: New York's Alfonse M. D'Amato and Pennsylvania's Arlen Specter. Two Southern Democrats, also seeking re-election Nov. 3, voted with Republicans to kill the amendment: Florida's Bob Graham and South Carolina's Ernest F. Hollings.

Amendment sponsor Edward M. Kennedy, D-Mass., said many cited local or election-year concerns this time, adding that "a lot of people say, 'Haven't we just done this?' "

Labor and Human Resources Committee Chairman James M. Jeffords, R-Vt., was one who felt that way. "We should give the last minimum wage increase some time to be absorbed into the economy," he said.

Congress raised the minimum wage in 1996 by 90 cents over two years, from $4.25 to $5.15 an hour. The 1998 plan by Kennedy and Paul Wellstone, D-Minn., would have raised it to $6.15 by 2000. *(1996 Almanac, p. 7-3)*

A business coalition aggressively courted swing senators this year as it lobbied to kill the proposal. GOP leaders said small businesses would be damaged by increasing the wage, and that some would have to trim their work forces to stay afloat. Some Republicans argued that no increase was needed so soon after the 1996 boost, particularly when inflation was low.

Kennedy, Minnesota's Paul Wellstone and other Democrats said there was no solid evidence that a higher minimum wage would result in job losses. Kennedy is expected to raise the issue again in 1999. ◆

Employment & Labor

Three Narrowly Written Worker Safety Bills Win Bipartisan Support

With major changes to worker safety laws pushed to the back burner, Congress cleared three less sweeping proposals that attracted bipartisan support.

SUMMARY

● The first (HR 2864 — PL 105-197) authorizes an existing program that allows state officials to offer advice to employers on improving worker safety without fear of federal penalties.

For more than two decades, the Occupational Safety and Health Administration (OSHA) has worked with states under authority provided by the Occupational Safety and Health Act (PL 91-596) to provide workplace consultants to businesses, particularly small employers, on how to meet OSHA standards. The bill formally authorizes the program and provides that if a state consultant finds a possible violation of federal worker safety laws, the employer would not suffer federal penalties if they quickly fix the problem.

The House passed the bill, sponsored by Cass Ballenger, R-N.C., on March 17, and the Senate cleared it June 24 — both on voice votes. President Clinton signed it July 16.

● A second measure (HR 2877 — PL 105-198), also sponsored by Ballenger, bars OSHA from including any reference in the job performance reviews of its inspectors to the the number of citations or enforcement actions they issue.

While the Clinton administration officially opposes using citations in performance reviews, Ballenger said he has heard that the agency has wrongly encouraged inspectors to take a harder line with employers by including the number of citations in annual performance reviews. Proponents of the bill said such a policy has forced inspectors to operate under a de facto quota system.

The House passed HR 2877 on March 17 by voice vote; the Senate cleared it June 24, also by voice vote. Clinton signed it July 16.

● A third bill (S 2112 — PL 105-241) allows enforcement of OSHA regulations in U.S. Postal Service facilities and offices. OSHA standards already applied to the Postal Service, but the Labor Department and many state agencies lacked authority to issue citations to the agency, making the regulations difficult to enforce.

In addition to facilitating enforcement, the measure prohibits the Postal Service from citing the cost of OSHA compliance as a factor in deciding whether to close or consolidate post offices, restrict or eliminate any service, or raise postal rates. It also requires the Postal Service to consider the effect of any closings or consolidations on the community, employees and economic savings.

The Senate passed the bill by voice vote July 31; the House cleared it Sept. 14, also by voice vote. Clinton signed it Sept. 28. ◆

Chapter 11
ENVIRONMENT

Nevada Nuclear Waste Site 11-3
Superfund Overhaul 11-5
National Parks 11-6
Forest Recovery 11-7
Grazing on Federal Land 11-8

Environment

Nevada Waste Site Falls In Election-Year Tussle Over Senate Seat

Box Score

- **Bills:** HR 1270; S 104
- **House action:** The House passed HR 1270 (H Rept 105-290, Parts 1 and 2), 307-120, on Oct. 30, 1997.
- **Senate action:** The Senate failed to invoke cloture on HR 1270 by a vote of 56-39 on June 2. The Senate passed S 104 (S Rept 105-10), 65-34, on April 15, 1997.

A proposal to open a temporary nuclear waste storage site 100 miles northwest of Las Vegas in the barren Nevada desert fell victim to election-year politics and continued opposition from the state's congressional delegation.

SUMMARY

The interim site, near Yucca Mountain, is a priority for nuclear power companies, which complain that waste is piling up at utility sites across the nation. Safety and environmental problems are expected to delay the opening of a permanent repository at Yucca Mountain until at least 2010.

The House and Senate passed bills (HR 1270, S 104) in 1997 to require the Department of Energy to build an interim storage site for spent fuel from commercial reactors. The House set a deadline of January 2002; the Senate, November 1999.

But Rep. John Ensign, R-Nev., was able to use a procedural move to insist that the Senate act on HR 1270, thereby exposing it to a filibuster. On June 2, the Senate came up four votes short of the 60 needed to shut off debate and move to a vote. The action followed a statement from House Speaker Newt Gingrich, R-Ga., that he did not expect to bring the bill before the House — a decision some Republicans complained was designed to boost Ensign in his Senate race against incumbent Democrat Harry Reid.

House-Senate Dispute Holds Up Nuclear Waste Site

FEBRUARY 28 — Senate, stymied by site opponents, says it is up to House to get legislation ready for conference

A procedural dispute between the House and Senate may have considerably dimmed prospects for legislation to store high-level nuclear waste at a temporary site in Nevada.

Both chambers passed bills (HR 1270, S 104) in 1997 requiring the Energy Department to build a temporary storage site for spent fuel from commercial nuclear reactors. The site, near Yucca Mountain, 100 miles northwest of Las Vegas, has been a priority for nuclear power plants in 35 states; they say the Energy Department is ignoring the problem of waste piling up at sites at the utilities.

For technical reasons, House members want the Senate to adopt the House version of the bill before a conference is held. But such a procedural move would allow Nevada Democratic Sens. Richard H. Bryan and Harry Reid to tie up the measure with objections on the floor.

"This is more than simply a delay on the nuclear waste bill — it's a potentially fatal blow," said Rep. John Ensign, R-Nev., who has joined Reid and Bryan in objecting to the proposal.

Bill supporters are optimistic that they have time to clear a measure this year. Nevertheless, they say the crowded election-year legislative calendar and the threat of delaying tactics from Reid and Bryan prevent prompt resolution.

"If we have to start the process over again [in the Senate], we're looking at a pretty slow process," said Senate Energy and Natural Resources Chairman Frank H. Murkowski, R-Alaska, who plans to meet with other supporters to develop a strategy for passage.

Whatever is decided, Senate Majority Leader Trent Lott, R-Miss., said no legislation would come before the Senate until late April or May at the earliest. "It needs to be done. It's overdue," Lott said. "It has cost billions of dollars and, in my mind, it's one of the biggest environmental issues in the country."

Congress called for a temporary storage site in Nevada after designating a permanent site at Yucca Mountain (PL 100 — 203). That site has run into safety and environmental problems expected to delay its opening at least until 2010. *(1995 Almanac, p. 5-27)*

Supporters said the temporary site would honor a commitment upheld by recent federal court decisions for the Energy Department to accept spent fuel from commercial plants.

But Nevada's congressional delegation and other elected officials in the state, including Democratic Gov. Bob Miller, have been unrelenting in arguing that their state should not store waste it has not generated. Environmentalists also have warned about the dangers of transporting radioactive materials across state borders.

President Clinton has sided with the Nevadans, promising to veto any bill to establish a temporary site. The bill the Senate passed in 1997 fell two votes short of the 67 votes needed to override a veto.

Murkowski and other supporters hold out hope that they could pick up two votes from senators who fear political repercussions. But the Nevada senators said they think that if it came to a veto override, they would gain the votes of some Democrats who initially supported the bill but would not be willing to vote against the president.

Both the Senate and House bills call for shipping waste to the Nevada site by rail. They also would establish user fees for utilities to replace the nearly $14 billion that electricity ratepayers have been paying utilities for waste storage over the past 15 years.

Slow Movement

Lott has been irritated with what he sees as the House's unwillingness to deal

Environment

with the problem quickly and come up with a compromise bill for House-Senate conference. He said in January that the House is "acting irresponsibly" by not clearing the way for action.

Some supporters privately have questioned whether the House's actions are part of an effort to boost Ensign's chances in his challenge to Reid for his Senate seat. They have accused House leaders of concluding it would be better for Ensign to claim credit for killing the bill than it would be to pass legislation that faced a presidential veto.

But Sen. Larry E. Craig, R-Idaho, discounted that idea, saying Reid and Ensign have been such forceful opponents of the bill that neither could use it to his political advantage.

With the outlook for waste legislation unclear, the nuclear industry has turned back to the courts to increase pressure on the Energy Department.

In November 1997, the U.S. Court of Appeals for the District of Columbia Circuit ruled that the department must begin to dispose of spent fuel by Jan. 31, but did not require spent fuel to be moved.

On Feb. 19, a coalition of 41 utilities asked the court to order the department to develop a program to dispose of used fuel "beginning immediately." The department said it is complying with court orders on commercial waste disposal.

Some proponents hope that a favorable court decision could increase the pressure on Congress to act. "The clock is ticking," Craig said. "But as far as I'm concerned, adjournment does not occur until October."

Senate Rejects Cloture Attempt

JUNE 6 — A proposal to store nuclear waste 100 miles from Las Vegas has long been opposed by Nevada's congressional delegation. But this time around, election-year politics helped contribute to the bill's demise.

The Senate on June 2 was four votes short of the 60 votes needed to invoke cloture and move to a vote on HR 1270. The bill would provide an interim storage site for high-level waste generated by nuclear power plants in 35 states. (*Vote 148, p. S-25*)

The vote came after Senate Democrats complained that taking up the nuclear waste bill would interrupt debate on, and possibly kill, the comprehensive tobacco proposal (S 1415 – S Rept 105-180) now being debated.

The Senate's action also followed a statement from House Speaker Newt Gingrich, R-Ga., who said he does not expect to bring the nuclear waste bill before the House this year.

Gingrich said his decision was the result of "the crowded calendar and the strong opposition of some members." But some lawmakers also saw it as a nod to Rep. John Ensign, R-Nev., in his challenge to Democratic Sen. Harry Reid. Ensign startled many senators by announcing the Speaker's decision even before Gingrich did.

After the Senate vote, representatives of the nuclear power industry vowed to continue exploring ways to clear the bill by the end of the 105th Congress. Issues that are "political rather than substantive" delayed the bill, said Joe Colvin, president and chief executive officer of the Nuclear Energy Institute, the Washington-based lobbying arm of the nuclear power industry.

But Senate Energy and Natural Resources Chairman Frank H. Murkowski, R-Alaska, said reviving the bill would not be possible this year.

"It looks like it's dead until Ensign's election comes up," Murkowski said in an interview. "It's a loss for the taxpayer, it's a loss for the industry and it's a loss for Congress, because it ain't going to go away."

Reid and Sen. Richard H. Bryan, D-Nev., declared victory. The Republicans, Reid said, were trying to drop tobacco and "trying to make nuclear waste the fall guy."

Temporary Site

The House and Senate passed bills (HR 1270, S 104) in 1997 requiring the Energy Department to build a temporary storage site for spent fuel from commercial nuclear reactors. The site has been a priority for nuclear power companies, which say the department is ignoring the waste piling up at utility company sites.

Congress called for a temporary storage site after designating a permanent site at Yucca Mountain (PL 100-203). That site has run into safety and environmental problems expected to delay its opening at least until 2010. (*1995 Almanac, p. 5-27*)

Supporters said a temporary site would honor a commitment by the federal government and upheld by recent federal court decisions for the Energy Department to accept spent fuel from commercial plants. But President Clinton has promised to veto any bill to establish such a site.

After weeks of speculation, Senate Majority Leader Trent Lott, R-Miss., scheduled a cloture vote during a break in the tobacco debate. Lott said June 1 that he had been told the nuclear waste bill had more than the 67 votes to override a presidential veto. The version the Senate passed in 1997 got 65 votes.

But some Democrats portrayed Lott's decision as a tactic to delay action on tobacco. Although the tobacco bill has bipartisan support, some Republicans have objected to the comprehensive bill, which would increase cigarette taxes and launch a campaign to cut teen smoking.

"In effect, a vote to invoke cloture is a vote to kill tobacco," Bryan said during floor debate on the nuclear waste bill.

Murkowski testily responded that Bryan and other Democrats were irresponsible in trying to combine the two topics. "This issue should stand on its own," he said during debate.

On the cloture vote, all 53 of the Republicans present supported limiting debate on the waste bill. They were joined by three of the 42 Democrats present: Carl Levin of Michigan, Ernest F. Hollings of South Carolina and Charles S. Robb of Virginia. Murkowski accused the other Democrats of uniting behind the bill to bolster Reid's chances. "It's crass politics to save Reid; that's what that caucus was all about," he said.

But among those who joined Reid and Bryan in opposing cloture was Bob Graham, D-Fla., a supporter of the storage proposal. Graham said before the vote that he was "unwilling to take the risk" of consuming floor time.

Reid also said Nevada voters recognize that he and Ensign are equally opposed to the storage site. "Nuclear waste has not been an issue in years gone by where people point to each other and say we [in the delegation] didn't do enough," he said. ◆

Superfund

Congress Unable To Resolve Partisan Differences On Superfund Overhaul

> **Box Score**
>
> - **Bills:** HR 2727, HR 3000; S 8
> - **House action:** The Transportation and Infrastructure Committee's Water Resources and Environment Subcommittee approved HR 2727, 18-12, on March 11.
> - **Senate action:** The Environment and Public Works Committee approved S 8 (S Rept 105-192), 11-7, on March 26.

SUMMARY

The effort to reauthorize the beleaguered superfund program remained buried amid sharp partisan differences in 1998. Neither the House nor the Senate was able to bridge long-standing concerns about the program (PL 96-510), the nation's primary tool for cleaning the most dangerous hazardous waste sites.

What progress there was came in the Senate, where the Environment and Public Works Committee finished work March 26 on a bill to update superfund. But the bill (S 8) was approved by a vote that broke mostly along party lines, and it went no further.

The bill called for $7.5 billion over five years to finance the program. The split vote, though expected, was still a disappointment to committee Chairman John H. Chafee, R-R.I., and Robert C. Smith, R-N.H., chairman of the superfund subcommittee, who tried to work out differences with Democrats.

Among the most difficult issues were questions about the roles to be played by states and the federal government. Republicans are determined to shift more power to states to decide how sites should be cleaned up, while Democrats believe the Environmental Protection Agency should have the leading role.

Things were more fractured in the House, where two bills were in play.

HR 2727, sponsored by moderate Sherwood Boehlert, R-N.Y., was approved in March by the House Water Resources and Environment Subcommittee. But the bill did not advance because the 18-12 vote did not meet the requirement of Transportation and Infrastructure Committee Chairman Bud Shuster, R-Pa., that no superfund bill would move forward unless it had overwhelming support.

The other bill, HR 3000, sponsored by Michael G. Oxley, R-Ohio, was discussed but never brought to a vote.

House Measure Fails To Garner Bipartisan Support

MARCH 14 — Rep. Sherwood Boehlert, R-N.Y., tried gallantly March 11 to put the best face on prospects for overhauling the superfund program this year.

But even after the House Transportation and Infrastructure Committee's Water Resources and Environment Subcommittee, which Boehlert chairs, approved HR 2727 by a vote of 18-12, the future looked anything but bright.

Only two Democrats voted for Boehlert's initiative, which is widely viewed as the most moderate of several superfund proposals put forth by Republicans.

The vote falls far short of the bipartisan package full committee Chairman Bud Shuster, R-Pa., said he wanted.

"We either move forward with a bipartisan bill, or we will not move forward," Shuster said March 4.

Full committee action has not been scheduled.

Boehlert was hoping his reputation as a pro-environment Republican and his warm relations with Democrats would bring all sides together and provide momentum for his bill.

Those goals were not realized, however, and that clearly left Boehlert disappointed. Superfund, the nation's primary tool for cleaning up the most dangerous waste sites, has been one of his highest priorities.

The outcome was all the more surprising because marathon negotiations between Boehlert and Democrats narrowed differences to the point where "our fingers were almost touching," Boehlert said.

But Democrats, complaining that negotiations were cut short, offered no amendments aiming to try to change the bill in full committee.

"We'd get up to the point of significant agreement and then there would be a backing away and we'd lose some ground. Then he set this arbitrary date for a markup. . . . We're not going to accept a bad bill," said James L. Oberstar of Minnesota, the full committee's ranking Democrat.

Still, some Democrats said that they believe the bill can be salvaged. "I think as the process moves forward, we will moderate some positions, we will look at compromises, continue to negotiate until we have something the administration feels comfortable with," said James A. Barcia of Michigan, one of the Democrats voting for HR 2727.

For that to happen, however, agreements will have to be brokered on such issues as liability, how to clean up damage to natural resources and protections for small businesses.

Accord Unlikely Despite Action By Senate Panel

MARCH 28 — Laying claim to the first significant movement on overhauling the beleaguered superfund program, the Senate Environment and Public Works Committee finished work March 26 on a bill to update the nation's primary tool for cleaning up toxic waste sites.

Environment

But while the bill (S 8) moved forward by an 11-7 mostly party-line vote, in reality, it has an uphill battle. The measure, designed to make superfund more efficient and effective, left the committee with sharp objections from Democrats and the administration that clouded prospects for passage this year.

"I believe the [bill] does have some serious flaws, even though there are provisions that are helpful," Max Baucus of Montana, the committee's ranking Democrat, told the panel. "Frankly, I believe you have not gone far enough."

The bill called for $7.5 billion over five years to finance the program.

The split vote, though expected, was still a disappointment to committee Chairman John H. Chafee, R-R.I., and Robert C. Smith, R-N.H., chairman of the superfund subcommittee, who tried to work out differences with Democrats.

Among the most difficult are questions about the roles to be played by states and the federal government. Republicans are determined to shift more power to states to decide how sites should be cleaned up, while Democrats believe the Environmental Protection Agency should have the leading role.

"We've come a long way toward getting together," Chafee said at the end of the three-day markup. "But I think this bill faces an uphill struggle."

Baucus, likewise, expressed regret that a compromise eluded the committee. "These are all issues [where] there could be bipartisan agreement," he said. "Without compromise . . . I fear this bill is a dead letter going no place."

Despite the overall failure, the committee agreed on some topics that only a year ago seemed beyond reach:

• Protections for small businesses with less than 75 employees or $3 million in annual revenues from shouldering excessive cleanup costs.

• Providing money for the economic redevelopment of so-called brownfields, industrial sites in cities that are not contaminated enough to be declared superfund sites but are too polluted to be used for any other purpose until cleaned.

The bill also would streamline the process for determining the best method for cleaning up a site and would set aside money to pay for cleaning up waste whose source could not be determined.

In negotiating changes, Republicans added incentives to clean up sites while protecting business interests and public health.

Superfund has been a widely supported goal because the program, which received $1.5 billion in 1997, is generally viewed as a failure, breeding lawsuits and lawyers' fees while sites take decades to clean up. ◆

House Defeats Parks Bill As Controversial Riders Sink Popular Projects

OCTOBER 10 — A sweeping parks and public lands bill studded with popular projects in 36 states went down to defeat Oct. 7 in the House, under the weight of a handful of controversial provisions.

By a lopsided margin of 123-302, the House rejected HR 4570, an omnibus parks bill that rolled nearly 100 bills into a giant piece of legislation. (*Vote 489, p. H-138*)

Critics argued during debate that the bill was designed to surround unpalatable measures with popular ones. Minnesota Democrat Bruce F. Vento described the bill as stuffed with "rancid pork."

Republican Sherwood Boehlert of New York, leader of pro-environment, moderate Republicans, derided the tactics, charging that sponsors decided to "hold perfectly good projects hostage in an attempt to jam through the Congress bad policies that don't have a prayer of passing independently."

Boehlert added that the arrangement is like giving a patient "90 percent penicillin laced with 10 percent arsenic."

Supporters, as well as the bill's sponsor, Republican James V. Hansen of Utah, urged lawmakers to pass the bill because 90 percent of the items were non-controversial. And the substitute bill that was the focus of the final vote, Hansen said, was stripped of the most objectionable items.

"Can anybody have a bill where everybody gets everything they want?" Hansen asked. "We have gone out of our way . . . to address concerns." Those concessions, however, came back to haunt Hansen.

A group of conservative members, led by Republican Richard W. Pombo of California, voted against the bill because Hansen "went way too far in accepting changes to try and make this bill work."

In all, 107 Republicans voted against the bill, pleasing environmental groups less than a month before the election.

While the bill included dozens of praised projects, such as authorization for the 6,000-mile cross-country American Discovery Trail, the expansion of the Fort Davis National Historic Site in Texas as well as creating national historic sites for Tuskegee airmen in Alabama and the birthplaces of Abraham Lincoln and George Washington, environmentalists said those items could not outweigh objectionable provisions.

Most troublesome, they said, was language that would limit new wilderness areas, accelerate timber harvests on federal lands and convey a road easement through a national forest in Alaska to the Chugach tribe. ◆

Forest Recovery

Lawmakers Include Forest Health Initiatives In Catch-All Spending Bill

Though an array of bills related to forest maintenance and management were introduced in 1998, the only significant measures related to forest health that survived were tucked deep within the omnibus fiscal 1999 spending package.

They include language to launch a pilot program for selective logging in three national forests in California — Plumas, Lassen and Tahoe — to help reduce the risk of catastrophic fires. It requires the Forest Service to start a five-year trial management plan based on principles developed by the Quincy Library Group, a panel of environmentalists, timber industry representatives and public officials.

The omnibus bill terminated the contentious forest road construction program, or "purchaser road credits," which allowed timber companies to cut more trees to offset the cost of roads they build on public land.

A stand-alone bill (HR 2515) that would have created a Forest Service program intended to clear dead and dying trees and otherwise improve forest health made it to the House floor, but it was defeated. Some Republicans said the bill would inhibit timber harvesting, while Democrats and other Republicans complained it would allow trees to be taken without restraint.

Fire Prevention Bill Sparks Debate

MARCH 28 — Moving to protect national forests from "catastrophic" fires, the House on March 27 was drawn into a sharp debate over how to best manage millions of acres of public woodland.

The differences were exposed during consideration of the Forest Recovery and Protection Act (HR 2515), legislation that sponsors said was crucial for protecting more than 40 million acres of overgrown national forests from wildfires, disease and loss of habitat.

Like previous debates over forest policy, consideration of HR 2515 brought out strong emotions. In this case, lawmakers' objections were enough to defeat the bill, 181-201. The bill was sponsored by Republican Bob Smith of Oregon.

The defeat was presaged when conservative Republicans — most of them from the West — could not turn back an amendment spearheaded by moderate, Eastern Republicans and Democrats to sharply limit new roads in areas of national forests with no roads.

The amendment, offered by Republican Sherwood Boehlert of New York, was attacked by conservative members of his party. Barbara Cubin, R-Wyo. called it part of an "extreme, radical environmental agenda."

The Boehlert amendment passed nonetheless by 200-187 before the bill was defeated.

Supporters said the legislation was needed to enhance the health of forests by allowing excess underbrush and decaying trees to be removed. Those materials, they said, are fuel for fires that are almost certain to ignite if left alone.

"We believe we have developed a common sense, science-based proposal for protecting forests," said Democrat Charles W. Stenholm of Texas.

Critics, however, characterized the legislation, known as the "Forest Health Bill," as false advertising. They said it is a mechanism for opening forest land to increased logging and road building.

"The philosophical assumption in this bill is, it's OK to cut down trees to save trees. I believe that is wrong. As long as we say, in order to preserve and protect trees we must cut down trees . . . this doesn't make sense," said Debbie Stabenow, D-Mich.

The bill would have established a five-year nationwide program to make forests more robust through such activities as thinning excess trees and underbrush; salvaging dead or dying trees; controlled fires; insects and disease control; and protecting seedlings.

The Forest Service would be responsible for carrying out the law, and it would be required to identify areas according to risk.

Despite the sober justification for the bill, debate soon veered into a more emotional realm, with opponents invoking the bruising 1995 fight over the timber salvage rider in the 1995 rescissions bill (PL 104–19). Virginia Republican Robert W. Goodlatte, a supporter, charged that the bill is being attacked by "misinformation put forth by irresponsible extremists." (1995 Almanac, p. 11-96)

Against that backdrop, Democrats and moderate Republicans, including Boehlert, moved to change the bill.

The bill, Boehlert said, "is an elaborate new program that could turn out to be just another road building and logging bill in disguise." ◆

Environment

Attempt To Revamp Fees For Grazing on Federal Land Draws Veto Threat

SUMMARY

A bill aimed at addressing one of the nation's most contentious regional land-use issues — fees for grazing on federal lands — was approved by the Senate Energy and Natural Resources Committee but went no further in the second session.

The House passed its version of the bill (HR 2493) on Oct. 20, 1997. Though a majority consensus on a modest rewrite of the fees developed in the House, the measure provoked a White House veto threat. It also pitted environmentalists and deficit hawks — who assert that the current fee structure amounts to a federal giveaway — against Western conservatives, who fought to preserve low fees for ranchers.

In contrast to 1996 attempts to advance a broad rewrite of rangeland management rules, House Agriculture Committee Chairman Bob Smith, R-Ore., had crafted a narrow bill (HR 2493 — H Rept 105-346, Parts 1 and 2) and worked diligently to resolve differences with Sherwood Boehlert, R-N.Y., the House GOP's leading moderate on environmental issues.

As a result, pro-environment Eastern Republicans, who otherwise might have sided with the Democrats against the bill, generally supported it. Only 22 Republicans voted against the bill in the House. (*1997 Almanac, p. 3-32; 1996 Almanac, p. 4-14*)

The cornerstone of the legislation was a new formula for calculating the fees for grazing on federal land. It would have increased the current fee from $1.35 to $1.84 per "animal unit month," the amount of acreage needed to feed a cow and her calf for a month.

Though many fiscal conservatives and environmentalists favored much higher fees, Boehlert's support for the measure proved pivotal in the defeat of floor amendments to increase the fees sharply. Those votes were close, though: An effort by Bruce F. Vento, D-Minn., to force big livestock producers to pay higher fees failed by a narrow, 208-212, vote in 1997.

The version of the bill approved by the Senate Energy and Natural Resources Committee (S Rept 105-338) was similar to the House measure but never made it to the floor for consideration. The White House maintained its adamant veto threat, criticizing the bill's complex grazing fee schedule and low return to the federal Treasury.

The Senate committee approved the bill July 28 by a vote of 11-9.

On a related issue, the final omnibus fiscal 1999 appropriations measure (HR 4328 — PL 105-277) included a provision that allows existing grazing permits on federal lands to be renewed without final completion of site-specific environmental reviews. Under the bill, roughly 5,000 permits set to expire in fiscal 1999 can be renewed while the site-specific reviews are still being processed. ◆

Chapter 12
EXECUTIVE BRANCH

Clinton Impeachment 12-3
   Chronology of Starr Investigation 12-4
   Ideological Leanings of House Judiciary Panel ... 12-11
   Perjury Charge 12-16
   Points of Contention 12-18
   History of Independent Counsel Law 12-21

Clinton Impeachment *(cont'd)*
   House Launches Inquiry 12-24
   Democrats Offer Censure Resolution 12-41
   Text of Impeachment Resolution 12-42
   Articles of Impeachment 12-46
   Those Who Voted Against Party Lines 12-48

House of Representatives Casts Historic Vote To Impeach Clinton

The House on Dec. 19 voted to impeach President Clinton despite nearly solid Democratic opposition and a last-minute upheaval in the Republican leadership.

SUMMARY

It was only the second time in U.S. history that a president had been impeached. The first was on Feb. 22, 1868, when the House voted to impeach President Andrew Johnson in a dispute that climaxed disagreements over Reconstruction. Johnson was subsequently acquitted by a single vote in a Senate trial.

The House adopted two of the four articles of impeachment recommended by the Judiciary Committee (H Res 611) one week earlier. The first accused Clinton of lying to a grand jury about his affair with White House intern Monica Lewinsky. The second charged him with obstructing justice in the Paula Jones sexual misconduct lawsuit by helping to conceal evidence and tampering with witnesses.

The articles that were rejected alleged that Clinton lied when he denied having a sexual relationship with Lewinsky or having spoken to her about her testimony in the Jones case, and accused the president of abuse of power for providing "false and misleading" answers to 81 written questions submitted to him as part of the Judiciary Committee's impeachment inquiry.

The Republican majority blocked Democratic efforts to vote on a proposal to censure Clinton rather than sending impeachment articles to the Senate for a trial.

Following the impeachment votes, the House adopted a resolution (H Res 614) notifying the Senate of the articles of impeachment and appointing 13 GOP members of the Judiciary Committee to serve as managers — the equivalent of prosecutors — in the Senate impeachment trial.

By the time the House took up the articles, the environment had become surreal. On the eve of the scheduled vote, Clinton had ordered a military strike against Iraq. That postponed debate for a day, enough time for Speaker-designate Robert L. Livingston, R-La., to publicly acknowledge that he, like Clinton, had been unfaithful to his wife.

When debate finally began Dec. 18, nerves were raw. Democrats bitterly complained that the votes should be delayed until hostilities with Iraq ended. Their anger was increased by Republicans' move to block consideration of a censure resolution.

"To be spending the time of this House to smear our commander in chief when brave men and women are risking their lives for their country shocks the conscience," John Conyers Jr. of Michigan, the Judiciary Committee's ranking Democrat, said on the floor.

Then came the bombshell from Livingston, who announced that he would not serve as Speaker and would leave Congress — setting an example for Clinton to follow, he said.

"Infidelity — adultery — is not a public act, it's a private act, and the government, the Congress, has no business intruding into private acts," Judiciary Chairman Henry J. Hyde, R-Ill., said in closing debate. "But it is our business, it is our duty to observe, to characterize public acts by public officials. ... And when you have a serial violator of the oath who is the chief law enforcement officer of the country — who appoints the judges and the Supreme Court, the attorney general — we have a problem."

Scandal Hangs Over Clinton's Address On State of Union

JANUARY 31 — If Bill Clinton survives what has become the greatest threat to his presidency, his Jan. 27 State of the Union address may well be viewed as the turning point back from the edge of the cliff.

The speech was remarkable not so much for what he said as for the chutzpah it took to say it. The address came at the end of a week of sensational news stories describing an alleged affair between the president and a 24-year-old former White House intern.

In 72 minutes, Clinton managed to remind the American people why they elected him twice, noting such successes as the first balanced federal budget in 30 years and the unbroken spell of economic bliss that has unfolded on his watch. *(Text, p. D-3)*

With that, he tapped into the public's tendency to judge elected officials not on their personal foibles but on a cold analysis of job performance. At least temporarily, Clinton managed to switch the debate from the issue of his character — which the public has long found wanting anyway — back to the fundamental question of leadership. His message was loud and clear: If you like what I've done as president, keep me around. I'm going to do more.

Several national opinion polls con-

Executive Branch

Box Score

- **Resolutions:** H Res 611, H Res 614.
- **House action:** The House on Dec. 19 adopted two articles of impeachment and rejected two. All were contained in H Res 611.

The House:
- Tabled (killed) a motion to substitute a resolution of censure, 230-204;
- Adopted Article I, 228-206;
- Rejected Article II, 205-229;
- Adopted Article III, 212-212;
- Rejected Article IV, 148-285.

The House also adopted H Res 614 notifying the Senate of its actions and appointing a team of "managers" to prosecute its case in the Senate trial. The vote was 228-190.

Investigation of the President

The following is a chronology of the Starr case:

Aug. 5, 1994: Kenneth W. Starr appointed independent counsel to investigate connections between the failed Madison Guaranty Savings and Loan and the Whitewater land deal that Bill and Hillary Clinton were involved in developing in Arkansas. Starr succeeded Robert B. Fiske, whom a U.S. Appeals Court refused to appoint because of possible conflicts of interest.

July 18, 1995: Senate Special Whitewater Committee begins hearings on Whitewater.

Aug. 17, 1995: Grand jury indicts Arkansas Democratic Gov. Jim Guy Tucker, James McDougal, the former owner of Madison Guaranty Savings and Loan, and his wife, Susan McDougal, on fraud and conspiracy charges.

May 26, 1966: Tucker and the McDougals are convicted.

April 22, 1997: Starr receives permission from U.S. District Court to extend Whitewater grand jury for six months.

May 27, 1997: U.S. Supreme Court rules that Paula Corbin Jones can pursue the sexual harassment lawsuit she filed against President Clinton on May 6, 1994, even though he is in office.

Jan. 12, 1998: Pentagon employee Linda Tripp provides Starr's office with tapes of conversations between her and former White House intern Monica Lewinsky, who describes her affair with Clinton and her discussions with Vernon A. Jordan about helping her find a job.

Jan. 16, 1998: Attorney General Janet Reno allows Starr to expand his investigation into whether Clinton and Jordan encouraged Lewinsky to lie under oath.

Jan. 17, 1998: Clinton testifies before grand jury in Jones case and denies a sexual relationship with Lewinsky.

Jan. 21, 1998: Lewinsky matter becomes public as media report that Starr is investigating whether Clinton perjured himself and urged others to lie.

Jan. 26, 1998: In White House news conference, Clinton emotionally declares, "I did not have sexual relations with that woman. . . . I never told anybody to lie."

Jan. 27, 1998: Grand jury begins questioning witnesses about Lewinsky matter

April 1, 1998: U.S. District Judge Susan Webber Wright dismisses Jones case.

May 5, 1998: Starr closes Arkansas phase of his investigation, and federal grand jury in Little Rock disbands.

May 22, 1998: Federal judge rules Secret Service agents can be called to testify about Clinton and Lewinsky's relationship.

July 17, 1998: In historic move, prosecutors subpoena Clinton.

July 28, 1998: Lewinsky is granted immunity from prosecution in exchange for testimony before the grand jury.

ducted after the public had learned details of the alleged affair and the supposed attempts to cover it up showed Clinton's approval rating still soaring in the range of 58 to 60 percent.

In his speech, Clinton unveiled a variety of proposals designed to seize control of the national agenda. They included a promise to set aside surplus federal revenues to preserve the Social Security program, tax breaks for child care and a bill of rights protecting consumers from the new vagaries of managed care medical systems.

"I think the American people have come to the conclusion that they do not want to drive the president out of office just because he's not faithful to his wife, and they turn off all the rest of it," said Republican Sen. Robert F. Bennett of Utah.

'A Boffo Performance'

Of course, Clinton's prospects could shift dramatically in the coming weeks if, for instance, Independent Counsel Kenneth W. Starr comes up with smoking-gun evidence that sets public opinion fatally against the president or forces him to resign rather than face a serious threat of impeachment by Congress. In that case, his State of the Union address will be remembered as a valiant last attempt to salvage his presidency.

But for the time being, he has managed to nudge open the door to political salvation a crack. Predictions by media commentators and former White House aides of a swift and ignominious end to his presidency proved to be grossly premature.

Even Republicans gave Clinton begrudging high marks for pulling off a politically potent speech against great odds. Though they objected to many of the new spending programs he outlined, some of them, for the first time since the scandal broke on Jan. 21, began to worry that Clinton might be able to rebound.

Senate Majority Leader Trent Lott, R-Miss., said afterward that Clinton gave "a boffo performance."

"The guy is incredible in his ability to come in there and act like everything is just hunky-dory, like there's nothing going on in the world but that speech," Lott said. "He should almost get an Academy Award."

GOP pollster Frank Luntz, who in the early days of the scandal had been urging Republicans to hold their fire and let the lurid news accounts do

Clinton Impeachment

July 29, 1998: Clinton agrees to testify before the grand jury via video from the White House.

Aug. 6, 1998: Lewinsky testifies before grand jury.

Aug. 17, 1998: Clinton testifies via video for more than four hours. Later, he admits in a brief, nationally televised speech to having had a relationship with Lewinsky that was "not appropriate" and says he "misled people."

Sept. 9, 1998: Starr's office delivers 36 boxes of documents, including two copies of his report and supporting evidence, to the House. His report outlines 11 possible grounds for impeachment.

Sept. 10, 1998: Clinton apologizes to congressional Democrats and Cabinet for misleading them about the affair.

Sept. 11, 1998: House votes 363-63 for resolution (H Res 525) approving release of 445 pages of Starr report. The report, containing lurid details of Clinton's encounters with Lewinsky, is posted on the World Wide Web.

Sept. 18, 1998: By a party-line vote, House Judiciary Committee decides to release Clinton's videotaped testimony before the grand jury and 2,800 additional pages of printed material.

Sept. 21, 1998: Four television networks broadcast Clinton's grand jury testimony.

Oct. 5, 1998: Judiciary Committee votes, 21-16, along party lines to recommend that the House begin formal impeachment proceedings.

Oct. 8, 1998: House votes, 258-176, for resolution (H Res 581) launching impeachment inquiry.

Oct. 30, 1998: U.S. District Judge Norma Holloway Johnson finds "a prima facie violation" of grand jury secrecy rules by Starr's office in the Lewinsky probe.

Nov. 3, 1998: Midterm elections increase Democrats' minority in the House by five members, giving Republicans a slim six-member majority in the 106th Congress. The election was seen as a rejection of the Republicans' focus on impeachment.

Nov. 5, 1998: House Judiciary Committee Chairman Henry J. Hyde, R-Ill., sends letter asking White House to verify or deny 81 assertions made in Starr report.

Nov. 6, 1998: Speaker Newt Gingrich, R-Ga., announces resignation in wake of election losses.

Nov. 13, 1998: Clinton agrees to $850,000 settlement in Jones suit but does not apologize.

Nov. 18, 1998: House Republicans pick Robert L. Livingston, R-La., as choice for next Speaker.

Nov. 19, 1998: Starr, first witness called before Judiciary Committee, testifies for 12 hours.

Dec. 8-9, 1998: Judiciary Committee hears testimony in Clinton's defense.

Dec. 11-12, 1998: Judiciary Committee approves four articles of impeachment (H Res 611).

Dec. 18, 1998: House impeachment debate opens, following one-day delay due to U.S. attack on Iraq.

Dec. 19, 1998: House adopts impeachment Articles I and III, by votes of 228-206 and 221-212. Two other articles are rejected, as is an attempt to substitute a resolution of censure. House then votes 228-190 to notify the Senate and appoint "managers" to prosecute the case in the Senate.

---

their work for them, switched gears immediately after the speech. He said he now believes the GOP should engage. "I think you'll see Republicans beginning to ask questions and demanding answers," he said.

On the night of the speech, Clinton called on his most valuable political asset: the ability to connect with an audience, especially a television audience, and to appear to be a commanding leader who nonetheless feels your pain. He mentioned not a word of the scandal, instead adhering to a just-policy-please script that his staff had thoroughly scrubbed for words or phrases that could be even remotely misconstrued as relating to sex or the president's personal conduct.

The one phrase that escaped the vetting was the line, "A strong nation rests on the rock of responsibility." Although it was a mere introduction to Clinton's thoughts on welfare overhaul and was not meant to be an applause line, Republicans broke in with long and loud applause in an apparent dig at Clinton's personal sense of responsibility.

Plenty of Applause

Clinton hit on themes that struck at the anxiety Americans feel about the future despite the rosy economic times. A speech that many believed might somehow be marred by the scandal was instead repeatedly interrupted by applause and by Democrats leaping to their feet more than 35 times to show support for the president's proposals.

He declared that the nation must move beyond the "sterile debate between those who say government is the enemy and those who say government is the answer." He said he envisioned a "third way" in which government "is leaner, more flexible, a catalyst for new ideas, and most of all, a government that gives the American people the tools they need to make the most of their own lives."

Putting to rest weeks of speculation about what the White House would propose to do with an expected budget surplus, Clinton announced that all of it should be earmarked to shore up the Social Security program. Clinton drew huge applause and a standing ovation when he declared his simple, four-word answer to the question of how to use the surplus: "Save Social Security first."

Executive Branch

He drew the biggest response of the night with a reference to the frustration many Americans feel with managed care plans that employ an army of non-medical personnel to keep costs down. "Medical decisions ought to be made by medical doctors, not insurance company accountants," Clinton said.

He called for a "Consumer Bill of Rights" for managed care patients to increase patients' access to doctors of their choosing and to emergency room care.

That is a far cry from Clinton's massive health industry overhaul proposal in 1993, which, ironically, was decried by Republicans and health experts as too bureaucratic and too likely to take decision-making away from doctors. (*1993 Almanac, p. 335*)

Among a slew of other domestic initiatives, Clinton proposed raising the minimum wage from the current $5.15 an hour, an idea sure to ignite partisan warfare. Republicans in 1996 fought a 90-cent hike in the wage but were forced to capitulate after Democrats tapped public sentiment favoring the increase for low wage-earners. (*1996 Almanac, p. 7-3*)

Clinton also said he would send to Congress legislation to allow early retirees and laid-off workers to buy into Medicare, the federal medical insurance program currently available to Americans age 65 and older. And he outlined a plan to spend $21.7 billion over five years on expanding tax credits for child care and related programs.

While proposing little that was new on the foreign affairs front, he delivered a strong warning to Iraqi President Saddam Hussein, one of the rare instances in which he brought Republicans in the chamber to their feet. Addressing Hussein directly, Clinton said: "You cannot defy the will of the world. . . . You have used weapons of mass destruction before; we are determined to deny you the capacity to use them again."

Though the first half of the speech was forceful and focused on his major initiatives, the latter half devolved into a Clintonesque to-do list, a lengthy recitation of programs and initiatives that often makes even his allies fidgety.

Foreshadowing the battles to come in Congress, Republicans decried the speech as promising much more than a government living within its means could deliver.

Sen. Connie Mack, R-Fla., said, "It's a staggering expansion of government." Idaho Republican Sen. Larry E. Craig said, "You can't declare the era of big government over and come up with new multibillion-dollar programs."

By contrast, Democrats were delighted, especially the liberals who dominate the House Caucus and who have long felt Clinton has abandoned their constituencies. Some congressional Democrats also ventured defenses of the president in the face of the scandal, which many had been reluctant to do earlier.

House Minority Leader Richard A. Gephardt, D-Mo., who has tangled with Clinton on trade and the budget, said, "The president has made a very emphatic statement, and until there is credible evidence or facts to the contrary, he deserves the benefit of the doubt."

But members of the president's party still worry about his future and the impact it may have on the Democratic agenda. Sen. Bob Kerrey, D-Neb., said: "It takes the heart out of you. I've only been here a day and I'm already losing my motivation."

Rep. Bruce F. Vento, D-Minn., bemoaned allegations that have "cast a cloud over policy programs."

Fighting Back

Clinton's speech was the highlight of a week in which the White House came out swinging, after several damaging days of fuzzy responses to allegations that he had had an affair with former intern Monica Lewinsky, then lied about it himself and encouraged her to lie about it as well. Both Clinton and Lewinsky reportedly denied the affair in depositions in a civil suit brought by Paula Jones, an Arkansas woman who says Clinton sexually harassed her when he was governor.

It was a marked reversal in both approach and psychology from the first few days of the scandal, when Clinton looked haggard and besieged and his aides seemed unsure of how to handle questions about his relationship with Lewinsky.

Clinton began the week with a brief but pointed denial of a sexual relationship with Lewinsky in 1996, who had by then become a full-time staff aide at the White House. "I did not have sexual relations with that woman, Miss Lewinsky. I never told anybody to lie. Not a single time, never," he said Jan. 26.

With that out of the way, first lady Hillary Rodham Clinton took charge of her husband's public-relations makeover, appearing on television news programs to field questions. As she has in the past during embarrassing controversies over Clinton's alleged womanizing, the first lady became the nation's first believer in his version of events. And she blamed the allegations on attempts by right-wing extremists to weaken him. "We can't afford to have a president distracted," she said.

Other events began to turn in the president's favor.

The media, digging into Lewinsky's life story, found not the frightened ingenue her lawyer had described in repeated interviews, but a woman from a privileged Beverly Hills background who seemed to friends and acquaintances to be flighty, star-struck and prone to talking openly about her sexual relationships with influential men.

Also, as the case against Clinton was examined more closely from a legal point of view, it seemed weaker than it had when the scandal broke. At that point, with Lewinsky's girl-talk confessions captured on tape by friend and confidante Linda Tripp, who delivered the tapes to Starr, the independent counsel seemed to hold all the cards.

But absent corroborating evidence Starr is still seeking, the legal issue could boil down to little more than a his-word-against-hers case that would probably be too weak to prove Clinton had lied when he denied the affair with Lewinsky.

"Any perjury case is a tough case," said Victoria Toensing, a Washington criminal defense lawyer. "You just don't go on 'he said-she said.' You have to find corroborating evidence."

Toensing said circumstantial evidence can suffice to build a case in some instances, such as when a witness sees a pair go into a room together and stay there alone — even if the witness does not observe the alleged act.

Former independent counsel James McKay, who investigated Attorney General Edwin Meese III and White House aide Lyn Nofziger during the Reagan administration, said: "If it's one person's word against another's, you have reasonable doubt built in right away. I think you will find that prosecutors won't bring a case in that kind of situation."

Starr is said to be in search of witnesses to support Lewinsky's claims, including presidential aides or Secret Service agents who may have seen the two together. Also under review is a document that Lewinsky allegedly gave Tripp that outlines how Tripp could lie to the grand jury about the events Lewinsky had confided in her.

Starr's difficulties were evident at week's end. Negotiations with Lewinsky's lawyers for her testimony broke down after Starr discovered that she was not offering prosecutors as much detail about her conversations with Clinton as she provided Tripp on tape, according to The New York Times.

Until the extent of the evidence gathered by Starr is known, the Lewinsky scandal continues to be a real threat to Clinton's presidency. Perhaps his most important solace comes from opinion polls that so far show the scandal having little impact on his job approval ratings.

"People do make a distinction between what someone does in his personal life and his ability to do his job," said Andrew Kohut, director of the Pew Research Center for the People and the Press. "However, if this involved perjury or obstruction of justice, which speaks to his role as president, the public has not come to any conclusion on that yet."

Clinton Address Fails To Defuse Ticking Time Bomb Of Starr Report

AUGUST 22 — President Clinton said he hoped his late-night mea culpa on Aug. 17 would put the Monica Lewinsky case behind him. But members of Congress, who will make the final determination, were not satisfied with what they heard.

The only certain result of Clinton's nationally televised speech was verification of what most Americans already assumed to be true — that he had had a sexual affair with the former White House intern and then lied about it.

A larger question remained: Was the president's explanation of his previous denials good enough to prevent Congress from initiating impeachment proceedings against him for perjury or obstruction of justice?

With members of his own Democratic Party expressing disappointment that the president lied about the case for seven months, it appears he still has some serious explaining to do before the Congress is willing to absolve him of a breach of trust.

In the coming weeks, according to a legal source with knowledge of the White House strategy, Clinton will privately explain to sympathetic members of Congress why he felt it was necessary to issue a false denial when the Lewinsky matter first came to light last January. And responsibility for his defense strategy, which until now has been controlled by his lawyers, will be assumed by political advisers who have experience in dealing with Congress.

Under the Constitution, "treason, bribery, or other high crimes and misdemeanors" are grounds for impeachment. That vague definition leaves wide latitude for lawmakers to insert their personal judgments into the impeachment process.

The subjective nature of the process was perhaps summed up best by Gerald R. Ford, R-Mich. (1949-73), when as House minority leader he led an effort in 1970 to impeach Supreme Court Justice William O. Douglas. "An impeachable offense is whatever a majority of the House of Representatives considers it to be at a given moment in history," Ford said. (1970 Almanac, p. 1025)

And along with their moral judgments, lawmakers also have to consider the long-term implications of the standard they may set for future presidential — as well as congressional — behavior.

Just hours before Clinton made his historic television address, Orrin G. Hatch, R-Utah, chairman of the Senate Judiciary Committee, admitted that impeachable offenses are in the eye of the beholder.

"It's not just law. It's politics. It's political as well once it hits the House," Hatch said. "And you have to combine those two and say — and this ought to be the prevailing question — what is in the best interest of our country, of our nation, of our people?"

Although some reports have predicted that Independent Counsel Kenneth W. Starr will hand a report over to Congress in September, there are indications that Starr may subpoena Clinton for another interview, which would cause a further delay.

Still, most lawmakers said they expect to receive Starr's report before the Nov. 3 elections. That does not leave them much time to soul-search and decide for themselves what offenses they think warrant impeachment.

Because the case Starr is compiling against Clinton apparently revolves around his efforts to conceal his sexual philandering, many members of Congress are reluctant to throw Clinton out of the White House for personal matters — even if he lied about them.

Others, however, feel it would be in the "best interest" of the country to kick out a president who cheated on his wife, publicly lied about it and may have encouraged others to lie as well.

Rep. George W. Gekas, R-Pa., fourth-ranking member on the Judiciary Committee, which would oversee an impeachment process, said he feels sexual misconduct alone is not grounds for impeachment. But lying about it could be.

"If it's just sex, that's not on any higher ground than getting drunk in the Oval Office," Gekas said. "But now Clinton's apologists are saying lying about sex isn't impeachable. I can't get past that. . . . If perjury is clearcut, we have a basis into an inquiry of impeachment."

Rep. Robert C. Scott, D-Va., who also sits on the Judiciary Committee, said lawmakers must stick to the Constitution, no matter how they may feel about Clinton's personal conduct.

"It's high crimes and misdemeanors [that are impeachable]. It's not misbehavior," said Scott. "I haven't seen anything that suggests there are impeachable offenses. Perjury is a crime with a legal definition. It's lying under oath about a material fact. Clinton's statement [in the Paula Jones case] was made about an immaterial fact in a case that was thrown out on summary judgment."

Most House members are publicly refusing to speculate on impeachment until they see the detailed allegations that Starr's report is expected to con-

Executive Branch

tain, but the range of potential charges is well-known.

Clinton has been accused of having a sexual affair with Lewinsky and lying about it during his deposition in the sexual harassment suit filed against him by former Arkansas state employee Paula Jones earlier this year. That suit has since been thrown out of court.

Starr is also probing whether Clinton obstructed justice by conspiring with others to cover up the affair.

In his speech, Clinton admitted he had an affair with Lewinsky and that he "misled" the public about it. But he insisted that his deposition in the Jones suit was "legally accurate."

During that deposition, Clinton denied having a sexual relationship with Lewinsky as defined by the lawyers in the case. That narrow definition, however, apparently did not cover the kind of sexual activity Clinton admitted to having engaged in with Lewinsky.

Clinton said he did not ask anyone else to lie or to destroy evidence.

Adding Fuel to the Fire

Many lawmakers expressed disappointment at what they called a lack of contrition in Clinton's four-minute televised speech. He never used the words "I'm sorry," and he spent much of the time attacking Starr and his four-year investigation.

Many Democrats, even those sympathetic to Clinton, found it hard to accept his defiant attitude.

"It wasn't his finest hour," said Rep. Charles W. Stenholm, D-Texas. "It would have been much better had he not gone on the attack, if he had been more sincerely contrite. He was more mad at Starr than sorry for what he had done."

Republicans say the criticism of Starr hurt the president more than it helped him.

"It was a little bit like a temper tantrum," said Rep. Curt Weldon, R-Pa. "If he had said he was sorry, that would have won him some support, but now he's caused the whole thing to be triggered to another level."

Weldon, who sits on the special committee investigating whether Clinton permitted the transfer of sensitive missile technology to China, said his colleagues were angered by Clinton's speech — and predicted that Starr and Republicans may now be even more motivated to go after the president.

"Clinton's arrogance was shining through, and it's being picked up by members I've talked to," Weldon said.

The Impeachment Process

House Judiciary Chairman Henry J. Hyde, R-Ill., has refused to speculate on when or how the House will take action in the wake of Clinton's speech. Earlier this summer, he said the House probably would not have time to take much action on the matter before the elections.

Hyde said his committee would first conduct its own investigation into the report — verifying or disproving Starr's findings — before proceeding to public hearings. Such an investigation could take months, and would likely be conducted behind closed doors.

The impeachment process would kick off when Starr notified Congress he had completed his report. Hyde would then introduce a "referral resolution" granting access to the report exclusively to members of the Judiciary Committee. That resolution would have to be approved by the committee and passed by the full House.

Once the resolution was passed, Starr's report would be handed over to the committee and its investigation would begin.

After a preliminary investigation, the committee could throw the case out or vote on a "resolution of inquiry" stating that there was substantial and credible evidence for impeachment.

If that resolution was passed, hearings would likely begin. During the hearings, additional information — possibly from other congressional probes looking into improper fund raising or other allegations — could be dumped into the mix.

Once the hearings were concluded, the committee and then the full House would vote on "bills of impeachment." If the House passed the bills of impeachment by a simple majority vote, the matter would move to the Senate, where it would be tried as if in a court of law.

A select group of members from the House Judiciary Committee would be named to serve as the prosecutors in the case; the president would be represented by his own defense team, and the chief justice of the Supreme Court would preside over the trial, with members of the Senate acting as jury.

Only once in history has a president been impeached. Andrew Johnson was impeached by the House in 1868, but he was subsequently acquitted by the Senate, which failed by one vote to reach the two-thirds majority required for conviction.

If the Senate does not convict, the president can remain in office.

Richard M. Nixon resigned from office on Aug. 9, 1974, days after the House Judiciary Committee voted out bills of impeachment but before the House took them up. *(1974 Almanac, p. 867)*

With the Clinton investigation, some members have talked of pursuing a lesser charge than impeachment, possibly a simple censure.

Political Implications

Regardless of whether Clinton goes on to face impeachment or other punishments, his admission of sexual wrongdoing has already begun to creep into political campaigns across the country.

Dozens of Republican candidates have issued statements calling for Clinton's resignation and linking their Democratic opponents to the White House.

"Our intention is to brand every single Democrat in the state with the scarlet 'C,'" said Trey Walker, executive director of the South Carolina state Republican Party. "What Bill Clinton has done . . . is, he has re-energized our base. . . . We will gratuitously use Clinton's face on all our literature."

Walker said in the hours after Clinton's speech that he was told two local Democratic officials were considering switching parties.

In races across the country, Republicans are also using Clinton's words against their Democratic candidates.

Matt Fong, who is challenging Sen. Barbara Boxer, D-Calif., is expected to make Clinton's admission an issue in his campaign. Boxer was one of the more outspoken critics of former Sen. Bob Packwood, R-Ore. (1969-95), when he was charged with sexually harassing female staffers. Boxer at the time said Packwood should resign immediately.

"She's just a total hypocrite," said Sal Russo, a media consultant working

Clinton Impeachment

with Fong's campaign. "This issue has shined the light on Boxer's pattern of putting partisanship first."

In the wake of Clinton's admission last week, Boxer was critical of him, but stopped short of calling for him to resign. "I think he should have told us the truth seven months ago, and we could have put this behind us," said Boxer, whose daughter is married to one of Hillary Rodham Clinton's brothers.

"That relationship was wrong, clear, black-and-white, no-room-for-ambiguity wrong."

Damaged Credibility

Sen. Dianne Feinstein, D-Calif., issued one of the harshest responses to the speech. "My trust in his credibility has been badly shattered," she said.

That damage was made obvious on Aug. 20 when Clinton announced that U.S. forces had attacked terrorist sites in Afghanistan and the Sudan.

The timing of the attack — just three days after he admitted misleading the American public — prompted suspicion from some lawmakers.

"The timing is so extraordinary that both friends and foes are going to conclude that it was done for the wrong motives," said Sen. Daniel R. Coats, R-Ind. "But even if it isn't, I believe people will use that as an excuse now to further put the United States' credibility and foreign leadership in question."

Sen. Rod Grams, R-Minn., said the president's lack of credibility was to blame for such questions. "When people begin to question their leaders, they begin to question those leaders' actions as well."

But most lawmakers were supportive. House Speaker Newt Gingrich, R-Ga., supported the attack and said he believed the "United States did exactly the right thing."

Congress Returns To Agenda in the Shadow of Scandal

SEPTEMBER 5 — The 105th Congress is returning for its final month to a political landscape that has been been transformed by the sex scandal that imperils Bill Clinton's presidency. Suddenly, traditional concerns over legislation and politics have been dwarfed by the overarching question of whether the president should step down.

The Senate came back from its summer recess Aug. 31 to face a long list of unfinished appropriations bills and partisan battles over health care, campaign finance and tax cuts. But the business of crafting bills and cutting deals has been overshadowed by the high drama of Independent Counsel Kenneth W. Starr's investigation of Clinton and the president's affair with former White House intern Monica S. Lewinsky.

Both Republicans and Democrats find themselves traversing unfamiliar, treacherous territory. The notion of Clinton's resignation or impeachment, which until his Aug. 17 address had been actively promoted only by a relatively small circle of the president's opponents, has come to confront members of both parties.

"There is no doubt that the environment in which we are legislating is vastly different than before the recess," said Idaho Republican Sen. Larry E. Craig, chairman of the Republican Policy Committee. "But no one knows how this is going to shake out."

What has become clear is the excruciating dilemma facing shell-shocked Democrats:

Do they abandon a popular president whose troubles stand to drag them down in November elections, or stick with the man whose personal behavior they find offensive and disturbing?

The rising anxiety among Democrats was underscored in the biting critique of the president delivered by Sen. Joseph I. Lieberman, D-Conn., an ideological ally of Clinton.

In a closely watched floor speech Sept. 3, Lieberman patiently and soberly described the damage Clinton's affair and deception had inflicted on the nation and his presidency. The president's behavior, Lieberman said, "is wrong and unacceptable and should be followed by some measure of public rebuke and accountability."

The White House could take cold comfort in Lieberman' position that it is premature to contemplate punishing the president until Starr delivers his report to Congress on the matter.

But in the wake of the speech, it seems inevitable that the House, which returns from its recess Sept. 9, will be consumed by such questions as whether a mere resolution of censure is the appropriate penalty for the president, or if the ultimate punishment of impeachment should be considered.

The Democrats' agony has been intensified by the mystery surrounding Starr's report. No one in Congress knows what will be in the report, or when it will arrive on Capitol Hill. Until it does, Democrats can count on a steady drip of press reports describing Clinton's relationship with Lewinsky in graphic and occasionally tawdry detail.

Members of both parties and outside political observers are reluctant to even hazard a guess as to the impact the scandal will have in the legislative arena. "This is kind of an X factor that a political scientist can't really calculate," said William F. Connelly, a professor of politics at Virginia's Washington & Lee University.

Still, some trends are emerging. Both parties appear to have incentive to pursue confrontation rather than compromise — Republicans because they smell Democratic weakness, and Democrats because they desperately want to change the subject from sex and scandal.

And Republicans, although they clearly hold the winning hand politically, face vexing tactical decisions. With some House conservatives determined to extract legislative concessions from Clinton in his time of troubles, and others notably Majority Whip Tom DeLay, R-Texas — pressing for the House to stay in session this fall to act on Starr's report, there is a danger the GOP will overplay its hand.

House Speaker Newt Gingrich, R-Ga., and other House leaders are getting ready for Starr's report. Gingrich and Minority Leader Richard A. Gephardt, D-Mo., scheduled a rare meeting on Sept. 9 to discuss, with other leaders, plans for receiving the report.

Thus far, Gingrich has adopted a cautious stance on the question of impeachment, stating that only a "pattern of felonies" and not a "single human mistake" should trigger impeachment proceedings. But Gingrich will come under intense pressure from conservatives to confront the White House — if not on impeachment, then in the legislative arena.

Executive Branch

All of this suggests that beyond the 13 annual appropriations bills, the only bit of must-pass legislation remaining, little will get accomplished. Democrats have been repeatedly stymied in advancing their priorities — proposals to crack down on managed care health plans, boost school construction and revamp the campaign finance system. Republicans still harbor hopes of producing a package of modest tax cuts, but time and the GOP's internal divisions are working against that effort.

Even Clinton's most bitter opponents say they are facing the last five weeks of this session with some trepidation. "I think it's going to be one of the toughest four to six weeks of the three-and-half years we've been in control," DeLay said in an interview. "It's going to be just brutal. The president feels like he's backed into a corner."

Birds on a Wire

Democrats spent the week of Aug. 31 trying to persuade everyone — most of all, themselves — that their agenda remains viable in spite of Clinton's woes. Senate Minority Leader Tom Daschle, D-S.D., repeatedly sought to make clear distinctions between the president, whose personal standing with congressional Democrats has never been lower, and his policies, which retain strong backing among the rank and file.

These days, Daschle seldom invokes Clinton's name, and he has noticeably cut back on his contact with reporters. In interviews, he typically expresses support for the Democratic agenda and the office of the presidency, without mentioning the man who currently holds that office.

Indeed, all Democrats are as skittish as birds on a wire. Rumors that Lieberman would call for censuring Clinton set off alarm bells in the White House. Lieberman has said that White House Chief of Staff Erskine Bowles had asked him to withhold comment until the president returned from his trip to Russia and Ireland.

While Lieberman stopped short of calling for an immediate censure, his speech seemed to touch a nerve among Democrats and sent an unmistakable signal to the White House just how precarious Clinton's standing is with members of his own party.

"The president apparently had extramarital sexual relations with an employee half his age and did so in the workplace," Lieberman said. Directly confronting Clinton's assertion that his affair with Lewinsky was "inappropriate," Lieberman added: "Such behavior is not just inappropriate. It is immoral."

Two leading Democratic senators, Bob Kerrey of Nebraska and Daniel Patrick Moynihan of New York, who were present for Lieberman's speech, echoed his sentiments. "We have to resolve this," Moynihan said.

Based on the initial reaction from the president and senior administration officials, Lieberman's broadside might prove to be a badly needed wake-up call underscoring the gravity of the president's situation. Traveling in Dublin, Ireland, the president for the first time used the words "I'm sorry" to express his regret for the scandal. "I've already said that I made a bad mistake, it was indefensible and I'm sorry about it," Clinton said.

Bowles said that Lieberman's criticism hit the president hard, in part because of the senator's close friendship with Clinton. "It's awfully tough — it's painful — when a friend gives you justifiable criticism, and that's what Joe did," Bowles said on CNN's "Evans, Novak, Hunt & Shields."

The question now is whether Lieberman's remarks trigger a flood of calls by Democrats for the president's resignation, censure or impeachment. So far, only a single Democrat — Rep. Paul McHale of Pennsylvania, who is retiring this year — has urged Clinton to resign. But with political experts predicting that the scandal could lead to a GOP rout in November, many House Democrats will be tempted to desert the president.

Connelly said it should not be surprising if Democrats abandon Clinton now, after the president maintained all year — falsely, as it turned out — that he had not had an affair with Lewinsky.

"For seven months he focused on self-preservation," Connelly said. "So it isn't surprising that for the next two months they'll focus on their self-preservation, too."

Some Republicans are convinced that, in order to turn the political tables on the GOP, Clinton will try to pick a fight over a popular issue by vetoing one or more of the remaining appropriations bills. That could undergird Democratic unity while conjuring up memories of the GOP's disastrous government shutdowns of 1995 and 1996.

On Sept. 2, the Senate sent the president the first of the 13 annual spending bills, a relatively uncontroversial measure (HR 4059) funding military construction. But with less than 20 voting days scheduled for the remainder of this session, it seems inevitable that several spending measures will be combined in a single omnibus bill.

In the past, the president has been able to seize the advantage in last-minute negotiations over such massive bills, using his veto to force concessions from Republicans. It remains to be seen whether he can still do so in his current predicament, but it might be one of the only actions he can take to revive his presidency.

Mindful of that history, DeLay and other Republicans are wary of predicting victory in this year's showdown. "We don't have a sense we can roll him," DeLay said. "It's too early to tell.'"

Reaching Out

What was somewhat surprising was how little Lott and other senior Republicans had to say about the scandal. In his first significant public comments on the matter, Lott told reporters Aug. 31 that he was "disgusted" by the circumstances surrounding Clinton's behavior. "There is a moral dimension to the American presidency," he said. "And today that dimension, that power has been lost in scandal and in deception."

But largely overlooked was an olive branch that Lott extended to Democrats. "Senate Democrats might not want to try to imitate General Custer," he said. "They might instead decide to work with us in a bipartisan way on those bills we can get completed."

That hoped-for bipartisanship was in evidence as the Senate Appropriations Committee began work on the remaining spending bills, including the $82.7 billion measure funding the Departments of Labor and Health and Human Services. The Senate measure was far more generous to Clinton's initiatives than the House version of the bill (HR 4274) and did not include several policy-related provisions opposed by the White House.

But Democrats are poised to block legislation toughening the nation's bankruptcy laws (S 1301) — a top priority of Lott's — in a bid to turn that bill into a vehicle for their pet proposals, including a boost in the minimum wage.

The relative calm that prevailed in the Senate during the week of Aug. 31 was somewhat deceptive. Publicly, senators and staffers stayed focused on legislative business while privately, they mused about the morality of adultery and the process of censuring a president, and quizzed reporters on the latest rumors on the scandal.

The distractions are likely to increase and intensify when the House comes back. After a long day fielding questions from reporters about Clinton's sexual peccadilloes and what action, if any, Congress should take in response, Maine Republican Sen. Olympia J. Snowe said with a sigh: "Everything's open to question, there's no way to read all of this. It's sort of surreal."

House Judiciary Committee Noted For Both Civility And Partisanship

SEPTEMBER 5 — If Independent Counsel Kenneth W. Starr submits a report to Congress this month on possible impeachable offenses committed by President Clinton, it will probably be referred to one of the most politically polarized panels in Congress: the House Judiciary Committee.

But, their differences aside, committee members assert that they can rise above partisan interests and give whatever evidence Starr submits a thorough and fair evaluation.

The 37-member committee matches old-line liberals such as ranking Democrat John Conyers Jr., D-Mich., and Barney Frank, D-Mass., with staunch conservatives such as Bob Barr, R-Ga., and Charles T. Canady, R-Fla. Democrats are expected to add Thomas M. Barrett of Wisconsin, another liberal, to the panel when the House reconvenes.

But in Henry J. Hyde, R-Ill., the committee has a chairman who enjoys respect on both sides of the aisle. And he has been able to maintain decorum and civility in the committee during even the most heated debates.

"There are people who talk about the committee as if it were a brawl," said Frank, the committee's second-ranking Democrat. "That's just not true."

Since the Republicans took control of the House in 1995, the committee has been a platform for advancing conservative causes. It has spent numerous days debating constitutional amendments on school prayer, congressional term limits and a balanced budget. It has approved legislation banning "partial-birth" abortions and taken on judges that members say have been overly liberal or "activist" in their rulings.

Along with the Government Reform and Oversight Committee, the committee has called on Attorney General Janet Reno to explain why she has not appointed an independent counsel to investigate the fundraising practices of the Clinton-Gore campaign in 1996.

But never has the committee's discourse been less than civil.

"We're used to each other," said Bill McCollum, R-Fla. "We've been involved in a number of critical matters over the years. There are a number of members that respect each other."

Sometimes the two sides seem to enjoy each other as sparring partners. Hyde and Frank in particular are known for their witty ripostes.

Earlier this year, for example, as Frank criticized Hyde for supporting a "sense of the Congress" resolution objecting to state laws allowing the medicinal use of marijuana, Hyde turned to Frank and said: "I yield to the gentleman's superior knowledge of marijuana."

Frank smiled broadly.

Few Options This Year

Starr is investigating events surrounding Clinton's affair with former White House intern Monica Lewinsky as well as a host of other issues going back to the Whitewater land deals Clinton was involved in while governor of Arkansas.

If he submits a report to Congress

Ideological Leanings

SEPTEMBER 5 — The House Judiciary Committee is a highly polarized group, as measured by the liberal Americans for Democratic Action (ADA), the American Conservative Union (ACU) and by the CQ rating that shows how often members voted with their party in 1997.

	ADA	ACU	CQ Party Unity
Republicans			
Hyde, Ill.	20	68	89
Sensenbrenner, Wis.	20	88	85
McCollum, Fla.	5	88	91
Gekas, Pa.	15	88	88
Coble, N.C.	5	88	93
L. Smith, Texas	0	88	92
Gallegly, Calif.	5	80	88
Canady, Fla.	10	92	93
Inglis, S.C.	5	100	93
Goodlatte, Va.	10	80	94
Buyer, Ind.	0	83	86
Bryant, Tenn.	5	100	94
Chabot, Ohio	20	96	87
Barr, Ga.	5	96	97
Jenkins, Tenn.	5	88	93
Hutchinson, Ark.	10	88	93
Pease, Ind.	15	96	93
Cannon, Utah	10	96	93
Rogan, Calif.	5	92	92
Graham, S.C.	5	92	93
Bono, Calif.	—	—	—
Democrats			
Conyers, Mich.	95	4	90
Frank, Mass.	100	4	91
Schumer, N.Y.	85	19	82
Berman, Calif.	80	9	81
Boucher, Va.	85	8	76
Nadler, N.Y.	100	4	93
Scott, Va.	90	8	87
Watt, N.C.	100	4	94
Lofgren, Calif.	95	8	92
Jackson-Lee, Texas	80	13	90
Waters, Calif.	95	8	92
Meehan, Mass.	90	20	92
Delahunt, Mass.	95	0	92
Wexler, Fla.	90	17	84
Rothman, N.J.	90	13	87

outlining possibly impeachable offenses, the House will forward it to a committee — presumably Judiciary — and write rules for the report's consideration. The committee's role is likely to be behind the scenes, at least initially. With just a month left before adjournment, the committee has few options on how to handle the report. It could launch into hearings in September but would have little chance of making much headway in such a

Executive Branch

short time. It could hold hearings after the elections or postpone all action until next year.

Already members are arguing over how to handle the report. Hyde is pushing for a resolution that would limit access to members of his committee. This approach has come under attack from Majority Whip Tom DeLay, R-Texas, and John D. Dingell, D-Mich., who support releasing it to the full House and to the public at large, for different reasons. DeLay's position is based on his underlying view that Clinton should be impeached, and that the Congress should stay in session as long as that takes. Dingell argues the public has a right to take a thorough look at all the evidence against the man they elected.

Starr's report may contain unredacted grand jury testimony, which is generally restricted from public view. For this reason, many members are hoping Starr submits an executive summary, which might satisfy members who want to see the report while not releasing sensitive documentation. Disputes over what to release and to whom could take weeks to resolve.

"There is no way, in my judgment, there [are] going to be hearings before the elections," McCollum said. "The later [Starr] sends it up, the less likely there will be any hearings this year."

Light on Moderates

The committee's reputation for partisanship comes from its almost complete lack of moderate members. Charged with debating controversial social policy issues including abortion and gun control, few moderates of either party have either sought appointment to the committee or been granted it if they did.

The Republicans, in particular, are a tightly knit and highly conservative lot, as measured by CQ Weekly's annual vote studies. In 1997, all GOP members of the committee voted with the party at least 85 percent of the time and as often as 97 percent of the time in the case of Barr. *(1997 Almanac, p. C-22)*

One moderate Republican who has sought a seat on the committee and been rebuffed is Tom Campbell, R-Calif. A former Stanford University law professor who served on the committee during his first tour in Congress (1989-1993), he has been deemed too likely to veer from party orthodoxy. In 1997, he voted with the party 75 percent of the time and has bucked his party on a number of issues, including his decision to vote against Newt Gingrich, R-Ga., for Speaker. *(1997 Almanac, p. 1-11)*

The Democrats are not as ideologically coordinated, but are still a generally liberal lot. Rick Boucher, D-Va., may be the most moderate member. Boucher has broken with fellow Democrats over the years on such issues as clamping down on terrorism and illegal immigration. He voted with the party 76 percent of the time in 1997.

Barrett, who had a party unity rating of 91, is more typical.

The importance of the committee to the future of the Clinton presidency is something of an open question. In 1974, the House Judiciary Committee's votes to impeach President Richard M. Nixon on three counts was enough to prompt Nixon to resign. Since the committee was the only congressional body to act in 1974, it will always be remembered as crucial in the history of Watergate. *(1974 Almanac, p. 903)*

But this time around, the case against Clinton may not even advance to the point of a committee vote. Or it may go further.

In the short term, many experts believe the crucial issue will not be what members of the committee think of Starr's report, but what the public and the House as a whole think.

So far a number of moderate Democrats have moved to distance themselves from Clinton. House Minority Leader Richard A. Gephardt, D-Mo., has said Clinton could be impeached, depending on what Starr's investigation has uncovered. Sen. Joseph I. Lieberman, D-Conn., was said to be considering offering a resolution censuring Clinton, but said in a Sept. 3 floor speech highly critical of the president that calls for resignation or censure should wait for the Starr report.

But the key will be what lawmakers say after the report is issued, says Marshall Wittmann, director of congressional relations at the Heritage Foundation, a conservative think tank. He says Democrats will be essential for any action, since Republicans are not likely to go forward with impeachment unless they have bipartisan support.

Starr Report Hits Capitol Hill, Drawing Outrage And Trepidation

SEPTEMBER 12 — Lawmakers reacted to the release of the long-anticipated report detailing President Clinton's illicit relationship with Monica Lewinsky with disgust, shock, outrage — and a wary eye to public opinion.

The documents from Independent Counsel Kenneth W. Starr, containing lurid details of White House liaisons, charged Clinton with perjury, obstruction of justice, witness tampering and abusing the power of his office in an effort to cover up an extramarital affair with the former intern.

It leveled 11 specific charges of wrongdoing against Clinton, including lying under oath, working with Lewinsky to conceal information about their relationship, and attempting to improperly influence the grand jury testimony of his personal secretary, Betty Currie.

In an effort to prove the president was untruthful when he testified in a civil deposition that he had never had sex with Lewinsky, Starr outlined their relationship at a level more suited to a pulp novel than a sober, legal report.

Based on testimony from Lewinsky, Starr said the former intern performed oral sex on the president nine times. Among the encounters were instances when Clinton was talking on the telephone to House members — a gesture of disrespect toward Congress that is not likely to go over well.

One of those involved, Sonny Callahan, R-Ala., chairman of the Appropriations Foreign Operations Subcommittee, said he could recall talking to the president about the deployment of U.S. troops in Bosnia.

"If it is true that my name is somehow mentioned in this report, I can say unequivocally and without hesitation that I had no knowledge I was sharing the president's time or attention with anyone else," Callahan said in a statement.

Asserting that the president knowingly and willingly violated the law and encouraged others to do so, the independent counsel said Congress was forced to consider issues far beyond a private, personal transgression.

"When such acts are committed by the president of the United States, we believe those acts 'may constitute grounds for impeachment,'" the report said.

A Political Decision

Members appeared dumbfounded by the speed with which Starr's investigation had concluded and uncertain what to do next. Like the American public, lawmakers were angered by Clinton's behavior but unsure whether his alleged transgressions were serious enough to merit the wrenching step of launching impeachment hearings.

"This could be a make-or-break weekend for the president," said Republican Rep. Peter T. King of New York as lawmakers left Washington on Sept. 11 with Starr's report in their briefcases.

With seven weeks until the midterm elections, one thing was clear: Not only Republicans but many Democrats were unwilling to go out on a political limb for a president they did not trust long before the Lewinsky scandal.

A senior Senate Republican aide said that a key factor in what happens next will be what Democrats heard during their weekend swings at home.

The decision whether to proceed to impeachment hearings or take some other action against Clinton, such as a censure, is in the end, a political, not a legal, determination. Congress' future course depends on whether the report produces an outcry from a public that, to date, has seemed as ambivalent as Congress — personally offended but leery of drastic measures.

The White House immediately began a counteroffensive, with Clinton's attorneys asserting that Starr had carried out a witch hunt, spending millions of dollars to rummage through Clinton's private life.

"This is personal and not impeachable," said Clinton's private attorney, David Kendall. "The amount of lurid, graphic detail here far exceeds any legal justification."

Earlier Friday, at a prayer breakfast, Clinton apologized for the first time to Lewinsky and her family. "I don't think there is a fancy way to say that I have sinned," he said.

But if a newly contrite Clinton, who spent the week begging forgiveness from lawmakers, his Cabinet and the public, was looking for signs that Democrats would rally 'round in his time of need, he did not find many.

Just hours after the prayer breakfast, the House passed a resolution (H Res 525) that authorized the public release of the report and laid out procedures for handling other evidence given to Congress by Starr. The resolution passed 363-63, with 138 Democrats voting yes.

Rep. James P. Moran, D-Va., said he was shocked by the number of Democrats who voted for the resolution. "Anxiety, nervousness, fear — all of those emotions play a role. And this [vote] was the easy one," he said.

Those Democrats who did speak out on the floor accused Republicans of reneging on a bipartisan deal worked out with House Speaker Newt Gingrich, R-Ga., that was to govern release of the thousands of pages of supporting materials delivered to the House on Sept. 9.

Others complained that the decision not to give the White House an advance copy of the report was unfair. Just a handful of liberals, including leaders of the Congressional Black Caucus, ventured so far to as defend the president.

Some Republicans who read portions of the report professed shock.

"We do not expect our presidents to lie under oath. We do not expect them to commit perjury," said Senate Judiciary Committee Chairman Orrin G. Hatch, R-Utah. "What I've read thus far bothers me greatly."

Charles T. Canady, R-Fla., chairman of the House Judiciary Committee's Constitution Subcommittee, said the report is "quite disturbing. . . . I believe there is evidence of perjury and obstruction of justice."

But he added that the Judiciary Committee cannot "rubber stamp" the report and must conduct its own review before deciding whether to proceed with an impeachment inquiry.

The Findings

The independent counsel's investigation began four years ago as a review of a questionable Arkansas land deal. It was later expanded to cover the 1995 firing of White House travel office personnel and improper White House use of confidential FBI files. The report before Congress deals solely with Clinton's relationship with Lewinsky.

Lawmakers had hoped to avoid such a situation. Gingrich last month said the House would likely seek evidence from all of Starr's investigations before deciding whether to proceed with an impeachment inquiry. The Speaker at that time said a "pattern of felonies" would be needed for the House to act.

In the report, Starr said it was his original desire to send up all findings at once, but as the information about the Lewinsky matter became overwhelming, it was apparent that delay "would be unwise." Decisions about what steps to take, if any, on the other matters are to be made "at the earliest practical time," it said.

The report leveled charges against Clinton in four areas:

● **Perjury.** It said Clinton, both in a civil deposition in a sexual harassment lawsuit brought by former Arkansas state employee Paula Corbin Jones and in testimony before a federal grand jury, lied numerous times about the nature of his relationship with Lewinsky and efforts to conceal their affair.

During that Jones deposition, Clinton denied that he had had a sexual relationship with Lewinsky. Clinton's legal team in their rebuttal said those statements were based on an ambiguous definition of sex.

To make the case that there could be little confusion about whether sex had taken place, Starr includes graphic descriptions of the physical relationship. Based on testimony from Lewinsky, White House personnel, official logs and transcripts, the report detailed encounters between Lewinsky and Clinton from Nov. 15, 1995, to Dec. 28, 1997.

Lewinsky said that while the two never had intercourse, she performed oral sex on the president nine times and that Clinton touched her breasts and genitals during some of their encounters. The report also said government-conducted DNA tests proved that semen stains on a blue dress owned by Lewinsky matched a blood

Executive Branch

sample taken from Clinton.

The report also said the two had engaged in sexually explicit conversations over the telephone on 10 to 15 occasions.

Clinton's lawyers said Starr had focused on the lurid details solely to humiliate Clinton: "The principal purpose of this investigation and the report is to embarrass the president and titillate the public."

The report further said Clinton was untruthful when he said he couldn't recall whether he had ever been alone with Lewinsky and or had exchanged gifts with her.

That leaves Congress faced with an earnest desire to muster up the dignity required by the historic situation — and the necessity of digging into the salacious details of the Starr report.

- **Obstruction of justice.** The Starr report said there was an understanding with Lewinsky to lie under oath in the Jones case. Lewinsky originally signed an affidavit denying that she had sex with Clinton. After a grant of immunity from Starr, she changed her story.

Starr charged that Clinton and Lewinsky also had an understanding to conceal gifts they had given each other instead of turning them over to lawyers in the Jones suit. He also said Clinton had not been truthful about discussions with his friend, lawyer Vernon Jordan, who tried to help Lewinsky find a job in New York.

He further charged that Clinton attempted to impede investigators by helping Lewinsky look for a job in New York, at a time when she would have been a witness harmful to him if she had testified in the Jones case.

Kendall denied that Clinton had tried to get Lewinsky a job in order to influence her testimony in the Paula Jones case: "Ms. Lewinsky was never offered a job at the White House after she left — and it's pretty apparent that if the president had ordered it, she would have been."

- **Witness tampering.** Starr charged that Clinton improperly tampered with a potential witness by attempting to influence the testimony of Currie, his secretary.

Starr said that Currie facilitated many of the meetings between Clinton and Lewinsky. She also collected gifts that Lewinsky said had come from Clinton after they were sought by subpoena.

On Dec. 28, 1997, Currie drove to Lewinsky's Watergate apartment and collected a box containing the gifts. She later turned them over to Starr.

The White House asserted that Currie said she was asked by Lewinsky to hold the gifts and that Clinton never asked Currie to get them.

- **Abuse of constitutional authority.** Starr said it was an abuse of power for Clinton to lie about the relationship to Congress and the public in January 1998; to promise to cooperate with the investigation and then refuse six invitations to voluntarily testify and invoke executive privilege; and to lie again in testimony in August.

It was, Starr said, "all as part of an effort to hinder, impede and deflect possible inquiry by the Congress."

What's Ahead

The report now launches Congress and the country on a politically perilous journey.

While there are some members who served in the House during the 1974 Watergate impeachment hearings, most lawmakers are heading into uncharted territory. Even for those who were then in the House, history is not a reliable guide to what lies ahead.

This is the first time Congress has faced the possibility of an impeachment inquiry based on the findings of an outside, independent counsel. The independent counsel is itself a relatively recent creation of Congress, a response to the Watergate scandal.

"This is a sacred process. This goes to the heart of our democracy," said House Minority Leader Richard A. Gephardt, D-Mo. "This is not politics. This is not spinning. This is not polling. This is not a lynch mob. This is not a witch hunt. This is not trying to find facts to support our already reached conclusions. This is a constitutional test."

But it was clear during debate on the rule to release the report, and from comments afterward, that Congress is going to have a tough time rising above partisanship.

Democrats accused Republicans of reneging on an agreement that only House Judiciary Committee Chairman Henry J. Hyde, R-Ill., and ranking Democrat John Conyers Jr. of Michigan would review boxes of supporting documents before they were released to the public.

Democratic Rep. David R. Obey of Wisconsin complained of "blatant disregard to fairness." Noting that he had served in Congress during Watergate, Obey said, "The reason, in the end, that the congressional process worked is that this was seen by the minority — then the Republicans — as being fundamentally fair to them."

Hyde insisted the debate on the first resolution did not presage partisan wrangling in the Judiciary Committee: "We won't be out on the floor where they can get some mileage out of it. This was spin, this morning. ... Their idea of bipartisanship is that we surrender on everything."

Democrats seemed willing to fight procedural, though not personal, battles for the president. But even then, only to a point. One great fear, beyond the impact on the November elections, is that any proceedings on the Lewinsky matter could stretch on for months.

Senate Minority Leader Tom Daschle, D-S.D., has publicly broached the idea of a lame-duck session after the elections to quickly dispose of the issue. "I don't think it's responsible for this Congress to leave on Oct. 9 [the target adjournment date] and expect this matter to be held over the country for the next three or four months without any action," Daschle said.

The White House appeared poised to mount a two-track counterattack against Starr and congressional Republicans: While Clinton apologizes repeatedly for his actions — and even admits that his first nationally televised mea culpa was not contrite enough — his lawyers and political aides denounce the report as factually flimsy and unnecessarily graphic.

In his original address to the nation, Clinton admitted that he had an improper relationship with Lewinsky but quickly turned to a denunciation of Starr and his lengthy investigation. After negative public reaction — and private confrontations with leaders of his own party and even his Cabinet members — Clinton has not repeated those attacks, instead talking about the biblical injunction to forgive one's enemies.

Clinton Impeachment

Judiciary Panel Votes To Release Clinton Video

SEPTEMBER 19 — Republicans by now had hoped to be gaining bipartisan approval for their handling of Independent Counsel Kenneth W. Starr's report to Congress on President Clinton's affair with Monica Lewinsky.

Instead, they now face the possibility of taking on one of the Constitution's most difficult tasks in an atmosphere of partisan acrimony.

This mood was illustrated by the rancorous, closed-door meetings of the House Judiciary Committee Sept. 17 and 18. The committee voted along party lines to release on Sept. 21 the videotape of Clinton testifying before the grand jury Aug. 17 and approximately 2,800 pages of printed material.

"It was strongly partisan, vigorously partisan," said Chairman Henry J. Hyde, R-Ill. "I prefer that it would go more smoothly."

What particularly disappointed members of both parties is that all of this quarrelling preceded the first real step — a formal vote of the House to initiate impeachment proceedings.

Republicans say the process has been driven by a belief that the public should know as much of the case against Clinton as possible. Democrats, however, say Republicans have designed the process solely to embarrass the president and sway public opinion.

"The public is not sufficiently anti-Clinton now," said committee member Barney Frank, D-Mass., characterizing the GOP's strategy, "This is designed to build up support for impeachment."

Republicans argued they were just trying to do their constitutional duty and examine the evidence supplied by Starr. They said they were complying with the spirit of a resolution (H Res 525) passed with bipartisan support Sept. 11 ordering Starr's material to be released no later than Sept. 28. (Vote 425, p. H-120)

"There was a general view among Democrats not to reveal anything, and a general view among Republicans to reveal as much as possible," Hyde said.

Nor was the rancor limited to the closed-door session. Democrats and Republicans engaged in a hostile exchange after the on-line magazine Salon published a story on a long-ago affair Hyde, who was married, had with a married woman. Speaker Newt Gingrich, R-Ga., and other members of the House Republican leadership asked FBI Director Louis J. Freeh to investigate whether any White House official was involved in leaking the story. The White House responded that anyone who was found to be involved would be fired, and attacked the letter to Freeh as an attempt by Republicans to use the story "for their own partisan interests."

The partisan disputes are only likely to continue as the process unfolds and Congress decides whether to formally commence an impeachment inquiry.

The committee still has to consider the release of enormous amounts of other materials. It will then turn to the issues of how to conduct an impeachment inquiry. That will address such questions as how to issue subpoenas, grant immunity and cite recalcitrant witnesses for contempt. It is still uncertain whether the committee would rely solely on Starr's evidence or seek testimony from Clinton, Lewinsky and others — and endure the embarrassing details again.

The House now appears likely to take a vote, before adjourning, on convening a formal inquiry. If it approves such an inquiry, the committee may hold hearings in a special session after the election. The committee could report articles of impeachment to the 106th Congress next year.

Comparisons With Watergate

As they move through the process, lawmakers of both parties refer to the only precedent they have — Watergate — and in that they have a selective memory.

Ranking Democrat John Conyers Jr. of Michigan, the only current member who was on the committee in 1974, remembers his fellow Democrats allowed Nixon's attorneys to review and rebut all materials before they were released. (*Watergate, 1974 Almanac, p. 903*)

"In 1974, we kept the records for seven weeks, going over them before there were any releases. This time we've dumped process and fairness on its head...." he said.

But Republicans remember that Watergate was not without its partisan sparring over procedural issues.

"I was there in 1973-74, and if that was bipartisan I would really like to see partisanship," said Senate Majority Leader Trent Lott, R-Miss.

In Watergate, Congress was not dealing with a report like Starr's, which Democrats contend is both overreaching and overly salacious. In March 1974, Watergate special prosecutor Leon Jaworski sent a 60-page "road map" and 800 pages of grand jury testimony and documents in what was referred to as a "bulging brief case."

Unlike Starr's 445-page report, the road map contained no narrative of events. Nor did it have any discussion of possible grounds of impeachment. It was merely an index to the most pertinent portions of the grand jury documents.

The Watergate-era Congress was also slower in releasing the material it received. Much of Jaworksi's report did not see the light of day until it was published at the end of August 1974. The committee did release material over the spring and summer of 1974, but the bulk of that came from its own investigation.

These types of differences have been central to Democratic claims of unfairness.

"I have to say with great remorse, and great disappointment, that we have here a Salem witch hunt, and I will not participate," said Rep. Sheila Jackson-Lee, D-Texas.

Jackson-Lee said Starr's material and the way it is being handled completely ignore principles of "due process" accorded defendants in a criminal proceeding.

This was a distinct minority position when the House voted 363-63 on Sept. 11 to release Starr's report. But as members read the report, heard from constituents and contemplated the release of more sexually explicit material, the initial bias toward openness was receiving a second look.

"I was so stunned by the graphic nature of it that I spent a good bit of the weekend wondering if I had cast the right vote," said David R. Obey of Wisconsin, a senior Democrat. "I'm not sure I would have voted to release that report if I had known the vulgari-

Legal Experts Say Perjury Charge Poses Greatest Peril to Clinton

SEPTEMBER 19 — Of the four grounds for impeachment enumerated by Independent Counsel Kenneth W. Starr, perjury strikes most legal experts as the most troublesome for President Clinton.

It also shows how the impeachment process differs from a criminal proceeding. Assertions by Clinton's attorneys that his statements under oath were technically not perjury might hold up in a court of law, where legalistic quibbling is commonplace.

In the court of public opinion, however, there is less tolerance for what Senate Minority Leader Tom Daschle, D-S.D., called "semantic tap-dancing" by the president and his lawyers.

The problem for Clinton is that he has to defend himself in both of these courts.

Daschle and other Democrats are clearly ambivalent about exploring whether the statements qualify as perjury. On Sept. 14, Daschle publicly advised Clinton to stop "hair-splitting over legal technicalities."

"It simply stands in the way of what we need to do: Move forward and let common sense guide us in doing what is best for the country," Daschle said in a statement at a news conference with House Minority Leader Richard A. Gephardt, D-Mo.

But Republicans may not want to drop the issue so quickly. It is clearly the one that resonates most with the public. While polls show that most Americans oppose impeachment, pollsters caution that might change if it is demonstrated that Clinton committed perjury.

In all likelihood, the Republican-controlled House Judiciary Committee will want to examine what Clinton said during his January deposition in the Paula Jones sexual harassment lawsuit and again during his grand jury testimony on Aug. 17. And even if it decides this qualifies as perjury, Congress will have to then determine whether it is an impeachable offense.

A Question of Interpretation

Both questions lend themselves to varying interpretations. Perjury is a criminal offense defined as knowingly giving false testimony in a legal proceeding when testimony is relevant to a material issue in the proceeding. The nation's founders set the standard for an impeachable offense as treason, bribery or "high crimes or misdemeanors."

If Congress wants to consider whether Clinton's testimony formally fits the definition of perjury, it would have to examine whether the statements were untrue, whether Clinton knew them to be and whether they were relevant to a material issue.

The first two lend themselves to an inquiry that could be highly embarrassing to the president. Some or all of the graphic descriptions of sex could be transformed from words on a page to live testimony.

The third — whether the testimony involved is a relevant issue — is unresolved in the case of the Jones deposition. In the case of Starr's criminal probe, it would be relevant, but by then Clinton was admitting inappropriate contact with Lewinsky.

The Jones case was dismissed in April by U.S. District Court Judge Susan Webber Wright. Prior to that, she had determined that the testimony pertaining to Clinton's relationship with Lewinsky was not crucial to Jones' sexual harassment suit. Her ruling came on a motion by Starr to halt the discovery process in the Jones case because it could interfere with his probe. She halted only the discovery related to Lewinsky.

Clinton supporters and a number of sympathetic legal scholars have taken this to mean his testimony does not relate to a material issue. Wright, however, still could decide that it does, and cite Clinton for contempt of court. In a footnote to a ruling on an appeal by Jones, she cited this possibility.

The other possible legal development is that the 8th Circuit Court of Appeals could reverse Wright's ruling and reinstate the Jones case.

An Impeachable Offense?

The larger question is whether perjury — especially this perjury, if it qualifies as such — would constitute an impeachable offense.

Perjury was grounds for the impeachments of two federal judges in 1989: Alcee L. Hastings (now a Democratic House member from Florida) and Walter L. Nixon Jr. What was an impeachable offense for a judge could also be for a president, says Joseph diGenova, a former federal prosecutor and independent counsel who probed the State Department's actions in the Bush administration. (1989 Almanac, p. 229)

"A prosecutor would bring this case in a minute," said diGenova. "Of course it's impeachable."

But others argue that it is one thing to commit perjury to hide official misconduct — which both Hastings and Nixon were accused of —and another to commit perjury about an extramarital affair.

"You need to consider the level of turpitude and the excuse, so to speak, which is that he was lying to protect his privacy and his family," said Mark M. Hager, law professor at American University in Washington.

Clinton Impeachment

ty," added John P. Murtha, D-Pa.

Constance A. Morella, R-Md., suggested that Clinton's videotaped testimony not be publicly released, saying it would only generate anger and fan partisan flames. "I think it would shed more heat than light," she said.

But Judiciary Committee Republicans argued they had little choice after the overwhelming vote to release the documents. "I would only remind you that 363 members voted to release this material," said a GOP committee aide.

The vote gave the panel the authority to withhold material, but little guidance on what grounds to use.

Some Republicans are also pushing to have the committee's inquiry go beyond issues related to Clinton's affair with Lewinsky. An inquiry dealing only with matters related to a sexual relationship has always made Gingrich uncomfortable.

He suggested earlier this summer that Starr send Congress material that he compiled on the Whitewater land deals, the White House's improper use of FBI files on Republicans and personnel changes in the White House travel office. When Starr provided nothing on these fronts, House Republicans immediately considered adding these matters to the impeachment inquiry on their own, using materials gleaned by the House Government Reform and Oversight Committee.

But expanding the probe faces skepticism not only from Democrats, but from some Republicans, who wonder if it would only complicate matters.

"That's within our purview, but the mechanism for this is more difficult," said committee member Asa Hutchinson, R-Ark. "What is in front of us is the Starr report."

Overriding Public Opinion

The Republicans' apparent determination to move toward impeachment against the polls represents something of a change in the GOP's attitudes.

Throughout their nearly four-year tenure at the House's helm, Republicans have often relied extensively on public opinion. Many of their most prominent policies — to overhaul welfare, balance the budget and cut taxes and spending, for example — have been justified at least partly on the grounds that they are the public's will.

But impeachment, some leading Republicans contend, is a serious, constitutional question that ought to be determined more by one's conscience than public opinion.

They have tended to discount the current polls, which show that while the scandal has ruined Clinton's personal standing and trustworthiness, about two-thirds of those surveyed still approve of his job performance. And about two-thirds say he should not be impeached.

To some extent, Republicans are anticipating a change in public attitudes as it digests the Starr report and its implications. "The impact of this still hasn't settled on the American people," said Republican E. Clay Shaw Jr. of Florida.

Many Republicans also report hearing a much more negative reaction to Clinton at town hall meetings in their districts and in phone calls. "That goes right in the face of what they see in the polls," said Michael Franc, vice president of government relations at the Heritage Foundation, a conservative think tank.

While some Republicans — particularly Majority Whip Tom DeLay, R-Texas, and a number of Judiciary Committee members — have expressed a strong resolve to move forward with an inquiry, others are reserved, especially in their public comments.

"There is no shortage of American people today that are eager for the chance to step up and yammer on this subject," said Majority Leader Dick Armey, R-Texas. "I think I have an obligation to hold my counsel."

Phil English, R-Pa., said that while Starr made a powerful case for impeachment, Clinton deserves a chance to respond. "I'm trying to puzzle this through," English said. "I'm not trying to draw any conclusions."

A House GOP leadership aide said that Republicans will move slowly, but deliberately, in the impeachment process. "We're going to move gingerly, one step at a time," he said, acknowledging that "our position is not without risks."

Republicans have strong incentives to "let this thing play out," said Roger Davidson, a professor of government and politics at the University of Maryland. "Public opinion hasn't jelled yet. And their core constituency would be furious if they thought that Republicans were somehow letting Clinton off the hook."

DeLay has promised to quash any attempt to forestall impeachment proceedings by censuring Clinton, saying such a punishment would be meaningless. However, that option may eventually gain popularity if Clinton's job approval ratings remain firm.

Democrats Go Slow

Democrats are also feeling their way. Most do not take solace in Clinton's relatively lofty job approval figure. They, too, figure that his support is soft and his presidency could easily implode with additional revelations.

The vast majority of Democrats are extremely critical of Clinton's having had an affair with Lewinsky and his misleading statements afterward, though uncertain whether the Starr report warrants an impeachment inquiry. But Clinton has never had close ties with congressional Democrats, especially those in the House, and they have not rushed to defend him.

For example, a majority of Democrats voted to publicly release the heart of Starr's report Sept. 11.

Members of the Congressional Black Caucus and some liberal stalwarts have demanded that Clinton be treated fairly. But many Democrats have been circumspect, wary of being seen as defending Clinton.

With the dearth of moderate Democrats on the Judiciary Committee, Republicans have to look elsewhere to find bipartisan support for impeachment. Moderate Democrats and those in competitive districts may be the most receptive to calls for resignation or impeachment, though most have held their fire so far.

Charles W. Stenholm of Texas, a conservative Democrat, said there is enough evidence to launch an impeachment inquiry. But he is uncertain whether Clinton ought to be impeached. He said he would judge cautiously, saying that his constituents want him to "act like a juror that they would want deciding their fate."

Tim Roemer, D-Ind., a moderate who blasted Clinton for his "recklessness" and "cavalier attitude with the truth," said lawmakers are proceeding carefully because "there are people all over the board back home." But Clin-

Points of Contention

Independent Counsel Kenneth W. Starr's report, released Sept. 11, contains 11 counts of alleged wrongdoing by President Clinton arising from his illicit affair with former White House intern Monica Lewinsky. The counts could be grounds for impeachment. Clinton's lawyers issued a point-by-point rebuttal Sept. 12. Following are the key issues in dispute:

ALLEGATION	STARR FINDINGS	CLINTON REBUTTAL
Perjury: Clinton lied about his relationship with Lewinsky in his Jan. 17, 1998, deposition in a sexual-harassment lawsuit filed by former Arkansas state employee Paula Corbin Jones.	Clinton denied having a "sexual relationship," a "sexual affair" or "sexual relations" with Lewinsky. She later testified to 10 sexual encounters.	The president's "good faith and reasonable interpretation" is that oral sex was not covered by the "special" definition presented by Jones' lawyers.
Perjury: Clinton lied again about Lewinsky when he testified on Aug. 17, 1998, before Starr's grand jury.	Clinton admitted an "inappropriate intimate relationship" but denied perjuring himself in his deposition in the Jones case. He contended oral sex was not covered by the definition offered by Jones' lawyers.	". . . False testimony provided as a result of confusion or mistake cannot as a matter of law constitute perjury."
Perjury: Clinton lied in the Jones case when he said he could not specifically recall being alone with Lewinsky or giving her gifts.	Clinton lied three times about time spent alone with Lewinsky, in one case repeating a "cover story" that she may have brought him "papers to sign."	Clinton did not deny meeting alone or exchanging gifts with Lewinsky; he simply could not recall specifics — and Jones' lawyers did not press him.
Perjury: Clinton lied about his conversations with Lewinsky regarding her testimony in the Jones case.	Clinton said "I'm not sure" that he discussed with Lewinsky her testimony in the Jones case beyond making jokes; she said they discussed it three times.	Differing recollections "cannot possibly support a perjury charge."
Obstruction of justice: Clinton concealed evidence of his involvement with Lewinsky, including gifts and an "intimate note" she sent him.	There is "a reasonable inference" that Clinton tried to conceal the gifts he gave Lewinsky by having his secretary retrieve them.	"This claim is wholly unfounded and simply absurd." The president "frequently exchanges gifts with friends" and did not try to conceal his gifts to Lewinsky.
Obstruction of justice: Clinton and Lewinsky agreed to lie about their relationship, and he instructed her to file a false affidavit in the Jones case.	Clinton and Lewinsky had an understanding that they would lie about their affair, and he knew her affidavit in the Jones case would be false.	"The use of 'cover stories' to conceal such a relationship, apart from any proceeding, is not unusual and not an obstruction of justice."
Obstruction of justice: Clinton tried to find Lewinsky a job in New York while she was a witness in the Jones case.	Hoping to ensure Lewinsky's silence, Clinton "devoted substantial time and attention" to help her find a private-sector job.	"There is no suggestion he ever ordered or directed anyone to assist Ms. Lewinsky or . . . give her special advantages," and his help was "insubstantial."
Perjury: Clinton lied about his conversations with lawyer Vernon Jordan regarding Lewinsky.	Clinton said he had not discussed Lewinsky's testimony with Jordan, but Jordan said they "absolutely" had talked about it.	"This allegation is a fabrication" because the testimony does not support Starr's version of events.
Obstruction of justice: Clinton attempted to influence the grand jury testimony of his secretary, Betty Currie.	Clinton improperly tried to influence her testimony by discussing his deposition with her the day after he gave it.	The charge is unfounded because "Currie was not a witness in any proceeding at the time he spoke with her."
Obstruction of justice: While Clinton refused to testify before the grand jury for seven months, he continued to lie to aides who were to testify.	Clinton's repeated denials of an affair — and the distribution of untrue "talking points" to his staff — caused top aides to mislead the grand jury.	Clinton "simply repeated to aides substantially the same statement he made to the whole country" in January; he did not attempt to corruptly influence them.
Abuse of power: Clinton's lies, refusals to testify for seven months and claims of executive privilege amounted to failure to "faithfully execute the laws."	Clinton's public denials, refusals of six invitations to testify before the grand jury and claims of executive privilege violated his oath of office.	Starr over-reached in an attempt to "transform personal misconduct into impeachable official malfeasance," especially when Clinton relied on legal advice.

ton's actions will not be easily dismissed, Roemer said, because "forgiveness to most Americans is not just to move on and forget about it."

Murtha, who took office in February 1974, in the midst of the Watergate scandal, said he has more immediate concerns than the possibility of impeachment, namely, "Can the president govern?" The first test, he said, is whether Clinton "has the ability to stand up to the pressure of a tax cut."

As long as Clinton can retain a favorable job approval rating and demonstrate that he has the capacity to govern, Murtha added, "as one of the senior Democrats, I wouldn't call on him for anything."

One Democratic aide said confidently that the impeachment threat has bound Clinton more closely than ever to congressional Democrats. "He can't make any deals with Republicans that we won't bless," the aide said.

Finding the political turf unsettled, many lawmakers in safe seats are concluding that there is comfort in hewing closely to their political base. Those who fail to do so are feeling the heat.

James P. Moran, D-Va., has been so outspoken in his criticism of Clinton that, he joked, "I'm basically making a safe Democratic district very competitive." He said he was asked not to speak at one gathering of local Democrats in his suburban Washington district and booed when introduced at another.

By the same token, Mark Souder, R-Ind., has drawn the ire of some of his constituents for saying he is unsure whether Clinton ought to be impeached. Souder, a member of the GOP's feisty Class of '94, is no Clinton ally. His votes are consistently conservative, and in February he called for Clinton's resignation.

But after reading Starr's report, Souder decided the case for impeachment based solely on the Lewinsky affair is inconclusive. Souder said he would vote to launch a formal impeachment inquiry and would welcome expanding it to include allegations on such matters as campaign finance abuses.

That is not tough enough for some of Souder's constituents. "A lot of our people want him impeached — then for the inquiry to start," said Souder, surprised at suddenly being accused of being a Clinton sympathizer. "It's 'Fire! Aim! Ready!'"

Braced for Inquiry, Democrats Still Lobby for a Deal

SEPTEMBER 26 — With Republicans moving inexorably toward a momentous vote authorizing an impeachment inquiry against President Clinton, Democrats and the White House have finally begun to fight back.

But the evolving Democratic strategy — to blame Republicans for dragging out the crisis engulfing the presidency and build support for a penalty less than impeachment — is not likely to save Clinton from that historic step.

Republican leaders have scheduled votes in the House Judiciary Committee and on the floor during the week of Oct. 5 on a resolution formally authorizing an impeachment inquiry, the first time since the Watergate affair that the House has done so.

The resolution will only establish ground rules for the process — it makes no recommendation on the question of impeachment.

For that reason, the floor vote should be a slam-dunk for Republicans. It is likely to be politically awkward for anyone but the most loyal Clinton supporters to object to the Judiciary Committee proceeding with an investigation into the long list of alleged impeachable offenses outlined by Independent Counsel Kenneth W. Starr.

"This will just say that there is a basis for going forward with an inquiry," said Rep. James E. Rogan, R-Calif., a Judiciary member. "It's essentially akin to a 'probable cause' determination in a criminal case."

But the White House, acutely aware that this might be its only chance to thwart a protracted impeachment probe that could produce embarrassing hearings and formal charges, is putting on a full-scale lobbying push against the resolution. Even first lady Hillary Rodham Clinton has entered the fray, calling lawmakers to shore up support for the president.

It would take a minor miracle for the administration to prevail in a contest over authorizing the investigation. But the White House is hoping for a sizable Democratic vote against the resolution, in part to buttress its claim that the entire exercise is being driven by politics.

Some Democrats who are facing tough re-election contests this fall have already signaled, however, that they might not be sympathetic to White House pleas. "I support opening an inquiry," said Rep. Charles W. Stenholm, D-Texas. A senior Democratic aide said that at this stage the leadership has no plans to take a formal position in opposition to the resolution.

"We're just too divided," the aide said. "A lot of our people want to vote for this."

For their part, Republicans claim not to be troubled by polls showing Clinton's support growing as the public has become disenchanted with the whole matter.

"There is an inevitability to this thing," said Rep. James C. Greenwood, a moderate Republican who represents a bellwether district near Philadelphia. "We will conduct an impeachment inquiry, and when it's done, we will vote out at least one article of impeachment."

Not all his colleagues are sure of that prediction, but most seem willing to risk it.

Coming Back?

Ever since Starr's report outlining grounds for Clinton's possible impeachment landed on Congress' doorstep Sept. 9, it has been clear that Democrats — not Republicans — will ultimately decide whether Clinton will hold onto his job.

Without significant Democratic backing, the GOP's drive to remove Clinton from office will inevitably come up short. As the Watergate affair proved, the political opposition can initiate an impeachment process — as Democrats did against President Richard M. Nixon in 1974. But because of the two-thirds majority needed in the Senate for conviction, members of the president's party will decide whether he actually leaves office.

Democrats are still struggling to regain their equilibrium after the Starr report. With all the humiliation Clinton's affair with former White House intern Monica Lewinsky has

Executive Branch

wreaked upon Democrats, their hostility toward the administration remains palpable.

Indeed, many Democrats say privately that they are still frustrated with Clinton's repeated resorts to hair-splitting in the Lewinsky matter. "There are people here who still want to see him leave," said one Democratic senator.

Several Democrats warn that Clinton's reservoir of Democratic backing on the Hill remains dangerously shallow. The fragile bonds between Democrats and the White House that seem to be re-forming in the wake of the Lewinsky debacle will be severely tested in the next several weeks.

Still, many Democrats found it encouraging that for the first time since the middle of August, the White House and Democrats seemed to be reading from the same script.

On the same day, Sept. 23, that House Minority Leader Richard A. Gephardt, D-Mo., slammed Republicans for dragging out impeachment proceedings for political gain, presidential spokesman Mike McCurry made the same point from the White House lectern, accusing GOP leaders of currying favor with their "jihad caucus" — the party's most extreme elements.

Clinton's standing in public opinion polls began to rise in the wake of the release of his videotaped testimony in the Lewinsky matter, which monopolized the airwaves during the morning of Sept. 21. Some Republicans had hoped that the videotape would deal Clinton a political death blow by portraying him as angry and even unstable.

Clinton went through rhetorical contortions to avoid disclosing details of his sexual activities with Lewinsky. But there were no fireworks, and even Republicans say the prevailing reaction from their constituents was one of sympathy for the president.

"Because of the advance buildup, people were let down," said Rep. Lindsey Graham, R-S.C., who is on the Judiciary panel. "They put themselves in his position, and they didn't like it."

Rogan, a former prosecutor, also was underwhelmed by what he saw: "I've seen more gripping testimony in purse-snatching cases."

Some Democrats, who have a tendency these days to ferret out any silver linings, say the GOP's decision to release the videotape, combined with other miscalculations, might even help the Democrats' bleak electoral prospects.

"I've seen a sea change in the past two weeks," said Rep. David R. Obey, D-Wis. "A lot of Democrats are mad as hell at how the Republicans are running impeachment."

The biggest challenge for the White House is to bring Democrats around to support some penalty short of impeachment for Clinton.

Several trial balloons were floated during the week of Sept. 21, all with the purpose of raising the possibility of an unprecedented presidential "plea bargain." Under these scenarios, Clinton would face censure or reprimand, perhaps combined with a financial penalty, in return for which Republicans would abandon efforts to impeach him.

In a sign of Clinton's desperation, he even reached out to former Senate Majority Leader Bob Dole, R-Kan. — whom he defeated in 1996 — to grease the wheels for such a deal. But on NBC's "Today" show on Sept. 24, Dole said it was "premature to talk about censure. We're in the very early stages of a proceeding that's going to last for a while."

For their part, Republican leaders quickly dismissed any suggestions of a plea agreement. "For anybody to start talking about doing anything before we finish the investigative process simply puts the cart before the horse," said House Speaker Newt Gingrich, R-Ga.

More ominously for the White House, several leading Democrats said the administration should approach the issue cautiously. "I'd be worried about the quality of mercy that abounds in these houses right now," said Sen. Dianne Feinstein, D-Calif., who has been a harsh critic of Clinton ever since it became clear that he lied about his affair with Lewinsky. Senate Minority Leader Tom Daschle, D-S.D., echoed Dole's comment that talk of a deal is premature.

But the White House appears to have no choice but to press for censure. "Democrats have to do more than criticize Republicans for how they are handling impeachment," said Thomas E. Mann, director of governmental studies at the Brookings Institution. "They have to present an alternative."

Familiar Challenge

Republicans face a depressingly familiar challenge. Unlike in past legislative showdowns with Clinton, they are trying not to overplay what is quite obviously a winning hand.

Their immediate task is to somehow ensure that the public views the impeachment process as fair, even if many Democrats do not. The pivotal player in this effort is House Judiciary Committee Chairman Henry J. Hyde, R-Ill., whose public statements have been aimed at showing that Republicans are not on a crusade to remove the president.

While the committee has at times resembled a war zone as members have scrapped over the release of documents, its biggest test — writing the rules for the impeachment inquiry — is looming.

"We're going to follow the Watergate model as much as we can," Hyde said Sept. 24. But it remains to be seen whether that can be achieved in the highly partisan atmosphere hanging over the committee.

Beyond that, impeachment hearings represent potentially dangerous territory for Republicans. "These hearings could come back to haunt them," Mann said. "If they get into questions about sex and body parts, it would demean the people asking the questions and be a disaster for our politics."

And on a political level, GOP leaders must somehow reconcile the demands of the party's conservative base — who want Clinton removed — and the general public, which has been more forgiving of the president.

That conflict is evident in the statements of Republicans, and in the mail and telephone traffic they get from constituents. In a recent appearance on CNN's "Late Edition," Rep. Bill McCollum, R-Fla., struggled to explain what he called the "dichotomy" between Clinton's persistently high job approval ratings and the seriousness of the allegations lodged by Starr.

"The country is basically at peace and not at war," he said. "The public does not want to see things changed or rattled right now."

But then McCollum ticked off Starr's bill of particulars — 15 counts of possible perjury and 11 counts of ob-

Independent Counsel Law Then and Now: Enough Irony for Both Parties

OCTOBER 3 — As Congress wends its way toward a presidential impeachment inquiry, it is worth noting a couple of important milestones. The 20th anniversary of the passage of the independent counsel law falls this month, as does the 25th anniversary of the event that precipitated it: the "Saturday Night Massacre" firing of Watergate Special Prosecutor Archibald Cox.

The ironies here are unavoidable. A scandal begets a law that begets (at least in part) a new scandal. A law created largely by Democrats comes back to haunt them. A system that may not have been broken then surely is now.

When historians look back on the current scandal they may well dub it "Nixon's Revenge." As president, Richard M. Nixon's attempts to attack his critics only backfired. His order that Cox be fired, far from saving his presidency, actually hastened its demise.

But in the years after Nixon left office, Democrats — it now appears to a growing number of people — seriously overplayed their hand. It was not enough that Nixon had resigned from office in great humiliation, or that Democrats scored big in the 1974 congressional elections, or that they regained the presidency in 1976. They had to prevent a Nixon from ever happening again. They had to come up with a highly complex — some would say quintessentially liberal — scheme for policing evil out of government.

Before 1978, when the independent counsel law (PL 95-521) was enacted, the system for limiting government corruption was based on the Founding Fathers' precepts about separation of powers, and checks and balances. While admittedly imperfect, the system dealt well with the most egregious abuses of office. It gave all prosecutorial power to the executive branch, which was kept in line through congressional pressure, judicial rulings and public opinion.

Since 1978, corruption in high office has been policed by an independent agent, divorced from any of the three branches, and more or less free to root out malfeasance where he sees fit.

The Democrats still in Congress who were involved in drafting the original statute and its various rewrites defend the law by arguing that it has been corrupted by Kenneth W. Starr. They point to the lengths to which Starr went to uncover evidence of criminality by Clinton.

But this argument overlooks the fact that, with the possible exception of alleged leaks of grand jury material, Starr has not done anything that the statute prohibits. Nowhere does it say he should exercise restraint, or put his decisions in broad perspective. Nowhere does it say he should not make the strongest case he can, given the evidence he has. Nowhere does it say charges related to sexual conduct or lying in a deposition for a dismissed civil case are not worthy of pursuit.

A more telling reaction to Starr comes from Democrats who have left office and have the luxury of public remorse. They have become something of a mea culpa caucus.

"I was a member of the Judiciary Committee then [in 1978]," said former Rep. Don Edwards, D-Calif. (1963-95). "I'm sorry I didn't pay more attention. It's a flawed law, and we are now paying the price."

"I don't know if anyone cares about old white males admitting their lack of foresight. But that's what we are," said Charles Tiefer, a former House deputy Democratic counsel who helped defend the statute when it was being challenged in court by Republicans.

The independent counsel statute, of course, is not solely responsible for the current state of affairs. The list of contributing factors is long. It includes the Supreme Court's decision that Paula Jones' sexual harassment suit could proceed while Clinton was in office. It includes U.S. District Judge Susan Webber Wright's decision that Monica Lewinsky was a suitable subject for pre-trial discovery in the Jones case. And, most important, it includes the conduct of Clinton, who could have spared himself and the nation considerable pain had he acted more decently to begin with or more truthfully in his Jones deposition.

But, for better or worse, the nation would not be in this situation today under the old system, in which special prosecutors were appointed on an ad hoc basis only when there was a public outcry for one.

Now it is the Republicans' turn. It would seem they are looking at a golden opportunity to overplay their hand. The public could judge them very harshly if it concludes they pushed the impeachment issue too far.

For much of the statute's 20-year history, Republicans have been the chief critics of the law as well as of the persons who have served as independent counsels, most notably Iran-contra investigator Lawrence E. Walsh. Now they are using the statute, which is up for reauthorization next year, as the rationale for an inquiry and defending Starr against attacks from Democrats. House Judiciary Committee Chairman Henry J. Hyde, R-Ill., insists that Democratic criticism of Starr is part of an effort to deflect attention from Clinton's misdeeds.

He and other Republicans would like to push forward with their inquiry without having to constantly evaluate Starr's actions. Perhaps they should look at the situation Democrats are now in and remember the old admonition: Be careful what you wish for, because you just might get it.

Executive Branch

struction of justice. "The maximum sentence for all that, if he were tried in court, would be something like 185 years in prison," he said. "He's not going to get that, but that's the serious nature of this."

Based on his contacts with constituents, Greenwood said that the public is also groping with questions of punishment and fairness. "If you ask my constituents, about one-third say impeach, one-third say drop it, and one-third say censure," he said.

Post-Election Deal?

Democratic partisans, such as Rep. Barney Frank of Massachusetts, have charged that the GOP's real purpose in extending the investigation through November is to fire up the party's conservative base. "They can't take the risk of Bill Clinton being unimpeached before the election," said Frank, a member of the Judiciary Committee.

GOP leaders have strenuously denied such charges, insisting they want a fair and careful probe. But some members concede that some sort of deal might be possible after the election. "The dynamic will shift," Graham said.

Such talk ignores the visceral desire of many House Republicans to follow the process all the way through to impeachment. If GOP leaders stop short, they could find themselves facing a backlash from their own members.

Rep. Robert L. Ehrlich Jr. of Maryland, one of the GOP's aggressive class of 1994, said: "There are a lot of people in my class who are simply not disposed to deal-making in this context." The determination of GOP leaders to hang tough, no matter what the polls might say, will be reinforced if Republicans make significant gains in the elections.

Greenwood cites the Constitution to suggest that the House should not do deals. "The Constitution doesn't empower us to criticize the president or fine the president," he said.

And that is why Democrats fear that no deal will be reached until after Clinton is formally impeached by the House. Hyde said Sept. 22 that it will be up to the Senate to negotiate any plea agreements.

To many Democrats, all of this seems to have an air of unreality. Clinton is rolling along with job approval ratings any second-term president would envy. The public has signaled repeatedly that it does not regard lying about sex — which may end up as Clinton's most serious transgression — as rising to the level of impeachment.

Perhaps more important, if the House approves one or more articles of an impeachment on a party-line basis, there is virtually no chance that the Senate will summon a two-thirds majority to convict Clinton and remove him from office.

Looking at the range of possible outcomes, there is little wonder why most Democrats and some Republicans are approaching the vote on the resolution of inquiry with apprehension.

Graham, normally an outspoken partisan, has been a model of restraint throughout this process. "I'm leaning 'yes' on the resolution," he said. "But I want to make sure that the substance of what we're looking into is serious enough to warrant putting the nation through more trauma."

Partisan Vote Sets Tone for House Inquiry On Impeachment

OCTOBER 10— Gerald D. Kleczka stood transfixed in the center of the House, voting card in hand and eyes on the tote board above him. Should he support the third presidential impeachment inquiry in the nation's history?

Kleczka, a seven-term Democrat from Milwaukee's South Side, hesitated for several minutes and talked to a couple of Judiciary Committee members. Finally, he punched in his card and cast his lot the same way as nearly every other Democratic lawmaker — hewing to the party line against an open-ended inquiry against President Clinton.

What it came down to, he said later, was, "Can I trust the Republicans to conduct this in a fair and expeditious manner?" His conclusion: "They are content to draw this out as far into next year as possible."

Republicans did not need the votes of Kleczka and the Democrats to move forward with the investigation. However, the Republicans dearly wanted more than 31 of them to revive the spirit of 1974 — when the House almost unanimously supported an impeachment investigation against Richard M. Nixon.

Instead, the flashes of anger, catcalls and party-line votes harked back to 1868. Then, the impeachment of Andrew Johnson fell one vote short of conviction in the Senate in a politically charged process that tarnished Congress' reputation as well as Johnson's.

But unless there is a bombshell from the Nov. 3 election, from the subsequent hearings or from Independent Counsel Kenneth W. Starr, there seems little chance that a bipartisan effort will develop to force Clinton from office. Nor is it clear how Republicans could put the brakes on this process without angering their most ardent supporters.

Indeed, the Oct. 8 vote may solidify a practice in which wavering members such as Kleczka side with their party when deciding how to handle the Clinton scandal — not because they want to defend him, but because it makes moral and political sense to them. So in the end, one of the most important votes of the decade was emblematic of a 105th Congress that has been riven by partisanship.

H Res 581, which directed the Judiciary Committee to conduct an open-ended impeachment investigation, was approved 258-176. The 31 Democrats who joined all Republicans in voting for the resolution were mostly conservatives and moderates. (Vote 498, p. H-142)

A Democratic alternative that would have limited the scope of the investigation and finished it by Dec. 31 lost, 198-236. (Vote 497, p. H-140)

The debate was curiously undramatic despite lawmakers' frequent references to history. There was no suspense to the proceedings, surprisingly little interest in them by many members, and periodically no decorum. Democrats accused Republicans of leading a witch hunt and short-circuiting the debate. Republicans taunted Democrats for not following the course laid down in Watergate.

Distractions abounded. The vote occurred less than a month before the election, as members scurried simultaneously to finish work on must-pass spending bills and head home to campaign.

The parties' sharply divergent views on how to proceed raise the stakes for November. Analysts will undoubtedly read the results as a referendum on how Congress ought to handle Clinton, regardless of the impact of other issues.

The partisan vote belied doubts on both sides of the aisle.

Democrats, whose allegiance to Clinton was always tenuous, have little affinity left for him. For a month now, many Democrats have eagerly blasted Republicans for the way in which they have conducted the investigation while studiously avoiding defending the president. Democrats who were undecided how to vote on an inquiry made clear that they were relying more on their instincts and feedback from their constituents than on any pleas from the White House.

And while Republicans uniformly supported an open-ended inquiry, several said they were unsure if what they now know of Clinton's misdeeds rose to the level of impeachment.

Both sides will doubtless be closely watching any shifts in public opinion. A CNN/USA Today/Gallup Poll released Oct. 7 showed that only 32 percent of those surveyed want Clinton impeached, while 65 percent do not.

Perhaps the inquiry will create a historical precedent of its own, for having started down the path to impeachment but turning aside to invent a reprimand short of removal from office.

Clinton himself was tight-lipped about his thoughts on what might lie ahead. "I hope that we can now move forward with this process in a way that is fair, that is constitutional and that is timely," he said. "Beyond that, I have nothing to say. It is not in my hands, it is in the hands of Congress and the people of this country — ultimately in the hands of God."

Alternative Rejected

The dynamics of the House vote were doubtlessly affected by the Judiciary Committee's action three days before. The panel divided along party lines after Democrats honed an alternative that let them go on record supporting an inquiry that was limited in scope and time.

As the vote neared, both Bill and Hillary Clinton spoke to wavering Democrats to minimize defections.

Several Democrats said that Clinton had frittered away whatever personal support he ever had by misleading the country for seven months about his affair. "People are going to vote their district, they're going to vote their conscience," said John P. Murtha, D-Pa., adding that Clinton's personal wishes were not part of the equation.

But neither were Democrats poised to throw Clinton overboard, as it seemed they might after the Starr report arrived Sept. 9. Many members said their constituents' anger had diminished since a videotape of his Aug. 17 testimony before a grand jury was broadcast Sept. 21.

Republicans tried to mitigate Democratic opposition by modeling rules on the Watergate inquiry. Democrats countered that there was little comparison between the two cases, either in how the evidence has emerged or in the nature of the president's mistakes.

James P. Moran, D-Va., an ideological ally of Clinton who has been unstinting in his criticism of the president's conduct in the Monica Lewinsky affair and who voted for H Res 851, fears that Democrats may be tying themselves too closely to Clinton. A partisan split and a November election focused on the president's fate was not in the long-term interest of the party, he said.

The morning began with good cheer as members posed in the chambers for a group photograph. But Democrats quickly expressed their displeasure that Republicans agreed to set aside only two hours to debate a matter of such import, though the time actually stretched well beyond that.

Republicans noted that 1974's debate on a resolution authorizing an inquiry of Richard M. Nixon was given only one hour of debate. But the vote in favor of the resolution that year was 410-4; this was obviously more contentious. *(1974 Almanac, p. 867)*

Conspicuous in his absence from the Oct. 8 debate was Speaker Newt Gingrich, R-Ga., who presided over it but offered no comment of his own. The White House has sought to tarnish the impeachment process by linking it to the unpopular Speaker.

The tepid aura surrounding the proceedings was underscored by the many empty seats in the chambers, especially on the Democratic side, until members were summoned to the floor shortly before the vote. At one point early in debate, David R. Obey, D-Wis., noted the importance of the moment and urged leaders of both parties to tell members to "get their tails here."

Judiciary Committee Chairman Henry J. Hyde, R-Ill., said the issue was simple: "Shall we look further or shall we look away?" He pledged "the fairest and most expeditious search for the truth that I can muster."

Democrats were skeptical.

Minority Whip David E. Bonior of Michigan said GOP leaders were determined to continue the investigation "not for the good of the country, but for their own partisan advantage."

Although Democrats condemned Clinton's actions, many said a lesser punishment than impeachment would fit his misdeeds. "Reprimand the president, condemn him, but let's move on," said Maxine Waters, D-Calif.

But Ileana Ros-Lehtinen, R-Fla., said the accusations against Clinton should not be so easily dismissed. "If we say that lying about sex in court is acceptable or even expected, then we have made our sexual harassment laws nothing more than a false promise — a fraud upon our society, upon our legal system and upon women," she said.

Among the Democrats voting for the GOP resolution was Paul McHale of Pennsylvania, who has also called for Clinton's resignation.

"Having deliberately provided false testimony under oath, the president, in my judgment, forfeited his right to office," McHale said. "His actions were not 'inappropriate'; they were predatory, reckless, breathtakingly arrogant for a man already a defendant in a sexual harassment suit."

Several other Democrats ominously warned the GOP of a backlash. "As you judge the president of the United States, the voters will be judging you on November the 3rd," said Charles B. Rangel, D-N.Y.

Hyde said Republicans were undeterred. "This is not about sexual misconduct any more than Watergate was about a third-rate burglary," he said. "If some people can lie under oath and others can't, let's find out."

Of the 31 Democrats who voted for the resolution, 24 are members either of the conservative "Blue Dog" coalition or moderate New Democrat coali-

Executive Branch

House Launches Inquiry

Text of H Res 581, adopted 258-176 by the House on Oct. 8.

Resolved, That the Committee on the Judiciary, acting as a whole or by any subcommittee thereof appointed by the chairman for the purposes hereof and in accordance with the rules of the committee, is authorized and directed to investigate fully and completely whether sufficient grounds exist for the House of Representatives to exercise its constitutional power to impeach William Jefferson Clinton, President of the United States of America. The committee shall report to the House of Representatives such resolutions, articles of impeachment, or other recommendations as it deems proper.

Sec. 2. (a) For the purpose of making such investigation, the committee is authorized to require —

(1) by subpoena or otherwise

(A) the attendance and testimony of any person (including at a taking of a deposition by counsel for the committee); and

(B) the production of such things; and

(2) by interrogatory, the furnishing of such information; as it deems necessary to such investigation.

(b) Such authority of the committee may be exercised

(1) by the chairman and the ranking minority member acting jointly, or, if either declines to act, by the other acting alone, except that in the event either so declines, either shall have the right to refer to the committee for decision the question whether such authority shall be so exercised and the committee shall be convened promptly to render that decision; or

(2) by the committee acting as a whole or by subcommittee. Subpoenas and interrogatories so authorized may be issued over the signature of the chairman, or ranking minority member, or any member designated by either of them, and may be served by any person designated by the chairman, or ranking minority member, or any member designated by either of them. The chairman, or ranking minority member, or any member designated by either of them (or, with respect to any deposition, answer to interrogatory, or affidavit, any person authorized by law to administer oaths) may administer oaths to any witness. For the purposes of this section, "things" includes, without limitation, books, records, correspondence, logs, journals, memorandums, papers, documents, writings, drawings, graphs, charts, photographs, reproductions, recordings, tapes, transcripts, printouts, data compilations from which information can be obtained (translated if necessary, through detection devices into reasonably usable form), tangible objects, and other things of any kind.

---

tion. A few others, including Leonard L. Boswell of Iowa and Lane Evans of Illinois, face particularly tough re-election campaigns.

All but 10 Democrats — and Jay Dickey, R-Ark. — also voted for the Democratic alternative, which enabled them to go on record favoring a more limited inquiry. Their proposal would have directed the Judiciary Committee to conduct an inquiry only after first determining whether the allegations presented by Starr, if true, constituted grounds for impeachment. If the allegations did not meet this standard, then the panel could consider other sanctions. The committee would have had to conclude in time for the House to consider its recommendations by Dec. 31.

Gene Taylor, D-Miss., who has also called on Clinton to resign, said relatively few Democrats joined him in the final vote because the Democrats found "a more viable alternative than was available just a few days ago."

Ellen O. Tauscher, D-Calif., said she voted for the resolution because she wanted the issue "off the table" while campaigning for re-election in her swing district.

Success Depends on Unity

Afterward, Hyde expressed disappointment that more Democrats did not vote for the resolution, though he expressed confidence that the panel's subsequent actions would be perceived as fair. "I think we'll see a better chance for nonpartisanship to rear its lovely head now that this is behind us," he said.

The ultimate success of his effort probably depends on it. "In the end, if there's going to be impeachment articles, it has to be bipartisan," said Ray LaHood, R-Ill., expressing confidence in Hyde. "With the absence of that, it's going to continue to look political."

Mark Souder, R-Ind., also believes that the inquiry must extend beyond the Lewinsky affair. "The general public views this as all about sex," he said. "Unless the investigation broadens beyond that, it's doubtful it will even come in front of the House, and it will never come before the Senate."

Some scholars are already wondering if the partisan atmosphere will diminish Congress's public standing, much as its statesmanlike efforts at dealing with Nixon improved Congress' standing 24 years ago.

"Public unhappiness with the whole thing is going to be so intense that no one is going to be impeached for a long time," predicted Gary C. Jacobsen, a political science professor at the University of California at San Diego.

The Republicans' task is made more difficult because of the relative lack of moderates in the House. That situation may be exacerbated next year, because moderate Democrats are among those most at risk of losing their seats.

"That makes it doubly difficult for a majority party to pursue an impeachment route," said Sarah Binder, a fellow at the Brookings Institution. "There is no center. That has to be crafted. And it's really hard to see where Republicans get it."

History may be unkind to both Clinton and Congress, said Ross K. Baker, a

Clinton Impeachment

political science professor at Rutgers University. He said for Clinton to be able to proclaim "I survived," as did Talleyrand after the French Revolution, is "not the legacy he was looking toward. Mere fortitude is not enough to get ranked among the greats."

But neither has Baker been impressed by Congress' deliberations. He said lawmakers have talked a lot about the solemnity of the occasion in "hushed and reverential terms. But it's largely to send a message that these are serious lawmakers embarking on a momentous deliberation. I just don't see that. I think it's a lot of maneuvering and partisan swordplay."

Voter Disapproval Moves Republicans To Expedite Inquiry

NOVEMBER 7 — By announcing plans for an impeachment inquiry consisting of a list of questions for President Clinton and just one witness — Independent Counsel Kenneth W. Starr — Judiciary Committee Chairman Henry J. Hyde of Illinois is attempting to provide something his Republican colleagues have lacked all year: a strategy.

To some viewers, the approach resembled a hastily organized retreat. Others said it seemed like an attempt to press forward with an impeachment resolution without adequately reviewing all the evidence. But it clearly reflects a post-election calculus that places great emphasis on dealing with impeachment quickly.

In the wake of an election in which voters clearly rejected the Republican focus on impeachment, the party now has to find a way out of the hole it has dug for itself. How far it can or should take the impeachment process has suddenly taken on new importance, even as it struggles with who should lead the party in the House.

It now appears considerably less likely that Republicans could muster a majority for impeachment in the House. Their showing on Election Day cost them five seats and considerable sway over moderates who have long questioned the wisdom of impeachment.

"Certainly there are going to be those members that might have been somewhat squishy in the first place and will use the election results as an excuse for not doing anything," said House Judiciary Committee member Bob Barr, R-Ga., the most vociferous proponent of impeachment.

Barr and a few ideologues remain unmoved, but most Republicans have concluded that their focus on impeachment, including an advertising campaign concentrating on the issue just before the election, hurt them badly because it overshadowed any other messages they had for voters.

This point was made by Hyde and by National Republican Senatorial Committee Chairman Mitch McConnell of Kentucky, among others. Rep. Steve Largent of Oklahoma left the strong impression that the GOP's lack of an agenda was a major reason he decided to challenge Rep. Dick Armey of Texas for the post of majority leader.

"I would tell you that I think one of the mandates for the leadership and for the 106th Congress is that we put together an agenda about what we're going to do for the American people," Largent said Nov. 6 in response to a question about the party's focus on impeachment before the election.

Still, Hyde insists that shutting down the process is not an option. Even in the face of a difficult election for Republicans, they have a duty to their conscience and to the Constitution to examine Starr's evidence, he said.

"I don't feel a groundswell of momentum behind us," he said in an Election Day interview. "But we still have a job to do, and we are going to do it."

Most Republican members of the committee, Hyde included, represent constituents who do not share the national inclination to drop the matter. They are not about to shut down the inquiry without giving Starr's charges a thorough evaluation.

"There aren't enough members who want to stop it," Hyde said. "I don't think there is a possibility of just dropping it."

Rep. Charles T. Canady, R-Fla., is one of the many conservatives still insistent that there be a vote, at least in committee, on whether to impeach Clinton. Canady argues that the committee needs a resolution of impeachment as a vehicle to handle the inquiry.

"We've got to have a way to bring the process to a conclusion, or move it forward," said Canady. "I think it would be wrong for us to simply cease doing things."

Reasserting Control

Republicans have spent much of the year reacting to events beyond their control — the unfolding in January of the presidential scandal involving former White House intern Monica Lewinsky, the legal maneuverings throughout the spring and summer, and the Sept. 9 arrival of Starr's report suggesting 11 possible grounds for impeachment.

Hyde's plan is an attempt to reassert some sense of control. One side effect is that it will force Democrats to leave their spectator position and make some tough decisions.

For example, it forces the White House to formulate a strategy and decide how cooperative to be with Hyde.

In addition to announcing an appearance by Starr on Nov. 19, Hyde on Nov. 5 sent a letter to the White House asking lawyers to agree to verify or deny 81 assertions made in Starr's report to Congress, including whether Clinton made false and misleading statements under oath. The White House was noncommittal in its response.

Committee Democrats, for their part, will have to decide whether to agree to a witness list limited to Starr. They want the inquiry to be concluded quickly. But if they sense that highly conservative Republicans on the committee will still press for a vote to impeach, they might want to hear from people other than Starr. Democrats believe Starr has been on a mission to bring down Clinton since not long after he was appointed independent counsel in 1994.

"We might want to have a witness or two," said Rep. Barney Frank of Massachusetts, the committee's second ranking Democrat. "But the general approach is right. We want to get this over with quickly."

If the White House balks at responding to questions, or if the Democrats balk at a short witness list, Hyde will be able to accuse Democrats of stringing out the impeachment inquiry.

A curtailed witness list may constitute a strategy, but it is not necessarily an exit strategy. At a news conference Nov. 5, Hyde for the first time entertained discussion of censuring Clinton. But in the same breath, he suggested pressing on with an impeachment.

To Hyde, the decision of whether to censure Clinton is best left to senators, and only if their House colleagues have first voted to impeach.

"If the bill of impeachment were to pass . . . then I think serious discussions of the nature you're suggesting might take place with the Senate," Hyde said. "They might want us at the table, I don't know. But I think it's right now premature."

The fact that Hyde is even now talking about impeachment is troubling to many Democrats. Frank argues that talk of impeachment is driven by the Republican need to play to their conservative core voters, many of whom would still like to see Clinton removed from office. Frank does not foresee the whole House voting to impeach Clinton, but he could envision the committee doing so as a sop to conservatives.

Many legal scholars also question Hyde's notion that an impeachment is a prerequisite to censure negotiations, particularly if impeachment is viewed as a merely preliminary move designed to open debate.

"I'm a little concerned that what it suggests is that the House's role is not very important," said Thomas Sargentich, a law professor at American University. "To the contrary, impeachment is a very grave threshold decision."

Legal scholars also question the notion that the House cannot initiate a censure or other form of rebuke. The idea is predicated on the notion that since the Senate is the only body that can strip the president of his office, it might be the only body that can devise a lesser punishment.

But Sargentich and others question this premise. Censure and rebuke are merely statements of congressional opinion. They do not require any action by the president. Their only effect comes from whatever moral authority they wield.

While censure and rebuke in this case may deal with the weighty topic of the indiscretion of the president, they are no different in substance from the many non-binding sense of the Congress resolutions that lawmakers routinely pass.

The House, for instance, recently passed a resolution praising St. Louis Cardinals home run king Mark McGwire. It is hard to imagine, legal experts say, that it would be constitutional for the House to praise a man for swatting baseballs over the fence but not to rebuke the president of the United States for bringing disgrace to the office.

Limiting testimony to Starr may spare the committee the soap opera that would result from full evidentiary hearings with testimony from Lewinsky and others.

Shifting the Focus

But testimony from the independent counsel is not without its potential flash points. Initially, Hyde had been reluctant to call Starr because he thought Democrats might try to shift the focus from Clinton's indiscretions and fabrications to Starr's methods and tactics.

In fact, Democrats are still likely to question Starr on how the Lewinsky case came to his attention, what contact he had with Clinton's political foes, and what evidence he used to persuade Attorney General Janet Reno to expand his jurisdiction to include Lewinsky.

They are also likely to ask about the pressure he brought to bear on Lewinsky, who was confronted in a Virginia hotel by Starr's agents and discouraged from talking to her attorney. Lewinsky testified that she was threatened with 27 years' imprisonment if she did not agree to secretly record conversations of others. She was told that her mother, Marcia Lewis, would be prosecuted if she did not testify. Her mother was forced to testify against her before a grand jury.

If they do not feel satisfied with the answers they get from Starr, Democrats may insist on calling Lewinsky herself. Hyde said the Democrats can call anyone they want but that he does not see the wisdom of calling Lewinsky to go over all the sordid details she testified to before Starr's grand jury.

In addition to their attempt to portray Starr in a bad light, Democrats are considering insisting on other witnesses on the grounds that it is not fair to conduct an impeachment inquiry against the president of the United States and hear only from his worst enemy.

Republicans, for their part, will try to use Starr to draw out damaging information about Clinton that he unearthed in his investigation but did not include in his report. These include the Whitewater land deals that formed the basis of Starr's appointment as independent counsel. They also include the "Travelgate" and "Filegate" operations at the White House, and allegations made by Kathleen Willey, a former White House aide who accused Clinton of groping her.

Many Republicans think Starr may even file a second report. In his initial report, and in correspondence with Hyde and ranking Democrat John Conyers Jr. of Michigan, Starr has said he is keeping his inquiry very active and would not rule out a further submission.

Hyde sees an even chance of another referral. He predicates this forecast on the fact that Starr continues to leave the committee hanging.

"I'm guessing 50-50," Hyde said. "He will not rule out that something is coming. He knows that we would like to know because we have a schedule we would like to meet, and our lives are made more complicated by piecemeal referrals."

In addition to the single-witness format, the 81 questions may cause some problems. The questions cover a number of topics raised throughout the Starr report, ranging from whether Clinton gave false or misleading testimony to whether he knew ahead of time that Lewinsky filed an untruthful affidavit in the Paula Jones case denying any sexual relations with Clinton. Some questions are fairly straightforward and technical in nature — such as whether he made a phone call to a certain person on a certain date — while others ask Clinton to make very damaging admissions.

The purpose, said Hyde, is to eliminate the areas that are not in dispute and concentrate on those that are. Failure of the White House to cooperate would prevent the timely completion of the inquiry, he said.

Publicly, at least, the White House is pledging cooperation. Clinton said his lawyers would "respond at the appropriate time, in the appropriate way."

But it is probably too much for Hyde to think that he is going to get straightforward, true-or-false answers.

He is more likely to get answers similar to those in Clinton's testimony in August before Starr's grand jury, in which he answered simple questions with nuanced, often hair-splitting responses.

Though the election results place Clinton in a much stronger position, he still cannot be perceived as uncooperative. He has so far done well by conveying a tone of contrition. A strident, uncooperative stance would make him vulnerable to attacks, even from fellow Democrats.

But it now appears he will not have to bend over backward to accommodate Hyde.

Starr's Testimony Changes Few Minds On Judiciary Panel

NOVEMBER 21 — Even though a majority of members now seem inclined to vote against the impeachment of President Clinton, the House appears increasingly likely to bring the matter to a vote later this year.

Independent Counsel Kenneth W. Starr's Nov. 19 appearance before the House Judiciary Committee demonstrated that there is still not a consensus on the committee, and reaction from members indicates that Republicans still cannot muster a majority to actually impeach the President.

But with a new slate of witnesses proposed, a grim determination on the part of Republicans to finish and vows not to carry the issue into the new year, lawmakers seem headed toward a vote against impeachment in the waning days of the 105th Congress.

Incoming Speaker Robert L. Livingston, R-La., has said in no uncertain terms that he does not want the issue to drag into January. And Committee Chairman Henry J. Hyde, R-Ill., repeated on numerous occasions his "fervent hope" to be finished by year's end. Lacking a mandate for impeachment from the public, these self-imposed deadlines now appear to be driving the process.

Republican Charles T. Canady of Florida said he anticipated the committee would vote on articles of impeachment the week of Dec. 7, with a vote by the full House coming the following week.

Plans to conclude the hearings by year's end could be complicated by the committee's decision to call additional witnesses and by expected fights over whether the panel should demand testimony from people, such as Clinton lawyer Robert Bennett, who might claim attorney-client privilege.

If the partisan nature of the Nov. 19 hearing is any indication, the committee is poised to vote the articles out along party lines. "I don't sense any reluctance to do our duty on the Republican side," Canady said.

But among the House rank and file, there is an expectation that Clinton would survive a floor vote. That may be a suitable outcome for many in GOP ranks who view impeachment as a political loser and want to move on.

"There's no good way out. You've got to play it out. You can't pull the plug," said one GOP strategist. "If 30 Republicans vote against it so be it. That's a short-term hit. We said from the outset that members would vote their consciences."

There is little chance the articles would win majority support on the House floor, since numerous Republicans are expected to break ranks and vote with Democrats against impeachment.

"Rock solid there are 15 or 20," Republican Peter T. King of New York said the day after the hearing. He said the total number of Republicans who would vote against impeachment could be "maybe 30 or 40, maybe more."

After the marathon Starr hearing, including a two-hour statement, cross-examination by lawyers for the committee and for Clinton, and questions from committee members, few, if any, minds were changed on the committee. The nation did not appear any more reconciled to the idea of impeaching the president. And a neat and clean resolution of the impeachment issue — one that would satisfy a broad range of lawmakers — did not appear any nearer.

When Starr finished, he was greeted with a standing ovation from Republicans and seated silence from Democrats — an almost perfect snapshot of a House divided. The following day, former Watergate investigator Samuel Dash, who had lent considerable credence and bipartisan cachet to Starr's probe as ethics adviser, resigned in protest, saying Starr overstepped his role in advocating impeachment and testifying to the committee.

If Starr did not nudge the Congress any closer to removing Clinton from office, Democrats were equally unsuccessful in painting Starr as a rogue prosecutor willing to use any tactics to bring down Clinton. With few exceptions, Starr was able to fend off hostile questions about his methods from Democrats, minority counsel Abbe D. Lowell and Clinton's attorney, David E. Kendall.

The hearing provided members a glimpse of Starr. But it did not give them what they most need to make an informed decision on impeachment — direct access to people with firsthand information about the accuracy of the assertions made in Starr's Sept. 9 referral to Congress offering grounds for impeachment.

Despite his title as independent counsel, which implies a lack of advocacy, Starr is a prosecutor and not an eyewitness to the events he presented in his referral.

As Republicans and Democrats struggle with the question of where the impeachment probe should go now, both sides seem almost paralyzed by fright at the notion of calling former White House intern Monica Lewinsky and other key witnesses to testify. The witness lists proposed by both sides consist of people who are not central to Starr's case.

Republicans insist they have all the material they need from the testimony given to the grand jury. On a matter as important as impeaching the president, they are content to rely heavily on Starr. Democrats, sensing the public is on their side, do not want to risk unpredictable testimony from Lewinsky or others.

No Significant Impact

The best indication of the hearing's minimal impact was that it had no effect on the normal cycle of spin and counter-spin by the two parties. Before and after the event, as well as during breaks, members scrambled to the television cameras and rushed to put out press releases. They reacted to events before they happened. They religiously stuck to scripts they had

Executive Branch

devised before Starr set foot in the Rayburn House Office Building. Depending on one's point of view, the hearing was either a watershed or a non-event. Starr's testimony was either compelling or frightening.

There was little in the way of sympathy for Starr in the Democratic ranks or weariness of him from Republicans.

The committee's most visibly uncertain member, Lindsey Graham, R-S.C., suggested he was willing to fall back in line with fellow Republicans, at least on the one issue of whether Clinton lied during his Aug. 17 grand jury testimony. The rest — including Clinton's alleged deceits in his Jan. 17 deposition in the Paula Corbin Jones sexual harassment case — Graham said was more like Peyton Place than Watergate.

The committee's most reserved member, Democrat Howard L. Berman of California, continued to play his cards close to his vest, though he consistently voted with Democrats.

The assessment of most Republicans was that Starr had recaptured the high ground in his testimony. "Today we are finally getting back to the facts in the case," Hyde said. "Judge Starr has set forth a clear, documented, compelling case against the president."

The line from Democrats was that they were less than impressed. "What we learned today was that Starr reads well and speaks slowly," said Barney Frank, D-Mass.

Starr did put to rest questions of whether Clinton was involved in the mishandling of sensitive FBI files or the mass firings of the staff of the White House travel office. In both cases, he exonerated Clinton. Starr also conceded that he was still lacking sufficient evidence to recommend impeachment stemming from Whitewater land deals that formed the initial focus of Starr's investigation when he was appointed in 1994.

Democrats complained that if Starr had reached a conclusion on these matters, he should have informed the Congress and the public earlier.

On the Lewinsky matter, which served as the basis for his impeachment referral, Starr added no new assertions or evidence. He did provide some context and rationale for his decisions. Starr made very clear in his presentation that he believes that a president violating the law is a potentially impeachable offense, even if the transgression might not involve his official capacity and stems from private conduct, such as a sexual affair.

"The offense is the despoiling and the attacks on the judicial system," Starr said.

But perhaps the main impact of his appearance was that it allowed Starr to make his case against the president in person. Like the tapes made of Lewinsky by her friend Linda Tripp, which were released two days before the hearing, Starr's testimony provided a voice. In his case it was a slow and quiet voice, measured out in almost perfectly even cadence.

Still Fighting

The hearing leaves members of the committee precisely where they were before: disagreeing over whether the assertions made by Starr, even if all true, would constitute impeachable offenses, and fighting over the process of the unfolding inquiry.

The committee now plans to turn to additional witnesses and possibly expand its inquiry well beyond the matters in Starr's referral.

After the Starr appearance, the committee voted to subpoena depositions from two people connected with allegations made by former White House volunteer Kathleen Willey that she was groped by the president: her lawyer, Daniel Gecker, and a Maryland state Democratic official, Nathan Landow, who, according to Willey, tried to influence her testimony. Robert Bennett was also subpoenaed, as was Clinton confidant Bruce Lindsey.

The Republican witnesses are an attempt to pick up where Starr left off. The two Willey witnesses touch on an area that Starr pursued, but did not mention in his referral.

Bennett is expected to address Clinton's deposition in the Jones case. Hyde said that even though impeachment hearings are not bound by claims of attorney-client privilege, his committee would not ask Bennett directly about his conversations with Clinton.

Lindsey potentially could provide a wealth of information as Clinton's closest confidant. He testified four times before Starr's grand jury but declined to answer questions about personal conversations he had with Clinton. He based his refusal on the grounds that he was covered by attorney-client privilege. On Nov. 9, the Supreme Court let stand a lower court ruling that such a privilege did not apply in Lindsey's case as a government lawyer.

As private lawyers, Gecker and Bennett clearly could assert attorney-client privilege. Nonetheless, Hyde said he was not interested in asking them about their confidential conversations.

Farther down the road, Republicans are considering expanding their inquiry well beyond Starr's referral, probing issues related to the campaign finance practices of the 1996 Clinton-Gore re-election team. They are considering calling former Democratic fundraiser John Huang.

The questioning of witnesses in private depositions raises questions about whether the public has a right to know their testimony, since they will speak to the issue of whether the nation's chosen leader should be removed. But given the public's professed revulsion to the scandal and the ensuing inquiry, Republicans do not expect much outrage about lack of access.

Democrats have not formally proposed anybody, but are considering a witness list that focuses on Starr's tactics, not his conclusions. They would like to get two of Starr's deputies, Jackie Bennett and Robert Bittman. They are also looking at Tripp, who secretly taped her, and book agent Lucianne Goldberg, who helped bring Tripp to the attention of prosecutors.

In Tripp and Goldberg, the Democrats have chosen two of the most unsympathetic figures in the entire scandal. By bringing them forward, Democrats want to emphasize an element of the scandal that has troubled the public from the beginning — the notion of a person betraying a friend by secretly taping their discussions about intensely private matters.

In Jackie Bennett and Bittman, Democrats have witnesses they want to press, under oath, to see if either were responsible for any of the leaks of grand jury material that were commonplace as the story unfolded.

Disputes Over Witnesses

The calling of the Republican witnesses set off a firestorm of protests from Democrats, who reiterated their argument that the committee would be negligent in its duties to simply accept Starr's version of events.

This point of view has some support among Republican members, who believe the committee is obliged to conduct a full evidence-gathering process before deciding whether to impeach the highest official in the country. "I think that we should still hear from other witnesses who can clear up existing conflicts of testimony," said Asa Hutchinson, R-Ark.

Even more vexing to Democrats was Hyde's apparent interest in expanding the inquiry. The financing of the 1996 campaign has been the subject of hearings in both Houses, has been under investigation by the Justice Department and is under consideration by Attorney General Janet Reno, who may recommend that it be subject to investigation by another independent counsel.

But to date no serious allegations have been made against Clinton or Vice President Al Gore. The possibility that Hyde would use Starr's referral dealing with Lewinsky as an avenue for re-examining the campaign finance issue drew a stream of protests from Democrats. Also high on their list of gripes was Starr's last-minute addition of material regarding Willey and former Associate Attorney General Webster Hubbell. Neither of these figures was central to Starr's referral, but he sent evidence for the committee to consider in the days leading up to the hearing.

The addition of new evidence and Hyde's apparent interest in jumping into campaign finance issues were enough to outrage Rick Boucher of Virginia, one of the least excitable Democratic members of the committee.

"I would suggest this is a matter of negligence," Boucher said. "I am dismayed by such a process, and I think the public should be dismayed by it as well."

Republicans insisted that all these complaints about process were merely a diversionary tactic to take the spotlight off Clinton's transgressions.

Party-Line Votes

The hearing was punctuated by partisan outbreaks. It started with Republicans and Democrats fighting over how long Kendall would be allowed to question Starr. Kendall had asked for 90 minutes and was granted 30. Bill Delahunt, D-Mass., opened the hearing by offering a resolution expanding the time to 90 minutes.

"This is meant to be the president's sole opportunity to confront his accuser during these proceedings," said Delahunt. "I submit this is a grave disservice not only to the president, but to the integrity of these proceedings. It is a complete and unwarranted departure from the precedents of this House."

Delahunt was defeated along party lines. In the end, however, Hyde gave Kendall, as well as Lowell, an additional 30 minutes. Republican counsel David P. Schippers took an additional 15 minutes.

The two sides also sparred over whether they would discuss future witnesses in public or in a closed-door hearing. Again, Republicans, who favored shutting the doors, won on party lines.

If the hearing was full of partisanship, it offered few moments of real drama. One of them was Graham's soliloquy on the nature of impeachment. For much of his presentation, he sounded as if he was willing to dismiss everything that Starr had asserted. He started by doubting whether an impeachment could be brought given the lack of public mandate for such action.

"Without public outrage, impeachment is hard to do, and it should be hard to do," Graham said. "And the truth of the matter is, Judge Starr, we may never get public outrage on behalf of what the president did."

He then noted that, on what would be the most troubling aspects of Clinton's presidency — the FBI file scandal, the White House travel office scandal and the Whitewater land deals — Starr did not have the evidence to recommend impeachment. Graham went on to repeat his queasiness about impeaching on the basis of Clinton's testimony in the Jan. 17 deposition in the Jones case — this time on the grounds that the president's testimony was not a material fact to the case. Dismissing these issues, he concluded: "It is Peyton Place that we're left with."

But just as soon as he looked as if he were willing to let Clinton off, Graham changed directions.

"But the cover-up of Peyton Place is going to the point that I no longer can ignore it and feel good about it," he said. "Because I believe the president of the United States went into a grand jury, in front of your grand jurors, took an oath, and six and seven months after this whole affair started, after being begged by everybody in this country to come clean, lied again."

Another dramatic moment came when Robert Wexler, D-Fla., delivered a fiery speech against impeachment. Throughout the day, the Democrats had little success in breaking Starr as a witness or challenging him on the facts. But Wexler ignored the specifics of Starr's case and appealed to broader issues of constitutional government and what the nation seems to think of impeaching the president.

"The American people do not approve, Mr. Starr," he said. "They know unfairness when they see it. They know injustice when they feel it. They know hypocrisy when they smell it, they know partisan politics when they are the victims of it. In their gut, they have figured this thing out. And still, this committee does not listen."

For the entire 12 hours of testimony, Starr remained unemotional in his presentation and unflappable under cross-examination.

The testiest moments came when Starr was questioned by his longtime adversary Kendall. The two clashed repeatedly over reported news leaks and other issues related to Starr's four-year probe of Clinton's behavior.

"We had been listening month after month to, 'it's a political witch hunt,' and that was unfair," Starr said.

Earlier in the day, committee Democratic lawyer Lowell made little headway in trying to contrast Starr to Watergate special prosecutor Leon Jaworski, who filed a report to Congress in 1974 that was long on evidence and short on conclusions. In fact, the Jaworski "road map" the committee used in 1974 was little more than an index to the relevant documents he was sending up.

Starr's report, on the other hand, was a no-holds-barred indictment of Clinton's behavior. All of the facts were carefully marshaled to support Starr's conclusions. And exculpatory facts — Democrats and Clinton lawyers argued — were ignored or downplayed.

Despite this, Starr did not come across as an overly aggressive prosecutor under questioning by Lowell.

Executive Branch

But Lowell's case was greatly enhanced Nov. 20 when Starr's ethics adviser resigned. Dash, who had served on the Senate Watergate Committee, was enraged by Starr's strong advocacy, saying he believes an independent counsel should take a neutral position and not testify directly to Congress.

"I resign for a fundamental reason," Dash said. "Against my strong advice, you decided to depart from your usual professional decision-making by accepting the invitation of the House Judiciary Committee to appear . . . and serve as an aggressive advocate for the proposition that the evidence . . . demonstrates that the president committed impeachable offenses."

GOP Pushes Toward a Vote On Articles of Impeachment

NOVEMBER 28 — With the end of the year at hand, Republicans and Democrats on the House Judiciary Committee are narrowing their options for bringing the impeachment inquiry to a close. The two sides still hold widely divergent views on the best exit strategy, but individual members have begun to float various proposals.

Increasingly confident that President Clinton would survive an impeachment vote, Democrats have turned again to discussing a resolution of censure or rebuke of the president for his efforts to conceal his affair with former White House intern Monica Lewinsky. Committee Democrats Bill Delahunt of Massachusetts and Rick Boucher of Virginia both say they plan to offer such a resolution during committee consideration. Off the committee, Paul McHale, D-Pa., has circulated a resolution of "condemnation and censure."

Republicans, meanwhile, are forging ahead with their plans for an impeachment vote in December. They are focusing intently on Independent Counsel Kenneth W. Starr's assertion that Clinton lied under oath, which may be the strongest case Starr presented and the one most likely to pick up support among moderate members outside the committee. Informal head counts show an impeachment article charging Clinton with perjury is still likely to fail on the floor, but would do better than one based on obstruction of justice.

Committee aides say they expect Chairman Henry J. Hyde, R-Ill., to call for committee action the week of Dec. 7, with floor action the following week. This could be delayed by difficulties in getting members back to Washington, though no such problems have surfaced yet.

Clinton's lawyers, meanwhile, on Nov. 27 were expected to send the panel answers to 81 questions submitted Nov. 5. In a Nov. 25 letter to Clinton, Hyde had threatened to subpoena the responses. Hyde also proposed allowing the Clinton's lawyers to address the panel Dec. 8.

The committee Republicans, who are a consistently conservative and partisan group, are likely to report an impeachment article charging Clinton with perjury and are considering additional articles based on other grounds, including obstruction of justice.

Bill McCollum of Florida, the third-ranking Republican on the committee, said he would be surprised if the panel went forward with only a perjury article, unless Clinton came forward with further evidence.

But even on the committee, perjury is considered the strongest case against the president. That is evident in the fact that Hyde has scheduled a Dec. 1 hearing dealing exclusively with perjury and its consequences to the justice system if it goes unpunished. The committee plans to hear from judges, military officers and convicted perjurers.

"If Democrats on the committee acknowledge that false statements were given under oath by the president, we want to help them understand what the consequences are," said committee member George W. Gekas, R-Pa.

According to legal experts, perjury is the closest thing Republicans have to a prima facie case — one that is so strong as to compel an expedited ruling from the judge or jury. Clinton himself provided strong evidence that he lied during his Jan. 17 deposition in the Paula Corbin Jones sexual harassment civil suit by later admitting to having inappropriate contact with Lewinsky, which he had denied under oath in the deposition. The perjury count for his Aug. 17 grand jury appearance is a bit more complex, but is predicated on the argument that Clinton simply repeated the alleged perjury in the earlier deposition.

Obstruction of justice, on the other hand, presents a much more complicated picture. It requires careful examination of more of the evidence, a comparison of statements of Lewinsky, presidential secretary Betty Currie and Clinton friend Vernon E. Jordan. It may require directly asking questions of each on matters where their accounts differ.

By pushing ahead with an obstruction charge, without hearing from witnesses, Republicans could be more vulnerable to complaints that they have not sufficiently examined the evidence.

Republicans continue to work behind the scenes in an attempt to find evidence not covered in Starr's Sept. 9 referral to Congress. To that end, they took a deposition Nov. 23 from Daniel Gecker, an attorney for Kathleen Willey, a former White House volunteer who alleges Clinton groped her. The committee also intends to depose Clinton confidant Bruce Lindsey; Robert Bennett, Clinton's lawyer in the Jones suit; and Maryland developer and Democratic fundraiser Nathan Landow.

But with only days remaining before they hope to go to markup, Republicans concede they are unlikely to find any smoking guns. No decision has been made whether there will be further public hearings. But many Republicans are treating the perjury hearing as their last chance to convince a skeptical public that the president should be impeached.

Consequences of Perjury

Democrats, meanwhile, openly mock the hearing as a tutorial on perjury when the committee should be either hearing witnesses or debating whether Clinton's liberties with the truth should be considered impeachable. Most Democrats are willing to concede Clinton lied, at least during his deposition. But they argue against impeachment on the grounds that the lies were an unfortunate attempt to conceal behavior that never should have been under investigation to begin with.

"I have no idea what this is supposed to be about," Delahunt, a former prosecutor, said of the proposed perjury hearing.

While Delahunt and his colleagues plan to offer a censure motion in committee as an alternative to impeachment articles, Hyde may rule that it is not germane. In any event, it is not likely to pick up many votes from Republicans on the committee.

Delahunt and Boucher have in mind a relatively short resolution that would condemn Clinton's behavior but would not read like an article of impeachment or an indictment.

McHale, one of Clinton's fiercest Democratic critics, has circulated a lengthy and highly damning resolution of censure and condemnation that concludes that Clinton lied under oath and impaired "the due and proper administration of justice in the conduct of lawful inquiries."

Many Democrats see his decision to support a resolution as an indication that very few conservative Democrats would join with Republicans in supporting articles of impeachment. But many are also likely to balk at its tough language. Most Democrats on the committee, while willing to concede that Clinton lied under oath, are far from conceding he obstructed justice.

A Delahunt aide said his resolution would be much less specific, in an attempt to gain maximum support from both sides of the aisle.

A resolution of censure or rebuke has been cited as a possibility since shortly after Starr sent his report to Congress. But the question of whether it would be appropriate or even constitutional has been the subject of considerable debate.

Even if the House is left with a choice of adopting either a resolution condemning Clinton's actions or nothing at all, such a resolution would not pass overwhelmingly. It is likely to pick up bipartisan support but would probably be rejected by hard-core Democratic Clinton supporters, and by Republicans and Democrats who think censure would be unconstitutional or an unwise precedent to set.

Rules Committee Chairman Gerald B.H. Solomon of New York, who is retiring at the end of the year, was one of the first Republicans to openly discuss the option of censure, suggesting the week of Nov. 23 a resolution crafted in such a way that it requires a presidential signature.

The Democratic interest in a resolution of censure comes as White House officials signal that they would probably not resist some sort of rebuke from Congress. Gregory B. Craig, special counsel to the president dealing with impeachment issues, reiterated such a position Nov. 22, three days after Starr's testimony to the House Judiciary Committee.

"The president has said, and I want to repeat, that we are in favor of any serious and reasonable proposition that has the promise of bringing this to a prompt and just conclusion," Craig said on NBC's "Meet the Press."

For Democrats, a censure or rebuke is not only a way of putting the impeachment issue to rest, it is a way to avoid a scenario that would do damage to the impeachment process.

They vehemently object to the committee's accepting the judgment of Starr without trying to directly corroborate his evidence by hearing from witnesses. They do not see the purpose in deposing witnesses, such as Gecker, who are not central to any of the charges suggested by Starr.

Many Democrats express bewilderment at the entire inquiry. "The truth is that there is no process," said Delahunt. "The process is in shambles."

Article II, Section 4 of the Constitution gives the House the power to impeach. Delahunt argues the hearing schedule seems to be an attempt to fill time before an expected impeachment vote in December and make it look as if the committee is undertaking an evaluation of the facts.

"The question I have is: What constitutes a process in which the Congress legitimately meets its responsibilities under Article II?" said Delahunt. "Clearly I think we're on very dangerous ground if we simply accept a written communication of an independent counsel, who falls within the executive branch of government."

This view gets some support from constitutional scholars, many of whom argue that the House needs to do significant fact finding of its own in impeachment proceedings if it is to fulfill its responsibilities.

"It does raise some potential constitutional problems," said Michael J. Gerhardt, law professor at the College of William and Mary. "Even if you recognize that making false statements under oath is an appropriate basis to investigate him, I think you'd still want to cross-examine people such as Monica Lewinsky, Betty Currie, possibly the president and the Secret Service people."

Hyde Leads Drive To Impeachment In Growing Isolation

DECEMBER 5 — This was supposed to be Henry J. Hyde's moment. The Illinois Republican and chairman of the House Judiciary Committee has always been regarded as one of the GOP's more thoughtful and fair-minded lawmakers and was considered the right person to undertake the momentous task of an impeachment inquiry.

But as his committee prepares to vote the week of Dec. 7 on articles impeaching President Clinton, Hyde finds himself presiding over a process that is increasingly chaotic, sometimes lacking in decorum and always riven by bitter partisanship. Along the way, he has abandoned his own admonitions that an impeachment cannot go forward without support from the other side of the aisle.

Hyde is relentlessly driving his committee — or at least its 21 Republicans — toward reporting articles of impeachment. He and colleagues are as unyielding in their push to impeach as the committee Democrats are in resistance.

When the committee meets Dec. 8 to begin the final phase of its inquiry, it will hear from Clinton's defense team — a presentation that was to take only one day. On Dec. 4, however, Clinton's attorneys proposed to call panels of witnesses whose testimony "will require no more than three to four days." Attorneys Gregory B. Craig and Charles F.C. Ruff said they wanted to call witnesses to testify on constitutional standards for impeachment, standards for prosecution, and prosecutorial misconduct.

But most, if not all, members on both sides have already made up their minds.

Hyde's inquiry has been unique in the annals of American history. Never before has a committee embarked on such a serious task in such a state of

Executive Branch

isolation. The public is unsympathetic to impeachment. The House is not in session, so member input is limited. And there has been a leadership vacuum since Speaker Newt Gingrich, R-Ga., announced he will leave.

Democrats, who once complained that Hyde was being micromanaged by Gingrich, are now pleading with incoming Speaker Robert L. Livingston, R-La., to step in to halt the process.

"I guess I'm making a plea here, and that is to Mr. Livingston to step in and take control of this runaway train before we go over a cliff," Charles E. Schumer of New York said.

After the White House presentations, the committee plans to hear again from its counsels, David P. Schippers for the Republicans and Abbe D. Lowell for the Democrats. Before the White House request, it had hoped debate and votes on articles of impeachment could be concluded by Dec. 12.

Leaders have been pressing this schedule in order to bring articles of impeachment to the full House the week of Dec. 14. Any delays would make it difficult to wrap up the matter before the 105th Congress expires Jan. 3.

With the outcome in committee all but certain, members of the panel are already beginning to look ahead to the expected floor vote. Committee members, who usually toil in the obscurity of arcane copyright issues or complex tort reform, are now regulars on an endless stream of talk shows about impeachment. All but a few have taken on the task of trying to build momentum for their party's cause when the vote comes to the floor.

"If you don't vote to impeach, you will be sending a message of toleration," said Bill McCollum, R-Fla., outlining the central Republican argument. "You will be undermining the justice system."

To build up support for impeachment, Republicans are using two tactics. First, they are expected to bar members from voting on an alternative, such as censure. Second, even as they push forward on bringing impeachment articles to the floor, they are downplaying its importance.

On the latter, Hyde often compares impeachment to an indictment, which does not require a demonstration of guilt, but rather the much lower threshold of "probable cause" that a law was broken. Others, such as McCollum, argue that, since the Senate is not likely to convict, an impeachment essentially is a form of censure because it amounts to an accusation without consequences.

These positions infuriate Democrats, who say Hyde and fellow Republicans seem intent on taking the Congress and the country into an abyss.

"I think that if the House votes to impeach the president, that becomes the most divisive event in United States history since the Vietnam War," said Rick Boucher of Virginia. "I'm not confident the enormity of that consequence is being appropriately considered by the people advocating impeachment."

Jerrold Nadler, a New York Democrat, adds a political element to his party's pleas. "If the Republicans vote to impeach," he says, "the voters will kill them."

Building Momentum

The action the week of the vote will be not only an attempt to bring the issue to a conclusion in the committee and build momentum for the following week, it will be a bid to reassert some order to a process that has been plagued by starts and stops, and sudden changes in direction.

The impeachment inquiry started this fall with a resounding whimper. Hyde's first decision after the House voted Oct. 8 to open the inquiry was to lay low until after the November election.

Since then, his committee has exploded into a frenzy of activity, with sudden, and short-lived, diversions into campaign finance issues and sexual misconduct allegations leveled against Clinton by former White House volunteer Kathleen Willey. In both cases, the committee voted to subpoena witnesses but never called them.

In the campaign finance case, the committee Republicans subpoenaed Justice Department memos Dec. 1 after receiving what they said was a tip that the documents directly implicated the president in criminal activity. After being allowed limited viewing of the memos by U.S. District Judge Norma Holloway Johnson, Republicans two days later concluded their investigation into the issue. Subpoenas for FBI Director Louis J. Freeh and former Justice Department investigator Charles G. LaBella were abruptly dropped. The same was true for subpoenas approved the previous week to Clinton confidant Bruce Lindsey and Clinton lawyer Robert Bennett, who were to be deposed on the Willey matter.

The inquiry's public hearings have ranged from thoughtful — though perhaps somewhat tangential — discourses by judges and scholars, to what Democrat Robert Wexler of Florida described as "theater of the absurd."

One such performance came Dec. 1 when two convicted perjurers, former basketball coach Pam Parsons and former psychologist Barbara Battalino, were called to testify. The two were chosen because their cases involved deceptions related to sex (oral sex in Battalino's case). A somber committee considered stories of sex and efforts to hide it. At one point, when asked by McCollum to describe the exact nature of her perjury, Parsons explained that she had lied in saying that she had not been to a gay bar called "Puss 'N Boots," when in fact, she had.

With all this, the impeachment inquiry will end precisely where it started. It has uncovered no new evidence and done little to explore the charges made in Independent Counsel Kenneth W. Starr's Sept. 9 impeachment referral. Unless they are called by Clinton's team, no witnesses with firsthand information will have come to testify. None of the assertions in Starr's report were either proved true or refuted.

With less than a week before a committee vote, Clinton's lawyers and committee Democrats complained that they did not know exactly what charges would be used for the basis of an impeachment article, or articles, and which portions of Starr's evidence would be used to support the accusations.

"The problem here is that there hasn't been any fashioning of what it is we are talking about," ranking Democrat John Conyers Jr. of Michigan said on CNN on Dec. 3. "They are going to vote out some articles that we have never had any notice about."

More broadly, they complain that Clinton is being asked to prove his innocence, rather than the committee prove his guilt. They point to Hyde's repeated suggestions that Clinton and the Democrats provide exculpatory ev-

Clinton Impeachment

idence, if they have it, to counter Starr's accusations.

"This is like a kangaroo court," Conyers said. "The presumption of innocence now has turned into a presumption of guilt. Due process is nonexistent."

Hyde denies both accusations, saying the committee does not need to cross-examine witnesses for two reasons. First, he says, the House's role is accusatory, not unlike a grand jury's. A full hearing of the evidence, including testimony from witnesses, is the responsibility of the Senate, which would try the case.

Second, he says, Republicans have not felt a need to call witnesses because no one has disputed any facts in the Starr report. "We haven't called a lot of witnesses because you've pled 'nolo contendere.' "

Passion But No Surprises

Despite the broadsides from Democrats, committee Republicans are not lacking in will to report articles of impeachment.

"If you were to draw a line right now and say there is no more argument, I would feel there is enough evidence to report articles on perjury and some derivation of obstruction of justice," said committee member Ed Bryant, R-Tenn.

There are a few committee Republicans, such as Mary Bono of California, who have declined to stake out a public position, but their colleagues expect they will fall in line when the final votes come.

Nor are committee Republicans in any mood to hear of a censure resolution. Democrats Boucher and Bill Delahunt of Massachusetts have been drafting one. And Republican staff director Thomas E. Mooney and his Democratic counterpart, Julian Epstein, met Dec. 2 to discuss the subject. But most Republicans remain staunchly opposed to censure, and Hyde is leaning against even allowing it to be brought up for a vote.

"I don't think it's germane," he said. "But we won't cross that bridge until we get to it."

By stopping a censure motion, Republicans hope to put pressure on undecided members to vote for impeachment. In fact, many are echoing McCollum's idea that in this case, impeachment amounts to a form of censure because it is an accusation unlikely to result in a conviction.

"There is nothing whatsoever about passing impeachment articles that forces a trial," McCollum said.

This view is not shared by many in the Senate, including Majority Leader Trent Lott, R-Miss., who conclude that a trial is inevitable for practical and political reasons, if not constitutional ones.

The partisan divide in the committee over impeachment and censure is so deep that the committee action may provide passion, but will probably offer little in the way of surprises. There are only a few real questions to be resolved. The first is how many articles will be drafted and how they will be structured. Perjury and obstruction of justice are a virtual certainty. A third dealing with abuse of power is possible as well.

The second question is whether any Republicans will break ranks on any of the articles other than perjury. The third is whom the Clinton legal team may call as witnesses.

Operating in Isolation

Hyde is quick to concede that he faces great difficulties. His image is almost the opposite of Peter W. Rodino, the undistinguished Democratic congressman from New Jersey (1949-89) who rose to prominence and won great respect for his conduct of the Watergate impeachment process. Hyde, in contrast, came into the process with a fair amount of respect on both sides of the aisle, but now has to defend himself and his committee as he pushes forward against a popular president.

He often finds himself in angry confrontations, such as one Dec. 1 with attorney and author Alan Dershowitz, who accused him of being on a mission to bring Clinton down.

"You haven't the slightest idea of the agony that many of us go through over this question," an angry Hyde fired back.

After Democrats ridiculed the idea of calling convicted perjurers to testify about the importance of telling the truth under oath, he felt compelled to explain its purpose.

"Why are we sitting here? Well, I can give you some reasons why we're sitting here," Hyde said. "We're exploring the double standard. We're exploring whether there's one rule of law for the powerful, for the rulers, and another one for the ruled."

Hyde also insists he never wanted to have the impeachment issue all to himself. He sometimes clashed with Gingrich. And, like many other committee chairmen, he chafed at Gingrich's policy of holding power close to the Speaker's office, assigning decisions to ad hoc task forces rather than to standing committees.

But on impeachment, he insists he always understood the importance of leadership input.

"There are some decisions that are so consequential that I would prefer having leadership [input]," he said before the leadership shake-up. "I don't want to be a one-man band."

While Hyde is no longer receiving guidance from the leadership, rank-and-file Republicans on the committee are in a similarly isolated position, having little contact with their colleagues, most of whom are at home in their districts while Congress is not in session.

Within the committee, members have been working at a frenzied pace attending hearings, granting media interviews and plotting strategies. Off the committee, there is an almost palpable sense of denial about the process. Livingston has steadfastly declined to jump into the fray, other than to let it be known he would like the process finished by the time he assumes his office in January. In meetings between House and Senate leaders, the subject has barely been broached. And when House Republicans convened in mid-November to elect new leaders, they remained silent on impeachment, even in informal conversations.

"It didn't come up one time," said Wayne T. Gilchrest, R-Md. "No one mentioned the elections; no one mentioned the impeachment process."

Ultimately, the biggest problem the Judiciary Committee has had with the impeachment inquiry is the same one that others have had with the underlying scandal: It inflicts misery on whomever it touches. Clinton's image has suffered greatly. Starr, despite his best efforts, has not shaken his image as a man intent on exposing Clinton's flaws. The media, which have breathlessly covered the scandal, have sometimes received loud complaints from their readers and viewers saying they are sick of the subject.

Executive Branch

Now the Congress is getting its turn to bask in the ugly light.

The current partisan bickering in the midst of a chaotic process is a natural outgrowth of the Founding Fathers' views on impeachment, said University of Virginia law professor A.E. Dick Howard. They intentionally handed the job to the House, rather than to the judicial branch, to make it difficult to impeach without a popular mandate.

"Impeachment strikes me as a terrain that invites chaotic proceedings," he said. "Unless the public is united in the view that the presidential behavior is so overwhelming that something has to be done, you're going to have this kind of near pandemonium."

Leaders Provide Little Guidance On Procedures

DECEMBER 5 — House Republican leaders have insisted for months that they must follow a prescribed and orderly process in their impeachment inquiry against President Clinton.

But as they are belatedly discovering, the process is dangerously murky when it comes to considering articles of impeachment on the House floor. The partisan hand-to-hand combat over procedures waged so far in the Judiciary Committee could rapidly escalate into all-out war.

The political pressures are immense, and the procedural challenges are daunting. The calendar requires leaders to act quickly and call a lame-duck session if they want to finish with the issue in the 105th Congress. But until rank-and-file GOP members made clear during the week of Nov. 30 their desire to dispense with the issue, GOP leaders were reluctant to even discuss a timetable.

Republicans are tentatively planning for a floor vote during the week of Dec. 14, predicated on the House Judiciary Committee approving at least one article of impeachment.

At least initially, the leaders favor a process that is normally reserved for routine legislation. With only an hour's debate and no consideration of amendments or alternatives, this approach would hardly reflect the historic nature of the vote. Nor would it allow for a full airing of the many opinions about how Clinton should be punished.

Speaker-designate Robert L. Livingston, R-La., and other GOP leaders believe they have no choice. They are being pushed by conservatives to seek the maximum penalty against Clinton. And they contend that the Constitution gives members no option to impose a lesser penalty such as censure, which Democrats and an undetermined number of Republicans favor.

This comes at an awkward time for Republicans. Since the leadership shake-up after the Nov. 3 election, Judiciary Committee Chairman Henry J. Hyde, R-Ill., has operated with little visible guidance from GOP leaders.

With outgoing Speaker Newt Gingrich, R-Ga., no longer interested in calling the shots, nobody but Livingston is in a position to give the GOP direction. Yet Livingston has been reluctant to provide leadership on this explosive matter.

He said he only briefly discussed impeachment in a Dec. 3 meeting with Majority Whip Tom DeLay, R-Texas. Then, facing a gantlet of reporters that morning after meeting with Senate Majority Leader Trent Lott, R-Miss., Livingston repeated his mantra: "I don't have any idea what we're going to do until the Judiciary Committee reports."

As a result, he is under fire from some of the same troops who nominated him as Speaker less than a month ago, for failing to exert control.

"We need to be able to tell the American people what the end game is and have a date certain when we're going to carry it out," said Rep. Ray LaHood, R-Ill. "And it's going to take the leadership to develop that."

Democrats put it more strongly. In a Dec. 1 letter to Gingrich, Minority Leader Richard A. Gephardt, D-Mo., protested: "I fear that this investigation is in chaos due to the lack of direction."

Livingston is not the only leader reluctant to plunge headlong into the impeachment process. Senators have been even less eager to wade into the thicket. At least they already have a set of rules specifically to deal with impeachment.

Even so, Lott and Minority Leader Tom Daschle, D-S.D., have maintained a respectful distance from the entire affair, saying it is premature to comment until the House Judiciary Committee completes its work.

If the House approves one or more articles of impeachment, the Senate will convene just the second presidential impeachment trial in history. Still, the subject barely came up as members of both parties met to elect their leaders during the week of Nov. 30.

Sen. Byron L. Dorgan, D-N.D., said his colleagues are mindful that under the Constitution, nothing can happen in the Senate until the House acts.

"You have a whole series of ifs," Dorgan said. "*If* the committee approves articles of impeachment, *if* the House goes along. We have not spent a lot of time and thought on what the House might or might not do."

Who's in Charge?

Any planning on impeachment is complicated by a number of other factors. The most prominent:

- The gradual transition from Gingrich to Livingston. Gingrich has been mostly away from Washington since he announced Nov. 6 his intention to step down, although he remains Speaker until the 105th Congress expires on Jan. 3. Livingston is still struggling with his preparations to be Speaker. GOP aides and strategists believe that Gingrich ultimately will follow Livingston's lead on impeachment.

The leadership holdovers lack Livingston's stature. Majority Leader Dick Armey, R-Texas, has had little to say publicly about impeachment all year, and his standing is suspect since he faced a stiff challenge to keep his leadership position. DeLay has called for Clinton's resignation and vociferously opposed considering any punishment short of impeachment, though he otherwise seems deferential to Livingston.

- Public opposition to impeachment, manifest in the GOP's poor showing in the Nov. 3 election. Leading Republicans have long conceded that an action as dramatic and historic as impeachment ought to be carried out in a bipartisan manner. But it now seems clear that hardly any Democrats will vote for impeachment, and they can point to several polls taken in late November that show support for impeachment running below one-third.

- Uncertainty about whether even a narrowly drawn article of impeachment focusing on perjury could pass the House. At least a handful of Republicans say they would vote against impeachment, and many others are noncommittal.

• Recognition that Senate Republicans are unlikely to find the two-thirds vote necessary to remove Clinton. Doing so would require about a dozen Senate Democrats to cross party lines.

• Indecision about whether to permit votes on censure. A censure resolution might pass. As many as 20 House Republicans are reportedly considering it, and a majority of Democrats would like to join them. But GOP leaders may not give them a chance to vote for such an alternative on the floor.

The leadership vacuum has given Hyde wide latitude in handling the impeachment process so far.

"Everything I can gather from both the old and new leadership is that they're following Henry's lead," said former Rep. Robert S. Walker, R-Pa. (1977-97), now president of The Wexler Group, a lobbying and consultant firm.

Added a GOP leadership aide: "If it wasn't always true that Henry Hyde was in charge, it's definitely true now."

Livingston noted that a month ago, Democrats "were condemning Speaker Gingrich for getting too involved, and now they seem to be mad at me for not getting involved enough."

But many Republicans believe that time demands decisions. DeLay told Livingston, based on a conference call with about 40 Republicans Dec. 2, that Republicans of all ideologies want to finish with impeachment this year.

Said LaHood: "The vast majority of members want this behind us before we're sworn in on Jan. 6 so we can begin anew with the issues the American people care about. I don't happen to believe this is one of them."

The effort is complicated by support for censure. Ken Johnson, communications director for W.J. "Billy" Tauzin, R-La., said some Republicans want to at least consider it, despite DeLay's opposition. "This notion you either give the president the death penalty or set him free isn't much of an option," Johnson said.

And Democrats likely will demand it. A Democratic leadership aide said his party will vigorously contest any attempt to deny a censure vote, adding that Democrats should be free to develop their own alternatives.

The Procedure

The resolution under which the House adjourned Oct. 21 allowed the Speaker to bring the chamber back for a lame-duck session "whenever, in his opinion, the public interest shall warrant it." Passing an impeachment resolution would require the approval of a simple majority of those present and voting, once a quorum of 218 is present.

The Speaker's gavel would be wielded by Gingrich or his designee.

How the House proceeds depends on whether the chamber approves a special procedural rule to guide its actions on impeachment. If so, that rule could stipulate the debate time, process for amendments and how a censure resolution would be considered.

If the House does not pass a special rule, it would follow regular parliamentary rules, under which an impeachment resolution would be brought to the floor as a privileged resolution, meaning that it would be accorded priority.

What follows are the procedures the House would use in an impeachment debate, based on interviews with congressional and outside experts.

Formal Process

If the House proceeds without special arrangements, it would act under bare-bones procedural rules.

This would enable the House to turn to an impeachment resolution immediately upon reconvening. Democrats could try to quash the effort through procedural motions — such as a motion to adjourn or a tabling motion, which would have the effect of killing the impeachment resolution. But they would be unlikely to succeed.

• **Debate time.** Only one hour would be allotted for debate. Hyde would control it. By custom, he would let John Conyers Jr. of Michigan, the committee's ranking Democrat, control a half-hour, but for debate only.

It is almost inconceivable that the House would consider taking the historic step of impeachment with only an hour of debate. The time could be extended with the consent of all members, as occurred Oct. 8, when the House directed the Judiciary Committee to consider impeachment (H Res 581).

• **Amendments.** None are likely to be allowed unless Hyde agrees. To foreclose the possibility of amendments once debate time expired, Hyde would "move the previous question," which would bring the House to a direct vote on the resolution as written. Only if such a motion failed would Democrats be able to offer amendments.

• **Voting.** Much would depend on how the Judiciary Committee wrote the impeachment resolution. Historical precedent would be for the panel to write one resolution with separate articles of impeachment, each of which could be voted on separately. If one or more articles pass, then the president is impeached and the resolution is sent to the Senate.

• **Alternatives.** Democrats would have an opportunity to offer a motion to recommit the resolution to the Judiciary Committee. Even if Democrats were able to direct the panel to report back a censure resolution, any Republican could object that it was not germane to impeachment. Democrats could fight any such ruling, but Republicans would defend it as a party vote over control.

Flexible Process

As it does with much regular legislation, the Rules Committee can send to the floor a free-standing rule setting the terms for floor debate. These special arrangements could describe everything from how much time would be allotted for each aspect of the debate to permitting certain amendments to be offered and blocking others.

The House could adopt an open rule, which would permit any germane amendment to be offered at the appropriate time and set no limits on debate. But a censure resolution would not be considered germane unless the rule specifically permitted it. In any event, it is highly unlikely that the GOP would relinquish control over a matter of such importance.

• **Debate time.** The allotted time for debate would be set by the rule. It could, for instance, set aside separate debate times for each article of impeachment.

• **Amendments.** The rule would determine whether and how the resolution could be amended.

Executive Branch

- **Alternatives.** The rule could specifically make in order a Democratic motion to send the resolution back to committee, with or without instructions. It could even allow Democrats to offer a censure resolution as a free-standing measure, or permit Republicans to do so in the event the impeachment resolution is defeated.

Censure

No matter how a censure resolution was written, members would have to make two basic decisions: Should they seek the Senate's imprimatur too? And should they try to get Clinton's signature on a censure resolution, as an admission of his wrongdoing?

If so, there is little time to waste — the Senate and Clinton would have to act before the 105th Congress expires Jan. 3, or start over in the 106th.

- **Senate and presidential action.** A censure resolution could be any one of three types. A simple resolution requires House action only. A concurrent resolution would require the Senate's approval as well. And a joint resolution would take effect only with the Senate's approval and the president's signature.

A joint resolution would exert public pressure on Clinton to sign it as an admission of misdeeds on his part. Also, a joint resolution would be the vehicle for "censure plus," provisions to impose a fine or reduction in his pension. Scholars have criticized a financial penalty as a bill of attainder, prohibited by the Constitution. But as long as the president signed it, no one else but Clinton would likely have the standing to sue.

- **Future votes.** If the House passes an impeachment resolution this month, the Senate can wait until it reconvenes in the 106th Congress to act. However, the House would have to act in the 106th to appoint managers to present the articles of impeachment to the Senate and to act as prosecution in a trial there.

This appointment of managers could be made in conjunction with the consideration of a larger rules package at the outset of the 106th Congress. It might still be subject to a separate vote. Republicans would probably portray this as a simple procedural vote and press their colleagues to toe the party line. But it could give Democrats another chance to trip up an impeachment effort.

Senate: Foregone Conclusion

Senate leaders, meanwhile, insist that no planning has taken place for a possible trial. "At the appropriate time, if need be, we will have a bipartisan effort to make sure that we know how to proceed if it's necessary," Lott said during his news conference with Livingston. "But we're not at that point."

Ironically, one of the few certainties in a Senate impeachment would be its outcome. Almost no one believes that, barring some new information showing criminal wrongdoing by the president, the Senate would be able to muster the two-thirds majority to convict Clinton and remove him from office.

Beyond that, senators and their aides are still wrestling with the most basic questions surrounding impeachment, including whether the Senate is actually required to hold a trial if the House approves one or more articles.

There is nothing in the Constitution that mandates a trial, although Senate rules explicitly call for such a proceeding to begin on 1 p.m. the day after the Senate formally is presented with articles of impeachment by the House.

But as a political matter, it is almost inconceivable that the Senate would not convene a trial if the House impeached the president. "I think that it would be very hard not to, if the House in fact acted," Lott said.

If the House votes for articles of impeachment later this month, Senate leaders would be able to delay the trial until next year in spite of the rule ordering a trial to start the day after the Senate receives articles of impeachment.

There is historical precedent in judicial cases for the Senate to try impeachments that were voted in a previous session of Congress, according to Senate parliamentarian Robert B. Dove.

Beyond that, it is unclear whether Senate leaders will modify or update the chamber's 26 rules on impeachment, which were last revised in 1986 to expedite judicial impeachments. For the most part, the rules are unchanged since the Senate acquitted Andrew Johnson in the only presidential impeachment trial 130 years ago.

While a trial might be lacking in suspense, it would be rich in historical drama. It quite literally would be the trial of the century, with Chief Justice William H. Rehnquist presiding. A contingent of House members — presumably led by Hyde — would act as prosecutors, while senators sit as a jury.

And in that role, senators would have to sit silently, not something that comes naturally to many senators. If during the trial, senators want to question a witness or offer motions, they must put them in writing and submit them to the chief justice. Rehnquist then would ask questions or make motions on behalf of the senators.

The timetable for a trial is impossible to predict. "It could last anywhere from a week to six months," said Judiciary Committee Chairman Orrin G. Hatch, R-Utah. The Senate could make time to conduct other legislative business as the trial proceeds, but in practical terms, that would be virtually impossible.

"My guess is that it would consume the Senate," Daschle said.

White House Launches Aggressive Defense

DECEMBER 12 — In court, it is not unusual for lawyers to try to wear down witnesses with lengthy examination before zeroing in on the toughest questions. In mounting its defense of President Clinton against a possible impeachment, White House lawyers turned this process on its head. It was the witnesses — 13 in all, plus two Clinton lawyers — who sought to wear down the president's accusers.

The president's defenders came to the House Judiciary Committee in waves, five panels in all, spread over two days. They included experts on the Constitution and prosecutorial standards, as well as the facts of the case against Clinton.

The defense counterattacked on multiple fronts. The constitutional experts argued that impeachment was out of proportion to allegations arising out of Clinton's sex life and would create national turmoil. A second set of experts dissected the allegations, attempting to poke holes in the case, show contradictions in the facts and provide alternative explanations for the president's behavior.

The arguments were sometimes provocative — such as that made by

Clinton Impeachment

Yale law Professor Bruce Ackerman that a lame-duck House vote for impeachment could create a constitutional morass — and sometimes highly technical.

The defense presented undecided House members — and likely would present senators — with a dilemma over how to frame the issues. Some may jump straight into the facts. For others, it will be a question of whether the alleged offenses, even if all true, warrant impeachment. Those in the latter category will have to balance the competing interests of the rule of law with the rights of the American people to choose their leaders.

For those most interested in the facts, the case is first and foremost about Clinton's alleged perjury — an attempt to conceal an affair with former White House intern Monica Lewinsky. Politically and legally, perjury is the linchpin of the case. The two articles of impeachment dealing with the subject — one pertaining to Clinton's Jan. 17 deposition in the Paula Corbin Jones sexual harassment suit and another in connection with his Aug. 17 grand jury testimony — are the most likely to pass the House.

Independent Counsel Kenneth W. Starr's investigation of the Lewinsky affair began, and ended, with these two episodes. He took on the case when he heard of evidence that would contradict Clinton's testimony in the Jones deposition. Starr ended his involvement, and sent an 11-count impeachment referral to the House, shortly after Clinton testified to Starr's grand jury on Aug. 17.

Anticipating the Charges

Tellingly, it was perjury that White House Counsel Charles F.C. Ruff turned to first in his presentation Dec. 9 to the Judiciary Committee.

Ruff's defense was not based on the four articles of impeachment drafted by the committee; those articles provided few specifics about which statements were perjurious and they were not released until the closing minutes of his testimony.

Rather, he based his arguments on the charges Starr suggested in his Sept. 9 referral to Congress. In that document, Starr focused on three instances in which he believed Clinton lied during his grand jury testimony:

- Clinton said his relationship with Lewinsky did not begin until early 1996, although she said it began in late 1995.
- Clinton stated that he believed — when he had given his testimony during the Jones sexual harassment deposition on Jan. 17 — that he had not perjured himself because oral sex performed on him was not covered by the definitions of sexual relations he was provided. This argument, Starr asserted, is implausible.
- Clinton engaged in another act of perjury before Starr's grand jury in stating that he did not think he had previously perjured himself. Starr argued that the evidence suggests that Clinton engaged in "sexual relations," even accepting his interpretation of the tortured definition worked out between the lawyers and the judge in the deposition. Oral sex performed on him may not have been covered under that definition, Starr asserted, but his reciprocation surely was. And Lewinsky testified that on multiple occasions, Clinton reciprocated.

On the first of these charges, Ruff argued it would be preposterous to impeach the president for admitting an affair, but getting its dates wrong.

On the second, Ruff said Starr did not provide sufficient reason why Clinton's testimony should be deemed non-credible.

The third count appeared to be the most difficult to rebut, evidenced by the fact that several Democrats on the committee had concluded they believe Lewinsky's version of events.

Ruff's approach was to ask members to step back and assess the overall significance of the charge. He suggested that committee members assume Lewinsky's testimony was true. Then, he said, lawmakers should ask the question: "Am I prepared to impeach the president because, after having admitted having engaged in egregiously wrongful conduct, he falsely described the particulars of that conduct?"

"The answer," he concluded, "must be no."

Republicans were in no mood to give Ruff much slack. As far as they were concerned, Lewinsky's detailed testimony about the sexual acts Clinton performed on her showed he had committed perjury.

"Monica Lewinsky described at least two things on several occasions the president did with her which would meet that definition [of sexual relations]," said Bill McCollum, R-Fla. "She's corroborated by having talked to seven different people — family members and friends — on several different occasions, at contemporaneous times to engaging in these relationships with the president, having told them precisely what she later told the grand jury."

From the grand jury perjury charges, Ruff looked back to the original charges that Clinton committed perjury in the Jones deposition in January. The question here was whether Clinton had been engaged in sexual relations based on the complex definitions provided by Jones' lawyers. Clinton denied that he had.

Ruff said, in response to a question from F. James Sensenbrenner Jr., R-Wis., that a person today might believe that Clinton lied. But Clinton thought — and thinks to this day — that he had done all he could to thwart the questions of Jones' lawyers without actually lying.

"I have no doubt that he walked up to a line that he thought he understood. Reasonable people — and you, maybe, have reached this conclusion — could determine that he crossed over that line and that what for him was truthful but misleading or non-responsive and misleading or evasive was, in fact, false," Ruff said. "But in his mind — and that's the heart and soul of perjury — he thought and he believed that what he was doing was being evasive but truthful."

This account went largely unchallenged by Republicans — perhaps because it is difficult to argue over what Clinton thought he was doing.

Other Charges

Ruff also addressed the obstruction of justice and witness-tampering charges made by Starr. On these issues, Starr's principal assertions were that Clinton:

- Conspired to conceal gifts he gave Lewinsky in an effort to thwart discovery of their relationship.
- Conspired to win Lewinsky's silence by helping her find a job.
- Encouraged Lewinsky to file a false affidavit and reached a tacit understanding with her that they would both lie if questioned in the Jones

Executive Branch

deposition about the nature of their relationship.
● Tried to coach secretary Betty Currie on her possible testimony in the Jones deposition.

On all of these fronts, Ruff said there were alternate interpretations to those presented by Starr. Here, too, he did not receive a lot of challenging questions from Republican members.

Ruff pointed out that on the very day that Clinton sought to have his gifts to Lewinsky retrieved, he gave her more. "Very strange conduct for a bunch of conspirators," Ruff said.

On the question of a job, he noted that Lewinsky testified that her job search began months before she was called to testify in the Jones case — a fact brought out under questioning by an alert grand juror, rather than by Starr's prosecutors. Ruff's fundamental point here is that Clinton had reasons independent of the Jones deposition to find Lewinsky a job. There is nothing illegal about trying to get someone to stay quiet about an embarrassing affair.

Ruff also noted that if Clinton really meant to obstruct justice by giving her a job to silence her, he could have easily found her a job at the White House. (At that time, she was working at the Pentagon.) Furthermore, he said Clinton was barely involved in efforts to find her a job in New York. That effort was led by Clinton friend Vernon Jordan.

No Republicans disputed the chronology Ruff presented. But Elton Gallegly of California challenged the suggestion that the president had no interest in the job search. He noted that Jordan called the White House after he had obtained Lewinsky a job offer and left the message: "Mission accomplished."

On the issue of Lewinsky's affidavit, Ruff referred to a statement from Lewinsky buried in Starr's referral: "There was no agreement to sign the affidavit in return for a job."

In his statement, Ruff did not address the charge that Clinton coached Betty Currie on her testimony. But Ruff did take up the issue in response to a question from McCollum. McCollum argued that Clinton had asked a number of leading questions about what Currie had seen, and what she knew of Clinton's relationship with Lewinsky strongly suggested he was tampering with potential testimony she might give.

"Betty Currie was not a witness," replied Ruff. "She was not on the witness list. The discovery process was closing down in Jones. Betty Currie had been known to the Jones lawyers for months. They could have put her on the list if they'd wanted to. They didn't. She was not on it."

Winnable in Court?

In addition to Ruff's testimony, a panel of former prosecutors was called in to give their views on whether Starr's referral, if it were to be tried in a court of law, would be winnable or even worth pursuing.

Impeachment is distinct from a criminal indictment and trial. But since there are so few impeachment precedents, and so many trials, lawmakers have traditionally used legal standards as a guideline in impeachments.

The prosecutors argued that if the case applied to an ordinary citizen, rather than the president, no responsible prosecutor would bother with it.

The argument was two-fold. First, panel members argued that no prosecutor would have time for such a trivial crime as lying about a consensual affair when there are more serious crimes to pursue.

This point was made by former prosecutor and former Massachusetts Republican Gov. William F. Weld, who said perjury is generally prosecuted as a way of getting at more serious underlying crimes. He cited a perjury case he had brought against a suspected arsonist. The perjury had to do with the defendant's whereabouts after a portion of downtown Lynn, Mass., was set ablaze. He used perjury as a "pass-through" to rattle the cage of a serious criminal.

In the absence of a serious underlying crime, neither he nor other federal prosecutors he oversaw as assistant attorney general under President Ronald Reagan would pursue a perjury charge, Weld said.

"It was also not the policy to seek an indictment based solely on evidence that a prospective defendant had falsely denied committing unlawful adultery or fornication," he said.

The second argument made by many of the prosecutors was that the facts were so murky that obtaining a conviction would be very difficult.

"Suffice it to say that, in my opinion, none [of the charges] is of the nature which a responsible federal prosecutor would present to a grand jury for indictment," said Thomas P. Sullivan, former U.S. Attorney for the Northern District of Illinois.

In addition to the largely factual presentations by the prosecutors and Ruff, a series of three panels of lawyers, academics and former members of Congress was called to attack the constitutionality of an impeachment.

The panelists included three former members who were on the House Judiciary Committee that voted to impeach President Richard M. Nixon in 1974 — Douglas Wayne Owens, D-Utah (1973-75; 1987-93), Elizabeth Holtzman, D-N.Y. (1973-81), and Robert Drinan, D-Mass. (1971-81). They also included a number of legal scholars, Watergate prosecutors and high-ranking government officials.

Several panelists cited William Pitt Fessenden, R-Maine, who in 1868 cast the crucial vote not to remove President Andrew Johnson from office. Impeachment, Fessenden said, is "to be exercised with extreme caution in extreme cases."

Most panelists argued that impeachment is a mechanism the people have to remove a president who is undermining their democratic form of government, rather than a judicial remedy to punish someone for wrongdoing.

"Impeachment," said former Attorney General Nicholas Katzenbach, "is a political process, a political remedy, to preserve confidence in that political process, not to punish a perpetrator."

Republicans, by and large, regarded this information as interesting academic discourse, but of little help to their inquiry. The Judiciary Constitution Subcommittee had already held one hearing on the constitutional standards of impeachment. They had little use for a second presentation, made entirely by experts opposed to impeachment.

"There's nothing new here — nothing new at all," said Bob Inglis, R-S.C.

Questions of Proportionality

A corollary of the argument that impeachment is too extreme a punishment is that it would set off a tumultuous trial in the Senate. Members of several panels argued that the government would be tied up for three months to a year. The president and the Senate, immersed in this trial, would be unable to work on any significant legislation. The president's jeopardy would hinder his foreign policy initiatives. And work at the Supreme Court would be greatly hampered by the fact that Supreme Court Chief Justice William H. Rehnquist would be called upon to preside at the trial.

The panel of former Democratic congressmen from the Judiciary Committee that voted to impeach Nixon said forcing a trial would be an even greater tragedy because the chances of attaining the two-thirds vote necessary for conviction and removal are extraordinarily remote.

Republicans countered that poor prospects in the Senate are no reason to abandon activity in the House.

"It would be in derogation of our constitutional responsibility to attempt to count noses in the Senate," said Charles T. Canady, R-Fla. "I will have to say that it's a very difficult thing to count noses in the Senate."

The entire two-day defense presentation was aimed less at committee members, most of whom seem to have made up their minds, than at other House members who are undecided.

But the plethora of witnesses underscored that the White House had come to the conclusion that it had to take the committee's role very seriously.

The previous week, the administration had toyed with the idea of presenting no defense — simply by insisting that the other side had failed to make a case because it had not called any witnesses with firsthand information about the facts.

But that strategy was abandoned when it became clear that GOP moderates would view it as an act of arrogance and a lack of contrition.

House Opens Historic Drama

DECEMBER 12 — The House gallery will be packed and a national television audience will be watching when Harris W. Fawell walks down to the well to cast the last, and perhaps the most difficult, vote of his 14-year congressional career.

The Illinois Republican went home to Naperville, Ill., when Congress adjourned in October, to retire and undergo heart surgery. He never figured he would be returning in December to cast a historic vote on impeaching a president.

After nearly 11 months of grave constitutional questions, X-rated presidential sex tales, high drama and low political farce, it has come to this: A lame-duck House is about to seize the national stage to determine the fate of Bill Clinton's presidency and its own place in history.

In the most closely watched vote since Congress authorized military action against Iraq in 1991, the House will vote during the week of Dec. 14 on whether to impeach Clinton. Passage would set the stage next year for the second Senate presidential impeachment trial in American history.

Lawmakers are struggling to come to grips with the implications of the vote. Mark Foley, R-Fla., said this was not merely the most important vote of his career. "It could be the most important thing I'll ever do," he said.

While the stakes could not be clearer, an air of political unreality hangs over the House proceedings. Almost no one believes the Senate will convict Clinton and remove him from office. Indeed, the president and key GOP leaders went ahead with an important meeting Dec. 8-9 on overhauling Social Security. There were no signs that an impeachment vote hung over Clinton's head.

Moreover, the American people have consistently demonstrated — by decisive majorities in poll after poll — that they are not ready to see the president forced from office.

Just six weeks ago, most lawmakers, Republicans and Democrats alike, were inclined to agree. The GOP's disappointing electoral showing Nov. 3 seemed to all but doom impeachment prospects.

Seldom has the conventional wisdom proven more unfounded. For conservatives, the goal of Clinton's impeachment long ago assumed all the elements of an ideological crusade. And it is the intensity that conservatives have brought to the debate — along with their perception of Clinton's arrogance and his array of misdeeds and miscalculations — that has helped make this vote too close to call.

There are some wild cards in this vote, including Fawell and 39 others who are departing Congress. It is unclear how their status as lame ducks will affect their thinking.

Even as the Judiciary Committee voted Dec. 11 to recommend impeachment, some members expressed hope that a deal could be struck at the highest levels of both parties. The goal would be to create an alternate punishment, such as censure, that would avoid a House showdown and calamitous Senate trial.

Clinton himself seemed increasingly determined to stave off a floor vote. On Dec. 11, he appeared in the White House Rose Garden to offer yet another apology for his behavior. "I never should have misled the country, the Congress, my friends or my family," the president said. "Quite simply, I gave into my shame. I have been condemned by my accusers with harsh words."

But the statement drew criticism from senior Republicans, and appeared not to change minds among the fence-sitters. Several Republicans expressed frustration that Clinton did not admit to lying or perjury.

"It's not enough to be apologetic. It's not enough to be remorseful. It's time for this president to tell the truth," said Rep. W. J. "Billy" Tauzin of Louisiana, one of the undecided Republicans.

Heavy Burden

All of this did nothing to ease the burden of Fawell and other lawmakers who prepared to return to Washington for the impeachment vote. While recuperating from his surgery, Fawell sporadically followed the Judiciary Committee's hearings on television. He is disturbed by the president's reckless behavior and dissembling, but equally troubled by the raw partisanship he observed at the hearings.

"This is a rough one," he said, although he is expected to vote for impeachment.

The political mathematics of this vote emerged slowly the week of Dec. 7. Any pretense of bipartisanship was abandoned long ago by both parties as they fought over the ground rules and then the standards for impeachment. The vast majority decided how they would vote well before the Judiciary Committee considered articles of impeachment, even if the members did

Executive Branch

not publicly declare their intentions.

The outcome will be decided by the approximately two dozen members — mostly moderate Republicans, many from the Northeast — who seemed genuinely uncertain how to vote as the floor vote loomed. And for those members, the political pressures have been particularly intense.

They are weighing wrenching questions of morality and conscience, politics and party loyalty. Many of the undecided GOP moderates weighed the risk of being defeated in the next general election if they supported impeachment against the risk of encouraging a conservative primary challenge if they did not.

"Washington is a place driven ultimately by politics, and that can never be taken out of the equation," said Mark Sanford, R-S.C., a conservative who almost certainly will vote to impeach Clinton. "But on this one, there is no free lunch."

One moderate Republican, who asked not to be identified, said he expected dire political consequences no matter how the impeachment saga finally ends.

"I've got two lousy options," he said. "Lousy option one is we don't impeach, and history records the chief law enforcement officer of the nation perjured himself and obstructed justice for months.

"Option two is we impeach knowing it's very unlikely that he will be removed from office, and we use the tool of impeachment for a case that's in some ways mundane and tawdry."

Political considerations will be placed alongside other, more personal factors, such as the desire of Brian P. Bilbray, R-Calif., to have a clear way to justify his vote to his five children.

How these individual mini-dramas are resolved could determine whether Clinton survives this formidable test. "Ultimately, while politics plays a role, it's going to be a gut check for these guys," said Marshall Wittmann, director of congressional relations at the conservative Heritage Foundation.

But Democrats and a number of Republicans were hoping for another option besides deciding whether to vote for impeachment. They wanted GOP leaders to permit a vote on a lesser penalty than impeachment — such as a sharply worded resolution condemning Clinton that Democrats have proposed.

"I feel it's wrong not to have the opportunity to vote for censure," said Michael N. Castle, R-Del., who agonized over the impending impeachment vote. "Republicans need to do this."

But it was uncertain whether a censure resolution would come to a vote on the floor. Leading conservatives, including Majority Whip Tom DeLay, R-Texas, denounced a censure as unconstitutional and meaningless. They also feared it would siphon off support for impeachment.

Even if a censure resolution were debated, GOP moderates were not unified whether to support it or what it should say. They seemed unlikely to simply embrace a resolution provided by Democratic lawmakers with Clinton's approval.

"I'm not too sure it shouldn't be our censure resolution, not what they agree to," Castle said.

Castle, for instance, wanted to include a fine against Clinton "of some great magnitude." Other Republicans wanted a more explicit admission of Clinton's wrongdoing in his affair with former White House intern Monica Lewinsky, namely lying under oath.

As the vote neared, the White House was reaching out to wavering members. A pair of undecided Republicans, Rick A. Lazio of New York and Jon D. Fox of Pennsylvania, were expected to accompany Clinton to the Middle East. The two will return to Washington with the president on Air Force One, which could give Clinton a chance to make his case.

GOP leaders, by contrast, were careful to avoid any perception that they were leaning on the rank-and-file. "I've gotten no phone calls, no comments from any members of the leadership," said Jim Kolbe of Arizona, who was still up in the air on his vote.

While undecided lawmakers confronted their individual agonies, Speaker-designate Robert L. Livingston, R-La., felt additional burdens.

Livingston's eagerness to take the House's reins in the 106th Congress is exceeded only by his desire to have the chamber dispense with impeachment before then. But he has been reluctant to exert his will on the matter. And outgoing Speaker Newt Gingrich, R-Ga., has been so determined to distance himself from the impeachment effort that he has declined to wield the gavel during the historic debate.

As a result, Livingston cannot escape the fact that the last vote of the 105th Congress will help shape how his Speakership is viewed in the 106th. Indeed, it may alter the legislative agenda and any prospects of bipartisanship for the next two years.

Inevitably, comparisons will be made to prior presidential impeachment efforts.

History has been kind to the ultimately bipartisan impeachment investigation of Richard M. Nixon that led to his 1974 resignation. But the partisan rhetoric of the Clinton impeachment effort seems more reminiscent of the 1868 impeachment and trial of Andrew Johnson, in which the politically charged process tarnished Congress' reputation as well as Johnson's.

Laying Low

Even as the Judiciary Committee's impeachment hearings commanded intense national attention, the real battle was being played out elsewhere for the hearts and minds of the undecided lawmakers.

The count was constantly in flux. Many who were considered undecided were merely undeclared. Some who were genuinely conflicted made a conscious effort to lay low. Banking Committee Chairman Jim Leach, R-Iowa, an independent sort who refused to vote for Gingrich for Speaker last year, was among those keeping mum.

While many members held off publicly declaring their position on impeachment during Judiciary Committee action, a stream of announcements were expected well before the floor vote.

Few wanted to prolong the intense scrutiny of their decision-making or to mull it over with their voting card in hand. "I have no interest in waking up that morning undecided or even unannounced," Castle said.

Republicans were being actively discouraged not to announce their positions without first consulting leaders of the Judiciary Committee. Two top Republicans on that panel, Chairman Henry J. Hyde, R-Ill., and Bill McCollum, R-Fla., circulated a letter asking colleagues to keep their options open.

"The temptation to follow public opinion and look for alternatives is

Democrats Offer Censure Resolution

Following is the text of the censure resolution proposed Dec. 9 by Democrats on the House Judiciary Committee:

It is the Sense of the Congress that:
On January 20, 1993, William Jefferson Clinton took the oath, prescribed by the Constitution of the United States, faithfully to execute the Office of President; implicit in that oath is the obligation that the President set an example of high moral standards and conduct himself in a manner that fosters respect for the truth; and William Jefferson Clinton has egregiously failed in this obligation, and through his actions has violated the trust of the American people, lessened their esteem for the office of President and dishonored the office which they have entrusted to him.

Be it resolved that:
1. The President made false statements concerning his reprehensible conduct with a subordinate;
2. The President wrongly took steps to delay discovery of the truth;
3. No person is above the law, and the President remains subject to criminal and civil penalties;
4. William Jefferson Clinton, President of the United States, by his conduct has brought upon himself and fully deserves the censure and condemnation of the American people and the Congress; and by his signature on this Joint Resolution, the President acknowledges this censure.

---

great," McCollum's letter concluded. "Please don't do so without letting the Judiciary Committee members make their case to you in the coming days."

Most of the undecided Republicans were moderates from competitive districts that Clinton carried in 1996. In the past, they have often broken with the top GOP leadership, which consists solely of Southern conservatives from safe GOP districts.

The New York delegation, whose 13 Republicans all come from districts that Clinton carried in 1996, has emerged as the hardest-fought battleground. Sen. Alfonse M. D'Amato, R-N.Y., who lost his re-election bid to Rep. Charles E. Schumer, D-N.Y., has been urging members to oppose impeachment.

Amo Houghton, R-N.Y., declared his opposition to impeachment in a Dec. 9 opinion article in The New York Times. He joined New York Republicans Peter T. King and Jack Quinn as declared opponents.

Charles B. Rangel, D-N.Y., said he had been in contact with some of the fence-sitters in the delegation. "It's very difficult for them," Rangel said. "It's becoming a litmus test for Republicans."

For their part, Democrats also faced the challenge of keeping defections to a minimum. Three Democrats were leaning strongly toward impeachment: Gene Taylor of Mississippi, Ralph M. Hall of Texas and Virgil H. Goode Jr. of Virginia.

But few, if any, were poised to join them, even among the 31 Democrats who voted on Oct. 8 for an open-ended impeachment inquiry.

Instead, House Minority Leader Richard A. Gephardt, D-Mo., signaled that Democrats would step up pressure on Livingston and DeLay to schedule a vote on censure. "What's important is that members are given a chance to vote on alternatives to impeachment," he said.

Three moderate Democrats — Tim Roemer of Indiana, Ellen O. Tauscher of California and James P. Moran of Virginia — circulated a letter to Livingston among the 31 Democrats asking for a censure vote.

But Taylor, who has emerged as Clinton's most passionate Democratic critic, brushed aside that approach: "I don't want there to be a lesser option because there really isn't a lesser option for people who perjure themselves."

How To Decide?

DeLay and other Republicans have billed impeachment as a "vote of conscience," along the lines of the vote authorizing the Persian Gulf War.

It is clear many members regard it that way. Ray LaHood, R-Ill., who was tapped by Gingrich to preside over the floor debate, said most members are deciding for themselves.

"This issue has to stand on its own," said LaHood, who was among the undecided. "It's not something that you stick your finger in the air and figure out where the wind is blowing."

It was also apparent that lawmakers consulted their constituents.

David L. Hobson, R-Ohio, has become so solicitous of the opinions of his constituents that his wife and children have temporarily refused to shop with him. With Hobson stopping to chat with people, it simply takes them too long to make it through a store.

While Hobson was sitting in his car parked outside a grocery store recently, a young woman with two small children thought she recognized him and tapped on the window.

"What do I tell my children?" she asked. Clinton "should be a role model," she said.

Other lawmakers are looking hard at how history will judge the Congress, and themselves. As retiring Rep. Bob Smith, R-Ore., watched the Judiciary Committee hearing from his office in Medford, he thought about the significance of his impending decision.

"It may be the most important vote I ever make, and it will be the last vote I will make," said Smith. "I worry if nothing is done, then in some backward way, we are supporting some actions of the president."

Several seemed to be basing their decision on whether Clinton has expressed adequate contrition for his misconduct. DeLay and other conservatives have touted impeachment as an end — a penalty in itself — rather than as the constitutionally prescribed means of moving toward a Senate trial.

'William Jefferson Clinton ... Warrants Impeachment and Trial'

Following is the text of the impeachment resolution proposed Dec. 9 by Republicans on the House Judiciary Committee:

A Resolution

Impeaching William Jefferson Clinton, President of the United States, for high crimes and misdemeanors.

Resolved, That William Jefferson Clinton, President of the United States, is impeached for high crimes and misdemeanors, and that the following articles of impeachment be exhibited to the United States Senate:

Articles of impeachment exhibited by the House of Representatives of the United States of America in the name of itself and of the people of the United States of America, against William Jefferson Clinton, President of the United States of America, in maintenance and support of its impeachment against him for high crimes and misdemeanors.

Article I

In his conduct while President of the United States, William Jefferson Clinton, in violation of his constitutional oath faithfully to execute the office of President of the United States and, to the best of his ability, preserve, protect, and defend the Constitution of the United States, and in violation of his constitutional duty to take care that the laws be faithfully executed, has willfully corrupted and manipulated the judicial process of the United States for his personal gain and exoneration, impeding the administration of justice, in that:

On August 17, 1998, William Jefferson Clinton swore to tell the truth, the whole truth, and nothing but the truth before a Federal grand jury of the United States. Contrary to that oath, William Jefferson Clinton willfully provided perjurious, false and misleading testimony to the grand jury concerning: (1) the nature and details of his relationship with a subordinate government employee; (2) prior perjurious, false and misleading testimony he gave in a Federal civil rights action brought against him; (3) prior false and misleading statements he allowed his attorney to make to a Federal judge in that civil rights action; and (4) his corrupt efforts to influence the testimony of witnesses and to impede the discovery of evidence in that civil rights action.

In doing this, William Jefferson Clinton has undermined the integrity of his office, has brought disrepute on the Presidency, has betrayed his trust as President, and has acted in a manner subversive of the rule of law and justice, to the manifest injury of the people of the United States.

Wherefore, William Jefferson Clinton, by such conduct, warrants impeachment and trial, and removal from office and disqualification to hold and enjoy any office of honor, trust or profit under the United States.

Article II

In his conduct while President of the United States, William Jefferson Clinton, in violation of his constitutional oath faithfully to execute the office of President of the United States and, to the best of his ability, preserve, protect, and defend the Constitution of the United States, and in violation of his constitutional duty to take care that the laws be faithfully executed, has willfully corrupted and manipulated the judicial process of the United States for his personal gain and exoneration, impeding the administration of justice, in that:

(1) On December 23, 1997, William Jefferson Clinton, in sworn answers to written questions asked as part of a Federal civil rights action brought against him, willfully provided perjurious, false and misleading testimony in response to questions deemed relevant by a Federal judge concerning conduct and proposed conduct with subordinate employees.

(2) On January 17, 1998, William Jefferson Clinton swore under oath to tell the truth, the whole truth, and nothing but the truth in a deposition given as part of a Federal civil rights action brought against him. Contrary to that oath, William Jefferson Clinton willfully provided perjurious, false and misleading testimony in response to questions deemed relevant by a Federal judge concerning the nature and details of his relationship with a subordinate government employee and his corrupt efforts to influence the testimony of that employee.

In all of this, William Jefferson Clinton has undermined the integrity of his office, has brought disrepute on the Presidency, has betrayed his trust as President, and has acted in a manner subversive of the rule of law and justice, to the manifest injury of the people of the United States.

Wherefore, William Jefferson Clinton, by such conduct, warrants impeachment and trial, and removal from office and disqualification to hold and enjoy any office of honor, trust or profit under the United States.

Article III

In his conduct while President of the United States, William Jefferson Clinton, in violation of his constitutional oath faithfully to execute the office of President of the United States and, to the best of his ability, preserve, protect, and defend the Constitution of the United States, and in violation of his constitutional duty to take care that the laws be faithfully executed, has prevented, obstructed, and impeded the administration of justice, and has to that end engaged personally, and through his subordinates and agents, in a course of conduct or scheme designed to delay, impede, cover up, and conceal the existence of evidence and testimony related to a Federal civil rights action brought against him in a duly instituted judicial proceeding.

The means used to implement this course of conduct or

scheme included one or more of the following acts:

(1) On or about December 17, 1997, William Jefferson Clinton corruptly encouraged a witness in a Federal civil rights action brought against him to execute a sworn affidavit in that proceeding that he knew to be perjurious, false and misleading.

(2) On or about December 17, 1997, William Jefferson Clinton corruptly encouraged a witness in a Federal civil rights action brought against him to give perjurious, false and misleading testimony if and when called to testify personally in that proceeding.

(3) On or about December 28, 1997, William Jefferson Clinton corruptly engaged in, encouraged, or supported a scheme to conceal evidence that had been subpoenaed in a Federal civil rights action brought against him.

(4) Beginning on or about December 7, 1997, and continuing through and including January 14, 1998, William Jefferson Clinton intensified and succeeded in an effort to secure job assistance to a witness in a Federal civil rights action brought against him in order to corruptly prevent the truthful testimony of that witness in that proceeding at a time when the truthful testimony of that witness would have been harmful to him.

(5) On January 17, 1998, at his deposition in a Federal civil rights action brought against him, William Jefferson Clinton corruptly allowed his attorney to make false and misleading statements to a Federal judge characterizing an affidavit, in order to prevent questioning deemed relevant by the judge. Such false and misleading statements were subsequently acknowledged by his attorney in a communication to that judge.

(6) On or about January 18 and January 20-21, 1998, William Jefferson Clinton related a false and misleading account of events relevant to a Federal civil rights action brought against him to a potential witness in that proceeding, in order to corruptly influence the testimony of that witness.

(7) On or about January 21, 23 and 26, 1998, William Jefferson Clinton made false and misleading statements to potential witnesses in a Federal grand jury proceeding in order to corruptly influence the testimony of those witnesses. The false and misleading statements made by William Jefferson Clinton were repeated by the witnesses to the grand jury, causing the grand jury to receive false and misleading information.

In all of this, William Jefferson Clinton has undermined the integrity of his office, has brought disrepute on the Presidency, has betrayed his trust as President, and has acted in a manner subversive of the rule of law and justice, to the manifest injury of the people of the United States.

Wherefore, William Jefferson Clinton, by such conduct, warrants impeachment and trial, and removal from office and disqualification to hold and enjoy any office of honor, trust or profit under the United States.

Article IV

Using the powers and influence of the office of President of the United States, William Jefferson Clinton, in violation of his constitutional oath faithfully to execute the office of President of the United States and, to the best of his ability, preserve, protect, and defend the Constitution of the United States, and in disregard of his constitutional duty to take care that the laws be faithfully executed, has repeatedly engaged in conduct that resulted in misuse and abuse of his high office, impaired the due and proper administration of justice and the conduct of lawful inquiries, and contravened the laws governing the integrity of the judicial and legislative branches and the truth-seeking purpose of coordinate investigative proceedings.

This misuse and abuse of office has included one or more of the following:

(1) As President, using the attributes of office, William Jefferson Clinton willfully made false and misleading public statements for the purpose of deceiving the people of the United States in order to continue concealing his misconduct and to escape accountability for such misconduct.

(2) As President, using the attributes of office, William Jefferson Clinton willfully made false and misleading statements to members of his Cabinet, and White House aides, so that these Federal employees would repeat such false and misleading statements publicly, thereby utilizing public resources for the purpose of deceiving the people of the United States, in order to continue concealing his misconduct and to escape accountability for such misconduct. The false and misleading statements made by William Jefferson Clinton to members of his Cabinet and White House aides were repeated by those members and aides, causing the people of the United States to receive false and misleading information from high government officials.

(3) As President, using the Office of White House Counsel, William Jefferson Clinton frivolously and corruptly asserted executive privilege, which is intended to protect from disclosure communications regarding the constitutional functions of the Executive, and which may be exercised only by the President, with respect to communications other than those regarding the constitutional functions of the Executive, for the purpose of delaying and obstructing a Federal criminal investigation and the proceedings of a Federal grand jury.

(4) As President, William Jefferson Clinton refused and failed to respond to certain written requests for admission and willfully made perjurious, false and misleading sworn statements in response to certain written requests for admission propounded to him as part of the impeachment inquiry authorized by the House of Representatives of the Congress of the United States. William Jefferson Clinton, in refusing and failing to respond and in making perjurious, false and misleading statements, assumed to himself functions and judgments necessary to the exercise of the sole power of impeachment vested by the Constitution in the House of Representatives and exhibited contempt for the inquiry.

In all of this, William Jefferson Clinton has undermined the integrity of his office, has brought disrepute on the Presidency, has betrayed his trust as President, and has acted in a manner subversive of the rule of law and justice, to the manifest injury of the people of the United States.

Wherefore, William Jefferson Clinton, by such conduct, warrants impeachment and trial, and removal from office and disqualification to hold and enjoy any office of honor, trust or profit under the United States.

Executive Branch

Playing to the Base

At first glance, the GOP's impeachment drive would appear to violate a cardinal rule of politics: If the American people oppose a high-profile issue by a 2-1 margin, it is time to back off.

And that is what the polls show on impeachment. A Dec. 8 poll by ABC News showed that 64 percent of Americans do not believe Clinton should be impeached. Only 33 percent favored impeachment.

What might be more striking is how Republicans who have been involved in the impeachment imbroglio have seen their own reputations tarnished.

For instance, a recent CNN/USA Today/Gallup poll showed that 56 percent of Americans still have a "favorable" opinion of Clinton, compared with 31 percent who view Hyde favorably.

So why are Republicans pressing forward? And will they pay a price?

Despite the national numbers, Republicans are paying closer attention to their own constituents, said independent pollster John Zogby.

Many Republicans are hearing from large and vocal groups of GOP voters who want Clinton ousted.

"Core Republicans are very intense about impeachment," Zogby said. "You have to take each district and measure the frequency and intensity of the calls for impeachment."

For many conservatives, Clinton has long been a despised figure, in the same way that Nixon was hated by liberals in the 1970s. Since Clinton admitted having an affair with Lewinsky, Republicans who identify themselves as moderates began turning against him.

While the public at large is currently opposed to impeachment, it is not a certainty that people will attach great importance to this vote in the 2000 elections. After the Gulf War, which most Democrats opposed, some in the party feared political fallout. But that never materialized.

"I think members' votes on impeachment in 1998 will have very little negative bearing on the elections two years hence," said Democratic pollster Alan Secrest. "This is an ideal time for an impeachment vote, whichever way you're going to vote."

But such predictions provide cold comfort to anti-impeachment Republicans such as King, who worries that the GOP's impeachment crusade will cost it control of the House.

The Arguments

Clinton's actions regarding his affair with Lewinsky and his attempt to conceal them will be roundly denounced on the House floor by both parties. But there will be sharp differences over the context of his actions.

Impeachment proponents will argue that Clinton clearly committed perjury, misleading the judicial system as well as the American people. This cannot be tolerated, his critics say, because the president cannot be above the law.

That the focus of the case is a private, extramarital affair, is not necessarily relevant to the merits of impeachment, advocates of impeachment say. What counts is the alleged lawbreaking that came with it.

They also argue that the president serves as a role model. Clinton's inability throughout the year to deliver a full account of his actions demonstrates to them that he does not comprehend the seriousness of his actions.

Censure is not a constitutional option, Clinton's most fervent critics say; the House's best and only recourse is to impeach him.

Opponents of impeachment also harshly condemn Clinton's behavior, but say that it does not rise to the level of impeachment — hardly comparing to the abuse of public power Nixon was responsible for in the Watergate affair.

At its heart, impeachment opponents say, the Clinton case involves conflicting stories related to an affair between two consenting adults. Clinton's attorneys and Judiciary Committee Democrats also insist that it would be hard to win a conviction if the case were presented in a court of law.

Impeachment is not tantamount to censure, Clinton's defenders say. There can be no guarantees that the Senate would quickly dispense with a trial and acquit him. A Senate trial could drag on for much of the year, even if a conviction was clearly unobtainable, needlessly tying Congress and the country in knots.

Those who oppose impeachment maintain that the process is and should be political, and as such ought not be attempted without strong support from both parties and the public.

Impact on the 106th

Almost any action the House takes on impeachment will have widespread implications for the 106th Congress.

If the House impeaches Clinton, then the Senate will prepare to try him. Convicting him and removing him from office would require 67 votes — posing the difficult challenge of holding all 55 Republicans and picking up the support of 12 Democrats.

But the impeachment process has already appeared to have a life of its own. Predicting what the Senate would do is perilous.

It is plausible that leading senators, recognizing the long odds against Clinton's conviction, would opt for a short trial and possibly mete out an alternative punishment. Some Senate Democrats have reportedly begun discussions on presenting a censure motion as a means to short-circuit a trial.

But a lengthy trial is also possible. If so, legislative activity may come to a standstill.

At the White House conference on Social Security, Republicans and Democrats agreed that an impeachment trial would probably doom efforts to shore up the nation's retirement system.

A House vote in favor of impeachment "reduces significantly" the prospects for a bipartisan deal on Social Security, said Judd Gregg, R-N.H., co-chairman of the Senate GOP task force addressing the issue.

Roemer said the House vote on impeachment may be "the only significant vote that takes place in the next two years, because we're caught like a deer in the headlights in an impeachment trial. Nothing happens."

House Accuses Clinton of Perjury, Obstruction

DECEMBER 22 — The Dec. 19 impeachment of William Jefferson Clinton culminated an era of intensely bitter partisanship in Washington and brought into sharp focus the public interest in the private lives of elected officials.

The votes occurred amid a bizarre juxtaposition of historic events, with the nation watching as television networks pre-empted regular programming.

Republicans pushed forward with impeachment as bombs rained down on Iraq and a few hours after their newly anointed leader, Speaker-in-waiting Robert L. Livingston of Louisiana, dropped a bombshell by announcing he would resign in response to a sex scandal of his own. A leaderless, lame-duck session of the 105th Congress impeached Clinton despite public opposition and with the concurrence of only a handful of Democrats.

The House approved two articles of impeachment — one on perjury, one on obstruction of justice — related to Clinton's affair with former White House intern Monica Lewinsky and his subsequent attempts to cover it up. It rejected two associated charges.

Clinton, who once claimed the mantle of a new generation of leaders, became only the second president to be impeached — and the first who had been elected to the presidency. A student of history, Clinton has indelibly stained his legacy with actions that even his most fervent supporters condemn. His fate now rests with the Senate.

Republicans crushed attempts to mete out a lesser penalty of censure. They argued that Clinton had lied under oath, and that impeachment was the only constitutional route to demonstrate that no one — not even the president — was above the law. Democrats responded that impeachment was too drastic for misdeeds emanating out of a desire to hide an extramarital affair.

Livingston provided an exclamation point to the arguments about the purity of public officials. After acknowledging his own sexual indiscretions two days earlier, he stunned colleagues by announcing that he would resign from the House rather than become its Speaker in the 106th Congress.

"Who can possibly absorb this?" asked Marge Roukema, R-N.J., who had strongly defended Livingston after he had acknowledged his affairs. "We're tortured — not only hearts, but souls."

Livingston suggested that Clinton take responsibility for his own actions and follow his example. But Clinton stood steadfast against talk of resignation. Two busloads of Democratic members joined him at a South Lawn ceremony shortly after the final vote. Standing with Vice President Al Gore and first lady Hillary Rodham Clinton, he pledged to serve "until the last hour of the last day of my term."

Public opinion, a fickle but potent ally in some of Clinton's darkest days, stood with him. An NBC News poll conducted Dec. 19 found that 72 percent of the public approved of his job performance. Only 34 percent said he should resign. Other quick polls showed that his approval ratings ticked upward after the vote.

The case now heads to the Senate and the second presidential impeachment trial in the nation's history. The first such trial, in 1868, ended one vote short of the two-thirds needed to remove Andrew Johnson.

The odds against Clinton's conviction are steep. Republicans seem unlikely to garner the necessary votes of at least 12 Democrats. Still, the outcome is unscripted as the chamber faces a maze of arcane rules and potentially torrid evidence.

The public's wide but shallow support for Clinton, combined with their distaste for a protracted trial steeped in the president's sexual proclivities, could play a role. The quest for a censure resolution could grow, but that would require Congress' diminishing ranks of centrists to reassert themselves.

Another obstacle to finding a middle ground is that conservatives have been loath to consider an alternative punishment short of impeachment. Republican senators likely will feel some of the same pressure from their right flank as their House colleagues did to advance the case against Clinton as far as possible.

The Republican drive to impeach Clinton is viewed by some historians as the latest example of a resurgent Congress eager to dominate the executive branch. Most agree that the threshold for impeachment has been lowered below the abuses of public power that led to the forced resignation of President Richard M. Nixon in 1974.

Fallout could be vast even in the 106th Congress. The fiery speeches on both sides, and the Democrats' characterization of the GOP-led effort as a "coup d'état," hardly portend the level of trust required to deal with such vexing issues as overhauling Social Security and protecting managed care patients.

The poisonous atmosphere prompted leading congressional Republicans to cast aspersions on the timing of Clinton's bombing of Iraq, which began on the eve of the scheduled impeachment debate and ended shortly after the last votes were cast.

The immediate task for Republicans is to find a new successor to outgoing Speaker Newt Gingrich, R-Ga., before the new Congress convenes Jan. 6. With Clinton's impeachment a foregone conclusion, Republicans engaged in a frenzied attempt to designate a new Speaker in the few hours before they left the Capitol — with all signs pointing to an affable, low-key conservative, Dennis Hastert, R-Ill. His selection would ratify the clout of his mentor, Majority Whip Tom DeLay, R-Texas, who rode herd on the GOP impeachment effort.

It was DeLay who, while choked with emotion during the floor debate, praised Livingston and his decision to resign. Livingston, he said, demonstrated that the decision to impeach Clinton was "a debate about relativism versus absolute truth."

That debate is destined to resound in the halls of the Capitol and the rest of the country for a long time. As Republican Richard H. Baker of Louisiana asked: "Where in God's name does the line of the private right to know end, and the individual right of personal liberty begin?"

Floor Dynamics

After weeks of buildup and days of frantic scrambling to keep up with events, members of both parties were somber as the day of the vote arrived.

Judiciary Committee Republicans kicked off the debate Dec. 18 with short speeches summarizing the charges against Clinton. "The president was obliged, under his sacred oath, to faithfully execute our nation's laws," said James E. Rogan, R-Calif. "Yet he repeatedly perjured himself and obstructed justice."

All was upstaged by Livingston's shocking announcement from the floor early the next day that he would abandon his quest for Speaker and resign from the House in six months.

It was a moment of high drama. Livingston began by describing the

Executive Branch

The Articles of Impeachment Considered by the House

Summaries of the articles of impeachment (H Res 611) against President Clinton as recommended by the House Judiciary Committee, followed by the Dec. 19 votes by the House:

ARTICLE I: Perjury before a federal grand jury on Aug. 17, 1998.

In its report (H Rept 105-830), the committee concluded Clinton lied about "the nature and details of his relationship" with former White House intern Monica Lewinsky; about his testimony in a Jan. 17 deposition in a sexual-harrassment suit filed by former Arkansas state employee Paula Corbin Jones; about statements he allowed his lawyer to make; and about "his corrupt efforts to influence the testimony of witnesses and to impede the discovery of evidence." Though he acknowledged an "improper relationship," Clinton resorted to "legal hairsplitting . . . to bypass the requirement of telling the complete truth."

Adopted: 228-206

ARTICLE II: Perjury in his Jan. 17 deposition in the Jones case.

The committee concluded that Clinton lied to Jones' lawyers about his relationship with Lewinsky, about gifts he had given her, and about efforts to conceal the relationship, including help given to Lewinsky in her pursuit of a job in New York.

Rejected: 205-229

ARTICLE III: Obstruction of justice.

The committee found that Clinton, "using the powers of his high office," engaged in a plan "to delay, impede, cover up and conceal" his involvement with Lewinsky and subsequent lies. The scheme included encouraging Lewinsky to file a false affidavit in the Jones case and making misleading statements to secretary Betty Currie when he knew she was likely to be a witness in the case.

Adopted: 221-212

ARTICLE IV: Abuse of power.

The committee said Clinton continued "a pattern of deceit and obstruction of duly authorized investigations" in his answers to 81 "requests for admission" that were submitted to him by the panel. "Several" of the president's answers "are clearly perjurious, false and misleading," the report says. It also accused Clinton of lying about his infidelities in six public statements, and of lying to Cabinet members and White House aides "knowing that they would repeat his false statements to the American public." His deceptions "caused millions of tax dollars to be spent by not only the Office of the Independent Counsel [Kenneth W. Starr] in its duly authorized investigation, but also by White House lawyers, communications employees and other government employees, who were utilized to help perpetuate the president's lies and defend him."

Rejected: 148-285.

case against Clinton and said the president had the power to heal the wounds he caused: "You, sir, may resign your post."

Democrats erupted at the frontal assault from a GOP leader. "No," they shouted repeatedly. A group, led by Maxine Waters, D-Calif., yelled, "You resign, you resign." Livingston held up his right hand as if to tell them to wait. He then delivered the body blow.

"I can only challenge you in such fashion if I am willing to heed my own words," he said. "I must set the example that I hope President Clinton will follow. I will not stand for Speaker of the House."

After listening to his last words in stunned silence, members of both parties gave Livingston a standing ovation as he left the floor. He strode to the sanctuary of his nearby office, followed by Republicans urging him to reconsider. They were joined by a number of Democrats who admired Livingston's bipartisan impulses as chairman of the Appropriations Committee and had looked forward to his speakership.

Livingston's mind was made up. Within minutes, the next campaign for Speaker was under way in earnest. Members huddled in lobbies and hallways to discuss the turn of events. During the vote on the first article of impeachment, DeLay and Bill Paxon, R-N.Y., were clearly working the floor, steering members to talk to Hastert at the back of the chamber.

Livingston's decision became as much a focus of debate as impeachment itself. Several Democrats, in a curious twist, said that Livingston's resignation was as misguided as the impeachment effort.

"It is a surrender to a developing sexual McCarthyism," said Jerrold Nadler, D-N.Y. "We are losing sight of the distinction between sins, which ought to be between a person and his family and his God, and crimes, which are the concern of the state and of society as a whole."

Judiciary Committee Chairman Henry J. Hyde, R-Ill., responded that the issue was indeed one of crimes — perjury and obstruction of justice, saying Clinton's impeachment grew out of "equal justice under the law, that's what we're fighting for."

The Democrats' most impassioned plea came from Minority Leader Richard A. Gephardt, D-Mo., who entwined Livingston's decision with Clinton's impeachment and said, "We are now rapidly descending into a politics where life imitates farce."

Clinton Impeachment

"Fratricide dominates our public debate and America is held hostage with tactics of smear and fear. Let all of us here today say no to resignation, no to impeachment, no to hatred, no to intolerance of each other, and no to vicious self-righteousness."

He, too, got a standing ovation, as well as bear hugs from fellow Democrats.

Republicans first prevailed on a procedural vote that prevented Democrats from offering a resolution to censure Clinton. That vote was 230-204. Democrats responded by briefly walking out in protest. *(Vote 542, p. H-154)*

They returned for the formal voting on H Res 611, which contained four articles of impeachment.

The first article, accusing Clinton of committing perjury in his Aug. 17 grand jury testimony, passed easily, 228-206. Five Democrats and five Republicans crossed party lines. Members had said this was the most likely to be approved because, unlike his deposition in the Paula Corbin Jones sexual harassment case, there was no question that his testimony was material to the investigation by Independent Counsel Kenneth W. Starr. *(Vote 543, p. H-154)*

The second article, charging Clinton with perjury in a deposition in the Jones lawsuit, failed, 205-229. Besides questions of its relevance to the case, the lawsuit was eventually dismissed. *(Vote 544, p. H-154)*

The third article, charging Clinton with obstructing justice, passed 221-212. Five Democrats voted for it, while 12 Republicans voted against. This charge was also seen as strong because it included Clinton's attempts to find Lewinsky a job, possibly in return for her silence, and his alleged witness tampering involving his secretary, Betty Currie. *(Vote 545, p. H-156)*

A fourth article, charging that Clinton violated his oath of office in providing misleading statements to 81 questions posed by the Judiciary Committee, failed, 148-285. A number of Republicans saw this as a reason to be angry at Clinton, but not to impeach him. *(Vote 546, p. H-156)*

After voting on the impeachment articles, the House authorized the appointment of 13 Republican Judiciary Committee members to prosecute the case in the Senate. The contingent walked across the Capitol, where Hyde presented a leather-bound parchment to Secretary of the Senate Gary Sisco. The House will have to reappoint managers in January, but that move is likely to be cast as procedural.

Republicans Unify

The vote to impeach Clinton represented a remarkable turnaround.

It occurred less than seven weeks after Democrats picked up a net of five House seats in the Nov. 3 election. Most observers cited the Republicans' disappointing showing — they had hoped to gain at least 20 seats — and public opposition to impeachment in declaring the effort all but dead.

Earlier in the month, the Judiciary Committee seemed to be lurching out of control with diversions into campaign finance issues and other sexual conduct allegations against Clinton. But by the time the panel voted for four articles of impeachment Dec. 11-12, it had become obvious that the effort was steaming ahead.

Perhaps the single biggest factor was the determination of the House Republican leadership to deny a floor vote on a resolution censuring Clinton.

Republican members denied that their arms were twisted.

Yet they were subjected to a fusillade of arguments by DeLay that nothing short of impeachment should be considered. Livingston, then in reluctant but firm control of the approaching session, picked up the call Dec. 12.

This decision had a direct impact on a group of 20 to 30 members, most of them moderates from districts that Clinton carried in 1996. Many of them were willing — some anxious to — consider something short of impeachment.

With censure foreclosed as an option, wavering Republicans were forced to confront the fact that if they voted against impeachment, it could appear as though they were defending Clinton. Each announcement in favor of impeachment increased pressure on other Republicans to follow suit or be left outside the GOP mainstream.

Efforts among some GOP moderates to push a censure alternative — backed, in one form or another, by Amo Houghton of New York and Michael N. Castle of Delaware, as well as by former President Gerald R. Ford and 1996 presidential nominee Bob Dole — fell flat. And some moderates — particularly Christopher Shays of Connecticut and Roukema — said censure was not a good option.

"Historically, moderate Republicans have placed special emphasis on ethics and honor," said John J. Pitney Jr., an associate professor of government at Claremont McKenna College in California. "So this is exactly the kind of issue on which they're likely to oppose Clinton."

House Republicans made a concerted effort to put impeachment in a particular context. Hyde said impeachment simply meant there was sufficient evidence to convene a Senate trial. Bill McCollum, R-Fla., argued that even if the Senate acquitted Clinton, impeachment would serve essentially as a censure.

The impeachment drive may have also picked up steam when Clinton's two most prominent and unpopular adversaries — Gingrich and Starr — faded from the scene.

Their absence made it harder for Democrats to demonize Republicans. It also put more focus on the actions that got Clinton into trouble.

Clinton's Mistakes

Clinton developed a well-earned reputation during his career for his astute political instincts, tapping into public support and disarming his enemies. But this failed him at key moments in the Lewinsky scandal, leading right up to floor debate.

Most troubling to the GOP moderates that Clinton had counted on were his responses Nov. 27 to the Judiciary Committee's 81 questions. His answers were carefully crafted in the same legalistic manner that marked his testimony. Many undecided Republicans wanted to hear not just another attempt at a heartfelt contrition from Clinton. They wanted a more open admission of his having lied under oath — regardless of how his opponents might use it, or if it would place him in greater jeopardy of criminal charges after he left the White House.

"What's more important — his presidency or the chance that he might at some time be prosecuted?" asked John Edward Porter, R-Ill.

Clinton may have also miscalculated in relying on public opinion, which for months showed overwhelming opposition to impeachment. A Washing-

Executive Branch

Against the Grain

Republicans who voted against impeachment:

Amo Houghton of New York: Houghton, a Rockefeller Republican, said on the House floor Dec. 18: "I'm proud of my party, but I'm opposed to impeachment.... When all the arguments are done and when the votes are taken, this is what we must work for: the humanity, the healing of this nation."

Peter T. King of New York: King has long tangled with the Republican Conference on leadership issues. Speaking on the House floor Dec. 18, he said, "I strongly believe that for a president of the United States to be impeached... for an election to be undone, there must be a direct abuse of presidential power.... How many of our former presidents would we have lost?"

Constance A. Morella of Maryland: Morella, who represents the affluent Washington-area Maryland suburbs, said in a written statement that the president would be remembered "not for the many accomplishments that have occurred during his term in office but for his sordid behavior and his failure to take responsibility for that behavior. However, putting the country through the turmoil and tumult of a Senate trial ... is wrong."

Christopher Shays of Connecticut: Perhaps the highest-profile House GOP moderate, Shays announced on the House floor Dec. 19 that "the impeachable offenses have not been proven, and the proven offenses are not impeachable. ... We've all tried to do our best, and we'll all have to live with our vote for the rest of our lives."

Mark Souder of Indiana: Souder, a steadfast conservative, considered changing his position under heavy pressure from constituents, but ultimately voted against all but the third article of impeachment. "My preference would be to combine the Starr report with additional evidence, when complete, of the campaign finance violations which the Justice Department continues to investigate," he said. "Impeachment is a rarely used, and extremely divisive, procedure."

Democrats who voted for impeachment:

Virgil H. Goode Jr. of Virginia: A freshman from southern Virginia's rural tobacco country, Goode supported the first three articles of impeachment. He said he "was always concerned about lying under oath by the president."

Ralph M. Hall of Texas: One of the few remaining old-style Southern Democrats, Hall voted for three articles of impeachment. "You just have to vote your conscience, and I did that," he said.

Paul McHale of Pennsylvania: After news of Clinton's relationship with Monica Lewinsky broke, McHale became the first Democrat to call for the president to resign. He said he voted in favor of the first three articles of impeachment after deciding "the evidence is overwhelming" that Clinton lied under oath and tried to obstruct justice.

Charles W. Stenholm of Texas: A well-liked fiscal conservative, Stenholm voted for the first three articles of impeachment. "The consequences of the president's actions go well beyond the details of perjury. They go to the heart of our national character."

Gene Taylor of Mississippi: Taylor, a renegade entering his sixth full term in the House, said he voted for all four counts of impeachment because "I think perjury is a very serious crime. And I believe it was intentional."

ton Post-ABC News poll released Dec. 15 showed respondents opposed impeaching and removing Clinton by 61 percent to 38 percent.

But the overall numbers masked the fact that, while Democrats opposed impeachment by 82 percent to 17 percent, Republicans endorsed it by 64 percent to 36 percent. And moderate Republicans began hearing from an increasing number of hard-core supporters demanding impeachment.

The approaching end of the 105th Congress at first appeared to hamper any GOP hopes of impeachment. Democrats complained about the timing, though Republicans were quick to note that until two months ago, Democrats were just as eager to wrap up the debate.

When Democrats picked up seats on Nov. 3, the roles switched. Democrats urged a go-slow approach while Republicans expressed a new determination to finish.

The result: Clinton's fate was decided by a lame-duck session, including outgoing members.

Many congressional and constitutional experts agreed that impeachment could carry over from one Congress to another, having done so in the cases of three federal judges. But the necessity of doing so was in some dispute.

Outgoing members, who had already lost their office space on Capitol Hill and were herded into temporary quarters, expressed disbelief at the action. "The idea of having your last vote be on impeachment is almost surrealistic," said Glenn Poshard, D-Ill., who lost a gubernatorial bid. "I can't believe it's gotten to this point."

Judiciary Committee

The historic vote came one week after the Judiciary Committee finished up work on the fourth and final article of impeachment. The fourth charge, approved 21-16, said that Clinton "willfully made perjurious, false and misleading sworn statements" when responding to the committee's questionnaire.

"At every turn when he was faced with the choice of answering questions honestly or deceitfully, the president has chosen deception," said Christopher B. Cannon, R-Utah.

But committee Republicans scaled

back the final article of impeachment by dropping charges that Clinton had lied to the American people, his Cabinet and staff, and frivolously asserted executive privilege when seeking to block testimony by Secret Service agents and White House lawyers.

An amendment by George Gekas, R-Pa., approved 29-5, jettisoned charges related to executive privilege and lying to the nation and his Cabinet. Several panel Republicans said those charges had not been sufficiently proved, especially the executive privilege claim.

After voting the final article, committee Republicans easily killed the Democrats' resolution to censure Clinton for making "false statements concerning his reprehensible conduct" with Lewinsky. It also said that he had "violated the trust of the American people, lessened their esteem for the office of the President, and dishonored" the presidency.

Clinton's misconduct, though "reprehensible," said Rick Boucher, D-Va., did not rise to the level required for impeachment. "In adopting this resolution of censure, we will give voice to the widely held public view that the president should not be removed from office but that he should be admonished by the Congress for his conduct."

Republicans countered that impeachment was the only appropriate step to condemn presidential misconduct and that there was no provision in the Constitution for censure.

Republicans defeated the censure resolution, 14-22. Robert C. Scott, D-Va., voted "nay," and Waters voted "present."

Announcements

Clinton's prospects for avoiding impeachment dwindled steadily in the ensuing days.

Livingston, who had lain low on impeachment for weeks, wrote Gephardt Dec. 12 to notify Democrats that they would not have an opportunity to offer a censure resolution on the floor.

"Censure of the president would violate the careful balance of separation of powers and the scheme laid out by the Framers to address the issue of executive misconduct," Livingston wrote.

A number of Republicans who had not previously declared their intentions did so Dec. 14. None had been regarded as likely candidates to oppose impeachment, and none did.

The news got worse for Clinton the following day, when several GOP moderates — including Jack Quinn of New York, who had previously opposed impeachment — announced they would vote to impeach. They included some of the White House's top prospects: Nancy L. Johnson, R-Conn.; Sue W. Kelly, R-N.Y.; and Fred Upton, R-Mich.

Clinton, Johnson said, "does not have the right to commit perjury when it is convenient or when he thinks the charges against him are frivolous."

By Dec. 16, Clinton's outlook had gone from critical to grave. Almost hourly, undecided Republicans stood before television cameras and microphones to say they would vote to impeach Clinton.

Porter, another GOP moderate who had once spoken against impeachment, switched in favor. The announcements of others, such as iconoclast Jim Leach of Iowa, as well as Sherwood L. Boehlert and Rick Lazio, both of New York, seemed to seal Clinton's fate. Lazio, who had just returned from a trip to the Middle East with Clinton, had earlier leaned against impeachment.

Debate Begins

The debate formally began at 9 a.m., Dec. 18, a cool, crisp day in Washington. Ray LaHood, R-Ill., widely respected for his fairness, wielded the gavel.

Members easily defeated a Democratic motion to adjourn, offered in protest of the GOP leadership's decision to vote on impeachment while the airstrikes against Iraq were under way. An almost full chamber then sat somberly as the clerk read the four articles of impeachment.

Hyde laid out the GOP position, saying, "The nation's chief executive has shown himself incapable of enforcing its laws, for he has corrupted the rule of law by his perjury and his obstruction of justice."

Gephardt attacked Republicans for staging the debate during the military action against Iraq and for blocking a vote on censure. "I can only conclude that this may be about winning a vote, not about high-minded ideals," he said.

Many members took pains to polish their words. Some spoke from notes or handwritten speeches they had revised on the floor.

Vic Fazio, D-Calif., said he was "sad that a reckless president and a Republican Congress driven by blind animus for him have brought us to this moment in history."

On the next morning, Democrats caucused to hear Hillary Rodham Clinton thank them for standing with her husband. Some members emerged from the meeting with moist eyes. For Democrats, the tumultuous week meant a full range of emotions: sadness, anger, frustration and defiance.

The decision by GOP leaders to block their effort to censure Clinton provoked genuine outrage among Democrats, who said that they had allowed the GOP, when it was in the minority, to present alternatives on momentous issues.

From a strictly partisan standpoint, said Chet Edwards, D-Texas, "We think it's going to thrust Democrats into the majority in the House and possibly the Senate in 2000."

Castle agreed that the Republicans were more downcast than Democrats after the vote and said that impeachment "has huge political ramifications." He predicted that people will revise their thoughts about the parties and individual lawmakers in ways "that will never go away."

Impeachment Raises Questions About Balance Of Power

DECEMBER 22— The House Judiciary Committee's report that accompanied the articles of impeachment against President Clinton began, curiously, with the phrase "equal justice under law."

The curious element is that this phrase is not generally associated with the legislative branch of government. Rather, it is a credo of the judicial branch. It was penned in 1935 by architect Cass Gilbert, and etched into the Supreme Court building he designed.

In the impeachment report (H Rept

Executive Branch

105-830), the words commence an argument that Clinton committed impeachable offenses, namely that he may have acted to pervert that equality of justice by lying under oath, obstructing justice and lying to Congress in an attempt to conceal his relationship with former White House intern Monica Lewinsky.

But "equal justice under law," as well as "the rule of law," a phrase favored by committee Chairman Henry J. Hyde, R-Ill., strike many constitutional scholars as odd in the context of impeachment. The prevailing, though not universal, view is that impeachment is primarily a political function, rather than a legal one.

In a presidential impeachment, most constitutional experts agree, lawmakers are asked whether they wish to claim a popular mandate to remove a popularly elected official. They are not called upon to don robes or wigs, or play jurors or grand jurors. They are not supposed to judge their political adversaries. They can set their own standards of evidence and are not required to follow the legal definition of crimes such as perjury.

To many experts, the Clinton impeachment has a deeply troubling element — an overreaching Congress taking on a quasi-judicial function from one branch of government to mount a political challenge to another. This, they say, could erode the separation of powers doctrine and make impeachments more common, especially in light of the voters' demonstrated preference for divided government.

"This concerns me a great deal, and it has nothing to do with who is president," said Thomas Sargentich, law professor at American University. "My concern is that for the integrity of a government, for a workable system of checks and balances, impeachment should largely stay in the background. Otherwise, we are changing our system of government and moving toward something that is more like a parliamentary system."

Lowering the Bar

If the Clinton impeachment appears as an overreach by Congress, it may also be seen as something of an act of desperation. One of the most unavoidable ironies of the year is that it was Clinton who was caught in an affair with a subordinate and a series of lies, but it was the House Republican leadership that imploded and the GOP that took losses at the polls in November.

Four years ago, when Republicans gained control of the House, they elected as Speaker a man who once spoke of making the House a "co-equal" to the White House. That vision, articulated by Newt Gingrich, R-Ga., in 1979, has all but vanished.

Yet, the Clinton impeachment may be the last desperate grasp at that dream. As it was done at great political risk to the party and at great damage to the House civility, the effort to impeach Clinton had an almost kamikaze element to it — as if House Republicans were so determined to bring the president down, they were willing to go down with him. The quintessential expression of this was Speaker-designate Robert L. Livingston, R-La., announcing his resignation in the well of the House, and demanding Clinton's as well.

In terms of audacity, this impeachment is unprecedented. There have been sixteen impeachments in all, including 13 judges, one president, one cabinet secretary and one senator.

Not since 1868 has a president been impeached. Not since then has a government official been impeached on a party-line vote. With the possible exception of Judge Harry E. Claiborne, who was found unfit for office in 1986 — he was in jail serving a sentence for tax fraud — no one has been impeached for something so far removed from his official duties.

No one has been impeached as the result of an independent counsel report to Congress. No one has been impeached in a lame duck session of Congress. And never before has an impeachment advanced on the argument that it is an end in itself — the ultimate censure, as Rep. Bill McCollum, R-Fla., termed it.

These precedents have already sparked a fierce debate over whether the action against Clinton will "lower the bar" for future impeachments.

"If we move from 'high crimes and misdemeanors' to 'we don't like the president; we think he lied,' we're going to have these things all the time," said Paul Finkelman, a University of Akron law professor and co-author of "Impeachable Offenses: A Documentary History from 1787 to the Present."

Because Clinton is a polarizing figure, there is a natural tendency for people to view the constitutional issues through the prism of Clinton. But Kathleen Clark, a Washington University law professor and critic of Clinton, says the two must be separated out, now matter how difficult that is.

"I'm of two minds on this," she said. "As it affects Clinton there's a kind of justice in this. It's not a very beautiful justice. It's a kind of retributive justice. But it's a justice."

On the other hand, she said, as this affects the institution of the presidency, it is a highly inappropriate, anti-democratic action.

The anti-democratic element is that not only was Clinton elected and reelected, he was elected by people fully aware of his history of half truths and sexual peccadilloes, Clark said. If they elected him under those circumstances, what right does Congress have to try to un-elect him?

Part of the trickiness of the Clinton case is that it was brought by Independent Counsel Kenneth W. Starr. It started out as a purely legal exercise, and when it was fully developed, it was thrust into the political arena.

Had it started in a more public way, it likely would not have advanced as far. It would have been politically difficult for congressional committees to play major roles in the investigation, as they did in Watergate. The pressure on them not to delve into such tawdry affairs would have great.

But Starr was shielded from such pressures. He was not himself accountable to voters. He gathered his information in private and was able to pressure Clinton before his grand jury. When he had gotten what he needed, he went to Congress.

'A Sorry Mess'

Many Republicans say broader arguments about the presidency miss the fundamental point that the Clinton impeachment is laced with allegations of serious violations of law — something most of Clinton's successors would presumably avoid.

Charles T. Canady, R-Fla., agreed that there is an "element of truth" to the argument that future presidents would always be "looking over their

Clinton Impeachment

shoulders" in fear of an impeachment.

But, he said, if future presidents lie under oath and obstruct justice, "I would like for them to be looking over their shoulders."

A number of Republicans make the argument that potential violations of law, even those limited to personal conduct, are impeachable since they undermine the president's authority as the chief law enforcement officer. The central premise behind the Clinton impeachment is that a president, who has great powers under his control, must demonstrate that he is accountable to the same justice that others are.

This is not universally accepted, even among Republicans, some of whom do not think any of the charges against Clinton warrant impeachment. And some see a mixed bag among the individual charges.

George Van Cleve, chief minority counsel on the committee that investigated the Iran-Contra scandal in 1987, said that of the two articles approved by the House, the obstruction of justice charge arising from the sexual harassment suit brought by Paula Corbin Jones is not "even in the zone" of an impeachable offense. But, he argues, the perjury charge stemming from Starr's investigation may well be.

"This whole thing is kind of a sorry mess," Van Cleve said. "I think personally I wish it hadn't come to this. But it's difficult for me to criticize people who say they are not going to tolerate [Clinton's] behavior."

An Emboldened Congress

If future presidents could be weakened by this impeachment, future Congresses may be emboldened.

The 105th Congress has shown a great deal of interest in expanding its prerogatives at the expense of other branches. Many of the same people who were early advocates of impeaching Clinton — most notably Majority Whip Tom DeLay, R-Texas — are advocates of widespread use of the impeachment process for judges whose rulings they do not favor.

Even those members with more restraint have backed restrictions on the powers and scope of the judicial branch that have provoked some unusually vocal complaints from judges. In April, the House passed a "judicial reform" measure (HR 1252) that would have limited judges' ability to overturn laws created through ballot initiatives. The Senate did not take up the measure.

Over the last four years, Congress has passed, or attempted to pass, a series of laws restricting judges from ruling in areas where civil liberties organizations frequently litigate — such as immigration and prison overcrowding — and forced them into areas favored by conservative groups, most notably adjudicating crime issues at the federal level.

On the presidential front, in addition to the impeachment, congressional Republicans have shown a new willingness to challenge the president on foreign policy issues, breaking a longtime America tradition that politics ends at the water's edge.

Angered by Clinton's decision Dec. 16 to bomb Iraq on the eve of an impeachment vote, delaying the vote, several Republicans, including Senate Majority Leader Trent Lott, R-Miss., and House Rules Committee Chairman Gerald B.H. Solomon, R-N.Y., expressed open dissension. DeLay announced in advance, on NBC's "Meet the Press" three days before the bombing, that he could not be supportive.

The dispute only intensified in the days that followed, as Republicans and Democrats fought bitterly over whether the debate should go forward with American troops in harm's way.

The Senate's Role

How the Senate treats the articles will bear heavily on the question of whether the impeachment bar will be lowered for future presidents.

"The Senate disposition will have a huge impact," said Michael Gerhardt, a law professor at the College of William and Mary in Virginia and an expert on impeachment. He said the acquittal of President Andrew Johnson in 1868 essentially "wiped the slate clean."

Particularly if Clinton is acquitted in trial, or if there is a bipartisan move to stop the proceedings before a full-blown evidentiary portion of the trial, the impact on future presidents could be mitigated. This would reinforce previously held views that impeachment should not be used for unlawful conduct that is private and does not subvert the government.

If the process ends in a harsh censure, the conclusions could be blurred. Would the lack of a conviction be a repudiation of the impeachment, or would the censure be a vindication of them? There would surely be a vigorous debate on this among the partisan interests on Capitol Hill, particularly if the impeachment trial was used as a tool to persuade Clinton to volunteer for some kind of penalty beyond censure.

The 2000 election also could be a determining factor on whether the Clinton impeachment is seen as vindicated or repudiated, or neither.

Damaging the Institution

In making the argument that removing Clinton from office would damage the presidency, Clinton supporters could gain backing even from senators who do not much like him personally.

They could combine that with an interest in averting the embarrassing spectacle of a Senate trial in winning the support of moderate Republicans who want an early way out. If this happens, Clinton should count himself lucky, say many experts.

"If a bipartisan Senate group spares the country from a six-month trial by arranging a censure deal, they'll do it for institutional respect for the presidency more than personal feeling for Bill Clinton," said Charles Tiefer, a University of Baltimore law professor and former House Democratic counsel.

Support for the institution of the presidency also provides a powerful counter-argument to those who say Clinton should resign now to spare the nation a Senate trial.

This analysis is rejected by many Republicans, who view appeals to the institution of the presidency in much the same way as writer Samuel Johnson saw patriotism: as the last refuge of scoundrels — or in this case the refuge of the defenders of scoundrels. During Watergate, many Republicans point out, President Richard M. Nixon made similar arguments about the impact of impeachment on future presidencies.

So far, Clinton himself has not made public appeals in behalf of the presidency. If he did, his sincerity would be in question, since his personal interests would coincide so neatly

Executive Branch

with his statements of principle.

"It's pretty tough to take as unbiased the position of a person who is literally in the position of saving his own skin," said Van Cleve.

The Andrew Johnson Legacy

Many historians believe Johnson's impeachment in 1868, even though it did not lead to a conviction, had a palpable impact on the presidency and Congress for years to come.

"The impeachment of Andrew Johnson in 1868 led to the most intense period of congressional domination and presidential weakness in American history," said Tiefer. "We may well move in that direction now."

The argument for this is the string of undistinguished presidents that followed Johnson and lasted until Theodore Roosevelt breathed new life into the office at the outset of the 20th century.

That argument may be a bit sweeping. In truth, the mediocre presidents may have started with Martin Van Buren in 1837 and lasted through the century, with the one stellar exception of Abraham Lincoln. But many scholars argue that the impeachment played a role.

In an ironic sense, however, the Johnson example may prove a boon to Clinton. The crisis could bring down the Clinton presidency. He could become a disgraced ex-president who lost the trust of an American public exhausted by months of scandal.

But in another sense, the impeachment could enhance his legacy.

Today, Johnson is not known as one of the most miserable presidents in American history. He is not remembered for his drunkenness during his swearing-in ceremony in 1865 as vice president, or his considerable lack of intellect. He is not remembered for his tolerance of slavery or his defiance of Congress. Rather, he is known as the president who weathered an unfortunate and ill-founded impeachment attempt.

By the same process, Clinton could be remembered as a persecuted president who withstood an onslaught, and defended the prerogatives of his office, even as he brought its dignity into question through his dalliances. For Clinton's harshest critics, this could be the ultimate indignity.

Vote Illustrates Power of GOP's Core Support

DECEMBER 22 — The historic Dec. 19 votes to impeach President Clinton were a stunning victory for social conservatives, who dominate the House Republican caucus and control the top leadership positions.

Defying overwhelming odds, they united their fractious party to — for only the second time in U.S. history — push an impeachment resolution through the House of Representatives.

To Democrats, the vote seemed an egregious example of the political overreaching that has characterized Republicans since they won control of Congress in 1994.

Conservatives, led by Majority Whip Tom DeLay, R-Texas, drove forward despite polls showing that two-thirds of Americans opposed impeachment. They risked further public opprobrium by proceeding with the vote while Clinton was overseeing military action against Iraq.

"So bent are [Republicans] on the destruction of this president that they would knock down the very pillars which support our constitutional system," John Lewis, D-Ga., said during the Dec. 18 House debate.

But the political dynamics of impeachment are complex. The vote was a testament to the power of the conservative movement that now dominates the Republicans' electoral base. It was an illustration of the bitter partisan split that has all but paralyzed the House, as well as a sign of deep cultural divisions over standards of personal behavior for public officials. Finally, the tally illustrated — and may have added to — the erosion of the political middle ground that has hamstrung moderates from both parties.

Republicans argued that they had no choice but to act, calling the debate principled, not political. Based on evidence gathered by Independent Counsel Kenneth W. Starr that Clinton may have committed perjury and obstructed justice, they said they were forced to take the somber step of impeachment.

"This is not the latest uninformed poll or the latest . . . talk show. It's a constitutional question, and it's our duty," said Marge Roukema, R-N.J.

In one sense, the GOP was responsive to the poll that, for them, mattered most — a clear demand from its conservative base for strong action against Clinton. "If Republicans are looking to bring their constituents to their side in the elections in 2000, they need to understand that they have to hold to principle," said Carmen Pate, president director of Concerned Women for America, a conservative group.

There was also a growing hope that Republicans could drive the broader electorate their way. Some analysts said they expected passage of the two articles of impeachment to force a shift in public opinion. Polls immediately after the votes did not bear that out.

That there were clear dangers for Republicans in defining themselves as the party of morality was evident on Dec. 19 when Speaker-elect Robert L. Livingston, R-La., announced on the House floor that he would resign after having admitted to extramarital affairs.

The announcement sucked the wind out of Republicans but energized Democrats. House Minority Leader Richard A. Gephardt, D-Mo., won bipartisan applause when he called for an end to the acidic personal attacks that were decimating politicians' careers. "We need to stop destroying imperfect people at the altar of unobtainable morality," Gephardt said. The White House quickly picked up the refrain.

A Venomous Atmosphere

The poisonous mood and lack of trust between Republicans and Democrats could make it much harder for Congress and the White House to compromise on legislation next year. If there is one thing both sides agreed on, it was that they needed action on issues such as education, tax cuts and Social Security to wash away the public's bitter aftertaste from impeachment.

The compromise choice to replace Livingston, Dennis Hastert of Illinois, must try to mend rifts with Democrats and within his own party even while working with a narrow, six-vote majority. It will not be easy. Democrats are already complaining that Hastert, a deputy of DeLay, was handpicked by the one person most responsible for the impeachment vote.

After creating momentum, House Republicans may have lost their ability

Clinton Impeachment

to steer the issue in the face of a seemingly inevitable, and unpredictable, Senate trial. "There is something about this whole process that shows a lack of judgment, a lack of proportionality, a lack of common sense," House Minority Whip David E. Bonior, D-Mich., complained on Dec. 18.

Unlike the 1974 debate during Watergate, there was virtually no effort to find bipartisan consensus this time around. *(1974 Almanac, p. 9-3)*

A Diminishing Middle

The stark partisanship was in part the result of a series of factors over the past several decades that have altered the tenor of American politics.

Changing demographics have shifted the Republican power base to the South and West, with a cluster of moderates huddled in the Northeast. There has also been a rise of religious and social conservatives who have agitated the party to emphasize issues such as abortion over economic policies that previously had primacy. Declines in overall voter participation have elevated the importance of those groups in many Republican districts.

At the same time, Democrats, just as united in their opposition to impeachment, increasingly represent urban, liberal districts. Their support is strong among minorities and labor unions, who are staunch backers of Clinton.

The ideological hardening has diminished the middle ground in the House and made bipartisan compromise an endangered art. Democrats themselves have pursued the politics of confrontation, filing ethics complaints against retiring House Speaker Newt Gingrich, R-Ga., and attempting to block Republican initiatives.

"We have seen ideology assert itself. Liberalism became strident; conservatism became strident," said Charles Dunn, a political analyst at Clemson University. "As a nation, historically we have not been a deep-set, ideological people. Ideology has been more a seasoning, and the mainstream in the middle the meat and potatoes of politics."

While there have been some bipartisan successes, moderates have often been marginalized as leaders of both parties have chosen conflict and stalemate over negotiation. Against this backdrop, impeachment was considered.

The charges against the president were leveled by the independent counsel, but the march to impeachment was nurtured and orchestrated by Republican conservatives. As recently as a month ago, after the GOP unexpectedly lost seats in the midterm elections, predictions held that as many as 40 party members would vote no.

Activists on the right, the conservative-dominated Judiciary Committee and DeLay quietly brought the party together. They painted Clinton's alleged perjury as not just a political or legal issue, but part of a pattern of lies and a sign of a moral decline in society that had to be checked.

Republicans were helped in no small measure by a White House and Democratic Party that did not dispute basic facts and used terms such as "reprehensible" to describe the president's behavior. To ease the pressure on wavering Republicans, leaders such as Judiciary Chairman Henry J. Hyde, R-Ill., emphasized that a vote for impeachment was not a vote to remove the president from office, but rather to send it to the Senate for trial.

A middle group in each party had sought a lesser censure resolution as a compromise to impeachment.

Underlining a national split between conservatives and moderates for control of the GOP, censure was supported by old-school Republicans such as former Senate Majority Leader and 1996 Republican presidential candidate Bob Dole, R-Kan., former President Gerald R. Ford and former Massachusetts Republican Gov. William F. Weld — whose nomination as ambassador to Mexico was blocked by his own party.

"There are some of us who would love to find a way out of this crisis," said Brian P. Bilbray, R-Calif., one House member who announced his position late in the game and who had advocated censure.

Citing concerns that such an effort was unconstitutional, DeLay and other House leaders refused to allow a vote on a censure resolution. Democrats called the move to block censure a bald-faced political tactic designed to increase the odds that impeachment would pass.

"This is the final defeat of the moderates," said a House Democratic aide.

The censure resolution was a factor, but far from the only reason moderates voted for impeachment. Increasingly angry about what they saw as Clinton's evasiveness and lies and getting clear signals from Livingston that party unity was expected, moderates came around.

Some argue that to the extent moderates stuck with the House leadership, they will gain more leverage on other issues in the next Congress.

"For the same reason that moderates are now caught between a rock and a hard place on this decision, they will in the future find themselves time and time again in the winning voting bloc in the 1999 Congress," said William F. Connelly Jr., a professor of politics at Washington and Lee University.

Where Next?

Many Republicans had been working on the premise that they could put this vote quickly behind them and move on, arguing that the Senate, with 55 Republicans and 45 Democrats, could not muster the two-thirds majority necessary to convict Clinton.

"The working assumption is that it will not get far in the Senate just because of the numbers over there and that . . . the next Congress will be dedicated to getting to issues like Social Security reform and tax cuts," said Ed Gillespie, a Republican consultant.

But the political calculation is quickly changing. The partisan dynamics in the Senate are much different than those in the House. The Senate is less polarized and an important unifying force may be a desire to protect the institution rather than the president.

Pressure for a trial, therefore, may come both from conservative Republicans and from Democrats, such as Robert C. Byrd, D-W.Va., who believe the Senate must follow the Constitution. As such, the White House could find it more difficult to portray the process as a partisan witch hunt. Already many Democrats have refused to rush to Clinton's side, saying they must act as impartial jurors.

While Senate Majority Leader Trent Lott, R-Miss., has said quick censure was not a possibility, others in the party are entertaining the idea. Just as Democrats have not embraced Clinton, Senate Republicans have not rushed to condemn him, and they may deem it in the best interest of the country to rise above the partisan fray and coalesce around a censure resolution. ◆

Chapter 13

GOVERNMENT

Year 2000 Census 13-3
Puerto Rico Plebiscite 13-6
Ronald Reagan National Airport 13-7

Government

From Courts to Congress, Battles Rage Over The 2000 Census

SUMMARY

Continuing a standoff over the conduct of the 2000 census, the omnibus fiscal 1999 spending bill funds the Commerce, Justice and State departments only through June 15, 1999, while Congress and President Clinton await a Supreme Court ruling on the legality of using statistical sampling to augment the traditional head count.

Arguments in the case of *House of Representatives v. Daley* are set for Nov. 30, and a decision is likely by March. The court's decision will influence but not necessarily determine the outcome of the tussle between Clinton and Congress on whether sampling should be used in the coming census.

Ultimately, that will require legislation. Billions of federal dollars are allocated on the basis of population data, and the 2000 census will determine the boundaries of House districts for the 2002 elections and beyond. Furthermore, House districts are drawn to reflect shifts in population. Sampling, which supporters say would correct a persistent undercount of low-income and minority Americans, is viewed as helpful to Democrats, and Republicans are going all out to block its use.

The court test was brought by House Republicans. A three-judge panel ruled Aug. 25 that existing law bars use of the sampling method. However, the panel avoided the question of whether sampling violates the constitutional requirement for an "actual enumeration" of the population. Census officials are making preparations to use either system for the 2000 count.

The House passed its version (HR 4276) of the Commerce-Justice-State bill on Aug. 6, but the bill drew a presidential veto threat over language that would have cut off funding for the Census Bureau as of March 31 unless Congress and the White House had agreed in a separate bill whether to allow the use of statistical sampling.

The census was not at issue in the Senate's debate on its version (S 2260) of the Commerce-Justice-State bill. But the controversy was one of the last resolved in the negotiations between the White House and Republicans on the omnibus spending bill.

Congress and Clinton will have to resolve the sampling issue between the time the Supreme Court rules next spring and June 15, when funding will run out for the three Cabinet departments and the entire federal judiciary.

House Panel OKs Bill To Halt Funds For Census Bureau

JULY 11 — The fight over the 2000 census may become the most bruising in recent history. That is no small achievement given the level of controversy surrounding almost every census since the first one was conducted in 1790.

Nearly two years before the next count is to begin, the battle over the 2000 census has already spawned two lawsuits, delayed passage of a disaster relief bill in 1997 (PL 105-18) because it contained a rider prohibiting the Census Bureau from using statistical sampling, and, in recent weeks, fueled an increasingly abrasive stream of words over the bureau's plan for conducting the census. Many believe the fight will continue even beyond April 1, 2000, when the count is to officially begin. (*1997 Almanac, p. 9-84*)

"It shouldn't be a surprise to anyone that the census is contentious because it's at the core of political representation. But the tenor of the debate has become more harsh," said TerriAnn Lowenthal, an independent consultant on census issues and former staff director of a House oversight panel on the 1990 census.

The latest twist occurred June 24 when a House Appropriations subcommittee approved a bill that would stop funding for the Census Bureau on March 31, 1999, unless a dispute is resolved over how the census will be conducted.

The agency proposes using statistical sampling on a large scale for the first time to improve the accuracy of the count. Critics, including many Republicans, vehemently oppose such a step, arguing that it would not necessarily improve accuracy and that the numbers could be manipulated. So broad are the differences that census officials are concerned the stalemate could directly affect the census by disrupting funding and distracting bureau officials with political concerns.

Commerce Secretary William M. Daley urged the House on July 8 not to allow political differences over the use of statistical sampling to interfere with the census, though he conceded that the battle lines are so hardened that his plea will likely be ignored.

"The success of census 2000 absolutely requires that there be no interruption in full funding," Daley said, noting that important preliminary work will begin this fall.

"This kind of living with a sword over the Census Bureau's head does not lend well to long-term planning. . . . If Congress is going to have a fight and vote over what method ought to be used . . . they should not hold hostage the census," Daley said.

And he said that if Congress failed to heed his warning, he would recommend that President Clinton veto not just the Census Bureau's $4 billion spending plan, but the entire fiscal 1999 $33 billion appropriations bill for the departments of Commerce, State and Justice that contains the funding for the decennial count.

Government

Republicans, most of whom oppose a census using sampling, are unlikely to be swayed by such threats. "It's very irresponsible to use a plan that is unproven and which has failed in the past," said Rep. Dan Miller of Florida, chairman of the House Government Reform and Oversight subcommittee on the census, who holds a doctorate in marketing and statistics.

Miller, like many of his Republican allies, objects to sampling on several levels. It is unconstitutional, he said, and it is too complicated to carry out on a large scale. Most important, it can be manipulated for political gain by a Democratic administration, he said.

"This should not be a partisan issue," Miller said. "But it is the administration that wants to make a change after 200 years that will benefit them."

History of Controversy

By now, however, the Census Bureau should be accustomed to living under a sword that has been dangling precariously for more than 200 years.

In 1792, George Washington issued the first presidential veto in history because he disagreed with the way Congress decided to apportion itself based on the 1790 census which put the population at 3.9 million.

According to the General Accounting Office, the experience in 1790 set the stage for the next two centuries.

"Ever since George Washington questioned the results of the first census in (1792), the accuracy of any given census has been in question," said a GAO report issued in May. "The questions have always been legitimate: The census has never counted 100 percent of those it should, in part, because American sensibilities would probably not tolerate more foolproof census-taking methods."

There are ways to ensure a better count using traditional practices, experts say, but Americans, not to mention Congress, would never accept the conditions that would have to be imposed. The census could be made precise if people were required to register with the government. Or, the country could follow the example set by Turkey, where a 14-hour mandatory curfew was imposed in December 1997 so census canvassers could easily count people.

Chronic Undercount

Doubts and disputes about the census have surfaced with regularity every 10 years, with much of the attention focused on the size of the undercount. As the GAO report pointed out, "The debates over the years about methods of apportionment focused on mathematics, but the crux of the matter was political power."

The pressure became even more acute in 1911 when Congress set the number of representatives at 435. After that action, a gain of representation in any one state came only at the loss of representation in another.

Concerns about the accuracy of the census crystallized in 1941 when the number of men turning out for the wartime draft was considerably higher than the number anticipated by the 1940 census.

There have been more recent controversies, too. Several states and cities sued the government in 1991 when Commerce Secretary Robert A. Mosbacher refused a Census Bureau request to adjust the 1990 census to compensate for an undercount. The case ended in 1996 when the Supreme Court ruled against the suit. *(1996 Almanac, p. 5-52)*

But this year, criticism has spilled beyond questions of how the count will be conducted to the motives of key officials to charges of racism from both sides.

The fights, says historian Margo J. Anderson of the University of Wisconsin at Milwaukee, "are structural to the process. The decision over how to count can be dressed up as science over politics, but the bottom line is, one side usually ends up with the advantage."

The struggle for advantage is being played out in full fury in the House where Democrats support the proposal as the best way to count every American, including minority populations that traditionally have been undercounted.

Embarrassed by missing an estimated 4 million Americans in the 1990 census, the Census Bureau recommended that statistical sampling be used in 2000 to ensure a more accurate count. Under the bureau's proposal, at least 90 percent of the people in every census tract (a geographic area) would be physically counted.

Sampling would then be used to fill in the statistical holes. Census officials insist sampling is a valid approach that will yield a more accurate census at a lower cost. Republicans, however, claim the technique is unconstitutional and open to political manipulation.

"It is a very risky approach," Miller said, voicing concerns by some statisticians that the Census Bureau may not have enough time to develop a fail-safe sampling program.

The Senate, meanwhile, has shown no interest in the debate.

"We represent the same amount of people, no matter how they count them," said Sen. Judd Gregg, R-N.H.

Money and Politics

The view is far different in the House, where the fight is being fueled by two of the most powerful forces in Washington — money and politics.

Census results help determine how $180 billion annually in federal spending is distributed through 20 grant programs, including such important ones as Medicaid and educational assistance to poor children.

And, most important for the political landscape, the results form the basis for redrawing boundary lines for congressional districts as well as those for state legislatures.

The Census Bureau, Miller said, "is one institution of government that should be above politics. Most elected officials in this country are dependent on a fair and accurate census, and if people don't trust it, it is a real threat to our democratic process."

With such high stakes comes sharp rhetoric.

One particularly acerbic display occurred June 23, when Miller derided Kenneth Prewitt, Clinton's choice to head the agency, as an academic who is ill-equipped to manage the logistics of the massive undertaking.

"The bureau needs a Gen. [H. Norman] Schwarzkopf, not a Professor Sherman Klunk, to save the census," Miller said on the House floor. "So why did the president nominate an academic? Because of politics."

That same day, Loretta Sanchez, D-Calif., proclaimed on the House floor: "The Republican leadership of the House fails to match their rhetoric in favor of a colorblind America with deeds. ... We who oppose government-sanctioned racism will not be silenced by these attacks. We will stand in this well as long as it takes to shed light and bring honest debate about the merits of an accurate census. ... Race became an issue by those who have turned this process into a fight over raw political power."

Two weeks earlier, on June 11, when a Republican-sponsored court challenge to the bureau's plans for the 2000 census was heard in U.S. District Court in Washington, D.C., Democrats had first unleashed their own tough talk.

"Shame on Newt Gingrich and other Republican extremists who want to pursue another racially exclusionary and inaccurate census in the year 2000," said J. Gerald Hebert, counsel to the Democratic Congressional Campaign Committee.

Driving the fight is the bureau's plan to break from tradition by using statistical sampling on a large scale to augment the physical count of the population.

Without sampling, supporters say, the 2000 census will be less accurate than the one conducted in 1990, which was the most inaccurate in decades. The 1990 census, which cost $2.6 billion, earned the dubious honor of being the first census in modern history to be less accurate than the one preceding it.

The 2000 census, by comparison, is projected to cost $4 billion if sampling is used. That is nearly twice the $2.6 billion spent in 1990 and four times the $1.1 billion cost in 1980. With costs so high, census officials say they feel pressure to deliver the most accurate count possible.

"You could end up spending $4.7 billion and have a worse census than you had in 1990," Daley said.

Counting Heads

The Census Bureau, backed by the National Academy of Sciences, proposed to increase accuracy by augmenting the traditional count with statistical sampling. Under the Census Bureau's proposal, most Americans would be counted the traditional way by tabulating surveys returned in the mail and follow-up interviews by census-takers for those who did not respond.

Even with such arduous work, census officials and other experts say it is impossible to count everybody using those methods.

Sampling would use the information gained from physically counting at least 90 percent of the people in a given census tract and project the remaining population. The accuracy of the projections would be buttressed by a separate survey of 750,000 households nationwide.

That approach has been deemed scientifically valid by the National Academy of Sciences, the General Accounting Office and the Commerce Department's inspector general.

But House Republicans, led by Speaker Gingrich, R-Ga., filed a lawsuit in U.S. District Court in Washington, arguing that sampling is illegal because the Constitution requires an "actual enumeration" every 10 years.

A second lawsuit was filed with a special three-judge federal panel in U.S. District Court in Alexandria, Va., on behalf of several plaintiffs led by Matthew Glavin, president of the Southeastern Legal Foundation of Atlanta. Both cases are pending.

When the Constitution was written, Maureen E. Mahoney, a lawyer representing House Republicans, told a special three-judge panel at the U.S. District Court in Washington on June 11, "The word 'enumerate,' in every dictionary at the time, said to count one-by-one or reckon singularly."

In other words, Mahoney said, the Constitution requires the census to be based on a physical counting of the population and not statistical extrapolation.

No matter what the court rules, an appeal to the Supreme Court is a virtual certainty, Republicans and Democrats agree.

Outside the courtroom, however, the legal arguments are supplanted by political realities. Democrats believe a more accurate count would help them because minorities, who tend to vote for Democrats, are the most-often-missed group. Republicans recognize the same phenomenon and charge that a census with sampling would be flawed.

"Having the power to define population as the basis both for representation and for federal funding is an enormous concentration of power," Gingrich wrote in his most recent book, "Lessons Learned the Hard Way."

In addition, Gingrich pointed out, the Census Bureau is part of Daley's Commerce Department. Daley is the son of the late mayor of Chicago Richard Daley, famed for creating a Democratic machine often accused of using unorthodox methods to ensure victory.

Gingrich wrote, "The specter of putting someone so closely connected to the Chicago Democratic machine in charge of the census with a statistical adjustment was too chilling even to contemplate."

Daley is fully aware of the tumultuous history of the census, but he believes the debate has gone beyond the normal bounds. "People's motives are being questioned; [critics ask] how are you going to politically cook the books? It's ridiculous," he said in a July 8 interview. "This is a career operation; we have more monitoring and oversight, and the idea that somebody is going to go in some room and cook some numbers just feeds an attitude, a cynicism that is distressing," Daley added.

Republican political operatives warn that sampling could make vulnerable 24 Republican House seats, a distressing prospect for a party with a thin, 228-206 majority.

Historians and other analysts, however, believe that number exaggerates the threat. Historically, about 10 seats shift after each census, but even that is a rough estimate.

"What the census does is count people. It has no correlation to voters," said Anderson, who wrote a respected history of the census. "The census does not count only the politically active." ◆

Government

House Narrowly Supports Puerto Rico Plebiscite; Senate Takes No Action

Box Score

- **Bills:** HR 856; S 472, S Res 279
- **House action:** The House passed HR 856 (H Rept 105-131, Part 1), 209-208, on March 4.
- **Senate action:** The Senate adopted S Res 279 by voice vote on Sept. 17. There were no votes on S 472.

SUMMARY

The House passed legislation (HR 856) by one vote that would require a plebiscite in Puerto Rico through which the island's residents could choose to remain a commonwealth, become the 51st state or declare independence. But the similar Senate bill (S 472) never made it to a markup.

The Senate adopted a non-binding resolution (S Res 279) expressing support for the citizens of Puerto Rico and their decision to hold a Dec. 13 referendum on their political status.

Supporters of Puerto Rican statehood believed that formal authorization of the plebiscite by Congress would give the balloting more legitimacy in Washington.

Backing the measure were House Resources Committee Chairman Don Young, R-Alaska, and Speaker Newt Gingrich, R-Ga. But Senate Majority Leader Trent Lott, R-Miss., told Puerto Rico Gov. Pedro Rossello that the Senate did not plan to act on the bill in 1998.

The bill ran into opposition both from advocates of the island's commonwealth status — who said the bill was stacked in favor of statehood — and from Republicans who feared Puerto Rican statehood would boost the number of Democrats in Congress.

Referendum Bill Skirts Trouble In the House

MARCH 7 — A bill to allow Puerto Ricans to vote on the island's political status barely stayed alive in the House on March 4.

On a dramatic 209-208 vote after more than 10 hours of debate, the House passed the bill (HR 856) to allow a referendum in Puerto Rico. First, however, it scuttled an amendment that would have made English the official language of the United States, including Puerto Rico if it chose statehood. Attachment of the language amendment had threatened to kill the bill in the House and prompted veto threats from the White House. (Vote 37, p. H-12)

The House action, though, does not guarantee that such a bill will become law. Senate Majority Leader Trent Lott, R-Miss., said March 3 that the legislation is not a priority this year.

The bill would require that a referendum be held in Puerto Rico this year offering three choices: commonwealth status, as the island has now; statehood; or independence.

Puerto Rico was ceded to the United States by Spain under the treaty ending the Spanish-American War in 1898. In 1952, it became a U.S. commonwealth, meaning its residents have some, but not all, the rights of U.S. citizens. Puerto Ricans are subject to the military draft but cannot vote in federal elections. They do not pay federal taxes if they live on the island.

"Puerto Rico's colonial status remains unchanged," said Democrat Carlos Romero-Barceló, Puerto Rico's non-voting House delegate. "This is defining legislation for my constituents. It is our future, and yet, I cannot vote," he said.

The first crucial test came when the House defeated on a 13-406 an amendment to keep Spanish as the official language in Puerto Rico. (Vote 28, p. H-10)

Lawmakers adopted, 238-182, a substitute to the amendment saying only that if Puerto Rico becomes a state, it will have to follow whatever official language policy applies to the rest of the country. (Vote 29, p. H-10)

"Our common language is the tie that binds us all," said Republican Robert L. Livingston of Louisiana. "The ability to communicate with a common tongue is the key to success."

But opponents argued that such a requirement would have been opposed by the framers of the Constitution, who designated neither an official religion nor an official language. "This is not a dictatorship," Romero-Barceló said, adding that he thinks such a requirement is unnecessary because Puerto Ricans want to learn and speak English.

The bill created some unusual alliances. Jose E. Serrano, D-N.Y., backed the bill. But others of Puerto Rican descent — Luis V. Gutierrez, D-Ill., and Nydia M. Velázquez, D-N.Y. — opposed it, as did Rules Committee Chairman Gerald B.H. Solomon, N.Y., who wrote the English-language amendment.

The opponents said the bill is written to stack the odds in favor of statehood and that those who favor commonwealth status were not consulted during the drafting. For instance, the bill would require that a new referendum be held in Puerto Rico every 10 years if neither statehood or independence is chosen. Those who favor the commonwealth option say the bill defines "commonwealth" in a way that could allow Congress to strip Puerto Ricans of their U.S. citizenship at some point in the future.

Other Amendments

The House defeated other amendments:

One, by Serrano, would have allowed Puerto Ricans who were born on the island but live in the U.S. mainland to vote in the referendum. It was defeated, 57-356. (Vote 32, p. H-12)

An amendment offered by Bob

Barr, R-Ga., would have required a three-quarters supermajority vote before Puerto Rico could become a state. It was defeated, 131-282. (Vote 34, p. H-12)

If the bill is enacted and a majority of Puerto Ricans choose either statehood or independence, the following process will be set in motion:

• The president will have six months to submit legislation to Congress that provides for a transition period of no longer than 10 years.

• A separate referendum will then be held in Puerto Rico to approve or reject the transition plan.

• Puerto Ricans will then have to vote a third time on the issue before statehood or independence can occur.

Statehood or continued commonwealth status would be the likely choice. In the last referendum on the issue, in 1993, 48 percent chose commonwealth status, and 46 percent, statehood. Only 4.4 percent chose independence.

Senate Declines To Take Up Bill On Island's Status

APRIL 4 — After narrowly surviving in the House, a bill for a referendum on statehood in Puerto Rico ran out of steam in the Senate on April 2.

Majority Leader Trent Lott, R-Miss., told Puerto Rico Gov. Pedro Rossello that the Senate does not plan to act this year on legislation to allow Puerto Ricans to decide their island's political status.

Lott has long said the issue was not a priority this year. Still, the announcement was a major setback for a cause that has lived on the edge for months. The matter came to the Senate only after the House approved HR 856 by a 209-208 vote on March 4.

The bill called for a referendum to be held in Puerto Rico this year offering three choices: commonwealth status, as the island has now; statehood; or independence.

Sen. Frank H. Murkowski, R-Alaska, chairman of the Committee on Energy and Natural Resources, agreed with Lott that there is not enough time to address the matter this year. Murkowski said there would have to be several hearings before a vote could be held.

"Growing up under territorial status in Alaska, I certainly support the right of residents to formulate what the vision of their future may be," Murkowski said in a statement.

But, he added, "I have no illusions about the time and effort that will be required." ◆

Partisan Rancor Flares In Debate To Rename Washington National Airport

Congress passed legislation to rename Washington National Airport in honor of President Reagan on Feb. 5, the day before his 87th birthday.

SUMMARY

President Clinton joined lawmakers in sending best wishes to the former president in a signing ceremony on Reagan's birthday. But the signing came only after a partisan feud.

The bill to rename the airport was the first legislation signed into law in 1998. It sparked criticism from Democrats that the Republican-controlled Congress was intent on pursuing a "do-nothing" agenda.

The bill also was criticized by some lawmakers representing the Maryland and Virginia suburbs, who said Congress was meddling in the jurisdiction of the Metropolitan Washington Airports Authority. Some Democrats also objected to naming the airport, which lawmakers of both parties use, for a GOP hero.

Democrats Resist Renaming Airport For Reagan

JANUARY 31 — Republicans saw the renaming of Washington National Airport for President Ronald Reagan as a perfect gift for his 87th birthday Feb. 6.

But after failed negotiations on a possible compromise — including a Democratic bid to name the Justice Department headquarters for former Attorney General Robert F. Kennedy — Democrats thwarted a Senate floor vote on the airport-naming bill (S 1297) Jan. 29.

Sponsor Paul Coverdell, R-Ga., accused Democrats of trying to "exact a quid pro quo" for the Reagan tribute. "Today a cynical attack was launched against a great national leader,"

Box Score

• **Bill:** S 1575 — PL 105-154

• **House action:** The House cleared the Senate version of the bill (S 1575) by voice vote on Feb. 5. The House passed its version of the bill (HR 2625), 240-186, on Feb. 4.

• **Senate action:** The Senate passed S 1575, by 76-22, on Feb. 4.

• **Presidential action:** Clinton signed S 1575 on Feb. 6.

Coverdell said. "It's a surprising way to start this new session."

Senate Minority Leader Tom Daschle, D-S.D., replied that Democrats would not agree to a GOP plan to permit only one amendment, which would revise the name to Ronald Reagan National Airport from Ronald Reagan Washington National Airport.

"I don't think it would be in our best interests to proceed today," Daschle said. A Senate Democratic leadership aide said Democrats wanted to propose a commission to recommend building names.

Democrats also want to propose as

Government

an amendment a bill (HR 2676) passed by the House last year to revamp the Internal Revenue Service.

Daschle said Reagan already had a namesake, a new Washington office complex. Democrats also argued that removal of "Washington" from the airport would be disrespectful to the nation's first president.

"There is some question as well whether the Reagan family even wants this done," Daschle said.

Michael Kamburowski, a spokesman for the Reagan Legacy Project of Americans for Tax Reform, a main proponent of the bill, replied that the bill reflects the public's high regard for Reagan. His group also wants to "Put Ron on the Rock" — carve Reagan's visage on Mount Rushmore.

The House Transportation and Infrastructure Committee on Jan. 27 voted 39-28 along party lines to approve a similar bill (HR 2625), over Democrats who said it defied wishes of local officials and Rep. James P. Moran, D-Va., whose district includes the airport.

James L. Oberstar of Minnesota, the panel's ranking Democrat, argued to "keep National truly national" and suggested naming the Pentagon for Reagan.

The lone Democrat who voted for the bill, Gene Taylor of Mississippi, offered an amendment to require private interests to pay half the expense of the renaming. It was defeated 28-38. Another amendment by Peter A. DeFazio, D-Ore., to require the airport authority's approval of the change, failed 30-37.

A committee aide said the panel's chairman, Bud Shuster, R-Pa., had discussed naming other buildings for Kennedy with his eldest son, Rep Joseph P. Kennedy II, D-Mass., including the Education Department and Union Station, without agreement.

Opponents Say Renaming Airport Undermines Local Decision-Making

FEBRUARY 7 — Congress put aside weighty matters of state — the budget, Iraq, the Asian financial crisis — to name the Ronald Reagan Washington National Airport on Feb. 5, a day before the former president's 87th birthday.

Democrats and Republicans wished Reagan the best, but only after a bruising battle over the airport. The House cleared the bill by voice vote Feb. 5. President Clinton signed the measure on Reagan's birthday, saying, "He is in our thoughts and prayers."

The bipartisan spirit of Clinton's birthday greetings followed long debate in which lawmakers pondered the question: To name or not to name?

The Senate passed the airport bill (S 1575) by a vote of 76-22 on Feb. 4. The House approved another version (HR 2625) the same day, 240-186, and moved quickly to adopt the Senate's slightly different version Feb. 5. (*Senate vote 7, p. S-4; House vote 6, p. H-4*)

For many Republicans, the campaign provided a chance to pay homage one more time to Reagan, who suffers from Alzheimer's disease.

House Speaker Newt Gingrich, R-Ga., said renaming the airport was an appropriate tribute for the man who gave America "freedom from fear, from insecurity, and finally from the emotional, physical and financial costs of the Cold War."

As sweet as the victory was for Republicans, it was a bitter loss for some Democrats who tried to block the bill. They saw the proposal as a blatant political act by Republicans.

"This was clearly part of a conservative ideological agenda. It was driven by conservative talk show hosts. The goal was to turn the airport into a political billboard to greet visitors to Washington," said Rep. James L. Oberstar, D-Minn., who led the opposition.

One More for "The Gipper"

The Reagan Legacy Project of the Americans for Tax Reform, a conservative group, launched the airport campaign last year as part of a wider effort to put his name on buildings and his face on Mount Rushmore.

Michael Reagan, the former president's son, joined the final push at a news conference with Gingrich on Feb. 4, urging Congress to "win just one more for the Gipper."

Some Democrats offered to name practically anything else for Reagan except that airport, suggesting the Pentagon or Dulles International Airport. Others suggested Reagan had been honored enough with a new office building and a new Nimitz-class aircraft carrier, both of which carry his name.

Senate Republican Leader Trent Lott of Mississippi cleared the way for a vote by agreeing to consider a bill to reform the Internal Revenue Service (HR 2676) by March 30.

In floor debate in both chambers, Democrats criticized the proposal for going against the wishes of local officials and ending the identification of the airport with the nation's first president, who lived nearby at Mount Vernon. They even questioned the $60,000 cost of new signs, to which Sen. John McCain, R-Ariz., replied by reading from a letter from a C-SPAN viewer who offered to foot the bill.

Democrats also raised the issue of names for other buildings. In the Senate, Harry Reid, D-Nev., proposed an amendment to remove J. Edgar Hoover's name from the headquarters of the Federal Bureau of Investigation.

"J. Edgar Hoover stands for what is bad about this country. This small man violated the rights of hundreds, if not thousands, of people, famous and not so famous," Reid said.

Sen. Orrin G. Hatch, R-Utah, opposed the amendment, saying Hoover had many accomplishments. "I have to say there is a raft of FBI agents who would be very offended by this," he said. The Senate voted 62-36 to table (kill) the amendment.

In the House, Minority Leader Richard A. Gephardt, D-Mo., tried unsuccessfully in January to broker a compromise on the airport bill that would have permitted consideration of legislation (HR 1383) to name the Justice Department headquarters after Robert F. Kennedy, the former attorney general and senator from New York. (*Vote 5, p. H-4*)

But when efforts at a compromise broke down, the fighting broke out. "It was partisanship to the max," said House Budget Committee Chairman John R. Kasich, R-Ohio.

The 10,500-member National Air Traffic Controllers Association joined Democrats in criticizing Reagan for firing 11,000 air-traffic controllers during a 1981 strike. Randy Schwitz, the association's executive vice president, said he would prefer to have a "hot poker in my eye" than an airport named for Reagan. (*1981 Almanac, p. 330*)

Renaming National Airport

Light Agenda

Democrats, with private agreement from some Republicans, questioned the amount of time spent debating the bill and the wisdom of making it the first bill passed this year. "It's indicative that they have nothing else to do," said Rep. Barney Frank, D-Mass.

The biggest challenge to the proposal came in the House, where Republicans Thomas M. Davis III of Virginia, and Constance A. Morella of Maryland joined Democrats James P. Moran of Virginia and Peter A. DeFazio of Oregon, in sponsoring an amendment to require approval of the local Metropolitan Washington Airports Authority.

Backers of the amendment argued that the bill would pre-empt local decision-making, which Reagan championed. The House voted narrowly, 206-215, to defeat the amendment. *(Vote 4, p. H-4)*

A last attempt to derail the bill failed when the House voted 186-237 against a motion to modify the bill and name one of the airport's terminals for Reagan. House Whip Tom DeLay, R-Texas, argued against the motion, pointing out that former presidents George Bush and John F. Kennedy both have entire airports named for them in Texas and New York. "To say that it is OK to name a terminal after Ronald Reagan is an insult to the name of one of the greatest presidents that has ever served this country," DeLay said. *(Vote 5, p. H-4)* ◆

Chapter 14
HEALTH

Managed Care 14-3
   Republican Plan 14-7
   Side-by-Side Comparison of Bills 14-10

Home Health Care 14-16

Lawmakers Agree on Need For Changes in Managed Care — But Only in Principle

Box Score

- **Bills:** HR 1415, HR 3605, HR 4250; S 644, S 2330, S 1890
- **House action:** The House passed HR 4250, 216-210, on July 24.
- **Senate action:** A motion by Daschle to bring HR 4250 to the Senate floor was tabled, or killed, 50-47, on Oct. 9.

SUMMARY

Despite sounding similar themes for months — emergency care should be covered; doctors, rather than insurers, should have control over patient care — Republicans and Democrats could not reach agreement on legislation to give patients more rights with their health insurers, especially managed care.

House and Senate Republicans developed separate legislation that looked mostly to the market to correct problems, while Democrats rallied behind a bill that would have had the government play a broader role in the nation's health care system. Democrats also said patients should have the right to sue their health plans in state courts.

Employers and insurers, especially managed care companies, lobbied vigorously against any federal legislation, fearing that mandates would drive up costs.

In fact, there was little chance that any legislation would become law. A deal on health care would have required all interests to compromise on the proper role and reach of government in health care, the extent to which people should have legal recourse over the outcome of care, and ability of free-market principles to work in a rapidly changing industry. Still, the managed care issue was one that neither Republicans nor Democrats could ignore.

Rep. Charlie Norwood, R-Ga., introduced his own managed care bill (HR 1415), which attracted more than 200 co-sponsors in the House. Alfonse M. D'Amato, R-N.Y., sponsored its Senate companion (S 644), but it had just five cosponsors. House GOP leaders assembled a managed care task force that produced a bill (HR 4250) that passed the House along mostly party lines.

Senate Republicans produced their own version (S 2330), which differed in several ways from the House bill. For example, the Senate plan did not allow for malpractice lawsuits, while the House plan gave patients limited recourse under federal law. Senate leaders, however, never brought their measure to a floor vote.

The Democrats' bill in the Senate (S 1890) never won a vote, though Senate Minority Leader Tom Daschle, D-S.D., and Sen. Edward M. Kennedy, D-Mass., tried many times to attach the proposal to must-pass legislation. In the House, a Democratic bill (HR 3605) sponsored by John D. Dingell of Michigan was rejected July 24 by a vote of 212-217. The American Medical Association, traditionally an ally of the Republican Party, backed the Democrats' measure due to their growing frustrations with managed care.

Members of both parties agreed that the patients' rights issue will resurface in the 106th Congress.

Clinton Pushes 'Bill of Rights' For Patients

MARCH 14 — President Clinton has turned up the pressure on Congress to enact a patients' "bill of rights" this year, but House Speaker Newt Gingrich, R-Ga., said such legislation would not cure the nation's ailing health care system.

Gingrich, in a speech delivered just hours after Clinton spoke before the American Medical Association on March 9, predicted that Congress would probably pass "some sort of patient-protection bill" this year. That assessment, coming from a member of the Republican leadership — which has strongly opposed such bills — reflects the increasing pressure lawmakers are under from constituents who want government regulation of managed care plans.

Gingrich said such legislation would simply "add a new layer of litigation and a new layer of regulation." He hinted that some change may be made to the Employee Retirement Income Security Act, known as ERISA (PL 93-406), a 1974 law that prevents employees from suing their health plans under state medical malpractice laws.

"So it will now be government bureaucrats watching corporate bureaucrats watching doctors. And the doctors will have greater access to trial lawyers to sue the corporate bureaucrats. That is not, in the long run, the solution," Gingrich said.

A Dominant Role

The issue of patients' rights in health care — particularly in managed care — is playing a dominant role on Capitol Hill, where dozens of bills have been introduced to place federal standards on health care insurers. Areas of concern among voters include access to emergency care, appeals processes and so-called gag clauses, which restrict physician-patient communications about issues such as treatments not covered by a patient's health plan.

Clinton called on the House and Senate "to go down in history as a Congress that saved lives by passing the patients' bill of rights. . . . It's just a question of mustering the will to get the job done and going through some of the very difficult issues around the edges that have to be resolved. But there is utterly no reason not to do this this year."

Added Pressures

Days after Gingrich and Clinton made their remarks, a presidential

Health

commission that last fall called for a consumer "bill of rights" released a final report that sidestepped the issue of federal legislation. While that outcome was widely expected, some critics said it was a blow to the president's push for congressional action.

The Advisory Commission on Consumer Protection and Quality in the Health Care Industry also avoided a specific recommendation on the complicated ERISA issue. After sharp and truncated debate, the group instead called for a "national dialogue" on the topic.

Despite those omissions, Health and Human Services Secretary Donna E. Shalala said the report would "shape the nation's health care agenda" and that it anticipated many changes that need to be made to the country's health care system.

Commission member Ron Pollack, executive director of the consumers group Families USA, called the panel's decision not to take a formal position on ERISA a "terrible abdication of their responsibilities."

But commission member J. Randall MacDonald, executive vice president of human resources and administration at GTE Corp., said, "We should do everything we can to stay out of the political process."

Industry Influence

A business group that has been lobbying against pending managed care bills said that the commission's reluctance to make legislative recommendations shows that proposals to establish government mandates are misguided.

Dan Danner, a spokesman for the Health Benefits Coalition, an alliance of insurers, manufacturers and other business organizations, said many lawmakers are beginning to "take a second look" at the legislation.

And even though Gingrich predicted Congress would pass a patients' rights bill, Danner was skeptical. "I don't think that's a foregone conclusion that there will be legislation, and if there is, we certainly don't think it will necessarily be onerous legislation that has a significant increase in costs," he said.

Danner's group, which includes the National Federation of Independent Business, the Health Insurance Association of America and Aetna U.S. Healthcare, has waged an all-out war against measures (HR 1415, S 644) sponsored by Rep. Charlie Norwood, R-Ga., and Sen. Alfonse M. D'Amato, R-N.Y.

The bills, which have garnered the most attention of the various efforts to regulate managed care, would allow patients to appeal denials of services, require plans to cover reasonable emergency care and prevent plans from limiting what doctors can tell patients about treatment options. The bills also would amend ERISA to allow patients to sue their health plans under state malpractice laws.

While many lawmakers like parts of the Norwood-D'Amato bill, some are looking for less far-reaching legislation. To that end, GOP-led House and Senate task forces have been working to develop alternative bills that could garner enough support for passage.

Democrats Seek To Give Patients More Power

APRIL 4 — As lawmakers struggled over whether the federal government should attempt to remedy consumers' concerns about managed care, Democrats stepped up pressure on Republicans to pass legislation that would give patients more power in dealing with their health insurance companies.

House and Senate Democrats on March 31 introduced a sweeping bill that would give consumers greater access to specialists, to emergency care and a speedy external appeals process when there is a dispute with insurers.

President Clinton has pushed Congress to enact a broad patients' rights bill this year, but GOP leaders in both chambers have signaled their displeasure with such measures. Business groups have waged an all-out fight against proposed mandates, saying they will drive up costs and curtail employees' coverage.

While Democrats looked to increase the government's role in health care, Ways and Means Committee Chairman Bill Archer, R-Texas, looked to the tax code. To help individuals without insurance afford it, Archer said Congress should use money from a possible federal tobacco settlement to expand the deductibility of health insurance benefits.

Archer's plan would allow small-business owners, the self-employed and workers whose employers do not provide health insurance to have the same full deductibility for health costs that many employers get. Archer also proposed lowering the threshold for deducting medical expenses from the current 7.5 percent of adjusted gross income to as low as 2.5 percent.

While the idea of allowing individuals the same deductibility for health costs as business has wide appeal among both Democrats and Republicans, tying it to the tobacco settlement may not. Many lawmakers want those funds to go exclusively to smoking-related illnesses.

Differentiating the Parties

The Archer plan underscored the big differences between the two parties, with Democrats calling for strong federal protections for patients and the GOP seeking to let the market work out glitches in the rapidly changing managed care industry.

In introducing their own legislation (S 1890, HR 3605), Democrats said they wanted to give consumers broad new protections, including the power to sue health plan providers for damages under state laws by amending the 1974 Employee Retirement Income Security Act (PL 93-406). The measures would also require that employees have the opportunity to see health care providers other than those on a plan's approved list.

Sen. Edward M. Kennedy, D-Mass., a leading sponsor, said the proposals "guarantee that families receive the health care they were promised when they bought an insurance policy and paid their premiums." John D. Dingell, D-Mich., the main House sponsor, said he hoped Congress could finish the bill by fall.

The legislation won immediate praise from Clinton and from two of Washington's most powerful lobbying groups, the American Medical Association and organized labor.

Business interests condemned the measures. Chip Kahn, chief operating officer and president-designate of the Health Insurance Association of

Managed Care

America, an industry group, said the legislation was "little more than a transparent, election-year guise of consumer protection."

Some consumers say Congress must act because insurers have harshly denied care, even in life-threatening situations. At the news conference to announce the Democratic leadership plan, David Garvey of Chicago said his wife, Barbara, became ill on a trip to Hawaii but was ordered by the family's Health Maintenance Organization (HMO) to return home for treatment, despite objections from Hawaii physicians who said she was too weak to travel. She suffered a stroke en route and died nine days later. "Our HMO was more interested in saving money than in saving her life," Garvey said.

Democrats have used such stories to put a human face on the issue and to intensify the move for federal regulation. On April 2, Kennedy tried unsuccessfully to force the Senate to vote on a non-binding resolution calling for enactment of a patients' bill of rights. His amendment was tabled (killed) on a vote of 51-47, allowing senators to avoid a test vote on the issue. The "sense of the Senate" amendment was one of several attached to the fiscal 1999 budget resolution (S Con Res 86). *(Vote 73, p. S-14)*

Lobbyists Rally Against High Cost Of Managed Care

APRIL 11 — For years, groups representing non-physician providers of medical services — such as podiatrists, chiropractors and optometrists — have accused managed care companies of trying to muscle them out of health plans. They are excluded, they say, just because they are not medical doctors even though they offer comparable services, often at lower costs.

Now they are fighting back with cash.

In 1997, members of the Patient Access to Responsible Care Alliance, a lobbying group fighting for legislation that would place federal standards on managed care plans, made contributions of nearly $1.6 million to political parties and congressional candidates, according to an analysis by the Center for Responsive Politics, a nonpartisan group that tracks campaign contributions. More than half of that money, 53 percent, went to Democrats who back efforts to broaden the federal government's role in managed care.

The giving is largely intended to bolster support for legislation (HR 1415, S 644) sponsored by Rep. Charlie Norwood, R-Ga., and Sen. Alfonse M. D'Amato, R-N.Y., that would establish standards for managed care companies, including provisions that would protect non-physician providers against discrimination and widen patient access to specialists.

The provider groups are up against formidable opposition. The managed care industry is working aggressively to prevent legislation such as the Norwood-D'Amato bills from passing. The industry gave nearly $1.1 million in 1997, with 64 percent of that going to Republicans, according to the center's analysis, which is based on Federal Election Commission data. Many insurers and employers oppose legislative fixes for managed care, saying federal mandates would be so costly that they would make health insurance unaffordable for employers and workers.

The totals include contributions to federal candidates by political action committees (PACs), individual contributions to candidates and to parties from people affiliated with these industries, and "soft money," which refers to unregulated, usually large contributions to political parties.

The issue cuts across party lines. Democrats more readily embrace sweeping legislation while Republicans are less interested in federal regulation of managed care. The GOP leadership in both chambers has said it will block bills that impose federal mandates on the industry.

Goliath vs. Goliath

While many of the provider groups say they cannot possibly compete with the deep pockets of powerful insurance companies and large employers, the flow of money so far in the managed care debate shows otherwise, according to Jennifer Shecter, who compiled the financial analysis for the center.

"I would in no way say this is a David versus Goliath battle; not in the least bit," she said. She said she expects contributions on both sides to accelerate as the managed care debate continues and as the campaign season swings into full gear.

Groups on both sides of the battle say their contributions are aimed not only at health care, which is a key priority for them, but also at issues such as Medicare, taxes, education and appropriations.

But they have focused much of their energy on the managed care debate. Already both sides have launched advertising campaigns in an attempt to influence the outcome. In January, the Health Benefits Coalition, an alliance of insurance and business groups, unveiled a $1 million advertising effort to stop legislation such as the Norwood-D'Amato bill. The provider alliance has waged a smaller-scale advertising campaign designed to convince people that their managed care companies are insensitive, overly powerful and concerned only about their bottom line.

Provider groups pushing for federal regulation of managed care plans say it is needed as much for consumers as it is to protect the providers' livelihoods.

"Our guys are not getting a fair chance to compete and consumers are not being served. The access is a big issue," said Alan Peterson, assistant director of government relations for the American Optometric Association, one of the provider groups operating within the alliance. He said "lots and lots" of plans are excluding optometrists from coverage just because they are not medical doctors.

The provider alliance, a coalition of 70 organizations, found an ally in Norwood, who was a dentist and has seen firsthand the problems that have arisen with the advent of managed care.

The problem, said David E. Hebert, director of federal government affairs for the American Association of Nurse Anesthetists and chairman of the provider alliance, is a "patchwork quilt" that now exists, with some health plans much more accepting of non-physician providers than others.

Groups such as Hebert's favor the Norwood-D'Amato measures because they would prevent health plans from

Health

discriminating against providers based on their "license or certification under applicable state law," according to the bills. The bills also would allow patients, at additional cost, to see providers outside the pre-approved health care network if they were unhappy with the options available under their plans.

More broadly, the measures would force health plans to cover emergency room care, provide a process for appeals of coverage decisions and allow patients to sue managed care health plans for malpractice.

Insurers say while the Norwood-D'Amato bills may be well intentioned, they would give health plans little latitude over screening and selecting providers.

"Policies that would make it more difficult for health plans to contract with selected providers and encourage patients to use those providers, or that would destroy incentives for innovation by micromanaging plan operations, would return us to the serious problems that brought on change in the first place," Karen Ignagni, president and chief executive officer of the American Association of Health Plans, a managed care trade group, told a House panel last October.

Money Talks

Several provider groups are pledging significant funds to back their battle against managed care. For example, the nurse anesthetists gave $135,396 in PAC contributions in 1997, with nearly $50,000 to Democrats and about $85,000 to Republicans. Hebert said that the group expects to spend $600,000 to $700,000 in the 1997-98 election cycle. The American Occupational Therapy Association, which gave $78,825 in 1997, is expected to give as much as $500,000 this election cycle, said Kathryn Pontzer, legislative counsel for the group.

The providers' group came together on the assumption that business and insurers would spend huge amounts of money to fight legislation setting mandates for managed care, as they did in fighting President Clinton's Health Security Act, which failed in 1994. (*1994 Almanac*, p. 319)

Last fall, Republican leaders urged business groups to get on board with the effort to block managed care overhaul legislation. Figures from the Center for Responsive Politics seem to suggest that several insurance and business groups, as well as the American Medical Association (AMA) are responding generously.

Ignagni's managed care group, for example, contributed $42,780 in 1997, with 83 percent of that total going to Republicans. The 1997 amount is nearly triple the group's 1995 tally of $14,597. The Health Insurance Association of America gave $117,015, which was 47 percent higher than 1995 contributions. In both years, Republicans received the major share of the take, receiving 67 percent in 1997 and 76 percent in 1995, according to the center.

While the AMA praised legislation (S 1890, HR 3605) from Sen. Edward M. Kennedy, D-Mass., and Rep. John D. Dingell, D-Mich., that includes many of the same provisions as the Norwood-D'Amato bills, the group and its state affiliates in 1997 gave 70 percent of its $442,682 contributions to Republicans.

Members of the Health Benefits Coalition also gave heavily to GOP candidates in 1997. Republicans received nearly all of the National Federation of Independent Business' contributions, taking home 86 percent of the group's $235,901 total, although the organization lobbies Congress on a host of issues, including taxes and the minimum wage, said Dan Danner, the federation's chief lobbyist. Insurers CIGNA and the Prudential Insurance Co. of America gave heavily as well, with 69 percent of companies' 1997 donations going to Republicans.

Both sides of the managed care issue are watching a House GOP task force led by Dennis Hastert, R-Ill., who hopes to release a bill by May. The measure will likely be the starting point for managed care legislation this year.

While Sen. Don Nickles, R-Okla., is leading a similar task force, he is extremely reluctant to pass legislation that includes any federal mandates on managed care, no matter how small.

At a time when constituents are complaining about managed care, many lawmakers feel they have to do something. Managed care companies may be feeling that pressure as well.

"A year ago, the industry was issuing a monolithic 'No. No. No.' to federal legislation, but now they're starting to appreciate the depth of concern people have about managed care," said Peterson, of the optometrists' group.

House Republicans Unveil Their Overhaul Plan

JUNE 27 — House Republicans' long-awaited health care proposal was intended to send the message that they have answered voters' concerns about managed care without abandoning core GOP goals such as reducing federal regulation and improving choices for individuals.

The outline, unveiled June 24, gives Republican lawmakers a plan they can take home over the July Fourth recess to answer months of criticism from Democrats that the GOP-led Congress was insensitive to calls for government remedies to abuses by managed care companies.

The question now, however, is whether the GOP plan will have credibility with voters after President Clinton and congressional Democrats have spent the better part of the past year calling for a "patients' bill of rights" — a neatly-packaged concept designed to play on voters' concerns about overly powerful health maintenance organization (HMO) bureaucracies.

Republicans are expected to attempt to reassure voters that they, too, have a health care solution that is focused on returning power to doctors and patients that has been stripped away as more Americans have moved into managed care.

Enacting a managed care bill this year is critical to Republicans, especially since many Democrats blame them for the demise of tobacco legislation in the Senate. A victory in health care may help the GOP avoid being seen as the party of obstruction.

By responding to patients' concerns, however, the party risks alienating the industry interests that have helped bring Republicans to power and keep them there. A leading business lobbying group on health care immediately condemned the GOP plan and promised a vigorous fight to defeat it.

As if to answer business concerns about federal interference, task force chairman Dennis Hastert, R-Ill., said the proposal would protect patients without expanding the reach of government.

"I'm proud to say that our plan provides patients with the necessary protections to get them well without new taxes, more bureaucracy or the heavy hand of government," Hastert said at a news conference attended by more industry lobbyists than journalists.

The plan represents a targeted approach that combines politically popular initiatives — allowing patients to appeal insurers' coverage decisions and giving them greater access to specialty care, for example — while including conservative, market-oriented proposals such as tax-exempt medical savings accounts and cooperatives that would allow small businesses to buy health coverage in purchasing pools.

Democrats said the plan would provide few true protections for patients, with Senate Minority Leader Tom Daschle, D-S.D., dubbing it "recycled rhetoric with one motive — political cover."

While some administration officials gave a warmer-than-expected response to the Republican health proposal, Democrats' pollster Celinda Lake said it reflected an overall strategy to "cooperate and not be confrontational," a tenor that would appeal to voters.

Just who voters believe is really answering their concerns on managed care depends on how both parties portray the issue over the recess and beyond, she said, adding that the next few months will bring a "real battle for credibility."

GOP Plan

The Republican proposal would allow consumers to appeal coverage decisions both to the insurer and to an outside panel of independent experts. But it is unclear if such appeals will be binding.

The task force also proposed modifications to the Employee Retirement Income Security Act (ERISA), a 1974 law (PL 93-406) governing health plans, to give consumers broader legal recourse. While the specifics were not spelled out, remedies would likely include a monetary penalty assessed on plans for each day they withheld care as a disincentive for plans to deny coverage. Patients also will be allowed to recover court costs plus receive the treatment they originally sought.

The task force proposal would permit women to designate gynecologists as their primary care physicians and pediatricians as the primary care doctors for children. The plan also would allow consumers in many cases to have the option — at an additional expense — to obtain care from a specialist not listed in an insurer's list of pre-approved providers. But there are exceptions. For example, if an employer offers an employee the option of a medical savings account — a tax-exempt account used for qualified medical expenses — then they would not be required to offer the additional choices, known as a point-of-service option. Or if employers could prove the point-of-service mandate increased their insurance costs by more than 1 percent —

GOP's Health Care Plan

JUNE 27 — The House Republican health care task force plan unveiled June 24 includes:

● Internal and external appeals processes that would give patients more power to challenge insurers' decisions about coverage. Internal appeals would be supervised by a plan's medical doctor and decided in a week to 10 days. External appeals would be judged by independent medical experts. Patients could choose to forgo the appeals and sue their provider.

● Changes to the 1974 Employee Retirement Income Security Act (ERISA) that would establish financial penalties for plans that were found to withhold medical care.

● Requirements that plans allow access to specialists not on a pre-approved list of providers.

● Coverage of emergency medical care when a "prudent layperson" would deem it necessary.

● Prohibitions on so-called gag clauses, which restrict communications between physicians and patients.

● Allowing women to see gynecologists and children to see pediatricians as their primary care physicians.

● Initiatives that would allow small businesses to pool resources to purchase coverage at more affordable rates than they could individually. The plan also would allow creation of nonprofit purchasing pools not subject to many state regulations now governing insurers.

● Initiatives that would protect the confidentiality of individual medical records while not inhibiting medical researchers' access to such data.

● Changes to current regulations governing tax-exempt medical savings accounts.

● A limitation on non-economic medical malpractice damage awards, to $250,000 unless a state already has a higher cap in place.

Hastert and others say it will not — they would also be exempt.

David E. Hebert, chairman of the Patient Access to Responsible Care Alliance, a coalition consisting primarily of non-physician health care provider groups that has backed a bill (HR 1415) sponsored by Rep. Charlie Norwood, R-Ga., complained that the provision to allow patients to see non-plan doctors "has enough exemptions that you could drive a Mack truck through it."

The GOP measure also would require plans to cover emergency medical care when a "prudent layperson" would deem it necessary and prohibit so-called gag clauses, which restrict communications between physicians and their patients.

Covering the Uninsured

The group incorporated into its proposal concepts that task force members have championed as ways to reduce the number of uninsured, especially those who work for small busi-

Health

nesses or who are self-employed and have difficulty finding coverage at affordable rates. They include a proposal from Commerce Committee Chairman Republican Thomas J. Bliley Jr. of Virginia, to create "HealthMarts," which would allow employers, insurers, providers and employees to develop packages that Bliley and other backers believe would give workers more choices for their health care.

Also included is an initiative from Education and the Workforce Employer-Employee Relations Subcommittee Chairman Harris W. Fawell, R-Ill., to allow church groups, trade associations and other organizations to form "association health plans," which would enable them to pool resources to purchase policies at more affordable rates than they could individually. Fawell, who is retiring this year, has tried several times to pass his concept into law.

While insurance groups including the Health Insurance Association of America (HIAA) and the National Association of Insurance Commissioners oppose the Bliley and Fawell initiatives, organizations such as the National Federation of Independent Business said the plans would make coverage affordable for small businesses.

A proposal championed by Commerce Health and Environment Subcommittee Chairman Michael Bilirakis, R-Fla., to promote the expansion of community health center networks — and to allow them to compete with other private health plans — is included as well.

Additional provisions of the GOP plan aim to protect confidentiality of individuals' medical information while allowing researchers necessary access so medical research will not be impeded.

The plan also pays homage to two GOP health staples: limiting medical malpractice awards and broader access to medical savings accounts. The proposal would place a $250,000 cap on non-economic malpractice (so-called pain and suffering) damage awards unless a state already has a higher cap in place. The proposal would lower the current deductibility levels of policies in the medical savings account demonstration project included in the insurance portability law (PL 104-191) Congress passed in 1996. (*1996 Almanac, p. 6-28*)

With lower deductibles in place, the policies may appeal to more people, task force members reasoned.

The panel also directed the House Ways and Means Committee to determine if "appropriate offsets" can be found to accelerate the 100 percent tax deductibility for the self-employed.

"This Republican plan is as good as it gets," said Ways and Means Health Subcommittee Chairman Bill Thomas, R-Calif., referring to the popular movie in which the character played by actress Helen Hunt made disparaging remarks about HMOs.

Developing the plan was a task that many Republicans had hoped to avoid. When President Clinton and congressional Democrats signaled last fall they would push for their "bill of rights" setting federal standards for managed care plans, GOP leaders dismissed it as just another attempt to resurrect Clinton's failed Health Security Act, which called for a mammoth overhaul of the nation's health care system. (*1994 Almanac, p. 319*)

Democrats have introduced legislation (S 1890, HR 3605) to put those intentions into law, including giving consumers more power to fight their health plans' coverage decisions and seek legal recourse over disputes. Norwood's bill, which has companion legislation in the Senate (S 944) sponsored by Alfonse M. D'Amato, R-N.Y., includes similar provisions.

Ron Pollack, executive director of the consumers group Families USA, said the GOP plan "has the odor of an election year public relations stunt. . . . The Gingrich task force offers us too little in any proposed details and too much in extraneous provisions that will kill any chances of managed care reform this year."

Republicans in both chambers, however, said action on managed care legislation could come as early as July. A Senate GOP task force is nearing completion of its own proposals.

Months in the Making

The House GOP plan came after four months of meetings, including 7:30 a.m. Thursday briefings where task force members nibbled on doughnuts and sipped coffee as they tried to understand what was wrong with the current health care system and how to fashion a cure.

As their discussions continued in Hastert's office, tucked in the Capitol suite designated for Majority Whip Tom DeLay, R-Texas, tensions increased, especially with Norwood, a former dentist who insisted that the final plan embrace his idea that patients should be able to sue their health plans for damages under state laws.

The differences seemed to have eased by the time the plan was released. At the news conference, Norwood thanked Hastert for his "tolerance of me over the last four months." While Norwood conceded the task force did not embrace his liability proposal, he said it does contain "75 percent" of what he sought.

"At some point, you have to stop fighting and declare victory," Norwood said, adding that he must see the legislative language before he gives his full support.

While Norwood is on board, Democrats and many industry groups are not. Even before Republicans made their plan public, the HIAA delivered harsh criticism.

"Its recommendations represent a mishmash of cobbled-together ideas that are guaranteed to raise consumers' costs, reduce choice and generate more federal bureaucracy," said Bill Gradison, a former Republican congressman from Ohio (1975-93) who serves as the group's president.

Gradison said no pending managed care bill would solve consumers' concerns about managed care more effectively than the marketplace.

"The market is moving in this direction, but not through some heavy, government-regulated scheme," he said. "We believe the public would be better served by no congressional action."

Democrats also pounced on the bill. Sen. Edward M. Kennedy, D-Mass., called it "a payback for health insurance industry support, not a serious effort to address the abuses of HMOs and managed care plans."

House Minority Leader Richard A. Gephardt, D-Mo., said that since the GOP proposal includes items that have already failed to pass Congress, such as the malpractice cap, the measure is "designed for show, not to become law."

Even interests usually friendly to the GOP criticized the plan. The Health Benefits Coalition, an alliance

Managed Care

of business and insurance groups that has been fighting the congressional momentum to regulate managed care, said the proposal was packed with "a broad array of big-government mandates that we will vigorously oppose."

And the American Medical Association, a longtime GOP ally that has thrown its support behind the Democrats' plan, said the Republican proposal "does not go far enough."

The Republicans' strategy in selling their plan over the next several months will be key to their ability to win points with voters in the November elections.

Important to Voters

Potential regulation of HMOs is one issue that a clear majority of the public sees as very important to both the country and to themselves personally, according to a recent poll conducted by Pew Research Center for the People & the Press.

When asked to rank a series of issues, 68 percent said the debate over HMO regulation is very important to the nation and 60 percent said it is very important personally. Andrew Kohut, director of the center, said the finding shows that "it's an opportunity for both sides to score points if they can do something on this because the public really wants something to happen."

For her part, Democratic strategist Lake is urging her clients to emphasize their traditional role as the party that voters can turn to for fighting big business and special interests. She said Democrats should do everything possible to link the GOP plan to House Speaker Newt Gingrich, R-Ga., since 73 percent of Americans she has polled said they do not trust him on HMO reform.

Republican pollster Kellyanne Fitzpatrick agreed that traditionally Democrats are trusted more than Republicans on the issue of health care, but she said they can battle back by pounding the key points of their plan — choice, access, quality and accountability.

"We need to start bragging about it a little bit more," she said.

Senate Assistant Majority Leader Don Nickles, R-Okla., agreed. "I do think it's important for our people to show that they are for something, not just against it."

Lobby Launches Ad Campaign To Discredit Bills

JULY 4 — As House Republicans begin pushing their proposal to give consumers more power with their managed care plans, a major industry group is firing back with a campaign of its own.

The American Association of Health Plans, which represents more than 1,000 managed care providers nationwide, recently began airing two television commercials in the Washington area to discredit legislative attempts to curb managed care.

The ads argue that such measures, including a House GOP plan unveiled June 24, will drive up costs and may cause people to lose their insurance. Both spots close with a chilling prediction: "When politicians play doctor, real people can get hurt."

While strategically timed to match the rollout of House Republican legislation, the ads are part of an ongoing strategy the group has used for months both inside the Beltway and beyond to battle back against political pressure for managed care legislation.

Since March the group's representatives have appeared at news events held in 10 targeted areas represented by lawmakers on both sides of the issue, said group spokesman John A. Murray.

Other groups on both sides of the debate have been running their own campaigns for months in hopes of winning support from the public as well as from legislators.

A Viable Strategy

Karen Ignagni, the association's president and chief executive officer, said the group's strategy of taking its message beyond the Beltway is working. The regional visits, combined with the group's lobbying and grassroots efforts, "are yielding political dividends throughout the nation," Ignagni wrote in a letter accompanying a compilation of press clippings sent to group members.

Those clippings showed that many newspapers ran articles and editorials that spelled out the industry's point of view. As the instigator of news conferences with local print and broadcast journalists, the group has often been able to make its arguments the main point of the article, with detractors lower in the story and often getting less attention.

Carter A. Eskew, partner with the public relations firm BSMG Worldwide agreed there are definite benefits to going outside the Beltway. Eskew, who is not involved in the managed care campaign, helped orchestrate a tobacco industry-sponsored nationwide advertising campaign credited with killing tobacco control legislation in the Senate (S 1415). He said there's "no question" those ads "helped change the dynamics of the [tobacco] debate."

Even with an unpopular industry such as tobacco, some people were still willing to listen to the industry's message, Eskew said. The resulting flurry of news reports boosts the spirits of trade group members, who "feel as if they're in the bunker" because their industry has been under attack. Washington lawmakers tend to pay more attention as well, Eskew said.

A big difference between tobacco and health care, however, is money. While tobacco interests spent $40 million on their campaign, the managed care group so far this year has spent $2 million, said Murray.

Adrienne Mitchem, legislative counsel for the advocacy group Consumers Union, said that no matter how much money the managed care industry spends, consumers will not buy the pitch.

Mitchem called the group's targeted press campaign "a last-ditch effort to turn back the tide" for congressional action this year. By now, she said, millions of Americans have become familiar with the problems of managed care and are not likely to be swayed by a media campaign to block federal protections.

Showdown Looms On Managed Care Legislation

JULY 18 — As President Clinton and congressional Democrats prepare for a showdown with Republicans over managed care legislation, both sides are trying to portray the issue as one that is so

Health

Side-by-Side Comparisons

Issue	Senate GOP (S 2330)	House-passed GOP (HR 4250)	Democrats (S 1890; HR 3605)
Malpractice lawsuits	No provision.	Modifies 1974 Employee Retirement Income Security Act (PL 93-406) to give patients broader legal recourse to collect damages from insurers. Health plans could be fined up to $250,000 for withholding coverage.	Amends ERISA to give patients ability to sue health plans under applicable state laws.
Malpractice damages cap	No cap.	Sets a $250,000 ceiling on non-economic (so-called pain and suffering) damages that a patient can be awarded in a lawsuit. Limit would not apply if a state already has a higher cap in place or enacts a new one.	No cap.
Primary care for women	Allows direct access to gynecologists without referral.	Similar provision.	Similar provision. Women may also choose gynecologists as their primary care physicians.
Mastectomies	Stipulates decisions regarding postoperative hospital stays be made by doctors and patients. Health plans that cover mastectomies must cover reconstructive breast surgery.	No provision.	Requires health plans to pay for a minimum 48-hour hospital stay. Requires coverage of post-mastectomy reconstructive breast surgery.
Internal appeals	Mandates an internal appeals process, giving patients more leverage to challenge a plan's coverage decision. Complaints must be addressed within 30 days, and in 72 hours for medical emergencies.	Establishes internal appeals process with same deadlines for decisions as the Senate plan.	Internal appeals must be decided within 15 business days, or 72 hours for emergencies.
External appeals	Mandates a binding external review process but limits those reviews to medical expenses exceeding $1,000 and procedures that are experimental, such as cancer treatments.	Does not limit appeals, but allows health plans to charge patients seeking an appeal between $25 and $100, or 10% of cost of medical procedure, whichever is less. Plans not complying with results of appeal could pay up to $250,000. Additional fines may be added by a judge.	Allows external appeals if care is denied because it is deemed medically unnecessary and the amount exceeds a "significant threshold," or if patient's life or health is in jeopardy. Decisions must be made within 60 days, or 72 hours for emergencies.

Side-by-Side Comparisons

Issue	Senate GOP (S 2330)	House-passed GOP (HR 4250)	Democrats (S 1890; HR 3605)
Medical savings accounts	Lifts many current restrictions on medical savings accounts (MSAs), tax-exempt savings accounts to pay medical expenses. Lifts cap on number of MSAs that can be sold nationwide.	Expands access to MSAs, with many similarities to the Senate plan.	No provision.
Gag rules	Prohibits health plans from dictating to health care providers what treatment options may or may not be discussed in conferences with patients.	Goes a step further than Senate bill, saying doctor-patient conversations could not be restricted by health plan.	Similar provision to House Republican bill.
HealthMarts	No provision.	Allows small businesses, insurers and health care providers to join forces and create purchasing pools to develop and administer health plans for workers. Effective date: Jan. 1, 2000.	No provision.
Association health plans	No provision.	Amends ERISA to allow church, trade and business organizations to form alliances and purchase insurance at rates lower than if they bought coverage individually.	No provision.
Point of service	Requires employers with more than 50 workers to offer the "point of service" option, which would permit employees to choose a health care provider from outside a pre-approved list. Employee would have to pay the difference.	Requires employers to offer the point of service option. Exceptions include companies that make health insurance available through a HealthMart or if insurance costs rise more than 1 percent.	Requires employers to offer point of service unless the employer offers at least one other health plan administered by a different company, or two or more health plans that have provider networks which "differ significantly."
Emergency care	Does not require pre-authorization for initial screenings if a "prudent layperson" would deem emergency care necessary or if patient is suffering "severe pain." For additional tests, approval of a "prudent emergency medical professional" would be required.	Uses prudent layperson definition for authorization of initial coverage. For additional tests, would require approval of a "prudent emergency medical professional."	Uses prudent layperson standard, but also includes requirement that emergency care be covered for "severe pain." Plans must cover post-stabilization and maintenance care when necessary.

Health

important it rises above politics.

"This should be a bipartisan issue," House Speaker Newt Gingrich, R-Ga., said at a July 16 rally at which House Republicans used the backdrop of a local emergency room to push their health care plan.

The same day, Clinton told a Democratic rally in a packed congressional hearing room that the managed care debate was a partisan issue only in Washington. "When you show up in an emergency room or when you test positive for a biopsy, no one asks you which political party you belong to," the president said.

Both Republicans and Democrats say there is ample room to put aside politics and compromise on legislation to provide patients with more protection from their managed care plans. In the Senate, both sides have even named their bill the "Patients' Bill of Rights," a fact sure to blur the lines in voters' minds about who is sponsoring what.

But as the proposals are compared and debated, differences between the two philosophies will become more apparent. Still unclear is whether the parties will find common ground on the issue or allow their differences to define them in the fall elections. Republicans will also have to resolve some intra-party differences over the issue before they can agree with Democrats.

An indication of the bill's prospects will become evident the week of July 20, when the House is scheduled to take action on a GOP bill (HR 4250) that Gingrich introduced July 16. The Senate also is likely to take action on its measure (S 2330) before Congress adjourns for the August recess.

Enactment before the break would likely mean that both chambers would sidestep the committee hearing process. But pressure is growing to act this year. The AFL-CIO July 16 kicked off a nationwide effort to push for action on patients' rights and announced an advertising campaign to prod lawmakers to enact the Democratic bill.

While there appear to be some areas of compromise — for example, both Democrats and Republicans would improve coverage of emergency medical care and force insurers to detail the type of medical treatments they cover — other issues have vast potential to sink any agreement. They include the dispute over whether patients should have the right to sue their health plans for damages and what restrictions, if any, should be placed on medical savings accounts, tax-exempt accounts to pay for qualified medical expenses.

At his appearance on Capitol Hill, Clinton said that, in the end, both sides will have to put "progress ahead of partisanship" in order to pass legislation this year. But Democrats have shown little willingness to give ground, insisting that their bill (S 1890; HR 3605) is the best way to remedy problems patients have with their health plans.

Dissent within Republican ranks caused Ways and Means Health Subcommittee Chairman Bill Thomas, R-Calif., to withdraw his support after the House GOP bill was changed at the last minute. Thomas declined to say why he dropped his support, but Republican aides said Thomas felt the changes made the bill too heavy with government regulation.

And pressure from Thomas and others caused Rep. Greg Ganske, R-Iowa, a former plastic surgeon who has adamantly backed the Democrats' managed care bill for months, to resign July 15 from a coveted spot on the bipartisan commission Congress created last year to help strengthen the long-term future of the Medicare program. House Republican leaders also may face opposition from members of the Conservative Action Team, known as CAT, who favor provisions in the House GOP plan that allow small businesses to pool resources and make health insurance coverage more affordable.

"Dropping or gutting these market-oriented provisions would tip this finely balanced package in favor of more mandates and government control," the group wrote in a letter to Gingrich.

Differences in the plans proposed by Senate and House Republicans underscore just how tough it will be for GOP leaders to develop a consensus within their own party on the managed care issue, as well as win support from both voters and the party's traditional business allies.

To be sure, some elements of both Republican proposals will be cast aside should the plans pass their respective chambers and reach a House-Senate conference committee. House Republicans will probably have to part with their proposal to cap non-economic damages in medical malpractice lawsuits at $250,000.

The liability issue is shaping up as a pivotal one. At his appearance on Capitol Hill, Clinton said that individual state laws could not solve the problems of managed care and that consumers should have the right to sue their health plans.

"It's not true that you can leave this issue up to the states. We've got to have comprehensive federal legislation," Clinton said. Many Republicans, including Gingrich and Senate Majority Leader Trent Lott, R-Miss., disagree with Clinton's assessment.

Senate GOP Plan

Senate Assistant Majority Leader Don Nickles, R-Okla., unveiled the broad outlines of the GOP plan on July 15, taking the same tack as House Republicans when they released their proposal June 24 — more choices without more government regulation. The bill was formally introduced July 17.

At first glance, many of the provisions of the Senate GOP bill appeared to be the same as its House counterpart. Emergency medical care would be covered when a "prudent layperson" deemed it necessary; women would have direct access to a gynecologist and be able to bypass a traditional managed care "gatekeeper"; and so-called gag clauses that restrict communications between insurers and patients would be abolished. Senate Republicans also would offer a "point of service" plan, requiring employers with 50 or more workers to permit employees to choose a health care provider from outside a pre-approved list, but the employee would have to bear the additional cost.

Under the Senate GOP plan, however, those and other provisions apply only to the 48 million Americans covered by self-insured health plans that fall under the Employee Retirement Income Security Act (ERISA), a 1974 law (PL 93-406) governing pension and health plans. Self-insured plans, in which an employer rather than an insurance company bears the financial risk, are exempt from state regulations.

Some parts of the Senate GOP

plan would apply to all 125 million Americans whose health plans are governed by ERISA but are not self-insured plans, and are therefore subject to state regulation.

The Senate bill would force all ERISA plans to have expedited internal and external review processes to appeal an insurer's decision on coverage. External appeals, however, would be granted only if the disputed coverage totalled $1,000 or more, or if the procedure in question was medically experimental, such as cancer treatment. The insurer would get to select the independent reviewer who would decide the appeal. Unlike the House GOP plan, the Senate proposal would require that the reviewer's decision be binding on the insurer.

But other provisions of the Senate bill, such as a requirement that health plans do not discriminate against healthy people based on genetics, apply to the approximately 160 million Americans who receive health coverage from employers. Other elements of the Senate GOP plan include a requirement that physicians and patients — not insurance companies — decide the length of a hospital stay after a mastectomy, and if plans cover mastectomies, they must also cover breast reconstruction.

Senate GOP aides said the bill's authors wanted to steer clear of interfering with state laws that apply to health plans and avoid an unnecessary layer of federal regulation. The aides also said that since so many states have enacted patients' rights laws, more will follow. A report released July 16 by the consumers group Families USA, however, found that no state offers the range of protections included in the Democrats' legislation.

Neither the House Republican managed care proposal nor the Democrats' proposals would make distinctions between ERISA plans. Both would set federal standards for health plans, but in dramatically different ways, with Democrats taking a far broader approach.

The Senate Republican plan would not amend ERISA to permit patients to sue their health plans for damages, while under the House plan patients could collect as much as $100,000 for denied treatment. The Senate plan also would include a variety of provisions backers say would expand medical research into women's illnesses, such as osteoporosis and breast and ovarian cancer. The Senate GOP plan faces scrutiny not only from House GOP members and Democrats, but also from Republican senators who fear it may not go far enough. Moderate Republican John H. Chafee of Rhode Island said he wants to review the bill's language before deciding if he will push his own alternative.

The Senate GOP plan is expected to draw fire from Democrats because of its provision to lift current federal restrictions governing medical savings accounts, which are tax-deductible accounts for medical expenses.

"They draw back from it like a vampire from a cross," Sen. Phil Gramm, R-Texas, said of Democrats' reaction to medical savings accounts, a Republican priority.

House GOP Plan

To promote their bill as a real-world alternative, members of the House GOP task force staged a news conference July 16 near the entrance to George Washington University Medical Center's emergency room, which is named for President Ronald Reagan, whose life was saved there after an assassination attempt in 1981.

In blistering heat, task force members stood with Gingrich to proclaim the merits of their approach. It should not matter, Gingrich said, that the GOP plan would not allow consumers to sue their health plans. Rather, he said, the focus is on getting patients medical care when they need it, rather than emphasizing litigation.

"We would like you to get the care faster than you can make an appointment with a lawyer," he said.

Although Thomas did not attend the event, other members of the task force supported Chairman Dennis Hastert of Illinois, as he praised the measure. In his prepared statement, Hastert also asked Democrats and other opponents of the bill not to "bog down the process now that it is within reach. I also must remind those who may want to demagogue this debate, kill it and make it a fall campaign issue, please think twice."

Democrats' Response

As Republicans released their proposals, Democrats continued to ride herd on the issue with press events that included a hearing in which witnesses' voices and pictures were garbled.

"Case Manager Y" told how his view of managed care changed from one of optimism to one of horror when he witnessed one HMO's medical director try to pressure a family into taking their loved one off a ventilator. While the family finally agreed, the hospital refused, citing a standard 24-hour waiting period. Within hours, the patient regained consciousness and survived.

Registered Nurse Carol Bragg told similar horror stories and said that the cost pressures of managed care were negatively affecting patient care. "It is heart-wrenching for all of us in the profession," she said.

Senate Minority Leader Tom Daschle, D-S.D., said the "clear message" garnered from the testimony was that "we need to hold HMOs accountable" for their decisions.

Democrats received a boost July 16 when the Congressional Budget Office said their bill would result in a 4 percent increase in premiums for employer-sponsored health insurance, an increase of about $7 per month per person. Democrats can use that analysis as a shield against charges that their plan will sharply increase premiums.

GOP Rushes Managed Care Bill Through House

JULY 25 — Attempting to take out a political insurance policy on one of the few issues that has resonated with voters this year, the House on July 24 passed a Republican bill (HR 4250) to strengthen consumer protections in managed care health plans.

Swift action on the bill — passed 216-210 only eight days after being introduced by Speaker Newt Gingrich, R-Ga. — demonstrated the Republicans' desire to fend off Democratic attacks that the GOP is insensitive to consumers' concerns about the quality of their health care.

"The patient protection act will ensure a better bill of health for millions of Americans," said House Commerce Committee Chairman Thomas J. Bliley

Health

Jr., R-Va. "It puts patients back in the driver's seat, where they belong."

Senate Republicans have introduced a similar, but more limited, plan. Senate Minority Leader Tom Daschle, D-S.D., who has long pushed for a vote on a Democratic alternative, said July 24 he was pessimistic that any health bill would come to the floor before the August recess.

The House measure includes many of the patient protections that both sides have been pushing, including broader rights to emergency-room care and easier access to gynecologist-obstetricians.

It would give patients expanded rights to appeal coverage decisions to an outside panel. It would not, however, allow consumers enrolled in managed care plans that are exempt from state regulation to sue their health plans under state laws, a key element of a competing Democratic bill.

Twelve Republicans voted against the GOP bill, joining nearly all the Democrats, who excoriated the measure as a political fig leaf that did not include enough patient protections and would, they argued, actually weaken the ability of consumers in some states to sue their health plans.

"This is a bill with rhetoric, but not a remedy," House Minority Leader Richard A. Gephardt, D-Mo., said during the debate.

The White House on July 23 threatened a presidential veto. The Office of Management and Budget said the legislation was "seriously flawed."

"It covers too few people, it provides too few patient protections and it contains unnecessary and irrelevant provisions that undermine the chances for a bipartisan agreement on a patients' bill of rights," the administration statement said.

For months President Clinton has been pushing a Democratic measure (HR 3605), sponsored by Rep. John D. Dingell of Michigan, that backers say would give patients broader rights, including the right to sue their plans for damages, than those in the GOP plan. Republicans criticized the Democratic plan as a costly creation of the trial lawyers' lobby.

Liability Debate

The House narrowly rejected the Dingell bill, which had the support of the American Medical Association and a host of consumer groups, 212-217. Breaking with his leadership, Greg Ganske, R-Iowa, a plastic surgeon, was a chief cosponsor of the bill. He was one of 10 Republicans voting for the plan.

"This is an issue of the trial lawyers seeking to enrich themselves at the expense of everyone else in the country," said Gingrich, inveighing against the Democratic alternative. Republicans charged that the Democratic bill would impose too much government regulation and drive up health care costs.

If, as Daschle predicted, the Senate waits weeks to act on the issue after House passage, Democrats are likely to use the intervening time to scrutinize the Republican plans — and to criticize them on the campaign trail.

Democrats charged that Republicans were in a rush to pass the bill but reluctant to have it dissected. No committee hearings were held, and the bill was drafted in closed-door meetings.

"This whole thing is designed not to have any discussion," said Rep. Jim McDermott, D-Wash.

Republicans countered that it was necessary to proceed quickly to floor action in order to stop Democrats' attempts to "demonize" the GOP managed care bill. "We knew early on that moving it through the committee process was not practical," said House GOP Conference Chairman John A. Boehner, R-Ohio.

In an effort to ensure the needed margin of victory, Republicans wrote a rule that implemented a series of last-minute changes, including increasing the maximum penalty for denial of benefits to $250,000 from $100,000 and expanding language that ensures doctors in managed care plans can inform patients of all their medical options. They also added a provision barring the Clinton administration from implementing a proposal for a national, medical identification number for each American unless such a plan was authorized by Congress.

Despite the controversy, the rule setting out debate on the measures passed, 279-143.

Senate Prospects

While both parties scrambled to round up votes for their bills, it was unclear whether either side wanted to move beyond rhetoric to produce a bipartisan compromise that could become law.

Rep. Dennis Hastert, R-Ill., chairman of the House Republican task force that designed the bill, said he wanted to deliver a measure that Clinton would sign.

In the Senate, Daschle insisted that Democrats be permitted to offer a series of amendments in hopes of changing the Republican plan.

"I'm very pessimistic about the prospects of legislation passing as we want it to pass," Daschle said July 24. The Senate had been expected to debate the bill the week of July 27.

"Our chances of getting a bill like that through a conference that involves members of the House Republican leadership is not very good. Optimistically, I'd say it's 50-50," he said.

Senate Majority Leader Trent Lott, R-Miss., urged Daschle and Democrats to instead accept an up-or-down vote on both plans, which would likely allow Republicans to prevail.

The Senate GOP plan, also developed by a task force, includes more limited protections than its counterpart in the House. Most provisions of the Senate Republican bill would apply only to the roughly 50 million Americans in plans covered by the Employee Retirement Income Security Act (ERISA), a 1974 law (PL 93-406) governing pensions and health plans.

Like the House bill, the Senate plan has not been debated by any committee.

Fueling House Republicans' rush to bring their bill to the floor was the fact that Democrats had filed a discharge petition for the Dingell plan, which had a growing number of signatures, including Ganske's. Had Democrats garnered 218 signatures, they could have forced their bill to the floor.

Some House Republicans complained during a July 22 GOP conference that there was not enough time for adequate examination of the 289-page document, and they asked for a week or two postponement in floor action.

Key Differences

Democrats delighted in the GOP confusion and speculated it might delay floor consideration. Republicans, Dingell said, were "twisting arms and disciplining their malcontents" in an attempt to emerge from "considerable disarray. . . . They're having trouble defining the bill and what the bill means."

The Dingell measure included provisions not in the Republican bill, such as ensuring that patients have continuity of care if their employers change health plans or their doctors leave their plans, and providing coverage for clinical trials for people with life-threatening or serious diseases.

One major difference is that the Democratic bill would allow individuals to sue their health plans under state law for "personal injury or wrongful death."

Currently, consumers who are covered by health plans regulated under ERISA can generally collect only the cost of the denied care. Democrats, including Dingell and Edward M. Kennedy, D-Mass., a leading Senate sponsor of the Democrats' plan, have said that they will fight any bill that does not permit patients to sue their health plans under state laws.

The GOP plan would set up an internal appeals process, allowing patients to challenge denials of care. It would also set up an appeal to an external panel of independent experts. Insurers could charge patients who use the external appeals process up to $100 or 10 percent of the cost of the procedure, whichever is less.

It also would establish purchasing cooperatives for small businesses and trade groups, designed to help them purchase coverage at the more affordable rates that larger businesses do. The cooperatives would be exempt from some state consumer protection laws.

The bill includes some hardy perennials from prior GOP health plans, including capping non-economic damages in medical malpractice suits at $250,000, unless a state already has a higher cap in place.

Even in areas where the Democratic and Republican bills set out to address the same issue, there are differences. For example, the Clinton administration complained that the GOP emergency medical care provision would not prohibit plans from limiting emergency room access in a hospital outside of a plan's network.

In addition, the White House also complained that the GOP bill did not go far enough to guarantee direct access to outside specialists.

Republicans countered that the Democratic plan merely substituted excessive government regulation for excessive private regulation and would drive up health care costs. They said that allowing individuals to sue was a cumbersome, costly provision and that their appeals plan was a more efficient way of providing recourse for patients.

Hastert and Charlie Norwood, R-Ga., a former dentist who has pushed GOP leaders to take comprehensive action on the managed care issue this year, defended the measure.

"All the way down the line, the medical necessity is determined by the physician," Norwood said, adding that the plan's internal and external appeals processes give consumers sufficient recourse to fight insurers' decisions. To resolve such concerns, Republican staff toughened the emergency medical care and "gag" provisions in their manager's amendment.

Prospects for Enactment

Public opinion polls show that voters are concerned that managed care companies, which cover 85 percent of people in employer-sponsored health plans, have too much power and ration coverage in order to save money.

Republicans have been loath to regulate the industry, and their plan relies heavily on market incentives such as expansion of medical savings accounts and small-business pooling that they say will give consumers more choice and more control.

Democrats say the answer must include tougher government regulations, an issue that has caused tensions among Republicans.

House Ways and Means Health Subcommittee Chairman Bill Thomas, R-Calif., who helped draft the plan, decided not to cosponsor it on the grounds that it was heavy on regulation. He rejoined his Republican colleagues and backed the bill when it became clear his support was necessary to garner the needed votes.

A group of House conservatives who thought the GOP leadership's plan contained too much government regulation unsuccessfully pushed an alternative that would allow a voucher system for employees who want to opt out of their employer-provided plans. Employees who used such vouchers would receive the same tax-deductibility as employers offering health coverage to employees. ◆

Health

Home Health Care Agencies Win Federal Payment Relief While New System Is Devised

Box Score

- **Bill:** HR 4328 — PL 105-277
- **House action:** The House adopted the conference report (H Rept 105-825) on HR 4328, 333-95, on Oct. 20. The House passed HR 4567 (H Rept 105-773, Part 1), 412-2, on Oct. 10.
- **Senate action:** The Senate cleared the conference report on HR 4328, 65-29, on Oct. 21.
- **Presidential action:** Clinton signed HR 4328 on Oct. 21.

SUMMARY

Complaining that an interim payment system Congress created as part of the 1997 balanced-budget law (PL 105-33) was forcing some home health agencies out of business, industry lobbyists pushed Congress to change the payment formula and postpone a 15 percent payment reduction for home health agencies scheduled to take effect Oct. 1, 1999. Supporters of the plan, originally HR 4567, said it will increase Medicare payments for more than 65 percent of all home health agencies. None will see a decrease.

The interim system was designed as a placeholder while the Health Care Financing Administration, which runs Medicare, develops a new payment system scheduled to be ready sometime in 2000.

While many members on both sides of the aisle agreed that the interim payment system needed adjustment, determining how to accomplish the task — and finance any fixes — proved troublesome.

Lawmakers turned their attention to the issue late in the 105th Congress, leaving little time for a separate bill to move through both chambers. As time passed, the omnibus spending bill became the obvious choice as a vehicle.

Republicans, Democrats and the White House struggled over budget offsets. Republicans tried to increase the number of people who could qualify for Roth Individual Retirement Accounts, named for Senate Finance Committee Chairman William V. Roth Jr., R-Del. When the White House objected, Republicans then tried to adjust the level at which individuals could convert funds they had accumulated in traditional IRAs to Roth IRAs. The White House, however, objected to both approaches, which were eventually scrapped.

Negotiators instead agreed to reduce payments based on a market basket of items or services used to determine payment increases to home health agencies. The reductions would be 1.1 percent in fiscal years 2000 through 2003. The National Association for Home Care, an industry organization, called the market basket reduction "a high price for the offered relief."

For additional financing, negotiators adopted a provision that would allow winners of prizes, such as casino jackpots or state lotteries, to determine whether they wanted an immediate payout, which would raise tax revenues.

House Panel Backs Revised Interim Payment System

SEPTEMBER 19 — Facing mounting pressure from home health agencies, the House Ways and Means Committee on Sept. 18 approved an interim payment system to ease the bite of changes made in the 1997 budget deal (PL 105-33).

The plan (HR 4567), which the panel approved by voice vote, would be in place until the Health Care Financing Administration (HCFA), the agency that oversees the federal Medicare and Medicaid programs, concludes work on a new payment system sometime in the year 2000.

The committee did not specify how the legislation, which would cost $1.4 billion, would be paid for. Several Democrats on the panel urged legislators not to use the budget surplus.

Chairman Bill Archer, R-Texas, said the measure would go to the House Commerce Committee for its consideration and assistance in identifying offsets.

Pete Stark, D-Calif., who supported the new formula, offered several alternatives for funding that he said would raise about $1.6 billion, but they were rejected mostly along party lines.

The Ways and Means Health Subcommittee had approved the new formula Sept. 15 by voice vote. At both the subcommittee and full committee markups, HCFA was criticized for not making specific recommendations on how to fix the interim payment system.

"You didn't want the responsibility for making the tough decisions. You just wanted to watch Congress," Archer told HCFA Deputy Administrator Michael Hash. But Democrats, such Charles B. Rangel of New York, said it was unfair to blame HCFA and that legislators — not the administration — should develop the solution.

The Senate is also working on the formula issue. Final action could occur before Congress adjourns for the year.

Critics argued that the interim payment system, as designed, was too harsh and had forced some agencies out of business. The new Ways and Means formula would raise slightly the per-cost limits for all agencies and increase per-beneficiary cost limits for low-cost agencies.

The formula would increase the aggregate limit on the costs per visit to 108 percent of the regional costs from 105 percent, and would raise the limit on costs per patient.

For agencies whose costs are below the national median, the new per-patient limit would be raised by half the difference between the agency's costs and the national median. Home health agencies created between 1994 and 1998 would get the national median payment, while those created after Oct. 1, 1998, would have a limit based upon 75 percent of the national median.

Subcommittee Chairman Bill Thomas, R-Calif., said the bill would "help those agencies that are at the lowest end of the reimbursement scale, while ensuring that no agencies will be negatively impacted."

Nancy L. Johnson, R-Conn., called the new formula "a very open-handed, fair approach to dealing with the problem on an interim basis."

Jim McCrery, R-La., said that while some agencies, including some in his state, "would be hurt" by the new formula, "it does provide relief to many agencies around the country."

The National Association for Home Care, which has been critical of the interim payment formula, said the new proposal was "an important step in bringing about fundamental . . . reform this year."

Heartstrings vs. Purse Strings: The Home Health Dilemma

SEPTEMBER 26 — In Anaconda, Mont., a down-on-its luck town, full of ghosts instead of promise, James T. Mills is running short of choices. An expert skier who was on the slopes just last winter, the 80-year-old is now wheelchair-bound after a debilitating stroke.

Mills' challenge these days is to remain in his tidy house in this once-bustling community. He has made it, so far, with around-the-clock care by a devoted family and visits from home health nurses.

"A lot of the healing is [in] being able to be here," said his wife, Jean Mills, 77, who has had to learn how to run the dizzying array of medical machinery that has replaced the mundane appliances on her kitchen counter.

Across town, Jane Anderson, administrator of the nonprofit home health agency treating Mills, has her own set of worries. She is afraid that Medicare changes approved by Congress in the 1997 balanced-budget law (PL 105-33) to save money and attack widespread fraud and abuse in the fast-growing industry will instead force her and other reputable providers to curtail services. For many seniors, the alternative to home health services is more expensive nursing home care. (1997 Almanac, p. 6-3)

Similar concerns are being voiced across the nation by the approximately 10,000 home health agencies that contract with Medicare — nearly double the number in 1990.

In an effort to save money and reduce incentives for agencies to overbill Medicare — a problem so rampant that a Senate committee last year held a hearing called "Jackpot: Gaming the Home Health Care System" — the budget law made a host of alterations.

Lawmakers placed an overall cap on reimbursement to individual agencies and froze payments per visit at 1994 levels. The cap was just an interim step while the Clinton administration designed a new, permanent system that would pay agencies a set amount per ailment, rather than per visit.

The changes have not worked out as planned. Industry officials said the law cut average payments by nearly a third — and slashed reimbursements to some agencies by as much as 81 percent.

Lawmakers were barraged with questions about the issue at town hall meetings during the August recess. Faced with worried senior citizens and an all-out industry lobbying blitz, including a Sept. 10 march on the Capitol, Congress is scrambling to partially roll back the changes.

"Something has to be done or we're going to lose home health care in this country," said Sen. Christopher S. Bond, R-Mo.

The abrupt about-face on home health care illustrates the political dilemma facing Congress as it tries to tame the fraud, waste and abuse that is estimated to eat up 11 percent, or about $20 billion, of annual spending on Medicare's fee-for-service program.

Lawmakers hope that targeted anti-fraud efforts will produce billions of dollars in savings, forestalling some of the politically painful spending cuts needed to ensure the long-term solvency of Medicare.

But as the home health imbroglio demonstrates, there is a catch: Going after waste and abuse requires Congress to make basic changes in how the program sets payment levels and reimburses care givers for the services Medicare provides to 38 million Americans. Those are precisely the kinds of difficult choices lawmakers had hoped to avoid.

"The biggest fraud in Medicare is the program design," said Thomas A. Scully, president and CEO of the Federation of American Health Systems, which represents private hospitals and health systems.

Scully and other experts argue that an irresistible invitation for abuse is embedded in the antiquated design of Medicare. Under the program, providers generally earn more by increasing the number of procedures, tests or home health visits they perform. Because of loose program controls, they are also able to boost profits by "upbilling" — charging Medicare for more expensive services or products than are warranted.

Lack of competitive bidding means that Medicare pays millions of dollars more than warranted for wheelchairs, hospital beds and other supplies. In one instance, Medicare paid $6 million to durable medical equipment companies that provided no services and whose false address was in the middle of a Miami airport runway.

The Health Care Financing Administration (HCFA), which oversees Medicare and Medicaid, is the world's largest purchaser of health care. More than 900 million Medicare claims are processed each year, and only about 10 percent are closely examined, according to HCFA.

In her 1997 annual audit of Medicare, June Gibbs Brown, inspector general for the Department of Health and Human Services (HHS), said waste, fraud and abuse totaled $20.3 billion of Medicare payments.

The estimate, extrapolated from a smaller audit of 8,048 claims, does not prove that the health industry intentionally bilked Medicare of more than $20 billion. Rather, Brown said, many claims were filled out incorrectly, did not include proper documentation, were medically unnecessary or were upbilled. She said it was impossible to pinpoint exactly how much came from intentional fraud.

An Inexact Science

Congress has tried to fix the system, with some success, by instituting more

Health

aggressive audits and investigations and tougher fines for those convicted of defrauding the system.

But that is only a partial answer that treats the symptoms, not the cause.

After stepping up enforcement, the government recovered about $1 billion in wrongful Medicare payments in fiscal 1997. That figure shows an improvement over recent years, but represents only a fraction of estimated waste and abuse. The fact that Congress was forced to cut projected Medicare spending by $112 billion over five years just to keep the program solvent through 2007 shows that more aggressive enforcement, so far, is no substitute for policy changes.

To prevent waste and abuse, and save big dollars, lawmakers have increasingly turned to managed care and the politically perilous tactic of up-front cost controls.

As the home health care fight shows, it is no easy task to clamp down on the powerful health industry, which already complains bitterly about budget cuts and the millions of dollars it spends each year to comply with complex federal laws. Further, lawmakers must weather the angst of seniors who worry that tighter rules mean reductions in care.

"Everybody is against fraud and abuse in general, but not when it involves someone they know," said Bruce Vladeck, a former HCFA administrator in the Clinton administration who is now professor of health policy at the Mt. Sinai School of Medicine in New York.

In fact, Congress and the Clinton administration have spent much of 1998 battling an industry backlash against recent investigations and legislation designed to crack down on fraud. Lawmakers have blocked proposed Clinton administration regulations to implement anti-fraud provisions of the 1997 budget law, debated a measure to weaken the Civil War-era False Claims Act that is one of the federal government's main prosecution tools, and are now grappling with the home health issue.

Health care analysts warn that the home health flap is just the beginning of a concerted industry effort to amend the budget law. Going far beyond the question of fraud, that law made a number of changes to reduce spending and keep the program solvent for 10 years. Hospitals are already complaining about cuts in reimbursement. Health maintenance organizations are unhappy with reduced payments and regulations they call confusing.

Home Health Conundrum

Home health care agencies, either private or nonprofit, provide nursing, physical therapy and other services to the homebound.

Home health care, which cost the federal government about $2.5 billion in fiscal 1989, zoomed to $18.1 billion in fiscal 1996 — about 10 percent of Medicare spending. Much of that growth was attributable to an increase in the number of visits per user, to 76 from 27. Unlike other Medicare outpatient services, recipients are not required to make copayments.

Home health was championed by lawmakers as a way to enable seniors to remain independent while at the same time providing a less costly alternative to nursing home care. While lawmakers have cracked down on home health, they still subscribe to the idea that it is beneficial to seniors.

The industry's rapid expansion was fueled by an aging population and a change made in 1983 in the way Medicare reimbursed hospitals. The 1983 law (PL 98-21) ended the practice of paying hospitals, within limits, whatever it cost to treat Medicare patients. It moved instead to a system that provided a set amount per diagnosis — a flat fee for an appendectomy, for example. (1983 Almanac, p. 391)

Analysts said the tighter payment system gave hospitals a financial incentive to discharge patients earlier. It was also pushed along by unscrupulous providers who took full advantage of Medicare program flaws.

An individual is not required to have a health care background to become a Medicare-certified provider, leading cab drivers, bartenders and convicted felons to open their own agencies. At a recent House Ways and Means Committee hearing, Bill Thomas, R-Calif., chairman of the Health Subcommittee, held up a copy of Entrepreneur magazine that contained an article telling how to strike it rich in home health.

One recent California case involved a home health care agency founded by a former nightclub owner. He and his administrator pleaded guilty to submitting false claims worth $2.5 million over a 17-month period and paying kickbacks for Medicare referrals.

Home health care agencies have low startup costs — many are family-run businesses — and can receive periodic, up-front Medicare payments that are only later reconciled with actual bills. That practice has resulted in overpayments to agencies that have later declared bankruptcy or simply vanished.

A 1988 decision by the U.S. District Court in Washington, D.C., overturned an HCFA effort to make it more difficult for individuals with chronic health conditions to qualify for home care. (1988 Almanac, p. 279)

Out of Control

George F. Grob, deputy inspector general for evaluation and inspections in HHS' Office of Inspector General, told the Senate Special Committee on Aging last year that home health care "is out of control, and very badly so."

One part of the problem, said Grob, is that the number of Medicare home health claims audited dropped significantly since 1988, when intermediaries were reviewing 50 percent of such billings. Only 2 to 3 percent are now audited, mostly because the number of claims processed has jumped significantly since 1988. In 1990, for example, beneficiaries received 70 million home health visits. By 1995, that figure was 250 million.

Two July 1997 reports by the HHS inspector general also detailed abuse.

One review of a randomly selected sample of home health agencies in California, Illinois, New York and Texas found that 40 percent of the total services provided did not meet Medicare payment rules. A second found that 25 percent of home health care agencies in five states were categorized as "problem providers," meaning their owners had questionable backgrounds or submitted multiple service claims.

To eliminate structural incentives for abuse, HCFA last year imposed a temporary moratorium on approving providers to participate in Medicare's home health care program.

The 1997 budget law required that agencies take out a surety bond, a financial instrument used to guarantee that individuals have a financial stake in a business and partially reimburse Medicare in the event of problems. Florida has used a similar system to weed out fly-by-night operators.

HCFA proposed that agencies take out a bond equal to 15 percent of their previous year's Medicare reimbursement. Officials estimate the average cost of such a bond at about $4,000. Due to pressure from Congress, which said the proposal was too onerous, the requirement is on hold pending a report from the General Accounting Office (GAO).

To limit incentives for overbilling, the law instituted the new, temporary payment system Oct. 1, 1997. The system bases payments on a blend of what Medicare paid for services in 1994 and agency-specific costs.

Agencies complained that the interim payment system rewarded inefficient agencies, which had high costs in 1994, while penalizing those who were more stringent. According to the National Association for Home Care, 1,240, or about 8 percent, of Medicare's 10,027 certified home health care agencies have either closed or withdrawn from the program due to the new system.

A report released Sept. 9 by the GAO, however, found that despite such closures, there were still more agencies to treat Medicare beneficiaries in August 1998 than in October 1996. Critics said the report was flawed because it focused on just seven states.

Complaints against the interim payment system got even louder when the Clinton administration announced in July that, because of a year 2000 computer problem, it could not complete the permanent payment plan on time. The Congressional Budget Office now estimates that home health care savings will be greater than the approximately $16 billion originally forecast over five years.

Fix It or Lose It?

Penny Thompson, director of HCFA's program integrity office, said that while officials in Washington understand agencies are upset about the new requirements, the changes are critical to preserving Medicare's home health benefits.

"If we don't do this, we won't have a benefit to protect. Manage it or you're not going to have it," she said.

Others point out that the intent of the budget changes was to close inefficient agencies. The question is whether Congress, in aiming at unscrupulous providers, hit some innocents as well.

With home health care agencies in every state, and intensive lobbying under way, Congress is now trying to figure out the exact impact of the budget law and some type of fix — within limits.

At a Sept. 18 markup, Thomas, Ways and Means Committee Chairman Bill Archer, R-Texas, and other members of the panel criticized Medicare administrators for not offering specific solutions. Archer said the agency "didn't want the responsibility for making the tough decisions."

Nancy L. Johnson, R-Conn., said HCFA was unable to deal with the problem as a result of "bureaucratic bungling" that plagues the agency. Several Democrats on the panel, however, said it was Congress' responsibility to come up with solutions.

Lawmakers may try to increase reimbursements to lower-cost providers or allow higher payments for more cost-intensive services. The House Ways and Means Committee on Sept. 18 approved a bill (HR 4567) to boost payments, but did not provide spending offsets. Archer and Thomas said the measure would go to the House Commerce Committee for consideration and assistance in identifying offsets.

At both an Aug. 6 hearing and the Sept. 18 markup, HCFA deputy administrator Michael Hash offered no alternatives to the current interim system but said the agency was willing to work with Congress to develop solutions. Hash said that while HCFA could implement the legislation, the agency had concerns about the proposal's $1.4 billion cost.

The White House has said it will accept only a budget-neutral bill, which would put Congress in the unhappy position of redistributing funds to create a new set of winners and losers.

In the Senate, the chairman of the Select Committee on Aging, Iowa Republican Charles E. Grassley, has offered his own bill (S 2323) to modify the interim system. He said he had "mixed feelings" about the Ways and Means plan because it "would not do much to address the reimbursement rates of high-cost agencies, and it also wouldn't eliminate the disparate treatment of older and newer agencies." Grassley said he also had "serious misgivings" about the price tag.

Finance Committee Chairman William V. Roth Jr., R-Del., and Daniel Patrick Moynihan, D-N.Y., circulated a "Dear Colleague" letter Sept. 17 referring to the GAO's findings and noting that "neither agency closures nor the interim payment system has significantly affected beneficiary access to care."

An Easy Target

William J. Mahon, executive director of the National Health Care Anti-Fraud Association, a group of private health insurers and government law enforcement officials, said Medicare has long been an easy target.

"Congress should know when it passes things, some people are going to scream," said Mahon. "Medicare has been perceived by some as the Mint."

Current HCFA administrator Nancy-Ann DeParle said her agency is making significant inroads against fraud and she does not anticipate pressure from Congress to curtail those efforts. "I haven't had any pushback from Congress with what we're trying to do here," she said in an interview.

The government recovered about $1 billion in wrongful Medicare payments in fiscal 1997, while HHS excluded more than 2,700 individuals and entities from doing business with Medicare, Medicaid and other federal and state programs for fraud or other professional misconduct. Also in fiscal 1997, federal prosecutors filed 282 criminal indictments in health care fraud cases, a 15 percent increase over the previous year, according to a 1997 report on the Health Care Fraud and Abuse Control Program, created by a 1996 law (PL 104-191) dealing with insurance portability. (*1996 Almanac*, p. 6-28)

Last year's budget bill gave HHS and HCFA more power to exclude providers convicted of felonies or health-related crimes and levy civil monetary penalties on providers who take kickbacks.

HHS says that a separate initiative that began in 1995 called Operation Restore Trust has found $23 in Medicare overpayments for every $1 spent on the effort. The program, originally conducted in five states, focused in on the fastest-growing areas of Medicare, in-

Health

cluding home health care, skilled nursing facilities and durable medical equipment providers. Due to its success, Operation Restore Trust has been expanded to 24 states.

The sweeping Justice Department investigation of health giant Columbia/HCA further illustrates the government's more aggressive approach. The company has been charged with misbilling Medicare, and the probe is continuing. As a result of the investigation, the company has made widespread management changes and beefed up compliance and auditing programs. A planned October trial of four Columbia/HCA officials was recently rescheduled until May 1999.

William J. Scanlon, director of health financing and systems issues for the GAO, said that HCFA still has significant obstacles ahead.

In testimony delivered Aug. 10 before the Medicare commission, Scanlon said HCFA's ability to avoid "inappropriate payments" was "still hampered" for several reasons, including the fact that even with increased resources, Medicare reviews less than 4 percent of claims. HCFA said the figure is about 10 percent.

Scanlon also said that Medicare's information systems do not allow easy profiling of claims to detect suspicious patterns of services. Even when inappropriate claims are found, there is almost no deterrent since most are simply returned unpaid with no fine.

"In the end, we are still going to be left with a loss of dollars to inappropriate payments," Scanlon said.

As home health illustrates, Congress has tried to get at fraud through policy changes, as well as tougher enforcement.

After intense, behind-the-scenes negotiations, Congress as part of the portability law gave HCFA and other agencies more enforcement tools.

The law moved money for anti-fraud efforts from the category of discretionary to mandatory spending, giving federal agencies new power to find and punish wrongdoers.

The 1997 budget law also included several pilot programs to test Medicare competitive bidding, changed the payment systems for skilled nursing care, and revamped Medicare payments for teaching hospitals and hospice care — two areas where the HHS inspector general had identified potential abuse.

Industry in the Middle

The push by HCFA, the Justice Department and the HHS inspector general to attack fraud has some industry groups complaining bitterly that they are being unfairly targeted by investigators more interested in winning convictions and fines than in distinguishing intentional fraud from honest mistakes.

The American Hospital Association recently led an attack against the agencies' aggressive use of the 1863 False Claims Act for what it called innocent billing errors. That action forced the Justice Department and the HHS in June to issue new guidelines under which the agencies would pursue fraud cases.

In an Aug. 5 letter to the American Academy of Family Physicians, Gibbs Brown said health providers, practitioners and suppliers would not be subject to civil monetary penalties or the False Claims Act for "billing errors, honest mistakes or negligence. . . . Our law enforcement efforts are focused on improper claims that are made intentionally, or with reckless disregard for the truth, or with deliberate ignorance of the truth," she wrote.

While the guidelines were a good step, congressional oversight is still necessary to make sure they are followed, said Robert R. Waller, president and CEO of the Mayo Foundation and chairman-elect of the Healthcare Leadership Council, a group of about 50 health insurers, drug manufacturers and other health companies.

"The government is having a hard time distinguishing between real fraud . . . and these differences in interpretation and honest clerical mistakes," Waller said.

With no one wanting to become the next Columbia/HCA, the health care industry has begun to put more effort into sophisticated up-front compliance and ethics programs to weed out billing errors and fraud. Compliance programs in place before an alleged illegal act are a mitigating factor at any sentencing.

Jefferson Government Relations, a Washington lobbying and consulting group, has created a 10-person subsidiary to help managed care entities contract with Medicare and set up compliance systems.

As Congress imposes tighter spending caps, officials are beginning to look at fraud differently. Managed care companies must guard against sanctions for providing too few, rather than too many, services to increase profits.

DeParle said she understands that some members of the health industry are unhappy. "This is a whole new world for them," she said. But she added that they are not under siege. "This is not Armageddon here for health care providers."

Vladeck said HCFA's fraud recovery efforts will continue to improve, and the claims error rate for Medicare will drop to the mid-to-low double digits within five to 10 years. Still, that is billions of dollars a year in fraud.

"But I don't think we're prepared to live in the kind of policy state that you would need to get below," that figure, Vladeck said.

DeParle wants to make substantial progress each year in cutting the rate, with the goal of reducing it to 5 percent by fiscal 2000, but she conceded that "that's probably too ambitious."

The reality that fraud will remain, at some level, within the Medicare program will continue to fuel the debate on Capitol Hill, said Mahon of the private anti-fraud group. "As long as the amount of money and the economic pressures of the system remain what they are, it will still be a fairly high-profile topic up there."

House, Senate Struggle Toward Compromise

OCTOBER 10 — House and Senate lawmakers inched toward compromise during the week of Oct. 5 on legislation to give home health agencies relief from an interim Medicare payment system Congress passed as part of the 1997 balanced-budget law (PL 105-33).

While the House was likely to approve the measure (HR 4567) during a scheduled Oct. 10 vote, the Senate worked to move its plan as either a free-standing measure or as part of an omnibus spending bill.

The interim payment system was designed as a placeholder while the Health Care Financing Administration, which runs Medicare, concludes work sometime in 2000 on a new payment system.

The lower payments in the interim system were part of Congress' effort to trim spending on home health, which has been one of the fastest growing programs in Medicare. But critics have argued that the system was too harsh and has forced some agencies to close, impelling lawmakers to alter the formula.

The House and Senate proposals have significant differences. For example, the Senate bill would delay for one year the proposed 15 percent payment reduction for home health agencies scheduled to take effect Oct. 1, 1999. The House bill does not address this.

House-Senate Differences

The bills also take different approaches to the funding dilemma. The Senate plan would shift money in the current interim payment system so that some agencies would see a reduction in their payments while others would see an increase. The House plan would provide money for a greater number of agencies than the Senate plan.

While home health agencies were glad that Congress was taking some action, neither bill would go far enough to remedy problems caused by the interim payment system, said Dayle Berke, director of government affairs for the National Association for Home Care, a trade group.

The largest obstacle between the two chambers may be how to pay for any remedy. The House plan, which is expected to cost about $2.5 billion over five years, would be funded by payments from increasing the number of people who could roll over savings into Roth IRAs, named for Senate Finance Committee Chairman William V. Roth Jr., R-Del. (*1997 Almanac, p. 2-30*)

The White House, however, has previously opposed such an expansion beyond those currently eligible: Single filers with adjusted gross annual incomes of $95,000 and joint filers with incomes up to $150,000. The bill would raise those limits to $145,000 for single taxpayers and married taxpayers filing separately and $290,000 for married taxpayers filing jointly.

Democrats objected. "You are creating a tax loophole for the very upper income that will cost billions and billions in the out years," said Rep. Pete Stark of California.

John M. Spratt Jr. of South Carolina, ranking Democrat on the House Budget Committee, said the plan dealt a "body blow to the deficit" because while it raises revenue from rollovers in the short term, it would cost nearly $12 billion over the next 10 years.

The Senate Finance panel also ran into trouble trying to find the approximately $1 billion needed to fund its plan. Staffers first looked to reduce the ability of some Medicare providers other than hospitals to write off bad debt — deductibles and copayments unpaid by Medicare beneficiaries. But when some senators objected, the committee instead turned to a set of tax-related offsets to fund their bill. The budget surplus may also provide funding.

Lawmakers and home health lobbyists alike expressed concern that a legislative fix not fall through the cracks as Congress rushed through its final days of legislative action. "We have to make sure something happens on this before we leave," said Rep. Tom Coburn, R-Okla.

Formula Changes

The House plan would raise payments for home health agencies that are now below the median payment to halfway between their current payment and the median payment, which is $3,465 per beneficiary. Agencies that currently receive that median, however, would get no increase.

Under the plan, backers said, more than 70 percent of all home health agencies will see an increase in their Medicare payments. Ways and Means Health Subcommittee Chairman Bill Thomas, R-Calif., said the bill "treats those who are most in need fairly."

In addition to its $2 billion for home health agencies, the House bill also provides $500 million for a program to allow Medicare-eligible veterans to receive Medicare coverage through medical facilities run by the Department of Veterans Affairs.

The Senate Finance plan, sponsored by Roth and Daniel Patrick Moynihan, D-N.Y., also aims to create more equity in payments given to home health agencies. The measure, backers said, would reduce extreme payment variations with a newer system designed to smooth out inequities and redistribute payments in a more fair manner.

In addition to its formula changes, the House bill would increase to 17 from 15 the number of members on the Medicare Payment Advisory Commission, which was created in last year's balanced-budget act.

The measure also would require that the secretary of Health and Human Services issue a report on the development and implementation schedule for the home health prospective payment system, as well as recommendations for alternatives to the 15 percent reduction in home health payment limits scheduled to go into effect on Oct. 1, 1999.

Home Health Care Relief Included In Omnibus Bill

OCTOBER 24 — Home health care agencies will soon see some relief from an interim Medicare payment system Congress passed as part of the 1997 balanced-budget law.

The relief measure, which was included in the omnibus spending bill (HR 4328) signed by President Clinton on Oct. 21, includes both an immediate increase in Medicare payments to home health agencies and postponement for one year of a scheduled 15 percent payment reduction that was to take effect Oct. 1, 1999.

Supporters of the plan said it will result in an increase of Medicare payments for more than 65 percent of all home health agencies. None will see a decrease.

The agreement was the product of tense, last-minute negotiations between congressional Republicans and the White House over how to finance the measure, which is expected to cost $1.7 billion over five years.

After administration objections, GOP leaders scrapped a proposal to adjust the level at which individuals could convert funds they had accu-

Health

mulated in traditional, tax-deferred Individual Retirement Accounts (IRAs) to Roth IRAs, named for Sen. Finance Committee Chairman William V. Roth Jr., R-Del. *(1997 Almanac, p. 2-30)*

Instead, negotiators adopted a provision that will allow winners of prizes, such as casino jackpots or state lotteries, to determine whether they want an immediate payout, which would raise tax revenues.

Additional financing will come from reductions in the so-called market basket, a select group of items or services used to determine payment increases to home health agencies. The market basket reductions would be 1.1 percent in fiscal years 2000 through 2003. The National Association for Home Care, an industry organization, called the market basket reduction "a high price for the offered relief."

While many legislators praised the deal, some said it provided too little additional money for low-cost agencies that keep their expenses to a minimum. "It does not level the playing field as much as it should between the low-cost states and the high-cost states," said Senate Special Aging Committee Chairman Charles E. Grassley, R-Iowa.

Besides adjustments in payments to home health agencies, the bill requires the secretary of Health and Human Services to report to Congress on HCFA's progress in developing the prospective payment system. Agency officials have said they expect to have the system ready sometime in the year 2000.

House, Senate Proposals

The House had passed its version of the home health care plan as a separate bill (HR 4567) on Oct. 10 by a vote of 412-2. The House bill called for $2 billion to be spent to increase payments to more than 70 percent of all home health agencies, with none seeing a decrease. *(Vote 516, p. H-146)*

It also included a variety of other provisions, such as $500 million for a program to allow eligible veterans to receive Medicare coverage through medical facilities run by the Department of Veterans Affairs.

The Senate version, which never came to the floor for a vote, would have redistributed money within the current system, boosting payments to about 85 percent of agencies but decreasing them for the rest. The Senate bill would have included a one-year delay in the 15 percent payment reduction for home health agencies scheduled to take effect on Oct. 1, 1999, at a cost of approximately $1 billion. The House bill did not address that issue. ◆

Chapter 15
INDUSTRY & REGULATION

Tobacco Settlement 15-3
   Settlement, Senate Bill Compared 15-4
   Senate Bill Highlights 15-8
Electricity Deregulation 15-16
Product Liability Overhaul 15-18

Regulatory Overhaul 15-20
   Overhaul Provisions 15-22
Property Rights 15-23
Baseball's Antitrust Exemption 15-25

Industry & Regulation

While Congress Debates Bill, Court Rules Against FDA's Power To Regulate Tobacco

Box Score

- **Bill:** S 1415
- **House action:** None.
- **Senate action:** The Senate failed, 53-46, to waive a budget point of order against S 1415 on June 17.

SUMMARY

The creation of a federal tobacco policy was supposed to be one of the main accomplishments of the 105th Congress, but it never came to fruition. An ambitious bill died under its own weight in the Senate in June, while House Republican leaders could never agree on legislation.

"I thought it was going to be probably the top issue of this legislative session," said Rep. Scott McInnis, R-Colo., who, along with Deborah Pryce, R-Ohio, was charged with crafting a House GOP tobacco package. "I think the tobacco bill fell apart primarily because you could not find enough votes here."

The tobacco issue had come to Congress through the offices of state attorneys general and cigarette makers, who reached a $368.5 billion legal settlement in June 1997 that needed Congress' imprimatur to become binding. The settlement aimed to reduce teen smoking and to require tobacco companies to foot some of the bill for smokers' health costs shouldered by the states in the past.

The Senate bill (S 1415 — S Rept 105-180) came to the floor May 18 with high hopes amid unusual circumstances. Rarely has a major piece of legislation reached such an advanced stage with its fate so uncertain.

John McCain, R-Ariz., chairman of the Senate Commerce, Science and Transportation Committee, had been charged with crafting a bill that could be a vehicle for further progress.

Both McCain and Senate Majority Leader Trent Lott, R-Miss., believed a House-Senate conference would be the true birthplace of federal tobacco policy. To keep the ball rolling toward that end, McCain was given control of a bill over which many committees would normally have shared jurisdiction.

S 1415, as approved by the Commerce Committee on April 1, would have raised the price of cigarettes by $1.10 per pack over five years, imposed multibillion-dollar "look-back" penalties on tobacco companies if youth smoking reduction targets were not met, and capped tobacco companies' legal liability at $6.5 billion per year if they met all the bill's conditions.

The industry found the terms too harsh and withdrew its support from the process, earning McCain a formidable enemy. Tobacco companies would spend upwards of $40 million on issue ads against S 1415 by the time the bill died.

Nevertheless, S 1415 seemed to gain momentum as it neared the Senate floor. Senators hostile to the bill, including Majority Whip Don Nickles, R-Okla., insisted on Finance Committee jurisdiction. But a May 14 Finance markup only served to demonstrate anti-tobacco sentiment, as an amendment passed to raise cigarette prices by $1.50 per pack over three years.

McCain brought to the floor May 18 a manager's amendment that was an amalgam of the Commerce bill, the Finance changes and input from the White House. McCain pleaded with his colleagues not to upset his "carefully balanced package" with amendments from the left or right.

But as opponents dragged out the debate to build time for their case, they succeeded in adding extraneous amendments offering tax breaks and increased funding for interdiction of illegal drugs. S 1415's supporters, meanwhile, helped make it unpassable with tough amendments to lift all legal liability caps and increase look-back penalties.

With hundreds of amendments still pending, a closed Senate GOP Conference meeting on June 17 led to a pair of procedural votes that brought the bill down a few hours later. The Senate failed by three votes to invoke cloture, and then 53 senators — seven shy of the 60 needed — voted to waive a budget point of order against S 1415, which violated spending limits allowed for the Commerce Committee.

Speaker Newt Gingrich, R-Ga., had declared a week earlier that he thought the House would never conference the McCain bill, and he had earlier popped a trial balloon floated by House Commerce Chairman Thomas J. Bliley Jr., R-Va., to introduce a McCain-style House bill.

Instead, Pryce and McInnis released an "outline of principles" after S 1415 died, promising a narrow bill that would create a model set of penalties that might be imposed by states on minors who smoke and create anti-tobacco public service announcements. But Democrats and public health groups opposed such a modest approach, and Republicans were split about the political wisdom of doing little versus doing nothing. The Pryce-McInnis plan was never introduced.

Heat Intensifies As McCain's Panel Raises the Stakes

APRIL 4 — Congress is taking its first step toward enacting sweeping tobacco legislation that gives the industry few of the benefits it wants.

The Senate Commerce Committee approved a bill (S 1415) by a vote of 19-1 on April 1 that would raise the price of cigarettes, restrict advertising of tobacco products in an effort to cut down on the 3,000 teenagers who start smoking each day, and cap liability claims against the industry at $6.5 billion a year.

Chairman John McCain, R-Ariz., told members not to be fooled by the

Industry & Regulation

Settlement, McCain Bill Compared

APRIL 4 — The Senate Commerce, Transportation and Science Committee approved a tobacco bill on April 1 that would raise the per-pack price of cigarettes and impose stiff regulations on the tobacco industry.

The impetus for the bill (S 1415) came from a settlement reached in June 1997 between the tobacco industry and 40 state attorneys general. That settlement would give the industry limited liability protection in civil lawsuits in exchange for paying $368.5 billion over the course of 25 years to settle legal claims, fund anti-smoking programs and reduce the number of teens who start smoking.

The bill, proposed by committee Chairman John McCain, R-Ariz., was crafted in collaboration with members on both sides of the aisle and attorneys general. Noticeably absent was the tobacco industry, which vowed to fight the legislation in court.

ISSUE	SETTLEMENT	S 1415
Industry payments	The industry would pay $368.5 billion over 25 years to settle claims and pay for cessation, education and anti-smoking campaigns.	Tobacco companies would pay $10 billion up front and $506 billion over 25 years to cover for legal claims and anti-smoking measures.
Price increase	The price of a pack of cigarettes would increase by $1.20 per pack over five years and $1.50 over 10 years. Tobacco companies would pay this money into a fund to settle claims and pay for anti-smoking campaigns.	The price would increase by $1.10 per pack fee over the next five years in payments to the government. The industry notes that price does not include retail markups, inflation and other cost increases. With those factors added, some Wall Street analysts predict the actual price increase would be $2.55 per pack over five years.
Liability protection	A $5 billion cap on annual payments for individual liability claims. A limit on punitive damages for past actions and class action suits would be banned.	A $6.5 billion cap on annual payments for individual liability claims. No other liability protections would be offered.
Advertising restrictions	It would ban outdoor and Internet advertising, use of characters such as the Marlboro Man or Joe Camel, and non-tobacco merchandise such as clothing decorated with tobacco logos. Tobacco companies would be prohibited from sponsoring outdoor sporting events. Placement, color, and size restrictions would be placed on over-the-counter advertising, with exceptions for companies with more than a 25 percent market share.	The bill would expand on these restrictions by including a prohibition on the use of animal figures and color ads on the back cover of adult magazines. Point-of-sale restrictions would apply to all companies regardless of market share.
Youth smoking reduction	The goal would be to reduce smoking among teenagers under 18 by 60 percent in 10 years. Tobacco companies that failed to meet target reduction rates the fifth year after enactment would have to pay a penalty of $80 million per percentage point by which the goal was missed.	The goal would be to reduce youth smoking by 60 percent over 10 years. It would increase the penalties the industry would pay for failing to meet the goals. It would increase the annual cap on penalty payments to $3.5 billion, up from $2 billion in the states' settlement.
FDA authority	The Food and Drug Administration (FDA) would be granted the authority to regulate nicotine as a drug, monitor new tobacco products and reduce levels of nicotine in products. The FDA would have the power to ban nicotine at the end of 12 years.	The FDA would be granted the authority to treat nicotine as its own class, rather than as a drug or medical device. If the FDA decides to ban nicotine, the president would be required to notify Congress, which would have two years to overturn the decsion.
Farmers	Tobacco farmers were not included in the settlement.	The bill would provide $28.5 billion in economic assistance for tobacco farmers and displaced workers. It would leave in place the federal price subsidy program that controls how much tobacco is grown and who can grow it.
Warning labels	Cigarette packs would display warning labels covering 25 percent of the package.	Same as settlement.

relative ease with which the bill cleared the committee. The fight is just beginning, he said.

"There is no doubt that this is the first round, and there are many rounds yet to fight," said McCain, who drafted the bill after round-the-clock meetings with lawmakers of both parties, White House aides, health care groups and state attorneys general who negotiated the proposed $368.5 billion deal with the tobacco industry in June 1997.

In an indication of what is to come on the Senate floor, Judd Gregg, R-N.H., sponsored an amendment to the budget resolution (S Con Res 86) opposing granting tobacco companies immunity from lawsuits.

"They just don't deserve any immunity," Gregg said after the amendment was approved, 79-19. (Vote 51, p. S-11)

Senators are gearing up for a floor battle over other issues, such as increasing the price of cigarettes by $1.10 per pack over five years, imposing penalties for failing to reduce the number of youths who smoke, and restricting the marketing of tobacco products overseas.

But swift committee approval of such a massive bill is a signal that Senate Republican leaders are placing tobacco legislation near the top of their priority list. Majority Leader Trent Lott, R-Miss., told reporters that it would come to the floor during the week of May 25.

The bill would have a big impact on the tobacco industry. It would force the companies to pay $10 billion up front and an additional $506 billion over the course of 25 years for a host of anti-smoking programs, legal damages, and advertising campaign and health care costs.

It would grant broad authority to the Food and Drug Administration (FDA) to regulate nicotine. It would impose multimillion-dollar penalties on the tobacco industry for failing to reduce the number of youths who smoke.

The bill drew criticism from the tobacco industry. Officials predicted that it would result in bankruptcy, and they vowed to fight it in court.

"This is a punitive and unrealistic assault on the industry," said tobacco lobbyist J. Phil Carlton, who predicted McCain bill would cause "certain bankruptcies."

Responding to reports that R.J. Reynolds Tobacco Co. intended to walk away from the states' settlement, McCain said the tobacco companies have a choice: accept this bill or face even tougher penalties. The tobacco company denied it would walk away, but said it opposed McCain's bill.

The White House made clear that tobacco legislation is among administration's top legislative priorities.

Returning from Africa, President Clinton told reporters April 3, "With each new revelation of the strategies which have been vigorously pursued to market cigarettes to children, I think they [tobacco companies] have an enormous interest in trying to reverse the record of the past, to try to put this unforgivable chapter behind them and to start off on a new path."

The Markup

Due to widespread interest in the bill, the committee moved the markup to the largest room in the Hart Senate Office Building. The hearing drew so many lobbyists that Democratic committee member Wendell H. Ford of Kentucky, who represents one of the largest tobacco-growing states, said he wanted to avoid a break because the lobbyists would approach members "like a duck on a June bug."

There was an air of comity throughout the daylong meeting as the committee picked its way through a spectrum of amendments, including how to spend new tobacco revenues to capping liability payments to limiting fees paid to lawyers.

In the end, the bill emerged largely unscathed because of a bipartisan consensus that the best place to debate controversial issues was the Senate floor.

"If we are ever to complete our mission, we have to move this through this committee," McCain told members at the start of the markup.

Ford, for example, agreed to hold off on most of his 47 amendments.

But that did not stop him from repeating his plea for aid for tobacco farmers. "If my farmers are not taken care of, this carpet is going to turn red," Ford declared during the hearing.

The bill included a proposal from Ford to provide $28.5 billion in economic assistance for tobacco farmers and displaced factory workers.

Olympia J. Snowe, R-Maine, offered an amendment suggesting in a "sense of the Senate" resolution that an unspecified amount of money from the bill be divided among health care programs such as Medicare, smoking prevention and cessation programs, aid to tobacco farmers, compensation for asbestos workers who smoke, aid to states for tobacco-related health care costs and the federal black lung program.

John D. Rockefeller IV, D-W.Va., successfully amended Snowe's measure to include money for veterans who smoke and for cancer research.

Objecting to Snowe's amendment, Sam Brownback, R-Kan., said it was not up to the Commerce Committee to divvy up the money pie.

The Snowe amendment as amended was adopted by voice vote.

Brownback sought an amendment that would have limited to $250 an hour the fees that lawyers who have waged lawsuits against the tobacco companies could receive. But he withdrew the amendment in an effort to get the bill to the floor. Fees paid to private attorneys who helped negotiate the settlement have become a major issue, with lawmakers objecting to fees as high as $2 billion in a single class-action suit.

But John Kerry, D-Mass., said it was "entirely inappropriate for the U.S. Congress to change private contracts after they've been made."

Kerry lost a bid to increase cigarette prices by $1.50 per pack, saying it would cut down on the number of teenagers who smoke. It was defeated by voice vote.

Republican John Ashcroft of Missouri lost on another voice vote on an amendment that would have granted liability protections to charitable organizations.

"It is remarkable that Congress would bow to the tobacco industry while refusing to allow reasonable limitations on liability for hard-working Americans who are making safe products — products that by their nature do not kill people, such as those sold by tobacco companies," said Ashcroft, the only member to vote against the bill.

John B. Breaux, D-La., and Slade Gorton, R-Wash., expressed worries that the price increase would prompt the industry to withdraw from partici-

Industry & Regulation

pating in the bill. If that happened, they argued, there would be no agreement from the companies to the stiff advertising restrictions, and the goal of reducing the number of youths who start smoking would be undermined.

"We are rushing to see who can be the toughest on tobacco companies," Breaux said. "I'm concerned that in trying to be tougher than the other guy, we will miss the target."

Breaux, whose mother died of lung cancer, said he has no sympathy for the tobacco companies, but without their consent, it would be impossible to win the advertising restrictions.

Ron Wyden, D-Ore., one of the most vocal tobacco opponents, sought to restrict tobacco companies from marketing their products overseas. He withdrew the amendment to allow the bill to move forward and allow more time to reach a consensus on the issue. Wyden said he does not want the bill to be "financed on the lungs of the children around the world."

How the Deal was Struck

In early March, McCain was summoned to a members-only meeting with the Senate's top Republican leaders to discuss a growing concern among the GOP: tobacco.

Fearful that Clinton and the Democratic Party had started to use tobacco as an election-year issue, Majority Whip Don Nickles, R-Okla., told McCain that he wanted the Commerce panel to produce a bill for the floor before the spring recess.

Already, there was strong opposition to granting the industry the legal protection later promised in the June 1997 agreement. There was also a fight brewing over how much authority to give the FDA. But the real trick was trying to figure out a way to increase the price of cigarettes without bankrupting the industry.

"The committee room became an open bazaar of public health officials, attorneys general, senate staffers and White House officials," said John Raidt, GOP staff director of the Commerce committee. "We tried to get a bipartisan coalition going on each contentious area of the bill."

On the issue of FDA authority, for example, commerce committee member Bill Frist, R-Tenn., hammered out an agreement with fellow Labor Committee members Edward M. Kennedy, D-Mass., and Vermont Republican James M. Jeffords, as well as with Judiciary Committee Chairman Orrin G. Hatch, R-Utah. Officials from the FDA and the White House also were on hand.

But the entire process is still shaky.

"Any threat to pull out of, or litigate, tobacco settlement legislation is the equivalent of Big Tobacco playing chicken with Congress," said Democrat Bob Graham of Florida. "Congress shouldn't blink."

Industry Exits From Tobacco Negotiations

APRIL 11 — In deciding to walk away from tobacco legislation, the nation's largest tobacco companies are betting they will be able to win a public relations blitz for their case, but lawmakers say the action only strengthens their resolve to pass a law that reduces the number of teen smokers.

The April 8 announcement by RJR Nabisco's chief executive officer, Steven F. Goldstone, angered many lawmakers. It raised questions about the future of legislation that would require the tobacco industry to pay billions for smoking-related illnesses. But it did not stop the process.

"We cannot be blackmailed or cajoled by the industry," said Senate Commerce Committee Chairman John McCain, R-Ariz., who drafted a bill (S 1415) that the Senate Commerce, Science and Transportation Committee approved in a bipartisan vote. He expects the bill to hit the Senate floor in late May.

House Speaker Newt Gingrich, R-Ga., agreed, saying the tobacco companies had no credibility left to stop Congress from passing a measure aimed at cutting down on teenage smoking.

But Sen. Wendell Ford, D-Ky., one of a handful of lawmakers to voice a different view, predicted the pullout would cause "the legislative process to disintegrate or inject some needed fiscal responsibility into the debate. Only time will tell."

Goldstone's announcement that the industry is pulling out of efforts to craft a tobacco policy was the latest salvo in an increasingly tense war over how to stop teenagers from smoking and how much money to force the tobacco industry to pay for treating smoking-related diseases.

Some lawmakers said it was a strategic move for the industry, which would be forced to pay as much as $516 billion over 25 years if S 1415 becomes law.

Sen. John H. Chafee, R-R.I., co-author of another bipartisan tobacco bill (S 1889), said Congress could end up gaining more flexibility if it does not try to reach agreement with the industry.

"I would suggest that Congress look at the possibility of imposing a direct increased tax on cigarettes to make up for the industry walking away from the bipartisan solutions we have proposed," Chafee said.

President Clinton said the industry's move is a "big mistake" and that the bill would move forward with or without the industry's consent.

Bombshell

Goldstone's announcement came during a quiet week in Washington. With most lawmakers out of town for the spring recess and little else going on, the timing of his speech put it on the front pages and network news shows.

Congress wants "to punish the tobacco industry, rather than take advantage of a historic opportunity to create a national tobacco policy," Goldstone said before the luncheon at the National Press Club. The other tobacco companies followed his lead and pulled out of negotiations, too.

The object of criticism by the companies is the McCain bill. It is much tougher on the industry and would cost them far more than the $368.5 billion proposed settlement the industry negotiated with 40 state attorneys general in June 1997.

"The legislative process, as far as tobacco is concerned, is broken beyond repair," Goldstone said. He and the other tobacco chiefs support the proposed settlement with the state attorneys general, but at this time, he said, "I have no hope of that happening."

Now, the tobacco companies say they will focus on generating support on Main Street by launching an advertising blitz. But few believe the companies will actually stop lobbying.

Tobacco Settlement

A Necessary Partner in Talks?

The loss of the tobacco industry at negotiations creates several nettlesome problems for lawmakers.

Congress cannot get what many health care experts say is crucial to cutting down teen smoking rates: voluntary advertising restrictions by the companies and penalties if they fail to reduce the number of teen smokers.

Some lawmakers say Congress can restrict advertising without the tobacco industry's permission. If that happens, tobacco officials say Congress must be prepared for a legal tangle in court.

That reply only heightened opposition to the industry on Capitol Hill.

"If tobacco companies are not willing to cooperate freely in the effort to protect our children from their deadly products, we might need to compel their assistance," said Sen. Bob Graham, D-Fla.

Bill's Rapid Pace Emboldens Backers, Confounds Foes

MAY 16 — A major anti-tobacco bill has gathered so much momentum as it heads to the Senate floor on May 18 that its opponents are struggling for a strategy to halt it.

"I want to kill this bill. I think it's a bad bill," Senate Majority Whip Don Nickles, R-Okla., said May 14.

But when asked about prospects for Senate passage of the measure (S 1415), Nickles reluctantly conceded that they are "too high."

Nickles spoke immediately after the Finance Committee approved, 13-6, language it will offer as an amendment to S 1415, a product of the Commerce, Science and Transportation Committee.

Finance wanted to assert its jurisdiction over the trade and revenue portions of the bill, which would raise at least $516 billion over 25 years. But in a blow to Republicans such as Nickles, who criticized S 1415 as a "tax and spend" package, the Finance Committee voted to boost the new taxes on a pack of cigarettes.

"Anybody who thinks they're going to keep a tough tobacco bill from passing in the Senate isn't living in the real world," said Charles E. Grassley, a Republican Finance member who said his Iowa constituents are demanding action.

Such talk has Democrats crowing. They are planning to turn tobacco into a major campaign issue if Congress fails to enact legislation.

"You saw what happened in the Finance Committee — they can't vote against it," said Edward M. Kennedy, D-Mass.

The Finance Committee voted, 10-9, to raise taxes by $1.50 per pack instead of $1.10. The vote came after a similar proposal failed, 9-10.

Alfonse M. D'Amato, R-N.Y., who voted "no" by proxy on the first version, was present to vote in support of the second. D'Amato then successfully attached, by an 11-9 vote, language that would require health insurers to let doctors decide how long a patient stays in the hospital after a mastectomy and to cover reconstructive surgery.

Finance Chairman William V. Roth Jr., R-Del., ended up voting against his committee's amendment because he thought its tax bill was too high.

But Roth nevertheless admitted that the positive vote of his committee, home to lawmakers who are warring factions on the tobacco debate, sent "a message that there is going to be significant legislation" passed.

Toughening the Bill

Democrats are going to offer floor amendments to make S 1415 tougher on the tobacco industry. This has left Commerce Chairman John McCain, R-Ariz., the bill's sponsor, striving for the political center.

McCain, who will partially rewrite his bill with a manager's amendment he is drafting in consultation with the White House, hopes to present his plan as a unified package that should not be picked apart.

Among other changes, the McCain rewrite will probably raise the tobacco industry's legal liability protection from his bill's current $6.5 billion annual cap to $8 billion.

But McCain knows it will be open season for disagreement on the floor. "I don't like it at all," McCain said of a $1.50 tax increase. "But we may not win there."

"Next week is not going to be for the faint-hearted," said Ron Wyden, D-Ore. Wyden said Democrats would offer amendments on secondhand smoke, minority health protections and exports.

Republicans plan amendments to use portions of the funds the bill would raise for tax cuts; lower its price tag; and tie it to efforts to combat illegal drugs.

If opponents of cigarette companies were emboldened by the moves at Finance, the markup was not all bad news for the tobacco industry.

The Finance amendment would soften or strike the Commerce bill's restrictions on exports. And, in place of the McCain bill's so-called lookback penalties, which would fine cigarette makers if reduction targets in youth smoking were not met, the Finance amendment would impose a non-deductible excise tax for the same purpose.

The change would afford the tobacco industry a volume adjustment, meaning the tax penalties they would have to pay would decrease if sales slackened.

Volume adjustment is one of the key provisions being sought by the tobacco industry, which the state attorneys general have been trying to woo back to the negotiating table.

Some senators, such as Judiciary Chairman Orrin G. Hatch, R-Utah, believe industry cooperation is essential to winning advertising restrictions and avoiding future legal challenges.

Defeat of Limits On Liability Hits Tobacco Bill Hard

MAY 23 — Tobacco legislation continues to swing on a pendulum ride between times when it appears to have the momentum to pass, and others when it looks ready for burial.

"On many occasions, people inside the media and outside the media have said this legislation is dead," Sen. John McCain, R-Ariz., said May 21. "I can assure you that this issue is not dead." McCain spoke minutes after suffering defeat on a key Senate vote that, in effect, lifted the cap on industry liability in his anti-tobacco bill (S 1415 — S Rept 105-180).

Industry & Regulation

Highlights Of S 1415

• Tobacco companies would pay at least $516 billion over 25 years to defray costs of smokers' illnesses and pay for a campaign to reduce smoking among teens.

• Cigarette fees would increase by $1.10 a pack over five years.

• Parent companies would be liable in civil lawsuits.

• Tobacco companies would face as much as $4 billion a year in fines if youth smoking did not decline by 60 percent in 10 years.

• The Food and Drug Administration would have the power to regulate nicotine.

• Tobacco advertising aimed at minors, including Internet advertising, may be banned.

A motion to table, or kill, an amendment by Judd Gregg, R-N.H., to strip the bill of any limits on legal liability for the tobacco industry failed, 37-61. *(Vote 145, p. S-24)*

The underlying bill would offer the tobacco industry an $8 billion annual cap on future lawsuits in exchange for agreeing to advertising restrictions and other provisions.

Although McCain expressed hope that the move would not prove fatal to S 1415, Senate Majority Leader Trent Lott, R-Miss., said, "There'll be liability provisions, or there'll be no bill. Period."

Such differences of opinion and spin were rife the week of May 18, much of which the Senate devoted to the bill. It was pulled shortly after the motion to table failed, but debate is scheduled to resume after the weeklong Memorial Day recess.

Until the vote on the Gregg amendment, McCain had succeeded in fending off floor changes to his bill. With the backing of the White House, McCain argued that S 1415 was a carefully crafted package that should not be picked apart.

In fact, the bill, originally approved by the Commerce, Science and Transportation Committee in April, had already been transformed by a manager's amendment into an amalgam of ideas from the Finance Committee and the Clinton administration, as well as pickings from other senators' bills.

The legislation has never been embraced as perfect, even by McCain; instead, it is widely characterized as a "vehicle" for further debate. McCain and Lott have both indicated that they believe the true birthplace of federal tobacco policy will be a House-Senate conference.

Still, McCain's pleas that the bill be accepted as a delicately balanced compromise swayed some votes on defeated amendments that would have capped attorneys' fees at $250 per hour and raised cigarette fees by $1.50 a pack, according to several senators.

Holding It All Together

But holding together what McCain has called "the great center" of support for S 1415 is going to be a more difficult chore when debate resumes in June.

Still pending are equally contentious plans to provide support payments to tobacco farmers and so-called look-back penalties that tobacco companies would pay if goals for reducing youth smoking are not met.

George Washington, discussing foreign policy in his farewell address, declared, " 'Tis our true policy to steer clear of permanent alliances," and senators have heeded his words on this bill. Support and opposition camps for the major provisions of the McCain bill are made up of kaleidoscopic coalitions.

The Gregg amendment drew its support from a rare alliance of bedrock conservatives who wish to sink the bill (or at least substitute something drastically smaller in price and reach) and the most liberal senators.

Democratic leaders appealed to their brethren to bear with them, saying an $8 billion annual liability cap was needed to lure tobacco companies back to the negotiating table.

But those pleas failed to sway two dozen Democrats who felt that the tobacco industry would not have agreed to the June 1997 settlement brokered with 40 state attorneys general if not for fear of big losses in court. Several senators switched their votes after it became clear that the motion to table the amendment would be defeated.

"There is not a feeling of trust for tobacco companies on the floor to save a deal they say they're walking away from," said Democratic Sen. Patrick J. Leahy of Vermont, who cosponsored the amendment to strip the bill of liability protections.

Feelings of distrust and questions about motives have seeped into the debate over tobacco, with some Republicans wishing to punt the issue entirely, and Democrats sensing political opportunity if they do so.

Tobacco companies and public health activists will redouble their efforts to sway public opinion during the interim with television and print ad campaigns. For now, political dynamics may ensure passage by coupling senators who support the bill with senators who are afraid to vote against it.

But like all coalitions on the bill, the "final passage" coalition is subject to change. And delay plays into the hands of those who wish to stop it, especially as an already-delayed appropriations season gets under way and the session's close starts to loom.

A stalemate in the Senate also would keep pressure off House Republican leaders, who have shown little enthusiasm for anti-tobacco legislation.

"Time is not on our side. There's no question about that," McCain said. "I think there's every likelihood, frankly, that this could be an election-year issue."

Stall and Destroy

S 1415's mere appearance on the Senate floor had been treated for weeks as a sort of holy grail by its supporters, who believed that senators could not risk voting against a popular bill.

"Anyone who opposes the bill knows that they are going to be tarred as being the spokesman for the tobacco industry, which in this debate has become the embodiment of all evil on this earth," said Phil Gramm, R-Texas.

Recognizing that they did not have the votes to stop S 1415, the bill's detractors made few attempts to hide their strategy of delaying it — either by stalling it to death, or at least buying time to build up support for their position in the court of public opinion.

"We're not going to ram this bill through just because that's what some people want to do," said Orrin G. Hatch, R-Utah. "This is a huge issue that deserves debate."

Engaging in lengthy colloquies and refusing to enter into unanimous consent agreements to limit the number of amendments or length of debate, opponents controlled the floor for hours, to the obvious frustration of the bill's managers.

But they failed on the two amendments they offered that came to a vote.

The Senate on May 19 tabled, 58-39, an amendment sponsored by Lauch Faircloth, R-N.C., to limit attorneys' fees to $250 per billable hour. *(Vote 142, p. S-24)*

On May 20, the Senate also tabled, 72-26, an amendment sponsored by John Ashcroft, R-Mo., that would have deleted the bill's revenue provisions, including the $1.10 per pack fee. *(Vote 143, p. S-24)*

The amendment's poor showing revealed the loneliness of its opponents. The solid core of senators who are likely to vote against final passage regardless of what shape the bill takes remains well below the 40-vote threshold needed to sustain a proper filibuster.

But the health care lobby has not yet matched the millions spent by the tobacco industry in its public relations effort to convince voters that the legislation represents what Gramm called "excruciating, bone-crushing tax increases" and poses the threat of a dangerous black market.

"I think as people realize what's in this bill, they like it less," said Majority Whip Don Nickles, R-Okla. "I've always said that a little time is a great disinfectant."

Strengthening the Bill

Senate allies of public health activists have vowed to toughen the bill at every turn. But McCain was able to keep them from checking off one top item on their list: raising fees from $1.10 per pack to $1.50. (The current federal excise tax on cigarettes is 24 cents per pack, increasing to 39 cents a pack in 2002).

"The most important part of reaching the goal of reducing teenage smoking is raising the price as high as possible," said Bob Graham, D-Fla.

Such rhetoric scared a majority of Republicans and some Democrats who maintained that the higher price tag on cigarettes would be borne disproportionately by lower-income workers.

Although the $1.50 rate had been approved by both the Finance and Budget committees, the amendment was tabled by a surprisingly strong 58-40 vote on May 20. *(Vote 144, p. S-24)*

After the vote that essentially lifted S 1415's liability cap, supporters of the bill hoped it could be made more punitive. Without the liability provisions, S 1415 is to a large extent dominated by the revenue provisions that the failed Ashcroft amendment sought to strip.

Because Ashcroft's amendment failed badly, and because conservatives went on record with the liability vote as being willing to take a tough stand against the tobacco industry, bill supporters remain optimistic that their side will retain the edge in vote tallies.

Down on the Farmers

In addition to the formality of passing Gregg's liability amendment, the Senate in June will confront a Gramm amendment to use the tobacco bill as the vehicle to eliminate the so-called marriage penalty for families earning less than $50,000 a year, and an amendment that would establish higher goals for reducing teen smoking and consequent look-back penalties.

Variations on the amendments on attorneys' fee and cigarette prices are also likely to be offered, and substitute amendments to limit the scope of the bill will also be the order of the day.

Perhaps the thorniest outstanding issue is the matter of providing some support to tobacco farmers. The Commerce-crafted bill contains provisions sponsored by Wendell H. Ford, D-Ky., that would offer $28.5 billion in assistance over 25 years to farmers and communities adversely affected by the bill, while leaving in place the federal price subsidy system.

But the manager's amendment also contains a farm buyout proposal, sponsored by Republicans Richard G. Lugar of Indiana and Mitch McConnell of Kentucky, that would pay holders of tobacco production quotas, and their tenants, $18 billion over three years.

The Lugar-McConnell proposal, a modification of S 1313, was included in the bill hours before floor debate began May 18 as part of the manager's amendment, much to the shock of Ford and other farm-state Democrats who felt betrayed by the move.

They argued that the Lugar-McConnell proposal, which would end the Depression-era tobacco support program, would imperil farmers and cost them dearly as production increased and prices dropped.

But Lugar said the proposal was consistent with the general move away from crop supports embodied in the 1996 "freedom to farm" law (PL 104-127). And McConnell defended the proposal, arguing that the support program is doomed given the political environment, so farmers should be compensated while there is tobacco money on the table. *(1996 Almanac, p. 3-15)*

But some Democrats saw the inclusion of the language as part of a divide and conquer strategy.

"There are a lot of folks that, in the absence of a better explanation, are concerned that it's designed to kill the bill," said Charles S. Robb, D-Va. "Any of the big pieces have the potential for taking the bill down."

Show Me the Money

Another thread that could tear apart the anti-tobacco coalition is the desire of the state attorneys general who looked to Congress to ratify their June 1997 settlement to bring this process to closure.

Richard Scruggs, a top plaintiffs' attorney in the state cases (and Lott's brother-in-law), said that if Congress fails to act this year, the tobacco companies might make individual states offers they could not refuse.

"That would invest the states in the money, instead of coming hat in hand to Congress," said Scruggs, who watched the debate from the Senate gallery.

McCain has warned repeatedly that if Congress fails to enact tobacco legislation, smoking will continue to be an issue in the courts, but there will not be the comprehensive prevention mechanisms available in his bill.

Tobacco companies have already settled cases in Mississippi, Florida, Texas and Minnesota for a total of $29.6 billion. Most other states have lawsuits pending, with cases on the docket in Washington, Oklahoma and Massachusetts.

Industry & Regulation

Cloture Vote Ahead As Senators Pile On Amendments

JUNE 6 — Supporters of tobacco legislation, who have watched two weeks of desultory Senate floor debate with mounting frustration, hope to get their revenge the week of June 8.

A motion to invoke cloture will come to a vote June 9; it is widely expected to fail. Nevertheless, Democrats believe that the motion has painted opponents of the bill (S 1415 — S Rept 105-180) into a corner.

Democrats still perceive cloture as inevitable on a second or third try. Because the next amendments on tap are GOP efforts to increase illegal drug interdiction and to offer some couples relief from the so-called marriage tax penalty, they entertain visions that it will become increasingly difficult for Republicans to vote against the popular tobacco package.

But Senate Majority Leader Trent Lott, R-Miss., took to the floor June 5 to warn that the Democratic strategy of trying to end debate could doom the package, signaling that he might join with those seeking to smother the bill through procedural means if they persist.

"At this point, it looks to me like it's over because of the games being played," Lott said.

Over the two weeks of Senate debate thus far, conservatives have become increasingly vocal about their opposition to the bill's bureaucratic reach and its $516 billion price tag over 25 years.

"This bill has no constituency except people who want to raise a whole lot of money," said Phil Gramm, R-Texas, in a June 4 interview.

Recognizing that they do not have the votes to block an up-or-down vote on final passage, Gramm and his allies have sought to delay that day of reckoning as long as possible.

But the cloture motion has put them in the position of having to unveil their amendments for floor action, or miss the opportunity to revise S 1415 before debate ends.

Democrats believe that enough Republicans are either sincere supporters of the bill or fear the political consequences of opposing it to join with them to provide the 60 votes necessary to invoke cloture on a subsequent try.

The bill is being heavily lobbied by a veritable who's who of Washington players, and the tobacco industry has poured tens of millions of dollars into a public relations campaign tarring the bill as a "big tax" proposal. Health groups have also advertised in swing senators' states.

Strategists in both parties say candidates who have accepted campaign contributions from tobacco companies and are perceived as having voted to block tobacco legislation may hand their opponents a winning issue.

"You put on this marriage penalty [amendment] and this drug proposal, and then see how many of them vote against it," said Edward M. Kennedy, D-Mass. "I'd love to write those ads."

A majority of married couples pay more in taxes than they would if they filed separately. The issue has become a prime concern for many Republicans and social conservatives. The House's troubled budget resolution (H Con Res 284) was propelled by a separate marriage penalty repeal proposal.

Still, even if supporters of the tobacco bill clear the hurdle of Senate passage, time is running short for enactment. Opponents and supporters alike expect tobacco legislation to be heavily rewritten in conference, but House GOP leaders have yet to show interest in taking up even a much narrower bill.

"The longer it takes, the more difficult it becomes," said Sen. Olympia J. Snowe, R-Maine.

The Tough Get Tougher

For all their criticism of the bill's size and scope, many conservatives have joined with liberals to support amendments that have made S 1415 tougher on tobacco interests.

"I think the legislation is in some real trouble because the people who want no legislation at all are trying to make it so good that it becomes bad," said Sen. Robert G. Torricelli, D-N.J., who favors a more modest approach.

On June 4, the Senate defeated a motion to table, or kill, an amendment by Richard J. Durbin, D-Ill., and Mike DeWine, R-Ohio, to stiffen the so-called look-back penalties on cigarette manufacturers who fail to reach goals for reducing youth smoking. The vote was 29-66. (Vote 149, p. S-25)

Twenty-eight Republicans joined 38 Democrats in support of the amendment. As with a May 21 vote that, in effect, eliminated the bill's cap on legal damages that tobacco companies could be forced to pay, several senators switched their votes in the waning minutes to line up on the prevailing side.

The Durbin-DeWine amendment would put the onus for reducing youth smoking on specific companies and brands, rather than setting mostly industry-wide standards, as in the underlying bill.

The amendment would require a 67 percent reduction over 10 years in smoking by minors, as opposed to the 60 percent reduction called for in S 1415. The amendment also would raise annual penalties to as much as $7 billion, up from $4 billion.

Supporters of the liability and look-back provisions said that making the bill tougher merely illustrates its momentum.

But bill sponsor John McCain, R-Ariz., complained that the amendments had upset his "carefully balanced package."

"If we fail to pass this bill, the states will go back to court to win in judgment or settlement what we might more efficiently accomplish with national legislation," he warned.

Slowing to a Crawl

For much of the week of June 1, the bill had little visible momentum. Debate dissolved into quorum calls as McCain and Democratic leaders sought a compromise with Gramm on the size of the marriage penalty proposal.

"What would be a reasonable amount?" Gramm asked McCain as they walked into a GOP policy luncheon June 2.

Gramm initially sought to give a tax deduction to all married couples earning less than $50,000 a year, at an estimated cost of $45 billion over five years. He subsequently agreed to lower his proposal's cost to $16.8 billion.

"What we're trying to do is take one-third of the money and give it back basically as a rebate," Gramm said. His proposal would have diverted about one-third of the amount S 1415 would raise for federal spending.

But Democrats argued that the revised tax break would still absorb too great a share of the money, particularly in the outlying years of the bill's 25-year lifespan, when it would gobble up closer to 75 percent of the total.

Their desire to offer a more narrowly targeted tax break brought negotiations with Gramm to an impasse that slowed the bill's movement for days.

"Their proposal is, they don't want my amendment," Gramm groused.

But Democrats, who want to offer a tax break only to those low-income couples who are actually penalized by the tax code for being married (some married couples do pay lower rates than they would if they filed as singles), recognize they do not have the votes to block the idea entirely. So negotiations were to continue over the weekend of June 6-7.

Losing Focus

In addition to growing partisan rancor, the bill's focus on teen smoking is being blurred by extraneous issues such as the marriage penalty.

The manager's amendment to S 1415 contains a provision to require health insurers to let doctors decide how long a patient stays in the hospital after a mastectomy and to cover reconstructive surgery.

The Senate on June 2 approved, by voice vote, an amendment offered by McCain to provide $3 billion over five years to treat veterans with smoking-related illnesses. Veterans may be stripped of their health benefits for such illnesses by the highway bill (HR 2400).

And a pending amendment offered by Paul Coverdell, R-Ga., and Larry E. Craig, R-Idaho, would not only move $16 billion over five years to drug interdiction accounts, but would allow federal funds to be spent on school vouchers for children who have been victims of violent crimes on school property as well.

The Coverdell-Craig amendment would also restrict convicted drug criminals from receiving federal student loans and would create a community registration bank for drug dealers, along the lines of the sex offender registry created by "Megan's law" (PL 104-145). (*1996 Almanac*, p. 5-45)

"I think it is critical that we remain focused on the smoking-related aspects of this legislation, rather than some of the other attempts to sort of grab some of the revenue and use it for worthy but nevertheless non-related causes," said John Kerry, D-Mass.

Kerry described the legislation as "a tax cut bill," arguing it would save billions of dollars in Medicare and Medicaid costs for treating smokers, as well as cutting down on lost productivity.

As it now stands, the bill would raise cigarette fees by $1.10 per pack and divide the resultant revenues as follows: States would receive $24.8 billion over the first five years in block grants for health and smoking programs; research efforts and public health programs would each receive $13.6 billion; and tobacco farmers would receive $9.9 billion.

Still To Come

Another thorny issue yet to be resolved concerns payments to farmers who hold tobacco quotas and their tenants. Two competing proposals continue to divide both caucuses: a three-year, $18 billion plan to buy out tobacco quota holders, offered by Richard G. Lugar, R-Ind., and Mitch McConnell, R-Ky.; and a package sponsored by Wendell H. Ford, D-Ky., that would pay farmers $16 billion over 25 years and offer $12.5 billion in aid to affected tobacco-raising communities.

Republicans are expected to offer at least two substitute amendments that would rein in the bill's size and price tag. And although an amendment to limit attorneys' fees to $250 per hour failed May 19, a fresh amendment capping their payments to $1,000 per hour is still expected to reach the floor.

A proposal to speed up the phase-in of 100 percent tax deductibility for health insurance purchased by self-employed workers and other people who do not receive insurance from employers will seek a second life on the floor, after having been killed in Finance Committee action May 14.

"I don't see any end at this point," said Minority Leader Tom Daschle, D-S.D., on June 5. He vowed to block movement to any other legislation until the tobacco debate is resolved, noting, "It's entirely possible we could be on this all the way through Independence Day."

Amendments, Ads Bury 'Inviolable' Tobacco Bill

JUNE 13 — The political games have begun. Calling the Republican Party a wholly owned subsidiary of the tobacco industry, President Clinton and other Democrats vowed to make GOP lawmakers pay for killing a sweeping anti-tobacco bill.

But Republicans said they derailed the $516 billion bill (S 1415 — S Rept 105-180) precisely because it had lost its focus on preventing tobacco addiction among teenagers.

Pledging to offer a trimmer bill to deal with the problem, Republicans believed they accomplished a remarkable feat of political jujitsu — turning the tobacco debate on its head by making the bill seem unattractive.

S 1415 was killed on a pair of procedural votes June 17. By that time, the tobacco industry and conservative opponents of the bill had succeeded in convincing a sufficient number of their fence-sitting colleagues that the debate was no longer about "big tobacco vs. kids," as advocates had long claimed, but about preventing a Washington "money grab" that would benefit lawyers and had no grass-roots constituency.

"What killed this bill was that the public never bought into the logic of it — they never saw this as a tool to fight teen smoking," said Sen. Phil Gramm, R-Texas. "This bill has no support in America, and it has lost its support in Congress."

Clinton called the Senate move "a vote against our children and for the tobacco lobby. It's as simple as that." He said he would not be satisfied by slimmed-down legislation.

"I am not going to participate in a charade which provides people with some cover to pretend that they did something they didn't. That would be wrong," Clinton said.

S 1415's high point may have been the Senate Commerce, Science and Transportation Committee markup

Industry & Regulation

April 1, when the bill was approved 19-1. Republicans and Democrats alike agreed that it was important to move a vehicle to the floor. But a similar argument, that the Senate should pass the bill in order to "fix" it in conference with the House, failed to sway the requisite 60 senators.

The committee version of the legislation lacked enough protection from legal liability to satisfy the tobacco industry, which withdrew its support for the legislation April 8. The tobacco companies, which would have been heavily penalized by S 1415, launched expensive advertising and public relations campaigns that helped kill the bill.

The Senate had given its strong endorsement to striking liability protections for the industry, a move that many Republicans supported, and GOP senators now hope will offer them some cover from Vice President Al Gore's charge June 18 that they are the "R.J. Reynolds Republican Party."

S 1415's sponsors, led by John McCain, R-Ariz., had banked on Majority Leader Trent Lott, R-Miss., stepping in at the last minute, like the town sheriff in an old movie, to bring order to the nearly four-week debate and push the bill to passage.

Instead, Lott filed a cloture motion that he opposed, signaling to Republicans that it was time to kill the bill.

"Nothing like the McCain bill is going to pass," Lott declared. "This bill that started out well-intentioned has grown like Topsy."

Lott filed the motion within hours of a closed-door meeting June 17 of about three-dozen Republican senators, by which time it had become clear that support was hemorrhaging for a bill that many had previously believed politically inviolable.

Lott's motion to invoke cloture failed, 57-42, with two tobacco-state Democrats (Wendell H. Ford of Kentucky and Charles S. Robb of Virginia) joining all but 14 of the 54 Republicans in opposition. (*Vote 161, p. H-48*)

S 1415 would have raised fees on cigarettes by $1.10 per pack over five years, given the federal government broad control over the distribution and marketing of tobacco products, and restricted tobacco advertising.

Speaker Newt Gingrich, R-Ga., promised that the House would take up a much smaller bill without new taxes, designed to fight teen smoking and drug addiction through incentives to states to create their own programs. But there appears little consensus for small-scale legislation, which Lott is also contemplating.

Other Playing Fields

And so the myriad players whose actions had been in a holding pattern during the Senate's consideration of S 1415 will resume fighting their own battles in the tobacco wars. At least 15 states will have their day in court to challenge tobacco companies to reimburse them for Medicaid expenses by the end of next year. The Food and Drug Administration and the tobacco companies will continue their appellate case to determine the agency's authority to regulate nicotine and tobacco advertising. And, of course, the issue will have a long half-life in the political sphere.

But in the Senate, fans and foes of the McCain bill declared comprehensive tobacco legislation dead for the year, defeating what may have been Clinton's last major domestic initiative of his presidency.

With chances that Congress will pass comprehensive tobacco legislation this year next to nil, state attorneys general, who had brought the issue to the fore with a June 1997 settlement with tobacco companies, fast-forwarded their plans to move ahead with individual lawsuits.

Four states have settled their suits, at an aggregate cost to the tobacco industry of more than $30 billion.

So the current state of affairs puts the tobacco industry back at square one. Tobacco companies pumped more than $40 million into an issue advertising campaign that helped kill the Senate bill, and they saw their stocks inch up the week of June 15 as a result. But they are left unsated in their desire for a legislative remedy for their legal woes.

"I think it's a big disappointment that a year after the June 20 agreement, which held great promise, we are not having a signing ceremony but a wake," said tobacco industry spokesman Scott Williams.

GOP Triumph?

But Gramm and his allies were not plagued by such second thoughts. They defeated a measure that proponents just weeks before had believed would pass with more than 70 votes.

As it happened, supporters of S 1415 were unable to muster the 60 votes necessary to prevail on the pair of procedural votes that brought the desultory Senate debate to its end.

After Lott's cloture motion failed, S 1415 was brought down when the Senate refused, 53-46, to waive budget rules violated by the bill's spending levels. (*Vote 162, p. H-48*)

Democratic threats to attach tobacco legislation "to every bill that comes down the pike," as Sen. Edward M. Kennedy, D-Mass., said, quickly rang hollow.

The Senate on June 18 tabled, or killed, 54-44, a motion to waive another budget point of order when Democrats sought to attach tobacco legislation to the fiscal 1999 energy and water spending bill (S 2138). Not a single Republican stayed with Democrats on the replay, and a tobacco amendment to the agriculture spending bill (S 2159) is likely to meet the same fate the week of June 22. (*Vote 164, p. H-48*)

Political Fallout

The much-anticipated legislation turned quickly into a strictly political issue. Democrats contended that one reason Senate Republicans iced the bill was to spare their House colleagues a contentious vote. But they argued that Republicans in both chambers would still be held accountable come November.

"I think the Republican Party has made a mistake of enormous proportions," said Robert G. Torricelli of New Jersey, vice chairman of the Democratic Senatorial Campaign Committee, after the decisive June 17 vote.

"I think some Republican senators will look back on this day as the day when they lost their seats."

Republicans have received the bulk of campaign contributions from tobacco companies in recent years. The Tobacco Institute contributed $50,000 to a Republican congressional fundraising dinner on the eve of the cloture vote.

Despite Democrats' predictions that Republicans will pay at election time, the GOP anticipates increasing its Senate majority by two to three seats for the 106th Congress. Mitch McConnell of Kentucky, chairman of the National Republican Senatorial Campaign Committee said, "If you look at the survey data I've been seeing, this bill is pretty unpopular."

Rep. Vic Fazio, D-Calif., suggested that the GOP is "misreading the polls," although he acknowledged that Republicans had some success in portraying the tobacco measure as a typical Democratic tax-and-spend proposal.

Point of Order

Republicans said S 1415 violated the spending limits allowed for the Commerce Committee under the Senate-passed budget resolution (S Con Res 86) even before the bill was amended on the floor to include more spending.

Asked why a point of order had not been raised earlier, Majority Whip Don Nickles, R-Okla., said, "I could have made a point of order at the start of the debate — I thought about that — but I wanted to be sure we had the votes."

The bill's opponents were able to gather force as debate dragged on, winning over colleagues who had been wavering. Some Republicans had worried that a vote against a bill to punish tobacco companies and cut down on teen smoking was tantamount to professional suicide.

But S 1415's opponents were able to convince their colleagues that casting the bill as a "massive tax increase" would inoculate them.

They were quick to blame the bill's proponents, such as public health organizations, for loading the bill with too many free-spending provisions.

Democrats, in turn, cried foul because Republicans loaded onto S 1415 amendments to cut taxes, fund drug interdiction efforts and cap attorneys' fees, proceeded to debate them at great length, and still opposed the overall product.

"What they did was spread DDT here — first delay, then destroy, then terminate any action on tobacco," said Frank R. Lautenberg, D-N.J., of S 1415's opponents, several of whom could be seen laughing in response on the Senate floor.

But political scientist William F. Connelly Jr. of Washington and Lee University in Virginia contended, "What you saw the last few weeks was the virtue of extended debate in the Senate."

"You saw Phil Gramm as Jimmy Stewart in 'Mr. Smith Goes to Washington,' getting his chance to stand up and say, 'This isn't big tobacco vs. kids, this is about big taxes and big government.'"

Although Gramm is no Hollywood casting director's ideal, his steady drumbeat, in tandem with Nickles and other conservatives such as John Ashcroft, R-Mo., helped convince wary colleagues that S 1415 was an expensive mess.

Impact of Ads

That characterization was more loudly broadcast by the tobacco industry's $40 million ad campaign. Many senators spoke of never hearing from constituents about the tobacco bill, except when they were echoing the ad blitz.

McCain related that during his frequent media appearances, he heard callers parrot the ads. "It's not intentional, but it's a kind of osmosis," he said.

But if the tobacco industry's splurge helped convince voters that S 1415 was bad medicine, Republicans maintain that the argument that the bill would raise taxes and expand government was not hard to make — much to the chagrin of Democrats and public health groups.

Confident that they had framed the terms of debate as a question of defending tobacco companies or fighting for children's health, the bill's champions never had a megaphone loud enough to compete with tobacco's megabucks.

According to Connelly, Republicans were also able to suggest that Democratic hands were not entirely clean, either, given their reliance on campaign contributions from trial lawyers — some of whom stood to reap a fortune under S 1415. This was a message propounded by an inside-the-Beltway ad campaign sponsored by the U.S. Chamber of Commerce.

After rejecting two earlier amendments that would have limited the pay of plaintiffs' lawyers, but not industry lawyers, to $250 or $1,000 per hour, the Senate on June 16 adopted, 49-48, an amendment that placed caps on fees. Lawyers would be paid on a sliding scale that reaches as high as $4,000 an hour, depending on when they filed their lawsuits. *(Vote 160, p. H-48)*

Some public health groups argued that the amendment's limitation on fees to $500 per hour for cases filed after June 15, 1998, would have a chilling effect on future litigation, effectively granting the industry limited liability protection.

But Democrats who defended S 1415's system of subjecting "outrageous" legal bills to arbitration found themselves hard pressed to argue against a cap of $4,000 per hour for lawyers who filed cases before 1994.

"Because this is arbitrary," suggested Democrat Kent Conrad of North Dakota, "in many cases, it may be way too much."

The amendment was adopted after the vote was held open for 40 minutes, more than twice the normal duration. Three senators changed their votes from "nay" to "aye," with Gordon H. Smith, R-Ore., providing the vote that put it over the top.

Race Against Time

With the House having failed as yet even to mark up a tobacco bill in committee, McCain and his Democratic confreres realized even as the Senate floor debate began May 18 that time was not on their side.

Their strategy of pushing S 1415 through the Senate in hopes of reaching a House-Senate conference was greatly imperiled by the hundreds of amendments filed on the bill and by their failure to reach time agreements on the few that were voted on.

By the week of June 15, Lott's impatience with the proceedings was heightened by the need to start moving long-delayed appropriations bills.

That goal was made real in the person of Appropriations Committee Chairman Ted Stevens, R-Alaska. Stevens had been counted on Democratic whip sheets as a vote for cloture, but he raised the budget point of order that killed S 1415.

"As a practical matter, we spent too much time on this bill," he said. "We must get back to our regular, ordinary drudge work of getting the 13 appropriations bills through the Senate."

Industry & Regulation

Ruling Throws FDA Jurisdiction Into Doubt

AUGUST 22 — For months, advocates of broad tobacco legislation have argued that lawmakers were missing their chance to give the federal government broad regulatory authority over tobacco. Congress should act, they warned, or risk a court decision that the Food and Drug Administration (FDA) has no business trying to control the marketing of tobacco products.

Now, a three-judge panel in the 4th U.S. Circuit Court of Appeals has ruled exactly that, overturning the Clinton administration's ambitious 1996 rules that gave the FDA the power to regulate the sale, distribution and use of cigarettes and other tobacco products.

The court's 2-1 decision, issued Aug. 14, is far from the final word on the matter. The government is appealing the case to the full circuit, and the case is expected to go all the way to the Supreme Court, where, legal experts say, there is still a reasonable chance the FDA rules will be reinstated.

But unless the appeals court is reversed, FDA regulatory control over tobacco will depend purely on Congress.

"The appeals court decision makes it even more imperative that Congress pass comprehensive legislation to address the problem of youth tobacco use and addiction," said Sen. John McCain, R-Ariz., the author of failed comprehensive legislation (S 1415) that would have granted the agency specific legal authority over tobacco.

Despite the court's decision, it appears unlikely that Congress will revive tobacco legislation before the end of the current legislative session.

In the House, the Republican leadership has never been enthusiastic about giving the FDA authority over tobacco. In 1995, when the Clinton administration first announced it was drafting the new rules, House Speaker Newt Gingrich, R-Ga., said the FDA had "lost its mind" and said the initiative was a "classic case of big government interference."

In the Senate, the McCain legislation died in June because Republican leaders contended it cost too much and went too far in expanding government controls over the industry.

Even before the favorable 4th Circuit decision, the tobacco companies had walked away from the negotiating table — and with the new opinion in their pocket they would appear to have little reason to return. Indeed, the ruling seems to bolster the tobacco industry's strategy of taking its chances with the courts and abandoning efforts to negotiate a compromise in Congress.

Given the uncertain legal situation, many public health groups continue to favor legislation along the lines of the McCain bill that would confirm the FDA's legal authority to regulate tobacco products.

Advocates of strong controls on tobacco say one of the few real options that remains available to them is to shine a spotlight on vulnerable incumbents, such as Sen. Ben Nighthorse Campbell, R-Colo., who have accepted political donations from tobacco companies, and to raise questions about undue influence.

If Republicans start feeling vulnerable from attacks that they are beholden to the industry, it could force the GOP leadership to provide political cover in the form of narrow legislation, although this course still appears unlikely.

"I think the only incentive would be public pressure," said John F. Banzhaf III, executive director of Action on Smoking and Health, a national anti-smoking group.

Congressional Intent

The key issue in the 4th Circuit case was whether Congress ever intended the FDA to regulate tobacco.

Federal agencies routinely respond to new public health threats without getting permission from Congress, whether they are battling an epidemic such as AIDS or proposing new regulations to reduce workplace hazards.

Indeed, Congress expects agencies, operating within the confines of their statutes, to exercise independent judgment, respond to problems that put the public at risk and establish regulations that carry out the law.

In the case of tobacco, the FDA issued the 1996 rules to regulate the sale and marketing of cigarettes as part of a broad effort to curb teenage smoking. Even though Congress never provided an explicit mandate, the agency contended that it had wide latitude to interpret its own statute.

But the 4th Circuit, based in Richmond, Va., ruled that Congress never intended the FDA to regulate tobacco, and therefore did not equip it with the laws to do so.

In its ruling, the court cited the 1984 Supreme Court decision in Chevron v. Natural Resources Defense Council, which lays out guidelines that courts use to determine agency jurisdiction.

Chevron established a two-part test to determine whether agencies overstep their legal mandates. The first part directed courts to decide whether Congress has spoken to the precise question at issue. If "the intent of Congress is clear," the matter is settled, and the court "must give effect to the unambiguously expressed intent of Congress."

But in cases where Congress has left provisions vague, courts are directed to give the agencies more leeway in interpreting their own statutes. As the Supreme Court put it in *Chevron*, "If the statute is silent or ambiguous with respect to the specific issue, the question for the court is whether the agency's answer is based on a permissible construction of the statute."

In its opinion, the 4th Circuit accepted the tobacco companies' argument that Congress never intended for FDA to regulate tobacco. The case, therefore, turned on the answer to the first part of the two-part test established in the *Chevron* case.

FDA officials say that the court probably chose to decide the case on the first test because otherwise it would have had to pay much greater deference to the agency and uphold the FDA rules.

While Congress never explicitly prohibited the agency from regulating tobacco products, the court determined that the agency attempted to "stretch the act beyond the scope intended by Congress."

Many public health advocates contend that Congress did not deliberately keep authority over tobacco from the FDA but simply avoided the issue because it lacked the political will to tackle it.

Jeff Nesbit, staff director for an anti-smoking task force headed by former FDA Commissioner David A. Kessler and former Surgeon General C. Everett Koop, pointed out that Kessler repeatedly asked Congress in letters and in testimony on Capitol Hill to weigh in on the issue, but that Congress declined, suggesting under the court's logic that Congress by its own inaction "acquiesced" in the FDA's rule-making.

"They totally missed the boat here," Nesbit said of the court. "It is not clear that Congress never intended FDA to regulate tobacco. What is clear is that they've never had the political courage to do anything about it."

Frist's Approach

At least implicitly, the decision validates the argument put forward by some Republicans, including Sen. Bill Frist of Tennessee, that tobacco products are unique and should be put in their own category in the law.

In the 1996 rules, the Clinton administration determined that cigarettes were a kind of hybrid of both drug (nicotine) and device (parts of the cigarette such as filters). During rule-making, the agency determined that tobacco products were unsafe.

But the court noted that the FDA's legal mission was to ensure that drugs are "safe and effective." In essence, the court found that the agency's rules contradicted the basic mission of the agency.

Frist, who wrote the FDA section of the McCain bill, was trying to avoid precisely the problem cited by the court: That the drug and device law's "safe use" provisions would in effect, "require prohibition of the distribution and marketing of tobacco products."

To avoid that problem, Frist proposed a "separate chapter" that would have created a whole new section of the law devoted to tobacco. Frist noted throughout the debate over the McCain bill that trying to regulate tobacco under the safe and effective standard was like trying "to take this square peg and fit it into a round hole."

Michael Pertschuk, a former chairman of the Federal Trade Commission, noted that the ruling could provide an opportunity for Republicans and the tobacco companies to draft narrow legislation that places clear limits on the agency's authority.

He said the companies could probably live with the teenage smoking rules. The White House has already gotten plenty of political mileage out of the children's health issue, and both the GOP and the companies would benefit from co-opting the cause.

What the companies would be reluctant to accept would be granting FDA broad clout to regulate nicotine — authority that could be used to control the levels of nicotine in cigarettes or even ban it. Once the agency is able to assert control over nicotine, the addictive substance in cigarettes, it potentially holds the power to make or break the industry. FDA officials say that was never their intent, because a blanket ban on nicotine could put millions of people in withdrawal and lead to a black market.

But the industry's fear of overregulation could lead the GOP — using the 4th Circuit decision as a backdrop — to embrace legislation that would enact regulations on teenage smoking, but make clear that Congress opposes granting the agency broader authority.

"I think [the case] actually opens the door for the Republican leadership and the tobacco lobby to shape legislation in the next Congress in which they say, 'We want to protect kids . . . and at the same time we're going to make sure FDA does not become a rogue agency on tobacco,'" said Pertschuk.

Implications for Agencies

Regulatory experts say that while the FDA case is fairly specific, it also raises broader questions about the ability of federal agencies to respond to public health threats when Congress fails to put specific directions into law.

One aspect of the case that is being watched closely by legal experts is the question of how much leeway courts allow agencies in interpreting their own statutes. The court itself acknowledged the implicit questions about the balance of power.

"This is not a case about whether additional or different regulations are needed to address legitimate concerns about the serious health problems related to tobacco use, and particularly youth tobacco use, in this country. At its core, this case is about who has the power to make this type of major policy decision," the court said. "As the Supreme Court has previously stated about a different agency and its enabling statute, neither federal agencies nor the courts can substitute their policy judgments for those of Congress."

In the decision, the court embraced an argument put forward by tobacco companies that the FDA repeatedly declined to claim any jurisdiction over cigarettes.

In turn, Congress declined over a period of 60 years to enact legislation providing the agency jurisdiction over tobacco products. By failing to act, the court found, Congress expressed its wishes through "legislative acquiescence."

Many legal experts said that this argument poses a potentially troublesome precedent for public health agencies that, if it were to stand up under appeal, could alter the relationship between Congress, the agencies and the courts.

The suggestion that Congress could express its intent through inaction on a particular piece of legislation is illogical, some regulatory experts say. The will of Congress can be discerned only through action rather than inaction.

To many legal experts, the decision threatens the notion that agencies must have the freedom to respond to developing health and other problems.

"I think the whole reason for administrative agencies is that they keep up with circumstances and fashion remedies much better than Congress," said Henry Geller, a Washington lawyer who served as general counsel to the Federal Communications Commission and is now a communications fellow at the Markle Foundation, a non-profit research organization. "The fact that Congress was asked to do something and failed to do it should not be determinative of the issue." ◆

Industry & Regulation

Bliley Pulls Plug On 1998 Effort To Deregulate Electricity

SUMMARY

The campaign on Capitol Hill to require states to deregulate the price of electricity came to an abrupt close in July when House Commerce Committee Chairman Thomas J. Bliley Jr., R-Va., pulled the plug.

While Bliley pledged to renew the push in 1999 for a federal mandate, other lawmakers backed narrower bills to increase federal oversight of reliability standards and clarify the role of federal and state regulators.

Electric rate deregulation ranked as a top priority at the start of the 105th Congress. Advocates argued that deregulation would allow utilities to sell to any customer, enabling consumers to select their electricity providers much the way they choose their long-distance phone carriers. Prices would be set by the market.

But reports of delays and mixed success in key states such as California that had adopted deregulation plans quickly deflated hopes for major legislation. *(1997 Almanac, p. 3-7)*

By the start of 1998, House Speaker Newt Gingrich, R-Ga., signaled that it would be problematic to pass a bill. In the Senate, Dale Bumpers, D-Ark., blocked a narrow bill (S 621) to repeal the Public Utilities Holding Company Act of 1935, which bars 16 big utility companies from entering new businesses and markets.

A last-ditch draft amendment to the bill Bliley supported (HR 655), delaying the federal mandate by one year from 2000 to 2001, failed to end a stalemate on the Commerce Committee's Energy and Power Subcommittee, chaired by Dan Schaefer, R-Colo.

Opposition came from lawmakers such as Michael D. Crapo, R-Idaho, representing regions with cheap hydropower and coal.

They warned that deregulation could hurt ratepayers if low-cost power was shipped to the highest bidder in other regions. Utilities with old debts from construction of nuclear plants also sought to delay a federal mandate.

The Clinton administration's bill (S 2287) to create a flexible mandate to encourage states to deregulate rates by 2003 was stymied in the Senate by Energy and Natural Resources Committee Chairman Frank H. Murkowski, R-Alaska, who opposed a federal mandate.

White House Plan Generates Scant Interest

MARCH 28 — Hoping to get the stalled debate on electricity deregulation moving, the Clinton administration offered its plan March 25 for opening the $208 billion industry to competition.

While the White House proposal allowing consumers to choose their electricity supplier by 2003 provided a momentary jolt, it may not be strong enough to support a legislative outcome this year. In an example of how the political lines are twisted, the administration plan was praised by some House Republicans and by at least one major interest group. But it was largely dismissed by a Republican senator key to the deregulation debate.

The administration's plan would allow consumers to pick their own electric utility service by 2003, which would increase competition and lower prices.

"We thought it was a positive movement on the part of the administration. It adds to our momentum," said Dana Perino, spokeswoman for Rep. Dan Schaefer, R-Colo., sponsor of one deregulation bill and chairman of the Commerce Committee's Energy and Power Subcommittee. The reaction was much the same from a trade group for investor-owned utilities.

The administration plan represents the final piece of the puzzle that Congress needed before it could seriously consider deregulation, said Paul J. Allen, a spokesman for the Alliance for Competitive Electricity, which is pushing for legislation.

"All the players are now on the field," Allen said. "Everything that happens this year is very important to the ultimate outcome because now everybody can settle into a position and the issue will get riper."

But the problem, according to some Republicans, is that the Clinton plan would cost consumers money.

"The administration's proposal is basically a new tax, a new tax of about $3 billion a year," said Sen. Frank H. Murkowski, R-Alaska, chairman of the Senate Energy and Natural Resources Committee.

Murkowski, whose committee oversees deregulation, said the administration did not provide a good starting point.

"The administration has come down, not with what I'd hoped, and that is legislative language, but what they refer to as a report," said Murkowski, who plans to start holding hearings on electric deregulation within a month. He also questioned the proposal's treatment of a tax dispute between public and private power. Equally disturbing, he said, was an absence of any reference to nuclear power and a more complete explanation of how renewable energy sources could be made competitive.

"Whether you like it or not, it [nuclear power] contributes about 22 percent of our total energy, and it's not mentioned in here, there's no reference to it in relationship to its significant contribution," he said.

Murkowski also was troubled by the administration's call that 5.5 percent of nation's power be supplied by renewable sources such as wind.

"What we've got before us is kind of a dilemma because the technology to achieve 51/2 percent isn't there. The question is, are consumers going to be willing to pay the cost? I'd say no, and then you'd have to consider a subsidy," Murkowski said.

Majority Leader Trent Lott, R-Miss., has not changed his view that tackling such a complex, politically volatile issue this late in a session already jammed with heavy legislation is not realistic, according to a spokeswoman.

According to the White House plan, competition among electric utilities would save the average family of four $232 annually and reduce emissions of greenhouse gases linked to global warming.

States, however, would be free to pursue their own deregulation plans. Sixteen states have deregulated electric rates or begun the process.

Consumers would pay $3 billion annually into a new federal fund for low-income energy assistance, energy efficiency and conservation. The proposal also calls for at least 5.5 percent of the nation's electricity to be generated from renewable sources by 2010.

At the center of the administration's plan is the advent of open competition nationwide among electricity suppliers by 2003. The proposal also contains a circuit breaker, allowing states to "opt out" if there is evidence competition would not yield positive results for consumers.

Vice President Al Gore said the administration's aim was that competition would spur broad benefits to consumers, environmental benefits and other advantages all at little risk.

"Competition already is beginning to reshape the way we generate and deliver electricity in America," he said. "It will spur innovation, create new incentives for energy efficiency and nearly triple our use of renewable energy."

For deregulation to become a reality, however, Congress will have to untangle competing bills and motives.

About a dozen bills have been introduced to restructure the electric power industry, either comprehensively or incrementally. But many utilities strongly oppose comprehensive bills such as the one proposed by Schaefer and soon to be by the administration, that require nationwide electric deregulation by a certain date.

Electricity Deregulation Dead for '98

JULY 25 — After months of private talks, House Commerce Committee Chairman Thomas J. Bliley Jr., R-Va., has reluctantly put a freeze on electric utility deregulation for 1998.

Once billed by House leaders as a priority of the 105th Congress, the push for a federal mandate to require states to deregulate the price of electricity for consumers nationwide ended in disarray.

Despite some signs of common ground between the Clinton administration and House Republicans (HR 655), Bliley pulled the plug after meeting with key Republicans on July 21. He found little support for a draft amendment that delayed by one year, from 2000 to 2001, the bill's mandate for states to deregulate.

Opposition came from Westerners fearful of losing cheap hydropower to other regions. Representatives of states where power is expensive warned that the influx of untested new suppliers could disrupt power and other services provided by local utilities. *(1997 Almanac, p. 3-7)*

A lobbyist familiar with the discussions said Republicans could muster only five firm votes in support of the bill, well short of the 15 needed to move it out of subcommittee.

Bliley summarized the failure to reach consensus in a letter July 22 to Energy and Power Subcommittee Chairman Dan Schaefer, R-Colo. Instead of focusing on division in the Republican camp, Bliley blamed Democrats.

"Unfortunately, a number of factors, including the calendar and a lack of support from the minority, have combined to make it highly unlikely your subcommittee will be able to hold a markup this year. Thus, I concur with your decision not to take that step this year," Bliley wrote to Schaefer.

Political Cost

Republicans privately fumed that Democrats were stalling negotiations in hopes of running in the November elections against a "do-nothing Congress." Democrats replied that Republicans failed to compromise among themselves and waited too long to attract Democrats.

Bliley's draft amendment did not fully resolve differences with potential allies in the Clinton administration and in the Senate. Energy and Natural Resources Committee Chairman Frank H. Murkowski, R-Alaska, continued to block efforts to move a deregulation bill (S 1401) in the Senate.

Utilities are divided over whether a federal mandate is needed. And even among supporters of a federal deadline for state action, there is disagreement on key issues such as the timing for the deadline and whether to allow states to craft their own reforms.

The Clinton administration stood behind its bill (S 2287) to create a flexible mandate in 2003, allowing states to opt out and use a different approach to energy deregulation.

"About eight of the top 10 issues have been resolved," said former Sen. J. Bennett Johnston, D-La., (1973-1997), a lobbyist for the Alliance for Competitive Electricity, which supports deregulation. The group represents 11 utilities, including New Jersey-based GPU Inc., owner of the Three Mile Island nuclear plant in Pennsylvania, the site of the worst nuclear accident in U.S. history, in 1979.

Johnston, a former chairman of the Energy and Natural Resources Committee, said Bliley made progress in resolving important issues. But he said the bill failed to assure utilities they could recover old debts and needed a broader "grandfather" provision to preserve state reforms.

"It never really got to arm-twisting level this year," said Tim Brown, spokesman for the Electric Power Supply Association, which represents 65 independent power producers and marketers supporting deregulation. "They will start from a good base in 1999."

Private utilities held out lingering hope for a bill (S 621) to repeal the Public Utilities Holding Company Act of 1935, which restricts 16 big utility companies from diversifying into new businesses. But Sen. Dale Bumpers, D-Ark., vowed to block narrow legislation, while promoting a deregulation bill (S 1401) that he cosponsored with Sen. Slade Gorton, R-Wash., to deregulate the price of electricity in 2002. ◆

Industry & Regulation

Product Liability Overhaul Dies in Senate; Sponsors Settle For Biomedical Bill

Box Score

- **Bill:** HR 872 — PL 105-230
- **House action:** The House passed HR 872 (H Rept 105-549) by voice vote July 30.
- **Senate action:** The Senate cleared HR 872 by voice vote July 30. The Senate on July 9 failed, 51-47, to invoke cloture on S 648.
- **Presidential action:** Clinton signed HR 872 on Aug. 13.

Supporters of legislation to overhaul the nation's laws governing faulty products got half a loaf from the 105th Congress. Although proponents of a broad overhaul (S 648) crafted a compromise deal with the White House, they could not shepherd it through the Senate. As a consolation prize, President Clinton signed into law a smaller bill (HR 872) that makes it more difficult to sue suppliers who provide raw materials for medical devices.

SUMMARY

Biomedical companies complained that they had trouble getting raw materials from suppliers wary of liability concerns, and the biomaterials legislation enjoyed the active or tacit support of many who opposed broader product liability overhaul.

The fight to ease product liability law is one of the longest-running shows on Capitol Hill, dating back to the 1980s. Clinton vetoed a GOP product liability bill in 1996, although he promised to support "common sense" product liability legislation.

The Senate Commerce, Science and Transportation Committee approved a version of S 648 (S Rept 105-32) on a party-line vote in May 1997, but that was seen as merely a starting point for negotiations with the White House. Conducted by Sens. John D. Rockefeller IV, D-W.Va., and Slade Gorton, R-Wash., those talks produced a less ambitious proposal that called for a $250,000 cap on punitive damages against small businesses, defined as those with fewer than 25 employees and less than $5 million in annual revenues. The 1996 bill would have covered big businesses as well.

Plaintiffs could only receive punitive damages if they showed "clear and convincing evidence" that a defendant acted with a "conscious, flagrant indifference" to the rights or safety of others. The deal also sought to place an 18-year limit on the filing of lawsuits relating to harm caused by goods used in the workplace.

Rockefeller warned fellow Democrats that any changes could unravel the package and prompt a veto, but they insisted on their right to try to amend the bill, specifically to exempt gun manufacturers from the proposed protections.

A motion to invoke cloture on S 648 failed in July, with longtime product liability legislation skeptics William V. Roth Jr., R-Del., and Richard C. Shelby, R-Ala., joining a unanimous Democratic Caucus to oppose shutting off debate.

With the broad bill dead for another year, Gorton and Rockefeller acquiesced in moving the biomaterials portion separately. "Product liability isn't going to happen," Rockefeller said. "I wanted both, but I'll go for one."

Under the biomaterials bill, civil action against a supplier must be dismissed if the material met the manufacturer's specifications and if the supplier did not make or market the final product. It also requires plaintiffs to submit an affidavit stating that the alleged harm was caused by the raw material used in the device. Passage of HR 872 came quickly. The House passed it late one evening in July; the Senate cleared it several hours later.

Medical Device Liability Measure Heads to House

JUNE 27 — Legislation to provide suppliers of raw materials for medical devices with some protection from legal liability cleared its last committee hurdle June 24 before heading to the House floor.

The House Commerce Committee approved the bill (HR 872 — H Rept 105-549, Part 2) by voice vote. Under the legislation, a supplier of raw materials could be dismissed from a lawsuit claiming harm caused by a medical device if it is shown that the supplier did not manufacture or sell the product and provided the materials as specified by the manufacturer.

Supporters say suppliers are becoming less willing to provide raw materials for medical devices because of the costs of fighting lawsuits for injury claims.

Democrats who back the bill have repeatedly warned that they will withdraw their support if it is attached to a broader product liability bill that would overhaul laws governing faulty products.

The House Judiciary Committee had give its voice vote approval to the bill April 1(H Rept 105-549, Part 1). In the Senate, supporters of limiting punitive damage awards against the makers of faulty products have included similar language in a compromise crafted last year by Sen. John D. Rockefeller IV, D-W.Va., and a high-level team of Clinton administration officials.

The compromise arose after Rockefeller expressed concerns about a broad product liability overhaul (S 648 — S Rept 105-32) that the Senate Commerce Committee approved last May. *(1997 Almanac, p. 3-12)*

Senate Vote Idles GOP Hopes For Liability Bill

JULY 11 — The fight to reduce manufacturers' legal liability for defective and dangerous products — a Republican priority since the Reagan administration and one of the longest running shows on Capitol Hill — has been extended for at least another year.

The Senate on July 9 turned back a cloture motion on a substitute amendment to the product liability bill (S 648 — S Rept 105-32). The 51-47 vote was well short of the 60 required to invoke cloture. *(Vote 188, p. S-30)*

"There is no next step," declared sponsor Slade Gorton, R-Wash. "It's not going to come up again" this year.

Two longtime Republican opponents of product liability legislation, William V. Roth Jr. of Delaware and Richard C. Shelby of Alabama, joined a unanimous Democratic Caucus in opposition to shutting off debate.

Democrats had framed the vote as a question of whether they would be allowed to amend the bill. A cloture motion to make S 648 the pending business on the floor had passed easily, 71-24, on July 7, but the Senate had quickly moved on to other legislation, effectively staving off Democratic amendments. *(Vote 184, p. S-30)*

"The right to offer amendments, to be heard, is sacrosanct when dealing with the U.S. Senate," said Democrat Christopher J. Dodd of Connecticut.

But Majority Leader Trent Lott, R-Miss., dismissed the Democratic complaint as a "smoke screen." Democrats have sought to offer unrelated amendments on tobacco and managed care to myriad bills on the floor, and Lott and Gorton were concerned S 648 would prove no exception.

"They were totally playing games with this," Lott said immediately after the July 9 vote. "It shows you how totally hypocritical and insincere Democrats have been on product liability since the beginning."

John McCain, R-Ariz., and Joseph I. Lieberman, D-Conn., who sponsored S 648's provisions that would have offered legal cover to suppliers of raw materials from which medical devices such as shunts, catheters and syringes are made, were hopeful that they could move a separate biomaterials bill (S 364).

The House Judiciary Committee approved biomaterials legislation (HR 872) in April. Such a measure has the active or tacit support of many opponents of broader product liability overhaul.

Lott's Maneuver

But the issue may have been made more complicated by Lott's last-minute, handwritten insertion of language into the S 648 substitute amendment that would have extended protections for suppliers of components of types of medical devices made by Baxter Healthcare Corp. and others.

Baxter has a plant in Cleveland, Miss., that employs about 1,000 people in making intravenous blood bags and other devices used in hospitals. Company officials have told Lott they had trouble getting raw materials from suppliers wary of liability concerns.

The family of a woman brain-damaged because of a Baxter-made tube received an $18 million verdict in February. The company would have been shielded against such damage awards as a result of Lott's language.

Lott insisted that the White House had signed off on his language and said that he would consider bringing up stand-alone biomaterials legislation only if Democrats would pass it by unanimous consent.

The product liability substitute would have capped punitive damages at $250,000 in cases against businesses with fewer than 25 employees and annual revenues less than $5 million.

S 648 would have specifically exempted tobacco companies and makers of silicone breast implants from its legal protections. Dow Corning Corp. on July 8 reached a tentative $3.2 billion settlement involving tens of thousands of women who claimed they were injured by silicone implants made by the company.

Democrats also wanted to exempt gun manufacturers from the bill's protections, estimating that 17 percent of the guns sold in the U.S. are made by small shops that would have been covered by S 648.

Cities such as Chicago and Philadelphia, and individuals such as parents of children slain with guns, are considering or pursuing lawsuits against gun manufacturers. They argue the companies should pay if they marketed their products in such a way that could create "foreseeable harm."

Although the jury is still out on the question of whether gun manufacturers should be held liable, Democrats refused to let debate be cut off without consideration of their gun amendment.

A scaled-back version of the amendment could still have been offered had cloture been invoked.

Congress OKs Bill To Protect Suppliers Of Biomaterials

AUGUST 1 — After years of delay, Congress gave quick assent to a bill providing legal protections to suppliers of raw materials used in medical devices.

The House passed the bill (HR 872) by voice vote July 30. The Senate cleared the measure by voice vote several hours later.

The bill requires dismissal of any civil case against a supplier if the material met the manufacturer's specifications and if the supplier did not make or market the final product.

It also orders the plaintiff to submit an affidavit stating that the alleged harm was caused by the raw material used in the device. Currently, both the manufacturer and supplier are sued in typical biomaterials product liability suits to avoid the need to determine which is responsible for the injuries. HR 872 would not shield companies that are intentionally negligent.

Biomedical companies had told lawmakers that they had trouble getting raw materials from suppliers wary of liability concerns. But supporters of broader product liability protection (S 648) for manufacturers had objected to a narrower biomedical bill.

Senate Majority Leader Trent Lott, R-Miss., whose attempt to amend S 648 to also protect suppliers of components of medical devices was controversial, said in an interview that HR 872 "doesn't satisfy me totally." But he added that the narrow measure had enough merit to warrant passage.

With the product liability overhaul (S 648) killed for the year by a Senate procedural vote July 9, its sponsors dropped their objections to the biomedical bill.

"Product liability isn't going to happen," said John D. Rockefeller IV, D-W.Va. "I wanted both, but I'll go for one." ◆

Industry & Regulation

Regulatory Overhaul Effort Generates Little Enthusiasm; Bill Stalls in Senate

Congress did not act on legislation to overhaul the federal regulatory process, despite efforts by Sens. Fred Thompson, R-Tenn., and Carl Levin, D-Mich., to develop and promote a bill they considered a middle-of-the-road alternative to more sweeping measures that had stalled in previous years.

SUMMARY

When Thompson, chairman of the Governmental Affairs Committee, and Levin introduced their bill (S 981) in February, the lack of support from either party's leadership was obvious. Their bill would have required government agencies to conduct in-depth analyses of the costs and benefits of proposed federal rules, but it would not have changed existing requirements in environmental laws that often result in costly regulations.

The bill's prospects became even dimmer the following month when Senate Majority Leader Trent Lott, R-Miss., introduced his own rival bill (S 1728). The more narrowly tailored Lott measure was referred to Thompson's committee, which did not take it up.

Though the Thompson-Levin bill was reported out of committee, its limited scope generated little enthusiasm among party conservatives, and the GOP leadership opted against bringing it to the floor. Most observers believed Lott had concluded that the bill's marginal benefits to the party's business constituency did not outweigh its substantial political costs, namely, environmental and labor groups' charges that it would undermine health and safety protections.

Reducing the burden of federal regulations has always been high on the agenda of congressional Republicans and their allies in the business community. In the 104th Congress, Senate Majority Leader Bob Dole, R-Kan., looking to solidify his base among conservative Republicans in anticipation of his 1996 presidential bid, pushed a far-reaching regulatory overhaul bill. It failed in a business-vs.-environmentalists showdown that led to bitter partisan recriminations over who was to blame.

Thompson and Levin introduced their more modest bill in hopes of avoiding a replay. Their measure would have required agencies to analyze the costs as well as the benefits of proposed regulations but would not allow cost considerations to trump health and safety. It would have required agencies to explain why they chose a rule if it were not the most cost-effective alternative.

House Republicans, many of whom favored a more sweeping overhaul, declined to act, acknowledging that with scant hope of comprehensive legislation passing the Senate, there was little reason to push a bill of their own.

Hill Would Get New Review Role Under House Plan

FEBRUARY 28 — Overhauling the federal rule-making process has long been a priority for Republicans. But sponsors of House and Senate bills are struggling to find the right political balance, and getting mixed results.

In the House, the Judiciary Subcommittee on Commercial and Administrative Law on Feb. 25 pushed through a bill (HR 1704) that would create a congressional office to analyze federal regulations. Approved 5-3 along party lines, the bill is intended to provide Congress with new oversight powers.

Under the bill, a new Congressional Office of Regulatory Analysis would study the costs and benefits of major regulations issued by agencies and submit annual reports on the total cost of such rules to the nation's economy.

Sue W. Kelly, R-N.Y., the sponsor of the bill, said the office would be a tool to rein in burdensome regulations and highlight the inefficiencies of the federal rule-making process.

Jerrold Nadler of New York, the ranking Democrat on the subcommittee, countered that the cost-benefit studies could be used by Republicans as ammunition to block rules that protect the environment and public health. "I'm not sure what this adds, other than another layer of bureaucracy," he said.

But by any measure, the House bill is a far cry from more sweeping legislation offered in the 104th Congress, and it represents the House GOP's more incremental approach.

Meanwhile, a more far-reaching regulatory overhaul bill in the Senate (S 981), by Republican Fred Thompson of Tennessee, chairman of the Governmental Affairs Committee, and Carl Levin of Michigan, a senior committee Democrat, continues to sputter.

The Thompson-Levin bill, the subject of a Feb. 24 hearing, would require that rules costing businesses more than $100 million annually be accompanied by an analysis of costs and benefits.

Levin said the bill is picking up momentum. Levin and Thompson announced Feb. 4 that they had made changes to the bill to answer environmental groups' objections that the original measure would have undermined health and safety regulations. Despite the changes, the bill continues to draw criticism from senators and interest groups on both ends of the political spectrum.

Senate Majority Leader Trent Lott, R-Miss., said in an interview that although he would eventually like to support the effort, the bill does not go far enough to overhaul the rule-making process, a view also expressed by Assistant Majority Leader Don Nickles, R-Okla.

Pushing in the other direction, a

long list of environmental and consumer groups attacked the Senate bill as a thinly veiled attempt to roll back health, safety and environmental laws.

Nancy Donley, president of Safe Tables Our Priority, a food safety group, testified in gripping detail about the death of her 6-year-old son, Alex, from food poisoning, saying the Thompson-Levin bill would further weaken food safety laws.

"This bill conducts a policy experiment on the public's health and safety," said Donley. "Our family and our entire community were sickened and destroyed by Alex's death, and these numbers aren't accounted for in a risk assessment or cost benefit analysis."

Outside Support

Thompson and Levin insist that their bill is more modest than past measures pushed by Senate Republicans.

It has been endorsed by the National Governors' Association and leading business groups, such as the National Federation of Independent Business.

But while the bill may be gaining momentum, its sponsors are finding it difficult to assemble a broad enough coalition to win passage in the Senate.

Lott said parts of the bill are simply too weak. He objected to a provision that would allow agencies to sidestep the cost-benefit analysis when impractical or contrary to the public interest. "That's ridiculous," he said. "Take that waiver out and you've got something."

Joseph I. Lieberman, D-Conn., who often casts swing votes on environmental issues, said he objects to the bill because it would undermine environmental laws. He said a better approach would be to include cost-benefit analyses in individual environmental laws rather than in a broad law covering all federal agencies.

"I'm worried that it sets up a series of hurdles that may have unintended consequences," said Lieberman.

Kelly said the intent of her more narrow House bill is to bolster Congress' authority to block regulations. So far, not a single rule has been challenged under the law. And Kelly said that the new office, modeled after the Congressional Budget Office, would help arm Congress with the information it needs to conduct in-depth studies of regulations.

As it stands now, the General Accounting Office routinely issues a report to Congress on whether an agency has complied with legal requirements, but it stops well short of conducting any independent studies of the rule.

But Nadler and other Democrats questioned whether the office would be effective. A recent Congressional Budget Office analysis found that the proposed regulatory office would need a staff of 135 and a budget of more than $35 million to keep up with the expected workload. Kelly's bill includes an authorization of about $5 million and envisions a staff of about 30 people.

Kelly countered, "We're shrinking rules and regulations by using this."

Rival Senate Bills Cloud the Scene

MARCH 14 — Just as his long-sought goal of advancing regulatory overhaul legislation seemed one step closer to reality, Sen. Fred Thompson, R-Tenn., received an unpleasant surprise, courtesy of Majority Leader Trent Lott, R-Miss.

Four days before Thompson's bill (S 981) was to be marked up by the Governmental Affairs Committee, Lott introduced his own bill, contending Thompson's did not go far enough to rein in burdensome government regulations.

Thompson's Governmental Affairs Committee approved S 981 on March 10, 8-4. But Lott's introduction of a rival measure (S 1728) clouded its fate considerably and further poisoned the already tense relationship between Thompson and Lott as the bill heads to the floor.

The Thompson bill, cosponsored by Carl Levin, D-Mich., would require that government agencies proposing regulations that would cost businesses more than $100 million conduct analyses of their costs and benefits.

After more far-reaching measures pushed by Senate Republicans set off a firestorm of opposition among many Democrats and environmental groups in the 104th Congress, Thompson and Levin were hoping their compromise bill would garner bipartisan support.

But it was the bill's moderation that drew Lott's opposition. His measure would place stronger limits on federal bureaucrats as they propose new regulations.

Overhauling the federal regulatory process has been a priority for Senate Republicans and their business allies ever since the GOP took control of Congress in 1995. And Lott may be calculating that it would best to hold off until Republicans command a stronger majority and can pass a bill without watering it down to get Democratic support.

At the same time, Lott held out the possibility that his own bill, which focuses on the arcane area of "risk assessment," could move either in place of the Thompson measure or as a floor amendment to it.

Lott noted that many of the provisions in his bill were included in the original version of S 981, which was modified in February to address concerns of environmentalists and win Democratic support.

'Nothing Nefarious'

Lott insisted that there is nothing "nefarious" about his bill or its timing. "I've been working on it for a long time," he said in an interview. "There is nothing sinister about it."

But the bill introduction caught Thompson off guard and raised question about whether Lott is trying to undercut him. It also raised questions of political payback: Thompson and Lott have had a rocky relationship ever since Thompson bucked the majority leader by insisting on a broad probe of 1996 campaign violations by both parties.

"I was surprised to learn that this other bill was being introduced," said Thompson, who has been laboring for months to secure Lott's support for his bill.

John Glenn of Ohio, the ranking Democrat on the Governmental Affairs panel and a supporter of S 981, said Lott further complicated already difficult negotiations on S 981.

"I didn't know there was going to be a separate bill," said Glenn. "I thought we were all working together on this. It doesn't help any."

Rocky Road

Even if Lott were to throw his support behind S 981, the outlook appears shaky at best. Granted, the bill is supported by an impressive coali-

Industry & Regulation

Overhaul Provisions

MARCH 14 — *Following are some main provisions of S 981, the Thompson-Levin regulatory overhaul bill:*

• Cost-benefit test: The bill would require agencies to conduct studies on the costs and benefits of the major rules they propose. Each analysis would explain how the benefits of the rule would be achieved, describe who might benefit from the standard and lay out compliance costs from the rulemaking and who would have to pay them. A major rule is defined as one that would cost $100 million or more, or one that the Office of Management and Budget determined would have a significant impact on the economy.

An agency would also have to issue a statement determining whether the rule would be likely to provide benefits that justify the costs and whether it would be more cost effective or have greater benefits than other alternatives considered by the agency. In a situation where the agency determines the rule would not likely provide benefits that justify the costs, the agency would have to explain why it selected the rule, including statutory provisions that required the agency to select the rule. An agency could bypass conducting a cost-benefit test if it found that it would be impractical or "contrary to an important public interest."

• Risk assessment: For major rules addressing health, safety or environmental risks, the bill would mandate an assessment of the risks affected by a rule. A risk assessment could also be conducted for agency decisions that would have a "substantial impact" on public policy or the economy. Each risk assessment would include descriptions of hazards addressed by the rule, the population or natural resources that would be the subject of the assessment and major uncertainties.

• Rule reviews: Agencies would be required to conduct periodic reviews of "economically significant rules" already on the books. One year after enactment, and every five years thereafter, agencies would be required to publish a list of rules it plans to review. In selecting rules, agencies are to pay close attention to rules that could be revised to be "substantially more cost effective" or increase the benefits.

• Peer review: The bill would mandate that cost-benefit examinations and risk assessments be reviewed by an independent panel of experts.

• Judicial review: The cost-benefit and risk assessments could be subject to court challenge only as part of a broader lawsuit against a final rule.

tion of business groups, from corporate giants such as General Motors Corp. to the National Federation of Independent Business (NFIB), the small-business lobby.

Thompson and Levin argue that their bill would apply greater common sense to the ways in which federal bureaucrats write regulations by requiring that they analyze the costs and benefits of the rules they are proposing.

They say the bill would simply put into law a longstanding practice endorsed by the Clinton administration in a 1993 executive order that requires agencies to conduct cost-benefit studies. S 981 would establish greater confidence in federal bureaucrats, they say.

Moreover, many Republicans as well as some Democrats who favor remaking the rule-making process are sure to provide plenty of support for the bill if it is considered on the floor.

Joseph I. Lieberman of Connecticut, who was one of the four Democrats who voted against the bill in committee, predicted that there is enough support in the Senate to pass the bill and overcome an expected Democratic-led filibuster. "I think we're fighting uphill," said Lieberman.

But to get the bill through the Senate, Republicans would face plenty of opposition.

In a March 6 letter, Office of Management and Budget Director Franklin D. Raines said the administration opposes the bill on the grounds that it might tie up the regulatory process by encouraging excessive legal challenges to rule-making.

Also in a March 6 letter to Thompson, Environment and Public Works Chairman John H. Chafee, R-R.I., and Max Baucus of Montana, the ranking Democrat on the committee, expressed strong concerns about the bill.

Chafee and Baucus said the best way to revamp the rule-making process would be through revising individual laws rather than applying a broad brush with an omnibus law.

Chafee and Baucus noted that they worked together on enactment of a Safe Drinking Water Law (PL 104-182) in 1996 that included a provision that required the Environmental Protection Agency to publish an analysis of the costs and benefits of many of the regulations it proposed. *(1996 Almanac, p. 4-4)*

"We generally believe such reforms are best accomplished within the framework of a specific regulatory statute, rather than in an-across-the board omnibus bill," Chafee and Baucus wrote.

Environmental groups have already spent months criticizing the bill as a thinly veiled attempt to roll back health, safety and environmental laws. They argue that the bill would give regulated industries more clout with federal regulators.

Picking up on that theme, Robert G. Torricelli, D-N.J., said at the markup that the bill would open the door to lawsuits from regulated industries, further slowing the rule-making process.

Torricelli and other Democratic opponents appear poised to hit the bill hard on the floor as a rollback of environment and other laws popular with much of the public.

Conservatives Not Enthused

While the bill is attracting much Republican support, it is apparent that Lott and other conservative Republicans are lukewarm at best.

Sam Brownback, R-Kan., voted for the bill in committee. But he said he still has reservations about it and favors the more far-reaching approach in legislation sponsored in 1995 by Bob Dole, R-Kan., the Senate majority leader at the time. (*1995 Almanac, p. 3-3*)

Brownback wants the courts to have greater power to review rule-making to give the bill some teeth. "I don't know if the bill's got support to make it on through without strengthening judicial review," Brownback said.

At the markup, the committee approved a series of minor amendments sponsored by Don Nickles, R-Okla., the assistant majority leader, aimed at tightening key provisions.

For example, one amendment, approved by voice vote, would require an explanation from agencies when they decide not to adopt a regulation that might have been a cost-effective alternative.

Nickles, who like Lott has been cool to the bill, said it is headed in the right direction and was improved at the markup, but he stopped short of a ringing endorsement.

"I think it's worth passing, but we'd maintain the right to strengthen it on the floor," he said.

Lott's bill is not a dramatic departure from S 981, but it would go further. Like S 981, it would require agencies to study the risks posed by such hazards as air pollution that rules are intended to address. "A lot of what was in my bill was in the original S 981," said Lott.

But the risk assessments would be more narrowly tailored than those in S 981 and would not take into account factors, such as human suffering, that are difficult to quantify, according to Gary D. Bass, executive director of OMB Watch, a public interest group opposed to S 981.

It would also appear to supersede provisions in existing statutes. "From a public interest standpoint it is worse than S 981 in several areas," said Bass.

Political Calculus

Lott is likely to continue to push for changes. But if he pushes too far, he risks alienating Democratic supporters of the bill, such as Levin and Glenn.

One leadership aide noted that the Republicans fought hard and lost a filibuster fight in 1995 to get the sweeping Dole bill through the floor. Passing the Thompson-Levin bill, the aide suggested, would represent a philosophical retreat from that position.

Lott must decide whether he wants to set aside floor time for a bill such as Thompson's that entails risks for politically vulnerable Republicans but does not go as far as he wants to address business groups' concerns about federal regulations.

Democrats in tough election races, such as Patty Murray, D-Wash., are sure to engage in lengthy floor speeches lambasting the bill for selling out to big business at the expense of environmental laws.

"This will take a lot of floor time," said Susan Eckerly, chief Senate lobbyist for the NFIB. "And it may mean some very tough votes for senators up for re-election. It's not a slam dunk." ◆

Property Rights Proponents Concede Defeat This Year But Say Victory Is in Sight

SUMMARY

After measures to establish broad new rights for property owners stalled in the 104th Congress, House Republicans promoted and passed a narrower measure (HR 1534). But the bill ran into opposition in the Senate, where a coalition of environmentalists, governors, and local and state elected officials said it would undermine the power of local zoning boards. The bill was also opposed by the Clinton administration, which threatened a veto.

Proponents of the legislation complained that local zoning panels unjustly delay building projects. Conservative activists and many developers contended that the boards often make decisions that amount to an uncompensated "taking" of property in violation of the Fifth Amendment. Currently, owners must exhaust their administrative and state appeals before going into federal court. Senate Judiciary Committee Chairman Orrin G. Hatch, R-Utah, sponsor of the Senate measure, argued that appeals can take up to a decade.

The legislation, which had the backing of the 190,000-member National Association of Home Builders, would have allowed builders to seek an expedited hearing in federal court, bypassing the time-consuming state court appeals process. The builders' association worked closely with the House Republican leadership in crafting the bill and mounted a major lobbying blitz in favor of it. The House easily passed the measure in October 1997.

The Senate Judiciary Committee approved its version of HR 1534 (S Rept 105-242) on Feb. 26, but Democrats vowed to filibuster the measure on the Senate floor. In July, the Republican leadership sought to bring a slightly modified version of the bill (S 2271) to the floor but lost a procedural vote to cut off debate.

Box Score

- **Bills:** HR 1534; S 2271
- **House action:** The House passed HR 1534 (H Rept 105-323) on Oct. 22, 1997, by a vote of 248-178.
- **Senate action:** The Senate failed to invoke cloture on S 2271 on July 13 by a vote of 52-42.

Stiff Opposition Greets Measure On Zoning Rights

FEBRUARY 28 — Senate proponents of legislation to provide property owners new legal rights to deal with local zoning and planning boards are running into a wall of opposition, and

Industry & Regulation

they concede that major revisions are needed to fend off a likely Democratic-led filibuster.

The bill (HR 1534) took a small step forward Feb. 26 when the Senate Judiciary Committee approved it, 10-8, on a straight party-line vote. But that slender margin of victory belied strong opposition from both sides of the aisle.

Among the opposition are administration officials who are threatening a veto, and Patrick J. Leahy of Vermont, the ranking Democrat on Judiciary, who has vowed to lead a filibuster against it. Some Republican senators who voted for HR 1534 in committee said their support is conditional on major revisions.

"I'm not at all sure it does what the proponents of this bill say that it does," said Fred Thompson, R-Tenn. Added Mike DeWine, R-Ohio, "I have serious reservations about this bill. This bill in its current form is not the solution."

Vice President Al Gore said in a statement: "This bill would radically change the American tradition of working out land disputes at the local level."

Faced with a chorus of criticism, Judiciary Chairman Orrin G. Hatch, R-Utah, said the bill needs major changes before it can be considered on the floor.

Proponents of HR 1534 complain that zoning boards unjustly delay building projects. HR 1534 would seek to correct this problem by allowing builders to seek a speedy hearing in federal court, bypassing a time-consuming state court appeals process that federal courts insist upon.

The bill is a priority of the 190,000-member National Association of Home Builders, which mounted a lobbying and grass-roots campaign to get it passed.

But the bill is facing a coalition of opposition from local officials, governors and environmental groups. They say HR 1534 would trample on local zoning and planning boards and give developers a legal tool with which to bludgeon localities into submission.

Losing Momentum

HR 1534 sailed through the House in the fall after the home builders' aggressive lobbying. The home builders sold the bill as a narrow procedural change, which convinced many members who had heard from constituents who could not get proposals acted on by local boards.

Under current law, developers must first exhaust appeals to a planning agency's decisions and be denied compensation before a federal court will hear a claim under the Fifth Amendment, which bars government from "taking" property without just compensation.

That process can go on for years, leaving homeowners and developers in limbo. As a remedy, HR 1534 would allow owners to take their cases directly to a federal court after filing at least two appeals to a planning board decision.

Hatch argued that the bill would give property owners a new avenue by which to get their claims heard in court.

But Leahy said the bill would upset a delicate balance between developers and average citizens. "We know this would just trample on the people of the state of Vermont," he said. "It's going to have to be changed considerably before it is considered on the floor."

House Passes Bill To Ease Property 'Takings' Claims

MARCH 14 — Property rights proponents applauded House passage March 12 of a bill (HR 992) that would provide land owners who challenge federal regulations with easier access to federal courts. But presidential opposition means the victory may be short lived.

The House passed the measure 230-180. But the comfortable margin belied strong opposition from a coalition of Democrats and some Republicans, and it would not be enough to override a threatened veto by President Clinton. *(Vote 52, p. H-16)*

While proponents of the bill say it would bring needed relief to property owners caught in legal limbo, opponents say the bill would give wealthy landowners and businesses new avenues with which to challenge environmental laws.

At issue is an 1887 statute known as the Tucker Act. Under the takings clause of the Fifth Amendment, the government cannot take a person's property without just compensation, such as fair market value. The Tucker Act provides jurisdiction over Fifth Amendment takings claims to the Court of Federal Claims in Washington, D.C. But any other challenges to agency action or regulation are filed in federal court.

That leaves a plaintiff "shuffling" between the Court of Claims to hear Fifth Amendment cases and a federal district court for other challenges to agency actions, such as a decision by the Corps of Engineers to deny a permit to build in an environmentally sensitive wetland.

Proponents of the bill, including sponsor Lamar Smith, R-Texas, said it is designed to correct the situation by allowing the Court of Claims to hear both takings claims as well as challenges to agency decisions.

"HR 992 seeks to provide a solution to an unfair judicial maze that often prevents private property owners from having their day in court," said Smith.

But opponents said the legislation is unnecessary and that its real intent is to allow property owners to shop around for a court likely to rule in their favor.

The House did adopt by voice vote a Smith amendment that narrowed the bill so that jurisdiction for certain claims under environmental laws, including some provisions of the Clean Water Act, would remain unchanged.

But it defeated, 206-206, an amendment by Melvin Watt, D-N.C., that would have allowed plaintiffs to hear takings and other claims in a federal district court, rather than the Court of Claims. Watt contended that the Court of Claims is stacked with Republican appointees hostile to environmental regulation. A no vote by House Speaker Newt Gingrich, R-Ga., killed the amendment. *(Vote 51, p. H-16)*

Opponents Block Senate Debate On Property Bill

JULY 18 — The Senate handed a big defeat to proponents of legislation that would provide new legal rights to property owners and big developers in disputes with local governments.

The key vote came July 13 on a procedural motion on whether to officially start debate on the bill. The 52-42 tally to invoke cloture, or cut off debate, on the motion fell short of the two-thirds required. *(Vote 197, p. S-32)*

With a packed legislative schedule ahead, Republican leaders said they had no plans to bring the bill (S 2271) back to the floor this year.

But proponents of the measure contended that their cause had reached a high-water mark in Congress, and vowed to return next year and push for enactment of the legislation.

"We moved the ball down the field further than it's ever been moved before," said Jerry Howard, senior staff vice president for the 190,000-member National Association of Homebuilders, which lobbied vigorously for the bill. "NAHB will not stop pushing this issue until the American people's rights are protected."

Proponents of the legislation, including Senate Majority Leader Trent Lott, R-Miss., and Judiciary Chairman Orrin G. Hatch, R-Utah, contend that federal courts often stomp on the legal rights of property owners.

They say that developers and small landowners alike cannot get adequate legal redress when local planning boards unjustly delay projects. The measure would seek to correct this problem by allowing builders to seek a speedy hearing in federal court, bypassing a time-consuming state appeals process on which federal courts insist.

"Many citizens who attempt to protect their property rights guaranteed by the Fifth Amendment of the Constitution are barred from the doors of the federal courthouse," said Hatch.

But the opponents, including most Democrats and many governors and mayors, countered that the bill would provide rich developers the legal club they need to pressure planning boards to approve their projects.

"This bill would federalize local zoning decisions," said Sen. Patrick J. Leahy of Vermont, the ranking Democrat on the Judiciary Committee. "Its unabashed purpose is to give wealthy developers increased power to short-circuit communities' decisions, those decisions made through the public processes of local government."

The bill was also strongly opposed by the Clinton administration, which threatened a veto, contending it would shift too much power away from local governments.

But even in defeat, the vote represented a step forward for the homebuilders and other proponents of property rights legislation. During the 104th Congress, Lott did not bring up property rights legislation for a vote on the floor, citing scheduling problems.

But this Congress, the homebuilders made the bill a top legislative priority and mounted a high-profile lobbying blitz to get a floor vote.

"We would do everything within the bounds of legality, ethics and morality to get this done," said Howard. ◆

Major League Baseball Loses Coveted Exemption From Antitrust Laws

Box Score

- **Bill:** S 53 — PL 105-297
- **Senate action:** The Senate passed S 53 by voice vote on July 30.
- **House action:** The House cleared the bill by voice vote on Oct. 7.
- **Presidential action:** Clinton signed S 53 on Oct. 27.

After a lengthy effort, Congress cleared legislation partially lifting Major League Baseball's 76-year antitrust exemption. President Clinton signed the bill into law Oct. 27 (S 53 — PL 105-297). The measure superseded a 1922 Supreme Court ruling that baseball was a sport rather than a business.

Because of that exemption, big-league ballplayers had not had some of the rights and protections enjoyed by other professional athletes. In labor disputes, players were unable to challenge owners' actions under antitrust laws. The lack of legal recourse contributed to the strike that ultimately led to the cancellation of the 1994 World Series.

The legislation had been bottled up in the Senate until two key senators, baseball owners and players struck a deal ensuring the bill would not apply to minor league teams. Baseball owners wanted to protect the system under which major-league clubs subsidize and transfer players among their farm teams, which represent a training and player selection system not found in most other professional sports.

The legislative path was essentially cleared July 29 when Senate Judiciary Chairman Orrin G. Hatch, R-Utah, and ranking Democrat Patrick J. Leahy of Vermont announced an agreement with professional baseball owners. The Senate passed the bill (S 53 — S Rept 105-118) by voice vote the next day.

In a statement, baseball commissioner Bud Selig said, "We are hopeful that this legislation will bring to an end the sort of acrimony that led to eight work stoppages over the last three decades."

Said Hatch: "With this agreement, I am confident that Congress will, once and for all, make clear that professional baseball players have the same rights as other professional athletes, and will help assure baseball fans across the United States that our national pastime will not again be interrupted by strikes."

The House cleared the bill Oct. 7 by voice vote. Leahy said it would restore "public confidence in the game after the breach of trust with fans that marked the cancellation of the 1994 World Series." ◆

Chapter 16

INTERNATIONAL AFFAIRS

State Department Authorization 16-3	**Relations With China** 16-23
Conference Report Highlights 16-6	Satellite Scandal 16-24
Religious Persecution 16-9	Top Campaign Donor 16-25
Iran Sanctions 16-16	Sanctions History 16-28
Iran Sanctions History 16-17	Trade Status 16-34
Current U.S. Global Sanctions 16-20	Clinton Trip 16-34
House Targets Nuclear Power 16-23	Human Rights 16-37
	International Monetary Fund 16-38

Anti-Abortion Language Dooms State Department Bill, U.N. Debt Repayment

The fiscal 1998-99 State Department authorization bill was originally advertised as a sign of bipartisanship between the Clinton administration and the Republican-controlled Congress. But it fell apart along the partisan divide on abortion and was vetoed by President Clinton.

SUMMARY

The core of the original bill (S 903), put together in the summer of 1997 by Senate Foreign Relations Committee Chairman Jesse Helms, R-N.C., administration officials, and the panel's ranking Democrat, Joseph R. Biden Jr. of Delaware, was an elaborate trade-off.

Helms agreed to allow payment of almost $1 billion in U.S. debts to the United Nations, while the administration pledged to insist on U.N. reforms and a reduction in the U.S. share of its budget, from 25 to 20 percent. The administration also agreed to Helms' proposal to merge several foreign affairs agencies into the State Department — ultimately the U.S. Information Agency, the Arms Control and Disarmament Agency and parts of the Agency for International Development.

The bill sailed through the Senate Foreign Relations Committee and the full Senate, which substituted its text for HR 1757, a House leadership bill that had won similarly quick approval. The resulting conference stalled, however, because of anti-abortion restrictions on international family planning aid added to the House bill by Christopher H. Smith, R-N.J., and bitterly opposed by Clinton. *(1997 Almanac, p. 8-32)*

House Speaker Newt Gingrich, R-Ga., and Helms revived the bill in March, linking the payment of U.N. debts and money Clinton wanted for the International Monetary Fund to Smith's abortion restrictions. The conference agreement was easily adopted by the House but barely cleared the Senate.

Buying time to change Clinton's mind about a veto, Senate leaders took the unusual step of holding on to the measure for nearly six months before sending it to the president. When they finally did, Clinton promptly vetoed the bill.

In the end, the foreign affairs reorganization and several other key provisions were included in an omnibus spending bill signed by Clinton (HR 4328 — PL 105-277). Only the U.N. funds were left out. Republicans continued to tie them to the anti-abortion restrictions. Democratic aides said that next year they would likely seek to renegotiate an agreement.

Seeking Showdown With Clinton, Gingrich Gets One With GOP Instead

MARCH 14 — House Speaker Newt Gingrich's strategy was simple: Get congressional Republicans to revive a dormant bill that would pay part of the U.S. debt to the United Nations and reorganize the foreign policy bureaucracy. Add abortion-related restrictions on U.S. aid to international family planning to ensure conservative support.

The result would be legislation that would serve as a politically charged ultimatum to President Clinton: Either accept our abortion policy or forget about old debts to the United Nations and, quite possibly, payments for the International Monetary Fund (IMF).

But to the embarrassment of the House leaders, they were tripped up by a faction of GOP conservatives who revile the United Nations.

More than 40 votes short of those necessary for passage, Republican leaders were forced to pull the conference report on the fiscal 1998-99 State Department authorization bill (HR 1757 — S Rept 105-432) from the House schedule March 13 and postpone action until March 18.

The GOP hierarchy plans a furious week of lobbying and arm-twisting, including a speech by Gingrich to the Republican Conference, in hopes of winning support for passage. The leaders' argument to conservatives will center on the bill's importance to the anti-abortion National Right to Life Committee, which is closely tracking how members vote.

"We'll sit down and level with every group" in the conference, said Rep. Gerald B.H. Solomon, R-N.Y., chairman of the House Rules Committee.

Party leaders have their work cut out. Their unenviable task is to convince rank-and-file Republicans to cast a vote fraught with political peril for legislation the White House has indicated Clinton will veto.

Democrats, who were frozen out of the Republican-only conference report, are unified in their opposition. Moderate Republicans, who favor abortion rights, will vote against the legislation based on the abortion provision.

The real test of the leaders' power of persuasion will come with the one group they took for granted: conservative Republicans who question giving a single dollar to the United Nations.

"If we owe them dues, subtract that from what they owe us," said Rep. Roscoe G. Bartlett, R-Md., who recently took his criticism to conserva-

---

Box Score

- **Bill:** HR 1757
- **House action:** The House adopted the conference report (H Rept 105-432) on HR 1757 on March 26, by voice vote. The House passed HR 1757 (H Rept 105-94) by voice vote on June 11, 1997.
- **Senate action:** The Senate cleared the conference report on HR 1757 on April 28 by a vote of 51-49. The Senate passed HR 1757 (S Rept 105-28), 90-5, on June 17, 1997.
- **Presidential action:** Clinton vetoed HR 1757 on Oct. 21.

International Affairs

tive talk radio shows and fired off faxes to conservative Republican groups.

Bartlett said congressional investigators have concluded that the United States spent $6.6 billion on peacekeeping from fiscal 1992 to fiscal 1995, erasing any outstanding debt the United States owes the world organization.

It is an argument that got 165 votes, including 157 Republicans, for a Bartlett amendment in the House last September and swayed several Republicans again in a closed-door meeting of the GOP on March 12.

"I just don't think that we owe them money for always engaging our forces in peacekeeping," said Rep. Helen Chenoweth, R-Idaho. "We pay an inordinate amount into the U.N."

"They have a pretty substantial debt with us," said Rep. J.C. Watts, R-Okla.

Even Rep. Dan Burton, R-Ind., who signed the conference report, had second thoughts about paying the U.N. money.

"There's no question that we're way in the black," he said.

The bill's stumble raises a larger question of why the GOP leadership decided to abandon a bipartisan approach and instead to try to ram a bill through the House despite its narrow majority.

The strategy rarely has worked in a closely divided Congress, but Republican leaders were intent on forcing a showdown with Clinton.

Gingrich Pressure

House and Senate negotiations on the State Department bill stalled last July over a House-passed provision barring U.S. aid to international family planning groups that use their own funds to perform or promote abortions.

In November, House Republican conservatives refused to let the bill move forward — as well as a $3.5 billion authorization for the International Monetary Fund — while the abortion impasse remained.

In the intervening months, the Clinton administration made little or no effort to negotiate with congressional Republicans on the abortion dispute, with the exception of an inconclusive meeting with Rep. Christopher H. Smith, R-N.J., who has spearheaded the House fight for the restrictions on family planning aid.

Last month, Gingrich instructed a reluctant Benjamin A. Gilman, R-N.Y., chairman of the House International Relations Committee, to resuscitate the authorization conference with Republicans only.

GOP senators, including Foreign Relations Committee Chairman Jesse Helms of North Carolina, had their doubts, but they eventually relented.

Several weeks of talks produced a conference report on March 10.

Gingrich averted a last-minute snag when faced with the opposition of conferee and GOP moderate Jim Leach, R-Iowa, who favors more money for the United Nations and opposes restrictions on family planning funds.

"I would like to have as much of the U.N. money as rapidly as possible," Leach said.

Short of the necessary Republican signatures to move the legislation, Gingrich yanked Leach off the conference and replaced him with Burton, who signed the report.

Bill's Provisions

The legislation would abolish the Arms Control and Disarmament Agency, the U.S. Information Agency (USIA) and parts of the Agency for International Development (AID), folding them into the State Department.

It would authorize $819 million from fiscal 1998 to fiscal 2000 to pay back U.S. dues to the United Nations and forgive $107 million in U.N. payments owed to the United States, in exchange for reforms at the international organization. Also authorized would be $100 million for the United Nations that was contained in the fiscal 1998 spending bill for the Commerce, Justice and State departments (PL 105-119).

The provisions largely are the work of Helms and Foreign Relations Committee ranking Democrat Joseph R. Biden Jr. of Delaware, who in a rare display of bipartisanship and pragmatism worked out the legislation with the White House.

The provision that Secretary of State Madeleine K. Albright has said the administration cannot accept would codify the ban on U.S. funds for international family planning groups that perform or advocate abortions and bar them from lobbying other countries on the issue.

The president would be allowed to waive the section of the bill related to groups that perform abortion, but if he chose to exercise that authority, the result would be a permanent spending cap of $356 million for family planning in any fiscal year, $29 million less than the current level.

The president would have no waiver authority on lobbying, a restriction Albright has labeled a "gag rule" and an affront to democracy.

But Republican leaders responded that the choice was clear for Clinton.

"This should be a no-brainer for the president," House Majority Leader Dick Armey, R-Texas, said in a statement. "Abandoning pro-abortion lobbying abroad in exchange for advancing his U.N. policy should be a welcomed compromise that allows him to address his highest priorities."

Said Gingrich in an interview with a handful of reporters March 11: "I refuse to contemplate that the president would veto legislation to pay the U.N. debt so taxpayers can pay for lobbying foreign countries on abortion."

Annan's Warning

Clinton renewed his plea to Congress for the U.N. money March 12 as U.N. Secretary General Kofi Annan traveled to Washington for meetings with the president and members of Congress. "If the United States expects to continue to exercise a leadership role in a way that benefits our own people in the 21st century, we have got to pay our U.N. dues and fulfill our responsibilities," the president said.

Annan warned that a deadbeat United States could lose its voting rights in the General Assembly if it fails to pay its arrears.

Republicans contend that the president could get his funds and a smooth course for the IMF money if he were willing to accept the abortion provision and that a veto would cost him dearly.

Rep. David M. McIntosh, R-Ind., chairman of the ad hoc Conservative Action Team, said that if the president vetoed the State Department bill, his group would pressure Gingrich to abandon a fiscal 1998 supplemental spending bill with the U.N. and IMF funds.

But it remains to be seen whether the bill will ever get to Clinton's desk. If the House leadership manages to round up enough votes to pass the legislation, it faces a tough fight in the

State Department Authorization

Senate, where Biden, despite his role in crafting parts of the legislation, is committed to defeating it.

Democrats would have to rely on moderate Republicans who back abortion rights and conservative GOP senators who have been outspoken in their criticism of the United Nations to produce a majority.

Senate Minority Leader Tom Daschle, D-S.D., said the prospects were good. Biden simply said, "We can defeat it."

Securing Support

The provisions of the legislation extend to perennial items that are popular with various ethnic groups and were included to gain support from various Republicans, including Gilman, who opposes the abortion provision.

The bill would authorize $100 million to move the U.S. Embassy in Israel from Tel Aviv to Jerusalem, which mirrors a 1995 law (PL 104-45) that requires the move to occur by 1999. *(1995 Almanac, p. 10-23)*

The bill also provides the House with an opportunity to express support for NATO expansion, which falls under the purview of the Senate. The conference report includes the European Security Act (HR 1758) that says emerging democracies in Central and Eastern Europe should be considered for membership.

The bill would authorize $38 million for efforts to undermine the current regime in Iraq, including $3 million to establish an international tribunal to indict, prosecute and punish Iraqi President Saddam Hussein, and $5 million for Radio Free Iraq.

The bill also authorizes $20 million for an international fund for Ireland and recommends that the money be disbursed in compliance with the so-called MacBride principles, which help businesses eliminate religious-based discrimination in recruitment and employment.

Abortion Curb Survives in House

MARCH 28 — No one was more surprised than Rep. Jack Kingston by the anti-climactic House vote on the long-delayed conference report for the fiscal 1998-99 State Department Authorization bill (HR 1757).

The Georgia Republican, presiding over the House debate the afternoon of March 26, was caught off guard when Democrats did not ask for a recorded vote on the controversial Republican bill, allowing it to pass by voice.

Perplexed, Kingston turned to the House parliamentarian. "There's no vote," Kingston said. "There's no one to recognize."

Majority Whip Tom DeLay, R-Texas, rushed to fill the gap, panting as he delivered an extemporaneous speech thanking everyone he could think of and preventing any attempt to reverse the voice vote in favor of the bill.

DeLay's effort was not strictly necessary. The 234-172 vote on the rule for debate told Democrats they did not have the votes to defeat the conference report. *(Vote 75, p. H-24)*

The bill includes abortion restrictions on international family planning aid, and Lee H. Hamilton of Indiana, the Democratic floor manager for the bill, decided that a recorded vote would only force anti-abortion Democrats to vote against their beliefs or against President Clinton.

Also, some Democrats were absent from the floor, accompanying Clinton on his trip to Africa.

But DeLay's rush to the floor showed the importance the House leadership attached to the vote and the hard work they had been forced to put into winning support for the measure.

It may not be enough to turn the bill into law, though. Democrats have vowed a tough fight in the Senate, and the White House has already promised to veto the legislation over the abortion-related restrictions.

The bill would authorize $819 million for U.S. payments to the United Nations, forgive $107 million in U.N. debts to the United States and consolidate several foreign affairs agencies. It also would make several controversial foreign policy directives.

Republicans had revived the dormant bill in an effort to challenge Clinton and force his hand on the abortion issue.

A House-Senate conference committee had bogged down for months because Senate members, prodded by Democrats, had refused to accept the abortion-related restrictions.

Last month, House Speaker Newt Gingrich, R-Ga., persuaded International Relations Committee Chairman Benjamin A. Gilman, R-N.Y., and Senate Foreign Relations Committee Chairman Jesse Helms, R-N.C., to report out a conference agreement, signed only by Republicans, that included the abortion restrictions.

Gingrich hoped to unite GOP conservatives and force Clinton to choose between accepting abortion provisions he has repeatedly threatened to veto and paying off U.S. debts to the United Nations.

But to the surprise of the GOP leadership, a large group of Republicans balked at paying any money to the United Nations, claiming that the United States was actually owed more money by the world body for peacekeeping expenses.

Their opposition forced GOP leaders to postpone votes on the measure March 13 and March 18, as Gingrich, Majority Leader Dick Armey, R-Texas, and other party officials pressed members one-on-one to vote for the legislation.

"I was seriously DeLayed," joked Mark Foley, R-Fla., of the majority whip's successful efforts to push the legislation.

Supporters of the legislation sought to convince recalcitrant members that the bill ultimately would accomplish their goals by tying U.S. payments to the United Nations to a series of reforms of the international organization and a decline in future U.S. contributions.

A Republican handout for party members emphasized that even the first $100 million contained in the fiscal 1998 spending bill for the Commerce, Justice, and State Departments (PL 105-119) could not be disbursed if the United Nations took actions considered to violate U.S. sovereignty.

And the GOP handout said that under the provisions drafted by Helms and ranking Foreign Relations Committee Democrat Joseph R. Biden Jr. of Delaware, Congress was not required to appropriate the rest of the money if the U.S. share of the regular U.N. budget and U.N. peacekeeping budgets did not decline.

The bill calls for scaling back the U.S. share of the U.N. budget from 25

International Affairs

Conference Report Highlights

MARCH 28 — Bogged down since last summer in a dispute over abortion restrictions on international family planning aid, the conference report on the State Department authorization bill (HR 1757 — conference report: H Rept 105-432) was finally sent to the House floor with only Republican signatures as a challenge to President Clinton. The report's key provisions:

U.N. debts: The United States would pay $819 million over fiscal years 1998-2000 in back dues to the United Nations while forgiving $107 million the organization owes the United States, mostly for peacekeeping. In return, the United Nations would have to reduce the U.S. share of its budget.

Abortion: For the first time, the "Mexico City" restrictions on international family planning aid would be written into law. (Presidents Ronald Reagan and George Bush used executive orders, which President Clinton rescinded.) No aid would be given to overseas family groups that use their own money to perform abortions or that lobby against abortion laws in other countries.

Agency consolidation: The Arms Control and Disarmament Agency and the U.S. Information Agency would be abolished and, along with some functions of the Agency for International Development, absorbed by the State Department.

Israel's capital: The U.S. Embassy in Israel would be moved from Tel Aviv to Jerusalem, and all government publications would identity Jerusalem as Israel's capital.

Cuban embargo: The secretary of State would have to report to Congress every three months on enforcement of a law prohibiting U.S. entry to anyone with property in Cuba that was confiscated from U.S. nationals. Clinton has waived the provision four times.

Iraqi Dissidents: The bill would authorize $15 million to help Iraqi groups opposed to President Saddam Hussein, and $3 million to establish an international tribunal to indict, prosecute and punish Saddam.

to 20 percent over three years and lowering the U.S. peacekeeping share from 31 to 25 percent.

To bolster their argument, Republicans brought in former U.N. Ambassador Jeane J. Kirkpatrick to talk to GOP dissidents.

"Conservatives, what more do we want?" asked Rules Committee Chairman Gerald B.H. Solomon, R-N.Y. "That is what we have been fighting for, to get a fair share of the burden shared by other countries throughout this world."

Republican supporters of the bill also reminded conservatives and anti-abortion Democrats that the legislation would reinstate the abortion control policy of the Reagan and Bush years.

That policy, known as the "Mexico City" policy after the 1984 U.N. population conference at which it was announced, would ban U.S. funds for international family planning groups that perform or advocate abortions or that lobby foreign governments on the issue. (1984 Almanac, p. 92)

In a relaxation of the Reagan/Bush standard, though, the president would be allowed to waive the section of the bill related to groups that perform abortions. But if he chose to exercise that authority, spending on family planning programs would be limited to $356 million a year, $29 million less than current spending.

Most Democrats argued that the restrictions were unnecessary because current U.S. law prevents federal dollars from being spent to provide or promote abortions.

They termed the lobbying restrictions a "gag rule" that would prevent family planning groups from even participating in conferences where abortion is mentioned. And they said that the potential cap on family planning funds would end up leading to unwanted births, increased abortions, and deaths of women and children.

"This bill seeks to send our nation's foreign policy back to the dark ages of women's reproductive health," said Louise M. Slaughter, D-N.Y. "This is a matter of life and death for many women."

But Judiciary Committee Chairman Henry J. Hyde, R-Ill., countered that "American money should not go to pay for killing unborn children, even if they are Third World unborn children."

Hyde added that the law that prevents U.S. aid money from being spent on abortions only leads to bookkeeping tricks.

"I wish my colleagues would stop insulting our intelligence," Hyde said. "My colleagues know and I know that if we give them [family planning groups] a million dollars, we free up their own money for other purposes."

Republican attempts to make the bill a test vote on the Mexico City policy appear to have succeeded, pushing 19 Democrats to support the rule governing debate, with more potentially supporting the legislation itself.

A knowledgeable House aide said that after that vote, Hamilton decided to yield to the pleas of Democratic members who did not want to buck Clinton but who knew that if they voted against the bill, they would be taken to task by anti-abortion groups.

Moreover, Democrats saw little need to challenge the bill since many, like Sam Gejdenson, D-Conn., believe that "this will never become law."

Even without the abortion language, administration officials have little love for the authorization bill, which they see as too stingy toward the United Nations.

They have also strongly objected to a provision in the bill that would authorize $100 million to move the U.S. Embassy in Israel from Tel Aviv to Jerusalem, mirroring a 1995 law (PL 104-45) that requires the move to occur by 1999. (1995 Almanac, p. 10-23)

State Department officials have said moving the mission to the disputed city would harm the U.S. role as an honest broker in the Middle East peace process.

In the Senate, Biden has pledged to defeat the legislation, which is scheduled to come up the week of March 30, despite having written the

State Department Authorization

U.N. provisions. He would have to rely on Republicans who support abortion rights, or are opposed to any U.N. funding, to put the minority Democrats over the top.

A Senate Republican source said Democrats would not be able to defeat the bill on a straight up-or-down vote, while Republicans lack the votes to stop a filibuster of the legislation.

In the past, Senate Minority Leader Tom Daschle, D-S.D., has also mentioned a third possibility: Democrats could simply agree to let the bill proceed to Clinton's desk for the inevitable veto. That does not appear to be an option now, though, because in recent weeks Daschle has said he would fight the legislation.

Republicans say that in some ways, the fate of the bill itself is beside the point. Republican leaders in both the House and Senate have vowed not to approve funds for the United Nations unless Clinton compromises on the abortion issue.

Awaiting the outcome of the debate on the authorization bill, the Senate approved fiscal 1998 supplemental spending bills (S 1768, S 1769) without U.N. funds. House leaders, meanwhile, have delayed consideration of a spending bill with the U.N. money and vowed to tie any funds to the anti-abortion language.

"We have a fair amount of options" to force Clinton to accept the Mexico City policy, said a Senate GOP source.

State Dept. Bill Depends in Senate On GOP Centrists

APRIL 25 — The fate of a bill that would repay most U.S. debts to the United Nations and consolidate several foreign affairs agencies is largely in the hands of a small group of Republican senators worried by the bill's anti-abortion provisions.

The Senate opened debate April 24 on the long-delayed conference report for the fiscal 1998-99 State Department authorization bill (HR 1757), with both Democrats and Republicans agreeing that the outcome of a vote scheduled for April 28 remained in doubt.

Senate Foreign Relations Committee Chairman Jesse Helms, R-N.C., said supporters are "facing a razor-thin majority in the Senate. We may not even have a majority."

Both sides were jockeying for the votes of about a dozen senators, mostly moderate Republicans, who might stray from their party's lines.

Secretary of State Madeleine K. Albright met with Senate Democrats April 21, urging all 45 to vote against the bill, which President Clinton has threatened to veto.

Republican leaders were urging potential dissidents — from abortion-rights supporters such as Susan Collins of Maine, to opponents of United Nations funding such as Ben Nighthorse Campbell of Colorado — to back the conference report.

The partisan split was a sharp change from last June when the Senate passed the bill, crafted by Helms and Joseph R. Biden Jr., D-Del., by 90-5.

The bill bogged down in conference over House-passed abortion restrictions on international family planning aid. In March, Republicans decided to move a unilateral conference report, without Democratic signatures, that included anti-abortion language.

The controversial provisions would reinstate portions of the "Mexico City" policy of the Reagan/Bush years that banned U.S. aid to family planning groups that use their own funds to perform or advocate abortions or that lobby foreign governments on the issue.

The president would be allowed to waive some restrictions, but then would have to settle for less family planning aid.

Senate Majority Leader Trent Lott, R-Miss., said the measure may be the administration's last chance to win congressional support for paying $819 million in U.S. debts to the U.N. and forgiving $107 million in U.N. debts to the United States.

Addressing Albright from the Senate floor, Lott said, "Madame Secretary, this is the last train out of Dodge on the U.N. arrearage. . . . If this bill doesn't pass in the Senate and isn't signed by the president, the U.N. issue is probably dead for this year."

Maine Republicans Collins and Olympia J. Snowe said they were torn between their desire to back the party leadership and pay off debts to the U.N. and their opposition to the abortion restrictions.

Snowe said the possibility of waiving some restrictions was a "positive departure" but indicated that she still might not vote for the bill. "Why make the distinctions on what private groups do with their money?" Snowe asked. "It's not our money, it's their money."

Collins said, "I'm not for Mexico City, but I'm in favor of money that's focused on paying off the United Nations."

Bill Clears Senate; Clinton Uncaps Veto Pen

MAY 2 — With President Clinton threatening to veto a key foreign policy bill because of its anti-abortion language, Republican leaders held off sending him the legislation that cleared the Senate April 28 in hopes of persuading him there was no other way to pay off U.S. debts to the United Nations, a White House priority.

"We're taking our time," said Senate Foreign Relations Committee Chairman Jesse Helms, R-N.C. "I want him to contemplate exactly what he's going to do to the U.N."

The Senate on April 28 narrowly adopted, 51-49, the conference report to the fiscal 1998-99 State Department authorization bill (HR 1757), which would respond to Clinton's pleas to pay nearly $1 billion in U.N. debts and consolidate several foreign affairs agencies. (Vote 105, p. S-18)

But White House officials have said Clinton would veto the legislation because it also includes abortion restrictions on international family planning aid.

"We hope they get it up here quickly so the president can veto it and we can get on with the process of passing a bill that the president can sign," White House spokesman Barry Toiv said after the Senate vote. "We can address the family planning issue separately."

Before the vote, Clinton criticized the bill, saying, "I don't think that is a responsible, mature message to send to the world by the leading country in the world. I think that if we want to lead,

International Affairs

we ought to lead, and we ought to lead by example by paying our way."

United States and U.N. officials have warned that this country could lose some of its influence, including its vote in the U.N. General Assembly, if it does not pay the back dues this year.

House Majority Leader Dick Armey, R-Texas, predicted that the pressures would force Clinton to sign the bill.

"Can you imagine vetoing 100 percent of what you want, because someone got 10 percent of what they want that you disagree with? That would be a foolish choice," Armey said.

The White House faced countervailing pressures from Democrats and family planning groups, leading White House Press Secretary Mike McCurry to rebuff GOP hopes.

"They ought to just send it down here so we can send it back to them in the same day's mail," McCurry said.

GOP leaders warned that if Clinton carried out his veto threat, they would not consider other legislation to pay the U.N. dues without the abortion restrictions.

"This is it," Senate Majority Leader Trent Lott, R-Miss., told reporters, blaming Clinton in an interview after the vote for being "willing to take down this carefully constructed package over abortion."

Helms added that if the president vetoed the bill "there will be no action on [U.N.] arrearages or anything else that the president is interested in. . . . This is the end of it, one way or another."

Some funds for the United Nations, along with money for the International Monetary Fund (IMF), are included in a supplemental appropriations bill (HR 3580 — H Rept 105-470) awaiting House floor consideration. But Republicans have threatened to add the abortion restrictions to that legislation as well.

The abortion issue dominated Senate debate on the conference report for the State Department bill. The legislation would authorize paying $819 million in U.S. debts to the United Nations and forgiving $107 million in U.N. debts to the United States in return for reforms of the international organization.

It also would merge the U.S. Information Agency, the Arms Control and Disarmament Agency and parts of the Agency for International Development into the State Department.

The bill would authorize $38 million to undermine the regime of Iraqi President Saddam Hussein and $100 million to move the U.S. Embassy in Israel from Tel Aviv to Jerusalem.

The most contentious provisions would reinstate, and for the first time write in law, portions of a policy from the Reagan and Bush administrations that banned U.S. aid to international family planning groups that perform, lobby for or otherwise advocate abortions, even if they use their own money.

In a relaxation of the Reagan/Bush standard, the president would be allowed to waive the section of the bill related to groups that perform abortions. But if he did, spending on family planning programs would be limited to $356 million a year, $29 million below current spending.

"What makes us think that we are so right on abortion, this administration's position is so right on abortion, we should be lobbying other countries to change their position?" asked Assistant Majority Leader Don Nickles, R-Okla.

Nickles was able to rally 48 of his GOP colleagues, including such previous holdouts as Ben Nighthorse Campbell, R-Colo., around his position.

Six Republicans and all but two Democrats — Minority Whip Wendell H. Ford of Kentucky and Deputy Minority Whip John B. Breaux of Louisiana — voted against the bill because of the abortion provisions.

GOP opponents, such as Olympia J. Snowe of Maine, said they voted against the measure because it would impose a "gag rule" on private groups by preventing them from lobbying, sponsoring conferences or distributing materials overseas on "alleged defects" in local abortion laws.

"This restriction on public debate is unhealthy for the democratic process and is something Americans would not tolerate if attempts were made to impose it here at home," Snowe said.

Joseph R. Biden Jr. of Delaware, the ranking Democrat on the Foreign Relations Committee, called the measure "legislative blackmail."

He and Helms had not included the restrictions in their original bill, which was approved last June by a 90-5 vote and was celebrated by both lawmakers and the administration as a sign of a new era of bipartisanship in foreign policy.

But House Republican conferees insisted on including some restrictions on abortion in the conference report, preventing the bill from moving forward since last year.

Helms eventually relented, and Republican conferees, without a single Democratic signature, reported the bill out in March. The House adopted the report on March 26.

John Kerry of Massachusetts, a member of the Senate Foreign Relations Committee, said the failure to pay off debts to the United Nations would make the United States a "scofflaw" in the organization, and hurt efforts to win support for policies in areas like Bosnia and Iraq.

"The reality is that the United States of America is going to lose significant prestige, significant leverage, and our interests are going to be set back in the international arena," Kerry said.

Clinton Swiftly Vetoes Bill; Cites Abortion Tie

OCTOBER 24 — It took congressional leaders nearly six months to send President Clinton a State Department authorization bill that passed in April, but only a few hours for the president to make good on his promise to veto it.

Clinton had pleaded with Congress for the nearly $1 billion in the bill to pay off U.S. debts to the United Nations, but he rejected the legislation Oct. 21 because it would have banned federal aid to international family planning groups that advocate or lobby on abortion.

The bill (HR 1757) cleared the Senate April 28, but Republican leaders hung on to it, hoping to change Clinton's mind about a veto.

Clinton said the bill "threatened our leadership in the world community by tying our payment of dues to the United Nations and other international organizations to these unrelated family planning issues."

The administration now will have to

scramble to find enough money to keep the debts from costing the United States its seat in the U.N. General Assembly.

Senate Foreign Relations Committee Chairman Jesse Helms, R-N.C., ranking Democrat Joseph R. Biden Jr. of Delaware, and the White House had reached a delicate compromise last year on payments to the United Nations based on reforms Helms wanted in the organization, and on reorganizing foreign policy agencies, but the bill fell hostage to anti-abortion forces in the House.

Not all of the work by Helms and Biden was in vain. A consolidation of several foreign policy agencies into the State Department and various foreign policy initiatives became law as part of the omnibus spending bill (HR 4328 — PL 105-277). ◆

Religious Persecution Bill Overcomes 11th-Hour Snags On Way to Enactment

Box Score

- **Bill:** HR 2431 — PL 105-292
- **House action:** The House cleared HR 2431 as amended by the Senate on Oct. 10 by voice vote. It passed the initial version of the bill (H Rept 105-480, Parts 1-3), 375-41, on May 14.
- **Senate action:** The Senate passed HR 2431, 98-0, on Oct. 9 after substituting the text of S 1868.
- **Presidential action:** Clinton signed HR 2431 on Oct. 27.

SUMMARY

With supporters such as House Speaker Newt Gingrich, R-Ga., and the Christian Coalition, legislation seeking to prevent religious persecution overseas seemed like a foregone conclusion. Yet with business groups worried about trade and the State Department worried about overseas relations, a behind-the-scenes campaign slowed down and then watered down the measure.

As introduced by Rep. Frank R. Wolf, R-Va., and Sen. Arlen Specter, R-Pa., in late 1997, the bill would have created a White House office to monitor religious persecution and impose tough economic sanctions on violators. The president could waive sanctions only in the interest of U.S. national security. The bill also would have increased the importance of religious persecution as a criterion for U.S. asylum. *(1997 Almanac, p. 8-41)*

The House International Relations Committee took the first cut at the bill, giving the State Department control over monitoring and agreeing to delete references in the bill to specific countries. The House Judiciary Committee effectively gutted the asylum and refugee provisions.

The House bill still was considered too strong for the Senate, so Majority Whip Don Nickles, R-Okla., produced his own measure (S 1868), which ultimately succeeded. It gives the president authority to impose diplomatic and economic sanctions against countries that consistently permit or endorse attacks against religious believers. The sanctions would expire after two years if not reauthorized and could be waived in the national interest or if they encouraged a backlash against members of a persecuted group. The measure creates an ambassador-at-large to assess and promote religious freedom overseas, as well as a 10-member commission to monitor progress. It requires annual State Department reports on religious freedom overseas.

Wolf's Faith in Bill Rewarded as Panel Gives Its Approval

MARCH 28 — Just before voting 31-5 to approve legislation that aims to reduce religious persecution overseas with sanctions on repressive regimes, members of the House International Relations Committee broke into a round of applause for Rep. Frank R. Wolf.

The Virginia Republican, who has a longtime interest in human rights issues, had managed to overcome strong initial opposition to craft a bill (HR 2431) that won the support of a wide range of religious groups and members of both parties.

Even the Clinton administration, which continues to oppose the legislation, acknowledged that it might rethink its initial threat of a presidential veto in light of changes made before and during the March 25 markup.

But in an interview, Wolf said it was too early to take a bow, noting that three other committees still must act on sections of the bill — Judiciary, Ways and Means, and Banking — and each has serious concerns.

And just as the International Relations panel was considering his legislation, Wolf learned that some powerful senators were championing an alternative that is more sweeping, though less strict.

Nonetheless, the International Relations vote was a victory for Wolf.

The bill, introduced last May as HR 1685 and revamped in September as HR 2431, had strong support from Republican leaders after the powerful Christian Coalition made the fight against religious persecution its top legislative priority. The bill became a subject of substantial interest from churches and religious broadcasters.

But the measure ran into a surprising amount of opposition from business groups and some religious organizations, leading the International Relations panel to delay consideration for six months as members tried to iron out differences.

As approved by International Relations, the measure would impose ex-

International Affairs

port and aid sanctions on countries that endorse or permit violent attacks on religious believers.

The sanctions would include a ban on U.S. imports from such countries, a prohibition on most U.S. aid, U.S. opposition to loans by multilateral development banks and the International Monetary Fund, and a denial of visas to those identified as persecutors.

The bill also would make it easier for victims of religious persecution overseas to qualify for asylum or refugee status under U.S. immigration law. And it would create a new Office of Religious Persecution Monitoring in the State Department to identify countries that should be subject to sanctions.

Averting 'Havoc'

Members of both parties and the administration had complained that despite its noble aspirations, the bill as originally drafted would have harmed U.S. foreign policy.

Stuart E. Eizenstat, under secretary of State for Economic Affairs, criticized the initial bill, telling the International Relations panel that it would "wreak havoc on U.S. foreign policy. . . . You will leave every country on tenterhooks for months and months."

Eizenstat particularly objected to a provision that would have allowed the director of a new Office of Religious Persecution, rather than the secretary of State or the president, to decide on sanctions — an unprecedented amount of power to give a low-level bureaucrat who was "almost unaccountable," Eizenstat said.

"This is a job many of us would like to have," he joked.

He also complained about provisions singling out Muslim countries and specific nations, such as Pakistan and China, as potential targets of sanctions.

Supporters countered that the legislation would allow the president to waive sanctions against any country for reasons of national security or if their imposition would serve only to increase, rather than decrease, religious persecution.

"The only way we could do more would be to give the president freedom to do absolutely nothing in the face of continuing religious persecution," said Rep. Christopher H. Smith, R-N.J., a key supporter of the legislation.

Nevertheless, Eizenstat's comments struck enough of a chord with committee members that Smith offered a compromise proposal to address some of the State Department's concerns.

Smith's amendment, approved on a voice vote, called for the secretary of State, rather than the director of the Office of Religious Persecution, to be responsible for determining which countries should be sanctioned.

It also eliminated from the bill a list of countries singled out as particularly worthy of attention because of alleged histories of religious persecution.

Still targeted, however, is Sudan, whose Muslim-dominated government has been engaged in a bloody civil war with Christians and animists.

The bill would ban trade and air travel with Sudan and prohibit new U.S. investment in the African nation.

But the panel opted to create one exception to this provision, voting 20-11 for an amendment offered by Robert Menendez, D-N.J., to allow American companies to participate in the Sudanese gum arabic industry until alternative sources for the material are found.

According to Menendez, Sudan supplies 90 percent of the world's reliable supply of gum arabic, a soluble gum from the acacia tree used in products ranging from medicine to diabetic candies. Grocery and pharmaceutical companies had lobbied for the exemption.

Second Look

Administration officials welcomed many of the changes made in the legislation, as well as an earlier substitute amendment by International Relations Committee Chairman Benjamin A. Gilman, R-N.Y., that moved the Office of Religious Persecution from the White House to the State Department and broadened the president's waiver authority.

Assistant Secretary of State for Legislative Affairs Barbara Mills Larkin said the changes made the measure "much better than before" and told panel members she was not certain whether Secretary of State Madeleine K. Albright would still recommend a presidential veto.

But she said State Department officials were still opposed to the measure because of the Sudan sanctions and the fact that sanctions were virtually automatic for countries considered to condone religious persecution.

They and other opponents worried that the measure could still hurt relations with key U.S. allies such as Saudi Arabia and give victims of religious persecution an immigration status denied to other human rights victims.

The panel's ranking Democrat, Lee H. Hamilton of Indiana, said that under the legislation "almost half the countries in the world" could still be subject to sanctions. He also expressed concern about the bill's asylum and refugee provisions, which he said would create "a hierarchy of human rights."

Some of those provisions may be struck by the Judiciary Committee. Its chairman, Henry J. Hyde, R-Ill., and Lamar Smith, R-Texas, chairman of the Immigration and Claims Subcommittee, wrote Gilman that they would surrender jurisdiction over the bill only if its asylum provisions were dropped.

Wolf's bill would make it easier for members of persecuted religious groups to qualify for asylum by essentially exempting them from a standard in a 1996 law (PL 104-208) to crack down on perceived abuses of the asylum process. (1996 Almanac, p. 5-3)

Under Wolf's bill, individual applicants would not have to demonstrate that they had a "credible fear of persecution." The 1996 law required such a demonstration if immigration officials were not to deport undocumented individuals who applied for asylum at airports and other points of entry.

Fear of a Deluge

At a March 24 International Relations hearing, Christopher Smith said creating a special status for religious refugees was "completely unnecessary and would encourage illegal immigration and fraudulent asylum claims."

And at the International Relations markup, Doug Bereuter, R-Neb., said that judgments on asylum needed to be made on a case-by-case basis, rather than by giving preference to particular groups.

"We have to keep the focus on the individual; we can't do it by class," Bereuter said. "Otherwise, there'll be tens of millions of people coming here."

But Smith said the legislation "sets a very high bar" for immigration, by limiting the benefits to groups that have been the victims of violent attacks. Besides, he asked "What does this language do? It doesn't generate a decision, it generates a hearing."

The asylum provisions have also received support from some lawmakers such as Rep. Howard L. Berman, D-Calif., who would like to repeal those portions of the 1996 law.

"I say undo everything. I don't want to stop anything from becoming undone," Berman said, a position supported by the Roman Catholic Church and some other refugee groups.

In addition to the asylum provisions, Lamar Smith, Melvin Watt, D-N.C., and other Judiciary Committee members have expressed concern about provisions of the bill that would give victims of religious persecution a leg up in winning permanent refugee status.

The bill may also encounter obstacles in the Ways and Means and Banking committees because of its provisions on trade and the Export-Import Bank.

Bill supporters said that they hope to push the full House to restore any provisions eliminated in the subsequent markups. But they are expecting a tough fight, particularly because many lawmakers, such as Elton Gallegly, R-Calif., say they are loath to tamper with current asylum law.

In the Senate, a companion bill by Arlen Specter, R-Pa., faces competition from alternative legislation introduced by Majority Whip Don Nickles, R-Okla.

Nickles' bill, which has the support of several other Republican senators, is both more comprehensive and less stringent than Wolf's legislation.

It would call on administration officials to take account of and address racial discrimination as well as violent racial attacks against religious groups.

But it would offer the president a broad menu of options to choose from when punishing foreign countries — from a diplomatic denunciation to the cutoff of exports, tariff benefits, or private U.S. loans. The president would still have the option of waiving any punishment.

Still, James M. Inhofe, R-Okla., who chaired a religious persecution task force for Senate Majority Leader Trent Lott, R-Miss., said that he expected the Senate would endorse whatever came out of the House.

Critics Make Headway Against Measure

MAY 2 — Facing a swirl of opposition, including that of President Clinton, lawmakers are watering down a bill (HR 2431) aimed at stemming religious persecution overseas.

Since it was introduced last year, the legislation, backed by the Christian Coalition and some other conservative religious groups, has come under attack from business associations, supporters of tighter immigration laws and lawmakers concerned that the bill would disrupt relations with key U.S. allies, such as Saudi Arabia.

The most recent attack came from Clinton.

In a meeting with about 60 evangelical Christian leaders at the White House April 27, Clinton asked the group to withdraw its support for the bill and an alternative Senate measure (S 1868).

He criticized both bills for requiring mandatory sanctions on countries that support or permit religious persecution.

The House bill would sanction offending countries by limiting U.S. exports, prohibiting most U.S. aid, requiring the U.S. government to oppose loans by multilateral development banks and the International Monetary Fund, and denying visas to those identified as persecutors.

The president would be allowed to waive the sanctions for reasons of national security or if their imposition would serve to increase, rather than decrease, religious persecution.

Clinton told the religious leaders that "what always happens if you have automatic sanctions legislation is it puts enormous pressure on whoever is in the executive branch to fudge an evaluation of the facts of what is going on. And that's not what you want. What you want is to leave the president some flexibility, including the ability to impose sanctions, some flexibility with a range of appropriate reactions."

A House Judiciary subcommittee on April 30 removed a key portion of the bill that would make it easier for members of persecuted religious minorities to qualify for asylum or refugee status in the United States.

The Immigration and Claims Subcommittee's changes came at the urging of Chairman Lamar Smith, R-Texas, who said that the provisions would undermine portions of the 1996 immigration law (PL 104-208) that sought to crack down on illegal immigration and false asylum claims. (1996 Almanac, p. 5-3)

Smith was particularly critical of a provision that would have allowed religious minorities deemed to be facing persecution to automatically qualify for an asylum hearing, exempting them from provisions of the 1996 law requiring applicants to first prove a "credible fear" of persecution or face deportation.

"It would encourage illegal immigration and fraudulent claims, opening up the floodgates for illegal aliens," Smith said.

Smith also criticized a provision that would grant additional refugee slots each year to victims of religious persecution, saying that "there is no reason to treat them better than other victims of religious, racial, ethnic or political persecution."

Rocky Road Ahead

If they are unable to work out a compromise, subcommittee Democrats and some Republicans are planning to try to reverse Smith's changes at a full Judiciary Committee markup May 6. But they did not force a roll-call vote.

The April 30 action was the second of several markups that are expected to water down the bill.

The House International Relations Committee voted March 25 to give the secretary of State greater control over which countries would be threatened with sanctions.

Soon, both the Ways and Means and Banking committees will take up the bill, with top lawmakers on those panels saying that they expect to remove potential sanctions that fall within their jurisdiction.

House supporters, such as Christopher H. Smith, R-N.J., and the bill's sponsor, Frank R. Wolf, R-Va., say they will try to reverse these decisions on the House floor, although it is not clear that the Rules Committee will permit such an attempt.

"If it's completely revamped, we will deal with it on the floor," said Wolf.

International Affairs

Even if supporters manage to reverse the changes, the Wolf bill is likely to be blended with a Senate bill that Wolf's allies view as a weaker alternative.

That bill, by Assistant Majority Leader Don Nickles, R-Okla., would address more forms of religious persecution than the House measure but would give the president a broader menu of options to choose from when punishing foreign countries.

House Committees Rip Into Bill

MAY 9 — Religious conservatives, who have focused almost exclusively on domestic issues since the end of the Cold War, are turning anew to foreign policy, saying America has lost its moral compass. But as they try to revive Ronald Reagan's approach to world affairs, they find it difficult to resurrect the political coalition that backed those policies.

As demonstrated by last year's battle over China's trade status and the current debate over a bill aimed at fighting religious persecution overseas (HR 2431), their traditional allies in the Republican Party are torn. Should the GOP support the goals of religious groups or other foreign policy objectives, from free trade to national security to limiting immigration?

The religious persecution bill, a top priority of the Christian Coalition and similar groups, is scheduled to be taken up by the House next week. Majority Leader Dick Armey, R-Texas, predicted May 5 that it would pass by "overwhelming numbers."

Yet, even though the legislation has won support from a range of religious and human rights groups and members of both parties, supporters will have trouble claiming a broad mandate for their legislation.

It took sponsors a year to fashion a bill— and enough compromises — to clear the principal committee involved, International Relations, on March 26.

As the legislation moved through two other committees, opponents watered down some of its strongest provisions, demonstrating the challenges religious conservatives might face as they seek to play a larger role on foreign policy issues. The bill still will have to be meshed with a Senate measure (S 1868) that some House members consider even less stringent.

"I think they have found out foreign policy is a little bit more complicated than they had believed," said Rep. Doug Bereuter, R-Neb. "You can't simply say, 'This is the bill we want, no changes.'"

Rep. Frank R. Wolf, R-Va., originally introduced the legislation with the strong backing of House Speaker Newt Gingrich, R-Ga. It included a list of provisions designed to punish countries that endorse or permit violent attacks against religious believers.

Some of these provisions remain in the bill, including restrictions on exports, a prohibition on all non-humanitarian aid, U.S. opposition to loans by multilateral development banks and the International Monetary Fund, and a denial of visas to those identified as persecutors.

But in recent weeks, three House panels, each concerned with different aspects of the legislation, have weakened portions of the bill.

Worried that the measure would undermine a 1996 immigration law (PL 104-208), the House Judiciary Committee on May 6 chose not to reinstate an important provision in the bill that had been deleted by its Immigration and Claims Subcommittee

That provision would have automatically granted members of persecuted religious groups an asylum hearing, exempting them from provisions of the 1996 law that require them to first prove a "credible fear" of persecution or face deportation.

Opponents of the provision, such as subcommittee Chairman Lamar Smith, R-Texas, had complained that the measure might encourage false asylum claims and illegal immigration.

The Judiciary Committee, however, endorsed a compromise that makes it more likely that victims of religious persecution will qualify as refugees and calls for additional training on religious discrimination for immigration judges and officers.

In another setback for supporters, the Ways and Means Committee, acting the same day, voted to strip out provisions banning trade with and investment in Sudan. Wolf and other supporters had singled out Sudan's government because of its "holy war" against Christians in the southern half of the country, including murder, crucifixions, torture and slavery.

But panel members objected, saying that imposing unilateral sanctions would not stem persecution and would harm other interests. "I see the bill as a legislative monster threatening U. S. national security and economic interests in a vain attempt to make the bill's sponsors look better than those opposing them," said Trade Subcommittee Chairman Philip M. Crane, R-Ill.

After removing the Sudan provisions, the panel took the unusual tack of voting out the bill without a recommendation to the House.

In March, the International Relations Committee, responding to administration concerns, voted to give the secretary of State, rather than the director of a new Office of Religious Persecution, greater control over which countries to threaten with sanctions.

Jim Leach, R-Iowa, chairman of the House Banking and Financial Services Committee, said that his panel will likely decline to act on the bill, but that he would recommend to congressional leaders that Export-Import Bank loans not be used as sanctions.

The Senate is soon to consider alternative legislation by Assistant Majority Leader Don Nickles, R-Okla., that would address more forms of religious persecution than the House measure but would give the president a broader menu of options when punishing foreign countries.

Strategic Interests

The fight over the bill is the latest round in a larger conflict.

Since the 1996 presidential election, some conservative religious groups have put a renewed emphasis on foreign policy, arguing that the United States in the post-Cold War era has lost its way, driven too much by business and short-term strategic interests.

As Gary L. Bauer, president of the Family Research Council, said in an April 13 speech at the Kennedy School of Government at Harvard University, "America's foreign and domestic policy are morally inseparable — what we do abroad will always reveal what we are at home."

Wolf and some other lawmakers agree.

"This country has been blessed by God," Wolf said. "We have to be faithful to our fundamental values of liberty. . . . We need to put back some morality in foreign policy."

Robert Kagan, a senior associate at the Carnegie Endowment for International Peace, said such views were intended to appeal to a Republican constituency that strongly supported Ronald Reagan's anti-communist foreign policy but that feels neglected by the current Republican leadership.

"They can get a lot of mileage out of the Reaganite stuff, out of the Reaganite impulse," Kagan said.

Religious conservatives say Republicans need their support on foreign policy legislation. "If they ignore our interests, they run the risk of alienating a constituency out there that makes up one-third of the electorate," said Randy Tate, executive director of the Christian Coalition.

But many Republicans remain unconvinced, saying that U.S. interests, even on human rights, are better served in the long term when subordinated to other foreign policy concerns.

"We simply cannot allow foreign policy to become an extension of domestic politics," Sen. Pat Roberts, R-Kan., said in an April 10 speech to the Kansas Press Association. "I am not saying these debates on the great moral and religious issues should not take place. I am merely arguing that we will not build successful foreign or trade policy by making the rest of the world conform to our way of life and our views of how we want things to be."

Sen. Chuck Hagel, R-Neb., said it was "a mindless way to approach foreign policy. . . . I am concerned that we are drifting in the direction of these religious groups that see the world in absolute black and white."

Caught in the crossfire are lawmakers such as Sen. Daniel R. Coats, R-Ind.

Coats is known on Capitol Hill for his adherence to conservative social causes, from opposing abortion to supporting school choice. But he said he has found it harder to line up with his religious conservative allies on some foreign policy issues, such as granting most-favored-nation trade status to China.

On that vote, some religious conservatives opposed allowing regular trade with China, because China is alleged to persecute Christians.

But Coats said he supported continued trade for its own benefits and because other religious groups said cutting off trade would cause China to restrict their missionary activities.

"It becomes a problem when religious conservatives take a specific issue and attach it to a broader agenda," Coats said. "I was torn, I was very torn."

After Hot Debate, House Passes Bill By Strong Margin

MAY 16 — After a year of twists and turns, the House on May 14 voted overwhelmingly to approve legislation aimed at punishing religious persecution overseas.

The 375-41 vote marked a vindication for the bill's author, Frank R. Wolf, R-Va., who had labored to move the bill through three committees and onto the House floor. *(Vote 155, p. H-46)*

It also marked a rare political victory for religious conservatives, who have complained in recent months that their agenda has been neglected by Republican leaders.

With the broad margin of victory, supporters would have the votes to override President Clinton's threatened veto of the legislation.

But there are more immediate obstacles. Supporters face the challenge of moving a quite different bill through the Senate, then meshing the two measures. Business groups and the Clinton administration are pushing to water down the Senate bill (S 1868), sponsored by Assistant Majority Leader Don Nickles, R-Okla., and Joseph I. Lieberman, D-Conn.

The House bill (HR 2431) would create an Office of Religious Persecution Monitoring in the State Department to address concerns worldwide.

The legislation would punish governments that carry out violent attacks against religious believers by banning U.S. exports to government agencies involved in persecution and exports of goods that could be used in persecution.

It would also prohibit non-humanitarian aid to such countries, require the U.S. government to oppose loans by multilateral development banks and the International Monetary Fund, and deny visas to those identified as persecutors.

Despite the lopsided vote, House debate on the measure was contentious.

Supporters cast the vote as a supreme moral choice. Wolf said that by voting for the bill, members would "send the message that we care for the least of us and it will show that the words of Jefferson hold true."

Lincoln Diaz-Balart, R-Fla., added, "We have to decide ultimately if what we accept and what we embrace as a society and as a world, as an international community, is ethics, as some sort of guide . . . or whether we are going to officially embrace the law of the jungle."

Critics said the bill would establish a "hierarchy of human rights" giving victims of religious persecution more protections than those who suffer because of their race or ethnicity.

Melvin Watt, D-N.C., complained that the Rules Committee had prevented him from offering an amendment applying the bill's protections to all forms of persecution.

"All forms of persecution should be protected against in a special way," Watt said.

In fact, Lee H. Hamilton of Indiana, the ranking Democrat on the International Relations Committee, charged that by passing the measure, "We invite other governments to test our tolerance for other forms of persecution."

The bill's supporters, however, said they would back Watt's approach in a separate bill. Passage of the religious persecution measure, they said, would build support for other human rights causes.

"Not every bill can address every problem," said Christopher H. Smith, R-N.J. "By not addressing this provision in the bill, we do not deny that there are other problems."

National Interests

Opponents also said that the measure would endanger U.S. diplomatic interests and commerce in countries such as Pakistan and Indonesia.

If Pakistan were punished because it carried out attacks against religious believers, Hamilton said, U.S. officials would lose the leverage of imposing sanctions on the country if it ex-

International Affairs

ploded a nuclear device in response to tests by India.

And Indonesia, in the middle of an economic and political crisis, could be dealt a further blow from sanctions because of its persecution of religious minorities.

"How would a financial collapse help religious tolerance?" Hamilton asked.

But supporters of the bill said such concerns paled in comparison to defending a basic moral principle.

"If you take away from me the right of my faith, can these other things even matter?" said House Majority Leader Dick Armey, R-Texas. "They will be lost, and in the end, so will we."

The bill's defenders noted that the president would have authority to waive any sanctions on the grounds of national security or because they are judged counterproductive in combatting religious persecution.

Linda Smith, R-Wash., said that although the bill "doesn't do a whole lot toward making the president do anything, it does make him break his silence on all of the things that are going on in the world."

For opponents on Capitol Hill and in the White House, the waiver does not solve the problems caused by the bill.

As the president's national security adviser, Samuel R. Berger, wrote in a May 14 op-ed piece in The Washington Post, "The bill's inclusion of a sanctions waiver does not address our fundamental concern, which is the automatic and compelled public censure that this exercise entails."

Berger said the bill would invite a backlash against minority religious groups who would be "accused of complicity in this uniquely American effort."

Amo Houghton, R-N.Y., made a similar point, saying he had not heard from a single missionary group overseas that supports the measure.

"When you want to help someone, you've got to make sure that the people you plan to help want to be helped," Houghton said. "Why are we superimposing our guilt on people who don't want to be helped?"

Defenders responded that they have the support of a broad range of religious groups such as the U.S. Catholic Bishop's Conference, the Southern Baptist Convention and B'nai B'rith.

Different Path

Despite the overwhelming House vote, the Senate is unlikely to consider companion legislation by Sen. Arlen Specter, R-Pa. That bill (S 772) is being held at the Senate desk by Majority Leader Trent Lott, R-Miss., while lawmakers seek to advance the bill by Nickles and Lieberman.

The Nickles-Lieberman measure had been slated to be taken up by the Senate Foreign Relations Committee on May 19, but aides said consideration would likely be delayed until after the Memorial Day recess.

Some senators are pressing for broader input from members of overseas religious groups before allowing Nickles' alternative to proceed to the Senate floor. Foreign Relations Chairman Jesse Helms, R-N.C., is hoping to work out a bipartisan compromise with ranking Democrat Joseph R. Biden Jr. of Delaware.

The Nickles-Lieberman bill would address non-violent forms of religious discrimination as well as the sort of violent attacks that would trigger sanctions in the House measure.

Under the Nickles-Lieberman legislation, administration officials could choose from a wide range of options in punishing countries that are not "gross violators" of religious freedom. These range from a private diplomatic protest to economic sanctions similar to those in the House bill.

However, the president would be required to punish countries judged to be gross violators with one of the more punitive sanctions.

According to Senate aides, only a few especially glaring violators, such as Sudan or Afghanistan, would likely face such sanctions.

"What are the chances of Egypt being punished? Zero," said one Senate aide. "What are the chances of Saudi Arabia being punished? Zero."

Like the House bill, the Senate measure would allow the president to waive the sanctions for national security grounds or if it is believed they would create a harmful backlash.

In addition, the measure would establish an ambassador-at-large for religious liberty at the State Department, a special adviser on religious persecution in the National Security Council and a seven-member outside commission on international religious liberty.

White House Moves

The administration likes the Nickles bill more than the House measure because it would give the president greater flexibility.

Nonetheless, John Shattuck, assistant secretary of State for Democracy, Human Rights and Labor, weighed in with several criticisms of the measure at a Senate Foreign Relations Committee hearing May 12.

Reciting a long list of initiatives that he said the administration is undertaking to protect religious freedom, Shattuck was particularly critical of the various institutions set up by the legislation.

"We believe that legislation best serves our mutual goal of promoting and upholding religious freedom when it consolidates and strengthens existing mechanisms rather than creating new ones in their stead," Shattuck said.

Shattuck pressed for relaxing the waiver standard from "national security" to "national interest."

On the other hand, the Christian Coalition and other religious groups are pushing to tighten the waiver standard. They would like the president to spell out publicly the rationale for any waivers he grants and make sure that there is an interval between the time when a country is deemed ripe for sanctions and when the president could waive them, so the groups can bring political pressure to bear.

GOP Deal Clears Path For Senate Action

SEPTEMBER 26 — A behind-the-scenes compromise among Republicans has cleared the way for Senate action on long-stalled legislation (S 1868) designed to discourage religious persecution overseas.

After months of negotiations, Rod Grams, R-Minn., and Chuck Hagel, R-Neb., both chairmen of Senate Foreign Relations subcommittees, persuaded Majority Whip Don Nickles, R-Okla., to water down his bill, which would have required the president to choose from a range of sanctions to punish countries that violate religious freedom.

Grams said the new version agreed to

Religious Persecution

Sept. 24 would minimize tensions with countries not considered major offenders. "We don't have to stand up and slap them in the face," he said.

Under the revised bill, an independent, nine-member commission and the State Department would produce an annual report on religious persecution worldwide. Unlike the earlier version, the report would no longer trigger presidential action. Instead, the president once a year would list countries he believes warrant sanctions.

Senate aides acknowledge the president could simply list countries that already have poor relations with the United States, such as Afghanistan. And even those named might not face sanctions, because the bill would give the president broad waiver authority.

The changes are a victory for business groups concerned that the measure would hurt exports. Hagel and Grams, both farm-state lawmakers, have been sympathetic to such business objections.

Still, Christian Coalition lobbyist Jeff Taylor said the group supports the bill, because it brings high-level attention to the issue of religious persecution. The legislation also calls for an ambassador-at-large to address the issue.

The House passed its own compromise bill (HR 2431 — H Rept 105-480, Parts I-III) in May, which is tougher than the Senate measure.

Compromise Improves Bill's Chances for Passage

OCTOBER 3 — A compromise bill stitched together by Senate Republican Whip Don Nickles of Oklahoma has increased the chance that Congress will pass and President Clinton will sign legislation designed to combat relgious persecution overseas. The measure unveiled Oct. 2 would put into law a deal reached among Republicans last month.

That deal watered down Nickles' original bill (S 1868), which would have given Congress and an independent nine-member commission a greater role in deciding whether to impose sanctions on countries that endorse or permit the persecution of religious believers.

The sanctions range from diplomatic protests to cutting off funds from international financial institutions, such as the World Bank or International Monetary Fund.

The latest version would leave decisions on sanctions largely to the president. But it would require the State Department to produce an annual report on religious persecution abroad and at least privately protest incidents in which governments tacitly or otherwise supported religious persecution.

The bill has been endorsed by major religious groups but still faces opposition from many Democrats and the White House. Hoping to win bipartisan support and avoid procedural hurdles, Nickles met several times with Senate Minority Leader Tom Daschle, D-S.D., and ranking Foreign Relations Committee Democrat Joseph R. Biden Jr. of Delaware.

In an Oct. 1 interview, Biden said they were "90 percent of the way there," but still had some disagreements about his call for requiring that the independent commission would have to be reauthorized in a few years to stay in existence.

Rep. Frank R. Wolf, R-Va., author of a stricter bill (HR 2431— H Rept 105-480, Parts 1-3) that passed the House on May 14, has agreed to let the House consider Nickles' bill in order to avoid convening a conference committee to reconcile the two measures.

Sen. Arlen Specter, R-Pa., who introduced a measure similar to Wolf's, said he would have liked the bill to be "significantly tougher."

"The reality is that we cannot get the president to sign a bill that has the toughness I would prefer," Specter said.

Senate Passes Final Measure By Wide Margin

OCTOBER 10 — After several last-minute concessions by Republicans, lawmakers sent the president a bill aimed at combating religious persecution overseas. The Senate passed the measure, 98-0, on Oct. 9, and the House cleared it by voice vote the following day. (Vote 310, S-48)

The measure (HR 2431) has these main features:

- An ambassador-at-large to monitor and promote religious freedom in other countries.
- A ten-member autonomous commission to monitor progress and advise Congress on efforts to counter religious persecution.
- Annual reports by the State Department examining religious freedom in countries around the globe.
- Authority for the president to invoke diplomatic and economic sanctions against countries that consistently permit or endorse attacks against religious believers.

The final legislation is far less stringent than bills introduced last year by Rep. Frank Wolf, R-Va., and Sen. Arlen Specter, R-Pa., that would have required tough economic sanctions against any country accused of religious persecution by a new White House monitor. The measure also is significantly weaker than the bill passed by the House May 14.

Presidential Discretion

In crafting a compromise, Senate Majority Whip Don Nickles, R-Okla., first had to win over the support of his fellow Republicans.

Under an agreement negotiated with Rod Grams, R-Minn., and Chuck Hagel, R-Neb., both chairmen of Senate Foreign Relations subcommittees, Nickles agreed that multilateral efforts should first be tried before unilateral sanctions were invoked.

Nickles also agreed to give the president much greater discretion in deciding which countries' behavior was so appalling that it would merit sanctions.

Under the legislation, the president would be required once a year to list "countries of concern" that warrant sanctions.

The president would be allowed to waive any sanctions that he believed:
- Were not in the national interest.
- Would actually encourage religious persecution by creating a backlash against members of minority religious groups.
- Were no longer needed because persecution had ended in the country.

The president's waiver authority was broadened Oct. 8 after Sens. Dianne Feinstein, D-Calif., and Max Baucus, D-Mont., threatened to prevent the Senate from taking up the

International Affairs

bill unless changes were made. The two Democrats forced Nickles to loosen the waiver standard from national security to steps "in the national interest."

That change, along with several other alterations to the bill, allowed Nickles to claim the support of Feinstein and Baucus, as well as that of Clinton, who had earlier threatened to veto the legislation.

Expressing Values

Some of the changes came at the prodding of Joseph R. Biden Jr. of Delaware, ranking Democrat on the Senate Foreign Relations Committee. Biden said one change would allow the State Department to hold off on sanctions for 90 days to allow for negotiations to end offensive practices. Another would require Congress to reauthorize the independent commission every four years.

In Senate debate Oct. 9, Joseph I. Lieberman of Connecticut, the bill's Democratic cosponsor, pointed to religious liberty as the cornerstone of the Bill of Rights and cited the support of a broad spectrum of religious groups.

"What we're saying here is that we have the right to express our values. We have the right to put our values at the center of American foreign policy," he said.

Nickles said, "Our purpose in this bill is not to punish any country. Our purpose in this bill is to modify behavior."

But with business groups still opposed to the legislation, even some of the bill's sponsors continued to have misgivings.

Grams, whose International Operations Subcommittee oversees the State Department, said he would carefully monitor how the measure was implemented to see if it damaged other foreign policy goals and ended up creating a backlash against missionaries.

"This is a dangerous area in which we are treading. It is full of pitfalls," Grams said. "We must pay attention to how it is working and have the good sense to end it if it is not." ◆

Clinton Vetoes Iran Sanctions But Vows To Punish Russians For Aiding Iranian Military

SUMMARY

Amid concerns about Iran's growing capability to launch ballistic missiles that could reach other areas of the Middle East and Europe, Congress moved to punish countries that offered technical assistance to Tehran. But the effort stalled after the Clinton administration announced its own steps against seven Russian companies.

Fears about Iran's progress were heightened July 22 when Iran tested the Shahab-3, an 800-mile rocket capable of reaching Israel, Saudi Arabia and U.S. forces in the Middle East.

Although the rocket exploded in flight, the test was successful enough to worry senior U.S. officials. Intelligence reports indicated Iran may be close to deploying missiles that could fly as far as 2,000 miles, congressional sources said.

Although the test missile was based largely on North Korean technology, Russian scientists played a part in its creation and also contributed to work on future missiles, administration officials said.

To cut off this aid, House International Relations Committee Chairman Benjamin A. Gilman, R-N.Y., drafted legislation, primarily aimed at Russia, that would have imposed sanctions on foreign entities helping Iran's missile program.

With the support of pro-Israel groups, the bill sailed through the House by voice vote in 1997. The Senate endorsed the bill overwhelmingly in May 1998, with one change — the House bill would have applied to those that had helped Iran since Aug. 8, 1995; the Senate set the date at Jan. 22, 1998. The House then endorsed the change.

Hoping to induce President Clinton to sign the bill, Gilman coupled it with a measure (S 610) to implement the treaty banning chemical weapons. Clinton, eager not to disturb relations with Moscow or the new more moderate government of Iranian President Mohammad Khatemi, nonetheless vetoed the measure.

Having cleared both chambers by far more than two-thirds majorities, the legislation seemed headed for an override. But House Speaker Newt Gingrich, R-Ga., decided to call off a scheduled vote after the administration announced it was using its own authority to punish seven Russian companies and laboratories for possible aid to Iran.

Box Score

- **Bill:** HR 2709
- **House action:** The House cleared the bill (HR 2709 — H Rept 105-375) on June 9, by agreeing, 392-22, to an amendment approved by the Senate. The House originally passed the bill by voice vote on Nov. 12, 1997.
- **Senate action:** The Senate passed HR 2709 on May 22, 90-4.
- **Presidential action:** Clinton vetoed HR 2709 on June 23, 1998.

Gilman aides said they intend to resurrect the bill — with certain changes — in the 106th Congress. One direction they may take is to tie the bill to U.S. aid to Russia for space station construction by including it in next year's NASA authorization bill.

Support in Senate For Iran Sanctions Still Strong

JANUARY 24 — When Congress was last in session, the Clinton administration persuaded Senate leaders to delay near-certain passage of tough economic sanctions aimed at halting Russian aid for Iranian development of long-range missiles.

Now it appears the administration may have only staved off the inevitable.

The Senate returns the week of Jan. 26, and support for the legislation remains strong; its 84 cosponsors include Majority Leader Trent Lott, R-Miss., and Minority Leader Tom Daschle, D-S.D.

The bill's prospects were further improved by warnings from Israeli Prime Minister Benjamin Netanyahu. During private meetings with Vice President Al Gore and members of Congress Jan. 20-21, he reiterated his concerns about Russian technology transfers to Tehran and the threat that new missiles would pose to Israel.

Senior administration officials, including national security adviser Samuel R. Berger and special envoy Frank G. Wisner, are talking to key members of the Senate about what progress the United States has made in getting Russia to rein in the companies and research institutes that have been assisting Iran with sensitive technology, high-strength metals and other material.

The assessment is certain to include Russia's announcement Jan. 22 that it would impose tighter restrictions on the export of materials that could be used to develop nuclear weapons.

But their effort to persuade lawmakers to give the administration more time to negotiate with the Russians may not be enough. In the first weeks of the session, Congress may hand the president a political and foreign policy nightmare.

The administration strongly opposes the bill, warning that it would jeopardize their delicate negotiations with the Russians to halt the trafficking of technology to Tehran. Senior officials have said they would recommend a presidential veto if the bill is passed.

The House further complicated matters by attaching to the sanctions bill (HR 2709 — H Rept 105-375) separate legislation the White House desperately wants, a Senate-passed bill (S 610) needed to implement the treaty banning chemical weapons. The Senate approved ratification of the treaty last year, but the United States is in violation of the accord until it passes legislation setting criminal penalties and the ground rules for international inspections.

If Clinton is willing to accept the sanctions bill in order to get the treaty legislation, that could exacerbate U.S.-Russian relations, already a bit rocky because of the proposed expansion of NATO to include three former Soviet-bloc nations.

If Clinton vetoes the sanctions legislation, he is certain to anger Israel and its U.S. supporters — the pro-Israel lobby, American Israel Public Affairs Committee (AIPAC), has pushed

18 Years of Punishment

MAY 16 — For the past 18 years, the United States has maintained an almost total ban on trade and financial dealings with Iran, originally because of its seizure of the U.S. Embassy and 52 hostages in Tehran and later due to its support of international terrorism.

Except for information and gifts worth less than $100, nothing may be imported from Iran, and nothing may be exported or sold to Iran, even through third countries, directly or indirectly. That includes overseas subsidiaries of U.S. companies.

Investments, banking or other financial transactions with Iran are prohibited.

The various degrees and types of sanctions have been imposed almost entirely by executive order. Congress has stepped in only once, passing a 1996 law (PL 104-172) that requires the president to impose sanctions on foreign companies that invest in the petroleum industries of Iran or Libya. President Clinton has yet to use the sanctions. (1996 Almanac, p. 9-5)

Ten days after Iranian militants stormed the U.S. Embassy on Nov. 4, 1979, President Jimmy Carter declared a national emergency to deal with the situation. Under the 1977 International Emergency Economic Powers Act (PL 95-223), that gave Carter authority to restrict commerce with Iran, he froze Iranian assets in the United States. The state of emergency has been renewed every year since by each president.

In April 1980, Carter broke diplomatic relations with Iran, banning imports and all exports except food and medicine. The day before President Ronald Reagan was inaugurated in 1981, Carter resumed communications with Tehran and partially lifted the economic embargo. (1980 Almanac, p. 352)

In January 1984, faced with evidence of Iran's complicity in the bombing of a U.S. Marine barracks in Beirut the previous October, Reagan strengthened export controls on Iran. Over the next two years, the Reagan administration became involved in an arms-for-hostages deal with Tehran, part of the Iran-contra scandal.

Reagan imposed new import and export controls on Iran in October 1987, using the anti-terrorism authority of the 1985 International Security and Development Cooperation Act (PL 99-83).

In the spring of 1995, Clinton issued orders banning U.S. involvement in Iran's oil development and tightening trade restrictions. In a 1997 order clarifying U.S. policy, Clinton banned virtually all trade and investment activity with Iran. Corporate criminal penalties for violations can reach half a million dollars.

hard for the sanctions bill — and raise questions about the hard-line U.S. policy toward Iran.

Earlier this month, Iranian President Mohammad Khatami appealed to the American people for a "crack in the wall of mistrust" between the two nations, but the message from Iran has been a mix of overture and attack.

A veto also would create a political opportunity for Republicans who have gone to great lengths to blame the president for the frayed relationship between the United States and its Mideast ally Israel.

International Affairs

Regional Threat

The administration recognizes that the stakes are high.

Gore telephoned Russian Prime Minister Victor Chernomyrdin on Jan. 17. They discussed the "continuing efforts to stop the flow of technology to Iran's ballistic missile program and agreed that both governments will intensify efforts to prevent these technology transfers from occurring," said Jonathan Spalter, the vice president's spokesman. "Both governments agreed that this problem poses a threat to regional stability and to the national interests of Russia and the United States," he said.

The sanctions bill would require the Clinton administration to publish periodic reports identifying overseas companies or research institutes that have transferred, or have attempted to transfer, prohibited missile-related technology to Iran since Aug. 8, 1995, the date Russia signed the Missile Technology Control Regime, a multilateral agreement to prevent the spread of ballistic missiles.

Though the bill does not specifically mention Russia, the companies and labs most frequently cited are all Russian.

Sanctions, including a ban on any U.S. economic aid, would be imposed for at least two years against any organization in violation.

The administration is particularly concerned about the low threshold that would trigger sanctions.

Under the bill, "credible information" of a violation would result in the penalties. Other laws that would require economic sanctions to deter weapons proliferation call for sanctions only if a "preponderance of the evidence" shows a violation.

The House-passed bill, which the Senate would consider when lawmakers return, would allow the president to waive the required sanctions on national security grounds.

The Senate version of the legislation (S 1311) does not include the waiver. That bill, sponsored by Lott and Sen. Joseph I. Lieberman, D-Conn., is pending before the Foreign Relations Committee.

Strong Sentiment

Spurred by published reports of the technology transfers and the assessment from Israeli intelligence of Russian help for Iran, the House moved quickly on the legislation. The International Relations Committee approved the measure Oct. 24, and the House passed it by voice vote Nov. 12.

Both House Speaker Newt Gingrich, R-Ga., and Minority Leader Richard A. Gephardt, D-Mo., were among more than 100 House cosponsors of the bill.

Lawmakers complained that the administration had the tools to punish those who aid Iran under other sanctions legislation but had failed to exercise its authority. The sentiment was the same in the Senate.

"An Iran with weapons of mass destruction is arguably the single biggest threat that faces the United States and its allies," Sen. Sam Brownback, R-Kan., chairman of the Foreign Relations Subcommittee on Near Eastern and South Asian Affairs, said Jan. 21. "Armed with weapons of mass destruction, Iran's rogue regime will be a menace to world security."

The Senate was poised to pass the sanctions bill Nov. 13, but an appeal from the administration to hold off persuaded Senate leaders to wait.

The White House argued that moving forward with the legislation before Wisner's trip to Moscow in January for talks with the Russians would undermine delicate negotiations. Clinton appointed Wisner, the former ambassador to India, in July 1997 to serve as a special envoy on the Russian weapons proliferation issue.

Critical Report

With Congress' return, the administration will have to come up with significant progress in the U.S.-Russian negotiations and the promise of more concessions by Russia to head off the legislation.

Lott was willing to give the administration some time to brief lawmakers on the situation before bringing the sanctions bill to a vote in the Senate.

Before Congress' return, the Republican majority on the Governmental Affairs Subcommittee on International Security, Proliferation and Federal Services issued a report sharply critical of the administration's effort to halt nuclear weapons proliferation.

"By speaking loudly but carrying a small stick, the Clinton administration risks its non-proliferation credibility and America's security," said the report, issued Jan. 12.

The report, based on the subcommittee's 1997 hearings under the chairmanship of Sen. Thad Cochran, R-Miss., examines the role of China, Russia, North Korea and the United States in providing technology and missile delivery systems that would allow rogue nations to develop weapons of mass destruction.

The subcommittee report said research institutes and companies that once were part of the military complex in the Soviet Union reportedly have provided equipment and material that can be used to develop ballistic missiles, including the Shahab-3, which could hit Israel, and the Shahab-4, which could strike targets in central Europe. The two reportedly are based on North Korean and Russian missiles.

"Most troubling," the report said, "is an assessment that if the flow of Russian missile technology to Iran is not stopped within a year, Tehran's missile program will become largely self-sufficient and less vulnerable to international pressures."

Republicans concluded that "the administration should do more than engage in discussions with Russia's leaders."

The GOP majority took a step toward punishing Russia in legislation the president did sign on Nov. 26, the fiscal 1998 foreign operations spending bill (HR 2159 — PL 105-118).

The bill contains a provision that would withhold 50 percent of aid to Russia if it fails to stop sharing sensitive military technology with Iran.

The president could waive the provision if he notifies Congress that the aid is in U.S. national security interests and that Russia is taking steps to curtail the transfer of technology to Iran.

Senate Votes To Impose Sanctions On Aid to Iran's Missile Program

MAY 23 — Despite a veto threat, the Senate on May 22 passed, 90-4, legislation that seeks to punish overseas companies and research labs that provide sophisticated missile technology to Iran.

The Clinton administration argued that the measure (HR 2709) could undermine relations with Russia, home to many of the companies and labs suspected of providing the technology to Iran.

The White House last year tried to delay action on the legislation, but support was broad in both chambers. The bill passed the House by voice vote in November, and a companion Senate version (S 1311) had 84 co-sponsors.

Majority Leader Trent Lott, R-Miss., said Iran's ability to procure weapons technology is "one of the most pressing international security questions we face." He also noted that the legislation would allow the president to waive sanctions for national security reasons. "We have tried to accommodate his concerns," Lott said.

The measure would require the administration to apply specific economic sanctions to companies trading arms technology to Iran.

Joseph I. Lieberman, D-Conn., said the measure would "delay the day rapidly approaching when Iran will have nuclear weapons."

In a May 21 policy statement on the bill, the administration said the standard of evidence of technology transfers is so low that sanctions might be applied against companies that had not aided Iran.

Joseph R. Biden Jr. of Delware, the ranking Democrat on the Foreign Relations Committee, said the bill could have the "exact opposite effect" sponsors wanted by hampering the administration's diplomatic leverage on Russia to institute a meaningful non-proliferation policy covering exports to Iran.

One argument against the bill was that companies that had shared technology with Iran in the past would have no incentive to refrain in the future, since the legislation would penalize those who transferred material after Aug. 8, 1995.

By voice vote, the Senate adopted an amendment by Carl Levin, D-Mich., that would move the date to Jan. 22, 1998. The bill must return to the House for consideration of the amendment.

Both the House and Senate versions of the bill include legislation (S 610) that would implement the treaty banning chemical weapons (Treaty Doc 103-21) that the Senate ratified last year.

Republican leaders added the chemical weapons provisions last year in an attempt to induce Clinton to sign the Iran sanctions measure.

House Clears Iran Sanctions Bill By Wide Margin

JUNE 13 — President Clinton might soon lose a veto battle with Congress for only the third time, in this case over economic sanctions.

The House on June 9 voted 392-22 to accept Senate amendments and thus clear legislation (HR 2709) that seeks to punish overseas research labs and companies that provide missile technology to Iran. *(Vote 211, p. H-62)*

Administration officials have recommended a veto, saying the bill could damage relations with Russia and undermine efforts to work with the Kremlin to prevent the leakage of missile technology. Several Russian companies and labs are suspected of helping Iran develop missiles.

If Clinton vetoes the bill, he will also reject attached legislation (S 610) that would implement a global treaty banning chemical weapons (Treaty Doc 103-21) that the Senate ratified last year. GOP leaders added the chemical weapons provisions in an attempt to induce Clinton to sign the Iran sanctions measure.

The bill passed both chambers by far more than the two-thirds necessary to override a veto. GOP leaders indicated that whether they attempt an override would depend on what Russia does in coming weeks to halt the transfers.

The House passed the bill by voice vote in November, but the Senate attached an amendment that would take into account a Russian decree earlier this year beefing up its export control regime. The bill would only punish those companies or labs that had transferred technology after Jan. 22, rather than since Aug. 8, 1995.

Supporters said the change showed Congress was making a good-faith effort to work with the Russian government.

"We are challenging them fairly and squarely to stop cheating, and we are saying to the Clinton administration, 'No more winking at violations, no more giving the benefit of the doubt to those who do not deserve it'," said House Intelligence Committee Chairman Porter J. Goss, R-Fla.

Some Democrats, such as Minority Leader Richard A. Gephardt of Missouri, argued that the legislation could harm efforts by Russia to crack down on the flow of missile technology.

"I am concerned that the passage of this legislation today will signal to Russia that we care more about sanctions than we do about the efforts it has made to address our concerns," Gephardt said.

Gephardt said his sentiments were shared by the Israeli government, a notion disputed by House International Relations Committee Chairman Benjamin A. Gilman, R-N.Y.

Pro-Israel groups have been prime movers behind the legislation, fearing that without U.S intervention, Iran will develop the capability to hit targets in the Middle East and Europe.

Iran Overtures Get Cold Shoulder On Capitol Hill

JUNE 20 — Secretary of State Madeleine K. Albright's vaunted relationship with Congress clearly has its limits, as her efforts to forge a new approach to Iran demonstrate.

Speaking June 17 at a dinner of the Asia Society in New York, Albright unveiled what was the administration's most direct overture to the government of Iran's moderate president, Mohammad Khatami.

The United States, Albright said, is ready to take steps toward normalizing relations between the countries, isolated from each other since the 1979 hostage crisis. "Obviously two decades of mistrust cannot be erased overnight. The gap between us remains wide," Albright said. "But it is time to test the possibilities of bridging this gap. Failure to do so would be irresponsible."

Albright noted that Khatami had moved toward several U.S. goals by publicly denouncing terrorism, softening Iran's opposition to the Middle

International Affairs

Current Sanctions

AUGUST 15 — Acting by itself or within an alliance, the United States has imposed a wide range of sanctions, from full economic embargoes to bans on military weapons sales, on dozens of countries. Below are some of the more significant sanctions now in effect and when the restrictions were first imposed. Most often, the president imposes the sanctions under the authority of previous law; those laws also are summarized below:

Angola, 1993
Type: Sanctions on the powerful UNITA faction are the only U.N. sanctions against a non-governmental entity. The embargo includes the sale of petroleum, arms, military equipment and restrictions on air travel.
Reason: Violence after U.N.-monitored elections in 1992. Failure to implement 1994 Lusaka protocol peace agreement.
Legislative authority: Executive Order in coordination with U.N. sanctions, Arms Export Control Act of 1968.

Azerbaijan, 1992
Type: Prohibits foreign assistance funds.
Reason: Azerbaijan's blockade against Armenia and Nagorno-Karabakh enclave.
Legislative authority: Arms Export Control Act, fiscal 1998 foreign operations appropriations act.

Cambodia, on/off since 1992
Type: Prohibits foreign assistance funds (except for humanitarian aid, elections or land mine removal).
Reason: Repression of opposition in election, failure to implement peace agreement.
Legislative authority: Fiscal 1998 foreign operations act.

China, 1989
Type: Export restrictions, restrictions on foreign assistance funds, prohibition on use of funds made available to the U.N. Population Fund for activities in China.
Reason: Tiananmen Square repression of democratic demonstrators.
Legislative authority: Export-Import Bank Act of 1945, Arms Export Control Act, fiscal 1998 foreign operations act.

Congo (formerly Zaire), 1990
Type: Aid restrictions.
Reason: U.S. opposition to regimes of Mobutu Sese Seko and Laurent Kabila.
Legislative authority: Arms Export Control Act, fiscal 1998 foreign operations act.

Cuba, 1960
Type: Broad sanctions on exports and imports; restrictions on travel; restrictions on investment in Cuba. Exceptions for journalists and diplomatic exchanges.
Reason: Takeover by Fidel Castro, repression of opposition, interventions in Africa in the 1980s.
Legislative authority: Trading with the Enemy Act, Foreign Assistance Act of 1961, Arms Export Control Act, Cuba Sanctions (Helms-Burton) Act, fiscal 1998 foreign operations act.

Gambia, 1994
Type: Aid restrictions with exceptions for humanitarian aid.
Reason: Military coup.
Legislative authority: Foreign Assistance Act of 1961.

Guatemala, 1990
Type: Prohibits foreign military financing funds.
Reason: Human rights violations.
Legislative authority: Fiscal 1998 foreign operations act.

Haiti, 1997
Type: Restrictions on aid (except humanitarian, election-related, antinarcotics, or law enforcement funds).
Reason: Political unrest.
Legislative authority: Fiscal 1998 foreign operations act.

India, 1998
Type: Restrictions on foreign assistance funds, bank loans to government or to finance trade.
Reason: Nuclear tests.
Legislative authority: Arms Export Control Act.

Iran, on/off since 1980
Type: Comprehensive trade and financial sanctions; ban on new investments.
Reason: Terrorist activities, efforts to acquire weapons of mass destruction, opposition to Middle East peace process.
Legislative authority: Foreign Assistance Act of 1961, International Security and Development Cooperation Act of 1985, Iran-Iraq Arms Nonproliferation Act of 1992, Iran-Libya Sanctions Act of 1996, fiscal 1998 foreign operations act.

Iraq, 1990
Type: Restrictions on commercial and financial activities, export and import sanctions; travel restrictions.
Reason: Attempt to acquire nuclear weapons, invasion of Kuwait.
Legislative authority: Foreign Assistance Act of 1961, International Emergency Economic Powers Act of 1977, International Security and Development Cooperation Act, Iran-Iraq Arms Non-proliferation Act of 1992, fiscal 1998 foreign operations act.

Liberia, 1992
Type: Arms embargo.
Reason: Civil war.
Legislative authority: Fiscal 1998 foreign operations act.

Libya, 1986
Type: Ban on economic and foreign assistance; ban on imports and exports, with exceptions for informational materials (books, magazines, films) and relief items. Travel ban for U.S. citizens.
Reason: Support for terrorism.
Legislative authority: Foreign Assistance Act of 1961, Internation-

al Emergency Economic Powers Act, International Security and Development Cooperation Act, Iran-Libya Sanctions Act, fiscal 1998 foreign operations act.

Myanmar (formerly Burma), 1988
Type: Prohibition against new investment and restrictions on government-to-government assistance; travel restrictions and ban on arms sales.
Reason: Failure to cooperate with international anti-narcotics efforts (in place since 1988) and repression of democratic opposition in elections (enacted in 1997).
Legislative authority: Foreign Assistance Act of 1961, Arms Export Control Act, International Emergency Economic Powers Act, Fiscal 1998 foreign operations act.

Niger, 1996
Type: Bans financial assistance, except for humanitarian aid.
Reason: Military coup.
Legislative authority: Foreign Assistance Act of 1961.

Nigeria, 1993
Type: Bans military training assistance and foreign aid; institutes travel ban.
Reason: Military suppression of democratization; failure to fully cooperate in counternarcotics efforts.
Legislative authority: Foreign Assistance Act of 1961.

North Korea, 1950
Type: Bans exports, except for informational materials, and all imports; relief aid approved on a case-by-case basis.
Reason: Korean War; suspected of stockpiling nuclear weapons.
Legislative authority: Trading with the Enemy Act, Foreign Assistance Act of 1961, fiscal 1998 foreign operations act.

Pakistan, 1979
Type: Ban on government loans, financial assistance, military and dual-use exports. Restrictions on private lending to Pakistani government. Ban on foreign assistance (imposed under previous sanctions). (Some sanctions have been periodically waived by presidential order.)
Reason: Nuclear weapons program, nuclear tests.
Legislative authority: Foreign Assistance Act of 1961, Arms Export Control Act.

Sudan, 1997
Type: Comprehensive economic and trade sanctions; ban on military financing.
Reason: Support for terrorism; human rights violations.
Legislative authority: International Emergency Economic Powers Act.

Syria, 1986
Type: Ban on bilateral and multilateral financial assistance, military sales; ban on dual-use exports, or anything that would enhance Syria's military capabilities.
Reason: Support for terrorism.
Legislative authority: Foreign Assistance Act of 1961, fiscal 1998 foreign operations act.

Yugoslavia (Republic of Serbia and Montenegro), 1992
Type: Full-scale trade embargo, currently suspended; assets blocked in United States; ban on investment in Serbia.
Reason: Civil war, political situation in Kosovo.
Legislative authority: International Emergency Economic Powers Act.

Laws:
Trading with the Enemy Act of 1917 (PL 65-91) World War I law allowed president to impose economic restrictions during war or national emergency. Provisions included authority to control foreign exchange, gold and foreign property.

Export-Import Bank Act of 1945 (PL 79-83) Prohibited the bank from supporting countries involved in terrorism, nuclear proliferation or human rights abuses.

Foreign Assistance Act of 1961 (PL 87-195) Allowed the restriction of foreign aid in cases of illegal activities, such as human rights violations, press censorship or limits on religious freedom. *(1961 Almanac, p. 293)*

Arms Export Control Act of 1968 (PL 90-629) Part of a supplemental appropriations act, it permitted sanctions against countries that spread nuclear arms or when the president deemed them necessary for world and U.S. security. *(1968 Almanac, p. 523)*

International Emergency Economic Powers Act of 1977 (PL 95-223) Amended the Trading with the Enemy Act to remove wartime as a necessary condition for the president to restrict overseas financial transactions or freeze foreign assets; allowed export embargoes during national emergency and economic embargoes. *(1977 Almanac, p. 412)*

International Security and Development Cooperation Act of 1985 (PL 99-83) Part of the fiscal 1986 foreign aid bill, it authorized the president to ban imports from countries involved in terrorism. *(1985 Almanac, p.41)*

Iran-Iraq Arms Non-Proliferation Act of 1992 (PL 102-484) Part of a defense authorization act, it imposed sanctions on governments and companies that transferred technology to Iran or Iraq that could be used to develop advanced weapons. *(1992 Almanac, p. 483)*

Cuba sanctions (Helms-Burton) Act of 1996 (PL 104-114) Codified U.S. economic embargo on Cuba. Effectively prohibited normal trade while Fidel Castro retains power. *(1996 Almanac, p. 9-6)*

Iran-Libya Sanctions Act of 1996 (PL 104-172) Imposed sanctions against foreign companies that invested in the oil industries of Iran or Libya or that sold goods such as weapons or oil equipment to Libya. *(1996 Almanac, p. 9-5)*

Fiscal 1998 Foreign Operations Appropriations Act (PL 105-118) Imposed a variety of restrictions on countries that include Cambodia, China and Guatemala. *(1997 Almanac, p. 9-37)*

International Affairs

East peace process and improving relations with Saudi Arabia and other Persian Gulf states.

Clinton echoed her comments June 18. "What we want," he said, "is a genuine reconciliation with Iran based on mutuality and reciprocity and a sense the Iranians are prepared to move away from support of terrorism and distribution of dangerous weapons, opposition to the peace process."

Albright's initiative is similar to one proposed in April by Lee H. Hamilton of Indiana, the ranking Democrat on the House International Relations Committee.

But it runs counter to the views of most lawmakers, who say there is little reason to improve relations because of Iran's support for terrorism and its efforts to acquire chemical, biological and nuclear weapons.

Congress recently approved legislation (HR 2709 — H Rept 105-375) that would impose sanctions on countries that supply missile technology to Iran to prevent the Islamic regime from threatening Israel and other Middle Eastern countries with weapons of mass destruction. Clinton is expected to veto the legislation, which he must do by June 23 or the bill will become law.

Lawmakers objected to a Clinton administration decision to waive sanctions under the 1996 Iran-Libya sanctions act (PL 104-172) against three foreign companies that invested in Iran's oil industry. They also objected to Albright's indications that the president would probably waive penalties for similar investments by European companies. (*1996 Almanac, p. 9-5*)

Sen. Alfonse M. D'Amato, R-N.Y., the chief sponsor of the sanctions law, said, "The administration can always be hopeful [about Iran], but first we've got to see some positive acts on their part."

Clinton Vetoes Sanctions on Iran Missile Aid

JUNE 27 — President Clinton will have to contend with a bipartisan effort to overturn one of his foreign policy vetoes when Congress returns from its July Fourth recess.

In an effort to maintain good relations with Russia and reach out to Iran, Clinton on June 23 vetoed legislation (HR 2709) primarily aimed at Russia that would impose sanctions on companies and research labs that provide missile technology to Iran. The bill passed both houses of Congress by overwhelming margins.

To induce Clinton to sign the bill, Congress included legislation that would implement the Chemical Weapons Convention the Senate ratified last year.

In his veto message, Clinton said the bill would make it harder to work with Russia on a range of issues, including nuclear proliferation and law enforcement. He discounted his ability to waive sanctions on national security grounds.

White House press secretary Mike McCurry said the White House did not want to undermine Secretary of State Madeleine K. Albright's recent overture to Iran's moderate president, Mohammad Khatami.

Clinton's decision drew bipartisan criticism on Capitol Hill, with some of the strongest attacks coming from members of his party.

"The president's veto of this bill will create the appearance that the administration is not as committed as it claims to be in preventing Iran from threatening the world with long-range missiles and nuclear, chemical, and biological weapons warheads," said Democratic Rep. Howard L. Berman of California.

Clinton Escapes Veto Override

JULY 18 — President Clinton may have narrowly averted the third veto override of his White House tenure.

House Speaker Newt Gingrich, R-Ga., postponed a July 17 attempt to overturn Clinton's veto of legislation (HR 2709 — H Rept 105-375) that would punish overseas research laboratories and companies that provide missile technology to Iran.

The bill includes legislation that would implement a treaty banning chemical weapons, something Clinton wants and which Republican leaders included as an inducement for him to sign the sanctions bill.

Republicans decided to put off the veto override vote after the Clinton administration announced July 15 it was taking steps to punish seven Russian companies and labs for possible aid to Iran's missile program.

The White House said it would cut off assistance to the labs, such as contracts for work on the international space station, a step called for in the bill.

Vice President Al Gore said the administration would go one step farther by banning those organizations from trading with the United States.

The White House announcement immediately followed what Gore termed an "encouraging step forward" by the Russian government commission on export controls.

Moscow announced that it was investigating the same organizations, as well as two others, and that they may face criminal and administrative charges for exporting goods and services that could have civilian and military uses. The Russian government also pledged to finish drafting a law to tighten export controls.

Russia is the principal target of the legislation, strongly backed by pro-Israel groups, which aims to prevent Iran from developing medium- and long-range missiles that could hit targets in the Middle East and Europe.

Nonetheless, Republicans were skeptical that the White House plan had any real teeth. GOP aides noted that several Russian entities that could have been sanctioned by the bill escaped punishment.

"They cut off nonexistent aid and barely existent trade, " said one Republican aide.

The bill's author, International Relations Committee Chairman Benjamin A. Gilman, R-N.Y., called the changes "a cynical effort to head off an override of the president's veto."

But the changes appeared to have made headway with congressional Democrats.

Placating Democrats

The bill passed both chambers of Congress with overwhelming bipartisan support. The House cleared the bill last month, 392-22, while the Senate passed the measure in May by a similarly lopsided 90-4 vote.

But GOP aides said that with the administration's announcement, they could no longer count on enough Democrats to garner the two-thirds majority needed to override a veto.

Howard L. Berman of California, a key Democratic supporter of the legislation, said he thought it was "best to leave the override aside and not take it up while we see the implementation of these announcements."

"I am very pleased that the Russian government has initiated an investigation and thrilled that the administration has said it will institute an embargo [on trade]," Berman said.

Republican aides, though, groused that any sanctions may have come too late to slow improvements in the range and accuracy of Iran's Shahab missiles.

Lawmakers were expected to hold the legislation in reserve in case the administration backslides on its promises to halt the proliferation of Russian technology.

"This will be hanging over their head like the sword of Damocles," said one GOP aide. ◆

House Bill Takes Aim At Iranian Reactor

AUGUST 8 — Concerned about Iran's efforts to develop nuclear weapons, the House voted overwhelmingly Aug. 3 to prevent the International Atomic Energy Agency from using U.S. money to aid nuclear power plant programs in that country.

The legislation (HR 3743), passed 405-13, would affect only a small portion of U.S. contributions to the agency, which tries to ensure compliance with the nuclear non-proliferation treaty. The bill would affect some of the $16 million the United States voluntarily contributes to the agency's technical assistance and cooperation fund. (Vote 377, p. H-106)

The measure targets the one-third U.S. share of the $1.6 million the fund will spend on the safety of a $1 billion nuclear power plant Iran is building with Russian help in Bushehr on the country's Persian Gulf coast. The regular $40 million U.S. contribution to the agency would be untouched.

The measure's sponsor, Robert Menendez, D-N.J., hinted that Iran might use the plant to develop nuclear weapons and said it is "ludicrous for the United States to support in any way a plant, even indirectly, which could pose a threat to the United States and to stability in the Middle East."

Lee H. Hamilton of Indiana, the ranking Democrat on the International Relations Committee, said the bill would have "zero impact on whether Iran builds a civilian nuclear reactor."

Republicans Voice Criticism Of White House Attempts To Warm Relations With China

President Clinton's nine-day trip to China in June and July highlighted a stormy year in U.S.-China relations: The administration moved toward closer ties with Beijing, while Republicans criticized from the sidelines but largely avoided actions that would have blocked better relations.

SUMMARY

The major fight was over Clinton's easing of restrictions on technology sales to China. In particular, Republicans criticized his efforts to make it easier for U.S. companies to launch satellites aboard Chinese rockets, saying he had allowed Beijing to acquire missile technology that could be used against the United States. And they claimed that big Democratic contributors such as Bernard L. Schwartz, former chief executive officer of satellite maker Loral Space and Communications, had helped influence Clinton's decision.

At one point, nearly a dozen congressional committees investigated the issue. But as time wore on and the Monica Lewinsky sex scandal took precedence, the work largely fell to the Senate Intelligence Committee and a special House committee set up to conduct the inquiry. Both were scheduled to release final reports by the end of the year. Congressional committees also continued to investigate whether the Chinese government had illegally attempted to influence U.S. political campaigns through campaign contributions.

Without waiting for the reports, lawmakers took steps in the fiscal 1999 defense authorization bill (HR 3616) to hinder the potential transfer of missile technology to China by shifting responsibility for satellite export licensing from the Commerce Department to the State Department.

They also took another slap at China by adopting an amendment by Sen. Tim Hutchinson, R-Ark., to the fiscal 1999 defense appropriations bill (HR 4103) primarily aimed at Beijing, that would deny U.S. visas to officials of

International Affairs

foreign governments directly involved in implementing policies of religious persecution, forced abortion or sterilization, or female genital mutilation.

In March, each chamber passed a resolution (S Res 187, H Res 364) urging the administration to pursue a resolution in the United Nations condemning China's human rights record.

Opponents of Clinton's China policy lost ground on the annual vote to maintain normal trade relations with Beijing. Seven fewer representatives than in 1997 voted for a resolution (H J Res 121) to overturn Clinton's decision to continue China's trade status, permitting non-discriminatory tariffs. Opponents also lost a lexicographic victory when China supporters were able to change most-favored-nation trade status to normal trade relations.

SATELLITE SCANDAL

Lawmakers Agree To Probe China's Export Waiver

MAY 23 — Democrats and Republicans who have been feuding over accusations of campaign finance improprieties moved quickly to support an investigation of allegations that President Clinton harmed national security when he waived tough export controls to allow U.S. companies to launch their satellites aboard inexpensive Chinese rockets.

The two parties also moved in unison in the House on May 20, voting to cut off the satellite trade with China.

Where they differ is on the broader foreign policy implications of Clinton's decision, the role played by campaign contributions and the extent of the president's personal responsibility for any security breaches that occurred.

Republicans charged that Clinton's decision was tied to campaign contributions by satellite executives and that it set off a chain of events that ended up giving China technology it could use to aim ballistic missiles more accurately at the United States. The GOP said those events frightened China's neighbors, leading India to test five nuclear bombs the week of May 11 as a deterrent.

"Our national security has been threatened by this Asian arms race, which has been unwittingly jump-started by the political hacks at the White House," said Majority Whip Tom DeLay, R-Texas, during a House debate May 19.

A group of 152 Republican House members and eight GOP senators wrote Clinton that the allegations required a reassessment of the entire U.S.-Beijing relationship, starting with cancellation of Clinton's planned visit to Beijing in June.

"He should not be going to China without a new American foreign policy towards China," said Rep. Duncan Hunter, R-Calif.

GOP support for China's most-favored-nation (MFN) trade status was also imperiled.

Democrats such as John P. Murtha of Pennsylvania, ranking member of the House Appropriations Committee's National Security Subcommittee, said that "the biggest mistake we could make is not to deal with China," even after the latest revelations.

Moreover, they said Republicans had likely exaggerated the damage to national security.

"Unbelievably wild charges have been made for political purposes," said Rep. Howard L. Berman, D-Calif. "It's going to take a long time to get to the bottom of this."

Many Democrats said that by waiving export controls, Clinton had done nothing more than Presidents George Bush and Ronald Reagan had done when Republicans controlled the White House.

They dismissed allegations that Clinton's February decision to license Loral Space & Communications to launch a satellite aboard a Chinese *Long March* rocket was influenced by generous campaign contributions to the Democratic Party from Loral board chairman Bernard Schwartz.

Rep. Paul E. Kanjorski, D-Pa., said he would resign if Republicans could prove that for campaign funds Clinton would "risk the country's security, violate his oath of office, commit treason, and subject not only every man, woman and child in America, but the 6 billion people of this world to nuclear war."

Still, Democrats approved a nonbinding, bipartisan resolution saying that Clinton had failed to act in "the national interest" and, over White House objections, supported efforts to cut off launches of U.S. satellites in China during debate on the fiscal 1999 defense authorization bill (HR 3616).

While Democrats argued over the format of the probes, they backed GOP plans to look into why Clinton approved the Loral satellite launch despite Justice Department concerns.

The department had warned administration officials that by granting a waiver, Clinton might interfere with an ongoing criminal investigation. That probe was looking into whether Loral and Hughes Electronics Corp. officials, in determining the cause of a 1996 launch rocket failure in China, had illegally shared information with Chinese officials on how to improve its civilian rockets — information that could also improve its military missile program. China's largest military and civilian rockets are essentially identical.

Over Democratic objections, House Speaker Newt Gingrich, R-Ga., called for the formation of a select committee of five Republicans and three Democrats to investigate the allegations. Senate Majority Leader Trent Lott, R-Miss., asked the Senate Intelligence Committee to play the lead role in a similar effort, and he assembled an eight-member GOP task force to coordinate the investigation with several other committees.

One of those panels, the Senate Governmental Affairs Subcommittee on International Security, Proliferation and Federal Services, held its first hearing May 21. The hearing revealed wide partisan rifts.

"It sounds to me like a situation where militarily significant technology transfer can occur and probably has occurred," said subcommittee Chairman Thad Cochran, R-Miss. "I think it's clear that the administration's export control policy for communications satellites isn't doing a good enough job of reducing the risk to American security."

Subcommittee Democrats said Clinton has only been continuing a procedure initiated by Reagan in 1988 and followed by Bush.

"It has made no difference whether the president was named Bush or Clinton — those waivers have been approved," said Carl Levin, D-Mich.

Top Individual Campaign Donor Is a Familiar Figure in Washington

MAY 23 — Bernard Schwartz was little known to most Americans before the publicity stemming from allegations that he helped hand over sensitive technology to the Chinese government and tried to buy political influence with campaign contributions. But Schwartz has long been known to Washington politicians.

The chairman of Loral Space and Communications Ltd., Schwartz was the biggest individual donor of campaign cash during the 1995-96 election cycle. He gave a total of $651,000 to individual candidates and the national parties — mainly Democrats. And Schwartz is well on his way to the top of the list again this election cycle. In 1997-98, Schwartz gave at least $393,000 to Democrats.

Loral's political action committee (PAC) — funded by Schwartz employees — also has been a player in political campaigns. In 1997, the Loral SpaceCom Civic Responsibility Fund gave $65,775 to mostly Democratic candidates, including Sen. Daniel Patrick Moynihan of New York, Sen. Barbara Boxer of California and Rep. Jane Harman of California, who is running for governor. So far in 1998, the PAC has contributed $22,500 to candidates from both parties, including Sen. John McCain, R-Ariz., Sen. Barbara A. Mikulski, D-Md., Rep. Robert L. Livingston, R-La., and Rep. John D. Dingell, D-Mich.

Such large campaign contributions have certainly caught the eye of political heavyweights. In the past six months, Schwartz has been to the White House three times for events with President Clinton. He attended two parties there in December — one a holiday event, the other a celebration for the Kennedy Center. Schwartz was also invited to the White House state dinner for British Prime Minister Tony Blair on Feb. 5. Later that month, Clinton signed a waiver allowing Loral to launch one of its satellites using a Chinese rocket. The waiver irked Justice Department officials, who were already investigating Loral for earlier dealings with the Chinese.

In August 1994, Schwartz was invited by the late Commerce Secretary Ronald H. Brown to travel on a department trade mission to China. Three months before the trip, Schwartz donated $100,000 to the Democratic National Committee.

Schwartz has even been considered on several occasions as a possible nominee for defense secretary.

But Schwartz and Loral strongly deny there is any connection between his contributions and his access to top government officials.

"Absolutely not," said Loral spokesman Tom Ross. "He contributes out of conviction, not because he's seeking favors."

The 72-year-old Schwartz took over Loral in 1972, when it was a small, struggling defense electronics company worth about $7 million. He eventually built it into a major player in the defense industry using shrewd business and investment skills. He sold most of the company to Lockheed Martin in 1996 for $9.1 billion, but held on to the portion of the business that dealt with telecommunications satellites.

Schwartz has always been a bit of an enigma in his business. Born to a working-class family in Brooklyn, N.Y., Schwartz, who is Jewish and a longtime Democrat, stood out in the defense industry, which is dominated by conservative Westerners. He attended City College of New York and later joined the Army during World War II — although he never served in battle. After his military service, Schwartz became an accountant.

When he finally entered the defense business in the 1970s, Schwartz was an outspoken opponent of the Vietnam War, even while he was winning contracts from the Pentagon.

"For him, one of the very satisfying aspects with the military as a defense contractor was that he felt they treated him with scrupulous fairness despite his feelings about Vietnam," Ross said.

Cochran's subcommittee plans to hold another hearing in June on the Commerce Department's procedures for granting licenses to U.S. satellite companies to launch from China. The May 21 hearing featured testimony from scientists about the many similarities between commercial satellite launchers and intercontinental ballistic missiles (ICBMs).

Governmental Affairs Chairman Fred Thompson, R-Tenn., acknowledged, however, that "no one here can know where technology has been transferred in a way that could compromise our interests."

Thompson said the administration should have been more cautious about how it licensed companies doing business with China. "There is no question that the standards have been relaxed with regard to the transfer of this technology and the export licensing," he said.

In September 1988, Reagan approved the launch of three communications satellites built by Hughes Aircraft on China's *Long March* rocket boosters, the first time the United States allowed a non-Western government to handle a U.S.-made satellite.

The decision was intended to keep the satellite industry competitive in the wake of the January 1986 explosion of the space shuttle *Challenger*. After the explosion, Reagan ordered the shuttle program to carry only military and scientific payloads and barred any commercial materials aboard.

International Affairs

To send satellites to countries such as China, companies must obtain an export license. Since the 1989 Tiananmen Square crackdown, commercial satellite shipments to China have been prohibited unless the president, on a case-by-case basis, issues a waiver determining that such shipments are in the national interest or that China has made political and human rights reforms.

In April 1995, Secretary of State Warren M. Christopher began an interagency review of restrictions on the export of communications satellites and recommended that satellites be kept under his department's purview. Commerce Secretary Ronald H. Brown appealed the decision to Clinton.

In March 1996, Clinton had the authority for issuing export licenses for satellites transferred to Commerce, a decision Thompson said exposed the administration's lack of regard for security.

"We saw the administration's national security process at work," he said. "Secretary Christopher convened an interagency group . . . and it was overridden on the recommendation of Ron Brown."

Levin produced a list of 20 waivers for exports of satellites launched by China since December 1989. Bush approved nine over three years and Clinton approved 11 in four and a half years.

Levin said all 20 waivers had been subject to National Security Council review. Clinton, at a May 22 news conference, said his waiver decisions were made "in the routine course of business, consistent with the 10-year-old policy" started by Reagan.

Thompson and Cochran said Clinton had not merely extended previous practice. "There is a transfer that contains militarily significant material," Thompson said, "and a transfer that does not."

Concern about the transfer of missile technology and new allegations of Chinese political contributions to U.S. campaigns spilled into the other areas of U.S.-China relations, with lawmakers showing stronger support for legislation taking a more confrontational stance towards Beijing.

"People seem more willing to act, now that they see blood in the water," said Sen. Tim Hutchinson, R-Ark., who has long championed a hard-line stance toward Beijing.

In one indication, the Senate Foreign Relations Committee May 19 approved three anti-China measures and said it planned to consider several others at a session the day before Clinton is to leave for Beijing.

Hutchinson said he would not wait that long and instead would offer the largely symbolic measures as amendments to the Senate version of the fiscal 1999 defense authorization bill (S 2057).

During debate on that measure, the Senate has already approved two anti-China amendments championed by hard-liners.

The controversy is also expected to renew a debate about granting China MFN trade status. Lott, for example, said he is reconsidering his support for the legislation.

"This really hurts," said Rep. Robert T. Matsui, ranking Democrat on the Ways and Means Trade Subcommittee, and a strong supporter of MFN. "The industry groups are in a panic."

Rep. Jim Kolbe, R-Ariz., said he planned to meet with Gingrich to try to persuade the Speaker — an MFN supporter — to make clear that the current controversy should not affect the U.S.-China trade relationship.

"We have to have a considered foreign policy relationship," Kolbe said. "We have to be very cautious."

Congress Fails To Set Policy On Export Controls

MAY 30 — Congressional Republicans have been quick to criticize President Clinton for allowing products with military potential — such as satellites — to be shipped to China and other countries but painfully slow to enact legislation setting export control policy.

Efforts to rewrite Cold War laws regulating "dual-use" exports — those with both commercial and military value — have been stymied for four years by congressional infighting and conflicting pressures from outside interests.

The latest bill (HR 1942), by Rep. Ileana Ros-Lehtinen, R-Fla., has been in a House International Relations subcommittee since July without even a hearing.

Since the most recent Export Control Administration Act (PL 96-72) expired in 1994, Clinton has set policy through executive orders and individual waivers, with little regular oversight and only occasional intervention from Capitol Hill.

Clinton has generally moved to make it easier for high-technology companies to sell their products overseas, while Congress has largely stayed silent, seldom objecting, sometimes even cheering from the sidelines.

The ad hoc process has satisfied neither business groups nor arms control advocates, Republicans nor Democrats. The lack of a clear policy, critics say, has fueled recent controversies over the sales of high-tech goods, such as satellites and supercomputers to China.

"We don't have any real guidelines, any rules of the road," said former Rep. Toby Roth, R-Wis. (1979-97), who drafted an export control bill in 1996 that passed the House but not the Senate. "Things are in limbo, and that leads to the problems we have today."

"Congress has fallen down on the job in terms of dealing with the issue responsibly," agreed Howard Diamond, senior research analyst at the private Arms Control Association.

Congress has generally stepped in only after particular transfers — from supercomputers to machine tools — have drawn lawmakers' attention. That has sent confusing signals to both exporters and foreign countries, critics say.

"We have spasmodic attempts to regulate high-technology products that have little concern for the potential use of the products and are more concerned with how to get mileage out of them politically," Diamond said.

Both the House and Senate are now investigating whether Clinton hurt national security when he allowed Loral Space & Communications to launch satellites aboard Chinese rockets even though the company was under investigation for allegedly sharing sensitive material with the Chinese after an earlier launch failure.

Christopher Cox, R-Calif., who chairs a special House panel on the case, said he will focus on the national security implications of the missile launching and technology transfers. "There's no question it helps U.S. business," Cox said May 24 on NBC's Meet the Press. "There is some question whether it has helped the People's Liberation Army."

Even before the investigation, and over White House objections, the House voted May 20 to ban the launching of U.S. satellites in China as an amendment to the fiscal 1999 defense authorization bill (HR 3616 — H Rept 105-532).

Several GOP senators have pledged to support suspending such launches when the Senate again takes up its own version of the defense bill (S 2057 — S Rept 105-189) the week of June 1.

Last November, after reports that U.S. supercomputers had turned up in Chinese and Russian missile labs, Congress insisted that Defense and State Department officials be given a stronger say on computer sales to either country.

Thad Cochran, R-Miss., who chairs a Senate Governmental Affairs subcommittee dealing with satellite issues, said Congress is likely to require a similar policy for satellites.

"People need to be paying greater attention to the national security consequences of dual-use exports," Cochran said. "Too much power to decide whether security interests are threatened has been handed to the companies and the Commerce Department."

Reliance on Business

During the last four years, Clinton has transferred primary responsibility over exports of many high-tech goods, from the combustion chambers of jet engines to satellites and supercomputers, from the State Department to the Commerce Department.

Republicans have complained that relying on companies, rather than U.S. government officials, to determine how U.S.-made products are being used by foreign buyers has made it easier for foreign weapons labs and other off-limits institutions to acquire U.S. technology.

Cochran said that because of these shifts, further restrictions on other dual-use items could be in the offing.

"Satellite technology transfer is something that has everyone's attention, so we want to strike while the iron's hot," Cochran said. "But there will be opportunities down the road to look at other dual-use items."

Business groups fret that efforts to further limit sales of machine tools and certain parts of commercial jet engines to countries such as China could be next on the critics' hit list.

Henry Sokolski of the Non-proliferation Policy Action Center, a private group that opposes the spread of nuclear and other weapons, said the Clinton administration's actions need a broad review.

Sokolski, who served as the Pentagon's deputy director of non-proliferation policy in the Bush administration, said Congress and the White House need to take a tougher stand on exports of dual-use items.

"You can't straddle it. You have to paint a bright yellow line down the middle and only allow those things on the right side of the road," he said.

Sokolski also pointed out that under Clinton, many items that may aid nuclear weapons programs, such as oscilloscopes that measure the force of an explosion, are no longer subject to individual licenses at all.

He urged that a computer registry of such exports be set up.

Business groups complain that such approaches are unrealistic. Howard Lewis, vice president for economic policy at the National Association of Manufacturers, said Congress should not be "micromanaging" rules on dual-use items, since the technology will change faster than any laws or regulations.

"The calculator my daughter used in high school is as powerful as anything J. Robert Oppenheimer used to design the atom bomb," Lewis said. "Trying to regulate the complex commercial world is a real neat trick — the devil is in the details."

Wassenaar Arrangement

Changes in the international environment since the end of the Cold War also make U.S. export controls less effective, business groups say.

"They are really trying to turn the clock back to the Cold War," said Edmund Rice, executive director for the Coalition for Employment through Exports, a coalition of major U.S. exporters. "But it's a different world. Unilateral controls by the United States are going to do absolutely nothing except hurt U.S. businesses."

Business groups note that unlike during the Cold War, there is little international coordination on the export of sensitive technology.

The Coordinating Committee on Multilateral Export Controls, which included NATO members and Japan, disbanded in 1994.

Since then, under a loose pact called the Wassenaar Arrangment, the United States and its allies have agreed to notify each other if they deny a license for exporting a particular product to a particular country. The agreement does not prevent another of the parties from then selling the same product to the country.

Industry groups and some lawmakers say the United States will hurt itself if it imposes export controls, because other countries will fill the void.

"If we re-create a set of Cold War standards for exports, then we will simply move American jobs overseas," said Rep. Sam Gejdenson, D-Conn.

Dueling on Dual Use

For nearly a decade, Gejdenson has been working with like-minded lawmakers to update the 1979 Export Administration Act, the latest in a series of export control laws dating back to 1940 that were used to keep sensitive products out of Soviet hands during the Cold War.

Even before the Berlin Wall fell nine years ago, Gejdenson and other lawmakers were complaining that the law's controls were hampering U.S. businesses.

They cited several studies by the National Academy of Sciences that showed U.S. competitiveness in the telecommunications, computer, and machine tool industries had been hurt because American companies were prevented from selling abroad.

After the Soviet Union collapsed, several attempts were made to overhaul the law, but they fell short, primarily because of opposition from the armed services committees.

The most serious attempt came in 1996. With the support of Clinton and House National Security Chairman Floyd D. Spence, R-S.C., Roth moved a bill through the House that would have streamlined the licensing of sensitive exports while giving the Pentagon

International Affairs

Satellite Sanctions on China Marked by Inconsistency

1988
Sept. 9: President Ronald Reagan agrees to license the export of U.S.-built satellites for launch in China for the first time.

1989
June 4: Crackdown on pro-democracy demonstrators in Tiananmen Square. The next day, President George Bush suspends military exports to China, including satellites.
December: Bush reinstates satellite export licenses.

1990
Feb. 16: Congress passes sanctions against China (PL 101-162 and 101-246), suspending export of satellites and products on State Department Munitions List; president may waive sanctions in the national interest.
April 7: China launches a foreign- built (Hughes Aircraft Co.) satellite for the first time.

1991
April 30: President Bush waives Tiananmen sanctions for export of three satellites to China.
June 16: With evidence that China transferred missile technology to Pakistan, Bush bans export of satellites and other high technology.

1992
March 23: Bush lifts missile proliferation sanctions after China agrees to abide by international pact on missile control.
Sept. 11: Bush waives Tiananmen sanctions for export of five satellites to China.
Dec. 21: Chinese rocket explodes and destroys Hughes satellite. China blames Hughes.

1993
July 2: President Clinton waives Tiananmen sanctions for export of two satellites to China.
Aug. 24: Clinton imposes sanctions, including a ban on some satellite-related equipment, on Chinese companies alleged to have transferred missile technology to Pakistan.
Oct. 20: The Washington Post reports that executives of Martin Marietta Corp. and Hughes are lobbying to waive latest ban on satellite exports. Hughes CEO C. Michael Armstrong later says he asked Clinton to review the policy.

1994
Jan. 6: Clinton administration exempts satellites from missile proliferation sanctions.

---

a say in dual-use exports, even if they are available from other countries.

But the bill ran aground in the waning days of the 104th Congress amid opposition from some defense committee members and Senate Banking Committee Chairman Alfonse M. D'Amato, R-N.Y.

The divisions in Congress largely mirror those between the State Department and Pentagon, on one side, and the Commerce Department on the other. State and Defense focus on preventing the proliferation of military technology, while Commerce supports business's efforts to promote exports of dual-use technologies.

"There is no center of gravity in Congress about what it wants to do on export controls," said Joel Johnson, vice president for international issues at the Aerospace Industries Association.

Select Committee To Investigate Sales to China

JUNE 20 — Gearing up for the long haul, the House on June 18 voted to spend up to $2.5 million investigating whether the Clinton administration permitted transfers of sensitive military technology to China.

A resolution (H Res 463), passed 409-10, set up the Select Committee on U.S. National Security and Military/Commercial Concerns with the People's Republic of China. Christopher Cox, R-Calif. will be the chairman.

Speaker Newt Gingrich, R-Ga., proposed such a panel last month, but debate between parties over the ratio of seats and the scope of the investigation held up agreement on its formation.

Gingrich proposed an eight-member committee of five Republicans and three Democrats. Democrats objected, saying they were underrepresented. Republicans said they would only increase the number if Democrats did not stack the panel with more partisan members.

The logjam broke when Minority Leader Richard A. Gephardt, D-Mo., chose Norm Dicks, a moderate Washington lawmaker, as the lead Democrat on the panel. Cox then agreed to consider either adding a Democrat or dropping a Republican from the panel.

After the House vote, Gephardt named the other Democratic members. They are: Robert C. Scott of Virginia, Lucille Roybal-Allard of California and John M. Spratt Jr. of South Carolina.

Relations With China

July 13: Clinton waives Tiananmen sanctions for export of a satellite to China.

September: Loral Chairman Bernard Schwartz joins trade mission to China led by Commerce Secretary Ronald H. Brown.

Oct. 4: Clinton waives missile proliferation sanctions in return for Chinese promise not to export ground-to-ground missiles.

1995

Jan. 26: Chinese rocket explodes and destroys Hughes satellite.

March 13: United States and China reach agreement on launch of 11 satellites over the next seven years at prices not less than 15 percent below competitors'.

July: China test-fires missiles near Taiwan.

July 25: Hughes and Chinese authorities issue separate findings on cause of Jan. 26 crash.

Oct. 9: Secretary of State Warren Christopher initials classified memo that State should retain licensing authority over satellite exports.

1996

Feb. 6: Clinton waives Tiananmen sanctions for export of three satellites to China.

Feb. 15: Chinese rocket explodes destroying satellite built by Loral and smashing into a village.

March: China test-fires missiles near Taiwan; Clinton sends two Navy carrier battle groups to the area.

March 14: Clinton administration announces it will move jurisdiction for licensing commercial satellites exports from State to Commerce Department.

April 10: China issues preliminary report that electrical joint failure caused Feb. 15 crash. Insurance companies demand Western review.

May: Committee headed by Loral executive Wah L. Lim agrees with Chinese report and shares findings with Chinese authorities. Loral notifies State and Defense departments of the actions.

1997

May: Defense Department classified report concludes that Loral and Hughes transferred technology to China that enhanced its ballistic missiles and harmed U.S. national security.

September: Justice Department begins criminal investigation of Loral and Hughes.

November: After a summit in Washington, Chinese President Jiang Zemin visits Hughes satellite plant in California.

1998

Feb. 18: Clinton waives Tiananmen sanctions for export of Loral satellite to China. Justice Department reportedly says that waiver could hamper any prosecution of the company.

March 16: Loral and China sign deal to launch five Loral satellites before 2002.

April 4: The New York Times reports that a federal grand jury is investigating Loral and Hughes for transferring missile guidance expertise to China. Investigations launched by Congress.

SOURCES: Congressional Research Service, newspaper accounts.

In addition to Cox, Gingrich named House Intelligence Committee Chairman Porter J. Goss Jr. of Florida; Doug Bereuter of Nebraska, chairman of the International Affairs subcommittee on Asia and the Pacific; Curt Weldon of Pennsylvania, chairman of the National Security subcommittee on Military Research and Development and House ethics committee Chairman James V. Hansen of Utah.

Multiple Probes Focus on Satellite Export Rules

JULY 11 — Did President Clinton, in his eagerness for more trade and better relations with Beijing, allow China to acquire sensitive missile technology that could be used against the United States?

That is the allegation that has touched off investigations and hearings by no fewer than 10 congressional committees and subcommittees this summer. The focus:

● Clinton's February decision to allow Loral Space and Communications to launch a satellite on a Chinese rocket even after he was warned the company might have violated national security in a previous launch.

● Clinton's decision in 1996 to shift the licensing of all satellite exports from the State Department to Commerce.

The committees also have been forced to confront a series of issues ranging from the approach the United States should take toward China, the role of foreign money in U.S. campaigns, the adequacy of export controls, the proliferation of weapons to countries such as Pakistan and Iran, and U.S. space policy.

Here are the issues so far:

Space Boom

The communications revolution produced a boom in satellites for telephone and computer communications and television transmission.

Since two of every three satellites are built in the United States, companies such as Hughes Space and Communications and Loral have prospered.

U.S. companies that launch satellites, such as Boeing and Lockheed Martin, also have benefited. But the demand for rockets and launching pads has outstripped the domestic supply, and the market share of U.S. companies has fallen from complete domination two decades ago to 40 percent today.

Changes in U.S. government policy also have had an impact on the

International Affairs

launch business.

Until 1984, all U.S.-built satellites were launched on U.S. spacecraft, principally the space shuttle. As the satellite industry grew, manufacturers looked for alternatives to the shuttle. At first, these included U.S. rockets, such as the Atlas, operated by Lockheed Martin, and the European Ariane.

Federal policy abruptly changed after the space shuttle Challenger exploded in 1986, killing seven astronauts. For more than two years, President Ronald Reagan banned all commercial cargo aboard the shuttle and then limited private payloads to those that could not be launched on other vehicles.

Eager to get their wares into space, satellite makers clamored to be allowed to launch their products on China's Long March rockets, which were both available and cheaper than U.S. or European launch providers.

In 1988, Reagan agreed, as long as the launches were approved by the State and Defense departments and included a series of safeguards. His decision was sealed in a bilateral agreement allowing China to launch no more than nine satellites between 1989 and 1994, a deal later extended to 11 more satellites by 2001. *(1988 Almanac, p. 642)*

The policy was temporarily derailed by the June 1989 Tiananmen Square massacre. In its wake, President Bush suspended all satellite launches until December, 1999. *(1989 Almanac, p. 518)*

Soon thereafter, Congress in the fiscal 1990-91 Foreign Relations Authorization Act (PL 101-246) banned the practice of launching satellites in China and the export to China of material on the State Department's munitions list, which included some satellite-related equipment. The president could issue waivers for individual satellite launches that he considered in the national interest. Manufacturers would have to obtain an export license from the State Department for each overseas launch. *(1990 Almanac, p. 799)*

As Bush prepared to leave office in 1992, his administration drafted a policy allowing the Commerce Department, with little input from Defense or State, to license the export of satellites devoid of technology that could have military use. The transfer of authority took place in 1993, the first year of the Clinton administration.

In 1995, the Commerce Department urged the White House to remove dual-use satellites from the State Department's munitions list and transfer them to the Commerce control list. Commerce officials argued that technology formerly judged to have military characteristics was now widely available in the commercial realm. The State Department agreed to some transfers, but resisted others, saying that some satellites still had substantial military applications.

Commerce appealed to the National Security Council, arguing that dual-use military technology was safe as long as it was embedded in the satellite and sealed off from foreign inspection.

Clinton resolved the dispute in March 1996, saying that he would authorize the transfer of licensing authority to the Commerce Department but with a new set of safeguards said to ensure the continued role of the State Department and the Pentagon in the decision-making process.

Under the rules, a five-member operating committee from the Arms Control and Disarmament Agency and the Energy, State, Commerce, and Defense departments must approve by majority vote every satellite export application. Dissenters can appeal any decision all the way to the oval office.

The Defense Department must approve a technology transfer control plan regulating the disclosure of technical information involved in each launch. And the Commerce Department now requires that Defense Department personnel be present at every launch.

Top officials in the State and Defense departments have testified that the changes guaranteed that national security would be protected when satellites are launched overseas.

But the General Accounting Office concluded in recent testimony that substantial differences exist in how satellite exports are treated under the old and new systems.

Under the new process, the GAO said, "technical information may not be as clearly controlled," because of a lack of explicit licensing requirements for technical data and a lack of Pentagon involvement in deciding which types of data are generally subject to licenses.

Moreover, Congress is no longer notified when an export license is considered, although it does receive notice when the president waives the Tiananmen sanctions.

Dr. Peter M. Leitner, a senior strategic adviser in the Pentagon's Defense Technology Security Administration, testified June 25 that the administration has further "neutered" the Defense Department's role by putting export control decisions in the hands of officials who don't agree with the controls.

Leitner said that politically motivated officials have pushed for licenses with little more information than contained on the license application, and that they have stifled dissent.

He and other critics also criticized the administration's pending shift of the Technology Security Administration within the Pentagon hierarchy.

Stephen D. Bryen, who headed the agency in the Reagan administration, told the Senate Armed Services Committee July 9 that the shift was a "very ill-advised and dangerous reorganization" that would have "an extraordinarily negative effect on export controls."

Missile Proliferation

These policy changes took place against a backdrop of U.S. concern over Chinese exports of missile technology to Pakistan and Iran.

Twice, from 1991 to 1992 and from 1993 to 1994, the State Department prohibited exports of U.S.-made satellites to China because Beijing exported technology for Pakistan's effort to develop a nuclear arsenal.

The sanctions cost U.S. satellite manufacturers hundreds of millions of dollars in business that went to European firms.

Subsequently, U.S. companies lobbied to have control over satellite exports moved to the Commerce Department. Under Commerce Department rules, China would have to transfer entire missiles or major missile components, rather than missile technology, to trigger a cutoff of U.S. exports. Past and current CIA officials have contended that the Chinese have, in fact, transferred complete missiles, but despite a four-year investigation, the administration has yet to make an official determination.

Last year, Arms Control and Disarmament Agency Director John Holum argued that such a determination should be made.

"History has proven that the only time we have gotten movement from the Chinese in missile proliferation has been in the case of a penalty being imposed," Holum said. "Carrots have gotten us nothing."

But now that he is also an undersecretary of State, Holum said he believes that the United States should have to provide a higher level of proof of proliferation before sanctions are imposed in order not to undermine the broader U.S.-China relationship.

Winter Crashes

Satellite export rules likely would have remained off the public radar were it not for two mid-winter launchpad accidents in China a year apart.

On Jan. 26, 1995, a Long March rocket exploded after liftoff and destroyed an Apstar-2 satellite built by Hughes, a division of General Motors.

In parallel six-month investigations, Chinese authorities and Hughes concluded the rocket was buffeted by high winds and shook itself apart. China said the satellite failed; Hughes blamed the rocket.

Justice Department officials are investigating whether Hughes violated the law in meetings with Chinese officials about the accident.

William Reinsch, undersecretary of Commerce for export administration, told a Senate Governmental Affairs Subcommittee July 8 that his department had cleared a report of the meetings, without sharing it with the Pentagon or State Department and that no Pentagon monitors had been present at the launch.

Reinsch told the committee that only on the day of the hearing and only after discussions with the National Security Council had he turned over the report to the Pentagon to determine if national security had been violated.

In retrospect, Reinsch said, "a better course of action would have been to refer it to the State Department for review."

Loss of Loral Satellite

On Feb. 14, 1996, another Long March rocket carrying an Intelsat satellite built by Loral went out of control after launch, crashed into a village in South China and killed an estimated 200 people.

For five hours, Chinese rescue crews kept the manufacturers and U.S. military officials from reaching the scene.

When they recovered the satellite, it was missing two circuit boards with encrypted signals, a loss that Rep. Curt Weldon, R-Pa., called a theft that should be a major focus of the congressional investigations.

A recent National Security Agency report concluded, however, that the circuit boards likely were destroyed in the crash. Even if they survived, the agency said, they were likely to prove of little value to the Chinese.

In the wake of the crash, insurance companies demanded a separate review of the Chinese explanation for the accident — a poorly soldered electrical connection — before they would ensure future flights.

A committee of U. S. and European experts met in Beijing and Palo Alto in April and May 1996. It included two scientists from Hughes, whose satellite was the next scheduled for launch in China. No U.S. government officials were included.

Because the satellite contained "militarily sensitive technologies," it had been exported under State Department guidelines requiring the presence of a Defense Department monitor at all such meetings.

The group was supposed to get government clearance for any correspondence that might help China's missile program. But as Loral officials acknowledged, before a final report was sent to U.S. government officials, a preliminary version was faxed to Chinese officials.

Loral officials soon confessed their error to the State and Defense departments. The Justice Department opened an investigation.

As prosecutors worked on the case, Loral launched a previously licensed satellite on a Chinese rocket in 1997, then sought another presidential waiver to launch a satellite.

National Security Adviser Sandy Berger advised Clinton to issue the waiver, saying it would offer China incentives to cooperate on missile exports, would benefit broader U.S.-China relations and would aid the U.S. satellite industry.

Berger urged a quick decision, noting that Loral could be subject to millions of dollars in penalties if there was a delay.

But Berger also warned the president that a waiver could undermine any legal case against Loral, since a jury would be reluctant to convict a company that had been granted a national security waiver by the president.

In fact, a 1997 Pentagon report concluded that Loral's actions after the 1996 crash had damaged national security. That report lies at the heart of the congressional investigation.

According to The New York Times, Pentagon officials determined that if they had seen the report first, they would not have cleared information that Loral provided China regarding its guidance and flight control systems and suggestions for diagnostic techniques that could be used to determine flaws in the launch vehicle.

China's Long March rockets are virtually identical to its ballistic missiles, the Pentagon said, so the information would prove valuable to its military efforts.

CIA officials, in their own report, disagreed, saying the technology used in the commercial rockets did not lend itself to ballistic missiles.

Claims that the technology transfers, if they occurred, damaged national security rest on China's increasing ability to launch sophisticated satellites without incident and on the close relationship between conventional rockets and nuclear missiles.

Henry Sokolski, executive director of the Nonproliferation Policy Education Center, said that through repeated launches and incremental improvements, China has accumulated knowledge that would allow it to deliver multiple-warhead intercontinental missiles in a fairly reliable manner.

He listed improvements in China's ability to protect fragile payloads against temperature changes, to control a rocket's altitude, to use "kick" motors to power a satellite to a particular point in space and to dispense multiple satellites from a single launcher.

Sokolski noted that since 1996, China has had 10 straight successful launches of increasing sophistication, while one in every four Chinese rock-

International Affairs

ets had crashed before then.

According to the Times, Wah Lim, a senior vice president at Loral who headed the independent review committee, wrote Chinese officials promising to work with them to make their launch vehicles as reliable as possible.

On the Hill

Congressional investigators have focused primarily on the Loral crash because of the subsequent Pentagon report and because of its political overtones.

Loral CEO Bernard L. Schwartz was the single largest contributor of campaign cash in the 1995-96 election cycle, and his money overwhelmingly went to Democrats. In the current election cycle, Schwartz has given about $400,000 to Democrats.

Investigators are also looking into another campaign finance tie. Johnny Chung, a key figure in a Justice Department investigation of illegal foreign campaign contributions, has admitted that $100,000 that he gave Democrats came from the Chinese government.

Chung said that he acted as a conduit for the money, which was given to him by the daughter of a top government official. The woman, Liu Chao-ying, is an executive of the state-run China Aerospace company, the parent of China Great Wall Industry Corp., which runs the commercial launch business.

The congressional committees are likely to meet through the summer and some, such as a select House committee headed by Christopher Cox, R-Calif. and Norm Dicks, D-Wash., are not expected to reach conclusions until the end of the year.

Lott Criticizes Clinton's Satellite Launch Policy

JULY 18 — Senate Majority Leader Trent Lott, R-Miss., has turned up the heat on the Clinton administration's policy that allows U.S. companies to launch satellites on Chinese rockets.

Issuing what he called an "interim report" on July 14, Lott said 13 Senate hearings in less than two months had demonstrated that controls to prevent China from learning military secrets from the satellite launches are "wholly inadequate" and that "national security concerns are regularly downplayed and even ignored."

Speaking on the Senate floor, Lott again called on Attorney General Janet Reno to appoint an independent counsel to investigate allegations of illegal Chinese contributions to U.S. political campaigns, saying that "new information has come to light" on these ties. He did not specify what the information was.

Lott said the administration's failure to cooperate with the Senate investigation would force him to delay Senate confirmation of any nominees from "non-cooperating agencies" that have been slow to respond to requests. He named the departments of State, Defense, Commerce and Justice, as well as the White House and Customs Service.

The Senate, Lott said, is "actively examining our subpoena options."

White House spokesman Mike McCurry said it was "ludicrous" of Lott to accuse the administration of not cooperating. "We've given hundreds, if not thousands, of pages of documentation to them," McCurry said.

He denounced Lott's "Alice in Wonderland" interim report "as a political argument made by a politician for political benefit."

"Sen. Lott today tried to connect a lot of dots that frankly don't connect," McCurry said. "And our judgment here is that that was not a serious statement by a serious person."

Senate Minority Leader Tom Daschle, D-S.D., joined the fight, calling Lott's comments "partisanship at its worst" and accusing him of recklessness.

And Sen. Bob Kerrey, D-Neb., vice-chairman of the Intelligence Committee, which has played the lead role in the investigations, said Lott's comments "threaten national security by pre-empting our ability to produce bipartisan conclusions."

Classified Remarks

Kerrey said the investigative committees have yet to reach any conclusions. GOP aides acknowledged that Lott's report was based on discussions with committee chairmen who are carrying out various aspects of the probe, rather than on committee reports.

Kerrey particularly criticized Lott for saying that he had new information that should prompt the appointment of an independent counsel, then refusing to release the information on the grounds that it was classified.

Calling Lott's remarks a misuse of classified information, Kerrey said, "The implication is that the [Intelligence] committee has reached some kind of conclusion. It most assuredly has not."

In the report, Lott drew five preliminary conclusions on the China satellite investigation:

- Transferring primary licensing authority for the export of U.S.-made satellites from the State Department to the Commerce Department had harmed U.S. export control efforts.
- In helping to improve the reliability of Chinese rockets after some failed launches, U.S. satellite companies had indirectly improved Beijing's ballistic missiles. Most experts say that missiles and booster rockets are virtually identical.
- Since China is using U.S. satellites for some of its military communications, the People's Liberation Army has clearly benefited from the export of American-made satellites.
- The Clinton administration has ignored Chinese transfers of missile and nuclear technology to other countries and adopted a policy to insulate China from potential sanctions under U.S. anti-proliferation laws.
- New information "should remove all resistance" to naming an independent counsel. Lott did not elaborate on this information in his speech or subsequent remarks to the press.

But at a July 15 Senate Judiciary Committee hearing, Fred Thompson, R-Tenn., implied that the new material was a copy of a memo that FBI Director Louis J. Freeh sent Reno in November recommending the appointment of an independent counsel to investigate campaign finance allegations.

Congressional investigators were briefed on the report last month. According to Thompson, Freeh said the independent counsel law not only allows but even requires appointment of an independent counsel because the investigation could involve President Clinton, Vice President Al Gore and other administration officials.

"It is difficult to imagine a more

compelling situation for appointing an independent counsel," Thompson quoted Freeh as writing.

Committee Chairman Orrin G. Hatch, R-Utah, said, "It is more clear than ever in my mind that the attorney general was and is required to seek an independent counsel in this area."

Conspicuous Targets

Hatch complained that the Justice Department has "been unable to do more than secure indictments against the most conspicuous targets, those who gave illegal donations to the DNC [Democratic National Committee] or re-election campaign. . . . The department appears to have come up empty on the complicity of others within the administration or the Democratic National Committee."

That result, Hatch said, should come as no surprise because "the [Justice] department has applied a different standard with respect to investigating possible violations of federal campaign fundraising laws involving senior administration officials than the standard that typically governs the commencement of ordinary criminal investigations."

Reno demurred, saying, "We've indicted 11 people in this investigation, and we're going to continue it wherever it takes us, no matter where it goes."

And she blasted Thompson for releasing a confidential memo: "I'm the one that you confirmed as attorney general. I've got to make the legal decisions. . . . If the Independent Counsel Act is triggered by any development, I'm going to do it."

Members Consider Incentives To Keep Launches at Home

SEPTEMBER 19 — Many Republicans agree with a decision by House and Senate negotiators to return responsibility for licensing satellite exports to the State Department, rather than the Commerce Department. They say it is essential for keeping sensitive technology out of foreign hands.

But some lawmakers and experts say the proposed transfer of authority does not address how Congress can keep the nation's satellite industry healthy.

As a result, those lawmakers and experts are calling for incentives and other programs to keep satellite companies from traveling to China and other countries that offer lower costs for launching and less red tape.

Republican John McCain of Arizona, chairman of the Senate Commerce, Science and Transportation Committee, promised at a Sept. 17 hearing to spend next year determining how to best control satellite launches.

"We've got to have an overall policy," he said. "And I don't know whether that requires legislation or not. But it certainly does require legislation to enhance the ability of U.S. industry to launch in the United States."

McCain's pledge came as House and Senate conferees on the fiscal 1999 defense authorization bill (HR 3616 — H Rept 105-532, S Rept 105-189) decided to include language returning authority for licensing satellites to the State Department.

McCain said in an interview Sept. 17 that a shift in jurisdiction between State and Commerce alone is not enough. "I'd like to see us address this in a more comprehensive fashion," he said. "What I don't want to do is make the change [from Commerce to State] and then have everybody say we've fixed the problem."

Several experts agreed that the conferees' decision should not be seen as a substitute for a broader technology transfer policy. They also said Congress must consider finding ways to assist and perhaps even subsidize U.S. launch capabilities.

"If Democrats and Republicans are serious about resolving the current controversy and truly want to make our commercial space industry not only profitable, but safe, bringing it back to the U.S. rather than trying to control [exports] to countries like China is the only way out," said Henry Sokolski, executive director of the Nonproliferation Policy Education Center, at the Commerce Committee hearing.

Starr Eclipse

The Commerce Committee is one of 11 congressional panels looking into the administration's handling of satellite exports to China. The key issues:

● President Clinton's 1996 decision to shift the licensing of satellite exports from the State Department to the Commerce Department after Commerce officials argued that technology once judged to have military characteristics was widely available commercially.

● Clinton's decision in February to allow Loral Space and Communications to launch a satellite on a Chinese rocket after the White House was warned the company might have previously transferred sensitive technology to China.

Republicans initially viewed the China developments as a promising election-year issue. They alleged the Loral decision was influenced by campaign contributions to the Democratic Party from former Loral CEO Bernard L. Schwartz.

But the issue has faded in the glare of Independent Counsel Kenneth W. Starr's report on Clinton's relationship with former White House intern Monica Lewinsky.

Market Pressures

Absent a clear export control policy — and Congress has not passed one since 1994 — several experts testified that moving licensing back to the State Department would make little difference.

They said the soaring global communications market and the rapid increase in the number of commercial satellites have left the United States unable to meet the demand.

"While I believe it is important that we restore export safeguards, as long as satellites are sent overseas for launch there is the risk of technology transfer," said Rep. Dave Weldon, R-Fla., whose district includes Cape Canaveral Air Station, one of the nation's two main commercial launch sites.

"Our best defense against such transfers," Weldon said, "is to enhance our domestic launch capacity."

Among the most important issues McCain wants to explore is how to limit liability in case of a rocket crash in the United States that causes death, injury or damage. Experts say liability is not as much of a problem overseas.

Both the House and Senate have passed legislation (HR 1702 — H Rept 105-347, S Rept 105-198) that would help the space launch industry in a limited way by requiring a Defense Department study of the nation's launch

International Affairs

infrastructure. The bill is awaiting a House-Senate conference.

Intelligence Estimates

At the Commerce Committee hearing, administration officials said the current licensing process for satellites is satisfactory.

Franklin C. Miller, principal deputy assistant secretary of Defense, said China's intercontinental ballistic missile program has not benefited from transfers of U.S. technology.

"I do not believe that the current generation of Chinese ICBMs' guidance capacity was improved through any of the China commercial space launch activities," Miller said.

McCain was unconvinced. "Air Force intelligence disagrees with you, Mr. Miller, and so does almost any expert in the area," he said.

TRADE STATUS

House Panel Backs China's Favored Trade Status

JUNE 27 — The House Ways and Means Committee June 25 backed President Clinton's decision to extend China's most-favored-nation trade status, giving the White House a boost before a battle next month on the House floor.

The committee by voice vote urged the House to disapprove a resolution (H J Res 121) by Rules Committee Chairman Gerald B.H. Solomon, R-N.Y., that would reverse Clinton's decision earlier this month to extend China's trade status for another year, allowing Beijing the same tariff treatment as nearly all other nations.

Solomon and other China critics want to drop MFN to express U.S. displeasure with China's occupation of Tibet, its human rights record, protectionist trade policies and proliferation of weapons of mass destruction.

At the markup, Jon Christensen, R-Neb., said he had backed away from his previous support of the trade status, particularly because of Beijing's persecution of Christians.

House Majority Leader Dick Armey, R-Texas, said June 23 that this year's battle over MFN would be more contentious than usual, partly because of investigations into China's role in U.S. political campaigns and its possible acquisition of U.S. missile technology.

Supporters are confident they have the votes to back Clinton.

Ways and Means Chairman Bill Archer, R-Texas, said that the debate had drifted far away from the original purpose of the 1974 law, under which Clinton had issued the annual waiver. He noted that law (PL 93-618), which he co-authored, was designed to punish communist countries that did not permit free emigration. *(1974 Almanac, p. 553)*

Normal Trade With China Wins Approval

JULY 25 — Despite the controversy surrounding U.S.-China relations this year — including charges that China tried to influence U.S. elections and that it improperly transferred sensitive missile technology — the House voted July 22 to continue normal trade relations between the two nations.

Opponents of the trade status raised familiar objections, including weapons proliferation and human rights abuses, but the House voted, 166-264, against a resolution (H J Res 121) that would have disapproved President Clinton's decision to extend the trade status for another year. *(Vote 317, p. H-92)*

That is seven fewer votes than China's opponents could muster last June, when a similar disapproval resolution was rejected 173-259. *(1997 Almanac, p. 8-37)*

The trade status, formerly known as "most favored nation" or MFN, was changed to "normal trade relations" by the Internal Revenue Service overhaul measure (PL 105-206) Clinton signed into law July 22.

The status allows Chinese goods to enter the United States at low, non-discriminatory tariff rates. Only seven countries do not enjoy a normal trade status. Both the House and Senate would have to pass disapproval legislation to change the status.

The House debate echoed the rhetoric of previous years. China's critics said normal trade has done little to improve the nation's record on human rights, weapons proliferation or other problems.

"If the policy was working, the record would be different. It is not," said House Minority Leader Richard A. Gephardt, D-Mo. "On every account, MFN has struck out," said Rules Committee Chairman Gerald B.H. Solomon, R-N.Y.

Those in favor of maintaining the trade status argued that to revoke it would prove disastrous to efforts to stabilize troubled Asian economies, calm disputes between India and Pakistan, and boost lagging U.S. exports.

CLINTON TRIP

GOP Mindful Of Contradictions In China Policy

JUNE 6 — With their harsh attacks on President Clinton's China policy, Republicans believe they have finally found a way to pierce the president's seemingly impenetrable political armor. But for an object lesson in the difficulties and dangers inherent in such a strategy, the Republicans need look no further than Bill Clinton.

As a presidential candidate in 1992, Clinton famously railed against President George Bush for "coddling tyrants" in China and conducting "business as usual with those who murdered freedom at Tiananmen Square."

But in politics, what goes around often comes around. Six years later, Clinton is under fire and facing multiple investigations by congressional Republicans for allegedly turning a blind eye to transfers of sensitive missile technology to Beijing. In part, Clinton's troubles stem from following the same sort of pro-business China policy for which he blasted Bush.

And in a twist of the rhetorical knife, Republicans have begun referring to the president's trip to China later this month as the "Tiananmen Square summit." It was the Chinese government's massacre of pro-democracy dissidents in Tiananmen Square in June 1989 that prompted candidate Clinton's condemnation of Bush in 1992.

Led by GOP critics, the House voted 305-116 on June 4 to approve a nonbinding resolution (H Con Res 285) that urges the president not to attend a welcoming ceremony in Tiananmen Square when he goes to China later this month. (*Vote 202, p. H-60*)

"We need to put pressure on communist China," said Rep. Dan Burton, R-Ind. "Are we supposed to turn our head and look the other way just for the almighty dollar?"

But Lee H. Hamilton of Indiana, the senior Democrat on the House International Relations Committee, said the largely symbolic resolution was a "superficial way to deal with a complex issue," and that it would do little to protect human rights in China.

When Clinton arrives in China on June 25, he will be at pains to demonstrate to American audiences that he is challenging China's leadership, while sending the message to China that he wants to maintain amicable relations. Even before the House vote, the administration was showing sensitivity to the questions of whether Clinton would meet Chinese leaders at Tiananmen Square. Presidential spokesman Mike McCurry noted that the meetings will be held at the Great Hall of the People, which is on the edge of the square and not technically in it.

GOP Vulnerabilities

But while Republicans have clearly put the administration and Democrats on the defensive over China, GOP leaders have their own vulnerabilities. For one thing, they are struggling to prevent the controversy over high-tech exports from triggering a wholesale re-examination of the longstanding U.S. policy of engagement with Beijing — a policy with which they generally agree.

House Speaker Newt Gingrich, R-Ga., who has led the charge in the technology imbroglio, is supporting the linchpin of the administration's China policy — renewal of Beijing's most-favored-nation (MFN) trade status, which ensures Chinese goods non-discriminatory tariffs. As expected, Clinton renewed China's MFN status June 3. Congress now has 90 days to vote to disapprove the renewal.

The apparent contradiction in Gingrich's stance has not been lost on conservative critics of Beijing. "After all this, he endorses the centerpiece of the Clinton China policy," said Robert Kagan, a former Reagan administration official and senior fellow at the Carnegie Endowment for International Peace.

At the same time, Republicans are also taking a risk in what looks like a promising investigation of the relationship between Democratic campaign contributions and the administration's approval of technology transfers to China. Previous campaign finance probes saw the GOP promise blockbuster revelations but fall short.

Four Senate committees and a House select committee will examine whether Clinton jeopardized national security by granting a waiver to Loral Space and Communications Ltd. to launch a commercial satellite on a Chinese rocket. Loral's chairman, Bernard Schwartz, was the largest individual contributor to Democrats during the last election cycle.

But the panels could have a tough time finding evidence to back up the charges being made by some GOP lawmakers. "Something terrible has happened," said Rep. Dana Rohrabacher, R-Calif., referring to the administration's satellite waivers. "And every man, woman and child may well have been jeopardized."

The Senate's investigation got off to a bumpy start June 4, as CIA Director George J. Tenet initially declined to share information related to the satellite controversy with the Intelligence Committee. Tenet reportedly refused to provide the information because it would jeopardize the Justice Department's ongoing probe of Loral.

The department, which has been investigating whether Loral illegally provided sensitive technology to China, later relented and agreed to the release of most of the disputed documents. But senators were taken aback by Tenet's refusal, and the incident might foreshadow future battles between the administration and Congress over the disclosure of key information.

Threat or Opportunity?

At the heart of all these issues are fundamental questions that have divided lawmakers ever since the Tiananmen Square massacre.

Can the United States maintain normal relations with the world's most populous nation? Or is China a retrograde communist dictatorship that represents an inevitable threat to U.S. interests?

There is ample evidence to support both points of view. Since 1989, China has engaged in a series of provocative actions that would seem to justify a more confrontational policy by the United States — including shipping nuclear bomb components to Pakistan in 1996 and threatening Taiwan the same year. All the while, thousands of political prisoners have languished in China's gulag. (*1996 Almanac, p. 9-9*)

But even China's harshest critics do not seem to want a return to the Cold War, when the United States and China were avowed enemies. With bilateral commerce booming — China was the United States' fourth-largest trading partner in 1997 — U.S. companies have worked furiously to ensure that does not happen.

Meanwhile, Americans seem conflicted in their views of China. There is still lingering suspicion of an old enemy. Kagan observed that the allegations over Chinese rockets caused such a stir simply because they involved China, which still aims missiles at the United States. "Would this have been as big a deal if it was Israel or Italy? I think not," he said.

"Basically, the center of gravity among the public tends to be that China is not a friend and not an enemy," said Steven Kull, director of the Program on International Attitudes at the University of Maryland.

On the big question — is China a threat or an opportunity? — Americans are almost evenly divided. In a poll conducted last fall by the Gallup Organization, 43 percent said China was a threat, while 45 percent felt it presented an opportunity.

The Wings Weigh In

Those who are most skeptical of the policy of engagement with China tend to come from the wings of both parties. In recent years, the effort to strip China of its MFN status has forged unusual alliances, joining liberals such as California Democratic Rep. Nancy Pelosi with conservatives such as Arkansas Republican Sen. Tim Hutchinson.

Because the wings in each party have a disproportionate impact on the

International Affairs

presidential nominating process, it is no surprise that China is getting a significant amount of attention from prospective presidential candidates.

Last year, for the first time, House Minority Leader Richard A. Gephardt, D-Mo., broke with Clinton in opposing the extension of MFN for China. When Clinton announced he was again seeking an MFN renewal this year, Gephardt fired off a stern rebuke of administration policy. "America must stand for more than money," he said.

Last year, House Budget Committee Chairman John R. Kasich, R-Ohio, also voted for the first time against renewing China's trade status. And in a recent speech, Malcolm S. "Steve" Forbes Jr. excoriated the administration's China policy.

"While commerce takes precedence over national security for this administration when it comes to China, the money that really talks is that which buys policy decisions," Forbes said in an address to the William J. Casey Institute of the Center for Security Policy.

But whenever possible, most politicians would prefer to have it both ways on China, registering concern over various Chinese policies while firmly embracing a productive, non-adversarial relationship.

Clinton performed his own 180-degree turn on the issue in 1994, when he effectively abandoned the idea that human rights should be linked to trade and instead endorsed the Bush administration policy he had hammered as a candidate two years earlier. (1994 Almanac, p. 137)

For his part, Gingrich has emphasized his outrage over the technology transfers and his objections to the president's trip, while downplaying his support for MFN. The Speaker signed a letter to Clinton urging that MFN be kept separate from the other China-related controversies.

Normally, Republicans would be scrambling to land a place in the president's delegation. But after the technology transfer controversy broke, interest dried up. "We have no takers," said Christina Martin, the Speaker's press secretary.

Senate Majority Leader Trent Lott, R-Miss., has taken a more cautious approach than Gingrich in criticizing the administration's China policy. He has vowed that the four Senate committees investigating U.S.-China policy would conduct vigorous, but nonpartisan, inquiries.

"This is a very serious matter that has affected my opinion of China," he told reporters June 2.

Still, while Lott has announced he is reconsidering his previous support for MFN, he said that the scandal should not prompt a full-scale reappraisal of the policy of engagement. "I wouldn't go that far," he said.

And Lott appeared skeptical of a House-backed proposal to prohibit the export of U.S. satellites to China, which passed overwhelmingly as an amendment to the fiscal 1999 defense authorization bill (HR 3616).

"We would not like to have a whole raft of amendments [to the bill]," he said. "We'll see what's most effective."

As in the House, interest among Senate Republicans in traveling to China with Clinton has waned considerably. But Democrats apparently had no qualms about joining the president's entourage. Aides to Senate Minority Leader Tom Daschle, D-S.D., said several Democrats had expressed interest in accompanying the president.

Referendum on Relations

As in recent years, the MFN debate will serve as something of a referendum on Sino-American relations. The House is expected to take up the issue after the July 4 congressional recess.

While the scandal over export technology transfers has alarmed business lobbyists — who annually enshrine MFN renewal as one of their top legislative priorities — no one seriously expects Congress to revoke MFN this year. Congress has never successfully moved to end China's special trade status since it began voting on the issue in 1980. It came close in 1992, however: Under fire from candidate Clinton and the Democratic Congress in 1992, Bush twice had to veto MFN disapproval measures, and only the Senate upheld his vetoes. (1992 Almanac, p. 157)

What is likely to be most significant about this year's battle is the prominent role taken by social conservative organizations such as the Family Research Council in opposing MFN. The Council's president, Gary L. Bauer, is a potential candidate for the GOP presidential nomination in 2000.

A spinoff of that group, called American Renewal Inc., has been running national television and newspaper advertisements that serve as a vivid reminder of the 1989 massacre. While showing the famous image of a lone protester standing up to a Chinese tank, Bauer urges Clinton: "Mr. President, don't go to Tiananmen Square."

With business groups pulling out all the stops to retain MFN, the debate promises to increase tensions between social and economic conservatives in the GOP. Those two factions have recently sparred over legislation to crack down on religious persecution abroad (HR 2431) and proposals to eliminate the so-called marriage tax penalty.

"This is the last thing we need," said Nebraska Republican Sen. Chuck Hagel, an unabashed free-trader who said he has no objections to the president visiting China. "We're playing a very dangerous game here, isolating ourselves."

But Hutchinson, a leading social conservative, said the controversy over high-tech exports has given his side new ammunition. "I think that multinational corporations have too much influence in the China debate," he said. "There has been an unholy alliance between big business, the Clinton administration and certain Republicans who have adopted the trade-at-any-price approach."

Republicans Call Clinton's Trip 'Disappointing'

JULY 4 — The good will generated by President Clinton's nine-day trip to China failed to impress GOP critics in Congress, who are still planning to move ahead with legislative measures designed to punish the Beijing regime for human rights abuses.

"I don't think this changes anything," said Sen. Tim Hutchinson of Arkansas, referring to an unprecedented televised appearance by the president. "Where's the substance? Where's the long-term benefits? . . . A verbal joust doesn't change Chinese policies or the repressive crackdown on the Chinese people."

Relations With China

To be sure, some Republicans acknowledged that positive feedback from the trip would likely create some political benefits for Clinton, particularly as he tries to persuade Congress to extend China's most-favored-nation trade status this month.

Speaker Newt Gingrich said Clinton had done "a good job" in China. "I think if you reach out to a billion people and talk about open markets and expand the zone of freedom on the planet, that's a pretty good investment for the world," he said.

But it did not sway those who felt the trip improperly rewarded China for squelching citizen dissent. "If I said his trip was disappointing, it would be an understatement," said Rep. Dana Rohrabacher of California.

Democrats, meanwhile, contend the GOP criticism of the trip will backfire on the Republican Party because most Americans approve of Clinton's efforts to improve relations with China. "It reinforces the image people see of the Republican Party as involving itself in partisan carping," said Democratic campaign consultant Mark Mellman. " . . . It makes them look small and partisan."

Congress Reiterates U.S. Commitment To Taiwan's Security

JULY 25 — The House July 20 reaffirmed the U.S. commitment to Taiwan's security, taking an indirect jab at some remarks President Clinton made on his recent trip to China.

By a vote of 390-1, the House approved a resolution (H Con Res 301), introduced by Majority Whip Tom DeLay, R-Texas, that restates longstanding U.S. policy as called for in the 1979 Taiwan Relations Act (PL 96-8). *(Vote 300, p. H-86; 1979 Almanac, p. 99)*

The Senate passed a similar resolution (S Con Res 107) July 10.

The Taiwan Relations Act acknowledges Beijing as the legitimate government of China but expresses a U.S. commitment to aid Taiwan's defense and ensure that its future is decided by peaceful means. It calls for Taiwan's membership in international financial institutions such as the World Bank and International Monetary Fund.

Rep. Doug Bereuter, R-Neb., said the resolution was intended to "repair the damage" some lawmakers said Clinton had caused with his comments.

Clinton largely restated U.S. policy that Taiwan is part of China but should only rejoin the mainland in a peaceful settlement. He did so in more explicit words than are usually used in the carefully constructed policy of "strategic ambiguity."

HUMAN RIGHTS

House Presses Clinton To Keep Pressure on China

MARCH 21 — The House has issued a unanimous rebuke to the Clinton administration for its decision not to seek a United Nations resolution condemning China's human rights practices.

By a vote of 397-0 on March 17, the House approved a non-binding resolution (H Res 364) by Rep. Christopher H. Smith, R-N.J., calling on the administration to introduce and support such a measure at the 54th session of the U.N. Commission on Human Rights taking place in Geneva. *(Vote 54, p. H-18)*

The House action followed the March 12 passage of a similar resolution (S Res 187) by the Senate.

Administration officials announced several days before the House vote that they would break with their past policy and no longer seek to condemn China at the U.N. conference.

They pointed to what they described as significant, positive strides that Beijing has made on human rights in the last year.

In particular, administration officials cited China's March 12 decision to sign the International Covenant on Civil and Political Rights. Signatories to the covenant promise to respect freedom of religion, thought, conscience and expression.

The administration also applauded Beijing's decision to release prominent dissident Wei Jingsheng in November and to pursue judicial reforms.

Both Democratic and Republican lawmakers said that Beijing's human rights record had not changed enough to justify the change in policy. Moreover, they said that China was unlikely to live up to its new commitments.

"The Beijing regime routinely ignores its legal promises, especially where human rights are concerned," Smith said.

Rep. Nancy Pelosi, D-Calif., pointed out that several notorious human rights violators, such as Sudan and Iraq, had also signed the covenant. ◆

International Affairs

Monetary Support for the IMF Hangs in the Balance For Much of the Year

SUMMARY

President Clinton's request to appropriate $17.9 billion for the International Monetary Fund (IMF) sparked a yearlong battle over issues as far-ranging as the global economy and overseas abortion policy. Under pressure from the business community, a reluctant Congress cleared the entire amount in the final days of the session after attaching language to revamp some IMF policies.

The tussle formally started in March in the House Banking and Financial Services Committee, when Chairman Jim Leach, R-Iowa, won approval of HR 3114 (H Rept 105-454). His measure would have provided the full $17.9 billion in funding — $3.4 billion for a new IMF lending program and $14.5 billion for a more controversial dues increase — along with general language to revamp IMF lending policies.

But Republican leaders never brought that measure to the floor. Leach's bill proved to be only a sideshow to a two-part appropriations battle over whether to include the funding in a fiscal 1998 supplemental spending bill (HR 3579) and, when it failed there, the fiscal 1999 foreign aid spending bill (HR 4569).

The Senate, friendly turf for IMF supporters throughout the year, approved funding with some conditions in its supplemental measure (S 1768). But the House Appropriations Committee split off the funding into a separate measure (HR 3580) that never made it to the floor. Conferees dropped IMF funding from the supplemental bill, saving the debate for the foreign aid measure.

For much of the spring and summer, funding for the 182-nation organization appeared to hang in the balance. Business and farm lobbyists joined the administration in a major lobbying campaign, contending the money was necessary to help stabilize overseas economies. But House Majority Leader Dick Armey, R-Texas, and other conservatives assailed the IMF for interfering with free markets, and liberals criticized it for pressuring nations to slash social and environmental programs.

The Senate, spurred by the decline of markets across the globe, included the funding in its version of the foreign aid bill (S 2334). But House members put just $3.4 billion in their version (HR 4569), and attached a provision to impose abortion restrictions on international family planning aid — a provision strongly opposed by the administration.

Unable to resolve their differences on a stand-alone bill, GOP leaders buckled under administration and business community pressure. In the final days of the session, they agreed to drop the abortion language and add the full $17.9 billion of funding to the omnibus appropriations bill (HR 4328). Congress attached conditions to the funding, but the language was of little importance because IMF was already doing what the legislation required. ◆

Chapter 17

LAW & JUDICIARY

Skilled Worker Visas 17-3	**Judicial Powers** 17-12
Immigration Initiatives 17-8	Justice Department Authorization 17-14
Prayer Amendment 17-9	**Juvenile Crime** 17-15
Flag Desecration Amendment 17-11	**Identity Theft** 17-16
	Assisted Suicide 17-18

Law & Judiciary

Protracted Negotiations Yield Increase In Number Of Visas for Skilled Workers

Box Score

- **Bill:** HR 4328 — PL 105-277
- **House action:** The House adopted the conference report (H Rept 105-825) on HR 4328, 333-95, on Oct. 20. It passed HR 3736 (H Rept 105-657) on Sept. 24, 288-133.
- **Senate action:** The Senate cleared the conference report on HR 4328, 65-29, on Oct. 21. It passed S 1723 (S Rept 105-186) on May 18 by a vote of 78-20.
- **Presidential action:** Clinton signed HR 4328 Oct. 21.

SUMMARY

At the beginning of 1998, high-tech companies hurting for technology-trained workers launched a lobbying campaign in favor of legislation to increase the number of temporary visas issued to highly skilled foreigners. The negotiations took all year and at one point appeared as if they would come to naught. But a provision temporarily increasing the number of "H-1B" visas from 65,000 to 115,000 was included in the omnibus spending package passed at the end of the 105th Congress.

From the outset, there was little doubt the Senate would try to aid the industry. Despite grumbling from labor-backed Democrats such as Edward M. Kennedy of Massachusetts, the majority of senators favored prompt action. A bill (S 1723) to increase the visas passed 78-20 in May.

But in the House, a similar measure faced opposition from both union-backed Democrats and Republican immigration hawks. The House Judiciary Committee reported a bill (HR 3736) to place new regulations on the program.

Under the bill, companies hoping to sponsor H-1B immigrants would have been required to show they had made good-faith efforts to find American workers before bringing in skilled foreigners and would have been prohibited from laying off existing workers with similar skills. Industry balked, and the bill stalled.

High-tech companies, the Clinton administration and Republicans led by Sen. Spencer Abraham of Michigan spent the summer working out a compromise. The deal materialized in a new version of HR 3736, which passed the House in September.

The Senate was then to take up the House-passed bill, but Kennedy and his allies were able to block consideration. To get around them, backers of the H-1B visa expansion added the provision to the omnibus spending package (HR 4328), and it sailed through.

The final version increases the number of H-1B visas to 115,000 in 1999 and 2000, then drops them to 107,500 in 2001. Thereafter, they would fall back to 65,000. It includes the House-passed requirements on businesses, but applies them only to a small class of employers that heavily depend on the H1-B program.

Senate Panel OKs Bill To Recruit Foreign Workers

APRIL 4 — With a robust economy, a huge lobbying effort from high-technology companies and a nation anxious about who will reprogram its computers to avoid a millennial crash, lawmakers are increasingly willing to allow companies to look beyond America's borders for skilled workers.

On April 2, the Senate Judiciary Committee approved a measure (S 1723) increasing the number of visas for skilled workers. The measure would increase the number of so-called H-1B visas from 65,000 to 95,000 per year, with a chance to grow to as much as 115,000 if other visa categories go unfilled. The bill, sponsored by Spencer Abraham, R-Mich., was approved 12-6, with the support of all 10 Republicans and two Democrats.

Opposition was muted as Democrats such as Dianne Feinstein of California and Edward M. Kennedy of Massachusetts struggled to balance the needs of their labor union supporters with the sizeable high-tech industries in their states. Union leaders say the visas depress wages. Rather than attack Abraham's proposal directly, the two offered their own, scaled-back proposal.

Under the Abraham measure, the visas would last for six years. Feinstein and Kennedy proposed they last for three. They also would have put more restrictions and regulations on the hiring of foreign workers.

When their effort failed 8-10, Feinstein chose to join one other Democrat, Herb Kohl of Wisconsin, in supporting Abraham, while Kennedy remained opposed. Both said they would work with Abraham to change the bill.

"I'm committed to support this bill," said Feinstein. "But I'd like to see it better than it is."

Democratic support for the Abraham bill was not the only sign of success for H-1B legislation. In the House, Rep. Lamar Smith, R-Texas, leader of a faction that takes a restrictive view toward immigration, has promised to move a bill this spring. Smith, though, may try to offset some of the new visas by cutting the number available to lesser-skilled workers.

The biggest obstacle for the H-1B legislation may be President Clinton. He opposed an earlier draft and has yet to take a position on the current approach.

Part of a Trend

The H-1B issue is part of a larger trend in which the Republicans have partially retreated from some of the strict immigration policies they adopted after taking control of Congress. First, they restored Supplemental Se-

Law & Judiciary

curity Income to legal immigrants who were cut off under the 1996 welfare law (PL 104-193). They are considering restoring food stamps to a portion of the 935,000 legal immigrants who lost nutrition benefits.

Second, they have allowed a category of illegal immigrants to adjust to legal status without having to leave the country. In passing the fiscal 1998 spending bill for the departments of Commerce Justice and State (PL 105-119), Congress terminated a provision known as 245(i) which allowed people to adjust their status from illegal to legal by paying a fine, but allowed people already in the country to continue to have that option.

That measure also granted amnesty to a class of refugees from Nicaragua and Cuba to stay in the country, while refugees from El Salvador, Guatemala and parts of Eastern Europe were allowed to apply for asylum under more liberal guidelines. This year, legislation giving Haitians similar treatment to the Guatemalans and Salvadorans is pending in Congress.

But nothing quite compares with the explosion of interest in the H-1B program. It became an issue almost impossible to ignore as computer industry stars such as Microsoft Corp. founder Bill Gates and Dell Computers Chairman Michael Dell personally lobbied the cause.

In letters and testimony, they told the subcommittee how thousands of jobs in their companies have gone unfilled for lack of skilled workers. They pointed to bulging help-wanted sections in newspapers, and to a Labor Department study estimating that over the next 10 years, 1.3 million new jobs related to computers and information technology will be created. The same study estimated that American universities would only produce about a quarter of that number of graduates immediately ready to fill the positions.

"It's a function of the high-tech worker shortage," said Scott Hoffman, director of American Business for Legal Immigration, the industry umbrella group lobbying the issue. "Companies are desperate for skilled workers. American colleges and universities are just not turning out enough people in these areas."

If the general shortages were not enough, the problem is compounded, industry experts say, by the necessary diversion of thousands of skilled computer programmers in the next two years to fix computer systems that were never programmed to deal with the year 2000 and beyond.

All these factors have combined to create a large and growing labor shortage, industry experts say. These conclusions have been echoed in studies by the Hudson Institute and Virginia Polytechnic University, among others. Somewhat contrary views have been forwarded by the General Accounting Office (GAO) and the Labor Department's inspector general. The GAO questioned whether there is sufficient data to conclude there is a shortage. Labor's inspector general concluded the H-1B program is poorly managed.

Democratic Opposition

The increased number of H-1B visas in Abraham's bill would last for five years, starting in the current fiscal year and ending in fiscal 2002. Originally, Abraham had made the increase permanent, but he agreed to the five-year period to mollify some Democrats. Also, in an attempt to answer critics who say high-tech jobs should go to Americans, the bill authorizes $50 million in matching grants to states for math, engineering and computer science scholarships.

Addressing a finding by the Labor Department that approximately 27 percent of current H-1B recipients are health care professionals, mostly nurses, nurses assistants and physical therapists, Abraham would cap visas for these professions at 10,000.

The H-1B visas last for six years, after which their holder has to return home or apply for a permanent visa. Currently, they are good for three years but can be easily extended for three more years.

The Kennedy-Feinstein alternative would have limited the duration of the program, and the visas, to three years. That proposal also called for a $250 application fee, tougher workplace enforcement and a ban on participating employers from laying off workers.

Much of the Democratic opposition was couched in terms of general observations. Feinstein, for instance, noted the H-1B program was a "massive indictment of our educational system."

She also argued that the program, though intended as temporary, was actually a foot in the door for immigrants hoping to come here permanently. About half the H-1B recipients, she said, eventually get permanent visas.

Abraham acknowledged that Feinstein had a legitimate argument on the shortcomings of the educational system. He said the money for American universities would lay the groundwork for a long-term solution. But he also conceded his measure was "just a Band-Aid, and a skimpy one at that."

As for the long-term intentions of H-1B visa holders, he said that his bill did not increase the number of permanent employment-related visas. Furthermore, he said he saw nothing wrong with awarding the lion's share of permanent visas to people who had six years in the U.S. to enhance their skills.

"If we don't, they will go overseas and work for our competitors," Abraham said.

The stiffest opposition to the Abraham bill came from the Federation for American Immigration Reform (FAIR), a group that advocates reducing legal immigration while beefing up efforts to block illegal immigration.

"It's amazing to see that Congress has fallen over so far for this massive public relations and propaganda campaign the industry has been mounting," said FAIR Deputy Director K. C. McAlpin.

He argued the shortages are greatly exaggerated and that high-tech industries, like others, are interested in exploiting cheap labor. Immigrants from developing countries are often willing to work for considerably less than their American counterparts since even a substandard wage in America allows them to live better than they did in their home countries, he said.

Furthermore, McAlpin argued, the visa situation is ripe for exploitation by employers. H-1B visa holders looking for sponsorship for a permanent visa would have very little negotiating leverage over employers they need to sponsor them, he said.

High-Tech Firms Cite Shortage Of Skilled Workers

MAY 23 — Though they are led by the same party, the House and Senate sometimes seem to operate in different universes, exhibiting different properties and governed by different laws of nature.

This was the case the week of May 18 when the Senate and the House Judiciary Committee took up legislation (S 1723, HR 3736) designed to increase the number of temporary visas for highly skilled workers. High-tech companies such as Intel Corp. and Microsoft Corp. have sought the increase to answer what they say is a shortage of skilled workers.

On the surface, the two chambers' actions seemed to be routine and similar. On May 18, the Senate passed its bill, by a vote of 78-20. (Vote 141, p. S-24)

Two days later, the Judiciary Committee approved the House measure, sponsored by Lamar Smith, R-Texas, by a vote of 23-4. Under the bills, the maximum annual allotment of H-1B visas would be increased from the current 65,000 to 115,000 by 2000.

But in the content of the legislation, as well as the politics surrounding it, the two chambers could not be further apart.

To try to protect American workers, Smith's bill in the House included two provisions that would set new criteria for businesses who want to sponsor H-1B immigrants. The same two provisions were met with something close to revulsion by Smith's Republican colleagues in the Senate.

The first would require businesses to show they have taken "good faith, timely and significant steps" to recruit equally qualified American workers. The second would bar companies from participating in the program if they had laid off any U.S. workers with skills equivalent to those of the foreign workers they brought in.

High-tech companies and their supporters in Congress said the provisions would greatly increase the regulatory burden on companies that have thrived because of their entrepreneurial, and to some extent, anti-Washington, attitudes.

They would "give the Department of Labor dramatic intrusive powers to intervene in hiring decisions of high-tech companies," said Spencer Abraham, R-Mich., sponsor of the Senate bill.

President Clinton does not accept this argument. He has threatened to veto Abraham's bill if it reaches his desk without the labor protections.

The Senate soundly rejected such provisions when they were offered as floor amendments by Edward M. Kennedy, D-Mass. An amendment prohibiting companies who had laid off workers from sponsoring H-1B workers was tabled (killed), 60-38, while the requirement that businesses attest to having made efforts to recruit American workers was also tabled, 59-39. (Votes 138 and 139, p. S-23)

In the House Judiciary Committee, the two issues were dealt with together in an amendment by Rep. James E. Rogan, R-Calif., that would have stripped them from the underlying bill. It was rejected, 7-24.

Those who voted against Rogan included some of the most conservative members of the committee, including Smith; Bill McCollum, R-Fla.; Bob Barr, R-Ga.; and Chairman Henry J. Hyde, R-Ill. They argued that the labor provisions were an important complement to a bill whose central purpose of increasing immigration could adversely affect American workers.

"I honestly don't think that either one of these things is unreasonable," said Hyde. "We ought to be trying to protect U.S. jobs."

Labor Shortages

Almost lost in the debate were the underlying bills, which were drafted at the urging of high-technology companies that say they face a significant temporary labor shortage. Newspaper classified sections around the country are bursting with ads for computer programmers and engineers, they point out. To make matters worse, some of the best and brightest programmers are needed to help companies avoid computer crashes associated with the year 2000. These pressures on the labor market resulted in the 65,000 cap for H-1B visas for the year 1998 being reached May 7, earlier than ever before.

Critics of the H-1B program say it is rife with abuse from companies known as "job shops" that do nothing but sponsor H-1B workers, then subcontract them to other companies. These companies, they argue, have enormous leverage over the immigrants because their sponsorship will be vital if they want to obtain permanent visas at the end of their H-1B term. For this reason, this system almost invites the employers to make unreasonable salary demands.

Critics also point out that not all the people brought in are overachievers that American industry desperately needs. Physical therapists, athletes, and even fashion models can obtain H-1B visas.

Aside from the labor provisions, the two bills are roughly equivalent. They would increase this year's allotment of H-1B visas to 95,000 and raise it to as high as 115,000 by fiscal 2000. The Senate bill would continue at that level until fiscal 2002. The House bill would drop back to 65,000 after fiscal 2000. Opponents of the legislation are dubious that these numbers will ever drop once companies put them into practice.

The Senate bill would provide matching grants to states for training American students in math, engineering and computer sciences. That provision is not in the House measure. In lieu of the labor provisions, the Abraham bill would greatly increase the penalties for knowingly abusing current labor policies in the H-1B program.

The House bill would limit the new visas to four years, rather than the six-year period under current law. Consistent with recent Judiciary Committee practice, the House bill requests two studies from the General Accounting Office. One would examine the high-tech labor market in general, and the other would look at age discrimination in high-tech employment.

House Amendments

Committee consideration of the House bill had a hurried and tentative quality to it, as if the members knew it was only a rough draft. Debate on the Rogan amendment to remove the labor provisions was given a 45-minute time limit. It was the only amendment to be given a recorded vote.

An amendment by Elton Gallegly,

Law & Judiciary

R-Calif., reducing the term of the new visas from six to four years — a significant policy change — was dispatched in a couple of minutes and by voice vote. The same action was taken on an amendment by Melvin Watt, D-N.C., giving universities and nonprofit research institutions an exemption from the layoff provisions. The same was the case with an amendment by Zoe Lofgren, D-Calif., reducing by more than half the number of temporary visas for unskilled workers. All were passed.

For a committee known for its political polarization, consideration of the bill was remarkably bipartisan. The labor provisions were supported by a majority of Republicans and by all voting Democrats, though Lofgren, who represents Silicon Valley, was absent at the time of the vote.

This was more the result of a confluence of interests than a cross-party accommodation. Labor-friendly Democrats supported the provisions as part of their alliance with unions. Some of the Republican support may have been driven by hostility or ambivalence toward increasing immigration.

Smith, Gallegly and other members have taken the view that U.S. immigration policy is already very generous and should not be further liberalized. Smith had tried to bargain with high-tech companies on the H-1B issue to get their support for restrictions in other categories of immigration. He added the labor provisions to his bill after they failed to support him.

Some of Smith's opponents believe the labor provisions were added as retribution against the companies. He denies this and points out that the provisions are consistent with his immigration views in general.

Bipartisan Amendments

Senate consideration was a fairly bipartisan affair as well, at least on final passage. The bill was supported by all but one Republican (Tim Hutchinson of Arkansas) and a majority of Democrats. Kennedy's bid to add the labor provisions was more partisan, but Republicans were still able to pick up a handful of Democrats.

The Senate considered only three amendments — Kennedy's two and one by Dale Bumpers, D-Ark., that would have eliminated another immigration program under which investors can be given visas, and ultimately citizenship, if they agree to keep at least 10 people employed in the United States. It was tabled by a 74-24 vote. (Vote 140, p. S-23)

The Senate debate was low-key and often postponed by consideration of other bills. It had been scheduled for the week of May 11. When it came up on Monday morning, May 18, the debate was on and off, as many senators were still in their home states. Many who were around were more interested in making statements about a proposed tobacco settlement, which was to be taken up later that day.

This lack of high-decibel debate did not deter the bill's supporters, who argued that it would be one of the most important pieces of legislation Congress considers this year.

"The ramifications are considerable," said Abraham, adding that major projects envisioned by companies such as Intel and Ford Motor Co., which is in his home state, could be put off for lack of skilled labor.

"It could cost us many American jobs," he said. "Layoffs could result and economic growth could be impacted."

Part of the difference in the two chambers' approaches may be attributable to their bills' sponsors. Unlike Smith, Abraham is an unapologetic supporter of immigration in all forms.

Furthermore, the Senate does not have people such as Smith and Gallegly, who have defined themselves in large part by their hawkish views on immigration. If there were many Republican senators uneasy with the new H-1B immigrants, they did not show it. As a result, the Senate bill had a relatively easy passage both in committee and on the floor.

The future of the Senate bill does not look quite so bright, however. If the House bill is passed as it is, the Senate bill will go into a contentious conference, with Clinton siding with the House conferees. The Clinton administration issued a veto threat against the Senate bill for not having adequate labor provisions.

The administration argues that the bill "emphasizes providing opportunities for foreign workers rather than providing opportunities for and protecting U.S. workers."

But the House bill, too, faces problems. Many pro-business Republicans think it is ludicrous that the party would back a bill expanding the Labor Department's purview over companies that are the epitome of free-enterprise success.

"I hope we can do something in advance of the floor debate or in conference to rectify what I think is a severe problem with this legislation," said republican Rep. Christopher B. Cannon of Utah.

In the end, lawmakers may have to strike a delicate balance to get the legislation enacted. Whatever labor provisions are included will have to be enough to assuage Clinton, while not as offensive to high-tech companies as are the Smith provisions.

Veto Talk Prompts Both Chambers To Postpone Votes

AUGUST 1 — Efforts to clear a bill that would increase the number of "H-1B" visas for foreign high-tech workers failed the week of July 27 when the Clinton administration signaled it was not happy with a proposed compromise. Scheduled for a vote in both chambers July 31, the measure (HR 3736) was pulled from the calendar under threat of a veto.

House and Senate leaders had hoped to pass a bill before the August recess to respond to pleas from the computer industry. Companies including Microsoft Corp. and Intel Corp. have been telling lawmakers they are facing a critical labor shortage that, in the short run at least, can only be addressed with foreign workers.

But with little chance the president would sign the measure, there was nothing to be gained by rushing it through. And late in the evening of July 30, Senate Minority Leader Tom Daschle, D-S.D., signaled that Democrats would stand by Clinton and block expedited consideration of the bill.

H-1B workers are sponsored by their employers, and their visas last for six years. No new H-1B visas have been issued since May 7, when this year's quota of 65,000 was met. The measure that lawmakers hoped to pass would increase the quota to 85,000 for

1998, and to 115,000 by 2001.

The House may vote on the bill the week of Aug. 3. But failure to act before the Senate left for recess means companies will have to wait until at least September before the spigot of H-1B workers could be turned on again.

How to handle the H-1B issue has caused two fissures: one between labor-backed Democrats and business-backed Republicans, and a second in House Republican ranks, between those who favor generous immigration policies and those who take a restrictive approach.

The divide in the Republican camp had been closed through a compromise reached July 23. The split between business and labor remains, however. And the administration announced July 30 that it was still firmly in labor's camp, despite the fact that Clinton counts on considerable support from Silicon Valley executives. The administration objected to the compromise on the same grounds that it opposed a version (S 1723) passed by the Senate on May 18: that it would not provide enough protection for American workers competing with the H-1B hires.

A Compromise Over Workers

The compromise language keeps the basic outline of the two requirements contained in an earlier House draft that had labor support, but scales back both considerably.

The first would require companies to go to considerable lengths to find American workers before looking overseas. The second would prevent companies from laying off workers with skills similar to those of the H-1B workers they bring in.

Under the compromise, those requirements would have applied only to companies of at least 51 people whose work force comprises at least 15 percent H-1B workers. The provision is an attempt to better police those companies that are highly dependent on foreign workers, including "job shops" that bring in foreign workers only to contract them out to other companies.

The layoff provision would be narrowed in another respect. It would apply only to people with virtually identical areas of expertise.

Furthermore, a role for the Labor Department, which under the earlier House bill would have certified that the companies had met the requirements, was deleted in the compromise.

Proponents of H-1B visas say they are a critical part of American business success in high-technology fields and that failing to provide ample numbers only encourages companies to relocate portions of their businesses overseas. Opponents argue the program is rife with abuse and that companies use the program to keep labor costs down.

House Passes Bill, Adds Safeguards For Americans

SEPTEMBER 26 — After months of lobbying by the high-tech industry, the House on Sept. 24 passed a compromise bill to increase the number of visas that allow highly skilled workers such as computer programmers to come to the United States for work.

The bill (HR 3736), which was passed on a 288-133 vote, was the product of negotiations earlier in the week between the White House and Spencer Abraham, R-Mich., the legislation's chief sponsor in the Senate. *(Vote 460, p. H-130)*

The measure would boost the number of temporary "H-1B" visas available each year from 65,000 to 115,000 in 1999 and 2000, and to 107,500 in 2001. Thereafter, the limit would return to 65,000.

The compromise came after the Clinton administration threatened to veto the Senate version of the bill (S 1723), which passed in May. The administration objected to that bill's lack of protections for American workers.

Administration officials and some Democrats were more supportive of a version approved by the House Judiciary Committee, also in May, because it included requirements that employers promise not to lay off Americans and replace them with H-1B visa holders and to recruit American employees before petitioning for foreign workers.

Under the House-passed compromise, these attestations would apply to businesses that had a certain percentage of H-1B workers and planned to hire workers who did not have master's degrees and who would be paid less than $60,000 a year. Employers would face stiff penalties and exclusion from the program if they violated the layoff rules.

Lamar Smith, R-Texas, sponsor of the House bill, said these provisions were designed to protect workers from companies most likely to abuse the system, so-called job shops. These are employers who hire a large number of H-1B employees, often merely to contract them out to other companies.

High-tech dependent firms would be defined as: companies with more than 50 employees, 15 percent of whom are H-1B workers; companies with 25 to 50 employees, 12 of whom are H-1B workers; and companies with up to 25 employees, seven of whom are H-1B workers.

The new version would also assess a $500 fee on employers for every visa application and renewal, raising about $75 million a year that would go to college scholarships and job training for low-income students studying math, engineering or computer sciences.

Senate Majority Leader Trent Lott, R-Miss., said Sept. 25 that the Senate would act on the bill "soon."

Balancing Interests

Proponents of the compromise argued that it struck the right balance between protecting American workers and making sure high-tech companies get the talent they need.

"Everyone loses when the private sector is denied access to skilled people," David Dreier, R-Calif., said during the House debate.

Many Democrats did not accept the deal between Abraham and the White House, saying that they were not brought into negotiations or given adequate time to review the changes.

"No one's read it. No one knows what's in the provisions of this bill," complained Ron Klink, of Pennsylvania, one of 98 Democrats to oppose the bill. "This is about giving away American jobs over the next three years."

Before the final vote, the House rejected, 177-242, a substitute offered by Democrat Melvin Watt of North Carolina that essentially was an earlier version of the bill that had been approved by the Judiciary Committee. *(Vote 459, p. H-130)*

That version would have required U.S. companies to promise that no American workers would be laid off to accommodate a foreign employee and

Law & Judiciary

Immigration Initiatives Catch Ride On Year-End Spending Bill

A handful of significant immigration provisions became law as part of the omnibus fiscal 1999 appropriations package (HR 4328 — PL 105-277) signed into law Oct. 21, including the following.

● **Haitian refugees.** The bill allowed nearly 50,000 Haitian refugees to remain in the United States permanently. Congress had agreed to a similar allowance last year for Nicaraguans and Cubans fleeing political turmoil in their homelands, but had not included Haitians, prompting a protest from the Black Caucus and others who decried what they considered a double standard. *(1997 Almanac, p. 5-11)*

The move to grant residency to the Haitians, most of whom are in South Florida, ran into strong opposition from some Californians and other House Republicans, who said it would send the wrong message to people considering immigrating to the country illegally. But Florida's senators, Republican Connie Mack and Democrat Bob Graham, led the ultimately successful fight to have the provision included in the catchall bill.

● **Border checks.** Another provision in the omnibus bill delayed through March 2001, the implementation of an automated system at the U.S. borders with Mexico and Canada to document the entry and departure of every non-citizen coming into and leaving the United States.

The system, which was required under a 1996 immigration law (PL 104-208), was intended to help the Immigration and Naturalization Service (INS) identify people who overstayed their visas. It was to be implemented by Oct. 1, 1998, but the INS was not ready to put it in place. In addition, Canadians and U.S. lawmakers representing areas along the northern border said that such a system would result in enormous traffic backups at the border.

Congress had made a temporary fix that postponed the deadline until Oct. 15. The House passed the interim bill (HR 4658) by voice vote Oct. 1, and the Senate cleared it Oct. 8, also by voice vote.

● **INS.** The INS received a boost in funding through the omnibus law, including $171 million designated to help it ease a backlog of naturalization and other immigration-related applications.

Overall, the INS received $3.86 billion for fiscal 1999, which was a 2 percent increase over fiscal 1998, though it still was $329 million, or 9 percent, less than the Clinton administration had requested.

Visa Compromise Wins Enactment In Omnibus Bill

OCTOBER 17 — A measure to significantly boost the number of visas allowing highly skilled workers, such as computer programmers, to immigrate to the United States for work arose from the legislative graveyard to be folded into the omnibus spending bill (HR 4328).

The legislation increases the number of six-year H-1B visas available from 65,000 to 115,000 in 1999 and 2000, and to 107,500 in 2001. Thereafter, the limit returns to 65,000.

The House had passed a compromise version of the bill (HR 3736) on Sept. 24, but Sen. Tom Harkin, D-Iowa, blocked the measure in the Senate, arguing that there was little evidence of a worker shortage and that the proposal might take jobs away from U.S. citizens.

At that point, lead sponsor, Sen. Spencer Abraham, R-Mich., declared the bill dead. But support from Republicans, Democrats and the White House helped revive it Oct. 13, and it became part of the negotiations on the omnibus spending bill.

The Clinton administration had threatened to veto an earlier, Senate-passed version of the bill (S 1723), saying it would not adequately protect American workers.

But the White House was more supportive of the House version, approved by the House Judiciary Committee in May, because it included requirements that employers promise not to lay off Americans and and replace them with H-1B visa holders. That version, sponsored by Lamar Smith, R-Texas, also required firms to recruit U.S. employees before petitioning for foreign workers. that they had made good-faith efforts to recruit domestic employees before looking abroad.

Under the compromise, those layoff and recruitment requirements would apply to H-1B dependent businesses — those that have a certain percentage of H-1B workers — and those that plan to hire workers who do not have master's degrees and who would be paid less than $60,000 a year. Employers face stiff penalties and exclusion from the program if they violate the layoff rules.

Those provisions were designed to protect workers from so-called job shops, firms that hire a large number of H-1B employees, often to simply contract them out to other companies.

Under the bill, H-1B dependent firms are defined as companies with more than 50 employees, 15 percent of whom are H-1B workers; companies with 25 to 50 employees, 12 of whom are H-1B workers; and companies with up to 25 employees, seven of whom are H-1B workers.

The compromise also assesses a $500 fee on employers for every visa application and renewal, raising about $75 million a year that would go to college scholarships and job training for low-income students studying math, engineering or computer sciences.

The visa issue was a difficult one for the White House because it had the potential to alienate key Democratic constituencies on opposite sides of the issue. The administration has traditionally been allied with organized labor but has not wanted to alienate its supporters in Silicon Valley.

Business groups had pushed for the extra visas, arguing that high-tech firms will face worker shortages unless they can import highly skilled talent. Companies including Microsoft Corp. and Intel Corp. told lawmakers they are facing a critical labor shortage that can only be addressed with foreign workers. Proponents of the compromise said it struck the right balance between protecting American workers and making sure high-tech companeis get the talent they need.

But unions said the measure would cost American jobs, saying the compromise still contained serious flaws and would exempt some employers from complying with the recruitment and layoff requirements.

Harkin said on Oct. 9 that the bill was unnecessary because there is no shortage of domestic computer programmers, engineers or other highly skilled workers.

"The programming shortage never materialized," he said. "And we don't need to pass this now. . . . We can always come back if there is a shortgage." To boost his case, Harkin cited an article in the San Jose (Calif.) Mercury News reporting an increase in layoffs in the high-tech sector.

But Abraham rejected Harkin's contention.

"Virtually every study I have seen . . . points to a very severe shortage," he said. Abraham said that a Commerce Department study projects there will be 130,000 new information technology jobs each year for the next few years. ◆

Constitutional Amendment On Religious Expression Meets Defeat in the House

Box Score

- **Bill:** H J Res 78
- **House action:** The House defeated the measure, 224-203, on June 4 — 61 votes short of the two-thirds necessary to pass a constitutional amendment.
- **Senate action:** None.

In early summer, lawmakers kicked off an election year season of constitutional debate with House consideration of a proposed amendment that would have expanded and clarified rights of religious expression.

SUMMARY

The measure gained a majority of votes in the House but fell well short of the two-thirds necessary for approval. The amendment would have guaranteed the right to pray and to recognize religious beliefs on public property — including schools — and would have prohibited the federal government or any state from establishing an official religion.

The measure was the ninth constitutional amendment considered in the House since the Republicans took control in 1995. It was sponsored by Rep. Ernest Istook, R-Okla., and backed by the Christian Coalition, which had been pushing for a floor vote since the summer of 1996.

Supporters said it was necessary because the First Amendment has been misinterpreted by the courts. Opponents contended that it would have destroyed the constitutional separation between church and state in America.

Prayer Amendment Advances Toward House Floor Vote

MARCH 7 — Proponents of a constitutional amendment to allow prayer and other forms of religious expression on public property advanced their cause March 4 when the House Judiciary Committee approved their measure on a 16-11 party-line vote.

Sponsors of H J Res 78 concede they are well short of the two-thirds majority needed for the resolution to pass the full House. But their short-term goal of getting the measure to the floor for a recorded vote now seems within reach.

Called the "religious freedom" constitutional amendment, the legislation is sponsored by Rep. Ernest Istook, R-Okla., and is backed by the Christian Coalition, which has been pushing for a floor vote since the summer of 1996.

The amendment would guarantee people's right to "pray and to recognize their religious beliefs, heritage, or traditions on public property." It would also provide public funding for religious schools and churches involved in social welfare programs.

Its supporters say a constitutional amendment is necessary not because the First Amendment's religion clauses are flawed, but because they have been misinterpreted by the courts. They argue court rulings have sometimes led local officials to adopt policies infringing on constitutionally protected religious expression.

Courts have walked a fine line in interpreting the First Amendment's two clauses, one prohibiting the establishment of a government-sanctioned religion and the other guaranteeing free expression of religion. Particularly in the context of public schools and courtrooms, where attendance is not always voluntary, free expression to one person can look like the government sanctioning of religion to another. The result has been a series of rulings that many conservatives say have overly secularized public life.

Law & Judiciary

"The First Amendment has been twisted beyond recognition time and time again by the Supreme Court," said Rep. Robert W. Goodlatte, R-Va.

But Democrats on the committee said the new language will complicate, not simplify, the courts' role in finding a proper balance. Furthermore, they added, language allowing public funding of religious schools and churches would make it almost impossible to keep the government out of religion.

"We are seeking to solve a problem that doesn't exist by creating problems that will exist," said Rep. Robert C. Scott, D-Va.

In 1993, Congress tried to clarify what it considered appropriate religious expression through passage of the Religious Freedom Restoration Act (PL 103-141). But that statute was struck down last year by the Supreme Court as unconstitutional.

The Istook measure has done much better in the 105th Congress than in the 104th, when proponents broke into two factions, one led by Istook and one led by Judiciary Committee Chairman Henry J. Hyde, R-Ill. With the two groups together, proponents may now muster a majority, but are still a long way from amending the Constitution. To do that, they would need a two-thirds vote in the House and Senate and ratification by 34 states.

House Vote Falls Short Of Needed Majority

JUNE 6 — Lawmakers kicked off an election-year season of constitutional debate and conservative legislation June 4 as the House took up a proposed amendment to the Constitution that would expand and clarify rights of religious expression. Although the House voted 224-203 for the measure (H J Res 78), the vote fell well short of the two-thirds necessary for approval. *(Vote 201, p. H-58)*

The vote marks the first time such an amendment reached the House floor since 1971, when the House defeated a narrower amendment covering only school prayer. This latest measure is a long way from ratification. Not only did it fall short of the two-thirds vote, it is not even being considered in the Senate. *(1971 Almanac, p. 624)*

If approved by Congress, it would have to be ratified by 38 states.

While this year's measure became known as a "school prayer" amendment, it contains broad language protecting religious expression on all kinds of public property. It also would allow government funding for religious institutions ranging from schools to social service agencies.

The vote was an inauspicious beginning to a string of election-year debates on amendments and legislative causes championed by religious conservatives. The Senate is planning to take up an amendment (S J Res 40) prohibiting flag desecration, starting in the Judiciary Committee, this summer. And both houses are considering amendments to bolster the rights of crime victims.

Also, Congress is considering other actions favored by religious conservatives, including a ban on crossing state lines to avoid parental notification laws restricting abortions (HR 3862, S 1645) and a possible attempt to override a presidential veto of legislation (HR 1122) banning so-called partial-birth abortions.

Voting on the religion amendment, sponsored by Ernest Istook, R-Okla., fell largely along party lines.

Istook said the measure was necessary not because the First Amendment's religion clauses — one prohibiting the establishment of a religion and the other guaranteeing individual rights to religious expression — are flawed but because judges have misinterpreted these two clauses, taking language restricting state-sponsored religion and turning it into jurisprudence that is openly hostile to personal expression of religion.

"The Supreme Court has twisted and distorted the plain and simple language of the Constitution," Istook said.

Opponents argued that if court interpretation is the problem, Istook's lengthy amendment would only complicate matters. Furthermore, they said, the section providing public funding for religious institutions raised the possibility of bizarre cults coming forward to demand their piece of the pie.

On a more fundamental level, opponents balked at amending the Constitution to alter the meaning of the original 10 amendments, which compose the Bill of Rights. This would have been the first time in American history such action was taken. "Where has the First Amendment failed us?" said David E. Skaggs, D-Colo. "I don't understand what we are doing here."

An Election Issue

Backers of the amendment knew they were well short of the votes they would need. But they were eager to get members on record. Indeed, the Christian Coalition plans to put the results into the voters' guides it distributes before the fall elections.

Going forward with a religion amendment and other conservative causes this close to the election may be the best expression yet of a sentiment often stated in GOP policy meetings: The party should concentrate more on getting loyal supporters to the polls than trying to win over swing voters.

The vote comes weeks after meetings between party leaders and James Dobson, president of a conservative religious group called Focus on the Family. Dobson had threatened to abandon the party if it did not return to issues of interest to religious conservatives.

Religious freedom is currently spelled out in the first sentence of the First Amendment, which says: "Congress shall make no law respecting an establishment of religion, or prohibiting the free exercise thereof."

But with its establishment and free-exercise clauses juxtaposed as they are, it leaves much room for interpretation. Indeed, the courts have been struggling for the proper balance of prohibiting an official religion while protecting the free exercise of private religion.

Nowhere is this conflict more evident than in public schools. Prayers and other forms of religious expression in publicly funded institutions, particularly those based on precepts of order and discipline, can obviously raise concerns about the establishment clause.

But since school is compulsory — and public school may be the only option for many families — limitations on religious expression at school can violate students' individual rights under the free-exercise clause.

The result of this conflict in the First Amendment has been a series of rulings striking a delicate balance. The Supreme Court started limiting school prayer in 1962 in *Engel v. Vitale*, and the following year in *Abington School District v. Schempp*. Both banned officially sanctioned prayers and religious exercise in schools.

The court broadened its approach in the 1971 case *Lemon v. Kurtzman*, which laid out general criteria for when it is appropriate for government to involve itself with religious institutions. This could come up in a variety of contexts — a city working with a church to provide a homeless shelter, for example, or a county providing special education to students in a religious school.

In *Lemon*, the court said that a government, in taking such action, must have a secular purpose, that it must neither advance nor inhibit religion, and must not foster excessive entanglement with religion.

Since then, the court has sought to elaborate on the decision with a series of rulings designed to address specific circumstances. In the 1985 *Wallace v. Jaffree* case, for instance, the court struck down compulsory moments of silence in public schools. The same year, in *Thornton v. Caldor, Inc.* it rejected a Connecticut law requiring companies to give employees time off on their Sabbath. And in *Lee v. Weisman* in 1992 it struck down non-denominational prayers at public school graduations.

In 1990, in *Employment Division v. Smith*, the court gave local governments considerable leeway to adopt laws violating free-exercise rights, as long as that was not the laws' primary purpose. Congress' attempt to correct this, a 1993 statute known as the Religious Freedom Restoration Act (PL 103-141), was struck down by the court in the 1997 ruling, *City of Boerne v. Flores*.

These rulings have convinced many religious conservatives that successive members of the Supreme Court are, almost without exception, anti-religion.

We seek "neutrality toward religion, not hostility to it," said Henry J. Hyde, R-Ill., chairman of the House Judiciary Committee.

But this argument did not come close to winning over the support necessary for passage. Republicans were unable to persuade their moderate wing to support the resolution, and even some conservatives opposed the

Flag Amendment Halted In the Senate

Despite overwhelming, bipartisan approval by the House in the first session of the 105th Congress, the Senate took no action on a proposed constitutional amendment to allow Congress to ban physical desecration of the U.S. flag. The strong House vote — on H J Res 54 (H Rept 105-126) — had buoyed supporters' hopes of winning passage in the Senate, where the real fight was expected to take place. (1997 Almanac, p. 5-10)

On June 24, 1998, the Senate Judiciary Committee approved two versions of the amendments that were virtually identical but for minor differences in their enacting clauses. H J Res 54 and S J Res 40 (S Rept 105-298) were approved, 10-7, with California Democrat Dianne Feinstein joining nine Republicans. Arlen Specter, R-Pa., was absent because of recent heart surgery.

The committee acted just before the Fourth of July recess in the hope of capitalizing on the upcoming patriotic holiday. However, the vote garnered almost no attention, and the measure was not taken up on the floor.

Judiciary Committee Chairman Orrin G. Hatch, R-Utah, argued that an amendment was necessary because of Supreme Court rulings in 1989 and 1990 protecting flag desecration as a form of free speech. Opponents of the measure, such as Joseph R. Biden Jr, D-Del., said it is impossible to legislate patriotic values.

The attempt in the 105th Congress marked the third time lawmakers had pushed a resolution to protect the flag since the earlier Supreme Court rulings. In 1990, the House fell 34 votes short of the two-thirds majority needed to approve a constitutional amendment. In 1995, the House easily passed a similar measure, but the Senate fell three votes short.

---

amendment on the grounds that the new language added to the Constitution would give the courts more, not less, opportunity for mischief.

Divisions Remain

But just getting a House vote was a victory for social conservatives. In 1996, they could not even move a measure out of the Judiciary Committee's Constitution subcommittee because they could not agree on its wording.

Istook led one faction, which supported an amendment not unlike H J Res 78. Hyde led another that advocated broader language with no specific mention of school prayer. The conservative religious advocacy groups were divided as well, with Dobson and his organization lining up with Istook and the Christian Coalition behind Hyde.

Those divisions remain. A number of backers of the original Hyde language still have problems with the Istook measure, said one GOP aide. But they have reasoned that it makes no sense to fight a pitched battle that would alienate some of their most loyal constituents over an amendment that stands little chance of passage.

Two proposed changes to this year's Istook amendment were offered by Sanford D. Bishop Jr., D-Ga. One would have deleted the word "God" from its preamble, on the grounds that Muslims and members of Eastern faiths consider it to be the name of the Judeo-Christian god, not a generic term for the creator of the universe. It was defeated, 6-419. (Vote 198, p. H-58)

A second would have deleted the portion dealing with public funding of religious institutions. It was defeated, 23-399. (Vote 199, p. H-58)

As the debate demonstrated, the issue can generate bitter exchanges.

In a speech May 5, Rep. Jack Kingston, R-Ga., declared: "There is no doubt in my mind that there is a special place in hell for a number of federal court judges, as I am sure there will be for members of Congress." ◆

Law & Judiciary

House-Passed Measure To Limit Judges' Powers Stalls in the Senate

Box Score

- **Bills:** HR 1252, HR 3718
- **House action:** The House passed HR 1252 (H Rept 105-478) by voice vote April 23. The House passed HR 3718, 352-53, on May 19.
- **Senate action:** None.

SUMMARY

A wide-ranging attempt by conservatives to deter "judicial activism," or the perceived tendency of judges to set policy from the bench, inched forward in the House last spring, only to die in the Senate. The bill (HR 1252) would have required three-judge panels, instead of a single federal judge, to hear challenges to state laws adopted by a referendum.

The measure's other provisions included a requirement that applications for writs of habeas corpus received in or transferred to a district court be randomly assigned to judges of a court, rather than delegated to a single judge. The controversial issue of allowing cameras in appellate courtrooms — and, on a temporary basis, in the courtrooms of trial judges — would have been resolved in the House-passed version by allowing coverage at a judge's discretion, with privacy protections for some witnesses if requested.

The bill also contained provisions to restrict federal judges from ordering the release of prisoners in state facilities to ease overcrowding. This provision was passed on May 19 as a freestanding bill (HR 3718), but it also died in the Senate.

House Committee Seeks Control Over Federal Judges

MARCH 28 — Constitutionally shut out of the process of confirming judges, the House is trying to put its imprint on the federal judiciary. On March 24, the Judiciary Committee approved a bill (HR 1252) that would restrict the power of federal judges.

Approved by a 12-8 vote, the bill is directed at "judicial activism," a trend perceived by many conservatives who argue that federal judges frequently go beyond their mandate.

Among other things, the measure would make it more difficult for judges to order tax increases to remedy problems such as a substandard school or an environmental hazard. It would also require that appeals of public referendums be heard by three-judge panels and give litigants in the 21 largest judicial districts the right to reject the first judge assigned to their case.

Though widely attacked by Democrats who say it would undercut judicial independence, the bill is less confrontational than an approach advocated by Majority Whip Tom DeLay, R-Texas, who has called for widespread judicial impeachments.

The measure includes some controversial provisions not connected with the overall theme of restraining activism. Judges' pay would no longer be linked to that of members of Congress, allowing them to get an automatic cost of living increase even if lawmakers blocked the increase for themselves.

As amended in committee, it would also allow cameras in district and appellate courts at the discretion of the presiding judge.

Charles T. Canady, R-Fla., sponsor of the bill, called the measure "balanced and sensible." He said there were numerous examples of judges acting as "quasi-lawmakers" or making up legal doctrine with no constitutional basis.

The U.S. Judicial Conference, the administrative arm of the judiciary, criticized much of the bill and urged "careful consideration."

Democrats argued that the legislation was little more than an attempt to bully judges into making rulings more in line with Republicans' conservative political goals. It would harm judicial independence without necessarily stopping judges from making unpopular rulings, said Barney Frank, D-Mass.

"It would do nothing in most cases to prevent the type of decisions we do not like," he said.

In the Senate, there is little interest in such legislation. Though some conservatives agree with its goals, the Senate has little impetus to act because it already exerts considerable control over the federal bench through the confirmation of judges.

Democratic Amendments

The markup was largely an exercise in partisanship, with Democrats proposing, and Republicans opposing, most of the amendments.

Howard L. Berman, D-Calif., offered an amendment striking the three-judge requirement for public referendums, arguing that it would be an inefficient use of scarce judicial resources. Republicans countered that the practice is currently mandated for hearing cases brought under voting rights laws. The amendment was rejected, 10-14.

Frank and James E. Rogan, R-Calif., offered an amendment to eliminate the provision allowing litigants to reject their first judge. They argued that the measure would only encourage litigants to go "judge shopping" to find one sympathetic to their cause. Their effort failed, 11-13.

The committee also reversed a subcommittee decision to soften the tax-increase provision. In subcommittee consideration June 10, Democrat Bill Delahunt of Massachussetts succeeded in replacing the original language of the bill that banned any ruling that "requires" a tax increase. His amendment changed "requires" to "expressly directs." He argued that, as written, the bill went too far. By voice vote, the committee reverted to the original concept.

Judicial Powers

The one amendment that was approved with bipartisan support was offered by Steve Chabot, R-Ohio, to allow television cameras in district courtrooms if the judge permitted it. The bill allowed this for appellate courts, where there are no witnesses, just legal discussions between lawyers and judges. Chabot's amendment extending coverage to trial courts was approved, 12-6.

An amendment to this amendment, offered by Jerrold Nadler, D-N.Y., to allow witnesses to have their voices and pictures scrambled to prevent recognition, was rejected, 9-9. It will likely resurface later in floor consideration.

What seemed like a united Republican front during most of the committee consideration, however, belied reservations some Republicans have about the bill. A number oppose the pay raise provision, a priority of Chairman Henry J. Hyde, R-Ill. The most vocal critic of this provision, F. James Sensenbrenner Jr., R-Wis., was angered that the subcommittee included the provision and declined to show up for any portion of the committee's consideration of the bill.

De-linking judges' pay from that of lawmakers is controversial in part because when Congress votes on whether to block automatic inflationary increases, some members are able to use the judges as political cover in casting their votes.

In December, a group of federal judges filed suit in federal court to remove the pay link with lawmakers. The judges argued that Congress' failure to keep their pay in line with inflation was an unconstitutional reduction in judicial pay.

House Strips Bill Of Strictest Limits On Judges' Powers

APRIL 25 — House Republicans had hoped to strike a blow against judicial activism through a bill they brought to the floor April 23. But by the time the debate was finished, they settled for a stern slap on the wrist.

The measure (HR 1252), passed by voice vote, would take a number of actions to restrain judges who conservative lawmakers believe have gone beyond their mandate.

The measure would deny federal judges the power to order prisoner releases to deal with overcrowding. It would attempt to limit their ability to block executions by granting death-row habeas corpus appeals. And it would require appeals of ballot initiatives to be heard by three-judge panels, rather than a single judge. Conservatives also took heart in the fact that the bill did not de-link judges' pay from lawmakers' pay.

But the two most controversial items were stripped from the bill. One would have prevented judges from forcing tax increases. The other would have given parties in civil lawsuits a right to reject the first judge assigned to their case.

The authors of these provisions either lost floor votes or foresaw they would if they had pressed their case.

"I caved," said Charles T. Canady, R-Fla., with a shrug and a smile, after he accepted an amendment by James E. Rogan, R-Calif., striking his provision allowing parties to reject their first judge. Rogan argued the Canady language would encourage litigants to shop around for a judge they deemed favorable to their cause. His arguments were winning over a number of fellow Republicans.

Donald Manzullo, R-Ill., sponsor of the tax-increase prohibition, removed the section after it was amended to his dislike. His language would have banned judges from making rulings that require a local jurisdiction to raise taxes.

By a 230-181 vote, the House adopted an amendment by Bill Delahunt, D-Mass., considerably narrowing the Manzullo provision. Delahunt's language said that judges could still issue stiff penalties against localities that would force them to raise taxes. They just could not "expressly direct" them to raise taxes. (*Vote 103, p. H-30*)

"It became meaningless in the end," said Manzullo of his provision. "Why have something that is meaningless?"

With the two most significant items gone, and with the bill facing an uphill battle in the Senate and a veto threat from President Clinton, Republicans chose to declare victory and move on.

"We brought this to the floor to begin the national debate," Manzullo said. "It was a great debate."

Checks and Balances

The bill, sponsored by Howard Coble, R-N.C., centered on the issue of the judicial branch of government and what its proper role should be. Conservative Republicans argued the third branch has gotten too arrogant, too powerful and too willing to thwart the will of the people.

"It has come down to re-establishing our system of checks and balances," said Majority Whip Tom DeLay, R-Texas.

The legislation responds to a number of rulings around the country that have angered local officials and conservative lawmakers.

Its provision on appeals of ballot initiatives was conceived by California lawmakers after federal judges there threw out the results of two successful ballot initiatives — one denying public services to illegal immigrants and another limiting affirmative action. (The latter was reversed on appeal.)

Anger at a federal judge in Tennessee, who has a long history of opposing the death penalty and who was the subject of an unsuccessful judicial misconduct suit, spawned two provisions in the bill. One would randomly assign death row appeals among judges so that one death penalty opponent could not repeatedly keep a prisoner from being executed. Another would require judicial misconduct cases to be heard by judges in other parts of the country.

The tax provision that Manzullo pulled from the bill owed its origin to rulings by a federal judge in Kansas City, Mo., and a federal magistrate in Rockford, Ill. forcing local school districts to raise taxes to improve facilities.

Democrats and moderate Republicans responded that this type of legislative response to specific rulings undermines, rather than restores, the checks and balances between elected and appointed branches. The judicial branch relies on independence from the whims of elected lawmakers, said Melvin Watt, D-N.C., and it needs to function under rules that do not change whenever some group is unhappy.

"Once we undermine those rules, which this bill does, we will undermine our system of justice," said Watt.

Law & Judiciary

House Passes Justice Dept. Authorization For First Time in Nearly a Decade

Serving notice that he wants to reassert control over the Department of Justice, Judiciary Chairman Henry J. Hyde, R-Ill., won House passage of a three-year reauthorization bill (HR 3303 — H Rept 105-526). Since 1979, the last time Congress cleared an authorization, Justice Department policy has been set by legislative "riders" on appropriations bills.

HR 3303 was Hyde's attempt to wrest control back to the Judiciary Committee and to signal his interest in greater scrutiny of the department's activities. The Senate Judiciary Committee approved a separate version of the bill, but the measure went no further in the Senate.

Passed by voice vote June 22 under suspension of the rules, the House bill proposed authorizing a total of $60 billion over three years for the Justice Department, and sought to make several substantial policy changes.

The bill also would have reauthorized for two years some programs set to expire at the end of fiscal 1998, including one regarding aliens who have been denied asylum and one providing additional training for law-enforcement officers.

The most controversial section would have allowed the attorney general to transfer 200 lawyers from the Washington, D.C., headquarters to federal district offices around the country.

Finally, the bill would have required the Justice Department to report to Congress each time the attorney general decides a provision of law is unconstitutional and, as a result, the Justice Department establishes a policy to refrain from enforcing the provision, or determines it will refrain from defending any federal statutory provision.

Intent on getting the bill to the House floor, Hyde kept off any items that could have derailed or delayed it. During the Judiciary Committee markup of the bill April 29, the provision on transferring lawyers from Washington to regional field offices was made optional after the department objected to language that would have made it mandatory.

Also kept off the bill was a proposal by Barney Frank, D-Mass., to restructure the program that administers prison industries. The one amendment that was approved aimed to give telephone companies more time to make their new digital systems accessible to FBI wiretaps.

The Senate Judiciary Committee approved a substitute version of HR 3303 by voice vote Sept. 17, removing language regarding certain FBI wiretapping requirements. But the measure did not go to the floor, and it died at the end of the session.

Aside from the stripping of the tax and judicial-assignment provisions, several major changes were made to the bill during floor consideration.

The provision de-linking federal judges' pay from that of members of Congress was stripped from the bill through a parliamentary maneuver.

Severing judicial salaries from congressional salaries has been a major cause for Judiciary Committee Chairman Henry J. Hyde, R-Ill., who had added language doing so when the bill was in subcommittee. Hyde argued that failing to give judges cost of living adjustments discourages highly skilled (and often highly paid) lawyers from becoming judges.

But Hyde faced too much resistance from within his own party. A number of Republicans either thought it would be inappropriate for judges to make more than members of Congress or wanted to use the salary issue to stress that they are unhappy with the performance of the federal bench.

Hyde countered that the opposition to judicial pay increases was driven by members who were "congenitally anti-judge." He had considered offering an amendment to restore his provision, but opted against it.

Other Changes

A second significant change was made in an amendment by DeLay barring federal judges from forcing state prisons to release prisoners to handle overcrowding. That measure was adopted, 367-52. (Vote 105, p. H-32)

A third change was made by a voice vote on an amendment by Democrat Jerrold Nadler of New York. The underlying bill would permit cameras in federal district and appellate courts at the discretion of the presiding judge. The Nadler amendment would allow witnesses in district courts to have their audio and video signals scrambled.

Nadler argued this was important to prevent witness intimidation. Proponents of televised trials argued the provision would all but assure that federal trials are not televised. Fred Graham, managing editor of Court TV, said scrambling audio feeds on live television is simply not practical.

With changes like these, the final House bill was considerably weaker than the one it started with. Liberal Massachusetts Democrat Barney Frank hinted at this near the end of debate when he said that changes in the bill might have allowed him to vote for it. But with the decision to keep judges' pay linked to lawmakers', he said, "Now I can vote against what I think is kind of a silly bill without any problem."

House Seeks Limits on Prison Jurisdiction

MAY 23 — For the second time in less than a month, the House voted May 19 to restrict federal judges from ordering

Juvenile Crime

the release of prisoners in state facilities to ease overcrowding.

The measure (HR 3718), which was sponsored by Majority Whip Tom DeLay, R-Texas, was passed 352-53. (Vote 163, p. H-48)

The same measure was incorporated into a larger bill (HR 1252) limiting judicial powers that the House passed April 23.

DeLay cited a number of judges he said had inappropriately involved themselves in the affairs of state prisons. The prison issue, he said, is part of a larger problem of "activist" judges going well beyond their mandate and interfering with the efforts of elected officials. ◆

Time Runs Out on Bills To Combat Violent Crimes Committed by Juveniles

Although combating juvenile crime was seen as a top Republican priority at the start of the 105th Congress, efforts to enact a juvenile crime bill fell by the wayside.

SUMMARY

The failure shows how crime has declined as an issue, at least at the federal level, despite some high-profile crimes committed by youth during the past year, including a shooting rampage in March by two boys outside a school in Jonesboro, Ark.

An overhaul of juvenile crime law was to be the last piece of the congressional crimefighting puzzle. Unlike adult crime rates, which began an impressive decline in the mid-1990s, youth crime remained stubbornly high until the past two years. The explanation for this, lawmakers asserted, was that states had not reformed their juvenile justice systems to take violent teenagers seriously.

The centerpiece of the most comprehensive House and Senate bills (HR 3, S 10) was a five-year, $500 million-per-year grant program for states that agreed to try violent teens as if they were adults. Both bills also included a number of record-keeping requirements for states, intended to help the states share information about violent teens as they move around the country. And both bills — particularly the Senate's — would have relaxed restrictions on housing teens and adults together in detention facilities.

The Senate bill also included a provision reauthorizing crime prevention programs. The House split this into a separate bill (HR 1818). (1997 Almanac, pp. 5-3, 5-4)

The House passed HR 3 and HR 1818 in 1997, but the Senate bill never made it to the floor. It came under fierce attack from liberals, who objected to its overall approach, and from conservatives, who saw in it a chance for the government to clamp down on gun sales. The Gun Owners of America opposed a provision that would have allowed the federal government to use the Racketeering Influenced and Corrupt Organizations statute to prosecute gangs. The group said it could be used to prosecute gun dealers.

With the Senate bill stalled, the House late in the session added the provisions of HR 3 to a much narrower, Senate-passed bill (S 2073) to reauthorize the National Center for Missing and Exploited Children. The move created the potential for the House to take the juvenile justice bill to conference with the Senate, even though the Senate had never taken action on its version. A conference would still have been a difficult one, with senators trying to add their pet provisions to the final product. Time simply ran out.

Senate Panel Tries Putting Bite Back Into Bill

MARCH 21 — The hearing before the Youth Violence Subcommittee of the Senate Judiciary Committee looked unexceptional in most respects. There

Box Score

- **Bills:** HR 3, HR 1818; S 2073; S 10
- **House action:** On Sept. 15, the House incorporated the provisions of HR 3 into an already-passed Senate bill (S 2073), passed it by a vote of 280-126 and sent it to a conference committee, which did not act. The House had passed HR 3 (H Rept 105-86) on May 8, 1997, by a vote of 286-132. The House passed HR 1818 (H Rept 105-155) on July 15, 1997, by a vote of 413-4.
- **Senate action:** The Senate Judiciary Committee approved S 10 (S Rept 105-108) on July 24, 1997, by a vote of 12-6.

was Chairman Jeff Sessions, R-Ala., several other senators and a panel of crime experts. Everybody was praising a bill (S 10) designed to clamp down on repeat juvenile offenders.

But in this case there was something very wrong with the picture. The March 2 session was an attempt not to move the bill — it had been out of committee and awaiting floor action since July 24 — but to save it.

During the past seven months, support for the measure, designed to encourage states to try some violent juvenile offenders as adults and to reorganize the system under which they are tried and punished, has been steadily eroding.

Three conservative senators, Robert C. Smith, R-N.H., Wayne Allard, R-Colo., and Conrad Burns, R-Mont., have withdrawn as cosponsors. Groups ranging from the Children's Defense Fund to Gun Owners of America have mobilized against it. Even Chief Justice of the United States William H. Rehnquist took a

Congress Clears Bill To Punish ID Theft

Congress cleared legislation (HR 4151) making it illegal to knowingly transfer or use someone else's personal identifying information, such as a Social Security number, with the intent of committing a federal crime or state felony. President Clinton signed the measure into law (PL 105-318) on Oct. 30.

The legislation was prompted by the increasing use of the Internet and other means to gain critical information about an individual. The information can be used by a criminal to essentially masquerade as that individual, borrowing money, using credit cards and going on spending sprees.

Under HR 4151, violators could face enhanced penalties of as much as 20 years in prison and a fine for certain offenses such as using the information in the commission of a violent crime. Other less serious crimes will carry a 15-year penalty or less.

Identity theft victims are also entitled to restitution for losses and costs they incurred. The Federal Trade Commission must give victims information on how to clear up problems caused by the theft.

Previously, federal law criminalized the fraudulent possession, transfer and production of identity documents, but it required law enforcement officials to catch the culprit in possession of those documents.

The Senate passed its own version of the legislation (S 512 — S Rept 105-274) July 30 and sent it to the House. House lawmakers inserted the text of S 512 into HR 4151, which had not been considered by any House committees, and passed it by voice vote Oct. 7.

The Senate then cleared the bill by voice vote Oct. 14.

swipe at it in his annual state of the judiciary speech in December, arguing the expansion of federal crimefighting would overly burden federal courts.

Yet the biggest obstacle to passage may be not in who is opposing it, but who is supporting it — namely, almost no one. "I don't know anybody, or any organization, that supports this legislation," said Vermont Sen. Patrick J. Leahy, ranking Democrat on the Judiciary Committee.

This is in sharp contrast to broad support that criminal justice measures received in the late 1980s and early 1990s, when crime issues made national headlines, were debated in communities around the country and helped shape electoral politics.

The juvenile crime legislation may yet pass, particularly if proponents move quickly to address the criticisms it is facing — that it is too harsh on teens or places too many demands on states.

But the fact that it is now in deep trouble shows how the politics of crime is changing. No longer must lawmakers stand enthusiastically behind crime measures in order to maintain their conservative credentials. Today there is simply not the hue and cry for crime legislation — at least not this legislation — that there once was.

Part of the GOP Agenda

George Bush used the crime issue in general — and a released Massachusetts inmate named Willie Horton in particular — to catapult himself beyond Michael Dukakis in the 1988 presidential race. President Clinton used crime proposals such as his "three strikes and you're out" law (PL 103-322) to reposition himself as a moderate and to take away a potent issue for Republicans. *(1994 Almanac, p. 273)*

Sessions and Judiciary Committee Chairman Orrin G. Hatch, R-Utah, the sponsor of S 10, have political aims for the bill as well. They hope it will help re-establish the GOP as the get-tough-on-crime party. In a Feb. 26 letter to their colleagues, they touted it as "an important component of the Republican anti-crime agenda."

There is little evidence they are succeeding. Arrest rates for violent crimes by juveniles are now down two years in a row. In 1996, they dropped 9.2 percent from 1995. The number of juveniles arrested on murder charges went down 10.7 percent during the same period and are down 31 percent from 1993.

Proponents of the measure point out youth violence rates are still significantly higher than they were in the early 1980s, before they spiked. They also argue this is just the lull before the storm and that the crime rate will rise again as a wave of children enters the teenage years, the time when they are most likely to commit violent crimes. But bill proponents are not getting this message across, and lawmakers are beginning to wonder whether crime rates may be entering a sustained decline.

Juvenile crime legislation was first conceived during the 104th Congress, but was not given high priority and was left unpassed in both houses when the Congress ended.

In the 105th, the leadership of both chambers made early commitments to the Hatch bill and two companion bills in the House. The main House bill (HR 3), sponsored by Republican Rep. Bill McCollum of Florida, was approved by the Judiciary Committee April 29 and passed by the full House May 8.

The Senate bill was slower off the mark, but Hatch pushed it through his panel before last year's August recess.

The Hatch-Sessions bill would authorize $500 million a year for five years to states for law enforcement and crime prevention, but only if they agree to a long list of conditions. Their worst juvenile offenders would have to be tried as adults, with much of the discretion on who to try as adults given to prosecutors, not judges.

States would have to fingerprint all juvenile offenders who commit a crime that would be a felony if they were older. And those fingerprints would have to be used to form a database that could be shared with law enforcement agents throughout the country.

Additionally, the bill would allow juveniles to be incarcerated in the same building as adults, though not in the same cell. It would crack down on gangs and other youth criminal activity through a series of stiffer penalties. And it would beef up federal enforcement of juvenile crime, including making it easier for federal prosecutors to take over cases from local authorities.

Juvenile Crime

An Upward Spiral

Broadly speaking, the Senate bill's goals are to get the most dangerous juvenile offenders off the streets and to send a message to all juveniles that their crimes will not go unpunished. The first of these is shared by virtually everyone. The latter is more controversial. But its proponents say it is vital because teens are coming to believe they can get away with anything. Currently, penalties for juveniles are minimal, often kept confidential and later expunged. This has sometimes meant an upward spiral in the severity of crimes that is not addressed until after the teen becomes an adult, said Sessions.

"The greatest [predictor] of adult crime is a juvenile criminal record," said Sessions, who called his bill "the most historic step forward in juvenile justice in 25 years."

Last spring, opposition to the House legislation was shrewdly kept under wraps by House Republicans. They drafted the bill and the accompanying rule for floor debate in such a way as to prevent Democrats from amending it.

In the Senate, sponsors of the bill have always known they face a more daunting task, with the Senate's more relaxed rules for floor debate.

But even they were surprised by the opposition that has developed. Critics say a downward spiral has developed: As the bill languishes, more people become familiar with its provisions and decide to oppose it.

Initially, the opposition came only from liberal Democratic senators such as Leahy and Edward M. Kennedy of Massachusetts, and from the criminal defense bar and liberal advocacy groups such as the Children's Defense Fund. Their principal objections were that the bill was overly harsh (they were especially concerned with the concept of housing youths with adults) and that it was mainly focused on punishing crime rather than preventing it.

Since then, opposition has developed from conservative groups and state law enforcement agencies. The conservative Gun Owners of America has turned against it for largely the same reason as the liberal groups. The group points to different crimes and different sets of circumstances, but it also argues the bill is too harsh and could lead to some heavy penalties for relatively minor infractions.

Gun Owners spokesman John Velleco cites the example of carrying a firearm within 1,000 feet of a school. The legislation increases penalties for such a crime, even making it punishable in certain cases under the Racketeer Influenced and Corrupt Organizations (RICO) law (PL 91-452), said Velleco. That means that one moment someone could be driving through a neighborhood carrying a firearm consistent with local laws, then the next moment turn a corner and unwittingly commit an offense prosecutable under RICO, he said.

"Everyone just wants to increase penalties on criminals," said Velleco. "What they are missing is that people who are supposed to be criminals are innocent people who just run afoul of some federal regulation."

State and local governments, meanwhile, have begun studying all the bill's fine print, especially record-keeping requirements they must comply with to receive the grant money. None of the current 50 states now is in compliance, according to a study by the National Center for Juvenile Justice, a non-profit research group. Some experts believe the states would have to spend a good deal of their grant money to comply.

Revisions Promised

With a perception they have little to gain from the measure and that federal agents may tread on their turf, many state and local government agencies have started to complain about the Hatch bill, either in public or privately to key senators.

The National District Attorneys Association is one of the more vocal opponents of the measure. Association President William L. Murphy calls it a "reckless" bill. The National Criminal Justice Association, a group of top state criminal justice officials appointed by their governors, is also on record against many of its provisions.

"We recognize the importance of federal assistance," said executive director Cabell C. Cropper. "But we advocate as much flexibility as possible."

Complaints from such groups led Sessions to hold his after-the-fact hearing, during which he promised to make three changes. He said he would eliminate a requirement that state records include photographs, as well as fingerprints. He also said he would clarify that only offenses that would have been felonies if committed by an adult need be recorded. Third, juvenile databases could be a subsection of the states' adult criminal databases.

Sessions hoped the hearing would allay fears about the bill and stress the importance of a good coast-to-coast system of records. His witnesses argued that it was in the states' interest to have good nationwide records so police could learn the criminal background of someone from another region.

But getting to that point is proving difficult. With opposition from so many quarters, not the least of which is state law enforcement, that nationwide system may not come into being any time soon.

House Makes Late Push for Bill On Juvenile Crime

SEPTEMBER 19 — In a move Democrats criticized as an end-of-session ploy, the House on Sept. 15 attached key provisions of its sweeping juvenile crime legislation (HR 3) to a much narrower bill (S 2073) reauthorizing the National Center for Missing and Exploited Children.

Sponsors said the House would request that the measure, passed 280-126, go directly to a conference committee even though the Senate has not acted on the broader juvenile crime overhaul. *(Vote 436, p. H-124)*

The House passed two juvenile crime measures last year. One (HR 3) would encourage states to make it easier for prosecutors to try juveniles as adults, and another (HR 1818) would combine several juvenile crime prevention programs into a block grant to the states. The former was opposed by Democrats; the latter passed with overwhelming bipartisan support. *(1997 Almanac, p. 5-3)*

A companion bill to both measures (S 10) has been stalled in the Senate, much to the disappointment of House Republicans, who have been pushing

Law & Judiciary

for a juvenile crime overhaul since taking control of Congress in 1995. (*1996 Almanac, p. 5-29*)

The Senate on June 26 passed by voice vote the measure reauthorizing funding for the center for missing and exploited children, providing it with $10 million a year for five years.

Republican Bill McCollum of Florida., who chairs the House Judiciary Subcommittee on Crime, said packaging the bills was intended to induce the Senate to take up all the proposals, including the contentious provisions contained in HR 3.

It is not clear whether the Senate would allow the measure to go directly to conference with the broader provisions attached or, if so, whether senators would agree to keep them there.

An Overstretched System

Advocates of attaching the juvenile crime legislation argued that recent school shootings demonstrate the need to curb crime among youths and said that lenient treatment of juveniles convicted of minor crimes emboldens them to commit more serious ones.

"We have spent too much time worrying about some of these juveniles on the street without thinking about the people, particularly in a lot of our urban centers, who are terrorized by these young people," said Mark Souder, R-Ind.

But opponents said the idea of trying children as young as age 14 as adults is a coldhearted and overly punitive approach to the problem. They also said the House action was an attempt to circumvent full Senate scrutiny of the measure.

Robert C. Scott, D-Va., said the Senate has not acted on its juvenile crime overhaul "because it cannot pass the 'light of day test.' . . . When daylight hits S 10, no one likes what they see."

The block grant bill would consolidate several prevention programs — including boot camps, treatment for abused and neglected children, and school-based gang prevention programs — into a single juvenile delinquency prevention block grant program.

"The combining of these bills is a Republican ploy to force members who already opposed HR 3 to vote for it now," said Democrat William L. Clay, of Missouri during the debate. ◆

Concerns of Doctors' Groups Undermine Support For Assisted Suicide Bill

Box Score

- **Bills:** HR 4006; S 2151
- **House action:** The House Judiciary Committee approved HR 4006 (H Rept 105-683, Part 1) by voice vote Aug. 4.
- **Senate action:** The Senate Judiciary Committee approved S 2151 (S Rept 105-372) by 11-6 Sept. 24.

An attempt by conservatives to deter physicians from helping patients use prescription drugs to commit suicide faltered late in the session.

SUMMARY

Senate Majority Whip Don Nickles, R-Okla., and House Judiciary Committee Chairman Henry J. Hyde, R-Ill., sponsors of the legislation (HR 4006, S 2151), vowed to revive the issue in the 106th Congress.

Support fractured when doctors and other health professionals protested the bill's potentially chilling effect on pain treatment for terminally ill patients.

The bill would have required revocation of a doctor's Drug Enforcement Administration (DEA) registration — the right to prescribe controlled drugs — if "clear and convincing evidence" showed that the physician dispensed or prescribed drugs to assist suicide.

Medical groups argued that the threat of such a penalty would make doctors reluctant to prescribe narcotics for pain relief.

The legislation arose from the Justice Department's reaction to an Oregon law that legalized assisted suicide under certain guidelines. In a 1997 letter, DEA Administrator Thomas A. Constantine agreed with congressional conservatives that giving a regulated drug to assist in suicide is not a "legitimate medical purpose," as the 1970 Controlled Substances Act requires.

Attorney General Janet Reno overturned Constantine's interpretation.

Nickles attempted to codify the Constantine letter through a "rider" to the omnibus appropriations law (PL 105-277). However, in the face of a filibuster threat, Nickles retreated.

Hyde Says Bill Aims To Reverse Reno Decision

JULY 25 — Doctors who prescribe drugs to help patients commit suicide would be penalized under a bill approved July 22, 6-5, by the House Judiciary Constitution Subcommittee. Judiciary Chairman Henry J. Hyde, R-Ill., said his bill (HR 4006) is designed to reverse a recent decision by Attorney General Janet Reno on the issue.

Following Oregon voters' approval of an initiative that allows physician-assisted suicide in some circumstances, the Drug Enforcement Administration prohibited doctors from dispensing drugs for assisted suicides. The agency held that the practice had no "legitimate medical purpose." But Reno said the ban exceeded the agency's authority, and she declined to join a challenge to the Oregon law.

Hyde said he wants to reverse her decision because it makes doctors "social engineers with a license to kill."

The bill would require the revocation of the federal prescription-writing license of a doctor who "intentionally dispensed or distributed a controlled substance with a purpose of causing, or assisting in causing, the suicide or euthanasia of any individual." The bill would exempt doctors whose patients accidentally die from drugs prescribed to relieve pain.

John Conyers Jr., D-Mich., said he opposed the bill because it would preempt state laws: "We are thwarting debate by imposing a single, Republican, Washington-knows-best solution."

By voice vote, the panel adopted an amendment by Republican Charles T. Canady of Florida that would require the government to prove through "clear and convincing evidence" that drugs were for anything other than pain management.

Judiciary Panel Backs Penalties On Suicide Aid

AUGUST 8 — Acting on a priority of Chairman Henry J. Hyde, R-Ill., the House Judiciary Committee on Aug. 4 approved a bill that would penalize doctors who prescribe controlled substances to help patients commit suicide.

The measure (HR 4006), approved by voice vote, would strip doctors of their ability to prescribe certain drugs if they were found to have used them in assisted suicides.

The measure was designed to reverse a recent determination by Attorney General Janet Reno that federal drug enforcement agents did not have authority over the use of such drugs in physician-assisted suicides.

Reno reversed a decision by the Drug Enforcement Administration that it would have such authority even in Oregon, where voters approved initiatives to prevent doctors from facing penalties for such acts in some narrow circumstances.

Under the bill, the Justice Department would be required to revoke physicians' licenses to write prescriptions for certain drugs if it found "clear and convincing" evidence that doctors intended to use such drugs to assist suicide.

Democrats said the bill could deter doctors from providing essential pain-killing drugs. Organizations such as the American Medical Association (AMA) oppose the bill, saying doctors might be forced to justify their prescriptions for legitimate pain-alleviating drugs.

"Patients who are in the most pain, and therefore in need of the largest doses of narcotics, are the most likely to be affected," the AMA and several other organizations wrote to the committee. Hyde said he trusted that doctors would not refrain from prescribing painkillers to people in severe pain.

Democrats' attempts to soften the bill failed. The panel defeated, 8-14, an amendment that would have exempted doctors in states with laws similar to Oregon's. Another amendment, defeated 6-14, would have protected doctors from federal civil or criminal penalties.

A similar bill (S 2151) is pending in the Senate Judiciary Committee.

Prospects Fade For Senate Passage Of Suicide Bill

SEPTEMBER 26 — Even as the Senate Judiciary Committee advanced a controversial bill (S 2151) aimed at ending physician-assisted suicide, supporters acknowledged the week of Sept. 21 that the measure was not likely to survive the session.

The bill, which was approved 11-6 by the committee Sept. 24, would penalize medical professionals who help patients commit suicide with controlled substances. The bill would require the Justice Department to revoke or deny the federal registration of medical professionals, who distribute drugs to help patients commit suicide. Such registrations allow medical professionals to prescribe or dispense federally controlled substances, a privilege doctors say is essential to their careers.

The measure has been the subject of growing criticism from medical professionals who say it would impede doctors' ability to control the pain of terminally ill patients.

"We're not going to get this through this year, obviously," because of time constraints, Committee Chairman Orrin G. Hatch, R-Utah, said after the panel voted.

Opposition from Doctors

In an effort to address criticism by doctors, Hatch added a requirement that before the department could initiate an investigation, the attorney general would have to determine that the medical professional dispensed a drug that caused a person's death, and that the professional did not prescribe the drug as medically needed. Hatch's substitute also would clarify that other medical professionals, such as pharmacists, could face penalties under the bill. Neither of these provisions is in the House bill.

The Hatch substitute also included a provision from the House bill that would require federal prosecutors to show "clear and convincing" evidence that the physician dispensed drugs to help a patient commit suicide.

Medical professionals were not impressed. "There have been no alternatives proposed that are satisfactory, although we are open to [discussing] proposals," said Dr. Thomas Reardon, chairman of the American Medical Association board. "If we knew of another option, we would offer it."

Amid doubts about its prospects for passage, a companion bill (HR 4006) was removed from the House calendar the week of Sept. 21.

"Clearly, they are running into trouble with the votes," said Barney Frank, D-Mass., a senior member of the House Judiciary Committee. "The overwhelming number of people in the medical community who oppose the substance of the bill are having an influence."

Charles T. Canady, R-Fla., chairman of the House Judiciary Subcommittee on the Constitution, said that "it's possible that it won't come up this year because of the press of events."

In the Senate, however, some Democrats pledged to block consideration of the bill if it ever came to the Senate floor. They said that the measure amounted to a federal intrusion into doctors' and pharmacists' professional decisions.

"This legislation, which has been touted as a way to reduce the number of physician-assisted suicides, may ultimately cause an increase in the number of patients who seek assistance from their physicians in ending their lives," said Patrick J. Leahy of Vermont, the Senate Judiciary Committee's ranking Democrat. ◆

Chapter 18
POLITICS & ELECTIONS

Campaign Finance 18-3
  Sanchez Probe Ends 18-4
  Bills Compared 18-8

Campaign Finance *(cont'd)*
  House Bill Highlights 18-15

McCain-Feingold Campaign Financing Bill Proves Dead on Revival

Box Score

- **Bills:** HR 2183; S 25
- **House action:** The House passed HR 2183, 252-179, on Aug. 6.
- **Senate action:** The Senate first failed to invoke cloture on Feb. 26, 51-48. The next attempt was on Sept. 10, when, on a 52-48 vote, it failed to invoke cloture when the measure was offered as an amendment to S 2237.

Long-suffering advocates of a campaign finance overhaul finally had a victory when the House voted to rewrite the laws. But the Senate remained resistant, and the effort died.

SUMMARY

The latest push was sparked in 1997 by investigations in both chambers that revealed campaign finance abuses by both parties. Supporters of an overhaul hoped the revelations would outrage the public sufficiently that voters would demand that Congress move legislation. But Republican leaders in both chambers focused instead on trying to pillory Democrats for alleged abuses.

However, a small group of Republicans in both chambers joined with Democrats to push an overhaul. The leaders were Sens. John McCain, R-Ariz., and Russell D. Feingold, D-Wis., and Reps. Christopher Shays, R-Conn., and Martin T. Meehan, D-Mass.

Their legislation would have banned national parties from receiving or spending "soft money," the unlimited and largely unregulated donations to political parties. State and local parties would no longer have been able to use soft money for federal election activity. And new restrictions would have been placed on campaign-related expenditures by third-party groups.

The Senate appeared to have buried the issue on Feb. 26, when it failed to muster the 60 votes needed to end a GOP filibuster on S 25. The vote, 51-48, was similar to a tally taken less than five months earlier. That vote, on Oct. 7, 1997, was 52-48.

In the House, GOP leaders tried several strategies to prevent a companion bill from stirring. First, they squelched debate by prohibiting the Shays-Meehan bill from coming to the floor during consideration of related legislation March 30. But the ploy encouraged the bill's supporters to embrace a procedural device that would have let them debate a variety of campaign finance bills on their own terms.

GOP leaders finally relented to an open debate in May. But they made sure Shays-Meehan was open to dozens of amendments, and they forced it to compete with 10 other substitute amendments to the underlying bill (HR 2183), a less sweeping alternative offered by a bipartisan group of freshmen. Whichever of the 11 substitute amendments got the most votes, and at least a majority, would have prevailed.

The other substitute amendments were either defeated or withdrawn in a prolonged process. The capstone was a 237-186 vote on Aug. 3 in favor of the Shays-Meehan amendment. Fifty-one Republicans voted for the measure, outweighing the 11 Democrats who voted against it. Three days later, the House passed the bill as amended. Advocates vowed to push the Senate to act after the August recess.

McCain and Feingold tried to revive the issue in the Senate by attaching S 25 to the Interior appropriations bill (S 2237). But they fell eight votes short of cutting off debate on Sept. 10, 52-48.

Senators' Votes Seem Set in Stone

FEBRUARY 28 — Arizona Republican Sen. John McCain can be excused if he is starting to feel a bit like the character portrayed by Bill Murray in the movie "Groundhog Day."

Like Murray's TV weatherman, who awakens each morning to live out the same day over and over again, McCain has been at the center of a campaign finance debate that never seems to change.

For the second time in less than five months, McCain's bill (S 25) to overhaul the nation's political fundraising laws, which he cosponsored with Wisconsin Democrat Russell D. Feingold, fell victim to a Republican-led filibuster. Because of a tangled procedural situation, the bill was offered as an amendment to an underlying GOP bill (S 1663) to restrict the use of union dues for political activities.

This latest drama was scripted well in advance. Before the debate, McCain and his allies acknowledged that they would not be able to garner the 60 votes needed to break the filibuster, which was led by Majority Leader Trent Lott, R-Miss., and Kentucky Republican Mitch McConnell.

Yet they were hoping to do better than in October, when they repeatedly fell eight votes shy of the 60 needed to overcome a filibuster.

Instead, they fared exactly the same, or would have if Iowa Democrat Tom Harkin, a McCain-Feingold supporter who missed the vote, had been present. On Feb. 26, the Senate failed, 51-48, to end the filibuster, as 44 Democrats and seven Republicans supported a motion to limit debate, while 48 Republicans opposed it. (*Vote 16, p. S-6*)

As he had last fall, McConnell immediately declared the bill finished for the year. "This undeserving legislation is dead," he said. Feingold vowed to try to keep the proposal's faint hopes alive by attempting to attach it to other legislation.

But with the divisions on this issue seemingly set in stone, McCain expressed little interest in pursuing guerrilla tactics to push the bill to yet another vote. "You risk, over time,

Politics & Elections

Sanchez Probe Ends

The House in February officially ended its prolonged and politically charged investigation of Democratic Rep. Loretta Sanchez's upset defeat of Republican Rep. Robert K. Dornan in California's 46th District in 1996.

By a 378-33 vote Feb. 12, the House accepted a recommendation (H Res 355) to drop the inquiry into Dornan's claims that the election was stolen through rampant voting by non-citizens. All 33 votes against the resolution were cast by Republicans. (Vote 16, p. H-6)

The recommendation came from from the contested-election task force of the House Oversight Committee, chaired by Vernon J. Ehlers, R-Mich.

The investigation focused particularly on Hermandad Mexicana Nacional, a group that helped register Hispanic voters in California in 1996. The task force found evidence of 748 illegal votes by non-citizens. Although that was not enough to negate Sanchez's 984-vote victory, Republicans said the results showed that Dornan's challenge was not frivolous and that the GOP was not unfairly targeting Hispanics.

Democrats disputed the task force's findings about election fraud and said Republicans were trying to intimidate Hispanic voters. "Racism is as real and persistent today as it was 100 years ago," Sanchez said.

Before voting to end the investigation, the House defeated, 194-215, a Democratic motion to return the resolution to the House Oversight Committee and strip most of its findings and conclusions. (Vote 15, p. H-6)

Dornan, who had been barred from the House floor until the issue was resolved, announced that he would try to regain his seat in the fall 1998 elections. But in a rematch Nov. 3, Sanchez beat Dornan by more than 12,000 votes.

alienating some of your supporters," he said.

Feingold and some of the bill's other supporters predicted that the GOP will pay a price in the fall elections for blocking the bill. "Somebody's going to get beat because of it," said Tennessee Republican Fred Thompson.

But if Republicans were worried about political fallout, most were not showing it. Among the 48 GOP senators who have consistently opposed McCain-Feingold were two potentially vulnerable incumbents: Sam Brownback of Kansas and Alfonse M. D'Amato of New York.

The McCain-Feingold bill would ban "soft money," the largely unregulated contributions to political parties that are meant for party-building activities, but which critics say find their way into campaigns. The bill would also curb "issue ads," which critics say often promote candidates more than issues. Both provisions are controversial, and the stalemate they have provoked has refocused attention on less sweeping alternatives that might break the deadlock.

But Sen. Robert F. Bennett, R-Utah, a key ally of McConnell's, said the political atmosphere has been so poisoned by the campaign finance battle that any sort of compromise is out of the question this year. Even proposals to require more timely and complete disclosure of contributions, which he and most other Republicans favor, have little chance of passing.

"This has become an ideological fight rather than a careful analysis of the problem," Bennett said. "It's a little like the health care debate in the 103rd Congress." That battle so deeply divided Congress that it took until the next session to enact a modest healthcare package. (1996 Almanac, p. 6-28)

Too Polarized To Pass Anything

The polarization of the campaign finance debate was underscored by the effort of moderate Republicans Olympia J. Snowe of Maine and James M. Jeffords of Vermont to soften the McCain-Feingold bill.

The amendment crafted by Snowe and Jeffords modified the bill's controversial provision on issue ads and would have barred unions and corporations from funding politically oriented ads 30 days before a primary election, or 60 days before a general election.

But even with those changes, which were deliberately designed to attract GOP support, not a single Republican changed sides. On a procedural vote to table, or kill, the modified measure, all 48 Republican opponents stayed "rock-solid," as McConnell put it. (Vote 15, p. S-6)

For his part, though, Lott failed to gain ground for his proposal to impose curbs on political activity by unions. Democrats filibustered that measure, and a motion to break the talkathon drew only 45 votes — all Republican. (Vote 17, p. S-6)

Attention now shifts to the House, where GOP leaders have scheduled a campaign finance debate for late next month. But the Senate stalemate promises to make any action taken by the House largely symbolic.

Having Something For Everyone Spells Trouble

MARCH 21 — The House is scheduled to take up a campaign finance bill the week of March 23 that would make most of the major changes advocated by partisans on both sides of the issue — thereby all but guaranteeing it will never be enacted as written.

The sweeping measure (HR 3485) includes almost every significant overhaul proposal that has been seriously debated since the issue took root last year. For example, it includes a "soft money" ban that is championed by many Democrats but which is anathema to most Republicans. And it includes restrictions on the political use of union dues that Republicans support, but which is a poison pill to most Democrats.

While the broad approach means the bill has something to please just about everyone, those pushing for change say that also means the measure has something for just about everyone to dislike.

The bill comes to the floor from the House Oversight Committee, which approved it March 18 on a 5-3, party-line vote after a markup that was often bitterly contentious. That final tally was symbolic of everything about the fiercely partisan session — from the votes on five failed Democratic amendments to the often accusatory debate — and paved the way for the House to pick up an issue that until now has been most prominently showcased in the Senate.

Twice in the last six months, the Senate has deadlocked over a major campaign finance bill (S 25) favored largely by Democrats and union-dues amendments forwarded by Republicans. Last October and again this February, neither side had the votes to overcome a filibuster by the other.

The House markup session March 18 set the stage for what could be another angry fight on the House floor.

Committee Democrats accused Republicans of including provisions in the bill that would clearly harm Democratic constituencies and of throwing in other measures intended to prevent the bill from picking up widespread support. "That's what this is all about," said Steny H. Hoyer, D-Md., "poison pills and getting enemies."

Republicans repeatedly countered that the bill was simply a beginning. "Everybody is going to have to give a little bit to get a better system," said Committee Chairman Bill Thomas, R-Calif.

Democrats said the bill would force them to turn their backs on a pair of influential constituencies. Unions, a key political ally of the Democrats, would be required to get prior written permission from every member before using their dues for political purposes. And the bill would allow citizenship verification programs that Democrats say are anti-Hispanic.

Heartburn for Both Sides

The bill will also give some Republicans heartburn by seeking to ban national political parties from receiving soft money, the unlimited, largely unregulated contributions that are intended for party-building activities. In another controversial move, the measure would regulate political advertisements by third-party groups in the final three months before an election. Both these provisions have been criticized by Republicans and some conservative groups as unacceptable attacks on free speech.

Other provisions would ban contributions by non-citizens, tighten reporting requirements, allow national parties to exceed contribution limits when a candidate faces a wealthy, self-financed opponent and increase the contribution limits imposed on individuals.

Democrats jumped on the latter provision in an attempt to paint Republicans as the party of the rich. The bill would double the amount of money individuals could give to a particular candidate for federal office (from $1,000 per election to $2,000). Total contributions by an individual to federal candidates and political parties would be capped at $75,000 a year.

The Democratic criticism did not sit well with Thomas, who aggressively accused Democrats of continually boiling issues down to "class warfare."

Democrats were most riled by the union and citizenship provisions, which stem from the 1996 election season.

Republican backers of the union-dues provision pointed to vast numbers of union workers - as well as non-members forced to pay dues - who are angered by union spending on political causes, or candidate campaigns, that they oppose.

Democrats complained that the requirement would paralyze unions with endless record-keeping, but Thomas dismissed the criticism. "The trade-off for a little bit more paperwork would be an excellent trade-off," he said, insisting the bill would guarantee that political spending is voluntary.

Democrats argued that the provision was nothing more than retaliation for organized labor's effective opposition to Republican candidates in the 1996 elections. Hoyer, who accused the GOP of "getting those who oppose them," said the plan would gag unions at election time. Unions, meanwhile, are fighting the initiative not only in Congress, but in California. There, voters in June will consider a referendum with similar language.

Democrats unsuccessfully offered amendments to remove the union restrictions and the citizenship verification program, which would allow at least five states - California, Florida, Illinois, New York and Texas - to check the citizenship of individuals before allowing them to vote.

The language stems from findings of illegal voting by non-citizens in the 1996 California congressional election in which Democrat Loretta Sanchez defeated Republican Robert K. Dornan. The provision led Democrats to charge Republicans with unfairly targeting and seeking to intimidate Hispanic-American voters.

GOP Leaders Maneuver To Block Democrats' Bill

APRIL 4 — In what may have been the year's last gasp for comprehensive campaign finance legislation, the House on March 30 overwhelmingly defeated a measure (HR 3581) that had elements disdained by both parties.

House Republican leaders had all but guaranteed the outcome by insisting that the legislation be considered under special rules that severely limited debate, prohibited amendments and required a two-thirds vote for passage — usually an impossible hurdle for all but the most non-controversial legislation.

Even the GOP leadership abandoned the final product, which had been approved in a preliminary form (as HR 3485) by the House Oversight Committee two weeks earlier. The vote was 74-337, with no Democrats and only about one-third of Republicans voting for it. (Vote 81, p. H-26)

But the bill's fate seemed less important to the GOP hierarchy than having prevented a bipartisan group from bringing its own broad rewrite of campaign finance legislation (HR 3526) to the floor. That leadership strategy provoked complaints from Republicans who have pushed for the bipartisan legislation and anger from Democrats.

There were frequent protests from Democrats that Speaker Newt Gingrich, R-Ga., had reneged on his pledge to conduct a fair and open debate on the issue. "This is a process the Politburo under Joseph Stalin would have been proud of," said Sam Gejdenson of Connecticut, the ranking Democrat on the Oversight Committee.

The House approved two small bills that would expand public disclosure of campaign contributions (HR 3582) and ban campaign contributions from non-citizens (HR 34).

The outlook for these bills is

Politics & Elections

murky, however. It may be impossible for the Senate to consider either of them without getting bogged down in the sort of broader dispute over campaign finance that tied the Senate in knots over the issue in October and again in February.

The Senate all but doomed prospects for enacting a major campaign finance bill this year through filibusters led by Senate GOP leaders twice in the last six months. The efforts blocked consideration of a bipartisan overhaul bill (S 25) sponsored by John McCain, R-Ariz., and Russell D. Feingold, D-Wis.

It was apparently out of fear that the House could pass a companion measure to McCain-Feingold — a bill (HR 3526) sponsored by Christopher Shays, R-Conn., and Martin T. Meehan, D-Mass. — that GOP leaders moved to ensure it could not be brought up.

Anger Over the Process

Democrats repeatedly called the process a "sham" and a "fraud." Meehan quoted Woody Allen in the movie "Bananas," in referring to the process as "a travesty of a mockery of a sham."

Some Republicans also expressed frustration that the House would not be considering HR 3526.

Asa Hutchinson, R-Ark., said the process "reflects the dark side of this institution, and both sides of the aisle have contributed to this darkness." He said it "sent a message to the American people that we are afraid of reform, and that we will undermine it at any price."

Matt Salmon, R-Ariz., said he was "ashamed to see how this is coming up tonight, that it is in the same manner as that of the leadership who ran the House for 40 years under the Democrats. It is wrong."

Oversight Committee Chairman Bill Thomas, R-Calif., offered few apologies for the GOP strategy. He said that if Democrats were so interested in campaign finance legislation, they could have enacted a bill without Republican support when Democrats controlled both chambers and the White House.

"Guess what happened?" Thomas asked. "Nothing. Nothing went to the president."

Thomas' bill, HR 3581, would require unions to get prior written permission from members before using their dues for political purposes. It would create experimental programs in five states to verify the citizenship of potential voters. And it would triple the amount of money individuals could contribute to federal candidates and political parties.

In addition, the measure would regulate political advertisements by third-party groups in the final three months before an election. And it would ban national political parties from receiving soft money — the unlimited, largely unregulated contributions that are intended for party-building activities.

The House also considered three other campaign finance bills offered by Thomas that were based on the broader legislation.

● It passed HR 34, to prohibit noncitizens from contributing to federal campaigns. The vote was 369-43. *(Vote 82, p. H-26)*

● It passed HR 3582, to strengthen reporting requirements for campaign contributions and expand the type of information that must be reported. The vote was 405-6. *(Vote 84, p. H-26)*

● The House rejected another bill, HR 2608, to prohibit labor unions or corporations from making campaign contributions on behalf of union members or stockholders without their approval. The vote was 166-246. *(Vote 83, p. H-26)*

Afterward, Democrats said they would turn their attention to advancing a discharge petition to force House action on comprehensive campaign finance legislation. To do so would require signatures from 218 members, and proponents were still 22 members short. Only seven Republicans had signed the petition as of April 1.

House Leadership Schedules Debate

APRIL 25 — Republican leaders who have tried to kill comprehensive campaign finance legislation in both chambers this year must now contend with an unexpected challenge — a protracted, election-year debate on the issue in the House.

Speaker Newt Gingrich, R-Ga., agreed to bring the matter to the floor in May after a small but growing group of Republican rebels joined with Democrats to force the action. Gingrich relented April 22 when it appeared that advocates of campaign finance legislation were moving toward the 218 signatures they needed on a discharge petition that would have cost GOP leaders control of the floor and allowed backers to debate a variety of campaign finance bills on their own terms.

"This is a great day for democracy," said Rep. Christopher Shays, R-Conn. Shays and other renegades had fought back after Gingrich prevented them from offering their own legislation during brief consideration of the issue March 30.

The show of strength in the petition drive made it likely that the House will pass something that overhaul proponents can cheer before members leave for the Memorial Day recess. "The public concern for this, the 'good government' groups who are fighting for it and the fact that it's an election year will probably apply enough pressure that it will pass the House," predicted Rep. Michael N. Castle, R-Del., who signed the petition.

But while Democrats and some Republicans hailed the decision to schedule a debate, there was no consensus on which overhaul proposal the House ought to pass. Any change in campaign finance laws threatens the way both parties now raise and spend money for elections. As if to underscore that uncertainty, neither Gingrich nor Minority Leader Richard A. Gephardt, D-Mo., would commit to backing a particular bill.

"I haven't decided yet," Gingrich said in an interview. "I am not ready to discuss this bill or that," Gephardt said.

And even if the House approves a measure, the Senate is unlikely to embrace it. Lately the Senate has been a graveyard for campaign finance legislation; GOP leaders there have mounted bill-killing filibusters twice in the past six months.

The most recent was Feb. 26, when backers of the Senate's leading overhaul proposal (S 25), sponsored by John McCain, R-Ariz., and Russell D. Feingold, D-Wis., fell nine votes short of the 60 needed to overcome a filibuster, 51-48.

But the equation could change if the House builds momentum by passing something like the McCain-Feingold measure. "If it comes out of there very strong, it puts added pressure here," McCain said. "But I still think we're in for the long haul."

Senate Majority Leader Trent Lott, R-Miss., an ardent foe of McCain-Feingold, said on "The NewsHour with Jim Lehrer" April 22 that the Senate is unlikely to revisit the issue. "I think it will not happen this year," he said.

But Lott also signaled that House action might change the dynamic. "You know, in Congress and in Washington," he said, "you never say 'never.'"

Looking Ahead in the House

The next step in the House will be for GOP leaders to decide how to structure the floor debate.

"We now have to work out an open rule that's fair," Gingrich said. "We have to have time for members to get educated. And then we'll go through, my guess is, a fairly protracted process of trying to write campaign law."

The starting point for floor debate will not be the widely known bill sponsored by overhaul advocates Shays and Martin T. Meehan, D-Mass., whose measure (HR 3526) is similar to the Senate's McCain-Feingold bill. Instead, House leaders will begin with a bill (HR 2183) developed by a bipartisan group of freshmen led by Asa Hutchinson, R-Ark., and Tom Allen, D-Maine. Gingrich said he chose that bill to reward the freshmen for acting in a bipartisan manner and for working with the Republican "team."

Among other things, the bill would:

- Prohibit national parties from accepting unregulated "soft money" contributions. State parties could continue to accept soft money.
- Increase the amount of money an individual could contribute to all candidates from $25,000 per election cycle to $25,000 per year.
- "Index" the federal limits on donations for individuals, political action committees and parties so that they rise with inflation.
- Require third-party groups — including nonprofit organizations and labor unions — that run issue-oriented TV and radio commercials to disclose the group's name, address and phone number to the Clerk of the House or Secretary of the Senate.
- Toughen candidate disclosure by requiring federal candidates to file electronic contribution reports monthly in election years.

There appeared to be at least two key differences between the freshmen-backed bill and the stricter Shays-Meehan and McCain-Feingold measures.

One is that Shays-Meehan would extend the ban on soft money to state parties. Some advocates of overhauling campaign finance laws contend that is the only way to assure that state parties do not serve as a conduit for injecting soft money into federal elections.

Another difference is that Shays-Meehan would require any issue-oriented ads that bear the name or likeness of a candidate and are aired within 60 days of an election to be paid for by "hard money" regulated by the Federal Election Commission.

GOP leaders are not about to cede the field to the Democrats, who have been the key proponents of campaign finance overhaul in the current Congress. "This is not going to be a win for the White House," said a leadership aide, predicting that Republicans could seek to restrict political contributions from labor unions, ban contributions from foreigners and prohibit fund-raising in the White House.

The House on March 30 voted 369-43 to prohibit non-citizens from contributing to federal campaigns (HR 34).

But it rejected another bill, HR 2608, that would have prohibited labor unions or corporations from making campaign contributions on behalf of union members or stockholders without their approval.

Gingrich Changes His Mind

Gingrich said his decision to reverse course was a manifestation of his "listen, learn, help and lead" philosophy of governing. "This was a good example of listening," he said.

Gephardt was less charitable. "Make no mistake, this was a retreat, not a conversion," he said. "The Republican leadership still opposes reform that reduces the role of money in politics."

The discharge petition — sponsored by Scotty Baesler, D-Ky., and a group of conservative Democrats known as the "Blue Dogs" — took on heightened visibility after the March 30 session in which leading supporters of an overhaul were muzzled.

By the time the House left for its spring recess on April 1, 196 members, including seven Republicans, had signed the petition. During the recess, backers of overhaul legislation put pressure on those who had not signed.

Newspapers, including The New York Times and The Boston Globe, named the holdouts in lead editorials. Common Cause tried to bring up the issue in town meetings with key members.

The result: Five more Republicans signed the petition when the House reconvened on April 21, raising the total to 204. One name that raised eyebrows among GOP leaders was Amo Houghton, R-N.Y., a former business executive whose support could have led to more defections among New York Republicans.

Houghton said he was determined to clamp down on soft money and that signing the petition was "the only way I could show my feelings."

In a bid to defuse the petition drive and retain control of the floor, Gingrich offered open floor debate, but asked Republicans to remove their names from the discharge petition.

In a contentious, closed-door caucus of House Republicans April 22, several overhaul opponents denounced the signers for end-running the regular process with the discharge petition and for supporting a measure that banned soft money without restricting labor contributions that overwhelmingly favor Democrats.

Later, Zach Wamp, R-Tenn., who signed the petition, said: "Sometimes conflict is the necessary companion with change, and it's not easy. This is not a process that any of us enjoyed."

Dueling Bills Threaten Chances For Overhaul

MAY 16 — Advocates of a campaign finance overhaul will finally get their wish the week of May 18 — a clear shot in the House at revamping the way campaigns are paid for.

The trouble is, they might be too divided to take advantage of the opportunity.

Politics & Elections

Comparison of Campaign Finance Bills

MAY 16 — Debate is set to begin in the House the week of May 18 on proposals to overhaul campaign finance law. The base bill will be a measure (HR 2183) drafted by a bipartisan group of freshmen led by Asa Hutchinson, R-Ark., and Tom Allen, D-Maine. The chief rival is likely to be another bipartisan bill (HR 3526) sponsored by Christopher Shays, R-Conn., and Martin T. Meehan, D-Mass.

Following is a comparison of some key provisions in current law and how the two bills would change them.

Category	Current law	Freshman bill	Shays-Meehan
"Soft money" for national parties	No limits on national parties' ability to receive soft money, which is funds restricted to party-building activities, and which cannot be used to promote an individual candidate.	Bans national parties from soliciting, receiving or spending soft money.	Bans national parties from soliciting, receiving or spending soft money.
Soft money for state parties	State parties must follow federal regulations for determining what proportion of their soft money can be spent on federal, state and local campaign activities.	Prohibits state parties from transferring soft money to parties in other states.	Prohibits state parties and local parties from using soft money for federal election activity.
Hard money	Contributions by political action committees, individuals and parties of hard money — the tightly regulated funds that can be used in individual campaigns — are limited by law.	Doubles the aggregate annual limit individuals may contribute and indexes all contribution limits to inflation. Removes limits on how much parties may spend.	Provides increases in limits on how much individuals can give to parties. Does not index contribution limits to inflation.
Issue advocacy	Only advertising that expressly advocates a candidate (such as those that say "vote for" or "defeat") is subject to full federal disclosure, contribution limits and other regulations. Advertising focused solely on issues is exempt.	Requires an organization to disclose its expenditures on issue-oriented advertisements that mention congressional candidates in any year that the group spends more than $25,000 on advertising that mentions one candidate or $100,000 on all candidates.	Expands full federal disclosure, contribution limits and other regulations to advertising that can be more broadly defined as advocating a candidate, and to paid broadcasts that cite a candidate within 60 days of an election.
Independent expenditures	Individuals or groups can spend as much as they want on advertising that urges voters to support or oppose a federal candidate as long as they do not consult with or coordinate with the candidate's campaign.	No provision.	Tightens the definition of what constitutes coordination and cooperation. Increases the frequency of disclosure of large amounts of money spent in independent campaigns close to an election.
Wealthy candidates	No limits imposed on how much candidates can spend from their personal funds.	No provision.	Bans parties from making coordinated expenditures for House candidates who exceed a $50,000 voluntary limit on using their personal or family funds.
Federal Election Commission (FEC)	The FEC may audit a candidate or initiate enforcement only if it has reason to believe a violation has occurred.	No provision.	Permits the FEC to conduct random campaign audits within 12 months after an election and allows more leeway to initiate enforcement.
Electronic filing	Candidates have an option to file their campaign forms electronically.	Requires electronic filing by campaign committees that exceed $50,000 in receipts and expenditures per year.	Requires electronic filing by all campaign committees that have receipts or expenditures above a level set by the FEC, which would post them on the Internet within 24 hours.

Source: Congressional Research Service

Two months ago, supporters of campaign finance legislation were united in their disdain for the way House Republican leaders stage-managed the debate. They demanded, and ultimately got, another chance to consider the issue more on their own terms.

This time, the biggest hurdle will be coalescing around one proposal before final votes are taken in June.

Instead of suppressing the would-be reformers, House leaders have pitted them against one another. Although strategists expect numerous proposals on the floor, the primary choice is between the most widely known campaign finance measure (HR 3526), sponsored by Christopher Shays, R-Conn., and Martin T. Meehan, D-Mass., and an upstart rival (HR 2183) fashioned by a bipartisan group of freshmen.

The Shays-Meehan bill takes a tougher stance against the unlimited contributions of party money and the independent issue advocacy ads that critics identify as the key problems with the current system.

Much is riding on the ability of the bills' backers to close ranks. Whatever slim hope they have of forcing the Senate to act on campaign finance legislation this year depends in large part on building momentum with overwhelming support for a bill in the House.

Merely passing such legislation in the House would be a milestone. It would mark the first time either chamber had approved a comprehensive campaign finance overhaul in the four years since the GOP took control of Congress.

Although the House and Senate have each passed campaign finance bills occasionally over the past two decades, it has been 19 years since Congress and the president last agreed to a significant revision of campaign finance laws. The last major change came at the end of a series of post-Watergate reforms that remain the basis of current law (PL 93-443). *(1974 Almanac, p. 611)*

The latest push for changing campaign laws was sparked last year by Senate and House campaign finance investigations that revealed abuses by both parties. Supporters of overhaul hoped the revelations would outrage the public and put irresistible pressure on Congress to move legislation.

But Republican leaders in both chambers focused instead on trying to pillory Democrats for alleged abuses of campaign finance laws. GOP leaders argue that only self-appointed watchdog groups and newspaper editorial boards are demanding wholesale changes to campaign law, and they note that the issue is a major concern in few congressional campaigns.

"The media is much more interested in this than the American people are, and some people like having media attention," said Anne M. Northup, R-Ky., who believes that the overhaul proposals would be particularly harmful to Republicans.

Shays and other overhaul backers are undaunted, however. "The American people are not apathetic, just frustrated," Shays said, explaining why attempts to rewrite the laws have had a hard time catching fire.

Rob Portman, R-Ohio, who is unsure which measure to support, said Congress' uncertainty mirrors the public's confusion about how to respond to abuses in raising and spending campaign funds.

"This is complicated stuff," he said. "There's no simple solution. Many people have ambivalent feelings about public financing and [spending] limits, and yet they know the current system doesn't work very well."

Which is the Real Reform?

With the House debate looming, supporters of the two competing bills have walked a fine line between pointing out flaws in their opponents' measures and alienating potential supporters, some of whom back both bills.

The measures have similarities. Both would stop national parties from raising or spending "soft money." These unrestricted donations to political parties are meant to be used only for party-building activities such as get-out-the-vote efforts. But critics say the money often finds its way into individual campaign activities in a manner technically forbidden by law.

Both bills would also impose new requirements on issue-advocacy ads paid for by third-party groups such as nonprofit organizations and labor unions. Critics contend that these ads are often little more than ill-disguised efforts to get around campaign restrictions.

The Shays-Meehan bill — a companion to the Senate proposal (S 25) sponsored by Sens. John McCain, R-Ariz., and Russell D. Feingold, D-Wis. — generally takes a tougher, more aggressive tack.

For one thing, Shays-Meehan would place more restrictions on the use of soft money by state and local parties than would the freshman bill. It would also take a harder line on issue-advocacy ads.

"There is only one meaningful campaign reform proposal," said Joan Claybrook, president of Public Citizen, one of a number of public interest groups that have endorsed Shays-Meehan.

But sponsors of the freshman bill bristle at the suggestion that their plan is merely a pale imitation. "It's very misleading, what they're saying," said Asa Hutchinson, R-Ark., a co-author of the freshman measure. "Both bills represent significant reform."

Critics of Shays-Meehan describe it as constitutionally dubious and politically untenable. The Senate version has withered under the weight of filibusters twice since October. Senate supporters will be hard-pressed to muster the eight additional votes they need to break the logjam there.

In addition, some Republicans complain that clamping down on soft money without inhibiting organized labor's ability to bankroll Democratic campaigns would amount to unilateral disarmament by the GOP.

Indeed, the reason it will be so difficult to assemble a large bipartisan coalition for any overhaul proposal is that there are so many different notions of reform. There is no shortage of ideas; at least 90 bills to change the campaign finance system have been introduced in the House during the 105th Congress.

While both major House bills reflect the view that only more and tighter restrictions can cure the system, a significant minority in the House takes exactly the opposite tack. John T. Doolittle, R-Calif., and 69 cosponsors hold that there ought to be fewer campaign finance limits, not more. Their bill (HR 965) would abolish contribution limits by individuals, parties and political action committees, and rely instead on quicker and fuller disclosure.

Republicans are likely to offer a controversial "paycheck protection" amendment that would require unions to get their members' prior permission every year before using their dues for political purposes. Democrats view the proposal as a poison pill, since it would threaten a chief source of their support, but the measure is also unpopular with some pro-labor Republicans. An attempt to pass a free-standing paycheck protection bill (HR 2608) failed March 30 when 52 Republicans abandoned the party line.

Members are so divided that Rick White, R-Wash., proposes simply creating a commission to recommend changes in election laws (HR 99).

Dividing the Reformers

House Republican leaders thought they had killed campaign finance legislation March 30 by strictly limiting debate and preventing a bipartisan group of lawmakers from bringing up their own legislation.

But the ploy backfired. A small but growing group of GOP renegades joined with Democrats to force action, closing in on the 218 signatures they needed for a discharge petition. That would have cost GOP leaders control of the floor and allowed backers to debate a variety of campaign finance bills on their own terms.

Finally, on April 22, House Speaker Newt Gingrich, R-Ga., agreed to hold a wide-open debate.

In doing so, Gingrich plucked the freshman bill from obscurity and made it the starting point for floor action, rather than the better-known Shays-Meehan. That forced self-styled reformers to spend time arguing about which of their proposals was best instead of moving as a united front.

"We better figure out what we want to do," said a Democratic aide. "There's a lot of conflict over whether people should back the freshman bill, Shays-Meehan or both."

Republicans also seemed uncertain. "I really don't know that there's going to be a groundswell of support behind anything," said Zach Wamp, R-Tenn., a Shays-Meehan supporter. He said it will be hard to persuade the GOP freshmen to back Shays-Meehan "and pull them off a product they worked so hard for."

Recognizing that only a narrow majority supports a comprehensive rewrite, proponents of both bills cannot afford to alienate potential supporters. "It's awkward," acknowledged Tom Allen, of Maine, the lead Democratic sponsor of the freshman bill.

"But if you believe in reform, you want both of these bills to be in play."

Actually, though Shays-Meehan supporters praise the freshmen for their efforts, they are eager for them to consolidate behind the better-known bill. In a letter to House members, Ann McBride, president of Common Cause, a citizens watchdog group that backs tighter campaign finance laws, said the freshman bill was "fatally flawed" in that it would not stop state parties from using soft money to influence federal elections.

The freshmen say they purposely sought to write legislation that was more limited than Shays-Meehan. Anything more ambitious, they argue, has no chance of drawing significant GOP support and runs a greater risk of being declared unconstitutional.

While public interest groups such as Common Cause, Public Citizen and the League of Women Voters have lined up behind Shays-Meehan, the freshman bill does command some support in the reform community.

Herb Alexander, director of the Citizens' Research Foundation at the University of Southern California and an expert on campaign finance, backs the measure partly because it has a better chance of being enacted.

"I believe the freshman bill offers the possibility of incremental change," he said, "and I think that's about as far as the Congress or even the House is willing to go."

Soft Money

Most of the attention in the campaign finance struggle has centered on soft money, the almost entirely unregulated funds currently raised by national, state and local party organizations. Overhaul groups have targeted soft money because they contend it is a chief way of evading campaign finance limits that apply to hard money, the tightly regulated contributions that can be used directly in federal election campaigns.

Soft money's role in financing elections has exploded in recent years: The national parties raised $262.1 million in soft money in 1996, three times more than the $86 million they raised in 1992.

Both Shays-Meehan and the freshman bill would ban national parties from soliciting, receiving or spending soft money. They would also prohibit federal candidates and officials from raising soft money for federal elections beyond their own.

But while Shays-Meehan would ban state and local parties from using soft money for federal election activities, the freshman bill contains no such restriction, though it would bar state parties from transferring soft money to parties in other states.

Shays-Meehan backers contend that this amounts to a huge loophole in the freshman bill that would allow state parties to use soft money to influence federal elections. Big contributors of soft money could give their funds directly to state parties instead of using national parties as a conduit.

On the flip side, critics of Shays-Meehan say that bill goes too far. For instance, they charge that it would block a state party's ability to run get-out-the-vote efforts for its gubernatorial candidate if the election coincided with the congressional election.

Said Michael J. Malbin, a political science professor at the State University of New York at Albany: "It's not the business of the federal government to take over all parties and make them national parties governed by national law."

Both parties stand to lose if soft money is restricted, though Republicans have raised the most vehement objections. But that is not because they collect vastly more soft money than Democrats.

The national Republican committees raised $138.2 million in soft money for the 1996 campaigns, not all that much more than the $123.9 million raised by Democrats. And soft money actually accounted for a higher percentage of all national party receipts among Democrats, 36 percent, compared with 25 percent for the GOP.

The margin widened somewhat in 1997, when national GOP committees raised $40.2 million in soft money compared with $33.9 million for Democrats, according to the Center for Responsive Politics.

Sheila Krumholz, the center's research director, speculated that Republicans are more concerned about a soft-money ban because they are looking ahead to the 2000 presidential election. "The degree to which Democrats were able to close in on Republican fundraising is demonstrative of [President] Clinton's fundraising prowess," she said. Put a Republican in the

White House, though, and the GOP margin could widen substantially.

John Linder, R-Ga., chairman of the National Republican Congressional Committee (NRCC), said he has more immediate objections to restricting soft money. He said the funds are vital to nourishing party-building activity in the states, and the only way to combat the edge Democrats get from independent spending by labor unions.

"They have a huge advantage with the unions," he said of the Democrats, "and they can live on that forever." Mary Mead Crawford, the NRCC's communications director, said that much of labor's campaign expenditures constitute neither hard nor soft money. While the spending is purportedly for get-out-the-vote efforts and internal communications among union members, it actually reaches a broader general audience, she contended.

"That's preposterous," said David Smith, the AFL-CIO's director of public policy. He said labor's campaign expenditures are dwarfed by corporate campaign contributions, advertising and lobbying efforts.

"Ordinary folks are overwhelmed by people who can afford to write big checks," Smith said. "That's why Republicans are so concerned about a big-money ban."

But Republicans are not alone in their concerns about the effect of banning soft money. While congressional Democrats ostensibly support a ban, the Idaho and Ohio Democratic parties have filed suit along with the Republican National Committee to try to force the Federal Election Commission to lift the existing limits on soft-money spending for issue advocacy advertising.

Issue Advocacy

Another major point of contention between the two leading campaign finance bills is the rapidly growing phenomenon of issue advocacy ads.

These advertisements often implicitly support the candidates of one political party. But since they nominally focus on an issue, campaign laws do not apply. As long as the ads do not expressly urge people to vote for or against a candidate, the groups paying for them can avoid disclosure or reporting requirements.

Shays-Meehan would expand the definition of ads covered by federal election laws to include those that have "no reasonable meaning" other than to advocate the election or defeat of a candidate. The definition would specifically include any ad broadcast within 60 days of an election that mentions a congressional candidate.

"Blatantly unconstitutional" is how Douglas Johnson, legislative director for the National Right to Life Committee, refers to the provision. "We believe members of Congress have no authority whatsoever to restrict speech merely because it mentions their names."

The anti-abortion group is one of many that asserts its views through independent expenditures.

"We do not believe that American voters need speech nannies," Johnson said. "Voters are grownups and ultimately can sort through competing political messages and reach their own judgment."

Numerous legal scholars are convinced that such a provision would not pass constitutional muster.

Although many of the issues in the House debate will echo those in the Senate earlier in the year, the political dynamics will be different.

The biggest difference will be a lower obstacle for passing something. In the Senate, Democrats — who have been the key proponents of a campaign finance overhaul in the current Congress — represent only 45 votes of the 60 needed to break a filibuster.

In the House, where filibusters are prohibited, Democrats can account for 205 of the 218 votes needed for passage. So it will be easier for supporters of an overhaul to prevail.

In addition, no one in the House has commanded a role opposing the sweeping changes in campaign finance laws the way Mitch McConnell, R-Ky., has in the Senate, where he has gone head-to-head with McCain and Feingold.

Linder conceded he is "concerned" about not having anyone of comparable stature or commitment opposing an overhaul in the House. "I pray for Mitch McConnell's health," he said.

To help fill the vacuum, Majority Whip Tom DeLay, R-Texas, announced May 14 that he had formed a "free speech coalition" of Republicans who oppose restricting the flow of campaign money.

"Money is not the root of all evil in politics," he said. "In fact, money is the lifeblood of politics."

There is a sharp contrast in the way the parties are handling campaign finance legislation. Virtually every House Democrat is expected to follow the lead of their Senate colleagues and vote for Shays-Meehan.

"If you're going to do campaign reform, you can't be timid," said Martin Frost of Texas, chairman of the Democratic Congressional Campaign Committee. "You have to take risks, and risk litigation."

Among Republicans, support for either Shays-Meehan or the freshman bill will probably be spotty. But strategists expect that enough Republicans will cross party lines to vote with Democrats to pass something.

Northup said she is "disgusted" with the two dozen Republicans she expects to join Democrats to pass a bill. She said the measure "will in no way make campaign finance more honest. It will just push the money underground, so the person who cheats the most has the best advantage."

But a narrow majority for passage probably would not be enough to move the Senate to act. Perhaps that is why Shays sounds frustrated.

"Republicans lost a tremendous amount of credibility," he said, "by saying, 'We're going to hold President Clinton accountable [for campaign finance abuses] . . . but none of these hearings, none of these investigations, should lead to reform.'"

Overhaul Backers Grow Wary As Leaders Signal Protracted Debate

MAY 23 — The House reopened a debate on campaign finance legislation May 21, with GOP leaders signaling that they may try to stall any final action this year by debating proposals at length throughout the summer.

Some backers of proposals to overhaul campaign finance laws immediately complained that this was an attempt by leaders to back out of a commitment to a fair debate.

"The good faith of the leaders will be tested by whether they deal with

Politics & Elections

this issue promptly, and whether they allocate enough time," said Tom Allen, D-Maine, co-author of one of the leading overhaul proposals.

Majority Whip Tom DeLay, R-Texas, denied that there was a conscious effort to try to sink the proposals through a protracted debate.

"But there's no other way" to handle all the different measures, said DeLay, who contended that the leading initiatives unconstitutionally infringe on an individual's right to make campaign contributions. "The proponents of eliminating free speech want an open and fair debate," he said. "And they're going to get it."

On March 30, House GOP leaders tried to kill campaign finance legislation by strictly limiting debate. That strategy blocked a bipartisan group of lawmakers from advancing their own bill to restrict the unlimited contributions of party money and the independent issue advocacy ads that critics identify as key problems with the current system.

A Reverse Tactic

Now GOP leaders may be attempting a reverse tactic — extending the debate so deep into the summer that no substantive action is possible this year.

Such a strategy would risk energizing overhaul proponents all over again, however. After the first debate, they were so unhappy with the way the issue had been handled that they threatened to force it back to the floor on their own terms through a discharge petition. House Speaker Newt Gingrich, R-Ga., relented on April 22, agreeing to hold a wide-open debate in May.

But Gingrich barely made good on the pledge. The only action the House took before the Memorial Day recess was to approve the procedural rule and begin the floor debate.

The rule makes a bill devised by a bipartisan group of freshmen (HR 2183) the starting point for debate. It also permits 11 substitute amendments to be considered, all of which would replace the underlying bill. Whichever gets the most votes (and at least a majority) prevails.

The rule also permits each of the substitute amendments to be further amended, and it allows a constitutional amendment to be offered as well.

In all, Rules Committee Chairman Gerald B. H. Solomon, R-N.Y., said that nearly 600 amendments had been filed. No other bill in the House's history has ever attracted so many proposed amendments, he said.

Overhaul backers fretted at the possibility that the issue would be used as filler, to be shoehorned into House floor debate for an hour or two at a time over a period of months.

"Once we start the debate we should take it up and finish it," said Christopher Shays, R-Conn., a co-author with Martin T. Meehan, D-Mass., of the most widely known campaign finance measure (HR 3526).

"If we have interruptions, it will be solely because we have a group of people trying to kill this bill," Shays said. "I think the Speaker does not want this to be a farce."

GOP Conference Chairman John A. Boehner of Ohio predicted that while the debate would be extensive, "I don't think we in the leadership want this hanging around for months."

Republican leaders can be confident that even if the House does pass a campaign finance overhaul, the Senate is unlikely to concur. Filibusters have stalled a bipartisan overhaul bill (S 25) there twice in the last eight months.

Key Amendments

Among the substitute amendments are those offered by:

● Shays and Meehan, based on HR 3526. The favorite measure of outside groups that advocate overhauling the campaign finance system, the bill would take an aggressive stance against "soft money" (the largely unregulated donations to political parties) and independent issue advocacy advertising.

● Asa Hutchinson, R-Ark., and Allen, based on the so-called freshman bill (HR 2183), which is also the base bill. For their bill to succeed, though, all the amendments to it would have to fail. To give themselves a fighting chance, they are offering their own bill as an amendment as well. It would take a somewhat less aggressive stance against soft money and issue advocacy advertising; its advocates say that gives it a greater chance of getting enacted.

● Rick White, R-Wash., based on HR 99. It would create an independent commission to recommend changes in campaign laws by next spring.

● John T. Doolittle, R-Calif., based on HR 965. It would abolish political contribution limits altogether, substituting quicker and fuller disclosure.

● David R. Obey, D-Wis., based on HR 243. It would finance campaigns with public money by combining public contributions with a 0.1 percent tax on corporate income above $10 million.

The rule also permits DeLay to offer a constitutional amendment (H J Res 119) that would allow Congress and the states to go beyond court-set limits on the government's right to regulate campaign expenditures. DeLay opposes the amendment, which is identical to one (H J Res 47) introduced by Minority Leader Richard A. Gephardt, D-Mo., but would offer it as proof that "reformers are trying to gut the First Amendment."

Bill Appears DOA, But Debate Lively

JUNE 13 — The latest chapter in the House's campaign finance odyssey began June 10 on the oddest of terms — debate on a constitutional amendment opposed by the member who offered it and by the vast majority of the House.

The measure (H J Res 119) would allow Congress and the states to go beyond court-set limits on the government's right to regulate campaign spending. Offered by Majority Whip Tom DeLay, R-Texas, it was identical to a measure (H J Res 47) introduced previously by Minority Leader Richard A. Gephardt, D-Mo.

DeLay had no interest in seeing it adopted; instead, he said he offered the amendment to show that "we have to manipulate and shred the First Amendment of the Constitution" in order to pave the way for the restrictive campaign finance overhaul bills offered by self-styled reformers.

Barney Frank, D-Mass., disputed DeLay, arguing that the contribution bans or limits in the proposed overhaul bills required no change to the Constitution. And he said that although he favors a constitutional amendment to allow limits on campaign spending as well as contributions, he does not back this one.

With both parties generally repudiating it, the proposed constitutional amendment fell far short of the two-thirds needed for adoption when the vote was taken the following day. The tally was 29-345, with 51 members voting "present." *(Vote 226, p. H-66)*

The three-hour debate frustrated overhaul advocates, who saw it as a time-wasting exercise that blocked action on bills that could pass. "The longer this debate goes on tonight, the weirder it gets," said Tom Allen, D-Maine, co-author of the so-called freshman bill (HR 2183), the base campaign finance overhaul measure.

Advocates of stricter fundraising laws have been hemmed in by the U.S. Supreme Court's landmark 1976 Buckley v. Valeo decision. The court ruled that reasonable limits on contributions were permissible but asserted that restrictions on spending by candidates or independent groups would impede constitutionally protected political speech.

Backers of overhaul measures argued that their bills proposed constitutionally permissible limits on contributions, not spending. "This is an attempt to drag a red herring across this discussion," said Allen.

But John T. Doolittle, R-Calif., insisted that "the so-called campaign finance issue is really about limiting our right to engage in political speech and participate in free elections."

The campaign finance debate is expected to begin in earnest during the week of June 15. The House is set to discuss the first of 11 substitute amendments to the freshman bill. Whichever substitute gets the most votes (and at least a majority) prevails.

The House will also consider a rule that would allow at least 258 amendments to the broader substitute proposals. These additional amendments run the gamut from making it more difficult for unions to solicit contributions from their members to prohibiting states from providing voter materials in any language but English.

Deliberate Stall?

Some overhaul advocates complain that GOP leaders are trying to sabotage their proposals through protracted debate. Majority Leader Dick Armey, R-Texas, said he hopes to complete debate by month's end, but would continue it after the July Fourth recess if necessary.

The most prominent substitute amendments are those offered by:

• Christopher Shays, R-Conn., and Martin T. Meehan, D-Mass., based on their bill (HR 3526), which would take an aggressive stance against "soft money" (the largely unregulated donations to political parties) and independent issue advocacy advertising.

• Asa Hutchinson, R-Ark., and Allen, based on the freshman bill, which is a somewhat less restrictive version of the Shays-Meehan measure. For their bill to succeed, all the other amendments to it would have to fail. To give themselves a fighting chance, they are offering their own bill as an amendment as well.

• Rick White, R-Wash., based on his bill (HR 99), which would create an independent commission to recommend changes in campaign laws by next spring.

Proposal Survives Key House Vote

JUNE 20 — The best-known House proposal to rewrite campaign finance laws survived its first test on the House floor with surprising ease June 19.

The House rejected, 155-254, a potentially crippling amendment to a campaign finance overhaul proposal by Christopher Shays, R-Conn., and Martin T. Meehan, D-Mass., based on their bill (HR 3526). The Shays-Meehan plan would ban national parties from receiving or spending "soft money" (the unlimited and largely unregulated donations to political parties) and set new restrictions on expenditures by third-party groups.

Backers of Shays-Meehan hope to ward off all major amendments in order to keep the proposal as close as possible to a Senate companion bill (S 25) sponsored by John McCain, R-Ariz., and Russell D. Feingold, D-Wis.

The first test came on an amendment by House Oversight Chairman Bill Thomas, R-Calif., to negate the entire act if any part of it were struck down by the courts. The amendment played to the members' fears that the courts might strike down the proposal's tough limits on third-party issue ads (ads touting issues, but which critics say effectively promote or attack individual candidates) while leaving the ban on soft money intact. Some members say that that would effectively limit political party spending while not restricting third-party groups.

Shays-Meehan backers countered that the amendment could ultimately kill their proposal, however, and the vote demonstrated their potential bipartisan strength. While Democrats were expected to vote strongly against the Thomas amendment (188 of 206 voted no), fully 65 of the House's 227 Republicans joined the measure's backers to vote no as well.

The vote came as the House continued a languid, on-again-off-again debate on campaign finance that had overhaul backers threatening to resurrect the procedural device they used to force floor action in the first place. GOP overhaul backers abandoned a discharge petition drive in April when GOP leaders agreed to hold a floor debate.

The threat caused Majority Leader Dick Armey, R-Texas, to pledge to wrap up debate by the Aug. 7 recess.

Democrats still objected, arguing that GOP leaders were engaging in a Senate-style filibuster. Republican leaders said they were only giving the matter the "free and open debate" that overhaul proponents had clamored for. "Apparently, the only kind of open debate they want is on their proposals," said Majority Whip Tom DeLay, R-Texas.

While Republicans defected from party orthodoxy on some votes, they stuck with the leadership on a crucial vote June 18 to set a second rule governing floor debate. The House voted 221-189 to approve the rule crafted by GOP leaders. *(Vote 247, p. H-72)*

The House had previously approved an initial rule that made a campaign finance proposal offered by a bipartisan group of freshmen (HR 2183) the base bill and permitted 11 substitute amendments to be considered, including Shays-Meehan. Whichever gets the most votes (and at least a majority) prevails.

The new rule allows at least 258 more amendments to the broader substitute proposals.

The first substitute to be considered was a proposal by Rick White, R-

Wash., to create an independent commission to recommend changes in campaign laws by next spring — a traditional way for members to defer difficult decisions. But with prospects improving for the House to approve a specific overhaul plan, support for a commission diminished, and the amendment failed, 156-201, on June 17. (*Vote 241, p. H-70*)

On June 19, the House voted 325-78 to accept a commission plan that would be added to — but not substitute for — Shays-Meehan.

House Debate Gathers Steam

JULY 25 — The slow-moving House debate about overhauling the nation's campaign finance laws is gaining momentum, but it remains uncertain whether GOP leaders will make good on their pledge to complete action on the issue before the August recess.

The House July 20 voted on nine amendments to the best-known campaign finance proposal, sponsored by Reps. Christopher Shays, R-Conn., and Martin T. Meehan, D-Mass. That marked progress in an off-again, on-again debate that began in May.

But the flurry of votes disposed of less than one-fifth of the 55 amendments originally made to the Shays-Meehan proposal. That number has been slowly dropping, as some lawmakers have withdrawn proposals and others have combined separate initiatives into a single amendment. Still, at least 30 amendments remain to be considered.

And beyond that, the proposal by Shays and Meehan, based on their bill (HR 3526) to eliminate unlimited "soft money" donations and place restrictions on so-called issue advocacy ads, is only the second of 11 major alternatives to the underlying campaign finance bill put forward by a bipartisan group of freshmen (HR 2183). Under the unusual procedures governing debate, the alternative that receives the most votes — and at least a majority — prevails.

The daunting array of amendments has prompted charges from advocates for overhauling the campaign fund-raising system that GOP leaders want to run out the clock and prevent the House from voting on meaningful political finance legislation this year.

But Shays insists that House Majority Leader Dick Armey, R-Texas, will fulfill his commitment to finish the bill by the start of the House recess Aug. 7. "I can't even contemplate the consequences of him not living up to his word," Shays said. "I believe he will." Rep. Bill Thomas, R-Calif., chairman of the House Oversight Committee, said July 17 that he feels "comfortable that that [promise] will be honored."

All along, the challenge for Shays and Meehan has been to steer their proposal through a gantlet of GOP-backed amendments that, if adopted, would make it all but impossible for Democrats to support the final product.

On July 21, the biggest test came in the form of an amendment by Bill Paxon, R-N.Y., that would have required labor unions to report in detail their expenditures on political activities. Democrats and pro-labor Republicans joined forces to defeat the amendment, 150-248. (*Vote 306, p. H-88*)

Several other amendments considered that day were aimed at highlighting well-chronicled Democratic fundraising excesses during the 1996 presidential campaign. For instance, House Majority Whip Tom DeLay, R-Texas, offered an amendment that tweaked Vice President Al Gore, whose legalistic defense of the fundraising calls he made from his office was that there was "no controlling legal authority" barring such fundraising.

The House approved DeLay's amendment, asserting that there is indeed such a controlling legal authority, on a vote of 360-36. (*Vote 304, p. H-88*)

Shays-Meehan Surviving

But DeLay's amendment and many others like it are essentially a sideshow to the main question of this convoluted and confusing debate — whether Republicans can cripple or kill the Shays-Meehan proposal.

So far, all evidence indicates they cannot, although Republicans have mounted formidable challenges and have more planned. When the House resumes debate on July 27, it is scheduled to vote on a pair of GOP-backed amendments chipping away at provisions in the so-called motor voter act, a 1993 law (PL 103-31) that made it easier for people to register to vote. (*1993 Almanac, p. 199*)

Many Republicans have long objected to the law, arguing it has led to vote fraud. Adoption of either of the amendments would represent a serious blow to supporters of Shays-Meehan.

There is a sense that the House might be moving to closure on the Shays-Meehan proposal. And if that occurs, Thomas said, the remainder of the debate might go more quickly.

"Given the pivotal role of [Shays-Meehan], whether it passes or fails will dictate clearly what is done with the rest of the campaign reform rule package," he said.

Legislation Nears Passage in House; Senate Still Unreceptive

AUGUST 1 — After months of delay and parliamentary obstruction, the House is set to pass a broad overhaul of the campaign finance system that would end unlimited "soft money" donations and place strict limits on so-called issue advocacy ads.

The vote, expected Aug. 3, comes after House members defeated a series of amendments July 30-31 that likely would have killed the overhaul bill (HR 3526) drafted by Christopher Shays, R-Conn., and Martin T. Meehan, D-Mass.

Fifteen amendments to Shays-Meehan were overwhelmingly defeated, paving the way for final passage. "Four or five months ago, nobody thought we would have gotten this far," Meehan said. "It will be a major story across the country when we pass the bill."

The bill would ban unlimited soft money donations to political parties from interest groups, businesses and wealthy individuals. It would also restrict political ads that advocate issues, but which critics say are often thinly veiled pitches for or against individual candidates.

While Shays and Meehan predicted that the House would easily pass their bill with 250 to 260 votes, there are still several more hurdles they must clear.

The Shays-Meehan bill is just the second of 11 substitutes to the underlying campaign finance bill (HR 2183) being debated by the House.

Under the rules set for debate, the substitute that passes with the most votes prevails. The House is expected to finish work on all the substitutes before its summer recess begins Aug. 7.

But the greatest hurdle the overhaul bill now faces is Senate action. Senate Majority Leader Trent Lott, R-Miss., has said he will not bring up the measure.

In February, a Senate filibuster killed a nearly identical campaign overhaul bill drafted by John McCain, R-Ariz., and Russell D. Feingold, D-Wis. Supporters of the bill fell eight votes short of ending that filibuster.

But campaign overhaul supporters say a strong House vote for Shays-Meehan will force the Senate to act.

"Passage is the 'big mo' [momentum] here," said Rep. Sander M. Levin, D-Mich. "What the senators who oppose campaign finance reform most fear is a vote in the House."

House opponents of the overhaul bill were more skeptical. They conceded that Shays-Meehan will likely pass with the largest majority of all substitutes, but predicted that the Senate will not have the time or the will to act on it.

"It's dead for this year. I am confident about that," said Republican Rep. John T. Doolittle of California, a Shays-Meehan opponent.

The Senate left town July 31 for its summer recess and will not return until Aug. 31. That leaves little more than a month for the Senate to act before Congress is set to adjourn for the year Oct. 9.

Although opponents pinned their hopes on the Senate, they predicted that the campaign finance debate will return again next year.

"This issue is not going to die. It was time for our members to come up to speed on this," Doolittle said. "This is just the beginning of the educational process."

'Poison Pill' Amendments

Shays-Meehan supporters defeated 15 amendments by wide margins July 30-31. Backers of the bill had characterized the amendments as "poison pills" that would dilute support for the measure and make it impossible to pass.

Among the amendments were several that would have rolled back provisions in the so-called motor voter act, a 1993 law (PL 103-31) that made it easier for people to register to vote. One amendment, offered by Robert W. Goodlatte, R-Va., would have required proof of citizenship and Social Security numbers to register and allowed states to require photo identification when voters went to the polls. That measure was defeated, 165 to 260. (*Vote 358, p. H-102*)

Another amendment by Rep. Ken Calvert, R-Calif., would have required candidates to raise at least 50 percent of their campaign contributions from within their home districts. It was defeated, 147 to 278. (*Vote 360, p. H-102*)

House Bill Gets Day in the Sun; Senate's Shadow Looms

AUGUST 8 — Defying the odds, advocates of a campaign finance overhaul pushed a sweeping bill (HR 2183) through the House on Aug. 6 and vowed to pressure the Senate to do the same.

But their chances of succeeding before Congress' scheduled adjournment Oct. 9 appeared not much better than winning the Powerball lottery.

Supporters of an overhaul cheered the House's 252-179 vote for the legislation, which previously had been amended largely along the lines of HR 3526, sponsored by Christopher Shays, R-Conn., and Martin T. Meehan, D-Mass. Sixty-one Republicans voted for the bill, more than making up for the 15 Democrats who voted against it. (*Vote 405, p. H-114*)

The legislation would ban national parties from receiving or spending "soft money" — unlimited and largely unregulated donations to political parties. It would also set new restrictions on campaign-related expenditures by third-party groups.

The vote represented the first time in six years that either chamber had passed a bill rewriting campaign fi-

Bill Highlights

AUGUST 8 — The House passed a campaign finance overhaul bill (HR 2183) on Aug. 6 that is based on a measure (HR 3526) by Christopher Shays, R-Conn., and Martin T. Meehan, D-Mass. That bill, in turn, is similar to the Senate proposal (S 25) sponsored by John McCain, R-Ariz., and Russell D. Feingold, D-Wis. In major provisions, HR 2183 would:

- **"Soft money" for national parties.** Ban national parties from soliciting, receiving or spending soft money, which is supposed to be used solely for party-building activities and not to promote individual candidates.
- **Soft money for state parties.** Prohibit state parties and local parties from using soft money for federal election activity.
- **"Hard money."** Increase the limits on how much individuals can give to parties.
- **Issue advocacy.** Expand full federal disclosure, contribution limits and other regulations to advertising that can be more broadly defined as advocating a candidate, and to paid broadcasts that cite a candidate within 60 days of an election.
- **Independent expenditures.** Tighten the definition of what expenditures by individuals and groups constitute coordination and cooperation with a campaign. The bill also would increase the frequency of disclosure of large amounts of money spent in independent campaigns close to an election.
- **Wealthy candidates.** Ban parties from making coordinated expenditures for House candidates who exceed a $50,000 voluntary limit on using their personal or family funds.
- **Federal Election Commission (FEC).** Permit the FEC to conduct random campaign audits within 12 months after an election and give the agency more leeway to initiate enforcement.

Politics & Elections

nance laws. The last significant revision of such laws was enacted 19 years ago. *(History, 1997 Almanac, p. 1-26)*

Its advocates endured numerous attempts by House GOP leaders to block or delay its passage over several months, most recently by forcing them to swat away a lengthy list of amendments. Majority Leader Dick Armey, R-Texas, paid grudging respect to Shays-Meehan's supporters, saying, "They did a good job of holding their mark and then passing their mark."

But it appears unlikely that overhaul supporters will be able to quickly translate their success in the Senate, which has twice rejected efforts to pass a similar bill in the 105th Congress. They would need to pick up the backing of eight additional senators to break a GOP-led filibuster. And if Republican leaders failed to kill the bill in the House, they at least postponed its passage so as to leave little time for the Senate to act.

"Obviously the clock is our worst enemy at this time," said Ann McBride, president of Common Cause, a citizens' watchdog group that backs tighter campaign finance laws. "We know it is an uphill, difficult fight. But no one said it could happen in the House, and it happened."

House Action

House Republican leaders tried several distinct strategies to discard a campaign finance overhaul, to no avail.

They squelched debate on campaign finance March 30 by prohibiting Shays-Meehan from coming to the House floor. But the ploy encouraged the bill's supporters to embrace a procedural device that would have let them debate a variety of campaign finance bills on their own terms.

GOP leaders finally relented to an open debate on the issue in May. But they made Shays-Meehan open to dozens of amendments, then forced it to compete with 10 other substitute amendments to the underlying bill, HR 2183. Whichever of the 11 substitute amendments got the most votes — and at least a majority — would prevail.

A crowning moment for the supporters of Shays-Meehan came Aug. 3, when the House voted for their substitute amendment, 237-186. Fifty-one Republicans voted for the measure, outweighing the 11 Democrats who voted against it. *(Vote 379, p. H-108)*

"This is truly an historic opportunity to restore integrity to the political process," Shays said.

Bill Thomas, R-Calif., complained that while the measure banned political parties from using soft money, "it in no way inhibits labor unions from influencing legislation and candidates with that same soft money."

Added Majority Whip Tom DeLay, R-Texas: "It is amazing to me that Republicans would support this disarmament bill."

GOP supporters responded that the legislation was fair to both parties. Zach Wamp, R-Tenn., asked fellow Republicans to "please put the public interest above their personal interest."

The relatively strong vote in favor of Shays-Meehan prompted the authors of several other substitute amendments to withdraw their measures.

One who persisted was John T. Doolittle, R-Calif., a stalwart critic of fundraising limits. His amendment, to abolish limits on campaign contributions and rely instead on quicker and fuller public disclosure, failed, 131-299. *(Vote 403, p. H-114)*

The final hurdle was a substitute amendment by Asa Hutchinson, R-Ark., and Tom Allen, D-Maine, based on the so-called freshman bill (HR 2183), which was also the base bill.

The freshman bill would take a somewhat less aggressive stance against soft money and issue advocacy advertising. Its advocates said that approach gave the legislation a better chance of passing in the Senate and surviving a constitutional challenge.

GOP leaders toyed with embracing the freshman proposal to get the 238 votes needed to topple Shays-Meehan. That prompted Shays-Meehan's supporters to elaborately praise the freshmen for their efforts but urge its defeat.

The freshman measure ultimately failed, 147-222, with 61 members voting "present." *(Vote 404, p. H-114)*

The Senate's Harsh Reality

Afterward, Shays-Meehan's supporters made a deceptively simple appeal to the Senate. "Why shouldn't a bill that has a majority of support in both houses become the law of the land?" asked Allen, a leader of the freshman effort who also supported Shays-Meehan.

But the peculiar rules of the Senate complicate matters. During the past year, GOP-led filibusters have twice stymied the companion bill to Shays-Meehan (S 25) sponsored by Sens. John McCain, R-Ariz., and Russell D. Feingold, D-Wis. While 52 senators — all 45 Democrats and seven Republicans — have supported the measure, they have repeatedly fallen eight votes short of the 60 needed to overcome the filibuster.

Majority Leader Trent Lott, R-Miss., indicated that the House vote had not changed the Senate's dynamics. "There is no more of a consensus than there was in the spring," said an aide to Lott.

Still, Democrats will undoubtedly try to move the bill again, most likely by trying to attach it to one of the several remaining fiscal 1999 appropriations bills. But McCain acknowledged that there were formidable obstacles.

"I'd love to see a vote this year," he said in a telephone interview. "But I understand the time constraints." The Senate returns from its summer recess Aug. 31 and is scheduled to adjourn Oct. 9.

Democrats have several higher priorities for the Senate's remaining weeks than overhauling campaign finance laws — including bills to regulate health maintenance organizations (S 1890) and to raise the minimum wage (S 1573).

Groups advocating an overhaul have signaled they will concentrate their lobbying efforts on a handful of GOP senators facing tough re-election races, such as Alfonse M. D'Amato of New York, as well as those who previously supported restrictions on fundraising, such as Tim Hutchinson, R-Ark.

A spokesman for Hutchinson, who was traveling in South Asia, said the senator had given no indication that he had softened his opposition to the bill.

An aide to Sen. Sam Brownback, R-Kan., who supported a sweeping overhaul when he served in the House, said Brownback's views were unchanged from a 1997 statement in which he asserted that the current legislation was "based on an unconstitutional premise of trying to restrict political speech."

And a House Republican who is close to D'Amato predicted that the New York senator would not drop his opposition. "One of the main reasons

Campaign Finance

he has been able to survive politically is that he has been able to raise more money than his opponents," said the lawmaker, who did not want to be identified.

Cloture Vote Fails in the Senate

SEPTEMBER 12 — The script was nearly the same and, to no one's surprise, so was the vote as the Senate again defeated efforts to tighten the nation's campaign finance laws.

With the outcome preordained, a motion Sept. 10 to cut off debate on campaign finance legislation failed by a vote of 52-48, eight votes shy of the 60 needed to invoke cloture. *(Vote 264, p. S-41)*

The action came as Sens. John McCain, R-Ariz., and Russell D. Feingold, D-Wis., tried to press forward with the campaign finance bill bearing their names. And as before, they failed. The Senate had voted 51-48 on Feb. 26 against cutting off debate, effectively killing the bill. *(Vote 16, p. S-6)*

This time, McCain and Feingold tried to revive the issue by attaching the legislation to the Senate interior appropriations bill (S 2237). Soon after the vote, McCain withdrew the amendment, though not his devotion to the cause. "We won't give up this fight," a clearly angered McCain said.

In urging his colleagues to support the measure, McCain portrayed the Senate as a barrier to the overhaul supported by the American public and the House. Failing to strengthen campaign finance laws, he said on the floor Sept. 10, would only inflame the public's low opinion of Congress.

Reno Decision

McCain and other supporters also hoped they would get a boost from Attorney General Janet Reno, who announced Sept. 8 that the Justice Department would launch yet another 90-day investigation of Democratic fundraising in the 1996 election cycle.

The latest investigation would specifically examine whether President Clinton was involved in the improper use of campaign money. If that probe finds sufficient evidence of such activity, it could lead to the appointment of an independent counsel to investigate Clinton.

The 90-day inquiry was triggered after a 30-day preliminary investigation found specific sufficient cause for a more detailed probe.

That investigation comes on the heels of two other 90-day inquiries into fundraising activities by Vice President Al Gore and former White House Deputy Chief of Staff Harold M. Ickes.

All the actions are centered on how the 1996 Clinton-Gore campaign solicited and distributed roughly $42 million in campaign funds. The question to be answered in the latest probe is whether the Clinton-Gore campaign used DNC funds to promote their re-election campaign instead of more general issues on behalf of the Democratic Party.

If investigators conclude that occurred, the Clinton-Gore campaign would have exceeded campaign spending limits established by federal law.

Clinton aides deny the money was used improperly and say that any investigation will reach a similar conclusion.

Whether that is the case or not, the news of the investigation failed to energize the Senate or swing the eight votes McCain needed to keep the campaign finance overhaul debate alive.

Opponents, including the Senate Republican leadership, said existing laws are sufficient if they are more aggressively enforced.

Changing campaign statutes, Larry E. Craig, R-Idaho, said just before the vote, "doesn't mean you'll get character change."

On Sept. 9, Slade Gorton, R-Wash., called McCain's effort "a modest step in the wrong direction."

Those were the arguments that won in February, and even though McCain and Feingold softened the bill in an effort to attract more Republican votes, they fell short once again. Among the most significant changes was language barring unions and corporations from funding politically oriented advertising within 60 days of an election.

Those provisions were coupled with language that bans "soft money" contributions and restricts issue advocacy advertising. The House-passed bill (HR 2183) has no such prohibition.

While disappointed by the defeat, McCain vowed to try again, although he indicated he is not likely to seek to attach campaign finance overhaul to another appropriations bill.

"I won't give up on the bill, but the question is, where can we make progress," McCain said.

That prospect is highly unlikely, said Majority Leader Trent Lott, R-Miss., who indicated supporters will have little chance of pressing their case again. "I've been patient, and I have tried to be cooperative," Lott said moments before McCain withdrew the amendment. "I do think now that the time is right to move on."

Mitch McConnell, R-Ky., the opposition's leader, was more blunt, suggesting that the issue is gone for good and would have an even more difficult time in the 106th Congress. "We hope to have an even more conservative Senate than we do now," after the election, McConnell told reporters after the vote.

As for McCain and his allies, McConnell was dismissive.

"Mysteriously, they must think this is a great political issue. . . . It seems to me we have demonstrated it won't pass," he said. "And anything else [such as adding it as an amendment] would be gamesmanship." ◆

Chapter 19
SCIENCE

Human Cloning 19-3
NASA Authorization 19-4
    Private Space Shuttles 19-9

Lawmakers Defer Legislative Action On Human Cloning

SUMMARY

A year after Scottish scientists announced that they had used cloning to produce a sheep named Dolly, proposals in Congress to stop the cloning of humans took on new urgency when Chicago physicist Richard Seed announced his determination to do so. But the debate ended in February after the Senate voted decisively against taking up a bill (S 1601) to ban human cloning.

Champions of the bill, such as Christopher S. Bond, R-Mo., and Bill Frist, R-Tenn., said the vote was the result of misinformation spread by rogue scientists and special interest groups. Opponents, such as the American Heart Association and the Cystic Fibrosis Foundation, said the measure could cut off entire avenues of research into cloning of individual cells to treat cancer, heart disease and other maladies.

Though there was a consensus that creating a carbon copy of any living or dead person is morally repugnant, the vote indicated that the Senate had serious reservations about the broadness of the bill. The outcome also suggested that opponents of the measure could have difficulty putting cloning into the context of the abortion debate.

The Senate voted 42-54 on Feb. 11 in favor of a motion to invoke cloture on a motion to proceed to S 1601 — or 18 votes short of the 60 required.

Senate Halts Debate On Cloning Bill

FEBRUARY 14 — After strong objections from advocacy groups such as the American Heart Association and the Cystic Fibrosis Foundation, the Senate on Feb. 11 blocked floor debate on a bill to ban human cloning.

The measure, S 1601, was stopped when a motion to proceed failed, 42-54, well short of the three-fifths needed. The action takes the bill off the fast track set by Senate Majority Leader Trent Lott, R-Miss. The bill has so far not been the subject of hearings. *(Vote 10, p. S-5)*

Dianne Feinstein, D-Calif., a main opponent of the bill, called the vote "a significant vote for common sense." Twelve Republicans joined 42 Democrats to thwart the measure.

S 1601 would ban a process known as somatic cell nuclear transfer to create a human embryo. In a series of letters and meetings with senators, medical groups said such language could cut off entire avenues of research into cloning individual cells to treat cancer, heart disease and other maladies.

Somatic cell nuclear transfer involves replacing the nucleus of an egg cell with the nucleus of some other cell — an adult cell that would not multiply if left in its original state. Scientists have found that the remaining part of the egg cell can somehow "reprogram" the new nucleus, causing it to multiply.

In theory, this organism could be implanted into a womb and allowed to develop into a human being. Hence, bill supporters Christopher S. Bond, R-Mo., and Bill Frist, R-Tenn., consider it an embryo, worthy of the same protection abortion opponents would accord to embryos conceived through fertilization.

But groups that fund medical research do not share that view. They see the organism as a growing mass of cells that could generate certain types of cells to treat specific diseases.

A leukemia patient, for instance, could receive bone marrow generated in a lab. A heart patient could receive new cells rather than an entire transplant. Burn victims could get new skin cells. Because the new cells would genetically match the patient's, rejection of the transplanted tissue would not be a problem.

Some of the 12 Republican "no" votes came from abortion rights supporters, such as Arlen Specter of Pennsylvania and Olympia J. Snowe of Maine. But they were joined by abortion foes such as Connie Mack of Florida and Strom Thurmond of South Carolina.

Mack was particularly outspoken. Noting that both his parents died of cancer, and that he, his wife, his brother and his daughter have all struggled with cancer, he said he would not do anything to jeopardize medical research. ◆

Science

Congressional Anger Over Russia's Space Station Role Snags NASA Authorization

Box Score

- **Bills:** HR 1275; S 1250
- **House action:** None in 1998.
- **Senate action:** The Senate Commerce, Science and Transportation Committee passed S 1250 (S Rept 105-195) by voice vote on March 12.

For the sixth year in a row, lawmakers were unable to send President Clinton a NASA authorization bill. This year's Senate version of the bill (S 1250) proposed placing financial limits on NASA's share of the space station, a joint laboratory for research in space being built by the United States, Russia and a partnership of 14 other countries.

After the House passed an authorization bill (HR 1275 — H Rept 105-65) in 1997, the Senate Commerce, Science and Transportation Committee approved S 1250 in March, but the measure never came to the floor. *(1997 Almanac, p. 3-44)*

Working separately, House and Senate appropriators required NASA to start developing plans on how to proceed on the space station if Russia could not continue to meet its financial obligations.

The appropriators allowed NASA in October to transfer $60 million in its fiscal 1998 budget to pay Russia for station goods and services on the condition that the agency submit a plan for minimizing reliance on Russia. They also required NASA to look at new ways to contract with the Russians.

Before the appropriators became involved, House Science Committee members held a series of hearings at which they berated the Clinton administration for allowing NASA to rely on Russia as a primary partner in building the station, whose initial components are set for launch in November. Their criticism intensified after an independent panel of experts concluded in May that the station's cost through assembly could reach $24 billion — $7 billion more than the agency projected in 1993 when it signed on with Russia.

NASA officials largely concurred with the panel's findings. After Russia's economic crisis worsened in late summer, they developed a proposal to spend as much as $660 million to buy new Russian vehicles to support the station, as well as spend up to $600 million more developing new U.S. hardware to reduce reliance on Russia in completing the project.

Senate Panel Clamps Price Cap On Space Station

MARCH 14 — Making clear the long-standing concern of lawmakers over the increasing cost of the international space station, the Senate Commerce, Science and Transportation Committee on March 12 clamped a price cap on NASA's share of the project.

The committee approved the spending limit as an amendment to legislation (S 1250) to reauthorize the space agency for fiscal years 1998 through 2000. Both the amendment and the bill passed by voice vote.

The committee also approved, again by voice vote, a separate bill (HR 1702 - H Rept 105-347) aimed at helping the commercial space industry by revising NASA's role to encourage private-sector involvement and competition in developing industrial space products. The House passed the commercial space bill last November.

Congress has not sent a NASA authorization bill to the White House since 1992, leaving funding and policy decisions since then largely in the hands of appropriators who provide money for the agency through annual spending bills for veterans and housing programs.

The Senate authorization bill, sponsored by Bill Frist, R-Tenn., calls for funding NASA at $13.63 billion for fiscal year 1998 and $13.46 billion in fiscal 1999, the level President Clinton has proposed.

It also includes a funding level of $13.68 billion in fiscal 2000. The House-passed authorization bill (HR 1275 - H Rept. 105-65) does not cover funding for that year.

Commerce Chairman John McCain, R-Ariz., said the space station cap is intended to signal that lawmakers will no longer tolerate the schedule slippages and cost overruns that have plagued the project. According to some agency estimates, the station is as much as $3.6 billion over budget.

Critics in both chambers have pointed to the station's problems as evidence that it should be killed, although they have failed to muster enough votes to do so over the last seven years.

McCain's amendment would limit NASA space station costs to $21.9 billion through the assembly phase. NASA currently estimates its share of the costs through assembly at around $21 billion, but has asked an independent appraiser to determine the true cost.

The amendment also would limit the U.S. share of transportation costs to assemble the complex to $17.7 billion. The figures were based on discussions with the General Accounting Office, which is conducting its own assessment of NASA's space station budget. "We need to have some kind of predictability associated with the project," said McCain, a supporter of the space station.

Sen. Kay Bailey Hutchison, R-Texas, agreed with McCain's concerns. Her support for the amendment is considered significant because her state is home to the Johnson Space Center, a major NASA site.

NASA Administrator Daniel S. Goldin declined to comment on the amendment, saying he had not had a chance to study it in detail. But he said he plans to work with McCain to come up with an agreement that Congress and NASA can live with.

To quell Congress' frustration over the space station's growing costs, Goldin and other agency officials have sought to emphasize that the project is a research and development program and that it has been difficult to anticipate future expenses.

"Any time you've got a constraint, you lose a little bit of flexibility," said Gretchen McClain, NASA's deputy associate administrator for the space station.

Some House Republican supporters of NASA said they also plan to study the legislative price cap idea. They said it is possible such a limit would be acceptable as long as the space agency is given enough flexibility.

The space station is a joint venture among the United States, Russia, Canada, Japan, Brazil and 11 European countries. It is scheduled to be fully operational by 2003. Supporters say it will advance scientific understanding, space exploration and international cooperation.

In 1993, the Clinton administration estimated that the project would cost $17.4 billion through assembly. But that amount began rising after Russia signed on as a partner the following year — a move that administration officials had initially said would reduce costs and speed up construction because Russia was the only other country with a manned space program.

In April 1997, the agency announced it was delaying the start of construction of the station because of Russia's failure to provide adequate funding for the space station service module, which would house astronauts and keep the station from falling out of orbit.

The Russian fiscal problems came in addition to a variety of other administrative difficulties. The situation led NASA to institute management controls on the station's prime contractor, Boeing. It did not award the company a bonus last year because of problems with program planning, cost estimation and hardware manufacturing.

McCain called on NASA last year to adopt a price cap on the space station and warned he would try to impose one if the agency could not keep its costs under control.

Because of the cost problems, NASA has had to transfer funds within its budget to keep the space station going. Last year, it was forced to use $200 million in space shuttle reserve funds, although Congress refused to let NASA transfer another $200 million from other internal accounts.

Last month, in a move that angered some lawmakers, the Clinton administration again asked Congress to approve transfer authority for another $200 million as part of the fiscal 1998 supplemental appropriations bill for disaster relief and U.S. military operations in Bosnia and Iraq.

House Science Committee Chairman F. James Sensenbrenner Jr., R-Wis., complained at a hearing last month that the agency's budget is "a mess" and that the Clinton administration has not been giving an accurate or honest accounting of the space agency's needs to Congress.

Sensenbrenner noted that hundreds of space shuttle workers were laid off after lawmakers balked at approving the $200 million transfer authority request last year. "NASA has done its best to juggle the conflicting science, technology, budgetary and foreign policy goals that the president keeps throwing it. But you can't juggle forever," Sensenbrenner said.

Goldin has warned lawmakers that it is "critical" his agency receive the transfer authority in order to avoid delays on the project.

Business of Space

The commercial space bill approved by the Commerce Committee has received strong support from space business groups who contend it would give the burgeoning industry more of an opportunity to grow.

The commercial space industry accounted for $7.5 billion in worldwide revenue in 1995, according to the Commerce Department. Frist said one estimate indicates that revenue could reach $120 billion by the year 2000.

The bill would set up a regulatory framework to license private reusable launch vehicles, or space shuttles, by giving the Federal Aviation Administration authority to issue licenses to private companies. Under current law, companies are not permitted to hold such licenses. In essence, they may launch vehicles into space but may not fly them back to Earth.

The bill also clarifies the Clinton administration's goal of making the Global Positioning System — a network of 24 satellites that can track objects on Earth from space — the international standard.

The legislation includes other provisions aimed at stimulating commercial growth, such as requiring the government to buy space-transportation services from private companies as often as is practical. And it would require NASA to study how companies could provide scientific data for satellites studying the atmosphere and environment.

The committee also incorporated provisions included in a separate commercial space bill (S 1473) sponsored by Democrat Bob Graham and Republican Connie Mack of Florida.

The Graham-Mack bill would authorize the conversion of surplus intercontinental ballistic missiles into launch vehicles. The missiles no longer can be used for defense under terms of the Strategic Arms Reduction Treaty.

Graham said he hoped the conversion would save money by eliminating storage costs and providing cost-effective launches for small scientific and commercial payloads.

Another key provision in the Graham-Mack bill would require the Department of Defense to conduct a comprehensive study of space launch infrastructure to address potential physical deficiencies and other problems at launch sites. Supporters say that if those problems are not addressed, the nation could lose commercial space business to other countries.

"We cannot afford to see these industries move overseas or be unable to compete in the worldwide market because we did not fulfill our responsibility here in the Congress," Frist said at a hearing on the issue March 5.

Higher Price Tag Clouds Future For Space Station

MARCH 28 — A new, higher cost estimate and a shake-up in the Russian government have cast doubt on the management and schedule of NASA's

Science

international space station, increasing congressional skepticism about the project.

A panel of outside experts picked by NASA to audit the space station project concluded in a preliminary report given to the agency March 19 that the total cost could be $24 billion, or $3 billion more than NASA has projected. The panel also determined that the station could take as much as three years longer to build than currently forecast.

Meanwhile, Russian President Boris Yeltsin on March 23 abruptly fired his top advisers, including Prime Minister Viktor Chernomyrdin, who a week before had assured Vice President Al Gore that Russia was committed to paying its share of the space station's cost.

NASA's handling of the space station project has been a frequent subject of criticism in Congress, but lawmakers recently have been calling for greater oversight. Some predicted that the audit will give them further political justification to impose tighter controls on the space agency.

The audit was prepared by a group of military and civilian space experts headed by Jay W. Chabrow, a retired TRW Inc. executive, aerospace consultant and member of the space station advisory committee. Senate Commerce Chairman John McCain, R-Ariz., and other lawmakers requested that the panel be formed last year to scrutinize the space station situation.

"It's another voice in the chorus, and it's a pretty authoritative, thoughtful voice," said John Logsdon, director of George Washington University's Space Policy Institute.

At McCain's urging, the Commerce Committee clamped a price cap on NASA's share of the project as part of legislation (S 1250) it approved March 12 to reauthorize the space agency for fiscal years 1998 through 2000.

McCain's amendment would limit space station costs to $21.9 billion through the assembly phase. NASA has estimated its share of the cost through assembly at about $21 billion.

The figures were based on discussions with the General Accounting Office, which conducted its own assessment of NASA's space station budget. Commerce Committee aides said they want to examine differences between the audit and the GAO report to determine whether the $24 billion number is highly probable or represents a worst-case scenario.

"It's very disturbing," McCain said of the audit's findings. "It argues for the cap I was talking about before. The result, obviously, is that NASA is being hurt politically and credibility-wise."

The Chabrow panel, however, concluded that an existing $2.1 billion annual price cap on the station has contributed to the project's problems by forcing managers to defer work. The Clinton administration imposed the cap in 1993, but it has not been written into law.

Critics of the space station have long pointed to its schedule slippages and cost overruns as evidence that it should be killed, although they have failed to muster enough votes to do so over the last seven years.

Leading opponents of the station in both chambers conceded that while the audit lends credibility to their cause, it is unlikely to gain them many new converts.

"I hate to denigrate my colleagues, but once they get committed to something like that, you couldn't get them off it with a cannon," said Sen. Dale Bumpers, D-Ark. "My guess is that I might pick up two or three votes."

Rep. Tim Roemer, D-Ind., said the space station appears to have too many powerful backers in states where NASA has contractors.

"We've got enough ammunition to kill almost any program to come before Congress except this one," Roemer said.

Russian Reliance

NASA announced a year ago it was delaying building the station because of Russia's failure to provide adequate funding for the service module.

Some lawmakers now worry that the Russian government shake-up could make it more difficult to deal with that country.

House Science Committee Chairman F. James Sensenbrenner Jr., R-Wis., said Chernomyrdin's departure "is bad news not only in the space area but in other areas as well." He plans to travel to Russia in April to meet with space officials.

A Russian spokesman dismissed the idea that Chernomyrdin's departure would cause problems.

"We believe that the Russian government crisis will not affect our participation in the project," spokesman Sergei Gorbunov told Reuters on March 23.

Still, some lawmakers fear that the station's schedule could be set back as it prepares its first launch in June. A NASA official told the House Space and Aeronautics subcommittee this month that the agency expects to decide by mid-May whether to re-evaluate Russia's role.

Republican Jerry Lewis of California., who chairs the House Appropriations subcommittee that funds NASA — Veterans Affairs, Housing and Urban Development, and Independent Agencies — said Gore assured him the week of March 16 that Russia would improve its performance. "I was very encouraged, and now it's back to square one," Lewis said.

NASA Cautioned To Bring Costs Down to Earth

MAY 9 — After months of venting anger over the rising cost of the international space station, supporters of the project in Congress are demanding that NASA develop a solution soon.

As a House Science Committee hearing on the space station May 6 made clear, such a solution presents both financial and diplomatic challenges. The Clinton administration must come up with a politically acceptable cost estimate for the station before the fiscal 1999 appropriations cycle gets under way, while at the same time coaxing Russia to honor its commitment to pay for part of the project.

The catalyst for the effort comes from a panel of outside experts picked by NASA to audit the space station project. The panel concluded in a report last month that the total cost through assembly of the station could be $24 billion — $3 billion more than the space agency now projects and $7 billion more than it predicted in 1993. The task force also determined that the station could take as much as three years longer to build than currently forecast — December 2006 rather than December 2003.

The panel of seven military and civilian experts, headed by aerospace consultant Jay W. Chabrow, estimated that NASA will need an extra $130 million to $250 million a year over the next seven years to cover the expected increased costs.

"Our finding is that cost and schedule projections provided by NASA are optimistic and consistent with our opinion that the program has been planned too aggressively for a technical task of this magnitude," Chabrow told the committee.

Critics of the space station have pointed to the report as further evidence that the project should be killed. Although they came within one vote of doing so in the House in 1993, they have failed to come close in either chamber since then. (1993 Almanac, p. 694)

Nevertheless, both Democratic and Republican backers of the station on the Science Committee fear dire consequences if NASA's problems continue.

"We've been resting on our laurels with rather comfortable margins in support of the station for the last couple of years," said committee Chairman F. James Sensenbrenner Jr., R-Wis. "Cost overruns erode that political support."

"It's time for us to get down to the nitty-gritty and correct these mistakes," agreed George E. Brown Jr. of California, the committee's ranking Democrat.

NASA Administrator Daniel S. Goldin promised to respond to the task force report by mid-June. He also said the agency is reviewing the extent of Russia's involvement in the project.

For now, Goldin acknowledged that his agency anticipates "some growth" in the space station's cost and schedule, but said "it will not be as large or as long" as the Chabrow panel forecast.

The Senate has joined the House in stepping up concern over the space station. In March, the Senate Commerce, Science and Transportation Committee clamped a $21.9 billion price cap on the project's cost in approving legislation (S 1250) to reauthorize NASA for fiscal years 1998 through 2000.

Rising Expectations

Described as the most complex structure ever put in orbit, the space station is a joint venture among the United States, Russia, Canada, Japan, Brazil and the 11 member nations of the European Space Agency. Supporters say it will advance scientific understanding, space exploration and international cooperation. The United States and Russia are handling the bulk of the project.

In 1993, the Clinton administration estimated that the station would cost $17.4 billion to develop, launch and assemble in orbit. That estimate began rising as Russia signed on as a partner the following year — a move administration officials initially said would reduce costs and speed up construction because Russia was the only other country with a manned space program.

Sensenbrenner, a space station supporter who has been among NASA's most vocal critics, laid down three major concerns for the agency and the Clinton administration to address before his committee holds another hearing on the project next month.

First, he said, the Office of Management and Budget must become "an active participant" in developing a solution. Outgoing budget director Franklin D. Raines did not accept a committee invitation to testify at the space station hearing, infuriating Sensenbrenner, who left an empty chair at the witness table with Raines' name on a placard.

Raines submitted written testimony pledging that if additional funding is needed, the administration will look first within NASA's human space flight account, which funds the space station and space shuttle programs.

Sensenbrenner called Raines' proposal unacceptable, saying it could lead to layoffs or cancellations of shuttle flights.

Earlier this year, after Congress refused to let NASA transfer $200 million from various internal accounts to the space station, the agency shifted money from the shuttle program, causing some layoffs.

"I don't want to see all the science and technology that is currently funded through the human space flight account be canceled out," Sensenbrenner said. "So in that case, somebody is going to have to step up to the plate and be honest in saying how we're going to get the money."

Russian Reliability

Sensenbrenner said NASA must develop a "credible plan" to deal with problems stemming from Russia's inability to live up to its commitment to build parts of the station. During a visit to Russia last month, Sensenbrenner said he learned that the Russian Space Agency has not yet received all funds expected for 1997 from the Russian government and has no firm commitment for this year.

Since then, Russian President Boris Yeltsin has ordered the government to fulfill its obligations to the space station project, his spokesman told Reuters on May 5. Representatives from Russia and other countries are expected to meet with NASA officials later this month to discuss a new launch timetable for the station.

Several committee members were openly skeptical that Russia will follow through. "Let's quit giving these fellows the benefit of the doubt," said Dana Rohrabacher, R-Calif., who chairs the Subcommittee on Space. "It's costing us so much money."

If Russia's financial problems persist, Sensenbrenner suggested, perhaps fewer of its crew members should be allowed aboard the station. "Why should they get the full benefits that were agreed to when they don't pay their share of the costs?" he asked.

Other committee members said they want the Clinton administration to show more vigilance in guarding against the sale of Russian missile technology to Iran. The House passed legislation (HR 2709 — H Rept 105-375) in November that would require economic sanctions against overseas companies or research institutes — mainly Russian — that have helped Iran develop ballistic missiles.

The Senate is expected to take up the bill this month. Some senators have expressed concern that further evidence of sales could jeopardize U.S.-Russian cooperation on the space station.

"If the Russians don't deliver on the station, how in the hell can we believe they're going to deliver on Iranian missile technology?" asked Sen. Barbara A. Mikulski, D-Md., at a NASA appropriations hearing April 23. The issue "could sink the space station, and it could create a very serious diplomatic situation," she warned.

Science

Sensenbrenner's final concern was that NASA avoid delays in developing an alternative for producing one of the station's first main components — the Russian-built service module, which would house astronauts and use small rockets to keep the station from falling out of orbit.

Goldin acknowledged that he made a mistake in allowing Russia to take on construction of the service module.

Although Goldin emphasized that he remains committed to keeping Russia as a partner in the station, he repeatedly assured Science Committee members that he shares their frustrations.

"We were too naive in expecting them to act like we act," Goldin said.

Space Station Support Rises As Confidence in Russia Plummets

AUGUST 8 — As recent votes in the House and Senate indicate, support in Congress for the international space station is on the rise. But congressional confidence in the Clinton administration's dealings with Russia on the project appears to have hit an all-time low.

At a House Science Committee hearing Aug. 5, members of both parties excoriated the administration for its willingness to keep Russia as a primary partner in the space station and its refusal to come up with a plan to solve the station's funding problems.

The hearing marked the third time in as many months that the committee has implored administration officials to develop a comprehensive response to a task force report indicating that the station's cost through assembly could be as high as $24.7 billion — $7 billion more than NASA predicted in 1993.

Much of the additional cost is attributed to Russia's inability to produce station components on time. A NASA report to Vice President Al Gore on July 30 said Russia's space agency has received only $20 million of the $340 million needed for the project this year.

The Science Committee's concerns come as White House officials are preparing for President Clinton's trip to Russia next month to meet with his counterpart, Boris Yeltsin.

The new director of the White House Office of Management and Budget, Jacob J. Lew, told the committee the administration "has spent considerable effort" addressing problems with the Russians. But he said it is "premature" to adjust the station's budget plans.

The White House is not yet ready to concede that Russia will fail to come through, Lew said.

But committee members did nothing to hide their skepticism. "They've broken every other commitment and missed every other deadline they've given us, so what leads you to believe anything's changed?" asked Science Chairman F. James Sensenbrenner Jr., R-Wis.

The committee's ranking Democrat, George E. Brown Jr. of California, echoed Sensenbrenner's concerns. He said NASA should be given more money for the station instead of taking funding from other parts of the space agency's budget.

But Lew said NASA's budget "is sufficient at this time" for fiscal 1999. He said officials are examining whether more money will be needed in fiscal 2000.

U.S.-Russian Partnership

The most complex structure ever planned for launch into orbit, the station would be a laboratory and living quarters the size of two football fields. It is being built by a partnership of the United States, Russia and 14 other nations, with initial launch of components for assembly in space scheduled for November 1998.

Critics have long pointed to the station's ballooning costs as evidence it should be killed. But an attempt in the Senate failed July 7 by a 2-to-1 margin. A similar effort in the House July 29 was beaten back by nearly a 3-to-1 margin — a victory supporters say is proof there is solid support for the station as NASA's centerpiece project.

In the Senate, Commerce, Science and Transportation Chairman John McCain, R-Ariz., has attached a legislative price cap on the station as part of a NASA authorization bill (S 1250).

McCain said in a July 29 interview the Senate may take up the measure in September with a possible separate vote on the price cap.

NASA has proposed a series of steps to solve the station's funding problems that would result in diminishing Russia's role. They would include modifications to its space shuttle as well as other changes to perform work intended for the Russians.

NASA Chief Says Space Station Needs Extra Funds

OCTOBER 10 — In his six years at the helm of NASA, Daniel S. Goldin has prided himself on accomplishing much while spending relatively little, running what he calls a "faster, better, cheaper" space agency.

But the severe financial crisis in Russia — a problem well beyond the scope of NASA's usual scientific and research mission — has thrust Goldin into the uncomfortable position of not only asking for but demanding more money.

Goldin bluntly warned the House Science Committee Oct. 7 that unless extra funding is provided over the next few years to help keep the International Space Station on track, the project should probably be abandoned.

Russia is the key partner in the station. NASA has developed a proposal to spend as much as $660 million to buy Russian space vehicles to support the station, as well as to spend up to $600 million more developing new U.S. hardware that would lessen reliance on Russia in completing the project.

NASA's budget has been flat in recent years, as the Clinton administration has chosen to concentrate on priorities other than space. The fiscal 1999 VA-HUD Appropriations conference report (HR 4194 — conference report: H Rept 105-769) that won House and Senate approval the week of Oct. 5 includes $13.7 billion for NASA, just $17 million more than the agency received in fiscal 1998.

The budget includes $2.27 billion for the space station, the amount President Clinton had sought for fiscal 1999. The project has operated under an informal $2.1 billion annual spending cap in recent years.

But in comments that appeared to be directed as much to the White House as to Congress, Goldin told Science Committee members that the Russian crisis warrants a new approach.

"It would be my vote as the NASA administrator that if we cannot fund this properly, because it would break the budget agreement, then maybe we ought to cancel the space station," he said.

Although the agency has tried to develop plans for dealing with Russia's problems, Goldin noted, "to carry out contingency plans takes money. We can't do it any other way. I'm saying, if we don't get additional resources, we cannot do what we say we're going to do."

Russian Dependence

As NASA's showcase project, the space station would be the most complex structure ever planned for launch into orbit. A laboratory and living quarters the size of two football fields, it is being built by a partnership of the United States, Russia and 14 other nations. The initial launch of components for assembly in space is scheduled for November.

Goldin's stance leaves many committee members in an uneasy position. As much as they deplore depending on Russia or spending more money, they consider it extremely important to see the station built after overcoming years of political and technical obstacles.

Many committee members criticized NASA for what they described as essentially a financial bailout of Russia. But they were even more openly frustrated with an administration they accused of refusing to give NASA the latitude and political support it needs to get the station built smoothly.

"The plain truth is that the White House is addicted to the Russians," said Science Committee Chairman F. James Sensenbrenner Jr., R-Wis. "I'm beginning to think it [the administration] doesn't care whether the space station gets built, as long as the Russians are happy.

"The problem," he said, "is that our relationship with the Russian space program is fundamentally flawed and is hurting our national interest."

The White House further incensed Sensenbrenner and other committee members by dispatching only Goldin to the Oct. 7 hearing. The committee had invited Office of Management and Budget Director Jacob Lew and Deputy Secretary of State Strobe Talbott to testify, but neither appeared.

Lew sent the committee a letter saying he could not appear because of budget matters.

A State Department spokesman said Talbott was in charge of the agency in the absence of Secretary of State Madeleine K. Albright.

In a direct challenge to the White House, Sensenbrenner warned that if the administration is not willing "to meet Congress in the middle," he may draft legislation to introduce in the 106th Congress that proposes changes in the space station arrangement.

"My colleagues and I may find a way to do that and keep Russia in the program; we might not," he said. "I would prefer to work with the administration, but we cannot keep waiting for leadership that hasn't come yet and may never come."

Sharing Space

The Clinton administration brought Russia into the space station program in 1993, contending that the move would promote greater international cooperation as well as save money because of Russia's considerable experience in space. (1993 Almanac, p. 249)

But in subsequent years, the project's cost rose from an estimated $17 billion to $21 billion. In April, a task force of experts led by aerospace consultant Jay W. Chabrow concluded that the total cost through assembly could reach $24 billion.

Since the report, Russia's economic crisis has left its space agency desperately strapped for cash. A NASA report to Vice President Al Gore in July said Russia's space program had received only $20 million of the $340 million needed for the space station this year.

Among Russia's main responsibilities is the station's service module, which would house astronauts and keep the station from falling out of orbit.

The service module had been scheduled to be launched in April 1999 but now is expected to be de-

Bill Boosts Private Shuttles

OCTOBER 10 — Moving to boost the U.S. commercial space industry, Congress cleared legislation that would allow the federal government to license private space shuttles.

The House approved the bill (HR 1702) by voice vote Oct. 5, and the Senate cleared it for the president, also by voice vote, Oct. 8.

Lawmakers worried by the number of U.S. companies launching satellites overseas, where costs are lower and red tape less prevalent, have become increasingly eager to aid the domestic launch industry.

The measure contains a regulatory framework to give the Federal Aviation Administration authority to issue licenses for private reusable launch vehicles. Supporters hope such vehicles, when developed, can significantly bring down the cost of putting satellites and other commercial payloads into orbit.

Under current law, companies are not permitted to hold such licenses. In essence, they may fly launch vehicles into space but may not return them to Earth.

The measure also calls for the Defense Department to conduct a comprehensive study of the nation's launch infrastructure. Many observers say the technology at U.S. launch sites is outdated.

To ensure President Clinton's support, Republicans removed language from the bill dealing with requirements for obtaining a license to own and operate a remote-sensing satellite, which can be run by remote control from Earth.

State Department officials had raised questions about remote-sensing and made it clear they did not want the process to compromise national security.

Science

layed until at least next summer.

In a move to help keep the project on schedule, conferees on the VA-HUD appropriations bill added language calling for NASA to study alternatives to contracting with Russia's government for space station parts and services.

Some station supporters have advocated bypassing the Russian government and dealing directly with its private space contractors.

But some experts contend that Russia's problems are so formidable that it is dangerous to continue to rely on that nation's help in building the station.

Systemic Problems

Russian space historian and author James Oberg told Science Committee members that Russia's inability to fulfill its commitments is not due to temporary conditions that will easily disappear. He also accused NASA of overlooking evidence of corruption in the Russian space program.

Some lawmakers were quick to concur with Oberg's assessment. Rep. Dave Weldon, R-Fla., pointed out a study by the Center for Strategic and International Studies detailing the impact of organized crime on Russia's economy.

"In many ways, I feel we're acting out a Greek tragedy here, talking about the same problem that has been besetting the space station effort for the past four years," Weldon said.

For now, at least, lawmakers appear willing to allow NASA to assist Russia in a limited fashion. An agency request to reprogram $60 million within its budget to bolster the space station met with a positive reaction from House VA-HUD Appropriations Chairman Jerry Lewis, R-Calif., and his Senate counterpart, Christopher S. Bond, R-Mo.

Goldin said the money would be used to pay for new goods and services. It would come from reducing the agency's obligations within its fiscal 1998 budget for station development and operations.

Chabrow told committee members the $24 billion cost estimate his task force developed could easily go higher unless the Russian government gets more money soon. He urged them to think twice about taking Russia out of the space station program.

"It would be a big mistake to throw them aside," he said. "They are there; all we need is cash flow."

case," said Amy E. Smithson, a senior associate at the Stimson Center who follows chemical weapons issues.

Appropriators OK Funds Transfer For Space Station

OCTOBER 17 — House and Senate appropriators agreed Oct. 15 to let NASA transfer $60 million within its budget to keep the International Space Station on schedule after the space agency submits a plan for how it expects to minimize Russia's future involvement in the project.

NASA Administrator Daniel S. Goldin had asked Congress in September to allow the transfer to purchase goods and services from Russia. The money would come from reducing the agency's obligations within its fiscal 1998 budget for station development and operations.

Russia is a main partner in the station, a joint endeavor under construction among the United States and 14 other nations. The station has suffered repeated cost overruns and schedule slippages because of Russia's inability to pay for its share of the project.

House Science Chairman F. James Sensenbrenner Jr., R-Wis., opposed the transfer. He said in an Oct. 9 letter to Goldin that the move "will further undermine our national interest by rewarding the Russian government for failing to fulfill its obligations."

But the chairmen and ranking members of the House and Senate VA-HUD Appropriations Subcommittees, not the Science Committee, had jurisdiction over the request. The appropriators said in an Oct. 13 letter to Goldin the money could be transferred if NASA submits a plan "which eliminates United States reliance on Russia at the earliest possible date."

Committee aides said the appropriators agreed to the transfer after the agency provided details on how it is working to lessen its dependence on Russia. The aides said NASA also promised to include a "definitive schedule" for reducing Russia's involvement on building the station in submitting its fiscal 2000 budget request next year.

NASA officials have warned they may need to spend as much as $660 million to buy Russian space vehicles to support the station over the next few years, as well as spend an additional $600 million to develop new U.S. hardware to reduce reliance on Russia.

Sentiment Soars As Glenn Leaves Senate Far Behind

OCTOBER 31 — As soon as Ohio's senior senator climbed from a plane at Kennedy Space Center before his historic Oct. 29 shuttle mission, he made himself clear: He was no longer a politician, but an astronaut again.

"I'm John Glenn. I'm PS-2 on this flight," the 77-year-old Democrat told the throng of reporters, referring to his job as second payload specialist aboard the shuttle *Discovery*. "I have been pleasantly surprised at the outpouring of interest in this flight. It's really gratifying to see people get so fired up about the space program once again."

Three days later, hundreds of thousands of spectators, including President Clinton and first lady Hillary Rodham Clinton, and a worldwide television audience of millions watched as the first American to orbit the Earth in 1962 became the oldest person ever sent into space. Glenn is to conduct a series of 10 experiments aboard *Discovery* until its scheduled Nov. 7 landing at the space center.

The launch on a sun-washed Florida afternoon was nearly flawless, the praise for Glenn and for NASA effusive, the mood distinctly nostalgic. Walter Cronkite came out of retirement to be a CNN commentator, along with former astronauts and early NASA engineers. Even legendary test pilot Chuck Yeager turned up on TV — albeit to criticize the idea of sending "old guys" into space. He is 75.

A unique blend of science, symbolism and spectacle, Glenn's mission touched a latent chord in the nation. It focused a torrent of attention on an earlier age when NASA's activities could unite and enthrall the nation like no other government agency.

The "Glennmania" raised hopes among NASA officials and lawmakers that at least some of the interest would rub off on the space agency as it moves beyond the shuttle into other projects, such as the forthcoming International Space Station.

"Our space program is good for the United States and good for the world," Clinton told launch workers after the liftoff. "America is very, very proud of you today."

Two hours before the launch, as the news media grandstands filled, Republican Rep. Dave Weldon was ecstatic. He represents Florida's "Space Coast."

"You can't buy publicity like this," Weldon said. "It's huge. It's beyond anything I expected."

Famous Phrases

On the roads and beaches, it was nearly impossible to spot a sign bearing anything other than the phrase "Godspeed, John Glenn" — the famous sendoff spoken just before his 1962 flight. The message adorned carpet stores, churches and even Cocoa Beach's Cabaret Lido topless bar, which added a "Welcome President Clinton" for good measure.

Tourists drove in from as far as Canada to witness *Discovery's* liftoff. With more than 3,000 journalists on hand to cover the launch — nearly 10 times as many as were present for Glenn's 1962 flight — and wall-to-wall television coverage, the launch took on the dimensions of a political convention or Super Bowl.

Reporters filled NASA's daily briefing rooms and scoured for details on everything from the food Glenn carried aboard *Discovery* — which included a supply of Metamucil wafers at his request — to the guest list, which included dignitaries ranging from former Ohio Democratic Sen. Howard M. Metzenbaum (1974-95) to socialite Ivana Trump.

One of the main focuses of media attention remained NASA's decision in late summer to remove Glenn from a key experiment in which he was to have taken the drug melatonin. Glenn was dropped because he did not meet the Food and Drug Administration's criteria for the experiment.

The decision to remove Glenn renewed criticism that the senator's trip was more a public relations stunt than a scientific mission. But Andrew Monjan, chief of the Neurobiology of Aging branch of the National Institute on Aging, asserted the mission would yield plenty of data.

"It's a wonderful opportunity we have [to conduct research] for whatever reason he's going up," Monjan told reporters Oct. 26.

Band of Brothers

Upon his arrival at the space center, Glenn remained in seclusion until the launch with his six fellow crew members to reduce exposure to germs. But he was clearly delighted to be the center of adulation as a member of the astronaut corps, the rarefied fraternity he abandoned three decades ago for business and politics.

Glenn was never able to turn his national celebrity to political advantage beyond his native Ohio. His 1984 presidential campaign as a moderate Democrat appealing to the South barely got off the ground.

A detail-oriented lawmaker who preferred such technical issues as nuclear non-proliferation, Glenn has relished being back in a world where actions are emphasized over words, where details are crucial and where everyone works cooperatively toward a common goal.

"He's very happy; he is a professional astronaut," James Wetherbee, director of NASA's flight crew operations, told reporters Oct. 28. "He's just a joy to be around, and I hope everybody who's watching him takes good notes and tries to follow him."

Sen. Patrick J. Leahy, D-Vt., among the dozens of lawmakers on hand for the launch, said Glenn "has gotten a lot more enjoyment in the last couple of years from being an astronaut than [from] being a senator."

Glenn announced in January 1997 he would not seek re-election to a fifth term. Like several other Senate veterans who have retired in recent years, he has spoken of the decline in cooperation and rise of partisanship in Congress.

"He does complain about the way things have gotten in the last few years, with more and more partisanship and head-butting," said Jack Sparks, Glenn's press secretary, who spent the week putting in 12-hour days. "And so, ending his career with this project, it's just been a great time for him."

Glenn was selected for the mission in January, after he spent two years lobbying NASA officials to allow him to help research the similarities between aging and space flight. "He is one stubborn man — or I should say astronaut," Annie Glenn said in an interview on NASA's internal cable television station that was broadcast Oct. 26.

In addition to providing regular blood and urine samples for analysis, Glenn will spend his time in space sleeping with electrodes attached to his scalp and swallowing a pill with a radio transmitter to monitor his temperature and circadian rhythms.

To many longtime NASA officials and followers of the space program, Glenn was the perfect choice to represent the last vestige of an era when space was an urgent, nonpartisan national priority of presidents and Congress.

In the days leading up to the launch, many of them went to great lengths to lament the agency's inability to find ways to sustain interest in its exploits except during rare peaks, such as last year's Mars Pathfinder mission.

"I personally have been very disappointed," said Walt Kapryan, who served as NASA spacecraft project engineer on Glenn's 1962 Project Mercury flight. "During Mercury and Gemini and Apollo, the public was behind us. After we got to the moon, the public lost interest in what was going on, and it's taken a while for that interest to come back."

To Glenn's fellow former Mercury astronaut Walter Schirra, such problems stem from NASA's inability to sustain public interest. "NASA has never been able to sell itself," he said.

Schirra and the other surviving Mercury astronauts, Gordon Cooper and Scott Carpenter, had their own brief return to the limelight during the week of Glenn's launch. They autographed copies of Tom Wolfe's book "The Right Stuff" and told reporters again and again they had no interest in trading places with their former crew member.

"Number one, I'm not that old," Schirra joked. "Number two, I don't need the flight time. And number three, I too would relish the chance to leave the U.S. Senate."

Schirra and Cooper appeared at an Oct. 27 reception for an hourlong tele-

Science

vision documentary on Glenn's life and exploits, "John Glenn: An American Hero." Its producer, Blaine Baggett, said in a speech that he has an even broader hope for Glenn's mission beyond reviving interest in space — providing an example in personal conduct.

"Many people, particularly younger people, confuse celebrity with heroism," Baggett said. "Who better to teach them than John Glenn?"

Selling the Station

In addition to detailing Glenn's storied career, Baggett's documentary featured a lengthy segment on the space station, an orbiting laboratory the size of two football fields, which is NASA's showcase project. Described as the most complex structure ever put in orbit, its initial element is scheduled to be launched next month in Russia.

Officials at Boeing Co., the station's main contractor, set up trailers offering information on the project at the Kennedy Space Center media site. They also handed out press packets and promotional items featuring the station's TV antennalike design.

The station already has broad support in Congress. But lawmakers have been highly critical of the project's spiralling cost, estimated as high as $24.7 billion. They also have attacked the Clinton administration's willingness to keep Russia as a primary partner in the project despite its ongoing financial crisis.

Increasing public support for the station "is not really rocket science," Kennedy Space Center Director Roy D. Bridges Jr. said in an Oct. 27 interview. "It's really just a matter of making it a national issue and then getting it funded."

Others are skeptical Glenn's launch can translate into broader support for the station.

"The public is fickle," said John M. Logsdon, director of George Washington University's Space Policy Institute, in an Oct. 27 interview. "Six weeks from now . . . this [flight] will be background." ◆

Chapter 20

SOCIAL POLICY

WIC Reauthorization 20-3	**Mortgage Insurance** 20-9
Child Support 20-6	**Government Help for Home Buyers** 20-11
Public Housing Overhaul 20-7	**Benefits for Immigrants** 20-16
Major Provisions 20-12	

Social Policy

WIC Reauthorized; Nutrition Aid Expanded For Low-Income Children

SUMMARY

Congress approved a five-year reauthorization of the school lunch, Women, Infants and Children (WIC), and other nutrition programs. The legislation was the first major expansion of such aid in decades and a sharp turnaround from House Republicans' 1995 effort to convert the school lunch program into a block grant.

The measure authorizes a new program to provide after-school snacks to teenagers in low-income areas, expands the availability of meals to low-income children in homeless shelters, authorizes a three-year study of the potential benefits of offering free school breakfast to all public school children and sets tougher penalties for individuals who defraud the WIC program.

Republicans, Democrats and the Clinton administration worked closely after some initial differences.

Michael N. Castle, R-Del., was in charge of drafting the legislation for the House Education and the Workforce Committee. Determined not to repeat the public relations disaster of 1995, when Republicans were harshly criticized for their proposed school lunch block grant, Castle refused to bring up a school nutrition bill until he reached consensus with Democrats, who initially wanted a $30 million school breakfast pilot program. Because the two parties had trouble reaching agreement on the issue, school nutrition was not debated at the subcommittee level.

The two sides came together at full committee markup, approving legislation including after-school aid, a five-state school breakfast pilot program, summer meals, WIC and other nutrition aid. The Senate Agriculture Committee unanimously approved its version of the bill, including a mandatory school breakfast pilot program.

The final bill contains a discretionary three-year, school breakfast pilot program in six school districts. It expands current programs, which already provide subsidies for after-school snacks to students age 12 and under. The measure covers students to age 18 in poor areas who attend programs sponsored by schools and outside groups such as the Boys and Girls Clubs. Teenagers in more affluent areas could qualify for school-sponsored programs.

The measure disqualifies grocers convicted of trafficking in WIC food vouchers and increases penalties for fraud. The WIC program provides food vouchers, nutrition and health services to low-income pregnant women and to children up to age 5.

House Committee Moves To Expand Nutrition Programs

JUNE 6 — After years of bickering and spending cuts, lawmakers have begun moving in bipartisan fashion to expand federal child nutrition programs.

Legislation (HR 3874) approved by the House Committee on Education and the Workforce on June 4 would provide snacks to teenagers in after-school programs and allow a five-state pilot project to test the effectiveness of providing free breakfasts to all students.

The bill also would reauthorize the Women, Infants and Children (WIC) nutrition and health program, while instituting tougher penalties for fraud. Private contractors would have more opportunity to participate in the federal summer meal program.

The 36-1 committee approval came after weeks of intense negotiations between sponsor Michael N. Castle, R-Del., and committee Democrats.

[The panel's Subcommittee on Early Childhood, Youth and Families had approved the bill by voice vote May 21.]

Box Score

- **Bill:** HR 3874 — PL 105-336
- **House action:** The House cleared the conference report (H Rept 105-786) on HR 3874, 422-1, on Oct. 9. The House passed HR 3874 (H Rept 105-633), 383-1, on July 20.
- **Senate action:** The Senate adopted the conference report on HR 3874 by unanimous consent on Oct. 7. On Sept. 17, the Senate adopted HR 3874 by unanimous consent in lieu of a committee-passed bill (S 2286 — S Rept 105-243).
- **Presidential action:** Clinton signed HR 3874 on Oct. 31.

Republicans were willing to agree to a Clinton administration plan to provide after-school snacks. Democrats and a coalition of nutrition and education groups wanted to broaden the administration proposal and pushed for a mandatory breakfast pilot program.

Republicans still feel the pain of the political pounding they took in the 1996 elections for their unsuccessful plan to turn the school lunch program into state block grants.

Castle told Democrats that he would not call up any school lunch legislation unless there was consensus between the two parties. He said Republicans did not want to leave themselves vulnerable to charges they were insensitive to children.

"They did not want to be 'school-lunched' on this, that's their term," said Lynn Woolsey, D-Calif. "Rather than grandstand, they came to the party, and we didn't 'school lunch' them."

The Senate Agriculture Committee may take up its version of the bill later this month.

After-School Aid

The House bill would build on programs that provide snacks to students up to age 12 in after-school education or enrichment programs.

It would expand both the school lunch and child and adult care food programs to pay for snacks for children

Social Policy

up to age 18 who participate in school-based activities or programs run by community groups such as the Boys Club. The aid to community groups would be targeted to low-income areas.

Noting that youths left unsupervised after school are the most likely to get into trouble, Castle said expanding the meal program would "contribute to efforts to reduce juvenile crime, drug and alcohol abuse, and teen pregnancy."

Woolsey said the expanded aid was more than just "Twinkies for teens," saying she hoped the federal government would eventually provide nutrition aid to for-profit child care centers.

The bill allows a five-state pilot program to assess the potential benefit of a federally funded, free school breakfast for all students. It did not provide mandatory funding, as Democrats had requested. Advocates of a universal school breakfast cite studies linking it to improved student achievement and discipline. Opponents say most students eat breakfast at home, and they call free meals a middle-class subsidy.

About 25 percent of children who eat subsidized school lunch now eat breakfast at school. Some states, such as Massachusetts, are moving toward universal breakfast programs using their own funds.

Toughening WIC

The bill would impose tougher penalties on individuals and grocers who defraud the WIC program.

The $4 billion program provides nutrition aid and health services to poor, pregnant women and to children up to age 5.

A recent study by the House Appropriations Committee said that hundreds of thousands of ineligible individuals were being served by WIC and that retail fraud was rampant. Advocates for the poor charged that the study was flawed but agreed that more stringent measures were needed.

The bill would disqualify grocers convicted of trafficking in WIC food vouchers, or who sell guns or drugs in exchange for vouchers. To qualify for the WIC program, individuals would have to personally apply at a WIC office and verify their income. Further, the bill would make it easier for states to crack down on grocers who attempt to price-gouge WIC participants.

At the request of General Mills Inc. and other food processors, the legislation calls for a federally funded study to determine whether efforts by state administrators to cut costs under WIC have had an adverse impact on participants.

General Mills is concerned that in cutting costs, some state WIC programs have barred Cheerios and other brand names in favor of lower-cost store brands.

Senate Panel OKs WIC Plan, With Measures To Curb Fraud

JUNE 27 — The Senate Agriculture Committee on June 25 approved a bill to reauthorize the Women, Infants and Children (WIC) nutrition program, provide after-school snacks to teenagers in low-income areas and institute a three-year pilot school breakfast pilot program. The votes was 17-0.

[The Senate subsequently passed the bill by voice vote September 17.]

"Nutrition programs in the Congress have a long history of bipartisan support, and I urge my Senate colleagues to continue in that tradition," said Agriculture Committee Chairman Richard G. Lugar, R-Ind.

The bill would extend the WIC program through 2003, while instituting new measures to weed out fraud, including requiring recipients to verify income and imposing tougher penalties on stores that traffic in WIC food vouchers.

It would provide after-school snacks to children age 13-18 in low-income areas, an idea proposed by the Clinton administration to both improve nutrition and help give children a safe place at the end of the day. Currently, snacks are given only to younger children.

Snacks would be offered through the National School Lunch program and the Child and Adult Care Food Program. The bill also calls for on-site inspections of providers in the Child and Adult Care Food Program to weed out fraud.

The legislation would require the Agriculture Department to carry out a three-year study to determine whether offering free school breakfasts has a positive impact on student nutrition, academic achievement, discipline and other factors.

The House bill allowed, but did not require, a five-state pilot program. Advocates of free school breakfast cite data showing it has far-reaching effects. Opponents say most students eat breakfast at home, and call free meals a middle-class subsidy.

House-Passed Bill Includes Trial Breakfast Program

JULY 25 — Three years after Republicans mounted an unsuccessful effort to turn the popular school lunch program into block grants to the states, the House on July 20 easily voted to expand child nutrition aid and experiment with free school breakfast.

By a vote of 383-1, lawmakers passed a measure (HR 3874) that would reauthorize the Women, Infants and Children (WIC) nutrition program through fiscal 2003, while tightening anti-fraud provisions. It would also provide after-school snacks to teenagers in low-income areas and extend the summer meals program through 2003. (Vote 297, p. H-86)

The bill would allow, but not require, a five-state pilot project to test the effectiveness of providing free breakfast to all children, regardless of income. About one-quarter of students who eat federally subsidized school lunches also eat breakfast at school.

The Senate Agriculture Committee on June 25 approved a companion bill (S 2286) that would require the Agriculture Department to carry out a three-year study to determine whether offering free school breakfast had a positive impact on student nutrition and academic achievement.

The House bill, written by Michael N. Castle, R-Del., was the product of intense negotiations. On one side were Clinton administration officials and some anti-poverty advocates who argued that expanding after-school aid should be a higher priority than providing breakfast. On the other side, many Democrats and nutrition groups pushed for mandatory school breakfast.

WIC Reauthorization

In the middle were House Republicans, stung by negative reaction to their leadership's 1995 plan to turn the school lunch program into block grants. Castle refused to mark up any plan until all parties reached a consensus. (*1995 Almanac, p. 7-35*)

"We ... have a good bill that will go a long way toward improving our nation's child nutrition program ... [and] ensuring our nation's children have access to healthy meals," Castle said.

Congress Clears Bill Reauthorizing, Expanding Child Nutrition Aid

OCTOBER 10 —The House on Oct. 9 cleared a five-year reauthorization of the school lunch, Women, Infants and Children (WIC) and other nutrition programs, marking the first significant expansion of such aid in decades.

The conference report on HR 3874, which the Senate adopted by unanimous consent on Oct. 7, would authorize a new program to provide after-school snacks to teenagers in low-income areas, to both improve nutrition and give students a safe place to go at the end of the day.

House passage came on a 422-1 vote; President Clinton is expected to sign it.

The measure would expand the availability of meals to poor children in homeless shelters, set tougher rules to guard against fraud in the $4 billion-a-year WIC program and extend the summer feeding program through 2003.

The legislation also would allow a three-year pilot program to gauge the potential benefit of providing free breakfast to school children regardless of income. During an Oct. 6 meeting, House and Senate conferees dropped a more stringent Senate provision that would have provided mandatory funding to carry out such a study.

Lawmakers and activists for the poor praised the measure, which marks a sharp reversal from Congress' last attempt to revise the school lunch program. House Republicans in 1995, as part of their "Contract With America," pushed unsuccessfully to turn the school lunch program into a state block grant. That sparked a public backlash. (*1995 Almanac, p . 7-35*)

Preventing Delinquency

Senate Agriculture Committee Chairman Richard G. Lugar, R-Ind., said the after-school program for teenagers would "aid welfare reform and combat juvenile delinquency."

William L. Clay of Missouri, the ranking Democrat on the House Education and the Workforce Committee, called the bill "an excellent example of what can be achieved when partisanship is put aside."

The bill would expand current child nutrition programs, which already provide subsidies for after-school snacks to students age 12 and under. The new program would cover students to age 18 in poor areas who attend programs sponsored by schools, groups such as the Boys and Girls Clubs, churches or other organizations. Teenagers in more affluent areas could qualify for school-sponsored programs.

The Food Research and Action Center, which lobbies to increase federal support for food aid, said the bill would make it easier for groups to set up or expand existing programs. Studies show that youth are most likely to get into trouble during after-school hours and before parents are home.

The bill would allow a pilot program in six school districts to test the effectiveness of providing free breakfast to all children, regardless of income. The number of children in school breakfast programs has gradually risen to about 7.1 million, from 3.6 million a decade ago. Some states and school districts are beginning to experiment with programs of universal free breakfast, citing studies that indicate such programs can have a positive impact on discipline, health and academic performance.

House Education and the Workforce Committee Chairman Bill Goodling, R-Pa., fought for a mandatory study, saying schools already have the option of expanding programs. Rep. Michael N. Castle, R-Del., said he feared that universal breakfast would primarily benefit middle- and upper-income students.

Sen. Tom Harkin, D-Iowa, said a controlled, mandatory study was necessary to provide concrete information about the possible benefits of such a program. Other lawmakers pointed out that the increased number of two-parent working families means more children are rushed to school, sometimes without breakfast.

The bill would reduce paperwork to make it easier for low-income school districts to set up universal breakfast programs. It also would disqualify grocers convicted of trafficking in WIC food vouchers and increase maximum penalties for fraud. The WIC program provides food vouchers, nutrition and health services to low-income, pregnant women and to children up to age 5.

The bill would authorize a study to determine whether the decision of some state WIC directors to require that recipients purchase cheaper store brand cereals and other foods, rather than name brands, has hurt the program. The conference report on the fiscal 1999 agriculture spending bill (HR 4101) has $1.5 million for the study. ◆

Social Policy

Lawmakers Clear Two Bills Aimed at Better Enforcement Of Child Support Payments

Congress cleared a pair of child-support measures that enjoyed wide bipartisan support.

● **Child support enforcement.** The first (HR 3130 — PL 105-200) reduced federal penalties on states that failed to meet a federal deadline for computerizing their child-support enforcement systems.

The bipartisan measure was intended to fix a problem arising from the 1988 Family Support Act (PL 100-485), which set an Oct. 1, 1995, deadline for all states to put in operation automated data processing systems to assist in child-support enforcement. The federal government agreed to pay 90 percent of administrative costs for creating the systems.

Most states missed that deadline, so Congress in 1995 extended it to Oct. 1, 1997 (PL 104-35). But 16 states and jurisdictions missed the new deadline.

Under the 1988 law, a state that missed the deadline faced the loss of all federal child-support payments and its Temporary Assistance for Needy Families welfare block grants. California, for example, stood to lose more than $4 billion, while Michigan could have lost $880 if the law were not changed. Lawmakers said penalties of that magnitude would jeopardize the very low-income families the 1988 law was intended to help. *(1988 Almanac, p. 352)*

HR 3130 created an alternative penalty system that is far less draconian but still imposes significant fines for those states that are behind schedule. The new law provides graduated penalties depending on how late a state is in complying with the automation requirement. A state that missed the October 1997 deadline would lose 4 percent of child-support funds, with the penalty increasing to 8 percent in the second year, 16 percent in the third year, 25 percent in the fourth year and 30 percent in the fifth and subsequent years.

The measure also replaces the existing child-support incentive program with a system rewarding states for efficient and effective performance in five areas of child-support enforcement.

The House passed the bill (H Rept 105-422) on March 5 by a vote of 414-1. "This bill strikes the right balance by penalizing states that missed the deadline for establishing effective computer systems while ensuring that these penalties don't hurt the very children we're trying to help," said E. Clay Shaw Jr., R-Fla. The lone dissenter was Ron Paul, R-Texas. *(Vote 39, p. H-14)*

The Senate passed its version of HR 3130 by unanimous consent April 2. The main difference between the two bills was the size of the proposed new penalties. Under the House bill, states that missed the October 1997 deadline would have lost 4 percent of their child support funds, with the penalty doubling each year up to a maximum of 20 percent. States could recoup three-quarters of an annual penalty if they put a system in place within one year of a missed deadline.

The Senate bill, too, started out with a 4 percent penalty, but increased it to 30 percent the fourth year. Further, states would get 100 percent forgiveness if they put a new system in place within one year of a missed deadline.

A compromise version of the bill was worked out informally, and the House approved it by voice vote June 25. The Senate cleared HR 3130 by voice vote June 26, and President Clinton signed it July 16.

● **Tougher penalties.** The second bill (HR 3811 — PL 105-187) created two new felony offenses for parents who willfully neglect making child-support payments. This was over and above existing federal penalties for first offenses of up to six months in prison and a $5,000 fine. Federal law comes into play when the deadbeat parent and his children reside in different states.

Under the legislation, sponsored by Judiciary Committee Chairman Henry J. Hyde, R-Ill., offenders who owed more than $10,000 in child support to children in another state could be jailed for up to two years. The same penalty would apply to those who cross state lines to avoid child-support obligations.

The House passed HR 3811 on May 12 by a vote of 402-16. The Senate cleared it by voice vote June 5. Clinton signed the bill into law June 24. *(Vote 139, p. H-42)* ◆

Public Housing

Three Years of Negotiations Yield a Housing Bill That Compromise Built

Box Score

- **Bill:** HR 4194 — PL 105-276
- **House action:** The House adopted the conference report (H Rept 105-769) on HR 4194, 409-14, on Oct. 6. The House passed HR 2 (H Rept 105-76) on May 14, 1997, by a vote of 293-132.
- **Senate action:** The Senate cleared the conference report on HR 4194, 96-1, on Oct. 8. It passed S 462 (S Rept 105-21) by voice vote Sept. 26, 1997.
- **Presidential action:** Clinton signed HR 4194 on Oct. 21.

SUMMARY

Proponents of overhauling the nation's public housing programs broke a three-year logjam and shepherded to enactment a measure that would transfer block grants and much decision-making to local public housing authorities.

The chief housing authorizers in the House and Senate — Rep. Rick A. Lazio, R-N.Y., and Sen. Connie Mack, R-Fla. — had failed to work out the differences between their two bills for years, despite a desire by some congressional leaders to showcase the measure as the second step, after the 1996 welfare overhaul (PL 104-193), toward revamping the social safety net.

Many thought the bill was dead, but the House revived it July 17 when it voted 230-181 to attach the chamber's version of the housing overhaul (HR 2) to the fiscal 1999 spending bill (HR 4194) for housing, veterans, space and science programs. Appropriators objected, but attaching the measure rejuvenated talks between Lazio, Mack, congressional Democrats and the Department of Housing and Urban Development, eventually leading to an agreement.

The provisions included in the final spending bill were an amalgam of the House, Senate and administration's proposals. Negotiators settled the biggest sticking point in the bill — how much of public and subsidized Section 8 housing to reserve for the very poor — by melding pieces of all three proposals. The measure would require that at least 40 percent of public housing units and 75 percent of Section 8 vouchers (used to help pay the rent in private apartments) be reserved for the very poor, those making less than 30 percent of median area income. The rest could be given to anyone making less than 80 percent of median area income. Housing authorities located in census tracts identified as poverty-stricken could admit 10 percent more higher-income residents if they gave more than 75 percent of vouchers to the very poor.

Republicans and most Democrats agreed that providing for a mix of incomes in public housing would improve conditions. But the changes the measure allows will not be fully implemented for eight to 10 years because changes will be made as current tenants move out and people who hold vouchers give up their assistance.

Housing Overhaul Still Seeks a Home In GOP Congress

FEBRUARY 21 — It had all the makings of a little-noticed bill that speeds through Congress with barely a blip and nary a detractor.

The bill (S 562) sought to prevent financial middlemen from charging elderly homeowners exorbitant fees for "reverse mortgages," which provide them with monthly income by drawing down their home equity.

Reverse mortgages were already commonplace, and cracking down on people who preyed on the elderly was not a controversial idea. Republicans and Democrats liked it. The Senate and the House liked it.

But those in charge of authorizing the nation's housing programs did not. Or more precisely, they did not like one another enough to let it clear.

Instead, authorizers amended the measure time and again at the end of 1997, volleying it from chamber to chamber, each time attaching unrelated riders dealing with the Section 8 subsidized housing program. Those provisions already had been signed into law in the appropriations measure (PL 105-65) funding the Department of Housing and Urban Development (HUD), but authorizers could not agree about them.

The result: a first-session death of the bill by ping-pong match. The defeat was not earth-shattering. Elderly homeowners, if bilked, could still turn to the criminal and civil courts. (*1997 Almanac, p. 7-12*)

But it was a supreme example of why, despite considerable effort, more far-reaching measures such as a sweeping rewrite of public housing laws (HR 2, S 462) and other smaller measures, such as bills to scale back private mortgage insurance (HR 607, S 318), have not gone far since Republicans took control of Congress in 1995. It is a story of apathy, missed opportunities and territorialism - somewhat like the problems plaguing public housing itself.

Compromise is elusive in part because some members have staked out territory mainly to prevent others from gaining a political foothold in the overhaul legislation. Some interest groups are not enthusiastic about change, preferring the devil they know to the one they don't. And issues such as how far to go in revamping the system continue to divide lawmakers and lobbyists.

To be sure, Congress has managed to reach beyond the authorizers to modernize housing laws, particularly laws on subsidized housing, through the appropriations process. And where appropriators have not acted, HUD has stepped in. Both have worked to

Social Policy

give local housing authorities more control over the tenants they choose, the rents they charge and the units they demolish.

But the failure to pass an overhaul measure has political and practical ramifications.

The Republican-led Congress has missed an opportunity to fulfill what Republican leaders once described as Step 2 — after the 1996 welfare overhaul (PL 104-193) — in transforming the nation's social policy by transferring power to states and localities.

And Congress' failure to act has kept in limbo those who provide and live in the nation's 1.3 million publicly funded housing units. Public housing authorities, continually strapped for money, find it more and more difficult to plan ahead. Residents face the same problem: One-third of welfare recipients live in public housing, and under the welfare law, most are now required to get jobs. What will happen to able-bodied residents who cannot find jobs and cannot pay their small rents? What will happen to their government landlords?

A New Deal Beginning

Public housing, a New Deal program created by the U.S. Housing Act of 1937, was envisioned to operate much like welfare, as a temporary home for those who found themselves briefly out of work. But in the decades since 1937, public housing has increasingly become a permanent warehouse for the poor, many of whom lack the training or skills needed to hold a job. Most public housing is located in inner cities or rural areas, both of which lack job opportunities.

Congressional authorizers, led by Rick A. Lazio, R-N.Y., chairman of the House Banking and Financial Services Subcommittee on Housing and Community Opportunity, and Sen. Connie Mack, R-Fla., chairman of the Senate Banking, Housing and Urban Affairs Subcommittee on Housing Opportunity and Community Development, have long wanted to change the public housing system.

Their bills differ in details but have the same overall aim: to transfer federal funding directly to local authorities and allow them to shake off federal dictates on who gets public housing and how much they should pay for it.

Despite past differences, Lazio and Mack say they will try again this year to clear the housing legislation that eluded them in 1996 and 1997. Many doubt they can, but the two offer some reasons for hope.

"It's an important political issue," Lazio said. "It would be an accomplishment that we would be proud to point to. I think there is also a sense that it is time."

Housing at a Crossroads

The impetus for revamping the housing system has built over the last decade, as housing authorities increasingly found themselves with growing federal mandates and shrinking operating funds.

Since the 1970s, the federal government has required that locally run public housing authorities, generally made up of community officials appointed by the city council, reserve public housing for their poorest citizens, charge rents no greater than 30 percent of income (which means those with no income pay no rent) and replace each housing unit they demolish.

When Democrats controlled Congress, subsidies to housing authorities increased or held steady, in part because most Democrats believed in paying the cost to make sure public housing went to the poorest people.

But Republicans, who saw HUD as wasteful, came to power in 1995 determined to make changes — or even abolish the Cabinet agency. One of the GOP Congress' first fiscal acts was to rescind $6.5 billion in housing funds to pay for California disaster relief and other emergencies. *(1995 Almanac, p. 11-96)*

Moderate Republicans and Democrats who supported public housing felt that with the loss of funds, already stringent federal housing guidelines would be a noose around housing authorities' necks. They moved to loosen them. The changes aimed to enable housing authorities to generate more cash from non-federal sources, such as their tenants.

For example, a 1996 appropriations measure required housing authorities to charge minimum rents of $25 to $50 per month, even for residents with no income. Another provision, also enacted in the stopgap spending bill (PL 104-99) for HUD, waived federal rules that required local authorities to give priority to applicants in the worst financial conditions.

But the changes, renewed in subsequent annual appropriations bills, suspended requirements only one year at a time. Some housing authorities, fearing a political turnover or change of heart, stuck to their old rules and saw their financial situations worsen.

And even housing authorities that made the changes still feel extremely strapped for cash, largely because of reduced federal subsidies.

In Richmond, Va., for example, the housing authority faces numerous demands for its money, and some services, such as litter control, can go wanting. But Richmond is fortunate. HUD ranks its housing authority's management in the top 1 percent in the nation. Units are well-maintained, if plain.

Richmond has mitigated some of the troubles plaguing other housing authorities by implementing spending law changes as soon as it could, said Richard C. Gentry, executive director of the Richmond Redevelopment and Housing Authority. He does not think a massive federal overhaul is needed to improve public housing, though he said, "You always want to have it wrapped up nice and tidy."

Gordon Cavanaugh, general counsel for the Council of Large Public Housing Authorities and the former head of Philadelphia's public housing system, insists that change is necessary.

"We've got the same old law but drastically reduced support for operations," he said. "Our plea to Sen. Mack and Chairman Lazio is to please give us relief," even a streamlined bill. "At least that would give the institution of public housing a fighting chance. Without changes, we do face bleeding to death. That's what's happening to us."

The Bills' Prescription

Lazio, sponsor of the pending overhaul bill (HR 2) as well as one the House passed in 1996, agrees with Cavanaugh's assessment that a broad overhaul is necessary if public housing is to survive.

"I think in my deep gut, that if we do not implement these reforms and

Public Housing

changes, we will play right into the hands of people who want to eliminate HUD," he said.

But finding a middle ground between his bill and the Senate's (S 462) has proved difficult. Both chambers passed bills in 1996 and 1997, but the measures never made it out of conference committee. (1996 Almanac, p. 7-21)

Though authorizers in both chambers agree that the way to save public housing is to loosen the federal government's grip, they have been unable to agree on how far to go in giving local authorities control.

In general, both bills would convert public housing programs into block grants to local authorities, which would have greater leeway in deciding how to spend money, which tenants to choose and how much rent to charge.

Besides allowing minimum rents — a provision temporarily in place through appropriations bills — the House and Senate bills would raise income caps on who can enter public housing, encouraging local authorities to attract more working-class, low-income families as tenants. These families now often pay as much as 50 percent of their income for their private apartments and could afford to pay more rent to public landlords than many current public housing tenants.

Sponsors of both bills agree in theory on such "income mixing," but they disagree on how many units should be made available to the working poor, with the Senate reserving more for the poor. The Clinton administration believes both bills would reserve too few units for the poorest people, though it prefers the Senate version.

The House bill would reserve at least 35 percent of public housing units for the very poor, those making less than 30 percent of an area's median income. Other units could be filled with those making up to 80 percent.

The Senate measure would reserve at least 40 percent of units for those making no more than 30 percent of median income, and would require that at least 70 percent of units be filled by those making no more than 60 percent. The rest could go to those making 80 percent.

Median area income varies from region to region. In Richmond, where median area income is $52,600, a family of four making 80 percent would earn $42,100. Median family income for the United States was estimated at $45,300 in 1998.

Many congressional Democrats worry that the change in income eligibility would entice cash-strapped public housing authorities to dump those families earning 30 percent and pick up more making 80 percent. The lower-income families will end up homeless, they say.

During the House's six-day debate on HR 2 in May, Joseph P. Kennedy II of Massachusetts, the ranking Democrat on the Housing Subcommittee, spoke out repeatedly against income mixing, saying the bill "will in fact in some ways fix public housing . . . by simply eliminating the poor from eligibility for these programs."

But Republicans and some housing authority directors say that the prospective working-class tenants are hardly wealthy. Instead, they are "that prototypical mother earning minimum wage with a kid or two," said Gentry of Richmond.

Besides differences over income mixing, the two bills differ in their approach to how much rent public housing authorities should be allowed to charge.

The House bill would allow tenants to pay a flat rent or current rents set by the so-called Brooke amendment, named for its sponsor, former Sen. Edward W. Brooke III, R-Mass. (1967-79), which guarantees that public housing residents pay no more than 30 percent of their incomes for rent. The bill would require local au-

House Clears Mortgage Insurance Bill

JULY 18 — A measure designed to ease the financial burden of homeownership by making it easier to cancel mortgage insurance was headed to the president's desk after the House cleared it by voice vote July 16.

The Senate first passed the bill (S 318 — S Rept 105-129) in November, but the House did not take it up before adjournment. The House had passed its own version of the measure (HR 607 — H Rept 105-55) in April 1997.

The House passed a compromise version of S 318 by voice vote July 14. The Senate took it up July 15 and passed it by voice vote with minor changes. That sent it back to the House for final action. President Clinton is expected to sign it.

Lenders often require potential homeowners to purchase private mortgage insurance if they cannot make a 20 percent down payment on the purchase price of the house. The insurance guarantees that the lender, or subsequent purchasers of the mortgage, will be paid if the homeowner defaults. But many homeowners, including James V. Hansen, R-Utah, who sponsored HR 607, complain that they cannot cancel the insurance policy once their equity in the home reaches 20 percent.

The bill the House passed July 14 would require lenders and insurance companies to notify homeowners about the process for canceling such policies. Once equity reaches 20 percent, homeowners could petition to cancel the policy. The bill would require insurance companies to automatically cancel the policy for most conventional mortgages if the homeowner's equity reaches 22 percent. Homeowners with high-risk mortgages generally could not cancel the insurance until midway through their loan — after 15 years, for example, on a 30-year mortgage.

In a compromise, the bill effectively would allow eight states to keep their stronger mortgage insurance laws. The states are California, Connecticut, Maryland, Massachusetts, Minnesota, Missouri, New York and Texas.

Social Policy

thorities to charge minimum monthly rents between $25 and $50, with some exemptions for hardship cases, and would allow them to set a rent ceiling so that residents who found jobs would not be penalized for increasing their incomes. The appropriations bills have given local officials one-year authority to implement such changes.

The Senate bill would retain the Brooke amendment, but would allow housing authorities to charge minimum rents of $25 per month — current law requires no minimum — and would allow them to establish rent ceilings.

A third area of disagreement is a House provision that would allow city governments to intercept HUD block grants designated for housing authorities. The proposal aims to improve housing in areas where housing authorities have not managed well. But many housing advocates believe it will set up a free-for-all between elected city officials and the housing boards they appointed but with which they do not always agree. The Senate bill does not contain the provision.

Another area of high volatility, and one that Lazio and Mack have spent a great deal of time debating, is a House provision that would repeal the bedrock of public housing, the 1937 Housing Act. The act established the nation's public housing system in an effort to eliminate tenements and blight.

Many involved in the debate say the provision is a political "scalp" some Republicans desperately want, but is otherwise unnecessary and harmless. Because the bills would change almost everything about the public housing programs established in 1937, it makes little difference whether the 1937 law stays on the books.

House Republicans, led by Lazio, have their minds set on the repeal of another New Deal-era social program to follow on repeal of the 1935 welfare program. Democrats do not want to give Republicans a chance to bash a program enacted under President Franklin D. Roosevelt. Senate Republicans are trapped between the two.

Housing advocates say the issue has taken far too much time. Said Rick Nelson, executive director of the National Association of Housing and Redevelopment Officials: "We are interested in having a reformed public housing program. I don't think there's a necessity to repeal the 1937 Housing Act, but if Congress wants to repeal it, let Congress repeal it."

Another controversial issue that has broken down more along party lines than House-Senate lines is a provision in both bills that would require able-bodied public housing residents who are not employed to perform eight hours of community service a month. Democrats say that amounts to a double standard because corporations and others who get government subsidies or assistance are not required to perform a similar service. Republicans say it is the least a person can do to receive low-cost housing.

New York Connection

Members in both chambers have dug deep trenches around the provisions in their bills, leaving others at a loss to explain why. "The chasm between the two bills doesn't seem all that non-negotiable to outsiders," Cavanaugh said. Observers are uncertain why members cannot split their differences, particularly on issues such as income mixing.

Part of the reason lies not so much in Washington as a few states to the North — in New York.

Three of the key figures in housing policy are from New York: Lazio; Senate Banking, Housing and Urban Affairs Committee Chairman Alfonse M. D'Amato, a Republican; and HUD Secretary Andrew M. Cuomo, a Democrat.

Their interest in housing is not peripheral. New York City is home to 12 percent of the nation's public housing and its housing authority has long prided itself on its ability to provide more safe and decent housing than many smaller communities.

One might think that a Lazio-D'Amato-Cuomo triumvirate could guarantee passage of a bill that New York constituents want.

One might be right if the three of them were mild-mannered folks from Minnesota. But some people say "there is an island thing" at play here. One staff member called it "a complex set of relationships . . . that I just don't understand and don't try to."

That "island thing" mostly involves Long Islanders D'Amato and Lazio, observers say, and adding Cuomo into the mix does not help. In part, it is a story of getting political power and keeping it.

D'Amato has it. He is the senator from New York, albeit the junior one. But the senior senator, Democrat Daniel Patrick Moynihan, 70, cannot stay in Congress forever. Lazio and Cuomo are often mentioned as candidates for Moynihan's seat. Cuomo, a former low-income housing developer in New York and the son of former Democratic Gov. Mario Cuomo, is also thought likely to win a prime spot in Vice President Al Gore's 2000 campaign for president.

Although D'Amato and Lazio come from the same place and the same party, their relationship has never been as a political father and son. Lazio and D'Amato have different legislative styles — Lazio tends to focus more on the details than does D'Amato — and Lazio showed early on in his political career that he would not follow D'Amato's lead, observers say. As a result, some believe D'Amato is suspicious of Lazio. The relationship may make it difficult for Mack — who has D'Amato's proxy on housing issues — and Lazio to work together, even though Mack and Lazio say they have a good relationship, and a common friendship with Speaker Newt Gingrich, R-Ga.

Lazio said of D'Amato: "I think we have high expectations of each other that have to be reconciled in order for us to come to an agreement. I like him, but I think that there are just nuances involved in coming from the same state that are not unique but that are reality. . . . There's a natural inclination to worry about everybody's agenda." Lazio said he would say the same about Cuomo.

A Senate Banking Committee spokesman said the relationship between D'Amato and Lazio has not derailed public housing. "It's not true. We work well with everybody and we'll continue to work well with everybody."

But the sometimes strained relationship among the three men has not gone unnoticed by the New York news media.

In an October column on subsidized housing, Marie Cocco of Long Island's

Newsday newspaper wrote, "Who can divine what forces conspired so that their political fortunes are bound together, linked by a peculiar affinity for the politics of housing and the knowledge that each must somehow maneuver around the other while making it appear they are cooperating in the best interests of New York state? . . . If this weren't politics, it would be opera." Cocco concluded that Cuomo and D'Amato were the "divas" and Lazio the "ingenue."

Lazio's supporters dislike the comparison and say the column was one of several "cheap shots" from the local news media. But many others say it is Lazio's agenda that most puzzles them.

Some observers say that he has been unwilling to give in on any major point, stalling the large public housing overhaul bill and keeping the VA-HUD Appropriations Subcommittee in knots over Section 8 housing changes throughout much of last summer.

Those close to him say he is reluctant to give up on principles he has fought hard for over the last three years, such as the repeal of the 1937 act and the minimum rent requirement. They add that he does not want to let down other Republicans who stood with him against a barrage of Democratic amendments.

Another reason may be that Lazio, who is 39, energetic and often described as boyish, wants to let his elders know that he is a force to be reckoned with. "On those issues of principle, I am not someone who caves easily," Lazio said.

But he added, "I think this is frankly a maturing process, when you realize that you cannot get the ideal bill . . . I am confident that we are moving in the direction for great success. Not everybody is going to agree with everything I suggest, so I understand that there is going to be reasonable compromise."

While others will wait to see what Lazio does, his talk of compromise offers some hope that the House and Senate may reach a consensus this session, if not on the grand public housing overhaul bill, then perhaps on a scaled-down version.

Mack and Lazio say they were moving closer to an agreement at the end of 1997 but ran out of time. They have not met since Congress returned in January.

Mack urged members and those affected by housing programs to remain patient. The issues, he said, "are much more complicated than meets the eye. . . . We're trying to find ways to compromise and get a bill but it's going to take some time."

But time is limited, he added. "The longer we wait into the year and if we can't come to a mutually accepted position, then trying to do something might become more difficult."

D'Amato said he is "hopeful" that what he termed "minor differences" will be resolved.

Outsiders Speak Up

While lawmakers are set to take another run at the legislation, staff members say the Clinton administration

Bill To Ease Home-Buying Stalls in Senate

OCTOBER 17 — The House passed a measure by voice vote Oct. 13 that aims to increase the number of people who own homes by providing more government help for home purchases and lessening regulatory burdens on builders.

The multifaceted bill (HR 3899) faced no vocal opposition from House members or the Department of Housing and Urban Development (HUD), but several senators had concerns, and the Senate never took it up. Bill sponsor Rick A. Lazio, R-N.Y., chairman of the House Banking Subcommittee on Housing and Community Opportunity, is expected to make another push for the legislation next year.

One of the bill's most contentious provisions would create a 25-member committee to propose new standards for manufactured housing, in consultation with HUD. The makers of mobile homes have long tried to budge HUD from 20-year-old standards that manufacturers believe are obsolete.

The issue is controversial because manufacturers and others in the mobile home industry would have 10 seats on the committee, a number some consumer groups fear would give makers and sellers too much control. Other seats would go to mobile home owners, consumer groups, local inspection officials and other experts.

The bill also would:

● Make several Federal Housing Administration (FHA) changes. It would allow HUD to increase the limits on the worth of mortgages the FHA could insure in some areas adjacent to higher-cost cities and suburbs. It would allow HUD to increase the number of adjustable rate mortgages it insures by up to 40 percent of the prior year's number. And it would require the General Accounting Office to study the effects of requiring inspections on all FHA homes before purchase.

● Require all federal regulations to include a "housing impact analysis" to ensure that the proposal would not make housing less affordable.

and some lobbying groups seem to have lost their enthusiasm.

"I haven't really seen any evidence that they are really dying to get a bill," said a Republican staff member. "They are very happy when the appropriators do what they do, [though] if push came to shove, they would prefer a bill."

Not so, Cuomo said. "We could do a lot of good with a good public housing bill, and we're going to work very hard for it," he said.

Added Kevin Marchman, HUD's assistant secretary for Public and Indian Housing: "I actually think they are going to come to an agreement."

But HUD is still concerned about changing the income requirements for public housing.

"We don't want to move away from our mission," Marchman said. "We want to make sure we reserve public

Social Policy

Public Housing Overhaul Provisions

The conference agreement on the spending bill for veterans, housing and science programs (HR 4194 — conference report: H Rept 105-769) includes provisions to overhaul public housing programs and give local housing authorities greater flexibility to choose tenants, set rents and make funding decisions.

Like the public housing overhaul bills (HR 2, S 462) that the House and Senate passed in 1997, the agreement replaces current public housing and low-income rental assistance programs with block grants to local housing authorities, which would be given greater latitude to use the funds for locally tailored housing programs. In making these changes, the measure amends but does not repeal the Housing Act of 1937. The House bill would have repealed it, but the Senate's bill amended it. (1997 Almanac, p. 7-12)

Local Housing Authorities

The agreement requires local housing authorities designated by the Department of Housing and Urban Development (HUD) as "troubled" to submit plans outlining specific goals for improving their projects and services. If the housing authority fails to meet those goals, HUD would be required to take over the authority, or seek appointment of a receiver.

The measure requires HUD to study the effectiveness of its current housing authority evaluations, as well as alternative methods of evaluating performance. This study must evaluate the merit of establishing an independent accreditation organization to assist or replace HUD's role in assessing housing authorities.

Public Housing Block Grants

The agreement converts federal funding for public housing into two block grants — one for capital improvements and the other for operating costs. The measure authorizes and appropriates $3 billion for public housing capital grants in fiscal 1999, and unspecified funds through fiscal 2003. For operating grants, the measure authorizes $2.9 billion and appropriates $2.8 billion in fiscal 1999, and unspecified sums through fiscal 2003.

Changes in Rent

Currently, the rent of public housing tenants and families receiving Section 8 assistance to live in private apartments is limited to 30 percent of adjusted income under the so-called Brooke amendment, named after former Sen. Edward W. Brooke, R-Mass. (1967-79). The Brooke amendment acts as both a "ceiling" and a "floor" for rents, so that the rent of most tenants is effectively set at 30 percent of income, and a tenant's rent automatically increases as earnings increase — which does not encourage a tenant to find work. In addition, because tenants are not subject to minimum rents and some renters have little or no income, some pay no rent.

The bill would change the system by:

• Restoring the Brooke amendment to its original intent, so that it acts only as a rent "ceiling" — allowing housing authorities to set rents at lower levels. Under the measure, a family's rent would be limited to no more than 30 percent of adjusted income, 10 percent of monthly income, or that portion of a welfare payment designated as housing assistance. Adjusted income is annual income minus exclusions allowed by HUD, such as medical expenses and child support payments.

• Allowing public housing tenants an alternative in calculating rents, giving them a choice between having their rent based on their income (limited to 30 percent of income), or set at a flat rate determined by the housing authority, based on the rental value of the housing. Such flat-rate rents could either be higher or lower than the rent level based on income, depending on the rental value of the unit. Tenants who choose such flat-rate rents would be permitted to switch back to income-based rents if they experienced financial hardship.

Minimum Rents

The bill generally requires local housing authorities to establish minimum rents for public housing and rental vouchers — with such minimum rents not to exceed $50 a month. Housing authorities would be allowed to grant hardship exemptions from minimum rent requirements.

Occupancy Changes

The agreement eliminates federal occupancy preference rules, and leaves it to local authorities to develop, based on local housing needs and priorities, their own guidelines for choosing tenants. These rules determine who may be granted public housing or housing subsidy assistance, and their priority in receiving such assistance.

The measure also aims to promote a greater mix of incomes in public and assisted housing.

As under current law, public housing assistance generally could be provided only to families making less than 80 percent of an area's median income. To ensure that housing authorities do not try to serve just the higher-income families in this low-income population, the agreement requires that at least 40 percent of public housing units available each year be reserved for very low-income families with incomes no higher than 30 percent of the area median income. At least 75 percent of the vouchers made available each year would have to be reserved for families with incomes at or below 30 percent of the median.

The measure includes a "fungibility" provision that allows housing authorities to reserve a lower portion (down to 30 percent of available units) of public housing units for the very poor if more than 75 percent of vouchers are provided for such poor families. The measure also includes provisions to ensure that local housing authorities do not concentrate low-income families in certain housing projects.

Under current law, 75 percent to 85 percent of public housing units must be provided to tenants with incomes at or below 50 percent of the area median, and all vouchers are reserved for such families.

Community Work Requirements

The agreement requires adult residents of public and assisted housing to contribute eight hours a month of service within their community, or to participate in an economic self-sufficiency program for eight hours a month. People who fail to do such community service work would have their lease terminated when it came up for annual renewal. Working adults, senior citizens, disabled people, and those in school or work training would be exempt from this requirement, as would people who are complying with work or training requirements under the 1996 welfare overhaul law (PL 104-193).

Other Occupancy Standards

The bill allows local housing authorities to deny public housing or rental assistance to people who are abusing drugs or alcohol, or whose history of drug and alcohol abuse provides reasonable cause for the authority to believe that the person may interfere with the health, safety, or right to peaceful surroundings of other residents. It also prohibits anyone classified as a "sexually violent predator" from receiving public housing assistance.

Leases for public housing and assisted housing would be modified to allow for the eviction of tenants who use illegal drugs, whose abusive use of alcohol interferes with the rights of other residents, or who engage in certain criminal activities. Tenants who are evicted because of drug-related crimes would be prohibited from receiving federal housing assistance for three years.

'Home Rule' Flexible Grants

The agreement establishes a four-year demonstration program under which local governments, if approved by HUD, could develop their own flexible low-income housing programs — generally receiving all the public housing and assisted housing funding that would otherwise be provided to the local housing authority.

Under the measure, only 100 local jurisdictions could participate in the program, which also would be limited to jurisdictions where local housing authorities scored in the lowest 40 percent nationwide in performance. No jurisdiction with a housing authority deemed to be a "high-performing" authority could participate. Of the 100, the measure further provides that no more than 55 authorities participating in the demonstration may be "troubled" (as designated by HUD), and no more than 45 may be "non-troubled."

Disposal of Obsolete Housing

The agreement eliminates requirements that housing authorities replace, on a one-for-one basis, every unit of public housing the housing authority disposes of or demolishes. It establishes the conditions under which housing authorities may demolish housing, requiring that it be obsolete, either in condition, location or other factors, and that rehabilitating it would not be cost effective.

The measure also reauthorizes through fiscal 2002 the HOPE VI program, which helps local authorities demolish dilapidated public housing units and replace many of them.

Section 8 Rental Assistance

The measure consolidates into a new block grant program the existing programs through which tenant-based rental assistance is provided through Section 8 certificates and vouchers. The measure authorizes unspecified sums in fiscal 2000 and fiscal 2001 to fund 100,000 new "incremental" vouchers each year. They would provide housing assistance to an additional 100,000 families each year. HUD already provides 1.4 million vouchers. The bill will add another 50,000 vouchers in fiscal 1999.

Other Provisions
Resident Management Activities

The bill authorizes public housing residents to form resident councils to consider issues affecting public housing developments and to consult with the local housing authority. Residents also would be authorized to create resident management corporations that could contract with a local housing authority to manage one or more public housing developments. The measure allows HUD, if requested by residents under certain circumstances, to transfer management of a public housing development or portion of one to an independent management entity.

'Reverse Mortgages'

The measure authorizes HUD to issue rules that would prohibit organizations from charging excessive fees for advising senior citizens on the availability of HUD-insured "reverse mortgages," as well as rules to prohibit lenders from dealing with organizations that charge such excessive fees. It also would expand and permanently authorize HUD's "reverse mortgages" program, called Home Equity Conversion Mortgages, which allows cash-strapped senior citizens to borrow against the equity in their homes for everyday expenses without having to make monthly interest or principal payments. The loan is repaid when the home is sold. The number of reverse mortgages would expand from 50,000 to 150,000. The provisions were also included in a bill (S 562) that passed both chambers in 1997 but was never cleared because of amendments attached during floor consideration.

The bill also:
- Prohibits HUD from establishing national occupancy standards, such as those established by some states to specify the maximum number of people who may live in a housing unit.
- Requires local housing authorities to inspect annually each public housing development and privately owned voucher-subsidized unit to ensure that such units are safe and clean.
- Permits housing authorities to remove a dilapidated or otherwise distressed public housing development, or a portion of one, from the available public housing stock, and provide housing vouchers to affected tenants.
- Allows residents of public housing to own one or more "common household pets," subject to "reasonable" requirements of the local housing authority and local laws or ordinances.
- Allows housing authorities to establish programs under which public housing residents, and families that are eligible for public housing, may purchase units of public housing or other low-income housing owned by the local housing authority.
- Reauthorizes the National Flood Insurance program through fiscal 2001. The program provides government-subsidized flood insurance policies to those who live in flood-prone areas.

---

housing units for the very poor."

In addition, public housing seems to be less of a focus at HUD these days. In the fiscal 1999 budget proposal President Clinton released Feb. 2, funding increases went to home ownership programs and vouchers. Operating and capital funds for traditional public housing would decrease.

HUD has already made changes to public housing programs, including stepped-up demolition of dilapidated units, and has worked with local authorities to implement the changes allowed in appropriations bills.

HUD officials say they can "come very close" to revamping public housing without changing any laws, March-

man said. In that regard, an overhaul bill "is not absolutely essential."

Some housing officials do not agree. Cavanaugh, who represents the large public housing authorities, said he thinks an overhaul bill is vital to the survival of public housing. "We're very desperate for the bills," he said.

Years of debate have taken their

Social Policy

toll on interest groups' enthusiasm, he added. "We assumed that somehow there would be the usual give and take and it would produce a bill. I think there's . . . depression" among concerned groups, he said. "If they don't hear us, it's because we're hoarse."

Final Housing Bill Cleared as Part Of VA-HUD Spending Measure

OCTOBER 10 — It took three years and countless negotiating sessions to get a measure to overhaul the nation's public housing system to President Clinton's desk.

He is expected to sign the legislation — now a 400-page section of the fiscal 1999 spending bill (HR 4194) for housing, veterans and science programs — the week of Oct. 12. The House adopted the conference report on the spending bill, 409-14, on Oct. 6 and the Senate cleared it, 96-1, on Oct. 8 after overcoming a last-minute objection. (House vote 483, p. H-138; Senate vote 307, p. S-47)

Coming as it did in the frenetic final days of the 105th Congress, proponents had to fight to draw attention to passage of the landmark housing measure (formerly HR 2, S 462). But for the 3 million Americans who count on federal assistance to provide an apartment or help them pay the rent, the bill makes significant changes — though the full effects may not be known for a decade.

Their rents may change, most likely becoming less burdensome if they are working but more so if they are not. Their neighbors may change as housing authorities are encouraged to break up concentrations of the very poor in certain buildings and to bring in more tenants who hold jobs. Their routines may change as those who are neither working, elderly or otherwise exempt are required to perform eight hours of community service a month. And their landlords may change, as housing authorities are required to give HUD detailed plans of how they will improve their projects in exchange for more freedom to make operating decisions and use block grants.

"This bill completely overhauls America's indefensible current public housing system," Speaker Newt Gingrich, R-Ga., said in a statement Oct. 6, adding, "This bill could almost be considered the second stage of the Republican welfare reform plan."

But congressional Democrats and the Clinton administration, who supported the final housing bill, were quick to dissociate it from the 1996 welfare overhaul, in part because that bill (PL 104-193) set time limits for receiving benefits, and the public housing overhaul bill does not. (Welfare overhaul, 1996 Almanac, p. 6-3)

"I would not use that analogy," said HUD Secretary Andrew M. Cuomo in a telephone news conference Oct. 5. "I would say this is only a change for the better. . . . It fundamentally transforms public housing."

Added Joseph P. Kennedy II of Massachusetts, the ranking Democrat on the House Banking and Financial Services Committee's Housing and Community Opportunity Subcommittee: "I think that this is the first major overhaul of the public housing of this country in 60 years and hopefully it creates a blueprint . . . where we will see finally eradicated from the landscape of America these monstrosities that have come to represent the idea of government-sponsored housing."

At an Oct. 6 news conference at the Capitol, Rep. Rick A. Lazio, R-N.Y., who sponsored the House version of the bill, said the final agreement was the "culmination of a three-year effort to transform public housing from a place of despair and decay." Appearing with House Majority Leader Dick Armey, R-Texas, and Majority Whip Tom DeLay, R-Texas, Lazio asked, "Who says the Republicans don't have an urban policy?"

In addition to touting the bill's achievements, Cuomo and Lazio used their news conferences to claim the measure was largely based on their own original, but divergent, proposals. That prompted questions about how the two up-and-coming New York politicians put aside their differences long enough to get the bill — an amalgam of the administration, House and Senate versions — through Congress.

Some staff members involved in negotiations and lobbyists following the process said that although Cuomo and Lazio deserved credit for their ideas and commitment, the credit for holding the bill together should largely go to two senators who stayed in the background — Connie Mack, R-Fla., and Paul S. Sarbanes, D-Md.

Patience of Job?

Mack, chairman of the Banking, Housing and Urban Affairs Subcommittee on Housing, is the author of the overhaul bills that the Senate passed in 1996 and 1997. Sarbanes is the Banking Committee's ranking Democrat. (1997 Almanac, p. 7-12)

According to staff members, they met on several occasions over the summer whenever it appeared that talks on the housing bill were collapsing. Time and again, each would agree to keep the process going; Mack would talk to Lazio and Sarbanes to Cuomo.

Mack and Lazio had tried to negotiate on their bills twice in as many years but could not bridge their differences. Lazio's bills would have changed the public housing system more quickly, allowing housing authorities to bring in more tenants with higher incomes. Mack's bills reserved more units for the very poor, who now occupy most units.

The lengthy but fruitless negotiations earned Mack a nickname from Senate Banking Chairman Alfonse M. D'Amato, R-N.Y.: "Job," the biblical man who endured much suffering but did not lose his faith.

Despite Mack and Sarbanes' efforts, summer negotiations fell apart several times. A major issue that held up Democratic and administration support for the plan was their wish to provide 100,000 more Section 8 vouchers to help low-income people pay their rents in private apartments. Currently, housing authorities distribute 1.4 million vouchers.

Everyone at the table, including Mack and Lazio, agreed that more vouchers were needed, but authorizers could not make that commitment. That was up to appropriators, who would have to find $500 million to pay for the new vouchers.

Appropriators finally came up with half that much, providing 50,000 new permanent vouchers and agreeing to drop a controversial pro-

Public Housing

vision that had been included in three previous VA-HUD bills. That provision imposed a three-month holdover period between the time that a previous tenant returned a voucher and a new tenant could receive it. The measure saved money because it kept 30,000 to 40,000 people a year on waiting lists for vouchers, according to Linda Couch, legislative liaison for the National Low Income Housing Coalition.

With the new funding and the changes, the bill essentially would provide 90,000 new vouchers in fiscal 1999, Cuomo said. The conference report also would authorize 100,000 vouchers each in fiscal 2000 and 2001.

That was enough to convince authorizers to settle their differences and allow the housing measure to move with the appropriations bill. It was not the first time appropriators would make major changes to public housing programs. Many of the changes made permanent by the public housing provision, such as allowing authorities to charge minimum rents, had been included in the last two HUD spending measures. Many housing authorities had been hesitant to use the new powers, though, because they did not know if the provisions would be changed in the following year's spending bill.

Among the last items to be settled were issues brought up by Cuomo and Lazio. Cuomo wanted to move "Operation Safe Home," a public housing anti-crime initiative, from the jurisdiction of HUD's inspector general to HUD or the Justice Department. Another was a Lazio plan to force HUD to raise income standards for the Community Development Block Grant (CDBG) program, often used to spruce up low-income neighborhoods, and the HOME program, which helps low-income people buy their own homes.

The inspector general provision was not included. The bill does contain language that would require HUD within 90 days to set new income limits for CDBG and HOME eligibility in at least 10 geographical areas.

Areas of Compromise

In several respects, the final bill includes parts of the administration, House and Senate measures.

The best example goes to the heart of the legislation: income targeting requirements. Both Democrats and Republicans believed that housing authorities and their tenants would be better off if public housing no longer served as a warehouse for the poorest of the poor. All sides agreed that a certain number of higher-income, working tenants should be allowed into public or subsidized housing. But they disagreed on how much should be reserved for the very poor, who now occupy most of that housing.

The final bill would require housing authorities to reserve at least 40 percent of public housing for the very poor — those making 30 percent or less of an area's median income. That provision is similar to the one in the Senate bill.

In the area of Section 8 vouchers, the bill would require that 75 percent be reserved for those making less than 30 percent of the median income. That is from the administration bill. But the bill also would allow public housing authorities that gave more than 75 percent of their vouchers to the very poor to bring in an additional 10 percent of higher-income tenants into public housing — raising the maximum percentage of higher-income tenants from 60 percent to 70 percent. This clause, known as "fungibility," would apply to housing authorities located in census tracts identified as poverty-stricken. The provision came from the House bill.

In addition to allowing a greater mix of incomes in public housing, the bill aims to increase the earning potential of those in public housing.

About 20 percent of public housing residents nationwide also receive welfare, and they would be required to follow the welfare overhaul law's work requirements. Others would have to perform community service, a requirement that sponsors hope would give them job skills. The elderly and disabled — who make up about 40 percent of public housing residents — and those already working would be exempt from service requirements.

By increasing tenants' income, the bill aims to increase the income of housing authorities, which are now so often strapped for cash that routine maintenance goes undone. The bill would allow housing authorities to take out mortgages on their buildings and otherwise contract with private or government entities to generate funds to build housing projects or rehabilitate existing ones.

It looked briefly as if the conference report might be held up in the Senate over a last-minute provision that would allow Freddie Mac, a government-sponsored enterprise that buys mortgages, to buy riskier loans not backed with private mortgage insurance. Lauch Faircloth, R-N.C., threatened to hold up the bill, but relented when leaders assured him the provision would be altered by language in the omnibus spending package. The lone senator to oppose the bill was Jon Kyl, R-Ariz., who said it provided too much money. ◆

Social Policy

Congress Clears Bill Restoring SSI Benefits To Certain Immigrants

SUMMARY

Moving once again to restore benefits eliminated by the 1996 welfare law, Congress in October cleared a bill (PL 105-306) continuing Medicaid and Supplemental Security Income (SSI) disability benefits for thousands of non-citizens whose immigration status was in doubt.

Earlier, in June, lawmakers cleared an agriculture research bill (PL 105-185) that included provisions restoring food stamp benefits to about 250,000 legal immigrants who were cut off by the welfare law.

The 1996 welfare law (PL 104-93) eliminated SSI, Medicaid and food stamp benefits to legal immigrants. After a public outcry and prodding from the Clinton administration, Congress voted in 1997 to restore SSI and Medicaid to most legal immigrants who were in the country in August 1996 when the welfare bill was signed. The provisions were part of the 1997 balanced-budget act (PL 105-33).

The budget act also allowed so-called non-qualified immigrants — meaning those whose immigration status was in doubt — to continue receiving aid through Sept. 30, 1998, while the Social Security Administration reviewed case files to weed out illegal immigrants.

Based on file reviews and statistical sampling, the Social Security Administration reported to Congress that the vast majority of the 16,438 non-qualified residents who were on the rolls when the welfare law was signed were either legal immigrants or had become citizens.

Rather than approve another short-term extension, the House passed a bill (HR 4558) by voice vote Sept. 23 to make all immigrants in the non-qualified category permanently eligible for benefits. The Senate cleared the bill by voice vote Oct. 8.

The Social Security Administration in a Sept. 18 statement estimated that the bill would guarantee benefits to 3,400 non-citizens who would have otherwise lost aid.

Dave Camp, R-Mich., said the House action would protect elderly disabled immigrants while "maintaining the underlying policy on welfare for newly arriving immigrants achieved in the welfare law, that those who arrived after 1996 must work or naturalize before becoming eligible."

The Clinton administration in a statement supporting the bill, said it would "further the president's efforts to reverse unduly harsh benefit restrictions on legal immigrants that have nothing to do with moving people from welfare to work."

The measure would also permanently extend a special program that helps individuals receiving federal unemployment assistance to begin their own businesses. The program allows individuals who are self-employed to keep their income but still draw unemployment benefits.

It clarifies that the 1996 welfare law did not bar foreign nationals from getting or renewing professional licenses in the United States.

The bill would make revisions to the SSI program to ensure that children with life-threatening illnesses who receive vacations or other gifts from nonprofit groups, such as the Make-a-Wish Foundation, do not lose their benefits.

The Make-a-Wish-Foundation, created in 1980, tries to fulfill the desires of critically ill children, such as arranging a trip to Disneyland or a visit with a celebrity. Wishes that call for travel require the foundation to give families spending money. Under SSI, such money is counted as income, making children ineligible for benefits.

To pay for the immigrant provisions and other changes, the bill lets the administration recoup SSI overpayments from Social Security checks. ◆

Chapter 21
TAXES

Internal Revenue Service Overhaul 21-3
  House, Senate Bills Compared 21-5
  Overhaul Provisions 21-9

Tax Credit Extensions 21-14
  Highlights of House Bill 21-16
Internet Tax Moratorium 21-19

Taxes

Clinton Signs Into Law IRS Overhaul Bill That 'Respects Taxpayers'

Box Score

- **Bill:** HR 2676 — PL 105-206
- **House action:** The House adopted the conference report (H Rept 105-599) on HR 2676, 402-8, on June 25. It passed HR 2676, 426-4, on Nov. 5, 1997.
- **Senate action:** The Senate cleared the conference report, 96-2, on July 9. It passed HR 2676, 97-0, on May 7.
- **Presidential action:** Clinton signed HR 2676 on July 22.

SUMMARY

With overwhelming bipartisan support, Congress cleared and President Clinton signed legislation to implement a top-to-bottom overhaul of the Internal Revenue Service.

The measure was designed to give taxpayers more rights and protections in their dealings with the tax-collection agency. In a key change, the overhaul shifts the burden of proof in many cases before U.S. Tax Court from the taxpayer to the agency. It also curbs interest charges and penalties in certain tax cases, establishes due-process requirements, gives taxpayers greater ability to sue the agency and places new restrictions on the agency's ability to seize property.

Congressional efforts to overhaul the IRS began in June 1997 with a lengthy report issued by a bipartisan commission chaired by Sen. Bob Kerrey, D-Neb., and Rep. Rob Portman, R-Ohio.

The Senate Finance Committee held a round of hearings in the fall of 1997 at which many taxpayers told horror stories of IRS abuse that produced a torrent of negative publicity for the agency.

The House passed its version (HR 2676) in the final days of the first session, but the Senate did not act until the second session, despite pressure from Senate Democrats, a handful of Republicans and Clinton to take up and pass the House bill in time for the 1998 tax season.

Many expected the Senate to take up the overhaul legislation in early 1998, but the committee instead held a second round of hearings featuring IRS whistleblowers who described an agency vastly out of control, where managers committed fraud without fear of punishment and heavily armed agents broke down the doors of innocent taxpayers.

Senate Republican leaders, however, ran into sharp criticism for trying to score political points by holding more hearings instead of fixing the problem. Lawmakers from both parties said it was time to move ahead with the long-delayed legislation instead of using the IRS as a punching bag for fundraising purposes.

Senate Committee OKs Bill Despite Cost Concerns

APRIL 4 — Based solely on the unanimous vote of approval by the Senate Finance Committee, it would be hard to believe that a bill to restructure the Internal Revenue Service is heading to the floor with its fate seriously jeopardized by a basic concern — money.

The committee's 20-0 vote March 31 masked the doubts held by many lawmakers over whether Senate leaders can find acceptable ways to fund the changes in the bill. While the tally signified the overwhelming desire in Congress to change the rules that govern the beleaguered tax collection agency, three hours of debate made it clear that the draft bill's success will be tied directly to the funding question. "The problem with it I see is we simply don't have enough money," said Bob Kerrey, D-Neb.

Nevertheless, Senate leaders predicted a floor vote on the bill no later than the first week in May.

After pushing the bill through his committee, Finance Chairman William V. Roth Jr., R-Del., said he would soon find the elusive funding sources. But like a man wheeling a shopping cart filled with groceries toward the check-out line, and carrying a wallet dreadfully short of cash, Roth is still looking for the $9.8 billion needed to fund the bill in the second five years.

"We expect by the time it comes to the Senate floor we will have it paid for," Roth said, without giving details.

Roth has regained the spotlight on an issue that caught fire last fall after his committee held high-profile hearings into often aggressive, and sometimes unethical, tactics that IRS agents have used to intimidate taxpayers. As the hearings further clouded the already tarnished image of the IRS, House Republicans seized the issue and produced a bill (HR 2676) to revamp the agency. The issue's power became clear when President Clinton reversed his initial opposition and the House overwhelmingly passed the measure Nov. 5.

Senate leaders, however, resisted pressures to act as expeditiously, and Roth held another round of hearings earlier this year to debate changes.

With nearly five months to contemplate the issue, Roth in late March unveiled a bill that, while based on the House legislation, veered greatly in scope and cost. Both bills would establish new taxpayer rights, including the right to sue the IRS for damages; both would create a new IRS governing board dominated by private-sector tax and management experts; and both would shift the burden of proof for wrongdoing from the taxpayer to the IRS. But the Senate bill's cost of $19.3 billion over 10 years would more than triple that of the House measure.

Like the House bill, Roth's measure

Taxes

would allow taxpayers to sue the IRS and recover attorneys' costs. But it goes further by allowing more people to claim "innocent spouse" relief in cases when a tax debt is determined to be the responsibility of an ex-spouse. That provision would cost $5.2 billion over 10 years, according to the Joint Committee on Taxation. The House bill offers mild relief for such spouses, but the Senate bill would hold taxpayers responsible only for their portion of the debt.

The reaction to Roth's bill was mixed, with virtually no outright opposition but plenty of lawmakers in both parties complaining that Roth had complicated what had promised to be an easy victory. Roth said his measure would not only change IRS rules but also affect agency culture. The House bill, he said, does not go far enough to improve taxpayers' ability to fight the agency or to hold the IRS accountable for its actions.

In other key differences from the House bill, the Senate's would reduce penalties and interest charges for certain delinquent taxpayers.

It would suspend interest charges and penalties after one year if the IRS had not yet notified a taxpayer of problems with a return. The charges could resume after the IRS notified the taxpayer of the debt. That lost revenue would cost the government about $5.3 billion over 10 years. Democrats say the IRS does not have the ability to notify all delinquent taxpayers of their debts within one year. Roth said the provision seeks to ensure that taxpayers do not suddenly find themselves facing years of penalties for taxes they did not know they owed.

Amendments

During the markup, members considered 10 amendments and adopted five of them. Democrats successfully teamed with some Republicans to change several sensitive provisions, while losing fights for more radical changes. The theme of many proposals: Make the Senate bill more like the House bill.

Kerrey offered an amendment to replace the bill's language with the text of the House bill. It was defeated, 8-12, with Bob Graham, D-Fla., joining all Republicans in opposing it. Kerrey said if the Senate bill went forward, Congress would have to either increase taxes, cut spending or waive spending caps agreed to in last year's budget deal (PL 105-33).

Roth rejected the idea, saying the differences in the bill were vital. "This bill goes so much further in favor of reform for the taxpayer," he said. Other Republicans said it would have left them in the position of rubber-stamping the House bill.

"The Senate should be a player in this," said Majority Whip Don Nickles, R-Okla.

Another 8-12 vote — with John B. Breaux of Louisiana as the only dissenting Democrat — came when Graham offered an amendment to fund the bill with an increase of 20 cents per pack in the cigarette tax. "There might be a right time to offer this amendment," Nickles said. "I don't think it is now."

The committee did make changes to Roth's bill, including voice vote approval of an amendment by Charles E. Grassley, R-Iowa, that would allow the IRS to seize homes and businesses only as a last resort.

Democrats helped Grassley push through an amendment, over Roth's objections, to reserve a spot on the proposed new IRS governing board for a representative from the agency's labor union. The vote was 12-8. Also by 12-8, the panel approved an amendment by Daniel Patrick Moynihan, D-N.Y., to grant the Treasury secretary a seat on the board.

Republican Phil Gramm of Texas said it would be "laughable" to include the two officials on the board, arguing that they would have conflicting interests in agency authority and work force issues that would steer them away from reform. Others said it makes sense to include on the board those who would be responsible for carrying out the changes.

After committee approval, many members continued to say the bill went too far. But one key House player — Republican Rob Portman of Ohio, who co-chaired with Kerrey a commission on restructuring the IRS — said he was disappointed that Roth weakened provisions seeking to force simpler tax legislation.

"It is a mistake to let Congress off the hook," Portman said, "since Congress is a major part of our problem."

IRS Overhaul Wins Big Approval From Senate

MAY 9 — With its resounding 97-0 vote on May 7, the Senate has removed any real doubt that the Internal Revenue Service will be restructured this year.

Senators of all political persuasions took to the floor over four days to debate, and largely praise, the ambitious bill (HR 2676) that would pare IRS powers to investigate taxpayers and put the embattled agency under the direction of a board of overseers dominated by private citizens. Senate Majority Leader Trent Lott, R-Miss., predicted that the measure would clear Congress by Memorial Day, and the Clinton administration expressed cautious backing.

Senate Finance Chairman William V. Roth Jr., R-Del., declared on the floor: "Americans, for the first time ever, will have a tax collection agency marked by a sincere dedication to service."

But the final form the bill will take is uncertain.

Despite the outpouring of support, the bill is drawing criticism from some experts, including business executives and a former IRS commissioner, who contend that it could undermine the agency's ability to collect revenue.

And senators may be in for a cold splash of fiscal reality when they go to conference.

The House version of the bill, passed in November, is much narrower in scope and about a third as expensive. House members are expected to balk at the Senate bill's estimated price tag of $18.3 billion over 10 years, possibly preferring to use some of that money to pay for election-year tax cuts.

In addition, Democrats are criticizing the Senate's main mechanism for offsetting the costs of its version of the bill: allowing more people to invest in a new type of Individual Retirement Account (IRA) that is named for Roth. The proposal would initially raise $8 billion through 2007 due to taxes on money converted from traditional IRAs, but would lose billions of

House and Senate IRS Overhaul Bills Propose More Oversight, Add Rights

MAY 9 — Both the House and Senate versions of a bill to overhaul the Internal Revenue Service (HR 2676) would greatly broaden taxpayers' rights and beef up oversight of the embattled agency.

The Senate version generally is more far-reaching than the House. It would make it more difficult for the IRS to collect penalties and would place the burden of proof in most disputes on the agency, rather than the taxpayer.

The Senate version would cost an estimated $18.3 billion over 10 years, mostly from lower tax collections, according to a revised estimate by the Joint Committee on Taxation. The House version would cost an estimated $6.2 billion over 10 years.

Here are the key provisions of the two versions:

● **Oversight board:** Each version would create a board that would oversee the administration and direction of the agency. The majorities of both the 11-member board in the House version and the nine-member board in the Senate version would be presidential appointees from the private sector.

● **Reorganization:** The Senate version would restructure the agency, eliminating geographical units in favor of units that serve taxpayers in similar situations. It also would transfer the IRS office of chief inspector to the Treasury inspector general's office.

Both versions would limit the IRS commissioner to a five-year term. The oversight board would recommend candidates for commissioner and could endorse the removal of a commissioner, but the president would not be bound by such recommendations.

● **Burden of Proof:** Both versions would place the legal burden of proof on the IRS in any court proceeding to prove taxpayer liability. This is a departure from present law, in which the commissioner's determination of tax liability is presumed correct unless proved otherwise. The taxpayer would still be required to keep receipts and other records, and would have to cooperate with reasonable requests by the IRS for information.

The Senate version would go somewhat further, requiring the government to show proof whenever it was using statistical information to reconstruct a taxpayer's income. The government would also have to produce evidence supporting a particular penalty before the court could impose the penalty.

● **"Innocent spouse:"** The Senate version would generally make the tax liability of spouses proportionate to their incomes, meaning a spouse with a low income would not be liable for all taxes owed by the couple. At present, spouses who sign a joint return are each responsible for the accuracy of the return and the full tax liability, even when only one spouse has earned all or most of the income.

The House version contains more limited spousal provisions, allowing the IRS to take into account "all the facts and circumstances" of a particular case.

● **Confidentiality:** Both versions would extend attorney-client confidentiality to include a taxpayer's dealings with a tax adviser, such as an accountant.

● **Lawsuits:** Both versions would allow a taxpayer to sue the government for up to $100,000 for civil damages caused by IRS negligence. As under present law, a taxpayer would still be able to sue for up to $1 million if the IRS "recklessly" or "intentionally" disregarded provisions of the tax code.

● **Interest and penalties:** The Senate version would suspend interest and certain penalties in cases when the IRS failed to provide appropriate notice of liability to a taxpayer within a year of the filing of a return.

● **Taxpayer rights:** Both versions would increase the amount of money that taxpayers could recover from the agency for legal fees and other costs, although they differ in some details. Both versions would also mandate that the IRS pay the same interest rate on money it owes taxpayers that taxpayers pay on money they owe the agency.

The Senate version would allow taxpayers 30 days to request a hearing before the IRS could take property. The IRS could not seize residences to satisfy unpaid liabilities of less than $5,000.

● **Role of Congress:** To coordinate oversight, the House bill would require two annual IRS hearings by a joint committee comprising senior members of the six House and Senate committees that oversee the agency.

In addition, the Joint Committee on Taxation would analyze proposed tax changes that would significantly complicate the code.

● **Offsets:** Both versions would raise about $4 billion over 10 years by restricting employer deductions for accrued vacation pay.

The Senate bill would raise additional revenue, largely by allowing taxpayers who were older than 70 years and six months to convert a portion of their traditional Individual Retirement Accounts to Roth IRAs beginning in 2005; taxes would have to be paid on any amount moved from a traditional IRA.

Taxes

dollars over the longer term because Roth IRAs feature tax-free interest and withdrawals.

Casting doubt on Lott's timeline, House Majority Leader Dick Armey, R-Texas, said the differing versions may consume negotiators until the Fourth of July recess. "There's a lot of detail stuff" to be resolved, Armey said.

One key difference is that the Senate version includes a provision that would suspend interest and certain penalties on a taxpayer who had not been notified of a deficiency by the IRS within 12 months of filing a return. Its estimated cost is $5.3 billion over 10 years.

Also at issue is whether to retain Senate language that would relieve some divorced taxpayers from being penalized for the tax debts of their former spouses. The Senate's "innocent spouse" provision would cost an estimated $5.2 billion over 10 years, while more limited language in the House version would cost $131 million.

Roth, who spent months writing additional taxpayer protections into the bill, said he has no intention of watering it down in conference. "We intend to stand firm," he said after the Senate vote.

Negotiable Points

Money aside, there are also some significant policy differences between the two bills. The Senate version, for example, contains somewhat broader language to put the legal burden of proof on the IRS, rather than the taxpayer, in cases that reach tax court. It also gives greater power to the IRS commissioner to hire and fire employees and determine the salaries of senior managers.

The House version contains language to coordinate congressional oversight of the IRS, thereby seeking to prevent as many as six House and Senate committees from giving conflicting directions to the agency.

But key lawmakers said they view the differences between the two bills as comparatively minor, and a final agreement within a month or two should be attainable.

"The major differences between the House and Senate bills are differences of degree, not of substance," said Rob Portman, R-Ohio, who helped write the House version. "I'm confident that we'll be able to iron out the minor differences quickly and deliver long-overdue IRS reform for the taxpayers."

The political tide against the IRS is so strong that not a single senator threatened to oppose the bill during the May 4-7 debate or offered amendments to slow it down. In the end, no one in the chamber voted against it. *(Vote 126, p. S-21)*

Outside the Capitol, however, there were serious reservations.

The administration's Office of Management and Budget warned against going too far in curbing the agency's legal powers. Provisions such as allowing taxpayers additional court challenges before paying the IRS may "unintentionally make it easier for non-compliant taxpayers to avoid paying their fair share of taxes," the OMB said in a May 5 statement.

The administration also opposes a provision in both versions that would make confidential any communications between taxpayers and their tax advisers, such as accountants. This provision, similar to an attorney-client privilege, could make it difficult to investigate fraud, OMB officials contended.

But President Clinton, who initially opposed IRS restructuring last year, appears to have limited leverage over the bill. Republicans could again cast him as a defender of the beleaguered agency if he were to issue a veto threat — a politically untenable position that caused Clinton to switch his position after dramatic hearings into allegations of mismanagement and abusive and illegal collection techniques.

Less bound by political concerns, some business executives say the measure is seriously flawed because it could pressure the IRS to collect more evidence against taxpayers in order to meet its burden of proof.

"You're sending a message that will do two things: undermine voluntary compliance and prompt the IRS to be even more intrusive," said Timothy J. McCormally, director of tax affairs for the Tax Executives Institute, an association of corporate tax executives.

Some of the harshest criticism came from Donald C. Alexander, who was IRS commissioner under Presidents Richard M. Nixon and Gerald R. Ford. Alexander is now a partner in the law and lobbying firm of Akin, Gump, Strauss, Hauer & Feld.

The measure, rather than striking a balance between the need of the IRS to investigate tax evasion and the right of taxpayers to a fair proceeding, would hamstring the agency and waive so many penalties that many people who underpay their taxes would effectively get the equivalent of interest-free government loans, Alexander said.

"The price tag is going to be far, far more than that [the $18.3 billion estimate] because this legislation is going to make it very, very difficult for the IRS to administer the laws reasonably and effectively," Alexander said.

Roth dismissed such concerns: "The reforms we are talking about should in no way interfere with the ability of the agency to collect funds."

The controversies aside, the bill would require many basic improvements in customer service, such as requiring the IRS to make it easier for taxpayers to contact agents by telephone. The agency would also have to keep taxpayers apprised of their rights and explain appeals procedures.

"All we are asking is that the agency treat people fairly and civilly," Roth said.

Banking on IRAs

Despite the sweeping nature of the bill, the only real suspense during the Senate debate was how the costs of the measure's provisions would be covered.

To offset most of the shortfall, Roth on May 5 proposed lifting restrictions in 2005 on Roth IRAs — created by last year's tax-cut bill (PL 105-34) — in order to extend eligibility to taxpayers who are at least 70 years and six months old and earn more than $100,000. An estimated $8 billion would be generated in 2005 to 2007 by taxes on the expected mass conversions from regular IRAs into Roth IRAs, which many investors prefer because neither contributions nor investment earnings are taxable when withdrawn upon retirement.

"The proposal will enlarge the group of taxpayers who can enjoy the benefits of the Roth IRA," said Roth.

Although Democrats expressed some concerns over the effects on the budget, the Senate on May 6 approved the proposal as an amendment to the bill, 56-42. *(Vote 120, p. S-21)*

By the next day, however, Democrats revved up the volume over the issue. They produced an analysis indicating that the bill would cost the Treasury a net $46 billion over 20 years because of the tax breaks for Roth IRA investors.

Minority Leader Tom Daschle, D-S.D., labeled the proposal "this crazy, half-baked offset." But he said Democrats would not try to block the bill over the issue — confirming the potency of IRS overhaul as a political issue in an election year.

"If it's not a poison pill, it is a distasteful pill," Daschle grumbled.

In addition to the Roth IRAs, the bill would be financed by a package of relatively minor revenue raisers, including cutting back the employer deduction for deferred vacation time.

By voice vote, the Senate rejected an amendment by Bob Kerrey, D-Neb., that would have helped offset the bill's costs by reinstating expired business taxes that pay for cleanups under the superfund hazardous waste program.

The Senate also rejected:

• An amendment by Christopher S. Bond, R-Mo., that would have replaced the nine-member, part-time oversight board with a five-member, full-time board. Bond contended that a part-time board would be unable to establish firm control over the agency. The vote was 25-74. *(Vote 121, p. S-21)*

• An amendment by Lauch Faircloth, R-N.C., that would have eliminated the requirement that the oversight board include a representative of the union for IRS workers. The vote was 35-64. *(Vote 123, p. S-21)*

• An amendment by Jeff Sessions, R-Ala., and Fred Thompson, R-Tenn., that would have removed a provision granting the oversight board's employee representative a waiver of conflict-of-interest laws. The waiver was added to address concerns that a board member who was also an employee would face inherent ethical conflicts, but Thompson, who chairs the Governmental Affairs Committee, argued that it would set a bad precedent. The vote was 42-57. *(Vote 122, p. S-21)*

• An amendment by Connie Mack, R-Fla., that would have removed the secretary of the Treasury from the board. The IRS falls under the Treasury Department. The vote was 40-59. *(Vote 124, p. S-21)*

The Senate also rejected, 37-60, a motion to override a budget point of order by Kerrey against an amendment by Paul Coverdell, R-Ga., that would have barred the IRS from conducting random audits. The amendment would have cost an estimated $1 billion a year, throwing the cost of the bill out of balance. *(Vote 125, p. S-21)*

Fine Tuning

By voice vote, the Senate adopted:

• An amendment by Harry Reid, D-Nev., and Byron L. Dorgan, D-N.D., to require the oversight board to study whether the IRS has the resources to prevent "transfer pricing" by foreign companies.

Dorgan said overseas companies are evading taxes by selling products to domestic subsidiaries at inflated prices, which enables the subsidiaries to claim a loss even when they do considerable business in this country.

• An amendment by Reid requiring the Treasury Department to conduct a study of the IRS practice of paying informants who "snitch" on people who underpay their taxes.

• An amendment by Phil Gramm, R-Texas, barring the IRS from pressuring people not to file lawsuits against the agency.

• Another Gramm amendment that would require the IRS to fire employees who threaten retaliatory audits or fail to file a return, and a third Gramm amendment shifting the burden of proof from the taxpayer to the government for certain taxes other than income taxes.

• An amendment by Rod Grams, R-Minn., to suspend interest on money owed to the IRS by taxpayers who live in presidentially declared disaster areas.

• An amendment by Bond and Carol Moseley-Braun, D-Ill., preventing the IRS from requiring taxpayers to file electronically.

• An amendment by Pete V. Domenici, R-N.M., to require all IRS recorded help lines to offer the option to talk to an employee.

• An amendment by Bob Graham, D-Fla., requiring the oversight board to include a small-business representative.

• An amendment by Herb Kohl and Russell D. Feingold, both Wisconsin Democrats, to require the IRS to appoint an independent expert to review an investigation of the equal employment opportunity practices of IRS offices in Milwaukee and Waukesha, Wis.

• An amendment by Susan Collins, R-Maine, and Mike DeWine, R-Ohio, to ease reporting requirements on colleges and universities that enroll students eligible for certain tax credits.

House Adopts Conference Report

JUNE 27 — A sweeping bill to restructure the Internal Revenue Service for the first time in four decades has rolled over potential roadblocks and is headed toward swift enactment.

With a wide-ranging group of supporters saying the legislation would not only alter the rules that govern the IRS but also change the culture at the agency, the House adopted the conference report on the bill June 25 by a resounding vote of 402-8. The legislation (HR 2676) is on target for Senate approval shortly after the July Fourth recess, and President Clinton has promised to sign it. *(Vote 274, p. H-80)*

"We need an IRS that reflects American values and respects American taxpayers," Clinton said June 24. "This bill goes a long way toward that goal, and I look forward to signing it."

Clinton's signature would cap a high-profile ride that was kicked into high gear last fall, when Senate Finance Chairman William V. Roth Jr., R-Del., held a series of emotionally tinged hearings featuring taxpayers who had been the focus of aggressive, abusive and sometimes misguided IRS agents. It will begin a new era of accountability and "customer service" for the nation's tax collector, said IRS Commissioner Charles O. Rossotti. "We have been given the tools; we have been given the direction," Rossotti said at a news conference with lawmakers June 24. "Now it is up to us to make it happen."

Republicans believe the bill's passage will represent both a major legislative accomplishment and a significant symbolic victory, moving forward their efforts to rip up the voluminous tax code. "This is a down payment on that," said House Majority Leader Dick Armey, R-Texas. "It shows again that we are committed to straightening out

Taxes

this system. Ultimately, the IRS and the taxpayers are handicapped by the complexity of this [code]."

The final version of the IRS bill was unveiled June 24 after months of public hearings and votes, and after a mad dash of political maneuvering at the end. With a frenzied series of closed-door meetings and phone conversations during the days leading up to the agreement, House leaders met their goal of holding a vote on the bill before heading home for the July Fourth recess.

But before they reached a deal, and after negotiators announced June 19 that they had worked out key issues, several extraneous issues worked their way into the debate and threatened to slow it down. At the same time, Republicans worked overtime to develop a funding plan for the measure, which would cost $12.9 billion over 10 years, mostly in reduced tax collections.

In the end, members included a controversial provision to expand a tax break on capital gains, prompting some of the Democrats' harshest criticisms of the bill.

"We're tucking in provisions that help the wealthiest of the wealthy," said House Minority Leader Richard A. Gephardt, D-Mo., who nevertheless voted for the bill. Jim McDermott, D-Wash., one of the few members to vote against the legislation, offered a motion to return the bill to conference to strip the capital gains provision. It was defeated 116-292. (Vote 273, p. H-78)

Taxpayer Rights

The bill is based on the premise that taxpayers should have more rights and protections in their dealings with the IRS. In a key change to a basic IRS principle, the bill seeks to shift the burden of proof in many cases before U.S. Tax Court from the taxpayer to the agency. Under existing law, taxpayers must disprove charges leveled against them by the IRS — unlike in criminal cases, where the burden of proof rests with the government. The legislation also would curb interest charges and penalties in certain tax cases, establish due-process requirements, give taxpayers greater abilities to sue the agency and place new restrictions on the agency's ability to seize property.

Bill drafters also hope to force change from within the agency. The legislation would create an independent board, drawn predominantly from the private sector, to oversee the IRS and direct strategic plans. It would grant increased flexibility to the commissioner, who could more freely move some employees into new positions and recruit private sector executives with higher salaries. Rossotti said he needs such flexibility to run the IRS like a business.

In response to public outrage over taxpayer abuse by IRS agents, the bill would mandate the firing of employees who violate a list of policies that includes the mistreatment of taxpayers. "The reforms will help create a culture where taxpayers and employees alike are protected from abuse," Roth said.

The organizational structure would also be altered at the mammoth agency, which has 102,000 employees. The bill seeks to replace the existing geographical units that determine who handles a taxpayer's case with a system based on serving taxpayers in similar situations.

Compromise

The bill has been changed significantly from the version passed by the House in November and the more far-reaching measure passed by the Senate in May. The final agreement generally expands on the House measure while retreating somewhat from the Senate's. It also includes significant provisions that were not in either bill.

The legislation's particulars evolved over several months, but lawmakers' desire to humble and revamp the agency never wavered. "This bill is necessary and exists and is successful because there was a culture of intimidation within the IRS," said Sen. Charles E. Grassley, R-Iowa. Grassley was a member of the congressional commission that two years ago began a one-year look at a potential restructuring of the IRS. The commission filed its report in June 1997, recommending improved customer service, a simpler tax code, and an oversight board. But it was Roth's committee hearings that captured headlines and the attention of congressional leaders.

House Republicans passed a bill easily in November. The Senate passed a broader bill in May that would have cost $18.3 billion over 10 years, about three times as much as the House version. The conference committee formally began work June 10, and within nine days Roth and Ways and Means Chairman Bill Archer, R-Texas, announced they had reached agreement on key points. But it would be five days before key players formally signed off on the deal. As negotiations intensified, the most prominent unresolved issue was the question of how to fund the bill.

"We're making significant progress," Roth said when he left a meeting of Senate conferees June 22. Democrats also appeared optimistic, but many — including Sen. Daniel Patrick Moynihan of New York, the top Democrat on the Finance Committee — continued to point to the funding issue. Two days later, members announced a final deal. The bill was to include a package of technical corrections to the new transportation funding law (PL 105-178), a change of the trade term "most favored nation" to "normal trade relations," and a provision to prohibit the IRS from taxing free meals given to some employees. The latter provision was pushed by Republican Rep. John Ensign, who is running for the Senate in Nevada, where casinos frequently provide their workers with free meals.

Capital Gains

The most notable addition to the bill seeks to give investors a break on capital gains taxes. The $2 billion provision would reduce from 18 months to 12 months the amount of time a person would have to hold investments before qualifying for the 20 percent tax rate established by the 1997 tax law (PL 105-34).

By including it, Republican lawmakers sought to let investors benefit more quickly from the stock market boom. Early in the negotiations, Roth shied away from the issue, which the Clinton administration had previously opposed. But Archer held firm, insisting on the change. With the popular bill on the verge of becoming law, Clinton stayed out of the way, though Gephardt and McDermott used the issue to paint Republicans as friends of the rich. Gephardt said June 25 the change would only help "fat cat speculators on Wall Street."

But by that time Roth and Archer had unveiled their funding plan and the bill was too attractive for more than a few members to oppose. The camaraderie was notable in that Republicans not only included a reduction in the capital gains holding period but also worked into their plan to fund the bill a measure to allow wealthy investors to roll over their traditional individual retirement accounts into new Roth IRAs, which allow tax-free withdrawals but disallow deferred taxes on deposits. The switch would raise $8 billion over 10 years, because investors would pay taxes on their traditional IRA withdrawals at the time of the rollover. But committee aides said after 10 years the change would cost the government about $1 billion a year in lost revenue.

Roth and Archer found the other $5 billion to cover the bill's cost by restricting employer deductions for vacation pay and altering the tax rules governing some real estate investment trusts and receivables.

The technical corrections to the $216 billion transportation law (PL 105-178) would restore two key provisions targeting drunken drivers that were inadvertently omitted. They would require a transfer of 1.5 percent of highway funds to safety programs for states that do not enact a ban on open containers of alcohol in automobiles or do not adopt minimum penalties for repeat drunken driving offenses. The transfer of funds would rise to 3 percent starting in fiscal 2003 for states that have not acted on either provision.

As IRS bill supporters stood outside announcing their deal to reporters June 24, lawmakers who had pushed hardest to revamp the IRS looked to Rossotti, who has received glowing reviews for bringing a business-first attitude to the agency. "We're throwing the ball now into your lap," Archer said.

IRS Bill Cleared, Sent to Clinton To Be Signed

JULY 11 — Despite considerable Democratic misgivings, the Senate cleared a bill (HR 2676) on July 8 to overhaul the Internal Revenue Service and bolster taxpayers' rights.

The 96-2 vote reflected the overpowering election year appeal of revamping an agency accused of using heavy-handed and even illegal tactics to collect revenue. The House resoundingly adopted the conference report (H Rept 105-599) on the bill June 25, and President Clinton, a one-time opponent of the overhaul, pledged to sign the measure. *(Vote 189, p. S-30)*

Democrats criticized language added in conference that would give investors a break on capital gains taxes by reducing from 18 months to 12 months the amount of time a person would have to hold investments before qualifying for the lower 20 percent tax rate established by the 1997 tax law (PL 105-34). The $2 billion provision would mostly benefit the wealthy, critics contended.

"Someone found $2 billion all on its lonesome in the legislative darkness to be stuck into a piece of legislation, without debate in the House or the Senate, in a manner that will benefit a very few," fumed Byron L. Dorgan, D-N.D.

Dorgan raised a point of order against the provision, saying it was not in the House or Senate bills. The chair denied the point of order, and a Dorgan motion to appeal the chair's ruling was tabled (killed), 76-22. *(Vote 186, p. S-30)*

Senators also clashed over an unrelated tax provision that would deny disability benefits to veterans whose illnesses resulted from smoking. The provision was part of a technical corrections package to the transportation law (PL 105-178), added by conferees to the IRS measure. Patty Murray, D-Wash., raised a point of order against it. The chair denied her point of order, and the Senate, 50-48, tabled her motion to appeal. *(Vote 187, p. S-30)* ◆

What the IRS Bill Does

JUNE 27 — Carrying through on promises to overhaul the Internal Revenue Service, the House adopted the conference report on the IRS Restructuring and Reform Act (HR 2676 — H Rept 105-599) just before departing for its July Fourth recess.

The vote on June 25 was 402-8. The Senate is expected to clear the bill after the recess. *(House vote 274, p. H-80)*

President Clinton has said he will sign the bill.

Despite years of complaints from taxpayers about the tactics of the IRS, overhaul efforts got off to a slow start in the 105th Congress. A bipartisan task force issued a 190-page report in June 1997 that recommended sweeping changes, but not much happened. Then the Senate Finance Committee held three days of hearings in late September that showcased aggrieved taxpayers complaining of their treatment at the hands of abusive tax-collection agents. The issue caught fire.

The House moved quickly, crafting a bill that won the Clinton administration's begrudging support. It was approved by the Ways and Means Committee, 33-4, on Oct. 22, and whizzed through the House, 426-4, on Nov. 5.

But the Senate Finance Committee did not vote on its version until March 31, 1998, after beefing up key provisions.

The bill reached the Senate floor on May 7, where it won a resounding 97-0 vote.

The conference agreement gives taxpayers new rights and protections when dealing with the IRS, curbs penalties and interest charges in some cases, allows taxpayers to sue the government for damages if IRS personnel disregard tax law, and makes it easier for a joint filer to be exempt from liability for the tax mistakes of his or her spouse.

It also restructures the management of the IRS by, among other steps, establishing an oversight board to help run the agency. Six of the board's nine members are to be drawn from the private sector.

The bill outlines a number of new offenses for which IRS employees will be fired, including falsifying or destroying documents to cover up mistakes.

Conferees included several provisions that were not in either the House or Senate bill, including one that reduces from 18 months to 12 months the time a taxpayer must hold an investment to be eligible for the 20 percent tax rate on the profit from its sale. It also includes a modified version of the House-passed bill making

Taxes

corrections to the recently enacted six-year transportation law (PL 105-178).

The measure's $12.9 billion cost is offset by revenue-raising provisions, including one that permits wealthy elderly persons to convert traditional Individual Retirement Accounts into the new Roth IRA and pay taxes on the converted money.

Agency Restructuring

Oversight Board

The bill would create an oversight board, to be established within the Treasury Department. The board would oversee IRS administration, management, conduct, direction and supervision of the execution and application of the tax code.

The board would not, however, have any responsibility or authority over the development and formulation of federal tax policy, nor over law enforcement activities of the IRS, including compliance activities such as criminal investigations, examination and collections, nor over specific procurement activities, such as selecting vendors and awarding contracts.

The bill directs the IRS commissioner to develop and implement a plan to reorganize the IRS to eliminate, or substantially modify, the existing national, regional and district structure of the IRS, and instead establish organizational units that assist particular groups of taxpayers with similar needs.

The bill would give the board the following specific responsibilities:

● **Strategic plans.** Reviewing and approving strategic plans, including establishing a mission statement and standards of performance, as well as annual and long-range plans.

● **Operational reviews.** Reviewing the operational functions of the IRS, including loans for modernization of the tax system, managed competition, and training and education.

● **Manager selection.** Reviewing the IRS commissioner's selection, evaluation and compensation of senior managers.

● **Reorganization.** Reviewing the commissioner's plans for major reorganization of the agency.

● The bill also directs the board to review the commissioner's annual budget request that is submitted to the Treasury secretary. The measure would give the board responsibility for ensuring that the budget request is in line with the annual and long-term strategic plans of the agency, as determined by the board.

Oversight Board Membership

Nine people would serve on the oversight board, six of whom are to be so-called "private life" members who are not federal employees.

Those private-sector members are to have expertise in management of large service organizations; customer service; federal tax laws, including administration and compliance; information technology; organization development; and the needs and concerns of taxpayers and small businesses.

The remaining three members would be the Treasury secretary (or if the Treasury secretary designates, the deputy Treasury secretary); the IRS commissioner; and an individual from a union representing a substantial number of IRS employees.

The members would be appointed by the president and would have to be confirmed by the Senate.

Under the agreement, the six private-sector members would serve no more than two five-year terms. The initial terms would be staggered, with two members serving for three years, two members serving for four years and two members serving for five years.

The Treasury secretary or deputy secretary, the IRS commissioner and the union representative would be removed from their positions on the oversight board upon termination of their employment.

The board is to select a chairman to serve a two-year term.

Appointment and Duties of IRS Commissioner

As under current law, the bill would allow the president to appoint — with the approval of the Senate — the IRS commissioner, and to remove the commissioner at will. A commissioner could be appointed to more than one five-year term.

The oversight board would have the authority to recommend candidates for commissioner to the president, but the president would not be required to follow the board's recommendations in appointing a commissioner.

As under current law, the commissioner would have "such duties as prescribed by the Treasury secretary." But the bill would define those duties to include the power to administer, conduct, direct and supervise the execution and application of the internal revenue laws or related statutes and tax conventions to which the federal government is a party.

Discipline of IRS Employees

The IRS would be required to fire an employee if any of the following conduct relating to the employee's official duties is proved in a disciplinary or other proceeding: perjury; falsifying or destroying documents to cover up mistakes; willful failure to obtain the required approval signatures on documents authorizing the seizure of a taxpayer's home, personal belongings or business assets; assault or battery on a taxpayer or other IRS employee; violations of IRS rules for the purpose of retaliating against a taxpayer or other IRS employee; or violations of the civil rights of a taxpayer.

Office of Taxpayer Advocate

The bill would change how the IRS taxpayer advocate is appointed. Under the measure, the taxpayer advocate would be appointed from among three individuals recommended by the oversight board.

The functions of the taxpayer advocate generally would be the same as in current law — assisting taxpayers who have problems with the IRS — and the candidate for that job would continue to be expected to have either substantial experience representing taxpayers before the IRS or have substantial experience with the IRS. The advocate would gain some new responsibilities, including monitoring the coverage and geographical allocation of problem resolution officers, as well as outlining criteria to be used by IRS employees in referring taxpayer inquiries to problem resolution officers.

The bill would expand the office to create a system of local taxpayer advocates who would report to the national taxpayer advocate. They would remain independent from the IRS examination, collection and appeals functions.

The national advocate's office would be expected to ensure easy access to the local taxpayer advocates, by, for example, making sure local phone numbers are published and made available in communities.

The national taxpayer advocate would be required to submit two annual reports to the House and Senate tax-writing committees. The year-end report must include information on areas of tax law that impose significant compliance burdens on taxpayers or the IRS, including specific recommendations for solving those problems. The national taxpayer advocate would be required to work with the national director of appeals to identify the 10 most litigated issues for each category of taxpayers. (Categories of taxpayers include, for example, individuals, self-employed and small businesses.) As under current law, the report would be submitted directly to the congressional tax-writing committees, with no in-

IRS Overhaul

tervening review by the commissioner, the oversight board or other government officials.

Prohibition on Politically Motivated Audits

The bill would make it a felony for executive branch officials to use IRS audits for political purposes. The bill would clarify current law to make it clear that the prohibition applies to direct or indirect requests for IRS audits. (Current law contains no explicit prohibition on high-level executive branch influence over taxpayer audits and collection activity, but the IRS does prohibit disclosure of tax returns and return information, except under specific circumstances. Unauthorized disclosure of tax return information is currently a felony, punishable by a fine not exceeding $5,000 and up to five years imprisonment, or both.)

Under the bill, an executive branch employee convicted of exerting undue influence over an IRS audit would receive the punishment as outlined in current law.

The bill includes three exceptions to the prohibitions. Under the bill, the prohibition would not apply to a request made to a specified person (executive branch employee) by a taxpayer or a taxpayer's representative; requests for disclosure of tax returns so long as the request is made in accordance with applicable law; and requests made by the Treasury secretary as a consequence of the implementation of a change in tax policy.

Electronic Filing

The bill states that it is the "policy of Congress to promote paperless filing," and sets a long-range goal of limiting paper returns to 20 percent of all tax returns by the year 2007. (Current law merely authorizes electronic filing of tax returns.)

The bill would require the Treasury secretary to establish a strategic plan to eliminate barriers and provide incentives to increase taxpayer use of electronic filing. The bill would direct the strategic plan to focus initially on tax returns that are prepared in an electronic format (on a computer using dedicated software), but then printed and mailed to the IRS for filing. Those tax returns would be filed electronically by 2002.

The bill would require the Treasury secretary to create an electronic commerce advisory group composed of tax practitioners, tax preparers who use electronic filing and other representatives from the electronic filing industry. The chairman of the electronic advisory group, the chairman of the oversight board and the Treasury secretary would be required to report annually to the congressional tax committees on IRS's programs in implementing its plan to meet the goal of 80 percent electronic filing by 2007.

Signatures on Tax Returns

The bill would direct the IRS to develop procedures to eliminate the need to file a paper form with a signature, and to allow signatures to be accepted digitally or in another electronic form. The bill would clarify that such "alternative signatures" are treated legally as signatures.

Return-Free System

The bill would require the IRS to study the feasibility of, and develop procedures for, the implementation of a return-free tax system after 2007. The agreement would require that an annual report be filed on the progress of the development of such a system, including what additional resources the IRS would need to implement the system, the changes to the tax code that would facilitate the system, the procedures developed to date, and the number and classes of taxpayers who would be permitted to use such a system. The first report would be to the congressional tax committees would be due on June 30, 1999.

Electronic Access to Accounts

The bill would require the IRS to establish, by 2007, a means by which taxpayers who file their tax returns electronically could access their accounts electronically, but it specifies that "all necessary privacy safeguards" must be in place by that date. The bill would require an interim progress report be issued to the congressional tax-writing committees by Dec. 31, 2003.

The Joint Committee on Taxation estimates that the above provisions will have no revenue effect.

Taxpayer Rights

Since 1995, Congress has enacted two so-called Taxpayer Bill of Rights. The bill includes provisions that would constitute the third in the progression, and under the House bill were labeled "Taxpayer Bill of Rights III."

Burden of Proof

Under current law, the taxpayer must prove that the claims of tax liability made by the IRS are not valid — that is, the burden of proof is on the taxpayer. The bill would shift the burden of proof to the IRS in disputes dealing with income, estate and gift taxes that come before the U.S. Tax Court.

Under the bill, the burden of proof would be on the IRS in tax court proceedings if the taxpayer has cooperated with the IRS by providing access to witnesses, information and documents within the control of the taxpayer. The bill specifies that corporations and partnerships whose net worth exceeds $7 million would not be eligible for the shift of burden of proof to the IRS.

Estimated cost: $2.7 billion over 10 years.

Innocent Spouse Relief

The bill would make it significantly easier for a joint filer to claim "innocent spouse" status when the IRS finds that his or her spouse has made mistakes on a tax return. (Under current law, spouses who file a joint return are each fully responsible for the accuracy of the return — and for the full tax liability — even when only one spouse has earned the income shown on the return. Relief from tax liability, interest and penalties is available for innocent spouses only in certain limited circumstances.)

The bill would effectively expand the number of instances in which a spouse can claim ignorance by, for example, allowing the IRS to take into account "all the facts and circumstances" of a particular case.

The bill also would limit a spouse's tax liability to the proportion of the couple's income for which the spouse is responsible — but only for those spouses who are no longer married, legally separated, or have been living apart for at least 12 months.

The bill would specifically provide the tax court with jurisdiction to review any IRS denial of, or its failure to rule on, an application for innocent spouse relief. A spouse whose application for relief is denied would be able file a petition for determination in tax court within 90 days of the denial. The bill also would direct the Treasury Department to develop a separate form with instructions for taxpayers to use in applying for innocent spouse relief.

Estimated cost: $1.4 billion over 10 years.

Filing of Refund Claims During Disability

The bill would suspend the statute of limitations on claims for refunds by taxpayers who are unable to manage their financial affairs due to "a medically determinable physical or mental impairment" of 12 months or more, unless the taxpayer's spouse or another person has been authorized to act on the taxpayer's behalf.

Estimated cost: $241 million over 10 years.

Taxes

Authority To Award Costs

The bill would expand IRS authority to award administrative and litigation costs to any person who prevails in a tax case. The bill would:

● **Reset the clock.** Change the point in time at which both the position of the government is determined and after which reasonable administrative costs can be awarded, to include the date on which the first letter of proposed tax deficiency (which allows the taxpayer an opportunity for administrative review) is sent.

● **Attorneys' fees.** Permit the award of attorneys' fees to specified persons who represent a taxpayer who is a prevailing party.

It also would provide for the awarding of reasonable costs and attorneys' fees to a taxpayer if the taxpayer makes an offer after he or she has a right to administrative review in the IRS Office of Appeals, the IRS rejects the offer, and later the IRS obtains a judgment against the taxpayer in an amount that is equal to or less than the taxpayer's offer for the amount of the liability (excluding interest).

And it would clarify that the award of attorneys' fees is permitted in action for civil damages for unauthorized inspection or disclosure of taxpayer returns and return information.

● **Equalize treatment by region.** Provide that in determining whether the government's position was substantially justified, the court shall take into account whether the government has lost in a court of appeal in other circuits on substantially similar issues.

Estimated cost: $145 million over 10 years.

Civil Damages for Negligence

The bill would expand current law to allow a taxpayer to sue the federal government for up to $100,000 in civil damages caused by IRS employees who "negligently" disregard provisions of the tax code. (Current law allows a taxpayer to sue the government for civil damages caused by an IRS employee who "recklessly" or "intentionally" disregards a provision of the tax code in connection with the collection of federal taxes; in those cases, the damages can be up to $1 million.)

The bill would specify that no one would be entitled to seek civil damages for negligence, or reckless or intentional disregard of the tax code or regulations, until all administrative remedies have been exhausted.

The bill also would permit a taxpayer to sue the federal government for up to $1 million in civil damages caused by an IRS employee who willfully violates provisions of bankruptcy law that allow automatic stays (non-collection of owed debts) or discharges.

And the bill would allow persons other than the taxpayer to sue the federal government for civil damages for unauthorized collection activities.

Estimated cost: $247 million over 10 years.

Taxpayer Audits/Collections

The bill would define what the taxpayer advocate must consider when issuing a "taxpayer assistance order" that, for example, would release property of the taxpayer that has been levied upon, or require the IRS to cease action against the taxpayer.

Before issuing the order, the taxpayer advocate would be required to consider whether there is an immediate threat of adverse actions; whether there has been a delay of more than 30 days in resolving the taxpayer's account problems; whether the taxpayer will have to pay significant costs, including fees for professional representation, if relief is not granted; and whether the taxpayer will suffer irreparable injury, or long-term adverse impact if relief is not granted.

The bill would prohibit the IRS from seizing residences to satisfy unpaid tax liabilities of less than $5,000, and prohibit the IRS from seizing a taxpayer's home without a court order.

The bill also would do the following with regard to taxpayer audits and IRS collection activities:

● **Accountant-client privilege.** Extend the common-law practice of attorney-client privilege to a taxpayer's dealings with any individual (generally tax accountants and advisers) authorized to practice before the IRS.

● **Extension of limits.** Require that each time the IRS asks a taxpayer to extend the statute of limitations on further assessment by the IRS (usually three years from first contact), that the taxpayer has the right to refuse any extension, or to limit the extension to particular issues.

● **Petition deadline.** Require the IRS to include on each deficiency notice to a taxpayer the date on which the taxpayer may file a petition with the Tax Court.

● **Third-party contact.** Prohibit the IRS from contacting any person other than the taxpayer with respect to the determination or collection of a tax liability, without providing reasonable notice to the taxpayer that third parties may be contacted.

● **Specified contacts.** Prohibit the IRS from issuing a summons for any third-party tax-related records, unless the IRS is unable to otherwise reasonably ascertain the correctness of an item on a return from the taxpayer's records, and the IRS first identifies with reasonable specificity where the information could be found.

● **Living allowance.** Direct the IRS to develop and publish a list of national and local allowances for living expenses to ensure that taxpayers who offer to settle an unpaid tax account retain adequate means to provide for basic living expenses, and require the IRS to prepare a statement of the rights of taxpayers and the obligations of the IRS relating to "offer in compromise."

● **Low-income settlements.** Prohibit the IRS from rejecting an offer of compromise from a low-income taxpayer solely on the basis of the amount of the offer.

● **Restaurant tipsters.** Prohibit the IRS from threatening to audit a restaurant because it does not enter into a Tip Reporting Alternative Commitment agreement, which obligates restaurant owners to educate their employees on tip-reporting obligations.

Estimated cost: $577 million over 10 years.

Penalty Relief for Taxpayers

The bill would suspend interest and certain penalties when the IRS does not provide appropriate notice to a taxpayer within 18 months after a return is filed; beginning in 2004, IRS must provide notice within 12 months.

The measure also would do the following relating to interest and penalty relief for taxpayers:

● **Installment penalty.** Reduce the "failure to pay" penalty by one-half while the taxpayer is paying off a tax liability in an installment agreement.

● **Payroll deposits.** Allow small businesses to designate deposits for each payroll period to prevent cascading penalties.

● **Penalty notices.** Require each penalty and interest notice to include a computation of the penalty or interest.

● **Management sign-off.** Require management approval of non-computer generated penalties.

Estimated cost: $5.2 billion over 10 years.

Disclosures to Taxpayers

The bill would require the IRS to print and make available to taxpayers explanations, definitions and clarifications on a variety of matters.

It would specify that the IRS must establish procedures to alert married taxpayers of their "joint and several" liability on all appropriate tax publications and instructions. (Joint and several liability means that spouses who file a joint tax return are each fully responsible for the accuracy of the return and for the full tax liability, even if only one spouse earned the income shown on the return.)

IRS Overhaul

The bill would require that general tax form instruction booklets include a description of conditions under which tax return information may be disclosed outside the IRS.

The bill would require that, no later than 180 days after the date of enactment, a description of the entire process from examination through collections — including the assistance available to taxpayers from the national taxpayer advocate at various points in the process — be provided with the first letter of proposed deficiency that allows a taxpayer an opportunity for administration review in the office of appeals.

It also would require the IRS to notify a taxpayer of the specific reasons for the disallowance, or partial disallowance, of a refund claim.

Estimated cost: less than $25 million over 10 years.

Low-Income Taxpayer Clinics

The bill would require the Treasury Department to make matching grants for the development, expansion or continuation of low-income taxpayer clinics.

Eligible clinics would be those that charge no more than a nominal fee to either represent low-income taxpayers in controversies with the IRS, or provide tax information to individuals for whom English is a second language. The bill would define "clinic" as a program at an accredited law school in which students represent low-income taxpayers, and as a nonprofit, tax-exempt organization that either represents low-income taxpayers or provides referral to qualified representatives.

The bill would limit the aggregate amount of grants to be awarded each year to $6 million, and no one taxpayer clinic could receive more than $100,000 a year. The clinics would have to provide matching funds on a dollar-for-dollar basis; the grants could pay for faculty and clinic administration salaries and clinic equipment costs.

The measure also would outline the criteria to be considered by the Treasury Department when making grant awards — the number of taxpayers served by the clinic, including the number of taxpayers in the geographical area for whom English is a second language; the existence of other taxpayer clinics serving the same population; the quality of the program; and alternative funding sources available to the clinic.

The Joint Committee on Taxation estimated that the above provisions would have no revenue effect.

Congressional Oversight

Reviews and Hearings

The bill would require the Joint Committee on Taxation to review all requests (other than requests by the chairman or ranking member of a committee or subcommittee of Congress) for investigations of the IRS by the General Accounting Office (GAO), and approve such requests when appropriate.

The bill would require two annual joint hearings of two majority members and one minority member of each of the House Ways and Means, Appropriations, and Government Reform and Oversight committees, and the Senate Finance, Appropriations, and Government Affairs committees. The bill would specify that the first annual meeting take place before April 1 each year, to review the strategic plans and budget for the IRS. The second annual meeting would be sometime after April 15, to review the strategic and business plans for the IRS; the budget for the IRS and whether it supports IRS objectives; the progress of the IRS in improving taxpayer service and compliance; and progress of the IRS in technology modernization.

The bill also would require the Joint Committee on Taxation to submit an annual report to the standing congressional tax committees on the overall status of the federal tax system, together with recommendations on possible simplification proposals.

Complexity Analysis

The bill states the sense of Congress that the IRS should provide the Congress with an independent view of tax administration, and that the tax-writing committees would hear analysis from IRS technical experts during the legislative process on how proposed tax provisions would be administered.

The bill also would require the Joint Committee on Taxation, in consultation with the IRS and the Treasury Department, to provide a "tax complexity analysis" for tax legislation that identifies those provisions in the bill or conference report that add significant complexity to the tax law, or that provide significant simplification.

Under the bill, a point of order could be raised in the House during floor consideration of a bill or conference report if the measure does not contain the required complexity analysis. The bill allows the point of order to be waived, however, by majority vote.

Miscellaneous Provisions

House-Senate conferees added several provisions to their report that were not in either the original House or Senate bill, including the following.

Capital Gains

The bill would reduce from 18 months to 12 months the time a taxpayer is required to hold investments before selling them in order to qualify for a reduced, 20 percent tax rate on the profits (capital gains). The provision would be effective beginning with gains realized Jan. 1, 1999.

Last year's tax bill (PL 105-34) had reduced the maximum tax rate on capital gains from the sale of stocks and other investments from 28 percent to 20 percent for investments held at least 18 months.

Estimated cost: $2.1 billion over 10 years.

Tax Treatment of Employer-Provided Meals

The bill would clarify that meals provided on the employer's premises, for the convenience of the employer, where more than half of the employees receive the meal, would not be taxable to the employees, and would be fully deductible to the employer. (Employer-provided, on-premises meals are commonly provided by casino operators.)

Estimated cost: $316 million over 10 years.

MFN Name Change

The bill would change the language in trade law regarding "most favored nation" trade status — a classification that currently applies to all but seven countries in the world. The term "most favored nation" would be replaced by the term "normal trade relation."

The Joint Committee on Taxation estimates that the above provision will have no revenue effect.

Surface Transportation Act Corrections

The bill includes provisions similar to HR 3978, which passed the House on June 3 by voice vote, and which would make numerous technical and other changes to the recently enacted six-year highway and transit law (PL 105-178). That corrections bill has not been considered separately in the Senate.

The transportation law contained a provision that would deny disability payments to veterans suffering from smoking-related ailments not directly related to their service. The provision was designed to generate $15.4 billion in savings to offset part of the cost of the transportation law.

Taxes

Among other provisions, the bill would clarify that those veterans provisions in PL 105-178 do not affect the disability payments of veterans who smoke, but whose illnesses result from other causes (such as herbicides and chemical weapons), and it would increase by 20 percent funding for Veterans Administration educational assistance for veterans' survivors and dependents.

The measure also would modify or clarify dozens of the 1,850 highway and other projects earmarked for the states and districts of specific members.

And it would enact two provisions to help prevent drunken driving that were inadvertently omitted from PL 105-178. Under the measure, states that fail to enact laws making it illegal to possess open containers of alcohol in a vehicle would be required to transfer 1.5 percent of their federal highway construction funds to highway safety programs. Similarly, states would have to transfer 1.5 percent of construction money to safety programs if they fail to adopt tougher penalties for repeat drunk-driving offenses.

No Joint Committee on Taxation estimate was immediately available.

Revenue-Raising Offsets

HR 2676 is projected to reduce federal revenues by $12.9 billion over 10 years. The major revenue-raising provisions that are intended to offset those revenue losses are described below.

Individual Retirement Accounts

The bill would raise an estimated $8 billion over 10 years by permitting wealthy elderly persons to convert traditional individual retirement accounts (IRAs) into so-called Roth IRAs, and pay taxes on the converted money.

Last year's tax law (PL 105-34) created a new IRA — known as the Roth IRA after its sponsor, Senate Finance Committee Chairman William V. Roth Jr., R-Del. — to which taxpayers may make contributions that are not tax deductible, but from which they may make tax-free withdrawals so long as certain conditions are met.

Individuals also were permitted to convert traditional IRAs into a Roth IRA — paying taxes on the converted amount — if their adjusted gross annual income was less than $100,000. Under current law, individuals over the age of 70 1/2 must withdraw a minimum amount from an IRA each year, and such withdrawals count toward the income threshold for converting a traditional IRA into a Roth IRA.

The conference agreement would provide that required annual withdrawals from IRAs would not count in calculating an individual's eligibility to convert traditional IRAs into Roth IRAs. If, for example, required annual withdrawals from IRAs push a couple's annual income to more than $100,000, the couple could still convert a traditional IRA into a Roth IRA, and take advantage of future tax-free withdrawals from the new Roth IRA.

Because they would pay taxes on the converted amount, federal revenues would increase. But, if the converted funds are left in the Roth IRA long enough, the revenue lost due to the tax-free withdrawals from the Roth IRA would be greater than the taxes paid on the converted IRA money.

Employer Deductions for Vacation Pay

The measure would raise an estimated $4.1 billion over 10 years by prohibiting employers from claiming deductions for vacation or severance pay that would be granted to employees in a tax year other than the one in which the dedication was made. ◆

GOP Reluctantly Agrees To Include Tax Provisions In Omnibus Spending Bill

Republican leaders began 1998 hoping for a major tax cut, perhaps on the order of $100 billion over five years. By the time Congress adjourned, they could barely eke out a $9.2 billion, largely housekeeping measure that extended expired tax credits and accelerated a health insurance deduction for the self-employed.

President Clinton set the tone for the year in his State of the Union address, in which he urged lawmakers to leave the projected budget surplus untouched until the government could ensure the long-term solvency of the Social Security Trust Fund. His simple refrain, "Save Social Security first," froze tax cutters in their tracks.

SUMMARY

In the months following the January speech, GOP leaders vacillated between taking on Clinton with a major tax cut, or assembling a comparatively minor tax package that would be offset with revenue raisers. The conflict torpedoed efforts to assemble a budget resolution, as Republicans could not bridge the gap between a House plan to cut taxes by $101 billion over five years, and the Senate version, which would have made no net cuts.

Giving up on a budget blueprint, the House in September passed an $80.1 billion, five-year tax cut (HR 4579 — H Rept 105-739). Assembled for maximum political appeal, the plan would have reduced taxes for certain married couples, farmers and the self-employed; granted deductions for interest on savings accounts, and provided new tax incentives for low-income areas.

Democrats praised many bill provisions. Yet they lined up against it because it would tap the projected budget surplus. The House passed the measure on a mostly partisan vote, giving it lit-

Box Score

● **Bill:** HR 4328 — PL 105-277

● **House action:** The House adopted the conference agreement on HR 4328, 333-95, on Oct. 20. It passed HR 4738 by voice vote Oct. 10, and passed HR 4579, 229-195, on Sept. 26.

● **Senate action:** The Senate cleared HR 4328 by voice vote Oct. 21.

● **Presidential action:** Clinton signed HR 4328 on Oct. 21.

tle momentum in the final weeks of the session.

With the Social Security issue exerting a powerful political pull, Senate Democrats and moderate Republicans opposed the bill. Unable to assemble a Finance Committee majority, and facing the prospect of Clinton scoring political points with an eventual veto if Congress ever cleared the bill, Senate Majority Leader Trent Lott, R-Miss., decided against bringing it to the floor.

But lawmakers came under heavy pressure from the business community to salvage one piece of the tax bill — a plan to extend expired tax credits, including one for corporate research and development. The House swiftly passed a nine-year, $9.2 billion plan (HR 4738 — H Rept 105-817) to extend the credits and give tax breaks to farmers and the self-employed.

The Finance Committee responded with an informal $8.5 billion package, which would have extended additional tax credits, but for shorter amounts of time. Unable to reach agreement on a stand-alone tax bill, leaders merged elements of the House and Senate plans and added them to the omnibus spending bill (HR 4328).

Archer's Tax Bill Moves in House; Democrats Dig In On Social Security

SEPTEMBER 19 — As end-of-session politics grow ever more surreal, a GOP-backed tax bill with Democratic provisions won House Ways and Means approval on Sept. 17, sparking rare harmony on tax policy but faint prospects of a change in law.

The $80.1 billion measure (HR 4579) may be considered by the full House as early as the week of Sept. 21. But with Senate Democrats lining up in opposition because the bill would tap the projected budget surplus, and the White House threatening a veto, the plan appears destined for campaign ads rather than the internal revenue code.

Democrats are opposing the bill to demonstrate that their top priority is preserving the solvency of the Social Security trust fund. Republicans are gearing up to batter incumbents who block tax cuts.

"Since the American people are paying too much in income taxes, I can't imagine why anyone would want to punish America's husbands and wives, farmers and ranchers, small-business people and senior citizens by denying them tax relief now," said committee Chairman Bill Archer, R-Texas, in his opening statement.

Signaling that the markup was primarily political theater, Ways and Means members refrained from offering any amendments to grant tax breaks to special interests. Instead, virtually the entire debate centered on a lone Democratic amendment, rejected on a party-line vote of 15-23, that would have delayed most of the tax cuts until the Social Security trust fund was certified as actuarially sound.

The committee then approved the measure by a mostly partisan vote, 23-15. One Democrat, Barbara B. Kennelly of Connecticut, joined Republicans in support.

Archer had designed the bill with an eye to wooing Democrats. The plan would grant tax breaks to local school boards and low-income communities, and primarily benefit the middle class, not the affluent.

But Democrats refused to take the bait, and the embattled White House, which some had thought would bow to GOP demands, instead dug in for a fight.

"The president will veto any tax cut or spending bill that changes the budget rules and drains the surplus before we have a bipartisan plan in place to strengthen Social Security," White House Chief of Staff Erskine B. Bowles wrote Archer just before the markup. The same day, President Clinton scoffed at GOP plans to tap the government's first surplus since 1969. "Shouldn't we see the ink turn from red to black and then watch it dry for a minute or two before we get carried away?" he asked.

It is unclear, however, whether Clinton will get a chance to break out his veto pen. The Archer plan faces opposition in the Senate from a coalition of Democrats and moderate Republicans reluctant to tap the surplus, and GOP leaders may lack the votes to steer any major tax-cut bill through the Finance Committee.

Instead, the leaders are considering attaching tax provisions to an appropriations measure, forcing Clinton into a choice between accepting the bill or vetoing popular spending measures. But such a showdown may be risky, because the president has nothing to lose by changing the subject away from his legal woes.

Also, with little time left this session, and 60 senators needed to overcome a filibuster, the prospects of Senate passage are uncertain. "We have a time factor here, and we have the procedural hurdles," said Finance Committee spokeswoman Ginny Flynn. "At this point, we don't know what's going to happen."

Democratic Appeal

The bill's demise, oddly, would be as much a disappointment to its Democratic opponents as to its GOP authors. That is because it would grant tax relief primarily to middle-income households earning from $30,000 to $100,000 annually, and targets traditional Democratic constituencies, including senior citizens and residents of low-income communities.

Indeed, Democrats at the markup heaped lavish praise on the measure. Pete Stark of California called it "great"; fellow Californian Robert T. Matsui called it "wonderful," and Benjamin L. Cardin of Maryland said: "The provisions are good provisions. I hope they become law."

Many people outside Congress also hailed the provisions. The bill would give an average annual tax cut of $243 to married couples, who frequently owe proportionately higher taxes than individuals; grant deductions to the self-employed, who are struggling with ever-higher health insurance premiums; and offer tax relief to farmers, who are facing a disastrous year.

But the rub is that, according to Democrats, the government lacks the money to pay for it. Of the projected $1.6 trillion surplus over the next 10 years, 98 percent is generated by payroll taxes for Social Security. Indeed, were it not for Social Security, the budget would be facing an estimated deficit in the next five years of $137 billion.

The Social Security trust fund is expected to run out of money by

Highlights of the House Tax Bill

The bill (HR 4579) approved Sept. 17 by the House Ways and Means Committee would cut taxes by $80.1 billion over five years. Most of that money would come from tapping the projected budget surplus, but $5.6 billion would be raised by closing a tax loophole for real estate investment trusts and regulated investment companies.

Following are highlights of the package, with five-year cost estimates by the Joint Committee on Taxation.

- **Married couples.** The bill would increase the standard deduction for married couples so that each spouse would have the same deduction as a single filer. As a result, the deduction for married couples would increase from $7,200 to $8,600 in 1999, reducing their taxes by an average of $243 per return. The deduction for singles would remain at $4,300.

  The intent is to pare back the "marriage penalty," a wrinkle in tax law that results in many married people owing higher taxes than they would owe if they were single. Cost: $28 billion.

- **Interest and dividends.** Individuals, regardless of their income, would be able to exclude up to $200 of combined interest and dividends from taxes. Married couples could exclude $400. Cost: $15 billion.

- **Estate tax.** The bill would provide an exemption from estate taxes of $1 million for deaths that occur or gifts that are made in 1999 and later. Under current law, the exemption is $600,000, and slated to increase gradually to $1 million in 2006. Cost: $17.9 billion.

- **Self-employed.** Beginning in 1999, the self-employed would be able to deduct 100 percent of their health insurance premiums. At present, they can deduct 45 percent, which is scheduled to increase to 100 percent in 2007 under current law. Cost: $5.1 billion.

- **Non-refundable personal credits.** Taxpayers would be able to claim certain personal credits (such as the dependent care credit, the adoption credit, the child tax credit and others) without having to face an additional individual minimum tax. Under the plan, the personal tax credits would offset the minimum tax liability as well as an individual's regular income tax liability, thereby preventing minimum tax liabilities from kicking in. Cost: $8.1 billion.

- **Social Security.** Senior citizens ages 65 to 69 would be able to earn up to $17,000 in 1999 without losing a portion of their Social Security benefits. The earnings limit would gradually rise to $30,000 in 2002 and $39,750 in 2008. Current law would permit the earnings limit to rise to $37,948 in 2008, but at a slower pace. Cost: $550 million.

  This proposal would be paid for by a one-year delay in reassessing — and raising — the Social Security benefits of a senior citizen who continues working, and earns increasingly higher salaries. The amount raised would be $570 million.

- **School construction.** The bill would liberalize the laws that cover tax exempt bonds issued to finance public school construction. School districts would have four years to spend the money after the bonds were issued, rather than the current requirement of two years. Cost: $1.4 billion.

- **Higher education.** The bill would grant a tax deferral to prepaid tuition programs that are established by private universities and other private higher education schools. This is an expansion of current law, which grants the tax exemption only to state-run higher education facilities. Cost: $572 million.

- **Government bonds.** States would be able to issue more private activity tax-exempt bonds, which typically finance privately owned transportation facilities, municipal services, economic development projects and social programs. The current annual limits of $50 per resident or $150 million (whichever is greater) would be increased to $75 per resident or $225 million. Cost: $1.1 billion.

- **Farmers.** The bill would permanently extend "income averaging" for farmers, which under current law would expire in 2000. Rather than pay high taxes in a good year, a farmer would have the option of paying a tax based on the average income of the preceding three years.

  Farmers also could reduce their tax burden by applying an operating loss in one year to their taxable income in any one of five past years, or to a future year. Under current law, they can apply it to two past years or to a future year. Cost: $126 million.

- **Business expensing.** Starting in 1999, small-business owners and farmers would be able to deduct up to $25,000 of the cost of business-related equipment. Under current law, the deduction is limited to $18,500 and is slated to rise to $25,000 in 2003. Cost: $1.1 billion.

- **Renewal communities.** To spur the revitalization of depressed areas, the proposal would grant a variety of tax incentives to businesses and individuals in 20 "renewal communities." These low-income areas would be designated by the secretary of Housing and Urban Development, and existing enterprise communities or empowerment zones could apply.

  The incentives would include a 100 percent capital gains exclusion on certain investments. Cost: $1 billion.

- **Expired credits.** Several tax credits that expired this year or would expire next year, including credits for research, work opportunity and welfare-to-work, would be extended through Feb. 29, 2000. The credit for contributions of stock to private foundations would be extended permanently. Cost: $6.2 billion.

about 2030 because of retiring Baby Boomers, so Democrats argued that tapping the surplus would amount to an unconscionable raid on the country's main retirement account. "Mr. Archer's proposal is clever, but it is not responsible," said Rep. Sander M. Levin, D-Mich.

Republicans retorted that their plan to cut taxes by $80.1 billion over five years (or $177 billion over 10 years) would take money only from general revenues, not the currently flush Social Security fund, and leave intact most of the surplus. In fact, Archer dubbed his bill the "90-10" plan because it would reserve about 90 percent of the surplus until lawmakers shored up Social Security.

"There is not one thing before the committee today that would impact upon the Social Security fund," said E. Clay Shaw Jr., R-Fla., chairman of the Human Resources Subcommittee. He added: "If you have a surplus and you fail to return it to the American people, Washington spends it."

Rather than trying to change the bill's tax provisions, Democrats united behind an amendment by ranking Democrat Charles B. Rangel of New York to defer most of the tax cuts until Congress took action to ensure the long-term solvency of Social Security. Only when the trust fund's board of trustees certified that the fund was in actuarial balance could the tax cuts take effect — a proposal that Republicans in unison decried as a poison pill.

The outcome was so pre-ordained that Democrats, prior to offering the amendment, distributed a news release assailing Republicans for successfully defeating it.

The debate did little to dispel the notion that Congress is mired in partisan deadlock. Rather than discuss bill provisions, members repeatedly went over technical budget matters outside the committee's normal purview, such as whether the bill's violation of "pay as you go" budget rules would cause a sequestration of Medicare funds.

"That discussion shed no light on anything," a frustrated Bill Thomas, R-Calif., said at the end of the markup.

The committee also approved, by voice vote, an Archer bill (HR 4578) that would give Republicans some political cover on Social Security. It would establish a reserve account within the Treasury to hold 90 percent of the budget surplus until Congress ensured the long-term solvency of the retirement fund. The committee rejected, 15-22, a Rangel amendment to wall off the entire surplus.

Chances Look Slim For House-Passed Tax Measure

OCTOBER 3 — With a GOP-backed tax bill apparently doomed, lawmakers are quietly beginning to talk about a much more modest goal: clearing a housekeeping measure that could cost up to $6.2 billion to extend expired tax provisions.

"Plan B is a narrow extenders package, fully paid for," said Ari Fleischer, spokesman for the House Ways and Means Committee.

Some of the provisions, such as a tax credit for research and development, are a top priority of business lobbyists. But in the final days of an election-year session, even a measure that has broad bipartisan support could run into trouble with last-minute Senate holds and amendments.

Before members can focus on such a minimal package, though, they need to fully expend their rhetoric on more ambitious election-year tax cut proposals. The partisan debate over the issue may last until the final days of the session, with the Senate expected to take up a bill (HR 4579) that would cut taxes by $80.1 billion over five years.

The House on Sept. 26 passed HR 4579 on a largely partisan vote of 229-195. All but 19 Democrats present voted against the bill, as did 11 Republicans, which gave the measure little momentum as it moved to the Senate. (Vote 469, p. H-134)

Most Senate Democrats, joined by a few moderate Republicans, oppose the plan. They say it would be wrong to tap the projected $1.6 trillion surplus until efforts are made to shore up the Social Security trust fund, which is expected to run out of money about 2030.

Even though bill supporters respond that they are reserving 90 percent of the projected surplus to protect Social Security, they are finding it hard to round up a 51-vote majority. A 60-vote supermajority to overcome a possible filibuster appears far out of reach.

Indeed, Democrats have such a strong hand that Senate Minority Leader Tom Daschle, D-S.D., said he may not even try to filibuster the bill. If Republicans can garner a majority vote, he said Sept. 29, then he is inclined to allow the bill to go through the Senate and let President Clinton score political points by vetoing it.

To prevent such a scenario, Senate Majority Leader Trent Lott, R-Miss., may decline to bring up the bill for a floor vote.

Democrats are floating a $25 billion plan that would be offset by revenue raisers, but Republicans dismissed it as far too small.

The Democrats have emphasized Social Security since Clinton urged Congress in his 1998 State of the Union address not to spend any of the projected surplus before safeguarding the Social Security trust fund. That strategy is working so well that White House spokesman Mike McCurry said Oct. 1: "It looks like we won that fight."

To Republicans, Clinton's position is hypocritical. After all, he has proposed tapping the surplus by billions of dollars to pay for emergency spending measures this year.

And if conservatives cannot get their tax cuts this year, then Clinton should be forced to give up on his supplemental spending requests as well, they say.

"Let's keep the president at his word," said a frustrated Sen. Phil Gramm, R-Texas. "Let's save Social Security next year, then have a tax cut. And let's also not spend $20 billion on supplemental spending."

Focus Shifts To Renewing Tax Credits

OCTOBER 10 — As lawmakers went down to the wire trying to clear a package of popular tax credit extensions, they put aside partisan rhetoric but faced nettlesome House-Senate differences.

The House Ways and Means Com-

Taxes

mittee took just 10 minutes Oct. 9 to give voice vote approval to a $9.2 billion, nine-year tax bill (HR 4738).

The plan would extend the research tax credit through 1999 and extend six other credits for varying lengths of time. It would also grant the self-employed a 100 percent deduction for health insurance premiums, beginning in 2003.

Instead of tapping the budget surplus, the bill would be fully offset with several revenue raisers, including the closing of a loophole for real estate investment trusts.

Trying to shepherd the bill through quickly, members gave voice vote approval to one amendment, offered by Chairman Bill Archer, R-Texas, that would give states from Jan. 1 to March 31, 1999, to decide whether to exempt students employed by schools from Social Security coverage.

But hours after the Ways and Means markup, the Senate Finance Committee met informally to assemble its own plan — casting grave doubt that lawmakers could clear a freestanding bill in the time remaining. However, one option would be to tack on tax provisions to an omnibus spending bill.

The Senate tax package, estimated at about $8.5 billion over nine years, would extend 10 expiring provisions, rather than the seven in the House plan. These would include the trade adjustment assistance program, which helps train U.S. workers who lose their jobs because of trade agreements.

To hold down costs, several credits, including the one for research, would expire June 30, 1999.

The Senate plan would make the deduction for the self-employed effective in 2002.

Thwarted by Split Over Taxes, GOP Looks to 1999

OCTOBER 17 — Their onetime goal of a $100 billion-plus tax cut shattered, Republicans agreed Oct. 15 to add a nine-year, $9.2 billion package of tax provisions to the omnibus spending bill.

The plan will extend popular expired tax credits, including a high-profile credit for business research. It will also accelerate a phase-in of health insurance deductions for the self-employed, grant a tax break to people claiming a child care tax credit and other deductions, and continue training for U.S. workers displaced by trade agreements.

Republicans put their best faces on the largely housekeeping plan, promising to make tax cuts a high priority in 1999.

"The reason why we didn't move tax cuts this year is because the Democrats don't like tax cuts," Senate Majority Leader Trent Lott, R-Miss., said Oct. 15. "But that's going to be right at the top of our priority list next year."

Since the research tax credit, a major issue for business lobbyists, will expire again on June 30, 1999, Congress appears certain to take up some type of tax legislation next year. Deductions for married couples and small businesses would likely be high on the GOP agenda, along with estate and capital gains tax cuts.

Whether Republicans have any more success next year depends on such factors as the outcome of the Nov. 3 elections and the state of the economy. Complicating matters, President Clinton and many lawmakers insist on shoring up the Social Security Trust Fund before tapping the budget surplus for tax cuts.

Blaming the other party for failed legislation is a hardy perennial of politics, but Republicans share much of the fault this year when it comes to taxes.

The GOP split hopelessly for months between conservatives who wanted to cut taxes by $101 billion or more over five years and moderates who would agree only to a comparatively minor tax cut that would not tap the budget surplus.

Up until the last two days of the session, the chairmen of the House and Senate tax-writing committees — Sen. William V. Roth Jr., R-Del., and Rep. Bill Archer, R-Texas — could not come to terms on even a bare-bones, bipartisan package of tax credit extensions.

Archer insisted on allowing Texas and other states to exempt students employed by schools from paying Social Security taxes, despite Roth's objections.

Archer rejected a Roth proposal to extend an alternative energy tax credit, and he opposed an extension of the Trade Adjustment Assistance Program, which retrains workers who lose their jobs due to trade agreements.

Like two 18th-century gentlemen turning their backs on each other to begin a duel, Archer and Roth ultimately gave up on their talks and pursued conflicting tax bills.

The House passed Archer's $9.2 billion plan Oct. 10 by voice vote. Roth countered by winning the informal approval of the Finance Committee for a nine-year, $8.5 billion plan that would extend eight tax credits and two trade provisions.

Over the next couple of days, the so-called tax extenders appeared in deep trouble because Senate leaders could not win a unanimous consent agreement to bring either plan to the floor. Several senators objected to the House plan because it did not include the trade assistance provision, and Sen. Phil Gramm, R-Texas, objected to the Senate plan because it did not include the Social Security provision for students.

But House and Senate negotiators ultimately split the difference, including both the Social Security language and the trade program in the tax package that they added to the omnibus spending bill (HR 4328).

The final plan will extend eight expiring tax and trade provisions, but not the alternative energy credit. The extensions are designed to help people who contribute stock to private foundations, U.S. shareholders of foreign corporations and employers of disadvantaged workers.

The plan will grant the self-employed a 100 percent deduction for health insurance premiums beginning in 2003. It will allow taxpayers to claim personal credits, such as the child tax credit, without facing an additional alternative minimum tax.

It will also increase the cap on private activity bonds, helping local governments fund various projects.

The $9.2 billion plan will be offset by several revenue raisers, including closing a loophole for real estate investment trusts. An additional $600 million of tax breaks for farmers, added to the omnibus spending bill, will be paid out of the surplus. ◆

Internet Tax Moratorium

High-Tech Industry Cheers Enactment of Moratorium On New Internet Taxes

Box Score

- **Bill:** HR 4328 — PL 105-277
- **House action:** The House adopted the conference report on HR 4328 (H Rept 105-825), 333-95, on Oct. 20. The House passed HR 4105 on June 23 by voice vote.
- **Senate action:** The Senate cleared HR 4328, 65-29, Oct. 21. The Senate passed S 442 (S Rept 105-276), 96-2, on Oct. 8.
- **Presidential action:** Clinton signed HR 4328 on Oct 21.

SUMMARY

After months of negotiations, the high-tech industry scored a major victory when the Senate cleared legislation placing a three-year moratorium on new taxes imposed on Internet access and commerce.

During the required timeout period, a 19-member commission will study how taxes should be applied to the Internet. The measure was included in the fiscal 1999 omnibus spending bill (HR 4328 — PL 105-277).

When the moratorium legislation was first introduced in 1997, it drew harsh criticism from state and local government leaders who said it would unfairly and unnecessarily pre-empt their taxing authority. They expressed particular concern about the potential impact on sales taxes, which the National Governors' Association said made up almost half of state revenues. But subsequent negotiations gave them enough concessions to withdraw their opposition. (1997 Almanac, p. 3-40)

Key changes included a grandfather clause allowing states that were collecting Internet access taxes before Oct. 1, 1998, to continue doing so, and a provision instructing the commission to examine whether states should be allowed to require companies to collect sales taxes from customers in states where the companies do not have a physical presence.

Under current law, companies are not required to collect such levies, a loophole that state and local officials say has cost them billions of dollars.

The House passed a revised bill (HR 4105) reflecting the negotiations in June. After a lengthy debate, the Senate passed its own carefully crafted compromise (S 442) on Oct. 8.

Rather than holding further negotiations to finalize a stand-alone measure, the Senate added S 442 to the year-end omnibus spending bill that was making its way through Congress.

House Commerce Committee OKs Moratorium

MAY 16 — Efforts to impose a moratorium on taxes aimed at the Internet have gained new life.

After months of negotiations between on-line industry representatives and state and local government officials, the House Commerce Committee on May 14 unanimously approved legislation (HR 3849) that would impose a three-year moratorium on Internet taxation.

An earlier version of the bill (HR 1054) had been stalled after being approved in October 1997 by subcommittees of the House Commerce and Judiciary committees.

HR 3849, approved 41-0, prohibits for three years taxes levied on Internet access or on-line services. It also bans the Federal Communications Commission from regulating the charges that subscribers pay for Internet access or on-line services.

The bill "is based on the simple principle that information should not be taxed," said Republican Rep. Christopher Cox of California.

The National Governors' Association (NGA), which has led negotiations on behalf of state and local officials, said it is "cautiously optimistic" about the latest version of the legislation but still has problems with parts of it.

The group said it still opposes a Senate version of the legislation (S 442), approved in November by the Commerce Committee.

However, S 442's sponsor, Ron Wyden, D-Ore., said the latest version of the House bill "looks promising," despite his earlier opposition to a compromise announced in March by Cox and the state and local officials, which formed the basis for HR 3849.

HR 3849 must still be approved by the Judiciary Committee and may be taken up by the Ways and Means Committee before it can reach the House floor. Cox said it is unlikely that the full House will act on HR 3849 before the chamber begins its Memorial Day recess May 25.

Searching for Compromise

State and local officials originally opposed a moratorium on Internet taxes, saying it would be an unfair pre-emption of state and local taxing authority.

However, the NGA, along with other state and local officials, reached a compromise with Cox on March 19.

One provision of the deal was an agreement to establish a commission to study ways to tax electronic commerce and to recommend legislation requiring companies to collect sales taxes from customers who live in states where a company does not have a physical presence.

The Supreme Court has said that under current law, a company does not have to collect sales taxes from customers in states where it does not have operations.

The issue of out-of-state sales taxes has been a growing concern for state officials, who have said their sales tax base could be threatened if companies that sell products over the Internet were allowed to take advantage of this law, used for years by mail-order companies.

In exchange for the agreement to

Taxes

address the sales tax issue in the bill, state and local officials agreed to refrain from imposing new taxes on Internet or on-line access for three years. Cox's original bill (HR 1054) called for a six-year moratorium.

But Internet service providers opposed a provision in the deal that grandfathered in existing taxes on Internet access. In addition, industry officials said state and local government officials had too much representation on the commission.

HR 3849 includes a number of concessions made by both sides:

● The grandfather clause was narrowed. States that have been enforcing taxes on Internet or other on-line access as of March 1, 1998, and want to continue doing so must pass a law specifically allowing such an action. The NGA said it opposes this provision and also expressed concern that HR 3849 does not grandfather in local taxes.

● The makeup of the commission was changed to meet the concerns of Internet and on-line industry officials. Instead of being led by someone recommended by the NGA, the 29-member commission established in HR 3849 would be headed by two people — one recommended by the NGA and the other from industry groups. At the same time, the number of commission members from the business sector would be increased from 12 to 13.

The legislation also addressed concerns of Edward J. Markey, D-Mass., that telecommunications carriers providing Internet access may try to use the bill to avoid taxes on telecommunications services.

The bill makes clear that telecommunications carriers that provide multiple services such as Internet access and cable television may exempt only Internet access or on-line services from taxes.

Second Panel Approves Ban On Internet Taxes

JUNE 20 — Legislation calling for a three-year moratorium on new Internet taxes has inched a step closer to House floor consideration, possibly before the July Fourth recess.

By voice vote, the House Judiciary Committee approved legislation (HR 3529) June 17 calling for a moratorium on new taxes such as those imposed on Internet access or on transactions that would not be taxed if conducted by telephone or mail.

During the markup, the committee, by voice vote, approved a substitute version of HR 3529 that is similar to a bill (HR 3849) approved by the House Commerce Committee in May.

HR 3849 was the result of months of negotiations among Republican Rep. Christopher Cox of California, the bill's sponsor, Internet industry representatives, and state and local government officials.

The committee, by voice vote, also approved HR 3849 after adopting an amendment striking the tax provisions from the bill. Panel members said they have jurisdiction over the tax-related provisions of the legislation and wanted to ensure they would maintain primary jurisdiction over the Internet tax measure when it moves to the floor.

The two bills approved by the Judiciary Committee could be combined by the House Rules Committee before legislation goes to the House floor, possibly as early as the week of June 22, according to a GOP aide.

Pushing for Time Out

Supporters of a moratorium say they are worried that new taxes might choke the growth of the Internet.

"I'm concerned . . . that many of the 30,000 state and local governments who are beginning to explore the possibility of imposing significant taxes and regulations on the Internet will do so," said Republican Steve Chabot of Ohio, HR 3529's sponsor.

State and local officials initially opposed the House legislation because they said it would unfairly pre-empt state and local taxing authority. But after securing some changes through negotiations with Cox, officials now say the legislation is more acceptable.

Among the key changes that state and local officials secured was the establishment of a commission, included in HR 3529, to study and make legislative recommendations on a uniform system for companies to collect sales taxes from out-of-state customers.

State and local officials have long sought to fix a loophole in existing law that does not require companies to collect sales taxes from customers in states where the companies do not have a physical presence.

But officials from the National Governors' Association (NGA) say the substitute version of HR 3529 approved by the Judiciary Committee is a step backward from legislation approved by the Commerce Committee.

Both versions included a provision grandfathering in existing taxes on Internet access, as long as states pass legislation one year after enactment.

The governors favored the grandfather clause but opposed the requirement that they pass new legislation incorporating the existing taxes. They offered to provide a list of states and cities that would be covered by the grandfather clause if this requirement were removed.

Instead, the Judiciary Committee added the list of eight states, a dozen cities in Colorado and the District of Columbia to the substitute but did not remove the provision requiring new legislation.

The panel also approved by voice vote an amendment to HR 3529 offered by Republican Robert W. Goodlatte of Virginia and backed by Internet industry groups to remove the District of Columbia and the cities in Colorado from the list of jurisdictions eligible to continue collecting Internet access taxes.

"Now we're in a worse state," said Tim Masanz, an NGA official.

Senate Action

Democratic Sen. Ron Wyden of Oregon is expected to offer a revamped version of his Internet tax moratorium bill (S 442) when it goes to the Senate floor. His bill was approved by the Commerce, Science and Transportation Committee in November.

The revised version of S 442 is likely to include a grandfather clause but would call for a six-year moratorium, according to a Senate aide.

It also may include a provision included in legislation (S 1888) introduced in March by Sens. Judd Gregg, R-N.H., and Joseph I. Lieberman, D-Conn., establishing a commission to study Internet taxation and regulation at the state and local levels but would not require the commission to study the matter of out-of-state sales taxes.

House Passes Bill; Senate Fight Lies Ahead

JUNE 27 — After securing key changes in the House to legislation that would impose a moratorium on new Internet taxes, state and local government officials will have to fight off Senate legislation that goes much further than the House bill.

The House passed legislation (HR 4105) by voice vote June 23 that would impose a three-year moratorium on new taxes on the Internet, such as those imposed on Internet access and on transactions not taxed if conducted by telephone or through the mail.

The Senate is likely to take up a bill (S 442) to double the moratorium to six years, and includes other items opposed by state and local officials.

The House legislation is the product of months of negotiations between the bill's sponsor, Christopher Cox, R-Calif., state and local governments and Internet industry representatives.

The bill "presents a balanced approach between regulation and taxation of Internet access, on-line services and electronic commerce," said Commerce Committee Chairman Thomas J. Bliley Jr., R-Va.

HR 4105, introduced June 22 by Cox, merges two bills (HR 3849 and HR 3529) approved by the House Commerce and Judiciary committees.

In addition to the moratorium, HR 4105 would create a 31-member commission to study taxation of the Internet and recommend whether companies should be required to collect sales taxes from out-of-state customers.

Such a commission is backed by state and local officials who would like to change current law, which does not require companies to collect sales taxes from customers in states where the companies do not have a physical presence. They fear their sales tax bases will continue to shrink as on-line and Internet shopping increases.

Taxing goods sold over the Internet is a potential gold mine for local governments. Electronic commerce is expected to reach $300 billion a year by 2002, according to a June study by the Business Software Alliance.

Despite the fragile compromise negotiated by Cox, both sides in the debate expressed continued concern about provisions in HR 4105.

In a joint statement, seven state and local government groups, including the National Governors' Association and the National League of Cities, said they support "the structure of this new bill."

But the groups said they are worried that consumers and "Main Street" businesses, those that do not do business over the Internet, would not be represented on the commission established to study Internet taxation.

Eight states currently collecting Internet access taxes would be required to pass new legislation in order to continue collecting the taxes.

Industry representatives said they want the state exemptions removed.

Senate Action

Both sides now shift their attention to the Senate bill on the Internet tax moratorium (S 442), approved by the Commerce, Science and Transportation Committee in November.

S 442's sponsor, Ron Wyden, D-Ore., said he is hopeful that the Senate will take up the bill soon after it returns from its July Fourth recess.

On the floor, Wyden is expected to offer a reworked version of his bill that includes some of the provisions added in HR 4105, such as allowing some states to continue collecting existing Internet access taxes.

Senate Plan Limits Tax Moratorium To Two Years

AUGUST 1 — Efforts to enact a moratorium on Internet taxation this session were complicated July 28 when a Senate panel voted to shorten the moratorium to two years.

The Senate Finance Committee approved, 19-1, a substitute of S 442 calling for the two-year tax time out.

It is at odds with a version of S 442 approved by the Senate Commerce, Transportation and Science Committee in November 1997 that would suspend Internet taxation until Jan. 1, 2004. *(1997 Almanac, p. 3-40)*

The moratorium places a hold on Internet access taxes and on other levies such as those imposed on transactons that would not otherwise be taxed.

As originally crafted, the Finance Committee's substitute would have cut the moratorium to three years, the same limit included in the House version of the bill (HR 4105).

But the panel adopted, 11-9, an amendment offered by Sens. John H. Chafee, R-R.I., and Bob Kerrey, D-Neb., to limit the time period to two years. During this period, the substitute calls for creation of a 16-member commission of state, local and federal government officials and business leaders to study and recommend rules for tax and tariff treatment of Internet commerce.

Democratic Sen. Ron Wyden of Oregon, the sponsor of S 442, said the Senate Finance Committee bill is "a mixed bag. Shortening the moratorium to two years is unfortunate."

With time running short and the Senate going on its summer recess without acting on the bill, supporters may have a difficult time reconciling the different versions and clearing a bill before the end of the 105th Congress.

But Senate Republican Leader Trent Lott of Mississippi said he still plans to move a bill to the floor this year. And President Clinton has said he would sign an Internet tax moratorium bill.

Governors Seek Changes

The legislation in both the House and Senate has gone through several revisions to satisfy state and local government officials who argued that the bills unfairly pre-empted state and local taxing authority.

After securing key changes in the House, state and local officials gave lukewarm support to HR 4105 when lawmakers passed the bill in June.

Before the Senate Finance markup, the National Governors' Association sent a letter July 27 to the committee urging the panel's leaders to take up HR 4105. The letter said that while the group would like some technical changes in HR 4105, it "represents a fair compromise."

The governors oppose the Commerce Committee's version of S 442 and have several problems with the Finance Committee's version as well.

Taxes

One of the governors' biggest complaints is that neither version includes a "grandfather" clause allowing states that currently impose and collect taxes on Internet access to continue doing so.

Under the Finance Committee's measure, states that currently collect taxes on Internet access would be prohibited from continuing to do so or imposing new Internet taxes after July 28, 1998.

In 1997, states collected about $53.4 million in Internet access taxes imposed on Internet service providers, according to the Federation of Tax Administrators.

HR 4105 grandfathers in Internet access taxes already in effect in eight states but also requires those states to pass legislation to re-enact those levies. The states are Connecticut, Iowa, New Mexico, North Dakota, Ohio, South Dakota, Tennessee and Wisconsin.

Although the governors oppose the stipulation that they pass new legislation to continue collecting current Internet access taxes, they would like to see a grandfather clause in some form added to the Senate legislation, said Tim Masanz, director of economic development for the governors' association.

"I don't think we have a reason for pre-empting the decisions of states that have already been made," said Sen. Kent Conrad, D-N.D.

Conrad offered an amendment to the Finance Committee's substitute to grandfather in states and cities that imposed and enforced Internet access taxes before July 28, 1998. It was rejected on a 10-10 vote.

"The mere fact that some states were aggressive in taxing Internet access does not mean they should be favored over others," said Finance Committee Chairman William V. Roth Jr., R-Del.

Even though they were pleased that the Finance Committee chose not to include a grandfather clause, some Internet industry representatives said they were afraid language in the bill might allow any state to collect back taxes on Internet access prior to July 28, 1998.

Sales Tax Loophole

The panel also defeated an amendment by Democrat Bob Graham of Florida that would have closed a loophole under current law that state and local officials have been trying to change for several years.

Current law does not require companies to collect sales taxes from customers in states where those companies do not have a physical presence.

The governors' association said states lose $4 billion a year in sales tax revenues because of this loophole. With Internet commerce expected to reach $300 billion by 2002, the governors estimate that states could lose at least $10 billion a year in sales tax revenues.

Graham's amendment, rejected 6-13, would have required companies to collect sales taxes from out-of-state customers when they solicit business and deliver products into a state.

A commission established in HR 4105 to study taxation of the Internet also would be required to propose legislative recommendations on a system for collecting sales taxes from out-of-state customers.

Cloture Motion Delays Action On Senate Floor

SEPTEMBER 26 — Efforts to begin Senate floor action on legislation to impose a moratorium on taxes aimed at the Internet were stymied Sept. 25, but supporters plan to make another push to move the measure the week of Sept. 28.

After overcoming a drive to add managed care legislation to the bill, backers of a moratorium on Internet taxes (S 442) were blocked by Sen. Bob Graham, D-Fla., who objected to a unanimous consent request to proceed to the bill.

Senate leaders filed a motion Sept. 25 to end debate on whether to proceed to S 442. The Senate is scheduled to vote on the cloture motion Sept. 29. But Sen. Ron Wyden, D-Ore., S 442's sponsor, was confident he had the votes to end debate.

The legislation calls for a time-out period on state Internet taxation to allow state, local and federal government officials working with industry representatives to figure out what type of tax treatment should be applied to Internet access and commerce.

But Graham said he believes that the commission created in the bill to study this issue should look at whether companies doing business via the Internet, mail or phone should have to collect sales taxes from customers in states where those companies do not have a physical presence. Current law does not require companies to do so.

Echoing an issue raised by state and local government officials, Graham, a former governor, said he is concerned about transferring this loophole to the Internet. The National Governors' Association has said that states lose about $4 billion a year in potential sales tax revenues because of this loophole.

Prior to Graham's objection, supporters were blocked twice from bringing the bill to the floor. Democrats, led by Edward M. Kennedy of Massachusetts, opposed the motion to begin action on the bill because it did not allow them to offer unrelated legislation, including a managed health care bill (S 1890), to S 442.

Since then, Kennedy has agreed to drop his effort to attach S 1890 to the Internet tax bill, according to a spokesman.

Supporters of S 442 say they have no problem with relevant amendments being offered to the bill.

In fact, Dale Bumpers, D-Ark., may offer an amendment that would require the commission to study the sales tax issue.

The commission included in the House bill (HR 4105), which was passed in June, would be required to study the issue and recommend legislation to Congress.

Bumpers also plans to offer an amendment to the bill that would require companies to collect sales taxes from out-of-state customers. His efforts to gain passage of such legislation in the past, however, have failed.

But Senate Commerce Committee Chairman John McCain, R-Ariz., whose panel has primary jurisdiction over the bill, said Graham wanted a guarantee that such amendments would succeed.

Graham "is insisting on a specific result. We do not insist on a specific result," McCain said.

Problems Ahead

Both McCain and Wyden appeared frustrated by the latest glitch to passing the tax moratorium.

They have spent weeks working with Sen. Byron L. Dorgan, D-N.D., and others who have raised concerns about the legislation.

"In the Senate you've got to have 100 or 102 votes," Wyden quipped.

Wyden worked out an agreement with Dorgan to add a provision to the bill to allow states that currently impose taxes on Internet access to continue doing so after the bill is enacted.

The House's version of the bill includes a similar provision but also would require those states to pass legislation within one year of the measure's enactment in order to continue imposing Internet access taxes, a requirement state and local officials opposed.

Meanwhile, if the Senate begins work on S 442, Wyden and McCain plan to offer an amendment extending the bill's moratorium to five years. As approved by the Senate Finance Committee in July, S 442 included a two-year moratorium.

The House bill has a three-year time-out period.

Senate Starts Work; Rejects Sales Tax Amendment

OCTOBER 3 — The Senate on Oct. 2 began work on a bill to place a moratorium on Internet taxes and rebuffed an attempt to allow states to require companies to collect sales taxes from out-of-state customers.

The bill (S 442) would impose a two-year moratorium on new taxes for Internet access or commerce. During this time-out period, a commission would study what type of tax treatment should be applied to the Internet.

After overcoming objections to bringing S 442 to the floor, the Senate voted, 65-30, to table (kill) the sales tax amendment offered by Sen. Dale Bumpers, D-Ark.

Under current law, companies do not have to collect sales taxes from customers who live in states where the companies do not have a physical presence. Bumpers' amendment would have authorized states to require such companies doing business via phone, mail or over the Internet to collect these taxes.

Bumpers said this loophole in the law has cost states billions of dollars, and the problem is going to get worse as more people turn to the Internet to shop. "What's going to happen to this country when schools close because their tax base is gone?" Bumpers asked.

S 442's sponsor, Democrat Ron Wyden of Oregon, has opposed linking the issue to his bill. He said S 442 has no impact on the current ability of states to collect taxes on Internet sales as long as they are taxed in the same way as goods or services purchased by other means.

Senate Commerce Committee Chairman John McCain, R-Ariz., argued that the amendment "represents a very large tax increase on the public."

Senate allies of state and local government officials, led by Sens. Bob Graham, D-Fla., and Byron L. Dorgan, D-N.D., were negotiating with the bill's supporters over provisions that might be included in an amendment offered by McCain and Wyden.

Among the items still under discussion is whether the commission established in the bill should study and make legislative recommendations on allowing states to require companies to collect sales taxes from out-of-state customers and whether the moratorium should be extended.

Senate Bill Places Three-Year Timeout On New Taxes

OCTOBER 10 — The Senate on Oct. 8 opened the door to enactment of legislation that would set a three-year moratorium on new state and local taxes imposed on Internet access and commerce.

Following the Senate's 96-2 passage of the bill (S 442), Senate supporters were looking to the House to clear the bill or make minor changes and send it back to the Senate for final action before Congress leaves for the year. The House approved its own version of the legislation in June. (Vote 308, p. S-47)

President Clinton has indicated that he will sign the legislation.

It took a week of debate before the Senate passed S 442. It would impose a timeout on new Internet taxes and establish a 19-member commission to study what type of tax treatment should be applied to the Internet.

States Win Concessions

When S 442 was first introduced in 1997 by Ron Wyden, D-Ore., state and local government officials, led by the National Governors' Association, complained that it was an attempt to pre-empt their taxing authority. (1997 Almanac, p. 3-40)

Since then, state and local leaders have gained concessions and no longer oppose the bill.

The Senate rebuffed, 45-52, an attempt by Wyden and Senate Commerce Committee Chairman John McCain, R-Ariz., to increase the moratorium to four years. (Vote 305, p. S-47)

But they did succeed in boosting the timeout to three years from the two-year moratorium included in the base bill sent to the Senate floor.

As part of that deal, however, supporters agreed to include a grandfather clause. That would allow at least a dozen states that currently collect taxes on Internet access to continue doing so after the bill is enacted. Both amendments were adopted by voice vote.

State and local officials also gained inclusion of a key amendment, offered by Republican Tim Hutchinson of Arkansas. It would require the commission established in S 442 to study whether states should be allowed to require companies to collect sales taxes from customers who live in states where the companies do not have a physical presence. Current law does not require them to collect sales taxes from those customers.

As a result, state and local officials say they have lost billions of dollars in sales tax revenues generated from mail order sales. They worry that if companies selling goods over the Internet are allowed to take advantage of this loophole, tax revenues will continue to decline as more consumers turn to the Internet to do their shopping.

"For the sake of small mom-and-pop businesses who find themselves in competition with Internet entities and other out-of-state sellers who do not have to collect sales taxes from out-of-state buy-

Taxes

ers, we should allow the commission" to study the issue, Hutchinson said.

But Judd Gregg, R-N.H., whose home state does not have a sales tax, said the amendment was aimed at "dramatically increasing taxes and the tax collection capacity of local communities and states across the country."

The Senate rejected, 30-68, a motion by McCain to kill Hutchinson's amendment. The amendment was then adopted by voice vote. *(Vote 304, p. S-47)*

Despite state and local officials' complaints, Wyden and others said current law relating to when companies have to collect sales taxes from out-of-state customers should not be applied differently to the Internet than it is to other ways of selling goods.

The legislation bans "discriminatory" treatment of Internet sales. But Wyden and McCain wanted to be sure that states do not try to say that the existence of a Web server in a state constitutes having a physical presence in the state. Such a claim would allow states to require companies to collect sales taxes from customers who live in those states.

Bob Graham, D-Fla., objected to the amendment and threatened to use a procedural maneuver to block it. He said he worried that some Internet companies now in litigation with states over the companies' sales tax liability might try to use the language to avoid paying back taxes.

The senators settled the dispute by adding language to the amendment to ensure that it could not be applied retroactively.

Meanwhile, senators voted, 98-1, to add legislation that would exempt from the moratorium commercial Web sites that failed to restrict access by children 17 and under to material on their sites that was deemed to be "harmful to minors." Similar legislation was passed by the House Oct. 7.

Under an amendment adopted by voice vote, Web sites would also be exempted from the moratorium if they failed to offer Internet users screening software to block out pornography or other objectionable material when browsing.

Tax Moratorium Enacted Within Spending Package

OCTOBER 17 — Concerned that Internet growth could be hampered by the imposition of a barrage of state and local taxes, lawmakers agreed late in the session to impose a moratorium on new state and local levies on Internet access and commerce. The provisions were enacted as part of the massive fiscal 1999 omnibus spending bill (PL 105-277) that cleared Oct. 21.

Supporters of a moratorium argue that the decentralized nature of the Internet makes it vulnerable to taxation from the 30,000 U.S. taxing jurisdictions. They say a timeout period is necessary to develop rational tax policies before state and local governments rush to profit from new Internet taxes. But state and local officials say that few states had imposed new Internet levies and that a moratorium was an unfair pre-emption of their taxing authority.

The legislation added to the omnibus spending bill mirrors a measure (S 442) passed by the Senate Oct. 8. It would impose a three-year moratorium on new state and local taxes targeted at Internet access and commerce. During the timeout period, a 19-member commission would be charged with studying what type of tax treatment should be applied to the Internet.

The measure also calls for the commission to examine whether states should be allowed to force companies to collect sales taxes from customers in states where the companies do not have a physical presence. Under current law, the companies are not required to do so. The provision was sought by state and local officials who say the current loophole in the law has cost them billions of dollars in lost sales tax revenues.

They also won another key concession from the measure's supporters: inclusion of a grandfather clause allowing at least a dozen states and those local jurisdictions that have been imposing Internet access taxes before Oct. 1, 1998, to continue doing so after the measure's enactment. In exchange, they agreed to back the three-year moratorium.

The legislation also includes a provision that would exempt from the moratorium Internet service providers who fail to offer customers filtering software that can be used to block out objectionable material when surfing the Internet. ◆

Chapter 22

TECHNOLOGY & COMMUNICATION

Digital Copyrights 22-3	**Encryption Exports** 22-19
Internet Gambling 22-7	Year 2000 Computer Glitch 22-21
On-Line Pornography 22-10	**Cellular Phone Fraud** 22-23
Satellite Fees/Cable TV Rates 22-14	**'Slamming,' 'Spamming' Restrictions** 22-24

Lawmakers Update Nations' Copyright Law For the Digital Age

Congress cleared a bill (HR 2281) updating protections for intellectual property in the digital age — the first significant rewrite of the nation's copyright laws in two decades. The legislation implements two international treaties aimed at improving protections for digital works such as computer software and compact discs. It also gives Internet and on-line service providers limited protection from liability for copyright infringement that takes place on their networks without their knowledge.

SUMMARY

A key provision bans the manufacture, use or sale of devices that are primarily designed to circumvent technology, such as encryption, used to protect copyrighted works from theft. Librarians and educators expressed concern that this would make it more difficult for people to access such works.

The House originally passed its version of HR 2281 (H Rept 105-551, Parts 1 and 2) by voice vote Aug. 4, after months of negotiations to resolve concerns raised by groups ranging from librarians to Internet service providers. The Senate had passed a similar bill (S 2037 — S Rept 105-190) on May 14 by a vote of 99-0.

House Panel Moves Copyright Bills; Debate Escalates

FEBRUARY 28 — A House panel on Feb. 26 took the first step in the 105th Congress on what could be a long journey toward updating the nation's copyright laws to reflect new technology and the growing popularity of the Internet.

The House Judiciary Committee's Courts and Intellectual Property Subcommittee approved by voice vote two copyright bills. Despite the panel's approval, the measures continue to be plagued by intense debate, which has raged for the past few years, over the best way to protect copyrighted materials in the information age.

"No one thinks this will be the last thing we do" on these issues, said Rep. Barney Frank of Massachusetts, the subcommittee's top Democrat.

The first bill (HR 2281) would outlaw the manufacture, importation or trafficking of devices "primarily designed or produced" to circumvent technology, such as encryption, aimed at preventing access to copyrighted materials. Encryption uses mathematical formulas to scramble information. The bill also would make it illegal under most circumstances to alter or remove copyright management information, such as the name of the author, from copyrighted materials.

The second bill (HR 3209) would provide on-line service providers with some protection from legal liability for copyrighted works stolen over their networks.

Circumventing the Law

HR 2281 was introduced to update U.S. law in response to two World Intellectual Property Organization treaties signed in December 1996 that established international recognition of copyrights for digitally produced goods such as movies and software.

The growth of the Internet has increased the ease and frequency with which copyrighted works can be stolen. The Internet allows thieves to send copies of software or music around the world with a click of a computer mouse. And digital technology allows for reproduction of identical copies.

The Judiciary subcommittee's debate on HR 2281 largely centered on the provision banning circumvention devices. Some lawmakers say banning such devices is the wrong approach. They argue that there are legitimate needs for such devices and say prohibiting them will slow development of new technology because manufacturers may be concerned that devices will be challenged in court as being primarily developed to infringe on copyrighted material.

Banning circumvention devices "is a quest, I think, that leads to untoward results," said Rep. Rick Boucher, D-Va., who has introduced an alternative bill (HR 3048) that would make it a crime to use such devices for the purpose of making an illegal copy.

He offered an amendment, which was rejected by voice vote, that would allow the manufacture of circumventing devices that have "substantial non-infringing uses" and double the fine established in the bill for using such technology to make illegal copies.

Howard Coble, R-N.C., the subcommittee chairman and sponsor of HR 2281, said he was concerned that Boucher's amendment would allow manufacturers to make devices that "purport" to be designed primarily for legitimate purposes but are instead intended for infringing copyrights.

But Boucher contended that because videocassette recorders and personal computers include circumventing technology, their use might also be challenged under the bill. He offered an amendment, which was rejected on a 2-10 vote, to make clear that VCRs and computers could still be manufactured for non-commercial use. But Frank and others dismissed the probability that the legislation could be used to ban VCRs and computers.

In response to concerns raised by librarians, the panel adopted by voice vote a Coble amendment to waive the

---

Box Score

- **Bill:** HR 2281 — PL 105-304
- **House action:** The House cleared the conference report (H Rept 105-796) on HR 2281 by voice vote Oct. 12.
- **Senate action:** The Senate adopted the conference report on HR 2281 by voice vote Oct. 8.
- **Presidential action:** Clinton signed HR 2281 on Oct. 28.

Technology & Communication

fines established in the bill against nonprofit libraries, archives and educational institutions for violating the ban on using circumventing technology if such institutions were unaware they were violating the law or were trying to examine the copyrighted works to determine whether they wanted to buy them.

The panel rejected, 6-7, a Frank amendment to exempt the institutions from the circumvention prohibitions altogether.

Rep. Howard L. Berman, D-Calif., questioned the need for either provision, saying most publishers will provide examples of their works to potential purchasers.

Liability Questions

The question of who should be responsible for copyright infringement on the Internet was far from settled with the panel's approval of HR 3209. Even the bill's authors said it was only a starting point for more negotiation.

Several questions were raised about the legislation. Rep. Zoe Lofgren, D-Calif., said she was concerned that Internet search engines, such as Yahoo, are not protected under the bill. Search engines allow Internet users to search for particular sites of interest.

Groups representing copyright holders, however, have raised concerns that the bill may go too far and exempt those service providers who may have more control over the information on their networks than they claim.

The panel rejected by voice vote a Frank amendment to limit the financial liability of on-line service providers that were unaware that infringement was taking place on their network to the amount of profit the provider made from the infringement.

House Judiciary Approves Update Of Copyright Laws

APRIL 4 — Taking a step toward bringing copyright laws into the computer age, the House Judiciary Committee approved legislation April 1 updating the laws for digitally produced products and offering some legal protection to those who transmit the copyrighted work of others on-line.

Committee members made it clear that more changes to copyright law are likely to be added when the bill reaches the House floor, as early as May. They said the changes would reflect an agreement struck March 31 among representatives of the telephone, computer, music publishing and other industries on a variety of copyright-related liability matters.

The Senate has yet to act on the copyright issue in the 105th Congress. Senate Judiciary Committee Chairman Orrin G. Hatch, R-Utah, indicated April 2 that action could occur after the spring recess. "We're close to writing a bill that all of us can support," he said.

The House committee approved, by voice vote, a bill (HR 2281) to revise U.S. copyright laws in response to two World Intellectual Property Organization treaties adopted in 1996 that established international recognition of copyrights for digitally produced goods such as movies and software.

The committee also added to the bill, by voice vote, a separate proposal (HR 3209) to give the nation's thousands of on-line service providers, such as America Online and Netcom, some liability protection for copyrighted works stolen over their networks.

Groups representing copyright holders have said HR 3209 may go too far and exempt those service providers who may have more control over the information on their networks than they claim.

Innovation Worries

Lengthy debate on the measure cut across party lines and centered on whether it would stifle technological innovation.

One critic of the bill, Rick Boucher, D-Va., accused the full committee of being too eager to approve the bill before Congress' adjournment for the spring recess. Boucher offered five amendments designed mainly to define legitimate uses for devices that could otherwise be used to make illegal digital copies. All were rejected by voice vote.

Other committee members disagreed with Boucher's assertion that they had not carefully considered the matter. Chairman Henry J. Hyde, R-Ill., said enactment of the legislation would cap "three and a half years of painful and painstaking discussions" over how to protect copyrighted materials in the information age.

Boucher said the proposal would slow development of new technology because manufacturers may be concerned that devices will be challenged in court as being primarily developed to infringe on copyrighted material. He said some videocassette recorders and personal computers could fall under the scope of HR 2281 — a concern that several of the bill's supporters dismissed.

"The argument that this is going to interfere with VCRs has no substance," said Barney Frank, D-Mass. The bill's sponsor, Courts and Intellectual Property Subcommittee Chairman Howard Coble, R-N.C., agreed with Frank. "No one is attempting to accelerate the path to a jail door on behalf of electronics manufacturers," Coble said.

On-Line Deal

Many committee members said they were encouraged by the prospect of the deal among on-line providers, telephone companies, libraries, universities and copyright holders. The groups have been meeting for months with Hatch and House Judiciary member Robert W. Goodlatte, R-Va.

Goodlatte said some provisions in the deal may be included in a manager's amendment offered on the House floor. But a Goodlatte aide said the committee already has incorporated some provisions that have emerged from the talks into the substitute amendment that merged the two bills.

One amendment included would allow a telephone company to claim that it was a "mere conduit" for stolen copyrighted material, providing only transmission lines. The amendment also would broaden an exemption for when Internet service providers would be liable for damages for contributing to copyright infringement.

The amendment also would shield providers who may be sued for removing on-line content later found not to be infringing on anyone's copyright.

Allan Adler, vice president for legal and government affairs for the Association of American Publishers, said the deal worked out with on-line service providers would allow copyright owners to obtain "injunctive relief" from those providers that are unwilling to cooperate. "The trade-off was for the [providers] to feel they got a better de-

Digital Copyrights

gree of certainty" for when they are liable for copyright infringement that takes place on their networks, he said.

Draft Measure Gets Boost From Senate Panel

MAY 2 — After a week of intense negotiations, a Senate panel made several changes April 30 to digital copyright legislation that boosts prospects for its passage by the Senate.

The draft legislation, approved unanimously by the Senate Judiciary Committee, would update the nation's copyright laws for the information age.

The bill, which has not been formally introduced, could go to the floor in mid-May when the Senate is expected to take up a package of technology bills.

The bill implements two international treaties that improve protection for copyrighted digital works such as computer software and movies. It also provides on-line service providers with some protection against liability for infringement that takes place on their networks without their knowledge.

By voice vote, the committee approved several amendments that resolved most of the outstanding issues plaguing the bill, such as providing remedies for on-line customers when information they have on an electronic site is unfairly taken down at the request of a copyright holder and addressing concerns about the bill's impact on technology aimed at blocking children's access to on-line pornography.

At the committee's April 23 markup, Committee Chairman Orrin G. Hatch, R-Utah, had given these parties until April 30 to work out their differences with the copyright holders.

The changes added to the bill April 30 brought John Ashcroft, R-Mo., who had championed many of the issues raised by such groups as the electronics manufacturers and educators, on board.

"We now have an agreement that almost all the interested parties can live with and a bill I can support," Ashcroft said.

Despite this, the parties were unable to work out a compromise on an issue raised by companies that make encryption products.

The companies argued that the bill would virtually ban research into new types of encryption, which scrambles information to prevent unauthorized access. They say the best way to test their encryption products is by trying to break the protections in existing encryption products.

"This will have a detrimental effect on the U.S. [encryption] industry," said John Scheibel, vice president and general counsel for the Computer and Communications Industry Association.

Committee leaders said they would try resolve the issue before the legislation goes to the Senate floor.

Several Issues Resolved

One of the major issues resolved relates to a provision in the bill banning the manufacture of devices primarily designed and marketed to circumvent technology aimed at preventing unauthorized access to copyrighted works.

Electronics manufacturers said this provision would have a chilling effect on the development of new technology by requiring companies to design their products to ensure they will not be sued for violating the legislation.

The committee adopted an amendment that makes clear that manufacturers do not have to design their products to work with certain technological safeguards used by copyright holders to protect their works from infringers.

For example, under the amendment, a manufacturer of video cassette recorders would not be required to ensure that its products are designed to work with technology included in some movie video tapes aimed at curbing illegal copying. At the same time, the amendment clarifies that companies cannot manufacture technology primarily designed to get around such a protection included in a videotape.

The committee also adopted an amendment requiring the Library of Congress' Copyright Office to study how current copyright laws relating to courses taught over long distances should be updated to reflect a desire by universities to teach more of these courses over the Internet.

The issue "is too difficult to solve" on this legislation, said Allan R. Adler, vice president for legal and government affairs at the Association of American Publishers.

A request by nonprofit educational institutions that they be given some protection from liability when someone using their on-line services infringes on a copyright was settled by calling for a Copyright Office study.

Among the other changes made to the bill was a clarification that the bill would have no impact on laws aimed at protecting people's personal privacy in on-line communications.

Senate Passes Bill To Protect Digital Copyrights

MAY 16 — The Senate passed legislation May 14 to bring the nation's copyright laws into the digital age.

The legislation (S 2037), passed 99-0, puts into effect two World Intellectual Property Organization treaties aimed at giving digital copyrighted works greater international protection. The bill also would shield online service providers from legal liability for infringement that takes place on their networks without their knowledge. (Vote 137, p. S-23)

"The United States started the Internet and remains its most significant hub," said Senate Judiciary Committee Chairman Orrin G. Hatch, R-Utah, the bill's chief sponsor. "No country comes close to the United States in creative output. ... This bill will help us maintain this edge in an increasingly competitive global market."

The bill had been plagued with controversy that was settled only after weeks of negotiations leading up to the Judiciary Committee's approval of the bill April 30. The only significant outstanding controversy has been over encryption products, which use mathematical formulas to scramble information to prevent unauthorized access.

Companies that make encryption products said a provision in the bill that would prohibit devices meant to circumvent technology used to protect copyrighted works from theft would virtually ban research into new encryption products.

Technology & Communication

S 2037's authors included language in the Judiciary Committee's report on the bill saying that "generally available encryption testing tools" would not be outlawed by the legislation. The companies say they would like a provision added to the bill specifically allowing encryption research.

Similar legislation (HR 2281), approved by the House Judiciary Committee on April 1 is awaiting action by the full House.

Copyright Bill Advances After Lengthy Markup

JUNE 20 — A House panel made progress June 18 toward resolving lingering problems with legislation aimed at protecting digitally produced works such as compact discs and computer software from copyright infringement.

After a lengthy markup spanning two days, the House Commerce Committee's Telecommunications, Trade and Consumer Protection Subcommittee approved legislation (HR 2281) by voice vote that implements two international treaties aimed at strengthening international copyright protection for digital works.

The bill also provides on-line and Internet service providers with some protection from liability when copyright infringement takes place on their networks without their knowledge.

The copyright legislation is a top priority for movie and record producers and software makers, who warned during a June 18 news conference before the panel's markup that one of the chief goals of the bill — protecting copyrighted works from piracy — would be compromised if too many changes were made to it.

"We're a victim of the 'what ifs' game," said Fritz Attaway, general counsel and senior vice president for government relations for the Motion Picture Association of America. "The answer to these 'what ifs' is to make this legislation totally ineffective."

The House Judiciary Committee approved HR 2281 in April.

The Commerce subcommittee, by voice vote, adopted a substitute version of HR 2281 on June 18 that mirrors a bill (S 2037) passed 99-0 by the Senate in May. Critics of the Senate measure used the subcommittee's markup as an opportunity to fix some problematic provisions that they say the Senate failed to address before passing its bill.

The panel approved a handful of amendments favored by equipment manufacturers and privacy advocates. Negotiations were expected to continue to resolve other issues, such as concerns that the measure would ban encryption research, before the full Commerce Committee acts on the bill, which it is expected to do the week of June 22.

Fair Balance?

Among the bill's most controversial provisions is one that would ban the manufacture, import and trafficking in devices primarily designed, produced and marketed to circumvent technology, such as encryption, aimed at protecting copyrighted works from theft.

"I have some reservations about whether a fair balance has been struck between the right of copyright owners to protect their works and the right of equipment manufacturers to engage freely in their trade," said John D. Dingell of Michigan, the top Democrat on the Commerce Committee.

Among the numerous amendments offered during the markup, the panel adopted by voice vote one that was offered by Scott L. Klug, R-Wis., and Rick Boucher, D-Va., to strengthen a provision in the Senate bill aimed at ensuring that equipment manufacturers will not be required to design their products to work with all types of technology used to protect copyrighted works.

The panel also approved by voice vote an amendment offered by the subcommittee's ranking Democrat, Edward J. Markey of Massachusetts, to make an exception to allow people to use circumvention devices to protect personal privacy.

Markey said the anti-circumvention language in the bill would prohibit people from taking steps to delete from their computers "cookies," bits of data put on a computer hard disk when someone visits a Web site. Some view them as an invasion of privacy because cookies can track what pages a user goes to on a Web site.

But James E. Rogan, R-Calif., argued that the amendment would create a "huge loophole" by allowing those who use circumvention devices to infringe copyrights to claim they were using the devices to protect their privacy.

In response to concerns raised by libraries and educators, Klug and Boucher also offered an amendment to ensure that Americans' legal right to "fair use" of copyrighted works would be protected under the bill.

Some lawmakers and library representatives say it should not be a crime for a library user or a student to circumvent technology aimed at protecting a copyrighted work from theft if their only purpose is to use it in a manner that does not infringe a copyright. "We're simply trying to take today's laws and apply them to the technology and the electronic equipment of the future," Klug said.

Boucher and Klug agreed to withdraw the amendment after the panel's chairman and others agreed to work on a compromise before the bill is marked up by the full committee.

House Measure Includes 'Fair Use' Assurances

JULY 18 — The House Commerce Committee approved legislation July 17 aimed at protecting digitally produced works such as computer software and compact discs from copyright infringement. Before approving the bill, the committee struck a deal over a contentious provision ensuring Americans' right to the "fair use" of copyrighted works.

The legislation (HR 2281), approved 41-0, implements two international treaties aimed at strengthening copyright protection for digital works. It also gives on-line and Internet service providers some protection from liability when copyright infringement takes place on their networks without their knowledge.

The issue has been a priority for movie and record producers and software makers. The Business Software Alliance said a recent study by its group and the Software Publishers Association shows that worldwide piracy of copyrighted software costs the industry an estimated $11.4 billion annually, with $2.7 billion of that in the United States alone.

Commerce Committee Chairman Thomas J. Bliley Jr., R-Va., called the bill "perhaps the most important piece of legislation related to electronic commerce that this Congress will consider."

The Senate passed its version of the bill (S 2037) in May, 99-0, one month after the House Judiciary Committee approved HR 2281.

The House Commerce Telecommunications, Trade and Consumer Protection Subcommittee also approved the bill last month. Since then, it had been the subject of intense negotiations over the use by libraries and others of copyrighted materials.

Some lawmakers and library representatives say it should not be a crime for a student or library user to circumvent technology aimed at protecting a copyrighted work if their only purpose is to use it in a manner that does not infringe on a copyright.

The Commerce Committee adopted by voice vote an amendment by Scott L. Klug, R-Wis., that Klug said creates a process "that doesn't short-circuit university and library research."

Waivers

Klug's amendment calls for the secretary of Commerce to issue regulations prohibiting the circumvention of technological protections two years after the bill becomes law.

During that two-year period, the amendment says, the secretary will conduct a study to determine whether the users of copyrighted works are being adversely affected by the fair use of those works.

The amendment also gives the secretary the authority to grant waivers for lawful uses of copyrighted works during that period.

"It's meant to be a real-world assessment of what's going on. . . . It's the result of a political process that library organizations and higher-education organizations have agreed not to oppose as [the bill] moves through the balance of the legislative process," said Adam M. Eisgrau, legislative counsel for the American Library Association's Washington office.

Eisgrau took part in discussions among interest groups, lawmakers and Commerce staff members that caused the markup to be postponed a day and ultimately culminated in a deal at 1:30 a.m. on July 17.

Many Commerce members said they were pleased that a deal could be struck. Even Rick Boucher, D-Va., who had pushed for more comprehensive fair-use language when the bill was before the subcommittee, said Klug's amendment represented an improvement over the bill's original language.

"This committee action creates the balance necessary to ensure that as new protections are extended to copyright owners, the rights of the users of intellectual property are not undermined," Boucher said.

The Commerce Committee also approved an amendment by W.J. "Billy" Tauzin, R-La., intended to address another controversial provision. That provision would ban the manufacture,

Internet Gambling

Efforts to crack down Internet gambling died after House and Senate negotiators declined to add it to the year-end omnibus spending bill because of differences between the chambers' versions that would have made enforcement difficult.

The legislation would have made Internet gambling a crime punishable by up to four years in prison and $20,000 in fines, or the total amount of gambling proceeds. It also would have required Internet service providers to cut off service to Internet gambling sites identified by authorities.

The House Judiciary Committee's Crime Subcommittee approved its version of the bill (HR 4427) by voice vote Sept. 14.

The bill sought to prohibit Internet gambling and allow law enforcement officials to direct Internet service providers to shut down gambling sites on their networks. Internet gambling site operators could be fined and jailed for up to four years under the bill. Those caught placing bets over the Internet also could face a fine and up to six months in jail.

The Senate had added similar legislation (S 474) to its Commerce-Justice-State spending bill (S 2260), by a vote of 90-10 on July 23. (Vote 229, p. S-36)

But the chief sponsor of the Senate measure, Republican Jon Kyl of Arizona, said the House version was "unacceptable" because it contained too many loopholes. For example, he objected to an exception in the House bill that would have allowed bets on parimutuel activities, such as horse racing, to be placed over the Internet as long as they were legal in the state or on the Indian reservation from which the bet was being sent and received.

Kyl's bill would only have allowed bets to be placed on such races over closed-loop networks other than the Internet. "If any one party can do it [gamble over the Internet], then there is no way to protect people anywhere in the country," he said.

In the absence of agreement, the provisions were dropped when the Commerce-Justice-State bill was folded into the omnibus appropriations measure (HR 4328) at the end of the session.

import and trafficking in devices primarily designed, produced and marketed to circumvent technology, such as encryption, aimed at protecting copyrighted works from theft.

Tauzin said he feared the ban would inhibit encryption research. His amendment clarifies that encryption research is still permissible as long as the encrypted materials were lawfully obtained.

Although the fair-use and encryption issues were resolved to the satisfaction of most members, at least one other matter will need to be addressed when the bill reaches the House floor.

Rep. Rick White, R-Wash., wants to extend some of the same legal protections currently available to radio stations transmitting copyrighted materials to those who use the Internet to broadcast those materials.

Technology & Communication

House Passes Bill Targeting Digital, On-Line Theft

AUGUST 8 — With limited debate, the House passed a major update of the nation's copyright laws Aug. 4 to include works produced for the digital age, sending the measure to a conference with the Senate.

By voice vote, the House passed the measure (HR 2281), which would implement two international treaties aimed at improving copyright protection for digital works such as compact discs and computer software.

The bill would provide some protection from legal liability to Internet service providers for infringement that takes place on their networks without their knowledge.

HR 2281's easy passage does not reflect the months of negotiations on the bill among copyright holders, librarians, educators, equipment manufacturers and Internet and on-line service providers or potential hurdles that may lie ahead in a conference with the Senate, which passed its own version (S 2037) in May.

Among the issues that will have to be sorted out by House and Senate conferees is whether to keep legislation, included in a substitute version of HR 2281 passed by the House, that would prohibit the use of most or part of information collections, such as databases, in a way that harms those collections' commercial marketability. The legislation (HR 2652) was passed as a separate bill in May by the House, but the Senate has not acted on it.

Fair Use

House lawmakers cleared the way for HR 2281's passage when the Commerce Committee approved a new version of the bill July 17, addressing librarians' concerns about the bill's effect on "fair use," a copyright principle that allows the limited use of products without permission for such purposes as education or research.

Concerns centered on a provision that would ban devices designed primarily to bypass technology aimed at preventing infringement. Librarians and some lawmakers said they feared the provision would create a "pay for use" system in which, for example, a student would be required to pay each time he copied a small portion of a work on the Internet for research.

The compromise worked out by the Commerce Committee calls for delaying the ban on circumvention devices for two years. During that time, the secretary of Commerce would be required to craft rules determining the effect the ban would have on fair use. The secretary could waive the ban in cases where fair use would be harmed. The rules and any waivers would be reviewed every three years after the initial two-year study.

One minor change that concerns copyright holders requires the secretary to determine the provision's impact on those who "gained initial lawful access" to a copyrighted work, such as by buying a subscription.

Copyright holders fear that the language would allow those who once held a subscription to an on-line magazine to continue to have access to that magazine long after their subscription expired.

Though many of the same groups that have been pushing for the digital copyright legislation also back the information collections legislation, they say they want to ensure that it not be an impediment to HR 2281's passage.

The information collections bill was opposed by librarians, researchers and some educators when it passed the House. These groups said the bill would limit or place new burdens on their ability to use such collections.

"The express linkage of the very sweeping database legislation to [HR 2281] cannot help the overall package's passage," said Adam M. Eisgrau, legislative counsel for the American Library Association.

House Judiciary Committee leaders also added a handful of other provisions to the substitute version of HR 2281 passed by the House that are not as controversial, including one to create an undersecretary of Commerce for intellectual property. They also included a bill (HR 2696) passed by the House in March to prevent some designs of shipbuilders from being copied by competitors for 10 years.

A spokeswoman for the Senate Judiciary Committee said the panel is still reviewing what was added to HR 2281 and may hold a hearing on the information collections legislation.

Piracy on the Rise

The bill has been a priority for copyright owners ranging from movie producers to software manufacturers.

Digital technology has made it possible for thieves to make perfect copies of works. And the Internet has made it easy for copies to be sent all over the world. For example, there are numerous Web sites that provide access to pirated music.

More than 40 percent of software used worldwide is illegally copied, according to the Business Software Alliance. The group said this kind of theft costs software companies $11.2 billion a year in lost revenues.

Conferees Remove Database Provision; Senate OKs Bill

OCTOBER 10 — The House was close to clearing legislation that would update legal protections for intellectual property in the digital age — the first significant rewrite of the nation's copyright laws in two decades.

The Senate adopted the conference report on HR 2281 by voice vote on Oct. 8. The House appeared likely to finish action before Congress leaves town and send the bill to President Clinton, who is expected to sign it.

The legislation would implement two international treaties to improve copyright protection for digital works, such as computer software and compact disks, and prevent the pirating of these products — a growing problem in the computer age.

It would also provide Internet and on-line service providers with some protection against liability for infringement that takes place on their networks without their knowledge.

One of the biggest sticking points settled by House and Senate conferees concerned language added by the House to its version of HR 2281 that would have provided legal protection for information collections such as computer databases.

The database legislation, approved

by the House in May as a separate bill (HR 2652), would have made it a crime to take all or most of an information collection and use it in a way that hurt the commercial marketability of that product.

Under current law, the facts in information collections cannot be copyrighted. Supporters say creators of information collections need protection to prevent competitors from taking their work and selling it as their own.

But a broad coalition of librarians, educators and researchers said the legislation was far too broad and would give producers of databases a "monopoly" over some facts. Several lawmakers echoed these concerns.

Given the controversy over the database legislation, which had not been acted on in the Senate, conferees agreed to remove the provision.

But Senate Judiciary Committee Chairman Orrin G. Hatch, R-Utah, promised supporters of the legislation that he would work in the 106th Congress to craft a compromise bill.

"We're pleased that a matter so serious and potentially so significant was not prematurely adopted," said Adam M. Eisgrau of the American Library Association.

Ensuring Fair Use

Another issue that needed to be settled by House and Senate conferees was differences in language aimed at protecting Americans' right to fair use of copyrighted material.

A key provision in the bill would ban the manufacture, use or sale of devices primarily designed to circumvent technology, such as encryption, used to protect a copyrighted work from theft. Librarians and educators worried that the provision would make it more difficult for people to access such works.

Both chambers included language aimed at addressing such concerns, but librarians favored the House's bill.

The House language would have required the secretary of Commerce to craft rules determining the impact the ban on circumvention technology would have on fair use and allow the secretary to waive the ban in cases where fair use would be affected. The conferees agreed to the House language but put the Library of Congress in charge of the rulemaking on the impact of the ban.

Hollywood Cheers As Measure Clears

OCTOBER 17 — On Oct. 12, lawmakers cleared a bill aimed at improving copyright protections for digital works such as computer software and compact discs, legislation that supporters say is essential to increase the availability of such materials on the Internet.

The legislation (HR 2281) would implement two international treaties aimed at improving worldwide protection for digital works. HR 2281's conference report was cleared Oct. 12 by the House on a voice vote. President Clinton said he would sign it.

Supporters say the bill would increase the amount of copyrighted works available on the Internet by providing creators of such materials with new protections against theft.

Pirates steal an estimated $20 billion worth of copyrighted materials a year, industry officials say. An average of 40 percent of computer software alone is pirated every year worldwide.

"Passage of the legislation brings us a step closer to being able to utilize the Internet as a means of providing information and entertainment to consumers," said Rich Taylor, spokesman for the Motion Picture Association of America. HR 2281 was a top priority for movie and record creators, software makers and publishers.

Hollywood alone contributed more than $2.5 million in individual and political action committee donations to members of Congress in the 1997-98 election cycle, according to the nonpartisan Center for Responsive Politics. Among the top recipients were key players on HR 2281: Rep. Howard Coble, R-N.C., the bill's sponsor; and Sens. Orrin G. Hatch, R-Utah, and Patrick J. Leahy, D-Vt., the top leaders on the Senate Judiciary Committee.

Even though various interest groups and lawmakers reached a compromise the week of Oct. 5, the legislation was held up briefly by House Majority Whip Tom DeLay, R-Texas, over an unrelated dispute concerning who should head an electronics industry group.

Angered by the appointment of former Rep. David McCurdy, D-Okla. (1981-1995), to head the Electronic Industries Alliance, DeLay yanked the bill from the House floor schedule Oct. 9 in protest. When asked about it, DeLay said, "We think it's an insult to the majority to hire a partisan Democrat" to head the organization.

However, pulling the bill was not much of a punishment for the alliance. "It was a piece of legislation that consumer [electronics] folks could live with. They were not championing this legislation," said alliance spokesman Mark Rosenker.

An alliance member, the Consumer Electronics Manufacturing Association, was among several groups critical of a key provision in the bill that would ban the use, manufacture or sale of devices primarily designed to circumvent technology aimed at protecting copyrighted material. They expressed concern that the provision would require them to design their products around anti-copying technology used by copyright holders.

In response to the association's concerns, the legislation includes language that says electronic, telecommunications or computer products do not have to be designed or built to work with anti-copying technology.

The legislation includes exceptions to the ban on circumvention technology for a few specific activities, including encryption research, computer security testing and reverse engineering, which would allow software creators to make sure their products work on certain types of computers.

HR 2281 also includes language aimed at ensuring that Americans will have "fair use" of copyrighted digital works. Librarians, educators and others feared the circumvention ban would jeopardize fair use of the material by punishing Americans even if they bypassed a technological protection only for the purpose of using a product in a non-infringing way.

The legislation requires the Librarian of Congress to waive the ban in cases where non-infringing use of a particular work would be adversely affected by the circumvention ban.

"We hope [the ban] will not prove in practice as potentially threatening as it does on its face," said Adam Eisgrau, legislative counsel for the American Library Association. But he added that "having a safety valve built into the bill is encouraging." ◆

Technology & Communication

Congress Takes Steps To Shield Children From Internet Porn, Predators

In a campaign against cyber-sin, lawmakers agreed to crack down on Web sites that allow children to access pornography, and to increase penalties for sex offenders who use the Internet to distribute child pornography. Both measures were enacted into law.

SUMMARY

● **Anti-pornography.** Despite objections from the Clinton administration, congressional leaders agreed to add the House-passed version of an anti-pornography bill (HR 3783) to the omnibus fiscal 1999 spending package (PL 105-277) that cleared Oct. 21. The House had passed HR 3783 (H Rept 105-775) in October, while the Senate included a similar measure legislation (S 1482 — S Rept 105-225) in its version of the Commerce-Justice-State spending bill (S 2260).

Under the legislation, Web sites must require proof that Web surfers are adults before providing access to material deemed "harmful to minors." Violators could face a $50,000 fine and six months in jail.

The White House opposed the bill, saying it preferred to promote the use of filtering software or other voluntary means to limit children's exposure to on-line smut. The Justice Department also questioned whether the legislation was constitutional.

● **Curbing pedophiles.** Lawmakers cleared a separate bill (HR 3494 — PL 105-314) targeting pedophiles who stalk children on the Internet. The bill, signed into law Oct. 30, prohibited knowingly transferring obscene materials to a minor over the Internet, or advertising information about a child to encourage or facilitate criminal sexual activity.

The measure doubled from 5 to 10 years the maximum prison sentence for enticing a minor to travel across state lines to engage in illegal sexual activity and increased from 10 to 15 years the maximum prison sentence for persuading a minor to engage in prostitution or a sexual act.

The House initially passed the bill in June. The Senate passed a revised version by voice vote Oct. 9. The House accepted the Senate changes Oct. 12, clearing the bill, 400-0. *(Vote 521, p. H-148)*

Asa Hutchinson, R-Ark., who managed the final debate in the House, praised the bill but decried some of the Senate changes, including a decision to drop a prohibition on contacting a minor over the Internet in order to engage in illegal sexual activity. Also dropped, he said, was language aimed at cracking down on serial rapists by mandating life in prison for such repeat offenders.

Senate Bills Seek To Limit Access To 'Cyberporn'

MARCH 14 — New legislation to limit children's access to pornography on the Internet is again raising constitutional questions about how to legally reduce children's exposure to on-line smut.

The Senate Commerce, Science and Transportation Committee approved two bills by voice vote on March 12 aimed at addressing the issue.

One of the bills, (S 1482), was introduced after the Supreme Court in 1997 struck down portions of the Communications Decency Act, included in the 1996 telecommunications law, (PL 104 – 104), that banned the dissemination to minors of "indecent" or "patently offensive" materials.

S 1482 would prohibit the commercial distribution on the World Wide Web to those under 17 of materials that are "harmful to minors."

The other bill (S 1619) approved by the committee would require schools and libraries to add filtering or blocking technology to their computers to keep children from accessing pornography on the Internet as a condition for receiving discounts to hook up to the Internet.

The discounts were mandated by the 1996 telecommunications overhaul through the universal service fund, which is supported by contributions from telecommunications carriers.

Carefully Crafted

Daniel R. Coats, R-Ind., S 1482's sponsor, said he used the Supreme Court's decision as a guide in writing his legislation and said it is carefully crafted to be constitutional.

Among other things, the legislation uses the "harmful to minors" standard, which has been upheld by the Supreme Court. It also limits the prohibition in the bill to commercial distribution, while the Communications Decency Act targeted both commercial and non-commercial dissemination.

"We believe we have corrected the constitutional problems," said Coats, one of the chief backers of the Communications Decency Act.

But critics such as the American Civil Liberties Union, one of several groups that challenged the Communications Decency Act, said in a letter to members of the committee that the government's interest in protecting children from harmful materials does not "justify the broad suppression of adult speech."

Daniel J. Weitzner, deputy director of the Center for Democracy and Technology, a group that promotes civil liberties in cyberspace, said he does not believe the Supreme Court will uphold efforts to mandate a national standard "harmful to minors" even though it has upheld the standard at the state level.

Weitzner said his group plans to launch a broad offensive against the bill before it goes to the Senate floor. But if Congress passes the bill, his group will challenge the measure in court.

Even those lawmakers who supported the legislation in committee were concerned about whether it could pass constitutional muster.

There are "concerns about its constitutionality," said committee Chairman John McCain, R-Ariz. "But more and more, parents are saying, 'this is terrible.' The question is how do we go about it in a constitutional fashion."

Some lawmakers said pornography on the Internet is so pervasive that Congress needs to do something to address the problem. "We're having such difficulty with pornography on the Web with children getting to it that I think we need to try something like this," said Sam Brownback, R-Kan.

Ron Wyden, D-Ore., was the only member to voice opposition to the bill, saying Congress should not mandate a "one size fits all" approach to the problem.

Ernest F. Hollings of South Carolina, the ranking Democrat on the Commerce Committee, predicted that there "will be enough holds on this bill that we can be done with it." A hold is a request — usually honored by the majority leader — by a senator to delay floor consideration of a measure.

Filtering Out Smut

McCain's legislation to tie the distribution of Internet subsidies to the use of filtering technology is also surrounded by controversy.

Educators and librarians are concerned about placing any new limits on the program to grant subsidies to schools, libraries and rural health care centers to hook up to the Internet and say decisions about the technology should be made at the local level.

They favor an approach proposed by Conrad Burns, R-Mont., that would require schools and libraries to adopt acceptable Internet use policies as a condition of receiving the subsidies.

By mandating the use of technology, "you give communities a false sense of security that government is taking care of it," Burns said. "That's not a good assumption."

Burns planned to offer his proposal as an amendment to S 1619 but withdrew it after Democrat John B. Breaux of Louisiana offered an amendment to require schools and libraries to select a blocking system that could be adjusted to suit the user by varying the degree of filtering.

Breaux withdrew his amendment after he and Burns agreed to work out a compromise before the legislation goes to the floor.

Internet Smut Curb Criticized As Too Tough

SEPTEMBER 19 — A Republican-led drive to protect children from smut on the Internet came under fire the week of Sept. 14 from opponents who questioned whether it would have barred the distribution of the graphic report on President Clinton's illicit affair by Independent Counsel Kenneth W. Starr.

The House Commerce Telecommunications, Trade and Consumer Protection Subcommittee passed by voice vote Sept. 17 a bill (HR 3783) to require distributors of on-line pornography to limit access to adult material.

The bill would set penalties of up to six months in prison and a fine of $50,000 for businesses that make any on-line communication for commercial purposes that is harmful to minors under the age of 17.

The American Civil Liberties Union opposed the bill, arguing the penalties could have applied to operators of Web sites that displayed Starr's report on Clinton.

"There is an irony that we're debating questions of how to protect children from graphic material on the Internet at the same time that Congress is voting on whether to release graphic material" sent to Capitol Hill by Starr, said Rep. Edward J. Markey, D-Mass., ranking member on the subcommittee.

Rep. Michael G. Oxley, R-Ohio, the bill's sponsor, disagreed, contending that the Starr report was not designed to appeal to prurient interests.

The Senate approved its version of measures to protect children from on-line pornography as part of a fiscal 1999 spending bill to fund the departments of Commerce, Justice and State on July 23.

Congress is working on new pornography legislation in the wake of a June 1997 Supreme Court ruling that struck down provisions of the 1996 telecommunications law (PL 104-104) barring "indecent" communications on the Internet. The court said the law was too broad.

House Panel Approves Internet Pornography Bill

SEPTEMBER 26 — The House Commerce Committee, trying to strike a delicate balance to protect both constitutional rights and children, approved a bill Sept. 24 to shield minors from pornography on the Internet.

Supporters of the bill (HR 3783), approved by voice vote, characterized it as a "minimal" attempt that does not prevent pornography from being put on the Internet. Content providers would be required to set up sturdy barriers to screen out children under age 17.

"HR 3783 does not burn the house to roast the pig," Committee Chairman Thomas J. Bliley Jr., R-Va., said. "Adults may still view any materials on the Internet they wish, with minimal inconvenience. ... HR 3783 merely requires adults to purchase adult material in cyberspace the same way they do in the real world."

Critics, however, repeated complaints that the bill is unconstitutional.

"At first glance," said Barry Steinhardt, president of the Electronic Frontier Foundation, a nonprofit group supporting free speech on the Internet, "it appears relatively benign with its sponsor's claim that it only applies to commercial pornographers who market their sites to minors, but when you look beneath the veneer, you quickly discover that it applies to any Web site that has a commercial component."

The bill would require Web sites containing material "harmful to minors" to use an adult verification method — such as a credit card, an adult access code or a personal identification number (PIN) — to keep children from accessing their sites. Failing to make "good faith" efforts to keep children out could result in fines up to $50,000 and imprisonment for up to six months.

The latest effort is in response to a 1997 Supreme Court ruling that struck down the Communications Decency

Technology & Communication

Act, a provision of the Telecommunications Act of 1996 (PL 104-104), which sought to ban indecent on-line speech. *(1997 Almanac, p. 5-25)*

House Passes Restrictions on Internet Smut

OCTOBER 10 — Concerned that children are being exposed to pornography with the click of a mouse, the House passed a bill Oct. 7 that would require companies to verify a person's age before he could view smut on the Internet.

By voice vote, the House passed HR 3783, which would require commercial Web sites to take steps to prevent those under 17 from gaining access to on-line material deemed "harmful to minors."

Under the bill, Web sites would be required to ask potential viewers for proof, such as a credit card or other means of identification, to ensure that only adults access on-line smut on their sites. Violators could face a $50,000 fine and six months in jail.

"Children cannot safely learn in a virtual red-light district," said Republican Rep. Michael G. Oxley of Ohio, the bill's sponsor.

The bill also includes a provision that would require Web sites to get parental consent before collecting personal data from children 12 or under.

But Rep. Barney Frank, D-Mass., and other critics say the bill's pornography section is unconstitutional because it may infringe on the rights of adults.

Daniel R. Coats, R-Ind., sponsor of the Senate version of the bill, said on Oct. 9 that it would likely be rolled into the omnibus spending bill.

The Supreme Court in 1997 struck down part of the Communications Decency Act (PL 104-104) that was aimed at restricting children's access to smut on-line, forcing Congress to write legislation that does not violate free speech rights. *(1997 Almanac, p. 5-25)*

In an Oct. 5 letter to Commerce Committee Chairman Thomas J. Bliley Jr., R-Va., the Justice Department questioned whether the bill violates the Constitution's free speech guarantee.

And the Motion Picture Association of America, led by Disney Co., said they had problems with the legislation. They said mainstream Internet sites could be subject to the bill's restrictions even if only one item, such as an R-rated movie available on-line, was objectionable.

Pornography Bill Rolled Into Spending Package

OCTOBER 17 — Congress added legislation to the omnibus spending bill (HR 4328), expected to be cleared the week of Oct. 19, that would require commercial Web site operators to take steps to keep children from accessing on their sites pornography or any other material deemed "harmful to minors."

On-line pornography was among the first issues Congress tried to tackle relating to the Internet, and is possibly the hardest to resolve.

With no hearings and little debate, Congress included legislation known as the Communications Decency Act in the 1996 telecommunications overhaul (PL 104-104) that banned on-line distribution to minors of indecent or "patently offensive" material. *(1996 Almanac, p. 3-46)*

The Supreme Court struck down part of the legislation in 1997, saying it was too broad and limited adults' free speech rights. *(1997 Almanac, p. 5-25)*

Sen. Daniel R. Coats, R-Ind., and Rep. Michael G. Oxley, R-Ohio, introduced new versions of the legislation (S 1482 and HR 3783) in this Congress, tailored to address many of the problems raised by the high court with the Communications Decency Act.

"We bent over backwards . . . to make it constitutional," Oxley said.

Despite objections from the administration, congressional leaders added Oxley's version of the legislation, which passed the House by voice vote Oct. 7, to the omnibus spending bill.

Oxley's measure would require commercial sites on the World Wide Web to ensure that only adults can access material deemed "harmful to minors." Web sites would have to require users to provide a credit card, password or other technologically feasible means of verifying that they are adults.

Violators could face a $50,000 fine and six months in prison. Web sites that fail to take the steps to keep children from accessing smut on their sites also would not benefit from the tax moratorium as stipulated by a provision added to that legislation.

Supporters pointed to several reasons why they believe the legislation is constitutional.

They noted that Oxley's bill is limited to commercial sites on the World Wide Web and does not apply to all speech on the entire Internet, addressing problems the high court raised in its decision on the Communications Decency Act. They also said the "harmful to minors" standard has been upheld by the Supreme Court for the state level.

Nonetheless, White House Internet policy adviser Ira Magaziner said the administration opposed the bill because the administration would prefer to promote the use of software filtering and other voluntary initiatives to limit children's exposure to on-line smut.

In addition, he said the Justice Department raised concerns about the bill's constitutionality, saying the court might not uphold the statute if it was too difficult and costly for Web site operators to comply with it without infringing on the protected speech of adults and minors.

The American Civil Liberties Union, the Electronic Privacy Information Center and Electronic Frontier Foundation have vowed to challenge the legislation in court. The groups were among those that filed suit against the Communications Decency Act.

"It is the height of irony that the same Congress that plastered the salacious Starr report all over the Internet now passes a plainly unconstitutional law to suppress a vaguely defined category of 'harmful' material," said Barry Steinhardt, president of the Electronic Frontier Foundation, a San Francisco-based think tank specializing in high-tech issues.

But some argue that there is less certainty this time around as to whether they will win such a fight.

The Supreme Court has "not spoken on whether a [federal] standard such as 'harmful to minors' is constitutional as a limitation on free expression," said David Cole, a law professor at Georgetown University.

Even David Sobel, general counsel for the Electronic Privacy Information Center, a Washington, D.C., public interest research institute focusing on electronic civil liberties issues, acknowledges that "it's a closer call" than the first legislation.

But Sobel said he believes there are at least two reasons the Oxley legislation will be struck down. First, he said, it is too difficult to determine the age of a Web surfer. Second, he does not believe the Supreme Court will endorse a national "harmful to minors" standard because states' views of what is harmful to minors often differ greatly, he added.

"The kind of material prosecuted in . . . Mississippi would not be prosecuted in New York City or San Francisco," Sobel said.

Meanwhile, the House on Oct. 12 cleared legislation (HR 3494) that would increase penalties for sex offenders who use the Internet to distribute child pornography.

While legislative efforts to crack down on pornography on the Web may have succeeded for now, a push to curb Internet gambling fell short.

The legislation was inserted into the Senate's Commerce, Justice, State spending bill (S 2260), by Jon Kyl, R-Ariz., during Senate floor consideration July 23.

But after the commerce spending measure was added to the omnibus bill, House and Senate negotiators chose not to keep the Internet gambling ban.

The legislation would have made Internet gambling a crime punishable by up to four years in prison and $20,000 in fines or the total amount of gambling proceeds.

It also would have required Internet service providers to cut service to gambling sites identified by law enforcement officials.

Kyl's ban was backed by a coalition that included the National Association of Attorneys General and conservative groups. But casinos and other groups supporting legalized gambling opposed any restrictions on the Internet.

Critics argued that the legislation would be impossible to enforce and would place unfair burdens on Internet service providers. Most Internet gambling operations are located outside the United States.

The House Judiciary Committee's Crime panel approved its own Internet gambling bill (HR 4427) Sept. 14. But Kyl said the legislation was "unacceptable" because that contained too many loopholes.

As a result, Kyl did not make a push to add the anti-gambling provision to the omnibus spending bill because of concerns that negotiators would try to compromise between the House and Senate measures and leave in parts of HR 4427 he opposes, according to a Senate aide.

Kyl plans to pursue an Internet gambling ban in the 106th Congress.

Meanwhile, another provision added to the Senate's commerce spending bill also was apparently deleted from the omnibus measure.

It would have required schools and libraries to add technology to their computers to block out pornography and other objectionable material as a condition for receiving federal subsidies for hooking up to the Internet.

However, privacy advocates succeeded in gaining inclusion in the omnibus bill of a measure that would require Web site operators to gain parental consent before collecting personal information from children, such as an electronic mail address.

Bill May Curb Internet Use By Pedophiles

MAY 9 — A House panel approved legislation May 6 to curb the growing use of the Internet by pedophiles to contact and distribute pornography to minors.

The legislation (HR 3494), approved by voice vote by the House Judiciary Committee, would establish a prison sentence of up to five years and fines for knowingly contacting a minor through an on-line service, such as the Internet, or through the mail for the purpose of engaging in sexual activity or transferring obscene materials.

Current law requires the federal government to prove that a pedophile "persuaded, induced, enticed or coerced" a child into a sexual act, according to the committee.

The Internet "is becoming the primary method [for pedophiles] for reaching kids," said Bill McCollum, R-Fla., the sponsor of HR 3494.

The bill also would increase penalties for other crimes against children, including a sentence of up to 15 years or a fine for transporting a child across state lines with the intent of forcing him or her to engage in prostitution or another illegal sexual activity.

The panel adopted by voice vote an amendment by McCollum that makes several changes to the legislation, including requiring a mandatory sentence of life in prison, unless the death penalty is imposed, for killing a child under age 14.

By voice vote, the committee approved an amendment offered by Republican Steve Chabot of Ohio that would prohibit federal prisons from allowing inmates to use an interactive computer service such as the Internet without supervision.

The amendment also would require the attorney general to conduct a survey of states to determine which ones allow unsupervised access to the Internet by inmates. The panel rejected, 7-17, an amendment by Democrat Barney Frank of Massachusetts to strike this provision.

House Approves Increased Penalties For Predators

JUNE 13 – Voting 416-0, the House approved legislation on June 11 that would create new penalties and expand others to crack down on pedophiles who use the Internet to contact or distribute pornography to minors. *(Vote 230, p. H-68)*

The bill (HR 3494) would subject adults to up to five years in prison and fines for using the Internet or the mail to contact a minor for the purpose of engaging in sexual activity or transferring obscene material.

"We will send a strong message to sexual predators and pedophiles across the nation," said Jennifer Dunn, R-Wash. "Make no mistake: You will be punished."

The measure would bolster several other penalties for crimes against children, including increasing to a maximum of 15 years the sentence for transporting a child across state lines with the intent of forcing him or her to engage in prostitution or other illegal sexual activity. ◆

Technology & Communication

House Bill Would Delay Increases in Fees For Some Satellite TV Transmissions

Box Score

- **Bills:** HR 2921, HR 3210; S 1422, S 2260
- **House action:** The House passed HR 2921 (H Rept 105-661, Parts 1-2) by voice vote Oct. 7. The Judiciary Subcommittee on Courts and Intellectual Property approved HR 3210 on March 18.
- **Senate action:** The Senate on July 21 added a revised version of S 1422 to S 2260 (S Rept 105-235). The Judiciary Committee approved S 1720 on Oct. 1.

The House passed a bill that would have delayed increases in copyright rates for satellite retransmissions of superstation and distant network signals to home satellite television subscribers.

SUMMARY

The bill (HR 2921) would have delayed until 2000 enforcement of a U.S. Copyright Office decision to raise those fees above the rates paid by cable TV for the same transmissions. Proponents contended the increase makes it more difficult for satellite companies to compete with cable, and the delay would give Congress time to consider more equitable treatment. Opponents, principally the Motion Picture Association of America, said the higher fees reflect the market value of those signals.

A revised version of the satellite fee legislation (S 1422) was incorporated into the Senate-passed Commerce-Justice-State Appropriations bill (S 2260), but was not in the final legislation.

A delay in the satellite fee increase also was included in a broader bill approved by the Senate Judiciary Committee (S 1720) that also would have allowed satellite TV companies to retransmit local broadcast signals to subscribers. But supporters were unable to move S 1720 to the floor before adjournment. The House counterpart, HR 3210, did not advance beyond subcommittee action.

Senate Panel OKs Bill To Promote Cable Competition

MARCH 14 — With growing concern over what some see as the slow development of competition to cable television, a Senate panel March 12 approved legislation that would delay a hefty increase in certain copyright fees on direct-broadcast satellite companies.

The Senate Commerce Committee approved legislation (S 1422) by voice vote that would prevent the Copyright Office from enforcing, collecting or awarding an increase in the fees that direct-broadcast satellite companies pay to downlink network and "superstation" signals to their customers.

In October, the Librarian of Congress, which has control over the copyright fees for satellite carriers, approved an increase to 27 cents a month per subscriber each for both network and superstation signals.

The fees had been 6 cents per subscriber for a network signal and 14 cents per subscriber for a superstation signal.

Direct-broadcast satellite is seen as the most viable competitor to cable. But some lawmakers, such as Commerce Committee Chairman John McCain, R-Ariz., say the fee increases — coupled with regulations that generally prohibit satellite operators from retransmitting local broadcast signals — will continue to hamper satellite companies' ability to compete. And some argue that the lack of robust competition has allowed cable operators to raise rates without having to worry about losing customers.

Cable companies say recent rate increases have been used to make necessary system upgrades and to pay for programming.

In addition to preventing the fee increases from going into effect, S 1422 also would require the Federal Communications Commission (FCC) to study the impact of the fee increases on competition in the multichannel video programming market.

The Motion Picture Association of America opposes the measure, saying the fee increases were based on the fair marketplace value for the signals.

House Bill Aims To Ease Licensing, Lower Fees

MARCH 21 — Direct-broadcast satellite companies are closer to getting rid of some legal impediments they claim are hampering their efforts to compete with cable television.

The House Judiciary Committee Subcommittee on Courts and Intellectual Property approved legislation (HR 3210) on March 18 that would, among other things, allow satellite broadcasters permanent licenses to retransmit signals without having to get the permission of every TV show they carry. The current license authority will expire at the end of 1999.

The legislation also would remove a prohibition against satellite companies' providing customers with local television station signals and against providing network signals to customers who have received the signals from a cable operator in the last 90 days. Under current law, satellite carriers can retransmit distant network signals only to homes that cannot obtain such signals over the air.

"I believe this is important legislation that sets a balanced approach with an eye at getting something passed and enacted this year," said Howard Coble, R-N.C., the bill's sponsor and the subcommittee's chairman.

In addition, the legislation also proposes a new board for determining the royalty fees paid by satellite carriers.

Several lawmakers have expressed concern about the slow development of competition in the multichannel video programming market and the pace at which cable rates have been increasing.

Direct-broadcast satellite has been seen as the most viable competitor to cable. But cable still controls 87 percent of the market as of July 1997, according to a report released in January by the Federal Communications Commission. The report found that cable's share of the market decreased only by 2 percent from the year before. The FCC's study also said that cable rates increased by 8.5 percent from July 1996 to July 1997, the period the report covered.

Going into the hearing, satellite companies were unhappy that the legislation did not address the royalty fees they pay to retransmit some signals.

Late last year, the Librarian of Congress, who enforces copyright law, adopted an arbitration panel's recommendation that the fees increase to 27 cents a month per subscriber for the signal from each network and "superstation," a local station whose signal is distributed nationwide. At the time, the rate for network signals was 6 cents, for superstations, as much as 17.5 cents.

The satellite industry and some lawmakers say the rate increase, which went into effect Jan. 1, places new obstacles in the way of satellite carriers, who must pay more than cable for the same signals. Satellite companies say cable is paying 2.45 cents for network signals, 9.8 cents for superstations.

Before the hearing, Coble proposed a compromise, offering to reduce the rates from 27 cents to 20 cents in his bill. A subcommittee aide said the satellite companies rejected the offer, but Andrew R. Paul, senior vice president for the Satellite Broadcasting and Communications Association, said he did not have time to talk to his members about the offer before the markup.

But in a surprising move, the panel adopted by voice vote an amendment offered by Rep. Rick Boucher, D-Va., that would roll back rates — for one year after enactment — to what they were before the increase took effect. "This is clearly hindering competition to cable," Boucher said of the rate hike.

But Howard L. Berman, D-Calif., argued — as the Motion Picture Association of America also has — that the higher fees reflect the fair market value of those signals. Berman conceded, though, that he does not understand why cable companies are paying so much less for the same signals. Rep. Barney Frank, D-Mass., countered, "This has nothing to do with the market rate. . . . We're in the land of arbitrary."

Rate Rollback

On March 12, the Senate Commerce Committee approved a stand-alone bill (S 1422) similar to the Boucher amendment that would have rolled back the fee increase until Jan. 1, 1999, and required the FCC during that time to study the impact the increase would have on competition to cable.

Paul said the satellite companies still have concerns with Coble's bill, particularly that it does not propose a solution for a long-running dispute over how to determine which customers cannot receive a local signal.

In addition, satellite companies such as Echostar Communications Corp. are worried about a provision in the House bill imposing a "must carry" requirement on satellite carriers, similar to one already applied to cable operators. The provision requires that satellite companies that want to retransmit a local station to a local market must carry all the stations in that market.

Time May Run Out On Move To Halt Rise in Rates

APRIL 11 — Wilfred C. Menard has had it with his cable television company.

Fed up with rates that have risen 50 percent over the past two years, Menard wrote the Federal Communications Commission (FCC) in January asking it to keep cable companies from using "every excuse in the book to raise prices."

"Every time I pay the bill, I think, 'Bring on the satellite,'" Menard said recently. But the 79-year-old military retiree in Lawrenceville, N.J., has been reluctant to switch. It is not the hassle of putting a dish on his roof to get satellite television service that bothers him. Rather, it is likelihood that the service, bound by a 1988 law, will not be able to send him local channels.

After a decade in which it has alternately deregulated and regulated the cable TV industry, Congress finds itself no closer to the competitive marketplace it has envisioned.

The 1996 telecommunications law (PL 104-104) was supposed to open up the vast market and lower rates. It has not worked as lawmakers hoped. (*1996 Almanac, p. 3-43*)

Local telephone companies were expected to invade the cable television business. So far, they have not moved quickly to provide cable. Direct broadcast satellite service was supposed to be the alternative to cable. It has been hobbled by other federal restrictions.

And cable rates are rising right along with the volume of angry mail to Congress.

"Overall, the rates are too high," said FCC Chairman William E. Kennard in an interview. "Many consumers are very upset about this."

It is, said Gene Kimmelman, co-director of Consumers Union's Washington office, the "Achilles' heel" of the 1996 telecommunications law.

"The fact that cable rates keep spiraling out of sight," Kimmelman said, "is a clear demonstration to the public that [the law] is failing."

Cable companies probably will keep raising prices unless the public rebels, said Bruce Leichtman, director of media strategies at the Yankee Group, a Boston-based company that analyzes the communications industry.

"People are not balking at these increases" by dropping their cable service, Leichtman said. The number of basic cable subscribers increased in 1997 by 1.2 million to 66 million.

Several bills have been introduced this year to ease restrictions on satellite services and make them more competitive with cable. But whether Congress will have time to tackle them in an abbreviated session is uncertain.

Congress is facing another deadline, too — on March 31, 1999, federal authority to regulate cable rates will expire.

Cable's share of the television market has declined by 2 percent in a one-year period ending in July 1997, but it

Technology & Communication

remained an overwhelming 87 percent, according to the FCC. More than two-thirds of households with a television also have cable.

Because most cable systems were built under franchises and the cost of building a competitor is now so high, most communities have only one cable service.

Critics say cable operators can raise rates without worrying consumers will flock to competitors.

Cable Dominates

Cable industry officials are defensive. Price increases are necessary, they say, to pay for programming — particularly for sporting events — to add channels and make improvements.

"We are a business just like anybody else," said David Krone, senior vice president for government relations for Tele-Communications Inc., the nation's biggest cable company with more than 17 million subscribers. "We raise rates because costs go up."

When Congress agreed in 1996 to remove price restrictions from the cable industry in three years, it figured that competition would hold rates down. (1996 Almanac, p. 3-43)

But local telephone companies have not been as aggressive in jumping into cable as some lawmakers had hoped, focusing more on trying to gain FCC approval to provide regional long-distance service.

"There is no prospect for [widespread] wire-based competition against cable in the next five years," said former FCC Chairman Reed Hundt.

Satellite services that provide channels directly to the home have more than 8.6 million subscribers as of February 1998 — an increase of nearly 2 million in the past year, according to the industry — but are not the sort of competition to cable that some lawmakers would like.

The up-front cost of buying a satellite dish and a receiver deters some consumers, although prices have been declining. Some electronics stores offer equipment starting at $99. And consumers must pay programming fees that run as low as $14.99 a month to get the signal.

Some members of Congress say they must remove legal obstacles before satellites can truly take on the cable industry.

One of the problems, they say, is a provision of the 1988 Home Satellite Viewers Act (PL 100-667), reauthorized in 1994, that allows satellite operators to retransmit network television signals to those viewers who cannot receive them from a standard antenna. (1988 Almanac, p. 584)

The law was written to protect local broadcasters from competing network signals that do not include local advertising, according to Rep. Rick Boucher, D-Va., a key player on the satellite legislation.

Beaming Local Channels

Satellite companies such as Echostar say eight out of 10 people who shop for a satellite dish do not get one after discovering they cannot receive local broadcasting.

Howard Coble, R-N.C., chairman of the House Judiciary Committee's Courts and Intellectual Property panel, has introduced a bill (HR 3210) that would allow satellite companies to deliver local broadcast stations to any customer.

The bill, approved by Coble's subcommittee March 18, also would make other changes to existing law to help satellite companies, including making permanent the license that allows satellite companies to transmit television programming without getting permission from every program developer. The license authority will expire at the end of 1999.

Similar legislation (S 1720) has been introduced in the Senate by Sen. Orrin G. Hatch, R-Utah.

But some satellite companies have opposed provisions in both bills that attempt to subject satellite companies to some of the same rules now applied to cable, including the requirement that if they carry any local stations, they must carry all.

Satellite companies also worry about a recent increase in copyright royalty fees they pay to retransmit signals of networks and superstations, local stations that are beamed nationwide. Some lawmakers argue that the increased rates put satellite companies at a disadvantage to cable companies, which pay much less.

Over the objections of Coble, his satellite bill now includes an amendment that would temporarily halt the rate increase. Coble said he may not support moving the bill unless he can find a compromise to the liking of television program developers, represented by the Motion Picture Association of America. A separate bill to roll back the rate increase has been introduced.

The Senate Commerce Committee approved one of those bills (S 1422) on March 12. Senate Majority Leader Trent Lott, R-Miss., has said S 1422 may be considered on the Senate floor in May.

Even with such legislation, there is little evidence that cable will be under enough competition any time soon to drive down rates.

Kennard told lawmakers March 31 that he does not believe "a year from now that we will have competition . . . to constrain rates."

Democratic Rep. Edward J. Markey of Massachusetts, a member of the Commerce panel's telecommunications subcommittee, said that if competition does not develop soon, "the only policy question we will need to answer is, 'Do our constituents prefer their monopolies unregulated or regulated?' "

He has introduced legislation (HR 3258) that would repeal the deadline that would end the FCC's authority over cable rates until more competition develops.

While most Republicans say they do not favor continuing regulation of the industry, they also say Congress may be left with little choice.

"Pressure is going to be put on Congress to do something," said Republican subcommittee member W. J. "Billy" Tauzin of Lousiana.

FCC Clout

Markey and others also say the FCC must be more aggressive in clamping down on the industry. "The FCC has rules in place that utterly fail to protect" consumers, Markey said.

The FCC's Kennard does not favor a freeze at this point but is studying cable rate regulation rules.

Kennard said it is unlikely that any changes to the current rules would be in place long enough to have an impact before the FCC's regulatory power over cable rates sunsets. He said extending the FCC's authority to regulate cable rates would give the commission time to assess the problem and propose a solution.

Decker Anstrom, president of the

National Cable Television Association, argues that extending the FCC's authority to regulate cable rates would stifle investment in cable systems.

After deregulating the cable industry in 1984, Congress reimposed rate regulation in 1992 because of consumer outrage over rate increases and poor service. *(1992 Almanac, p. 171)*

Anstrom acknowledged that the industry "didn't have a very good case to make" when Congress reimposed regulation in 1992. But he and other cable industry officials insist that the situation is far different today, noting that customer service has improved and that cable operators now face competition.

"It's an outdated solution," Anstrom said of regulation of his industry. "This is a very different marketplace."

Satellite TV Bill Wins Approval Of House Panel

JUNE 20 — With time running out for lawmakers to enact a broader bill aimed at removing barriers to competition, a House panel approved a narrow measure June 17 to roll back an increase in fees that satellite TV companies pay to retransmit some programming to their subscribers.

Responding to concerns about the slow development of competition to cable television, the House Commerce Committee's Telecommunications, Trade and Consumer Protection Subcommittee approved the bill (HR 2921) by voice vote.

The bill stems from the decision by the librarian of Congress in October 1997 to boost the copyright royalty fees that direct-broadcast satellite operators pay to retransmit network and superstation signals. The librarian oversees the Copyright Office, which administers the royalties.

The fees, imposed per subscriber per month, went from 6 cents for network signals and as much as 17.5 cents for superstation signals to 27 cents each.

The bill would prohibit officials from collecting the fee increase for seven months while the Federal Communications Commission (FCC) conducts a study on the impact the increase may have on competition to cable.

HR 2921's opponents say the increase reflects the fair market value of the signals.

Supporters, however, say cable operators pay much less for the same signals. They say the increase, which went into effect Jan. 1 and is being passed on to customers, adds to the hurdles that satellite operators face in their efforts to compete with cable.

Edward J. Markey of Massachusetts, the panel's top Democrat, tried unsuccessfully to offer an amendment that would have extended the FCC's authority to regulate cable rates one year beyond the time that the FCC submits its report on the fee increase. Under the 1996 telecommunications law (PL 104-104), the FCC's authority to regulate rates will sunset in March 1999.

Commerce Panel Votes To Delay Fees Increase

JUNE 27— The House Commerce Committee approved legislation June 24 to roll back an increase in the fees that satellite television companies pay to retransmit superstation and network programming.

Approved by voice vote, the bill (HR 2921) would delay the increase, approved in October 1997 and in effect since January, while the Federal Communications Commission (FCC) studies the impact that the higher fees may have on competition in the multichannel video programming market.

The panel adopted by voice vote an amendment by the bill's sponsor, W. J. "Billy" Tauzin, R-La., to extend the period during which the fee increase would not be in effect, from seven months to one year.

HR 2921's backers said the fee increase has added a hurdle in the efforts of satellite TV companies such as DIRECTV to compete with cable television. The fee increases "are excessive and are totally out of proportion to the fees for exactly the same programming that are paid by cable systems," said Rick Boucher, D-Va.

Boucher and others said the lack of competition has allowed cable companies to raise rates without losing customers. Lawmakers are particularly interested in removing competitive barriers facing satellite companies before March 1999, when the FCC's authority to regulate cable rates ends.

The bill now heads to the House Judiciary Committee for consideration, which could prove problematic for the bill's supporters.

Howard Coble, R-N.C., chairman of the Judiciary Committee's subcommittee with jurisdiction over the legislation, opposes the bill and hopes to make it more acceptable to television programming owners.

Critics such as the Motion Picture Association of America said higher fees better reflect the fair market value of network and superstation signals.

An amendment similar to HR 2921 was added to a broader satellite bill (HR 3910) approved by Coble's subcommittee in March. Coble has been reluctant to move HR 3910 because of the amendment but is considering adding provisions from that bill to HR 2921, according to a committee aide.

House Committee Adds Controversy To Satellite Bill

AUGUST 8 — One of the easiest steps many lawmakers thought they could take in 1998 to boost competition to cable television was to roll back a sharp increase in the rates that satellite TV companies pay for some programming.

But efforts to clear a bill before the end of the 105th Congress were impeded Aug. 4 when the House Judiciary Committee added a controversial provision to the legislation (HR 2921) as part of an amendment adopted by voice vote.

The provision, offered by Howard Coble, R-N.C., would allow satellite operators to provide customers with their local broadcast stations only if they carry all the stations in that local market. This "must carry" provision, as it is known, was included in a bill (HR 3210) approved in March by House Judiciary's Courts and Intellectual Property Subcommittee.

As approved by voice vote by the Judiciary Committee, HR 2921 would

Technology & Communication

roll back until Dec. 31, 1999, an increase in the royalty fees that satellite television operators pay to retransmit network and superstation signals.

The Commerce Committee's version, approved in June, would delay the fee increase for one year after the bill's enactment and require the Federal Communications Commission to study the effect the hike would have on competition.

Supporters of a rollback say the increase, which has been in place since January, added a hurdle to the efforts of satellite operators to cut into cable's dominance in the multichannel video programming market because cable operators pay much less for the same signals. Many members say competition is key to keeping cable operators from continuing to increase rates, which have risen 7.3 percent in the past year.

Under current law, satellite TV companies can provide network signals only to viewers who cannot receive them from an over-the-air antenna. Some satellite operators and lawmakers say this is one of the reasons why some viewers have been reluctant to drop cable.

Echostar Communications Corp., which has been the most aggressive in pushing to provide customers with local broadcast stations, said the company only has the satellite capacity to serve a few markets if it had to carry all the stations in each market it wanted to serve and that it would not be economically feasible.

The company has been urging legislators to phase in the must-carry requirement, an approach favored by W. J. "Billy" Tauzin, R-La., chairman of the House Commerce Committee's Telecommunications panel and HR 2921's sponsor. "It's as if someone was looking for a way" to derail the bill by adding the must-carry provision, Tauzin said.

A House Judiciary aide said Coble has no intention of derailing the bill but thought the issue should be addressed sooner rather than later.

Cable companies are subject to must-carry rules, and they say satellite companies should play by the same rules if they want the same privileges.

Even if the bill is stymied, satellite companies could get a shorter reprieve under a provision added to the Senate's Commerce, State and Justice spending bill (S 2260). It would roll back the fee increase until March 31, 1999.

Senate Bill Leaves Local Programming Up in the Air

OCTOBER 3 — The Senate Judiciary Committee approved a bill (S 1720) Oct. 1 to keep about 1 million satellite viewers from losing some broadcast programming and make satellite providers more competitive with cable television.

But efforts to move related legislation (S 2494) through the Senate Commerce Committee broke down the same day in a dispute between satellite companies and broadcasters.

S 1720, approved by the Senate Judiciary Committee on a voice vote, would allow satellite companies to provide customers with their local programming.

Under current law, companies can only provide network programming to customers who cannot receive such signals through an antenna.

Supporters say the legislation is necessary to help satellite companies compete more effectively with cable. Many viewers are unwilling to switch to satellite because they cannot receive local broadcast station signals as part of their satellite programming package.

S 1720 would reduce, beginning Jan. 1, 1999, the copyright fees satellite companies pay to beam network and superstation signals to viewers. The fees increased on Jan. 1, 1998, forcing satellite companies to pay more for the same signals than cable companies.

The bill also would provide temporary relief for satellite viewers who could lose their ability to receive some network programming by Oct. 8 because of a federal court's ruling in a lawsuit brought by broadcasters.

S 1720 would extend the shutoff date until Feb. 28, 1999. The lawsuit charged that many viewers are illegally receiving network signals via satellite.

Under S 2494, the Federal Communications Commission would be required during this time to develop new rules to determine which viewers can receive network signals.

Senate Commerce and Judiciary Committee leaders had agreed to combine S 2494 and S 1720 before they reached the floor. Efforts to clear a comprehensive satellite measure are in doubt because of problems with S 2494.

House Passes Bill To Delay Increase In Satellite Fees

OCTOBER 10 — The House on Oct. 7 passed a measure (HR 2921) by voice vote that aims to boost competition between the cable and satellite television industries, by delaying until Dec. 31, 1999, a copyright fee increase that satellite companies would pay to transmit some programming.

Supporters said the delay would provide more time for consideration of how to fairly treat satellite and cable companies with future legislation.

Current law mandates that satellite companies can provide network signals only to viewers who cannot receive them from an antenna. Some satellite operators and lawmakers say this is one reason some viewers have been reluctant to drop cable service.

Because cable companies pay less than satellite companies for the same transmissions, bill supporters say that satellites face a sharp competitive disadvantage.

The Copyright Office in the Library of Congress recommended increasing the rates that took effect in January, to 27 cents a month for superstation and distant network signals.

In 1994, Congress had increased copyright payment rates through 1997 to 6 cents a month per subscriber for each distant network signal and to 14 cents for most superstation signals. ◆

Encryption

Lawmakers, White House Remain Conflicted About Encryption Export Restrictions

SUMMARY

Lawmakers failed to settle the long-running policy dispute over encryption, technology that scrambles data or communications for privacy. High-tech industry leaders say current export restrictions put them at a competitive disadvantage to foreign firms. But the Clinton administration has been reluctant to lift export controls because of concerns that increasing the availability of encryption will hamper law enforcement and intelligence gathering.

In 1997, five House committees approved a bill (HR 695 — H Rept 105-108) backed by industry leaders that would have allowed for the export of encryption products that are generally available overseas. (*1997 Almanac, p. 3-36*)

But Rules Committee Chairman Gerald B.H. Solomon, R-N.Y., insisted that any bill that went to the House floor include restrictions favored by the FBI and other law-enforcement agencies. Because HR 695's chief sponsors and industry officials opposed this version, the stalemate did not get settled.

Congress Calls For Tighter Limits On Encryption

JULY 11 — Demands for more action from Congress met the Clinton administration's July 7 announcement that it would allow U.S. companies to sell strong encryption products to banks and financial institutions in 45 countries without previously proposed restrictions.

The new guidelines will allow U.S. companies, after a one-time review, to export products with encryption — technology that scrambles computer data or electronic communications for privacy — of any strength level to banks or financial institutions.

The companies would not have to develop new products that include a feature giving law enforcement access to the "key" needed to decode encrypted data or communications.

When the Commerce Department first announced in May 1997 that it was loosening export restrictions on encryption products used by banks and financial institutions, it required companies that sold those products to have a key recovery plan. Companies that want to export stronger encryption products to anyone else must still agree to submit a plan for making products that include a key recovery feature.

The policy change will affect 70 percent of the world's financial institutions, but it only applies to 45 countries that have acceptable money-laundering laws, the Commerce Department said.

Industry officials said current export restrictions put U.S. companies at a disadvantage against some foreign competitors who can export and sell much stronger encryption products.

While acknowledging that the administration's latest move is a step in the right direction, some lawmakers and a coalition of high-tech industry interests and privacy advocates said it does not go far enough.

Rep. Rick White, R-Wash., and other lawmakers said Congress still needs to act to provide broader relief. "It's clear there won't be the liberalization of encryption policy needed" by the administration, White said. "It's high time to bring this issue to the [House] floor."

"We don't like this piecemeal approach," said Sue Richard, a spokeswoman for Americans for Computer Privacy, which represents high-tech companies that favor lifting export restrictions on encryption.

White and Richard's group back legislation (HR 695) that would allow the export of encryption products generally available overseas and would ban efforts to require that U.S. encryption products include a key recovery feature.

Efforts to move HR 695 received a boost in June when House Majority Leader Dick Armey, R-Texas, threw his support behind the bill and promised to bring it to the House floor this session.

13 Companies Offer Proposal On Encryption

JULY 18 — A group of computer companies unveiled a proposal July 13 to give their industry relief from restrictions on the export of encryption devices while addressing law enforcement concerns about such technology.

Cisco Systems Inc. and 12 other companies said the plan may help resolve the dispute over how much control the government should retain over encryption, technology that scrambles information to prevent unauthorized access.

The administration has been reluctant to relax export controls on encryption unless the products include a way for law enforcement to gain access to an unscrambled version of encrypted information. Legal and national security officials fear the export of unbreakable encryption would lead to its widespread use by criminals as camouflage.

The plan calls for the use of technology that would allow law enforcement officials with a court order to gain access to the information before it is encrypted. The technology may be included in a network router, which controls the flow of traffic over the Internet, and would allow access before the data is encrypted.

Ten of the companies, which include Hewlett-Packard and Novell,

Technology & Communication

have applied for permission to sell strong encryption products that include this technology. The administration praised the initiative but did not say whether it would agree to the companies' requests. The companies say they would still push for legislation that would relax export controls for all encryption products.

Administration Eases Rules On Encryption

SEPTEMBER 19 — The Clinton administration's latest effort to provide some relief from export restrictions on data scrambling technology has not assuaged those who have been pushing for more decisive action from Congress.

Even though the prospect of legislation clearing Congress this year is all but dead, the administration announced Sept. 16 that it will relax its current regulations over the export of encryption, technology that uses mathematical formulas to scramble data and communications in order to block access from unauthorized users.

While welcoming the administration's announcement as a step in the right direction, industry officials, privacy advocates and some lawmakers say they will continue to push next year for legislation that provides broader relief.

"We still have a long way to go, but this is a good start," said Rep. Zoe Lofgren, D-Calif.

Many industry officials back legislation (HR 695) co-sponsored by Lofgren and Robert W. Goodlatte, R-Va., that would allow for the export of encryption products that are generally available overseas. HR 695 has been approved by five House committees since 1997, but critics, including Rules Committee Chairman Gerald B.H. Solomon, R-N.Y., have been successful in keeping the bill from moving to the floor.

Industry officials say strong, unbreakable encryption is widely available around the world, and U.S. policies have done little but hurt American companies that sell encryption products or include it in other products such as software in their efforts to compete with foreign firms.

Some lawmakers and industry officials say they believe the threat of legislation has helped move the administration. Continued congressional pressure is needed to force the administration to lift the remaining restrictions opposed by industry, they say.

"Progress wouldn't have occurred without the legislative effort," Goodlatte said.

Administration officials say their policies have been designed to balance the needs of industry while also ensuring that strong, unbreakable encryption is not widely used by criminals or terrorists to hide their illegal activities.

"We must ensure that new technology does not mean new and sophisticated criminal and terrorist activity which leaves law enforcement outmatched," said Vice President Al Gore, who joined several other administration officials in announcing the new policies at a news conference at the White House. "And we must ensure that the sensitive financial and business transactions that now cruise along the information superhighway are 100 percent safe in cyberspace. Balancing these needs is no simple task, to say the least."

Piecemeal Relief

The new rules, which will be formally crafted later this year, are part of a piecemeal approach the administration has taken in providing industry some relief from export restrictions.

The current regulations are set to expire at the end of 1998. They allow for the export of products with a strength of 56 bits under controlled circumstances. But companies must agree to develop products in the future that include a key recovery feature that law enforcement can use to unscramble encrypted information. (A bit is a digit in a binary system; the longer the bit string, the greater the number of possible "keys" needed to unscramble the encrypted data or communications.)

Companies would be allowed to export their products as long as they included a recovery feature allowing law enforcement officials, with a court order, to gain access to the needed keys.

Many high-tech companies and privacy advocates oppose a key-recovery requirement, saying it provides a back door into encrypted information.

The new regulations would allow companies to export 56-bit products without having to agree to develop key-recovery products in the future.

These exports, however, would be prohibited to seven countries suspected of supporting terrorist activities: Iran, Iraq, Libya, Syria, Sudan, North Korea and Cuba.

The legislation would also allow the export of products of unlimited strength, with or without a key-recovery feature, to a handful of specific industries in 45 nations, an exception similar to one granted earlier this year for export to banking and financial institutions.

The industries include insurance companies, subsidiaries of U.S. firms, health and medical organizations except biochemical and pharmaceutical manufacturers, and foreign on-line merchants who sell products or services over the Internet to customers in the United States.

Industry Looks to Hill

While praising the administration's moves, Democratic Sen. Patrick J. Leahy of Vermont, who has co-sponsored legislation (S 2067) to relax U.S. encryption export controls beyond what the administration has proposed, said 56-bit products are quickly becoming outdated and that "128-bit encryption is now the preferred encryption strength."

Privacy advocates complain that the new policies provide little relief for individuals who want to use strong encryption for overseas transactions.

"Our big concern is that it leaves the little guy out," said Alan Davidson, staff counsel for the Center for Democracy and Technology, a group that promotes civil liberties in cyberspace.

At the same time, the administration has refused to rule out imposing controls on domestic use of encryption, which the FBI has advocated. Under current law, it is legal to use any type of encryption in the United States.

An FBI official said the agency still believes that encryption products sold in this country should include a mechanism for law enforcement officials to gain access to an unscrambled version of data or communications. ◆

Year 2000 Computer Glitch

Congress Clears Three Bills To Address Potential Chaos Created by 'Year 2000' Glitch

Box Score

- **Bills:** HR 4328 — PL 105-277; S 2392 — PL 105-271; HR 3116 — PL 105-164
- **House action:** The House adopted the conference report (H Rept 105-825) on HR 4328, 333-95, on Oct. 20. The House cleared S 2392 by voice vote on Oct. 1. It passed HR 3116 (H Rept 105-417) by voice vote on Feb. 24.
- **Senate action:** The Senate cleared the conference report on HR 4328, 65-29, on Oct. 21. The Senate passed S 2392 on Sept. 28 by voice vote. It cleared HR 3116 on March 6 by voice vote.
- **Presidential action:** Clinton signed HR 4328 on Oct. 21. He signed S 2392 on Oct. 19. He signed HR 3116 March 20.

SUMMARY

A new century is approaching, and with it, growing concern that the federal government and key private industries may not be able to solve what is widely referred to as the Year 2000 computer problem.

The problem stems from computer software that was written to assume the first two digits of a year are "19." If uncorrected, the glitch may cause computers to malfunction or shut down on Jan. 1, 2000, with potential massive disruptions to commerce, government and public utilities.

Congressional committees held numerous hearings in 1998 to review public and private-sector efforts to address the problem. But President Clinton's requests for emergency funding to speed Year 2000 work on federal computer systems ran into trouble when House GOP conservatives demanded that such funding be offset by spending cuts elsewhere.

They stripped emergency funds from the defense (HR 4103) and Treasury-Postal (HR 4104) appropriations bills, contributing to delays in approving those and other funding measures.

Ultimately, Republican leaders and the White House negotiated the inclusion of $3.35 billion in emergency funding to fix government computers in the fiscal 1999 omnibus appropriations package (HR 4328).

Separately, Congress cleared legislation (S 2392) to encourage corporations to disclose information about their compliance efforts by limiting their liability for statements concerning such efforts. Companies had been reluctant to share information because of concerns that any disclosure they made could be used against them in court.

The compromise version of S 2392 bars, with a few exceptions, the use in court of a company's year 2000 "readiness disclosure statement" to prove the accuracy of the company's assertions about how it is dealing with the problem, except in cases where the court finds fraud.

The measure also protects companies from liability for Year 2000 statements that are alleged to be false, misleading or inaccurate, unless it is proved that the company knowingly made false statements with intent to deceive or mislead.

And the legislation establishes a government Year 2000 Web site that will post information about the latest solutions available for consumers, businesses and local governments.

Finally, Congress also cleared legislation (HR 3116) that requires federal banking agencies to offer suggestions to banks and other financial institutions on fixing their computers, and to monitor companies performing services for banks to ensure that they, too, address the problem.

House Panel OKs Plan To Address Banking Problems

FEBRUARY 7 — The House Banking and Financial Services Committee approved legislation by voice vote Feb. 5 aimed at shoring up the financial community's efforts to fix the Year 2000 problem.

Among the numerous problems banks could encounter if they fail to fix their Year 2000 problems are errors in checking account transactions and interest calculations. Among the problems consumers could encounter are malfunctions with automated teller machines, which may assume all bank cash cards have expired.

The legislation (HR 3116) requires federal banking agencies and the National Credit Union Administration, which regulates all federally chartered credit unions, to conduct seminars for financial institutions on the implications of the Year 2000 problem and provide suggestions for solving problems associated with it.

HR 3116 also gives the Office of Thrift Supervision and the credit union administration the authority to examine the operations of service providers who contract with financial institutions to perform such tasks as data processing and information system management. This extension of authority would give the two agencies the same statutory authority enjoyed by the Federal Reserve, the Comptroller of the Currency and the Federal Deposit Insurance Corporation.

The bill's supporters say this extension of authority is necessary to ensure that service providers that contract with thrifts and credit unions are taking the steps to be Year 2000 compliant.

Under current law, the two agencies have to gain the permission of the service providers to examine their operations but not all have been willing to cooperate, officials said.

Some committee members and industry officials expressed concern about broadening the credit union administration's regulatory authority.

Technology & Communication

They said unlike the thrift office, the credit union administration has not made a case for permanently extending its authority.

The committee adopted by voice vote an amendment, offered by Republican Reps. Richard H. Baker of Lousiana and Spencer Bachus of Alabama, to sunset the credit union administration's authority over service providers on Dec. 31, 2001.

Senate Clears Bill, Extends Review To Financial Service Providers

MARCH 7 — The Senate cleared legislation March 6 aimed at ensuring that companies that provide services to thrifts and credit unions are addressing the Year 2000 computer problem.

The legislation (HR 3116 — H Rept 105-417) cleared by voice vote. It would extend authority to the Office of Thrift Supervision and the National Credit Union Administration to examine the operations of companies that perform services, such as data processing or information systems management, to ensure they are taking steps to address the Year 2000 computer glitch.

The bill would make the additional oversight authority permanent for the thrift office but would sunset the credit union administration's authority after Dec. 31, 2001.

In addition, the bill would require federal financial regulatory agencies to offer seminars to financial institutions on the implications of the Year 2000 problem and provide suggestions for how to fix it.

The problem stems from the practice of using just two digits instead of four to represent the year in computer date fields. Unless the problem is fixed, computers will be unable to distinguish the year 2000 from the year 1900, which could cause computer systems to malfunction or shut down.

The legislation was passed by the House on Feb. 24, also by voice vote. The Clinton administration said at the time that it supported the bill.

Clinton's Speech On Y2K Glitch Heartens GOP

JULY 18 — President Clinton's call for quick action on the Year 2000 computer problem encouraged congressional Republicans and business groups that have been clamoring for White House leadership on the looming technical glitch.

But Republicans also stressed that they want Clinton to continue keeping the issue in front of the public while ensuring his administration gets its own house in order.

Clinton announced a series of initiatives July 14 to combat the Year 2000 problem, including sending legislation to Congress seeking to immunize businesses from lawsuits that share information about it. Business executives historically have been fearful to disclose details to each other, fearing it could expose them to lawsuits while affecting their bottom lines.

The computer problem stems from using two digits instead of four to represent the year in computer programs. As a result, many systems may be unable to distinguish 2000 from 1900, which may cause computers to go haywire or break down.

In his most extensive public comments on the subject to date, Clinton warned that the problem could have disastrous consequences for government as well as banks, airlines and other computer-dependent sectors.

"Any business that approaches the new year armed only with a bottle of champagne and a noisemaker is likely to have a very big hangover on New Year's morning," Clinton said in a speech to the National Academy of Sciences.

Robert F. Bennett, R-Utah, who heads a Year 2000 task force in the Senate, praised the president's statement as "a stirring call to arms." The Information Technology Association of America, a leading group on business-related computer policy, described it as "a sign that this administration is ready to engage on this difficult situation."

Steve Horn, R-Calif., chairman of the House Government Reform and Oversight subcommittee with jurisdiction over Year 2000 matters, called on Clinton to make it an ongoing focal point of his agenda.

"I hope he just doesn't make one speech about this," Horn said. "He needs to repeat that message in every major city in America."

Last month, in his latest report card on the government's progress in addressing the problem, Horn said the departments of Transportation, State, Energy and Health and Human Services were not moving fast enough.

"I hope the president's message means he will finally direct his administration to join Congress in a concerted effort to deal with this important national challenge," said House Republican Conference Chairman John A. Boehner of Ohio.

Deadline Approaches

Clinton said he expects all federal agencies and the White House to complete work on making their computers Year 2000-compliant by March 1999.

At the same time, the president challenged businesses to take responsibility for compliance, to keep customers informed and to share information among themselves.

Clinton's Year 2000 adviser, John A. Koskinen, said the White House is sending Congress a proposal to encourage companies to share information on the best ways to make repairs.

Horn said he hopes such a bill can clear Congress soon. He and Constance A. Morella, R-Md., who chairs the House Science Technology Subcommittee, met with Democrats to discuss moving the legislation without becoming bogged down over partisan politics.

Horn added, however, that he prefers Congress wait until next year before considering any controversial proposals addressing the legal liability of companies targeted with lawsuits stemming from the Year 2000 problem.

Although business groups have sought legislative relief from large damage awards in lawsuits, Congress has been unable to pass broad liability legislation acceptable to members of both parties and the White House.

"We've got to keep the heat on," Horn said.

Congress Approves Limited Protections For Firms That Share Information

OCTOBER 3 — Congress cleared legislation that would make it easier for companies to share information about fixing their Year 2000 computer glitches without the fear of a lawsuit.

The legislation (S 2392), passed by the Senate on Sept. 28 by voice vote, would provide companies with limited protection from the use of statements concerning Year 2000 remedies or companies' progress in correcting the problem.

Bypassing the committee process, the House cleared S 2392 on Oct. 1 by voice vote, and President Clinton is expected to sign the legislation.

Supporters of S 2392 say many companies have been reluctant to share information about how to repair the problem or provide status reports on their efforts to fix their own systems out of fear that such data could be used against them in a lawsuit by disgruntled customers or competitors.

The computer problem stems from the use of two digits instead of four to represent the date in computers or devices with computer chips embedded in them. If left uncorrected, computer systems may not be able to distinguish between 2000 and 1900, causing some systems to malfunction or shut down.

S 2392 bans, with a few exceptions, the use of "Year 2000 readiness disclosure" statements by plaintiffs as evidence in court to prove the truth or accuracy of a company's assertions about dealing with the problem.

The bill also protects companies from liability for Year 2000 statements they made that are alleged to be false, inaccurate or misleading unless it is proven the company knew it was false, inaccurate or misleading and made it with an intent to deceive or mislead.

"No bill can magically solve the Y2K problem, but this bill greatly increases the chances that people will come forward more readily with solutions," said Patrick J. Leahy of Vermont, the top Democrat on the Senate Judiciary Committee. ◆

Lawmakers Clear Legislation Aimed at Curbing Cell Phone Fraud

SUMMARY

Congress cleared legislation (S 493) making it a federal crime to use computer software to copy, or "clone," the electronic serial numbers of legal cellular phone users, then use the numbers to charge calls to the legal user's account.

Previously, prosecutors had to prove an "intent to defraud" in the use of such cloning devices, which they said was difficult unless an offender was caught in the act.

The electronic serial numbers are transmitted to gain access to a telecommunications network. Thieves use scanners to pick up the serial numbers, which can then be electronically copied into another cellular phone. Calls made from those doctored phones are then charged to the account of the phone from which the serial number was stolen.

The Senate first passed the anti-cloning bill on Nov. 10, 1997, in response to increasing reports of cell phone crime. (*1997 Almanac, p. 3-42*)

On Feb. 26, the House passed its own version of the bill (HR 2460) by a vote of 414-1. The measure proposed to ban the production, trafficking and possession of "copycat" machines that allow thieves to clone cellular phones. Violators could face a fine and 15 years in prison for a first offense. Ron Paul, R-Texas, was the lone vote against the bill. (*Vote 25, p. H-10*)

The House also approved by voice vote a substitute amendment, crafted in consultation with senators and the Justice Department, to among other things, allow the government to seize property used to commit the crimes outlawed under the bill.

After approving HR 2460, the House inserted the text into S 493 and sent it back to the Senate. The move was intended to allow the Senate to clear the legislation without going to conference.

The anti-cloning bill cleared its final congressional hurdle April 1, when the Senate accepted the amended House version by voice vote, clearing it for the president. President Clinton signed the bill April 24 (PL 105-172).

The administration supported the bill, in part because of the House amendment allowing the government to seize property used to commit the crimes outlawed under the legislation.

Cellular Phone Privacy Bill Dies

The Senate never acted on separate House-passed legislation (HR 2369) that would have made illegal the simple interception of cellular calls, a response to the 1996 interception of a cellular phone call between House Speaker Newt Gingrich, R-Ga., and members of the GOP leadership. Under existing law, the action is illegal only if a call is intentionally intercepted and disclosed.

The House had passed HR 2369 by a vote of 414-1 on March 5. (*Vote 38, p. H-12*) ◆

Technology & Communication

Congress Seeks Restrictions On Unauthorized Switching Of Long-Distance Carriers

> **Box Score**
>
> • **Bills:** HR 3888; S 1618
> • **House action:** The House passed HR 3888 (H Rept 105-801) by voice vote on Oct. 12.
> • **Senate action:** The Senate passed S 1618 (S Rept 105-183), 99-0, on May 12.

SUMMARY

Legislators sought to crack down on telecommunications companies that change a customer's long-distance service without permission, a practice known as "slamming." But the legislation died on the final day of the session, entangled in an unrelated dispute.

Backers of the legislation (HR 3888, S 1618) said slamming was a growing problem, one that generated more than 14,000 complaints to the Federal Communications Commission (FCC) in 1998. They vowed to revive a bill in 1999 unless the FCC takes stronger action on its own.

By voice vote, the House passed a version of HR 3888 on Oct. 12 that called for giving telecommunications companies a choice: abide by a voluntary anti-slamming rule that would be developed by the FCC, the industry and consumer groups, or be subject to tougher FCC regulations.

Republican Sen. Susan Collins of Maine, voiced concerns that the legislation would pre-empt tougher state laws and would not give states adequate authority to allow consumers to "freeze" their choice of a long-distance carrier.

But AT&T and some House members objected that some companies might use freeze language to lock in customers and thwart competition.

On Oct. 20, one day before Congress adjourned, Senate Commerce Committee Chairman John McCain, R-Ariz., and House Commerce Committee Chairman Thomas J. Bliley Jr., R-Va., announced that they had agreed on language requiring the FCC to develop rules that would prevent companies from marketing freezes in an unfair or deceptive manner.

However, Senate floor action on the legislation was blocked after Wendell H. Ford, D-Ky., tried to add an unrelated provision naming a federal courthouse after a Kentucky judge.

Senate Panel Seeks To Curb 'Slamming'

MARCH 14 — The Senate Commerce Committee took aim March 12 at the unauthorized switching of a consumer's long-distance carrier.

The committee approved a bill (S 1618) that would require companies to gain verbal, written or electronic verification of a consumer's authorization for a change in his long-distance carrier.

The committee adopted by voice vote an amendment offered by Conrad Burns, R-Mont., requiring the FCC to submit a report to Congress identifying the telephone companies that were the subject of the most slamming complaints. "It's a very pervasive and extensive problem," said Olympia J. Snowe, R-Maine, one of the bill's cosponsors.

Among the verification methods the FCC requires is a letter of authorization before switching a consumer's long-distance carrier.

But such letters are sometimes drafted in a way that make it difficult for consumers to know they are agreeing to switch carriers by signing the letters, according to the FCC.

Senate Passes Bill To End 'Slamming,' 'Spamming'

MAY 16 — Responding to growing complaints from consumers, the Senate unanimously passed a bill May 12 to crack down on the unauthorized switching of a customer's provider of long-distance telephone service.

The legislation (S 1618), passed 99-0, would prohibit a company from changing a subscriber's long-distance provider without the customer's permission. And it would require a company to notify customers within 15 days that their provider has been changed. (Vote 130, p. S-22)

Supporters of S 1618 said subscribers often receive lower-quality service and higher rates from companies that switch their long-distance service without permission.

The Senate adopted by voice vote an amendment offered by the bill's chief sponsor, Commerce Committee Chairman John McCain, R-Ariz., that would set penalties of $40,000 for a first-time offense and $150,000 for a repeat offense.

In addition, the amendment also included a provision to curb "spamming," the practice of sending unsolicited electronic mail.

Those sending unsolicited e-mail would be required to provide a valid return e-mail address and inform recipients that they can stop future messages by typing "remove" in the subject line.

House Panel Marks Up Bill

AUGUST 8 — House lawmakers took steps Aug. 6 to crack down on two byproducts of the information age.

The House Commerce Committee's Telecommunications, Trade and Consumer Protection subcommittee approved by voice vote a bill (HR 3888) to curb "slamming," the unauthorized switching of a customer's long-distance provider, and "spamming," unsolicited e-mail.

Subcommittee Chairman W.J. "Billy" Tauzin, R-La., HR 3888's sponsor, cited a company that would phone consumers and ask during the sales pitch, "Can I put you on hold?" After this, customers were switched to the company because "hold" was its name.

HR 3888 would require companies to gain verbal, written or electronic consent from customers before switching their long-distance carriers and to notify them of the change in writing.

The panel approved, by voice vote, a substitute version of the bill by Tauzin and John D. Dingell of Michigan, the top Democrat on the full committee. It would allow consumers who said they had been slammed to be immediately switched to their original providers and to receive a credit for charges they paid to the unauthorized company.

Long-distance providers that lost customers to an unauthorized company could file a complaint with the FCC. The FCC could order the slammer to pay those providers the amount of their lost revenues and $500. If the FCC found that a company did not switch a customer's service, that company would be entitled to the credit paid to the customer or allowed to bill the customer for charges it was owed. Under the original bill, consumers would be required to pursue a complaint with the FCC on their own.

Those who violated the provisions could face a fine of at least $40,000 for the first offense.

Michael G. Oxley, R-Ohio, said he feared that the FCC would be overwhelmed with complaints from providers. He offered an amendment, which he withdrew, that would have required providers to instead seek damages in court. "Our goal should be less bureaucracy and reliance on the FCC, not more," Oxley said.

The 1996 telecommunications law (PL 104-104) called on the FCC to adopt rules to curb slamming, but some members say the commission has not done enough. In the past year, however, the FCC has levied big fines against two companies accused of the practice.

Blocking Junk E-Mail

HR 3888 also would require those who send unsolicited e-mail to include their name and e-mail address in the message and would allow recipients to stop new messages from being sent to them by typing "remove" in the subject line. Violators could face a $15,000 fine.

Rick White, R-Wash., and a few others were wary of the provisions. White said Congress should consider alternatives to legislation. "We may not know as much about this issue as we would like to know," he said.

He offered an amendment that would prohibit junk e-mail from being sent through Internet service providers that post policies prohibiting it. He withdrew the amendment after Tauzin agreed to work on a compromise.

House Commerce Approves Measure

SEPTEMBER 26 — Standing united against a growing problem in the Information Age, the House Commerce Committee Sept. 24 approved a bill to protect consumers from having their long-distance provider switched without permission.

The bill (HR 3888) would make it illegal for a long-distance company to change a person's service without the person's authorization, a practice known as "slamming." Companies could face a $40,000 fine for the first offense and a $150,000 fine for subsequent violations.

The bill, approved by voice vote, is similar to legislation (S 1618) the Senate passed in May. It is expected to win final approval before Congress adjourns.

Slamming has become more commonplace and indiscriminate as competition for customers intensifies in the telecommunications industry.

"While it is true that competition has resulted in numerous benefits for consumers, competition also has its darker side. And slamming is proof of that," said Thomas J. Bliley Jr., R-Va., Commerce Committee chairman.

The bill would require the FCC and the Federal Trade Commission to develop rules to prevent slamming. But in a change to make the bill more palatable, the rules would go into effect if companies failed to police themselves.

In order to change providers, customers would have to give direct consent. Long-distance carriers would be required to notify them of the switch in writing.

The bill also aims to corral a growing problem on the Internet known as "spamming" — sending unsolicited e-mail. It would require those sending unsolicited e-mails to include their names and e-mail addresses in their messages. Recipients could stop new e-mail by typing "remove" in the subject line.

House Sends Modified Bill To Senate

OCTOBER 17 — The House Oct. 12 passed legislation to protect consumers from a growing problem in the marketplace — the unauthorized switching of their long-distance phone service.

But the chances of the Senate clearing the legislation (HR 3888) before Congress adjourns for the year appear dim.

The bill has been blocked in the Senate by those who complain that it does not go far enough to reduce the problem known as "slamming," and that the bill no longer includes a provision to crack down on unsolicited e-mail.

HR 3888, passed by the House by voice vote, would give telecommunications companies the option of complying with a voluntary code for switching consumers' long-distance service or being subject to more stringent regulation. Those who do not follow the code could face tougher penalties.

An earlier version of HR 3888 was tougher, imposing new regulations on telecommunications companies, regardless of their efforts to self-regulate.

Before bringing HR 3888 to the House floor, supporters removed a controversial provision on spectrum licenses that were won by some companies that have since filed for bankruptcy.

Rep. W.J. "Billy" Tauzin, R-La., HR 3888's sponsor, and others have criticized the FCC's handling of the licenses. Tauzin added a provision to the bill that would have forgiven the debts owed to the government for the licenses if the companies that received them returned the spectrum so it could be re-auctioned.

The Clinton administration and

others objected because of the possible costs to the federal government, estimated at as much as $1 billion.

'Slamming' Bill Dies in Senate

OCTOBER 24 — Despite agreement on a compromise, legislation to crack down on companies that change consumers' long-distance phone service without permission died in the Senate Oct. 21.

The bill (HR 3888) was derailed by an unrelated dispute over an attempt by Wendell H. Ford, D-Ky., to add a provision to the measure naming a federal courthouse after a Kentucky judge.

But Ken Johnson, spokesman for HR 3888 sponsor Rep. W.J. "Billy" Tauzin, R-La., complained the bill was delayed by "last-minute interference of powerful telecommunications companies."

In an effort to move the bill through the Senate, House and Senate lawmakers worked for more than a week to address the concerns of Sen. Susan Collins, R-Maine, that the bill would pre-empt tougher state laws and not give states clear authority to let consumers freeze their choice of long-distance provider.

However, AT&T and some House lawmakers said some companies might use the freeze language to lock in customers and thwart competition.

Senate and House Commerce Committee leaders reached a deal Oct. 20 to settle the issue by adding language requiring the FCC to develop rules to prevent companies from marketing the freezes in an unfair or deceptive way.

Senate Commerce Committee Chairman John McCain, R-Ariz., and Tauzin said they would urge the FCC to craft its own rules to combat slamming. If the FCC did not, they said they will be back in 1999 with new legislation. ◆

Chapter 23

TRADE

Fast-Track Trade Authority 23-3
  Main Provisions of Trade Bill 23-5

Relations With Vietnam 23-9
Africa Trade, Investment 23-10

Lawmakers Again Reject President's Attempt To Regain Fast-Track Trade Authority

> **Box Score**
>
> ● **Bills:** HR 2621; S 2400
>
> ● **House action:** The House defeated HR 2621 (H Rept 105-341, Part 1), 180-243, on Sept. 25.
>
> ● **Senate action:** The Senate Finance Committee approved S 2400 (S Rept 105-280), 18-2, on July 21.

SUMMARY

For the second time in two years, Congress denied President Clinton the renewal of authority to negotiate trade agreements and submit them to Congress for expedited approval — so-called fast track.

But unlike in 1997, when the president was fully engaged in lobbying to regain that authority, this year's bill was brought to the House floor by the Republican leadership in large measure as a means to highlight divisions in Democratic ranks.

In the end, the House voted on the legislation (HR 2621) after its defeat was seen as a foregone conclusion. But the decisiveness of the 180-243 vote — 71 Republicans voted "nay," while only 29 Democrats voted "aye" — signaled that Congress was leading the United States away from its half-century pursuit of global free trade.

Some House GOP leaders said they would not revive the issue in the 106th Congress.

Fast-track authority, granted to every president since Gerald R. Ford, means that Congress must take up proposed trade agreements within 90 days and cast up-or-down votes with no amendments allowed. Since that authority expired in 1994, Canada, the European Union, Latin countries and others have been cutting a new wave of trade accords without U.S. involvement.

Reauthorization of fast track was originally attempted in November 1997. However, faced with the prospect of defeat — largely because of strong Democratic opposition in the House — Republican leaders and Clinton decided to cancel a vote on the bill at the end of the first session of the 105th Congress.

Opponents had turned the debate into a referendum on the 1993 North American Free Trade Agreement which, critics said, failed to live up to promises of job creation. In addition, most Democrats insisted that labor and environmental guarantees should play a central role in trade negotiations — conditions that Republicans and their business supporters successfully limited to those having a direct impact on trade.

This year, administration officials objected to the timing of the vote, claiming that the GOP leadership was attempting to widen rifts between free-traders and organized labor and environmentalists in the Democratic Party in the weeks before Election Day.

Republicans countered that many exporters, particularly hard-pressed farmers, need new trade agreements to ensure that overseas markets are open. U.S. exports were sharply declining because of the Asian financial crisis. Still, in the days leading up to the vote, free-trade advocates urged GOP leaders to defer the issue until 1999, out of fear that defeat of the measure would roil already jittery global financial markets.

The full Senate never considered the issue, although a renewal of fast-track authority was included in omnibus trade legislation (S 2400) that the Finance Committee approved in July. That bill did not move further.

Pointing to Farmers' Plight, Gingrich Calls For New Vote

JUNE 27 — Citing a pressing need to help farmers reach overseas markets, Speaker Newt Gingrich, R-Ga., promised June 25 that the House would vote in September on renewal of "fast track" negotiating authority for the president to pursue trade agreements.

But House Democrats, who joined with their allies in organized labor last fall to stall fast-track legislation (HR 2621), predicted that Gingrich and the White House would again fail to come up with the votes needed to adopt the controversial measure.

Gingrich's decision to revive fast track came as he threw his support behind other initiatives aimed at addressing the trade concerns of both agriculture and business. They included efforts to reach a bipartisan agreement on funding the International Monetary Fund (IMF) and granting China most-favored-nation trade status.

At a news conference with the bipartisan leadership of the House Agriculture Committee, Gingrich said it is "very important for the United States to continue to open markets" for U.S. agricultural products. "There is, I think, a real need for very specific action to improve American access to the world market and to ensure that American farmers, the most productive in the world, are able to actually sell that produce around the world," he said.

Other lawmakers agreed, pointing to growing troubles in rural areas that are expected to reduce farm income by 8 percent from last year. Although many Democrats blame the situation on the 1996 farm law (PL 104-127) that deregulated commodity programs in favor of giving farmers fixed, declining payments over time, Republicans have contended trade barriers are the real problem. *(Farm law, 1996 Almanac, p. 3-15)*

House Agriculture Chairman Bob Smith, R-Ore., has warned of a possible repeat of the 1980s farm crisis this fall if prompt action is not taken. "This Congress must give farmers and ranchers a square deal," said Smith, who touted Gingrich's announcement as "a

Trade

historic day for agriculture."

Nevertheless, there were immediate signs that the effort faces a formidable struggle on several fronts, especially since it will unfold in the tight time period leading up to congressional elections in November.

IMF funding has stalled in the House, where members have criticized the IMF from the left for not backing labor protections and from the right for interfering with the free market.

The fiscal 1998 supplemental appropriations bill (PL 105-174) did not contain a requested $17.9 billion in IMF funding, which had been a top White House priority. Supporters say bolstering the IMF is necessary to safeguard the U.S. economy from significant fallout from the Asian crisis.

House Majority Whip Tom DeLay, R-Texas, a leading conservative critic of the IMF, issued a statement after Gingrich's news conference that raised strong objections to funding the agency.

"The agriculture community is right when it asks that we support policies that promote free trade and open markets," DeLay said. "But supporting the IMF is not necessarily the best way to achieve those goals, and we need to be very careful before we give the IMF more of the taxpayers' hard-earned money."

Fast-Track Prospects

Meanwhile, other lawmakers who fought the fast-track proposal last year predicted supporters would have an even more difficult time in the House attempting to pass the measure again.

Fast track guarantees that once the president submits a trade agreement to Congress for ratification, lawmakers must take an up-or-down vote within 90 days, with amendments prohibited. Foreign countries are reluctant to begin serious trade negotiations unless fast-track rules are in place for fear that Congress will force a second round of negotiations to seek parochial concerns.

Gingrich estimated that supporters were "about eight votes" shy of winning approval last fall, and predicted that the recent decline in farm prices and the financial crisis in Asia would influence lawmakers. "My instinct is that a lot of members who were wavering last fall now realize that it's important for us to pass this and send the right signal to the world markets," he said.

But Sherrod Brown, D-Ohio, who helped lead the fight against fast track last fall, predicted the issue has even less of a chance this year. He contended Gingrich needs "more like 28 votes" instead of eight.

"There's no reason it will pass now," Brown said. "Here's why they're weaker than they were before — they said the stock market would plunge and a recession would occur if we defeated fast track. Well, the stock market kept going up, and the economy has kept going. . . . Gingrich is just using fast track to raise money from the business community."

In addition to the fast-track and IMF issues, Gingrich said the House is taking three other steps to assist agriculture:

● A vote on most-favored-nation status for China, which the Speaker said should be divorced from the recent controversy over whether the Clinton administration's export policies allowed the Chinese to improve their missile technology.

● Reforming sanctions policy to exempt financial assistance for exports of agricultural commodities. The fiscal 1999 agriculture appropriations bill (HR 4101) passed by the House on June 24 includes an amendment lifting agriculture sanctions on Pakistan after that country's recent nuclear tests.

● Pushing the administration to negotiate with European Union countries to persuade them to reduce farm subsidies and anti-competitive trade practices.

Finance Committee Sends Bill To Senate Floor

JULY 25 — As the Senate Finance Committee completed work on a bill that includes the politically volatile issue of "fast track" trade negotiating authority, the panel's top Democrat and its Republican chairman thanked each other for a two-hour meeting that had been downright cordial.

But the kind words exchanged by Daniel Patrick Moynihan, D-N.Y., and Chairman William V. Roth Jr., R-Del., hid the divisions that turned fast track into one of the most contentious issues of 1997, and which threaten to have the same effect this year. In sending the draft bill to the Senate floor by a convincing vote of 18-2, the committee officially returned to Congress' front burner an effort to give the president authority to send trade agreements to Congress for expedited up-or-down votes.

Eight months ago, President Clinton and GOP leaders were left defeated after failing to secure the votes needed to pass fast-track legislation in the House. Until recently, it was considered a dead issue in Washington, and the House Democrats who played key roles in defeating it liked it that way. Now business leaders and union officials are preparing for another full-fledged debate, and House Democrats are preparing for legislative battle. (*Fast track, 1997 Almanac, p. 2-85*)

This time, however, Roth has sought to expand the debate beyond fast track. He included in the bill an array of trade measures with support from various factions in Congress. The most prominent is an initiative to promote trade with 48 nations of sub-Saharan Africa. "We feel by putting this package together, we improved the chances of getting it all approved," he said.

Perhaps setting the tone for things to come, grumbles emanated from those who oppose fast track and those who had hoped for relatively calm passage of the Africa trade measure (HR 1432), which Clinton touted in his State of the Union address. Supporters say the Africa initiative, which seeks to reduce tariffs and expand free-trade areas with qualified countries, would boost the African countries' economies, reduce their dependence on aid and forge important trading alliances. William E. Bucknam, co-chairman of a coalition of businesses pushing the measure, said the addition of fast track to the bill has left the group "concerned but optimistic."

Carol Moseley-Braun, D-Ill., who pointed out that she was the only African-American committee member, was less diplomatic. "I am saddened by the fact that, by my perspective, a poison pill has been placed in the legislation — and that is fast track," she said. She and Kent Conrad, D-N.D., opposed the bill.

After the markup, reaction from all

Trade Bill: Not Just 'Fast Track'

The draft trade bill approved July 21 by the Senate Finance Committee includes provisions from several trade measures, as follows:

● **Fast track.** The key element would renew "fast track" negotiating authority for the president to pursue trade agreements. It would allow the president to submit such agreements to Congress for up-or-down votes with no amendments. Supporters say it is needed to ensure competitiveness with countries whose leaders have similar powers. Critics fear it would mute Congress' role and put American workers and companies in jeopardy. It has strong backing from the business community but fierce opposition from organized labor.

American presidents had this authority from 1974 to 1994. Last year President Clinton and Republican leaders led efforts to renew it, but failed when a bloc of House Democrats and Republicans refused to give their support. *(Fast track, 1997 Almanac, p. 2-85)*

● **Africa trade.** The draft includes language from a House-passed bill (HR 1432) that would allow many products from sub-Saharan Africa to be imported duty free. For apparel, duty-free benefits generally would be extended only to products made with U.S. fabric, thread and yarn. The bill would waive rules that cut off tariff benefits for one year to countries whose annual exports of a particular product to the United States exceed either $85 million or 50 percent of U.S. imports.

● **Generalized System of Preferences (GSP).** The bill seeks to extend the president's ability to grant GSP status — duty-free benefits to developing countries on certain products — through Dec. 31, 2000. The president's authority to grant such preferences expired June 30.

● **Caribbean Basin Initiative.** The program was enacted in 1983 to grant tariff benefits to Central American and Caribbean countries with economic problems. The bill would expand the number of products that could be targeted for tariff benefits to include items such as canned tuna, petroleum and some textiles. The provision is narrower than a bill (HR 2644) defeated in the House last year. *(Caribbean trade, 1997 Almanac, p. 2-88)*

● **Trade Adjustment Assistance programs.** Several trade bills have included provisions to assist workers, companies and communities adversely affected by trade agreements. The bill would reauthorize through Sept. 30, 2000, three programs set to expire this fall. The programs provide technical assistance for businesses, training and income support for workers who lose their jobs because of new competition from foreign countries, and similar assistance for workers displaced by factory shifts to Canada or Mexico after the 1993 North American Free Trade Agreement. *(1993 Almanac, p. 171)*

● **Agriculture.** The measure includes language from a bill (S 219) that would identify foreign countries that move to prevent the United States from exporting agriculture products.

● **Shipbuilding.** The measure would incorporate a bill (S 1216) to ratify a shipbuilding agreement the United States has reached with the European Union, Japan, South Korea and Norway. The agreement, ratified by all parties except the United States, would eliminate most shipbuilding subsidies and allow countries to fine foreign shipyards for selling ships at "unfair" prices.

● **Mongolia.** The bill includes a measure (S 343) to permanently grant normal trade relations status to Mongolia, which has received such status — formerly known as "most favored nation" — since 1991.

● **Wool.** The bill would reduce the approximately 31 percent tariff on wool fabric. Suit manufacturers say that would lower their costs for obtaining wool and help them compete with Canadian and Mexican manufacturers, who can export to the United States without facing high duties on their finished suits.

---

corners of Washington was swift. Some Democrats objected to Roth's decision to combine the trade measures, accusing Republicans of trying to force House Democrats to take a potentially party-dividing vote on the trade package just before the November elections.

"It's an underhanded way to force on the American people a trade agreement that they don't like," said Sherrod Brown, D-Ohio, who strongly opposed fast track last year. "This will only bury fast track deeper than it was buried last year."

Clinton has publicly cooled to the idea of reviving the fast-track bill in this Congress. Clinton spokesman Mike McCurry called the resurrection of the issue "political mischief-making and not international economic policy-making," and did little to brush aside speculation that Democrats hope to avoid a vote on an initiative that divided their party last year.

"I didn't say that," he said in response to such a question. "But you can easily surmise that, couldn't you?"

The Senate is expected to pass the bill with broad bipartisan support. The House is an obstacle.

"Mr. Gephardt is opposed to the bill," said Erik Smith, spokesman for Minority Leader Richard A. Gephardt, D-Mo., who led the 1997 effort against the legislation. "He believes it will fail again. Nothing has happened to merit a shift in our members' opinions."

Business groups continue to support the measure, arguing that the United States is losing ground because of the president's inability to easily negotiate trade agreements. "The longer we

Trade

wait, the more we're going to get our clock cleaned in the global marketplace," said John Howard, director of international policy for the U.S. Chamber of Commerce.

On the opposite side of the issue, organized labor officials are repeating last year's mantra: The bill would allow trade agreements with potentially harmful consequences for American workers to quietly take effect. David Smith, public policy director for the AFL-CIO, said he has heard nothing to suggest the votes of Democrats who opposed the bill last year will change. Moreover, he said, efforts by Republicans to force a vote could backfire.

"Any vote on fast track will energize the unions," he said.

Senate Majority Leader Trent Lott, R-Miss., said he thinks the trade legislation, which he called "monumental," could be considered on the Senate floor in September. House Speaker Newt Gingrich, R-Ga., promised last month that the House will consider fast-track legislation this fall but said he wants the Senate to act first. Supporters are pointing with excitement to Senate approval July 16 of a nonbinding amendment to the fiscal 1999 Agriculture spending bill (S 2159) that called on the Senate to vote on fast track this year.

Amendments

The Finance markup, attended by more than 200 lobbyists, reporters and administration officials, moved smoothly. Lawmakers readied 20 amendments, but the panel voted on only three, soundly defeating them.

The panel rejected, 5-15, an amendment by John H. Chafee, R-R.I., to remove a provision to lower tariffs on wool fabric.

It also defeated two amendments by Conrad. One, rejected 6-14, would have required the administration to consider the potential economic consequences of trade agreements and allowed the United States to renegotiate agreements that had adverse effects. The other, rejected 4-16, would have required the president to assess the currency stability of other parties to any fast-track agreement.

Roth told the committee that passing fast track is the right message to send to America's trading partners.

"What is needed is a strong statement of the United States' commitment to a free and open trading system," he said.

Moynihan agreed, but joined other Democrats who expressed doubt about the bill's prospects in the House. Phil Gramm, R-Texas, said such doubts may be justified. Still, by moving it through the Senate, "at least we made the effort," Gramm said.

Besides fast track and Africa trade, the bill embraces several other measures, including:

- The text of a Senate bill (S 1216) to implement an international shipbuilding trade agreement.
- A provision to permanently grant Mongolia "normal trade relations" status, a term that replaced "most favored nation" on July 22 when Clinton signed into law a bill (HR 2676) to overhaul the Internal Revenue Service.
- An extension through 2000 of the Trade Adjustment Assistance program, which provides training to workers in industries that lose jobs because of trade agreements.
- A provision to allow Caribbean and Central American nations covered by the Caribbean Basin Initiative (CBI) to export some products to the United States free of duties and quotas.
- Reauthorization through 2000 of the Generalized System of Preferences (GSP), which allows the president to extend duty-free treatment to imports from certain developing nations.
- Reduced tariffs on imported wool.

The committee spent almost as much time debating the wool tariff as it did talking about fast track, but it was clear the bill will live or die with the latter issue. "In the newspaper headlines," Brown said, "it will be seen only as fast track."

House Vote Signals Reversal of Support For Free Trade

SEPTEMBER 26 — The House on Sept. 25 delivered a severe blow to the nation's longstanding free-trade policy, decisively rejecting a proposal to renew fast-track trade authority. The vote was 180-243.

The outcome leaves U.S. trade policy in apparent disarray and the House as torn as ever by partisan warfare.

"We're really going to have to redefine where we're going on trade," said a dejected Rep. Robert T. Matsui, D-Calif., a leading free-trader. "It's in shambles."

With members on record against the fast-track bill (HR 2621), GOP Conference Chairman John A. Boehner of Ohio said the House may not bring up the issue again until 2001. That would further hobble President Clinton, already weakened by an impeachment inquiry and widespread distrust.

Some supporters, however, said they hoped to revive the issue in 1999.

The vote, although distorted considerably by pre-election politics, signaled that the United States is turning away from its 50-year pursuit of global free trade. Attempts to renew fast track have foundered for several years, but the Sept. 25 vote was the first time the GOP-led Congress firmly rejected a major free-trade initiative.

For many businesses that rely on exports, the impact will be costly.

Fast-track trade authority, granted to every president since Gerald R. Ford, means Congress must take up proposed trade agreements within 90 days in an up-or-down vote; no amendments are allowed. Since fast track expired in 1994, other nations have refused to work out trade deals with the United States for fear they will be amended by Congress, and instead are negotiating agreements with U.S. competitors such as Canada and the European Union.

"We need fast track to get to the negotiating table," said William J. Morley, a lobbyist with the U.S. Chamber of Commerce. "Every day we don't have it is a loss for business."

Even before the Sept. 25 vote, U.S. exports were sharply declining because of the Asian financial crisis. In the days leading up to the vote, Democratic free-trade advocates urged GOP leaders to defer the issue until 1999, for fear of roiling the already unsettled global financial markets.

"Should HR 2621 fail on the floor of the House, it will send further shock waves to already fragile world markets," Democratic fast-track supporters wrote House Speaker Newt Gingrich, R-Ga., on Sept. 17. "We urge you to postpone the vote so that both our parties can maximize votes and ensure fast track passage."

Confident labor supporters, on the other hand, welcomed the showdown as a repudiation of expanded free-trade agreements. They blamed the 1993 North American Free Trade Agreement (NAFTA) for costing U.S. workers as many as 420,000 jobs, and wanted to amend the bill to put a greater emphasis on human rights overseas. (NAFTA, 1993 Almanac, p. 171)

Prior to the vote, members on both sides agreed that fast-track support had slipped since 1997, when supporters believed they were within about a dozen votes of victory.

This time, with Election Day looming, more Republicans sounded protectionist arguments that have resonated with the public. More Democrats took up the cause of labor unions, which are major campaign contributors. Furthermore, Matsui and other Democratic free-trade supporters voted against the bill to protest Republican tactics.

In such a charged atmosphere, Democrats said the only reason GOP leaders were taking the unusual step of bringing up a bill certain to lose was to rake in business contributions and embarrass Clinton, a free-trader.

"He [Gingrich] is using the issue as a sacrificial lamb for his own political purposes," said Democratic Rep. Barney Frank of Massachussetts.

Indeed, Republicans began blaming Clinton for the bill's demise even before the debate began, contending he should have bucked labor and rallied the Democrats behind the measure.

Denying partisan motives, however, GOP leaders also said the only sure way of testing fast-track support was to take a vote — especially since members would want to avoid voting no and disturbing the global economy. The leaders tried to pick up support by adopting last-minute changes in the Rules Committee, such as giving the House and Senate Agriculture committees an advisory roll in trade agreements.

"We'll never know where the votes are unless we move ahead," Boehner said.

And Gingrich, on the morning of the vote, shrugged off the dire financial predictions. Asked if he was concerned about the impact of the vote on financial markets, he said: "Nope."

The only ray of light for free-trade advocates came from the Senate, where members have maintained a more internationalist outlook. On the day of the fast-track vote, Senate Majority Leader Trent Lott, R-Miss., said the issue would be "high on the agenda" in 1999 — a scant boost to trade if the House remains opposed.

Partisan Meltdown

In the next few weeks, the biggest effect of the vote may be on Clinton's requested $17.9 billion for the International Monetary Fund (IMF).

Business leaders are pressing for congressional approval of the full amount, contending that it is needed to prevent the Asian economic crisis from spreading to regions such as Latin America. The Senate has included the $17.9 billion in its version of the fiscal 1999 foreign operations spending bill (S 2334), but the House, led by Republican IMF opponents such as Majority Leader Dick Armey of Texas, has drawn the line at $3.4 billion.

Now, with a partisan meltdown over trade issues, some lawmakers speculate it will be even harder to pass the full IMF funding request. "Some of the Republicans who support this bill [fast track] may now vote against IMF because they can say to the business community: 'Yeah, but I voted for fast track,'" said Rep. Barney Frank, D-Mass.

In the long term, the impact on U.S. trade policy may be substantial.

In the 1992 and 1996 presidential campaigns, Republican candidate Pat Buchanan and independent candidate Ross Perot whipped up isolationist sentiment. At the same time, human rights advocates and environmentalists began lobbying for trade provisions that would advance overseas living conditions.

But before the Sept. 25 vote, Congress, pressed by Clinton, had generally hewed to the free-trade policies that dated back to the end of World War II.

Bipartisan majorities narrowly cleared major agreements such as NAFTA in 1993, and gave annual approval to continued trade with China. When fast-track legislation appeared to lack House support in 1997, House GOP leaders pulled the bill rather than risk a "no" vote.

But after the Sept. 25 vote, the House may not be able to pass fast track for years, even if leaders are inclined to try. That is partly because members who voted no could not easily reverse their votes, and partly because of the political acrimony that has swept aside the longstanding bipartisan trade consensus.

California's Matsui said he may step down from the Ways and Means Trade Subcommittee, where he is the ranking Democrat. In the partisan atmosphere that has overtaken trade policy, there is little good he can do anyway, he said.

"Legislating is a little like being a craftsman. You need to work through it," he said. "You don't just barrel through and throw something out, and say 'take it or leave it.' ... In 20 years, I have never seen trade issues handled like Republicans are handling fast track."

Two Free-Traders Helped Set Back 'Fast Track'

OCTOBER 3 — There was nothing gentle about House Speaker Newt Gingrich, R-Ga., when he took to the floor Sept. 25 to blast Democrats for opposing fast-track trade legislation.

In a remarkably biting speech even for the combative conservative, Gingrich implied that Democrats were willing to let the world sink into an economic recession to appease their supporters in the labor movement.

"It is sad to see the partisan politics of the unions and the Democratic Party, and, yes, this [measure] may go down," he said. "But if this goes down and we end up in a steep worldwide recession, some of us will have had the comfort of knowing we cast the right vote."

Blunt as his words were, Gingrich, a longtime advocate of free trade, found himself playing anything but a straightforward role on that Sept. 25 vote. By allowing the House to take up a fast-track bill (HR 2621) that had little chance to pass, Gingrich may have damaged prospects that lawmakers would give the president expanded trade negotiating authority in the next few years.

As expected, the House decisively defeated the proposal, 180-243, min-

Trade

utes after Gingrich's speech. Business leaders lobbied hard for the bill, contending they needed more access to overseas markets, but they could not overcome the combined forces of labor opposition and bitter partisan bickering. (Vote 466, p. H-132)

Gingrich was not the only free-trader who would compromise his own policy beliefs that day. The leading Democratic advocate of expanding international commerce, Robert T. Matsui of California, found himself leading the opposition to a proposal he had strongly supported as recently as 1997.

As different as they are in temperament and background, the two veteran lawmakers — the caustic Georgian and the cerebral Californian — found themselves under irresistible pressure to advance the interests of their own political parties, rather than adhere to their free-trade instincts.

The story of how the two men would temporarily bury the very thing they believed in illustrates how partisan and self-destructive the legislative process has become in this election year. Furthermore, the overwhelming bipartisan margin by which the House rejected the proposal — just 151 Republicans and 29 Democrats voted aye — indicates that fast-track supporters face a tough battle if they try to revive the measure in 1999.

"It's a very sad day for America, and it's a sad day for economies around the world," said a dejected Ways and Means Chairman Bill Archer, R-Texas, minutes after the vote.

Trying to salvage the measure, however, Archer wrote a letter to President Clinton on Sept. 29 asking him to set a "date certain" for a fast-track vote in 1999. "We can begin today by working together toward passing fast-track legislation in the 106th Congress," he wrote.

'Vital to National Security'

It would be hard to overstate the importance that GOP leaders and their business allies place on giving the president fast-track negotiating authority. The preamble to HR 2621, written by Archer, declares: "The expansion of international trade is vital to the national security of the United States. . . . Trade agreements today serve the same purposes that security pacts played during the Cold War, binding nations together through a series of mutual rights and obligations."

Fast-track trade authority, granted to every president since Gerald R. Ford, means Congress must take up proposed trade agreements within 90 days in an up-or-down vote without amendments. Since a 1988 fast-track measure (PL 100-418) expired in 1994, economically growing countries such as Chile have refused to wrap up major trade deals with the United States because Congress could amend them.

"Chile . . . has a trade deal with every major economy in this hemisphere except us, giving each of our competitors an 11 percent tariff advantage, costing our citizens extra taxes on imported goods and costing our American workers jobs," said Jennifer Dunn, R-Wash., in the Sept. 25 debate. "The world is not waiting for the United States."

Even though the nation is losing business overseas, House Republican leaders have been stymied in their efforts to pass fast-track legislation. They pulled the measure from the floor in November 1997 when they appeared to lack at least 10 votes, and have been unsuccessful since in picking up additional support.

The reasons are many: opposition by labor and environmental groups, protectionist sentiment among many conservatives, a reluctance among some Republicans to give any more power to Clinton, and mixed feelings about the 1993 North American Free Trade Agreement.

Matsui and other Democrats warn that fast track may remain in limbo indefinitely unless Republicans add compromise language encouraging trade negotiations to focus more on overseas labor and environmental issues.

In contrast, the Senate, which is often seen as having a more internationalist outlook, likely has the votes for passage. (1997 Almanac, p. 2-85)

An Awkward Position

Frustrated by the continued liberal opposition and sensing a chance to score political points weeks before Election Day, Gingrich announced in July that the House would vote on the measure in late September. He suspected the issue would put many Democrats in the uncomfortable position of trying to stand by labor unions — a vital source of campaign contributions and volunteers — without casting a vote against well-heeled businesses. Indeed, he even baited the Democrats in his floor speech: "The real issue is: Your union will not let you vote for free trade."

The conflicting political currents left Clinton, who made fast-track passage a priority in his January State of the Union address, in the awkward position of asking GOP leaders to put off the vote until early 1999. The alternative would have been to break with a majority of congressional Democrats just a few weeks before elections.

The decision to go to the floor also alienated Democratic free-traders — especially when Republican campaign officials said the vote would be used to target some Democratic fast-track opponents in the fall elections.

"If they were using the issue of free trade to defeat my Democratic colleagues, I wasn't going to let myself be used as an agent in that process, and I resent it," Matsui said.

Free-trade Democrats, including Matsui, Steny H. Hoyer of Maryland and Vic Fazio of California, pleaded with Gingrich to postpone the vote until 1999. Otherwise, they said, many members recorded as voting no before November could not easily change their positions in the future.

Republicans acknowledged the danger. Before the vote, GOP Conference Chairman John A. Boehner of Ohio said that if members voted it down, the House likely would not take up fast-track legislation again until 2001.

Although leaders hardly ever schedule a floor debate on a bill that lacks a majority, Gingrich decided to forge ahead. If Democrats such as Matsui voted against the bill, then they — not GOP leaders — would be seen as the ones playing politics with vital trade issues, he reasoned.

"In the middle of this level of instability, you yell partisan politics, and then you vote partisan against your own rhetoric?" Gingrich said on the floor as a grim and weary Matsui sat silently.

For the Speaker, seeking to bolster the slender 11-member House Republican majority, the fast-track vote may pay political dividends. That is because business organizations, frustrated all year by Republican inattention to their issues, are now training their fire on Democrats. "American business will hold fast-track opponents accountable for their actions," warned U.S. Chamber of Commerce Executive Vice President Bruce Josten in a written statement.

But infuriated Democrats accused the Speaker of selling out the nation's long-term economic interest.

Matsui said before the vote that next year he may give up his position as the ranking member on the Ways and Means Trade Subcommittee because the once-bipartisan consensus on trade has become so poisoned by political intrigue. Then the 20-year congressional veteran, widely lauded for taking a thoughtful approach to trade and tax issues, managed the opposition to fast track in the floor debate and assailed Republicans with unusually harsh rhetoric.

"Today's exercise in this legislation soils our national trade policy with the mud of partisan politics," he said. "It shows a disdain for the legislative process and it threatens to disrupt international markets and quite possibly our national economy."

Matsui's opposition could serve two purposes. It may help shield more junior Democrats in tough races who voted against the bill, while also giving Matsui more leverage with the party if he wants to drum up support for fast track in 1999.

The effect of the Sept. 25 vote is uncertain. Predictions that it would unsettle world markets proved unfounded, perhaps because the business community did not take the vote seriously. "The thing was dead as a doornail and everybody knew that," said I.M. Destler, a professor and trade expert at the University of Maryland's School of Public Affairs.

Furthermore, Destler and other economists said they doubted the lack of fast track would have much effect on U.S. trade in the next year, in part because negotiators can do some preliminary work even without that authority.

However, if Clinton still lacks fast-track authority by the time of World Trade Organization negotiations in late 1999 on boosting trade, that would begin to undermine the 50-year global trend toward free trade, they warned.

Disappointing as the partisan meltdown was to fast-track supporters, it did give them a consolation prize. The more lawmakers used trade to grapple for partisan advantage, the more they were forced to concede the wisdom of the bill's central tenet: limiting the congressional role on trade agreements.

"I believe that our president, as other presidents, should have the right to negotiate trade contracts, and it should not be the House or the Senate that is going to dot every 'i' or cross every 't,' " said Rep. Charles B. Rangel of New York. But Rangel, a loyal Democrat, criticized the bill for failing to protect workers or the environment. He voted against it. ◆

House Backs Clinton On Efforts To Continue Normalization With Vietnam

Endorsing President Clinton's policy of expanding relations with Vietnam, the House defeated a measure (H J Res 120) that would have prevented Vietnam's participation in U.S. trade financing programs.

SUMMARY

On June 3, Clinton asked Congress to extend for another year his authority to exempt Vietnam from the Jackson-Vanik amendments to the 1974 Trade Law (PL 93-618), which restricts trade with communist governments that limit emigration. The last waiver had been issued in April 1997.

An attempt by Dana Rohrabacher, R-Calif., to block the waiver failed July 30. The House defeated his resolution by a vote of 163-260. (*Vote 356, p. H-100*)

U.S. Ambassador to Vietnam Pete Peterson, a former prisoner of war in that country and three-term congressman from Florida (1991-97), had returned to Capitol Hill to help persuade his former colleagues to continue Clinton's policy of gradually normalizing political and economic relations with Vietnam.

Clinton's decision allowed U.S. exporters and investors to obtain loans, loan guarantees and political risk insurance from the Export-Import Bank, Overseas Private Investment Corporation and Agriculture Department.

It marked a step toward granting Hanoi normal trade benefits, an action that Clinton cannot take until the two countries negotiate a comprehensive trade agreement and submit it for congressional approval.

Opponents called the funds "corporate welfare for communists," particularly given Hanoi's poor record of economic management.

Rohrabacher said Hanoi had not earned a waiver from the Jackson-Vanik restrictions. Other critics said Vietnam has not fully accounted for missing U.S. servicemen.

Supporters of Clinton's policy said Hanoi has stepped up its efforts to determine the fate of American soldiers still unaccounted for since the war. And they said that closer relations were in the national interest.

The United States has worked to improve relations with Vietnam since the early 1990s. Clinton lifted the U.S. trade embargo in 1994 and established diplomatic relations in 1995. ◆

Trade

Clinton Gets Mixed Results On Sub-Saharan Trade, Investment Initiatives

President Clinton's efforts to spur private investment and trade with Africa prompted several initiatives, but only one bill cleared. That legislation (HR 4283) addresses Africa's agriculture needs while providing markets for U.S. farmers.

SUMMARY

The legislation directs the Agency for International Development, the Overseas Private Investment Corporation and the Agriculture Department (USDA) to oversee programs that encourage agriculture and rural development in sub-Saharan Africa, particularly micro-enterprises, assistance to women, farmers and rural entrepreneurs. It also instructs the USDA to hold $20 million worth of reserves of U.S. farm products, such as wheat, rice and corn, for distribution to Africa.

The White House pushed bills (S 778, HR 1432) encouraging free trade and private investment in Africa. And the Senate Finance Committee included Africa trade provisions in a trade package (S 2400) it approved in July. But Southeastern lawmakers and Senate Majority Leader Trent Lott, R-Miss., killed the measures because of provisions that essentially would have granted some countries duty-free and quota-free treatment for textiles and apparel exports.

Sub-Saharan Bill Moves Quickly To House Floor

FEBRUARY 28 — Bipartisan legislation that seeks to stimulate economic development and investment in sub-Saharan Africa is on its way to the House floor after swift voice vote approval Feb. 25 by the Ways and Means Committee. Sponsors said one long-range goal is to reduce Africa's dependence on U.S. aid.

The legislation (HR 1432) would include the 48-nation region of sub-Saharan Africa in the generalized system of preferences (GSP) until 2008, allowing eligible developing countries in the region to export certain products to the United States duty-free. It also would establish a U.S.-Africa Trade and Economic Cooperation Forum and direct the president to establish a free-trade area to encourage commerce between the United States and sub-Saharan Africa.

The bill, sponsored by Rep. Philip M. Crane, R-Ill., chairman of the Ways and Means Subcommittee on Trade, has the support of the full committee's ranking Democrat, Charles B. Rangel of New York, who held a news conference after the markup to praise it.

U.S. Trade Representative Charlene Barshefsky appeared briefly before the committee to convey the Clinton administration's support for the bill. "American interests are best served if we view African countries as partners in trade, not simply recipients of aid," Barshefsky told the panel. President Clinton will make his first presidential visit to Africa in March.

The panel approved by voice vote an amendment by Jim Nussle, R-Iowa, stipulating that no money authorized in the bill would finance any non-governmental organizations.

As part of a substitute amendment approved by voice vote, the bill would strengthen punishments against countries that attempted to illegally transship textile and apparel products through sub-Saharan Africa to avoid U.S. quotas. The provision is part of an effort to assuage the concerns of lawmakers from districts with textile and apparel interests, who are worried about job losses. If the bill is enacted, exports of those goods from Africa will be exempt from duties and quotas.

A study by the U.S. International Trade Commission concluded that the impact on American jobs would be minimal, because Africa currently accounts for less than 1 percent of U.S. textile and apparel imports.

Panel members such as John Lewis, D-Ga., who expressed concern about human rights violations in African nations, received assurances that the president would have discretion in granting trade privileges to those countries.

The Trade Subcommittee approved the bill Oct. 23, 1997.

Box Score

- **Bills:** HR 4283 — PL 105-385; HR 1432, S 778, S 2400
- **House action:** The House cleared HR 4283 (H Rept 105-681, Part 1) by voice vote Oct. 20. The House passed the bill by voice vote Sept. 28. The House passed HR 1432, 233-186, on March 11. The Ways and Means Committee approved HR 1432 by voice vote Feb. 25.
- **Senate action:** The Senate amended and passed HR 4283 on Oct. 20. The Finance Committee approved S 2400, carrying Africa trade provisions, by 18-2 on July 21.
- **Presidential action:** Clinton signed HR 4283 on Nov. 13.

House Passes Bill To Promote Sub-Saharan Trade

MARCH 14 — A bill that aims to promote trade and private-sector investment in sub-Saharan Africa passed the House on March 11 by a vote of 233-186. Supporters hailed the measure (HR 1432) as the first step in changing U.S. relations with the 48-country region from one based on foreign aid to one based on trade. The region is made up of the African countries south of the Sahara. It does not include North African, Arab-majority countries such as Egypt, Algeria or Morocco. (*Vote 47, p. H-16*)

"It's been too long that Africa has been shut out of international trade," said Rep. Charles B. Rangel of New York, ranking Democrat on the Ways and Means Committee.

The vote came after the House turned back attempts by members whose districts include clothing and textile plants to add provisions protecting those industries from imports.

Sen. Richard G. Lugar, R-Ind., has introduced a companion measure (S 778) that is awaiting action in the Senate Finance Committee.

The House bill directs the president to develop a plan within a year to establish one or more free-trade areas with qualified sub-Saharan countries. Among the requirements for participation is certification from the president that the country is moving toward a market economy and does not abuse human rights.

The bill would extend duty-free treatment under the generalized system of preferences (GSP) through June 2008 for African countries already participating in the GSP, which allows developing countries to export certain products to the United States duty-free. Beginning in July, the president could extend duty-free treatment to textiles and other products now excluded from the GSP program, after determining that allowing duty-free export of the products would not threaten domestic industries.

Most opposition to the bill came from Southeastern lawmakers who feared it would allow Asian and other countries to illegally "transship" textile and clothing products to the United States through African nations participating in the bill's programs. They feared that would undermine American jobs. Opponents complained about a provision that would require that at least 35 percent of products shipped duty-free to the United States be produced in Africa. That, they argue, would allow duty-free imports of goods produced outside Africa.

Republicans Howard Coble of North Carolina and Mac Collins of Georgia, and Democrats Sanford D. Bishop Jr. of Georgia, Melvin Watt of North Carolina and John M. Spratt Jr. of South Carolina had hoped to offer a substitute measure that would have added extra protections for the domestic garment and apparel industries. It was effectively defeated when the House voted 227-190 to adopt a rule governing floor debate that prohibited the substitute version from coming to a vote. (*Vote 43, p. H-14*)

The House adopted by voice vote an amendment by Linda Smith, R-Wash., to expand the measure's eligibility requirements to assure that any participating country is cooperating in the fight to eliminate slavery.

The House defeated, 156-258, an amendment by Doug Bereuter, R-Neb., to add Morocco to the list of countries that could participate in the bill's programs. (*Vote 45, p. H-14*)

It also defeated by voice vote an amendment by Democrat Maxine Waters of California to set minimum funding for the Development Fund for Africa at the fiscal 1998 level — about $700 million.

Clinton Hopes Africa Trip Will Rally Support From the Hill

APRIL 4 — President Clinton spent much of the past two weeks trying to raise the profile of Africa at home, but many members of Congress are paying scant attention to the continent, dimming chances that the administration will win support for initiatives designed to reorient U.S. policy on the region.

Speaking to the South African Parliament on March 26, Clinton said that in going to Africa "my motive in part was to help the American people see the new Africa with new eyes, and to focus our own efforts on new policies suited to the new reality."

In particular, Clinton said he wanted to stop policy-makers from asking, "What can we do for Africa?" and ask instead, "What can we do with Africa?"

Changes that Clinton proposes include a bill aimed at spurring free trade and private-sector investment in sub-Saharan Africa, as well as several targeted assistance programs.

But lawmakers said that if Clinton is to see these initiatives enacted this year, he and other administration officials will need to devote considerable time to lobbying Congress.

Legislators said Clinton will have to put particular effort into pushing the centerpiece of his legislative agenda: trade and investment legislation for the 48 nations of sub-Saharan Africa (S 778; HR 1432 — H Rept 105-423, Parts 1 and 2).

Sen. John B. Breaux, D-La., said of Clinton, "I hope that after he gets back, it will start picking up, but the bill has not yet generated the discussion that is necessary to get these things done."

The bill's Senate sponsor, Richard G. Lugar, R-Ind., said it "needs to be a priority of the administration" if it is to pass this year. The Senate Finance Committee hopes to take up his bill later this year.

The companion measures would direct the president to develop a plan within a year to spur free trade with qualified sub-Saharan countries.

To participate, countries would be required to be moving toward a market economy while not engaging in "gross violations" of human rights. North African, Arab-majority countries such as Egypt, Algeria and Morocco are excluded from the program.

The bill would urge the Overseas Private Investment Corporation to spend $650 million for two new programs designed to improve infrastructure and encourage equity investments in the sub-Saharan region. It also would extend until 2008 current duty-free treatment under the Generalized System of Preferences for imports from Africa that do not threaten U.S. industries.

But its most controversial provision would effectively grant qualified countries duty-free and quota-free treatment for exports of textiles and apparel.

Opponents worry that Asian nations will take advantage of the special trade benefits to illegally ship goods through Africa, and they complain that the bill's efforts to control such shipments are inadequate.

Apparel Opposition

Earlier this month, House supporters of the measure managed to overcome opposition from Southeastern lawmakers to pass the bill, 233-186.

But supporters acknowledge they face more determined opposition in

Trade

the Senate, where textile-state lawmakers such as Ernest F. Hollings, D-S.C., and textile groups and labor unions have vowed to defeat the bill.

In addition, Senate Majority Leader Trent Lott, R-Miss., has made clear that the Africa bill ranks low on his list of trade priorities.

In a March 31 interview, Lott said he would support passing the Africa bill only if it was part of a package that included the stalled fast-track trade negotiating legislation and the granting of North American Free Trade Agreement benefits to Caribbean countries.

"The president should be here and pushing fast track and enhanced NAFTA for the Caribbean countries," Lott said. "When we deal with those countries, we can deal with the third [Africa]."

A key supporter, Rep. Robert T. Matsui, D-Calif., ranking member of the Ways and Means Trade Subcommittee, said such a combination would kill any eventual agreement in the House. He noted that neither of the other two measures Lott mentioned had passed the House. "If you put all of these in one bill, that would be enough opposition. Anyone who opposes any of these measures will vote against it," Matsui said.

But he and Senate aides involved with the issue said the bill might still be passed in tandem with other legislation, such as efforts to extend the Generalized System of Preferences or trade adjustment assistance programs.

"There's interest in the bill as a vehicle for other legislation," said a knowledgeable Senate aide.

Mandela's Reservations

Another obstacle was thrown in the bill's path during Clinton's visit to Africa. At a March 27 news conference, South African President Nelson Mandela criticized the bill while Clinton stood by his side. "This is a matter over which we have serious reservations, this legislation," Mandela said. "To us it is not acceptable."

Mandela said he thought the bill would require African countries to adopt economic and political reforms that are too stringent before being eligible for trade and investment benefits. Clinton and some other African leaders disagree with Mandela's assessment.

Mandela's stand has been endorsed by some prominent liberals, such as Randall Robinson, president of the lobbying association TransAfrica, and consumer advocate Ralph Nader, who have been making a similar case to Congress.

Opponents say they expect to benefit from Mandela's moral stature as a leader of the anti-apartheid movement. "He's one of the most widely respected human beings in the world," said Ann Hoffman of the Union of Needletrades, Industrial and Textile Employees, which has pushed hard against the bill. "It cannot but help our cause."

Mandela and other African leaders also fret that U.S. policy-makers will use the trade legislation as an excuse to further cut American aid to the region.

Direct U.S. assistance to sub-Saharan Africa, aside from food aid and limited balance-of-payments support, has fallen from $840 million in fiscal 1992 to about $700 million in the current fiscal year.

The Clinton administration is seeking to raise that total by only about $30 million in the fiscal 1999 budget, according to officials from the U.S. Agency for International Development.

But the administration has proposed several new programs for the continent, including $35 million to forgive debts owed by African nations to the U.S. government, $30 million in funds designed to spur trade and investment, $26 million in additional educational funds, and a $30 million program to bolster the judicial system in the central African countries of Rwanda, Burundi, and the Democratic Republic of Congo.

And in an effort to reassure African nations that the United States remains committed to the region, Clinton unveiled a series of modest programs and grants during his six-nation tour.

In Ghana, for example, he pledged a half-million dollars to teach crowd control techniques to the national police force, offered a $67 million loan to help the African nation buy two power plants fueled by natural gas and pledged $1 million over three years to link African schools to those in the United States over the Internet.

It was not entirely clear how many of these new initiatives will require congressional approval, since some programs may be funded by shuffling current appropriations.

But Sonny Callahan, R-Ala., who chairs the House Appropriations Foreign Operations Subcommittee, said that before Clinton's departure he had warned the president to steer clear of new commitments during his trip. He was "irritated" by Clinton's apparent failure to heed his admonition.

John Ashcroft, R-Mo., chairman of the Senate Foreign Relations Subcommittee on African Affairs, said he generally supported Clinton's approach but was concerned about the aid pledges.

"I'm not prepared to sign off on the president's promises in Africa," Ashcroft said.

Patrick J. Leahy, D-Vt., ranking member of the Senate Appropriations Foreign Operations Subcommittee, said that such sentiment is widespread in Congress and he expects Clinton's trip to have little effect.

"I see Congress being absolutely irresponsible in dealing with Africa," Leahy said, noting that the whole continent receives far less aid than either Egypt or Israel. "I don't think it will change. I hope it does." ◆

Chapter 24

TRANSPORTATION & INFRASTRUCTURE

Surface Transportation 24-3
   House, Senate Bills Compared 24-5
   Ethanol Proposal 24-18
   Highlights of Conference Report 24-22

Surface Transportation *(cont'd)*
   Bill Provisions 24-27
FAA Reauthorization 24-34

Transportation Law Benefits Those Who Held The Purse Strings

SUMMARY

With deficit concerns melting, lawmakers approved a big increase in spending on the nation's roads and mass transit systems with passage of a six-year, $217.9 billion surface transportation reauthorization bill (HR 2400).

Overall, the Transportation Equity Act for the 21st Century provided a 40 percent increase over its predecessor, the Intermodal Surface Transportation Efficiency Act of 1991. The new law included $174.6 billion for highways, $41 billion for mass transit and $2 billion for safety programs. Most of the highway and mass transit funding is guaranteed.

While the 1991 law emphasized support for alternatives to highways and building links between different modes of transportation, the 1998 reauthorization was notable for its huge increase in funding for both highways and mass transit. Lawmakers gave states and local government more flexibility to use federal funds to help them reduce a backlog of repairs and needed projects. The law also provides support for innovative financing, or loans and lines of credit, designed to encourage a mixture of private and public funding to help pay for big construction projects.

Lawmakers resolved a long battle over transportation spending caps in the Taxpayer Relief Act of 1997 (PL 105-34) by agreeing to $17.7 billion in offsets. The package included $15.4 billion from denying veterans' disability payments for smoking-related ailments and $2.3 billion from paring social service block grants.

The passage of HR 2400 marked a reversal of fortune for House Transportation and Infrastructure Committee Chairman Bud Shuster, R-Pa., whose proposal to cut other discretionary programs in order to increase transportation funding was defeated, 214-216, in 1997. A stalemate in the first year of the 105th Congress forced lawmakers to pass a $9.8 billion short-term extension (PL 105-130) of transportation funding to keep money flowing to states.

Armed with budget-surplus projections at the start of 1998, Shuster found broad, bipartisan support for his proposal to set the level of highway spending at the level of the prior year's gasoline tax receipts. Governors backed his efforts and urged quick action to avert a funding cutoff.

In the Senate, Phil Gramm, R-Texas, and Robert C. Byrd, D-W.Va., led the fight to spend the 4.3 cent share of the gas tax once used for deficit reduction. The Senate approved by voice vote on March 5 a compromise amendment to its version of the bill (S 1173) to increase highway spending by $25.8 billion. The amendment closed a wide gap in spending levels in the Senate and House versions of the bill. The Senate-passed amendment included $18.9 billion for states, and $6.9 billion targeted to programs including highways in the Appalachian region, trade corridor projects near the Mexican or Canadian borders, and highways on public land.

After the short-term funding expired at the end of April, Shuster and other negotiators came under heavy pressure to reach a deal, while states relied on prior federal funding and their own resources to continue work on road projects. Negotiators worked out key disputes before final House and Senate passage of HR 2400 on May 22. Negotiators deleted a key Senate provision to withhold a share of federal funding from states that did not adopt a new lower blood-alcohol content threshold of 0.08 percent for drunken driving violations.

President Clinton supported the drunken driving provision and criticized 1,850 highway projects worth $9.35 billion. The bill contains $8.2 billion for mass transit projects and $3 billion in bus projects. Despite objections, Clinton said the bill did "a lot more good than harm, much more."

The conference report on HR 2400 contained Shuster's top priority, a guarantee to spend on transportation all revenue collected from the 18.3-cents-per-gallon gas tax, including the 4.3-cent share formerly devoted to deficit reduction. Shuster did not succeed in his effort to push the Highway Trust Fund off-budget, but the bill did put a "firewall," or guarantee, around most funding for highway and mass transit. The guarantee, designed to protect overall funding and specific projects, sparked a turf war with appropriators, who complained the guarantee left little room for revisions or more projects.

Donor states, which receive less than a dollar of federal funding for each dollar paid in federal gas taxes, won support from key leaders including Speaker Newt Gingrich, R-Ga., and House Majority Whip Tom DeLay, R-Texas. The negotiators agreed to guarantee each state 90.5 percent of its transportation funding allocation based on gas tax payments.

The mass transit portion of the bill includes $5 billion that was added to match the Senate's level of spending,

Box Score

- **Bill:** HR 2400 — PL 105-178
- **House action:** The House cleared the conference report (H Rept 105-550) on HR 2400, 297-86, on May 22. The House approved its version of HR 2400 (H Rept 105-467), 337-80, on April 1.
- **Senate action:** The Senate adopted the conference report on HR 2400, 88-5, on May 22. The final version of the Senate bill (S 1173 — S Rept 105-95) was approved March 12, 96-4, in the form of a manager's amendment. The Senate agreed by unanimous consent to consider the bill passed as soon as the House passed its version of the bill.
- **Presidential action:** Clinton signed HR 2400 on June 9.

Transportation & Infrastructure

at the insistence of Banking and Urban Development Chairman Alfonse M. D'Amato, R-N.Y., who faced a tough re-election fight. The package includes funding for mass transit projects at the Salt Lake City Winter Olympics in 2002.

A bill (HR 3978) containing technical corrections to the transportation law was blocked by Democratic Sen. John D. Rockefeller IV of West Virginia who wanted to restore veterans' disability payments for smoking-related ailments. The corrections were then added to the conference report on a bill (HR 2676 — PL 105-206) to restructure the Internal Revenue Service. The House adopted the conference report (H Rept 105-559) on HR 2676 on June 25, and the Senate cleared it by a 96-2 vote on July 9.

The bill restores several accidentally deleted measures to deter drunken driving, including $500 million in incentives for states that enact the new blood-alcohol standard of 0.08 percent.

Budget Surplus Whets Debate On More Highway Spending

JANUARY 10 — The battle over reauthorization of highway and transportation programs in 1998 will be closely tied to the debate over the fast-shrinking budget deficit.

Advocates of increased transportation spending, including House Speaker Newt Gingrich, R-Ga., were encouraged the week of Jan. 5 by projected increases in tax revenues and President Clinton's pledge to propose a balanced budget for fiscal 1999.

The bottom line: A balanced budget will free up transportation money.

Gingrich, R-Ga., said he is targeting transportation, paying down the debt and repairing the Social Security retirement fund for extra money expected to be generated by the shrinking deficit.

He wants to use the surplus revenue to "pay off the transportation trust fund," which is estimated to contain $20 to $30 billion in unspent gasoline taxes that help to offset the deficit.

Deficit reduction was one of a nest of thorny issues, including campaign finance reform, that delayed reauthorization of the transportation bill last year.

But now that projections show rosy economic prospects and rising tax revenues, the case is growing for using the trust funds.

House Transportation and Infrastructure Chairman Bud Shuster, R-Pa., said Gingrich's comments and near-term prospects for a balanced budget would help him make the case for his bill (HR 2400), which calls for $218.3 billion in highway and mass transit funding over six-years, well above limits set in last year's balanced-budget deal.

"I am very encouraged by Speaker Gingrich's statement," Shuster said in a Jan. 7 interview.

Gingrich and other House leaders blocked Shuster from moving forward with the bill in 1997 because it exceeded spending limits in the balanced-budget agreement. Shuster said he had an agreement to bring his bill to the House floor after an agreement on a fiscal 1999 budget resolution.

"We will have a fair shot, and fight this battle out in the spring," Shuster said.

Battle Lines Drawn

Battle lines are already forming in the Senate, where Environment and Public Works Committee Chairman John H. Chafee, R-R.I., has tried to hold the line in defending the limits set in the balanced-budget deal.

Chafee is urging an early Senate floor vote, perhaps in February, on a "fiscally responsible" reauthorization bill (S 1173) that complies with budget authority caps set in the balanced-budget agreement.

Senate Majority Leader Trent Lott, R-Miss., who backs Chafee's efforts, has settled a controversy with Democrats by agreeing to allow a vote this year on campaign finance reform, ending what had been a roadblock late last year to Senate consideration of the six-year reauthorization of highway spending.

But Chafee and Lott face a groundswell of support for an amendment by Sens. Robert C. Byrd, D-W.Va., and Phil Gramm, R-Texas, to boost highway spending by $6 billion to $30 billion a year.

The Gramm-Byrd amendment, which has 48 other co-sponsors, calls for spending a 4.3-cent portion of the federal gasoline tax that was reserved for deficit reduction in the highway trust fund under the balanced-budget amendment.

Lott and Chafee continue to push for early consideration of the reauthorization. The bill (S 1173) was approved on an 18-0 vote by Chafee's committee on Sept. 17.

The Senate bill calls for $145 billion in highway funding over six years. It is expected that provisions of a public transportation measure that was approved by the Banking, Housing and Urban Affairs Committee on Sept. 25 will be added by amendment to S 1173, providing $35.7 billion in mass transit funding over six years.

Just before adjourning last year, House and Senate negotiators reached agreement on a temporary spending bill that kept $5.5 billion in transportation money flowing to the states over the winter, based on the funding formula used in fiscal 1997. The plan also allowed states to spend reserve funds.

Tough Act

The short-term bill did not resolve problems that stymied Congress in 1997, and Congress will be under pressure to complete work quickly before the end of the six-month extension on May 1.

The top issue to be resolved remains the overall amount of highway spending to be authorized as part of the six-year reauthorization of the highway bill.

While the Senate prepared to consider S 1173, Shuster, who once predicted that the highway reauthorization could turn into a "nuclear war," said things may go more smoothly than he expected. His efforts could be complicated by possible demands to respond to two investigations — one by the House ethics committee and the other by a federal grand jury in Boston.

The bill would authorize average annual funding of about $36 billion over six years for highways and mass transit. That compares with limits on transportation budget authority contained in the balanced-budget agreement of roughly $29.5 billion per year.

Rep. James L. Oberstar of Minnesota, ranking Democrat on the Transportation Committee, said: "Democrats and Republicans on the committee are united on this bill. It will be up to Chairman Shuster to win the support of Speaker Gingrich and the Republican House leadership to get our bill to the floor."

Members Want Piece of Pie

While waiting for the budget debate to ripen, Shuster confirmed that his staff has been sifting nominations from about 400 House members for a piece of the $9 billion in the bill for special projects.

The projects, which have not been selected yet, amount to 5 percent of the highway portion of the bill's funding.

The Clinton administration has criticized special projects and praised the Senate bill for not including any.

Shuster defended the special projects and predicted that senators would seek money for some of their own in a conference committee. "Angels in heaven do not decide where highways and transit systems are going to be built. It's a political process," Shuster said.

While Shuster prepares a raft of special projects, floor amendments are being lined up in the Senate.

The Gramm-Byrd amendment has gained strong bipartisan support. Assistant Majority Leader Don Nickles, R-Okla., became a co-sponsor this month. Democratic leader Tom Daschle of South Dakota, another cosponsor, noted that the proposal would be good for his state as well as good policy.

"Gas taxes were designed to fund highway projects," he said. "The Byrd-Gramm amendment allows all gas taxes to be spent on highways."

But the proposal prompted countermeasures by opponents. Budget Committee Chairman Pete V. Domenici, R-N.M., pledged to raise a point of order that would require Gramm-Byrd supporters to get 60 votes.

Chafee and Domenici have sent a letter to colleagues saying the Gramm-Byrd amendment would result in more than 40 states, in effect, getting less funding than otherwise, because of money earmarked for the Appalachian Regional Commission and a program that supports projects in trade corridors or near the Canadian and Mexican borders.

"The Gramm-Byrd amendment would take money away from Rhode Island and other New England states, and use it to build highways in Appalachia and other areas," Chafee said last week.

A competing Chafee-Domenici amendment calls for "fast track" procedures to increase transportation funding if projected tax revenues increase.

Other Issues

Other controversial issues are waiting in the wings in the Senate.

An early battle on affirmative action is brewing over an amendment sponsored by Mitch McConnell, R-Ky., and Jeff Sessions, R-Ala., calling for an end to a program that has set a goal of giving at least 10 percent of construction contracts to businesses owned by women and minorities.

Transportation Secretary Rodney Slater has strongly opposed the amendment because it would make it "difficult to recommend" the Senate bill to President Clinton. The amendment also faces opposition from Chafee.

In other anticipated amendments:

- Craig Thomas, R-Wyo., wants to require a minimum allocation of mass transit funds for each state.
- Connie Mack, R-Fla., wants to give states ways to "opt out" of portions of federal transportation programs and directly receive some federal gasoline taxes.
- Frank R. Lautenberg, D-N.J., wants to hold back highway funds from states that do not lower the standard for drunken-driving violations from 0.10 percent blood-alcohol content to 0.08 percent.
- James M. Inhofe, R-Okla., wants to bar the Environmental Protection Agency (EPA) from implementing strict new clean air standards until an independent panel can review their effect on pollution.

House, Senate Bills Compared

JANUARY 10 — Here is a comparison of provisions in the Senate bill (S 1173) and the House bill (HR 2400) for the six-year reauthorization of the Intermodal Surface Transportation Efficiency Act. The Senate bill is awaiting a floor vote, and the House bill is in the Transportation and Infrastructure Committee.

- **Highways:** The Senate bill would authorize $145 billion for highways, highway safety and other surface transportation, roughly a 20 percent increase in the current level of spending. The House bill would authorize $181.9 billion for highways and highway safety.
- **Donor states:** The House bill would guarantee states no less than 95 percent of their proportional contributions to the highway trust fund for all formula programs. The Senate bill, using different calculations, includes a guarantee of 90 percent. The provisions are aimed at about 30 donor states that receive less than a dollar of highway funding for each dollar they pay in gasoline taxes.
- **Flexibility:** The Senate bill would authorize $43 billion over six years for the surface transportation program and would expand eligibility to include intercity passenger service by bus or rail, public and private vehicles, and public rail safety infrastructure. The House bill would authorize $40 billion over six years for the same program and would expand eligibility to include anti-icing and de-icing programs and certain environmental projects.
- **Tolls:** The House bill would establish a new pilot program to permit toll booths on three free interstate highways as part of reconstruction projects. The Senate bill would keep the current prohibition on tolls for interstate highways.
- **Gasoline taxes:** Both bills would retain the current 18.3-cent per gallon federal gasoline tax.

Transportation & Infrastructure

Governors' Pleas Nudge Senate Into Action

FEBRUARY 28 — Senate Majority Leader Trent Lott unlocked the stalled debate on the six-year highway reauthorization bill Feb. 26 after the nation's governors complained that the delay in releasing transportation funds threatens thousands of jobs.

Lott, R-Miss., pushed the bill (S 1173) to the floor while continuing negotiations with other senators over the size of the highway spending legislation and how to fit it under spending caps contained in the 1997 balanced-budget agreement.

Though the negotiations did not reach a conclusion, Lott came away with a deal to delay for one week amendments that could exceed the funding caps. Republican leaders in both the House and Senate said they would try to speed up action to pass reauthorization of the 1991 Intermodal Surface Transportation Efficiency Act and move away from past pledges to delay action until after the fiscal 1999 budget agreement.

With demands for quick action coming from the National Governors' Association during its annual winter meeting in Washington which started Feb. 21, Lott rolled out his plan to push forward debate on the bill. And he began negotiations aimed at reaching a compromise with Sens. Robert C. Byrd, D-W.Va., and Phil Gramm, R-Texas, and supporters of their proposed amendment to spend 4.3 cents of the gasoline tax earmarked for deficit reduction on highways and mass transit. The federal gas tax is 18.3 cents per gallon, of which 14 cents goes into the Highway Trust Fund for transportation projects.

Governors Lobby Hill

The governors carried their demands for fast action in personal visits on Capitol Hill. In a litany of public statements, they warned that highway contracts are threatened because Congress is not moving quickly enough to approve the bill before a short-term extension of highway funds runs out at the end of April.

Governors were armed with a new survey by the American Association of State Highway and Transportation Officials projecting that 42,100 jobs could be lost for each $1 billion in road contracts canceled because of delays. The Senate bill currently would provide $180.7 billion for highways and mass transit over six years; the House bill would provide $218.3 billion.

The study found that delay in the six-year highway reauthorization bill has already forced Connecticut to cut back programs targeting drunken drivers and Illinois to defer for one year the rehabilitation of the Stevenson Expressway in Chicago, a priority project.

"If we don't get action before the [April 30] deadline, we could lose the whole road construction season," said Republican Gov. Jim Edgar of Illinois.

After a series of meetings between governors and lawmakers on Capitol Hill, support for quick action grew both in the House and Senate.

House Transportation and Infrastructure Committee Chairman Bud Shuster, R-Pa., told several governors in a private meeting that he would move his own highway reauthorization bill (HR 2400) to the House floor "within 72 hours" of agreement on a funding amount with Republican leaders on a House task force.

In the Senate, supporters of the Gramm-Byrd amendment initially sought a $30 billion increase over five years. Budget Committee Chairman Pete V. Domenici, R-N.M., offered about $18 billion over five years.

The increases were to be tacked on to the $180.7 billion in spending over six years authorized in S 1173. Gramm told governors that Domenici offered "half a loaf," and argued for more.

The dilemma for Senate Republican leaders was to find other cuts to pay for any increase in transportation spending above the 1997 balanced-budget caps.

Lott declined to specify how he would pay for increased highway spending. He pointed to savings mentioned in President Clinton's fiscal 1999 budget, including as much as $17 billion in veterans benefits if a policy were changed to limit aid for smoking-related ailments to only those illnesses directly connected to smoking during military service.

"We're going to say 'Mr. President, you have an excellent list. But we're going to spend it here,' " Lott said.

Senate Minority Leader Tom Daschle, D-S.D., said veterans' groups would oppose the idea.

Besides the spending level, negotiations on the Gramm-Byrd amendment also hinged on another provision, which earmarked funding from the gas tax for road construction in the Appalachian region and another program to build more roads connecting Canada and Mexico to the United States.

Givers and Takers

One of the key issues to be resolved in the Senate and House was an ongoing disagreement on the formula used to divide transportation funding among the states.

Governors were unified in pushing for a multiyear highway reauthorization bill. But without enough money to go around and to meet all the needs for road repairs and improvements, they were divided on how to distribute the money.

There are more than 20 states across the Sun Belt and in parts of the West, including California, that are called "donor states" because they receive less than $1 of highway and mass transit funding for each $1 their residents pay in federal gasoline taxes into the highway fund.

The donor states argue they are unfairly subsidizing other states, mainly in the Northeast, parts of the Midwest, and sparsely populated areas in the West, that receive more highway funding than their residents pay in gas taxes.

The gap varies from Alaska which receives the most — $5.02 from the Highway Trust Fund for every $1 of gasoline taxes paid by its residents, to South Carolina which receives the least — 71 cents for every $1, according to Department of Transportation figures compiled between 1992 and 1996.

House Majority Whip Tom DeLay, R-Texas, praised the House bill at a rally with several governors, including Republican David Beasley of South Carolina. DeLay said the bill moves in the right direction to alter the formula for dividing highway money, but he added that he plans to push for more revisions. "I think we can do better," he said.

The House bill would guarantee states no less than a 95 percent return on their contributions to the highway trust fund for most programs.

The Senate bill would use different calculations and guarantee states a 90 percent return on their contributions for most highway projects.

In the Senate, Lott and John W. Warner, R-Va., have urged more funding for donor states.

"We will have a more equitable formula, or we will have no bill," Lott said. "Mississippi is getting tired of dirt roads. We want some asphalt. . . . I also want more asphalt for my buddies in Florida, Texas and Alabama." Mississippi received 82 cents for each $1 of gasoline taxes it paid in 1992 to 1996.

Lawmakers from the Northeast seemed willing to give some ground to donor states, but were adamant in defending the interests of their states.

Senate Environment and Public Works Committee Chairman John H. Chafee, R-R.I., stressed that S 1173 would provide big increases for all states.

While states were divided on the issue of how to distribute highway money, many lawmakers and governors agreed that highway spending deserves a big increase.

The governors estimated that the current level of highway spending by all levels of government, about $40 billion a year, would need to grow by 50 percent each year to stop deterioration.

They cited a 1995 Transportation Department study showing one of every 10 miles of most major roads in the United States is in poor condition, and that approximately 25 percent of bridges are either overly worn, too narrow or weak, including the heavily traveled Woodrow Wilson Bridge that brings commuters from Virginia across the Potomac River to the nation's capital every day.

Robert L. Darbelnet, president of the American Automobile Association, said deteriorating roads cause 30 percent of all traffic accidents. The crashes kill approximately 42,000 people every year.

In a joint statement, Beasley and Democratic Gov. Jeanne Shaheen of New Hampshire said, "It is unconscionable that highway trust funds are being used for anything but transportation at a time when everyone can see that our roads and bridges desperately need repair."

Opening Debate

As floor debate opened Feb. 26, Chafee said the Senate bill provides money for a mix of transportation, including mass transit and alternatives to automobiles.

The Senate took only one vote, on Feb. 27, adopting by voice vote an amendment by Christopher S. Bond, R-Mo., to promote private sector programs to mitigate the loss of wetlands from road construction by creating other protected wetlands.

Other key issues to be debated include new clean air standards set by the Environmental Protection Agency and proposals to give states more flexibility to build roads with money targeted for transit. "It's full speed ahead for Senate debate," Chafee said.

The debate, expected to last more than a week, also will include an amendment by Sen. Frank R. Lautenberg, D-N.J., to hold back highway funds from states that do not lower the standard for drunken-driving violations from 0.1 percent blood-alcohol content to 0.08 percent blood-alcohol content. Sen. Byron L. Dorgan, D-N.D., supports a related proposal to ban open alcohol containers in cars.

One controversial amendment is sponsored by Republican Sens. Mitch McConnell of Kentucky and Jeff Sessions of Alabama to end a program that has set a goal of giving 10 percent of construction contracts to businesses owned by women and minorities. Chafee and Transportation Secretary Rodney Slater oppose the program.

As the Senate moved forward on its bill, the governors left town. "I'm glad Congress is moving," said Republican Gov. Edward T. Schafer of North Dakota, co-chairman of a governors' transportation task force. "There's no doubt in my mind we helped get things moving."

Senate's Solution To Road Wars: More Money

MARCH 7 — The Senate approved a simple solution to a long-simmering dispute over the division of federal transportation money among states: a bigger pot of funds.

The $25.8 billion increase, approved by voice vote March 5, was part of a deal brokered earlier in the week by Senate Majority Leader Trent Lott, R-Miss., to win support for the six-year surface transportation reauthorization bill (S 1173). The increase also averted an amendment for an even bigger spending increase proposed by Sens. Robert C. Byrd, D-W.Va., and Phil Gramm, R-Texas, and promoted strongly by governors.

The deal cleared the way for lawmakers to work on other key details, including complaints by some states that they do not receive a fair share of transportation money, proposals to speed up projects by streamlining environmental requirements, a proposal to end a program that sets a goal of giving 10 percent of construction contracts to businesses owned by women and minorities and measures to toughen laws against drunken driving.

Lott and Senate Minority Leader Tom Daschle, D-S.D., both called for efforts to expedite passage and send legislation to a conference committee that must work out differences with a pending House bill (HR 2400).

While strong consensus for more funding has emerged in Congress, disagreement continues on the exact amount and the division of the money. The Senate bill would provide about $173 billion for highways, including about $1.7 billion for highway safety. The House bill would provide about $181.9 billion for highways.

And both chambers have problems. Neither has decided how to pay for the increased spending and remain under spending caps in last year's balanced-budget agreement.

Senate Budget Committee Chairman Pete V. Domenici, R-N.M., said he would look at savings identified in President Clinton's 1999 budget to offset the increases.

"I believe we will be able to meet the caps and do this, but it may very well be that in a few years we will not be able to do that," he said. "I do not think it is going to be a big disparity."

The Senate's plan won praise from the Clinton administration and from House Republican leaders including Transportation and Infrastructure Committee Chairman Bud Shuster of Pennsylvania, although he said he still prefers the House bill and its higher

Transportation & Infrastructure

spending level.

House Republican leaders have not publicly identified what programs they would cut to pay for the boost in spending; Domenici has mentioned only savings of between $10 billion to $17 billion from a change in Clinton's budget to deny benefits to veterans for smoking-related ailments not related to smoking during military service.

Environment and Public Works Committee Chairman John H. Chafee, R-R.I., won approval of the deal by an 18-0 committee vote March 3. The deal sparked a flurry of private meetings aimed at resolving continuing questions about the division of money and other issues.

With the Senate moving to complete its bill, House Republican leaders agreed to try to quickly settle a dispute over the spending level in HR 2400 and send final legislation to the president before a short-term extension of transportation funding runs out April 30.

"I'm ready to move tomorrow," Shuster said March 4, as House negotiators continued meetings before deciding when floor debate would start.

Battle Among the States

While House leaders tried to settle their differences, Senate Republican leaders tried to remove obstacles to passage. Sen. Alfonse M. D'Amato, R-N.Y., facing re-election this fall, won an agreement to increase mass transit funding by $5 billion, to $41.3 billion, after Rep. Charles E. Schumer, D-N.Y., said New York subway riders were "getting mugged" by the Senate's preference for roads. Schumer is running for the Democratic nomination to challenge D'Amato.

The $25.8 billion increase offers something for most regions of the country. It includes $18.9 billion in additional spending over six years, providing an increase for every state.

The plan provides $6.9 billion over five years for specific programs, including $1.8 billion requested by Byrd to complete highways in the Appalachian region. Gramm won $450 million for highways in trade corridors that carry traffic from the Canadian and Mexican borders. About $1.8 billion went to 10 states with high-density populations, including California and Florida. And $1.9 billion went to 18 "donor" states, mainly in the South, to increase the guarantee of funds they receive from the highway trust fund to 91 percent from 90 percent of their contributions.

The Senate deal also would provide $850 million for several programs related to federal lands, concentrated in the West, including roads on Indian reservations, national parks and wildlife refuges.

Despite the geographic reach of the agreement, members from donor states, which receive less than $1 in transportation funding for each $1 they pay in gasoline taxes, vowed to seek more money.

Shuster predicted that the Senate would settle on an apportionment plan favoring "little states," while the House would favor "big states" with bigger delegations.

Other Issues

The Senate also waded into a debate on racial and gender preferences and settled several environmental battles.

The Senate voted 58-37 on March 6 to table, or kill, a proposal by Sen. Mitch McConnell, R-Ky., to end a program that sets a goal of giving 10 percent of construction contracts to businesses owned by women and minorities, and promote efforts to help small businesses without regard to race or gender.

Defenders of the program, including Carol Moseley-Braun, D-Ill., charged that elimination of the program would "leave a legacy of no economic opportunity" for women and minorities. Transportation Secretary Rodney Slater opposed the amendment, saying it might cause him to recommend that Clinton veto the bill.

With Clinton's support, the Senate voted 62-32 to approve an amendment to require states to enact a new law to require a lower standard of 0.08 percent blood-alcohol content for drunken-driving violations. It was one of several measures aimed at curbing traffic accidents linked to drunken drivers. (*Vote 20, p. S-6*)

The Senate approved by voice vote March 5 a proposal by Ron Wyden, D-Ore., and Robert C. Smith, R-N.H., to require environmental reviews in early stages of a construction project.

And the Senate approved by voice vote March 4 a proposal by James M. Inhofe, R-Okla., to put in law the federal requirement for three years of monitoring to determine whether an area meets new standards for particulate matter and ozone, and to require the EPA to pay for monitoring equipment.

Senate Completes Floor Action On Highway Bill

MARCH 14 — Facing pressure from governors to renew funding by the end of April, the Senate on March 12 reached agreement on a long-delayed $214.3 billion six-year reauthorization of highway and mass transit programs, while House Republican leaders tried to reach final agreement on their own transportation spending plan.

The final version of the Senate bill (S 1173), was approved, 96-4, in the form of a managers' amendment. Senators agreed by unanimous consent to consider the bill passed as soon as the House passed its version. [That occurred on April 2.] (*Vote 30, p. S-8*)

The Senate bill would provide an approximately 40 percent increase in overall spending, including $173 billion for highways and $41.3 billion for mass transit. Senate and House Republican leaders have both pledged to send a bill to President Clinton by the end of April, when a short-term extension of transportation funding will expire.

Sen. John H. Chafee, R-R.I., the bill's floor manager, said it "perpetuates the critical central ideals" of the ground-breaking national policy established in the Intermodal Surface Transportation Efficiency Act of 1991. Like the earlier law, he said, his bill would encourage links between roads and other forms of transportation, and relieve congestion, improve road safety and reduce pollution. (*1991 Almanac, p. 147*)

A dispute over the division of money among states dominated two weeks of debate on the bill, which provides the framework for the nation's transportation policy.

The final bill is designed to shift more money to states in the South and West, where fast growth in urban areas has driven increased demand for funding.

"We have crafted a bill that is responsive to the vastly different conditions in each region," Chafee said.

With the Senate bill now headed to a conference committee, that battle over money will move to the House. Republican leaders announced March 12 that they are working on the "framework of an agreement" on transportation funding that could unlock a stalemate on consideration of the House reauthorization bill (HR 2400).

Among key issues to be resolved between the Senate and House are the overall level of funding — set at $214.3 billion in the Senate bill and at $218.3 billion in the current version of HR 2400. The most difficult question is how to apportion the money.

Sen. John W. Warner, R-Va., said he believes the Senate will prevail in conference with its apportionment plan, which guarantees each state at least a 90 percent return on its gasoline-tax contributions to the highway trust fund. Other provisions in the Senate bill are designed to increase the minimum return to each state to 91 percent of gas tax contributions.

A key dispute looms on the issue of whether to extend that guarantee to discretionary spending, and whether the Senate will agree to House demonstration projects, which were begun in the 1980s to develop new ways of building transportation systems.

For his part, House Transportation and Infrastructure Chairman Bud Shuster, R-Pa., continued to defend his plan to use $9 billion on demonstration projects to be inserted in the House bill based on lawmakers' recommendations. The Senate took aim at Shuster's plan by voting 78-22 on March 12 to approve an amendment that would require demonstration projects to be paid for from a state's overall allocation based on formula, rather than separate appropriations. (Vote 29, p. S-8)

'Highway Pork'

Sen. John McCain, R-Ariz., the amendment's sponsor, urged an end to "highway pork" and the unfair practice of making his own state "pay the price for other states' earmarked projects."

The Senate and House also must reach agreement on how they will pay for increased transportation spending above limits set in last year's balanced-budget agreement (PL 105-33). Senate Budget Committee Chairman Pete V. Domenici, R-N.M., said he would reveal his own budget proposal March 17 and has focused on finding spending cuts to offset more transportation spending.

House Speaker Newt Gingrich, R-Ga., and a Republican leadership task force discussed the framework of a plan that includes several spending options and the possibility — strongly backed by Shuster — of moving the highway trust fund off budget, to permit spending increases not subject to spending caps. Domenici, Chafee and the Clinton administration strongly opposed Shuster's proposal.

Shuster said his committee planned a markup of HR 2400 on March 24, saying Republican leaders including House Budget Committee Chairman John R. Kasich, R-Ohio, were near agreement on transportation funding. His tough negotiations echoed the successful strategy of Sens. Robert C. Byrd, D-W.Va., and Phil Gramm, R-Texas, to virtually compel Republican leaders to accept a $25.8 billion increase in highway spending by building strong support among colleagues for an even bigger spending increase.

"I know my friend John Kasich can count," Shuster told the American Public Transit Association on March 10. "He knows I have the votes."

Division of Money

Once Shuster and Kasich find common ground on the spending level in HR 2400, the House will begin the next round of the long-simmering dispute over apportionment that was at the heart of the Senate's debate.

Chafee helped clear the way for passage by winning voice vote approval March 11 to a plan to shift about $350 million to seven states that were unhappy with the division of the $25.8 billion spending increase negotiated by Byrd, Gramm and the Republican leadership. The $25.8 billion was given to Appalachian regional roads, to highways in trade corridors carrying traffic to the Canadian and Mexican borders, to 10 states with high-density populations, and to 18 "donor states" that receive less than $1 in transportation funding for each $1 they pay in gasoline taxes.

The increased funding helped win overwhelming support for the bill, but did not end the donor state battle.

Sen. Connie Mack, R-Fla., led a last-ditch effort by donor states to repeal the 4.3-cents-per-gallon increase in the gasoline tax that was created in 1993 and dedicated to deficit reduction. S 1173 will dedicate the 4.3 cents to transportation funding, but Mack argued that states could get more for that money if they collected it as a state gasoline tax rather than receiving it through a federal trust fund formula.

The amendment failed when the Senate voted 18-80 to reject a procedural motion vote that would have allowed the amendment to be put to a vote. (Vote 26, p. S-7)

William D. Fay, president of the American Highway Users Alliance, representing transportation companies and motorists groups that pay the gasoline tax, said his organization opposed the repeal of the 4.3-cent tax and urged donor states not to expect a 100 percent return on federal gas taxes that support a "national system with national needs and priorities."

In the end, compromises cleared the way for final passage. Senate Banking, Housing and Urban Affairs Committee Chairman Alfonse M. D'Amato, R-N.Y., won approval, 96-4, of an amendment that added $41.3 billion in mass transit funding. It included a $5 billion increase in funding to be divided among mass transit programs in cities and rural areas. Nearly half the $5 billion went to "new starts" of mass transit systems or extensions. (Vote 25, p. S-7)

While compromises satisfied most demands of lawmakers, not all of them came away pleased with the final bill. The four senators who opposed the final bill came from Wisconsin and Pennsylvania, states unhappy with the final division of money. "The formula did not provide us with adequate funding," said Sen. Arlen Specter, R-Pa.

"It was old-fashioned log-rolling," said Sen. Judd Gregg, R-N.H., who voted for the final bill despite his reservations. He strongly opposed the $5 billion increase in mass transit funding won by D'Amato, because it was not clear what revenues or spending cuts would be used to pay for it. Gregg was one of four senators who

Transportation & Infrastructure

voted against the mass transit spending package.

With the dispute in the Senate now over, Chafee said senators would prepare for a conference committee where many issues must be resolved.

New Policy Initiatives

The Senate bill would withhold a share of highway funding from states that do not ban open containers of alcohol in moving automobiles or do not lower the blood-alcohol content standard for drunken-driving violations to 0.08 percent from 0.1 percent.

House Republicans leaders, including Shuster, have said they support an alternative approach that would provide incentives to states that take steps against drunken drivers.

Other Senate initiatives that will face attack in the House include a provision to extend the gasoline tax exemption for gasoline mixed with ethanol beyond 2000, when it will expire, to 2007. The Senate voted 71-26 on March 11 to table (kill) an amendment to delete that extension. *(Vote 27, p. S-7)*

Many provisions in the Senate bill echo and strengthen policies laid out in earlier legislation. The bill continues to give priority to the 44,000-mile network of Interstate highways and to the National Highway System, the 160,000-mile network of major roads specified by the National Highway System Designation Act (PL 104-59). *(1995 Almanac, 3-60)*

The Senate bill would streamline existing programs, reducing the number of major highway program categories from five to three. It would provide annual funding over the next six years for two of the centerpieces of the 1991 reauthorization law: about $1.3 billion for a program to reduce traffic congestion and air pollution and about $631.8 million to build car pool parking, bicycle trails, pedestrian walkways and other commuter improvements.

The Senate bill would allow states to use some federal funding for enhancements to Amtrak, the federally owned passenger railway, and other private rail terminals and publicly owned bus terminals.

The bill would establish a new financing program to provide lines of credit worth an estimated $10 billion to new transportation programs. It would permit employers to give employees $65 in cash for monthly tax-free mass transit, and provide for "welfare to work" assistance for welfare recipients to use transit systems to get to jobs.

As part of a plan to prevent injuries from automobile accidents, the bill would provide incentive grants to states that increase their annual rates of seat belt usage or surpass the national average for seat belt usage. It would also provide for new federal tests to develop safer airbags.

A federal freeze on bigger trucks would continue, limiting the use of larger-combination trucks to 22 states.

The bill contains tough new criminal penalties backed by the Clinton administration for terrorist acts involving railroads: life prison sentences for causing train wrecks. To help relieve traffic and improve safety, it authorizes the use of highway money to provide for traffic warnings and navigational aids.

Shuster Prepares For Onslaught Against Members' Pet Projects

MARCH 21 — House Transportation and Infrastructure Committee Chairman Bud Shuster, R-Pa., plans to defend a precious House perquisite the week of March 22 when he unveils his $9 billion list of highway projects designated for the districts of some lucky House colleagues.

Lawmakers are still vying to get their pet projects included on the list, which would be added to the House version of the surface transportation reauthorization bill (HR 2400) when it is marked up March 24.

But Shuster will be up against critics, including Sen. John McCain, R-Ariz., who said his list amounts to a big helping of "highway pork." Shuster predicted he would win against opposition in the Senate and from the Clinton administration.

To pay for his bill, Shuster would still need unspecified offsets. The bill would move the Highway Trust Fund off budget and provide about $3.7 billion more for transportation than the bill approved by the Senate (S 1173) on March 12.

Shuster predicted his bill would easily pass through the House by early April. The key battle over Shuster's $9 billion list is expected in mid-April in a conference committee that will try to resolve differences between House and Senate bills while racing to send final legislation to President Clinton. Lawmakers are trying to beat an April 30 deadline for the end of a short-term extension of transportation funding.

Shuster pledged to preserve the earmarked projects against an expected heavy attack. "These are high-priority projects,'" Shuster said in an interview. "We are vetting them carefully. The vetting process will be done soon."

Shuster declined to release the list of projects proposed by his colleagues but did confirm that he received 1,600 requests — about four per member.

McCain's Complaint

The Senate squared off for a confrontation March 12 by voting 78-22 to approve McCain's amendment requiring that special projects be paid for out of allocation to the trust fund allocation and not require extra money authorized by Congress. The amendment would give states the option of paying for the projects.

McCain said Shuster's planned $9 billion in demonstration projects, which are supposed to develop new ways of building transportation systems, exceeds the total $8 billion authorized for projects in three prior reauthorization bills dating back to 1982.

"This is offensive," McCain said. "I'll do everything in my power to make sure that such outlandish action is not condoned by the Senate."

Transportation Secretary Rodney Slater lined up against special projects in September 1997.

But Slater left unclear how far the Clinton administration would go in trying to kill individual projects. President Ronald Reagan vetoed the 1987 reauthorization bill [PL 100 — 17], criticizing "pork barrel" projects, but Congress voted to override him. *(1987 Almanac, p. 331)*

Criticism about the special projects comes at a time when Shuster faces an

Surface Transportation

investigation by the House ethics committee into his ties to a lobbyist, Ann Eppard, who is his former aide. A federal grand jury in Boston has been examining his connections to two campaign contributors with an interest in a federal highway project.

Gary Ruskin, director of the Congressional Accountability Project and author of the House ethics complaint questioning Shuster's ties to Eppard, has criticized Shuster for raising money from contributors who want his support for projects. Ruskin also has questioned whether Shuster's power over projects sought by members would give him the "ability to influence the ethics committee investigation." Ruskin's nonprofit group is affiliated with consumer advocate Ralph Nader.

For his part, Shuster has denied trying to influence other members or to use his power to raise campaign money. He moved to deflect the Senate criticism March 18 by reaching agreement with House Majority Whip Tom DeLay, R-Texas, and with members of his panel to include the funding for special projects under a provision of HR 2400 that guarantees each state a 95 percent return on its contributions to the highway trust fund.

"It will be in the bill," Shuster said. "It will make it fairer for all the states."

Unlike McCain's amendment, Shuster would continue to give lawmakers the final decision on whether to pay for earmarked projects.

Shuster said he was trying to respond to critics by evaluating projects proposed by 400 House members according to a cost-benefit analysis. A bipartisan group of senior committee members is reviewing the proposals.

But critics charge that his efforts to be fair fall short.

"Congress should not be in the business of earmarking. These decisions should be made by states, cities and planning organizations," said David Hirsch, transportation policy coordinator for Friends of the Earth, a Washington-based environmental advocacy group.

Little Payoff for Projects

A study by the General Accounting Office warned in 1995 that earmarked projects often "yield a low payoff for a variety of reasons, including the fact that they frequently are not aligned with the states' transportation priorities, can languish in the early stages of project development, or may never get started at all."

House Transportation Appropriations Subcommittee Chairman Frank R. Wolf, R-Va., praised Shuster's plans to evaluate project request, but remains critical. For three years, Wolf has refused to include them in appropriations bills. "If we did not have these projects, states would receive more money," he said.

Demonstration projects were begun in the 1970s, when Shuster and other lawmakers began inserting projects for their home districts that were ostensibly intended to demonstrate new road-building techniques. One of the first demonstration projects, proposed by Shuster, provided $25 million from 1976 to 1980 for a bypass on U.S. Route 20 around Everett, Pa. It was built with new construction techniques.

But critics, including Hirsch and Wolf, question whether many projects were justified. Stung by criticism, lawmakers in 1991 renamed the road projects and began referring to designated items as high-priority projects.

Battle With the States

The battle over special road projects pits the House, whose members want projects for their home districts, against state and federal transportation departments and senators, who tend to defer to the states.

Francis B. Francois, executive director of the American Association of State Highway and Transportation Officials, said that states should make the decision on where federal money should be spent on highway projects because "they are in the best position to weigh all the merits."

Members of Shuster's committee are resolute in defending their project-picking power. "Why should we accept that the center of all wisdom is in the state capital with the state department of transportation? Sometimes they don't divide money fairly. They tend to favor urban areas. When that happens, we hear about it from our constituents," said James L. Oberstar of Minnesota, the ranking Democrat on the panel.

He and other members of the committee point out that, while the Senate Environment and Public Works Committee has no formal program through which to solicit nominations from every senator, individual senators seek and get targeted money in other ways.

In the past, senators have objected to the highway bill and then at the last minute "compromised" by adding a list of their own projects and not killing any in the House.

This year, Sen. John W. Warner, R-Va., has secured $900 million for repairs to the federal government-owned Woodrow Wilson Bridge near Washington in the Senate reauthorization bill (S 1173).

As part of a deal increasing highway funding by $25.8 billion to clear the way for Senate passage, Robert C. Byrd, D-W.Va., won $1.8 billion to complete roads in the Appalachian region.

Shuster said he saw little difference between his $9 billion plan and efforts by senators to fund specific projects of their own.

"The Senate castigates projects. . . . But when they come to conference at about 2 a.m. on the 21st day, they reach in their pocket and pull out a list," Shuster said.

Competition for Money

While Shuster parries Senate efforts to kill House projects, he faces heavy lobbying from individual lawmakers and states supporting specific projects.

Indiana state officials have been conferring with lawmakers such as Rep. Lee H. Hamilton, D-Ind., who wants money for a bridge across the Ohio River to Kentucky.

Illinois hopes to snag money to help pay the $500 million cost of repairing a 12-mile stretch of Interstate 55, the Stevenson Expressway south of Chicago.

Some states are hoping transportation funding will help provide for new interstate highways.

Nevada has been working with Rep. Jim Gibbons, R-Nev., in seeking funding for a proposed stretch of Interstate 395 between Reno and Carson City, Nev., has one of the only state capitals in the country not served by an interstate highway.

And some states, including Indiana, are promoting plans to build parts of new transcontinental highways to help nurture economic development.

Transportation & Infrastructure

The fight for money has prompted a few states, including California, to publicly state they are not seeking money for projects, even though the state is certain to get extra money for road projects because of the work of individual lawmakers such as Frank Riggs, R-Calif., who sits on Shuster's committee. He wants money to widen the Pacific Coast Highway, U.S. 101.

Not all states are participating. Delaware said it is not expecting to be on Shuster's list.

That is because Delaware's lone House member, Republican Michael N. Castle, is opposed to designating federal money for roads that may not be needed.

"We should not be doing this. It comes down to political favoritism, not transportation needs," Castle said."

Road Wars, Special Projects Ensure Rough Ride In House

MARCH 28 — The House is racing to act on a $218.3 billion surface transportation reauthorization bill (HR 2400)the week of March 30 after months of wrangling over the division of money among states and coveted special road projects.

Debate on the bill is set to begin on April 1 on the House floor, where at least one major battle looms: a bruising fight over a proposal by Rep. Nita M.Lowey, D-N.Y., to pressure states to enact a lower blood-alcohol content threshold of 0.08 percent for drunken driving violations. The battle pits advocates of states' rights, including the National Governors' Association and the beer industry, against safety advocates, including Mothers Against Drunk Driving, who have mounted a strong lobbying effort on Capitol Hill.

With little debate and virtually no discord, the House Transportation and Infrastructure Committee voted 69-0 on March 24 to approve the bill, which included a deal on spending that GOP Chairman Bud Shuster of Pennsylvania cut with House Republican leaders. It also approved a plan to move the transportation trust fund off-budget in fiscal 1999.

The Ways and Means Committee gave voice vote approval to the bill two days later, with provisions that would allow the current 5.4-cents-per-gallon gasoline tax credit for fuel mixed with ethanol to expire in 2000. That would bring in $900 million over two years, enough to pay for repeal of a tax on heavy truck tires, repeal of a 4.3-cents-per-gallon share of tax on railroad diesel fuel and transfer from the General Fund to the Aquatic Resources Trust Fund of a 3.4-cent share of the tax on motorboat and small-engine gasoline.

The panel voted 11-22 to reject an amendment by Sander M. Levin, D-Mich., to extend the ethanol tax credit to 2007.

House Speaker Newt Gingrich pledged to fight for the ethanol tax credit. "It's a program that I am very deeply committed to."

Both chambers are trying to expedite passage before a short-term extension of transportation funding expires April 30. Shuster said he expected the bill to sail through the House. "I would be surprised if it did not get 400 votes," he said at the markup.

James L. Oberstar of Minnesota, the panel's ranking Democrat, embraced Shuster after the committee vote and said he expected the bill to win strong bipartisan support on floor. The bill has been nicknamed the Building Efficient Surface Transportation and Equity Act (BESTEA), but Oberstar joked it should be called the "Bud E. Shuster Transportation for Eternity Act."

The bill bears the unmistakable imprint of Shuster, who shaped the legislation and worked out a deal with House Republican leaders to pay for the spending increases with offsets that will be identified later when a House and Senate conference committee meets to work out the final bill.

It was a sweet victory for Shuster, and a bitter loss for House Budget Committee Chairman John R. Kasich, R-Ohio, who said the spending level was too high. He plans to propose a floor amendment to slash the federal gasoline tax from18.3 cents per gallon to a maximum of 7.4 cents over four years, starting in October. He would allow states to increase their own gasoline tax to pay for roads and other transportation projects.

Kasich was concerned that the bill would require about $26 billion in unspecified offsets. The outlays required by the bill would exceed spending caps in the 1997 balanced-budget agreement by that amount.

The legislation is the biggest highway and mass transit bill in history. It provides a 40 percent increase in overall funding and exceeds the Senate bill in funding by $4 billion. Oberstar called it "the king of transportation bills."

Package of Projects

Despite Kasich's strong opposition, the Transportation and Infrastructure Committee approved by voice vote a substitute amendment by Shuster that incorporated terms of the House Republican deal and a controversial package of $9.3 billion in funding for more than 1,467 projects requested by more than 300 House members.

Sen. John McCain, R-Ariz., who opposed special projects, pledged to continue his fight to eliminate them. "I find it amazing that as the House struggles to find money to pay for an emergency disaster supplemental bill, they see fit to waste more than $9 billion," he said.

Shuster sought to defuse criticism this year by adopting a new procedure that required lawmakers to show that most projects were considered appropriate by state transportation agencies. But the projects have remained controversial because in many cases they are not considered priorities by the states.

Three critics of the special projects included Reps. Sue Myrick, R-N.C., and Oklahoma Republicans Tom Coburn and Steve Largent, said they objected to the committee's procedure for specifically asking each of them to request targeted funding for road projects.

They said that calls made by committee staff asking them to specifically accept money seemed like a tacit request for a commitment to support the bill. "The process stinks," Coburn said.

Coburn and Largent both rejected $15 million in funding offered for projects in their districts. "People on the committee don't know Oklahoma and should not be making these decisions," Coburn said.

Other critics of the projects included Gary Ruskin, director of the Congressional Accountability Project, whose ethics complaint prompted a pending House ethics committee investigation of Shuster, focusing on his ties to lobbyist Ann Eppard, who is his former top aide.

Ruskin said the awarding of projects to members of the ethics committee, whether or not they actively lobbied for the funding, created the potential for Shuster to exercise influence on the committee. And Ruskin called on the ethics panel to look into projects awarded to clients of Eppard as part of its investigation of Shuster.

"I think members of the ethics subcommittee were neck deep in a conflict of interest when they elected not to appoint outside counsel to investigate this case," Ruskin said.

Special Projects

Several special projects were within the jurisdiction of Eppard's clients or members of the ethics panel:

• The Harlingen (Texas) Area Chamber of Commerce won support for efforts to develop the U.S. 77 corridor to provide a link to the proposed Interstate 69 in Houston. The committee provided $7.5 million for an interchange on U.S. 77 in Harlingen. The chamber is one of Eppard's clients.

• Another lobbying client, the San Juan Tren Urbano, a mass-transit system in Puerto Rico's capital city, won two of the 98 project slots eligible for a share of $6 billion final design and construction of new mass-transit systems or extensions.

• The committee provided $15 million for a road extension and widening Interstate 25 in the district of Joel Hefley, R-Colo., chairman of the ethics subcommittee handling the Shuster case.

• It made available $10 million for two improvement projects on Interstate 49 in the district of Jim McCrery, R-La., who also sits on the four-member ethics subcommittee.

Zoe Lofgren of California, ranking Democrat on the subcommittee, did not request any special projects, but the bill nonetheless cleared the way for funding for a light-rail line in her district.

McCrery said he did not believe the awarding of funding amounted to a conflict because he requested a list of projects before he was appointed to the ethics subcommittee and did not actively lobby for funding. "I took care to make sure there was not a conflict," McCrery said.

Hefley said he did not actively lobby for projects, and Chet Edwards, D-Texas, the fourth member of the panel, said he did not lobby for funding for any projects in his district, although he was part of a coalition that supported funding for Interstate 35 in Texas, which was funded by the committee.

"No project would influence my decisions on the committee," Edwards said.

In response to critics of special projects, Shuster defended his role on the House floor March 26.

He denied trying to use his power to grant projects to put pressure on House members to support the bill.

"I challenge these members to name one person, one person, whom I went to and said, 'You will get a project in exchange for your vote,' " Shuster said. He said the charges that he tried to influence votes or threatened to withhold funding were a "blatant falsehood."

More Battles

While Shuster tried to answer critics of special projects, other key House battles began to take shape, with some Democrats, including Edwards and David R. Obey of Wisconsin, lining up against consideration of HR 2400 until offsets are provided for the spending increase above limits.

"It's putting the cart before the horse," said Robert T. Matsui, D-Calif. He was concerned that the bill would be considered before a budget resolution on specific spending cuts to keep the budget in balance.

For his part, Shuster said offsets would likely be worked out in conference committee before the legislation becomes law.

Shuster defused one potential battle in negotiations with House Majority Whip Tom DeLay of Texas, who has been a leader in pushing for an increased share of money for donor states — those that receive less than a dollar of transportation funding for each dollar they pay in gasoline taxes.

Under the substitute amendment adopted by Shuster's committee, the special projects would be included as part of the calculation of a minimum allocation guarantee that provides for each state to receive at least 90 percent of its contributions to the Highway Trust Fund.

DeLay said he may continue his efforts to press for a minimum guarantee of 95 percent for each state, but he will likely wait until Senate and House conferees are working on the final bill.

Another possible floor amendment was being considered by Rep. Frank Riggs, R-Calif., to eliminate a Transportation Department program that sets a goal of giving 10 percent of construction contracts to businesses owned by women and minorities. A similar amendment offered by GOP Sen. Mitch McConnell of Kentucky was tabled, or killed, in the Senate by a 58-37 vote on March 6.

Several members on the committee said they expected that relatively few amendments would be offered on the floor, in part to help speed the legislation toward final passage before the April 30 deadline.

Quick passage by the House would leave time after the Easter recess for the conference committee to resolve differences in the House and Senate bills and settle disputes. It "could very well be a contentious conference," said Nick J. Rahall II, D-W.Va.

The main battles in the conference committee will include the fate of the ethanol tax credit, which extend to 2007. The committee will also determine the fate of the $9.3 billion in special projects in the House bill.

Other key issues are expected to include differences in the formulas for dividing money and guarantees in both bills designed to increase the share of funding for more than 20 donor states.

Both the Senate and House bills revamp the current formulas used to apportion money, which were based on a historic share of funding that incorporated outdated population figures from the 1980 census and outdated factors, including the land area of each state and postal road mileage in each state. The revised formulas in both bills incorporate the latest census estimates of population and statistical measures of road systems and road usage in states, including the length in miles of all lanes of traffic in each state and mileage driven by vehi-

Transportation & Infrastructure

cles on highways.

But the formulas in the House and Senate bills differ in the weight they place on different measures of highway usage. Based on House committee staff estimates, about 14 states — mainly those with small populations, such as Wyoming, Rhode Island and Nevada — would fare better under the formulas used in the Senate bill than under HR 2400.

Both bills would guarantee that each state receive about 90 percent of the gas taxes it contributes to the Highway Trust Fund. But the guarantees would be calculated in different ways.

Doug Callaway, Washington representative for the Florida Department of Transportation, said he believed the minimum allocation provisions in both bills now appeared to be roughly the same. "We want to make sure the guarantees are strengthened in conference committee and are not eroded," Callaway said.

House Passes $219 Billion Highway Bill

APRIL 4 — The House set the stage for a tug-of-war with the Senate over building roads and fixing bridges by passing a six-year, $219 billion highway and mass transit bill packed with special projects for lawmakers.

After a bitter battle on the House floor over $9 billion in pet projects added to the bill in committee, the House voted 337-80 on April 1 to pass it. Now it goes to a conference committee to work out differences with a similar bill (S 1173) approved by the Senate on March 12. The administration said the legislation is a budget buster. (Vote 98, p. H-30)

Among the funding tucked into the bill is $3 million over three years for a public television documentary on "infrastructure awareness," a $97 million crosstown bridge in Oklahoma City and $12 million over six years for an Appalachian Transportation Institute at Marshall University.

Many issues remain outstanding for the House-Senate conference, which begins its work April 21 and has nine days to reach a compromise before temporary funding runs out on April 30. Negotiators must find the money for the biggest public works bill in history, decide how to crack down on drunken driving and determine the future of a tax credit for gasoline mixed with ethanol.

Republican Bud Shuster of Pennsylvania, chairman of the House Transportation and Infrastructure Committee, which engineered the legislation (HR 2400), said it would provide a historic funding boost at a time when many roads and bridges in the United States are in dire need of repairs.

Shuster compared the cost of the bill with other expensive transportation projects in U.S. history, including construction of the Panama Canal and the Interstate Highway System started in 1956.

"Save our roads, improve mass transit, job creation and environmental preservation. That is what this bill is all about," said Shuster, whose Pennsylvania district is the recipient of $25 million in special projects.

But Bob Inglis, R-S.C., who voted against the bill, said: "This is probably the most embarrassing night that I have ever spent in this Congress. We came to change things and we are not. We are participating in the big old trough that has characterized this place in the past."

The conference committee must settle on an overall spending level and handle the crucial task of identifying offsets, or spending cuts, to pay for an approximately 40 percent increase in transportation spending in both bills. Though the House and Senate bills are similar in scope, there are key differences.

The House bill would provide about $5 billion more in funding and includes formulas to apportion money that would not be as favorable as the Senate legislation to about 14 states with small populations, mainly in the West and Northeast.

Crucial Battles

The search to find the money for the transportation bill began March 31 when the House Rules Committee approved a rule that specified veterans programs should not be cut to pay for transportation projects.

"To pave roads you need hot asphalt," said Lindsey Graham, R-S.C. "Right now, Congress' preferred method of payment is a hot check."

On April 2, Senate Budget Committee Chairman Pete V. Domenici, R-N.M., defended $18.5 billion in offsets for transportation in his budget plan, including $10 billion in revenue from a potential change in federal policy to deny veterans health benefits for treating smoking-related illnesses that did not occur during military service.

But Sen. John D. Rockefeller IV said, "It is outrageous that veterans' programs are being looted in this way." In response to such criticism, the Senate passed by voice vote on April 2 an amendment to the 1999 budget resolution (S Con Res 86) that called for a one-year study of health benefits for veterans with smoking-related ailments.

Another potential battle in coming weeks will be over how to satisfy more than 20 states that receive less than $1 in highway funding for each $1 they pay in gas taxes. Both bills guarantee about a 90 percent return on contributions to the Highway Trust Fund, but they use different calculations to measure the amount each state is guaranteed.

Clinton's Dissatisfaction

President Clinton continued to express dissatisfaction with the spending level in the House bill, which would soak up funding he wants for other programs. The bill would require about $26 billion in offsets because it exceeds spending caps in the 1997 balanced-budget agreement. (PL 105 — 33)

Returning from a 12-day trip to Africa, Clinton said on April 3 that he was "determined that highway spending, though it is quite important . . . must be within the balanced budget and should not crowd out critical investments in education, child care, health care, or threaten our budget discipline."

Opponents of the bill, including David R. Obey, D-Wis., and Vic Fazio, D-Calif., predicted Clinton would give serious thought to a veto.

"I pray to God that the president of the United States vetoes it," said Mike Parker, R-Miss.

Fight Over 'Highway Pork'

The biggest eruption came over the projects costing about $9 billion that were inserted in the bill by Shuster's committee and approved on March 24.

The project list remained in flux until the final vote. The House approved by voice vote an amendment by Shuster, increasing the number of special projects from 1,466 to 1,506.

In addition to the projects, the bill provided for a wide range of other items, including grants for universities and mass transit projects.

Critics said that much of the spending in the bill would pay for "highway pork," projects that they said could hardly be considered essential.

Matt Salmon, R-Ariz., accused Shuster and his supporters of being "Republicrats" and big spenders.

Rep. Nick J. Rahall II, D-W.Va., a supporter of Shuster's bill, shot back that Salmon and his colleagues are their own party of "right wing wacko kids for some of the philosophy they are espousing."

Kasich's Rebellion

House Budget Committee Chairman John R. Kasich, R-Ohio, helped lead the unsuccessful uprising against Shuster's bill. Kasich had been defeated earlier at the Republican caucus when leaders backed Shuster and opposed Kasich's efforts to cut the bill.

Instead of trying to cut funding in the bill, Kasich proposed an alternative — trying to revamp the nation's transportation funding system and return more control over transportation funding to states.

His proposal would have cut the federal gasoline tax of 18.3 cents per gallon to 7.4 cents per gallon at the end of a four-year transition period. He encouraged states to raise their own gasoline taxes to balance the cut in the federal tax. His amendment was defeated, 98-318, with two members voting present. *(Vote 97, p. H-30)*

Kasich's proposal was doomed, with little support from states or from groups such as truckers that pay gasoline taxes. Opponents of his measure charged that it would turn back the clock on transportation funding to a time before the Interstate Highway System was launched.

Kasich and other critics of the spending level in the bill faced a phalanx of opposition from House members who stood up to defend individual projects that went to their districts.

For example, Lloyd Doggett, D-Texas, said a $16 million project to build a bypass for trucks around Austin would remove traffic from the "most dangerous section of Interstate 35" between the Mexican border and Minnesota. He said the bill would provide support for projects backed by House members and assure their priorities are addressed by state and transportation bureaucrats.

"These bureaucracies are not the know-all and be-all on planning transportation," Doggett said.

With a broad base of support, Shuster easily defeated two other efforts to cut funding in the bill. The House voted 79-337 to defeat an amendment by Graham to delete funding for special highway projects and funding for other mass transit and bus projects. *(Vote 95, p. H-28)*

The House voted 106-312 to defeat an amendment offered by Rep. John M. Spratt Jr., D-S.C., to allow more time to identify offsets or cut transportation spending by continuing for two more months the temporary extension of highway spending that expires April 30. The amendment was backed by the Clinton administration. *(Vote 96, p. H-30)*

In the end, Shuster won broad support on final passage. Three members voted present — Joel Hefley, R-Colo.; Zoe Lofgren, D-Calif.; and Jim McCrery, R-La. — all members of the ethics subcommittee examining ties between Shuster and Ann Eppard, a lobbyist who is his former top aide. The fourth member of the panel, Chet Edwards, D-Texas, voted against the bill.

A Range of Battles To Come

The contentious floor debate left unresolved a spectrum of issues that must still be settled in conference.

They include a battle over a proposed Senate extension of the tax credit for gasoline mixed with ethanol and pilot projects in the House bill that would allow states to be certified to conduct environmental reviews of road projects.

Shuster put off the debate on a number of key issues by reaching a "Big Four" deal with three other senior members of his committee — James L. Oberstar of Minnesota, the ranking Democrat; Rahall; and Tom Petri, R-Wis. — to stand together against any amendment that any one of them opposed.

That agreement helped prevent some controversial proposals from reaching the floor, where debate could have delayed efforts to send legislation to Clinton before the April 30 deadline.

As part of efforts to expedite the House vote, the Rules Committee crafted a narrow plan for floor debate that winnowed about 30 proposed amendments down to six, including three aimed at the controversial core of the bill: the big increase in spending without specific offsets, which must be decided in conference.

The Rules Committee refused to allow an amendment offered Rep. Nita M. Lowey, D-N.Y., that mirrored language adopted by the Senate in March to withhold a share of federal funding from states that do not enact a lower blood-alcohol content threshold of .08 percent for drunken-driving violations. The House bill would provide incentives, in the form of highway safety funding, to states that lower the threshold and take other steps to encourage safety and driver sobriety.

Sen. Frank R. Lautenberg, D-N.J., a backer of the Senate provision, charged that the House was influenced by campaign donations.

A study by the Center for Responsive Politics found that the alcohol industry accounted for $734,000 in donations to political action committees and $989,000 in soft money contributions to political parties in 1997 and so far in 1998.

Shuster and other backers of the House approach to curbing drunken driving said the Senate provision would impinge on states' rights.

For now, Shuster appears to have won the key battle in defense of special projects.

Rahall said he doubts that senators would mount a strong attack on special projects in conference and would instead focus on pushing their own projects.

"In the past, they have come into conference with proposals for projects of their own tucked in their pockets and tucked in their socks," Rahall said.

For one, Sen. John W. Warner, R-Va., wants to defend and perhaps increase the $900 million in funding in the Senate bill to replace the

Transportation & Infrastructure

Woodrow Wilson Bridge near Washington, D.C. The House bill would not provide any funding for the project.

It remains unclear how strongly Shuster and others would fight for a provision in the House bill that would take the Highway Trust Fund off budget. Republican John H. Chafee of Rhode Island and other senators have vowed opposition, and some supporters of the House bill have speculated that the trust fund provision could be dropped in negotiations.

In other floor action, the House debated and rejected, 194-225, an amendment by Republican Rep. Marge Roukema of New Jersey to replace a Transportation Department program that sets a goal of providing 10 percent of transportation projects to businesses owned by women and minorities with another program that would recruit and provide assistance to such businesses. *(Vote 93, p. H-28)*

"I know of course that discrimination exists," Roukema said. "But we cannot attack discrimination with a different style of discrimination."

House Speaker Newt Gingrich, R-Ga., supported the amendment. "The taxpayers of the United States should expect that the lowest competitive bidder will get the grant," he said.

Democrat Eleanor Holmes Norton, the delegate for the District of Columbia, defended the program and warned that Republicans would face retaliation by women voters who own businesses.

"Hundreds of thousands of women's faces are trained on us now," Norton said. "They are taking names, and they are counting votes."

For Conferees, Debate Is Where To Spend Money, Where To Find It

APRIL 25 — Money and offsets will be at the heart of efforts of House and Senate negotiators who began April 22 trying to reconcile two broad surface transportation reauthorization bills.

The six-year, $219 billion House bill (HR 2400) and the six-year, $217.3 billion Senate version would each boost spending on highways and mass transit by about 40 percent. While the bills are tantalizingly similar, they diverge on such crucial questions as how much should be spent on key programs, and how the mammoth increase should be offset with spending cuts or new revenue-raising proposals. Such offsets are needed for the bill to comply with the 1997 balanced-budget agreement (PL 105-33).

Rep. Bud Shuster, R-Pa., chairman of the House Transportation and Infrastructure Committee, opened the first meeting as chairman of the conference April 22 by promising motorists a greater return on gas taxes they pay into the Highway Trust Fund.

"I will make every effort to make sure that when you fill up at the pump, the gas taxes you pay will go to make your roads and bridges smoother and safer," Shuster said.

His opening remarks followed a behind-the-scenes tug of war with Environment and Public Works Chairman John H. Chafee, R-R.I., over who should wield the gavel during the conference. Shuster prevailed after reaching an agreement with Chafee that would allow a senator to chair the conference committee for the next six-year transportation reauthorization bill and a "midcourse correction bill" that may be required in three years.

Shuster begins the conference with strong support from House Speaker Newt Gingrich, R-Ga., and personal ties to Senate Majority Leader Trent Lott, R-Miss., a "close friend from when we came into the House together" in 1973. Shuster also carries into the debate a reputation as an aggressive negotiator and a champion of the transportation and construction industry and of higher funding for states.

"Shuster is a bulldog. Chafee is a gentleman," said one Senate aide, describing the contrasting personalities of the two men who will play key roles in shaping final legislation.

Shuster moved quickly to work out an agreement on a number of non-controversial surface transportation issues approved by voice vote of the conference committee April 24.

Shuster acknowledged big obstacles to a final agreement on how pay for the sharp spending increase in the bill, but he dismissed hints that the Clinton administration is considering a veto because of the high level of spending and lack of offsets.

Rep. David Minge, D-Minn., began circulating a letter in the House the week of April 20 seeking signatures urging Clinton to veto HR 2400.

Minge said the letter was to support Clinton's efforts to make sure there are offsets to pay for the bill.

"We simply cannot end up with a budget-buster bill," said Sen. John W. Warner, R-Va., who pointed to $9 billion in highway projects for specific members' districts in the House bill and a matching amount for mass transit programs. Nevertheless, Warner is seeking as much as $1.6 billion to replace the Woodrow Wilson Bridge, which spans the Potomac River and is a major commuter path between Virginia and Maryland.

Philadelphia Mayor Edward Rendell offered support to Shuster in a speech at the National Press Club on April 22, saying that provisions in the House bill "routinely referred to as pork are extraordinarily important."

While the conference committee appeared to be reaching agreement on non-financial issues, negotiators predicted that disputes over money and offsets would almost certainly stretch beyond the April 30 expiration of a temporary extension of transportation funding (PL 105-33).

Ethanol Battle

Another key fight remained unresolved and delayed appointment of the last conferees from the Ways and Means Committee. Bill Archer, R-Texas, the committee chairman, wants to appoint conferees who support expiration of a 5.4-cents-per-gallon gas tax exemption for fuel mixed with ethanol as planned in 2000. Gingrich wants to appoint conferees who support a Senate provision to extend the exemption to 2007.

Shuster predicted the conference could last well beyond the two weeks that it took Senate and House negotiators to produce the 1991 surface transportation bill, in 1991 (PL 102-240). *(1991 Almanac, p. 137)*

"I would be happy if we send final legislation to President Clinton by Memorial Day," said Shuster. He strongly opposed an idea floated by Senate Appropriations Committee

Chairman Ted Stevens, R-Alaska, to pass another short-term funding extension as part of a supplemental appropriations bill.

"States are running out of money. My state is one of them," Stevens said, adding that he had not discussed his idea with other senators.

"I'm opposed to an extension. I think extensions are going to go nowhere," Shuster quickly replied. "We need to keep the pressure on."

While Shuster batted away talk of another extension, he went on the offensive against the Clinton administration in response to its pointed attacks on the House bill as a budget-buster.

Clinton vs. Shuster

Transportation Secretary Rodney Slater attacked Shuster's plan to take the Highway Trust Fund off budget in an April 23 speech at the National Press Club:

"We have worked too hard to balance the budget and to put our economic house in order. We cannot allow this action to negate that kind of achievement."

He said the administration would stick to its intention not to permit any budget surplus to be earmarked for transportation infrastructure.

"What we need to keep in mind is that the surplus is not for transportation. We said that the surplus should be reserved for Social Security first," said Slater.

Shuster fired back by releasing a videotape of Clinton who, as governor of Arkansas in 1991, criticized use of the Highway Trust Fund for deficit reduction instead of transportation.

"The Congress took that money from us under a solemn contract to turn right around and give it back to be spent only on roads — federal highways," Clinton said on the tape. "Instead they are hoarding it, they are keeping it up there, and the only reason is to make the federal deficit look smaller than it is. It is just as wrong as it can be, and we ought to stop it."

Shuster showed the video and offered a punch line: "I agree with the president."

Search for Offsets

While the White House and Shuster fought over Shuster's off-budget proposal, Gingrich and Lott met April 23 to discuss another potentially explosive topic: how to involve committees with jurisdiction in decisions that will result in spending cuts needed to pay for the bill.

They were joined by Shuster and Chafee to discuss how to pick offsets without violating the turf of key committees.

"It is clear that all the relevant committees need to be involved. We were talking about what can be done to achieve this," Shuster said.

The Congressional Budget Office estimates that the House bill would exceed the baseline budget by $33 billion, and the Senate bill by $34 billion, over six years.

Senate Budget Chairman Pete V. Domenici, R-N.M., warned other negotiators that offsets would probably have to exceed the $18.5 billion in offsets specified in the Senate-passed budget resolution (S Con Res 86), which was aimed at keeping the budget in balance over the next five years. Based on more recent projections, Domenici said April 22 that necessary offsets could amount to "more like $25 to $30 billion."

Domenici said the failure to find off-sets would imperil the appropriations process this year, because it would effectively violate provisions of the balanced-budget agreement.

"Some people do not think this is important," Domenici said. "It is important."

Chafee said a key decision would be what baseline budget to use in determining how much the bills would actually increase spending over current programs required by law over the next six years. The size of the increase will determine how much is needed in offsets.

"We will have to determine how much we can spend," Chafee said.

House negotiators began the conference hoping to reach an early decision to ensure the survival of the special projects for their districts. Senators want to focus on the overall spending level and on determining how money will be distributed to the states. The House bill would provide more money for most states, while the Senate bill would favor states with smaller populations.

Privately, staff aides traded barbs over provisions included in both bills that would pay for special projects or devote funding to specific states. In one meeting, a coffee cup was used to collect quarters for each "disparaging remark" aimed at the other side. It soon filled up.

The States' Share

One obstacle involves working out a compromise on apportioning money to the states.

Chafee is expected to help lead efforts to preserve funding for Northeastern states, including his own, that have traditionally received more than $1 in transportation funding for each $1 they pay in gas taxes. Gingrich and Lott want to increase the share of funding for more than 20 "donor states" in the South, Midwest and West that receive less in transportation funding than they pay in gas taxes.

"This is more than a regional issue. We need to ensure that the needs of densely populated and congested states are fairly treated," said Sen. Frank R. Lautenberg, D-N.J.

The Southern Governors Association circulated a letter urging negotiators to consider the needs of donor states and to preserve provisions in both bills that would ensure states receive at least a 90 percent return on contributions to the Highway Trust Fund.

Some senators grumbled that Shuster would be likely to favor House provisions and questioned whether the unusual agreement that allowed him to take the gavel was fair to the Senate.

"It was supposed to be a quid pro quo," said one senator. "I wish there was more quid for the quo."

Chafee replied that he had wanted to be chairman and discussed the matter with Lott, but he denied rumors that Lott had declined to go to bat for him because Shuster would be a stronger advocate for donor states. "It was never elevated to that level," Chafee said.

Chafee said he concluded it was Shuster's turn, even though the House chaired the 1991 transportation bill conference committee. He said he agreed with Shuster's argument that the Senate chaired another conference committee in 1995 on a bill to designate the National Highway System (PL 104-59).

Shuster said he would work hard to reach compromises, stressing that his

Transportation & Infrastructure

Industries Take Sides in Ethanol Battle

MAY 2 — Major industries are lining up on opposite sides of a House proposal to let a $900 million tax exemption for the ethanol industry die.

On one side is Ways and Means Chairman Bill Archer, R-Texas, an opponent of the gasoline substitute made primarily from corn that accounts for 1 percent of the nation's energy consumption. On the other are lawmakers from the Corn Belt and presidential hopefuls who are seeking the votes of Iowa corn farmers in the nation's first caucuses in 2000.

Archer might appear to be at a big disadvantage in a tussle with the top Republican and Democratic leaders and the White House. But he has an equalizer: a coalition of allies that includes oil, railroad and trucking businesses and even recreational groups.

Archer calls the tax break "a violation of the free market" and has pledged to resist any extension. He and others have tried to kill the subsidy since it was first approved to deal with the oil shortages of the 1970s.

The debate over ethanol is spilling into the House-Senate conference committee considering the surface transportation bill (HR 2400), which will decide whether to keep the ethanol program alive.

Six conferees from the House and Senate tax-writing committees will probably make the final decision. The appointment of three Ways and Means conferees has been delayed because of a sharp split on ethanol between Archer and House Speaker Newt Gingrich, R-Ga., who supports the program.

The House version of the bill contains Archer's proposal to allow the tax break to expire in 2000 and raise $900 million over two years from new gas tax revenue. That would be enough to pay for the repeal of a 4.3 cents-per-gallon tax on railroad diesel fuel, repeal of a tax on heavy truck tires and a transfer from the General Fund to the Aquatic Resources Trust Fund of a 3.4-cent share of the tax on motorboat and small-engine gasoline.

The Senate version of the bill would continue the tax break to 2007, but reduce it gradually to 5.1 cents-per-gallon from the current 5.4 cents on gasoline mixed with ethanol. The exemption was extended to 2000 by the Omnibus Budget Reconciliation Act of 1990. (1990 Almanac, p. 160)

Archer's plan has been under attack by farmers who say killing the program would hurt crop prices and end a program that reduces the nation's reliance on imported oil.

"Not since the days of the robber barons have Big Oil and Big Railroads teamed up so effectively at the expense of the American farmer," said Ryland Utlaut, a Missouri corn farmer who is head of the 30,000-member National Corn Growers Association.

Critics of the ethanol tax break say it is wasteful. A 1997 General Accounting Office study concluded that the ethanol tax break had cost the government $7.1 billion in gas tax revenue from 1979 to 1995 and found that ethanol had little effect on the environment.

Besides railroad and truck interests, which would benefit from continued tax cuts, Archer's plan has tacit support from the oil industry, which makes a petroleum derivative used as a gasoline additive that competes with ethanol in cities where air quality standards require cleaner fuels.

Archer Daniels Midland Co., the nation's biggest ethanol producer with an estimated 40 percent market share, is influential in Washington. In the 1997-98 election cycle, the company's political action committee has contributed $94,500 to congressional candidates, roughly evenly divided between the two parties.

By contrast, the nation's five Fortune 500 railroads have given six times as much money to congressional candidates, mostly Republican.

Presidential Politics

Despite its mixed record, ethanol has become intertwined in presidential politics.

Gingrich recently joked to reporters that his strong support for ethanol might be linked to an aspiration to run for president. "None of you should draw any particular conclusion from my long commitment to ethanol. It's sound energy policy. It's a renewable resource. And it helps protect the environment, especially in Iowa," Gingrich said.

In a more serious moment, Gingrich flatly predicted the final bill would continue the ethanol tax break.

Derrick A. Crandall, co-chairman of the American League of Anglers and Boaters, a coalition of boating, fishing and environmental groups, predicted a compromise.

"What ties us to ethanol is not logic, but the budget process and the need for offsets," Crandall said.

No. 1 goal is to ensure gas taxes will be reserved for transportation. He hinted he would be open to compromising on a gamut of other issues, including the Senate's proposal to lower the blood-alcohol content threshold to 0.08 percent for drunken driving violations.

"We're talking about all the options with everybody," Shuster said.

Conferees Struggle To Make Painful Choices

MAY 2 — Federal highway funding went into a deep freeze on May 1.

The inability of Congress to pass a surface transportation bill before the expiration of a short-term extension of federal funding at the end of April left states scrambling to cancel contracts and find emergency sources of money for new projects.

Missouri state officials told road contractors they could not count on getting contracts because of delays in Washington. Illinois decided to wait until fiscal 1999 — when funding doubts are resolved — on a traffic-snarling reconstruction plan for the Stevenson Expressway, Interstate 55 in Chicago.

The six-year highway and mass transit funding bill (HR 2400) has hardly steamrolled through Congress. The long delays have sent ripples across the heartland.

A big roadblock stands in the way of final passage: a battle over money that shows no sign of being resolved. The bill would bust the budget baseline by more than $30 billion, according to the Congressional Budget Office. While lawmakers agree on the need for a big increase in highway and mass transit funding, they have not agreed on how to pay for it with cuts in other programs. The alternative — passing a bill without such offsets — would be political poison in an election year and possibly invite a veto by President Clinton.

House and Senate negotiators moved quickly to resolve technical differences in a conference committee, approving an initial package of highway provisions April 24. They followed up by approving dozens of highway, mass transit and safety provisions on April 28 and April 30.

But there was no sign of a consensus on the crucial issue of how much to spend on transportation overall. Lawmakers must make a painful choice between scaling back the bill or cutting other programs.

Bud Shuster, R-Pa., chairman of the House Transportation and Infrastructure Committee and the conference, said the decision would be made at a level "above our pay grade" by Republican leaders, including House Speaker Newt Gingrich, R-Ga., and Senate Majority Leader Trent Lott, R-Miss. Shuster said he would take "the happy elephant approach: leaning and smiling, smiling and leaning."

Lott said he discussed new offsets with Senate Budget Committee Chairman Pete V. Domenici, R-N.M., on April 28. He said they went beyond the short list of $18.5 billion in offsets mentioned in the Senate-passed budget resolution (S Con Res 86), including elimination of veterans health benefits for smoking-related ailments not connected to military service and a possible increase in the limit for loans insured by the Federal Housing Administration. But Lott declined to specify what the new offsets were.

Trouble for States

Francis B. Francois, executive director of the American Association of State Highway and Transportation Officials, said the federal funding freeze would have the biggest effect in about 30 states with shorter construction seasons, and among smaller states, with less financial resources of their own.

"Many of these states do not have enough money to continue to fund programs on their own while they wait for federal funding," Francois said.

Other states took the end of the temporary authorization (PL 105-130) in stride but warned that their mood might change.

"Nevada and other states are going out on a limb by spending their own money in place of federal money. But patience will begin to wear out in June if Congress does not conclude this," said Leo Penne, director of Nevada's Washington, D.C., office.

Senate Appropriations Committee Chairman Ted Stevens, R-Alaska, called for adding a short-term extension to a fiscal 1998 supplemental spending bill (HR 3579) to help states in dire straits.

"Many states are running out of money," Stevens said. "And my state is one of them."

The delays hit Alaska particularly hard because they prevent new road projects and effectively shorten what is already a short building season because of the long Arctic winter.

But strong opposition blocked Stevens from moving on his idea. Phil Gramm, R-Texas, said an extension would ensure that completing final legislation would "take a very long period of time."

Shuster joined other House members in signing a letter written by ranking committee Democrat James L. Oberstar of Minnesota opposing an extension.

The letter was sent to Rep. David R. Obey of Wisconsin, ranking Democrat on the Appropriations Committee, who serves on the conference committee considering the supplemental fiscal 1998 spending bill (HR 3579).

"We need to keep the pressure on to pass a bill," Oberstar said in an interview.

House Appropriations Committee Chairman Robert L. Livingston, R-La., said there is "sufficient opposition from the leadership and from ranking members" to prevent him from supporting an extension in the supplemental spending bill.

House Majority Leader Dick Armey, R-Texas, said the leadership would let Shuster decide on the need for an extension. "We've talked to Bud Shuster about that, and right now he sees no sense of urgency," Armey told reporters at his weekly news briefing on April 28.

Lott would not rule out a short-term extension. "We could do that," Lott said. "But what we really want to do is to get [the bill] done." He remained optimistic that a bill could be completed "within the next week or two."

Budget Battle

While states continued to urge quick action by Congress, the White House pressed for cuts in the transportation bill.

Transportation Secretary Rodney Slater said he wanted to increase transportation spending but "not at the expense of the good school, the good job, the good home that has to be at the end of the transportation journey."

The administration began privately discussing its views on a wide range of key budget-related issues. It strongly opposed Shuster's proposal to take the Highway Trust Fund off budget but has been studying other alternatives to satisfy Shuster's demand for a mechanism to ensure all gas tax revenues are spent on transportation projects and not kept in reserve.

Gas Tax Revenues

The National Governors' Association has strongly supported a similar mechanism to make sure gas tax revenues are distributed to states soon after they are collected.

One alternative approach was contained in a bill (S 404) sponsored by Sens. John H. Chafee, R-R.I., and Christopher S. Bond, R-Mo., to set the level of transportation funding at the level of gas tax revenues collected in the prior year. It would ensure that gas taxes are distributed and not kept in the highway or mass transit accounts of the Highway Trust Fund.

Transportation & Infrastructure

Another idea being studied would set up another category of funding, reserved for transportation, similar to the Violent Crime Reduction Trust Fund, without specifically setting a deadline for when gas taxes must be spent.

Shuster said he regards the issue of reserving gas taxes for transportation as crucial and hinted he would be willing to work out trades on other issues if he could get a pledge on reserving funds.

Shuster's position raised questions about whether he might work out a grand compromise in which he agreed to accept a wide range of demands from the Senate — including a big cut in $9 billion earmarked for special projects for congressional districts and lowering the blood-alcohol content threshold to 0.08 percent for drunken driving violations.

Chafee said he would be willing to discuss a trade to settle the sharp division on the tougher drunken driving standard that opponents portray as an unfunded mandate. "By its very nature, it becomes a trade item," he said. "For what, we don't know. We have a long way to go in this conference yet."

The conference committee approved three packages of mainly technical provisions on April 28 and April 30, reconciling differences in the two versions of the bill.

They included a guarantee of motorcycle access to federal roads and an end to required durability testing for all road projects that would cost $25 million.

The motorcycle proposal was supported by Rep. Don Young, R-Alaska, who used to race motorcycles. He said the proposal was in response to efforts by community groups in Chicago to ban motorcycles from some main roads.

Sen. Bob Graham, D-Fla., questioned whether the provision would effectively give motorcycles special status not given to other vehicles. But guaranteed equal access for motorcycles was adopted on April 28 as part of the package after an amendment was approved by unanimous consent to ensure that the provision would not limit the ability of states to regulate road safety.

The conferees also agreed on provisions that would:

● Permit contractors to do the environmental analysis as well as subsequent design work on projects.

● Allow urban areas with populations of less than 200,000 to use grants on both projects and operations.

● Require financing plans for all highway and mass transit projects costing more than $1 billion.

● Reduce from 16 to seven the goals for planning organizations that develop transportation plans.

White House Offers a Road Plan Of Its Own

MAY 9 — The Clinton administration made its own bid to break the stalemate between House and Senate conferees over the surface transportation bill.

The administration on May 6 sent Congress a seven-year, $218.9 billion highway and mass transit plan, renewing hope for a final agreement before the Memorial Day recess.

In a key concession to Congress, the administration agreed with the Senate plan to use some veterans' health care benefits to pay for highways and mass transit.

The administration also backed a proposal to set annual highway spending at the level of federal gas tax receipts in the prior year. It warned Congress to keep its hands off the projected budget surplus of $43 billion to $63 billion in fiscal 1998, provide full offsets for highway spending and set a sustainable spending level.

The overall plan drew a lukewarm response. "We love their spending level. But we would like it in six years," said Scott Brenner, communications director of the House Transportation and Infrastructure Committee.

Senators privately grumbled about the lack of proposals from the House to pay for its six-year, $219 billion version. It would cost $1.7 billion more than the Senate bill. House Budget Committee Chairman John R. Kasich, R-Ohio, opposed the bill on the House floor, and bill backers questioned any role for him in negotiations.

Opening Volley

President Clinton's proposal prompted a flurry of talks among congressional leaders. Senate Majority Leader Trent Lott, R-Miss., held meetings with other Senate leaders and finally pulled House Speaker Newt Gingrich, R-Ga., aside for a few minutes May 6.

Senate Environment and Public Works Committee Chairman John H. Chafee, R-R.I., quickly pitched his own plan to Gingrich: reserve transportation money in a fund similar to the Violent Crime Reduction Trust Fund, set annual spending at the level of the prior year's gas tax receipts and include $18.5 billion in offsets specified in the Senate-passed budget resolution (S Con Res 86). Senators also discussed another offset of about $1.5 billion from increased cuts in Medicaid administration.

Gingrich made no commitment before going back to his office, then to the airport to fly to New Hampshire for a speech. A Senate aide compared the meeting to "a serve in tennis."

Lott confirmed that he is considering a plan to link $18.5 billion in offsets to more unspecified cuts by appropriators. "That is one option, but we haven't made a final decision," he said.

"We made an interesting proposal," Chafee said. "Obviously, it's a package deal. ... We want other provisions in the bill that don't necessarily deal specifically with this issue." In addition to the offsets, the Senate wants a lower national blood-alcohol content standard of 0.08 percent for drunken driving violations.

"When we get to a major concession on our part in connection with the funding, obviously there are other issues that we want to work out at the same time," Chafee said. His proposal sparked a rush of staff meetings. "Things are moving quickly," a House aide said May 7.

Chafee acceded to House Transportation and Infrastructure Committee Chairman Bud Shuster, R-Pa., by guaranteeing that all gas taxes would be spent on transportation. "If we can make progress on budget issues in the next day or two, I believe the conference committee will be able to resolve the remaining issues quickly," Chafee said.

The key issues were offsets and the spending level.

Aides for both Shuster and Chafee were trying to work out details of a proposal to ensure that all gas taxes are spent on highway and mass transit projects. Shuster said he wants "a commitment that the revenue coming in is spent."

While senators negotiated with Gingrich, the ethanol industry won a bitter battle. Gingrich appointed Reps. Jim Nussle, R-Iowa, and Kenny Hulshof, R-Mo., as tax-writing conferees on the bill. House Ways and Means Chairman Bill Archer, R-Texas, said the move would "stack the deck" in favor of a Senate provision to extend an ethanol tax break from 2000 until 2007.

The tax break, created in 1978, amounts to a 5.4 cents-per-gallon exemption on the gas tax for fuel mixed with ethanol. *(1978 Almanac, p. 646)*

The appointments killed Archer's House-passed plan to eliminate some excise taxes on truckers and railroads. While farmers and ethanol makers hailed Gingrich's move, Archer pledged to oppose the bill.

On May 6, the conferees approved about 20 road provisions. One would let states permit low-emission vehicles to use high-occupancy vehicle lanes. Another calls for a study to improve access to the John F. Kennedy Center for the Performing Arts in Washington, D.C.

Veto Threat Looms As Conferees Near Agreement

MAY 16 — House and Senate negotiators unveiled a pared-down, $167 billion six-year deal on highway funding in the surface transportation reauthorization bill (HR 2400) on May 13, while facing a veto threat from the Clinton administration.

The agreement emerged from a bicameral summit May 13 that included a general agreement on the spending level and a package of about $20 billion in offsets.

"This is a very important breakthrough in terms of guaranteeing highway funding," said Environment and Public Works Committee Chairman John H. Chafee, R-R.I.

Funding for mass transit remained unresolved, with House Republicans pushing for about $33 billion over six years and senators pushing for about $2 billion more.

Transportation and Infrastructure Committee Chairman Bud Shuster, R-Pa., said a deal was imminent. "We're very close," Shuster said. "It is our objective to not only have agreements but to have legislation on the floor next week [week of May 18]. I think it's possible."

But Office of Management and Budget Director (OMB) Franklin D. Raines threatened a veto May 14, saying the deal did not meet White House demands for a bill fully paid for with acceptable offsets. "We have yet to see a proposal from the conferees that meets those tests. We are prepared to work with them as we have in the last few days to come up with a bill before Congress goes home," for the Memorial Day recess, Raines said.

The administration set the stage for a deal by offering its own plan May 6 to stretch money in the legislation over seven instead of six years, cutting spending by about 15 percent.

Lawmakers spurned the proposal, but it contained seeds of compromise, including general support for a proposal in a bill (S 404) sponsored by Chafee and Sen. Christopher S. Bond, R-Mo., to set highway spending at the level of the prior year's gas tax receipts.

Tailoring Offsets

The deal would provide about $200 billion to about $202 billion in outlays over six years, depending on whether the House or Senate proposal on mass transit prevails. Of the $167 billion in highway spending, about $162 billion would be mandatory spending, protected by a firewall that Shuster demanded.

The spending bill represents a scaling down of the $204 billion in outlays in the House version and $206 billion in outlays in the Senate version. The deal would include $20 billion in offsets.

The key offset, endorsed by the administration, was a policy change to deny veterans disability compensation for smoking-related ailments not associated with military service. The deal calls for OMB scoring to peg savings from the change at $15.5 billion instead of $10.5 billion, as estimated in the Senate budget resolution (S Con Res 86). The other offsets are $3 billion in cuts to social service block grants and about $2 billion in housing

program reductions. The list did not include a proposed increase in the present Federal Housing Administration loan limit of $170,362 for cities. It would have raised $1 billion over five years in interest payments.

Lawmakers canceled another offset, a $2 billion cut in reimbursements to states for administering Medicaid. Another offset, food stamp savings, was spent on other programs with Senate passage May 12 of an agriculture research bill (S 1150).

With Republican leaders nearing agreement on financing the bill, Shuster tried to sell the package to Democrats and the White House.

Shuster met May 13 with three administration officials — Raines, Transportation Secretary Rodney Slater, and Gene Sperling, chairman of the National Economic Council. Raines had sent a letter May 12 to Shuster threatening a presidential veto if lawmakers did not scale back spending or find acceptable offsets.

But Shuster said the gap with the White House is narrowing: "We've got to move toward them, and they've got to move toward us."

Other Issues

Negotiators also sought agreement on other matters, including projects earmarked for members' districts, including $9 billion in House road projects.

Vice President Al Gore called for public pressure on conferees to agree to a Senate provision for a national 0.08 percent blood-alcohol standard for drunken driving violations.

"The whole country knows exactly what the right thing to do is and will judge your actions on the basis of whether or not you comply with what's the clearly felt will of the American people," Gore warned lawmakers at a White House ceremony May 13.

Congress Clears $216 Billion Highway Bill

MAY 23 — Congress sent President Clinton on May 22 a $216 billion, six-year surface transportation plan, increasing spending 40 percent to repair cracked asphalt and expand the

Transportation & Infrastructure

Highlights: How the Bill Would Affect Drivers, Mass Transit Passengers

MAY 23 — Following are key provisions of the conference report on the $216 billion, six-year surface transportation reauthorization bill (HR 2400 — H Rept 105-550). The bill would:

- **Highways.** Provide $173 billion in funding for highways and $2 billion for highway safety. Of the highway funding, about $163 billion would be protected by a firewall, meaning that it could not be used for other purposes, and about $4 billion would be mandatory spending. The rest of the highway funding would be discretionary.
- **Highway Trust Fund.** Dedicate the trust fund to transportation projects and keep it on budget. The bill would set annual highway spending at roughly the level of the prior year's gas tax receipts.
- **Motor fuels tax reauthorization.** Continue the current gas tax of 18.3 cents per gallon. A 4.3 cent share of the tax, formerly devoted to deficit reduction, would be spent on transportation as well as the remainder of the tax.
- **Minimum guarantee.** Guarantee states a return of 90.5 cents back in transportation funding for each $1 they pay in gas taxes.
- **Special projects.** Provide $7 billion for 1,506 special projects in House members' districts and about $2.35 billion for 300 Senate projects.
- **Interstate highways.** Support extensions of some existing interstate highways, such as Interstate 69 in Indiana, between Bloomington and Indianapolis. The interstate era officially ended in 1996 when the 45,744-mile system was completed, but there are continuing demands to build more extensions and connections between interstate highways.
- **Bridges.** Provide continued support for repairs of bridges. The bill would include money to retrofit bridges to prevent earthquake damage and would provide support for preservation of national historic covered bridges.
- **Woodrow Wilson Memorial Bridge.** Provide $900 million for the replacement of the bridge on the Capital Beltway, Interstate 495, near Washington, D.C. The money would cover slightly more than half the $1.6 billion needed to replace the drawbridge, which spans the Potomac River.
- **Mass transit.** Provide $41 billion in funding over six years for mass transit, including commuter rail lines and bus lines.
- **Ethanol.** Extend a partial gas tax exemption for fuel mixed with ethanol until 2007. The tax break, previously scheduled to expire in 2000, exempts gas mixed with ethanol from 5.4 cents per gallon of the gas tax. The exemption would be reduced to 5.3 cents per gallon in 2001, 5.2 cents in 2003 and 5.1 cents in 2005.
- **Drunken driving prevention.** Provide $500 million in incentive grants to states if they adopt a lower, 0.08 percent blood-alcohol content standard for drunken driving violations. States would also be able to tap $140 million in incentive grants if they adopted five of eight safety measures, including the new blood-alcohol content standard. A portion of federal funding would be withheld from states that did not enact laws to punish repeat drunken driving offenses or did not bar open containers of alcohol in automobiles.
- **Offsets.** Provide for $20 billion in offsets, including a policy change to deny veterans disability payments for ailments caused by smoking and not related to military service. The veterans policy change would be valued at $15.4 billion.
- **Safety belts.** Provide $500 million in performance grants to states to increase the percentage of residents using seat belts or that exceed the national average for seat belt use.
- **Olympic assistance.** Authorize support for transportation projects in cities that will be home to the winter or summer Olympics. The first beneficiary would be Salt Lake City, where the 2002 games will be held.
- **Air bags.** Encourage development of new airbags to avert deaths of children or small adults linked to the powerful force of the devices when they deploy in automobile accidents.
- **Trucking.** Continue a ban on longer-combination trucks in most states. The bigger trucks would be allowed in 22 states that permitted them before June 1, 1991.

nation's network of highways and mass transit.

The final bill took shape in a late-night session on May 21 with leaders of the conference committee and Transportation Secretary Rodney Slater, in which negotiators put the final touches on the deal, including a $41 billion package for mass transit.

The linchpin of the deal was a menu of $17.7 billion in offsets, including $15.4 billion from denying veterans' disability payments for smoking-related ailments and $2.3 billion in cuts in social service block grants.

Lawmakers had been hesitant about voting to take away veterans' benefits on the eve of the Memorial Day holiday honoring America's war dead but agreed to do so after solid backing from the White House.

With states clamoring for transportation funding that was cut off May 1 when a temporary extension expired, the threat of a potential veto by Clinton vanished after lawmakers agreed not to go after the budget surplus or

Surface Transportation

other offsets to pay for the bill, such as cuts in Medicaid administrative costs and housing programs.

The bill would provide the nation's biggest investment in transportation construction for the 45,744-mile Interstate Highway System since the 1950s. For the first time, it would tie annual highway funding directly to the previous year's gas tax receipts, assuring that they are not diverted to deficit reduction.

The bill would create 400,000 jobs in construction, maintenance and operation of the nation's highways and mass transit systems, while continuing to support a base of more than 1.6 million jobs, according to transportation economists. The money will help states and local governments make needed repairs for deteriorating highways and aging bridges.

"It's a good bill," said Slater on May 21. "It's a major jobs bill."

The Senate adopted the conference report, 88-5, on May 22. Hours later, the House cleared the conference report, 297-86, and sent it to President Clinton who was expected to sign it.

The votes came at the end of a monthlong negotiating conference in which policy issues were overshadowed by a bitter struggle over the division of money. The fight was finally resolved with a deal between the House and Senate to share $9.35 billion in money for specially designated programs and projects.

The proposed funding formula will replace calculations based on long-standing historical allocations with usage factors such as vehicle-miles and lane-miles and guarantee each state a return of 90.5 cents in transportation funding for each dollar of gas taxes paid.

House Transportation and Infrastructure Committee Chairman Bud Shuster, R-Pa., and Senate Environment and Public Works Chairman John H. Chafee, R-R.I., began the final week of talks May 18 by announcing a deal on several key issues, including a plan for guaranteed highway spending.

It included a key Chafee concession: killing a Senate provision to withhold a share of federal funding from states that did not adopt a new lower blood-alcohol standard of 0.08 percent for drunken driving violations. Instead, the bill offers $500 million in incentive grants to states observing that standard.

Chafee agreed after he found he did not have support from key Senate conferees, including John W. Warner, R-Va., or from Senate Majority Leader Trent Lott, R-Miss. Opponents charged that the measure was an unfunded mandate on states, and they were backed by heavy lobbying from the beer and restaurant industries.

Administration Response

President Clinton supported the failed drunken driving sanctions and was sharply critical of earmarked special projects in the bill.

But the administration gave its tacit support to the overall spending plan after lawmakers agreed to scale down a list of offsets, including changes in housing programs that the administration hopes to use for other priorities.

Lawmakers raced to complete the bill which would restore federal transportation funding to states that was cut off May 1 after a temporary extension expired.

The bill's passage came nearly eight months after the Sept. 30, 1997, expiration of its predecessor, the Intermodal Surface Transportation and Efficiency Act of 1991 (PL 102–240).

It marked a personal triumph for Shuster, who hammered out the final compromise, including a new name for the legislation: the Transportation Equity Act for the 21st Century, TEA 21.

"For too long we have neglected our nation's infrastructure, and now we are paying the price. We are spending too much time in traffic. Too many people are dying on bad roads. And too much highway money has been siphoned off for other federal spending," said Shuster.

Special Projects

The Pennsylvania lawmaker, who remains under a federal grand jury investigation in Boston for ties to two political contributors who had an interest in a federal road project, fended off criticism that the bill was a budget-buster bloated with special projects.

"In my view, the pork-barrel funding spree in this bill is going to make Congress the laughingstock of America," said Rep. David R. Obey, D-Wis.

But Shuster replied that special projects were supported by state transportation officials. The bill would provide $7 billion for 1,506 House earmarked road projects, about 25 percent less than the original House version of the bill after an across-the-board cut in funding.

The amount cut from House projects, about $2.35 billion, would go to Senate programs mainly to provide adjustment payments to donor states that receive less than a dollar in transportation funding for each dollar they pay in gas taxes and about 300 special projects.

The projects range from a bike path in Washington, D.C., to reconstruction of the Stevenson Expressway, Interstate 55, in Chicago and $900 million to replace the aging Woodrow Wilson Memorial Bridge that spans the Potomac River near Washington, D.C.

Shuster fell short of his original objective of pushing the Highway Trust Fund off budget, but he succeeded in building bipartisan support for putting a "firewall" around most highway and mass transit funding.

The firewall would effectively turn highways and mass transit into mandatory programs similar to entitlements such as Social Security and Medicare. It would ensure that gas taxes could not be diverted to other domestic programs and would set annual spending at roughly the level of the previous year's gas tax receipts.

"Once this bill is signed, every time you pay your gas taxes at the pump, that money will go to make your roads and bridges smoother and safer," Shuster said.

The bill would provide about 90% in mandatory or guaranteed funding. The remainder would be discretionary.

Cutting a Deal

The final big obstacle to completing the bill was a dispute over mass transit funding. The $5 billion in discretionary extra transit funding was added to match the level of spending in the Senate version of the bill and to mollify Senate Banking and Urban Development Chairman Alfonse M. D'Amato, R-N.Y., who faces a tough re-election campaign this year.

While D'Amato held out for more money, negotiators tried to resolve the issue of offsets and to tweak the highway funding formula, using computer

Transportation & Infrastructure

runs, to push some states from about 90 to 91 cents in return on gas taxes.

"We're struggling to get that extra penny," Shuster said.

In the final rush, negotiators slipped extra provisions into the bill including a revised version of a proposal (HR 1739) by Rep. James L. Oberstar, D-Minn., to allow motorized vehicles to be used on two boat portage routes in the Boundary Waters Canoe Area Wilderness.

And they agreed to a provision that would connect efforts to deal with regional haze to target dates for dealing with a new Environmental Protection Agency standard for particulate matter.

A bitter battle between business and labor unions ended with a decision not to specifically expand the Davis-Bacon Act of 1931 requiring that prevailing wages must be paid on construction projects.

After Coaxing House To Cut Pork From Bill, Senate Piles It On

MAY 30 — Traffic backs up in the hometown of Senate Majority Leader Trent Lott when a 50-year-old drawbridge over the Pascagoula River rises for a ship or shrimp boat.

But relief may soon be on its way. At the last minute, the Mississippi Republican inserted an authorization for $38 million in the six-year surface transportation bill (HR 2400) to build a high-rise span to carry traffic overhead while ships ply the river.

In the dash to complete the bill before the Memorial Day recess, Lott and other senators managed to insert more than 300 special highway and bridge projects worth nearly $2 billion. They did it by cajoling the House to cut its list of about 1,500 projects by the same amount, or 25 percent, to $7 billion.

Senators also added about $3 billion for mass transit projects, including $640 million for rail projects, intermodal facilities and buses for Salt Lake City, Utah, which is hosting the 2002 Winter Olympics.

The Senate voted 88-5 to adopt the conference report (H Rept 105-550) on May 22, and the House cleared it, 297-86, hours later. (*Senate vote 147, p. S-24; House vote 192, p. H-56*)

The legislation awaits the expected signature of President Clinton, but it has been temporarily snagged by the discovery of inadvertent omissions of several key provisions from the bill. A corrections bill is expected to move quickly when Congress returns the week of June 1.

Then, for design work to be completed and concrete to be poured, the authorization bill's projects will need to be funded in annual appropriations bills, starting with fiscal 1999.

The effort by senators to insert take-home projects came in the final week of hurried, closed-door negotiations by leaders of the House-Senate conference committee.

The scramble for projects came just two months after Lott and 77 other senators lined up to pass an amendment March 12 to curb earmarked projects in the surface transportation bill. The amendment to the Senate version of the bill (S 1173) would have required governors and state legislatures, not members of Congress, to grant money for special projects from formula funds distributed to states.

Battle Over Pork

Sen. John McCain, R-Ariz., who sponsored the March 12 amendment, said the final version of the bill ignored the intent of his proposal. He called on Clinton to veto "the largest pork barrel spending bill ever written."

McCain charged that the long list of special projects took money away from 20 "donor" states, mainly in the South, Midwest and West, that receive less than $1 back in funding for each $1 paid in federal gas taxes. The bill would guarantee each state a return of 90.5 cents on the dollar.

"The only guarantee that donor states should expect from this legislation is that they will continue to subsidize road projects in other states for the next six years," McCain said.

Rep. David Minge, D-Minn., charged that the bill was veiled in a "shroud of secrecy" to protect projects. "It is nearly impossible to separate the good from the bad," he said.

House Transportation and Infrastructure Committee Chairman Bud Shuster, R-Pa., defended the projects as a rightful prerogative for members of Congress, who know the needs of communities as well as or better than state officials.

Dividing the Pot

The final list of special projects was assembled after Shuster and Environment and Public Works Committee Chairman John H. Chafee, R-R.I., agreed to split the House's $9.35 billion pot for special road projects. Their deal cut total funding for House projects by $2.35 billion and devoted that money to unnamed Senate projects.

Of the Senate's amount, about $710 million was directed by about 40 senators to lump-sum payments to states to use for unspecified projects. The rest went to lists provided by Lott and others. "The senators always come up with projects," a matter-of-fact Shuster said afterward.

Of Lott, one of the prime recipients of project money, Shuster said: "Compared to him, I'm a cream puff."

In addition to getting authorization to replace the functionally obsolete bridge on the Pascagoula River, which would allow unimpeded river traffic to and from the sprawling Ingalls Shipbuilding Inc. yard not far from Lott's home, the senator also won a provision for one of his dream projects: completion of a stretch of Interstate 69 in Mississippi.

The bill also designates $8 million to pay for seismic design and engineering of a Great River bridge that may be part of Interstate 69. That bridge would cost $180 million.

Jerril Newell, program director for the Mississippi Transportation Department, said the Pascagoula bridge is the state's top priority road project. "With Sen. Lott being from Mississippi, we feel like we did get preferential treatment," Newell said.

Other senators who earmarked special projects included Chafee, a bicycling enthusiast, who inserted $11.9 million for two bikeways in Rhode Island.

Senate Minority Leader Tom Daschle, D-S.D., designated $35 million for the Eastern Dakota Expressway, which connects his hometown, Aberdeen, with Interstate 29. Daschle said the money would pay for raising the highway and solving problems caused by flooding over the past year.

He also won $6 million for two bridges and $500,000 to pay for land to enhance a scenic road in Rapid City.

The final bill also includes $12 billion for bus and rail projects, about $3 billion more than was contained in the House's version of the bill.

Senators staked claim to the extra $3 billion, earmarking it for bus and rail projects, and Shuster said Banking Committee Chairman Alfonse M. D'Amato, R-N.Y., proposed the offset for the increase: a cut in social service block grants. D'Amato designated $353 million for the Long Island Railroad and $76 million for three ferry terminals. Richard C. Shelby, R-Ala., diverted $87.5 million to a transit corridor in Birmingham, Ala.

Winners and Losers

A study by Citizens Against Government Waste, a nonprofit advocacy group, concluded that the biggest winners of special projects — designated by both House members and senators — included states that are home to influential lawmakers.

Comparing state shares of special road project funding to population, the study found five states received more than double the national average of about $34 per capita spent on the 1,850 designated road projects in the bill.

The top five were Alaska ($113 per capita), South Dakota ($113), Idaho ($94), West Virginia ($85) and Wyoming ($71). Pennsylvania, Shuster's home state, ranked 10th ($57). Mississippi ranked 17th ($42).

The bottom-ranked states were Delaware ($12), Arizona ($14), Colorado ($18) and Florida ($19).

Environmental Objections

As lawmakers touted the projects they brought home, environmentalists took aim at a provision added in conference that would delay efforts to cut regional haze that obscures vistas in some national parks and wilderness areas.

The provision, backed by House Commerce Committee Chairman Thomas J. Bliley Jr., R-Va., Rep. John D. Dingell, D-Mich., and Sen. James M. Inhofe, R-Okla., would give states up to nine years to solve the problem of haze by tying deadlines to target dates by which they must deal with the related problem of particulates in the air. Particulates and haze are linked to pollution from automobiles, factories and coal-fired power plants.

A dozen groups, including the Natural Resources Defense Council and League of Conservation Voters, wrote to Clinton on May 22 requesting a veto. They said the haze provision was one of a series of attempts by Congress to undermine environmental programs.

"We respectfully urge you to say no to these unconscionable attacks on our National Parks and clean air programs," the groups wrote to Clinton.

Despite objections, the president is expected to sign the bill. But his approval is not likely to come until lawmakers meet to agree on corrections.

Meanwhile, state transportation officials continue to wait for renewal of funding that ended May 1, after a temporary extension (PL 105-130) expired.

"It's been a long wait. Now it looks like we'll have to wait a little while longer," said Billy Higgins, a lobbyist for the American Association of State Highway and Transportation Officials.

Dispute Over Veterans' Benefits, Slows Roads Bill

JUNE 6 — A bitter battle over highway and transit spending continued in the Senate after the House passed a bill to correct technical flaws in the six-year $216 billion surface transportation spending bill (HR 2400).

The House approved the corrections bill (HR 3978) by voice vote June 3, but final passage was stymied in the Senate by a renewed battle over a key $15.4 billion offset that would help pay for the spending bill.

John D. Rockefeller IV, D-W.Va., pledged to offer an amendment to the corrections bill that would kill the offset, which would end disability payments for veterans with smoking-related ailments not directly related to military service.

Lawmakers hoped President Clinton would be able to sign both bills by June 9, the deadline for approving the legislation. But Rockefeller forced Senate Majority Leader Trent Lott, R-Miss., to hold back the corrections bill in order to avoid a messy debate pitting highway interests against veterans.

"We're not going to be able to do that," Lott said of Rockefeller's amendment. He said he was looking for legislation in which to insert the corrections bill.

The battle over the surface transportation bill seemed over when Congress cleared HR 2400 May 22, just before the Memorial Day recess.

But the discovery of a number of flaws, including the omission of provisions to prevent drunken driving, required that a corrections bill be drafted.

Another War for Veterans

Rockefeller seized the opportunity June 4, vowing to offer the amendment to the corrections bill the week of June 7 to save the veterans' benefits.

The cut in benefits for tobacco-related illnesses had bipartisan support and the blessing of the Clinton administration. But support wavered because lawmakers did not want to return home for the Memorial Day weekend after voting to strip a benefit from the nation's veterans. On May 22, the House barely defeated, 190-195, a proposal to delete the offset.

Veterans' groups staunchly opposed the cut, saying it wrongly took away a needed benefit. They were not mollified by a provision in the corrections bill to ensure that veterans' disability benefits would continue for smokers who develop diseases such as lung cancer from non-tobacco causes such as herbicides and chemical weapons.

Jockeying for Dollars

While a final battle over the benefits offset took shape, House and Senate members pored over special projects. Lawmakers described revisions as attempts to "restore" accidental deletions.

The technical corrections bill dealt with 65 of the 1,850 special road projects in the transportation bill. One correction moved the start from 1999 to 1998 for a $94 million upgrade to a 325-mile stretch of a highway tying the lower 48 states to Alaska.

One part of the "national defense highway" drew fire because it sits in the sparsely populated Yukon Territory of Canada.

"I think the national defense of the United States needs a new highway in Canada about as much as each of us

Transportation & Infrastructure

needs a case of pneumonia," scoffed Rep. David R. Obey, D-Wis.

Other corrections would restore two provisions on drunken driving. States that did not ban open containers of alcohol in cars or adopt tougher penalties for drunken driving would be required to spend 1.5 percent of construction funding on safety programs.

Rep. James L. Oberstar, D-Minn., got one of the biggest insertions in the corrections bill: $5 million over five years for a Minnesota Transportation History project coordinated by the Minnesota Historical Society. Oberstar was one of the negotiators who played a leading role in earmarking projects.

Separately, another home-state provision was inserted in the conference report for HR 2400 by Tom Petri, R-Wis., at the request of Wisconsin officials. It set off a brief floor fight June 3. The proposal redirected $241 million from Milwaukee area transit projects to projects selected by Republican Gov. Tommy G. Thompson.

The money was provided in the 1991 reauthorization law (PL 102–240) but was not spent because of a dispute over whether to spend it on a light-rail project in Milwaukee County.

Rep. Thomas M. Barrett, D-Wis., said he was concerned about Thompson's control of money, then withdrew his objection to the bill. House Transportation and Infrastructure Committee Chairman Bud Shuster, R-Pa., rejected an amendment by Barrett to keep funding in the Milwaukee area. But Petri said he was assured the money would go there.

Clinton Signs Highway Bill, Says 'It's Paid For'

JUNE 13 — An abandoned stretch of the Pennsylvania Turnpike got a second life from the six-year federal highway law, courtesy of House Transportation and Infrastructure Committee Chairman Bud Shuster, R-Pa. The weed-dotted section of old pavement will become a federally funded training ground for truck drivers, likely to benefit a company run by Shuster's son-in-law and a campaign contributor.

Shuster inserted the provision in the $216 billion highway bill (PL 105-178), signed by President Clinton on June 9, turning the road into a truck driving school, one of two dozen special projects designated for his district.

Shuster, whose panel controlled the budget for transportation spending, earmarked $3 million for the school, not far from his farmhouse in central Pennsylvania.

The school's beneficiaries will probably include Smith Transport Inc., a thriving trucking company in Roaring Spring, Pa., headed by Barry F. Smith, who gave $2,000 to Shuster's 1998 re-election campaign. The company's managers include Charles Grove Dixon, a vice president who is married to Shuster's daughter, Virginia.

When Shuster stepped up on a stage in the Old Executive Office Building on June 9 to be the first of 40 lawmakers to greet President Clinton at the bill-signing ceremony, he had good reason to celebrate.

The highway bill he crafted as the chairman of a panel of House and Senate negotiators will deliver about $110 million in road projects for his district.

That pot represents about eight times the amount that Shuster offered to most individual House members to direct at their discretion to local road projects that had been vetted by his committee. The members of his committee got more money, about $40 million apiece, except for senior members on the panel who got more.

In Shuster's district, the money will pay for more than 20 road projects, including $22 million for an access road to a resort hotel being developed by Mark Langdale, president of the U.S. subsidiary of Mexico's largest hotel chain.

The projects in Shuster's district represent just one example of long lists of items inserted in the bill by powerful lawmakers.

The largess of the highway bill and its principal author prompted rebukes from budget hawks in Congress and taxpayer groups that urged Clinton to veto it. House Budget Committee John R. Kasich, R-Ohio, called the bill "a hog."

The Clinton administration publicly opposed earmarked projects as a waste of money. But in the end, Clinton decided to accept the projects as part of a bargain to preserve some of his own spending priorities. A technical corrections bill (HR 3978) needed to fix flaws in the law remains stalled in the Senate.

Sen. John D. Rockefeller IV, D-W.Va., continued to prevent simple voice vote passage of the corrections bill by insisting on offering an amendment that would kill a $15.4 billion offset needed to pay for the transportation bill. The offset would eliminate disability benefits for veterans who have smoking-related ailments.

At a news conference, Clinton joked that Transportation Secretary Rodney Slater sounded like a preacher in extolling the bill. "I thought he was going to pass the plate," Clinton said. "Then I realized you had already given him all the money."

After signing the bill, Clinton defended his decision not to veto the projects for individual members' districts. In all, the law contained $21.35 billion in such earmarked projects, with $9.35 billion directed to roads and the rest to mass transit.

"It spends a little more than I wanted to," Clinton said in an interview with Congressional Quarterly after signing the bill. "But unlike the original bill, it's paid for.

"And they paid for it in a way that doesn't get into the surplus and doesn't erode the budgets I recommended for education, the environment and research. That's why I signed it," he said. "It's not the same as the bill I recommended. But it does a lot more good than harm, much more."

Policy Changes

The law made significant changes in policy, including a pledge to spend all federal gas tax revenues on transportation and not divert a portion to deficit reduction. New formulas for highway funding will be based on road usage factors such as lane-miles and vehicle-miles rather than historic state allotments. And each state received a minimum guarantee of at least a 90.5 percent return on gas taxes paid into the Highway Trust Fund.

While Clinton pledged to continue a fight for sanctions on states to get tough on drunken driving, a mandate dropped in conference, state officials and public watchdog groups continued to scrutinize the provisions of the law, which was hastily cleared May 22 before most lawmakers could read it.

In Pennsylvania, the state Department of Transportation was still scratching its head over Shuster's truck driving school.

"Frankly, I can't tell you much more than what's in the provision," said Larry King, deputy secretary for planning in the state transportation department.

Shuster's provision said simply that the Transportation secretary would make grants to the state to establish an "advanced tractor trailer safety and operator training facility," using the empty highway and Letterkenny Army Depot in Chambersburg, Pa.

The provision does not say who will operate the school or which companies will send drivers to it. But the nearest headquarters for a sizable trucking operation is Smith's company, about 40 miles away in Roaring Spring, Pa. Smith did not return phone calls seeking his comments.

The highway legislation also includes $1.5 million for an improved access road to the Bedford County Business Park, near where Smith Transport is planning to open an office, about a dozen miles away from the highway that will be used as the school.

Resort Hotel

In 1976, Shuster delivered one of the nation's first demonstration projects, providing $25 million from 1976 to 1980 for a highway bypass to divert traffic around his hometown, Everett, Pa., which has 1,800 residents.

One of the major projects in the new law will be $22 million to pay for an access road, a parking facility and other road projects related to the proposed redevelopment of the resort hotel about two miles south of the hamlet of Bedford, which has 3,000 residents.

The Shober's Run Development Co. bought the 192-year-old Bedford Springs Hotel for $1 from the Redevelopment Authority of Bedford County on May 21. The deal came the day before Congress passed the transportation bill, containing funding for the new access road and parking facility.

The development company is headed by Langdale, top executive of Posadas USA Inc., a Texas-based subsidiary of Grupo Posadas, Mexico's biggest hotel operator.

Shober's Run Development has promised to spend $56 million to renovate the 165-room hotel, which closed 10 years ago. It plans to add 60 rooms.

The resort hotel represents one of the newest and most striking examples of what amounts to a building boom in Bedford County and neighboring Blair County, which encompasses the biggest town, Altoona, in Shuster's district.

While taxpayer groups criticize Shuster as a pork-barrel politician, constituents see him as a hero.

"He's really making our area come alive," said Rosalind Sky, a longtime resident of Altoona, whose family once had a financial interest in the Bedford Springs Hotel.

As Sky and other residents see it, Shuster has helped to integrate his district into a development corridor between Pittsburgh and State College, home of Pennsylvania State University. The centerpiece of Shuster's work is Interstate 99, dubbed the Bud Shuster Highway, linking Altoona to the Pennsylvania Turnpike

'Pigskin Parkway'

Shuster also cemented one of the last links in the Pittsburgh-State College corridor running through his district by inserting a provision to designate a 31-mile stretch of Pennsylvania 26 as the Nittany Parkway. The designation will help the highway get additional funding and relieve traffic that is particularly bad on Saturdays in the fall when fans clog the road to attend football games at Penn State.

Environmental groups nicknamed the project the "Pigskin Parkway," saying the money would be better spent on mass transit. ◆

What the Highway Bill Does

JULY 11 — The sweeping, six-year, $217.9 billion Transportation Equity Act for the 21st Century (PL 105-178), nicknamed TEA 21, provides a 40 percent increase in spending over six years from current levels to improve the nation's aging highways and mass transit systems.

The debate on Capitol Hill involved prolonged wrangling over the size of the increase and the division of money among states.

The law set highway spending at the level of the previous year's gasoline tax revenue, assuring that all gasoline taxes are expended and not retained for deficit reduction. Lawmakers also included $17.7 billion in offsets to make up for the increase above baseline budget projections, including a reduction in disability compensation for veterans who have smoking-related illnesses and a cut in social service block grants.

The law won strong backing from the construction industry, and from states that face mounting costs for road repairs and demands for new transportation projects. It is expected to create thousands of new jobs as well.

Supporters said the law will help make up for delayed improvements in the national grid of asphalt and concrete.

Although the bill included more than $100 billion for road repairs and maintenance, that amount was less than one-quarter of the amount needed to improve the condition of aging roads and crumbling bridges, based on a study by the American Society of Civil Engineers.

To make up for the backlog of repairs and new projects, the legislation increased flexibility in state and local use of federal funds. It also provided $530 million for a new, innovative financing program that will back lending and lines of credit worth $10 billion for large-scale transportation projects.

Critics charged that the law was simply too big and dubbed it a prime example of "pork barrel" spending, with nearly $18 billion, devoted to specifically designated highway, rail and bus projects requested by members of Congress for their districts. Budget hawks led a mostly unsuccessful effort to scale back the increase and the special projects for districts.

House Transportation and Infrastructure Committee Chairman Bud Shuster, R-Pa., lost a key battle early in the debate. His amendment to the fiscal 1998 budget resolution (H Con Res 84) to sharply increase transportation funding and cut other discre-

Transportation & Infrastructure

tionary spending failed by a 214-216 vote on the House floor on May 21, 1997. The narrow defeat prompted Shuster and his allies to delay further work on the reauthorization until 1998, hoping that rosier revenue projections would erase opposition to increased transportation spending.

A year later, with the looming promise of a budget surplus, the political tide moved in Shuster's favor.

In the Senate, Robert C. Byrd, D-W.Va., and Phil Gramm, R-Texas, led a push to spend on transportation a 4.3-cent share of the 18.3-cents-per-gallon gasoline tax, which was formerly dedicated to deficit reduction. Their push resulted in Senate passage by voice vote March 5 of a compromise amendment that increased highway spending by $25.8 billion.

The deal closed a gap between Senate and House versions of the legislation. In conference committee, negotiators worked out other differences. The House prevailed on a crucial issue, deletion of a Senate provision backed by the Clinton administration to withhold a share of highway funding from states that do not enact a blood-alcohol content limit of 0.08 percent for drunken driving violations. Negotiators agreed to a compromise that required states to enact tougher penalties for repeat drunken driving offenders and provided $500 million in incentive grants to states that enact the new blood-alcohol standard.

The Senate adopted and the House cleared the conference report on the bill (HR 2400 — H Rept 105-550) on May 22. The Senate voted 88-5; the House voted 297-86.

President Clinton signed the bill into law June 9, surrounded by 40 lawmakers.

Although the administration was opposed to special projects in the legislation and wanted tougher provisions aimed at drunken driving, Clinton said the law would pay for needed transportation improvements without threatening other spending priorities.

"It does a lot more good than harm, much more," Clinton said.

Following are the main provisions of the law. The provisions include technical corrections to the law that were inserted in the conference report for the Internal Revenue Service restructuring bill (HR 2676 – H Rept 105-599), which was adopted by the House by 402-8 on June 25 and cleared the Senate on July 9, 96-2. Spending numbers were provided by the Department of Transportation. Congressional Budget Office estimates are not yet available. The law:

Spending and Finances

Spending Levels

● **Scope and cost.** Authorizes $217.9 billion for surface transportation, representing a 40 percent increase over current funding. The law includes $174.6 billion for highways, $41 billion for mass transit programs and $2 billion for safety programs. Of the total authorized, $198 billion is guaranteed funding.

● **Declaration of policy.** Continues the policy set in the 1991 law (PL 102-240) of connecting highways to other modes of transportation to create an intermodal system. TEA 21 promotes the goal of providing more equity in the distribution of formula funds among states.

● **Guaranteed funding.** Authorizes $162 billion in guaranteed funding for highways and $36 billion for mass transit.

● **Obligation ceiling.** Provides that obligations shall not exceed $21.5 billion in fiscal 1998, $25.4 billion in fiscal 1999, $26.2 billion in fiscal 2000, $26.7 billion in fiscal 2001, $27.2 billion in fiscal 2002 and $27.7 billion in fiscal 2003.

● **Federal matching share.** Retains the current 80 percent federal share for many transportation projects. The law gives states flexibility to calculate their 20 percent non-federal share for enhancement projects as a program-wide average or for multiple projects. The law allows fair market value of land obtained by the state or local government to be included in the non-federal share of project costs.

● **Administrative costs.** Reduces from 3.75 percent to 1.5 percent the share of highway funds used for administrative costs of the Transportation Department. The law provides separate funding for research costs, which were separated from administrative costs.

Financing

● **Motor fuels tax reauthorization.** Extends the current tax of 18.3 cents per gallon through fiscal 2005. The share of the tax devoted to the Transit Account of the Highway Trust Fund increases to 2.86 cents from 2.85 cents to correct an error in previous legislation. The law provides for use on transportation programs of 4.3 cents of the 18.3-cents-per-gallon gas tax formerly set aside for deficit reduction.

The law reduces from 5.55 cents to 4.3 cents per gallon the tax on railroad diesel fuel devoted to deficit reduction.

● **Ethanol.** Extends partial gas tax exemption for fuel mixed with ethanol, formerly scheduled to expire in 2000, until 2007. The law reduces the exemption from 5.4 cents per gallon to 5.3 cents in fiscal 2001, 5.2 cents in fiscal 2003, and 5.1 cents in fiscal 2005.

● **Funding offsets.** Provides two offsets worth $17.7 billion to pay for the law, which exceeds baseline budget projections. The law cut veterans' disability payments for smoking-related ailments, saving $15.4 billion based on directed scoring of the Office of Management and Budget. It cuts $2.3 billion in social service block grants. The law repeals the highway spending limit set in the Taxpayer Relief Act of 1997 (PL 105-34).

● **Highway Trust Fund.** Sets annual highway spending at the level of previous year's gas tax receipts. The law provides that any balance of more than $8 billion in the highway account of the Highway Trust Fund would be put into the General Fund on Sept. 30. The law provides that interest would no longer accrue on money in the Highway Trust Fund. The law exempts receipts and expenditures of the trust fund from budgetary restrictions under the 1985 Balanced Budget and Emergency Deficit Control Act (PL 99-177).

● **Davis-Bacon guarantee.** Retains a requirement under the Davis-Bacon Act of 1931 that prevailing wage rates in an area must be paid on federal construction projects. Contractors on federally funded projects are covered by this requirement.

● **State infrastructure banks.** Reduces pilot program permitting federal funds to be used in infrastructure bank programs that lend money for toll road projects from a maximum of 10 to four states: Missouri, California, Florida and Rhode Island.

● **Loans.** Provides $530 million for an innovative finance program to pay for loans, loan guarantees and lines of credit for transportation projects that cost at least $100 million or consume 50 percent of a state's annual apportionment of federal highway funds. The money is available to finance loans, loan guarantees and lines of credit worth $10.6 billion. The report cited three examples of eligible projects: Woodrow Wilson Memorial Bridge near Washington, D.C., Pennsylvania Station in New York City, and a proposed high-speed rail line connecting Tampa, Orlando and Miami in Florida.

Highways

● **Highway and surface transportation.** Authorizes $23.8 billion for the interstate maintenance program; $28.6 billion for the National Highway System; $20.4 billion for the bridge program; $33.3 billion for the surface transportation program; $8.1 billion for the congestion mitigation and air quality improvement program; $5.8 billion for the high-risk road safety improvement program; $4.6 billion for the high-cost interstate system reconstruction and improvement program; $4.0 billion for transportation education, research, technology innovation and demonstration, including intelligent technology systems.

Surface Transportation

- **Interstate maintenance.** Provides $23.8 billion for maintenance of the Interstate Highway System, restoring reconstruction as an eligible activity.
- **National Highway System.** Provides $28.6 billion for the National Highway System. The law allows a 15 percent increase in the limit on mileage in the National Highway System, to 178,250 miles from 155,000 miles. The limit covers the nation's systems of interstate highways, major arterial routes and routes important to the defense of the United States. The law provides for interstate system routes to be chosen by the Transportation secretary based on joint action of transportation officials of the state in which the route is located and officials from adjoining states, in cooperation with local and regional officials.
- **Surface transportation.** Provides $33.3 billion for the surface transportation program. The law sets aside 10 percent of surface transportation program funding for enhancements such as pedestrian walkways and preservation activities, and expands eligibility to welcome centers and transportation museums. The law also sets aside another 10 percent of surface transportation funding for safety-related construction to be apportioned to hazard elimination and railroad crossing improvements.

The law increases flexibility by allowing states to calculate their 20 percent non-federal share of projects on a single-project, multiple-project or program basis. The law makes certain environmental and pollution abatement projects eligible for funding under the program, as well as programs aimed at reducing vehicle emissions that result from extremely cold starts, and projects utilizing environmentally acceptable anti-icing and de-icing compositions.

The law allows up to 15 percent of surface transportation funds to be allocated to areas of less than 5,000 in population to be used on roads classified as rural minor connectors.

- **Bridge program.** Provides $20.4 billion for the bridge replacement and rehabilitation program. The law sets aside $525 million for high-cost bridge projects and requires use of a portion of these funds for seismic retrofit of bridges. The law makes certain icing and de-icing compositions used on bridges eligible for funding under the bridge program. The law allows states to transfer up to 50 percent of bridge funds to national highway or surface transportation programs, but provides that the amount transferred would be deducted from national bridge needs in calculating funding for the next fiscal year.
- **Minimum guarantee.** Provides that each state receives a share of the total annual Highway Trust Fund apportionments based on the state's estimated gas tax payments. The law guarantees that each state receives at least 90.5 percent of its share of total apportionments based on gas tax payments. Funding for special projects is included in the calculation, along with other program and formula funding for interstate maintenance, the National Highway System, surface transportation program, metropolitan planning, congestion mitigation, air quality program and bridge program.

The law provides $33.6 billion to provide payments to states to make sure they receive their minimum guarantee. The law lists the percentage share of trust fund apportionments for each state and the District of Columbia as follows:

Alabama, 2.03; Alaska, 1.19; Arizona, 1.56; Arkansas, 1.32; California, 9.20; Colorado, 1.17; Connecticut, 1.52; Delaware, 0.44; District of Columbia, 0.40; Florida, 4.62; Georgia, 3.51; Hawaii, 0.52; Idaho, 0.77; Illinois, 3.38; Indiana, 2.36; Iowa, 1.20; Kansas, 1.17; Kentucky, 1.74; Louisiana, 1.59; Maine, 0.53; Maryland, 1.51; Massachusetts, 1.86; Michigan, 3.15; Minnesota, 1.50; Mississippi, 1.22; Missouri, 2.36; Montana, 0.99; Nebraska, 0.78; Nevada, 0.72; New Hampshire, 0.52; New Jersey, 2.58; New Mexico, 0.99; New York, 5.16; North Carolina, 2.83; North Dakota, 0.66; Ohio, 3.43; Oklahoma, 1.54; Oregon, 1.22; Pennsylvania, 4.99; Rhode Island, 0.60; South Carolina, 1.59; South Dakota, 0.71; Tennessee, 2.26; Texas, 7.21; Utah, 0.78; Vermont, 0.46; Virginia, 2.56; Washington, 1.79; West Virginia, 1.13; Wisconsin, 1.99; Wyoming, 0.70.

- **High-priority projects.** Provides for about 1,850 high-priority highway and surface transportation projects worth $9.35 billion, of which $7 billion in projects were selected by House members and $2.35 billion designated by senators. The projects for senators include lump sums apportioned to states to ensure they receive their minimum guarantee of 90.5 percent return on gas taxes.

Projects were earmarked for 49 states. No road projects are designated for Delaware. The law provides for $8.2 billion in earmarked mass transit projects. It also provides $3 billion for bus programs.

- **Disadvantaged Business Enterprise.** Continues the current Transportation Department program that sets a goal of giving 10 percent of construction contracts to disadvantaged businesses, including businesses owned by minorities and women.

The law requires a study evaluating the program by the General Accounting Office. The measure clarifies that state and local governments may continue to receive federal transportation funds, even if a court rules that the program is unconstitutional. The law requires a review by the General Accounting Office.

- **Allocation formulas.** Allocates funds for different programs based on formulas that employ usage factors such as vehicle miles and lane miles in urban and rural areas and measures of gasoline consumption, including contributions to the Highway Trust Fund. For example, interstate maintenance funding to each state is distributed according to a ratio based one-third on interstate vehicle miles, one-third on interstate lane miles and one-third on contributions to the trust fund attributed to commercial vehicles.
- **Woodrow Wilson Bridge.** Provides $900 million for replacement of the bridge, which crosses the Potomac River on the Capital Beltway, Interstate 495, just outside Washington, D.C.
- **Federal lands highways.** Authorizes $4.1 billion for the federal lands highway program, including $1.6 billion for American Indian reservation roads; $1.4 billion for public lands highways; $940 million for park roads; and $100 million for a new category called refuge roads, which provide access to lands in National Wildlife Refuge Areas.
- **High-risk roads.** Creates a high-risk road safety improvement program that provides funds for construction and other projects, including pavement marking and road sign projects. The law requires the Transportation Department to contract with a private, nonprofit organization to help collect data on high-risk roads and develop a public awareness campaign.
- **Appalachian roads.** Provides $2.25 billion for Appalachian Development Highway System, which covers 13 states. The law gives eligibility under this program to two counties in Georgia, two counties in Alabama, two counties in Virginia and one county in Mississippi. The law bases distribution of the money on cost-to-complete estimates for new roads in the system.
- **Emergency relief.** Continues the emergency relief program, providing $600 million for grants to state and local government to pay for damage to roads from natural disasters.
- **Olympics assistance.** Authorizes transportation assistance for U.S. cities that will host the summer or winter Olympics, Paralympics or Special Olympics international events. The law provides $640 million for rail, bus and intermodal facility projects for the Salt Lake City Winter Olympics of 2002.
- **National corridors.** Provides $700 million for efforts to develop transportation corridors of national significance and develop coordinated border infrastructure to improve movement of people and goods across the Canadian and Mexican borders. The law provides that up to $30 million would be used for construction related to law enforcement at the border. The border infrastructure program is designed to deal with increased truck traffic since passage of the North

Transportation & Infrastructure

American Free Trade Agreement (PL 103-182).

• **Funding flexibility.** Gives states greater flexibility to use federal funds. The law caps the transfer of transportation enhancement funds to other programs at an amount that matches the difference between current enhancement funding and funding under the same program in fiscal 1997. The transfer may not exceed 25 percent of a state's current transportation enhancement funding. The law limits the transfer of congestion mitigation and air quality improvement funding to no more than 50 percent of the increase in funding in this program provided to states under the law.

• **Agency streamlining.** Consolidates and streamlines current practices of the Federal Highway Administration to oversee federal aid highway projects. The law requires elimination of the highway administration's regional offices and delegation of responsibilities to the agency's state offices. The law creates technical resource centers and gives siting preference to cities that currently have regional offices. The law permits states to assume responsibility for approval of plans, estimates, contract awards and inspections. It requires the Transportation Department and states to enter into agreements to establish the appropriate level of federal oversight of National Highway System projects.

• **Headquarters.** Requires the Transportation Department to consult authorizing committees before buying a new headquarters office to replace its current leased quarters in Washington, D.C.

• **Metric system.** Gives states the option to use the metric system on roads.

• **Year 2000.** Directs the Transportation secretary to develop a plan and budget to deal with date-related computer problems to assure that systems operate effectively in the year 2000 and beyond. The law also directs the secretary to make contingency plans for problems that cannot be corrected.

• **Transportation statistics.** Provides $186 million for the Bureau of Transportation Statistics for studies including analysis of transportation and the flow of commodities.

• **Infrastructure video.** The law authorizes $2.9 million to pay 60 percent of the cost of producing a video documentary about infrastructure in cooperation with a nonprofit national public television station and the National Academy of Engineering.

• **Ferries.** Provides $220 million for construction of ferries and ferry terminals. Of the total, $50 million would go to Alaska, $25 million to New Jersey and $25 million to Washington. The transit portion of the law provides another $14 million in each of six years for ferries and ferry facilities in Alaska and Hawaii. The Transportation secretary was directed to conduct a study of ferry transportation.

• **Motorcycles.** Prevents state or local governments from barring motorcycles from federal roads.

• **Tolls.** Provides $51 million for value-pricing pilot programs. The law increases from five to 15 state pilot programs for value pricing, or toll, projects aimed at relieving congestion. The law permits single-occupant cars on high-occupancy vehicle lanes as part of a value-pricing program. The law provides for a study of the impact of the program on low-income drivers. It also permits tolls to be collected as a pilot program on three interstate highways to pay for reconstruction and rehabilitation.

• **Property acquisition.** Increases flexibility for state and local governments to compete for land purchases. They would receive a credit for the value of publicly owned lands incorporated in federally funded projects. The law requires states to charge the fair market value for land and airspace acquired in federally funded projects, unless the property is turned into a park or put to other public use.

• **State oversight**. Gives states responsibility for the design, award and inspection of projects unless states opt out. States may also assume responsibility for projects on the National Highway System, not including interstate highways unless the states or the Transportation secretary determine otherwise.

• **Combined contracts.** Allows contracts combining responsibility for design and construction phases of projects to help increase accountability and accelerate completion. The law also allows states to hire under a single contract consultant services that involve environmental analysis and subsequent engineering and design for a project.

• **Pavement life analysis.** Deletes a requirement for life-cycle cost analysis for large project segments on the National Highway System. The law directs the Transportation secretary to develop guidelines for states to conduct their own studies of life-cycle costs of projects in order to help cut maintenance costs and improve quality.

• **Canadian highway.** Provides $94 million for upgrading a 325-mile stretch of highway in the Yukon Territory of Canada. The road is part of a national defense highway connecting Alaska to the lower 48 states.

• **High-priority corridors.** Designates or expands about 20 high-priority highway corridors that are deemed regionally or nationally important. They include a corridor from Sarnia, Ontario, Canada, along Interstate 94 to the Ambassador Bridge in Detroit; U.S. 90 from Lafayette, La., to New Orleans; portions of a corridor from Batesville to Fulton, Miss.; a corridor from Fulton, Miss., to Birmingham, Ala.; and a corridor from Everett to Tacoma, Wash.

• **Congestion mitigation.** Provides $8.1 billion in funds to areas with air pollution problems to reduce traffic congestion (such as construction of carpooling lanes, expansion of transit, emissions testing programs and other such projects). The measure makes programs that reduce motor vehicle emissions caused by extreme cold start conditions eligible for funding under the congestion mitigation and air quality improvement program, and it requires the National Academy of Sciences to conduct a study on the effectiveness of the program in improving the air quality in non-attainment areas.

Environmental Issues

• **Environmental reviews.** Reduces paperwork and aims to speed up environmental review of projects to permit quicker completion of projects. The law streamlines environmental reviews by requiring cooperation and concurrent, rather than sequential, evaluation of projects. The law permits the Transportation secretary to meet with counterparts in other federal agencies to resolve project-related environmental issues.

• **National scenic byways.** Provides $148 million for technical assistance and grants to states under the national scenic byways program. The Transportation secretary designates national scenic byways or all-American roads that would be nominated by states or federal land-management agencies. The roads must have outstanding scenic, historic, cultural, natural, recreational and archeological qualities. The law provides $9 million to establish a national center in Duluth, Minn., to help local organizations put together applications for grants under the scenic byways program; and $4 million to develop the Coal Heritage Scenic Byway in West Virginia.

• **Bicycles.** Continues support for efforts to improve bike paths and other facilities for both bicycles and pedestrians. The law requires states to consider bicycle safety in planning and completing transportation projects.

• **Recreational Trails Program.** Provides $270 million to build and maintain trails. States must use at least 30 percent of funding to support non-motorized use of recreational trails.

The law reactivates the Recreational Trails Advisory Commission until the end of fiscal 2000 and continues state advisory committees that implement the trails program. The law encourages use of youth conservation or service corps members in completing trail projects.

Surface Transportation

● **One call.** Provides $6 million for grants to states that operate one-call notification programs to prevent unintentional damage to underground pipelines and cables. The law encourages states to develop programs that require excavators to notify the state about excavation plans so they provide advance notice to pipeline and cable operators. The program provides grants to states that show their one-call notification systems meet minimum standards.

● **Particulate matter monitoring.** Requires the Environmental Protection Agency to designate areas that do not meet federal particulate matter standards within about four years, based on air quality monitoring data. The law codifies a timetable that has been used by regulators. The law requires that the agency pay for the cost of equipment for monitoring particulate matter.

● **Regional haze.** Ties compliance deadlines for reducing haze that limits visibility in national parks and wilderness areas to the deadlines for meeting new federal standards for fine particles and ambient air quality.

● **Community and system preservation program.** Authorizes $120 million for a pilot program to provide grants to states, local government and metropolitan planning organizations to make transportation systems more efficient and reduce environmental effects.

Mass Transit

● **Transit program.** Provides $41 billion over six years for transit programs, including $29.3 billion from the mass transit account of the Highway Trust Fund and $12.7 billion from the General Fund, subject to appropriation.

● **Capital investment.** Provides $9.1 billion for new starts of mass transit systems or extensions of existing ones, including 96 earmarked fixed guideway projects for final design and construction and 71 fixed guideway projects for analysis and preliminary engineering; $6.6 billion for fixed guideway modernization and $3.5 billion bus capital projects, including 149 earmarked projects. The law permits the federal government to pay 100 percent of the cost of transit vehicles. The law revises the definition of capital project to include preventive maintenance, leasing of equipment, safety equipment, transit enhancements, non-fixed route transit service and facilities that include community services such as child care and health care.

● **Transit benefits.** Increases limit on non-taxable mass transit benefits that employers may give each employee to $100 a month in 2002 from the current $65 a month. The law clarifies employers' plans to make sure that giving employees the option of taxable cash compensation in lieu of transportation benefits will not affect the tax-free status of transit benefits.

● **Welfare to work.** Provides $750 million over six years, including $350 million from the general fund, to help low-income persons commute to jobs. About 60 percent of the total is directed to projects in cities with more than 200,000 residents, and $60 million is set aside to help city dwellers make a "reverse commute" to jobs in the suburbs. The law broadens job training programs and assistance and allows states to reserve slots in job training on road projects for welfare recipients.

● **Agency reauthorization.** Reauthorizes mass transportation programs of the Federal Transit Administration.

● **Formula grants.** Authorizes $20 billion over six years for transit formula grants — including urban formula grants, rural formula grants and $456 million for transportation services for the elderly and disabled. Beginning in fiscal 2000, formula grants would be funded entirely from the mass transit account of the Highway Trust Fund.

● **Urban formula grants.** Authorizes $18 billion over six years (91 percent of available formula grant funding each year) for urban formula grants. The law requires that 1 percent of the formula grant funding provided to large urbanized areas be used for transit "enhancement" activities. Bicycle access projects are eligible for 95 percent of federal cost sharing.

● **Rural formula grants.** Authorizes $1.2 billion over six years. For the final five years of the law, rural formula grants receive 6.37 percent of total mass transit funding. The law provides $17.5 million for intercity, fixed-route, over-the road bus services as part of the program to increase rural transportation accessibility for disabled persons.

The law eliminates operating assistance for large urbanized areas (those with populations over 200,000), but it expands the definition of "capital project" to include preventive maintenance and certain leasing of equipment or facilities, thereby making those activities eligible for funding with capital grants. Smaller urbanized areas continue to be eligible for operating assistance — however, the law limited to $400 million in any one year the total amount of formula grants that may be used for operating assistance and preventive maintenance, combined (in both large and small urban areas).

● **Fuel-efficient trucks.** Provides $250 million in grants to be matched with private funding for fuel-efficient, low-polluting trucks and other heavy vehicles.

● **Clean fuels.** Provides $500 million for grants to purchase or lease buses that run on low-polluting fuels. The buses run on electricity and clean fuels including biodiesel, a fuel typically made from methanol and soybean oil. Two-thirds of the money will go to areas with a population of more than 1 million.

● **New grant procedures.** Establishes new procedures that the Federal Transit Administration must follow before approving a grant or loan for the construction of new fixed-rail transit systems, requiring among other things that the agency develop public guidelines for evaluating and rating the merits of proposals. These new procedures are not applied to projects requiring less than $25 million in federal funding.

● **Other provisions.** Establishes a pilot program for the testing and deployment of new bus technologies, which focuses on low-emission technology engines (including those powered by natural gas, batteries, fuel cell, biodiesel fuel, alcohol-based fuel and hybrid electric).

● **Accessibility.** Provides $3 million annual funding to help transit systems comply with the Americans With Disabilities Act (PL 101-336). The law permits use of surface transportation funds to make sidewalks accessible. The law requires that a study be conducted on the effect the privatization of mass transit services has on transit-dependent populations.

Highway Safety

● **Safety programs.** Provides $933 million for the highway safety programs of the National Highway Traffic Safety Administration.

● **Construction.** Provides $3 billion for safety construction, including removal of road hazards and improvements in rail-highway grade crossings.

● **Drunken driving prevention.** Provides $500 million in incentive grants to states that meet a new standard of 0.08 percent blood-alcohol content for drunken driving violations. The law provides for $219.5 million in incentive grants to states that enact a list of measures meant to curb drunken driving. The criteria include adoption of a program to prevent drivers under the age of 21 from drinking alcoholic beverages and a program to punish persons convicted of repeat drunken driving offenses. Two other provisions require the transfer to safety programs of 1.5 percent of road construction funds for states that do not enact bans on open containers of alcohol in automobiles or do not enact tougher penalties for second drunken driving offenses. The transfer of funds rises to 3 percent starting in fiscal 2002.

Transportation & Infrastructure

• **National driver register.** Continues the national driver register managed by the National Highway Traffic Safety Administration. The law permits certain functions to be transferred to a non-federal manager.

• **Safety set-aside.** Requires states to set aside 2 percent of the surface transportation program funding for railway-highway crossings, 2 percent for hazard elimination and 6 percent for railway-highway crossings or hazard elimination. The law allows federal safety officials to testify as invited witnesses but prevents them from lobbying for or against bills in state legislatures.

• **Safety belt incentives.** Authorizes $500 million in safety belt incentive grants for states that meet criteria such as enactment of a safety belt use law and rules on child seats or restraining systems. The program is designed to decrease federal medical costs related to injuries in traffic accidents. The law provides $68 million for occupant protection incentive grants to states to encourage increased use of safety belts and provides $15 million for educational programs to encourage use of child safety seats.

• **Airbags.** Requires the Transportation secretary to issue a final rule no later than March 1, 2000, to improve safety of airbags for children and adults. The rule takes effect no sooner than 2002 and no later than 2006.

• **U.S. content.** Revises regulations for consumer labeling showing the percentage of a new automobile's value attributable to work in America. In calculating American content for labeling purposes, the law requires the share of the value of each automobile component attributable to American workers to be rounded to the nearest 5 percentage points. Currently, only parts with 70 percent or greater American content are counted for labeling purposes.

• **Odometer.** Retains the current 300-mile limit as the maximum odometer reading for new automobiles offered for sale, but provides an exemption for automobiles sold to companies that specialize in renting or leasing cars for 30 days or less. The law gives the Transportation secretary authority to grant other exemptions.

• **Data improvement.** Provides $32 million for incentive grants to encourage states to improve timeliness, accuracy and accessibility of highway safety data.

Research and Technology

• **Transportation research.** Provides $592 million for research and development, including testing of new technology. The law establishes a new cooperative research program to address transportation-related environmental issues and authorizes a program jointly under the Transportation and Energy departments to develop fuel-efficient vehicles.

• **Safety research.** Provides support for research to reduce drunken driving, reduce tire blowouts, improve school bus occupant safety and improve training in vehicle pursuit for police.

• **Statistics.** Expands the role of the Bureau of Transportation Statistics, directing it to establish and maintain transportation-related databases and a National Transportation Library.

• **University transportation centers.** Authorizes funding for 10 regional university transportation centers and 23 other centers. The law consolidates university transportation centers and research institute programs. The law provides $192 million for university transportation research.

• **Intelligent transportation systems.** Provides about $1.3 billion to develop and implement intelligent transportation system (ITS) technologies, including automatic braking systems and new electronic signs to improve safety and relieve congestion. The law requires the Transportation secretary to update the national plan and list standards starting in 1999 to promote widespread use of the new technology. The law permits use of national highway, surface transportation and congestion mitigation funding for some ITS projects.

• **Technology initiatives.** Provides $250 million for transportation technology deployment, including $108 million for innovative bridge research and construction.

• **Other grants.** Provides grants of $4 million for seismic research at the University of California at San Diego: $1 million for global climate research at the University of Alabama at Huntsville; $1.25 million for asphalt research at Auburn University; $2 million for advanced vehicle research at the University of Alabama at Tuscaloosa; $6 million for the research projects related to bridges at the University of Oklahoma and Oklahoma State University; and $18.25 million for medical research related to injuries from traffic accidents at the University of Alabama at Birmingham, Calspan University of Buffalo, N.Y., Louisiana State University and George Washington University in Washington, D.C.

Railroads

• **High-speed rail.** Authorizes $40 million for high-speed rail corridor planning and provides $150 million to develop improved technology. The law also authorizes $100 million for pilot program grants to support light rail projects, and $31.5 million for grants to the Alaska Railroad. The law modifies the railroad rehabilitation financing program to acquire or improve intermodal and rail equipment and facilities, limiting to $3.5 billion the amount of loans that may be outstanding at any one time. Of that amount, $1 billion in loans is reserved for small freight railroads.

• **Railroad rehabilitation.** Provides for up to $3.5 billion in loans for private or public sponsor of rail projects, including $1 billion reserved for projects benefiting certain freight railroads.

• **Amtrak.** Continues to permit use of some congestion mitigation and air quality funds for Amtrak. The law broadens eligibility to include harbor projects and certain highway projects for funding provided by Amtrak to non-Amtrak states under the Taxpayer Relief Act of 1997 (PL 105-34).

• **Rail crossings.** Provides $120 million for safety improvements at rail grade crossings, including a set-aside of about $30 billion of surface transportation funds, to target railway-highway crossing hazards on existing high-speed rail corridors and on other corridors to be selected in the future. The corridors include San Diego to Sacramento, Calif.; Detroit to Milwaukee; Miami to Tampa, Fla.; Washington, D.C., to Charlotte, N.C.; Vancouver, B.C., Canada, to Eugene, Ore.; and Minneapolis to Chicago. The law provides for $500,000 a year in funding for the Operation Lifesaver program to eliminate accidents at crossings.

Metropolitan and State Planning

• **Metropolitan planning.** Streamlines 16 metropolitan planning categories into seven. Metropolitan planning organizations are required to evaluate whether plans support economic vitality, increase safety, increase mobility of people and freight, improve energy conservation, protect the environment, enhance links in transportation system, promote efficiency and preserve the existing transportation system.

• **Statewide planning.** Streamlines the number of statewide planning factors from 20 to seven and clarifies that failure to consider any specific factor is not reviewable in court. The law gives states flexibility to move projects within a three-year transportation improvement program if the metropolitan planning organization concurs. The states must consult with local transportation officials on plans.

• **Designation of planning organizations.** Retain current law that permits designation of a metropolitan planning organization if the governor and local government entities representing 75 percent of the population of the metropolitan area agree.

Surface Transportation

● **Freight shippers.** Adds freight shippers to the list of stakeholders who must be consulted as part of the metropolitan and statewide planning process.

● **Double and triple trailers.** Continues to limit use of longer-combination trucks on the interstate system to states that allowed them before June 1, 1991. The limit covers trucks that have two or more trailers that weigh more than 80,000 pounds, including so-called Rocky Mountain doubles, which consist of one long and one short trailer.

● **Motor carrier safety grants.** Authorizes $579 million over six years to support state enforcement of commercial motor safety and other related regulations. The law provides set-asides of up to 5 percent for national safety priorities and 5 percent for border safety enforcement.

● **Motor carrier hotline.** Authorizes $1.5 million over six years to establish a nationwide, toll-free hotline that truck drivers and others may use to report motor carrier safety violations.

● **Exemptions.** Authorizes the Transportation secretary to develop a process for granting short-term regulatory exemptions from federal motor carrier safety requirements.

● **Information systems.** Provides $65 million for motor carrier information analysis and for improvements in information systems that contain carrier, vehicle and driver safety records.

● **Penalties.** Establishes a maximum penalty of $10,000 for violations of most motor carrier safety regulations. The law increases authority of the Transportation secretary to order unsafe motor carriers to stop operations.

Boating

● **Boating safety.** Provides more than $300 million for grants to states for boating safety programs. Provides apportionments from the boating safety account, permitting the Coast Guard to use 2 percent for administering state boating safety programs; 2 percent for inspection and regulation of recreational boats; and 3 percent for maintaining aids to navigation that primarily promote recreational boating safety, with the remainder to be appropriated as grants to states for their boating safety programs. The law provides that 5 percent of any amounts appropriated each year in excess of $35 million for state boating safety programs be used for the development and maintenance of public access facilities.

● **Aquatic trust fund.** Increases the share of the 18.3-cent-per-gallon gas tax for motorboat users paid into the Aquatic Resources Trust Fund from 11.5 cents to 13.5 cents in 2003. The change reduces the share of the tax paid into the general fund by 2 cents.

● **Boating promotion.** Provides $36 million for a national outreach and communications program to promote boating and fishing.

● **Boundary Waters.** Permits mechanized vehicles on four boat portage routes in the Boundary Waters Canoe Area Wilderness in Minnesota.

Miscellaneous Provisions

● **Student loans.** Specifies an interest rate subsidy of about one-half of 1 percentage point for student loans made over three months, starting July 1.

● **Veterans' aid.** Increases by 20 percent the rate of basic educational assistance to veterans under the Montgomery GI bill. The law also increases assistance for specially equipped homes and automobiles for disabled veterans. It provides that certain remarried surviving spouses of veterans may be reinstated for dependency and indemnity compensation upon termination of a remarriage. The law includes a sense of the Congress resolution that the secretary of Veterans Affairs should recover from tobacco companies the cost of caring for tobacco-related illnesses of veterans.

● **Kennedy Center.** Provides for a $500,000 study of the methods to improve pedestrian and vehicular access to the John F. Kennedy Center for the Performing Arts in Washington, D.C.

● **Wetlands.** Provides $100 million for wetlands restoration pilot program.

● **Commercial zone.** Designates commercial zone in Dona Ana and Luna counties in New Mexico to encourage cross-border trade. The law permits Mexican trucks to carry products across the border into the new commercial zone and to pick up American cargo there to carry back to Mexico.

● **Minnesota history.** Provides $5 million for the Minnesota Transportation History Network to support museum exhibits and programs at national historic landmarks in Minnesota, emphasizing the theme of transportation history.

● **Driving schools.** Provides $7.5 million for a driver training and safety center in Connellsville, Pa.; $3 million for a motor carrier operator vehicle and training facility to be operated on an unused stretch of the Pennsylvania Turnpike near Breezewood, Pa., and at Letterkenny Army Depot near Chambersburg, Pa.; and $1 million for a heavy equipment operator training facility at Hibbing, Minn.

● **Visitor centers.** Provides $12.4 million for a visitor center near Interstate 64 in West Virginia to provide information about the New River Gorge, $6 million for a visitor center and museum at Fort Peck, Mont., and $600,000 for an interpretive center for the Blue Ridge Parkway in Virginia. The law provides $5 million for transportation history exhibits as part of the Minnesota Transportation History Network and permits Georgia to conduct a pilot program to operate an information center along Interstate 75 in Cobb County. The law provides $4 million for a visitor center for the Rhode Island National Wildlife Refuge, $500,000 for a visitor center at the Sachuest Point National Wildlife Refuge and funding for entrance paving and removal of an old runway at Ninigret National Wildlife Refuge, both in Rhode Island.

● **Smithsonian Institution program.** Authorizes $5 million for the Smithsonian Institution to pay for transportation-related exhibits, and educational and research programs.

● **Covered bridges.** Provides $50 million for protection of historic covered bridges. The law calls for grants to states to cover the cost of rehabilitation, relocation, repair and fire protection system installation.

● **Bridge projects.** Provides $10 million for rehabilitation of the highway bridge on U.S. 13 near St. Georges, Del., to demonstrate new bridge technology; $15 million for seismic design and deployment of the Great River Bridge between Mississippi and Arkansas; $5 million for replacement and widening of box bridges on the Natchez Trace Parkway and in Madison County in Mississippi; and $2 million for preservation of the Chain of Rocks Bridge in Missouri. The law provides funding eligibility for the Cuyahoga River Bridge in Ohio and permits continuation of toll collection for fund improvements for the International Bridge in Sault Ste. Marie, Mich.

● **Civil War projects.** Provides $1 million to revitalize a former iron works as a visitor center for the Richmond National Battlefield Park in Virginia; $500,000 to the Shenandoah Valley Battlefield National Historic District Commission to develop a plan to protect 10 Civil War battlefields in the area.

● **Winter heating oil pilot program.** Establishes a pilot program to permit the Transportation secretary to grant waivers from maximum on-duty hours for winter heating oil delivery drivers during an 18-month period starting Nov. 1. The law directs the secretary to report to Congress on the pilot program, including an assessment of the impact on public safety.

● **Reports.** Requires 75 reports and studies on transportation issues, including the safety research and assessments of the Disadvantaged Business Enterprise program and the congestion mitigation air quality improvement program. ◆

Transportation & Infrastructure

Dispute Over Competition Leads to Interim Six-Month Reauthorization of FAA

Box Score

- **Bill:** HR 4328 — PL 105-277
- **House action:** The House adopted the conference report (H Rept 105-825) on HR 4328, 333-95, on Oct. 20. It passed HR 4057 (H Rept 105-639) by voice vote on Aug. 4.
- **Senate action:** The Senate cleared the conference report on HR 4328, 65-29, on Oct. 21. It passed HR 4057, 92-1, on Sept. 25 after substituting the text of S 2279.
- **Presidential action:** Clinton signed HR 4328 on Oct. 21.

Efforts to pass free-standing legislation (HR 4057, S 2279) reauthorizing Federal Aviation Administration (FAA) programs fell apart late in the session because House and Senate negotiators were unable to agree upon provisions to eliminate flight restrictions at several airports.

SUMMARY

Consequently, provisions were included in the omnibus appropriations law (HR 4328) to fund FAA airport improvement grants for the first six months of fiscal 1999. That forces Congress to revisit the issue early next year.

The most intractable disputes centered on the length of the authorization and on efforts by Senate Commerce Chairman John McCain, R-Ariz., to loosen Ronald Reagan Washington National Airport's "perimeter" rule — which limits flights to 1,250 miles — and to increase the number of landing and takeoff "slots" at National, O'Hare International airport in Chicago and John F. Kennedy and LaGuardia airports in New York.

House Panel Votes For Competition; Hands Setback To Major Airlines

JUNE 27 — The House Transportation and Infrastructure Committee approved June 25 a three-month delay in adopting proposed federal guidelines aimed at nurturing competition at regional hub airports.

A bipartisan compromise brokered by Chairman Bud Shuster, R-Pa., marked a setback for major airlines. They had tried to kill or block the proposed guidelines that would make it harder for big airlines to cut their prices and keep smaller rivals from launching new routes to regional airports such as Pittsburgh or St. Louis.

The panel approved an amendment to the airline service improvement bill (HR 2748) that would provide for three months of congressional review of the guidelines, delaying their adoption until early 1999.

In another jab at big airlines, the amendment called for the Transportation Department to review joint business ventures by major airlines involving the sharing of passenger reservation information, aircraft leasing and frequent-flier programs.

The bill would provide grants to support increased air service to small communities and encourage competition by permitting exemptions to airline slot limits that restrict the number of flights at New York's Kennedy and LaGuardia Airports, Chicago's O'Hare Airport and Ronald Reagan Washington National Airport.

"It's a big win for us because it does not substantially delay our ability to come forth with guidelines," said William Schulz, a spokesman for the Transportation Department.

Major airlines refused to concede defeat, saying they would press forward to kill the guidelines and expressing confidence that studies would support their view that guidelines would be unfair.

"We think once Congress sees what the guidelines will do, it will kill the guidelines," said David A. Fuscus, a spokesman for the Air Transport Association of America, which represents about 20 U.S. airlines. "We don't think Congress will put up with these re-regulation efforts."

What the Deal Would Do

The compromise emerged after long negotiations, more than two months after the Department of Transportation unveiled the proposed guidelines April 6.

Transportation Secretary Rodney Slater sat in on one key meeting involving Shuster and James L. Oberstar of Minnesota, the committee's ranking Democrat. And the administration put its stamp of approval on the deal before it was made public.

The bill would require a study of airline competition by the Transportation Department and a separate six-month study by the National Research Council of the National Academy of Sciences.

The pending agreement would require the Transportation Department to review airline alliances, which stop short of business mergers but involve the sharing of passenger reservation information to coordinate connection flights and provide for cooperation in other activities such as mileage awards for frequent fliers.

The deal emerged after heavy lobbying and an advertising blitz by major airlines opposing the guidelines.

The lobbying came to a head on June 11 when top airline executives met with House Speaker Newt Gingrich, R-Ga., and Shuster and other Republican leaders. The meeting was attended by executives of American, United, Delta, Northwest, Continental and Alaska airlines, and by Carol Hallett, the president and CEO of the Air Transport Association. The airline officials said they opposed the guidelines.

The big airlines wanted to kill the guidelines outright, but they threw their support behind the proposals to require studies of airline competition, which would delay the guidelines and allow them more time to mount opposition.

"We had to recognize political realities," said one airline industry official.

With lobbying from airlines and differing views among industry experts and scholars about the effectiveness of the proposed guidelines, lawmakers could have justified derailing the guidelines.

But they have been under pressure from rural constituents to take action against big airlines. Small airports have seen a decline in service. Business travelers, angered by rising prices for business-class and unrestricted fares, have also demanded action.

In the key June 11 summit with top industry executives, Shuster said that Gingrich did not buckle to the airlines in the meeting and elected not to intervene in their behalf.

"The Speaker really took a strong stand in favor of competition," said Shuster.

The battle over the guidelines now moves to the House floor and to the Senate, where more skirmishes are expected. The aviation industry is deeply divided on the proposed competition guidelines, which would rein in major airlines and help smaller, lower-cost rivals pick up business.

The Big Boys' Argument

Big airlines say the guidelines would create a double standard by allowing small airlines to offer low fares when entering a market but preventing big airlines from matching them.

While several lawmakers praised the deal made by Shuster's committee, many of them stopped short of embracing the guidelines.

Since they were issued April 6, the guidelines have been criticized in the Senate and House as hard to enforce. In the Senate, several committees have held hearings on airline competition.

"I think it's good they are looking at guidelines. But I don't think they got it right on the first try," said Republican Slade Gorton of Washington, chairman of the Senate Commerce Subcommittee on Aviation.

Gorton and other legislators say the guidelines would be hard to interpret and to enforce, requiring several tests to determine whether price wars between big airlines and new competitors at regional hubs involves unfair competition.

One proposed guideline would prohibit big airlines from cutting fares sharply and increasing seat capacity only if these actions would reduce local revenues.

On the 20th anniversary of the airline deregulation act of 1978 (PL 95–504), there is widespread discontent on Capitol Hill over the effects of the spoke-and-hub system, developed by big airlines to provide more efficient service. (1978 Almanac, p. 496)

While the 1978 law is widely regarded as a success for reducing average airfares and saving consumers more than $10 billion a year, critics charge that the hub-and-spoke system effectively gives big airlines market shares of well over 50 percent at certain regional airport hubs.

Alfred Kahn, a retired Cornell University economics professor who oversaw airline deregulation in the 1970s as chairman of the Civil Aeronautics Board, charged that further delay would result in more closures by small, lower-cost airlines that are trying to challenge major airlines at regional hubs.

"It's outrageous to wait," Kahn said of the proposed study approved by the House committee. "It's disgraceful. The lawmakers will postpone this until all these smaller airlines are dead."

A United Lobbying Front

Against the litany of complaints from business lobby groups, rural towns and consumer groups, major airlines have formed a united front against the guidelines.

The big airlines have an extensive lobbying operation in Washington, and they have pledged to continue the campaign to educate the public about airline competition and to fight the guidelines, which they portray as an attempt by the Clinton administration to "re-regulate" the airline industry.

A study by the Center for Responsive Politics, which monitors campaign contributions, found that the airline industry has contributed about $2 million to candidates and party committees in the 1997-98 election cycle, with 60 percent going to Republicans.

The industry gave $427,623 to Senate candidates and $574,262 to House candidates. In addition, the industry donated $1.1 million to party committees, with Republicans receiving about 70 percent.

While the administration has pushed for adoption of guidelines on anti-competitive practices, key legislators have been asking for modifications to make the guidelines easier to enforce.

Clifford Winston, an economist at the Brookings Institution, said airlines are fighting the guidelines because they fear a loss of business.

In addition, he said, "they are nervous that this is going to establish a precedent. They really don't want the government to make a habit of intervening in their activities."

Winston and some other airline industry experts say there is a lack of clear evidence to support the guidelines. "It's premature to do anything," he said. "Now we can find out the truth. The evidence will lead one way or the other."

Winston said he doubts that the administration will move forward with guidelines before both studies are completed.

Slater agreed to cooperate with lawmakers: "We welcome the call for a study of the broader issues of aviation competition and look forward to providing the Congress with this information."

Other Issues

The committee also approved by voice vote a one-year fiscal 1999 reauthorization bill (HR 4057) to provide $2.3 billion for the airport improvement program and $5.6 billion for FAA operations.

Shuster said the one-year reauthorization bill is part of his plan to push next year for legislation to require that all money in the Aviation Trust Fund be used on transportation projects.

The legislation included provisions to protect airline employees who reveal safety problems and a 3 percent airport improvement set-aside for airport security, including equipment to detect explosive devices.

Transportation & Infrastructure

Senate Committee's FAA Bill Praised As Pro-Competitive, Criticized as Perk

JULY 11 — The Senate Commerce Committee opened a new fight over the Reagan Washington National Airport by approving a bill that would erase a distance limit on direct flights to airports in fast-growing Western states — allowing many members to fly home more easily.

The panel approved by voice vote July 9 a four-year $42.4 billion reauthorization for the Federal Aviation Administration (FAA) containing the Reagan airport provision. The bill is subject to amendments that will be considered at a markup the week of July 13.

Commerce Chairman John McCain, R-Ariz., won a battle in defeating by an 8-11 committee vote a proposal to raise the current cap, from $3 to $4, on charges that airports assess on travelers.

McCain also predicted he could defeat a draft amendment by Wendell H. Ford, D-Ky., to shrink the reauthorization to one year. A shorter period would match a bill (HR 2748) backed by House Transportation and Infrastructure Committee Chairman Bud Shuster, R-Pa., who plans to seek increased expenditures from the Aviation Trust Fund next year.

Perimeter Rule Battle

The panel approved the bill with little dissent, but McCain faced opposition in the Washington area to his proposal, which would allow flights beyond a 1,250-mile radius from the Reagan National Airport.

The bill would permit 24 exemptions to daily flight limits at the airport, including 12 for flights beyond 1,250 miles. Currently, there are 550 flights a day. The bill also would permit conversion of 100 unused military flight slots to commercial air carriers over three years at O'Hare International Airport in Chicago. It also would permit exemptions to flight limits at two crowded New York airports, LaGuardia and John F. Kennedy.

Local officials in Maryland and Virginia opposed action by Congress to lengthen flights at Reagan National Airport, saying lawmakers had already pre-empted local decision-making by passing a law (PL 105-154) to rename the airport for former President Ronald Reagan.

Critics charged that McCain was trying to help legislators save time on their commutes home by offering more direct flights. McCain vowed not to take any direct flight to Phoenix from the airport "if there ever is one."

He said he is trying to increase airline competition and denied that his proposal was intended to benefit Arizona-based America West Airlines, which hopes to offer direct flights to Phoenix.

McCain has collected $78,115 from political action committees and employees of the air transport industry between 1991 and 1996, according to the Center for Responsive Politics. America West accounted for $4,900.

John W. Timmons, a lobbyist for America West, said the distance limit is a "considerable disadvantage."

"We are the only major carrier that does not have direct access from our principal hub to Washington National Airport," Timmons said.

McCain said his proposal was intended to help airlines formed since the beginning of airline deregulation in the 1970s, not just America West.

"I resent any implication that I am helping any particular airline," he said.

McCain's proposal is likely to face opposition in the House, where members from the Washington suburbs have urged colleagues to defeat any bill affecting operations at the airport.

McCain moved to build support for the overall bill, which he said is meant to provide stable funding for federal regulators and promote airline competition.

He supports proposed Transportation Department guidelines meant to nurture competition at regional hub airports. He said he opposes a provision in the House bill calling for congressional review and a three-month delay in implementing the guidelines.

The bill would provide $23.5 billion for the FAA, $8.9 billion for facilities and equipment and $10 billion for airport improvement.

Senate Majority Leader Trent Lott, R-Miss., backed a narrow bill on airport changes but said he does not think the Senate will get involved in the matter of competition at hubs.

Bill Advances, Burdened With Added Flights At Busy Airports

JULY 18 — A crucial aviation bill, designed to spur consumer choice and competition, took flight from the Senate Commerce Committee on July 14 with controversial provisions to increase the number of commercial flights at four of the nation's busiest airports.

The bill (S 2279), approved by voice vote, would set broad national policy for commercial aviation and airport construction for the next four years, as well as provide $23.5 billion in funding for the Federal Aviation Administration and $18.9 billion for airport construction over four years.

Its fate could depend on resolving controversies over adding flights at four crowded airports in New York, Chicago and Washington. But its prospects improved on July 16 when Senate negotiators agreed to slash the number of potential new flights at O'Hare International Airport, from 100 flights daily to 30.

Local officials in each city are adamantly opposed to extra flights because of the noise and congestion they would bring. Critics also worry about the safety of adding flights to jammed airspace.

Supporters, including Commerce, Science and Transportation Committee Chairman John McCain, R-Ariz., stress that greater capacity is the way to inject competition into the airline industry, which is consolidating and may become dominated by a handful of major carriers that could drive prices up.

The push for more flights came primarily from McCain, who said he thinks that added competition would force fares down and who wants to add flights to underserved cities, including several in his home state.

At least 15 senators support efforts to limit the number of flights. Their

FAA Authorization

reasons vary from worries about noise and safety to the belief that local officials should have been consulted.

Another factor in cutting down the increased number of flights is that the House version (HR 2748) calls for 29 additional flights at Chicago's O'Hare International Airport, where there are 2,400 flights a day. The last minute change brings the Senate bill nearly in line with the House version.

The issue is important to Sen. Carol Moseley-Braun, D-Ill., who is in a tough re-election race. Reducing the extra flights would be hailed by 400,000 people who live near O'Hare, but it could anger residents in smaller, underserved cities, such as Springfield, who have been pushing for improved local service.

In addition to the 30 flights at O'Hare, the Senate legislation would open 24 at Reagan Washington National Airport and an unspecified number at New York's Kennedy and LaGuardia airports.

Moseley-Braun and Richard J. Durbin, D-Ill., also secured better service to smaller cities under the agreement. At least 18 of the 30 daily flights from O'Hare must fly into underserved areas.

House Passes Bill, Leaves Conflicts For Conference

AUGUST 8 — The House passed by voice vote Aug. 4 a one-year Federal Aviation Administration (FAA) reauthorization bill (HR 4057), setting the stage for a confrontation with the Senate over aviation funding and airline competition.

The bill, providing $5.6 billion for FAA operations and $2.3 billion for the airport improvement program, generated little debate on the floor. But battle lines formed behind the scenes over the one-year scope of the House bill, compared with the four-year Senate version (S 2279), is expected on the Senate floor in September.

Bud Shuster, R-Pa., limited the House reauthorization bill to one year in order to mount a campaign next year to revamp aviation spending.

"Approximately $10 billion is being paid into the Aviation Trust Fund each year, yet we are spending only about $5.6 billion of that," Shuster said. The trust fund collects revenue from taxes on airline tickets to pay for aviation services and airport improvements.

Senate Commerce, Science and Transportation Committee Chairman John McCain, R-Ariz., opposed Shuster's campaign. He backed a four-year reauthorization of aviation programs.

Another battle is brewing over provisions on airline competition in the Senate reauthorization bill and in a separate House bill (HR 2748) to improve service.

Fight Over Flights

While lawmakers raced to complete work before the August recess, a feud broke out over proposals in the Senate reauthorization bill and in HR 2748 to increase flights at four big-city airports: LaGuardia and Kennedy in New York, O'Hare in Chicago and Ronald Reagan Washington National Airport.

The battle divided state delegations, with members from rural areas and small towns supporting new flights to major cities and those from communities near big airports opposed to increased air traffic and noise.

In the Senate, McCain quietly reached a compromise with Illinois Democrats Carol Moseley-Braun and Richard J. Durbin to reduce a proposed increase of 100 flights a day at O'Hare to 30 flights. But that deal still faced attack by House Judiciary Committee Chairman Henry J. Hyde, R-Ill.

Hyde also opposed a similar proposal for 29 new flights at O'Hare in HR 2748. He blocked that bill with a July 16 letter to Speaker Newt Gingrich, R-Ga., asking for it to be referred to his Judiciary Committee because several antitrust-related provisions fell under his panel's purview.

For example, one provision would require the Justice Department's antitrust division to sign off on Transportation Department reviews of pending airline mergers.

Hyde told Gingrich he was "very concerned that the practical effect of this provision may be to limit the vigorous enforcement of the antitrust laws in this industry."

Hyde said his panel should have jurisdiction over the proposed flight increases because they would change the "current rules of competition."

Hyde staunchly opposed any increase in flights that pass near the west and northwest Chicago suburbs in his district. A deal was expected to either kill increased traffic at O'Hare or remove antitrust-related provisions, which would be added later as floor amendments or in conference committee.

But making a deal with Hyde on O'Hare could unravel changes at other airports. Fourteen House members, including Hyde, wrote a July 16 letter to Majority Leader Dick Armey, R-Texas, opposing increased traffic at "four of the most congested airports in the country" and demanding a floor vote on HR 2748. They said Congress should stay out of local decisions on airport growth.

Perimeter Rule Targeted

McCain faces a barrage of criticism over his proposal to end a ban on flights from Reagan National Airport that extend beyond 1,250 miles.

Rep. James P. Moran, D-Va., charged that the change in the so-called perimeter rule limiting long-distance flight at National could hurt nearby Dulles International Airport, where local businesses and big carriers have investments.

Meanwhile, a group of 25 state attorneys general lined up to promote quick adoption of pending Transportation Department guidelines. HR 2748 would delay by at least three months implementation of the guidelines, aimed at curbing alleged anti-competitive practices by major airlines, to allow for a congressional review of the new policy.

Iowa Attorney General Tom Miller said, "The airline industry wants to delay things. Our position is there should be no delay."

Senate Passes FAA Authorization Amid Doubts About Deregulation

SEPTEMBER 26 — While the aviation industry prepared to celebrate the 20th anniversary of airline deregulation, the

Transportation & Infrastructure

Senate passed a two-year Federal Aviation Administration authorization bill on Sept. 25, setting the stage for a contentious debate in conference committee over proposals to increase airline competition.

The Senate voted 92-1 to approve HR 4057, providing for fiscal 1999 $5.6 billion for FAA operations and $2.4 billion for airport improvement grants. Charles S. Robb, D-Va., voted against the bill because he opposes a provision that would increase flights at Ronald Reagan Washington National Airport.

The lure of airport grants helped propel the bill through a thicket of controversy over the issue of airline competition. Passage came as the Transportation Department prepared final guidelines to forbid predatory pricing tactics allegedly used by major airlines to attack smaller rivals such as Southwest and AirTran and protect hub airports in such big cities as Detroit and Denver. Major airlines use connections through hub airports to fill seats and cut costs.

While lawmakers did not enact heavy restrictions on big airlines, they endorsed modest measures to help smaller communities and small airlines, including $30 million to provide grants of up to $500,000 a year to small towns to support local efforts to assess air service needs and improve service.

The Senate also approved by voice vote Sept. 25 an amendment to forbid discrimination by big airlines in making cooperative agreements with regional carriers to coordinate ticketing, baggage services and gate access at large airports where a single carrier has more than half the total passengers.

The measure's sponsor, Byron L. Dorgan, D-N.D., charged that big airlines had "retreated into these regional monopolies because they don't want to compete with one another."

Commerce Committee Chairman John McCain, R-Ariz., said the bill contained "essential provisions to promote a competitive aviation industry."

At a ceremony celebrating the 20th anniversary of deregulation, Transportation Secretary Rodney Slater praised Congress for tackling airline competition and predicted that final guidelines would be issued in the first quarter of 1999.

"There is no question the Airline Deregulation Act of 1978 has been an overwhelming success — average airfares have declined and more people are flying," he said Sept. 23 at a Washington, D.C., ceremony marking the anniversary. "Yet the benefits of deregulation have not been evenly distributed."

On Capitol Hill, lawmakers disagreed on how to nurture more competition and improve service to crowded airports and rural areas. The bill included compromise amendments to resolve a dispute over a provision backed by McCain to add 24 daily flights at National Airport, including 12 flights that would be exempt from a ban on flights beyond a radius of 1,250 miles.

The bill would also add flights at three other airports where flights currently are limited: O'Hare International Airport in Chicago and John F. Kennedy and LaGuardia airports in New York.

The added flights were intended to spur the entry of new rivals to challenge major carriers, while also improving access from rural areas to big cities.

Airline Competition

While the Senate prepared to resolve differences with the House version of the FAA bill (HR 4057), House members hoped to revive proposals from another stalled bill (HR 2748) dealing with airline competition and rural air service. HR 2748 has been blocked by an objection to increasing the number of daily flights at O'Hare airport from Rep. Henry J. Hyde, R-Ill., whose congressional district is nearby.

Rep. James L. Oberstar, of Minnesota, ranking Democrat on the Transportation and Infrastructure Committee, said he would try to insert in the FAA bill a provision of HR 2748 that calls for federal aid to help finance acquisition of jets by regional airlines.

While Transportation Department officials moved forward on guidelines, they offered to cooperate with Congress if it wants to review them.

Deregulation: a Mixed Record

While lawmakers applaud the success of deregulation in allowing airlines to cut fares, they are under pressure from rural communities unhappy with sparse choices and from consumer groups angered by high prices for tickets purchased on short notice. The complaints raised questions about the overall success of deregulation (PL 95-504). *(1978 Almanac, p. 496)*

Richard Branson, chairman of Virgin Group Ltd., opened a new front in the deregulation debate the week of Sept. 21 by urging Congress to relax a requirement that U.S. citizens hold at least 75 percent of the voting stock in a domestic airline. Branson, a British citizen, wants to launch a low-fare alternative to major U.S. airlines.

Branson won applause from consumer groups and a provision to require a Transportation Department study of the issue by December.

He and other critics contend that big airlines are now taking advantage of their strength to squeeze out rivals.

"Instead of competing, the majors are falling all over themselves to arrange cooperation deals," Branson said in a Sept. 24 speech to the International Aviation Club in Washington, D.C., referring to global alliances involving major carriers. "At the very same time, the lifeblood of competition — start-up airlines — is no longer flowing the way it should."

Alfred Kahn, a retired Cornell University economics professor who headed the former Civil Aeronautics Board under President Jimmy Carter, has become a sharp critic of aggressive tactics used by big airlines to cut prices when rivals launch new service.

Kahn said in a Sept. 23 speech to a deregulation group in Washington that guidelines were needed to "encourage the contestability of markets."

Based on industry statistics, airline travel is booming under deregulation. Revenue from tickets has increased more than 75 percent since 1987, and miles traveled by passengers on domestic flights have risen by 50 percent.

Deregulation has been credited with saving consumers $10 billion a year by permitting cost savings by airlines and lower fares for travelers.

But the critics on Capitol Hill say that new measures are needed to help challengers compete with major airlines at hub airports and improve service to rural airports.

"Increasingly, we in Congress hear, not praise for deregulation, but criticism of its inadequacies," Oberstar said.

FAA Authorization

Campaign Against Guidelines

With the clamor for action growing on Capitol Hill, airlines responded with an advertising campaign against the guidelines being developed by the Transportation Department, arguing that the provisions would put bureaucrats in charge of air service and restrict the ability of major airlines to offer deep discounts at hub airports where they are competing with a rival's new service.

In response to attacks by consumer groups, the industry also released results of two studies that raised questions about the rationale for the guidelines and their potential effect.

Brian Campbell, president of Campbell-Hill Aviation Group, an Alexandria, Va.-based industry consulting group, said major airlines would see a big cut in revenue and demand labor concessions if they were forced to reduce fares to match the low fares of smaller rivals.

"The end result will be less capacity [fewer seats] as well as higher fares for consumers — the opposite result that [the Transportation Department] claims it wants to achieve," said Robert Gallo, vice president of the Airline Planning Group, an Arlington, Va., consulting firm.

While major airlines attacked the guidelines, several consumer groups warned that they would falter without support from Congress. The Aviation Consumer Action Project, an advocacy group founded by Ralph Nader, urged lawmakers to monitor guidelines.

Paul Hudson, the group's executive director, endorsed efforts to revive a proposal in HR 2748 to require congressional review of Transportation Department guidelines to ensure that they are strengthened and enforced. "History shows that when consumer-oriented regulations come out, the industry opposes them, and the regulations are buried or weakened to the point of being meaningless," Hudson said.

National Airport Dispute

While the fight over guidelines simmered, the Senate approved several amendments offered jointly by the four senators from Maryland and Virginia to limit the effect of adding flights at National Airport. The Senate approved by voice vote provisions to set aside at least 10 percent of FAA grants for the airport authority to pay for noise abatement, to stagger flights throughout the day and to require an environmental assessment before flights are added.

The Senate approved by voice vote a manager's amendment that reduced the duration of the bill from four to two years, bringing it closer to the House bill's one-year length. The shorter term would leave room for lawmakers to move forward on a plan to consider major changes in aviation funding next year.

The manager's amendment also included a compromise on a provision modifying the 1920 Death on the High Seas Act. The bill would permit families of victims of airline crashes in the ocean to collect non-economic damages for loss of care, comfort and companionship but cap them at $750,000 per case.

The Senate voted 69-27 to table an amendment by Robert G. Torricelli, D-N.J., to target airport noise by establishing an office of noise abatement and control in the Environmental Protection Agency. (Vote 287, p. S-44)

House Panel Strips Out Added Flights

OCTOBER 10 — The House blocked a plan the week of Oct. 5 to add more flights to four crowded big-city airports.

House Transportation and Infrastructure Committee Chairman Bud Shuster, R-Pa., insisted on a stripped-down one-year Federal Aviation Administration (FAA) authorization bill (HR 4057) that cut out non-essential provisions, including adding slots at the airports.

The Senate's version of the bill had called for a two-year authorization and included the flight additions.

Rep. Constance A. Morella, R-Md., said House Judiciary Committee Chairman Henry J. Hyde, R-Ill., played a key role in persuading House leaders to oppose Senate provisions calling for additional flights at Reagan Washington National Airport, O'Hare International Airport in Chicago and LaGuardia and John F. Kennedy airports in New York.

"Henry Hyde is a champion," Morella said. Hyde opposed the proposed addition of 30 additional daily flights at O'Hare, which is near his congressional district.

The House also blocked a provision by Senate Commerce Committee Chairman John McCain, R-Ariz., to allow some flights to and from Reagan Airport to fly more than 1,250 miles without stopping. Current FAA rules cap how far these flights can travel nonstop.

With time running out, lawmakers were prepared to delete non-essential provisions to clear the way for passage of the bill, which contains airport improvement grants and funding for FAA operations.

The bill included a House provision calling for a 12-week congressional review of pending Transportation Department guidelines aimed at increasing competition at hub airports.

Pared-Back FAA Reauthorization Could Kick Off 'Year of Aviation'

OCTOBER 17 — House and Senate leaders ended a rancorous dispute over airline competition by agreeing to a stripped, six-month reauthorization of the Federal Aviation Administration.

The short-term reauthorization, needed to provide airport improvement grants, would be inserted in the omnibus spending bill (HR 4328).

Republican Bud Shuster of Pennsylvania, chairman of the Transportation and Infrastructure Committee, has pledged to make 1999 the "year of aviation" and to seek changes in management of the Aviation Trust Fund. The House originally supported a one-year reauthorization, while the Senate backed a two-year bill.

Senate Commerce Committee Chairman John McCain, R-Ariz., said the reauthorization would set the stage for a new round of debate on airline competition, including his pet proposal: exemptions to the perimeter rule that prevents flights to and from Ronald Reagan Washington National Airport

Transportation & Infrastructure

from extending beyond 1,250 miles.

Negotiators deleted his proposed perimeter rule exemptions and other proposals for increased flights at O'Hare International Airport in Chicago and LaGuardia and John F. Kennedy airports in New York.

"I am deeply disturbed that the House leadership has killed aviation competition legislation this session of Congress," McCain said.

He criticized "the utter intransigence on the part of the major airlines, and the unmitigated gall that they exhibit in defending the anti-competitive status quo." He accused House lawmakers from Illinois and Virginia of pursuing "parochial interests."

Judiciary Committee Chairman Henry J. Hyde, R-Ill., whose district is near O'Hare airport, helped kill the flight increases in the House.

The bill would require a congressional review of proposed federal guidelines aimed at increasing competition at regional hub airports. Major airlines have strongly opposed the new guidelines, which would restrict their ability to cut prices in order to compete with new rivals at hub airports. ◆

Appendix A

CONGRESS AND ITS MEMBERS

Glossary of Congressional Terms .... A-3 **List of Members, 105th Congress, 2nd Session** .. A-14

Glossary of Congressional Terms

Act — The term for legislation once it has passed both chambers of Congress and has been signed by the president or passed over his veto, thus becoming law. Also used in parliamentary terminology for a bill that has been passed by one house and engrossed. *(Also see engrossed bill.)*

Adjournment sine die — Adjournment without a fixed day for reconvening — literally, "adjournment without a day." Usually used to connote the final adjournment of a session of Congress. A session can continue until noon Jan. 3 of the following year, when, under the 20th Amendment to the Constitution, it automatically terminates. Both chambers must agree to a concurrent resolution for either chamber to adjourn for more than three days.

Adjournment to a day certain — Adjournment under a motion or resolution that fixes the next time of meeting. Under the Constitution, neither chamber can adjourn for more than three days without the concurrence of the other. A session of Congress is not ended by adjournment to a day certain.

Amendment — A proposal by a member of Congress to alter the language, provisions or stipulations in a bill or in another amendment. An amendment usually is printed, debated and voted upon in the same manner as a bill.

Amendment in the nature of a substitute — Usually an amendment that seeks to replace the entire text of a bill by striking out everything after the enacting clause and inserting a new version of the bill. An amendment in the nature of a substitute can also refer to an amendment that replaces a large portion of the text of a bill.

Appeal — A member's challenge of a ruling or decision made by the presiding officer of the chamber. A senator can appeal to members of the Senate to override the decision. If carried by a majority vote, the appeal nullifies the chair's ruling. In the House, the decision of the Speaker traditionally has been final; seldom are there appeals to the members to reverse the Speaker's stand. To appeal a ruling is considered an attack on the Speaker.

Appropriations bill — A bill that gives legal authority to spend or obligate money from the Treasury. The Constitution disallows money to be drawn from the Treasury "but in Consequence of Appropriations made by Law."

By congressional custom, an appropriations bill originates in the House. It is not supposed to be considered by the full House or Senate until a related measure authorizing the funding is enacted. An appropriations bill grants the actual budget authority approved by the authorization bill, though not necessarily the full amount permissible under the authorization.

If the 13 regular appropriations bills are not enacted by the start of the fiscal year, Congress must pass a stopgap spending bill or the departments and agencies covered by the unfinished bills must shut down.

About half of all budget authority, notably that for Social Security and interest on the federal debt, does not require annual appropriations; those programs exist under permanent appropriations. *(Also see authorization bill, budget authority, budget process, supplemental appropriations bill.)*

Authorization bill — Basic, substantive legislation that establishes or continues the legal operation of a federal program or agency either indefinitely or for a specific period of time, or which sanctions a particular type of obligation or expenditure. Under the rules of both chambers, appropriations for a program or agency may not be considered until the program has been authorized, although this requirement is often waived.

An authorization sets the maximum amount of funds that can be given to a program or agency, although sometimes it merely authorizes "such sums as may be necessary." *(Also see backdoor spending authority.)*

Backdoor spending authority — Budget authority provided in legislation outside the normal appropriations process. The most common forms of backdoor spending are borrowing authority, contract authority, entitlements and loan guarantees that commit the government to payments of principal and interest on loans — such as guaranteed student loans — made by banks or other private lenders. Loan guarantees result in actual outlays only when there is a default by the borrower.

In some cases, such as interest on the public debt, a permanent appropriation is provided that becomes available without further action by Congress.

Bills — Most legislative proposals before Congress are in the form of bills and are designated according to the chamber in which they originate — HR in the House of Representatives or S in the Senate — and by a number assigned in the order in which they are introduced during the two-year period of a congressional term.

"Public bills" deal with general questions and become public laws if they are cleared by Congress and signed by the president. "Private bills" deal with individual matters, such as claims against the government, immigration and naturalization cases or land titles, and become private laws if approved and signed. *(Also see private bills, resolution.)*

Bills introduced — In both the House and Senate, any number of members may join in introducing a single bill or resolution. The first member listed is the sponsor of the bill, and all subsequent members listed are cosponsors.

Many bills are committee bills and are introduced under the name of the chairman of the committee or subcommittee. All appropriations bills fall into this category. A committee frequently holds hearings on a number of related bills and may agree to one of them or to an entirely new bill. *(Also see clean bill.)*

Bills referred — After a bill is introduced, it is referred to the committee or committees that have jurisdiction over the subject with which the bill is concerned. Under the standing rules of the House and Senate, bills are referred by the Speaker in the House and by the presiding officer in the Senate. In practice, the House and Senate parliamentarians act for these officials and refer the vast majority of bills. *(Also see discharge a committee.)*

Borrowing authority — Statutory authority that permits a federal agency to incur obligations and make payments for specified purposes with borrowed money.

Budget — The document sent to Congress by the president early each year estimating government revenue and expenditures for the ensuing fiscal year.

Budget Act — The common name for the Congressional Budget and Impoundment Control Act of 1974, which established the current budget process and created the Congressional Budget Office. The act also put limits on presidential authority to spend ap-

Congress and Its Members

propriated money. It has undergone several major revisions since 1974. (Also see budget process, impoundments.)

Budget authority — Authority for federal agencies to enter into obligations that result in immediate or future outlays. The basic forms of budget authority are appropriations, contract authority and borrowing authority. Budget authority may be classified by (1) the period of availability (one-year, multiple-year or without a time limitation), (2) the timing of congressional action (current or permanent) or (3) the manner of determining the amount available (definite or indefinite). (Also see appropriations, outlays.)

Budget process — The annual budget process was created by the Congressional Budget and Impoundment Control Act of 1974, with a timetable that was modified in 1990. Under the law, the president must submit his proposed budget by the first Monday in February. Congress is supposed to complete an annual budget resolution by April 15, setting guidelines for congressional action on spending and tax measures.

Budget rules enacted in the 1990 Budget Enforcement Act and updated in 1993 and 1997 set caps on discretionary spending through fiscal 2002. The caps can be adjusted annually to account for changes in the economy and other limited factors. In addition, pay-as-you-go (PAYGO) rules require that any tax cut, new entitlement program or expansion of existing entitlement benefits that would increase a deficit be offset by an increase in taxes or a cut in entitlement spending.

The rules hold Congress harmless for budget-deficit increases that lawmakers do not explicitly cause — for example, increases due to a recession or to an expansion in the number of beneficiaries qualifying for Medicare or food stamps. PAYGO does not apply if there is a budget surplus.

If Congress exceeds the discretionary spending caps in its appropriations bills, the law requires an across-the-board cut — known as a sequester — in non-exempt discretionary spending accounts. If Congress violates the PAYGO rules, entitlement programs are subject to a sequester. Supplemental appropriations are subject to similar controls, with the proviso that if both Congress and the president agree, spending designated as an emergency can exceed the caps.

Budget resolution — A concurrent resolution that is passed by both chambers of Congress but does not require the president's signature. The measure sets a strict ceiling on discretionary budget authority, along with non-binding recommendations about how the spending should be allocated. The budget resolution may also contain "reconciliation instructions" requiring authorizing and tax-writing committees to propose changes in existing law to meet deficit-reduction goals. The Budget Committee in each chamber then bundles those proposals into a reconciliation bill and sends it to the floor. (Also see reconciliation.)

By request — A phrase used when a senator or representative introduces a bill at the request of an executive agency or private organization but does not necessarily endorse the legislation.

Calendar — An agenda or list of business awaiting possible action by each chamber. The House uses six legislative calendars. They are the Consent, Corrections, Discharge, House, Private and Union calendars. (Also see individual listings.)

In the Senate, all legislative matters reported from committee go on one calendar. They are listed there in the order in which committees report them or the Senate places them on the calendar, but they may be called up out of order by the majority leader, either by obtaining unanimous consent of the Senate or by a motion to call up a bill. The Senate also has one non-legislative calendar, which is used for treaties and nominations. (Also see executive calendar.)

Call of the calendar — Senate bills that are not brought up for debate by a motion, unanimous consent or a unanimous consent agreement are brought before the Senate for action when the calendar listing them is "called." Bills must be called in the order listed. Measures considered by this method usually are non-controversial, and debate on the bill and any proposed amendments is limited to five minutes for each senator.

Chamber — The meeting place for the membership of either the House or the Senate; also the membership of the House or Senate meeting as such.

Clean bill — Frequently after a committee has finished a major revision of a bill, one of the committee members, usually the chairman, will assemble the changes and what is left of the original bill into a new measure and introduce it as a "clean bill." The revised measure, which is given a new number, is referred back to the committee, which reports it to the floor for consideration. This often is a timesaver, as committee-recommended changes in a clean bill do not have to be considered and voted on by the chamber. Reporting a clean bill also protects committee amendments that could be subject to points of order concerning germaneness.

Clerk of the House — An officer of the House of Representatives who supervises its records and legislative business. Many former administrative duties were transferred in 1992 to a new position, the director of non-legislative and financial services.

Cloture — The process by which a filibuster can be ended in the Senate other than by unanimous consent. A motion for cloture can apply to any measure before the Senate, including a proposal to change the chamber's rules. A cloture motion requires the signatures of 16 senators to be introduced. To end a filibuster, the cloture motion must obtain the votes of three-fifths of the entire Senate membership (60 if there are no vacancies), except when the filibuster is against a proposal to amend the standing rules of the Senate and a two-thirds vote of senators present and voting is required.

The cloture request is put to a roll call vote one hour after the Senate meets on the second day following introduction of the motion. If approved, cloture limits each senator to one hour of debate. The bill or amendment in question comes to a final vote after 30 hours of consideration, including debate time and the time it takes to conduct roll calls, quorum calls and other procedural motions. (Also see filibuster.)

Committee — A division of the House or Senate that prepares legislation for action by the parent chamber or makes investigations as directed by the parent chamber.

There are several types of committees. Most standing committees are divided into subcommittees, which study legislation, hold hearings and report bills, with or without amendments, to the full committee. Only the full committee can report legislation for action by the House or Senate. (Also see standing, oversight, select and special committees.)

Committee of the Whole — The working title of what is formally "The Committee of the Whole House [of Representatives] on the State of the Union." The membership is composed of all House members sitting as a committee. Any 100 members who are present on the floor of the chamber to consider legislation comprise a quorum of the committee. Any legislation, however, must first have passed through the regular legislative or appropriations committee and have been placed on the calendar.

Technically, the Committee of the Whole considers only bills directly or indirectly appropriating money, authorizing appropriations or involving taxes or charges on the public. Because the Committee of the Whole need number only 100 representatives, a quorum is more readily attained and legislative business is expedited. Before 1971, members' positions were not individually recorded on votes taken in the Committee of the Whole.

When the full House resolves itself into the Committee of the Whole, it replaces the Speaker with a "chairman." A measure is debated and amendments may be proposed, with votes on amendments as needed. *(Also see five-minute rule.)*

When the committee completes its work on the measure, it dissolves itself by "rising." The Speaker returns, and the chairman of the Committee of the Whole reports to the House that the committee's work has been completed. At this time, members may demand a roll call vote on any amendment adopted in the Committee of the Whole. The final vote is on passage of the legislation.

In 1993 and 1994, the four delegates from the territories and the resident commissioner of Puerto Rico were allowed to vote on questions before the Committee of the Whole. If their votes were decisive in the outcome, however, the matter was automatically re-voted, with the delegates and resident commissioner ineligible. They could vote on final passage of bills or on separate votes demanded after the Committee of the Whole rises. This limited voting right was rescinded in 1995.

Committee veto — A requirement added to a few statutes directing that certain policy directives by an executive department or agency be reviewed by certain congressional committees before they are implemented. Under common practice, the government department or agency and the committees involved are expected to reach a consensus before the directives are carried out. *(Also see legislative veto.)*

Concurrent resolution — A concurrent resolution, designated H Con Res or S Con Res, must be adopted by both chambers, but it is not sent to the president for approval and, therefore, does not have the force of law. A concurrent resolution, for example, is used to fix the time for adjournment of a Congress. It is also used to express the sense of Congress on a foreign policy or domestic issue. The annual budget resolution is a concurrent resolution.

Conference — A meeting between representatives of the House and the Senate to reconcile differences between the two chambers on provisions of a bill. Members of the conference committee are appointed by the Speaker and the presiding officer of the Senate.

A majority of the conferees for each chamber must agree on a compromise, reflected in a "conference report" before the final bill can go back to both chambers for approval. When the conference report goes to the floor, it is difficult to amend. If it is not approved by both chambers, the bill may go back to conference under certain situations, or a new conference may be convened. Many rules and informal practices govern the conduct of conference committees.

Bills that are passed by both chambers with only minor differences need not be sent to conference. Either chamber may "concur" with the other's amendments, completing action on the legislation. Sometimes leaders of the committees of jurisdiction work out an informal compromise instead of having a formal conference. *(Also see custody of the papers.)*

Confirmations — *(See nominations.)*

Congressional Record — The daily, printed account of proceedings in both the House and Senate chambers, showing substantially verbatim debate, statements and a record of floor action. Highlights of legislative and committee action are given in a Daily Digest section of the Record, and members are entitled to have their extraneous remarks printed in an appendix known as "Extension of Remarks." Members may edit and revise remarks made on the floor during debate, although the House in 1995 limited members to technical or grammatical changes.

The Congressional Record provides a way to distinguish remarks spoken on the floor of the House and Senate from undelivered speeches. In the Senate, all speeches, articles and other matter that members insert in the Record without actually reading them on the floor are set off by large black dots, or bullets. However, a loophole allows a member to avoid the bulleting if he or she delivers any portion of the speech in person. In the House, undelivered speeches and other material are printed in a distinctive typeface. The record is also available in electronic form. *(Also see Journal.)*

Congressional terms of office — Terms normally begin on Jan. 3 of the year following a general election. Terms are two years for representatives and six years for senators. Representatives elected in special elections are sworn in for the remainder of a term. Under most state laws, a person may be appointed to fill a Senate vacancy and serve until a successor is elected; the successor serves until the end of the term applying to the vacant seat.

Consent Calendar — Members of the House may place on this calendar most bills on the Union or House Calendar that are considered non-controversial. Bills on the Consent Calendar normally are called on the first and third Mondays of each month. On the first occasion that a bill is called in this manner, consideration may be blocked by the objection of any member. The second time, if there are three objections, the bill is stricken from the Consent Calendar. If fewer than three members object, the bill is given immediate consideration.

A member may also postpone action on the bill by asking that the measure be passed over "without prejudice." In that case, no objection is recorded against the bill and its status on the Consent Calendar remains unchanged. A bill stricken from the Consent Calendar remains on the Union or House Calendar. The Consent Calendar has seldom been used in recent years.

Continuing resolution — A joint resolution, cleared by Congress and signed by the president, to provide new budget authority for federal agencies and programs until the regular appropriations bills have been enacted. Also known as "CRs" or continuing appropriation, continuing resolutions are used to keep agencies operating when, as often happens, Congress fails to finish the regular appropriations process by the start of the new fiscal year.

The CR usually specifies a maximum rate at which an agency may incur obligations, based on the rate of the prior year, the president's budget request or an appropriations bill passed by either or both chambers of Congress but not yet enacted.

Contract authority — Budget authority contained in an authorization bill that permits the federal government to enter into contracts or other obligations for future payments from funds not yet appropriated by Congress. The assumption is that funds will be provided in a subsequent appropriations act. *(Also see budget authority.)*

Corrections Calendar, Corrections Day — A House calendar established in 1995 to speed consideration of bills aimed at eliminating burdensome or unnecessary regulations. Bills on the Corrections Calendar can be called up on the second and fourth Tuesday of each month, called Corrections Day. They are subject to

Congress and Its Members

one hour of debate without amendment, and require a three-fifths majority for passage. *(Also see calendar.)*

Correcting recorded votes — Rules prohibit members from changing their votes after the result has been announced. Occasionally, however, a member may announce hours, days or months after a vote has been taken that he or she was "incorrectly recorded." In the Senate, a request to change one's vote almost always receives unanimous consent, so long as it does not change the outcome. In the House, members are prohibited from changing votes if they were tallied by the electronic voting system.

Cosponsor — *(See bills introduced.)*

Current services estimates — Estimated budget authority and outlays for federal programs and operations for the forthcoming fiscal year based on continuation of existing levels of service without policy changes but with adjustments for inflation and for demographic changes that affect programs. These estimates, accompanied by the underlying economic and policy assumptions upon which they are based, are transmitted by the president to Congress when the budget is submitted.

Custody of the papers — To reconcile differences between the House and Senate versions of a bill, a conference may be arranged. The chamber with "custody of the papers" — the engrossed bill, engrossed amendments, messages of transmittal — is the only body empowered to request the conference. By custom, the chamber that asks for a conference is the last to act on the conference report.

Custody of the papers sometimes is manipulated to ensure that a particular chamber acts either first or last on the conference report. *(Also see conference.)*

Deferral — Executive branch action to defer, or delay, the spending of appropriated money. The 1974 Congressional Budget and Impoundment Control Act requires a special message from the president to Congress reporting a proposed deferral of spending. Deferrals may not extend beyond the end of the fiscal year in which the message is transmitted. A federal district court in 1986 struck down the president's authority to defer spending for policy reasons; the ruling was upheld by a federal appeals court in 1987. Congress can prohibit proposed deferrals by enacting a law doing so; most often, cancellations of proposed deferrals are included in appropriations bills. *(Also see rescission.)*

Dilatory motion — A motion made for the purpose of killing time and preventing action on a bill or amendment. House rules outlaw dilatory motions, but enforcement is largely within the discretion of the Speaker or chairman of the Committee of the Whole. The Senate does not have a rule barring dilatory motions except under cloture.

Discharge a committee — Occasionally, attempts are made to relieve a committee of jurisdiction over a bill that is before it. This is attempted more often in the House than in the Senate, and the procedure rarely is successful.

In the House, if a committee does not report a bill within 30 days after the measure is referred to it, any member may file a discharge motion. Once offered, the motion is treated as a petition needing the signatures of a majority of members (218 if there are no vacancies). After the required signatures have been obtained, there is a delay of seven days.

Thereafter, on the second and fourth Mondays of each month, except during the last six days of a session, any member who has signed the petition must be recognized, if he or she so desires, to move that the committee be discharged. Debate on the motion to discharge is limited to 20 minutes. If the motion is carried, consideration of the bill becomes a matter of high privilege.

If a resolution to consider a bill is held up in the Rules Committee for more than seven legislative days, any member may enter a motion to discharge the committee. The motion is handled like any other discharge petition in the House. Occasionally, to expedite non-controversial legislative business, a committee is discharged by unanimous consent of the House, and a petition is not required. In 1993, the signatures on pending discharge petitions — previously kept secret — were made a matter of public record. *(For Senate procedure, see discharge resolution.)*

Discharge Calendar — The House calendar to which motions to discharge committees are referred when they have the required number of signatures (218) and are awaiting floor action. *(Also see calendar.)*

Discharge petition — *(See discharge a committee.)*

Discharge resolution — In the Senate, a special motion that any senator may introduce to relieve a committee from consideration of a bill before it. The resolution can be called up for Senate approval or disapproval in the same manner as any other Senate business. *(For House procedure, see discharge a committee.)*

Discretionary spending caps — *(See budget process.)*

Division of a question for voting — A practice that is more common in the Senate but also used in the House whereby a member may demand a division of an amendment or a motion for purposes of voting. Where an amendment or motion can be divided, the individual parts are voted on separately when a member demands a division. This procedure occurs most often during the consideration of conference reports.

Enacting clause — Key phrase in bills beginning, "Be it enacted by the Senate and House of Representatives . . ." A successful motion to strike it from legislation kills the measure.

Engrossed bill — The final copy of a bill as passed by one chamber, with the text as amended by floor action and certified by the clerk of the House or the secretary of the Senate.

Enrolled bill — The final copy of a bill that has been passed in identical form by both chambers. It is certified by an officer of the chamber of origin (clerk of the House or secretary of the Senate) and then sent on for the signatures of the House Speaker, the Senate president pro tempore and the president of the United States. An enrolled bill is printed on parchment.

Entitlement program — A federal program that guarantees a certain level of benefits to people or other entities who meet requirements set by law. Examples include Social Security and unemployment benefits. Some entitlements have permanent appropriations; others are funded under annual appropriations bills. In either case, it is mandatory for Congress to provide the money.

Executive Calendar — A non-legislative calendar in the Senate that lists presidential documents such as treaties and nominations. *(Also see calendar.)*

Executive document — A document, usually a treaty, sent to the Senate by the president for consideration or approval. Executive documents are referred to committee in the same manner as other measures. Unlike legislative documents, treaties do not die at the end of a Congress but remain "live" proposals until acted on by the Senate or withdrawn by the president.

Executive session — A meeting of a Senate or House committee (or occasionally of either chamber) that only its members may attend. Witnesses regularly appear at committee meetings in executive session — for example, Defense Department officials during presentations of classified defense information. Other members of Congress may be invited, but the public and news media are not allowed to attend.

Filibuster — A time-delaying tactic associated with the Senate and used by a minority in an effort to prevent a vote on a bill or amendment that probably would pass if voted upon directly. The most common method is to take advantage of the Senate's rules permitting unlimited debate, but other forms of parliamentary maneuvering may be used.

The stricter rules of the House make filibusters more difficult, but delaying tactics are employed occasionally through various procedural devices allowed by House rules. (*Also see cloture.*)

Fiscal year — Financial operations of the government are carried out in a 12-month fiscal year, beginning on Oct. 1 and ending on Sept. 30. The fiscal year carries the date of the calendar year in which it ends. (From fiscal 1844 to fiscal 1976, the fiscal year began July 1 and ended the following June 30.)

Five-minute rule — A debate-limiting rule of the House that is invoked when the House sits as the Committee of the Whole. Under the rule, a member offering an amendment and a member opposing it are each allowed to speak for five minutes. Debate is then closed. In practice, amendments regularly are debated for more than 10 minutes, with members gaining the floor by offering pro forma amendments or obtaining unanimous consent to speak longer than five minutes. (*Also see Committee of the Whole, hour rule, strike out the last word.*)

Floor manager — A member who has the task of steering legislation through floor debate and amendment to a final vote in the House or the Senate. Floor managers usually are chairmen or ranking members of the committee that reported the bill. Managers are responsible for apportioning the debate time granted to supporters of the bill. The ranking minority member of the committee normally apportions time for the minority party's participation in the debate.

Frank — A member's facsimile signature, which is used on envelopes in lieu of stamps for the member's official outgoing mail. The "franking privilege" is the right to send mail postage-free.

Germane — Pertaining to the subject matter of the measure at hand. All House amendments must be germane to the bill being considered. The Senate requires that amendments be germane when they are proposed to general appropriations bills or to bills being considered once cloture has been adopted or, frequently, when the Senate is proceeding under a unanimous consent agreement placing a time limit on consideration of a bill. The 1974 budget act also requires that amendments to concurrent budget resolutions be germane.

In the House, floor debate must be germane, and the first three hours of debate each day in the Senate must be germane to the pending business.

Gramm-Rudman-Hollings Deficit Reduction Act — (*See sequester.*)

Grandfather clause — A provision that exempts people or other entities already engaged in an activity from rules or legislation affecting that activity.

Hearings — Committee sessions for taking testimony from witnesses. At hearings on legislation, witnesses usually include specialists, government officials and spokesmen for individuals or entities affected by the bill or bills under study. Hearings related to special investigations bring forth a variety of witnesses. Committees sometimes use their subpoena power to summon reluctant witnesses. The public and news media may attend open hearings but are barred from closed, or "executive," hearings. The vast majority of hearings are open to the public. (*Also see executive session.*)

Hold-harmless clause — A provision added to legislation to ensure that recipients of federal funds do not receive less in a future year than they did in the current year if a new formula for allocating funds authorized in the legislation would result in a reduction to the recipients. This clause has been used most often to soften the impact of sudden reductions in federal grants.

Hopper — Box on House clerk's desk into which members deposit bills and resolutions to introduce them.

Hour rule — A provision in the rules of the House that permits one hour of debate time for each member on amendments debated in the House of Representatives sitting as the House. Therefore, the House normally amends bills while sitting as the Committee of the Whole, where the five-minute rule on amendments operates.

House as in the Committee of the Whole — A procedure that can be used to expedite consideration of certain measures such as continuing resolutions and, when there is debate, private bills. The procedure can be invoked only with the unanimous consent of the House or a rule from the Rules Committee and has procedural elements of both the House sitting as the House of Representatives, such as the Speaker presiding and the previous question motion being in order, and the House sitting as the Committee of the Whole, with the five-minute rule being in order. (*See Committee of the Whole.*)

House Calendar — A listing for action by the House of public bills that do not directly or indirectly appropriate money or raise revenue. (*Also see calendar.*)

Immunity — The constitutional privilege of members of Congress to make verbal statements on the floor and in committee for which they cannot be sued or arrested for slander or libel. Also, freedom from arrest while traveling to or from sessions of Congress or on official business. Members in this status may only be arrested for treason, felonies or a breach of the peace, as defined by congressional manuals.

Joint committee — A committee composed of a specified number of members of both the House and Senate. A joint committee may be investigative or research-oriented, an example of the latter being the Joint Economic Committee. Others have housekeeping duties; examples include the joint committees on Printing and on the Library of Congress.

Joint resolution — Like a bill, a joint resolution, designated H J Res or S J Res, requires the approval of both chambers and the signature of the president, and has the force of law if approved. There is no practical difference between a bill and a joint resolution. A joint resolution generally is used to deal with a limited matter such as a single appropriation.

Joint resolutions are also used to propose amendments to the Constitution. In that case they require a two-thirds majority in both chambers. They do not require a presidential signature, but they must be ratified by three-fourths of the states to become a part of the Constitution. *(Also see concurrent resolution, resolution.)*

Journal — The official record of the proceedings of the House and Senate. The Journal records the actions taken in each chamber, but, unlike the Congressional Record, it does not include the substantially verbatim report of speeches, debates, statements and the like.

Law — An act of Congress that has been signed by the president or passed, over his veto, by Congress. Public bills, when signed, become public laws and are cited by the letters PL and a hyphenated number. The number before the hyphen corresponds to the Congress, and the one or more digits after the hyphen refer to the numerical sequence in which the president signed the bills during that Congress. Private bills, when signed, become private laws. *(Also see bills, private bills.)*

Legislative day — The "day" extending from the time either chamber meets after an adjournment until the time it next adjourns. Because the House normally adjourns from day to day, legislative days and calendar days usually coincide. But in the Senate, a legislative day may, and frequently does, extend over several calendar days. *(Also see recess.)*

Line-item veto — Presidential authority to strike individual items from appropriations bills, which presidents since Ulysses S. Grant have sought. Congress gave the president a form of the power in 1996 (PL 104-130), but this "enhanced rescission authority" was struck down by the Supreme Court in 1998 as unconstitutional because it allowed the president to change laws on his own.

Loan guarantees — Loans to third parties for which the federal government guarantees the repayment of principal or interest, in whole or in part, to the lender in the event of default.

Lobby — A group seeking to influence the passage or defeat of legislation. Originally the term referred to people frequenting the lobbies or corridors of legislative chambers to speak to lawmakers.

The definition of a lobby and the activity of lobbying is a matter of differing interpretation. By some definitions, lobbying is limited to direct attempts to influence lawmakers through personal interviews and persuasion. Under other definitions, lobbying includes attempts at indirect, or "grass-roots," influence, such as persuading members of a group to write or visit their district's representative and state's senators or attempting to create a climate of opinion favorable to a desired legislative goal.

The right to attempt to influence legislation is based on the First Amendment to the Constitution, which says Congress shall make no law abridging the right of the people "to petition the government for a redress of grievances."

Majority leader — Floor leader for the majority party in each chamber. In the Senate, in consultation with the minority leader, the majority leader directs the legislative schedule for the chamber. He or she is also his party's spokesperson and chief strategist. In the House, the majority leader is second to the Speaker in the majority party's leadership and serves as the party's legislative strategist. *(Also see Speaker, whip.)*

Manual — The official handbook in each chamber prescribing in detail its organization, procedures and operations.

Marking up a bill — Going through the contents of a piece of legislation in committee or subcommittee to, for example, consider the provisions, act on amendments to provisions and proposed revisions to the language, and insert new sections and phraseology. If the bill is extensively amended, the committee's version may be introduced as a separate (or "clean") bill, with a new number, before being considered by the full House or Senate. *(Also see clean bill.)*

Minority leader — Floor leader for the minority party in each chamber.

Morning hour — The time set aside at the beginning of each legislative day for the consideration of regular, routine business. The "hour" is of indefinite duration in the House, where it is rarely used. In the Senate, it is the first two hours of a session following an adjournment, as distinguished from a recess. The morning hour can be terminated earlier if the morning business has been completed.

Business includes such matters as messages from the president, communications from the heads of departments, messages from the House, the presentation of petitions, reports of standing and select committees and the introduction of bills and resolutions.

During the first hour of the morning hour in the Senate, no motion to proceed to the consideration of any bill on the calendar is in order except by unanimous consent. During the second hour, motions can be made but must be decided without debate. Senate committees may meet while the Senate conducts the morning hour.

Motion — In the House or Senate chamber, a request by a member to institute any one of a wide array of parliamentary actions. He or she "moves" for a certain procedure, such as the consideration of a measure. The precedence of motions, and whether they are debatable, is set forth in the House and Senate manuals.

Nominations — Presidential appointments to office subject to Senate confirmation. Although most nominations win quick Senate approval, some are controversial and become the topic of hearings and debate. Sometimes senators object to appointees for patronage reasons — for example, when a nomination to a local federal job is made without consulting the senators of the state concerned. In some situations a senator may object that the nominee is "personally obnoxious" to him. Usually other senators join in blocking such appointments out of courtesy to their colleagues. *(Also see senatorial courtesy.)*

One-minute speeches — Addresses by House members at the beginning of a legislative day. The speeches may cover any subject but are limited to one minute's duration.

Outlays — Actual spending that flows from the liquidation of budget authority. Outlays associated with appropriations bills and other legislation are estimates of future spending made by the Congressional Budget Office (CBO) and the White House's Office of Management and Budget (OMB). CBO's estimates govern bills for the purpose of congressional floor debate, while OMB's numbers govern when it comes to determining whether legislation exceeds spending caps.

Outlays in a given fiscal year may result from budget authority provided in the current year or in previous years. *(Also see budget authority, budget process.)*

Override a veto — If the president vetoes a bill and sends it back to Congress with his objections, Congress may try to override his veto and enact the bill into law. Neither chamber is required to attempt to override a veto. The override of a veto requires a recorded vote with a two-thirds majority of those present and voting in each chamber. The question put to each chamber is: "Shall the bill pass, the objections of the president to the contrary notwithstanding?" *(Also see pocket veto, veto.)*

Oversight committee — A congressional committee or designated subcommittee that is charged with general oversight of one or more federal agencies' programs and activities. Usually, the oversight panel for a particular agency is also the authorizing committee for that agency's programs and operations.

Pair — A voluntary, informal arrangement that two lawmakers, usually on opposite sides of an issue, make on recorded votes. In many cases the result is to subtract a vote from each side, with no effect on the outcome.

Pairs are not authorized in the rules of either chamber, are not counted in tabulating the final result and have no official standing. However, members pairing are identified in the Congressional Record, along with their positions on such votes, if known. A member who expects to be absent for a vote can pair with a member who plans to vote, with the latter agreeing to withhold his or her vote.

There are three types of pairs:

(1) A live pair involves a member who is present for a vote and another who is absent. The member in attendance votes and then withdraws the vote, announcing that he or she has a live pair with colleague "X" and stating how the two members would have voted, one in favor, the other opposed. A live pair may affect the outcome of a closely contested vote, since it subtracts one "yea" or one "nay" from the final tally. A live pair may cover one or several specific issues.

(2) A general pair, widely used in the House, does not entail any arrangement between two members and does not affect the vote. Members who expect to be absent notify the clerk that they wish to make a general pair. Each member then is paired with another desiring a pair, and their names are listed in the Congressional Record. The member may or may not be paired with another taking the opposite position, and no indication of how the members would have voted is given.

(3) A specific pair is similar to a general pair, except that the opposing stands of the two members are identified and printed in the Congressional Record.

Pay-as-you go (PAYGO) rules — *(See budget process.)*

Petition — A request or plea sent to one or both chambers from an organization or private citizens' group seeking support for particular legislation or favorable consideration of a matter not yet receiving congressional attention. Petitions are referred to appropriate committees. In the House, a petition signed by a majority of members (218) can discharge a bill from a committee. *(Also see discharge a committee.)*

Pocket veto — The act of the president in withholding his approval of a bill after Congress has adjourned. When Congress is in session, a bill becomes law without the president's signature if he does not act upon it within 10 days, excluding Sundays, from the time he receives it. But if Congress adjourns sine die within that 10-day period, the bill will die even if the president does not formally veto it.

The Supreme Court in 1986 agreed to decide whether the president could pocket veto a bill during recesses and between sessions of the same Congress or only between Congresses. The justices in 1987 declared the case moot, however, because the bill in question was invalid once the case reached the court. *(Also see adjournment sine die, veto.)*

Point of order — An objection raised by a member that the chamber is departing from rules governing its conduct of business. The objector cites the rule violated, with the chair sustaining his or her objection if correctly made. Order is restored by the chair's suspending proceedings of the chamber until it conforms to the prescribed "order of business."

Both chambers have procedures for overcoming a point of order, either by vote or, what is most common in the House, by including language in the rule for floor consideration that waives a point of order against a given bill. *(Also see rules.)*

President of the Senate — Under the Constitution, the vice president of the United States presides over the Senate. In his absence, the president pro tempore, or a senator designated by the president pro tempore, presides over the chamber.

President pro tempore — The chief officer of the Senate in the absence of the vice president — literally, but loosely, the president for a time. The president pro tempore is elected by his fellow senators. Recent practice has been to elect the senator of the majority party with the longest period of continuous service.

Previous question — A motion for the previous question, when carried, has the effect of cutting off all debate, preventing the offering of further amendments and forcing a vote on the pending matter. In the House, a motion for the previous question is not permitted in the Committee of the Whole, unless a rule governing debate provides otherwise. The motion for the previous question is a debate-limiting device and is not in order in the Senate.

Printed amendment — A House rule guarantees five minutes of floor debate in support and five minutes in opposition, and no other debate time, on amendments printed in the Congressional Record at least one day prior to the amendment's consideration in the Committee of the Whole.

In the Senate, while amendments may be submitted for printing, they have no parliamentary standing or status. An amendment submitted for printing in the Senate, however, may be called up by any senator.

Private bill — A bill dealing with individual matters such as claims against the government, immigration or land titles. When a private bill is before the chamber, two members may block its consideration, thereby recommitting the bill to committee. The backers still have recourse, however. The measure can be put into an "omnibus claims bill" — several private bills rolled into one. As with any bill, no part of an omnibus claims bill may be deleted without a vote. When the private bill goes back to the House floor in this form, it can be deleted from the omnibus bill only by majority vote.

Private Calendar — The House calendar for private bills. The Private Calendar must be called on the first Tuesday of each month, and the Speaker may call it on the third Tuesday of each month as well. *(Also see calendar, private bill.)*

Privileged questions — The order in which bills, motions and other legislative measures are considered on the floor of the Senate and House is governed by strict priorities. A motion to table, for instance, is more privileged than a motion to recommit. Thus, if a member moves to recommit a bill to committee for further consideration, another member can supersede the first action by moving to table it, and a vote will occur first on the motion to table (or kill) the motion to recommit. A motion to adjourn is considered "of the highest privilege" and must be considered before virtually any other motion.

Congress and Its Members

Pro forma amendment — (*See strike out the last word.*)

Public Laws — (*See law.*)

Questions of privilege — These are matters affecting members of Congress individually or collectively. Matters affecting the rights, safety, dignity and integrity of proceedings of the House or Senate as a whole are questions of privilege in both chambers.

Questions involving individual members are called questions of "personal privilege." A member rising to ask a question of personal privilege is given precedence over almost all other proceedings. For instance, if a member feels that he or she has been improperly impugned in comments by another member, he or she can immediately demand to be heard on the floor on a question of personal privilege. An annotation in the House rules points out that the privilege rests primarily on the Constitution, which gives members a conditional immunity from arrest and an unconditional freedom to speak in the House.

In 1993, the House changed its rules to allow the Speaker to delay for two legislative days the floor consideration of a question of the privileges of the House unless it is offered by the majority leader or minority leader.

Quorum — The number of members whose presence is necessary for the transaction of business. In the Senate and House, it is a majority of the membership. In the Committee of the Whole House, a quorum is 100. If a point of order is made that a quorum is not present, the only business that is in order is either a motion to adjourn or a motion to direct the sergeant-at-arms to request the attendance of absentees. In practice, however, both chambers conduct much of their business without a quorum present. (*Also see Committee of the Whole House.*)

Reading of bills — Traditional parliamentary procedure required bills to be read three times before they were passed. This custom is of little modern significance. Normally a bill is considered to have its first reading when it is introduced and printed, by title, in the Congressional Record. In the House, a bill's second reading comes when floor consideration begins. (The actual reading of a bill is most likely to occur at this point, if at all.) The second reading in the Senate is supposed to occur on the legislative day after the measure is introduced, but before it is referred to committee. The third reading (again, usually by title) takes place when floor action has been completed on amendments.

Recess — A recess, as distinguished from adjournment, does not end a legislative day and therefore does not interrupt unfinished business. (The rules in each chamber set forth certain matters to be taken up and disposed of at the beginning of each legislative day.) The House usually adjourns from day to day. The Senate often recesses, thus meeting on the same legislative day for several calendar days or even weeks at a time.

Recognition — The power of recognition of a member is lodged in the Speaker of the House and the presiding officer of the Senate. The presiding officer names the member to speak first when two or more members simultaneously request recognition. The order of recognition is governed by precedents and tradition for many situations. In the Senate, for instance, the majority leader has the right to be recognized first.

Recommit to committee — A motion, made on the floor after a bill has been debated, to return it to the committee that reported it. If approved, recommittal usually is considered a death blow to the bill. In the House, the right to offer a motion to recommit is guaranteed to the minority leader or someone he or she designates.

A motion to recommit may include instructions to the committee to report the bill again with specific amendments or by a certain date. Or the instructions may direct that a particular study be made, with no definite deadline for further action.

If the recommittal motion includes instructions to "report the bill back forthwith" and the motion is adopted, floor action on the bill continues with the changes directed by the instructions automatically incorporated into the bill; the committee does not actually reconsider the legislation.

Reconciliation — The 1974 budget act created a "reconciliation" procedure for bringing existing tax and spending laws into conformity with ceilings set in the congressional budget resolution. Under the procedure, the budget resolution sets specific deficit-reduction targets and instructs tax-writing and authorizing committees to propose changes in existing law to meet those targets. Those recommendations are consolidated without change by the Budget committees into an omnibus reconciliation bill, which then must be considered and approved by both chambers of Congress.

Special rules in the Senate limit debate on a reconciliation bill to 20 hours and bar extraneous or non-germane amendments. (*Also see budget resolution, sequester.*)

Reconsider a vote — Until it is disposed of, a motion to reconsider the vote by which an action was taken has the effect of putting the action in abeyance. In the Senate, the motion can be made only by a member who voted on the prevailing side of the original question or by a member who did not vote at all. In the House, it can be made only by a member on the prevailing side.

A common practice in the Senate after close votes on an issue is a motion to reconsider, followed by a motion to table the motion to reconsider. On this motion to table, senators vote as they voted on the original question, which allows the motion to table to prevail, assuming there are no switches. That closes the matter, and further motions to reconsider are not entertained.

In the House, as a routine precaution, a motion to reconsider usually is made every time a measure is passed. Such a motion almost always is tabled immediately, thus shutting off the possibility of future reconsideration except by unanimous consent.

Motions to reconsider must be entered in the Senate within the next two days the Senate is in session after the original vote has been taken. In the House, they must be entered either on the same day or on the next succeeding day the House is in session. Sometimes on a close vote, a member will switch his or her vote to be eligible to offer a motion to reconsider.

Recorded vote — A vote upon which each member's stand is individually made known. In the Senate, this is accomplished through a roll call of the entire membership, to which each senator on the floor must answer "yea," "nay" or "present." Since January 1973, the House has used an electronic voting system for recorded votes, including yea-and-nay votes formerly taken by roll calls.

When not required by the Constitution, a recorded vote can be obtained on questions in the House on the demand of one-fifth (44 members) of a quorum or one-fourth (25) of a quorum in the Committee of the Whole. Recorded votes are required in the House for appropriations, budget and tax bills. (*Also see yeas and nays.*)

Report — Both a verb and a noun as a congressional term. A committee that has been examining a bill referred to it by the parent chamber "reports" its findings and recommendations to the chamber when it completes consideration and returns the measure. The process is called "reporting" a bill. In some cases, a bill is reported without a written report.

A "report" is the document setting forth the committee's explanation of its action. Senate and House reports are numbered separately and are designated S Rept or H Rept. When a committee report is not unanimous, the dissenting committee members may file a statement of their views, called minority or dissenting views and referred to as a minority report. Members in disagreement with some provisions of a bill may file additional or supplementary views. Sometimes a bill is reported without a committee recommendation.

Legislative committees occasionally submit adverse reports. However, when a committee is opposed to a bill, it usually fails to report the bill at all. Some laws require that committee reports — favorable or adverse — be made.

Rescission — Cancellation of budget authority that was previously appropriated but has not yet been spent.

Resolution — A "simple" resolution, designated H Res or S Res, deals with matters entirely within the prerogatives of a single chamber. It requires neither passage by the other chamber nor approval by the president, and it does not have the force of law. Most resolutions deal with the rules or procedures of one chamber. They are also used to express the sentiments of a single chamber, such as condolences to the family of a deceased member, or to comment on foreign policy or executive business. A simple resolution is the vehicle for a "rule" from the House Rules Committee. *(Also see concurrent and joint resolutions, rules.)*

Rider — An amendment, usually not germane, that its sponsor hopes to get through more easily by including it in other legislation. A rider becomes law if the bill to which it is attached is enacted. Amendments providing legislative directives in appropriations bills are examples of riders, though technically legislation is banned from appropriations bills.

The House, unlike the Senate, has a strict germaneness rule; thus, riders usually are Senate devices to get legislation enacted quickly or to bypass lengthy House consideration and, possibly, opposition.

Rules — Each chamber has a body of rules and precedents that govern the conduct of business. These rules deal with issues such as duties of officers, the order of business, admission to the floor, parliamentary procedures on handling amendments and voting, and jurisdictions of committees. They are normally changed only at the start of each Congress.

In the House, a rule may also be a resolution reported by the Rules Committee to govern the handling of a particular bill on the floor. The committee may report a rule, also called a special order, in the form of a simple resolution. If the House adopts the resolution, the temporary rule becomes as valid as any standing rule and lapses only after action has been completed on the measure to which it pertains.

The rule sets the time limit on general debate. It may also waive points of order against provisions of the bill in question such as non-germane language or against certain amendments expected on the floor. It may even forbid all amendments or all amendments except those proposed by the legislative committee that handled the bill. In this instance, it is known as a "closed" rule as opposed to an "open" rule, which puts no limitation on floor amendments, thus leaving the bill completely open to alteration by the adoption of germane amendments. *(Also see point of order.)*

Secretary of the Senate — Chief administrative officer of the Senate, responsible for overseeing the duties of Senate employees, educating Senate pages, administering oaths, overseeing the registration of lobbyists and handling other tasks necessary for the continuing operation of the Senate. *(Also see Clerk of the House.)*

Select or special committee — A committee set up for a special purpose and, usually, for a limited time by resolution of either the House or Senate. Most special committees are investigative and lack legislative authority: Legislation is not referred to them, and they cannot report bills to their parent chambers. The House in 1993 terminated its four select committees.

Senatorial courtesy — A general practice with no written rule — sometimes referred to as "the courtesy of the Senate" — applied to consideration of executive nominations. Generally, it means that nominations from a state are not to be confirmed unless they have been approved by the senators of the president's party of that state, with other senators following their colleagues' lead in the attitude they take toward consideration of such nominations. *(Also see nominations.)*

Sequester — Automatic, across-the-board spending cuts, generally triggered after the close of a session by a report issued by the Office of Management and Budget. Under the 1985 Gramm-Rudman anti-deficit law, modified in 1987, a year-end sequester was triggered if the deficit exceeded a pre-set maximum. However, the Budget Enforcement Act of 1990, updated in 1993 and 1997, effectively replaced that procedure through fiscal 2002.

Instead, if Congress exceeds an annual cap on discretionary budget authority or outlays, a sequester is triggered for all eligible discretionary spending to make up the difference. If Congress violates pay-as-you-go rules by allowing the net effect of legislated changes in mandatory spending and taxes to increase the deficit, a sequester is triggered for all non-exempt entitlement programs. Similar procedures apply to supplemental appropriations bills. *(Also see budget process.)*

Sine die — *(See adjournment sine die.)*

Speaker — The presiding officer of the House of Representatives, selected by his party caucus and formally elected by the whole House. While both parties nominate candidates, choice by the majority party is tantamount to election. In 1995, House rules were changed to limit the Speaker to four consecutive terms.

Special session — A session of Congress after it has adjourned sine die, completing its regular session. Special sessions are convened by the president.

Spending authority — The 1974 budget act defines spending authority as borrowing authority, contract authority and entitlement authority for which budget authority is not provided in advance by appropriation acts.

Sponsor — *(See bills introduced.)*

Standing committees — Committees that are permanently established by House and Senate rules. The standing committees of the House were reorganized in 1974, with some changes in jurisdictions and titles made when Republicans took control of the House in 1995. The last major realignment of Senate committees was in 1977. The standing committees are legislative committees: Legislation may be referred to them, and they may report bills and resolutions to their parent chambers.

Standing vote — A non-recorded vote used in both the House and Senate. (A standing vote is also called a division vote.) Members in favor of a proposal stand and are counted by the presiding

Congress and Its Members

officer. Then members opposed stand and are counted. There is no record of how individual members voted.

Statutes at large — A chronological arrangement of the laws enacted in each session of Congress. Though indexed, the laws are not arranged by subject matter, and there is no indication of how they changed previously enacted laws. (*Also see law, U.S. Code.*)

Strike from the Record — A member of the House who is offended by remarks made on the House floor may move that the offending words be "taken down" for the Speaker's cognizance and then expunged from the debate as published in the Congressional Record.

Strike out the last word — A motion whereby a House member is entitled to speak for five minutes on an amendment then being debated by the chamber. A member gains recognition from the chair by moving to "strike out the last word" of the amendment or section of the bill under consideration. The motion is pro forma, requires no vote and does not change the amendment being debated. (*Also see five-minute rule.*)

Substitute — A motion, amendment or entire bill introduced in place of the pending legislative business. Passage of the substitute kills the original measure by supplanting it. The substitute may also be amended. (Also see amendment in the nature of a substitute.)

Supplemental appropriations bill — Legislation appropriating funds after the regular annual appropriations bill for a federal department or agency has been enacted. Supplemental appropriations bills often arrive about halfway through the fiscal year, when needs that Congress and the president did not anticipate (or may not have wanted to fund) become pressing. In recent years, supplementals have been driven by spending to help victims of natural disasters and to carry out peacekeeping commitments.

Suspend the rules — A time-saving procedure for passing bills in the House. The wording of the motion, which may be made by any member recognized by the Speaker, is: "I move to suspend the rules and pass the bill . . ." A favorable vote by two-thirds of those present is required for passage. Debate is limited to 40 minutes, and no amendments from the floor are permitted. If a two-thirds favorable vote is not attained, the bill may be considered later under regular procedures. The suspension procedure is in order every Monday and Tuesday and is intended to be reserved for non-controversial bills.

Table a bill — Motions to table, or to "lay on the table," are used to block or kill amendments or other parliamentary questions. When approved, a tabling motion is considered the final disposition of that issue. One of the most widely used parliamentary procedures, the motion to table is not debatable, and adoption requires a simple majority vote.

In the Senate, however, different language sometimes is used. The motion may be worded to let a bill "lie on the table," perhaps for subsequent "picking up." This motion is more flexible, keeping the bill pending for later action, if desired. Tabling motions on amendments are effective debate-ending devices in the Senate.

Treaties — Executive proposals — in the form of resolutions of ratification — which must be submitted to the Senate for approval by two-thirds of the senators present. Treaties are normally sent to the Foreign Relations Committee for scrutiny before the Senate takes action. Foreign Relations has jurisdiction over all treaties, regardless of the subject matter. Treaties are read three times and debated on the floor in much the same manner as legislative proposals. After approval by the Senate, treaties are formally ratified by the president.

Trust funds — Funds collected and used by the federal government for carrying out specific purposes and programs according to terms of a trust agreement or statute such as the Social Security and unemployment compensation trust funds. Such funds are administered by the government in a fiduciary capacity and are not available for the general purposes of the government.

Unanimous consent — A procedure used to expedite floor action. Proceedings of the House or Senate and action on legislation often take place upon the unanimous consent of the chamber, whether or not a rule of the chamber is being violated. It is frequently used in a routine fashion, such as by a senator requesting the unanimous consent of the Senate to have specified members of his or her staff present on the floor during debate on a specific amendment. A single member's objection blocks a unanimous consent request.

Unanimous consent agreement — A device used in the Senate to expedite legislation. Much of the Senate's legislative business, dealing with both minor and controversial issues, is conducted through unanimous consent or unanimous consent agreements. On major legislation, such agreements usually are printed and transmitted to all senators in advance of floor debate. Once agreed to, they are binding on all members unless the Senate, by unanimous consent, agrees to modify them. An agreement may list the order in which various bills are to be considered; specify the length of time for debate on bills and contested amendments and when they are to be voted upon; and, frequently, require that all amendments introduced be germane to the bill under consideration.

In this regard, unanimous consent agreements are similar to the "rules" issued by the House Rules Committee for bills pending in the House.

Union Calendar — Bills that directly or indirectly appropriate money or raise revenue are placed on this House calendar according to the date they are reported from committee. (*Also see calendar.*)

U.S. Code — A consolidation and codification of the general and permanent laws of the United States arranged by subject under 50 titles, the first six dealing with general or political subjects, and the other 44 alphabetically arranged from agriculture to war. The U.S. Code is updated annually, and a new set of bound volumes is published every six years. (Also see law, statutes at large.)

Veto — Disapproval by the president of a bill or joint resolution (other than one proposing an amendment to the Constitution). When Congress is in session, the president must veto a bill within 10 days, excluding Sundays, after he has received it; otherwise, it becomes law without his signature. When the president vetoes a bill, he returns it to the chamber of origin along with a message stating his objections. (*Also see pocket veto, override a veto.*)

Voice vote — In either the House or Senate, members answer "aye" or "no" in chorus, and the presiding officer decides the result. The term is also used loosely to indicate action by unanimous consent or without objection. (Also see yeas and nays.)

Whip — In effect, the assistant majority or minority leader, in either the House or Senate. His or her job is to help marshal votes in support of party strategy and legislation.

Glossary

Without objection — Used in lieu of a vote on non-controversial motions, amendments or bills that may be passed in either chamber if no member voices an objection.

Yeas and nays — The Constitution requires that yea-and-nay votes be taken and recorded when requested by one-fifth of the members present. In the House, the Speaker determines whether one-fifth of the members present requested a vote. In the Senate, practice requires only 11 members. The Constitution requires the yeas and nays on a veto override attempt. *(Also see recorded vote.)*

Yielding — When a member has been recognized to speak, no other member may speak unless he or she obtains permission from the member recognized. This permission is called yielding and usually is requested in the form, "Will the gentleman (or gentlelady) yield to me?" While this activity occasionally is seen in the Senate, the Senate has no rule or practice to parcel out time.

In the House, the floor manager of a bill usually apportions debate time by yielding specific amounts of time to members who have requested it. ◆

Congress and Its Members

Members of the 105th Congress, 2nd Session . . .

(As of Dec. 19, 1998, when the second session of the 105th Congress adjourned sine die.)

Representatives
R 228; D 206; I 1;
2 vacancies

— A —

Abercrombie, Neil, D-Hawaii (1)
Ackerman, Gary L., D-N.Y. (5)
Aderholt, Robert B., R-Ala. (4)
Allen, Tom, D-Maine (1)
Andrews, Robert E., D-N.J. (1)
Archer, Bill, R-Texas (7)
Armey, Dick, R-Texas (26)

— B —

Bachus, Spencer, R-Ala. (6)
Baesler, Scotty, D-Ky. (6)
Baker, Richard H., R-La. (6)
Baldacci, John, D-Maine (2)
Ballenger, Cass, R-N.C. (10)
Barcia, James A., D-Mich. (5)
Barr, Bob, R-Ga. (7)
Barrett, Bill, R-Neb. (3)
Barrett, Thomas M., D-Wis. (5)
Bartlett, Roscoe G., R-Md. (6)
Barton, Joe L., R-Texas (6)
Bass, Charles, R-N.H. (2)
Bateman, Herbert H., R-Va. (1)
Becerra, Xavier, D-Calif. (30)
Bentsen, Ken, D-Texas (25)
Bereuter, Doug, R-Neb. (1)
Berman, Howard L., D-Calif. (26)
Berry, Marion, D-Ark. (1)
Bilbray, Brian P., R-Calif. (49)
Bilirakis, Michael, R-Fla. (9)
Bishop, Sanford D. Jr., D-Ga. (2)
Blagojevich, Rod R., D-Ill. (5)
Bliley, Thomas J. Jr., R-Va. (7)
Blumenauer, Earl, D-Ore. (3)
Blunt, Roy, R-Mo. (7)
Boehlert, Sherwood, R-N.Y. (23)
Boehner, John A., R-Ohio (8)
Bonilla, Henry, R-Texas (23)
Bonior, David E., D-Mich. (10)
Bono, Mary, R-Calif. (44)
Borski, Robert A., D-Pa. (3)
Boswell, Leonard L., D-Iowa (3)
Boucher, Rick, D-Va. (9)
Boyd, Allen, D-Fla. (2)
Brady, Kevin, R-Texas (8)
Brady, Robert A., D-Pa. (1)
Brown, Corrine, D-Fla. (3)
Brown, George E. Jr., D-Calif. (42)
Brown, Sherrod, D-Ohio (13)
Bryant, Ed, R-Tenn. (7)
Bunning, Jim, R-Ky. (4)
Burr, Richard M., R-N.C. (5)
Burton, Dan, R-Ind. (6)
Buyer, Steve, R-Ind. (5)

— C —

Callahan, Sonny, R-Ala. (1)
Calvert, Ken, R-Calif. (43)
Camp, Dave, R-Mich. (4)
Campbell, Tom, R-Calif. (15)
Canady, Charles T., R-Fla. (12)
Cannon, Christopher B., R-Utah (3)
Capps, Lois, D-Calif. (22)
Cardin, Benjamin L., D-Md. (3)
Carson, Julia, D-Ind. (10)
Castle, Michael N., R-Del. (AL)
Chabot, Steve, R-Ohio (1)
Chambliss, Saxby, R-Ga. (8)
Chenoweth, Helen, R-Idaho (1)
Christensen, Jon, R-Neb. (2)
Clay, William L., D-Mo. (1)
Clayton, Eva, D-N.C. (1)
Clement, Bob, D-Tenn. (5)
Clyburn, James E., D-S.C. (6)
Coble, Howard, R-N.C. (6)
Coburn, Tom, R-Okla. (2)
Collins, Mac, R-Ga. (3)
Combest, Larry, R-Texas (19)
Condit, Gary A., D-Calif. (18)
Conyers, John Jr., D-Mich. (14)
Cook, Merrill, R-Utah (2)
Cooksey, John, R-La. (5)
Costello, Jerry F., D-Ill. (12)
Cox, Christopher, R-Calif. (47)
Coyne, William J., D-Pa. (14)
Cramer, Robert E. "Bud," D-Ala. (5)
Crane, Philip M., R-Ill. (8)
Crapo, Michael D., R-Idaho (2)
Cubin, Barbara, R-Wyo. (AL)
Cummings, Elijah E., D-Md. (7)
Cunningham, Randy "Duke," R-Calif. (51)

— D —

Danner, Pat, D-Mo. (6)
Davis, Danny K., D-Ill. (7)
Davis, Jim, D-Fla. (11)
Davis, Thomas M. III, R-Va. (11)
Deal, Nathan, R-Ga. (9)
DeFazio, Peter A., D-Ore. (4)
DeGette, Diana, D-Colo. (1)
Delahunt, Bill, D-Mass. (10)
DeLauro, Rosa, D-Conn. (3)
DeLay, Tom, R-Texas (22)
Deutsch, Peter, D-Fla. (20)
Diaz-Balart, Lincoln, R-Fla. (21)
Dickey, Jay, R-Ark. (4)
Dicks, Norm, D-Wash. (6)
Dingell, John D., D-Mich. (16)
Dixon, Julian C., D-Calif. (32)
Doggett, Lloyd, D-Texas (10)
Dooley, Cal, D-Calif. (20)
Doolittle, John T., R-Calif. (4)
Doyle, Mike, D-Pa. (18)
Dreier, David, R-Calif. (28)
Duncan, John J. "Jimmy" Jr., R-Tenn. (2)
Dunn, Jennifer, R-Wash. (8)

— E —

Edwards, Chet, D-Texas (11)
Ehlers, Vernon J., R-Mich. (3)
Ehrlich, Robert L. Jr., R-Md. (2)
Emerson, Jo Ann, R-Mo. (8)
Engel, Eliot L., D-N.Y. (17)
English, Phil, R-Pa. (21)
Ensign, John, R-Nev. (1)
Eshoo, Anna G., D-Calif. (14)
Etheridge, Bob, D-N.C. (2)
Evans, Lane, D-Ill. (17)
Everett, Terry, R-Ala. (2)
Ewing, Thomas W., R-Ill. (15)

— F —

Farr, Sam, D-Calif. (17)
Fattah, Chaka, D-Pa. (2)
Fawell, Harris W., R-Ill. (13)
Fazio, Vic, D-Calif. (3)
Filner, Bob, D-Calif. (50)
Foley, Mark, R-Fla. (16)
Forbes, Michael P., R-N.Y. (1)
Ford, Harold E. Jr., D-Tenn. (9)
Fossella, Vito J., R-N.Y. (13)
Fowler, Tillie, R-Fla. (4)
Fox, Jon D., R-Pa. (13)
Frank, Barney, D-Mass. (4)
Franks, Bob, R-N.J. (7)
Frelinghuysen, Rodney, R-N.J. (11)
Frost, Martin, D-Texas (24)
Furse, Elizabeth, D-Ore. (1)

— G —

Gallegly, Elton, R-Calif. (23)
Ganske, Greg, R-Iowa (4)
Gejdenson, Sam, D-Conn. (2)
Gekas, George W., R-Pa. (17)
Gephardt, Richard A., D-Mo. (3)
Gibbons, Jim, R-Nev. (2)
Gilchrest, Wayne T., R-Md. (1)
Gillmor, Paul E., R-Ohio (5)
Gilman, Benjamin A., R-N.Y. (20)
Gingrich, Newt, R-Ga. (6)
Gonzalez, Henry B., D-Texas (20)
Goode, Virgil H. Jr., D-Va. (5)
Goodlatte, Robert W., R-Va. (6)
Goodling, Bill, R-Pa. (19)
Gordon, Bart, D-Tenn. (6)
Goss, Porter J., R-Fla. (14)
Graham, Lindsey, R-S.C. (3)
Granger, Kay, R-Texas (12)

Green, Gene, D-Texas (29)
Greenwood, James C., R-Pa. (8)
Gutierrez, Luis V., D-Ill. (4)
Gutknecht, Gil, R-Minn. (1)

— H —

Hall, Ralph M., D-Texas (4)
Hall, Tony P., D-Ohio (3)
Hamilton, Lee H., D-Ind. (9)
Hansen, James V., R-Utah (1)
Harman, Jane, D-Calif. (36)
Hastert, Dennis, R-Ill. (14)
Hastings, Alcee L., D-Fla. (23)
Hastings, Richard "Doc", R-Wash. (4)
Hayworth, J.D., R-Ariz. (6)
Hefley, Joel, R-Colo. (5)
Hefner, W.G. "Bill," D-N.C. (8)
Herger, Wally, R-Calif. (2)
Hill, Rick, R-Mont. (AL)
Hilleary, Van, R-Tenn. (4)
Hilliard, Earl F., D-Ala. (7)
Hinchey, Maurice D., D-N.Y. (26)
Hinojosa, Rubén, D-Texas (15)
Hobson, David L., R-Ohio (7)
Hoekstra, Peter, R-Mich. (2)
Holden, Tim, D-Pa. (6)
Hooley, Darlene, D-Ore. (5)
Horn, Steve, R-Calif. (38)
Hostettler, John, R-Ind. (8)
Houghton, Amo, R-N.Y. (31)
Hoyer, Steny H., D-Md. (5)
Hulshof, Kenny, R-Mo. (9)
Hunter, Duncan, R-Calif. (52)
Hutchinson, Asa, R-Ark. (3)
Hyde, Henry J., R-Ill. (6)

— I —

Inglis, Bob, R-S.C. (4)
Istook, Ernest, R-Okla. (5)

— J —

Jackson, Jesse Jr., D-Ill. (2)
Jackson-Lee, Sheila, D-Texas (18)
Jefferson, William J., D-La. (2)
Jenkins, Bill, R-Tenn. (1)
John, Chris, D-La. (7)
Johnson, Eddie Bernice, D-Texas (30)
Johnson, Jay W., D-Wis. (8)
Johnson, Nancy L., R-Conn. (6)
Johnson, Sam, R-Texas (3)
Jones, Walter B. Jr., R-N.C. (3)

— K —

Kanjorski, Paul E., D-Pa. (11)
Kaptur, Marcy, D-Ohio (9)
Kasich, John R., R-Ohio (12)
Kelly, Sue W., R-N.Y. (19)
Kennedy, Joseph P. II, D-Mass. (8)
Kennedy, Patrick J., D-R.I. (1)
Kennelly, Barbara B., D-Conn. (1)
Kildee, Dale E., D-Mich. (9)
Kilpatrick, Carolyn Cheeks, D-Mich. (15)
Kim, Jay C., R-Calif. (41)
Kind, Ron, D-Wis. (3)
King, Peter T., R-N.Y. (3)
Kingston, Jack, R-Ga. (1)
Kleczka, Gerald D., D-Wis. (4)
Klink, Ron, D-Pa. (4)
Klug, Scott L., R-Wis. (2)
Knollenberg, Joe, R-Mich. (11)
Kolbe, Jim, R-Ariz. (5)
Kucinich, Dennis J., D-Ohio (10)

— L —

LaFalce, John J., D-N.Y. (29)
LaHood, Ray, R-Ill. (18)
Lampson, Nick, D-Texas (9)
Lantos, Tom, D-Calif. (12)
Largent, Steve, R-Okla. (1)
Latham, Tom, R-Iowa (5)
LaTourette, Steven C., R-Ohio (19)
Lazio, Rick A., R-N.Y. (2)
Leach, Jim, R-Iowa (1)
Lee, Barbara, D-Calif. (9)
Levin, Sander M., D-Mich. (12)
Lewis, Jerry, R-Calif. (40)
Lewis, John, D-Ga. (5)
Lewis, Ron, R-Ky. (2)

Linder, John, R-Ga. (11)
Lipinski, William O., D-Ill. (3)
Livingston, Robert L., R-La. (1)
LoBiondo, Frank A., R-N.J. (2)
Lofgren, Zoe, D-Calif. (16)
Lowey, Nita M., D-N.Y. (18)
Lucas, Frank D., R-Okla. (6)
Luther, William P. "Bill," D-Minn. (6)

— M —

Maloney, Carolyn B., D-N.Y. (14)
Maloney, Jim, D-Conn. (5)
Manton, Thomas J., D-N.Y. (7)
Manzullo, Donald, R-Ill. (16)
Markey, Edward J., D-Mass. (7)
Martinez, Matthew G., D-Calif. (31)
Mascara, Frank R., D-Pa. (20)
Matsui, Robert T., D-Calif. (5)
McCarthy, Carolyn, D-N.Y. (4)
McCarthy, Karen, D-Mo. (5)
McCollum, Bill, R-Fla. (8)
McCrery, Jim, R-La. (4)
McDade, Joseph M., R-Pa. (10)
McDermott, Jim, D-Wash. (7)
McGovern, Jim, D-Mass. (3)
McHale, Paul, D-Pa. (15)
McHugh, John M., R-N.Y. (24)
McInnis, Scott, R-Colo. (3)
McIntosh, David M., R-Ind. (2)
McIntyre, Mike, D-N.C. (7)
McKeon, Howard P. "Buck," R-Calif. (25)
McKinney, Cynthia A., D-Ga. (4)
McNulty, Michael R., D-N.Y. (21)
Meehan, Martin T., D-Mass. (5)
Meek, Carrie P., D-Fla. (17)
Meeks, Gregory W., D-N.Y. (6)
Menendez, Robert, D-N.J. (13)
Metcalf, Jack, R-Wash. (2)
Mica, John L., R-Fla. (7)
Millender-McDonald, Juanita, D-Calif. (37)
Miller, Dan, R-Fla. (13)
Miller, George, D-Calif. (7)
Minge, David, D-Minn. (2)
Mink, Patsy T., D-Hawaii (2)
Moakley, Joe, D-Mass. (9)
Mollohan, Alan B., D-W.Va. (1)
Moran, James P., D-Va. (8)
Moran, Jerry, R-Kan. (1)
Morella, Constance A., R-Md. (8)
Murtha, John P., D-Pa. (12)
Myrick, Sue, R-N.C. (9)

— N —

Nadler, Jerrold, D-N.Y. (8)
Neal, Richard E., D-Mass. (2)
Nethercutt, George, R-Wash. (5)
Neumann, Mark W., R-Wis. (1)
Ney, Bob, R-Ohio (18)
Northup, Anne M., R-Ky. (3)
Norwood, Charlie, R-Ga. (10)
Nussle, Jim, R-Iowa (2)

— O —

Oberstar, James L., D-Minn. (8)
Obey, David R., D-Wis. (7)
Olver, John W., D-Mass. (1)
Ortiz, Solomon P., D-Texas (27)
Owens, Major R., D-N.Y. (11)
Oxley, Michael G., R-Ohio (4)

— P —

Packard, Ron, R-Calif. (48)
Pallone, Frank Jr., D-N.J. (6)
Pappas, Michael, R-N.J. (12)
Parker, Mike, R-Miss. (4)
Pascrell, Bill Jr., D-N.J. (8)
Pastor, Ed, D-Ariz. (2)
Paul, Ron, R-Texas (14)
Paxon, Bill, R-N.Y. (27)
Payne, Donald M., D-N.J. (10)
Pease, Ed, R-Ind. (7)
Pelosi, Nancy, D-Calif. (8)
Peterson, Collin C., D-Minn. (7)
Peterson, John E., R-Pa. (5)
Petri, Tom, R-Wis. (6)
Pickering, Charles W. "Chip" Jr., R-Miss. (3)
Pickett, Owen B., D-Va. (2)
Pitts, Joseph R., R-Pa. (16)

... Governors, Justices, Cabinet-Rank Officers

Pombo, Richard W., R-Calif. (11)
Pomeroy, Earl, D-N.D. (AL)
Porter, John Edward, R-Ill. (10)
Portman, Rob, R-Ohio (2)
Poshard, Glenn, D-Ill. (19)
Price, David E., D-N.C. (4)
Pryce, Deborah, R-Ohio (15)

— Q —

Quinn, Jack, R-N.Y. (30)

— R —

Radanovich, George P., R-Calif. (19)
Rahall, Nick J. II, D-W.Va. (3)
Ramstad, Jim, R-Minn. (3)
Rangel, Charles B., D-N.Y. (15)
Redmond, Bill, R-N.M. (3)
Regula, Ralph, R-Ohio (16)
Reyes, Silvestre, D-Texas (16)
Riggs, Frank, R-Calif. (1)
Riley, Bob, R-Ala. (3)
Rivers, Lynn, D-Mich. (13)
Rodriguez, Ciro D., D-Texas (28)
Roemer, Tim, D-Ind. (3)
Rogan, James E., R-Calif. (27)
Rogers, Harold, R-Ky. (5)
Rohrabacher, Dana, R-Calif. (45)
Ros-Lehtinen, Ileana, R-Fla. (18)
Rothman, Steven R., D-N.J. (9)
Roukema, Marge, R-N.J. (5)
Royal-Allard, Lucille, D-Calif. (33)
Royce, Ed, R-Calif. (39)
Rush, Bobby L., D-Ill. (1)
Ryun, Jim, R-Kan. (2)

— S —

Sabo, Martin Olav, D-Minn. (5)
Salmon, Matt, R-Ariz. (1)
Sanchez, Loretta, D-Calif. (46)
Sanders, Bernard, I-Vt. (AL)
Sandlin, Max, D-Texas (1)
Sanford, Mark, R-S.C. (1)
Sawyer, Tom, D-Ohio (14)
Saxton, H. James, R-N.J. (3)
Scarborough, Joe, R-Fla. (1)
Schaefer, Dan, R-Colo. (6)
Schaffer, Bob, R-Colo. (4)
Schumer, Charles E., D-N.Y. (9)
Scott, Robert C., D-Va. (3)
Sensenbrenner, F. James Jr., R-Wis. (9)
Serrano, Jose E., D-N.Y. (16)
Sessions, Pete, R-Texas (5)
Shadegg, John, R-Ariz. (4)
Shaw, E. Clay Jr., R-Fla. (22)
Shays, Christopher, R-Conn. (4)
Sherman, Brad, D-Calif. (24)
Shimkus, John, R-Ill. (20)
Shuster, Bud, R-Pa. (9)
Sisisky, Norman, D-Va. (4)
Skaggs, David E., D-Colo. (2)
Skeen, Joe, R-N.M. (2)
Skelton, Ike, D-Mo. (4)
Slaughter, Louise M., D-N.Y. (28)
Smith, Adam, D-Wash. (9)
Smith, Bob, R-Ore. (2)
Smith, Christopher H., R-N.J. (4)
Smith, Lamar, R-Texas (21)
Smith, Linda, R-Wash. (3)
Smith, Nick, R-Mich. (7)
Snowbarger, Vince, R-Kan. (3)
Snyder, Vic, D-Ark. (2)
Solomon, Gerald B.H., R-N.Y. (22)
Souder, Mark, R-Ind. (4)
Spence, Floyd D., R-S.C. (2)
Spratt, John M. Jr., D-S.C. (5)
Stabenow, Debbie, D-Mich. (8)
Stark, Pete, D-Calif. (13)
Stearns, Cliff, R-Fla. (6)
Stenholm, Charles W., D-Texas (17)
Stokes, Louis, D-Ohio (11)
Strickland, Ted, D-Ohio (6)
Stump, Bob, R-Ariz. (3)
Stupak, Bart, D-Mich. (1)
Sununu, John E., R-N.H. (1)

— T —

Talent, James M., R-Mo. (2)
Tanner, John, D-Tenn. (8)
Tauscher, Ellen O., D-Calif. (10)
Tauzin, W.J. "Billy," R-La. (3)
Taylor, Charles H., R-N.C. (11)
Taylor, Gene, D-Miss. (5)
Thomas, Bill, R-Calif. (21)
Thompson, Bennie, D-Miss. (2)
Thornberry, William M. "Mac," R-Texas (13)
Thune, John, R-S.D. (AL)
Thurman, Karen L., D-Fla. (5)
Tiahrt, Todd, R-Kan. (4)
Tierney, John F., D-Mass. (6)
Torres, Esteban E., D-Calif. (34)
Towns, Edolphus, D-N.Y. (10)
Traficant, James A. Jr., D-Ohio (17)
Turner, Jim, D-Texas (2)

— U —

Upton, Fred, R-Mich. (6)

— V —

Velázquez, Nydia M., D-N.Y. (12)
Vento, Bruce F., D-Minn. (4)
Visclosky, Peter J., D-Ind. (1)

— W —

Walsh, James T., R-N.Y. (25)
Wamp, Zach, R-Tenn. (3)
Waters, Maxine, D-Calif. (35)
Watkins, Wes, R-Okla. (3)
Watt, Melvin, D-N.C. (12)
Watts, J.C., R-Okla. (4)
Waxman, Henry A., D-Calif. (29)
Weldon, Curt, R-Pa. (7)
Weldon, Dave, R-Fla. (15)
Weller, Jerry, R-Ill. (11)
Wexler, Robert, D-Fla. (19)
Weygand, Bob, D-R.I. (2)
White, Rick, R-Wash. (1)
Whitfield, Edward, R-Ky. (1)
Wicker, Roger, R-Miss. (1)
Wilson, Heather, R-N.M. (1)
Wise, Bob, D-W.Va. (2)
Wolf, Frank R., R-Va. (10)
Woolsey, Lynn, D-Calif. (6)
Wynn, Albert R., D-Md. (4)

— Y —

Yates, Sidney R., D-Ill. (9)
Young, C.W. Bill, R-Fla. (10)
Young, Don, R-Alaska (AL)

Delegates

Christian-Green, Donna M., D-Virgin Is.
Faleomavaega, Eni F.H., D-Am. Samoa
Norton, Eleanor Holmes, D-D.C.
Romero-Barceló, Carlos, D-P.R.
Underwood, Robert A., D-Guam

Senators
R 55; D 45

Abraham, Spencer, R-Mich.
Akaka, Daniel K., D-Hawaii
Allard, Wayne, R-Colo.
Ashcroft, John, R-Mo.
Baucus, Max, D-Mont.
Bennett, Robert F., R-Utah
Biden, Joseph R. Jr., D-Del.
Bingaman, Jeff, D-N.M.
Bond, Christopher S., R-Mo.
Boxer, Barbara, D-Calif.
Breaux, John B., D-La.
Brownback, Sam, R-Kan.
Bryan, Richard H., D-Nev.
Bumpers, Dale, D-Ark.
Burns, Conrad, R-Mont.
Byrd, Robert C., D-W.Va.
Campbell, Ben Nighthorse, R-Colo.
Chafee, John H., R-R.I.
Cleland, Max, D-Ga.
Coats, Daniel R., R-Ind.
Cochran, Thad, R-Miss.
Collins, Susan, R-Maine
Conrad, Kent, D-N.D.
Coverdell, Paul, R-Ga.
Craig, Larry E., R-Idaho
D'Amato, Alfonse M., R-N.Y.
Daschle, Tom, D-S.D.
DeWine, Mike, R-Ohio
Dodd, Christopher J., D-Conn.
Domenici, Pete V., R-N.M.
Dorgan, Byron L., D-N.D.
Durbin, Richard J., D-Ill.
Enzi, Michael B., R-Wyo.
Faircloth, Lauch, R-N.C.
Feingold, Russell D., D-Wis.
Feinstein, Dianne, D-Calif.
Ford, Wendell H., D-Ky.
Frist, Bill, R-Tenn.
Glenn, John, D-Ohio
Gorton, Slade, R-Wash.
Graham, Bob, D-Fla.
Gramm, Phil, R-Texas
Grams, Rod, R-Minn.
Grassley, Charles E., R-Iowa
Gregg, Judd, R-N.H.
Hagel, Chuck, R-Neb.
Harkin, Tom, D-Iowa
Hatch, Orrin G., R-Utah
Helms, Jesse, R-N.C.
Hollings, Ernest F., D-S.C.
Hutchinson, Tim, R-Ark.
Hutchison, Kay Bailey, R-Texas
Inhofe, James M., R-Okla.
Inouye, Daniel K., D-Hawaii
Jeffords, James M., R-Vt.
Johnson, Tim, D-S.D.
Kempthorne, Dirk, R-Idaho
Kennedy, Edward M., D-Mass.
Kerrey, Bob, D-Neb.
Kerry, John, D-Mass.
Kohl, Herb, D-Wis.
Kyl, Jon, R-Ariz.
Landrieu, Mary L., D-La.
Lautenberg, Frank R., D-N.J.
Leahy, Patrick J., D-Vt.
Levin, Carl, D-Mich.
Lieberman, Joseph I., D-Conn.
Lott, Trent, R-Miss.
Lugar, Richard G., R-Ind.
Mack, Connie, R-Fla.
McCain, John, R-Ariz.
McConnell, Mitch, R-Ky.
Mikulski, Barbara A., D-Md.
Moseley-Braun, Carol, D-Ill.
Moynihan, Daniel Patrick, D-N.Y.
Murkowski, Frank H., R-Alaska
Murray, Patty, D-Wash.
Nickles, Don, R-Okla.
Reed, Jack, D-R.I.
Reid, Harry, D-Nev.
Robb, Charles S., D-Va.
Roberts, Pat, R-Kan.
Rockefeller, John D. IV, D-W.Va.
Roth, William V. Jr., R-Del.
Santorum, Rick, R-Pa.
Sarbanes, Paul S., D-Md.
Sessions, Jeff, R-Ala.
Shelby, Richard C., R-Ala.
Smith, Gordon H., R-Ore.
Smith, Robert C., R-N.H.
Snowe, Olympia J., R-Maine
Specter, Arlen, R-Pa.
Stevens, Ted, R-Alaska
Thomas, Craig, R-Wyo.
Thompson, Fred, R-Tenn.
Thurmond, Strom, R-S.C.
Torricelli, Robert G., D-N.J.
Warner, John W., R-Va.
Wellstone, Paul, D-Minn.
Wyden, Ron, D-Ore.

Governors
R 32; D 17; I 1

Ala. — Fob James Jr., R
Alaska — Tony Knowles, D
Ariz. — Fife Symington, R
Ark. — Mike Huckabee, R
Calif. — Pete Wilson, R
Colo. — Roy Romer, D
Conn. — John G. Rowland, R
Del. — Thomas R. Carper, D
Fla. — Lawton Chiles, D
Ga. — Zell Miller, D
Hawaii — Benjamin J. Cayetano, D
Idaho — Phil Batt, R
Ill. — Jim Edgar, R
Ind. — Frank L. O'Bannon, D
Iowa — Terry E. Branstad, R
Kan. — Bill Graves, R
Ky. — Paul E. Patton, D
La. — Mike Foster, R
Maine — Angus King, I
Md. — Parris N. Glendening, D
Mass. — Paul Cellucci, R
Mich. — John Engler, R
Minn. — Arne Carlson, R
Miss. — Kirk Fordice, R
Mo. — Mel Carnahan, D
Mont. — Marc Racicot, R
Neb. — Ben Nelson, D
Nev. — Bob Miller, D
N.H. — Jeanne Shaheen, D
N.J. — Christine Todd Whitman, R
N.M. — Gary E. Johnson, R
N.Y. — George E. Pataki, R
N.C. — James B. Hunt Jr., D
N.D. — Edward T. Schafer, R
Ohio — George V. Voinovich, R
Okla. — Frank Keating, R
Ore. — John Kitzhaber, D
Pa. — Tom Ridge, R
R.I. — Lincoln C. Almond, R
S.C. — David Beasley, R
S.D. — William J. Janklow, R
Tenn. — Don Sundquist, R
Texas — George W. Bush, R
Utah — Michael O. Leavitt, R
Vt. — Howard Dean, D
Va. — James S. Gilmore III, R
Wash. — Gary Locke, D
W.Va. — Cecil H. Underwood, R
Wis. — Tommy G. Thompson, R
Wyo. — Jim Geringer, R

Supreme Court

Rehnquist, William H. — Va., Chief Justice
Breyer, Stephen G. — Mass.
Ginsburg, Ruth Bader — N.Y.
Kennedy, Anthony M. — Calif.
O'Connor, Sandra Day — Ariz.
Scalia, Antonin — Va.
Souter, David H. — N.H.
Stevens, John Paul — Ill.
Thomas, Clarence — Ga.

Cabinet

Albright, Madeleine K. — State
Babbitt, Bruce — Interior
Brown, Jesse — Veterans Affairs
Cohen, William S. — Defense
Cuomo, Andrew M. — HUD
Daley, William M. — Commerce
Glickman, Dan — Agriculture
Herman, Alexis — Labor
Peña, Federico F. — Energy
Reno, Janet — Attorney General
Richardson, Bill — U.N. Representative
Riley, Richard W. — Education
Rubin, Robert E. — Treasury
Shalala, Donna E. — HHS
Slater, Rodney — Transportation
West, Togo D. Jr. — Veterans Affairs

Other Executive Branch Officers

Gore, Al — Vice President
Barshefsky, Charlene — U.S. Trade Representative (nominee)
Berger, Samuel R. — National Security Adviser
Bowles, Erskine — Chief of Staff
Browner, Carol M. — EPA Administrator
Raines, Franklin D. — OMB Director
Sperling, Gene — Chairman, National Economic Council
Tenet, George J. — Director of Central Intelligence
Yellen, Janet — Chairman, Council of Economic Advisers

Appendix B
VOTE STUDIES

Voting Analyses
  Presidential Support B-3
    History, Definition B-4
    Leading Scorers B-5
  Party Unity B-6
    Definition B-6
    History, ... B-7
    Leading Scorers B-8
  Conservative Coalition B-9
    History, Definition B-9
    Leading Scorers B-10
  Voting Participation B-11
    History, Definition B-11
  Guide to Voting Analyses B-12

Background Material
  Presidential Support
    Definitions and Data B-13

Background Material *(cont'd)*
  Presidential Support *(cont'd)*
    List of Votes B-14
    Individual House Members' Scores B-16
    Individual Senators' Scores B-18
  Party Unity
    Definitions and Data B-19
    List of Votes B-20
    Individual Senators' Scores B-21
    Individual House Members' Scores B-22
  Conservative Coalition
    Definitions and Data B-24
    List of Votes B-25
    Individual House Members' Scores B-26
    Individual Senators' Scores B-28
  Voting Participation
    Individual Senators' Scores B-29
    Individual House Members' Scores B-30

President's Success Score Droops As White House Priorities Make Scant Headway

President Clinton's historic defeat on two articles of impeachment in the House on Dec. 19 dwarfs all other votes when it comes to assessing his success in the 1998 session of Congress.

In fact, even without the votes that made him the first elected president in U.S. history to be impeached, Clinton's legislative year has to be scored as a failure — if the goal was to advance a policy agenda. Virtually all of his major proposals died.

But if — as cynics would have it — the main thing in politics is to triumph over one's political adversaries, then Clinton performed rather well. He effectively shut down the Republican agenda, including tax cuts and reduced regulations, helped deliver unexpected Democratic victories at the polls in November and, indirectly, contributed to the stunning downfall of then-House Speaker Newt Gingrich, R-Ga.

On paper, Clinton ended the year with a 51 percent success score, according to Congressional Quarterly's annual study of voting patterns. This means he prevailed on 51 percent of the 154 House and Senate floor votes on which he took a position.

That is, on the surface, a fairly low score. It is lower than the scores of Presidents Dwight D. Eisenhower (76 percent) and Ronald Reagan (56.1 percent) in their sixth years in office. It is lower, even, than President Richard M. Nixon's (59.6 percent) in his sixth year — the year he resigned rather than face impeachment.

In fact, Clinton's score was the sixth lowest of any president since Congressional Quarterly began keeping track of such things at the beginning of the Eisenhower administration 46 years ago.

Almost none of the priorities that Clinton set at the beginning of the year became law, and few of them even got a floor vote. Tobacco legislation, campaign finance overhaul, "fast track" trade legislation and a "bill of rights" for patients in managed health care all fell far short of enactment.

But Clinton seems to resist being judged by ordinary standards.

Like a clutch quarterback in the final seconds of play, he came through when he had to. After losing a series of House appropriations floor votes, he managed to recover most of his losses when eight of the measures were folded into a massive end-of-session omnibus bill.

The resulting package (PL 105-277) funded several Democratic priorities, including increased spending for teachers, while excluding most of the conservative policy "riders" added in the House.

And with the Republicans in post-election disarray, it was Clinton — despite his lame-duck status — who set much of the legislative tone for this year. His call to save Social Security first, for example, continues to undercut Republican efforts to cut taxes.

In that sense, Clinton fared better than Eisenhower and Reagan, both of whom suffered big congressional setbacks at the polls at this point in their presidencies and saw their power wane.

"Given the partisan tensions that culminated in the impeachment vote, it's quite surprising that Clinton did as well as he did in Congress," said Norman J. Ornstein, a congressional scholar at the American Enterprise Institute, a Washington think tank.

Personal Scandal

For Clinton to merely survive the year in office, let alone win enactment of any major initiatives, was a kind of victory. He was haunted by charges of lying under oath about a sexual liaison with a White House intern, leading members of both parties to support an impeachment inquiry.

Although Clinton took no formal position on early House votes related to the scandal, such as a Sept. 11 vote to publicly release a sexually explicit report by Independent Counsel Kenneth W. Starr, the issue dominated the landscape, giving Clinton scarce chance to pursue his vigorous agenda.

On the other hand, it meant he had nothing to lose by battling GOP initiatives, thereby turning the subject away from scandal. By threatening vetoes on a battery of issues from tax cuts to restrictions on overseas family planning funds, the president stymied congressional conservatives just when it seemed that they should be piling up political points.

When threats were not enough, Clinton wielded his veto pen to stop five bills.

The measures would have expanded the tax benefits of education savings accounts (HR 2646); created school vouchers in the District of Columbia (S 1502); punished countries that offered technical assistance to Iran's missile program (HR 2709); appropriated less money than Clinton wanted for agriculture programs in fiscal 1999 (HR 4101); and tied reauthorization of State Department programs to anti-abortion restrictions in international family planning (HR 1757).

In a year marked by sharply drawn

CQ Vote Studies

Presidential Support	B-3
History, Definition	B-4
Leading Scorers	B-5
Party Unity	B-6
Definition	B-6
History	B-7
Leading Scorers	B-8
Conservative Coalition	B-9
History, Definition	B-9
Leading Scorers	B-10
Voting Participation	B-11
History, Definition	B-11
Background Materials	B-13

Vote Studies

Presidential Success > History

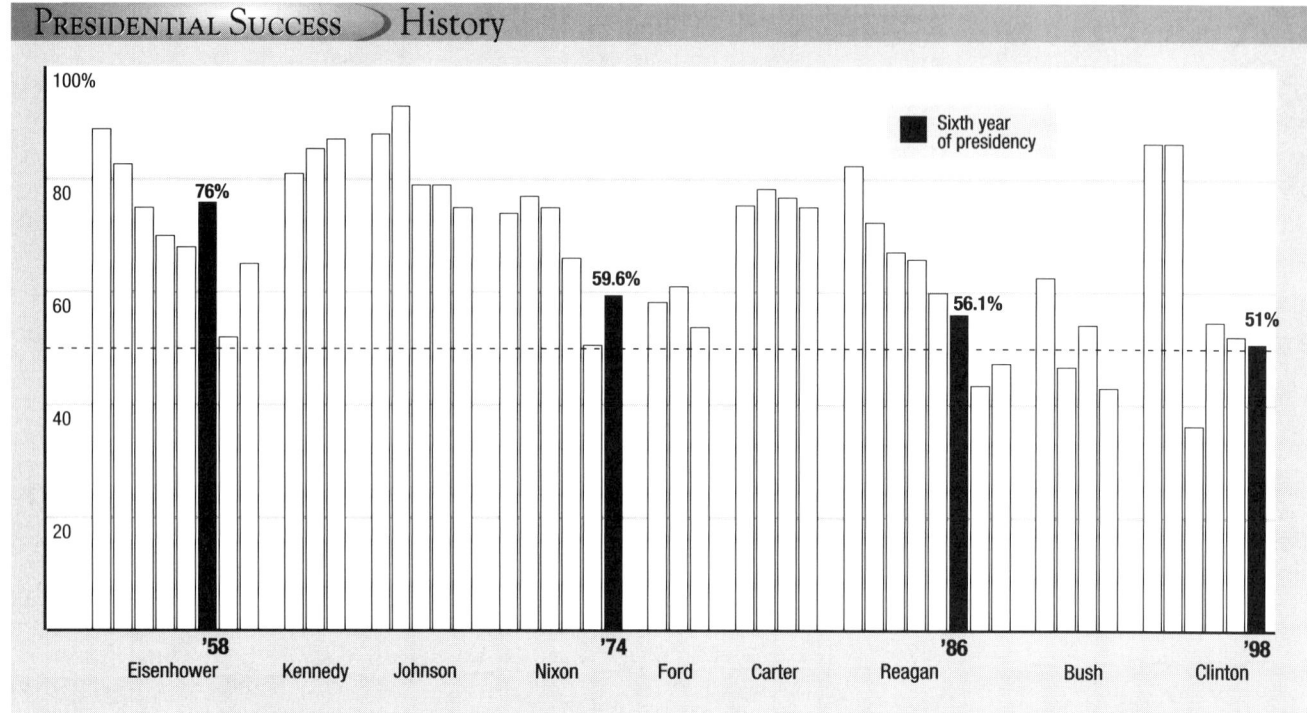

partisan lines, House Democrats supported Clinton 74 percent of the time; Senate Democrats averaged 82 percent support. Regionally, Clinton fared best with Eastern Senate Democrats (84 percent support) and worst with Southern House Republicans (22 percent support).

His most reliable Republican supporters in the Senate were John H. Chafee of Rhode Island (77 percent) and James M. Jeffords of Vermont (69 percent). In the House, the most GOP support came from Constance A. Morella of Maryland (71 percent) and Sherwood Boehlert of New York (60 percent).

Domestic Setbacks

In his 1998 State of the Union address, Clinton laid out an ambitious domestic agenda. He called for a health care bill of rights to protect consumers; comprehensive regulation of tobacco; tightened campaign finance laws; expanded Medicare benefits; an increased minimum wage; expanded child care programs; and the hiring of 100,000 new teachers.

He got virtually nothing.

Most of his proposals, such as permitting uninsured people as young as 55 to enroll in Medicare, never made it out of the gate. Other plans, including tobacco and campaign finance legislation, were extensively debated in Congress before falling to Senate procedural motions.

Clinton also failed on environmental issues. Proposals to create tax credits to promote energy efficiency and launch clean water initiatives received scant attention on the Hill, and the administration was unable to generate enthusiasm for ratifying a global warming treaty.

The president did somewhat better on his proposal for $7.4 billion over five years to hire 100,000 new teachers. After an extensive appropriations battle, he won the $1.2 billion needed for the first year — but no authorizing language that would give momentum for additional funding.

"Clinton had a big agenda, and it just didn't happen," said George C. Edwards III, director of the Center for Presidential Studies at Texas A&M University. "It's very difficult to point to a very important piece of legislation that has Bill Clinton's stamp on it."

Overall, on domestic issues, Clinton lost on 43 of 69 House votes, and 19 of 36 Senate votes, not counting nominations. Many of his defeats came on conservative-backed policy riders to appropriations bills, such as proposals to limit access to abortion or create vouchers for private schools.

In the end, however, most of those

Definition

How often the president won his way on roll call votes on which he took a clear position.

1998 Data

Senate	48 victories
	24 defeats
House	30 victories
	52 defeats

Total Clinton success rate: 51%

For More Information

Individual leaders	B-5
Background and data	B-13
List of votes	B-14
House members' scores	B-16
Senators' scores	B-18

riders fell by the wayside. Demonstrating that even an embattled White House wields considerable clout, Clinton carried the day on much of the end-of-session negotiating on fiscal 1999 spending.

The omnibus appropriations bill opened the gates for a flood of new spending, giving the president victories for such items as funding for the Bosnia peacekeeping mission, Year 2000 computer fixes, anti-terrorism efforts and farm relief.

Although Republicans also scored a

Presidential Support

Leading Scorers: Presidential Support

Support indicates those who in 1998 voted most often for President Clinton's position; **opposition** shows those who voted most often against the president's position.

Scores are based on actual votes cast; members are listed alphabetically when their scores are tied. Members who missed half or more of the votes are not listed.

Support / Opposition

SENATE

Republicans (Support)		Democrats (Support)		Republicans (Opposition)		Democrats (Opposition)	
Chafee, R.I.	77%	Glenn, Ohio	96%	Inhofe, Okla.	86%	Byrd, W.Va.	26%
Jeffords, Vt.	69	Kennedy, Mass.	96	Smith, N.H.	81	Hollings, S.C.	26
Roth, Del.	64	Kerry, Mass.	94	Nickles, Okla.	77	Conrad, N.D.	25
Collins, Maine	63	Rockefeller, W.Va.	94	Ashcroft, Mo.	76	Dorgan, N.D.	24
D'Amato, N.Y.	60	Dodd, Conn.	93	Hutchinson, Ark.	74	Ford, Ky.	23
Specter, Pa.	60	Levin, Mich.	93	Allard, Colo.	72	Moynihan, N.Y.	22
Domenici, N.M.	57	Sarbanes, Md.	92	Sessions, Ala.	72	Torricelli, N.J.	22
Smith, Ore.	55	Akaka, Hawaii	91	Craig, Idaho	71	Breaux, La.	21
Snowe, Maine	55	Biden, Del.	91	Faircloth, N.C.	71	Reid, Nev.	21
Lugar, Ind.	54	Mikulski, Md.	91	Enzi, Wyo.	69	Baucus, Mont.	19
Stevens, Alaska	54			Helms, N.C.	68	Murray, Wash.	18
Bennett, Utah	53			Gramm, Texas	67	Feingold, Wis.	17
Cochran, Miss.	53			Kyl, Ariz.	67	Graham, Fla.	17
DeWine, Ohio	51			Kempthorne, Idaho	66	Leahy, Vt.	17
Mack, Fla.	50			Shelby, Ala.	66	Lieberman, Conn.	17

HOUSE

Republicans (Support)		Democrats (Support)		Republicans (Opposition)		Democrats (Opposition)	
Morella, Md.	71%	McDermott, Wash.	95%	Collins, Ga.	88%	Goode, Va.	74%
Boehlert, N.Y.	60	Skaggs, Colo.	93	Coble, N.C.	84	Hall, Texas	70
Johnson, Conn.	57	Watt, N.C.	91	Coburn, Okla.	84	Taylor, Miss.	67
Shays, Conn.	57	Conyers, Mich.	90	Deal, Ga.	84	Danner, Mo.	54
Leach, Iowa	53	Eshoo, Calif.	90	Schaefer, Colo.	84	Traficant, Ohio	53
Campbell, Calif.	52	Hastings, Fla.	90	Weldon, Fla.	84	Stenholm, Texas	51
Castle, Del.	51	Meeks, N.Y.	90	Blunt, Mo.	83	John, La.	50
Houghton, N.Y.	49	Wexler, Fla.	90	Christensen, Neb.	83	Lipinski, Ill.	50
Gilman, N.Y.	46	Barrett, Wis.	89	Doolittle, Calif.	83	Condit, Calif.	49
Ramstad, Minn.	43	Carson, Ind.	89	Istook, Okla.	83	McIntyre, N.C.	48
Forbes, N.Y.	41	Obey, Wis.	89	Solomon, N.Y.	83	Turner, Texas	47
Kelly, N.Y.	41	Payne, N.J.	89			Cramer, Ala.	46
Porter, Ill.	41	Sabo, Minn.	89			Peterson, Minn.	45
Kolbe, Ariz.	40	Scott, Va.	89				
		Yates, Ill.	89				

few victories, they never recovered from the eleventh-hour negotiations, which took place just weeks before their Nov. 3 electoral setbacks. "We have failed in this process," said a disheartened Rep. Jon Christensen, R-Neb.

Foreign Policy

Presidents traditionally do best in the foreign policy and defense arena, and Clinton has been no exception.

In 1998, he prevailed in the Senate on 15 of 20 foreign policy and defense votes. In the House, however, which proved more difficult terrain for the president across the board, Clinton won on just four of 13 votes.

One of Clinton's biggest victories came when the Senate voted to open the doors of the North Atlantic Treaty Organization, allowing Hungary, Poland and the Czech Republic to join the strategic alliance (Treaty Doc 105-36).

Clinton also won on repeated votes to fund the U.S. mission in Bosnia. And after a yearlong battle, he prevailed upon lawmakers to appropriate $18 billion for the International Monetary Fund, which he considered an essential step in staving off a global economic downturn.

Yet the president failed to win rati-

Vote Studies

fication of a comprehensive nuclear test ban treaty. Lawmakers also refused his repeated requests to pay off debts to the United Nations.

The House twice voted to restrict technology transfers to China, despite administration opposition. It also rebuffed Clinton by passing a bill (HR 2709) that would have punished overseas research laboratories and companies that provided missile technology to Iran. Clinton vetoed the measure.

Taxes and Trade

Clinton may have scored his most resounding victories on an issue that Republicans had hoped to convert into Election Day gains: tax cuts.

By urging Congress to set aside the budget surplus for the Social Security trust fund, rather than use it for tax reduction, he divided conservatives and ultimately paralyzed GOP efforts to cut taxes by $100 billion or more.

To some GOP leaders, it was Clinton's use of the Social Security debate, as much as any issue, that fueled Democratic gains at the polls. "We should have been more aggressive," Gingrich said after the elections.

But for Clinton, the tax issue proved a rather hollow victory. He failed to stir much debate about ways to ensure the future solvency of Social Security, meaning that both he and Congress will have to wrestle with the "third rail" of politics this year.

The president could also point to victories on other tax-related issues. The House failed to pass a constitutional amendment, opposed by the White House, that would have made it more difficult for Congress to impose new taxes. And the Senate turned back a plan that would have terminated the internal revenue code.

In addition, Clinton claimed victory when Congress cleared a measure (PL 105-206) to overhaul the IRS. However, GOP lawmakers also took credit for the bill, which was one of the few concrete achievements that elected officials of either party could point to in 1998.

Clinton's biggest economic setback may have come Sept. 25, when the House voted overwhelmingly against giving him fast-track trade negotiating authority. The White House took no formal position on that vote because of unusual political currents, but urged GOP leaders to hold off until early 1999 before bringing the top administration priority to the floor.

With many House lawmakers going on record to oppose the plan, GOP leaders are skeptical about reviving the issue before 2001. That would leave Clinton with greatly reduced leverage when he tries to negotiate overseas trade agreements in his final two years in office. ◆

Partisan Voting on the Rise: Ideology Impedes Bills; Some Welcome the Contrast

The end-of-session decision in the House to impeach the president on a pair of party-line votes brought an emotionally draining end to a year marked throughout by a rise in partisan voting.

An analysis of 1998 roll call votes compiled by Congressional Quarterly found that 56 percent of the votes in each chamber (55.7 percent in the Senate; 55.5 percent in the House) pitted a majority of one party against a majority of the other. That is an increase of about 5 percentage points over 1997 party-unity vote ratios, reversing a two-year decline in the proportion of such votes.

Roger Davidson, a congressional scholar at the University of Maryland, says even those figures did not fully reflect the depth of differences between the two parties, because Congress passed relatively few major bills.

"It was a low workload year. You could argue that both parties were distracted by impeachment in 1998," he said. Yet the parties continued to have passionate differences on emotional issues such as abortion, school vouchers, gay rights, affirmative action and the minimum wage.

In fact, Davidson argues, Congress is in the midst of the most partisan era since Reconstruction at the end of the Civil War. "There is a very deep chasm between the parties," he said.

Whether the emotions unleashed in the impeachment fight will spill over into other issues in 1999 is unclear. While members of both parties decried the acrid tone of the impeachment debate, there were differing views on whether the rising tide of party-unity votes in 1998 was a troubling development or a welcome one.

For moderates such as Rep. David E. Price, D-N.C., the increase in partisanship was worrisome because it could hinder agreement in 1999 on key issues including education funding and a Social Security overhaul.

"Partisan feelings have been rubbed

Definition

The percentage of recorded floor votes in each chamber on which a majority of one party voted against a majority of the other party.

1998 Data

	Partisan Votes	Total Votes	Percent
Senate	175	314	55.7%
House	296	533	55.5%

For More Information

Individual leaders	B-8
Background and data	B-19
List of votes	B-20
Senators' scores	B-21
House members' scores	B-22

raw. We're just going to have to see what will happen in 1999," Price said in an interview. "Voters want issues resolved. There is not a lot of sympathy for excessive partisanship."

But for some lawmakers who had partisan political objectives, and less compromising legislative goals, 1998 was, if anything, not partisan enough.

"We failed to put bills on the floor with more of a partisan pattern to define differences," said Rep. Tom

Coburn, R-Okla.

Coburn said it was important for parties to stake out positions in 1999 on abortion, proposals to cut government and other issues.

Reversing a Trend

Partisan voting spiked in 1995, when more than two of every three votes were party-unity votes, but it declined over the next two years. In 1997, party-unity votes accounted for 50 percent of votes in either chamber, the lowest level since 1990 in the House and 1991 in the Senate. (*1997 Almanac, p. C-7; 1995 Almanac, p. C-8*)

The balanced-budget agreement of 1997, in which Democrats and Republicans agreed on a plan to eliminate the deficit in five years, was emblematic of the spirit of bipartisanship that marked the first year of the 105th Congress. But that tone changed quickly in 1998.

Joseph Cooper, a Johns Hopkins University political scientist, says Independent Counsel Kenneth W. Starr's investigation of Clinton's sexual relationship with a White House intern prodded both parties to form battle lines in 1998. "Republicans thought the Monica Lewinsky case would be a silver bullet," he said. "They became rigid in their policy goals."

In one of the first floor votes of the year, Republicans on Feb. 5 backed legislation to rename Washington National Airport after a GOP hero, former President Ronald Reagan. Democrats were strongly opposed to the measure in the House, and evenly split in the Senate. Supporters said the legislation would honor Reagan, but opponents said it was a blatant political act.

Skirmishing continued to erupt periodically through the rest of 1998.

Bitter disputes over policy "riders" contributed to long delays in the passage of major appropriations bills, culminating in the late-October rush to wrap eight unfinished spending bills into a huge omnibus measure (PL 105-277).

Battle Over Riders

Typical of the partisan trench warfare on spending bill riders was the dispute over the Census Bureau proposal, supported by Democrats, to use statistical sampling in the 2000 census in

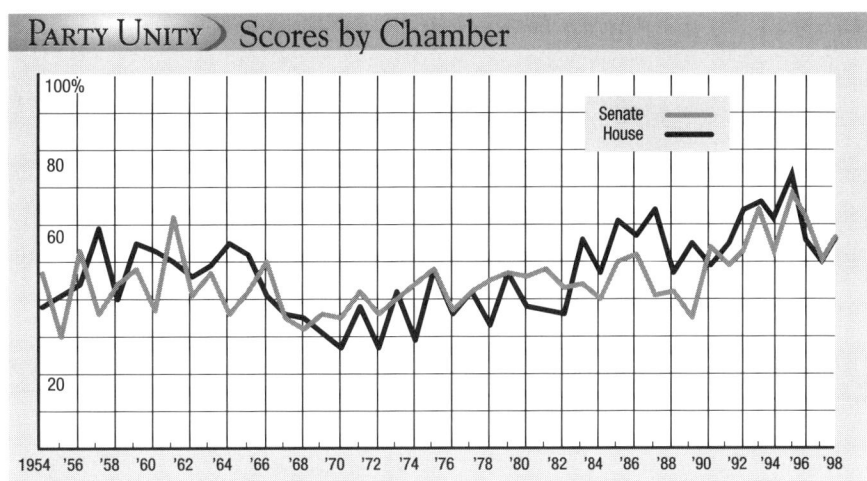

Party Unity Scores by Chamber

order to improve the accuracy of the count and include citizens who might otherwise be missed because of poor English, the lack of a permanent residence or other reasons. Results of the census will determine House district boundaries for the 2002 election.

In a party-line floor vote Aug. 5, Republicans defeated a Democratic amendment to permit sampling. The omnibus spending bill ultimately provided funding for the departments of Commerce, Justice and State only through June 15, 1999, in order to provide more time to work out the sampling dispute.

Social issues, such as abortion, provided fertile ground for other disputes in 1998. The House voted to override Clinton's veto of a bill (HR 1122) to ban "partial birth" abortion, but the Senate failed by three votes to follow suit.

Republicans elected to cut short some other abortion battles to clear the way for the omnibus spending bill. For example, they agreed to strip from the agricultural appropriations bill a House floor amendment approved along party lines that would have barred the Food and Drug Administration from using funds to test or approve the French abortion pill, RU-486.

Despite the increase in partisan voting in 1998, Congress reached bipartisan agreement on significant legislation, including the $217.9 billion surface transportation reauthorization law (PL 105-178), an overhaul of housing programs (PL 105-276), Internal Revenue Service reforms (PL 105-206), and reauthorization of Head Start (PL 105-285).

Some of the biggest partisan battles were fought over bills that were designed to delineate clear political differences. For example, Republicans forced a showdown on education policy and won passage of a bill (HR 2646) to create tax-preferred savings accounts for elementary and secondary school expenses, including private school tuition — a bill that Clinton vetoed.

Democrats also sought confrontation. For example, Sen. Richard J. Durbin of Illinois said Democrats wanted Republicans to take a stand on managed care. While a House-passed GOP bill (HR 4250) encouraged increased patient protections, it stopped short of a Democratic proposal to allow patients to sue health plans in state courts. The House bill was tabled, or killed, in the Senate. "We wanted there to be a clear message showing what the parties were for in the election," Durbin said.

A $368.5 billion settlement reached by state attorneys general with cigarette makers to resolve tobacco-related lawsuits fell apart in the Senate, after the two parties staked out divergent positions. A number of Democrats joined John McCain, R-Ariz., to support a broad bill (S 1415) to raise the price of a pack of cigarettes by $1.10 and require "lookback" penalties if cigarette companies failed to meet youth smoking reduction targets. GOP leaders backed a narrower approach for reducing teen smoking. The Senate fell three votes short of invoking cloture on the McCain bill.

Campaign finance was another

Vote Studies

Leading Scorers: Party Unity

Support indicates those who in 1998 voted most consistently with their party's majority against the other party; **opposition** shows how often members voted against their party's majority. Scores are based on votes cast; members are listed alphabetically when their scores are tied. Members who missed half or more of the votes are not listed.

Support — SENATE

Republicans		Democrats	
Craig, Idaho	99%	Kennedy, Mass.	100%
Smith, N.H.	99	Glenn, Ohio	99
Ashcroft, Mo.	98	Sarbanes, Md.	99
Hutchinson, Ark.	98	Wellstone, Minn.	99
Nickles, Okla.	98	Harkin, Iowa	98
Sessions, Ala.	98	Levin, Mich.	98
Allard, Colo.	97	Reed, R.I.	98
Gramm, Texas	97	Lautenberg, N.J.	97
Grams, Minn.	97	Mikulski, Md.	97
Helms, N.C.	97	Akaka, Hawaii	96
Inhofe, Okla.	97		

Opposition — SENATE

Republicans		Democrats	
Jeffords, Vt.	51%	Byrd, W.Va.	28%
Specter, Pa.	51	Breaux, La.	27
Chafee, R.I.	43	Lieberman, Conn.	20
D'Amato, N.Y.	38	Hollings, S.C.	19
Snowe, Maine	35	Reid, Nev.	19
Collins, Maine	33	Ford, Ky.	17
Roth, Del.	21	Robb, Va.	17
Campbell, Colo.	18	Baucus, Mont.	16
DeWine, Ohio	18	Graham, Fla.	15
Stevens, Alaska	18	Torricelli, N.J.	15

Support — HOUSE

Republicans		Democrats	
Paxon, N.Y.	98%	Becerra, Calif.	99%
Archer, Texas	97	Lee, Calif.	99
Armey, Texas	97	Lewis, Ga.	99
Hastings, Wash.	97	Olver, Mass.	99
Sessions, Texas	97	Roybal-Allard, Calif.	99
Shadegg, Ariz.	97	Clay, Mo.	98
Snowbarger, Kan.	97	Furse, Ore.	98
		Stark, Calif.	98
		Tierney, Mass.	98

Opposition — HOUSE

Republicans		Democrats	
Morella, Md.	60%	Hall, Texas	77%
Shays, Conn.	42	Goode, Va.	72
Boehlert, N.Y.	41	Traficant, Ohio	67
Gilman, N.Y.	38	Taylor, Miss.	59
Johnson, Conn.	38	Stenholm, Texas	50
Castle, Del.	37	Peterson, Minn.	46
Leach, Iowa	37	John, La.	44
Campbell, Calif.	36	Lipinski, Ill.	42
Forbes, N.Y.	35	Turner, Texas	42
Houghton, N.Y.	34	Danner, Tenn.	41
Kelly, N.Y.	34		

battleground. Reps. Christopher Shays, R-Conn., and Martin T. Meehan, D-Mass., overcame obstacles erected by the leadership to win House passage of legislation (an amended version of HR 2183) to ban "soft money" contributions in federal elections and expand regulation of advertising. But the drive foundered Sept. 10 when the Senate came eight votes short of ending debate on a proposal to attach a bill (S 25) sponsored by McCain and Russell D. Feingold, D-Wis., to the Interior appropriations bill (S 2237).

The lack of a broad consensus on partisan issues such as campaign finance changes gave a minority of members a powerful tool to block legislation in the Senate. Of 29 cloture motions considered — including the failed attempt to end debate on McCain's campaign finance bill — only 11 were approved. On the 18 defeated cloture motions, Democrats cast 755 votes in line with their own caucus, and 30 votes in agreement with Republicans.

While Democrats were often a frustrated minority in Congress, they won enough Republican support to win 61 of 175 party-unity votes in the Senate, and 80 of 296 such votes in the House. Many of the votes amounted to Pyrrhic victories, however. For example, while Democrats were able to marshall enough GOP support to defeat two the four articles of impeachment against Clinton Dec. 19, they could not attract enough Republicans to defeat the other two.

In recent years, both parties have shown a high degree of loyalty on votes when the parties disagree, and that pattern continued in 1998 as Republicans succeeded in keeping an average of 86 percent of their conference in line on party-unity votes in both the House and Senate. Democrats kept an average of 87 percent of caucus members unified on these votes in the Senate, and 82 percent in the House.

Crossing Party Lines

Lawmakers who voted most often against their caucus tended to be Republican moderates, mainly from the Northeast, and conservative Democrats, typically from that party's former stronghold in the South.

In the Senate, no Republican voted with Democrats more often than any Democrat. And no Democrat voted against his party more often than any Republican did.

Republicans who voted in agreement most often with the other party were James M. Jeffords of Vermont and Arlen Specter of Pennsylvania in the Senate, and Constance A. Morella of Maryland and Christopher Shays of Connecticut in the House.

Democrats who voted most often with Republicans were Robert C. Byrd of West Virginia and John B. Breaux of Louisiana in the Senate, and Ralph M. Hall of Texas and Virgil H. Goode Jr. of Virginia in the House.

While the ongoing impeachment proceeding may spawn further division in the Senate this year, in the House, some members said emotions may cool.

"We are at the point where we hit rock bottom, and I now hope we are coming back," Appropriations Committee Chairman C.W. "Bill" Young, R-Fla., said Dec. 19. ◆

Influential Since the 1940s, The Conservative Coalition Limps Into History in 1998

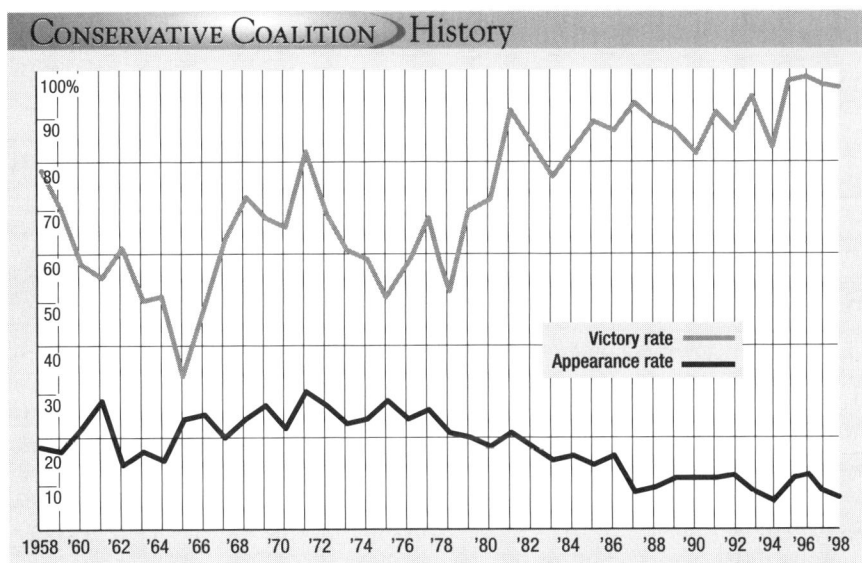

Definition

A voting bloc in the House and Senate consisting of a majority of Republicans and majority of Southern Democrats, combined against a majority of Northern Democrats.

Appearance indicates how often the coalition voted as a group. Victory indicates how often the coalition prevailed on these votes.

1998 Data

Senate	8 victories
	0 defeats
	8 appearances in 314 votes
House	40 victories
	2 defeats
	42 appearances in 533 votes

Total Congress appearance rate: 6%
Total Congress victory rate: 96%

For More Information

Individual leaders	B-10
Background and data	B-24
List of votes	B-25
House members' scores	B-26
Senators' scores	B-28

Eclipsed by rigid partisanship and the shift of the South toward the Republican Party, the conservative coalition — a tool of political analysis for much of the century — became moribund in 1998.

The voting alliance of Republicans and Southern Democrats, which once determined the outcome of major civil rights, labor and economic legislation, finally ran out of steam. Specifically:

• In the Senate, Southern Democrats left their party on only eight votes, too few to be statistically significant.

• No significant bill was enacted because of the votes of the coalition.

• The House showed that it could take the most momentous step possible, impeachment of the president, with the votes of only four Southern Democrats.

Accordingly, Congressional Quarterly, which has maintained the conservative coalition vote study since 1957, is downgrading it. In future years, CQ will collect and publish members' scores for purposes of continuity and research, but will not write about them — unless the North-South axis reasserts itself as a significant factor on more than regional issues. In a chamber as closely divided as the current House, any bloc of votes that develops cohesion could become significant.

The coalition has been on life support since the mid-1980s. In 1995, it became largely irrelevant as a political force because Republicans no longer needed the votes of Southern Democrats to pass their legislation.

Coalition scores retained some use-

Leading Scorers: Conservative Coalition

Support indicates those who in 1998 voted most often with the conservative coalition. **Opposition** indicates those who voted most often against the coalition. Scores are based on votes cast, and members are listed alphabetically when scores are tied. Members who missed half the votes are not listed.

HOUSE *

Support						Opposition					
Republican		**Southern Democrat**		**Northern Democrat**		**Republican**		**Southern Democrat**		**Northern Democrat**	
Baker, La.	100%	John, La.	100%	Traficant, Ohio	95%	Morella, Md.	61%	Lewis, Ga.	93%	Jackson, Ill.	100%
Boehner, Ohio	100	Cramer, Ala.	98	Boswell, Iowa	93	Shays, Conn.	50	McKinney, Ga.	90	Gutierrez, Ill.	98
Brady, Texas	100	Stenholm, Texas	98	Skelton, Mo.	93	Paul, Texas	44	Watt, N.C.	81	Tierney, Mass.	98
Calvert, Calif.	100	Hall, Texas	95	Danner, Mo.	88	Boehlert, N.Y.	36	Hastings, Fla.	80	Lee, Calif.	97
Cannon, Utah	100	Turner, Texas	95	Condit, Calif.	80	Campbell, Calif.	36	Hilliard, Ala.	78	Payne, N.J.	97
Chambliss, Ga.	100	McIntyre, N.C.	93	Pomeroy, N.D.	79	Johnson, Conn.	33	Doggett, Texas	76	Davis, Ill.	95
DeLay, Texas	100	Goode, Va.	90			Sensenbrenner, Wis.	31	Brown, Fla.	71	Owens, N.Y.	95
Granger, Texas	100	Pickett, Va.	90					Meek, Fla.	71	Roybal-Allard, Calif.	95
Hastings, Wash.	100	Tanner, Tenn.	90							Rush, Ill.	95
Lewis, Ky.	100	Sandlin, Texas	88							Stark, Calif.	95
McCrery, La.	100	Sisisky, Va.	88							Meeks, N.Y.	94
Oxley, Ohio	100										
Packard, Calif.	100										
Pickering, Miss.	100										
Redmond, N.M.	100										
Rogers, Ky.	100										
Sessions, Texas	100										
Smith, Ore.	100										
Smith, Texas	100										
Tauzin, La.	100										
Taylor, N.C.	100										
Wicker, Miss.	100										
Wilson, N.M.	100										
Young, Fla.	100										

*Note: CQ's statistical methodology did not yield enough Senate votes in 1998 to serve as a reliable way to align members on a liberal-conservative spectrum.

fulness to political scientists because they constituted a statistically derived scale of political ideology. But in 1998, they became too rare in the Senate, and the votes were often on issues without clear ideological coloration.

A Powerful Force

The occasional alliance of Southern Democrats with conservative Republicans first became a force in President Franklin D. Roosevelt's second term, when it stopped his plan to "pack" the Supreme Court. In the 1940s and '50s, it blocked Democratic initiatives on civil rights, education and labor bills. In 1981, it passed President Ronald Reagan's budget. As recently as 1993, it formed to win approval of the North American Free Trade Agreement.

As a concept, the term also referred to the clout of Southern committee chairmen, who used the one-party dominance of their region to amass seniority. This reached its zenith in the 1950s, as Virginia Democrat Howard W. Smith (1931-67) refused to convene the House Rules Committee, which he chaired, to consider legislation he did not like.

But Smith lost his autonomy in 1961, and three years later, Arizona Sen. Barry Goldwater's presidential campaign gave Republicans a foothold in the South. Thirty years later, Republicans took a majority of Southern seats for the first time since Reconstruction on their way to control of Congress.

Not only are there fewer Democrats from the South, there is also greater diversity among them. Many House districts have been drawn to elect black (or, in Texas, Hispanic) members who are less conservative, and the urbanization of Southern cities has added a few white liberals. Southern is no longer a synonym for conservative.

CQ's statistical methodology did not yield enough Senate votes in 1998 to serve as a reliable way to align members on a liberal-conservative spectrum. While proud liberals Edward M. Kennedy, D-Mass., and Paul Wellstone, D-Minn., scored 0 percent support, those scoring 100 percent included several Republicans (such as William V. Roth Jr. of Delaware and Slade Gorton of Washington) who scored in the 60 percent to 70 percent range on the more subjective ratings of the American Conservative Union (ACU).

And none of the eight Senate votes on which the coalition formed are included in the votes chosen for ratings by the ACU or the liberal Americans for Democratic Action. None are CQ key votes.

In the House, the only CQ conservative coalition vote that was chosen by the ideological groups was a July 23 vote on overriding President Clinton's veto of an abortion-procedure bill. Without the formation of the coalition, the vote probably would not have hit the two-thirds majority needed for overrides. The bill died in the Senate in September on a key vote when the coalition did not form to pass it.

The 42 votes in the House database (7.9 percent of all House roll call votes) are more in line with prior years, and they yield results that seem to track with other ideological measuring sticks.

Three of the four Southern Democrats who voted for impeachment (Ralph M. Hall and Charles W. Stenholm of Texas and Virgil H. Goode Jr. of Virginia) rank among those voting with the coalition 90 percent of the time.

Those voting in opposition to the coalition rank high in other indices, and GOP opponents such as Constance A. Morella of Maryland and Christopher Shays of Connecticut voted against impeachment.

The one anomaly is Ron Paul of Texas, who ranked third in opposition and yet is considered one of the most conservative members. But the former Libertarian Party candidate for president is a maverick who led his party in opposition to the coalition in 1997. ◆

Lawmakers Sustain Historically High Voting Participation Rate

Definition

How often a member voted yea or nay on roll call votes on the floor of the House or Senate.

1998 Data

	Recorded Votes	Percent
Senate	314	97.4%
House	533	95.5%
Total Congress	847	95.7%

For More Information

Senators' scores B-29
House members' scores B-30

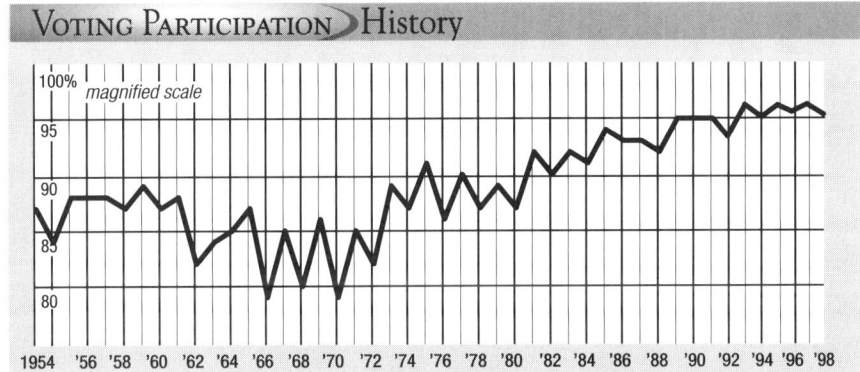

Members of Congress continued to rack up strong voting records in 1998 with a 95.7 percent overall participation rate. That was only slightly lower than the previous election-year record of 95.8 percent set two years earlier.

In a repeat of the pattern set in 1995-96, however, 1998 saw a drop from the preceding year, due in significant part to campaign demands and retirements. The overall participation rate in 1997, as in 1995, was 96.5.

Voting participation — measured by how often members vote yea or nay on roll call votes — has climbed during the past decade, reaching at least 95 percent in every year but one. Members' voting diligence stems in part from a desire to avoid the kind of ugly campaign brawls seen most recently in last fall's race between Sen. Alfonse M. D'Amato, R-N.Y., and his challenger, Rep. Charles E. Schumer, D-N.Y.

D'Amato targeted Schumer's voting record, accusing him of failing to represent his constituents by missing more than 100 floor votes and posting a 79 percent voting participation rate in 1998 — in contrast to D'Amato's 97 percent score. Schumer argued that his 1998 record was out of line with his usual voting diligence and that his previous participation scores had regularly been over 90 percent.

D'Amato's strategy backfired, however, when his own voting record as a member of supervisory boards for Nassau County and the Town of Hempstead was examined. It was reported that in 1980, while D'Amato was running for the U.S. Senate, he missed more than 900 votes before the two boards. He went on to win his race for the Senate that year.

In the end, voters were not as impressed with D'Amato's Senate attendance record as he would have liked, and he lost his re-election bid to Schumer. While the race may not have hinged on the attendance issue, the negative campaign is a continuing reminder of the potential cost of missing a large number of roll call votes.

Sixteen senators maintained 100 percent voting scores in 1998. Nine had perfect scores for both sessions of the 105th Congress, including Charles E. Grassley, R-Iowa, who currently has the longest streak of perfect attendance of any member in Congress. Grassley has not missed a vote since July 1993.

Few members had an absence excuse as airtight as that of Sen. John Glenn, D-Ohio, whose participation rate of 76.4 percent was the lowest in the Senate. After casting his last vote Sept. 29, he began preparations with NASA to serve as a payload specialist aboard the space shuttle Discovery. Only four other senators had scores lower than 90 percent: Ernest F. Hollings, D-S.C., Arlen Specter, R-Pa., Daniel K. Inouye, D-Hawaii, and

Vote Studies

Jesse Helms, R-N.C. Helms and Specter underwent surgery in 1998.

Overall, the average Senate participation rate was 97.4 percent, lower than last year's rate of 98.7 percent, which was the highest recorded for either chamber in the 46 years that Congressional Quarterly has been tracking participation levels.

The average in the House was 95.5 percent, also lower than last year's 96.3 percent rate. Nine members had perfect attendance, including three freshmen.

Only three House members had a 100 percent attendance rate for the entire 105th Congress: Jim Ramstad, R-Minn., Michael Pappas, R-N.J., and Jesse L. Jackson Jr., D-Ill. Pappas, however, will not be able to add to his streak; he lost his bid for re-election to Democratic challenger Rush D. Holt.

Thirty-four House members fell below 90 percent, compared with 19 members in 1997. Of the 10 members below 80 percent, five were running for higher offices: Jane Harman, D-Calif., Frank Riggs, R-Calif., Glenn Poshard, D-Ill., Barbara B. Kennelly, D-Conn., and Schumer. All five had participated in more than 90 percent of the roll call votes in 1997. Of the five, only Schumer was successful in his race.

Jackson, with a three-year streak that began Jan. 3, 1996, has the longest perfect attendance record of any House member. But he has more than three decades to go before he nears the record of former Rep. William Natcher, D-Ky. (1953-94), who did not miss a roll call vote in 40 years. ◆

Guide to CQ's Voting Analyses

Since 1945, Congressional Quarterly has analyzed the voting behavior of members of Congress. These studies have become references for academics, journalists, politicians and students who want information on how Congress behaves as an institution and how individual members vote.

What votes are used: CQ bases its vote studies on all roll call votes in which members were asked to vote "yea" or "nay." In 1998 there were 533 such votes in the House and 314 in the Senate.

Those totals include votes in the House to approve the Journal (11 in 1998) and in the Senate to instruct the sergeant at arms to request members' presence in the chamber (three in 1998). They do not include quorum calls, which require only that members vote "present." The House held 14 such votes in 1998.

The separate studies on presidential support, party unity and the conservative coalition cover specific votes selected from the total according to the criteria described on pp. B-4, B-6 and B-9.

Individual scores: In most of the charts that follow, a member's scores are calculated two ways: the first based on all votes, regardless of whether the member voted; the second based only on the votes the individual member actually cast.

The lists of leading scorers on pp. B-5, B-8 and B-10 are based on votes cast, not counting absences.

Overall scores: For consistency with previous years, graphs and breakdowns of chambers, parties and regions are based on the first set of scores. (*Methodology, 1987 Almanac, p. 22-C*)

Rounding: Scores are rounded to the nearest percentage point, except that rounding is not used to bring any score up to 100 percent.

Regions: Congressional Quarterly defines regions of the United States as follows: **East:** Conn., Del., Maine, Md., Mass., N.H., N.J., N.Y., Pa., R.I., Vt., W.Va. **West:** Alaska, Ariz., Calif., Colo., Hawaii, Idaho, Mont., Nev., N.M., Ore., Utah, Wash., Wyo. **South:** Ala., Ark., Fla., Ga., Ky., La., Miss., N.C., Okla., S.C., Tenn., Texas, Va. **Midwest:** Ill., Ind., Iowa, Kan., Mich., Minn., Mo., Neb., N.D., Ohio, S.D., Wis.

References to Northern Democrats and Northern Republicans include all members who do not represent the 13 Southern states, as defined by CQ.

Presidential Support Background

Congressional Quarterly determines presidential positions on congressional votes by examining the statements made by President Clinton or his authorized spokesmen.

Support measures the percentage of the time members voted in accord with the position of the president.

Opposition measures the percentage of the time members voted against the president's position. **Success** measures the percentage of the contested votes on which the president prevailed. Absences lowered parties' scores. Scores for 1997 are given for comparison.

National Security vs. Domestic Issues

Following are presidential success scores broken down into domestic and national security issues, with national security comprising votes on issues of foreign policy and defense.

	National Security		Domestic		Average	
	1998	1997	1998	1997	1998	1997
Senate	75%	58%	63%	75%	67%	71%
House	31	18	38	47	37	39
Average	**58**	**32**	**49**	**61**	**51**	**54**

Average Scores

	Support					Opposition			
	Republicans		Democrats			Republicans		Democrats	
	1998	1997	1998	1997		1998	1997	1998	1997
Senate	41%	60%	82%	85%	Senate	56%	39%	13%	13%
House	26	30	74	71	House	71	68	21	26

Regional Averages

	Support									Opposition							
	East		West		South		Midwest			East		West		South		Midwest	
	1998	1997	1998	1997	1998	1997	1998	1997		1998	1997	1998	1997	1998	1997	1998	1997
Republicans									**Republicans**								
Senate	53%	66%	41%	60%	35%	56%	40%	58%	Senate	43%	31%	55%	39%	61%	42%	59%	41%
House	34	39	24	28	22	27	26	31	House	64	60	72	68	74	71	72	68
Democrats									**Democrats**								
Senate	84	84	81	87	81	83	83	86	Senate	12	12	14	12	17	17	13	13
House	77	73	79	77	68	66	73	69	House	19	24	16	20	27	31	23	28

Success Rate History

Average score for both chambers of Congress:

Eisenhower	
1953	89.0%
1954	82.8
1955	75.0
1956	70.0
1957	68.0
1958	76.0
1959	52.0
1960	65.0

Kennedy	
1961	81.0%
1962	85.4
1963	87.1

Johnson	
1964	88.0%
1965	93.0
1966	79.0
1967	79.0
1968	75.0

Nixon	
1969	74.0%
1970	77.0
1971	75.0
1972	66.0
1973	50.6
1974	59.6

Ford	
1974	58.2%
1975	61.0
1976	53.8

Carter	
1977	75.4%
1978	78.3
1979	76.8
1980	75.1

Reagan	
1981	82.4%
1982	72.4
1983	67.1
1984	65.8
1985	59.9
1986	56.1
1987	43.5
1988	47.4

Bush	
1989	62.6%
1990	46.8
1991	54.2
1992	43.0

Clinton	
1993	86.4%
1994	86.4
1995	36.2
1996	55.1
1997	53.6
1998	50.6

1998 House Presidential Position Votes

The following is a list of House votes in 1998 on which there was a clear presidential position. Votes are categorized by topic and listed by roll call number with a brief description.

Domestic Policy

21 Victories

Vote Number	Description
17	Voter identification
25	Telecommunications
37	Puerto Rico
38	Telecommunications
39	Child support
80	Environment
100	Law enforcement
101	Federal courts
133	Affirmative action
139	Child support
140	Law enforcement
197	Vocational aid
201	Religious freedom amendment
204	Legal immigrants
297	Nutrition
312	NEA
398	Executive orders
426	Head Start
489	National parks
544	Impeachment
546	Impeachment

38 Defeats

Vote Number	Description
9	Education
24	Federal agencies
50	Federal agencies
51	Property rights
52	Property rights
74	Small business
78	Union organizing
96	Transportation
114	Needle exchange
119	Education
151	Financial services
160	Federal mandates
163	Federal courts
171	Abortion
225	Bankruptcy law
228	Minimum wage
243	Education
280	Abortion
282	Environment
296	Housing
325	Abortion (veto override)
327	Environment
336	Health care
339	Health care
349	Domestic partners
388	Census sampling
411	Education
412	Needle exchange
414	Adoption
416	D.C. appropriations
424	Education
451	Education
452	Education
479	Agriculture appropriations
506	Bankruptcy law
542	Censure
543	Impeachment
545	Impeachment

Defense and Foreign Policy

4 Victories

Vote Number	Description
58	Bosnia policy
71	Visas
317	China MFN
356	Vietnam policy

9 Defeats

Vote Number	Description
155	Religious persecution
168	China policy
169	China policy
170	China policy
181	Nuclear exports
211	Iran sanctions
377	Iran sanctions
442	Drug interdiction
449	Foreign aid

Economic Affairs and Trade

5 Victories

Vote Number	Description
47	Trade
63	International environment
102	Tax limit amendment
274	IRS overhaul
538	Omnibus appropriations

5 Defeats

Vote Number	Description
10	Line item veto (veto override)
88	Supplemental appropriations
239	Tax code
464	Budget
469	Tax code

House Success Score

Victories 30
Defeats 52
Total 82
Success rate 36.6%

Background Material

1998 Senate Presidential Position Votes

The following is a list of Senate votes in 1998 on which there was a clear presidential position. Votes are categorized by topic and listed by roll call number with a brief description.

Domestic Policy

14 Victories

Vote Number	Description
20	Transportation
23	Affirmative action
119	Job training
128	Legal immigrants
129	Legal immigrants
130	Telecommunications
137	Digital copyright
148	Nuclear waste (cloture)
197	Property rights (cloture)
238	Banking
239	Credit unions
266	Union organizing (cloture)
277	Abortion (veto override)
290	Education

18 Defeats

Vote Number	Description
86	Education
90	Education
91	Education
94	Education
102	Education
138	Immigration
139	Immigration
141	Immigration
145	Tobacco policy
161	Tobacco policy (cloture)
162	Tobacco policy
169	Education
176	Abortion
192	Education
194	Education
268	Mining
294	Environment
298	Agriculture appropriations

Defense and Foreign Policy

15 Victories

Vote Number	Description
47	Mexico drug policy
106	NATO expansion
109	NATO expansion
110	Bosnia policy
111	NATO expansion
112	NATO expansion
117	NATO expansion
131	Anti-missile defense (cloture)
171	Bosnia policy
172	Women in the military
180	Women in the military
249	Bosnia policy
254	Nuclear test ban
256	International Monetary Fund
262	Anti-missile defense (cloture)

5 Defeats

Vote Number	Description
24	Intelligence policy
105	Family planning
146	Iran sanctions
174	Base closures
257	North Korea policy

Economic Affairs and Trade

3 Victories

Vote Number	Description
189	IRS overhaul
241	Tax code
314	Omnibus appropriations

1 Defeat

Vote Number	Description
13	Line-Item veto (veto override)

Nominations

16 Victories

Vote Number	Description
1	Ann L. Aiken
2	Carlos R. Moreno
3	Christine O.C. Miller
9	Dr. David Satcher
11	Margaret M. Morrow
18	Richard L. Young
33	Jeremy D. Fogel
35	Susan Graber
48	M. Margaret McKeown
61	G. Patrick Murphy
104	Scott Snyder Fleming
166	Susan Oki Mollway
182	A. Howard Matz
183	Victoria A. Roberts
295	Sonia Sotomayor
309	William A. Fletcher

Senate Success Score

Victories	48
Defeats	24
Total	**72**
Success rate	67%

Vote Studies

Presidential Support and Opposition: House

1. Clinton Support Score. Percentage of 82 recorded votes in 1998 on which President Clinton took a position and on which a representative voted "yea" or "nay" in agreement with the president's position. Failures to vote lowered both support and opposition scores.

2. Clinton Opposition Score. Percentage of 82 recorded votes in 1998 on which President Clinton took a position and on which a representative voted "yea" or "nay" in disagreement with the president's position. Failures to vote lowered both support and opposition scores.

3. Clinton Support Score (adjusted for absences). Percentage of 82 recorded votes in 1998 on which President Clinton took a position and on which a representative was present and voted "yea" or "nay" in agreement with the president's position. In this version of the study, absences were not counted; therefore, failures to vote did not lower support or opposition scores. Opposition scores, not listed here, are the inverse of the support score; i.e., the opposition score is equal to 100 percent minus the individual's support score.

[1] Barbara Lee, D-Calif., was sworn in April 21, replacing Ronald V. Dellums, D-Calif., who resigned Feb. 6. Lee was eligible for 62 presidential support votes in 1998. Dellums was eligible for two presidential support votes in 1998 but did not vote on either of them.

[2] Lois Capps, D-Calif., was sworn in March 17, replacing Walter Capps, D-Calif., who died Oct. 28, 1997. Lois Capps was eligible for 70 presidential support votes in 1998.

[3] Mary Bono, R-Calif., was sworn in April 21, replacing Sonny Bono, R-Calif., who died Jan. 5. Mary Bono was eligible for 62 presidential support votes in 1998. Sonny Bono was eligible for no presidential support votes in 1998.

[4] Newt Gingrich, R-Ga., as Speaker of the House, voted at his discretion on 30 presidential support votes in 1998.

[5] Heather Wilson, R-N.M., was sworn in June 25, replacing Stephen H. Schiff, R-N.M., who died March 25. Wilson was eligible for 37 presidential support votes in 1998. Schiff was eligible for 14 presidential support votes in 1998 but did not vote on any of them.

[6] Gregory W. Meeks, D-N.Y., was sworn in Feb. 5, replacing Floyd H. Flake, D-N.Y., who resigned on Nov. 15, 1997. Meeks was eligible for 80 presidential support votes in 1998.

[7] Robert A. Brady, D-Pa., was sworn in May 21, replacing Thomas M. Foglietta, D-Pa., who resigned Nov. 11, 1997. Brady was eligible for 46 presidential support votes in 1998.

Democrats *Republicans*
Independent

		1	2	3
ALABAMA				
1	*Callahan*	23	72	24
2	*Everett*	20	79	20
3	*Riley*	18	82	18
4	*Aderholt*	21	79	21
5	Cramer	52	44	54
6	*Bachus*	20	79	20
7	Hilliard	84	13	86
ALASKA				
AL	*Young*	27	70	28
ARIZONA				
1	*Salmon*	26	73	26
2	Pastor	82	18	82
3	*Stump*	20	80	20
4	*Shadegg*	22	77	22
5	*Kolbe*	40	60	40
6	*Hayworth*	23	77	23
ARKANSAS				
1	Berry	61	35	63
2	Snyder	80	18	81
3	*Hutchinson*	26	72	26
4	*Dickey*	24	74	25
CALIFORNIA				
1	*Riggs*	20	66	23
2	*Herger*	22	76	23
3	Fazio	77	18	81
4	*Doolittle*	16	79	17
5	Matsui	82	18	82
6	Woolsey	84	15	85
7	Miller	74	15	84
8	Pelosi	80	16	84
9	Lee[1]	85	11	85
10	Tauscher	77	23	77
11	*Pombo*	23	77	23
12	Lantos	80	18	81
13	Stark	82	12	87
14	Eshoo	87	10	90
15	*Campbell*	51	48	52
16	Lofgren	84	11	88
17	Farr	84	12	87
18	Condit	50	49	51
19	*Radanovich*	20	79	20
20	Dooley	80	20	80
21	*Thomas*	28	71	28
22	*Capps*[2]	73	23	73
23	*Gallegly*	21	78	21
24	Sherman	72	28	72
25	*McKeon*	23	74	24
26	Berman	76	13	85
27	*Rogan*	27	73	27
28	*Dreier*	26	73	26
29	Waxman	84	15	85
30	Becerra	82	11	88
31	Martinez	77	16	83
32	Dixon	76	13	85
33	Roybal-Allard	80	13	86
34	Torres	77	11	88
35	Waters	76	13	85
36	Harman	52	15	78
37	Millender-McD.	78	15	84
38	Horn	34	63	35
39	*Royce*	20	73	21
40	*Lewis*	32	65	33
41	*Kim*	28	72	28
42	Brown	77	13	85
43	*Calvert*	24	76	24
44	*Bono*[3]	23	59	23
45	*Rohrabacher*	26	74	26
46	Sanchez	71	20	78
47	*Cox*	26	70	27
48	*Packard*	20	74	21
49	*Bilbray*	34	65	35
50	Filner	84	15	85
51	*Cunningham*	22	67	25
52	*Hunter*	20	78	20
COLORADO				
1	DeGette	85	13	86
2	Skaggs	83	6	93
3	*McInnis*	26	72	26
4	*Schaffer*	18	82	18
5	*Hefley*	21	78	21
6	*Schaefer*	16	80	16
CONNECTICUT				
1	Kennelly	70	17	80
2	Gejdenson	83	17	83
3	DeLauro	82	18	82
4	*Shays*	57	43	57
5	Maloney	66	32	68
6	*Johnson*	57	43	57
DELAWARE				
AL	*Castle*	51	49	51
FLORIDA				
1	*Scarborough*	24	71	26
2	Boyd	61	38	62
3	Brown	77	15	84
4	*Fowler*	26	71	27
5	Thurman	77	23	77
6	*Stearns*	18	82	18
7	*Mica*	22	73	23
8	*McCollum*	26	73	26
9	*Bilirakis*	20	78	20
10	*Young*	20	61	24
11	Davis	73	26	74
12	*Canady*	22	78	22
13	*Miller*	30	66	32
14	*Goss*	28	59	32
15	*Weldon*	16	80	16
16	*Foley*	38	61	38
17	Meek	80	12	87
18	*Ros-Lehtinen*	27	65	29
19	Wexler	88	10	90
20	Deutsch	79	17	82
21	*Diaz-Balart*	32	66	33
22	*Shaw*	34	66	34
23	Hastings	84	10	90
GEORGIA				
1	*Kingston*	20	80	20
2	Bishop	57	41	58
3	*Collins*	12	87	12
4	McKinney	87	13	87
5	Lewis	74	11	87
6	*Gingrich*[4]	5	32	13
7	*Barr*	20	77	20
8	*Chambliss*	22	78	22
9	*Deal*	16	84	16
10	*Norwood*	17	78	18
11	*Linder*	20	76	21
HAWAII				
1	Abercrombie	82	18	82
2	Mink	83	15	85
IDAHO				
1	*Chenoweth*	29	71	29
2	*Crapo*	29	67	30
ILLINOIS				
1	Rush	79	15	84
2	Jackson	83	17	83
3	Lipinski	48	48	50
4	Gutierrez	80	17	83
5	Blagojevich	74	22	77
6	*Hyde*	20	79	20
7	Davis	84	15	85
8	*Crane*	23	74	24
9	Yates	68	9	89
10	*Porter*	39	57	41
11	*Weller*	26	72	26
12	Costello	67	32	68
13	*Fawell*	35	56	39

ND Northern Democrats SD Southern Democrats

Background Material

Member			
14 Hastert	21	78	21
15 Ewing	27	66	29
16 Manzullo	21	78	21
17 Evans	82	17	83
18 LaHood	28	71	28
19 Poshard	52	20	73
20 Shimkus	24	72	25

INDIANA
1 Visclosky	79	21	79
2 McIntosh	23	73	24
3 Roemer	61	39	61
4 Souder	24	73	25
5 Buyer	23	73	24
6 Burton	20	72	21
7 Pease	23	74	24
8 Hostettler	24	76	24
9 Hamilton	77	22	78
10 Carson	83	10	89

IOWA
1 Leach	51	46	53
2 Nussle	27	72	27
3 Boswell	65	35	65
4 Ganske	33	63	34
5 Latham	24	76	24

KANSAS
1 Moran	29	71	29
2 Ryun	21	77	21
3 Snowbarger	22	77	22
4 Tiahrt	20	79	20

KENTUCKY
1 Whitfield	23	74	24
2 Lewis	20	80	20
3 Northup	24	74	25
4 Bunning	20	77	20
5 Rogers	22	76	23
6 Baesler	60	38	61

LOUISIANA
1 Livingston	23	74	24
2 Jefferson	73	15	83
3 Tauzin	22	73	23
4 McCrery	24	71	26
5 Cooksey	23	71	25
6 Baker	20	79	20
7 John	43	43	50

MAINE
1 Allen	82	16	84
2 Baldacci	79	20	80

MARYLAND
1 Gilchrest	37	61	38
2 Ehrlich	24	73	25
3 Cardin	74	21	78
4 Wynn	82	17	83
5 Hoyer	80	18	81
6 Bartlett	18	80	19
7 Cummings	82	17	83
8 Morella	71	29	71

MASSACHUSETTS
1 Olver	85	12	88
2 Neal	77	20	80
3 McGovern	78	20	80
4 Frank	80	18	81
5 Meehan	82	11	88
6 Tierney	80	17	83
7 Markey	76	17	82
8 Kennedy	78	17	82
9 Moakley	67	18	79
10 Delahunt	83	17	83

MICHIGAN
1 Stupak	73	24	75
2 Hoekstra	24	76	24
3 Ehlers	33	67	33
4 Camp	27	73	27
5 Barcia	60	39	60
6 Upton	33	67	33
7 Smith	26	73	26
8 Stabenow	73	21	78
9 Kildee	74	26	74
10 Bonior	80	16	84
11 Knollenberg	24	76	24
12 Levin	83	17	83
13 Rivers	76	24	76
14 Conyers	79	9	90
15 Kilpatrick	77	11	88
16 Dingell	77	17	82

MINNESOTA
1 Gutknecht	24	76	24
2 Minge	71	28	72
3 Ramstad	43	57	43
4 Vento	85	15	85
5 Sabo	88	11	89
6 Luther	71	23	75
7 Peterson	55	45	55
8 Oberstar	83	15	85

MISSISSIPPI
1 Wicker	23	74	24
2 Thompson	77	17	82
3 Pickering	20	77	20
4 Parker	24	65	27
5 Taylor	33	66	33

MISSOURI
1 Clay	73	10	88
2 Talent	20	79	20
3 Gephardt	73	16	82
4 Skelton	57	41	58
5 McCarthy	80	18	81
6 Danner	45	52	46
7 Blunt	17	83	17
8 Emerson	22	78	22
9 Hulshof	24	74	25

MONTANA
AL Hill	27	68	28

NEBRASKA
1 Bereuter	28	72	28
2 Christensen	16	76	17
3 Barrett	27	73	27

NEVADA
1 Ensign	27	73	27
2 Gibbons	22	78	22

NEW HAMPSHIRE
1 Sununu	24	74	25
2 Bass	33	66	33

NEW JERSEY
1 Andrews	77	23	77
2 LoBiondo	35	65	35
3 Saxton	30	66	32
4 Smith	27	72	27
5 Roukema	34	66	34
6 Pallone	78	22	78
7 Franks	38	62	38
8 Pascrell	70	29	70
9 Rothman	80	17	83
10 Payne	82	10	89
11 Frelinghuysen	37	63	37
12 Pappas	23	77	23
13 Menendez	74	21	78

NEW MEXICO
1 Wilson[5]	22	35	22
2 Skeen	27	73	27
3 Redmond	24	68	26

NEW YORK
1 Forbes	41	59	41
2 Lazio	37	63	37
3 King	30	67	31
4 McCarthy	68	32	68
5 Ackerman	82	13	86
6 Meeks[6]	79	9	90
7 Manton	71	20	78
8 Nadler	76	20	79
9 Schumer	67	12	85
10 Towns	76	13	85
11 Owens	83	11	88
12 Velázquez	79	18	81
13 Fossella	23	77	23
14 Maloney	79	17	82
15 Rangel	77	11	88
16 Serrano	80	15	85
17 Engel	79	17	82
18 Lowey	82	17	83
19 Kelly	41	59	41
20 Gilman	45	54	46
21 McNulty	65	21	76
22 Solomon	17	82	17
23 Boehlert	60	40	60
24 McHugh	34	65	35
25 Walsh	35	63	36
26 Hinchey	82	17	83
27 Paxon	17	76	18
28 Slaughter	82	18	82
29 LaFalce	82	17	83
30 Quinn	30	65	32
31 Houghton	44	46	49

NORTH CAROLINA
1 Clayton	80	17	83
2 Etheridge	71	27	73
3 Jones	21	79	21
4 Price	77	23	77
5 Burr	23	73	24
6 Coble	16	83	16
7 McIntyre	51	46	52
8 Hefner	70	18	79
9 Myrick	18	77	19
10 Ballenger	22	77	22
11 Taylor	17	80	18
12 Watt	89	9	91

NORTH DAKOTA
AL Pomeroy	72	24	75

OHIO
1 Chabot	27	73	27
2 Portman	29	71	29
3 Hall	65	33	66
4 Oxley	24	72	25
5 Gillmor	28	70	29
6 Strickland	66	34	66
7 Hobson	28	71	28
8 Boehner	24	74	25
9 Kaptur	67	28	71
10 Kucinich	78	22	78
11 Stokes	82	12	87
12 Kasich	24	73	25
13 Brown	82	17	83
14 Sawyer	88	12	88
15 Pryce	26	59	30
16 Regula	28	72	28
17 Traficant	46	52	47
18 Ney	27	73	27
19 LaTourette	38	61	38

OKLAHOMA
1 Largent	26	71	27
2 Coburn	16	80	16
3 Watkins	23	73	24
4 Watts	21	79	21
5 Istook	16	77	17
6 Lucas	22	78	22

OREGON
1 Furse	74	11	87
2 Smith	17	72	19
3 Blumenauer	83	15	85
4 DeFazio	77	20	80
5 Hooley	77	22	78

PENNSYLVANIA
1 Brady[7]	83	6	88
2 Fattah	80	11	88
3 Borski	78	21	79
4 Klink	70	23	75
5 Peterson	24	76	24
6 Holden	61	39	61
7 Weldon	28	71	28
8 Greenwood	35	57	38
9 Shuster	24	71	26
10 McDade	18	55	25
11 Kanjorski	82	18	82
12 Murtha	72	27	73
13 Fox	34	66	34
14 Coyne	82	17	83
15 McHale	73	27	73
16 Pitts	21	78	21
17 Gekas	21	77	21
18 Doyle	66	30	68
19 Goodling	18	77	19
20 Mascara	73	27	73
21 English	35	63	36

RHODE ISLAND
1 Kennedy	79	21	79
2 Weygand	73	27	73

SOUTH CAROLINA
1 Sanford	33	67	33
2 Spence	18	82	18
3 Graham	22	78	22
4 Inglis	18	78	19
5 Spratt	71	27	73
6 Clyburn	83	17	83

SOUTH DAKOTA
AL Thune	23	77	23

TENNESSEE
1 Jenkins	20	80	20
2 Duncan	22	78	22
3 Wamp	18	82	18
4 Hilleary	20	79	20
5 Clement	65	34	65
6 Gordon	61	38	62
7 Bryant	20	79	20
8 Tanner	55	39	58
9 Ford	61	21	75

TEXAS
1 Sandlin	61	37	63
2 Turner	52	46	53
3 Johnson	20	78	20
4 Hall	29	70	30
5 Sessions	20	78	20
6 Barton	20	78	20
7 Archer	21	77	21
8 Brady	20	77	20
9 Lampson	80	18	81
10 Doggett	80	18	81
11 Edwards	80	18	81
12 Granger	28	72	28
13 Thornberry	23	77	23
14 Paul	30	67	31
15 Hinojosa	76	20	79
16 Reyes	73	21	78
17 Stenholm	49	51	49
18 Jackson-Lee	78	16	83
19 Combest	22	78	22
20 Gonzalez	12	1	91
21 Smith	22	74	23
22 DeLay	20	78	20
23 Bonilla	29	67	30
24 Frost	71	26	73
25 Bentsen	78	22	78
26 Armey	22	77	22
27 Ortiz	66	30	68
28 Rodriguez	78	18	81
29 Green	68	28	71
30 Johnson	79	13	86

UTAH
1 Hansen	18	72	20
2 Cook	18	78	19
3 Cannon	17	72	19

VERMONT
AL Sanders	83	15	85

VIRGINIA
1 Bateman	21	57	27
2 Pickett	60	39	60
3 Scott	89	11	89
4 Sisisky	63	37	63
5 Goode	26	74	26
6 Goodlatte	23	77	23
7 Bliley	23	77	23
8 Moran	80	18	81
9 Boucher	77	21	79
10 Wolf	74	76	24
11 Davis	33	65	34

WASHINGTON
1 White	29	70	30
2 Metcalf	21	79	21
3 Smith	20	77	20
4 Hastings	22	76	23
5 Nethercutt	27	73	27
6 Dicks	84	15	85
7 McDermott	89	5	95
8 Dunn	23	76	23
9 Smith	79	20	80

WEST VIRGINIA
1 Mollohan	63	28	69
2 Wise	74	21	78
3 Rahall	74	22	77

WISCONSIN
1 Neumann	22	77	22
2 Klug	33	62	35
3 Kind	77	23	77
4 Kleczka	74	24	75
5 Barrett	88	11	89
6 Petri	30	68	31
7 Obey	88	11	89
8 Johnson	72	27	73
9 Sensenbrenner	22	78	22

WYOMING
AL Cubin	21	79	21

Southern states - Ala., Ark., Fla., Ga., Ky., La., Miss., N.C., Okla., S.C., Tenn., Texas, Va.

Vote Studies

	1	2	3
ALABAMA			
Shelby	33	65	34
Sessions	28	71	28
ALASKA			
Stevens	53	44	54
Murkowski	38	51	42
ARIZONA			
McCain	46	47	49
Kyl	31	61	33
ARKANSAS			
Hutchinson	24	68	26
Bumpers	85	13	87
CALIFORNIA			
Feinstein	88	13	88
Boxer	85	10	90
COLORADO			
Campbell	47	53	47
Allard	28	72	28
CONNECTICUT			
Dodd	93	7	93
Lieberman	83	17	83
DELAWARE			
Roth	58	33	64
Biden	83	8	91
FLORIDA			
Mack	50	50	50
Graham	83	17	83
GEORGIA			
Coverdell	39	58	40
Cleland	86	13	87
HAWAII			
Inouye	75	11	87
Akaka	81	8	91
IDAHO			
Craig	29	71	29
Kempthorne	33	65	34
ILLINOIS			
Moseley-Braun	75	13	86
Durbin	86	10	90
INDIANA			
Lugar	54	46	54
Coats	39	56	41
IOWA			
Grassley	39	61	39
Harkin	81	11	88
KANSAS			
Brownback	36	63	37
Roberts	35	64	35
KENTUCKY			
McConnell	39	61	39
Ford	75	22	77
LOUISIANA			
Breaux	78	21	79
Landrieu	85	14	86
MAINE			
Snowe	54	44	55
Collins	63	38	63
MARYLAND			
Sarbanes	92	8	92
Mikulski	86	8	91
MASSACHUSETTS			
Kennedy	92	4	96
Kerry	90	6	94
MICHIGAN			
Abraham	46	54	46
Levin	88	7	93
MINNESOTA			
Grams	39	61	39
Wellstone	85	13	87
MISSISSIPPI			
Cochran	53	47	53
Lott	39	60	39
MISSOURI			
Bond	38	61	38
Ashcroft	24	76	24
MONTANA			
Burns	38	63	38
Baucus	71	17	81
NEBRASKA			
Hagel	42	57	42
Kerrey	89	10	90
NEVADA			
Reid	76	21	79
Bryan	88	13	88
NEW HAMPSHIRE			
Smith	19	81	19
Gregg	42	54	43
NEW JERSEY			
Lautenberg	90	10	90
Torricelli	75	21	78
NEW MEXICO			
Domenici	53	40	57
Bingaman	81	13	87
NEW YORK			
D'Amato	56	38	60
Moynihan	71	19	78
NORTH CAROLINA			
Helms	25	53	32
Faircloth	25	63	29
NORTH DAKOTA			
Conrad	75	25	75
Dorgan	75	24	76
OHIO			
DeWine	51	49	51
Glenn	72	3	96
OKLAHOMA			
Nickles	22	76	23
Inhofe	13	76	14
OREGON			
Smith	54	44	55
Wyden	79	14	85
PENNSYLVANIA			
Specter	49	32	60
Santorum	40	60	40
RHODE ISLAND			
Chafee	76	22	77
Reed	90	10	90
SOUTH CAROLINA			
Thurmond	44	56	44
Hollings	67	24	74
SOUTH DAKOTA			
Daschle	90	10	90
Johnson	89	11	89
TENNESSEE			
Thompson	42	58	42
Frist	44	54	45
TEXAS			
Gramm	32	64	33
Hutchison	35	60	37
UTAH			
Hatch	47	51	48
Bennett	47	42	53
VERMONT			
Jeffords	68	31	69
Leahy	81	17	83
VIRGINIA			
Warner	38	58	39
Robb	90	10	90
WASHINGTON			
Gorton	49	51	49
Murray	82	18	82
WEST VIRGINIA			
Byrd	74	26	74
Rockefeller	82	6	94
WISCONSIN			
Kohl	85	14	86
Feingold	83	17	83
WYOMING			
Thomas	39	60	39
Enzi	31	68	31

Democrats *Republicans*

ND Northern Democrats   SD Southern Democrats

Southern states - Ala., Ark., Fla., Ga., Ky., La., Miss., N.C., Okla., S.C., Tenn., Texas, Va.

Presidential Support and Opposition: Senate

1. Clinton Support Score. Percentage of 72 recorded votes in 1998 on which President Clinton took a position and on which a senator voted "yea" or "nay" in agreement with the president's position. Failures to vote lowered both support and opposition scores.

2. Clinton Opposition Score. Percentage of 72 recorded votes in 1998 on which President Clinton took a position and on which a senator voted "yea" or "nay" in disagreement with the president's position. Failures to vote lowered both support and opposition scores.

3. Clinton Support Score (adjusted for absences). Percentage of 72 recorded votes in 1998 on which President Clinton took a position and on which a senator was present and voted "yea" or "nay" in agreement with the president's position. In this version of the study, absences were not counted; therefore, failures to vote did not lower support or opposition scores. Opposition scores, not listed here, are the inverse of the support score; i.e., the opposition score is equal to 100 percent minus the individual's support score.

Party Unity Background

Party unity votes. Recorded votes that split the parties, with a majority of voting Democrats opposing a majority of voting Republicans. Members who switched parties are accounted for.

Party unity support. Percentage of party unity votes on which members voted "yea" or "nay" *in agreement* with a majority of their party. Failures to vote lowered scores for chambers and parties.

Opposition to party. Percentage of party unity votes on which members voted "yea" or "nay" *in disagreement* with a majority of their party. Failures to vote lowered scores for chambers and parties.

Average Scores by Chamber

	Republicans		Democrats			Republicans		Democrats	
	1998	1997	1998	1997		1998	1997	1998	1997
Party Unity	**86%**	**88%**	**83%**	**82%**	**Opposition**	**12%**	**9%**	**13%**	**15%**
Senate	86	87	87	85	Senate	12	12	10	14
House	86	88	82	82	House	11	9	13	15

Sectional Support, Opposition

Senate	Support	Opposition	House	Support	Opposition
Northern Republicans	84	15	Northern Republicans	84	13
Southern Republicans	91	7	Southern Republicans	88	8
Northern Democrats	88	9	Northern Democrats	85	11
Southern Democrats	83	15	Southern Democrats	74	20

1998 Victories, Defeats

	Senate	House	Total
Republicans won, Democrats lost	114	216	330
Democrats won, Republicans lost	61	80	141

Unanimous Voting by Parties

The number of times each party voted unanimously on party unity votes:

	Senate		House		Total	
	1998	1997	1998	1997	1998	1997
Republicans voted unanimously	33	38	42	63	75	101
Democrats voted unanimously	46	35	8	11	54	46

Party Unity Average Scores

Average score for each party in both chambers of Congress:

Year	Republicans	Democrats	Year	Republicans	Democrats
1963	72%	71%	1981	76%	69%
1964	69	67	1982	71	72
1965	70	69	1983	74	76
1966	67	61	1984	72	74
1967	71	66	1985	75	79
1968	63	57	1986	71	78
1969	62	62	1987	74	81
1970	59	57	1988	73	79
1971	66	62	1989	73	81
1972	64	57	1990	74	81
1973	68	68	1991	78	81
1974	62	63	1992	79	79
1975	70	69	1993	84	85
1976	66	65	1994	83	83
1977	70	67	1995	91	80
1978	67	64	1996	87	80
1979	72	69	1997	88	82
1980	70	68	1998	86	83

1998 Party Unity Votes

Following are the votes, by roll call number, on which a majority of Democrats voted against a majority of Republicans.

House
(296 of 533 "yea/nay" votes)

2	37	85	120	160	216	244	280	311	347	384	406	447	481	514
3	43	86	121	165	217	246	281	312	349	385	407	448	484	520
4	45	87	123	166	218	247	282	313	351	386	408	449	485	522
5	46	88	124	171	219	248	283	315	352	387	409	450	488	523
6	47	91	130	173	220	249	284	320	356	388	411	451	489	530
7	50	93	132	176	221	259	285	321	357	389	412	452	490	534
8	51	94	133	179	222	260	286	325	358	390	413	459	493	535
9	52	102	134	180	223	263	287	327	359	391	414	461	494	537
12	58	103	136	182	224	265	288	328	360	392	415	462	497	540
15	68	104	137	186	225	267	290	329	362	393	416	463	498	541
17	69	106	145	188	227	269	291	330	365	394	421	464	500	542
19	72	107	146	191	228	270	292	331	366	395	422	465	501	543
20	73	108	147	196	234	271	293	332	367	396	423	466	502	544
22	74	109	150	200	235	272	295	334	368	398	424	468	503	545
23	75	113	151	201	236	273	296	335	370	400	433	469	504	546
24	76	114	153	202	238	275	302	336	375	401	436	470	505	547
29	78	115	156	205	239	276	306	337	376	402	439	473	506	
30	79	117	157	208	241	277	307	338	379	403	440	476	508	
34	80	118	158	209	242	278	308	339	381	404	443	478	512	
36	83	119	159	210	243	279	310	343	382	405	446	480	513	

Senate
(175 of 314 "yea/nay" votes)

1	19	52	68	82	96	125	153	169	194	216	230	249	277	296
4	21	53	69	83	97	131	154	171	197	217	231	254	278	298
5	22	54	70	84	98	133	155	172	198	218	233	258	279	300
6	23	55	71	86	99	134	156	174	200	219	236	262	280	305
9	34	56	73	87	100	138	157	175	201	220	237	264	281	309
10	36	57	74	88	102	139	158	176	204	221	238	266	282	311
11	38	58	76	89	105	142	159	177	205	222	240	267	283	312
12	42	60	77	90	109	144	160	180	207	223	241	268	286	
14	45	62	78	91	120	148	161	187	208	224	242	272	287	
15	46	64	79	93	122	150	162	188	210	225	243	273	289	
16	47	65	80	94	123	151	164	191	212	226	244	274	294	
17	50	67	81	95	124	152	166	192	215	227	246	275	295	

Proportion of Partisan Roll Calls

How often a majority of Democrats voted against a majority of Republicans:

Year	House	Senate	Year	House	Senate	Year	House	Senate	Year	House	Senate
1955	41%	30%	1966	41%	50%	1977	42%	42%	1988	47%	42%
1956	44	53	1967	36	35	1978	33	45	1989	55	35
1957	59	36	1968	35	32	1979	47	47	1990	49	54
1958	40	44	1969	31	36	1980	38	46	1991	55	49
1959	55	48	1970	27	35	1981	37	48	1992	64	53
1960	53	37	1971	38	42	1982	36	43	1993	65	67
1961	50	62	1972	27	36	1983	56	44	1994	62	52
1962	46	41	1973	42	40	1984	47	40	1995	73	69
1963	49	47	1974	29	44	1985	61	50	1996	56	62
1964	55	36	1975	48	48	1986	57	52	1997	50	50
1965	52	42	1976	36	37	1987	64	41	1998	56	56

Background Material

	1	2	3
ALABAMA			
Shelby	91	9	91
Sessions	98	2	98
ALASKA			
Stevens	82	18	82
Murkowski	91	7	93
ARIZONA			
McCain	81	15	84
Kyl	93	4	96
ARKANSAS			
Hutchinson	94	2	98
Bumpers	95	5	95
CALIFORNIA			
Feinstein	87	13	87
Boxer	88	10	90
COLORADO			
Campbell	82	18	82
Allard	96	3	97
CONNECTICUT			
Dodd	90	9	91
Lieberman	80	20	80
DELAWARE			
Roth	75	21	79
Biden	85	13	87
FLORIDA			
Mack	86	13	87
Graham	85	15	85
GEORGIA			
Coverdell	90	8	92
Cleland	87	13	87
HAWAII			
Inouye	79	6	93
Akaka	89	4	96
IDAHO			
Craig	99	1	99
Kempthorne	96	4	96
ILLINOIS			
Moseley-Braun	85	8	91
Durbin	94	5	95
INDIANA			
Lugar	84	16	84
Coats	87	10	89

	1	2	3
IOWA			
Grassley	86	14	86
Harkin	92	2	98
KANSAS			
Brownback	96	4	96
Roberts	94	5	95
KENTUCKY			
McConnell	95	5	95
Ford	82	17	83
LOUISIANA			
Breaux	73	27	73
Landrieu	88	11	89
MAINE			
Snowe	65	35	65
Collins	67	33	67
MARYLAND			
Sarbanes	99	1	99
Mikulski	94	3	97
MASSACHUSETTS			
Kennedy	98	0	100
Kerry	95	5	95
MICHIGAN			
Abraham	91	9	91
Levin	95	2	98
MINNESOTA			
Grams	97	3	97
Wellstone	98	1	99
MISSISSIPPI			
Cochran	86	14	86
Lott	94	4	96
MISSOURI			
Bond	86	12	88
Ashcroft	98	2	98
MONTANA			
Burns	94	6	94
Baucus	80	15	84
NEBRASKA			
Hagel	89	11	89
Kerrey	88	11	89
NEVADA			
Reid	78	19	81
Bryan	90	10	90

	1	2	3
NEW HAMPSHIRE			
Smith	98	1	99
Gregg	90	9	91
NEW JERSEY			
Lautenberg	97	3	97
Torricelli	83	14	85
NEW MEXICO			
Domenici	81	16	83
Bingaman	83	13	87
NEW YORK			
D'Amato	60	37	62
Moynihan	83	10	89
NORTH CAROLINA			
Helms	75	2	97
Faircloth	89	9	91
NORTH DAKOTA			
Conrad	87	13	87
Dorgan	87	13	87
OHIO			
DeWine	82	18	82
Glenn	77	1	99
OKLAHOMA			
Nickles	98	2	98
Inhofe	95	3	97
OREGON			
Smith	85	15	85
Wyden	86	12	88
PENNSYLVANIA			
Specter	41	43	49
Santorum	91	9	91
RHODE ISLAND			
Chafee	57	42	57
Reed	98	2	98
SOUTH CAROLINA			
Thurmond	91	9	91
Hollings	74	17	81
SOUTH DAKOTA			
Daschle	90	10	90
Johnson	93	7	93
TENNESSEE			
Thompson	87	13	87
Frist	94	6	94

Democrats **Republicans**

	1	2	3
TEXAS			
Gramm	97	3	97
Hutchison	89	8	92
UTAH			
Hatch	87	13	87
Bennett	81	15	84
VERMONT			
Jeffords	49	50	49
Leahy	86	13	87
VIRGINIA			
Warner	83	14	85
Robb	83	17	83
WASHINGTON			
Gorton	83	17	83
Murray	91	9	91
WEST VIRGINIA			
Byrd	72	28	72
Rockefeller	88	7	93
WISCONSIN			
Kohl	87	13	87
Feingold	86	14	86
WYOMING			
Thomas	94	5	95
Enzi	96	4	96

ND Northern Democrats   SD Southern Democrats

Southern states - Ala., Ark., Fla., Ga., Ky., La., Miss., N.C., Okla., S.C., Tenn., Texas, Va.

Party Unity and Party Opposition: Senate

1. Party Unity. Percentage of 175 party unity recorded votes in 1998 on which a senator voted "yea" or "nay" in agreement with a majority of his or her party. (Party unity roll calls are those on which a majority of voting Democrats opposed a majority of voting Republicans.) Failures to vote lowered both party unity and party opposition scores.

2. Party Opposition. Percentage of 175 party unity recorded votes in 1998 on which a senator voted "yea" or "nay" in disagreement with a majority of his or her party. Failures to vote lowered both party unity and party opposition scores.

3. Party Unity (adjusted for absences). Percentage of 175 party unity recorded votes in 1998 on which a senator was present and voted "yea" or "nay" in agreement with a majority of his or her party. In this version of the study, absences were not counted; therefore, failures to vote did not lower unity or opposition scores. Opposition scores, not listed here, are the inverse of the unity score; i.e., the opposition score is equal to 100 percent minus the individual's unity score.

Vote Studies

Party Unity and Party Opposition: House

1. Party Unity. Percentage of 296 party unity recorded votes in 1998 on which a representative voted "yea" or "nay" in agreement with a majority of his or her party. (Party unity roll calls are those on which a majority of voting Democrats opposed a majority of voting Republicans.) Failures to vote lowered both party unity and party opposition scores.

2. Party Opposition. Percentage of 296 party unity recorded votes in 1998 on which a representative voted "yea" or "nay" in disagreement with a majority of his or her party. Failures to vote lowered both party unity and party opposition scores.

3. Party Unity (adjusted for absences). Percentage of 296 party unity recorded votes in 1998 on which a representative was present and voted "yea" or "nay" in agreement with a majority of his or her party. In this version of the study, absences were not counted; therefore, failures to vote did not lower unity or opposition scores. Opposition scores, not listed here, are the inverse of the unity score; i.e., the opposition score is equal to 100 percent minus the individual's unity score.

---

[1] Barbara Lee, D-Calif., was sworn in April 21, replacing Ronald V. Dellums, D-Calif., who resigned Feb. 6. Lee was eligible for 249 party unity votes in 1998. Dellums was eligible for eight party unity votes in 1998. His support score was 75 percent; opposition score, zero; support score adjusted for absences 100 percent.

[2] Lois Capps, D-Calif., was sworn in March 17, replacing Walter Capps, D-Calif., who died Oct. 28, 1997. Lois Capps was eligible for 268 party unity votes in 1998.

[3] Mary Bono, R-Calif., was sworn in April 21, replacing Sonny Bono, R-Calif., who died Jan. 5. Mary Bono was eligible for 249 party unity votes in 1998. Sonny Bono was eligible for no party unity votes in 1998.

[4] Newt Gingrich, R-Ga., as Speaker of the House, voted at his discretion on 61 party unity votes in 1998.

[5] Heather Wilson, R-N.M., was sworn in June 25, replacing Stephen H. Schiff, R-N.M., who died March 25. Wilson was eligible for 162 party unity votes in 1998. Schiff was eligible for 29 party unity votes in 1998 but did not vote on any of them.

[6] Gregory W. Meeks, D-N.Y., was sworn in Feb. 5, replacing Floyd H. Flake, D-N.Y., who resigned on Nov. 15, 1997. Meeks was eligible for 288 party unity votes in 1998.

[7] Robert A. Brady, D-Pa., was sworn in May 21, replacing Thomas M. Foglietta, D-Pa., who resigned Nov. 11, 1997. Brady was eligible for 211 party unity votes in 1998.

Democrats *Republicans*
Independent

	1	2	3
ALABAMA			
1 *Callahan*	89	6	93
2 *Everett*	94	6	94
3 *Riley*	93	6	94
4 *Aderholt*	90	9	91
5 Cramer	58	39	60
6 *Bachus*	89	10	89
7 Hilliard	90	5	94
ALASKA			
AL *Young*	84	11	89
ARIZONA			
1 *Salmon*	93	6	94
2 Pastor	91	9	91
3 *Stump*	93	7	93
4 *Shadegg*	97	3	97
5 *Kolbe*	80	19	81
6 *Hayworth*	94	6	94
ARKANSAS			
1 Berry	68	29	70
2 Snyder	79	20	80
3 *Hutchinson*	85	10	90
4 *Dickey*	91	7	93
CALIFORNIA			
1 *Riggs*	74	6	92
2 *Herger*	93	4	96
3 Fazio	88	10	90
4 *Doolittle*	91	6	94
5 Matsui	92	7	92
6 Woolsey	95	5	95
7 Miller	90	2	97
8 Pelosi	94	3	97
9 Lee[1]	98	1	99
10 Tauscher	79	19	81
11 *Pombo*	92	7	93
12 Lantos	92	5	95
13 Stark	92	2	98
14 Eshoo	92	5	95
15 *Campbell*	64	36	64
16 Lofgren	90	8	92
17 Farr	90	5	95
18 Condit	62	37	63
19 *Radanovich*	90	4	96
20 Dooley	79	19	80
21 *Thomas*	89	10	90
22 Capps[2]	90	8	91
23 *Gallegly*	90	10	90
24 Sherman	82	17	83
25 *McKeon*	94	5	95
26 Berman	83	4	95
27 *Rogan*	88	8	92
28 *Dreier*	90	9	91
29 Waxman	94	3	97
30 Becerra	90	1	99
31 Martinez	77	15	84
32 Dixon	85	5	95
33 Roybal-Allard	91	1	99
34 Torres	81	4	95
35 Waters	85	5	94
36 Harman	63	13	83
37 Millender-McD.	89	4	96
38 *Horn*	73	27	73
39 *Royce*	83	9	90
40 *Lewis*	86	12	88
41 *Kim*	84	15	85
42 Brown	90	6	94
43 *Calvert*	93	6	94
44 *Bono*[3]	92	7	92
45 *Rohrabacher*	90	10	90
46 Sanchez	86	9	90
47 *Cox*	89	7	92
48 *Packard*	91	6	94
49 *Bilbray*	73	26	74
50 Filner	94	3	97
51 *Cunningham*	82	6	93
52 *Hunter*	91	7	93
COLORADO			
1 DeGette	96	3	97
2 Skaggs	84	5	94
3 *McInnis*	89	8	92
4 *Schaffer*	89	11	89
5 *Hefley*	91	8	92
6 *Schaefer*	90	4	96
CONNECTICUT			
1 Kennelly	68	8	90
2 Gejdenson	93	5	94
3 DeLauro	96	3	97
4 *Shays*	58	42	58
5 Maloney	79	21	79
6 *Johnson*	62	38	62
DELAWARE			
AL *Castle*	63	36	63
FLORIDA			
1 *Scarborough*	85	8	91
2 Boyd	68	31	69
3 Brown	89	4	95
4 *Fowler*	87	9	91
5 Thurman	86	13	87
6 *Stearns*	91	8	92
7 *Mica*	89	8	92
8 *McCollum*	90	7	92
9 *Bilirakis*	89	9	91
10 *Young*	77	7	92
11 Davis	80	19	81
12 *Canady*	93	6	94
13 *Miller*	87	9	90
14 *Goss*	84	6	93
15 *Weldon*	91	6	94
16 *Foley*	82	16	84
17 Meek	86	6	93
18 *Ros-Lehtinen*	76	18	81
19 Wexler	90	8	92
20 Deutsch	84	11	88
21 *Diaz-Balart*	79	20	80
22 *Shaw*	86	12	88
23 Hastings	85	5	95
GEORGIA			
1 *Kingston*	94	6	94
2 Bishop	70	29	71
3 *Collins*	93	5	95
4 McKinney	92	8	92
5 Lewis	82	1	99
6 *Gingrich*[4]	21	0	100
7 *Barr*	90	7	93
8 *Chambliss*	94	5	95
9 *Deal*	93	5	94
10 *Norwood*	91	3	96
11 *Linder*	92	4	96
HAWAII			
1 Abercrombie	91	8	92
2 Mink	93	5	95
IDAHO			
1 *Chenoweth*	88	11	89
2 *Crapo*	86	10	89
ILLINOIS			
1 Rush	93	4	95
2 Jackson	96	4	96
3 Lipinski	55	40	58
4 Gutierrez	92	6	93
5 Blagojevich	85	11	88
6 *Hyde*	91	7	92
7 Davis	93	4	95
8 *Crane*	93	4	96
9 Yates	72	4	95
10 *Porter*	69	30	69
11 *Weller*	86	12	88
12 Costello	75	24	76
13 *Fawell*	75	19	80

ND Northern Democrats   SD Southern Democrats

Background Material

		1	2	3
14	*Hastert*	95	4	96
15	Ewing	86	10	90
16	*Manzullo*	95	5	95
17	Evans	91	8	92
18	LaHood	83	17	83
19	Poshard	63	13	83
20	*Shimkus*	91	7	93

INDIANA
1	Visclosky	82	17	83
2	McIntosh	91	6	94
3	Roemer	66	33	66
4	Souder	89	9	90
5	Buyer	85	8	91
6	Burton	86	6	93
7	Pease	91	8	91
8	Hostettler	91	9	91
9	Hamilton	70	27	72
10	Carson	92	4	96

IOWA
1	Leach	62	36	63
2	Nussle	89	11	89
3	Boswell	65	35	65
4	*Ganske*	75	23	76
5	Latham	94	6	94

KANSAS
1	Moran	90	10	90
2	Ryun	94	4	96
3	Snowbarger	96	3	97
4	Tiahrt	96	4	96

KENTUCKY
1	Whitfield	88	10	90
2	Lewis	93	6	94
3	Northup	91	8	91
4	Bunning	90	8	92
5	Rogers	90	8	92
6	Baesler	65	32	67

LOUISIANA
1	Livingston	92	5	95
2	Jefferson	82	8	91
3	Tauzin	87	7	92
4	McCrery	90	5	94
5	Cooksey	88	5	95
6	Baker	92	5	94
7	John	48	39	56

MAINE
1	Allen	91	7	93
2	Baldacci	91	8	92

MARYLAND
1	*Gilchrest*	71	29	71
2	Ehrlich	85	12	87
3	Cardin	86	9	91
4	Wynn	91	6	93
5	Hoyer	88	11	89
6	Bartlett	94	5	95
7	Cummings	95	5	95
8	*Morella*	39	60	40

MASSACHUSETTS
1	Olver	96	1	99
2	Neal	91	5	95
3	McGovern	93	3	97
4	Frank	90	6	94
5	Meehan	93	3	97
6	Tierney	96	2	98
7	Markey	85	4	95
8	Kennedy	90	6	93
9	Moakley	73	5	94
10	Delahunt	95	3	97

MICHIGAN
1	Stupak	80	17	83
2	Hoekstra	93	7	93
3	Ehlers	77	21	78
4	Camp	91	8	92
5	Barcia	66	32	67
6	*Upton*	79	21	79
7	*Smith*	87	11	88
8	Stabenow	85	13	87
9	Kildee	84	16	84
10	Bonior	94	6	95
11	Knollenberg	94	6	94
12	Levin	93	7	93
13	Rivers	89	10	90
14	Conyers	84	5	95
15	Kilpatrick	90	3	96
16	Dingell	82	10	89

MINNESOTA
1	*Gutknecht*	91	8	92
2	Minge	80	19	81
3	*Ramstad*	68	32	68
4	Vento	97	3	97
5	Sabo	89	10	90
6	Luther	85	10	89
7	Peterson	53	46	54
8	Oberstar	89	10	90

MISSISSIPPI
1	*Wicker*	91	6	94
2	Thompson	89	5	95
3	*Pickering*	90	4	95
4	Parker	76	9	89
5	Taylor	41	58	41

MISSOURI
1	Clay	83	2	98
2	Talent	93	7	93
3	Gephardt	85	6	93
4	Skelton	63	36	64
5	McCarthy	88	8	92
6	Danner	58	40	59
7	Blunt	93	4	95
8	Emerson	91	8	92
9	Hulshof	87	11	89

MONTANA
AL	Hill	87	8	92

NEBRASKA
1	*Bereuter*	83	16	84
2	*Christensen*	88	5	95
3	*Barrett*	87	13	87

NEVADA
1	Ensign	81	18	82
2	Gibbons	93	7	93

NEW HAMPSHIRE
1	Sununu	89	9	91
2	Bass	78	22	78

NEW JERSEY
1	Andrews	84	14	86
2	LoBiondo	75	25	75
3	Saxton	79	20	80
4	*Smith*	78	21	79
5	Roukema	74	26	74
6	Pallone	92	7	92
7	Franks	72	27	73
8	Pascrell	85	14	86
9	Rothman	84	13	87
10	Payne	88	2	97
11	*Frelinghuysen*	76	23	77
12	Pappas	85	15	85
13	Menendez	90	10	90

NEW MEXICO
1	*Wilson* [5]	86	13	87
2	Skeen	89	11	89
3	Redmond	87	10	90

NEW YORK
1	Forbes	63	34	65
2	Lazio	72	27	73
3	King	80	17	82
4	McCarthy	82	18	82
5	Ackerman	94	3	97
6	*Meeks* [6]	86	3	97
7	Manton	81	11	88
8	Nadler	94	4	96
9	Schumer	79	5	94
10	Towns	82	6	93
11	Owens	95	3	97
12	Velázquez	93	3	96
13	*Fossella*	90	9	91
14	Maloney	91	7	93
15	Rangel	85	5	95
16	Serrano	91	4	95
17	Engel	93	3	97
18	Lowey	93	6	94
19	*Kelly*	66	34	66
20	Gilman	61	38	62
21	McNulty	72	8	89
22	*Solomon*	93	4	96
23	Boehlert	58	41	58
24	McHugh	78	20	80
25	Walsh	73	27	73
26	Hinchey	94	4	96
27	Paxon	90	2	98
28	Slaughter	92	4	96
29	LaFalce	88	10	90

30	Quinn	74	23	76
31	Houghton	63	32	66

NORTH CAROLINA
1	Clayton	90	5	95
2	Etheridge	79	18	81
3	*Jones*	92	8	92
4	Price	86	13	87
5	Burr	89	8	92
6	Coble	91	6	93
7	McIntyre	60	39	61
8	Hefner	80	8	91
9	Myrick	92	5	94
10	Ballenger	92	6	94
11	*Taylor*	93	4	95
12	Watt	95	4	96

NORTH DAKOTA
AL	Pomeroy	78	20	80

OHIO
1	*Chabot*	91	9	91
2	Portman	91	9	91
3	Hall	74	24	76
4	Oxley	89	8	91
5	Gillmor	85	13	87
6	Strickland	84	15	85
7	Hobson	90	9	91
8	Boehner	95	4	96
9	Kaptur	80	15	95
10	Kucinich	83	16	84
11	Stokes	91	3	97
12	*Kasich*	92	6	93
13	Brown	94	3	97
14	Sawyer	93	6	94
15	Pryce	70	10	88
16	Regula	86	13	87
17	Traficant	32	66	33
18	Ney	82	15	85
19	LaTourette	78	22	78

OKLAHOMA
1	Largent	87	8	91
2	Coburn	91	6	94
3	Watkins	93	6	94
4	Watts	91	8	92
5	Istook	89	4	96
6	Lucas	95	5	95

OREGON
1	Furse	86	2	98
2	*Smith*	82	7	92
3	Blumenauer	91	8	92
4	DeFazio	89	7	93
5	Hooley	88	12	88

PENNSYLVANIA
1	*Brady* [7]	92	2	97
2	Fattah	91	3	96
3	Borski	89	9	91
4	Klink	80	17	82
5	*Peterson*	93	5	95
6	Holden	73	27	73
7	Weldon	77	18	81
8	Greenwood	64	31	68
9	Shuster	90	4	95
10	McDade	58	11	84
11	Kanjorski	86	14	86
12	Murtha	71	26	73
13	Fox	71	27	72
14	Coyne	95	5	95
15	McHale	83	16	84
16	Pitts	96	4	96
17	Gekas	90	7	93
18	Doyle	76	21	79
19	*Goodling*	90	6	94
20	Mascara	80	20	80
21	English	81	19	81

RHODE ISLAND
1	Kennedy	90	9	91
2	Weygand	87	13	87

SOUTH CAROLINA
1	Sanford	76	23	76
2	Spence	95	5	95
3	Graham	89	8	92
4	Inglis	89	6	93
5	Spratt	77	18	81
6	Clyburn	93	5	95

SOUTH DAKOTA
AL	*Thune*	95	5	95

TENNESSEE
1	*Jenkins*	94	5	95
2	Duncan	88	13	88
3	Wamp	89	10	89
4	Hilleary	91	7	93
5	Clement	74	24	76
6	Gordon	72	25	74
7	Bryant	95	4	96
8	Tanner	65	29	69
9	Ford	76	7	91

TEXAS
1	Sandlin	70	27	72
2	Turner	56	41	58
3	Johnson	91	4	96
4	Hall	23	75	23
5	*Sessions*	97	3	97
6	Barton	92	6	94
7	*Archer*	95	3	97
8	*Brady*	90	5	94
9	Lampson	84	14	86
10	Doggett	91	8	92
11	Edwards	83	16	84
12	Granger	90	9	91
13	Thornberry	92	8	92
14	Paul	74	23	76
15	Hinojosa	85	9	91
16	Reyes	81	12	87
17	Stenholm	49	50	50
18	Jackson-Lee	90	6	94
19	*Combest*	95	5	95
20	Gonzalez	16	0	98
21	*Smith*	93	5	95
22	DeLay	93	4	95
23	Bonilla	83	15	85
24	Frost	80	5	84
25	Bentsen	85	15	85
26	Armey	94	3	97
27	Ortiz	72	23	76
28	Rodriguez	88	2	92
29	Green	81	14	86
30	Johnson	87	6	93

UTAH
1	Hansen	92	4	96
2	Cook	87	10	90
3	Cannon	87	5	94

VERMONT
AL	*Sanders*	94	5	95

VIRGINIA
1	Bateman	77	6	92
2	Pickett	59	40	60
3	Scott	91	9	91
4	Sisisky	64	35	65
5	Goode	27	71	28
6	*Goodlatte*	92	8	92
7	*Bliley*	93	6	94
8	Moran	78	20	79
9	Boucher	78	18	81
10	Wolf	88	11	88
11	Davis	80	19	81

WASHINGTON
1	White	87	13	87
2	Metcalf	85	14	86
3	*Smith*	83	14	86
4	Hastings	97	3	97
5	Nethercutt	93	5	95
6	Dicks	84	15	85
7	McDermott	92	4	96
8	Dunn	93	5	94
9	Smith	83	17	83

WEST VIRGINIA
1	Mollohan	70	25	74
2	Wise	81	14	85
3	Rahall	76	21	78

WISCONSIN
1	Neumann	83	14	86
2	Klug	76	19	80
3	Kind	84	14	86
4	Kleczka	84	15	85
5	Barrett	93	7	93
6	*Petri*	85	14	86
7	Obey	91	8	92
8	Johnson	83	15	85
9	*Sensenbrenner*	84	14	86

WYOMING
AL	*Cubin*	95	4	96

Southern states - Ala., Ark., Fla., Ga., Ky., La., Miss., N.C., Okla., S.C., Tenn., Texas, Va.

Conservative Coalition Background

Conservative coalition. As used in this study, "conservative coalition" means a voting alliance of Republicans and Southern Democrats against the Northern Democrats in Congress. This meaning, rather than any philosophic definition of the "conservative coalition" position, is the basis for CQ's selection of coalition votes.

Conservative coalition vote. Any vote in the Senate or the House on which a majority of voting Southern Democrats and a majority of voting Republicans opposed a majority of voting Northern Democrats. Votes on which there was an even division within the ranks of voting Northern Democrats, Southern Democrats or Republicans are not included.

Conservative coalition support score. Percentage of conservative coalition votes on which a member voted "yea" or "nay" *in agreement* with the position of the conservative coalition. Failures to vote, even if a member announced a stand, lower the score.

Conservative coalition opposition score. Percentage of conservative coalition votes on which a member voted "yea" or "nay" *in disagreement* with the position of the conservative coalition. Failures to vote, even if a member announced a stand, lower the score.

Average Scores

In percentages

	Support							Opposition					
	Southern Democrats		Republicans		Northern Democrats			Southern Democrats		Republicans		Northern Democrats	
	1998	1997	1998	1997	1998	1997		1998	1997	1998	1997	1998	1997
Senate	74	73	85	87	34	32	Senate	24	27	13	12	61	67
House	59	63	88	86	31	33	House	35	34	10	10	65	64

Regional Averages

In percentages

	Support								Opposition							
	East		West		South		Midwest			East		West		South		Midwest	
	1998	1997	1998	1997	1998	1997	1998	1997		1998	1997	1998	1997	1998	1997	1998	1997
Republicans									**Republicans**								
Senate	68	70	91	91	91	95	81	94	Senate	24	30	10	9	6	5	20	15
House	78	82	89	86	91	89	88	86	House	19	16	9	9	6	7	10	12
Democrats									**Democrats**								
Senate	32	27	47	37	74	73	28	34	Senate	67	72	45	65	24	27	67	62
House	27	31	26	27	59	63	40	40	House	68	66	70	69	35	34	58	57

Conservative Coalition History

Following is the percentage of the recorded votes on which the coalition appeared and its percentage of victories on those votes.

Year	Appearance	Victories	Year	Appearance	Victories
1971	30%	83%	1985	14%	89%
1972	27	69	1986	16	87
1973	23	61	1987	8	93
1974	24	59	1988	9	89
1975	28	50	1989	11	87
1976	24	58	1990	11	82
1977	26	68	1991	11	91
1978	21	52	1992	12	87
1979	20	70	1993	9	94
1980	18	72	1994	8	82
1981	21	92	1995	11	98
1982	18	85	1996	12	99
1983	15	77	1997	9	98
1984	16	83	1998	6	96

1998 Conservative Coalition Votes

The following is a list of votes cast in 1998 on which a majority of Southern Democrats and a majority of Republicans voted against a majority of all other Democrats.

House Victories & Defeats

40 Victories

Vote Number	Description
20	Law enforcement
68	Copyright
69	Copyright
74	Small business
113	Needle exchange
114	Needle exchange
137	Intelligence authorization
144	Financial services
160	Federal mandates
166	Defense policy
180	Border control
219	Bankruptcy law
221	Bankruptcy law
222	Bankruptcy law
223	Bankruptcy law
225	Bankruptcy law
252	Nuclear energy
258	Price supports
263	Agriculture appropriations
273	IRS overhaul
286	Gun control
308	Campaign finance
321	Abortion
325	Abortion
328	Environment
343	Radioactive waste
344	Environment
346	Veterans' funding
351	Consumer protection
352	VA/HUD appropriations
389	Environment
401	Federal powers
415	Tobacco policy
420	Hunting
435	Drug policy
436	Law enforcement
440	Border control
460	Immigration
494	Treasury/Postal appropriations
520	Consumer protection

2 Defeats

Vote Number	Description
259	Agriculture appropriations
447	Foreign aid

Senate Victories & Defeats

8 Victories

Vote Number	Description
144	Tobacco policy
174	Base closures
178	Defense policy
185	Space station
204	Foreign aid
233	Immigration
275	Bankruptcy law
287	Transportation

0 Defeats

House Victory Score

Victories	40
Defeats	2
Total	**42**
Success rate	95%

Senate Victory Score

Victories	8
Defeats	0
Total	**8**
Success rate	100%

Vote Studies

Conservative Coalition Support and Opposition: House

1. Conservative Coalition Support. Percentage of 42 recorded votes in 1998 on which the conservative coalition appeared and on which a representative voted "yea" or "nay" in agreement with the position of the conservative coalition. Failures to vote lowered both support and opposition scores.

2. Conservative Coalition Opposition. Percentage of 42 recorded votes in 1998 on which the conservative coalition appeared and on which a representative voted "yea" or "nay" in disagreement with the position of the conservative coalition. Failures to vote lowered both support and opposition scores.

3. Conservative Coalition Support (adjusted for absences). Percentage of 42 recorded votes in 1998 on which the conservative coalition appeared and on which a representative was present and voted "yea" or "nay" in agreement with the position of the conservative coalition. In this version of the study, absences were not counted; therefore, failures to vote did not lower support or opposition scores. Opposition scores, not listed here, are the inverse of the support score; i.e., the opposition score is equal to 100 percent minus the individual's support score.

[1] Barbara Lee, D-Calif., was sworn in April 21, replacing Ronald V. Dellums, D-Calif., who resigned Feb. 6. Lee was eligible for 38 conservative coalition votes in 1998. Dellums was eligible for no conservative coalition votes in 1998.

[2] Lois Capps, D-Calif., was sworn in March 17, replacing Walter Capps, D-Calif., who died Oct. 28, 1997. Lois Capps was eligible for 41 conservative coalition votes in 1998.

[3] Mary Bono, R-Calif., was sworn in April 21, replacing Sonny Bono, R-Calif., who died Jan. 5. Mary Bono was eligible for 38 conservative coalition votes in 1998. Sonny Bono was eligible for no conservative coalition votes in 1998.

[4] Newt Gingrich, R-Ga., as Speaker of the House, voted at his discretion on five conservative coalition votes in 1998.

[5] Heather Wilson, R-N.M., was sworn in June 25, replacing Stephen H. Schiff, R-N.M., who died March 25. Wilson was eligible for 22 conservative coalition votes in 1998. Schiff was eligible for one conservative coalition vote in 1998 but did not vote.

[6] Gregory W. Meeks, D-N.Y., was sworn in Feb. 5, replacing Floyd H. Flake, D-N.Y., who resigned on Nov. 15, 1997. Meeks was eligible for 42 conservative coalition votes in 1998.

[7] Robert A. Brady, D-Pa., was sworn in May 21, replacing Thomas M. Foglietta, D-Pa., who resigned Nov. 11, 1997. Brady was eligible for 32 conservative coalition votes in 1998.

Democrats   *Republicans*
Independent

		1	2	3
ALABAMA				
1	*Callahan*	98	2	98
2	*Everett*	98	2	98
3	*Riley*	93	5	95
4	*Aderholt*	95	5	95
5	Cramer	95	2	98
6	*Bachus*	88	12	88
7	Hilliard	19	69	22
ALASKA				
AL	*Young*	90	7	93
ARIZONA				
1	*Salmon*	93	7	93
2	Pastor	45	55	45
3	*Stump*	93	7	93
4	*Shadegg*	90	7	93
5	*Kolbe*	83	17	83
6	*Hayworth*	88	12	88
ARKANSAS				
1	Berry	79	17	83
2	Snyder	57	43	57
3	*Hutchinson*	81	12	87
4	*Dickey*	93	2	98
CALIFORNIA				
1	Riggs	74	7	91
2	*Herger*	98	2	98
3	Fazio	45	52	46
4	*Doolittle*	90	10	90
5	Matsui	31	69	31
6	Woolsey	17	83	17
7	Miller	10	86	10
8	Pelosi	12	83	13
9	Lee[1]	3	97	3
10	Tauscher	62	36	63
11	*Pombo*	88	12	88
12	Lantos	24	76	24
13	Stark	5	88	5
14	Eshoo	21	79	21
15	Campbell	64	36	64
16	Lofgren	24	76	24
17	Farr	19	69	22
18	Condit	79	19	80
19	*Radanovich*	83	12	88
20	Dooley	62	38	62
21	*Thomas*	93	5	95
22	Capps[2]	29	71	29
23	*Gallegly*	90	10	90
24	Sherman	38	62	38
25	*McKeon*	98	2	98
26	Berman	10	74	11
27	*Rogan*	83	17	83
28	*Dreier*	88	12	88
29	Waxman	14	86	14
30	Becerra	7	88	8
31	Martinez	45	50	48
32	Dixon	17	71	19
33	Roybal-Allard	5	90	5
34	Torres	12	74	14
35	Waters	12	79	13
36	Harman	40	31	57
37	Millender-McD.	14	74	16
38	*Horn*	83	17	83
39	*Royce*	64	24	73
40	*Lewis*	95	2	98
41	*Kim*	95	5	95
42	Brown	21	79	21
43	*Calvert*	100	0	100
44	*Bono*[3]	95	5	95
45	*Rohrabacher*	79	21	79
46	Sanchez	43	52	45
47	*Cox*	81	14	85
48	*Packard*	95	0	100
49	*Bilbray*	83	17	83
50	Filner	7	93	7
51	*Cunningham*	90	2	97
52	*Hunter*	88	10	90
COLORADO				
1	DeGette	14	86	14
2	Skaggs	21	71	23
3	*McInnis*	88	7	93
4	*Schaffer*	88	12	88
5	*Hefley*	88	12	88
6	*Schaefer*	90	2	97
CONNECTICUT				
1	Kennelly	26	55	32
2	Gejdenson	19	79	20
3	DeLauro	10	88	10
4	*Shays*	50	50	50
5	Maloney	55	45	55
6	*Johnson*	67	33	67
DELAWARE				
AL	*Castle*	76	24	76
FLORIDA				
1	*Scarborough*	83	17	83
2	Boyd	86	14	86
3	Brown	26	64	29
4	*Fowler*	95	5	95
5	Thurman	57	43	57
6	*Stearns*	90	7	93
7	*Mica*	88	10	90
8	*McCollum*	86	12	88
9	*Bilirakis*	90	7	93
10	*Young*	76	0	100
11	Davis	69	31	69
12	*Canady*	95	5	95
13	*Miller*	88	12	88
14	*Goss*	81	7	92
15	*Weldon*	95	2	98
16	*Foley*	88	10	90
17	Meek	29	69	29
18	*Ros-Lehtinen*	76	24	76
19	Wexler	31	69	31
20	Deutsch	52	48	52
21	*Diaz-Balart*	83	17	83
22	*Shaw*	90	10	90
23	Hastings	19	79	20
GEORGIA				
1	*Kingston*	86	14	86
2	Bishop	83	17	83
3	*Collins*	90	7	93
4	McKinney	10	90	10
5	Lewis	5	67	7
6	*Gingrich*[4]	100	0	100
7	*Barr*	86	10	90
8	*Chambliss*	95	0	100
9	*Deal*	90	7	93
10	*Norwood*	90	5	95
11	*Linder*	95	5	95
HAWAII				
1	Abercrombie	24	76	24
2	Mink	14	86	14
IDAHO				
1	*Chenoweth*	86	14	86
2	*Crapo*	90	7	93
ILLINOIS				
1	Rush	5	88	5
2	Jackson	0	100	0
3	Lipinski	57	40	59
4	Gutierrez	2	95	2
5	Blagojevich	36	60	38
6	*Hyde*	83	12	88
7	Davis	5	95	5
8	*Crane*	86	10	90
9	Yates	10	74	11
10	*Porter*	79	21	79
11	*Weller*	86	14	86
12	Costello	57	43	57
13	*Fawell*	81	14	85

ND Northern Democrats   SD Southern Democrats

Background Material

		1	2	3
14	Hastert	98	2	98
15	Ewing	90	5	95
16	Manzullo	93	7	93
17	Evans	19	81	19
18	LaHood	86	14	86
19	Poshard	29	45	39
20	Shimkus	98	2	98

INDIANA

		1	2	3
1	Visclosky	48	52	48
2	McIntosh	81	17	83
3	Roemer	71	29	71
4	Souder	83	14	85
5	Buyer	88	10	90
6	Burton	93	5	95
7	Pease	90	10	90
8	Hostettler	88	12	88
9	Hamilton	64	31	68
10	Carson	17	79	18

IOWA

		1	2	3
1	Leach	90	10	90
2	Nussle	98	2	98
3	Boswell	93	7	93
4	Ganske	86	12	88
5	Latham	98	2	98

KANSAS

		1	2	3
1	Moran	98	2	98
2	Ryun	90	7	93
3	Snowbarger	95	5	95
4	Tiahrt	98	2	98

KENTUCKY

		1	2	3
1	Whitfield	86	12	88
2	Lewis	100	0	100
3	Northup	93	7	93
4	Bunning	98	2	98
5	Rogers	100	0	100
6	Baesler	76	21	78

LOUISIANA

		1	2	3
1	Livingston	93	2	98
2	Jefferson	45	45	50
3	Tauzin	90	0	100
4	McCrery	95	0	100
5	Cooksey	98	2	98
6	Baker	95	0	100
7	John	98	0	100

MAINE

		1	2	3
1	Allen	19	81	19
2	Baldacci	33	67	33

MARYLAND

		1	2	3
1	Gilchrest	79	19	80
2	Ehrlich	79	14	85
3	Cardin	33	60	36
4	Wynn	38	57	40
5	Hoyer	50	50	50
6	Bartlett	93	5	95
7	Cummings	26	74	26
8	Morella	38	60	39

MASSACHUSETTS

		1	2	3
1	Olver	7	93	7
2	Neal	19	74	21
3	McGovern	7	93	7
4	Frank	19	76	20
5	Meehan	10	83	10
6	Tierney	2	98	2
7	Markey	10	74	11
8	Kennedy	10	86	10
9	Moakley	14	64	18
10	Delahunt	7	93	7

MICHIGAN

		1	2	3
1	Stupak	40	57	41
2	Hoekstra	83	17	83
3	Ehlers	74	26	74
4	Camp	93	7	93
5	Barcia	69	29	71
6	Upton	79	21	79
7	Smith	88	12	88
8	Stabenow	48	50	49
9	Kildee	40	60	40
10	Bonior	7	93	7
11	Knollenberg	95	5	95
12	Levin	31	69	31
13	Rivers	19	81	19
14	Conyers	7	86	8
15	Kilpatrick	12	86	12
16	Dingell	40	52	44

MINNESOTA

		1	2	3
1	Gutknecht	90	10	90
2	Minge	69	31	69
3	Ramstad	79	21	79
4	Vento	14	86	14
5	Sabo	36	64	36
6	Luther	40	57	41
7	Peterson	76	24	76
8	Oberstar	26	74	26

MISSISSIPPI

		1	2	3
1	Wicker	98	0	100
2	Thompson	31	60	34
3	Pickering	95	0	100
4	Parker	90	2	97
5	Taylor	86	14	86

MISSOURI

		1	2	3
1	Clay	10	76	11
2	Talent	93	5	95
3	Gephardt	38	57	40
4	Skelton	90	7	93
5	McCarthy	36	64	36
6	Danner	86	12	88
7	Blunt	95	2	98
8	Emerson	93	7	93
9	Hulshof	86	12	88

MONTANA

		1	2	3
AL	Hill	95	2	98

NEBRASKA

		1	2	3
1	Bereuter	93	7	93
2	Christensen	88	7	93
3	Barrett	95	2	98

NEVADA

		1	2	3
1	Ensign	76	21	78
2	Gibbons	86	14	86

NEW HAMPSHIRE

		1	2	3
1	Sununu	81	19	81
2	Bass	81	19	81

NEW JERSEY

		1	2	3
1	Andrews	40	57	41
2	LoBiondo	71	29	71
3	Saxton	81	17	83
4	Smith	69	29	71
5	Roukema	79	21	79
6	Pallone	31	69	31
7	Franks	71	29	71
8	Pascrell	45	52	46
9	Rothman	29	64	31
10	Payne	2	83	3
11	Frelinghuysen	83	17	83
12	Pappas	76	24	76
13	Menendez	29	71	29

NEW MEXICO

		1	2	3
1	Wilson [5]	100	0	100
2	Skeen	93	7	93
3	Redmond	98	0	100

NEW YORK

		1	2	3
1	Forbes	71	26	73
2	Lazio	83	17	83
3	King	88	10	90
4	McCarthy	36	64	36
5	Ackerman	14	81	15
6	Meeks [6]	5	79	6
7	Manton	33	55	38
8	Nadler	10	83	10
9	Schumer	14	57	20
10	Towns	17	67	20
11	Owens	5	88	5
12	Velázquez	7	83	8
13	Fossella	86	14	86
14	Maloney	21	74	23
15	Rangel	14	74	16
16	Serrano	12	79	13
17	Engel	10	81	11
18	Lowey	29	71	29
19	Kelly	74	26	74
20	Gilman	74	26	74
21	McNulty	29	62	32
22	Solomon	90	5	95
23	Boehlert	64	36	64
24	McHugh	83	12	88
25	Walsh	86	12	88
26	Hinchey	7	90	7
27	Paxon	86	5	95
28	Slaughter	21	77	23
29	LaFalce	36	62	37

		1	2	3
30	Quinn	86	10	90
31	Houghton	79	14	85

NORTH CAROLINA

		1	2	3
1	Clayton	33	55	38
2	Etheridge	76	19	80
3	Jones	88	12	88
4	Price	64	31	68
5	Burr	93	5	95
6	Coble	86	12	88
7	McIntyre	88	7	93
8	Hefner	43	38	53
9	Myrick	95	2	98
10	Ballenger	93	2	98
11	Taylor	95	0	100
12	Watt	19	81	19

NORTH DAKOTA

		1	2	3
AL	Pomeroy	79	21	79

OHIO

		1	2	3
1	Chabot	81	19	81
2	Portman	95	2	98
3	Hall	60	40	60
4	Oxley	98	0	100
5	Gillmor	93	5	95
6	Strickland	50	50	50
7	Hobson	90	7	93
8	Boehner	100	0	100
9	Kaptur	48	50	49
10	Kucinich	29	71	29
11	Stokes	17	79	18
12	Kasich	88	10	90
13	Brown	12	88	12
14	Sawyer	33	67	33
15	Pryce	76	5	94
16	Regula	95	5	95
17	Traficant	93	5	95
18	Ney	88	12	88
19	LaTourette	81	19	81

OKLAHOMA

		1	2	3
1	Largent	93	5	95
2	Coburn	95	2	98
3	Watkins	95	2	98
4	Watts	95	5	95
5	Istook	95	5	95
6	Lucas	98	2	98

OREGON

		1	2	3
1	Furse	10	88	10
2	Smith	88	0	100
3	Blumenauer	24	74	24
4	DeFazio	14	86	14
5	Hooley	36	64	36

PENNSYLVANIA

		1	2	3
1	Brady [7]	9	84	10
2	Fattah	7	90	7
3	Borski	29	71	29
4	Klink	48	50	49
5	Peterson	95	5	95
6	Holden	67	33	67
7	Weldon	76	19	80
8	Greenwood	76	21	78
9	Shuster	90	2	97
10	McDade	64	10	87
11	Kanjorski	36	64	36
12	Murtha	67	29	70
13	Fox	79	21	79
14	Coyne	21	79	21
15	McHale	45	52	46
16	Pitts	90	10	90
17	Gekas	95	5	95
18	Doyle	57	38	60
19	Goodling	81	14	85
20	Mascara	62	38	62
21	English	81	19	81

RHODE ISLAND

		1	2	3
1	Kennedy	26	71	27
2	Weygand	45	55	45

SOUTH CAROLINA

		1	2	3
1	Sanford	74	26	74
2	Spence	95	5	95
3	Graham	95	5	95
4	Inglis	86	12	88
5	Spratt	83	17	83
6	Clyburn	33	62	35

SOUTH DAKOTA

		1	2	3
AL	Thune	98	2	98

TENNESSEE

		1	2	3
1	Jenkins	93	5	95
2	Duncan	76	24	76
3	Wamp	86	14	86
4	Hilleary	90	10	90
5	Clement	86	14	86
6	Gordon	71	24	75
7	Bryant	98	2	98
8	Tanner	90	10	90
9	Ford	36	40	47

TEXAS

		1	2	3
1	Sandlin	83	12	88
2	Turner	93	5	95
3	Johnson	90	2	97
4	Hall	95	5	95
5	Sessions	100	0	100
6	Barton	95	5	95
7	Archer	93	5	95
8	Brady	93	0	100
9	Lampson	62	36	63
10	Doggett	24	76	24
11	Edwards	69	31	69
12	Granger	98	0	100
13	Thornberry	98	2	98
14	Paul	55	43	56
15	Hinojosa	55	38	59
16	Reyes	64	33	66
17	Stenholm	98	2	98
18	Jackson-Lee	29	62	32
19	Combest	98	2	98
20	Gonzalez	0	7	0
21	Smith	98	0	100
22	DeLay	100	0	100
23	Bonilla	86	12	88
24	Frost	79	19	80
25	Bentsen	67	33	67
26	Armey	93	2	98
27	Ortiz	64	33	66
28	Rodriguez	50	48	51
29	Green	62	36	63
30	Johnson	38	52	42

UTAH

		1	2	3
1	Hansen	95	2	98
2	Cook	93	5	95
3	Cannon	83	0	100

VERMONT

		1	2	3
AL	Sanders	17	83	17

VIRGINIA

		1	2	3
1	Bateman	81	2	97
2	Pickett	90	10	90
3	Scott	43	57	43
4	Sisisky	88	12	88
5	Goode	90	10	90
6	Goodlatte	93	7	93
7	Bliley	93	7	93
8	Moran	67	33	67
9	Boucher	67	29	70
10	Wolf	86	14	86
11	Davis	90	10	90

WASHINGTON

		1	2	3
1	White	95	5	95
2	Metcalf	81	19	81
3	Smith	83	10	90
4	Hastings	100	0	100
5	Nethercutt	90	5	95
6	Dicks	60	40	60
7	McDermott	14	79	15
8	Dunn	93	5	95
9	Smith	45	45	55

WEST VIRGINIA

		1	2	3
1	Mollohan	67	33	67
2	Wise	52	48	52
3	Rahall	52	48	52

WISCONSIN

		1	2	3
1	Neumann	74	24	76
2	Klug	86	12	88
3	Kind	57	43	57
4	Kleczka	48	48	50
5	Barrett	26	74	26
6	Petri	71	29	71
7	Obey	31	69	31
8	Johnson	55	45	55
9	Sensenbrenner	69	31	69

WYOMING

		1	2	3
AL	Cubin	95	2	98

Southern states - Ala., Ark., Fla., Ga., Ky., La., Miss., N.C., Okla., S.C., Tenn., Texas, Va.

Vote Studies

	1	2	3
ALABAMA			
Shelby	100	0	100
Sessions	100	0	100
ALASKA			
Stevens	88	13	88
Murkowski	88	13	88
ARIZONA			
McCain	75	25	75
Kyl	88	13	88
ARKANSAS			
Hutchinson	63	13	83
Bumpers	25	75	25
CALIFORNIA			
Feinstein	50	50	50
Boxer	38	63	38
COLORADO			
Campbell	100	0	100
Allard	100	0	100
CONNECTICUT			
Dodd	38	63	38
Lieberman	38	63	38
DELAWARE			
Roth	75	0	100
Biden	50	50	50
FLORIDA			
Mack	100	0	100
Graham	88	13	88
GEORGIA			
Coverdell	88	0	100
Cleland	88	13	88
HAWAII			
Inouye	50	38	57
Akaka	38	38	50
IDAHO			
Craig	100	0	100
Kempthorne	100	0	100
ILLINOIS			
Moseley-Braun	25	63	29
Durbin	13	88	13
INDIANA			
Lugar	50	50	50
Coats	75	25	75
IOWA			
Grassley	75	25	75
Harkin	13	88	13
KANSAS			
Brownback	88	13	88
Roberts	88	13	88
KENTUCKY			
McConnell	100	0	100
Ford	88	13	88
LOUISIANA			
Breaux	100	0	100
Landrieu	75	25	75
MAINE			
Snowe	75	25	75
Collins	88	13	88
MARYLAND			
Sarbanes	25	75	25
Mikulski	38	63	38
MASSACHUSETTS			
Kennedy	0	100	0
Kerry	38	63	38
MICHIGAN			
Abraham	88	13	88
Levin	13	88	13
MINNESOTA			
Grams	75	25	75
Wellstone	0	88	0
MISSISSIPPI			
Cochran	88	13	88
Lott	88	0	100
MISSOURI			
Bond	100	0	100
Ashcroft	75	25	75
MONTANA			
Burns	100	0	100
Baucus	38	38	50
NEBRASKA			
Hagel	88	13	88
Kerrey	75	25	75
NEVADA			
Reid	63	38	63
Bryan	38	63	38
NEW HAMPSHIRE			
Smith	88	0	100
Gregg	88	13	88
NEW JERSEY			
Lautenberg	25	75	25
Torricelli	63	38	63
NEW MEXICO			
Domenici	88	13	88
Bingaman	50	38	57
NEW YORK			
D'Amato	63	38	63
Moynihan	25	75	25
NORTH CAROLINA			
Helms	100	0	100
Faircloth	100	0	100
NORTH DAKOTA			
Conrad	50	50	50
Dorgan	50	50	50
OHIO			
DeWine	88	13	88
Glenn	13	38	25
OKLAHOMA			
Nickles	100	0	100
Inhofe	100	0	100
OREGON			
Smith	75	25	75
Wyden	50	38	57
PENNSYLVANIA			
Specter	25	38	40
Santorum	88	13	88
RHODE ISLAND			
Chafee	50	50	50
Reed	25	75	25
SOUTH CAROLINA			
Thurmond	88	13	88
Hollings	50	25	67
SOUTH DAKOTA			
Daschle	38	63	38
Johnson	13	88	13
TENNESSEE			
Thompson	88	13	88
Frist	100	0	100

Democrats   **Republicans**

	1	2	3
TEXAS			
Gramm	88	13	88
Hutchison	88	13	88
UTAH			
Hatch	100	0	100
Bennett	100	0	100
VERMONT			
Jeffords	38	50	43
Leahy	13	88	13
VIRGINIA			
Warner	63	38	63
Robb	75	25	75
WASHINGTON			
Gorton	100	0	100
Murray	50	50	50
WEST VIRGINIA			
Byrd	25	75	25
Rockefeller	38	38	50
WISCONSIN			
Kohl	25	75	25
Feingold	38	63	38
WYOMING			
Thomas	75	25	75
Enzi	75	25	75

ND Northern Democrats   SD Southern Democrats

Southern states - Ala., Ark., Fla., Ga., Ky., La., Miss., N.C., Okla., S.C., Tenn., Texas, Va.

Conservative Coalition Support and Opposition: Senate

1. Conservative Coalition Support. Percentage of 8 recorded votes in 1998 on which the conservative coalition appeared and on which a senator voted "yea" or "nay" in agreement with the position of the conservative coalition. Failures to vote lowered both support and opposition scores.

2. Conservative Coalition Opposition. Percentage of 8 recorded votes in 1998 on which the conservative coalition appeared and on which a senator voted "yea" or "nay" in disagreement with the position of the conservative coalition. Failures to vote lowered both support and opposition scores.

3. Conservative Coalition Support (adjusted for absences). Percentage of 8 recorded votes in 1998 on which the conservative coalition appeared and on which a senator was present and voted "yea" or "nay" in agreement with the position of the conservative coalition. In this version of the study, absences were not counted; therefore, failures to vote did not lower support or opposition scores. Opposition scores, not listed here, are the inverse of the support score; i.e., the opposition score is equal to 100 percent minus the individual's support score.

Background Material

	1	2
ALABAMA		
Shelby	98	99
Sessions	97	98
ALASKA		
Stevens	99	99
Murkowski	96	95
ARIZONA		
McCain	94	96
Kyl	94	94
ARKANSAS		
Hutchinson	95	95
Bumpers	98	98
CALIFORNIA		
Feinstein	99	99
Boxer	97	98
COLORADO		
Campbell	99	99
Allard	99	99
CONNECTICUT		
Dodd	99	99
Lieberman	100	100
DELAWARE		
Roth	96	96
Biden	96	96
FLORIDA		
Mack	99	99
Graham	100	100
GEORGIA		
Coverdell	97	97
Cleland	99	99
HAWAII		
Inouye	85	85
Akaka	93	93
IDAHO		
Craig	100	100
Kempthorne	99	99
ILLINOIS		
Moseley-Braun	92	92
Durbin	98	98
INDIANA		
Lugar	100	100
Coats	97	97

	1	2
IOWA		
Grassley	100	100
Harkin	96	95
KANSAS		
Brownback	99	99
Roberts	99	99
KENTUCKY		
McConnell	99	99
Ford	99	99
LOUISIANA		
Breaux	99	99
Landrieu	99	99
MAINE		
Snowe	99	99
Collins	100	100
MARYLAND		
Sarbanes	99	99
Mikulski	96	96
MASSACHUSETTS		
Kennedy	97	96
Kerry	98	98
MICHIGAN		
Abraham	100	100
Levin	97	97
MINNESOTA		
Grams	99	99
Wellstone	97	97
MISSISSIPPI		
Cochran	100	100
Lott	98	100
MISSOURI		
Bond	98	98
Ashcroft	99	99
MONTANA		
Burns	99	99
Baucus	95	95
NEBRASKA		
Hagel	99	99
Kerrey	98	98
NEVADA		
Reid	98	98
Bryan	99	99

	1	2
NEW HAMPSHIRE		
Smith	99	99
Gregg	98	98
NEW JERSEY		
Lautenberg	99	99
Torricelli	98	98
NEW MEXICO		
Domenici	95	95
Bingaman	95	95
NEW YORK		
D'Amato	97	97
Moynihan	93	93
NORTH CAROLINA		
Helms	78	78
Faircloth	96	96
NORTH DAKOTA		
Conrad	99	99
Dorgan	99	99
OHIO		
DeWine	100	100
Glenn	76	76
OKLAHOMA		
Nickles	99	99
Inhofe	95	95
OREGON		
Smith	99	99
Wyden	96	96
PENNSYLVANIA		
Specter	86	86
Santorum	99	99
RHODE ISLAND		
Chafee	99	99
Reed	100	100
SOUTH CAROLINA		
Thurmond	99	99
Hollings	89	90
SOUTH DAKOTA		
Daschle	100	100
Johnson	100	100
TENNESSEE		
Thompson	100	100
Frist	99	99

Democrats   ***Republicans***

	1	2
TEXAS		
Gramm	99	99
Hutchison	96	95
UTAH		
Hatch	99	99
Bennett	95	95
VERMONT		
Jeffords	99	99
Leahy	99	99
VIRGINIA		
Warner	97	97
Robb	100	100
WASHINGTON		
Gorton	99	99
Murray	99	99
WEST VIRGINIA		
Byrd	100	100
Rockefeller	93	93
WISCONSIN		
Kohl	99	99
Feingold	100	100
WYOMING		
Thomas	99	99
Enzi	99	99

ND Northern Democrats   SD Southern Democrats

Southern states - Ala., Ark., Fla., Ga., Ky., La., Miss., N.C., Okla., S.C., Tenn., Texas, Va.

Voting Participation: Senate

1. Voting Participation. Percentage of 314 recorded votes in 1998 on which a senator voted "yea" or "nay."

2. Voting Participation (without motions to instruct). Percentage of 311 recorded votes in 1998 on which a senator voted "yea" or "nay." In this version of the study, three votes to instruct the sergeant at arms to request the attendance of absent senators are not included.

Absences due to illness. Congressional Quarterly no longer designates members who missed votes due to illness. In the past, notations to that effect were based on official statements published in the Congressional Record, but these were found to be inconsistently used.

Rounding. Scores are rounded to nearest percentage, except that no scores are rounded up to 100 percent. Members with a 100 percent score participated in all recorded votes for which they were eligible.

Vote Studies

Voting Participation: House

1. **Voting Participation.** Percentage of 533 recorded votes in 1998 on which a representative voted "yea" or "nay."

2. **Voting Participation (without Journal votes).** Percentage of 522 recorded votes in 1998 on which a representative voted "yea" or "nay." In this version of the study, 11 votes on approval of the House Journal were not included.

Absences due to illness. Congressional Quarterly no longer designates members who missed votes due to illness. In the past, notations to that effect were based on official statements published in the Congressional Record, but these were found to be inconsistently used.

Rounding. Scores are rounded to the nearest percentage, except that no scores are rounded up to 100 percent. Members with a 100 percent score participated in all recorded votes for which they were eligible.

[1] Barbara Lee, D-Calif., was sworn in April 21, replacing Ronald V. Dellums, D-Calif., who resigned Feb. 6. Lee was eligible for 438 votes in 1998. Dellums was eligible for 10 votes in 1998. His voting participation score was 67 percent, both with and without the inclusion of Journal votes.

[2] Lois Capps, D-Calif., was sworn in March 17, replacing Walter Capps, D-Calif., who died Oct. 28, 1997. Lois Capps was eligible for 482 votes in 1998.

[3] Mary Bono, R-Calif., was sworn in April 21, replacing Sonny Bono, R-Calif., who died Jan. 5. Mary Bono was eligible for 438 votes in 1998. Sonny Bono was eligible for no votes in 1998.

[4] Newt Gingrich, R-Ga., as Speaker of the House, voted at his discretion on 73 votes in 1998.

[5] Heather Wilson, R-N.M., was sworn in June 25, replacing Stephen H. Schiff, R-N.M., who died March 25. Wilson was eligible for 267 votes in 1998. Schiff was eligible for 64 votes in 1998 but cast no votes.

[6] Gregory W. Meeks, D-N.Y., was sworn in Feb. 5, replacing Floyd H. Flake, D-N.Y., who resigned on Nov. 15, 1997. Meeks was eligible for 523 votes in 1998.

[7] Robert A. Brady, D-Pa., was sworn in May 21, replacing Thomas M. Foglietta, D-Pa., who resigned Nov. 11, 1997. Brady was eligible for 362 votes in 1998.

Democrats — *Republicans* — **Independent**

		1	2
ALABAMA			
1	Callahan	95	95
2	*Everett*	99	99
3	*Riley*	99	99
4	*Aderholt*	99	99
5	Cramer	98	98
6	*Bachus*	99	99
7	Hilliard	94	94
ALASKA			
AL	*Young*	94	95
ARIZONA			
1	*Salmon*	97	97
2	Pastor	99	99
3	*Stump*	99	99
4	*Shadegg*	99	99
5	*Kolbe*	98	98
6	*Hayworth*	99	99
ARKANSAS			
1	Berry	98	98
2	Snyder	99	99
3	*Hutchinson*	94	94
4	*Dickey*	97	98
CALIFORNIA			
1	*Riggs*	75	75
2	*Herger*	96	96
3	Fazio	97	97
4	*Doolittle*	95	95
5	Matsui	99	99
6	Woolsey	99	99
7	Miller	92	92
8	Pelosi	94	94
9	Lee[1]	99	99
10	Tauscher	98	98
11	*Pombo*	99	99
12	Lantos	96	96
13	Stark	93	93
14	Eshoo	96	96
15	*Campbell*	99	99
16	Lofgren	95	96
17	Farr	95	95
18	Condit	99	99
19	*Radanovich*	93	93
20	Dooley	99	99
21	*Thomas*	99	99
22	Capps[2]	99	99
23	*Gallegly*	99	99
24	Sherman	99	99
25	*McKeon*	99	99
26	Berman	87	87
27	*Rogan*	96	96
28	*Dreier*	99	99
29	Waxman	94	94
30	Becerra	92	92
31	Martinez	88	89
32	Dixon	89	89
33	Roybal-Allard	93	93
34	Torres	81	81
35	Waters	89	89
36	Harman	68	69
37	Millender-McD.	92	92
38	*Horn*	99	99
39	*Royce*	92	92
40	*Lewis*	97	97
41	*Kim*	99	99
42	Brown	96	96
43	*Calvert*	99	99
44	*Bono*[3]	99	99
45	*Rohrabacher*	99	99
46	Sanchez	95	95
47	*Cox*	95	95
48	*Packard*	97	97
49	*Bilbray*	97	98
50	Filner	98	98
51	*Cunningham*	91	91
52	*Hunter*	95	95
COLORADO			
1	DeGette	99	99
2	Skaggs	88	88
3	*McInnis*	96	96
4	*Schaffer*	100	100
5	*Hefley*	98	98
6	*Schaefer*	93	93
CONNECTICUT			
1	Kennelly	77	76
2	Gejdenson	98	98
3	DeLauro	99	99
4	*Shays*	99	99
5	Maloney	97	98
6	*Johnson*	99	99
DELAWARE			
AL	*Castle*	99	99
FLORIDA			
1	*Scarborough*	92	93
2	Boyd	99	99
3	Brown	93	93
4	*Fowler*	95	95
5	Thurman	99	99
6	*Stearns*	98	98
7	*Mica*	97	98
8	*McCollum*	97	97
9	*Bilirakis*	97	97
10	*Young*	83	83
11	Davis	99	99
12	*Canady*	99	99
13	*Miller*	97	97
14	*Goss*	89	89
15	*Weldon*	95	95
16	*Foley*	96	96
17	Meek	94	94
18	*Ros-Lehtinen*	92	91
19	Wexler	95	95
20	Deutsch	93	93
21	*Diaz-Balart*	96	97
22	*Shaw*	98	98
23	Hastings	91	90
GEORGIA			
1	*Kingston*	99	99
2	Bishop	99	99
3	*Collins*	97	97
4	McKinney	99	99
5	Lewis	81	81
6	*Gingrich*[4]	14	14
7	*Barr*	95	95
8	*Chambliss*	99	99
9	*Deal*	98	98
10	*Norwood*	93	93
11	*Linder*	96	96
HAWAII			
1	Abercrombie	99	99
2	Mink	98	98
IDAHO			
1	*Chenoweth*	98	98
2	*Crapo*	96	96
ILLINOIS			
1	Rush	93	93
2	Jackson	100	100
3	Lipinski	93	93
4	Gutierrez	96	96
5	Blagojevich	95	95
6	*Hyde*	95	96
7	Davis	96	96
8	*Crane*	94	95
9	Yates	75	75
10	*Porter*	98	98
11	*Weller*	98	99
12	Costello	98	99
13	*Fawell*	92	92

ND Northern Democrats   SD Southern Democrats

Background Material

		1	2
14	*Hastert*	98	99
15	*Ewing*	95	95
16	*Manzullo*	98	98
17	Evans	99	99
18	*LaHood*	99	99
19	Poshard	65	65
20	*Shimkus*	98	98

INDIANA

		1	2
1	Visclosky	97	98
2	McIntosh	96	96
3	Roemer	99	99
4	*Souder*	96	97
5	*Buyer*	92	93
6	*Burton*	92	93
7	*Pease*	99	99
8	*Hostettler*	99	99
9	Hamilton	97	97
10	Carson	93	93

IOWA

		1	2
1	*Leach*	98	98
2	*Nussle*	99	99
3	Boswell	99	99
4	*Ganske*	98	98
5	*Latham*	99	99

KANSAS

		1	2
1	*Moran*	100	100
2	*Ryun*	98	98
3	*Snowbarger*	99	99
4	*Tiahrt*	98	98

KENTUCKY

		1	2
1	*Whitfield*	97	97
2	*Lewis*	99	99
3	*Northup*	99	99
4	*Bunning*	99	99
5	*Rogers*	97	98
6	Baesler	96	96

LOUISIANA

		1	2
1	*Livingston*	96	97
2	Jefferson	88	88
3	*Tauzin*	93	93
4	*McCrery*	92	92
5	*Cooksey*	91	91
6	*Baker*	95	95
7	John	86	86

MAINE

		1	2
1	Allen	98	98
2	Baldacci	99	99

MARYLAND

		1	2
1	*Gilchrest*	97	98
2	*Ehrlich*	95	95
3	Cardin	95	95
4	Wynn	96	96
5	Hoyer	98	99
6	*Bartlett*	99	99
7	Cummings	99	99
8	*Morella*	98	98

MASSACHUSETTS

		1	2
1	Olver	98	98
2	Neal	95	95
3	McGovern	96	96
4	Frank	95	95
5	Meehan	94	94
6	Tierney	98	98
7	Markey	91	91
8	Kennedy	93	93
9	Moakley	79	79
10	Delahunt	99	99

MICHIGAN

		1	2
1	Stupak	97	97
2	*Hoekstra*	99	99
3	*Ehlers*	98	98
4	*Camp*	99	99
5	Barcia	98	98
6	*Upton*	100	100
7	*Smith*	98	98
8	Stabenow	97	97
9	Kildee	99	99
10	Bonior	99	99
11	Knollenberg	99	100
12	Levin	99	99
13	Rivers	99	99
14	Conyers	90	90
15	Kilpatrick	90	90
16	Dingell	94	94

MINNESOTA

		1	2
1	*Gutknecht*	98	98
2	Minge	99	99
3	*Ramstad*	100	100
4	Vento	99	99
5	Sabo	98	98
6	Luther	96	96
7	Peterson	99	99
8	Oberstar	98	98

MISSISSIPPI

		1	2
1	*Wicker*	96	96
2	Thompson	94	94
3	*Pickering*	94	95
4	*Parker*	84	84
5	Taylor	98	99

MISSOURI

		1	2
1	Clay	87	87
2	*Talent*	99	99
3	Gephardt	90	90
4	Skelton	99	99
5	McCarthy	96	96
6	Danner	97	97
7	*Blunt*	96	96
8	*Emerson*	99	99
9	*Hulshof*	98	98

MONTANA

		1	2
AL	*Hill*	96	96

NEBRASKA

		1	2
1	*Bereuter*	99	99
2	*Christensen*	90	90
3	*Barrett*	99	99

NEVADA

		1	2
1	*Ensign*	97	98
2	*Gibbons*	99	99

NEW HAMPSHIRE

		1	2
1	*Sununu*	98	98
2	*Bass*	99	99

NEW JERSEY

		1	2
1	Andrews	98	98
2	*LoBiondo*	99	99
3	*Saxton*	98	98
4	*Smith*	98	98
5	*Roukema*	98	98
6	Pallone	99	99
7	*Franks*	99	99
8	Pascrell	98	98
9	Rothman	96	96
10	Payne	91	91
11	*Frelinghuysen*	99	99
12	*Pappas*	100	100
13	Menendez	98	98

NEW MEXICO

		1	2
1	*Wilson* [5]	99	98
2	*Skeen*	99	100
3	Redmond	98	98

NEW YORK

		1	2
1	*Forbes*	96	96
2	*Lazio*	99	99
3	*King*	97	97
4	McCarthy	99	99
5	Ackerman	92	92
6	Meeks [6]	86	86
7	Manton	92	92
8	Nadler	94	94
9	Schumer	79	79
10	Towns	82	82
11	Owens	94	94
12	Velázquez	94	94
13	*Fossella*	98	98
14	Maloney	94	94
15	Rangel	86	86
16	Serrano	95	95
17	Engel	93	93
18	Lowey	97	97
19	*Kelly*	99	99
20	*Gilman*	99	99
21	McNulty	83	83
22	*Solomon*	97	97
23	*Boehlert*	99	99
24	*McHugh*	98	98
25	*Walsh*	98	98
26	Hinchey	98	98
27	*Paxon*	92	91
28	Slaughter	96	97
29	LaFalce	98	98

		1	2
30	Quinn	95	95
31	*Houghton*	94	94

NORTH CAROLINA

		1	2
1	Clayton	94	94
2	Etheridge	98	98
3	*Jones*	99	99
4	Price	99	99
5	*Burr*	97	97
6	*Coble*	96	96
7	McIntyre	97	97
8	*Hefner*	81	81
9	*Myrick*	97	97
10	*Ballenger*	97	97
11	*Taylor*	94	94
12	Watt	98	98

NORTH DAKOTA

		1	2
AL	Pomeroy	97	98

OHIO

		1	2
1	*Chabot*	99	99
2	*Portman*	98	98
3	Hall	96	97
4	*Oxley*	96	96
5	*Gillmor*	98	98
6	Strickland	99	99
7	*Hobson*	99	99
8	*Boehner*	99	99
9	Kaptur	94	94
10	Kucinich	99	99
11	Stokes	93	93
12	*Kasich*	98	98
13	Brown	97	97
14	Sawyer	98	98
15	*Pryce*	77	77
16	*Regula*	99	99
17	Traficant	97	97
18	*Ney*	97	97
19	*LaTourette*	99	99

OKLAHOMA

		1	2
1	*Largent*	94	94
2	*Coburn*	97	97
3	*Watkins*	98	98
4	*Watts*	99	99
5	*Istook*	93	93
6	*Lucas*	100	100

OREGON

		1	2
1	Furse	86	87
2	*Smith*	89	89
3	Blumenauer	98	98
4	DeFazio	95	96
5	Hooley	97	98

PENNSYLVANIA

		1	2
1	Brady [7]	96	96
2	Fattah	92	93
3	Borski	97	97
4	Klink	97	97
5	*Peterson*	98	98
6	Holden	99	99
7	*Weldon*	96	96
8	*Greenwood*	94	94
9	*Shuster*	94	94
10	*McDade*	67	68
11	Kanjorski	99	99
12	Murtha	95	96
13	*Fox*	99	99
14	Coyne	99	99
15	McHale	99	99
16	*Pitts*	99	99
17	*Gekas*	97	97
18	Doyle	97	97
19	*Goodling*	95	95
20	Mascara	100	100
21	*English*	98	98

RHODE ISLAND

		1	2
1	Kennedy	99	99
2	Weygand	99	99

SOUTH CAROLINA

		1	2
1	*Sanford*	98	98
2	*Spence*	99	99
3	*Graham*	95	95
4	*Inglis*	89	90
5	Spratt	94	94
6	Clyburn	97	98

SOUTH DAKOTA

		1	2
AL	*Thune*	99	99

TENNESSEE

		1	2
1	*Jenkins*	98	98
2	*Duncan*	99	99
3	*Wamp*	98	98
4	*Hilleary*	99	99
5	Clement	97	98
6	Gordon	97	97
7	*Bryant*	99	99
8	Tanner	96	96
9	Ford	85	84

TEXAS

		1	2
1	Sandlin	97	97
2	Turner	97	97
3	*Johnson*	92	92
4	Hall	99	99
5	*Sessions*	98	98
6	*Barton*	97	98
7	*Archer*	97	97
8	*Brady*	95	96
9	Lampson	95	96
10	Doggett	99	99
11	Edwards	99	99
12	*Granger*	98	99
13	*Thornberry*	99	99
14	*Paul*	98	98
15	Hinojosa	95	95
16	Reyes	92	93
17	Stenholm	99	99
18	Jackson-Lee	97	97
19	*Combest*	99	99
20	Gonzalez	16	16
21	*Smith*	98	98
22	*DeLay*	96	96
23	*Bonilla*	98	98
24	Frost	94	94
25	Bentsen	99	100
26	*Armey*	97	97
27	Ortiz	94	94
28	Rodriguez	97	97
29	Green	94	93
30	Johnson	94	94

UTAH

		1	2
1	*Hansen*	96	96
2	*Cook*	97	97
3	*Cannon*	89	89

VERMONT

		1	2
AL	*Sanders*	98	98

VIRGINIA

		1	2
1	*Bateman*	81	81
2	*Pickett*	98	98
3	Scott	100	100
4	Sisisky	99	99
5	Goode	98	98
6	*Goodlatte*	99	99
7	*Bliley*	99	99
8	Moran	97	97
9	Boucher	94	94
10	*Wolf*	99	99
11	*Davis*	98	98

WASHINGTON

		1	2
1	*White*	98	98
2	*Metcalf*	99	99
3	*Smith*	94	94
4	*Hastings*	99	99
5	*Nethercutt*	98	98
6	Dicks	98	98
7	McDermott	96	96
8	*Dunn*	98	98
9	Smith	98	99

WEST VIRGINIA

		1	2
1	Mollohan	93	93
2	Wise	96	96
3	Rahall	97	97

WISCONSIN

		1	2
1	*Neumann*	97	97
2	*Klug*	95	95
3	Kind	99	99
4	Kleczka	99	99
5	Barrett	99	99
6	*Petri*	99	99
7	Obey	98	98
8	Johnson	98	98
9	*Sensenbrenner*	99	99

WYOMING

		1	2
AL	*Cubin*	98	98

Southern states - Ala., Ark., Fla., Ga., Ky., La., Miss., N.C., Okla., S.C., Tenn., Texas, Va.

Appendix C

KEY VOTES

Key Votes
Senate C-3
House C-9

Individual Members' Votes
Senate C-16
House C-18

Key Votes

Distracted by Impeachment, Republicans Hand Clinton A Few Legislative Victories

Since 1945, Congressional Quarterly has selected a series of key votes on major issues of the year. An issue is judged by the extent to which it represents:
- A matter of major controversy.
- A matter of presidential or political power.
- A matter of potentially great impact on the nation and lives of Americans.

For each group of related votes on an issue, one key vote is usually chosen — one that, in the opinion of CQ editors, was most improtant in determining the outcome.

Charts showing how each member of Congress voted on these key issues begin on p. C-16.

10 CLONING BAN

After scientists in Scotland announced in 1997 that they had cloned a sheep named Dolly, legislation to ban human cloning was put on a fast track. For much of 1997 and early 1998, it looked as if a broad cloning ban would pass the Senate. But a Feb. 11 decision to block debate on an anti-cloning bill (S 1601) showed how medical research groups and biotech companies were able to make their case, even amid the clamor over Dolly.

It also showed how the cloning issue would not be fought along the same battle lines as abortion. Anti-abortion forces entered the debate on cloning early, hoping to have some products of genetic manipulation defined as human life even though scientists disagreed. They lost when not only Democrats, but also abortion opponents such as Sens. Connie Mack, R-Fla., and Strom Thurmond, R-S.C., sided with researchers and cited their own experiences with serious diseases in concluding that there is a huge gray area that could be valuable ground for advances in medical knowledge.

The measure was halted when Dianne Feinstein, D-Calif., objected to bringing it up. Sixty votes are necessary to overcome such an objection; the vote on the motion to proceed failed, 42-54: R 42-12; D 0-42 (ND 0-34; SD 0-8).

There was, and is, consensus in Congress that human cloning is morally repugnant. But medical groups and many senators contended that the measure, sponsored by Republicans Bill Frist of Tennessee and Christopher S. Bond of Missouri, was too broad and could interfere with research. For example, they argued that reproducing masses of human cells for the purposes of replacing badly burned skin could be halted by the legislation. The same could be true of an experimental process of cloning human cells into animals for the purposes of having the animals produce human antibodies.

The measure would have banned a process known as somatic cell nuclear transfer for the purposes of creating a human embryo. The process involves replacing the nucleus of an egg cell with the nucleus of some other cell — an adult cell that would not multiply if left in its original state. Scientists have found that the remaining portion of the cell can somehow "reprogram" the new nucleus into multiplying.

Bond and Frist argued that this new cell could be considered an embryo, and thus worthy of the same protection as an embryo created through sexual intercourse. They were backed by The National Right to Life Committee and other groups opposed to abortion.

But scientific groups said the language was too broad. Feinstein offered an alternative that would have banned creating a human being through the somatic cell transfer process. It was opposed by anti-abortion groups and by some medical organizations.

16 CAMPAIGN FINANCE

In October 1997, Senate Democrats put heavy pressure on Majority Leader Trent Lott, R-Miss., to schedule a vote on a campaign finance bill that he and most of his GOP colleagues vehemently opposed. Democrats threatened to bring the Senate to a halt in the session's closing days unless they got their way.

Displaying his pragmatic streak, Lott acceded to the Democrats' demands and agreed to permit a debate on the matter in early 1998. But Lott could afford to be magnanimous: He had the votes.

Joined by Mitch McConnell, R-Ky., Lott led a successful filibuster against the campaign finance proposal, which was sponsored by John McCain, R-Ariz., and Russell D. Feingold, D-Wis.

The outcome was scripted in advance. Before the debate, McCain acknowledged that his side would not be able to amass the 60 votes needed to break the filibuster. But campaign finance advocates were hoping to do better than they had in October 1997, when they managed to garner 52. *(1997 Almanac, p. 1-26)*

Instead, they fared exactly the same — or would have, had all members been present. Tom Harkin, D-Iowa, a supporter of the McCain-Feingold proposal, was absent. On the key vote, which occurred Feb. 26, the Senate failed to end the filibuster, 51-48. Forty-four Democrats and seven Republicans supported a motion to limit debate; 48 Republicans opposed it.

The vote came on an amendment to a GOP bill (S 1663) that would have limited the use of union dues for political activity. The amendment,

Key Votes

proposed by McCain and Feingold, was a modified version of their campaign finance bill (S 25).

The decisive factor was the willingness of GOP senators who faced reelection in 1998 — such as Alfonse M. D'Amato of New York, Christopher S. Bond of Missouri and Sam Brownback of Kansas — to stand with Lott and McConnell. McConnell said that the 48 Republicans who opposed the bill the previous autumn remained "rock solid."

The McCain-Feingold bill would have banned "soft money," unregulated donations to political parties by unions, corporations and wealthy individuals. It also would have imposed new restrictions on issue-oriented television ads run by interest groups.

The legislation had picked up momentum in 1997 as Congress probed fundraising excesses in the 1996 presidential campaign. But opponents charged that the measure infringed on constitutionally protected political speech. And many Republicans feared that it would diminish their substantial fundraising advantage over Democrats.

The vote of Feb. 26 took much of the steam out of the Senate's campaign finance debate. McConnell was gleeful in declaring victory. "This undeserving legislation is dead," he said after the vote. But Lott's bill on union dues also was defeated. The Senate failed to end a Democratic filibuster on that bill, 45-54.

There were efforts to revive the McCain-Feingold bill later in 1998, but they also failed. On Sept. 10, Democrats again fell short of closing debate on the proposal by the same 52-48 vote.

44 IMF FUNDING

The Senate's strong early vote — 84-16 on March 26 — to appropriate $17.9 billion for the International Monetary Fund (IMF) set the tone for months of high-stakes maneuvering between pro-trade business interests and an unlikely array of environmentalists, free-trade conservatives and others opposed to the funding.

Early in 1998, President Clinton requested the appropriation as part of an emergency supplemental bill (PL 105-174) to shore up IMF reserves, which had been drawn down by massive loans to economically troubled Asian nations. Clinton and many top lawmakers in both parties said the money was necessary to stabilize economies across much of the world.

But House leaders turned a cool shoulder to the request. Majority Leader Dick Armey, R-Texas, denounced the IMF for interfering with free markets, while critics on the left blamed the organization for contributing to deteriorating labor and environmental conditions overseas.

When the House Appropriations Committee on March 24 split IMF funding off from the main supplemental bill (HR 3579), all eyes turned to the Senate. The upper chamber had historically been a bastion of support for trade and international commerce measures, and if the IMF appropriation was to have any chance of reaching the president's desk, it needed a strong Senate vote.

But Senate appropriators also had given IMF a rough ride. The Senate Appropriations Committee approved the funding, but attached such contentious provisions that it was unclear whether the 182-nation organization would be able to comply. For example, the committee insisted that the IMF make loans only to countries that honored certain trade agreements.

When the supplemental bill (S 1768) went to the floor, Mitch McConnell, R-Ky., proposed an amendment that would ease the IMF conditions. It would require that the United States and its major "G-7" industrial partners agree to push for such IMF measures as requiring borrowing countries to abide by international trade agreements.

McConnell's conditions fell far short of what IMF critics demanded. Conservatives such as Connie Mack, R-Fla., and Spencer Abraham, R-Mich., assailed the IMF for pressuring governments to raise taxes, devalue currencies and delay regulatory changes, and said the organization would have to be completely revamped before getting their support.

On the left, Democrats such as Paul Wellstone, D-Minn., criticized the international organization for promoting austerity policies that reduced the standard of living in recipient countries.

But funding supporters such as Chuck Hagel, R-Neb., and Patrick J. Leahy, D-Vt., carried the day by contending that the funding was needed to restore confidence in the global economy.

The Senate passed the amendment on March 26 by a vote of 84-16: R 41-14, D 43-2 (ND 35-2, SD 8-0). The overwhelming vote gave considerable momentum to the administration's funding request.

Still skeptical, House leaders refused to include the funding in the supplemental bill. Instead, the IMF issue lingered all year, as appropriators wrestled with the issue in the fiscal 1999 foreign operations spending bill (HR 4328 — PL 105-277).

But with the resounding Senate vote echoing throughout the negotiations, Congress finally cleared the IMF funding in the final days of the session.

112 NATO EXPANSION

The Senate strongly endorsed admitting Poland, Hungary and the Czech Republic to NATO on April 30, but only after sending a clear signal that the alliance should not rush to invite any more former Soviet satellites to join.

Expansion of the alliance had a powerful head of steam by the time it reached the Senate floor in the spring. It was strongly backed by President Clinton and most Republican and Democratic congressional leaders. And the Clinton administration orchestrated support from labor, veterans and ethnic groups with ties to the three countries.

Opponents of expansion were a politically diverse lot. Conservative isolationists warned that expanding the alliance would overextend U.S. overseas commitments. Some liberals argued that for Poland, Hungary and the Czech Republic to meld their armed forces into NATO would distract them from needed economic reforms. And several foreign policy experts worried that adding the three countries to NATO would exacerbate relations with Russia.

The critics faced an uphill fight from the beginning. And it was apparent by April 27, when the Senate began its final four days of debate, that they had no momentum. For instance, the argument that expansion would undermine relations with Russia was blunted by Moscow's public acquiescence.

It was clear that the protocol amending the treaty to add the three new countries (Treaty Doc 105-36) would be supported by considerably more than the required two-thirds majority of the Senate. But the critics by then had shifted their focus to delaying, at least for a few years, any invitations to other countries.

The leading candidates for a second round of expansion were Romania and Slovenia. But nine other countries also had applied for NATO membership, including the three Baltic republics — Estonia, Latvia and Lithuania.

The Baltic states posed a particularly awkward problem for NATO. On the one hand, all three had made progress in establishing democratic institutions and free-market economies, which are among the prerequisites of membership. But all three would be difficult to defend, because they are small and adjacent to Russia. Moreover, the Soviet Union had annexed all three in 1940. Although the United States never recognized the annexation, it was widely believed that Russia would object strenuously to NATO membership for countries it deemed former Soviet republics.

For months, even some staunch supporters of admitting the first three countries made it clear they wanted to see how that phase of expansion panned out before admitting additional countries.

The test came on an amendment to the treaty protocol offered by John W. Warner of Virginia, the second-ranking Republican on the Senate Armed Services Committee. Warner's proposal would have barred any additional invitations for three years after the first group was admitted. The amendment was rejected, 41-59. But it garnered more "yea" votes than the one-third that would be needed to block admission a second group of countries, if they were invited too quickly.

Both parties split on the Warner amendment, Republicans opposing it, 24-31, and Democrats, 17-28 (ND 15-22, SD 2-6).

The Senate also rejected several other amendments that would have made admission of Poland, Hungary and the Czech Republic dependent on various developments. But it adopted, by voice vote, two amendments by Ted Stevens, R-Alaska, chairman of the Appropriations Committee. One required congressional authorization of any U.S. spending related to NATO enlargement. The other urged the president to propose to other alliance members a gradual reduction in the U.S. share of NATO's budget.

The Senate than approved the treaty amendment, 80-19. The three countries are to formally join NATO April 4 at a 50th anniversary meeting of the alliance in Washington.

141 SKILLED-WORKER VISAS

In 1996, Congress greatly restricted immigration policy, cutting off welfare benefits to legal immigrants and passing tough new provisions against illegal immigration. The Senate's May 18 vote to expand the so-called H-1B visa program was perhaps the best evidence of how much things had changed in two years.

The vote was 78-20: R 51-2; D 27-18 (ND 20-17, SD 7-1).

The H-1B program is for skilled immigrants, most of whom go to work in the computer industry, but many of whom fill medium-skilled jobs as medical technicians, physical therapists, even fashion models.

Unlike lesser-skilled immigrants, H-1B recipients had business lobbies, particularly Silicon Valley, arguing their case. But they are still immigrants, and they touch a nerve among groups that argue the country is already swamped with too many foreigners. Groups such as the Federation for American Immigration Reform argued that the program is a way for companies to import cheap labor instead of hiring equally skilled American workers. Labor unions said the program is a ruse for depressing wages.

The overwhelming vote in the Senate showed the increasingly strong nexus between a pro-business stance and a pro-immigration stance. It also showed that taking an anti-immigration position is increasingly difficult.

The vote created the momentum for an H-1B expansion to be enacted. A similar bill ran into some trouble in the House, but was eventually included in the omnibus spending package (HR 4328 — PL 105-277) passed at year's end.

The Senate bill, increasing the annual allotment of H-1B visas from 65,000 to 115,000, sailed through both the Judiciary Committee and full Senate. Only two Republicans, and fewer than half the Democrats, voted against it.

In committee, and on the floor, Edward M. Kennedy, D-Mass., tried to amend the measure with labor-backed provisions that would have made it much harder for employers to participate in the program. They would have been required to demonstrate their efforts to attract American workers before being allowed to go into the H-1B program. They would have been barred from it if they had laid off any U.S. workers with skills comparable to those of foreigners they wanted to sponsor.

But even these provisions got little Senate support. Both were voted down with near unanimous Republican opposition and a handful Democratic defections.

Later in the legislative process, Republican immigration hard-liners would emerge in the House. The vote put the Senate clearly on the pro-immigration side.

The vote was a significant victory for a new lobby — high-technology companies. Many of the companies that pushed hard for the H-1B expansion were small businesses just a few years ago. Today, these companies, including Sun Microsystems Inc., Intel Corp. and Microsoft Corp., have grown into corporate giants.

Their lobbying and political contributions had not grown as fast as their profits, however. Many of them had a corporate culture that was somewhat anti-Washington; they saw it necessary to open D.C. offices only in the last few years.

The H-1B debate was their first industry-wide cooperative effort, and it was a resounding success. At the beginning of 1998, few members outside of those who represent high-tech states had given much thought to the issue. But by spring the high-tech lobby had put it squarely on senators' agendas. They aggressively argued that they could not continue to grow as fast as they had if they could not get their hands on the skilled workers they needed. They implicitly threatened to

Key Votes

take jobs overseas if overseas workers could not be brought here.

The lopsided vote showed how effectively the lobby had done its homework. Even some Democratic senators had a hard time fighting them. Many, like Dianne Feinstein of California, chose their business constituents over their labor union backers, after some attempts to mollify both sides.

161 TOBACCO LEGISLATION

By the time the Senate floor debate on tobacco legislation (S 1415) reached its fourth week, the action had come to resemble an old serial drama at the movies, complete with cliffhanger moments of suspense, its audience unsure what would happen from one week to the next.

Finally, on June 17, Majority Leader Trent Lott, R-Miss., had seen enough. He shut down the Senate in the morning to convene in his office a meeting of some three dozen Republicans. The decision was made to hold a cloture vote later in the day and, when that failed, to bring the bill down.

During the meeting, Mitch McConnell of Kentucky, chairman of the National Republican Senatorial Committee, reportedly assured nervous colleagues that the tobacco industry would run ads against the bill for their political protection.

The tobacco industry had spent more than $40 million on issue ads that attacked S 1415, and a like amount on lobbying. S 1415 would have raised fees on cigarettes by $1.10 per pack over five years, given the federal government broad control over the distribution and marketing of tobacco products, and restricted tobacco advertising.

"I've never discounted the effect of a lot of money on ads," bill sponsor John McCain, R-Ariz., told a news conference. "If cloture is not invoked, tobacco companies have made a wise investment, and they have won because they have changed the views of a significant number of Americans."

The creation of a federal tobacco policy had seemed almost a foregone conclusion at earlier stages of the legislative process. But as the bill bogged down in the Senate and both its friends and enemies bloated it with big-dollar amendments, it became clear that there was no longer a clear political consensus to lend the effort momentum.

"What killed this bill was that the public never bought into the logic of it — they never saw this as a tool to fight teen smoking," Phil Gramm, R-Texas, told a gaggle of reporters after Lott's meeting broke up. "This bill has no support in America, and it has lost its support in Congress."

There had been three previous cloture votes on the bill, but those had been filed by Democrats and were seen more as maneuvering over control of the schedule than about the bill. As Lott's strategy became clear, the bill's strongest supporters were angered.

"What they did was spread DDT here — first delay, then destroy, then terminate any action on tobacco," Frank R. Lautenberg, D-N.J., said of S 1415's opponents, several of whom could be seen laughing in response on the Senate floor.

Senators for and against the bill had spent the better part of the day counting noses. Asked by a reporter whether his side didn't enjoy a three-vote cushion, Majority Whip Don Nickles, R-Okla., a leading opponent of the bill, replied, "I wouldn't say that yet."

But that is just how the vote turned out. The motion to invoke cloture fell three votes short of the 60 required, 57-42: R 14-40; D 43-2 (ND 37-0, SD 6-2). S 1415 was then taken down on a budget point of order.

169 EDUCATION SAVINGS ACCOUNTS

Opinion polls show that Americans are worried about school quality. Unfortunately for Republicans, the surveys also show that voters believe Democrats do a better job on education issues.

Trying to assuage public concern on both counts, congressional Republicans pushed legislation (HR 2646) that would have allowed families to contribute up to $2,000 per child per year in special savings accounts for private school tuition, tutoring, computer equipment and other education expenses. The legislation passed the House, 230-198, on Oct. 23, 1997, and was taken up by the Senate this year.

Despite White House veto threats and a determined effort by Minority Leader Tom Daschle, D-S.D., to persuade Democrats not to vote for the legislation, the Senate approved the final conference report on June 24, by a vote of 59-36: R 51-2; D 8-34 (ND 6-28, SD 2-6).

The vote indicated a growing willingness among Democrats to buck the White House and search for new ways to give parents more control over their childrens' education. But it also showed the two parties were still far from consensus, a fact that the White House exploited later in the year, when Clinton browbeat Republicans into adding $1.2 billion to the omnibus spending bill (HR 4328 — PL 105-277) as a down payment on his plan to hire 100,000 new teachers.

The savings account bill, sponsored by Paul Coverdell, R-Ga., was designed to move Republicans beyond their narrow emphasis on federally funded vouchers for private schools. Because parents, rather than the government, could choose how to manage the accounts, Republicans hoped they would appeal to Democrats. Robert G. Torricelli, D-N.J., was a chief cosponsor of the bill.

The middle ground turned out to be elusive. The Clinton administration charged that the legislation would mainly benefit upper-income taxpayers. Democrats used debate on the Coverdell bill to force votes on Clinton's proposals to hire teachers and allow local governments to issue $22 billion in federally backed bonds for school construction. Both those initiatives were defeated.

Senate Republicans offered competing amendments that they said would limit the federal role in education and return more power to the states. In a surprise vote, the Senate by 50-49 adopted an amendment by Slade Gorton, R-Wash., that would turn $10.3 billion in annual elementary and secondary programs into broad block grants.

The Senate also adopted an amendment by John Ashcroft, R-Mo., to bar Clinton from proceeding with his plans for voluntary math and reading tests.

With those provisions attached, several Democrats who had said they might have voted for the underlying Coverdell bill decided to vote "nay."

In the end, five Democrats voted for the measure, which passed the Senate, 56-43, on April 23.

House-Senate conferees dropped the proposals on testing and block grants. The final bill retained some bipartisan sweeteners attached in the Senate, including making prepaid college tuition completely tax free. The conference report passed the House, 225-197, on June 18. Twelve Democrats voted for it, 10 Republicans against. Republicans did not even attempt an override after Clinton, as promised, vetoed the bill July 21. They have promised to revive the legislation next year.

180 SAME-SEX TRAINING

Hoping to capitalize on support from a national commission, social conservatives tried to force the Army, Navy and Air Force to follow the Marine Corps' example and segregate male and female recruits during training. But the effort, which came to a head in amendments to the fiscal 1999 defense authorization bill (HR 3616), was rejected by the Senate.

The underlying issue, a battle more than two decades old, was the proper role of women in the armed forces. Starting in 1975, when an amendment to the fiscal 1976 defense bill (PL 94-106) required the admission of women to the national military academies, Congress and successive administrations had eliminated or scaled back rules intended to keep women out of jobs involving any risk of combat. Women's rights groups and female officers vigorously promoted these changes, contending that excluding women from combat jobs — the most prestigious in the services — effectively barred them from rising to the highest ranks.

Social conservatives, however, argued that allowing women into more jobs had undermined combat readiness by lowering standards for physical strength and creating sexual tensions in small units.

The long-running debate gained new urgency in 1996 following allegations of sexual abuse by drill sergeants at some Army training bases. Although the incidents occurred at advanced training facilities, conservatives seized on them to push for legislation that would require the services to organize new recruits in separate units and to house men and women in separate barracks.

Efforts to pass such a bill yielded nothing in 1997, partly because those who challenged mixed-gender training did not want to appear to be condoning the abusive behavior.

But in December 1997, a special commission created by Defense Secretary William S. Cohen and chaired by former Kansas Republican Sen. Nancy Kassebaum Baker (1978-97), recommended separate housing and training units for male and female recruits. The change, Baker said, would reduce distractions for recruits and drill instructors.

The Army, Navy and Air Force vigorously objected, arguing that training men and women together helped acclimate them to working in mixed-gender teams.

Cohen adopted several other recommendations by the Baker panel aimed at making basic training more rigorous and improving the quality of the sergeants and petty officers who supervise recruits. But he allowed the services to continue mixing men and women in the same small units and allowed them to be housed in the same barracks, with physical barriers and supervision.

The House version of the fiscal 1999 defense authorization bill (H Rept 105-532) included a requirement that men and women recruits be housed in separate buildings and trained in separate small units. The House debated the bill under a rule that prohibited any amendments dealing with the issue.

The version of the bill drafted by the Senate Armed Services Committee (S 2057 — S Rept 105-189) would have required only that current policies remain until a commission mandated by Congress in the fiscal 1998 defense authorization bill (PL 105-85) completed its review in 1999.

The issue arose on the Senate floor in a flurry of votes. But in the most sweeping decision, the Senate on June 25 rejected, 39-53, an amendment by Robert C. Byrd, D-W. Va., that would have barred the services from putting male and female recruits in the same small unit, or housing them in the same building. Republicans supported the amendment, but not overwhelmingly, 31-21, while Democrats opposed it, 8-32 (ND 5-27, SD 3-5).

The conference report on the bill (H Rept 105-736) required only that sleeping areas for male and female recruits housed in the same building be separated by permanent walls. In an unusual move, the conference report also included a non-binding expression of the sense of the House that men and women should be trained in separate small units.

201 SANCTIONS

For months, Richard G. Lugar of Indiana, a senior Republican on the Senate Foreign Relations Committee, had been waging an often lonely and seemingly hopeless fight to slow down the use of overseas economic sanctions by Congress and the executive branch.

Despite the cost of sanctions to U.S. businesses and the restrictions they impose on the administration's diplomatic flexibility, many lawmakers came to believe sanctions are an effective and relatively painless way of exerting influence over other nations and the conduct of U.S foreign policy.

Lugar and influential Reps. Lee H. Hamilton, D-Ind., and Philip M. Crane, R-Ill., believed otherwise, arguing that while some sanctions might have merit, their cumulative weight had partially crippled American foreign policy, harmed U.S. exporters and had little substantive effect on the behavior of foreign countries. The three were supported by USA Engage, an influential coalition of businesses that had joined together expressly to overturn sanctions that critics contended cost the U.S. economy as much as $20 billion a year.

Lugar introduced a bill (S 1413) that would have slowed down the imposition of new sanctions by instituting a formal process under which lawmakers would have to weigh the costs and benefits of new restrictions on aid and trade. The bill also would have put a two-year limit on any sanctions unless Congress renewed them.

But their arguments made little headway until India and Pakistan tested nuclear weapons in May. The tests triggered automatic sanctions under the Arms Export Control Act, contained in the 1994 State Department authorization bill (PL 103-236).

The Arms Export Control Act, originally sponsored by Sen. John Glenn, D-Ohio, cuts off non-humanitarian aid, bars the export of defense material and certain other technology, and halts U.S. credit and loan guarantees to non-nuclear nations that detonate nuclear weapons. It does not permit a presidential waiver.

The sanctions hit Pakistan, a poorer, smaller country, much harder than they hit India. U.S. farmers also were threatened when the Clinton administration decided that the law's credit ban would prevent the United States from guaranteeing bank loans on exports of wheat and other crops to Pakistan.

With U.S wheat farmers about to be squeezed out of a major wheat auction, the Senate unanimously approved legislation (S 2282) allowing India and Pakistan to continue to use guaranteed loans to import American food, fertilizer and other agricultural commodities.

Congress later allowed Clinton to waive sanctions against the two South Asian countries for a year.

But with farmers up in arms about the sanctions and other restrictions on trade, Lugar saw an opportunity to advance his broader bill. On July 15, he introduced it as an amendment to the agriculture appropriations bill (S 2159).

Lugar tried to use the pressure of the farm lobby to make his case, noting that the measure was backed by the American Farm Bureau Federation. "There is a passionate cry of farmers to take this action — that they are being thought of," Lugar said.

Lugar was opposed by Senate Foreign Relations Committee Chairman Jesse Helms, R-N.C., the co-author of a 1996 law (PL 104-114) that tightened the decades-old U.S. embargo on trade with Cuba, as well as other sanctions laws.

Helms argued that sanctions often were a crucial tool in addressing issues such as terrorism, drugs, and nuclear proliferation. "Obviously, sanctions are not always the answer," Helms said. "But we cannot escape the conclusion that sometimes they are the only answer."

Although a majority of GOP senators voted with him, Lugar's amendment was tabled (killed), 53-46: R 27-28; D 26-18 (ND 22-14, SD 4-4).

277 'PARTIAL BIRTH' ABORTION

Call it the showdown that never happened. For months, opponents of abortion rights had hoped to gain support in their effort to override President Clinton's veto of legislation (HR 1122) to ban a procedure they refer to as "partial birth" abortion.

Despite such efforts, the tally when they finally voted Sept. 18 was the same as in May 1997, when the Senate failed to override Clinton's veto by three votes. The outcome indicated that in a year when both sides had hoped to capitalize on the 25th anniversary of the Supreme Court's affirmation of the right to an abortion, neither side had gained ground, leaving the battle lines fairly static. The vote on passage was 64-36: R 51-4; D 13-32 (ND 9-28, SD 4-4).

Clinton vetoed the bill on Oct. 10, 1997, because he said it did not provide exceptions to permit the procedure when necessary to protect a woman's health. Under the legislation, doctors who performed the abortion procedure could have been sentenced to two years in prison and could have faced fines and lawsuits for civil damages. The measure would have exempted the woman from criminal penalties. The House voted, 296-132, on July 23 to override the veto.

Rick Santorum, R-Pa., the leader of the override effort, called the procedure "infanticide." Bill Frist, R-Tenn., a heart surgeon, said the procedure is dangerous for women and inhumane to the fetus.

Abortion-rights supporters such as Barbara Boxer, D-Calif., said the bill would "force doctors to make decisions that jeopardize women's health" because they could perform the procedure only to save the woman's life, not just to protect her health.

Carol Moseley-Braun, D-Ill., and others urged Congress to allow doctors and their patients — rather than legislators — to make decisions about abortion. Congress "does not have the right to practice medicine," said Moseley-Braun.

As in 1997, a bipartisan group of senators proposed an alternative they hoped would provide a middle ground. The backers said their proposal, which never received a floor vote, would have outlawed the procedure on a viable fetus — one that can live outside the womb — except when necessary to prevent "grievous injury" to the woman's physical health. Minority Leader Tom Daschle, D-S.D., proposed a similar measure in 1997, but it was rejected, 36-64.

Even though abortion opponents lost their battle to override Clinton's veto, John Ashcroft, R-Mo., said the issue will return. "This will not be the end of the debate," he said. "We will come back; we will vote again."

314 OMNIBUS APPROPRIATIONS

Senate leaders had hoped there would not be a recorded vote on the $500 billion-plus omnibus spending bill for fiscal 1999. Most senators had already left for home as congressional leaders and the White House hashed out a deal.

But the end product — which busted the 1997 balanced-budget agreement — doled out hundreds of hometown projects and served as the engine to drive unrelated bills into law. It was thus deemed either too important to pass without putting members on record — or too offensive, which was why several senators demanded a recorded vote.

For many fiscal conservatives, the Senate's final vote of the 105th Congress was a dismaying retreat from fiscal discipline, as President Clinton and congressional Democrats won billions of dollars in late-stage concessions from Republicans eager to go home and campaign.

Democrats were energized by the opportunity to trumpet their education priorities and portray a scandal-plagued Clinton as strong.

The bill (HR 4328 — PL 105-277) combined eight of the 13 annual spending bills. It contained $21 billion in "emergency" spending that was not subject to budget "caps" set in place under the 1997 balanced-budget law (PL 105-33). Some of this emergency spending, such as financing for the Bosnia peacekeeping mission and year 2000 computer fixes, had already been passed by the Senate. Veterans such as Budget Committee Chairman Pete V. Domenici, R-N.M., and Appropriations Committee Chairman Ted Stevens, R-Alaska, felt the caps were too tight.

Senators generally are more permissive on spending than House members, and getting federal spending for one's state is part of a senator's job description. But the process that produced the bill — with decisions made by a small group of GOP leaders and administration aides — earned withering criticism from many, especially the top Democrat on the Appropriations Committee, Robert C. Byrd of West Virginia. He particularly bristled at the presence of administration aides in negotiating sessions to which he was excluded.

"Now someone said . . . that making legislation is like making sausage," Byrd said. "Don't kid yourself. I have made sausage, and I can tell you that what we did this year was significantly more sloppy." After giving a classic stemwinder in which he said he would hold his nose and vote for the bill, Byrd decided that he had given such a good speech that he had changed his own mind. He voted "nay."

The Senate's No. 2 Republican, Don Nickles of Oklahoma, also was dismayed by the spending orgy and boycotted a Republican pep rally for the measure.

When Republicans failed to make gains in the Nov. 3 elections, disappointment among core voters over the omnibus bill was deemed one of the reasons.

GOP leaders had hoped to pass the bill by voice vote, but several dissatisfied senators called for a recorded vote to register their opposition. The bill passed easily, however, on Oct. 21 by a vote of 65-29: R 33-20; D 32-9 (ND 26-9, SD 6-0).

The Senate had been in this position before, most notably in 1996, when Clinton extracted almost $7 billion in late-stage talks over a comparable omnibus bill. Those talks occurred in the Senate Appropriations Committee offices in the Capitol, which prompted Stevens to declare he would never again permit White House aides in his office to help write bills. So the 1998 sessions took place in the suite of House Speaker Newt Gingrich, R-Ga. *(1996 Almanac, p. 10-3)*

The bills had been delayed by troubles in the House as well as by political gamesmanship by Senate Democrats, who on several occasions used the spending bills to force votes on their election year agenda.

The must-pass bill also became loaded with lawmakers' pet initiatives. It contained non-spending items that were of little interest to voters but that represented major accomplishments for lawmakers who had toiled for years on relatively obscure issues. For example, the bill reorganized U.S. foreign policy agencies, increased the number of visas for high-tech workers, curbed minors' access to pornography on the Internet and implemented the recently passed Chemical Weapons Convention. It included an extension of popular corporate tax breaks, such as the research and development tax credit.

Clinton won a $1.2 billion down payment on his initiative to subsidize the hiring of 100,000 new teachers, obtained his full $17.9 billion request for the International Monetary Fund and got many "emergency" spending items, including financing for the Bosnia peacekeeping mission and $5.9 billion in farm disaster aid. ◆

10 LINE-ITEM VETOES

The House set the stage Feb. 5 for the final act in Congress' experiment with the line-item veto as it restored funding for 38 military construction projects that President Clinton had killed in 1997 by exercising his short-lived but historic power.

The 1996 line-item veto law (PL 104-130) set forth a complicated mechanism for permitting the president to eliminate individual projects from spending bills that he otherwise had little choice but to sign. Under the law, which raised questions about the separation of power between the executive and legislative branches of government, the president's line-item vetoes would automatically take effect unless Congress passed a bill to void them.

The president could then veto that "disapproval" bill, which would require a two-thirds vote to overturn.

The fiscal 1998 military construction spending bill (PL 105-45) was the first appropriations bill to be presented to a president wielding the line-item veto. Clinton enraged members on both sides of the aisle by carving $287 million in projects from the low-profile bill. Most of the 38 projects were included in the Pentagon's long-term plans, though none were included in Clinton's fiscal 1998 budget. The White House later admitted that Clinton vetoed some projects based on faulty information about them, which added momentum to the drive to roll back the vetoes.

The House and Senate passed the disapproval bill (HR 2631) in November 1997, and Clinton promptly vetoed it just as the House adjourned. It was one of the few items in line for an early vote in 1998. *(1997 Almanac, p. 2-63)*

The House overrode Clinton's veto 347-69: R 197-23; D 149-46 (ND 100-41, SD 49-5); I 1-0. The Senate cleared the bill Feb. 25 in a 78-20 vote.

By the time Congress was ready to overturn the veto, much of Capitol Hill's trepidation over potential abuse of the new power had faded. When applying the veto to spending bills that came after the military construction bill, Clinton had used a much lighter hand.

The successful override came as a constitutional challenge to the 1996 law was poised to erase Clinton's 1997 vetoes anyway. The Supreme Court struck down the law in a 6-3 ruling in June.

95 TRANSPORTATION PROJECTS

House Transportation and Infrastructure Committee Chairman Bud Shuster, R-Pa., had patiently waited to reverse a bitter 1997 defeat at the hands of "deficit hawks."

On April 1, he got his chance. He cleared the way for passage of the $219 billion House version of the six-year surface transportation reauthorization bill (HR 2400) by defeating a campaign led by Lindsey Graham, R-S.C., to strip members' designated projects, known as

Key Votes

earmarks, from the bill. Graham's amendment would have deleted $9 billion in road projects and erased money for specified transit and bus projects.

For Shuster, it was a sweet victory. In May 1997, the House had scrapped by a two-vote margin his proposal to pare tax cuts and slice discretionary spending across the board in order to raise transportation spending by $12 billion over five years. A stalemate ensued, and Congress passed a temporary extension of funding (PL 105-130). (1997 *Almanac*, p. 3-18)

For Graham and many other members of the GOP Class of 1994, the vote was a clash between old-fashioned "pork barrel" politics and the budget-balancing spirit of the House GOP's "Contract With America."

Shuster turned the tide against less senior rivals with the help of economic projections showing a likely budget surplus. His bill called for a 40 percent increase in spending and required unspecified offsets because it exceeded the budget caps set in the balanced-budget deal by about $20 billion.

Shuster said the payoff would come in new jobs and economic growth. And he offered a tempting sweetener: a project selection process that guaranteed each member a shot at earmarking $15 million in highway funds.

At a GOP Conference meeting before the vote, Shuster was tacitly supported by House leaders, who hoped projects would help win elections. But House Budget Committee Chairman John R. Kasich, R-Ohio, spoke in opposition, arguing that the bill spent too much money. On the floor, Kasich offered an amendment to cut the federal gasoline tax from 18.3 cents to 7.4 cents a gallon over four years; it was defeated.

But the most pitched battle was fought over the project-killing Graham amendment. Shuster said the alternative to projects was to give money to states, and, he argued, "It is not reasonable to believe somehow there is a non-political, pure process back in the statehouses, as compared to the decisions made here." He suggested that Graham's opposition was "mystifying" because Graham had requested project funding in a letter.

Graham replied that he had decided to reject the $15 million for his district. He said the bill made a "sham" of the balanced-budget agreement.

Bob Inglis, R-S.C., summed up the feelings of many: "This is probably the most embarrassing night that I have ever spent in this Congress. We came here to change things, and we are not. We are participating in the big old trough that has characterized this place in the past."

In the end, Shuster won big. The final vote on the Graham amendment was 79-337: R 67-152; D 12-184 (ND 6-137, SD 6-47); I 0-1.

133 AFFIRMATIVE ACTION

The Republican Party has been deeply divided about whether to push for elimination of race- or sex-based preferences in education and hiring. From presidential elections to House campaigns, the GOP has been unable to reconcile its objection to what some term special treatment with a political need to reach out to women and minorities.

The House GOP leadership decided to support an amendment to the Higher Education Act reauthorization (HR 6) by Frank Riggs of California that would have eliminated affirmative action at public colleges and universities.

The Riggs amendment, modeled after California's 1996 Proposition 209, would have ended admissions preferences based on race, sex, ethnicity or national origin. "I believe we must focus on equality of opportunity in this country, not mandate equality of results," Riggs said.

Rather than serving to make affirmative action a defining issue between the Republican and Democratic parties, however, the amendment exposed internal fissures within the GOP. It was rejected by a vote of 171-249: R: 166-55; D: 5-193 (ND 2-143; SD 3-50); I: 0-1.

House Republican leaders voted for the amendment, but in a move that likely ensured its demise, J.C. Watts of Oklahoma, the House's only African-American Republican, joined John Lewis, D-Ga., a noted civil rights leader, in a letter to colleagues urging them to vote against the amendment.

Top Democrats spoke out against the measure. "This amendment would travel us down the retrograde road of racial divisiveness," said Minority Leader Richard A. Gephardt, D-Mo.

The House on April 1 defeated a similar amendment by Marge Roukema, R-N.J., to the surface transportation reauthorization bill (HR 2400) that would have softened requirements that the Transportation Department use female- or minority-owned businesses for 10 percent of construction projects.

151 BANKING

With the securities and insurance industries pressuring Congress to take another run at overhauling Depression-era financial services laws, House Republican leaders launched an all-out effort May 13 to pass a bill that would allow cross-ownership of banks, brokerages and insurance firms.

Speaker Newt Gingrich, R-Ga., and GOP Conference Chairman John A. Boehner of Ohio, the House leaders most active in crafting the bill (HR 10), knew that without their pressure, the measure would never make it past strong opposition from all but the largest banks. That opposition had contributed to a hasty decision to pull the bill from floor consideration in late March, after it became clear that the legislation, then attached to a credit union expansion measure (HR 1151), would not pass.

History was also against them: The House had never passed a bill to tear down the 1933 Glass-Steagall Act and subsequent laws aimed at keeping securities and insurance separate from banking.

Because the House had not considered a measure like HR 10 since 1991 and had never passed one, many members found themselves faced with a complex bill they did not fully understand. In addition, many banks lobbied hard against the measure, and the Clinton administration expressed concern about core provisions.

As the voting began May 13, Republican leaders appeared uncertain what the final outcome would be. With the regular 15-minute voting period coming to a close, a defeat seemed imminent, as "nays" outnumbered "yeas."

But when the deficit reached more than a dozen votes, Gingrich emerged and began methodically working the GOP side of the chamber, persuading members one by one to support the measure. After talking to Gingrich, several Republicans went to the well to cast an "yea" vote or to change their vote from "nay" to "yea."

Among the last to switch were four Florida Republicans — Michael Bilirakis, Dan Miller, Cliff Stearns and Dave Weldon — leading to speculation that Gingrich had promised benefits for the Sunshine State. But members and lobbyists said the four did not appear to receive any special guarantees. Their conversions brought the "yeas" and "nays" to a tie, until Connecticut Democrat Jim Maloney switched his vote from "yea" to "nay."

Then Gingrich called on Education Committee Chairman Bill Goodling, R-Pa., a moderate facing a tight election, to cast the deciding vote. Goodling had stood near the well for several minutes holding both a red "nay" card and a green "yea" card. He cast the deciding "yea" vote. The vote was 214-213: R 153-73, D 61-139 (ND 47-100, SD 14-39), I 0-1.

Opponents scoffed at the one-vote victory, saying the bill was as good as dead because Senate Banking Committee Chairman Alfonse M. D'Amato, R-N.Y., had pledged to bring it up only if it received broad bipartisan support in the House.

But supporters said the vote was nothing short of historic. Given the House's history of refusing to even bring such bills to the floor, "a one-vote victory looks like a landslide," Boehner said.

Despite skepticism that the vote would spur Senate action on the bill, D'Amato — facing a tough re-election battle he would eventually lose — moved the measure through his committee. It eventually died on the Senate floor, as conservatives Phil Gramm, R-Texas, and Richard C. Shelby, R-Ala., held it up, demanding changes to community investment provisions.

188 FOOD STAMPS FOR LEGAL IMMIGRANTS

Even before he signed a broad welfare overhaul (PL 104-193) in August 1996, President Clinton warned that he would seek to reverse provisions of the measure that eliminated federal benefits to legal immigrants.

In the 1997 budget law (PL 105-33), Congress restored disability aid to legal immigrants. This year, Republicans and the White House sparred over Clinton's request to re-instate food stamps.

The White House insisted that legislation (S 1150) to create new mandatory spending programs for agriculture research also include funding to restore nutrition aid to many of the 935,000 legal immigrants dropped from the food stamp rolls under the welfare law.

The White House and Democrats chose the research bill as their vehicle in part because the agriculture program was to be funded by reducing federal payments to states to administer the food stamp program.

The initial Senate version of the bill focused on agriculture research. After Democrats and the White House weighed in, House and Senate negotiators worked out a conference report (H Rept 105-492) that included $818 million over five years to restore food stamps to elderly and disabled legal immigrants who were in the country when the welfare law was signed, as well as children under age 18.

Overall, the legislation would restore benefits to an estimated 250,000 legal immigrants. The conference report included $600 million for agriculture research programs and $1 billion in mandatory crop insurance funding over five years.

Sen. Phil Gramm, R-Texas, held up the consideration of the measure for weeks. When it finally got to the Senate floor on May 12, the bill passed by a vote of 92-8.

In the House, a determined group of conservatives, led by Majority Leader Dick Armey, R-Texas, opposed restoration of food stamp benefits. Despite a deteriorating farm economy, some lawmakers also opposed the agriculture spending.

When the bill came to the House floor on May 22, Republican leaders brought it up under a rule that would have automatically stripped the food stamp provisions. Nearly 100 Republicans voted against the rule, which was defeated 120-289: R 118-98; D 2-190 (ND 1-140, SD 1-50); I 0-1.

The defeat of the rule marked a turning point. With the House at an impasse, farm-state lawmakers were forced to go home for the Memorial Day recess without the promised agriculture and food stamp legislation.

Under pressure from their rank and file, House GOP leaders were forced to stage a quick political turnabout. The House took up the bill again June 4 under a rule that protected the immigrant provisions. The conference report passed, 364-50, with Armey among those voting yea.

In the weeks that followed, Republicans also backed off their opposition to expanding aid to farmers affected by drought and falling prices. Congress ultimately approved a fiscal 1998 omnibus spending bill (105-277) that included nearly $6 billion in emergency agriculture aid.

290 CONTRACEPTIVE COVERAGE

For years, abortion rights supporters have pushed unsuccessfully to require health plans that cover prescription drugs to also cover contraceptives.

Rep. Nita M. Lowey, D-N.Y., scored a partial victory on that issue as part of the House debate over legislation (HR 4104) to fund the Treasury Department, Postal Service and general government spending for fiscal 1999.

After several attempts, Lowey pushed through an amendment requiring health care plans for federal workers to provide coverage for contraceptives if they also cover other prescription drugs. The vote, which splintered Republicans and Democrats, illustrated that the GOP may have more flexibility than in previous years on family planning issues. It also provided lawmakers with one of the year's few floor votes on the politically sensitive topic.

Before that victory, however, Lowey had to fend off attacks from several abortion rights opponents.

First, Todd Tiahrt, R-Kan., succeeded in striking Lowey's contraceptive language, which had been inserted into the legislation in committee, because it sought to legislate on an appropriations bill. Since the Treasury-Postal measure had been brought to the House floor under a rule that protected only one provision in the bill — language to block an annual cost of living increase for members of Congress — measures such as Lowey's were left vulnerable to deletion.

Tiahrt and Christopher H. Smith, R-N.J., one of Congress' most vocal

Key Votes

abortion opponents, objected to federal funding for contraceptives. Smith contended that some of them can be used to chemically induce abortions.

But Democrats, led by Lowey, outmaneuvered Smith and his allies, scoring a surprising victory when they returned to the floor with a slightly reworded version of the amendment. The new language barred federal funds from being used to renew contracts with health care plans for federal employees that provide coverage for prescription drugs but do not include coverage for contraceptives. That new language made the amendment in line with House rules, which allow for limitations on how money is spent. Lowey also added language to exempt five health care plans with a religious orientation that opposed her amendment.

The vote on passage was 224-198: R 48-177; D 175-21 (ND 130-17, SD 45-4); I 1-0.

Smith then countered with an amendment seeking to bar the use of contraceptives that chemically induce abortions. Lowey charged that Smith was trying to outlaw funding for all contraceptives.

"The gentleman from New Jersey is saying to every woman who may take a birth control pill or use another one of the five accepted methods of contraception that they are abortionists," Lowey said, to applause from many female lawmakers. Smith's amendment was rejected, 198-222.

296 PUBLIC HOUSING OVERHAUL

Twice in two years the House and Senate had passed measures to overhaul the nation's public housing system as part of the GOP's effort to remake government social programs.

So when House Banking and Financial Services Committee Chairman Jim Leach, R-Iowa, and Rick A. Lazio, R-N.Y., chairman of the committee's housing panel, appealed to Republican leaders to attach their bill (HR 2) to the fiscal 1999 spending measure for housing, veterans, and science programs, they were given a chance to make their case on the House floor.

On July 17, Leach and Lazio offered HR 2 as an amendment to the spending bill (HR 4194) and argued that a ride on the appropriations measure offered the best chance for their bill to become law.

Lazio and his Senate counterpart, Housing Subcommittee Chairman Connie Mack, R-Fla., had not been able to agree on the details of a bill, despite consensus on broad concepts, during more than three years of negotiating. Both chambers' bills sought to transfer block grants and most operating decisions to local authorities. Both aimed to allow authorities to break up welfare dependence in housing projects by enticing higher-income tenants. But Lazio and Mack could not agree on the specific number of units to reserve for the very poor, nor on a handful of other issues.

Leach and Lazio believed that attaching the measure to the spending bill would rejuvenate talks and provide an extra incentive for another principal, Housing and Urban Development (HUD) Secretary Andrew M. Cuomo, to negotiate.

But the amendment was not without detractors. Both the chairman and ranking Democrat on the VA-HUD Appropriations Subcommittee vociferously opposed joining the bills, saying that attaching the 400-page bill made a mockery of House rules prohibiting authorization provisions on spending legislation.

Ranking Democrat Louis Stokes of Ohio abandoned his usual reserved manner and complained that the Banking Committee had "not been able to do their job. This year, they seem to be admitting defeat earlier than usual."

Not all Banking panel members wanted to combine the housing measure and spending bill. The panel's ranking Democrat, John J. LaFalce of New York, and top Housing Subcommittee Democrat Joseph P. Kennedy II of Massachusetts argued that Lazio and Leach should consent to convene a separate conference on HR 2 and the Senate housing overhaul measure (S 462).

Kennedy said Republicans were trying to "jam" the bill "down the throat of the administration." Cuomo released a statement calling HR 2 "repugnant."

Nonetheless, the House voted to attach HR 2 to the spending measure. The vote was 230-181: R 215-4; D 15-176 (ND 8-136, SD 7-40); I 0-1.

As Leach and Lazio had predicted, pressure to complete work on the spending bill eventually forced a compromise. The final version was more moderate than the House bill, reserving more of public and subsidized housing for those with the lowest incomes, but it contained elements of the House and Senate bills and the administration's proposals.

339 MANAGED CARE REGULATIONS

Trying to wrest momentum away from Democrats on the politically explosive issue of regulating managed health care was no easy task for the GOP, especially for House Republicans eager to gain cover on the issue before the fall elections.

The solution came in the form of a package of changes developed by a House Republican task force after meeting for months behind closed doors. The group produced a bill (HR 4250) that allowed GOP members to say they had supported a managed care overhaul. But it split the House, mostly along party lines, and provided a glimpse of where members stood on one of the most controversial issues of the year. The White House threatened a veto.

The task force, led by Dennis Hastert, R-Ill., included many of the patient protections that both sides of the managed care debate had endorsed, such as giving broader rights to emergency-room care and allowing patients to appeal coverage decisions to an outside panel. The GOP bill would not, however, have allowed consumers in managed care plans that are exempt from state regulation to sue their health plans under state laws, a key element of a competing Democratic bill.

Commerce Committee Chairman Thomas J. Bliley Jr., R-Va., a member of the task force, said the proposal would put "patients back in the driver's seat, where they belong." Minority Leader Richard A. Gephardt, D-Mo., dismissed the bill as "rhetoric but not a remedy."

Gephardt and other Democrats blasted the GOP leadership for not holding committee hearings on the proposal, but instead taking it directly to the House floor for a vote. "This whole thing is designed not to have any discussion," said Jim McDermott, D-Wash.

GOP leaders, citing the fact that many chairman of committees with jurisdiction for health care were on the task force, said such hearings were unnecessary. They also charged that Democrats would attempt to "demonize" the GOP managed care bill. "We knew early on that moving it through the committee process was not practical," said GOP Conference Chairman John A. Boehner, R-Ohio.

The administration said the legislation was "seriously flawed." A statement from the Office of Management and Budget said the bill would cover too few people, provide too few patient protections and "contains unnecessary and irrelevant provisions that undermine the chances for a bipartisan agreement on a patients' bill of rights."

Despite such objections, the bill passed July 24. The vote was 216-210: R 213-12; D 3-197 (ND 2-147, SD 1-50); I 0-1.

Shortly before that vote, the House turned back a Democratic alternative (HR 3605) on a tally of 212-217. Supporters of Democratic bill, including the American Medical Association and a host of provider and consumer groups, said it would have given patients broader rights than the GOP plan, such as the ability to sue their plans for damages. Republicans criticized the Democratic plan as a costly creation of the trial lawyers' lobby.

Ten Republicans, however, broke with the GOP leadership to endorse the Democrats' measure, including plastic surgeon Greg Ganske, R-Iowa.

405 CAMPAIGN FINANCE OVERHAUL

The House vote on Aug. 6 to overhaul campaign finance laws marked the first time in six years that either chamber had acted to rewrite the laws.

Although the effort died in the Senate, the House's action raised the prospect that Congress was inching closer to its first significant revision of campaign finance laws in nearly 20 years.

House passage of HR 2183 came only after an arduous process. Its advocates endured numerous attempts by GOP leaders to block or delay its passage over several months.

From the outset, the leading vehicle of overhaul advocates was a bipartisan measure (HR 3526), sponsored by Christopher Shays, R-Conn., and Martin T. Meehan, D-Mass. It was based on a similar Senate plan (S 25) by John McCain, R-Ariz., and Russell D. Feingold, D-Wis.

The legislation would ban national parties from receiving or spending "soft money" — unlimited and largely unregulated donations to political parties. It also would set new restrictions on campaign-related expenditures by third-party groups.

GOP leaders initially squelched debate on campaign finance March 30 by prohibiting the Shays-Meehan measure from coming to the House floor. But the ploy only encouraged the bill's supporters to embrace a procedural device that would have let them debate a variety of campaign finance bills on their own terms.

GOP leaders finally relented to an open debate on the issue in May. But they made the bill open to dozens of amendments, then forced it to compete with 10 other substitute amendments to the underlying bill. Whichever of the 11 substitute amendments got the most votes — and at least a majority — would prevail.

A crowning moment for supporters of the Shays-Meehan measure came Aug. 3, when the House voted for their substitute amendment, 237-186. Fifty-one Republicans voted for the measure, outweighing the 11 Democrats who voted against it.

The relatively strong vote prompted the authors of several other substitute amendments to withdraw their measures.

The final hurdle was a substitute amendment by Asa Hutchinson, R-Ark., and Tom Allen, D-Maine, based on the so-called freshman bill.

The freshman bill would have taken a somewhat less aggressive stance against soft money and issue advocacy advertising. Its advocates said that approach gave the legislation a better chance of passing in the Senate and surviving a constitutional challenge.

GOP leaders toyed with embracing the freshman proposal to get the 238 votes needed to top — and topple — the Shays-Meehan bill. That prompted supporters of the proposal to elaborately praise the freshmen for their efforts but urge its defeat. The freshman measure ultimately failed, 147-222, with 61 members voting "present."

That cleared the way for final passage of the bill, amended along the lines of the Shays-Meehan proposal, by a vote of 252-179: R 61-164; D 190-15 (ND 142-9, SD 48-6); I 1-0.

Advocates of a campaign finance overhaul vowed afterward to push the Senate to act after the August recess.

McCain and Feingold tried to revive the issue in the Senate by attaching S 25 to the Interior appropriations bill (S 2237). But they fell eight votes short of cutting off debate on Sept. 10, 52-48. It marked the third time in less than a year that the Senate stymied overhaul advocates.

425 RELEASE OF STARR REPORT

Within the White House, the week of Sept. 7 must have felt like one of the lowest points of Bill Clinton's presidency. On Sept. 9, Independent Counsel Kenneth W. Starr sent a report to the House suggesting that Clinton be impeached. Two days later, the House voted to release the report to the public.

The report gave Starr's version of Clinton's affair with former intern Monica Lewinsky and subsequent events, and Clinton's representatives cautioned that it should be viewed as a one-sided document. But the vote on the resolution to release the report (H Res 525) signaled that Republicans, in their effort to impeach Clinton, were willing to accept Starr's allegations and move forward despite a lack of public support. The resolution was adopted by a vote of 363-63: R 224-0; D 138-63 (ND 102-46, SD 36-17); I 1-0.

However, rather than reading the salacious details of the Starr report as evidence of Clinton's immorality and lack of respect for laws, much of the public was repulsed by the fact that these details were released, polls showed. The vote also represented the last time GOP plans for investigating Clinton were able to pick up Democratic support.

No one in Congress had read the report before it was released, and many felt blindsided when they learned of its explicit descriptions of Clinton's liaisons with Lewinsky. The report was posted on the Internet and became the subject of voluminous media coverage. The report was lampooned as X-rated; numerous observers argued that the vote to release it would have been a vi-

Key Votes

olation of the Congress' own Communications Decency Act — a portion of the 1996 telecommunications overhaul (PL 104-104) bill limiting indecent content on the Internet that was declared unconstitutional by the Supreme Court. Starr and his prosecutors insisted the details were necessary to document Clinton's lies and efforts to get others to lie.

Supporting material, including a videotape of Clinton's Aug. 17 testimony before a grand jury, was released in subsequent weeks, after having been screened — and to some extent, redacted — by committee members.

When the dust cleared, the public was clearly still opposed to impeachment and vehemently objected to being subjected to all of the details of the relationship.

The fact that most Democrats joined in the vote was lost on the public. The most vocal Democrats were those on the Judiciary Committee who voted against the release, on the grounds it violated due process and basic fairness. Those Democrats who voted for the release generally declined to defend their vote, and in some cases expressed remorse.

The vote to release was a turning point in the Republican impeachment effort, one that Democrats say vividly demonstrated how out of step the GOP was with popular sentiment. And within days, bipartisan cooperation on impeachment began eroding. By the time a vote authorizing an impeachment inquiry was taken Oct. 8, the two parties had separated like oil and water.

460 SKILLED-WORKER VISAS

The House in 1998 was a major stumbling block for legislation designed to increase the number of skilled temporary workers allowed to immigrate to the United States.

While a bill (S 1723) increasing the number of so-called H-1B visas sailed through the Senate, an unlikely coalition of labor-backed Democrats and Republican immigration hard-liners held up the House bill (HR 3736) for most of the year. But behind-the-scenes negotiating helped get the measure enacted.

The major turning point was House passage Sept. 24, by a vote of 288-133: R 189-34; D 99-98 (ND 66-76; SD 33-22); I 0-1.

The vote represented a big success for a new lobby — the high-tech industry. It also represented a major departure from the anti-immigration policies pushed by House hard-liners in 1996. Since that year, Congress has voted to restore welfare benefits to legal immigrants, loosen requirements on immigrants waiting for permanent visas, and give partial or complete amnesty to a category of Central American refugees who came to America to escape civil wars in the 1980s.

The vote to expand the number of skilled immigrant visas was more than merely a retreat from previous policies. It was an affirmative decision to expand immigration, at least for skilled workers.

The vote was not the last chapter in the year's debate. With the House acting so late, a handful of senators was able to block action on a conference report. In the end, the measure was added to the omnibus spending package (HR 4328 — PL 105-277) passed at the end of the year. But the House vote was clearly the highest hurdle in a difficult year.

The legislation will increase the number of H-1B visas allotted each year from 65,000 to as many as 115,000. The measure was the principal 1998 legislative goal of a new lobby — high-tech companies.

At the beginning of the year, few lawmakers had given much thought to the issue of these visas. But by spring, companies such as Microsoft Corp., Sun Microsystems Inc. and Intel Corp. made them take notice. They persuasively argued that their phenomenal rates of growth would be stymied if they could not find enough programmers and other skilled workers. They implicitly threatened to take plants overseas if they could not get enough workers from overseas to come here.

But it was a difficult lobbying job. In the House Judiciary Committee's Immigration Subcommittee on April 30, Chairman Lamar Smith, R-Texas, a leader among immigration hawks, added two provisions the high-tech lobby found unacceptable. One would have required companies hoping to sponsor H-1B immigrants to show that they had gone to great lengths to find American workers first. The second would have barred companies from using the H-1B program if they had laid off any workers with comparable skills.

The industry spent the summer trying to round up support from the GOP leadership and sympathetic senators in an effort to pressure Smith to relent. Shortly before the August recess, he agreed to a compromise that would keep the requirements, but apply them to only a certain percentage of companies.

The measure, however, was left to languish over the August recess after President Clinton objected. By late September, though, a new compromise — similar to Smith's bill — was developed. The revised bill passed with relatively little floor debate.

538 OMNIBUS APPROPRIATIONS

Republican leaders portrayed the massive, year-end omnibus spending bill as a win for their party and an inevitable result of divided government, but many in the rank and file saw it as an embarrassing retreat from GOP principles.

For Democrats, the vote — and behind-the-scenes negotiations that led up to it — provided a rejuvenating breather. They got to change the subject from impeachment to their election year agenda, especially education.

The vote capped a year of gridlock on the budget after President Clinton and congressional Republicans spent months talking past each other and trying to use the budget to score political points, mostly in vain. Action on most of the 13 annual appropriations bills for fiscal 1999 — the approximately one-third of the budget upon which Congress and Clinton must agree each year — slid past deadline, and eight of the measures were lumped together into an everything-but-the-kitchen-sink bill (HR 4328 — PL 105-277) that broke through budget targets set only a year earlier.

The eight bills had been slowed by numerous disagreements among Republicans, and between them and the White House.

Despite the impeachment inquiry hanging over his head, Clinton entered the talks with a strong hand. Ever since

Republicans took the political fallout for the 1995-96 partial government shutdowns and for a vetoed 1997 flood aid bill, Clinton had used veto threats to extract concessions from them on spending bills. *(1997 Almanac, p. 9-84; 1996 Almanac, p. 10-3)*

The talks started Oct. 7 but moved slowly as White House Chief of Staff Erskine Bowles, under pressure from Democrats in Congress, played hard ball. As negotiations dragged on, Democrats took delight in having a forum for their election year agenda.

Clinton won a $1.2 billion down payment on his initiative to subsidize the hiring of 100,000 new teachers, obtained his full $17.9 billion request for the International Monetary Fund, and got many "emergency" spending items, including financing for the Bosnia peacekeeping mission and $5.9 billion in farm disaster aid.

Such emergency spending did not count against budget "caps" set in place in 1997. By the time such add-ons were totaled — including GOP-sought money for drug interdiction, intelligence and missile defense — the emergency spending took a $21 billion bite from future budget surpluses.

Republican conservatives were appalled. "At a time when we are dealing with a weakened president . . . you would think that our leadership, who professed to be conservatives leading this revolution, could stand tough within that budget cap and stay true to the commitment that we . . . came here for in 1994," said Jon Christensen, R-Neb.

Democrats were generally pleased with the bill's spending provisions, but they railed against the chaotic process that produced the 16-inch thick, 40-pound, nearly 4,000- page measure. It was also filled with many parochial projects of the kind that Republicans had criticized under Democratic-controlled congresses.

House Speaker Newt Gingrich, R-Ga., fired back in an impassioned speech criticizing the "perfectionist caucus" in his own party, saying that concessions were necessary to obtain Clinton's signature. But the bill was far larger than it would have been had the 13 annual spending bills been negotiated individually.

Despite grumbling from junior GOP conservatives, the bill passed Oct. 20 by a vote of 333-95: R 162-64; D 170-31 (ND 120-26, SD 50-5); I 1-0.

After the agreement was sealed, Democrats and Republicans staged competing pep rallies. Clinton and the Democrats seemed happy while Republicans seemed to be putting on a brave face. The GOP chairmen of the Budget and Appropriations committees were notably absent.

543 IMPEACHMENT

By the time the House was ready to vote Dec. 19 to make Bill Clinton only the second president ever to be impeached, the environment had become surreal.

On the eve of the scheduled vote, Clinton had ordered a military strike against Iraq. That postponed debate for a day, enough time for Speaker-designate Robert L. Livingston, R-La., to publicly acknowledge that he, like Clinton, had been unfaithful to his wife.

When debate finally began Dec. 18 on the four articles of impeachment, nerves were raw. The articles, approved Dec. 11 and 12 by the House Judiciary Committee along party lines, accused the president of two counts of perjury, one count of obstruction of justice and one count of abuse of power.

Through it all, Democrats bitterly complained that the votes should be delayed until hostilities with Iraq ended. Their anger was increased by Republicans' move to block consideration of a censure resolution.

"To be spending the time of this House to smear our commander in chief when brave men and women are risking their lives for their country shocks the conscience," John Conyers Jr. of Michigan, the Judiciary Committee's ranking Democrat, said on the floor.

Then came the bombshell from Livingston that he would not serve as Speaker and would leave Congress — setting an example for Clinton to follow, he said.

"Infidelity — adultery — is not a public act, it's a private act, and the government, the Congress, has no business intruding into private acts," Judiciary Chairman Henry J. Hyde, R-Ill., said in closing debate. "But it is our business, it is our duty to observe, to characterize public acts by public officials. . . . And when you have a serial violator of the oath who is the chief law enforcement officer of the country — who appoints the judges and the Supreme Court, the attorney general — we have a problem."

The House adopted the first article, which accuses Clinton of lying to a grand jury about his affair with Monica Lewinsky, by a vote of 228-206: R 223-5; D 5-200 (ND 1-149, SD 4-51); I 0-1. A second count, accusing Clinton of obstructing justice, was also adopted, 221-212.

The two other recommended articles were rejected. ◆

Senate Key Votes 1, 2, 3, 4, 5, 6

	1	2	3	4	5	6
ALABAMA						
Sessions	Y	N	N	Y	Y	N
Shelby	Y	N	Y	Y	N	N
ALASKA						
Murkowski	Y	N	Y	N	Y	N
Stevens	Y	N	Y	Y	Y	N
ARIZONA						
Kyl	Y	N	N	N	Y	N
McCain	Y	Y	Y	N	Y	Y
ARKANSAS						
Hutchinson	Y	N	Y	Y	N	N
Bumpers	N	Y	Y	Y	N	Y
CALIFORNIA						
Boxer	N	Y	Y	N	Y	Y
Feinstein	N	Y	Y	Y	Y	Y
COLORADO						
Allard	Y	N	N	N	Y	N
Campbell	N	N	N	N	Y	N
CONNECTICUT						
Dodd	N	Y	Y	N	Y	Y
Lieberman	N	Y	Y	N	Y	Y
DELAWARE						
Roth	N	N	Y	N	Y	Y
Biden	N	Y	Y	N	N	Y
FLORIDA						
Mack	N	N	N	N	Y	N
Graham	N	Y	Y	Y	Y	Y
GEORGIA						
Coverdell	Y	N	N	N	Y	N
Cleland	N	Y	Y	N	Y	Y
HAWAII						
Akaka	N	Y	Y	N	N	Y
Inouye	N	Y	Y	N	Y	Y
IDAHO						
Craig	Y	N	Y	Y	Y	N
Kempthorne	Y	N	Y	Y	Y	N
ILLINOIS						
Durbin	N	Y	Y	N	N	Y
Moseley-Braun	N	Y	Y	N	N	Y
INDIANA						
Coats	Y	N	Y	N	Y	N
Lugar	N	N	Y	N	Y	N
IOWA						
Grassley	Y	N	Y	N	Y	Y
Harkin	N	?	Y	Y	N	Y
KANSAS						
Brownback	Y	N	Y	N	Y	N
Roberts	Y	N	Y	Y	Y	N
KENTUCKY						
McConnell	Y	N	Y	N	Y	N
Ford	N	Y	Y	N	Y	N
LOUISIANA						
Breaux	N	Y	Y	N	Y	Y
Landrieu	N	Y	Y	Y	N	Y
MAINE						
Collins	N	Y	Y	N	Y	Y
Snowe	N	Y	Y	Y	Y	Y
MARYLAND						
Mikulski	N	Y	Y	N	N	Y
Sarbanes	N	Y	Y	Y	N	Y
MASSACHUSETTS						
Kennedy	N	Y	Y	N	N	Y
Kerry	N	Y	Y	N	N	Y
MICHIGAN						
Abraham	Y	N	N	N	Y	Y
Levin	?	Y	Y	N	N	Y
MINNESOTA						
Grams	Y	N	Y	N	Y	N
Wellstone	N	Y	N	Y	N	Y
MISSISSIPPI						
Cochran	Y	N	Y	N	Y	N
Lott	Y	N	Y	N	Y	N
MISSOURI						
Ashcroft	Y	N	N	N	Y	N
Bond	Y	N	Y	Y	Y	N
MONTANA						
Burns	Y	N	Y	N	Y	N
Baucus	N	Y	Y	N	Y	Y
NEBRASKA						
Hagel	Y	N	Y	Y	Y	N
Kerrey	N	Y	Y	N	Y	Y
NEVADA						
Bryan	–	Y	Y	N	Y	Y
Reid	?	Y	Y	Y	Y	Y
NEW HAMPSHIRE						
Gregg	Y	N	Y	Y	Y	Y
Smith	Y	N	N	Y	N	N
NEW JERSEY						
Lautenberg	N	Y	Y	Y	N	Y
Torricelli	N	Y	Y	Y	N	Y
NEW MEXICO						
Domenici	Y	N	Y	N	Y	Y
Bingaman	N	Y	Y	Y	Y	Y
NEW YORK						
D'Amato	Y	N	Y	N	?	Y
Moynihan	N	Y	Y	Y	N	Y
NORTH CAROLINA						
Faircloth	Y	N	N	Y	?	N
Helms	Y	N	N	Y	Y	N
NORTH DAKOTA						
Conrad	N	Y	Y	N	N	Y
Dorgan	N	Y	Y	Y	Y	Y
OHIO						
DeWine	Y	N	Y	N	Y	Y
Glenn	N	Y	Y	N	N	Y
OKLAHOMA						
Inhofe	Y	N	Y	N	Y	N
Nickles	Y	N	N	Y	N	N
OREGON						
Smith	N	N	Y	N	Y	Y
Wyden	N	Y	Y	Y	Y	Y
PENNSYLVANIA						
Santorum	Y	N	Y	N	Y	N
Specter	N	Y	Y	Y	Y	?
RHODE ISLAND						
Chafee	N	Y	Y	Y	Y	Y
Reed	N	Y	Y	Y	Y	Y
SOUTH CAROLINA						
Thurmond	N	N	Y	Y	Y	N
Hollings	N	Y	Y	N	N	Y
SOUTH DAKOTA						
Daschle	N	Y	Y	N	Y	Y
Johnson	N	Y	Y	N	Y	Y
TENNESSEE						
Frist	Y	N	Y	N	Y	Y
Thompson	Y	Y	N	N	Y	N

	1	2	3	4	5	6
TEXAS						
Gramm	Y	N	Y	N	Y	N
Hutchison	Y	N	Y	Y	Y	N
UTAH						
Bennett	N	N	Y	N	Y	Y
Hatch	Y	N	Y	N	Y	N
VERMONT						
Jeffords	N	Y	Y	Y	Y	Y
Leahy	N	Y	Y	Y	Y	Y
VIRGINIA						
Warner	?	N	Y	Y	Y	Y
Robb	N	Y	Y	N	Y	Y
WASHINGTON						
Gorton	Y	N	Y	N	Y	N
Murray	N	Y	Y	Y	Y	Y
WEST VIRGINIA						
Byrd	N	Y	Y	Y	N	Y
Rockefeller	N	Y	Y	N	N	Y
WISCONSIN						
Feingold	N	Y	N	N	N	Y
Kohl	N	Y	Y	Y	Y	Y
WYOMING						
Enzi	Y	N	Y	Y	Y	N
Thomas	Y	N	Y	N	N	N

Key

- Y Voted for (yea).
- # Paired for.
- + Announced for.
- N Voted against (nay).
- X Paired against.
- – Announced against.
- P Voted "present."
- C Voted "present" to avoid possible conflict of interest.
- ? Did not vote or otherwise make a position known.

Democrats •   *Republicans*

ND Northern Democrats   SD Southern Democrats

Southern states - Ala., Ark., Fla., Ga., Ky., La., Miss., N.C., Okla., S.C., Tenn., Texas, Va.

Following are Senate votes from 1998 selected by Congressional Quarterly as key votes. Original vote numbers are in parentheses.

1. S 1601. Human Cloning Ban. Motion to invoke cloture (thus limiting debate) on the motion to proceed to the bill banning creation of a human embryo through cloning. Motion rejected 42-54: R 42-12; D 0-42 (ND 0-34, SD 0-8). Feb. 11, 1998. Three-fifths of the total Senate (60) is required to invoke cloture. (*Senate vote 10*)

2. S 1663. Campaign Finance Overhaul. Motion to invoke cloture (thus limiting debate) on the McCain, R-Ariz., substitute amendment that would revise financing of federal political campaigns. Motion rejected 51-48: R 7-48; D 44-0 (ND 36-0, SD 8-0). Feb. 26, 1998. Three-fifths of the total Senate (60) is required to invoke cloture. (*Senate vote 16*)

3. S 1768. IMF Funding. McConnell, R-Ky., amendment to provide $17.9 billion for the International Monetary Fund, including $3.4 billion for a new program aimed at preventing global financial crises and $14.5 billion for the U.S. "quota" to the international agency. The amendment would prohibit release of the quota funds unless the IMF agrees to certain conditions, including restricting aid to nations that do not conform to trade agreements. Adopted 84-16: R 41-14; D 43-2 (ND 35-2, SD 8-0). March 26, 1998. (*Senate vote 44*)

4. S 1768. NATO Expansion. Warner, R-Va., amendment to add language to the resolution of ratification that would require the president to certify to Congress that the United States will not support any further NATO expansion for three years from the date Poland, Hungary and the Czech Republic join the alliance. Rejected 41-59: R 24-31; D 17-28 (ND 15-22, SD 2-6). April 30, 1998. A "nay" was a vote in support of the president's position. (*Senate vote 112*)

5. S 1723. Skilled-Worker Visas. Passage of the bill to increase the number of so-called H-1B visas, which allow highly skilled immigrants to work in the United States for six years, from the current cap of 65,000 per year to 95,000 for the remainder of fiscal 1998. The measure also would increase the cap on the visas to 105,000 for fiscal 1999 and 115,000 for the following three fiscal years, but would sunset the cap to its original level at the end of fiscal 2002. The bill also would increase the authorization for certain educational grants, authorize funding for an Internet job bank and authorize funding to provide training opportunities in information technology. Passed 78-20: R 51-2; D 27-18 (ND 20-17, SD 7-1). May 18, 1998. A "nay" was a vote in support of the president's position. (*Senate vote 141*)

6. S 1415. Tobacco Restrictions. Motion to invoke cloture (thus limiting debate) on the modified Senate Commerce, Science and Transportation Committee substitute amendment to the bill to increase tobacco restrictions. The substitute would require the tobacco industry to pay $516 billion over 25 years for anti-smoking, education and research programs; raise taxes on cigarettes by $1.10 per pack over five years; and impose penalties on the tobacco industry if youth smoking does not decrease by 60 percent over 10 years. Motion rejected 57-42: R 14-40; D 43-2 (ND 37-0, SD 6-2). June 17, 1998. Three-fifths of the total Senate (60) is required to invoke cloture. A "yea" was a vote in support of the president's position. (*Senate vote 161*)

Senate Key Votes 7, 8, 9, 10, 11

	7 8 9 10 11
ALABAMA	
Sessions	Y Y N Y N
Shelby	Y Y Y Y Y
ALASKA	
Murkowski	Y Y N Y ?
Stevens	Y Y Y Y Y
ARIZONA	
Kyl	Y Y Y Y N
McCain	Y N Y Y N
ARKANSAS	
Hutchinson	Y ? Y Y Y
Bumpers	N Y N N ?
CALIFORNIA	
Boxer	N N Y N Y
Feinstein	Y N N N Y
COLORADO	
Allard	Y N N Y N
Campbell	Y Y Y Y Y
CONNECTICUT	
Dodd	N N N N Y
Lieberman	Y N Y N Y
DELAWARE	
Roth	Y ? N Y Y
Biden	Y N N Y Y
FLORIDA	
Mack	Y N Y Y Y
Graham	N N Y N Y
GEORGIA	
Coverdell	Y Y Y Y Y
Cleland	Y N N N Y
HAWAII	
Akaka	? ? Y N Y
Inouye	N Y Y N ?
IDAHO	
Craig	Y Y N Y Y
Kempthorne	Y N N Y Y
ILLINOIS	
Durbin	N N N N Y
Moseley-Braun	N N N N Y
INDIANA	
Coats	Y Y N Y N
Lugar	Y N N Y N

	7 8 9 10 11
IOWA	
Grassley	Y Y Y Y N
Harkin	N N Y N Y
KANSAS	
Brownback	Y Y N Y Y
Roberts	Y Y N Y Y
KENTUCKY	
McConnell	Y Y Y Y Y
Ford	N Y Y Y Y
LOUISIANA	
Breaux	Y N Y Y Y
Landrieu	N N N Y Y
MAINE	
Collins	Y N Y N N
Snowe	Y N Y N N
MARYLAND	
Mikulski	N N Y N Y
Sarbanes	N N Y N Y
MASSACHUSETTS	
Kennedy	N N N N Y
Kerry	N N N Y N
MICHIGAN	
Abraham	Y Y Y Y Y
Levin	N N Y N N
MINNESOTA	
Grams	Y Y N Y N
Wellstone	N N Y N N
MISSISSIPPI	
Cochran	Y N N Y Y
Lott	Y Y Y Y Y
MISSOURI	
Ashcroft	Y Y Y Y N
Bond	Y N N Y Y
MONTANA	
Burns	Y Y N Y Y
Baucus	? ? N N N
NEBRASKA	
Hagel	Y N Y Y N
Kerrey	N N N N N
NEVADA	
Bryan	N N Y N Y
Reid	N N Y N Y

	7 8 9 10 11
NEW HAMPSHIRE	
Gregg	Y Y N Y Y
Smith	Y Y Y Y N
NEW JERSEY	
Lautenberg	N N Y N Y
Torricelli	Y Y Y N Y
NEW MEXICO	
Domenici	+ N N Y Y
Bingaman	N N Y N Y
NEW YORK	
D'Amato	Y N Y Y Y
Moynihan	N Y N Y N
NORTH CAROLINA	
Faircloth	Y Y Y Y Y
Helms	Y Y Y Y ?
NORTH DAKOTA	
Conrad	N Y N Y Y
Dorgan	N N N Y Y
OHIO	
DeWine	Y Y Y N Y
Glenn	N ? ? N ?
OKLAHOMA	
Inhofe	Y Y Y Y N
Nickles	Y Y Y Y N
OREGON	
Smith	Y N N Y Y
Wyden	N – Y N Y
PENNSYLVANIA	
Santorum	Y Y Y Y N
Specter	? ? Y Y N
RHODE ISLAND	
Chafee	N N N N Y
Reed	N N Y N Y
SOUTH CAROLINA	
Thurmond	Y N Y Y Y
Hollings	N Y Y Y ?
SOUTH DAKOTA	
Daschle	N N Y Y Y
Johnson	N N N Y Y
TENNESSEE	
Frist	Y Y N Y N
Thompson	Y N Y Y Y

Key

Y	Voted for (yea).
#	Paired for.
+	Announced for.
N	Voted against (nay).
X	Paired against.
–	Announced against.
P	Voted "present."
C	Voted "present" to avoid possible conflict of interest.
?	Did not vote or otherwise make a position known.

Democrats • *Republicans*

	7 8 9 10 11
TEXAS	
Gramm	Y N N Y N
Hutchison	Y N N Y Y
UTAH	
Bennett	Y Y Y Y Y
Hatch	Y Y Y Y Y
VERMONT	
Jeffords	N N N N Y
Leahy	N N Y Y Y
VIRGINIA	
Warner	Y N Y N Y
Robb	N N N N Y
WASHINGTON	
Gorton	Y Y N Y Y
Murray	N N Y N Y
WEST VIRGINIA	
Byrd	Y Y N Y N
Rockefeller	? ? N N Y
WISCONSIN	
Feingold	N N Y N N
Kohl	Y N Y N N
WYOMING	
Enzi	Y Y N Y N
Thomas	Y N N Y N

ND Northern Democrats   SD Southern Democrats

Southern states - Ala., Ark., Fla., Ga., Ky., La., Miss., N.C., Okla., S.C., Tenn., Texas, Va.

7. HR 2646. Education Savings Accounts. Adoption of the conference report on the bill to allow individuals to contribute up to $2,000 a year of after-tax funds in tax-sheltered savings accounts that may be used to pay for educational expenses. Adopted (thus cleared for the president) 59-36: R 51-2; D 8-34 (ND 6-28, SD 2-6). June 24, 1998. A "nay" was a vote in support of the president's position. (*Senate vote 169*)

8. S 2057. Same-Sex Military Training. Byrd, D-W.Va., amendment to the Gramm, R-Texas, amendment. The Byrd amendment would prohibit the armed forces from housing male and female recruits in the same barracks and would prohibit them from conducting gender-integrated basic training. The Gramm amendment would remove restrictions on recipients of Naval Reserve Officers' Training Corps scholarships. Rejected 39-53: R 31-21; D 8-32 (ND 5-27, SD 3-5). June 25, 1998. (Subsequently, the Gramm amendment was adopted by voice vote.) A "nay" was a vote in support of the president's position. (*Senate vote 180*)

9. S 2159. Economic Sanctions. Stevens, R-Alaska, motion to table (kill) the Lugar, R-Ind., amendment that would revise the process the president and Congress use to impose unilateral economic sanctions by establishing guidelines for future sanctions and setting up procedures for consideration and implementation of sanctions proposals. The amendment would prohibit the president from implementing any unilateral economic sanction without 45 days' notice, and it would express the sense of Congress that all future unilateral sanctions end within two years of their enactment unless extended by law. Motion agreed to 53-46: R 27-28; D 26-18 (ND 22-14, SD 4-4). July 15, 1998. (*Senate vote 201*)

10. HR 1122. "Partial-Birth" Abortion. Passage, over President Clinton's Oct. 10, 1997, veto, of the bill to ban a certain late-term abortion procedure, in which the physician partially delivers the fetus before completing the abortion. Anyone convicted of performing such an abortion would be subject to a fine and up to two years in prison. Rejected 64-36: R 51-4; D 13-32 (ND 9-28, SD 4-4). Sept. 18, 1998. A two-thirds majority of those present and voting (67 in this case) of both houses is required to override a veto. A "nay" was a vote in support of the president's position. (*Senate vote 277*)

11. HR 4328. Fiscal 1999 Omnibus Appropriations. Adoption of the conference report on the bill to provide almost $500 billion in new budget authority for those Cabinet departments and federal agencies whose fiscal 1999 appropriations bills were never enacted. The measure incorporates eight previously separate appropriations bills: Labor-HHS-Education, Interior, Treasury-Postal, Foreign Operations, Commerce-Justice-State, District of Columbia, Agriculture and Transportation. In addition, the bill provides $20.8 billion in "emergency" supplemental spending, including $6.8 billion for military spending ($1.9 billion of it for Bosnia operations), $5.9 billion for relief to farmers, $2.4 billion for anti-terrorism programs, $3.35 billion to address Year 2000 computer problems and $1.55 billion for disaster relief from Hurricane Georges. The measure also contains language to extend expiring tax provisions (at a cost of $9.7 billion over nine years). Adopted (thus cleared for the president) 65-29: R 33-20; D 32-9 (ND 26-9, SD 6-0). Oct. 21, 1998. A "yea" was a vote in support of the president's position. (*Senate vote 314*)

House Key Votes 1, 2, 3, 4, 5

Following are House votes from 1998 selected by Congressional Quarterly as key votes. Original vote number in parentheses.

1. HR 2631. Line-item vetoes. Passage, over President Clinton's Nov. 13, 1997, veto, of the bill to disapprove Clinton's line-item vetoes of 38 projects, totaling $287 million, in the fiscal 1998 military construction appropriations bill (HR 2016 — PL 105-45). Passed 347-69: R 197-23; D 149-46 (ND 100-41, SD 49-5); I 1-0. Feb. 5, 1998. A two-thirds majority of those present and voting (277 in this case) of both chambers is required to override a veto. A "nay" was a vote in support of the president's position. *(House vote 10)*

2. HR 2400. Special Transportation Projects. Graham, R-S.C., amendment to strike provisions that provide funds for specified projects, including about $9 billion for highway projects, and other funding for specified transit and bus projects. Rejected 79-337: R 67-152; D 12-184 (ND 6-137, SD 6-47); I 0-1. April 1, 1998. *(House vote 95)*

3. HR 6. Affirmative Action. Riggs, R-Calif., amendment to prohibit any public institution of higher education that participates in any Higher Education Act program from discriminating against, or granting preferential treatment to any person or group in admissions based in whole or in part on race, sex, color, ethnicity or national origin. Rejected 171-249: R 166-55; D 5-193 (ND 2-143, SD 3-50); I 0-1. May 6, 1998. A "nay" was a vote in support of the president's position. *(House vote 133)*

4. HR 10. Financial Services Overhaul. Passage of the bill to eliminate current Glass-Steagall Act and Bank Holding Company Act barriers against affiliations between banking, securities, insurance and other firms. Passed 214-213: R 153-73; D 61-139 (ND 47-100, SD 14-39); I 0-1. May 13, 1998. A "nay" was a vote in support of the president's position. *(House vote 151)*

5. S 1150. Food Stamps for Legal Immigrants. Adoption of the rule (H Res 446) to dispose of the conference report on the bill to reauthorize agricultural research and education programs through fiscal 2002. The rule would have allowed a point of order to strike $818 million in funding in the conference report to restore food stamps to 250,000 legal immigrants. Rejected 120-289: R 118-98; D 2-190 (ND 1-140, SD 1-50); I 0-1. May 22, 1998. *(House vote 188)*

[1] Barbara Lee, D-Calif., was sworn in April 21, replacing Ronald V. Dellums, D-Calif., who resigned Feb. 6.

[2] Lois Capps, D-Calif., was sworn in March 17, replacing Walter Capps, D-Calif., who died Oct. 28, 1997.

[3] Mary Bono, R-Calif., was sworn in April 21, replacing Sonny Bono, R-Calif., who died Jan. 5.

[4] Newt Gingrich, R-Ga., as Speaker of the House, voted at his discretion.

[5] Heather Wilson, R-N.M., was sworn in June 25, replacing Stephen H. Schiff, R-N.M., who died March 25.

[6] Gregory W. Meeks, D-N.Y., was sworn in Feb. 5, replacing Floyd H. Flake, D-N.Y., who resigned Nov. 15, 1997.

[7] Robert A. Brady, D-Pa., was sworn in May 21, replacing Thomas M. Foglietta, D-Pa., who resigned Nov. 11, 1997.

Key

Y	Voted for (yea).
#	Paired for.
+	Announced for.
N	Voted against (nay).
X	Paired against.
–	Announced against.
P	Voted "present."
C	Voted "present" to avoid possible conflict of interest.
?	Did not vote or otherwise make a position known.

Democrats **Republicans** Independent

	1	2	3	4	5
ALABAMA					
1 Callahan	Y	N	Y	N	N
2 Everett	Y	N	Y	N	N
3 Riley	Y	N	Y	N	N
4 Aderholt	Y	N	Y	N	N
5 Cramer	Y	N	N	N	N
6 Bachus	Y	N	Y	N	N
7 Hilliard	Y	N	N	N	N
ALASKA					
AL Young	Y	N	N	N	N
ARIZONA					
1 Salmon	N	Y	Y	Y	Y
2 Pastor	Y	N	N	N	N
3 Stump	Y	Y	Y	Y	N
4 Shadegg	Y	Y	Y	Y	Y
5 Kolbe	Y	Y	Y	Y	Y
6 Hayworth	Y	Y	Y	Y	N
ARKANSAS					
1 Berry	Y	N	N	N	N
2 Snyder	Y	N	N	N	N
3 Hutchinson	Y	N	Y	N	N
4 Dickey	N	N	N	N	N
CALIFORNIA					
1 Riggs	Y	N	Y	Y	?
2 Herger	?	N	Y	Y	Y
3 Fazio	Y	N	N	Y	N
4 Doolittle	Y	N	Y	N	N
5 Matsui	Y	N	N	N	N
6 Woolsey	Y	N	N	N	N
7 Miller	Y	N	N	N	?
8 Pelosi	Y	N	N	N	N
9 Lee[1]			N	N	N
9 Dellums	?				
10 Tauscher	Y	N	N	N	N
11 Pombo	Y	N	Y	N	Y
12 Lantos	Y	N	N	N	N
13 Stark	N	N	N	N	?
14 Eshoo	?	N	N	N	N
15 Campbell	Y	Y	N	Y	N
16 Lofgren	N	P	N	N	N
17 Farr	Y	N	N	N	N
18 Condit	Y	Y	N	Y	N
19 Radanovich	Y	N	?	Y	Y
20 Dooley	N	N	N	Y	N
21 Thomas	Y	Y	Y	Y	Y
22 Capps, L.[2]			N	N	N
23 Gallegly	Y	N	Y	Y	Y
24 Sherman	N	N	N	N	N
25 McKeon	+	N	Y	Y	Y
26 Berman	Y	N	N	N	N
27 Rogan	Y	Y	Y	Y	Y
28 Dreier	Y	N	Y	N	Y
29 Waxman	N	N	N	N	N
30 Becerra	+	N	N	N	N
31 Martinez	N	N	N	N	N
32 Dixon	Y	N	N	N	N
33 Roybal-Allard	Y	N	N	N	N
34 Torres	Y	?	N	N	N
35 Waters	Y	?	N	Y	N
36 Harman	N	N	N	?	?
37 Millender-McD.	Y	N	N	N	N

	1	2	3	4	5
38 Horn	Y	N	Y	Y	N
39 Royce	N	?	Y	Y	Y
40 Lewis	Y	N	N	Y	Y
41 Kim	Y	N	Y	Y	Y
42 Brown	Y	N	N	N	N
43 Calvert	Y	N	Y	N	Y
44 Bono, M.[3]			Y	Y	Y
45 Rohrabacher	N	Y	Y	Y	Y
46 Sanchez	N	N	N	N	N
47 Cox	Y	Y	Y	Y	Y
48 Packard	Y	N	Y	N	Y
49 Bilbray	Y	N	Y	Y	N
50 Filner	N	N	N	N	N
51 Cunningham	Y	N	Y	Y	Y
52 Hunter	Y	Y	Y	N	Y
COLORADO					
1 DeGette	N	N	N	Y	N
2 Skaggs	N	Y	–	–	–
3 McInnis	Y	N	Y	N	Y
4 Schaffer	Y	Y	Y	Y	Y
5 Hefley	Y	N	Y	N	Y
6 Schaefer	Y	N	?	Y	Y
CONNECTICUT					
1 Kennelly	Y	N	N	N	N
2 Gejdenson	Y	N	N	Y	N
3 DeLauro	Y	N	N	N	N
4 Shays	N	Y	N	Y	N
5 Maloney	Y	N	N	N	N
6 Johnson	Y	N	N	Y	N
DELAWARE					
AL Castle	Y	Y	N	Y	N
FLORIDA					
1 Scarborough	Y	Y	Y	N	Y
2 Boyd	Y	N	N	Y	N
3 Brown	Y	N	N	N	N
4 Fowler	Y	N	Y	Y	Y
5 Thurman	Y	N	N	N	N
6 Stearns	Y	N	Y	Y	Y
7 Mica	Y	N	Y	Y	Y
8 McCollum	Y	Y	Y	Y	Y
9 Bilirakis	Y	N	Y	Y	Y
10 Young	Y	Y	Y	Y	Y
11 Davis	N	N	N	N	N
12 Canady	Y	N	Y	Y	Y
13 Miller	N	Y	Y	Y	Y
14 Goss	Y	Y	Y	Y	Y
15 Weldon	Y	N	Y	N	Y
16 Foley	Y	Y	Y	Y	?
17 Meek	Y	N	N	N	N
18 Ros-Lehtinen	Y	?	N	Y	Y
19 Wexler	N	Y	N	Y	N
20 Deutsch	N	Y	N	Y	?
21 Diaz-Balart	Y	N	N	Y	N
22 Shaw	Y	N	Y	Y	Y
23 Hastings	Y	N	?	N	N
GEORGIA					
1 Kingston	Y	Y	Y	Y	Y
2 Bishop	Y	N	N	Y	N
3 Collins	Y	N	Y	Y	Y
4 McKinney	N	N	N	N	N
5 Lewis	Y	Y	N	N	N
6 Gingrich[4]				Y	Y
7 Barr	Y	Y	Y	Y	Y
8 Chambliss	Y	N	Y	N	N
9 Deal	Y	Y	Y	Y	Y
10 Norwood	Y	N	Y	N	Y
11 Linder	Y	N	Y	Y	Y
HAWAII					
1 Abercrombie	Y	N	N	N	N
2 Mink	Y	N	N	N	N
IDAHO					
1 Chenoweth	Y	N	Y	N	Y
2 Crapo	Y	N	Y	N	Y
ILLINOIS					
1 Rush	Y	N	N	N	N
2 Jackson	Y	N	N	N	N
3 Lipinski	Y	N	N	N	N
4 Gutierrez	N	N	N	N	N
5 Blagojevich	Y	N	N	N	N
6 Hyde	Y	Y	Y	Y	Y
7 Davis	Y	N	N	N	N
8 Crane	Y	N	Y	Y	Y
9 Yates	N	?	?	?	N
10 Porter	+	Y	Y	Y	N
11 Weller	Y	N	Y	Y	N
12 Costello	Y	N	N	N	N

ND Northern Democrats   SD Southern Democrats

	1	2	3	4	5
13 ***Fawell***	Y	N	Y	Y	Y
14 ***Hastert***	Y	N	Y	Y	Y
15 ***Ewing***	N	N	Y	N	N
16 ***Manzullo***	Y	N	Y	N	Y
17 Evans	Y	N	N	N	N
18 ***LaHood***	Y	N	N	N	N
19 Poshard	Y	N	N	N	N
20 ***Shimkus***	Y	N	Y	Y	N
INDIANA					
1 Visclosky	Y	N	N	N	N
2 ***McIntosh***	Y	?	Y	Y	Y
3 Roemer	Y	N	N	N	N
4 ***Souder***	Y	Y	N	Y	N
5 ***Buyer***	Y	N	N	N	Y
6 ***Burton***	+	N	Y	Y	N
7 ***Pease***	Y	N	Y	Y	N
8 ***Hostettler***	Y	N	Y	Y	Y
9 Hamilton	Y	N	N	N	N
10 Carson	N	N	–	N	N
IOWA					
1 ***Leach***	N	Y	N	Y	N
2 ***Nussle***	N	N	N	Y	N
3 Boswell	N	N	N	N	N
4 ***Ganske***	N	N	Y	Y	N
5 ***Latham***	Y	N	Y	Y	N
KANSAS					
1 ***Moran***	Y	N	N	N	N
2 ***Ryun***	Y	N	Y	N	N
3 ***Snowbarger***	Y	N	N	N	Y
4 ***Tiahrt***	Y	N	Y	N	Y
KENTUCKY					
1 ***Whitfield***	Y	N	Y	Y	Y
2 ***Lewis***	Y	N	Y	N	Y
3 ***Northup***	Y	N	Y	Y	N
4 ***Bunning***	Y	N	Y	Y	N
5 ***Rogers***	Y	N	Y	N	Y
6 Baesler	Y	N	Y	N	N
LOUISIANA					
1 ***Livingston***	Y	N	Y	Y	N
2 Jefferson	Y	?	N	N	N
3 ***Tauzin***	Y	N	Y	Y	Y
4 ***McCrery***	Y	P	Y	Y	Y
5 ***Cooksey***	Y	N	Y	Y	N
6 ***Baker***	Y	N	Y	Y	N
7 John	Y	N	N	Y	N
MAINE					
1 Allen	Y	N	N	N	N
2 Baldacci	Y	N	N	N	N
MARYLAND					
1 ***Gilchrest***	Y	N	N	Y	N
2 ***Ehrlich***	Y	Y	Y	Y	Y
3 Cardin	Y	N	N	N	N
4 Wynn	?	N	N	N	N
5 Hoyer	Y	N	N	N	N
6 ***Bartlett***	Y	N	Y	Y	Y
7 Cummings	Y	N	N	N	N
8 ***Morella***	Y	Y	N	Y	N
MASSACHUSETTS					
1 Olver	Y	N	N	N	N
2 Neal	Y	N	N	Y	N
3 McGovern	Y	N	N	Y	N
4 Frank	N	N	N	N	N
5 Meehan	N	N	N	N	N
6 Tierney	Y	N	N	N	N
7 Markey	N	N	N	Y	N
8 Kennedy	Y	N	N	N	N
9 Moakley	Y	N	N	N	N
10 Delahunt	Y	N	N	Y	N
MICHIGAN					
1 Stupak	N	N	N	Y	N
2 ***Hoekstra***	Y	Y	Y	Y	Y
3 ***Ehlers***	Y	N	Y	N	N
4 ***Camp***	Y	N	Y	N	Y
5 Barcia	Y	N	N	Y	N
6 ***Upton***	N	N	N	Y	N
7 ***Smith***	N	Y	N	Y	N
8 Stabenow	Y	N	N	Y	N
9 Kildee	Y	N	N	N	N
10 Bonior	Y	N	N	N	N
11 ***Knollenberg***	Y	N	Y	Y	Y
12 Levin	Y	N	N	Y	N
13 Rivers	N	N	N	N	N
14 Conyers	N	N	N	N	?
15 Kilpatrick	Y	N	N	N	N
16 Dingell	Y	N	N	Y	N

	1	2	3	4	5
MINNESOTA					
1 ***Gutknecht***	Y	Y	Y	N	N
2 Minge	N	Y	N	N	N
3 ***Ramstad***	N	N	Y	N	N
4 Vento	N	N	N	N	N
5 Sabo	Y	N	N	N	N
6 Luther	N	N	N	N	N
7 Peterson	Y	N	N	N	N
8 Oberstar	Y	N	N	N	N
MISSISSIPPI					
1 ***Wicker***	Y	N	Y	N	?
2 Thompson	Y	N	N	N	N
3 ***Pickering***	Y	N	Y	N	Y
4 ***Parker***	Y	Y	Y	Y	?
5 Taylor	Y	N	Y	N	N
MISSOURI					
1 Clay	Y	N	N	N	N
2 ***Talent***	Y	N	Y	Y	N
3 Gephardt	Y	N	N	N	N
4 Skelton	Y	N	N	N	N
5 McCarthy	N	N	N	N	N
6 Danner	Y	N	N	N	N
7 ***Blunt***	Y	N	Y	N	Y
8 ***Emerson***	Y	N	Y	Y	Y
9 ***Hulshof***	Y	N	Y	N	Y
MONTANA					
AL ***Hill***	Y	Y	Y	Y	N
NEBRASKA					
1 ***Bereuter***	Y	N	Y	N	N
2 ***Christensen***	Y	Y	?	N	N
3 ***Barrett***	Y	Y	N	N	N
NEVADA					
1 ***Ensign***	N	N	N	Y	Y
2 ***Gibbons***	Y	N	N	Y	Y
NEW HAMPSHIRE					
1 ***Sununu***	Y	N	Y	Y	Y
2 ***Bass***	Y	N	Y	Y	Y
NEW JERSEY					
1 Andrews	N	N	N	Y	N
2 ***LoBiondo***	Y	N	Y	Y	N
3 ***Saxton***	Y	N	N	Y	Y
4 ***Smith***	Y	N	Y	Y	N
5 ***Roukema***	Y	N	Y	Y	Y
6 Pallone	Y	N	N	Y	N
7 ***Franks***	N	N	Y	Y	N
8 Pascrell	Y	N	N	Y	N
9 Rothman	N	N	N	N	N
10 Payne	N	?	N	N	N
11 ***Frelinghuysen***	Y	Y	Y	Y	Y
12 ***Pappas***	Y	Y	Y	Y	N
13 Menendez	Y	N	N	N	N
NEW MEXICO					
1 ***Schiff*** [5]	?				
2 ***Skeen***	Y	N	N	N	N
3 ***Redmond***	Y	N	N	N	N
NEW YORK					
1 ***Forbes***	Y	N	N	Y	N
2 ***Lazio***	Y	N	N	Y	N
3 ***King***	Y	N	N	Y	?
4 McCarthy	Y	N	N	Y	N
5 Ackerman	N	N	N	Y	N
6 Meeks [6]		N	N	Y	?
7 Manton	Y	N	N	Y	N
8 Nadler	Y	N	N	Y	N
9 Schumer	Y	N	N	Y	N
10 Towns	N	N	N	Y	?
11 Owens	N	N	N	N	N
12 Velázquez	Y	N	N	N	N
13 ***Fossella***	Y	N	Y	Y	N
14 Maloney	Y	N	N	Y	N
15 Rangel	N	?	N	Y	N
16 Serrano	Y	N	N	N	N
17 Engel	N	N	N	Y	N
18 Lowey	Y	N	N	Y	N
19 ***Kelly***	Y	N	N	Y	N
20 ***Gilman***	Y	N	N	Y	N
21 McNulty	Y	N	?	Y	N
22 ***Solomon***	Y	N	Y	Y	Y
23 ***Boehlert***	Y	N	N	Y	N
24 ***McHugh***	Y	N	Y	N	N
25 ***Walsh***	Y	N	N	Y	N
26 Hinchey	Y	N	N	N	N
27 ***Paxon***	Y	N	Y	Y	Y
28 Slaughter	Y	N	N	N	N
29 LaFalce	Y	N	N	N	N

	1	2	3	4	5
30 ***Quinn***	Y	N	N	Y	–
31 ***Houghton***	Y	N	N	Y	Y
NORTH CAROLINA					
1 Clayton	Y	N	N	N	N
2 Etheridge	Y	N	N	N	N
3 ***Jones***	Y	Y	Y	N	Y
4 Price	Y	N	N	Y	N
5 ***Burr***	Y	Y	N	N	Y
6 ***Coble***	Y	N	Y	Y	Y
7 McIntyre	Y	N	N	N	N
8 Hefner	Y	N	N	?	N
9 ***Myrick***	Y	Y	N	Y	Y
10 ***Ballenger***	Y	Y	Y	Y	Y
11 ***Taylor***	Y	Y	Y	Y	?
12 Watt	Y	N	N	N	N
NORTH DAKOTA					
AL Pomeroy	Y	Y	N	Y	N
OHIO					
1 ***Chabot***	N	Y	Y	Y	Y
2 ***Portman***	Y	N	Y	Y	Y
3 Hall	+	N	N	Y	N
4 ***Oxley***	Y	N	Y	Y	N
5 ***Gillmor***	Y	N	Y	Y	N
6 Strickland	N	N	N	Y	N
7 ***Hobson***	Y	Y	N	Y	Y
8 ***Boehner***	Y	Y	Y	Y	Y
9 Kaptur	Y	N	N	N	N
10 Kucinich	Y	N	N	N	N
11 Stokes	Y	N	N	N	N
12 ***Kasich***	Y	Y	Y	Y	N
13 Brown	N	N	N	Y	N
14 Sawyer	Y	N	N	Y	N
15 ***Pryce***	Y	N	N	Y	N
16 ***Regula***	Y	N	N	Y	N
17 Traficant	Y	N	N	N	Y
18 ***Ney***	Y	N	N	Y	N
19 ***LaTourette***	Y	N	N	Y	N
OKLAHOMA					
1 ***Largent***	Y	Y	N	N	Y
2 ***Coburn***	Y	Y	Y	N	Y
3 ***Watkins***	Y	N	N	N	N
4 ***Watts***	Y	N	N	N	N
5 ***Istook***	Y	Y	Y	N	Y
6 ***Lucas***	Y	N	Y	N	N
OREGON					
1 Furse	?	N	N	N	?
2 ***Smith***	Y	N	Y	N	P
3 Blumenauer	Y	N	N	N	N
4 DeFazio	N	N	N	N	?
5 Hooley	Y	N	N	N	N
PENNSYLVANIA					
1 Brady [7]					N
2 Fattah	Y	N	N	N	N
3 Borski	Y	N	N	N	N
4 Klink	?	N	N	N	N
5 ***Peterson***	Y	N	Y	N	N
6 Holden	Y	N	N	Y	N
7 ***Weldon***	Y	N	N	Y	N
8 ***Greenwood***	N	N	Y	Y	Y
9 ***Shuster***	Y	N	?	N	Y
10 ***McDade***	Y	N	N	Y	N
11 Kanjorski	N	N	N	N	N
12 Murtha	Y	N	N	Y	N
13 ***Fox***	Y	N	N	Y	N
14 Coyne	Y	N	N	Y	N
15 McHale	Y	N	N	N	N
16 ***Pitts***	Y	N	Y	Y	Y
17 ***Gekas***	Y	N	Y	Y	Y
18 Doyle	Y	N	?	Y	N
19 ***Goodling***	Y	N	Y	Y	Y
20 Mascara	Y	N	N	N	N
21 ***English***	Y	N	N	Y	Y
RHODE ISLAND					
1 Kennedy	Y	N	N	N	N
2 Weygand	Y	N	N	N	N
SOUTH CAROLINA					
1 ***Sanford***	N	Y	N	Y	Y
2 ***Spence***	Y	N	Y	Y	Y
3 ***Graham***	Y	Y	Y	N	Y
4 ***Inglis***	Y	Y	Y	Y	Y
5 Spratt	Y	N	N	Y	N
6 Clyburn	Y	N	N	N	N
SOUTH DAKOTA					
AL ***Thune***	Y	N	Y	N	N

	1	2	3	4	5
TENNESSEE					
1 ***Jenkins***	Y	N	Y	N	Y
2 ***Duncan***	N	N	Y	N	Y
3 ***Wamp***	Y	Y	Y	Y	Y
4 ***Hilleary***	Y	Y	Y	N	Y
5 Clement	Y	N	N	N	N
6 Gordon	Y	N	N	Y	N
7 ***Bryant***	Y	N	Y	Y	N
8 Tanner	Y	N	N	Y	N
9 Ford	Y	N	N	Y	N
TEXAS					
1 Sandlin	Y	N	N	N	N
2 Turner	Y	N	N	N	N
3 ***Johnson, Sam***	Y	Y	Y	N	?
4 Hall	Y	Y	Y	N	N
5 ***Sessions***	Y	Y	Y	N	Y
6 ***Barton***	Y	Y	Y	N	Y
7 ***Archer***	Y	Y	Y	Y	Y
8 ***Brady***	Y	N	Y	N	Y
9 Lampson	Y	N	N	N	N
10 Doggett	N	N	N	N	N
11 Edwards	Y	Y	N	N	N
12 ***Granger***	Y	N	Y	N	N
13 ***Thornberry***	Y	Y	Y	N	N
14 ***Paul***	Y	N	Y	N	Y
15 Hinojosa	Y	N	N	N	N
16 Reyes	Y	N	N	N	?
17 Stenholm	Y	Y	N	N	N
18 Jackson-Lee	Y	N	N	N	N
19 ***Combest***	Y	N	Y	N	N
20 Gonzalez	?	?	?	?	?
21 ***Smith***	Y	N	Y	N	Y
22 ***DeLay***	Y	N	Y	Y	Y
23 ***Bonilla***	Y	Y	N	N	N
24 Frost	Y	N	N	Y	N
25 Bentsen	Y	N	N	N	N
26 ***Armey***	?	N	Y	Y	Y
27 Ortiz	Y	N	N	N	N
28 Rodriguez	Y	N	N	N	N
29 Green	Y	N	N	N	?
30 Johnson, E.B.	Y	N	N	Y	N
UTAH					
1 ***Hansen***	Y	N	Y	Y	N
2 ***Cook***	Y	N	Y	Y	N
3 ***Cannon***	Y	?	Y	N	Y
VERMONT					
AL *Sanders*	Y	N	N	N	N
VIRGINIA					
1 ***Bateman***	Y	N	+	+	–
2 Pickett	Y	N	N	N	N
3 Scott	Y	N	N	N	N
4 Sisisky	Y	N	N	N	N
5 Goode	Y	N	N	N	Y
6 ***Goodlatte***	Y	N	Y	Y	Y
7 ***Bliley***	Y	N	Y	Y	Y
8 Moran	Y	N	N	Y	N
9 Boucher	Y	N	N	N	N
10 ***Wolf***	Y	Y	N	Y	N
11 ***Davis***	Y	N	N	N	N
WASHINGTON					
1 ***White***	Y	Y	N	Y	Y
2 ***Metcalf***	Y	N	Y	Y	Y
3 ***Smith, Linda***	Y	N	Y	Y	N
4 ***Hastings***	Y	N	Y	Y	Y
5 ***Nethercutt***	Y	Y	Y	Y	N
6 Dicks	Y	N	N	Y	N
7 McDermott	N	N	N	N	N
8 ***Dunn***	Y	N	Y	Y	Y
9 Smith, Adam	Y	N	N	Y	N
WEST VIRGINIA					
1 Mollohan	Y	N	N	Y	N
2 Wise	Y	N	N	Y	N
3 Rahall	Y	N	N	Y	N
WISCONSIN					
1 ***Neumann***	N	Y	?	Y	Y
2 ***Klug***	N	?	N	Y	Y
3 Kind	N	Y	N	N	N
4 Kleczka	Y	N	N	N	N
5 Barrett	N	Y	N	N	N
6 ***Petri***	N	N	N	Y	Y
7 Obey	Y	N	N	N	N
8 Johnson	N	N	N	N	N
9 ***Sensenbrenner***	N	Y	Y	Y	Y
WYOMING					
AL ***Cubin***	Y	Y	Y	Y	Y

Southern states - Ala., Ark., Fla., Ga., Ky., La., Miss., N.C., Okla., S.C., Tenn., Texas, Va.

House Key Votes 6, 7, 8, 9

Key

Y	Voted for (yea).
#	Paired for.
+	Announced for.
N	Voted against (nay).
X	Paired against.
−	Announced against.
P	Voted "present."
C	Voted "present" to avoid possible conflict of interest.
?	Did not vote or otherwise make a position known.

Democrats **Republicans** *Independent*

6. HR 4104. Contraceptive Coverage. Lowey, D-N.Y., amendment to prohibit the Office of Personnel Management from accepting a contract that provides coverage for prescription drugs unless the plan also provides equivalent coverage for prescription contraception drugs. Adopted 224-198: R 48-177; D 175-21 (ND 130-17, SD 45-4); I 1-0. July 16, 1998. *(House vote 290)*

7. HR 4194. Public Housing Overhaul. Lazio, R-N.Y., amendment to overhaul public housing management and allow increased local control over rents and occupancy standards. Adopted 230-181: R 215-4; D 15-176 (ND 8-136, SD 7-40); I 0-1. July 17, 1998. *(House vote 296)*

8. HR 4250. Managed Care Regulations. Passage of the bill to revise managed care and medical insurance regulations. The bill would provide a range of patient protections, create a two-step appeals process for challenging a health plan administrator's decisions and expand the availability of medical savings accounts. Passed 216-210: R 213-12; D 3-197 (ND 2-147, SD 1-50); I 0-1. July 24, 1998. A "nay" was a vote in support of the president's position. *(House vote 339)*

9. HR 2183. Campaign Finance Overhaul. Passage of the bill to ban soft money contributions for federal elections, expand regulations on advertising that advocates a candidate and tighten the definition of what constitutes coordination with a federal candidate. The text of the bill is the Shays-Meehan substitute adopted by the House on Aug. 3. Passed 252-179: R 61-164; D 190-15 (ND 142-9, SD 48-6); I 1-0. Aug. 6, 1998. *(House vote 405)*

---

[1] Barbara Lee, D-Calif., was sworn in April 21, replacing Ronald V. Dellums, D-Calif., who resigned Feb. 6.

[2] Lois Capps, D-Calif., was sworn in March 17, replacing Walter Capps, D-Calif., who died Oct. 28, 1997.

[3] Mary Bono, R-Calif., was sworn in April 21, replacing Sonny Bono, R-Calif., who died Jan. 5.

[4] Newt Gingrich, R-Ga., as Speaker of the House, voted at his discretion.

[5] Heather Wilson, R-N.M., was sworn in June 25, replacing Steven H. Schiff, R-N.M., who died March 25.

[6] Gregory W. Meeks, D-N.Y., was sworn in Feb. 5, replacing Floyd H. Flake, D-N.Y., who resigned Nov. 15, 1997.

[7] Robert A. Brady, D-Pa., was sworn in May 21, replacing Thomas M. Foglietta, D-Pa., who resigned Nov. 11, 1997.

		6	7	8	9
ALABAMA					
1	Callahan	N	?	Y	N
2	Everett	N	Y	Y	N
3	Riley	N	Y	Y	N
4	Aderholt	N	Y	Y	N
5	Cramer	Y	N	N	Y
6	Bachus	N	Y	Y	N
7	Hilliard	Y	N	N	Y
ALASKA					
AL	Young	N	Y	Y	N
ARIZONA					
1	Salmon	N	Y	Y	N
2	Pastor	Y	N	N	Y
3	Stump	N	Y	Y	N
4	Shadegg	N	Y	Y	N
5	Kolbe	Y	Y	Y	N
6	Hayworth	N	Y	Y	N
ARKANSAS					
1	Berry	Y	N	N	Y
2	Snyder	Y	?	N	Y
3	Hutchinson	N	Y	Y	N
4	Dickey	N	Y	Y	N
CALIFORNIA					
1	Riggs	Y	Y	Y	Y
2	Herger	N	Y	Y	N
3	Fazio	Y	N	N	Y
4	Doolittle	N	+	Y	N
5	Matsui	Y	N	N	Y
6	Woolsey	Y	N	N	Y
7	Miller	Y	N	N	Y
8	Pelosi	Y	N	N	Y
9	Lee[1]	Y	N	N	Y
10	Tauscher	Y	N	N	Y
11	Pombo	N	Y	Y	N
12	Lantos	Y	N	N	Y
13	Stark	Y	N	N	Y
14	Eshoo	Y	N	N	Y
15	Campbell	Y	Y	N	Y
16	Lofgren	Y	N	N	Y
17	Farr	Y	N	N	Y
18	Condit	Y	Y	N	Y
19	Radanovich	N	Y	Y	N
20	Dooley	Y	N	N	Y
21	Thomas	Y	Y	Y	N
22	Capps, L.[2]	Y	N	N	Y
23	Gallegly	Y	Y	Y	Y
24	Sherman	Y	N	N	Y
25	McKeon	N	Y	Y	N
26	Berman	Y	N	N	Y
27	Rogan	N	Y	Y	N
28	Dreier	N	Y	Y	N
29	Waxman	Y	N	N	Y
30	Becerra	Y	N	N	Y
31	Martinez	Y	N	N	N
32	Dixon	Y	N	N	Y
33	Roybal-Allard	+	−	N	Y
34	Torres	Y	N	N	Y
35	Waters	Y	N	N	Y
36	Harman	Y	?	N	Y
37	Millender-McD.	Y	−	N	Y
38	Horn	Y	Y	Y	Y

		6	7	8	9
39	Royce	N	Y	Y	N
40	Lewis	N	Y	Y	N
41	Kim	N	Y	Y	Y
42	Brown	Y	N	N	Y
43	Calvert	Y	Y	Y	N
44	Bono, M.[3]	Y	Y	Y	N
45	Rohrabacher	N	Y	Y	N
46	Sanchez	Y	N	N	Y
47	Cox	N	Y	Y	N
48	Packard	N	Y	Y	Y
49	Bilbray	Y	Y	Y	Y
50	Filner	#	−	N	Y
51	Cunningham	N	Y	Y	?
52	Hunter	N	Y	Y	N
COLORADO					
1	DeGette	Y	N	N	Y
2	Skaggs	Y	N	N	Y
3	McInnis	N	Y	Y	N
4	Schaffer	N	Y	Y	N
5	Hefley	N	Y	Y	N
6	Schaefer	N	Y	Y	N
CONNECTICUT					
1	Kennelly	?	?	N	Y
2	Gejdenson	Y	N	Y	Y
3	DeLauro	Y	N	N	Y
4	Shays	Y	Y	Y	Y
5	Maloney	Y	N	N	Y
6	Johnson	Y	Y	Y	Y
DELAWARE					
AL	Castle	Y	Y	Y	Y
FLORIDA					
1	Scarborough	N	Y	Y	N
2	Boyd	Y	N	N	Y
3	Brown	Y	N	N	Y
4	Fowler	Y	Y	Y	Y
5	Thurman	Y	N	N	Y
6	Stearns	N	Y	Y	N
7	Mica	N	+	Y	N
8	McCollum	N	Y	Y	N
9	Bilirakis	N	Y	Y	N
10	Young	N	Y	?	N
11	Davis	Y	N	N	Y
12	Canady	N	Y	Y	N
13	Miller	N	Y	Y	N
14	Goss	N	Y	Y	N
15	Weldon	N	Y	Y	N
16	Foley	Y	Y	Y	Y
17	Meek	Y	N	N	Y
18	Ros-Lehtinen	N	Y	Y	N
19	Wexler	Y	N	N	Y
20	Deutsch	Y	N	N	Y
21	Diaz-Balart	N	Y	Y	N
22	Shaw	Y	Y	Y	N
23	Hastings	Y	N	N	N
GEORGIA					
1	Kingston	N	Y	Y	N
2	Bishop	Y	N	N	N
3	Collins	N	Y	Y	N
4	McKinney	Y	N	N	Y
5	Lewis	?	?	N	Y
6	Gingrich[4]				Y
7	Barr	N	Y	N	N
8	Chambliss	N	Y	Y	N
9	Deal	N	Y	Y	Y
10	Norwood	N	Y	Y	N
11	Linder	N	Y	?	N
HAWAII					
1	Abercrombie	Y	N	N	N
2	Mink	Y	N	N	N
IDAHO					
1	Chenoweth	N	Y	N	N
2	Crapo	N	Y	N	N
ILLINOIS					
1	Rush	Y	N	N	Y
2	Jackson	Y	N	N	Y
3	Lipinski	N	N	N	Y
4	Gutierrez	Y	N	N	Y
5	Blagojevich	Y	N	N	Y
6	Hyde	N	Y	Y	N
7	Davis	Y	N	N	Y
8	Crane	N	Y	Y	N
9	Yates	Y	N	?	Y
10	Porter	Y	Y	Y	Y
11	Weller	N	Y	Y	N
12	Costello	N	N	N	Y
13	Fawell	Y	Y	Y	N

ND Northern Democrats   SD Southern Democrats

	6	7	8	9
14 Hastert	N	Y	Y	N
15 Ewing	N	Y	Y	N
16 Manzullo	Y	Y	Y	N
17 Evans	Y	N	N	Y
18 LaHood	N	Y	Y	N
19 Poshard	Y	N	N	Y
20 Shimkus	N	Y	Y	Y

INDIANA

	6	7	8	9
1 Visclosky	Y	N	N	Y
2 McIntosh	N	Y	Y	N
3 Roemer	Y	N	N	Y
4 Souder	N	Y	Y	N
5 Buyer	N	Y	Y	N
6 Burton	N	Y	Y	N
7 Pease	N	Y	Y	N
8 Hostettler	N	Y	Y	N
9 Hamilton	Y	N	N	Y
10 Carson	Y	N	N	Y

IOWA

	6	7	8	9
1 Leach	Y	Y	Y	Y
2 Nussle	N	Y	Y	N
3 Boswell	Y	N	N	Y
4 Ganske	Y	Y	N	Y
5 Latham	N	Y	Y	N

KANSAS

	6	7	8	9
1 Moran	N	Y	Y	N
2 Ryun	N	Y	Y	N
3 Snowbarger	N	Y	Y	N
4 Tiahrt	N	Y	Y	N

KENTUCKY

	6	7	8	9
1 Whitfield	N	Y	Y	N
2 Lewis	N	Y	Y	N
3 Northup	N	Y	Y	N
4 Bunning	N	Y	Y	N
5 Rogers	N	Y	Y	N
6 Baesler	Y	Y	N	Y

LOUISIANA

	6	7	8	9
1 Livingston	N	?	Y	N
2 Jefferson	Y	?	N	Y
3 Tauzin	N	Y	Y	N
4 McCrery	N	Y	Y	N
5 Cooksey	N	Y	Y	N
6 Baker	N	Y	Y	N
7 John	?	?	?	N

MAINE

	6	7	8	9
1 Allen	Y	N	N	Y
2 Baldacci	Y	N	N	Y

MARYLAND

	6	7	8	9
1 Gilchrest	Y	Y	Y	Y
2 Ehrlich	Y	Y	Y	N
3 Cardin	Y	N	N	Y
4 Wynn	Y	N	N	Y
5 Hoyer	Y	N	N	Y
6 Bartlett	N	Y	Y	N
7 Cummings	Y	N	N	Y
8 Morella	Y	Y	N	Y

MASSACHUSETTS

	6	7	8	9
1 Olver	Y	N	N	Y
2 Neal	Y	N	N	Y
3 McGovern	Y	N	N	Y
4 Frank	Y	N	N	Y
5 Meehan	Y	N	N	Y
6 Tierney	Y	N	N	Y
7 Markey	Y	N	?	Y
8 Kennedy	Y	N	N	Y
9 Moakley	Y	?	N	Y
10 Delahunt	Y	N	N	Y

MICHIGAN

	6	7	8	9
1 Stupak	N	N	N	N
2 Hoekstra	N	Y	Y	N
3 Ehlers	N	Y	Y	N
4 Camp	N	Y	Y	N
5 Barcia	N	N	N	N
6 Upton	Y	Y	Y	Y
7 Smith	N	Y	Y	N
8 Stabenow	Y	N	N	Y
9 Kildee	N	N	N	Y
10 Bonior	Y	N	N	Y
11 Knollenberg	N	Y	Y	N
12 Levin	Y	N	N	Y
13 Rivers	Y	N	N	Y
14 Conyers	Y	N	N	Y
15 Kilpatrick	Y	N	N	Y
16 Dingell	Y	N	N	Y

MINNESOTA

	6	7	8	9
1 Gutknecht	N	Y	Y	N
2 Minge	Y	N	N	Y
3 Ramstad	Y	Y	Y	Y
4 Vento	Y	N	N	Y
5 Sabo	Y	N	N	Y
6 Luther	Y	Y	N	Y
7 Peterson	N	N	N	N
8 Oberstar	Y	N	N	Y

MISSISSIPPI

	6	7	8	9
1 Wicker	N	Y	Y	N
2 Thompson	Y	N	N	Y
3 Pickering	N	Y	Y	N
4 Parker	?	?	Y	Y
5 Taylor	N	N	N	Y

MISSOURI

	6	7	8	9
1 Clay	Y	N	N	Y
2 Talent	N	Y	Y	N
3 Gephardt	N	N	N	Y
4 Skelton	N	N	N	Y
5 McCarthy	Y	N	N	Y
6 Danner	Y	Y	N	Y
7 Blunt	N	Y	Y	N
8 Emerson	N	Y	Y	N
9 Hulshof	N	Y	Y	N

MONTANA

	6	7	8	9
AL Hill	?	?	Y	Y

NEBRASKA

	6	7	8	9
1 Bereuter	Y	Y	Y	Y
2 Christensen	N	Y	Y	N
3 Barrett	N	Y	Y	N

NEVADA

	6	7	8	9
1 Ensign	Y	Y	Y	N
2 Gibbons	Y	Y	Y	N

NEW HAMPSHIRE

	6	7	8	9
1 Sununu	N	Y	Y	N
2 Bass	Y	Y	Y	Y

NEW JERSEY

	6	7	8	9
1 Andrews	Y	N	N	Y
2 LoBiondo	N	Y	Y	Y
3 Saxton	N	Y	Y	Y
4 Smith	N	Y	N	Y
5 Roukema	Y	Y	N	Y
6 Pallone	Y	N	N	Y
7 Franks	Y	Y	Y	Y
8 Pascrell	Y	N	N	Y
9 Rothman	Y	N	N	Y
10 Payne	Y	N	N	Y
11 Frelinghuysen	Y	Y	Y	Y
12 Pappas	N	Y	Y	N
13 Menendez	Y	N	N	Y

NEW MEXICO

	6	7	8	9
1 Wilson[5]	Y	Y	Y	N
2 Skeen	N	Y	Y	N
3 Redmond	N	Y	Y	N

NEW YORK

	6	7	8	9
1 Forbes	N	Y	N	Y
2 Lazio	Y	Y	Y	Y
3 King	N	Y	Y	N
4 McCarthy	Y	N	N	Y
5 Ackerman	Y	N	N	Y
6 Meeks[6]	Y	N	N	Y
7 Manton	Y	N	N	Y
8 Nadler	Y	N	N	Y
9 Schumer	Y	N	N	Y
10 Towns	Y	N	N	Y
11 Owens	Y	N	N	Y
12 Velázquez	Y	N	N	Y
13 Fossella	N	Y	Y	N
14 Maloney	Y	N	N	Y
15 Rangel	Y	N	N	Y
16 Serrano	Y	N	N	Y
17 Engel	Y	N	N	Y
18 Lowey	Y	N	N	Y
19 Kelly	Y	Y	Y	Y
20 Gilman	Y	Y	Y	Y
21 McNulty	?	?	N	Y
22 Solomon	N	Y	Y	N
23 Boehlert	Y	Y	Y	Y
24 McHugh	N	Y	Y	N
25 Walsh	N	N	Y	Y
26 Hinchey	Y	N	N	Y
27 Paxon	N	Y	Y	N
28 Slaughter	Y	N	N	Y
29 LaFalce	N	N	N	Y

NORTH CAROLINA

	6	7	8	9
1 Clayton	?	N	N	Y
2 Etheridge	Y	N	N	Y
3 Jones	N	Y	Y	N
4 Price	Y	N	N	Y
5 Burr	N	Y	Y	N
6 Coble	N	Y	Y	N
7 McIntyre	Y	Y	N	Y
8 Hefner	Y	N	N	Y
9 Myrick	N	Y	Y	N
10 Ballenger	N	Y	Y	N
11 Taylor	N	Y	Y	N
12 Watt	Y	N	N	Y

NORTH DAKOTA

	6	7	8	9
AL Pomeroy	Y	N	N	Y

OHIO

	6	7	8	9
1 Chabot	N	Y	Y	N
2 Portman	N	Y	Y	N
3 Hall	N	N	N	Y
4 Oxley	Y	Y	Y	N
5 Gillmor	N	Y	Y	N
6 Strickland	Y	N	N	Y
7 Hobson	Y	Y	Y	N
8 Boehner	N	Y	Y	N
9 Kaptur	Y	N	N	Y
10 Kucinich	N	N	N	Y
11 Stokes	Y	N	N	Y
12 Kasich	N	Y	Y	N
13 Brown	Y	N	N	Y
14 Sawyer	Y	N	N	Y
15 Pryce	Y	Y	Y	N
16 Regula	N	Y	Y	N
17 Traficant	Y	N	N	Y
18 Ney	N	Y	Y	N
19 LaTourette	N	Y	Y	N

OKLAHOMA

	6	7	8	9
1 Largent	N	Y	Y	N
2 Coburn	N	Y	Y	N
3 Watkins	N	Y	Y	N
4 Watts	N	Y	Y	N
5 Istook	N	Y	Y	N
6 Lucas	N	Y	Y	N

OREGON

	6	7	8	9
1 Furse	Y	N	N	Y
2 Smith	N	Y	Y	N
3 Blumenauer	Y	N	N	Y
4 DeFazio	Y	N	N	Y
5 Hooley	Y	N	N	Y

PENNSYLVANIA

	6	7	8	9
1 Brady[7]	Y	N	N	Y
2 Fattah	Y	N	N	Y
3 Borski	Y	Y	Y	Y
4 Klink	N	Y	N	Y
5 Peterson	N	Y	Y	N
6 Holden	N	N	N	Y
7 Weldon	N	Y	Y	N
8 Greenwood	Y	Y	Y	Y
9 Shuster	N	Y	Y	N
10 McDade	N	Y	Y	N
11 Kanjorski	Y	N	N	Y
12 Murtha	Y	N	N	Y
13 Fox	Y	Y	Y	Y
14 Coyne	Y	N	N	Y
15 McHale	Y	N	N	Y
16 Pitts	N	Y	Y	N
17 Gekas	N	Y	Y	N
18 Doyle	N	N	N	Y
19 Goodling	N	Y	Y	N
20 Mascara	N	N	N	Y
21 English	N	Y	Y	N

RHODE ISLAND

	6	7	8	9
1 Kennedy	Y	N	N	Y
2 Weygand	Y	N	N	Y

SOUTH CAROLINA

	6	7	8	9
1 Sanford	N	Y	Y	N
2 Spence	N	Y	Y	N
3 Graham	N	Y	Y	N
4 Inglis	N	Y	Y	?
5 Spratt	Y	N	N	Y
6 Clyburn	Y	N	N	Y

SOUTH DAKOTA

	6	7	8	9
AL Thune	N	Y	Y	Y

TENNESSEE

	6	7	8	9
1 Jenkins	N	Y	Y	N
2 Duncan	N	Y	Y	Y
3 Wamp	N	Y	Y	N
4 Hilleary	N	Y	Y	N
5 Clement	Y	N	N	Y
6 Gordon	Y	N	N	Y
7 Bryant	N	Y	Y	N
8 Tanner	Y	?	N	Y
9 Ford	+	–	–	Y

TEXAS

	6	7	8	9
1 Sandlin	Y	N	N	Y
2 Turner	Y	N	N	Y
3 Johnson, Sam	N	Y	Y	N
4 Hall	N	N	N	Y
5 Sessions	N	Y	Y	N
6 Barton	N	?	Y	N
7 Archer	N	Y	Y	N
8 Brady	N	Y	Y	N
9 Lampson	Y	N	N	Y
10 Doggett	Y	N	N	Y
11 Edwards	Y	N	N	Y
12 Granger	N	Y	Y	N
13 Thornberry	N	Y	Y	N
14 Paul	N	N	N	N
15 Hinojosa	Y	N	N	Y
16 Reyes	Y	N	N	Y
17 Stenholm	N	Y	N	Y
18 Jackson-Lee	Y	N	N	Y
19 Combest	N	Y	Y	N
20 Gonzalez	?	?	?	?
21 Smith	N	Y	Y	N
22 DeLay	N	Y	Y	N
23 Bonilla	N	Y	Y	N
24 Frost	Y	N	N	Y
25 Bentsen	Y	N	N	Y
26 Armey	N	Y	Y	N
27 Ortiz	X	–	N	Y
28 Rodriguez	Y	N	?	Y
29 Green	Y	N	N	Y
30 Johnson, E.B.	Y	N	N	Y

UTAH

	6	7	8	9
1 Hansen	N	Y	Y	N
2 Cook	Y	Y	Y	Y
3 Cannon	N	Y	Y	N

VERMONT

	6	7	8	9
AL Sanders	Y	N	N	Y

VIRGINIA

	6	7	8	9
1 Bateman	N	Y	Y	N
2 Pickett	Y	N	N	Y
3 Scott	Y	N	N	Y
4 Sisisky	Y	N	N	Y
5 Goode	N	Y	Y	N
6 Goodlatte	N	Y	Y	N
7 Bliley	N	Y	Y	N
8 Moran	Y	N	N	Y
9 Boucher	Y	N	N	Y
10 Wolf	N	Y	Y	N
11 Davis	Y	Y	Y	Y

WASHINGTON

	6	7	8	9
1 White	N	Y	Y	N
2 Metcalf	N	Y	Y	Y
3 Smith, Linda	N	Y	Y	Y
4 Hastings	N	Y	Y	N
5 Nethercutt	Y	N	Y	N
6 Dicks	Y	N	N	Y
7 McDermott	Y	N	N	Y
8 Dunn	Y	?	Y	N
9 Smith, Adam	Y	N	N	Y

WEST VIRGINIA

	6	7	8	9
1 Mollohan	N	N	N	N
2 Wise	Y	N	N	Y
3 Rahall	N	N	N	N

WISCONSIN

	6	7	8	9
1 Neumann	N	Y	Y	N
2 Klug	Y	Y	?	Y
3 Kind	Y	N	N	Y
4 Kleczka	Y	N	N	Y
5 Barrett	Y	N	N	Y
6 Petri	N	Y	Y	Y
7 Obey	Y	N	N	Y
8 Johnson	Y	N	N	Y
9 Sensenbrenner	N	Y	Y	N

WYOMING

	6	7	8	9
AL Cubin	N	Y	Y	N

Southern states - Ala., Ark., Fla., Ga., Ky., La., Miss., N.C., Okla., S.C., Tenn., Texas, Va.

House Key Votes 10, 11, 12, 13

10. H Res 525. Release of Starr Report. Adoption of the resolution to provide for the release and distribution of the report from Independent Counsel Kenneth W. Starr regarding allegations of criminal offenses and other misconduct by President Clinton. Under the resolution, the Judiciary Committee will review the materials to determine whether they contain grounds for impeachment. It also requires the committee to immediately release the initial 445-page report, and release other documents to the public on Sept. 28 unless the committee votes not to release certain materials. Adopted 363-63: R 224-0; D 138-63 (ND 102-46, SD 36-17); I 1-0. Sept. 11, 1998. (House vote 425)

11. HR 3736. Skilled-Worker Visas. Passage of the bill to increase the number of six-year H-1B skill- and profession-based visas for foreign workers from 65,000 to 115,000 in fiscal 1999 and 2000 and 107,500 in fiscal 2001. The bill also would require some employers using H-1B workers to prove they have tried to recruit qualified U.S. workers and have not laid off U.S. workers. Passed 288-133: R 189-34; D 99-98 (ND 66-76, SD 33-22); I 0-1. Sept. 24, 1998. A "nay" was a vote in support of the president's position. (House vote 460)

12. HR 4328. Fiscal 1999 Omnibus Appropriations. Adoption of the conference report on the bill to provide almost $500 billion in new budget authority for those Cabinet departments and federal agencies whose fiscal 1999 appropriations bills were never enacted. The measure incorporates eight previously separate appropriations bills: Labor-HHS-Education, Interior, Treasury-Postal, Foreign Operations, Commerce-Justice-State, District of Columbia, Agriculture and Transportation. In addition, the bill provides $20.8 billion in "emergency" supplemental spending, including $6.8 billion for military spending ($1.9 billion of it for Bosnia operations), $5.9 billion for relief to farmers, $2.4 billion for anti-terrorism programs, $3.35 billion to address Year 2000 computer problems and $1.55 billion for disaster relief from Hurricane Georges. The measure also contains language to extend expiring tax provisions (at a cost of $9.7 billion over nine years), increase the number of H-1B visas for high-tech foreign workers, impose a three-year moratorium on new taxes on Internet access, implement the Chemical Weapons Convention and extend for six months Chapter 12 of the bankruptcy code, which is designed to help struggling farmers. Adopted 333-95: R 162-64; D 170-31 (ND 120-26, SD 50-5); I 1-0. Oct. 20, 1998. (HR 4328 was originally the fiscal 1999 Transportation appropriations bill.) A "yea" was a vote in support of the president's position. (House vote 538)

13. H Res 611. Impeachment of President Clinton/Article I — Grand Jury Perjury. Adoption of Article I of the resolution, which would impeach President Clinton for "perjurious, false and misleading testimony" during his Aug. 17, 1998, federal grand jury testimony about his relationship with former White House intern Monica Lewinsky, his prior testimony in the Paula Jones sexual harassment lawsuit and his attempts to influence others' testimony in both. Adopted 228-206: R 223-5; D 5-200 (ND 1-149, SD 4-51); I 0-1. Dec. 19, 1998. A "nay" was a vote in support of the president's position. (House vote 543)

[1] Barbara Lee, D-Calif., was sworn in April 21, replacing Ronald V. Dellums, D-Calif., who resigned Feb. 6.

[2] Lois Capps, D-Calif., was sworn in March 17, replacing Walter Capps, D-Calif., who died Oct. 28, 1997.

[3] Mary Bono, R-Calif., was sworn in April 21, replacing Sonny Bono, R-Calif., who died Jan. 5.

[4] Newt Gingrich, R-Ga., as Speaker of the House, voted at his discretion.

[5] Heather Wilson, R-N.M., was sworn in June 25, replacing Stephen H. Schiff, R-N.M., who died March 25.

[6] Gregory W. Meeks, D-N.Y., was sworn in Feb. 5, replacing Floyd H. Flake, D-N.Y., who resigned Nov. 15, 1997.

[7] Robert A. Brady, D-Pa., was sworn in May 21, replacing Thomas M. Foglietta, D-Pa., who resigned Nov. 11, 1997.

Key

Y	Voted for (yea).
#	Paired for.
+	Announced for.
N	Voted against (nay).
X	Paired against.
–	Announced against.
P	Voted "present."
C	Voted "present" to avoid possible conflict of interest.
?	Did not vote or otherwise make a position known.

Democrats **Republicans**
Independent

	10	11	12	13
ALABAMA				
1 *Callahan*	Y	Y	Y	Y
2 *Everett*	Y	Y	Y	Y
3 *Riley*	Y	Y	Y	Y
4 *Aderholt*	Y	Y	Y	Y
5 Cramer	Y	Y	N	Y
6 *Bachus*	Y	N	N	Y
7 Hilliard	N	N	Y	N
ALASKA				
AL *Young*	?	N	Y	Y
ARIZONA				
1 *Salmon*	Y	Y	N	Y
2 Pastor	Y	Y	Y	N
3 *Stump*	Y	N	N	Y
4 *Shadegg*	Y	Y	Y	Y
5 *Kolbe*	Y	Y	Y	Y
6 *Hayworth*	Y	Y	Y	Y
ARKANSAS				
1 Berry	Y	N	Y	N
2 Snyder	Y	Y	Y	N
3 *Hutchinson*	Y	N	Y	Y
4 *Dickey*	Y	Y	Y	Y
CALIFORNIA				
1 *Riggs*	Y	N	N	Y
2 *Herger*	Y	Y	Y	Y
3 Fazio	Y	Y	?	N
4 *Doolittle*	Y	Y	Y	Y
5 Matsui	Y	Y	Y	N
6 Woolsey	N	Y	Y	N
7 Miller	N	Y	N	?
8 Pelosi	N	Y	Y	N
9 Lee[1]	N	N	N	N
10 Tauscher	Y	Y	Y	N
11 *Pombo*	Y	Y	Y	Y
12 Lantos	Y	Y	Y	N
13 Stark	N	N	?	N
14 Eshoo	Y	Y	Y	N
15 *Campbell*	Y	Y	N	Y
16 Lofgren	N	Y	N	N
17 Farr	Y	Y	Y	N
18 Condit	Y	N	N	Y
19 *Radanovich*	Y	Y	Y	Y
20 Dooley	Y	Y	Y	N
21 *Thomas*	Y	Y	Y	Y
22 Capps, L.[2]	Y	Y	Y	N
23 *Gallegly*	Y	N	Y	Y
24 Sherman	Y	N	Y	N
25 *McKeon*	Y	Y	Y	Y
26 Berman	Y	Y	Y	N
27 *Rogan*	Y	Y	Y	Y
28 *Dreier*	Y	Y	Y	Y
29 Waxman	Y	Y	Y	N
30 Becerra	N	Y	Y	N
31 Martinez	N	N	Y	N
32 Dixon	Y	Y	Y	N
33 Roybal-Allard	N	N	Y	N
34 Torres	N	?	Y	N
35 Waters	N	?	Y	N
36 Harman	Y	N	Y	N
37 Millender-McD.	Y	N	Y	N
38 Horn	Y	N	Y	N
39 *Royce*	Y	N	N	Y
40 *Lewis*	Y	Y	Y	Y
41 *Kim*	Y	Y	Y	Y
42 Brown	N	N	Y	N
43 *Calvert*	Y	Y	Y	Y
44 *Bono, M.*[3]	Y	Y	Y	Y
45 *Rohrabacher*	Y	Y	Y	Y
46 Sanchez	Y	+	Y	N
47 *Cox*	Y	Y	Y	Y
48 *Packard*	Y	Y	Y	Y
49 *Bilbray*	Y	Y	N	Y
50 Filner	N	N	N	N
51 *Cunningham*	Y	Y	Y	Y
52 *Hunter*	Y	N	Y	Y
COLORADO				
1 DeGette	Y	N	N	N
2 Skaggs	N	Y	N	N
3 *McInnis*	Y	Y	N	Y
4 *Schaffer*	Y	Y	N	Y
5 *Hefley*	Y	N	N	Y
6 *Schaefer*	Y	?	Y	Y
CONNECTICUT				
1 Kennelly	Y	?	Y	N
2 Gejdenson	Y	N	Y	N
3 DeLauro	Y	N	Y	N
4 *Shays*	Y	Y	N	N
5 Maloney	Y	Y	Y	N
6 *Johnson*	Y	Y	Y	Y
DELAWARE				
AL *Castle*	Y	Y	N	Y
FLORIDA				
1 *Scarborough*	?	Y	N	Y
2 Boyd	Y	Y	N	N
3 Brown	N	N	Y	N
4 *Fowler*	Y	Y	Y	Y
5 Thurman	Y	N	N	N
6 *Stearns*	Y	Y	Y	Y
7 *Mica*	Y	Y	Y	Y
8 *McCollum*	Y	Y	Y	Y
9 *Bilirakis*	Y	Y	Y	Y
10 *Young*	Y	Y	Y	Y
11 Davis	Y	Y	Y	N
12 *Canady*	Y	Y	Y	Y
13 *Miller*	Y	Y	N	Y
14 *Goss*	Y	+	Y	Y
15 *Weldon*	Y	Y	Y	Y
16 *Foley*	Y	Y	Y	Y
17 Meek	N	Y	Y	N
18 *Ros-Lehtinen*	Y	Y	Y	Y
19 Wexler	N	N	Y	N
20 Deutsch	N	N	Y	N
21 *Diaz-Balart*	Y	Y	Y	Y
22 *Shaw*	Y	Y	Y	Y
23 Hastings	N	Y	Y	N
GEORGIA				
1 *Kingston*	Y	N	Y	Y
2 Bishop	Y	Y	Y	N
3 *Collins*	Y	N	Y	Y
4 *McKinney*	Y	N	Y	N
5 Lewis	N	N	Y	N
6 *Gingrich*[4]	Y	Y	Y	Y
7 *Barr*	Y	N	N	Y
8 *Chambliss*	Y	Y	Y	Y
9 *Deal*	Y	N	Y	Y
10 *Norwood*	Y	N	Y	Y
11 *Linder*	Y	Y	Y	Y
HAWAII				
1 Abercrombie	Y	N	Y	N
2 Mink	Y	N	Y	N
IDAHO				
1 *Chenoweth*	Y	N	Y	Y
2 *Crapo*	Y	Y	Y	Y
ILLINOIS				
1 Rush	N	N	Y	N
2 Jackson	N	N	Y	N
3 Lipinski	Y	N	Y	N
4 Gutierrez	Y	N	Y	N
5 Blagojevich	Y	N	Y	N
6 *Hyde*	Y	Y	N	Y
7 Davis	N	N	Y	N
8 *Crane*	Y	Y	N	Y
9 Yates	N	?	N	N
10 *Porter*	Y	Y	Y	Y
11 *Weller*	Y	Y	Y	Y
12 Costello	Y	N	N	N
13 *Fawell*	Y	Y	Y	Y

ND Northern Democrats SD Southern Democrats

	10	11	12	13
14 Hastert	Y	Y	Y	Y
15 Ewing	Y	Y	Y	Y
16 *Manzullo*	Y	Y	N	Y
17 Evans	Y	N	Y	N
18 LaHood	Y	Y	N	Y
19 Poshard	?	?	?	N
20 *Shimkus*	Y	Y	Y	Y
INDIANA				
1 Visclosky	Y	N	Y	N
2 *McIntosh*	Y	Y	N	Y
3 Roemer	Y	Y	Y	N
4 *Souder*	Y	Y	Y	Y
5 *Buyer*	Y	Y	Y	Y
6 *Burton*	Y	+	Y	Y
7 Pease	Y	Y	Y	Y
8 *Hostettler*	Y	N	N	Y
9 Hamilton	Y	Y	N	N
10 Carson	N	N	Y	N
IOWA				
1 Leach	Y	Y	Y	Y
2 *Nussle*	Y	Y	Y	Y
3 Boswell	Y	Y	Y	N
4 *Ganske*	Y	Y	Y	Y
5 *Latham*	Y	Y	Y	Y
KANSAS				
1 *Moran*	Y	Y	Y	Y
2 *Ryun*	Y	Y	Y	Y
3 *Snowbarger*	Y	Y	Y	Y
4 *Tiahrt*	Y	Y	Y	Y
KENTUCKY				
1 *Whitfield*	Y	N	Y	Y
2 *Lewis*	Y	Y	Y	Y
3 *Northup*	Y	Y	Y	Y
4 *Bunning*	Y	Y	Y	Y
5 *Rogers*	Y	Y	Y	Y
6 Baesler	Y	N	Y	N
LOUISIANA				
1 *Livingston*	Y	Y	Y	Y
2 Jefferson	N	N	Y	N
3 *Tauzin*	Y	Y	Y	Y
4 *McCrery*	Y	Y	Y	Y
5 *Cooksey*	Y	Y	Y	Y
6 *Baker*	Y	Y	Y	Y
7 John	Y	Y	Y	N
MAINE				
1 Allen	Y	Y	Y	N
2 Baldacci	Y	Y	Y	N
MARYLAND				
1 *Gilchrest*	Y	Y	Y	Y
2 *Ehrlich*	Y	Y	Y	Y
3 Cardin	Y	N	N	N
4 Wynn	Y	N	Y	N
5 Hoyer	Y	Y	Y	N
6 *Bartlett*	Y	N	Y	Y
7 Cummings	N	N	Y	N
8 *Morella*	Y	Y	Y	N
MASSACHUSETTS				
1 Olver	Y	N	Y	N
2 Neal	N	Y	Y	N
3 McGovern	Y	Y	Y	N
4 Frank	N	Y	Y	N
5 Meehan	N	Y	?	N
6 Tierney	Y	Y	Y	N
7 Markey	N	Y	Y	N
8 Kennedy	N	Y	Y	N
9 Moakley	Y	N	Y	N
10 Delahunt	N	Y	Y	N
MICHIGAN				
1 Stupak	Y	N	N	N
2 *Hoekstra*	Y	Y	N	Y
3 *Ehlers*	Y	Y	N	N
4 *Camp*	Y	Y	Y	Y
5 Barcia	?	N	Y	N
6 *Upton*	Y	Y	N	Y
7 *Smith*	Y	N	N	N
8 Stabenow	Y	Y	Y	N
9 Kildee	Y	N	Y	N
10 Bonior	Y	N	Y	N
11 *Knollenberg*	Y	Y	Y	Y
12 Levin	Y	Y	Y	N
13 Rivers	Y	N	N	N
14 Conyers	Y	N	Y	N
15 Kilpatrick	N	N	Y	N
16 Dingell	Y	N	Y	N

	10	11	12	13
MINNESOTA				
1 *Gutknecht*	Y	Y	Y	Y
2 Minge	Y	N	N	N
3 *Ramstad*	Y	Y	Y	Y
4 Vento	Y	Y	Y	N
5 Sabo	N	Y	Y	N
6 Luther	Y	Y	N	N
7 Peterson	Y	N	N	N
8 Oberstar	Y	N	N	N
MISSISSIPPI				
1 *Wicker*	Y	Y	Y	Y
2 Thompson	N	N	Y	N
3 *Pickering*	Y	Y	Y	Y
4 *Parker*	Y	Y	Y	Y
5 Taylor	Y	N	N	Y
MISSOURI				
1 Clay	N	N	Y	N
2 *Talent*	Y	Y	Y	Y
3 Gephardt	Y	Y	Y	Y
4 Skelton	Y	?	Y	N
5 McCarthy	Y	Y	Y	N
6 Danner	Y	N	N	N
7 *Blunt*	Y	Y	Y	Y
8 *Emerson*	Y	Y	N	Y
9 Hulshof	Y	Y	Y	Y
MONTANA				
AL *Hill*	Y	Y	Y	Y
NEBRASKA				
1 *Bereuter*	Y	Y	Y	Y
2 *Christensen*	Y	Y	N	Y
3 *Barrett*	Y	Y	Y	Y
NEVADA				
1 *Ensign*	Y	Y	N	Y
2 *Gibbons*	Y	Y	Y	Y
NEW HAMPSHIRE				
1 Sununu	Y	Y	Y	Y
2 *Bass*	Y	Y	Y	Y
NEW JERSEY				
1 Andrews	Y	N	Y	N
2 *LoBiondo*	Y	N	Y	Y
3 *Saxton*	Y	Y	Y	Y
4 *Smith*	Y	N	N	Y
5 *Roukema*	Y	N	Y	N
6 Pallone	Y	N	Y	N
7 *Franks*	Y	Y	Y	Y
8 Pascrell	Y	N	Y	N
9 Rothman	Y	N	Y	N
10 Payne	Y	N	Y	N
11 *Frelinghuysen*	Y	Y	N	Y
12 *Pappas*	Y	Y	N	Y
13 Menendez	Y	Y	Y	N
NEW MEXICO				
1 *Wilson*[5]	Y	Y	Y	Y
2 *Skeen*	Y	Y	Y	Y
3 *Redmond*	Y	Y	Y	Y
NEW YORK				
1 *Forbes*	Y	Y	Y	Y
2 *Lazio*	Y	Y	Y	Y
3 *King*	Y	Y	N	N
4 McCarthy	Y	Y	Y	N
5 Ackerman	N	Y	Y	N
6 Meeks[6]	N	N	Y	N
7 Manton	Y	?	Y	N
8 Nadler	N	Y	Y	N
9 Schumer	Y	Y	Y	N
10 Towns	N	N	Y	N
11 Owens	N	Y	Y	N
12 Velázquez	N	N	Y	N
13 *Fossella*	Y	Y	Y	Y
14 Maloney	Y	N	Y	N
15 Rangel	Y	N	Y	N
16 Serrano	N	N	Y	N
17 Engel	N	N	N	N
18 Lowey	Y	Y	Y	N
19 *Kelly*	Y	Y	Y	Y
20 *Gilman*	Y	Y	Y	Y
21 McNulty	Y	N	Y	N
22 *Solomon*	Y	N	Y	Y
23 *Boehlert*	Y	Y	Y	Y
24 *McHugh*	Y	Y	Y	Y
25 *Walsh*	Y	Y	Y	Y
26 Hinchey	N	N	Y	N
27 *Paxon*	Y	Y	Y	Y
28 Slaughter	Y	Y	Y	N
29 LaFalce	Y	Y	Y	N

	10	11	12	13
30 *Quinn*	Y	Y	Y	Y
31 *Houghton*	Y	Y	Y	N
NORTH CAROLINA				
1 Clayton	N	Y	Y	N
2 Etheridge	Y	Y	Y	N
3 *Jones*	Y	Y	N	Y
4 Price	Y	Y	Y	N
5 *Burr*	Y	Y	Y	Y
6 *Coble*	Y	Y	N	Y
7 McIntyre	Y	Y	Y	N
8 Hefner	N	Y	Y	N
9 *Myrick*	Y	Y	N	Y
10 *Ballenger*	Y	Y	N	Y
11 *Taylor*	Y	Y	Y	Y
12 Watt	N	Y	Y	N
NORTH DAKOTA				
AL Pomeroy	Y	Y	Y	N
OHIO				
1 *Chabot*	Y	Y	N	Y
2 *Portman*	Y	Y	N	Y
3 Hall	Y	Y	N	N
4 *Oxley*	Y	Y	Y	Y
5 *Gillmor*	Y	Y	Y	Y
6 Strickland	Y	N	N	N
7 *Hobson*	Y	Y	Y	Y
8 *Boehner*	Y	Y	Y	Y
9 Kaptur	Y	N	N	N
10 Kucinich	Y	N	Y	N
11 Stokes	N	N	Y	N
12 *Kasich*	Y	Y	Y	Y
13 Brown	Y	N	Y	N
14 Sawyer	Y	Y	Y	N
15 *Pryce*	+	+	+	Y
16 *Regula*	Y	Y	Y	Y
17 Traficant	Y	N	Y	Y
18 *Ney*	Y	N	Y	Y
19 *LaTourette*	Y	Y	Y	Y
OKLAHOMA				
1 *Largent*	Y	Y	N	Y
2 *Coburn*	Y	Y	N	Y
3 *Watkins*	Y	Y	Y	Y
4 *Watts*	Y	N	Y	Y
5 *Istook*	Y	Y	N	Y
6 *Lucas*	Y	Y	Y	Y
OREGON				
1 Furse	?	Y	N	N
2 *Smith*	Y	Y	Y	Y
3 Blumenauer	Y	Y	N	N
4 DeFazio	Y	N	N	N
5 Hooley	Y	Y	Y	N
PENNSYLVANIA				
1 Brady[7]	N	N	Y	N
2 Fattah	N	N	Y	N
3 Borski	Y	N	Y	N
4 Klink	Y	N	N	N
5 *Peterson*	Y	Y	Y	Y
6 Holden	Y	N	N	N
7 *Weldon*	Y	Y	N	Y
8 *Greenwood*	Y	Y	Y	Y
9 *Shuster*	Y	Y	Y	Y
10 *McDade*	Y	Y	Y	Y
11 Kanjorski	Y	N	N	N
12 Murtha	Y	?	Y	N
13 *Fox*	Y	Y	Y	Y
14 Coyne	Y	N	Y	N
15 McHale	Y	Y	Y	N
16 *Pitts*	Y	Y	Y	Y
17 *Gekas*	Y	Y	Y	Y
18 Doyle	Y	N	Y	N
19 *Goodling*	Y	Y	N	Y
20 Mascara	Y	N	Y	N
21 *English*	Y	Y	Y	Y
RHODE ISLAND				
1 Kennedy	N	Y	Y	N
2 Weygand	Y	Y	Y	N
SOUTH CAROLINA				
1 *Sanford*	Y	Y	N	Y
2 *Spence*	Y	N	Y	Y
3 *Graham*	Y	Y	N	Y
4 *Inglis*	Y	Y	N	Y
5 Spratt	Y	Y	Y	N
6 Clyburn	N	N	Y	N
SOUTH DAKOTA				
AL *Thune*	Y	Y	Y	Y

	10	11	12	13
TENNESSEE				
1 *Jenkins*	+	Y	Y	Y
2 *Duncan*	Y	N	N	Y
3 *Wamp*	Y	N	N	Y
4 *Hilleary*	Y	N	Y	Y
5 Clement	Y	Y	Y	N
6 Gordon	Y	Y	Y	N
7 *Bryant*	Y	Y	Y	Y
8 Tanner	Y	Y	Y	N
9 Ford	N	Y	Y	N
TEXAS				
1 Sandlin	Y	N	Y	N
2 Turner	Y	Y	Y	N
3 *Johnson, Sam*	Y	Y	N	Y
4 Hall	Y	Y	Y	Y
5 *Sessions*	Y	Y	Y	Y
6 *Barton*	Y	Y	Y	Y
7 *Archer*	Y	Y	Y	Y
8 *Brady*	Y	+	N	Y
9 Lampson	Y	N	Y	N
10 Doggett	Y	Y	N	N
11 Edwards	Y	Y	Y	N
12 *Granger*	Y	Y	Y	Y
13 *Thornberry*	Y	Y	N	Y
14 *Paul*	Y	Y	N	Y
15 Hinojosa	Y	Y	Y	N
16 Reyes	Y	Y	Y	N
17 Stenholm	Y	Y	Y	N
18 Jackson-Lee	N	Y	Y	N
19 *Combest*	Y	N	Y	Y
20 Gonzalez	?	N	Y	N
21 *Smith*	Y	Y	Y	Y
22 *DeLay*	Y	Y	Y	Y
23 *Bonilla*	Y	Y	Y	Y
24 Frost	Y	Y	Y	N
25 Bentsen	Y	Y	Y	N
26 *Armey*	Y	Y	Y	Y
27 Ortiz	Y	Y	Y	N
28 Rodriguez	Y	N	Y	N
29 Green	Y	N	Y	N
30 Johnson, E.B.	–	Y	Y	N
UTAH				
1 *Hansen*	Y	Y	?	Y
2 *Cook*	Y	Y	Y	Y
3 *Cannon*	Y	Y	Y	Y
VERMONT				
AL *Sanders*	Y	N	Y	N
VIRGINIA				
1 *Bateman*	Y	Y	Y	Y
2 Pickett	Y	Y	Y	N
3 Scott	N	Y	Y	N
4 Sisisky	Y	Y	Y	N
5 Goode	Y	N	N	Y
6 *Goodlatte*	Y	Y	Y	Y
7 *Bliley*	Y	Y	Y	Y
8 Moran	N	Y	Y	N
9 Boucher	Y	N	Y	N
10 *Wolf*	Y	Y	N	Y
11 *Davis*	Y	Y	Y	Y
WASHINGTON				
1 *White*	Y	Y	Y	N
2 *Metcalf*	Y	N	Y	Y
3 *Smith, Linda*	Y	Y	N	Y
4 *Hastings*	Y	Y	Y	Y
5 *Nethercutt*	Y	Y	Y	Y
6 Dicks	Y	Y	Y	N
7 McDermott	N	Y	N	N
8 *Dunn*	Y	Y	Y	Y
9 Smith, Adam	Y	Y	N	N
WEST VIRGINIA				
1 Mollohan	N	N	?	N
2 Wise	Y	N	Y	N
3 Rahall	Y	N	N	N
WISCONSIN				
1 *Neumann*	Y	Y	N	Y
2 *Klug*	Y	Y	Y	Y
3 Kind	Y	Y	N	N
4 Kleczka	N	N	N	N
5 Barrett	N	N	Y	N
6 *Petri*	Y	Y	N	Y
7 Obey	Y	N	Y	N
8 Johnson	Y	N	N	N
9 *Sensenbrenner*	Y	Y	N	Y
WYOMING				
AL *Cubin*	Y	Y	Y	Y

Southern states - Ala., Ark., Fla., Ga., Ky., La., Miss., N.C., Okla., S.C., Tenn., Texas, Va.

Appendix D

TEXTS

State of the Union Address D-3
   Republican Response D-8
Agriculture Appropriations Veto Message D-11
State Dept. Authorization Veto Message D-12
Clinton Impeachment
   Presidential Address D-13
     Senators Respond D-13
     Gingrich Calls for Decorum D-14
   Independent Counsel's Report D-15
     White House Response D-22

Clinton Impeachment *(cont'd)*
   Clinton's Grand Jury Testimony D-23
   Judiciary Committee's Opening Statements D-29
   Judiciary Committee Counsels' Statements D-34
   Hyde, Conyers, Starr Statements D-37
   Articles of Impeachment D-40
   Judiciary Committee's Report D-42
   Democratic Reaction to Impeachment Vote D-46

Clinton Stresses Accomplishments, Calls State of the Union 'Strong'

Following is a transcript of President Clinton's State of the Union message, delivered to Congress on Jan. 27, as provided by the Federal News Service:

PRESIDENT CLINTON: Thank you. Mr. Speaker, Mr. Vice President, members of the 105th Congress, distinguished guests, my fellow Americans:

Since the last time we met in this chamber, America has lost two patriots and fine public servants. Though they sat on opposite sides of the aisle, Reps. Walter Capps [D-Calif.] and Sonny Bono [R-Calif.] shared a deep love for this House and an unshakable commitment to improving the lives of all our people.

In the past few weeks, they have both been eulogized. Tonight, I think we should begin by sending a message to their families and their friends that we celebrate their lives, and give thanks for their service to our nation.

For 209 years it has been the president's duty to report to you on the state of the union. Because of the hard work and high purpose of the American people, these are good times for America. We have more than 14 million new jobs, the lowest unemployment in 24 years, the lowest inflation in 30 years, incomes are rising, and we have the highest home ownership in history. Crime has dropped for a record five years in a row, and the welfare rolls are at their lowest levels in 27 years. Our leadership in the world is unrivaled. Ladies and gentlemen, the state of our union is strong.

But with barely 700 days left in the 20th century, this is not a time to rest. It is a time to build — to build the America within reach, an America where everybody has a chance to get ahead, with hard work; where every citizen can live in a safe community; where families are strong, schools are good, and all our young people can go on to college; an America where scientists find cures for diseases from diabetes to Alzheimer's to AIDS; an America where every child can stretch a hand across a keyboard and reach every book ever written, every painting ever painted, every symphony ever composed; where government provides opportunity and citizens honor the responsibility to give something back to their communities; an America which leads the world to new heights of peace and prosperity.

This is the America we have begun to build. This is the America we can leave to our children — if we join together to finish the work at hand. Let us strengthen our nation for the 21st century.

Rarely have Americans lived through so much change in so many ways in so short a time. Quietly, but with gathering force, the ground has shifted beneath our feet as we have moved into an information age, a global economy, a truly new world.

For five years now, we have met the challenge of these changes as Americans have at every turning point in our history, by renewing the very idea of America, widening the circle of opportunity, deepening the meaning of our freedom, forging a more perfect union. We shaped a new kind of government for the information age.

I thank the vice president for his leadership, and the Congress for its support, in building a government that is leaner, more flexible, a catalyst for new ideas, and most of all, a government that gives the American people the tools they need to make the most of their own lives.

We have moved past the sterile debate between those who say government is the enemy and those who say government is the answer. My fellow Americans, we have found a third way. We have the smallest government in 35 years, but a more progressive one. We have a smaller government but a stronger nation.

We are moving steadily toward an even stronger America in the 21st century — an economy that offers opportunity, a society rooted in responsibility, and a nation that lives as a community.

Balanced Budget

First, Americans in this chamber and across this nation have pursued a new strategy for prosperity: fiscal discipline to cut interest rates and spur growth; investments in education and skills, in science and technology and transportation, to prepare our people for the new economy; new markets for American products and American workers.

When I took office, the deficit for 1998 was projected to be $357 billion, and heading higher. This year, our deficit is projected to be $10 billion, and heading lower.

For three decades, six presidents have come before you to warn of the damage deficits pose to our nation. Tonight I come before you to announce that the federal deficit, once so incomprehensibly large that it had 11 zeros, will be simply zero. I will submit to Congress, for 1999, the first balanced budget in 30 years.

And if we hold fast to fiscal discipline, we may balance the budget this year — four years ahead of schedule. You can all be proud of that, because turning a sea of red ink into black is no miracle. It is the product of hard work by the American people, and of two visionary actions in Congress: the courageous vote in 1993 that led to a cut in the deficit of 90 percent and the truly historic bipartisan balanced-budget agreement passed by this Congress.

Here's the really good news. If we maintain our resolve, we will produce balanced budgets as far as the eye can see. We must not go back to unwise spending or untargeted tax cuts that risk reopening the deficit.

Last year, together we enacted targeted tax cuts so that the typical middle-class family will now have the lowest tax rates in 20 years.

My plan to balance the budget next year includes both new investments and new tax cuts targeted to the needs of working families, for education, for child care, for the environment. But whether the issue is tax cuts or spending, I ask all of you to meet this test: approve only those priorities that can actually be accomplished without adding a dime to the deficit.

Social Security

Now, if we balance the budget for next year, it is projected that we'll then have a sizable surplus in the years that immediately follow. What should we do with this projected surplus? I have a simple four-word answer: Save Social Security first.

Tonight I propose that we reserve 100 percent of the surplus — that's every penny of any surplus — until we have taken all the necessary measures to strengthen the Social Security system for the 21st century.

Let us say to all Americans watching tonight, whether you're 70 or 50, or whether you just started paying into the system, Social Security will be there when you need it. Let us make this commitment: Social Security first. Let's do that — together.

I also want to say that all the American people who are watching us tonight should be invited to join in this discussion, in facing these issues squarely and forming a true consensus on how we should proceed. We'll start by conducting nonpartisan forums in every region of the country, and I hope that lawmakers of both parties will participate. We'll hold a White House conference on Social Security in December. And one year from now, I will convene the leaders of Congress to craft historic bipartisan legislation to achieve a landmark for our generation, a Social Security system that is strong in the 21st century.

Minimum Wage

In an economy that honors opportunity, all Americans must be able to reap the rewards of prosperity. Because these times are good, we can afford to take one simple, sensible step to help millions of workers struggling to provide for their families: We should raise the minimum wage.

Education

The information age is first and foremost an education age, in which education will start at birth and continue throughout a lifetime. Last year, from this podium, I said that education has to be our highest priority. I laid out a 10-point plan to move us forward, and urged all of us to let politics stop at the schoolhouse door.

Since then, this Congress — across party lines — and the American people have responded, in the most important year for education in a generation — expanding public school choice, opening the way to 3,000 charter schools, working to connect every classroom in the country to the information superhighway, committing to expand Head Start to a million children, launching America Reads, sending literally thousands of college students into our elementary schools to make sure all our 8-year-olds can read.

Last year I proposed — and you passed — 220,000 new Pell grant scholarships for deserving students. Student loans, already less expensive and easier to repay — now you get to deduct the interest. Families all over America now can put their savings into new, tax-free education IRAs. And this year, for the first two years of college, families will get a $1,500 tax credit — a Hope scholarship that will cover the cost of most community college tuition. And for junior and senior year, graduate school, and job training, there is a lifetime learning credit. You did that, and you should be very proud of it.

College for All

And because of these actions, I have something to say to every family listening to us tonight: Your children can go on to college. If you know a child from a poor family, tell her not to give up, she can go on to college. If you know a young couple struggling with bills, worried they won't be able to send their children to college, tell them not to give up, their children can go on to college. If you know somebody who's caught in a dead-end job and afraid he can't afford the classes necessary to get better jobs for the rest of his life, tell him not to give up, he can go on to college.

Because of the things that have been done, we can make college as universal in the 21st century as high school is today. And, my friends, that will change the face and future of America.

We have opened wide the doors of the world's best system of higher education. Now we must make our public elementary and secondary schools the world's best as well — by raising standards, raising expectations and raising accountability.

Thanks to the actions of this Congress last year, we will soon have, for the very first time, a voluntary national test based on national standards in fourth-grade reading and eighth-grade math. Parents have a right to know whether their children are mastering the basics. And every parent already knows the key: good teachers and small classes.

Smaller Classrooms

Tonight, I propose the first-ever national effort to reduce class size in the early grades. My balanced budget will help to hire a hundred thousand new teachers who have passed the state competency tests. Now with these teachers — listen — with these teachers, we will actually be able to reduce class size in the first, second and third grades to an average of 18 students a class all across America. Now if I've got the math right, more teachers teaching smaller classes requires more classrooms. So I also propose a school construction tax cut to help communities modernize or build 5,000 schools.

We must also demand greater accountability.

When we promote a child from grade to grade who hasn't mastered the work, we don't do that child any favors. It is time to end social promotion in America's schools.

Last year in Chicago they made that decision — not to hold our children back, but to lift them up. Chicago stopped social promotion and started mandatory summer school to help students who are behind to catch up.

I propose to help other communities follow Chicago's lead. Let's say to them: Stop promoting children who don't learn, and we will give you the tools to make sure they do.

I also ask this Congress to support our efforts to enlist colleges and universities to reach out to disadvantaged children starting in the sixth grade so that they can get the guidance and hope they need so they can know that they, too, will be able to go on to college.

Global Economics

As we enter the 21st century, the global economy requires us to seek opportunity not just at home, but in all the markets of the world. We must shape this global economy, not shrink from it.

In the last five years we have led the way in opening new markets, with 240 trade agreements that remove foreign barriers to products bearing the proud stamp "Made in the U.S.A." Today record high exports account for fully one-third of our economic growth. I want to keep them going, because that's the way to keep America growing and to advance a safer, more stable world.

Now all of you know, whatever your views are, that I think this is a great opportunity for America. I know there is opposition to more comprehensive trade agreements. I have listened carefully, and I believe that the opposition is rooted in two fears.

First, that our trading partners will have lower environmental and labor standards, which will give them an unfair advantage in our market and do their own people no favors, even if there's more business. And second, that if we have more trade, more of our workers will lose their jobs and have to start over.

I think we should seek to advance worker and environmental standards around the world.

I have made it abundantly clear that it should be a part of our trade agenda, but we cannot influence other countries' decisions if we send them a message that we're backing away from trade with them.

This year I will send legislation to Congress, and ask other nations to join us, to fight the most intolerable labor practice of all — abusive child labor.

Job Training

We should also offer help and hope to those Americans temporarily left behind with the global marketplace or by the march of technology, which may have nothing to do with trade. That's why we have more than doubled funding for training dislocated workers since 1993. And if my new budget is adopted, we will triple funding. That's why we must do more, and more quickly, to help workers who lose their jobs for whatever reason. You know, we help communities in a special way when their military base closes. We ought to help them in the same way if their factory closes.

Again, I ask the Congress to continue its bipartisan work to consolidate the tangle of training programs we have today into one single GI Bill for workers, a simple skills grant so people can, on their own, move quickly to new jobs, to higher incomes and brighter futures.

Now, we all know in every way in life, change is not always easy, but we have to decide whether we're going to try to hold it back and hide from it, or reap its benefits. And remember the big picture here: While we've been entering into hundreds of new trade agreements, we've been creating millions of new jobs. So this year we will forge new partnerships with Latin America, Asia and Europe, and we should pass the new African Trade Act. It has bipartisan support.

Fast Track

I will also renew my request for the fast-track negotiating authority necessary to open more new markets, create more new jobs, which every president has had for two decades.

You know, whether we like it or not, in ways that are mostly positive, the world's economies are more and more interconnected and interdependent. Today, an economic crisis anywhere can affect economies everywhere. Recent months have brought serious financial problems to Thailand, Indonesia, South Korea and beyond.

Now why should Americans be concerned about this? First, these countries are our customers. If they sink into recession, they won't be able to buy the goods we'd like to sell them. Second, they're also our competitors, so if their currencies lose their value and go down, then the price of their goods will drop, flooding our market and others with much cheaper goods, which makes it a lot tougher for our people to compete. And finally, they are our strategic partners. Their stability bolsters our security.

The American economy remains sound and strong, and I want to keep it that way. But because the turmoil in Asia will have an impact on all the world's economies, including ours, making that negative impact as small as possible is the right thing to do for America, and the right thing to do for a safer world.

Our policy is clear: No nation can recover if it does not reform itself, but when nations are willing to undertake serious economic reform, we should help them do it. So I call on Congress to renew America's commitment to the International Monetary Fund. And I think we should say to all the people we're trying to represent here, that preparing for a far-off storm that may reach our shores is far wiser than ignoring the thunder till the clouds are just overhead.

Welfare to Work

A strong nation rests on the rock of responsibility. A society rooted in responsibility must first promote the value of work, not welfare. We could be proud that after decades of finger-pointing and failure, together we ended the old welfare system. And we're now replacing welfare checks with paychecks. Last year, after a record four-year decline in welfare rolls, I challenged our nation to move 2 million more Americans off welfare by the year 2000. I'm pleased to report we have also met that goal two full years ahead of schedule. This is a grand achievement, the sum of many acts of individual courage, persistence and hope.

For 13 years, Elaine Kinslow of Indianapolis, Ind., was on and off welfare. Today she's a dispatcher with a van company. She's saved enough money to move her family into a good neighborhood. And she's helping other welfare recipients go to work. Elaine Kinslow and all those like her are the real heroes of the welfare revolution. There are millions like her all across America, and I am happy she could join the first lady tonight. Elaine, we're very proud of you. Please stand up.

We still have a lot more to do, all of us, to make welfare reform a success — providing child care, helping families move closer to available jobs, challenging more companies to join our Welfare to Work Partnership, increasing child-support collections from deadbeat parents who have a duty to support their own children. I also want to thank Congress for restoring some of the benefits to immigrants who are here legally and working hard, and I hope you will finish that job this year.

Health Care

We have to make it possible for all hard-working families to meet their most important responsibilities. Two years ago, we helped guarantee that Americans can keep their health insurance when they change jobs. Last year, we extended health care to up to 5 million children. This year, I challenge Congress to take the next historic steps.

One hundred and sixty million of our fellow citizens are in managed-care plans. These plans save money, and they can improve care. But medical decisions ought to be made by medical doctors, not insurance company accountants. I urge this Congress to reach across the aisle and write into law a consumer bill of rights that says this: You have the right to know all your medical options, not just the cheapest. You have the right to choose the doctor you want for the care you need. You have the right to emergency room care wherever and whenever you need it. You have the right to keep your medical records confidential. Now, traditional care or managed care, every American deserves quality care.

Millions of Americans between the ages of 55 and 65 have lost their health insurance. Some are retired. Some are laid off. Some lose their coverage when their spouses retire. After a lifetime of work, they're left with nowhere to turn. So I ask the Congress: Let these hard-working Americans buy into the Medicare system. It won't add a dime to the deficit, but the peace of mind it will provide will be priceless.

Teen Smoking

Next, we must help parents protect their children from the gravest health threat that they face: an epidemic of teen smoking spread by multimillion-dollar marketing campaigns. I challenge Congress: Let's pass bipartisan, comprehensive legislation that will improve public health, protect our tobacco farmers, and change the way tobacco companies do business forever. Let's do what it takes to bring teen smoking down. Let's raise the price of cigarettes by up to $1.50 a pack over the next 10 years, with penalties on the tobacco industry if it keeps marketing to our children.

Now tomorrow, like every day, 3,000 children will start smoking, and a thousand will die early as a result. Let this Congress be remembered as the Congress that saved their lives.

In the new economy, most parents work harder than ever. They face a constant struggle to balance their obligations to be good workers, and their even more important obligations to be good parents.

The Family and Medical Leave Act was the very first bill I was privileged to sign into law as president in 1993. Since then, about 15 million people have taken advantage of it, and I've met a lot of them all across this country. I ask you to extend the law to cover 10 million more workers, and to give parents time off when they have to go see their children's teachers or take them to the doctor.

Child Care

Child care is the next frontier we must face to enable people to succeed at home and at work. Last year, I co-hosted the very first White House Conference on Child Care with one of our foremost experts, America's first lady. From all corners of America, we heard the same message — without regard to region or income or political affiliation — we've got to raise the quality of child care, we've got to make it safer, we've got to make it more affordable. So here's my plan.

Help families to pay for child care for a million more children; scholarships and background checks for child-care workers, and a new emphasis on early learning; tax credits for businesses that provide child care for their employees; and a larger child-care tax credit for working families.

Now, if you pass my plan, what this means is that a family of four with an income of $35,000 and high child-care costs will no longer pay a single penny of federal income tax.

You know, I think this is such a big issue with me because of my own personal experience. I have often wondered how my mother, when she was a young widow, would have been able to go away to school and get an education and come back and support me, if my grandparents hadn't been able to take care of me. She and I were really very lucky. How many other families have never had that same opportunity? The truth is, we don't know the answer to that question, but we do know what the answer should be. Not a single American family should ever have to choose between the job they need and the child they love.

Law Enforcement

A society rooted in responsibility must provide safe streets, safe schools, and safe neighborhoods. We pursued a strategy of more police, tougher punishment, smarter prevention with crime-fighting partnerships, with local law enforcement and citizen groups, where the rubber hits the road. I can report to you tonight that it's working. Violent crime is down, robbery is down, assault is down, burglary is down for five years in a row all across America. Now, we need to finish the job of putting 100,000 more police on our streets.

Again, I ask Congress to pass a juvenile crime bill that provides more prosecutors and probation officers to crack down on gangs and guns and drugs and bar violent juveniles from buying guns for life. And I ask you to dramatically expand our support for after-school programs. I think every American should know that most juvenile crime is committed between the hours of 3:00 in the afternoon and 8:00 at night. We can keep so many of our children out of trouble in the first place if we give them some place to go other than the streets, and we ought to do it.

Drug use is on the decline. I thank Gen. [Barry] McCaffrey for his leadership, and I thank this Congress for passing the largest antidrug budget in history. Now I ask you to join me in a ground-breaking effort to hire a thousand new Border Patrol agents and to deploy the most sophisticated available new technologies to help close the door on drugs at our borders.

Police, prosecutors, and prevention programs — good as they are, they can't work if our court system doesn't work. Today there are large numbers of vacancies in our federal courts. Here is what the Chief Justice of the United States wrote: "Judicial vacancies cannot remain at such high levels indefinitely without eroding the quality of justice." I simply ask the United States Senate to heed this plea and vote on the highly qualified nominees before you, up or down.

Foreign Friends and Foes

We must exercise responsibility not just at home but around the world. On the eve of a new century, we have the power and the duty to build a new era of peace and security. But make no mistake about it, today's possibilities are not tomorrow's guarantees. America must stand against the poisoned appeals of extreme nationalism. We must combat an unholy axis of new threats from terrorists, international criminals and drug traffickers.

These 21st century predators feed on technology and the free flow of information and ideas and people, and they will be all the more lethal if weapons of mass destruction fall into their hands. To meet these challenges, we are helping to write international rules of the road for the 21st century, protecting those who join the family of nations and isolating those who do not.

Within days, I will ask the Senate for its advice and consent to make Hungary, Poland and the Czech Republic the newest members of NATO. For 50 years, NATO contained communism and kept America and Europe secure. Now these three formerly communist countries have said yes to democracy. I ask the Senate to say yes to them, our new allies. By taking in new members and working closely with new partners, including Russia and Ukraine, NATO can help to assure that Europe is a stronghold for peace in the 21st century.

Bosnia Mission

Next, I will ask Congress to continue its support for our troops and their mission in Bosnia. This Christmas, Hillary and I traveled to Sarajevo with [former] Sen. and Mrs. [Bob] Dole and a bipartisan congressional delegation. We saw children playing in the streets where, two years ago, they were hiding from snipers and shells. The shops were filled with food. The cafes were alive with conversation. The progress there is unmistakable, but it is not yet irreversible.

To take firm root, Bosnia's fragile peace still needs the support of American and allied troops when the current NATO mission ends in June. I think Sen. Dole actually said it best. He said, "This is like being ahead in the fourth quarter of a football game. Now is not the time to walk off the field and forfeit the victory."

I wish all of you could have seen our troops in Tuzla. They're very proud of what they are doing in Bosnia, and we're all very proud of them. One of those brave soldiers is sitting with the first lady tonight — Army Sgt. Michael Tolbert. His father was a decorated Vietnam vet. After college in Colorado, he joined the Army. Last year he led an infantry unit that stopped a mob of extremists from taking over a radio station that is a voice of democracy and tolerance in Bosnia. Thank you very much, Sergeant, for what you represent.

In Bosnia and around the world, our men and women in uniform always do their mission well. Our mission must be to keep them well-trained and ready, to improve their quality of life, and to provide the 21st century weapons they need to defeat any enemy.

Weapons Treaties

I ask Congress to join me in pursuing an ambitious agenda to reduce the serious threat of weapons of mass destruction. This year, four decades after it was first proposed by President Eisenhower, a Comprehensive Nuclear Test Ban is within reach. By ending nuclear testing, we can help to prevent the development of new and more dangerous weapons, and make it more difficult for non-nuclear states to build them. I am pleased to announce that four former chairmen of the Joint Chiefs of Staff — Gens. John Shalikashvili, Colin Powell and David Jones, and Adm. William Crowe — have endorsed this treaty, and I ask the Senate to approve it this year.

Together we must also confront the new hazards of chemical and biological weapons, and the outlaw states, terrorists and organized criminals seeking to acquire them.

Saddam Hussein

[Iraqi leader] Saddam Hussein has spent the better part of this decade, and much of his nation's wealth, not on providing for the Iraqi people, but on developing nuclear, chemical and biological weapons and the missiles to deliver them. The United Nations weapons inspectors have done a truly remarkable job, finding and destroying more of Iraq's arsenal than was destroyed during the entire gulf war. Now, Saddam Hussein wants to stop them from completing their mission.

I know I speak for everyone in this chamber, Republicans and Democrats, when I say to Saddam Hussein, "You cannot defy the will of the world." And when I say to him, "You have used weapons of mass destruction before; we are determined to deny you the capacity to use them again."

Last year the Senate ratified the Chemical Weapons Convention to protect our soldiers and citizens from poison gas. Now we must act to prevent the use of disease as a weapon of war and terror. The Biological Weapons Convention has been in effect for 23 years now. The rules are good, but the enforcement is weak. We must strengthen it with a new international inspection system to detect and deter cheating.

In the months ahead I will pursue our security strategy with old allies in Asia and Europe, and new partners from Africa to India and Pakistan, from South America to China. And from Belfast to Korea to the Middle East, America will continue to stand with those who stand for peace.

United Nations

Finally, it's long past time to make good on our debt to the United Nations. More and more we are working with other nations to achieve common goals. If we want America to lead, we've got to set a good example. As we see so clearly in Bosnia, allies who share our goals can also share our burdens. In this new era, our freedom and independence are actually enriched, not weakened, by our increasing interdependence with other nations. But we have to do our part.

Our founders set America on a permanent course toward a more perfect union. To all of you, I say, it is a journey we can only make together, living as one community.

Campaign Finance

First, we have to continue to reform our government, the instrument of our national community. Everyone knows elections have become too expensive, fueling a fundraising arms race. This year, by March the 6th, at long last the Senate will actually vote on bipartisan campaign finance reform proposed by Sens. [John] McCain [R-Ariz.] and [Russell D.] Feingold [D-Wis.]. Let's be clear: A vote against McCain-Feingold is a vote for soft money and for the status quo. I ask you to strengthen our democracy and pass campaign finance reform this year.

But at least equally important, we have to address the real reason for the explosion in campaign costs: the high cost of media advertising. I will — for the folks watching at home, those were the groans of pain in the audience — I will formally request that the Federal Communications Commission act to provide free or reduced-cost television time for candidates who observe spending limits voluntarily. The airwaves are a public trust, and broadcasters also have to help us in this effort to strengthen our democracy.

Under the leadership of Vice President [Al] Gore, we have reduced the federal payroll by 300,000 workers, cut 16,000 pages of regulation, eliminated hundreds of programs and improved the operations of virtually every government agency. But we can do more.

IRS Overhaul

Like every taxpayer, I'm outraged by the reports of abuses by the IRS. We need some changes there: new citizen advocacy panels, a stronger taxpayer advocate, phone lines open 24 hours a day, relief for innocent taxpayers.

Last year, by an overwhelming bipartisan margin, the House of Representatives passed sweeping IRS reforms. This bill must not now languish in the Senate. Tonight I ask the Senate: Follow the House; pass the bipartisan package as your first order of business.

I hope to goodness before I finish I can think of something to say follow the Senate on, so I'll be out of trouble!

A nation that lives as a community must value all its communities. For the past five years, we have worked to bring the spark of private enterprise to inner-city and poor rural areas with community development banks, more commercial loans into poor neighborhoods, cleanup of polluted sites for development. Under the continued leadership of the vice president, we propose to triple the number of empowerment zones to give business incentives to invest in those areas.

We should also give poor families more help to move into homes of their own, and we should use tax cuts to spur the construction of more low-income housing.

Last year this Congress took strong action to help the District of Columbia. Let us renew our resolve to make our capital city a great city for all who live and visit here.

Our cities are the vibrant hubs of great metropolitan areas. They are still the gateway for new immigrants from every continent who come here to work for their own American dreams. Let's keep our cities going strong into the 21st century. They're a very important part of our future.

Environmental Challenges

Our communities are only as healthy as the air our children breathe, the water they drink, the Earth they will inherit. Last year we put in place the toughest-ever controls on smog and soot. We moved to protect Yellowstone, the Everglades, Lake Tahoe. We expanded every community's right to know about toxics that threaten their children.

Just yesterday, our food safety plan took effect, using new science to protect consumers from dangers like *E coli* and salmonella.

Tonight, I ask you to join me in launching a new Clean Water initiative, a far-reaching effort to clean our rivers, our lakes and our coastal waters for our children.

Our overriding environmental challenge tonight is the worldwide problem of climate change, global warming, the gathering crisis that requires worldwide action. The vast majority of scientists have concluded unequivocally that if we don't reduce the emission of greenhouse gases at some point in the next century, we'll disrupt our climate and put our children and grandchildren at risk. This past December, America led the world to reach a historic agreement committing our nation to reduce greenhouse gas emissions through market forces, new technologies, energy efficiency.

We have it in our power to act right here, right now. I propose $6 billion in tax cuts, in research and development, to encourage innovation, renewable energy, fuel-efficient cars, energy-efficient homes. Every time we have acted to heal our environment, pessimists have told us it would hurt the economy. Well, today our economy is the strongest in a generation, and our environment is the cleanest in a generation. We have always found a way to clean the environment and grow the economy at the same time. And when it comes to global warming, we'll do it again.

Racial Discrimination

Finally, community means living by the defining American value, the ideal heard 'round the world: that we're all created equal. Throughout our history, we haven't always honored that ideal, and we've never fully lived up to it. Often it's easier to believe that our differences matter more than what we have in common. It may be easier, but it's wrong. . . .

In our day and generation to make sure that America truly becomes one nation, what do we have to do? We're becoming more and more and more diverse. Do you believe we can become one nation? The answer cannot be to dwell on our differences, but to build on our shared values. And we all cherish family and faith, freedom and responsibility. We all want our children to grow up in the world where their talents are matched by their opportunities. I've launched this national initiative on race to help us recognize our common interests and to bridge the opportunity gaps that are keeping us from becoming one America. Let us begin by recognizing what we still must overcome: Discrimination against any American is un-American. We must vigorously enforce the laws that make it illegal. I ask your help to end the backlog at the Equal Employment Opportunity Commission. Sixty thousand of our fellow citizens are waiting in line for justice, and we should act now to end their wait.

We should also recognize that the greatest progress we can make toward building one America lies in the progress we make for all Americans, without regard to race. When we open the doors of college to all Americans, when we rid all our streets of crime, when there are jobs available to people from all our neighborhoods, when we make sure all parents have the child care they need, we're helping to build one nation.

We in this chamber and in this government must do all we can to address the continuing American challenge to build one America. But we'll only move forward if all our fellow citizens, including every one of you at home watching tonight, is also committed to this cause.

We must work together, learn togeth-

Texts

er, live together, serve together. On the forge of common enterprise, Americans of all backgrounds can hammer out a common identity.

We see it today in the United States military, in the Peace Corps, in AmeriCorps. Wherever people of all races and backgrounds come together in a shared endeavor and get a fair chance, we do just fine. With shared values and meaningful opportunities and honest communications and citizen service, we can unite a diverse people in freedom and mutual respect. We are many; we must be one.

In that spirit, let us lift our eyes to the new millennium. How will we mark that passage? It just happens once every thousand years. This year, Hillary and I launched the White House Millennium Program to promote America's creativity and innovation and to preserve our heritage and culture into the 21st century. Our culture lives in every community, and every community has places of historic value that tell our stories as Americans. We should protect them. I am proposing a public-private partnership to advance our arts and humanities and to celebrate the millennium by saving America's treasures great and small.

Scientific Research

And while we honor the past, let us imagine the future. Now, think about this. The entire store of human knowledge now doubles every five years. In the 1980s, scientists identified the gene causing cystic fibrosis; it took nine years. Last year, scientists located the gene that causes Parkinson's disease — in only nine days! Within a decade, "gene chips" will offer a road map for prevention of illnesses throughout a lifetime. Soon, we'll be able to carry all the phone calls on Mother's Day on a single strand of fiber the width of a human hair. A child born in 1998 may well live to see the 22nd century. Tonight, as part of our gift to the millennium, I propose a 21st century research fund for path-breaking scientific inquiry, the largest funding increase in history for the National Institutes of Health, the National Science Foundation, and the National Cancer Institute. We have already discovered genes for breast cancer and diabetes. I ask you to support this initiative so ours will be the generation that finally wins the war against cancer and begins a revolution in our fight against all deadly diseases.

As important as all this scientific progress is, we must continue to see that science serves humanity, not the other way around. We must prevent the misuse of genetic tests to discriminate against any American; and we must ratify the ethical consensus of the scientific and religious communities and ban the cloning of human beings.

We should enable all the world's people to explore the far reaches of cyberspace. Think of this: The first time I made a State of the Union speech to you, only a handful of physicists used the World Wide Web — literally just a handful of people. Now in schools and libraries, homes and businesses, millions and millions of Americans surf the Net every day.

We must give parents the tools they need to help protect their children from inappropriate material on the Net, but we also must make sure that we protect the exploding, global commercial potential of the Internet. We can do the kinds of things that we need to do and still protect our kids. For one thing, I ask Congress to step up support for building the next generation Internet. It's getting kind of clogged, you know. And the next generation Internet will operate at speeds up to a thousand times faster than today.

Space Exploration

Even as we explore this inner space, in the new millennium we're going to open new frontiers in outer space. Throughout all history, humankind has had only one place to call home — our planet Earth. Beginning this year, 1998, men and women from 16 countries will build a foothold in the heavens — the international space station. With its vast expanses, scientists and engineers will actually set sail on an uncharted sea of limitless mystery and unlimited potential. And this October, a true American hero, a veteran pilot of 149 combat missions and one five-hour space flight that changed the world, will return to the heavens. Godspeed, John Glenn!

John, you will carry with you America's hopes, and on your uniform once again you will carry America's flag, marking the unbroken connection between the deeds of America's past and the daring of America's future. Nearly 200 years ago, a tattered flag, its broad stripes and bright stars still gleaming through the smoke of a fierce battle, moved Francis Scott Key to scribble a few words on the back of an envelope, the words that became our national anthem. Today that Star-Spangled Banner, along with the Declaration of Independence, the Constitution and the Bill of Rights, are on display just a short walk from here. They are America's treasures. And we must also save them for the ages. I ask all Americans to support our project to restore all our treasures so that the generations of the 21st century can see for themselves the images and the words that are the old and continuing glory of America, an America that has continued to rise through every age against every challenge, a people of great works and greater possibilities, who have always, always found the wisdom and strength to come together as one nation, to widen the circle of opportunity, to deepen the meaning of our freedom, to form that more perfect union.

Let that be our gift to the 21st century.

God bless you, and God bless the United States. ◆

Republican Response

Lott: Fighting for the Family Is GOP's Top Priority

Following is a transcript of the Jan. 27 Republican response to the State of the Union address by Senate Majority Leader Trent Lott, R-Miss., as provided by the Federal News Service:

MAJORITY LEADER TRENT LOTT: Tonight I'd like to share with you our plans here in the Congress for a safer, stronger and more prosperous America. Those plans are shaped by our commitment to family, to faith and to freedom. And they highlight some real differences between the Republican Party and the president concerning what government should do and how much of your money government should take; big government or families, more taxes or more freedom.

We believe the choice is clear. The first priority of your representatives in Washington must be to fight for the interests of the American family. That's one of the first things — that's why one of the first things we'll tackle is the real reform that's necessary for the IRS. I'll have more to say about IRS later on, but the bottom line is this: We're going to stop the abuses the IRS has been inflicting on the American taxpayers. You've got our word on it.

Also, we'll be building on the progress of the last few years, when our Republican Congress, working with the nation's governors, took some historic first steps. We took the first step in transforming welfare into workfare. We started reducing taxes, especially for families with children. And, with considerable difficulty, we finally worked out a long-term agreement with the president for a balanced budget.

We protected Medicare. And in that same way, we're going to protect Medicare this year against any changes that would imperil its financial stability. We strengthened education opportunities for disabled youngsters, launched a long-overdue reform of the nation's troubled foster care system, made adoption easier and encouraged alternatives to abortion.

We proved that people of goodwill and of strong faith can work together to deal with the problems that face our nation and our neighborhoods. But we have only just begun the difficult job of stopping big government, making it more responsive and, perhaps hardest of all, rebuilding the trust you used to have in your elected officials.

That's especially important when it comes to education, to taxes, and to the twin plagues of drugs and crime. Those are the three areas where the American people are most dissatisfied and where our freedom is most threatened.

Parents and good teachers as well are dissatisfied with schools where kids don't learn, and in many cases where they aren't even safe. When one-quarter of our children — one out of every four in the high schools — can barely read, isn't it obvious that the current system just isn't working?

I know we're all fed up with the criminal justice system that has tragically failed to halt the poisonous epidemic of drugs that is undermining family life in our country. Violent crime is turning the land of the free into the land of the fearful.

Today's workers and today's savers are angry and disillusioned with a tax code that benefits only tax lawyers and big government. Let's take a look at the typical family budget. The typical family pays more than 38 percent in its income in taxes. That's nearly 40 cents of every dollar. That's not just bad policy; it's immoral.

Our tax system should not penalize marriage, hard work or savings, not to mention your efforts just to keep up with the cost of living. We believe these high taxes mean less freedom overall. And yet President Clinton now wants the government to spend billions of dollars more. But I don't have to tell you; if government spends more, you'll wind up getting taxed more. You know that. He knows that.

Instead, Republicans want you, the people who work hard for the money, to keep more of what you earn. The president seems to think that big government can solve all your children's problems if you'll just give government more of your money and more control over your lives. I think that's nonsense.

We think the best things for safe, healthy children are healthy, stable families, not more government programs that require parents to work longer, to take home less and to spend less time with their children. That's why we fought for the $500-per-child tax credit last year.

Once again, the choice is really quite clear: Big government or families; more taxes or more freedom. The American people elected us in the Congress to listen to you and then to lead. So while we listen respectfully to the president's ideas, we cannot wait on them.

One example is the drug crisis. With all due respect, for the past five years we've had all of the wrong kinds of signals. It took the president four years to admit the need to reduce the tax burden on the American people, as we finally did in the Balanced Budget Act in 1997. That was a welcome reversal of the pile-on-the-taxes approach in his first four years in office.

Overtaxed, Overgoverned

But you know that Americans are still overtaxed, overregulated and overgoverned. This chart shows how the income of the federal government over the last 30 years has gone up almost 1,000 percent. But during the same period, family incomes rose only half as much. Government has gotten fat while families are working overtime just to stay where they were.

We believe hard-working Americans deserve a break. So our focus in 1998 will be to increase family income by cutting taxes and making government more accountable for the way it spends your money. But tax relief is only the first step.

As I said earlier, the only way to limit government and expand individual freedom is to eliminate the IRS as we know it today. It is morally wrong for a free people to live in fear of any government agency. It is morally wrong for a citizen in a democracy to be presumed guilty until proven innocent. And that's the way it is at IRS.

Tax Code Changes

But IRS reform also is not enough by itself. The real problem lies with the tax code. It's too long, it is too complicated, and it's simply unfair. It punishes you if you are achieving things. It discourages work and savings and innovation.

As Republicans, we pledge to replace the tax code with a new system that is fair, consistent, easy to understand, and less frightening to the American taxpayer, a tax code that will end the fear and encourage more savings and investment.

Because the Republican balanced-budget plan is working now, we should commit here and now not to spend any budget surplus on unnecessary government programs. If there is a surplus, our priority should be to use part of that to pay down the national debt and return the rest to you, the taxpayer. After all, it is your money.

Like those proposals, our education plan proposes fundamental change from what we now have. As a father and as a prospective grandfather, I realize that nothing is more important than education of our young people. Washington today has more than 750 education programs in 39 different bureaucracies. That just doesn't make sense. And it doesn't make sense for Washington to tax the people in your community and then give the money back, with strings attached, of course.

We want to cut those strings and remove the out-of-date rules and restrictions that hold back our schools from the future. For example, if your community needs to build new schools or rehabilitate old ones, you should be able to do that. If you want to offer merit pay for great teachers, you should be able to do that, too.

State Education Testing

We've heard a lot from the president about testing. But he thinks Washington should administer the tests. Wrong again. We think that you — the parents, the teachers, the local officials — should do the job. Republicans in Congress strongly support that kind of state testing, just as we support an even more important kind: periodic testing for teachers.

Now, you won't hear much about that from the president. On this subject, the president disagrees with us and we disagree with him. But good teachers, like my mother, bless her heart, who taught public school for 19 years, don't object to testing. They want it.

They say teacher testing will be a key step in implementing the kind of merit pay program that attracts star teachers.

They also say even the best teachers can't get good results when their school is a dangerous and violent place. We hope the president this year will finally see the wisdom in our proposal to give freedom of choice to low-income families whose children are stuck in dead-end, drug-ridden schools. Because we care so deeply about those families, we want them to have the same option exercised by President Clinton and Vice President Gore, who chose the schools for their children.

Parental choice and involvement are absolutely essential. But choice in education doesn't mean abandoning our public schools. It simply means moving decision-making away from Washington and back to you, at your family's kitchen table. That's the first and most important step to launch in an era of education renewal that will equip our schools and our students to lead America and the world into the new century.

But don't forget, today's young people confront a danger even worse than poor

Texts

education. Teen drug abuse has become epidemic, and there are no safe havens from this insidious modern plague. Overall, teenage drug use has nearly doubled since 1992. And perhaps most frightening of all, nearly half of all 17-year-olds say they could buy marijuana in just an hour's time. Like the president, I want to stop youth smoking. But narcotics is a problem that is a far greater threat to teenagers.

First, to solve the drug crisis, we have to start with the family, the school, and with our churches and synagogues. Studies clearly show that teens in families that eat together, play together and, yes, pray together, are the ones least likely to try drugs. When the battle against drug abuse is first waged at home, the war is half-won.

Second, schools must be drug-free. We must demand absolute accountability and zero tolerance for any drug abuse on school grounds.

And third, there is the critical role for the federal government. We simply have got to be more aggressive in guarding our national borders. Along with that, we must be more vigilant in arresting and prosecuting anyone — yes, anyone — who sells this poison to our young people.

And fourth, it's time to get tough on society's predators. We must end parole for violent criminals, crack down on juvenile criminals, increase prison capacity and make the death penalty a real threat. And we need to impose mandatory penalties for crimes committed with a gun.

If we're honestly committed to protecting the innocent, we must do more to punish the guilty. By combining national leadership here in Washington with community activism, we can and we will save America one child and one neighborhood at a time.

Child Care

We don't pretend to have all the answers here in Washington. In fact, we don't have them. But I guarantee you we will ask the right questions this time. For example, there is the issue of child care. We say give families more flexibility in the way they work and care for their children. But how do we do it?

Well, first and foremost, cut tax burdens on the American family. Don't force both parents to work, and work longer hours, when they could have more time at home with their kids. Give stay-at-home parents the same tax breaks and benefits available to parents who use day care. After all, all moms work, whether at home or in an outside job.

Let employers negotiate with their employees for flex time and comp time arrangements. Help small businesses provide on-site day care. And make it easier and more profitable for older Americans to provide child care for growing families.

We're talking about common-sense approaches here because, as parents and grandparents ourselves, we've learned it takes parents and parental choice to raise a child in today's world.

Foreign Affairs

Of course, there are dangers in today's world that demand strong national leadership. You know, just last week Pope John Paul's visit to Cuba reminded us once again that despite the collapse of communism, the future remains very uncertain over much of the globe.

And let me make one thing perfectly clear tonight to [Iraqi leader] Saddam Hussein or anyone else who needs to be told: Despite any current controversy, this Congress will vigorously support the president in full defense of America's interests throughout the world.

By the same token, though, we ask the president to work with us in considering ways to stop the threats of terrorism, international narcotics and the spread of weapons of mass destruction. You know, as hard as it is to believe, right now our country has no national defense against missiles carrying nuclear, chemical or biological warheads. Those who hate America most in Iraq, in Iran and elsewhere, they know that.

President Clinton, I urge you to reconsider your opposition to having a national missile defense for America. Join us in taking the steps that will actually deploy a national missile defense system for the United States.

More Reforms

Now, there are at least a dozen other important subjects the Congress will deal with in the months ahead; for example, ending the dreadful practice of "partial birth" abortions. I urge our Democratic colleagues in the Senate to help us override the president's second veto of that legislation.

In addition, we're committed to more positive reforms in health care, protection of workers' rights and their pay checks, reform of bankruptcy pay check laws, and legislation to combat teen smoking. All the while, we're going to concentrate on what we call oversight in the Congress, which means finding out why you aren't getting your money's worth from government and why so much of your hard-earned money goes for programs filled with fraud and abuse.

For instance, last year the administration admitted it paid out $23 billion in ineligible Medicare claims — that's in one year alone — and spent another $5 billion in improper payments in just one welfare program. That's intolerable. We intend to make government accountable from the classrooms to the courts, from the clerks to the president's cabinet, from the post office to the presidency.

Now, this isn't a matter of Republicans vs. Democrats. No, it's a question of whether we will learn from past mistakes in order to restore the great institutions and cherished values — family, faith and freedom — that for so long have held us together as a nation.

The president was right tonight to point out our heroes. But there are some others we should not forget about. Twenty-five years ago next month, a small band of Americans returned home after long captivity in Southeast Asia. Some were broken in body, but never broken in spirit. Those returning prisoners of war reminded us, through our cheers and our tears, just how precious we hold our freedom.

Now the world has changed greatly, and greatly for the better, in those 25 years. But we must remember why it changed, why we can now look to the century ahead with high hopes, and just why we are the envy of the world. The reason is that Americans — we, the people — have been willing to sacrifice everything to protect our families, to practice our faith and to defend our freedom.

What those heroes fought to preserve, we must now work to recover and to strengthen by renewing American education, restoring the security of the American family, and rebuilding the kind of government that works with you and for you, the kind of government you can trust.

Thank you for listening. Good night, and bless you all. ◆

Clinton, in Veto Message, Calls for Better Safety Net For Farmers

Following is the text of President Clinton's Oct. 7 veto message on HR 4101, the agriculture appropriations bill.

TO THE HOUSE OF REPRESENTATIVES:

I am returning herewith without my approval, HR 4101, the "Agriculture, Rural Development, Food and Drug Administration, and Related Agencies Appropriations Act, 1999." I am vetoing this bill because it fails to address adequately the crisis now gripping our Nation's farm community.

I firmly believe and have stated often that the Federal Government must play an important role in strengthening the farm safety net. This appropriations bill provides an opportunity each year for the government to take steps to help hardworking farmers achieve a decent living, despite the misfortune of bad weather, crop disease, collapsing markets, or other forces that affect their livelihoods. It is especially necessary for the government to act this year, with prices dropping precipitously, crops destroyed by flood, drought, and disease, and where many farmers will see their net income drop by as much as 40 percent below a 5-year average.

Two years ago, when I signed the "Freedom to Farm Bill" [PL 104-127], I made clear that it did not provide an adequate safety net for our nation's farmers. There is no better proof of that bill's shortcomings than the hardship in America's farm country this year. Our farm families are facing their worst crisis in a decade.

My administration has already taken steps to address this crisis. In July, we announced the purchase of $250 million of wheat to export to hungry people around the world. In August, I signed legislation to speed up farm program payments. But in the face of a growing emergency for our nation's farmers, we must do more to ensure that American farmers can continue to provide, for years to come, the safest and least expensive food in the world. Last month, I sent to the Congress a request for $2.3 billion in emergency aid for our farmers, and I supported Senator [Tom] Daschle's [D-S.D.] and [Tom] Harkin's [D-Iowa] proposal to boost farm income by lifting the cap on marketing loan rates.

I am extremely disappointed that the Congress has reacted to this agriculture emergency situation by sending me a bill that fails to provide an adequate safety net for our farmers. I have repeatedly stated that I would veto any emergency farm assistance bill if it did not adequately address our farmers' immediate needs, and this bill does not do enough.

The lack of sufficient emergency aid for farmers in this bill is particularly problematic in light of the bill's other provisions that affect farmers and their rural communities. Cutting edge agricultural research is absolutely essential to improve our farmers' productivity and to maintain their advantage over our competitors around the world. But this bill eliminates the $120 million in competitive research grants for this year that I strongly supported and signed into law just last June.

It also blocks the $60 million from the Fund for Rural America provided through that same bill, preventing needed additional rural development funds that would help our nation's rural communities to diversify their economies and improve their quality of life. The bill also cuts spending for our food safety initiative in half, denying funds for research, public education, and other food safety improvements.

Many of our most vulnerable farmers have also had to face an obstacle that no one in America ever should have to confront: racial discrimination. Over 1,000 minority farmers have filed claims of discrimination by USDA's farm loan programs in the 1980s and early 1990s that the statute of limitations bars from being addressed. While I am pleased that this legislation contains a provision waiving the statute of limitations, I am disappointed that it does not contain the language included in the Senate's version of this bill, which accelerates the resolution of the cases, provides claimants with a fair and full court review if they so choose, and covers claims stemming from USDA's housing loan programs.

Therefore, as I return this bill, I again call on the Congress to send me a comprehensive plan, before this session ends, that adequately responds to the very real needs of our farmers at this difficult time.

WILLIAM J. CLINTON
THE WHITE HOUSE,
October 7, 1998

Linking Payment of U.N. Dues With Curbs on Family Planning Is 'Unacceptable,' Clinton Says

Following is the text of President Clinton's Oct. 21 veto message on HR 1757, the State Department authorization bill.

TO THE HOUSE OF REPRESENTATIVES:

I am returning herewith without my approval HR 1757, the "Foreign Affairs Reform and Restructuring Act of 1998."

I take this action for several reasons, most importantly, because the Congress has included in this legislation unacceptable restrictions on international family planning programs and threatened our leadership in the world community by tying our payment of dues to the United Nations and other international organizations to these unrelated family planning issues.

Current law, with which Administration policy is fully consistent, already prohibits the use of Federal funds to pay for abortions abroad and for lobbying on abortion issues. This bill would go beyond those limits. One provision would deny U.S. Government funding for family planning programs carried out by foreign non-governmental organizations (NGOs) that use their own funds to perform abortions even though the overall result of these NGO family planning programs is to reduce the incidence of abortion. Although the bill allows the President to waive this restriction, use of the waiver would also cripple many programs by limiting annual spending for international family planning to $356 million, $44 million below the amount available for Fiscal Year 1998.

A second provision would attempt to restrict the free speech of foreign NGOs by prohibiting funding for those that use their own funds to engage in any activity intended to alter the laws of a foreign country either to promote or to deter abortion. The bill would even ban drafting and distributing material or public statements on abortion. The bill does not contain a waiver for this restriction.

These restrictions and the funding limit would severely jeopardize the ability of the United States to meet the growing demand for family planning and other critical health services in developing countries. By denying funding to organizations that offer a wide range of safe and effective family planning services, the bill would increase unwanted pregnancies and lead to more abortions than would otherwise be the case.

I am also deeply concerned that the Congress has effectively tied these unacceptable restrictions on international family planning to payment of legitimate U.S. arrears to the United Nations and other international organizations. A strong United Nations, with the United States playing a leadership role, is in our national interest. Payment of our dues to the United Nations is essential to our ability to lead. There are strongly held beliefs on both sides of the debate over international population policy. These issues ought to be considered separately on their own merits; they should not be permitted to hinder U.S. obligations to the world community.

The package authorizing arrears payments linked to U.N. reforms was the result of good-faith negotiations between my Administration and the Congress more than a year and a half ago. Unfortunately, due to the passage of time, some of these conditions are now outdated and are no longer achievable. In particular, the fact that the U.N. has concluded negotiations on assessment rates for the next 3 years has significantly decreased our ability to negotiate a limitation on the U.S. assessed share of the U.N. regular budget below 22 percent. Furthermore, the increase in contested arrears during this period requires that the United States have additional flexibility in obtaining a contested arrears account. While many of the U.N. reform benchmarks in the package remain acceptable, significant revisions are required, and I look forward to working with the Congress next year to secure the payment of our arrears and an achievable package of U.N. reforms.

The Bill contains important and carefully negotiated authority to reorganize the foreign affairs agencies and other basic authorities for these agencies. Many of these provisions were supported by my Administration, and I am pleased that they have been included in the Omnibus Consolidated and Emergency Supplemental Appropriations Act for FY 1999.

For the foregoing reasons, I am compelled to return HR 1757 without my approval.

WILLIAM J. CLINTON
THE WHITE HOUSE,
October 21, 1998

'Critical Lapse in Judgment'

Following is the text of President Clinton's Aug. 17 address to the nation, as transcribed by the Federal Document Clearing House:

Good evening.

This afternoon, in this room, from this chair, I testified before the Office of Independent Counsel and the grand jury.

I answered their questions truthfully, including questions about my private life, questions no American citizen would ever want to answer.

Still, I must take complete responsibility for all my actions, both public and private. And that is why I am speaking to you tonight.

As you know, in a deposition in January, I was asked questions about my relationship with Monica Lewinsky. While my answers were legally accurate, I did not volunteer information.

Indeed, I did have a relationship with Ms. Lewinsky that was not appropriate. In fact, it was wrong. It constituted a critical lapse in judgment and a personal failure on my part for which I am solely and completely responsible.

But I told the grand jury today, and I say to you now that at no time did I ask anyone to lie, to hide or destroy evidence or to take any other unlawful action.

I know that my public comments and my silence about this matter gave a false impression. I misled people, including even my wife. I deeply regret that.

I can only tell you I was motivated by many factors. First, by a desire to protect myself from the embarrassment of my own conduct.

I was also very concerned about protecting my family. The fact that these questions were being asked in a politically inspired lawsuit, which has since been dismissed, was a consideration too.

In addition, I had real and serious concerns about an independent counsel investigation that began with private business dealings 20 years ago, dealings, I might add, about which an independent federal agency found no evidence of any wrongdoing by me or my wife over two years ago.

The independent counsel investigation moved on to my staff and friends, then into my private life. And now the investigation itself is under investigation.

This has gone on too long, cost too much and hurt too many innocent people.

Now, this matter is between me, the two people I love most — my wife and our daughter — and our God. I must put it right, and I am prepared to do whatever it takes to do so.

Nothing is more important to me personally. But it is private, and I intend to reclaim my family life for my family. It's nobody's business but ours.

Even presidents have private lives. It is time to stop the pursuit of personal destruction and the prying into private lives and get on with our national life.

Our country has been distracted by this matter for too long, and I take my responsibility for my part in all of this. That is all I can do.

Now it is time — in fact, it is past time — to move on.

We have important work to do — real opportunities to seize, real problems to solve, real security matters to face.

RELATED TEXTS

Independent Counsel's Report	D-15
White House Response	D-22
Clinton Grand Jury Testimony	D-23
Judiciary Panel Statements	D-29
Counsels' Statements	D-34
Hyde, Conyers, Starr Statements	D-37
Democratic Reaction to Vote	D-40
Articles of Impeachment	D-42
Judiciary Panel's Report	D-44

And so tonight, I ask you to turn away from the spectacle of the past seven months, to repair the fabric of our national discourse and to return our attention to all the challenges and all the promise of the next American century.

Thank you for watching. And good night. ◆

Lieberman, Colleagues Respond

From the Sept. 3 floor statement of Sen. Joseph I. Lieberman, D-Conn.:

"Whether he or we think it fair or not, the reality is in 1998 that a president's private life is public. . . . The president is not just the elected leader of our country. He is, as presidential scholar Clinton Rossiter observed, 'the one-man distillation of the American people. . . .' The president is a role model who, because of his prominence and the moral authority that emanates from his office, sets standards of behavior for the people he serves. . . .

"In this case, the president apparently had extramarital relations with an employee half his age and did so in the workplace, in the vicinity of the Oval Office. Such behavior is not just inappropriate. It is immoral. And it is harmful, for it sends a message of what is acceptable behavior to the larger American family, particularly to our children, which is as influential as the negative message that is communicated by the entertainment culture. . . .

"I believe that the president could have lessened the harm his relationship with Ms. Lewinsky has caused if he had acknowledged his mistake and spoken with candor about it to the American people shortly after it became public in January. But, as we now know, he chose not to do this.

"This deception is particularly troubling because it was not just a reflexive and, in many ways, understandable human act of concealment to protect himself and his family from what he called the embarrassment of his own conduct . . . but rather it was the intentional and premeditated decision to do so. . . .

"The transgressions the president has admitted to are too consequential for us to walk away and leave the impression for our children today and for our posterity tomorrow that what he acknowledges he did within the White House is acceptable behavior for our nation's leader. On the contrary, as I have said, it is wrong and unacceptable, and should be followed by some measure of public rebuke and accountability.

"We in Congress, elected representatives of all the American people, are surely capable institutionally of expressing such disapproval through a resolution of reprimand or censure of the president for his misconduct. But it is premature to do so, as my colleagues of both parties seem to agree, until we have received the report of the independent counsel and the White House's response to it.

"In the same way, it seems to me that talk of impeachment and resignation at this time is unjust and unwise. . . ."

Sen. Bob Kerrey, D-Neb., immediately after Lieberman's speech:

"I wish to join him and say that the president has got to go far further than he did in his speech to the nation. This is not just inappropriate behavior. This is not a private matter."

Texts

Sen. Daniel Patrick Moynihan, D-N.Y., following Kerrey:

"In the aftermath of the president's speech on Aug. 17, I commented that it was not adequate. But it was not until just this moment that the full measure of that inadequacy was presented to us in the context of the needs of the nation, of the profound moral consequences that will arise not just from what has happened but from what might happen if we do not proceed with the measure of moral compass, but also with a capacity to understand we are all sinners."

President Clinton was asked at a photo opportunity Sept. 4 in Dublin, Ireland, if he had any comments on Lieberman's remarks. His response:

"I've been briefed on them, and basically I agree with what he said. I've already said that I made a bad mistake, it was indefensible, and I'm sorry about it. So I have nothing else to say except that I can't disagree with anyone else who wants to be critical of what I have already acknowledged was indefensible."

'Reaping the Whirlwind'

Excerpts of the Sept. 9 floor speech of Sen. Robert C. Byrd, D-W.Va.:

"The pressure on the Congress is escalating. Talk of impeachment is in the air, along with suggestions of resolutions of reprimand and censure. Some have even suggested that we ought to get on with impeachment and get this thing behind us.

"There had to come a time sooner or later when the boil would be lanced. The problem is that with the lancing a hemorrhaging may be only one of those continuing symptoms of an even greater lancing, perhaps even an amputation, that still lurks in the shadows up ahead.

"There is no question but that the president himself has sown the wind and he is reaping the whirlwind. His televised speech of Aug. 17 heaped hot coals upon himself — coals causing wounds that continue to inflame and burn ever more deeply. Coming as the speech did so soon after the president's appearance before the grand jury, his words were ill-timed, ill-formed and ill-advised. . . .

"In this instance, the president himself has by his own actions and his own words thrown the first stone at himself, and thus, made himself vulnerable to the stoning by others.

"What a sorrowful spectacle!

"To maintain that presidents have private lives is, of course, not to be denied. But the Oval Office of the White House is not a private office. It is where much of the business of the nation is conducted daily. . . .

"Former President Nixon, in an earlier tragedy for the nation and for all of us who were here and lived through it, tried the same thing — delay, delay, delay and counterattack, attack, attack. . . . Time seems to be turning backwards in its flight. And many of the mistakes that President Nixon made are being made all over again.

"As we find ourselves being brought nearer and nearer, as it would seem, to a yawning abyss, I urge that we all step back, and give ourselves and the country a little pause in which to reflect and meditate before we cast ourselves headlong over the precipice. To say we ought to get on with impeachment and get this thing behind us is a bold thing to say. But boldness to the point of cavalierness can come back to haunt us. . . .

"I also suggest that putting this thing behind us is not going to be an easy thing to do. If Congress reaches that stage of voting on articles of impeachment, it is going to be a traumatic experience for all of us, both here in this city and throughout the country. . . .

"There is a constitutional process in place. We should let it work. It is my suggestion that everyone should exercise some self-restraint against calling for impeachment or censure or for the president's resignation. Who knows? I may do that before it's all over. But not now. . . .

"Let us, as senators, remember that if the House ultimately votes to impeach this president, then we all should be careful not to attempt to influence the other body — and when I say we all, I have reference to ourselves and to the executive branch and to the media. . . .

"We must not compromise any final decision by rushing to judgment in advance. I trust that we all will weigh carefully in our own minds and hearts the possible consequences to the nation of our words and actions and judgments if that duty ultimately should beckon us. . . .

"And so I respectfully urge everyone in this town to calm down for a little while and contemplate with seriousness the impact that our actions may have on the well-being of the nation — your children, my grandchildren, our children, our grandchildren — and the paralysis we may be spawning if we continue to be mesmerized with each new rumor and each new titillating whisper." ◆

Gingrich Calls for Decorum

On Sept. 10, House Speaker Newt Gingrich, R-Ga., took the chair to remind members of the House's rules regarding references to the president. He did so, he said, because this was the first time the House had considered an impeachment-related matter since proceedings were first broadcast in 1978. Excerpts follow:

"Members engaging in debate must abstain from language that is personally offensive toward the president, including references to various types of unethical behavior. Rulings in this Congress, which will be annotated in the accompanying Section 370 of the House Rules and Manual, include references to alleged criminal conduct. This documented restriction extends to referencing extraneous material personally abusive of the president that would be improper if spoken as the member's own words. . . .

"On Jan. 27, 1909, the House adopted a report in response to improper references in debate to the president. That report read, in part, as follows: 'The freedom of speech in debate in the House of Representatives should never be denied or abridged. But freedom of speech in debate does not mean license to indulge in personal abuses or ridicule. The right of members of the two houses of Congress to criticize the official acts of the president and other executive officers is beyond question. But this right is subject to proper rules requiring decorum in debate.' . . .

"In addition to relying on the precedents of the House, the chair would comment on the importance of comity and integrity of debate in the House and in an electronic age. . . . In 1974 there were no allegations of personal misconduct on the part of the president called to order on the floor before or during proceedings in executive session of the Committee on the Judiciary.

"Indeed, it is only during the actual pendency of proceedings in impeachment as the pending business on the floor of the House that remarks in debate may include references to personal misconduct on the part of the president. While an inquiry is under way in committee, the committee is the proper forum for examination and debate of such allegations. . . .

"This is not to say that the president is beyond criticism in debate or that members are prohibited from expressing opinions about executive policy or competence to hold office. It is permissible in debate to challenge the president on matters of policy; the difference is one between political criticism and personally offensive criticism. . . ." ◆

Independent Counsel's Report: Clinton 'Lied Under Oath And Obstructed Justice'

The following are excerpts from the report submitted by Independent Counsel Kenneth W. Starr to the House on Sept. 9 and released Sept. 11. The excerpts are taken from the section laying out "eleven possible grounds for impeachment" of President Clinton.

Pursuant to Section 595(c) of Title 28, the Office of Independent Counsel hereby submits substantial and credible information that President Clinton obstructed justice during the *Jones v. Clinton* sexual harassment lawsuit by lying under oath and concealing evidence of his relationship with a young White House intern and federal employee, Monica Lewinsky.

After a federal criminal investigation of the President's actions began in January 1998, the President lied under oath to the grand jury and obstructed justice during the grand jury investigation. There also is substantial and credible information that the President's actions with respect to Monica Lewinsky constitute an abuse of authority inconsistent with the President's constitutional duty to faithfully execute the laws.

There is substantial and credible information supporting the following eleven possible grounds for impeachment:

1. President Clinton lied under oath in his civil case when he denied a sexual affair, a sexual relationship, or sexual relations with Monica Lewinsky.

2. President Clinton lied under oath to the grand jury about his sexual relationship with Ms. Lewinsky.

3. In his civil deposition, to support his false statement about the sexual relationship, President Clinton also lied under oath about being alone with Ms. Lewinsky and about the many gifts exchanged between Ms. Lewinsky and him.

4. President Clinton lied under oath in his civil deposition about his discussions with Ms. Lewinsky concerning her involvement in the *Jones* case.

5. During the *Jones* case, the President obstructed justice and had an understanding with Ms. Lewinsky to jointly conceal the truth about their relationship by concealing gifts subpoenaed by Ms. Jones's attorneys.

6. During the *Jones* case, the President obstructed justice and had an understanding with Ms. Lewinsky to jointly conceal the truth of their relationship from the judicial process by a scheme that included the following means: (i) Both the President and Ms. Lewinsky understood that they would lie under oath in the Jones case about their sexual relationship; (ii) the President suggested to Ms. Lewinsky that she prepare an affidavit that, for the President's purposes, would memorialize her testimony under oath and could be used to prevent questioning of both of them about their relationship; (iii) Ms. Lewinsky signed and filed the false affidavit; (iv) the President used Ms. Lewinsky's false affidavit at his deposition in an attempt to head off questions about Ms. Lewinsky; and (v) when that failed, the President lied under oath at his civil deposition about the relationship with Ms. Lewinsky.

7. President Clinton endeavored to obstruct justice by helping Ms. Lewinsky obtain a job in New York at a time when she would have been a witness harmful to him were she to tell the truth in the Jones case.

8. President Clinton lied under oath in his civil deposition about his discussions with Vernon Jordan concerning Ms. Lewinsky's involvement in the Jones case.

9. The President improperly tampered with a potential witness by attempting to corruptly influence the testimony of his personal secretary, Betty Currie, in the days after his civil deposition.

10. President Clinton endeavored to obstruct justice during the grand jury investigation by refusing to testify for seven months and lying to senior White House aides with knowledge that they would relay the President's false statements to the grand jury — and did thereby deceive, obstruct, and impede the grand jury.

11. President Clinton abused his constitutional authority by (i) lying to the public and the Congress in January 1998 about his relationship with Ms. Lewinsky; (ii) promising at that time to cooperate fully with the grand jury investigation; (iii) later refusing six invitations to testify voluntarily to the grand jury; (iv) invoking Executive Privilege; (v) lying to the grand jury in August 1998; and (vi) lying again to the public and Congress on August 17, 1998 — all as part of an effort to hinder, impede, and deflect possible inquiry by the Congress of the United States.

The first two possible grounds for impeachment concern the President's lying under oath about the nature of his relationship with Ms. Lewinsky. The details associated with those grounds are, by their nature, explicit. The President's testimony unfortunately has rendered the details essential with respect to those two grounds, as will be explained in those grounds.

Jones v. Clinton

I. **There is substantial and credible information that President Clinton lied under oath as a defendant in *Jones v. Clinton* regarding his sexual relationship with Monica Lewinsky.**

(1) He denied that he had a 'sexual relationship' with Monica Lewinsky.

(2) He denied that he had a "sexual affair" with Monica Lewinsky.

(3) He denied that he had "sexual relations" with Monica Lewinsky.

(4) He denied that he engaged in or caused contact with the genitalia of "any person" with an intent to arouse or gratify (oral sex performed on him by Ms. Lewinsky).

(5) He denied that he made contact with Monica Lewinsky's breasts or genitalia with an intent to arouse or gratify. . . .

On May 6, 1994, former Arkansas state employee Paula Corbin Jones filed a federal civil rights lawsuit against President Clinton claiming that he had sexually harassed her on May 8, 1991, by requesting her to perform oral sex on him in a suite at the Excelsior Hotel in Little Rock. . . .

On January 17, 1998, Ms. Jones' lawyers deposed President Clinton under oath with Judge Wright present and presiding over the deposition. . . .

The term "sexual relations" was defined: For the purposes of this deposition, a person engages in "sexual relations" when the person knowingly engages in or causes . . . contact with the genitalia, anus, groin, breast, inner thigh, or buttocks of any person with an intent to arouse or gratify the sexual desire of any person. . . . "Contact" means intentional touching, either directly or through clothing.

President Clinton answered a series of questions about Ms. Lewinsky, including:

Q: Did you have an extramarital sexual affair with Monica Lewinsky?

WJC: No. . . . I have never had sexual relations with Monica Lewinsky. I've never had an affair with her.

President Clinton reiterated his denial under questioning by his own attorney. . . .

Monica Lewinsky testified under oath before the grand jury that, beginning in November 1995, when she was a 22-year-old White House intern, she had a lengthy relationship with the President that included substantial sexual activity. She testified

Texts

in detail about the times, dates, and nature of ten sexual encounters that involved some form of genital contact. ... White House records corroborate Ms. Lewinsky's testimony in that the President was in the Oval Office area during the encounters. The records of White House entry and exit are incomplete for employees, but they do show her presence in the White House on eight of those occasions. ...

Ms. Lewinsky testified that she and the President engaged in 'phone sex' approximately fifteen times. The President initiated each phone sex encounter by telephoning Ms. Lewinsky. ...

Ms. Lewinsky produced to OIC [Office of Independent Counsel] investigators a dress she wore during the encounter on February 28, 1997, which she believed might be stained with the President's semen. At the request of the OIC, the FBI Laboratory examined the dress and found semen stains.

At that point, the OIC requested a DNA sample from the President. On August 3, 1998, two weeks before the President's grand jury testimony, a White House physician drew blood from the President in the presence of a senior OIC attorney and a FBI special agent. Through the most sensitive DNA testing, RFLP testing, the FBI Laboratory determined conclusively that the semen on Ms. Lewinsky's dress was, in fact, the President's. The chance that the semen is not the President's is one in 7.87 trillion. ...

During her relationship with the President, Monica Lewinsky spoke contemporaneously to several friends, family members, and counselors about the relationship. Their testimony corroborates many of the details of the sexual activity provided by Ms. Lewinsky to the OIC.

Sexual Relationship

II. There is substantial and credible information that President Clinton lied under oath to the grand jury about his sexual relationship with Monica Lewinsky. ...

The President was largely aware [of the substantial body assembled by the OIC] before he testified to the grand jury on August 17, 1998. Not only did the President know that Ms. Lewinsky had reached an immunity agreement with this Office in exchange for her truthful testimony, but the President knew from public reports and his own knowledge that his semen might be on one of Ms. Lewinsky's dresses. ...

The President admitted to an "inappropriate intimate" relationship, but he maintained that he had not committed perjury in the Jones case when he denied having a sexual relationship, sexual affair, or sexual relations with her. The President contended that he had believed his various statements in the Jones case to be legally accurate. He also testified that the inappropriate relationship began not in November 1995 when Ms. Lewinsky was an intern, as Ms. Lewinsky and other witnesses have testified, but in 1996.

During his grand jury testimony, the President was asked whether Monica Lewinsky performed oral sex on him and, if so, whether he had committed perjury in his civil deposition by denying a sexual relationship, sexual affair, or sexual relations with her. The President refused to say whether he had oral sex. Instead, the President said (i) that the undefined terms 'sexual affair,' 'sexual relationship,' and 'sexual relations' necessarily require sexual intercourse, that he had not engaged in intercourse with Ms. Lewinsky, and that he therefore had not committed perjury in denying a sexual relationship, sexual affair, or sexual relations. ...

In the foregoing testimony to the grand jury, the President lied under oath three times.

1. The President testified that he believed oral sex was not covered by any of the terms and definitions for sexual activity used at the Jones deposition. That testimony is not credible: At the Jones deposition, the President could not have believed that he was telling "the truth, the whole truth, and nothing but the truth" in denying a sexual relationship, sexual relations, or a sexual affair with Monica Lewinsky.

2. In all events, even putting aside his definitional defense, the President made a second false statement to the grand jury. The President's grand jury testimony contradicts Ms. Lewinsky's grand jury testimony on the question whether the President touched Ms. Lewinsky's breasts or genitalia during their sexual activity. There can be no contention that one of them has a lack of memory or is mistaken. On this issue, either Monica Lewinsky lied to the grand jury, or President Clinton lied to the grand jury. Under any rational view of the evidence, the President lied to the grand jury. ...

First, Ms. Lewinsky's testimony about these encounters is detailed and specific. She described with precision nine incidents of sexual activity in which the President touched and kissed her breasts and four incidents involving contacts with her genitalia.

Second, Ms. Lewinsky has stated repeatedly that she does not want to hurt the President by her testimony. Thus, if she had exaggerated in her many prior statements, she presumably would have said as much, rather than adhering to those statements. She has confirmed those details, however, even though it clearly has been painful for her to testify to the details of her relationship with the President.

Third, the testimony of many of her friends, family members, and counselors corroborate her testimony in important detail. ... These statements were made well before the President's grand jury testimony rendered these precise details important. Ms. Lewinsky had no motive to lie to these individuals (and obviously not to counselors). Indeed, she pointed out to many of them that she was upset that sexual intercourse had not occurred, an unlikely admission if she were exaggerating the sexual aspects of their relationship.

Fourth, a computer file obtained from Ms. Lewinsky's home computer contained a draft letter that referred in one place to their sexual relationship. The draft explicitly refers to "watching your mouth on my breast" and implicitly refers to direct contact with Ms. Lewinsky's genitalia. This draft letter further corroborates Ms. Lewinsky's testimony and indicates that the President's grand jury testimony is false.

Fifth, as noted above, the President's "hands-off" scenario — in which he would have received oral sex on nine occasions from Ms. Lewinsky but never made direct contact with Ms. Lewinsky's breasts or genitalia — is implausible. As Ms. Lewinsky herself testified, it suggests that she and the President had some kind of 'service contract — that all I did was perform oral sex on him and that's all this relationship was.' But as the above descriptions and the [preceding] Narrative explain, the nature of the relationship, including the sexual relationship, was far more than that. ...

3. Finally, the President made a third false statement to the grand jury about his sexual relationship with Monica Lewinsky. He contended that the intimate contact did not begin until 1996. Ms. Lewinsky has testified that it began November 15, 1995, during the government shutdown — testimony corroborated by statements she made to friends at the time. A White House photograph of the evening shows the President and Ms. Lewinsky eating pizza. White House records show that Ms. Lewinsky did not depart the White House until 12:18 a.m. and show that the President was in the Oval Office area until 12:35 a.m.

Ms. Lewinsky was still an intern when she says the President began receiving oral sex from her, whereas she was a full-time employee by the time that the President admits they began an "inappropriate intimate" relationship. ...

Civil Deposition

III. There is substantial and credible information that President Clinton lied under oath during his civil deposition when he stated that he could not recall being alone with Monica Lewinsky and when he minimized the number of gifts they had exchanged. ...

Substantial and credible information

demonstrates that the President made three false statements under oath in his civil deposition regarding whether he had been alone with Ms. Lewinsky.

First, the President lied when he said 'I don't recall' in response to the question whether he had ever been alone with Ms. Lewinsky. The President [subsequently] admitted to the grand jury that he had been alone with Ms. Lewinsky. It is not credible that he actually had no memory of this fact six months earlier, particularly given that they were obviously alone when engaging in sexual activity.

Second, when asked whether he had been alone with Ms. Lewinsky in the hallway in the Oval Office, the President answered, 'I don't believe so, unless we were walking back to the back dining room with the pizza.' That statement, too, was false: Most of the sexual encounters between the President and Ms. Lewinsky occurred in that hallway (and on other occasions, they walked through the hallway to the dining room or study), and it is not credible that the President would have forgotten this fact.

Third, the President suggested at his civil deposition that he had no specific recollection of being alone with Ms. Lewinsky in the Oval Office, but had a general recollection that Ms. Lewinsky may have brought him 'papers to sign' on certain occasions when she worked at the Legislative Affairs Office.

This statement was false. Ms. Lewinsky did not bring him papers for official purposes. To the contrary, 'bringing papers' was one of the sham "cover stories" that the President and Ms. Lewinsky had originally crafted to conceal their sexual relationship. The fact that the President resorted to a previously designed cover story when testifying under oath at the Jones deposition confirms that he made these false denials in a calculated manner with the intent and knowledge that they were false. . . .

The President stated in his civil deposition that he could not recall whether he had ever given any gifts to Ms. Lewinsky; that he could not remember whether he had given her a hat pin although "certainly, I could have"; and that he had received a gift from Ms. Lewinsky only "once or twice." In fact, the evidence demonstrates that they exchanged numerous gifts of various kinds at many points over a lengthy period of time. Indeed, on December 28, only three weeks before the deposition, they had discussed the hat pin. Also on December 28, the President had given Ms. Lewinsky a number of gifts, more than he had ever given her before.

A truthful answer to the questions about gifts at the Jones deposition would have raised further questions about the President's relationship with Monica Lewinsky. The number itself would raise questions about the relationship and prompt further questions about specific gifts; some of the specific gifts (such as . . . *Leaves of Grass*) would raise questions whether the relationship was sexual and whether the President had lied in denying that their relationship was sexual. Ms. Lewinsky explained the point: Had they admitted the gifts, it would 'at least prompt [the *Jones* attorneys] to want to question me about what kind of friendship I had with the President and they would want to speculate and they'd leak it and my name would be trashed and he [the President] would be in trouble.'

Clinton-Lewinsky Conversations

IV. **There is substantial and credible information that the President lied under oath during his civil deposition concerning conversations he had with Monica Lewinsky about her involvement in the *Jones* case.**

Ms. Lewinsky testified that she spoke three times to President Clinton about the prospect of testifying in the *Jones* lawsuit — once (December 17, 1997) after she was on the witness list and twice more (December 28, 1997, and January 5, 1998) after she had been subpoenaed. . . .

There is substantial and credible information that President Clinton lied under oath in his civil deposition in answering 'I'm not sure' when asked whether he had talked to Ms. Lewinsky about the prospect of her testifying. In fact, he had talked to Ms. Lewinsky about it on three occasions in the month preceding his civil deposition, as Ms. Lewinsky's testimony makes clear. . . .

There is substantial and credible information that the President lied under oath in his civil deposition when he denied knowing that Ms. Lewinsky had received her subpoena at the time he had last talked to her. . . . In fact, he knew that she had been subpoenaed. Given that the conversation with Ms. Lewinsky occurred in the few weeks immediately before the President's civil deposition, he could not have forgotten the conversation. As a result, there is no plausible conclusion except that the President intentionally lied in this answer.

During the civil deposition, the President also falsely dated his last conversation with Ms. Lewinsky as 'probably sometime before Christmas,' which implied that it might have been before the December 19 subpoena. Because Ms. Lewinsky had been subpoenaed on December 19, that false statement about the date of the conversation was a corollary to his other false statement (that he did not know she had been subpoenaed at the time of their last conversation). . . .

Concealment of Evidence

V. **There is substantial and credible information that President Clinton endeavored to obstruct justice by engaging in a pattern of activity to conceal evidence regarding his relationship with Monica Lewinsky from the judicial process in the Jones case.** The pattern included:

(i) concealment of gifts that the President had given Ms. Lewinsky and that were subpoenaed from Ms. Lewinsky in the Jones case; and

(ii) concealment of a note sent by Ms. Lewinsky to the President on January 5, 1998.

From the beginning, President Clinton and Monica Lewinsky hoped and expected that their relationship would remain secret. They took active steps, when necessary, to conceal the relationship. The President testified that "I hoped that this relationship would never become public." . . .

The uncontroverted evidence demonstrates that the President had given gifts to Ms. Lewinsky before December 28, 1997; that the President told Ms. Lewinsky on the phone on December 17, 1997, that he had more gifts for her; that Ms. Lewinsky met with the President at the White House on December 28; that on the 28th, Ms. Lewinsky was concerned about retaining possession of the gifts the President had previously given her because they were under subpoena; that on the 28th, the President gave several Christmas gifts to Ms. Lewinsky; and that after that meeting, Ms. Lewinsky transferred some gifts (including one of the new gifts) to the President's personal secretary, Ms. Currie, who stored them under her bed in her home. . . .

The testimony conflicts as to what happened when Ms. Lewinsky raised the subject of gifts with the President and what happened later that day. The President testified that he told Ms. Lewinsky that 'you have to give them whatever you have.' According to Ms. Lewinsky, she raised the possibility of hiding the gifts, and the President offered a somewhat neutral response.

Ms. Lewinsky testified that Betty Currie called her to retrieve the gifts soon after Ms. Lewinsky's conversation with the President. Ms. Currie says that she believes that Ms. Lewinsky called her about the gifts, but she says she has a dim memory of the events.

The central factual question is whether the President orchestrated or approved the concealment of the gifts. The reasonable inference from the evidence is that he did.

The witnesses disagree about whether Ms. Currie called Ms. Lewinsky or Ms. Lewinsky called Ms. Currie. That issue is relevant because Ms. Currie would not have called Ms. Lewinsky about the gifts unless the President directed her to do so. Indeed, because she did not know of the gifts issue, there is no other way that Ms. Currie could have known to make such a

Texts

call unless the President told her to do so.

Ms. Lewinsky's testimony on the issue is consistent and unequivocal. In her February 1, 1998, handwritten statement, she wrote: "Ms. Currie called Ms. L later that afternoon a[nd] said that the Pres. had told her Ms. L wanted her to hold onto something for her." In her grand jury testimony, Ms. Lewinsky said that several hours after she left the White House, Ms. Currie called and said something along the lines of 'The President said you have something to give me.'

Ms. Currie's testimony is contrary but less clear. Ms. Currie has stated that Ms. Lewinsky called her, but her memory of the conversation, in contrast to Ms. Lewinsky's, generally has been hazy and uncertain. As to whether she had talked to the President about the gifts, for example, Ms. Currie initially said she had not, but then said that Ms. Lewinsky (who said that Ms. Currie had talked to the President) 'may remember better than I. I don't remember.'

Ms. Lewinsky's testimony makes more sense than Ms. Currie's testimony. First, Ms. Lewinsky stated that if Ms. Currie had not called, Ms. Lewinsky simply would have kept the gifts (and perhaps thrown them away). She would not have produced the gifts to Ms. Jones' attorneys. And she would not have given them to a friend or mother because she did not want to get anyone else involved. She was not looking for someone else to take them.

Also, Ms. Currie drove to Ms. Lewinsky's house to pick up the gifts. That was only the second time that Ms. Currie had ever gone there. More generally, the person making the extra effort (in this case, Ms. Currie) is ordinarily the person requesting the favor.

2. Even if Ms. Lewinsky is mistaken and she did call Ms. Currie first, the evidence still leads clearly to the conclusion that the President orchestrated this transfer. . . .

3. Even if the President did not orchestrate the transfer to Ms. Currie, there is still substantial evidence that he encouraged the concealment and non-production of the gifts by Ms. Lewinsky. The President 'hoped that this relationship would never become public.' The President gave Ms. Lewinsky new gifts on December 28, 1997. Given his desire to conceal the relationship, it makes no sense that the President would have given Ms. Lewinsky more gifts on the 28th unless he and Ms. Lewinsky understood that she would not produce all of her gifts in response to her subpoena. . . .

On January 4, 1998, Ms. Lewinsky left a book for the President with Ms. Currie. Ms. Lewinsky had enclosed in the book a romantic note that she had written, inspired by a recent viewing of the movie "Titanic." In the note, Ms. Lewinsky told the President that she wanted to have sexual intercourse with him, at least once.

On January 5, in the course of discussing her affidavit and possible testimony in a phone conversation with the President, Ms. Lewinsky says she told the President, 'I shouldn't have written some of those things in the note.' According to Ms. Lewinsky, the President said that he agreed and that she should not write those kinds of things on paper.

On January 15, President Clinton served responses to Ms. Jones' second set of document requests, which again asked for documents that related to 'Monica Lewisky.' The President stated that he had 'no documents' responsive to this request.

The President remembered the book Ms. Lewinsky had given him about the Presidents and testified that he 'did like it a lot.' President Clinton testified that he did not recall a romantic note enclosed in the book or when he had received it.

The request for production of documents that the President received from Ms. Jones' attorneys called for all documents reflecting communications between him and Ms. Lewinsky. The note given to him by Ms. Lewinsky on January 5, 1998, fell within that category and would have been revealing about the relationship. Indeed, had the note been produced, the President might have been foreclosed from denying a sexual relationship at his deposition. Based on Ms. Lewinsky's testimony, there is substantial and credible information that the President concealed or destroyed this note at a time when such documents were called for by the request for production of documents.

False Affidavit

VI. There is substantial and credible information that (i) President Clinton and Ms. Lewinsky had an understanding that they would lie under oath in the *Jones* case about their relationship; and (ii) President Clinton endeavored to obstruct justice by suggesting that Ms. Lewinsky file an affidavit so that she would not be deposed, she would not contradict his testimony, and he could attempt to avoid questions about Ms. Lewinsky at his deposition.

Based on their conversations and their past practice, both the President and Ms. Lewinsky understood that they would lie under oath in the *Jones* case about their sexual relationship, as part of a scheme to obstruct justice in the *Jones* case. In pursuing this effort:

The President suggested that Monica Lewinsky file an affidavit, which he knew would be false;

The President had an interest in Ms. Lewinsky's false affidavit because it would "lock in" her testimony, allowing the President to deny the sexual relationship under oath without fear of contradiction;

Ms. Lewinsky signed and, on January 16, sent to the Court the false affidavit denying a sexual relationship with the President as part of a motion to quash her deposition subpoena;

The President's attorney used the affidavit to object to questions about Ms. Lewinsky at his January 17 deposition; and

When that failed, the President also lied under oath about the relationship with Ms. Lewinsky at his civil deposition, including by the use of 'cover stories' that he and Ms. Lewinsky had devised. . . .

There is substantial and credible information that the President and Ms. Lewinsky reached an understanding that both of them would lie under oath when asked whether they had a sexual relationship (a conspiracy to obstruct justice or to commit perjury, in criminal law terms). Indeed, a tacit or express agreement to make false statements would have been an essential part of their December and January discussions, lest one of the two testify truthfully in the *Jones* case and thereby incriminate the other as a perjurer.

There also is substantial and credible information that President Clinton endeavored to obstruct justice by suggesting that Ms. Lewinsky file an affidavit to avoid her deposition, which would "lock in" her testimony under oath, and to attempt to avoid questions at his own deposition — all to impede the gathering of discoverable evidence in the *Jones v. Clinton* litigation.

During the course of their relationship, the President and Ms. Lewinsky also discussed and used cover stories to justify her presence in and around the Oval Office area.

The evidence indicates — given Ms. Lewinsky's unambiguous testimony and the President's lack of memory, as well as the fact that they both planned to lie under oath — that the President suggested the continued use of the cover stories even after Ms. Lewinsky was named as a potential witness in the *Jones* litigation. At no time did the President tell Ms. Lewinsky to abandon these stories and to tell the truth about her visits, nor did he ever indicate to her that she should tell the truth under oath about the relationship.

While the President testified that he could not remember such conversations about the cover stories, he had repeated the substance of the cover stories in his *Jones* deposition. The President's use of false cover stories in testimony under oath in his *Jones* deposition strongly corroborates Ms. Lewinsky's testimony that he suggested them to her on December 17 as a means of avoiding disclosure of the truth of their relationship.

Lewinsky Job Search

VII. There is substantial and credible information that President Clinton en-

deavored to obstruct justice by helping Ms. Lewinsky obtain a job in New York at a time when she would have been a witness against him were she to tell the truth during the *Jones* case.

The President had an incentive to keep Ms. Lewinsky from jeopardizing the secrecy of the relationship. That incentive grew once the Supreme Court unanimously decided in May 1997 that the case and discovery process were to go forward.

At various times during the Jones discovery process, the President and those working on his behalf devoted substantial time and attention to help Ms. Lewinsky obtain a job in the private sector. . . .

On October 1, the President was served with interrogatories asking about his sexual relationships with women other than Mrs. Clinton. On October 7, 1997, Ms. Lewinsky couriered a letter expressing dissatisfaction with her job search to the President. In response, Ms. Lewinsky said she received a late-night call from President Clinton on October 9, 1997. She said that the President told her he would start helping her find a job in New York.

The following Saturday, October 11, 1997, Ms. Lewinsky met with President Clinton alone in the Oval Office dining room from 9:36 a.m. until about 10:54 a.m. In that meeting, she furnished the President a list of New York jobs in which she was interested. Ms. Lewinsky mentioned to the President that she would need a reference from someone in the White House; the President said he would take care of it. Ms. Lewinsky also suggested to the President that Vernon Jordan might be able to help her, and President Clinton agreed. Immediately after the meeting, President Clinton spoke with Mr. Jordan by telephone.

According to White House Chief of Staff Erskine Bowles, at some time in the summer or fall of 1997, President Clinton raised the subject of Monica Lewinsky and stated that 'she was unhappy where she was working and wanted to come back and work at the OEOB [Old Executive Office Building]; and could we take a look.' Mr. Bowles referred the matter to Deputy Chief of Staff John Podesta.

Mr. Podesta said he asked Betty Currie to have Ms. Lewinsky call him, but heard nothing until about October 1997, when Ms. Currie told him that Ms. Lewinsky was looking for opportunities in New York. The Ambassador to the United Nations, Bill Richardson, said that Mr. Podesta told him that Ms. Currie had a friend looking for a position in New York.

According to Ms. Lewinsky, Ambassador Richardson called her on October 21, 1997, and interviewed her soon thereafter. She was then offered a position at the U.N. Ms. Lewinsky was unenthusiastic. During the latter part of October 1997, the President and Ms. Lewinsky discussed enlisting Vernon Jordan to aid in pursuing private-sector possibilities.

On November 5, 1997, Ms. Lewinsky met Mr. Jordan in his law office. Mr. Jordan told Ms. Lewinsky that she came "highly recommended." Ms. Lewinsky explained that she hoped to move to New York, and went over her list of possible employers. Mr. Jordan telephoned President Clinton shortly after the meeting.

Ms. Lewinsky had no contact with the President or Mr. Jordan for another month. On December 5, 1997, however, the parties in the Jones case exchanged witness lists. Ms. Jones's attorneys listed Ms. Lewinsky as a potential witness. The President testified that he learned that Ms. Lewinsky was on the list late in the day on December 6.

The effort to obtain a job for Ms. Lewinsky then intensified. On December 7, President Clinton met with Mr. Jordan at the White House. Ms. Lewinsky met with Mr. Jordan on December 11 to discuss specific job contacts in New York. Mr. Jordan gave her the names of some of his business contacts. He then made calls to contacts at MacAndrews & Forbes (the parent corporation of Revlon), American Express, and Young & Rubicam.

Mr. Jordan also telephoned President Clinton to keep him informed of the efforts to help Ms. Lewinsky. Mr. Jordan testified that President Clinton was aware that people were trying to get jobs for her, that Mr. Podesta was trying to help her, that Bill Richardson was trying to help her, but that she wanted to work in the private sector. . . .

On December 17, 1997, according to Ms. Lewinsky, President Clinton called her in the early morning and told her that she was on the witness list [in the *Jones* case], and they discussed their cover stories. On December 18 and December 23, she interviewed for jobs with New York-based companies that had been contacted by Mr. Jordan. On December 19, Ms. Lewinsky was served with a deposition subpoena by Ms. Jones's lawyers. On December 22, 1997, Mr. Jordan took her to her new attorney; she and Mr. Jordan discussed the subpoena, the Jones case, and her job search during the course of the ride. . . .

On Sunday, December 28, 1997, Monica Lewinsky and the President met in the Oval Office. During that meeting, the President and Ms. Lewinsky discussed both her move to New York and her involvement in the Jones suit.

On January 5, 1998, Ms. Lewinsky declined the United Nations offer. On January 7, 1998, Ms. Lewinsky signed the affidavit denying the relationship with President Clinton (she had talked on the phone to the President on January 5 about it). Mr. Jordan informed the President of her action. . . .

One can draw inferences about the party's intent from circumstantial evidence. In this case, the President assisted Ms. Lewinsky in her job search in late 1997, at a time when she would have become a witness harmful to him in the Jones case were she to testify truthfully. The President did not act half-heartedly. His assistance led to the involvement of the Ambassador to the United Nations, one of the country's leading business figures (Mr. Perelman), and one of the country's leading attorneys (Vernon Jordan).

The question, therefore, is whether the President's efforts in obtaining a job for Ms. Lewinsky were to influence her testimony or simply to help an ex-intimate without concern for her testimony. Three key facts are essential in analyzing his actions: the chronology of events, the fact that the President and Ms. Lewinsky both intended to lie under oath about the relationship, and the fact that it was critical for the President that Ms. Lewinsky lie under oath.

There is substantial and credible information that the President assisted Ms. Lewinsky in her job search motivated at least in part by his desire to keep her "on the team" in the *Jones* litigation.

Vernon Jordan and Lewinsky

VIII. There is substantial and credible information that the President lied under oath in describing his conversations with Vernon Jordan about Ms. Lewinsky.

President Clinton was asked during his civil deposition whether he had talked to Mr. Jordan about Ms. Lewinsky's involvement in the Jones case. The President stated that he knew Mr. Jordan had talked to Ms. Lewinsky about her move to New York, but stated that he did not recall whether Mr. Jordan had talked to Ms. Lewinsky about her involvement in the *Jones* case. The testimony was false. A lie under oath about these conversations was necessary to avoid inquiry into whether Ms. Lewinsky's job and her testimony were improperly related. . . .

Vernon Jordan testified that his conversations with the President about Ms. Lewinsky's subpoena were, in fact, 'a continuing dialogue.' When asked if he had kept the President informed about Ms. Lewinsky's status in the Jones case in addition to her job search, Mr. Jordan responded: 'The two — absolutely.'

On December 19, Ms. Lewinsky phoned Mr. Jordan and told him that she had been subpoenaed in the Jones case. Following that call, Mr. Jordan telephoned the President to inform him 'that Monica Lewinsky was coming to see me, and that she had a subpoena' — but the President was unavailable. Later that day, at 5:01

Texts

p.m., Mr. Jordan had a seven-minute telephone conversation with the President:

I said to the President, 'Monica Lewinsky called me up. She's upset. She's gotten a subpoena. She is coming to see me about this subpoena. I'm confident that she needs a lawyer, and I will try to get her a lawyer.'

Later on December 19, after meeting with Ms. Lewinsky, Mr. Jordan went to the White House and met with the President alone in the Residence. Mr. Jordan testified: "I told him that Monica Lewinsky had been subpoenaed, came to me with a subpoena." According to Mr. Jordan, the President 'thanked me for my efforts to get her a job and thanked me for getting her a lawyer.'

According to Mr. Jordan, on January 7, 1998, Ms. Lewinsky showed him a copy of her signed affidavit denying any sexual relationship with the President. He testified that he told the President about the affidavit, probably in one of his two logged calls to the White House that day. . . .

In his civil deposition, the President stated that he had talked to Vernon Jordan about Ms. Lewinsky's job. But as the testimony of Mr. Jordan reveals, and as the President as much as conceded in his subsequent grand jury appearance, the President did talk to Mr. Jordan about Ms. Lewinsky's involvement in the *Jones* case — including that she had been subpoenaed, that Mr. Jordan had helped her obtain a lawyer, and that she had signed an affidavit denying a sexual relationship with the President.

Given their several communications in the weeks before the deposition, it is not credible that the President forgot the subject of their conversations during his civil deposition. His statements [Clinton had said: I knew that he met with her. I think Betty suggested that he meet with her. Anyway, he met with her. I, I thought that he talked to her about something else. I didn't know that — I thought he had given her some advice about her move to New York. Seems like that's what Betty said.] were more than mere omissions; they were affirmative misstatements. . . .

The President's motive for making false and misleading statements about this subject in his civil deposition was straightforward. If the President admitted that he had talked with Vernon Jordan both about Monica Lewinsky's involvement in the *Jones* case and about her job, questions would inevitably arise about whether Ms. Lewinsky's testimony and her future job were connected. Such an admission by the President in his civil deposition likely would have prompted Ms. Jones' attorneys to inquire further into the subject. And such an admission in his deposition would have triggered public scrutiny when the deposition became public.

Betty Currie's Testimony

IX. **There is substantial and credible information that President Clinton endeavored to obstruct justice by attempting to influence the testimony of Betty Currie.**

In a meeting with Betty Currie on the day after his deposition and in a separate conversation a few days later, President Clinton made statements to her that he knew were false. The contents of the statements and the context in which they were made indicate that President Clinton was attempting to influence the testimony that Ms. Currie might have been required to give in the *Jones* case or in a grand jury investigation. . . .

The President referred to Ms. Currie on multiple occasions in his civil deposition when describing his relationship with Ms. Lewinsky. As he himself recognized, a large number of questions about Ms. Lewinsky were likely to be asked in the very near future. The President thus could foresee that Ms. Currie either might be deposed or questioned or might need to prepare an affidavit.

The President called her shortly after the deposition and met with Ms. Currie the next day. The President appeared "concerned," according to Ms. Currie. He then informed Ms. Currie that questions about Ms. Lewinsky had been asked at the deposition.

The statements the President made to her on January 18 and again on January 20 or 21 — that he was never alone with Ms. Lewinsky, that Ms. Currie could always hear or see them and that he never touched Ms. Lewinsky — were false, but consistent with the testimony that the President provided under oath at his deposition. The President knew that the statements were false at the time he made them to Ms. Currie. The President's suggestion that he was simply trying to refresh his memory when talking to Ms. Currie conflicts with common sense: Ms. Currie's confirmation of false statements could not in any way remind the President of the facts. Thus, it is not plausible that he was trying to refresh his recollection.

The President's grand jury testimony reinforces that conclusion. He testified that in asking questions of Ms. Currie such as 'We were never alone, right' and 'Monica came on to me, and I never touched her, right,' he intended a date restriction on the questions. But he did not articulate a date restriction in his conversations with Ms. Currie.

Moreover, with respect to some aspects of this incident, the President was unable to devise any innocent explanation, testifying that he did not know why he had asked Ms. Currie some questions and admitting that he was 'just trying to reconcile the two statements as best [he could].' On the other hand, if the most reasonable inference from the President's conduct is drawn — that he was attempting to enlist a witness to back up his false testimony from the day before — his behavior with Ms. Currie makes complete sense.

The content of the President's statements and the context in which those statements were made provide substantial and credible information that President Clinton sought improperly to influence Ms. Currie's testimony. Such actions constitute an obstruction of justice and improper influence on a witness.

Lying to Grand Jury Witnesses

X. **There is substantial and credible information that President Clinton endeavored to obstruct justice during the federal grand jury investigation. While refusing to testify for seven months, he simultaneously lied to potential grand jury witnesses knowing that they would relay the falsehoods to the grand jury.**

The President's grand jury testimony followed seven months of investigation in which he had refused six invitations to testify before the grand jury. During this period, there was no indication that the President would admit any sexual relationship with Ms. Lewinsky. To the contrary, the President vehemently denied the allegations.

Rather than lie to the grand jury himself, the President lied about his relationship with Ms. Lewinsky to senior aides, and those aides then conveyed the President's false story to the grand jury.

In this case, the President lied to, among others, three current senior aides — John Podesta, Erskine Bowles, and Sidney Blumenthal — and one former senior aide, Harold Ickes. The President denied any kind of sexual relationship with Monica Lewinsky; said that Ms. Lewinsky had made a sexual demand on him; and denied multiple telephone conversations with Monica Lewinsky. The President, by his own later admission, was aware that his aides were likely to convey the President's version of events to the grand jury.

The President's aides took the President at his word when he made these statements. Each aide then testified to the nature of the relationship between Monica Lewinsky and the President based on those statements — without knowing that they were calculated falsehoods by the President designed to perpetuate the false statements that the President made during his deposition in the *Jones* case.

The aides' testimony provided the grand jury a false account of the relationship between the President and Ms. Lewinsky. Their testimony thus had the potential to affect the investigation — including decisions by the OIC and grand jury about how to conduct the investigation (for example, whether to subpoena Secret Service agents) and whether to indict particular individuals. . . .

The President made the following misleading statements to his aides:

The President told Mr. Podesta that he had not engaged in sex 'in any way whatsoever' with Ms. Lewinsky, 'including oral sex.'

The President told Mr. Podesta, Mr. Bowles, and Mr. Ickes that he did not have a 'sexual relationship' with Ms. Lewinsky.

The President told Mr. Podesta that 'when [Ms. Lewinsky] came by, she came by to see Betty [Currie].'

The President told Mr. Blumenthal that Ms. Lewinsky 'came on to him and that he had told her he couldn't have sexual relations with her and that she threatened him.'

The President told Mr. Blumenthal that he couldn't remember making any calls to Ms. Lewinsky other than once when he left a message on her answering machine.

During the President's grand jury testimony, the President admitted that his statements to aides denying a sexual relationship with Ms. Lewinsky 'may have been misleading.' The President also knew his aides likely would be called to testify regarding any communications with him about Ms. Lewinsky. And he presumably expected his aides to repeat his statements regarding Ms. Lewinsky to all questioners, including to the grand jury. Finally, he himself refused to testify for many months. The combination of the President's silence and his deception of his aides had the effect of presenting a false view of events to the grand jury.

The President says that at the time he spoke to his aides, he chose his words with great care so that, in his view, his statements would be literally true because he was referring only to intercourse.

That explanation is undermined by the President's testimony before the grand jury that his denials 'may have been misleading' and by the contradictory testimony by the aides themselves — particularly John Podesta, who says that the President specifically denied oral sex with Ms. Lewinsky. Moreover, on January 24, 1998, the White House issued talking points for its staff, and those talking points refute the President's literal truth argument: The talking points state as the President's view the belief that a relationship that includes oral sex is "of course" a "sexual relationship."

For all of these reasons, there is substantial and credible information that the President improperly tampered with witnesses during the grand jury investigation.

Constitutional Duty

XI. There is substantial and credible information that President Clinton's actions since January 17, 1998, regarding his relationship with Monica Lewinsky have been inconsistent with the President's constitutional duty to faithfully execute the laws.

Before, during, and after his January 17, 1998, civil deposition, the President attempted to conceal the truth about his relationship with Ms. Lewinsky from the judicial process in the Jones case. Furthermore, the President has since lied under oath to the grand jury and facilitated the provision of false information to the grand jury by others.

The President also misled the American people and the Congress in his public statement of January 26, 1998, in which he denied "sexual relations" with Ms. Lewinsky. The President misled his Cabinet and his senior aides by denying the relationship to them. The Cabinet and senior aides in turn misled the American people and the Congress by conveying the President's denials and professing their belief in the credibility of those denials.

The President promised in January 1998 to cooperate fully with the grand jury investigation and to provide 'more rather than less, sooner rather than later.' At that time, the OIC was conducting a criminal investigation and was obligated to report to Congress any substantial and credible information that may constitute grounds for an impeachment.

The President's conduct delayed the grand jury investigation (and thereby delayed any potential congressional proceedings). He asserted, appealed, withdrew, and reasserted Executive Privilege (and asserted other governmental privileges never before applied in federal criminal proceedings against the government). The President asserted these privileges concerning the investigation of factual questions about which the President already knew the answers.

The President refused six invitations to testify voluntarily before the grand jury. At the same time, the President's aides and surrogates argued publicly that the entire matter was frivolous and that any investigation of it should cease.

After being subpoenaed in July, the President made false statements to the grand jury on August 17, 1998. That night, the President again made false statements to the American people and Congress, contending that his answers in his civil deposition had been 'legally accurate.' The President then made an implicit plea for Congress to take no action: 'Our country has been distracted by this matter for too long.'

The President has pursued a strategy of deceiving the American people and Congress in January 1998, delaying and impeding the criminal investigation for seven months, and deceiving the American people and Congress again in August 1998. . . . ◆

Texts

White House Response: 'Private Mistake [Not] an Impeachable Action'

The following are excerpts from the preliminary response issued by the White House Sept. 11 shortly after the House vote to release Independent Counsel Kenneth W. Starr's report:

The President has acknowledged a serious mistake — an inappropriate relationship with Monica Lewinsky. He has taken responsibility for his actions, and he has apologized to the country, to his friends, leaders of his party, the cabinet and most importantly, his family.

This private mistake does not amount to an impeachable action. A relationship outside one's marriage is wrong — and the President admits that. It is not a high crime or misdemeanor. The Constitution specifically states that Congress shall impeach only for "treason, bribery or other high crimes and misdemeanors."...

"High crimes and misdemeanors" had a fixed meaning to the Framers of our Constitution — it meant wrongs committed against our system of government. The impeachment clause was designed to protect our country against a President who was using his official powers against the nation, against the American people, against our society. It was never designed to allow a political body to force a President from office for a very personal mistake....

[Starr's] report is based entirely on allegations obtained by a grand jury . . . that would never be admitted in court, that has never been seen by the President or his lawyers, and that was not subject to cross-examination or any other traditional safeguards to ensure its credibility....

The President did not commit perjury. Most of the illegal leaks suggesting his testimony was perjurious falsely describe his testimony. First of all, the President never testified in the Jones deposition that he was not alone with Ms. Lewinsky. The President never testified that his relationship with Ms. Lewinsky was the same as with any other intern. To the contrary, he admitted exchanging gifts with her, knowing about her job search, receiving cards and notes from her, and knowing other details of her personal life that made it plain he had a special relationship with her.

The President has admitted he had an improper sexual relationship with Ms. Lewinsky. In a civil deposition, he gave narrow answers to ambiguous questions. As a matter of law, those answers could not give rise to a criminal charge of perjury. In the face of the President's admission of his relationship, the disclosure of lurid and salacious allegations can only be intended to humiliate the President and force him from office.

There was no obstruction of justice. We believe [Clinton personal secretary] Betty Currie testified that Ms. Lewinsky asked her to hold the gifts and that the President never talked to her about the gifts. The President admitted giving and receiving gifts from Ms. Lewinsky when he was asked about it. The President never asked Ms. Lewinsky to get rid of the gifts and he never asked Ms. Currie to get them. We believe that Ms. Currie's testimony supports the President's.

The President never tried to get Ms. Lewinsky a job after she left the White House in order to influence her testimony in the Paula Jones case. The President knew Ms. Lewinsky was unhappy in her Pentagon job after she left the White House and did ask the White House personnel office to treat her fairly in her job search. He never instructed anyone to hire her, or even indicated that he very much wanted it to happen....

The President did not facilitate Ms. Lewinsky's interview with [cabinet member] Bill Richardson, or her discussions with [Clinton friend and adviser] Vernon Jordan. Betty Currie asked [Deputy Chief of Staff] John Podesta if he could help her with her New York job search which led to an interview with Bill Richardson, and Ms. Currie also put her in touch with her longtime friend, Mr. Jordan. Mr. Jordan has made it clear that this is the case, and, as a private individual, he is free to offer job advice wherever he sees fit.

There was no witness tampering. Betty Currie was not supposed to be a witness in the Paula Jones case. If she was not called or going to be called, it was impossible for any conversations the President had with her to be witness tampering. The President testified that he did not in any way attempt to influence her recollection....

Invocation of privileges was not an abuse of power. The President's lawful assertion of privileges in a court of law was only made on the advice of his Counsel, and was in significant measure validated by the courts. The legal claims were advanced sparingly and as a last resort after all attempts at compromise by the White House Counsel's office were rejected to protect the core constitutional and institutional interests of this and future presidencies.

Neither the President nor the White House played a role in the Secret Service's lawful efforts to prevent agents from testifying to preserve its protective function. The President never asked, directed or participated in any decision regarding the protective function privilege. Neither did any White House official. The Treasury and Justice departments independently decided to respond to the historically unprecedented subpoenas of Secret Service personnel and to pursue the privilege to ensure the protection of this and future presidents.

The President did not abuse his power by permitting White House staff to comment on the investigation. The President has acknowledged misleading his family, staff and the country about the nature of his relationship with Ms. Lewinsky.... However, this personal failing does not constitute a criminal abuse of power. If allowing aides to repeat misleading statements is a crime, then any number of public officials are guilty of misusing their office for as long as they fail to admit wrongdoing in response to any allegation about their activities.

The actions of White House attorneys were completely lawful. The White House Counsel attorneys provided the President and White House officials with informed, candid advice on issues raised during this investigation that affected the President's official duties. This was especially necessary given the fact that impeachment proceedings against the President were a possible result of the OIC's [Office of the Independent Counsel] investigation from Day One....

This means that the OIC report is left with nothing but the details of a private sexual relationship.... Given the flimsy and unsubstantiated basis for the accusations, there is a complete lack of any credible evidence to initiate an impeachment inquiry concerning the President....

Where's Whitewater? The OIC's allegations reportedly include no suggestion of wrongdoing by the President in any of the areas which Mr. Starr spent four years investigating: Whitewater, the FBI files and the White House travel office. What began as an inquiry into a 24-year-old land deal in Arkansas has ended as an inquest into brief, improper personal encounters between the President and Monica Lewinsky. Despite the exhaustive nature of the OIC's investigation into the Whitewater, FBI files and travel office matters . . . to this day the OIC has never exonerated the President or the First Lady of wrongdoing. ◆

Congress Releases Clinton's Testimony About His Relationship With Intern

The following are excerpts from the official transcript of President Clinton's grand jury testimony videotaped Aug. 17 and made public Sept. 21. Clinton was questioned by lawyers for the Office of the Independent Counsel, including Kenneth W. Starr, Robert Bittman and Solomon L. Wisenberg. The excerpts also include comments by Clinton lawyer David E. Kendall.

BITTMAN: Mr. President, we are first going to turn to some of the details of your relationship with Monica Lewinsky that follow up on your deposition that you provided in the Paula Jones case, as was referenced, on January 17th, 1998.

The questions are uncomfortable, and I apologize for that in advance. I will try to be as brief and direct as possible.

Mr. President, were you physically intimate with Monica Lewinsky?

PRESIDENT CLINTON: Mr. Bittman, I think maybe I can save the — you and the grand jurors a lot of time if I read a statement, which I think will make it clear what the nature of my relationship with Ms. Lewinsky was and how it related to the testimony I gave, what I was trying to do in that testimony. . . .

Q: Absolutely. Please, Mr. President.

C: When I was alone with Ms. Lewinsky on certain occasions in early 1996 and once in early 1997, I engaged in conduct that was wrong. These encounters did not consist of sexual intercourse. They did not constitute sexual relations as I understood that term to be defined at my January 17th, 1998, deposition. But they did involve inappropriate intimate contact. These inappropriate encounters ended, at my insistence, in early 1997. I also had occasional telephone conversations with Ms. Lewinsky that included inappropriate sexual banter.

I regret that what began as a friendship came to include this conduct, and I take full responsibility for my actions. While I will provide the grand jury whatever other information I can, because of privacy considerations affecting my family, myself, and others, and in an effort to preserve the dignity of the office I hold, this is all I will say about the specifics of these particular matters. I will try to answer, to the best of my ability, other questions including questions about my relationship with Ms. Lewinsky; questions about my understanding of the term: "sexual relations," as I understood it to be defined at my January 17th, 1998, deposition; and questions concerning alleged subornation of perjury, obstruction of justice, and intimidation of witnesses.

That, Mr. Bittman, is my statement. . . .

'Sexual Relations'

Q: Let us then move to the definition [of sexual relations] that was provided you during your deposition [in the Paula Jones case]. . . .

C: I can tell you what my understanding of the definition is, if you want me to.

. . . My understanding of this definition is it covers contact by the person being deposed with the enumerated areas [genitalia, anus, groin, breast, inner thigh or buttocks], if the contact is done with an intent to arouse or gratify. That's my understanding of the definition.

Q: What did you believe the definition to include and exclude? What kinds of activities?

C: I thought the definition included any activity by the person being deposed, where the person was the actor and came in contact with those parts of the bodies with the purpose or intent or gratification, and excluded any other activity. For example, kissing is not covered by that, I don't think.

Q: Did you understand the definition to be limited to sexual activity?

C: Yes, I understood the definition to be limited to, to physical contact with those areas of the bodies with the specific intent to arouse or gratify. That's what I understood it to be.

Q: What specific acts did the definition include, as you understood the definition on January 17, 1998?

C: Any contact with the areas there mentioned, sir. . . . If the person being deposed contacted those parts of another person's body with an intent to arouse or gratify, that was covered. . . .

Q: [In the Paula Jones deposition] your attorney, Mr. Bennett, objected to any questions about Ms. Lewinsky. . . . I will read the portion that I am referring to. . . . "Counsel is fully aware that Ms. Lewinsky has filed, has an affidavit which they are in possession of saying that there is absolutely no sex of any kind in any manner, shape or form, with President Clinton". . . .

C: Well, actually, in the present tense that is an accurate statement. . . .

Q: And do you remember in the deposition that Mr. Bennett asked you about that. This is at the end of the — towards the end of the deposition. And you indicated, he asked you whether the statement that Ms. Lewinsky made in her affidavit was —

C: Truthful.

Q: — true. And you indicated that it was absolutely correct.

C: I did. . . . I believe at the time that she filled out this affidavit, if she believed that the definition of sexual relationship was two people having intercourse, then this is accurate. And I believe that is the definition that most ordinary Americans would give it.

If you said Jane and Harry have a sexual relationship, and you're not talking about people being drawn into a lawsuit and being given definitions, and then a great effort to trick them in some way, but you are just talking about people in ordinary conversations, I'll bet the grand jurors, if they were talking about two people they know, and said they have a sexual relationship, they meant they were sleeping together; they meant they were having intercourse together.

So, I'm not at all sure that this affidavit is not true and was not true in Ms. Lewinsky's mind at the time she swore it out.

Q: Did you talk with Ms. Lewinsky about what she meant to write in her affidavit?

C: I didn't talk to her about her definition. I did not know what was in this affidavit before it was filled out specifically. I did not know what words were used specifically before it was filled out, or what meaning she gave to them. But I'm just telling you that it's certainly true what she says here. . . .

Q: Do you agree with me that if [Bennett] misled Judge Wright in some way that you would have corrected the record and said, excuse me, Mr. Bennett, think the judge is getting a misimpression by what you're saying?

C: Mr. Bennett was representing me. I wasn't representing him. And I wasn't even paying much attention to this conversation, which is why, when you started asking me about this, I asked to see the deposition, I was focusing on my answers to the questions. And I've told you what I believe about this deposition, which I believe to be true. And it's obvious, and I think by your questions you have betrayed that the Jones lawyers' strategy in this case had nothing to do with uncovering or proving sexual harassment.

By the time this discovery started, they knew they had a bad case on the law and

Texts

they knew what our evidence was. They knew they had a lousy case on the facts. And so their strategy, since they were being funded by my political opponents, was to have this dragnet of discovery. They wanted to cover everybody. And they convinced the Judge, because she gave them strict orders not to leak, that they should be treated like other plaintiffs in other civil cases, and how could they ever know whether there had been any sexual harassment, unless they first knew whether there had been any sex.

And so, with that broad mandate limited by time and employment in the federal or state government, they proceeded to cross the country and try to turn up whatever they could; not because they thought it would help their case. By the time they did this discovery, they knew what this deal was in their case, and they knew what was going to happen. And Judge Wright subsequently threw it out. . . .

Lewinsky Meetings

Q: If I could summarize your testimony [on the number of times you were alone with Lewinsky], approximately five times you saw her before she left the White House, and approximately nine times after she left the employment of the White House?

C: I know there were several times in '97. I've told you that I've looked at my calendar and I tell you what I think the outer limits are. I would think that would sound about right. . . .

Q: Do you believe that Ms. Lewinsky was at the White House and saw you on December 28th, 1997?

C: Yes, sir, I do.

Q: And do you remember talking with Ms. Lewinsky about her subpoena that she received for the Paula Jones case on that day?

C: I remember talking with Ms. Lewinsky about her testimony, or about the prospect that she might have to give testimony. And she, she talked to me about that. I remember that.

Q: And you also gave her Christmas gifts, is that not correct, Mr. President?

C: That is correct. They were Christmas gifts and they were going-away gifts. She was moving to New York taking a new job, starting a new life. And I gave her some gifts.

Q: And you actually requested this meeting, is that not correct?

C: I don't remember that, Mr. Bittman, but it's quite possible that I invited her to come by before she left town. But usually when we met, she requested the meetings. . . .

Q: You mentioned that you discussed her subpoena in the Paula Jones case. Tell us specifically, what did you discuss?

C: No, sir, that's not what I said. I said, my recollection is I knew by then, of course, that she had gotten a subpoena. And I knew that she was, therefore, was slated to testify. And she mentioned to me — and I believe it was at this meeting.

She mentioned — I remember a conversation about the possibility of her testifying. I believe it must have occurred on the 28th.

She mentioned to me that she did not want to testify. So, that's how it came up. Not in the context of, I heard you have a subpoena, let's talk about it. She raised the issue with me in the context of her desire to avoid testifying, which I certainly understood; not only because there were some embarrassing facts about our relationship that were inappropriate, but also because a whole lot of innocent people were being traumatized and dragged through the mud by these Jones lawyers . . . and since she didn't know Paula Jones and knew nothing about sexual harassment, and certainly had no experience with that, I, I clearly understood why she didn't want to be a part of it. . . .

Q: Did anyone, as far as you knew, know about your embarrassing, inappropriate intimate relationship that you had with Ms. Lewinsky?

C: At that time, I was unaware that she had told anyone else about it. But if, if I had known that, it would not have surprised me.

Q: Had you told anyone?

C: Absolutely not.

Q: Had you tried, in fact, not to let anyone else know about this relationship?

C: Well, of course.

Q: What did you do?

C: Well, I never said anything about it, for one thing. And I did what people do when they do the wrong thing. I tried to do it where nobody else was looking at it.

Q: How many times did you do that?

C: Well, if you go back to my statement, I remember there were a few times in '96, I can't say with any certainty. There was once in early '97. After she left the White House, I do not believe I ever had any inappropriate contact with her in the rest of '96. There was one occasion in '97 when, regrettably, that we were together for a few minutes, I think about 20 minutes, and there was inappropriate contact. And after that, to the best of my memory and belief it did not occur again. . . .

Q: Getting back to your meeting with Ms. Lewinsky on December 28, you are aware that she's been subpoenaed. You are aware, are you not, Mr. President, that the subpoena called for the production of, among other things, all the gifts that you had given Ms. Lewinsky? You were aware of that on December 28th, weren't you?

C: I'm not sure. And I understand this is an important question. I did have a conversation with Ms. Lewinsky at some time about gifts, the gifts I'd given her. I do not know whether it occurred on the 28th, or whether it occurred earlier. I do not know whether it occurred in person or whether it occurred on the telephone. I have searched my memory for this, because I know it's an important issue. . . .

The reason I'm not sure it happened on the 28th is that my recollection is that Ms. Lewinsky said something to me like, what if they ask me about the gifts you've given me. That's the memory I have. That's why I question whether it happened on the 28th, because she had a subpoena with her, request for production. And I told her that if they asked her for gifts, she'd have to give them whatever she had, that that's what the law was. . . . And I think, Mr. Bittman, it must have happened before then, because — either that, or Ms. Lewinsky didn't want to tell me that she had the subpoena, because that was the language I remember her using. . . .

Q: Mr. President, if your intent was, as you have earlier testified, that you didn't want anybody to know about this relationship you had with Ms. Lewinsky, why would you feel comfortable giving her gifts in the middle of discovery in the Paula Jones case?

C: Well, sir, for one thing, there was no existing improper relationship at that time. I had, for nearly a year, done my best to be a friend to Ms. Lewinsky, to be a counselor to her, to give her good advice, and to help her. She had, for her part, most of the time, accepted the changed circumstances. She talked to me a lot about her life, her job ambitions, and she continued to give me gifts. And I felt that it was a right thing to do to give her gifts. . . .

Currie's Role

Q: After you gave her the gifts on December 28th, did you speak with your secretary, Ms. Currie, and ask her to pick up a box of gifts that were some compilation of gifts that Ms. Lewinsky would have —

C: No, sir, I didn't do that.

Q: — to give to Ms. Currie?

C: I did not do that.

Q: When you testified in the Paula Jones case, this was only two-and-a-half weeks after you had given her these six gifts, you were asked, at page 75 in your deposition, lines 2 through 5, "Well, have you ever given any gifts to Monica Lewinsky?" And you answer, "I don't recall." And you were correct. You pointed out that you actually asked them, for prompting, "Do you know what they were?"

C: I think what I meant there was — don't recall what they were, not that I don't recall whether I had given them. And then if you see, they did give me these specifics, and I gave them quite a good explanation here. . . . I had no interest in not answering their questions about these gifts. I do not believe that gifts are incriminating, nor do I think they are wrong, I think it was a good thing to do. I'm not, I'm still not sorry I gave Monica Lewinsky gifts. . . .

Currie Testimony

Q: Let me ask you about the meeting you had with Betty Currie at the White House on Sunday, January 18 of this year, the day after your deposition. First of all, you didn't — Mrs. Currie, your secretary of six-some years, you never allowed her, did you, to watch whatever intimate activity you did with Ms. Lewinsky, did you?

C: No, sir, not to my knowledge.

Q: And as far as you know, she couldn't hear anything either, is that right?

C: There were a couple of times when Monica was there when I asked Betty to be places where she could hear, because Monica was upset and I — this was after there was — all the inappropriate contact had been terminated.

Q: No, I'm talking . . . about the times that you actually had the intimate contact.

C: She was — I believe that — well, first of all, on that one occasion in 1997, I do not know whether Betty was in the White House after the radio [Feb. 28] address in the Oval Office complex. I believe she probably was, but I'm not sure. But I'm certain that someone was there. I always — always someone was there. In 1996, I think most of the times that Ms. Lewinsky was there, there may not have been anybody around except maybe coming in and out, but not permanently so. I — that's correct. I never — I didn't try to involve Betty in that in any way.

Q: Well, not only did you not try to involve her, you specifically tried to exclude her and everyone else, isn't that right?

C: Well, yes. . . .

Q: So, if Ms. Currie testified that you approached her on the 18th, or you spoke with her and you said, you were always there when she was there, she wasn't, was she? That is, Mrs. Currie?

C: She was always there in the White House, and I was concerned — let me back up and say. . . . I was more concerned about the times after [the final sexual encounter] when Ms. Lewinsky was upset, and I wanted to establish at least that I had not — because these questions were — some of them were off the wall. Some of them were way out of line, I thought.

And what I wanted to establish was that Betty was there at all other times in the complex, and I wanted to know what Betty's memory was about what she heard, what she could hear. And what I did not know was — I did not know that. And I was trying to figure out, and I was trying to figure out in a hurry because I knew something was up.

Q: So, you wanted . . . to check her memory for what she remembered, and that is —

C: That's correct.

Q: — whether she remembered nothing, or whether she remembered an inappropriate intimate relationship?

C: Oh, no, no, no, no. No. I didn't ask her about it in that way. I asked her about what the — what I was trying to determine was whether my recollection was right and that she was always in the office complex when Monica was there, and whether she thought she could hear any conversations we had, or did she hear any.

And then I asked her specifically about a couple of times when — once when I asked her to remain in the dining room, Betty, while I met with Monica in my study. And once when I took Monica in the, the small office Nancy Hernreich occupies right next to Betty's and talked to her there for a few minutes. That's my recollection of that. . . .

Q: If Ms. Currie testified that these were not really questions to her, that they were more like statements, is that not true?

C: Well, I can't testify as to what her perception was. I can tell you this. I was trying to get information in a hurry. I was downloading what I remembered. I think Ms. Currie would also testify that I explicitly told her, once I realized that you were involved in the Jones case — you, the Office of Independent Counsel — and that she might have to be called as a witness, that she should just go in there and tell the truth, tell what she knew, and be perfectly truthful. So, I was not trying to get Betty Currie to say something that was untruthful. I was trying to get as much information as quickly as I could.

Q: What information were you trying to get from her when you said, I was never alone with her, right?

C: I don't remember exactly what I did say with her. That's what you say I said.

Q: If Ms. Currie testified to that, if she says you told her, I was never alone with her, right? . . .

C: Mr. Bittman, just a minute. I was never alone with her, right, might be a question. And what I might have meant by that is, in the Oval Office complex. . . .

Endorsing Lewinsky's Testimony

SOLOMON WISENBERG: Mr. President, I want to, before I go into a new subject area, briefly go over something you were talking about with Mr. Bittman. The statement of your attorney, Mr. Bennett, at Paula Jones deposition, "Counsel is fully aware" — it's page 54, line 5 — "Counsel is fully aware that Ms. Lewinsky has filed, has an affidavit which they are in possession of saying that there is absolutely no sex of any kind in any manner, shape or form, with President Clinton." That statement is made by your attorney in front of Judge Susan Webber Wright, correct?

C: That's correct.

Q: That statement is a completely false statement. Whether or not Mr. Bennett knew of your relationship with Ms. Lewinsky, the statement that there was "no sex of any kind in any manner, shape or form, with President Clinton," was an utterly false statement. Is that correct?

C: It depends on what the meaning of the word "is" is. If the — if he — if "is" means is and never has been that is not — that is one thing. If it means there is none, that was a completely true statement.

But, as I have testified, and I'd like to testify again, this is — it is somewhat unusual for a client to be asked about his lawyer's statements, instead of the other way around. I was not paying a great deal of attention to this exchange. I was focusing on my own testimony.

And if you go back and look at the sequence of this, you will see that the Jones lawyers decided that this was going to be the Lewinsky deposition, not the Jones deposition. . . . But that is not how I prepared for it. That is not how I was thinking about it. And I am not sure, Mr. Wisenberg, as I sit here today, that I sat there and followed all these interchanges between the lawyers. I'm quite sure that I didn't follow all the interchanges between the lawyers all that carefully.

And I don't really believe, therefore, that I can say Mr. Bennett's testimony or statement is testimony and is imputable to me. I didn't — I don't know that I was even paying that much attention to it. . . .

Q: You are the President of the United States and your attorney tells a United States District Court Judge that there is no sex of any kind, in any way, shape or form, whatsoever. And you feel no obligation to do anything about that at that deposition, Mr. President?

C: I have told you, Mr. Wisenberg, I will tell you for a third time. I am not even sure that when Mr. Bennett made that statement that I was concentrating on the exact words he used. Now, if someone had asked me on that day, are you having any kind of sexual relations with Ms. Lewinsky, that is, asked me a question in the present tense, I would have said no. And it would have been completely true. . . .

Q: I just want to make sure I understand, Mr. President. Do you mean today that because you were not engaging in sexual activity with Ms. Lewinsky during the deposition that the statement of Mr. Bennett might be literally true?

C: No, sir. . . . I wasn't trying to give you a cute answer, that I was obviously not involved in anything improper during a deposition. I was trying to tell you that generally

Texts

speaking in the present tense, if someone said that, that would be true. But I don't know what Mr. Bennett had in his mind. I don't know. I didn't pay any attention to this colloquy that went on. I was waiting for my instructions as a witness to go forward I was worried about my own testimony. . . .

Jordan's Role

Q: If Mr. Jordan has told us that he visited you in the Residence on the night of the 19th [Dec. 19, 1997], after a White House holiday dinner, to discuss Monica Lewinsky and her subpoena with you, do you have any reason to doubt it?

C: No. . . .

Q: If Mr. Jordan has told us that he spoke with you over the phone within about an hour of Monica receiving her subpoena, and later visited you that very day, the night at the White House, to discuss it, again you'd have no reason to doubt him, is that correct?

C: I've already — I believe I've already testified about that here today, that I had lots of conversations with Vernon. I'm sure that I had lots of conversations with him that included comments about this. And if he has a specific memory of when I had some conversation on a certain day, [I] would be inclined to trust his memory over mine, because under the present circumstances my head's probably more cluttered than his, and my schedule is probably busier. He's probably got better records.

Q: And when Mr. Jordan met with you at the Residence that night, sir, he asked you if you'd been involved in a sexual relationship with Monica Lewinsky, didn't he?

C: I do not remember exactly what the nature of the conversation was. I do remember that I told him that there was no sexual relationship between me and Monica Lewinsky, which was true. . . .

Q: Mr. President, if Mr. Jordan has told us that he had a very disturbing conversation with Ms. Lewinsky that day, then went over to visit you at the White House, and that before he asked you the question about a sexual relationship, related that disturbing conversation to you, the conversation being that Ms. Lewinsky had a fixation on you and thought that perhaps the First Lady would leave you at the end of — that you would leave the First Lady at the end of your term and come be with Ms. Lewinsky, do you have any reason to doubt him that it was on that night that that conversation happened?

C: All I can tell you, sir, is I, I certainly don't remember him saying that. Now, he could have said that because, as you know, a great many things happened in the ensuing two or three days. And I could have just forgotten it. But I don't remember him ever saying that.

Q: At any time?

C: No, I don't remember him saying that. What I remember was that he said that Monica came to see him, that she was upset that she was going to have to testify, that he had referred her to a lawyer. . . .

Q: That is something that one would be likely to remember, don't you think, Mr. President?

C: I think I would, and I'd be happy to share it with you if I did. I only had one encounter with Ms. Lewinsky, I seem to remember, which was somewhat maybe reminiscent of that. But not that, if you will, obsessive, if that's the way you want to use that word. . . .

Q: Mr. President, you swore under oath in the Jones case that you didn't think anyone other than your lawyers had ever told you that Monica Lewinsky had been subpoenaed. . . . Here's the testimony, sir:

"Question — we've gone over it a little bit before: 'Did anyone other than your attorneys ever tell you that Monica Lewinsky had been served with a subpoena in this case?' Answer, 'I don't think so.' " Now, this deposition was taken just three-and-a-half weeks after, by your own testimony, Vernon Jordan made a trip at night to the White House to tell you, among other things, that Monica Lewinsky had been subpoenaed and was upset about it. Why did you give that testimony under oath in the Jones case, sir?

C: Well, Mr. Wisenberg, I think you have to — again, you have to put this in the context of the flow of questions, and I've already testified to this once today, I will testify to it again. My answer to the next question, I think, is a way of finishing my answer to the question and the answer you've said here. I was trying to remember who the first person, other than Mr. Bennett — I don't think Mr. Bennett — who the first person told me that, who told me Paula Jones had, I mean, excuse me, Monica Lewinsky had a subpoena. And I thought that Bruce Lindsey was the first person. And that's how I was trying to remember that.

Keep in mind, sort of like today, these questions are being kind of put at me rapid-fire. But, unlike today, I hadn't had the opportunity to prepare at this level of detail. . . . Several of my answers are somewhat jumbled. But this is an honest attempt here — if you read both these answers, it's obviously they were both answers to that question you quoted, to remember the first person, who was not Mr. Bennett, who told me. And I don't believe Vernon was the first person who told me. I believe Bruce Lindsey was.

Q: Let me read the question, because I want to talk about the first person issue. The question on line 25 of page 68 is, "Did anyone other than your attorneys ever tell you that Monica Lewinsky had been served with a subpoena in this case?" Answer, "I don't think so." You would agree with me, sir, that the question doesn't say, the question doesn't say anything about who was the first person. It just says, did anyone tell you. Isn't that correct?

C: That's right. And I said Bruce Lindsey, because I was trying to struggle with who — where I had heard this. And they were free to ask a follow-up question, and they didn't. . . .

Q: If Vernon Jordan has told us that you have an extraordinary memory, one of the greatest memories he's ever seen in a politician, would that be something you would care to dispute?

C: No, I do have a good memory. At least, I have had a good memory in my life. . . . Now, I have been shocked, and so have members of my family and friends of mine, at how many things that I have forgotten in the last six years, I think because of the pressure and the pace and the volume of events in the president's life, compounded by the pressure of your four-year inquiry, and all the other things that have happened, I'm amazed there are lots of times when I literally can't remember last week. . . .

Q: If he's told us that he notified you around January 7th, when [Lewinsky] signed her affidavit, and that you generally understood that it would deny a sexual relationship, do you have any reason to doubt that?

C: No.

Q: . . . And yet when you were asked, sir, at the Jones deposition about Vernon Jordan, and specifically about whether or not he had discussed the lawsuit with you, didn't reveal that to the Court. . . . This is your answer, or a portion of it: "I knew that he met with her. I think Betty suggested that he meet with her. Anyway, he met with her. I, I thought that he talked to her about something else."

Why didn't you tell the Court, when you were under oath and sworn to tell the truth, the whole truth, and nothing but the truth, that you had been talking with Vernon Jordan about the case, about the affidavit, the lawyer, the subpoena?

C: Well, that's not the question I was asked. I was not asked any question about — I was asked, "Has it ever been reported to you that he met with Monica Lewinsky and talked about this case." I believe — I may be wrong about this — my impression was that at the time, I was focused on the meetings. I believe the meetings he had were meetings about her moving to New York and getting a job. I knew at some point that she had told him that she needed some help, because she had gotten a subpoena. I'm not sure I know whether she did that in a meeting or a phone call. And I was not, I was not focused on that.

I know that, I know Vernon helped her to get a lawyer, Mr. Carter. And I, I believe that he did it after she had called him, but I'm not sure. But I knew that the main source of their meetings was about her move to New York and her getting a job.

Q: Are you saying, sir, that you forgot when you were asked this question that Vernon Jordan had come on December 19th, just three-and-a-half weeks before, and said that he had met that day, the day that Monica got the subpoena?

C: It's quite possible — it's a sort of a jumbled answer. It's quite possible that I had gotten mixed up between whether she had met with him or talked to him on the telephone in those three and a half weeks.

Again, I say, sir, just from the tone of your voice and the way you are asking questions here, it's obvious that this is the most important thing in the world, and that everybody was focused on all the details at the time. But that's not the way it worked. I was, I was doing my best to remember. . . .

Clinton's Responsibility

Q: Mr. President, the next series of questions are from the grand jurors. And let me tell you that the grand jurors want you to be more specific about the inappropriate conduct. The first question was, one of the grand jurors has said that you referred to what you did with Ms. Lewinsky as inappropriate contact; what do you mean by that?

C: . . . What I meant was, and what they can infer that I meant was, that I did things that were — when I was alone with her, that were inappropriate and wrong. But that they did not include any activity that was within the definition of sexual relations that I was given by Judge Wright in the deposition. I said that I did not do those things that were in that, within that definition, and I testified truthfully to that. And that's all I can say about it. . . .

Q: Well, I have a question regarding your definition then. And my question is, is oral sex performed on you within that definition as you understood it, the definition in the Jones —

C: As I understood it, it was not, no. . . .

Q: If a person touched another person, if you touched another person on the breast, would that be, in your view, and was it within your view, when you took the deposition, within the definition of sexual relations?

C: If the person being deposed?

Q: Yes.

C: — in this case, me, directly touched the breast of another person, with the purpose to arouse or gratify, under that definition that would be included.

Q: Only directly, sir, or would it be directly or through clothing?

C: Well, I would — I think the common sense definition would be directly. That's how I would infer what it means.

Q: If the person being deposed kissed the breast of another person, would that be in the definition of sexual relations as you understood it when you were under oath in the Jones case?

C: Yes, that would constitute contact. I think that would. If it were direct contact, I believe it would. I — maybe I should read it again, just to make sure. Because this basically says if there was any direct contact with an intent to arouse or gratify, if that was the intent of the contact, then that would fall within the definition. That's correct.

Q: So, touching, in your view then and now — the person being deposed touching or kissing the breast of another person would fall within the definition?

C: That's correct, sir.

Q: And you testified that you didn't have sexual relations with Monica Lewinsky in the Jones deposition, under that definition, correct?

C: That's correct, sir.

Q: If the person being deposed touched the genitalia of another person, would that be — and with the intent to arouse the sexual desire, arouse or gratify, as defined in [the operative definition in the Jones case], would that be, under your understanding then and now sexual relations? . . .

C: Yes, it would. If you had a direct contact with any of these places in the body, if you had direct contact with intent to arouse or gratify, that would fall within the definition.

Q: So, you didn't do any of those three things — with Monica Lewinsky?

C: You are free to infer that my testimony is that I did not have sexual relations, as I understood this term to be defined.

Q: Including touching her breast, kissing her breast, or touching her genitalia?

C: That's correct. . . .

Q: Oral sex, in your view, is not covered, correct?

C: If performed on the deponent.

Q: Is not covered, correct?

C: That's my reading of this number (1).

Q: And you are declining to answer the hypothetical about insertion of an object. I need to inform you, Mr. President — we'll go on, at least for now. But I need to inform you that the grand jury will consider your not answering the questions more directly in their determination of whether or not they are going to issue another subpoena. . . .

Lying to Staff

Q: Do you recall denying any sexual relationship with Monica Lewinsky to the following people: Harry Thomasson, Erskine Bowles, Harold Ickes, [John] Podesta, Mr. Blumenthal, Mr. Jordan, Ms. Betty Currie? Do you recall denying any sexual relationship with Monica Lewinsky to those individuals?

C: I recall telling a number of those people that I didn't have, either I didn't have an affair with Monica Lewinsky or didn't have sex with her. And I believe, sir, that — you'll have to ask them what they thought. But I was using those terms in the normal way people use them. You'll have to ask them what they thought I was saying. . . .

Did I hope that I would never have to be here on this day giving this testimony? Of course. But I also didn't want to do anything to complicate this matter further. So, I said things that were true. They may have been misleading, and if they were I have to take responsibility for it, and I'm sorry.

Q: After January 21st when The [Washington] Post article broke and said that Judge Starr was looking into this, you knew that they might be witnesses. You knew that they might be called into a grand jury, didn't you?

C: That's right. I think I was quite careful what I said after that. I may have said something to all these people to that effect, but I'll also — whenever anybody asked me any details, I said, look, I don't want you to be a witness or I turn you into a witness or give you information that could get you in trouble. I just wouldn't talk. I, by and large, didn't talk to people about this.

Q: If all of these people — let's leave out Mrs. Currie for a minute. Vernon Jordan, Sid Blumenthal, John Podesta, Harold Ickes, Erskine Bowles, Harry Thomasson, after the story broke, after Judge Starr's involvement was known on January 21st, have said that you denied a sexual relationship with them. Are you denying that?

C: No.

Q: And you've told us that you —

C: I'm just telling you what I meant by it.

Job for Lewinsky

Q: Did you, on or about January the 13th, 1998, Mr. President, ask Erskine Bowles to ask John Hilley if he would give a recommendation for Monica Lewinsky?

C: In 1998?

Q: Yes. On or about January 13th, 1998, did you ask Erskine Bowles, your Chief of Staff, if he would ask John Hilley to give a recommendation for Monica Lewinsky?

C: At some point, sir, I believe I talked to Erskine Bowles about whether Monica Lewinsky could get a recommendation that was not negative from the Legislative Affairs Office. I believe I did. . . . I do not know what the date was. At some point I did talk to him. . . .

My recollection is, sir, that Ms. Lewinsky was moving to New York, wanted to get a job in the private sector; was confident she would get a good recommendation from the Defense Department; and was concerned that because she had been moved from the Legislative Affairs Office,

Texts

transferred to the Defense Department, that her ability to get a job might be undermined by a bad recommendation from the Legislative Affairs Office.

So, I asked Erskine if we could get her a recommendation that just was at least neutral, so that if she had a good recommendation from the Defense Department it wouldn't prevent her from getting a job in the private sector. . . .

Q: And who was it that asked you to do that on Monica Lewinsky's behalf?

C: I think she did. You know, she tried for months and months to get a job back in the White House, not so much in the West Wing but somewhere in the White House complex, including the Old Executive Office Building. And she talked to Marsha Scott, among others.

She very much wanted to come back. And she interviewed for some jobs but never got one.

She was, from time to time, upset about it. And I think what she was afraid of is that she couldn't get a — from the minute she left the White House she was worried about this. That if she didn't come back to the White House and work for awhile and get a good job recommendation, that no matter how well she had done at the Pentagon it might hurt her future employment prospects.

Well, it became obvious that, you know, her mother had moved to New York. She wanted to go to New York. She wasn't going to get a job in the White House. So, she wanted to get a job in the private sector, and said, I hope that I won't get a letter out of the Legislative Affairs Office that will prevent my getting a job in the private sector. And that's what I talked to Erskine about. Now, that's my entire memory of this.

Hiding the Gifts

Q: All right. I want to go back briefly to the December 28th conversation with Ms. Lewinsky. I believe you testified to the effect that she asked you, what if they ask me about gifts you gave me. My question to you is, after that statement by her, did you ever have a conversation with Betty Currie about gifts, or picking something up from Monica Lewinsky?

C: I don't believe I did, sir. No.

Q: You never told her anything to this effect, that Monica has something to give you?

C: No, sir. . . .

Q: And so you have no knowledge that, or you had no knowledge at the time, that Betty Currie went and picked up, your secretary went and picked up from Monica Lewinsky items that were called for by the Jones subpoena and hid them under her bed? You had no knowledge that anything remotely like that was going to happen?

C: I did not. I did not know she had those items, I believe, until that was made public.

Q: And you agree with me that that would be a very wrong thing to do, to hide evidence in a civil case, or any case? Isn't that true?

C: Yes. I don't know that, that Ms. Currie knew that that's what she had at all. But —

Q: I'm not saying she did. . . .

Q: Did you ever say anything like that, you can always say that you were coming to see Betty or bringing me letters? Was that part of any kind of a, anything you said to [Lewinsky] or a cover story, before you had any idea she was going to be part of Paula Jones?

C: I might well have said that.

Q: Okay.

C: Because I certainly didn't want this to come out, if I could help it. And I was concerned about that. I was embarrassed about it. I knew it was wrong. And, you know, of course, I didn't want it to come out. But —

Q: But you are saying that you didn't say anything — I want to make sure I understand. Did you say anything like that once you knew or thought she might be a witness in the Jones case? Did you repeat that statement, or something like it to her?

C: Well, again, I don't recall, and I don't recall whether I might have done something like that, for example, if somebody says, what if the reporters ask me this, that or the other thing. I can tell you this: In the context of whether she could be a witness, I have a recollection that she asked me, well, what do I do if I get called as a witness, and I said you have to get a lawyer. And that's all I said. And I never asked her to lie.

Q: Did you tell her to tell the truth?

C: Well, I think the implication was she would tell the truth. I've already told you that I felt strongly that she could issue, that she could execute an affidavit that would be factually truthful, that might get her out of having to testify. . . .

Getting a Job

Q: I want to go back to a question about Vernon Jordan. I want to go back to late December and early January, late December of '97 and early January of '98. During this time, Mr. President, you are being sued for sexual harassment by a woman who claims, among other things, that others got benefits that she didn't because she didn't [have] sex [with] you. While this is happening, your powerful friend, Vernon Jordan, is helping to get Monica Lewinsky a job and a lawyer. He's helping to get a job and a lawyer for someone who had some kind of sex with you, and who has been subpoenaed in the very case, the Jones case. Don't you see a problem with this? Didn't you see a problem with this?

C: No. . . . I don't think it was wrong to be helping her. Look —

Q: A subpoenaed witness in a case against you?

C: Absolutely. Look, for one thing, I had already proved in two ways that I was not trying to influence her testimony. I didn't order her to be hired at the White House. I could have done so. I wouldn't do it. She tried for months to get in. She was angry. Secondly, after I —

Q: Wasn't she kept —

C: After I terminated the improper contact with her, she wanted to come in more than she did. She got angry when she didn't get in sometimes. I knew that that might make her more likely to speak, and I still did it because I had to limit the contact.

And, thirdly, let me say, I formed an opinion really early in 1996 . . . once I got into this unfortunate and wrong conduct, that when I stopped it, which I knew I'd have to do and which I should have done a long time before I did, that she would talk about it. Not because Monica Lewinsky is a bad person. . . . But I knew that the minute there was no longer any contact, she would talk about this. She would have to. She couldn't help it. It was, it was a part of her psyche. So, I had put myself at risk, sir. I was not trying to buy her silence or get Vernon Jordan to buy her silence. I thought she was a good person. She had not been involved with me for a long time in any improper way, months, and I wanted to help her get on with her life. It's just as simple as that. . . .

Defining Sex

Q: Well, the grand jury would like to know, Mr. President, why it is that you think that oral sex performed on you does not fall within the definition of sexual relations as used in your deposition.

C: Because that is — if the deponent is the person who has oral sex performed on him, then the contact is with — not with anything on that list, but with the lips of another person. It seems to be self-evident that that's what it is. And I thought it was curious. Let me remind you, sir, I read this carefully. . . . And I had to admit under this definition that I'd actually had sexual relations with Gennifer Flowers. Now, I would rather have taken a whipping than done that, after all the trouble I'd been through with Gennifer Flowers. . . .

Q: Would you have been prepared, if asked by the Jones lawyers, would you have been prepared to answer a question directly asked about oral sex performed on you by Monica Lewinsky?

C: If the Judge had required me to answer it, of course, I would have answered it. And I would have answered it truthfully. . . . ◆

'Do We Have a Duty To Look Further Or To Look Away?'

The following are excerpts from opening statements made Oct. 5 by the members of the House Judiciary Committee as it considered whether to recommend opening a full impeachment inquiry. From transcripts provided by Federal News Service.

Chairman Henry J. Hyde, R-Ill.

. . . On Sept. 11, the Office of Independent Counsel transmitted materials to the House of Representatives that, in his opinion, constituted substantial and credible evidence that may constitute grounds for impeachment of the president of the United States. . . .

Today it's our responsibility and our constitutional duty to review those materials referred to us and recommend to the House of Representatives whether the matter merits a further inquiry. Let me be clear about this. We are not here today to decide whether or not to impeach Mr. Clinton. We are not here to pass judgment on anyone. We are here to ask and answer this one simple question: Based upon what we now know, do we have a duty to look further or to look away?

We are constantly reminded how weary America is of this whole situation, and I dare say most of us share that weariness. But we members of Congress took an oath that we would perform all of our constitutional duties, not just the pleasant ones . . . .

We are going to work expeditiously and fairly. When we have completed our inquiry, whatever the result, we will make our recommendations to the House. We will do so as soon as we can, consistent with principles of fairness and completeness.

I anticipate several objections to our procedures from our Democratic friends, the first of which deals with their demand that we establish first, before proceeding with any inquiry, what the standards are for impeachment. We don't propose, however, to deviate from the wise counsel of former Chairman Peter Rodino who during the Nixon impeachment inquiry, published a staff report rejecting the establishment of a particular standard for impeachment before inquiring into the facts of the case.

Let me quote from Chairman Rodino's report: "Delicate issues of basic constitutional law are involved. Those issues cannot be defined in detail in advance of full investigation of the facts. The Supreme Court of the United States does not reach out in the abstract to rule on the constitutionality of statutes or of conduct.

"Cases must be brought and adjudicated on particular facts in terms of the Constitution. Similarly, the House does not engage in abstract, advisory or hypothetical debates about the precise nature of conduct that calls for the exercise of its constitutional powers. Rather, it must await full development of the facts and understanding of the events to which those facts relate."

The 20th century has been referred to often as the American century. It is imperative we be able to look back at this episode with dignity and pride, knowing we have performed our duty in the best interests of the entire country. In this difficult moment in our history lies the potential for our finest achievement: proof that democracy works.

Ranking Democrat John Conyers Jr., Mich.

We meet today for only the third time in the history of our nation to consider whether or not to open an inquiry of impeachment against the president of the United States. For more than 200 years, we have been guided by that brilliant legacy of our Founding Fathers and of our Constitution, which, generation after generation, has helped us endure the difficult political and social questions that face us. . . .

This committee was called upon to consider the standard for impeachment of a president in 1974. And at the risk of dating myself, I remain the only member of the committee serving today who was there then. Our staff issued a report in February of that year that has become a model for scholars and historians alike. The report concluded that "impeachment is a constitutional remedy addressed to serious offenses against the system of government. And it is directed at constitutional wrongs that subvert the structure of government or undermine the integrity of office and even the Constitution itself."

Those words are as true today as they were in 1974. An impeachment is only for a serious abuse of official power or a serious breach of official duties. On that, the constitutional scholars are in overwhelming agreement.

The failure to even articulate a standard of impeachment against which the evidence can be measured, a step the 1974 committee took prior to any investigation, is not [the] only failure of this investigation into the president. The tactics of the investigation into the president have also, in my judgment, been an offense to the tradition of this great country and to the common sense of the American people. . . .

Our review of the evidence sent with the referral convinces many of us of one thing: There is no support for any suggestion that the president obstructed justice, or that he tampered with witnesses or abused the power of his office. . . . This is not Watergate; it is an extramarital affair. Americans know [that] and want to finish this.

And 99 percent of the facts are already on the table. The investigatory phase will be far less significant than in previous congressional inquiries. There are only a handful of witnesses that can provide us probative information, all of whom have been before the grand jury three, four, five and six times. . . .

The open-ended Republican proposal [is] a means for dragging this matter out well past the [November] elections. . . . There is no need for this investigation to be open-ended when we can, because of its limited factual predicate, close it down within six weeks. . . .

F. James Sensenbrenner Jr., R-Wis.

Today we begin a task second only in gravity to Congress' power to declare war. It is important at the outset to note that this debate is not about the fact that President Clinton had an affair with Monica Lewinsky and then lied about it to his family, his staff, his Cabinet and to the American public. It is about Judge Starr's finding that the president violated his oath "to tell the truth, the whole truth and nothing but the truth" in a successful attempt to defeat Paula Jones' civil-rights suit against him. . . .

The president denies all the allegations. Someone is lying, and someone is telling the truth. An impeachment inquiry is the only way to get to the bottom of this mess. . . .

Barney Frank, D-Mass.

. . . The chairman said we shouldn't look away, we should look further. I agree. What we shouldn't do, however, is adopt a resolution which says, "Let's look around. Let's see what we can find. Let's see if we can find something in Whitewater and the FBI files and the travel office and the campaign finance office." . . .

I don't think much of the job [Starr has] done, but he's there and he has that statutory responsibility and, therefore, I think we have to look at what he said. But let's look at what he said; let us not turn this into an impeachment inquiry in search of a

Texts

high crime. Let's look at what Mr. Starr charged the president with and decide. . . .

Bill McCollum, R-Fla.

. . . This is not about jaywalking, it's not about driving under the influence. Those are not major crimes for which any president would be impeached.

But I would suggest to you that what it's about is whether or not we can sustain the constitutional form of our government without going forward at this point. It's about the separation of powers in the three branches of government: the legislative, the executive and judicial. It's about whether or not what the president may have done, if gone without punishment, without being impeached, without being removed from office, would undermine the judicial system, the third branch of our government. . . .

Even if it were only shown to us that the president of the United States lied under oath and committed perjury in the civil deposition he took or, even more seriously, before the grand jury when he testified just a month or so ago, if that is all that's proven, that's enough for us to impeach and enough for him to be thrown out of office. And if we were not to do that, I submit, it would undermine our constitutional system and destroy the foundation of our judicial system. . . .

Charles E. Schumer, D-N.Y.

. . . Whether you cite The Federalist Papers or legal scholars like Justice [Joseph] Story, the president's actions, while wrong and inappropriate and possibly illegal, are clearly not impeachable. . . .

I'd support a motion of censure or a motion to rebuke, as President Ford suggested yesterday, not because it is politically expedient to do but because the president's actions cry out for punishment and because censure or rebuke, not impeachment, is the right punishment.

It is time to move forward and not have the Congress and the American people endure a specter of what could be a yearlong focus on a tawdry, but not impeachable, affair. The world economy is in crisis and cries out for American leadership. . . . The American people cry out for us to solve the problems facing America like health care, education and ensuring that seniors have a decent retirement. This investigation, now it its fifth year, has run its course. It's time to move on.

George W. Gekas, R-Pa.

. . . Reviewing and re-reviewing the referral by the independent counsel . . . is a duty imposed upon us by statute and by the Constitution. In the referral, there are allegations, again, for the evaluation of this committee. I have had difficulty, for instance, in one allegation in which the independent counsel says, "The president repeatedly and unlawfully invoked the executive privilege to conceal evidence of his personal misconduct from the grand jury." . . . But that is not for me to conclude . . . simply because I have doubts about it. . . . I have to inquire further into what justification there is for the allegation. . . .

I am not yet satisfied that there's guilt or innocence with respect to the perjury allegations, but, by darn, it is worth a fuller inquiry by this body.

Howard L. Berman, D-Calif.

. . . Let's seek some common ground. First, every four years the people vote for president. This popular decision is a defining moment of our constitutional system. The people's vote is almost sacred and should not be altered except under the most extreme circumstances.

Secondly, the impeachment process is a constitutionally mandated procedure for undoing the people's will, but only when the president is found guilty of treason, bribery, or other high crimes and misdemeanors. Third, the impeachment process is not a legal proceeding. We are not a courtroom. The impeachment process should not be used as a legislative vote of no confidence on the president's conduct or policies. We are not governed by a parliamentary system. . . .

The majority party has an obligation to recognize that "high crimes and misdemeanors" has a meaning. All felonies are not high crimes and misdemeanors. All high crimes and misdemeanors are not felonies. Because of the deference the Constitution gives to the person who wins a presidential Electoral College vote, the standard for impeachment is far more complicated and subtle than a straight reading of a criminal statute. . . .

The minority party has an obligation to recognize that a Democratically controlled Congress, at the urging of President Clinton, passed a statute that allowed for the naming of an independent counsel by a three-judge panel. The independent counsel was in turn given the approval by a Democratic attorney general to pursue the Monica Lewinsky matter. . . .

I may . . . regret my vote for the independent counsel statute. But the fact remains, no matter what I think, that statute is the law. . . . The same statute requires the independent counsel to report what he believes are grounds for impeachment to the House. It is our obligation to proceed to decide whether the independent counsel's contentions are in fact grounds for impeachment. . . .

I suggest that whatever rules of procedure are adopted, our first order of business is to resolve if the events portrayed in the Starr report's narrative rise to the level of an impeachable offense. . . .

Howard Coble, R-N.C.

. . . A society founded upon the rule of law is one which values truth. Without it, we have no courts which will function. In its absence, we have no civil society. This ultimately means that citizens in our republic, regardless of the power they have or the position they hold, must make an obligatory commitment to observe the law. As Theodore Roosevelt once said, obedience to the law is demanded as a right, not asked as a favor. . . .

Rick Boucher, D-Va.

. . . The rules we set, the process that we employ, the balances we achieve to assure that the rights of all are protected and that the nation's interests are served, will influence not just the course of this investigation but future impeachment investigations, as well. . . .

Before the investigation phase of our work begins, we should establish a shared understanding . . . of the fact that the framers of the Constitution did not intend for impeachment to be a punishment for individual misconduct; of the fact that they intended for impeachment to occur only when that misconduct is substantial and is so important to the functioning of the office of the president that it is absolutely incompatible with our constitutional system of government.

Our process will then require that the allegations of the independent counsel each be compared to the historical constitutional standard, and that only those allegations that meet that threshold test become the subject of our formal inquiry. . . .

Lamar Smith, R-Texas

. . . The inquiry into the president's conduct must go on for one simple reason: The truth matters.

The president holds a public office we rightly regard as the most powerful in the world. The president serves as a role model for us and for our children. He influences the lives of millions of people. That is why no president should tarnish our values and our ideals. Actions do have consequences. The difference between right and wrong still exists, and honesty always counts.

We should not underestimate the gravity of the case against the president. When he put his hand on the Bible and recited his oath of office, he swore to faithfully uphold the laws of the United States — not some laws, all laws. . . .

Jerrold Nadler, D-N.Y.

The work of this committee during the Nixon impeachment investigation commanded the respect and the support of the

American people. A broad consensus that Mr. Nixon had to go was developed precisely because the process was seen to be fair and deliberate. If our conduct in this matter does not earn the confidence of the American people, then any action we take, especially if we seek to overturn the result of a free election, will be viewed with great suspicion and could divide our nation for years to come. . . .

[In 1974] the committee stated the issue clearly: "The crucial factor is not the intrinsic quality of behavior but the significance of its effect upon our constitutional system or the functioning of government."

We should, therefore, first determine the standard we will use to determine what is an impeachable offense. As far as I am concerned, we could simply reaffirm the report of this committee adopted by the House in 1974.

Then we should inquire which of the 11 allegations, if proven to be true, would meet the standard and would be, therefore, impeachable offenses. Only then would it make sense to examine the evidence relating to those allegations, if any, determined to constitute impeachable offenses in order to determine whether there is sufficient evidence to justify going forward with formal impeachment proceedings. . . .

Elton Gallegly, R-Calif.

. . . In my 12 years in Congress, this is undoubtedly the most serious issue I've ever had to deal with and, without question, the most serious issue that any of us on this committee will likely ever have to deal with. . . . I would appeal to all my colleagues to concentrate on the facts. So far, this whole matter has been a contest of spin. . . . We should get back to the hard work of analyzing the evidence for the purpose of reaching a just result.

If at the end of our inquiry the facts do not support the charges, the president should be fully exonerated. On the other hand, if the facts support the allegations, we have a duty to move forward. . . .

Robert C. Scott, D-Va.

. . . I am not aware of any constitutional scholar who believes that all of the allegations before us are impeachable offenses, as intended by the framers of the Constitution. In fact, half of the leading authorities interviewed by the International Law Journal said that not only did none of the allegations reach that level, but also said that the question wasn't even close.

And so it is in that light that . . . we ask to consider the standards of impeachment before we go further. And even if we don't adopt a standard, we should at least take a moment to consider the history in prior cases of impeachments, rather than simply blurt out unreasoned, partisan feelings about whether or not we want the president to continue in office. . . .

Charles T. Canady, R-Fla.

. . . In the Nixon case, this committee never adopted a fixed definition or standard for impeachable offenses, not before the inquiry, not during the inquiry, not at the end of the inquiry. . . . After the House had voted to commence an impeachment inquiry, the staff of the Judiciary Committee prepared a report on constitutional grounds for presidential impeachment.

But that report itself acknowledged that it offered "no fixed standards for determining whether grounds for impeachment exist." The staff recognized, as Mr. Hyde noted earlier, that judgments concerning application of the constitutional standard must await full development of the facts.

More importantly, the inappropriateness of attempts to articulate a fixed standard for impeachable offenses was recognized by the Founders. Alexander Hamilton in The Federalist No. 65, stated that, "Impeachment proceedings cannot be tied down by strict rules in the delineation of impeachable offenses." . . .

Melvin Watt, D-N.C.

. . . There's nothing in our Constitution which mandates that Congress weigh in on the political judgment about whether the president should or should not resign. . . . But what our Constitution does mandate us to do is to make a constitutional judgment based on a constitutional standard. . . .

In meeting and honoring that mandate, it seems to me that the starting place should be putting politics aside and having a clear understanding of what our Founding Fathers and our historical precedents say the constitutional standard means. Without that, we have no standards and the process will become majority rule and partisan politics as usual. . . .

Bob Inglis, R-S.C.

. . . The question is whether the truth matters, and there are some who seem to be saying that the truth really doesn't matter. It doesn't matter whether the president lied under oath . . . whether the president obstructed justice . . . whether the president tampered with witnesses.

Basically, I think what those people who would assert that have to be saying is that power is what matters, power unconstrained by principle. And the risk for us there is that that seems to me to be the sure prescription for tyranny and what the Founders wanted to avoid. They wanted a constitutional republic where power was constrained by truth. . . .

Zoe Lofgren, D-Calif.

. . . In England, impeachment was used as a tool by Parliament to tame the King. But it was altered when our Constitution was written because we don't need to tame the king. We have three branches of government that are ruled by laws. . . . George Mason and James Madison said on Sept. 8, 1787: ". . . We need to have a specific form of reference for the use of impeachment, and it is very limited. It is limited to those actions that are so serious, that so threaten our constitutional system of government that we may not wait for the next election to take action." Ben Franklin referred to it as "the alternative to assassination."

So we believe that before we begin chasing facts, we ought to know what is the relevance of the facts we are chasing? . . . We need a common understanding of what is an impeachable offense. . . .

Robert W. Goodlatte, R-Va.

. . . The charges against the president include perjury, witness tampering and obstruction of justice. These are serious charges, charges that cannot be wiped away by a mere wink and a nod, an apology, or someone's interpretation of the latest public opinion poll. The standard that we follow and the standard we teach our children is that no person is above the law, including the president of the United States. . . .

If we did not proceed with this inquiry of impeachment, the committee would be doing a grave disservice to our Constitution, our House of Representatives and our sacred trust with the American people.

Sheila Jackson-Lee, D-Texas

. . . The Founding Fathers included impeachment as a constitutional remedy because they were worried about presidential tyranny and gross abuse of power. They did not intend impeachment or the threat of impeachment to serve as a device for denouncing the president for private misbehavior or for transforming the United States into a parliamentary form of government in which Congress can vote no confidence in an executive whose behavior it dislikes. . . .

The framers of the Constitution never intended the availability of impeachment as a license for a fishing expedition. Never before has this House authorized a free-ranging, potentially endless investigation [into] a public official's private behavior or his behavior before he attained federal office. . . .

Steve Buyer, R-Ind.

. . . While acting in his role as commander-in-chief of the military, it is alleged that [the president] was on the telephone with a subcommittee chairman of the Appropriations Committee discussing sending troops to Bosnia when he had a subordinate perform a sex act upon him. . . .

While I recognize that the Uniform Code of Military Justice does not apply to the president, clearly his conduct, at a minimum, would be unbecoming of an officer and a gentleman. In the military, even a consensual relationship between a superior and a subordinate is unacceptable behavior, prejudicial to good order and discipline. . . .

Should we ask the members of the armed forces to accept a code of conduct that is higher for troops than for the commander in chief? . . .

Maxine Waters, D-Calif.

. . . Democracy is threatened when a fair legal process is sacrificed to appease the passions of a few. After all the pontificating, posturing and debating, let's think about what is happening to the rights of individuals. Let's take a look at the actions of the independent counsel, who appears to be gathering evidence by any means necessary. . . .

Let's have a review of what the majority has done to date. First, it dumped 445 pages of a report needlessly filled with explicit sexual details on the public. Next, they released the president's videotaped grand jury testimony along with more than 3,000 pages of similar materials. When that fizzled, the Republicans then released 4,600 pages of transcripts and other grand jury testimony.

The Republicans did this without giving the president the opportunity to review the materials prior to their release. . . . The power to impeach a president should not be casually used to remove a president, overturn an election, simply because we don't like him or his policies. . . .

Ed Bryant, R-Tenn.

. . . The president of our country has been accused of 11 counts of violating the provisions of our Constitution as defined by the standards "high crimes and misdemeanors," many of which if true, would have disastrous effects on our third branch of government, the judiciary. . . .

My experience as one of three former federal prosecutors on this panel has taught me that some matters cannot be rushed to judgment. Justice cannot be rushed. And we should not place arbitrary timetables on such an important task as this. . . . We must work as a committee to preserve the integrity of that third branch of government, the judiciary. We must also set an example that truth is what we seek, and lying, especially under oath, is not permissible. . . .

Martin T. Meehan, D-Mass.

. . . The committee should first ascertain reasonably specific constitutional standards for impeachment and then ask ourselves whether Ken Starr's best case against the president surpasses or falls short of that standard.

If we fail to ask ourselves this fundamental question at the beginning of our inquiry, we fail the American people. Prolonging an impeachment investigation that inflicts daily damage to our country, where the independent counsel's case on its face fell short of high crimes and misdemeanors, would be a wholesale abdication of our responsibility to pursue the public interest. . . .

The reality is that the committee already has all the evidence it needs to resolve the Lewinsky matter. . . . Leaving the timing and scope of this inquiry open-ended is certain to permit excursions into far-flung matters . . .

Steve Chabot, R-Ohio

. . . Those who would urge an end to this inquiry before it even starts frequently argue that impeachable offenses are only those which result in an injury to the state. They contend that perjury, or at least perjury relating to sexual matters in a civil action that was subsequently dismissed, results only in an injury to a private litigant and is not impeachable. That argument is wrong. It is a misstatement of the historic record. . . .

Perjury has long been considered a crime against the state. By committing perjury, a person has interfered with the administration of justice. In 1890, the Supreme Court said in [*In Re Loney*] that, "Perjury is an offense against the public justice of the United States." . . .

As a crime against the state, perjury was directly described as a higher misdemeanor at its inception in 15th century England. . . .

When state governments were first being established in the early days of the American republic, perjury also was regularly listed in their constitutions as a "high crime or misdemeanor" or in some varied phrase of that nature. The Kentucky Constitution, ratified in 1792, for example, stated that, "Laws shall be made to exclude from suffrage . . . those who shall thereafter be convicted of bribery, perjury, forgery or other high crimes or misdemeanors." The House and the Senate have impeached federal judges for perjury. . . .

Bill Delahunt, D-Mass.

. . . I am profoundly disturbed at the thought that this committee would base its determination solely on the Starr referral. Never before in our history has the House proceeded with a presidential impeachment inquiry premised exclusively on the raw allegations of a single prosecutor, nor should it now. It is the committee's responsibility to conduct our own preliminary review to determine whether the information from the independent counsel is sufficient to warrant a full-blown investigation, and we have not done that.

If we abdicate that responsibility, we will turn the independent counsel statute into a political weapon with an automatic trigger aimed at every future president. And in the process, we will have turned the United States Congress into a rubberstamp. . . .

That is the difference between the two resolutions before us today: The majority version permits no independent assessment by the committee and asks us instead to accept the referral purely on faith. Our alternative ensures that there is a process, one that is orderly, deliberative and expeditious for determining whether the referral is a sound basis for an inquiry. . . .

Bob Barr, R-Ga.

. . . As we so quickly . . . forget in times of stability and prosperity, our system is a fragile one, a brief flicker of light in an otherwise dark march of human political history. If we drop our guard, even for a moment, and allow a president to demand citizens gratify his personal desires and let him place himself in the way of laws designed to prevent such conduct, that light will be greatly dimmed, if not snuffed out. . . .

We are witnessing nothing less than the symptoms of a cancer on the American presidency. If we fail to remove it, it will expand to destroy the principles that matter most to all of us. Any system of government can choose to perpetuate virtue or vice. If this president is allowed to use the presidency to gratify his personal desires in the same way a corrupt county or parish boss solicits money for votes, future occupants will, sadly, do the same. If the proposition that perjury is sometimes acceptable is allowed to stand, in the blink of an eye it will become acceptable in every case. . . .

The president of the United States controls at his fingertips the greatest arsenal of destructive power ever assembled in human history. . . . He is the singular individual charged with the constitutional duty of faithfully enforcing the laws, all the laws, of the United States. When evidence emerges that he would abuse that power or fail in that duty, it is a matter of gravest constitutional importance. If we fail to address such charges, we will soon be left standing dazed and befuddled among the smoldering ruins of a great democracy. . . . History is littered with the wreckage of nations whose leaders buried their heads in the sand as adversity appeared on the horizon. . . .

Robert Wexler, D-Fla.

. . . Impeachment is not about adultery; it is rooted in a constitutional standard that has met the test of time. It is about subversion of government. The president had an affair. He lied about it. He didn't want anyone to know about it. Does anyone reasonably believe that this amounts to subversion of government?

Does anyone reasonably believe that this is what the Founding Fathers were talking about? For more than 200 years since that convention in Philadelphia, Congress has never, never removed a president from office. Is this where we want to set the bar for future presidents? I plead with this committee to end this nonsense. We have real work to do for the people who sent us.

Bill Jenkins, R-Tenn.

... In my mind, the task, although painful, is simple. We're bound by the Constitution and the laws. We have information, we have evidence, we have recent precedents. These are ingredients that make up all the trials that have been conducted in the courts of our land for as long as we've been a nation. ...

Our role today, and it's been said many times in this hearing, is elementary. It is much like a preliminary hearing. It is to determine if we should recommend to the House of Representatives whether an inquiry should take place. The burden required for this is far less than will be required at other stages, if any, of this proceeding. ...

Steven R. Rothman, D-N.J.

... After a four-year investigation, the independent counsel Mr. Starr has presented the House with 11 allegations of presidential misconduct. Our goal should be to resolve these 11 charges without further delay. However, I will not give my consent to another blank-check, open-ended investigation of the president. That is not the role of our committee. It is not fair to the president, it is not fair to the country, and it is not in our national interest.

If Mr. Starr has more charges, let him bring them forth now, or else we should resolve these Lewinsky charges before the end of this year.

President Clinton engaged in a morally wrong relationship with Ms. Lewinsky and engaged in highly inappropriate conduct in trying to hide that relationship. He must be given an appropriate punishment that fits his offenses. ...

Asa Hutchinson, R-Ark.

... I know many are saying, "This is not Watergate," and I agree. The facts are different. But are not the important questions the same? Is the rule of law less significant today than 25 years ago? Is unchecked perjury, if proven, less of a threat to our judicial system today than when Watergate was the example? In my judgment, these are not insignificant questions that our committee and the American people must answer. ...

I do not know the conclusion of this matter. I do not have all the answers. But in my judgment, the first step is clear; we must seek out those answers. And based upon my own independent review of the evidence, it appears there exists reasonable cause to conduct a formal inquiry that is independent, that is fair and leads to a speedy resolution. ...

Thomas M. Barrett, D-Wis.

... President Clinton's conduct was wrong, and he must be held accountable. But it would hurt our country in the long run to drag this matter out endlessly.

It's time, Mr. Chairman, therefore, for a focused and fair inquiry, and there must be finality to this process, for if there is one common thread tying the views of virtually every American together, it is this: The time has come to put this chapter of our history behind us and move on to the matters that affect the lives of citizens throughout our country.

Ed Pease, R-Ind.

... As a people, we share a heritage which provides a system for the determination of truth, where everyone who has an interest also has the opportunity to be heard. Our duty, as members, in the matter before us is to ensure that this heritage is sustained and enhanced here. It can only be so if we remain firm in our resolve to find the truth, no matter the political consequences. The Constitution provides our compass. I intend to follow it wherever it may take us. ...

Christopher B. Cannon, R-Utah

... Our debate is just beginning as to whether [the president's] conduct ... is so reckless as to justify impeachment. And yet my colleagues on the other side are demanding ad nauseam a clear standard for what constitutes an impeachable offense. They speak of the rule of law as requiring such a standard because they apparently misunderstand the meaning of the core concept of the rule of law. ...

In opposition to the clarity necessary in criminal matters, the rule of law is simple; that no person or position or organization is above the law. Here we are burdened to determine, each according to his conscience, after the facts are as clear as we can make them, if the president's conduct falls short of the standard the Founding Fathers left intentionally vague. ...

James E. Rogan, R-Calif.

... I enter these proceedings with no fixed conclusions as to whether the president committed potentially impeachable offenses. As a former gang-murder prosecutor and trial court judge, I know the presumption of innocence is not a courtesy we grant to the president; it is his as a matter of right. ...

If this president or any president has engaged in marital indiscretions, this appropriately is the concern of a limited universe of people. ... It is not the concern of the House Judiciary Committee, nor is it the concern of the Congress of the United States. ...

However, it is both our purpose and our legal obligation to review the president's alleged conduct within the framework of the rule of law and whether such conduct violated his obligation to faithfully execute the law. This is a very critical distinction, because up until now, the heritage of American jurisprudence has been that no person is above the law. ...

Theodore Roosevelt understood this when he said that "no man is above the law and no man is below it, nor do we ask any man's permission when we require him to obey it." His words are important because Roosevelt made no exception to this ideal for those who happen to share his party affiliation or his political agenda. Roosevelt knew the rule of law had to apply to all men, or it would apply to no man.

President Kennedy echoed that sentiment shortly before his death, when he said that "for one man to defy a law or court order he does not like is to invite others to do the same. This leads to a breakdown of all justice. Some societies respect the rule of force. America respects the rule of law." ...

Lindsey Graham, R-S.C.

... Nobody can tell me yet whether this is part of a criminal enterprise or a bunch of lies that built upon themselves based on not wanting [to] embarrass your family. If that's what it is, about an extramarital affair with an intern, and that's it, I will not vote to impeach this president no matter if 82 percent of the people [at] home want me to, because we will destroy this country.

If it is about a criminal enterprise where the operatives of the president at every turn confront witnesses against him in illegal ways, threaten people, extort them, if there's a secret police unit in this White House that goes after women or anybody else that gets in the way of this president, that is Richard Nixon times 10, and I will vote to impeach him.

Mary Bono, R-Calif.

... There are too many questions that need to be answered. ... I would just like to know whether the president committed perjury ... obstructed justice ... [or] abused power. ... Without this process, none of us will ever know the answers to these questions, and without these answers, our country cannot put this issue behind us. ... ◆

Texts

GOP Cites 15 Possible Felonies By Clinton; Democrats Say Case Is 'Overstated'

Following are excerpts from statements made Oct. 5 to the House Judiciary Committee by majority counsel David P. Schippers and minority counsel Abbe D. Lowell, as provided by the Federal News Service.

SCHIPPERS: Members of the committee, as the chief investigative counsel for the majority, I've been called upon to advise the Judiciary Committee of the results of our analysis and review of the Sept. 9, 1998, referral from the Office of the Independent Counsel in which there was a conclusion that there is substantial and credible information that President William Jefferson Clinton committed acts that may constitute grounds for an impeachment. . . .

The standard of review was set by me in our very first meeting after the delivery of the materials. I reminded the staff that we are not advocates, that we are professionals asked to perform a professional, albeit distasteful, duty. Therefore, I asked them to review the referral and supporting data in the light most favorable to the president.

Throughout this effort, we have been determined to avoid even the suggestion of preference because we view our responsibility as requiring an unbiased, full and expeditious review, untrammeled by any preconceived notions or opinions. Our approach has been solely in keeping with constitutional and legal standards of fairness and impartiality.

Before moving on to the substantive areas of the report, I would like to address two elementary but basic concepts of our constitutional government. These will serve to put our conclusions in the proper perspective.

First, the president of the United States enjoys a singular and appropriately lofty position in our system of government. But that position, by its very nature, involves equally unique and onerous responsibilities among which are included affirmative obligations that apply to no other citizen.

Specifically, the Constitution of the United States imposes upon the president the explicit and affirmative duty to take care that the laws be faithfully executed. Moreover, before entering upon the duties of his office, the president is constitutionally commanded to take the following oath: "I do solemnly swear or affirm that I will faithfully execute the office of president of the United States and will, to the best of my ability, preserve, protect and defend the Constitution of the United States."

The president, then, is the chief law enforcement officer of the United States. Although he is neither above nor below the law, he is, by virtue of his office, held to a higher standard than any other American. Furthermore, as chief executive officer and commander in chief, he is the repository of a special trust.

Second, many defendants who face legal action, whether it be civil or criminal, can honestly believe that the case against them is unwarranted and factually deficient. It is not, however, in the discretion of the litigant to decide that any tactics are justified to defeat the lawsuit in that situation; rather, it is incumbent upon that individual to testify fully and truthfully during the truth-seeking phase. It is then the function of our system of law to expose the frivolous cases. The litigant may not with impunity mislead, deceive or lie under oath in order to prevail in the lawsuit or for other personal gain. Any other result would be subversive of the American rule of law. The principle that every witness in every case must tell the truth, the whole truth and nothing but the truth is the foundation of the American system of justice, which is the envy of every civilized nation.

The sanctity of the oath taken by a witness is the most essential bulwark of the truth-seeking function of a trial, which is the American method of ascertaining the facts. If lying under oath is tolerated, and when exposed is not visited with immediate and substantial adverse consequences, the integrity of this country's entire judicial process is fatally compromised and that process will inevitably collapse.

The subject matter of the underlying case, whether civil or criminal, and the circumstances under which the testimony is given, are of no significance whatever. It is the oath itself that is sacred and must be enforced.

Committee Staff's Task

The independent counsel act provides in relevant part that an independent counsel shall advise the House of Representatives of any substantial and credible information that may constitute grounds for an impeachment. In compliance with the statutory mandate, the Office of the Independent Counsel, Kenneth Starr, informed the House of Representatives on Sept. 9, 1998, that it was prepared to submit a referral under that statute.

On that day, the independent counsel's office delivered to the House the following material: A) a referral consisting of an introduction, a narrative of relevant events, and an identification and analysis of the substantial and credible information that may support grounds for impeachment of William Jefferson Clinton; B) an appendix in six three-ring binders totaling in excess of 2,500 pages of the most relevant testimony and other material cited in the referral; and C) 17 transmittal boxes containing grand jury transcripts, deposition transcripts, FBI reports, reports of interviews and thousands of pages of incidental back-up documents.

Pursuant to H Res 525, all of this material was turned over to the Committee on the Judiciary to be held in executive session until Sept. 28, 1998, and at that time, the House ordered that all materials be released to the public except those which were withheld by action of the committee.

My staff and the minority staff were then instructed by the committee to review the referral together with all the other evidence and testimony that had been submitted for the purposes of determining whether there actually existed substantial and credible evidence that President William Jefferson Clinton may have committed acts that may constitute grounds to proceed to a resolution for an impeachment inquiry.

Because of the narrow scope of our directive, the investigation and analysis was necessarily circumscribed by the information delivered with the referral. We also considered some information and analysis that was furnished by the counsel for the president. . . .

At the suggestion of the minority counsel, the [material that remained in the possession of the Office of the Independent Counsel] was later reviewed by members of both staffs. The material was, as anticipated, irrelevant.

To support the referral, the House has been furnished with grand jury transcripts, FBI interview memoranda, transcripts of depositions, other interview memoranda, statements, audio recordings and, where available, video recordings of all persons named in the referral. In addition, the House was provided with a copy of every document cited and a mass of documentary and other evidence produced by witnesses, the White House, the president, the Secret Service and the Department of Defense.

This report is confined solely to that referral and supporting evidence and the testimonies supplied to the House and then to this committee, supplemented only by the information provided by the president's counsel. . . .

We are fully aware that the purpose of this hearing is solely for the committee to decide whether there is sufficient, credible and substantial evidence to proceed to an impeachment inquiry — this and nothing more. . . . My report, then, represents only a distillation and consensus of the staff's efforts and conclusions for your guidance and consideration.

At the outset, one point needs to be made. The witness, Monica Lewinsky's, credibility may be subject to some skepticism. At an appropriate stage of the proceedings, that credibility will, of necessity, be assessed together with the credibility of all other witnesses in the light of all the other evidence.

Ms. Lewinsky admitted to having lied on occasion to Miss Tripp, and she also admitted to having executed and caused to be filed a false affidavit in the Paula Jones case.

On the other hand, Ms. Lewinsky obtained a grant of immunity for her testimony before the grand jury and therefore has no reason to lie thereafter.

Furthermore, the witness's account of the relevant events could well have been much more damaging. For the most part, though, the record reflects that she was an embarrassed and reluctant witness who actually downplayed her White House encounters. In testifying, Ms. Lewinsky demonstrated a remarkable memory supported by her personal diary concerning dates and events.

Finally, the record includes ample corroboration of her testimony by independent and disinterested witnesses, by documentary evidence, and in part, by the grand jury testimony of the president himself.

Consequently, for the limited purpose of this report, we suggest that Monica Lewinsky's testimony is both substantial and credible. . . .

Majority Lists 15 Counts

The assertions of presidential misconduct cited in the referral, though arising initially out of sexual indiscretions, are completely distinct and involve allegations of an ongoing series of deliberate and direct assaults by Mr. Clinton upon the justice system of the United States and upon the judicial branch of our government which holds a place in the constitutional framework of checks and balances equal to that of the executive and the legislative branches.

As a result of our research and review of the referral and supporting documentation, we respectfully submit that there exists substantial and credible evidence of 15 separate events directly involving President William Jefferson Clinton that could — could — constitute felonies which, in turn, may constitute grounds to proceed with an impeachment inquiry.

I will now present the catalog of those charges together with a brief statement of the evidence supporting each. Please understand that nothing contained in this report is intended to constitute an accusation against the president or anyone else, and it should not be construed as such by anyone. What follows is nothing more than a litany of the crimes that might have been committed based upon the substantial and credible evidence provided by the independent counsel and reviewed, tested and analyzed by my staff.

With that caution in mind, I will proceed.

First, there is substantial and credible evidence that the president may have been part of a conspiracy with Monica Lewinsky and others to obstruct justice and the due administration of justice by: A) providing false and misleading testimony under oath in a civil deposition and before the grand jury; B) withholding evidence and causing evidence to be withheld and concealed; and C) tampering with prospective witnesses in a civil lawsuit and before a federal grand jury. . . .

Second, there is substantial and credible evidence that the president may have aided and abetted, counseled and procured Monica Lewinsky to file and cause to be filed a false affidavit in the case of Jones v. Clinton. . . .

Third, there is substantial and credible evidence that the president may have aided, abetted, counseled and procured Monica Lewinsky in obstruction of justice when she executed and caused to be filed a false affidavit in the case of Jones v. Clinton with knowledge of the pending proceedings and with the intent to influence, obstruct or impede that proceeding in the due administration of justice. . . .

Four, there is substantial and credible evidence that the president may have engaged in misprision of Monica Lewinsky's felonies, of submitting a false affidavit, and of obstructing the due administration of justice both by taking affirmative steps to conceal those felonies and by failing to disclose the felonies, though under a constitutional and statutory duty to do so. . . .

Five, there is substantial and credible evidence that the president may have testified falsely under oath in his deposition in Jones v. Clinton regarding his relationship with Monica Lewinsky. . . .

Six, there is substantial and credible evidence that the president may have given false testimony under oath before the federal grand jury on Aug. 17th, 1998, concerning his relationship with Monica Lewinsky. . . .

Seven, there is substantial and credible evidence that the president may have given false testimony under oath in his deposition given in Jones v. Clinton regarding a statement that he could not recall being alone with Monica Lewinsky and regarding his minimizing the number of gifts that they had exchanged. . . .

Eight, there is substantial and credible evidence that the president may have testified falsely under oath in his deposition concerning conversations with Monica Lewinsky about her involvement in the Jones case. . . .

Nine, there is substantial and credible evidence that the president may have endeavored to obstruct justice by engaging in [a] pattern of activity calculated to conceal evidence from the judicial proceedings regarding his relationship with Monica Lewinsky. . . .

Ten, there is substantial and credible evidence that the president himself may have endeavored to obstruct justice in the case of Jones v. Clinton by agreeing with Monica Lewinsky on a cover story about their relationship, by causing a false affidavit to be filed and by getting false and misleading testimony in his deposition. . . .

Eleven, there is substantial and credible evidence that the president may have endeavored to obstruct justice by helping Monica Lewinsky to obtain a job in New York City at a time when she would have given evidence adverse to Mr. Clinton, if she told the truth. . . .

Twelve, there is substantial and credible evidence that the president may have testified falsely under oath in his deposition concerning his conversations with Vernon Jordan about Ms. Lewinsky. The record tends to establish that Mr. Jordan and the president discussed Ms. Lewinsky on various occasions from the time she was served until she fired Mr. [Francis] Carter and hired Mr. [William] Ginsburg. . . .

Thirteen, there is substantial and credible evidence that the president may have endeavored to obstruct justice and engage in witness tampering in attempting to coach and influence the testimony of Betty Currie before the grand jury. . . .

Fourteen, there is substantial and credible evidence that the president may have engaged in witness tampering by coaching perspective witnesses and by narrating elaborate detailed false accounts of his relationship with Ms. Lewinsky as if those stories were true, intending that those witnesses believe the story and testify to it before a grand jury. . . .

Fifteen, there is substantial and credible evidence that the president may have given false testimony under oath before the federal grand jury concerning his knowledge of the contents of Monica Lewinsky's affidavit and his knowledge of remarks made in his presence by his counsel. . .

Minority Counsel's Statement

LOWELL: In the time that I have, I will set out the enormous differences in approach between the majority staff's and the minority staff's analysis. I will point to

Texts

some of the problems caused by the committee's not having begun this process with a discussion of a constitutional standard of impeachment. I will bring the committee's attention to why the huge gaps between the charges in the referral, and now as proposed by majority counsel, and the actual evidence support the type of fair, focused and expeditious review being proposed by the Democratic members. And we will recommend that part of the committee's work should include evaluating the weight and the credibility of the evidence because of the conduct of the independent counsel.

To begin with, we differ from our staff colleagues as we do not believe that this committee or the House of Representatives is supposed to be an extension of the Office of the Independent Counsel. . . . The evidence that Congress has received from the independent counsel on the Lewinsky matter alone comes after he spent nine months with a large staff of trained investigators and prosecutors and $4 million. It is a one-sided presentation by a prosecutor. . . .

If after this much time, by this many experienced attorneys, spending this much money, and conducting these many interviews, the evidence he sent does not support the charges he makes, how does renaming or relisting or further subdividing the grounds using that same evidence as majority counsel has just done make the case any stronger or the issues any clearer?

We also seem to differ because we see the committee's constitutional and historic task quite differently from the type of listing of laws and statutes that the independent counsel's referral contains and as majority counsel has just done. . . .

Initiating an impeachment process for only the third time in American history takes a far higher threshold than simply making a laundry list of laws a president may have violated. As [Rep. Howard L.] Berman said this morning, not all offenses are high crimes and misdemeanors, and not all high crimes and misdemeanors come from criminal conduct.

In our review of the evidence . . . we have been particularly guided by the gravity impressed on us by our own staff predecessors 24 years ago, when they wrote: "Because the impeachment of the president is a grave step for the nation, it is to be predicated upon conduct seriously incompatible with either the constitutional form and principles of government or the proper performance of constitutional duties of the presidential office."

. . . We have reviewed the referral as it was sent, not as a set of theoretical questions about what is or is not an impeachable offense in a vacuum, but a specific set of 11 grounds tied closely with the facts as the independent counsel has presented them. . . . The question the committee will be called upon to answer is whether the allegations of lying under oath, obstruction and tampering — or even as majority counsel renames them as misprision of a crime, false statements or even conspiracy — tied to the specific facts alleged in the referral and the evidence constitute grounds for proceeding, because wrenching the individual words "perjury," "false statements," "obstruction" or "tampering" from their factual context is not consistent with the historical precedence concerning the constitutional framework defining a proceeding. . . .

We agree with our Democratic members who have stated so articulately that the process thus far is backwards. The committee is considering whether to open what type of actual impeachment inquiry without having spent a single minute discussing what conduct by a president rises to an impeachable offense. . . .

Were the committee to proceed as the Democratic members have been urging, to develop a shared understanding of what constitutes an impeachable offense, the committee might save time and resources, because at the end of that consideration the committee might find that none of the alleged violations . . . all of which are based on the president's private relationship with Monica Lewinsky, would rise to the constitutional threshold.

Without having what will be the committee's deliberations on this important issue, the staff simply kept in mind the broadest and the least-forgiving definition of the constitutional definition of high crimes and misdemeanors. And when we did that, this is what we saw: From the beginning, the framers said that they had to involve, "great and dangerous offenses to subvert the Constitution," the quote from George Mason.

Or that as Alexander Hamilton stated, they require there to be, "injuries done immediately to the society itself." . . .

In our law, there is a prosecutor strategy which courts routinely disapprove by which they divide what they believe to be a single offense into many different charges. They do this to make a case look more serious or foreboding. . . .

But no matter how many different grounds were sent by the independent counsel, and no matter how many majority counsel may further divide them up or rename them to be in order to pile on additional charges, they fit into three distinct claims: First, that the president lied under oath about the nature of a sexual relationship with Monica Lewinsky; second, that he committed obstruction when he sought others to help him conceal that inappropriate relationship; and third, that he abused the office of the presidency by taking steps to hide that relationship. . . .

One basic allegation — that is, that the president was engaged in an improper relationship which he did not want disclosed — is the core charge that Mr. Starr and the majority suggest triggers this constitutional crisis. . . .

Some have raised the impeachment of judges . . . for perjury, as a precedent for this committee. But members of this committee especially know that the lies in those cases had to do with the discharge of those judges' duties, and that the standards for impeaching judges appointed for life are not the same as for reversing presidential elections. . . .

As the committee decides on the scope of its work, one other issue should be included . . . We have pointed to just some of the times when the independent counsel makes a statement not supported by the evidence he sent or then jumps to a guilty inference when a more innocent explanation was far more obvious. A full and fair inquiry should therefore consider whether numerous actions by the independent counsel undermine his claim to impartiality and fairness.

Considering this would not be an attempt to divert attention from the president's conduct or for delay.

When Monica Lewinsky's testimony was released by the committee, it was Mr. Starr himself who wrote the committee on Sept. 25, 1998. And this is what he said: "At the time we submitted our referral, we reviewed these questions about his conduct as incidental and tangential. Nonetheless, the issue has now been raised publicly and appears to bear on the substantiality and credibility of the information we've provided to the House in our referral."

We agree with the independent counsel that his conduct bears on the substantiality and credibility of the information he gathered and transmitted. Consequently, on the independent counsel's own invitation to the committee, this, too, should be the subject of its review. . . .

Chairman Hyde, ranking member Conyers and members, for only the third time in the 200-year history of our country has an impeachment process been invoked. As members on both sides of the aisle have said, this is not a step that should be undertaken lightly and it is one, as the Democratic members have argued, that should not [turn into] a fishing expedition to find something better than that which has been sent in the original referral.

The staff has been asked to make a preliminary evaluation of the charges and of the evidence. This preliminary review indicates that the charges are often overstated; based on strained definitions of what is an offense under the law; are often not supported by the actual evidence in the boxes; and are sometimes, as with the case of counts 10 [lying to potential grand jury witnesses to affect their testimony] and 11 [abuse of power] in the referral, the product of zeal to make the case rather than to state the law. . . . ◆

Hyde Launches 'Search for Truth'; Conyers Denounces 'Obsession'

Excerpts of the Nov. 19 opening statement by House Judiciary Committee Chairman Henry J. Hyde, R-Ill., as transcribed by Federal News Service:

This morning, we commence our second public hearing in fulfillment of the mandate imposed on us in House Resolution 581. While the business of impeachment is rare, and happily so, it becomes necessary from time to time when circumstances require that it be exercised as a constitutional counterbalance to allegations of serious abuse of presidential power. . . .

Throughout our history, we've had a number of impeachment inquiries, but this one represents a historical first. Never before has an impeachment inquiry arisen because of a referral from an independent counsel under Section 595(C) of the statute. For that reason, we have no precedent to follow on the involvement of the independent counsel in our proceedings. However, it seems both useful and instructive that we should hear from him since he is the person most familiar with the complicated matters the House has directed us to review.

We're holding this hearing to learn the facts surrounding this situation, including those in the referral that Judge [Kenneth W.] Starr sent us Sept. 9, 1998, and to determine whether those facts justify our voting on articles of impeachment. . . .

We began our work on Nov. 9 at the hearing when we were enlightened by the testimony of two panels of outstanding academics about the history and nature of the impeachment process. Today, the search for the truth continues as we turn to the underlying facts. . . .

As we announced earlier this week, we will hear from other witnesses in live hearings and in depositions as we move toward a final resolution.

In addition, we have yet to hear from the president. And I can assure my colleagues, if and when the president would want to testify, he may have unlimited time to do so. In any event, we are hopeful that the pledge of cooperation we received from his attorneys will soon be fulfilled.

Let me repeat my New Year's resolution. It's my fervent hope we will be able to conclude this inquiry before the new year turns. I'm hopeful that all members will bear this in mind as we conduct this search for truth with all deliberate speed.

There are many voices telling us to halt this debate, that the people are weary of it all. There are other voices suggesting we have a duty to debate the many questions raised by the circumstances in which we find ourselves, questions of high consequence for constitutional government.

David Broder, writing in The Washington Post yesterday, suggested that in our hearings, "We will define as a nation the standard of honesty we're going to impose on our president."

What is the significance of a false statement under oath? Is it essentially different from a garden-variety lie? A mental reservation? A fib? An evasion? A little white lie? Hyperbole?

In a court proceeding, do you assume some trivial responsibility when you raise your right hand and swear to God to tell the truth, the whole truth, and nothing but the truth?

And what of the rule of law — that unique aspect of a free society that protects you from the fire on your roof or the knock on your door at 3 a.m.? What does lying under oath do to the rule of law?

Do we still have a government of laws and not of men? Does the law apply to some people with force and ferocity while the powerful are immune? Do we have one set of laws for the officers and another for the enlisted? Should we?

These are but a few questions these hearings are intended to explore. And just perhaps, when the debate is over, the rationalizations and the distinctions and the semantic gymnastics are put to rest, we may be closer to answering for our generation the haunting question asked 139 years ago in a small military cemetery in Pennsylvania — whether a nation conceived in liberty and dedicated to the proposition that all men are created equal can long endure.

Conyers Statement

Excerpts of the Nov. 19 opening statement of Rep. John Conyers Jr., D-Mich., as transcribed by Federal News Service:

. . . Today's witness, Kenneth W. Starr, wrote the tawdry, salacious and unnecessarily graphic referral that he delivered to us in September with so much drama and fanfare. And now the majority members of this committee have called that same prosecutor forward to testify in an unprecedented desperation effort to breathe new life into a dying inquiry.

It is fundamental to the integrity of this inquiry to examine whether the independent counsel's evidence is tainted, whether conclusions are colored by improper motive. In short, it is relevant to examine the conduct of the independent counsel and his staff, where their behavior impacts directly on the credibility of the evidence in the referral.

For example, the committee must understand whether Mr. Starr improperly threatened witnesses if they did not provide incriminating evidence against the president of the United States, whether Mr. Starr's partisan interests affected the collection and presentation of evidence, and whether Mr. Starr himself violated the law by leaking uncensored grand jury material to humiliate the president.

Mr. Chairman and members, contrary to the views that have been expressed by Chairman Hyde . . . these are not collateral issues at all. They go to the very heart of Mr. Starr's referral. To turn a blind eye to these is to continue an unfair and partisan process.

Now, no one defends the president's conduct, but even Republican witnesses at our hearing only last week testified that even if the alleged facts are proven true, they simply do not amount to impeachable offenses. The idea of a federally paid sex policeman spending millions of dollars to trap an unfaithful spouse . . . would have been unthinkable prior to the Starr investigation. Let there be no mistake, it is not now acceptable in America to investigate a person's private sexual activity, it is not acceptable to force mothers to testify against their daughters, to make lawyers testify against their clients, to require Secret Service agents to testify against the people they protect, or to make bookstores tell what books people read. It is not acceptable for rogue attorneys and investigators to trap a young woman in a hotel room, discourage her from calling her lawyer, ridicule her when she asked to call her mother. But the record suggests, I'm sorry to say, that is precisely how Kenneth W. Starr has conducted this investigation.

An independent counsel must do justice both in the specific matter he's investigating and to the system of justice as a whole. While an independent counsel can and should pursue a case with vigor, I and many others believe that Mr. Starr has crossed that line into obsession.

And when I talk about obsession, sir, I wonder why Mr. Starr encouraged Linda Tripp to continue to betray and entrap her

Texts

young, unsuspecting friend, and to allow her to continue her illegal tape recording without court approval.

And when I talk about obsession, I wonder why Mr. Starr ignored his ethical obligations and failed to disclose his involvement in the Paula Jones case, which could have disqualified him from this point of the investigation. . . .

Is it just a coincidence that the independent counsel failed to provide this committee with important exculpatory evidence in his referral, casually glossing over the central part of Monica Lewinsky's testimony, when she clearly stated that, quote, "No one promised me a job; no one asked me to lie," unquote, about her relationship. Perhaps Mr. Starr will persuade us not to be concerned about these matters, but he surely carries the burden of showing us and the American people that these things did not affect his fairness nor his impartiality. . . .

Over the course of this investigation, the independent counsel complained publicly and still does that a lack of cooperation was impeding his investigation, and yet he has now afforded members of the committee the same treatment about which he has complained. . . .

Finally, Mr. Chairman, I would be remiss in my duties if I did not observe that to date our committee process has not been bipartisan nor fair. All this committee has done since Sept. 9 is to, in a partisan manner, dump salacious grand jury material on a public that doesn't want it. . . .

We need to do better than 11th-hour unilateral decisions to subpoena witnesses having little to do with the underlying referral. We need to do better in offering the president a full and fair opportunity to participate in these hearings. . . .

Starr Statement

Excerpts of the Nov. 19 opening statement of Independent Counsel Kenneth W. Starr before the House Judiciary Committee, as transcribed by Federal News Service:

Let me say at the outset that I recognize that it is the House of Representatives, and not an independent counsel, which enjoys the sole power to impeach. My role today is to discuss our referral and the underlying investigation. . . .

As our referral explains, the evidence suggests that the president made false statements under oath and thwarted the search for truth in *Jones v. Clinton*. The evidence further suggests that the president made false statements under oath to the grand jury on Aug. 17 of this year.

That same night, the president publicly acknowledged an inappropriate relationship, but maintained that his testimony had been legally accurate. The president also declared that all inquiries into the matter should end because, he said, it was private. But shortly after the president's Aug. 17 speech, Sens. [Joseph I.] Lieberman [D-Conn.], [Bob] Kerrey [D-Neb.] and [Daniel Patrick] Moynihan [D-N.Y.] stated that the president's actions were not a private matter. In our view, they were correct.

Indeed, the evidence suggests that the president repeatedly tried to thwart the legal process in the Jones matter and in the grand jury investigation. That is not a private matter. The evidence further suggests that the president, in the course of these efforts, misused his authority and his power as president and contravened his duty to faithfully execute the laws. That, too, is not a private matter. . . .

The evidence suggests that the misuse of presidential authority occurred in the following 10 ways:

First, the evidence suggests that the president made a series of premeditated false statements in his civil deposition on Jan. 17, 1998. Those were statements under oath. The president had taken an oath to tell the truth, the whole truth, and nothing but the truth.

By making false statements under oath, the president, the chief executive of our nation, failed to adhere to that oath and to his presidential oath to faithfully execute the laws.

Second, the evidence suggests that apart from making false statements under oath, the president engaged in a pattern of behavior during the Jones litigation to thwart the judicial process. The president reached an agreement with Ms. Lewinsky that each would make false statements under oath. He provided job assistance to Ms. Lewinsky at a time when the Jones case was proceeding and Ms. Lewinsky's truthful testimony would have been harmful. He engaged in an apparent scheme to conceal gifts that had been subpoenaed from Ms. Lewinsky. He coached a potential witness, his own secretary Mrs. Currie, with a false account of relevant events.

Those acts constitute a pattern of obstruction that is fundamentally inconsistent with the president's duty to faithfully execute the law.

Third, the evidence suggests that the president participated in a scheme at his civil deposition in which his attorney, in his presence, deceived a U.S. district judge in an effort to cut off questioning about Ms. Lewinsky. The president did not correct his attorney's statement. A false statement to a federal judge in order to shortcut and to prevent relevant questioning is an obstruction of the judicial process.

Fourth, the evidence suggests that on Jan. 23, 1998, after the criminal investigation had become public, the president made false statements to his Cabinet and used his Cabinet as unwitting surrogates to publicly support the president's false story.

Fifth, the evidence suggests that the president, acting in a premeditated and calculated fashion, deceived the American people on Jan. 26 and on other occasions when he denied a relationship with Ms. Lewinsky.

Sixth, the evidence suggests that the president, after the criminal investigation became public, made false statements to his aides and concocted false alibis that these government employees repeated to the grand jury sitting at the U.S. courthouse. As a result, the grand jury here in Washington received inaccurate information.

Seventh, having promised the American people to cooperate with the investigation, the president refused six invitations to testify before the grand jury. Refusing to cooperate with a duly authorized federal criminal investigation is inconsistent with the general statutory duty of all executive-branch employees to cooperate with criminal investigations. It also is inconsistent with the president's duty to faithfully execute the laws.

Eighth, the president and his administration asserted three different governmental privileges to conceal relevant information from the grand jury. The privilege assertions were legally baseless in these circumstances. They were inconsistent with the actions of Presidents [Jimmy] Carter and [Ronald] Reagan in similar circumstances. And they delayed and impeded the investigation.

Ninth, the president made false statements under oath to the grand jury on Aug. 17, 1998. The president again took an oath to tell the truth, the whole truth and nothing but the truth. The evidence demonstrates that the president failed to adhere to that oath and thus to his presidential oath to faithfully execute the laws.

Tenth, the evidence suggests that the president deceived the American people in his speech on Aug. 17 by stating that his testimony had been legally accurate.

In addition to these 10 points, it bears mention that well before January of 1998, the president used governmental resources and prerogatives to pursue his relationship. The evidence suggests that the president used his secretary, Betty Currie, a government employee, to facilitate and to conceal the relationship with Ms. Lewinsky. The president used White House aides and the U.S. ambassador to the United Nations in his effort to find Ms. Lewinsky a job at a time when it was foreseeable, even likely, that she would be a witness in the Jones case. And the president used a governmental attorney, Bruce Lindsey, to assist his personal legal defense during the Jones case.

In short, the evidence suggests that the president repeatedly used the machinery of government and the powers of his high office to conceal his relationship — to conceal the relationship from the American people, from the judicial process in the Jones case, and from the grand jury.

Let me turn, then, to the legal context in which these issues first arose. At the outset, I want to emphasize that our referral never suggests that the relationship between the president and Ms. Lewinsky in and of itself could constitute a high crime or misdemeanor. Indeed, the referral never passes judgment on the president's relationship with Ms. Lewinsky. The propriety of a relationship is not the concern of our office. The referral is instead about obstruction of justice, lying under oath, tampering with witnesses and the misuse of power. The referral cannot be understood without appreciating this vital distinction. . . .

Let me summarize the five points that explain how the president's relationship with Ms. Lewinsky — what was otherwise private conduct — became a matter of concern to the courts. This is critical to fully understand the nature of the committee's inquiry. One: The president was sued for sexual harassment in federal court, and the Supreme Court ruled in that case that the case should go forward.

Two: The law of sexual harassment and the law of evidence allow the plaintiff to inquire into the defendant's relationships with other women — with women in the workplace, which in this case included the president's relationship with Ms. Lewinsky.

Three: Applying those settled legal principles, [U.S. District] Judge Susan Webber Wright repeatedly rejected the president's objections to such inquiries. The judge, instead, ordered the president to answer the questions.

Four: It is a federal crime to commit perjury and obstruct justice in civil cases, including sexual harassment cases. Violators are subject to a sentence of up to 10 years imprisonment for obstruction, and 5 years for perjury.

Five: The evidence suggests that the president and Ms. Lewinsky made false statements under oath and obstructed the judicial process in the Jones case by preventing the court from obtaining the truth about the relationship. . . .

The key point about the president's conduct is this: On at least six different occasions from Dec. 17, 1997, through Aug. 17, 1998, the president had to make a decision. He could choose truth, or he could choose deception. On all six occasions, the president chose deception, a pattern of calculated behavior over a span of months. . . .

Perjury and obstruction of justice are, of course, serious crimes. In 1790, the first Congress, sitting in New York, passed a criminal law that banned perjury. A violator was subject to three years' imprisonment. Today, federal criminal law makes perjury a felony punishable by five years' imprisonment.

In cases involving public officials, courts treat false statements with special condemnation. U.S. District Judge Royce Lamberth, here in Washington, recently sentenced Ronald Blackley, the former chief of staff to the former secretary of agriculture, to 37 months' imprisonment for false statements. The District Court, Judge Lamberth, stated — in his words — "The court has a duty to send a message to other high-level government officials that there is a severe penalty to be paid for providing false information under oath."

Although perjury and obstruction of justice are serious federal crimes, some have suggested that they are not high crimes or misdemeanors when the underlying events concern the president's private actions. Under this theory, a president's obstruction and perjury must involve concealment of official actions.

This interpretation does not appear in the Constitution itself. Moreover, the Constitution lists bribery as a high crime or misdemeanor. And if a president involved in a civil suit bribed the judge to rule in his favor or bribed a witness to provide favorable testimony, there could be no textual question that he had committed a high crime or misdemeanor under the plain language of Article II, even though the underlying events would not have involved his official duties. In addition, virtually everyone agrees that serious crimes, such as murder and rape, would be impeachable even though they do not involve official duties.

Justice Story, in the last century, stated in his famous Commentaries that there is not a syllable in the Constitution which confines impeachment to official acts. With all respect, an absolute and inflexible requirement of a connection to official duties appears, fairly viewed, to be an incorrect interpretation of the Constitution.

History and practice support the conclusion that perjury, in particular, is a high crime and misdemeanor. Perjury has been the basis, as the committee knows, for the removal of several judges. As far as we know, no one has questioned whether perjury was a high crime or misdemeanor in those cases.

In addition, as several of the scholars who appeared before you testified and to whom the chairman referred, perjury seems to have been recognized as a high crime or misdemeanor at the time of the founding of our republic. And the House manager's report in the impeachment of Judge Walter Nixon, for perjury, stated, "It is difficult to imagine an act more subversive to the legal process than lying from the witness stand."

And finally, I note that the federal sentencing guidelines include bribery and perjury in the same guideline, reflecting the common-sense conclusion that bribery and perjury are equivalent means of interfering with the governmental process. For these reasons, we concluded that perjury and obstruction of justice, like bribery, "may constitute grounds for an impeachment." Having said that, let me again emphasize my role here. We had a judgment to make. But whether the president's actions are, in fact, grounds for an impeachment or some other sanction is a decision in the sole discretion of the Congress.

A final point warrants mention in this respect. Criminal prosecution and punishment are not the same as, or a substitute for, congressionally imposed sanctions. As the Supreme Court stated in a 1993 case, the framers recognized that most likely there would be two sets of proceedings for individuals who committed impeachable offenses — the impeachment trial and a separate criminal trial. In fact, the Constitution explicitly provides for two separate proceedings. The framers deliberately separated the two forums to avoid raising the specter of bias and to ensure independent judgment. . . . ◆

'William Jefferson Clinton ... Is Impeached For High Crimes And Misdemeanors'

Following is the text of H Res 611, the articles of impeachment against President Clinton:

Resolution, Impeaching William Jefferson Clinton, President of the United States, for high crimes and misdemeanors.

Resolved, that William Jefferson Clinton, President of the United States, is impeached for high crimes and misdemeanors, and that the following articles of impeachment be exhibited to the United States Senate:

Articles of impeachment exhibited by the House of Representatives of the United States of America in the name of itself and of the people of the United States of America, against William Jefferson Clinton, President of the United States of America, in maintenance and support of its impeachment against him for high crimes and misdemeanors.

Article I

In his conduct while President of the United States, William Jefferson Clinton, in violation of his constitutional oath faithfully to execute the office of the President of the United States, and to the best of his ability, preserve, protect, and defend the Constitution of the United States, and in violation of his constitutional duty to take care that the laws be faithfully executed, has willfully corrupted and manipulated the judicial process of the United States for his personal gain and exoneration, impeding the administration of justice, in that:

On August 17, 1998, William Jefferson Clinton swore to tell the truth, the whole truth and nothing but the truth before a Federal grand jury of the United States. Contrary to that oath, William Jefferson Clinton willfully provided perjurious, false and misleading testimony to the grand jury concerning one or more of the following: (1) the nature and details of his relationship with a subordinate government employee; (2) prior perjurious, false and misleading testimony he gave in a Federal civil rights action brought against him; (3) prior false and misleading statements he allowed his attorney to make to a Federal judge in that civil rights action; and (4) his corrupt efforts to influence the testimony of witnesses and to impede the discovery of evidence in that civil rights action.

In doing this, William Jefferson Clinton has undermined the integrity of his office, has brought disrepute on the Presidency, has betrayed his trust as President, and has acted in a manner subversive of the rule of law and justice, to the manifest injury of the people of the United States.

Wherefore, William Jefferson Clinton, by such conduct, warrants impeachment and trial, and removal from office and disqualification to hold and enjoy any office of honor, trust or profit under the United States.

Article II

In his conduct while President of the United States, William Jefferson Clinton, in violation of his constitutional oath faithfully to execute the office of President of the United States, and, to the best of his ability, preserve, protect, and defend the Constitution of the United States, and in violation of his constitutional duty to take care that the laws be faithfully executed, has willfully corrupted and manipulated the judicial process of the United States for his personal gain and exoneration, impeding the administration of justice, in that:

(1) On December 23, 1997, William Jefferson Clinton, in sworn answers to written questions asked as part of a Federal civil rights action brought against him, willfully provided perjurious, false and misleading testimony in response to questions deemed relevant by a Federal judge concerning conduct and proposed conduct with subordinate employees.

(2) On January 17, 1998, William Jefferson Clinton swore under oath to tell the truth, the whole truth, and nothing but the truth in a deposition given as part of a Federal civil rights action brought against him. Contrary to that oath, William Jefferson Clinton willfully provided perjurious, false and misleading testimony in response to questions deemed relevant by a Federal judge concerning the nature and details of his relationship with a subordinate government employee, his knowledge of that employee's involvement and participation in the civil rights action brought against him, and his corrupt efforts to influence the testimony of that employee.

In all of this, William Jefferson Clinton has undermined the integrity of his office, has brought disrepute on the Presidency, has betrayed his trust as president, and has acted in a manner subversive of the rule of law and justice, to the manifest injury of the people of the United States.

Wherefore William Jefferson Clinton, by such conduct, warrants impeachment and trial, and removal from office and disqualification to hold and enjoy any office of honor, trust or profit under the United States.

Article III

In his conduct, while President of the United States, William Jefferson Clinton, in violation of his constitutional oath faithfully to execute the office of President of the United States and, to the best of his ability, preserve, protect, and defend the Constitution of the United States, and in violation of his constitutional duty to take care that the laws be faithfully executed, has prevented, obstructed, and impeded the administration of justice, and has to that end engaged personally, and through his subordinates and agents, in a course of conduct or scheme designed to delay, impede, cover up, and conceal the existence of evidence and testimony related to a Federal civil rights action brought against him in a duly instituted judicial proceeding.

The means used to implement this course of conduct or scheme included one or more of the following acts:

(1) On or about December 17, 1997, William Jefferson Clinton corruptly encouraged a witness in a Federal civil rights action brought against him to execute a sworn affidavit in that proceeding that he knew to be perjurious, false and misleading.

(2) On or about December 17, 1997, William Jefferson Clinton corruptly encouraged a witness in a Federal civil rights action brought against him to give perjurious, false and misleading testimony if and when called to testify personally in that proceeding.

(3) On or about December 28, 1997, William Jefferson Clinton corruptly engaged in, encouraged, or supported a scheme to conceal evidence that had been subpoenaed in a Federal civil rights action brought against him.

(4) Beginning on or about December 7, 1997, and continuing through and including January 14, 1998, William Jefferson Clinton intensified and succeeded in an effort to secure job assistance to a witness in a Federal civil rights action brought against him in order to corruptly prevent the truthful testimony of that witness in that proceeding at a time when the truthful testimony of that witness would have been harmful to him.

(5) On January 17, 1998, at his deposition in a Federal civil rights action brought

against him, William Jefferson Clinton corruptly allowed his attorney to make false and misleading statements to a Federal judge characterizing an affidavit, in order to prevent questioning deemed relevant by the judge. Such false and misleading statements were subsequently acknowledged by his attorney in a communication to that judge.

(6) On or about January 18 and January 20-21, 1998, William Jefferson Clinton related a false and misleading account of events relevant to a Federal civil rights action brought against him to a potential witness in that proceeding, in order to corruptly influence the testimony of that witness.

(7) On or about January 21, 23, and 26, 1998, William Jefferson Clinton made false and misleading statements to potential witnesses in a Federal grand jury proceeding in order to corruptly influence the testimony of those witnesses. The false and misleading statements made by William Jefferson Clinton were repeated by witnesses to the grand jury, causing the grand jury to receive false and misleading information.

In all of this, William Jefferson Clinton has undermined the integrity of his office, has brought disrepute on the Presidency, has betrayed his trust as President, and has acted in a manner subversive to the rule of law and justice, to the manifest injury to the people of the United States.

Wherefore, William Jefferson Clinton, by such conduct, warrants impeachment and trial, and removal from office and disqualification to hold and enjoy any office of honor, trust or profit under the United States.

Article IV

Using the powers and influence of the office of the President of the United States, William Jefferson Clinton, in violation of his constitutional oath faithfully to execute the office of President of the United States and, to the best of his ability, preserve, protect, and defend the Constitution of the United States, and in disregard of his constitutional duty to take care that the laws be faithfully executed, has engaged in conduct that resulted in misuse and abuse of his high office, impaired the due and proper administration of justice and the conduct of lawful inquiries, and contravened the authority of the legislative branch and the truth-seeking purpose of a coordinate investigative proceeding, in that, as President, William Jefferson Clinton refused and failed to respond to certain written requests for admission and willfully made perjurious, false and misleading sworn statements in response to certain written requests for admission propounded to him as part of the impeachment inquiry authorized by the House of Representatives of the Congress of the United States.

William Jefferson Clinton, in refusing and failing to respond and in making perjurious, false and misleading statements, assumed to himself functions and judgments necessary to the exercise of the sole power of impeachment vested by the Constitution in the House of Representatives and exhibited contempt for the inquiry.

In doing this, William Jefferson Clinton has undermined the integrity of his office, has brought disrepute on the Presidency, has betrayed his trust as President, and has acted in a manner subversive of the rule of law and justice, to the manifest injury of the people of the United States.

Wherefore, William Jefferson Clinton, by such conduct, warrants impeachment and trial, and removal from office and disqualification to hold and enjoy any office of honor, trust or profit under the United States. ◆

Texts

Principle of Equal Justice Under Law 'Lies at the Heart of This Matter'

Following are excerpts of the House Judiciary Committee's report (H Rept 105-830) accompanying its resolution of impeachment (H Res 611):

Introduction

"Equal Justice Under Law." That principle so embodies the American constitutional order that we have carved it in stone on the front of our Supreme Court. The carving shines like a beacon from the highest sanctum of the Judicial Branch across to the Capitol, the home of the Legislative Branch, and down Pennsylvania Avenue to the White House, the home of the Executive Branch. It illuminates our national life and reminds those other branches that despite the tumbling tides of politics, ours is a government of laws and not of men. It was the inspired vision of our founders and framers that the Judicial, Legislative, and Executive branches would work together to preserve the rule of law.

But Equal Justice Under Law amounts to much more than a stone carving. Although we cannot see or hear it, this living, breathing force has real consequences in the lives of average citizens every day. Ultimately, it protects us from the knock on the door in the middle of the night. More commonly, it allows us to claim the assistance of the government when someone has wronged us — even if that person is stronger or wealthier or more popular than we are. In America, unlike other countries, when the average citizen sues the Chief Executive of our nation, they stand equal before the bar of justice. The Constitution requires the judicial branch of our government to apply the law equally to both. That is the living consequence of Equal Justice Under Law.

The President of the United States must work with the Judicial and Legislative branches to sustain that force. The temporary trustee of that office, William Jefferson Clinton, worked to defeat it. When he stood before the bar of justice, he acted without authority to award himself the special privileges of lying and obstructing to gain an advantage in a federal civil rights action in the United States District Court for the Eastern District of Arkansas, in a federal grand jury investigation in the United States District Court for the District of Columbia, and in an impeachment inquiry in the United States House of Representatives. His resistance brings us to this most unfortunate juncture.

So Equal Justice Under Law lies at the heart of this matter. It rests on three essential pillars: an impartial judiciary, an ethical bar, and a sacred oath. If litigants profane the sanctity of the oath, Equal Justice Under Law loses its protective force. Against that backdrop, consider the actions of President Clinton.

On May 27, 1997, the nine justices of the Supreme Court of the United States unanimously ruled that Paula Corbin Jones could pursue her federal civil rights actions against William Jefferson Clinton. . . . On December 11, 1997, United States District Judge Susan Webber Wright ordered President Clinton to provide Ms. Jones with answers to certain routine questions relevant to the lawsuit. Acting under the authority of these court orders, Ms. Jones exercised her rights — rights that every litigant has under our system of justice. She sought answers from President Clinton to help her prove her case against him, just as President Clinton sought and received answers from her.

President Clinton used numerous means to prevent her from getting truthful answers. On December 17, 1997, he encouraged a witness, whose truthful testimony would have helped Ms. Jones, to file a false affidavit in the case and to testify falsely if she were called to testify in the case. On December 23, 1997, he provided, under oath, false written answers to Ms. Jones's questions. On December 28, 1997, he began an effort to get the witness to conceal evidence that would have helped Ms. Jones. Throughout this period, he intensified efforts to provide the witness with help in getting a job to ensure that she carried out his designs. On January 17, 1998, President Clinton provided, under oath, numerous false answers to Ms. Jones's questions during his deposition. In the days immediately following the deposition, he provided a false and misleading account to another witness, Betty Currie, in hopes that she would substantiate the false testimony he gave in the deposition.

These actions denied Ms. Jones her rights as a litigant, subverted the fundamental truth-seeking function of the United States District Court for the Eastern District of Arkansas, and violated President Clinton's constitutional oath to preserve, protect and defend the Constitution of the United States and his constitutional duty to take care that the laws be faithfully executed. Beginning shortly after his deposition, President Clinton became aware that a federal grand jury empaneled by the United States District Court for the District of Columbia was investigating his actions before and during his civil deposition. President Clinton made numerous false statements to potential grand jury witnesses in hopes that they would repeat these statements to the grand jury. On August 17, 1998, President Clinton appeared before the grand jury by video and, under oath, provided numerous false answers to the questions asked. These actions impeded the grand jury's investigation, subverted the fundamental truth-seeking function of the United States District Court for the District of Columbia, and violated President Clinton's constitutional oath to preserve, protect and defend the Constitution of the United States and his constitutional duty to take care that the laws be faithfully executed. . . .

On October 8, 1998, the United States House of Representatives passed House Resolution 581 directing the Committee on the Judiciary to begin an inquiry to determine whether President Clinton should be impeached. As part of that inquiry, the Committee sent written requests for admission to him. On November 27, 1998, President Clinton provided, under oath, numerous false statements to this Committee in response to the requests for admission. These actions impeded the committee's inquiry, subverted the fundamental truth-seeking function of the United States House of Representatives in exercising the sole power of impeachment, and violated President Clinton's constitutional oath to preserve, protect and defend the Constitution of the United States and his constitutional duty to take care that the laws be faithfully executed.

By these actions, President Clinton violated the sanctity of the oath without which Equal Justice Under Law cannot survive. . . . He has disgraced himself and the high office he holds. His high crimes and misdemeanors undermine our Constitution. They warrant his impeachment, his removal from office, and his disqualification from holding further office. . . .

Explanation of Articles

Article I: Perjury in the Civil Case

On August 17, 1998, William Jefferson Clinton swore to tell the truth, the whole truth, and nothing but the truth before a federal grand jury of the United States. Contrary to that oath, William Jefferson Clinton willfully provided perjurious, false and misleading testimony to the grand jury concerning one or more of the following: (1) the nature and details of his relationship with a subordinate government employee; (2) prior perjurious, false and misleading testimony he gave in a federal civil rights action brought against him; (3) prior false and misleading statements he allowed his attorney to make to a Federal judge in that civil rights action; and (4) his corrupt efforts to influence the testimony of witnesses and to impede the discovery of evidence in that civil rights action. . . .

[T]he fact that he provided to the grand jury a half-true, incomplete and misleading statement as a true and complete characterization of his conduct (as required by the oath), and used that statement as a response to direct questions going to the heart of the investigation into whether he committed perjury and obstructed justice related to his deposition, constitutes a premeditated effort to thwart the investigation and to justify prior criminal wrongdoing. . . .

At the deposition of the President, his attorney Mr. [Robert] Bennett, in characterizing the affidavit of Monica Lewinsky in which she stated that she did not have sexual relations with the President, stated that sexual relations in that affidavit meant there is no sex of any kind in any manner, shape or form. The President would have the grand jury, and now the House of Representatives, believe that the purposely broad definition of sexual relations, meant to address the affidavit filed, and chosen by the court in the Jones case, meant something different than the same words in Ms. Lewinsky's affidavit, and that it took into account contorted and strained interpretations of words and meanings. It is unrealistic to contemplate that the President, at his deposition, honestly and without a desire to mislead, gave the meaning to the definition of sexual relations that he testified to before the grand jury. . . .

The [Office of Independent Counsel] proceeded to gather a substantial body of evidence proving that the President did indeed subvert the judicial system by lying under oath in his deposition and obstructing justice. This evidence includes Ms. Lewinsky's consistent and detailed testimony given under oath regarding 11 specific sexual encounters with the President, confirmation of the President's semen stain on Monica Lewinsky's dress, and the testimony of Monica Lewinsky's friends, family members and counselors to whom she made near contemporaneous statements about the relationship. Ms. Lewinsky's memory and accounts were further corroborated by her recollection of times and phone calls which were shown to be correct with entrance logs and phone records. . . .

As indicated, contrary to this compelling corroborated evidence, President Clinton testified before the grand jury that he did not have sexual relations with Ms. Lewinsky. The Committee has concluded that the President lied under oath in making this statement. The obligation to tell the truth, the whole truth, and nothing but the truth requires a complete answer and does not allow a deponent to hide behind twisted interpretations that a reasonable person would not draw. . . . Legal hairsplitting used to bypass the requirement of telling the complete truth directly challenges the deterrence factor of the nation's perjury laws, denying a citizen her right to a constitutional orderly disposition of her claims in a court of law. . . .

The President . . . testified that even under his strained and unrealistic interpretation of the definition of sexual relationship, intended to cover that term as used in Ms. Lewinsky's false affidavit, the touching of her breasts and genitalia would fall under that definition and thus would constitute sexual relations. While it is curious that the President would assert that oral sex would not constitute sexual relations, but the touching of breasts would constitute such relations, even under his tortured reconstruction of the definition, the President committed perjury. . . . Ms. Lewinsky testified under oath on several occasions that the President and she did engage in conduct that involved the touching of breasts and genitalia. . . .

The President did not have to answer untruthfully in the grand jury. The Constitution provided him with the opportunity to assert his Fifth Amendment right to refuse to respond, based on his opinion that a completely truthful answer would tend to incriminate him for prior acts of perjury and obstruction of justice. . . .

The Committee concluded that the President provided perjurious, false and misleading testimony to a Federal grand jury concerning prior perjurious, false and misleading testimony. . . .

The President did not believe that he had given truthful answers in his deposition testimony. If he had, he would not have related a false account of events to Betty Currie, his secretary, who he knew, according to his own statements in the deposition, might be called as a witness in the Jones case. He would not have told false accounts to his aides who, he admitted, he knew would be called to testify before the grand jury. . . . Rather than tell the complete truth, the President lied about his relationship, the cover stories, the affidavit, the subpoena and the search for a job for Ms. Lewinsky at his deposition. He then denied committing perjury at his deposition before the grand jury. The President thus engaged in a series of lies and obstruction, each one calculated to cover the one preceding it. . . .

The Committee concluded that the President provided perjurious, false, and misleading testimony to a Federal grand jury concerning prior false and misleading statements he allowed his attorney to make to a Federal judge in that civil rights action. . . .

At the President's deposition on January 17, 1998, an attorney for Paula Jones began to ask the President questions about his relationship with Ms. Lewinsky. Mr. Bennett objected to the innuendo of the questions and he pointed out that Ms. Lewinsky had signed an affidavit denying a sexual relationship with the President. Mr. Bennett asserted that this indicated there is no sex of any kind in any manner, shape or form, between the President and Ms. Lewinsky, and after a warning from Judge Wright he stated that, "I am not coaching the witness. In preparation of the witness for this deposition, the witness is fully aware of [Lewinsky's] affidavit, so I have not told him a single thing he doesn't know." . . . The President did not say anything to correct Mr. Bennett, even though he knew the affidavit was false. . . .

Later in the deposition, Mr. Bennett read the President the portion of Ms. Lewinsky's affidavit in which she denied having a sexual relationship with the President and asked the President if Ms. Lewinsky's statement was true and accurate. The President responded: "That is absolutely true." . . .

The Committee concluded that the President provided perjurious, false, and misleading testimony to a Federal grand jury concerning his corrupt efforts to influence the testimony of witnesses and to impede the discovery of evidence in that civil rights action. . . .

On December 19, 1997, Monica Lewinsky was served with a subpoena in connection with the case of *Jones* v. *Clinton*. The subpoena required her to testify at a deposition on January 23, 1998. The subpoena also required her to produce each and every gift given to her by President Clinton. On the morning of December 28, 1997, Ms. Lewinsky met with the President for about 45 minutes in the Oval Office. . . . At this meeting they discussed the fact that the gifts had been subpoenaed, including a hat pin, the first gift Clinton had given Lewinsky. Monica Lewinsky testified that at some point in this meeting she said to the President, " 'Well, you know, I — maybe I should put the gifts away outside my house somewhere or give them to someone, maybe Betty.' And he sort of said, I think he responded, 'I don't know' or 'Let me think about that.' And left that topic."

President Clinton provided the following explanation to the grand jury and this Committee regarding this conversation: "Ms. Lewinsky said something to me like, 'What if they ask me about the gifts you've

Texts

given me?' but I do not know whether that conversation occurred on December 28, 1997, or earlier. Whenever this conversation occurred, I testified, I told her that if they asked her for gifts, she'd have to give them whatever she had. I simply was not concerned about the fact that I had given her gifts. Indeed, I gave her additional gifts on December 28, 1997." . . .

It simply strains logic to believe the President would encourage Monica Lewinsky to turn over the gifts. To do so would have raised questions about their relationship and would have been contrary to all of their other efforts to conceal the relationship, including the filing of an affidavit denying a sexual relationship. . . .

The record reflects that President Clinton attempted to influence the testimony of Betty Currie, his personal secretary, by coaching her to recite inaccurate answers to possible questions that might be asked of her if called to testify in the Paula Jones case. . . .

The record reflects that President Clinton met with a total of five aides who would later be called to testify before the grand jury shortly after the President's deposition in the Paula Jones case and following a Washington Post story, published on January 21, 1998, which detailed the relationship between the President and Monica Lewinsky. During the meetings the President made untrue statements to his aides. . . .

Article II: Perjury in the Civil Case

On December 23, 1997, William Jefferson Clinton, in sworn answers to written questions asked as part of a Federal civil rights action brought against him, willfully provided perjurious, false and misleading testimony in response to questions deemed relevant by a Federal judge concerning conduct and proposed conduct with subordinate employees. . . .

According to the sworn testimony of Monica Lewinsky, she and the President had 11 [sic] sexual encounters, eight while she worked at the White House and two thereafter. The sexual encounters generally occurred in or near the Oval Office private study. . . . According to Ms. Lewinsky, she performed oral sex on the President; he never performed oral sex on her.

The record indicates an agreement to deny the conduct and that a relationship existed between the President and Monica Lewinsky. . . . The President lied in his deposition about his being alone or in certain locations with a subordinate federal employee who was a witness in the action brought against him. . . .

The President lied in his deposition about his knowledge of gifts exchanged between himself and a subordinate federal employee who was a witness in the action brought against him. The record indicates that the President did present each of these items as gifts to Monica Lewinsky: 1. A lithograph; 2. A hatpin; 3. A large "Black Dog" canvas bag; 4. A large "Rockettes" blanket; 5. A pin of the New York skyline; 6. A box of "cherry chocolates"; 7. A pair of novelty sunglasses; 8. A stuffed animal from the "Black Dog"; 9. A marble bear's head; 10. A London pin; 11. A shamrock pin; 12. An Annie Lennox compact disc; 13. Davidoff cigars.

The record indicates that the President gave false and misleading testimony in his deposition when he responded "once or twice" to the question "has Monica Lewinsky ever given you any gifts?" The evidence shows that Ms. Lewinsky gave the President approximately a total of 38 gifts presented on numerous occasions. . . .

Monica Lewinsky was served with a subpoena on December 19, 1997, a subpoena that commanded her to appear for a deposition on January 23, 1998, and to produce certain documents and gifts. Monica Lewinsky talked to Vernon Jordan about it that day, and Mr. Jordan spoke to the President shortly thereafter. The President and Ms. Lewinsky met on December 28th and discussed the subpoena. . . .

When asked in the Jones deposition about his last meeting with Ms. Lewinsky, the President remembered only that she stopped by "probably sometime before Christmas" and he "stuck his head out [of the office], said hello to her." . . .

Article III: Obstruction of Justice

. . . President Clinton, using the powers of his high office, engaged personally and through his subordinates and agents, in a course of conduct or plan designed to delay, impede, cover up, and conceal the existence of evidence and testimony related to the duly instituted federal civil rights lawsuit of *Jones v. Clinton* and the duly instituted investigation of Independent Counsel Kenneth Starr.

Although the actions of President Clinton do not have to rise to the level of violating the federal statute regarding obstruction of justice in order to justify impeachment, some if not all of his actions clearly do. . . .

The Committee concluded that on or about December 17, 1997, William Jefferson Clinton . . . corruptly encouraged a witness in a Federal civil rights action brought against him to give perjurious, false and misleading testimony if and when called to testify personally in that proceeding. Prior to December 17, 1997, the record demonstrates that the President and Monica Lewinsky had discussed the use of fabricated stories to conceal their relationship. The record also reveals that the President revisited this same topic in a telephone conversation with Monica Lewinsky on December 17, 1997; in fact, she was encouraged to repeat these fabrications if called to testify in the Paula Jones case. . . .

The Committee concluded that on or about December 28, 1997, William Jefferson Clinton corruptly engaged in, encouraged, or supported a scheme to conceal evidence that had been subpoenaed in a Federal civil rights action brought against him. . . . The concealment and non-production of the gifts to the attorneys for Paula Jones allowed the President to provide false and misleading statements about the gifts at his deposition in the case of *Jones v. Clinton*. . . .

The Committee concluded that beginning on or about December 7, 1997, and continuing through and including January 14, 1998, William Jefferson Clinton intensified and succeeded in an effort to secure job assistance to a witness in a Federal civil rights action brought against him in order to corruptly prevent the truthful testimony of that witness. . . .

The Committee concluded that on or about January 18 and January 20-21, 1998, William Jefferson Clinton related a false and misleading account of events relevant to a Federal civil rights action brought against him to a potential witness in that proceeding, in order to corruptly influence the testimony of that witness [Currie]. . . .

The President's public apology occurred on August 17, 1998, during a nationally televised broadcast in which he confessed having made misleading statements about the nature of his relationship with Monica Lewinsky. It should be noted, however, that the apology was delivered [on the same day that] the FBI released its DNA report that linked the President (based on his blood sample) to a semen stain on one of Ms. Lewinsky's dresses. . . .

Article IV: Abuse of Power

The President abused his power by refusing and failing to respond to certain written requests for admission and willfully made perjurious, false, and misleading sworn statements in response to certain written requests for admission propounded to him by the Committee. . . .

On November 5, 1998, the Committee presented President Clinton with 81 requests for admission. The requests were made in order to allow the President to candidly dispute or affirm key sworn evidence before the Committee by admitting or denying certain facts. The President responded to the requests on November 27, 1998. After a thorough review . . . the Committee concluded that several of the President's answers to the 81 questions asked of him by the Committee are clearly perjurious, false, and misleading. . . . His answers are a continuation of a pattern of deceit and obstruction of duly authorized investigations. . . .

President Clinton made six public statements denying allegations that he had an improper sexual relationship with Monica Lewinsky or obstructed justice in the federal civil rights case of *Jones v. Clinton*. The Committee concluded that the public trust, which is held by the President of the United States, was deliberately abused by President Clinton when he made these false statements. . . .

The Committee concluded that President Clinton consciously misled several aides and Cabinet members knowing that they would repeat his false statements to the American public. These officials are all federally paid civil servants who have used their positions in the White House as a pulpit to repeat President Clinton's false statements to the American public. The Committee believes that use of these advisors in an attempt to mislead the American public and beat his criminal allegations was an abuse of the office of the President and his position as head of the executive branch of government. The President's continued deceptions caused millions of tax dollars to be spent by not only the Office of Independent Counsel in its duly authorized investigation, but also by White House lawyers, communications employees and other government employees, who were utilized to help perpetuate the President's lies and defend him from his criminal conduct.

Minority Dissent

Following are excerpts of the Democratic dissent:

For only the second time in the history of our Nation, the House is poised to impeach a sitting President. The Judiciary Committee Democrats uniformly and resoundingly dissent.

We believe that the President's conduct was wrongful in attempting to conceal an extramarital relationship. But we do not believe that the allegations that the President violated criminal laws in attempting to conceal that relationship — even if proven true — amount to the abuse of official power, which is an historically rooted prerequisite for impeaching a President. Nor do we believe that the Majority has come anywhere close to establishing the impeachable misconduct alleged. . . .

Impeachment is like a wall around the fort of the separation of powers fundamental to our Constitution; the crack we put in the wall today becomes the fissure tomorrow, which ultimately destroys the wall entirely. This process is that serious. It is so serious the wall was not even approached when President Lincoln suspended the writ of habeas corpus, nor when President Roosevelt misled the public in the lend-lease program, nor when there was evidence that Presidents [Ronald] Reagan and [George] Bush gave misleading evidence in the Iran-contra affair. . . .

Without any independent examination of fact witnesses, this Committee essentially rubber-stamped a September 9th Referral from the Office of Independent Counsel (OIC).

That Referral contained largely unproven allegations based on grand jury testimony — often inadmissible hearsay evidence — which was never subject to cross examination. Indeed, the Committee's investigation of this material amounted to nothing more than simply releasing to the public the Referral and tens of thousands of accompanying pages of confidential grand jury material.

In this regard, we decry the partisanship that accompanied this sad three-month process at nearly every turn, and point out its unfortunate departure from the experience of Watergate in 1974. ◆

President Vows To Stay in Office 'Until the Last Hour of the Last Day'

Following is a transcript of remarks made at the White House following the Dec. 19 House vote to impeach President Clinton. The speakers are House Minority Leader Richard A. Gephardt, D-Mo., Vice President Al Gore and Clinton. Transcript provided by Federal News Service.

GEPHARDT: Mr. President, Mr. Vice President, First Lady Hillary Clinton, we've just witnessed a partisan vote that was a disgrace to our country and our Constitution. [Judiciary Committee] Chairman Henry Hyde [R-Ill.] once called impeachment the ultimate weapon, and said that for it to succeed, ultimately, it has to be bipartisan. The fact that a vote as important as this occurred in such a partisan way violated the spirit of our democracy.

We must turn away now from the politics of personal destruction, and return to a politics of values. The American people deserve better than what they've received over these long five months. They want their Congress to bring this issue to a speedy compromise, closure. And they want their president, twice elected to his office, to continue his work fighting for their priorities.

The Democratic Caucus in the House will continue to stand alongside our president, and we will work to enact the agenda that we were sent here to pass.

We look forward to supporting his agenda in the upcoming session of Congress. The president has demonstrated his effectiveness as a national and world leader in the face of intense and unprecedented negative attacks by his opponents. I'm confident that he will continue to do so for the rest of his elected term of office.

Despite the worst efforts of the Republican leadership in the House, the Constitution will bear up under the strain, and our nation will survive. The constitutional process about to play out in the United States Senate will hopefully, finally, be fair, and allow us to put an end to this sad chapter of our history.

Ladies and gentlemen, it is now my honor to present our great vice president of these United States, Al Gore.

GORE: Thank you very much, Mr. Leader. To you and to David [E.] Bonior [D-Mich.] and to the entire Democratic Caucus leadership, thank you for what you have done for our country. I would also like to single out for special thanks and praise Congressman John Conyers [Jr., D-Mich.] and all of the members of the Judiciary Committee who are present here today.

And to you, Dick Gephardt, I would like to repeat a judgment that I made to the smaller group earlier. You and I came here on the same day 22 years ago, and in all that time, I don't believe I have heard a finer speech on the floor of the House of Representatives than the one that you delivered this morning.

But in all that time, I do believe this is the saddest day I have seen in our nation's capital, because today's vote in the House of Representatives disregarded the plain wishes and goodwill of the American people, and the plain meaning of our Constitution. Let me say simply, the president has acknowledged that what he did was wrong, but we must all acknowledge that invoking the solemn power of impeachment in the cause of partisan politics is wrong — wrong for our Constitution, wrong for the United States of America.

Republican leaders would not even allow the members of the House of Representatives to cast the vote they wanted to. They were not allowed to vote their conscience. What happened as a result does a great disservice to a man I believe will be regarded in the history books as one of our greatest presidents.

There is no doubt in my mind that the verdict of history will undo the unworthy judgment rendered a short while ago in the United States Capitol. But we do not have to wait for history. Instead, let us live up to the ideals of this season. Let us reach out to one another, and reach out for what is best in ourselves, our history, and our country. Let us heal this land, not tear it apart. Let us move forward, not toward bitter and angry division.

Our founders anticipated that there might be a day like this one, when excessive partisanship unlocked a form of vitriol and vehemence that hurts our nation. We all know that a process that wounds good people in both parties does no service to this country. What America needs is not resignations, but the renewal of civility, respect for one another, decency toward each other, and the certain belief that together we can serve this land and make a better life for all of our people.

That is what President Clinton has done. That is what he is doing, and that is what he will continue to do for the next two years. I feel extremely privileged to have been able to serve with him as his partner for the past six years. And I look forward to serving with him for the next two years. I have seen him close at hand, day after day, making the most important decisions about peace, prosperity, and our future, and making them always by asking what is right for the American people, what is right for all of the American people. I know him. I know his wonderful first lady. I know his heart, and his will, and I have seen his work.

Six years ago, he was left with the highest budget deficit in history, and he ended it. Six years ago, he was handed a failing economy. Today, because of his leadership, we are on the verge of the longest period of peacetime prosperity in all of American history. And I know nothing will stop him from doing the job that the American people sent him here to do.

I say to you today, President William Jefferson Clinton will continue and will complete his mission on behalf of the American people.

I'm proud to present to you my friend, America's great president, Bill Clinton.

CLINTON: Thank you very much. Thank you. Good afternoon.

Let me begin by expressing my profound and heartfelt thanks to Congressman Gephardt and the leadership and all the members of the Democratic Caucus for what they did today. I thank the few brave Republicans who withstood enormous pressure to stand with them for the plain meaning of the Constitution, and for the proposition that we need to pull together to move beyond partisanship, to get on with the business of our country. I thank the millions upon millions of American citizens who have expressed their support and their friendship to Hillary, to me, to our family and to our administration during these last several weeks.

The words of the members here with me and others who were a part of their endeavor in defense of our Constitution were powerful and moving, and I will never forget them. The question is, what are we going to do now?

I have accepted responsibility for what I did wrong in my personal life, and I have invited members of Congress to work with us to find a reasonable, bipartisan, and proportionate response. That approach was rejected today by Republicans in the House.

But I hope it will be embraced in the Senate. I hope there will be a constitutional and fair means of resolving this matter in a prompt manner.

Meanwhile, I will continue to do the work of the American people. We still, after all, have to save Social Security, and Medicare for the 21st century. We have to give all our children world- class schools. We have to pass a patient's bill of rights, we have to make sure the economic turbulence around the world does not curb our economic opportunity here at home. We have to keep America the world's strongest force for peace and freedom. In short, we have a lot to do before we enter the 21st century.

And we still have to keep working to build that elusive one America I have talked so much about. For six years now I have done everything I could to bring our country together across the lines that divide us, including bringing Washington together across party lines. Out in the country people are pulling together, but just as America is coming together, it must look from the country's point of view like Washington is coming apart.

I want to echo something Mr. Gephardt said. It is something I have felt strongly all my life. We must stop the politics of personal destruction. We must get rid of the poisonous venom of excessive partisanship, obsessive animosity, and uncontrolled anger. That is not what America deserves. That is not what America is about. We are doing well now. We are a good and decent country. But, we have significant challenges we have to face. In order to do it right, we have to have some atmosphere of decency and civility, some presumption of good faith, some sense of proportionality and balance in bringing judgment against those who are in different parties. We have important work to do.

We need a constructive debate that has all the different voices in this country heard in the halls of Congress. I want the American people to know today that I am still committed to working with people of good faith, and good will of both parties to do what's best for our country, to bring our nation together, to lift our people up, to move us all forward together. It's what I've tried to do for six years. It's what I intend to do for two more, until the last hour of the last day of my term.

So with profound gratitude for the defense of the Constitution and the best in America that was raised today by the members here and those who joined them, I ask the American people to move with me, to go on from here, to rise above the rancor, to overcome the pain and division, to be a repairer of the breach, all of us, to make this country as one America, what it can and must be for our children in the new century about to dawn.

Thank you very much. ◆

Appendix E
PUBLIC LAWS

Public Laws

Public Laws 105-1 through 105-153 were enacted in the first session of the 105th Congress. (1997 Almanac, p. E-3)

PL 105-154 (S 1575) Rename the Washington National Airport located in the District of Columbia and Virginia as the "Ronald Reagan Washington National Airport." Introduced by COVERDELL, R-Ga., Jan. 27, 1998. Senate passed Feb. 4. House passed Feb. 5. President signed Feb. 6, 1998.

PL 105-155 (HR 1271) Authorize the Federal Aviation Administration's research, engineering, and development programs for fiscal years 1998 through 2000, and for other purposes. Introduced by MORELLA, R-Md., April 10, 1997. House Science reported, amended, April 21 (H Rept 105-61). House passed, amended, April 29. Senate Commerce, Science and Transportation reported, amended, Nov. 9 (S Rept 105-152). Senate passed, amended, Nov. 13. House agreed to amendments, under suspension of the rules, Feb. 3, 1998. President signed Feb. 11, 1998.

PL 105-156 (HR 3042) Amend the Morris K. Udall Scholarship and Excellence in National Environmental and Native American Public Policy Act of 1992 to establish the United States Institute for Environmental Conflict Resolution to conduct environmental conflict resolution and training, and for other purposes. Introduced by KOLBE, R-Ariz., on Nov. 13, 1997. House Education and the Workforce and Resources discharged. House passed Nov. 13. Senate passed Jan. 29, 1998. President signed Feb. 11, 1998.

PL 105-157 (S 1349) Authorize the Secretary of Transportation to issue a certificate of documentation with appropriate endorsement for employment in the coastwise trade for the vessel Prince Nova, and for other purposes. Introduced by DODD, D-Conn., on Oct. 30, 1997. Senate Commerce, Science and Transportation discharged. Senate passed Nov. 13. House passed Feb. 3, 1998. President signed Feb. 11, 1998.

PL 105-158 (S 1564) Provide redress for inadequate restitution of assets, seized by the U.S. Government during World War II, which belonged to victims of the Holocaust, and for other purposes. Introduced by D'AMATO, R-N.Y., on Nov. 13, 1997. Senate passed Nov. 13. House International Relations discharged. House passed Jan. 27, 1998. President signed Feb. 13, 1998.

PL 105-159 (HR 2631) Disapprove the cancellations transmitted by the president Oct. 6, 1997, regarding PL 105-45, fiscal 1998 military construction appropriations. Introduced by SKEEN, R-N.M., on Oct. 7, 1997. House passed, under suspension of the rules, Nov. 8. Senate passed Nov. 9. President vetoed Nov. 13, 1997. House Appropriations discharged Feb. 5, 1998. House overrode president's veto Feb. 5. Senate overrode president's veto Feb. 25. Bill became law Feb. 25, 1998.

PL 105-160 (S 927) Reauthorize the Sea Grant Program. Introduced by SNOWE, R-Maine, on June 17, 1997. Senate Commerce, Science and Transportation reported Nov. 8 (S Rept 105-150). Senate passed, amended, Nov. 13. House passed, amended, under suspension of the rules, Feb. 11, 1998. Senate agreed to House amendment Feb. 12. President signed March 6, 1998.

PL 105-161 (S 916) Designate the U.S. Post Office building located at 750 Highway 28 East in Taylorsville, Miss., as the "Blaine H. Eaton Post Office Building." Introduced by COCHRAN, R-Miss., on June 17, 1997. Senate Government Affairs discharged. Senate passed Oct. 9. House passed, under suspension of the rules, Feb. 24, 1998. President signed March 9, 1998.

PL 105-162 (S 985) Designate the post office located at 194 Ward St. in Patterson, N.J., as the "Larry Doby Post Office." Introduced by TORRICELLI, D-N.J., on June 27, 1997. Senate Government Affairs discharged. Senate passed, amended, Oct. 9. House passed, under suspension of the rules, Feb. 24, 1998. President signed March 9, 1998.

PL 105-163 (HR 595) Designate the federal building and U.S. courthouse located at 475 Mulberry Street in Macon, Ga., as the "William Augustus Bootle Federal Building and United States Courthouse." Introduced by CHAMBLISS, R-Ga., on Feb. 5, 1997. House Transportation and Infrastructure reported July 31 (H Rept 105-233). House passed, under suspension of the rules, Nov. 13. Senate passed March 6, 1998. President signed March 20, 1998.

PL 105-164 (HR 3116) Address the Year 2000 computer problems with regard to financial institutions, to extend examination parity to the Director of the Office of Thrift Supervision and the National Credit Union Administration, and for other purposes. Introduced by LEACH, R-Iowa, on Jan. 28, 1998. House Banking and Financial Services reported, amended, Feb. 24 (H Rept 105-417). Senate passed March 6. President signed March 20, 1998.

PL 105-165 (S 347) Designate the federal building located at 61 Forsyth Street S.W., in Atlanta, Ga., as the "Sam Nunn Atlanta Federal Center." Introduced by CLELAND, D-Ga., on Feb. 24, 1997. Senate Environment and Public Works reported June 5 (no written report). Senate passed June 12. House Transportation and Infrastructure discharged. House passed, amended, March 3, 1998. Senate agreed to House amendments March 6. President signed March 20, 1998.

PL 105-166 (S 758) Make certain technical corrections to the Lobbying Disclosure Act of 1995. Introduced by LEVIN, D-Mich., on May 16, 1997. Senate Governmental Affairs reported Nov. 8, 1997 (S Rept 105-147). Senate passed Nov. 13. House passed, under suspension of the rules, March 18, 1998. President signed April 6, 1998.

PL 105-167 (S 750) Consolidate certain mineral interests in the National Grasslands in Billings County, N.D., through the exchange of federal and private mineral interests to enhance land management capabilities and environmental and wildlife protection, and for other purposes. Introduced by DORGAN, D-N.D., on May 15, 1997. Senate Energy and Natural Resources reported, amended, Sept. 30 (S Rept 105-92). Senate passed, amended, Oct. 6. House passed, under suspension of the rules, March 30, 1998. President signed April 13, 1998.

Public Laws

PL 105-168 (S 419) Provide surveillance, research, and services aimed at prevention of birth defects, and for other purposes. Introduced by BOND, R-Mo., on March 11, 1997. Senate Labor and Human Resources discharged. Senate passed, amended, June 12. House passed, under suspension of the rules, March 10, 1998. President signed April 21, 1998.

PL 105-169 (HR 1116) Provide for the conveyance of the reversionary interest of the United States in certain lands to the Clint Independent School District and the Fabens Independent School District. Introduced by REYES, D-Texas, on March 18, 1997. House passed, under suspension of the rules, Sept. 29. Senate Foreign Relations reported March 3, 1998 (no written report). Senate passed April 1. President signed April 24, 1998.

PL 105-170 (HR 2843) Direct the administrator of the Federal Aviation Administration to re-evaluate the equipment in medical kits carried on, and to make a decision regarding requiring automatic external defibrillators to be carried on, aircraft operated by air carriers, and for other purposes. Introduced by DUNCAN, R-Tenn., on Nov. 6, 1997. House Transportation and Infrastructure reported March 20, 1998 (H Rept 105-456). House passed, amended, under suspension of the rules, March 24. Senate Commerce, Science and Transportation discharged. Senate passed April 3. President signed April 24, 1998.

PL 105-171 (HR 3226) Authorize the secretary of Agriculture to convey certain lands and improvements in the state of Virginia, and for other purposes. Introduced by GOODLATTE, R-Va., on Feb. 12, 1998. House passed under suspension of the rules, March 24. Senate passed April 3. President signed April 24, 1998.

PL 105-172 (S 493) Amend title 18, United States Code, with respect to scanning receivers and similar devices. Introduced by KYL, R-Ariz., on March 20, 1997. Senate Judiciary reported, amended, Sept. 18 (no written report). Senate passed, amended, Nov. 10. House Judiciary discharged. House passed, amended, Feb. 26, 1998. Senate agreed to House amendments April 1. President signed April 24, 1998.

PL 105-173 (S 1178) Amend the Immigration and Nationality Act to modify and extend the visa waiver pilot program, and to provide for the collection of data with respect to the number of non-immigrants who remain in the United States after the expiration of the period of stay authorized by the attorney general. Introduced by ABRAHAM, R-Mich., on Sept. 15, 1997. Senate passed, amended, Sept. 26. House passed, amended, March 25, 1998. Senate agreed to House amendments April 1. President signed April 27, 1998.

PL 105-174 (HR 3579) Make emergency supplemental appropriations for the fiscal year ending Sept. 30, 1998, and for other purposes. Introduced by LIVINGSTON, R-La., on March 27, 1998. Appropriations reported March 27 (H Rept 105-469). House passed, amended, March 31. Senate passed, amended, March 31. Senate asked for conference March 31. House agreed to conference April 23. Conference report filed in the House on April 30 (H Rept 105-504). House agreed to conference report April 30. Senate agreed to conference report April 30. President signed May 1, 1998.

PL 105-175 (H J Res 102) Express the sense of the Congress on the occasion of the 50th anniversary of the founding of the modern state of Israel and reaffirming the bonds of friendship and cooperation between the United States and Israel. Introduced by LANTOS, D-Calif., on Nov. 7, 1997. House passed, under suspension of the rules, April 28, 1998. Senate passed April 29. President signed May 11, 1998.

PL 105-176 (HR 3301) Amend chapter 51 of title 31, United States Code, to allow the secretary of the Treasury greater discretion with regard to the placement of the required inscriptions on quarter dollars issued under the 50 States Commemorative Coin Program. Introduced by CASTLE, R-Del., on March 2, 1998. House Banking and Financial Services discharged. House passed March 27. Senate passed May 19. President signed May 29, 1998.

PL 105-177 (HR 2472) Extend certain programs under the Energy Policy and Conservation Act. Introduced by SCHAEFER, R-Colo., on Sept. 15, 1997. Commerce reported Sept. 26 (H Rept 105-275). House passed, under suspension of the rules, Sept. 29. Senate passed, amended, Sept. 30. House agreed to Senate amendment Nov. 9. Senate agreed to House amendment Feb. 12, 1998. Senate insisted on its amendment and asked for conference Feb. 12. House agreed to Senate amendment, under suspension of the rules, May 19. President signed June 1, 1998.

PL 105-178 (HR 2400) Authorize funds for federal-aid highways, highway safety programs and transit programs, and for other purposes. Introduced by SHUSTER, R-Pa., on Sept. 4, 1997. House Transportation and Infrastructure reported, amended, March 25, 1998 (H Rept 105-467, Part I). House Transportation and Infrastructure filed supplemental report March 27 (Part II). House Ways and Means reported, amended, March 27 (Part III). House Budget discharged. House passed, amended, April 1. Senate passed, amended, April 2. Senate asked for conference April 2. House disagreed with Senate amendment and agreed to conference April 3. Conference report filed May 22 (H Rept 105-550). House agreed to conference report May 22. Senate agreed to conference report May 22. President signed June 9, 1998.

PL 105-179 (HR 824) Redesignate the federal building located at 717 Madison Place, N.W., in the District of Columbia, as the "Howard T. Markey National Courts Building," introduced by HYDE, R-Ill., on Feb. 25, 1997. House Transportation and Infrastructure reported July 28, 1997 (H Rept 105-211). House passed, under suspension of the rules, Sept. 23, 1997. Senate Environment and Public Works reported May 21, 1998 (no written report). Senate passed June 2. President signed June 16, 1998.

PL 105-180 (HR 3565) Amend Part L of the Omnibus Crime Control and Safe Streets Act of 1968. Introduced by McCOLLUM, R-Fla., on March 26, 1998. House Judiciary reported April 21 (H Rept 105-486). House passed, under suspension of the rules, April 21. Senate passed May 15. President signed June 16, 1998.

PL 105-181 (S 1605) Establish a matching grant program to help state and local jurisdictions purchase armor vests for use by law enforcement departments. Introduced by CAMPBELL, R-Colo., on Feb. 4, 1998. Senate Judiciary reported, amended, Feb. 26 (no written report). Senate passed, amended, March 11. House Judiciary discharged. House passed, amended, May 12. Senate agreed to House amendments May 15. President signed June 16, 1998.

Public Laws

PL 105-182 (S 423) Extend the legislative authority for the Board of Regents of Gunston Hall to establish a memorial to honor George Mason. Introduced by ROBB, D-Va., on March 11, 1997. Senate Energy and Natural Resources reported June 26 (S Rept 105-38). Senate passed July 11. House Resources reported Oct. 31 (H Rept 105-363). House passed, under suspension of the rules, June 9, 1998. President signed June 19, 1998.

PL 105-183 (S 1244) Amend title 11, United States Code, to protect certain charitable contributions, and for other purposes. Introduced by GRASSLEY, R-Iowa, on Oct. 1, 1997. House Judiciary reported, amended, Feb. 26, 1998 (no written report). Senate passed, amended, May 13. House passed June 3. President signed June 19, 1998.

PL 105-184 (HR 1847) Improve the criminal law relating to fraud against consumers. Introduced by GOODLATTE, R-Va., on June 10, 1997. House Judiciary reported, amended, June 26 (H Rept 105-158). House passed, amended, under suspension of the rules, July 8. Senate Judiciary reported, amended, Oct. 9 (no written report). Senate passed, amended, Nov. 9. House agreed to Senate amendment, under suspension of the rules, June 16, 1998. President signed June 23, 1998.

PL 105-185 (S 1150) Ensure that federally funded agricultural research, extension and education address high-priority concerns with national or multistate significance, to reform, extend and eliminate certain agricultural research programs, and for other purposes. Introduced by LUGAR, R-Ind., on Sept. 5, 1997. Senate Agriculture, Nutrition and Forestry reported Sept. 5 (S Rept 105-73). Senate passed, amended, Oct. 29. House passed, amended, Feb. 24, 1998. House asked for conference Feb. 24. Senate disagreed with House amendment and agreed to conference Feb. 27. Conference report filed April 22 (H Rept 105-492). Senate agreed to conference report May 12. House agreed to conference report June 4. President signed June 23, 1998.

PL 105-186 (S 1900) Establish a commission to examine issues pertaining to the disposition of Holocaust-era assets in the United States before, during and after World War II, and to make recommendations to the president on further action, and for other purposes. Introduced by D'AMATO, R-N.Y., on April 1, 1998. Senate Banking, Housing and Urban Affairs reported, amended, April 30 (no written report). Senate passed, amended, May 1. House passed, amended, June 9. Senate agreed to House amendment June 10. President signed June 23, 1998.

PL 105-187 (HR 3811) Establish felony violations for the failure to pay legal child support obligations, and for other purposes. Introduced by HYDE, R-Ill., on May 7, 1998. House passed, under suspension of the rules, May 12. Senate passed June 5. President signed June 24, 1998.

PL 105-188 (S 2069) Permit the mineral leasing of American Indian land located within the Fort Berthold Indian Reservation in any case in which there is consent from a majority interest in the parcel of land under consideration for lease. Introduced by DORGAN, D-N.D., on May 12, 1998. Senate Indian Affairs reported, amended, June 5 (S Rept 105-205). Senate passed, amended, June 10. House passed June 24. President signed July 7, 1998.

PL 105-189 (HR 651) Extend the deadline under the Federal Power Act for the construction of a hydroelectric project located in the state of Washington, and for other purposes. Introduced by WHITE, R-Wash., on Feb. 6, 1997. House Commerce reported March 11 (H Rept 105-12). House passed, under suspension of the rules, March 11. Senate Energy and Natural Resources reported Nov. 4 (S Rept 105-133). Senate passed June 25, 1998. President signed July 14, 1998.

PL 105-190 (HR 652) Extend the deadline under the Federal Power Act for the construction of a hydroelectric project located in the state of Washington, and for other purposes. Introduced by WHITE, R-Wash., on Feb. 6, 1997. House Commerce reported March 11 (H Rept 105-13). House passed, under suspension of the rules, March 11. Senate Energy and Natural Resources reported Nov. 4 (S Rept 105-134). Senate passed June 25, 1998. President signed July 14, 1998.

PL 105-191 (HR 848) Extend the deadline under the Federal Power Act applicable to the construction of the AuSable Hydroelectric Project in New York, and for other purposes. Introduced by McHUGH, R-N.Y., on Feb. 26, 1997. House Commerce reported June 7 (H Rept 105-122). House passed, under suspension of the rules, June 10. Senate Energy and Natural Resources reported Nov. 4 (S Rept 105-135). Senate passed June 25, 1998. President signed July 14, 1998.

PL 105-192 (HR 1184) Extend the deadline under the Federal Power Act for the construction of the Bear Creek Hydroelectric Project in the state of Washington, and for other purposes. Introduced by METCALF, R-Wash., on March 20, 1997. House Commerce reported June 7 (H Rept 105-123). House passed, amended, under suspension of the rules, June 10. Senate Energy and Natural Resources reported Nov. 4 (S Rept 105-136). Senate passed June 25, 1998. President signed July 14, 1998.

PL 105-193 (HR 1217) Extend the deadline under the Federal Power Act for the construction of a hydroelectric project located in the state of Washington, and for other purposes. Introduced by METCALF, R-Wash., on March 21, 1997. House Commerce reported June 7 (H Rept 105-124). House passed, under suspension of the rules, June 10. Senate Energy and Natural Resources reported Nov. 4 (S Rept 105-137). Senate passed June 25, 1998. President signed July 14, 1998.

PL 105-194 (S 2282) Amend the Arms Export Control Act, and for other purposes. Introduced by McCONNELL, R-Ky., on July 9, 1998. Senate passed, amended, July 9. House passed, amended, under suspension of the rules, July 14. Senate agreed to House amendment July 14. President signed July 14, 1998.

PL 105-195 (HR 960) Validate certain conveyances in the City of Tulare, Tulare County, Calif., and for other purposes. Introduced by THOMAS, R-Calif., March 5, 1997. House passed, amended, July 8. Senate Energy and Natural Resources reported Oct. 31. Senate passed June 25, 1998. President signed July 16, 1998.

PL 105-196 (HR 2202) Amend the Public Health Service Act to revise and extend the bone marrow donor program, and for other purposes. Introduced by YOUNG, R-Fla., July 17, 1997. House Commerce reported, amended, May 18, 1998

Public Laws

(H Rept 105-538). House passed, amended, May 19. Senate Labor and Human Resources discharged. Senate passed June 24. President signed July 16, 1998.

PL 105-197 (HR 2864) Require the secretary of Labor to establish a program under which employers may consult with state officials respecting compliance with occupational safety and health requirements. Introduced by BALLENGER, R-N.C., Nov. 7, 1997. House Education and the Workforce reported, amended, March 17, 1998 (H Rept 105-444). House passed, amended, March 17. Senate passed June 24. President signed July 16, 1998.

PL 105-198 (HR 2877) Amend the Occupational Safety and Health Act of 1970. Introduced by BALLENGER, R-N.C., Nov. 7, 1997. House Education and the Workforce reported, amended, March 17, 1998 (H Rept 105-445). House passed, amended, March 17. Senate passed June 24. President signed July 16, 1998.

PL 105-199 (HR 3035) Establish an advisory commission to provide advice and recommendations on the creation of an integrated, coordinated federal policy designed to prepare for and respond to serious drought emergencies. Introduced by SKEEN, R-N.M., Nov. 12, 1997. House Transportation and Infrastructure reported, amended, May 22, 1998 (H Rept 105-554, Part 1). House Resources discharged. House Agriculture discharged. House passed, amended, under suspension of the rules June 16. Senate passed June 24. President signed July 16, 1998.

PL 105-200 (HR 3130) Provide for an alternative penalty procedure for states that fail to meet federal child support data processing requirements, to reform federal incentive payments for effective child support performance and to provide for a more flexible penalty procedure for states that violate interjurisdictional adoption requirements. Introduced by SHAW, R-Fla., Jan. 28, 1998. House Ways and Means reported, amended, Feb. 27 (H Rept 105-422). House passed, amended, March 5. Senate Finance discharged. Senate passed, amended, April 2. House agreed to Senate amendments, with amendments, June 25. Senate agreed to House amendments to Senate amendments June 26. President signed July 16, 1998.

PL 105-201 (HJ Res 113) Approve the location of a Martin Luther King, Jr. memorial in the nation's capital. Introduced by MORELLA, R-Md., March 4, 1998. House Resources reported June 22 (H Rept 105-589). House passed June 22. Senate passed June 25. President signed July 16, 1998.

PL 105-202 (S 731) Extend the legislative authority for construction of the National Peace Garden memorial, and for other purposes. Introduced by BUMPERS, D-Ark., May 8, 1997. Senate Energy and Natural Resources reported June 26, 1997 (S Rept 105-40). Senate passed July 11. House Resources reported Oct. 31 (H Rept 105-362). House passed, amended, Nov. 13. Senate agreed to House amendment June 25, 1998. President signed July 16, 1998.

PL 105-203 (HR 1635) Establish within the U.S. National Park Service the National Underground Railroad Network to Freedom program, and for other purposes. Introduced by STOKES, D-Ohio, May 15, 1997. House Resources reported, amended, June 3, 1998 (H Rept 105-559). House passed, amended, under suspension of the rules June 9. Senate Energy and Natural Resources discharged. Senate passed June 25. President signed July 21, 1998.

PL 105-204 (S 2316) Require the secretary of Energy to submit to Congress a plan to ensure that all amounts accrued on the books of the U.S. Enrichment Corp. for the disposition of depleted uranium hexafluoride will be used to treat and recycle depleted uranium hexafluoride. Introduced by McCONNELL, R-Ky., July 15, 1998. Senate passed, amended, July 16. House passed by unanimous consent July 20. President signed July 21, 1998.

PL 105-205 (HR 1316) Amend chapter 87 of title 5, U.S. Code, with respect to the order of precedence to be applied in the payment of life insurance benefits. Introduced by COLLINS, R-Ga., April 14, 1997. House Government Reform and Oversight reported, amended, June 18 (H Rept 105-134). House passed, amended, June 24. Senate Governmental Affairs reported Nov. 6 (no written report). Senate passed June 18, 1998. President signed July 22, 1998.

PL 105-206 (HR 2676) Amend the Internal Revenue Code of 1986 to restructure and reform the IRS, and for other purposes. Introduced by ARCHER, R-Texas, Oct. 21, 1997. House Ways and Means reported, amended, Oct. 31 (H Rept 105-364, Part 1). House Government Reform and Oversight discharged. House Rules discharged. House passed, amended, Nov. 5. Senate Finance reported, amended, April 22, 1998 (S Rept 105-174). Senate passed, amended, May 7. Conference report filed in House June 24 (H Rept 105-599). House agreed to conference report June 25. Senate agreed to conference report July 9. President signed July 22, 1998.

PL 105-207 (HR 1273) Authorize appropriations for fiscal years 1998 and 1999 for the National Science Foundation. Introduced by SCHIFF, R-N.M., April 10, 1997. House Science reported, amended, April 21 (H Rept 105-63). House passed, amended, April 24. Senate Labor and Human Resources discharged. Senate passed, amended, May 12, 1998. House agreed to Senate amendment, under suspension of the rules, July 14. President signed July 29, 1998.

PL 105-208 (HR 1439) Facilitate the sale of certain land in Tahoe National Forest, in the state of California to Placer County, California. Introduced by DOOLITTLE, R-Calif., April 24, 1997. House Resources reported, amended, June 3 (H Rept 105-114). House passed, amended, under suspension of the rules, June 3. Senate Energy and Natural Resources reported June 26, 1998 (S Rept 105-231). Senate passed July 17. President signed July 29, 1998.

PL 105-209 (HR 1460) Allow for election of the delegate from Guam by other than separate ballot. Introduced by UNDERWOOD, D-Guam, April 24, 1997. House Resources reported, amended, Sept. 18 (H Rept 105-253). House passed, amended, under suspension of the rules, Sept. 23. Senate Energy and Natural Resources reported June 5, 1998 (S Rept 105-203). Senate passed July 17. President signed July 29, 1998.

PL 105-210 (HR 1779) Make a minor adjustment in the exterior boundary of the Devil's Backbone Wilderness in the Mark Twain National Forest, Missouri, to exclude a small parcel of land containing improvements. Intro-

Public Laws

duced by BLUNT, R-Mo., June 4, 1997. House Agriculture reported Oct. 2 (H Rept 105-295, Part 1). House Resources discharged Oct. 2. House passed, under suspension of the rules, Oct. 21. Senate Energy and Natural Resources reported June 26, 1998 (S Rept 105-232). Senate passed July 17. President signed July 29, 1998.

PL 105-211 (HR 2165) Extend the deadline under the Federal Power Act applicable to the construction of FERC Project Number 3862 in the state of Iowa. Introduced by LEACH, R-Iowa, July 15, 1997. House Commerce reported Sept. 26 (H Rept 105-273). House passed, under suspension of the rules, Nov. 13. Senate Energy and Natural Resources reported July 2, 1998 (S Rept 105-237). Senate passed July 17. President signed July 29, 1998.

PL 105-212 (HR 2217) Extend the deadline under the Federal Power Act applicable to the construction of FERC Project Number 9248 in the state of Colorado. Introduced by McINNIS, R-Colo., July 22, 1997. House Commerce reported May 6, 1998 (H Rept 105-509). House passed, under suspension of the rules, May 12. Senate Energy and Natural Resources reported July 2 (S Rept 105-238). Senate passed July 17. President signed July 29, 1998.

PL 105-213 (HR 2841) Extend the time required for the construction of a hydroelectric project. Introduced by BUNNING, R-Ky., Nov. 6, 1997. House Commerce reported May 6, 1998 (H Rept 105-510). House passed, amended, under suspension of the rules, May 12. Senate Energy and Natural Resources reported July 2 (S Rept 105-239). Senate passed July 17. President signed July 29, 1998.

PL 105-214 (HR 2870) Amend the Foreign Assistance Act of 1961 to facilitate protection of tropical forests through debt reduction with developing countries with tropical forests. Introduced by PORTMAN, R-Ohio, Nov. 7, 1997. House International Relations reported, amended, March 13, 1998 (H Rept 105-443). House passed, amended, March 19. Senate Foreign Relations discharged. Senate passed, amended, July 14. House agreed to Senate amendment July 15. President signed July 29, 1998.

PL 105-215 (HR 3156) Present a congressional gold medal to Nelson Rolihlahla Mandela. Introduced by HOUGHTON, R-N.Y., Feb. 4, 1998. House passed, under suspension of the rules, June 16. Senate passed July 14. President signed July 29, 1998.

PL 105-216 (S 318) Require automatic cancellation and notice of cancellation rights with respect to private mortgage insurance, which is required as condition for entering into a residential mortgage transaction, to abolish the Thrift Depositor Protection Oversight Board. Introduced by D'AMATO, R-N.Y., Feb. 12, 1997. House Banking, Housing, and Urban Affairs reported, amended, Oct. 31 (H Rept 105-129). Senate passed, amended, Nov. 9. Senate passed, amended, Nov. 9. House passed, amended, under suspension of the rules, July 14, 1998. Senate agreed to House amendments, with amendment, July 15. House agreed to Senate amendments, amended, July 16. President signed July 29, 1998.

PL 105-217 (HR 39) Reauthorize the African Elephant Conservation Act. Introduced by YOUNG, R-Alaska, Jan. 7, 1997. House Resources reported April 21 (H Rept 105-59). House passed, under suspension of the rules, April 23. Senate Environment and Public Works reported June 25, 1998 (no written report). Senate passed July 23. President signed Aug. 5.

PL 105-218 (HR 643) Designate the United States courthouse to be constructed at the corner of Superior and Huron Roads, in Cleveland, Ohio, as the "Carl B. Stokes United States Courthouse." Introduced by LaTOURETTE, R-Ohio, Feb. 6, 1997. House Transportation and Infrastructure reported July 31 (H Rept 105-231). House passed, under suspension of the rules, Sept. 23. Senate Environment and Public Works reported July 22, 1998 (no written report). Senate passed July 31. President signed Aug. 7, 1998.

PL 105-219 (HR 1151) Amend the Federal Credit Union Act to clarify existing law and ratify the longstanding policy of the National Credit Union Administration Board with regard to field of membership of federal credit unions. Introduced by LaTOURETTE, R-Ohio, March 20, 1997. House Banking and Financial Services reported, amended, March 30, 1998 (H Rept 105-472). House passed, amended, under suspension of the rules, April 1. Senate Banking, Housing, and Urban Affairs reported, amended, May 21 (S Rept 105-193). Senate passed, amended, July 28. House agreed to Senate amendment under suspension of the rules Aug. 4. President signed Aug. 7, 1998.

PL 105-220 (HR 1385) Consolidate, coordinate, and improve employment, training, literacy, and vocational rehabilitation programs in the United States. Introduced by McKEON, R-Calif., April 17, 1997. House Education and the Workforce reported, amended, May 8 (H Rept 105-93). House passed, amended, May 16. Senate Labor and Human Resources discharged May 1, 1998. Senate passed, amended, May 5. House disagreed to Senate amendment and agreed to a conference May 22. Conference report filed in House July 29 (H Rept 105-659). Senate agreed to conference report July 30. House agreed to conference report July 31. President signed Aug. 7, 1998.

PL 105-221 (HR 3152) Provide that certain volunteers at private nonprofit food banks are not employees for purposes of the Fair Labor Standards Act of 1938. Introduced by CAMPBELL, R-Calif., Feb. 4, 1998. House Education and the Workforce discharged. House passed, amended, June 25. Senate Labor and Human Resources discharged. Senate passed July 29. President signed Aug. 7, 1998.

PL 105-222 (HR 3731) Designate the auditorium located within the Sandia Technology Transfer Center in Albuquerque, N.M., as the "Steve Schiff Auditorium." Introduced by SKEEN, R-N.M., April 23, 1998. National Security discharged July 15. House passed July 16. Senate passed July 30. President signed Aug. 7, 1998.

PL 105-223 (HR 4354) Establish the United States Capitol Police Memorial Fund on behalf of the families of Detective John Michael Gibson and Private First Class Jacob Joseph Chestnut of the United States Capitol Police. Introduced by GINGRICH, R-Ga., July 30, 1998. House Oversight and Ways and Means discharged. House passed, amended, July 31. Senate passed July 31. President signed Aug. 7, 1998.

PL 105-224 (HR 434) Provide for the conveyance of small parcels of land in the Carson National Forest and the Santa Fe National Forest, New Mexico, to the village of El Rito and the town of Jemez Springs, N.M. Introduced

Public Laws

by RICHARDSON, D-N.M., Jan. 9, 1997. House Resources reported, amended, Oct. 30 (H Rept 105-359). House passed, amended, under suspension of the rules, Nov. 4. Senate Energy and Natural Resources reported, amended, July 2, 1998 (S Rept 105-236). Senate passed, amended, July 17. House agreed to Senate amendment under suspension of the rules Aug. 3. President signed Aug. 12, 1998.

PL 105-225 (HR 1085) Revise, codify, and enact without substantive change certain general and permanent laws, related to patriotic and national observances, ceremonies, and organizations, as Title 36, U.S. Code, "Patriotic and National Observances, Ceremonies and Organizations." Introduced by HYDE, R-Ill., March 17, 1997. House Judiciary reported, amended, Oct. 21 (H Rept 105-326). House passed, amended, Feb. 3, 1998. Senate Judiciary reported July 16 (no written report). Senate passed July 30. President signed Aug. 12, 1998.

PL 105-226 (HR 3504) Amend the John F. Kennedy Center Act to authorize appropriations for the John F. Kennedy Center for the Performing Arts and to further define the criteria for capital repair and operation and maintenance. Introduced by SHUSTER, R-Pa., March 19, 1998. Transportation and Infrastructure reported, amended, May 13 (H Rept 105-533). House passed, amended, under suspension of the rules, June 3. Senate Environment and Public Works reported July 22 (no written report). Senate passed July 31. President signed Aug. 12, 1998.

PL 105-227 (HR 4237) Amend the District of Columbia Convention Center and Sports Arena Authorization Act of 1995 to revise the revenues and activities covered under such act. Introduced by NORTON, D-D.C., July 16, 1998. House Government Reform and Oversight and Rules discharged. House passed July 30. Senate passed July 31. President signed Aug. 4, 1998.

PL 105-228 (S 2344) Amend the Agricultural Market Transition Act to provide for the advance payment, in full, of the fiscal year 1999 payments otherwise required under production flexibility contracts. Introduced by COVERDELL, R-Ga., July 22, 1998. Senate Agriculture, Nutrition and Forestry discharged. Senate passed July 30. House passed, under suspension of the rules, Aug. 3. President signed Aug. 12, 1998.

PL 105-229 (HR 765) Ensure maintenance of a herd of wild horses in Cape Lookout National Seashore. Introduced by JONES, R-N.C., Feb. 13, 1997. House Resources reported July 14 (H Rept 105-179). House passed, under suspension of the rules, July 22. Senate Energy and Natural Resources reported, amended, Oct. 28 (S Rept 105-115). Senate passed, amended, July 17, 1998. House agreed to Senate amendment, under suspension of the rules, Aug. 3. President signed Aug. 13, 1998.

PL 105-230 (HR 872) Establish rules governing product liability actions against raw materials and bulk component suppliers to medical device manufacturers. Introduced by GEKAS, R-Pa., Feb. 27, 1997. House Judiciary reported, amended, May 22, 1998 (H Rept 105-549, Part 1). House Commerce reported, amended, July 14 (Part 2). House passed, amended, July 30. Senate passed July 30. President signed Aug. 13, 1998.

PL 105-231 (S 1759) Grant a federal charter to the American GI Forum of the United States. Introduced by HATCH, R-Utah, March 13, 1998. Senate Judiciary discharged. Senate passed, amended, July 31. House passed, under suspension of the rules, Aug. 3. President signed Aug. 13, 1998.

PL 105-232 (S 1800) Designate the federal building and U.S. courthouse located at 85 Marconi Boulevard in Columbus, Ohio, as the "Joseph P. Kinneary United States Courthouse." Introduced by GLENN, D-Ohio, March 19, 1998. Senate Environment and Public Works reported May 21 (no written report). Senate passed June 2. House Transportation and Infrastructure reported July 14 (H Rept 105-619). House passed, under suspension of the rules, Aug. 4. President signed Aug. 13, 1998.

PL 105-233 (S 2143) Amend Chapter 45 of Title 28, U.S. Code to authorize the administrative assistant to the Chief Justice to accept voluntary services. Introduced by HATCH, R-Utah, June 9, 1998. Senate Judiciary reported, amended, July 9 (no written report). Senate passed, amended, July 16. House passed, amended, under suspension of the rules, Aug. 3. President signed Aug. 13, 1998.

PL 105-234 (HR 3824) Amend the Fastener Quality Act to exempt from its coverage certain fasteners approved by the Federal Aviation Administration for use in aircraft. Introduced by SENSENBRENNER, R-Wis., May 11, 1998. House Science reported, amended, June 9 (H Rept 105-574, Part 1). House Commerce discharged. House passed, amended, under suspension of the rules, June 16. Senate Commerce, Science and Transportation reported, amended, July 27 (S Rept 105-267). Senate passed, amended, July 31. House agreed to Senate amendments Aug. 6. President signed Aug. 14, 1998.

PL 105-235 (S J Res 54) Find the government of Iraq in unacceptable and material breach of its international obligations. Introduced by LOTT, R-Miss., June 25, 1998. Senate Foreign Relations reported July 27 (no written report). Senate passed, amended, July 31. House passed, under suspension of the rules, Aug. 3. President signed Aug. 14, 1998.

PL 105-236 (HR 629) Grant the consent of the Congress to the Texas Low-Level Radioactive Waste Disposal Compact. Introduced by BARTON, R-Texas, Feb. 6, 1997. House Commerce reported July 15 (H Rept 105-181). House passed, amended, Oct. 7. Senate passed, amended, April 1, 1998. Conference report filed in the House July 16 (H Rept 105-630). House agreed to conference report July 29. Senate agreed to conference report Sept. 2. President signed Sept. 20, 1998.

PL 105-237 (HR 4059) Make appropriations for military construction, family housing, and base realignment and closure for the Department of Defense for the fiscal year ending September 30, 1999. Introduced by PACKARD, R-Calif., June 16, 1998. House Appropriations reported June 16 (H Rept 105-578). House passed June 22. Senate passed, amended, June 25. Conference report filed in the House on July 24 (H Rept 105-647). House agreed to conference report July 29. Senate agreed to conference report Sept. 1. President signed Sept. 20, 1998.

PL 105-238 (S 1683) Transfer administrative jurisdiction over part of the Lake Chelan National Recreation Area from the secretary of the Interior to the secretary of Agriculture for inclusion in the Wenatchee National Forest. Introduced by GORTON, R-Wash., Feb. 26, 1998. Senate Energy and Natural Resources reported, amended, June 10 (S Rept 105-228). Senate passed, amended, July 17. House passed, under suspension of the rules, Sept. 9. President signed Sept. 23, 1998.

PL 105-239 (S 1883) Direct the secretary of the Interior to convey the Marion National Fish Hatchery and the Claude Harris National Aquacultural Research Center to the state of Alabama. Introduced by SHELBY, R-Ala., March 31, 1998. Senate Environment and Public Works reported, amended, July 24 (S Rept 105-263). Senate passed, amended, July 31. House passed, under suspension of the rules, Sept. 9. President signed Sept. 23, 1998.

PL 105-240 (H J Res 128) Make continuing appropriations for fiscal year 1999. Introduced by LIVINGSTON, R-La., Sept. 16, 1998. House passed Sept. 17. Senate passed Sept. 17. President signed Sept. 25, 1998.

PL 105-241 (S 2112) Make the Occupational Safety and Health Act of 1970 applicable to the United States Postal Service in the same manner as any other employer. Introduced by ENZI, R-Wyo., May 22, 1998. Senate Labor and Human Resources reported July 28 (no written report). Senate passed July 31. House passed, under suspension of the rules, Sept. 14. President signed Sept. 28, 1998.

PL 105-242 (HR 1856) Amend the Fish and Wildlife Act of 1956 to direct the Secretary of the Interior to conduct a volunteer pilot project at one national wildlife refuge in each U.S. Fish and Wildlife Service region. Introduced by SAXTON, R-N.J., June 10, 1997. House Resources reported, amended, Oct. 21 (H Rept 105-329). House passed, amended, under suspension of the rules, Nov. 4. Senate Environment and Public Works reported, amended, July 28, 1998 (no written report). Senate passed, amended, Sept. 11. House agreed to Senate amendments Sept. 18. President signed Oct. 5, 1998.

PL 105-243 (S 1695) Authorize the secretary of the Interior to study the suitability and feasibility of designating the Sand Creek Massacre National Historic Site in the state of Colorado as a unit of the National Park System. Introduced by CAMPBELL, R-Colo., March 2, 1998. Senate Energy and Natural Resources reported, amended, July 10 (S Rept 105-244). Senate passed, amended, July 17. House Resources reported Sept. 9 (H Rept 105-687). House passed Sept. 18. President signed Oct. 6, 1998.

PL 105-244 (HR 6) Extend the authorization of programs under the Higher Education Act of 1965. Introduced by McKEON, R-Calif., on Jan. 7, 1997. House Education and the Workforce reported, amended, April 17, 1998 (H Rept 105-481). House passed, amended, May 6. Senate Labor and Human Resources discharged May 7. Senate passed, amended, July 9. Conference report filed in the House on Sept. 25 (H Rept 105-750). House agreed to conference report Sept. 28. Senate agreed to conference report Sept. 29. President signed Oct. 7, 1998.

PL 105-245 (HR 4060) Make appropriations for energy and water development for the fiscal year ending Sept. 30, 1999. Introduced by McDADE, R-Pa., June 16, 1998. House Appropriations reported June 16 (H Rept105-581). House passed, amended, June 22. Senate passed, amended, June 23. Conference report filed in the House on Sept. 25 (H Rept 105-749). House agreed to conference report Sept. 28. Senate agreed to conference report Sept. 29. President signed Oct. 7, 1998.

PL 105-246 (S 1379) Amend Section 552 of Title 5, U.S. Code, and the National Security Act of 1947 to require disclosure under the Freedom of Information Act regarding certain persons and to disclose Nazi war criminal records without impairing any investigation or prosecution conducted by the Department of Justice or certain intelligence matters. Introduced by DeWINE, R-Ohio, Nov. 5, 1997. Senate Judiciary reported, amended, March 5, 1998 (no written report). Senate passed, amended, June 19. House passed Aug. 6. President signed Oct. 8, 1998.

PL 105-247 (HR 3096) Correct a provision relating to termination of benefits for convicted persons. Introduced by GREENWOOD, R-Pa., Jan. 27, 1998. House Education and the Workforce reported March 17 (H Rept 105-446). House passed March 24. Senate Governmental Affairs reported Aug. 25 (S Rept 105-296). Senate passed Sept. 28. President signed Oct. 9, 1998.

PL 105-248 (HR 4382) Amend the Public Health Service Act to revise and extend the program for mammography quality standards. Introduced by BLILEY, R-Va., Aug. 3, 1998. House Commerce reported, amended, Sept. 14 (H Rept 105-713). House passed, amended, under suspension of the rules, Sept. 15. Senate passed Sept. 25. President signed Oct. 9, 1998.

PL 105-249 (H J Res 133) Make further continuing appropriations for fiscal year 1999. Introduced by LIVINGSTON, R-La., Oct. 9, 1998. House Appropriations discharged. House passed Oct. 9. Senate passed Oct. 9. President signed Oct. 9, 1998.

PL 105-250 (S 1355) Designate the United States courthouse located at 141 Church Street in New Haven, Conn. as the "Richard C. Lee United States Courthouse." Introduced by LIEBERMAN, D-Conn., Oct. 31, 1997. Senate Environment and Public Works reported May 21, 1998 (no written report). Senate passed June 2. House passed, amended, under suspension of the rules, Sept. 23. Senate agreed to House amendments Sept. 30. President signed Oct. 9, 1998.

PL 105-251 (S 2022) Provide for the improvement of interstate criminal justice identification, information, communications and forensics. Introduced by DeWINE, R-Ohio, April 3, 1998. Senate Judiciary reported, amended, May 21 (no written report). Senate passed, amended, July 13. House passed, amended, under suspension of the rules, Oct. 7. Senate agreed to House amendments Oct. 8. President signed Oct. 9, 1998.

PL 105-252 (S 2071) Extend a quarterly financial report program administered by the secretary of Commerce. Introduced by THOMPSON, R-Tenn., May 13, 1998. Senate Governmental Affairs reported July 8 (S Rept 105-241). Senate passed Sept. 10. House Government Reform and Oversight discharged. House passed Sept. 28. President signed Oct. 9, 1998.

PL 105-253 (H J Res 131) Waive certain enrollment requirements for the remainder of the 105th Congress with respect to any bill or joint resolution making general or

Public Laws

continuing appropriations for fiscal year 1999. Introduced by SOLOMON, R-N.Y., Oct. 7, 1998. House Oversight discharged. House passed Oct. 8. Senate passed Oct. 9. President signed Oct. 12, 1998, 1998.

PL 105-254 (H J Res 134) Make further continuing appropriations for fiscal year 1999. Introduced by LIVINGSTON, R-La., Oct. 12, 1998. House Appropriations discharged. House passed Oct. 12. Senate passed Oct. 12. President signed Oct. 12, 1998.

PL 105-255 (HR 3007) Establish the Commission on the Advancement of Women in Science, Engineering, and Technology Development. Introduced by MORELLA, R-Md., Nov. 9, 1997. House Science reported, amended, June 3, 1998 (H Rept 105-562, Part 1). House passed, amended, under suspension of the rules, Sept. 14. Senate passed Oct. 1. President signed Oct. 14, 1998.

PL 105-256 (HR 4068) Make certain technical corrections in laws relating to Native Americans. Introduced by YOUNG, R-Alaska, June 16, 1998. House Resources reported, amended, Sept. 18 (H Rept 105-733). House passed, amended, under suspension of the rules, Sept. 23. Senate passed Oct. 1. President signed Oct. 14, 1998.

PL 105-257 (H J Res 135) Make further continuing appropriations for fiscal year 1999. Introduced by LIVINGSTON, R-La., Oct. 14, 1998. Appropriations discharged. House passed Oct. 14. Senate passed Oct. 14. President signed Oct. 14, 1998.

PL 105-258 (S 414) Amend the Shipping Act of 1984 to encourage competition in international shipping and growth of United States exports. Introduced by HUTCHISON, R-Texas, March 10, 1997. Senate Commerce, Science and Transportation reported, amended, July 31 (S Rept 105-61). Senate passed, amended, April 22, 1998. House passed, amended, under suspension of the rules, Aug. 4. Senate agreed to House amendment Oct. 1. President signed Oct. 14, 1998.

PL 105-259 (HR 4658) Extend the date by which an automated entry-exit control system must be developed. Introduced by SMITH, R-Texas, Oct. 1, 1998. House Judiciary discharged. House passed Oct. 1. Senate passed Oct. 8. President signed Oct. 15, 1998.

PL 105-260 (H J Res 136) Make further continuing appropriations for fiscal year 1999. Introduced by LIVINGSTON, R-La., Oct. 16, 1998. House Appropriations discharged. House passed Oct. 16. Senate passed Oct. 16. President signed Oct. 16, 1998.

PL 105-261 (HR 3616) Authorize appropriations for fiscal year 1999 for military activities of the Department of Defense and prescribe military personnel strengths for fiscal year 1999. Introduced by SPENCE, R-S.C., April 1, 1998. House National Security reported, amended, May 12 (H Rept 105-532). House passed, amended, May 21. Senate passed, with amendments, June 25. Conference report filed in the House on Sept. 22 (H Rept 105-736). House agreed to conference report Sept. 24. Senate agreed to conference report Oct. 1. President signed Oct. 17, 1998.

PL 105-262 (HR 4103) Make appropriations for the Department of Defense for the fiscal year ending Sept. 30, 1999. Introduced by YOUNG, R-Fla., June 22, 1998. House Appropriations reported June 22 (H Rept 105-591). House passed, amended, June 24. Senate passed, amended, July 30. Conference report filed in the House Sept. 25 (H Rept 105-746). House agreed to conference report Sept. 28. Senate agreed to conference report Sept. 29. President signed Oct. 17, 1998.

PL 105-263 (HR 449) Provide for the orderly disposal of certain federal lands in Clark County, Nevada, and provide for the acquisition of environmentally sensitive lands in the state of Nevada. Introduced by ENSIGN, R-Nev., Jan. 20, 1997. House Resources reported, amended, April 23 (H Rept 105-68). House passed, amended, under suspension of the rules April 23. Senate Energy and Natural Resources reported Aug. 25, 1998 (S Rept 105-291). Senate passed Oct. 2. President signed Oct. 19, 1998.

PL 105-264 (HR 930) Require federal employees to use federal travel charge cards for all payments of expenses of official government travel; amend Title 31, U.S. Code, to establish requirements for prepayment audits of federal agency transportation expenses; authorize reimbursement of federal agency employees for taxes incurred on travel or transportation reimbursements; and authorize test programs for the payment of federal employee travel and relocation expenses. Introduced by HORN, R-Calif., March 5, 1997. House passed, amended, under suspension of the rules, April 16. Senate Governmental Affairs reported, amended, Aug. 25, 1998 (S Rept 105-295). Senate passed, with amendments, Sept. 1. House agreed to Senate amendments under suspension of the rules Oct. 5. President signed Oct. 19, 1998.

PL 105-265 (HR 1481) Amend the Great Lakes Fish and Wildlife Restoration Act of 1990 to provide for implementation of recommendations of the U.S. Fish and Wildlife Service contained in the Great Lakes Fishery Restoration Study Report. Introduced by LaTOURETTE, R-Ohio, on April 29, 1997. House Resources reported, amended, Sept. 15, 1998 (H Rept 105-715). House passed, amended, under suspension of the rules Sept. 23. Senate passed Oct. 2. President signed Oct. 19, 1998.

PL 105-266 (HR 1836) Amend Chapter 89 of Title 5, U.S. Code, to improve administration of sanctions against unfit health care providers under the Federal Employees Health Benefits Program. Introduced by BURTON, R-Ind., June 10, 1997. House Government Reform and Oversight reported, amended, Nov. 4 (H Rept 105-374). House passed, amended, under suspension of the rules Nov. 4. Senate Governmental Affairs reported, amended, July 21, 1998 (S Rept 105-257). Senate passed, amended, Sept. 30. House agreed to Senate amendments under suspension of the rules Oct. 5. President signed Oct. 19, 1998.

PL 105-267 (HR 3381) Direct the secretaries of Agriculture and the Interior to exchange land and other assets with Big Sky Lumber Co. Introduced by HILL, R-Mont., March 5, 1998. House Resources reported, amended, Sept. 16 (H Rept 105-723, Part 1). House Agriculture discharged. House passed, amended, under suspension of the rules, Sept. 23. Senate passed Oct. 2. President signed Oct. 19, 1998.

PL 105-268 (HR 3790) Require the secretary of the Treasury to mint coins in commemoration of the bicentennial of the Library of Congress. Introduced by THOMAS, R-Calif., May 5, 1998. House passed under suspension of the rules Aug. 4. Senate Banking, Housing, and Urban

Affairs discharged. Senate passed Oct. 6. President signed Oct. 19, 1998.

PL 105-269 (HR 4248) Authorize the use of receipts from the sale of the Migratory Bird Hunting and Conservation Stamp to promote additional stamp purchases. Introduced by CUNNINGHAM, R-Calif., July 16, 1998. House passed, amended, under suspension of the rules, Sept. 28. Senate passed Oct. 6. President signed Oct. 19, 1998.

PL 105-270 (S 314) Provide a process for identifying the functions of the federal government that are not inherently governmental. Introduced by THOMAS, R-Wyo., Feb. 12, 1997. Senate Governmental Affairs reported, amended, July 28, 1998 (S Rept 105-269). Senate passed, amended, July 30. House passed under suspension of the rules Oct. 5. President signed Oct. 19, 1998.

PL 105-271 (S 2392) Encourage the disclosure and exchange of information about computer processing problems, solutions, test practices and test results in connection with the transition to the year 2000. Introduced by BENNETT, R-Utah, July 30, 1998. Senate Judiciary reported, amended, Sept. 17 (no written report). Senate passed, amended, Sept. 28. House passed Oct. 1. President signed Oct. 19, 1998.

PL 105-272 (HR 3694) Authorize appropriations for fiscal year 1999 for intelligence and intelligence-related activities of the U.S. government, the Community Management Account, and the Central Intelligence Agency Retirement and Disability System. Introduced by GOSS, R-Fla., April 21, 1998. House Intelligence reported, amended, May 5 (H Rept 105-508). House passed, amended, May 7. Senate Intelligence discharged. Senate passed, with amendment, June 26. Conference report filed in the House Oct. 5 (H Rept 105-780). House agreed to conference report Oct. 7. Senate agreed to conference report Oct. 8. President signed Oct. 20, 1998.

PL 105-273 (H J Res 137) Make further continuing appropriations for the fiscal year 1999. Introduced by LIVINGSTON, R-La., Oct. 19, 1998. House Appropriations discharged. House passed Oct. 19. Senate passed Oct. 20. President signed Oct. 20, 1998.

PL 105-274 (HR 4566) Make technical and clarifying amendments to the National Capital Revitalization and Self-Government Improvement Act of 1997. Introduced by DAVIS, R-Va., Sept. 15, 1998. House passed, amended, Oct. 10, under suspension of the rules. Senate passed Oct. 14. President signed Oct. 21, 1998.

PL 105-275 (HR 4112) Make appropriations for the legislative branch for the fiscal year ending Sept. 30, 1999. Introduced by WALSH, R-N.Y., June 23, 1998. House Appropriations reported June 23 (H Rept 105-595). House passed, amended, June 25. Senate passed, amended, July 21. Conference report filed in the House Sept. 22 (H Rept 105-734). House agreed to conference report Sept. 24. Senate agreed to conference report Sept. 25. President signed Oct. 21, 1998.

PL 105-276 (HR 4194) Make appropriations for the departments of Veterans Affairs and Housing and Urban Development, and for sundry independent agencies, boards, commissions, corporations, and offices for the fiscal year ending Sept. 30, 1999. Introduced by LEWIS, R-Calif., July 8, 1998. House Appropriations reported July 8, 1998 (H Rept 105-610). House passed, amended, July 29. Senate passed, amended, July 30. Conference report filed in the House Oct. 5 (H Rept 105-769). House agreed to conference report Oct. 6. Senate agreed to conference report Oct. 8. President signed Oct. 21, 1998.

PL 105-277 (HR 4328) Make appropriations for the department of Transportation and related agencies for the fiscal year ending Sept. 30, 1999. Introduced by WOLF, R-Va., July 24, 1998. House Appropriations reported July 24 (H Rept 105-648). House passed, amended, July 30. Senate passed, amended, July 30. Conference report filed in the House Oct. 19 (H Rept 105-825). House agreed to conference report Oct. 20. Senate agreed to conference report Oct. 21. President signed Oct. 21, 1998.

PL 105-278 (HR 2616) Amend Titles VI and X of the Elementary and Secondary Education Act of 1965 to improve and expand charter schools. Introduced by RIGGS, R-Calif., Oct. 6, 1997. House Education and the Workforce reported, amended, Oct. 14 (H Rept 105-321). House passed, amended, Nov. 7. Senate Labor and Human Resources discharged. Senate passed, amended, Oct. 8, 1998. House agreed to Senate amendment, under suspension of the rules, Oct. 10. President signed Oct. 22, 1998.

PL 105-279 (HR 1659) Provide for the expeditious completion of the acquisition of private mineral interests within the Mount St. Helens National Volcanic Monument mandated by the 1982 act that established the monument. Introduced by SMITH, R-Wash., May 16, 1997. House Resources reported, amended, Sept. 11, 1998 (H Rept 105-704). House passed, amended, under suspension of the rules, Sept. 23. Senate passed Oct. 7. President signed Oct. 23, 1998.

PL 105-280 (HR 2411) Provide for a land exchange involving the Cape Cod National Seashore and extend the authority for the Cape Cod National Seashore Advisory Commission. Introduced by DELAHUNT, D-Mass., Sept. 5, 1997. House Resources reported, amended, June 5, 1998 (H Rept 105-568). House passed, amended, June 22, under suspension of the rules. Senate Energy and Natural Resources reported Sept. 25 (S Rept 105-392). Senate passed Oct. 7. President signed Oct. 26, 1998.

PL 105-281 (HR 2886) Provide for a demonstration project in the Stanislaus National Forest, Calif., under which a private contractor will perform multiple resource management activities for that unit of the National Forest System. Introduced by DOOLITTLE, R-Calif., on Nov. 7, 1997. House Resources reported, amended, May 12, 1998 (H Rept 105-527). House passed, amended, under suspension of the rules May 12. Senate Energy and Natural Resources reported, amended, Aug. 25 (S Rept 105-292). Senate passed, amended, Oct. 2. House agreed to Senate amendment Oct. 10. President signed Oct. 26, 1998.

PL 105-282 (HR 3796) Authorize the secretary of Agriculture to convey the administrative site for the Rogue River National Forest and use the proceeds for the construction or improvement of offices and support buildings for the Rogue River National Forest and the Bureau of Land Management. Introduced by SMITH, R-Ore., on May 5, 1998. House Resources reported June 3 (H Rept 105-561). House passed June 16 under suspension of the rules. Senate Energy and Natural Resources reported, with

Public Laws

amendment, Aug. 25 (S Rept 105-293). Senate passed, amended, Oct. 2. House agreed to Senate amendment Oct. 10. President signed Oct. 26, 1998.

PL 105-283 (HR 4081) Extend the deadline under the Federal Power Act applicable to the construction of a hydroelectric project in the state of Arkansas. Introduced by HUTCHINSON, R-Ark., on June 18, 1998. House Commerce reported Sept. 25 (H Rept 105-748). House passed Sept. 28 under suspension of the rules. Senate passed Oct. 7. President signed Oct. 26, 1998.

PL 105-284 (HR 4284) Authorize the government of India to establish a memorial to honor Mahatma Gandhi in the District of Columbia. Introduced by McCOLLUM, R-Fla., on July 21, 1998. House Resources reported July 31 (H Rept 105-666). House passed Sept. 15, under suspension of the rules. Senate Energy and Natural Resources discharged. Senate passed Oct. 8. President signed Oct. 26, 1998.

PL 105-285 (S 2206) Amend the Head Start Act, the Low-Income Home Energy Assistance Act of 1981, and the Community Services Block Grant Act to reauthorize and make improvements to those acts and to establish demonstration projects that provide an opportunity for persons with limited means to accumulate assets. Introduced by COATS, R-Ind., on June 23, 1998. Senate Labor and Human Resources reported, amended, July 21 (S Rept 105-256). Senate passed, amended, July 27. House passed, with amendment, under suspension of the rules, Sept. 14. Conference report filed in the House Oct. 6, (H Rept 105-788). Senate agreed to conference report Oct. 8. House agreed to conference report, under suspension of the rules, Oct. 9. President signed Oct. 27, 1998.

PL 105-286 (HR 8) Amend the Clean Air Act to deny entry into the United States of certain foreign motor vehicles that do not comply with state laws governing motor vehicles emissions. Introduced by BILBRAY, R-Calif., on Jan. 7, 1997. House Commerce reported, amended, July 20, 1998 (H Rept 105-634). House passed, amended, under suspension of the rules, July 20. Senate Environment and Public Works reported Sept. 28 (S Rept 105-355). Senate passed, with amendment, Oct. 5. House agreed to Senate amendment under suspension of the rules, Oct. 7. President signed Oct. 27, 1998.

PL 105-287 (HR 624) Amend the Armored Car Industry Reciprocity Act of 1993 to clarify certain requirements and to improve the flow of interstate commerce. Introduced by WHITFIELD, R-Ky., on Feb. 6, 1997. House Commerce reported Feb. 25 (H Rept 105-6). House passed Feb. 26 under suspension of the rules. Senate Commerce, Science and Transportation reported Sept. 1, 1998 (S Rept 105-297). Senate passed Oct. 9. President signed Oct. 27, 1998.

PL 105-288 (HR 1021) Provide for a land exchange involving certain National Forest System lands within the Routt National Forest in the state of Colorado. Introduced by McINNIS, R-Colo., on March 11, 1997. House Resources reported May 5, 1998 (H Rept 105-506). House passed May 12 under suspension of the rules. Senate passed Oct. 9. President signed Oct. 27, 1998.

PL 105-289 (HR 1197) Amend Title 35, U.S. Code, to protect patent owners against the unauthorized sale of plant parts taken from plants illegally reproduced. Introduced by SMITH, R-Ore., on March 20, 1997. House passed Oct. 9, 1998, under suspension of the rules. Senate passed, with amendment, Oct. 15. House agreed to Senate amendment under suspension of the rules Oct. 16. President signed Oct. 27, 1998.

PL 105-290 (HR 2186) Authorize the secretary of the Interior to provide assistance to the National Historic Trails Interpretive Center in Casper, Wyo. Introduced by CUBIN, R-Wyo., on July 17, 1997. House Resources reported March 24, 1998 (H Rept 105-459). House passed March 30 under suspension of the rules. Senate Energy and Natural Resources reported Sept. 9 (S Rept 105-323). Senate passed, with amendments, Oct. 2. House agreed to Senate amendments Oct. 10. President signed Oct. 27, 1998.

PL 105-291 (HR 2370) Amend the Organic Act of Guam for the purposes of clarifying the local judicial structure and the Office of Attorney General. Introduced by UNDERWOOD, D-Guam, on July 31, 1997. House Resources reported, amended, Sept. 24, 1998 (H Rept 105-742). House passed, amended, under suspension of the rules Oct. 5. Senate passed Oct. 15. President signed Oct. 27, 1998.

PL 105-292 (HR 2431) Establish an Office of Religious Persecution Monitoring and provide for the imposition of sanctions against countries engaged in a pattern of religious persecution. Introduced by WOLF, R-Va., Sept. 8, 1997. House International Relations reported, amended, April 1, 1998 (H Rept 105-480, Part 1). House Ways and Means reported, amended, May 8 (Part 2). House Judiciary reported, amended, May 8 (Part 3). House Banking and Financial Services and House Rules discharged. House passed, amended, May 14. Senate passed, with amendments, Oct. 9. House agreed to Senate amendments under suspension of the rules Oct. 10. President signed Oct. 27, 1998.

PL 105-293 (HR 2795) Extend certain contracts between the Bureau of Reclamation and irrigation water contractors in Wyoming and Nebraska that receive water from Glendo Reservoir. Introduced by BARRETT, R-Neb., Nov. 4, 1997. House Resources reported, amended, June 25, 1998 (H Rept 105-604). House passed, amended, under suspension of the rules Sept. 15. Senate passed Oct. 7. President signed Oct. 27, 1998.

PL 105-294 (HR 3069) Extend the Advisory Council on California Indian Policy to allow it to advise Congress on the implementing of the council's proposals and recommendations. Introduced by MILLER, D-Calif., Nov. 13, 1997. House Resources reported June 9, 1998 (H Rept 105-571). House passed under suspension of the rules June 16, 1998. Senate Indian Affairs reported, with amendment, Sept. 22 (S Rept 105-342). Senate passed Oct. 9. President signed Oct. 27, 1998.

PL 105-295 (HR 4079) Authorize the construction of temperature control devices at Folsom Dam in California. Introduced by DOOLITTLE, R-Calif., June 18, 1998. House Resources reported Sept. 15 (H Rept 105-717). House passed, amended, under suspension of the rules Sept. 15. Senate Energy and Natural Resources reported Sept. 25 (S Rept 105-378). Senate passed Oct. 7. President signed Oct. 27, 1998.

PL 105-296 (HR 4166) Amend the Idaho Admission Act regarding the sale or lease of school land. Introduced by

CRAPO, R-Idaho, June 25, 1998. House Resources reported Sept. 11 (H Rept 105-705). House passed under suspension of the rules Sept. 15. Senate Energy and Natural Resources reported Sept. 25 (S Rept 105-393). Senate passed Oct. 7. President signed Oct. 27, 1998.

PL 105-297 (S 53) Require the general application of the antitrust laws to major league baseball. Introduced by HATCH, R-Utah, Jan. 21, 1997. Senate Judiciary reported, amended, Oct. 29 (S Rept 105-118). Senate passed, amended, July 30, 1998. House passed Oct. 7 under suspension of the rules. President signed Oct. 27, 1998.

PL 105-298 (S 505) Amend the provisions of Title 17, U.S. Code, with respect to the duration of copyright. Introduced by HATCH, R-Utah, March 20, 1997. Senate Judiciary discharged. Senate passed, amended, Oct. 7, 1998. House passed under suspension of the rules Oct. 7. House passed under suspension of the rules Oct. 7. President signed Oct. 27, 1998.

PL 105-299 (S 1298) Designate a federal building located in Florence, Ala., as the "Justice John McKinley Federal Building." Introduced by SHELBY, R-Ala., Oct. 20, 1997. Senate Environment and Public Works reported May 21, 1998 (no written report). Senate passed June 2. House passed, under suspension of the rules, Oct. 9. President signed Oct. 27, 1998.

PL 105-300 (S 1892) Provide that a person closely related to a judge of a court exercising judicial power under article III of the U.S. Constitution (other than the Supreme Court) may not be appointed as a judge of the same court. Introduced by KYL, R-Ariz., March 31, 1998. Senate Judiciary reported May 21 (no written report). Senate passed Oct. 6. House passed, under suspension of the rules, Oct. 7. President signed Oct. 27, 1998.

PL 105-301 (S 1976) Increase public awareness of the plight of victims of crime with developmental disabilities, collect data to measure the magnitude of the problem, and develop strategies to address the safety and justice needs of victims of crime with developmental disabilities. Introduced by DeWINE, R-Ohio, April 23, 1998. Senate Judiciary reported, amended, June 25 (no written report). Senate passed, amended, July 13. House passed, under suspension of the rules, Oct. 7. President signed Oct. 27, 1998.

PL 105-302 (S 2235) Amend Part Q of the Omnibus Crime Control and Safe Streets Act of 1968 to encourage the use of school resource officers. Introduced by CAMPBELL, R-Colo., June 25, 1998. Senate Judiciary reported Sept. 24 (no written report). Senate passed Oct. 7. House passed, under suspension of the rules, Oct. 9. President signed Oct. 27, 1998.

PL 105-303 (HR 1702) Encourage the development of a commercial space industry in the United States. Introduced by SENSENBRENNER, R-Wis., May 22, 1997. House Science reported, amended, Oct. 24 (H Rept 105-347). House passed, amended, Nov. 4. Senate Commerce, Science and Transportation reported, amended, June 2, 1998 (S Rept 105-198). Senate passed, amended, July 30. House agreed to Senate amendment with an amendment pursuant to H. Res. 572 Oct. 5. Senate agreed to House amendment to Senate amendment Oct. 8. President signed Oct. 28, 1998.

PL 105-304 (HR 2281) Amend Title 17, U.S. Code, to implement the World Intellectual Property Organization Copyright Treaty and Performances and Phonograms Treaty. Introduced by COBLE, R-N.C., July 29, 1997. House Judiciary reported, amended, May 22, 1998 (H Rept 105-551, Part 1). House Commerce reported, amended, July 22 (Part 2). House Ways and Means discharged. House passed, amended, under suspension of the rules, Aug. 4. Senate passed, amended, Sept. 17. Conference report filed in the House Oct. 8 (H Rept 105-796). Senate agreed to conference report Oct. 8. House agreed to conference report under suspension of the rules Oct. 12. President signed Oct. 28, 1998.

PL 105-305 (HR 3332) Amend the High-Performance Computing Act of 1991 to authorize appropriations for fiscal years 1999 and 2000 for the Next Generation Internet program, to require the Advisory Committee on High-Performance Computing and Communications, Information Technology, and the Next Generation Internet to monitor and give advice concerning the development and implementation of the Next Generation Internet program and report to the president and the Congress on its activities. Introduced by SENSENBRENNER, R-Wis., March 4, 1998. House passed, amended, under suspension of the rules, Sept. 14. Senate Commerce, Science and Transportation discharged. Senate passed Oct. 8. President signed Oct. 28, 1998.

PL 105-306 (HR 4558) Make technical amendments to clarify the provision of benefits for noncitizens, and to improve the provision of unemployment insurance, child support and supplemental security income benefits. Introduced by SHAW, R-Fla., Sept. 14, 1998. House Ways and Means reported, amended, Sept. 22 (H Rept 105-735, Part 1). House passed, amended, under suspension of the rules, Sept. 23. Senate passed Oct. 8. President signed Oct. 28, 1998.

PL 105-307 (S 2468) Designate the Biscayne National Park Visitor Center as the Dante Fascell Visitor Center. Introduced by GRAHAM, D-Fla., Sept. 14, 1998. Senate Energy and Natural Resources reported, amended, Sept. 25 (S Rept 105-407). Senate passed, amended, Oct. 7. House Resources discharged. House passed Oct. 10. President signed Oct. 29, 1998.

PL 105-308 (HR 700) Remove the restriction on the distribution of certain revenues from the Mineral Springs parcel to certain members of the Agua Caliente Band of Cahuilla Indians. Introduced by S. BONO, R-Calif., Feb. 12, 1997. House Resources reported, amended, Sept. 3 (H Rept 105-241). House passed, amended, under suspension of the rules Sept. 8. Senate Indian Affairs reported, with amendment, Sept. 28, 1998 (S Rept 105-349). Senate passed, amended, Oct. 12. House agreed to Senate amendment under suspension of the rules Oct. 15. President signed Oct. 30, 1998.

PL 105-309 (HR 1274) Authorize appropriations for the National Institute of Standards and Technology for fiscal years 1998 and 1999. Introduced by MORELLA, R-Md., April 10, 1997. House Science reported, amended, April 21 (H Rept 105-64). House passed, amended, April 24. Senate Commerce, Science and Transportation discharged. Senate passed, with amendment, Oct. 9, 1998. House agreed to Senate amendment under suspension of the rules Oct. 13. President signed Oct. 30, 1998.

Public Laws

PL 105-310 (HR 1756) Amend Chapter 53 of Title 31, U.S. Code, to require the development and implementation by the secretary of the Treasury of a national strategy to combat money laundering and related financial crimes. Introduced by VELÁZQUEZ, D-N.Y., June 3, 1997. House Banking and Financial Services reported, amended, June 25, 1998 (H Rept 105-608, Part 1). House Judiciary discharged. House passed, amended, under suspension of the rules Oct. 5. Senate passed, with amendment, Oct. 15. House agreed to Senate amendment under suspension of the rules Oct. 16. President signed Oct. 30, 1998.

PL 105-311 (HR 2675) Require that the Office of Personnel Management submit proposed legislation under which group universal life insurance and group variable universal life insurance would be available under Chapter 87 of Title 5, U.S. Code. Introduced by MICA, R-Fla., Oct. 21, 1997. House Government Reform and Oversight reported, amended, Nov. 4. (H Rept 105-373). House passed, amended, under suspension of the rules, Nov. 4. Senate Governmental Affairs reported, with amendments, Sept. 21, 1998 (S Rept 105-337). Senate passed, with amendments, Oct. 5. House agreed to Senate amendments under suspension of the rules Oct. 8. President signed Oct. 30, 1998.

PL 105-312 (HR 2807) Amend the Rhinoceros and Tiger Conservation Act of 1994 to prohibit the selling, importing or exporting of products labeled as containing substances derived from rhinoceros or tiger. Introduced by SAXTON, R-N.J., Nov. 4, 1997. House Resources reported, amended, April 28, 1998 (H Rept 105-495). House passed, amended, under suspension of the rules April 28. Senate Environment and Public Works discharged. Senate passed, with amendment, Oct. 13. House agreed to Senate amendment, with amendments, Oct. 14. Senate agreed to House amendments to Senate amendment Oct. 15. President signed Oct. 30, 1998.

PL 105-313 (HR 3055) Deem the activities of the Miccosukee Tribe on the Tamiami Indian Reservation to be consistent with the purposes of the Everglades National Park. Introduced by HASTINGS, D-Fla., Nov. 13, 1997. House Resources reported, amended, Sept. 11, 1998 (H Rept 105-708, Part 1). House passed, amended, under suspension of the rules, Oct. 12. Senate passed Oct. 15. President signed Oct. 30, 1998.

PL 105-314 (HR 3494) Amend Title 18, U.S. Code, with respect to violent sex crimes against children. Introduced by McCOLLUM, R-Fla., March 18, 1998. House Judiciary reported, amended, June 3 (H Rept 105-557). House passed, amended, June 11. Senate Judiciary reported, with amendments, Sept. 17 (no written report). Senate passed, with amendments, Oct. 9. House agreed to Senate amendments under suspension of the rules Oct. 12. President signed Oct. 30, 1998.

PL 105-315 (HR 3528) Amend Title 28, U.S. Code, with respect to the use of alternative dispute resolution processes in United States district courts. Introduced by COBLE, R-N.C., March 23, 1998. House Judiciary reported, amended, April 21 (H Rept 105-487). House passed, amended, under suspension of the rules April 21. Senate Judiciary reported, with amendments, July 30 (no written report). Senate passed, with amendments, Oct. 7. House agreed to Senate amendments under suspension of the rules Oct. 10. President signed Oct. 30, 1998.

PL 105-316 (HR 3687) Authorize prepayment of amounts due under a water reclamation project contract for the Canadian River Project, Texas. Introduced by THORNBERRY, R-Texas, April 1, 1998. House Resources discharged. House passed, amended, Aug. 7. Senate Energy and Natural Resources reported, with amendment, Sept. 25 (S Rept 105-410). Senate passed Oct. 14. President signed Oct. 30, 1998.

PL 105-317 (HR 3903) Provide for an exchange of lands located near Gustavus, Alaska. Introduced by YOUNG, R-Alaska, May 19, 1998. House Resources reported, amended, Sept. 11 (H Rept 105-706, Part 1). House Commerce discharged. House passed, amended, under suspension of the rules Sept. 15. Senate passed Oct. 2. Senate passed, amended, Oct. 8. House agreed to Senate amendments Oct. 10. President signed Oct. 30, 1998.

PL 105-318 (HR 4151) Amend Chapter 47 of Title 18, U.S. Code, relating to identity fraud. Introduced by SHADEGG, R-Ariz., June 25, 1998. House passed, amended, under suspension of the rules, Oct. 7. Senate passed Oct. 14. President signed Oct. 30, 1998.

PL 105-319 (HR 4293) Establish a cultural and training program for disadvantaged individuals from Northern Ireland and the Republic of Ireland. Introduced by WALSH, R-N.Y., July 21, 1998. House passed, amended, under suspension of the rules Oct. 7. Senate passed Oct. 8. President signed Oct. 30, 1998.

PL 105-320 (HR 4309) Provide a comprehensive program of support for victims of torture. Introduced by SMITH, R-N.J., July 22, 1998. House International Relations reported, amended, Sept. 14 (H Rept 105-709, Part 1). House Commerce discharged. House passed, amended, under suspension of the rules Sept. 14. Senate passed, amended, Oct. 8. House agreed to Senate amendment under suspension of the rules Oct. 10. President signed Oct. 30, 1998.

PL 105-321 (HR 4326) Transfer administrative jurisdiction over certain federal lands located within or adjacent to the Rogue River National Forest and to clarify the authority of the Bureau of Land Management to sell and exchange other federal lands in Oregon. Introduced by SMITH, R-Ore., July 24, 1998. House Resources reported Oct. 12 (H Rept 105-810). House passed, amended, Oct. 12. Senate passed Oct. 14. President signed Oct. 30, 1998.

PL 105-322 (HR 4337) Authorize the secretary of the Interior to provide financial assistance to the state of Maryland for a pilot program to develop measures to eradicate or control nutria and restore marshland damaged by nutria. Introduced by GILCREST, R-Md., July 27, 1998. House passed under suspension of the rules Sept. 28. Senate passed Oct. 9. President signed Oct. 30, 1998.

PL 105-323 (HR 4660) Amend the State Department Basic Authorities Act of 1956 to provide rewards for information leading to the arrest or conviction of any individual for the commission of an act, or conspiracy to commit an act, of international terrorism, narcotics related offenses, or for serious violations of international humanitarian law relating to the former Yugoslavia. Introduced by GILMAN, R-N.Y., Oct. 1, 1998. House passed, amended, under suspension of the rules Oct. 8. Senate passed, with amendment, Oct. 14. House agreed to Senate amend-

Public Laws

ment under suspension of the rules Oct. 15. President signed Oct. 30, 1998.

PL 105-324 (HR 4679) Amend the Federal Food, Drug, and Cosmetic Act to clarify the circumstances in which a substance is considered to be a pesticide chemical for purposes of such act. Introduced by BLILEY, R-Va., Oct. 2, 1998. House passed under suspension of the rules Oct. 7. Senate passed Oct. 9. President signed Oct. 30, 1998.

PL 105-325 (S 231) Establish the National Cave and Karst Research Institute in the state of New Mexico. Introduced by BINGAMAN, D-N.M., Jan. 29, 1997. Senate Energy and Natural Resources reported June 26 (S Rept 105-37). Senate passed July 11. House Resources reported April 28, 1998 (H Rept 105-496). House passed Oct. 10. President signed Oct. 30, 1998.

PL 105-326 (S 890) Dispose of certain federal properties located in Dutch John, Utah, and assist the local government in the interim delivery of basic services to the Dutch John community. Introduced by BENNETT, R-Utah, June 12, 1997. Senate Energy and Natural Resources reported, amended, July 27, 1998 (S Rept 105-264). Senate passed, amended, Oct. 2. House passed Oct. 8. President signed Oct. 30, 1998.

PL 105-327 (S 1333) Amend the Land and Water Conservation Fund Act of 1965 to allow national park units that cannot charge an entrance or admission fee to retain other fees and charges. Introduced by FRIST, R-Tenn., Oct. 29, 1997. Senate Energy and Natural Resources reported, amended, Sept. 8, 1998 (S Rept 105-311). Senate passed, amended, Oct. 2. House Resources discharged. House passed Oct. 10. President signed Oct. 30, 1998.

PL 105-328 (S 2094) Amend the Fish and Wildlife Improvement Act of 1978 to enable the secretary of the Interior to more effectively use the proceeds of sales of certain items. Introduced by ALLARD, R-Colo., May 20, 1998. Senate Environment and Public Works reported, amended, July 31 (S Rept 105-285). Senate passed, amended, Sept. 11. House passed under suspension of the rules Oct. 9. President signed Oct. 30, 1998.

PL 105-329 (S 2106) Expand the boundaries of Arches National Park, Utah, to include portions of certain drainages that are under the jurisdiction of the Bureau of Land Management, and to include a portion of Fish Seep Draw owned by the state of Utah. Introduced by BENNETT, R-Utah, May 21, 1998. Senate Energy and Natural Resources reported, amended Sept. 14 (S Rept 105-330). Senate passed, amended Oct. 2. House passed Oct. 10, 1998. President signed Oct. 30, 1998.

PL 105-330 (S 2193) Implement the provisions of the Trademark Law Treaty. Introduced by HATCH, R-Utah, June 18, 1998. Senate Judiciary reported July 16 (no written report). Senate passed, amended, Sept. 17. House passed, under suspension of the rules, Oct. 9. President signed Oct. 30, 1998.

PL 105-331 (HR 678) Require the secretary of the Treasury to mint coins in commemoration of the sesquicentennial of the birth of Thomas Alva Edison and to redesign the half dollar circulating coin for 1997 to commemorate Edison. Introduced by GILLMOR, R-Ohio, Feb. 11, 1997. House passed, amended, under suspension of the rules Sept. 9, 1998. Senate passed Oct. 7. President signed Oct. 31, 1998.

PL 105-332 (HR 1853) Amend the Carl D. Perkins Vocational and Applied Technology Education Act. Introduced by RIGGS, R-Calif., June 10, 1997. House Education and the Workforce reported, amended, July 14 (H Rept 105-177). House passed, amended, July 22. Senate Labor and Human Resources discharged. Senate passed, with amendment, June 12, 1998. Senate agreed to conference report (H Rept 105-800) Oct. 8. House agreed to conference report Oct. 9. President signed Oct. 31, 1998.

PL 105-333 (HR 2000) Amend the Alaska Native Claims Settlement Act to make certain clarifications to the land bank protection provisions. Introduced by YOUNG, R-Alaska, June 19, 1997. House Resources reported, amended, Aug. 5, 1998 (H Rept 105-677). House passed, amended, under suspension of the rules Sept. 23. Senate passed Oct. 7. President signed Oct. 31, 1998.

PL 105-334 (HR 2327) Provide for a change in the exemption from the child labor provisions of the Fair Labor Standards Act of 1938 for minors between 16 and 18 years of age who engage in the operation of automobiles and trucks. Introduced by COMBEST, R-Texas, July 31, 1997. House passed, amended, under suspension of the rules Sept. 28, 1998. Senate passed, with amendment, Oct. 12. House agreed to Senate amendment under suspension of the rules Oct. 13. President signed Oct. 31, 1998.

PL 105-335 (HR 3830) Provide for the exchange of certain lands within the state of Utah. Introduced by HANSEN, R-Utah, May 12, 1998. House Resources reported June 24 (H Rept 105-598). House passed June 24. Senate Energy and Natural Resources reported Sept. 14 (S Rept 105-331). Senate passed Oct. 9. President signed Oct. 31, 1998.

PL 105-336 (HR 3874) Amend the Child Nutrition Act of 1966 to make improvements to the special supplemental nutrition program for women, infants and children and to extend the authority of that program through fiscal year 2003. Introduced by CASTLE, R-Del., May 14, 1998. House Education and the Workforce reported, amended, July 20 (H Rept 105-633). House passed, amended, under suspension of the rules July 20. Senate passed, amended, Sept. 17. Conference report filed in the House Oct. 6 (H Rept 105-786). Senate agreed to conference report Oct. 7. House agreed to conference report under suspension of the rules Oct. 9. President signed Oct. 31, 1998.

PL 105-337 (HR 4259) Allow Haskell Indian Nations University and the Southwestern Indian Polytechnic Institute each to conduct a demonstration project to test the feasibility and desirability of new personnel management policies and procedures. Introduced by SNOWBARGER, R-Kan., July 16, 1998. House Government Reform and Oversight reported Sept. 9 (H Rept 105-700, Part 1. House passed Oct. 6. Senate passed Oct. 14. President signed Oct. 31, 1998.

PL 105-338 (HR 4655) Establish a program to support a transition to democracy in Iraq. Introduced by GILMAN, R-N.Y., Sept. 29, 1998. House passed under suspension of the rules Oct. 5. Senate passed Oct. 7. President signed Oct. 31, 1998.

Public Laws

PL 105-339 (S 1021) Amend Title 5, U.S. Code, to provide that consideration may not be denied to preference eligibles applying for certain positions in the competitive service. Introduced by HAGEL, R-Neb., July 16, 1997. Senate Veterans' Affairs reported, amended, Sept. 21, 1998 (S Rept 105-340). Senate passed, amended, Oct. 5. House passed under suspension of the rules Oct. 8. President signed Oct. 31, 1998.

PL 105-340 (S 1722) Amend the Public Health Service Act to revise and extend certain programs with respect to women's health research and prevention activities at the National Institutes of Health and the Centers for Disease Control and Prevention. Introduced by FRIST, R-Tenn., March 6, 1998. Senate Labor and Human Resources discharged. Senate passed, amended, Oct. 12. House passed under suspension of the rules Oct. 13. President signed Oct. 31, 1998.

PL 105-341 (S 2285) Establish a commission, in honor of the 150th Anniversary of the Seneca Falls Convention, to further protect sites of historic importance in the efforts to secure equal rights for women. Introduced by DODD, D-Conn., July 10, 1998. Senate Energy and Natural Resources reported Sept. 25 (S Rept 105-396). Senate passed Oct. 7. House Resources discharged. House passed Oct. 10. President signed Oct. 31, 1998.

PL 105-342 (S 2240) Establish the Adams National Historical Park in the Commonwealth of Massachusetts. Introduced by MURKOWSKI, R-Alaska, June 26, 1998. Senate Energy and Natural Resources reported, amended, Sept. 25 (S Rept 105-404). Senate passed, amended, Oct. 7. House Resources discharged. House passed Oct. 10. President signed Nov. 2, 1998.

PL 105-343 (S 2246) Amend the act that established the Frederick Law Olmsted National Historic Site, in the Commonwealth of Massachusetts, by modifying the boundary. Introduced by MURKOWSKI, R-Alaska, June 26, 1998. Senate Energy and Natural Resources reported Sept. 25 (S Rept 105-405). Senate passed Oct. 7. House Resources discharged. House passed Oct. 10. President signed Nov. 2, 1998.

PL 105-344 (S 2413) Prohibit the conveyance of Woodland Lake Park tract in Apache-Sitgreaves National Forest in the state of Arizona unless the conveyance is made to the town of Pinetop-Lakeside or authorized by act of Congress. Introduced by McCAIN, R-Ariz., July 31, 1998. Senate Energy and Natural Resources reported, amended, Oct. 6 (S Rept 105-384). Senate passed, amended, Oct. 9. House passed Oct. 10. President signed Nov. 2, 1998.

PL 105-345 (S 2427) Amend the Omnibus Parks and Public Lands Management Act of 1996 to extend the legislative authority for the Black Patriots Foundation to establish a commemorative work. Introduced by CAMPBELL, R-Colo., Aug. 31, 1998. Senate Energy and Natural Resources discharged. Senate passed Oct. 8. House Resources discharged. House passed Oct. 10. President signed Nov. 2, 1998.

PL 105-346 (S 2505) Direct the secretary of the Interior to convey title to the Tunnison Lab Hagerman Field Station in Gooding County, Idaho, to the University of Idaho. Introduced by CRAIG, R-Idaho, Sept. 21, 1998. Senate Environment and Public Works reported, amended, Sept. 28 (S Rept 105-354). Senate passed, amended, Oct. 5. House passed under suspension of the rules Oct. 9. President signed Nov. 2, 1998.

PL 105-347 (S 2561) Amend the Fair Credit Reporting Act with respect to furnishing and using consumer reports for employment purposes. Introduced by NICKLES, R-Okla., Oct. 6, 1998. Senate passed Oct. 6. House passed Oct. 9. President signed Nov. 2, 1998.

PL 105-348 (S J Res 51) Grant the consent of Congress to the Potomac Highlands Airport Authority Compact entered into between the states of Maryland and West Virginia. Introduced by SARBANES, D-Md., June 10, 1998. Senate Judiciary reported July 30 (no written report). Senate passed July 31. House passed under suspension of the rules Oct. 9. President signed Nov. 2, 1998.

PL 105-349 (S J Res 58) Recognize the accomplishments of inspectors general since their creation in 1978 in preventing and detecting waste, fraud, abuse, and mismanagement, and in promoting economy, efficiency, and effectiveness in the federal government. Introduced by GLENN, D-Ohio, Oct. 1, 1998. Senate passed Oct. 1. House passed under suspension of the rules Oct. 10. President signed Nov. 2, 1998.

PL 105-350 (H J Res 138) Appoint the day for the convening of the first session of the 106th Congress. Introduced by SOLOMON, R-N.Y., Oct. 20, 1998. House passed Oct. 20. Senate passed Oct. 21. President signed Nov. 3, 1998.

PL 105-351 (S 538) Authorize the secretary of the Interior to convey certain facilities of the Minidoka project to the Burley Irrigation District. Introduced by CRAIG, R-Idaho, April 9, 1997. Senate Energy and Natural Resources reported, amended, Nov. 3 (S Rept 105-131). Senate passed, amended June 25, 1998. House passed Oct. 12. President signed Nov. 3, 1998.

PL 105-352 (S 744) Authorize the construction of the Fall River Water Users District Rural Water System and authorize financial assistance to the Fall River Water Users District, a nonprofit corporation, in the planning and construction of the water supply system. Introduced by JOHNSON, D-S.D., May 14, 1997. Senate Energy and Natural Resources reported, amended, Sept. 25, 1998 (S Rept 105-369). Senate passed, amended Oct. 7. House Resources discharged. House passed Oct. 12. President signed Nov. 3, 1998.

PL 105-353 (S 1260) Amend the Securities Act of 1933 and the Securities Exchange Act of 1934 to limit the conduct of securities class actions under state law. Introduced by GRAMM, R-Texas, Oct. 7, 1997. Senate Banking, Housing, and Urban Affairs reported, amended, May 4, 1998 (S Rept 105-182). Senate passed, amended, May 13. House passed, amended, July 22. Conference report filed in House Oct. 9 (H Rept 105-803). Senate agreed to conference report Oct. 13. House agreed to conference report, under suspension of the rules, Oct. 13. President signed Nov. 3, 1998.

PL 105-354 (S 2524) Clarify without substantive change laws related to Patriotic and National Observances, Ceremonies, and Organizations and to improve the U.S. Code. Introduced by HATCH, R-Utah, Sept. 28, 1998. Senate Judiciary reported Oct. 1 (no written report). Senate passed Oct. 8. House passed, under suspension of the rules, Oct. 12. President signed Nov. 3, 1998.

Public Laws

PL 105-355 (HR 3910) Authorize the Automobile National Heritage Area. Introduced by DINGELL, D-Mich., May 20, 1998. House Resources discharged. House passed, amended, Oct. 10. Senate passed Oct. 14. President signed Nov. 6, 1998.

PL 105-356 (S 2232) Establish the Little Rock Central High School National Historic Site in the state of Arkansas. Introduced by BUMPERS, D-Ark., June 25, 1998. Senate Energy and Natural Resources reported, amended, Sept. 8 (S Rept 105-307). Senate passed, amended, Oct. 2. House Resources discharged. House passed Oct. 8. President signed Nov. 6, 1998.

PL 105-357 (HR 3633) Amend the Controlled Substances Import and Export Act to place limitations on controlled substances brought into the United States from Mexico. Introduced by CHABOT, R-Ohio, April 1, 1998. House Judiciary reported July 16 (H Rept 105-629, Part 1). House Commerce discharged. House passed, amended, under suspension of the rules, Aug. 3. Senate passed Oct. 20. President signed Nov. 10, 1998.

PL 105-358 (HR 3723) Authorize funds for the payment of salaries and expenses of the Patent and Trademark Office. Introduced by COBLE, R-N.C., April 23, 1998. House Judiciary reported, amended, May 12 (H Rept 105-528). House passed, amended, under suspension of the rules, May 12. Senate Judiciary discharged. Senate passed Oct. 14. President signed Nov. 10, 1998.

PL 105-359 (HR 4501) Require the secretary of Agriculture and the secretary of the Interior to conduct a study to improve the access for persons with disabilities to outdoor recreational opportunities made available to the public. Introduced by SCHAFFER, R-Colo., Aug. 6, 1998. House passed, under suspension of the rules, Oct. 14. Senate passed Oct. 20. President signed Nov. 10, 1998.

PL 105-360 (HR 4821) Extend into fiscal year 1999 the visa processing period for diversity applicants whose visa processing was suspended during fiscal year 1998 due to embassy bombings. Introduced by SMITH, R-Texas, Oct. 13, 1998. House passed, under suspension of the rules, Oct. 15. Senate passed Oct. 21. President signed Nov. 10, 1998.

PL 105-361 (S 459) Amend the Native American Programs Act of 1974 to extend certain authorizations. Introduced by CAMPBELL, R-Colo., March 18, 1997. Senate Indian Affairs reported, amended, May 21 (S Rept 105-20). Senate passed, amended, Sept. 29. House Education and the Workforce discharged. House passed with amendments Oct. 9, 1998. Senate agreed to House amendments Oct. 14. President signed Nov. 10, 1998.

PL 105-362 (S 1364) Eliminate unnecessary and wasteful federal reports. Introduced by McCAIN, R-Ariz., Nov. 4, 1997. Senate Governmental Affairs reported, amended, May 11, 1998 (S Rept 105-187). Senate passed, amended June 10. House passed with amendment, under suspension of the rules, Oct. 13. Senate agreed to House amendment with amendment Oct. 21. House agreed to Senate amendment to House amendment Oct. 21. President signed Nov. 10, 1998.

PL 105-363 (S 1718) Amend the Weir Farm National Historic Site Establishment Act of 1990 to authorize the acquisition of additional acreage for the historic site to permit the development of visitor and administrative facilities and to authorize the appropriation of additional amounts for the acquisition of real and personal property. Introduced by LIEBERMAN, D-Conn., March 5, 1998. Senate Energy and Natural Resources reported, amended, Sept. 14 (S Rept 105-328). Senate passed, amended Oct. 2. House Resources discharged. House passed with amendments Oct. 10. Senate agreed to House amendments Oct. 14. President signed Nov. 10, 1998.

PL 105-364 (S 2241) Provide for the acquisition of lands formerly occupied by the Franklin D. Roosevelt family at Hyde Park, N.Y. Introduced by MURKOWSKI, R-Alaska, June 26, 1998. Senate Energy and Natural Resources reported Sept. 25 (S Rept 105-400). Senate passed Oct. 7. House Resources discharged. House passed Oct. 15. President signed Nov. 10, 1998.

PL 105-365 (S 2272) Amend the boundaries of Grant-Kohrs Ranch National Historic Site in the state of Montana. Introduced by BURNS, R-Mont., July 8, 1998. Senate Energy and Natural Resources reported Sept. 9 (S Rept 105-324). Senate passed Oct. 2. House passed, under suspension of the rules, Oct. 15. President signed Nov. 10, 1998.

PL 105-366 (S 2375) Amend the Securities Exchange Act of 1934 and the Foreign Corrupt Practices Act of 1977, to strengthen prohibitions on international bribery and other corrupt practices. Introduced by D'AMATO, R-N.Y., July 30, 1998. Senate Banking, Housing, and Urban Affairs reported July 30, 1998 (S Rept 105-277). Senate passed July 31. House passed with amendments Oct. 9. Senate agreed to House amendments with amendments Oct. 14. House disagreed to Senate amendments Nos. 2 through 6 and agreed to Senate amendment No. 1, with an amendment Oct. 20. Senate receded from its amendments Nos. 2 through 6 Oct. 21. Senate agreed to House amendment to Senate amendment No. 1 Oct. 21. President signed Nov. 10, 1998.

PL 105-367 (S 2500) Protect the sanctity of contracts and leases entered into by surface patent holders with respect to coalbed methane gas. Introduced by ENZI, R-Wyo., Sept. 18, 1998. Senate Energy and Natural Resources reported amended Sept. 25 (S Rept 105-408). Senate passed, amended, Oct. 9. House passed, under suspension of the rules, Oct. 15. President signed Nov. 10, 1998.

PL 105-368 (HR 4110) Provide a cost of living adjustment in rates of compensation paid to veterans with service-connected disabilities, to make various improvements in education, housing, and cemetery programs of the Department of Veterans Affairs. Introduced by STUMP, R-Ariz., June 23, 1998. House Veterans' Affairs reported July 15 (H Rept 105-627). House passed, amended under suspension of the rules, Aug. 3. Senate Veterans' Affairs discharged. Senate passed with amendment Sept. 30. House agreed to Senate amendment with amendments Oct. 10. Senate agreed to House amendments to Senate amendment Oct. 21. President signed Nov. 11, 1998.

PL 105-369 (HR 1023) Provide for compassionate payments with regard to individuals with blood-clotting disorders, such as hemophilia, who contracted human immuno deficiency virus due to contaminated blood products. Introduced by GOSS, R-Fla., March 11, 1997. House Judiciary reported, amended, March 25, 1998 (H Rept 105-465,

Public Laws

Part 1). House Ways and Means reported, amended May 7 (Part 2). House Commerce discharged. House passed, amended, under suspension of the rules, May 19. Senate Labor and Human Resources reported Oct. 7 (no written report). Senate passed Oct. 21. President signed Nov. 12, 1998.

PL 105-370 (HR 2070) Amend Title 18, U. S. Code, to provide for the mandatory testing for serious transmissible diseases of incarcerated persons whose bodily fluids come into contact with corrections personnel and notice to those persons of the results of the tests. Introduced by SOLOMON, R-N.Y., June 25, 1997. House Judiciary reported, amended, July 31, 1998 H Rept 105-665). House passed, amended, under suspension of the rules Aug. 3. Senate Judiciary discharged. Senate passed, amended, Oct. 20. House agreed to Senate amendment Oct. 21. President signed Nov. 12, 1998.

PL 105-371 (HR 2263) Authorize and request the president to award the Medal of Honor posthumously to Theodore Roosevelt for his gallant and heroic actions in the attack on San Juan Heights, Cuba, during the Spanish-American War. Introduced by McHALE, D-Pa., July 25, 1997. House passed, under suspension of the rules, Oct. 8, 1998. Senate passed Oct. 21, 1998. President signed Nov. 12, 1998.

PL 105-372 (HR 3267) Direct the secretary of the Interior, acting through the Bureau of Reclamation, to conduct a feasibility study and construct a project to reclaim the Salton Sea. Introduced by HUNTER, R-Calif., Feb. 25, 1998. House Resources reported, amended, July 14 (H Rept 105-621, Part 1). House Transportation and Infrastructure discharged. House passed, amended July 15. Senate passed, amended Oct. 13. House agreed to Senate amendments Oct. 21. President signed Nov. 12, 1998.

PL 105-373 (HR 4083) Make available to the Ukrainian Museum and Archives the USIA television program "Window on America." Introduced by KUCINICH, D-Ohio, June 18, 1998. House passed, amended, under suspension of the rules Sept. 14. Senate Foreign Relations discharged. Senate passed Oct. 21. President signed Nov. 12, 1998.

PL 105-374 (HR 4164) Amend Title 28, U.S. Code, with respect to the enforcement of child custody and visitation orders. Introduced by COBLE, R-N.C., June 25, 1998. House passed, under suspension of the rules, July 14. Senate Judiciary discharged. Senate passed, amended, Oct. 21. House agreed to Senate amendment Oct. 21. President signed Nov. 12, 1998.

PL 105-375 (S 759) Amend the State Department Basic Authorities Act of 1956 to require the secretary of State to submit an annual report to Congress concerning diplomatic immunity. Introduced by COVERDELL, R-Ga., May 16, 1997. Senate Foreign Relations reported, amended, Nov. 4 (no written report). Senate passed, amended, Nov. 8. House passed, under suspension of the rules, Oct. 14, 1998. President signed Nov 12, 1998.

PL 105-376 (S 1132) Modify the boundaries of the Bandelier National Monument to include the lands within the headwaters of the Upper Alamo Watershed that drain into the monument and that are not currently within the jurisdiction of a federal land management agency, to authorize purchase or donation of those lands. Introduced by BINGAMAN, D-N.M., July 31, 1997. Senate Energy and Natural Resources reported, amended April 29, 1998 (S Rept 105-178). Senate passed, amended, July 17. House passed Oct. 20. President signed Nov. 12, 1998.

PL 105-377 (S 1134) Grant the consent and approval of Congress to an interstate forest fire protection compact. Introduced by MURRAY, D-Wash., July 31, 1997. Senate Judiciary reported July 16, 1998 (no written report). Senate passed July 30. House passed, under suspension of the rules, Oct. 15. President signed Nov. 12, 1998.

PL 105-378 (S 1408) Establish the Lower East Side Tenement National Historic Site. Introduced by D'AMATO, R-N.Y., Nov. 7, 1997. Senate Energy and Natural Resources reported Sept. 8, 1998 (S Rept 105-303). Senate passed Oct. 2. House Resources discharged. House passed, amended, Oct. 10. Senate agreed to House amendment Oct. 14. President signed Nov. 12, 1998.

PL 105-379 (S 1733) Amend the Food Stamp Act of 1977 to require food stamp state agencies to take certain actions to ensure that food stamp coupons are not issued for deceased individuals, and to require the secretary of Agriculture to conduct a study of options for the design, development, implementation, and operation of a national database to track participation in federal means-tested public assistance programs. Introduced by LUGAR, R-Ind., March 10, 1998. Senate Agriculture, Nutrition, and Forestry discharged. Senate passed, amended, Oct. 14. House passed, under suspension of the rules, Oct. 15. President signed Nov.12, 1998.

PL 105-380 (S 2129) Eliminate restrictions on the acquisition of certain land contiguous to Hawaii Volcanoes National Park. Introduced by AKAKA, D-Hawaii, June 2, 1998. Senate Energy and Natural Resources reported Sept. 8 (S Rept 105-313). Senate passed Oct. 2. House Resources discharged. House passed Oct. 14. President signed Nov. 12, 1998.

PL 105-381 (S J Res 35) Grant the consent of Congress to the Pacific Northwest Emergency Management Arrangement. Introduced by CRAIG, R-Idaho, July 21, 1997. Senate Judiciary reported July 16, 1998 (no written report). Senate passed July 31. House passed, under suspension of the rules, Oct. 15. President signed Nov. 12, 1998.

PL 105-382 (HR 633) Amend the Foreign Service Act of 1980 to provide that the annuities of certain special agents and security personnel of the Department of State be computed in the same way as applies generally with respect to federal law enforcement officers. Introduced by DAVIS, R-Va., Feb. 6, 1997. House International Relations reported, amended, Sept. 28, 1998 (H Rept 105-755, Part 1). House Government Reform and Oversight discharged. House passed, amended, under suspension of the rules Oct. 5. Senate passed Oct. 20. President signed Nov. 13, 1998.

PL 105-383 (HR 2204) Authorize appropriations for fiscal years 1998 and 1999 for the Coast Guard. Introduced by SHUSTER, R-Pa., July 24, 1997. House Transportation and Infrastructure reported, amended, July 31 (H Rept 105-236). House passed, amended Oct. 21. Senate passed, amended, Oct. 12, 1998. House agreed to Senate amendment with an amendment Oct. 15. Senate agreed to House amendment to Senate amendment Oct. 21. President signed Nov. 13, 1998.

Public Laws

PL 105-384 (HR 3461) Approve a governing international fishery agreement between the United States and the Republic of Poland. Introduced by SAXTON, R-N.J., March 12, 1998. House Resources discharged. House passed, amended, Oct. 12. Senate passed Oct. 21. President signed Nov. 13, 1998.

PL 105-385 (HR 4283) Support sustainable and broad-based agricultural and rural development in sub-Saharan Africa. Introduced by BEREUTER, R-Neb., July 21, 1998. House International Relations reported Aug. 6 (H Rept 105-681, Part 1). House Agriculture discharged. House passed, under suspension of the rules, Sept. 28. Senate passed, amended, Oct. 20. House agreed to Senate amendment Oct. 20. President signed Nov. 13, 1998.

PL 105-386 (S 191) Throttle criminal use of guns. Introduced by HELMS, R-N.C., Jan. 22, 1997. Senate Judiciary reported, amended, Nov. 6 (no written report). Senate passed, amended, Nov. 13. House passed, amended, under suspension of the rules, Oct. 9, 1998. Senate agreed to House amendment Oct. 15. President signed Nov. 13, 1998.

PL 105-387 (S 391) Provide for the disposition of certain funds appropriated to pay judgment in favor of the Mississippi Sioux Indians. Introduced by DORGAN, D-N.D., March 4, 1997. Senate Indian Affairs reported, amended Oct. 7, 1998 (S Rept 105-379). Senate passed, amended, Oct. 9. House passed, amended, under suspension of the rules, Oct. 10. Senate agreed to House amendment Oct. 14. President signed Nov. 13, 1998.

PL 105-388 (S 417) Extend energy conservation programs under the Energy Policy and Conservation Act through Sept. 30, 2002. Introduced by MURKOWSKI, R-Alaska, March 10, 1997. Senate Energy and Natural Resources reported, amended, June 11 (S Rept 105-25). Senate passed, amended, June 27. House passed, amended, Sept. 28, 1998. Senate agreed to House amendments, with amendment, Oct. 8. House agreed to Senate amendment to House amendments under suspension of the rules, Oct. 15. President signed Nov. 13, 1998.

PL 105-389 (S 1397) Establish a commission to assist in commemoration of the centennial of powered flight and the achievements of the Wright brothers. Introduced by HELMS, R-N.C., Nov. 7, 1997. Senate Governmental Affairs reported, amended, Aug. 25, 1998 (S Rept 105-294). Senate passed, amended, Sept. 22. House passed under suspension of the rules, Oct. 14. President signed Nov. 13, 1998.

PL 105-390 (S 1525) Provide financial assistance for higher education to the dependents of federal, state and local public safety officers who are killed or permanently and totally disabled as the result of a traumatic injury sustained in the line of duty. Introduced by SPECTER, R-Pa., Nov. 12, 1997. Senate Judiciary reported May 7, 1998 (no written report). Senate passed May 15. House Judiciary discharged. House passed, amended, Oct. 10. Senate agreed to House amendment Oct. 15. President signed Nov. 13, 1998.

PL 105-391 (S 1693) Provide for improved management and increased accountability for certain National Park Service programs. Introduced by THOMAS, R-Wyo., Feb. 27, 1998. Senate Energy and Natural Resources reported, amended, June 5 (S Rept 105-202). Senate passed, amended, June 11. House Resources reported, amended, Oct. 2 (H Rept 105-767). House passed, under suspension of the rules, Oct. 13. Senate agreed to House amendment Oct. 14. President signed Nov. 13, 1998.

PL 105-392 (S 1754) Amend the Public Health Service Act to consolidate and reauthorize health professions and minority and disadvantaged health professions and disadvantaged health education programs. Introduced by FRIST, R-Tenn., March 12, 1998. Senate Labor and Human Resources reported, amended June 23 (S Rept 105-220). Senate passed, amended July 31. House passed, amended, under suspension of the rules, Oct. 13. Senate agreed to House amendment Oct. 14. President signed Nov. 13, 1998.

PL 105-393 (S 2364) Reauthorize and make reforms to programs authorized by the Public Works and Economic Development Act of 1965 and the Appalachian Regional Development Act of 1965. Introduced by CHAFEE, R-R.I., July 28, 1998. Senate Environment and Public Works reported Sept. 14 (S Rept 105-332). Senate passed, amended, Oct. 12. House passed, under suspension of the rules, Oct. 13. President signed Nov. 13, 1998.

PL 105-394 (S 2432) Support programs of grants to states to address the assistive technology needs of individuals with disabilities. Introduced by JEFFORDS, R-Vt., Sept. 2, 1998. Senate Labor and Human Resources reported, amended, Sept. 15 (S Rept 105-334). Senate passed, amended, Oct. 5. House passed, amended, under suspension of the rules, Oct. 9. Senate agreed to House amendment Oct. 14. President signed Nov. 13, 1998. ◆

Appendix H

HOUSE ROLL CALL VOTES

Bill Number Index H-3
Individual Roll Call Votes H-4

Subject Index H-158

House Roll Call Votes By Bill Number

House Bills

H Con Res 152, H-18
H Con Res 185, H-122
H Con Res 202, H-6
H Con Res 206, H-14
H Con Res 208, H-86
H Con Res 213, H-108
H Con Res 218, H-32
H Con Res 220, H-38
H Con Res 227, H-18
H Con Res 235, H-18
H Con Res 254, H-122
H Con Res 270, H-62
H Con Res 284, H-60, H-62
H Con Res 285, H-60
H Con Res 288, H-74
H Con Res 301, H-86
H Con Res 304, H-122
H Con Res 311, H-98
H Con Res 315, H-130
H Con Res 320, H-146
H Con Res 331, H-144
H Con Res 334, H-146

H J Res 78, H-58
H J Res 102, H-34
H J Res 107, H-4
H J Res 111, H-30
H J Res 117, H-124
H J Res 119, H-66
H J Res 120, H-100
H J Res 121, H-92
H J Res 128, H-126

H Res 144, H-128
H Res 267, H-38
H Res 352, H-6
H Res 355, H-6
H Res 361, H-18
H Res 364, H-18
H Res 392, H-86
H Res 401, H-68
H Res 414, H-36
H Res 417, H-62
H Res 422, H-42
H Res 423, H-40
H Res 432, H-52
H Res 433, H-52
H Res 440, H-48
H Res 447, H-62
H Res 452, H-74
H Res 459, H-118
H Res 463, H-70
H Res 494, H-148
H Res 505, H-130
H Res 507, H-102
H Res 525, H-120
H Res 545, H-128
H Res 552, H-130, H-132
H Res 557, H-144
H Res 565, H-144
H Res 575, H-138

H Res 581, H-140, H-142
H Res 598, H-150
H Res 604, H-152
H Res 611, H-154, H-156

HR 6, H-36, H-38, H-40
HR 10, H-42, H-44
HR 34, H-26
HR 217, H-10
HR 424, H-8
HR 559, H-150
HR 629, H-98
HR 678, H-118
HR 856, H-10, H-12
HR 992, H-16
HR 1122, H-92, H-94
HR 1151, H-28
HR 1154, H-136
HR 1252, H-30, H-32
HR 1260, H-150
HR 1428, H-8
HR 1432, H-14, H-16
HR 1544, H-8, H-10
HR 1560, H-118
HR 1635, H-62
HR 1689, H-92
HR 1722, H-150
HR 1754, H-150
HR 1757, H-24
HR 1847, H-68
HR 1872, H-38
HR 2181, H-8
HR 2183, H-54, H-70, H-72, H-80, H-86, H-88, H-102, H-104, H-106, H-108, H-114
HR 2348, H-140
HR 2369, H-12
HR 2400, H-28, H-30, H-52, H-54, H-56
HR 2431, H-46
HR 2460, H-10
HR 2515, H-24
HR 2538, H-120
HR 2578, H-22
HR 2589, H-22
HR 2608, H-26
HR 2616, H-148
HR 2621, H-132
HR 2625, H-4
HR 2631, H-6
HR 2646, H-40, H-68, H-70
HR 2676, H-56, H-78, H-80
HR 2709, H-62
HR 2829, H-42
HR 2846, H-4, H-6
HR 2863, H-120
HR 2870, H-18, H-20
HR 2883, H-16
HR 2888, H-66
HR 3039, H-48
HR 3096, H-22
HR 3097, H-68, H-70
HR 3130, H-14

HR 3150, H-64, H-66, H-134, H-144
HR 3211, H-20
HR 3246, H-24
HR 3248, H-128
HR 3267, H-82
HR 3310, H-22, H-24
HR 3412, H-20
HR 3433, H-58
HR 3494, H-66, H-68, H-148
HR 3528, H-30
HR 3534, H-46, H-48
HR 3546, H-34
HR 3565, H-30
HR 3579, H-26, H-28, H-32, H-36
HR 3616, H-48, H-50, H-52, H-54, H-92, H-130
HR 3630, H-58
HR 3682, H-80
HR 3694, H-40, H-138
HR 3717, H-34
HR 3718, H-48
HR 3731, H-84
HR 3736, H-130
HR 3743, H-106
HR 3808, H-56
HR 3809, H-48
HR 3811, H-42
HR 3853, H-74
HR 3874, H-86
HR 3875, H-144
HR 3891, H-134
HR 3892, H-120
HR 3963, H-150
HR 3989, H-60
HR 4059, H-72, H-74, H-100
HR 4060, H-72, H-74, H-134
HR 4101, H-74, H-76, H-122, H-136
HR 4103, H-76, H-122, H-134
HR 4104, H-78, H-82, H-84, H-134, H-140
HR 4110, H-146
HR 4112, H-78, H-130
HR 4193, H-90, H-92, H-94
HR 4194, H-82, H-86, H-96, H-98, H-100, H-124, H-138
HR 4250, H-96
HR 4259, H-138
HR 4274, H-136, H-142
HR 4276, H-108, H-110, H-112, H-114
HR 4300, H-124, H-126
HR 4328, H-100, H-122, H-152
HR 4380, H-116, H-118
HR 4382, H-124
HR 4550, H-126
HR 4567, H-146
HR 4569, H-126, H-128
HR 4570, H-138
HR 4578, H-132
HR 4579, H-132, H-134
HR 4614, H-136

HR 4616, H-140
HR 4655, H-136
HR 4756, H-150

Senate Bills

S 419, H-14
S 852, H-148
S 1132, H-152
S 1150, H-56, H-60
S 1364, H-148
S 1502, H-34, H-36
S 1733, H-152
S 2073, H-124, H-134
S 2095, H-148
S 2133, H-152
S 2206, H-120

S Con Res 37, H-34

S J Res 54, H-108

House Votes 2, 3, 4, 5, 6, 7, 8 *

1. Quorum Call.* 364 Responded. Jan. 27, 1998.

2. Robert K. Dornan Election Challenge/Motion To Table. Solomon, R-N.Y., motion to table the Gephardt, D-Mo., privileged resolution to dismiss the complaint by former Rep. Robert K. Dornan, R-Calif., contesting the election of Loretta Sanchez, D-Calif. Motion agreed to 214-189: R 213-1; D 1-187 (ND 1-136, SD 0-51); I 0-1. Jan. 28, 1998.

3. HR 2625. Renaming National Airport/Previous Question. Solomon, R-N.Y., motion to order the previous question (thus ending debate and the possibility of amendment) on adoption of the rule (H Res 344) to provide for House floor consideration of the bill to rename Washington National Airport the Ronald Reagan National Airport. Motion agreed to 227-189: R 222-0; D 5-188 (ND 3-136, SD 2-52); I 0-1. Feb. 4, 1998.

4. HR 2625. Renaming National Airport/Local Authority. Davis, R-Va., amendment to make renaming Washington National Airport located in Virginia the Ronald Reagan National Airport contingent on the approval of the Metropolitan Washington Airports Authority. Rejected 206-215: R 10-214; D 195-1 (ND 141-1, SD 54-0); I 1-0. Feb. 4, 1998.

5. HR 2625. Renaming National Airport/Recommit. Oberstar, D-Minn., motion to recommit the bill to the Transportation and Infrastructure Committee with instructions to report it back with an amendment to name the terminal at Washington National Airport, instead of the airport itself, after Ronald Reagan. Motion rejected 186-237: R 0-223; D 185-14 (ND 136-9, SD 49-5); I 1-0. Feb. 4, 1998.

6. HR 2625. Renaming National Airport/Passage. Passage of the bill to rename Washington National Airport located in Virginia the Ronald Reagan National Airport. Passed 240-186: R 222-3; D 18-182 (ND 14-132, SD 4-50); I 0-1. Feb. 4, 1998.

7. H J Res 107. Health Care Task Force Sanctions/Passage. Passage of the joint resolution to express the sense of Congress that public funds should not be used to pay a $285,865 sanction a federal judge imposed after ruling that Clinton Administration officials misled the courts regarding the makeup of a 1993 health care reform task force. Passed 273-126: R 209-3; D 64-122 (ND 41-93, SD 23-29); I 0-1. Feb. 4, 1998.

8. HR 2846. National Education Testing Curbs/Previous Question. Linder, R-Ga., motion to order the previous question (thus ending debate and the possibility of amendment) on adoption of the rule (H Res 348) to provide for House floor consideration of the bill to prohibit the use of federal education funds for any federally-sponsored national test in reading, math, or any other subject that is not specifically authorized by federal statute. Motion agreed to 220-185: R 214-0; D 6-184 (ND 3-134, SD 3-50); I 0-1. Feb. 5, 1998.

* CQ does not include quorum calls in its vote charts.

Key

- **Y** Voted for (yea).
- **#** Paired for.
- **+** Announced for.
- **N** Voted against (nay).
- **X** Paired against.
- **−** Announced against.
- **P** Voted "present."
- **C** Voted "present" to avoid possible conflict of interest.
- **?** Did not vote or otherwise make a position known.

Democrats **Republicans** *Independent*

	2	3	4	5	6	7	8
ALABAMA							
1 *Callahan*	Y	Y	N	N	Y	Y	Y
2 *Everett*	Y	Y	N	N	Y	Y	Y
3 *Riley*	Y	Y	N	N	Y	Y	Y
4 *Aderholt*	Y	Y	N	N	Y	+	Y
5 Cramer	N	N	Y	N	Y	Y	N
6 *Bachus*	Y	Y	N	N	Y	Y	Y
7 Hilliard	N	N	Y	Y	N	N	N
ALASKA							
AL *Young*	?	Y	N	N	Y	Y	Y
ARIZONA							
1 *Salmon*	Y	Y	N	N	Y	Y	Y
2 Pastor	N	N	Y	Y	N	N	N
3 *Stump*	Y	Y	N	N	Y	Y	Y
4 *Shadegg*	Y	Y	N	N	Y	Y	Y
5 *Kolbe*	Y	Y	N	N	Y	Y	Y
6 *Hayworth*	Y	Y	N	N	Y	Y	Y
ARKANSAS							
1 Berry	N	N	Y	Y	N	N	N
2 Snyder	N	N	Y	Y	N	Y	N
3 *Hutchinson*	?	Y	N	N	Y	Y	Y
4 *Dickey*	Y	Y	N	N	Y	Y	Y
CALIFORNIA							
1 *Riggs*	Y	?	N	N	Y	Y	?
2 *Herger*	Y	?	?	?	?	?	?
3 Fazio	N	N	Y	Y	N	N	N
4 *Doolittle*	Y	Y	N	N	Y	Y	Y
5 Matsui	N	N	Y	Y	N	N	N
6 Woolsey	N	N	Y	Y	N	N	N
7 Miller	N	N	Y	Y	N	N	N
8 Pelosi	N	N	Y	Y	N	N	N
9 Dellums	N	N	Y	Y	N	?	N
10 Tauscher	N	N	Y	Y	N	N	N
11 *Pombo*	Y	Y	N	N	Y	Y	Y
12 Lantos	N	N	Y	Y	N	N	N
13 Stark	N	N	Y	Y	N	N	N
14 Eshoo	N	?	?	?	?	?	?
15 *Campbell*	Y	Y	N	N	Y	N	Y
16 Lofgren	N	N	Y	Y	N	N	N
17 Farr	N	N	Y	Y	N	?	N
18 Condit	N	N	Y	Y	N	N	N
19 *Radanovich*	Y	Y	N	N	Y	Y	Y
20 Dooley	?	N	Y	Y	N	N	N
21 *Thomas*	Y	Y	N	N	Y	Y	Y
22 Vacant							
23 *Gallegly*	?	Y	N	N	Y	Y	Y
24 Sherman	N	N	Y	Y	N	N	N
25 *McKeon*	Y	Y	N	N	Y	+	+
26 Berman	?	N	Y	Y	N	N	N
27 *Rogan*	Y	Y	N	N	Y	Y	?
28 *Dreier*	Y	Y	N	N	Y	Y	Y
29 Waxman	N	N	Y	Y	N	N	N
30 Becerra	−	−	+	+	−	−	−
31 Martinez	N	N	Y	Y	N	Y	N
32 Dixon	N	?	Y	Y	N	N	N
33 Roybal-Allard	N	N	Y	Y	N	N	N
34 Torres	N	?	?	?	N	N	N
35 Waters	N	N	Y	Y	N	N	N
36 Harman	N	N	Y	Y	N	N	N
37 Millender-McD.	N	N	Y	Y	N	N	N
38 *Horn*	Y	Y	N	N	Y	Y	Y
39 *Royce*	Y	Y	N	N	Y	Y	Y
40 *Lewis*	Y	Y	N	N	Y	Y	Y
41 *Kim*	Y	Y	N	N	Y	Y	Y
42 Brown	N	N	Y	Y	N	N	N
43 *Calvert*	Y	Y	N	N	Y	Y	Y
44 Vacant							
45 *Rohrabacher*	Y	Y	N	N	Y	Y	Y
46 Sanchez	N	N	Y	Y	N	+	N
47 *Cox*	Y	Y	N	N	Y	Y	Y
48 *Packard*	Y	Y	N	N	Y	Y	Y
49 *Bilbray*	Y	Y	N	N	Y	Y	Y
50 Filner	N	N	Y	N	N	N	N
51 *Cunningham*	Y	Y	N	N	Y	Y	Y
52 *Hunter*	Y	Y	N	N	Y	Y	Y
COLORADO							
1 DeGette	?	N	Y	Y	N	N	N
2 Skaggs	N	N	Y	Y	N	N	N
3 *McInnis*	Y	Y	N	N	Y	Y	Y
4 *Schaffer*	Y	Y	N	N	Y	Y	Y
5 *Hefley*	Y	Y	N	N	Y	Y	Y
6 *Schaefer*	Y	Y	N	N	Y	Y	Y
CONNECTICUT							
1 Kennelly	?	N	Y	Y	N	N	N
2 Gejdenson	N	N	Y	Y	N	N	N
3 DeLauro	N	N	Y	Y	N	N	N
4 *Shays*	Y	Y	N	N	Y	Y	Y
5 Maloney	N	N	Y	Y	N	Y	N
6 *Johnson*	?	Y	N	N	Y	Y	Y
DELAWARE							
AL *Castle*	Y	Y	N	N	Y	Y	Y
FLORIDA							
1 *Scarborough*	?	Y	N	N	Y	Y	Y
2 Boyd	N	N	Y	N	Y	Y	N
3 Brown	N	N	N	N	N	N	N
4 *Fowler*	Y	Y	N	N	Y	Y	Y
5 Thurman	N	N	N	N	N	Y	N
6 *Stearns*	Y	Y	N	N	Y	Y	Y
7 *Mica*	Y	Y	N	N	Y	Y	Y
8 *McCollum*	Y	Y	N	N	Y	Y	Y
9 *Bilirakis*	Y	Y	N	N	Y	Y	Y
10 *Young*	Y	Y	N	N	Y	Y	Y
11 Davis	N	N	Y	N	Y	Y	N
12 *Canady*	Y	Y	N	N	Y	Y	Y
13 *Miller*	Y	Y	N	N	Y	Y	Y
14 *Goss*	Y	Y	N	N	Y	Y	Y
15 *Weldon*	Y	Y	N	N	Y	Y	Y
16 *Foley*	Y	Y	N	N	Y	Y	Y
17 Meek	N	N	Y	Y	N	N	N
18 *Ros-Lehtinen*	?	Y	N	N	Y	Y	Y
19 Wexler	N	N	Y	Y	N	N	N
20 Deutsch	N	N	Y	Y	N	N	N
21 *Diaz-Balart*	Y	Y	N	N	Y	Y	Y
22 *Shaw*	Y	Y	N	N	Y	Y	Y
23 Hastings	N	N	Y	Y	N	N	N
GEORGIA							
1 *Kingston*	Y	Y	N	N	Y	Y	Y
2 Bishop	N	N	Y	Y	N	N	N
3 *Collins*	Y	Y	N	N	Y	Y	Y
4 McKinney	N	N	Y	Y	N	N	N
5 Lewis	N	N	Y	Y	N	N	N
6 *Gingrich*		N	N	Y			
7 *Barr*	Y	Y	N	N	Y	Y	Y
8 *Chambliss*	Y	Y	N	N	Y	Y	Y
9 *Deal*	?	Y	N	N	Y	Y	Y
10 *Norwood*	Y	Y	N	N	Y	Y	Y
11 *Linder*	Y	Y	N	N	Y	Y	Y
HAWAII							
1 Abercrombie	N	N	?	N	N	?	N
2 Mink	N	N	Y	Y	N	Y	N
IDAHO							
1 *Chenoweth*	Y	Y	N	N	Y	Y	?
2 *Crapo*	Y	Y	N	N	Y	Y	Y
ILLINOIS							
1 Rush	N	N	Y	N	N	N	N
2 Jackson	N	N	Y	N	N	N	N
3 Lipinski	?	N	Y	N	Y	N	N
4 Gutierrez	N	N	Y	Y	N	N	N
5 Blagojevich	N	N	Y	Y	N	N	N
6 *Hyde*	Y	Y	N	N	Y	Y	Y
7 Davis	N	N	Y	Y	N	N	N
8 *Crane*	Y	Y	N	N	Y	Y	Y
9 Yates	N	N	Y	Y	N	?	N
10 *Porter*	Y	Y	N	N	Y	Y	Y
11 *Weller*	Y	Y	N	N	Y	Y	Y
12 Costello	N	N	Y	Y	N	N	N

ND Northern Democrats   SD Southern Democrats

	2	3	4	5	6	7	8
13 ***Fawell***	Y	Y	N	N	Y	Y	Y
14 ***Hastert***	Y	Y	N	N	Y	Y	Y
15 ***Ewing***	?	Y	N	N	Y	Y	Y
16 ***Manzullo***	Y	Y	N	N	Y	Y	Y
17 Evans	N	Y	Y	N	Y	Y	N
18 ***LaHood***	Y	Y	N	N	Y	Y	Y
19 Poshard	N	N	Y	Y	N	Y	N
20 ***Shimkus***	Y	Y	N	N	Y	Y	Y

INDIANA

	2	3	4	5	6	7	8
1 Visclosky	N	N	Y	Y	N	Y	?
2 ***McIntosh***	Y	Y	N	N	Y	Y	Y
3 Roemer	N	N	Y	Y	N	Y	N
4 ***Souder***	Y	Y	N	N	Y	?	Y
5 ***Buyer***	Y	Y	N	N	Y	Y	Y
6 ***Burton***	Y	Y	N	N	Y	Y	+
7 ***Pease***	Y	Y	N	N	Y	Y	Y
8 ***Hostettler***	Y	Y	N	N	Y	Y	Y
9 Hamilton	N	N	Y	Y	N	Y	N
10 Carson	N	N	Y	Y	N	N	N

IOWA

	2	3	4	5	6	7	8
1 ***Leach***	Y	Y	?	N	Y	Y	Y
2 ***Nussle***	Y	Y	Y	N	Y	Y	Y
3 Boswell	N	N	Y	Y	N	Y	N
4 ***Ganske***	Y	Y	N	N	Y	Y	Y
5 ***Latham***	Y	Y	N	N	Y	Y	Y

KANSAS

	2	3	4	5	6	7	8
1 ***Moran***	Y	Y	N	N	Y	Y	Y
2 ***Ryun***	Y	Y	N	N	Y	Y	Y
3 ***Snowbarger***	Y	Y	N	N	Y	Y	Y
4 ***Tiahrt***	Y	Y	N	N	Y	Y	Y

KENTUCKY

	2	3	4	5	6	7	8
1 ***Whitfield***	Y	Y	N	N	Y	?	Y
2 ***Lewis***	Y	Y	N	N	Y	Y	Y
3 ***Northup***	Y	Y	N	N	Y	Y	Y
4 ***Bunning***	Y	Y	N	N	Y	Y	Y
5 ***Rogers***	Y	Y	N	N	Y	Y	Y
6 Baesler	N	N	Y	N	Y	Y	N

LOUISIANA

	2	3	4	5	6	7	8
1 ***Livingston***	Y	Y	N	N	Y	Y	Y
2 Jefferson	N	N	Y	Y	N	N	N
3 ***Tauzin***	Y	Y	N	N	Y	Y	Y
4 ***McCrery***	Y	Y	N	N	Y	Y	Y
5 ***Cooksey***	Y	Y	N	N	Y	Y	Y
6 ***Baker***	Y	Y	N	N	Y	Y	Y
7 John	N	N	Y	Y	N	Y	N

MAINE

	2	3	4	5	6	7	8
1 Allen	N	N	Y	Y	N	N	N
2 Baldacci	N	N	Y	Y	N	Y	N

MARYLAND

	2	3	4	5	6	7	8
1 ***Gilchrest***	Y	Y	Y	N	Y	Y	Y
2 ***Ehrlich***	Y	Y	N	N	Y	Y	Y
3 Cardin	N	N	Y	Y	N	N	N
4 Wynn	N	N	Y	Y	N	Y	N
5 Hoyer	N	N	Y	?	N	N	N
6 ***Bartlett***	Y	Y	N	N	Y	?	Y
7 Cummings	N	N	Y	Y	N	N	N
8 ***Morella***	?	Y	Y	N	N	Y	Y

MASSACHUSETTS

	2	3	4	5	6	7	8
1 Olver	N	N	Y	Y	N	N	N
2 Neal	N	N	Y	Y	N	N	?
3 McGovern	N	N	Y	Y	N	N	N
4 Frank	N	N	Y	Y	N	?	N
5 Meehan	N	N	Y	Y	Y	N	N
6 Tierney	N	N	Y	Y	N	N	N
7 Markey	N	N	Y	Y	N	N	?
8 Kennedy	N	N	Y	Y	Y	N	N
9 Moakley	N	N	Y	Y	N	N	N
10 Delahunt	N	N	Y	Y	N	?	N

MICHIGAN

	2	3	4	5	6	7	8
1 Stupak	N	N	Y	Y	N	N	?
2 ***Hoekstra***	Y	Y	N	N	Y	Y	Y
3 ***Ehlers***	Y	Y	N	?	Y	Y	Y
4 ***Camp***	Y	Y	N	N	Y	Y	Y
5 Barcia	N	N	?	Y	N	Y	N
6 ***Upton***	Y	Y	N	N	Y	Y	Y
7 ***Smith***	Y	Y	N	N	Y	Y	Y
8 Stabenow	N	N	Y	N	N	Y	N
9 Kildee	N	N	Y	Y	N	Y	N
10 Bonior	N	N	Y	Y	N	?	N
11 ***Knollenberg***	Y	Y	N	N	Y	Y	Y
12 Levin	N	N	Y	Y	N	Y	N
13 Rivers	N	N	Y	Y	N	Y	N
14 Conyers	N	N	Y	Y	N	N	N
15 Kilpatrick	N	N	Y	Y	N	N	N
16 Dingell	N	N	Y	Y	N	N	N

MINNESOTA

	2	3	4	5	6	7	8
1 ***Gutknecht***	Y	Y	N	N	Y	Y	Y
2 Minge	N	N	Y	Y	N	Y	N
3 ***Ramstad***	Y	Y	N	N	Y	Y	Y
4 Vento	N	N	Y	Y	Y	N	N
5 Sabo	N	N	Y	Y	N	N	Y
6 Luther	–	–	Y	Y	N	Y	N
7 Peterson	N	N	Y	Y	N	Y	N
8 Oberstar	N	N	Y	Y	N	N	N

MISSISSIPPI

	2	3	4	5	6	7	8
1 ***Wicker***	Y	Y	N	N	Y	Y	Y
2 Thompson	N	N	Y	Y	N	N	N
3 ***Pickering***	Y	Y	N	N	Y	?	Y
4 ***Parker***	Y	Y	N	N	Y	Y	Y
5 Taylor	N	N	Y	N	Y	Y	N

MISSOURI

	2	3	4	5	6	7	8
1 Clay	N	N	Y	Y	N	N	N
2 ***Talent***	Y	Y	N	N	Y	?	Y
3 Gephardt	N	N	Y	Y	N	N	N
4 Skelton	N	N	Y	Y	N	Y	Y
5 McCarthy	N	–	Y	Y	N	N	N
6 Danner	N	N	Y	Y	N	Y	N
7 ***Blunt***	Y	Y	N	N	Y	Y	Y
8 ***Emerson***	Y	Y	N	N	Y	Y	Y
9 ***Hulshof***	Y	Y	N	N	Y	Y	Y

MONTANA

	2	3	4	5	6	7	8
AL ***Hill***	Y	Y	N	N	Y	Y	Y

NEBRASKA

	2	3	4	5	6	7	8
1 ***Bereuter***	Y	Y	N	N	Y	?	Y
2 ***Christensen***	Y	Y	N	N	Y	Y	Y
3 ***Barrett***	Y	Y	Y	N	Y	Y	Y

NEVADA

	2	3	4	5	6	7	8
1 ***Ensign***	Y	Y	N	N	Y	Y	Y
2 ***Gibbons***	Y	Y	N	N	Y	Y	Y

NEW HAMPSHIRE

	2	3	4	5	6	7	8
1 ***Sununu***	Y	Y	N	N	Y	Y	Y
2 ***Bass***	Y	Y	N	N	Y	Y	Y

NEW JERSEY

	2	3	4	5	6	7	8
1 Andrews	N	N	Y	Y	N	N	N
2 ***LoBiondo***	Y	Y	N	N	Y	Y	Y
3 ***Saxton***	Y	Y	N	N	Y	Y	Y
4 ***Smith***	Y	Y	N	N	Y	Y	Y
5 ***Roukema***	Y	Y	N	N	Y	Y	Y
6 Pallone	N	N	Y	Y	N	N	N
7 ***Franks***	Y	?	N	N	Y	Y	Y
8 Pascrell	N	N	Y	Y	N	Y	N
9 Rothman	N	N	Y	Y	N	N	N
10 Payne	N	?	Y	Y	N	N	N
11 ***Frelinghuysen***	Y	Y	N	N	Y	Y	Y
12 ***Pappas***	Y	Y	N	N	Y	Y	Y
13 Menendez	N	N	Y	Y	N	N	N

NEW MEXICO

	2	3	4	5	6	7	8
1 ***Schiff***	?	?	?	?	?	?	?
2 ***Skeen***	Y	Y	N	N	Y	Y	Y
3 ***Redmond***	Y	Y	N	N	Y	Y	Y

NEW YORK

	2	3	4	5	6	7	8
1 ***Forbes***	N	Y	Y	N	Y	Y	Y
2 ***Lazio***	Y	Y	N	N	Y	Y	Y
3 ***King***	Y	Y	N	N	Y	N	?
4 McCarthy	N	N	Y	Y	Y	Y	N
5 Ackerman	N	N	Y	Y	N	N	N
6 Vacant							
7 Manton	N	N	Y	Y	N	N	N
8 Nadler	N	N	Y	Y	N	N	N
9 Schumer	N	N	Y	Y	N	N	N
10 Towns	N	N	Y	Y	N	N	N
11 Owens	N	N	Y	Y	N	N	N
12 Velázquez	N	N	Y	Y	N	N	N
13 ***Fossella***	Y	Y	N	N	Y	Y	Y
14 Maloney	N	N	Y	Y	N	Y	N
15 Rangel	N	N	Y	Y	N	N	N
16 Serrano	N	N	Y	Y	N	N	N
17 Engel	N	N	Y	Y	N	N	?
18 Lowey	N	N	Y	Y	N	N	N
19 ***Kelly***	Y	Y	N	N	Y	Y	Y
20 ***Gilman***	Y	Y	N	N	Y	Y	Y
21 McNulty	N	N	Y	Y	N	N	N
22 ***Solomon***	Y	Y	N	N	Y	Y	Y
23 ***Boehlert***	Y	Y	N	N	Y	Y	Y
24 ***McHugh***	Y	Y	N	N	Y	Y	Y
25 ***Walsh***	Y	Y	N	N	Y	Y	Y
26 Hinchey	N	N	Y	Y	N	N	N
27 ***Paxon***	Y	Y	N	N	Y	Y	Y
28 Slaughter	N	N	Y	Y	N	N	N
29 LaFalce	N	N	Y	Y	N	N	N
30 ***Quinn***	Y	Y	N	N	Y	Y	Y
31 ***Houghton***	Y	Y	N	N	Y	N	Y

NORTH CAROLINA

	2	3	4	5	6	7	8
1 Clayton	N	N	Y	Y	N	N	N
2 Etheridge	N	N	Y	Y	N	Y	N
3 ***Jones***	Y	Y	N	N	Y	Y	Y
4 Price	N	N	Y	Y	N	Y	N
5 ***Burr***	Y	Y	N	N	Y	Y	Y
6 ***Coble***	Y	Y	N	N	Y	Y	Y
7 McIntyre	N	N	Y	Y	N	Y	N
8 Hefner	?	N	Y	Y	N	N	N
9 ***Myrick***	Y	Y	N	N	Y	Y	Y
10 ***Ballenger***	Y	Y	N	N	Y	Y	Y
11 ***Taylor***	Y	Y	N	N	Y	Y	?
12 Watt	N	N	Y	Y	N	N	N

NORTH DAKOTA

	2	3	4	5	6	7	8
AL Pomeroy	N	N	Y	Y	N	N	?

OHIO

	2	3	4	5	6	7	8
1 ***Chabot***	Y	Y	N	N	Y	Y	Y
2 ***Portman***	Y	Y	N	N	Y	Y	Y
3 Hall	N	N	Y	Y	N	?	–
4 ***Oxley***	Y	Y	N	N	Y	Y	Y
5 ***Gillmor***	Y	Y	N	N	Y	Y	Y
6 Strickland	N	N	Y	Y	N	Y	N
7 ***Hobson***	Y	Y	N	N	Y	Y	Y
8 ***Boehner***	Y	Y	N	N	Y	Y	Y
9 Kaptur	N	N	Y	Y	N	N	N
10 Kucinich	N	N	Y	Y	Y	N	N
11 Stokes	N	?	Y	Y	N	N	N
12 ***Kasich***	Y	Y	N	N	Y	Y	Y
13 Brown	N	N	Y	Y	N	N	N
14 Sawyer	N	N	Y	Y	N	N	N
15 ***Pryce***	Y	Y	N	N	Y	Y	Y
16 ***Regula***	Y	Y	N	N	Y	Y	Y
17 Traficant	Y	Y	N	N	Y	Y	Y
18 ***Ney***	Y	Y	N	?	Y	?	Y
19 ***LaTourette***	Y	Y	N	N	Y	Y	Y

OKLAHOMA

	2	3	4	5	6	7	8
1 ***Largent***	Y	Y	N	N	Y	Y	?
2 ***Coburn***	Y	Y	N	N	Y	Y	Y
3 ***Watkins***	Y	Y	N	N	Y	Y	Y
4 ***Watts***	Y	Y	N	N	Y	Y	Y
5 ***Istook***	Y	Y	N	N	Y	Y	Y
6 ***Lucas***	Y	Y	N	N	Y	Y	Y

OREGON

	2	3	4	5	6	7	8
1 Furse	N	N	Y	Y	N	N	N
2 ***Smith***	?	Y	N	N	Y	Y	Y
3 Blumenauer	N	N	Y	Y	N	N	?
4 DeFazio	N	N	Y	Y	N	N	N
5 Hooley	N	N	Y	Y	N	Y	N

PENNSYLVANIA

	2	3	4	5	6	7	8
1 Vacant							
2 Fattah	N	?	?	Y	N	?	N
3 Borski	?	N	Y	Y	N	?	N
4 Klink	N	N	Y	Y	N	Y	?
5 ***Peterson***	Y	Y	N	N	Y	Y	Y
6 Holden	N	N	Y	Y	Y	Y	N
7 ***Weldon***	Y	Y	N	N	Y	Y	Y
8 ***Greenwood***	Y	Y	N	N	Y	Y	Y
9 ***Shuster***	Y	Y	N	N	Y	Y	Y
10 ***McDade***	?	Y	N	N	Y	Y	Y
11 Kanjorski	N	N	Y	Y	N	N	N
12 Murtha	N	N	Y	Y	N	Y	N
13 ***Fox***	Y	Y	N	N	Y	Y	Y
14 Coyne	N	N	Y	Y	N	N	N
15 McHale	N	N	Y	N	N	Y	N
16 ***Pitts***	Y	Y	N	N	Y	Y	Y
17 ***Gekas***	Y	Y	N	N	Y	?	Y
18 Doyle	N	N	Y	Y	Y	Y	N
19 ***Goodling***	Y	Y	N	N	Y	+	Y
20 Mascara	N	N	Y	Y	N	Y	N
21 ***English***	Y	Y	N	N	Y	Y	Y

RHODE ISLAND

	2	3	4	5	6	7	8
1 Kennedy	N	N	Y	Y	Y	N	N
2 Weygand	N	N	Y	Y	N	N	N

SOUTH CAROLINA

	2	3	4	5	6	7	8
1 ***Sanford***	Y	Y	Y	N	N	Y	Y
2 ***Spence***	Y	Y	N	N	Y	Y	Y
3 ***Graham***	Y	Y	N	N	Y	Y	Y
4 ***Inglis***	Y	Y	N	N	Y	Y	Y
5 Spratt	N	N	Y	Y	N	?	N
6 Clyburn	N	N	Y	Y	N	N	N

SOUTH DAKOTA

	2	3	4	5	6	7	8
AL ***Thune***	Y	Y	N	N	Y	Y	Y

TENNESSEE

	2	3	4	5	6	7	8
1 ***Jenkins***	Y	Y	N	N	Y	Y	Y
2 ***Duncan***	Y	Y	N	N	Y	Y	Y
3 ***Wamp***	Y	Y	N	N	Y	Y	Y
4 ***Hilleary***	Y	Y	N	N	Y	Y	Y
5 Clement	N	N	Y	Y	N	Y	N
6 Gordon	N	N	Y	Y	N	N	N
7 ***Bryant***	Y	Y	N	N	Y	Y	Y
8 Tanner	?	N	Y	Y	N	Y	N
9 Ford	N	N	Y	Y	N	N	N

TEXAS

	2	3	4	5	6	7	8
1 Sandlin	N	N	Y	Y	N	N	N
2 Turner	N	Y	Y	N	Y	Y	Y
3 ***Johnson, Sam***	Y	Y	N	N	Y	Y	?
4 Hall	N	Y	Y	N	Y	Y	Y
5 ***Sessions***	Y	Y	N	N	Y	Y	Y
6 ***Barton***	Y	Y	N	N	Y	Y	Y
7 ***Archer***	Y	Y	N	N	Y	Y	Y
8 ***Brady***	Y	Y	N	N	Y	Y	Y
9 Lampson	N	N	Y	Y	N	N	N
10 Doggett	N	N	Y	Y	N	N	?
11 Edwards	N	N	Y	Y	N	Y	N
12 ***Granger***	Y	Y	N	N	Y	Y	Y
13 ***Thornberry***	Y	Y	N	N	Y	Y	Y
14 ***Paul***	Y	Y	Y	N	N	Y	Y
15 Hinojosa	N	N	Y	Y	N	?	N
16 Reyes	N	N	Y	Y	N	N	N
17 Stenholm	N	N	Y	Y	N	Y	N
18 Jackson-Lee	N	N	Y	Y	N	N	N
19 ***Combest***	Y	Y	N	N	Y	Y	Y
20 Gonzalez	?	?	?	?	?	?	?
21 ***Smith***	Y	Y	N	N	Y	Y	Y
22 ***DeLay***	Y	Y	N	N	Y	Y	Y
23 ***Bonilla***	Y	Y	N	N	Y	Y	Y
24 Frost	N	N	Y	Y	N	N	N
25 Bentsen	N	N	Y	Y	N	N	N
26 ***Armey***	Y	Y	N	N	Y	Y	Y
27 Ortiz	?	N	Y	Y	N	Y	N
28 Rodriguez	N	N	Y	Y	N	Y	N
29 Green	N	N	Y	Y	N	Y	N
30 Johnson, E.B.	N	N	Y	Y	N	N	N

UTAH

	2	3	4	5	6	7	8
1 ***Hansen***	Y	Y	N	N	Y	Y	Y
2 ***Cook***	Y	Y	N	N	Y	Y	Y
3 ***Cannon***	Y	Y	N	N	Y	Y	Y

VERMONT

	2	3	4	5	6	7	8
AL *Sanders*	N	N	Y	Y	N	N	N

VIRGINIA

	2	3	4	5	6	7	8
1 ***Bateman***	Y	Y	N	N	Y	Y	Y
2 Pickett	N	N	Y	Y	N	Y	N
3 Scott	N	N	Y	Y	N	N	N
4 Sisisky	N	N	Y	Y	N	Y	N
5 Goode	N	N	Y	Y	N	Y	Y
6 ***Goodlatte***	Y	Y	N	N	Y	Y	Y
7 ***Bliley***	Y	Y	N	N	Y	Y	Y
8 Moran	N	N	Y	Y	N	N	N
9 Boucher	N	N	Y	Y	N	N	N
10 ***Wolf***	Y	Y	Y	N	Y	Y	Y
11 ***Davis***	Y	Y	Y	N	Y	Y	Y

WASHINGTON

	2	3	4	5	6	7	8
1 ***White***	Y	Y	N	N	Y	Y	Y
2 ***Metcalf***	Y	Y	N	N	Y	Y	Y
3 ***Smith, Linda***	Y	Y	N	N	Y	Y	Y
4 ***Hastings***	Y	Y	N	N	Y	Y	Y
5 ***Nethercutt***	Y	Y	N	N	Y	?	Y
6 Dicks	N	Y	Y	Y	N	?	N
7 McDermott	N	N	Y	Y	N	N	N
8 ***Dunn***	Y	Y	N	N	Y	Y	Y
9 Smith, Adam	N	N	Y	Y	N	N	N

WEST VIRGINIA

	2	3	4	5	6	7	8
1 Mollohan	?	?	Y	Y	N	N	N
2 Wise	?	N	Y	Y	N	Y	N
3 Rahall	N	N	Y	Y	N	Y	N

WISCONSIN

	2	3	4	5	6	7	8
1 ***Neumann***	Y	Y	N	N	Y	Y	Y
2 ***Klug***	Y	Y	N	N	Y	Y	Y
3 Kind	?	N	Y	Y	N	Y	N
4 Kleczka	N	N	Y	Y	N	Y	N
5 Barrett	N	N	Y	Y	N	Y	N
6 ***Petri***	Y	Y	N	N	Y	Y	Y
7 Obey	N	N	Y	Y	N	Y	N
8 Johnson	N	N	Y	Y	N	Y	N
9 ***Sensenbrenner***	Y	Y	N	N	Y	Y	Y

WYOMING

	2	3	4	5	6	7	8
AL ***Cubin***	Y	Y	N	N	Y	Y	Y

Southern states - Ala., Ark., Fla., Ga., Ky., La., Miss., N.C., Okla., S.C., Tenn., Texas, Va.

House Votes 9, 10, 12, 13, 14, 15, 16 *

9. HR 2846. National Education Testing Curbs/Passage. Passage of the bill to prohibit the use of federal education funds for any federally-sponsored national test in reading, math, or any other subject that is not specifically authorized by federal statute. Passed 242-174: R 217-2; D 25-171 (ND 16-126, SD 9-45); I 0-1. Feb. 5, 1998. A "nay" was a vote in support of the president's position.

10. HR 2631. Military Construction Line-Item Veto Disapproval/Veto Override. Passage, over President Clinton's Nov. 13, 1997, veto, of the bill to disapprove Clinton's line-item vetoes of 38 projects, totaling $287 million, in the fiscal 1998 military construction appropriations bill (HR2016 — PL105-45). Passed 347-69: R 197-23; D 149-46 (ND 100-41, SD 49-5); I 1-0. Feb. 5, 1998. A two-thirds majority of those present and voting (277 in this case) of both chambers is required to override a veto. A "nay" was a vote in support of the president's position.

11. Quorum Call.* 356 Responded. Feb. 5, 1998.

12. H Res 352. Suspension of the Rules/Rule. Adoption of the rule (H Res 352) to provide for House floor consideration of bills on Wednesday, February 11 and Thursday, February 12 under suspension of the rules. Adopted 217-191: R 213-0; D 4-190 (ND 2-138, SD 2-52); I 0-1. Feb. 11, 1998.

13. H Con Res 202. Child Care Funds for Parents Staying Home/Adoption. Goodling, R-Pa., motion to suspend the rules and adopt the concurrent resolution to express the sense of Congress recognizing the importance of parents who forgo a second income to stay at home to raise children, and that Congress should not discriminate against these families. Motion agreed to 409-0: R 219-0; D 189-0 (ND 135-0, SD 54-0); I 1-0. Feb. 11, 1998. A two-thirds majority of those present and voting (273 in this case) is required for adoption under suspension of the rules.

14. Procedural Motion/Journal. Approval of the House Journal of Wednesday, Feb. 11, 1998. Approved 353-43: R 198-12; D 154-31 (ND 114-22, SD 40-9); I 1-0. Feb. 12, 1998.

15. H Res 355. Dornan Election Challenge/Recommit. Hoyer, D-Md., motion to recommit the privileged resolution to the House Oversight Committee with instructions to report it back with an amendment to include only the dismissal of the complaint by former Rep. Robert K. Dornan, R-Calif., contesting the election of Loretta Sanchez, D-Calif. Motion rejected 194-215: R 1-214; D 192-1 (ND 140-1, SD 52-0); I 1-0. Feb. 12, 1998.

16. H Res 355. Dornan Election Challenge/Adoption. Adoption of the privileged resolution to dismiss the complaint by former Rep. Robert K. Dornan, R-Calif., contesting the election of Loretta Sanchez, D-Calif. Adopted 378-33: R 184-33; D 193-0 (ND 141-0, SD 52-0); I 1-0. Feb. 12, 1998.

* CQ does not include quorum calls in its vote charts.

[1] Ronald V. Dellums, D-Calif., resigned Feb. 6.

[2] Gregory W. Meeks, D-N.Y., was sworn in Feb. 5, replacing Floyd H. Flake, D-N.Y., who resigned Nov. 15, 1997.

Key

Y	Voted for (yea).
#	Paired for.
+	Announced for.
N	Voted against (nay).
X	Paired against.
−	Announced against.
P	Voted "present."
C	Voted "present" to avoid possible conflict of interest.
?	Did not vote or otherwise make a position known.

Democrats **Republicans** Independent

	9	10	12	13	14	15	16
ALABAMA							
1 **Callahan**	Y	Y	?	?	?	?	?
2 **Everett**	Y	Y	Y	Y	Y	N	Y
3 **Riley**	Y	Y	Y	Y	Y	N	Y
4 **Aderholt**	Y	Y	Y	Y	Y	N	Y
5 Cramer	N	Y	N	Y	Y	Y	Y
6 **Bachus**	Y	Y	Y	Y	Y	N	Y
7 Hilliard	N	Y	N	Y	N	Y	Y
ALASKA							
AL **Young**	Y	Y	Y	Y	?	N	Y
ARIZONA							
1 **Salmon**	Y	N	Y	Y	Y	N	Y
2 Pastor	N	Y	N	Y	Y	Y	Y
3 **Stump**	Y	Y	Y	Y	Y	N	N
4 **Shadegg**	Y	Y	Y	Y	Y	N	Y
5 **Kolbe**	Y	Y	Y	Y	Y	N	Y
6 **Hayworth**	Y	Y	Y	Y	Y	N	Y
ARKANSAS							
1 Berry	N	Y	N	Y	?	Y	Y
2 Snyder	N	Y	N	Y	Y	Y	Y
3 **Hutchinson**	Y	Y	Y	Y	Y	N	Y
4 **Dickey**	Y	N	Y	Y	Y	N	Y
CALIFORNIA							
1 **Riggs**	Y	Y	Y	Y	?	?	?
2 **Herger**	?	?	Y	Y	Y	N	N
3 Fazio	N	Y	N	Y	Y	Y	Y
4 **Doolittle**	Y	Y	?	?	Y	N	N
5 Matsui	N	Y	N	Y	Y	Y	Y
6 Woolsey	N	Y	N	Y	Y	Y	Y
7 Miller	N	Y	N	Y	Y	Y	Y
8 Pelosi	Y	Y	N	Y	Y	Y	Y
9 Dellums[1]	?	?					
10 Tauscher	N	Y	Y	Y	Y	Y	Y
11 **Pombo**	Y	Y	Y	Y	Y	N	N
12 Lantos	N	Y	?	?	?	?	?
13 Stark	N	N	N	Y	Y	Y	Y
14 Eshoo	?	?	?	?	?	?	?
15 **Campbell**	Y	Y	Y	Y	Y	N	Y
16 Lofgren	N	N	N	Y	Y	Y	Y
17 Farr	N	Y	N	Y	Y	Y	Y
18 Condit	Y	Y	Y	Y	Y	Y	Y
19 **Radanovich**	Y	Y	Y	Y	Y	N	Y
20 Dooley	N	N	N	Y	Y	Y	Y
21 **Thomas**	Y	Y	Y	Y	Y	N	Y
22 Vacant							
23 **Gallegly**	Y	Y	Y	Y	Y	N	Y
24 Sherman	N	N	N	Y	Y	Y	Y
25 **McKeon**	+	+	Y	Y	Y	N	Y
26 Berman	N	Y	N	Y	Y	Y	Y
27 **Rogan**	Y	Y	Y	Y	Y	N	N
28 **Dreier**	Y	Y	Y	Y	Y	N	Y
29 Waxman	N	N	N	Y	Y	Y	Y
30 Becerra	−	+	N	Y	Y	Y	Y
31 Martinez	N	N	N	P	Y	Y	Y
32 Dixon	N	Y	N	Y	Y	Y	Y
33 Roybal-Allard	N	Y	N	Y	Y	Y	Y
34 Torres	N	N	Y	Y	Y	Y	Y
35 Waters	N	Y	Y	Y	Y	Y	Y
36 Harman	N	N	?	?	?	?	?
37 Millender-McD.	N	Y	N	Y	Y	Y	Y
38 **Horn**	Y	Y	Y	Y	Y	N	Y
39 **Royce**	Y	Y	Y	Y	Y	N	N
40 **Lewis**	Y	Y	Y	Y	Y	N	Y
41 **Kim**	Y	Y	Y	Y	Y	N	Y
42 Brown	N	Y	N	Y	Y	Y	Y
43 **Calvert**	Y	Y	Y	Y	Y	N	N
44 Vacant							
45 **Rohrabacher**	Y	N	Y	Y	Y	N	Y
46 Sanchez	N	N	N	Y	Y	Y	Y
47 **Cox**	Y	Y	Y	Y	Y	N	Y
48 **Packard**	Y	Y	Y	Y	Y	N	Y
49 **Bilbray**	Y	Y	Y	Y	Y	N	Y
50 Filner	N	N	N	Y	Y	Y	Y
51 **Cunningham**	Y	Y	Y	Y	Y	N	Y
52 **Hunter**	Y	Y	Y	Y	?	N	N
COLORADO							
1 DeGette	N	N	N	Y	Y	Y	Y
2 Skaggs	N	N	N	Y	Y	Y	Y
3 **McInnis**	Y	Y	Y	Y	Y	N	Y
4 **Schaffer**	Y	Y	Y	Y	N	N	N
5 **Hefley**	Y	Y	Y	Y	Y	N	Y
6 **Schaefer**	Y	Y	Y	Y	Y	N	Y
CONNECTICUT							
1 Kennelly	N	Y	N	Y	Y	Y	Y
2 Gejdenson	N	Y	N	Y	Y	Y	Y
3 DeLauro	N	Y	N	Y	Y	Y	Y
4 **Shays**	Y	N	Y	Y	Y	N	Y
5 Maloney	N	Y	N	Y	Y	Y	Y
6 **Johnson**	N	Y	Y	Y	N	Y	Y
DELAWARE							
AL **Castle**	Y	Y	Y	Y	Y	N	Y
FLORIDA							
1 **Scarborough**	Y	Y	Y	Y	Y	?	Y
2 Boyd	Y	Y	N	Y	Y	Y	Y
3 Brown	N	Y	N	Y	Y	Y	Y
4 **Fowler**	Y	Y	Y	Y	Y	N	Y
5 Thurman	N	Y	N	Y	Y	Y	Y
6 **Stearns**	Y	Y	?	Y	Y	N	Y
7 **Mica**	Y	Y	Y	Y	Y	N	Y
8 **McCollum**	Y	Y	Y	Y	Y	N	Y
9 **Bilirakis**	Y	Y	Y	Y	Y	N	Y
10 **Young**	Y	Y	Y	Y	Y	N	Y
11 Davis	N	N	N	Y	Y	Y	Y
12 **Canady**	Y	Y	Y	Y	Y	N	Y
13 **Miller**	Y	N	?	?	?	?	?
14 **Goss**	Y	Y	Y	Y	Y	N	Y
15 **Weldon**	Y	Y	Y	Y	Y	N	Y
16 **Foley**	Y	Y	Y	Y	Y	N	Y
17 Meek	N	Y	N	Y	Y	Y	Y
18 **Ros-Lehtinen**	Y	Y	+	Y	Y	N	Y
19 Wexler	N	N	N	Y	Y	Y	Y
20 Deutsch	N	N	N	Y	N	Y	Y
21 **Diaz-Balart**	Y	Y	?	Y	Y	N	Y
22 **Shaw**	Y	Y	Y	Y	Y	N	Y
23 Hastings	N	Y	N	Y	Y	Y	Y
GEORGIA							
1 **Kingston**	Y	Y	Y	Y	Y	N	N
2 Bishop	N	Y	N	Y	Y	Y	Y
3 **Collins**	Y	Y	Y	Y	Y	N	Y
4 McKinney	N	N	N	Y	Y	Y	Y
5 Lewis	N	Y	N	Y	Y	Y	Y
6 **Gingrich**							
7 **Barr**	Y	Y	Y	Y	Y	N	N
8 **Chambliss**	Y	Y	Y	Y	Y	N	Y
9 **Deal**	Y	Y	Y	Y	Y	N	Y
10 **Norwood**	Y	Y	Y	Y	?	N	N
11 **Linder**	Y	?	?	?	Y	N	Y
HAWAII							
1 Abercrombie	N	Y	N	Y	N	Y	Y
2 Mink	N	Y	−	+	+	+	+
IDAHO							
1 **Chenoweth**	Y	Y	Y	Y	Y	N	N
2 **Crapo**	Y	Y	Y	Y	?	N	Y
ILLINOIS							
1 Rush	N	Y	N	Y	?	Y	Y
2 Jackson	N	Y	N	Y	Y	Y	Y
3 Lipinski	Y	Y	Y	Y	Y	Y	Y
4 Gutierrez	N	N	N	Y	Y	Y	Y
5 Blagojevich	N	Y	N	Y	Y	Y	Y
6 **Hyde**	Y	Y	Y	Y	?	N	Y
7 Davis	N	Y	N	Y	Y	Y	Y
8 **Crane**	Y	Y	Y	Y	?	?	N
9 Yates	N	N	N	?	Y	Y	Y
10 **Porter**	Y	+	Y	Y	Y	Y	Y
11 **Weller**	Y	Y	Y	Y	N	N	Y
12 Costello	N	Y	N	Y	N	Y	Y

ND Northern Democrats   SD Southern Democrats

	9	10	12	13	14	15	16
13 ***Fawell***	Y	Y	Y	Y	Y	N	Y
14 ***Hastert***	Y	Y	Y	Y	Y	N	Y
15 ***Ewing***	Y	N	Y	Y	Y	N	Y
16 ***Manzullo***	Y	Y	Y	Y	Y	N	Y
17 Evans	Y	Y	N	Y	Y	Y	Y
18 ***LaHood***	Y	Y	Y	Y	Y	N	Y
19 Poshard	N	Y	?	?	N	Y	Y
20 ***Shimkus***	Y	Y	Y	Y	Y	N	Y
INDIANA							
1 Visclosky	N	Y	N	Y	N	Y	Y
2 ***McIntosh***	Y	Y	Y	Y	Y	N	N
3 Roemer	Y	Y	N	Y	Y	Y	Y
4 ***Souder***	Y	Y	Y	Y	Y	N	Y
5 ***Buyer***	Y	Y	Y	Y	Y	?	?
6 ***Burton***	+	+	Y	Y	Y	N	N
7 ***Pease***	Y	Y	Y	Y	Y	N	Y
8 ***Hostettler***	Y	Y	Y	Y	Y	N	N
9 Hamilton	Y	Y	Y	Y	Y	Y	Y
10 Carson	N	N	N	Y	Y	Y	Y
IOWA							
1 ***Leach***	Y	N	Y	Y	Y	N	Y
2 ***Nussle***	Y	N	Y	Y	Y	N	Y
3 Boswell	N	N	N	Y	Y	Y	Y
4 ***Ganske***	Y	N	Y	Y	Y	N	Y
5 ***Latham***	Y	Y	Y	Y	Y	N	Y
KANSAS							
1 ***Moran***	Y	Y	Y	Y	N	N	Y
2 ***Ryun***	Y	Y	Y	Y	Y	N	Y
3 ***Snowbarger***	Y	Y	Y	Y	?	N	Y
4 ***Tiahrt***	Y	Y	Y	Y	Y	N	N
KENTUCKY							
1 ***Whitfield***	Y	Y	Y	Y	Y	N	Y
2 ***Lewis***	Y	Y	Y	Y	Y	N	N
3 ***Northup***	Y	Y	Y	Y	Y	N	Y
4 ***Bunning***	Y	Y	Y	Y	Y	N	Y
5 ***Rogers***	Y	Y	Y	Y	Y	N	Y
6 Baesler	N	Y	N	Y	Y	Y	Y
LOUISIANA							
1 ***Livingston***	Y	Y	Y	Y	Y	N	?
2 Jefferson	N	Y	N	Y	Y	Y	Y
3 ***Tauzin***	Y	Y	Y	Y	Y	N	Y
4 ***McCrery***	Y	Y	Y	Y	Y	N	Y
5 ***Cooksey***	Y	Y	Y	Y	Y	N	Y
6 ***Baker***	Y	Y	Y	Y	Y	N	Y
7 John	Y	Y	N	Y	?	Y	Y
MAINE							
1 Allen	N	Y	N	Y	Y	Y	Y
2 Baldacci	N	Y	N	Y	N	Y	Y
MARYLAND							
1 ***Gilchrest***	Y	Y	Y	Y	Y	N	Y
2 ***Ehrlich***	Y	Y	Y	Y	Y	N	Y
3 Cardin	N	Y	N	Y	Y	Y	Y
4 Wynn	N	?	N	Y	Y	Y	Y
5 Hoyer	N	Y	N	Y	Y	Y	Y
6 ***Bartlett***	Y	Y	Y	Y	Y	N	N
7 Cummings	N	Y	N	Y	Y	Y	Y
8 ***Morella***	Y	Y	Y	Y	Y	N	Y
MASSACHUSETTS							
1 Olver	N	Y	N	Y	N	Y	Y
2 Neal	N	Y	N	Y	Y	Y	Y
3 McGovern	N	Y	N	Y	Y	Y	Y
4 Frank	N	N	N	P	Y	Y	Y
5 Meehan	N	N	N	Y	Y	Y	Y
6 Tierney	N	Y	N	Y	Y	Y	Y
7 Markey	N	N	N	Y	Y	Y	Y
8 Kennedy	N	Y	N	Y	Y	Y	Y
9 Moakley	N	Y	N	Y	Y	Y	Y
10 Delahunt	N	Y	N	Y	Y	Y	Y
MICHIGAN							
1 Stupak	N	N	N	Y	N	Y	Y
2 ***Hoekstra***	Y	Y	Y	Y	Y	N	Y
3 ***Ehlers***	Y	Y	Y	Y	Y	N	Y
4 ***Camp***	Y	Y	Y	Y	Y	N	Y
5 Barcia	N	Y	N	Y	Y	Y	Y
6 ***Upton***	Y	N	Y	Y	Y	N	Y
7 ***Smith***	Y	N	Y	Y	Y	N	Y
8 Stabenow	N	Y	N	Y	Y	Y	Y
9 Kildee	N	Y	N	Y	Y	Y	Y
10 Bonior	N	Y	N	Y	Y	Y	Y
11 ***Knollenberg***	Y	Y	Y	Y	Y	N	Y
12 Levin	N	Y	N	Y	Y	Y	Y
13 Rivers	N	N	N	Y	Y	Y	Y
14 Conyers	N	N	N	?	Y	?	Y
15 Kilpatrick	?	Y	N	Y	Y	Y	Y
16 Dingell	N	Y	N	Y	Y	Y	Y

	9	10	12	13	14	15	16
MINNESOTA							
1 ***Gutknecht***	Y	Y	Y	Y	N	N	N
2 Minge	N	N	N	Y	Y	Y	Y
3 ***Ramstad***	Y	N	Y	Y	N	N	Y
4 Vento	N	N	N	Y	?	Y	Y
5 Sabo	N	Y	N	Y	Y	Y	Y
6 Luther	N	N	N	Y	Y	Y	Y
7 Peterson	Y	Y	N	Y	Y	Y	Y
8 Oberstar	N	Y	N	Y	?	Y	Y
MISSISSIPPI							
1 ***Wicker***	Y	Y	Y	Y	Y	N	Y
2 Thompson	N	Y	N	Y	N	Y	Y
3 ***Pickering***	?	Y	Y	Y	Y	N	Y
4 ***Parker***	Y	Y	Y	Y	Y	N	Y
5 Taylor	Y	Y	N	Y	N	Y	Y
MISSOURI							
1 Clay	N	Y	N	Y	N	Y	Y
2 ***Talent***	Y	Y	Y	Y	?	N	Y
3 Gephardt	N	Y	N	Y	N	Y	Y
4 Skelton	N	Y	N	Y	Y	Y	Y
5 McCarthy	N	N	N	Y	Y	Y	Y
6 Danner	Y	Y	N	Y	Y	Y	Y
7 ***Blunt***	Y	Y	Y	Y	Y	N	Y
8 ***Emerson***	Y	Y	Y	Y	Y	N	Y
9 ***Hulshof***	Y	Y	Y	Y	Y	N	Y
MONTANA							
AL ***Hill***	Y	Y	Y	Y	Y	N	Y
NEBRASKA							
1 ***Bereuter***	Y	Y	Y	Y	Y	N	Y
2 ***Christensen***	Y	Y	Y	Y	Y	N	Y
3 ***Barrett***	Y	Y	Y	Y	Y	N	Y
NEVADA							
1 ***Ensign***	Y	N	Y	Y	?	?	Y
2 ***Gibbons***	Y	Y	Y	Y	N	N	Y
NEW HAMPSHIRE							
1 ***Sununu***	Y	Y	Y	Y	Y	N	Y
2 ***Bass***	Y	Y	Y	Y	Y	N	Y
NEW JERSEY							
1 Andrews	N	N	N	Y	Y	Y	Y
2 ***LoBiondo***	Y	Y	Y	Y	N	N	Y
3 ***Saxton***	Y	Y	Y	Y	Y	N	Y
4 ***Smith***	Y	Y	Y	Y	Y	N	Y
5 ***Roukema***	Y	Y	Y	Y	Y	N	Y
6 Pallone	N	Y	N	Y	Y	Y	Y
7 ***Franks***	Y	N	Y	Y	Y	N	Y
8 Pascrell	N	Y	N	Y	N	Y	Y
9 Rothman	N	N	N	Y	Y	Y	Y
10 Payne	N	N	N	P	Y	Y	Y
11 ***Frelinghuysen***	Y	Y	Y	Y	Y	N	Y
12 ***Pappas***	Y	Y	Y	Y	Y	N	Y
13 Menendez	N	Y	N	Y	N	Y	Y
NEW MEXICO							
1 ***Schiff***	?	?	?	?	?	?	?
2 ***Skeen***	Y	Y	Y	Y	Y	N	Y
3 ***Redmond***	Y	Y	Y	Y	Y	N	Y
NEW YORK							
1 ***Forbes***	N	Y	Y	Y	Y	Y	Y
2 ***Lazio***	Y	Y	Y	Y	Y	N	Y
3 ***King***	Y	Y	Y	Y	Y	N	Y
4 McCarthy	N	N	N	Y	Y	Y	Y
5 Ackerman	N	N	N	Y	Y	Y	Y
6 Meeks [2]			N	Y	Y	Y	Y
7 Manton	N	Y	N	Y	Y	Y	Y
8 Nadler	N	Y	?	?	?	Y	Y
9 Schumer	N	Y	N	Y	Y	Y	Y
10 Towns	N	N	N	Y	Y	Y	Y
11 Owens	N	N	N	Y	Y	Y	Y
12 Velázquez	N	N	N	Y	N	Y	Y
13 ***Fossella***	Y	Y	Y	Y	Y	N	Y
14 Maloney	N	Y	N	Y	Y	Y	Y
15 Rangel	N	N	N	Y	Y	Y	Y
16 Serrano	N	N	N	Y	Y	Y	Y
17 Engel	N	N	N	Y	Y	Y	Y
18 Lowey	N	Y	N	Y	Y	Y	Y
19 ***Kelly***	Y	Y	Y	Y	Y	N	Y
20 ***Gilman***	Y	Y	Y	Y	Y	Y	Y
21 McNulty	N	Y	N	Y	N	Y	Y
22 ***Solomon***	Y	Y	Y	Y	Y	?	?
23 ***Boehlert***	Y	Y	Y	Y	Y	N	Y
24 ***McHugh***	Y	Y	Y	Y	Y	N	Y
25 ***Walsh***	Y	Y	Y	Y	Y	N	Y
26 Hinchey	N	Y	N	Y	N	Y	Y
27 ***Paxon***	Y	Y	Y	Y	Y	N	Y
28 Slaughter	N	Y	N	Y	Y	Y	Y
29 LaFalce	N	Y	N	Y	Y	Y	Y

	9	10	12	13	14	15	16
30 ***Quinn***	Y	Y	Y	Y	Y	N	Y
31 ***Houghton***	Y	Y	Y	Y	Y	N	Y
NORTH CAROLINA							
1 Clayton	N	Y	N	Y	Y	Y	Y
2 Etheridge	N	Y	N	Y	Y	Y	Y
3 ***Jones***	Y	Y	Y	Y	Y	N	N
4 Price	N	Y	N	Y	Y	Y	Y
5 ***Burr***	Y	Y	Y	Y	Y	N	Y
6 ***Coble***	Y	Y	Y	Y	Y	N	Y
7 McIntyre	N	Y	N	Y	Y	Y	Y
8 Hefner	N	Y	N	Y	Y	Y	Y
9 ***Myrick***	Y	Y	?	?	Y	N	Y
10 ***Ballenger***	Y	Y	Y	Y	Y	N	N
11 ***Taylor***	Y	Y	Y	Y	Y	N	N
12 Watt	N	Y	N	Y	Y	Y	Y
NORTH DAKOTA							
AL Pomeroy	N	Y	N	Y	Y	Y	Y
OHIO							
1 ***Chabot***	Y	N	Y	Y	Y	N	N
2 ***Portman***	Y	Y	Y	Y	Y	N	Y
3 Hall	–	+	N	Y	Y	Y	Y
4 ***Oxley***	Y	Y	Y	Y	Y	N	Y
5 ***Gillmor***	Y	Y	Y	Y	Y	N	Y
6 Strickland	Y	N	N	Y	Y	Y	Y
7 ***Hobson***	Y	Y	Y	Y	Y	N	Y
8 ***Boehner***	Y	Y	Y	Y	Y	N	Y
9 Kaptur	Y	Y	N	Y	Y	Y	Y
10 Kucinich	N	Y	N	Y	N	Y	Y
11 Stokes	N	Y	N	Y	Y	Y	Y
12 ***Kasich***	Y	Y	Y	Y	Y	N	Y
13 Brown	N	N	N	Y	Y	Y	Y
14 Sawyer	N	Y	?	Y	Y	Y	Y
15 ***Pryce***	Y	Y	Y	Y	Y	N	Y
16 ***Regula***	Y	Y	Y	Y	Y	N	Y
17 Traficant	Y	Y	Y	Y	Y	N	Y
18 ***Ney***	Y	Y	Y	Y	Y	N	Y
19 ***LaTourette***	Y	Y	Y	Y	Y	N	Y
OKLAHOMA							
1 ***Largent***	Y	Y	Y	Y	Y	N	Y
2 ***Coburn***	Y	Y	Y	Y	Y	N	Y
3 ***Watkins***	Y	Y	Y	Y	Y	N	Y
4 ***Watts***	Y	Y	Y	Y	Y	N	Y
5 ***Istook***	+	Y	Y	Y	Y	N	Y
6 ***Lucas***	Y	Y	Y	Y	Y	N	Y
OREGON							
1 Furse	N	?	N	Y	?	?	?
2 ***Smith***	Y	Y	?	?	?	?	?
3 Blumenauer	N	Y	N	Y	Y	Y	Y
4 DeFazio	Y	N	N	Y	N	Y	Y
5 Hooley	N	Y	N	Y	Y	Y	Y
PENNSYLVANIA							
1 Vacant							
2 Fattah	N	Y	N	Y	Y	Y	Y
3 Borski	N	Y	N	Y	N	Y	Y
4 Klink	?	?	N	Y	Y	Y	Y
5 ***Peterson***	Y	Y	Y	Y	Y	?	Y
6 Holden	Y	Y	N	Y	Y	Y	Y
7 ***Weldon***	Y	Y	Y	Y	?	N	Y
8 ***Greenwood***	Y	N	Y	Y	Y	N	Y
9 ***Shuster***	Y	Y	Y	Y	Y	N	Y
10 ***McDade***	Y	Y	Y	Y	?	N	Y
11 Kanjorski	N	N	N	Y	Y	Y	Y
12 Murtha	N	Y	N	Y	Y	Y	Y
13 ***Fox***	Y	Y	Y	Y	N	N	Y
14 Coyne	N	Y	N	Y	Y	Y	Y
15 McHale	N	Y	N	Y	Y	Y	Y
16 ***Pitts***	Y	Y	Y	Y	Y	N	Y
17 ***Gekas***	Y	Y	Y	Y	Y	N	N
18 Doyle	Y	Y	N	Y	Y	Y	Y
19 ***Goodling***	Y	Y	Y	Y	Y	N	Y
20 Mascara	N	Y	N	Y	Y	Y	Y
21 ***English***	Y	Y	Y	Y	N	N	Y
RHODE ISLAND							
1 Kennedy	N	Y	N	Y	Y	Y	Y
2 Weygand	N	Y	N	Y	Y	Y	Y
SOUTH CAROLINA							
1 ***Sanford***	Y	N	Y	Y	Y	N	Y
2 ***Spence***	Y	Y	Y	Y	Y	N	N
3 ***Graham***	Y	Y	Y	Y	Y	N	Y
4 ***Inglis***	Y	Y	Y	Y	Y	N	Y
5 Spratt	N	Y	N	Y	P	Y	Y
6 Clyburn	N	Y	N	Y	N	Y	Y
SOUTH DAKOTA							
AL ***Thune***	Y	Y	Y	Y	Y	N	Y

	9	10	12	13	14	15	16
TENNESSEE							
1 ***Jenkins***	Y	Y	Y	Y	Y	N	Y
2 ***Duncan***	Y	N	Y	Y	Y	N	Y
3 ***Wamp***	Y	Y	Y	Y	Y	N	Y
4 ***Hilleary***	Y	Y	Y	Y	N	N	Y
5 Clement	N	Y	N	Y	+	+	+
6 Gordon	N	Y	N	Y	Y	Y	Y
7 ***Bryant***	Y	Y	Y	Y	Y	N	Y
8 Tanner	N	Y	N	Y	Y	Y	Y
9 Ford	N	Y	N	Y	Y	Y	Y
TEXAS							
1 Sandlin	N	Y	N	Y	Y	Y	Y
2 Turner	Y	Y	N	Y	Y	Y	Y
3 ***Johnson, Sam***	Y	Y	Y	Y	Y	N	Y
4 Hall	Y	Y	Y	Y	Y	Y	Y
5 ***Sessions***	Y	Y	Y	Y	N	N	Y
6 ***Barton***	Y	Y	Y	Y	Y	N	Y
7 ***Archer***	Y	Y	Y	Y	Y	N	Y
8 ***Brady***	Y	Y	Y	Y	Y	N	Y
9 Lampson	N	Y	N	Y	Y	Y	Y
10 Doggett	N	N	N	Y	Y	Y	Y
11 Edwards	N	Y	N	Y	?	Y	?
12 ***Granger***	Y	Y	Y	Y	Y	N	Y
13 ***Thornberry***	Y	Y	Y	Y	Y	N	Y
14 ***Paul***	Y	Y	Y	Y	Y	N	N
15 Hinojosa	N	Y	N	Y	Y	Y	Y
16 Reyes	N	Y	N	Y	Y	Y	Y
17 Stenholm	Y	Y	N	Y	Y	Y	Y
18 Jackson-Lee	N	Y	N	Y	Y	Y	Y
19 ***Combest***	Y	Y	Y	Y	Y	N	Y
20 Gonzalez	?	?	?	?	?	?	?
21 ***Smith***	Y	Y	Y	Y	Y	N	Y
22 ***DeLay***	Y	Y	Y	Y	Y	N	Y
23 ***Bonilla***	Y	Y	Y	Y	Y	N	Y
24 Frost	N	Y	N	Y	Y	Y	Y
25 Bentsen	N	Y	N	Y	Y	Y	Y
26 ***Armey***	Y	?	Y	Y	Y	N	Y
27 Ortiz	N	Y	N	Y	Y	Y	Y
28 Rodriguez	N	Y	N	Y	Y	?	Y
29 Green	N	Y	N	Y	N	Y	Y
30 Johnson, E.B.	N	Y	N	Y	Y	Y	Y
UTAH							
1 ***Hansen***	Y	Y	Y	Y	Y	N	Y
2 ***Cook***	Y	Y	Y	Y	Y	N	Y
3 ***Cannon***	?	Y	Y	Y	Y	N	Y
VERMONT							
AL *Sanders*	N	Y	N	Y	Y	Y	Y
VIRGINIA							
1 ***Bateman***	Y	Y	Y	Y	Y	N	Y
2 Pickett	Y	Y	N	Y	N	Y	Y
3 Scott	N	Y	N	Y	N	Y	Y
4 Sisisky	Y	Y	N	Y	Y	Y	Y
5 Goode	Y	Y	Y	Y	Y	Y	Y
6 ***Goodlatte***	Y	Y	Y	Y	Y	N	Y
7 ***Bliley***	Y	Y	Y	Y	Y	N	Y
8 Moran	N	Y	N	Y	Y	Y	Y
9 Boucher	N	Y	N	Y	Y	Y	Y
10 ***Wolf***	Y	Y	Y	Y	Y	N	Y
11 ***Davis***	Y	Y	Y	Y	Y	N	Y
WASHINGTON							
1 ***White***	Y	Y	?	Y	Y	N	Y
2 ***Metcalf***	Y	Y	Y	Y	Y	N	Y
3 ***Smith, Linda***	Y	Y	?	Y	Y	N	?
4 ***Hastings***	Y	Y	Y	Y	Y	N	Y
5 ***Nethercutt***	Y	Y	Y	Y	Y	N	Y
6 Dicks	N	Y	N	Y	Y	Y	Y
7 McDermott	N	N	N	Y	N	Y	Y
8 ***Dunn***	Y	Y	Y	Y	Y	N	Y
9 Smith, Adam	N	Y	N	Y	Y	Y	Y
WEST VIRGINIA							
1 Mollohan	Y	Y	N	Y	Y	Y	Y
2 Wise	N	Y	N	+	Y	Y	?
3 Rahall	N	Y	N	Y	Y	Y	Y
WISCONSIN							
1 ***Neumann***	Y	N	Y	Y	Y	N	Y
2 ***Klug***	Y	N	Y	Y	Y	N	Y
3 Kind	N	N	N	Y	Y	Y	Y
4 Kleczka	Y	Y	N	Y	Y	Y	Y
5 Barrett	N	N	N	Y	Y	Y	Y
6 ***Petri***	Y	N	Y	Y	Y	N	Y
7 Obey	N	Y	N	?	N	Y	Y
8 Johnson	N	N	N	Y	?	?	?
9 ***Sensenbrenner***	Y	N	?	Y	Y	N	N
WYOMING							
AL ***Cubin***	Y	Y	Y	Y	Y	N	N

Southern states - Ala., Ark., Fla., Ga., Ky., La., Miss., N.C., Okla., S.C., Tenn., Texas, Va.

House Votes 17, 18, 19, 20, 21, 22, 23

17. HR 1428. Voter Eligibility Verification/Passage. Pease, R-Ind., motion to suspend the rules and pass, as amended, the bill to establish a pilot program in the five largest states, under which state and local officials could require Social Security numbers from voting applicants. It also directs the Justice Department, in consultation with the Social Security Administration and the Immigration and Naturalization Service, to set up a system in which local officials could seek verification of the citizenship of those attempting to vote. Motion rejected 210-200: R 203-13; D 7-186 (ND 1-140, SD 6-46); I 0-1. Feb. 12, 1998. A two-thirds majority of those present and voting (273 in this case) is required for passage under suspension of the rules.

18. HR 424. Mandatory Minimum Sentences for Gun Crimes/Passage. McCollum, R-Fla., motion to suspend the rules and pass the bill to impose mandatory minimum sentences for possession of a gun while committing a violent crime or drug trafficking offense. Motion agreed to 350-59: R 219-4; D 130-55 (ND 91-45, SD 39-10); I 1-0. Feb. 24, 1998. A two-thirds majority of those present and voting (273 in this case) is required for passage under suspension of the rules.

19. HR 1544. Federal Agency Compliance/Internal Revenue Service. Nadler, D-N.Y., amendment to limit the bill to require federal agencies to follow appellate court precedents to affect only the Internal Revenue Service, and those agencies dealing with benefits. Rejected 172-238: R 8-212; D 163-26 (ND 128-11, SD 35-15); I 1-0. Feb. 25, 1998.

20. HR 2181. Witness Protection/Death Penalty. Conyers, D-Mich., amendment to give courts the ability to reduce death penalty sentences that are provided in the bill to make it a federal offense to travel across state or international borders to intimidate a witness in a state criminal proceeding. Rejected 113-300: R 7-214; D 105-86 (ND 91-49, SD 14-37); I 1-0. Feb. 25, 1998.

21. HR 2181. Witness Protection/Passage. Passage of the bill to make it a federal offense to travel across state or international borders to intimidate a witness in a state criminal proceeding. Passed 366-49: R 221-2; D 144-47 (ND 101-38, SD 43-9); I 1-0. Feb. 25, 1998.

22. HR 1544. Federal Agency Compliance/Civil Rights. Jackson-Lee, D-Texas, amendment to prevent the bill to require federal agencies to follow appellate court precedents from applying to issues dealing with civil, labor and environmental rights. Rejected 164-253: R 2-220; D 161-33 (ND 128-15, SD 33-18); I 1-0. Feb. 25, 1998.

23. HR 1544. Federal Agency Compliance/Foreign Entities. Jackson-Lee, D-Texas, amendment to prevent the bill to require federal agencies to follow appellate court precedents from applying to cases involving foreign entities. Rejected 154-258: R 1-217; D 152-41 (ND 119-22, SD 33-19); I 1-0. Feb. 25, 1998.

Key

- **Y** Voted for (yea).
- **#** Paired for.
- **+** Announced for.
- **N** Voted against (nay).
- **X** Paired against.
- **−** Announced against.
- **P** Voted "present."
- **C** Voted "present" to avoid possible conflict of interest.
- **?** Did not vote or otherwise make a position known.

Democrats   **Republicans**
Independent

	17	18	19	20	21	22	23
ALABAMA							
1 *Callahan*	?	Y	N	N	Y	N	N
2 *Everett*	?	Y	N	N	Y	N	N
3 *Riley*	Y	Y	N	N	Y	N	N
4 *Aderholt*	Y	Y	N	N	Y	N	N
5 Cramer	N	Y	N	N	Y	N	N
6 *Bachus*	Y	Y	N	N	Y	N	N
7 Hilliard	N	N	Y	Y	N	Y	Y
ALASKA							
AL *Young*	?	?	N	N	Y	N	N
ARIZONA							
1 *Salmon*	Y	Y	N	N	Y	N	N
2 Pastor	N	Y	Y	N	Y	Y	Y
3 *Stump*	Y	Y	N	N	Y	N	N
4 *Shadegg*	?	Y	N	N	Y	N	N
5 *Kolbe*	Y	Y	N	N	Y	N	N
6 *Hayworth*	Y	Y	N	N	Y	N	N
ARKANSAS							
1 Berry	N	Y	N	N	Y	N	Y
2 Snyder	N	Y	Y	Y	N	Y	Y
3 *Hutchinson*	N	Y	N	N	Y	N	N
4 Dickey	Y	Y	N	N	Y	N	N
CALIFORNIA							
1 *Riggs*	?	Y	−	−	Y	N	−
2 *Herger*	Y	Y	N	N	Y	N	N
3 Fazio	N	N	Y	N	Y	Y	Y
4 *Doolittle*	Y	Y	N	N	Y	N	N
5 Matsui	N	N	Y	Y	N	Y	Y
6 Woolsey	N	Y	Y	Y	Y	Y	Y
7 Miller	N	Y	?	?	?	?	?
8 Pelosi	N	?	?	?	?	?	?
9 Vacant							
10 Tauscher	N	Y	Y	N	Y	N	Y
11 *Pombo*	Y	Y	N	N	Y	N	N
12 Lantos	?	?	Y	N	Y	Y	Y
13 Stark	N	Y	Y	Y	N	Y	Y
14 Eshoo	?	Y	Y	Y	Y	Y	Y
15 *Campbell*	Y	Y	N	N	Y	N	N
16 Lofgren	N	N	Y	N	Y	Y	Y
17 Farr	N	Y	Y	N	Y	Y	Y
18 Condit	Y	Y	N	N	Y	N	N
19 *Radanovich*	Y	Y	N	N	Y	N	N
20 Dooley	N	N	Y	N	Y	N	Y
21 *Thomas*	Y	Y	N	N	Y	N	N
22 Vacant							
23 *Gallegly*	Y	Y	N	N	Y	N	N
24 Sherman	N	Y	Y	Y	Y	Y	Y
25 *McKeon*	Y	Y	N	N	Y	N	N
26 Berman	N	N	Y	Y	Y	Y	Y
27 *Rogan*	Y	Y	N	N	Y	N	N
28 *Dreier*	Y	Y	N	N	Y	N	N
29 Waxman	N	N	Y	Y	Y	Y	Y
30 Becerra	N	Y	Y	Y	Y	Y	Y
31 Martinez	N	N	Y	N	Y	Y	Y
32 Dixon	N	N	Y	Y	Y	Y	Y
33 Roybal-Allard	N	N	Y	Y	Y	Y	Y
34 Torres	N	Y	Y	Y	Y	Y	Y
35 Waters	N	N	Y	Y	N	Y	Y
36 Harman	?	Y	Y	N	Y	N	Y
37 Millender-McD.	N	N	Y	Y	Y	Y	Y

	17	18	19	20	21	22	23
38 *Horn*	Y	Y	N	N	Y	N	N
39 *Royce*	Y	Y	N	N	Y	N	N
40 *Lewis*	Y	Y	N	N	Y	N	N
41 *Kim*	Y	Y	N	N	Y	N	N
42 Brown	N	?	Y	Y	Y	Y	Y
43 *Calvert*	Y	Y	N	N	Y	N	N
44 Vacant							
45 *Rohrabacher*	Y	Y	N	N	Y	N	N
46 Sanchez	N	Y	Y	N	+	Y	Y
47 *Cox*	Y	Y	N	N	N	N	N
48 *Packard*	Y	Y	N	N	Y	N	N
49 *Bilbray*	Y	Y	N	N	Y	N	N
50 Filner	N	N	Y	Y	Y	Y	Y
51 *Cunningham*	Y	Y	N	N	Y	N	N
52 *Hunter*	Y	Y	N	N	Y	N	N
COLORADO							
1 DeGette	N	N	Y	Y	N	Y	Y
2 Skaggs	N	N	Y	Y	Y	Y	Y
3 *McInnis*	Y	Y	N	N	Y	N	N
4 *Schaffer*	N	Y	N	N	Y	N	N
5 *Hefley*	Y	Y	N	N	Y	N	N
6 *Schaefer*	Y	Y	N	N	Y	N	N
CONNECTICUT							
1 Kennelly	N	Y	?	?	Y	Y	Y
2 Gejdenson	N	Y	+	+	Y	Y	Y
3 DeLauro	N	Y	?	?	Y	Y	Y
4 *Shays*	N	N	Y	N	Y	N	N
5 Maloney	N	Y	Y	N	Y	Y	Y
6 *Johnson*	Y	Y	N	N	Y	N	N
DELAWARE							
AL *Castle*	Y	Y	N	N	Y	N	N
FLORIDA							
1 *Scarborough*	Y	N	N	Y	N	N	N
2 Boyd	N	Y	N	N	Y	N	N
3 Brown	N	N	+	+	+	+	+
4 *Fowler*	Y	Y	N	N	Y	N	N
5 Thurman	N	Y	Y	Y	Y	Y	Y
6 *Stearns*	Y	Y	N	N	Y	N	N
7 *Mica*	Y	Y	−	−	+	−	−
8 *McCollum*	Y	Y	N	N	Y	N	N
9 *Bilirakis*	Y	Y	N	N	Y	N	N
10 *Young*	Y	Y	N	N	Y	N	N
11 Davis	N	Y	Y	N	Y	N	N
12 *Canady*	Y	Y	N	N	Y	N	N
13 *Miller*	?	Y	N	N	Y	N	N
14 *Goss*	Y	Y	N	N	Y	N	N
15 *Weldon*	Y	Y	N	N	Y	N	N
16 *Foley*	Y	Y	N	N	Y	N	N
17 Meek	N	N	Y	N	Y	Y	Y
18 *Ros-Lehtinen*	N	Y	N	N	Y	N	N
19 Wexler	N	Y	Y	Y	Y	Y	Y
20 Deutsch	Y	Y	Y	N	Y	Y	Y
21 *Diaz-Balart*	Y	Y	N	N	Y	N	N
22 *Shaw*	Y	Y	N	N	Y	N	N
23 Hastings	N	N	Y	N	Y	Y	Y
GEORGIA							
1 *Kingston*	Y	Y	N	N	Y	N	N
2 Bishop	N	N	Y	N	Y	N	N
3 *Collins*	Y	Y	N	N	Y	N	N
4 McKinney	N	N	Y	Y	N	Y	Y
5 Lewis	N	N	Y	Y	N	Y	Y
6 *Gingrich*	Y						
7 *Barr*	Y	Y	N	N	Y	N	N
8 *Chambliss*	Y	Y	N	N	Y	N	N
9 *Deal*	Y	Y	N	N	Y	N	N
10 *Norwood*	Y	Y	N	N	Y	N	N
11 *Linder*	Y	Y	N	N	Y	N	N
HAWAII							
1 Abercrombie	N	Y	Y	Y	Y	Y	Y
2 Mink	−	N	Y	Y	N	Y	Y
IDAHO							
1 *Chenoweth*	Y	Y	N	N	Y	N	N
2 *Crapo*	Y	Y	N	N	Y	N	N
ILLINOIS							
1 Rush	N	?	Y	Y	N	Y	Y
2 Jackson	N	N	Y	Y	N	Y	Y
3 Lipinski	Y	Y	N	N	Y	N	N
4 Gutierrez	N	?	Y	Y	Y	Y	Y
5 Blagojevich	N	Y	Y	Y	Y	Y	Y
6 *Hyde*	Y	Y	N	N	Y	N	N
7 Davis	N	N	Y	N	Y	Y	Y
8 *Crane*	Y	Y	N	N	Y	N	N
9 Yates	N	Y	Y	Y	Y	Y	Y
10 *Porter*	Y	Y	N	N	Y	N	N
11 *Weller*	Y	Y	N	N	Y	N	N
12 Costello	N	Y	N	N	Y	N	N

ND Northern Democrats   SD Southern Democrats

	17	18	19	20	21	22	23
13 ***Fawell***	Y	Y	N	N	Y	N	N
14 ***Hastert***	Y	Y	N	N	Y	N	N
15 ***Ewing***	Y	Y	N	N	Y	N	N
16 ***Manzullo***	Y	Y	N	N	Y	N	N
17 Evans	N	Y	Y	Y	Y	Y	Y
18 ***LaHood***	Y	Y	N	N	Y	N	N
19 Poshard	N	?	?	?	?	?	?
20 ***Shimkus***	Y	Y	N	N	Y	N	N
INDIANA							
1 Visclosky	N	Y	Y	N	Y	Y	N
2 ***McIntosh***	Y	Y	N	N	Y	N	N
3 Roemer	N	Y	N	N	Y	N	N
4 ***Souder***	Y	Y	N	N	Y	N	N
5 ***Buyer***	?	Y	N	N	Y	N	N
6 ***Burton***	Y	Y	N	N	Y	N	N
7 ***Pease***	Y	Y	N	N	Y	N	N
8 ***Hostettler***	Y	Y	N	N	Y	N	N
9 Hamilton	N	Y	Y	Y	Y	Y	N
10 Carson	N	N	Y	Y	Y	Y	Y
IOWA							
1 ***Leach***	Y	Y	N	N	Y	N	N
2 ***Nussle***	Y	Y	N	N	Y	N	N
3 Boswell	N	Y	N	N	Y	N	N
4 ***Ganske***	Y	Y	N	N	Y	N	N
5 ***Latham***	Y	Y	N	N	Y	N	N
KANSAS							
1 ***Moran***	Y	Y	N	N	Y	N	N
2 ***Ryun***	Y	Y	N	N	Y	N	N
3 ***Snowbarger***	Y	Y	N	N	Y	N	N
4 ***Tiahrt***	Y	Y	N	N	Y	N	N
KENTUCKY							
1 ***Whitfield***	Y	Y	N	N	Y	N	N
2 ***Lewis***	Y	Y	?	N	Y	N	N
3 ***Northup***	Y	Y	N	N	Y	N	N
4 ***Bunning***	Y	Y	N	N	Y	N	N
5 ***Rogers***	Y	Y	N	N	Y	N	N
6 Baesler	N	Y	Y	N	Y	Y	Y
LOUISIANA							
1 ***Livingston***	Y	Y	N	N	Y	N	N
2 Jefferson	?	Y	Y	N	Y	Y	Y
3 ***Tauzin***	Y	Y	N	N	Y	N	N
4 ***McCrery***	Y	Y	N	N	Y	N	N
5 ***Cooksey***	Y	Y	N	N	Y	N	N
6 ***Baker***	Y	Y	N	N	Y	N	N
7 John	N	Y	N	N	Y	N	N
MAINE							
1 Allen	N	Y	Y	Y	Y	Y	Y
2 Baldacci	N	Y	Y	Y	Y	Y	Y
MARYLAND							
1 ***Gilchrest***	Y	Y	N	N	Y	N	N
2 ***Ehrlich***	Y	Y	N	N	Y	N	N
3 Cardin	N	Y	Y	N	Y	Y	Y
4 Wynn	N	N	Y	N	Y	Y	Y
5 Hoyer	N	Y	Y	N	Y	Y	Y
6 ***Bartlett***	Y	Y	N	N	Y	N	N
7 Cummings	N	N	Y	Y	N	N	Y
8 ***Morella***	N	Y	Y	N	Y	N	N
MASSACHUSETTS							
1 Olver	N	N	Y	Y	Y	Y	Y
2 Neal	N	Y	Y	Y	Y	Y	Y
3 McGovern	N	Y	Y	Y	N	Y	Y
4 Frank	N	Y	Y	Y	Y	Y	N
5 Meehan	N	Y	Y	Y	Y	Y	Y
6 Tierney	N	Y	Y	Y	Y	Y	Y
7 Markey	N	Y	Y	Y	Y	Y	Y
8 Kennedy	N	Y	Y	Y	Y	Y	Y
9 Moakley	N	N	Y	Y	Y	Y	Y
10 Delahunt	N	N	Y	Y	N	Y	Y
MICHIGAN							
1 Stupak	N	?	Y	Y	Y	Y	Y
2 ***Hoekstra***	Y	Y	N	Y	Y	N	N
3 ***Ehlers***	Y	Y	N	N	Y	N	N
4 ***Camp***	Y	Y	N	N	Y	N	N
5 Barcia	N	Y	Y	N	Y	Y	Y
6 ***Upton***	Y	Y	N	N	Y	N	N
7 ***Smith***	Y	Y	N	N	Y	N	N
8 Stabenow	N	Y	Y	Y	N	Y	Y
9 Kildee	N	Y	Y	Y	Y	Y	Y
10 Bonior	N	N	Y	Y	N	Y	Y
11 ***Knollenberg***	Y	Y	N	N	Y	N	N
12 Levin	N	Y	Y	Y	Y	Y	Y
13 Rivers	N	Y	Y	Y	N	Y	Y
14 Conyers	N	N	Y	Y	N	Y	?
15 Kilpatrick	N	N	Y	Y	N	Y	Y
16 Dingell	N	Y	Y	N	Y	Y	Y

	17	18	19	20	21	22	23
MINNESOTA							
1 ***Gutknecht***	Y	Y	N	Y	Y	N	N
2 Minge	N	N	N	Y	Y	N	N
3 ***Ramstad***	Y	Y	N	N	Y	N	N
4 Vento	N	N	Y	Y	Y	Y	Y
5 Sabo	N	N	Y	Y	N	N	Y
6 Luther	N	Y	–	+	+	–	–
7 Peterson	N	N	N	N	Y	N	N
8 Oberstar	N	N	Y	Y	N	Y	Y
MISSISSIPPI							
1 ***Wicker***	Y	Y	N	N	Y	N	N
2 Thompson	N	Y	Y	Y	Y	N	Y
3 ***Pickering***	Y	Y	N	N	Y	N	N
4 ***Parker***	Y	Y	N	N	Y	N	N
5 Taylor	Y	Y	N	N	Y	N	N
MISSOURI							
1 Clay	N	N	Y	Y	N	Y	Y
2 ***Talent***	Y	Y	N	N	Y	N	N
3 Gephardt	N	Y	?	N	Y	Y	Y
4 Skelton	N	Y	Y	N	Y	N	N
5 McCarthy	N	+	Y	Y	Y	Y	Y
6 Danner	N	Y	Y	N	Y	Y	Y
7 ***Blunt***	Y	Y	N	N	Y	N	N
8 ***Emerson***	Y	Y	N	N	Y	N	N
9 ***Hulshof***	Y	Y	N	N	Y	N	N
MONTANA							
AL ***Hill***	Y	Y	N	N	Y	N	N
NEBRASKA							
1 ***Bereuter***	Y	Y	N	N	Y	N	N
2 ***Christensen***	Y	Y	N	N	Y	N	N
3 ***Barrett***	Y	Y	N	N	Y	N	N
NEVADA							
1 ***Ensign***	Y	Y	N	N	Y	N	N
2 ***Gibbons***	Y	Y	N	N	Y	N	N
NEW HAMPSHIRE							
1 ***Sununu***	Y	Y	N	N	Y	N	N
2 ***Bass***	Y	Y	N	N	Y	N	N
NEW JERSEY							
1 Andrews	N	Y	Y	N	Y	Y	Y
2 ***LoBiondo***	Y	Y	Y	N	Y	N	N
3 ***Saxton***	Y	Y	N	N	Y	N	N
4 ***Smith***	Y	Y	N	?	Y	N	?
5 ***Roukema***	Y	Y	N	N	Y	N	N
6 Pallone	N	Y	Y	N	Y	Y	Y
7 ***Franks***	Y	Y	N	N	Y	N	N
8 Pascrell	N	Y	Y	N	Y	Y	Y
9 Rothman	N	Y	Y	N	Y	Y	Y
10 Payne	N	N	Y	Y	N	Y	Y
11 ***Frelinghuysen***	Y	Y	N	N	Y	N	?
12 ***Pappas***	Y	Y	N	Y	Y	N	N
13 Menendez	N	Y	Y	N	Y	Y	Y
NEW MEXICO							
1 ***Schiff***	?	?	?	?	?	?	?
2 ***Skeen***	Y	Y	N	N	Y	N	N
3 ***Redmond***	Y	Y	–	N	Y	N	N
NEW YORK							
1 ***Forbes***	N	Y	N	N	Y	N	N
2 ***Lazio***	Y	Y	N	N	Y	N	N
3 ***King***	Y	Y	N	N	Y	N	N
4 McCarthy	N	Y	Y	Y	Y	Y	Y
5 Ackerman	N	Y	Y	Y	Y	Y	Y
6 Meeks	N	N	Y	Y	N	Y	Y
7 Manton	N	Y	Y	N	Y	Y	N
8 Nadler	N	N	Y	Y	?	Y	Y
9 Schumer	N	Y	Y	N	Y	Y	Y
10 Towns	?	Y	Y	Y	N	Y	Y
11 Owens	N	Y	Y	Y	N	Y	Y
12 Velázquez	N	Y	Y	Y	Y	Y	Y
13 ***Fossella***	Y	Y	N	N	Y	N	N
14 Maloney	N	Y	Y	Y	Y	Y	Y
15 Rangel	N	N	Y	Y	N	Y	Y
16 Serrano	N	N	Y	Y	N	Y	Y
17 Engel	N	Y	Y	Y	Y	Y	Y
18 Lowey	N	Y	Y	Y	Y	Y	Y
19 ***Kelly***	Y	Y	N	N	Y	N	N
20 ***Gilman***	Y	?	Y	N	Y	N	N
21 McNulty	N	N	Y	Y	Y	Y	Y
22 ***Solomon***	Y	Y	N	N	Y	N	N
23 ***Boehlert***	N	Y	N	N	Y	N	N
24 ***McHugh***	Y	Y	Y	N	Y	N	N
25 ***Walsh***	N	Y	Y	N	Y	N	N
26 Hinchey	N	N	Y	Y	Y	Y	Y
27 ***Paxon***	Y	Y	?	?	?	?	?
28 Slaughter	N	Y	Y	Y	Y	Y	Y
29 LaFalce	N	N	Y	Y	N	Y	Y

	17	18	19	20	21	22	23
30 ***Quinn***	Y	Y	Y	N	Y	N	N
31 ***Houghton***	N	Y	N	N	Y	N	N
NORTH CAROLINA							
1 Clayton	N	N	Y	Y	N	Y	Y
2 Etheridge	N	Y	Y	N	Y	Y	Y
3 ***Jones***	Y	Y	N	N	Y	N	N
4 Price	N	Y	Y	N	Y	Y	Y
5 ***Burr***	Y	Y	N	N	Y	N	N
6 ***Coble***	Y	Y	N	N	Y	N	N
7 McIntyre	N	?	Y	N	Y	Y	Y
8 Hefner	N	?	Y	Y	Y	Y	Y
9 ***Myrick***	Y	Y	N	N	Y	N	N
10 ***Ballenger***	Y	Y	N	N	Y	N	N
11 ***Taylor***	Y	Y	N	N	Y	N	N
12 Watt	N	N	Y	Y	N	Y	Y
NORTH DAKOTA							
AL Pomeroy	N	Y	Y	N	Y	Y	Y
OHIO							
1 ***Chabot***	N	Y	N	N	Y	N	N
2 ***Portman***	Y	Y	N	N	Y	N	N
3 Hall	N	Y	Y	Y	?	N	N
4 ***Oxley***	?	Y	N	N	Y	N	N
5 ***Gillmor***	Y	Y	N	N	Y	N	N
6 Strickland	N	Y	Y	N	Y	Y	Y
7 ***Hobson***	Y	Y	N	N	Y	N	?
8 ***Boehner***	Y	Y	N	N	Y	N	N
9 Kaptur	N	Y	Y	N	Y	Y	Y
10 Kucinich	N	Y	Y	Y	P	Y	Y
11 Stokes	N	N	Y	Y	N	Y	?
12 ***Kasich***	Y	Y	N	N	Y	N	N
13 Brown	N	?	Y	Y	N	Y	Y
14 Sawyer	N	N	Y	Y	Y	Y	Y
15 ***Pryce***	Y	Y	N	N	Y	N	N
16 ***Regula***	Y	Y	N	N	Y	N	N
17 Traficant	N	Y	N	N	Y	N	Y
18 ***Ney***	Y	Y	N	N	Y	N	N
19 ***LaTourette***	Y	Y	N	N	Y	N	N
OKLAHOMA							
1 ***Largent***	?	Y	N	N	Y	N	N
2 ***Coburn***	Y	Y	N	N	Y	N	N
3 ***Watkins***	Y	Y	N	N	Y	N	N
4 ***Watts***	Y	N	N	N	Y	N	N
5 ***Istook***	Y	Y	N	N	Y	N	N
6 ***Lucas***	Y	Y	N	N	Y	N	N
OREGON							
1 Furse	?	?	Y	Y	N	Y	Y
2 ***Smith***	?	Y	N	N	Y	N	N
3 Blumenauer	N	Y	Y	Y	Y	Y	Y
4 DeFazio	N	Y	Y	Y	Y	Y	Y
5 Hooley	N	Y	Y	Y	Y	Y	Y
PENNSYLVANIA							
1 Vacant							
2 Fattah	N	N	Y	Y	N	Y	Y
3 Borski	N	Y	Y	N	Y	Y	Y
4 Klink	N	?	?	?	?	?	?
5 ***Peterson***	Y	Y	N	N	Y	N	N
6 Holden	N	Y	Y	N	Y	Y	Y
7 ***Weldon***	Y	Y	N	N	Y	N	N
8 ***Greenwood***	Y	Y	N	N	Y	Y	N
9 ***Shuster***	Y	Y	N	N	Y	N	N
10 ***McDade***	Y	Y	N	N	Y	N	N
11 Kanjorski	N	Y	Y	N	Y	N	N
12 Murtha	N	Y	Y	N	Y	N	N
13 ***Fox***	Y	Y	Y	N	Y	Y	N
14 Coyne	N	N	Y	Y	Y	Y	Y
15 McHale	N	Y	Y	N	Y	Y	Y
16 ***Pitts***	Y	Y	N	N	Y	N	N
17 ***Gekas***	Y	Y	N	N	Y	N	N
18 Doyle	N	Y	Y	N	Y	Y	Y
19 ***Goodling***	Y	Y	N	Y	Y	N	N
20 Mascara	N	Y	Y	N	Y	Y	Y
21 ***English***	Y	Y	N	N	Y	N	N
RHODE ISLAND							
1 Kennedy	N	Y	Y	Y	N	Y	Y
2 Weygand	N	Y	Y	Y	N	Y	Y
SOUTH CAROLINA							
1 ***Sanford***	Y	Y	N	N	Y	N	N
2 ***Spence***	Y	Y	N	N	Y	N	N
3 ***Graham***	Y	Y	N	N	Y	N	?
4 ***Inglis***	Y	Y	N	N	Y	N	N
5 Spratt	N	Y	Y	N	Y	Y	N
6 Clyburn	N	Y	Y	Y	N	Y	Y
SOUTH DAKOTA							
AL ***Thune***	Y	Y	N	N	Y	N	N

	17	18	19	20	21	22	23
TENNESSEE							
1 ***Jenkins***	Y	Y	N	N	Y	N	N
2 ***Duncan***	Y	Y	N	N	Y	N	N
3 ***Wamp***	Y	Y	N	N	Y	N	N
4 ***Hilleary***	Y	Y	N	N	Y	N	N
5 Clement	–	Y	N	N	Y	N	N
6 Gordon	N	Y	N	N	Y	N	N
7 ***Bryant***	Y	Y	N	N	Y	N	N
8 Tanner	N	Y	N	N	Y	N	N
9 Ford	N	?	?	?	?	?	?
TEXAS							
1 Sandlin	N	Y	Y	N	Y	Y	Y
2 Turner	Y	Y	Y	N	Y	N	N
3 ***Johnson, Sam***	Y	Y	N	N	Y	N	N
4 Hall	Y	Y	N	N	Y	N	N
5 ***Sessions***	Y	Y	N	N	Y	N	N
6 ***Barton***	Y	Y	N	N	Y	N	N
7 ***Archer***	Y	Y	N	N	Y	N	N
8 ***Brady***	Y	Y	N	N	Y	–	N
9 Lampson	N	+	Y	N	Y	Y	Y
10 Doggett	N	Y	Y	N	Y	Y	N
11 Edwards	N	Y	Y	N	Y	Y	Y
12 ***Granger***	Y	Y	N	N	Y	N	N
13 ***Thornberry***	Y	Y	N	N	Y	N	N
14 ***Paul***	N	N	N	Y	N	N	N
15 Hinojosa	N	Y	Y	N	Y	Y	Y
16 Reyes	N	Y	Y	N	Y	Y	Y
17 Stenholm	N	Y	N	N	Y	N	N
18 Jackson-Lee	N	?	Y	Y	Y	Y	Y
19 ***Combest***	Y	Y	N	N	Y	N	N
20 Gonzalez	?	?	?	?	?	?	?
21 ***Smith***	Y	Y	N	N	Y	N	N
22 ***DeLay***	Y	Y	N	N	Y	N	N
23 ***Bonilla***	Y	Y	N	N	Y	N	N
24 Frost	N	Y	Y	N	Y	+	Y
25 Bentsen	N	Y	Y	N	Y	Y	N
26 ***Armey***	Y	Y	N	N	Y	N	N
27 Ortiz	N	Y	Y	N	Y	Y	Y
28 Rodriguez	N	Y	?	?	Y	Y	Y
29 Green	N	Y	Y	N	Y	Y	Y
30 Johnson, E.B.	N	Y	Y	Y	Y	Y	Y
UTAH							
1 ***Hansen***	Y	Y	N	N	Y	N	N
2 ***Cook***	Y	Y	N	N	Y	N	N
3 ***Cannon***	Y	Y	N	N	Y	N	N
VERMONT							
AL *Sanders*	N	Y	Y	Y	Y	Y	Y
VIRGINIA							
1 ***Bateman***	Y	Y	N	N	Y	N	N
2 Pickett	Y	Y	N	N	Y	N	N
3 Scott	N	N	Y	Y	N	Y	Y
4 Sisisky	N	Y	N	N	Y	N	N
5 Goode	Y	N	N	N	Y	N	N
6 ***Goodlatte***	Y	Y	N	N	Y	N	N
7 ***Bliley***	Y	Y	N	N	Y	N	N
8 Moran	N	Y	Y	N	Y	Y	Y
9 Boucher	N	Y	?	N	Y	Y	Y
10 ***Wolf***	Y	Y	N	N	Y	N	N
11 ***Davis***	Y	Y	N	N	Y	N	N
WASHINGTON							
1 ***White***	Y	Y	N	N	Y	N	N
2 ***Metcalf***	Y	Y	N	N	Y	N	N
3 ***Smith, Linda***	N	N	N	N	Y	N	N
4 ***Hastings***	Y	Y	N	N	Y	N	N
5 ***Nethercutt***	Y	Y	N	N	Y	N	N
6 Dicks	N	Y	Y	N	Y	Y	N
7 McDermott	N	N	Y	Y	N	Y	Y
8 ***Dunn***	Y	Y	N	N	Y	N	N
9 Smith, Adam	N	Y	N	N	Y	N	N
WEST VIRGINIA							
1 Mollohan	N	N	Y	Y	N	Y	Y
2 Wise	N	Y	Y	Y	Y	Y	Y
3 Rahall	N	Y	Y	Y	Y	Y	Y
WISCONSIN							
1 ***Neumann***	Y	Y	N	N	Y	N	N
2 ***Klug***	Y	Y	N	Y	Y	N	N
3 Kind	N	Y	Y	N	Y	Y	Y
4 Kleczka	N	Y	Y	Y	Y	Y	Y
5 Barrett	N	Y	Y	Y	N	Y	Y
6 ***Petri***	Y	Y	Y	N	Y	N	N
7 Obey	N	Y	Y	Y	Y	Y	Y
8 Johnson	?	Y	Y	Y	Y	Y	Y
9 ***Sensenbrenner***	Y	Y	N	N	Y	N	N
WYOMING							
AL ***Cubin***	Y	Y	N	N	Y	N	N

Southern states - Ala., Ark., Fla., Ga., Ky., La., Miss., N.C., Okla., S.C., Tenn., Texas, Va.

House Votes 24, 25, 26, 27, 28, 29, 30

24. HR 1544. Federal Agency Compliance/Passage. Passage of the bill to require federal agencies to follow appellate court precedents when administering policies or regulations. Passed 241-176: R 191-31; D 50-144 (ND 29-114, SD 21-30); I 0-1. Feb. 25, 1998. A "nay" was a vote in support of the president's position.

25. HR 2460. Wireless Telephone Protection/Passage. Passage of the bill to prohibit the production, trafficking in and possession of devices used to reprogram cellular telephones with unauthorized identification numbers, and could impose a penalty of 15 years imprisonment if convicted. Passed 414-1: R 220-1; D 194-0 (ND 142-0, SD 52-0); I 0-0. Feb. 26, 1998. Subsequently, S493, a similar Senate-passed bill was passed in lieu after being amended to contain the text of HR2460 as passed by the House; HR2460 was laid on the table. A "yea" was a vote in support of the president's position.

26. HR 217. Homeless Housing Programs Consolidation/Passage. Lazio, R-N.Y., motion to suspend the rules and pass the bill to consolidate into a single block grant program seven homeless housing programs authorizing $1 billion a year through fiscal 2002. Motion agreed to 386-23: R 195-19; D 190-4 (ND 137-4, SD 53-0); I 1-0. March 3, 1998. A two-thirds majority of those present and voting (273 in this case) is required for passage under suspension of the rules.

27. HR 856. Puerto Rico Political Status/Rule. Adoption of the rule (H Res 376) to provide for House floor consideration of the bill to establish a process to determine and implement a permanent political status for Puerto Rico, including referenda in Puerto Rico and subsequent action by Congress. Adopted 370-41: R 180-36; D 189-5 (ND 137-3, SD 52-2); I 1-0. March 4, 1998.

28. HR 856. Puerto Rico Political Status/Spanish Language. Gutierrez, D-Ill., amendment to the Solomon, R-N.Y., amendment to maintain Spanish as an official language in Puerto Rico. The Solomon amendment would establish that English is the official language of the United States, and that if Puerto Rico chooses statehood, English would be the sole official language of all federal government activities in Puerto Rico. Rejected 13-406: R 0-223; D 13-182 (ND 12-129, SD 1-53); I 0-1. March 4, 1998.

29. HR 856. Puerto Rico Political Status/Languages. Burton, R-Ind., amendment to the Solomon, R-N.Y., amendment to treat Puerto Rico the same as the states and recognize the primary role of English in national affairs, but not preclude the use of other languages in government functions when appropriate. The Solomon amendment would establish that English is the official language of the United States, and that if Puerto Rico chooses statehood English would be the sole official language of all federal government activities in Puerto Rico. Adopted 238-182: R 55-168; D 182-14 (ND 134-8, SD 48-6); I 1-0. March 4, 1998.

30. HR 856. Puerto Rico Political Status/English Language. Solomon, R-N.Y., amendment to treat Puerto Rico the same as the states, recognizing the primary role of English in national affairs, but not preclude the use of other languages in government functions when appropriate. Adopted 265-153: R 85-138; D 179-15 (ND 132-8, SD 47-7); I 1-0. March 4, 1998.

Key

- **Y** Voted for (yea).
- **#** Paired for.
- **+** Announced for.
- **N** Voted against (nay).
- **X** Paired against.
- **−** Announced against.
- **P** Voted "present."
- **C** Voted "present" to avoid possible conflict of interest.
- **?** Did not vote or otherwise make a position known.

Democrats **Republicans** *Independent*

	24	25	26	27	28	29	30
ALABAMA							
1 *Callahan*	Y	Y	Y	Y	N	N	N
2 *Everett*	Y	Y	Y	N	N	N	N
3 *Riley*	Y	Y	Y	N	N	N	N
4 *Aderholt*	Y	Y	Y	N	N	N	N
5 Cramer	Y	Y	Y	N	N	Y	Y
6 *Bachus*	Y	Y	Y	N	N	N	N
7 Hilliard	N	Y	Y	Y	N	Y	Y
ALASKA							
AL *Young*	Y	Y	Y	Y	N	Y	Y
ARIZONA							
1 *Salmon*	N	Y	?	N	N	N	N
2 Pastor	N	Y	Y	Y	Y	Y	Y
3 *Stump*	Y	Y	Y	Y	N	N	N
4 *Shadegg*	N	Y	N	Y	N	N	N
5 *Kolbe*	Y	Y	Y	Y	N	Y	Y
6 *Hayworth*	N	Y	Y	Y	N	N	N
ARKANSAS							
1 Berry	Y	Y	Y	Y	N	Y	Y
2 Snyder	Y	Y	Y	Y	Y	Y	Y
3 *Hutchinson*	Y	Y	Y	Y	N	N	N
4 *Dickey*	Y	Y	Y	Y	N	N	N
CALIFORNIA							
1 *Riggs*	N	Y	Y	Y	N	Y	Y
2 *Herger*	N	Y	Y	Y	N	N	N
3 Fazio	Y	Y	Y	Y	N	Y	Y
4 *Doolittle*	N	Y	?	?	?	?	?
5 Matsui	Y	Y	Y	Y	N	Y	Y
6 Woolsey	N	Y	Y	Y	Y	Y	Y
7 Miller	?	?	Y	Y	Y	Y	Y
8 Pelosi	?	?	Y	Y	N	Y	Y
9 Vacant							
10 Tauscher	Y	Y	Y	Y	N	Y	Y
11 *Pombo*	Y	Y	Y	Y	N	N	N
12 Lantos	N	Y	Y	Y	Y	Y	Y
13 Stark	N	Y	?	Y	N	Y	Y
14 Eshoo	N	Y	Y	Y	N	Y	Y
15 *Campbell*	N	?	Y	Y	N	Y	Y
16 Lofgren	Y	Y	Y	Y	N	Y	Y
17 Farr	N	Y	Y	Y	N	Y	Y
18 Condit	Y	Y	Y	Y	N	Y	Y
19 *Radanovich*	N	Y	Y	Y	N	N	N
20 Dooley	Y	Y	Y	Y	N	Y	Y
21 *Thomas*	N	Y	Y	Y	N	N	Y
22 Vacant							
23 *Gallegly*	Y	Y	Y	Y	N	Y	Y
24 Sherman	Y	Y	Y	Y	N	Y	Y
25 *McKeon*	Y	Y	Y	Y	N	Y	Y
26 Berman	N	Y	Y	Y	N	Y	?
27 *Rogan*	N	Y	Y	+	N	N	N
28 *Dreier*	N	Y	Y	Y	N	N	N
29 Waxman	N	Y	Y	Y	N	Y	Y
30 Becerra	N	Y	Y	Y	N	Y	Y
31 Martinez	N	Y	Y	Y	N	Y	Y
32 Dixon	N	Y	Y	Y	N	Y	Y
33 Roybal-Allard	N	Y	Y	Y	N	Y	Y
34 Torres	N	Y	?	?	?	?	?
35 Waters	N	Y	Y	Y	P	Y	Y
36 Harman	Y	Y	?	?	?	?	?
37 Millender-McD.	N	Y	Y	Y	N	Y	Y

	24	25	26	27	28	29	30
38 *Horn*	Y	Y	Y	Y	N	N	N
39 *Royce*	N	Y	N	N	N	N	N
40 *Lewis*	N	Y	Y	N	N	N	N
41 *Kim*	Y	Y	Y	N	N	Y	Y
42 Brown	N	Y	Y	Y	N	Y	Y
43 *Calvert*	N	Y	Y	N	N	N	N
44 Vacant							
45 *Rohrabacher*	N	Y	Y	N	N	N	N
46 Sanchez	Y	Y	Y	Y	N	N	N
47 *Cox*	N	Y	N	Y	N	N	N
48 *Packard*	Y	Y	Y	Y	N	N	N
49 *Bilbray*	Y	Y	Y	Y	N	N	N
50 Filner	N	Y	Y	Y	N	Y	Y
51 *Cunningham*	Y	Y	Y	Y	N	N	N
52 *Hunter*	Y	Y	Y	Y	N	N	Y
COLORADO							
1 DeGette	N	Y	Y	Y	N	Y	Y
2 Skaggs	N	Y	Y	Y	N	Y	Y
3 *McInnis*	Y	Y	?	Y	N	Y	Y
4 *Schaffer*	Y	Y	Y	N	N	N	Y
5 *Hefley*	Y	Y	Y	N	N	N	N
6 *Schaefer*	Y	Y	Y	Y	N	N	N
CONNECTICUT							
1 Kennelly	N	Y	Y	Y	N	Y	Y
2 Gejdenson	N	Y	Y	Y	N	Y	Y
3 DeLauro	N	Y	Y	Y	N	Y	Y
4 *Shays*	Y	Y	Y	Y	N	N	N
5 Maloney	N	Y	?	Y	N	Y	Y
6 *Johnson*	Y	Y	Y	Y	N	N	N
DELAWARE							
AL *Castle*	Y	Y	Y	Y	N	Y	Y
FLORIDA							
1 *Scarborough*	N	?	?	?	N	N	N
2 Boyd	Y	Y	Y	Y	N	Y	Y
3 Brown	−	?	Y	Y	N	Y	Y
4 *Fowler*	Y	Y	Y	Y	N	Y	Y
5 Thurman	N	Y	Y	Y	N	Y	Y
6 *Stearns*	Y	Y	Y	Y	N	N	N
7 *Mica*	+	Y	Y	Y	N	N	N
8 *McCollum*	Y	Y	Y	Y	N	Y	Y
9 *Bilirakis*	Y	Y	Y	Y	N	N	N
10 *Young*	Y	Y	Y	Y	N	N	N
11 Davis	Y	Y	Y	Y	N	Y	Y
12 *Canady*	Y	Y	Y	Y	N	N	Y
13 *Miller*	Y	N	Y	N	N	N	N
14 *Goss*	Y	Y	Y	Y	N	N	N
15 *Weldon*	Y	Y	Y	N	N	N	N
16 *Foley*	Y	Y	Y	Y	N	N	N
17 Meek	N	Y	Y	Y	N	Y	Y
18 *Ros-Lehtinen*	Y	Y	?	Y	N	Y	Y
19 Wexler	N	Y	Y	Y	N	Y	Y
20 Deutsch	N	Y	Y	Y	N	Y	Y
21 *Diaz-Balart*	Y	Y	N	Y	N	Y	Y
22 *Shaw*	Y	Y	Y	Y	N	Y	Y
23 Hastings	N	Y	Y	Y	N	Y	Y
GEORGIA							
1 *Kingston*	N	Y	Y	N	N	N	N
2 Bishop	Y	Y	Y	Y	N	Y	Y
3 *Collins*	Y	Y	Y	Y	N	N	N
4 *McKinney*	N	Y	Y	Y	Y	Y	Y
5 Lewis	N	Y	Y	Y	N	Y	Y
6 *Gingrich*							
7 *Barr*	N	Y	Y	N	N	N	N
8 *Chambliss*	Y	Y	Y	N	N	N	N
9 *Deal*	Y	Y	Y	Y	N	Y	Y
10 *Norwood*	Y	Y	Y	N	N	N	N
11 *Linder*	Y	Y	Y	Y	N	N	N
HAWAII							
1 Abercrombie	N	Y	Y	Y	N	Y	Y
2 Mink	N	Y	Y	Y	N	Y	Y
IDAHO							
1 *Chenoweth*	Y	Y	N	?	N	N	N
2 *Crapo*	Y	Y	Y	Y	N	N	N
ILLINOIS							
1 Rush	N	Y	?	Y	Y	Y	Y
2 Jackson	N	Y	Y	Y	N	Y	Y
3 Lipinski	N	Y	Y	Y	N	N	N
4 Gutierrez	N	Y	Y	Y	Y	Y	Y
5 Blagojevich	N	Y	Y	Y	N	Y	Y
6 *Hyde*	Y	Y	Y	Y	N	N	N
7 Davis	N	Y	Y	Y	N	Y	Y
8 *Crane*	Y	N	N	N	N	N	N
9 Yates	N	Y	Y	Y	N	Y	Y
10 *Porter*	Y	Y	Y	Y	N	Y	Y
11 *Weller*	Y	Y	Y	Y	N	N	N
12 Costello	N	Y	N	N	N	Y	Y

ND Northern Democrats   SD Southern Democrats

	24	25	26	27	28	29	30
13 ***Fawell***	Y	Y	Y	Y	N	N	N
14 ***Hastert***	Y	Y	Y	Y	N	N	N
15 ***Ewing***	Y	Y	Y	?	N	N	Y
16 ***Manzullo***	Y	Y	N	Y	N	N	N
17 Evans	N	Y	Y	Y	N	Y	Y
18 ***LaHood***	Y	Y	Y	N	N	N	N
19 Poshard	?	?	?	?	?	?	?
20 ***Shimkus***	Y	Y	?	?	?	?	?
INDIANA							
1 Visclosky	N	Y	Y	Y	N	Y	Y
2 ***McIntosh***	Y	Y	N	Y	N	N	N
3 Roemer	Y	Y	Y	Y	N	Y	Y
4 ***Souder***	Y	Y	Y	Y	N	N	N
5 ***Buyer***	Y	Y	Y	Y	N	Y	Y
6 ***Burton***	N	Y	Y	Y	N	Y	Y
7 ***Pease***	Y	Y	Y	Y	N	N	Y
8 ***Hostettler***	N	Y	N	Y	N	Y	Y
9 Hamilton	Y	Y	Y	Y	N	Y	Y
10 Carson	N	Y	Y	N	N	Y	Y
IOWA							
1 ***Leach***	Y	Y	Y	Y	N	Y	Y
2 ***Nussle***	Y	Y	Y	Y	N	N	Y
3 Boswell	Y	Y	Y	Y	N	Y	Y
4 ***Ganske***	Y	Y	Y	Y	N	N	N
5 ***Latham***	Y	Y	Y	N	N	N	N
KANSAS							
1 ***Moran***	Y	Y	Y	Y	N	N	Y
2 ***Ryun***	Y	Y	N	Y	N	N	Y
3 ***Snowbarger***	Y	Y	Y	Y	N	N	N
4 ***Tiahrt***	Y	Y	Y	+	N	N	N
KENTUCKY							
1 ***Whitfield***	Y	Y	Y	N	N	N	N
2 ***Lewis***	Y	Y	Y	N	N	N	N
3 ***Northup***	Y	+	Y	Y	N	N	Y
4 ***Bunning***	N	Y	Y	Y	N	N	N
5 ***Rogers***	Y	Y	Y	N	N	N	N
6 Baesler	N	Y	Y	Y	N	N	N
LOUISIANA							
1 ***Livingston***	Y	Y	Y	Y	N	N	N
2 Jefferson	N	Y	Y	Y	N	Y	Y
3 ***Tauzin***	Y	Y	Y	Y	N	Y	Y
4 ***McCrery***	Y	Y	Y	Y	N	N	Y
5 ***Cooksey***	Y	Y	Y	Y	N	N	N
6 ***Baker***	Y	Y	Y	Y	N	N	N
7 John	Y	Y	Y	Y	N	Y	Y
MAINE							
1 Allen	N	Y	Y	Y	N	Y	Y
2 Baldacci	N	Y	Y	Y	N	Y	Y
MARYLAND							
1 ***Gilchrest***	Y	Y	Y	Y	N	Y	Y
2 ***Ehrlich***	Y	Y	Y	Y	N	Y	Y
3 Cardin	Y	Y	Y	Y	N	Y	Y
4 Wynn	N	Y	Y	Y	N	Y	Y
5 Hoyer	Y	Y	Y	Y	N	Y	Y
6 ***Bartlett***	Y	Y	Y	Y	N	N	N
7 Cummings	N	Y	Y	Y	N	Y	Y
8 ***Morella***	Y	Y	Y	Y	N	Y	Y
MASSACHUSETTS							
1 Olver	N	Y	Y	Y	N	Y	Y
2 Neal	N	Y	?	Y	N	Y	Y
3 McGovern	N	Y	Y	Y	N	Y	Y
4 Frank	N	Y	Y	?	N	Y	Y
5 Meehan	N	Y	Y	Y	N	Y	Y
6 Tierney	N	Y	Y	Y	N	Y	Y
7 Markey	N	Y	Y	Y	N	Y	Y
8 Kennedy	N	Y	Y	Y	Y	Y	Y
9 Moakley	N	Y	Y	Y	N	Y	Y
10 Delahunt	N	Y	Y	Y	N	Y	Y
MICHIGAN							
1 Stupak	N	Y	Y	Y	N	Y	Y
2 ***Hoekstra***	Y	Y	Y	Y	N	N	N
3 ***Ehlers***	Y	Y	Y	Y	N	Y	Y
4 ***Camp***	Y	Y	Y	Y	N	Y	Y
5 Barcia	N	Y	Y	Y	N	Y	Y
6 ***Upton***	Y	Y	Y	Y	N	N	N
7 ***Smith***	Y	Y	Y	Y	N	N	N
8 Stabenow	N	Y	Y	Y	N	Y	Y
9 Kildee	N	Y	Y	Y	N	Y	Y
10 Bonior	N	Y	Y	Y	N	Y	Y
11 ***Knollenberg***	Y	Y	Y	Y	N	N	N
12 Levin	N	Y	Y	Y	N	Y	Y
13 Rivers	N	Y	N	Y	N	Y	Y
14 Conyers	N	Y	Y	Y	Y	N	N
15 Kilpatrick	N	Y	Y	Y	–	+	+
16 Dingell	N	Y	Y	Y	N	Y	Y
MINNESOTA							
1 ***Gutknecht***	Y	Y	+	Y	N	N	N
2 Minge	Y	Y	Y	Y	N	Y	Y
3 ***Ramstad***	Y	Y	Y	Y	N	N	Y
4 Vento	N	Y	Y	Y	N	Y	Y
5 Sabo	N	Y	Y	Y	N	Y	Y
6 Luther	+	+	+	+	–	+	+
7 Peterson	Y	Y	Y	Y	N	Y	Y
8 Oberstar	N	Y	Y	Y	N	Y	Y
MISSISSIPPI							
1 ***Wicker***	Y	Y	Y	N	N	N	N
2 Thompson	N	Y	Y	Y	N	Y	Y
3 ***Pickering***	Y	Y	Y	Y	N	N	Y
4 ***Parker***	Y	Y	Y	Y	N	N	N
5 Taylor	Y	Y	Y	Y	N	Y	Y
MISSOURI							
1 Clay	N	Y	Y	Y	N	Y	Y
2 ***Talent***	Y	Y	Y	Y	N	N	N
3 Gephardt	N	Y	Y	Y	N	Y	Y
4 Skelton	Y	Y	Y	Y	N	Y	Y
5 McCarthy	N	Y	Y	Y	N	Y	Y
6 Danner	Y	Y	Y	Y	N	Y	Y
7 ***Blunt***	Y	Y	Y	Y	N	N	N
8 ***Emerson***	Y	Y	Y	N	N	N	N
9 ***Hulshof***	Y	Y	Y	Y	N	Y	Y
MONTANA							
AL ***Hill***	Y	Y	Y	Y	N	N	N
NEBRASKA							
1 ***Bereuter***	Y	Y	Y	Y	N	N	Y
2 ***Christensen***	Y	Y	?	Y	N	N	Y
3 ***Barrett***	Y	Y	Y	Y	N	N	Y
NEVADA							
1 ***Ensign***	N	Y	Y	Y	N	Y	Y
2 ***Gibbons***	Y	Y	Y	?	N	Y	Y
NEW HAMPSHIRE							
1 ***Sununu***	Y	Y	Y	Y	N	N	N
2 ***Bass***	Y	Y	Y	Y	N	N	N
NEW JERSEY							
1 Andrews	N	Y	Y	Y	N	Y	Y
2 ***LoBiondo***	N	Y	Y	Y	N	N	N
3 ***Saxton***	Y	Y	Y	Y	N	Y	Y
4 ***Smith***	?	Y	Y	Y	N	Y	Y
5 ***Roukema***	Y	Y	?	Y	N	N	N
6 Pallone	N	Y	Y	Y	N	Y	Y
7 ***Franks***	Y	Y	Y	Y	N	N	N
8 Pascrell	Y	Y	Y	Y	N	Y	Y
9 Rothman	N	Y	Y	Y	N	Y	Y
10 Payne	N	Y	Y	Y	Y	Y	Y
11 ***Frelinghuysen***	Y	Y	Y	Y	N	N	N
12 ***Pappas***	Y	Y	Y	Y	N	N	N
13 Menendez	N	Y	Y	Y	N	N	N
NEW MEXICO							
1 ***Schiff***	?	?	?	?	?	?	?
2 ***Skeen***	Y	Y	Y	Y	N	Y	Y
3 ***Redmond***	Y	Y	Y	Y	N	Y	Y
NEW YORK							
1 ***Forbes***	Y	Y	Y	Y	N	Y	Y
2 ***Lazio***	Y	Y	Y	Y	N	Y	Y
3 ***King***	Y	Y	Y	Y	N	N	Y
4 McCarthy	Y	Y	Y	Y	N	Y	Y
5 Ackerman	N	Y	Y	Y	N	Y	Y
6 Meeks	N	Y	Y	Y	Y	Y	Y
7 Manton	N	Y	Y	Y	N	Y	Y
8 Nadler	N	Y	Y	Y	N	Y	Y
9 Schumer	N	Y	Y	Y	–	+	–
10 Towns	N	Y	Y	?	Y	N	N
11 Owens	N	Y	Y	Y	Y	Y	Y
12 Velázquez	N	Y	Y	Y	Y	N	N
13 ***Fossella***	N	Y	Y	Y	N	N	Y
14 Maloney	N	Y	Y	Y	N	Y	Y
15 Rangel	N	Y	Y	Y	N	Y	Y
16 Serrano	N	Y	Y	Y	Y	Y	Y
17 Engel	N	Y	Y	Y	N	Y	Y
18 Lowey	N	Y	Y	Y	N	Y	Y
19 ***Kelly***	Y	Y	Y	Y	N	Y	Y
20 ***Gilman***	Y	Y	Y	Y	N	Y	Y
21 McNulty	N	Y	Y	Y	N	Y	Y
22 ***Solomon***	Y	Y	Y	Y	N	N	N
23 ***Boehlert***	Y	Y	Y	Y	N	Y	Y
24 ***McHugh***	Y	Y	Y	Y	N	N	Y
25 ***Walsh***	Y	Y	Y	Y	N	Y	Y
26 Hinchey	N	Y	Y	Y	N	Y	Y
27 ***Paxon***	?	Y	Y	Y	N	N	N
28 Slaughter	N	Y	Y	Y	N	Y	Y
29 LaFalce	N	Y	Y	Y	N	Y	Y
30 ***Quinn***	N	Y	Y	Y	N	N	Y
31 ***Houghton***	Y	Y	Y	Y	N	Y	Y
NORTH CAROLINA							
1 Clayton	N	Y	Y	Y	N	Y	Y
2 Etheridge	N	Y	Y	Y	N	Y	Y
3 ***Jones***	Y	Y	N	N	N	N	N
4 Price	N	Y	Y	Y	N	Y	Y
5 ***Burr***	Y	Y	Y	Y	N	N	N
6 ***Coble***	Y	Y	N	Y	N	N	N
7 McIntyre	N	Y	Y	Y	N	Y	Y
8 Hefner	N	Y	?	Y	N	Y	Y
9 ***Myrick***	Y	Y	Y	Y	N	N	N
10 ***Ballenger***	Y	Y	Y	Y	N	Y	Y
11 ***Taylor***	Y	Y	Y	Y	N	N	N
12 Watt	N	Y	Y	Y	N	Y	Y
NORTH DAKOTA							
AL Pomeroy	N	Y	Y	Y	N	Y	Y
OHIO							
1 ***Chabot***	Y	Y	Y	N	N	N	N
2 ***Portman***	N	Y	Y	Y	N	Y	Y
3 Hall	Y	Y	Y	Y	N	Y	Y
4 ***Oxley***	Y	Y	Y	Y	N	Y	Y
5 ***Gillmor***	Y	Y	Y	Y	N	N	Y
6 Strickland	Y	Y	Y	Y	N	Y	Y
7 ***Hobson***	Y	Y	Y	Y	N	N	N
8 ***Boehner***	Y	Y	Y	Y	N	N	N
9 Kaptur	N	Y	Y	Y	N	Y	Y
10 Kucinich	N	Y	Y	Y	N	Y	Y
11 Stokes	N	Y	Y	Y	N	Y	Y
12 ***Kasich***	Y	Y	Y	Y	N	N	N
13 Brown	N	Y	Y	Y	N	Y	Y
14 Sawyer	N	Y	N	Y	N	Y	Y
15 ***Pryce***	Y	Y	Y	Y	N	N	N
16 ***Regula***	Y	Y	Y	N	N	N	N
17 Traficant	Y	Y	Y	Y	N	N	N
18 ***Ney***	Y	Y	Y	Y	N	N	N
19 ***LaTourette***	Y	Y	Y	Y	N	N	N
OKLAHOMA							
1 ***Largent***	Y	Y	Y	Y	N	N	N
2 ***Coburn***	Y	Y	Y	Y	N	N	N
3 ***Watkins***	Y	Y	Y	Y	N	N	N
4 ***Watts***	Y	Y	Y	Y	N	N	N
5 ***Istook***	Y	Y	Y	N	N	N	Y
6 ***Lucas***	Y	Y	Y	Y	N	N	Y
OREGON							
1 Furse	Y	Y	Y	Y	N	Y	?
2 ***Smith***	Y	Y	Y	Y	N	N	N
3 Blumenauer	N	Y	N	Y	N	Y	N
4 DeFazio	Y	Y	N	Y	N	Y	Y
5 Hooley	N	Y	Y	Y	N	Y	Y
PENNSYLVANIA							
1 Vacant							
2 Fattah	N	?	Y	Y	N	Y	Y
3 Borski	N	Y	Y	Y	N	Y	Y
4 Klink	?	?	Y	Y	N	Y	Y
5 ***Peterson***	Y	Y	Y	Y	N	N	Y
6 Holden	Y	Y	Y	Y	N	N	Y
7 ***Weldon***	Y	Y	Y	Y	N	N	N
8 ***Greenwood***	Y	Y	Y	Y	N	Y	Y
9 ***Shuster***	Y	Y	Y	Y	N	N	N
10 ***McDade***	N	Y	Y	Y	N	N	Y
11 Kanjorski	N	Y	Y	Y	N	Y	Y
12 Murtha	Y	Y	Y	Y	N	Y	Y
13 ***Fox***	Y	Y	Y	Y	N	Y	Y
14 Coyne	N	Y	Y	Y	N	Y	Y
15 McHale	N	Y	Y	Y	N	Y	Y
16 ***Pitts***	Y	Y	Y	Y	N	N	N
17 ***Gekas***	Y	Y	Y	Y	N	N	Y
18 Doyle	Y	Y	Y	Y	N	Y	Y
19 ***Goodling***	Y	Y	Y	N	N	N	N
20 Mascara	N	Y	Y	Y	N	Y	Y
21 ***English***	Y	Y	Y	Y	N	Y	Y
RHODE ISLAND							
1 Kennedy	N	Y	Y	?	N	Y	Y
2 Weygand	N	Y	Y	Y	N	Y	Y
SOUTH CAROLINA							
1 ***Sanford***	Y	Y	Y	Y	N	N	N
2 ***Spence***	Y	Y	Y	N	N	N	N
3 ***Graham***	Y	Y	Y	N	N	N	N
4 ***Inglis***	Y	Y	Y	Y	N	N	N
5 Spratt	N	Y	Y	Y	N	Y	Y
6 Clyburn	N	Y	Y	Y	N	Y	Y
SOUTH DAKOTA							
AL ***Thune***	Y	Y	Y	Y	N	N	N
TENNESSEE							
1 ***Jenkins***	Y	Y	Y	N	N	N	Y
2 ***Duncan***	Y	Y	N	N	N	N	Y
3 ***Wamp***	N	Y	N	N	N	N	Y
4 ***Hilleary***	Y	Y	Y	N	N	N	N
5 Clement	Y	Y	Y	Y	N	Y	Y
6 Gordon	?	Y	Y	Y	N	Y	Y
7 ***Bryant***	Y	Y	Y	N	N	N	N
8 Tanner	Y	Y	Y	Y	N	Y	Y
9 Ford	?	?	Y	Y	N	Y	Y
TEXAS							
1 Sandlin	Y	Y	Y	Y	N	Y	Y
2 Turner	Y	Y	Y	Y	N	Y	Y
3 ***Johnson, Sam***	Y	Y	Y	Y	N	N	N
4 Hall	Y	Y	Y	N	N	N	N
5 ***Sessions***	Y	Y	Y	N	N	N	N
6 ***Barton***	Y	Y	Y	Y	N	Y	Y
7 ***Archer***	Y	Y	Y	N	N	N	N
8 ***Brady***	Y	Y	Y	Y	N	N	N
9 Lampson	N	Y	Y	Y	N	Y	Y
10 Doggett	N	Y	Y	Y	N	Y	Y
11 Edwards	N	Y	Y	Y	N	Y	Y
12 ***Granger***	Y	Y	Y	Y	N	Y	Y
13 ***Thornberry***	Y	Y	Y	Y	N	Y	Y
14 ***Paul***	Y	N	N	Y	N	N	N
15 Hinojosa	N	Y	Y	Y	N	Y	Y
16 Reyes	N	Y	Y	Y	N	Y	Y
17 Stenholm	Y	Y	Y	Y	N	N	N
18 Jackson-Lee	N	Y	Y	Y	N	Y	Y
19 ***Combest***	Y	Y	Y	Y	N	N	N
20 Gonzalez	?	?	?	?	?	?	?
21 ***Smith***	Y	Y	Y	Y	N	N	Y
22 ***DeLay***	N	Y	N	Y	N	N	N
23 ***Bonilla***	Y	Y	Y	Y	N	Y	Y
24 Frost	N	Y	Y	Y	N	Y	Y
25 Bentsen	Y	Y	Y	Y	N	Y	Y
26 ***Armey***	Y	Y	Y	Y	N	N	N
27 Ortiz	Y	Y	Y	Y	N	Y	Y
28 Rodriguez	N	Y	Y	Y	N	Y	Y
29 Green	N	Y	Y	Y	N	Y	Y
30 Johnson, E.B.	N	Y	Y	Y	N	Y	Y
UTAH							
1 ***Hansen***	Y	Y	Y	Y	N	Y	Y
2 ***Cook***	Y	Y	Y	Y	N	Y	Y
3 ***Cannon***	Y	Y	N	Y	N	Y	Y
VERMONT							
AL *Sanders*	N	?	Y	Y	N	Y	Y
VIRGINIA							
1 ***Bateman***	Y	Y	Y	Y	N	N	N
2 Pickett	Y	Y	Y	Y	N	N	N
3 Scott	N	Y	Y	Y	N	Y	N
4 Sisisky	Y	Y	Y	Y	N	N	N
5 Goode	Y	Y	Y	N	N	N	N
6 ***Goodlatte***	Y	Y	Y	Y	N	N	N
7 ***Bliley***	Y	Y	Y	Y	N	N	N
8 Moran	Y	Y	Y	Y	N	Y	Y
9 Boucher	Y	Y	Y	Y	N	Y	Y
10 ***Wolf***	Y	Y	Y	Y	N	N	N
11 ***Davis***	Y	Y	Y	Y	N	N	N
WASHINGTON							
1 ***White***	Y	Y	?	Y	N	N	N
2 ***Metcalf***	Y	Y	Y	Y	N	N	N
3 ***Smith, Linda***	Y	Y	?	N	N	N	N
4 ***Hastings***	Y	?	Y	Y	N	N	N
5 ***Nethercutt***	Y	Y	Y	Y	N	N	N
6 Dicks	N	Y	Y	Y	N	Y	Y
7 McDermott	N	Y	Y	Y	N	Y	Y
8 ***Dunn***	Y	Y	Y	Y	N	N	N
9 Smith, Adam	Y	Y	Y	Y	N	Y	Y
WEST VIRGINIA							
1 Mollohan	N	Y	Y	Y	N	Y	Y
2 Wise	N	Y	Y	Y	N	Y	Y
3 Rahall	N	Y	Y	Y	N	Y	Y
WISCONSIN							
1 ***Neumann***	Y	Y	Y	Y	N	N	N
2 ***Klug***	Y	Y	Y	Y	N	Y	Y
3 Kind	N	Y	Y	Y	N	Y	Y
4 Kleczka	N	Y	Y	Y	N	Y	Y
5 Barrett	N	Y	Y	Y	N	Y	Y
6 ***Petri***	Y	Y	Y	N	N	N	N
7 Obey	N	Y	Y	N	N	Y	Y
8 Johnson	N	Y	Y	Y	N	Y	Y
9 ***Sensenbrenner***	Y	Y	N	N	N	N	N
WYOMING							
AL ***Cubin***	Y	Y	Y	Y	N	N	N

Southern states - Ala., Ark., Fla., Ga., Ky., La., Miss., N.C., Okla., S.C., Tenn., Texas, Va.

House Votes 32, 33, 34, 35, 36, 37, 38 *

Key

- **Y** Voted for (yea).
- **#** Paired for.
- **+** Announced for.
- **N** Voted against (nay).
- **X** Paired against.
- **−** Announced against.
- **P** Voted "present."
- **C** Voted "present" to avoid possible conflict of interest.
- **?** Did not vote or otherwise make a position known.

Democrats   **Republicans**   *Independent*

31. Quorum Call.* 405 Responded. March 4, 1998.

32. HR 856. Puerto Rico Political Status/Voter Eligibility. Serrano, D-N.Y., amendment to permit individuals who were born in Puerto Rico, but who do not currently reside on the island, to vote in the referenda authorized by the bill. Rejected 57-356: R 9-208; D 47-148 (ND 42-99, SD 5-49); I 1-0. March 4, 1998.

33. HR 856. Puerto Rico Political Status/Second Referendum. Stearns, R-Fla., amendment to strike the provision authorizing a referendum every 10 years if the voters fail to approve statehood or independence by a majority, and instead authorize a second referendum no later than 90 days after the initial ballot to vote on the two status options that received the most votes in the first referendum. Rejected 28-384: R 26-190; D 2-193 (ND 2-139, SD 0-54); I 0-1. March 4, 1998.

34. HR 856. Puerto Rico Political Status/Supermajority. Barr, R-Ga., amendment to require a 75 percent supermajority in the third referendum that would be held to approve or disapprove a statehood or independence plan enacted by Congress. Rejected 131-282: R 124-95; D 7-186 (ND 3-137, SD 4-49); I 0-1. March 4, 1998.

35. HR 856. Puerto Rico Political Status/Olympics. Gutierrez, D-Ill., amendment to permit Puerto Rico to compete as an independent nation in the Olympics even if it becomes a state. Rejected 2-413: R 0-219; D 2-193 (ND 2-139, SD 0-54); I 0-1. March 4, 1998.

36. HR 856. Puerto Rico Political Status/English Language. Separate vote at the request of Solomon, R-N.Y., on the Solomon amendment, as amended, to treat Puerto Rico the same as the states with regard to language, recognizing the primary role of English in national affairs, but not preclude the use of other languages in government functions when appropriate. Adopted 240-177: R 56-164; D 183-13 (ND 135-7, SD 48-6); I 1-0. March 4, 1998.

37. HR 856. Puerto Rico Political Status/Passage. Passage of the bill to establish a process for determining and implementing a permanent political status for Puerto Rico, including referenda in Puerto Rico and subsequent action by Congress. Passed 209-208: R 43-177; D 165-31 (ND 121-21, SD 44-10); I 1-0. March 4, 1998. A "yea" was a vote in support of the president's position.

38. HR 2369. Wireless Privacy/Passage. Passage of the bill to require the Federal Communications Commission to step up enforcement against violators of wireless telephone privacy, and make illegal any modification of scanners to receive private wireless communications. Passed 414-1: R 219-1; D 194-0 (ND 143-0, SD 51-0); I 1-0. March 5, 1998. A "yea" was a vote in support of the president's position.

* CQ does not include quorum calls in its vote charts.

	32	33	34	35	36	37	38
ALABAMA							
1 Callahan	N	N	Y	N	N	N	Y
2 Everett	N	N	Y	N	N	N	Y
3 Riley	N	N	N	N	N	N	Y
4 Aderholt	N	N	Y	N	N	N	Y
5 Cramer	N	N	N	N	Y	N	Y
6 Bachus	N	Y	N	N	N	N	Y
7 Hilliard	N	N	N	Y	Y	Y	Y
ALASKA							
AL Young	Y	N	N	N	Y	Y	Y
ARIZONA							
1 Salmon	N	N	Y	N	N	N	Y
2 Pastor	Y	N	N	N	Y	Y	Y
3 Stump	N	N	Y	N	N	N	Y
4 Shadegg	N	Y	N	N	N	N	Y
5 Kolbe	N	N	N	N	Y	Y	Y
6 Hayworth	N	N	Y	N	N	N	Y
ARKANSAS							
1 Berry	N	N	N	N	Y	N	Y
2 Snyder	N	N	N	N	Y	Y	Y
3 Hutchinson	N	N	N	N	N	N	Y
4 Dickey	N	N	Y	N	N	N	Y
CALIFORNIA							
1 Riggs	N	?	?	?	?	X	Y
2 Herger	N	Y	Y	N	N	N	Y
3 Fazio	N	N	N	N	Y	Y	Y
4 Doolittle	?	?	?	?	?	?	?
5 Matsui	N	N	N	N	Y	Y	Y
6 Woolsey	N	N	N	N	Y	Y	Y
7 Miller	Y	N	N	N	N	Y	Y
8 Pelosi	N	N	N	N	Y	Y	Y
9 Vacant							
10 Tauscher	N	N	N	N	Y	Y	Y
11 Pombo	N	N	N	N	N	N	Y
12 Lantos	N	N	N	N	Y	Y	Y
13 Stark	N	N	N	N	Y	Y	Y
14 Eshoo	N	N	N	N	Y	Y	Y
15 Campbell	N	Y	N	N	Y	Y	Y
16 Lofgren	N	N	N	N	Y	Y	+
17 Farr	N	N	?	N	Y	Y	Y
18 Condit	N	N	N	N	Y	N	Y
19 Radanovich	N	Y	N	N	Y	N	Y
20 Dooley	N	N	N	N	Y	Y	Y
21 Thomas	N	N	N	N	N	N	Y
22 Vacant							
23 Gallegly	N	N	N	N	Y	Y	Y
24 Sherman	N	Y	Y	N	Y	Y	Y
25 McKeon	N	N	N	N	Y	Y	Y
26 Berman	N	?	?	?	?	?	Y
27 Rogan	N	Y	N	N	N	N	Y
28 Dreier	N	N	N	N	N	N	Y
29 Waxman	N	N	N	N	Y	Y	Y
30 Becerra	N	N	N	N	N	Y	Y
31 Martinez	N	N	N	N	N	Y	Y
32 Dixon	N	N	N	N	Y	Y	Y
33 Roybal-Allard	N	N	N	N	Y	Y	Y
34 Torres	?	?	?	?	?	?	Y
35 Waters	Y	N	N	P	N	Y	Y
36 Harman	?	?	?	?	?	?	?
37 Millender-McD.	N	N	N	N	Y	Y	Y

	32	33	34	35	36	37	38
38 Horn	N	Y	Y	N	N	N	Y
39 Royce	N	N	Y	N	N	N	Y
40 Lewis	N	N	N	N	N	N	Y
41 Kim	N	N	N	N	Y	Y	Y
42 Brown	Y	N	N	N	Y	Y	Y
43 Calvert	N	N	N	N	Y	N	Y
44 Vacant							
45 Rohrabacher	Y	Y	Y	N	N	N	Y
46 Sanchez	N	N	N	Y	Y	Y	Y
47 Cox	Y	N	N	N	N	N	Y
48 Packard	N	N	N	N	Y	N	Y
49 Bilbray	N	?	N	N	Y	Y	Y
50 Filner	N	N	N	N	Y	Y	Y
51 Cunningham	N	N	Y	N	N	N	Y
52 Hunter	N	Y	Y	N	N	N	Y
COLORADO							
1 DeGette	N	N	N	N	Y	Y	Y
2 Skaggs	N	N	N	N	Y	Y	−
3 McInnis	N	N	N	N	Y	N	−
4 Schaffer	N	Y	Y	N	N	N	−
5 Hefley	N	N	N	N	N	N	−
6 Schaefer	?	?	?	?	?	?	Y
CONNECTICUT							
1 Kennelly	Y	N	N	N	Y	Y	Y
2 Gejdenson	Y	N	N	N	Y	Y	Y
3 DeLauro	Y	N	N	N	Y	Y	Y
4 Shays	Y	N	Y	N	N	N	Y
5 Maloney	Y	N	N	N	Y	Y	Y
6 Johnson	Y	N	N	N	Y	N	Y
DELAWARE							
AL Castle	N	N	Y	N	Y	N	Y
FLORIDA							
1 Scarborough	N	N	Y	N	N	N	Y
2 Boyd	N	N	N	N	Y	Y	Y
3 Brown	N	N	N	N	Y	Y	Y
4 Fowler	N	Y	Y	N	N	N	Y
5 Thurman	N	N	N	N	Y	Y	Y
6 Stearns	N	Y	N	N	N	N	Y
7 Mica	N	N	N	N	Y	Y	Y
8 McCollum	N	N	N	N	N	N	Y
9 Bilirakis	N	N	N	N	N	N	Y
10 Young	N	N	N	N	N	N	Y
11 Davis	N	N	N	N	Y	Y	Y
12 Canady	N	N	N	N	N	N	Y
13 Miller	N	Y	N	N	N	N	Y
14 Goss	N	N	N	N	N	N	Y
15 Weldon	N	N	N	N	N	N	Y
16 Foley	N	?	N	N	Y	Y	Y
17 Meek	N	N	N	N	Y	Y	Y
18 Ros-Lehtinen	Y	N	N	N	Y	Y	+
19 Wexler	N	N	N	N	Y	Y	Y
20 Deutsch	N	N	N	N	Y	Y	Y
21 Diaz-Balart	Y	N	N	N	Y	Y	Y
22 Shaw	N	N	Y	N	N	N	Y
23 Hastings	N	N	N	N	Y	Y	Y
GEORGIA							
1 Kingston	N	Y	Y	N	N	N	Y
2 Bishop	N	N	N	N	Y	Y	Y
3 Collins	N	N	N	N	Y	Y	Y
4 McKinney	Y	N	N	N	Y	Y	Y
5 Lewis	Y	N	N	N	Y	Y	Y
6 Gingrich							
7 Barr	N	N	Y	N	N	N	Y
8 Chambliss	N	N	N	N	N	N	Y
9 Deal	N	N	N	N	N	N	Y
10 Norwood	N	N	Y	N	N	N	Y
11 Linder	N	Y	N	N	N	N	Y
HAWAII							
1 Abercrombie	N	N	N	N	Y	Y	Y
2 Mink	N	N	N	N	Y	Y	Y
IDAHO							
1 Chenoweth	N	N	Y	N	N	N	Y
2 Crapo	N	N	Y	N	N	N	Y
ILLINOIS							
1 Rush	Y	N	N	Y	N	Y	Y
2 Jackson	Y	N	N	N	Y	Y	Y
3 Lipinski	Y	N	N	N	N	N	Y
4 Gutierrez	Y	N	N	Y	N	N	Y
5 Blagojevich	Y	N	N	N	Y	Y	Y
6 Hyde	N	N	N	N	Y	N	Y
7 Davis	Y	N	N	N	Y	N	Y
8 Crane	N	N	N	N	N	N	Y
9 Yates	N	?	?	?	?	?	Y
10 Porter	N	N	N	N	Y	Y	Y
11 Weller	Y	N	N	N	N	N	Y
12 Costello	N	N	N	N	Y	N	Y

ND Northern Democrats   SD Southern Democrats

	32	33	34	35	36	37	38
13 *Fawell*	N	N	Y	N	N	N	Y
14 *Hastert*	N	N	N	N	N	N	Y
15 *Ewing*	N	N	Y	N	Y	N	Y
16 *Manzullo*	N	N	N	N	N	N	Y
17 Evans	N	N	N	N	Y	Y	Y
18 *LaHood*	N	N	N	N	N	N	Y
19 Poshard	?	?	?	?	?	?	?
20 *Shimkus*	?	?	?	?	?	?	?
INDIANA							
1 Visclosky	N	N	N	N	Y	Y	Y
2 *McIntosh*	N	Y	Y	N	N	N	Y
3 Roemer	N	N	N	N	Y	Y	Y
4 *Souder*	N	Y	Y	N	N	N	Y
5 *Buyer*	N	N	N	N	N	Y	Y
6 *Burton*	N	N	N	N	Y	Y	Y
7 *Pease*	N	N	Y	N	N	N	Y
8 *Hostettler*	N	N	Y	N	Y	N	Y
9 Hamilton	N	N	N	N	Y	Y	Y
10 Carson	Y	Y	N	N	Y	Y	Y
IOWA							
1 *Leach*	N	N	N	N	Y	Y	Y
2 *Nussle*	N	N	N	N	Y	N	Y
3 Boswell	N	N	N	N	Y	Y	Y
4 *Ganske*	N	N	N	N	N	N	Y
5 *Latham*	N	N	N	N	N	N	Y
KANSAS							
1 *Moran*	N	Y	N	N	N	N	Y
2 *Ryun*	N	N	Y	N	N	N	Y
3 *Snowbarger*	N	Y	Y	N	N	N	Y
4 *Tiahrt*	N	N	Y	N	N	N	Y
KENTUCKY							
1 *Whitfield*	N	N	N	N	N	N	Y
2 *Lewis*	N	N	Y	N	N	N	Y
3 *Northup*	N	N	Y	N	N	N	Y
4 *Bunning*	N	N	Y	N	N	N	Y
5 *Rogers*	N	N	Y	N	N	N	Y
6 Baesler	N	N	N	N	N	N	Y
LOUISIANA							
1 *Livingston*	N	N	Y	N	N	N	Y
2 Jefferson	Y	N	N	N	Y	Y	Y
3 *Tauzin*	N	N	N	N	Y	Y	Y
4 *McCrery*	N	N	Y	N	N	N	Y
5 *Cooksey*	N	N	N	N	N	Y	Y
6 *Baker*	N	N	N	N	N	N	Y
7 John	N	N	N	N	Y	Y	Y
MAINE							
1 Allen	N	N	N	N	Y	Y	Y
2 Baldacci	N	N	N	N	Y	Y	Y
MARYLAND							
1 *Gilchrest*	N	N	Y	N	Y	Y	Y
2 *Ehrlich*	N	N	N	N	Y	N	Y
3 Cardin	N	N	N	N	Y	Y	Y
4 Wynn	Y	N	N	N	Y	Y	Y
5 Hoyer	Y	N	N	N	Y	Y	Y
6 *Bartlett*	N	N	Y	N	N	N	Y
7 Cummings	N	N	N	N	Y	Y	Y
8 *Morella*	N	N	N	N	Y	Y	Y
MASSACHUSETTS							
1 Olver	Y	N	N	N	Y	Y	Y
2 Neal	Y	N	N	N	Y	Y	Y
3 McGovern	Y	N	N	N	Y	Y	Y
4 Frank	N	N	N	N	Y	Y	Y
5 Meehan	Y	N	N	N	Y	Y	Y
6 Tierney	Y	N	N	N	Y	Y	Y
7 Markey	Y	N	N	N	Y	Y	Y
8 Kennedy	Y	N	N	N	Y	Y	Y
9 Moakley	Y	N	N	N	Y	Y	Y
10 Delahunt	Y	N	N	N	Y	Y	Y
MICHIGAN							
1 Stupak	N	N	N	N	Y	Y	Y
2 *Hoekstra*	N	N	Y	N	N	N	Y
3 *Ehlers*	N	N	N	N	Y	Y	Y
4 *Camp*	N	N	N	N	N	N	Y
5 Barcia	N	N	N	N	Y	Y	Y
6 *Upton*	N	N	Y	N	N	N	Y
7 *Smith*	N	N	Y	N	N	N	Y
8 Stabenow	N	N	N	N	Y	N	Y
9 Kildee	N	N	N	N	Y	Y	Y
10 Bonior	Y	N	N	N	Y	Y	Y
11 *Knollenberg*	N	N	Y	N	N	N	Y
12 Levin	N	N	N	N	Y	Y	Y
13 Rivers	N	N	N	N	Y	N	Y
14 Conyers	N	N	N	N	Y	Y	Y
15 Kilpatrick	–	–	–	?	+	+	+
16 Dingell	?	N	N	N	Y	Y	Y

	32	33	34	35	36	37	38
MINNESOTA							
1 *Gutknecht*	N	N	Y	N	N	N	Y
2 Minge	N	N	N	N	Y	Y	Y
3 *Ramstad*	N	N	N	N	N	N	Y
4 Vento	N	N	N	N	Y	Y	Y
5 Sabo	N	N	N	N	Y	Y	Y
6 Luther	–	–	–	?	+	+	+
7 Peterson	N	N	N	N	Y	N	Y
8 Oberstar	N	N	N	N	Y	Y	Y
MISSISSIPPI							
1 *Wicker*	N	N	Y	N	N	N	Y
2 Thompson	N	N	N	N	Y	Y	Y
3 *Pickering*	N	N	N	N	N	N	Y
4 *Parker*	N	N	N	N	N	Y	Y
5 Taylor	N	N	N	N	Y	Y	Y
MISSOURI							
1 Clay	N	N	N	N	Y	Y	Y
2 *Talent*	N	N	N	N	N	N	Y
3 Gephardt	N	N	N	N	Y	Y	Y
4 Skelton	N	N	N	N	Y	N	Y
5 McCarthy	N	N	N	N	Y	Y	Y
6 Danner	N	N	Y	N	Y	N	Y
7 *Blunt*	N	N	N	N	N	N	Y
8 *Emerson*	N	N	Y	N	N	N	Y
9 *Hulshof*	N	N	N	N	Y	N	Y
MONTANA							
AL *Hill*	N	N	Y	N	N	N	Y
NEBRASKA							
1 *Bereuter*	N	N	Y	N	Y	N	Y
2 *Christensen*	N	N	Y	N	Y	N	Y
3 *Barrett*	N	N	Y	N	Y	N	Y
NEVADA							
1 *Ensign*	N	N	N	N	N	N	Y
2 *Gibbons*	N	N	Y	N	N	N	Y
NEW HAMPSHIRE							
1 *Sununu*	N	N	Y	N	N	N	Y
2 *Bass*	N	N	N	N	N	N	Y
NEW JERSEY							
1 Andrews	N	N	N	N	Y	Y	Y
2 *LoBiondo*	N	N	N	N	N	N	Y
3 *Saxton*	N	N	N	N	Y	Y	Y
4 *Smith*	N	N	N	N	Y	Y	Y
5 *Roukema*	N	N	N	N	N	N	Y
6 Pallone	Y	N	N	N	Y	Y	Y
7 *Franks*	?	N	N	N	N	Y	Y
8 Pascrell	N	N	N	N	Y	Y	Y
9 Rothman	N	N	N	N	Y	Y	Y
10 Payne	Y	N	N	N	Y	Y	Y
11 *Frelinghuysen*	N	N	N	N	Y	Y	Y
12 *Pappas*	N	N	N	N	N	N	Y
13 Menendez	Y	N	N	N	N	N	Y
NEW MEXICO							
1 *Schiff*	?	?	?	?	?	?	?
2 *Skeen*	N	N	N	N	Y	Y	Y
3 *Redmond*	N	N	N	N	Y	Y	Y
NEW YORK							
1 *Forbes*	N	N	N	N	Y	Y	Y
2 *Lazio*	N	N	Y	N	Y	Y	Y
3 *King*	N	N	N	N	Y	Y	Y
4 McCarthy	N	N	N	N	Y	Y	Y
5 Ackerman	Y	N	N	N	Y	Y	Y
6 Meeks	Y	N	N	N	Y	Y	Y
7 Manton	N	N	N	N	Y	Y	Y
8 Nadler	Y	N	N	N	Y	Y	Y
9 Schumer	+	N	N	N	Y	Y	Y
10 Towns	Y	N	N	N	N	N	Y
11 Owens	Y	N	N	N	Y	Y	Y
12 Velázquez	Y	N	N	Y	N	N	Y
13 *Fossella*	N	N	Y	N	Y	N	Y
14 Maloney	N	N	N	N	Y	Y	Y
15 Rangel	Y	N	N	N	Y	Y	Y
16 Serrano	Y	N	N	N	Y	Y	Y
17 Engel	Y	N	N	N	Y	Y	Y
18 Lowey	N	N	N	N	Y	Y	Y
19 *Kelly*	N	N	N	N	Y	Y	Y
20 *Gilman*	Y	N	N	N	Y	Y	Y
21 McNulty	Y	N	N	N	Y	Y	Y
22 *Solomon*	N	N	Y	N	N	N	Y
23 *Boehlert*	N	N	N	N	Y	Y	Y
24 *McHugh*	N	N	Y	N	Y	N	Y
25 *Walsh*	N	N	N	N	Y	Y	Y
26 Hinchey	Y	N	N	N	Y	Y	Y
27 *Paxon*	N	N	Y	N	N	N	Y
28 Slaughter	N	N	N	N	Y	Y	Y
29 LaFalce	N	N	N	N	Y	Y	Y

	32	33	34	35	36	37	38
30 *Quinn*	N	N	N	N	Y	Y	?
31 *Houghton*	N	N	N	N	Y	N	?
NORTH CAROLINA							
1 Clayton	N	N	N	N	Y	Y	Y
2 Etheridge	N	N	N	N	Y	Y	Y
3 *Jones*	N	Y	Y	N	N	N	Y
4 Price	N	N	N	N	Y	Y	Y
5 *Burr*	N	N	N	N	N	N	Y
6 *Coble*	N	N	Y	N	N	N	Y
7 McIntyre	N	N	N	N	Y	N	Y
8 Hefner	N	N	N	N	Y	Y	Y
9 *Myrick*	N	N	Y	N	N	N	Y
10 *Ballenger*	N	N	Y	N	N	N	Y
11 *Taylor*	N	Y	Y	N	N	N	Y
12 Watt	N	N	N	N	Y	Y	Y
NORTH DAKOTA							
AL Pomeroy	N	N	N	N	Y	Y	Y
OHIO							
1 *Chabot*	N	N	N	N	N	N	Y
2 *Portman*	?	N	Y	N	N	N	Y
3 Hall	N	N	N	N	Y	Y	Y
4 *Oxley*	N	N	Y	N	Y	N	Y
5 *Gillmor*	N	N	N	N	Y	N	Y
6 Strickland	N	N	N	N	Y	N	Y
7 *Hobson*	N	N	Y	N	N	N	Y
8 *Boehner*	N	N	Y	N	N	N	Y
9 Kaptur	N	N	N	N	Y	N	Y
10 Kucinich	N	N	N	N	Y	Y	Y
11 Stokes	N	N	N	N	Y	Y	Y
12 *Kasich*	N	N	N	N	N	N	Y
13 Brown	N	N	N	N	Y	Y	Y
14 Sawyer	N	N	N	N	Y	Y	Y
15 *Pryce*	N	N	Y	N	N	N	Y
16 *Regula*	N	N	Y	N	N	N	Y
17 Traficant	N	N	N	N	N	N	Y
18 *Ney*	N	N	Y	N	N	N	Y
19 *LaTourette*	?	N	N	N	N	N	Y
OKLAHOMA							
1 *Largent*	N	N	N	N	N	N	Y
2 *Coburn*	N	N	Y	N	N	N	Y
3 *Watkins*	N	N	N	N	N	N	Y
4 *Watts*	N	N	N	N	N	N	Y
5 *Istook*	N	Y	Y	N	N	N	Y
6 *Lucas*	N	N	N	N	N	N	Y
OREGON							
1 Furse	Y	N	N	N	Y	Y	Y
2 *Smith*	N	?	?	?	N	N	Y
3 Blumenauer	N	N	N	N	Y	Y	Y
4 DeFazio	N	N	N	N	Y	Y	Y
5 Hooley	N	N	N	N	Y	Y	Y
PENNSYLVANIA							
1 Vacant							
2 Fattah	N	N	N	N	Y	Y	Y
3 Borski	N	N	N	N	Y	Y	Y
4 Klink	N	N	N	N	Y	Y	Y
5 *Peterson*	?	N	Y	N	N	Y	Y
6 Holden	N	N	N	N	N	Y	Y
7 *Weldon*	N	N	Y	N	N	N	Y
8 *Greenwood*	N	N	Y	N	Y	N	Y
9 *Shuster*	N	N	Y	N	N	N	Y
10 *McDade*	N	?	?	?	?	#	Y
11 Kanjorski	N	N	N	N	Y	Y	Y
12 Murtha	N	N	N	N	Y	Y	Y
13 *Fox*	N	N	N	N	Y	N	Y
14 Coyne	N	N	N	N	Y	Y	Y
15 McHale	N	N	N	N	Y	Y	Y
16 *Pitts*	N	N	Y	N	N	N	Y
17 *Gekas*	?	N	N	N	Y	Y	Y
18 Doyle	N	N	N	N	Y	Y	Y
19 *Goodling*	N	N	Y	N	N	N	Y
20 Mascara	N	N	N	N	Y	Y	Y
21 *English*	N	N	N	N	Y	Y	Y
RHODE ISLAND							
1 Kennedy	N	N	N	N	Y	Y	Y
2 Weygand	N	N	N	N	Y	Y	Y
SOUTH CAROLINA							
1 *Sanford*	N	Y	Y	N	N	N	Y
2 *Spence*	N	N	Y	N	N	N	Y
3 *Graham*	N	N	Y	N	N	N	Y
4 *Inglis*	N	N	Y	N	N	N	Y
5 Spratt	N	N	Y	N	Y	Y	Y
6 Clyburn	N	N	N	N	Y	Y	Y
SOUTH DAKOTA							
AL *Thune*	N	N	N	N	N	N	Y

	32	33	34	35	36	37	38
TENNESSEE							
1 *Jenkins*	N	N	Y	N	N	N	Y
2 *Duncan*	N	Y	Y	N	N	N	Y
3 *Wamp*	N	N	Y	N	N	N	Y
4 *Hilleary*	N	N	Y	N	N	N	Y
5 Clement	N	N	N	N	Y	Y	Y
6 Gordon	N	N	N	N	Y	N	Y
7 *Bryant*	N	N	Y	N	N	N	Y
8 Tanner	N	N	N	N	Y	N	Y
9 Ford	N	N	N	N	Y	Y	Y
TEXAS							
1 Sandlin	N	N	N	N	Y	Y	Y
2 Turner	N	N	N	N	Y	Y	Y
3 *Johnson, Sam*	N	N	Y	N	N	N	Y
4 Hall	N	N	Y	N	N	N	Y
5 *Sessions*	N	N	N	N	N	N	Y
6 *Barton*	N	N	Y	N	Y	N	Y
7 *Archer*	N	N	Y	N	N	N	Y
8 *Brady*	N	N	Y	N	N	N	Y
9 Lampson	N	N	N	N	Y	Y	Y
10 Doggett	N	N	N	N	Y	Y	Y
11 Edwards	N	N	N	N	Y	Y	Y
12 *Granger*	N	?	Y	N	Y	Y	Y
13 *Thornberry*	N	N	Y	N	N	N	Y
14 *Paul*	N	Y	Y	N	N	N	N
15 Hinojosa	N	N	N	N	Y	Y	Y
16 Reyes	N	N	N	N	Y	Y	Y
17 Stenholm	N	N	N	N	N	Y	Y
18 Jackson-Lee	Y	N	N	N	Y	Y	+
19 *Combest*	N	Y	Y	N	N	N	Y
20 Gonzalez	?	?	?	?	?	?	?
21 *Smith*	N	N	Y	N	Y	N	Y
22 *DeLay*	N	N	N	N	N	Y	Y
23 *Bonilla*	N	N	N	N	Y	Y	Y
24 Frost	N	N	?	N	Y	Y	Y
25 Bentsen	N	N	N	N	Y	Y	Y
26 *Armey*	N	N	Y	N	N	N	Y
27 Ortiz	N	N	N	N	Y	Y	Y
28 Rodriguez	N	N	N	N	Y	Y	?
29 Green	N	N	N	N	Y	Y	Y
30 Johnson, E.B.	Y	N	N	N	Y	Y	+
UTAH							
1 *Hansen*	N	N	N	N	N	N	Y
2 *Cook*	N	N	N	N	Y	N	Y
3 *Cannon*	N	N	N	N	Y	Y	Y
VERMONT							
AL *Sanders*	Y	N	N	N	Y	Y	Y
VIRGINIA							
1 *Bateman*	N	N	Y	N	N	N	Y
2 Pickett	N	N	N	N	N	N	Y
3 Scott	N	N	N	N	Y	Y	Y
4 Sisisky	N	N	Y	N	N	N	Y
5 Goode	N	N	Y	N	N	N	Y
6 *Goodlatte*	N	N	Y	N	N	N	Y
7 *Bliley*	N	N	N	N	N	N	Y
8 Moran	N	N	N	N	Y	Y	Y
9 Boucher	N	N	N	N	Y	Y	Y
10 *Wolf*	N	N	Y	N	N	N	Y
11 *Davis*	N	N	N	N	N	Y	Y
WASHINGTON							
1 *White*	N	N	N	N	N	N	Y
2 *Metcalf*	N	N	Y	N	N	N	Y
3 *Smith, Linda*	N	Y	N	N	N	N	Y
4 *Hastings*	N	N	Y	N	N	N	Y
5 *Nethercutt*	N	N	N	N	N	N	Y
6 Dicks	N	N	N	N	Y	Y	Y
7 McDermott	N	N	N	N	Y	Y	Y
8 *Dunn*	N	N	N	N	N	N	Y
9 Smith, Adam	N	N	N	N	Y	Y	Y
WEST VIRGINIA							
1 Mollohan	N	N	N	N	Y	Y	Y
2 Wise	N	N	N	N	Y	Y	Y
3 Rahall	N	N	N	N	Y	Y	Y
WISCONSIN							
1 *Neumann*	N	N	Y	N	N	N	Y
2 *Klug*	N	N	Y	N	N	N	Y
3 Kind	N	N	N	N	Y	N	Y
4 Kleczka	N	N	N	N	Y	N	Y
5 Barrett	N	N	N	N	Y	Y	Y
6 *Petri*	N	Y	Y	N	N	N	Y
7 Obey	Y	N	N	N	Y	N	Y
8 Johnson	N	N	N	N	Y	N	Y
9 *Sensenbrenner*	N	Y	Y	N	N	N	Y
WYOMING							
AL *Cubin*	N	Y	Y	N	N	N	Y

Southern states - Ala., Ark., Fla., Ga., Ky., La., Miss., N.C., Okla., S.C., Tenn., Texas, Va.

House Votes 39, 40, 41, 42, 43, 44, 45

39. HR 3130. Child Support Performance/Passage. Passage of the bill to establish a new alternative penalty for states failing to meet the October 1, 1997 deadline to establish a computer system to assist in child support enforcement. The bill also would create a new federal incentive system to reward states with effective child support enforcement programs. Passed 414-1: R 218-1; D 195-0 (ND 141-0, SD 54-0); I 1-0. March 5, 1998. A "yea" was a vote in support of the president's position.

40. Procedural Motion/Journal. Approval of the House Journal of Monday, March 9, 1998. Approved 365-39: R 196-19; D 168-20 (ND 124-14, SD 44-6); I 1-0. March 10, 1998.

41. H Con Res 206. Use of Rotunda for Holocaust Remembrance/Passage. Thomas, R-Calif., motion to suspend the rules and adopt the resolution to permit the use of the Capitol Rotunda for a ceremony as part of the commemoration to remember victims of the Holocaust. Motion agreed to 406-0: R 215-0; D 190-0 (ND 140-0, SD 50-0); I 1-0. March 10, 1998. A two-thirds majority of those present and voting (271 in this case) is required for adoption under suspension of the rules.

42. S 419. Birth Defects Prevention/Passage. Bilirakis, R-Fla., motion to suspend the rules and pass the bill to authorize $30 million in fiscal 1998, $40 million in fiscal 1999, and such sums as may be necessary in fiscal 2000 and 2001 for programs intended to collect data on birth defects and prevention, conduct research on birth defects and broaden public awareness of birth defects. Motion agreed to 405-2: R 213-2; D 191-0 (ND 140-0, SD 51-0); I 1-0. March 10, 1998. A two-thirds majority of those present and voting (272 in this case) is required for passage under suspension of the rules.

43. HR 1432. Trade with sub-Saharan Africa/Rule. Adoption of the rule (H Res 383) to provide floor consideration of the bill to set a new trade and investment policy toward the countries of sub-Saharan Africa. Adopted 227-190: R 172-48; D 55-141 (ND 43-100, SD 12-41); I 0-1. March 11, 1998.

44. HR 1432. Trade with sub-Saharan Africa/Eligibility. Waters, D-Calif., amendment to clarify the eligibility provisions to state that countries need not meet every one of the bill's enumerated requirements. Rejected 81-334: R 3-218; D 77-116 (ND 58-84, SD 19-32); I 1-0. March 11, 1998.

45. HR 1432. Trade with sub-Saharan Africa/Morocco. Bereuter, R-Neb., amendment that would give the president discretion, subject to congressional approval, to designate Morocco as eligible to participate in the programs established by the bill if the country otherwise meets the eligibility requirements and if that designation is in the national interest of the United States. Rejected 156-258: R 131-91; D 25-166 (ND 19-122, SD 6-44); I 0-1. March 11, 1998.

Key

- **Y** Voted for (yea).
- **#** Paired for.
- **+** Announced for.
- **N** Voted against (nay).
- **X** Paired against.
- **−** Announced against.
- **P** Voted "present."
- **C** Voted "present" to avoid possible conflict of interest.
- **?** Did not vote or otherwise make a position known.

Democrats **Republicans** Independent

	39	40	41	42	43	44	45
ALABAMA							
1 *Callahan*	Y	Y	Y	Y	N	N	Y
2 *Everett*	Y	Y	Y	Y	N	N	N
3 *Riley*	Y	Y	Y	Y	N	N	N
4 *Aderholt*	Y	Y	Y	Y	N	N	N
5 Cramer	Y	Y	Y	Y	N	N	N
6 *Bachus*	Y	Y	Y	Y	N	N	N
7 Hilliard	Y	N	Y	Y	N	Y	N
ALASKA							
AL *Young*	Y	Y	Y	Y	N	N	Y
ARIZONA							
1 *Salmon*	Y	Y	Y	Y	Y	N	Y
2 Pastor	Y	Y	Y	Y	N	Y	N
3 *Stump*	Y	Y	Y	Y	N	N	N
4 *Shadegg*	Y	Y	Y	Y	Y	N	Y
5 *Kolbe*	Y	Y	Y	Y	Y	N	N
6 *Hayworth*	Y	Y	Y	Y	Y	N	Y
ARKANSAS							
1 Berry	Y	Y	Y	Y	N	N	N
2 Snyder	Y	Y	Y	Y	N	Y	N
3 *Hutchinson*	Y	Y	Y	Y	N	N	N
4 *Dickey*	Y	N	Y	Y	N	N	N
CALIFORNIA							
1 *Riggs*	Y	?	?	?	?	N	N
2 *Herger*	Y	Y	Y	Y	Y	N	N
3 Fazio	Y	N	Y	Y	Y	N	N
4 *Doolittle*	?	Y	Y	Y	Y	N	Y
5 Matsui	Y	Y	Y	Y	Y	Y	N
6 Woolsey	Y	Y	Y	Y	N	Y	N
7 Miller	Y	Y	Y	Y	N	Y	N
8 Pelosi	Y	Y	Y	Y	N	Y	N
9 Vacant							
10 Tauscher	Y	Y	Y	Y	Y	N	N
11 *Pombo*	Y	Y	Y	Y	Y	N	N
12 Lantos	Y	Y	Y	Y	N	N	N
13 Stark	Y	Y	Y	Y	N	Y	?
14 Eshoo	Y	Y	Y	Y	Y	N	N
15 *Campbell*	Y	Y	Y	Y	Y	Y	Y
16 Lofgren	Y	Y	Y	Y	N	N	N
17 Farr	Y	Y	Y	Y	Y	Y	N
18 Condit	Y	Y	Y	Y	N	N	N
19 *Radanovich*	Y	Y	Y	Y	Y	?	?
20 Dooley	Y	Y	Y	Y	Y	N	N
21 *Thomas*	?	Y	Y	Y	Y	N	N
22 *Gallegly*	Y	Y	Y	Y	N	N	N
23 Sherman	Y	Y	Y	Y	N	N	N
24 *McKeon*	Y	Y	Y	Y	Y	N	N
25 Berman	Y	Y	Y	Y	N	N	N
26 *Rogan*	Y	Y	Y	Y	Y	N	Y
27 *Dreier*	Y	Y	Y	Y	Y	N	N
28 Waxman	Y	Y	Y	Y	N	?	?
29 Becerra	Y	N	Y	Y	N	Y	N
30 Martinez	Y	Y	Y	Y	N	N	N
31 Dixon	Y	Y	Y	Y	N	N	N
32 Roybal-Allard	Y	Y	Y	Y	N	N	N
33 Torres	Y	Y	Y	Y	N	?	N
34 Waters	Y	N	Y	Y	N	Y	N
35 Harman	?	?	?	?	?	?	?
36 Millender-McD.	Y	Y	Y	Y	N	N	N
37 *Horn*	Y	Y	Y	Y	N	Y	N

	39	40	41	42	43	44	45
39 *Royce*	Y	Y	Y	Y	Y	N	N
40 *Lewis*	Y	Y	Y	Y	Y	N	N
41 *Kim*	Y	Y	Y	Y	Y	N	Y
42 Brown	Y	N	Y	Y	N	Y	N
43 *Calvert*	Y	Y	Y	Y	Y	N	Y
44 Vacant							
45 *Rohrabacher*	Y	Y	Y	Y	Y	N	N
46 Sanchez	Y	Y	Y	Y	N	Y	N
47 *Cox*	Y	Y	Y	Y	Y	N	N
48 *Packard*	Y	Y	Y	Y	Y	N	N
49 *Bilbray*	Y	Y	Y	Y	Y	N	Y
50 Filner	Y	N	Y	Y	N	Y	N
51 *Cunningham*	Y	Y	Y	Y	N	N	N
52 *Hunter*	Y	Y	Y	Y	N	N	N
COLORADO							
1 DeGette	Y	Y	Y	Y	N	N	N
2 Skaggs	Y	Y	Y	Y	N	Y	N
3 *McInnis*	Y	Y	Y	Y	Y	N	N
4 *Schaffer*	Y	N	Y	Y	Y	N	N
5 *Hefley*	Y	N	Y	Y	Y	N	N
6 *Schaefer*	Y	?	?	?	Y	N	N
CONNECTICUT							
1 Kennelly	Y	Y	Y	Y	N	N	N
2 Gejdenson	Y	Y	Y	Y	N	Y	N
3 DeLauro	Y	Y	Y	Y	N	Y	N
4 *Shays*	Y	Y	Y	Y	Y	N	N
5 Maloney	Y	Y	Y	Y	N	Y	N
6 *Johnson*	Y	Y	Y	Y	Y	N	Y
DELAWARE							
AL *Castle*	Y	Y	Y	Y	Y	N	N
FLORIDA							
1 *Scarborough*	Y	Y	Y	Y	N	N	N
2 Boyd	Y	Y	Y	Y	N	N	N
3 Brown	Y	Y	Y	Y	Y	Y	N
4 *Fowler*	Y	Y	Y	Y	N	N	N
5 Thurman	Y	Y	Y	Y	N	N	N
6 *Stearns*	Y	Y	Y	Y	N	N	N
7 *Mica*	Y	Y	Y	Y	N	N	N
8 *McCollum*	Y	Y	Y	Y	Y	N	N
9 *Bilirakis*	?	Y	Y	Y	Y	N	N
10 *Young*	Y	?	?	?	N	N	N
11 Davis	Y	Y	Y	Y	Y	N	N
12 *Canady*	Y	Y	Y	Y	Y	N	N
13 *Miller*	Y	Y	Y	Y	N	N	N
14 *Goss*	Y	Y	Y	Y	Y	N	N
15 *Weldon*	Y	Y	Y	Y	N	N	N
16 *Foley*	Y	Y	Y	Y	Y	N	N
17 Meek	Y	Y	Y	Y	Y	Y	?
18 *Ros-Lehtinen*	Y	Y	Y	Y	Y	N	Y
19 Wexler	Y	Y	Y	Y	N	Y	N
20 Deutsch	Y	Y	Y	Y	N	−	−
21 *Diaz-Balart*	Y	Y	Y	Y	Y	N	Y
22 *Shaw*	Y	Y	Y	Y	Y	N	N
23 Hastings	Y	N	Y	Y	Y	Y	N
GEORGIA							
1 *Kingston*	Y	N	Y	Y	Y	N	N
2 Bishop	Y	Y	Y	Y	N	N	N
3 *Collins*	Y	Y	Y	Y	N	N	N
4 McKinney	Y	Y	Y	Y	N	Y	N
5 Lewis	Y	N	Y	Y	N	Y	N
6 *Gingrich*							
7 *Barr*	Y	Y	Y	Y	N	N	N
8 *Chambliss*	Y	Y	Y	Y	N	N	N
9 *Deal*	Y	Y	Y	Y	N	N	N
10 *Norwood*	Y	Y	Y	Y	N	N	N
11 *Linder*	Y	Y	Y	Y	Y	N	N
HAWAII							
1 Abercrombie	Y	Y	Y	Y	N	Y	N
2 Mink	Y	Y	Y	Y	N	Y	N
IDAHO							
1 *Chenoweth*	Y	N	Y	Y	Y	?	?
2 *Crapo*	Y	Y	Y	Y	N	N	N
ILLINOIS							
1 Rush	Y	?	Y	Y	Y	Y	N
2 Jackson	Y	Y	Y	Y	N	Y	N
3 Lipinski	Y	Y	Y	Y	N	N	N
4 Gutierrez	Y	Y	Y	Y	N	Y	N
5 Blagojevich	Y	?	?	?	N	N	N
6 *Hyde*	Y	Y	Y	Y	Y	N	N
7 Davis	Y	Y	Y	Y	N	Y	N
8 *Crane*	Y	N	Y	Y	Y	Y	Y
9 Yates	Y	Y	Y	Y	N	N	N
10 *Porter*	Y	Y	Y	Y	Y	N	N
11 *Weller*	Y	?	?	?	Y	N	N
12 Costello	Y	N	Y	Y	N	N	N
13 *Fawell*	Y	Y	Y	Y	N	Y	N

ND Northern Democrats SD Southern Democrats

	39	40	41	42	43	44	45
14 ***Hastert***	Y	Y	Y	Y	Y	N	Y
15 ***Ewing***	Y	Y	Y	Y	Y	N	Y
16 ***Manzullo***	Y	Y	Y	Y	Y	N	Y
17 Evans	Y	Y	Y	Y	N	N	N
18 ***LaHood***	Y	Y	Y	Y	Y	N	Y
19 Poshard	?	?	?	?	?	?	?
20 ***Shimkus***	?	Y	Y	Y	Y	N	Y
INDIANA							
1 Visclosky	Y	Y	Y	Y	N	N	N
2 ***McIntosh***	Y	Y	Y	Y	Y	N	Y
3 Roemer	Y	Y	Y	Y	Y	N	N
4 ***Souder***	Y	Y	Y	Y	Y	N	N
5 ***Buyer***	Y	?	?	?	Y	N	Y
6 ***Burton***	Y	Y	Y	Y	Y	N	N
7 ***Pease***	Y	Y	Y	Y	Y	N	Y
8 ***Hostettler***	Y	Y	Y	Y	N	N	Y
9 Hamilton	Y	Y	Y	Y	Y	N	Y
10 Carson	Y	Y	Y	Y	N	Y	N
IOWA							
1 ***Leach***	Y	Y	Y	Y	Y	N	Y
2 ***Nussle***	Y	N	Y	Y	Y	N	N
3 Boswell	Y	Y	Y	Y	N	N	N
4 ***Ganske***	?	N	Y	Y	Y	N	N
5 ***Latham***	Y	Y	Y	Y	Y	N	Y
KANSAS							
1 ***Moran***	Y	N	Y	Y	N	N	Y
2 ***Ryun***	Y	Y	Y	Y	Y	N	Y
3 ***Snowbarger***	Y	Y	Y	Y	Y	N	Y
4 ***Tiahrt***	Y	Y	Y	Y	Y	N	Y
KENTUCKY							
1 ***Whitfield***	Y	Y	Y	Y	Y	N	Y
2 ***Lewis***	Y	Y	Y	Y	N	N	N
3 ***Northup***	Y	Y	Y	Y	Y	N	Y
4 ***Bunning***	Y	Y	Y	Y	N	N	N
5 ***Rogers***	Y	Y	Y	Y	N	N	N
6 Baesler	Y	Y	Y	Y	N	N	N
LOUISIANA							
1 ***Livingston***	Y	Y	Y	Y	Y	N	N
2 Jefferson	Y	Y	Y	Y	Y	Y	N
3 ***Tauzin***	Y	Y	Y	Y	Y	N	N
4 ***McCrery***	Y	Y	Y	Y	Y	N	N
5 ***Cooksey***	Y	Y	Y	Y	N	N	Y
6 ***Baker***	Y	Y	Y	Y	Y	N	N
7 John	Y	Y	Y	Y	N	?	?
MAINE							
1 Allen	Y	Y	Y	Y	Y	N	N
2 Baldacci	Y	Y	Y	Y	N	N	N
MARYLAND							
1 ***Gilchrest***	Y	?	?	?	Y	N	Y
2 ***Ehrlich***	Y	Y	Y	Y	N	N	Y
3 Cardin	Y	Y	Y	Y	Y	N	N
4 Wynn	Y	Y	Y	Y	Y	Y	N
5 Hoyer	Y	Y	Y	Y	N	Y	Y
6 ***Bartlett***	Y	Y	Y	Y	Y	N	N
7 Cummings	Y	Y	Y	Y	N	Y	N
8 ***Morella***	Y	Y	Y	Y	Y	N	Y
MASSACHUSETTS							
1 Olver	Y	Y	Y	Y	N	Y	N
2 Neal	Y	Y	Y	Y	N	N	N
3 McGovern	Y	Y	Y	Y	N	N	N
4 Frank	Y	Y	Y	Y	N	Y	N
5 Meehan	Y	Y	Y	Y	N	Y	N
6 Tierney	Y	Y	Y	Y	N	N	N
7 Markey	Y	Y	Y	Y	Y	Y	N
8 Kennedy	Y	?	?	?	N	Y	N
9 Moakley	Y	Y	Y	Y	N	N	N
10 Delahunt	Y	Y	Y	Y	N	Y	N
MICHIGAN							
1 Stupak	Y	Y	Y	Y	N	N	N
2 ***Hoekstra***	Y	Y	Y	Y	Y	N	Y
3 ***Ehlers***	Y	Y	Y	Y	Y	N	Y
4 ***Camp***	Y	Y	Y	Y	Y	N	Y
5 Barcia	Y	Y	Y	Y	N	N	N
6 ***Upton***	Y	Y	Y	Y	Y	N	N
7 ***Smith***	Y	Y	Y	Y	Y	N	Y
8 Stabenow	Y	Y	Y	Y	N	N	N
9 Kildee	Y	Y	Y	Y	N	Y	N
10 Bonior	Y	N	Y	Y	N	Y	N
11 ***Knollenberg***	Y	Y	Y	Y	Y	N	Y
12 Levin	Y	Y	Y	Y	Y	N	N
13 Rivers	Y	Y	Y	Y	N	Y	Y
14 Conyers	Y	Y	Y	Y	N	Y	N
15 Kilpatrick	+	Y	Y	Y	Y	Y	N
16 Dingell	?	Y	Y	Y	N	N	N

	39	40	41	42	43	44	45
MINNESOTA							
1 ***Gutknecht***	Y	N	Y	Y	N	N	Y
2 Minge	Y	Y	Y	Y	N	N	Y
3 ***Ramstad***	Y	N	Y	Y	N	Y	Y
4 Vento	Y	Y	Y	Y	Y	N	N
5 Sabo	Y	N	Y	Y	N	N	N
6 Luther	+	+	Y	Y	N	N	Y
7 Peterson	Y	Y	Y	Y	N	N	?
8 Oberstar	Y	Y	Y	Y	N	N	N
MISSISSIPPI							
1 ***Wicker***	Y	N	Y	Y	N	N	Y
2 Thompson	Y	N	Y	Y	N	Y	N
3 ***Pickering***	Y	Y	Y	Y	N	N	N
4 ***Parker***	Y	Y	Y	Y	Y	N	N
5 Taylor	Y	N	Y	Y	N	N	N
MISSOURI							
1 Clay	Y	N	Y	Y	N	Y	N
2 ***Talent***	Y	Y	Y	Y	Y	N	N
3 Gephardt	Y	N	Y	Y	N	Y	N
4 Skelton	Y	Y	Y	Y	Y	N	N
5 McCarthy	Y	Y	Y	Y	N	N	N
6 Danner	Y	Y	Y	Y	N	N	N
7 ***Blunt***	Y	Y	Y	Y	Y	N	N
8 ***Emerson***	Y	Y	Y	Y	N	N	N
9 ***Hulshof***	Y	Y	Y	Y	Y	N	N
MONTANA							
AL ***Hill***	Y	Y	Y	Y	Y	N	Y
NEBRASKA							
1 ***Bereuter***	Y	Y	Y	Y	Y	N	Y
2 ***Christensen***	Y	Y	Y	Y	Y	N	Y
3 ***Barrett***	Y	Y	Y	Y	Y	N	Y
NEVADA							
1 ***Ensign***	Y	N	Y	Y	Y	N	N
2 ***Gibbons***	Y	Y	Y	Y	Y	N	Y
NEW HAMPSHIRE							
1 ***Sununu***	Y	Y	Y	Y	Y	N	Y
2 ***Bass***	Y	Y	Y	Y	Y	N	Y
NEW JERSEY							
1 Andrews	Y	Y	Y	Y	N	N	N
2 ***LoBiondo***	Y	N	Y	Y	N	N	N
3 ***Saxton***	Y	Y	Y	Y	Y	N	Y
4 ***Smith***	Y	Y	Y	Y	Y	N	Y
5 ***Roukema***	Y	Y	Y	Y	Y	N	Y
6 Pallone	Y	Y	Y	Y	N	N	N
7 ***Franks***	Y	Y	Y	Y	Y	N	Y
8 Pascrell	Y	Y	Y	Y	?	N	N
9 Rothman	Y	Y	Y	Y	N	N	N
10 Payne	Y	Y	Y	Y	Y	Y	N
11 ***Frelinghuysen***	Y	Y	Y	Y	Y	N	Y
12 ***Pappas***	Y	Y	Y	Y	Y	N	Y
13 Menendez	Y	Y	Y	Y	Y	N	N
NEW MEXICO							
1 ***Schiff***	?	?	?	?	?	?	?
2 ***Skeen***	Y	Y	Y	Y	Y	N	Y
3 ***Redmond***	Y	Y	Y	Y	+	−	+
NEW YORK							
1 ***Forbes***	Y	Y	Y	Y	Y	N	Y
2 ***Lazio***	Y	Y	Y	Y	Y	N	Y
3 ***King***	Y	Y	Y	Y	Y	N	N
4 McCarthy	Y	+	+	+	Y	N	N
5 Ackerman	Y	Y	Y	Y	Y	N	N
6 Meeks	Y	Y	Y	Y	Y	Y	N
7 Manton	Y	Y	Y	Y	N	?	?
8 Nadler	Y	Y	Y	Y	N	Y	N
9 Schumer	Y	?	?	?	N	N	N
10 Towns	Y	Y	Y	Y	Y	Y	N
11 Owens	Y	Y	Y	Y	N	Y	N
12 Velázquez	Y	Y	Y	Y	N	Y	N
13 ***Fossella***	Y	Y	Y	Y	Y	N	Y
14 Maloney	Y	Y	Y	Y	N	N	N
15 Rangel	Y	Y	Y	Y	Y	Y	N
16 Serrano	Y	Y	Y	Y	N	Y	N
17 Engel	Y	Y	Y	Y	Y	Y	N
18 Lowey	Y	Y	Y	Y	Y	N	N
19 ***Kelly***	Y	Y	Y	Y	Y	N	Y
20 ***Gilman***	Y	Y	Y	Y	N	N	Y
21 McNulty	Y	Y	Y	Y	Y	N	N
22 ***Solomon***	Y	Y	Y	Y	Y	N	Y
23 ***Boehlert***	Y	Y	Y	Y	Y	N	Y
24 ***McHugh***	Y	Y	Y	Y	Y	N	Y
25 ***Walsh***	Y	Y	Y	Y	Y	N	Y
26 Hinchey	Y	N	Y	Y	N	N	N
27 ***Paxon***	Y	Y	Y	Y	Y	N	Y
28 Slaughter	Y	Y	Y	Y	N	N	N
29 LaFalce	Y	Y	Y	Y	N	N	Y

	39	40	41	42	43	44	45
30 ***Quinn***	?	Y	Y	Y	Y	N	Y
31 ***Houghton***	Y	Y	Y	Y	Y	N	Y
NORTH CAROLINA							
1 Clayton	Y	Y	Y	Y	N	Y	N
2 Etheridge	Y	Y	Y	Y	N	N	N
3 ***Jones***	Y	Y	Y	Y	N	N	N
4 Price	Y	Y	Y	Y	N	N	N
5 ***Burr***	Y	Y	Y	Y	Y	N	N
6 ***Coble***	Y	Y	Y	Y	N	N	N
7 McIntyre	Y	Y	Y	Y	N	N	N
8 Hefner	Y	?	?	?	N	Y	N
9 ***Myrick***	Y	Y	Y	Y	N	N	N
10 ***Ballenger***	Y	Y	Y	Y	N	N	N
11 ***Taylor***	Y	Y	Y	Y	N	N	N
12 Watt	Y	Y	Y	Y	N	Y	N
NORTH DAKOTA							
AL Pomeroy	Y	Y	Y	Y	Y	N	Y
OHIO							
1 ***Chabot***	Y	Y	Y	Y	Y	N	Y
2 ***Portman***	Y	Y	Y	Y	Y	N	Y
3 Hall	Y	Y	Y	Y	Y	N	Y
4 ***Oxley***	Y	Y	Y	Y	Y	N	Y
5 ***Gillmor***	Y	Y	Y	Y	Y	N	Y
6 Strickland	Y	Y	Y	Y	N	N	N
7 ***Hobson***	Y	Y	Y	Y	Y	N	Y
8 ***Boehner***	Y	Y	Y	Y	Y	N	Y
9 Kaptur	Y	Y	Y	Y	N	Y	N
10 Kucinich	Y	N	Y	Y	N	Y	N
11 Stokes	Y	Y	Y	Y	N	Y	N
12 ***Kasich***	Y	Y	Y	Y	Y	N	Y
13 Brown	Y	Y	Y	Y	N	Y	N
14 Sawyer	Y	Y	Y	Y	N	N	N
15 ***Pryce***	Y	Y	Y	Y	Y	N	Y
16 ***Regula***	Y	Y	Y	Y	Y	N	N
17 Traficant	Y	Y	Y	Y	N	N	N
18 ***Ney***	Y	Y	Y	Y	N	N	N
19 ***LaTourette***	Y	Y	Y	Y	Y	N	Y
OKLAHOMA							
1 ***Largent***	Y	Y	Y	Y	Y	N	N
2 ***Coburn***	Y	Y	Y	Y	N	N	Y
3 ***Watkins***	Y	Y	Y	Y	Y	N	Y
4 ***Watts***	Y	N	Y	Y	Y	N	N
5 ***Istook***	Y	Y	Y	Y	N	N	N
6 ***Lucas***	Y	Y	Y	Y	Y	N	Y
OREGON							
1 Furse	Y	?	?	?	?	?	?
2 ***Smith***	Y	Y	Y	Y	Y	N	Y
3 Blumenauer	Y	Y	Y	Y	Y	N	Y
4 DeFazio	Y	N	Y	Y	N	Y	N
5 Hooley	Y	Y	Y	Y	N	N	N
PENNSYLVANIA							
1 Vacant							
2 Fattah	Y	?	?	?	?	Y	N
3 Borski	Y	N	Y	Y	N	N	N
4 Klink	?	Y	Y	Y	N	N	N
5 ***Peterson***	Y	Y	Y	Y	Y	N	Y
6 Holden	Y	Y	Y	Y	N	N	N
7 ***Weldon***	Y	Y	Y	Y	?	N	N
8 ***Greenwood***	Y	Y	Y	Y	Y	N	Y
9 ***Shuster***	Y	Y	Y	Y	Y	N	Y
10 ***McDade***	Y	Y	Y	Y	Y	N	Y
11 Kanjorski	Y	Y	Y	Y	N	N	N
12 Murtha	Y	Y	Y	Y	N	N	N
13 ***Fox***	Y	N	Y	Y	Y	N	Y
14 Coyne	Y	Y	Y	Y	Y	N	N
15 McHale	Y	Y	Y	Y	N	N	N
16 ***Pitts***	Y	Y	Y	Y	Y	N	Y
17 ***Gekas***	Y	Y	Y	Y	?	N	Y
18 Doyle	Y	Y	Y	Y	N	N	N
19 ***Goodling***	Y	Y	Y	Y	Y	N	N
20 Mascara	Y	Y	Y	Y	N	N	N
21 ***English***	Y	N	Y	Y	Y	N	Y
RHODE ISLAND							
1 Kennedy	Y	Y	Y	Y	N	Y	N
2 Weygand	Y	Y	Y	Y	N	N	N
SOUTH CAROLINA							
1 ***Sanford***	Y	Y	Y	Y	N	N	N
2 ***Spence***	Y	Y	Y	Y	N	?	N
3 ***Graham***	Y	Y	Y	Y	N	N	Y
4 ***Inglis***	Y	?	?	?	N	N	N
5 Spratt	Y	Y	Y	Y	N	N	N
6 Clyburn	Y	N	Y	Y	N	Y	N
SOUTH DAKOTA							
AL ***Thune***	Y	Y	Y	Y	Y	N	Y

	39	40	41	42	43	44	45
TENNESSEE							
1 ***Jenkins***	Y	Y	Y	Y	Y	N	N
2 ***Duncan***	Y	Y	Y	Y	N	N	N
3 ***Wamp***	Y	Y	Y	Y	Y	N	N
4 ***Hilleary***	Y	N	Y	Y	N	N	N
5 Clement	Y	Y	Y	Y	N	N	Y
6 Gordon	Y	Y	Y	Y	N	N	N
7 ***Bryant***	Y	Y	Y	Y	Y	N	N
8 Tanner	Y	Y	Y	Y	N	N	N
9 Ford	Y	Y	Y	Y	Y	Y	N
TEXAS							
1 Sandlin	Y	Y	Y	Y	N	N	N
2 Turner	Y	Y	Y	Y	N	N	N
3 ***Johnson, Sam***	Y	Y	Y	N	Y	N	N
4 Hall	Y	Y	Y	Y	N	N	N
5 ***Sessions***	Y	N	Y	Y	Y	N	Y
6 ***Barton***	Y	?	?	?	?	N	N
7 ***Archer***	Y	Y	Y	Y	Y	N	N
8 ***Brady***	Y	+	+	+	+	N	N
9 Lampson	Y	Y	Y	Y	N	N	N
10 Doggett	Y	Y	Y	?	Y	N	Y
11 Edwards	Y	Y	Y	Y	N	N	N
12 ***Granger***	Y	Y	Y	Y	Y	N	N
13 ***Thornberry***	Y	Y	Y	Y	N	N	N
14 ***Paul***	N	Y	Y	N	Y	N	N
15 Hinojosa	Y	+	+	Y	N	N	N
16 Reyes	Y	Y	Y	Y	N	N	N
17 Stenholm	Y	Y	Y	Y	N	N	N
18 Jackson-Lee	Y	Y	Y	Y	Y	Y	N
19 ***Combest***	Y	Y	Y	Y	N	N	N
20 Gonzalez	?	?	?	?	?	?	?
21 ***Smith***	Y	Y	Y	Y	Y	N	Y
22 ***DeLay***	Y	Y	Y	Y	Y	N	Y
23 ***Bonilla***	Y	Y	Y	Y	N	N	N
24 Frost	Y	Y	Y	Y	N	N	N
25 Bentsen	Y	Y	Y	Y	Y	N	N
26 ***Armey***	Y	Y	Y	Y	Y	N	Y
27 Ortiz	Y	Y	Y	Y	N	N	N
28 Rodriguez	Y	?	?	?	?	?	?
29 Green	Y	Y	Y	Y	N	N	N
30 Johnson, E.B.	Y	Y	Y	Y	Y	Y	N
UTAH							
1 ***Hansen***	Y	Y	Y	Y	Y	N	N
2 ***Cook***	Y	Y	Y	Y	Y	N	N
3 ***Cannon***	Y	Y	Y	Y	Y	N	Y
VERMONT							
AL *Sanders*	Y	Y	Y	Y	N	Y	N
VIRGINIA							
1 ***Bateman***	Y	Y	Y	Y	Y	N	Y
2 Pickett	Y	?	?	Y	N	N	Y
3 Scott	Y	Y	Y	Y	N	Y	N
4 Sisisky	Y	Y	Y	Y	N	N	N
5 Goode	Y	Y	Y	Y	N	N	N
6 ***Goodlatte***	Y	Y	Y	Y	Y	N	Y
7 ***Bliley***	Y	Y	Y	Y	Y	N	Y
8 Moran	Y	Y	Y	Y	Y	Y	Y
9 Boucher	Y	Y	Y	Y	N	N	N
10 ***Wolf***	Y	Y	Y	Y	Y	N	N
11 ***Davis***	Y	?	?	?	Y	Y	Y
WASHINGTON							
1 ***White***	Y	Y	Y	Y	Y	N	Y
2 ***Metcalf***	Y	Y	Y	Y	N	N	N
3 ***Smith, Linda***	Y	Y	Y	Y	Y	N	N
4 ***Hastings***	Y	Y	Y	Y	Y	N	Y
5 ***Nethercutt***	Y	Y	Y	Y	Y	N	Y
6 Dicks	Y	Y	Y	Y	Y	N	N
7 McDermott	+	Y	Y	Y	Y	N	N
8 ***Dunn***	Y	Y	Y	Y	Y	N	Y
9 Smith, Adam	Y	Y	Y	Y	Y	N	N
WEST VIRGINIA							
1 Mollohan	Y	Y	Y	Y	N	N	N
2 Wise	Y	Y	Y	Y	N	N	N
3 Rahall	Y	Y	Y	Y	N	N	N
WISCONSIN							
1 ***Neumann***	Y	Y	Y	Y	Y	N	Y
2 ***Klug***	Y	Y	Y	Y	Y	N	Y
3 Kind	Y	Y	Y	Y	Y	N	Y
4 Kleczka	Y	Y	Y	Y	N	N	N
5 Barrett	Y	Y	Y	Y	N	Y	N
6 ***Petri***	Y	Y	Y	Y	Y	N	Y
7 Obey	Y	Y	Y	Y	N	N	N
8 Johnson	Y	Y	Y	Y	Y	N	N
9 ***Sensenbrenner***	Y	Y	Y	Y	Y	N	Y
WYOMING							
AL ***Cubin***	Y	Y	Y	Y	Y	N	N

Southern states - Ala., Ark., Fla., Ga., Ky., La., Miss., N.C., Okla., S.C., Tenn., Texas, Va.

House Votes 46, 47, 48, 49, 50, 51, 52

46. HR 1432. Trade with sub-Saharan Africa/Recommit. Bishop, D-Ga., motion to recommit the bill to the Ways and Means Committee with instructions to declare that the president should investigate, rather than develop, the establishment of a free trade area, and that the access program established by the president should be modeled on the program now in effect for the countries of the Caribbean. Motion rejected 193-224: R 66-157; D 126-67 (ND 98-44, SD 28-23); I 1-0. March 11, 1998.

47. HR 1432. Trade with sub-Saharan Africa/Passage. Passage of the bill to set a new trade and investment policy towards the countries of sub-Saharan Africa, including authorizing the president to grant duty-free treatment to, and requiring the development of, a plan to enter into one or more free trade agreements with eligible sub-Saharan African countries. The bill also would strengthen punishment against countries that attempt to illegally transship textile and apparel through sub-Saharan Africa to avoid U.S. quotas. Passed 233-186: R 141-84; D 92-101 (ND 68-74, SD 24-27); I 0-1. March 11, 1998. A "yea" was a vote in support of the president's position.

48. HR 2883. Government Performance and Results/Rule. Adoption of the rule (HRes 384) to provide for House floor consideration of the bill to require federal agencies to revise and resubmit to Congress, by the end of fiscal 1998, their "strategic plans" to outline their mission, general goals and objectives, and describe how those goals and objectives will be achieved. Adopted 412-0: R 218-0; D 193-0 (ND 141-0, SD 52-0); I 1-0. March 12, 1998.

49. Procedural Motion/Journal. Approval of the House Journal of Wednesday, March 11, 1998. Approved 368-43: R 205-14; D 162-29 (ND 118-22, SD 44-7); I 1-0. March 12, 1998.

50. HR 2883. Government Performance and Results/Passage. Passage of the bill to require federal agencies to revise and resubmit to Congress, by the end of fiscal 1998, their "strategic plans" to outline their mission, general goals and objectives, and describe how those goals and objectives will be achieved. The bill also requires agency inspectors general to annually audit agency performance reports and submit the results to Congress. Passed 242-168: R 221-0; D 21-167 (ND 10-127, SD 11-40); I 0-1. March 12, 1998.

51. HR 992. Private Property Rights/U.S. District Courts. Watt, D-N.C., amendment to grant the U.S. District Courts jurisdiction to determine all claims arising out of disputes over government seizure of private property. Rejected 206-206: R 36-185; D 169-21 (ND 128-10, SD 41-11); I 1-0. March 12, 1998.

52. HR 992. Private Property Rights/Passage. Passage of the bill to give landowners greater leeway in suing the federal government for disputes over government seizure of private property, by allowing such suits to be heard either in the U.S. District Court or the U.S. Court of Federal Claims. Passed 230-180: R 184-36; D 46-143 (ND 21-116, SD 25-27); I 0-1. March 12, 1998. A "nay" was a vote in support of the president's position.

Key

- Y Voted for (yea).
- # Paired for.
- + Announced for.
- N Voted against (nay).
- X Paired against.
- − Announced against.
- P Voted "present."
- C Voted "present" to avoid possible conflict of interest.
- ? Did not vote or otherwise make a position known.

Democrats **Republicans** *Independent*

		46	47	48	49	50	51	52
ALABAMA								
1	*Callahan*	Y	N	Y	Y	Y	N	Y
2	*Everett*	Y	N	Y	Y	Y	N	Y
3	*Riley*	Y	N	Y	Y	Y	N	Y
4	*Aderholt*	Y	N	Y	Y	Y	N	Y
5	Cramer	Y	N	Y	Y	Y	N	Y
6	*Bachus*	Y	N	Y	Y	Y	N	Y
7	Hilliard	N	Y	Y	N	N	Y	N
ALASKA								
AL	*Young*	N	N	Y	Y	Y	N	Y
ARIZONA								
1	*Salmon*	N	Y	Y	Y	Y	N	Y
2	Pastor	Y	N	Y	Y	N	Y	N
3	*Stump*	Y	N	Y	Y	Y	N	Y
4	*Shadegg*	N	Y	Y	Y	Y	N	Y
5	*Kolbe*	N	Y	Y	Y	Y	Y	Y
6	*Hayworth*	Y	Y	Y	Y	Y	N	Y
ARKANSAS								
1	Berry	Y	N	Y	Y	N	Y	N
2	Snyder	N	Y	Y	Y	N	Y	N
3	*Hutchinson*	N	Y	Y	?	N	Y	
4	*Dickey*	Y	N	Y	Y	Y	N	Y
CALIFORNIA								
1	*Riggs*	N	Y	Y	Y	Y	N	Y
2	*Herger*	N	Y	Y	Y	Y	N	Y
3	Fazio	N	Y	Y	N	N	Y	N
4	*Doolittle*	N	Y	Y	Y	Y	N	Y
5	Matsui	N	Y	Y	Y	N	N	N
6	Woolsey	Y	N	Y	Y	N	Y	N
7	Miller	Y	N	N	N	N	Y	N
8	Pelosi	Y	Y	Y	Y	N	Y	N
9	Vacant							
10	Tauscher	N	Y	Y	Y	N	Y	N
11	*Pombo*	N	Y	Y	Y	Y	N	Y
12	Lantos	Y	N	Y	Y	N	Y	N
13	Stark	Y	N	Y	N	N	Y	N
14	Eshoo	N	Y	Y	Y	N	Y	N
15	*Campbell*	N	Y	Y	Y	Y	Y	Y
16	Lofgren	N	Y	?	?	?	?	?
17	Farr	Y	N	Y	Y	N	Y	N
18	Condit	Y	Y	Y	Y	Y	N	Y
19	*Radanovich*	N	Y	Y	Y	Y	N	Y
20	Dooley	N	Y	Y	Y	N	Y	Y
21	*Thomas*	N	Y	Y	Y	Y	N	Y
22	*Gallegly*	N	Y	Y	Y	Y	N	Y
23	Sherman	Y	N	Y	Y	N	Y	N
24	*McKeon*	N	Y	Y	Y	Y	N	Y
25	Berman	N	Y	Y	Y	?	?	?
26	Rogan	N	Y	N	Y	N	Y	N
27	*Dreier*	N	Y	Y	Y	Y	N	Y
28	Waxman	N	Y	Y	Y	N	Y	N
29	Becerra	Y	Y	N	N	N	Y	N
30	Martinez	Y	Y	Y	N	Y	Y	Y
31	Dixon	Y	Y	Y	Y	N	Y	N
32	Roybal-Allard	Y	N	Y	N	Y	Y	?
33	Torres	Y	N	Y	N	Y	Y	?
34	Waters	Y	Y	Y	N	N	Y	N
35	Harman	?	?	?	?	?	?	?
36	Millender-McD.	N	Y	Y	Y	N	Y	N
37	*Horn*	N	Y	Y	Y	Y	Y	Y
39	*Royce*	N	Y	Y	Y	Y	N	Y
40	*Lewis*	N	Y	Y	Y	Y	N	Y
41	*Kim*	N	Y	Y	Y	Y	N	Y
42	Brown	Y	N	Y	N	?	?	?
43	*Calvert*	N	Y	Y	Y	Y	N	Y
44	Vacant							
45	*Rohrabacher*	Y	N	Y	Y	Y	N	Y
46	Sanchez	Y	?	?	?	?	?	?
47	*Cox*	N	Y	Y	Y	Y	N	Y
48	*Packard*	N	Y	Y	Y	Y	N	Y
49	*Bilbray*	N	Y	Y	Y	Y	N	Y
50	Filner	Y	N	N	N	N	Y	N
51	*Cunningham*	Y	N	Y	Y	Y	N	?
52	*Hunter*	Y	N	Y	Y	Y	N	Y
COLORADO								
1	DeGette	N	Y	Y	Y	N	Y	N
2	Skaggs	N	Y	Y	Y	N	Y	N
3	*McInnis*	N	Y	Y	Y	Y	N	Y
4	*Schaffer*	N	N	Y	N	Y	N	Y
5	*Hefley*	N	N	Y	N	Y	N	Y
6	*Schaefer*	N	N	Y	Y	Y	?	Y
CONNECTICUT								
1	Kennelly	Y	Y	Y	Y	N	Y	N
2	Gejdenson	Y	N	Y	Y	N	Y	N
3	DeLauro	Y	N	Y	Y	N	Y	N
4	*Shays*	N	Y	Y	Y	Y	Y	Y
5	Maloney	N	Y	Y	Y	Y	Y	Y
6	*Johnson*	N	Y	?	?	Y	N	
DELAWARE								
AL	*Castle*	N	Y	Y	Y	Y	Y	N
FLORIDA								
1	*Scarborough*	N	Y	Y	?	Y	N	Y
2	Boyd	Y	N	Y	Y	Y	N	Y
3	Brown	N	Y	Y	Y	N	Y	N
4	*Fowler*	Y	N	Y	Y	Y	N	Y
5	Thurman	N	Y	Y	Y	Y	N	Y
6	*Stearns*	Y	N	Y	Y	Y	N	Y
7	*Mica*	N	Y	Y	Y	Y	N	Y
8	*McCollum*	N	Y	Y	Y	Y	N	Y
9	*Bilirakis*	N	N	Y	Y	Y	N	Y
10	*Young*	N	Y	Y	Y	Y	N	Y
11	Davis	N	Y	?	N	Y	Y	
12	*Canady*	Y	N	Y	Y	Y	N	Y
13	*Miller*	N	Y	Y	Y	Y	N	Y
14	*Goss*	N	Y	Y	+	−	+	
15	*Weldon*	N	Y	Y	Y	Y	N	Y
16	*Foley*	N	Y	Y	Y	Y	N	Y
17	Meek	N	Y	Y	N	Y	Y	Y
18	*Ros-Lehtinen*	Y	Y	Y	Y	Y	Y	Y
19	Wexler	N	Y	Y	N	Y	N	
20	Deutsch	+	+	Y	N	Y	N	
21	*Diaz-Balart*	N	N	Y	Y	Y	Y	Y
22	*Shaw*	N	Y	Y	Y	Y	N	Y
23	Hastings	N	Y	Y	N	N	Y	N
GEORGIA								
1	*Kingston*	Y	N	Y	Y	Y	N	Y
2	Bishop	Y	N	Y	N	Y	Y	
3	*Collins*	Y	N	Y	Y	Y	N	Y
4	McKinney	N	Y	Y	Y	N	Y	N
5	Lewis	Y	Y	Y	N	N	Y	N
6	*Gingrich*			Y			N	
7	*Barr*	Y	N	Y	Y	N	Y	
8	*Chambliss*	Y	N	Y	Y	Y	N	Y
9	*Deal*	Y	N	Y	Y	Y	N	Y
10	*Norwood*	Y	N	Y	Y	Y	N	Y
11	*Linder*	N	Y	Y	Y	Y	N	Y
HAWAII								
1	Abercrombie	Y	N	Y	N	N	Y	N
2	Mink	Y	N	Y	N	Y	N	
IDAHO								
1	*Chenoweth*	N	N	Y	Y	Y	N	Y
2	*Crapo*	N	N	Y	Y	Y	N	Y
ILLINOIS								
1	Rush	Y	N	Y	Y	Y	N	Y
2	Jackson	N	N	Y	Y	N	Y	N
3	Lipinski	N	N	Y	N	N	N	
4	Gutierrez	Y	N	N	N	N	Y	N
5	Blagojevich	Y	N	Y	Y	N	Y	N
6	*Hyde*	N	Y	Y	Y	Y	N	Y
7	Davis	N	N	Y	N	N	Y	N
8	*Crane*	N	Y	?	Y	Y	N	Y
9	Yates	Y	Y	Y	N	N	Y	N
10	*Porter*	N	Y	Y	Y	Y	N	Y
11	*Weller*	N	Y	?	Y	N	Y	
12	Costello	Y	N	Y	Y	N	Y	N
13	*Fawell*	N	Y	Y	Y	Y	N	Y

ND Northern Democrats SD Southern Democrats

	46	47	48	49	50	51	52
14 **Hastert**	N	Y	Y	Y	Y	?	Y
15 **Ewing**	N	Y	Y	Y	Y	Y	Y
16 **Manzullo**	N	Y	Y	Y	Y	N	Y
17 Evans	Y	N	Y	Y	N	Y	N
18 **LaHood**	N	Y	Y	Y	Y	Y	Y
19 Poshard	?	?	?	?	?	?	?
20 **Shimkus**	N	Y	Y	Y	Y	N	Y
INDIANA							
1 Visclosky	N	N	Y	N	N	Y	N
2 **McIntosh**	Y	Y	Y	Y	Y	N	Y
3 Roemer	N	Y	Y	Y	N	N	Y
4 **Souder**	N	N	?	Y	Y	N	Y
5 **Buyer**	N	N	Y	Y	Y	N	Y
6 **Burton**	Y	N	Y	Y	Y	N	Y
7 **Pease**	N	Y	Y	Y	Y	N	Y
8 **Hostettler**	N	N	Y	Y	Y	N	Y
9 Hamilton	N	Y	Y	Y	N	Y	N
10 Carson	Y	N	Y	Y	N	Y	N
IOWA							
1 **Leach**	N	Y	Y	Y	Y	Y	N
2 **Nussle**	N	Y	Y	N	Y	N	Y
3 Boswell	Y	Y	Y	Y	N	N	Y
4 **Ganske**	Y	Y	Y	Y	Y	N	Y
5 **Latham**	N	Y	Y	Y	Y	N	Y
KANSAS							
1 **Moran**	Y	N	Y	N	Y	N	Y
2 **Ryun**	N	Y	Y	Y	Y	N	Y
3 **Snowbarger**	N	Y	Y	Y	Y	N	Y
4 **Tiahrt**	N	Y	Y	Y	Y	N	Y
KENTUCKY							
1 **Whitfield**	N	N	Y	Y	Y	N	Y
2 **Lewis**	Y	N	Y	Y	Y	N	Y
3 **Northup**	N	Y	Y	Y	Y	N	Y
4 **Bunning**	Y	N	Y	Y	?	?	Y
5 **Rogers**	Y	N	Y	Y	Y	N	Y
6 Baesler	Y	N	Y	Y	Y	Y	Y
LOUISIANA							
1 **Livingston**	N	Y	?	?	Y	N	Y
2 Jefferson	N	Y	Y	Y	N	Y	N
3 **Tauzin**	Y	Y	Y	Y	Y	N	Y
4 **McCrery**	N	Y	Y	Y	Y	N	Y
5 **Cooksey**	Y	N	Y	Y	Y	N	Y
6 **Baker**	Y	Y	Y	Y	Y	N	Y
7 John	?	?	?	?	?	?	?
MAINE							
1 Allen	N	Y	Y	Y	N	Y	N
2 Baldacci	Y	N	Y	Y	N	Y	N
MARYLAND							
1 **Gilchrest**	N	Y	Y	Y	Y	Y	N
2 **Ehrlich**	N	Y	Y	Y	Y	N	Y
3 Cardin	Y	Y	Y	Y	N	Y	N
4 Wynn	N	Y	Y	Y	N	Y	N
5 Hoyer	N	Y	Y	Y	N	Y	N
6 **Bartlett**	N	N	Y	Y	Y	N	Y
7 Cummings	N	Y	Y	P	–	Y	N
8 **Morella**	N	Y	Y	Y	Y	Y	N
MASSACHUSETTS							
1 Olver	Y	N	Y	Y	N	Y	N
2 Neal	Y	Y	Y	Y	N	Y	N
3 McGovern	Y	N	Y	Y	N	Y	N
4 Frank	Y	N	Y	Y	N	Y	N
5 Meehan	Y	Y	Y	Y	N	Y	N
6 Tierney	Y	N	Y	Y	N	Y	N
7 Markey	Y	Y	Y	Y	N	Y	?
8 Kennedy	Y	Y	Y	Y	N	Y	N
9 Moakley	Y	N	Y	Y	N	Y	N
10 Delahunt	Y	N	Y	Y	N	Y	N
MICHIGAN							
1 Stupak	Y	N	Y	N	N	Y	N
2 **Hoekstra**	N	Y	Y	Y	Y	N	Y
3 **Ehlers**	N	Y	Y	Y	Y	Y	N
4 **Camp**	N	Y	Y	Y	Y	N	Y
5 Barcia	Y	N	Y	Y	N	N	Y
6 **Upton**	N	Y	Y	Y	Y	Y	N
7 **Smith**	N	Y	Y	Y	Y	N	Y
8 Stabenow	+	Y	Y	Y	Y	Y	N
9 Kildee	Y	N	Y	Y	N	Y	N
10 Bonior	Y	N	Y	Y	N	Y	N
11 **Knollenberg**	N	Y	Y	Y	Y	N	Y
12 Levin	N	Y	Y	Y	N	Y	N
13 Rivers	Y	Y	Y	Y	Y	Y	N
14 Conyers	Y	N	Y	Y	N	Y	N
15 Kilpatrick	N	Y	Y	Y	N	Y	N
16 Dingell	Y	N	Y	Y	N	Y	N

	46	47	48	49	50	51	52
MINNESOTA							
1 **Gutknecht**	N	Y	Y	Y	Y	N	Y
2 Minge	N	Y	Y	Y	N	Y	Y
3 **Ramstad**	N	Y	Y	N	Y	Y	N
4 Vento	Y	Y	Y	Y	N	Y	N
5 Sabo	N	Y	Y	N	N	Y	N
6 Luther	Y	Y	Y	Y	Y	Y	N
7 Peterson	Y	N	Y	N	N	N	Y
8 Oberstar	Y	N	Y	N	N	Y	N
MISSISSIPPI							
1 **Wicker**	Y	N	Y	Y	Y	N	Y
2 Thompson	Y	N	Y	N	N	Y	N
3 **Pickering**	Y	N	Y	Y	Y	N	Y
4 **Parker**	N	Y	Y	Y	Y	N	?
5 Taylor	Y	N	Y	N	Y	N	Y
MISSOURI							
1 Clay	Y	N	Y	N	N	Y	N
2 **Talent**	Y	N	Y	Y	Y	N	Y
3 Gephardt	Y	Y	Y	N	?	?	N
4 Skelton	Y	N	Y	Y	Y	Y	Y
5 McCarthy	Y	Y	Y	Y	Y	Y	N
6 Danner	Y	N	Y	Y	Y	N	Y
7 **Blunt**	N	N	Y	Y	Y	N	Y
8 **Emerson**	Y	N	Y	Y	Y	N	Y
9 **Hulshof**	N	Y	Y	Y	Y	N	Y
MONTANA							
AL **Hill**	N	Y	Y	Y	Y	N	Y
NEBRASKA							
1 **Bereuter**	N	Y	Y	Y	Y	N	Y
2 **Christensen**	N	Y	Y	Y	Y	N	Y
3 **Barrett**	N	Y	Y	Y	Y	N	Y
NEVADA							
1 **Ensign**	N	N	Y	N	Y	N	Y
2 **Gibbons**	Y	N	Y	N	Y	N	Y
NEW HAMPSHIRE							
1 **Sununu**	N	Y	Y	Y	Y	N	Y
2 **Bass**	Y	Y	Y	Y	Y	Y	N
NEW JERSEY							
1 Andrews	Y	N	Y	Y	N	Y	N
2 **LoBiondo**	N	N	Y	N	Y	Y	N
3 **Saxton**	N	N	?	Y	Y	Y	N
4 **Smith**	N	N	Y	Y	Y	Y	N
5 **Roukema**	N	Y	Y	Y	Y	Y	N
6 Pallone	Y	N	Y	Y	N	Y	N
7 **Franks**	N	Y	Y	Y	Y	N	N
8 Pascrell	Y	N	Y	N	N	Y	N
9 Rothman	N	Y	Y	Y	N	Y	N
10 Payne	N	Y	Y	Y	N	Y	N
11 **Frelinghuysen**	N	Y	Y	Y	Y	Y	N
12 **Pappas**	Y	N	Y	Y	Y	Y	N
13 Menendez	N	Y	Y	Y	N	Y	N
NEW MEXICO							
1 **Schiff**	?	?	?	?	?	?	?
2 **Skeen**	N	Y	Y	Y	Y	N	Y
3 **Redmond**	–	+	+	+	+	–	+
NEW YORK							
1 **Forbes**	Y	N	Y	Y	Y	Y	N
2 **Lazio**	N	Y	Y	Y	Y	N	N
3 **King**	N	Y	Y	Y	Y	N	Y
4 McCarthy	N	Y	Y	Y	N	Y	N
5 Ackerman	Y	Y	?	?	N	Y	N
6 Meeks	N	Y	Y	Y	N	Y	N
7 Manton	?	?	Y	N	N	Y	N
8 Nadler	Y	N	Y	Y	?	?	?
9 Schumer	?	?	?	Y	N	Y	N
10 Towns	N	Y	Y	Y	N	Y	N
11 Owens	N	Y	Y	Y	N	Y	N
12 Velázquez	Y	N	Y	Y	N	Y	N
13 **Fossella**	N	Y	Y	Y	Y	N	Y
14 Maloney	Y	Y	Y	Y	N	Y	N
15 Rangel	N	Y	Y	Y	N	?	N
16 Serrano	Y	N	Y	Y	N	Y	N
17 Engel	Y	Y	Y	Y	N	Y	N
18 Lowey	N	Y	Y	Y	N	Y	N
19 **Kelly**	N	Y	Y	Y	Y	Y	N
20 **Gilman**	N	Y	Y	Y	Y	Y	N
21 McNulty	Y	Y	Y	Y	N	Y	N
22 **Solomon**	?	N	Y	Y	Y	N	Y
23 **Boehlert**	N	Y	Y	Y	Y	Y	N
24 **McHugh**	Y	N	?	?	Y	N	Y
25 **Walsh**	N	N	Y	Y	Y	Y	N
26 Hinchey	Y	Y	Y	N	N	Y	N
27 **Paxon**	N	Y	Y	Y	Y	N	Y
28 Slaughter	Y	N	Y	Y	N	Y	N
29 LaFalce	Y	N	Y	Y	N	Y	N

	46	47	48	49	50	51	52
30 **Quinn**	N	N	Y	Y	Y	N	N
31 **Houghton**	N	Y	Y	Y	Y	N	Y
NORTH CAROLINA							
1 Clayton	Y	N	Y	Y	N	Y	N
2 Etheridge	Y	N	Y	Y	N	Y	N
3 **Jones**	Y	N	Y	Y	Y	N	Y
4 Price	Y	N	Y	Y	N	Y	N
5 **Burr**	Y	N	Y	Y	Y	N	Y
6 **Coble**	Y	N	Y	Y	Y	N	Y
7 McIntyre	Y	N	Y	Y	Y	Y	Y
8 Hefner	Y	N	Y	Y	N	Y	N
9 **Myrick**	Y	N	Y	Y	Y	N	Y
10 **Ballenger**	Y	N	Y	Y	Y	N	Y
11 **Taylor**	N	N	Y	Y	Y	N	Y
12 Watt	Y	N	Y	Y	N	Y	N
NORTH DAKOTA							
AL Pomeroy	Y	Y	Y	Y	N	Y	N
OHIO							
1 **Chabot**	N	Y	Y	Y	Y	N	Y
2 **Portman**	N	Y	Y	Y	Y	N	N
3 Hall	N	Y	Y	Y	Y	Y	Y
4 **Oxley**	N	Y	Y	Y	Y	N	Y
5 **Gillmor**	N	Y	Y	N	Y	N	Y
6 Strickland	Y	N	Y	Y	N	Y	N
7 **Hobson**	N	Y	Y	Y	Y	N	Y
8 **Boehner**	N	Y	Y	Y	Y	N	Y
9 Kaptur	Y	N	Y	Y	N	Y	N
10 Kucinich	Y	N	Y	N	N	Y	N
11 Stokes	Y	N	Y	Y	N	Y	N
12 **Kasich**	N	Y	Y	Y	Y	N	Y
13 Brown	Y	N	Y	Y	N	Y	N
14 Sawyer	Y	Y	Y	Y	N	Y	N
15 **Pryce**	N	Y	Y	Y	Y	N	Y
16 **Regula**	N	Y	Y	Y	Y	N	N
17 Traficant	Y	N	Y	Y	Y	N	Y
18 **Ney**	Y	N	Y	Y	Y	N	Y
19 **LaTourette**	N	Y	Y	Y	Y	N	N
OKLAHOMA							
1 **Largent**	Y	Y	Y	Y	Y	N	Y
2 **Coburn**	Y	N	Y	Y	Y	N	Y
3 **Watkins**	Y	Y	Y	Y	Y	N	Y
4 **Watts**	Y	Y	Y	Y	Y	N	Y
5 **Istook**	N	Y	Y	Y	Y	N	Y
6 **Lucas**	Y	N	Y	Y	Y	N	Y
OREGON							
1 Furse	?	?	?	?	?	?	?
2 **Smith**	N	N	Y	Y	Y	N	Y
3 Blumenauer	N	Y	Y	Y	N	Y	N
4 DeFazio	Y	N	Y	N	N	Y	N
5 Hooley	N	Y	Y	Y	N	Y	N
PENNSYLVANIA							
1 Vacant							
2 Fattah	N	Y	Y	Y	N	Y	N
3 Borski	Y	N	Y	N	N	Y	N
4 Klink	Y	N	Y	Y	N	Y	N
5 **Peterson**	N	Y	Y	Y	Y	N	Y
6 Holden	Y	N	Y	Y	N	Y	Y
7 **Weldon**	N	N	Y	Y	Y	Y	N
8 **Greenwood**	N	N	Y	Y	Y	Y	N
9 **Shuster**	N	Y	Y	Y	Y	N	Y
10 **McDade**	Y	Y	Y	Y	Y	N	Y
11 Kanjorski	Y	N	Y	Y	N	Y	N
12 Murtha	Y	N	Y	?	N	Y	N
13 **Fox**	N	Y	Y	N	Y	Y	N
14 Coyne	Y	Y	Y	Y	N	Y	N
15 McHale	Y	N	Y	Y	N	Y	N
16 **Pitts**	N	Y	Y	Y	Y	N	Y
17 **Gekas**	N	Y	Y	Y	Y	N	Y
18 Doyle	Y	N	Y	Y	?	Y	Y
19 **Goodling**	Y	N	Y	Y	Y	N	Y
20 Mascara	Y	N	Y	Y	N	Y	Y
21 **English**	N	Y	Y	N	Y	N	Y
RHODE ISLAND							
1 Kennedy	Y	N	Y	Y	N	Y	N
2 Weygand	Y	N	Y	Y	N	Y	Y
SOUTH CAROLINA							
1 **Sanford**	Y	N	Y	Y	Y	Y	N
2 **Spence**	Y	N	Y	Y	Y	N	Y
3 **Graham**	Y	N	Y	Y	Y	N	Y
4 **Inglis**	Y	N	Y	Y	Y	N	Y
5 Spratt	Y	N	Y	Y	N	Y	N
6 Clyburn	Y	N	Y	N	N	Y	N
SOUTH DAKOTA							
AL **Thune**	N	Y	Y	Y	Y	N	Y

	46	47	48	49	50	51	52
TENNESSEE							
1 **Jenkins**	Y	N	Y	Y	Y	N	Y
2 **Duncan**	Y	N	Y	Y	Y	N	Y
3 **Wamp**	Y	N	Y	Y	Y	N	Y
4 **Hilleary**	Y	N	Y	N	Y	N	Y
5 Clement	Y	N	Y	Y	N	N	Y
6 Gordon	Y	N	Y	Y	N	Y	Y
7 **Bryant**	Y	N	Y	Y	Y	N	Y
8 Tanner	Y	N	?	?	?	?	?
9 Ford	N	Y	Y	Y	N	Y	Y
TEXAS							
1 Sandlin	N	Y	Y	Y	N	Y	Y
2 Turner	N	Y	Y	Y	N	N	Y
3 **Johnson, Sam**	N	Y	Y	Y	Y	N	Y
4 Hall	Y	N	Y	Y	Y	N	Y
5 **Sessions**	N	Y	Y	N	Y	N	Y
6 **Barton**	N	Y	Y	Y	Y	N	Y
7 **Archer**	N	Y	Y	Y	Y	N	Y
8 **Brady**	N	Y	Y	Y	Y	N	Y
9 Lampson	N	Y	Y	Y	N	Y	N
10 Doggett	N	Y	Y	Y	Y	Y	N
11 Edwards	N	Y	Y	Y	N	N	Y
12 **Granger**	N	Y	Y	Y	Y	N	Y
13 **Thornberry**	Y	N	Y	Y	Y	N	Y
14 **Paul**	N	N	Y	Y	Y	N	Y
15 Hinojosa	N	Y	Y	Y	–	Y	Y
16 Reyes	Y	N	Y	Y	N	Y	Y
17 Stenholm	Y	N	Y	Y	Y	N	Y
18 Jackson-Lee	N	Y	Y	Y	N	Y	N
19 **Combest**	Y	N	Y	Y	Y	N	Y
20 Gonzalez	?	?	?	?	?	?	?
21 **Smith**	N	Y	Y	Y	Y	N	Y
22 **DeLay**	N	Y	Y	Y	Y	N	Y
23 **Bonilla**	Y	N	Y	Y	Y	N	Y
24 Frost	N	Y	Y	Y	N	Y	Y
25 Bentsen	N	Y	Y	Y	N	Y	N
26 **Armey**	N	Y	Y	Y	Y	N	Y
27 Ortiz	Y	N	Y	Y	Y	N	Y
28 Rodriguez	?	?	Y	Y	N	Y	N
29 Green	Y	N	Y	Y	Y	Y	Y
30 Johnson, E.B.	N	Y	Y	Y	N	Y	N
UTAH							
1 **Hansen**	N	Y	Y	Y	Y	N	Y
2 **Cook**	N	Y	Y	Y	Y	N	Y
3 **Cannon**	N	Y	Y	Y	Y	N	Y
VERMONT							
AL *Sanders*	Y	N	Y	Y	N	Y	N
VIRGINIA							
1 **Bateman**	N	Y	Y	Y	Y	N	Y
2 Pickett	Y	N	Y	N	Y	N	Y
3 Scott	N	Y	Y	Y	N	Y	N
4 Sisisky	Y	N	Y	Y	Y	N	Y
5 Goode	Y	N	Y	Y	Y	N	Y
6 **Goodlatte**	Y	Y	Y	Y	Y	N	Y
7 **Bliley**	N	Y	Y	Y	Y	N	Y
8 Moran	N	Y	Y	Y	N	Y	N
9 Boucher	Y	N	Y	Y	N	Y	N
10 **Wolf**	N	Y	Y	Y	Y	N	Y
11 **Davis**	N	Y	Y	Y	Y	N	Y
WASHINGTON							
1 **White**	N	Y	Y	Y	Y	N	Y
2 **Metcalf**	N	N	Y	Y	Y	N	Y
3 **Smith, Linda**	N	Y	Y	Y	Y	N	Y
4 **Hastings**	N	Y	Y	Y	Y	N	Y
5 **Nethercutt**	N	Y	Y	Y	Y	N	Y
6 Dicks	N	Y	Y	Y	N	Y	N
7 McDermott	N	Y	Y	Y	N	Y	N
8 **Dunn**	N	Y	Y	Y	Y	N	Y
9 Smith, Adam	N	Y	Y	Y	N	Y	N
WEST VIRGINIA							
1 Mollohan	Y	N	Y	Y	N	Y	N
2 Wise	N	Y	Y	Y	N	Y	N
3 Rahall	Y	N	Y	Y	N	Y	N
WISCONSIN							
1 **Neumann**	N	N	Y	Y	Y	N	Y
2 **Klug**	N	Y	Y	Y	Y	Y	N
3 Kind	N	Y	Y	Y	N	Y	Y
4 Kleczka	Y	N	Y	Y	N	Y	N
5 Barrett	Y	Y	Y	Y	N	Y	N
6 **Petri**	N	Y	Y	Y	Y	N	Y
7 Obey	Y	N	Y	Y	N	Y	N
8 Johnson	Y	N	Y	Y	N	Y	N
9 **Sensenbrenner**	N	N	Y	Y	Y	N	Y
WYOMING							
AL **Cubin**	N	Y	Y	Y	Y	N	Y

Southern states - Ala., Ark., Fla., Ga., Ky., La., Miss., N.C., Okla., S.C., Tenn., Texas, Va.

House Votes 53, 54, 55, 56, 57, 58, 59

53. Procedural Motion/Journal. Approval of the House Journal of Monday, March 16, 1998. Approved 359-38: R 194-15; D 164-23 (ND 121-13, SD 43-10); I 1-0. March 17, 1998.

54. H Res 364. Human Rights in China/Passage. Smith, R-N.J., motion to suspend the rules and adopt the resolution to urge President Clinton to initiate a resolution in the United Nations to condemn human rights violations in China. Motion agreed to 397-0: R 209-0; D 187-0 (ND 134-0, SD 53-0); I 1-0. March 17, 1998. A two-thirds majority of those present and voting (265 in this case) is required for adoption under suspension of the rules.

55. H Res 361. Human Rights in Cambodia/Passage. Bereuter, R-Neb., motion to suspend the rules and adopt the resolution to call upon the government in Cambodia to enforce the rule of law, protect human rights, and allow exiled opposition leaders to return to with full political rights. Motion agreed to 393-1: R 205-1; D 187-0 (ND 134-0, SD 53-0); I 1-0. March 17, 1998. A two-thirds majority of those present and voting (263 in this case) is required for adoption under suspension of the rules.

56. H Con Res 152. Northern Ireland Peace Talks/Passage. Smith, R-N.J., motion to suspend the rules and adopt the resolution to call on all parties in the Northern Ireland peace talks to condemn violence and address outstanding human rights violations as part of the peace process. Motion agreed to 407-2: R 213-2; D 193-0 (ND 141-0, SD 52-0); I 1-0. March 18, 1998. A two-thirds majority of those present and voting (274 in this case) is required for adoption under suspension of the rules.

57. H Con Res 235. Violence in Kosovo/Passage. Gilman, R-N.Y., motion to suspend the rules and adopt the resolution to condemn violence against ethnic Albanians in Kosovo by Serbian authorities, and call for a dialogue between the Serbian government and the leaders of the ethnic Albanians in Kosovo to end the violence by all parties. Motion agreed to 406-1: R 211-1; D 194-0 (ND 142-0, SD 52-0); I 1-0. March 18, 1998. A two-thirds majority of those present and voting (272 in this case) is required for adoption under suspension of the rules.

58. H Con Res 227. Withdrawal of U.S. Forces from Bosnia/Adoption. Adoption of the concurrent resolution to invoke the authority granted by the War Powers Resolution of 1973 to direct the president to remove U.S. armed forces from the Republic of Bosnia and Herzegovina within 60 days after a final court judgment is entered determining the constitutional validity of the concurrent resolution, unless a declaration of war or specific authorization for such use of U.S. armed forces has been enacted. Rejected 193-225: R 180-43; D 13-181 (ND 10-131, SD 3-50); I 0-1. March 18, 1998. A "nay" was a vote in support of the president's position.

59. HR 2870. Tropical Forest Conservation/Rule. Adoption of the rule (H Res 388) to provide for floor consideration of the bill to authorize the president to forgive or reduce debts of developing countries to the United States in exchange for protection of tropical forests in those countries. Adopted 411-0: R 216-0; D 194-0 (ND 143-0, SD 51-0); I 1-0. March 19, 1998.

[1] Lois Capps, D-Calif., was sworn in March 17, replacing Walter Capps, D. Calif., who died Oct. 28, 1997.

Key

- Y Voted for (yea).
- # Paired for.
- + Announced for.
- N Voted against (nay).
- X Paired against.
- – Announced against.
- P Voted "present."
- C Voted "present" to avoid possible conflict of interest.
- ? Did not vote or otherwise make a position known.

Democrats **Republicans** Independent

	53	54	55	56	57	58	59
ALABAMA							
1 *Callahan*	Y	Y	Y	Y	Y	N	Y
2 *Everett*	Y	Y	Y	Y	Y	Y	Y
3 *Riley*	Y	Y	Y	Y	Y	Y	Y
4 *Aderholt*	Y	Y	Y	Y	Y	Y	Y
5 Cramer	Y	Y	Y	Y	Y	N	Y
6 *Bachus*	Y	Y	Y	Y	Y	Y	Y
7 Hilliard	N	Y	Y	Y	Y	N	Y
ALASKA							
AL *Young*	Y	Y	Y	Y	Y	N	?
ARIZONA							
1 *Salmon*	?	?	?	Y	Y	Y	Y
2 Pastor	Y	Y	Y	Y	Y	N	Y
3 *Stump*	Y	Y	Y	Y	Y	Y	Y
4 *Shadegg*	Y	Y	Y	Y	Y	Y	Y
5 *Kolbe*	Y	Y	Y	Y	Y	N	Y
6 *Hayworth*	Y	Y	Y	Y	Y	Y	Y
ARKANSAS							
1 Berry	Y	Y	Y	Y	Y	N	Y
2 Snyder	Y	Y	Y	Y	Y	Y	Y
3 *Hutchinson*	Y	Y	?	Y	Y	Y	Y
4 *Dickey*	N	Y	Y	Y	?	Y	Y
CALIFORNIA							
1 *Riggs*	Y	Y	Y	Y	Y	Y	?
2 *Herger*	Y	Y	Y	?	Y	Y	Y
3 Fazio	N	Y	Y	Y	Y	N	Y
4 *Doolittle*	?	Y	Y	?	?	Y	Y
5 Matsui	Y	Y	Y	Y	Y	N	Y
6 Woolsey	Y	Y	Y	Y	Y	Y	Y
7 Miller	Y	Y	Y	Y	Y	N	Y
8 Pelosi	Y	Y	Y	Y	Y	N	Y
9 Vacant							
10 Tauscher	Y	Y	Y	Y	Y	N	Y
11 *Pombo*	Y	Y	Y	Y	Y	Y	Y
12 Lantos	Y	Y	Y	Y	Y	N	Y
13 Stark	Y	Y	Y	Y	Y	N	Y
14 Eshoo	Y	Y	Y	Y	Y	N	Y
15 *Campbell*	Y	Y	Y	Y	Y	Y	Y
16 Lofgren	Y	Y	Y	Y	Y	N	Y
17 Farr	Y	Y	Y	Y	Y	N	Y
18 Condit	Y	Y	Y	Y	Y	Y	Y
19 *Radanovich*	Y	Y	Y	Y	Y	Y	Y
20 Dooley	Y	Y	Y	Y	Y	N	Y
21 *Thomas*	Y	Y	Y	Y	Y	Y	Y
22 Capps, L.[1]		Y	Y	Y	Y	Y	Y
23 *Gallegly*	Y	Y	Y	Y	Y	Y	?
24 Sherman	Y	Y	Y	Y	Y	N	Y
25 *McKeon*	Y	Y	Y	Y	Y	Y	Y
26 Berman	Y	Y	Y	Y	Y	Y	Y
27 *Rogan*	N	Y	Y	Y	Y	Y	Y
28 *Dreier*	Y	Y	Y	Y	Y	Y	Y
29 Waxman	Y	Y	Y	Y	Y	N	Y
30 Becerra	N	Y	Y	Y	Y	N	Y
31 Martinez	?	?	?	?	?	?	?
32 Dixon	Y	Y	Y	Y	Y	N	Y
33 Royal-Allard	Y	Y	Y	Y	Y	N	Y
34 Torres	Y	Y	Y	Y	Y	Y	Y
35 Waters	N	Y	Y	Y	Y	N	Y
36 Harman	Y	?	Y	Y	Y	N	Y
37 Millender-McD.	Y	Y	Y	Y	Y	N	Y

	53	54	55	56	57	58	59
38 *Horn*	Y	Y	Y	Y	Y	Y	Y
39 *Royce*	Y	Y	Y	Y	Y	Y	Y
40 *Lewis*	Y	Y	Y	Y	Y	N	Y
41 *Kim*	Y	Y	Y	Y	Y	N	Y
42 Brown	N	Y	Y	Y	Y	N	Y
43 *Calvert*	Y	Y	Y	Y	Y	Y	Y
44 Vacant							
45 *Rohrabacher*	Y	Y	Y	Y	Y	Y	Y
46 Sanchez	Y	Y	Y	Y	Y	N	Y
47 *Cox*	Y	Y	Y	Y	Y	Y	Y
48 *Packard*	Y	Y	Y	Y	Y	Y	Y
49 *Bilbray*	?	?	?	Y	Y	Y	Y
50 Filner	N	Y	Y	Y	Y	Y	Y
51 *Cunningham*	Y	Y	Y	Y	Y	Y	?
52 *Hunter*	?	?	?	Y	Y	N	Y
COLORADO							
1 DeGette	Y	Y	Y	Y	Y	N	Y
2 Skaggs	Y	Y	Y	Y	Y	N	Y
3 *McInnis*	?	?	?	Y	Y	Y	Y
4 *Schaffer*	N	Y	Y	Y	Y	Y	Y
5 *Hefley*	N	Y	Y	Y	Y	Y	Y
6 *Schaefer*	Y	Y	Y	Y	Y	Y	Y
CONNECTICUT							
1 Kennelly	Y	Y	Y	Y	Y	N	Y
2 Gejdenson	Y	Y	Y	Y	Y	N	Y
3 DeLauro	Y	Y	Y	Y	Y	N	Y
4 *Shays*	Y	Y	Y	Y	Y	Y	Y
5 Maloney	Y	Y	Y	Y	Y	N	Y
6 *Johnson*	Y	Y	Y	Y	Y	Y	Y
DELAWARE							
AL *Castle*	Y	Y	Y	Y	Y	N	Y
FLORIDA							
1 *Scarborough*	Y	Y	Y	Y	+	Y	Y
2 Boyd	Y	Y	Y	Y	Y	N	Y
3 Brown	Y	Y	Y	Y	Y	N	Y
4 *Fowler*	Y	Y	Y	Y	Y	Y	Y
5 Thurman	Y	Y	Y	Y	Y	N	Y
6 *Stearns*	Y	Y	Y	Y	Y	Y	Y
7 *Mica*	Y	Y	Y	Y	Y	Y	Y
8 *McCollum*	Y	Y	Y	Y	Y	Y	Y
9 *Bilirakis*	Y	Y	Y	Y	Y	Y	Y
10 *Young*	Y	Y	Y	Y	Y	N	Y
11 Davis	Y	Y	Y	Y	Y	N	Y
12 *Canady*	Y	Y	Y	Y	Y	Y	Y
13 *Miller*	Y	Y	Y	Y	Y	Y	Y
14 *Goss*	Y	Y	Y	Y	Y	N	Y
15 *Weldon*	Y	Y	Y	Y	Y	Y	Y
16 *Foley*	Y	Y	Y	Y	Y	Y	Y
17 Meek	Y	Y	Y	Y	Y	N	Y
18 *Ros-Lehtinen*	Y	Y	Y	Y	Y	Y	Y
19 Wexler	Y	Y	Y	Y	Y	N	Y
20 Deutsch	Y	Y	Y	Y	Y	N	Y
21 *Diaz-Balart*	?	+	+	Y	Y	Y	Y
22 *Shaw*	Y	Y	Y	Y	Y	Y	Y
23 Hastings	N	Y	Y	Y	Y	N	Y
GEORGIA							
1 *Kingston*	Y	Y	Y	Y	Y	Y	Y
2 Bishop	Y	Y	Y	Y	Y	N	Y
3 *Collins*	Y	?	?	Y	Y	Y	Y
4 McKinney	Y	Y	Y	Y	Y	N	Y
5 Lewis	N	Y	Y	Y	Y	N	?
6 *Gingrich*							
7 *Barr*	Y	Y	Y	P	P	Y	Y
8 *Chambliss*	Y	Y	Y	Y	Y	N	Y
9 *Deal*	Y	Y	Y	Y	Y	Y	Y
10 *Norwood*	Y	Y	Y	Y	Y	Y	Y
11 *Linder*	Y	Y	Y	Y	Y	Y	Y
HAWAII							
1 Abercrombie	Y	Y	Y	Y	Y	N	Y
2 Mink	Y	Y	Y	Y	Y	N	Y
IDAHO							
1 *Chenoweth*	Y	Y	Y	Y	Y	Y	Y
2 *Crapo*	Y	Y	Y	Y	Y	Y	Y
ILLINOIS							
1 Rush	?	?	?	Y	Y	N	Y
2 Jackson	Y	Y	Y	Y	Y	N	Y
3 Lipinski	?	?	?	?	?	?	Y
4 Gutierrez	?	?	?	?	?	?	Y
5 Blagojevich	Y	Y	Y	Y	Y	N	Y
6 *Hyde*	Y	Y	Y	Y	Y	Y	Y
7 Davis	?	?	?	?	?	?	Y
8 *Crane*	?	+	+	?	?	Y	Y
9 Yates	?	?	Y	Y	Y	N	Y
10 *Porter*	Y	?	?	Y	Y	Y	Y
11 *Weller*	N	Y	Y	Y	Y	Y	Y
12 Costello	?	?	?	Y	Y	N	Y

ND Northern Democrats   SD Southern Democrats

	53	54	55	56	57	58	59
13 ***Fawell***	?	?	?	Y	?	N	Y
14 ***Hastert***	+	+	+	Y	Y	Y	Y
15 ***Ewing***	Y	Y	Y	?	Y	Y	Y
16 ***Manzullo***	Y	Y	Y	Y	Y	Y	Y
17 Evans	Y	Y	Y	Y	Y	N	Y
18 ***LaHood***	Y	Y	Y	Y	Y	Y	Y
19 Poshard	?	?	?	?	?	?	?
20 ***Shimkus***	Y	Y	Y	Y	Y	Y	Y
INDIANA							
1 Visclosky	N	Y	Y	Y	Y	N	Y
2 ***McIntosh***	Y	Y	Y	?	Y	Y	Y
3 Roemer	Y	Y	Y	Y	Y	N	Y
4 ***Souder***	Y	Y	Y	Y	Y	Y	Y
5 ***Buyer***	Y	Y	Y	Y	Y	N	Y
6 ***Burton***	Y	Y	Y	Y	Y	Y	Y
7 ***Pease***	Y	Y	Y	Y	Y	Y	Y
8 ***Hostettler***	Y	Y	Y	Y	Y	N	Y
9 Hamilton	Y	Y	Y	Y	Y	N	Y
10 Carson	Y	Y	Y	Y	Y	N	Y
IOWA							
1 ***Leach***	Y	Y	Y	Y	Y	N	Y
2 ***Nussle***	Y	Y	Y	Y	Y	Y	Y
3 Boswell	Y	Y	Y	Y	Y	N	Y
4 ***Ganske***	Y	Y	Y	Y	Y	Y	Y
5 ***Latham***	Y	Y	Y	Y	Y	Y	Y
KANSAS							
1 ***Moran***	N	Y	Y	Y	Y	Y	Y
2 ***Ryun***	Y	Y	Y	Y	Y	Y	Y
3 ***Snowbarger***	Y	Y	Y	Y	Y	Y	Y
4 ***Tiahrt***	Y	Y	Y	Y	Y	N	Y
KENTUCKY							
1 ***Whitfield***	Y	Y	Y	Y	Y	Y	Y
2 ***Lewis***	Y	Y	Y	Y	Y	Y	Y
3 ***Northup***	Y	Y	Y	Y	Y	N	Y
4 ***Bunning***	Y	Y	Y	Y	Y	Y	Y
5 ***Rogers***	Y	Y	Y	Y	Y	Y	Y
6 Baesler	Y	Y	Y	Y	Y	N	Y
LOUISIANA							
1 ***Livingston***	Y	Y	Y	Y	Y	Y	?
2 Jefferson	N	Y	Y	Y	Y	N	Y
3 ***Tauzin***	Y	Y	Y	Y	Y	Y	Y
4 ***McCrery***	Y	Y	Y	Y	Y	Y	Y
5 ***Cooksey***	Y	Y	Y	Y	Y	Y	Y
6 ***Baker***	Y	Y	Y	Y	Y	Y	Y
7 John	Y	Y	Y	Y	Y	N	Y
MAINE							
1 Allen	Y	Y	Y	Y	Y	N	Y
2 Baldacci	Y	Y	Y	Y	Y	N	Y
MARYLAND							
1 ***Gilchrest***	Y	Y	Y	Y	Y	N	Y
2 ***Ehrlich***	Y	Y	Y	Y	Y	Y	Y
3 Cardin	Y	Y	Y	Y	Y	N	Y
4 Wynn	Y	Y	Y	Y	Y	N	Y
5 Hoyer	Y	Y	Y	Y	Y	N	Y
6 ***Bartlett***	Y	Y	Y	Y	Y	Y	Y
7 Cummings	Y	Y	Y	Y	Y	N	Y
8 ***Morella***	Y	Y	Y	Y	Y	N	Y
MASSACHUSETTS							
1 Olver	Y	Y	Y	Y	Y	N	Y
2 Neal	Y	Y	Y	Y	Y	N	Y
3 McGovern	Y	Y	Y	Y	Y	N	Y
4 Frank	Y	Y	Y	Y	Y	N	Y
5 Meehan	Y	Y	Y	Y	Y	N	Y
6 Tierney	Y	Y	Y	Y	Y	?	Y
7 Markey	Y	Y	Y	Y	Y	Y	Y
8 Kennedy	?	?	?	Y	Y	N	Y
9 Moakley	?	?	?	Y	Y	N	Y
10 Delahunt	Y	Y	Y	Y	Y	N	Y
MICHIGAN							
1 Stupak	?	?	?	?	?	?	Y
2 ***Hoekstra***	Y	Y	Y	Y	Y	Y	Y
3 ***Ehlers***	Y	Y	Y	Y	Y	Y	Y
4 ***Camp***	Y	Y	Y	Y	Y	Y	Y
5 Barcia	Y	Y	Y	Y	Y	N	Y
6 ***Upton***	Y	Y	Y	Y	Y	Y	Y
7 ***Smith***	Y	Y	Y	Y	Y	Y	Y
8 Stabenow	Y	Y	Y	Y	Y	N	Y
9 Kildee	Y	Y	Y	Y	Y	N	Y
10 Bonior	Y	Y	Y	Y	Y	N	Y
11 ***Knollenberg***	Y	Y	Y	Y	Y	N	Y
12 Levin	Y	Y	Y	Y	Y	N	Y
13 Rivers	Y	Y	Y	Y	Y	N	Y
14 Conyers	Y	Y	Y	Y	Y	N	Y
15 Kilpatrick	Y	Y	Y	Y	Y	N	Y
16 Dingell	Y	Y	Y	Y	Y	N	Y

	53	54	55	56	57	58	59
MINNESOTA							
1 ***Gutknecht***	Y	Y	Y	Y	Y	Y	?
2 Minge	Y	Y	Y	Y	Y	N	Y
3 ***Ramstad***	N	Y	Y	Y	Y	Y	Y
4 Vento	Y	Y	Y	Y	Y	N	Y
5 Sabo	N	Y	Y	Y	Y	N	Y
6 Luther	Y	Y	Y	Y	Y	N	Y
7 Peterson	Y	Y	Y	Y	Y	Y	Y
8 Oberstar	N	Y	Y	Y	Y	N	Y
MISSISSIPPI							
1 ***Wicker***	Y	Y	Y	Y	Y	N	Y
2 Thompson	N	Y	Y	Y	Y	N	Y
3 ***Pickering***	?	Y	Y	Y	Y	Y	Y
4 ***Parker***	?	?	?	?	?	?	?
5 Taylor	N	Y	Y	Y	Y	N	Y
MISSOURI							
1 Clay	N	Y	Y	Y	Y	N	Y
2 ***Talent***	Y	Y	Y	Y	Y	Y	Y
3 Gephardt	Y	Y	Y	?	?	?	?
4 Skelton	Y	Y	Y	Y	Y	N	Y
5 McCarthy	Y	Y	Y	Y	Y	N	Y
6 Danner	Y	Y	Y	Y	Y	Y	Y
7 ***Blunt***	Y	Y	Y	Y	Y	Y	Y
8 ***Emerson***	Y	Y	Y	Y	Y	Y	Y
9 ***Hulshof***	Y	Y	Y	Y	Y	Y	Y
MONTANA							
AL ***Hill***	Y	Y	Y	Y	Y	Y	Y
NEBRASKA							
1 ***Bereuter***	Y	Y	Y	Y	Y	Y	Y
2 ***Christensen***	Y	Y	Y	Y	Y	Y	Y
3 ***Barrett***	Y	Y	Y	Y	Y	Y	Y
NEVADA							
1 ***Ensign***	N	Y	Y	Y	Y	Y	Y
2 ***Gibbons***	Y	Y	Y	Y	Y	Y	Y
NEW HAMPSHIRE							
1 ***Sununu***	Y	Y	Y	Y	Y	Y	Y
2 ***Bass***	Y	Y	Y	Y	Y	Y	Y
NEW JERSEY							
1 Andrews	?	?	?	Y	Y	N	Y
2 ***LoBiondo***	N	Y	Y	Y	Y	Y	Y
3 ***Saxton***	Y	Y	Y	Y	Y	Y	Y
4 ***Smith***	Y	Y	Y	Y	Y	N	Y
5 ***Roukema***	Y	Y	Y	Y	Y	Y	Y
6 Pallone	Y	Y	Y	Y	Y	N	Y
7 ***Franks***	Y	Y	Y	Y	Y	Y	Y
8 Pascrell	Y	Y	Y	Y	Y	N	Y
9 Rothman	Y	Y	Y	Y	Y	N	Y
10 Payne	Y	Y	Y	Y	Y	N	Y
11 ***Frelinghuysen***	Y	Y	Y	Y	Y	Y	Y
12 ***Pappas***	Y	Y	Y	Y	Y	Y	Y
13 Menendez	Y	Y	Y	Y	Y	N	Y
NEW MEXICO							
1 ***Schiff***	?	?	?	?	?	?	?
2 ***Skeen***	Y	Y	Y	Y	Y	Y	Y
3 ***Redmond***	Y	Y	Y	Y	Y	Y	Y
NEW YORK							
1 ***Forbes***	Y	Y	Y	Y	Y	Y	Y
2 ***Lazio***	Y	Y	Y	Y	Y	N	Y
3 ***King***	Y	Y	Y	Y	Y	N	Y
4 McCarthy	Y	Y	Y	Y	Y	N	Y
5 Ackerman	Y	Y	Y	Y	Y	N	Y
6 Meeks	Y	Y	Y	Y	Y	N	Y
7 Manton	Y	Y	Y	Y	Y	N	Y
8 Nadler	Y	Y	Y	Y	Y	N	Y
9 Schumer	Y	Y	Y	Y	Y	N	Y
10 Towns	Y	Y	Y	Y	Y	N	Y
11 Owens	Y	Y	Y	Y	Y	N	Y
12 Velázquez	Y	Y	Y	Y	Y	N	Y
13 ***Fossella***	Y	Y	Y	Y	Y	Y	Y
14 Maloney	Y	Y	Y	Y	Y	N	Y
15 Rangel	Y	Y	Y	Y	Y	N	?
16 Serrano	Y	Y	Y	Y	Y	N	Y
17 Engel	Y	Y	Y	Y	Y	N	?
18 Lowey	Y	Y	Y	Y	Y	N	Y
19 ***Kelly***	Y	Y	Y	Y	Y	Y	Y
20 ***Gilman***	Y	Y	Y	Y	Y	N	Y
21 McNulty	+	+	+	Y	Y	N	Y
22 ***Solomon***	Y	Y	Y	Y	Y	N	Y
23 ***Boehlert***	Y	Y	Y	Y	Y	N	Y
24 ***McHugh***	Y	Y	Y	Y	Y	Y	Y
25 ***Walsh***	Y	Y	Y	Y	Y	Y	Y
26 Hinchey	N	Y	Y	Y	Y	N	Y
27 ***Paxon***	Y	Y	Y	Y	Y	Y	Y
28 Slaughter	Y	Y	Y	Y	Y	N	Y
29 LaFalce	Y	Y	Y	Y	Y	N	Y

	53	54	55	56	57	58	59
30 ***Quinn***	Y	Y	Y	Y	Y	N	Y
31 ***Houghton***	Y	Y	Y	N	Y	N	Y
NORTH CAROLINA							
1 Clayton	Y	Y	Y	Y	Y	N	Y
2 Etheridge	Y	Y	Y	Y	Y	N	Y
3 ***Jones***	Y	Y	Y	Y	Y	Y	Y
4 Price	Y	Y	Y	Y	Y	N	Y
5 ***Burr***	Y	Y	Y	Y	Y	Y	Y
6 ***Coble***	Y	Y	Y	Y	Y	Y	Y
7 McIntyre	Y	Y	Y	Y	Y	N	Y
8 Hefner	Y	Y	Y	?	?	?	?
9 ***Myrick***	Y	Y	Y	Y	Y	Y	Y
10 ***Ballenger***	Y	Y	Y	Y	Y	Y	Y
11 ***Taylor***	Y	Y	Y	Y	Y	Y	Y
12 Watt	Y	Y	Y	Y	Y	N	Y
NORTH DAKOTA							
AL Pomeroy	Y	Y	Y	Y	Y	N	Y
OHIO							
1 ***Chabot***	Y	Y	Y	Y	Y	Y	Y
2 ***Portman***	Y	Y	Y	Y	Y	N	Y
3 Hall	Y	Y	Y	Y	Y	N	Y
4 ***Oxley***	Y	Y	Y	Y	Y	N	Y
5 ***Gillmor***	N	Y	Y	Y	Y	N	Y
6 Strickland	Y	Y	Y	Y	Y	N	?
7 ***Hobson***	Y	Y	Y	Y	?	Y	Y
8 ***Boehner***	Y	Y	Y	Y	Y	N	Y
9 Kaptur	Y	Y	Y	Y	Y	N	Y
10 Kucinich	N	Y	Y	Y	Y	N	Y
11 Stokes	Y	Y	Y	Y	Y	N	Y
12 ***Kasich***	Y	Y	Y	Y	Y	Y	Y
13 Brown	Y	Y	Y	Y	Y	N	Y
14 Sawyer	Y	Y	Y	Y	Y	N	Y
15 ***Pryce***	Y	Y	Y	Y	Y	Y	Y
16 ***Regula***	Y	Y	Y	Y	Y	Y	Y
17 Traficant	Y	Y	Y	Y	Y	Y	Y
18 ***Ney***	Y	Y	Y	Y	Y	Y	Y
19 ***LaTourette***	Y	Y	Y	Y	Y	N	Y
OKLAHOMA							
1 ***Largent***	Y	Y	?	Y	Y	N	Y
2 ***Coburn***	Y	Y	Y	Y	Y	Y	Y
3 ***Watkins***	Y	Y	Y	Y	Y	Y	Y
4 ***Watts***	N	Y	Y	Y	Y	Y	Y
5 ***Istook***	Y	Y	Y	Y	Y	Y	Y
6 ***Lucas***	Y	Y	Y	Y	Y	Y	Y
OREGON							
1 Furse	Y	Y	Y	Y	Y	N	Y
2 ***Smith***	Y	Y	Y	Y	Y	Y	Y
3 Blumenauer	Y	Y	Y	Y	Y	N	Y
4 DeFazio	N	Y	Y	Y	Y	Y	Y
5 Hooley	Y	Y	Y	Y	Y	N	Y
PENNSYLVANIA							
1 Vacant							
2 Fattah	Y	Y	Y	Y	Y	N	Y
3 Borski	?	?	?	Y	Y	N	Y
4 Klink	Y	Y	Y	Y	Y	N	Y
5 ***Peterson***	Y	Y	Y	Y	Y	Y	Y
6 Holden	Y	Y	Y	Y	Y	N	Y
7 ***Weldon***	Y	Y	Y	Y	Y	Y	Y
8 ***Greenwood***	Y	Y	Y	Y	Y	Y	Y
9 ***Shuster***	Y	Y	Y	Y	Y	Y	Y
10 ***McDade***	?	?	?	?	?	?	?
11 Kanjorski	Y	Y	Y	Y	Y	N	Y
12 Murtha	Y	Y	Y	Y	Y	N	Y
13 ***Fox***	N	Y	Y	Y	Y	Y	Y
14 Coyne	Y	Y	Y	Y	Y	N	Y
15 McHale	Y	Y	Y	Y	Y	N	Y
16 ***Pitts***	Y	Y	Y	Y	Y	Y	Y
17 ***Gekas***	Y	Y	Y	Y	?	Y	Y
18 Doyle	Y	Y	Y	Y	Y	N	Y
19 ***Goodling***	Y	Y	Y	Y	Y	Y	Y
20 Mascara	Y	Y	Y	Y	Y	N	Y
21 ***English***	N	?	Y	Y	Y	Y	Y
RHODE ISLAND							
1 Kennedy	Y	Y	Y	Y	Y	N	Y
2 Weygand	Y	Y	Y	Y	Y	N	Y
SOUTH CAROLINA							
1 ***Sanford***	?	?	?	Y	Y	Y	Y
2 ***Spence***	Y	Y	Y	Y	Y	Y	Y
3 ***Graham***	Y	Y	Y	Y	?	Y	Y
4 ***Inglis***	?	?	?	?	?	Y	Y
5 Spratt	Y	Y	Y	Y	Y	N	Y
6 Clyburn	N	Y	Y	Y	Y	N	Y
SOUTH DAKOTA							
AL ***Thune***	Y	Y	Y	Y	Y	Y	Y

	53	54	55	56	57	58	59
TENNESSEE							
1 ***Jenkins***	Y	Y	Y	Y	Y	Y	Y
2 ***Duncan***	Y	Y	Y	Y	Y	Y	Y
3 ***Wamp***	Y	Y	Y	Y	Y	Y	Y
4 ***Hilleary***	N	Y	Y	Y	Y	Y	Y
5 Clement	Y	Y	Y	Y	Y	N	Y
6 Gordon	Y	Y	Y	Y	Y	N	Y
7 ***Bryant***	Y	Y	Y	Y	Y	Y	Y
8 Tanner	Y	Y	Y	Y	Y	N	Y
9 Ford	Y	Y	Y	Y	Y	N	Y
TEXAS							
1 Sandlin	Y	Y	Y	Y	Y	N	Y
2 Turner	?	?	?	?	?	N	Y
3 ***Johnson, Sam***	Y	Y	Y	Y	Y	Y	Y
4 Hall	Y	Y	Y	Y	Y	Y	Y
5 ***Sessions***	N	Y	Y	Y	Y	Y	Y
6 ***Barton***	Y	Y	Y	Y	Y	Y	Y
7 ***Archer***	Y	Y	Y	Y	Y	Y	Y
8 ***Brady***	Y	Y	Y	Y	Y	Y	Y
9 Lampson	Y	Y	Y	Y	Y	N	Y
10 Doggett	Y	Y	Y	Y	Y	Y	Y
11 Edwards	Y	Y	Y	Y	Y	N	Y
12 ***Granger***	Y	Y	Y	Y	Y	Y	Y
13 ***Thornberry***	Y	Y	Y	Y	Y	N	Y
14 ***Paul***	Y	Y	N	N	N	Y	Y
15 Hinojosa	Y	Y	Y	Y	Y	N	Y
16 Reyes	Y	Y	Y	Y	Y	N	Y
17 Stenholm	N	Y	Y	Y	Y	N	Y
18 Jackson-Lee	Y	Y	Y	Y	Y	N	Y
19 ***Combest***	Y	Y	Y	Y	Y	Y	Y
20 Gonzalez	?	?	?	?	?	?	?
21 ***Smith***	Y	Y	Y	Y	Y	Y	Y
22 ***DeLay***	Y	Y	Y	Y	Y	Y	Y
23 ***Bonilla***	Y	Y	Y	Y	Y	Y	Y
24 Frost	Y	Y	Y	Y	Y	N	?
25 Bentsen	Y	Y	Y	Y	Y	N	Y
26 ***Armey***	Y	Y	Y	?	Y	Y	Y
27 Ortiz	Y	Y	Y	Y	Y	N	Y
28 Rodriguez	Y	Y	Y	Y	Y	N	Y
29 Green	Y	Y	Y	Y	Y	N	Y
30 Johnson, E.B.	N	Y	Y	Y	Y	N	Y
UTAH							
1 ***Hansen***	Y	Y	Y	Y	Y	Y	Y
2 ***Cook***	Y	Y	Y	Y	Y	Y	Y
3 ***Cannon***	?	?	?	Y	Y	Y	Y
VERMONT							
AL *Sanders*	Y	Y	Y	Y	Y	N	Y
VIRGINIA							
1 ***Bateman***	Y	Y	Y	Y	Y	N	Y
2 Pickett	N	Y	Y	Y	Y	N	Y
3 Scott	Y	Y	Y	Y	Y	N	Y
4 Sisisky	Y	Y	Y	Y	Y	N	Y
5 Goode	Y	Y	Y	Y	Y	Y	Y
6 ***Goodlatte***	Y	Y	Y	Y	Y	Y	Y
7 ***Bliley***	Y	Y	Y	Y	Y	N	Y
8 Moran	Y	Y	Y	Y	Y	N	Y
9 Boucher	Y	Y	Y	Y	Y	N	Y
10 ***Wolf***	Y	Y	Y	Y	Y	N	Y
11 ***Davis***	Y	Y	Y	Y	Y	N	Y
WASHINGTON							
1 ***White***	Y	Y	Y	Y	Y	Y	Y
2 ***Metcalf***	Y	Y	Y	Y	Y	Y	Y
3 ***Smith, Linda***	Y	Y	Y	Y	Y	Y	Y
4 ***Hastings***	Y	Y	Y	?	Y	N	Y
5 ***Nethercutt***	Y	Y	Y	Y	Y	Y	Y
6 Dicks	Y	Y	Y	Y	Y	N	Y
7 McDermott	N	Y	Y	Y	Y	N	Y
8 ***Dunn***	?	?	?	Y	Y	N	Y
9 Smith, Adam	Y	Y	Y	Y	Y	N	Y
WEST VIRGINIA							
1 Mollohan	Y	Y	Y	Y	Y	N	Y
2 Wise	Y	Y	Y	Y	Y	N	Y
3 Rahall	Y	Y	Y	Y	Y	N	Y
WISCONSIN							
1 ***Neumann***	Y	Y	Y	Y	Y	Y	Y
2 ***Klug***	Y	Y	Y	Y	Y	Y	Y
3 Kind	Y	Y	Y	Y	Y	N	Y
4 Kleczka	Y	Y	Y	Y	Y	N	Y
5 Barrett	Y	Y	Y	Y	Y	N	Y
6 ***Petri***	Y	Y	Y	Y	Y	Y	Y
7 Obey	Y	Y	?	Y	Y	N	Y
8 Johnson	Y	Y	Y	Y	Y	N	Y
9 ***Sensenbrenner***	Y	Y	Y	Y	Y	Y	Y
WYOMING							
AL ***Cubin***	Y	Y	Y	Y	Y	Y	Y

Southern states - Ala., Ark., Fla., Ga., Ky., La., Miss., N.C., Okla., S.C., Tenn., Texas, Va.

House Votes 60, 61, 62, 63, 64, 65, 66

60. Procedural Motion/Journal. Approval of the House Journal of Wednesday, March 18, 1998. Approved 359-49: R 194-19; D 164-30 (ND 120-23, SD 44-7); I 1-0. March 19, 1998.

61. HR 2870. Tropical Forest Conservation/Notification. Gilman, R-N.Y., amendment to require the Clinton administration to notify Congress prior to finalizing any debt reduction transaction. Adopted 416-1: R 220-0; D 195-1 (ND 144-0, SD 51-1); I 1-0. March 19, 1998.

62. HR 2870. Tropical Forest Conservation/Medicinal Uses. Vento, D-Minn., amendment to expand the list of activities that could be supported with tropical forest protection funds to include research and identification of medical uses of tropical forest plant life, and require that indigenous leaders be consulted. Adopted 335-79: R 139-79; D 195-0 (ND 143-0, SD 52-0); I 1-0. March 19, 1998.

63. HR 2870. Tropical Forest Conservation/Passage. Passage of the bill to authorize the president to forgive or reduce debts of developing countries in exchange for protection of tropical forests in those countries. The bill would authorize the president to forgive up to $325 million of debt over the next three years for such projects and target debts to the United States incurred through the Agency for International Development and the Agriculture Department. Passed 356-61: R 161-60; D 194-1 (ND 142-1, SD 52-0); I 1-0. March 19, 1998. A "yea" was a vote in support of the president's position.

64. Procedural Motion/Journal. Approval of the House Journal of Monday, March 23, 1998. Approved 368-40: R 200-16; D 167-24 (ND 122-17, SD 45-7); I 1-0. March 24, 1998.

65. HR 3211. Arlington Cemetery Burials/Passage. Stump, R-Ariz., motion to suspend the rules and pass the bill to codify eligibility criteria for burial at Arlington National Cemetery to include individuals in the military who die on active duty, and most retired members of the armed forces. Motion agreed to 412-0: R 220-0; D 191-0 (ND 139-0, SD 52-0); I 1-0. March 24, 1998. A two-thirds majority of those present and voting (275 in this case) is required for passage under suspension of the rules.

66. HR 3412. Small Business Loans/Passage. Talent, R-Mo., motion to suspend the rules and pass the bill to reauthorize the activities of the Small Business Investment Companies program, which uses Small Business Administration guarantees to leverage private capital for investment in small businesses. Motion agreed to 407-0: R 215-0; D 191-0 (ND 139-0, SD 52-0); I 1-0. March 24, 1998. A two-thirds majority of those present and voting (272 in this case) is required for passage under suspension of the rules.

Key

- Y Voted for (yea).
- # Paired for.
- + Announced for.
- N Voted against (nay).
- X Paired against.
- − Announced against.
- P Voted "present."
- C Voted "present" to avoid possible conflict of interest.
- ? Did not vote or otherwise make a position known.

Democrats **Republicans** *Independent*

	60	61	62	63	64	65	66
ALABAMA							
1 *Callahan*	Y	Y	N	Y	Y	Y	Y
2 *Everett*	Y	Y	N	Y	Y	Y	Y
3 *Riley*	Y	Y	N	N	Y	Y	Y
4 *Aderholt*	Y	Y	N	N	Y	Y	Y
5 Cramer	Y	Y	Y	Y	Y	Y	Y
6 *Bachus*	Y	Y	N	Y	Y	Y	Y
7 Hilliard	N	N	Y	Y	N	Y	Y
ALASKA							
AL *Young*	?	Y	N	N	Y	Y	Y
ARIZONA							
1 *Salmon*	Y	Y	N	N	Y	Y	Y
2 Pastor	Y	Y	Y	Y	Y	Y	Y
3 *Stump*	Y	Y	N	N	Y	Y	Y
4 *Shadegg*	Y	Y	N	N	Y	Y	Y
5 *Kolbe*	Y	Y	Y	Y	Y	Y	Y
6 *Hayworth*	Y	Y	N	Y	Y	Y	Y
ARKANSAS							
1 Berry	Y	Y	Y	Y	Y	Y	Y
2 Snyder	Y	Y	Y	Y	Y	Y	Y
3 *Hutchinson*	?	Y	N	Y	Y	Y	Y
4 Dickey	N	Y	Y	Y	Y	Y	Y
CALIFORNIA							
1 *Riggs*	?	?	?	?	Y	Y	Y
2 *Herger*	N	Y	N	N	Y	Y	?
3 Fazio	N	Y	Y	Y	N	Y	Y
4 *Doolittle*	Y	Y	N	N	Y	Y	Y
5 Matsui	Y	Y	Y	Y	Y	Y	Y
6 Woolsey	Y	Y	Y	Y	Y	Y	Y
7 Miller	N	Y	Y	Y	Y	Y	Y
8 Pelosi	Y	Y	Y	Y	Y	Y	Y
9 Vacant							
10 Tauscher	Y	Y	Y	Y	Y	Y	Y
11 *Pombo*	Y	Y	N	Y	Y	Y	Y
12 Lantos	Y	Y	Y	Y	Y	Y	Y
13 Stark	N	Y	Y	?	?	?	?
14 Eshoo	Y	Y	Y	Y	Y	Y	Y
15 *Campbell*	Y	Y	Y	Y	Y	Y	Y
16 Lofgren	Y	Y	Y	Y	Y	Y	Y
17 Farr	Y	Y	Y	Y	Y	Y	Y
18 Condit	Y	Y	Y	Y	Y	Y	Y
19 *Radanovich*	Y	Y	N	Y	Y	Y	Y
20 Dooley	Y	Y	Y	Y	Y	Y	Y
21 *Thomas*	Y	Y	N	Y	Y	Y	Y
22 Capps, L.	Y	Y	Y	Y	+	+	Y
23 *Gallegly*	?	?	?	?	Y	Y	Y
24 Sherman	Y	Y	Y	Y	Y	Y	Y
25 *McKeon*	Y	Y	N	Y	Y	Y	Y
26 Berman	Y	Y	Y	Y	Y	Y	Y
27 *Rogan*	N	Y	N	Y	N	Y	Y
28 *Dreier*	Y	Y	Y	Y	Y	Y	Y
29 Waxman	Y	Y	Y	Y	Y	Y	Y
30 Becerra	N	Y	Y	Y	N	Y	?
31 Martinez	?	?	?	?	Y	Y	Y
32 Dixon	Y	Y	Y	Y	Y	Y	Y
33 Roybal-Allard	Y	Y	Y	Y	Y	Y	Y
34 Torres	Y	Y	Y	Y	Y	Y	Y
35 Waters	N	Y	Y	Y	?	?	Y
36 Harman	Y	Y	Y	Y	?	?	Y
37 Millender-McD.	Y	Y	Y	Y	Y	Y	Y

	60	61	62	63	64	65	66
38 *Horn*	Y	Y	Y	Y	Y	Y	Y
39 *Royce*	Y	Y	?	Y	?	?	?
40 *Lewis*	Y	Y	Y	Y	Y	Y	Y
41 *Kim*	Y	Y	Y	Y	Y	Y	Y
42 Brown	N	Y	Y	Y	N	Y	Y
43 *Calvert*	?	Y	Y	Y	Y	Y	Y
44 Vacant							
45 *Rohrabacher*	Y	Y	Y	Y	Y	Y	Y
46 Sanchez	Y	Y	Y	Y	Y	Y	Y
47 *Cox*	Y	Y	Y	Y	Y	Y	Y
48 *Packard*	Y	Y	Y	Y	Y	Y	Y
49 *Bilbray*	Y	Y	Y	Y	Y	Y	Y
50 Filner	N	Y	Y	Y	N	Y	Y
51 *Cunningham*	Y	Y	Y	Y	Y	Y	Y
52 *Hunter*	Y	Y	Y	Y	Y	Y	Y
COLORADO							
1 DeGette	Y	Y	Y	Y	Y	Y	Y
2 Skaggs	Y	Y	Y	Y	Y	Y	Y
3 *McInnis*	Y	Y	Y	Y	Y	Y	Y
4 *Schaffer*	N	Y	N	N	N	Y	Y
5 *Hefley*	Y	Y	Y	Y	Y	Y	Y
6 *Schaefer*	Y	Y	Y	N	Y	Y	Y
CONNECTICUT							
1 Kennelly	Y	Y	Y	Y	Y	Y	Y
2 Gejdenson	Y	Y	Y	Y	Y	Y	Y
3 DeLauro	Y	Y	Y	Y	Y	Y	Y
4 *Shays*	Y	Y	Y	Y	Y	Y	Y
5 Maloney	Y	Y	Y	Y	Y	Y	Y
6 *Johnson*	Y	Y	Y	Y	Y	Y	Y
DELAWARE							
AL *Castle*	Y	Y	Y	Y	Y	Y	Y
FLORIDA							
1 *Scarborough*	Y	Y	Y	Y	Y	Y	Y
2 Boyd	Y	Y	Y	Y	Y	Y	Y
3 Brown	Y	Y	Y	Y	Y	Y	Y
4 *Fowler*	Y	Y	Y	Y	Y	Y	Y
5 Thurman	Y	Y	Y	Y	Y	Y	Y
6 *Stearns*	Y	Y	N	N	Y	Y	Y
7 *Mica*	Y	Y	N	Y	Y	Y	Y
8 *McCollum*	Y	Y	Y	Y	Y	Y	Y
9 *Bilirakis*	Y	Y	Y	Y	Y	Y	Y
10 *Young*	Y	Y	Y	Y	Y	Y	?
11 Davis	Y	Y	Y	Y	Y	Y	Y
12 *Canady*	Y	Y	Y	Y	Y	Y	Y
13 *Miller*	Y	Y	Y	Y	Y	Y	Y
14 *Goss*	Y	Y	Y	Y	Y	Y	Y
15 *Weldon*	Y	Y	Y	Y	Y	Y	Y
16 *Foley*	Y	+	+	Y	Y	Y	Y
17 Meek	Y	Y	Y	Y	Y	Y	Y
18 *Ros-Lehtinen*	Y	Y	Y	Y	Y	Y	Y
19 Wexler	Y	Y	Y	Y	Y	Y	Y
20 Deutsch	Y	Y	Y	Y	Y	Y	Y
21 *Diaz-Balart*	Y	Y	Y	Y	?	Y	Y
22 *Shaw*	Y	Y	Y	Y	Y	Y	Y
23 Hastings	N	Y	Y	Y	Y	Y	Y
GEORGIA							
1 *Kingston*	Y	Y	Y	Y	Y	Y	Y
2 Bishop	Y	Y	Y	Y	Y	Y	Y
3 *Collins*	Y	Y	N	N	Y	Y	Y
4 *McKinney*	Y	Y	Y	Y	Y	Y	Y
5 Lewis	?	?	?	?	N	Y	Y
6 *Gingrich*							
7 *Barr*	Y	Y	N	N	Y	Y	Y
8 *Chambliss*	Y	Y	Y	Y	Y	Y	Y
9 *Deal*	Y	Y	Y	Y	?	Y	Y
10 *Norwood*	Y	Y	Y	Y	Y	Y	Y
11 *Linder*	Y	Y	Y	Y	Y	Y	Y
HAWAII							
1 Abercrombie	N	Y	Y	Y	Y	Y	Y
2 Mink	Y	Y	Y	Y	Y	Y	Y
IDAHO							
1 *Chenoweth*	N	Y	N	N	+	+	+
2 *Crapo*	Y	Y	N	Y	Y	Y	Y
ILLINOIS							
1 Rush	Y	Y	Y	Y	Y	Y	Y
2 Jackson	Y	Y	Y	Y	Y	Y	Y
3 Lipinski	Y	Y	Y	Y	Y	Y	Y
4 Gutierrez	Y	Y	Y	Y	N	Y	Y
5 Blagojevich	Y	Y	Y	Y	Y	Y	Y
6 *Hyde*	Y	Y	Y	Y	Y	Y	Y
7 Davis	Y	Y	Y	Y	Y	Y	Y
8 *Crane*	?	Y	N	N	N	Y	Y
9 Yates	N	Y	Y	?	?	?	Y
10 *Porter*	Y	Y	Y	Y	Y	Y	Y
11 *Weller*	N	Y	Y	N	Y	Y	Y
12 Costello	N	Y	Y	N	Y	Y	Y

ND Northern Democrats   SD Southern Democrats

	60	61	62	63	64	65	66
13 ***Fawell***	N	Y	Y	Y	Y	Y	Y
14 ***Hastert***	Y	Y	Y	Y	Y	Y	Y
15 ***Ewing***	Y	Y	Y	Y	Y	Y	Y
16 ***Manzullo***	?	Y	Y	Y	?	?	?
17 Evans	Y	Y	Y	Y	Y	Y	Y
18 ***LaHood***	Y	Y	Y	Y	Y	Y	Y
19 Poshard	?	?	?	?	Y	Y	Y
20 ***Shimkus***	Y	Y	Y	Y	Y	Y	Y
INDIANA							
1 Visclosky	N	Y	Y	Y	Y	Y	Y
2 ***McIntosh***	Y	Y	Y	Y	Y	Y	Y
3 Roemer	Y	Y	Y	Y	Y	Y	Y
4 ***Souder***	Y	Y	N	Y	Y	Y	Y
5 ***Buyer***	Y	Y	Y	Y	?	Y	Y
6 ***Burton***	Y	Y	N	N	Y	Y	Y
7 ***Pease***	Y	Y	Y	Y	Y	Y	Y
8 ***Hostettler***	Y	Y	N	N	Y	Y	Y
9 Hamilton	Y	Y	Y	Y	Y	Y	Y
10 Carson	N	Y	Y	Y	Y	Y	Y
IOWA							
1 ***Leach***	Y	Y	Y	Y	Y	Y	Y
2 ***Nussle***	Y	Y	Y	Y	Y	Y	Y
3 Boswell	Y	Y	Y	Y	Y	Y	Y
4 ***Ganske***	Y	Y	Y	Y	Y	Y	Y
5 ***Latham***	Y	Y	Y	Y	Y	Y	Y
KANSAS							
1 ***Moran***	N	Y	N	Y	N	Y	Y
2 ***Ryun***	Y	Y	N	N	Y	Y	Y
3 ***Snowbarger***	Y	Y	N	N	Y	Y	Y
4 ***Tiahrt***	Y	Y	N	N	Y	Y	Y
KENTUCKY							
1 ***Whitfield***	Y	Y	Y	Y	Y	Y	Y
2 ***Lewis***	Y	Y	–	N	Y	Y	Y
3 ***Northup***	Y	Y	Y	Y	Y	Y	Y
4 ***Bunning***	Y	Y	N	Y	Y	Y	Y
5 ***Rogers***	Y	Y	Y	Y	Y	Y	Y
6 Baesler	Y	Y	Y	Y	Y	Y	Y
LOUISIANA							
1 ***Livingston***	?	Y	Y	Y	Y	Y	Y
2 Jefferson	Y	Y	Y	Y	?	?	?
3 ***Tauzin***	Y	Y	Y	Y	Y	Y	Y
4 ***McCrery***	Y	Y	Y	Y	Y	Y	Y
5 ***Cooksey***	Y	Y	Y	Y	?	Y	Y
6 ***Baker***	Y	Y	N	Y	Y	Y	Y
7 John	Y	Y	Y	Y	Y	Y	Y
MAINE							
1 Allen	Y	Y	Y	Y	Y	Y	Y
2 Baldacci	Y	Y	Y	Y	Y	Y	Y
MARYLAND							
1 ***Gilchrest***	Y	Y	Y	Y	Y	Y	Y
2 ***Ehrlich***	Y	Y	Y	Y	N	Y	Y
3 Cardin	Y	Y	Y	Y	Y	Y	Y
4 Wynn	Y	Y	Y	Y	Y	Y	Y
5 Hoyer	?	Y	Y	Y	Y	Y	Y
6 ***Bartlett***	Y	Y	N	N	Y	Y	Y
7 Cummings	Y	Y	Y	Y	Y	Y	Y
8 ***Morella***	Y	Y	Y	Y	Y	Y	Y
MASSACHUSETTS							
1 Olver	Y	Y	Y	Y	Y	Y	Y
2 Neal	Y	Y	Y	Y	Y	Y	Y
3 McGovern	Y	Y	Y	Y	Y	Y	Y
4 Frank	Y	Y	Y	Y	Y	Y	Y
5 Meehan	Y	Y	Y	Y	Y	Y	Y
6 Tierney	Y	Y	Y	Y	Y	Y	Y
7 Markey	Y	Y	Y	Y	Y	Y	Y
8 Kennedy	Y	Y	Y	Y	Y	Y	Y
9 Moakley	Y	Y	Y	Y	Y	Y	Y
10 Delahunt	Y	Y	Y	Y	Y	Y	Y
MICHIGAN							
1 Stupak	N	Y	Y	Y	N	Y	Y
2 ***Hoekstra***	Y	Y	N	Y	Y	Y	Y
3 ***Ehlers***	Y	Y	Y	Y	Y	Y	Y
4 ***Camp***	Y	Y	Y	Y	Y	Y	Y
5 Barcia	Y	Y	Y	Y	Y	Y	Y
6 ***Upton***	Y	Y	Y	Y	Y	Y	Y
7 ***Smith***	Y	Y	Y	Y	Y	Y	Y
8 Stabenow	Y	Y	Y	Y	Y	Y	Y
9 Kildee	Y	Y	Y	Y	Y	Y	Y
10 Bonior	Y	Y	Y	?	Y	Y	Y
11 ***Knollenberg***	Y	Y	Y	Y	Y	Y	Y
12 Levin	Y	Y	Y	Y	Y	Y	Y
13 Rivers	Y	Y	Y	Y	Y	Y	Y
14 Conyers	Y	Y	Y	Y	Y	Y	Y
15 Kilpatrick	Y	Y	Y	Y	Y	Y	Y
16 Dingell	Y	Y	Y	Y	Y	Y	Y

	60	61	62	63	64	65	66
MINNESOTA							
1 ***Gutknecht***	?	Y	Y	Y	N	Y	Y
2 Minge	Y	Y	Y	Y	Y	Y	Y
3 ***Ramstad***	N	Y	Y	Y	N	Y	Y
4 Vento	Y	Y	Y	Y	Y	Y	Y
5 Sabo	N	Y	Y	Y	N	Y	Y
6 Luther	Y	Y	Y	Y	Y	Y	Y
7 Peterson	Y	Y	Y	Y	Y	Y	Y
8 Oberstar	N	Y	Y	Y	N	Y	Y
MISSISSIPPI							
1 ***Wicker***	N	Y	N	Y	N	Y	Y
2 Thompson	N	Y	Y	Y	N	Y	Y
3 ***Pickering***	Y	Y	N	Y	Y	Y	Y
4 ***Parker***	?	?	N	N	Y	Y	Y
5 Taylor	N	Y	Y	Y	N	Y	Y
MISSOURI							
1 Clay	N	Y	Y	Y	N	Y	Y
2 ***Talent***	Y	Y	Y	Y	Y	Y	Y
3 Gephardt	?	?	?	?	Y	Y	Y
4 Skelton	Y	Y	Y	Y	Y	Y	Y
5 McCarthy	Y	Y	Y	Y	Y	Y	Y
6 Danner	Y	Y	Y	N	Y	Y	Y
7 ***Blunt***	Y	Y	Y	Y	Y	Y	Y
8 ***Emerson***	Y	Y	N	N	Y	Y	Y
9 ***Hulshof***	Y	Y	Y	Y	Y	Y	Y
MONTANA							
AL ***Hill***	Y	Y	Y	Y	N	Y	Y
NEBRASKA							
1 ***Bereuter***	Y	Y	Y	Y	Y	Y	Y
2 ***Christensen***	Y	Y	Y	Y	Y	Y	Y
3 ***Barrett***	Y	Y	Y	Y	Y	Y	Y
NEVADA							
1 ***Ensign***	N	Y	Y	Y	N	Y	Y
2 ***Gibbons***	N	Y	N	Y	Y	Y	Y
NEW HAMPSHIRE							
1 ***Sununu***	Y	Y	N	Y	Y	Y	Y
2 ***Bass***	Y	Y	Y	Y	Y	Y	?
NEW JERSEY							
1 Andrews	Y	Y	Y	Y	Y	Y	Y
2 ***LoBiondo***	N	Y	Y	Y	N	Y	Y
3 ***Saxton***	Y	Y	Y	Y	Y	Y	Y
4 ***Smith***	Y	Y	Y	Y	Y	Y	Y
5 ***Roukema***	Y	Y	Y	Y	Y	Y	Y
6 Pallone	Y	Y	Y	Y	Y	Y	Y
7 ***Franks***	Y	Y	Y	Y	Y	Y	Y
8 Pascrell	Y	Y	Y	Y	Y	Y	Y
9 Rothman	Y	Y	Y	Y	Y	Y	Y
10 Payne	Y	Y	Y	Y	?	?	?
11 ***Frelinghuysen***	Y	Y	Y	Y	Y	Y	Y
12 ***Pappas***	Y	Y	Y	Y	Y	Y	Y
13 Menendez	Y	Y	Y	Y	N	Y	Y
NEW MEXICO							
1 ***Schiff***	?	?	?	?	?	?	?
2 ***Skeen***	Y	Y	Y	Y	Y	Y	Y
3 ***Redmond***	Y	Y	Y	Y	Y	Y	Y
NEW YORK							
1 ***Forbes***	Y	Y	Y	Y	Y	Y	Y
2 ***Lazio***	Y	Y	Y	Y	Y	Y	Y
3 ***King***	Y	Y	Y	Y	Y	Y	Y
4 McCarthy	Y	Y	Y	Y	Y	Y	Y
5 Ackerman	Y	Y	Y	Y	Y	Y	Y
6 Meeks	Y	Y	Y	Y	Y	Y	Y
7 Manton	Y	Y	Y	Y	Y	Y	Y
8 Nadler	Y	Y	Y	Y	Y	Y	Y
9 Schumer	Y	Y	Y	Y	?	?	?
10 Towns	Y	Y	Y	Y	Y	Y	Y
11 Owens	Y	Y	Y	Y	Y	Y	Y
12 Velázquez	N	Y	Y	Y	Y	Y	Y
13 ***Fossella***	Y	Y	N	N	Y	Y	Y
14 Maloney	Y	Y	Y	Y	N	Y	Y
15 Rangel	?	?	?	?	?	?	?
16 Serrano	Y	Y	Y	Y	Y	Y	Y
17 Engel	?	Y	Y	Y	Y	Y	Y
18 Lowey	Y	Y	Y	Y	Y	Y	Y
19 ***Kelly***	Y	Y	Y	Y	Y	Y	Y
20 ***Gilman***	Y	Y	Y	Y	Y	Y	Y
21 McNulty	N	Y	Y	Y	N	Y	Y
22 ***Solomon***	Y	Y	N	N	Y	Y	Y
23 ***Boehlert***	Y	Y	Y	Y	Y	Y	Y
24 ***McHugh***	Y	Y	Y	Y	Y	Y	Y
25 ***Walsh***	Y	Y	Y	Y	Y	Y	Y
26 Hinchey	N	Y	Y	Y	Y	Y	Y
27 ***Paxon***	Y	Y	N	N	Y	Y	Y
28 Slaughter	Y	Y	Y	Y	N	Y	Y
29 LaFalce	Y	Y	Y	Y	Y	Y	Y

	60	61	62	63	64	65	66
30 ***Quinn***	Y	Y	Y	Y	Y	Y	Y
31 ***Houghton***	Y	Y	?	Y	Y	Y	Y
NORTH CAROLINA							
1 Clayton	Y	Y	Y	Y	Y	Y	Y
2 Etheridge	Y	Y	Y	Y	Y	Y	Y
3 ***Jones***	Y	Y	N	N	Y	Y	Y
4 Price	Y	Y	Y	Y	Y	Y	Y
5 ***Burr***	Y	Y	Y	Y	Y	Y	Y
6 ***Coble***	Y	Y	N	N	Y	Y	Y
7 McIntyre	Y	Y	Y	Y	Y	Y	Y
8 Hefner	?	Y	Y	Y	Y	Y	Y
9 ***Myrick***	Y	Y	N	Y	Y	Y	Y
10 ***Ballenger***	Y	Y	Y	Y	Y	Y	Y
11 ***Taylor***	Y	Y	N	N	Y	Y	Y
12 Watt	Y	Y	Y	Y	Y	Y	Y
NORTH DAKOTA							
AL Pomeroy	Y	Y	Y	Y	Y	Y	Y
OHIO							
1 ***Chabot***	Y	Y	N	Y	Y	Y	Y
2 ***Portman***	Y	Y	Y	Y	Y	Y	Y
3 Hall	Y	Y	Y	Y	Y	Y	Y
4 ***Oxley***	Y	Y	Y	Y	Y	Y	Y
5 ***Gillmor***	Y	Y	Y	Y	Y	Y	Y
6 Strickland	Y	Y	Y	Y	Y	Y	Y
7 ***Hobson***	Y	Y	Y	Y	Y	Y	Y
8 ***Boehner***	Y	Y	Y	Y	Y	Y	Y
9 Kaptur	Y	Y	Y	Y	Y	Y	Y
10 Kucinich	N	Y	Y	Y	N	Y	Y
11 Stokes	Y	Y	Y	Y	Y	Y	Y
12 ***Kasich***	?	Y	Y	Y	Y	Y	Y
13 Brown	Y	Y	Y	Y	Y	Y	Y
14 Sawyer	Y	Y	Y	Y	Y	Y	Y
15 ***Pryce***	Y	Y	Y	Y	Y	Y	Y
16 ***Regula***	Y	Y	Y	Y	Y	Y	Y
17 Traficant	Y	Y	Y	Y	Y	Y	Y
18 ***Ney***	Y	Y	Y	N	Y	Y	Y
19 ***LaTourette***	Y	Y	Y	Y	Y	Y	Y
OKLAHOMA							
1 ***Largent***	Y	Y	Y	Y	Y	Y	Y
2 ***Coburn***	Y	Y	N	N	Y	Y	?
3 ***Watkins***	Y	Y	Y	N	Y	Y	Y
4 ***Watts***	Y	Y	Y	N	Y	Y	Y
5 ***Istook***	Y	Y	Y	Y	Y	Y	Y
6 ***Lucas***	Y	Y	Y	N	Y	Y	Y
OREGON							
1 Furse	Y	?	?	Y	Y	Y	Y
2 ***Smith***	Y	Y	N	N	Y	Y	?
3 Blumenauer	Y	Y	Y	Y	Y	Y	Y
4 DeFazio	N	Y	Y	Y	N	Y	Y
5 Hooley	Y	Y	Y	Y	+	+	+
PENNSYLVANIA							
1 Vacant							
2 Fattah	Y	Y	Y	Y	Y	Y	Y
3 Borski	N	Y	Y	Y	N	Y	Y
4 Klink	Y	Y	Y	Y	Y	Y	Y
5 ***Peterson***	Y	Y	N	N	Y	Y	Y
6 Holden	Y	Y	Y	Y	Y	Y	Y
7 ***Weldon***	?	Y	Y	Y	Y	Y	Y
8 ***Greenwood***	Y	Y	Y	Y	Y	Y	Y
9 ***Shuster***	Y	Y	Y	Y	Y	Y	Y
10 ***McDade***	Y	Y	Y	Y	Y	Y	Y
11 Kanjorski	Y	Y	Y	Y	Y	Y	Y
12 Murtha	Y	Y	Y	Y	Y	Y	Y
13 ***Fox***	N	Y	Y	Y	N	Y	Y
14 Coyne	Y	Y	Y	Y	Y	Y	Y
15 McHale	Y	Y	Y	Y	Y	Y	Y
16 ***Pitts***	Y	Y	Y	Y	Y	Y	Y
17 ***Gekas***	Y	?	?	N	Y	Y	Y
18 Doyle	Y	Y	?	?	Y	Y	Y
19 ***Goodling***	Y	Y	Y	Y	Y	Y	Y
20 Mascara	Y	Y	Y	Y	Y	Y	Y
21 ***English***	N	Y	Y	Y	Y	Y	Y
RHODE ISLAND							
1 Kennedy	Y	Y	Y	Y	Y	Y	Y
2 Weygand	Y	Y	Y	Y	Y	Y	Y
SOUTH CAROLINA							
1 ***Sanford***	Y	Y	N	N	Y	Y	Y
2 ***Spence***	Y	Y	Y	Y	Y	Y	Y
3 ***Graham***	Y	Y	N	Y	Y	Y	Y
4 ***Inglis***	Y	Y	N	Y	?	?	?
5 Spratt	Y	Y	Y	Y	?	?	?
6 Clyburn	N	Y	Y	Y	N	Y	Y
SOUTH DAKOTA							
AL ***Thune***	Y	Y	Y	Y	Y	Y	Y

	60	61	62	63	64	65	66
TENNESSEE							
1 ***Jenkins***	Y	Y	N	N	Y	Y	Y
2 ***Duncan***	Y	Y	Y	N	Y	Y	Y
3 ***Wamp***	Y	Y	N	N	N	Y	Y
4 ***Hilleary***	N	Y	N	N	N	Y	Y
5 Clement	Y	Y	Y	Y	Y	Y	Y
6 Gordon	Y	Y	Y	Y	Y	Y	Y
7 ***Bryant***	Y	Y	Y	Y	Y	Y	Y
8 Tanner	Y	Y	Y	Y	Y	Y	Y
9 Ford	N	Y	Y	Y	Y	Y	Y
TEXAS							
1 Sandlin	Y	Y	Y	Y	Y	Y	Y
2 Turner	Y	Y	Y	Y	Y	Y	Y
3 ***Johnson, Sam***	Y	Y	N	N	Y	Y	Y
4 Hall	Y	Y	Y	Y	Y	Y	Y
5 ***Sessions***	N	Y	N	N	N	Y	Y
6 ***Barton***	Y	Y	N	Y	Y	Y	Y
7 ***Archer***	Y	Y	Y	Y	Y	Y	Y
8 ***Brady***	N	Y	N	N	Y	Y	Y
9 Lampson	Y	Y	Y	Y	Y	Y	Y
10 Doggett	Y	Y	Y	Y	Y	Y	Y
11 Edwards	Y	Y	Y	Y	Y	Y	Y
12 ***Granger***	Y	Y	N	Y	Y	Y	Y
13 ***Thornberry***	Y	Y	N	N	Y	Y	Y
14 ***Paul***	Y	Y	N	N	Y	Y	Y
15 Hinojosa	Y	Y	Y	Y	Y	Y	Y
16 Reyes	Y	Y	Y	Y	Y	Y	Y
17 Stenholm	Y	Y	Y	Y	Y	Y	Y
18 Jackson-Lee	Y	Y	Y	Y	Y	Y	Y
19 ***Combest***	Y	Y	N	N	Y	Y	Y
20 Gonzalez	?	?	?	?	?	?	?
21 ***Smith***	Y	Y	Y	Y	Y	Y	Y
22 ***DeLay***	N	Y	N	N	Y	Y	Y
23 ***Bonilla***	Y	Y	N	N	Y	Y	Y
24 Frost	?	?	?	?	Y	Y	Y
25 Bentsen	Y	Y	Y	Y	Y	Y	Y
26 ***Armey***	Y	Y	N	Y	Y	Y	Y
27 Ortiz	Y	Y	Y	Y	Y	Y	Y
28 Rodriguez	Y	Y	Y	Y	Y	Y	Y
29 Green	Y	Y	Y	Y	Y	Y	Y
30 Johnson, E.B.	Y	Y	Y	Y	N	Y	Y
UTAH							
1 ***Hansen***	Y	Y	N	N	Y	Y	Y
2 ***Cook***	Y	Y	Y	Y	Y	Y	Y
3 ***Cannon***	Y	Y	N	N	?	?	?
VERMONT							
AL *Sanders*	Y	Y	Y	Y	Y	Y	Y
VIRGINIA							
1 ***Bateman***	Y	Y	Y	Y	Y	Y	Y
2 Pickett	N	Y	Y	Y	N	Y	Y
3 Scott	Y	Y	Y	Y	Y	Y	Y
4 Sisisky	Y	Y	Y	Y	Y	Y	Y
5 Goode	Y	Y	Y	Y	Y	Y	Y
6 ***Goodlatte***	Y	Y	Y	Y	Y	Y	Y
7 ***Bliley***	Y	Y	Y	Y	Y	Y	Y
8 Moran	Y	Y	Y	Y	Y	Y	Y
9 Boucher	Y	Y	Y	Y	Y	Y	Y
10 ***Wolf***	Y	Y	Y	Y	Y	Y	Y
11 ***Davis***	Y	Y	Y	Y	Y	Y	Y
WASHINGTON							
1 ***White***	Y	Y	Y	?	Y	Y	Y
2 ***Metcalf***	Y	Y	Y	Y	Y	Y	Y
3 ***Smith, Linda***	Y	Y	Y	?	Y	Y	Y
4 ***Hastings***	Y	Y	N	Y	Y	Y	Y
5 ***Nethercutt***	Y	Y	N	Y	Y	Y	Y
6 Dicks	Y	Y	Y	Y	Y	Y	Y
7 McDermott	N	Y	Y	Y	+	+	+
8 ***Dunn***	Y	Y	Y	Y	Y	Y	Y
9 Smith, Adam	Y	Y	Y	Y	Y	Y	Y
WEST VIRGINIA							
1 Mollohan	Y	Y	Y	Y	Y	Y	Y
2 Wise	Y	Y	Y	Y	Y	Y	Y
3 Rahall	Y	Y	Y	Y	Y	Y	Y
WISCONSIN							
1 ***Neumann***	Y	Y	N	N	Y	Y	Y
2 ***Klug***	Y	Y	Y	Y	Y	Y	Y
3 Kind	Y	Y	Y	Y	Y	Y	Y
4 Kleczka	Y	Y	Y	Y	Y	Y	Y
5 Barrett	Y	Y	Y	Y	Y	Y	Y
6 ***Petri***	Y	Y	N	N	Y	Y	Y
7 Obey	Y	Y	Y	Y	Y	Y	Y
8 Johnson	Y	Y	Y	Y	Y	Y	Y
9 ***Sensenbrenner***	Y	Y	N	N	Y	Y	Y
WYOMING							
AL ***Cubin***	Y	Y	N	N	Y	Y	Y

Southern states - Ala., Ark., Fla., Ga., Ky., La., Miss., N.C., Okla., S.C., Tenn., Texas, Va.

House Votes 67, 68, 69, 70, 71, 72, 73

Key
- Y Voted for (yea).
- # Paired for.
- + Announced for.
- N Voted against (nay).
- X Paired against.
- − Announced against.
- P Voted "present."
- C Voted "present" to avoid possible conflict of interest.
- ? Did not vote or otherwise make a position known.

Democrats **Republicans** *Independent*

---

67. HR 3096. Fraudulent Disability Claims Correction/Passage. Greenwood, R-Pa., motion to suspend the rules and pass the bill to correct current law to clarify that a person convicted of fraud in the initial application for federal employees' workers compensation benefits, or in any subsequent application for continuation of benefits, would lose those benefits. Motion agreed to 408-0: R 216-0; D 191-0 (ND 140-0, SD 51-0); I 1-0. March 24, 1998. Bills on the corrections calendar require a three-fifths majority of those present and voting (245 in this case) for passage.

68. HR 2589. Copyright Term Extension/Small Business. McCollum, R-Fla., amendment to the Sensenbrenner, R-Wis., amendment to limit the exemption from music licensing fees to cover restaurants of 3,500 square feet or less which play radio or television broadcasts. The Sensenbrenner amendment would exempt restaurants, bars, and coffee shops from having to pay licensing fees for retransmission of radio and television broadcasts. Rejected 150-259: R 34-187; D 115-72 (ND 97-41, SD 18-31); I 1-0. March 25, 1998.

69. HR 2589. Copyright Term Extension/Music Licensing Fees. Sensenbrenner, R-Wis., amendment to exempt restaurants, bars, and coffee shops from having to pay licensing fees for retransmission of radio and television broadcasts. Adopted 297-112: R 205-16; D 92-95 (ND 57-81, SD 35-14); I 0-1. March 25, 1998. Subsequently, HR2589 was passed by voice vote.

70. HR 2578. Traveler Visa Waivers/Greece and Portugal. Pombo, R-Calif., amendment to increase the visa refusal rate (the number of citizens refused visas to the United States from their home consulates) from 2 percent to 3 percent to allow citizens of Portugal and Greece to take part with the other Europeans Union countries in the tourist visa waiver program. Adopted 360-46: R 179-41; D 180-5 (ND 136-0, SD 44-5); I 1-0. March 25, 1998.

71. HR 2578. Traveler Visa Waivers/Passage. Passage of the bill to extend through April 2000 the visa waiver pilot program which allows most Western Europeans, Japanese and Australians to travel to the United States for 90 days without a visa. Passed 407-0: R 221-0; D 185-0 (ND 136-0, SD 49-0); I 1-0. March 25, 1998. A "yea" was a vote in support of the president's position.

72. HR 3310. Small Business Paperwork Reduction/Agency Discretion. Kucinich, D-Ohio., amendment to require agencies to establish policies to waive, delay or reduce civil penalties for first-time violations in appropriate circumstances, including whether the business has been acting in good faith to comply, and whether the business has obtained significant economic benefit from the violation. Rejected 183-221: R 7-209; D 175-12 (ND 135-4, SD 40-8); I 1-0. March 26, 1998.

73. HR 3310. Small Business Paperwork Reduction/State-Run Federal Programs. McIntosh, R-Ind., amendment to apply the bill's suspension of fines provision to state-run federal enforcement programs. Adopted 224-179: R 203-12; D 21-167 (ND 7-132, SD 14-35); I 0-0. March 26, 1998.

---

[1] Stephen H. Schiff, R-N.M., died March 25.

	67	68	69	70	71	72	73
ALABAMA							
1 **Callahan**	Y	Y	Y	Y	Y	N	Y
2 Everett	Y	N	Y	Y	Y	N	Y
3 **Riley**	Y	N	Y	Y	Y	N	Y
4 **Aderholt**	Y	N	Y	N	Y	N	Y
5 Cramer	Y	N	Y	Y	Y	Y	Y
6 **Bachus**	Y	N	Y	Y	Y	N	Y
7 Hilliard	Y	N	N	Y	Y	Y	N
ALASKA							
AL **Young**	Y	N	Y	Y	Y	N	Y
ARIZONA							
1 **Salmon**	Y	N	Y	Y	Y	N	Y
2 Pastor	Y	N	Y	Y	Y	Y	N
3 **Stump**	Y	N	Y	N	Y	N	Y
4 **Shadegg**	Y	N	Y	Y	Y	N	Y
5 **Kolbe**	Y	N	Y	Y	Y	N	Y
6 **Hayworth**	Y	N	Y	Y	Y	N	Y
ARKANSAS							
1 Berry	?	N	Y	N	Y	Y	N
2 Snyder	Y	N	Y	Y	Y	Y	N
3 **Hutchinson**	Y	Y	Y	N	Y	N	Y
4 Dickey	Y	N	Y	Y	Y	N	Y
CALIFORNIA							
1 **Riggs**	Y	−	+	Y	Y	?	?
2 **Herger**	?	N	Y	Y	Y	N	Y
3 Fazio	Y	N	Y	Y	Y	Y	N
4 **Doolittle**	Y	N	Y	Y	Y	N	Y
5 Matsui	Y	Y	N	Y	Y	Y	N
6 Woolsey	Y	N	Y	Y	Y	Y	N
7 Miller	Y	Y	N	Y	Y	Y	N
8 Pelosi	Y	Y	N	Y	Y	Y	N
9 Vacant							
10 Tauscher	Y	Y	N	Y	Y	Y	N
11 **Pombo**	Y	N	N	Y	Y	N	Y
12 Lantos	Y	Y	N	Y	Y	Y	N
13 Stark	?	?	?	Y	Y	Y	N
14 Eshoo	Y	Y	N	Y	Y	Y	N
15 **Campbell**	Y	N	Y	N	Y	N	Y
16 Lofgren	Y	Y	N	Y	Y	Y	N
17 Farr	Y	N	Y	Y	Y	Y	N
18 Condit	Y	N	Y	Y	Y	Y	N
19 **Radanovich**	Y	Y	N	Y	Y	N	Y
20 Dooley	Y	Y	N	Y	Y	Y	N
21 **Thomas**	Y	Y	Y	Y	Y	N	Y
22 Capps, L.	Y	Y	N	Y	Y	Y	N
23 **Gallegly**	Y	N	Y	N	Y	N	Y
24 Sherman	Y	Y	N	Y	Y	Y	N
25 **McKeon**	Y	N	Y	Y	Y	N	Y
26 Berman	Y	Y	N	Y	Y	Y	N
27 **Rogan**	Y	Y	N	Y	Y	N	Y
28 **Dreier**	Y	N	Y	Y	Y	N	Y
29 Waxman	Y	Y	N	Y	Y	Y	N
30 Becerra	Y	Y	N	Y	Y	?	?
31 Martinez	Y	Y	N	Y	Y	Y	N
32 Dixon	Y	Y	N	Y	Y	Y	N
33 Roybal-Allard	Y	Y	N	Y	Y	Y	N
34 Torres	Y	Y	Y	Y	Y	Y	N
35 Waters	?	?	?	?	?	?	?
36 Harman	?	?	?	?	?	?	?
37 Millender-McD.	Y	?	?	?	?	?	?

	67	68	69	70	71	72	73
38 **Horn**	Y	N	Y	Y	Y	N	Y
39 **Royce**	?	?	?	?	?	?	?
40 **Lewis**	Y	N	Y	Y	Y	N	Y
41 **Kim**	Y	Y	N	Y	N	N	Y
42 Brown	Y	Y	N	Y	Y	Y	N
43 **Calvert**	Y	N	Y	Y	Y	N	Y
44 Vacant							
45 **Rohrabacher**	Y	N	Y	Y	Y	N	Y
46 Sanchez	Y	Y	N	Y	Y	Y	N
47 **Cox**	Y	N	Y	Y	Y	N	Y
48 **Packard**	Y	N	Y	Y	Y	N	Y
49 **Bilbray**	Y	N	Y	Y	Y	N	Y
50 Filner	Y	Y	N	Y	Y	Y	N
51 **Cunningham**	Y	N	Y	Y	Y	N	Y
52 **Hunter**	Y	Y	Y	Y	Y	N	Y
COLORADO							
1 DeGette	Y	Y	N	Y	Y	Y	N
2 Skaggs	Y	Y	N	Y	Y	Y	N
3 **McInnis**	Y	N	Y	Y	Y	N	Y
4 **Schaffer**	Y	N	Y	Y	Y	N	Y
5 **Hefley**	Y	N	Y	Y	Y	N	Y
6 **Schaefer**	Y	N	Y	Y	Y	N	Y
CONNECTICUT							
1 Kennelly	Y	Y	N	Y	Y	Y	N
2 Gejdenson	Y	Y	Y	Y	Y	Y	N
3 DeLauro	Y	Y	N	Y	Y	Y	N
4 **Shays**	Y	Y	N	Y	Y	Y	N
5 Maloney	Y	N	Y	Y	Y	Y	N
6 **Johnson**	Y	N	Y	Y	Y	N	N
DELAWARE							
AL **Castle**	Y	N	Y	Y	Y	N	Y
FLORIDA							
1 **Scarborough**	Y	N	Y	Y	Y	N	Y
2 Boyd	Y	N	Y	Y	Y	N	Y
3 Brown	Y	+	−	+	+	Y	−
4 **Fowler**	Y	N	Y	Y	Y	N	Y
5 Thurman	Y	Y	Y	Y	Y	Y	N
6 **Stearns**	Y	N	Y	N	Y	N	Y
7 **Mica**	Y	Y	Y	Y	Y	N	Y
8 **McCollum**	Y	Y	N	N	Y	N	Y
9 **Bilirakis**	Y	N	Y	Y	Y	N	Y
10 **Young**	?	N	Y	Y	Y	N	Y
11 Davis	Y	N	Y	Y	Y	Y	N
12 **Canady**	Y	Y	N	Y	Y	N	Y
13 **Miller**	Y	N	Y	Y	Y	N	Y
14 **Goss**	Y	N	Y	Y	Y	N	Y
15 **Weldon**	Y	N	Y	Y	Y	N	Y
16 **Foley**	Y	Y	Y	Y	Y	N	Y
17 Meek	Y	Y	N	Y	Y	Y	N
18 **Ros-Lehtinen**	Y	N	Y	Y	Y	N	Y
19 Wexler	Y	Y	N	Y	Y	Y	N
20 Deutsch	Y	Y	N	Y	Y	Y	N
21 **Diaz-Balart**	Y	N	Y	Y	Y	Y	Y
22 **Shaw**	Y	N	Y	Y	Y	N	Y
23 Hastings	Y	Y	N	Y	Y	Y	N
GEORGIA							
1 **Kingston**	Y	N	Y	Y	Y	N	Y
2 Bishop	Y	N	Y	Y	Y	Y	Y
3 **Collins**	Y	N	Y	N	Y	N	Y
4 **McKinney**	Y	Y	N	Y	Y	Y	N
5 Lewis	Y	Y	N	Y	Y	Y	N
6 **Gingrich**							
7 **Barr**	Y	N	Y	Y	Y	N	Y
8 **Chambliss**	Y	N	Y	Y	Y	N	Y
9 **Deal**	Y	N	Y	N	Y	N	Y
10 **Norwood**	Y	N	Y	Y	Y	N	Y
11 **Linder**	Y	N	Y	Y	Y	N	Y
HAWAII							
1 Abercrombie	Y	Y	N	Y	Y	Y	N
2 Mink	Y	Y	N	Y	Y	Y	N
IDAHO							
1 **Chenoweth**	+	N	Y	Y	Y	N	Y
2 **Crapo**	Y	N	Y	Y	Y	?	?
ILLINOIS							
1 Rush	Y	Y	N	Y	Y	Y	N
2 Jackson	Y	Y	N	Y	Y	N	N
3 Lipinski	Y	Y	Y	Y	Y	Y	N
4 Gutierrez	Y	Y	Y	Y	Y	Y	N
5 Blagojevich	Y	N	Y	Y	Y	Y	N
6 **Hyde**	Y	Y	N	Y	Y	N	Y
7 Davis	Y	Y	N	Y	Y	Y	N
8 **Crane**	Y	N	Y	Y	Y	N	Y
9 Yates	?	Y	N	?	?	Y	N
10 **Porter**	Y	N	Y	Y	Y	N	Y
11 **Weller**	Y	N	Y	Y	Y	N	Y
12 Costello	Y	Y	Y	Y	Y	Y	N

ND Northern Democrats SD Southern Democrats

	67	68	69	70	71	72	73
13 ***Fawell***	Y	N	Y	N	Y	N	Y
14 ***Hastert***	Y	N	Y	Y	Y	N	Y
15 ***Ewing***	Y	N	Y	Y	Y	N	Y
16 ***Manzullo***	?	N	Y	Y	Y	N	Y
17 Evans	Y	Y	Y	Y	Y	Y	N
18 ***LaHood***	Y	Y	N	Y	Y	N	Y
19 Poshard	Y	Y	Y	Y	Y	Y	N
20 ***Shimkus***	Y	N	Y	Y	Y	N	Y
INDIANA							
1 Visclosky	Y	N	Y	Y	Y	Y	N
2 ***McIntosh***	Y	N	Y	Y	Y	N	Y
3 Roemer	Y	N	Y	Y	Y	N	N
4 ***Souder***	Y	N	Y	Y	Y	N	Y
5 ***Buyer***	Y	N	Y	Y	Y	N	Y
6 ***Burton***	Y	N	Y	Y	Y	N	Y
7 ***Pease***	Y	Y	N	N	Y	N	Y
8 ***Hostettler***	Y	N	Y	Y	Y	N	Y
9 Hamilton	Y	N	Y	Y	Y	N	N
10 Carson	Y	Y	Y	Y	Y	Y	N
IOWA							
1 ***Leach***	Y	N	Y	Y	Y	N	Y
2 ***Nussle***	Y	N	Y	Y	Y	N	Y
3 Boswell	Y	N	Y	Y	Y	Y	N
4 ***Ganske***	Y	N	Y	Y	Y	N	Y
5 ***Latham***	Y	N	Y	Y	Y	N	Y
KANSAS							
1 ***Moran***	Y	N	Y	Y	Y	N	Y
2 ***Ryun***	Y	N	Y	Y	Y	N	Y
3 ***Snowbarger***	Y	N	Y	N	Y	N	Y
4 ***Tiahrt***	Y	N	Y	Y	Y	N	Y
KENTUCKY							
1 ***Whitfield***	Y	N	Y	Y	Y	N	Y
2 ***Lewis***	Y	N	Y	N	Y	N	Y
3 ***Northup***	Y	N	Y	Y	Y	N	Y
4 ***Bunning***	Y	N	Y	N	Y	N	Y
5 ***Rogers***	Y	N	Y	N	Y	N	Y
6 Baesler	Y	N	Y	N	Y	Y	N
LOUISIANA							
1 ***Livingston***	Y	Y	Y	Y	Y	N	Y
2 Jefferson	?	?	?	?	?	?	?
3 ***Tauzin***	Y	N	Y	Y	Y	N	Y
4 ***McCrery***	Y	N	Y	Y	Y	N	Y
5 ***Cooksey***	Y	N	Y	Y	Y	N	Y
6 ***Baker***	Y	N	Y	N	Y	N	Y
7 John	Y	N	Y	Y	Y	Y	Y
MAINE							
1 Allen	Y	Y	N	Y	Y	Y	N
2 Baldacci	Y	Y	Y	Y	Y	Y	N
MARYLAND							
1 ***Gilchrest***	Y	Y	Y	N	Y	Y	Y
2 ***Ehrlich***	Y	N	Y	Y	Y	N	Y
3 Cardin	Y	?	?	?	?	?	?
4 Wynn	Y	N	Y	Y	Y	Y	N
5 Hoyer	Y	Y	N	Y	Y	Y	N
6 ***Bartlett***	Y	N	Y	Y	Y	N	Y
7 Cummings	Y	N	N	Y	Y	Y	N
8 ***Morella***	Y	Y	N	Y	Y	Y	N
MASSACHUSETTS							
1 Olver	Y	Y	N	Y	Y	?	?
2 Neal	Y	Y	Y	Y	Y	Y	N
3 McGovern	Y	Y	N	Y	Y	Y	N
4 Frank	Y	Y	N	Y	Y	Y	N
5 Meehan	Y	Y	N	Y	Y	Y	N
6 Tierney	Y	Y	N	Y	Y	Y	N
7 Markey	Y	Y	N	Y	Y	Y	N
8 Kennedy	Y	Y	N	Y	Y	Y	N
9 Moakley	Y	Y	N	Y	Y	Y	N
10 Delahunt	Y	Y	N	Y	Y	Y	N
MICHIGAN							
1 Stupak	Y	Y	N	Y	Y	Y	N
2 ***Hoekstra***	Y	N	Y	Y	Y	N	Y
3 ***Ehlers***	Y	N	Y	Y	Y	N	Y
4 ***Camp***	Y	N	Y	Y	Y	N	Y
5 Barcia	Y	N	Y	Y	Y	Y	N
6 ***Upton***	Y	N	Y	Y	Y	N	Y
7 ***Smith***	Y	N	Y	Y	Y	N	Y
8 Stabenow	Y	N	Y	Y	Y	Y	N
9 Kildee	Y	Y	N	Y	Y	Y	N
10 Bonior	Y	Y	N	Y	Y	Y	N
11 ***Knollenberg***	Y	N	Y	Y	Y	N	Y
12 Levin	Y	Y	N	Y	Y	Y	N
13 Rivers	Y	Y	N	Y	Y	Y	N
14 Conyers	Y	+	−	+	+	+	−
15 Kilpatrick	Y	Y	N	Y	Y	Y	N
16 Dingell	Y	Y	N	Y	Y	Y	N

	67	68	69	70	71	72	73
MINNESOTA							
1 ***Gutknecht***	Y	N	Y	Y	Y	N	Y
2 Minge	Y	N	Y	Y	Y	Y	Y
3 ***Ramstad***	Y	N	Y	Y	Y	N	Y
4 Vento	Y	Y	N	Y	Y	Y	N
5 Sabo	Y	Y	N	Y	Y	Y	N
6 Luther	Y	Y	N	Y	Y	Y	N
7 Peterson	Y	N	Y	Y	Y	Y	N
8 Oberstar	Y	Y	N	Y	Y	Y	N
MISSISSIPPI							
1 ***Wicker***	Y	N	Y	Y	Y	N	Y
2 Thompson	Y	N	Y	Y	Y	Y	N
3 ***Pickering***	Y	N	Y	Y	Y	N	Y
4 ***Parker***	Y	N	Y	Y	Y	N	Y
5 Taylor	Y	N	Y	N	Y	N	Y
MISSOURI							
1 Clay	Y	Y	N	Y	Y	Y	N
2 ***Talent***	Y	N	Y	Y	Y	N	Y
3 Gephardt	Y	Y	N	Y	Y	Y	N
4 Skelton	Y	N	Y	Y	Y	Y	Y
5 McCarthy	Y	Y	N	Y	Y	Y	N
6 Danner	Y	N	Y	Y	Y	N	Y
7 ***Blunt***	Y	N	Y	N	Y	N	Y
8 ***Emerson***	Y	N	Y	N	Y	N	Y
9 ***Hulshof***	Y	N	Y	Y	Y	N	Y
MONTANA							
AL ***Hill***	Y	N	Y	Y	Y	N	Y
NEBRASKA							
1 ***Bereuter***	Y	N	Y	Y	Y	N	Y
2 ***Christensen***	Y	N	Y	Y	Y	N	Y
3 ***Barrett***	Y	N	Y	Y	Y	N	Y
NEVADA							
1 ***Ensign***	Y	N	Y	Y	Y	N	Y
2 ***Gibbons***	Y	N	Y	Y	Y	N	Y
NEW HAMPSHIRE							
1 ***Sununu***	Y	N	Y	Y	Y	N	Y
2 ***Bass***	Y	N	Y	Y	Y	N	Y
NEW JERSEY							
1 Andrews	Y	N	Y	Y	Y	Y	N
2 ***LoBiondo***	Y	N	Y	Y	Y	N	N
3 ***Saxton***	Y	N	Y	?	?	N	N
4 ***Smith***	Y	N	Y	Y	Y	N	N
5 ***Roukema***	Y	N	Y	N	Y	N	N
6 Pallone	Y	N	Y	Y	Y	Y	N
7 ***Franks***	Y	N	Y	Y	Y	N	N
8 Pascrell	Y	Y	Y	Y	Y	Y	N
9 Rothman	Y	?	?	?	?	?	N
10 Payne	?	?	?	?	?	?	?
11 ***Frelinghuysen***	Y	N	Y	Y	Y	N	?
12 ***Pappas***	Y	N	Y	Y	Y	N	Y
13 Menendez	Y	Y	N	Y	Y	Y	N
NEW MEXICO							
1 ***Schiff*** [1]	?	?	?	?			
2 ***Skeen***	Y	N	Y	Y	Y	N	Y
3 ***Redmond***	Y	N	Y	Y	Y	Y	Y
NEW YORK							
1 ***Forbes***	Y	Y	N	Y	Y	N	N
2 ***Lazio***	Y	Y	Y	Y	Y	Y	Y
3 ***King***	Y	N	Y	Y	Y	N	N
4 McCarthy	Y	Y	N	Y	Y	Y	N
5 Ackerman	Y	Y	N	Y	Y	Y	N
6 Meeks	Y	Y	N	Y	Y	Y	N
7 Manton	Y	Y	N	Y	Y	Y	N
8 Nadler	Y	Y	N	Y	Y	Y	N
9 Schumer	?	Y	N	?	?	Y	N
10 Towns	Y	Y	N	?	?	Y	N
11 Owens	Y	Y	N	Y	Y	Y	N
12 Velázquez	Y	Y	N	Y	Y	Y	N
13 ***Fossella***	Y	N	Y	Y	Y	N	Y
14 Maloney	Y	Y	N	Y	Y	Y	N
15 Rangel	?	X	?	?	?	?	?
16 Serrano	Y	Y	N	Y	Y	Y	N
17 Engel	Y	Y	N	Y	Y	Y	N
18 Lowey	Y	Y	N	Y	Y	Y	N
19 ***Kelly***	Y	Y	N	Y	Y	N	Y
20 ***Gilman***	Y	N	Y	Y	Y	N	Y
21 McNulty	Y	N	Y	Y	Y	Y	N
22 ***Solomon***	Y	N	Y	N	Y	N	Y
23 ***Boehlert***	Y	N	Y	Y	Y	Y	N
24 ***McHugh***	Y	N	Y	Y	Y	N	Y
25 ***Walsh***	Y	N	Y	Y	Y	N	Y
26 Hinchey	Y	Y	N	Y	Y	Y	N
27 ***Paxon***	Y	N	Y	Y	Y	?	?
28 Slaughter	Y	Y	N	Y	Y	Y	N
29 LaFalce	Y	Y	N	Y	Y	Y	N

	67	68	69	70	71	72	73
30 ***Quinn***	Y	N	Y	Y	Y	N	Y
31 ***Houghton***	Y	?	?	?	?	?	?
NORTH CAROLINA							
1 Clayton	Y	Y	Y	Y	Y	Y	N
2 Etheridge	Y	N	Y	Y	Y	Y	N
3 ***Jones***	Y	N	Y	Y	Y	N	Y
4 Price	Y	N	Y	Y	Y	Y	N
5 ***Burr***	Y	N	Y	Y	Y	N	Y
6 ***Coble***	Y	Y	N	Y	Y	N	Y
7 McIntyre	Y	N	Y	Y	Y	Y	N
8 Hefner	Y	Y	Y	Y	Y	Y	N
9 ***Myrick***	Y	N	Y	Y	Y	N	Y
10 ***Ballenger***	Y	N	Y	N	Y	N	Y
11 ***Taylor***	Y	N	Y	Y	Y	N	Y
12 Watt	Y	Y	N	Y	Y	Y	N
NORTH DAKOTA							
AL Pomeroy	Y	N	Y	Y	Y	Y	N
OHIO							
1 ***Chabot***	Y	N	Y	Y	Y	N	Y
2 ***Portman***	Y	N	Y	Y	Y	N	Y
3 Hall	Y	Y	Y	Y	Y	Y	N
4 ***Oxley***	Y	N	Y	Y	Y	N	Y
5 ***Gillmor***	Y	N	Y	Y	Y	?	?
6 Strickland	Y	N	Y	Y	Y	Y	N
7 ***Hobson***	Y	N	Y	Y	Y	N	Y
8 ***Boehner***	Y	N	Y	Y	Y	N	Y
9 Kaptur	Y	Y	Y	Y	Y	Y	N
10 Kucinich	Y	Y	Y	Y	Y	Y	N
11 Stokes	Y	Y	N	Y	Y	Y	N
12 ***Kasich***	Y	N	Y	Y	Y	N	Y
13 Brown	Y	Y	N	Y	Y	Y	N
14 Sawyer	Y	N	Y	Y	Y	Y	N
15 ***Pryce***	Y	N	Y	Y	Y	N	Y
16 ***Regula***	Y	N	Y	Y	Y	N	Y
17 Traficant	Y	N	Y	Y	Y	Y	Y
18 ***Ney***	Y	N	Y	Y	Y	N	Y
19 ***LaTourette***	Y	N	Y	Y	Y	N	Y
OKLAHOMA							
1 ***Largent***	Y	N	Y	Y	Y	N	Y
2 ***Coburn***	Y	N	Y	Y	Y	N	Y
3 ***Watkins***	Y	N	Y	Y	Y	N	Y
4 ***Watts***	Y	N	Y	N	Y	N	Y
5 ***Istook***	Y	N	Y	N	Y	N	Y
6 ***Lucas***	Y	N	Y	Y	Y	N	Y
OREGON							
1 Furse	Y	Y	N	Y	Y	Y	N
2 ***Smith***	Y	N	Y	Y	Y	N	Y
3 Blumenauer	Y	N	Y	Y	Y	Y	N
4 DeFazio	Y	Y	N	Y	Y	Y	N
5 Hooley	+	N	Y	Y	Y	Y	N
PENNSYLVANIA							
1 Vacant							
2 Fattah	Y	Y	N	Y	Y	Y	N
3 Borski	Y	Y	Y	Y	Y	Y	N
4 Klink	Y	N	Y	Y	Y	Y	N
5 ***Peterson***	Y	N	Y	Y	Y	N	Y
6 Holden	Y	N	Y	Y	Y	Y	Y
7 ***Weldon***	Y	N	Y	Y	Y	N	N
8 ***Greenwood***	Y	N	Y	Y	Y	N	N
9 ***Shuster***	Y	N	Y	Y	Y	N	Y
10 ***McDade***	Y	Y	Y	?	Y	N	Y
11 Kanjorski	Y	N	Y	Y	Y	Y	N
12 Murtha	Y	N	Y	Y	Y	Y	Y
13 ***Fox***	Y	N	Y	Y	Y	N	Y
14 Coyne	Y	N	Y	Y	Y	Y	N
15 McHale	Y	N	Y	Y	Y	Y	N
16 ***Pitts***	Y	N	Y	Y	Y	N	Y
17 ***Gekas***	Y	N	Y	Y	Y	N	Y
18 Doyle	Y	N	Y	Y	Y	Y	N
19 ***Goodling***	Y	N	Y	N	Y	N	Y
20 Mascara	Y	N	Y	Y	Y	Y	N
21 ***English***	Y	N	Y	Y	Y	N	Y
RHODE ISLAND							
1 Kennedy	Y	Y	N	Y	Y	Y	N
2 Weygand	Y	N	Y	Y	Y	Y	N
SOUTH CAROLINA							
1 ***Sanford***	Y	N	Y	N	Y	N	Y
2 ***Spence***	Y	N	Y	Y	Y	N	Y
3 ***Graham***	Y	N	Y	Y	Y	N	Y
4 ***Inglis***	?	N	Y	Y	Y	N	Y
5 Spratt	?	N	Y	Y	Y	Y	N
6 Clyburn	Y	N	Y	Y	Y	Y	N
SOUTH DAKOTA							
AL ***Thune***	Y	N	Y	Y	Y	N	Y

	67	68	69	70	71	72	73
TENNESSEE							
1 ***Jenkins***	Y	Y	Y	Y	Y	N	Y
2 ***Duncan***	Y	N	Y	Y	Y	N	Y
3 ***Wamp***	Y	Y	Y	Y	Y	N	Y
4 ***Hilleary***	Y	Y	Y	Y	Y	N	Y
5 Clement	Y	Y	N	Y	Y	Y	Y
6 Gordon	Y	Y	N	Y	Y	Y	Y
7 ***Bryant***	Y	Y	Y	N	Y	N	Y
8 Tanner	Y	Y	N	Y	Y	Y	Y
9 Ford	Y	+	−	+	+	+	−
TEXAS							
1 Sandlin	Y	N	Y	Y	Y	Y	N
2 Turner	Y	N	Y	Y	Y	N	Y
3 ***Johnson, Sam***	Y	N	Y	N	Y	N	Y
4 Hall	Y	N	Y	N	Y	N	Y
5 ***Sessions***	Y	N	Y	Y	Y	N	Y
6 ***Barton***	?	N	Y	N	Y	N	Y
7 ***Archer***	Y	N	Y	Y	Y	N	Y
8 ***Brady***	Y	N	Y	N	Y	N	Y
9 Lampson	Y	Y	N	Y	Y	Y	N
10 Doggett	Y	Y	N	Y	Y	Y	N
11 Edwards	Y	N	Y	Y	Y	Y	N
12 ***Granger***	Y	N	Y	N	Y	N	Y
13 ***Thornberry***	Y	N	Y	Y	Y	N	Y
14 ***Paul***	Y	Y	N	Y	Y	N	Y
15 Hinojosa	Y	N	Y	Y	Y	Y	N
16 Reyes	Y	N	Y	Y	Y	?	N
17 Stenholm	Y	N	Y	Y	Y	N	Y
18 Jackson-Lee	Y	?	?	?	?	?	?
19 ***Combest***	Y	N	Y	N	Y	N	Y
20 Gonzalez	?	?	?	?	?	?	?
21 ***Smith***	Y	N	Y	N	Y	N	Y
22 ***DeLay***	Y	N	Y	Y	Y	?	Y
23 ***Bonilla***	Y	N	Y	Y	Y	N	?
24 Frost	Y	Y	Y	Y	Y	Y	N
25 Bentsen	Y	N	Y	Y	Y	Y	N
26 ***Armey***	?	N	Y	Y	Y	N	Y
27 Ortiz	Y	Y	N	Y	Y	Y	N
28 Rodriguez	Y	N	Y	Y	Y	Y	N
29 Green	Y	N	Y	N	Y	Y	N
30 Johnson, E.B.	Y	?	?	?	?	?	?
UTAH							
1 ***Hansen***	Y	Y	Y	Y	Y	N	Y
2 ***Cook***	Y	N	Y	Y	Y	−	+
3 ***Cannon***	?	?	?	?	?	?	?
VERMONT							
AL *Sanders*	Y	Y	N	Y	Y	Y	?
VIRGINIA							
1 ***Bateman***	Y	N	Y	Y	Y	N	Y
2 Pickett	Y	N	Y	Y	Y	N	Y
3 Scott	Y	N	Y	Y	Y	Y	N
4 Sisisky	Y	N	Y	Y	Y	N	Y
5 Goode	Y	N	Y	Y	Y	N	Y
6 ***Goodlatte***	Y	Y	Y	N	Y	N	Y
7 ***Bliley***	Y	Y	Y	Y	Y	N	Y
8 Moran	Y	N	Y	Y	Y	Y	N
9 Boucher	Y	Y	Y	Y	Y	Y	N
10 ***Wolf***	Y	N	Y	Y	Y	N	Y
11 ***Davis***	Y	N	Y	Y	Y	N	Y
WASHINGTON							
1 ***White***	Y	N	Y	N	Y	N	Y
2 ***Metcalf***	Y	N	Y	Y	Y	N	Y
3 ***Smith, Linda***	Y	N	Y	Y	Y	N	Y
4 ***Hastings***	Y	N	Y	N	Y	N	Y
5 ***Nethercutt***	Y	N	Y	Y	Y	N	Y
6 Dicks	Y	N	Y	Y	Y	Y	N
7 McDermott	+	#	X	+	+	+	−
8 ***Dunn***	Y	N	Y	Y	Y	N	Y
9 Smith, Adam	Y	N	Y	Y	Y	Y	N
WEST VIRGINIA							
1 Mollohan	Y	Y	Y	Y	Y	N	Y
2 Wise	Y	Y	Y	Y	Y	Y	N
3 Rahall	Y	Y	Y	Y	Y	Y	N
WISCONSIN							
1 ***Neumann***	Y	N	Y	Y	Y	N	Y
2 ***Klug***	Y	N	Y	Y	Y	N	Y
3 Kind	Y	N	Y	Y	Y	Y	N
4 Kleczka	Y	−	#	+	+	Y	N
5 Barrett	Y	N	Y	Y	Y	Y	N
6 ***Petri***	Y	N	Y	Y	Y	N	Y
7 Obey	Y	Y	Y	Y	Y	Y	N
8 Johnson	Y	N	Y	Y	Y	Y	N
9 ***Sensenbrenner***	Y	N	Y	Y	Y	N	Y
WYOMING							
AL ***Cubin***	Y	N	Y	Y	Y	N	Y

Southern states - Ala., Ark., Fla., Ga., Ky., La., Miss., N.C., Okla., S.C., Tenn., Texas, Va.

House Votes 74, 75, 76, 77, 78, 79, 80

74. HR 3310. Small Business Paperwork Reduction/Passage. Passage of the bill to suspend most civil fines on small-businesses for first-time paperwork violations. Under the bill, the federal regulating agency could choose to suspend the fine if the violation had not caused actual harm to the public health or safety, and the business corrects the violation within six months. Passed 267-140: R 213-4; D 54-135 (ND 27-113, SD 27-22); I 0-1. March 26, 1998. A "nay" was a vote in support of the president's position.

75. HR 1757. Fiscal 1998 State Department Authorization/Rule. Adoption of the rule (H Res 385) to provide for floor consideration of the conference report on the bill to authorize $1.75 billion in fiscal 1998 and $1.69 billion in fiscal 1999 for State Department diplomatic and consular functions, authorize $819 million over fiscal years 1998 through 2000 to pay back U.S. dues to the United Nations, codify restrictions on U.S. funds for international family planning and reorganize U.S. foreign policy agencies. Adopted 234-172: R 215-4; D 19-167 (ND 14-124, SD 5-43); I 0-1. March 26, 1998. (Subsequently, the conference report was adopted by voice vote.)

76. HR 3246. Labor Union Organizing Curbs/Rule. Adoption of the rule (H Res 393) to provide for floor consideration of the bill to permit employers to refuse to hire, or fire, those who seek employment with the primary intent of organizing workers to join a union. Adopted 220-185: R 216-1; D 4-183 (ND 1-137, SD 3-46); I 0-1. March 26, 1998.

77. HR 3246. Labor Union Organizing Curbs/Bona Fide Applicants. Goodling, R-Pa., amendment to clarify that any "bona fide" applicant would continue to enjoy every right provided by the National Labor Relations Act, including the right to form, join, or assist labor organizations. Adopted 398-0: R 214-0; D 183-0 (ND 135-0, SD 48-0); I 1-0. March 26, 1998.

78. HR 3246. Labor Union Organizing Curbs/Passage. Passage of the bill to permit employers to refuse to hire, or fire, those who seek employment to organize workers to join a union. Passed 202-200: R 194-20; D 8-179 (ND 0-138, SD 8-41); I 0-1. March 26, 1998. A "nay" was a vote in support of the president's position.

79. HR 2515. Forest Recovery/Road Construction. Boehlert, R-N.Y., amendment to the Smith, R-Ore., amendment to prohibit the building of roads under the bill in roadless areas. The Smith amendment would prohibit the construction of roads under the bill that are not allowed under current law. Adopted 200-187: R 52-156; D 147-31 (ND 117-17, SD 30-14); I 1-0. March 27, 1998. (Subsequently, the Smith amendment, as amended, was rejected by voice vote).

80. HR 2515. Forest Recovery/Passage. Passage of the bill to direct the Agriculture Department to establish a five-year nationwide program to restore and protect public forests from fire, disease and infestation through forest recovery projects. Rejected 181-201: R 153-51; D 28-149 (ND 12-123, SD 16-26); I 0-1. March 27, 1998. A "nay" was a vote in support of the president's position.

Key

- **Y** Voted for (yea).
- **#** Paired for.
- **+** Announced for.
- **N** Voted against (nay).
- **X** Paired against.
- **−** Announced against.
- **P** Voted "present."
- **C** Voted "present" to avoid possible conflict of interest.
- **?** Did not vote or otherwise make a position known.

Democrats **Republicans** Independent

	74	75	76	77	78	79	80
ALABAMA							
1 *Callahan*	Y	Y	Y	Y	Y	Y	N
2 *Everett*	Y	Y	Y	Y	Y	N	Y
3 *Riley*	Y	Y	Y	Y	Y	N	Y
4 *Aderholt*	Y	Y	Y	Y	Y	N	Y
5 Cramer	Y	N	N	Y	N	N	Y
6 *Bachus*	Y	Y	Y	Y	Y	N	Y
7 Hilliard	N	N	N	Y	N	N	Y
ALASKA							
AL *Young*	Y	Y	Y	Y	N	?	?
ARIZONA							
1 *Salmon*	Y	Y	Y	Y	Y	N	Y
2 Pastor	N	N	N	Y	N	Y	N
3 *Stump*	Y	Y	Y	Y	Y	N	Y
4 *Shadegg*	Y	Y	Y	Y	Y	N	Y
5 *Kolbe*	Y	Y	Y	Y	Y	N	Y
6 *Hayworth*	Y	Y	Y	Y	Y	N	Y
ARKANSAS							
1 Berry	Y	Y	N	Y	N	−	+
2 Snyder	N	N	N	Y	N	Y	N
3 *Hutchinson*	Y	Y	Y	Y	Y	N	Y
4 *Dickey*	Y	Y	Y	Y	Y	N	Y
CALIFORNIA							
1 *Riggs*	Y	Y	Y	Y	Y	N	Y
2 *Herger*	Y	Y	Y	Y	Y	N	Y
3 Fazio	N	N	N	Y	N	Y	N
4 *Doolittle*	Y	Y	Y	Y	Y	N	Y
5 Matsui	N	N	N	Y	N	Y	N
6 Woolsey	N	N	N	Y	N	Y	N
7 Miller	N	N	N	Y	N	Y	N
8 Pelosi	N	N	N	Y	N	Y	N
9 Vacant							
10 Tauscher	Y	N	N	Y	N	Y	N
11 *Pombo*	Y	Y	Y	Y	Y	N	Y
12 Lantos	N	N	N	Y	N	Y	N
13 Stark	N	N	N	Y	N	Y	N
14 Eshoo	N	N	N	Y	N	Y	N
15 *Campbell*	Y	Y	Y	Y	N	N	N
16 Lofgren	N	N	N	Y	N	Y	N
17 Farr	N	N	N	Y	N	Y	N
18 Condit	Y	N	N	Y	N	Y	N
19 *Radanovich*	Y	Y	Y	Y	Y	N	Y
20 Dooley	Y	N	N	Y	N	N	Y
21 *Thomas*	Y	Y	Y	Y	Y	N	Y
22 Capps, L.	Y	N	N	Y	N	Y	N
23 *Gallegly*	Y	Y	Y	Y	Y	N	Y
24 Sherman	N	N	N	+	N	Y	N
25 *McKeon*	Y	Y	Y	Y	Y	N	Y
26 Berman	N	N	N	Y	N	Y	N
27 *Rogan*	Y	Y	Y	Y	Y	N	Y
28 *Dreier*	Y	Y	Y	Y	Y	N	Y
29 Waxman	N	N	N	Y	N	Y	N
30 Becerra	?	N	N	Y	N	+	−
31 Martinez	N	N	N	Y	N	Y	N
32 Dixon	N	N	N	Y	N	Y	N
33 Roybal-Allard	N	N	N	Y	N	Y	N
34 Torres	N	N	N	N	Y	Y	N
35 Waters	?	?	?	?	?	?	?
36 Harman	?	?	?	?	?	?	?
37 Millender-McD.	?	?	?	?	?	?	?

	74	75	76	77	78	79	80
38 *Horn*	Y	Y	Y	Y	Y	Y	N
39 *Royce*	#	?	?	?	?	?	?
40 *Lewis*	Y	Y	Y	Y	Y	N	Y
41 *Kim*	Y	Y	Y	Y	Y	N	Y
42 Brown	N	N	N	Y	N	Y	N
43 *Calvert*	Y	Y	Y	Y	Y	N	Y
44 Vacant							
45 *Rohrabacher*	Y	Y	Y	Y	Y	N	Y
46 Sanchez	Y	N	N	Y	N	+	−
47 *Cox*	Y	Y	Y	Y	Y	N	Y
48 *Packard*	Y	Y	Y	Y	Y	N	Y
49 *Bilbray*	Y	Y	Y	Y	Y	Y	N
50 Filner	N	N	N	Y	N	Y	N
51 *Cunningham*	Y	Y	Y	Y	Y	N	?
52 *Hunter*	Y	Y	Y	?	Y	N	Y
COLORADO							
1 DeGette	N	N	N	Y	N	Y	N
2 Skaggs	N	N	N	Y	N	Y	N
3 *McInnis*	Y	Y	Y	Y	Y	N	Y
4 *Schaffer*	Y	Y	Y	Y	Y	N	Y
5 *Hefley*	Y	Y	Y	Y	Y	N	Y
6 *Schaefer*	Y	Y	Y	Y	Y	Y	Y
CONNECTICUT							
1 Kennelly	N	N	N	Y	N	Y	N
2 Gejdenson	N	N	N	Y	N	Y	N
3 DeLauro	N	N	N	Y	N	Y	N
4 *Shays*	N	Y	Y	Y	N	Y	N
5 Maloney	Y	N	N	Y	N	Y	N
6 *Johnson*	Y	Y	Y	Y	N	Y	N
DELAWARE							
AL *Castle*	Y	N	Y	Y	Y	Y	N
FLORIDA							
1 *Scarborough*	Y	Y	Y	Y	Y	N	Y
2 Boyd	Y	N	N	Y	Y	N	Y
3 Brown	−	−	−	+	−	+	−
4 *Fowler*	Y	Y	Y	Y	Y	N	Y
5 Thurman	Y	N	N	N	N	N	Y
6 *Stearns*	Y	Y	Y	Y	Y	N	Y
7 *Mica*	Y	Y	Y	Y	Y	N	Y
8 *McCollum*	Y	Y	Y	Y	Y	?	?
9 *Bilirakis*	Y	Y	Y	Y	Y	N	Y
10 *Young*	Y	Y	Y	Y	Y	N	Y
11 Davis	Y	N	N	Y	N	Y	N
12 *Canady*	Y	Y	Y	Y	Y	N	Y
13 *Miller*	Y	Y	Y	Y	Y	N	?
14 *Goss*	Y	Y	Y	Y	Y	Y	N
15 *Weldon*	Y	Y	Y	Y	Y	N	Y
16 *Foley*	Y	Y	Y	Y	Y	Y	N
17 Meek	N	N	N	Y	N	?	N
18 *Ros-Lehtinen*	N	Y	Y	−	Y	Y	Y
19 Wexler	N	N	N	Y	N	Y	N
20 Deutsch	Y	N	N	Y	N	Y	N
21 *Diaz-Balart*	Y	Y	?	Y	N	Y	Y
22 *Shaw*	Y	Y	Y	Y	Y	Y	Y
23 Hastings	N	N	N	Y	N	Y	N
GEORGIA							
1 *Kingston*	Y	N	Y	Y	Y	N	Y
2 Bishop	Y	N	N	Y	N	N	Y
3 *Collins*	Y	Y	Y	Y	Y	N	Y
4 McKinney	N	N	N	Y	N	Y	N
5 Lewis	N	N	N	Y	N	Y	N
6 *Gingrich*					Y		
7 *Barr*	Y	Y	Y	Y	Y	N	Y
8 *Chambliss*	Y	Y	Y	Y	Y	N	Y
9 *Deal*	Y	Y	Y	Y	Y	N	Y
10 *Norwood*	Y	Y	Y	Y	Y	N	Y
11 *Linder*	Y	Y	Y	Y	Y	N	Y
HAWAII							
1 Abercrombie	N	N	N	Y	N	Y	N
2 Mink	N	N	N	Y	N	Y	N
IDAHO							
1 *Chenoweth*	Y	Y	Y	Y	Y	N	N
2 *Crapo*	?	?	?	?	?	N	N
ILLINOIS							
1 Rush	N	N	N	Y	N	Y	N
2 Jackson	N	N	N	Y	N	Y	N
3 Lipinski	N	Y	N	Y	N	?	?
4 Gutierrez	N	N	N	Y	N	Y	N
5 Blagojevich	N	Y	N	Y	N	Y	N
6 *Hyde*	Y	Y	Y	Y	Y	N	Y
7 Davis	N	N	N	Y	N	Y	N
8 *Crane*	Y	Y	Y	Y	Y	N	Y
9 Yates	N	N	?	?	?	Y	N
10 *Porter*	Y	Y	Y	Y	Y	N	Y
11 *Weller*	Y	Y	Y	Y	Y	N	Y
12 Costello	N	N	Y	Y	N	N	Y

ND Northern Democrats   SD Southern Democrats

	74	75	76	77	78	79	80
13 ***Fawell***	Y	Y	Y	Y	Y	Y	N
14 ***Hastert***	Y	Y	Y	Y	Y	N	Y
15 ***Ewing***	Y	Y	Y	Y	Y	N	Y
16 ***Manzullo***	Y	Y	Y	Y	Y	N	Y
17 Evans	N	N	N	Y	N	Y	N
18 ***LaHood***	Y	Y	Y	Y	N	N	Y
19 Poshard	N	Y	N	Y	N	Y	N
20 ***Shimkus***	Y	Y	Y	Y	N	N	Y
INDIANA							
1 Visclosky	N	N	N	Y	N	Y	N
2 ***McIntosh***	Y	Y	Y	Y	Y	N	Y
3 Roemer	Y	N	N	Y	N	Y	N
4 ***Souder***	Y	Y	Y	Y	Y	N	Y
5 ***Buyer***	Y	Y	Y	Y	Y	N	Y
6 ***Burton***	Y	Y	Y	Y	Y	N	Y
7 ***Pease***	Y	Y	Y	Y	Y	N	Y
8 ***Hostettler***	Y	Y	Y	Y	Y	N	Y
9 Hamilton	Y	N	N	Y	N	Y	N
10 Carson	N	N	N	Y	N	Y	N
IOWA							
1 ***Leach***	Y	N	Y	Y	Y	Y	N
2 ***Nussle***	Y	Y	Y	Y	Y	Y	Y
3 Boswell	Y	N	N	Y	N	Y	N
4 ***Ganske***	Y	Y	Y	Y	Y	Y	N
5 ***Latham***	Y	Y	Y	Y	Y	N	Y
KANSAS							
1 ***Moran***	Y	Y	Y	Y	Y	N	Y
2 ***Ryun***	Y	Y	Y	Y	Y	N	Y
3 ***Snowbarger***	Y	Y	Y	Y	Y	N	Y
4 ***Tiahrt***	Y	Y	Y	Y	Y	N	Y
KENTUCKY							
1 ***Whitfield***	Y	Y	Y	Y	Y	N	Y
2 ***Lewis***	Y	Y	Y	Y	Y	N	Y
3 ***Northup***	Y	Y	Y	Y	Y	N	Y
4 ***Bunning***	Y	Y	Y	Y	Y	N	Y
5 ***Rogers***	Y	Y	Y	?	?	?	?
6 Baesler	N	N	N	Y	N	Y	Y
LOUISIANA							
1 ***Livingston***	Y	Y	Y	Y	Y	N	Y
2 Jefferson	?	?	?	?	?	?	?
3 ***Tauzin***	Y	Y	Y	Y	Y	N	Y
4 ***McCrery***	Y	Y	Y	Y	Y	N	Y
5 ***Cooksey***	Y	Y	+	+	+	−	+
6 ***Baker***	Y	Y	Y	Y	Y	N	Y
7 John	Y	Y	N	Y	Y	N	Y
MAINE							
1 Allen	N	N	N	Y	N	Y	N
2 Baldacci	N	N	N	Y	N	Y	N
MARYLAND							
1 ***Gilchrest***	Y	Y	Y	Y	Y	Y	Y
2 ***Ehrlich***	Y	Y	Y	Y	Y	N	Y
3 Cardin	?	?	?	?	?	?	?
4 Wynn	N	N	N	Y	N	Y	N
5 Hoyer	N	N	N	Y	N	Y	N
6 ***Bartlett***	Y	Y	Y	Y	Y	N	Y
7 Cummings	N	N	N	Y	N	Y	N
8 ***Morella***	Y	Y	Y	Y	Y	Y	N
MASSACHUSETTS							
1 Olver	N	N	N	Y	N	Y	N
2 Neal	N	N	N	Y	N	Y	N
3 McGovern	N	?	N	Y	N	Y	N
4 Frank	N	N	N	Y	N	Y	N
5 Meehan	N	N	N	Y	N	Y	N
6 Tierney	N	N	N	Y	N	Y	N
7 Markey	N	N	N	?	N	Y	N
8 Kennedy	N	N	N	Y	N	Y	N
9 Moakley	N	?	N	Y	N	Y	N
10 Delahunt	N	N	N	Y	N	N	N
MICHIGAN							
1 Stupak	N	Y	N	Y	N	N	Y
2 ***Hoekstra***	Y	Y	Y	Y	Y	N	Y
3 ***Ehlers***	Y	Y	Y	Y	Y	Y	N
4 ***Camp***	Y	Y	Y	Y	Y	N	Y
5 Barcia	N	Y	N	Y	N	N	Y
6 ***Upton***	Y	Y	Y	Y	Y	N	Y
7 ***Smith***	Y	Y	Y	Y	Y	N	Y
8 Stabenow	Y	N	N	Y	N	Y	N
9 Kildee	N	Y	N	Y	N	Y	N
10 Bonior	N	N	N	Y	N	Y	N
11 ***Knollenberg***	Y	Y	Y	Y	Y	N	Y
12 Levin	N	N	N	Y	N	Y	N
13 Rivers	N	N	N	Y	N	Y	N
14 Conyers	−	−	−	+	−	+	−
15 Kilpatrick	N	N	N	Y	N	Y	N
16 Dingell	N	N	N	Y	N	Y	N

	74	75	76	77	78	79	80
MINNESOTA							
1 ***Gutknecht***	Y	Y	Y	Y	Y	N	Y
2 Minge	Y	N	N	Y	N	N	N
3 ***Ramstad***	Y	Y	Y	Y	Y	N	Y
4 Vento	N	N	N	Y	N	Y	N
5 Sabo	N	N	N	Y	N	Y	N
6 Luther	Y	N	N	Y	N	Y	N
7 Peterson	N	Y	N	Y	N	N	Y
8 Oberstar	N	Y	N	Y	N	N	Y
MISSISSIPPI							
1 ***Wicker***	Y	Y	Y	Y	Y	?	?
2 Thompson	N	N	N	Y	N	Y	N
3 ***Pickering***	Y	Y	Y	Y	Y	N	Y
4 ***Parker***	Y	Y	Y	Y	Y	N	?
5 Taylor	Y	Y	N	Y	Y	Y	Y
MISSOURI							
1 Clay	N	N	N	Y	N	?	?
2 ***Talent***	Y	Y	Y	Y	Y	N	Y
3 Gephardt	N	N	N	Y	N	Y	N
4 Skelton	Y	N	N	Y	N	Y	Y
5 McCarthy	N	N	N	Y	N	Y	N
6 Danner	Y	N	N	Y	N	N	Y
7 ***Blunt***	Y	Y	Y	Y	Y	N	Y
8 ***Emerson***	Y	Y	Y	Y	Y	N	Y
9 ***Hulshof***	Y	Y	Y	Y	Y	Y	Y
MONTANA							
AL ***Hill***	Y	Y	Y	Y	Y	N	Y
NEBRASKA							
1 ***Bereuter***	Y	Y	Y	Y	Y	N	Y
2 ***Christensen***	Y	Y	Y	Y	Y	?	?
3 ***Barrett***	Y	Y	Y	Y	Y	N	Y
NEVADA							
1 ***Ensign***	Y	Y	Y	Y	Y	N	Y
2 ***Gibbons***	Y	Y	Y	Y	Y	N	Y
NEW HAMPSHIRE							
1 ***Sununu***	Y	Y	Y	Y	Y	Y	Y
2 ***Bass***	Y	Y	Y	Y	Y	Y	N
NEW JERSEY							
1 Andrews	N	N	N	Y	N	Y	N
2 ***LoBiondo***	Y	Y	Y	Y	Y	Y	N
3 ***Saxton***	Y	Y	Y	Y	Y	Y	N
4 ***Smith***	N	Y	Y	Y	N	Y	N
5 ***Roukema***	Y	Y	Y	Y	Y	Y	N
6 Pallone	N	N	N	Y	N	Y	N
7 ***Franks***	Y	Y	Y	Y	N	Y	N
8 Pascrell	N	N	N	Y	N	Y	N
9 Rothman	N	N	N	Y	N	Y	N
10 Payne	?	?	?	?	?	?	?
11 ***Frelinghuysen***	Y	Y	Y	Y	Y	Y	N
12 ***Pappas***	Y	Y	Y	Y	Y	Y	N
13 Menendez	N	N	N	Y	N	Y	N
NEW MEXICO							
1 Vacant							
2 ***Skeen***	Y	Y	Y	Y	Y	N	Y
3 ***Redmond***	Y	Y	Y	Y	Y	N	Y
NEW YORK							
1 ***Forbes***	Y	Y	N	Y	N	Y	N
2 ***Lazio***	Y	Y	Y	Y	Y	Y	N
3 ***King***	Y	Y	Y	Y	N	N	Y
4 McCarthy	N	N	N	Y	N	Y	N
5 Ackerman	N	N	N	Y	N	Y	N
6 Meeks	N	N	N	Y	N	Y	N
7 Manton	N	N	N	Y	N	Y	N
8 Nadler	N	N	N	Y	N	Y	N
9 Schumer	N	N	N	Y	N	Y	N
10 Towns	N	N	N	Y	N	Y	N
11 Owens	N	N	N	Y	N	Y	N
12 Velázquez	N	N	N	Y	N	Y	N
13 ***Fossella***	Y	Y	Y	Y	Y	N	Y
14 Maloney	N	N	N	Y	N	?	N
15 Rangel	X	?	?	?	?	?	?
16 Serrano	N	N	N	Y	N	Y	N
17 Engel	N	N	−	+	−	Y	N
18 Lowey	N	N	N	Y	N	Y	N
19 ***Kelly***	Y	Y	Y	Y	Y	Y	N
20 ***Gilman***	Y	Y	Y	Y	−	Y	N
21 McNulty	N	−	−	+	−	+	−
22 ***Solomon***	Y	Y	Y	Y	?	N	Y
23 ***Boehlert***	N	Y	Y	Y	N	Y	N
24 ***McHugh***	Y	Y	Y	Y	N	N	Y
25 ***Walsh***	Y	Y	Y	Y	Y	Y	N
26 Hinchey	N	N	N	Y	N	Y	N
27 ***Paxon***	Y	Y	Y	Y	Y	?	Y
28 Slaughter	N	N	N	Y	N	Y	N
29 LaFalce	N	N	N	Y	N	Y	N

	74	75	76	77	78	79	80
30 ***Quinn***	Y	Y	Y	Y	N	Y	N
31 ***Houghton***	?	?	?	?	?	?	?
NORTH CAROLINA							
1 Clayton	Y	N	N	Y	N	Y	N
2 Etheridge	Y	N	N	Y	N	Y	N
3 ***Jones***	Y	Y	Y	Y	Y	N	Y
4 Price	Y	N	N	Y	N	Y	N
5 ***Burr***	Y	Y	Y	Y	Y	N	Y
6 ***Coble***	Y	Y	Y	Y	Y	N	Y
7 McIntyre	Y	N	N	Y	Y	Y	N
8 Hefner	N	N	N	?	N	Y	N
9 ***Myrick***	Y	Y	Y	Y	Y	N	Y
10 ***Ballenger***	Y	Y	Y	Y	Y	N	+
11 ***Taylor***	Y	Y	Y	Y	Y	N	Y
12 Watt	N	N	N	Y	N	?	?
NORTH DAKOTA							
AL Pomeroy	Y	N	N	Y	N	?	?
OHIO							
1 ***Chabot***	Y	Y	Y	Y	Y	Y	N
2 ***Portman***	Y	Y	Y	Y	Y	N	N
3 Hall	Y	Y	N	Y	N	Y	N
4 ***Oxley***	Y	Y	Y	Y	Y	N	Y
5 ***Gillmor***	?	?	?	Y	Y	Y	Y
6 Strickland	N	N	N	Y	N	Y	N
7 ***Hobson***	Y	Y	Y	Y	Y	N	Y
8 ***Boehner***	Y	Y	Y	Y	Y	N	Y
9 Kaptur	N	N	N	Y	N	Y	N
10 Kucinich	N	Y	N	Y	N	Y	N
11 Stokes	N	N	N	Y	N	Y	N
12 ***Kasich***	?	Y	Y	Y	Y	N	Y
13 Brown	N	N	N	Y	N	Y	N
14 Sawyer	N	N	N	Y	N	Y	N
15 ***Pryce***	Y	Y	Y	Y	Y	N	Y
16 ***Regula***	Y	Y	Y	Y	Y	N	Y
17 Traficant	Y	Y	Y	Y	N	N	Y
18 ***Ney***	Y	Y	Y	Y	Y	N	Y
19 ***LaTourette***	Y	Y	Y	Y	N	N	N
OKLAHOMA							
1 ***Largent***	Y	Y	Y	Y	Y	N	Y
2 ***Coburn***	Y	Y	Y	Y	Y	?	?
3 ***Watkins***	Y	Y	Y	Y	Y	?	?
4 ***Watts***	Y	Y	Y	Y	Y	N	Y
5 ***Istook***	Y	Y	Y	Y	Y	N	Y
6 ***Lucas***	Y	Y	Y	Y	Y	N	Y
OREGON							
1 Furse	N	N	N	Y	N	Y	N
2 ***Smith***	Y	Y	Y	?	Y	N	Y
3 Blumenauer	N	N	N	Y	N	Y	N
4 DeFazio	N	N	N	Y	N	Y	N
5 Hooley	N	N	N	Y	N	Y	N
PENNSYLVANIA							
1 Vacant							
2 Fattah	N	N	N	Y	N	Y	N
3 Borski	N	N	N	Y	N	Y	N
4 Klink	Y	N	N	Y	N	N	N
5 ***Peterson***	Y	Y	Y	Y	Y	N	Y
6 Holden	Y	N	N	Y	N	Y	N
7 ***Weldon***	Y	Y	Y	Y	Y	N	Y
8 ***Greenwood***	Y	N	Y	Y	Y	Y	N
9 ***Shuster***	Y	Y	Y	Y	Y	N	Y
10 ***McDade***	Y	Y	Y	?	?	N	Y
11 Kanjorski	N	N	N	Y	N	Y	N
12 Murtha	Y	N	N	Y	N	Y	N
13 ***Fox***	Y	Y	Y	Y	Y	Y	N
14 Coyne	N	N	N	Y	N	Y	N
15 McHale	Y	N	N	Y	N	Y	N
16 ***Pitts***	Y	Y	Y	Y	Y	N	Y
17 ***Gekas***	Y	Y	Y	Y	Y	N	Y
18 Doyle	Y	N	N	Y	N	N	Y
19 ***Goodling***	Y	Y	Y	Y	Y	Y	Y
20 Mascara	N	N	N	Y	N	N	Y
21 ***English***	Y	Y	Y	Y	Y	Y	Y
RHODE ISLAND							
1 Kennedy	N	N	N	Y	N	Y	N
2 Weygand	Y	N	N	Y	N	Y	N
SOUTH CAROLINA							
1 ***Sanford***	Y	Y	Y	Y	Y	Y	N
2 ***Spence***	Y	Y	Y	Y	Y	N	Y
3 ***Graham***	Y	Y	Y	Y	Y	N	Y
4 ***Inglis***	Y	Y	Y	Y	Y	N	Y
5 Spratt	Y	N	N	Y	N	Y	N
6 Clyburn	N	N	N	Y	N	Y	N
SOUTH DAKOTA							
AL ***Thune***	Y	Y	Y	Y	Y	N	Y

	74	75	76	77	78	79	80
TENNESSEE							
1 ***Jenkins***	Y	Y	Y	Y	Y	N	Y
2 ***Duncan***	Y	Y	Y	Y	Y	N	Y
3 ***Wamp***	Y	Y	Y	Y	Y	N	N
4 ***Hilleary***	Y	Y	Y	Y	Y	N	N
5 Clement	Y	N	N	Y	N	Y	N
6 Gordon	Y	N	N	Y	N	Y	N
7 ***Bryant***	Y	Y	Y	Y	Y	?	?
8 Tanner	Y	N	N	Y	Y	Y	Y
9 Ford	−	−	−	+	−	+	−
TEXAS							
1 Sandlin	Y	N	N	Y	N	N	Y
2 Turner	Y	N	N	Y	N	N	Y
3 ***Johnson, Sam***	Y	Y	Y	Y	Y	N	Y
4 Hall	Y	Y	Y	Y	Y	N	Y
5 ***Sessions***	Y	Y	Y	Y	Y	N	Y
6 ***Barton***	Y	Y	Y	Y	Y	N	Y
7 ***Archer***	?	Y	Y	Y	Y	N	Y
8 ***Brady***	Y	Y	Y	Y	Y	N	Y
9 Lampson	N	N	N	Y	N	Y	N
10 Doggett	N	N	N	Y	N	Y	N
11 Edwards	N	?	N	Y	N	N	?
12 ***Granger***	Y	Y	Y	Y	Y	N	Y
13 ***Thornberry***	Y	Y	Y	Y	Y	N	Y
14 ***Paul***	Y	Y	Y	Y	Y	N	N
15 Hinojosa	N	N	N	Y	N	?	?
16 Reyes	N	N	N	Y	N	Y	N
17 Stenholm	Y	N	Y	Y	Y	N	Y
18 Jackson-Lee	?	?	?	?	?	?	?
19 ***Combest***	Y	Y	Y	Y	Y	N	Y
20 Gonzalez	?	?	?	?	?	?	?
21 ***Smith***	Y	Y	Y	?	?	?	?
22 ***DeLay***	Y	Y	Y	Y	Y	N	?
23 ***Bonilla***	#	?	?	?	?	?	?
24 Frost	Y	N	N	Y	N	?	?
25 Bentsen	N	N	N	Y	N	Y	N
26 ***Armey***	Y	Y	Y	Y	Y	N	Y
27 Ortiz	N	N	N	Y	N	Y	N
28 Rodriguez	N	N	N	Y	N	Y	N
29 Green	Y	N	N	Y	N	Y	?
30 Johnson, E.B.	?	?	?	?	?	?	?
UTAH							
1 ***Hansen***	Y	Y	Y	Y	Y	?	?
2 ***Cook***	Y	Y	Y	Y	Y	?	?
3 ***Cannon***	?	?	?	?	?	?	?
VERMONT							
AL *Sanders*	N	N	N	Y	N	Y	N
VIRGINIA							
1 ***Bateman***	Y	Y	Y	Y	Y	N	Y
2 Pickett	Y	N	N	Y	N	N	Y
3 Scott	N	N	N	Y	N	Y	N
4 Sisisky	Y	N	N	Y	N	N	Y
5 Goode	Y	Y	Y	Y	Y	N	Y
6 ***Goodlatte***	Y	Y	Y	Y	Y	N	Y
7 ***Bliley***	Y	Y	Y	Y	Y	N	Y
8 Moran	Y	N	N	Y	N	Y	N
9 Boucher	N	N	N	Y	N	Y	?
10 ***Wolf***	Y	Y	Y	Y	Y	N	Y
11 ***Davis***	Y	Y	Y	Y	Y	Y	N
WASHINGTON							
1 ***White***	Y	Y	Y	Y	Y	Y	N
2 ***Metcalf***	Y	Y	Y	Y	N	N	Y
3 ***Smith, Linda***	Y	Y	Y	Y	Y	N	Y
4 ***Hastings***	Y	Y	Y	Y	Y	N	Y
5 ***Nethercutt***	Y	Y	Y	Y	Y	N	Y
6 Dicks	N	N	N	Y	N	N	N
7 McDermott	X	−	−	−	−	+	−
8 ***Dunn***	Y	Y	Y	Y	Y	N	Y
9 Smith, Adam	Y	N	N	Y	N	Y	N
WEST VIRGINIA							
1 Mollohan	Y	Y	N	Y	N	N	N
2 Wise	N	N	N	Y	N	N	Y
3 Rahall	N	Y	N	Y	N	N	Y
WISCONSIN							
1 ***Neumann***	Y	Y	Y	Y	Y	N	N
2 ***Klug***	Y	Y	Y	Y	Y	Y	N
3 Kind	Y	N	N	Y	N	Y	N
4 Kleczka	N	N	N	Y	N	Y	N
5 Barrett	N	N	N	Y	N	Y	N
6 ***Petri***	Y	Y	Y	Y	Y	Y	N
7 Obey	N	N	N	Y	N	Y	N
8 Johnson	Y	N	N	?	N	Y	N
9 ***Sensenbrenner***	Y	Y	Y	Y	Y	Y	N
WYOMING							
AL ***Cubin***	Y	Y	Y	Y	Y	N	Y

Southern states - Ala., Ark., Fla., Ga., Ky., La., Miss., N.C., Okla., S.C., Tenn., Texas, Va.

House Votes 81, 82, 83, 84, 85, 86, 87

81. Campaign Finance Overhaul/Passage. Thomas, R-Calif., motion to suspend the rules and pass the bill to ban raising or spending "soft money" contributions by federal candidates and state and national political parties, require unions to obtain written consent from workers before they spend dues revenue, and to establish a voter eligibility confirmation pilot program. Motion rejected 74-337: R 74-140; D 0-196 (ND 0-143, SD 0-53); I 0-1. March 30, 1998. A two-thirds majority of those present and voting (275 in this case) is required for passage under suspension of the rules.

82. HR 34. Non-Citizens Contributions Ban/Passage. Thomas, R-Calif., motion to suspend the rules and pass the bill to clarify that non-citizens are prohibited from contributing to federal campaigns. Motion agreed to 369-43: R 209-6; D 159-37 (ND 112-31, SD 47-6); I 1-0. March 30, 1998. A two-thirds majority of those present and voting (276 in this case) is required for passage under suspension of the rules.

83. HR 2608. Involuntary Contributions Ban/Passage. Thomas, R-Calif., motion to suspend the rules and pass the bill to prohibit involuntary use of funds of employees and shareholders of corporations, and of labor union members, for political activities. Motion rejected 166-246: R 163-52; D 3-193 (ND 0-143, SD 3-50); I 0-1. March 30, 1998. A two-thirds majority of those present and voting (276 in this case) is required for passage under suspension of the rules.

84. Campaign Reporting and Disclosure/Passage. Thomas, R-Calif., motion to suspend the rules and pass the bill to overhaul the reporting of campaign contribution information to the Federal Election Commission by tightening reporting requirements and expanding the type of information reported. Motion agreed to 405-6: R 213-1; D 191-5 (ND 138-5, SD 53-0); I 1-0. March 30, 1998. A two-thirds majority of those present and voting (275 in this case) is required for passage under suspension of the rules.

85. HR 3579. Fiscal 1998 Supplemental Appropriations/Rule. Adoption of the rule (H Res 402) to provide for floor consideration of the bill to provide $2.9 billion in supplemental appropriations, including $2.3 billion for the military, primarily to support military operations in Iraq and Bosnia, and $575 million for disaster relief. Adopted 220-199: R 218-3; D 2-195 (ND 0-145, SD 2-50); I 0-1. March 31, 1998.

86. Procedural Motion/Secret Session. Obey, D-Wis., motion that the House resolve into secret session to discuss intelligence budget issues relating to HR3579, which provides supplemental appropriations for the military and disaster relief. Motion rejected 194-227: R 0-223; D 193-4 (ND 143-1, SD 50-3); I 1-0. March 31, 1998.

87. HR 3579. Fiscal 1998 Supplemental Appropriations/Recommit. Murtha, D-Pa., motion to recommit the bill to the House Appropriations Committee with instructions to report it back with an amendment to strike the bill's offsets of $2.9 billion. Motion rejected 195-224: R 0-220; D 194-4 (ND 146-0, SD 48-4); I 1-0. March 31, 1998.

Key

- **Y** Voted for (yea).
- **#** Paired for.
- **+** Announced for.
- **N** Voted against (nay).
- **X** Paired against.
- **−** Announced against.
- **P** Voted "present."
- **C** Voted "present" to avoid possible conflict of interest.
- **?** Did not vote or otherwise make a position known.

Democrats   **Republicans**   *Independent*

	81	82	83	84	85	86	87
ALABAMA							
1 Callahan	N	Y	Y	Y	Y	N	N
2 Everett	N	Y	Y	Y	Y	N	N
3 Riley	N	Y	Y	Y	Y	N	N
4 Aderholt	N	Y	N	Y	Y	N	N
5 Cramer	N	Y	N	Y	N	Y	Y
6 Bachus	Y	Y	N	Y	Y	N	N
7 Hilliard	N	Y	N	Y	N	Y	Y
ALASKA							
AL Young	N	Y	N	Y	Y	N	N
ARIZONA							
1 Salmon	Y	Y	Y	Y	Y	N	N
2 Pastor	N	Y	N	Y	N	Y	Y
3 Stump	N	Y	Y	Y	Y	N	N
4 Shadegg	Y	Y	Y	N	Y	N	N
5 Kolbe	Y	Y	Y	Y	Y	N	N
6 Hayworth	Y	Y	Y	Y	Y	N	N
ARKANSAS							
1 Berry	N	Y	N	Y	N	Y	+
2 Snyder	N	Y	N	Y	N	Y	Y
3 Hutchinson	Y	Y	Y	Y	Y	N	N
4 Dickey	N	Y	Y	Y	Y	N	N
CALIFORNIA							
1 Riggs	−	+	+	+	+	−	−
2 Herger	Y	Y	Y	Y	Y	N	N
3 Fazio	N	N	N	Y	N	Y	Y
4 Doolittle	N	N	Y	N	Y	N	N
5 Matsui	N	Y	N	Y	N	Y	Y
6 Woolsey	N	Y	N	Y	N	Y	Y
7 Miller	N	Y	N	Y	N	Y	Y
8 Pelosi	N	N	N	Y	N	Y	Y
9 Vacant							
10 Tauscher	N	Y	N	Y	N	Y	Y
11 Pombo	N	N	Y	Y	Y	N	N
12 Lantos	N	Y	N	Y	N	Y	Y
13 Stark	N	Y	N	Y	N	Y	Y
14 Eshoo	N	Y	N	Y	N	Y	Y
15 Campbell	Y	Y	Y	Y	N	N	N
16 Lofgren	N	N	N	Y	N	Y	Y
17 Farr	N	N	N	Y	N	Y	Y
18 Condit	N	Y	N	Y	N	Y	Y
19 Radanovich	Y	Y	Y	Y	Y	N	N
20 Dooley	N	Y	N	Y	N	Y	Y
21 Thomas	Y	Y	Y	Y	N	N	N
22 Capps, L.	N	Y	N	Y	N	Y	Y
23 Gallegly	N	Y	Y	Y	Y	N	N
24 Sherman	N	Y	N	Y	N	Y	Y
25 McKeon	Y	Y	Y	Y	Y	N	N
26 Berman	N	N	N	Y	N	Y	Y
27 Rogan	Y	Y	Y	Y	Y	N	N
28 Dreier	N	Y	Y	Y	Y	N	N
29 Waxman	N	N	N	Y	N	Y	Y
30 Becerra	N	N	N	Y	N	?	Y
31 Martinez	N	N	N	N	N	Y	Y
32 Dixon	N	N	N	Y	N	Y	Y
33 Roybal-Allard	N	N	N	Y	N	Y	Y
34 Torres	N	N	N	Y	N	Y	Y
35 Waters	?	?	?	?	?	?	?
36 Harman	N	Y	N	Y	N	Y	Y
37 Millender-McD.	N	Y	N	Y	N	Y	Y

	81	82	83	84	85	86	87
38 Horn	Y	Y	N	Y	Y	N	N
39 Royce	?	?	?	?	?	?	?
40 Lewis	N	Y	Y	Y	Y	N	N
41 Kim	P	P	P	P	Y	N	N
42 Brown	N	Y	N	Y	N	Y	Y
43 Calvert	N	Y	Y	Y	Y	N	N
44 Vacant							
45 Rohrabacher	Y	Y	Y	Y	Y	N	N
46 Sanchez	N	Y	N	Y	N	Y	Y
47 Cox	?	Y	Y	Y	Y	N	N
48 Packard	N	Y	Y	Y	Y	N	N
49 Bilbray	N	Y	Y	Y	Y	N	N
50 Filner	N	N	N	Y	N	Y	Y
51 Cunningham	N	Y	Y	Y	Y	N	N
52 Hunter	?	?	?	?	Y	N	N
COLORADO							
1 DeGette	N	Y	N	Y	N	Y	Y
2 Skaggs	N	N	Y	Y	N	Y	Y
3 McInnis	N	Y	Y	Y	Y	N	N
4 Schaffer	N	Y	Y	Y	Y	N	N
5 Hefley	N	Y	Y	Y	Y	N	N
6 Schaefer	Y	Y	Y	Y	Y	N	N
CONNECTICUT							
1 Kennelly	N	Y	N	Y	N	Y	Y
2 Gejdenson	N	Y	N	Y	N	Y	Y
3 DeLauro	N	Y	N	Y	N	Y	Y
4 Shays	N	Y	Y	Y	Y	N	N
5 Maloney	N	Y	N	Y	N	Y	Y
6 Johnson	N	Y	N	Y	Y	N	N
DELAWARE							
AL Castle	Y	Y	N	Y	Y	N	N
FLORIDA							
1 Scarborough	Y	Y	Y	Y	Y	N	N
2 Boyd	N	Y	N	Y	N	Y	Y
3 Brown	N	N	N	Y	N	Y	Y
4 Fowler	Y	Y	Y	Y	Y	N	N
5 Thurman	N	Y	N	Y	N	Y	Y
6 Stearns	N	Y	Y	Y	Y	N	N
7 Mica	Y	Y	Y	Y	Y	N	N
8 McCollum	Y	Y	Y	Y	Y	N	N
9 Bilirakis	N	Y	Y	Y	Y	N	N
10 Young	N	Y	Y	Y	Y	N	N
11 Davis	N	N	N	Y	N	Y	Y
12 Canady	N	Y	Y	Y	Y	N	N
13 Miller	Y	Y	Y	Y	Y	N	N
14 Goss	Y	Y	Y	Y	Y	N	N
15 Weldon	Y	Y	Y	Y	Y	N	N
16 Foley	N	Y	Y	Y	Y	N	N
17 Meek	N	N	N	Y	N	Y	Y
18 Ros-Lehtinen	N	N	N	Y	Y	N	N
19 Wexler	N	Y	N	Y	N	Y	Y
20 Deutsch	N	Y	N	Y	N	Y	Y
21 Diaz-Balart	N	N	N	Y	Y	N	N
22 Shaw	N	Y	Y	Y	Y	N	N
23 Hastings	N	Y	N	Y	N	Y	Y
GEORGIA							
1 Kingston	Y	Y	Y	Y	Y	N	N
2 Bishop	N	Y	N	Y	N	Y	Y
3 Collins	N	Y	Y	Y	Y	N	N
4 McKinney	N	N	N	Y	N	Y	Y
5 Lewis	N	Y	N	Y	N	Y	Y
6 Gingrich		Y			Y	N	
7 Barr	N	Y	Y	Y	Y	N	N
8 Chambliss	Y	Y	Y	Y	Y	N	N
9 Deal	N	Y	Y	Y	Y	N	N
10 Norwood	N	Y	Y	Y	Y	N	N
11 Linder	N	Y	Y	Y	Y	N	N
HAWAII							
1 Abercrombie	N	Y	N	Y	N	Y	Y
2 Mink	N	N	N	Y	N	Y	Y
IDAHO							
1 Chenoweth	Y	N	Y	N	Y	N	N
2 Crapo	N	Y	N	Y	N	N	N
ILLINOIS							
1 Rush	N	Y	N	Y	N	Y	Y
2 Jackson	N	Y	N	Y	N	Y	Y
3 Lipinski	N	Y	N	Y	Y	Y	Y
4 Gutierrez	N	N	N	Y	N	Y	Y
5 Blagojevich	N	Y	N	Y	N	Y	Y
6 Hyde	N	Y	Y	Y	Y	N	N
7 Davis	N	N	N	Y	?	Y	Y
8 Crane	N	Y	Y	Y	Y	N	N
9 Yates	?	?	?	?	N	Y	Y
10 Porter	Y	Y	Y	Y	Y	N	N
11 Weller	Y	Y	Y	Y	Y	N	N
12 Costello	N	Y	N	Y	N	Y	Y

ND Northern Democrats   SD Southern Democrats

	81	82	83	84	85	86	87
13 ***Fawell***	Y	Y	Y	Y	Y	N	?
14 ***Hastert***	N	Y	Y	Y	Y	N	N
15 ***Ewing***	Y	Y	Y	Y	Y	N	N
16 ***Manzullo***	N	Y	Y	Y	Y	N	N
17 Evans	N	Y	N	Y	N	Y	Y
18 ***LaHood***	N	Y	N	Y	Y	N	N
19 Poshard	N	Y	N	Y	N	Y	Y
20 ***Shimkus***	Y	Y	N	Y	Y	N	N
INDIANA							
1 Visclosky	N	Y	N	Y	N	Y	Y
2 ***McIntosh***	N	Y	Y	Y	Y	N	N
3 Roemer	N	Y	N	Y	N	Y	Y
4 ***Souder***	Y	Y	Y	Y	Y	N	N
5 ***Buyer***	Y	Y	Y	Y	Y	N	N
6 ***Burton***	N	Y	Y	Y	Y	N	N
7 ***Pease***	N	Y	N	Y	Y	N	N
8 ***Hostettler***	N	Y	Y	Y	Y	N	N
9 Hamilton	N	Y	N	Y	N	Y	Y
10 Carson	N	Y	N	Y	N	Y	Y
IOWA							
1 ***Leach***	N	Y	N	Y	Y	N	N
2 ***Nussle***	N	Y	Y	Y	Y	N	N
3 Boswell	N	Y	N	Y	N	Y	Y
4 ***Ganske***	N	Y	Y	Y	Y	N	N
5 ***Latham***	N	Y	Y	Y	Y	N	N
KANSAS							
1 ***Moran***	N	Y	Y	Y	Y	N	N
2 ***Ryun***	N	Y	Y	Y	Y	N	N
3 ***Snowbarger***	N	Y	Y	Y	Y	N	N
4 ***Tiahrt***	N	Y	Y	Y	Y	N	N
KENTUCKY							
1 ***Whitfield***	N	Y	N	Y	Y	N	N
2 ***Lewis***	N	Y	Y	Y	Y	N	N
3 ***Northup***	N	Y	N	Y	Y	N	N
4 ***Bunning***	N	Y	Y	Y	Y	N	N
5 ***Rogers***	N	Y	Y	Y	Y	N	N
6 Baesler	N	Y	N	Y	?	Y	Y
LOUISIANA							
1 ***Livingston***	Y	Y	Y	Y	Y	N	N
2 Jefferson	?	?	?	?	?	?	?
3 ***Tauzin***	Y	Y	Y	Y	Y	N	N
4 ***McCrery***	N	Y	Y	Y	Y	N	N
5 ***Cooksey***	–	+	+	+	Y	N	N
6 ***Baker***	N	Y	Y	Y	Y	N	N
7 John	N	Y	N	Y	N	Y	Y
MAINE							
1 Allen	N	Y	N	Y	N	Y	Y
2 Baldacci	N	Y	N	Y	N	Y	Y
MARYLAND							
1 ***Gilchrest***	Y	Y	Y	Y	Y	N	N
2 ***Ehrlich***	Y	Y	Y	Y	Y	N	N
3 Cardin	?	?	?	?	N	Y	Y
4 Wynn	N	N	N	Y	N	Y	Y
5 Hoyer	N	N	N	Y	N	?	Y
6 ***Bartlett***	Y	Y	Y	Y	Y	N	N
7 Cummings	N	Y	N	Y	N	Y	Y
8 ***Morella***	N	N	N	Y	N	N	N
MASSACHUSETTS							
1 Olver	N	Y	N	Y	N	Y	Y
2 Neal	N	Y	N	Y	N	Y	Y
3 McGovern	N	Y	N	Y	N	Y	Y
4 Frank	N	Y	N	Y	N	Y	Y
5 Meehan	N	Y	N	Y	N	Y	Y
6 Tierney	N	Y	N	Y	N	Y	Y
7 Markey	N	Y	N	Y	N	Y	Y
8 Kennedy	N	Y	N	Y	N	Y	Y
9 Moakley	N	Y	N	Y	N	Y	Y
10 Delahunt	N	Y	N	Y	N	Y	Y
MICHIGAN							
1 Stupak	N	Y	N	Y	N	Y	Y
2 ***Hoekstra***	N	Y	Y	Y	Y	N	N
3 ***Ehlers***	N	N	N	Y	Y	N	N
4 ***Camp***	Y	Y	Y	Y	Y	N	N
5 Barcia	N	Y	N	Y	N	Y	Y
6 ***Upton***	Y	Y	Y	Y	Y	N	N
7 ***Smith***	Y	Y	Y	Y	Y	N	N
8 Stabenow	N	Y	N	Y	N	Y	Y
9 Kildee	N	Y	N	Y	N	Y	Y
10 Bonior	N	Y	N	Y	N	Y	Y
11 ***Knollenberg***	N	Y	Y	Y	Y	N	N
12 Levin	N	Y	N	Y	N	Y	Y
13 Rivers	N	Y	N	Y	N	Y	Y
14 Conyers	N	Y	N	Y	N	Y	Y
15 Kilpatrick	N	Y	N	Y	N	Y	Y
16 Dingell	N	N	N	N	N	Y	Y
MINNESOTA							
1 ***Gutknecht***	Y	Y	Y	Y	Y	N	N
2 Minge	N	Y	N	Y	N	Y	Y
3 ***Ramstad***	N	Y	Y	Y	Y	N	N
4 Vento	N	Y	N	Y	N	Y	Y
5 Sabo	N	N	N	N	N	Y	Y
6 Luther	N	Y	N	Y	N	Y	Y
7 Peterson	N	Y	N	Y	N	Y	Y
8 Oberstar	N	N	N	Y	N	Y	Y
MISSISSIPPI							
1 ***Wicker***	N	Y	Y	Y	Y	N	N
2 Thompson	N	Y	N	Y	N	Y	Y
3 ***Pickering***	N	Y	Y	Y	Y	N	N
4 ***Parker***	N	Y	Y	Y	Y	N	N
5 Taylor	N	Y	Y	Y	Y	N	N
MISSOURI							
1 Clay	N	Y	N	Y	N	Y	Y
2 ***Talent***	N	Y	Y	Y	Y	N	N
3 Gephardt	N	Y	N	Y	N	Y	Y
4 Skelton	N	Y	N	Y	N	Y	Y
5 McCarthy	–	+	–	+	N	Y	Y
6 Danner	N	Y	N	Y	N	Y	Y
7 ***Blunt***	N	Y	Y	Y	Y	N	N
8 ***Emerson***	N	Y	Y	Y	Y	N	N
9 ***Hulshof***	Y	Y	Y	Y	Y	N	N
MONTANA							
AL ***Hill***	Y	Y	Y	Y	Y	N	N
NEBRASKA							
1 ***Bereuter***	?	?	?	?	Y	N	N
2 ***Christensen***	N	Y	Y	Y	Y	N	N
3 ***Barrett***	N	Y	Y	Y	Y	N	N
NEVADA							
1 ***Ensign***	N	Y	Y	Y	Y	N	N
2 ***Gibbons***	N	Y	Y	Y	Y	N	N
NEW HAMPSHIRE							
1 ***Sununu***	Y	Y	Y	Y	Y	N	N
2 ***Bass***	Y	Y	N	Y	Y	N	N
NEW JERSEY							
1 Andrews	N	Y	N	Y	N	Y	Y
2 ***LoBiondo***	N	Y	N	Y	Y	N	N
3 ***Saxton***	N	Y	N	Y	Y	N	N
4 ***Smith***	N	Y	N	Y	Y	N	N
5 ***Roukema***	Y	Y	Y	Y	Y	N	N
6 Pallone	N	Y	N	Y	N	Y	Y
7 ***Franks***	N	Y	N	Y	Y	N	N
8 Pascrell	N	Y	N	Y	N	Y	Y
9 Rothman	N	Y	N	Y	N	Y	Y
10 Payne	?	?	?	?	?	?	?
11 ***Frelinghuysen***	Y	Y	Y	Y	Y	N	N
12 ***Pappas***	N	Y	N	Y	Y	N	N
13 Menendez	N	Y	N	Y	N	Y	Y
NEW MEXICO							
1 Vacant							
2 ***Skeen***	N	Y	Y	Y	Y	N	N
3 ***Redmond***	N	Y	Y	Y	Y	N	N
NEW YORK							
1 ***Forbes***	N	Y	N	Y	Y	N	N
2 ***Lazio***	N	Y	N	Y	Y	N	N
3 ***King***	N	Y	N	Y	Y	N	N
4 McCarthy	N	Y	N	Y	N	Y	Y
5 Ackerman	N	Y	N	Y	N	Y	Y
6 Meeks	N	N	N	Y	N	Y	Y
7 Manton	N	Y	N	Y	N	Y	Y
8 Nadler	N	Y	N	Y	N	Y	Y
9 Schumer	N	Y	N	Y	N	Y	Y
10 Towns	N	N	N	Y	N	Y	Y
11 Owens	N	N	N	Y	N	Y	Y
12 Velázquez	N	N	N	Y	N	Y	Y
13 ***Fossella***	N	Y	Y	Y	Y	N	N
14 Maloney	N	Y	N	Y	N	Y	Y
15 Rangel	?	?	?	?	?	?	?
16 Serrano	N	N	N	Y	N	Y	Y
17 Engel	N	Y	N	Y	N	Y	Y
18 Lowey	N	Y	N	Y	N	Y	Y
19 ***Kelly***	N	Y	N	Y	Y	N	N
20 ***Gilman***	N	Y	N	Y	Y	N	N
21 McNulty	N	Y	N	Y	N	Y	Y
22 ***Solomon***	?	?	?	?	Y	N	N
23 ***Boehlert***	N	Y	N	Y	Y	N	N
24 ***McHugh***	N	Y	N	Y	Y	N	N
25 ***Walsh***	N	Y	N	Y	Y	N	N
26 Hinchey	N	Y	N	Y	N	Y	Y
27 ***Paxon***	N	Y	Y	Y	?	N	N
28 Slaughter	N	Y	N	Y	N	Y	Y
29 LaFalce	N	Y	N	Y	N	Y	Y
30 ***Quinn***	N	Y	N	Y	N	N	N
31 ***Houghton***	N	Y	N	Y	Y	N	N
NORTH CAROLINA							
1 Clayton	N	Y	N	Y	N	Y	Y
2 Etheridge	N	Y	N	Y	N	Y	Y
3 ***Jones***	N	Y	Y	Y	Y	N	N
4 Price	N	Y	N	Y	N	Y	Y
5 ***Burr***	N	Y	Y	Y	Y	N	N
6 ***Coble***	+	+	+	+	Y	N	N
7 McIntyre	N	Y	N	Y	N	Y	Y
8 Hefner	N	Y	N	Y	N	Y	Y
9 ***Myrick***	N	Y	Y	Y	Y	N	N
10 ***Ballenger***	Y	Y	Y	Y	Y	N	N
11 ***Taylor***	Y	Y	N	Y	Y	N	N
12 Watt	N	N	N	Y	N	Y	Y
NORTH DAKOTA							
AL Pomeroy	N	Y	N	Y	N	Y	Y
OHIO							
1 ***Chabot***	N	Y	Y	Y	Y	N	N
2 ***Portman***	N	Y	Y	Y	Y	N	N
3 Hall	N	Y	N	Y	N	Y	Y
4 ***Oxley***	N	Y	Y	Y	Y	N	N
5 ***Gillmor***	Y	Y	Y	Y	Y	N	N
6 Strickland	N	Y	N	Y	N	Y	Y
7 ***Hobson***	N	Y	Y	Y	Y	N	N
8 ***Boehner***	N	Y	Y	Y	Y	N	N
9 Kaptur	N	N	N	Y	N	Y	Y
10 Kucinich	N	Y	N	Y	N	Y	Y
11 Stokes	N	Y	N	Y	N	Y	Y
12 ***Kasich***	Y	Y	Y	Y	Y	N	N
13 Brown	N	Y	N	Y	N	Y	Y
14 Sawyer	N	Y	N	Y	N	Y	Y
15 ***Pryce***	Y	Y	Y	Y	Y	N	N
16 ***Regula***	N	Y	N	Y	Y	N	N
17 Traficant	N	Y	N	Y	N	N	Y
18 ***Ney***	N	Y	N	Y	Y	N	N
19 ***LaTourette***	N	Y	N	Y	Y	N	N
OKLAHOMA							
1 ***Largent***	N	Y	Y	Y	Y	N	N
2 ***Coburn***	Y	Y	N	Y	Y	N	N
3 ***Watkins***	Y	Y	Y	Y	Y	N	N
4 ***Watts***	N	Y	Y	Y	Y	N	N
5 ***Istook***	N	Y	Y	Y	Y	N	N
6 ***Lucas***	Y	Y	Y	Y	Y	N	N
OREGON							
1 Furse	N	Y	N	Y	N	Y	Y
2 ***Smith***	N	Y	Y	Y	Y	N	N
3 Blumenauer	N	Y	N	Y	N	Y	Y
4 DeFazio	N	Y	N	Y	N	Y	Y
5 Hooley	N	Y	N	Y	N	Y	Y
PENNSYLVANIA							
1 Vacant							
2 Fattah	N	N	N	Y	N	Y	Y
3 Borski	N	Y	N	Y	N	Y	Y
4 Klink	N	Y	N	Y	N	Y	Y
5 ***Peterson***	N	Y	Y	Y	Y	N	N
6 Holden	N	Y	N	Y	N	Y	Y
7 ***Weldon***	Y	Y	N	Y	Y	N	N
8 ***Greenwood***	Y	Y	N	Y	Y	N	N
9 ***Shuster***	Y	Y	Y	Y	Y	N	N
10 ***McDade***	N	Y	N	Y	Y	N	N
11 Kanjorski	N	Y	N	Y	N	Y	Y
12 Murtha	N	N	N	N	N	Y	Y
13 ***Fox***	Y	Y	N	Y	Y	N	N
14 Coyne	N	Y	N	Y	N	Y	Y
15 McHale	N	Y	N	Y	N	Y	Y
16 ***Pitts***	N	Y	Y	Y	Y	N	N
17 ***Gekas***	N	Y	?	Y	Y	N	N
18 Doyle	N	Y	N	Y	N	Y	Y
19 ***Goodling***	N	Y	Y	Y	Y	N	N
20 Mascara	N	Y	N	Y	N	Y	Y
21 ***English***	Y	Y	N	Y	Y	N	N
RHODE ISLAND							
1 Kennedy	N	N	N	Y	N	Y	Y
2 Weygand	N	Y	N	Y	N	Y	Y
SOUTH CAROLINA							
1 ***Sanford***	Y	Y	Y	Y	Y	N	N
2 ***Spence***	Y	Y	Y	Y	Y	N	N
3 ***Graham***	N	Y	Y	Y	Y	N	N
4 ***Inglis***	N	Y	Y	Y	Y	N	N
5 Spratt	N	Y	N	Y	N	Y	Y
6 Clyburn	N	Y	N	Y	N	Y	Y
SOUTH DAKOTA							
AL ***Thune***	N	Y	Y	Y	Y	N	N
TENNESSEE							
1 ***Jenkins***	N	Y	Y	Y	Y	N	N
2 ***Duncan***	Y	Y	Y	Y	Y	N	N
3 ***Wamp***	N	Y	Y	Y	Y	N	N
4 ***Hilleary***	Y	Y	Y	Y	Y	N	N
5 Clement	N	Y	N	Y	N	Y	Y
6 Gordon	N	Y	N	Y	N	Y	Y
7 ***Bryant***	Y	Y	Y	Y	Y	N	N
8 Tanner	N	Y	N	Y	N	Y	Y
9 Ford	N	Y	N	Y	N	Y	Y
TEXAS							
1 Sandlin	N	Y	N	Y	N	Y	Y
2 Turner	N	Y	N	Y	N	Y	Y
3 ***Johnson, Sam***	N	Y	Y	Y	Y	N	?
4 Hall	N	Y	Y	Y	Y	N	N
5 ***Sessions***	N	Y	Y	Y	Y	N	N
6 ***Barton***	N	Y	Y	Y	Y	N	N
7 ***Archer***	Y	Y	Y	?	Y	N	N
8 ***Brady***	N	Y	Y	Y	Y	N	N
9 Lampson	N	Y	N	Y	N	Y	Y
10 Doggett	N	Y	N	Y	N	Y	Y
11 Edwards	N	Y	N	Y	N	Y	Y
12 ***Granger***	Y	Y	Y	Y	Y	N	N
13 ***Thornberry***	Y	Y	Y	Y	Y	N	N
14 ***Paul***	N	Y	N	Y	Y	N	N
15 Hinojosa	N	Y	N	Y	N	Y	Y
16 Reyes	N	Y	N	Y	N	Y	Y
17 Stenholm	N	Y	N	Y	N	Y	N
18 Jackson-Lee	N	N	N	Y	N	Y	Y
19 ***Combest***	N	Y	Y	Y	Y	N	N
20 Gonzalez	?	?	?	?	?	?	?
21 ***Smith***	N	Y	Y	Y	Y	N	N
22 ***DeLay***	N	Y	Y	Y	Y	N	N
23 ***Bonilla***	N	Y	Y	Y	Y	N	N
24 Frost	N	Y	N	Y	N	Y	Y
25 Bentsen	N	Y	N	Y	N	Y	Y
26 ***Armey***	N	Y	Y	Y	Y	N	N
27 Ortiz	N	Y	N	Y	N	Y	Y
28 Rodriguez	N	Y	N	Y	N	Y	Y
29 Green	N	Y	N	Y	N	Y	Y
30 Johnson, E.B.	N	N	N	Y	N	Y	Y
UTAH							
1 ***Hansen***	Y	Y	Y	Y	Y	N	N
2 ***Cook***	Y	Y	Y	Y	Y	N	N
3 ***Cannon***	?	?	?	?	?	?	?
VERMONT							
AL *Sanders*	N	Y	N	Y	N	Y	Y
VIRGINIA							
1 ***Bateman***	N	Y	Y	Y	Y	N	N
2 Pickett	N	Y	N	Y	N	Y	Y
3 Scott	N	N	N	Y	N	Y	Y
4 Sisisky	N	Y	N	Y	N	Y	Y
5 Goode	N	Y	Y	Y	N	N	N
6 ***Goodlatte***	N	Y	Y	Y	Y	N	N
7 ***Bliley***	?	?	?	?	Y	N	N
8 Moran	N	Y	N	Y	N	Y	Y
9 Boucher	N	Y	N	Y	N	Y	Y
10 ***Wolf***	N	Y	Y	Y	Y	N	N
11 ***Davis***	N	Y	N	Y	Y	N	N
WASHINGTON							
1 ***White***	Y	Y	Y	Y	Y	N	N
2 ***Metcalf***	Y	Y	N	Y	Y	N	N
3 ***Smith, Linda***	N	Y	Y	Y	Y	N	N
4 ***Hastings***	N	Y	Y	Y	Y	N	N
5 ***Nethercutt***	N	Y	Y	Y	Y	N	N
6 Dicks	N	Y	N	Y	N	Y	Y
7 McDermott	N	N	N	Y	N	Y	Y
8 ***Dunn***	N	Y	Y	Y	Y	N	N
9 Smith, Adam	N	Y	N	Y	N	Y	Y
WEST VIRGINIA							
1 Mollohan	N	N	N	N	N	Y	Y
2 Wise	N	Y	N	Y	N	Y	Y
3 Rahall	N	Y	N	Y	N	Y	Y
WISCONSIN							
1 ***Neumann***	N	Y	N	Y	Y	N	N
2 ***Klug***	N	Y	Y	Y	Y	N	N
3 Kind	N	Y	N	Y	N	Y	Y
4 Kleczka	N	Y	N	Y	N	Y	Y
5 Barrett	N	Y	N	Y	N	Y	Y
6 ***Petri***	Y	Y	N	Y	Y	N	N
7 Obey	N	Y	N	Y	N	Y	Y
8 Johnson	N	Y	N	Y	N	Y	Y
9 ***Sensenbrenner***	Y	Y	Y	Y	Y	N	N
WYOMING							
AL ***Cubin***	N	Y	Y	Y	Y	N	N

Southern states - Ala., Ark., Fla., Ga., Ky., La., Miss., N.C., Okla., S.C., Tenn., Texas, Va.

House Votes 88, 90, 91, 92, 93, 94, 95 *

Key

Y	Voted for (yea).
#	Paired for.
+	Announced for.
N	Voted against (nay).
X	Paired against.
–	Announced against.
P	Voted "present."
C	Voted "present" to avoid possible conflict of interest.
?	Did not vote or otherwise make a position known.

Democrats **Republicans** Independent

---

88. HR 3579. Fiscal 1998 Supplemental Appropriations/Passage. Passage of the bill to provide $2.9 billion in supplemental appropriations, including $2.3 billion for the military, primarily to support military operations in Iraq and Bosnia, and $575 million for disaster relief. Passed 212-208: R 205-17; D 7-190 (ND 2-143, SD 5-47); I 0-1. March 31, 1998. A "nay" was a vote in support of the president's position.

89. Quorum Call.* 387 Responded. March 31, 1998.

90. HR 2400. Surface Transportation Reauthorization/Rule. Adoption of the rule (H Res 405) to provide for floor consideration of the bill to authorize $218.3 billion over six years for federal highway and mass transit programs. Adopted 357-61: R 203-16; D 153-45 (ND 118-27, SD 35-18); I 1-0. April 1, 1998.

91. Adjournment Resolution/Adoption. Adoption of the concurrent resolution to adjourn the House from April 1, 1998 until 12:30 p.m. on April 21, 1998, and the Senate until noon on April 20, 1998. Adopted 223-187: R 212-2; D 11-184 (ND 9-134, SD 2-50); I 0-1. April 1, 1998.

92. HR 1151. Credit Union Membership Rules/Passage. Leach, R-Iowa, motion to suspend the rules and pass the bill to allow credit unions to expand beyond their original membership base. Motion agreed to 411-8: R 213-8; D 197-0 (ND 144-0, SD 53-0); I 1-0. April 1, 1998. A two-thirds majority of those present and voting (280 in this case) is required for passage under suspension of the rules.

93. HR 2400. Surface Transportation Reauthorization/Affirmative Action. Roukema, R-N.J., amendment to end the Transportation Department's program that sets a goal of providing at least 10 percent of transportation contracts to small businesses owned by women and minorities and replace it with a program encouraging affirmative action and discouraging preferential treatment in relation to government transportation contracts. Rejected 194-225: R 191-29; D 3-195 (ND 0-145, SD 3-50); I 0-1. April 1, 1998.

94. HR 2400. Surface Transportation Reauthorization/Welfare to Work Transportation. Davis, D-Ill., amendment to increase from $42 million to $150 million per year the authorization for a new welfare-to-work transportation program, which would finance services that transport current and former welfare recipients to and from jobs, and job-related activities. Adopted 242-175: R 48-171; D 193-4 (ND 145-0, SD 48-4); I 1-0. April 1, 1998.

95. HR 2400. Surface Transportation Reauthorization/Specified Projects. Graham, R-S.C., amendment to strike provisions that provide funds for specified projects, including about $9 billion for highway projects, and other funding for specified transit and bus projects. Rejected 79-337: R 67-152; D 12-184 (ND 6-137, SD 6-47); I 0-1. April 1, 1998.

* CQ does not include quorum calls in its vote charts.

	88	90	91	92	93	94	95
ALABAMA							
1 *Callahan*	Y	Y	Y	Y	Y	N	N
2 *Everett*	Y	Y	Y	Y	Y	N	N
3 *Riley*	Y	Y	Y	Y	Y	N	N
4 *Aderholt*	Y	Y	Y	Y	Y	N	N
5 Cramer	N	N	N	Y	N	Y	N
6 *Bachus*	Y	Y	Y	N	Y	N	N
7 Hilliard	N	Y	N	Y	N	Y	N
ALASKA							
AL *Young*	Y	Y	Y	Y	Y	N	N
ARIZONA							
1 *Salmon*	Y	N	Y	Y	Y	N	Y
2 Pastor	N	Y	N	Y	N	Y	N
3 *Stump*	Y	Y	Y	Y	Y	N	Y
4 *Shadegg*	Y	N	Y	Y	Y	N	Y
5 *Kolbe*	Y	Y	Y	Y	N	Y	N
6 *Hayworth*	Y	Y	Y	Y	N	Y	N
ARKANSAS							
1 Berry	–	Y	N	Y	N	Y	N
2 Snyder	N	Y	N	Y	N	Y	N
3 *Hutchinson*	Y	Y	Y	Y	?	Y	N
4 *Dickey*	Y	Y	Y	Y	Y	Y	N
CALIFORNIA							
1 *Riggs*	+	+	+	Y	Y	N	N
2 *Herger*	Y	Y	Y	Y	Y	N	N
3 Fazio	N	N	N	Y	N	Y	N
4 *Doolittle*	Y	Y	Y	Y	Y	N	N
5 Matsui	N	Y	N	Y	N	Y	N
6 Woolsey	N	Y	N	Y	N	Y	N
7 Miller	N	Y	N	Y	N	Y	N
8 Pelosi	N	N	N	Y	N	Y	N
9 Vacant							
10 Tauscher	N	Y	N	Y	N	Y	N
11 *Pombo*	Y	Y	Y	Y	Y	N	N
12 Lantos	N	Y	N	Y	N	Y	N
13 Stark	N	Y	N	Y	N	Y	N
14 Eshoo	N	Y	N	Y	N	Y	N
15 *Campbell*	N	Y	Y	Y	Y	N	Y
16 Lofgren	N	Y	N	Y	N	Y	P
17 Farr	N	Y	N	Y	N	Y	N
18 Condit	N	Y	N	+	N	Y	N
19 *Radanovich*	Y	Y	Y	Y	P	N	N
20 Dooley	N	N	N	Y	N	Y	N
21 *Thomas*	N	Y	Y	Y	N	Y	N
22 Capps, L.	N	Y	N	Y	N	Y	N
23 *Gallegly*	Y	Y	Y	Y	Y	N	N
24 Sherman	N	Y	N	Y	N	Y	N
25 *McKeon*	Y	Y	Y	Y	Y	N	N
26 Berman	N	Y	N	Y	N	Y	N
27 *Rogan*	Y	Y	N	Y	N	Y	N
28 *Dreier*	Y	Y	Y	Y	Y	N	N
29 Waxman	N	Y	N	Y	N	Y	N
30 Becerra	N	N	N	Y	N	Y	N
31 Martinez	N	Y	N	Y	N	Y	N
32 Dixon	Y	N	N	Y	N	Y	N
33 Roybal-Allard	N	N	N	Y	N	Y	N
34 Torres	N	N	N	Y	N	Y	?
35 Waters	?	?	?	?	?	?	?
36 Harman	N	N	N	Y	N	Y	N
37 Millender-McD.	N	Y	N	Y	N	Y	N
38 *Horn*	Y	Y	Y	Y	Y	Y	N
39 *Royce*	?	?	?	?	?	?	?
40 *Lewis*	Y	Y	Y	Y	Y	N	N
41 *Kim*	Y	Y	Y	N	N	N	N
42 Brown	N	N	N	Y	N	Y	N
43 *Calvert*	Y	Y	Y	Y	Y	Y	N
44 Vacant							
45 *Rohrabacher*	N	Y	Y	Y	Y	N	Y
46 Sanchez	N	Y	N	Y	N	Y	N
47 *Cox*	Y	?	?	Y	Y	N	Y
48 *Packard*	Y	Y	Y	Y	Y	N	N
49 *Bilbray*	Y	Y	Y	Y	Y	N	N
50 Filner	N	N	N	Y	N	Y	N
51 *Cunningham*	Y	Y	Y	Y	Y	N	N
52 *Hunter*	Y	Y	Y	Y	Y	N	Y
COLORADO							
1 DeGette	N	Y	N	Y	N	Y	N
2 Skaggs	N	N	N	Y	N	Y	Y
3 *McInnis*	Y	Y	Y	Y	Y	N	N
4 *Schaffer*	Y	Y	N	Y	Y	N	Y
5 *Hefley*	Y	Y	Y	Y	Y	N	N
6 *Schaefer*	Y	Y	Y	N	Y	N	N
CONNECTICUT							
1 Kennelly	N	Y	N	Y	N	Y	N
2 Gejdenson	N	Y	N	Y	N	Y	N
3 DeLauro	N	Y	N	Y	N	Y	N
4 *Shays*	N	N	Y	Y	N	Y	N
5 Maloney	N	Y	N	Y	N	Y	N
6 *Johnson*	Y	Y	Y	Y	N	Y	N
DELAWARE							
AL *Castle*	N	N	Y	Y	N	N	Y
FLORIDA							
1 *Scarborough*	Y	Y	Y	Y	Y	?	Y
2 Boyd	N	Y	N	Y	N	Y	N
3 Brown	N	N	N	Y	N	Y	N
4 *Fowler*	Y	Y	Y	Y	Y	N	N
5 Thurman	N	Y	N	Y	N	Y	N
6 *Stearns*	Y	Y	Y	Y	Y	N	Y
7 *Mica*	Y	Y	Y	Y	Y	N	N
8 *McCollum*	Y	Y	Y	Y	Y	N	Y
9 *Bilirakis*	Y	Y	Y	Y	Y	N	N
10 *Young*	Y	N	Y	Y	Y	N	N
11 Davis	N	N	N	Y	N	Y	N
12 *Canady*	Y	N	Y	Y	Y	N	N
13 *Miller*	Y	N	Y	Y	Y	N	N
14 *Goss*	Y	Y	Y	Y	Y	N	N
15 *Weldon*	Y	Y	Y	Y	Y	N	N
16 *Foley*	Y	Y	Y	Y	Y	N	N
17 Meek	N	N	N	Y	N	Y	N
18 *Ros-Lehtinen*	Y	Y	Y	Y	?	?	?
19 Wexler	N	N	N	Y	N	Y	N
20 Deutsch	N	N	N	Y	N	Y	N
21 *Diaz-Balart*	Y	Y	Y	Y	N	N	N
22 *Shaw*	Y	Y	Y	Y	Y	N	N
23 Hastings	N	N	N	Y	N	Y	N
GEORGIA							
1 *Kingston*	Y	Y	Y	Y	Y	Y	Y
2 Bishop	Y	Y	N	Y	N	Y	N
3 *Collins*	Y	Y	Y	Y	N	N	N
4 McKinney	N	Y	N	Y	N	Y	N
5 Lewis	N	N	N	Y	N	Y	Y
6 *Gingrich*				Y			
7 *Barr*	Y	Y	Y	Y	N	Y	N
8 *Chambliss*	Y	Y	Y	Y	Y	N	N
9 *Deal*	Y	Y	Y	Y	Y	N	Y
10 *Norwood*	Y	Y	Y	Y	Y	N	N
11 *Linder*	Y	Y	?	Y	Y	N	N
HAWAII							
1 Abercrombie	N	Y	N	Y	N	Y	N
2 Mink	N	Y	N	Y	N	Y	N
IDAHO							
1 *Chenoweth*	N	Y	Y	Y	Y	N	N
2 *Crapo*	N	Y	Y	Y	Y	N	N
ILLINOIS							
1 Rush	N	Y	N	Y	N	Y	N
2 Jackson	N	Y	N	Y	N	Y	N
3 Lipinski	Y	Y	N	Y	N	Y	N
4 Gutierrez	N	Y	N	Y	N	Y	N
5 Blagojevich	N	Y	N	Y	N	Y	N
6 *Hyde*	Y	Y	Y	Y	Y	Y	N
7 Davis	N	N	N	Y	N	Y	N
8 *Crane*	Y	Y	N	N	Y	N	N
9 Yates	N	N	Y	Y	N	Y	?
10 *Porter*	Y	Y	Y	Y	N	Y	N
11 *Weller*	Y	Y	Y	Y	Y	N	N
12 Costello	N	Y	N	Y	N	Y	N

ND Northern Democrats   SD Southern Democrats

	88	90	91	92	93	94	95
13 ***Fawell***	Y	Y	?	Y	Y	Y	N
14 ***Hastert***	Y	Y	Y	Y	Y	N	N
15 ***Ewing***	Y	Y	Y	Y	Y	N	N
16 ***Manzullo***	Y	Y	Y	Y	Y	N	N
17 Evans	N	Y	N	Y	N	Y	N
18 ***LaHood***	Y	Y	Y	Y	N	Y	N
19 Poshard	N	Y	N	Y	N	Y	N
20 ***Shimkus***	Y	Y	Y	Y	Y	Y	N
INDIANA							
1 Visclosky	N	Y	N	Y	N	Y	N
2 ***McIntosh***	Y	Y	Y	Y	Y	N	?
3 Roemer	N	Y	N	Y	N	Y	N
4 ***Souder***	N	Y	Y	Y	N	Y	Y
5 ***Buyer***	Y	Y	Y	Y	Y	N	N
6 ***Burton***	Y	Y	Y	Y	Y	N	N
7 ***Pease***	Y	Y	Y	Y	Y	N	N
8 ***Hostettler***	Y	Y	Y	N	Y	N	N
9 Hamilton	N	Y	N	Y	N	Y	N
10 Carson	N	Y	Y	Y	N	Y	N
IOWA							
1 ***Leach***	Y	Y	Y	Y	N	Y	Y
2 ***Nussle***	N	Y	Y	Y	Y	Y	N
3 Boswell	N	Y	Y	Y	N	Y	N
4 ***Ganske***	Y	Y	Y	Y	Y	N	N
5 ***Latham***	Y	Y	Y	Y	Y	N	N
KANSAS							
1 ***Moran***	N	Y	Y	Y	Y	N	N
2 ***Ryun***	Y	Y	Y	Y	Y	N	N
3 ***Snowbarger***	Y	Y	Y	Y	Y	N	N
4 ***Tiahrt***	Y	Y	Y	Y	Y	N	N
KENTUCKY							
1 ***Whitfield***	Y	Y	Y	Y	Y	N	N
2 ***Lewis***	Y	Y	Y	Y	Y	N	N
3 ***Northup***	Y	Y	Y	Y	Y	N	N
4 ***Bunning***	Y	Y	Y	Y	Y	N	N
5 ***Rogers***	Y	Y	Y	Y	Y	Y	N
6 Baesler	N	Y	N	Y	N	Y	N
LOUISIANA							
1 ***Livingston***	Y	Y	Y	Y	Y	N	N
2 Jefferson	?	?	?	?	?	?	?
3 ***Tauzin***	Y	Y	Y	Y	Y	N	N
4 ***McCrery***	Y	Y	Y	Y	Y	N	P
5 ***Cooksey***	Y	Y	Y	Y	Y	N	N
6 ***Baker***	Y	Y	Y	Y	Y	N	N
7 John	N	Y	N	Y	N	Y	N
MAINE							
1 Allen	Y	Y	N	Y	N	Y	N
2 Baldacci	Y	Y	N	Y	N	Y	N
MARYLAND							
1 ***Gilchrest***	Y	?	?	Y	N	Y	N
2 ***Ehrlich***	Y	Y	Y	Y	Y	N	Y
3 Cardin	N	N	N	Y	N	Y	N
4 Wynn	N	Y	N	Y	N	Y	N
5 Hoyer	N	N	N	Y	N	Y	N
6 ***Bartlett***	Y	Y	Y	Y	Y	Y	N
7 Cummings	N	Y	N	Y	N	Y	N
8 ***Morella***	N	N	Y	Y	N	Y	Y
MASSACHUSETTS							
1 Olver	N	Y	N	Y	N	Y	N
2 Neal	N	Y	N	Y	N	Y	N
3 McGovern	N	Y	N	Y	N	Y	N
4 Frank	N	Y	N	Y	N	Y	N
5 Meehan	N	Y	N	Y	N	Y	N
6 Tierney	N	Y	N	Y	N	Y	N
7 Markey	N	Y	N	Y	N	Y	N
8 Kennedy	N	?	?	?	N	Y	N
9 Moakley	N	Y	N	Y	N	Y	N
10 Delahunt	N	Y	N	Y	N	Y	N
MICHIGAN							
1 Stupak	N	Y	N	Y	N	Y	N
2 ***Hoekstra***	Y	Y	Y	Y	Y	N	Y
3 ***Ehlers***	Y	Y	Y	Y	Y	N	N
4 ***Camp***	Y	Y	Y	Y	Y	N	N
5 Barcia	N	Y	N	Y	N	Y	N
6 ***Upton***	N	Y	Y	Y	Y	Y	N
7 ***Smith***	Y	Y	Y	Y	Y	?	Y
8 Stabenow	N	Y	N	Y	N	Y	N
9 Kildee	N	Y	N	Y	N	Y	N
10 Bonior	N	Y	N	Y	N	Y	N
11 ***Knollenberg***	Y	Y	Y	Y	Y	N	N
12 Levin	N	Y	N	Y	N	Y	N
13 Rivers	N	Y	N	Y	N	Y	N
14 Conyers	N	N	N	Y	N	Y	N
15 Kilpatrick	N	Y	N	Y	N	Y	N
16 Dingell	N	Y	N	Y	N	Y	N

	88	90	91	92	93	94	95
MINNESOTA							
1 ***Gutknecht***	Y	Y	Y	Y	Y	N	Y
2 Minge	N	N	N	Y	N	Y	Y
3 ***Ramstad***	Y	Y	Y	Y	Y	N	N
4 Vento	N	Y	N	Y	N	Y	N
5 Sabo	N	N	N	Y	N	Y	N
6 Luther	N	N	N	Y	N	Y	N
7 Peterson	N	Y	N	Y	N	Y	N
8 Oberstar	N	Y	N	Y	N	Y	N
MISSISSIPPI							
1 ***Wicker***	Y	Y	Y	Y	Y	N	N
2 Thompson	N	Y	N	Y	N	Y	N
3 ***Pickering***	Y	Y	Y	Y	Y	N	N
4 ***Parker***	Y	Y	Y	Y	Y	N	Y
5 Taylor	Y	Y	N	Y	Y	N	N
MISSOURI							
1 Clay	N	Y	N	Y	N	Y	N
2 ***Talent***	Y	Y	Y	Y	Y	N	N
3 Gephardt	N	N	N	Y	N	Y	N
4 Skelton	N	Y	N	Y	N	Y	N
5 McCarthy	N	Y	N	Y	N	Y	N
6 Danner	N	Y	N	Y	N	Y	N
7 ***Blunt***	Y	Y	Y	Y	Y	N	N
8 ***Emerson***	Y	Y	Y	Y	Y	Y	N
9 ***Hulshof***	Y	Y	Y	Y	Y	Y	N
MONTANA							
AL ***Hill***	Y	Y	Y	Y	Y	N	Y
NEBRASKA							
1 ***Bereuter***	Y	Y	Y	Y	Y	N	N
2 ***Christensen***	Y	N	Y	Y	Y	N	Y
3 ***Barrett***	Y	N	Y	Y	Y	N	Y
NEVADA							
1 ***Ensign***	Y	Y	Y	Y	Y	Y	N
2 ***Gibbons***	Y	Y	Y	Y	N	N	N
NEW HAMPSHIRE							
1 ***Sununu***	Y	Y	Y	Y	Y	N	N
2 ***Bass***	Y	Y	Y	Y	Y	N	N
NEW JERSEY							
1 Andrews	N	Y	?	Y	N	Y	N
2 ***LoBiondo***	Y	Y	Y	Y	Y	Y	N
3 ***Saxton***	Y	Y	Y	Y	Y	N	N
4 ***Smith***	Y	Y	Y	Y	Y	Y	N
5 ***Roukema***	Y	Y	Y	Y	Y	N	N
6 Pallone	N	Y	N	Y	N	Y	N
7 ***Franks***	Y	Y	Y	Y	Y	Y	N
8 Pascrell	N	Y	N	Y	N	Y	N
9 Rothman	N	Y	N	Y	N	Y	N
10 Payne	?	?	?	?	?	?	?
11 ***Frelinghuysen***	Y	Y	Y	Y	Y	N	Y
12 ***Pappas***	Y	Y	Y	Y	Y	Y	Y
13 Menendez	N	Y	N	Y	N	Y	N
NEW MEXICO							
1 Vacant							
2 ***Skeen***	Y	Y	Y	Y	Y	Y	N
3 ***Redmond***	Y	Y	Y	Y	Y	Y	N
NEW YORK							
1 ***Forbes***	Y	Y	Y	Y	N	Y	N
2 ***Lazio***	Y	Y	Y	Y	N	Y	N
3 ***King***	Y	Y	Y	Y	Y	N	N
4 McCarthy	N	Y	N	Y	N	Y	N
5 Ackerman	N	Y	N	Y	N	Y	N
6 Meeks	N	Y	N	Y	N	Y	N
7 Manton	N	Y	N	Y	N	Y	N
8 Nadler	N	Y	N	Y	N	Y	N
9 Schumer	?	N	N	Y	N	Y	N
10 Towns	N	Y	N	Y	N	Y	N
11 Owens	N	Y	N	Y	N	Y	N
12 Velázquez	N	Y	N	Y	N	Y	N
13 ***Fossella***	Y	Y	Y	Y	Y	N	N
14 Maloney	N	N	N	Y	N	Y	N
15 Rangel	?	?	?	?	?	?	?
16 Serrano	N	Y	N	Y	N	Y	N
17 Engel	N	Y	N	Y	N	Y	N
18 Lowey	N	N	N	Y	N	Y	N
19 ***Kelly***	Y	Y	Y	Y	N	Y	N
20 ***Gilman***	Y	Y	Y	Y	N	Y	N
21 McNulty	N	Y	N	Y	N	Y	N
22 ***Solomon***	Y	Y	Y	Y	Y	N	N
23 ***Boehlert***	Y	Y	Y	Y	N	Y	N
24 ***McHugh***	Y	Y	Y	Y	Y	Y	N
25 ***Walsh***	Y	Y	Y	Y	N	Y	N
26 Hinchey	N	Y	N	Y	N	Y	N
27 ***Paxon***	Y	Y	Y	N	Y	N	N
28 Slaughter	N	Y	N	Y	N	Y	N
29 LaFalce	N	N	N	Y	?	?	N

	88	90	91	92	93	94	95
30 ***Quinn***	Y	Y	Y	Y	N	Y	N
31 ***Houghton***	Y	Y	Y	Y	N	Y	N
NORTH CAROLINA							
1 Clayton	N	N	N	Y	N	Y	N
2 Etheridge	N	N	N	Y	N	Y	N
3 ***Jones***	Y	Y	Y	Y	Y	N	Y
4 Price	N	N	N	Y	N	Y	N
5 ***Burr***	Y	Y	Y	Y	Y	N	Y
6 ***Coble***	Y	Y	Y	Y	Y	N	N
7 McIntyre	N	Y	N	Y	N	Y	N
8 Hefner	N	Y	N	Y	N	Y	N
9 ***Myrick***	Y	N	Y	Y	Y	N	Y
10 ***Ballenger***	Y	Y	Y	Y	Y	N	Y
11 ***Taylor***	Y	Y	Y	Y	Y	N	Y
12 Watt	N	N	N	Y	N	Y	N
NORTH DAKOTA							
AL Pomeroy	N	N	N	Y	N	Y	Y
OHIO							
1 ***Chabot***	Y	Y	Y	Y	Y	N	Y
2 ***Portman***	Y	Y	Y	Y	Y	N	N
3 Hall	N	Y	N	Y	N	Y	N
4 ***Oxley***	Y	Y	Y	Y	Y	N	N
5 ***Gillmor***	Y	Y	Y	N	Y	Y	N
6 Strickland	N	Y	N	Y	N	Y	N
7 ***Hobson***	Y	Y	Y	Y	Y	N	Y
8 ***Boehner***	Y	Y	Y	Y	Y	N	Y
9 Kaptur	N	Y	N	Y	N	Y	N
10 Kucinich	N	Y	N	Y	N	Y	N
11 Stokes	N	Y	N	Y	N	Y	N
12 ***Kasich***	Y	Y	Y	Y	Y	N	Y
13 Brown	N	N	N	Y	N	Y	N
14 Sawyer	N	Y	N	Y	N	Y	N
15 ***Pryce***	Y	Y	Y	Y	Y	N	N
16 ***Regula***	Y	Y	Y	Y	Y	N	N
17 Traficant	N	Y	Y	Y	N	Y	N
18 ***Ney***	Y	Y	Y	Y	Y	N	N
19 ***LaTourette***	Y	Y	Y	Y	N	N	N
OKLAHOMA							
1 ***Largent***	Y	Y	Y	Y	Y	N	Y
2 ***Coburn***	Y	Y	P	Y	Y	N	Y
3 ***Watkins***	Y	Y	Y	N	Y	N	N
4 ***Watts***	Y	Y	Y	Y	N	N	N
5 ***Istook***	Y	Y	Y	Y	Y	N	Y
6 ***Lucas***	Y	Y	Y	Y	Y	N	N
OREGON							
1 Furse	N	Y	N	Y	N	Y	N
2 ***Smith***	Y	Y	Y	?	N	Y	N
3 Blumenauer	N	Y	N	Y	N	Y	N
4 DeFazio	N	Y	N	Y	N	Y	N
5 Hooley	N	Y	N	Y	N	Y	N
PENNSYLVANIA							
1 Vacant							
2 Fattah	N	Y	N	Y	N	Y	N
3 Borski	N	Y	?	Y	N	Y	N
4 Klink	N	Y	N	Y	N	Y	N
5 ***Peterson***	Y	Y	Y	Y	Y	N	N
6 Holden	N	Y	Y	Y	N	Y	N
7 ***Weldon***	Y	Y	Y	Y	Y	Y	N
8 ***Greenwood***	Y	Y	?	Y	Y	N	N
9 ***Shuster***	Y	Y	Y	Y	N	N	N
10 ***McDade***	Y	Y	Y	Y	N	N	N
11 Kanjorski	N	Y	N	Y	N	Y	N
12 Murtha	N	Y	Y	Y	N	Y	N
13 ***Fox***	Y	Y	Y	Y	Y	Y	N
14 Coyne	N	Y	N	Y	N	Y	N
15 McHale	N	Y	N	Y	N	Y	N
16 ***Pitts***	Y	Y	Y	Y	Y	N	N
17 ***Gekas***	Y	Y	Y	Y	Y	N	N
18 Doyle	N	Y	Y	Y	N	Y	N
19 ***Goodling***	Y	Y	Y	Y	Y	N	N
20 Mascara	N	Y	Y	Y	N	Y	N
21 ***English***	Y	Y	Y	Y	N	Y	N
RHODE ISLAND							
1 Kennedy	N	Y	N	Y	N	Y	N
2 Weygand	N	Y	N	Y	N	Y	N
SOUTH CAROLINA							
1 ***Sanford***	Y	N	Y	Y	Y	N	Y
2 ***Spence***	Y	Y	Y	Y	Y	N	N
3 ***Graham***	Y	N	Y	Y	Y	N	Y
4 ***Inglis***	Y	N	Y	Y	Y	N	Y
5 Spratt	N	N	N	Y	N	?	N
6 Clyburn	N	Y	N	Y	N	Y	N
SOUTH DAKOTA							
AL ***Thune***	Y	Y	Y	Y	Y	N	N

	88	90	91	92	93	94	95
TENNESSEE							
1 ***Jenkins***	Y	Y	Y	Y	Y	N	N
2 ***Duncan***	N	Y	Y	Y	Y	N	N
3 ***Wamp***	Y	Y	Y	Y	Y	N	Y
4 ***Hilleary***	Y	Y	Y	Y	Y	N	Y
5 Clement	N	Y	N	Y	N	Y	N
6 Gordon	N	Y	N	Y	N	Y	N
7 ***Bryant***	Y	Y	Y	Y	Y	N	N
8 Tanner	N	N	N	Y	N	Y	N
9 Ford	N	N	N	Y	N	Y	N
TEXAS							
1 Sandlin	N	Y	N	Y	N	Y	N
2 Turner	N	Y	N	Y	N	Y	N
3 ***Johnson, Sam***	Y	Y	Y	Y	Y	N	Y
4 Hall	Y	Y	N	Y	Y	N	Y
5 ***Sessions***	Y	Y	Y	Y	Y	N	Y
6 ***Barton***	Y	Y	Y	N	Y	N	Y
7 ***Archer***	Y	Y	Y	Y	Y	N	Y
8 ***Brady***	Y	Y	Y	Y	Y	N	N
9 Lampson	N	Y	N	Y	N	Y	N
10 Doggett	N	Y	N	Y	N	Y	N
11 Edwards	N	N	N	Y	N	Y	Y
12 ***Granger***	Y	Y	Y	Y	Y	N	N
13 ***Thornberry***	Y	Y	Y	Y	Y	N	Y
14 ***Paul***	N	Y	Y	N	Y	N	N
15 Hinojosa	N	Y	N	Y	N	Y	N
16 Reyes	N	Y	N	Y	N	Y	N
17 Stenholm	N	N	N	Y	Y	Y	Y
18 Jackson-Lee	N	Y	N	Y	N	Y	N
19 ***Combest***	Y	Y	Y	Y	Y	N	N
20 Gonzalez	?	?	?	?	?	?	?
21 ***Smith***	Y	Y	Y	Y	Y	Y	N
22 ***DeLay***	Y	Y	Y	Y	Y	N	N
23 ***Bonilla***	Y	Y	Y	Y	Y	N	Y
24 Frost	N	Y	N	Y	N	Y	N
25 Bentsen	N	N	N	Y	N	Y	N
26 ***Armey***	Y	Y	Y	Y	Y	N	N
27 Ortiz	N	Y	N	Y	N	Y	N
28 Rodriguez	N	Y	N	Y	N	Y	N
29 Green	N	Y	N	Y	N	Y	N
30 Johnson, E.B.	N	Y	N	Y	N	Y	N
UTAH							
1 ***Hansen***	Y	Y	Y	Y	Y	N	N
2 ***Cook***	Y	Y	Y	Y	Y	N	N
3 ***Cannon***	?	?	?	?	?	?	?
VERMONT							
AL *Sanders*	N	Y	N	Y	N	Y	N
VIRGINIA							
1 ***Bateman***	Y	Y	Y	Y	Y	N	N
2 Pickett	Y	Y	Y	Y	N	Y	N
3 Scott	N	Y	N	Y	N	Y	N
4 Sisisky	N	Y	N	Y	N	Y	N
5 Goode	Y	Y	?	Y	N	N	N
6 ***Goodlatte***	Y	Y	Y	Y	Y	N	N
7 ***Bliley***	Y	Y	Y	Y	Y	N	N
8 Moran	N	N	N	Y	N	Y	N
9 Boucher	N	Y	Y	Y	N	Y	N
10 ***Wolf***	Y	N	Y	Y	Y	N	Y
11 ***Davis***	Y	Y	Y	Y	N	N	N
WASHINGTON							
1 ***White***	Y	Y	Y	Y	Y	N	Y
2 ***Metcalf***	Y	Y	Y	Y	Y	N	N
3 ***Smith, Linda***	Y	Y	Y	Y	Y	Y	N
4 ***Hastings***	Y	Y	Y	Y	Y	N	N
5 ***Nethercutt***	Y	Y	Y	Y	Y	N	Y
6 Dicks	N	Y	N	Y	N	Y	N
7 McDermott	N	N	N	Y	N	Y	N
8 ***Dunn***	Y	Y	Y	Y	Y	N	N
9 Smith, Adam	N	N	N	Y	N	Y	N
WEST VIRGINIA							
1 Mollohan	N	Y	N	Y	N	Y	N
2 Wise	N	Y	N	Y	N	Y	N
3 Rahall	N	Y	N	Y	N	Y	N
WISCONSIN							
1 ***Neumann***	Y	Y	Y	Y	Y	N	Y
2 ***Klug***	N	?	?	?	?	?	?
3 Kind	N	N	N	Y	N	Y	Y
4 Kleczka	N	Y	N	Y	N	Y	N
5 Barrett	N	N	N	Y	N	Y	Y
6 ***Petri***	N	Y	?	Y	N	N	N
7 Obey	N	N	N	Y	N	Y	N
8 Johnson	N	Y	N	Y	N	Y	N
9 ***Sensenbrenner***	N	Y	Y	Y	Y	N	Y
WYOMING							
AL ***Cubin***	Y	Y	Y	Y	Y	N	Y

Southern states - Ala., Ark., Fla., Ga., Ky., La., Miss., N.C., Okla., S.C., Tenn., Texas, Va.

House Votes 96, 97, 98, 100, 101, 102, 103 *

96. HR 2400. Surface Transportation Reauthorization/Extend ISTEA. Spratt, D-S.C., amendment to eliminate all the bill's provisions and instead extend the existing short-term ISTEA reauthorization until July 1, 1998. Rejected 106-312: R 51-169; D 55-142 (ND 32-112, SD 23-30); I 0-1. April 1, 1998. A "yea" was a vote in support of the president's position.

97. HR 2400. Surface Transportation Reauthorization/State Transition. Kasich, R-Ohio, amendment to eliminate all of the bill's provisions, and instead turn over more control of transportation projects to the states and reduce the federal gas tax over a four-year period. Rejected 98-318: R 82-138; D 16-179 (ND 8-134, SD 8-45); I 0-1. April 1, 1998.

98. HR 2400. Surface Transportation Reauthorization/Passage. Passage of the bill to authorize $219 billion over six years for federal highway and mass transit programs. The bill's transportation funding represents a 40 percent increase in spending over the next six years. The bill also modifies highway funding formulas. Passed 337-80: R 165-54; D 171-26 (ND 129-15, SD 42-11); I 1-0. April 1, 1998.

99. Quorum Call.* 389 Responded. April 21, 1998.

100. HR 3565. Assistance for Police Survivors/Passage. McCollum, R-Fla., motion to suspend the rules and pass the bill to authorize the Bureau of Justice Assistance to spend no less than $150,000 each year to provide counseling and peer support programs for families of public safety officers killed in the line of duty. Motion agreed to 403-8: R 208-8; D 194-0 (ND 142-0, SD 52-0); I 1-0. April 21, 1998. A two-thirds majority of those present and voting (274 in this case) is required for passage under suspension of the rules. A "yea" was a vote in support of the president's position.

101. HR 3528. Dispute Resolution Alternatives/Passage. Coble, R-N.C., motion to suspend the rules and pass the bill to direct federal district courts to devise and implement their own alternative dispute resolution programs or to examine and improve any such existing programs. Motion agreed to 405-2: R 211-1; D 193-1 (ND 142-1, SD 51-0); I 1-0. April 21, 1998. A two-thirds majority of those present and voting (272 in this case) is required for passage under suspension of the rules. A "yea" was a vote in support of the president's position.

102. H J Res 111. Tax Limitation Constitutional Amendment/Passage. Passage of the joint resolution proposing a constitutional amendment requiring a two-thirds majority vote in both the House and the Senate in order to raise taxes. Rejected 238-186: R 213-12; D 25-173 (ND 14-133, SD 11-40); I 0-1. April 22, 1998. A two-thirds majority of those present and voting (283 in this case) is required to pass a joint resolution proposing an amendment to the Constitution. A "nay" was a vote in support of the president's position.

103. HR 1252. Limits on Federal Judges' Power/Tax Increases. Delahunt, D-Mass., amendment to provide that the limitation on judicial imposition of remedies that require a tax increase shall apply only where the court "expressly directs" that a tax be imposed. Adopted 230-181: R 47-168; D 182-13 (ND 140-4, SD 42-9); I 1-0. April 23, 1998. (Subsequently, the section containing this provision was removed by unanimous consent.)

* *CQ does not include quorum calls in its vote charts.*

[1] *Barbara Lee, D-Calif., was sworn in April 21, replacing Ronald V. Dellums, D-Calif., who resigned Feb. 6.*

[2] *Mary Bono, R-Calif., was sworn in April 21, replacing Sonny Bono, R-Calif., who died Jan. 5.*

Key

Y	Voted for (yea).
#	Paired for.
+	Announced for.
N	Voted against (nay).
X	Paired against.
–	Announced against.
P	Voted "present."
C	Voted "present" to avoid possible conflict of interest.
?	Did not vote or otherwise make a position known.

Democrats **Republicans** Independent

		96	97	98	100	101	102	103
ALABAMA								
1	**Callahan**	N	N	Y	Y	Y	Y	N
2	**Everett**	N	N	Y	Y	Y	Y	N
3	**Riley**	N	N	Y	Y	Y	Y	N
4	**Aderholt**	N	N	Y	Y	Y	Y	N
5	Cramer	N	N	Y	Y	Y	Y	N
6	**Bachus**	N	Y	Y	Y	Y	Y	N
7	Hilliard	N	N	Y	Y	Y	N	N
ALASKA								
AL	**Young**	N	N	Y	Y	Y	Y	N
ARIZONA								
1	**Salmon**	Y	Y	N	Y	Y	Y	N
2	Pastor	N	N	Y	Y	Y	N	Y
3	**Stump**	N	Y	N	Y	Y	Y	N
4	**Shadegg**	Y	Y	N	Y	Y	Y	N
5	**Kolbe**	Y	N	Y	Y	Y	Y	N
6	**Hayworth**	Y	Y	N	Y	Y	Y	N
ARKANSAS								
1	Berry	N	N	Y	Y	Y	Y	Y
2	Snyder	Y	N	Y	Y	Y	N	Y
3	**Hutchinson**	N	N	Y	Y	Y	Y	N
4	**Dickey**	N	N	Y	Y	Y	Y	N
CALIFORNIA								
1	**Riggs**	N	N	Y	Y	Y	Y	N
2	**Herger**	N	Y	N	Y	Y	Y	N
3	Fazio	Y	N	Y	Y	Y	N	Y
4	**Doolittle**	N	N	N	Y	Y	Y	N
5	Matsui	N	N	Y	Y	Y	N	?
6	Woolsey	N	N	Y	Y	Y	N	Y
7	Miller	N	Y	Y	Y	Y	N	?
8	Pelosi	N	N	Y	Y	Y	N	Y
9	Lee [1]				Y	Y	N	Y
10	Tauscher	N	N	Y	Y	Y	N	Y
11	**Pombo**	N	Y	Y	Y	Y	Y	N
12	Lantos	N	N	Y	Y	Y	N	Y
13	Stark	Y	N	Y	N	Y	N	Y
14	Eshoo	Y	N	Y	Y	Y	N	Y
15	**Campbell**	Y	Y	N	N	Y	N	Y
16	Lofgren	Y	P	P	Y	Y	N	Y
17	Farr	N	N	Y	Y	Y	N	Y
18	Condit	Y	Y	Y	Y	Y	Y	N
19	**Radanovich**	N	Y	N	Y	Y	Y	?
20	Dooley	Y	Y	N	Y	Y	N	Y
21	**Thomas**	N	N	Y	Y	Y	Y	N
22	Capps, L.	N	N	Y	Y	Y	N	Y
23	**Gallegly**	N	N	Y	Y	Y	Y	N
24	Sherman	N	N	Y	Y	Y	N	Y
25	**McKeon**	N	N	Y	Y	Y	Y	N
26	Berman	Y	N	Y	Y	Y	N	Y
27	**Rogan**	Y	Y	Y	Y	Y	Y	N
28	**Dreier**	N	Y	Y	Y	Y	Y	N
29	Waxman	Y	N	Y	Y	Y	N	Y
30	Becerra	Y	N	Y	Y	Y	N	?
31	Martinez	N	N	Y	Y	Y	N	Y
32	Dixon	N	N	Y	?	?	?	?
33	Roybal-Allard	Y	N	Y	Y	Y	N	Y
34	Torres	?	?	?	Y	Y	N	Y
35	Waters	?	?	?	Y	Y	?	Y
36	Harman	Y	Y	Y	Y	Y	Y	Y
37	Millender-McD.	N	N	Y	Y	Y	N	Y

		96	97	98	100	101	102	103
38	**Horn**	N	N	Y	Y	Y	Y	Y
39	**Royce**	?	?	?	Y	Y	Y	N
40	**Lewis**	N	N	Y	Y	Y	Y	N
41	**Kim**	N	N	Y	?	?	?	Y
42	Brown	N	N	Y	?	?	?	Y
43	**Calvert**	N	N	Y	Y	Y	Y	N
44	**Bono, M.** [2]				Y	Y	Y	Y
45	**Rohrabacher**	Y	Y	N	Y	Y	Y	Y
46	Sanchez	Y	N	Y	Y	Y	Y	Y
47	**Cox**	Y	Y	N	Y	Y	Y	N
48	**Packard**	N	N	Y	Y	Y	Y	N
49	**Bilbray**	N	Y	Y	Y	Y	Y	Y
50	Filner	N	N	Y	Y	Y	N	Y
51	**Cunningham**	N	N	Y	Y	Y	Y	N
52	**Hunter**	N	Y	N	Y	Y	Y	N
COLORADO								
1	DeGette	N	N	Y	Y	Y	N	Y
2	Skaggs	Y	N	N	Y	Y	N	Y
3	**McInnis**	N	N	Y	Y	Y	Y	N
4	**Schaffer**	N	Y	N	Y	Y	Y	N
5	**Hefley**	N	Y	P	Y	Y	Y	N
6	**Schaefer**	N	N	Y	Y	Y	Y	N
CONNECTICUT								
1	Kennelly	N	N	Y	Y	Y	N	Y
2	Gejdenson	N	N	Y	Y	Y	N	Y
3	DeLauro	N	N	Y	Y	Y	N	Y
4	**Shays**	Y	N	N	Y	Y	Y	Y
5	Maloney	N	N	Y	Y	Y	N	Y
6	**Johnson**	N	N	Y	Y	Y	N	Y
DELAWARE								
AL	**Castle**	Y	N	N	Y	Y	Y	Y
FLORIDA								
1	**Scarborough**	Y	Y	N	N	Y	Y	N
2	Boyd	Y	Y	Y	Y	Y	N	?
3	Brown	N	N	Y	Y	Y	N	Y
4	**Fowler**	N	N	Y	Y	Y	Y	N
5	Thurman	Y	Y	Y	Y	Y	N	Y
6	**Stearns**	Y	N	Y	Y	Y	Y	N
7	**Mica**	N	N	Y	Y	Y	Y	N
8	**McCollum**	N	Y	Y	Y	Y	Y	N
9	**Bilirakis**	N	Y	Y	Y	Y	Y	N
10	**Young**	N	Y	Y	?	?	Y	N
11	Davis	Y	N	N	Y	Y	N	Y
12	**Canady**	N	Y	Y	Y	Y	Y	N
13	**Miller**	Y	Y	N	Y	Y	Y	N
14	**Goss**	N	Y	N	Y	Y	Y	N
15	**Weldon**	N	N	Y	Y	?	Y	N
16	**Foley**	N	Y	Y	Y	Y	Y	N
17	Meek	N	N	Y	Y	Y	N	Y
18	**Ros-Lehtinen**	?	?	#	Y	Y	Y	N
19	Wexler	Y	N	Y	Y	Y	N	Y
20	Deutsch	Y	N	Y	Y	Y	N	Y
21	**Diaz-Balart**	N	N	Y	Y	Y	Y	N
22	**Shaw**	N	N	Y	Y	N	N	N
23	Hastings	Y	N	N	Y	Y	?	?
GEORGIA								
1	**Kingston**	Y	Y	N	N	Y	Y	N
2	Bishop	N	N	Y	Y	Y	N	Y
3	**Collins**	N	N	Y	Y	Y	Y	N
4	**McKinney**	N	N	Y	Y	Y	N	Y
5	Lewis	Y	N	Y	Y	Y	N	Y
6	**Gingrich**						Y	
7	**Barr**	Y	Y	N	Y	Y	Y	?
8	**Chambliss**	N	N	Y	Y	Y	Y	N
9	**Deal**	Y	Y	Y	Y	Y	Y	N
10	**Norwood**	N	N	Y	Y	Y	Y	N
11	**Linder**	N	Y	Y	Y	Y	Y	N
HAWAII								
1	Abercrombie	N	N	Y	Y	Y	N	Y
2	Mink	N	N	Y	Y	Y	N	Y
IDAHO								
1	**Chenoweth**	N	Y	N	Y	Y	Y	N
2	**Crapo**	N	Y	Y	Y	Y	Y	N
ILLINOIS								
1	Rush	N	N	Y	?	?	N	Y
2	Jackson	N	N	Y	Y	Y	N	Y
3	Lipinski	N	Y	Y	Y	Y	N	Y
4	Gutierrez	N	N	Y	Y	Y	N	Y
5	Blagojevich	N	N	Y	Y	Y	N	Y
6	**Hyde**	N	N	Y	Y	Y	Y	N
7	Davis	N	N	Y	Y	Y	N	Y
8	**Crane**	Y	Y	N	Y	Y	Y	N
9	Yates	?	?	X	Y	Y	N	Y
10	**Porter**	Y	N	Y	Y	Y	Y	N
11	**Weller**	N	N	Y	Y	Y	Y	N
12	Costello	N	N	Y	Y	Y	N	Y

ND Northern Democrats SD Southern Democrats

		96	97	98	100	101	102	103
13	**Fawell**	N	N	Y	Y	Y	Y	Y
14	**Hastert**	N	N	Y	Y	Y	Y	N
15	**Ewing**	N	N	Y	Y	Y	Y	Y
16	**Manzullo**	N	N	Y	Y	Y	Y	N
17	Evans	N	N	Y	Y	Y	N	Y
18	**LaHood**	N	N	Y	Y	Y	Y	Y
19	Poshard	N	N	Y	Y	Y	N	Y
20	**Shimkus**	N	N	Y	Y	Y	Y	N
INDIANA								
1	Visclosky	N	N	Y	Y	Y	N	Y
2	**McIntosh**	N	Y	Y	Y	Y	Y	N
3	Roemer	Y	N	Y	Y	Y	Y	Y
4	**Souder**	Y	Y	N	Y	Y	Y	N
5	**Buyer**	N	N	Y	Y	Y	Y	N
6	**Burton**	N	N	Y	Y	Y	Y	N
7	**Pease**	N	N	Y	Y	Y	Y	N
8	**Hostettler**	N	N	Y	Y	Y	N	N
9	Hamilton	N	N	Y	Y	Y	N	Y
10	Carson	N	N	Y	Y	Y	N	Y
IOWA								
1	**Leach**	N	N	Y	Y	Y	Y	Y
2	**Nussle**	N	N	Y	Y	Y	Y	N
3	Boswell	N	N	Y	Y	Y	Y	Y
4	**Ganske**	N	N	Y	Y	Y	Y	Y
5	**Latham**	N	N	Y	Y	Y	Y	N
KANSAS								
1	**Moran**	N	N	Y	Y	Y	Y	N
2	**Ryun**	N	N	Y	Y	Y	Y	N
3	**Snowbarger**	N	N	Y	Y	Y	Y	N
4	**Tiahrt**	N	N	Y	Y	Y	Y	N
KENTUCKY								
1	**Whitfield**	Y	N	Y	Y	Y	Y	Y
2	**Lewis**	N	N	Y	Y	Y	Y	N
3	**Northup**	N	N	Y	Y	Y	Y	N
4	**Bunning**	N	N	Y	Y	Y	Y	?
5	**Rogers**	N	N	Y	Y	Y	Y	N
6	Baesler	N	N	Y	Y	Y	N	Y
LOUISIANA								
1	**Livingston**	Y	Y	Y	Y	Y	Y	N
2	Jefferson	?	?	?	Y	Y	N	Y
3	**Tauzin**	N	N	Y	Y	Y	Y	N
4	**McCrery**	P	P	P	Y	?	Y	N
5	**Cooksey**	N	N	Y	Y	Y	Y	?
6	**Baker**	N	N	Y	Y	Y	Y	N
7	John	N	N	Y	?	?	Y	Y
MAINE								
1	Allen	N	N	Y	Y	Y	N	Y
2	Baldacci	N	N	Y	Y	Y	N	Y
MARYLAND								
1	**Gilchrest**	N	N	Y	Y	Y	Y	Y
2	**Ehrlich**	N	N	Y	Y	Y	Y	N
3	Cardin	Y	N	N	Y	Y	N	Y
4	Wynn	N	N	Y	Y	Y	N	Y
5	Hoyer	Y	N	N	Y	Y	N	Y
6	**Bartlett**	Y	Y	Y	Y	Y	Y	N
7	Cummings	N	N	Y	Y	Y	N	Y
8	**Morella**	N	N	N	Y	Y	N	Y
MASSACHUSETTS								
1	Olver	N	N	Y	Y	Y	N	?
2	Neal	N	N	Y	Y	Y	N	Y
3	McGovern	N	N	Y	Y	Y	N	Y
4	Frank	N	N	Y	Y	Y	N	Y
5	Meehan	N	N	Y	?	?	N	Y
6	Tierney	N	N	Y	Y	Y	N	Y
7	Markey	N	N	Y	Y	Y	N	Y
8	Kennedy	N	N	Y	?	?	N	Y
9	Moakley	N	N	Y	Y	Y	N	Y
10	Delahunt	N	N	Y	Y	Y	N	Y
MICHIGAN								
1	Stupak	N	N	Y	Y	Y	N	Y
2	**Hoekstra**	N	Y	N	Y	Y	Y	N
3	**Ehlers**	N	N	Y	Y	Y	Y	Y
4	**Camp**	N	N	Y	Y	Y	Y	Y
5	Barcia	N	N	Y	Y	Y	Y	Y
6	**Upton**	N	N	Y	Y	Y	Y	Y
7	**Smith**	N	Y	Y	Y	Y	Y	N
8	Stabenow	N	N	Y	Y	Y	N	Y
9	Kildee	N	N	Y	Y	Y	N	Y
10	Bonior	N	N	Y	Y	Y	N	Y
11	**Knollenberg**	N	N	Y	Y	Y	Y	N
12	Levin	N	N	Y	Y	Y	N	Y
13	Rivers	N	N	Y	Y	Y	N	Y
14	Conyers	N	N	Y	Y	?	N	Y
15	Kilpatrick	N	N	Y	Y	Y	N	Y
16	Dingell	N	N	Y	Y	Y	N	Y
MINNESOTA								
1	**Gutknecht**	N	N	Y	Y	Y	Y	Y
2	Minge	Y	N	N	Y	Y	N	Y
3	**Ramstad**	N	N	Y	Y	Y	Y	Y
4	Vento	N	N	Y	Y	Y	N	Y
5	Sabo	Y	N	N	Y	Y	N	Y
6	Luther	Y	N	Y	Y	Y	N	Y
7	Peterson	Y	N	Y	Y	Y	N	N
8	Oberstar	N	N	Y	Y	Y	N	Y
MISSISSIPPI								
1	**Wicker**	N	N	Y	Y	Y	Y	N
2	Thompson	N	N	Y	Y	Y	N	Y
3	**Pickering**	N	N	Y	Y	Y	Y	N
4	**Parker**	Y	Y	N	Y	Y	Y	N
5	Taylor	Y	N	Y	Y	Y	Y	N
MISSOURI								
1	Clay	N	N	Y	Y	Y	N	?
2	**Talent**	N	N	Y	Y	Y	Y	N
3	Gephardt	N	N	Y	Y	Y	N	Y
4	Skelton	N	N	Y	Y	Y	Y	Y
5	McCarthy	N	N	Y	Y	Y	N	Y
6	Danner	N	N	Y	Y	Y	Y	N
7	**Blunt**	N	N	Y	Y	Y	Y	N
8	**Emerson**	N	N	Y	Y	Y	Y	N
9	**Hulshof**	N	N	Y	Y	Y	Y	N
MONTANA								
AL	**Hill**	Y	N	N	Y	Y	N	N
NEBRASKA								
1	**Bereuter**	N	N	Y	Y	Y	N	N
2	**Christensen**	Y	Y	N	?	?	Y	N
3	**Barrett**	Y	Y	N	Y	Y	Y	N
NEVADA								
1	**Ensign**	N	N	Y	Y	Y	Y	N
2	**Gibbons**	N	N	Y	Y	Y	Y	N
NEW HAMPSHIRE								
1	**Sununu**	Y	N	Y	Y	Y	Y	Y
2	**Bass**	N	N	Y	Y	Y	Y	Y
NEW JERSEY								
1	Andrews	N	N	Y	Y	Y	Y	Y
2	**LoBiondo**	N	N	Y	Y	Y	Y	Y
3	**Saxton**	N	N	Y	Y	Y	Y	Y
4	**Smith**	N	N	Y	Y	Y	Y	Y
5	**Roukema**	N	N	Y	Y	Y	Y	Y
6	Pallone	N	N	Y	Y	Y	Y	Y
7	**Franks**	N	N	Y	Y	Y	Y	Y
8	Pascrell	N	N	Y	Y	Y	N	Y
9	Rothman	N	N	Y	Y	Y	N	Y
10	Payne	?	?	?	Y	Y	N	Y
11	**Frelinghuysen**	N	N	Y	Y	Y	Y	N
12	**Pappas**	N	N	Y	Y	Y	Y	Y
13	Menendez	N	N	Y	Y	Y	N	Y
NEW MEXICO								
1	Vacant							
2	**Skeen**	N	N	Y	Y	Y	Y	N
3	**Redmond**	N	N	Y	Y	?	Y	N
NEW YORK								
1	**Forbes**	N	N	Y	Y	Y	Y	Y
2	**Lazio**	N	N	Y	Y	Y	Y	Y
3	**King**	N	N	Y	Y	Y	Y	N
4	McCarthy	N	?	Y	Y	Y	Y	Y
5	Ackerman	N	N	Y	?	?	N	Y
6	Meeks	N	N	Y	Y	Y	N	Y
7	Manton	N	N	Y	Y	Y	N	Y
8	Nadler	N	N	Y	Y	Y	N	Y
9	Schumer	N	N	Y	Y	Y	?	Y
10	Towns	N	N	Y	?	Y	N	Y
11	Owens	N	N	Y	Y	Y	N	Y
12	Velázquez	N	N	Y	Y	Y	N	Y
13	**Fossella**	N	N	Y	Y	Y	Y	N
14	Maloney	Y	N	Y	?	Y	N	Y
15	Rangel	?	?	?	Y	Y	N	Y
16	Serrano	N	N	Y	Y	Y	N	Y
17	Engel	N	N	Y	Y	Y	N	Y
18	Lowey	N	N	Y	Y	Y	N	Y
19	**Kelly**	N	N	Y	Y	Y	Y	Y
20	**Gilman**	N	N	Y	Y	Y	Y	Y
21	McNulty	N	N	Y	Y	Y	N	Y
22	**Solomon**	N	N	Y	Y	Y	Y	N
23	**Boehlert**	N	N	Y	Y	N	N	Y
24	**McHugh**	N	N	Y	Y	Y	Y	N
25	**Walsh**	N	N	Y	Y	Y	Y	Y
26	Hinchey	N	N	Y	Y	Y	N	Y
27	**Paxon**	N	N	Y	?	?	Y	?
28	Slaughter	N	N	Y	Y	N	N	Y
29	LaFalce	Y	N	N	Y	Y	N	Y
30	**Quinn**	N	N	Y	Y	Y	Y	Y
31	**Houghton**	N	N	Y	Y	Y	N	Y
NORTH CAROLINA								
1	Clayton	Y	N	Y	Y	Y	N	Y
2	Etheridge	Y	N	Y	Y	Y	Y	Y
3	**Jones**	Y	Y	N	Y	Y	Y	N
4	Price	Y	N	Y	Y	Y	N	Y
5	**Burr**	Y	Y	N	Y	Y	Y	Y
6	**Coble**	N	N	Y	Y	Y	Y	N
7	McIntyre	N	N	Y	Y	Y	Y	Y
8	Hefner	N	N	Y	?	?	?	Y
9	**Myrick**	Y	Y	N	Y	Y	Y	N
10	**Ballenger**	Y	Y	N	Y	Y	Y	N
11	**Taylor**	N	Y	Y	Y	Y	Y	N
12	Watt	Y	N	Y	Y	Y	N	Y
NORTH DAKOTA								
AL	Pomeroy	Y	N	N	Y	Y	N	Y
OHIO								
1	**Chabot**	Y	Y	N	Y	Y	Y	N
2	**Portman**	Y	Y	N	Y	Y	Y	N
3	Hall	N	N	Y	Y	Y	N	Y
4	**Oxley**	N	N	Y	Y	Y	Y	N
5	**Gillmor**	Y	N	Y	Y	Y	N	N
6	Strickland	N	N	Y	Y	Y	N	Y
7	**Hobson**	Y	Y	N	Y	Y	Y	Y
8	**Boehner**	Y	Y	N	Y	Y	Y	N
9	Kaptur	N	N	Y	Y	Y	N	Y
10	Kucinich	N	N	Y	Y	Y	N	Y
11	Stokes	N	N	Y	Y	Y	N	Y
12	**Kasich**	Y	Y	N	Y	Y	Y	N
13	Brown	Y	Y	N	Y	Y	N	Y
14	Sawyer	Y	N	Y	Y	Y	N	Y
15	**Pryce**	N	Y	Y	Y	Y	Y	Y
16	**Regula**	N	N	Y	Y	Y	Y	Y
17	Traficant	N	N	Y	Y	Y	Y	N
18	**Ney**	N	N	Y	Y	Y	Y	Y
19	**LaTourette**	N	N	Y	Y	Y	Y	Y
OKLAHOMA								
1	**Largent**	Y	Y	N	Y	Y	Y	N
2	**Coburn**	Y	Y	N	N	Y	Y	N
3	**Watkins**	N	Y	Y	?	?	Y	?
4	**Watts**	N	N	Y	Y	Y	Y	N
5	**Istook**	N	Y	Y	?	?	+	?
6	**Lucas**	N	Y	Y	Y	Y	Y	N
OREGON								
1	Furse	N	N	Y	Y	Y	N	Y
2	**Smith**	N	N	Y	?	?	Y	N
3	Blumenauer	N	N	Y	Y	Y	N	Y
4	DeFazio	N	N	Y	Y	Y	N	Y
5	Hooley	N	N	Y	Y	Y	N	Y
PENNSYLVANIA								
1	Vacant							
2	Fattah	N	N	Y	Y	Y	N	Y
3	Borski	N	N	Y	Y	Y	N	Y
4	Klink	N	N	Y	Y	Y	N	Y
5	**Peterson**	N	N	Y	Y	Y	Y	N
6	Holden	N	N	Y	Y	Y	N	Y
7	**Weldon**	N	N	Y	Y	Y	Y	?
8	**Greenwood**	N	N	Y	?	?	Y	Y
9	**Shuster**	N	N	Y	Y	Y	Y	N
10	**McDade**	N	N	Y	Y	Y	Y	Y
11	Kanjorski	N	N	Y	Y	Y	N	Y
12	Murtha	N	N	Y	Y	Y	N	Y
13	**Fox**	N	N	Y	Y	Y	Y	Y
14	Coyne	N	N	Y	Y	Y	N	Y
15	McHale	N	N	Y	Y	Y	N	Y
16	**Pitts**	N	N	Y	Y	Y	Y	N
17	**Gekas**	N	N	Y	Y	Y	Y	N
18	Doyle	N	N	Y	Y	Y	N	Y
19	**Goodling**	N	N	Y	Y	Y	Y	N
20	Mascara	N	N	Y	Y	Y	N	Y
21	**English**	N	N	Y	Y	Y	Y	N
RHODE ISLAND								
1	Kennedy	Y	N	Y	Y	Y	N	Y
2	Weygand	Y	N	Y	Y	Y	N	Y
SOUTH CAROLINA								
1	**Sanford**	Y	Y	N	N	Y	Y	N
2	**Spence**	N	N	Y	Y	Y	Y	N
3	**Graham**	Y	Y	N	Y	Y	Y	N
4	**Inglis**	Y	Y	N	?	?	Y	N
5	Spratt	Y	N	N	Y	Y	N	Y
6	Clyburn	N	N	Y	Y	Y	N	Y
SOUTH DAKOTA								
AL	**Thune**	N	N	Y	Y	Y	Y	N
TENNESSEE								
1	**Jenkins**	N	N	Y	Y	Y	Y	N
2	**Duncan**	N	N	Y	Y	Y	Y	N
3	**Wamp**	N	Y	Y	N	Y	Y	N
4	**Hilleary**	N	Y	Y	Y	Y	Y	N
5	Clement	N	N	Y	Y	Y	N	Y
6	Gordon	N	N	Y	Y	Y	Y	Y
7	**Bryant**	N	N	Y	Y	Y	Y	N
8	Tanner	Y	N	Y	Y	Y	?	?
9	Ford	N	N	Y	Y	?	N	Y
TEXAS								
1	Sandlin	N	N	Y	Y	Y	Y	Y
2	Turner	N	N	Y	Y	Y	N	N
3	**Johnson, Sam**	N	Y	N	Y	Y	Y	N
4	Hall	Y	Y	N	Y	Y	Y	N
5	**Sessions**	Y	Y	N	Y	Y	Y	N
6	**Barton**	Y	Y	N	Y	Y	Y	N
7	**Archer**	N	Y	Y	Y	Y	Y	N
8	**Brady**	N	Y	Y	Y	Y	Y	N
9	Lampson	N	N	Y	Y	Y	N	Y
10	Doggett	Y	N	Y	Y	Y	N	Y
11	Edwards	Y	N	N	Y	Y	N	Y
12	**Granger**	N	N	Y	Y	Y	Y	N
13	**Thornberry**	Y	Y	N	Y	Y	Y	N
14	**Paul**	Y	Y	N	N	Y	Y	N
15	Hinojosa	N	N	Y	Y	Y	N	Y
16	Reyes	N	N	Y	Y	Y	N	Y
17	Stenholm	Y	Y	N	Y	Y	N	N
18	Jackson-Lee	N	N	Y	Y	Y	N	Y
19	**Combest**	N	N	Y	Y	Y	Y	N
20	Gonzalez	?	?	?	?	?	?	?
21	**Smith**	N	N	Y	Y	Y	Y	N
22	**DeLay**	N	Y	Y	Y	Y	Y	N
23	**Bonilla**	Y	Y	N	Y	Y	Y	N
24	Frost	N	N	Y	Y	Y	N	Y
25	Bentsen	Y	N	N	Y	Y	N	Y
26	**Armey**	N	Y	Y	Y	Y	Y	N
27	Ortiz	N	N	Y	Y	Y	N	Y
28	Rodriguez	N	N	Y	Y	Y	N	Y
29	Green	N	N	Y	Y	Y	Y	Y
30	Johnson, E.B.	N	N	Y	Y	Y	N	Y
UTAH								
1	**Hansen**	N	N	Y	Y	Y	Y	N
2	**Cook**	N	N	Y	Y	Y	Y	?
3	**Cannon**	?	?	?	?	?	Y	N
VERMONT								
AL	*Sanders*	N	N	Y	Y	Y	N	Y
VIRGINIA								
1	**Bateman**	N	N	Y	+	+	–	–
2	Pickett	N	N	Y	Y	Y	N	N
3	Scott	Y	N	Y	Y	Y	N	Y
4	Sisisky	Y	Y	Y	Y	Y	N	N
5	Goode	N	N	Y	Y	Y	N	Y
6	**Goodlatte**	N	Y	Y	Y	Y	Y	N
7	**Bliley**	N	N	Y	Y	Y	Y	N
8	Moran	Y	Y	N	Y	Y	N	Y
9	Boucher	N	N	Y	Y	Y	N	Y
10	**Wolf**	Y	Y	N	Y	Y	Y	N
11	**Davis**	N	N	Y	Y	?	Y	N
WASHINGTON								
1	**White**	Y	Y	N	Y	Y	Y	Y
2	**Metcalf**	N	N	Y	Y	Y	Y	N
3	**Smith, Linda**	N	N	Y	Y	Y	Y	N
4	**Hastings**	N	Y	Y	Y	Y	Y	N
5	**Nethercutt**	Y	N	N	Y	Y	Y	N
6	Dicks	Y	N	Y	Y	Y	N	Y
7	McDermott	N	N	Y	Y	Y	N	Y
8	**Dunn**	N	N	Y	Y	Y	Y	N
9	Smith, Adam	Y	N	N	Y	Y	N	Y
WEST VIRGINIA								
1	Mollohan	N	N	Y	Y	Y	N	Y
2	Wise	N	N	Y	Y	Y	N	Y
3	Rahall	N	N	Y	Y	Y	N	Y
WISCONSIN								
1	**Neumann**	Y	Y	Y	Y	Y	Y	N
2	**Klug**	?	?	?	Y	Y	Y	Y
3	Kind	Y	Y	N	Y	Y	N	Y
4	Kleczka	N	N	Y	Y	Y	N	Y
5	Barrett	Y	N	N	Y	Y	N	Y
6	**Petri**	N	N	Y	Y	Y	Y	?
7	Obey	Y	Y	N	Y	Y	N	Y
8	Johnson	N	N	Y	Y	Y	N	Y
9	**Sensenbrenner**	N	Y	N	Y	Y	Y	N
WYOMING								
AL	**Cubin**	N	N	N	Y	Y	Y	N

Southern states - Ala., Ark., Fla., Ga., Ky., La., Miss., N.C., Okla., S.C., Tenn., Texas, Va.

House Votes 104, 105, 106, 107, 108, 109, 110

Key

- Y Voted for (yea).
- # Paired for.
- + Announced for.
- N Voted against (nay).
- X Paired against.
- − Announced against.
- P Voted "present."
- C Voted "present" to avoid possible conflict of interest.
- ? Did not vote or otherwise make a position known.

Democrats **Republicans** *Independent*

104. HR 1252. Limits on Federal Judges' Power/Restricting Disclosure. Jackson-Lee, D-Texas, amendment to permit a federal court to enter an order restricting the disclosure of information obtained through discovery or an order restricting access to court records in a civil case only after making a finding of fact that such an order would not restrict the disclosure of information that is relevant to protecting the public health or safety. Rejected 177-242: R 9-211; D 167-31 (ND 129-18, SD 38-13); I 1-0. April 23, 1998.

105. HR 1252. Limits on Federal Judges' Power/Prisoner Release. DeLay, R-Texas, amendment to prohibit federal judges from allowing the early release from prison of any prisoner on the basis of prison conditions. Adopted 367-52: R 220-2; D 147-49 (ND 104-42, SD 43-7); I 0-1. April 23, 1998.

106. HR 1252. Limits on Federal Judges' Power/Parent Testimony. Lofgren, D-Calif., amendment to establish a privilege under the Federal Rules of Evidence to prevent parents and children from being compelled to testify against one another. Rejected 162-256: R 10-211; D 151-45 (ND 118-29, SD 33-16); I 1-0. April 23, 1998.

107. HR 1252. Limits on Federal Judges' Power/Jurisdiction. Conyers, D-Mich., amendment to provide for jurisdiction, service of process and discovery in civil actions brought against defendants located outside the United States. Rejected 200-216: R 18-201; D 181-15 (ND 142-4, SD 39-11); I 1-0. April 23, 1998.

108. HR 1252. Limits on Federal Judges' Power/Disburse Funds. Aderholt, R-Ala., amendment to prohibit federal judges from ordering state and local governments to disburse any funds to enforce a federal or state law. Rejected 174-236: R 162-53; D 12-182 (ND 4-140, SD 8-42); I 0-1. April 23, 1998. (Subsequently, the bill passed by voice vote).

109. HR 3579. Fiscal 1998 Supplemental Appropriations/Motion to Instruct. Obey, D-Wis., motion to instruct the House conferees to support the Clinton administration's request for $18 billion for the International Monetary Fund. Rejected 186-222: R 22-193; D 164-28 (ND 123-20, SD 41-8); I 0-1. April 23, 1998.

110. H Con Res 218. Cease Fire in Afghanistan/Adoption. Bereuter, R-Neb., motion to suspend the rules and adopt the concurrent resolution to express the sense of Congress to call upon all warring factions and national powers in Afghanistan to participate in a dialogue and to actively cooperate in the acceleration of endeavors for peace. Motion agreed to 391-1: R 205-1; D 185-0 (ND 136-0, SD 49-0); I 1-0. April 28, 1998. A two-thirds majority of those present and voting (262 in this case) is required for adoption under suspension of the rules.

	104	105	106	107	108	109	110
ALABAMA							
1 Callahan	N	Y	N	N	Y	N	Y
2 Everett	N	Y	N	N	Y	N	Y
3 *Riley*	N	Y	N	N	Y	N	+
4 *Aderholt*	N	Y	N	N	Y	N	Y
5 Cramer	N	Y	N	N	Y	Y	Y
6 Bachus	N	Y	N	N	Y	N	Y
7 Hilliard	Y	N	Y	N	N	Y	Y
ALASKA							
AL *Young*	N	Y	N	N	Y	N	Y
ARIZONA							
1 *Salmon*	N	Y	N	N	Y	Y	N
2 Pastor	Y	Y	Y	Y	N	Y	Y
3 *Stump*	N	Y	N	N	Y	N	Y
4 *Shadegg*	N	Y	N	N	Y	N	Y
5 *Kolbe*	N	Y	N	Y	Y	Y	Y
6 *Hayworth*	N	Y	N	N	Y	N	Y
ARKANSAS							
1 Berry	Y	Y	Y	Y	N	N	Y
2 Snyder	Y	N	Y	Y	N	Y	Y
3 *Hutchinson*	N	Y	N	N	Y	N	Y
4 *Dickey*	N	Y	N	N	Y	N	Y
CALIFORNIA							
1 Riggs	N	Y	N	?	?	N	?
2 *Herger*	N	Y	N	N	Y	N	Y
3 Fazio	Y	Y	Y	Y	N	Y	Y
4 *Doolittle*	N	Y	N	N	Y	N	Y
5 Matsui	N	Y	Y	Y	N	Y	Y
6 Woolsey	Y	Y	Y	Y	N	Y	Y
7 Miller	Y	N	Y	Y	N	N	Y
8 Pelosi	Y	N	Y	Y	N	Y	Y
9 Lee	Y	N	Y	Y	N	Y	Y
10 Tauscher	Y	Y	Y	Y	N	Y	Y
11 *Pombo*	N	Y	N	N	Y	N	Y
12 Lantos	Y	Y	Y	Y	N	Y	Y
13 Stark	Y	N	Y	Y	N	?	Y
14 Eshoo	Y	Y	Y	Y	N	Y	+
15 *Campbell*	N	Y	N	N	N	N	Y
16 Lofgren	N	Y	Y	Y	N	Y	+
17 Farr	Y	Y	Y	Y	N	Y	Y
18 Condit	N	Y	N	Y	Y	N	Y
19 *Radanovich*	N	Y	N	N	Y	N	Y
20 Dooley	N	Y	Y	Y	N	Y	Y
21 *Thomas*	N	Y	N	N	Y	N	Y
22 Capps, L.	Y	Y	Y	Y	N	Y	Y
23 *Gallegly*	N	Y	N	N	Y	N	Y
24 Sherman	Y	Y	N	Y	N	Y	Y
25 *McKeon*	N	Y	N	N	Y	N	Y
26 Berman	Y	Y	Y	Y	N	Y	Y
27 *Rogan*	N	Y	N	N	Y	N	Y
28 *Dreier*	N	Y	N	N	Y	N	Y
29 Waxman	Y	N	Y	Y	N	Y	Y
30 Becerra	Y	Y	Y	Y	N	Y	Y
31 Martinez	Y	N	Y	N	Y	Y	?
32 Dixon	?	?	?	?	?	?	?
33 Roybal-Allard	Y	Y	Y	Y	N	Y	Y
34 Torres	Y	Y	Y	Y	N	Y	Y
35 Waters	Y	Y	Y	Y	N	Y	Y
36 Harman	Y	Y	Y	Y	N	Y	+
37 Millender-McD.	Y	N	Y	N	Y	N	+

	104	105	106	107	108	109	110
38 *Horn*	Y	Y	N	N	N	N	Y
39 *Royce*	N	Y	N	N	Y	N	Y
40 *Lewis*	N	Y	N	N	Y	N	Y
41 *Kim*	N	Y	N	N	Y	N	Y
42 Brown	Y	N	Y	Y	N	Y	Y
43 *Calvert*	N	Y	N	N	Y	N	Y
44 *Bono, M.*	N	Y	N	N	Y	N	Y
45 *Rohrabacher*	Y	Y	N	N	Y	N	Y
46 Sanchez	Y	Y	Y	N	Y	N	Y
47 *Cox*	N	Y	N	N	?	N	Y
48 *Packard*	N	Y	N	N	Y	N	Y
49 *Bilbray*	N	Y	N	N	N	N	?
50 Filner	Y	N	Y	N	Y	N	Y
51 *Cunningham*	N	Y	N	N	Y	N	Y
52 *Hunter*	N	Y	N	Y	Y	N	Y
COLORADO							
1 DeGette	Y	N	Y	N	Y	Y	Y
2 Skaggs	N	N	N	Y	N	Y	Y
3 *McInnis*	N	Y	N	N	Y	N	Y
4 *Schaffer*	N	Y	N	N	Y	N	Y
5 *Hefley*	N	Y	N	N	Y	N	Y
6 *Schaefer*	N	Y	N	N	Y	N	Y
CONNECTICUT							
1 Kennelly	Y	Y	Y	Y	N	Y	Y
2 Gejdenson	Y	Y	Y	Y	N	Y	Y
3 DeLauro	Y	Y	Y	Y	N	Y	Y
4 *Shays*	Y	Y	N	N	N	Y	Y
5 Maloney	Y	Y	Y	Y	N	Y	Y
6 *Johnson*	N	Y	N	N	N	Y	Y
DELAWARE							
AL *Castle*	N	Y	N	N	N	Y	Y
FLORIDA							
1 *Scarborough*	N	Y	N	N	Y	N	Y
2 Boyd	N	Y	N	N	Y	Y	Y
3 Brown	Y	Y	Y	Y	N	Y	Y
4 *Fowler*	N	Y	N	N	Y	N	Y
5 Thurman	Y	Y	N	Y	N	Y	Y
6 *Stearns*	N	Y	N	N	Y	N	Y
7 *Mica*	N	Y	N	N	Y	N	Y
8 *McCollum*	N	Y	N	N	Y	N	Y
9 *Bilirakis*	N	Y	N	N	Y	N	Y
10 *Young*	N	Y	N	N	Y	N	Y
11 Davis	Y	Y	+	Y	N	Y	Y
12 *Canady*	N	Y	N	N	Y	N	Y
13 *Miller*	?	?	?	?	?	?	?
14 *Goss*	N	Y	N	N	Y	N	Y
15 *Weldon*	N	Y	N	N	Y	N	Y
16 *Foley*	N	Y	N	N	Y	N	?
17 Meek	Y	?	?	?	?	?	?
18 *Ros-Lehtinen*	N	Y	N	N	N	N	Y
19 Wexler	Y	Y	N	N	N	Y	Y
20 Deutsch	Y	Y	Y	Y	N	Y	Y
21 *Diaz-Balart*	N	Y	N	N	Y	N	Y
22 *Shaw*	N	Y	N	N	Y	N	Y
23 Hastings	?	?	?	?	?	?	Y
GEORGIA							
1 *Kingston*	N	Y	N	N	Y	N	Y
2 Bishop	Y	Y	Y	Y	N	N	Y
3 *Collins*	N	Y	N	N	Y	N	Y
4 *McKinney*	Y	Y	Y	Y	N	N	Y
5 Lewis	Y	N	Y	Y	N	Y	Y
6 *Gingrich*							
7 *Barr*	N	Y	N	N	Y	N	?
8 *Chambliss*	N	Y	N	N	Y	N	Y
9 *Deal*	N	Y	N	N	Y	N	Y
10 *Norwood*	N	Y	N	N	Y	N	Y
11 *Linder*	N	Y	N	N	Y	N	Y
HAWAII							
1 Abercrombie	Y	Y	Y	Y	N	Y	Y
2 Mink	Y	Y	Y	Y	N	Y	Y
IDAHO							
1 *Chenoweth*	N	Y	N	N	Y	N	Y
2 *Crapo*	N	Y	N	N	Y	N	Y
ILLINOIS							
1 Rush	Y	N	Y	N	Y	Y	Y
2 Jackson	Y	N	Y	N	Y	Y	Y
3 Lipinski	Y	Y	N	N	N	Y	Y
4 Gutierrez	?	Y	Y	Y	N	Y	Y
5 Blagojevich	Y	Y	Y	Y	N	Y	Y
6 *Hyde*	N	Y	N	N	Y	N	?
7 Davis	Y	N	Y	Y	?	Y	Y
8 *Crane*	N	N	N	N	Y	N	Y
9 Yates	Y	N	Y	Y	N	?	Y
10 *Porter*	N	Y	N	N	N	Y	Y
11 *Weller*	N	Y	N	N	Y	N	Y
12 Costello	Y	Y	Y	N	N	Y	Y

ND Northern Democrats SD Southern Democrats

	104	105	106	107	108	109	110
13 ***Fawell***	N	N	N	N	N	Y	Y
14 ***Hastert***	N	Y	N	N	Y	?	Y
15 ***Ewing***	N	Y	N	N	N	N	Y
16 ***Manzullo***	N	Y	N	N	Y	N	Y
17 Evans	Y	N	Y	Y	N	N	Y
18 ***LaHood***	N	Y	N	N	N	Y	Y
19 Poshard	Y	Y	Y	?	?	?	?
20 ***Shimkus***	N	Y	N	N	Y	N	Y
INDIANA							
1 Visclosky	Y	Y	Y	Y	N	Y	Y
2 ***McIntosh***	N	Y	N	N	Y	N	Y
3 Roemer	N	Y	N	Y	N	Y	Y
4 ***Souder***	N	Y	N	N	?	N	Y
5 ***Buyer***	N	Y	N	N	?	N	Y
6 ***Burton***	N	Y	N	N	Y	N	Y
7 ***Pease***	N	Y	N	N	Y	N	Y
8 ***Hostettler***	N	Y	N	N	Y	N	Y
9 Hamilton	N	Y	N	Y	N	Y	Y
10 Carson	Y	N	Y	Y	N	N	Y
IOWA							
1 ***Leach***	Y	Y	Y	N	N	Y	Y
2 ***Nussle***	N	Y	N	N	Y	Y	Y
3 Boswell	Y	Y	N	Y	N	Y	Y
4 ***Ganske***	N	Y	N	N	N	N	?
5 ***Latham***	N	Y	N	N	Y	Y	Y
KANSAS							
1 ***Moran***	N	Y	N	N	Y	N	Y
2 ***Ryun***	N	Y	N	N	Y	N	+
3 ***Snowbarger***	N	Y	?	N	Y	N	Y
4 ***Tiahrt***	N	Y	N	N	Y	N	Y
KENTUCKY							
1 ***Whitfield***	N	Y	N	N	N	N	Y
2 ***Lewis***	N	Y	N	N	Y	N	Y
3 ***Northup***	N	Y	N	N	Y	N	Y
4 ***Bunning***	N	Y	N	N	Y	N	Y
5 ***Rogers***	N	Y	N	N	Y	N	Y
6 Baesler	Y	Y	Y	Y	N	Y	?
LOUISIANA							
1 ***Livingston***	N	Y	N	N	Y	N	Y
2 Jefferson	Y	Y	Y	Y	N	?	?
3 ***Tauzin***	N	Y	N	N	Y	N	Y
4 ***McCrery***	?	Y	N	N	Y	N	Y
5 ***Cooksey***	N	Y	N	N	Y	N	Y
6 ***Baker***	N	Y	N	N	Y	N	Y
7 John	N	Y	N	Y	N	Y	Y
MAINE							
1 Allen	Y	Y	N	Y	N	Y	Y
2 Baldacci	Y	Y	Y	Y	N	Y	Y
MARYLAND							
1 ***Gilchrest***	N	Y	N	N	N	Y	Y
2 ***Ehrlich***	N	Y	N	Y	Y	N	Y
3 Cardin	Y	Y	N	Y	N	Y	Y
4 Wynn	Y	Y	Y	Y	N	Y	Y
5 Hoyer	Y	Y	N	Y	N	Y	Y
6 ***Bartlett***	N	Y	N	N	Y	N	Y
7 Cummings	Y	Y	Y	Y	N	Y	Y
8 ***Morella***	Y	Y	N	Y	N	?	Y
MASSACHUSETTS							
1 Olver	Y	N	Y	Y	N	Y	Y
2 Neal	Y	Y	Y	Y	N	Y	Y
3 McGovern	Y	Y	N	Y	N	Y	Y
4 Frank	Y	N	N	Y	N	Y	Y
5 Meehan	Y	Y	N	Y	N	Y	Y
6 Tierney	Y	N	N	Y	N	Y	Y
7 Markey	Y	Y	Y	Y	N	Y	Y
8 Kennedy	Y	N	Y	Y	N	Y	Y
9 Moakley	Y	Y	N	Y	N	Y	Y
10 Delahunt	Y	N	Y	Y	N	Y	Y
MICHIGAN							
1 Stupak	Y	Y	Y	Y	N	Y	Y
2 ***Hoekstra***	N	Y	N	N	Y	N	Y
3 ***Ehlers***	N	Y	N	N	N	N	Y
4 ***Camp***	N	Y	N	N	–	N	Y
5 Barcia	Y	Y	Y	Y	N	N	Y
6 ***Upton***	N	Y	N	N	N	N	Y
7 ***Smith***	N	Y	N	Y	Y	N	Y
8 Stabenow	Y	Y	Y	Y	N	Y	Y
9 Kildee	Y	Y	Y	Y	N	Y	Y
10 Bonior	Y	N	Y	Y	N	Y	Y
11 ***Knollenberg***	N	Y	N	N	Y	N	Y
12 Levin	Y	Y	N	Y	N	Y	Y
13 Rivers	Y	Y	N	Y	N	Y	Y
14 Conyers	Y	N	Y	Y	N	N	Y
15 Kilpatrick	Y	N	Y	Y	N	Y	Y
16 Dingell	Y	Y	N	Y	N	Y	Y
MINNESOTA							
1 ***Gutknecht***	N	Y	N	N	N	N	Y
2 Minge	Y	Y	Y	Y	N	Y	Y
3 ***Ramstad***	N	Y	N	N	N	N	Y
4 Vento	Y	Y	Y	Y	N	Y	Y
5 Sabo	Y	N	Y	Y	N	Y	Y
6 Luther	Y	Y	Y	Y	N	Y	Y
7 Peterson	N	Y	Y	N	Y	N	Y
8 Oberstar	Y	N	Y	Y	N	Y	Y
MISSISSIPPI							
1 ***Wicker***	N	Y	N	N	Y	N	Y
2 Thompson	Y	N	Y	Y	N	N	Y
3 ***Pickering***	N	Y	N	N	Y	N	Y
4 ***Parker***	N	Y	N	N	Y	N	Y
5 Taylor	N	Y	Y	Y	N	N	Y
MISSOURI							
1 Clay	?	?	?	?	?	?	Y
2 ***Talent***	N	Y	N	N	Y	N	Y
3 Gephardt	Y	Y	Y	Y	N	Y	Y
4 Skelton	N	Y	Y	Y	N	Y	Y
5 McCarthy	Y	Y	N	Y	N	Y	Y
6 Danner	N	Y	N	Y	Y	N	Y
7 ***Blunt***	N	Y	N	N	Y	N	?
8 ***Emerson***	Y	Y	N	N	Y	N	Y
9 ***Hulshof***	N	Y	N	N	Y	N	Y
MONTANA							
AL ***Hill***	N	Y	N	N	Y	N	Y
NEBRASKA							
1 ***Bereuter***	Y	Y	N	N	Y	Y	Y
2 ***Christensen***	N	Y	N	N	Y	Y	?
3 ***Barrett***	N	Y	N	N	Y	Y	Y
NEVADA							
1 ***Ensign***	N	Y	N	Y	Y	N	?
2 ***Gibbons***	N	Y	N	N	Y	N	Y
NEW HAMPSHIRE							
1 ***Sununu***	N	Y	N	N	N	N	Y
2 ***Bass***	N	Y	N	N	N	N	Y
NEW JERSEY							
1 Andrews	Y	Y	Y	Y	N	Y	Y
2 ***LoBiondo***	N	Y	Y	Y	N	N	Y
3 ***Saxton***	N	Y	N	N	N	N	Y
4 ***Smith***	N	Y	N	N	N	N	Y
5 ***Roukema***	N	Y	N	N	N	N	Y
6 Pallone	Y	Y	Y	Y	N	Y	Y
7 ***Franks***	N	Y	N	Y	N	N	Y
8 Pascrell	Y	Y	Y	Y	N	Y	Y
9 Rothman	N	Y	Y	N	N	Y	Y
10 Payne	Y	N	Y	Y	N	Y	Y
11 ***Frelinghuysen***	N	Y	N	N	N	N	Y
12 ***Pappas***	N	Y	N	Y	N	N	Y
13 Menendez	Y	Y	Y	Y	N	Y	Y
NEW MEXICO							
1 Vacant							
2 ***Skeen***	N	Y	N	N	Y	Y	Y
3 ***Redmond***	N	Y	N	N	Y	N	Y
NEW YORK							
1 ***Forbes***	N	Y	N	N	N	?	Y
2 ***Lazio***	N	Y	N	N	N	Y	Y
3 ***King***	N	Y	N	N	Y	N	Y
4 McCarthy	Y	Y	Y	Y	N	Y	Y
5 Ackerman	Y	Y	Y	Y	N	Y	Y
6 Meeks	Y	N	Y	Y	N	Y	+
7 Manton	Y	Y	N	Y	N	Y	Y
8 Nadler	Y	Y	Y	Y	N	Y	Y
9 Schumer	Y	Y	Y	Y	N	Y	Y
10 Towns	Y	N	N	Y	N	Y	?
11 Owens	Y	N	Y	Y	N	Y	Y
12 Velázquez	Y	N	Y	Y	N	Y	Y
13 ***Fossella***	N	Y	N	N	N	Y	Y
14 Maloney	N	Y	Y	Y	N	Y	?
15 Rangel	Y	N	Y	Y	N	Y	?
16 Serrano	Y	N	Y	Y	N	Y	?
17 Engel	Y	Y	Y	Y	N	Y	+
18 Lowey	Y	Y	Y	Y	N	Y	Y
19 ***Kelly***	N	Y	N	N	N	N	Y
20 ***Gilman***	N	Y	N	N	N	Y	Y
21 McNulty	Y	Y	Y	Y	N	Y	Y
22 ***Solomon***	N	Y	N	N	Y	N	Y
23 ***Boehlert***	N	Y	N	N	N	N	Y
24 ***McHugh***	N	Y	N	N	Y	N	Y
25 ***Walsh***	N	Y	N	N	N	N	Y
26 Hinchey	Y	N	Y	Y	N	Y	Y
27 ***Paxon***	?	?	?	?	?	?	Y
28 Slaughter	Y	Y	Y	Y	N	Y	Y
29 LaFalce	Y	Y	Y	Y	N	Y	Y
30 ***Quinn***	N	Y	N	N	N	N	Y
31 ***Houghton***	N	Y	N	N	N	Y	Y
NORTH CAROLINA							
1 Clayton	Y	Y	Y	Y	N	Y	Y
2 Etheridge	Y	Y	Y	Y	N	Y	Y
3 ***Jones***	N	Y	N	N	Y	N	Y
4 Price	Y	Y	Y	Y	N	Y	Y
5 ***Burr***	N	Y	N	N	Y	?	Y
6 ***Coble***	N	Y	N	?	?	?	Y
7 McIntyre	Y	Y	N	Y	Y	Y	Y
8 Hefner	Y	Y	Y	Y	Y	Y	Y
9 ***Myrick***	N	Y	N	N	Y	N	Y
10 ***Ballenger***	N	Y	N	Y	Y	N	Y
11 ***Taylor***	N	Y	N	N	Y	N	+
12 Watt	N	N	Y	Y	N	Y	Y
NORTH DAKOTA							
AL Pomeroy	N	Y	Y	Y	N	Y	Y
OHIO							
1 ***Chabot***	N	Y	N	Y	Y	N	Y
2 ***Portman***	N	Y	N	N	Y	N	Y
3 Hall	Y	Y	Y	Y	N	Y	Y
4 ***Oxley***	N	Y	N	N	N	N	Y
5 ***Gillmor***	N	Y	N	N	N	N	Y
6 Strickland	Y	Y	Y	Y	N	N	Y
7 ***Hobson***	N	Y	N	N	N	N	Y
8 ***Boehner***	N	Y	N	N	Y	?	Y
9 Kaptur	Y	Y	Y	Y	?	?	Y
10 Kucinich	Y	Y	N	Y	N	N	Y
11 Stokes	Y	N	Y	Y	N	Y	Y
12 ***Kasich***	N	Y	N	N	Y	N	Y
13 Brown	Y	Y	Y	Y	N	Y	Y
14 Sawyer	Y	Y	N	Y	N	Y	Y
15 ***Pryce***	N	Y	N	N	N	N	Y
16 ***Regula***	N	Y	N	N	N	N	Y
17 Traficant	N	Y	Y	Y	Y	N	Y
18 ***Ney***	N	Y	N	N	N	Y	Y
19 ***LaTourette***	N	Y	N	N	N	Y	Y
OKLAHOMA							
1 ***Largent***	N	Y	N	N	Y	N	Y
2 ***Coburn***	N	Y	N	N	Y	N	Y
3 ***Watkins***	N	Y	N	N	Y	N	Y
4 ***Watts***	N	Y	N	N	Y	N	Y
5 ***Istook***	?	?	?	?	?	–	Y
6 ***Lucas***	N	Y	N	N	Y	N	Y
OREGON							
1 Furse	Y	N	Y	Y	N	Y	Y
2 ***Smith***	N	Y	N	N	Y	N	?
3 Blumenauer	Y	Y	Y	Y	N	Y	Y
4 DeFazio	Y	Y	Y	Y	N	N	Y
5 Hooley	Y	Y	Y	Y	N	Y	Y
PENNSYLVANIA							
1 Vacant							
2 Fattah	Y	?	?	?	?	?	Y
3 Borski	Y	Y	Y	Y	N	Y	Y
4 Klink	Y	Y	Y	Y	N	N	Y
5 ***Peterson***	N	Y	N	N	Y	N	Y
6 Holden	Y	Y	N	Y	N	Y	Y
7 ***Weldon***	N	Y	N	N	N	N	Y
8 ***Greenwood***	N	Y	N	N	N	N	?
9 ***Shuster***	N	Y	N	N	Y	N	Y
10 ***McDade***	N	Y	Y	N	N	N	Y
11 Kanjorski	N	Y	Y	Y	N	Y	Y
12 Murtha	N	Y	Y	N	N	Y	Y
13 ***Fox***	Y	Y	Y	?	?	?	Y
14 Coyne	Y	Y	Y	Y	N	Y	Y
15 McHale	Y	Y	N	Y	N	Y	Y
16 ***Pitts***	N	Y	N	N	Y	N	Y
17 ***Gekas***	N	Y	N	N	Y	N	Y
18 Doyle	N	Y	Y	Y	N	N	Y
19 ***Goodling***	N	Y	N	N	Y	N	Y
20 Mascara	Y	Y	Y	Y	N	Y	Y
21 ***English***	N	Y	N	Y	N	N	Y
RHODE ISLAND							
1 Kennedy	Y	N	Y	Y	N	Y	Y
2 Weygand	Y	Y	Y	Y	N	Y	Y
SOUTH CAROLINA							
1 ***Sanford***	N	Y	Y	N	Y	N	Y
2 ***Spence***	N	Y	N	N	Y	N	Y
3 ***Graham***	N	Y	N	N	Y	N	Y
4 ***Inglis***	N	Y	N	N	Y	N	?
5 Spratt	Y	?	?	Y	N	Y	Y
6 Clyburn	Y	N	Y	Y	N	Y	Y
SOUTH DAKOTA							
AL ***Thune***	N	Y	N	N	Y	N	Y
TENNESSEE							
1 ***Jenkins***	N	Y	N	N	Y	N	Y
2 ***Duncan***	N	Y	N	Y	Y	N	Y
3 ***Wamp***	N	Y	N	Y	Y	N	Y
4 ***Hilleary***	N	Y	N	Y	Y	N	Y
5 Clement	Y	Y	Y	Y	N	Y	Y
6 Gordon	N	Y	Y	N	N	Y	Y
7 ***Bryant***	N	Y	N	N	Y	N	Y
8 Tanner	?	?	?	?	?	?	?
9 Ford	Y	Y	Y	Y	N	Y	Y
TEXAS							
1 Sandlin	N	Y	Y	Y	N	Y	?
2 Turner	N	Y	N	N	N	Y	Y
3 ***Johnson, Sam***	N	Y	N	N	Y	N	Y
4 Hall	?	Y	N	N	Y	N	Y
5 ***Sessions***	N	Y	N	N	Y	N	Y
6 ***Barton***	N	Y	N	N	Y	N	Y
7 ***Archer***	N	Y	N	N	Y	N	Y
8 ***Brady***	N	Y	N	N	Y	N	Y
9 Lampson	Y	Y	Y	Y	N	Y	Y
10 Doggett	Y	Y	N	Y	N	Y	Y
11 Edwards	Y	Y	Y	Y	N	Y	Y
12 ***Granger***	N	Y	N	N	Y	N	Y
13 ***Thornberry***	N	Y	N	N	Y	N	Y
14 ***Paul***	N	Y	Y	N	Y	N	N
15 Hinojosa	Y	Y	Y	+	–	Y	Y
16 Reyes	Y	Y	Y	Y	N	?	Y
17 Stenholm	N	Y	N	N	Y	Y	Y
18 Jackson-Lee	Y	N	Y	Y	N	Y	Y
19 ***Combest***	N	Y	N	N	Y	N	Y
20 Gonzalez	?	?	?	?	?	?	?
21 ***Smith***	N	Y	N	N	Y	N	Y
22 ***DeLay***	N	Y	N	N	Y	N	Y
23 ***Bonilla***	N	Y	N	N	Y	N	Y
24 Frost	Y	Y	Y	Y	N	Y	Y
25 Bentsen	Y	Y	N	Y	N	Y	Y
26 ***Armey***	N	Y	N	N	Y	N	Y
27 Ortiz	Y	Y	Y	Y	N	N	Y
28 Rodriguez	Y	Y	Y	Y	N	Y	Y
29 Green	Y	Y	Y	Y	N	Y	Y
30 Johnson, E.B.	Y	Y	Y	Y	N	Y	Y
UTAH							
1 ***Hansen***	N	Y	N	N	Y	N	Y
2 ***Cook***	?	Y	N	N	Y	N	?
3 ***Cannon***	N	Y	N	N	Y	N	Y
VERMONT							
AL *Sanders*	Y	N	Y	Y	N	N	Y
VIRGINIA							
1 ***Bateman***	–	–	–	+	+	–	+
2 Pickett	N	Y	N	N	Y	Y	Y
3 Scott	Y	N	N	Y	N	Y	Y
4 Sisisky	N	Y	N	N	Y	Y	Y
5 Goode	N	Y	N	N	Y	N	?
6 ***Goodlatte***	N	Y	N	N	Y	N	Y
7 ***Bliley***	N	Y	N	N	Y	N	Y
8 Moran	Y	Y	N	Y	N	Y	Y
9 Boucher	Y	Y	Y	Y	N	Y	Y
10 ***Wolf***	N	Y	N	N	Y	N	Y
11 ***Davis***	N	Y	N	N	N	Y	Y
WASHINGTON							
1 ***White***	N	Y	N	N	N	N	?
2 ***Metcalf***	N	Y	N	N	Y	N	Y
3 ***Smith, Linda***	N	Y	N	N	Y	N	Y
4 ***Hastings***	N	Y	N	N	Y	N	Y
5 ***Nethercutt***	N	Y	N	N	Y	N	Y
6 Dicks	N	Y	N	Y	N	Y	Y
7 McDermott	Y	N	Y	Y	N	Y	Y
8 ***Dunn***	N	Y	N	N	Y	N	Y
9 Smith, Adam	Y	Y	N	Y	N	Y	Y
WEST VIRGINIA							
1 Mollohan	Y	Y	Y	Y	N	N	Y
2 Wise	Y	Y	N	Y	N	Y	Y
3 Rahall	Y	Y	Y	Y	N	N	Y
WISCONSIN							
1 ***Neumann***	N	Y	N	N	Y	N	Y
2 ***Klug***	N	Y	N	N	N	N	Y
3 Kind	Y	Y	Y	Y	N	Y	Y
4 Kleczka	Y	Y	N	Y	N	Y	Y
5 Barrett	Y	N	N	Y	N	Y	Y
6 ***Petri***	N	Y	N	N	N	N	Y
7 Obey	Y	?	Y	Y	N	Y	Y
8 Johnson	Y	Y	Y	Y	N	Y	Y
9 ***Sensenbrenner***	N	Y	N	N	Y	N	Y
WYOMING							
AL ***Cubin***	N	Y	N	N	Y	N	Y

Southern states - Ala., Ark., Fla., Ga., Ky., La., Miss., N.C., Okla., S.C., Tenn., Texas, Va.

House Votes 111, 112, 113, 114, 115, 116, 117

111. S Con Res 37. International Character of Little League Baseball, Inc/Adoption. Smith, R-N.J., motion to suspend the rules and adopt the concurrent resolution to express the sense of Congress that Little League Baseball, Inc. was established to support and develop Little League Baseball worldwide. Motion agreed to 398-0: R 210-0; D 187-0 (ND 137-0, SD 50-0); I 1-0. April 28, 1998. A two-thirds majority of those present and voting (266 in this case) is required for adoption under suspension of the rules.

112. H J Res 102. 50th Anniversary of Modern State of Israel/Adoption. Gilman, R-N.Y., motion to suspend the rules and adopt the joint resolution to commend the people of Israel for their achievements in building a new state and a pluralistic democratic society in the Middle East, and reaffirm the bonds of friendship which have existed between the United States and Israel for the past half-century. Motion agreed to 402-0: R 211-0; D 190-0 (ND 139-0, SD 51-0); I 1-0. April 28, 1998. A two-thirds majority of those present and voting (268 in this case) is required for adoption under suspension of the rules.

113. HR 3717. Needle Distribution Programs/Recommit. Pelosi, D-Calif., motion to recommit the bill to the Commerce Committee with instructions to report it back with an amendment to allow lifting the ban on federal funds for needle distribution in cases where state or municipal health officials certify that needle distribution reduces the spread of AIDS, does not increase illegal drug use and is acceptable to the locality involved. Motion rejected 149-277: R 7-216; D 141-61 (ND 115-34, SD 26-27); I 1-0. April 29, 1998.

114. HR 3717. Needle Distribution Programs/Passage. Passage of the bill to prohibit the use of federal funds for needle distribution programs. Passed 287-140: R 213-11; D 74-128 (ND 42-107, SD 32-21); I 0-1. April 29, 1998. A "nay" was a vote in support of the president's position.

115. HR 3546. National Dialogue on Social Security/Recommit. Pomeroy, D-N.D., motion to recommit the bill to the Ways and Means Committee with instructions to report it back with an amendment to reserve the budget surplus until Congress has taken comprehensive action to assure that Social Security is solvent for the future. Motion rejected 197-223: R 0-223; D 196-0 (ND 144-0, SD 52-0); I 1-0. April 29, 1998.

116. HR 3546. National Dialogue on Social Security/Passage. Passage of the bill to create an eight-member bipartisan panel to recommend long-range changes to keep Social Security from going bankrupt, and direct the president and Congress to convene a national dialogue on the future of Social Security with help from members of private public interest groups. Passed 413-8: R 222-1; D 191-6 (ND 139-6, SD 52-0); I 0-1. April 29, 1998.

117. S 1502. District of Columbia Student Scholarships/Rule. Adoption of the rule (H Res 413) to provide for House floor consideration of the bill to create a $7 million school scholarship program for low-income elementary and secondary students living in Washington, D.C. Adopted 224-199: R 223-1; D 1-197 (ND 1-147, SD 0-50); I 0-1. April 30, 1998.

Key

Y	Voted for (yea).
#	Paired for.
+	Announced for.
N	Voted against (nay).
X	Paired against.
–	Announced against.
P	Voted "present."
C	Voted "present" to avoid possible conflict of interest.
?	Did not vote or otherwise make a position known.

Democrats **Republicans** *Independent*

	111	112	113	114	115	116	117
ALABAMA							
1 Callahan	N	Y	N	N	Y	N	Y
2 Everett	N	Y	N	N	Y	N	Y
3 Riley	N	Y	N	N	Y	N	+
4 Aderholt	N	Y	N	N	Y	N	Y
5 Cramer	N	Y	N	N	Y	Y	Y
6 Bachus	N	Y	N	N	Y	N	Y
7 Hilliard	Y	N	Y	N	N	Y	Y
ALASKA							
AL Young	N	Y	N	N	Y	N	Y
ARIZONA							
1 Salmon	N	Y	N	Y	Y	N	Y
2 Pastor	Y	Y	Y	Y	N	Y	Y
3 Stump	N	Y	N	N	Y	N	Y
4 Shadegg	N	Y	N	N	Y	N	Y
5 Kolbe	N	Y	N	N	Y	Y	Y
6 Hayworth	N	Y	N	N	Y	N	Y
ARKANSAS							
1 Berry	Y	Y	Y	Y	N	N	Y
2 Snyder	N	Y	N	Y	N	Y	Y
3 Hutchinson	Y	Y	N	N	Y	N	Y
4 Dickey	N	Y	N	N	Y	N	Y
CALIFORNIA							
1 Riggs	N	Y	?	?	N	?	
2 Herger	N	Y	N	N	Y	N	Y
3 Fazio	Y	Y	Y	Y	N	Y	Y
4 Doolittle	N	Y	N	N	Y	N	Y
5 Matsui	N	Y	Y	Y	N	Y	N
6 Woolsey	Y	Y	Y	Y	N	Y	Y
7 Miller	Y	Y	Y	Y	N	Y	N
8 Pelosi	Y	N	Y	Y	N	Y	N
9 Lee	Y	Y	Y	N	Y	Y	Y
10 Tauscher	Y	Y	Y	Y	N	Y	Y
11 Pombo	N	Y	N	N	Y	N	Y
12 Lantos	Y	Y	Y	Y	N	Y	Y
13 Stark	Y	N	Y	N	Y	?	Y
14 Eshoo	Y	Y	Y	Y	N	Y	N
15 Campbell	Y	N	Y	N	N	N	Y
16 Lofgren	N	Y	Y	Y	Y	Y	+
17 Farr	Y	Y	Y	Y	N	Y	Y
18 Condit	N	Y	Y	Y	Y	N	Y
19 Radanovich	N	Y	N	N	N	Y	N
20 Dooley	N	Y	Y	Y	N	N	Y
21 Thomas	N	Y	N	N	Y	N	Y
22 Capps, L.	Y	Y	Y	Y	N	Y	Y
23 Gallegly	N	Y	N	N	Y	N	Y
24 Sherman	Y	Y	Y	Y	N	Y	Y
25 McKeon	N	Y	N	N	Y	N	Y
26 Berman	Y	Y	Y	Y	N	Y	Y
27 Rogan	N	Y	N	N	Y	N	Y
28 Dreier	N	Y	N	N	Y	N	Y
29 Waxman	Y	Y	Y	Y	N	Y	Y
30 Becerra	Y	Y	Y	Y	N	Y	Y
31 Martinez	Y	N	Y	Y	N	Y	?
32 Dixon	?	?	?	?	?	?	?
33 Roybal-Allard	Y	Y	Y	Y	N	Y	Y
34 Torres	Y	Y	Y	Y	N	Y	Y
35 Waters	Y	Y	Y	Y	N	Y	Y
36 Harman	Y	Y	Y	Y	N	Y	+
37 Millender-McD.	Y	N	Y	N	Y	Y	+

	111	112	113	114	115	116	117
38 Horn	Y	Y	N	N	N	N	Y
39 Royce	N	Y	N	N	Y	N	Y
40 Lewis	N	Y	N	N	Y	N	Y
41 Kim	N	Y	N	N	Y	N	Y
42 Brown	Y	N	Y	N	Y	Y	Y
43 Calvert	N	Y	N	N	Y	N	Y
44 Bono, M.	N	Y	N	N	Y	N	Y
45 Rohrabacher	Y	N	N	N	Y	N	?
46 Sanchez	Y	Y	Y	Y	Y	Y	Y
47 Cox	N	Y	N	N	?	N	Y
48 Packard	N	Y	N	N	Y	N	Y
49 Bilbray	N	Y	N	N	N	Y	Y
50 Filner	Y	N	Y	Y	N	Y	Y
51 Cunningham	N	Y	N	N	Y	N	Y
52 Hunter	N	Y	N	Y	Y	N	Y
COLORADO							
1 DeGette	Y	N	Y	Y	N	Y	Y
2 Skaggs	N	N	Y	N	Y	Y	Y
3 McInnis	N	Y	N	N	Y	N	Y
4 Schaffer	N	Y	N	N	Y	N	Y
5 Hefley	N	Y	N	N	Y	N	Y
6 Schaefer	N	Y	N	N	Y	N	Y
CONNECTICUT							
1 Kennelly	Y	Y	Y	Y	N	Y	Y
2 Gejdenson	Y	Y	Y	Y	N	Y	Y
3 DeLauro	Y	Y	Y	Y	N	Y	Y
4 Shays	Y	Y	N	N	Y	N	Y
5 Maloney	Y	Y	Y	Y	N	Y	Y
6 Johnson	N	Y	N	N	N	N	Y
DELAWARE							
AL Castle	N	Y	N	N	N	N	Y
FLORIDA							
1 Scarborough	N	Y	N	N	Y	N	Y
2 Boyd	N	Y	N	N	N	N	Y
3 Brown	Y	Y	Y	Y	N	Y	Y
4 Fowler	N	Y	N	N	Y	N	Y
5 Thurman	Y	Y	Y	Y	N	Y	Y
6 Stearns	N	Y	N	N	Y	N	Y
7 Mica	N	Y	N	N	Y	N	Y
8 McCollum	N	Y	N	N	Y	N	Y
9 Bilirakis	N	Y	N	N	Y	N	Y
10 Young	N	Y	N	N	Y	N	Y
11 Davis	Y	Y	+	Y	N	Y	Y
12 Canady	N	Y	N	N	Y	N	Y
13 Miller	?	?	?	?	?	?	?
14 Goss	N	Y	N	N	Y	N	Y
15 Weldon	N	Y	N	N	Y	N	?
16 Foley	N	Y	N	N	Y	N	Y
17 Meek	Y	?	Y	?	?	?	Y
18 Ros-Lehtinen	N	Y	N	N	Y	N	Y
19 Wexler	Y	Y	N	N	Y	Y	Y
20 Deutsch	Y	Y	Y	Y	N	Y	Y
21 Diaz-Balart	N	Y	N	N	Y	N	Y
22 Shaw	N	Y	N	N	Y	N	Y
23 Hastings	?	?	?	?	?	?	Y
GEORGIA							
1 Kingston	N	Y	N	N	Y	N	Y
2 Bishop	Y	Y	Y	Y	N	N	Y
3 Collins	N	Y	N	N	Y	N	Y
4 McKinney	Y	Y	Y	Y	N	Y	Y
5 Lewis	Y	N	Y	Y	N	Y	Y
6 Gingrich							
7 Barr	N	Y	N	N	Y	N	?
8 Chambliss	N	Y	N	N	Y	N	Y
9 Deal	N	Y	N	N	Y	N	Y
10 Norwood	N	Y	N	N	Y	N	Y
11 Linder	N	Y	N	N	Y	N	Y
HAWAII							
1 Abercrombie	Y	Y	Y	Y	N	Y	Y
2 Mink	Y	Y	Y	Y	N	Y	Y
IDAHO							
1 Chenoweth	N	Y	N	N	Y	N	Y
2 Crapo	N	Y	N	N	Y	N	Y
ILLINOIS							
1 Rush	Y	N	Y	N	Y	Y	Y
2 Jackson	Y	N	Y	N	Y	Y	Y
3 Lipinski	Y	Y	N	N	N	N	Y
4 Gutierrez	?	Y	Y	Y	N	Y	Y
5 Blagojevich	Y	Y	Y	Y	N	Y	Y
6 Hyde	N	Y	N	N	Y	N	?
7 Davis	Y	N	Y	Y	?	Y	Y
8 Crane	N	Y	N	N	Y	N	Y
9 Yates	Y	N	Y	Y	N	?	Y
10 Porter	N	Y	N	N	N	N	Y
11 Weller	N	Y	N	N	Y	N	Y
12 Costello	Y	Y	Y	Y	N	N	Y

ND Northern Democrats   SD Southern Democrats

	111	112	113	114	115	116	117
13 ***Fawell***	N	N	N	N	N	Y	Y
14 ***Hastert***	N	Y	N	N	Y	?	Y
15 ***Ewing***	N	Y	N	N	N	N	Y
16 ***Manzullo***	N	Y	N	N	N	Y	Y
17 Evans	Y	N	Y	Y	N	N	Y
18 ***LaHood***	N	Y	N	N	N	Y	Y
19 Poshard	Y	Y	Y	?	?	?	?
20 ***Shimkus***	N	Y	N	N	Y	N	Y
INDIANA							
1 Visclosky	Y	Y	Y	Y	N	Y	Y
2 ***McIntosh***	N	Y	N	N	Y	N	Y
3 Roemer	N	Y	N	Y	N	Y	Y
4 ***Souder***	N	Y	N	N	?	N	Y
5 ***Buyer***	N	Y	N	N	?	N	Y
6 ***Burton***	N	Y	N	N	Y	N	Y
7 ***Pease***	N	Y	N	N	Y	N	Y
8 ***Hostettler***	N	Y	N	N	Y	N	Y
9 Hamilton	N	Y	N	Y	N	Y	Y
10 Carson	Y	N	Y	Y	N	N	Y
IOWA							
1 ***Leach***	Y	Y	Y	N	N	Y	Y
2 ***Nussle***	N	Y	N	N	Y	Y	Y
3 Boswell	Y	Y	N	Y	N	Y	Y
4 ***Ganske***	N	Y	N	N	N	N	?
5 ***Latham***	N	Y	N	N	Y	Y	Y
KANSAS							
1 ***Moran***	N	Y	N	N	Y	N	Y
2 ***Ryun***	N	Y	N	N	Y	N	+
3 ***Snowbarger***	N	Y	?	N	Y	N	Y
4 ***Tiahrt***	N	Y	N	N	Y	N	Y
KENTUCKY							
1 ***Whitfield***	N	Y	N	N	N	N	Y
2 ***Lewis***	N	Y	N	N	Y	N	Y
3 ***Northup***	N	Y	N	N	Y	N	Y
4 ***Bunning***	N	Y	N	N	Y	N	Y
5 ***Rogers***	N	Y	N	N	Y	N	Y
6 Baesler	Y	Y	Y	Y	N	Y	?
LOUISIANA							
1 ***Livingston***	N	Y	N	N	Y	N	Y
2 Jefferson	Y	Y	Y	Y	N	?	?
3 ***Tauzin***	N	Y	N	N	Y	N	Y
4 ***McCrery***	?	Y	N	N	Y	N	Y
5 ***Cooksey***	N	Y	N	N	Y	N	Y
6 ***Baker***	N	Y	N	N	Y	N	Y
7 John	N	Y	N	Y	N	Y	Y
MAINE							
1 Allen	Y	Y	N	Y	N	Y	Y
2 Baldacci	Y	Y	Y	Y	N	Y	Y
MARYLAND							
1 ***Gilchrest***	N	Y	N	N	N	Y	Y
2 ***Ehrlich***	N	Y	N	Y	Y	N	Y
3 Cardin	Y	Y	N	Y	N	Y	Y
4 Wynn	Y	Y	Y	Y	N	Y	Y
5 Hoyer	Y	Y	N	Y	N	Y	Y
6 ***Bartlett***	N	Y	N	N	Y	N	Y
7 Cummings	Y	Y	Y	Y	N	Y	Y
8 ***Morella***	Y	Y	N	Y	N	?	Y
MASSACHUSETTS							
1 Olver	Y	N	Y	Y	N	Y	Y
2 Neal	Y	Y	Y	Y	N	Y	Y
3 McGovern	Y	Y	N	Y	N	Y	Y
4 Frank	Y	N	N	Y	N	Y	Y
5 Meehan	Y	N	Y	Y	N	Y	Y
6 Tierney	Y	N	N	Y	N	Y	Y
7 Markey	Y	Y	Y	Y	N	Y	Y
8 Kennedy	Y	N	Y	Y	N	Y	Y
9 Moakley	Y	Y	N	Y	N	Y	Y
10 Delahunt	Y	N	Y	Y	N	Y	Y
MICHIGAN							
1 Stupak	Y	Y	Y	Y	N	Y	Y
2 ***Hoekstra***	N	Y	N	N	Y	N	Y
3 ***Ehlers***	N	Y	N	N	N	N	Y
4 ***Camp***	N	Y	N	N	–	N	Y
5 Barcia	Y	Y	Y	Y	N	Y	Y
6 ***Upton***	N	Y	N	N	N	N	Y
7 ***Smith***	N	Y	N	Y	Y	N	Y
8 Stabenow	Y	Y	Y	Y	N	Y	Y
9 Kildee	Y	Y	Y	Y	N	Y	Y
10 Bonior	Y	N	Y	Y	N	Y	Y
11 ***Knollenberg***	N	Y	N	N	Y	N	Y
12 Levin	Y	Y	N	Y	N	Y	Y
13 Rivers	Y	Y	N	Y	N	Y	Y
14 Conyers	Y	N	Y	Y	N	N	Y
15 Kilpatrick	Y	N	Y	Y	N	Y	Y
16 Dingell	Y	Y	N	Y	N	Y	Y

	111	112	113	114	115	116	117
MINNESOTA							
1 ***Gutknecht***	N	Y	N	N	N	N	Y
2 Minge	Y	Y	Y	Y	N	Y	Y
3 ***Ramstad***	N	Y	N	N	N	N	Y
4 Vento	Y	Y	Y	Y	N	Y	Y
5 Sabo	Y	N	Y	Y	N	Y	Y
6 Luther	Y	Y	Y	Y	N	Y	Y
7 Peterson	N	Y	Y	N	Y	N	Y
8 Oberstar	Y	N	Y	Y	N	Y	Y
MISSISSIPPI							
1 ***Wicker***	N	Y	N	N	Y	N	Y
2 Thompson	Y	N	Y	Y	N	N	Y
3 ***Pickering***	N	Y	N	N	Y	N	Y
4 ***Parker***	N	Y	N	N	Y	N	Y
5 Taylor	N	Y	Y	Y	N	N	Y
MISSOURI							
1 Clay	?	?	?	?	?	?	Y
2 ***Talent***	N	Y	N	N	Y	N	Y
3 Gephardt	Y	Y	Y	Y	N	Y	Y
4 Skelton	N	Y	Y	Y	N	Y	Y
5 McCarthy	Y	Y	N	Y	N	Y	Y
6 Danner	N	Y	N	Y	Y	N	Y
7 ***Blunt***	N	Y	N	N	Y	N	?
8 ***Emerson***	Y	Y	N	N	Y	N	Y
9 ***Hulshof***	N	Y	N	N	Y	N	Y
MONTANA							
AL ***Hill***	N	Y	N	N	Y	N	Y
NEBRASKA							
1 ***Bereuter***	Y	Y	N	N	Y	Y	Y
2 ***Christensen***	N	Y	N	N	Y	Y	?
3 ***Barrett***	N	Y	N	N	Y	Y	Y
NEVADA							
1 ***Ensign***	N	Y	N	Y	Y	N	?
2 ***Gibbons***	N	Y	N	N	Y	N	Y
NEW HAMPSHIRE							
1 ***Sununu***	N	Y	N	N	N	N	Y
2 ***Bass***	N	Y	N	N	N	N	Y
NEW JERSEY							
1 Andrews	Y	Y	Y	Y	N	Y	Y
2 ***LoBiondo***	N	Y	Y	N	N	N	Y
3 ***Saxton***	N	Y	N	N	N	N	Y
4 ***Smith***	N	Y	N	N	N	N	Y
5 ***Roukema***	N	Y	N	N	N	Y	Y
6 Pallone	Y	Y	Y	Y	N	Y	Y
7 ***Franks***	N	Y	N	Y	N	N	Y
8 Pascrell	Y	Y	Y	Y	N	Y	Y
9 Rothman	N	Y	Y	N	N	Y	Y
10 Payne	Y	N	Y	Y	N	Y	Y
11 ***Frelinghuysen***	N	Y	N	N	N	N	Y
12 ***Pappas***	N	Y	N	Y	N	N	Y
13 Menendez	Y	Y	Y	Y	N	Y	Y
NEW MEXICO							
1 Vacant							
2 ***Skeen***	N	Y	N	N	Y	Y	Y
3 ***Redmond***	N	Y	N	N	Y	N	Y
NEW YORK							
1 ***Forbes***	N	Y	N	N	N	?	Y
2 ***Lazio***	N	Y	N	N	N	Y	Y
3 ***King***	N	Y	Y	N	Y	N	Y
4 McCarthy	Y	Y	Y	Y	N	Y	Y
5 Ackerman	Y	Y	Y	Y	N	Y	Y
6 Meeks	Y	N	Y	Y	N	Y	+
7 Manton	Y	Y	N	Y	N	Y	Y
8 Nadler	Y	Y	Y	Y	N	Y	Y
9 Schumer	Y	Y	Y	Y	N	Y	Y
10 Towns	Y	N	N	Y	N	Y	?
11 Owens	Y	N	Y	Y	N	Y	Y
12 Velázquez	Y	N	Y	Y	N	Y	Y
13 ***Fossella***	N	Y	N	N	Y	N	Y
14 Maloney	N	Y	Y	Y	N	Y	?
15 Rangel	Y	N	Y	Y	N	Y	?
16 Serrano	Y	N	Y	Y	N	Y	?
17 Engel	Y	Y	Y	Y	N	Y	+
18 Lowey	Y	Y	Y	Y	N	Y	Y
19 ***Kelly***	N	Y	N	N	N	N	Y
20 ***Gilman***	N	Y	N	N	N	Y	Y
21 McNulty	Y	Y	Y	Y	N	Y	Y
22 ***Solomon***	N	Y	N	N	Y	N	Y
23 ***Boehlert***	N	Y	N	N	N	N	Y
24 ***McHugh***	N	Y	N	Y	Y	N	Y
25 ***Walsh***	N	Y	N	N	N	N	Y
26 Hinchey	Y	N	Y	Y	N	Y	Y
27 ***Paxon***	?	?	?	?	?	?	Y
28 Slaughter	Y	Y	Y	Y	N	Y	Y
29 LaFalce	Y	Y	Y	Y	N	Y	Y

	111	112	113	114	115	116	117
30 ***Quinn***	N	Y	N	N	N	N	Y
31 ***Houghton***	N	Y	N	N	N	Y	Y
NORTH CAROLINA							
1 Clayton	Y	Y	Y	Y	N	Y	Y
2 Etheridge	Y	Y	Y	Y	N	Y	Y
3 ***Jones***	N	Y	N	N	Y	N	Y
4 Price	Y	Y	Y	Y	N	Y	Y
5 ***Burr***	N	Y	N	N	Y	?	Y
6 ***Coble***	N	Y	N	?	?	?	Y
7 McIntyre	Y	Y	N	Y	Y	Y	Y
8 Hefner	Y	Y	Y	Y	Y	Y	Y
9 ***Myrick***	N	Y	N	N	Y	N	Y
10 ***Ballenger***	N	Y	N	Y	Y	N	Y
11 ***Taylor***	N	Y	N	N	Y	N	+
12 Watt	N	N	Y	Y	N	Y	Y
NORTH DAKOTA							
AL Pomeroy	N	Y	Y	Y	N	Y	Y
OHIO							
1 ***Chabot***	N	Y	N	Y	Y	N	Y
2 ***Portman***	N	Y	N	N	Y	N	Y
3 Hall	Y	Y	Y	Y	N	Y	Y
4 ***Oxley***	N	Y	N	N	N	N	Y
5 ***Gillmor***	N	Y	N	N	Y	N	Y
6 Strickland	Y	Y	Y	Y	N	N	Y
7 ***Hobson***	N	Y	N	N	N	N	Y
8 ***Boehner***	N	Y	N	N	Y	?	Y
9 Kaptur	Y	Y	Y	Y	?	?	Y
10 Kucinich	Y	Y	N	Y	N	N	Y
11 Stokes	Y	N	Y	Y	N	Y	Y
12 ***Kasich***	N	Y	N	N	Y	N	Y
13 Brown	Y	Y	Y	Y	N	N	Y
14 Sawyer	Y	Y	N	Y	N	Y	Y
15 ***Pryce***	N	Y	N	N	N	N	Y
16 ***Regula***	N	Y	N	N	N	N	Y
17 Traficant	N	Y	Y	Y	Y	N	Y
18 ***Ney***	N	Y	N	N	N	Y	Y
19 ***LaTourette***	N	Y	N	N	N	Y	Y
OKLAHOMA							
1 ***Largent***	N	Y	N	N	Y	N	Y
2 ***Coburn***	N	Y	N	N	Y	N	Y
3 ***Watkins***	N	Y	N	N	Y	N	Y
4 ***Watts***	N	Y	N	N	Y	N	Y
5 ***Istook***	?	?	?	?	?	–	Y
6 ***Lucas***	N	Y	N	N	Y	N	Y
OREGON							
1 Furse	Y	N	Y	Y	N	Y	Y
2 ***Smith***	N	Y	N	N	Y	N	?
3 Blumenauer	Y	Y	Y	Y	N	Y	Y
4 DeFazio	Y	Y	Y	Y	N	N	Y
5 Hooley	Y	Y	Y	Y	N	Y	Y
PENNSYLVANIA							
1 Vacant							
2 Fattah	Y	?	?	?	?	?	Y
3 Borski	Y	Y	Y	Y	N	Y	Y
4 Klink	Y	Y	Y	Y	N	N	Y
5 ***Peterson***	N	Y	N	N	Y	N	Y
6 Holden	Y	Y	N	Y	N	Y	Y
7 ***Weldon***	N	Y	N	N	N	N	Y
8 ***Greenwood***	N	Y	N	N	N	N	?
9 ***Shuster***	N	Y	N	N	Y	N	Y
10 ***McDade***	N	Y	Y	N	N	N	Y
11 Kanjorski	N	Y	Y	Y	N	Y	Y
12 Murtha	N	Y	Y	N	N	Y	Y
13 ***Fox***	Y	Y	Y	?	?	?	Y
14 Coyne	Y	Y	Y	Y	N	Y	Y
15 McHale	Y	Y	N	Y	N	Y	Y
16 ***Pitts***	N	Y	N	N	Y	N	Y
17 ***Gekas***	N	Y	N	N	Y	N	Y
18 Doyle	N	Y	Y	Y	N	N	Y
19 ***Goodling***	N	Y	N	N	Y	N	Y
20 Mascara	Y	Y	Y	Y	N	Y	Y
21 ***English***	N	Y	N	Y	N	N	Y
RHODE ISLAND							
1 Kennedy	Y	N	Y	Y	N	Y	Y
2 Weygand	Y	Y	Y	Y	N	Y	Y
SOUTH CAROLINA							
1 ***Sanford***	N	Y	Y	N	Y	N	Y
2 ***Spence***	N	Y	N	N	Y	N	Y
3 ***Graham***	N	Y	N	N	Y	N	Y
4 ***Inglis***	N	Y	N	N	Y	N	?
5 Spratt	Y	?	?	Y	N	Y	Y
6 Clyburn	Y	N	Y	Y	N	Y	Y
SOUTH DAKOTA							
AL ***Thune***	N	Y	N	N	Y	N	Y

	111	112	113	114	115	116	117
TENNESSEE							
1 ***Jenkins***	N	Y	N	N	Y	N	Y
2 ***Duncan***	N	Y	N	Y	Y	N	Y
3 ***Wamp***	N	Y	N	Y	Y	N	Y
4 ***Hilleary***	N	Y	N	Y	Y	N	Y
5 Clement	Y	Y	Y	Y	N	Y	Y
6 Gordon	N	Y	Y	N	N	Y	Y
7 ***Bryant***	N	Y	N	N	Y	N	Y
8 Tanner	?	?	?	?	?	?	?
9 Ford	Y	Y	Y	Y	N	Y	Y
TEXAS							
1 Sandlin	N	Y	Y	Y	N	Y	?
2 Turner	N	Y	N	N	N	Y	Y
3 ***Johnson, Sam***	N	Y	N	N	Y	N	Y
4 Hall	?	Y	N	N	Y	N	Y
5 ***Sessions***	N	Y	N	N	Y	N	Y
6 ***Barton***	N	Y	N	N	Y	N	Y
7 ***Archer***	N	Y	N	N	Y	N	Y
8 ***Brady***	N	Y	N	N	Y	N	Y
9 Lampson	Y	Y	Y	Y	N	Y	Y
10 Doggett	Y	Y	N	Y	N	Y	Y
11 Edwards	Y	Y	Y	Y	N	Y	Y
12 ***Granger***	N	Y	N	N	Y	N	Y
13 ***Thornberry***	N	Y	N	N	Y	N	Y
14 ***Paul***	N	Y	Y	N	Y	N	N
15 Hinojosa	Y	Y	Y	+	–	Y	Y
16 Reyes	Y	Y	Y	Y	N	?	Y
17 Stenholm	N	Y	N	N	Y	Y	Y
18 Jackson-Lee	Y	N	Y	Y	N	Y	Y
19 ***Combest***	N	Y	N	N	Y	N	Y
20 Gonzalez	?	?	?	?	?	?	?
21 ***Smith***	N	Y	N	N	Y	N	Y
22 ***DeLay***	N	Y	N	N	Y	N	Y
23 ***Bonilla***	N	Y	N	N	Y	N	Y
24 Frost	Y	Y	Y	Y	N	Y	Y
25 Bentsen	Y	Y	N	Y	N	Y	Y
26 ***Armey***	N	Y	N	N	Y	N	Y
27 Ortiz	Y	Y	Y	Y	N	N	Y
28 Rodriguez	Y	Y	Y	Y	N	Y	Y
29 Green	Y	Y	Y	Y	N	Y	Y
30 Johnson, E.B.	Y	Y	Y	Y	N	Y	Y
UTAH							
1 ***Hansen***	N	Y	N	N	Y	N	Y
2 ***Cook***	?	Y	N	N	Y	N	?
3 ***Cannon***	N	Y	N	N	Y	N	Y
VERMONT							
AL *Sanders*	Y	N	Y	Y	N	N	Y
VIRGINIA							
1 ***Bateman***	–	–	–	+	+	–	+
2 Pickett	N	Y	N	N	Y	Y	Y
3 Scott	Y	N	N	Y	N	Y	Y
4 Sisisky	N	Y	N	N	Y	Y	Y
5 Goode	N	Y	N	N	Y	N	?
6 ***Goodlatte***	N	Y	N	N	Y	N	Y
7 ***Bliley***	N	Y	N	N	Y	N	Y
8 Moran	Y	Y	N	Y	N	Y	Y
9 Boucher	Y	Y	Y	Y	N	Y	Y
10 ***Wolf***	N	Y	N	N	Y	N	Y
11 ***Davis***	N	Y	N	N	N	Y	Y
WASHINGTON							
1 ***White***	N	Y	N	N	N	N	?
2 ***Metcalf***	N	Y	N	N	Y	N	Y
3 ***Smith, Linda***	N	Y	N	N	Y	N	Y
4 ***Hastings***	N	Y	N	N	Y	N	Y
5 ***Nethercutt***	N	Y	N	N	Y	N	Y
6 Dicks	N	Y	N	Y	N	Y	Y
7 McDermott	Y	N	Y	Y	N	Y	Y
8 ***Dunn***	N	Y	N	N	Y	N	Y
9 Smith, Adam	Y	Y	N	Y	N	Y	Y
WEST VIRGINIA							
1 Mollohan	Y	Y	Y	Y	N	N	Y
2 Wise	Y	Y	N	Y	N	Y	Y
3 Rahall	Y	Y	Y	Y	N	N	Y
WISCONSIN							
1 ***Neumann***	N	Y	N	N	Y	N	Y
2 ***Klug***	N	Y	N	N	N	N	Y
3 Kind	Y	Y	Y	Y	N	Y	Y
4 Kleczka	Y	Y	N	Y	N	Y	Y
5 Barrett	Y	N	N	Y	N	Y	Y
6 ***Petri***	N	Y	N	N	N	N	Y
7 Obey	Y	?	Y	Y	N	Y	Y
8 Johnson	Y	Y	Y	Y	N	Y	Y
9 ***Sensenbrenner***	N	Y	N	N	Y	N	Y
WYOMING							
AL ***Cubin***	N	Y	N	N	Y	N	Y

Southern states - Ala., Ark., Fla., Ga., Ky., La., Miss., N.C., Okla., S.C., Tenn., Texas, Va.

House Votes 118, 119, 120, 121, 122, 123, 124

118. S 1502. District of Columbia Student Scholarships/Commit. Norton, D-D.C., motion to commit the bill to the Government Reform and Oversight Committee with instructions to authorize $3.5 million for the District of Columbia control board to fund reading tutors in the District's 73 lowest performing schools, and authorize $3.5 million for the Education Department to fund reforms at the District's 70 lowest performing schools to be administered under the Comprehensive School Reform Demonstration education program. Motion rejected 198-224: R 2-219; D 195-5 (ND 148-0, SD 47-5); I 1-0. April 30, 1998.

119. S 1502. District of Columbia Student Scholarships/Passage. Passage of the bill to create a $7 million school scholarship program for low-income elementary and secondary students living in Washington, D.C. Passed 214-206: R 208-13; D 6-192 (ND 2-145, SD 4-47); I 0-1. April 30, 1998. Thus cleared for the president. A "nay" was a vote in support of the president's position.

120. H Res 414. Waiving Requirements for Considering a Rule/Adoption. Adoption of the resolution to waive the two-thirds majority required for considering a rule on the same day it is reported from the Rules Committee. Adopted 211-196: R 211-0; D 0-195 (ND 0-144, SD 0-51); I 0-1. April 30, 1998.

121. HR 3579. Fiscal 1998 Emergency Supplemental Appropriations/Conference Report. Adoption of the conference report on the bill to appropriate $6.1 billion in supplemental spending, including $2.6 billion for disaster relief to states, and $2.9 billion for operations in Bosnia and other overseas operations. Adopted 242-163: R 192-21; D 50-141 (ND 26-116, SD 24-25); I 0-1. April 30, 1998.

122. HR 6. Higher Education Act Reauthorization/Personal Identifier. Paul, R-Texas, amendment to prohibit the Education Department from using a student's Social Security number or any other identifier used in any federal program as the electronic personal identifier required under the bill. Rejected 112-286: R 93-122; D 19-163 (ND 15-115, SD 4-48); I 0-1. May 5, 1998.

123. HR 6. Higher Education Act Reauthorization/Information Technology. Owens, D-N.Y., amendment to establish a $100 million grant program for colleges and universities that will be used to establish and oversee information technology education recruitment projects. Rejected 172-234: R 4-213; D 167-21 (ND 127-9, SD 40-12); I 1-0. May 5, 1998.

124. HR 6. Higher Education Act Reauthorization/Achievement Awards. McGovern, D-Mass., amendment to authorize an achievement award to students eligible for Pell Grants who graduate in the top 10 percent of their high school class. Adopted 220-187: R 33-184; D 186-3 (ND 135-2, SD 51-1); I 1-0. May 5, 1998.

Key

Y	Voted for (yea).
#	Paired for.
+	Announced for.
N	Voted against (nay).
X	Paired against.
–	Announced against.
P	Voted "present."
C	Voted "present" to avoid possible conflict of interest.
?	Did not vote or otherwise make a position known.

Democrats **Republicans** *Independent*

	118	119	120	121	122	123	124
ALABAMA							
1 *Callahan*	Y	Y	N	Y	N	Y	Y
2 *Everett*	Y	Y	N	Y	N	Y	Y
3 *Riley*	Y	Y	N	Y	N	Y	Y
4 *Aderholt*	Y	Y	N	Y	N	Y	Y
5 Cramer	Y	Y	N	Y	Y	Y	N
6 *Bachus*	Y	Y	N	Y	N	Y	Y
7 Hilliard	Y	Y	N	Y	Y	Y	Y
ALASKA							
AL *Young*	Y	Y	N	Y	N	Y	Y
ARIZONA							
1 *Salmon*	Y	Y	N	Y	N	Y	Y
2 Pastor	Y	Y	Y	N	Y	Y	N
3 *Stump*	Y	Y	N	Y	N	Y	Y
4 *Shadegg*	Y	Y	N	Y	N	Y	Y
5 *Kolbe*	Y	Y	N	Y	N	Y	Y
6 *Hayworth*	Y	Y	N	Y	N	Y	Y
ARKANSAS							
1 Berry	Y	Y	N	Y	Y	Y	N
2 Snyder	Y	Y	Y	N	Y	Y	N
3 *Hutchinson*	Y	Y	N	Y	N	Y	Y
4 *Dickey*	Y	Y	N	Y	N	Y	Y
CALIFORNIA							
1 *Riggs*	?	?	N	Y	N	Y	Y
2 *Herger*	Y	Y	N	Y	N	Y	Y
3 Fazio	Y	Y	N	Y	N	Y	N
4 *Doolittle*	Y	Y	N	Y	N	Y	Y
5 Matsui	Y	Y	Y	N	Y	Y	N
6 Woolsey	Y	?	Y	N	Y	Y	N
7 Miller	Y	Y	Y	N	Y	Y	N
8 Pelosi	Y	Y	Y	N	Y	Y	N
9 Lee	Y	Y	Y	N	Y	Y	N
10 Tauscher	Y	N	Y	N	Y	Y	N
11 *Pombo*	Y	Y	N	Y	N	Y	Y
12 Lantos	Y	Y	Y	N	Y	Y	N
13 Stark	Y	Y	Y	N	Y	Y	N
14 Eshoo	+	Y	Y	N	Y	Y	N
15 *Campbell*	Y	Y	N	Y	N	Y	Y
16 Lofgren	+	Y	Y	N	Y	Y	N
17 Farr	Y	Y	Y	N	Y	Y	N
18 Condit	Y	Y	N	Y	Y	Y	N
19 *Radanovich*	Y	?	N	Y	N	Y	Y
20 Dooley	Y	Y	N	Y	Y	Y	N
21 *Thomas*	Y	Y	N	Y	N	Y	Y
22 Capps, L.	Y	Y	Y	N	Y	Y	N
23 *Gallegly*	Y	Y	N	Y	N	Y	Y
24 Sherman	Y	Y	Y	N	Y	Y	N
25 *McKeon*	Y	Y	N	Y	N	Y	Y
26 Berman	Y	Y	Y	N	Y	Y	N
27 *Rogan*	Y	Y	N	Y	N	Y	Y
28 *Dreier*	Y	Y	N	Y	N	Y	Y
29 Waxman	Y	Y	Y	N	Y	Y	N
30 Becerra	Y	Y	N	Y	N	Y	N
31 Martinez	?	?	Y	N	Y	N	N
32 Dixon	?	?	?	?	?	?	?
33 Royal-Allard	Y	Y	Y	N	Y	Y	N
34 Torres	Y	Y	Y	N	Y	Y	N
35 Waters	Y	Y	Y	N	Y	Y	N
36 Harman	+	Y	Y	N	Y	Y	N
37 Millender-McD.	+	+	Y	N	Y	Y	N

	118	119	120	121	122	123	124
38 *Horn*	Y	Y	N	Y	N	Y	Y
39 *Royce*	Y	Y	N	Y	N	Y	Y
40 *Lewis*	Y	Y	N	N	N	Y	Y
41 *Kim*	Y	Y	N	Y	N	Y	Y
42 Brown	Y	Y	Y	N	?	?	N
43 *Calvert*	Y	Y	N	Y	N	Y	Y
44 *Bono, M.*	Y	Y	N	Y	N	Y	Y
45 *Rohrabacher*	Y	Y	Y	Y	N	Y	Y
46 Sanchez	Y	Y	N	Y	Y	Y	N
47 *Cox*	Y	Y	N	Y	N	Y	Y
48 *Packard*	Y	Y	N	Y	N	Y	Y
49 *Bilbray*	?	?	N	Y	N	Y	Y
50 Filner	Y	Y	Y	N	Y	Y	N
51 *Cunningham*	Y	Y	N	Y	N	Y	Y
52 *Hunter*	Y	Y	N	Y	N	Y	Y
COLORADO							
1 DeGette	Y	Y	Y	N	Y	Y	N
2 Skaggs	Y	Y	N	Y	Y	Y	N
3 *McInnis*	Y	Y	N	Y	N	Y	Y
4 *Schaffer*	Y	Y	N	Y	N	Y	Y
5 *Hefley*	Y	Y	N	Y	N	Y	Y
6 *Schaefer*	Y	Y	N	Y	N	Y	Y
CONNECTICUT							
1 Kennelly	Y	Y	Y	N	Y	Y	?
2 Gejdenson	?	?	Y	N	Y	Y	N
3 DeLauro	Y	Y	Y	N	Y	?	N
4 *Shays*	Y	Y	N	N	Y	Y	Y
5 Maloney	Y	Y	Y	N	Y	Y	N
6 *Johnson*	Y	Y	N	N	N	Y	Y
DELAWARE							
AL *Castle*	Y	Y	N	Y	N	Y	Y
FLORIDA							
1 *Scarborough*	Y	Y	N	Y	N	Y	Y
2 Boyd	Y	Y	Y	Y	Y	Y	N
3 Brown	Y	Y	Y	N	Y	Y	N
4 *Fowler*	Y	Y	N	Y	N	Y	Y
5 Thurman	Y	Y	Y	N	Y	Y	N
6 *Stearns*	Y	Y	N	Y	N	Y	Y
7 *Mica*	Y	Y	N	Y	N	Y	Y
8 *McCollum*	Y	Y	N	Y	N	Y	Y
9 *Bilirakis*	Y	Y	N	Y	N	Y	Y
10 *Young*	Y	Y	N	Y	N	Y	Y
11 Davis	Y	Y	Y	N	Y	Y	N
12 *Canady*	Y	Y	N	Y	N	Y	Y
13 *Miller*	Y	Y	N	Y	N	Y	Y
14 *Goss*	Y	Y	N	Y	N	Y	Y
15 *Weldon*	Y	Y	N	Y	N	Y	Y
16 *Foley*	?	?	N	Y	N	Y	Y
17 Meek	Y	Y	Y	N	?	?	?
18 *Ros-Lehtinen*	Y	Y	N	Y	N	Y	Y
19 Wexler	Y	Y	Y	N	Y	Y	N
20 Deutsch	Y	Y	Y	N	Y	Y	N
21 *Diaz-Balart*	Y	Y	N	Y	N	Y	Y
22 *Shaw*	Y	Y	N	Y	N	Y	Y
23 Hastings	Y	Y	Y	N	Y	Y	N
GEORGIA							
1 *Kingston*	Y	Y	N	Y	N	Y	Y
2 Bishop	Y	Y	N	Y	Y	Y	N
3 *Collins*	Y	Y	N	Y	N	Y	Y
4 *McKinney*	Y	Y	N	Y	Y	Y	N
5 Lewis	Y	Y	N	Y	N	Y	N
6 *Gingrich*	N	Y					
7 *Barr*	?	?	?	?	?	?	Y
8 *Chambliss*	Y	Y	N	Y	N	Y	Y
9 *Deal*	Y	Y	N	Y	N	Y	Y
10 *Norwood*	Y	Y	N	Y	N	Y	Y
11 *Linder*	Y	Y	N	Y	N	Y	Y
HAWAII							
1 Abercrombie	Y	Y	Y	N	Y	Y	N
2 Mink	Y	Y	Y	N	Y	Y	N
IDAHO							
1 *Chenoweth*	Y	Y	N	Y	N	Y	Y
2 *Crapo*	Y	Y	N	Y	N	Y	Y
ILLINOIS							
1 Rush	Y	Y	Y	N	Y	Y	N
2 Jackson	Y	Y	Y	N	Y	Y	N
3 Lipinski	Y	Y	N	Y	Y	Y	N
4 Gutierrez	Y	Y	Y	N	Y	Y	N
5 Blagojevich	Y	Y	Y	N	Y	Y	N
6 *Hyde*	?	?	N	Y	N	Y	Y
7 Davis	Y	Y	Y	N	Y	Y	N
8 *Crane*	Y	Y	N	Y	N	Y	Y
9 Yates	Y	Y	Y	N	Y	Y	N
10 *Porter*	Y	Y	N	Y	N	Y	Y
11 *Weller*	Y	Y	N	Y	N	Y	Y
12 Costello	Y	Y	Y	N	Y	Y	N

ND Northern Democrats   SD Southern Democrats

	118	119	120	121	122	123	124
13 ***Fawell***	Y	Y	N	Y	N	Y	Y
14 ***Hastert***	Y	Y	N	Y	N	Y	Y
15 ***Ewing***	Y	Y	N	Y	N	Y	Y
16 ***Manzullo***	Y	Y	N	Y	N	Y	Y
17 Evans	Y	Y	Y	N	Y	Y	N
18 ***LaHood***	Y	Y	N	Y	N	Y	Y
19 Poshard	?	?	N	Y	Y	Y	N
20 ***Shimkus***	Y	Y	N	Y	N	Y	Y
INDIANA							
1 Visclosky	Y	Y	N	Y	Y	Y	N
2 ***McIntosh***	Y	Y	N	Y	N	Y	Y
3 Roemer	Y	Y	N	Y	Y	Y	N
4 ***Souder***	Y	Y	N	Y	N	Y	Y
5 ***Buyer***	Y	Y	N	Y	N	Y	Y
6 ***Burton***	Y	Y	N	Y	N	Y	Y
7 ***Pease***	Y	Y	N	Y	N	Y	Y
8 ***Hostettler***	Y	Y	N	Y	N	Y	Y
9 Hamilton	Y	Y	N	Y	Y	Y	N
10 Carson	Y	Y	Y	N	Y	Y	N
IOWA							
1 ***Leach***	Y	Y	N	Y	N	Y	Y
2 ***Nussle***	Y	Y	N	Y	N	Y	Y
3 Boswell	Y	Y	N	Y	Y	Y	N
4 ***Ganske***	Y	Y	N	N	N	Y	Y
5 ***Latham***	Y	Y	N	Y	N	Y	Y
KANSAS							
1 ***Moran***	Y	Y	N	Y	N	Y	Y
2 ***Ryun***	+	+	N	Y	N	Y	Y
3 ***Snowbarger***	Y	Y	N	Y	N	Y	Y
4 ***Tiahrt***	Y	Y	N	Y	N	Y	Y
KENTUCKY							
1 ***Whitfield***	Y	Y	N	Y	N	Y	Y
2 ***Lewis***	Y	Y	N	Y	N	Y	Y
3 ***Northup***	Y	Y	N	Y	N	Y	Y
4 ***Bunning***	Y	Y	N	Y	N	Y	Y
5 ***Rogers***	Y	Y	N	Y	N	Y	Y
6 Baesler	?	?	N	Y	Y	Y	N
LOUISIANA							
1 ***Livingston***	Y	Y	N	Y	N	Y	Y
2 Jefferson	?	?	Y	N	Y	Y	?
3 ***Tauzin***	Y	Y	N	Y	N	Y	Y
4 ***McCrery***	Y	Y	N	Y	N	Y	Y
5 ***Cooksey***	Y	Y	N	N	N	Y	Y
6 ***Baker***	Y	Y	N	Y	N	Y	Y
7 John	Y	Y	N	Y	Y	Y	N
MAINE							
1 Allen	Y	Y	Y	N	Y	Y	N
2 Baldacci	Y	Y	Y	Y	Y	Y	N
MARYLAND							
1 ***Gilchrest***	Y	Y	N	Y	N	Y	Y
2 ***Ehrlich***	Y	Y	N	Y	N	Y	Y
3 Cardin	Y	Y	Y	N	Y	Y	N
4 Wynn	Y	Y	Y	N	Y	Y	N
5 Hoyer	Y	Y	Y	N	Y	Y	N
6 ***Bartlett***	Y	Y	N	Y	N	Y	Y
7 Cummings	Y	Y	Y	N	Y	Y	N
8 ***Morella***	Y	Y	Y	N	N	Y	N
MASSACHUSETTS							
1 Olver	Y	Y	Y	N	Y	Y	N
2 Neal	Y	Y	Y	N	Y	Y	N
3 McGovern	Y	Y	Y	N	Y	Y	N
4 Frank	Y	Y	Y	N	Y	N	N
5 Meehan	Y	Y	Y	N	Y	Y	N
6 Tierney	Y	Y	Y	N	Y	Y	N
7 Markey	Y	Y	Y	N	Y	Y	N
8 Kennedy	Y	Y	Y	N	Y	Y	N
9 Moakley	Y	Y	Y	N	Y	Y	N
10 Delahunt	Y	Y	Y	N	Y	Y	N
MICHIGAN							
1 Stupak	Y	Y	Y	Y	Y	Y	N
2 ***Hoekstra***	Y	Y	N	Y	N	Y	Y
3 ***Ehlers***	Y	Y	N	Y	N	Y	Y
4 ***Camp***	Y	Y	N	Y	N	Y	Y
5 Barcia	Y	Y	N	Y	Y	Y	N
6 ***Upton***	Y	Y	N	Y	N	Y	Y
7 ***Smith***	Y	Y	N	Y	N	Y	Y
8 Stabenow	Y	Y	Y	N	Y	Y	N
9 Kildee	Y	Y	N	Y	Y	Y	N
10 Bonior	Y	Y	Y	N	Y	Y	N
11 ***Knollenberg***	Y	Y	N	Y	N	Y	Y
12 Levin	Y	Y	Y	N	Y	Y	N
13 Rivers	Y	Y	Y	N	Y	Y	N
14 Conyers	Y	Y	Y	N	Y	N	N
15 Kilpatrick	Y	Y	Y	N	Y	Y	N
16 Dingell	Y	Y	Y	N	Y	Y	N

	118	119	120	121	122	123	124
MINNESOTA							
1 ***Gutknecht***	Y	Y	N	Y	N	Y	Y
2 Minge	Y	Y	N	Y	Y	Y	N
3 ***Ramstad***	Y	Y	N	Y	N	Y	Y
4 Vento	Y	Y	Y	N	Y	Y	N
5 Sabo	Y	Y	Y	N	Y	Y	N
6 Luther	Y	Y	N	Y	Y	Y	N
7 Peterson	Y	Y	N	Y	Y	Y	N
8 Oberstar	Y	Y	Y	N	Y	N	N
MISSISSIPPI							
1 ***Wicker***	Y	Y	N	Y	N	Y	Y
2 Thompson	Y	Y	Y	N	Y	Y	N
3 ***Pickering***	Y	Y	N	Y	N	Y	Y
4 ***Parker***	Y	Y	N	Y	N	Y	Y
5 Taylor	Y	Y	N	Y	Y	Y	N
MISSOURI							
1 Clay	Y	Y	Y	N	Y	Y	N
2 ***Talent***	Y	Y	N	Y	N	Y	Y
3 Gephardt	Y	Y	Y	N	?	?	N
4 Skelton	Y	Y	N	Y	Y	Y	N
5 McCarthy	Y	Y	Y	Y	Y	Y	N
6 Danner	Y	Y	N	Y	Y	Y	N
7 ***Blunt***	?	?	N	Y	N	Y	Y
8 ***Emerson***	Y	Y	N	Y	N	Y	Y
9 ***Hulshof***	Y	Y	N	Y	N	Y	Y
MONTANA							
AL ***Hill***	Y	Y	N	Y	N	Y	Y
NEBRASKA							
1 ***Bereuter***	Y	Y	N	Y	N	Y	Y
2 ***Christensen***	?	?	N	Y	N	Y	Y
3 ***Barrett***	Y	Y	N	Y	N	Y	Y
NEVADA							
1 ***Ensign***	?	Y	N	Y	N	Y	Y
2 ***Gibbons***	Y	Y	N	Y	N	Y	Y
NEW HAMPSHIRE							
1 ***Sununu***	Y	Y	N	Y	N	Y	Y
2 ***Bass***	Y	Y	N	Y	N	Y	Y
NEW JERSEY							
1 Andrews	Y	Y	N	Y	Y	Y	N
2 ***LoBiondo***	Y	Y	N	Y	N	Y	Y
3 ***Saxton***	Y	Y	N	Y	N	Y	Y
4 ***Smith***	Y	Y	N	Y	N	Y	Y
5 ***Roukema***	Y	Y	N	Y	N	Y	Y
6 Pallone	Y	Y	Y	Y	Y	Y	N
7 ***Franks***	Y	Y	N	Y	N	Y	Y
8 Pascrell	Y	Y	N	Y	Y	Y	N
9 Rothman	Y	Y	Y	N	Y	Y	N
10 Payne	Y	Y	Y	N	Y	Y	N
11 ***Frelinghuysen***	Y	Y	N	Y	N	Y	Y
12 ***Pappas***	Y	Y	N	Y	N	Y	Y
13 Menendez	Y	Y	Y	N	Y	Y	N
NEW MEXICO							
1 Vacant							
2 ***Skeen***	Y	Y	N	Y	N	Y	Y
3 ***Redmond***	Y	Y	N	Y	N	Y	Y
NEW YORK							
1 ***Forbes***	Y	Y	N	Y	N	Y	Y
2 ***Lazio***	Y	Y	N	Y	N	Y	Y
3 ***King***	Y	Y	N	Y	N	Y	Y
4 McCarthy	Y	Y	Y	N	Y	Y	N
5 Ackerman	Y	Y	Y	N	Y	Y	N
6 Meeks	Y	Y	Y	N	Y	Y	N
7 Manton	Y	Y	Y	N	Y	Y	N
8 Nadler	Y	Y	Y	N	Y	N	N
9 Schumer	Y	Y	Y	N	?	?	N
10 Towns	?	?	Y	N	Y	Y	N
11 Owens	Y	Y	Y	N	Y	Y	N
12 Velázquez	Y	Y	Y	N	Y	Y	N
13 ***Fossella***	Y	Y	N	Y	N	Y	Y
14 Maloney	?	?	Y	N	Y	Y	N
15 Rangel	?	?	Y	N	Y	Y	N
16 Serrano	?	?	Y	N	Y	Y	N
17 Engel	+	+	Y	N	Y	Y	N
18 Lowey	Y	Y	Y	N	Y	Y	N
19 ***Kelly***	Y	Y	N	Y	N	Y	Y
20 ***Gilman***	Y	Y	N	Y	N	Y	Y
21 McNulty	Y	Y	N	Y	Y	Y	N
22 ***Solomon***	Y	Y	N	Y	N	Y	Y
23 ***Boehlert***	Y	Y	Y	N	N	Y	Y
24 ***McHugh***	Y	Y	N	Y	N	Y	Y
25 ***Walsh***	Y	Y	N	Y	N	Y	Y
26 Hinchey	Y	Y	Y	N	Y	Y	N
27 ***Paxon***	Y	Y	N	Y	N	Y	Y
28 Slaughter	Y	Y	Y	N	Y	Y	N
29 LaFalce	Y	Y	N	Y	Y	Y	N

	118	119	120	121	122	123	124
30 ***Quinn***	Y	Y	N	Y	N	Y	Y
31 ***Houghton***	Y	Y	N	Y	N	Y	Y
NORTH CAROLINA							
1 Clayton	Y	Y	Y	N	Y	Y	N
2 Etheridge	Y	Y	N	Y	Y	Y	N
3 ***Jones***	Y	Y	N	Y	N	Y	Y
4 Price	Y	Y	Y	Y	Y	Y	N
5 ***Burr***	Y	Y	N	Y	N	Y	Y
6 ***Coble***	Y	Y	N	Y	N	Y	Y
7 McIntyre	Y	Y	N	Y	Y	Y	N
8 Hefner	Y	Y	Y	Y	Y	Y	N
9 ***Myrick***	Y	Y	N	Y	N	Y	Y
10 ***Ballenger***	Y	Y	N	Y	N	Y	Y
11 ***Taylor***	+	+	N	Y	N	Y	Y
12 Watt	Y	Y	Y	N	Y	Y	N
NORTH DAKOTA							
AL Pomeroy	Y	Y	Y	Y	Y	Y	N
OHIO							
1 ***Chabot***	Y	Y	N	Y	N	Y	Y
2 ***Portman***	Y	Y	N	Y	N	Y	Y
3 Hall	Y	Y	N	Y	Y	Y	N
4 ***Oxley***	Y	Y	N	Y	N	Y	Y
5 ***Gillmor***	Y	Y	N	Y	N	Y	Y
6 Strickland	Y	Y	N	Y	Y	Y	N
7 ***Hobson***	Y	Y	N	Y	N	Y	Y
8 ***Boehner***	Y	Y	N	Y	N	Y	Y
9 Kaptur	Y	Y	N	Y	Y	Y	N
10 Kucinich	Y	Y	Y	N	Y	N	N
11 Stokes	Y	Y	Y	N	Y	Y	N
12 ***Kasich***	Y	Y	N	Y	N	Y	Y
13 Brown	Y	Y	Y	N	Y	Y	N
14 Sawyer	Y	Y	Y	N	Y	Y	N
15 ***Pryce***	Y	Y	N	Y	N	Y	Y
16 ***Regula***	Y	Y	N	Y	N	Y	Y
17 Traficant	Y	Y	N	Y	Y	Y	Y
18 ***Ney***	Y	Y	N	Y	N	Y	Y
19 ***LaTourette***	Y	Y	N	Y	N	Y	Y
OKLAHOMA							
1 ***Largent***	Y	Y	N	Y	N	Y	Y
2 ***Coburn***	Y	Y	N	Y	N	Y	Y
3 ***Watkins***	Y	Y	N	Y	N	Y	Y
4 ***Watts***	Y	Y	N	Y	N	Y	Y
5 ***Istook***	Y	Y	N	Y	N	Y	Y
6 ***Lucas***	Y	Y	N	Y	N	Y	Y
OREGON							
1 Furse	Y	Y	Y	N	Y	Y	N
2 ***Smith***	?	?	?	?	?	?	?
3 Blumenauer	Y	Y	Y	N	Y	Y	N
4 DeFazio	Y	Y	Y	N	Y	Y	N
5 Hooley	Y	Y	Y	N	Y	Y	N
PENNSYLVANIA							
1 Vacant							
2 Fattah	Y	Y	Y	N	Y	Y	N
3 Borski	Y	Y	Y	N	Y	Y	N
4 Klink	Y	Y	Y	Y	Y	Y	N
5 ***Peterson***	Y	Y	N	Y	N	Y	Y
6 Holden	Y	Y	N	Y	Y	Y	N
7 ***Weldon***	Y	Y	N	Y	N	Y	Y
8 ***Greenwood***	Y	Y	Y	N	N	Y	Y
9 ***Shuster***	Y	Y	N	Y	N	Y	Y
10 ***McDade***	Y	Y	N	Y	N	Y	Y
11 Kanjorski	Y	Y	Y	N	Y	Y	N
12 Murtha	Y	Y	N	Y	Y	Y	N
13 ***Fox***	Y	Y	N	Y	N	Y	Y
14 Coyne	Y	Y	Y	N	Y	Y	N
15 McHale	Y	Y	Y	N	Y	Y	N
16 ***Pitts***	Y	Y	N	Y	N	Y	Y
17 ***Gekas***	?	Y	N	Y	N	Y	Y
18 Doyle	Y	Y	N	Y	Y	Y	N
19 ***Goodling***	Y	Y	N	Y	N	Y	Y
20 Mascara	Y	Y	N	Y	Y	Y	N
21 ***English***	Y	Y	N	Y	N	Y	Y
RHODE ISLAND							
1 Kennedy	Y	Y	Y	N	Y	Y	N
2 Weygand	Y	Y	Y	N	Y	Y	N
SOUTH CAROLINA							
1 ***Sanford***	Y	Y	N	Y	N	Y	Y
2 ***Spence***	Y	Y	N	Y	N	Y	Y
3 ***Graham***	Y	Y	N	Y	N	Y	Y
4 ***Inglis***	?	?	N	Y	N	Y	Y
5 Spratt	Y	Y	N	Y	Y	Y	N
6 Clyburn	Y	Y	Y	N	Y	Y	N
SOUTH DAKOTA							
AL ***Thune***	Y	Y	N	Y	N	Y	Y

	118	119	120	121	122	123	124
TENNESSEE							
1 ***Jenkins***	Y	Y	N	Y	N	Y	Y
2 ***Duncan***	Y	Y	N	Y	N	Y	Y
3 ***Wamp***	Y	Y	N	Y	N	Y	Y
4 ***Hilleary***	Y	Y	N	Y	N	Y	Y
5 Clement	Y	Y	N	Y	Y	Y	N
6 Gordon	Y	Y	N	Y	Y	Y	N
7 ***Bryant***	Y	Y	N	Y	N	Y	Y
8 Tanner	?	Y	N	Y	Y	Y	N
9 Ford	Y	Y	N	Y	Y	Y	N
TEXAS							
1 Sandlin	?	?	?	?	?	?	?
2 Turner	Y	Y	N	Y	Y	Y	N
3 ***Johnson, Sam***	Y	Y	N	Y	N	Y	Y
4 Hall	Y	Y	N	Y	Y	Y	?
5 ***Sessions***	Y	Y	N	Y	N	Y	Y
6 ***Barton***	Y	Y	N	Y	N	Y	Y
7 ***Archer***	Y	Y	N	Y	N	Y	Y
8 ***Brady***	Y	Y	N	Y	N	Y	Y
9 Lampson	Y	Y	N	Y	Y	Y	N
10 Doggett	Y	Y	Y	N	Y	Y	N
11 Edwards	Y	Y	N	Y	Y	Y	N
12 ***Granger***	Y	Y	N	Y	N	Y	Y
13 ***Thornberry***	Y	Y	N	Y	N	Y	Y
14 ***Paul***	Y	Y	N	Y	N	N	Y
15 Hinojosa	Y	Y	Y	N	Y	Y	N
16 Reyes	Y	Y	Y	Y	Y	Y	N
17 Stenholm	Y	Y	N	Y	Y	Y	N
18 Jackson-Lee	Y	Y	Y	N	Y	Y	N
19 ***Combest***	Y	Y	N	Y	N	Y	Y
20 Gonzalez	?	?	?	?	?	?	?
21 ***Smith***	Y	Y	N	Y	N	Y	Y
22 ***DeLay***	Y	Y	N	Y	N	Y	Y
23 ***Bonilla***	Y	Y	N	Y	N	Y	Y
24 Frost	Y	Y	N	Y	Y	Y	N
25 Bentsen	Y	Y	N	Y	Y	Y	N
26 ***Armey***	Y	Y	N	Y	N	Y	Y
27 Ortiz	Y	Y	N	Y	Y	Y	N
28 Rodriguez	Y	Y	Y	Y	Y	Y	N
29 Green	Y	Y	N	Y	Y	Y	N
30 Johnson, E.B.	Y	Y	Y	N	Y	Y	N
UTAH							
1 ***Hansen***	Y	Y	N	Y	N	Y	Y
2 ***Cook***	?	?	?	Y	N	Y	Y
3 ***Cannon***	Y	Y	N	Y	N	Y	Y
VERMONT							
AL *Sanders*	Y	Y	Y	N	Y	N	N
VIRGINIA							
1 ***Bateman***	+	+	–	+	–	+	+
2 Pickett	Y	Y	N	Y	Y	Y	N
3 Scott	Y	Y	Y	N	Y	Y	N
4 Sisisky	Y	Y	N	Y	Y	Y	N
5 Goode	Y	Y	N	Y	Y	Y	N
6 ***Goodlatte***	Y	Y	N	Y	N	Y	Y
7 ***Bliley***	Y	Y	N	Y	N	Y	Y
8 Moran	Y	Y	Y	N	Y	Y	N
9 Boucher	Y	Y	N	Y	Y	Y	N
10 ***Wolf***	Y	Y	N	Y	N	Y	Y
11 ***Davis***	Y	Y	N	Y	N	Y	Y
WASHINGTON							
1 ***White***	?	?	N	Y	N	Y	Y
2 ***Metcalf***	Y	Y	N	Y	N	Y	Y
3 ***Smith, Linda***	Y	Y	N	Y	N	Y	Y
4 ***Hastings***	Y	Y	N	Y	N	Y	Y
5 ***Nethercutt***	Y	Y	N	Y	N	Y	Y
6 Dicks	Y	Y	Y	N	Y	Y	N
7 McDermott	Y	Y	Y	N	Y	Y	N
8 ***Dunn***	Y	Y	N	Y	N	Y	Y
9 Smith, Adam	Y	Y	Y	N	Y	Y	N
WEST VIRGINIA							
1 Mollohan	Y	Y	N	Y	Y	Y	N
2 Wise	Y	Y	N	Y	+	+	N
3 Rahall	Y	Y	N	Y	Y	Y	N
WISCONSIN							
1 ***Neumann***	Y	Y	N	Y	N	Y	Y
2 ***Klug***	Y	Y	N	Y	N	Y	Y
3 Kind	Y	Y	N	Y	Y	Y	N
4 Kleczka	Y	Y	N	Y	Y	Y	N
5 Barrett	Y	Y	Y	N	Y	Y	N
6 ***Petri***	Y	Y	N	Y	N	Y	Y
7 Obey	Y	Y	Y	N	Y	Y	N
8 Johnson	Y	Y	N	Y	Y	Y	N
9 ***Sensenbrenner***	Y	Y	N	Y	N	Y	Y
WYOMING							
AL ***Cubin***	Y	Y	N	Y	N	Y	Y

Southern states - Ala., Ark., Fla., Ga., Ky., La., Miss., N.C., Okla., S.C., Tenn., Texas, Va.

House Votes 125, 126, 127, 128, 129, 130, 131

Key

- Y Voted for (yea).
- # Paired for.
- + Announced for.
- N Voted against (nay).
- X Paired against.
- − Announced against.
- P Voted "present."
- C Voted "present" to avoid possible conflict of interest.
- ? Did not vote or otherwise make a position known.

Democrats **Republicans** *Independent*

---

125. H Con Res 220. Extradite Palestinian Terrorists/Adoption. Gilman, R-N.Y., motion to suspend the rules and adopt the resolution to express the sense of Congress that the United States should demand that Yasir Arafat and the Palestinian Authority transfer to the United States for prosecution those residents of its territory who are suspected in the killings of American citizens. Motion agreed to 406-0: R 216-0; D 189-0 (ND 137-0, SD 52-0); I 1-0. May 5, 1998. A two-thirds majority of those present and voting (271 in this case) is required for adoption under suspension of the rules.

126. H Res 267. Drug-Free Schools/Adoption. Souder, R-Ind., motion to suspend the rules and adopt the resolution to express the sense of the House that all schools should be drug-free. Motion agreed to 408-1: R 218-1; D 189-0 (ND 137-0, SD 52-0); I 1-0. May 5, 1998. A two-thirds majority of those present and voting (273 in this case) is required for adoption under suspension of the rules.

127. HR 1872. Communications Satellite Privatization/Takings. Morella, R-Md., amendment to require that in implementing market access restrictions the FCC does not restrict Comsat in a manner that would create a liability under the takings clause of the Constitution. Rejected 111-304: R 50-167; D 61-136 (ND 47-97, SD 14-39); I 0-1. May 6, 1998.

128. HR 1872. Communications Satellite Privatization/Fresh Look. Tauzin, R-La., amendment to eliminate the "fresh look" provisions of the bill that permit a customer that is locked into a long-term business agreement with a telecommunications carrier to take a fresh look at more competitive alternatives. Rejected 80-339: R 41-179; D 39-159 (ND 29-116, SD 10-43); I 0-1. May 6, 1998.

129. HR 1872. Communications Satellite Privatization/Passage. Passage of the bill to establish a timeline and conditions for the privatization of Intelsat and Inmarsat, calling for Inmarsat to be privatized by 2001 and Intelsat by 2002. Passed 403-16: R 219-1; D 183-15 (ND 133-12, SD 50-3); I 1-0. May 6, 1998.

130. HR 6. Higher Education Act Reauthorization/College Sports. Roemer, D-Ind., amendment to eliminate the provision of the bill that requires colleges and universities to report planned elimination of college sport four years in advance of the reduction and to justify that decision. Adopted 292-129: R 98-124; D 193-5 (ND 141-5, SD 52-0); I 1-0. May 6, 1998.

131. HR 6. Higher Education Act Reauthorization/Labor Codes. Miller, D-Calif., amendment to state the sense of Congress that all American colleges and universities should adopt rigorous labor codes of conduct to assure that university and college licensed merchandise is not made by sweatshop and exploited adult or child labor either domestically or abroad. Adopted 393-28: R 195-27; D 197-1 (ND 146-0, SD 51-1); I 1-0. May 6, 1998.

	125	126	127	128	129	130	131
ALABAMA							
1 **Callahan**	N	Y	Y	Y	Y	N	N
2 **Everett**	N	Y	Y	Y	Y	N	N
3 **Riley**	N	Y	Y	Y	Y	N	Y
4 **Aderholt**	N	Y	Y	Y	Y	N	N
5 Cramer	Y	N	N	Y	N	Y	Y
6 **Bachus**	N	Y	Y	Y	Y	N	N
7 Hilliard	Y	N	N	N	N	Y	Y
ALASKA							
AL **Young**	X	N	Y	Y	Y	N	N
ARIZONA							
1 **Salmon**	N	Y	Y	Y	Y	N	N
2 Pastor	Y	N	N	Y	Y	Y	Y
3 **Stump**	N	Y	Y	Y	Y	N	N
4 **Shadegg**	N	Y	Y	Y	Y	N	N
5 **Kolbe**	N	Y	Y	Y	Y	N	N
6 **Hayworth**	N	Y	Y	Y	Y	N	N
ARKANSAS							
1 Berry	Y	N	N	N	Y	Y	Y
2 Snyder	Y	N	N	Y	Y	Y	Y
3 **Hutchinson**	N	Y	Y	Y	Y	N	N
4 **Dickey**	N	Y	Y	Y	Y	N	N
CALIFORNIA							
1 **Riggs**	N	Y	Y	Y	Y	N	N
2 **Herger**	N	Y	Y	Y	Y	N	N
3 Fazio	Y	N	N	N	N	Y	Y
4 **Doolittle**	N	Y	Y	Y	Y	N	N
5 Matsui	Y	N	N	N	N	Y	Y
6 Woolsey	Y	N	N	Y	Y	Y	Y
7 Miller	Y	N	?	?	N	Y	Y
8 Pelosi	Y	N	N	N	N	Y	Y
9 Lee	Y	N	N	N	N	Y	Y
10 Tauscher	Y	N	N	Y	Y	Y	Y
11 **Pombo**	N	Y	Y	Y	Y	N	N
12 Lantos	Y	N	N	?	?	?	?
13 Stark	Y	N	N	N	Y	Y	Y
14 Eshoo	Y	N	N	N	N	Y	Y
15 **Campbell**	N	Y	Y	Y	Y	Y	Y
16 Lofgren	Y	N	N	Y	Y	Y	Y
17 Farr	Y	N	N	N	Y	Y	Y
18 Condit	Y	N	N	N	Y	N	Y
19 **Radanovich**	N	Y	?	Y	N	N	N
20 Dooley	Y	N	N	Y	Y	N	Y
21 **Thomas**	N	Y	Y	Y	Y	N	N
22 Capps, L.	Y	N	N	P	Y	Y	Y
23 **Gallegly**	N	Y	Y	Y	Y	N	N
24 Sherman	Y	N	N	Y	Y	N	N
25 **McKeon**	N	Y	Y	Y	Y	N	N
26 Berman	Y	N	N	?	N	Y	Y
27 **Rogan**	N	Y	Y	Y	Y	N	Y
28 **Dreier**	N	Y	Y	Y	Y	N	N
29 Waxman	Y	N	N	N	?	Y	Y
30 Becerra	Y	N	N	N	?	Y	Y
31 Martinez	Y	N	N	N	N	Y	Y
32 Dixon	?	?	?	?	?	Y	Y
33 Roybal-Allard	Y	N	N	N	N	Y	Y
34 Torres	Y	N	N	N	N	Y	Y
35 Waters	Y	N	N	N	N	Y	Y
36 Harman	Y	N	Y	N	?	?	?
37 Millender-McD.	Y	N	N	N	N	Y	Y

	125	126	127	128	129	130	131
38 **Horn**	N	Y	Y	Y	N	N	Y
39 **Royce**	N	Y	Y	Y	N	N	N
40 **Lewis**	N	Y	Y	Y	N	N	N
41 **Kim**	N	Y	Y	Y	N	N	N
42 Brown	Y	?	N	N	N	Y	Y
43 **Calvert**	N	Y	Y	Y	Y	N	N
44 **Bono, M.**	N	Y	Y	P	N	N	N
45 **Rohrabacher**	N	Y	Y	Y	N	N	N
46 Sanchez	Y	N	N	Y	N	Y	Y
47 **Cox**	N	Y	Y	Y	Y	N	N
48 **Packard**	N	Y	Y	Y	Y	N	N
49 **Bilbray**	N	Y	Y	Y	N	N	N
50 Filner	Y	N	N	Y	N	Y	Y
51 **Cunningham**	N	Y	Y	Y	Y	N	N
52 **Hunter**	N	Y	Y	Y	Y	N	N
COLORADO							
1 DeGette	Y	N	N	N	N	Y	Y
2 Skaggs	Y	N	N	N	−	+	−
3 **McInnis**	N	Y	Y	Y	Y	N	N
4 **Schaffer**	N	Y	Y	Y	Y	N	N
5 **Hefley**	N	Y	Y	Y	Y	N	N
6 **Schaefer**	N	Y	?	?	?	?	?
CONNECTICUT							
1 Kennelly	#	X	?	?	Y	Y	Y
2 Gejdenson	Y	N	N	N	Y	Y	Y
3 DeLauro	Y	N	N	N	N	Y	Y
4 **Shays**	N	Y	Y	Y	Y	Y	Y
5 Maloney	Y	N	N	N	Y	Y	Y
6 **Johnson**	N	N	Y	N	N	Y	Y
DELAWARE							
AL **Castle**	N	Y	Y	N	N	N	N
FLORIDA							
1 **Scarborough**	N	Y	Y	Y	Y	Y	N
2 Boyd	Y	Y	N	Y	Y	N	N
3 Brown	Y	N	N	N	N	Y	Y
4 **Fowler**	N	Y	Y	Y	Y	N	N
5 Thurman	Y	N	N	N	Y	N	N
6 **Stearns**	N	Y	Y	Y	Y	N	N
7 **Mica**	N	Y	Y	Y	Y	N	N
8 **McCollum**	N	Y	Y	Y	Y	N	N
9 **Bilirakis**	N	Y	Y	Y	Y	N	N
10 **Young**	N	Y	Y	Y	Y	N	N
11 Davis	Y	N	N	Y	Y	Y	Y
12 **Canady**	N	Y	Y	Y	Y	N	N
13 **Miller**	N	Y	Y	Y	Y	N	N
14 **Goss**	N	Y	Y	Y	Y	N	N
15 **Weldon**	N	Y	Y	Y	Y	N	N
16 **Foley**	N	Y	Y	Y	Y	N	N
17 Meek	#	X	?	?	Y	Y	Y
18 **Ros-Lehtinen**	N	Y	Y	Y	N	N	Y
19 Wexler	Y	N	N	N	Y	Y	Y
20 Deutsch	Y	N	N	N	N	Y	Y
21 **Diaz-Balart**	N	Y	Y	Y	N	N	N
22 **Shaw**	N	Y	Y	Y	Y	N	N
23 Hastings	Y	N	N	N	?	?	?
GEORGIA							
1 **Kingston**	N	Y	Y	Y	Y	N	N
2 Bishop	Y	N	N	Y	N	Y	Y
3 **Collins**	N	Y	Y	N	Y	N	N
4 McKinney	Y	N	N	Y	Y	Y	Y
5 Lewis	Y	N	N	N	N	Y	Y
6 **Gingrich**	N	Y					
7 **Barr**	N	Y	Y	Y	Y	N	N
8 **Chambliss**	N	Y	Y	Y	Y	N	N
9 **Deal**	N	Y	Y	Y	Y	N	N
10 **Norwood**	N	Y	Y	Y	Y	N	N
11 **Linder**	N	Y	Y	Y	Y	N	N
HAWAII							
1 Abercrombie	Y	N	N	N	Y	Y	Y
2 Mink	Y	N	N	N	N	Y	Y
IDAHO							
1 **Chenoweth**	N	Y	Y	Y	Y	N	Y
2 **Crapo**	N	N	?	N	Y	Y	Y
ILLINOIS							
1 Rush	Y	N	N	N	N	Y	Y
2 Jackson	Y	N	N	N	N	Y	Y
3 Lipinski	Y	Y	N	N	Y	N	N
4 Gutierrez	Y	N	N	N	N	Y	Y
5 Blagojevich	Y	N	N	N	?	Y	Y
6 **Hyde**	N	Y	Y	Y	Y	N	N
7 Davis	Y	N	N	N	−	+	+
8 **Crane**	N	Y	Y	Y	Y	N	N
9 Yates	Y	N	N	N	N	Y	Y
10 **Porter**	N	Y	Y	N	N	Y	Y
11 **Weller**	N	Y	Y	Y	Y	N	N
12 Costello	Y	N	N	N	N	N	Y

ND Northern Democrats   SD Southern Democrats

	125	126	127	128	129	130	131
13 ***Fawell***	N	N	?	Y	N	N	N
14 ***Hastert***	N	Y	Y	Y	N	N	N
15 ***Ewing***	N	Y	Y	Y	N	N	N
16 ***Manzullo***	N	Y	Y	Y	Y	N	N
17 Evans	Y	N	N	Y	N	Y	Y
18 ***LaHood***	N	Y	Y	Y	N	N	N
19 Poshard	Y	N	N	N	N	Y	Y
20 ***Shimkus***	N	Y	Y	Y	Y	N	N
INDIANA							
1 Visclosky	Y	N	N	N	–	+	+
2 ***McIntosh***	N	Y	Y	Y	Y	N	N
3 Roemer	Y	N	N	N	N	Y	Y
4 ***Souder***	N	Y	Y	N	Y	N	N
5 ***Buyer***	N	Y	Y	Y	N	N	Y
6 ***Burton***	N	Y	Y	Y	N	N	N
7 ***Pease***	N	Y	Y	Y	Y	N	Y
8 ***Hostettler***	N	Y	Y	Y	Y	N	N
9 Hamilton	Y	N	N	N	N	Y	Y
10 Carson	Y	N	N	N	–	+	+
IOWA							
1 ***Leach***	N	N	Y	Y	N	N	Y
2 ***Nussle***	N	Y	Y	N	Y	N	Y
3 Boswell	Y	N	N	N	N	N	Y
4 ***Ganske***	N	Y	Y	Y	N	N	N
5 ***Latham***	N	Y	Y	Y	?	N	N
KANSAS							
1 ***Moran***	N	Y	Y	Y	Y	N	N
2 ***Ryun***	N	Y	Y	Y	Y	N	N
3 ***Snowbarger***	N	Y	Y	Y	Y	N	N
4 ***Tiahrt***	N	Y	Y	Y	Y	N	N
KENTUCKY							
1 ***Whitfield***	N	Y	Y	Y	N	N	N
2 ***Lewis***	N	Y	Y	Y	Y	N	N
3 ***Northup***	N	Y	Y	Y	N	N	N
4 ***Bunning***	?	#	?	#	Y	N	N
5 ***Rogers***	N	Y	Y	Y	N	N	N
6 Baesler	Y	N	N	N	N	Y	Y
LOUISIANA							
1 ***Livingston***	N	Y	Y	Y	Y	N	N
2 Jefferson	Y	N	N	Y	N	Y	Y
3 ***Tauzin***	N	Y	Y	Y	?	?	?
4 ***McCrery***	N	Y	Y	Y	N	N	N
5 ***Cooksey***	N	Y	Y	Y	Y	N	N
6 ***Baker***	N	Y	Y	?	N	N	N
7 John	Y	N	N	Y	N	N	Y
MAINE							
1 Allen	Y	N	N	Y	N	Y	Y
2 Baldacci	Y	N	N	Y	N	Y	Y
MARYLAND							
1 ***Gilchrest***	N	Y	Y	Y	N	N	Y
2 ***Ehrlich***	N	Y	Y	Y	N	N	N
3 Cardin	Y	N	N	N	N	Y	Y
4 Wynn	Y	N	N	N	N	Y	Y
5 Hoyer	Y	N	N	N	N	Y	Y
6 ***Bartlett***	N	Y	Y	Y	Y	N	N
7 Cummings	Y	N	N	N	N	Y	Y
8 ***Morella***	Y	N	Y	N	N	Y	Y
MASSACHUSETTS							
1 Olver	Y	N	N	N	N	Y	Y
2 Neal	Y	N	N	N	N	Y	Y
3 McGovern	Y	N	N	N	N	Y	Y
4 Frank	Y	N	N	N	Y	Y	Y
5 Meehan	Y	N	?	?	N	Y	Y
6 Tierney	Y	N	N	N	N	Y	Y
7 Markey	Y	N	N	N	N	Y	Y
8 Kennedy	Y	N	N	N	N	Y	Y
9 Moakley	Y	N	N	N	N	Y	Y
10 Delahunt	Y	N	N	N	N	Y	Y
MICHIGAN							
1 Stupak	Y	N	N	N	N	Y	Y
2 ***Hoekstra***	N	Y	Y	N	Y	N	N
3 ***Ehlers***	N	Y	Y	N	Y	N	N
4 ***Camp***	N	Y	Y	N	Y	N	N
5 Barcia	Y	N	N	N	Y	Y	Y
6 ***Upton***	N	Y	Y	N	N	N	N
7 ***Smith***	X	#	?	?	Y	N	N
8 Stabenow	Y	N	N	N	N	Y	Y
9 Kildee	Y	N	N	N	N	Y	Y
10 Bonior	Y	N	N	N	Y	Y	Y
11 ***Knollenberg***	N	Y	Y	Y	N	N	N
12 Levin	Y	N	N	N	N	Y	Y
13 Rivers	Y	N	N	N	N	Y	Y
14 Conyers	Y	N	N	N	N	Y	Y
15 Kilpatrick	Y	N	N	N	N	Y	Y
16 Dingell	Y	N	N	N	N	Y	N

	125	126	127	128	129	130	131
MINNESOTA							
1 ***Gutknecht***	N	Y	Y	Y	N	N	N
2 Minge	Y	N	N	Y	N	Y	Y
3 ***Ramstad***	Y	N	Y	Y	N	N	Y
4 Vento	Y	N	N	N	N	Y	Y
5 Sabo	Y	N	N	N	N	N	Y
6 Luther	Y	N	N	N	N	Y	Y
7 Peterson	Y	N	N	Y	N	N	Y
8 Oberstar	Y	N	N	N	N	Y	Y
MISSISSIPPI							
1 ***Wicker***	N	Y	Y	Y	Y	N	N
2 Thompson	Y	N	N	?	N	Y	Y
3 ***Pickering***	N	Y	Y	Y	Y	N	N
4 ***Parker***	?	?	?	?	?	?	?
5 Taylor	N	Y	N	Y	N	N	Y
MISSOURI							
1 Clay	Y	N	N	N	N	Y	Y
2 ***Talent***	N	Y	Y	Y	N	N	N
3 Gephardt	Y	N	N	N	Y	Y	Y
4 Skelton	Y	N	N	N	N	N	Y
5 McCarthy	Y	N	N	N	N	Y	Y
6 Danner	Y	N	N	N	N	Y	Y
7 ***Blunt***	N	Y	Y	Y	N	N	N
8 ***Emerson***	N	Y	Y	Y	Y	N	Y
9 ***Hulshof***	N	Y	Y	Y	Y	N	N
MONTANA							
AL ***Hill***	N	Y	Y	Y	Y	N	N
NEBRASKA							
1 ***Bereuter***	N	Y	Y	Y	N	N	N
2 ***Christensen***	N	Y	Y	Y	?	?	?
3 ***Barrett***	N	Y	Y	Y	N	N	N
NEVADA							
1 ***Ensign***	N	Y	Y	Y	Y	N	N
2 ***Gibbons***	N	Y	Y	Y	Y	N	N
NEW HAMPSHIRE							
1 ***Sununu***	N	Y	Y	Y	Y	N	N
2 ***Bass***	N	Y	Y	Y	N	N	Y
NEW JERSEY							
1 Andrews	Y	N	N	N	N	Y	Y
2 ***LoBiondo***	N	N	Y	Y	N	N	Y
3 ***Saxton***	N	Y	Y	Y	N	N	N
4 ***Smith***	N	Y	Y	Y	N	N	Y
5 ***Roukema***	N	N	Y	Y	N	N	N
6 Pallone	Y	N	N	N	N	Y	Y
7 ***Franks***	N	Y	Y	Y	N	N	N
8 Pascrell	Y	N	N	N	N	Y	Y
9 Rothman	Y	N	N	N	N	Y	Y
10 Payne	Y	N	N	N	N	Y	Y
11 ***Frelinghuysen***	N	Y	Y	Y	N	N	N
12 ***Pappas***	N	Y	Y	Y	N	N	Y
13 Menendez	Y	N	N	N	?	Y	Y
NEW MEXICO							
1 Vacant							
2 ***Skeen***	N	Y	Y	Y	N	N	Y
3 ***Redmond***	N	Y	Y	Y	Y	N	Y
NEW YORK							
1 ***Forbes***	N	Y	Y	Y	–	–	–
2 ***Lazio***	N	Y	Y	Y	N	N	Y
3 ***King***	N	Y	Y	Y	N	N	N
4 McCarthy	Y	N	N	Y	N	Y	Y
5 Ackerman	Y	N	N	N	N	Y	Y
6 Meeks	Y	N	N	N	?	?	?
7 Manton	Y	N	N	Y	N	Y	Y
8 Nadler	Y	N	N	N	N	Y	Y
9 Schumer	Y	N	N	N	N	Y	Y
10 Towns	Y	N	N	N	Y	Y	Y
11 Owens	Y	N	N	N	N	Y	Y
12 Velázquez	Y	N	N	N	N	Y	Y
13 ***Fossella***	N	Y	Y	Y	?	?	?
14 Maloney	Y	N	N	?	N	Y	Y
15 Rangel	Y	N	N	N	N	Y	Y
16 Serrano	Y	N	N	N	N	Y	Y
17 Engel	Y	N	N	N	N	Y	Y
18 Lowey	Y	N	N	N	?	?	?
19 ***Kelly***	N	Y	Y	Y	Y	N	N
20 ***Gilman***	N	Y	Y	Y	N	N	N
21 McNulty	Y	N	N	N	?	?	?
22 ***Solomon***	N	Y	Y	Y	N	N	N
23 ***Boehlert***	N	N	Y	Y	N	N	N
24 ***McHugh***	?	N	Y	Y	N	N	N
25 ***Walsh***	N	Y	Y	Y	N	N	N
26 Hinchey	Y	N	N	N	Y	Y	Y
27 ***Paxon***	N	Y	Y	?	N	N	N
28 Slaughter	Y	N	N	N	N	Y	Y
29 LaFalce	Y	N	N	N	N	Y	Y

	125	126	127	128	129	130	131
30 ***Quinn***	N	Y	Y	Y	N	N	N
31 ***Houghton***	N	Y	Y	Y	N	N	N
NORTH CAROLINA							
1 Clayton	Y	N	N	N	N	Y	Y
2 Etheridge	Y	N	N	Y	N	Y	Y
3 ***Jones***	N	Y	Y	Y	N	N	N
4 Price	Y	N	N	N	N	Y	Y
5 ***Burr***	N	Y	Y	Y	N	N	N
6 ***Coble***	N	Y	Y	Y	N	N	N
7 McIntyre	Y	N	N	Y	N	Y	Y
8 Hefner	Y	N	N	N	N	Y	Y
9 ***Myrick***	N	Y	Y	Y	N	N	N
10 ***Ballenger***	N	Y	Y	Y	N	N	N
11 ***Taylor***	N	Y	Y	Y	N	N	N
12 Watt	Y	N	N	N	N	Y	Y
NORTH DAKOTA							
AL Pomeroy	Y	N	N	Y	N	Y	Y
OHIO							
1 ***Chabot***	N	Y	Y	Y	Y	N	N
2 ***Portman***	N	Y	Y	Y	Y	N	N
3 Hall	Y	N	N	N	N	Y	Y
4 ***Oxley***	N	Y	Y	Y	N	N	N
5 ***Gillmor***	N	Y	Y	Y	Y	N	N
6 Strickland	Y	N	N	Y	N	Y	Y
7 ***Hobson***	N	Y	Y	Y	Y	N	N
8 ***Boehner***	N	+	Y	Y	Y	N	N
9 Kaptur	Y	N	?	N	?	?	?
10 Kucinich	Y	N	N	N	Y	Y	Y
11 Stokes	Y	N	N	N	?	?	?
12 ***Kasich***	N	Y	Y	Y	Y	N	N
13 Brown	Y	N	N	N	N	Y	Y
14 Sawyer	Y	N	N	N	N	Y	Y
15 ***Pryce***	N	Y	Y	Y	Y	N	N
16 ***Regula***	N	Y	Y	Y	Y	N	N
17 Traficant	Y	N	N	Y	N	N	Y
18 ***Ney***	N	Y	Y	Y	Y	N	N
19 ***LaTourette***	N	Y	Y	Y	N	N	N
OKLAHOMA							
1 ***Largent***	N	Y	Y	Y	Y	N	N
2 ***Coburn***	N	Y	Y	Y	Y	N	N
3 ***Watkins***	N	Y	Y	Y	Y	N	Y
4 ***Watts***	N	Y	Y	Y	Y	N	Y
5 ***Istook***	N	Y	Y	Y	N	N	N
6 ***Lucas***	N	Y	Y	Y	Y	N	N
OREGON							
1 Furse	Y	N	N	N	?	?	?
2 ***Smith***	N	Y	?	Y	N	N	N
3 Blumenauer	Y	N	N	N	N	Y	Y
4 DeFazio	Y	N	?	X	Y	Y	Y
5 Hooley	Y	N	N	N	N	Y	Y
PENNSYLVANIA							
1 Vacant							
2 Fattah	Y	N	N	N	N	Y	Y
3 Borski	Y	N	N	Y	N	Y	Y
4 Klink	Y	N	N	N	N	Y	Y
5 ***Peterson***	N	Y	Y	Y	Y	N	N
6 Holden	Y	N	N	Y	N	Y	Y
7 ***Weldon***	N	Y	?	Y	N	N	N
8 ***Greenwood***	N	Y	?	?	N	N	N
9 ***Shuster***	N	Y	Y	Y	N	N	N
10 ***McDade***	N	Y	Y	Y	N	N	N
11 Kanjorski	Y	N	N	N	Y	N	Y
12 Murtha	Y	N	N	Y	N	N	Y
13 ***Fox***	N	Y	Y	Y	N	N	Y
14 Coyne	Y	N	N	N	N	Y	Y
15 McHale	Y	N	N	N	Y	N	Y
16 ***Pitts***	N	Y	Y	Y	N	N	N
17 ***Gekas***	N	Y	Y	Y	N	N	N
18 Doyle	Y	N	N	Y	N	Y	Y
19 ***Goodling***	N	Y	Y	Y	N	N	N
20 Mascara	Y	N	N	Y	N	Y	Y
21 ***English***	N	N	Y	Y	N	N	N
RHODE ISLAND							
1 Kennedy	Y	N	N	N	N	Y	Y
2 Weygand	Y	N	N	N	N	Y	Y
SOUTH CAROLINA							
1 ***Sanford***	N	Y	Y	N	Y	N	N
2 ***Spence***	N	Y	Y	Y	N	N	N
3 ***Graham***	N	Y	Y	Y	N	N	N
4 ***Inglis***	N	Y	Y	N	Y	N	N
5 Spratt	Y	N	N	N	N	Y	Y
6 Clyburn	Y	N	N	N	?	?	?
SOUTH DAKOTA							
AL ***Thune***	N	Y	Y	Y	Y	N	N

	125	126	127	128	129	130	131
TENNESSEE							
1 ***Jenkins***	N	Y	Y	Y	N	N	N
2 ***Duncan***	N	Y	Y	N	Y	N	N
3 ***Wamp***	N	Y	Y	Y	Y	N	N
4 ***Hilleary***	N	Y	Y	Y	N	N	N
5 Clement	Y	N	N	Y	N	Y	Y
6 Gordon	Y	N	N	Y	N	Y	Y
7 ***Bryant***	N	Y	Y	Y	N	N	N
8 Tanner	Y	N	N	Y	N	N	Y
9 Ford	Y	N	N	N	N	Y	Y
TEXAS							
1 Sandlin	?	?	?	?	N	Y	Y
2 Turner	Y	N	N	Y	N	N	Y
3 ***Johnson, Sam***	N	Y	?	Y	Y	N	N
4 Hall	N	?	?	?	Y	N	N
5 ***Sessions***	N	Y	Y	Y	Y	N	N
6 ***Barton***	N	Y	Y	Y	Y	N	N
7 ***Archer***	N	Y	Y	Y	Y	N	N
8 ***Brady***	N	Y	Y	Y	Y	N	N
9 Lampson	Y	N	N	N	N	Y	Y
10 Doggett	Y	N	N	N	N	Y	Y
11 Edwards	Y	N	N	Y	N	N	Y
12 ***Granger***	N	Y	Y	Y	N	N	N
13 ***Thornberry***	N	Y	Y	Y	Y	N	N
14 ***Paul***	N	P	Y	N	Y	N	N
15 Hinojosa	Y	N	N	N	N	Y	Y
16 Reyes	Y	N	N	Y	N	Y	Y
17 Stenholm	Y	N	N	Y	N	N	Y
18 Jackson-Lee	Y	N	N	N	N	Y	Y
19 ***Combest***	N	Y	Y	Y	N	N	N
20 Gonzalez	?	?	?	?	?	?	?
21 ***Smith***	N	Y	Y	Y	N	N	N
22 ***DeLay***	N	Y	Y	Y	Y	N	N
23 ***Bonilla***	N	Y	Y	Y	Y	N	N
24 Frost	Y	N	N	Y	N	Y	Y
25 Bentsen	Y	N	N	N	N	Y	Y
26 ***Armey***	N	Y	Y	Y	Y	N	N
27 Ortiz	Y	N	N	Y	N	Y	Y
28 Rodriguez	Y	N	N	Y	N	Y	Y
29 Green	Y	N	N	X	N	Y	Y
30 Johnson, E.B.	Y	N	N	N	N	Y	Y
UTAH							
1 ***Hansen***	N	Y	Y	Y	N	N	N
2 ***Cook***	N	Y	Y	Y	N	N	N
3 ***Cannon***	N	Y	Y	Y	Y	N	N
VERMONT							
AL *Sanders*	Y	N	N	N	N	Y	Y
VIRGINIA							
1 ***Bateman***	–	+	+	+	–	–	–
2 Pickett	N	N	N	Y	N	N	Y
3 Scott	Y	N	N	N	N	Y	Y
4 Sisisky	Y	N	N	Y	N	N	Y
5 Goode	N	N	N	Y	N	Y	Y
6 ***Goodlatte***	N	Y	Y	Y	Y	N	Y
7 ***Bliley***	N	Y	?	#	N	N	Y
8 Moran	N	Y	N	Y	N	Y	Y
9 Boucher	Y	N	N	N	N	Y	Y
10 ***Wolf***	N	Y	Y	Y	N	N	N
11 ***Davis***	N	Y	Y	Y	N	N	N
WASHINGTON							
1 ***White***	N	Y	Y	Y	Y	N	N
2 ***Metcalf***	N	Y	Y	?	Y	N	N
3 ***Smith, Linda***	N	Y	Y	Y	?	?	?
4 ***Hastings***	N	Y	Y	Y	Y	N	N
5 ***Nethercutt***	N	Y	Y	Y	Y	N	N
6 Dicks	Y	N	N	Y	N	Y	Y
7 McDermott	Y	N	N	N	Y	Y	Y
8 ***Dunn***	N	Y	?	?	N	N	N
9 Smith, Adam	Y	N	N	N	N	Y	Y
WEST VIRGINIA							
1 Mollohan	Y	N	N	Y	?	Y	Y
2 Wise	Y	N	N	N	N	Y	Y
3 Rahall	Y	N	N	N	?	?	?
WISCONSIN							
1 ***Neumann***	N	Y	Y	N	?	?	?
2 ***Klug***	N	Y	Y	N	N	N	N
3 Kind	Y	N	N	N	N	Y	Y
4 Kleczka	Y	N	N	N	Y	Y	Y
5 Barrett	Y	N	N	N	N	Y	Y
6 ***Petri***	N	Y	Y	Y	Y	N	N
7 Obey	Y	N	N	N	Y	Y	Y
8 Johnson	Y	N	N	N	N	Y	Y
9 ***Sensenbrenner***	N	Y	?	?	Y	N	N
WYOMING							
AL ***Cubin***	N	Y	Y	Y	?	N	N

Southern states - Ala., Ark., Fla., Ga., Ky., La., Miss., N.C., Okla., S.C., Tenn., Texas, Va.

House Votes 132, 133, 134, 135, 136, 137, 138

132. HR 6. Higher Education Act Reauthorization/Olympic Scholarships. Stupak, D-Mich., amendment to authorize $5 million for each of five fiscal years for the Olympic Scholarship program, which provides college scholarships for Olympic athletes while they train. Adopted 219-200: R 37-183; D 181-17 (ND 137-9, SD 44-8); I 1-0. May 6, 1998.

133. HR 6. Higher Education Act Reauthorization/Preferential Treatment. Riggs, R-Calif., amendment to prohibit any public institution of higher education that participates in any Higher Education Act program from discriminating against, or granting preferential treatment to any person or group in admissions based in whole or in part on race, sex, color, ethnicity or national origin. Rejected 171-249: R 166-55; D 5-193 (ND 2-143, SD 3-50); I 0-1. May 6, 1998. A "nay" was a vote in support of the president's position.

134. HR 6. Higher Education Act Reauthorization/Race. Campbell, R-Calif., amendment to provide that no person shall be excluded from, or have a diminished chance of acceptance to, the minority science and engineering improvement program of the Higher Education Act because of the applicant's race, color, religion or national origin. Rejected 189-227: R 184-34; D 5-192 (ND 1-144, SD 4-48); I 0-1. May 6, 1998.

135. HR 6. Higher Education Act Reauthorization/Passage. Passage of the bill to reauthorize federal student financial aid programs and other federal assistance to institutions of higher education through fiscal 2003. Passed 414-4: R 215-4; D 198-0 (ND 145-0, SD 53-0); I 1-0. May 6, 1998.

136. HR 2646. Education Savings Accounts/Motion to Instruct. Rangel, D-N.Y., motion to instruct the House conferees to agree to provisions relating to tax-favored financing for public school construction consistent, to the maximum extent possible, with the approach taken in HR 3320, the Public School Modernization Act of 1998. Motion rejected 192-222: R 5-214; D 186-8 (ND 139-5, SD 47-3); I 1-0. May 7, 1998.

137. HR 3694. Fiscal 1999 Intelligence Authorization/Authorization Reduction. Sanders, I-Vt., amendment to reduce the bill's authorization by 5 percent. The bill authorizes classified amounts in fiscal 1999 for U.S. intelligence agencies and intelligence-related activities of the U.S. government. Rejected 120-291: R 21-196; D 98-95 (ND 85-56, SD 13-39); I 1-0. May 7, 1998. (Subsequently, the bill passed by voice vote).

138. H Res 423. Drugs and Children/Adoption. Hastert, R-Ill., motion to suspend the rules and adopt the resolution to express the sense of the House that it is committed to working toward making America drug-free. Motion agreed to 412-2: R 217-2; D 194-0 (ND 141-0, SD 53-0); I 1-0. May 12, 1998. A two-thirds majority of those present and voting (276 in this case) is required for adoption under suspension of the rules.

Key

- Y Voted for (yea).
- # Paired for.
- + Announced for.
- N Voted against (nay).
- X Paired against.
- − Announced against.
- P Voted "present."
- C Voted "present" to avoid possible conflict of interest.
- ? Did not vote or otherwise make a position known.

Democrats   **Republicans**
Independent

	132	133	134	135	136	137	138
ALABAMA							
1 *Callahan*	Y	Y	N	Y	N	Y	Y
2 *Everett*	Y	Y	N	Y	N	Y	Y
3 *Riley*	Y	Y	N	Y	N	Y	Y
4 *Aderholt*	Y	Y	N	Y	Y	Y	Y
5 Cramer	Y	Y	N	Y	Y	Y	Y
6 *Bachus*	Y	Y	N	Y	N	Y	Y
7 Hilliard	Y	Y	N	Y	Y	Y	Y
ALASKA							
AL *Young*	Y	Y	Y	Y	Y	N	Y
ARIZONA							
1 *Salmon*	Y	Y	Y	N	Y	Y	Y
2 *Pastor*	Y	Y	N	Y	Y	Y	Y
3 *Stump*	Y	Y	N	Y	N	Y	N
4 *Shadegg*	Y	Y	Y	N	Y	Y	N
5 *Kolbe*	Y	Y	N	Y	N	Y	Y
6 *Hayworth*	Y	Y	N	Y	N	Y	Y
ARKANSAS							
1 Berry	Y	Y	Y	Y	N	Y	Y
2 Snyder	Y	Y	N	Y	Y	Y	Y
3 *Hutchinson*	Y	Y	?	Y	N	Y	Y
4 Dickey	Y	Y	N	Y	Y	Y	N
CALIFORNIA							
1 *Riggs*	Y	Y	−	−	Y	Y	Y
2 *Herger*	Y	Y	N	Y	N	Y	N
3 Fazio	Y	Y	N	Y	Y	Y	Y
4 *Doolittle*	Y	Y	Y	Y	Y	N	Y
5 Matsui	Y	Y	N	Y	Y	Y	Y
6 Woolsey	Y	Y	N	Y	Y	Y	Y
7 Miller	Y	Y	N	Y	Y	Y	Y
8 Pelosi	Y	Y	?	N	Y	Y	Y
9 Lee	Y	Y	N	Y	Y	Y	Y
10 Tauscher	Y	Y	N	Y	Y	Y	Y
11 *Pombo*	Y	Y	Y	Y	N	N	Y
12 Lantos	?	?	N	Y	Y	Y	Y
13 Stark	Y	Y	N	Y	Y	Y	Y
14 Eshoo	Y	Y	N	Y	Y	Y	Y
15 *Campbell*	Y	Y	N	Y	Y	Y	Y
16 Lofgren	Y	Y	N	Y	Y	Y	Y
17 Farr	Y	Y	N	Y	Y	Y	Y
18 Condit	Y	Y	Y	Y	N	Y	Y
19 *Radanovich*	Y	Y	?	?	?	?	?
20 Dooley	Y	Y	Y	Y	Y	Y	Y
21 *Thomas*	Y	Y	N	Y	N	Y	Y
22 Capps, L.	Y	Y	N	Y	Y	Y	Y
23 *Gallegly*	Y	Y	N	Y	N	Y	Y
24 Sherman	Y	Y	N	Y	Y	Y	Y
25 *McKeon*	Y	Y	N	Y	N	Y	Y
26 Berman	Y	Y	N	Y	Y	Y	Y
27 *Rogan*	Y	Y	?	N	Y	N	Y
28 *Dreier*	Y	Y	N	Y	N	Y	Y
29 Waxman	Y	Y	N	Y	Y	Y	Y
30 Becerra	Y	Y	N	Y	Y	Y	Y
31 Martinez	Y	Y	Y	Y	N	Y	Y
32 Dixon	Y	Y	N	Y	Y	Y	Y
33 Royal-Allard	Y	Y	N	Y	Y	Y	Y
34 Torres	Y	Y	N	Y	Y	Y	Y
35 Waters	Y	Y	N	Y	Y	Y	Y
36 Harman	?	?	N	N	Y	Y	Y
37 Millender-McD.	Y	Y	N	Y	Y	Y	Y

	132	133	134	135	136	137	138
38 *Horn*	Y	Y	Y	Y	Y	Y	Y
39 *Royce*	Y	Y	N	Y	Y	Y	Y
40 *Lewis*	Y	Y	N	Y	N	Y	Y
41 *Kim*	Y	Y	N	Y	N	Y	Y
42 Brown	Y	Y	N	Y	Y	Y	Y
43 *Calvert*	Y	Y	Y	Y	Y	Y	Y
44 *Bono, M.*	Y	Y	N	Y	Y	Y	Y
45 *Rohrabacher*	Y	Y	Y	Y	Y	Y	N
46 Sanchez	Y	Y	N	Y	Y	Y	Y
47 *Cox*	Y	Y	N	Y	N	Y	Y
48 *Packard*	Y	Y	N	Y	N	N	N
49 *Bilbray*	Y	Y	N	Y	Y	Y	Y
50 Filner	Y	Y	Y	Y	Y	Y	Y
51 *Cunningham*	Y	Y	N	Y	N	Y	Y
52 *Hunter*	Y	Y	N	N	Y	N	Y
COLORADO							
1 DeGette	Y	Y	N	Y	Y	Y	Y
2 Skaggs	+	+	−	+	−	+	+
3 *McInnis*	Y	Y	Y	Y	N	Y	Y
4 *Schaffer*	Y	Y	Y	N	Y	N	Y
5 *Hefley*	Y	Y	N	N	Y	Y	Y
6 *Schaefer*	?	?	Y	Y	Y	N	Y
CONNECTICUT							
1 Kennelly	Y	Y	N	Y	Y	Y	Y
2 Gejdenson	Y	Y	N	Y	Y	Y	Y
3 DeLauro	Y	Y	N	Y	Y	Y	Y
4 *Shays*	Y	Y	N	Y	N	Y	Y
5 Maloney	Y	Y	N	Y	Y	Y	Y
6 *Johnson*	Y	Y	N	Y	Y	Y	Y
DELAWARE							
AL *Castle*	Y	Y	N	Y	Y	Y	Y
FLORIDA							
1 *Scarborough*	Y	Y	N	Y	Y	Y	Y
2 Boyd	Y	Y	N	Y	Y	Y	Y
3 Brown	Y	Y	N	Y	Y	Y	Y
4 *Fowler*	Y	Y	N	Y	N	Y	Y
5 Thurman	Y	Y	N	Y	Y	Y	Y
6 *Stearns*	Y	Y	Y	Y	Y	Y	Y
7 *Mica*	Y	Y	N	Y	N	Y	Y
8 *McCollum*	Y	Y	?	N	N	N	Y
9 *Bilirakis*	Y	N	Y	Y	Y	N	Y
10 *Young*	Y	Y	N	Y	N	N	Y
11 Davis	Y	Y	N	Y	Y	Y	Y
12 *Canady*	Y	Y	N	Y	N	Y	Y
13 *Miller*	Y	Y	N	Y	N	N	N
14 *Goss*	Y	Y	N	Y	N	Y	Y
15 *Weldon*	Y	Y	N	Y	N	Y	Y
16 *Foley*	Y	Y	N	Y	Y	Y	Y
17 Meek	Y	Y	N	Y	Y	Y	Y
18 *Ros-Lehtinen*	Y	Y	N	Y	Y	Y	Y
19 Wexler	Y	Y	N	Y	Y	Y	Y
20 Deutsch	Y	Y	N	Y	Y	Y	Y
21 *Diaz-Balart*	Y	Y	N	Y	N	Y	Y
22 *Shaw*	Y	Y	N	Y	N	Y	Y
23 Hastings	?	?	?	?	?	?	?
GEORGIA							
1 *Kingston*	Y	Y	N	Y	N	Y	Y
2 Bishop	Y	Y	N	Y	Y	Y	Y
3 *Collins*	Y	Y	N	Y	Y	N	N
4 McKinney	Y	Y	N	Y	Y	Y	Y
5 Lewis	Y	Y	N	N	Y	Y	Y
6 *Gingrich*							
7 *Barr*	Y	Y	N	Y	N	N	Y
8 *Chambliss*	Y	Y	N	Y	N	Y	Y
9 *Deal*	Y	Y	N	Y	Y	Y	Y
10 *Norwood*	Y	Y	N	N	Y	Y	Y
11 *Linder*	Y	Y	N	Y	N	Y	Y
HAWAII							
1 Abercrombie	Y	Y	N	N	Y	Y	Y
2 Mink	Y	Y	Y	Y	Y	Y	Y
IDAHO							
1 *Chenoweth*	Y	Y	Y	N	?	N	Y
2 *Crapo*	Y	Y	N	Y	N	Y	Y
ILLINOIS							
1 Rush	Y	Y	N	Y	Y	Y	Y
2 Jackson	Y	Y	N	N	Y	Y	Y
3 Lipinski	Y	Y	N	N	Y	Y	Y
4 Gutierrez	Y	Y	N	N	Y	Y	Y
5 Blagojevich	Y	Y	Y	Y	Y	Y	Y
6 *Hyde*	Y	Y	N	Y	N	Y	Y
7 Davis	+	+	Y	Y	Y	Y	Y
8 *Crane*	Y	Y	N	Y	N	Y	Y
9 Yates	Y	Y	N	N	Y	Y	Y
10 *Porter*	Y	Y	N	Y	Y	Y	Y
11 *Weller*	Y	Y	N	Y	N	Y	Y
12 Costello	Y	Y	N	Y	Y	Y	Y

ND Northern Democrats   SD Southern Democrats

	132	133	134	135	136	137	138
13 ***Fawell***	Y	Y	N	N	Y	N	Y
14 ***Hastert***	Y	Y	N	N	Y	N	Y
15 ***Ewing***	Y	Y	N	N	Y	Y	Y
16 ***Manzullo***	Y	Y	N	N	Y	N	Y
17 Evans	Y	Y	N	N	Y	Y	Y
18 ***LaHood***	Y	Y	N	N	Y	Y	Y
19 Poshard	Y	Y	N	N	Y	Y	Y
20 ***Shimkus***	Y	Y	N	N	Y	N	Y
INDIANA							
1 Visclosky	+	+	N	N	Y	Y	Y
2 ***McIntosh***	Y	Y	Y	N	Y	N	Y
3 Roemer	Y	Y	N	N	Y	Y	Y
4 ***Souder***	Y	Y	N	N	Y	N	Y
5 ***Buyer***	Y	Y	N	N	Y	Y	Y
6 ***Burton***	Y	Y	N	N	Y	N	Y
7 ***Pease***	Y	Y	N	N	Y	Y	Y
8 ***Hostettler***	Y	Y	N	N	Y	Y	Y
9 Hamilton	Y	Y	Y	Y	N	Y	Y
10 Carson	+	+	–	–	+	+	+
IOWA							
1 ***Leach***	Y	Y	N	N	Y	N	Y
2 ***Nussle***	Y	Y	Y	Y	Y	N	Y
3 Boswell	Y	Y	N	N	Y	Y	Y
4 ***Ganske***	Y	Y	N	N	Y	N	Y
5 ***Latham***	Y	Y	N	N	Y	N	Y
KANSAS							
1 ***Moran***	Y	Y	N	N	Y	Y	Y
2 ***Ryun***	Y	Y	N	N	Y	N	Y
3 ***Snowbarger***	Y	Y	N	Y	Y	N	Y
4 ***Tiahrt***	Y	Y	N	N	Y	N	N
KENTUCKY							
1 ***Whitfield***	Y	Y	N	N	Y	Y	Y
2 ***Lewis***	Y	Y	N	N	Y	N	Y
3 ***Northup***	Y	Y	Y	N	Y	N	Y
4 ***Bunning***	Y	Y	N	N	Y	N	Y
5 ***Rogers***	Y	Y	N	N	Y	Y	Y
6 Baesler	Y	Y	N	N	Y	Y	Y
LOUISIANA							
1 ***Livingston***	Y	Y	Y	Y	Y	N	Y
2 Jefferson	Y	Y	N	N	Y	Y	Y
3 ***Tauzin***	?	?	Y	Y	Y	Y	Y
4 ***McCrery***	Y	Y	N	Y	Y	Y	Y
5 ***Cooksey***	Y	Y	N	N	Y	N	Y
6 ***Baker***	Y	Y	Y	Y	Y	Y	Y
7 John	Y	Y	Y	Y	N	Y	Y
MAINE							
1 Allen	Y	Y	N	N	Y	Y	Y
2 Baldacci	Y	Y	N	N	Y	Y	Y
MARYLAND							
1 ***Gilchrest***	Y	Y	Y	Y	Y	N	Y
2 ***Ehrlich***	Y	Y	Y	N	Y	N	Y
3 Cardin	Y	Y	P	P	P	Y	Y
4 Wynn	Y	Y	Y	Y	Y	Y	Y
5 Hoyer	Y	Y	Y	Y	N	Y	Y
6 ***Bartlett***	Y	Y	Y	Y	Y	Y	Y
7 Cummings	Y	Y	Y	Y	Y	Y	Y
8 ***Morella***	Y	Y	Y	Y	N	Y	Y
MASSACHUSETTS							
1 Olver	Y	Y	N	N	Y	Y	Y
2 Neal	Y	Y	N	N	Y	Y	Y
3 McGovern	Y	Y	N	N	Y	Y	Y
4 Frank	Y	Y	N	N	Y	Y	Y
5 Meehan	Y	Y	N	N	Y	Y	Y
6 Tierney	Y	Y	N	N	Y	Y	Y
7 Markey	Y	Y	N	N	Y	Y	Y
8 Kennedy	Y	Y	N	N	Y	Y	Y
9 Moakley	Y	Y	N	N	Y	Y	Y
10 Delahunt	Y	Y	N	N	Y	Y	Y
MICHIGAN							
1 Stupak	Y	Y	N	N	Y	Y	Y
2 ***Hoekstra***	Y	Y	N	N	Y	N	Y
3 ***Ehlers***	Y	Y	N	N	Y	Y	Y
4 ***Camp***	Y	Y	N	N	Y	Y	Y
5 Barcia	Y	Y	Y	Y	Y	Y	Y
6 ***Upton***	Y	Y	Y	Y	Y	Y	Y
7 ***Smith***	Y	Y	N	Y	Y	Y	N
8 Stabenow	Y	Y	N	N	Y	Y	Y
9 Kildee	Y	Y	N	N	Y	Y	Y
10 Bonior	Y	Y	Y	Y	Y	Y	Y
11 ***Knollenberg***	Y	Y	N	N	Y	N	Y
12 Levin	Y	Y	N	Y	Y	Y	Y
13 Rivers	Y	Y	Y	Y	Y	Y	Y
14 Conyers	Y	Y	Y	Y	N	Y	Y
15 Kilpatrick	Y	Y	Y	N	Y	Y	Y
16 Dingell	Y	Y	Y	Y	N	Y	Y
MINNESOTA							
1 ***Gutknecht***	Y	Y	Y	N	Y	N	Y
2 Minge	Y	Y	Y	N	Y	Y	Y
3 ***Ramstad***	Y	Y	N	N	Y	Y	Y
4 Vento	Y	Y	N	N	Y	Y	Y
5 Sabo	Y	Y	Y	Y	Y	N	Y
6 Luther	Y	Y	N	N	Y	Y	Y
7 Peterson	Y	Y	Y	Y	N	Y	Y
8 Oberstar	Y	Y	Y	N	N	Y	Y
MISSISSIPPI							
1 ***Wicker***	Y	Y	N	N	Y	N	N
2 Thompson	Y	Y	Y	Y	Y	Y	Y
3 ***Pickering***	Y	Y	N	N	Y	N	Y
4 ***Parker***	?	?	N	N	Y	N	Y
5 Taylor	Y	Y	N	N	N	Y	Y
MISSOURI							
1 Clay	Y	Y	N	N	Y	Y	Y
2 ***Talent***	Y	Y	N	N	Y	Y	Y
3 Gephardt	Y	Y	N	N	Y	Y	Y
4 Skelton	Y	Y	Y	N	Y	Y	Y
5 McCarthy	Y	Y	Y	N	Y	Y	Y
6 Danner	Y	Y	N	N	Y	Y	Y
7 ***Blunt***	Y	Y	N	N	Y	Y	Y
8 ***Emerson***	Y	Y	N	Y	Y	Y	Y
9 ***Hulshof***	Y	Y	N	N	Y	Y	Y
MONTANA							
AL ***Hill***	Y	Y	N	N	Y	N	Y
NEBRASKA							
1 ***Bereuter***	Y	Y	N	N	Y	Y	Y
2 ***Christensen***	?	?	?	?	?	?	?
3 ***Barrett***	Y	Y	Y	Y	Y	Y	Y
NEVADA							
1 ***Ensign***	Y	Y	Y	N	Y	Y	Y
2 ***Gibbons***	Y	Y	N	N	Y	Y	Y
NEW HAMPSHIRE							
1 ***Sununu***	Y	Y	N	N	Y	N	Y
2 ***Bass***	Y	Y	N	N	Y	N	Y
NEW JERSEY							
1 Andrews	Y	Y	Y	N	Y	Y	Y
2 ***LoBiondo***	Y	Y	N	N	Y	N	Y
3 ***Saxton***	Y	Y	N	N	Y	Y	Y
4 ***Smith***	Y	Y	N	N	Y	Y	Y
5 ***Roukema***	Y	Y	N	N	Y	Y	Y
6 Pallone	Y	Y	N	N	Y	Y	Y
7 ***Franks***	Y	Y	N	N	Y	Y	Y
8 Pascrell	Y	Y	Y	Y	N	Y	Y
9 Rothman	Y	Y	N	N	Y	Y	Y
10 Payne	Y	Y	Y	N	Y	Y	Y
11 ***Frelinghuysen***	Y	Y	N	N	Y	Y	Y
12 ***Pappas***	Y	Y	N	N	Y	Y	Y
13 Menendez	Y	Y	Y	Y	N	Y	Y
NEW MEXICO							
1 Vacant							
2 ***Skeen***	Y	Y	N	N	Y	N	Y
3 ***Redmond***	Y	Y	Y	Y	Y	N	Y
NEW YORK							
1 ***Forbes***	+	Y	N	N	Y	N	Y
2 ***Lazio***	Y	Y	N	N	Y	N	Y
3 ***King***	Y	Y	N	N	Y	Y	Y
4 McCarthy	Y	Y	Y	N	Y	Y	Y
5 Ackerman	Y	Y	N	N	Y	Y	Y
6 Meeks	?	?	Y	Y	Y	Y	Y
7 Manton	Y	Y	N	N	Y	Y	Y
8 Nadler	Y	Y	N	N	Y	Y	Y
9 Schumer	Y	Y	Y	N	Y	Y	Y
10 Towns	Y	Y	Y	Y	Y	Y	Y
11 Owens	Y	Y	Y	N	Y	Y	Y
12 Velázquez	Y	Y	N	N	Y	Y	Y
13 ***Fossella***	+	+	?	+	?	N	Y
14 Maloney	Y	Y	Y	N	Y	Y	Y
15 Rangel	Y	Y	Y	N	Y	Y	Y
16 Serrano	Y	Y	N	N	Y	Y	Y
17 Engel	Y	Y	N	N	Y	Y	Y
18 Lowey	?	?	N	N	Y	Y	Y
19 ***Kelly***	Y	Y	N	N	Y	N	Y
20 ***Gilman***	Y	Y	N	N	Y	N	Y
21 McNulty	?	?	?	?	?	?	?
22 ***Solomon***	Y	Y	N	N	Y	N	Y
23 ***Boehlert***	Y	Y	N	N	Y	N	Y
24 ***McHugh***	Y	Y	N	N	Y	Y	Y
25 ***Walsh***	Y	Y	N	N	Y	Y	Y
26 Hinchey	Y	Y	N	N	Y	Y	Y
27 ***Paxon***	Y	Y	N	N	Y	Y	Y
28 Slaughter	Y	Y	N	N	Y	Y	Y
29 LaFalce	Y	Y	N	N	Y	Y	Y
30 ***Quinn***	Y	Y	N	N	Y	Y	Y
31 ***Houghton***	Y	Y	N	N	Y	Y	Y
NORTH CAROLINA							
1 Clayton	Y	Y	Y	N	Y	Y	Y
2 Etheridge	Y	Y	N	N	Y	Y	Y
3 ***Jones***	Y	Y	N	Y	Y	Y	Y
4 Price	Y	Y	N	N	Y	Y	Y
5 ***Burr***	Y	Y	N	N	Y	N	Y
6 ***Coble***	Y	Y	N	N	Y	N	Y
7 McIntyre	Y	Y	N	N	Y	Y	Y
8 Hefner	Y	Y	N	N	Y	Y	Y
9 ***Myrick***	Y	Y	N	N	Y	Y	Y
10 ***Ballenger***	Y	Y	N	N	Y	N	Y
11 ***Taylor***	Y	Y	Y	N	Y	Y	N
12 Watt	Y	Y	Y	Y	Y	Y	Y
NORTH DAKOTA							
AL Pomeroy	Y	Y	N	N	Y	Y	Y
OHIO							
1 ***Chabot***	Y	Y	N	N	Y	Y	Y
2 ***Portman***	Y	Y	N	N	Y	Y	Y
3 Hall	Y	Y	Y	N	Y	Y	Y
4 ***Oxley***	Y	Y	Y	Y	Y	Y	Y
5 ***Gillmor***	Y	Y	N	N	Y	N	Y
6 Strickland	Y	Y	N	N	Y	Y	Y
7 ***Hobson***	Y	Y	N	N	Y	N	Y
8 ***Boehner***	Y	Y	Y	Y	Y	N	Y
9 Kaptur	?	?	Y	N	Y	Y	Y
10 Kucinich	Y	Y	Y	Y	N	Y	Y
11 Stokes	?	?	Y	N	Y	Y	Y
12 ***Kasich***	Y	Y	N	N	Y	N	Y
13 Brown	Y	Y	N	Y	Y	Y	Y
14 Sawyer	Y	Y	P	P	P	Y	Y
15 ***Pryce***	Y	Y	Y	N	Y	N	Y
16 ***Regula***	Y	Y	Y	N	Y	N	Y
17 Traficant	Y	Y	Y	Y	Y	N	Y
18 ***Ney***	Y	Y	N	N	Y	N	Y
19 ***LaTourette***	Y	Y	N	N	Y	N	Y
OKLAHOMA							
1 ***Largent***	Y	Y	N	N	Y	N	N
2 ***Coburn***	Y	Y	N	N	Y	N	N
3 ***Watkins***	Y	Y	N	N	Y	Y	Y
4 ***Watts***	Y	Y	N	N	Y	Y	Y
5 ***Istook***	Y	Y	N	N	Y	Y	Y
6 ***Lucas***	Y	Y	N	N	Y	N	Y
OREGON							
1 Furse	Y	Y	Y	Y	Y	Y	Y
2 ***Smith***	Y	Y	N	N	Y	Y	Y
3 Blumenauer	Y	Y	N	N	Y	Y	Y
4 DeFazio	Y	Y	N	N	Y	Y	Y
5 Hooley	Y	Y	N	N	Y	Y	Y
PENNSYLVANIA							
1 Vacant							
2 Fattah	?	?	N	N	Y	Y	Y
3 Borski	Y	Y	N	N	Y	Y	Y
4 Klink	Y	Y	Y	Y	N	Y	Y
5 ***Peterson***	Y	Y	N	N	Y	Y	Y
6 Holden	Y	Y	N	N	Y	Y	Y
7 ***Weldon***	Y	Y	N	N	Y	Y	Y
8 ***Greenwood***	Y	Y	N	N	Y	Y	Y
9 ***Shuster***	Y	Y	N	N	Y	N	Y
10 ***McDade***	Y	Y	N	N	Y	N	Y
11 Kanjorski	Y	Y	N	N	Y	Y	Y
12 Murtha	Y	Y	N	N	Y	Y	Y
13 ***Fox***	Y	Y	N	N	Y	N	Y
14 Coyne	Y	Y	N	N	Y	Y	Y
15 McHale	Y	Y	N	N	Y	Y	Y
16 ***Pitts***	Y	Y	N	N	Y	N	Y
17 ***Gekas***	Y	Y	Y	Y	Y	N	Y
18 Doyle	Y	Y	Y	Y	Y	?	?
19 ***Goodling***	?	Y	N	N	Y	N	Y
20 Mascara	Y	Y	Y	Y	Y	Y	Y
21 ***English***	Y	Y	N	N	Y	Y	Y
RHODE ISLAND							
1 Kennedy	Y	Y	N	N	Y	Y	Y
2 Weygand	Y	Y	N	N	Y	Y	Y
SOUTH CAROLINA							
1 ***Sanford***	Y	Y	N	N	Y	Y	N
2 ***Spence***	Y	Y	N	N	Y	Y	Y
3 ***Graham***	Y	Y	N	N	Y	Y	Y
4 ***Inglis***	Y	Y	N	N	Y	N	Y
5 Spratt	Y	Y	N	N	Y	?	?
6 Clyburn	?	?	Y	Y	Y	Y	Y
SOUTH DAKOTA							
AL ***Thune***	Y	Y	N	N	Y	Y	Y
TENNESSEE							
1 ***Jenkins***	Y	Y	N	N	Y	Y	Y
2 ***Duncan***	Y	Y	N	N	Y	Y	Y
3 ***Wamp***	Y	Y	N	N	Y	Y	Y
4 ***Hilleary***	Y	Y	N	N	Y	Y	Y
5 Clement	Y	Y	N	N	Y	Y	Y
6 Gordon	Y	Y	N	N	Y	Y	Y
7 ***Bryant***	Y	Y	N	N	Y	Y	Y
8 Tanner	Y	Y	N	N	Y	Y	Y
9 Ford	Y	Y	N	Y	Y	Y	Y
TEXAS							
1 Sandlin	Y	Y	N	Y	Y	Y	Y
2 Turner	Y	Y	N	N	Y	Y	Y
3 ***Johnson, Sam***	Y	Y	Y	Y	Y	N	N
4 Hall	Y	Y	Y	Y	Y	Y	N
5 ***Sessions***	Y	Y	Y	Y	Y	N	N
6 ***Barton***	Y	Y	N	N	Y	Y	Y
7 ***Archer***	Y	Y	Y	N	Y	N	Y
8 ***Brady***	Y	Y	N	Y	Y	N	Y
9 Lampson	Y	Y	N	N	Y	Y	Y
10 Doggett	Y	Y	N	N	Y	Y	Y
11 Edwards	Y	Y	N	N	Y	Y	Y
12 ***Granger***	Y	Y	Y	N	Y	N	Y
13 ***Thornberry***	Y	Y	N	N	Y	N	N
14 ***Paul***	Y	N	Y	N	Y	Y	N
15 Hinojosa	Y	Y	N	N	Y	Y	Y
16 Reyes	Y	Y	N	N	Y	Y	Y
17 Stenholm	Y	Y	Y	N	Y	Y	Y
18 Jackson-Lee	Y	Y	N	N	Y	Y	Y
19 ***Combest***	Y	Y	N	N	Y	Y	Y
20 Gonzalez	?	?	?	?	?	?	?
21 ***Smith***	Y	Y	N	N	Y	Y	Y
22 ***DeLay***	Y	Y	Y	Y	Y	N	Y
23 ***Bonilla***	Y	Y	N	N	Y	Y	N
24 Frost	Y	Y	Y	N	Y	Y	Y
25 Bentsen	Y	Y	N	N	Y	Y	Y
26 ***Armey***	Y	Y	N	N	Y	N	Y
27 Ortiz	Y	Y	N	N	Y	Y	Y
28 Rodriguez	Y	Y	N	N	Y	Y	Y
29 Green	Y	Y	N	N	Y	Y	Y
30 Johnson, E.B.	Y	Y	Y	Y	Y	Y	Y
UTAH							
1 ***Hansen***	Y	Y	N	Y	Y	N	Y
2 ***Cook***	Y	Y	N	N	Y	N	Y
3 ***Cannon***	Y	Y	N	Y	Y	N	N
VERMONT							
AL *Sanders*	Y	Y	N	N	Y	Y	Y
VIRGINIA							
1 ***Bateman***	+	+	+	+	+	+	+
2 Pickett	Y	Y	N	N	Y	Y	Y
3 Scott	Y	Y	N	N	Y	Y	Y
4 Sisisky	Y	Y	N	N	Y	Y	Y
5 Goode	Y	Y	N	N	Y	Y	Y
6 ***Goodlatte***	Y	Y	N	N	Y	Y	Y
7 ***Bliley***	Y	Y	N	N	Y	N	Y
8 Moran	Y	Y	N	N	Y	Y	Y
9 Boucher	Y	Y	Y	Y	Y	Y	Y
10 ***Wolf***	Y	Y	N	N	Y	Y	Y
11 ***Davis***	Y	Y	N	N	Y	N	Y
WASHINGTON							
1 ***White***	Y	Y	N	N	Y	Y	Y
2 ***Metcalf***	Y	Y	N	N	Y	N	Y
3 ***Smith, Linda***	Y	Y	N	Y	Y	N	Y
4 ***Hastings***	Y	Y	N	N	Y	N	Y
5 ***Nethercutt***	Y	Y	Y	N	Y	Y	Y
6 Dicks	Y	Y	N	N	Y	Y	Y
7 McDermott	Y	Y	N	N	Y	Y	Y
8 ***Dunn***	?	Y	N	N	Y	N	Y
9 Smith, Adam	Y	Y	N	N	Y	Y	Y
WEST VIRGINIA							
1 Mollohan	Y	Y	N	N	Y	N	Y
2 Wise	Y	Y	N	N	Y	Y	Y
3 Rahall	?	?	N	N	Y	Y	Y
WISCONSIN							
1 ***Neumann***	?	?	?	?	?	?	?
2 ***Klug***	Y	Y	N	N	Y	Y	Y
3 Kind	Y	Y	N	N	Y	Y	Y
4 Kleczka	Y	Y	N	N	Y	Y	Y
5 Barrett	Y	Y	N	N	Y	Y	Y
6 ***Petri***	Y	Y	Y	Y	Y	N	Y
7 Obey	Y	Y	N	Y	Y	Y	Y
8 Johnson	Y	Y	N	N	Y	Y	Y
9 ***Sensenbrenner***	Y	Y	Y	Y	Y	Y	N
WYOMING							
AL ***Cubin***	Y	Y	N	Y	Y	N	N

Southern states - Ala., Ark., Fla., Ga., Ky., La., Miss., N.C., Okla., S.C., Tenn., Texas, Va.

House Votes 139, 140, 141, 142, 143, 144, 145

Key

Y Voted for (yea).
Paired for.
+ Announced for.
N Voted against (nay).
X Paired against.
− Announced against.
P Voted "present."
C Voted "present" to avoid possible conflict of interest.
? Did not vote or otherwise make a position known.

Democrats **Republicans**
Independent

139. HR 3811. Deadbeat Parents Punishment/Passage. McCollum, R-Fla., motion to suspend the rules and pass the bill to increase penalties on parents who willfully fail to pay court-ordered child support for a child living in another state. Motion agreed to 402-16: R 213-8; D 188-8 (ND 136-7, SD 52-1); I 1-0. May 12, 1998. A two-thirds majority of those present and voting (279 in this case) is required for passage under suspension of the rules.

140. HR 2829. Bulletproof Vest Grants/Passage. McCollum, R-Fla., motion to suspend the rules and pass the bill to authorize a $25 million federal grant program to help local police departments purchase bulletproof vests. Motion agreed to 412-4: R 216-4; D 195-0 (ND 143-0, SD 52-0); I 1-0. May 12, 1998. A two-thirds majority of those present and voting (278 in this case) is required for passage under suspension of the rules.

141. H Res 422. Honoring Slain Law Enforcement Officers/Adoption. McCollum, R-Fla., motion to suspend the rules and adopt the resolution to express the sense of the House that law enforcement officers killed in the line of duty should be honored. Motion agreed to 416-0: R 220-0; D 195-0 (ND 143-0, SD 52-0); I 1-0. May 12, 1998. A two-thirds majority of those present and voting (278 in this case) is required for adoption under suspension of the rules.

142. HR 10. Financial Services Overhaul/Rule. Adoption of the rule (H Res 428) to provide for House floor consideration of the bill to eliminate barriers against affiliations between banking, securities, insurance and other firms. Adopted 311-105: R 201-18; D 109-87 (ND 75-69, SD 34-18); I 1-0. May 13, 1998.

143. HR 10. Financial Services Overhaul/Consumer Provisions. Bliley, R-Va., manager's amendment to add consumer protection provisions that allow federal banking regulators to preempt state bank insurance sales laws that conflict with federal rules, require federal banking and securities regulators to review existing consumer fee disclosure requirements, and require the General Accounting Office to report on concentration in the financial services industry and its impact on consumers. Adopted 407-11: R 210-10; D 196-1 (ND 145-0, SD 51-1); I 1-0. May 13, 1998.

144. HR 10. Financial Services Overhaul/National Bank Subsidiaries. LaFalce, D-N.Y., amendment to allow national bank subsidiaries to engage in any activity that is financial in nature, with the exception of underwriting insurance or engaging in real estate investment activities, even if it is not a permissible activity for the national bank itself. Rejected 115-306: R 15-207; D 99-99 (ND 76-70, SD 23-29); I 1-0. May 13, 1998.

145. HR 10. Financial Services Overhaul/Bank Holding Companies. Baker, R-La., amendment to expand the allowable activities of national bank subsidiaries, allowing subsidiaries to engage in activities that are generally allowable to bank holding companies, but which are not permissible for national banks. Rejected 140-281: R 133-89; D 7-191 (ND 1-147, SD 6-44); I 0-1. May 13, 1998.

	139	140	141	142	143	144	145
ALABAMA							
1 *Callahan*	Y	Y	Y	Y	Y	N	Y
2 Everett	Y	Y	Y	N	Y	N	Y
3 *Riley*	Y	Y	Y	N	N	N	Y
4 *Aderholt*	Y	Y	Y	Y	Y	N	Y
5 Cramer	Y	Y	Y	N	Y	N	Y
6 *Bachus*	Y	Y	Y	N	N	N	Y
7 Hilliard	Y	Y	Y	?	?	?	?
ALASKA							
AL *Young*	Y	Y	Y	Y	Y	N	N
ARIZONA							
1 *Salmon*	Y	Y	Y	Y	Y	N	N
2 Pastor	Y	Y	Y	Y	Y	Y	N
3 *Stump*	Y	Y	Y	Y	Y	N	Y
4 *Shadegg*	Y	Y	Y	Y	Y	N	Y
5 *Kolbe*	Y	Y	Y	Y	Y	N	N
6 *Hayworth*	Y	Y	Y	Y	Y	N	Y
ARKANSAS							
1 Berry	Y	Y	Y	Y	Y	N	N
2 Snyder	Y	Y	Y	Y	Y	Y	N
3 *Hutchinson*	Y	Y	Y	Y	Y	N	Y
4 *Dickey*	Y	Y	Y	N	Y	N	Y
CALIFORNIA							
1 *Riggs*	Y	Y	Y	?	Y	N	N
2 *Herger*	Y	Y	Y	Y	Y	N	N
3 Fazio	Y	Y	Y	Y	Y	N	N
4 *Doolittle*	Y	Y	Y	Y	Y	N	N
5 Matsui	Y	Y	Y	N	Y	N	N
6 Woolsey	Y	Y	Y	N	Y	Y	N
7 Miller	Y	Y	Y	N	Y	Y	N
8 Pelosi	Y	Y	Y	N	Y	N	N
9 Lee	N	Y	Y	N	Y	N	N
10 Tauscher	Y	Y	Y	Y	Y	N	N
11 *Pombo*	Y	Y	Y	Y	Y	N	Y
12 Lantos	Y	Y	Y	N	Y	N	N
13 Stark	N	Y	Y	Y	Y	Y	N
14 Eshoo	Y	Y	Y	Y	Y	N	N
15 *Campbell*	Y	N	Y	Y	N	N	N
16 Lofgren	Y	Y	Y	N	Y	N	N
17 Farr	Y	Y	Y	N	Y	N	N
18 Condit	Y	Y	Y	Y	Y	N	N
19 *Radanovich*	Y	Y	Y	?	?	?	?
20 Dooley	Y	Y	Y	Y	Y	N	N
21 *Thomas*	Y	Y	Y	Y	Y	N	N
22 Capps, L.	Y	Y	Y	N	Y	N	N
23 *Gallegly*	Y	Y	Y	Y	Y	N	Y
24 Sherman	Y	Y	Y	N	Y	N	N
25 *McKeon*	Y	Y	Y	Y	Y	N	Y
26 Berman	Y	Y	Y	N	Y	N	N
27 *Rogan*	Y	Y	Y	Y	Y	N	N
28 *Dreier*	Y	Y	Y	Y	N	Y	Y
29 Waxman	Y	Y	Y	N	Y	N	N
30 Becerra	Y	Y	Y	N	Y	N	N
31 Martinez	Y	Y	Y	N	Y	N	N
32 Dixon	Y	Y	Y	N	Y	N	N
33 Royal-Allard	Y	Y	Y	N	Y	N	N
34 Torres	Y	Y	Y	N	Y	N	N
35 Waters	N	Y	Y	N	Y	Y	N
36 Harman	?	?	?	?	?	?	?
37 Millender-McD.	Y	Y	Y	N	Y	N	N
38 *Horn*	Y	Y	Y	Y	Y	N	Y
39 *Royce*	Y	Y	Y	Y	Y	N	N
40 *Lewis*	Y	Y	Y	Y	Y	N	N
41 *Kim*	Y	Y	Y	Y	Y	N	N
42 Brown	Y	Y	Y	N	Y	N	N
43 *Calvert*	Y	Y	Y	Y	Y	N	Y
44 *Bono, M.*	Y	Y	Y	Y	Y	N	Y
45 *Rohrabacher*	Y	Y	Y	Y	Y	N	N
46 Sanchez	Y	Y	Y	Y	Y	N	Y
47 *Cox*	Y	Y	Y	Y	Y	N	Y
48 *Packard*	Y	Y	Y	Y	Y	N	Y
49 *Bilbray*	Y	Y	Y	Y	Y	N	N
50 Filner	Y	Y	Y	N	Y	N	N
51 *Cunningham*	Y	Y	Y	Y	Y	N	N
52 *Hunter*	Y	Y	Y	Y	Y	N	Y
COLORADO							
1 DeGette	Y	Y	Y	Y	Y	N	N
2 Skaggs	+	+	+	+	+	−	−
3 *McInnis*	Y	Y	Y	Y	Y	Y	Y
4 *Schaffer*	Y	Y	Y	Y	N	N	N
5 *Hefley*	Y	Y	N	Y	N	Y	N
6 *Schaefer*	Y	Y	Y	Y	Y	N	N
CONNECTICUT							
1 Kennelly	Y	Y	Y	Y	Y	N	N
2 Gejdenson	Y	Y	Y	Y	Y	N	N
3 DeLauro	Y	Y	Y	Y	Y	N	N
4 *Shays*	Y	Y	Y	Y	Y	N	N
5 Maloney	Y	Y	Y	N	Y	Y	N
6 *Johnson*	Y	Y	Y	Y	Y	N	N
DELAWARE							
AL *Castle*	Y	Y	Y	Y	Y	Y	Y
FLORIDA							
1 *Scarborough*	Y	Y	Y	N	N	N	N
2 Boyd	Y	Y	Y	Y	Y	N	N
3 Brown	Y	Y	Y	N	Y	N	N
4 *Fowler*	Y	Y	Y	Y	Y	N	N
5 Thurman	Y	Y	Y	Y	Y	Y	N
6 *Stearns*	Y	Y	Y	Y	Y	N	Y
7 *Mica*	Y	Y	Y	Y	Y	N	N
8 *McCollum*	Y	Y	Y	N	N	N	Y
9 *Bilirakis*	Y	Y	Y	Y	Y	N	N
10 *Young*	Y	Y	Y	Y	Y	N	N
11 Davis	Y	Y	Y	Y	Y	N	N
12 *Canady*	Y	Y	Y	Y	Y	N	Y
13 *Miller*	Y	Y	Y	Y	Y	N	N
14 *Goss*	Y	Y	Y	Y	Y	N	N
15 *Weldon*	Y	Y	Y	Y	Y	N	N
16 *Foley*	Y	Y	Y	Y	Y	N	N
17 Meek	Y	Y	N	Y	Y	N	N
18 *Ros-Lehtinen*	Y	Y	Y	Y	Y	N	N
19 Wexler	Y	?	Y	Y	Y	N	N
20 Deutsch	Y	Y	Y	Y	Y	N	N
21 *Diaz-Balart*	Y	Y	Y	Y	Y	N	N
22 *Shaw*	Y	Y	Y	Y	Y	N	N
23 Hastings	N	Y	Y	N	Y	N	N
GEORGIA							
1 *Kingston*	Y	Y	Y	Y	Y	N	N
2 Bishop	Y	Y	Y	Y	Y	N	N
3 *Collins*	Y	Y	Y	Y	Y	N	Y
4 McKinney	Y	Y	Y	Y	Y	N	N
5 Lewis	Y	Y	Y	N	Y	N	N
6 *Gingrich*							
7 *Barr*	N	Y	Y	Y	Y	N	N
8 *Chambliss*	Y	Y	Y	Y	Y	N	Y
9 *Deal*	Y	Y	Y	Y	Y	N	Y
10 *Norwood*	Y	Y	Y	Y	Y	N	Y
11 *Linder*	Y	?	Y	Y	Y	N	N
HAWAII							
1 Abercrombie	Y	Y	Y	Y	Y	N	N
2 Mink	Y	Y	Y	?	Y	N	N
IDAHO							
1 *Chenoweth*	Y	Y	Y	Y	Y	N	N
2 *Crapo*	Y	Y	Y	Y	Y	N	Y
ILLINOIS							
1 Rush	Y	Y	Y	Y	Y	N	N
2 Jackson	N	Y	Y	N	Y	N	N
3 Lipinski	Y	Y	Y	N	Y	N	N
4 Gutierrez	Y	Y	Y	N	Y	N	N
5 Blagojevich	Y	Y	Y	Y	Y	N	N
6 *Hyde*	Y	Y	Y	Y	Y	N	N
7 Davis	Y	Y	Y	N	Y	N	N
8 *Crane*	Y	Y	Y	Y	Y	N	Y
9 Yates	Y	Y	Y	N	N	N	N
10 *Porter*	Y	Y	Y	Y	Y	N	N
11 *Weller*	Y	Y	Y	Y	Y	N	N
12 Costello	Y	Y	Y	N	Y	N	N

ND Northern Democrats   SD Southern Democrats

	139	140	141	142	143	144	145
13 **Fawell**	Y	Y	Y	Y	Y	N	Y
14 **Hastert**	Y	Y	Y	Y	Y	N	N
15 **Ewing**	Y	Y	Y	?	Y	N	Y
16 **Manzullo**	N	Y	Y	Y	Y	N	N
17 Evans	Y	Y	Y	N	Y	Y	N
18 **LaHood**	N	Y	Y	N	N	N	N
19 Poshard	Y	Y	Y	N	Y	N	N
20 **Shimkus**	Y	Y	Y	Y	Y	N	N
INDIANA							
1 Visclosky	Y	Y	Y	Y	Y	Y	N
2 **McIntosh**	Y	Y	Y	Y	Y	Y	Y
3 Roemer	Y	Y	Y	Y	Y	N	N
4 **Souder**	Y	Y	Y	Y	Y	Y	Y
5 **Buyer**	Y	Y	?	Y	Y	N	Y
6 **Burton**	Y	Y	Y	Y	Y	N	N
7 **Pease**	Y	Y	Y	Y	Y	N	Y
8 **Hostettler**	Y	Y	Y	Y	Y	Y	Y
9 Hamilton	Y	Y	Y	Y	Y	N	N
10 Carson	Y	Y	Y	N	Y	Y	N
IOWA							
1 **Leach**	Y	Y	Y	Y	Y	N	N
2 **Nussle**	Y	Y	Y	Y	Y	N	Y
3 Boswell	Y	Y	Y	N	Y	Y	N
4 **Ganske**	Y	Y	Y	Y	Y	N	N
5 **Latham**	Y	Y	Y	Y	Y	N	Y
KANSAS							
1 **Moran**	Y	Y	Y	Y	Y	N	Y
2 **Ryun**	Y	Y	Y	Y	Y	N	Y
3 **Snowbarger**	Y	Y	Y	Y	Y	N	Y
4 **Tiahrt**	Y	Y	Y	N	N	N	Y
KENTUCKY							
1 **Whitfield**	Y	Y	Y	Y	Y	N	N
2 **Lewis**	Y	Y	Y	N	Y	N	N
3 **Northup**	Y	Y	Y	Y	Y	N	N
4 **Bunning**	Y	Y	Y	Y	Y	N	Y
5 **Rogers**	Y	Y	Y	Y	Y	N	Y
6 Baesler	Y	Y	Y	N	Y	Y	N
LOUISIANA							
1 **Livingston**	Y	Y	Y	Y	Y	N	N
2 Jefferson	Y	Y	Y	Y	Y	Y	N
3 **Tauzin**	Y	Y	Y	Y	Y	N	Y
4 **McCrery**	Y	Y	Y	Y	Y	N	Y
5 **Cooksey**	Y	Y	Y	Y	Y	N	Y
6 **Baker**	Y	Y	Y	Y	Y	N	Y
7 John	Y	Y	Y	Y	Y	N	N
MAINE							
1 Allen	Y	Y	Y	Y	Y	Y	N
2 Baldacci	Y	Y	Y	N	Y	N	N
MARYLAND							
1 **Gilchrest**	?	?	?	?	?	?	Y
2 **Ehrlich**	Y	Y	Y	Y	Y	N	Y
3 Cardin	Y	Y	Y	N	Y	Y	N
4 Wynn	Y	Y	Y	Y	Y	N	N
5 Hoyer	Y	Y	Y	N	Y	Y	N
6 **Bartlett**	Y	Y	Y	Y	Y	N	Y
7 Cummings	Y	Y	Y	Y	Y	N	N
8 **Morella**	Y	Y	Y	Y	Y	N	N
MASSACHUSETTS							
1 Olver	Y	Y	Y	N	Y	Y	N
2 Neal	Y	Y	Y	Y	Y	N	N
3 McGovern	Y	Y	Y	Y	Y	N	N
4 Frank	Y	Y	Y	N	Y	Y	N
5 Meehan	Y	Y	Y	N	Y	Y	N
6 Tierney	Y	Y	Y	N	Y	Y	N
7 Markey	Y	Y	Y	Y	Y	N	N
8 Kennedy	Y	Y	Y	N	Y	Y	N
9 Moakley	Y	Y	Y	Y	Y	Y	N
10 Delahunt	Y	Y	Y	N	Y	N	N
MICHIGAN							
1 Stupak	Y	Y	Y	Y	Y	N	N
2 **Hoekstra**	Y	Y	Y	Y	Y	N	Y
3 **Ehlers**	Y	Y	Y	Y	Y	N	N
4 **Camp**	Y	Y	Y	Y	Y	N	Y
5 Barcia	Y	Y	Y	Y	Y	N	N
6 **Upton**	Y	Y	Y	Y	Y	N	N
7 **Smith**	Y	Y	Y	Y	Y	N	Y
8 Stabenow	Y	Y	Y	Y	Y	N	N
9 Kildee	Y	Y	Y	Y	Y	N	N
10 Bonior	Y	Y	Y	Y	Y	Y	N
11 **Knollenberg**	Y	Y	Y	Y	Y	N	N
12 Levin	Y	Y	Y	Y	Y	N	N
13 Rivers	Y	Y	Y	Y	Y	N	N
14 Conyers	N	Y	Y	N	Y	Y	N
15 Kilpatrick	+	?	+	–	+	+	N
16 Dingell	Y	Y	Y	Y	Y	N	N

	139	140	141	142	143	144	145
MINNESOTA							
1 **Gutknecht**	Y	Y	Y	Y	Y	N	Y
2 Minge	Y	Y	Y	Y	Y	N	N
3 **Ramstad**	Y	Y	Y	Y	Y	Y	Y
4 Vento	Y	Y	Y	N	Y	Y	N
5 Sabo	N	Y	Y	Y	Y	Y	N
6 Luther	Y	Y	Y	N	Y	Y	N
7 Peterson	Y	Y	Y	Y	Y	N	Y
8 Oberstar	Y	Y	Y	Y	Y	Y	N
MISSISSIPPI							
1 **Wicker**	Y	Y	Y	Y	Y	N	Y
2 Thompson	Y	Y	Y	N	Y	Y	N
3 **Pickering**	Y	Y	Y	Y	Y	N	Y
4 **Parker**	Y	Y	Y	Y	Y	N	N
5 Taylor	Y	Y	Y	N	Y	N	Y
MISSOURI							
1 Clay	Y	Y	Y	?	?	?	N
2 **Talent**	Y	Y	Y	Y	Y	N	Y
3 Gephardt	Y	Y	Y	N	Y	N	N
4 Skelton	Y	Y	Y	N	Y	N	N
5 McCarthy	Y	Y	Y	N	Y	N	N
6 Danner	Y	Y	Y	N	Y	N	N
7 **Blunt**	Y	N	Y	Y	Y	N	N
8 **Emerson**	Y	Y	Y	Y	Y	N	Y
9 **Hulshof**	Y	Y	Y	Y	Y	N	Y
MONTANA							
AL **Hill**	Y	Y	Y	Y	Y	N	Y
NEBRASKA							
1 **Bereuter**	Y	Y	Y	Y	Y	N	Y
2 **Christensen**	?	?	?	?	?	?	?
3 **Barrett**	Y	Y	Y	Y	Y	N	Y
NEVADA							
1 **Ensign**	Y	Y	Y	Y	Y	N	Y
2 **Gibbons**	Y	Y	Y	Y	?	Y	N
NEW HAMPSHIRE							
1 **Sununu**	Y	Y	Y	Y	Y	N	Y
2 **Bass**	Y	Y	Y	Y	Y	N	N
NEW JERSEY							
1 Andrews	Y	Y	Y	Y	Y	N	N
2 **LoBiondo**	Y	Y	Y	Y	Y	N	N
3 **Saxton**	Y	Y	Y	Y	Y	N	N
4 **Smith**	Y	Y	Y	Y	Y	N	N
5 **Roukema**	Y	Y	Y	Y	Y	N	N
6 Pallone	Y	Y	Y	Y	Y	N	N
7 **Franks**	Y	Y	Y	Y	Y	N	N
8 Pascrell	Y	Y	Y	Y	Y	N	N
9 Rothman	Y	Y	Y	N	Y	N	N
10 Payne	Y	Y	Y	N	Y	Y	N
11 **Frelinghuysen**	Y	Y	Y	Y	Y	N	N
12 **Pappas**	Y	Y	Y	Y	Y	N	N
13 Menendez	?	?	?	N	Y	N	N
NEW MEXICO							
1 Vacant							
2 **Skeen**	Y	Y	Y	Y	Y	N	N
3 **Redmond**	Y	Y	Y	Y	Y	N	Y
NEW YORK							
1 **Forbes**	Y	Y	Y	Y	Y	N	N
2 **Lazio**	Y	Y	Y	Y	Y	N	N
3 **King**	Y	Y	Y	Y	Y	N	Y
4 McCarthy	Y	Y	Y	Y	Y	N	N
5 Ackerman	Y	Y	Y	Y	Y	N	N
6 Meeks	Y	Y	Y	Y	Y	N	N
7 Manton	Y	Y	Y	Y	Y	N	N
8 Nadler	Y	Y	Y	Y	Y	N	N
9 Schumer	?	?	?	N	Y	Y	N
10 Towns	Y	Y	Y	Y	Y	N	N
11 Owens	Y	Y	Y	N	Y	Y	N
12 Velázquez	Y	Y	Y	Y	Y	Y	N
13 **Fossella**	Y	Y	Y	Y	Y	N	N
14 Maloney	Y	Y	Y	Y	Y	N	N
15 Rangel	Y	Y	Y	Y	Y	N	N
16 Serrano	Y	Y	Y	N	Y	Y	N
17 Engel	Y	Y	Y	Y	Y	N	N
18 Lowey	Y	Y	Y	N	Y	N	N
19 **Kelly**	Y	Y	Y	Y	Y	Y	Y
20 **Gilman**	Y	Y	Y	Y	Y	N	N
21 McNulty	Y	Y	Y	Y	Y	N	N
22 **Solomon**	Y	Y	Y	Y	Y	N	N
23 **Boehlert**	Y	Y	Y	Y	Y	Y	Y
24 **McHugh**	Y	Y	Y	Y	Y	N	N
25 **Walsh**	Y	Y	Y	Y	Y	N	N
26 Hinchey	Y	Y	Y	N	Y	Y	N
27 **Paxon**	Y	Y	Y	Y	Y	N	?
28 Slaughter	Y	Y	Y	N	Y	Y	N
29 LaFalce	Y	Y	Y	N	Y	Y	N

	139	140	141	142	143	144	145
30 **Quinn**	Y	Y	Y	Y	Y	N	N
31 **Houghton**	Y	Y	Y	Y	Y	N	N
NORTH CAROLINA							
1 Clayton	Y	Y	Y	Y	Y	Y	N
2 Etheridge	Y	Y	Y	Y	Y	N	N
3 **Jones**	Y	Y	Y	N	Y	N	Y
4 Price	Y	Y	Y	N	Y	Y	N
5 **Burr**	Y	Y	Y	Y	Y	N	N
6 **Coble**	Y	Y	Y	Y	Y	N	Y
7 McIntyre	Y	Y	Y	N	Y	N	N
8 Hefner	?	?	?	?	?	?	?
9 **Myrick**	+	+	+	Y	Y	Y	Y
10 **Ballenger**	Y	Y	Y	Y	Y	N	N
11 **Taylor**	Y	Y	Y	Y	Y	N	Y
12 Watt	Y	Y	Y	N	Y	Y	N
NORTH DAKOTA							
AL Pomeroy	Y	Y	Y	Y	Y	N	N
OHIO							
1 **Chabot**	Y	Y	Y	Y	Y	N	N
2 **Portman**	Y	Y	Y	Y	Y	N	Y
3 Hall	Y	Y	Y	?	Y	Y	N
4 **Oxley**	Y	Y	Y	Y	Y	N	N
5 **Gillmor**	Y	Y	Y	Y	Y	N	N
6 Strickland	Y	Y	Y	Y	Y	N	N
7 **Hobson**	Y	Y	Y	Y	Y	N	N
8 **Boehner**	Y	Y	Y	Y	Y	N	Y
9 Kaptur	Y	Y	Y	Y	Y	Y	N
10 Kucinich	Y	Y	Y	N	Y	Y	N
11 Stokes	Y	Y	Y	N	Y	Y	N
12 **Kasich**	Y	Y	Y	Y	Y	N	N
13 Brown	Y	Y	Y	Y	Y	N	N
14 Sawyer	Y	Y	Y	N	Y	N	N
15 **Pryce**	Y	Y	Y	Y	Y	N	Y
16 **Regula**	Y	Y	Y	Y	Y	N	Y
17 Traficant	Y	Y	Y	Y	Y	N	N
18 **Ney**	Y	Y	Y	Y	Y	N	N
19 **LaTourette**	Y	Y	Y	Y	Y	Y	Y
OKLAHOMA							
1 **Largent**	Y	Y	Y	Y	Y	N	Y
2 **Coburn**	Y	Y	Y	N	Y	N	Y
3 **Watkins**	Y	Y	Y	Y	Y	N	Y
4 **Watts**	N	Y	Y	Y	Y	N	Y
5 **Istook**	Y	Y	Y	N	Y	N	Y
6 **Lucas**	Y	Y	Y	Y	Y	N	Y
OREGON							
1 Furse	N	Y	Y	Y	Y	N	N
2 **Smith**	Y	Y	Y	Y	Y	N	N
3 Blumenauer	Y	Y	Y	Y	Y	Y	N
4 DeFazio	Y	Y	Y	N	Y	Y	N
5 Hooley	Y	Y	Y	Y	Y	Y	N
PENNSYLVANIA							
1 Vacant							
2 Fattah	Y	Y	Y	N	?	Y	N
3 Borski	Y	Y	Y	N	Y	Y	N
4 Klink	Y	Y	Y	Y	Y	N	N
5 **Peterson**	Y	Y	Y	Y	Y	N	Y
6 Holden	Y	Y	Y	Y	Y	N	N
7 **Weldon**	Y	Y	Y	Y	Y	N	N
8 **Greenwood**	?	?	?	Y	Y	N	N
9 **Shuster**	Y	Y	Y	Y	Y	N	N
10 **McDade**	Y	Y	Y	Y	Y	N	N
11 Kanjorski	Y	Y	Y	N	Y	Y	N
12 Murtha	Y	Y	Y	Y	Y	N	N
13 **Fox**	Y	Y	Y	Y	Y	N	Y
14 Coyne	Y	Y	Y	Y	Y	N	N
15 McHale	Y	Y	Y	N	Y	Y	N
16 **Pitts**	Y	Y	Y	Y	Y	N	Y
17 **Gekas**	Y	Y	Y	?	Y	N	N
18 Doyle	Y	Y	Y	Y	Y	N	N
19 **Goodling**	Y	Y	Y	Y	Y	N	N
20 Mascara	Y	Y	Y	Y	Y	N	N
21 **English**	Y	Y	Y	Y	Y	N	Y
RHODE ISLAND							
1 Kennedy	Y	Y	Y	Y	Y	Y	N
2 Weygand	Y	Y	Y	Y	Y	Y	N
SOUTH CAROLINA							
1 **Sanford**	Y	N	Y	Y	Y	N	N
2 **Spence**	Y	Y	Y	Y	Y	N	N
3 **Graham**	Y	Y	Y	Y	Y	N	Y
4 **Inglis**	Y	Y	Y	Y	Y	N	Y
5 Spratt	Y	Y	Y	Y	Y	N	N
6 Clyburn	Y	Y	Y	N	Y	Y	N
SOUTH DAKOTA							
AL **Thune**	Y	Y	Y	N	N	N	Y

	139	140	141	142	143	144	145
TENNESSEE							
1 **Jenkins**	Y	Y	Y	Y	Y	N	Y
2 **Duncan**	Y	Y	Y	N	Y	N	Y
3 **Wamp**	Y	Y	Y	N	Y	N	Y
4 **Hilleary**	Y	Y	Y	N	Y	N	Y
5 Clement	Y	Y	Y	Y	Y	N	N
6 Gordon	Y	Y	Y	Y	Y	N	N
7 **Bryant**	Y	Y	Y	Y	Y	N	Y
8 Tanner	Y	Y	Y	Y	Y	N	N
9 Ford	Y	Y	Y	Y	Y	N	N
TEXAS							
1 Sandlin	Y	Y	Y	N	Y	Y	N
2 Turner	Y	Y	Y	N	Y	N	N
3 **Johnson, Sam**	Y	Y	Y	Y	N	N	Y
4 Hall	Y	Y	Y	Y	Y	N	P
5 **Sessions**	N	Y	Y	Y	Y	N	Y
6 **Barton**	Y	Y	Y	Y	Y	N	Y
7 **Archer**	Y	Y	Y	Y	Y	N	Y
8 **Brady**	Y	Y	Y	Y	Y	N	Y
9 Lampson	Y	Y	Y	N	Y	Y	N
10 Doggett	Y	Y	Y	Y	Y	N	N
11 Edwards	Y	Y	Y	Y	Y	N	N
12 **Granger**	Y	Y	Y	Y	Y	N	Y
13 **Thornberry**	Y	Y	Y	Y	Y	N	Y
14 **Paul**	N	N	Y	Y	Y	N	Y
15 Hinojosa	Y	Y	Y	Y	Y	N	N
16 Reyes	Y	Y	Y	Y	Y	N	N
17 Stenholm	Y	Y	Y	Y	Y	N	Y
18 Jackson-Lee	Y	Y	Y	Y	Y	Y	N
19 **Combest**	Y	Y	Y	Y	Y	N	Y
20 Gonzalez	?	?	?	?	?	?	?
21 **Smith**	Y	Y	Y	Y	Y	N	Y
22 **DeLay**	Y	Y	Y	Y	Y	N	Y
23 **Bonilla**	Y	Y	Y	Y	Y	N	Y
24 Frost	Y	Y	Y	Y	Y	N	N
25 Bentsen	Y	Y	Y	N	Y	Y	N
26 **Armey**	Y	Y	Y	Y	Y	N	Y
27 Ortiz	Y	Y	Y	Y	Y	Y	N
28 Rodriguez	Y	Y	Y	Y	Y	N	N
29 Green	Y	Y	Y	Y	Y	Y	–
30 Johnson, E.B.	Y	Y	Y	Y	Y	Y	N
UTAH							
1 **Hansen**	Y	Y	Y	Y	Y	N	Y
2 **Cook**	Y	Y	Y	Y	Y	N	Y
3 **Cannon**	N	Y	Y	Y	Y	N	Y
VERMONT							
AL *Sanders*	Y	Y	Y	Y	Y	Y	N
VIRGINIA							
1 **Bateman**	+	+	+	+	+	+	+
2 Pickett	Y	Y	Y	Y	Y	N	N
3 Scott	Y	Y	Y	N	Y	N	N
4 Sisisky	Y	Y	Y	Y	Y	N	N
5 Goode	Y	Y	Y	N	N	Y	Y
6 **Goodlatte**	Y	Y	Y	Y	Y	Y	Y
7 **Bliley**	Y	Y	Y	Y	Y	N	N
8 Moran	Y	Y	Y	Y	Y	Y	Y
9 Boucher	Y	Y	Y	Y	Y	N	Y
10 **Wolf**	Y	Y	Y	Y	Y	N	N
11 **Davis**	Y	Y	Y	N	Y	Y	Y
WASHINGTON							
1 **White**	Y	Y	Y	Y	?	N	N
2 **Metcalf**	Y	Y	Y	Y	Y	N	N
3 **Smith, Linda**	Y	Y	Y	Y	Y	N	N
4 **Hastings**	Y	Y	Y	Y	Y	N	N
5 **Nethercutt**	Y	Y	Y	Y	Y	N	Y
6 Dicks	Y	Y	Y	N	Y	N	N
7 McDermott	Y	Y	Y	N	Y	Y	N
8 **Dunn**	Y	Y	Y	Y	Y	N	N
9 Smith, Adam	Y	Y	Y	N	Y	Y	N
WEST VIRGINIA							
1 Mollohan	?	?	?	Y	Y	Y	N
2 Wise	Y	Y	Y	Y	Y	N	N
3 Rahall	?	?	?	Y	Y	N	N
WISCONSIN							
1 **Neumann**	Y	Y	Y	Y	Y	N	Y
2 **Klug**	Y	Y	Y	Y	Y	N	Y
3 Kind	Y	Y	Y	Y	Y	Y	N
4 Kleczka	Y	Y	Y	Y	Y	Y	N
5 Barrett	Y	Y	Y	N	Y	Y	N
6 **Petri**	Y	Y	Y	Y	Y	Y	Y
7 Obey	Y	Y	Y	N	Y	Y	N
8 Johnson	Y	Y	Y	N	Y	Y	N
9 **Sensenbrenner**	N	Y	Y	Y	Y	N	Y
WYOMING							
AL **Cubin**	Y	Y	Y	Y	Y	N	N

Southern states - Ala., Ark., Fla., Ga., Ky., La., Miss., N.C., Okla., S.C., Tenn., Texas, Va.

House Votes 146, 147, 148, 149, 150, 151, 152

Key

Y Voted for (yea).
Paired for.
+ Announced for.
N Voted against (nay).
X Paired against.
− Announced against.
P Voted "present."
C Voted "present" to avoid possible conflict of interest.
? Did not vote or otherwise make a position known.

Democrats **Republicans** *Independent*

---

146. HR 10. Financial Services Overhaul/Financial Holding Company. Leach, R-Iowa, amendment to the Roukema amendment, to delete provisions of the bill that allow financial holding companies and wholesale financial holding companies to earn up to 5 percent of their revenues from commercial activities. The Roukema amendment would increase from 5 percent to 10 percent the amount of total financial holding company revenues that may be earned each year through commercial, non-financial activity. Adopted 229-193: R 138-83; D 90-110 (ND 72-75, SD 18-35); I 1-0. May 13, 1998.

147. HR 10. Financial Services Overhaul/Financial Holding Companies. Roukema, R-N.J., amendment, as amended, to delete provisions of the bill that allow financial holding companies and wholesale financial holding companies to earn up to 5 percent of their revenues from commercial activities. Adopted 218-204: R 131-91; D 86-113 (ND 67-79, SD 19-34); I 1-0. May 13, 1998.

148. HR 10. Financial Services Overhaul/Economic Impact. Kingston, R-Ga., amendment to require the General Accounting Office to conduct a study on the projected economic impact the bill will have on banks and other financial institutions that have total assets of $100 million or less. Adopted 404-18: R 221-2; D 182-16 (ND 129-16, SD 53-0); I 1-0. May 13, 1998.

149. HR 10. Financial Services Overhaul/Bank Insurance Fund. Roukema, R-N.J., amendment to require the FDIC to conduct a study on the Bank Insurance Fund and the Savings Association Insurance Fund to examine their safety and soundness in light of bank and thrift mergers and consolidations that have occurred since 1984. Adopted 406-13: R 212-7; D 193-6 (ND 141-5, SD 52-1); I 1-0. May 13, 1998.

150. HR 10. Financial Services Overhaul/Federal Savings Association. Metcalf, R-Wash., amendment to allow any federal savings association that converts to a national bank charter or state bank charter to retain the word "Federal" in its name, provided it remains an insured depository institution. Adopted 256-166: R 211-11; D 44-155 (ND 31-115, SD 13-40); I 1-0. May 13, 1998.

151. HR 10. Financial Services Overhaul/Passage. Passage of the bill to eliminate current Glass-Steagall Act and Bank Holding Company Act barriers against affiliations between banking, securities, insurance and other firms. Passed 214-213: R 153-73; D 61-139 (ND 47-100, SD 14-39); I 0-1. May 13, 1998.

152. Procedural Motion/Adjourn. Serrano, D-N.Y., motion to adjourn. Motion rejected 15-379: R 0-206; D 15-172 (ND 13-124, SD 2-48); I 0-1. May 14, 1998.

	146	147	148	149	150	151	152
ALABAMA							
1 *Callahan*	N	N	Y	Y	Y	N	N
2 *Everett*	N	N	Y	Y	Y	N	N
3 *Riley*	Y	Y	Y	Y	Y	N	N
4 *Aderholt*	Y	Y	Y	Y	Y	N	N
5 Cramer	Y	Y	Y	Y	N	Y	N
6 *Bachus*	Y	Y	Y	Y	Y	N	N
7 Hilliard	N	N	Y	Y	N	N	N
ALASKA							
AL *Young*	N	N	Y	Y	Y	N	?
ARIZONA							
1 *Salmon*	N	N	Y	Y	Y	Y	N
2 Pastor	N	N	Y	Y	N	N	N
3 *Stump*	N	N	Y	N	Y	Y	N
4 *Shadegg*	Y	Y	Y	Y	Y	Y	N
5 *Kolbe*	Y	Y	Y	Y	N	Y	?
6 *Hayworth*	N	N	Y	Y	Y	Y	N
ARKANSAS							
1 Berry	Y	Y	Y	Y	N	N	N
2 Snyder	Y	Y	Y	Y	N	N	N
3 *Hutchinson*	Y	Y	Y	Y	Y	N	N
4 *Dickey*	N	N	Y	N	Y	N	N
CALIFORNIA							
1 *Riggs*	N	N	Y	Y	Y	Y	?
2 *Herger*	Y	Y	Y	Y	Y	N	N
3 Fazio	N	N	N	Y	N	Y	N
4 *Doolittle*	Y	Y	Y	?	Y	Y	N
5 Matsui	Y	Y	Y	Y	N	N	N
6 Woolsey	Y	Y	Y	Y	N	N	N
7 Miller	Y	Y	Y	Y	N	N	N
8 Pelosi	Y	Y	Y	Y	N	N	N
9 Lee	N	N	Y	Y	N	N	N
10 Tauscher	N	N	Y	Y	Y	N	N
11 *Pombo*	Y	N	Y	N	Y	N	N
12 Lantos	N	N	Y	Y	N	N	N
13 Stark	N	Y	N	Y	N	Y	N
14 Eshoo	N	N	Y	Y	N	N	Y
15 *Campbell*	Y	Y	Y	Y	Y	N	N
16 Lofgren	Y	Y	Y	Y	N	N	N
17 Farr	N	N	Y	Y	N	N	N
18 Condit	Y	Y	Y	Y	N	Y	N
19 *Radanovich*	?	?	?	?	?	Y	?
20 Dooley	N	N	N	Y	N	N	N
21 *Thomas*	Y	Y	Y	Y	Y	N	N
22 Capps, L.	N	N	Y	Y	N	N	N
23 *Gallegly*	Y	Y	Y	Y	Y	N	N
24 Sherman	N	N	Y	N	N	N	N
25 *McKeon*	Y	Y	Y	Y	Y	Y	N
26 Berman	Y	Y	Y	Y	N	Y	N
27 *Rogan*	N	N	Y	Y	Y	N	N
28 *Dreier*	N	N	Y	Y	Y	N	N
29 Waxman	Y	Y	Y	Y	N	N	N
30 Becerra	Y	Y	Y	Y	N	N	?
31 Martinez	Y	Y	Y	Y	N	N	Y
32 Dixon	Y	Y	Y	Y	N	N	?
33 Royal-Allard	Y	Y	Y	Y	N	N	N
34 Torres	Y	Y	N	Y	N	N	?
35 Waters	Y	Y	Y	Y	N	N	N
36 Harman	?	?	?	?	?	?	?
37 Millender-McD.	Y	Y	Y	Y	N	N	N

	146	147	148	149	150	151	152
38 *Horn*	Y	Y	Y	Y	Y	Y	N
39 *Royce*	N	N	Y	Y	N	Y	N
40 *Lewis*	Y	N	Y	?	Y	Y	N
41 *Kim*	Y	N	Y	Y	Y	Y	N
42 Brown	N	N	Y	Y	N	N	Y
43 *Calvert*	Y	Y	Y	Y	Y	Y	N
44 *Bono, M.*	N	Y	Y	Y	Y	Y	N
45 *Rohrabacher*	N	N	Y	N	N	N	N
46 Sanchez	N	N	Y	N	N	N	N
47 *Cox*	Y	Y	Y	Y	?	Y	N
48 *Packard*	Y	N	Y	Y	Y	N	N
49 *Bilbray*	N	N	Y	Y	Y	Y	N
50 Filner	Y	Y	Y	N	N	N	Y
51 *Cunningham*	N	N	Y	Y	Y	Y	N
52 *Hunter*	N	Y	Y	Y	Y	N	N
COLORADO							
1 DeGette	N	N	Y	Y	Y	Y	N
2 Skaggs	+	+	+	+	−	−	−
3 *McInnis*	Y	Y	Y	Y	N	N	N
4 *Schaffer*	N	N	Y	Y	Y	N	N
5 *Hefley*	N	N	Y	N	Y	N	N
6 *Schaefer*	Y	Y	Y	Y	Y	Y	N
CONNECTICUT							
1 Kennelly	N	N	Y	Y	N	N	N
2 Gejdenson	Y	Y	Y	Y	N	Y	N
3 DeLauro	N	N	Y	Y	N	Y	N
4 *Shays*	N	N	Y	Y	N	N	N
5 Maloney	N	N	Y	Y	N	N	N
6 *Johnson*	Y	Y	Y	Y	N	Y	N
DELAWARE							
AL *Castle*	N	N	Y	Y	Y	Y	N
FLORIDA							
1 *Scarborough*	Y	Y	Y	Y	Y	N	N
2 Boyd	Y	Y	Y	Y	N	N	N
3 Brown	N	N	Y	N	N	N	N
4 *Fowler*	Y	Y	Y	Y	Y	N	?
5 Thurman	N	N	Y	Y	N	N	N
6 *Stearns*	N	N	Y	Y	N	N	?
7 *Mica*	Y	Y	Y	Y	Y	Y	N
8 *McCollum*	N	N	Y	Y	N	N	N
9 *Bilirakis*	Y	Y	Y	Y	Y	Y	N
10 *Young*	Y	Y	Y	Y	Y	Y	N
11 Davis	N	N	Y	Y	N	N	?
12 *Canady*	Y	Y	Y	Y	N	N	N
13 *Miller*	Y	Y	Y	Y	Y	Y	N
14 *Goss*	Y	Y	Y	Y	Y	Y	N
15 *Weldon*	N	N	Y	Y	N	N	N
16 *Foley*	N	Y	Y	Y	Y	N	N
17 Meek	N	N	Y	N	N	N	N
18 *Ros-Lehtinen*	Y	N	Y	Y	Y	Y	N
19 Wexler	N	N	Y	Y	N	N	N
20 Deutsch	N	N	Y	Y	N	N	N
21 *Diaz-Balart*	Y	Y	Y	Y	Y	Y	N
22 *Shaw*	Y	Y	Y	Y	Y	Y	N
23 Hastings	N	N	Y	N	N	N	N
GEORGIA							
1 *Kingston*	Y	Y	Y	Y	Y	Y	N
2 Bishop	Y	Y	Y	Y	N	Y	N
3 *Collins*	Y	Y	Y	Y	Y	Y	N
4 McKinney	N	N	Y	N	N	N	N
5 Lewis	N	N	Y	Y	N	N	Y
6 *Gingrich*						Y	
7 *Barr*	Y	Y	Y	Y	Y	Y	N
8 *Chambliss*	Y	Y	Y	Y	Y	Y	N
9 *Deal*	Y	Y	Y	Y	Y	Y	N
10 *Norwood*	Y	Y	Y	Y	Y	Y	?
11 *Linder*	N	N	Y	Y	Y	Y	N
HAWAII							
1 Abercrombie	Y	Y	N	Y	N	N	N
2 Mink	N	N	N	Y	N	N	N
IDAHO							
1 *Chenoweth*	Y	Y	Y	Y	Y	N	N
2 *Crapo*	Y	Y	?	Y	Y	Y	N
ILLINOIS							
1 Rush	Y	N	Y	Y	Y	N	N
2 Jackson	Y	Y	Y	Y	N	N	N
3 Lipinski	Y	Y	Y	Y	N	N	N
4 Gutierrez	Y	Y	Y	Y	N	N	N
5 Blagojevich	Y	N	Y	N	Y	N	N
6 *Hyde*	Y	N	Y	Y	Y	N	N
7 Davis	N	N	Y	Y	N	N	N
8 *Crane*	Y	Y	Y	N	Y	Y	N
9 Yates	?	?	?	?	?	?	?
10 *Porter*	N	N	Y	Y	Y	N	N
11 *Weller*	Y	Y	Y	Y	Y	Y	N
12 Costello	Y	Y	Y	Y	N	N	N

ND Northern Democrats   SD Southern Democrats

	146	147	148	149	150	151	152
13 ***Fawell***	Y	Y	Y	Y	Y	Y	N
14 ***Hastert***	N	N	?	Y	Y	Y	N
15 ***Ewing***	Y	Y	Y	Y	Y	N	N
16 ***Manzullo***	Y	Y	Y	Y	Y	N	N
17 Evans	Y	Y	Y	Y	N	N	N
18 ***LaHood***	N	N	N	N	N	N	N
19 Poshard	Y	Y	Y	Y	N	N	N
20 ***Shimkus***	Y	N	Y	Y	N	Y	N
INDIANA							
1 Visclosky	N	N	Y	Y	Y	N	N
2 ***McIntosh***	Y	Y	Y	Y	Y	Y	N
3 Roemer	N	N	Y	Y	N	N	N
4 ***Souder***	Y	Y	Y	Y	Y	Y	N
5 ***Buyer***	N	Y	Y	Y	Y	Y	N
6 ***Burton***	N	Y	Y	Y	Y	Y	N
7 ***Pease***	Y	Y	Y	Y	Y	Y	N
8 ***Hostettler***	Y	Y	Y	N	Y	Y	N
9 Hamilton	Y	Y	Y	Y	N	N	N
10 Carson	N	N	Y	Y	N	N	N
IOWA							
1 ***Leach***	Y	Y	Y	Y	Y	Y	N
2 ***Nussle***	Y	Y	Y	Y	Y	Y	N
3 Boswell	Y	Y	Y	Y	Y	N	N
4 ***Ganske***	Y	Y	Y	Y	Y	Y	N
5 ***Latham***	Y	Y	Y	Y	Y	Y	N
KANSAS							
1 ***Moran***	Y	Y	Y	Y	Y	N	N
2 ***Ryun***	N	N	Y	Y	Y	N	N
3 ***Snowbarger***	N	N	Y	Y	Y	N	N
4 ***Tiahrt***	N	N	Y	Y	Y	N	N
KENTUCKY							
1 ***Whitfield***	Y	Y	Y	Y	Y	Y	N
2 ***Lewis***	N	N	Y	Y	Y	Y	N
3 ***Northup***	Y	Y	Y	Y	Y	Y	N
4 ***Bunning***	N	N	Y	Y	Y	Y	N
5 ***Rogers***	Y	Y	Y	Y	Y	N	N
6 Baesler	Y	Y	Y	Y	N	N	N
LOUISIANA							
1 ***Livingston***	N	N	Y	Y	Y	Y	N
2 Jefferson	N	N	Y	Y	N	N	N
3 ***Tauzin***	N	N	Y	Y	Y	Y	N
4 ***McCrery***	Y	Y	Y	Y	Y	Y	N
5 ***Cooksey***	Y	Y	Y	Y	Y	Y	N
6 ***Baker***	N	N	Y	Y	Y	Y	N
7 John	Y	N	Y	Y	Y	Y	N
MAINE							
1 Allen	N	N	Y	Y	N	N	N
2 Baldacci	Y	Y	Y	Y	N	N	N
MARYLAND							
1 ***Gilchrest***	Y	Y	Y	Y	Y	Y	N
2 ***Ehrlich***	N	N	Y	Y	Y	Y	N
3 Cardin	Y	Y	Y	Y	N	N	N
4 Wynn	N	N	Y	Y	N	N	N
5 Hoyer	Y	Y	Y	Y	N	N	Y
6 ***Bartlett***	N	N	Y	Y	Y	Y	N
7 Cummings	Y	N	Y	Y	N	N	N
8 ***Morella***	N	N	Y	Y	Y	Y	N
MASSACHUSETTS							
1 Olver	Y	Y	Y	Y	N	N	N
2 Neal	N	N	Y	Y	N	Y	N
3 McGovern	N	N	Y	Y	Y	Y	N
4 Frank	N	N	?	?	?	N	Y
5 Meehan	N	N	Y	Y	N	N	N
6 Tierney	Y	Y	Y	Y	N	N	N
7 Markey	Y	Y	Y	Y	N	Y	N
8 Kennedy	Y	Y	Y	Y	N	N	N
9 Moakley	N	N	Y	Y	N	N	N
10 Delahunt	Y	Y	Y	Y	N	Y	N
MICHIGAN							
1 Stupak	N	N	Y	Y	Y	Y	N
2 ***Hoekstra***	N	N	Y	Y	Y	Y	N
3 ***Ehlers***	Y	Y	Y	Y	Y	Y	N
4 ***Camp***	Y	Y	Y	Y	Y	N	N
5 Barcia	N	N	Y	Y	Y	Y	N
6 ***Upton***	Y	Y	Y	Y	Y	Y	N
7 ***Smith***	N	N	Y	Y	Y	Y	N
8 Stabenow	N	N	Y	Y	Y	Y	N
9 Kildee	Y	Y	Y	Y	N	N	N
10 Bonior	Y	Y	N	Y	N	N	N
11 ***Knollenberg***	N	N	Y	Y	Y	Y	N
12 Levin	N	N	Y	Y	N	Y	N
13 Rivers	Y	Y	Y	Y	Y	N	N
14 Conyers	Y	N	N	N	N	N	Y
15 Kilpatrick	N	N	Y	Y	Y	N	N
16 Dingell	N	N	Y	Y	Y	Y	N

	146	147	148	149	150	151	152
MINNESOTA							
1 ***Gutknecht***	Y	Y	Y	Y	Y	N	N
2 Minge	Y	Y	Y	Y	N	N	N
3 ***Ramstad***	N	N	Y	Y	Y	N	N
4 Vento	N	N	N	Y	N	N	N
5 Sabo	Y	Y	N	N	N	N	Y
6 Luther	Y	Y	Y	Y	N	N	N
7 Peterson	Y	Y	Y	N	Y	N	N
8 Oberstar	Y	Y	N	N	N	N	N
MISSISSIPPI							
1 ***Wicker***	Y	Y	Y	Y	Y	N	N
2 Thompson	N	N	Y	Y	N	N	N
3 ***Pickering***	Y	Y	Y	Y	Y	N	N
4 ***Parker***	Y	Y	N	N	Y	Y	N
5 Taylor	N	Y	Y	Y	N	N	N
MISSOURI							
1 Clay	N	N	Y	Y	N	N	N
2 ***Talent***	N	N	Y	Y	Y	Y	?
3 Gephardt	Y	Y	Y	Y	N	N	N
4 Skelton	Y	Y	Y	Y	N	N	N
5 McCarthy	Y	Y	Y	Y	N	N	N
6 Danner	Y	Y	Y	Y	N	N	N
7 ***Blunt***	Y	Y	Y	Y	N	N	N
8 ***Emerson***	Y	Y	Y	Y	Y	Y	N
9 ***Hulshof***	Y	Y	Y	Y	Y	N	N
MONTANA							
AL ***Hill***	N	N	Y	Y	Y	Y	N
NEBRASKA							
1 ***Bereuter***	Y	Y	Y	Y	N	N	N
2 ***Christensen***	?	?	Y	Y	Y	N	?
3 ***Barrett***	Y	Y	Y	Y	Y	N	N
NEVADA							
1 ***Ensign***	Y	Y	Y	Y	Y	Y	N
2 ***Gibbons***	Y	Y	Y	Y	Y	Y	N
NEW HAMPSHIRE							
1 ***Sununu***	Y	Y	Y	Y	Y	Y	N
2 ***Bass***	Y	Y	Y	?	Y	Y	N
NEW JERSEY							
1 Andrews	Y	Y	Y	Y	N	Y	N
2 ***LoBiondo***	Y	N	Y	Y	Y	Y	N
3 ***Saxton***	Y	Y	Y	Y	Y	Y	N
4 ***Smith***	Y	Y	Y	Y	Y	Y	N
5 ***Roukema***	N	N	Y	Y	Y	Y	N
6 Pallone	Y	Y	Y	Y	Y	Y	N
7 ***Franks***	Y	Y	Y	Y	Y	Y	N
8 Pascrell	N	N	Y	Y	N	Y	N
9 Rothman	Y	Y	Y	Y	N	N	?
10 Payne	N	N	Y	Y	N	N	N
11 ***Frelinghuysen***	Y	Y	Y	Y	Y	Y	N
12 ***Pappas***	Y	N	Y	Y	Y	Y	N
13 Menendez	Y	Y	Y	Y	N	N	N
NEW MEXICO							
1 Vacant							
2 ***Skeen***	Y	Y	Y	Y	Y	N	N
3 ***Redmond***	Y	Y	Y	Y	Y	N	N
NEW YORK							
1 ***Forbes***	?	N	Y	Y	Y	Y	N
2 ***Lazio***	N	N	Y	Y	Y	Y	N
3 ***King***	N	N	Y	Y	Y	Y	N
4 McCarthy	N	N	Y	Y	Y	Y	N
5 Ackerman	N	N	Y	Y	N	Y	Y
7 Manton	N	N	Y	Y	Y	N	N
6 Meeks	N	N	Y	Y	N	Y	?
8 Nadler	Y	N	Y	Y	N	Y	N
9 Schumer	N	N	Y	Y	N	Y	N
10 Towns	N	N	Y	Y	N	Y	N
11 Owens	N	N	Y	Y	N	N	N
12 Velázquez	N	N	N	Y	N	N	N
13 ***Fossella***	N	N	Y	Y	Y	Y	N
14 Maloney	Y	Y	Y	Y	N	Y	N
15 Rangel	N	N	Y	Y	Y	Y	N
16 Serrano	N	N	Y	Y	N	N	Y
17 Engel	N	N	Y	Y	N	Y	?
18 Lowey	N	N	Y	Y	N	Y	N
19 ***Kelly***	N	N	Y	Y	Y	Y	N
20 ***Gilman***	Y	Y	Y	Y	Y	Y	N
21 McNulty	N	N	Y	Y	N	Y	Y
22 ***Solomon***	N	N	Y	Y	Y	Y	N
23 ***Boehlert***	Y	Y	Y	Y	Y	Y	N
24 ***McHugh***	Y	Y	Y	Y	Y	N	N
25 ***Walsh***	N	N	Y	Y	Y	Y	N
26 Hinchey	Y	Y	Y	Y	N	N	N
27 ***Paxon***	N	N	Y	Y	Y	Y	N
28 Slaughter	Y	N	Y	Y	N	N	Y
29 LaFalce	N	N	Y	Y	N	N	N

	146	147	148	149	150	151	152
30 ***Quinn***	Y	N	Y	Y	Y	Y	?
31 ***Houghton***	Y	Y	Y	Y	Y	Y	N
NORTH CAROLINA							
1 Clayton	N	N	Y	Y	N	N	N
2 Etheridge	N	N	Y	Y	Y	N	N
3 ***Jones***	N	Y	Y	Y	Y	N	?
4 Price	N	N	Y	Y	N	Y	N
5 ***Burr***	N	N	Y	Y	Y	N	N
6 ***Coble***	Y	Y	Y	Y	Y	Y	N
7 McIntyre	Y	Y	Y	Y	Y	N	N
8 Hefner	?	?	?	?	?	?	?
9 ***Myrick***	N	N	Y	Y	Y	Y	?
10 ***Ballenger***	Y	Y	Y	Y	Y	Y	N
11 ***Taylor***	Y	Y	Y	Y	Y	Y	N
12 Watt	N	N	Y	Y	N	N	N
NORTH DAKOTA							
AL Pomeroy	Y	Y	Y	Y	N	Y	N
OHIO							
1 ***Chabot***	Y	Y	Y	Y	Y	Y	N
2 ***Portman***	Y	Y	Y	Y	Y	Y	N
3 Hall	N	Y	Y	Y	Y	Y	N
4 ***Oxley***	Y	Y	Y	Y	Y	Y	N
5 ***Gillmor***	Y	Y	Y	Y	N	Y	N
6 Strickland	N	N	Y	Y	N	Y	N
7 ***Hobson***	Y	Y	Y	Y	Y	Y	N
8 ***Boehner***	N	N	Y	Y	Y	Y	N
9 Kaptur	Y	?	Y	Y	N	N	?
10 Kucinich	Y	Y	Y	Y	N	N	N
11 Stokes	N	N	Y	Y	N	N	N
12 ***Kasich***	Y	Y	Y	Y	Y	Y	N
13 Brown	N	N	Y	Y	Y	Y	N
14 Sawyer	N	N	Y	Y	Y	Y	N
15 ***Pryce***	Y	N	Y	Y	Y	Y	N
16 ***Regula***	Y	Y	Y	Y	Y	Y	N
17 Traficant	Y	Y	Y	Y	Y	N	?
18 ***Ney***	N	N	Y	Y	Y	Y	N
19 ***LaTourette***	N	N	Y	Y	Y	Y	N
OKLAHOMA							
1 ***Largent***	N	N	Y	Y	Y	N	N
2 ***Coburn***	Y	Y	Y	Y	Y	N	N
3 ***Watkins***	Y	Y	Y	Y	Y	N	N
4 ***Watts***	N	N	Y	Y	Y	N	N
5 ***Istook***	Y	Y	Y	Y	Y	N	N
6 ***Lucas***	Y	Y	Y	Y	Y	N	N
OREGON							
1 Furse	N	N	Y	Y	N	N	N
2 ***Smith***	Y	N	Y	Y	Y	N	N
3 Blumenauer	N	N	N	Y	N	N	N
4 DeFazio	Y	Y	P	Y	N	N	P
5 Hooley	N	N	Y	Y	Y	N	N
PENNSYLVANIA							
1 Vacant							
2 Fattah	N	N	Y	Y	N	N	?
3 Borski	Y	Y	Y	Y	N	N	N
4 Klink	N	N	Y	Y	N	N	N
5 ***Peterson***	Y	Y	Y	Y	Y	N	N
6 Holden	N	N	Y	Y	N	Y	N
7 ***Weldon***	N	N	Y	Y	Y	Y	?
8 ***Greenwood***	N	N	Y	Y	Y	Y	?
9 ***Shuster***	N	N	Y	Y	Y	Y	N
10 ***McDade***	Y	Y	Y	Y	Y	Y	?
11 Kanjorski	Y	Y	N	N	N	N	N
12 Murtha	N	Y	Y	Y	N	Y	N
13 ***Fox***	Y	Y	Y	Y	Y	Y	N
14 Coyne	N	N	Y	Y	N	Y	N
15 McHale	N	N	Y	Y	N	N	N
16 ***Pitts***	N	N	Y	Y	Y	Y	N
17 ***Gekas***	N	Y	Y	Y	Y	Y	N
18 Doyle	N	N	Y	Y	N	Y	N
19 ***Goodling***	Y	Y	Y	Y	Y	Y	?
20 Mascara	N	N	Y	Y	N	N	N
21 ***English***	N	N	Y	Y	Y	Y	N
RHODE ISLAND							
1 Kennedy	Y	Y	Y	Y	N	N	N
2 Weygand	N	N	Y	Y	N	N	N
SOUTH CAROLINA							
1 ***Sanford***	Y	Y	Y	Y	Y	Y	N
2 ***Spence***	?	?	Y	Y	Y	Y	N
3 ***Graham***	Y	Y	Y	Y	Y	N	N
4 ***Inglis***	Y	Y	Y	Y	Y	Y	N
5 Spratt	N	N	Y	Y	N	Y	N
6 Clyburn	N	N	Y	Y	N	N	N
SOUTH DAKOTA							
AL ***Thune***	Y	Y	Y	Y	Y	N	N

	146	147	148	149	150	151	152
TENNESSEE							
1 ***Jenkins***	Y	Y	Y	Y	Y	N	N
2 ***Duncan***	Y	Y	Y	Y	Y	N	N
3 ***Wamp***	Y	Y	Y	Y	Y	Y	N
4 ***Hilleary***	Y	Y	Y	Y	Y	N	N
5 Clement	Y	Y	Y	Y	N	N	N
6 Gordon	N	N	Y	Y	N	Y	N
7 ***Bryant***	N	N	Y	Y	Y	Y	?
8 Tanner	N	N	Y	Y	N	Y	N
9 Ford	N	N	Y	Y	N	Y	N
TEXAS							
1 Sandlin	Y	Y	Y	Y	N	N	N
2 Turner	N	N	Y	Y	Y	N	N
3 ***Johnson, Sam***	N	N	Y	Y	Y	N	N
4 Hall	N	N	Y	Y	Y	N	N
5 ***Sessions***	N	N	Y	Y	Y	N	N
6 ***Barton***	Y	Y	Y	Y	Y	N	?
7 ***Archer***	Y	Y	Y	Y	Y	Y	N
8 ***Brady***	Y	Y	Y	Y	Y	N	N
9 Lampson	N	Y	Y	Y	N	N	N
10 Doggett	N	N	Y	Y	N	N	N
11 Edwards	Y	N	Y	Y	N	N	N
12 ***Granger***	N	N	Y	Y	Y	N	N
13 ***Thornberry***	N	N	Y	Y	Y	N	N
14 ***Paul***	N	N	Y	Y	Y	N	N
15 Hinojosa	Y	Y	Y	Y	N	N	N
16 Reyes	Y	Y	Y	Y	N	N	?
17 Stenholm	N	N	Y	N	Y	N	?
18 Jackson-Lee	N	N	Y	Y	Y	N	N
19 ***Combest***	Y	Y	Y	Y	Y	N	N
20 Gonzalez	?	?	?	?	?	?	?
21 ***Smith***	Y	Y	Y	Y	Y	N	N
22 ***DeLay***	N	N	Y	Y	Y	N	N
23 ***Bonilla***	Y	N	Y	Y	Y	N	N
24 Frost	N	N	Y	Y	Y	Y	N
25 Bentsen	N	Y	Y	Y	N	N	N
26 ***Armey***	N	N	Y	?	Y	Y	N
27 Ortiz	Y	Y	Y	Y	N	N	N
28 Rodriguez	Y	Y	Y	Y	N	N	N
29 Green	N	N	Y	Y	N	N	N
30 Johnson, E.B.	N	N	Y	Y	N	Y	Y
UTAH							
1 ***Hansen***	Y	Y	Y	Y	Y	Y	N
2 ***Cook***	N	N	Y	Y	N	Y	N
3 ***Cannon***	Y	N	Y	Y	Y	N	N
VERMONT							
AL *Sanders*	Y	Y	Y	Y	Y	N	N
VIRGINIA							
1 ***Bateman***	–	–	+	+	+	+	–
2 Pickett	Y	Y	Y	Y	N	N	N
3 Scott	N	N	Y	Y	Y	N	N
4 Sisisky	Y	Y	Y	Y	Y	N	N
5 Goode	Y	Y	Y	Y	Y	N	N
6 ***Goodlatte***	N	N	Y	Y	Y	Y	N
7 ***Bliley***	Y	Y	Y	Y	Y	Y	N
8 Moran	N	N	Y	Y	N	Y	N
9 Boucher	N	N	Y	Y	Y	N	N
10 ***Wolf***	Y	Y	Y	Y	Y	Y	N
11 ***Davis***	Y	N	Y	Y	Y	N	N
WASHINGTON							
1 ***White***	N	N	Y	Y	Y	Y	N
2 ***Metcalf***	Y	Y	Y	Y	Y	Y	N
3 ***Smith, Linda***	Y	Y	Y	Y	Y	Y	N
4 ***Hastings***	Y	Y	Y	Y	Y	Y	N
5 ***Nethercutt***	Y	Y	Y	?	Y	Y	N
6 Dicks	Y	Y	Y	Y	Y	Y	N
7 McDermott	Y	Y	Y	Y	Y	N	Y
8 ***Dunn***	N	Y	Y	Y	Y	Y	N
9 Smith, Adam	N	N	Y	Y	Y	Y	N
WEST VIRGINIA							
1 Mollohan	N	N	Y	Y	N	Y	N
2 Wise	N	N	Y	Y	N	Y	N
3 Rahall	N	N	Y	Y	Y	Y	N
WISCONSIN							
1 ***Neumann***	N	N	Y	Y	Y	Y	N
2 ***Klug***	Y	Y	Y	Y	Y	Y	N
3 Kind	N	N	N	Y	N	N	N
4 Kleczka	Y	Y	Y	Y	N	N	N
5 Barrett	Y	Y	Y	Y	N	N	N
6 ***Petri***	Y	Y	Y	Y	Y	N	N
7 Obey	Y	Y	Y	Y	N	N	N
8 Johnson	Y	Y	Y	Y	N	N	N
9 ***Sensenbrenner***	N	N	Y	Y	Y	Y	N
WYOMING							
AL ***Cubin***	Y	N	Y	Y	Y	Y	N

Southern states - Ala., Ark., Fla., Ga., Ky., La., Miss., N.C., Okla., S.C., Tenn., Texas, Va.

House Votes 153, 154, 155, 156, 157, 158, 159

Key

- Y Voted for (yea).
- # Paired for.
- + Announced for.
- N Voted against (nay).
- X Paired against.
- − Announced against.
- P Voted "present."
- C Voted "present" to avoid possible conflict of interest.
- ? Did not vote or otherwise make a position known.

Democrats **Republicans** *Independent*

153. Disapproval of Dan Burton/Motion to Table. Armey, R-Texas, motion to table (kill) the Gephardt, D-Mo., privileged resolution to disapprove of the way Dan Burton, R-Ind., has handled his role as chairman of the House Government Reform and Oversight Committee. Motion agreed to 223-196: R 220-0; D 3-195 (ND 0-146, SD 3-49); I 0-1. May 14, 1998.

154. HR 2431. Religious Persecution/Policy Recommendations. Hastings, D-Fla., amendment to allow the director of the Office of Religious Persecution Monitoring, in conjunction with the secretary of State, to make policy recommendations that emphasize the promotion and development of legal protections and respect for religious freedom in U.S. development programs. Adopted 415-3: R 216-2; D 198-1 (ND 145-1, SD 53-0); I 1-0. May 14, 1998.

155. HR 2431. Religious Persecution/Passage. Passage of the bill to establish a new office in the State Department to monitor religious persecution overseas, and to direct U.S. sanctions against countries and individuals determined to have engaged in religious persecution. Passed 375-41: R 206-14; D 169-27 (ND 123-20, SD 46-7); I 0-0. May 14, 1998.

156. HR 3534. Mandates Information/Tax Revenues. Moakley, D-Mass., amendment to strike provisions which exempt from points of order measures resulting in net decreases in tax revenue over five years. Rejected 176-233: R 1-212; D 174-21 (ND 132-10, SD 42-11); I 1-0. May 19, 1998.

157. HR 3534. Mandates Information/Public Health. Waxman, D-Calif., amendment to permit points of order against provisions in legislation which remove or make less stringent private sector mandates established to protect public health and the environment. Rejected 190-221: R 22-192; D 167-29 (ND 133-10, SD 34-19); I 1-0. May 19, 1998.

158. HR 3534. Mandates Information/Points of Order. Boehlert, R-N.Y., amendment to prohibit points of order to be raised against amendments offered on the floor. Rejected 189-223: R 27-188; D 161-35 (ND 130-13, SD 31-22); I 1-0. May 19, 1998.

159. HR 3534. Mandates Information/Civil Rights. Becerra, D-Calif., amendment to permit points of order against provisions which remove or make less stringent private sector mandates established to protect civil rights. Rejected 180-231: R 6-208; D 173-23 (ND 133-10, SD 40-13); I 1-0. May 19, 1998.

	153	154	155	156	157	158	159
ALABAMA							
1 *Callahan*	Y	Y	Y	N	N	N	N
2 *Everett*	Y	Y	Y	N	N	N	N
3 *Riley*	Y	Y	Y	N	N	N	N
4 *Aderholt*	Y	Y	Y	N	N	N	N
5 Cramer	N	Y	Y	N	N	N	N
6 *Bachus*	Y	Y	Y	N	N	N	N
7 Hilliard	N	Y	N	Y	Y	Y	Y
ALASKA							
AL *Young*	Y	Y	Y	N	N	N	N
ARIZONA							
1 *Salmon*	Y	Y	N	N	N	N	N
2 Pastor	N	Y	Y	Y	Y	Y	Y
3 *Stump*	Y	Y	N	N	N	N	N
4 *Shadegg*	Y	Y	N	N	N	N	N
5 *Kolbe*	Y	Y	N	N	N	N	N
6 *Hayworth*	Y	Y	Y	N	N	N	N
ARKANSAS							
1 Berry	N	Y	Y	Y	N	N	Y
2 Snyder	N	Y	N	Y	N	N	N
3 *Hutchinson*	Y	Y	Y	N	N	N	N
4 Dickey	Y	Y	?	N	?	N	N
CALIFORNIA							
1 *Riggs*	?	?	?	N	N	N	N
2 *Herger*	Y	Y	N	N	N	N	N
3 Fazio	N	Y	N	Y	Y	Y	Y
4 *Doolittle*	Y	Y	N	N	N	N	N
5 Matsui	N	Y	N	Y	Y	Y	Y
6 Woolsey	N	Y	Y	Y	Y	Y	Y
7 Miller	N	Y	Y	Y	Y	Y	Y
8 Pelosi	N	Y	Y	Y	Y	Y	Y
9 Lee	N	Y	Y	Y	Y	Y	Y
10 Tauscher	N	Y	N	Y	Y	Y	Y
11 *Pombo*	?	Y	N	N	N	N	N
12 Lantos	N	Y	Y	Y	Y	Y	Y
13 Stark	N	Y	Y	Y	Y	Y	Y
14 Eshoo	N	Y	Y	Y	Y	Y	Y
15 *Campbell*	Y	Y	Y	N	N	N	N
16 Lofgren	N	Y	Y	Y	Y	Y	Y
17 Farr	N	Y	Y	Y	Y	Y	Y
18 Condit	N	Y	Y	N	N	N	N
19 *Radanovich*	?	Y	Y	N	N	N	N
20 Dooley	N	Y	N	N	N	N	Y
21 *Thomas*	Y	Y	Y	N	N	N	N
22 Capps, L.	N	Y	Y	Y	Y	Y	Y
23 *Gallegly*	Y	Y	Y	N	N	N	N
24 Sherman	N	Y	Y	N	Y	N	N
25 *McKeon*	Y	Y	Y	N	N	N	N
26 Berman	N	Y	Y	Y	Y	Y	Y
27 *Rogan*	Y	Y	Y	−	−	−	−
28 *Dreier*	Y	Y	Y	N	N	N	N
29 Waxman	N	Y	Y	Y	Y	Y	Y
30 Becerra	N	Y	Y	Y	Y	Y	Y
31 Martinez	N	Y	Y	Y	Y	Y	Y
32 Dixon	N	Y	Y	Y	Y	Y	Y
33 Royal-Allard	N	Y	Y	Y	Y	Y	Y
34 Torres	?	?	?	Y	Y	Y	Y
35 Waters	N	Y	N	Y	Y	Y	Y
36 Harman	?	?	?	?	?	?	?
37 Millender-McD.	N	Y	Y	Y	Y	Y	Y

	153	154	155	156	157	158	159
38 *Horn*	Y	Y	Y	N	Y	N	N
39 *Royce*	Y	Y	Y	N	N	N	N
40 *Lewis*	Y	?	?	N	N	N	N
41 *Kim*	Y	Y	Y	N	N	N	N
42 Brown	N	Y	N	Y	Y	Y	Y
43 *Calvert*	Y	Y	Y	N	N	N	N
44 *Bono, M.*	Y	Y	Y	N	N	N	N
45 *Rohrabacher*	Y	Y	Y	N	N	N	N
46 Sanchez	N	Y	Y	Y	Y	Y	Y
47 *Cox*	Y	Y	Y	N	N	N	N
48 *Packard*	Y	Y	Y	N	N	N	N
49 *Bilbray*	Y	Y	Y	N	N	N	N
50 Filner	N	Y	Y	Y	Y	Y	Y
51 *Cunningham*	Y	Y	Y	N	N	N	N
52 *Hunter*	Y	Y	Y	N	N	N	N
COLORADO							
1 DeGette	N	Y	N	Y	Y	Y	Y
2 Skaggs	−	+	−	+	+	+	+
3 *McInnis*	Y	Y	Y	N	N	N	N
4 *Schaffer*	Y	Y	N	N	N	N	N
5 *Hefley*	Y	Y	Y	N	N	N	N
6 *Schaefer*	Y	Y	Y	N	N	N	N
CONNECTICUT							
1 Kennelly	N	Y	Y	Y	Y	Y	Y
2 Gejdenson	N	Y	Y	Y	Y	Y	Y
3 DeLauro	N	Y	Y	Y	Y	Y	Y
4 *Shays*	Y	Y	N	Y	N	Y	Y
5 Maloney	N	Y	Y	Y	N	Y	N
6 *Johnson*	Y	Y	N	N	Y	N	N
DELAWARE							
AL *Castle*	Y	Y	Y	N	N	Y	N
FLORIDA							
1 *Scarborough*	Y	Y	Y	N	N	N	N
2 Boyd	N	Y	Y	Y	N	N	N
3 Brown	N	Y	Y	Y	Y	Y	Y
4 *Fowler*	?	?	Y	N	N	N	N
5 Thurman	N	Y	Y	Y	Y	Y	Y
6 *Stearns*	Y	Y	Y	N	N	N	N
7 *Mica*	Y	Y	Y	N	N	N	N
8 *McCollum*	Y	Y	Y	N	N	N	N
9 *Bilirakis*	Y	Y	Y	N	N	N	N
10 *Young*	Y	Y	Y	N	N	N	N
11 Davis	N	Y	Y	N	N	N	Y
12 *Canady*	Y	Y	Y	N	N	N	N
13 *Miller*	Y	Y	Y	N	N	N	?
14 *Goss*	Y	Y	Y	N	N	N	N
15 *Weldon*	Y	Y	Y	N	N	N	N
16 *Foley*	Y	Y	Y	N	N	N	N
17 Meek	N	Y	Y	Y	Y	Y	Y
18 *Ros-Lehtinen*	Y	Y	Y	N	N	N	N
19 Wexler	N	Y	Y	Y	Y	Y	Y
20 Deutsch	N	Y	Y	Y	Y	Y	Y
21 *Diaz-Balart*	Y	Y	Y	N	N	N	N
22 *Shaw*	Y	Y	Y	N	N	N	N
23 Hastings	N	Y	N	Y	Y	Y	Y
GEORGIA							
1 *Kingston*	Y	Y	Y	N	N	N	N
2 Bishop	N	Y	Y	Y	N	N	Y
3 *Collins*	Y	Y	Y	N	N	N	N
4 McKinney	N	Y	Y	Y	Y	Y	Y
5 Lewis	N	Y	Y	Y	Y	Y	Y
6 *Gingrich*							
7 *Barr*	Y	Y	N	N	N	N	N
8 *Chambliss*	Y	Y	Y	N	N	N	N
9 *Deal*	Y	Y	Y	N	N	N	N
10 *Norwood*	Y	Y	Y	N	N	N	N
11 *Linder*	Y	Y	Y	N	N	N	N
HAWAII							
1 Abercrombie	N	Y	Y	Y	Y	Y	Y
2 Mink	N	Y	N	Y	Y	Y	Y
IDAHO							
1 *Chenoweth*	Y	N	N	N	N	N	Y
2 *Crapo*	Y	Y	N	N	N	N	N
ILLINOIS							
1 Rush	N	Y	Y	Y	Y	Y	Y
2 Jackson	N	Y	Y	Y	Y	Y	Y
3 Lipinski	N	Y	Y	Y	Y	Y	N
4 Gutierrez	N	Y	Y	Y	Y	Y	Y
5 Blagojevich	N	Y	Y	Y	Y	Y	Y
6 *Hyde*	Y	Y	Y	N	N	N	N
7 Davis	N	Y	Y	Y	Y	Y	Y
8 *Crane*	Y	Y	N	?	?	?	?
9 Yates	N	Y	Y	Y	Y	Y	Y
10 *Porter*	Y	Y	Y	N	N	N	N
11 *Weller*	Y	Y	Y	N	N	N	N
12 Costello	N	Y	Y	Y	Y	Y	Y

ND Northern Democrats   SD Southern Democrats

	153	154	155	156	157	158	159
13 ***Fawell***	Y	Y	Y	N	N	Y	N
14 ***Hastert***	Y	Y	Y	N	N	N	N
15 ***Ewing***	Y	Y	Y	–	–	–	–
16 ***Manzullo***	Y	Y	Y	N	N	N	N
17 Evans	N	Y	Y	Y	Y	Y	Y
18 ***LaHood***	Y	Y	Y	N	N	N	N
19 Poshard	N	Y	Y	Y	Y	Y	Y
20 ***Shimkus***	Y	Y	Y	N	N	N	N
INDIANA							
1 Visclosky	N	Y	Y	Y	Y	Y	Y
2 ***McIntosh***	Y	Y	Y	N	N	N	N
3 Roemer	N	Y	Y	N	N	N	N
4 ***Souder***	Y	?	Y	N	N	N	N
5 ***Buyer***	Y	Y	Y	N	N	N	N
6 ***Burton***	Y	Y	Y	N	N	N	N
7 ***Pease***	Y	Y	Y	N	N	N	N
8 ***Hostettler***	Y	Y	Y	N	N	N	N
9 Hamilton	N	Y	N	N	N	N	N
10 Carson	N	Y	Y	Y	Y	Y	Y
IOWA							
1 ***Leach***	Y	Y	Y	N	Y	Y	N
2 ***Nussle***	Y	Y	Y	N	N	N	N
3 Boswell	N	Y	Y	N	Y	Y	N
4 ***Ganske***	Y	Y	Y	?	?	?	?
5 ***Latham***	Y	Y	Y	N	N	N	N
KANSAS							
1 ***Moran***	Y	Y	Y	N	N	N	N
2 ***Ryun***	Y	Y	Y	–	–	–	–
3 ***Snowbarger***	Y	Y	Y	N	N	N	N
4 ***Tiahrt***	Y	Y	Y	N	N	N	N
KENTUCKY							
1 ***Whitfield***	Y	Y	Y	N	N	N	N
2 ***Lewis***	Y	Y	Y	N	N	N	N
3 ***Northup***	Y	Y	Y	N	N	N	N
4 ***Bunning***	Y	Y	Y	N	N	N	N
5 ***Rogers***	Y	Y	Y	N	N	N	N
6 Baesler	N	Y	Y	?	?	?	?
LOUISIANA							
1 ***Livingston***	Y	Y	Y	–	–	–	–
2 Jefferson	N	Y	N	Y	Y	Y	Y
3 ***Tauzin***	Y	Y	Y	N	N	N	N
4 ***McCrery***	Y	Y	Y	N	N	N	N
5 ***Cooksey***	Y	Y	Y	N	N	N	N
6 ***Baker***	Y	Y	Y	N	N	N	N
7 John	?	Y	Y	N	N	N	N
MAINE							
1 Allen	N	Y	Y	Y	Y	Y	Y
2 Baldacci	N	Y	Y	Y	Y	Y	Y
MARYLAND							
1 ***Gilchrest***	Y	Y	Y	N	Y	Y	N
2 ***Ehrlich***	Y	Y	Y	N	N	N	N
3 Cardin	N	Y	Y	Y	Y	Y	Y
4 Wynn	N	Y	Y	Y	Y	Y	Y
5 Hoyer	N	Y	Y	Y	Y	Y	Y
6 ***Bartlett***	Y	Y	Y	N	N	N	N
7 Cummings	N	Y	Y	Y	Y	Y	Y
8 ***Morella***	Y	Y	Y	Y	Y	Y	Y
MASSACHUSETTS							
1 Olver	N	Y	Y	Y	Y	Y	Y
2 Neal	N	Y	Y	Y	Y	Y	Y
3 McGovern	N	Y	Y	Y	Y	Y	Y
4 Frank	N	Y	Y	Y	Y	Y	Y
5 Meehan	N	Y	Y	Y	Y	Y	Y
6 Tierney	N	Y	Y	Y	Y	Y	Y
7 Markey	N	Y	Y	Y	Y	Y	Y
8 Kennedy	N	Y	Y	Y	Y	Y	Y
9 Moakley	N	Y	Y	Y	Y	Y	Y
10 Delahunt	N	Y	Y	Y	Y	Y	Y
MICHIGAN							
1 Stupak	N	Y	Y	Y	Y	Y	Y
2 ***Hoekstra***	Y	Y	Y	N	N	N	N
3 ***Ehlers***	Y	Y	Y	N	N	Y	N
4 ***Camp***	Y	Y	Y	N	N	N	N
5 Barcia	N	Y	Y	Y	Y	N	Y
6 ***Upton***	Y	Y	Y	N	N	Y	N
7 ***Smith***	Y	Y	Y	N	N	N	N
8 Stabenow	N	Y	Y	Y	Y	Y	Y
9 Kildee	N	Y	Y	Y	Y	Y	Y
10 Bonior	N	Y	P	Y	Y	Y	Y
11 ***Knollenberg***	Y	Y	Y	N	N	N	N
12 Levin	N	Y	Y	Y	Y	Y	Y
13 Rivers	N	Y	Y	Y	Y	Y	Y
14 Conyers	N	Y	N	Y	Y	Y	Y
15 Kilpatrick	N	Y	Y	Y	Y	Y	Y
16 Dingell	N	Y	N	Y	Y	Y	Y

	153	154	155	156	157	158	159
MINNESOTA							
1 ***Gutknecht***	Y	Y	Y	N	N	N	N
2 Minge	N	Y	Y	Y	N	N	Y
3 ***Ramstad***	Y	Y	Y	N	Y	Y	N
4 Vento	N	Y	Y	Y	Y	Y	Y
5 Sabo	N	Y	N	Y	Y	Y	Y
6 Luther	N	Y	Y	Y	Y	Y	Y
7 Peterson	N	Y	Y	N	N	N	N
8 Oberstar	N	Y	N	Y	Y	Y	Y
MISSISSIPPI							
1 ***Wicker***	Y	Y	Y	N	N	N	N
2 Thompson	N	Y	Y	Y	Y	Y	Y
3 ***Pickering***	Y	Y	Y	N	N	N	N
4 ***Parker***	Y	Y	Y	N	N	N	N
5 Taylor	Y	Y	Y	Y	N	N	Y
MISSOURI							
1 Clay	N	Y	N	?	?	?	?
2 ***Talent***	Y	Y	Y	N	N	N	N
3 Gephardt	N	Y	Y	Y	Y	Y	Y
4 Skelton	N	Y	Y	Y	N	N	Y
5 McCarthy	N	Y	Y	Y	Y	Y	Y
6 Danner	N	Y	Y	N	N	N	N
7 ***Blunt***	Y	Y	Y	N	N	N	N
8 ***Emerson***	Y	Y	Y	N	N	N	N
9 ***Hulshof***	Y	Y	Y	N	N	N	N
MONTANA							
AL ***Hill***	Y	Y	Y	N	N	N	N
NEBRASKA							
1 ***Bereuter***	Y	Y	Y	N	N	N	N
2 ***Christensen***	Y	Y	Y	N	N	N	N
3 ***Barrett***	Y	Y	Y	N	N	N	N
NEVADA							
1 ***Ensign***	Y	Y	Y	N	N	N	N
2 ***Gibbons***	Y	Y	N	–	N	N	N
NEW HAMPSHIRE							
1 ***Sununu***	Y	Y	Y	N	N	N	N
2 ***Bass***	Y	Y	Y	N	N	N	N
NEW JERSEY							
1 Andrews	N	Y	Y	Y	Y	Y	Y
2 ***LoBiondo***	Y	Y	Y	N	Y	Y	N
3 ***Saxton***	Y	Y	Y	N	Y	Y	N
4 ***Smith***	Y	Y	Y	N	Y	Y	N
5 ***Roukema***	Y	Y	Y	N	Y	Y	N
6 Pallone	N	Y	Y	Y	Y	Y	Y
7 ***Franks***	Y	Y	Y	N	Y	Y	N
8 Pascrell	N	Y	Y	Y	Y	Y	Y
9 Rothman	N	Y	Y	N	Y	Y	Y
10 Payne	N	Y	Y	Y	Y	Y	Y
11 ***Frelinghuysen***	Y	Y	Y	N	Y	Y	N
12 ***Pappas***	Y	Y	Y	N	N	N	N
13 Menendez	N	Y	Y	Y	Y	Y	Y
NEW MEXICO							
1 Vacant							
2 ***Skeen***	Y	Y	Y	N	N	N	N
3 ***Redmond***	Y	Y	Y	N	N	N	N
NEW YORK							
1 ***Forbes***	Y	Y	Y	N	Y	Y	Y
2 ***Lazio***	Y	Y	Y	N	Y	Y	N
3 ***King***	Y	Y	Y	N	N	N	N
4 McCarthy	N	Y	Y	N	Y	Y	N
5 Ackerman	N	Y	Y	Y	Y	Y	Y
6 Meeks	N	Y	Y	?	?	?	?
7 Manton	N	Y	Y	Y	Y	Y	Y
8 Nadler	N	Y	Y	Y	Y	Y	Y
9 Schumer	N	Y	Y	?	?	?	?
10 Towns	N	Y	Y	Y	Y	Y	Y
11 Owens	N	Y	Y	Y	Y	Y	Y
12 Velázquez	N	Y	Y	Y	Y	Y	Y
13 ***Fossella***	Y	Y	Y	N	N	N	N
14 Maloney	N	Y	Y	Y	Y	Y	Y
15 Rangel	N	Y	N	Y	Y	Y	Y
16 Serrano	N	Y	Y	Y	Y	Y	Y
17 Engel	N	Y	Y	Y	Y	Y	Y
18 Lowey	N	Y	Y	Y	Y	Y	Y
19 ***Kelly***	Y	Y	Y	N	Y	Y	N
20 ***Gilman***	Y	Y	Y	N	Y	Y	N
21 McNulty	N	Y	Y	?	?	?	?
22 ***Solomon***	Y	Y	Y	N	N	N	N
23 ***Boehlert***	Y	Y	Y	N	Y	Y	N
24 ***McHugh***	Y	Y	Y	N	N	N	N
25 ***Walsh***	Y	Y	Y	N	Y	Y	N
26 Hinchey	N	Y	Y	Y	Y	Y	Y
27 ***Paxon***	Y	Y	Y	?	?	?	?
28 Slaughter	N	Y	Y	Y	Y	Y	Y
29 LaFalce	N	Y	Y	Y	Y	Y	Y

	153	154	155	156	157	158	159
30 ***Quinn***	?	?	?	N	N	Y	N
31 ***Houghton***	Y	Y	N	N	N	N	N
NORTH CAROLINA							
1 Clayton	N	Y	Y	Y	Y	Y	Y
2 Etheridge	N	Y	Y	Y	Y	Y	Y
3 ***Jones***	Y	Y	Y	N	N	N	N
4 Price	N	Y	Y	Y	Y	N	Y
5 ***Burr***	Y	Y	Y	N	N	N	N
6 ***Coble***	Y	Y	Y	N	N	N	N
7 McIntyre	N	Y	Y	N	N	N	N
8 Hefner	?	?	?	Y	Y	Y	Y
9 ***Myrick***	Y	Y	Y	N	N	N	N
10 ***Ballenger***	Y	Y	Y	N	N	N	N
11 ***Taylor***	Y	Y	Y	N	N	N	N
12 Watt	N	Y	N	Y	Y	Y	Y
NORTH DAKOTA							
AL Pomeroy	N	Y	Y	Y	N	Y	Y
OHIO							
1 ***Chabot***	Y	Y	Y	N	N	N	N
2 ***Portman***	Y	Y	Y	N	N	N	N
3 Hall	N	Y	Y	Y	Y	N	Y
4 ***Oxley***	Y	Y	Y	N	N	N	N
5 ***Gillmor***	Y	Y	Y	N	N	N	N
6 Strickland	N	Y	Y	Y	Y	Y	Y
7 ***Hobson***	Y	Y	Y	N	N	N	N
8 ***Boehner***	Y	Y	Y	N	N	N	N
9 Kaptur	N	Y	Y	Y	Y	Y	Y
10 Kucinich	N	Y	Y	Y	Y	Y	Y
11 Stokes	N	Y	N	Y	Y	Y	Y
12 ***Kasich***	Y	Y	Y	N	N	N	N
13 Brown	N	Y	Y	Y	Y	Y	Y
14 Sawyer	N	Y	Y	Y	Y	Y	Y
15 ***Pryce***	Y	Y	Y	N	N	N	N
16 ***Regula***	Y	Y	Y	N	N	N	N
17 Traficant	?	?	?	Y	N	N	N
18 ***Ney***	Y	Y	Y	N	N	N	N
19 ***LaTourette***	Y	Y	Y	N	N	Y	N
OKLAHOMA							
1 ***Largent***	Y	Y	Y	N	N	N	N
2 ***Coburn***	Y	Y	Y	N	N	N	N
3 ***Watkins***	Y	Y	Y	N	N	N	N
4 ***Watts***	Y	Y	Y	N	N	N	N
5 ***Istook***	Y	Y	Y	N	N	N	N
6 ***Lucas***	Y	Y	Y	N	N	N	N
OREGON							
1 Furse	N	Y	Y	Y	Y	Y	Y
2 ***Smith***	Y	Y	Y	N	N	N	N
3 Blumenauer	N	Y	N	Y	Y	Y	Y
4 DeFazio	N	Y	Y	Y	Y	Y	Y
5 Hooley	N	Y	Y	Y	Y	Y	Y
PENNSYLVANIA							
1 Vacant							
2 Fattah	N	Y	Y	?	?	?	?
3 Borski	N	Y	Y	Y	Y	Y	Y
4 Klink	N	Y	Y	Y	Y	Y	Y
5 ***Peterson***	Y	Y	Y	N	N	N	N
6 Holden	N	Y	Y	Y	Y	Y	Y
7 ***Weldon***	Y	?	Y	N	N	Y	N
8 ***Greenwood***	Y	Y	Y	?	?	?	?
9 ***Shuster***	Y	Y	Y	?	?	?	?
10 ***McDade***	Y	Y	Y	N	N	Y	N
11 Kanjorski	N	Y	Y	Y	Y	Y	Y
12 Murtha	N	Y	Y	Y	Y	Y	Y
13 ***Fox***	Y	Y	Y	N	Y	N	Y
14 Coyne	N	Y	Y	Y	Y	Y	Y
15 McHale	N	Y	Y	Y	Y	Y	Y
16 ***Pitts***	Y	Y	Y	N	N	N	N
17 ***Gekas***	Y	Y	Y	N	N	N	N
18 Doyle	N	Y	Y	Y	Y	Y	Y
19 ***Goodling***	Y	Y	Y	–	–	–	–
20 Mascara	N	Y	Y	Y	Y	Y	Y
21 ***English***	Y	Y	N	N	N	N	N
RHODE ISLAND							
1 Kennedy	N	Y	Y	Y	Y	Y	Y
2 Weygand	N	Y	Y	Y	Y	Y	Y
SOUTH CAROLINA							
1 ***Sanford***	Y	Y	N	N	N	N	N
2 ***Spence***	Y	Y	Y	N	N	N	N
3 ***Graham***	Y	Y	Y	N	N	N	N
4 ***Inglis***	Y	Y	Y	–	N	N	N
5 Spratt	N	Y	Y	Y	Y	Y	Y
6 Clyburn	N	Y	Y	Y	Y	Y	Y
SOUTH DAKOTA							
AL ***Thune***	Y	Y	Y	N	N	N	N

	153	154	155	156	157	158	159
TENNESSEE							
1 ***Jenkins***	Y	Y	Y	N	N	N	N
2 ***Duncan***	Y	Y	Y	N	N	N	N
3 ***Wamp***	Y	Y	Y	N	N	N	N
4 ***Hilleary***	Y	Y	Y	N	N	N	N
5 Clement	N	Y	Y	Y	Y	Y	Y
6 Gordon	N	Y	Y	Y	N	N	Y
7 ***Bryant***	Y	Y	Y	N	N	N	N
8 Tanner	N	Y	Y	N	N	N	N
9 Ford	N	Y	Y	Y	Y	Y	Y
TEXAS							
1 Sandlin	N	Y	Y	N	N	N	Y
2 Turner	N	Y	Y	N	N	N	N
3 ***Johnson, Sam***	Y	Y	Y	N	N	N	N
4 Hall	Y	Y	Y	Y	N	N	N
5 ***Sessions***	Y	Y	Y	N	N	N	N
6 ***Barton***	Y	Y	Y	N	N	N	N
7 ***Archer***	Y	Y	Y	N	N	N	N
8 ***Brady***	Y	Y	Y	N	N	N	N
9 Lampson	N	Y	Y	Y	Y	Y	Y
10 Doggett	N	Y	Y	Y	Y	Y	Y
11 Edwards	N	Y	Y	N	N	N	Y
12 ***Granger***	Y	Y	Y	N	N	N	N
13 ***Thornberry***	Y	Y	Y	N	N	N	N
14 ***Paul***	Y	N	N	N	N	N	N
15 Hinojosa	N	Y	Y	Y	Y	Y	Y
16 Reyes	N	Y	Y	Y	Y	N	Y
17 Stenholm	N	Y	Y	N	N	N	N
18 Jackson-Lee	N	Y	Y	Y	Y	Y	Y
19 ***Combest***	Y	Y	Y	N	N	N	N
20 Gonzalez	?	?	?	?	?	?	?
21 ***Smith***	Y	Y	Y	N	N	N	N
22 ***DeLay***	Y	Y	Y	N	N	N	N
23 ***Bonilla***	Y	Y	N	N	N	N	N
24 Frost	N	Y	Y	Y	Y	Y	Y
25 Bentsen	N	Y	Y	Y	Y	Y	Y
26 ***Armey***	Y	Y	Y	N	N	N	N
27 Ortiz	N	Y	Y	Y	Y	N	Y
28 Rodriguez	N	Y	Y	Y	Y	Y	Y
29 Green	N	Y	Y	Y	Y	Y	Y
30 Johnson, E.B.	N	Y	Y	Y	Y	Y	Y
UTAH							
1 ***Hansen***	Y	Y	Y	N	N	N	N
2 ***Cook***	Y	Y	Y	N	N	N	N
3 ***Cannon***	Y	?	Y	N	N	N	N
VERMONT							
AL *Sanders*	N	Y	+	Y	Y	Y	Y
VIRGINIA							
1 ***Bateman***	+	+	–	–	–	–	–
2 Pickett	N	Y	N	N	N	N	N
3 Scott	N	Y	Y	Y	Y	Y	Y
4 Sisisky	N	Y	Y	N	N	N	Y
5 Goode	Y	Y	Y	N	N	N	N
6 ***Goodlatte***	Y	Y	Y	N	N	N	N
7 ***Bliley***	Y	Y	Y	N	N	N	N
8 Moran	N	Y	N	Y	Y	Y	N
9 Boucher	N	Y	Y	Y	Y	Y	Y
10 ***Wolf***	Y	Y	Y	N	N	N	N
11 ***Davis***	Y	Y	Y	N	Y	N	N
WASHINGTON							
1 ***White***	Y	Y	Y	N	N	N	N
2 ***Metcalf***	Y	Y	Y	N	N	N	N
3 ***Smith, Linda***	Y	Y	Y	N	N	N	N
4 ***Hastings***	Y	Y	Y	N	N	N	N
5 ***Nethercutt***	Y	Y	Y	N	N	N	N
6 Dicks	N	Y	N	Y	Y	Y	Y
7 McDermott	N	Y	N	Y	Y	Y	Y
8 ***Dunn***	Y	Y	Y	N	N	N	N
9 Smith, Adam	N	Y	N	Y	Y	Y	Y
WEST VIRGINIA							
1 Mollohan	N	Y	?	Y	Y	Y	Y
2 Wise	N	Y	Y	Y	Y	Y	Y
3 Rahall	N	Y	Y	Y	Y	Y	Y
WISCONSIN							
1 ***Neumann***	Y	Y	Y	N	N	N	N
2 ***Klug***	Y	Y	Y	N	N	N	N
3 Kind	N	Y	Y	Y	Y	Y	Y
4 Kleczka	N	Y	Y	Y	Y	Y	Y
5 Barrett	N	Y	Y	Y	Y	Y	Y
6 ***Petri***	Y	Y	Y	N	N	Y	N
7 Obey	N	Y	?	Y	Y	Y	Y
8 Johnson	N	N	Y	?	Y	Y	Y
9 ***Sensenbrenner***	Y	Y	Y	N	N	N	N
WYOMING							
AL ***Cubin***	Y	Y	Y	N	N	N	N

Southern states - Ala., Ark., Fla., Ga., Ky., La., Miss., N.C., Okla., S.C., Tenn., Texas, Va.

House Votes 160, 161, 162, 163, 164, 165, 166

160. HR 3534. Mandates Information/Passage. Passage of the bill to require congressional committees to include in their reports on legislation detailed information on potential private sector mandates in excess of $100 million that result from the legislation. The bill also provides for points of order to be used to block consideration of legislation which contains such private sector mandates or whose committee reports lack the required information on the mandate. Passed 279-132: R 205-9; D 74-122 (ND 40-103, SD 34-19); I 0-1. May 19, 1998. A "nay" was a vote in support of the president's position.

161. H Res 440. Foreign Fundraising Resolution/Adoption. Adoption of the resolution to express the sense of the Congress that the Committee on Government Reform and Oversight should confer immunity from prosecution for information and testimony concerning illegal foreign fundraising activities. Adopted 402-0: R 210-0; D 191-0 (ND 139-0, SD 52-0); I 1-0. May 19, 1998.

162. HR 3039. Veterans Transitional Housing/Passage. Stump, R-Ariz., motion to suspend the rules and pass the bill to authorize the Veterans Affairs Department to guarantee loans for the development of transitional housing for homeless veterans. Motion agreed to 405-1: R 212-1; D 192-0 (ND 140-0, SD 52-0); I 1-0. May 19, 1998. A two-thirds majority of those present and voting (271 in this case) is required for passage under suspension of the rules.

163. HR 3718. Prison Release Orders/Passage. Coble, R-N.C., motion to suspend the rules and pass the bill to prohibit a federal court from carrying out any felony prisoner release order on the basis of prison conditions. Motion agreed to 352-53: R 211-2; D 141-50 (ND 99-40, SD 42-10); I 0-1. May 19, 1998. A two-thirds majority of those present and voting (270 in this case) is required for passage under suspension of the rules.

164. HR 3809. Drug Interdiction/Passage. Archer, R-Texas, motion to suspend the rules and pass the bill to authorize $2 billion in fiscal 1999 and $2.2 billion in fiscal 2000 for drug interdiction activities of the U.S. Customs Service. Motion agreed to 320-86: R 208-4; D 112-81 (ND 75-66, SD 37-15); I 0-1. May 19, 1998. A two-thirds majority of those present and voting (271 in this case) is required for passage under suspension of the rules.

165. HR 3616. Fiscal 1999 Defense Authorization/Previous Question. Frank, D-Mass., motion to order the previous question (thus ending debate and the possibility of amendment) on adoption of the rule (H Res 441) to provide for House floor consideration of the bill to authorize $270.4 billion for defense programs. Motion agreed to 281-134: R 216-1; D 65-132 (ND 38-105, SD 27-27); I 0-1. May 20, 1998.

166. HR 3616. Fiscal 1999 Defense Authorization/Rule. Adoption of the rule (H Res 441) to provide for House floor consideration of the bill to authorize $270.4 billion for defense programs. Adopted 304-108: R 213-3; D 91-104 (ND 0-141, SD 0-54); I 0-1. May 20, 1998.

Key

Y Voted for (yea).
Paired for.
+ Announced for.
N Voted against (nay).
X Paired against.
− Announced against.
P Voted "present."
C Voted "present" to avoid possible conflict of interest.
? Did not vote or otherwise make a position known.

Democrats **Republicans** *Independent*

	160	161	162	163	164	165	166
ALABAMA							
1 *Callahan*	Y	Y	Y	Y	Y	Y	Y
2 *Everett*	Y	Y	Y	Y	Y	Y	Y
3 *Riley*	Y	Y	Y	Y	Y	Y	+
4 *Aderholt*	Y	Y	Y	Y	Y	Y	Y
5 Cramer	Y	Y	Y	Y	Y	Y	Y
6 *Bachus*	Y	Y	Y	Y	Y	Y	Y
7 Hilliard	N	Y	Y	N	N	N	N
ALASKA							
AL *Young*	Y	Y	Y	Y	Y	Y	Y
ARIZONA							
1 *Salmon*	Y	Y	Y	Y	Y	Y	Y
2 Pastor	N	Y	Y	N	N	Y	Y
3 *Stump*	Y	Y	Y	Y	Y	Y	Y
4 *Shadegg*	Y	Y	Y	Y	Y	Y	Y
5 *Kolbe*	Y	Y	Y	Y	Y	Y	Y
6 *Hayworth*	Y	Y	Y	Y	Y	Y	Y
ARKANSAS							
1 Berry	Y	Y	Y	Y	Y	N	N
2 Snyder	Y	Y	Y	Y	Y	Y	Y
3 *Hutchinson*	Y	Y	Y	Y	Y	Y	Y
4 Dickey	Y	Y	Y	Y	Y	Y	Y
CALIFORNIA							
1 *Riggs*	Y	Y	Y	Y	Y	Y	Y
2 *Herger*	Y	Y	Y	Y	Y	Y	Y
3 Fazio	Y	Y	Y	N	Y	Y	Y
4 *Doolittle*	Y	Y	Y	Y	Y	Y	Y
5 Matsui	N	Y	Y	Y	N	N	N
6 Woolsey	N	Y	Y	?	Y	N	N
7 Miller	N	Y	Y	N	N	N	N
8 Pelosi	N	Y	Y	N	N	N	Y
9 Lee	N	Y	N	N	N	N	N
10 Tauscher	Y	Y	Y	Y	Y	N	Y
11 *Pombo*	Y	Y	Y	Y	Y	Y	Y
12 Lantos	N	Y	Y	Y	N	N	N
13 Stark	N	Y	N	N	N	Y	Y
14 Eshoo	N	Y	Y	Y	N	N	N
15 *Campbell*	Y	Y	Y	N	Y	N	N
16 Lofgren	Y	Y	Y	Y	Y	N	N
17 Farr	N	Y	Y	Y	N	Y	Y
18 Condit	Y	Y	Y	Y	Y	N	N
19 *Radanovich*	Y	Y	Y	Y	Y	Y	Y
20 Dooley	Y	Y	Y	Y	Y	N	Y
21 *Thomas*	Y	Y	Y	Y	Y	Y	?
22 Capps, L.	Y	Y	Y	Y	Y	N	N
23 *Gallegly*	Y	Y	Y	Y	Y	Y	Y
24 Sherman	Y	Y	Y	Y	Y	N	Y
25 *McKeon*	Y	Y	Y	Y	Y	Y	Y
26 Berman	N	Y	Y	N	N	N	N
27 *Rogan*	Y	Y	Y	Y	Y	Y	Y
28 *Dreier*	Y	Y	Y	Y	Y	Y	Y
29 Waxman	N	Y	Y	N	N	Y	Y
30 Becerra	N	Y	Y	N	N	N	N
31 Martinez	N	Y	Y	N	Y	N	Y
32 Dixon	N	Y	Y	N	Y	N	Y
33 Roybal-Allard	N	Y	Y	N	N	N	N
34 Torres	N	Y	Y	N	N	N	N
35 Waters	N	?	Y	?	N	N	Y
36 Harman	?	?	?	?	?	?	?
37 Millender-McD.	N	Y	Y	N	Y	N	Y

	160	161	162	163	164	165	166
38 *Horn*	Y	Y	Y	Y	Y	Y	Y
39 *Royce*	Y	Y	Y	Y	Y	Y	Y
40 *Lewis*	Y	Y	Y	Y	Y	Y	Y
41 *Kim*	Y	Y	Y	Y	Y	Y	Y
42 Brown	N	Y	Y	Y	Y	N	N
43 *Calvert*	Y	Y	Y	Y	Y	Y	Y
44 *Bono, M.*	Y	Y	Y	Y	Y	Y	Y
45 *Rohrabacher*	Y	Y	Y	Y	Y	Y	Y
46 Sanchez	Y	Y	Y	Y	Y	N	Y
47 *Cox*	Y	Y	Y	Y	Y	Y	Y
48 *Packard*	Y	Y	Y	Y	Y	Y	Y
49 *Bilbray*	N	+	Y	Y	Y	Y	Y
50 Filner	N	Y	Y	N	N	N	N
51 *Cunningham*	Y	Y	Y	Y	Y	Y	Y
52 *Hunter*	Y	Y	Y	Y	Y	Y	Y
COLORADO							
1 DeGette	N	Y	Y	N	N	N	N
2 Skaggs	−	+	+	−	?	N	N
3 *McInnis*	?	Y	Y	Y	Y	Y	Y
4 *Schaffer*	Y	Y	Y	Y	Y	Y	Y
5 *Hefley*	Y	Y	Y	Y	Y	Y	Y
6 *Schaefer*	Y	Y	Y	Y	Y	Y	Y
CONNECTICUT							
1 Kennelly	N	Y	Y	Y	Y	Y	Y
2 Gejdenson	N	Y	Y	Y	N	N	N
3 DeLauro	N	Y	Y	Y	N	N	N
4 *Shays*	N	Y	Y	Y	Y	Y	N
5 Maloney	Y	Y	Y	Y	Y	Y	Y
6 *Johnson*	Y	Y	Y	Y	Y	Y	Y
DELAWARE							
AL *Castle*	Y	Y	Y	Y	Y	Y	Y
FLORIDA							
1 *Scarborough*	Y	Y	Y	Y	Y	Y	Y
2 Boyd	Y	Y	Y	Y	Y	N	N
3 Brown	N	Y	Y	Y	N	N	N
4 *Fowler*	Y	Y	Y	Y	Y	Y	Y
5 Thurman	Y	Y	Y	Y	Y	N	N
6 *Stearns*	Y	Y	Y	Y	Y	Y	Y
7 *Mica*	Y	Y	Y	Y	Y	Y	Y
8 *McCollum*	Y	Y	Y	Y	Y	Y	Y
9 *Bilirakis*	Y	Y	Y	Y	Y	Y	Y
10 *Young*	Y	Y	Y	Y	Y	Y	Y
11 Davis	Y	Y	Y	Y	Y	N	N
12 *Canady*	Y	Y	Y	Y	Y	Y	Y
13 *Miller*	Y	Y	Y	Y	Y	Y	Y
14 *Goss*	Y	Y	Y	Y	Y	Y	Y
15 *Weldon*	Y	Y	Y	Y	Y	Y	Y
16 *Foley*	Y	Y	Y	Y	Y	Y	Y
17 Meek	N	?	?	?	?	N	Y
18 *Ros-Lehtinen*	N	Y	Y	Y	Y	Y	Y
19 Wexler	N	Y	Y	Y	N	N	N
20 Deutsch	N	Y	Y	N	N	N	N
21 *Diaz-Balart*	N	Y	Y	Y	Y	Y	Y
22 *Shaw*	Y	Y	Y	Y	Y	Y	Y
23 Hastings	N	Y	Y	N	N	N	N
GEORGIA							
1 *Kingston*	Y	Y	Y	Y	Y	Y	Y
2 Bishop	Y	Y	Y	Y	Y	Y	Y
3 *Collins*	Y	Y	Y	Y	Y	Y	Y
4 McKinney	N	Y	N	N	N	N	N
5 Lewis	N	Y	Y	N	N	N	N
6 *Gingrich*							
7 *Barr*	Y	?	Y	Y	Y	Y	Y
8 *Chambliss*	Y	Y	Y	Y	Y	Y	Y
9 *Deal*	Y	Y	Y	Y	Y	Y	Y
10 *Norwood*	Y	Y	Y	Y	Y	Y	Y
11 *Linder*	Y	Y	Y	Y	Y	Y	Y
HAWAII							
1 Abercrombie	N	Y	Y	Y	Y	Y	Y
2 Mink	N	Y	Y	Y	Y	N	Y
IDAHO							
1 *Chenoweth*	Y	Y	Y	Y	Y	Y	Y
2 *Crapo*	Y	Y	Y	Y	Y	Y	Y
ILLINOIS							
1 Rush	N	Y	Y	N	N	N	N
2 Jackson	N	Y	Y	N	N	N	N
3 Lipinski	Y	Y	Y	Y	Y	Y	Y
4 Gutierrez	N	Y	Y	N	N	N	N
5 Blagojevich	N	Y	Y	Y	N	N	N
6 *Hyde*	Y	Y	Y	Y	Y	Y	Y
7 Davis	N	Y	Y	N	N	N	N
8 *Crane*	?	?	?	?	?	?	?
9 Yates	N	Y	Y	Y	N	N	N
10 *Porter*	Y	Y	Y	Y	Y	Y	Y
11 *Weller*	Y	Y	Y	Y	Y	Y	Y
12 Costello	Y	Y	Y	Y	N	N	N

ND Northern Democrats   SD Southern Democrats

	160	161	162	163	164	165	166
13 ***Fawell***	Y	?	?	?	?	Y	Y
14 ***Hastert***	Y	Y	Y	Y	Y	Y	Y
15 ***Ewing***	+	+	+	+	+	+	+
16 ***Manzullo***	Y	Y	Y	Y	Y	Y	Y
17 Evans	N	Y	Y	N	N	N	N
18 ***LaHood***	Y	Y	Y	Y	Y	Y	Y
19 Poshard	Y	Y	Y	Y	N	N	N
20 ***Shimkus***	Y	Y	Y	Y	Y	Y	Y
INDIANA							
1 Visclosky	N	Y	Y	Y	N	Y	Y
2 ***McIntosh***	Y	?	?	?	?	Y	Y
3 Roemer	Y	Y	Y	Y	Y	Y	Y
4 ***Souder***	Y	Y	Y	Y	Y	Y	Y
5 ***Buyer***	?	Y	Y	Y	Y	Y	Y
6 ***Burton***	Y	Y	Y	Y	Y	Y	Y
7 ***Pease***	Y	Y	Y	Y	Y	Y	Y
8 ***Hostettler***	Y	Y	Y	Y	Y	Y	Y
9 Hamilton	Y	Y	Y	Y	Y	N	N
10 Carson	N	Y	Y	N	N	–	–
IOWA							
1 ***Leach***	Y	Y	Y	N	Y	Y	Y
2 ***Nussle***	Y	Y	Y	Y	Y	Y	Y
3 Boswell	Y	Y	Y	Y	Y	Y	Y
4 ***Ganske***	?	?	?	?	?	Y	Y
5 ***Latham***	Y	Y	Y	Y	Y	Y	Y
KANSAS							
1 ***Moran***	Y	Y	Y	Y	Y	Y	Y
2 ***Ryun***	+	Y	Y	Y	Y	Y	Y
3 ***Snowbarger***	Y	Y	Y	Y	Y	Y	Y
4 ***Tiahrt***	Y	Y	Y	Y	Y	Y	Y
KENTUCKY							
1 ***Whitfield***	Y	Y	Y	Y	Y	Y	Y
2 ***Lewis***	Y	Y	Y	Y	Y	Y	Y
3 ***Northup***	Y	Y	Y	Y	Y	?	Y
4 ***Bunning***	Y	Y	Y	Y	Y	Y	Y
5 ***Rogers***	Y	Y	Y	Y	Y	Y	Y
6 Baesler	?	?	?	?	?	N	N
LOUISIANA							
1 ***Livingston***	+	+	Y	Y	Y	Y	Y
2 Jefferson	N	Y	Y	Y	Y	N	Y
3 ***Tauzin***	Y	Y	Y	Y	Y	Y	Y
4 ***McCrery***	Y	Y	Y	Y	Y	Y	?
5 ***Cooksey***	Y	?	?	?	?	Y	Y
6 ***Baker***	Y	Y	Y	Y	Y	Y	Y
7 John	Y	Y	Y	Y	Y	Y	Y
MAINE							
1 Allen	N	Y	Y	Y	N	Y	Y
2 Baldacci	N	Y	Y	Y	N	Y	Y
MARYLAND							
1 ***Gilchrest***	N	Y	Y	Y	Y	Y	Y
2 ***Ehrlich***	Y	Y	Y	Y	Y	Y	Y
3 Cardin	N	Y	Y	Y	Y	N	N
4 Wynn	N	Y	Y	Y	Y	N	Y
5 Hoyer	N	Y	Y	Y	N	Y	Y
6 ***Bartlett***	Y	Y	Y	Y	Y	Y	Y
7 Cummings	N	?	Y	Y	Y	N	N
8 ***Morella***	N	Y	Y	Y	Y	Y	Y
MASSACHUSETTS							
1 Olver	N	Y	Y	N	N	N	N
2 Neal	N	Y	Y	Y	N	N	N
3 McGovern	N	Y	Y	Y	N	N	N
4 Frank	N	Y	Y	N	N	N	N
5 Meehan	N	Y	Y	Y	N	N	N
6 Tierney	N	Y	Y	N	N	N	N
7 Markey	N	Y	Y	Y	N	Y	Y
8 Kennedy	N	Y	?	Y	N	N	N
9 Moakley	N	Y	Y	Y	N	N	N
10 Delahunt	N	Y	Y	N	N	N	N
MICHIGAN							
1 Stupak	N	Y	Y	N	Y	N	N
2 ***Hoekstra***	Y	Y	Y	Y	Y	Y	Y
3 ***Ehlers***	Y	Y	Y	Y	Y	Y	Y
4 ***Camp***	Y	Y	Y	Y	Y	Y	Y
5 Barcia	Y	Y	Y	Y	Y	Y	Y
6 ***Upton***	Y	Y	Y	Y	Y	Y	Y
7 ***Smith***	Y	Y	Y	Y	Y	Y	Y
8 Stabenow	Y	Y	Y	Y	Y	–	–
9 Kildee	Y	Y	Y	Y	Y	N	Y
10 Bonior	N	Y	Y	N	N	N	N
11 ***Knollenberg***	Y	Y	Y	Y	Y	Y	Y
12 Levin	N	Y	Y	Y	Y	N	N
13 Rivers	Y	Y	Y	Y	Y	N	N
14 Conyers	N	Y	Y	N	N	N	N
15 Kilpatrick	N	Y	Y	N	N	N	Y
16 Dingell	N	Y	Y	N	N	N	N

	160	161	162	163	164	165	166
MINNESOTA							
1 ***Gutknecht***	Y	Y	Y	Y	Y	Y	Y
2 Minge	Y	Y	Y	Y	Y	Y	N
3 ***Ramstad***	Y	Y	Y	Y	Y	Y	Y
4 Vento	N	Y	Y	Y	N	N	N
5 Sabo	N	Y	Y	N	N	Y	Y
6 Luther	Y	Y	Y	Y	Y	N	N
7 Peterson	Y	Y	Y	Y	N	Y	Y
8 Oberstar	N	Y	Y	N	N	N	N
MISSISSIPPI							
1 ***Wicker***	Y	Y	Y	Y	Y	Y	Y
2 Thompson	N	Y	Y	N	N	Y	N
3 ***Pickering***	Y	Y	Y	Y	Y	Y	Y
4 ***Parker***	Y	Y	Y	Y	Y	Y	Y
5 Taylor	Y	Y	Y	Y	Y	Y	Y
MISSOURI							
1 Clay	?	?	?	?	?	?	?
2 ***Talent***	Y	Y	Y	Y	Y	Y	Y
3 Gephardt	N	Y	Y	Y	Y	N	N
4 Skelton	Y	Y	Y	Y	Y	Y	Y
5 McCarthy	Y	Y	Y	Y	Y	Y	Y
6 Danner	Y	Y	Y	Y	Y	Y	Y
7 ***Blunt***	Y	Y	Y	Y	Y	Y	Y
8 ***Emerson***	Y	Y	Y	Y	Y	Y	Y
9 ***Hulshof***	Y	Y	Y	Y	Y	Y	Y
MONTANA							
AL ***Hill***	Y	Y	Y	Y	Y	Y	Y
NEBRASKA							
1 ***Bereuter***	Y	Y	Y	Y	Y	Y	Y
2 ***Christensen***	Y	Y	Y	Y	Y	Y	Y
3 ***Barrett***	Y	Y	Y	Y	Y	Y	Y
NEVADA							
1 ***Ensign***	Y	Y	Y	Y	Y	Y	Y
2 ***Gibbons***	Y	Y	Y	Y	Y	Y	Y
NEW HAMPSHIRE							
1 ***Sununu***	Y	Y	Y	Y	Y	Y	Y
2 ***Bass***	Y	Y	Y	Y	Y	Y	Y
NEW JERSEY							
1 Andrews	N	Y	Y	Y	Y	?	?
2 ***LoBiondo***	Y	Y	Y	Y	Y	Y	Y
3 ***Saxton***	N	Y	Y	Y	Y	Y	Y
4 ***Smith***	Y	Y	Y	Y	Y	Y	Y
5 ***Roukema***	Y	Y	Y	Y	Y	Y	Y
6 Pallone	N	Y	Y	Y	Y	N	Y
7 ***Franks***	Y	Y	Y	Y	Y	Y	Y
8 Pascrell	N	Y	Y	Y	Y	Y	Y
9 Rothman	N	Y	Y	Y	Y	N	Y
10 Payne	N	Y	Y	N	N	N	?
11 ***Frelinghuysen***	Y	Y	Y	Y	Y	Y	Y
12 ***Pappas***	Y	Y	Y	Y	Y	Y	Y
13 Menendez	N	Y	Y	Y	Y	N	Y
NEW MEXICO							
1 Vacant							
2 ***Skeen***	Y	Y	Y	Y	Y	Y	Y
3 ***Redmond***	Y	Y	Y	Y	Y	Y	Y
NEW YORK							
1 ***Forbes***	N	Y	Y	Y	Y	Y	Y
2 ***Lazio***	Y	Y	Y	Y	Y	Y	Y
3 ***King***	Y	Y	Y	Y	Y	Y	Y
4 McCarthy	Y	Y	Y	Y	Y	Y	Y
5 Ackerman	N	Y	Y	Y	Y	N	N
6 Meeks	?	?	?	?	?	?	?
7 Manton	N	Y	Y	Y	N	N	?
8 Nadler	N	Y	Y	Y	N	N	N
9 Schumer	?	?	?	?	?	N	N
10 Towns	N	Y	Y	N	N	N	Y
11 Owens	N	Y	Y	N	N	N	N
12 Velázquez	N	Y	Y	N	N	N	N
13 ***Fossella***	Y	Y	Y	Y	Y	Y	Y
14 Maloney	N	Y	Y	Y	Y	N	N
15 Rangel	N	Y	Y	N	Y	N	N
16 Serrano	N	Y	Y	N	N	N	N
17 Engel	N	Y	Y	Y	N	N	N
18 Lowey	N	Y	Y	Y	Y	N	N
19 ***Kelly***	Y	Y	Y	Y	Y	Y	Y
20 ***Gilman***	Y	Y	Y	Y	Y	Y	Y
21 McNulty	?	?	?	?	?	N	N
22 ***Solomon***	Y	Y	Y	Y	Y	Y	Y
23 ***Boehlert***	N	Y	Y	Y	Y	Y	Y
24 ***McHugh***	Y	Y	Y	Y	Y	Y	Y
25 ***Walsh***	Y	Y	Y	Y	Y	Y	Y
26 Hinchey	N	?	?	?	?	?	?
27 ***Paxon***	?	?	?	?	?	?	?
28 Slaughter	N	Y	Y	Y	Y	N	Y
29 LaFalce	Y	Y	Y	Y	Y	N	N

	160	161	162	163	164	165	166
30 ***Quinn***	Y	Y	Y	Y	Y	Y	Y
31 ***Houghton***	Y	Y	Y	Y	Y	Y	Y
NORTH CAROLINA							
1 Clayton	Y	Y	Y	Y	Y	N	Y
2 Etheridge	Y	Y	Y	Y	Y	N	N
3 ***Jones***	Y	Y	Y	Y	Y	Y	Y
4 Price	Y	Y	Y	Y	Y	N	Y
5 ***Burr***	Y	Y	Y	Y	Y	Y	?
6 ***Coble***	Y	Y	Y	Y	Y	Y	Y
7 McIntyre	Y	Y	Y	Y	Y	Y	Y
8 Hefner	N	Y	Y	Y	Y	Y	Y
9 ***Myrick***	Y	Y	Y	Y	Y	Y	Y
10 ***Ballenger***	Y	Y	Y	Y	Y	Y	Y
11 ***Taylor***	Y	Y	Y	Y	Y	Y	Y
12 Watt	N	Y	Y	N	N	N	N
NORTH DAKOTA							
AL Pomeroy	Y	Y	Y	Y	Y	Y	Y
OHIO							
1 ***Chabot***	Y	Y	Y	Y	Y	Y	Y
2 ***Portman***	Y	Y	Y	Y	Y	Y	Y
3 Hall	Y	Y	Y	Y	Y	Y	Y
4 ***Oxley***	Y	Y	Y	Y	Y	Y	Y
5 ***Gillmor***	Y	Y	Y	Y	Y	Y	Y
6 Strickland	Y	Y	Y	Y	Y	N	N
7 ***Hobson***	Y	Y	Y	Y	Y	Y	Y
8 ***Boehner***	Y	Y	Y	Y	Y	Y	Y
9 Kaptur	N	Y	Y	Y	Y	N	N
10 Kucinich	N	Y	Y	Y	N	N	N
11 Stokes	N	Y	Y	N	N	N	N
12 ***Kasich***	Y	Y	Y	Y	Y	Y	Y
13 Brown	N	Y	Y	Y	N	N	N
14 Sawyer	N	Y	Y	Y	N	N	N
15 ***Pryce***	Y	Y	Y	Y	Y	Y	Y
16 ***Regula***	Y	Y	Y	Y	Y	Y	Y
17 Traficant	Y	Y	Y	Y	Y	Y	Y
18 ***Ney***	Y	Y	Y	Y	Y	?	Y
19 ***LaTourette***	Y	Y	Y	Y	Y	Y	Y
OKLAHOMA							
1 ***Largent***	Y	Y	Y	Y	Y	Y	Y
2 ***Coburn***	Y	Y	Y	Y	Y	Y	Y
3 ***Watkins***	Y	Y	Y	Y	Y	Y	Y
4 ***Watts***	Y	Y	Y	Y	Y	Y	Y
5 ***Istook***	Y	Y	Y	Y	Y	Y	Y
6 ***Lucas***	Y	Y	Y	Y	Y	Y	Y
OREGON							
1 Furse	N	Y	Y	N	N	N	N
2 ***Smith***	Y	Y	Y	Y	Y	Y	Y
3 Blumenauer	N	Y	Y	N	N	N	N
4 DeFazio	N	Y	Y	Y	N	N	N
5 Hooley	Y	Y	Y	Y	Y	N	N
PENNSYLVANIA							
1 Vacant							
2 Fattah	?	?	?	?	?	N	N
3 Borski	N	Y	Y	Y	Y	Y	Y
4 Klink	N	Y	Y	Y	Y	Y	Y
5 ***Peterson***	Y	Y	Y	Y	Y	Y	Y
6 Holden	Y	Y	Y	Y	Y	Y	Y
7 ***Weldon***	Y	Y	Y	Y	Y	Y	Y
8 ***Greenwood***	?	?	?	?	?	?	Y
9 ***Shuster***	?	?	?	?	?	Y	Y
10 ***McDade***	Y	?	?	?	?	Y	Y
11 Kanjorski	N	Y	Y	Y	Y	N	Y
12 Murtha	Y	Y	Y	Y	Y	Y	Y
13 ***Fox***	Y	Y	Y	Y	Y	Y	Y
14 Coyne	N	Y	Y	Y	Y	N	N
15 McHale	N	Y	Y	Y	Y	Y	Y
16 ***Pitts***	Y	Y	Y	Y	Y	Y	Y
17 ***Gekas***	Y	Y	Y	Y	Y	Y	Y
18 Doyle	Y	Y	Y	Y	Y	Y	Y
19 ***Goodling***	–	+	+	+	+	+	+
20 Mascara	N	Y	Y	Y	Y	Y	Y
21 ***English***	Y	Y	Y	Y	Y	Y	Y
RHODE ISLAND							
1 Kennedy	N	Y	Y	N	N	Y	Y
2 Weygand	Y	Y	Y	Y	Y	N	Y
SOUTH CAROLINA							
1 ***Sanford***	Y	Y	N	Y	N	Y	Y
2 ***Spence***	Y	Y	Y	Y	Y	Y	Y
3 ***Graham***	Y	Y	Y	Y	Y	Y	Y
4 ***Inglis***	Y	Y	Y	Y	Y	Y	Y
5 Spratt	Y	Y	Y	Y	Y	Y	Y
6 Clyburn	N	Y	Y	N	N	Y	Y
SOUTH DAKOTA							
AL ***Thune***	Y	Y	Y	Y	Y	Y	Y

	160	161	162	163	164	165	166
TENNESSEE							
1 ***Jenkins***	Y	Y	Y	Y	Y	Y	Y
2 ***Duncan***	Y	Y	Y	Y	Y	Y	Y
3 ***Wamp***	Y	Y	Y	Y	Y	Y	Y
4 ***Hilleary***	Y	Y	Y	Y	Y	Y	Y
5 Clement	Y	Y	Y	Y	Y	Y	Y
6 Gordon	Y	Y	Y	Y	Y	Y	Y
7 ***Bryant***	Y	Y	Y	Y	Y	Y	Y
8 Tanner	Y	Y	Y	Y	Y	Y	Y
9 Ford	Y	Y	Y	N	Y	N	Y
TEXAS							
1 Sandlin	Y	Y	Y	Y	Y	N	Y
2 Turner	Y	Y	Y	Y	Y	Y	Y
3 ***Johnson, Sam***	Y	Y	Y	Y	Y	Y	Y
4 Hall	Y	Y	Y	Y	Y	Y	Y
5 ***Sessions***	Y	Y	Y	Y	Y	Y	Y
6 ***Barton***	Y	Y	Y	Y	Y	Y	Y
7 ***Archer***	Y	?	?	?	?	Y	Y
8 ***Brady***	Y	Y	Y	Y	Y	Y	Y
9 Lampson	N	Y	Y	Y	Y	Y	Y
10 Doggett	N	Y	Y	Y	Y	N	N
11 Edwards	Y	Y	Y	Y	Y	Y	Y
12 ***Granger***	Y	Y	Y	Y	Y	Y	Y
13 ***Thornberry***	Y	Y	Y	Y	Y	Y	Y
14 ***Paul***	Y	Y	Y	Y	N	Y	Y
15 Hinojosa	Y	Y	Y	Y	Y	N	N
16 Reyes	Y	Y	Y	Y	N	Y	Y
17 Stenholm	Y	Y	Y	Y	Y	Y	Y
18 Jackson-Lee	N	Y	Y	Y	Y	N	N
19 ***Combest***	Y	Y	Y	Y	Y	Y	Y
20 Gonzalez	?	?	?	?	?	?	?
21 ***Smith***	Y	Y	Y	Y	Y	Y	Y
22 ***DeLay***	Y	Y	Y	Y	Y	Y	Y
23 ***Bonilla***	Y	Y	Y	Y	N	Y	Y
24 Frost	Y	Y	Y	Y	Y	Y	Y
25 Bentsen	Y	Y	Y	Y	Y	N	N
26 ***Armey***	Y	Y	Y	Y	+	?	?
27 Ortiz	Y	Y	Y	Y	N	Y	Y
28 Rodriguez	Y	Y	Y	Y	N	N	N
29 Green	Y	Y	Y	Y	N	N	N
30 Johnson, E.B.	N	Y	Y	N	N	N	N
UTAH							
1 ***Hansen***	Y	Y	Y	Y	Y	Y	Y
2 ***Cook***	Y	Y	Y	Y	Y	Y	Y
3 ***Cannon***	Y	Y	Y	Y	Y	Y	Y
VERMONT							
AL *Sanders*	N	Y	Y	N	N	N	N
VIRGINIA							
1 ***Bateman***	+	+	+	+	+	+	+
2 Pickett	Y	Y	Y	Y	Y	Y	Y
3 Scott	N	Y	Y	N	N	Y	Y
4 Sisisky	Y	Y	Y	Y	Y	Y	Y
5 Goode	Y	Y	Y	Y	Y	Y	Y
6 ***Goodlatte***	Y	Y	Y	Y	Y	Y	Y
7 ***Bliley***	Y	Y	Y	Y	Y	Y	Y
8 Moran	Y	Y	Y	Y	Y	Y	Y
9 Boucher	N	Y	Y	Y	Y	Y	Y
10 ***Wolf***	Y	Y	Y	Y	Y	Y	Y
11 ***Davis***	Y	Y	Y	Y	Y	Y	Y
WASHINGTON							
1 ***White***	Y	Y	Y	Y	Y	Y	Y
2 ***Metcalf***	Y	Y	Y	Y	Y	Y	Y
3 ***Smith, Linda***	Y	Y	Y	Y	Y	Y	Y
4 ***Hastings***	Y	Y	Y	Y	Y	Y	Y
5 ***Nethercutt***	Y	Y	Y	Y	Y	Y	Y
6 Dicks	N	?	?	?	?	Y	Y
7 McDermott	N	Y	Y	N	N	N	N
8 ***Dunn***	Y	Y	Y	Y	Y	Y	Y
9 Smith, Adam	Y	Y	Y	Y	N	Y	Y
WEST VIRGINIA							
1 Mollohan	N	Y	Y	Y	N	Y	Y
2 Wise	N	Y	Y	Y	Y	Y	Y
3 Rahall	N	Y	Y	Y	Y	N	N
WISCONSIN							
1 ***Neumann***	Y	Y	Y	Y	Y	Y	Y
2 ***Klug***	Y	Y	Y	Y	Y	Y	Y
3 Kind	Y	Y	Y	Y	Y	N	N
4 Kleczka	Y	Y	Y	N	Y	N	N
5 Barrett	N	Y	Y	N	N	N	N
6 ***Petri***	Y	Y	Y	Y	Y	Y	Y
7 Obey	N	Y	Y	N	N	N	N
8 Johnson	Y	Y	Y	Y	Y	N	N
9 ***Sensenbrenner***	Y	Y	Y	Y	Y	Y	Y
WYOMING							
AL ***Cubin***	Y	Y	Y	Y	Y	Y	Y

Southern states - Ala., Ark., Fla., Ga., Ky., La., Miss., N.C., Okla., S.C., Tenn., Texas, Va.

House Votes 167, 168, 169, 170, 171, 172, 173

Key

- Y Voted for (yea).
- # Paired for.
- + Announced for.
- N Voted against (nay).
- X Paired against.
- − Announced against.
- P Voted "present."
- C Voted "present" to avoid possible conflict of interest.
- ? Did not vote or otherwise make a position known.

Democrats   **Republicans**   *Independent*

167. HR 3616. Fiscal 1999 Defense Authorization/Business Interests. Spence, R-S.C., amendment to express the sense of Congress that U.S. business interests should not be placed above U.S. national security interests and that during President Clinton's upcoming trip to China he should not conclude certain types of international agreements. Adopted 417-4: R 223-0; D 193-4 (ND 141-2, SD 52-2); I 1-0. May 20, 1998.

168. HR 3616. Fiscal 1999 Defense Authorization/Government Representative. Bereuter, R-Neb., amendment to prohibit the participation of U.S. citizens in the investigation of a failed launch of a U.S. satellite on a foreign launch vehicle. Adopted 414-7: R 220-1; D 193-6 (ND 142-3, SD 51-3); I 1-0. May 20, 1998. A "nay" was a vote in support of the president's position.

169. HR 3616. Fiscal 1999 Defense Authorization/Missile Equipment. Hefley, R-Colo., amendment to prevent the transfer of any U.S. missile equipment or technology that could be used by the People's Republic of China for strategic purposes. Adopted 412-6: R 217-1; D 194-5 (ND 143-2, SD 51-3); I 1-0. May 20, 1998. A "nay" was a vote in support of the president's position.

170. HR 3616. Fiscal 1999 Defense Authorization/U.S. Satellites. Hunter, R-Calif., amendment to prohibit the export or re-export of any U.S. satellites, including commercial satellites and their components, to the People's Republic of China. Adopted 364-54: R 210-10; D 153-44 (ND 110-34, SD 43-10); I 1-0. May 20, 1998. A "nay" was a vote in support of the president's position.

171. HR 3616. Fiscal 1999 Defense Authorization/Abortion. Lowey, D-N.Y., amendment to repeal provisions of current law that prohibit privately-funded abortions at overseas Defense Department medical facilities. Rejected 190-232: R 30-194; D 159-38 (ND 114-29, SD 45-9); I 1-0. May 20, 1998. A "yea" was a vote in support of the president's position.

172. HR 3616. Fiscal 1999 Defense Authorization/Kyoto Protocol. Gilman, R-N.Y., amendment to state that no provision of the Kyoto Protocol on global warming will restrict the procurement, training, operation or maintenance of U.S. armed forces. Adopted 420-0: R 223-0; D 196-0 (ND 142-0, SD 54-0); I 1-0. May 20, 1998.

173. HR 3616. Fiscal 1999 Defense Authorization/United Nations. Hefley, R-Colo., amendment to prohibit the assignment of any member of the U.S. armed services to duty with the United Nations Rapidly Deployable Mission Headquarters, or any other standing army under command of the U.N. Adopted 250-172: R 213-11; D 37-160 (ND 20-123, SD 17-37); I 0-1. May 20, 1998.

	167	168	169	170	171	172	173
ALABAMA							
1 *Callahan*	Y	Y	Y	Y	N	Y	Y
2 *Everett*	Y	Y	Y	Y	N	Y	Y
3 *Riley*	Y	Y	Y	Y	N	Y	Y
4 *Aderholt*	Y	Y	Y	Y	N	Y	Y
5 Cramer	Y	Y	Y	Y	Y	Y	Y
6 *Bachus*	Y	Y	Y	Y	N	Y	Y
7 Hilliard	Y	Y	Y	Y	Y	Y	N
ALASKA							
AL *Young*	Y	Y	Y	Y	N	Y	Y
ARIZONA							
1 *Salmon*	Y	Y	Y	N	N	Y	Y
2 Pastor	Y	Y	Y	Y	Y	Y	N
3 *Stump*	Y	Y	Y	N	N	Y	Y
4 *Shadegg*	Y	Y	Y	Y	N	Y	Y
5 *Kolbe*	Y	Y	Y	N	Y	Y	N
6 *Hayworth*	Y	Y	Y	Y	N	Y	Y
ARKANSAS							
1 Berry	Y	Y	Y	N	N	Y	Y
2 Snyder	Y	Y	Y	Y	Y	Y	Y
3 *Hutchinson*	Y	Y	Y	Y	N	Y	Y
4 *Dickey*	Y	Y	Y	Y	N	Y	Y
CALIFORNIA							
1 *Riggs*	Y	Y	Y	Y	N	Y	Y
2 *Herger*	Y	Y	Y	Y	N	Y	Y
3 Fazio	Y	Y	Y	N	Y	Y	N
4 *Doolittle*	Y	Y	Y	Y	N	Y	Y
5 Matsui	Y	Y	Y	N	Y	Y	N
6 Woolsey	Y	Y	Y	Y	Y	Y	N
7 Miller	Y	Y	Y	Y	Y	Y	N
8 Pelosi	Y	Y	Y	Y	Y	Y	N
9 Lee	Y	Y	Y	N	Y	Y	N
10 Tauscher	Y	Y	Y	Y	Y	Y	N
11 *Pombo*	Y	Y	Y	Y	N	Y	Y
12 Lantos	Y	Y	Y	Y	Y	Y	N
13 Stark	?	Y	Y	Y	Y	Y	N
14 Eshoo	Y	Y	Y	N	Y	Y	N
15 *Campbell*	Y	N	N	N	Y	Y	Y
16 Lofgren	Y	Y	Y	Y	Y	Y	N
17 Farr	Y	Y	Y	N	Y	Y	N
18 Condit	Y	Y	Y	Y	Y	Y	Y
19 *Radanovich*	Y	Y	Y	Y	N	Y	Y
20 Dooley	Y	Y	Y	N	Y	Y	N
21 *Thomas*	Y	Y	Y	Y	N	Y	Y
22 Capps, L.	Y	Y	Y	Y	Y	Y	Y
23 *Gallegly*	Y	Y	Y	Y	N	Y	Y
24 Sherman	Y	Y	Y	Y	Y	Y	N
25 *McKeon*	Y	Y	Y	Y	N	Y	Y
26 Berman	Y	Y	Y	Y	Y	Y	N
27 *Rogan*	Y	Y	Y	Y	N	Y	Y
28 *Dreier*	Y	Y	Y	N	N	Y	Y
29 Waxman	Y	Y	Y	N	Y	Y	N
30 Becerra	Y	Y	Y	N	Y	Y	N
31 Martinez	Y	Y	Y	Y	Y	Y	Y
32 Dixon	Y	Y	Y	Y	Y	Y	N
33 Roybal-Allard	Y	Y	Y	N	Y	Y	N
34 Torres	Y	Y	Y	Y	Y	Y	N
35 Waters	Y	Y	Y	N	Y	Y	N
36 Harman	?	?	?	?	?	?	?
37 Millender-McD.	Y	Y	Y	Y	Y	Y	N
38 *Horn*	Y	Y	Y	Y	Y	Y	Y
39 *Royce*	Y	Y	Y	Y	N	Y	Y
40 *Lewis*	Y	Y	Y	Y	N	Y	Y
41 *Kim*	Y	Y	Y	N	Y	Y	Y
42 Brown	Y	Y	Y	N	Y	Y	N
43 *Calvert*	Y	Y	Y	Y	N	Y	Y
44 *Bono, M.*	Y	Y	Y	Y	Y	Y	Y
45 *Rohrabacher*	Y	Y	Y	Y	Y	Y	Y
46 Sanchez	Y	Y	Y	N	Y	Y	N
47 *Cox*	Y	?	?	Y	N	Y	Y
48 *Packard*	Y	Y	Y	Y	N	Y	Y
49 *Bilbray*	Y	Y	Y	Y	Y	Y	Y
50 Filner	Y	Y	Y	Y	Y	Y	N
51 *Cunningham*	Y	Y	Y	Y	N	Y	Y
52 *Hunter*	Y	Y	Y	Y	N	Y	Y
COLORADO							
1 DeGette	Y	Y	Y	Y	Y	Y	N
2 Skaggs	Y	Y	Y	N	Y	Y	N
3 *McInnis*	Y	Y	Y	Y	N	Y	Y
4 *Schaffer*	Y	Y	Y	Y	N	Y	Y
5 *Hefley*	Y	Y	Y	Y	N	Y	Y
6 *Schaefer*	Y	Y	Y	Y	N	Y	Y
CONNECTICUT							
1 Kennelly	Y	Y	Y	Y	Y	Y	N
2 Gejdenson	Y	Y	Y	Y	Y	Y	Y
3 DeLauro	Y	Y	Y	Y	Y	Y	N
4 *Shays*	Y	Y	Y	Y	Y	Y	Y
5 Maloney	Y	Y	Y	Y	Y	Y	Y
6 *Johnson*	Y	Y	Y	N	Y	Y	N
DELAWARE							
AL *Castle*	Y	Y	Y	Y	Y	Y	Y
FLORIDA							
1 *Scarborough*	Y	Y	Y	Y	N	Y	Y
2 Boyd	Y	Y	Y	Y	Y	Y	N
3 Brown	Y	Y	Y	Y	Y	Y	N
4 *Fowler*	Y	Y	Y	Y	N	Y	N
5 Thurman	Y	Y	Y	Y	Y	Y	N
6 *Stearns*	Y	Y	Y	Y	N	Y	Y
7 *Mica*	Y	Y	Y	Y	N	Y	Y
8 *McCollum*	Y	Y	Y	Y	N	Y	Y
9 *Bilirakis*	Y	Y	Y	Y	N	Y	Y
10 *Young*	Y	Y	Y	Y	N	Y	Y
11 Davis	Y	Y	Y	Y	Y	Y	N
12 *Canady*	Y	Y	Y	Y	N	Y	Y
13 *Miller*	Y	Y	Y	Y	N	Y	Y
14 *Goss*	Y	Y	Y	Y	N	Y	Y
15 *Weldon*	Y	Y	+	Y	N	Y	Y
16 *Foley*	Y	Y	Y	Y	Y	Y	Y
17 Meek	Y	Y	Y	Y	Y	Y	N
18 *Ros-Lehtinen*	Y	Y	Y	Y	N	Y	Y
19 Wexler	N	N	N	N	Y	Y	N
20 Deutsch	Y	Y	Y	Y	Y	Y	N
21 *Diaz-Balart*	Y	+	Y	Y	N	Y	Y
22 *Shaw*	Y	Y	Y	Y	Y	Y	Y
23 Hastings	N	N	N	N	Y	Y	N
GEORGIA							
1 *Kingston*	Y	Y	Y	Y	N	Y	Y
2 Bishop	Y	Y	Y	Y	Y	Y	N
3 *Collins*	Y	Y	Y	Y	N	Y	Y
4 McKinney	Y	Y	Y	Y	Y	Y	Y
5 Lewis	Y	Y	Y	N	Y	Y	N
6 *Gingrich*							
7 *Barr*	Y	Y	Y	Y	N	Y	Y
8 *Chambliss*	Y	Y	Y	Y	N	Y	Y
9 *Deal*	Y	Y	Y	Y	N	Y	Y
10 *Norwood*	Y	?	Y	Y	N	Y	Y
11 *Linder*	Y	Y	Y	Y	N	Y	Y
HAWAII							
1 Abercrombie	Y	Y	Y	Y	Y	Y	N
2 Mink	Y	Y	Y	Y	Y	Y	N
IDAHO							
1 *Chenoweth*	Y	Y	Y	N	Y	Y	Y
2 *Crapo*	Y	Y	Y	Y	N	Y	Y
ILLINOIS							
1 Rush	Y	Y	Y	Y	Y	Y	N
2 Jackson	Y	Y	Y	Y	Y	Y	N
3 Lipinski	Y	Y	Y	Y	N	Y	Y
4 Gutierrez	Y	Y	Y	N	Y	Y	Y
5 Blagojevich	Y	Y	Y	Y	Y	Y	Y
6 *Hyde*	Y	Y	Y	Y	N	Y	Y
7 Davis	Y	Y	Y	Y	Y	Y	N
8 *Crane*	Y	Y	Y	N	N	Y	Y
9 Yates	Y	N	Y	N	Y	Y	N
10 *Porter*	Y	Y	Y	Y	Y	Y	Y
11 *Weller*	Y	Y	Y	Y	N	Y	Y
12 Costello	Y	Y	Y	Y	N	Y	N

ND Northern Democrats   SD Southern Democrats

	167	168	169	170	171	172	173
13 ***Fawell***	Y	Y	?	Y	Y	Y	Y
14 ***Hastert***	Y	Y	Y	Y	N	Y	Y
15 ***Ewing***	+	+	+	+	X	+	+
16 ***Manzullo***	Y	Y	Y	N	N	Y	Y
17 Evans	Y	Y	Y	Y	Y	Y	N
18 ***LaHood***	Y	Y	Y	Y	N	Y	Y
19 Poshard	Y	Y	Y	Y	N	Y	Y
20 ***Shimkus***	Y	Y	Y	Y	N	Y	Y
INDIANA							
1 Visclosky	Y	Y	Y	Y	Y	Y	N
2 ***McIntosh***	Y	Y	?	Y	N	Y	Y
3 Roemer	Y	Y	Y	Y	N	Y	Y
4 ***Souder***	Y	Y	Y	?	N	Y	Y
5 ***Buyer***	Y	Y	Y	Y	N	Y	Y
6 ***Burton***	Y	Y	Y	Y	N	Y	Y
7 ***Pease***	Y	Y	Y	Y	N	Y	Y
8 ***Hostettler***	Y	Y	Y	Y	N	Y	Y
9 Hamilton	N	N	N	N	N	Y	N
10 Carson	+	+	+	+	+	+	–
IOWA							
1 ***Leach***	Y	Y	Y	Y	Y	Y	N
2 ***Nussle***	Y	Y	Y	Y	N	Y	Y
3 Boswell	Y	Y	Y	Y	Y	Y	Y
4 ***Ganske***	Y	Y	Y	Y	N	Y	Y
5 ***Latham***	Y	Y	Y	Y	N	Y	Y
KANSAS							
1 ***Moran***	Y	Y	Y	Y	N	Y	Y
2 ***Ryun***	Y	Y	Y	Y	N	Y	Y
3 ***Snowbarger***	Y	Y	Y	Y	N	Y	Y
4 ***Tiahrt***	Y	Y	Y	Y	N	Y	Y
KENTUCKY							
1 ***Whitfield***	Y	Y	Y	Y	N	Y	Y
2 ***Lewis***	Y	Y	Y	Y	N	Y	Y
3 ***Northup***	Y	Y	Y	Y	N	Y	Y
4 ***Bunning***	Y	Y	Y	Y	N	Y	Y
5 ***Rogers***	Y	Y	Y	Y	N	Y	Y
6 Baesler	Y	Y	Y	Y	Y	Y	N
LOUISIANA							
1 ***Livingston***	Y	Y	Y	Y	N	Y	Y
2 Jefferson	Y	Y	Y	Y	Y	Y	N
3 ***Tauzin***	Y	Y	Y	Y	N	Y	Y
4 ***McCrery***	Y	Y	Y	Y	N	Y	Y
5 ***Cooksey***	Y	Y	Y	Y	N	Y	Y
6 ***Baker***	Y	Y	Y	Y	N	Y	Y
7 John	Y	Y	Y	Y	N	Y	N
MAINE							
1 Allen	Y	Y	Y	N	Y	Y	N
2 Baldacci	Y	Y	Y	Y	Y	Y	N
MARYLAND							
1 ***Gilchrest***	Y	Y	Y	Y	Y	Y	Y
2 ***Ehrlich***	Y	Y	Y	Y	Y	Y	Y
3 Cardin	Y	Y	Y	Y	Y	Y	N
4 Wynn	Y	Y	Y	Y	Y	Y	N
5 Hoyer	Y	Y	Y	Y	Y	Y	N
6 ***Bartlett***	Y	Y	Y	Y	N	Y	Y
7 Cummings	Y	Y	Y	Y	Y	Y	N
8 ***Morella***	Y	Y	Y	Y	Y	Y	N
MASSACHUSETTS							
1 Olver	Y	Y	Y	N	Y	Y	N
2 Neal	Y	Y	Y	Y	Y	Y	N
3 McGovern	Y	Y	Y	Y	Y	Y	N
4 Frank	Y	Y	Y	Y	Y	P	N
5 Meehan	Y	Y	Y	Y	Y	Y	N
6 Tierney	Y	Y	Y	Y	Y	Y	N
7 Markey	Y	Y	Y	Y	Y	Y	N
8 Kennedy	Y	Y	Y	Y	Y	Y	N
9 Moakley	Y	Y	Y	Y	N	Y	N
10 Delahunt	Y	Y	Y	Y	Y	Y	N
MICHIGAN							
1 Stupak	Y	Y	Y	Y	N	Y	N
2 ***Hoekstra***	Y	Y	Y	Y	N	Y	Y
3 ***Ehlers***	Y	Y	Y	N	N	Y	N
4 ***Camp***	Y	Y	Y	Y	N	Y	Y
5 Barcia	Y	Y	Y	Y	N	Y	Y
6 ***Upton***	Y	Y	Y	Y	N	Y	Y
7 ***Smith***	Y	Y	Y	Y	N	Y	Y
8 Stabenow	+	+	+	–	#	+	+
9 Kildee	Y	Y	Y	Y	N	Y	N
10 Bonior	Y	Y	Y	Y	Y	Y	N
11 ***Knollenberg***	Y	Y	Y	Y	N	Y	Y
12 Levin	Y	Y	Y	Y	Y	Y	N
13 Rivers	Y	Y	Y	Y	Y	Y	N
14 Conyers	Y	Y	Y	N	Y	Y	N
15 Kilpatrick	Y	Y	Y	N	Y	Y	N
16 Dingell	Y	Y	Y	Y	Y	Y	N
MINNESOTA							
1 ***Gutknecht***	Y	Y	Y	Y	N	Y	Y
2 Minge	Y	Y	Y	Y	Y	Y	N
3 ***Ramstad***	Y	Y	Y	Y	Y	Y	Y
4 Vento	Y	Y	Y	Y	Y	Y	N
5 Sabo	Y	Y	Y	N	Y	Y	N
6 Luther	Y	Y	Y	Y	Y	Y	N
7 Peterson	Y	Y	Y	Y	N	Y	Y
8 Oberstar	Y	Y	Y	Y	N	Y	N
MISSISSIPPI							
1 ***Wicker***	Y	Y	Y	Y	N	Y	Y
2 Thompson	Y	Y	Y	Y	Y	Y	N
3 ***Pickering***	Y	Y	Y	Y	N	Y	Y
4 ***Parker***	Y	Y	Y	Y	N	Y	Y
5 Taylor	Y	Y	Y	Y	N	Y	Y
MISSOURI							
1 Clay	?	?	?	?	?	?	?
2 ***Talent***	Y	Y	Y	Y	N	Y	Y
3 Gephardt	Y	Y	Y	Y	Y	Y	N
4 Skelton	Y	Y	Y	Y	N	Y	N
5 McCarthy	Y	Y	Y	N	Y	Y	N
6 Danner	Y	Y	Y	Y	N	Y	Y
7 ***Blunt***	Y	Y	Y	Y	N	Y	Y
8 ***Emerson***	Y	Y	Y	Y	N	Y	Y
9 ***Hulshof***	Y	Y	Y	Y	N	Y	Y
MONTANA							
AL ***Hill***	Y	Y	?	Y	N	Y	Y
NEBRASKA							
1 ***Bereuter***	Y	Y	Y	Y	N	Y	Y
2 ***Christensen***	Y	Y	Y	Y	N	Y	Y
3 ***Barrett***	Y	Y	Y	Y	N	Y	Y
NEVADA							
1 ***Ensign***	Y	Y	Y	Y	N	Y	Y
2 ***Gibbons***	Y	Y	Y	Y	N	Y	Y
NEW HAMPSHIRE							
1 ***Sununu***	Y	Y	Y	Y	N	Y	Y
2 ***Bass***	Y	Y	Y	+	Y	Y	Y
NEW JERSEY							
1 Andrews	Y	Y	Y	Y	Y	Y	Y
2 ***LoBiondo***	Y	Y	Y	Y	N	Y	Y
3 ***Saxton***	Y	Y	Y	Y	N	Y	Y
4 ***Smith***	Y	Y	Y	Y	N	Y	Y
5 ***Roukema***	Y	Y	Y	Y	Y	Y	Y
6 Pallone	Y	Y	Y	Y	Y	Y	N
7 ***Franks***	Y	Y	Y	Y	Y	Y	Y
8 Pascrell	Y	Y	Y	Y	Y	Y	N
9 Rothman	Y	Y	Y	Y	Y	Y	N
10 Payne	Y	Y	Y	Y	Y	Y	N
11 ***Frelinghuysen***	Y	Y	Y	Y	Y	Y	Y
12 ***Pappas***	Y	Y	Y	Y	N	Y	Y
13 Menendez	Y	Y	Y	Y	Y	Y	N
NEW MEXICO							
1 Vacant							
2 ***Skeen***	Y	Y	Y	Y	N	Y	Y
3 ***Redmond***	Y	Y	Y	Y	N	Y	Y
NEW YORK							
1 ***Forbes***	Y	Y	Y	Y	N	Y	Y
2 ***Lazio***	Y	Y	Y	Y	N	Y	Y
3 ***King***	Y	Y	Y	Y	N	Y	N
4 McCarthy	Y	Y	Y	Y	Y	Y	N
5 Ackerman	Y	Y	Y	N	Y	Y	N
6 Meeks	?	?	?	?	?	?	?
7 Manton	Y	Y	Y	Y	N	Y	N
8 Nadler	Y	Y	Y	Y	Y	Y	N
9 Schumer	Y	Y	Y	Y	Y	Y	N
10 Towns	Y	Y	Y	Y	Y	Y	N
11 Owens	Y	Y	Y	?	Y	Y	N
12 Velázquez	Y	Y	Y	Y	Y	Y	N
13 ***Fossella***	Y	Y	Y	Y	N	Y	Y
14 Maloney	Y	Y	Y	Y	Y	Y	N
15 Rangel	Y	Y	Y	Y	Y	Y	N
16 Serrano	Y	Y	Y	N	Y	Y	N
17 Engel	Y	Y	Y	Y	Y	Y	N
18 Lowey	Y	Y	Y	Y	Y	Y	N
19 ***Kelly***	Y	Y	Y	Y	Y	Y	Y
20 ***Gilman***	Y	Y	Y	Y	Y	Y	Y
21 McNulty	Y	Y	Y	Y	N	Y	Y
22 ***Solomon***	Y	Y	Y	Y	N	Y	Y
23 ***Boehlert***	Y	Y	Y	Y	Y	Y	Y
24 ***McHugh***	Y	Y	Y	Y	N	Y	Y
25 ***Walsh***	Y	Y	Y	Y	N	Y	Y
26 Hinchey	Y	Y	Y	Y	Y	Y	N
27 ***Paxon***	Y	Y	Y	Y	N	Y	Y
28 Slaughter	Y	Y	Y	Y	Y	Y	N
29 LaFalce	Y	Y	Y	N	N	Y	N
30 ***Quinn***	Y	Y	Y	Y	N	Y	Y
31 ***Houghton***	Y	Y	Y	N	Y	Y	N
NORTH CAROLINA							
1 Clayton	Y	Y	Y	N	Y	Y	N
2 Etheridge	Y	Y	Y	Y	Y	Y	Y
3 ***Jones***	Y	Y	Y	Y	N	Y	Y
4 Price	Y	Y	Y	Y	Y	Y	N
5 ***Burr***	Y	Y	Y	Y	N	Y	Y
6 ***Coble***	Y	Y	Y	Y	N	Y	Y
7 McIntyre	Y	Y	Y	Y	N	Y	Y
8 Hefner	Y	Y	Y	Y	Y	Y	Y
9 ***Myrick***	Y	Y	Y	Y	N	Y	Y
10 ***Ballenger***	Y	Y	Y	Y	N	Y	Y
11 ***Taylor***	Y	Y	Y	Y	N	Y	Y
12 Watt	Y	N	Y	N	Y	Y	N
NORTH DAKOTA							
AL Pomeroy	Y	Y	Y	Y	Y	Y	Y
OHIO							
1 ***Chabot***	Y	Y	Y	Y	N	Y	Y
2 ***Portman***	Y	Y	Y	Y	N	Y	Y
3 Hall	Y	Y	Y	Y	N	Y	N
4 ***Oxley***	Y	Y	Y	Y	N	Y	Y
5 ***Gillmor***	Y	Y	Y	Y	N	Y	Y
6 Strickland	Y	Y	Y	Y	Y	Y	Y
7 ***Hobson***	Y	Y	Y	Y	N	Y	Y
8 ***Boehner***	Y	Y	Y	Y	N	Y	Y
9 Kaptur	Y	Y	Y	Y	N	Y	Y
10 Kucinich	Y	Y	Y	Y	N	Y	N
11 Stokes	Y	Y	Y	Y	Y	Y	N
12 ***Kasich***	Y	Y	Y	?	N	Y	Y
13 Brown	Y	Y	Y	Y	Y	Y	N
14 Sawyer	Y	Y	Y	N	Y	Y	N
15 ***Pryce***	Y	Y	Y	Y	Y	Y	Y
16 ***Regula***	Y	Y	Y	Y	N	Y	Y
17 Traficant	Y	Y	Y	Y	N	Y	Y
18 ***Ney***	Y	Y	Y	Y	N	Y	Y
19 ***LaTourette***	Y	Y	Y	Y	N	Y	Y
OKLAHOMA							
1 ***Largent***	Y	Y	Y	Y	N	Y	Y
2 ***Coburn***	Y	Y	Y	Y	N	Y	Y
3 ***Watkins***	Y	Y	Y	Y	N	Y	Y
4 ***Watts***	Y	Y	Y	Y	N	Y	Y
5 ***Istook***	Y	Y	Y	Y	N	Y	Y
6 ***Lucas***	Y	Y	Y	Y	N	Y	Y
OREGON							
1 Furse	Y	Y	Y	N	Y	Y	N
2 ***Smith***	Y	Y	Y	Y	N	Y	Y
3 Blumenauer	Y	Y	Y	Y	Y	Y	N
4 DeFazio	Y	Y	Y	Y	Y	Y	Y
5 Hooley	Y	Y	Y	Y	Y	Y	N
PENNSYLVANIA							
1 Vacant							
2 Fattah	Y	Y	Y	N	Y	Y	N
3 Borski	Y	Y	Y	Y	N	Y	N
4 Klink	Y	Y	Y	Y	N	Y	N
5 ***Peterson***	Y	Y	Y	Y	N	Y	Y
6 Holden	Y	Y	Y	Y	N	Y	N
7 ***Weldon***	Y	Y	Y	Y	N	Y	Y
8 ***Greenwood***	Y	Y	Y	Y	Y	Y	N
9 ***Shuster***	Y	Y	Y	Y	N	Y	Y
10 ***McDade***	Y	Y	Y	Y	N	?	Y
11 Kanjorski	Y	Y	Y	Y	N	Y	N
12 Murtha	Y	Y	Y	Y	?	?	?
13 ***Fox***	Y	Y	Y	Y	N	Y	Y
14 Coyne	Y	Y	Y	Y	Y	Y	N
15 McHale	Y	Y	Y	Y	Y	Y	N
16 ***Pitts***	Y	Y	Y	Y	N	Y	Y
17 ***Gekas***	Y	Y	Y	Y	N	Y	Y
18 Doyle	Y	Y	Y	Y	N	Y	N
19 ***Goodling***	Y	Y	Y	Y	N	Y	Y
20 Mascara	Y	Y	Y	Y	N	Y	N
21 ***English***	Y	Y	Y	Y	N	Y	Y
RHODE ISLAND							
1 Kennedy	Y	Y	Y	Y	Y	Y	N
2 Weygand	Y	Y	Y	Y	N	Y	N
SOUTH CAROLINA							
1 ***Sanford***	Y	Y	Y	Y	N	Y	Y
2 ***Spence***	Y	Y	Y	Y	N	Y	Y
3 ***Graham***	Y	Y	Y	Y	N	Y	Y
4 ***Inglis***	Y	Y	Y	Y	N	Y	Y
5 Spratt	Y	Y	Y	?	Y	Y	N
6 Clyburn	Y	Y	Y	Y	Y	Y	N
SOUTH DAKOTA							
AL ***Thune***	Y	Y	Y	Y	N	Y	Y
TENNESSEE							
1 ***Jenkins***	Y	Y	Y	Y	N	Y	Y
2 ***Duncan***	Y	Y	Y	Y	N	Y	Y
3 ***Wamp***	Y	Y	Y	Y	N	Y	Y
4 ***Hilleary***	Y	Y	Y	Y	N	Y	Y
5 Clement	Y	Y	Y	Y	Y	Y	Y
6 Gordon	Y	Y	Y	Y	Y	Y	Y
7 ***Bryant***	Y	Y	Y	Y	N	Y	Y
8 Tanner	Y	Y	Y	Y	Y	Y	Y
9 Ford	Y	Y	Y	Y	Y	Y	N
TEXAS							
1 Sandlin	Y	Y	Y	Y	Y	Y	Y
2 Turner	Y	Y	Y	Y	Y	Y	Y
3 ***Johnson, Sam***	Y	Y	Y	Y	N	Y	Y
4 Hall	Y	Y	Y	Y	N	Y	Y
5 ***Sessions***	Y	Y	Y	Y	N	Y	Y
6 ***Barton***	Y	Y	Y	Y	N	Y	Y
7 ***Archer***	Y	Y	Y	Y	N	Y	Y
8 ***Brady***	Y	Y	?	Y	N	Y	Y
9 Lampson	Y	Y	Y	Y	Y	Y	N
10 Doggett	Y	Y	Y	Y	Y	Y	N
11 Edwards	Y	Y	Y	Y	Y	Y	N
12 ***Granger***	Y	Y	Y	Y	N	Y	Y
13 ***Thornberry***	Y	Y	Y	Y	N	Y	Y
14 ***Paul***	Y	Y	Y	Y	N	Y	Y
15 Hinojosa	Y	Y	Y	Y	Y	Y	N
16 Reyes	Y	Y	Y	N	Y	Y	N
17 Stenholm	Y	Y	Y	Y	N	Y	Y
18 Jackson-Lee	Y	Y	Y	Y	Y	Y	N
19 ***Combest***	Y	Y	Y	Y	N	Y	Y
20 Gonzalez	?	?	?	?	?	?	?
21 ***Smith***	Y	Y	Y	Y	N	Y	Y
22 ***DeLay***	Y	Y	Y	Y	N	Y	Y
23 ***Bonilla***	Y	Y	Y	Y	N	Y	Y
24 Frost	Y	Y	Y	Y	Y	Y	N
25 Bentsen	Y	Y	Y	Y	Y	Y	N
26 ***Armey***	Y	Y	Y	Y	N	Y	Y
27 Ortiz	Y	Y	Y	N	N	Y	N
28 Rodriguez	Y	Y	Y	Y	Y	Y	N
29 Green	Y	Y	Y	Y	Y	Y	Y
30 Johnson, E.B.	Y	Y	Y	Y	Y	Y	N
UTAH							
1 ***Hansen***	Y	Y	Y	Y	N	Y	Y
2 ***Cook***	Y	Y	Y	Y	N	Y	Y
3 ***Cannon***	?	Y	Y	Y	N	Y	Y
VERMONT							
AL *Sanders*	Y	Y	Y	Y	Y	Y	N
VIRGINIA							
1 ***Bateman***	+	+	+	+	–	+	+
2 Pickett	Y	Y	Y	N	N	Y	N
3 Scott	Y	Y	Y	Y	Y	Y	N
4 Sisisky	Y	Y	Y	Y	Y	Y	N
5 Goode	Y	Y	Y	Y	N	Y	Y
6 ***Goodlatte***	Y	Y	Y	Y	N	Y	Y
7 ***Bliley***	Y	Y	Y	Y	N	Y	Y
8 Moran	Y	Y	N	N	Y	Y	N
9 Boucher	Y	Y	Y	Y	Y	Y	N
10 ***Wolf***	Y	Y	Y	Y	N	Y	Y
11 ***Davis***	Y	Y	Y	Y	N	Y	Y
WASHINGTON							
1 ***White***	Y	Y	Y	Y	Y	Y	Y
2 ***Metcalf***	Y	Y	Y	Y	N	Y	Y
3 ***Smith, Linda***	Y	Y	Y	Y	N	Y	Y
4 ***Hastings***	Y	Y	Y	Y	N	Y	Y
5 ***Nethercutt***	Y	Y	Y	Y	N	Y	Y
6 Dicks	Y	Y	Y	N	Y	Y	N
7 McDermott	N	N	N	N	Y	Y	N
8 ***Dunn***	Y	Y	Y	Y	N	Y	Y
9 Smith, Adam	Y	Y	Y	N	Y	Y	N
WEST VIRGINIA							
1 Mollohan	?	Y	Y	Y	N	Y	N
2 Wise	Y	Y	Y	Y	?	?	?
3 Rahall	Y	Y	Y	Y	N	Y	N
WISCONSIN							
1 ***Neumann***	Y	Y	Y	Y	N	Y	Y
2 ***Klug***	Y	Y	Y	Y	N	Y	Y
3 Kind	Y	Y	Y	Y	Y	Y	N
4 Kleczka	Y	Y	Y	Y	Y	Y	N
5 Barrett	Y	Y	Y	N	Y	Y	N
6 ***Petri***	Y	Y	Y	Y	N	Y	Y
7 Obey	Y	Y	Y	N	Y	Y	N
8 Johnson	Y	Y	Y	Y	Y	Y	Y
9 ***Sensenbrenner***	Y	Y	Y	Y	N	Y	Y
WYOMING							
AL ***Cubin***	Y	Y	Y	Y	N	Y	Y

Southern states - Ala., Ark., Fla., Ga., Ky., La., Miss., N.C., Okla., S.C., Tenn., Texas, Va.

House Votes 174, 175, 176, 177, 178, 179, 180

Key

- Y Voted for (yea).
- # Paired for.
- + Announced for.
- N Voted against (nay).
- X Paired against.
- − Announced against.
- P Voted "present."
- C Voted "present" to avoid possible conflict of interest.
- ? Did not vote or otherwise make a position known.

Democrats **Republicans** *Independent*

174. HR 2400. Surface Transportation Reauthorization/Motion to Instruct. Obey, D-Wis., motion to instruct the House conferees to oppose provisions which prohibit or reduce service-connected disability compensation to veterans for smoking-related illnesses. Motion agreed to 422-0: R 224-0; D 197-0 (ND 143-0, SD 54-0); I 1-0. May 20, 1998.

175. Procedural Motion/Journal. Approval of the House Journal of Wednesday, May 20, 1998. Approved 339-58: R 188-17; D 150-41 (ND 108-30, SD 42-11); I 1-0. May 21, 1998.

176. H Res 432. President's Assertions of Executive Privilege/Adoption. Adoption of the resolution to express the sense of the House that all documents relating to any claims of executive privilege asserted by the president should be immediately made publicly available. Adopted 259-157: R 223-1; D 36-155 (ND 21-116, SD 15-39); I 0-1. May 21, 1998.

177. H Res 433. Presidential Cooperation with Investigation/Adoption. Adoption of the resolution to call on the president to immediately call upon his friends, former associates and appointees, and their associates, who have asserted their Fifth Amendment rights or left the country to avoid testifying in congressional investigations, to testify fully and truthfully before the relevant congressional committee. Adopted 342-69: R 221-0; D 120-69 (ND 86-52, SD 34-17); I 1-0. May 21, 1998.

178. HR 3616. Fiscal 1999 Defense Authorization/Military Retirees. Thornberry, R-Texas, amendment to authorize a demonstration program to offer enrollment in the Federal Employees Health Benefits Program to military Medicare-eligible retirees. Adopted 420-1: R 220-1; D 199-0 (ND 146-0, SD 53-0); I 1-0. May 21, 1998.

179. HR 3616. Fiscal 1999 Defense Authorization/U.S. Borders. Reyes, D-Texas, amendment to the Traficant, D-Ohio, amendment, to require the attorney general or the secretary of the Treasury to submit a formal request to the Defense Department asking for the deployment of troops along the border. The Traficant amendment would authorize the Defense Department to assign members of the armed forces to assist in patrolling U.S. borders. Rejected 179-243: R 9-210; D 169-33 (ND 126-22, SD 43-11); I 1-0. May 21, 1998.

180. HR 3616. Fiscal 1999 Defense Authorization/U.S. Border. Traficant, D-Ohio, amendment to authorize the Defense Department to assign members of the armed forces to assist the Immigration and Naturalization Service and the Customs Service in monitoring and patrolling U.S. borders. Adopted 288-132: R 203-14; D 85-117 (ND 57-91, SD 28-26); I 0-1. May 21, 1998.

[1] Robert A. Brady, D-Pa., was sworn in May 21, replacing Thomas M. Foglietta, D-Pa., who resigned Nov. 11, 1997.

	174	175	176	177	178	179	180
ALABAMA							
1 *Callahan*	Y	Y	Y	Y	Y	N	Y
2 *Everett*	Y	Y	Y	Y	Y	N	Y
3 *Riley*	Y	Y	Y	Y	Y	N	Y
4 *Aderholt*	Y	N	Y	Y	Y	N	Y
5 Cramer	Y	Y	Y	Y	Y	N	Y
6 *Bachus*	Y	Y	Y	Y	Y	N	Y
7 Hilliard	Y	N	N	N	Y	Y	N
ALASKA							
AL *Young*	Y	?	Y	Y	Y	N	Y
ARIZONA							
1 *Salmon*	Y	Y	Y	Y	Y	N	Y
2 Pastor	Y	N	N	N	Y	Y	N
3 *Stump*	Y	Y	Y	Y	Y	N	N
4 *Shadegg*	Y	Y	Y	Y	Y	N	Y
5 *Kolbe*	Y	?	Y	Y	Y	N	Y
6 *Hayworth*	Y	Y	Y	Y	Y	N	N
ARKANSAS							
1 Berry	Y	Y	Y	Y	Y	Y	N
2 Snyder	Y	Y	N	Y	Y	Y	N
3 *Hutchinson*	Y	Y	Y	Y	Y	N	Y
4 *Dickey*	Y	Y	Y	Y	Y	N	Y
CALIFORNIA							
1 *Riggs*	Y	Y	Y	Y	Y	N	Y
2 *Herger*	Y	Y	Y	Y	Y	N	Y
3 Fazio	Y	N	N	N	Y	Y	N
4 *Doolittle*	Y	Y	Y	Y	Y	N	Y
5 Matsui	Y	Y	N	N	Y	Y	N
6 Woolsey	Y	Y	N	P	Y	Y	N
7 Miller	Y	Y	N	N	Y	Y	N
8 Pelosi	?	Y	N	?	Y	Y	N
9 Lee	Y	Y	N	N	Y	Y	N
10 Tauscher	Y	Y	N	P	Y	Y	Y
11 *Pombo*	Y	Y	Y	Y	Y	N	Y
12 Lantos	Y	Y	Y	Y	Y	Y	Y
13 Stark	Y	Y	N	N	Y	Y	N
14 Eshoo	Y	Y	N	Y	Y	Y	N
15 *Campbell*	Y	Y	Y	Y	Y	N	Y
16 Lofgren	Y	Y	N	Y	Y	Y	N
17 Farr	Y	Y	?	Y	Y	Y	Y
18 Condit	Y	Y	Y	Y	Y	Y	Y
19 *Radanovich*	Y	Y	Y	Y	Y	N	Y
20 Dooley	Y	Y	N	Y	Y	Y	N
21 *Thomas*	Y	Y	Y	Y	N	N	Y
22 Capps, L.	Y	Y	N	Y	Y	Y	N
23 *Gallegly*	Y	Y	Y	Y	Y	N	Y
24 Sherman	Y	Y	Y	Y	Y	Y	N
25 *McKeon*	Y	Y	Y	Y	Y	N	Y
26 Berman	Y	Y	P	P	Y	Y	N
27 *Rogan*	Y	Y	Y	Y	Y	N	Y
28 *Dreier*	Y	Y	Y	Y	Y	N	Y
29 Waxman	Y	Y	N	Y	Y	Y	N
30 Becerra	Y	N	N	N	Y	Y	N
31 Martinez	Y	Y	N	N	Y	N	N
32 Dixon	Y	?	N	Y	Y	Y	N
33 Roybal-Allard	Y	Y	N	N	Y	Y	N
34 Torres	Y	?	?	?	?	?	?
35 Waters	Y	N	N	N	N	N	N
36 Harman	?	?	?	?	?	?	?
37 Millender-McD.	Y	Y	N	Y	Y	Y	N
38 *Horn*	Y	Y	Y	Y	Y	N	Y
39 *Royce*	Y	Y	Y	Y	Y	N	Y
40 *Lewis*	Y	Y	Y	Y	Y	N	Y
41 *Kim*	Y	Y	Y	Y	Y	N	Y
42 Brown	Y	N	N	N	Y	Y	N
43 *Calvert*	Y	Y	Y	Y	Y	N	Y
44 *Bono, M.*	Y	?	Y	Y	Y	N	Y
45 *Rohrabacher*	Y	Y	Y	Y	Y	N	Y
46 Sanchez	Y	Y	N	P	Y	Y	Y
47 *Cox*	Y	?	Y	Y	Y	N	Y
48 *Packard*	Y	Y	Y	Y	Y	N	Y
49 *Bilbray*	Y	Y	Y	Y	Y	N	Y
50 Filner	Y	N	N	N	Y	Y	N
51 *Cunningham*	Y	Y	Y	Y	Y	N	Y
52 *Hunter*	Y	Y	Y	Y	Y	N	Y
COLORADO							
1 DeGette	Y	Y	N	N	Y	Y	N
2 Skaggs	Y	+	N	N	+	Y	N
3 *McInnis*	Y	Y	Y	Y	Y	N	Y
4 *Schaffer*	Y	N	Y	Y	Y	N	Y
5 *Hefley*	Y	N	Y	Y	Y	N	Y
6 *Schaefer*	Y	Y	Y	Y	Y	N	Y
CONNECTICUT							
1 Kennelly	Y	Y	N	Y	Y	Y	N
2 Gejdenson	Y	Y	N	Y	Y	Y	N
3 DeLauro	Y	Y	N	Y	Y	Y	N
4 *Shays*	Y	Y	Y	Y	Y	N	Y
5 Maloney	Y	Y	Y	Y	Y	Y	Y
6 *Johnson*	Y	Y	Y	Y	Y	Y	Y
DELAWARE							
AL *Castle*	Y	Y	Y	Y	Y	N	Y
FLORIDA							
1 *Scarborough*	Y	Y	Y	Y	Y	N	Y
2 Boyd	Y	Y	N	Y	Y	N	Y
3 Brown	Y	Y	N	N	Y	Y	N
4 *Fowler*	Y	Y	Y	Y	Y	N	Y
5 Thurman	Y	N	N	N	Y	Y	Y
6 *Stearns*	Y	Y	Y	Y	Y	N	Y
7 *Mica*	Y	Y	Y	Y	Y	N	Y
8 *McCollum*	Y	?	Y	Y	Y	N	Y
9 *Bilirakis*	Y	Y	Y	Y	Y	N	Y
10 *Young*	Y	Y	Y	Y	Y	N	Y
11 Davis	Y	Y	N	Y	Y	Y	N
12 *Canady*	Y	Y	Y	Y	Y	N	Y
13 *Miller*	Y	Y	Y	Y	Y	N	Y
14 *Goss*	Y	Y	Y	Y	Y	N	Y
15 *Weldon*	Y	Y	Y	Y	Y	N	Y
16 *Foley*	Y	Y	Y	Y	Y	?	?
17 Meek	Y	Y	N	N	Y	Y	N
18 *Ros-Lehtinen*	Y	Y	Y	Y	Y	N	Y
19 Wexler	Y	N	N	N	Y	Y	N
20 Deutsch	Y	N	N	N	Y	Y	N
21 *Diaz-Balart*	Y	Y	Y	Y	Y	N	Y
22 *Shaw*	Y	Y	Y	Y	Y	N	Y
23 Hastings	Y	N	N	N	Y	Y	N
GEORGIA							
1 *Kingston*	Y	Y	Y	Y	Y	N	Y
2 Bishop	Y	Y	N	P	Y	Y	Y
3 *Collins*	Y	Y	Y	Y	Y	N	Y
4 *McKinney*	Y	Y	Y	Y	Y	Y	N
5 Lewis	Y	N	N	N	Y	Y	N
6 *Gingrich*							
7 *Barr*	Y	?	Y	Y	Y	N	Y
8 *Chambliss*	Y	?	Y	Y	Y	N	Y
9 *Deal*	Y	Y	Y	Y	Y	N	Y
10 *Norwood*	Y	Y	Y	Y	Y	N	Y
11 *Linder*	Y	Y	Y	Y	Y	N	Y
HAWAII							
1 Abercrombie	Y	Y	Y	Y	Y	Y	N
2 Mink	Y	Y	Y	Y	Y	Y	N
IDAHO							
1 *Chenoweth*	Y	Y	Y	Y	Y	N	Y
2 *Crapo*	Y	?	?	Y	Y	N	Y
ILLINOIS							
1 Rush	Y	Y	N	N	Y	N	N
2 Jackson	Y	Y	N	N	Y	Y	N
3 Lipinski	Y	Y	Y	Y	Y	N	Y
4 Gutierrez	Y	N	?	Y	Y	N	N
5 Blagojevich	Y	Y	Y	Y	Y	Y	N
6 *Hyde*	Y	?	Y	Y	Y	N	Y
7 Davis	Y	Y	N	Y	Y	N	N
8 *Crane*	Y	Y	Y	Y	Y	N	Y
9 Yates	Y	N	N	N	Y	Y	N
10 *Porter*	Y	Y	Y	Y	Y	N	Y
11 *Weller*	Y	N	Y	Y	Y	N	Y
12 Costello	Y	N	N	Y	N	Y	N

ND Northern Democrats   SD Southern Democrats

	174	175	176	177	178	179	180
13 ***Fawell***	Y	Y	Y	Y	Y	N	Y
14 ***Hastert***	Y	Y	Y	Y	Y	N	Y
15 ***Ewing***	Y	Y	Y	Y	Y	N	Y
16 ***Manzullo***	Y	Y	Y	Y	Y	N	Y
17 Evans	Y	Y	Y	Y	Y	Y	N
18 ***LaHood***	Y	Y	Y	Y	Y	N	Y
19 Poshard	Y	N	N	Y	Y	Y	Y
20 ***Shimkus***	Y	Y	Y	Y	Y	N	Y
INDIANA							
1 Visclosky	Y	N	N	N	Y	N	Y
2 ***McIntosh***	Y	Y	Y	Y	Y	N	Y
3 Roemer	Y	Y	Y	Y	Y	N	Y
4 ***Souder***	Y	Y	Y	Y	Y	N	Y
5 ***Buyer***	Y	?	Y	Y	Y	N	N
6 ***Burton***	Y	Y	Y	Y	Y	N	Y
7 ***Pease***	Y	Y	Y	Y	Y	N	Y
8 ***Hostettler***	Y	Y	Y	Y	Y	N	Y
9 Hamilton	Y	Y	Y	Y	Y	Y	N
10 Carson	+	P	N	N	Y	N	Y
IOWA							
1 ***Leach***	Y	Y	Y	Y	Y	N	Y
2 ***Nussle***	Y	N	Y	Y	Y	N	Y
3 Boswell	Y	Y	Y	Y	Y	N	Y
4 ***Ganske***	Y	Y	Y	Y	P	N	Y
5 ***Latham***	Y	Y	Y	Y	Y	N	Y
KANSAS							
1 ***Moran***	Y	N	Y	Y	Y	N	Y
2 ***Ryun***	Y	Y	Y	Y	Y	N	N
3 ***Snowbarger***	Y	Y	Y	Y	Y	N	Y
4 ***Tiahrt***	Y	Y	Y	Y	Y	N	Y
KENTUCKY							
1 ***Whitfield***	Y	N	Y	Y	Y	Y	N
2 ***Lewis***	Y	?	Y	Y	Y	N	Y
3 ***Northup***	Y	Y	Y	Y	Y	N	Y
4 ***Bunning***	Y	Y	Y	Y	Y	N	Y
5 ***Rogers***	Y	Y	Y	Y	Y	N	Y
6 Baesler	Y	Y	Y	Y	Y	N	Y
LOUISIANA							
1 ***Livingston***	Y	Y	Y	Y	Y	N	Y
2 Jefferson	Y	Y	N	N	Y	Y	Y
3 ***Tauzin***	Y	Y	Y	Y	Y	N	Y
4 ***McCrery***	Y	Y	Y	Y	Y	N	Y
5 ***Cooksey***	Y	Y	Y	Y	Y	N	Y
6 ***Baker***	Y	?	Y	Y	Y	N	Y
7 John	Y	Y	Y	Y	Y	Y	Y
MAINE							
1 Allen	Y	Y	N	Y	Y	Y	N
2 Baldacci	Y	N	N	Y	Y	Y	N
MARYLAND							
1 ***Gilchrest***	Y	Y	Y	Y	Y	N	Y
2 ***Ehrlich***	Y	Y	Y	Y	Y	N	N
3 Cardin	Y	Y	N	Y	Y	Y	N
4 Wynn	Y	Y	N	N	Y	Y	N
5 Hoyer	Y	Y	N	Y	Y	Y	N
6 ***Bartlett***	Y	Y	Y	Y	Y	N	Y
7 Cummings	Y	Y	N	N	Y	Y	N
8 ***Morella***	Y	Y	Y	Y	Y	Y	N
MASSACHUSETTS							
1 Olver	Y	Y	N	N	Y	Y	N
2 Neal	Y	Y	N	Y	Y	Y	N
3 McGovern	Y	Y	N	P	?	Y	N
4 Frank	Y	Y	N	P	Y	Y	N
5 Meehan	Y	Y	N	Y	Y	Y	Y
6 Tierney	Y	?	N	Y	Y	Y	N
7 Markey	Y	N	N	N	Y	Y	N
8 Kennedy	Y	Y	N	N	Y	Y	N
9 Moakley	Y	Y	N	Y	Y	N	Y
10 Delahunt	Y	Y	N	N	Y	Y	N
MICHIGAN							
1 Stupak	Y	N	N	Y	Y	Y	N
2 ***Hoekstra***	Y	Y	Y	Y	Y	N	Y
3 ***Ehlers***	Y	Y	Y	Y	Y	Y	N
4 ***Camp***	Y	Y	Y	Y	Y	N	Y
5 Barcia	Y	Y	Y	Y	Y	Y	Y
6 ***Upton***	Y	Y	Y	Y	Y	N	Y
7 ***Smith***	Y	Y	Y	Y	Y	N	Y
8 Stabenow	+	Y	Y	Y	Y	Y	Y
9 Kildee	Y	Y	Y	Y	Y	Y	Y
10 Bonior	Y	N	N	N	Y	Y	N
11 ***Knollenberg***	Y	Y	Y	Y	Y	N	Y
12 Levin	Y	Y	N	N	Y	Y	Y
13 Rivers	Y	Y	P	Y	Y	N	Y
14 Conyers	Y	Y	N	N	Y	Y	N
15 Kilpatrick	Y	Y	N	Y	Y	Y	N
16 Dingell	Y	Y	N	Y	Y	Y	N

	174	175	176	177	178	179	180
MINNESOTA							
1 ***Gutknecht***	Y	N	Y	Y	Y	N	Y
2 Minge	Y	Y	N	Y	Y	Y	N
3 ***Ramstad***	Y	N	Y	Y	Y	N	Y
4 Vento	Y	N	N	N	Y	Y	N
5 Sabo	Y	N	N	Y	Y	Y	N
6 Luther	Y	Y	N	Y	Y	Y	Y
7 Peterson	Y	Y	Y	Y	Y	N	Y
8 Oberstar	Y	N	N	N	Y	Y	N
MISSISSIPPI							
1 ***Wicker***	Y	N	Y	Y	?	?	?
2 Thompson	Y	N	N	N	Y	Y	N
3 ***Pickering***	Y	Y	Y	Y	Y	N	Y
4 ***Parker***	Y	Y	Y	?	?	?	?
5 Taylor	Y	N	Y	Y	Y	N	Y
MISSOURI							
1 Clay	?	N	N	N	Y	Y	N
2 ***Talent***	Y	Y	Y	Y	Y	N	Y
3 Gephardt	Y	N	N	Y	Y	Y	Y
4 Skelton	Y	Y	N	Y	Y	Y	Y
5 McCarthy	Y	Y	N	Y	Y	Y	Y
6 Danner	Y	Y	Y	Y	Y	Y	Y
7 ***Blunt***	Y	Y	Y	Y	Y	N	Y
8 ***Emerson***	Y	Y	Y	Y	Y	N	Y
9 ***Hulshof***	Y	Y	Y	Y	Y	N	Y
MONTANA							
AL ***Hill***	Y	Y	Y	Y	Y	N	Y
NEBRASKA							
1 ***Bereuter***	Y	Y	Y	Y	Y	N	Y
2 ***Christensen***	Y	Y	Y	Y	Y	N	Y
3 ***Barrett***	Y	Y	Y	Y	Y	N	?
NEVADA							
1 ***Ensign***	Y	N	Y	Y	Y	N	Y
2 ***Gibbons***	Y	N	Y	Y	Y	N	Y
NEW HAMPSHIRE							
1 ***Sununu***	Y	Y	Y	Y	Y	N	Y
2 ***Bass***	Y	?	Y	Y	Y	N	Y
NEW JERSEY							
1 Andrews	Y	Y	N	N	Y	N	Y
2 ***LoBiondo***	Y	N	Y	Y	Y	N	Y
3 ***Saxton***	Y	Y	Y	Y	Y	N	Y
4 ***Smith***	Y	Y	Y	Y	Y	N	Y
5 ***Roukema***	Y	Y	Y	Y	Y	N	Y
6 Pallone	Y	N	N	Y	Y	Y	Y
7 ***Franks***	Y	Y	Y	?	Y	N	Y
8 Pascrell	Y	Y	Y	Y	Y	N	Y
9 Rothman	Y	Y	N	Y	Y	Y	N
10 Payne	Y	Y	N	N	Y	Y	N
11 ***Frelinghuysen***	Y	?	Y	Y	Y	N	Y
12 ***Pappas***	Y	Y	Y	Y	Y	N	Y
13 Menendez	Y	N	N	Y	Y	Y	N
NEW MEXICO							
1 Vacant							
2 ***Skeen***	Y	Y	Y	Y	Y	N	Y
3 ***Redmond***	Y	Y	Y	Y	Y	N	Y
NEW YORK							
1 ***Forbes***	Y	Y	Y	Y	Y	N	Y
2 ***Lazio***	Y	Y	Y	Y	Y	N	Y
3 ***King***	Y	Y	Y	Y	Y	N	Y
4 McCarthy	Y	Y	Y	Y	Y	N	Y
5 Ackerman	Y	Y	N	N	Y	Y	N
6 Meeks	?	?	?	?	?	?	?
7 Manton	Y	Y	N	Y	Y	N	Y
8 Nadler	Y	Y	N	N	Y	Y	N
9 Schumer	?	?	?	Y	Y	Y	Y
10 Towns	Y	Y	N	N	Y	Y	Y
11 Owens	Y	?	N	N	Y	N	Y
12 Velázquez	Y	N	N	N	Y	Y	N
13 ***Fossella***	Y	Y	Y	Y	Y	N	Y
14 Maloney	Y	Y	N	P	Y	Y	Y
15 Rangel	Y	Y	N	N	Y	Y	N
16 Serrano	Y	Y	N	N	Y	Y	N
17 Engel	Y	Y	N	N	Y	Y	Y
18 Lowey	Y	N	N	Y	Y	Y	Y
19 ***Kelly***	Y	Y	Y	Y	Y	N	Y
20 ***Gilman***	Y	Y	Y	Y	Y	N	Y
21 McNulty	Y	Y	N	Y	Y	Y	Y
22 ***Solomon***	Y	Y	Y	Y	Y	N	Y
23 ***Boehlert***	Y	Y	Y	Y	Y	N	Y
24 ***McHugh***	Y	Y	Y	Y	Y	N	Y
25 ***Walsh***	Y	Y	Y	Y	Y	N	Y
26 Hinchey	Y	N	N	N	Y	Y	N
27 ***Paxon***	Y	Y	Y	Y	Y	N	Y
28 Slaughter	Y	N	N	N	Y	Y	N
29 LaFalce	Y	Y	N	Y	Y	Y	Y

	174	175	176	177	178	179	180
30 ***Quinn***	Y	Y	Y	Y	Y	?	?
31 ***Houghton***	Y	Y	N	Y	Y	Y	N
NORTH CAROLINA							
1 Clayton	Y	Y	N	P	Y	Y	N
2 Etheridge	Y	Y	Y	Y	Y	Y	Y
3 ***Jones***	Y	Y	Y	Y	Y	N	Y
4 Price	Y	Y	Y	Y	Y	Y	Y
5 ***Burr***	Y	?	Y	Y	Y	N	Y
6 ***Coble***	Y	Y	Y	Y	Y	N	Y
7 McIntyre	Y	Y	Y	Y	Y	N	Y
8 Hefner	Y	Y	N	Y	Y	Y	Y
9 ***Myrick***	Y	Y	Y	Y	Y	N	Y
10 ***Ballenger***	Y	Y	Y	Y	Y	N	Y
11 ***Taylor***	Y	Y	Y	Y	Y	N	Y
12 Watt	Y	Y	N	P	Y	N	N
NORTH DAKOTA							
AL Pomeroy	Y	?	N	Y	Y	Y	Y
OHIO							
1 ***Chabot***	Y	Y	Y	Y	Y	N	Y
2 ***Portman***	Y	Y	Y	Y	Y	N	Y
3 Hall	Y	?	N	Y	Y	Y	Y
4 ***Oxley***	Y	Y	Y	Y	Y	N	Y
5 ***Gillmor***	Y	Y	Y	Y	Y	N	Y
6 Strickland	Y	Y	Y	Y	Y	Y	Y
7 ***Hobson***	Y	Y	Y	Y	Y	N	Y
8 ***Boehner***	Y	Y	Y	Y	Y	N	Y
9 Kaptur	Y	Y	?	Y	Y	Y	Y
10 Kucinich	Y	N	N	Y	Y	N	Y
11 Stokes	Y	Y	N	N	Y	Y	N
12 ***Kasich***	Y	Y	Y	Y	Y	N	Y
13 Brown	Y	Y	N	N	Y	Y	N
14 Sawyer	Y	Y	N	Y	Y	Y	N
15 ***Pryce***	?	Y	Y	Y	Y	N	Y
16 ***Regula***	Y	Y	Y	Y	Y	N	Y
17 Traficant	Y	Y	Y	Y	Y	N	Y
18 ***Ney***	Y	Y	Y	Y	Y	N	Y
19 ***LaTourette***	Y	Y	Y	Y	Y	N	Y
OKLAHOMA							
1 ***Largent***	Y	Y	Y	Y	Y	N	Y
2 ***Coburn***	Y	Y	Y	Y	Y	N	Y
3 ***Watkins***	Y	Y	Y	Y	Y	N	Y
4 ***Watts***	Y	Y	Y	Y	Y	N	Y
5 ***Istook***	Y	Y	Y	Y	Y	N	Y
6 ***Lucas***	Y	Y	Y	Y	Y	N	Y
OREGON							
1 Furse	Y	Y	N	N	Y	Y	N
2 ***Smith***	Y	Y	Y	Y	Y	N	Y
3 Blumenauer	Y	Y	N	Y	Y	Y	N
4 DeFazio	Y	N	N	P	Y	Y	N
5 Hooley	Y	Y	N	Y	Y	Y	N
PENNSYLVANIA							
1 Brady [1]			N	N	Y	Y	N
2 Fattah	Y	Y	N	N	Y	Y	N
3 Borski	Y	N	N	Y	Y	Y	N
4 Klink	Y	Y	N	Y	Y	N	Y
5 ***Peterson***	Y	Y	Y	Y	Y	N	Y
6 Holden	Y	Y	Y	Y	Y	N	Y
7 ***Weldon***	Y	Y	Y	Y	Y	N	Y
8 ***Greenwood***	Y	Y	Y	Y	Y	N	Y
9 ***Shuster***	Y	Y	Y	Y	Y	N	Y
10 ***McDade***	Y	Y	Y	?	Y	?	?
11 Kanjorski	Y	Y	N	Y	Y	Y	N
12 Murtha	Y	Y	N	N	Y	Y	Y
13 ***Fox***	Y	N	Y	Y	Y	N	Y
14 Coyne	Y	Y	N	Y	Y	Y	N
15 McHale	Y	Y	Y	Y	Y	Y	N
16 ***Pitts***	Y	Y	Y	Y	Y	N	Y
17 ***Gekas***	Y	Y	Y	Y	Y	N	Y
18 Doyle	Y	Y	N	Y	Y	Y	Y
19 ***Goodling***	Y	P	Y	Y	Y	N	Y
20 Mascara	Y	Y	N	Y	Y	Y	Y
21 ***English***	Y	N	Y	Y	Y	N	Y
RHODE ISLAND							
1 Kennedy	Y	Y	N	Y	Y	Y	N
2 Weygand	Y	Y	N	Y	Y	Y	N
SOUTH CAROLINA							
1 ***Sanford***	Y	Y	Y	Y	Y	N	N
2 ***Spence***	Y	Y	Y	Y	Y	N	Y
3 ***Graham***	Y	Y	Y	Y	Y	N	Y
4 ***Inglis***	Y	Y	Y	Y	Y	N	Y
5 Spratt	Y	Y	N	Y	Y	Y	N
6 Clyburn	Y	Y	N	N	Y	Y	N
SOUTH DAKOTA							
AL ***Thune***	Y	Y	Y	Y	Y	N	Y

	174	175	176	177	178	179	180
TENNESSEE							
1 ***Jenkins***	Y	Y	Y	Y	Y	N	Y
2 ***Duncan***	Y	Y	Y	Y	Y	N	Y
3 ***Wamp***	Y	N	Y	Y	Y	N	Y
4 ***Hilleary***	Y	N	Y	Y	Y	N	Y
5 Clement	Y	Y	N	Y	Y	Y	Y
6 Gordon	Y	Y	N	Y	Y	N	Y
7 ***Bryant***	Y	Y	Y	Y	Y	N	Y
8 Tanner	Y	Y	N	Y	Y	Y	Y
9 Ford	Y	Y	N	Y	Y	Y	N
TEXAS							
1 Sandlin	Y	Y	N	Y	Y	Y	Y
2 Turner	Y	?	Y	Y	Y	N	Y
3 ***Johnson, Sam***	Y	?	?	?	?	?	?
4 Hall	Y	Y	Y	Y	Y	N	Y
5 ***Sessions***	Y	Y	Y	Y	Y	N	Y
6 ***Barton***	Y	?	Y	Y	Y	Y	Y
7 ***Archer***	Y	Y	Y	Y	Y	N	Y
8 ***Brady***	Y	Y	Y	Y	Y	N	Y
9 Lampson	Y	Y	N	Y	Y	Y	N
10 Doggett	Y	Y	N	Y	Y	Y	N
11 Edwards	Y	Y	N	Y	Y	Y	N
12 ***Granger***	Y	?	Y	Y	Y	N	Y
13 ***Thornberry***	Y	Y	Y	Y	Y	N	Y
14 ***Paul***	Y	Y	Y	Y	Y	Y	N
15 Hinojosa	Y	Y	N	Y	Y	Y	N
16 Reyes	Y	Y	N	Y	Y	Y	N
17 Stenholm	Y	Y	Y	Y	Y	Y	Y
18 Jackson-Lee	Y	Y	N	N	Y	Y	N
19 ***Combest***	Y	Y	Y	Y	Y	N	Y
20 Gonzalez	?	?	?	?	?	?	?
21 ***Smith***	Y	Y	Y	Y	Y	N	Y
22 ***DeLay***	Y	Y	Y	Y	Y	N	Y
23 ***Bonilla***	Y	Y	Y	Y	Y	Y	N
24 Frost	Y	Y	N	Y	Y	Y	Y
25 Bentsen	Y	Y	N	Y	Y	Y	N
26 ***Armey***	Y	Y	Y	Y	Y	N	?
27 Ortiz	Y	Y	N	Y	Y	Y	N
28 Rodriguez	Y	Y	N	N	Y	Y	N
29 Green	Y	N	Y	Y	Y	Y	N
30 Johnson, E.B.	Y	N	N	N	Y	Y	Y
UTAH							
1 ***Hansen***	Y	Y	Y	Y	Y	N	Y
2 ***Cook***	Y	Y	Y	Y	Y	N	Y
3 ***Cannon***	Y	Y	Y	Y	Y	Y	Y
VERMONT							
AL *Sanders*	Y	Y	N	Y	Y	Y	N
VIRGINIA							
1 ***Bateman***	+	+	+	+	+	+	−
2 Pickett	Y	N	N	N	?	Y	Y
3 Scott	Y	N	N	N	Y	Y	N
4 Sisisky	Y	Y	Y	Y	Y	Y	Y
5 Goode	Y	Y	Y	Y	Y	N	Y
6 ***Goodlatte***	Y	Y	Y	Y	Y	N	Y
7 ***Bliley***	Y	Y	Y	Y	Y	N	Y
8 Moran	Y	Y	N	N	Y	Y	Y
9 Boucher	Y	Y	N	Y	Y	Y	Y
10 ***Wolf***	Y	Y	Y	Y	Y	N	Y
11 ***Davis***	Y	Y	Y	Y	Y	N	Y
WASHINGTON							
1 ***White***	Y	Y	Y	Y	Y	N	Y
2 ***Metcalf***	Y	Y	Y	Y	Y	N	Y
3 ***Smith, Linda***	Y	Y	Y	Y	Y	N	Y
4 ***Hastings***	Y	Y	Y	Y	Y	N	Y
5 ***Nethercutt***	Y	Y	Y	Y	Y	N	Y
6 Dicks	Y	Y	N	N	Y	Y	N
7 McDermott	Y	N	?	N	Y	Y	N
8 ***Dunn***	Y	Y	Y	Y	Y	N	Y
9 Smith, Adam	Y	Y	N	Y	Y	Y	N
WEST VIRGINIA							
1 Mollohan	Y	Y	N	Y	Y	Y	N
2 Wise	Y	Y	N	Y	Y	Y	N
3 Rahall	Y	Y	N	Y	Y	N	Y
WISCONSIN							
1 ***Neumann***	Y	Y	Y	Y	Y	N	Y
2 ***Klug***	Y	Y	Y	Y	Y	N	Y
3 Kind	Y	Y	P	P	Y	Y	Y
4 Kleczka	Y	Y	N	Y	Y	Y	Y
5 Barrett	Y	Y	P	Y	Y	Y	N
6 ***Petri***	Y	Y	Y	Y	Y	N	Y
7 Obey	Y	N	P	Y	Y	Y	Y
8 Johnson	Y	?	P	Y	Y	Y	N
9 ***Sensenbrenner***	Y	Y	Y	Y	Y	N	Y
WYOMING							
AL ***Cubin***	Y	Y	Y	Y	Y	N	Y

Southern states - Ala., Ark., Fla., Ga., Ky., La., Miss., N.C., Okla., S.C., Tenn., Texas, Va.

House Votes 181, 182, 183, 184, 185, 186, 187

181. HR 3616. Fiscal 1999 Defense Authorization/Nuclear Exports. Gilman, R-N.Y., amendment to establish reporting requirements for nuclear exports comparable to those in existing law for conventional arms. Adopted 405-9: R 217-0; D 187-9 (ND 136-7, SD 51-2); I 1-0. May 21, 1998. A "nay" was a vote in support of the president's position.

182. HR 3616. Fiscal 1999 Defense Authorization/Motion to Recommit. Frank, D-Mass., motion to recommit the bill to the National Security Committee with instructions to report it back with an amendment that no funds appropriated for the Department of Defense for fiscal year 1999 may be used for the deployment of the U.S. armed forces in the Republic of Bosnia and Herzegovina after December 31, 1998, unless a law has been enacted that explicitly authorizes the deployment of such armed forces. Motion rejected 167-251: R 129-89; D 38-161 (ND 32-114, SD 6-47); I 0-1. May 21, 1998.

183. HR 3616. Fiscal 1999 Defense Authorization/Passage. Passage of the bill to authorize $270.4 billion for defense programs, including $49.1 billion for weapons procurement, $36.2 billion for research and development, $94.5 billion for operations and maintenance, $8.2 billion for military construction, and $11.9 billion for defense-related activities of the Department of Energy. Passed 357-60: R 207-10; D 150-49 (ND 100-46, SD 50-3); I 0-1. May 21, 1998.

184. HR 2400. Surface Transportation Reauthorization/Motion to Instruct. Obey, D-Wis., motion to instruct the House conferees to limit the aggregate number of earmarked demonstration projects to a number that does not exceed the aggregate number of projects earmarked during the 42 years since enactment of the Highway Trust Fund in 1956. Motion rejected 77-332: R 52-163; D 25-168 (ND 17-124, SD 8-44); I 0-1. May 21, 1998.

185. HR 2400. Surface Transportation Reauthorization/Motion to Instruct. Minge, D-Minn., motion to instruct the House conferees to ensure that spending in the conference agreement is fully paid for using Congressional Budget Office estimates. Motion rejected 156-251: R 92-122; D 64-128 (ND 41-99, SD 23-29); I 0-1. May 21, 1998.

186. HR 2183. Campaign Finance Revisions/Previous Question. Linder, R-Ga., motion to order the previous question (thus ending debate and the possibility of amendment) on adoption of the rule (H Res 442) to provide for House floor consideration of the bill to prohibit national political parties from accepting the largely unregulated "soft money" contributions, ban state parties from transferring soft money to parties in other states, double the aggregate annual limits that individuals can contribute to campaigns, index contribution limits to inflation and require third-parties to disclose their expenditures on issue-oriented advertisements once they reach a certain threshold. Motion agreed to 208-190: R 205-0; D 3-189 (ND 1-139, SD 2-50); I 0-1. May 21, 1998.

187. Procedural Motion/Adjourn. Stenholm, D-Texas, motion to adjourn. Motion rejected 59-304: R 3-191; D 56-113 (ND 37-84, SD 19-29); I 0-0. May 22, 1998.

Key

- **Y** Voted for (yea).
- **#** Paired for.
- **+** Announced for.
- **N** Voted against (nay).
- **X** Paired against.
- **−** Announced against.
- **P** Voted "present."
- **C** Voted "present" to avoid possible conflict of interest.
- **?** Did not vote or otherwise make a position known.

Democrats **Republicans** *Independent*

	181	182	183	184	185	186	187
ALABAMA							
1 Callahan	Y	N	Y	N	N	Y	?
2 Everett	Y	N	Y	N	Y	Y	N
3 Riley	Y	N	Y	N	N	Y	N
4 Aderholt	Y	N	Y	N	Y	Y	N
5 Cramer	Y	N	N	N	N	Y	N
6 Bachus	Y	Y	Y	N	Y	Y	N
7 Hilliard	Y	N	N	N	N	N	N
ALASKA							
AL Young	Y	Y	Y	N	N	Y	?
ARIZONA							
1 Salmon	Y	Y	Y	Y	Y	Y	N
2 Pastor	Y	N	Y	N	N	N	N
3 Stump	Y	Y	Y	Y	Y	Y	N
4 Shadegg	Y	N	Y	Y	Y	Y	N
5 Kolbe	Y	N	Y	N	Y	Y	N
6 Hayworth	Y	Y	Y	Y	Y	Y	N
ARKANSAS							
1 Berry	Y	N	N	N	N	N	N
2 Snyder	Y	N	Y	N	Y	N	N
3 Hutchinson	Y	Y	Y	N	Y	Y	N
4 Dickey	Y	N	Y	N	N	Y	?
CALIFORNIA							
1 Riggs	Y	N	Y	N	N	Y	?
2 Herger	Y	Y	Y	N	Y	?	?
3 Fazio	N	N	N	N	N	N	Y
4 Doolittle	Y	N	Y	N	N	Y	Y
5 Matsui	Y	N	N	N	N	N	N
6 Woolsey	Y	N	N	N	N	N	N
7 Miller	Y	N	N	N	N	N	?
8 Pelosi	Y	N	N	N	N	N	?
9 Lee	Y	N	N	N	N	N	N
10 Tauscher	N	N	Y	N	Y	N	Y
11 Pombo	Y	Y	Y	N	Y	Y	N
12 Lantos	Y	N	N	N	Y	N	N
13 Stark	Y	Y	N	?	?	?	N
14 Eshoo	Y	N	N	Y	N	N	N
15 Campbell	Y	Y	N	Y	N	Y	N
16 Lofgren	Y	Y	N	P	Y	N	N
17 Farr	Y	Y	Y	Y	N	Y	N
18 Condit	Y	Y	Y	Y	N	Y	N
19 Radanovich	Y	N	Y	N	Y	Y	N
20 Dooley	N	N	Y	N	N	Y	N
21 Thomas	Y	Y	Y	N	N	Y	N
22 Capps, L.	Y	N	N	N	N	N	N
23 Gallegly	Y	N	Y	N	N	Y	N
24 Sherman	Y	N	N	Y	Y	N	N
25 McKeon	Y	Y	Y	N	N	Y	N
26 Berman	Y	N	Y	?	?	?	N
27 Rogan	Y	N	Y	N	Y	?	?
28 Dreier	Y	N	Y	N	Y	Y	N
29 Waxman	Y	N	?	?	?	?	?
30 Becerra	Y	N	N	N	Y	?	?
31 Martinez	Y	N	N	N	?	?	Y
32 Dixon	?	N	Y	N	N	Y	N
33 Roybal-Allard	Y	N	N	N	N	N	Y
34 Torres	?	?	?	?	?	?	?
35 Waters	Y	Y	Y	Y	N	N	Y
36 Harman	?	?	?	?	?	?	?
37 Millender-McD.	Y	N	Y	N	N	N	Y

	181	182	183	184	185	186	187
38 Horn	Y	N	Y	N	N	Y	N
39 Royce	Y	Y	N	Y	Y	Y	Y
40 Lewis	Y	N	Y	N	N	Y	N
41 Kim	Y	N	Y	N	N	Y	N
42 Brown	N	Y	N	N	N	N	N
43 Calvert	Y	N	Y	N	N	Y	N
44 Bono, M.	Y	N	Y	N	N	Y	?
45 Rohrabacher	Y	Y	Y	Y	Y	Y	N
46 Sanchez	Y	N	Y	N	Y	N	N
47 Cox	Y	N	Y	N	Y	Y	N
48 Packard	Y	N	Y	N	N	Y	N
49 Bilbray	Y	Y	Y	Y	Y	Y	N
50 Filner	Y	Y	N	N	N	N	Y
51 Cunningham	Y	N	Y	N	Y	Y	N
52 Hunter	Y	N	Y	N	Y	Y	?
COLORADO							
1 DeGette	Y	N	N	N	Y	N	Y
2 Skaggs	+	−	+	+	+	−	−
3 McInnis	Y	Y	Y	N	N	Y	N
4 Schaffer	Y	Y	Y	Y	Y	Y	N
5 Hefley	Y	Y	Y	N	N	?	N
6 Schaefer	Y	Y	Y	N	N	Y	N
CONNECTICUT							
1 Kennelly	Y	N	N	N	Y	N	Y
2 Gejdenson	Y	N	Y	N	N	N	Y
3 DeLauro	Y	N	Y	N	N	N	Y
4 Shays	Y	Y	N	Y	N	N	N
5 Maloney	Y	N	N	N	N	N	N
6 Johnson	Y	Y	Y	Y	Y	Y	N
DELAWARE							
AL Castle	Y	N	Y	Y	Y	Y	Y
FLORIDA							
1 Scarborough	Y	Y	Y	Y	Y	?	N
2 Boyd	Y	N	Y	N	Y	N	Y
3 Brown	Y	N	N	N	N	N	N
4 Fowler	Y	N	Y	N	N	Y	N
5 Thurman	Y	N	Y	N	N	N	N
6 Stearns	Y	Y	Y	Y	Y	Y	N
7 Mica	Y	Y	Y	Y	Y	Y	N
8 McCollum	Y	Y	Y	Y	Y	Y	N
9 Bilirakis	Y	Y	Y	N	N	Y	?
10 Young	Y	N	Y	N	N	Y	N
11 Davis	Y	N	Y	N	N	N	N
12 Canady	Y	Y	Y	N	Y	?	N
13 Miller	Y	Y	Y	Y	Y	Y	N
14 Goss	Y	N	Y	N	N	Y	N
15 Weldon	Y	N	Y	N	N	Y	N
16 Foley	?	?	?	?	?	?	?
17 Meek	Y	N	N	N	N	N	Y
18 Ros-Lehtinen	Y	N	Y	N	N	Y	N
19 Wexler	Y	N	Y	Y	Y	N	N
20 Deutsch	Y	N	Y	?	?	?	?
21 Diaz-Balart	Y	N	Y	N	N	Y	N
22 Shaw	Y	N	Y	N	N	?	N
23 Hastings	Y	N	Y	N	N	N	Y
GEORGIA							
1 Kingston	Y	Y	Y	N	Y	Y	Y
2 Bishop	Y	N	Y	N	N	N	Y
3 Collins	Y	N	Y	N	N	Y	N
4 McKinney	Y	N	N	Y	N	N	Y
5 Lewis	Y	N	Y	Y	Y	N	Y
6 Gingrich							
7 Barr	Y	Y	Y	Y	Y	Y	Y
8 Chambliss	Y	N	Y	N	Y	Y	N
9 Deal	Y	Y	Y	N	Y	Y	N
10 Norwood	Y	Y	Y	Y	Y	Y	N
11 Linder	Y	Y	Y	N	Y	Y	N
HAWAII							
1 Abercrombie	Y	N	N	N	N	N	Y
2 Mink	Y	Y	Y	N	N	N	Y
IDAHO							
1 Chenoweth	Y	Y	Y	N	Y	Y	N
2 Crapo	Y	Y	Y	N	Y	Y	N
ILLINOIS							
1 Rush	Y	Y	N	N	N	N	Y
2 Jackson	Y	Y	N	N	N	N	N
3 Lipinski	Y	Y	Y	N	N	N	N
4 Gutierrez	Y	N	N	N	N	N	N
5 Blagojevich	Y	N	Y	N	N	N	N
6 Hyde	Y	N	Y	N	N	Y	N
7 Davis	Y	Y	N	N	N	N	?
8 Crane	Y	Y	Y	Y	Y	Y	N
9 Yates	?	?	X	?	?	?	N
10 Porter	Y	N	Y	Y	Y	Y	?
11 Weller	Y	Y	Y	N	Y	Y	N
12 Costello	Y	Y	Y	N	N	N	N

ND Northern Democrats   SD Southern Democrats

	181	182	183	184	185	186	187
13 ***Fawell***	Y	N	Y	N	N	Y	?
14 ***Hastert***	Y	Y	Y	N	N	Y	N
15 ***Ewing***	Y	Y	Y	N	N	Y	N
16 ***Manzullo***	Y	Y	Y	?	?	?	?
17 Evans	Y	N	Y	N	Y	N	N
18 ***LaHood***	Y	Y	Y	N	N	Y	N
19 Poshard	Y	Y	Y	N	Y	N	N
20 ***Shimkus***	Y	Y	Y	N	N	Y	N
INDIANA							
1 Visclosky	Y	N	Y	N	N	N	N
2 ***McIntosh***	Y	Y	Y	N	Y	Y	N
3 Roemer	Y	Y	Y	N	Y	N	N
4 ***Souder***	Y	Y	Y	Y	Y	Y	?
5 ***Buyer***	Y	N	Y	N	N	Y	N
6 ***Burton***	Y	Y	Y	N	N	?	N
7 ***Pease***	Y	Y	Y	N	N	Y	N
8 ***Hostettler***	Y	N	Y	N	N	Y	N
9 Hamilton	Y	N	Y	N	N	N	N
10 Carson	Y	N	Y	N	Y	N	N
IOWA							
1 ***Leach***	Y	N	Y	Y	Y	Y	N
2 ***Nussle***	Y	Y	Y	N	Y	Y	N
3 Boswell	Y	N	Y	N	N	N	N
4 ***Ganske***	Y	Y	Y	N	N	Y	N
5 ***Latham***	Y	Y	Y	N	N	Y	N
KANSAS							
1 ***Moran***	Y	Y	Y	N	N	Y	N
2 ***Ryun***	Y	Y	Y	N	N	Y	N
3 ***Snowbarger***	Y	Y	Y	N	N	Y	N
4 ***Tiahrt***	Y	Y	Y	N	N	Y	N
KENTUCKY							
1 ***Whitfield***	Y	Y	Y	N	?	Y	Y
2 ***Lewis***	Y	Y	Y	N	N	Y	N
3 ***Northup***	Y	N	Y	N	N	Y	N
4 ***Bunning***	Y	Y	Y	N	N	Y	N
5 ***Rogers***	Y	Y	Y	N	N	Y	N
6 Baesler	Y	N	Y	N	N	N	N
LOUISIANA							
1 ***Livingston***	Y	N	Y	N	N	Y	N
2 Jefferson	Y	N	Y	N	N	N	?
3 ***Tauzin***	Y	N	Y	N	N	Y	N
4 ***McCrery***	Y	N	Y	?	?	?	?
5 ***Cooksey***	Y	N	Y	N	N	Y	N
6 ***Baker***	Y	Y	Y	N	Y	Y	N
7 John	Y	N	Y	N	N	N	N
MAINE							
1 Allen	Y	N	Y	N	N	N	Y
2 Baldacci	Y	N	Y	N	N	N	N
MARYLAND							
1 ***Gilchrest***	Y	N	Y	N	N	Y	N
2 ***Ehrlich***	Y	N	Y	N	Y	Y	N
3 Cardin	Y	N	Y	N	Y	N	N
4 Wynn	Y	N	Y	N	Y	N	N
5 Hoyer	Y	N	Y	N	Y	N	N
6 ***Bartlett***	Y	Y	Y	N	Y	Y	N
7 Cummings	Y	N	Y	N	N	N	N
8 ***Morella***	Y	N	N	Y	Y	Y	?
MASSACHUSETTS							
1 Olver	Y	N	Y	N	N	N	Y
2 Neal	Y	N	Y	N	N	N	N
3 McGovern	Y	N	N	N	N	N	Y
4 Frank	N	Y	N	N	N	N	N
5 Meehan	Y	N	Y	Y	Y	N	N
6 Tierney	Y	Y	Y	N	N	N	N
7 Markey	Y	N	N	N	N	N	?
8 Kennedy	Y	N	Y	N	N	N	N
9 Moakley	Y	N	Y	N	N	N	N
10 Delahunt	Y	N	N	N	N	N	Y
MICHIGAN							
1 Stupak	Y	N	Y	N	N	N	N
2 ***Hoekstra***	Y	N	N	Y	Y	Y	N
3 ***Ehlers***	Y	N	N	N	N	Y	N
4 ***Camp***	Y	Y	Y	N	N	Y	N
5 Barcia	Y	N	Y	N	N	N	N
6 ***Upton***	Y	Y	Y	N	N	Y	N
7 ***Smith***	Y	Y	Y	N	Y	Y	N
8 Stabenow	Y	N	Y	N	N	N	N
9 Kildee	Y	N	Y	N	N	N	N
10 Bonior	Y	N	N	N	N	N	Y
11 ***Knollenberg***	Y	N	Y	N	N	Y	N
12 Levin	Y	N	Y	N	Y	N	N
13 Rivers	Y	N	N	N	Y	N	N
14 Conyers	Y	Y	N	N	N	N	?
15 Kilpatrick	Y	N	Y	N	N	N	N
16 Dingell	Y	N	Y	N	N	N	N

	181	182	183	184	185	186	187
MINNESOTA							
1 ***Gutknecht***	Y	N	Y	N	N	Y	?
2 Minge	Y	N	N	Y	Y	N	N
3 ***Ramstad***	Y	Y	Y	N	N	Y	N
4 Vento	Y	N	N	Y	N	N	N
5 Sabo	Y	N	Y	N	P	N	Y
6 Luther	Y	N	N	N	Y	N	N
7 Peterson	Y	Y	Y	N	P	N	N
8 Oberstar	Y	N	N	N	N	N	N
MISSISSIPPI							
1 ***Wicker***	?	?	?	?	?	?	?
2 Thompson	Y	N	Y	N	N	N	N
3 ***Pickering***	Y	Y	Y	N	N	Y	N
4 ***Parker***	?	?	?	?	?	?	?
5 Taylor	Y	N	Y	N	Y	N	N
MISSOURI							
1 Clay	Y	N	Y	N	N	N	Y
2 ***Talent***	Y	Y	Y	N	N	Y	N
3 Gephardt	Y	N	Y	N	Y	N	Y
4 Skelton	N	N	Y	N	N	N	N
5 McCarthy	Y	N	N	N	Y	N	–
6 Danner	Y	Y	Y	N	N	N	N
7 ***Blunt***	Y	Y	Y	N	N	Y	N
8 ***Emerson***	Y	Y	Y	N	Y	Y	N
9 ***Hulshof***	Y	Y	Y	N	Y	Y	N
MONTANA							
AL ***Hill***	Y	Y	Y	Y	Y	Y	N
NEBRASKA							
1 ***Bereuter***	Y	N	Y	N	N	Y	N
2 ***Christensen***	Y	Y	Y	Y	Y	Y	N
3 ***Barrett***	Y	Y	Y	N	Y	Y	N
NEVADA							
1 ***Ensign***	Y	Y	Y	N	Y	Y	N
2 ***Gibbons***	Y	Y	Y	Y	N	Y	N
NEW HAMPSHIRE							
1 ***Sununu***	Y	Y	Y	N	Y	Y	N
2 ***Bass***	Y	Y	Y	N	N	Y	N
NEW JERSEY							
1 Andrews	Y	N	Y	N	Y	N	N
2 ***LoBiondo***	Y	Y	Y	N	N	Y	N
3 ***Saxton***	Y	N	Y	N	N	Y	N
4 ***Smith***	Y	N	Y	N	N	Y	N
5 ***Roukema***	Y	Y	Y	N	N	Y	N
6 Pallone	Y	N	Y	N	N	N	Y
7 ***Franks***	Y	Y	N	N	N	Y	N
8 Pascrell	Y	N	Y	N	N	N	?
9 Rothman	Y	N	Y	N	N	N	N
10 Payne	Y	N	N	N	N	N	Y
11 ***Frelinghuysen***	Y	N	Y	N	N	Y	N
12 ***Pappas***	Y	N	Y	N	N	Y	N
13 Menendez	Y	N	Y	N	N	N	N
NEW MEXICO							
1 Vacant							
2 ***Skeen***	Y	N	Y	N	N	Y	N
3 ***Redmond***	Y	N	Y	N	N	Y	N
NEW YORK							
1 ***Forbes***	Y	Y	Y	N	N	Y	N
2 ***Lazio***	Y	N	Y	N	N	Y	N
3 ***King***	Y	N	Y	N	N	Y	N
4 McCarthy	Y	N	Y	N	N	N	N
5 Ackerman	Y	N	Y	N	N	N	?
6 Meeks	?	?	?	?	?	?	?
7 Manton	Y	N	Y	N	N	N	Y
8 Nadler	Y	N	N	N	N	N	?
9 Schumer	Y	N	Y	Y	Y	N	?
10 Towns	Y	Y	Y	?	?	?	?
11 Owens	Y	Y	N	N	N	N	?
12 Velázquez	Y	N	N	N	N	N	N
13 ***Fossella***	Y	N	Y	N	N	Y	N
14 Maloney	Y	N	Y	Y	Y	N	N
15 Rangel	Y	Y	Y	Y	N	N	?
16 Serrano	Y	Y	N	N	N	N	?
17 Engel	Y	N	N	N	N	N	N
18 Lowey	Y	N	N	N	N	N	N
19 ***Kelly***	Y	Y	Y	N	N	Y	N
20 ***Gilman***	Y	N	Y	N	N	Y	N
21 McNulty	Y	N	Y	N	N	N	N
22 ***Solomon***	Y	N	Y	N	N	Y	N
23 ***Boehlert***	Y	N	Y	N	N	Y	N
24 ***McHugh***	Y	N	Y	N	N	Y	N
25 ***Walsh***	Y	N	Y	N	N	Y	N
26 Hinchey	Y	N	N	N	N	N	?
27 ***Paxon***	Y	Y	Y	N	N	Y	N
28 Slaughter	Y	N	N	N	N	N	Y
29 LaFalce	Y	N	Y	N	Y	N	N

	181	182	183	184	185	186	187
30 ***Quinn***	?	?	#	?	?	?	–
31 ***Houghton***	Y	N	Y	N	N	Y	N
NORTH CAROLINA							
1 Clayton	Y	N	Y	N	Y	N	Y
2 Etheridge	Y	N	Y	N	Y	N	N
3 ***Jones***	Y	N	Y	Y	Y	Y	N
4 Price	Y	N	Y	N	Y	N	N
5 ***Burr***	Y	N	Y	N	Y	?	N
6 ***Coble***	Y	Y	Y	N	Y	Y	N
7 McIntyre	N	N	Y	N	Y	N	Y
8 Hefner	Y	N	Y	N	Y	N	?
9 ***Myrick***	Y	Y	Y	Y	Y	Y	N
10 ***Ballenger***	Y	Y	Y	Y	Y	Y	N
11 ***Taylor***	?	?	?	?	?	?	?
12 Watt	Y	Y	Y	N	N	N	Y
NORTH DAKOTA							
AL Pomeroy	Y	N	Y	N	Y	N	Y
OHIO							
1 ***Chabot***	Y	Y	Y	Y	Y	Y	N
2 ***Portman***	Y	N	Y	Y	Y	Y	N
3 Hall	Y	N	Y	N	N	N	Y
4 ***Oxley***	?	N	Y	N	N	?	?
5 ***Gillmor***	Y	Y	Y	N	N	Y	N
6 Strickland	Y	N	Y	N	N	N	?
7 ***Hobson***	Y	N	Y	Y	Y	Y	N
8 ***Boehner***	Y	N	Y	N	N	?	N
9 Kaptur	Y	Y	Y	Y	N	N	?
10 Kucinich	Y	N	N	N	N	N	N
11 Stokes	Y	Y	Y	N	N	N	N
12 ***Kasich***	Y	Y	Y	Y	Y	Y	N
13 Brown	Y	N	N	Y	Y	N	Y
14 Sawyer	N	N	Y	N	Y	N	Y
15 ***Pryce***	Y	Y	Y	N	Y	Y	N
16 ***Regula***	Y	Y	Y	N	N	Y	N
17 Traficant	Y	Y	Y	N	N	Y	N
18 ***Ney***	Y	Y	Y	?	?	Y	N
19 ***LaTourette***	Y	N	Y	N	Y	Y	N
OKLAHOMA							
1 ***Largent***	Y	Y	Y	Y	Y	Y	N
2 ***Coburn***	Y	Y	Y	Y	Y	?	N
3 ***Watkins***	Y	Y	Y	N	Y	Y	N
4 ***Watts***	Y	Y	Y	N	Y	Y	N
5 ***Istook***	Y	Y	Y	Y	N	Y	N
6 ***Lucas***	Y	Y	Y	N	Y	Y	N
OREGON							
1 Furse	Y	Y	N	N	N	N	?
2 ***Smith***	Y	N	Y	N	N	Y	N
3 Blumenauer	?	N	Y	N	N	N	N
4 DeFazio	Y	Y	N	N	N	?	?
5 Hooley	Y	Y	N	N	Y	N	N
PENNSYLVANIA							
1 Brady	Y	N	Y	N	N	N	?
2 Fattah	Y	N	Y	N	N	N	Y
3 Borski	Y	N	Y	N	N	N	N
4 Klink	Y	N	Y	N	N	N	N
5 ***Peterson***	Y	Y	Y	N	N	Y	N
6 Holden	Y	N	Y	N	N	N	N
7 ***Weldon***	Y	Y	Y	N	N	Y	N
8 ***Greenwood***	Y	Y	Y	N	N	Y	N
9 ***Shuster***	Y	N	Y	N	N	Y	N
10 ***McDade***	?	?	?	?	?	?	?
11 Kanjorski	Y	N	Y	N	N	N	N
12 Murtha	Y	N	Y	N	N	N	N
13 ***Fox***	Y	Y	Y	N	Y	Y	N
14 Coyne	?	N	Y	N	N	N	Y
15 McHale	Y	N	Y	N	N	N	N
16 ***Pitts***	Y	Y	Y	N	N	Y	N
17 ***Gekas***	Y	N	Y	N	N	Y	N
18 Doyle	Y	N	Y	N	N	N	N
19 ***Goodling***	Y	N	+	N	N	Y	N
20 Mascara	Y	N	Y	N	N	N	N
21 ***English***	Y	Y	Y	N	N	Y	N
RHODE ISLAND							
1 Kennedy	Y	N	Y	N	Y	N	N
2 Weygand	Y	N	Y	N	Y	N	?
SOUTH CAROLINA							
1 ***Sanford***	Y	Y	Y	Y	Y	Y	N
2 ***Spence***	Y	N	Y	N	N	Y	?
3 ***Graham***	Y	Y	Y	Y	Y	Y	?
4 ***Inglis***	Y	Y	Y	Y	Y	Y	?
5 Spratt	?	?	?	N	Y	N	N
6 Clyburn	Y	N	Y	N	N	N	N
SOUTH DAKOTA							
AL ***Thune***	Y	Y	Y	N	N	Y	N

	181	182	183	184	185	186	187
TENNESSEE							
1 ***Jenkins***	Y	N	Y	N	N	Y	N
2 ***Duncan***	Y	Y	Y	N	N	Y	N
3 ***Wamp***	Y	Y	Y	N	Y	Y	N
4 ***Hilleary***	Y	Y	Y	Y	Y	Y	N
5 Clement	Y	N	Y	N	N	?	?
6 Gordon	Y	N	Y	N	N	N	N
7 ***Bryant***	Y	Y	Y	N	N	Y	N
8 Tanner	Y	N	Y	N	Y	N	Y
9 Ford	Y	N	Y	N	N	N	Y
TEXAS							
1 Sandlin	Y	N	Y	N	N	N	N
2 Turner	Y	N	Y	N	Y	N	N
3 ***Johnson, Sam***	?	?	?	?	?	?	?
4 Hall	Y	Y	Y	Y	Y	Y	N
5 ***Sessions***	Y	Y	Y	Y	Y	Y	?
6 ***Barton***	Y	N	Y	Y	Y	Y	N
7 ***Archer***	Y	Y	Y	Y	Y	Y	N
8 ***Brady***	Y	Y	Y	N	Y	Y	N
9 Lampson	Y	N	Y	N	N	N	N
10 Doggett	Y	Y	N	N	Y	N	N
11 Edwards	Y	N	Y	Y	Y	N	Y
12 ***Granger***	Y	Y	Y	N	N	Y	N
13 ***Thornberry***	Y	Y	Y	Y	Y	Y	N
14 ***Paul***	Y	Y	N	N	Y	?	N
15 Hinojosa	Y	N	Y	N	N	N	N
16 Reyes	Y	N	Y	N	N	N	?
17 Stenholm	Y	N	Y	Y	Y	N	Y
18 Jackson-Lee	Y	N	Y	N	N	N	N
19 ***Combest***	Y	Y	Y	N	Y	Y	N
20 Gonzalez	?	?	?	?	?	?	?
21 ***Smith***	Y	Y	Y	N	N	Y	N
22 ***DeLay***	Y	N	Y	N	N	Y	?
23 ***Bonilla***	Y	Y	Y	N	N	Y	N
24 Frost	Y	N	Y	N	N	N	N
25 Bentsen	Y	N	Y	N	Y	N	N
26 ***Armey***	Y	N	Y	N	N	Y	N
27 Ortiz	Y	N	Y	N	N	N	Y
28 Rodriguez	Y	N	Y	N	N	N	N
29 Green	Y	Y	Y	N	N	N	?
30 Johnson, E.B.	Y	N	Y	N	N	N	N
UTAH							
1 ***Hansen***	Y	N	Y	N	N	Y	N
2 ***Cook***	Y	Y	Y	N	N	Y	N
3 ***Cannon***	Y	Y	Y	N	Y	Y	N
VERMONT							
AL *Sanders*	Y	N	N	N	N	N	?
VIRGINIA							
1 ***Bateman***	+	–	+	–	–	+	–
2 Pickett	N	N	Y	N	Y	N	Y
3 Scott	Y	N	Y	N	Y	N	Y
4 Sisisky	Y	N	Y	Y	N	N	Y
5 Goode	Y	Y	Y	N	Y	N	Y
6 ***Goodlatte***	Y	Y	Y	N	Y	Y	N
7 ***Bliley***	Y	N	Y	N	N	Y	N
8 Moran	Y	N	Y	?	?	N	N
9 Boucher	Y	N	Y	N	N	N	N
10 ***Wolf***	Y	N	Y	Y	Y	Y	N
11 ***Davis***	Y	N	Y	N	Y	Y	N
WASHINGTON							
1 ***White***	Y	N	Y	N	N	Y	N
2 ***Metcalf***	Y	Y	Y	N	N	Y	N
3 ***Smith, Linda***	Y	Y	Y	N	Y	Y	N
4 ***Hastings***	Y	Y	Y	Y	Y	Y	N
5 ***Nethercutt***	Y	Y	Y	Y	Y	Y	N
6 Dicks	Y	N	Y	N	N	N	N
7 McDermott	Y	N	N	N	Y	N	?
8 ***Dunn***	Y	N	Y	N	N	Y	N
9 Smith, Adam	Y	N	Y	N	Y	N	N
WEST VIRGINIA							
1 Mollohan	Y	N	Y	N	N	N	?
2 Wise	Y	N	Y	N	N	N	N
3 Rahall	Y	N	N	N	N	N	N
WISCONSIN							
1 ***Neumann***	Y	Y	Y	Y	Y	Y	N
2 ***Klug***	Y	Y	Y	Y	Y	Y	N
3 Kind	Y	N	N	Y	Y	N	N
4 Kleczka	Y	N	Y	Y	Y	N	N
5 Barrett	Y	N	N	Y	Y	N	N
6 ***Petri***	Y	Y	N	N	N	Y	N
7 Obey	Y	N	N	Y	N	Y	Y
8 Johnson	Y	N	Y	N	N	N	N
9 ***Sensenbrenner***	Y	Y	N	Y	Y	Y	N
WYOMING							
AL ***Cubin***	Y	Y	Y	Y	Y	Y	?

Southern states - Ala., Ark., Fla., Ga., Ky., La., Miss., N.C., Okla., S.C., Tenn., Texas, Va.

House Votes 188, 189, 190, 191, 192, 193, 194

Key

- Y Voted for (yea).
- # Paired for.
- + Announced for.
- N Voted against (nay).
- X Paired against.
- − Announced against.
- P Voted "present."
- C Voted "present" to avoid possible conflict of interest.
- ? Did not vote or otherwise make a position known.

Democrats **Republicans** *Independent*

---

188. S 1150. Agriculture Reauthorization Conference Report/Rule. Adoption of the rule (H Res 446) to dispose of the conference report on the bill to reauthorize agricultural research and education programs through fiscal 2002. The rule would have allowed a point of order to strike $818 million in funding in the conference report to restore food stamps to 250,000 legal immigrants. Rejected 120-289: R 118-98; D 2-190 (ND 1-140, SD 1-50); I 0-1. May 22, 1998.

189. HR 2676. Internal Revenue Service Overhaul/Motion to Instruct. Coyne, D-Pa., motion to instruct the House conferees to insist on the provisions in the House bill and thereby not further delay restructuring of the Internal Revenue Service. Motion agreed to 388-1: R 200-1; D 187-0 (ND 137-0, SD 50-0); I 1-0. May 22, 1998.

190. HR 2400. Surface Transportation Reauthorization Conference Report/Rule. Adoption of the rule (H Res 449) to waive points of order against the conference report on the bill to reauthorize federal highway and mass transit programs. Adopted 359-29: R 192-11; D 166-18 (ND 126-9, SD 40-9); I 1-0. May 22, 1998.

191. HR 2400. Surface Transportation Reauthorization/Motion to Recommit. Obey, D-Wis., motion to recommit the conference report to the Committee of Conference with instructions to strike those provisions of the conference report that prohibit or reduce service-connected disability compensation to veterans relating to use of tobacco products. Motion rejected 190-195: R 87-114; D 102-81 (ND 70-65, SD 32-16); I 1-0. May 22, 1998.

192. HR 2400. Surface Transportation Reauthorization/Conference Report. Adoption of the conference report on the bill to authorize $216 billion over six years for federal highway and mass transit programs. Adopted (thus cleared for the president) 297-86: R 143-56; D 153-30 (ND 116-19, SD 36-12); I 1-0. May 22, 1998.

193. Procedural Motion/Journal. Approval of the House Journal of Friday, May 22, 1998. Approved 354-35: R 188-14; D 165-21 (ND 121-14, SD 44-7); I 1-0. June 03, 1998.

194. HR 3808. Carl D. Pursell Post Office/Passage. McHugh, R-N.Y., motion to suspend the rules and pass the bill to designate a U.S. post office in Plymouth, Mich., as the "Carl D. Pursell Post Office." Motion agreed to 389-0: R 201-0; D 187-0 (ND 136-0, SD 51-0); I 1-0. June 03, 1998. A two-thirds majority of those present and voting (260 in this case) is required for passage under suspension of the rules.

		188	189	190	191	192	193	194
ALABAMA								
1	**Callahan**	N	Y	?	?	Y	Y	Y
2	**Everett**	N	Y	N	Y	Y	Y	Y
3	**Riley**	N	Y	N	Y	Y	Y	Y
4	**Aderholt**	N	Y	Y	Y	Y	Y	Y
5	Cramer	N	Y	N	Y	Y	Y	Y
6	**Bachus**	N	Y	N	Y	Y	Y	Y
7	Hilliard	N	Y	Y	N	Y	N	Y
ALASKA								
AL	**Young**	N	Y	Y	Y	Y	Y	?
ARIZONA								
1	**Salmon**	Y	Y	Y	Y	N	?	?
2	Pastor	N	Y	Y	Y	Y	Y	Y
3	**Stump**	N	Y	Y	Y	N	Y	Y
4	**Shadegg**	Y	Y	N	Y	N	?	?
5	**Kolbe**	Y	Y	Y	N	N	?	?
6	**Hayworth**	N	Y	Y	N	+	+	
ARKANSAS								
1	Berry	N	Y	Y	N	Y	Y	Y
2	Snyder	N	Y	Y	Y	Y	Y	Y
3	**Hutchinson**	N	?	Y	N	Y	Y	Y
4	Dickey	N	Y	Y	N	Y	?	?
CALIFORNIA								
1	**Riggs**	?	?	?	?	?	Y	Y
2	**Herger**	Y	Y	Y	N	Y	Y	Y
3	Fazio	N	Y	Y	?	?	N	Y
4	**Doolittle**	Y	Y	Y	N	Y	?	Y
5	Matsui	N	Y	Y	N	Y	Y	Y
6	Woolsey	N	Y	Y	Y	Y	Y	Y
7	Miller	?	?	?	?	?	Y	Y
8	Pelosi	N	Y	Y	Y	Y	Y	Y
9	Lee	N	Y	Y	N	Y	?	Y
10	Tauscher	N	Y	Y	N	Y	Y	Y
11	**Pombo**	Y	Y	Y	N	Y	Y	Y
12	Lantos	N	Y	Y	Y	Y	Y	Y
13	Stark	?	Y	Y	Y	N	Y	Y
14	Eshoo	N	Y	Y	N	Y	Y	Y
15	**Campbell**	N	Y	Y	N	Y	Y	Y
16	Lofgren	N	?	?	?	?	Y	Y
17	Farr	N	Y	Y	N	Y	Y	Y
18	Condit	N	Y	Y	Y	Y	Y	Y
19	**Radanovich**	Y	Y	Y	N	Y	Y	Y
20	Dooley	N	Y	Y	Y	Y	Y	Y
21	**Thomas**	Y	Y	Y	Y	Y	Y	Y
22	Capps, L.	N	Y	Y	Y	Y	Y	Y
23	**Gallegly**	Y	Y	Y	N	Y	Y	Y
24	Sherman	N	Y	Y	Y	Y	Y	Y
25	**McKeon**	Y	Y	Y	N	Y	Y	Y
26	Berman	N	Y	Y	Y	Y	N	Y
27	**Rogan**	N	Y	Y	Y	N	Y	Y
28	**Dreier**	Y	Y	Y	N	Y	Y	Y
29	Waxman	N	Y	?	Y	N	Y	Y
30	Becerra	N	Y	N	Y	Y	Y	Y
31	Martinez	N	Y	Y	Y	Y	?	?
32	Dixon	N	Y	Y	N	+	Y	Y
33	Roybal-Allard	N	Y	Y	Y	Y	Y	Y
34	Torres	?	?	?	?	?	?	?
35	Waters	N	Y	Y	Y	Y	Y	Y
36	Harman	?	?	?	?	?	Y	Y
37	Millender-McD.	N	Y	Y	N	Y	Y	Y

		188	189	190	191	192	193	194
38	**Horn**	N	Y	N	Y	Y	Y	Y
39	**Royce**	Y	Y	Y	Y	?	Y	Y
40	**Lewis**	N	Y	Y	N	Y	Y	Y
41	**Kim**	N	Y	N	Y	Y	Y	Y
42	Brown	N	Y	Y	N	Y	N	Y
43	**Calvert**	N	Y	Y	N	Y	Y	Y
44	**Bono, M.**	Y	Y	Y	N	Y	+	+
45	**Rohrabacher**	Y	Y	Y	N	N	?	?
46	Sanchez	N	Y	Y	Y	Y	Y	Y
47	**Cox**	Y	Y	Y	N	N	?	?
48	**Packard**	Y	Y	Y	Y	Y	Y	Y
49	**Bilbray**	N	Y	Y	N	Y	Y	Y
50	Filner	N	Y	Y	N	Y	N	Y
51	**Cunningham**	Y	Y	Y	Y	Y	Y	Y
52	**Hunter**	Y	Y	Y	N	N	Y	Y
COLORADO								
1	DeGette	N	Y	?	Y	Y	Y	Y
2	Skaggs	−	+	+	+	−	Y	Y
3	**McInnis**	Y	Y	Y	N	Y	?	?
4	**Schaffer**	Y	Y	Y	Y	N	N	Y
5	**Hefley**	Y	?	?	?	?	N	Y
6	**Schaefer**	Y	Y	Y	N	Y	Y	Y
CONNECTICUT								
1	Kennelly	N	Y	Y	Y	Y	Y	Y
2	Gejdenson	N	Y	Y	Y	Y	Y	Y
3	DeLauro	N	Y	Y	Y	Y	Y	Y
4	**Shays**	N	Y	N	Y	N	Y	Y
5	Maloney	N	Y	Y	Y	Y	Y	Y
6	**Johnson**	N	Y	Y	N	Y	Y	Y
DELAWARE								
AL	**Castle**	N	Y	Y	Y	N	Y	Y
FLORIDA								
1	**Scarborough**	Y	Y	Y	Y	Y	Y	Y
2	Boyd	N	Y	N	Y	N	Y	Y
3	Brown	N	Y	Y	N	Y	Y	Y
4	**Fowler**	Y	Y	Y	N	Y	Y	Y
5	Thurman	N	Y	N	Y	N	Y	Y
6	**Stearns**	Y	Y	Y	Y	Y	Y	Y
7	**Mica**	Y	Y	Y	N	Y	+	+
8	**McCollum**	Y	Y	Y	Y	Y	Y	Y
9	**Bilirakis**	Y	Y	Y	Y	Y	Y	Y
10	**Young**	Y	Y	Y	Y	Y	Y	Y
11	Davis	N	Y	Y	Y	Y	Y	Y
12	**Canady**	Y	N	Y	N	Y	Y	Y
13	**Miller**	Y	Y	Y	Y	Y	Y	Y
14	**Goss**	Y	Y	Y	Y	Y	Y	Y
15	**Weldon**	N	Y	Y	N	Y	Y	Y
16	**Foley**	?	?	?	?	?	Y	Y
17	Meek	N	Y	Y	N	Y	Y	Y
18	**Ros-Lehtinen**	N	Y	Y	Y	?	Y	Y
19	Wexler	N	Y	N	?	Y	Y	Y
20	Deutsch	?	?	?	?	?	Y	Y
21	**Diaz-Balart**	N	Y	N	Y	?	?	+
22	**Shaw**	Y	Y	N	Y	Y	Y	Y
23	Hastings	N	Y	N	Y	N	N	Y
GEORGIA								
1	**Kingston**	Y	?	?	?	X	Y	Y
2	Bishop	N	Y	Y	N	Y	Y	Y
3	**Collins**	Y	Y	Y	Y	Y	Y	Y
4	**McKinney**	N	Y	Y	N	Y	Y	Y
5	Lewis	N	N	Y	N	Y	Y	Y
6	**Gingrich**				N			
7	**Barr**	Y	Y	Y	Y	Y	Y	Y
8	**Chambliss**	N	Y	Y	N	Y	Y	Y
9	**Deal**	Y	Y	Y	Y	Y	Y	Y
10	**Norwood**	Y	Y	Y	Y	Y	Y	Y
11	**Linder**	Y	Y	N	Y	Y	Y	Y
HAWAII								
1	Abercrombie	N	Y	Y	N	Y	Y	Y
2	Mink	N	Y	Y	N	Y	Y	Y
IDAHO								
1	**Chenoweth**	N	Y	Y	N	Y	Y	Y
2	**Crapo**	N	Y	Y	Y	Y	Y	Y
ILLINOIS								
1	Rush	N	Y	Y	N	Y	Y	Y
2	Jackson	N	Y	Y	N	Y	Y	Y
3	Lipinski	N	Y	Y	N	Y	Y	Y
4	Gutierrez	N	Y	Y	N	Y	Y	Y
5	Blagojevich	N	Y	Y	N	Y	?	?
6	**Hyde**	N	?	?	?	?	Y	Y
7	Davis	N	Y	Y	N	Y	Y	Y
8	**Crane**	Y	Y	Y	N	Y	?	?
9	Yates	N	Y	N	Y	N	Y	Y
10	**Porter**	N	Y	Y	N	Y	+	+
11	**Weller**	N	Y	Y	N	Y	Y	Y
12	Costello	N	Y	Y	N	Y	N	Y

ND Northern Democrats   SD Southern Democrats

	188	189	190	191	192	193	194
13 **Fawell**	Y	?	?	?	?	Y	Y
14 **Hastert**	Y	Y	Y	N	Y	Y	Y
15 **Ewing**	N	Y	Y	N	Y	Y	Y
16 **Manzullo**	Y	Y	Y	N	Y	N	Y
17 Evans	N	Y	Y	Y	Y	Y	Y
18 **LaHood**	N	Y	Y	N	Y	Y	Y
19 Poshard	N	Y	Y	Y	Y	?	?
20 **Shimkus**	N	Y	Y	N	Y	Y	Y
INDIANA							
1 Visclosky	N	Y	Y	N	Y	N	Y
2 **McIntosh**	Y	Y	Y	Y	Y	Y	Y
3 Roemer	N	Y	Y	N	Y	Y	Y
4 **Souder**	N	Y	N	Y	N	Y	Y
5 **Buyer**	Y	Y	Y	N	Y	Y	?
6 **Burton**	N	?	?	?	#	?	?
7 **Pease**	N	Y	Y	N	Y	Y	Y
8 **Hostettler**	Y	Y	Y	N	Y	Y	Y
9 Hamilton	N	Y	Y	N	Y	Y	Y
10 Carson	N	Y	Y	Y	Y	Y	Y
IOWA							
1 **Leach**	N	Y	Y	Y	Y	Y	Y
2 **Nussle**	N	Y	Y	N	Y	N	Y
3 Boswell	N	Y	Y	Y	Y	Y	Y
4 **Ganske**	N	Y	Y	N	Y	Y	Y
5 **Latham**	N	Y	Y	N	Y	Y	Y
KANSAS							
1 **Moran**	N	Y	Y	N	Y	N	Y
2 **Ryun**	N	Y	Y	N	Y	Y	Y
3 **Snowbarger**	Y	Y	Y	N	Y	Y	Y
4 **Tiahrt**	Y	Y	Y	Y	Y	Y	?
KENTUCKY							
1 **Whitfield**	Y	Y	Y	Y	Y	Y	Y
2 **Lewis**	Y	Y	Y	Y	Y	Y	Y
3 **Northup**	N	Y	Y	N	Y	Y	Y
4 **Bunning**	N	Y	Y	Y	Y	Y	Y
5 **Rogers**	Y	Y	Y	N	+	Y	Y
6 Baesler	N	Y	Y	Y	Y	Y	?
LOUISIANA							
1 **Livingston**	N	Y	Y	N	Y	Y	Y
2 Jefferson	N	Y	Y	Y	Y	Y	Y
3 **Tauzin**	Y	Y	Y	N	Y	Y	Y
4 **McCrery**	Y	?	?	?	?	Y	Y
5 **Cooksey**	N	Y	Y	N	Y	Y	Y
6 **Baker**	N	Y	Y	Y	Y	Y	Y
7 John	N	Y	Y	N	Y	Y	Y
MAINE							
1 Allen	N	Y	Y	N	Y	Y	Y
2 Baldacci	N	Y	Y	N	Y	Y	Y
MARYLAND							
1 **Gilchrest**	N	Y	Y	N	Y	Y	Y
2 **Ehrlich**	Y	Y	Y	N	Y	Y	Y
3 Cardin	N	Y	Y	Y	N	Y	Y
4 Wynn	N	Y	Y	Y	Y	Y	Y
5 Hoyer	N	Y	Y	Y	N	Y	Y
6 **Bartlett**	Y	Y	Y	Y	N	Y	Y
7 Cummings	N	Y	Y	N	Y	Y	Y
8 **Morella**	N	?	Y	Y	N	Y	Y
MASSACHUSETTS							
1 Olver	N	Y	Y	Y	Y	Y	Y
2 Neal	N	Y	Y	?	?	Y	Y
3 McGovern	N	Y	Y	Y	Y	Y	Y
4 Frank	N	Y	Y	N	Y	Y	Y
5 Meehan	N	Y	?	?	?	?	?
6 Tierney	N	Y	N	Y	N	Y	Y
7 Markey	N	Y	Y	N	Y	Y	Y
8 Kennedy	N	Y	Y	Y	Y	Y	Y
9 Moakley	N	Y	Y	Y	Y	?	?
10 Delahunt	N	Y	Y	Y	Y	Y	Y
MICHIGAN							
1 Stupak	N	Y	Y	Y	Y	Y	Y
2 **Hoekstra**	Y	?	?	?	?	Y	Y
3 **Ehlers**	N	Y	Y	N	Y	Y	Y
4 **Camp**	Y	Y	Y	N	Y	Y	Y
5 Barcia	N	Y	Y	N	Y	?	Y
6 **Upton**	N	Y	Y	N	Y	Y	Y
7 **Smith**	N	Y	Y	Y	Y	Y	Y
8 Stabenow	N	Y	Y	Y	Y	Y	Y
9 Kildee	N	Y	Y	Y	Y	Y	Y
10 Bonior	N	Y	Y	N	Y	Y	Y
11 **Knollenberg**	Y	Y	Y	N	Y	Y	Y
12 Levin	N	Y	Y	N	Y	Y	Y
13 Rivers	N	Y	Y	Y	Y	Y	Y
14 Conyers	?	?	?	?	?	Y	Y
15 Kilpatrick	N	Y	Y	N	Y	Y	Y
16 Dingell	N	Y	Y	N	Y	Y	Y
MINNESOTA							
1 **Gutknecht**	N	Y	Y	N	Y	Y	Y
2 Minge	N	Y	N	Y	N	Y	Y
3 **Ramstad**	N	Y	Y	N	Y	Y	Y
4 Vento	N	Y	Y	N	Y	Y	Y
5 Sabo	N	Y	N	Y	N	N	Y
6 Luther	N	Y	Y	Y	Y	Y	Y
7 Peterson	N	Y	Y	Y	Y	Y	Y
8 Oberstar	N	Y	Y	N	Y	N	Y
MISSISSIPPI							
1 **Wicker**	?	?	?	?	#	N	Y
2 Thompson	N	Y	Y	Y	Y	N	Y
3 **Pickering**	Y	Y	Y	N	Y	Y	Y
4 **Parker**	?	?	?	?	X	?	Y
5 Taylor	N	Y	Y	Y	N	N	Y
MISSOURI							
1 Clay	N	Y	Y	N	Y	N	Y
2 **Talent**	N	Y	Y	Y	Y	Y	Y
3 Gephardt	N	?	?	?	Y	N	Y
4 Skelton	N	Y	Y	N	Y	Y	Y
5 McCarthy	N	Y	Y	Y	Y	Y	Y
6 Danner	N	Y	Y	N	Y	Y	Y
7 **Blunt**	Y	?	Y	?	?	Y	Y
8 **Emerson**	Y	Y	Y	Y	N	Y	Y
9 **Hulshof**	Y	Y	Y	Y	Y	Y	Y
MONTANA							
AL **Hill**	N	Y	Y	Y	Y	Y	Y
NEBRASKA							
1 **Bereuter**	N	Y	Y	N	Y	Y	Y
2 **Christensen**	N	Y	N	Y	N	Y	Y
3 **Barrett**	N	Y	N	Y	N	Y	Y
NEVADA							
1 **Ensign**	Y	Y	Y	Y	Y	N	Y
2 **Gibbons**	Y	Y	Y	Y	Y	Y	Y
NEW HAMPSHIRE							
1 **Sununu**	Y	Y	Y	N	Y	Y	Y
2 **Bass**	Y	Y	Y	N	Y	Y	Y
NEW JERSEY							
1 Andrews	N	Y	Y	N	Y	Y	Y
2 **LoBiondo**	N	Y	Y	N	Y	N	Y
3 **Saxton**	Y	Y	Y	N	Y	Y	Y
4 **Smith**	N	Y	Y	Y	Y	Y	Y
5 **Roukema**	Y	Y	Y	Y	N	?	?
6 Pallone	N	Y	Y	N	Y	Y	Y
7 **Franks**	N	Y	Y	N	Y	Y	Y
8 Pascrell	N	Y	Y	N	Y	Y	Y
9 Rothman	N	Y	Y	N	Y	+	+
10 Payne	N	Y	Y	N	Y	Y	Y
11 **Frelinghuysen**	Y	Y	Y	N	N	Y	Y
12 **Pappas**	N	Y	Y	Y	Y	Y	Y
13 Menendez	N	Y	Y	N	Y	N	Y
NEW MEXICO							
1 Vacant							
2 **Skeen**	N	Y	Y	N	Y	Y	Y
3 **Redmond**	N	Y	Y	N	Y	Y	Y
NEW YORK							
1 **Forbes**	N	Y	Y	N	Y	?	?
2 **Lazio**	N	Y	Y	N	Y	Y	Y
3 **King**	?	?	?	?	?	Y	Y
4 McCarthy	N	Y	Y	N	Y	Y	Y
5 Ackerman	N	Y	Y	N	Y	Y	Y
6 Meeks	?	?	?	?	?	Y	Y
7 Manton	N	Y	Y	Y	Y	Y	Y
8 Nadler	N	Y	Y	N	Y	Y	Y
9 Schumer	N	Y	Y	N	Y	Y	Y
10 Towns	?	?	?	?	?	Y	Y
11 Owens	N	Y	Y	N	Y	Y	Y
12 Velázquez	N	Y	Y	N	Y	N	Y
13 **Fossella**	N	Y	Y	N	Y	Y	Y
14 Maloney	N	Y	N	Y	N	Y	Y
15 Rangel	N	?	?	?	?	Y	Y
16 Serrano	N	Y	Y	N	Y	Y	Y
17 Engel	N	Y	Y	Y	Y	Y	Y
18 Lowey	N	Y	Y	Y	Y	Y	Y
19 **Kelly**	N	Y	Y	Y	Y	Y	Y
20 **Gilman**	N	Y	Y	Y	N	Y	Y
21 McNulty	N	Y	Y	Y	N	Y	Y
22 **Solomon**	Y	Y	Y	N	Y	Y	Y
23 **Boehlert**	N	Y	Y	N	Y	Y	Y
24 **McHugh**	N	Y	Y	N	Y	Y	Y
25 **Walsh**	N	Y	Y	N	Y	Y	Y
26 Hinchey	N	Y	Y	N	Y	Y	Y
27 **Paxon**	Y	Y	Y	N	Y	Y	Y
28 Slaughter	N	Y	Y	Y	Y	Y	Y
29 LaFalce	N	Y	Y	Y	Y	?	?
30 **Quinn**	–	+	+	+	#	Y	Y
31 **Houghton**	Y	Y	Y	N	Y	Y	Y
NORTH CAROLINA							
1 Clayton	N	Y	Y	Y	Y	Y	Y
2 Etheridge	N	Y	Y	Y	Y	N	Y
3 **Jones**	Y	Y	Y	Y	N	Y	Y
4 Price	N	Y	Y	Y	N	Y	Y
5 **Burr**	Y	?	?	?	X	Y	Y
6 **Coble**	Y	Y	Y	N	Y	Y	Y
7 McIntyre	N	Y	Y	Y	Y	Y	Y
8 Hefner	N	Y	Y	Y	Y	Y	Y
9 **Myrick**	Y	Y	Y	Y	N	Y	Y
10 **Ballenger**	Y	Y	Y	Y	N	Y	Y
11 **Taylor**	?	?	?	?	?	Y	Y
12 Watt	N	Y	Y	N	Y	Y	Y
NORTH DAKOTA							
AL Pomeroy	N	Y	Y	Y	Y	Y	Y
OHIO							
1 **Chabot**	Y	Y	N	Y	N	Y	Y
2 **Portman**	Y	Y	Y	N	N	Y	Y
3 Hall	N	Y	Y	N	Y	Y	Y
4 **Oxley**	N	Y	Y	N	Y	Y	Y
5 **Gillmor**	N	Y	Y	Y	Y	Y	Y
6 Strickland	N	Y	Y	Y	N	Y	Y
7 **Hobson**	Y	Y	N	Y	N	Y	Y
8 **Boehner**	Y	Y	N	N	N	Y	Y
9 Kaptur	N	Y	Y	Y	Y	Y	Y
10 Kucinich	N	Y	Y	N	Y	N	Y
11 Stokes	N	Y	Y	N	Y	?	?
12 **Kasich**	N	Y	Y	Y	N	Y	Y
13 Brown	N	Y	Y	Y	N	Y	Y
14 Sawyer	N	Y	Y	Y	Y	?	?
15 **Pryce**	N	Y	Y	Y	Y	Y	Y
16 **Regula**	N	Y	Y	Y	Y	Y	Y
17 Traficant	Y	Y	Y	N	Y	Y	Y
18 **Ney**	N	Y	Y	N	Y	Y	Y
19 **LaTourette**	N	Y	Y	N	Y	Y	Y
OKLAHOMA							
1 **Largent**	Y	Y	N	Y	N	Y	Y
2 **Coburn**	Y	Y	N	Y	N	Y	Y
3 **Watkins**	N	Y	Y	Y	Y	Y	Y
4 **Watts**	N	Y	Y	Y	Y	N	Y
5 **Istook**	Y	Y	Y	N	Y	Y	Y
6 **Lucas**	N	Y	Y	Y	Y	Y	Y
OREGON							
1 Furse	?	?	?	?	?	?	?
2 **Smith**	P	?	?	?	?	?	Y
3 Blumenauer	N	Y	Y	N	Y	Y	Y
4 DeFazio	?	?	?	?	?	N	Y
5 Hooley	N	Y	Y	N	Y	?	?
PENNSYLVANIA							
1 Brady	N	Y	Y	N	Y	Y	Y
2 Fattah	N	Y	Y	N	Y	Y	Y
3 Borski	N	Y	Y	N	Y	Y	Y
4 Klink	N	Y	Y	N	Y	Y	Y
5 **Peterson**	N	Y	Y	N	Y	Y	Y
6 Holden	N	Y	Y	N	Y	Y	Y
7 **Weldon**	N	Y	Y	Y	Y	Y	Y
8 **Greenwood**	Y	Y	Y	N	Y	Y	Y
9 **Shuster**	Y	Y	Y	N	Y	Y	Y
10 **McDade**	N	?	?	?	#	Y	Y
11 Kanjorski	N	Y	Y	N	Y	Y	Y
12 Murtha	N	Y	Y	N	Y	Y	Y
13 **Fox**	N	Y	Y	Y	Y	N	Y
14 Coyne	N	Y	Y	N	Y	Y	Y
15 McHale	N	Y	Y	Y	Y	Y	Y
16 **Pitts**	Y	Y	Y	N	Y	Y	Y
17 **Gekas**	Y	Y	Y	N	Y	Y	Y
18 Doyle	N	Y	Y	N	Y	Y	Y
19 **Goodling**	Y	Y	Y	N	Y	Y	Y
20 Mascara	N	Y	Y	N	Y	Y	Y
21 **English**	Y	Y	Y	Y	Y	N	Y
RHODE ISLAND							
1 Kennedy	N	Y	N	Y	N	Y	Y
2 Weygand	N	Y	Y	Y	Y	Y	Y
SOUTH CAROLINA							
1 **Sanford**	Y	?	?	?	X	Y	Y
2 **Spence**	Y	Y	Y	N	N	Y	Y
3 **Graham**	Y	Y	?	?	–	Y	Y
4 **Inglis**	Y	Y	Y	Y	N	?	?
5 Spratt	N	Y	Y	Y	Y	Y	Y
6 Clyburn	N	Y	Y	N	Y	?	?
SOUTH DAKOTA							
AL **Thune**	N	Y	Y	N	Y	+	+
TENNESSEE							
1 **Jenkins**	Y	Y	Y	N	Y	Y	Y
2 **Duncan**	Y	Y	Y	N	Y	Y	Y
3 **Wamp**	Y	?	?	?	#	?	?
4 **Hilleary**	Y	Y	Y	Y	Y	Y	Y
5 Clement	N	Y	Y	N	Y	Y	Y
6 Gordon	N	Y	Y	Y	Y	Y	Y
7 **Bryant**	N	Y	Y	N	Y	Y	Y
8 Tanner	N	Y	Y	Y	Y	Y	Y
9 Ford	N	Y	Y	N	Y	N	Y
TEXAS							
1 Sandlin	N	Y	Y	Y	Y	Y	Y
2 Turner	N	Y	Y	Y	Y	Y	Y
3 **Johnson, Sam**	?	?	?	?	X	Y	Y
4 Hall	N	Y	N	Y	N	Y	Y
5 **Sessions**	Y	Y	Y	Y	N	N	Y
6 **Barton**	Y	Y	Y	Y	N	Y	Y
7 **Archer**	Y	?	?	?	X	Y	Y
8 **Brady**	Y	Y	Y	Y	Y	Y	Y
9 Lampson	N	Y	Y	Y	Y	?	Y
10 Doggett	N	Y	N	Y	Y	Y	Y
11 Edwards	N	Y	N	Y	N	Y	Y
12 **Granger**	N	Y	Y	N	Y	Y	Y
13 **Thornberry**	N	Y	Y	Y	N	Y	Y
14 **Paul**	Y	Y	Y	N	N	Y	Y
15 Hinojosa	N	Y	Y	N	Y	Y	Y
16 Reyes	?	?	?	?	?	Y	Y
17 Stenholm	N	?	?	?	?	Y	Y
18 Jackson-Lee	N	Y	Y	Y	Y	Y	Y
19 **Combest**	N	Y	Y	N	Y	Y	Y
20 Gonzalez	?	?	?	?	?	?	?
21 **Smith**	Y	Y	Y	N	Y	Y	Y
22 **DeLay**	Y	Y	Y	N	Y	?	?
23 **Bonilla**	N	Y	Y	Y	N	Y	Y
24 Frost	N	Y	Y	N	Y	Y	Y
25 Bentsen	N	Y	N	Y	N	Y	Y
26 **Armey**	Y	Y	Y	N	Y	Y	Y
27 Ortiz	N	Y	Y	N	Y	Y	Y
28 Rodriguez	N	Y	Y	Y	Y	Y	Y
29 Green	?	?	?	?	#	Y	Y
30 Johnson, E.B.	N	Y	Y	N	Y	Y	Y
UTAH							
1 **Hansen**	N	Y	Y	N	Y	Y	Y
2 **Cook**	N	Y	Y	N	Y	Y	Y
3 **Cannon**	Y	Y	Y	Y	Y	Y	Y
VERMONT							
AL *Sanders*	N	Y	Y	Y	Y	Y	Y
VIRGINIA							
1 **Bateman**	–	+	+	+	+	Y	Y
2 Pickett	N	Y	Y	Y	Y	N	Y
3 Scott	N	Y	Y	Y	Y	Y	Y
4 Sisisky	N	Y	Y	Y	Y	Y	Y
5 Goode	Y	Y	Y	Y	Y	Y	Y
6 **Goodlatte**	Y	Y	Y	Y	Y	Y	Y
7 **Bliley**	Y	Y	Y	N	Y	Y	Y
8 Moran	N	Y	Y	Y	N	Y	Y
9 Boucher	N	Y	?	?	?	?	?
10 **Wolf**	N	Y	Y	Y	N	Y	Y
11 **Davis**	N	Y	Y	N	Y	Y	Y
WASHINGTON							
1 **White**	Y	Y	Y	N	N	Y	Y
2 **Metcalf**	Y	Y	Y	Y	Y	Y	Y
3 **Smith, Linda**	N	Y	Y	Y	N	?	?
4 **Hastings**	Y	Y	Y	Y	N	Y	Y
5 **Nethercutt**	N	Y	Y	Y	N	Y	Y
6 Dicks	N	?	Y	Y	N	Y	Y
7 McDermott	N	Y	Y	Y	Y	N	Y
8 **Dunn**	Y	Y	Y	N	Y	Y	Y
9 Smith, Adam	N	Y	Y	Y	N	Y	Y
WEST VIRGINIA							
1 Mollohan	N	?	?	?	?	Y	Y
2 Wise	N	Y	Y	N	Y	Y	Y
3 Rahall	N	Y	Y	N	Y	Y	Y
WISCONSIN							
1 **Neumann**	Y	Y	Y	Y	Y	Y	Y
2 **Klug**	Y	Y	Y	N	Y	Y	Y
3 Kind	N	Y	Y	Y	Y	Y	Y
4 Kleczka	N	Y	Y	Y	Y	Y	Y
5 Barrett	N	Y	N	Y	Y	Y	Y
6 **Petri**	Y	Y	Y	N	Y	Y	Y
7 Obey	N	Y	N	Y	N	?	?
8 Johnson	N	Y	Y	Y	Y	Y	Y
9 **Sensenbrenner**	Y	Y	Y	Y	N	Y	Y
WYOMING							
AL **Cubin**	Y	Y	Y	N	Y	Y	Y

Southern states - Ala., Ark., Fla., Ga., Ky., La., Miss., N.C., Okla., S.C., Tenn., Texas, Va.

House Votes 195, 196, 197, 198, 199, 200, 201

195. HR 3630. Steven Schiff Post Office/Passage. McHugh, R-N.Y., motion to suspend the rules and pass the bill to designate a U.S. post office in Albuquerque, N.M., as the "Steven Schiff Post Office." Motion agreed to 391-0: R 202-0; D 188-0 (ND 136-0, SD 52-0); I 1-0. June 3, 1998. A two-thirds majority of those present and voting (261 in this case) is required for passage under suspension of the rules.

196. H J Res 78. Religious Freedom Constitutional Amendment/Rule. Adoption of the rule (H Res 453) to provide for House floor consideration of a constitutional amendment that would guarantee an individual's right to pray and recognize their religious beliefs on public property, including schools. Adopted 248-169: R 221-1; D 27-167 (ND 11-132, SD 16-35); I 0-1. June 4, 1998.

197. HR 3433. Vocational Rehabilitation Services/Passage. Passage of the bill to restructure the system under which individuals collecting disability benefits under the Social Security and Supplemental Security Income programs receive vocational rehabilitation services by providing a voucher that beneficiaries may use to obtain such services. Passed 410-1: R 218-0; D 191-1 (ND 138-1, SD 53-0); I 1-0. June 4, 1998. A "yea" was a vote in support of the president's position.

198. H J Res 78. Religious Freedom Constitutional Amendment/Reference to God. Bishop, D-Ga., amendment to delete the measure's reference to God, adding instead language stating that the measure's intent is "to secure the people's right to freedom of religion." Rejected 6-419: R 1-223; D 5-195 (ND 3-146, SD 2-49); I 0-1. June 4, 1998.

199. H J Res 78. Religious Freedom Constitutional Amendment/Equal Access to Benefits. Bishop, D-Ga., amendment to strike language at the end of the measure regarding equal access to benefits on account of religion. Rejected 23-399: R 5-217; D 18-181 (ND 5-142, SD 13-39); I 0-1. June 4, 1998.

200. H J Res 78. Religious Freedom Constitutional Amendment/Recommit. Scott, D-Va., motion to recommit the bill to the Judiciary Committee with instructions to report it back with a substitute amendment reaffirming the First Amendment to the Constitution. Motion rejected 203-223: R 23-201; D 179-22 (ND 141-8, SD 38-14); I 1-0. June 4, 1998.

201. H J Res 78. Religious Freedom Constitutional Amendment/Passage. Passage of the joint resolution to propose a constitutional amendment to guarantee an individual's right to pray and recognize their religious beliefs on public property, including schools. It also would bar governments from requiring anyone to participate in any religious activity or to deny benefits on the basis of religion. Rejected 224-203: R 197-28; D 27-174 (ND 9-140, SD 18-34); I 0-1. June 4, 1998. A two-thirds majority vote of those present and voting (285 in this case) is required to pass a joint resolution proposing an amendment to the Constitution.

Key

- Y Voted for (yea).
- \# Paired for.
- \+ Announced for.
- N Voted against (nay).
- X Paired against.
- – Announced against.
- P Voted "present."
- C Voted "present" to avoid possible conflict of interest.
- ? Did not vote or otherwise make a position known.

Democrats **Republicans** *Independent*

		195	196	197	198	199	200	201
ALABAMA								
1	Callahan	Y	Y	Y	N	N	N	Y
2	Everett	Y	Y	Y	N	N	N	Y
3	Riley	Y	Y	Y	N	N	N	Y
4	Aderholt	Y	Y	Y	N	N	N	Y
5	Cramer	Y	Y	Y	N	N	N	Y
6	Bachus	Y	Y	Y	N	N	N	Y
7	Hilliard	Y	N	Y	N	N	Y	N
ALASKA								
AL	Young	Y	Y	Y	N	N	N	Y
ARIZONA								
1	Salmon	?	Y	Y	N	N	N	Y
2	Pastor	Y	N	Y	N	N	Y	N
3	Stump	Y	Y	Y	N	N	N	Y
4	Shadegg	?	Y	Y	N	N	N	Y
5	Kolbe	?	Y	Y	N	N	N	Y
6	Hayworth	+	Y	Y	N	N	N	Y
ARKANSAS								
1	Berry	Y	Y	Y	N	Y	N	Y
2	Snyder	Y	N	Y	N	N	Y	N
3	Hutchinson	Y	Y	Y	N	N	N	Y
4	Dickey	?	Y	Y	N	N	N	Y
CALIFORNIA								
1	Riggs	Y	Y	Y	N	N	N	Y
2	Herger	Y	?	Y	N	N	N	Y
3	Fazio	Y	N	Y	N	N	Y	N
4	Doolittle	?	Y	Y	N	N	N	Y
5	Matsui	Y	N	Y	N	N	Y	N
6	Woolsey	Y	N	Y	N	N	Y	N
7	Miller	Y	N	Y	N	N	Y	N
8	Pelosi	Y	N	Y	N	N	Y	N
9	Lee	?	N	Y	N	N	Y	N
10	Tauscher	Y	N	Y	N	N	Y	N
11	Pombo	Y	Y	Y	N	N	N	Y
12	Lantos	Y	N	Y	N	Y	N	N
13	Stark	Y	N	Y	N	N	Y	N
14	Eshoo	Y	N	Y	N	N	Y	N
15	Campbell	Y	Y	Y	N	N	N	Y
16	Lofgren	Y	N	Y	N	N	Y	N
17	Farr	Y	N	Y	N	N	Y	N
18	Condit	Y	Y	Y	N	N	N	Y
19	Radanovich	Y	Y	Y	N	N	N	Y
20	Dooley	Y	N	Y	N	N	Y	N
21	Thomas	Y	Y	Y	N	N	N	Y
22	Capps, L.	Y	N	Y	N	N	Y	N
23	Gallegly	Y	Y	Y	N	N	N	Y
24	Sherman	Y	N	Y	N	N	Y	N
25	McKeon	Y	Y	Y	N	N	N	Y
26	Berman	Y	N	Y	N	N	Y	N
27	Rogan	Y	Y	Y	N	N	N	Y
28	Dreier	Y	Y	Y	N	?	N	Y
29	Waxman	Y	N	Y	N	N	Y	N
30	Becerra	Y	N	Y	N	N	Y	N
31	Martinez	?	N	Y	N	Y	N	N
32	Dixon	Y	N	Y	N	N	Y	N
33	Roybal-Allard	Y	N	Y	N	N	Y	N
34	Torres	?	N	Y	N	N	Y	N
35	Waters	Y	N	Y	N	N	Y	N
36	Harman	?	N	Y	N	N	Y	N
37	Millender-McD.	Y	N	Y	N	N	Y	N

		195	196	197	198	199	200	201
38	Horn	Y	Y	Y	N	N	Y	N
39	Royce	Y	Y	Y	N	N	Y	Y
40	Lewis	Y	Y	Y	N	N	Y	Y
41	Kim	Y	Y	Y	N	N	Y	Y
42	Brown	Y	N	Y	N	N	Y	N
43	Calvert	Y	Y	Y	N	N	N	Y
44	Bono, M.	+	Y	Y	N	N	N	Y
45	Rohrabacher	?	Y	Y	N	N	N	Y
46	Sanchez	Y	N	Y	N	Y	N	N
47	Cox	?	Y	Y	N	N	N	Y
48	Packard	Y	Y	Y	N	N	N	Y
49	Bilbray	Y	Y	Y	N	N	Y	Y
50	Filner	Y	N	Y	N	N	Y	N
51	Cunningham	Y	Y	Y	N	N	N	Y
52	Hunter	Y	Y	Y	N	?	N	Y
COLORADO								
1	DeGette	Y	N	?	N	N	Y	N
2	Skaggs	Y	–	+	N	N	Y	N
3	McInnis	?	Y	Y	N	N	N	Y
4	Schaffer	Y	Y	Y	N	N	N	Y
5	Hefley	Y	Y	Y	N	N	N	Y
6	Schaefer	Y	Y	Y	N	N	N	Y
CONNECTICUT								
1	Kennelly	Y	N	Y	N	N	Y	N
2	Gejdenson	Y	N	Y	N	N	Y	N
3	DeLauro	Y	N	Y	N	N	Y	N
4	Shays	Y	Y	Y	N	N	N	Y
5	Maloney	Y	N	Y	N	N	Y	N
6	Johnson	Y	Y	Y	N	N	N	Y
DELAWARE								
AL	Castle	Y	Y	Y	N	N	Y	N
FLORIDA								
1	Scarborough	Y	Y	Y	N	N	N	Y
2	Boyd	Y	N	Y	N	N	N	Y
3	Brown	Y	?	Y	N	N	Y	N
4	Fowler	Y	Y	Y	N	Y	N	Y
5	Thurman	Y	?	Y	N	N	Y	N
6	Stearns	Y	Y	Y	N	N	N	Y
7	Mica	+	Y	Y	N	N	N	Y
8	McCollum	Y	Y	Y	N	N	N	Y
9	Bilirakis	Y	Y	Y	N	N	N	Y
10	Young	Y	Y	Y	N	N	N	Y
11	Davis	Y	N	Y	N	N	Y	N
12	Canady	Y	Y	Y	N	N	N	Y
13	Miller	Y	Y	Y	N	N	N	Y
14	Goss	Y	Y	Y	N	N	N	Y
15	Weldon	Y	Y	Y	N	N	N	Y
16	Foley	Y	Y	Y	N	N	N	Y
17	Meek	Y	N	Y	N	N	Y	N
18	Ros-Lehtinen	Y	Y	Y	?	?	?	#
19	Wexler	Y	N	Y	N	N	Y	N
20	Deutsch	Y	N	Y	N	N	Y	N
21	Diaz-Balart	+	Y	Y	N	N	N	Y
22	Shaw	Y	Y	Y	N	N	N	Y
23	Hastings	Y	N	Y	N	N	Y	N
GEORGIA								
1	Kingston	Y	Y	Y	N	N	N	Y
2	Bishop	Y	Y	Y	Y	Y	N	Y
3	Collins	Y	Y	?	N	N	N	Y
4	McKinney	Y	N	Y	?	N	Y	N
5	Lewis	Y	N	Y	?	?	–	?
6	Gingrich							Y
7	Barr	Y	Y	Y	N	N	N	Y
8	Chambliss	Y	Y	Y	N	N	N	Y
9	Deal	Y	Y	Y	N	N	N	Y
10	Norwood	Y	Y	Y	N	N	N	Y
11	Linder	Y	Y	Y	N	N	N	Y
HAWAII								
1	Abercrombie	Y	N	Y	N	N	Y	N
2	Mink	Y	N	P	N	N	Y	N
IDAHO								
1	Chenoweth	Y	Y	Y	N	N	N	Y
2	Crapo	Y	Y	Y	N	N	N	Y
ILLINOIS								
1	Rush	Y	N	Y	N	N	Y	N
2	Jackson	Y	N	Y	N	N	Y	N
3	Lipinski	Y	N	Y	N	N	N	Y
4	Gutierrez	Y	N	Y	N	N	Y	N
5	Blagojevich	?	N	Y	N	N	Y	N
6	Hyde	Y	Y	Y	N	N	N	Y
7	Davis	Y	N	Y	N	Y	N	N
8	Crane	?	Y	Y	N	N	N	Y
9	Yates	Y	N	Y	N	N	Y	N
10	Porter	+	Y	Y	N	N	N	Y
11	Weller	Y	Y	Y	N	N	N	Y
12	Costello	Y	N	Y	N	N	N	Y

ND Northern Democrats SD Southern Democrats

	195	196	197	198	199	200	201
13 ***Fawell***	Y	?	?	Y	Y	Y	N
14 ***Hastert***	Y	Y	Y	N	N	N	Y
15 ***Ewing***	Y	Y	Y	N	N	N	Y
16 ***Manzullo***	Y	Y	Y	N	N	N	Y
17 Evans	Y	N	Y	N	N	Y	N
18 ***LaHood***	Y	Y	Y	N	N	N	Y
19 Poshard	?	N	Y	N	N	Y	N
20 ***Shimkus***	Y	Y	Y	N	N	N	Y
INDIANA							
1 Visclosky	Y	N	Y	N	N	Y	N
2 ***McIntosh***	Y	Y	Y	N	N	N	Y
3 Roemer	Y	Y	Y	N	N	N	Y
4 ***Souder***	Y	Y	Y	N	N	N	Y
5 ***Buyer***	Y	Y	Y	N	N	N	Y
6 ***Burton***	?	Y	Y	N	N	N	Y
7 ***Pease***	Y	Y	Y	N	N	N	Y
8 ***Hostettler***	?	Y	Y	N	N	N	N
9 Hamilton	Y	Y	Y	N	N	Y	N
10 Carson	Y	N	Y	N	N	Y	N
IOWA							
1 ***Leach***	Y	Y	Y	N	N	Y	N
2 ***Nussle***	Y	Y	Y	N	N	N	Y
3 Boswell	Y	N	Y	N	N	Y	N
4 ***Ganske***	Y	Y	Y	N	N	N	Y
5 ***Latham***	Y	Y	Y	N	N	N	Y
KANSAS							
1 ***Moran***	Y	Y	Y	N	N	N	Y
2 ***Ryun***	Y	Y	Y	N	N	N	Y
3 ***Snowbarger***	Y	Y	Y	N	N	N	Y
4 ***Tiahrt***	Y	Y	Y	N	N	N	Y
KENTUCKY							
1 ***Whitfield***	Y	Y	Y	N	N	N	Y
2 ***Lewis***	Y	Y	Y	N	N	N	Y
3 ***Northup***	Y	Y	Y	N	N	Y	N
4 ***Bunning***	Y	Y	Y	N	N	N	Y
5 ***Rogers***	Y	Y	Y	N	N	N	Y
6 Baesler	Y	Y	Y	N	N	N	Y
LOUISIANA							
1 ***Livingston***	Y	Y	Y	N	N	N	Y
2 Jefferson	Y	N	Y	Y	Y	Y	N
3 ***Tauzin***	Y	Y	Y	N	N	N	Y
4 ***McCrery***	Y	Y	Y	N	N	N	Y
5 ***Cooksey***	Y	Y	Y	N	N	N	Y
6 ***Baker***	Y	Y	Y	N	N	N	Y
7 John	Y	Y	?	N	N	N	Y
MAINE							
1 Allen	Y	N	Y	N	N	Y	N
2 Baldacci	Y	N	Y	N	N	Y	N
MARYLAND							
1 ***Gilchrest***	Y	Y	Y	N	N	Y	N
2 ***Ehrlich***	Y	Y	Y	N	Y	N	N
3 Cardin	Y	N	Y	N	N	Y	N
4 Wynn	Y	N	Y	N	Y	Y	N
5 Hoyer	Y	N	Y	Y	N	Y	N
6 ***Bartlett***	Y	Y	Y	N	N	N	Y
7 Cummings	Y	N	Y	N	N	Y	N
8 ***Morella***	Y	Y	Y	N	N	Y	N
MASSACHUSETTS							
1 Olver	Y	N	Y	N	N	Y	N
2 Neal	?	N	Y	N	N	Y	N
3 McGovern	Y	?	?	N	N	Y	N
4 Frank	Y	N	N	N	N	Y	N
5 Meehan	?	?	?	N	N	Y	N
6 Tierney	Y	N	Y	N	N	Y	N
7 Markey	Y	N	Y	N	?	Y	N
8 Kennedy	Y	N	Y	N	N	Y	N
9 Moakley	?	N	Y	N	N	Y	N
10 Delahunt	Y	N	Y	N	N	Y	N
MICHIGAN							
1 Stupak	Y	N	Y	N	N	Y	N
2 ***Hoekstra***	Y	Y	Y	N	N	N	Y
3 ***Ehlers***	Y	Y	Y	N	N	N	Y
4 ***Camp***	Y	Y	Y	N	N	N	Y
5 Barcia	Y	Y	Y	N	N	N	Y
6 ***Upton***	Y	Y	Y	N	N	N	Y
7 ***Smith***	Y	Y	Y	N	N	N	Y
8 Stabenow	Y	N	Y	N	N	Y	N
9 Kildee	Y	N	Y	N	N	Y	N
10 Bonior	Y	N	Y	N	N	Y	N
11 ***Knollenberg***	Y	Y	Y	N	N	N	Y
12 Levin	Y	N	Y	N	N	Y	N
13 Rivers	Y	N	Y	N	N	Y	N
14 Conyers	Y	N	Y	N	N	Y	N
15 Kilpatrick	Y	N	Y	N	N	Y	N
16 Dingell	Y	N	Y	N	N	Y	N

	195	196	197	198	199	200	201
MINNESOTA							
1 ***Gutknecht***	Y	Y	Y	N	N	N	Y
2 Minge	Y	N	Y	N	N	Y	N
3 ***Ramstad***	Y	Y	Y	N	N	N	Y
4 Vento	Y	N	Y	N	N	Y	N
5 Sabo	Y	N	Y	N	N	Y	N
6 Luther	Y	N	Y	N	N	Y	N
7 Peterson	Y	Y	Y	N	N	N	Y
8 Oberstar	Y	N	Y	N	N	Y	N
MISSISSIPPI							
1 ***Wicker***	Y	Y	Y	N	N	N	Y
2 Thompson	Y	N	Y	N	N	Y	Y
3 ***Pickering***	Y	Y	Y	N	N	N	Y
4 ***Parker***	Y	Y	Y	N	N	N	Y
5 Taylor	Y	Y	Y	N	N	N	Y
MISSOURI							
1 Clay	Y	?	?	N	N	Y	N
2 ***Talent***	Y	?	Y	N	N	N	Y
3 Gephardt	Y	N	Y	N	N	Y	N
4 Skelton	Y	Y	?	N	N	N	Y
5 McCarthy	Y	N	Y	N	N	Y	N
6 Danner	Y	Y	Y	N	Y	Y	Y
7 ***Blunt***	Y	Y	Y	N	N	N	Y
8 ***Emerson***	Y	Y	Y	N	N	N	Y
9 ***Hulshof***	Y	Y	Y	N	N	N	Y
MONTANA							
AL ***Hill***	Y	Y	Y	N	N	N	Y
NEBRASKA							
1 ***Bereuter***	Y	Y	Y	N	N	N	Y
2 ***Christensen***	Y	Y	Y	N	N	N	Y
3 ***Barrett***	Y	Y	Y	N	N	N	Y
NEVADA							
1 ***Ensign***	Y	?	Y	N	N	Y	Y
2 ***Gibbons***	+	Y	Y	N	N	N	Y
NEW HAMPSHIRE							
1 ***Sununu***	Y	Y	Y	N	N	N	Y
2 ***Bass***	Y	Y	Y	N	N	N	Y
NEW JERSEY							
1 Andrews	Y	N	Y	N	N	Y	N
2 ***LoBiondo***	Y	Y	Y	N	N	N	Y
3 ***Saxton***	Y	Y	Y	N	N	Y	N
4 ***Smith***	Y	Y	Y	N	N	N	Y
5 ***Roukema***	?	Y	Y	N	N	N	Y
6 Pallone	Y	N	Y	N	N	Y	N
7 ***Franks***	Y	Y	Y	N	N	Y	N
8 Pascrell	Y	N	Y	N	N	Y	N
9 Rothman	+	N	Y	N	N	Y	N
10 Payne	Y	?	?	N	Y	Y	N
11 ***Frelinghuysen***	Y	Y	Y	N	N	Y	N
12 ***Pappas***	Y	Y	Y	N	N	N	Y
13 Menendez	Y	N	Y	N	N	Y	N
NEW MEXICO							
1 Vacant							
2 ***Skeen***	Y	Y	Y	N	N	N	Y
3 ***Redmond***	Y	Y	Y	N	N	N	Y
NEW YORK							
1 ***Forbes***	?	Y	Y	N	N	Y	Y
2 ***Lazio***	Y	Y	Y	N	Y	N	Y
3 ***King***	Y	Y	Y	N	N	N	Y
4 McCarthy	Y	N	Y	N	N	Y	N
5 Ackerman	Y	N	Y	N	N	Y	N
6 Meeks	Y	N	?	N	N	Y	N
7 Manton	Y	N	Y	N	N	Y	N
8 Nadler	Y	N	Y	N	N	Y	N
9 Schumer	Y	N	Y	N	N	Y	N
10 Towns	Y	N	Y	N	N	Y	N
11 Owens	Y	N	P	N	N	Y	N
12 Velázquez	Y	N	Y	N	N	Y	N
13 ***Fossella***	Y	Y	Y	N	N	N	Y
14 Maloney	Y	N	Y	N	N	Y	N
15 Rangel	Y	N	Y	N	N	Y	N
16 Serrano	Y	N	Y	N	N	Y	N
17 Engel	Y	N	Y	N	N	Y	N
18 Lowey	Y	N	Y	N	N	Y	N
19 ***Kelly***	Y	Y	Y	N	N	Y	N
20 ***Gilman***	Y	Y	Y	N	N	Y	N
21 McNulty	Y	N	Y	N	N	Y	N
22 ***Solomon***	Y	Y	Y	N	N	N	Y
23 ***Boehlert***	Y	Y	Y	N	N	Y	N
24 ***McHugh***	Y	Y	Y	N	N	N	Y
25 ***Walsh***	Y	Y	Y	N	N	N	Y
26 Hinchey	Y	N	Y	N	N	Y	N
27 ***Paxon***	Y	Y	Y	N	N	N	Y
28 Slaughter	Y	N	Y	N	N	Y	N
29 LaFalce	?	N	Y	N	N	Y	N

	195	196	197	198	199	200	201
30 ***Quinn***	Y	Y	Y	N	N	N	Y
31 ***Houghton***	Y	Y	?	N	N	N	N
NORTH CAROLINA							
1 Clayton	Y	N	Y	N	Y	Y	N
2 Etheridge	Y	N	Y	N	N	Y	N
3 ***Jones***	Y	Y	Y	N	N	N	Y
4 Price	Y	N	Y	N	N	Y	N
5 ***Burr***	Y	Y	Y	N	N	N	Y
6 ***Coble***	Y	Y	Y	N	N	N	Y
7 McIntyre	Y	Y	Y	N	N	N	Y
8 Hefner	Y	N	Y	N	N	Y	N
9 ***Myrick***	Y	Y	Y	N	N	N	Y
10 ***Ballenger***	Y	Y	Y	N	N	N	Y
11 ***Taylor***	Y	Y	Y	N	N	N	Y
12 Watt	Y	N	Y	N	Y	Y	N
NORTH DAKOTA							
AL Pomeroy	Y	N	Y	N	N	Y	N
OHIO							
1 ***Chabot***	Y	Y	Y	N	N	N	Y
2 ***Portman***	Y	Y	Y	N	N	N	Y
3 Hall	Y	Y	Y	N	N	Y	N
4 ***Oxley***	Y	Y	Y	N	N	N	Y
5 ***Gillmor***	Y	Y	Y	N	N	N	Y
6 Strickland	Y	N	Y	N	N	Y	N
7 ***Hobson***	Y	Y	Y	N	N	N	Y
8 ***Boehner***	Y	Y	Y	N	N	N	Y
9 Kaptur	Y	N	Y	N	N	Y	N
10 Kucinich	Y	N	Y	N	N	Y	N
11 Stokes	?	?	Y	N	N	Y	N
12 ***Kasich***	Y	Y	Y	N	N	N	Y
13 Brown	Y	N	Y	N	?	Y	N
14 Sawyer	?	N	Y	N	N	Y	N
15 ***Pryce***	Y	Y	Y	N	N	N	Y
16 ***Regula***	Y	Y	Y	N	N	N	Y
17 Traficant	Y	Y	Y	N	N	N	Y
18 ***Ney***	Y	Y	Y	N	N	N	Y
19 ***LaTourette***	Y	Y	Y	N	N	N	N
OKLAHOMA							
1 ***Largent***	Y	Y	?	N	N	N	Y
2 ***Coburn***	Y	Y	?	N	N	N	Y
3 ***Watkins***	Y	Y	Y	N	N	N	Y
4 ***Watts***	Y	Y	Y	N	N	N	Y
5 ***Istook***	Y	Y	Y	N	N	N	Y
6 ***Lucas***	Y	Y	Y	N	N	N	Y
OREGON							
1 Furse	?	?	?	?	?	?	X
2 ***Smith***	Y	Y	?	N	N	N	Y
3 Blumenauer	Y	N	Y	N	N	Y	N
4 DeFazio	Y	N	Y	N	N	Y	N
5 Hooley	Y	N	Y	N	N	Y	N
PENNSYLVANIA							
1 Brady	Y	N	Y	N	N	Y	N
2 Fattah	Y	N	Y	N	N	Y	N
3 Borski	Y	N	Y	N	N	Y	N
4 Klink	Y	N	Y	N	Y	Y	N
5 ***Peterson***	Y	Y	Y	N	N	N	Y
6 Holden	Y	N	Y	N	N	Y	N
7 ***Weldon***	Y	Y	Y	N	N	N	Y
8 ***Greenwood***	Y	Y	Y	N	N	Y	N
9 ***Shuster***	Y	Y	Y	N	N	N	Y
10 ***McDade***	Y	Y	?	?	?	?	?
11 Kanjorski	Y	N	Y	N	N	Y	N
12 Murtha	Y	Y	Y	N	N	Y	N
13 ***Fox***	Y	Y	Y	N	N	Y	N
14 Coyne	Y	N	Y	N	N	Y	N
15 McHale	Y	N	Y	N	N	Y	N
16 ***Pitts***	Y	Y	Y	N	N	N	Y
17 ***Gekas***	Y	Y	?	N	N	N	Y
18 Doyle	Y	N	Y	N	N	Y	N
19 ***Goodling***	Y	Y	Y	N	N	N	Y
20 Mascara	Y	N	Y	N	N	Y	N
21 ***English***	Y	N	Y	N	N	N	Y
RHODE ISLAND							
1 Kennedy	Y	N	Y	N	N	Y	N
2 Weygand	Y	N	Y	N	N	Y	N
SOUTH CAROLINA							
1 ***Sanford***	Y	Y	Y	N	N	N	Y
2 ***Spence***	Y	Y	Y	N	N	N	Y
3 ***Graham***	Y	Y	Y	N	N	N	Y
4 ***Inglis***	?	Y	Y	N	N	N	Y
5 Spratt	Y	?	Y	N	Y	Y	N
6 Clyburn	?	Y	Y	N	Y	Y	N
SOUTH DAKOTA							
AL ***Thune***	+	Y	Y	N	N	N	Y

	195	196	197	198	199	200	201
TENNESSEE							
1 ***Jenkins***	Y	Y	Y	N	N	N	Y
2 ***Duncan***	Y	Y	Y	N	N	N	Y
3 ***Wamp***	?	Y	Y	N	N	N	Y
4 ***Hilleary***	Y	Y	Y	N	N	N	Y
5 Clement	Y	Y	Y	N	N	N	Y
6 Gordon	Y	N	Y	N	N	N	Y
7 ***Bryant***	Y	Y	Y	N	N	N	Y
8 Tanner	Y	Y	Y	N	Y	Y	Y
9 Ford	Y	N	Y	N	N	Y	Y
TEXAS							
1 Sandlin	Y	Y	Y	N	N	N	Y
2 Turner	Y	Y	Y	N	N	N	Y
3 ***Johnson, Sam***	Y	Y	Y	N	N	N	Y
4 Hall	Y	Y	Y	N	N	N	Y
5 ***Sessions***	Y	Y	Y	N	N	N	Y
6 ***Barton***	Y	Y	Y	N	N	N	Y
7 ***Archer***	Y	Y	Y	N	N	N	Y
8 ***Brady***	Y	Y	Y	N	N	N	Y
9 Lampson	Y	N	Y	N	N	Y	N
10 Doggett	Y	N	Y	N	N	Y	N
11 Edwards	Y	N	Y	N	N	Y	N
12 ***Granger***	Y	Y	Y	N	N	N	Y
13 ***Thornberry***	Y	Y	Y	N	N	N	Y
14 ***Paul***	Y	Y	Y	N	Y	N	N
15 Hinojosa	Y	N	Y	N	N	Y	N
16 Reyes	Y	N	Y	?	?	?	?
17 Stenholm	Y	Y	Y	N	N	N	Y
18 Jackson-Lee	Y	N	Y	N	N	Y	N
19 ***Combest***	Y	Y	Y	N	N	N	Y
20 Gonzalez	?	?	?	?	?	?	?
21 ***Smith***	Y	Y	Y	N	N	N	Y
22 ***DeLay***	?	Y	Y	N	N	N	Y
23 ***Bonilla***	Y	Y	Y	N	N	N	Y
24 Frost	Y	N	Y	N	N	Y	N
25 Bentsen	Y	N	Y	N	N	Y	N
26 ***Armey***	?	Y	Y	N	N	N	Y
27 Ortiz	Y	Y	Y	N	Y	Y	Y
28 Rodriguez	Y	N	Y	N	N	Y	N
29 Green	Y	N	Y	N	Y	Y	N
30 Johnson, E.B.	Y	N	Y	N	Y	Y	N
UTAH							
1 ***Hansen***	Y	Y	Y	N	N	N	Y
2 ***Cook***	Y	Y	Y	N	N	N	Y
3 ***Cannon***	Y	Y	Y	N	N	N	Y
VERMONT							
AL *Sanders*	Y	N	Y	N	N	Y	N
VIRGINIA							
1 ***Bateman***	Y	Y	Y	N	N	N	Y
2 Pickett	Y	N	Y	N	N	Y	N
3 Scott	Y	N	Y	N	Y	Y	N
4 Sisisky	Y	N	Y	N	N	Y	N
5 Goode	Y	Y	Y	N	N	N	Y
6 ***Goodlatte***	Y	Y	Y	N	N	N	Y
7 ***Bliley***	Y	Y	Y	N	N	N	Y
8 Moran	Y	N	Y	N	N	Y	N
9 Boucher	?	N	Y	N	Y	Y	N
10 ***Wolf***	Y	Y	Y	N	N	N	Y
11 ***Davis***	Y	Y	Y	N	N	N	Y
WASHINGTON							
1 ***White***	Y	Y	Y	N	N	N	N
2 ***Metcalf***	Y	Y	Y	N	N	N	Y
3 ***Smith, Linda***	Y	Y	Y	N	N	N	Y
4 ***Hastings***	Y	Y	Y	N	N	N	Y
5 ***Nethercutt***	Y	Y	Y	N	N	N	Y
6 Dicks	Y	N	Y	N	N	Y	N
7 McDermott	Y	N	Y	N	N	Y	N
8 ***Dunn***	Y	Y	Y	N	N	N	Y
9 Smith, Adam	Y	N	Y	N	N	Y	N
WEST VIRGINIA							
1 Mollohan	Y	?	?	?	?	?	#
2 Wise	Y	N	Y	N	N	Y	N
3 Rahall	Y	Y	Y	N	N	N	Y
WISCONSIN							
1 ***Neumann***	Y	Y	Y	N	N	N	Y
2 ***Klug***	Y	Y	Y	N	N	N	Y
3 Kind	Y	N	Y	N	N	Y	N
4 Kleczka	Y	N	Y	N	N	Y	N
5 Barrett	Y	N	Y	N	N	Y	N
6 ***Petri***	Y	Y	Y	N	N	N	Y
7 Obey	?	N	Y	N	N	Y	N
8 Johnson	Y	N	Y	N	N	Y	N
9 ***Sensenbrenner***	Y	Y	Y	N	N	N	Y
WYOMING							
AL ***Cubin***	Y	Y	Y	N	N	N	Y

Southern states - Ala., Ark., Fla., Ga., Ky., La., Miss., N.C., Okla., S.C., Tenn., Texas, Va.

House Votes 202, 203, 204, 205, 206, 207, 208

202. H Con Res 285. Tiananmen Square Resolution/Adoption. Adoption of the concurrent resolution to express the sense of the Congress that the president should reconsider his decision to be formally received in Tiananmen Square. Adopted 305-116: R 219-4; D 85-112 (ND 64-82, SD 21-30); I 1-0. June 4, 1998.

203. S 1150. Agriculture Reauthorization Conference Report/Consideration. Judgment of the House on proceeding to the consideration of the conference report on the bill to reauthorize agricultural research and education programs through fiscal 2002, despite the Solomon, R-N.Y., point of order regarding intergovernmental unfunded mandates. Agreed to consider the conference report 324-91: R 135-86; D 188-5 (ND 139-3, SD 49-2); I 1-0. June 4, 1998.

204. S 1150. Agricultural Reauthorization Conference Report/Adoption. Adoption of the conference report on the bill to reauthorize agricultural research and education programs through fiscal 2002. The conference report restores about $800 million over five years in funding for food stamp benefits for certain legal immigrants; directs about $500 million in mandatory funding for crop insurance programs; and directs about $600 million over five years to a new, mandatory agricultural research program. Adopted (thus cleared for the president) 364-50: R 170-48; D 193-2 (ND 144-0, SD 49-2); I 1-0. June 4, 1998.

205. H Con Res 284. Fiscal 1999 Budget Resolution/Rule. Adoption of the rule (H Res 455) to provide for House floor consideration of the concurrent resolution to adopt a five-year budget plan to reduce federal spending over 1999-2003 by $101 billion below levels provided under the Balanced Budget Act of 1997. Savings from the spending cuts would finance tax cuts, including an elimination of the so-called marriage penalty. Adopted 216-197: R 215-4; D 1-192 (ND 1-140, SD 0-52); I 0-1. June 4, 1998.

206. HR 3989. User Fee Authorization/Recommit. Moakley, D-Mass., motion to recommit the bill to the Ways and Means Committee with instructions to report it back with a substitute amendment to express the sense of the House that user fees in the Fiscal 1999 Budget Resolution (HConRes284) should be enacted as soon as possible. Motion rejected 0-416: R 0-221; D 0-194 (ND 0-143, SD 0-51); I 0-1. June 5, 1998.

207. HR 3989. User Fee Authorization/Passage. Passage of the bill to authorize the 36 user fee proposals contained in President Clinton's fiscal 1999 budget proposal. Rejected 0-421: R 0-223; D 0-197 (ND 0-145, SD 0-52); I 0-1. June 5, 1998.

208. H Con Res 284. Fiscal 1999 Budget Resolution/Conservative Action Team Substitute. Neumann, R-Wis., substitute amendment to adopt a five-year budget plan that would seek to limit the growth of government spending to the rate of inflation, while calling for $150 billion in tax reductions over five years, and increasing defense spending above current levels by $56 billion over five years. Rejected 158-262: R 155-67; D 3-194 (ND 0-146, SD 3-48); I 0-1. June 5, 1998.

Key

- **Y** Voted for (yea).
- **#** Paired for.
- **+** Announced for.
- **N** Voted against (nay).
- **X** Paired against.
- **−** Announced against.
- **P** Voted "present."
- **C** Voted "present" to avoid possible conflict of interest.
- **?** Did not vote or otherwise make a position known.

Democrats **Republicans** *Independent*

		202	203	204	205	206	207	208
ALABAMA								
1	*Callahan*	Y	Y	Y	Y	N	N	Y
2	*Everett*	Y	Y	Y	Y	N	N	Y
3	*Riley*	Y	Y	Y	Y	N	N	Y
4	*Aderholt*	Y	Y	Y	Y	N	N	Y
5	Cramer	N	Y	Y	N	N	N	N
6	*Bachus*	Y	Y	Y	Y	N	N	Y
7	Hilliard	N	Y	Y	N	N	N	N
ALASKA								
AL	*Young*	Y	Y	Y	?	N	N	Y
ARIZONA								
1	*Salmon*	Y	N	N	Y	N	N	Y
2	Pastor	N	Y	Y	N	N	N	N
3	*Stump*	Y	N	N	Y	N	N	Y
4	*Shadegg*	Y	N	N	Y	N	N	Y
5	*Kolbe*	Y	Y	Y	Y	N	N	N
6	*Hayworth*	Y	Y	Y	Y	N	N	Y
ARKANSAS								
1	Berry	N	Y	Y	N	N	N	N
2	Snyder	Y	Y	Y	N	N	N	N
3	*Hutchinson*	Y	Y	Y	Y	N	N	Y
4	*Dickey*	Y	Y	Y	Y	N	N	Y
CALIFORNIA								
1	*Riggs*	Y	Y	Y	Y	N	N	Y
2	*Herger*	Y	N	N	Y	N	N	Y
3	Fazio	N	Y	Y	N	N	N	N
4	*Doolittle*	Y	N	N	Y	N	N	Y
5	Matsui	N	Y	Y	N	N	N	N
6	Woolsey	Y	Y	Y	N	N	N	N
7	Miller	Y	Y	Y	N	N	N	N
8	Pelosi	Y	?	Y	N	?	N	N
9	Lee	Y	Y	Y	N	N	N	N
10	Tauscher	Y	Y	Y	N	N	N	N
11	*Pombo*	Y	N	Y	Y	N	N	Y
12	Lantos	Y	Y	Y	N	N	N	N
13	Stark	Y	Y	Y	?	N	N	N
14	Eshoo	N	Y	Y	N	N	N	N
15	*Campbell*	Y	Y	Y	N	N	N	N
16	Lofgren	N	Y	Y	N	N	N	N
17	Farr	N	Y	Y	N	N	N	N
18	Condit	N	N	Y	N	N	N	N
19	*Radanovich*	Y	Y	Y	Y	N	N	Y
20	Dooley	N	Y	Y	N	N	N	N
21	*Thomas*	Y	Y	Y	Y	N	N	Y
22	Capps, L.	Y	Y	Y	N	N	N	N
23	*Gallegly*	Y	N	Y	Y	N	N	Y
24	Sherman	Y	Y	Y	N	N	N	N
25	*McKeon*	Y	Y	Y	Y	N	N	Y
26	Berman	N	Y	Y	N	N	N	N
27	*Rogan*	Y	Y	Y	Y	N	N	Y
28	*Dreier*	Y	N	Y	Y	N	N	Y
29	Waxman	N	Y	Y	N	N	N	N
30	Becerra	N	Y	Y	N	N	N	N
31	Martinez	N	Y	?	N	N	N	N
32	Dixon	Y	Y	Y	N	N	N	N
33	Roybal-Allard	N	Y	Y	N	N	N	N
34	Torres	N	Y	Y	N	N	N	N
35	Waters	N	Y	Y	N	N	N	N
36	Harman	Y	+	+	?	?	N	N
37	Millender-McD.	N	Y	Y	N	N	N	N

		202	203	204	205	206	207	208
38	Horn	Y	Y	Y	Y	N	N	N
39	*Royce*	Y	N	N	Y	N	N	Y
40	*Lewis*	Y	Y	Y	Y	N	N	Y
41	*Kim*	N	Y	Y	Y	N	N	N
42	Brown	N	Y	Y	N	N	N	N
43	*Calvert*	Y	Y	Y	Y	N	N	Y
44	*Bono, M.*	Y	Y	Y	Y	N	N	Y
45	*Rohrabacher*	Y	N	N	Y	N	N	Y
46	Sanchez	Y	Y	Y	N	N	N	N
47	*Cox*	Y	Y	Y	Y	N	N	Y
48	*Packard*	Y	Y	Y	Y	N	N	Y
49	*Bilbray*	Y	N	Y	Y	N	N	N
50	Filner	N	Y	Y	N	N	N	N
51	*Cunningham*	Y	N	Y	Y	N	N	Y
52	*Hunter*	Y	Y	N	Y	N	N	Y
COLORADO								
1	DeGette	N	Y	Y	N	N	N	N
2	Skaggs	N	Y	Y	N	N	N	N
3	*McInnis*	Y	Y	Y	Y	N	N	Y
4	*Schaffer*	Y	Y	Y	Y	N	N	Y
5	*Hefley*	Y	N	N	?	N	N	Y
6	*Schaefer*	Y	N	N	Y	N	N	Y
CONNECTICUT								
1	Kennelly	Y	Y	Y	N	N	N	N
2	Gejdenson	Y	Y	Y	N	?	?	?
3	DeLauro	Y	Y	Y	N	N	N	N
4	*Shays*	Y	Y	Y	N	N	N	N
5	Maloney	Y	Y	Y	N	N	N	N
6	*Johnson*	Y	Y	Y	Y	N	N	N
DELAWARE								
AL	*Castle*	Y	Y	Y	N	N	N	N
FLORIDA								
1	*Scarborough*	Y	N	Y	Y	N	N	Y
2	Boyd	Y	Y	Y	N	N	N	N
3	Brown	N	Y	Y	N	N	N	N
4	*Fowler*	Y	Y	Y	Y	N	N	Y
5	Thurman	N	Y	Y	N	N	N	N
6	*Stearns*	Y	Y	N	Y	N	N	Y
7	*Mica*	Y	N	Y	Y	N	N	Y
8	*McCollum*	Y	Y	Y	Y	N	N	Y
9	*Bilirakis*	Y	N	Y	Y	N	N	Y
10	*Young*	Y	N	Y	Y	N	N	Y
11	Davis	N	Y	Y	N	N	N	N
12	*Canady*	Y	Y	Y	Y	N	N	Y
13	*Miller*	Y	N	N	Y	N	N	Y
14	*Goss*	Y	N	N	Y	N	N	Y
15	*Weldon*	Y	N	N	Y	N	N	Y
16	*Foley*	Y	Y	Y	Y	N	N	Y
17	Meek	N	Y	N	N	N	N	N
18	*Ros-Lehtinen*	?	?	?	?	?	?	?
19	Wexler	N	Y	Y	N	N	N	N
20	Deutsch	N	Y	Y	N	N	N	N
21	*Diaz-Balart*	Y	Y	Y	Y	N	N	Y
22	*Shaw*	Y	N	Y	Y	N	N	N
23	Hastings	N	Y	Y	N	N	N	N
GEORGIA								
1	*Kingston*	Y	N	N	Y	N	N	Y
2	Bishop	N	Y	Y	N	N	N	N
3	*Collins*	Y	N	Y	Y	N	N	Y
4	*McKinney*	Y	Y	Y	N	N	N	N
5	Lewis	?	?	?	?	?	?	?
6	*Gingrich*	Y			N	N		
7	*Barr*	Y	N	N	Y	N	N	Y
8	*Chambliss*	Y	Y	Y	Y	N	N	Y
9	*Deal*	Y	N	N	Y	N	N	Y
10	*Norwood*	Y	Y	Y	Y	N	N	Y
11	*Linder*	Y	Y	Y	Y	N	N	?
HAWAII								
1	Abercrombie	Y	Y	Y	N	N	N	N
2	Mink	N	Y	Y	N	N	N	N
IDAHO								
1	*Chenoweth*	Y	N	Y	Y	N	N	Y
2	*Crapo*	Y	N	Y	Y	N	N	N
ILLINOIS								
1	Rush	N	Y	N	N	N	N	N
2	Jackson	Y	Y	Y	N	N	N	N
3	Lipinski	Y	Y	Y	N	N	N	N
4	Gutierrez	Y	Y	Y	N	N	N	N
5	Blagojevich	N	Y	Y	N	N	N	N
6	*Hyde*	Y	Y	Y	Y	N	N	N
7	Davis	N	Y	N	N	N	N	N
8	*Crane*	Y	N	N	Y	N	N	Y
9	Yates	N	?	?	?	N	N	N
10	*Porter*	Y	N	Y	Y	N	N	N
11	*Weller*	Y	Y	Y	Y	N	N	Y
12	Costello	Y	Y	Y	N	N	N	N

ND Northern Democrats   SD Southern Democrats

	202	203	204	205	206	207	208
13 ***Fawell***	Y	N	Y	Y	N	N	N
14 ***Hastert***	Y	N	Y	Y	N	N	Y
15 ***Ewing***	Y	Y	Y	Y	N	N	Y
16 ***Manzullo***	Y	N	N	Y	N	N	Y
17 Evans	Y	Y	Y	N	N	N	N
18 ***LaHood***	Y	Y	Y	Y	N	N	Y
19 Poshard	Y	Y	Y	N	N	N	N
20 ***Shimkus***	Y	Y	Y	Y	N	N	Y
INDIANA							
1 Visclosky	Y	Y	Y	N	N	N	N
2 ***McIntosh***	Y	N	Y	Y	N	N	Y
3 Roemer	N	Y	Y	N	N	N	N
4 ***Souder***	Y	Y	Y	Y	N	N	N
5 ***Buyer***	Y	Y	Y	Y	?	N	N
6 ***Burton***	Y	Y	Y	Y	N	N	Y
7 ***Pease***	Y	Y	Y	Y	N	N	Y
8 ***Hostettler***	Y	N	N	Y	N	N	Y
9 Hamilton	N	Y	Y	N	N	N	N
10 Carson	N	Y	Y	N	N	N	N
IOWA							
1 ***Leach***	N	Y	Y	Y	N	N	N
2 ***Nussle***	Y	Y	Y	Y	N	N	N
3 Boswell	Y	Y	Y	N	N	N	N
4 ***Ganske***	Y	Y	Y	N	N	N	N
5 ***Latham***	Y	Y	Y	Y	N	N	N
KANSAS							
1 ***Moran***	Y	Y	Y	Y	N	N	Y
2 ***Ryun***	Y	Y	Y	Y	N	N	Y
3 ***Snowbarger***	Y	Y	Y	Y	N	N	Y
4 ***Tiahrt***	Y	N	N	Y	N	N	Y
KENTUCKY							
1 ***Whitfield***	Y	N	Y	?	N	N	N
2 ***Lewis***	Y	Y	Y	Y	N	N	Y
3 ***Northup***	Y	Y	Y	Y	N	N	N
4 ***Bunning***	Y	Y	Y	Y	N	N	Y
5 ***Rogers***	Y	Y	Y	Y	N	N	N
6 Baesler	Y	Y	Y	N	N	N	N
LOUISIANA							
1 ***Livingston***	Y	N	Y	Y	N	N	Y
2 Jefferson	N	Y	Y	N	N	N	N
3 ***Tauzin***	Y	Y	Y	Y	N	N	N
4 ***McCrery***	Y	Y	Y	Y	N	N	Y
5 ***Cooksey***	Y	Y	Y	Y	?	N	Y
6 ***Baker***	Y	Y	Y	Y	N	N	Y
7 John	N	Y	Y	N	N	N	N
MAINE							
1 Allen	N	Y	Y	N	N	N	N
2 Baldacci	N	Y	Y	N	N	N	N
MARYLAND							
1 ***Gilchrest***	Y	Y	Y	Y	N	N	N
2 ***Ehrlich***	Y	N	Y	Y	N	N	Y
3 Cardin	Y	Y	Y	N	N	N	N
4 Wynn	N	Y	Y	N	N	N	N
5 Hoyer	N	?	Y	N	N	N	N
6 ***Bartlett***	Y	N	?	Y	N	N	Y
7 Cummings	N	Y	Y	N	N	N	N
8 ***Morella***	Y	Y	Y	N	N	N	N
MASSACHUSETTS							
1 Olver	N	Y	Y	N	N	N	N
2 Neal	N	Y	Y	N	N	N	N
3 McGovern	N	Y	Y	N	N	N	N
4 Frank	?	?	?	?	N	N	N
5 Meehan	N	Y	Y	N	N	N	N
6 Tierney	N	Y	Y	N	N	N	N
7 Markey	N	?	Y	N	N	N	N
8 Kennedy	N	Y	Y	N	?	?	?
9 Moakley	N	Y	Y	N	N	N	N
10 Delahunt	Y	Y	Y	N	N	N	N
MICHIGAN							
1 Stupak	N	Y	Y	N	N	N	N
2 ***Hoekstra***	Y	Y	Y	Y	N	N	Y
3 ***Ehlers***	Y	Y	Y	Y	N	N	N
4 ***Camp***	Y	Y	Y	Y	N	N	Y
5 Barcia	Y	Y	Y	N	N	N	N
6 ***Upton***	Y	Y	Y	Y	N	N	N
7 ***Smith***	Y	Y	Y	Y	N	N	Y
8 Stabenow	Y	Y	Y	N	N	N	N
9 Kildee	Y	Y	Y	N	N	N	N
10 Bonior	Y	Y	Y	N	N	N	N
11 ***Knollenberg***	Y	Y	Y	Y	N	N	Y
12 Levin	Y	Y	Y	N	N	N	N
13 Rivers	Y	Y	Y	N	N	N	N
14 Conyers	N	Y	Y	?	N	N	N
15 Kilpatrick	N	Y	Y	N	N	N	N
16 Dingell	N	Y	Y	N	N	N	N
MINNESOTA							
1 ***Gutknecht***	Y	Y	Y	Y	N	N	N
2 Minge	Y	Y	Y	N	N	N	N
3 ***Ramstad***	Y	Y	Y	Y	N	N	N
4 Vento	N	Y	Y	N	N	N	N
5 Sabo	N	Y	Y	N	N	N	?
6 Luther	N	Y	Y	N	N	N	N
7 Peterson	Y	Y	Y	N	N	N	N
8 Oberstar	N	Y	Y	N	N	N	N
MISSISSIPPI							
1 ***Wicker***	Y	Y	Y	Y	N	N	Y
2 Thompson	Y	Y	Y	N	N	N	N
3 ***Pickering***	Y	Y	Y	Y	N	N	Y
4 ***Parker***	Y	Y	Y	Y	N	N	Y
5 Taylor	Y	N	N	N	N	N	Y
MISSOURI							
1 Clay	Y	Y	Y	N	N	N	N
2 ***Talent***	Y	Y	?	Y	N	N	Y
3 Gephardt	Y	Y	Y	N	N	N	N
4 Skelton	N	Y	Y	N	N	N	N
5 McCarthy	N	Y	Y	N	N	N	N
6 Danner	N	Y	Y	N	N	N	N
7 ***Blunt***	Y	Y	N	Y	N	N	Y
8 ***Emerson***	Y	Y	Y	N	N	N	Y
9 ***Hulshof***	Y	Y	Y	Y	N	N	Y
MONTANA							
AL ***Hill***	Y	Y	Y	Y	N	N	N
NEBRASKA							
1 ***Bereuter***	Y	Y	Y	Y	N	N	N
2 ***Christensen***	Y	Y	Y	Y	N	N	Y
3 ***Barrett***	Y	Y	Y	Y	N	N	N
NEVADA							
1 ***Ensign***	Y	N	N	Y	N	N	Y
2 ***Gibbons***	Y	N	Y	Y	N	N	Y
NEW HAMPSHIRE							
1 ***Sununu***	Y	N	N	Y	N	N	Y
2 ***Bass***	Y	N	N	Y	N	N	N
NEW JERSEY							
1 Andrews	N	Y	Y	N	N	N	N
2 ***LoBiondo***	Y	Y	Y	Y	N	N	N
3 ***Saxton***	Y	N	N	Y	N	N	Y
4 ***Smith***	Y	Y	Y	Y	N	N	N
5 ***Roukema***	Y	N	N	Y	N	N	N
6 Pallone	Y	Y	Y	N	N	N	N
7 ***Franks***	Y	Y	Y	Y	N	N	N
8 Pascrell	Y	Y	Y	N	N	N	N
9 Rothman	Y	Y	Y	N	N	N	N
10 Payne	Y	Y	Y	N	N	N	N
11 ***Frelinghuysen***	Y	Y	Y	Y	N	N	N
12 ***Pappas***	Y	N	N	Y	N	N	Y
13 Menendez	Y	Y	Y	N	N	N	N
NEW MEXICO							
1 Vacant							
2 ***Skeen***	Y	Y	Y	Y	N	N	N
3 ***Redmond***	Y	Y	Y	Y	N	N	Y
NEW YORK							
1 ***Forbes***	Y	Y	Y	Y	N	N	N
2 ***Lazio***	Y	Y	Y	Y	N	N	N
3 ***King***	Y	Y	Y	Y	N	N	N
4 McCarthy	Y	Y	Y	N	N	N	N
5 Ackerman	N	Y	Y	N	N	N	N
6 Meeks	Y	Y	Y	N	N	N	N
7 Manton	Y	Y	Y	N	N	N	N
8 Nadler	Y	Y	Y	N	N	N	N
9 Schumer	Y	Y	Y	?	?	?	N
10 Towns	N	Y	Y	N	N	N	N
11 Owens	N	Y	Y	N	N	N	N
12 Velázquez	N	Y	Y	N	N	N	N
13 ***Fossella***	Y	N	Y	Y	N	N	N
14 Maloney	Y	Y	Y	N	N	N	N
15 Rangel	N	Y	Y	N	N	N	N
16 Serrano	–	Y	Y	N	N	N	N
17 Engel	?	+	+	–	N	N	N
18 Lowey	Y	Y	Y	N	N	N	N
19 ***Kelly***	Y	Y	Y	Y	N	N	N
20 ***Gilman***	Y	N	Y	Y	N	N	N
21 McNulty	Y	Y	Y	N	N	N	N
22 ***Solomon***	Y	N	N	Y	N	N	Y
23 ***Boehlert***	Y	Y	Y	Y	N	N	N
24 ***McHugh***	Y	N	Y	Y	N	N	N
25 ***Walsh***	Y	Y	Y	Y	N	N	N
26 Hinchey	N	N	Y	N	N	N	N
27 ***Paxon***	Y	N	Y	Y	N	N	Y
28 Slaughter	Y	Y	Y	N	N	N	N
29 LaFalce	N	Y	Y	N	N	N	N
30 ***Quinn***	Y	Y	Y	Y	N	N	N
31 ***Houghton***	N	Y	Y	Y	?	?	N
NORTH CAROLINA							
1 Clayton	N	Y	Y	N	N	N	N
2 Etheridge	Y	Y	Y	N	N	N	N
3 ***Jones***	Y	N	Y	Y	N	N	Y
4 Price	Y	Y	Y	N	N	N	N
5 ***Burr***	?	?	?	Y	N	N	Y
6 ***Coble***	Y	N	Y	Y	N	N	Y
7 McIntyre	Y	Y	Y	N	N	N	N
8 Hefner	N	Y	Y	N	N	N	N
9 ***Myrick***	+	–	–	Y	N	N	Y
10 ***Ballenger***	Y	Y	Y	Y	N	N	+
11 ***Taylor***	Y	N	Y	Y	N	N	Y
12 Watt	N	Y	Y	N	N	N	N
NORTH DAKOTA							
AL Pomeroy	Y	Y	Y	N	N	N	N
OHIO							
1 ***Chabot***	Y	N	N	Y	N	N	Y
2 ***Portman***	Y	Y	Y	Y	N	N	Y
3 Hall	Y	Y	Y	N	N	N	N
4 ***Oxley***	Y	Y	Y	Y	N	N	Y
5 ***Gillmor***	N	N	Y	Y	N	N	Y
6 Strickland	Y	Y	Y	N	N	N	N
7 ***Hobson***	Y	Y	Y	Y	N	N	N
8 ***Boehner***	Y	Y	Y	Y	N	N	Y
9 Kaptur	N	Y	Y	N	N	N	N
10 Kucinich	Y	Y	Y	N	N	N	N
11 Stokes	N	Y	Y	N	N	N	N
12 ***Kasich***	Y	Y	Y	Y	N	N	Y
13 Brown	N	Y	Y	N	N	N	N
14 Sawyer	N	Y	Y	N	N	N	N
15 ***Pryce***	Y	Y	+	Y	N	N	N
16 ***Regula***	Y	Y	Y	Y	N	N	N
17 Traficant	Y	N	Y	Y	N	N	N
18 ***Ney***	Y	?	Y	Y	N	N	N
19 ***LaTourette***	Y	Y	Y	Y	N	N	N
OKLAHOMA							
1 ***Largent***	Y	N	N	Y	N	?	Y
2 ***Coburn***	Y	N	N	Y	N	N	Y
3 ***Watkins***	Y	Y	Y	Y	N	N	Y
4 ***Watts***	Y	Y	Y	Y	N	N	Y
5 ***Istook***	Y	N	N	Y	N	N	Y
6 ***Lucas***	Y	Y	Y	Y	N	N	Y
OREGON							
1 Furse	?	?	?	?	?	?	?
2 ***Smith***	Y	Y	Y	?	N	N	Y
3 Blumenauer	N	Y	Y	N	P	P	N
4 DeFazio	Y	Y	Y	N	N	N	N
5 Hooley	Y	Y	Y	N	N	N	N
PENNSYLVANIA							
1 Brady	N	Y	Y	N	N	N	N
2 Fattah	N	Y	Y	N	N	N	N
3 Borski	N	Y	Y	N	N	N	N
4 Klink	N	Y	Y	N	N	N	N
5 ***Peterson***	Y	Y	Y	Y	N	N	Y
6 Holden	Y	Y	Y	N	N	N	N
7 ***Weldon***	Y	Y	Y	Y	N	N	Y
8 ***Greenwood***	Y	N	N	Y	N	N	N
9 ***Shuster***	Y	N	Y	Y	N	N	Y
10 ***McDade***	?	?	?	?	?	?	?
11 Kanjorski	N	Y	Y	N	N	N	N
12 Murtha	N	Y	Y	N	N	N	N
13 ***Fox***	Y	Y	Y	Y	N	N	Y
14 Coyne	N	Y	Y	N	N	N	N
15 McHale	Y	Y	Y	N	N	N	N
16 ***Pitts***	Y	Y	Y	Y	N	N	Y
17 ***Gekas***	Y	Y	Y	Y	N	N	N
18 Doyle	Y	Y	Y	N	N	N	N
19 ***Goodling***	Y	Y	Y	Y	N	N	Y
20 Mascara	Y	Y	Y	N	N	N	N
21 ***English***	Y	N	Y	Y	N	N	N
RHODE ISLAND							
1 Kennedy	Y	Y	Y	N	N	N	N
2 Weygand	N	Y	Y	N	N	N	N
SOUTH CAROLINA							
1 ***Sanford***	Y	N	N	Y	N	N	Y
2 ***Spence***	Y	N	Y	Y	N	N	Y
3 ***Graham***	Y	Y	Y	Y	N	N	Y
4 ***Inglis***	Y	N	Y	Y	N	N	Y
5 Spratt	Y	Y	Y	N	N	N	N
6 Clyburn	N	Y	Y	N	N	N	N
SOUTH DAKOTA							
AL ***Thune***	Y	Y	Y	Y	N	N	Y
TENNESSEE							
1 ***Jenkins***	Y	Y	Y	Y	N	N	Y
2 ***Duncan***	Y	N	Y	Y	N	N	Y
3 ***Wamp***	Y	N	Y	Y	N	N	Y
4 ***Hilleary***	Y	Y	Y	Y	N	N	Y
5 Clement	N	Y	Y	N	N	N	N
6 Gordon	N	Y	Y	N	N	N	N
7 ***Bryant***	Y	N	Y	Y	N	N	Y
8 Tanner	Y	Y	Y	N	N	N	?
9 Ford	N	Y	Y	N	N	N	N
TEXAS							
1 Sandlin	Y	Y	Y	N	N	N	N
2 Turner	Y	Y	Y	N	N	N	N
3 ***Johnson, Sam***	Y	N	N	Y	N	N	Y
4 Hall	Y	Y	Y	N	N	N	Y
5 ***Sessions***	Y	N	Y	Y	?	N	Y
6 ***Barton***	Y	N	N	Y	N	N	Y
7 ***Archer***	Y	N	N	Y	N	N	Y
8 ***Brady***	Y	Y	N	Y	N	N	Y
9 Lampson	Y	Y	Y	N	N	N	N
10 Doggett	Y	Y	Y	N	N	N	N
11 Edwards	N	Y	Y	N	N	N	N
12 ***Granger***	Y	Y	Y	Y	N	N	N
13 ***Thornberry***	Y	Y	Y	Y	N	N	Y
14 ***Paul***	Y	N	N	Y	N	N	Y
15 Hinojosa	Y	Y	Y	N	N	N	N
16 Reyes	?	?	?	?	?	N	N
17 Stenholm	Y	Y	Y	N	N	N	N
18 Jackson-Lee	N	Y	Y	N	N	N	N
19 ***Combest***	Y	Y	Y	Y	N	N	Y
20 Gonzalez	?	?	?	?	?	?	?
21 ***Smith***	Y	N	Y	Y	N	N	Y
22 ***DeLay***	Y	N	N	Y	N	N	Y
23 ***Bonilla***	Y	Y	Y	Y	N	N	Y
24 Frost	N	Y	Y	N	N	N	N
25 Bentsen	N	Y	Y	N	N	N	N
26 ***Armey***	Y	N	Y	Y	N	N	Y
27 Ortiz	N	Y	Y	N	N	N	N
28 Rodriguez	N	Y	Y	N	N	N	N
29 Green	N	Y	Y	N	N	N	N
30 Johnson, E.B.	N	Y	Y	N	?	?	?
UTAH							
1 ***Hansen***	Y	Y	Y	Y	N	N	Y
2 ***Cook***	Y	Y	Y	Y	N	N	Y
3 ***Cannon***	Y	N	N	Y	N	N	Y
VERMONT							
AL *Sanders*	Y	Y	Y	N	N	N	N
VIRGINIA							
1 ***Bateman***	Y	Y	+	+	N	N	Y
2 Pickett	N	Y	Y	N	N	N	N
3 Scott	Y	Y	Y	N	N	N	N
4 Sisisky	Y	Y	Y	N	N	N	N
5 Goode	Y	N	N	N	N	N	Y
6 ***Goodlatte***	Y	N	N	Y	N	N	Y
7 ***Bliley***	Y	N	N	Y	N	N	Y
8 Moran	?	?	?	N	N	N	N
9 Boucher	N	Y	Y	N	N	N	N
10 ***Wolf***	Y	Y	Y	Y	N	N	N
11 ***Davis***	Y	Y	Y	Y	N	N	N
WASHINGTON							
1 ***White***	Y	Y	Y	Y	N	N	Y
2 ***Metcalf***	Y	Y	Y	Y	N	N	Y
3 ***Smith, Linda***	Y	Y	Y	Y	N	N	N
4 ***Hastings***	Y	N	Y	Y	N	N	Y
5 ***Nethercutt***	Y	Y	Y	Y	N	N	Y
6 Dicks	N	Y	Y	N	N	N	N
7 McDermott	N	Y	Y	N	N	N	N
8 ***Dunn***	Y	Y	Y	Y	N	N	Y
9 Smith, Adam	N	Y	Y	N	N	N	N
WEST VIRGINIA							
1 Mollohan	?	?	?	?	?	?	?
2 Wise	N	Y	Y	N	N	N	N
3 Rahall	N	Y	Y	N	N	N	N
WISCONSIN							
1 ***Neumann***	Y	N	N	Y	N	N	Y
2 ***Klug***	Y	Y	Y	Y	N	N	Y
3 Kind	N	Y	Y	N	N	N	N
4 Kleczka	N	Y	Y	N	N	N	N
5 Barrett	N	Y	Y	N	N	N	N
6 ***Petri***	Y	N	Y	Y	N	N	Y
7 Obey	Y	Y	Y	N	N	N	N
8 Johnson	Y	Y	Y	N	N	N	N
9 ***Sensenbrenner***	Y	N	N	Y	N	N	N
WYOMING							
AL ***Cubin***	Y	N	Y	Y	N	N	Y

Southern states - Ala., Ark., Fla., Ga., Ky., La., Miss., N.C., Okla., S.C., Tenn., Texas, Va.

House Votes 209, 210, 211, 212, 213, 214, 215

209. H Con Res 284. Fiscal 1999 Budget Resolution/Democratic Substitute. Spratt, D-S.C., substitute amendment to adopt a five-year budget plan that would provide budget authority for discretionary spending at the levels agreed to in the 1997 Balanced Budget Act and provide for $30 billion in tax reductions over five years by closing so-called tax loopholes. The amendment would provide for $10 billion in new mandatory spending initiatives, including funds to reduce classroom sizes and child care. Rejected 164-257: R 0-223; D 164-33 (ND 128-19, SD 36-14); I 0-1. June 5, 1998.

210. H Con Res 284. Fiscal 1999 Budget Resolution/Adoption. Adoption of the concurrent resolution to adopt a five-year budget plan that would create a surplus of $63.4 billion by 2003, by cutting spending by $101 billion over five years and using the funds to finance tax reduction which would include the elimination of the so-called marriage penalty. The plan calls for an increase, by $5 billion, in defense spending, over the caps agreed to under the Balanced Budget Act of 1997. The resolution sets binding levels for the fiscal year ending Sept. 30, 1999: budget authority, $1,730.4 billion; outlays, $1,721.9 billion; revenues, $1,755.6 billion; and surplus, $33.7 billion. Adopted 216-204: R 213-9; D 3-194 (ND 1-145, SD 2-49); I 0-1. June 5, 1998.

211. HR 2709. Iran Missile Sanctions/Agreeing to Senate Amendment. Gilman, R-N.Y., motion to agree to the Senate amendment changing the effective date for sanctionable activities from Aug. 8, 1995, to Jan. 22, 1998. The bill would require economic sanctions against overseas companies and research institutes that have aided Iranian efforts to develop ballistic missiles that could reach Israel, U.S. forces in the Persian Gulf or Europe. It also contains provisions needed to implement a treaty banning chemical weapons that was approved by the Senate in 1997. Motion agreed to (thus clearing the bill for the president) 392-22: R 216-3; D 175-19 (ND 129-15, SD 46-4); I 1-0. June 9, 1998. A "nay" was a vote in support of the president's position.

212. H Res 417. Importance of Fathers/Adoption. McIntosh, R-Ind., motion to suspend the rules and adopt the resolution to express the sense of the House that a better America depends in large part on the active involvement of fathers in raising their children. The resolution encourages each father to accept this responsibility. Motion agreed to 415-0: R 217-0; D 197-0 (ND 146-0, SD 51-0); I 1-0. June 9, 1998. A two-thirds majority of those present and voting (277 in this case) is required for adoption under suspension of the rules.

213. H Res 447. Financial Management by Federal Agencies/Adoption. Horn, R-Calif., motion to suspend the rules and adopt the resolution to express the sense of the House that Congress must impose consequences on federal agencies that fail their annual financial audits and must conduct more vigorous oversight of these agencies. Motion agreed to 415-0: R 217-0; D 197-0 (ND 146-0, SD 51-0); I 1-0. June 9, 1998. A two-thirds majority of those present and voting (277 in this case) is required for adoption under suspension of the rules.

214. HR 1635. Underground Railroad Program/Passage. Hansen, R-Utah, motion to suspend the rules and pass the bill to direct the National Park Service to create a nationwide network of historic buildings, routes, projects and museums, which would be known as the "National Underground Railroad Network to Freedom Program." Motion agreed to 415-2: R 217-2; D 197-0 (ND 146-0, SD 51-0); I 1-0. June 9, 1998. A two-thirds majority of those present and voting (278 in this case) is required for passage under suspension of the rules.

215. H Con Res 270. U.S. Support for Taiwan/Adoption. Gilman, R-N.Y., motion to suspend the rules and adopt the concurrent resolution that would call on President Clinton, during his upcoming trip to China, to secure a commitment from the Chinese to stop threatening to use force against Taiwan and express the sense of the Congress that Taiwan should be commended for its recent economic success and democratic elections. Motion agreed to 411-0: R 216-0; D 194-0 (ND 143-0, SD 51-0); I 1-0. June 9, 1998. A two-thirds majority of those present and voting (274 in this case) is required for adoption under suspension of the rules.

Key

- **Y** Voted for (yea).
- **#** Paired for.
- **+** Announced for.
- **N** Voted against (nay).
- **X** Paired against.
- **−** Announced against.
- **P** Voted "present."
- **C** Voted "present" to avoid possible conflict of interest.
- **?** Did not vote or otherwise make a position known.

Democrats   **Republicans**   *Independent*

		209	210	211	212	213	214	215
ALABAMA								
1	Callahan	N	Y	Y	Y	Y	Y	Y
2	Everett	N	Y	Y	Y	Y	Y	Y
3	Riley	N	Y	Y	Y	Y	Y	?
4	Aderholt	N	Y	Y	Y	Y	Y	Y
5	Cramer	N	N	Y	Y	Y	Y	Y
6	Bachus	N	Y	Y	Y	Y	Y	Y
7	Hilliard	Y	N	Y	Y	Y	Y	Y
ALASKA								
AL	Young	N	Y	Y	Y	Y	Y	Y
ARIZONA								
1	Salmon	N	Y	Y	Y	Y	Y	Y
2	Pastor	Y	N	Y	Y	Y	Y	Y
3	Stump	N	Y	Y	Y	Y	Y	Y
4	Shadegg	N	Y	Y	Y	Y	Y	Y
5	Kolbe	N	Y	Y	Y	Y	Y	Y
6	Hayworth	N	Y	Y	Y	Y	Y	Y
ARKANSAS								
1	Berry	N	N	Y	Y	Y	Y	Y
2	Snyder	Y	N	Y	Y	Y	Y	Y
3	Hutchinson	N	Y	Y	Y	Y	Y	Y
4	Dickey	N	Y	Y	Y	Y	Y	Y
CALIFORNIA								
1	Riggs	N	Y	Y	Y	Y	Y	Y
2	Herger	N	Y	Y	Y	Y	Y	Y
3	Fazio	Y	N	P	Y	Y	Y	Y
4	Doolittle	N	Y	Y	Y	Y	Y	Y
5	Matsui	Y	N	Y	Y	Y	Y	Y
6	Woolsey	Y	N	Y	Y	Y	Y	Y
7	Miller	Y	N	Y	Y	Y	Y	?
8	Pelosi	Y	N	Y	Y	Y	Y	Y
9	Lee	Y	N	Y	Y	Y	Y	Y
10	Tauscher	Y	N	Y	Y	Y	Y	Y
11	Pombo	N	Y	Y	Y	Y	Y	Y
12	Lantos	Y	N	Y	Y	Y	Y	Y
13	Stark	Y	N	Y	Y	Y	Y	Y
14	Eshoo	Y	N	Y	Y	Y	Y	Y
15	Campbell	N	N	Y	Y	Y	Y	Y
16	Lofgren	Y	N	N	Y	Y	Y	Y
17	Farr	Y	N	+	+	+	+	+
18	Condit	Y	N	Y	Y	Y	Y	Y
19	Radanovich	N	Y	Y	Y	Y	Y	Y
20	Dooley	Y	N	N	Y	Y	Y	Y
21	Thomas	N	Y	Y	Y	Y	Y	Y
22	Capps, L.	Y	N	Y	Y	Y	Y	Y
23	Gallegly	N	Y	Y	Y	Y	Y	Y
24	Sherman	Y	N	Y	Y	Y	Y	Y
25	McKeon	N	Y	Y	Y	Y	Y	Y
26	Berman	Y	N	Y	Y	Y	Y	Y
27	Rogan	N	Y	Y	Y	Y	Y	Y
28	Dreier	N	Y	Y	Y	Y	Y	Y
29	Waxman	Y	N	?	?	?	?	?
30	Becerra	Y	N	Y	Y	Y	Y	Y
31	Martinez	Y	N	Y	Y	Y	Y	Y
32	Dixon	Y	N	Y	Y	Y	Y	Y
33	Roybal-Allard	Y	N	Y	Y	Y	Y	Y
34	Torres	Y	N	Y	Y	Y	Y	Y
35	Waters	Y	N	Y	Y	Y	Y	Y
36	Harman	Y	N	Y	Y	Y	Y	Y
37	Millender-McD.	Y	N	Y	Y	Y	Y	Y
38	Horn	N	Y	Y	Y	Y	Y	Y
39	Royce	N	Y	Y	Y	Y	Y	Y
40	Lewis	N	Y	Y	Y	Y	Y	Y
41	Kim	N	Y	Y	Y	N	Y	Y
42	Brown	Y	N	Y	Y	Y	Y	Y
43	Calvert	N	Y	Y	Y	Y	Y	Y
44	Bono, M.	N	Y	Y	Y	Y	Y	Y
45	Rohrabacher	N	Y	Y	Y	Y	Y	Y
46	Sanchez	Y	N	Y	Y	Y	Y	?
47	Cox	N	Y	Y	Y	Y	Y	Y
48	Packard	N	Y	Y	Y	Y	Y	Y
49	Bilbray	?	N	Y	Y	Y	Y	Y
50	Filner	Y	N	Y	Y	Y	Y	Y
51	Cunningham	N	Y	Y	Y	Y	Y	Y
52	Hunter	N	Y	?	?	?	Y	Y
COLORADO								
1	DeGette	Y	N	Y	Y	Y	Y	Y
2	Skaggs	Y	N	Y	Y	Y	Y	Y
3	McInnis	N	Y	Y	Y	?	Y	Y
4	Schaffer	N	Y	Y	Y	Y	Y	Y
5	Hefley	N	N	Y	Y	Y	Y	Y
6	Schaefer	N	Y	Y	Y	Y	Y	Y
CONNECTICUT								
1	Kennelly	Y	N	Y	Y	Y	Y	Y
2	Gejdenson	Y	N	Y	Y	Y	Y	Y
3	DeLauro	Y	N	Y	Y	Y	Y	Y
4	Shays	N	Y	Y	Y	Y	Y	Y
5	Maloney	Y	N	Y	Y	Y	Y	Y
6	Johnson	N	N	Y	Y	Y	Y	Y
DELAWARE								
AL	Castle	N	N	Y	Y	Y	Y	Y
FLORIDA								
1	Scarborough	N	Y	Y	Y	Y	Y	Y
2	Boyd	N	N	Y	Y	Y	Y	Y
3	Brown	Y	N	Y	Y	Y	Y	Y
4	Fowler	N	Y	Y	Y	Y	Y	Y
5	Thurman	Y	N	Y	Y	Y	Y	Y
6	Stearns	N	Y	Y	Y	Y	Y	Y
7	Mica	N	Y	Y	Y	Y	Y	Y
8	McCollum	N	Y	Y	Y	Y	Y	Y
9	Bilirakis	N	Y	Y	Y	Y	Y	Y
10	Young	N	Y	?	?	?	?	?
11	Davis	N	N	Y	Y	Y	Y	Y
12	Canady	N	Y	Y	Y	Y	Y	Y
13	Miller	N	Y	Y	Y	Y	Y	Y
14	Goss	N	Y	Y	Y	Y	Y	Y
15	Weldon	N	Y	Y	Y	Y	Y	Y
16	Foley	N	Y	Y	Y	Y	Y	Y
17	Meek	?	N	Y	Y	Y	Y	Y
18	Ros-Lehtinen	?	?	Y	Y	Y	Y	Y
19	Wexler	Y	N	+	+	+	+	+
20	Deutsch	Y	N	+	+	+	+	+
21	Diaz-Balart	N	Y	Y	Y	Y	Y	Y
22	Shaw	N	Y	Y	Y	Y	Y	Y
23	Hastings	Y	N	N	Y	Y	Y	Y
GEORGIA								
1	Kingston	N	Y	Y	Y	Y	Y	Y
2	Bishop	Y	N	?	Y	Y	Y	Y
3	Collins	N	Y	Y	Y	Y	Y	Y
4	McKinney	N	N	Y	Y	Y	Y	Y
5	Lewis	?	−	?	?	?	?	?
6	Gingrich	N	Y					
7	Barr	N	Y	Y	Y	Y	Y	Y
8	Chambliss	N	Y	Y	Y	Y	Y	Y
9	Deal	N	Y	Y	Y	Y	Y	Y
10	Norwood	N	Y	Y	Y	Y	Y	Y
11	Linder	N	Y	Y	Y	Y	Y	Y
HAWAII								
1	Abercrombie	Y	N	Y	Y	Y	Y	Y
2	Mink	Y	N	N	Y	Y	Y	Y
IDAHO								
1	Chenoweth	N	Y	Y	Y	Y	Y	Y
2	Crapo	N	Y	Y	Y	Y	Y	Y
ILLINOIS								
1	Rush	N	N	?	?	?	?	?
2	Jackson	N	N	Y	Y	Y	Y	Y
3	Lipinski	N	N	Y	Y	Y	Y	Y
4	Gutierrez	Y	N	Y	Y	Y	Y	Y
5	Blagojevich	Y	N	Y	Y	Y	Y	Y
6	Hyde	N	Y	Y	Y	Y	Y	?
7	Davis	Y	N	Y	Y	Y	Y	Y
8	Crane	N	Y	Y	Y	Y	Y	Y
9	Yates	Y	N	N	Y	Y	Y	Y
10	Porter	N	Y	Y	Y	Y	Y	Y
11	Weller	N	Y	Y	Y	Y	Y	Y
12	Costello	Y	N	Y	Y	Y	Y	Y

ND Northern Democrats   SD Southern Democrats

	209	210	211	212	213	214	215
13 ***Fawell***	N	Y	Y	?	Y	Y	Y
14 ***Hastert***	N	Y	Y	Y	Y	Y	Y
15 ***Ewing***	N	Y	Y	Y	Y	Y	Y
16 ***Manzullo***	N	Y	Y	Y	Y	Y	Y
17 Evans	Y	N	Y	Y	Y	Y	Y
18 ***LaHood***	N	Y	Y	Y	Y	Y	Y
19 Poshard	Y	N	Y	Y	Y	Y	Y
20 ***Shimkus***	N	Y	Y	Y	Y	Y	Y
INDIANA							
1 Visclosky	N	N	Y	Y	Y	Y	Y
2 ***McIntosh***	N	Y	Y	Y	Y	Y	Y
3 Roemer	N	N	Y	Y	Y	Y	Y
4 ***Souder***	N	P	Y	Y	Y	Y	Y
5 ***Buyer***	N	Y	Y	Y	Y	Y	Y
6 ***Burton***	N	Y	Y	Y	Y	Y	Y
7 ***Pease***	N	Y	Y	Y	Y	Y	Y
8 ***Hostettler***	N	Y	N	Y	Y	Y	Y
9 Hamilton	Y	N	N	Y	Y	Y	Y
10 Carson	Y	N	Y	Y	Y	Y	Y
IOWA							
1 ***Leach***	N	Y	?	Y	Y	Y	Y
2 ***Nussle***	N	Y	Y	Y	Y	Y	Y
3 Boswell	Y	N	Y	Y	Y	Y	Y
4 ***Ganske***	N	N	Y	Y	Y	Y	Y
5 ***Latham***	N	Y	Y	Y	Y	Y	Y
KANSAS							
1 ***Moran***	N	Y	N	Y	Y	Y	Y
2 ***Ryun***	N	Y	Y	Y	Y	Y	Y
3 ***Snowbarger***	N	Y	Y	?	Y	Y	Y
4 ***Tiahrt***	N	Y	Y	Y	Y	Y	Y
KENTUCKY							
1 ***Whitfield***	N	Y	Y	Y	Y	Y	Y
2 ***Lewis***	N	Y	Y	Y	Y	Y	Y
3 ***Northup***	N	Y	Y	Y	Y	Y	Y
4 ***Bunning***	N	Y	Y	Y	Y	Y	Y
5 ***Rogers***	N	Y	Y	Y	Y	Y	Y
6 Baesler	N	N	Y	Y	Y	Y	Y
LOUISIANA							
1 ***Livingston***	N	Y	Y	Y	Y	Y	Y
2 Jefferson	Y	N	N	Y	Y	Y	Y
3 ***Tauzin***	N	Y	Y	Y	Y	Y	Y
4 ***McCrery***	N	Y	Y	Y	Y	Y	Y
5 ***Cooksey***	N	Y	Y	Y	Y	Y	Y
6 ***Baker***	N	Y	Y	Y	Y	Y	Y
7 John	N	N	Y	Y	Y	Y	Y
MAINE							
1 Allen	Y	N	Y	Y	Y	Y	Y
2 Baldacci	Y	N	Y	Y	Y	Y	Y
MARYLAND							
1 ***Gilchrest***	N	Y	Y	Y	Y	Y	Y
2 ***Ehrlich***	N	Y	Y	Y	Y	Y	Y
3 Cardin	Y	N	Y	Y	Y	Y	Y
4 Wynn	Y	N	Y	Y	Y	Y	Y
5 Hoyer	Y	N	Y	Y	Y	Y	Y
6 ***Bartlett***	N	Y	Y	Y	Y	Y	Y
7 Cummings	Y	N	Y	Y	Y	Y	Y
8 ***Morella***	N	N	Y	Y	Y	Y	Y
MASSACHUSETTS							
1 Olver	Y	N	Y	Y	Y	Y	Y
2 Neal	Y	N	Y	Y	Y	Y	Y
3 McGovern	Y	N	Y	Y	Y	Y	Y
4 Frank	Y	N	Y	Y	Y	Y	Y
5 Meehan	N	N	Y	Y	Y	Y	Y
6 Tierney	Y	N	Y	Y	Y	Y	Y
7 Markey	Y	N	Y	Y	Y	Y	Y
8 Kennedy	?	?	N	Y	Y	Y	Y
9 Moakley	Y	N	Y	Y	Y	Y	Y
10 Delahunt	Y	N	Y	Y	Y	Y	Y
MICHIGAN							
1 Stupak	N	N	Y	Y	Y	Y	Y
2 ***Hoekstra***	N	Y	Y	Y	Y	Y	Y
3 ***Ehlers***	N	Y	Y	Y	Y	Y	Y
4 ***Camp***	N	Y	Y	Y	Y	Y	Y
5 Barcia	Y	N	Y	Y	Y	Y	Y
6 ***Upton***	N	Y	Y	Y	Y	Y	Y
7 ***Smith***	N	Y	Y	Y	Y	Y	Y
8 Stabenow	Y	N	Y	Y	Y	Y	Y
9 Kildee	Y	N	Y	Y	Y	Y	Y
10 Bonior	Y	N	P	Y	Y	Y	Y
11 ***Knollenberg***	N	Y	Y	Y	Y	Y	Y
12 Levin	Y	N	Y	Y	Y	Y	Y
13 Rivers	Y	N	Y	Y	Y	Y	Y
14 Conyers	Y	N	N	Y	Y	Y	Y
15 Kilpatrick	Y	N	Y	Y	Y	Y	Y
16 Dingell	Y	N	Y	Y	Y	Y	Y

	209	210	211	212	213	214	215
MINNESOTA							
1 ***Gutknecht***	N	Y	Y	Y	Y	Y	Y
2 Minge	N	N	Y	Y	Y	Y	Y
3 ***Ramstad***	N	Y	Y	Y	Y	Y	Y
4 Vento	Y	N	Y	Y	Y	Y	Y
5 Sabo	?	?	?	?	?	?	?
6 Luther	Y	N	Y	Y	Y	Y	Y
7 Peterson	N	N	Y	Y	Y	Y	Y
8 Oberstar	Y	N	Y	Y	Y	Y	Y
MISSISSIPPI							
1 ***Wicker***	N	Y	Y	Y	?	?	?
2 Thompson	Y	N	Y	Y	Y	Y	Y
3 ***Pickering***	N	Y	Y	Y	Y	Y	Y
4 ***Parker***	N	Y	Y	Y	Y	Y	Y
5 Taylor	N	N	Y	Y	Y	Y	Y
MISSOURI							
1 Clay	Y	N	Y	Y	Y	Y	Y
2 ***Talent***	N	Y	Y	Y	Y	Y	?
3 Gephardt	Y	N	P	Y	Y	Y	Y
4 Skelton	Y	N	Y	Y	Y	Y	Y
5 McCarthy	Y	N	Y	Y	Y	Y	Y
6 Danner	N	N	Y	Y	Y	Y	Y
7 ***Blunt***	N	Y	Y	Y	Y	Y	Y
8 ***Emerson***	N	Y	Y	Y	Y	Y	Y
9 ***Hulshof***	N	Y	Y	Y	Y	Y	Y
MONTANA							
AL ***Hill***	N	Y	Y	Y	Y	Y	Y
NEBRASKA							
1 ***Bereuter***	N	Y	Y	Y	Y	Y	Y
2 ***Christensen***	N	Y	Y	Y	Y	Y	Y
3 ***Barrett***	N	Y	Y	Y	Y	Y	Y
NEVADA							
1 ***Ensign***	N	Y	Y	Y	Y	Y	Y
2 ***Gibbons***	N	Y	Y	Y	Y	Y	Y
NEW HAMPSHIRE							
1 ***Sununu***	N	Y	Y	Y	Y	Y	Y
2 ***Bass***	N	Y	Y	Y	Y	Y	Y
NEW JERSEY							
1 Andrews	Y	N	Y	Y	Y	Y	Y
2 ***LoBiondo***	N	Y	Y	Y	Y	Y	Y
3 ***Saxton***	N	Y	Y	Y	Y	Y	Y
4 ***Smith***	N	Y	Y	Y	Y	Y	Y
5 ***Roukema***	N	Y	Y	Y	Y	?	?
6 Pallone	Y	N	Y	Y	Y	Y	Y
7 ***Franks***	N	Y	Y	Y	Y	Y	Y
8 Pascrell	Y	N	Y	Y	Y	Y	Y
9 Rothman	Y	N	Y	Y	Y	Y	Y
10 Payne	Y	N	Y	Y	Y	Y	Y
11 ***Frelinghuysen***	N	Y	Y	Y	Y	Y	Y
12 ***Pappas***	N	Y	Y	Y	Y	Y	Y
13 Menendez	Y	N	Y	Y	Y	Y	Y
NEW MEXICO							
1 Vacant							
2 ***Skeen***	N	Y	Y	Y	Y	Y	Y
3 ***Redmond***	N	Y	Y	Y	Y	Y	Y
NEW YORK							
1 ***Forbes***	N	Y	Y	Y	Y	Y	Y
2 ***Lazio***	N	Y	Y	Y	Y	Y	Y
3 ***King***	N	Y	Y	Y	Y	Y	Y
4 McCarthy	Y	N	Y	Y	Y	Y	Y
5 Ackerman	Y	N	Y	Y	Y	Y	Y
6 Meeks	N	N	Y	Y	Y	Y	Y
7 Manton	Y	N	Y	Y	Y	Y	Y
8 Nadler	Y	N	Y	Y	Y	Y	Y
9 Schumer	Y	N	?	?	?	?	?
10 Towns	Y	N	Y	Y	Y	Y	Y
11 Owens	Y	N	Y	Y	Y	Y	Y
12 Velázquez	Y	N	Y	Y	Y	Y	Y
13 ***Fossella***	N	Y	Y	Y	Y	Y	Y
14 Maloney	Y	N	Y	Y	Y	Y	Y
15 Rangel	Y	N	Y	Y	Y	Y	Y
16 Serrano	Y	N	Y	Y	Y	Y	Y
17 Engel	Y	N	Y	Y	Y	Y	Y
18 Lowey	Y	N	Y	Y	Y	Y	Y
19 ***Kelly***	N	Y	Y	Y	Y	Y	Y
20 ***Gilman***	N	Y	Y	Y	Y	Y	Y
21 McNulty	Y	N	Y	Y	Y	Y	Y
22 ***Solomon***	N	Y	Y	Y	Y	Y	Y
23 ***Boehlert***	N	Y	Y	Y	Y	Y	Y
24 ***McHugh***	N	Y	Y	Y	Y	Y	Y
25 ***Walsh***	N	Y	Y	Y	Y	Y	Y
26 Hinchey	Y	N	Y	Y	Y	Y	Y
27 ***Paxon***	N	Y	Y	Y	Y	Y	Y
28 Slaughter	Y	N	Y	Y	Y	Y	Y
29 LaFalce	Y	?	N	Y	Y	Y	Y

	209	210	211	212	213	214	215
30 ***Quinn***	N	N	Y	Y	Y	Y	Y
31 ***Houghton***	N	Y	?	?	?	?	?
NORTH CAROLINA							
1 Clayton	Y	N	Y	Y	Y	Y	Y
2 Etheridge	Y	N	Y	Y	Y	Y	Y
3 ***Jones***	N	Y	Y	Y	Y	Y	Y
4 Price	Y	N	Y	Y	Y	Y	Y
5 ***Burr***	N	Y	Y	Y	Y	Y	Y
6 ***Coble***	N	Y	Y	Y	Y	Y	Y
7 McIntyre	Y	N	Y	Y	Y	Y	Y
8 Hefner	Y	N	Y	Y	Y	Y	Y
9 ***Myrick***	N	Y	Y	Y	Y	Y	Y
10 ***Ballenger***	–	+	Y	+	+	+	+
11 ***Taylor***	N	Y	Y	Y	Y	Y	Y
12 Watt	Y	N	Y	Y	Y	Y	Y
NORTH DAKOTA							
AL Pomeroy	Y	N	Y	Y	Y	Y	Y
OHIO							
1 ***Chabot***	N	Y	Y	Y	Y	Y	Y
2 ***Portman***	N	Y	Y	Y	Y	Y	Y
3 Hall	Y	N	Y	Y	Y	Y	Y
4 ***Oxley***	N	Y	Y	Y	Y	Y	Y
5 ***Gillmor***	N	Y	Y	Y	Y	Y	Y
6 Strickland	Y	N	Y	Y	Y	Y	Y
7 ***Hobson***	N	Y	Y	Y	Y	Y	Y
8 ***Boehner***	N	Y	Y	Y	Y	Y	Y
9 Kaptur	Y	N	Y	Y	Y	Y	Y
10 Kucinich	N	N	Y	Y	Y	Y	Y
11 Stokes	Y	N	Y	Y	Y	Y	Y
12 ***Kasich***	N	Y	Y	Y	Y	Y	Y
13 Brown	Y	N	Y	Y	Y	Y	Y
14 Sawyer	Y	N	Y	Y	Y	Y	Y
15 ***Pryce***	N	Y	Y	Y	Y	Y	Y
16 ***Regula***	N	Y	Y	Y	Y	Y	Y
17 Traficant	N	N	Y	Y	Y	Y	Y
18 ***Ney***	N	Y	Y	Y	Y	Y	Y
19 ***LaTourette***	N	Y	Y	Y	Y	Y	Y
OKLAHOMA							
1 ***Largent***	N	Y	Y	Y	Y	Y	Y
2 ***Coburn***	N	Y	Y	Y	Y	Y	Y
3 ***Watkins***	N	Y	Y	Y	Y	Y	Y
4 ***Watts***	N	Y	Y	Y	Y	Y	Y
5 ***Istook***	N	Y	Y	Y	Y	Y	Y
6 ***Lucas***	N	Y	Y	Y	Y	Y	Y
OREGON							
1 Furse	?	?	N	Y	Y	Y	Y
2 ***Smith***	N	Y	Y	Y	Y	Y	Y
3 Blumenauer	Y	N	Y	Y	Y	Y	Y
4 DeFazio	N	N	Y	Y	Y	Y	Y
5 Hooley	Y	N	Y	Y	Y	Y	Y
PENNSYLVANIA							
1 Brady	Y	N	Y	Y	Y	Y	Y
2 Fattah	N	N	Y	Y	Y	Y	Y
3 Borski	Y	N	Y	Y	Y	Y	Y
4 Klink	Y	N	Y	Y	Y	Y	Y
5 ***Peterson***	N	Y	Y	Y	Y	Y	Y
6 Holden	Y	N	Y	Y	Y	Y	Y
7 ***Weldon***	N	Y	Y	Y	Y	Y	Y
8 ***Greenwood***	N	Y	Y	Y	Y	Y	Y
9 ***Shuster***	N	Y	Y	Y	Y	Y	Y
10 ***McDade***	?	?	Y	?	Y	Y	Y
11 Kanjorski	Y	N	N	Y	Y	Y	Y
12 Murtha	N	N	N	Y	Y	Y	?
13 ***Fox***	N	Y	Y	Y	Y	Y	Y
14 Coyne	Y	N	Y	Y	Y	Y	Y
15 McHale	Y	N	Y	Y	Y	Y	Y
16 ***Pitts***	N	Y	Y	Y	Y	Y	Y
17 ***Gekas***	N	Y	Y	Y	?	Y	Y
18 Doyle	Y	N	Y	Y	Y	Y	Y
19 ***Goodling***	N	Y	?	Y	Y	Y	Y
20 Mascara	N	N	Y	Y	Y	Y	Y
21 ***English***	N	Y	Y	Y	Y	Y	Y
RHODE ISLAND							
1 Kennedy	Y	N	Y	Y	Y	Y	Y
2 Weygand	Y	N	Y	Y	Y	Y	Y
SOUTH CAROLINA							
1 ***Sanford***	N	Y	Y	Y	Y	N	Y
2 ***Spence***	N	Y	Y	Y	Y	Y	Y
3 ***Graham***	N	Y	Y	Y	Y	Y	Y
4 ***Inglis***	N	Y	?	?	?	?	?
5 Spratt	Y	N	Y	Y	Y	Y	Y
6 Clyburn	Y	N	Y	Y	Y	Y	Y
SOUTH DAKOTA							
AL ***Thune***	N	Y	Y	Y	Y	Y	Y

	209	210	211	212	213	214	215
TENNESSEE							
1 ***Jenkins***	N	Y	Y	Y	Y	Y	Y
2 ***Duncan***	N	Y	Y	Y	Y	Y	Y
3 ***Wamp***	N	Y	Y	Y	Y	Y	Y
4 ***Hilleary***	N	Y	Y	Y	Y	Y	Y
5 Clement	Y	N	Y	Y	Y	Y	Y
6 Gordon	Y	N	Y	Y	Y	Y	Y
7 ***Bryant***	N	Y	Y	Y	Y	Y	Y
8 Tanner	?	?	Y	Y	Y	Y	Y
9 Ford	Y	N	Y	Y	Y	Y	Y
TEXAS							
1 Sandlin	N	N	Y	Y	Y	Y	Y
2 Turner	N	N	Y	Y	Y	Y	Y
3 ***Johnson, Sam***	N	Y	?	?	?	?	?
4 Hall	N	Y	Y	Y	Y	Y	Y
5 ***Sessions***	N	Y	Y	Y	Y	Y	Y
6 ***Barton***	N	Y	Y	Y	Y	Y	Y
7 ***Archer***	N	Y	Y	Y	Y	Y	Y
8 ***Brady***	N	Y	Y	Y	Y	Y	Y
9 Lampson	Y	N	Y	Y	Y	Y	Y
10 Doggett	Y	N	Y	Y	Y	Y	Y
11 Edwards	Y	N	Y	Y	Y	Y	Y
12 ***Granger***	N	Y	Y	Y	Y	Y	Y
13 ***Thornberry***	N	Y	Y	Y	Y	Y	Y
14 ***Paul***	N	?	N	Y	Y	N	Y
15 Hinojosa	Y	N	Y	Y	Y	Y	Y
16 Reyes	Y	N	Y	Y	Y	Y	Y
17 Stenholm	Y	N	Y	Y	Y	Y	Y
18 Jackson-Lee	Y	N	Y	Y	Y	Y	Y
19 ***Combest***	N	Y	Y	Y	Y	Y	Y
20 Gonzalez	?	?	?	?	?	?	?
21 ***Smith***	N	Y	Y	Y	Y	Y	Y
22 ***DeLay***	N	Y	Y	Y	Y	Y	Y
23 ***Bonilla***	N	Y	Y	Y	Y	Y	Y
24 Frost	Y	N	Y	Y	Y	Y	Y
25 Bentsen	Y	N	Y	Y	Y	Y	Y
26 ***Armey***	N	Y	Y	Y	Y	Y	Y
27 Ortiz	Y	N	Y	Y	Y	Y	Y
28 Rodriguez	Y	N	Y	Y	Y	Y	Y
29 Green	Y	N	Y	Y	Y	Y	Y
30 Johnson, E.B.	?	?	N	Y	Y	Y	Y
UTAH							
1 ***Hansen***	N	Y	Y	Y	Y	Y	Y
2 ***Cook***	N	Y	Y	Y	Y	Y	Y
3 ***Cannon***	N	Y	Y	Y	Y	Y	Y
VERMONT							
AL *Sanders*	N	N	Y	Y	Y	Y	Y
VIRGINIA							
1 ***Bateman***	N	Y	Y	Y	Y	Y	Y
2 Pickett	N	N	Y	Y	Y	Y	Y
3 Scott	Y	N	Y	Y	Y	Y	Y
4 Sisisky	Y	N	Y	Y	Y	Y	Y
5 Goode	N	Y	Y	Y	Y	Y	Y
6 ***Goodlatte***	N	Y	Y	Y	Y	Y	Y
7 ***Bliley***	N	Y	Y	Y	Y	Y	Y
8 Moran	Y	N	N	Y	Y	Y	Y
9 Boucher	N	N	Y	Y	Y	Y	Y
10 ***Wolf***	N	Y	Y	Y	Y	Y	Y
11 ***Davis***	N	Y	Y	Y	Y	Y	Y
WASHINGTON							
1 ***White***	N	Y	Y	Y	Y	Y	Y
2 ***Metcalf***	N	Y	Y	Y	Y	Y	Y
3 ***Smith, Linda***	N	N	Y	Y	Y	Y	Y
4 ***Hastings***	N	Y	Y	Y	Y	Y	Y
5 ***Nethercutt***	N	Y	Y	Y	Y	Y	Y
6 Dicks	Y	N	Y	Y	Y	Y	Y
7 McDermott	Y	N	N	Y	Y	Y	Y
8 ***Dunn***	N	Y	Y	Y	Y	Y	Y
9 Smith, Adam	Y	N	Y	Y	Y	Y	Y
WEST VIRGINIA							
1 Mollohan	?	?	Y	Y	Y	Y	Y
2 Wise	Y	N	Y	Y	Y	Y	Y
3 Rahall	N	N	N	Y	Y	Y	Y
WISCONSIN							
1 ***Neumann***	N	Y	Y	Y	Y	Y	Y
2 ***Klug***	N	Y	Y	Y	Y	Y	Y
3 Kind	Y	N	Y	Y	Y	Y	Y
4 Kleczka	Y	N	Y	Y	Y	Y	Y
5 Barrett	Y	N	Y	Y	Y	Y	Y
6 ***Petri***	N	Y	Y	Y	Y	Y	Y
7 Obey	Y	N	N	Y	Y	Y	Y
8 Johnson	Y	N	Y	Y	Y	Y	Y
9 ***Sensenbrenner***	N	Y	Y	Y	Y	Y	Y
WYOMING							
AL ***Cubin***	N	Y	Y	Y	Y	Y	Y

Southern states - Ala., Ark., Fla., Ga., Ky., La., Miss., N.C., Okla., S.C., Tenn., Texas, Va.

House Votes 216, 217, 218, 219, 220, 221, 222

216. HR 3150. Bankruptcy Overhaul/Consideration of Rule. Judgment of the House on proceeding to the consideration of the rule (H Res 462) to provide for House floor consideration of the bill to overhaul the nation's bankruptcy laws, despite the Nadler, D-N.Y., point of order regarding unfunded mandates. Agreed to consider the rule 248-166: R 215-1; D 33-164 (ND 19-125, SD 14-39); I 0-1. June 10, 1998.

217. HR 3150. Bankruptcy Overhaul/Previous Question. McInnis, R-Colo., motion to order the previous question (thus ending debate and the possibility of amendment) on adoption of the rule (H Res 462) to provide for House floor consideration of the bill to overhaul the nation's bankruptcy laws. Motion agreed to 236-183: R 217-0; D 19-182 (ND 12-135, SD 7-47); I 0-1. June 10, 1998.

218. HR 3150. Bankruptcy Overhaul/Rule. Adoption of the rule (H Res 462) to provide for House floor consideration of the bill to overhaul the nation's bankruptcy laws by barring individuals with average incomes or higher from filing for bankruptcy under Chapter 7 and thus walking away from most debts. Adopted 251-172: R 222-1; D 29-170 (ND 19-127, SD 10-43); I 0-1. June 10, 1998.

219. HR 3150. Bankruptcy Overhaul/Small Businesses. Nadler, D-N.Y., amendment to modify the bill's provisions related to small businesses, so as to eliminate added paperwork requirements and the definition that a small business is an entity with $5 million or less in debt. The amendment also would exclude from the calculation of a debtor's income that must be made available to repay unsecured creditors any expenditure necessary for the continuing operation of the debtor's business. Rejected 136-290: R 4-222; D 131-68 (ND 107-40, SD 24-28); I 1-0. June 10, 1998.

220. HR 3150. Bankruptcy Overhaul/Means-Testing Costs. Delahunt, D-Mass., amendment to authorize the U.S. Judicial Conference to reduce disbursements to unsecured non-priority creditors payable in Chapter 13 cases to cover the increased costs of implementing the bill's means-testing provisions. Rejected 149-278: R 2-224; D 146-54 (ND 118-29, SD 28-25); I 1-0. June 10, 1998.

221. HR 3150. Bankruptcy Overhaul/Homestead Property. Gekas, R-Pa., amendment to prohibit the conversion of non-exempt assets into exempt homestead property within one year of filing for bankruptcy. Adopted 222-204: R 181-44; D 41-159 (ND 9-139, SD 32-20); I 0-1. June 10, 1998.

222. HR 3150. Bankruptcy Overhaul/Recording Contracts. Scott, D-Va., amendment to strike provisions that prevent recording artists from discharging their obligations under contracts with recording companies when they file for bankruptcy. Rejected 111-316: R 4-222; D 106-94 (ND 84-63, SD 22-31); I 1-0. June 10, 1998.

Key

- **Y** Voted for (yea).
- **#** Paired for.
- **+** Announced for.
- **N** Voted against (nay).
- **X** Paired against.
- **−** Announced against.
- **P** Voted "present."
- **C** Voted "present" to avoid possible conflict of interest.
- **?** Did not vote or otherwise make a position known.

Democrats **Republicans** Independent

		216	217	218	219	220	221	222
ALABAMA								
1	*Callahan*	Y	Y	Y	N	N	Y	N
2	*Everett*	Y	Y	Y	N	N	N	N
3	*Riley*	Y	Y	Y	N	N	N	N
4	*Aderholt*	Y	Y	Y	N	N	N	N
5	Cramer	Y	Y	Y	N	N	Y	N
6	*Bachus*	Y	?	Y	N	N	N	N
7	Hilliard	N	N	N	Y	N	N	Y
ALASKA								
AL	*Young*	Y	Y	Y	N	N	Y	N
ARIZONA								
1	*Salmon*	Y	Y	Y	N	N	Y	N
2	Pastor	N	N	N	Y	Y	N	N
3	*Stump*	Y	Y	Y	N	N	Y	N
4	*Shadegg*	Y	Y	Y	N	N	Y	N
5	*Kolbe*	Y	Y	Y	N	N	N	N
6	Hayworth	Y	Y	Y	N	N	Y	N
ARKANSAS								
1	Berry	N	Y	N	N	N	N	N
2	Snyder	Y	N	N	N	N	N	N
3	*Hutchinson*	Y	Y	Y	N	N	Y	N
4	*Dickey*	Y	Y	Y	N	N	Y	N
CALIFORNIA								
1	*Riggs*	Y	Y	Y	N	N	N	N
2	*Herger*	Y	Y	Y	N	N	Y	N
3	Fazio	N	N	N	Y	Y	N	N
4	*Doolittle*	Y	Y	Y	N	N	N	N
5	Matsui	N	N	N	Y	N	N	N
6	Woolsey	N	N	N	Y	Y	N	Y
7	Miller	N	N	?	Y	Y	N	Y
8	Pelosi	N	N	N	Y	Y	N	Y
9	Lee	N	N	N	Y	Y	N	Y
10	Tauscher	Y	Y	Y	N	N	Y	N
11	*Pombo*	Y	Y	Y	N	N	Y	N
12	Lantos	N	N	N	Y	Y	N	N
13	Stark	N	N	N	Y	Y	N	N
14	Eshoo	N	N	N	Y	Y	N	N
15	*Campbell*	Y	Y	Y	Y	Y	Y	N
16	Lofgren	?	N	N	Y	Y	N	N
17	Farr	−	−	−	+	+	−	−
18	Condit	N	N	Y	N	N	Y	N
19	*Radanovich*	Y	Y	Y	N	N	Y	N
20	Dooley	Y	Y	Y	N	N	N	N
21	*Thomas*	Y	Y	Y	N	N	Y	N
22	Capps, L.	N	N	N	Y	Y	N	Y
23	*Gallegly*	Y	Y	Y	N	N	N	N
24	Sherman	Y	Y	Y	N	N	N	N
25	*McKeon*	Y	Y	Y	N	N	Y	N
26	Berman	N	?	?	?	?	?	?
27	*Rogan*	Y	Y	Y	N	N	Y	N
28	*Dreier*	Y	Y	Y	N	N	Y	Y
29	Waxman	N	N	N	Y	Y	N	N
30	Becerra	N	N	N	Y	Y	N	Y
31	Martinez	N	N	N	Y	N	N	Y
32	Dixon	N	N	N	Y	Y	N	N
33	Royall-Allard	N	N	N	Y	Y	N	Y
34	Torres	N	N	?	Y	Y	N	Y
35	Waters	N	N	N	Y	Y	N	Y
36	Harman	?	N	N	?	Y	N	N
37	Millender-McD.	N	N	N	Y	Y	N	Y

		216	217	218	219	220	221	222
38	*Horn*	Y	Y	Y	N	N	Y	N
39	*Royce*	Y	Y	Y	N	N	N	N
40	*Lewis*	Y	Y	Y	N	N	N	N
41	*Kim*	Y	Y	Y	N	N	Y	N
42	Brown	N	?	?	Y	N	Y	N
43	*Calvert*	Y	Y	Y	N	N	N	N
44	*Bono, M.*	Y	Y	Y	N	N	N	N
45	*Rohrabacher*	Y	Y	Y	N	N	N	N
46	Sanchez	N	N	N	Y	N	N	N
47	*Cox*	Y	Y	Y	N	N	N	N
48	*Packard*	Y	Y	Y	N	N	N	N
49	*Bilbray*	Y	Y	Y	N	N	N	N
50	Filner	N	N	N	Y	Y	N	Y
51	*Cunningham*	Y	Y	Y	N	N	Y	N
52	*Hunter*	Y	Y	Y	N	N	Y	N
COLORADO								
1	DeGette	N	N	N	Y	Y	N	N
2	Skaggs	Y	N	N	Y	Y	N	Y
3	*McInnis*	Y	Y	Y	N	N	Y	N
4	*Schaffer*	Y	Y	Y	N	N	N	N
5	*Hefley*	Y	Y	Y	N	N	Y	N
6	*Schaefer*	Y	Y	Y	N	N	Y	N
CONNECTICUT								
1	Kennelly	N	N	N	Y	Y	N	N
2	Gejdenson	N	N	N	Y	Y	N	N
3	DeLauro	N	N	N	Y	Y	N	N
4	*Shays*	Y	Y	Y	N	N	N	N
5	Maloney	Y	Y	Y	N	N	Y	N
6	*Johnson*	Y	Y	Y	N	N	N	N
DELAWARE								
AL	*Castle*	Y	Y	Y	N	N	N	N
FLORIDA								
1	*Scarborough*	Y	?	Y	N	N	Y	N
2	Boyd	Y	Y	Y	N	N	Y	N
3	Brown	N	N	?	Y	Y	N	Y
4	*Fowler*	Y	Y	Y	N	N	N	N
5	Thurman	N	N	N	Y	Y	N	N
6	*Stearns*	Y	Y	Y	N	N	Y	N
7	*Mica*	Y	Y	Y	N	N	N	N
8	*McCollum*	Y	Y	Y	N	N	Y	N
9	*Bilirakis*	Y	Y	Y	N	N	Y	N
10	*Young*	?	Y	Y	N	N	Y	N
11	Davis	Y	N	N	Y	N	Y	Y
12	*Canady*	Y	Y	Y	N	N	Y	N
13	*Miller*	Y	Y	Y	N	N	Y	N
14	*Goss*	Y	Y	Y	N	N	Y	N
15	*Weldon*	Y	Y	Y	N	N	Y	N
16	*Foley*	Y	Y	Y	N	N	Y	N
17	Meek	N	N	N	Y	Y	N	Y
18	*Ros-Lehtinen*	Y	Y	Y	N	N	Y	N
19	Wexler	N	N	N	Y	Y	N	Y
20	Deutsch	Y	N	N	Y	N	Y	N
21	*Diaz-Balart*	Y	Y	Y	N	N	Y	N
22	*Shaw*	Y	Y	Y	N	N	Y	N
23	Hastings	N	N	N	Y	Y	Y	N
GEORGIA								
1	*Kingston*	Y	Y	Y	N	N	N	N
2	Bishop	N	N	N	N	N	Y	Y
3	*Collins*	Y	Y	Y	N	N	N	N
4	McKinney	N	N	N	Y	Y	N	Y
5	Lewis	N	N	N	?	?	?	?
6	*Gingrich*							
7	*Barr*	Y	Y	Y	N	N	N	N
8	*Chambliss*	Y	Y	Y	N	N	Y	N
9	*Deal*	Y	Y	Y	N	N	Y	N
10	*Norwood*	Y	Y	Y	N	N	Y	N
11	*Linder*	?	Y	Y	N	N	Y	N
HAWAII								
1	Abercrombie	N	N	N	Y	Y	N	Y
2	Mink	N	N	N	Y	Y	N	Y
IDAHO								
1	*Chenoweth*	Y	Y	Y	N	N	Y	N
2	*Crapo*	Y	Y	Y	N	N	Y	N
ILLINOIS								
1	Rush	N	N	N	Y	Y	N	Y
2	Jackson	N	N	N	Y	Y	N	Y
3	Lipinski	N	N	N	N	N	N	N
4	Gutierrez	N	N	N	Y	Y	N	Y
5	Blagojevich	N	N	N	N	N	N	N
6	*Hyde*	Y	Y	Y	N	N	Y	N
7	Davis	N	N	N	Y	Y	N	Y
8	*Crane*	Y	Y	Y	N	N	Y	N
9	Yates	N	N	N	Y	Y	N	Y
10	*Porter*	Y	Y	Y	N	N	N	N
11	*Weller*	Y	Y	Y	N	N	Y	N
12	Costello	N	N	N	N	N	N	N

ND Northern Democrats   SD Southern Democrats

	216	217	218	219	220	221	222
13 ***Fawell***	Y	Y	Y	N	N	?	N
14 ***Hastert***	Y	Y	Y	N	N	Y	N
15 ***Ewing***	Y	Y	Y	N	N	Y	N
16 ***Manzullo***	Y	Y	Y	N	N	Y	N
17 Evans	N	N	N	Y	Y	N	N
18 ***LaHood***	Y	Y	Y	N	N	Y	N
19 Poshard	N	N	N	Y	Y	N	N
20 ***Shimkus***	Y	Y	Y	N	N	Y	N
INDIANA							
1 Visclosky	N	N	N	Y	Y	N	Y
2 ***McIntosh***	Y	Y	Y	N	N	N	N
3 Roemer	Y	Y	Y	N	N	N	N
4 ***Souder***	Y	Y	Y	Y	N	N	N
5 ***Buyer***	Y	Y	Y	N	N	N	N
6 ***Burton***	Y	Y	Y	N	N	Y	N
7 ***Pease***	Y	Y	Y	N	N	Y	N
8 ***Hostettler***	Y	Y	Y	N	N	Y	N
9 Hamilton	N	N	Y	N	N	N	Y
10 Carson	N	N	N	Y	Y	N	Y
IOWA							
1 ***Leach***	?	Y	Y	N	N	Y	N
2 ***Nussle***	Y	Y	Y	N	N	Y	N
3 Boswell	Y	Y	Y	N	N	Y	N
4 ***Ganske***	Y	Y	Y	N	N	Y	N
5 ***Latham***	Y	Y	Y	N	N	Y	N
KANSAS							
1 ***Moran***	Y	Y	Y	N	N	Y	N
2 ***Ryun***	Y	Y	Y	N	N	Y	N
3 ***Snowbarger***	Y	Y	Y	N	N	Y	N
4 ***Tiahrt***	Y	Y	Y	N	N	Y	N
KENTUCKY							
1 ***Whitfield***	Y	Y	Y	N	N	Y	N
2 ***Lewis***	Y	Y	Y	N	N	Y	N
3 ***Northup***	Y	Y	Y	N	N	Y	N
4 ***Bunning***	Y	Y	Y	N	N	Y	N
5 ***Rogers***	Y	Y	Y	N	N	Y	N
6 Baesler	Y	Y	Y	N	N	N	N
LOUISIANA							
1 ***Livingston***	Y	Y	Y	N	N	Y	N
2 Jefferson	N	N	N	N	Y	N	N
3 ***Tauzin***	Y	Y	Y	N	N	Y	N
4 ***McCrery***	Y	Y	Y	N	N	Y	N
5 ***Cooksey***	Y	Y	Y	N	N	Y	N
6 ***Baker***	Y	Y	Y	N	N	Y	N
7 John	N	N	N	N	Y	Y	N
MAINE							
1 Allen	N	N	N	Y	N	N	Y
2 Baldacci	N	N	N	Y	N	N	Y
MARYLAND							
1 ***Gilchrest***	Y	Y	Y	N	N	N	N
2 ***Ehrlich***	Y	Y	Y	N	N	Y	N
3 Cardin	Y	N	N	Y	N	N	N
4 Wynn	N	N	N	Y	Y	N	N
5 Hoyer	N	N	N	N	Y	N	N
6 ***Bartlett***	Y	Y	Y	N	N	Y	N
7 Cummings	N	N	N	Y	Y	N	N
8 ***Morella***	Y	Y	Y	N	N	N	N
MASSACHUSETTS							
1 Olver	N	?	N	Y	Y	N	Y
2 Neal	N	N	N	Y	Y	N	Y
3 McGovern	N	N	N	Y	Y	N	Y
4 Frank	Y	N	N	N	?	N	N
5 Meehan	N	N	N	Y	Y	N	Y
6 Tierney	N	N	N	Y	Y	N	Y
7 Markey	N	N	N	N	Y	N	Y
8 Kennedy	N	N	N	Y	Y	N	N
9 Moakley	?	N	N	Y	Y	N	Y
10 Delahunt	N	N	N	Y	Y	N	Y
MICHIGAN							
1 Stupak	N	N	N	Y	Y	N	Y
2 ***Hoekstra***	Y	Y	Y	N	N	N	N
3 ***Ehlers***	Y	Y	Y	N	N	N	N
4 ***Camp***	Y	Y	Y	N	N	Y	N
5 Barcia	N	N	Y	Y	Y	Y	N
6 ***Upton***	Y	Y	Y	N	N	N	N
7 ***Smith***	Y	Y	Y	N	N	Y	N
8 Stabenow	N	N	N	N	N	N	N
9 Kildee	N	N	N	Y	Y	N	N
10 Bonior	N	N	N	Y	Y	N	Y
11 ***Knollenberg***	Y	Y	Y	N	N	Y	N
12 Levin	N	N	N	Y	Y	N	N
13 Rivers	N	N	N	Y	N	N	Y
14 Conyers	?	N	N	Y	Y	N	Y
15 Kilpatrick	N	N	N	Y	Y	N	Y
16 Dingell	Y	N	Y	Y	N	N	N

	216	217	218	219	220	221	222
MINNESOTA							
1 ***Gutknecht***	Y	Y	Y	N	N	Y	N
2 Minge	N	N	Y	N	Y	N	N
3 ***Ramstad***	Y	Y	Y	N	N	Y	N
4 Vento	N	N	N	Y	Y	N	Y
5 Sabo	N	N	N	N	Y	N	Y
6 Luther	N	N	N	N	Y	N	Y
7 Peterson	Y	Y	Y	N	N	N	N
8 Oberstar	N	N	N	Y	Y	N	N
MISSISSIPPI							
1 ***Wicker***	Y	Y	Y	N	N	Y	N
2 Thompson	N	N	N	Y	Y	N	N
3 ***Pickering***	Y	Y	Y	N	N	Y	N
4 ***Parker***	Y	Y	Y	N	N	Y	N
5 Taylor	N	N	N	N	Y	N	N
MISSOURI							
1 Clay	N	N	N	Y	Y	N	Y
2 ***Talent***	Y	Y	Y	N	N	Y	N
3 Gephardt	N	N	N	Y	Y	N	Y
4 Skelton	N	N	N	N	Y	N	N
5 McCarthy	N	N	N	N	Y	N	Y
6 Danner	N	N	Y	N	Y	N	N
7 ***Blunt***	Y	Y	Y	N	N	Y	N
8 ***Emerson***	Y	Y	Y	N	N	N	N
9 ***Hulshof***	Y	Y	Y	N	N	Y	N
MONTANA							
AL ***Hill***	Y	Y	Y	N	N	Y	N
NEBRASKA							
1 ***Bereuter***	Y	Y	Y	N	N	N	N
2 ***Christensen***	Y	Y	Y	N	N	Y	N
3 ***Barrett***	Y	Y	Y	N	N	Y	N
NEVADA							
1 ***Ensign***	N	Y	Y	N	N	Y	N
2 ***Gibbons***	Y	Y	Y	N	N	Y	N
NEW HAMPSHIRE							
1 ***Sununu***	Y	Y	Y	N	N	Y	Y
2 ***Bass***	Y	Y	Y	N	N	Y	N
NEW JERSEY							
1 Andrews	N	N	N	N	N	Y	N
2 ***LoBiondo***	Y	Y	Y	N	N	Y	N
3 ***Saxton***	Y	Y	Y	N	N	N	N
4 ***Smith***	Y	Y	Y	N	N	Y	N
5 ***Roukema***	Y	Y	Y	N	N	N	N
6 Pallone	N	N	N	Y	Y	N	Y
7 ***Franks***	Y	Y	Y	N	N	N	N
8 Pascrell	N	N	N	Y	Y	N	Y
9 Rothman	Y	Y	Y	N	N	N	Y
10 Payne	N	N	N	Y	Y	N	Y
11 ***Frelinghuysen***	Y	Y	Y	N	N	N	N
12 ***Pappas***	Y	Y	Y	N	N	Y	N
13 Menendez	N	N	N	N	N	N	Y
NEW MEXICO							
1 Vacant							
2 ***Skeen***	Y	Y	Y	N	N	Y	N
3 ***Redmond***	Y	Y	Y	N	N	Y	N
NEW YORK							
1 ***Forbes***	Y	Y	Y	N	N	Y	N
2 ***Lazio***	Y	Y	Y	N	N	Y	N
3 ***King***	Y	Y	Y	N	N	Y	N
4 McCarthy	N	N	N	Y	Y	N	Y
5 Ackerman	N	N	N	Y	Y	N	Y
6 Meeks	N	N	N	Y	Y	N	Y
7 Manton	N	N	N	Y	Y	N	Y
8 Nadler	N	N	N	Y	Y	N	N
9 Schumer	N	N	N	?	?	?	?
10 Towns	N	N	N	Y	Y	N	N
11 Owens	N	N	N	Y	Y	N	Y
12 Velázquez	N	N	N	Y	Y	N	Y
13 ***Fossella***	Y	Y	Y	N	N	Y	N
14 Maloney	N	N	N	Y	Y	N	N
15 Rangel	N	N	N	N	Y	N	N
16 Serrano	N	N	N	Y	Y	N	N
17 Engel	N	N	N	Y	Y	N	Y
18 Lowey	N	N	N	Y	Y	N	N
19 ***Kelly***	Y	Y	Y	N	N	N	N
20 ***Gilman***	+	Y	Y	N	N	Y	N
21 McNulty	N	N	N	Y	Y	N	Y
22 ***Solomon***	Y	Y	Y	N	N	Y	N
23 ***Boehlert***	Y	Y	Y	N	N	N	N
24 ***McHugh***	Y	Y	Y	N	N	Y	N
25 ***Walsh***	Y	Y	Y	N	N	Y	N
26 Hinchey	N	N	N	Y	Y	N	Y
27 ***Paxon***	Y	Y	Y	N	N	Y	N
28 Slaughter	N	N	N	Y	Y	N	N
29 LaFalce	N	N	N	Y	Y	N	Y

	216	217	218	219	220	221	222
30 ***Quinn***	Y	Y	Y	N	N	Y	N
31 ***Houghton***	?	?	?	N	N	N	N
NORTH CAROLINA							
1 Clayton	N	N	N	?	Y	N	Y
2 Etheridge	N	N	N	N	Y	N	N
3 ***Jones***	Y	Y	Y	N	N	Y	N
4 Price	N	N	N	Y	Y	N	N
5 ***Burr***	Y	Y	Y	N	N	Y	N
6 ***Coble***	Y	Y	Y	N	N	Y	N
7 McIntyre	N	N	Y	N	N	Y	N
8 Hefner	N	N	N	Y	Y	N	Y
9 ***Myrick***	Y	Y	Y	N	N	Y	N
10 ***Ballenger***	Y	Y	Y	N	N	Y	N
11 ***Taylor***	Y	Y	Y	N	N	Y	N
12 Watt	N	N	N	Y	Y	N	Y
NORTH DAKOTA							
AL Pomeroy	N	N	N	N	N	N	Y
OHIO							
1 ***Chabot***	Y	Y	Y	N	N	N	N
2 ***Portman***	Y	Y	Y	N	N	Y	N
3 Hall	N	N	N	Y	N	N	N
4 ***Oxley***	?	Y	Y	N	N	Y	N
5 ***Gillmor***	Y	Y	Y	N	N	Y	N
6 Strickland	N	N	N	Y	Y	N	Y
7 ***Hobson***	Y	Y	Y	N	N	N	N
8 ***Boehner***	Y	Y	Y	N	N	Y	N
9 Kaptur	N	N	N	Y	Y	N	Y
10 Kucinich	N	N	N	Y	Y	N	N
11 Stokes	N	N	N	Y	Y	N	Y
12 ***Kasich***	Y	Y	Y	N	N	N	N
13 Brown	N	N	N	Y	Y	N	N
14 Sawyer	Y	N	N	Y	Y	N	N
15 ***Pryce***	Y	Y	Y	N	N	N	N
16 ***Regula***	Y	Y	Y	N	N	N	N
17 Traficant	Y	Y	Y	N	N	Y	N
18 ***Ney***	Y	Y	Y	N	N	Y	N
19 ***LaTourette***	Y	Y	Y	N	N	N	N
OKLAHOMA							
1 ***Largent***	Y	Y	Y	N	N	N	N
2 ***Coburn***	Y	Y	Y	N	Y	Y	N
3 ***Watkins***	Y	Y	Y	N	N	Y	N
4 ***Watts***	Y	Y	Y	N	N	Y	N
5 ***Istook***	Y	Y	Y	N	N	N	N
6 ***Lucas***	Y	Y	Y	N	N	Y	N
OREGON							
1 Furse	N	N	N	Y	Y	N	Y
2 ***Smith***	Y	Y	Y	N	N	Y	N
3 Blumenauer	N	N	N	N	Y	N	?
4 DeFazio	N	N	N	Y	Y	N	Y
5 Hooley	N	N	N	Y	N	N	Y
PENNSYLVANIA							
1 Brady	N	N	N	Y	Y	N	Y
2 Fattah	N	N	N	Y	Y	N	Y
3 Borski	?	N	N	Y	Y	N	N
4 Klink	N	N	N	Y	Y	N	Y
5 ***Peterson***	Y	Y	Y	N	N	Y	N
6 Holden	Y	N	N	N	N	N	Y
7 ***Weldon***	Y	Y	Y	N	N	Y	N
8 ***Greenwood***	Y	Y	Y	N	N	Y	N
9 ***Shuster***	Y	Y	Y	N	N	Y	N
10 ***McDade***	Y	Y	Y	N	N	Y	N
11 Kanjorski	N	N	N	Y	Y	N	Y
12 Murtha	N	N	N	N	Y	N	Y
13 ***Fox***	Y	Y	Y	N	N	N	N
14 Coyne	N	N	N	Y	Y	N	Y
15 McHale	N	N	N	N	N	N	N
16 ***Pitts***	Y	Y	Y	N	N	Y	N
17 ***Gekas***	Y	Y	Y	N	N	Y	N
18 Doyle	N	N	N	Y	Y	N	N
19 ***Goodling***	Y	?	Y	N	N	Y	N
20 Mascara	N	N	N	Y	Y	N	Y
21 ***English***	Y	Y	Y	N	N	Y	N
RHODE ISLAND							
1 Kennedy	Y	N	Y	N	Y	N	N
2 Weygand	Y	N	N	N	Y	N	N
SOUTH CAROLINA							
1 ***Sanford***	Y	Y	Y	Y	N	Y	N
2 ***Spence***	Y	Y	Y	N	N	Y	N
3 ***Graham***	Y	Y	Y	N	N	Y	N
4 ***Inglis***	?	?	?	N	N	Y	N
5 Spratt	N	N	N	N	N	N	Y
6 Clyburn	N	N	N	Y	Y	N	N
SOUTH DAKOTA							
AL ***Thune***	Y	Y	Y	N	N	Y	N

	216	217	218	219	220	221	222
TENNESSEE							
1 ***Jenkins***	Y	Y	Y	N	N	Y	N
2 ***Duncan***	Y	Y	Y	N	N	Y	N
3 ***Wamp***	Y	Y	Y	N	N	Y	N
4 ***Hilleary***	Y	Y	Y	N	N	Y	N
5 Clement	N	N	N	N	N	N	N
6 Gordon	Y	N	N	N	N	N	N
7 ***Bryant***	Y	Y	Y	N	N	Y	N
8 Tanner	N	N	N	N	N	N	N
9 Ford	N	N	N	N	Y	?	Y
TEXAS							
1 Sandlin	N	N	N	N	N	Y	Y
2 Turner	Y	N	N	N	N	Y	N
3 ***Johnson, Sam***	Y	Y	Y	N	N	Y	N
4 Hall	Y	N	N	N	N	Y	N
5 ***Sessions***	Y	Y	Y	N	N	Y	N
6 ***Barton***	Y	Y	Y	N	N	Y	N
7 ***Archer***	Y	Y	Y	N	N	Y	N
8 ***Brady***	Y	+	Y	N	N	Y	N
9 Lampson	N	N	N	Y	Y	Y	Y
10 Doggett	N	N	N	Y	N	Y	Y
11 Edwards	N	N	N	Y	Y	Y	N
12 ***Granger***	Y	Y	Y	N	N	Y	N
13 ***Thornberry***	Y	Y	Y	N	N	Y	N
14 ***Paul***	Y	Y	Y	N	N	Y	N
15 Hinojosa	N	N	N	Y	Y	Y	Y
16 Reyes	N	N	N	Y	Y	Y	Y
17 Stenholm	N	N	N	N	N	Y	N
18 Jackson-Lee	N	N	N	Y	Y	Y	Y
19 ***Combest***	Y	Y	Y	N	N	Y	N
20 Gonzalez	?	?	?	?	?	?	?
21 ***Smith***	Y	Y	Y	N	N	Y	N
22 ***DeLay***	Y	Y	Y	N	N	Y	N
23 ***Bonilla***	Y	Y	Y	N	N	Y	N
24 Frost	Y	N	Y	N	N	Y	N
25 Bentsen	N	N	N	N	N	Y	Y
26 ***Armey***	Y	Y	Y	N	N	Y	N
27 Ortiz	N	N	N	Y	Y	Y	Y
28 Rodriguez	N	N	N	Y	Y	Y	Y
29 Green	N	N	N	Y	Y	Y	Y
30 Johnson, E.B.	N	N	N	Y	Y	Y	N
UTAH							
1 ***Hansen***	Y	Y	Y	N	N	Y	N
2 ***Cook***	?	Y	Y	N	N	Y	N
3 ***Cannon***	Y	Y	Y	N	N	Y	N
VERMONT							
AL *Sanders*	N	N	N	Y	Y	N	Y
VIRGINIA							
1 ***Bateman***	Y	Y	Y	N	N	Y	N
2 Pickett	?	N	N	N	N	Y	Y
3 Scott	N	N	N	Y	Y	N	Y
4 Sisisky	Y	N	Y	N	N	Y	Y
5 Goode	Y	Y	Y	N	N	Y	N
6 ***Goodlatte***	Y	Y	Y	N	N	Y	N
7 ***Bliley***	Y	Y	Y	N	N	Y	N
8 Moran	Y	Y	Y	N	N	N	N
9 Boucher	Y	Y	Y	N	N	Y	N
10 ***Wolf***	Y	Y	N	N	N	Y	N
11 ***Davis***	Y	Y	Y	N	N	Y	N
WASHINGTON							
1 ***White***	Y	Y	Y	N	N	Y	N
2 ***Metcalf***	Y	Y	Y	N	N	N	N
3 ***Smith, Linda***	Y	Y	Y	N	N	Y	N
4 ***Hastings***	Y	Y	Y	N	N	Y	N
5 ***Nethercutt***	Y	Y	Y	N	N	Y	N
6 Dicks	N	N	Y	Y	Y	N	N
7 McDermott	–	N	N	Y	Y	N	N
8 ***Dunn***	Y	?	Y	N	N	N	N
9 Smith, Adam	Y	Y	Y	N	N	N	Y
WEST VIRGINIA							
1 Mollohan	N	N	N	Y	Y	Y	Y
2 Wise	N	N	N	Y	Y	N	N
3 Rahall	N	N	N	Y	Y	Y	N
WISCONSIN							
1 ***Neumann***	Y	Y	Y	N	N	Y	N
2 ***Klug***	?	?	?	N	N	Y	N
3 Kind	N	Y	Y	N	N	Y	N
4 Kleczka	Y	Y	Y	N	N	N	Y
5 Barrett	N	N	N	N	Y	N	Y
6 ***Petri***	Y	Y	Y	N	N	N	N
7 Obey	N	N	N	N	Y	N	N
8 Johnson	N	N	N	N	Y	N	N
9 ***Sensenbrenner***	?	?	Y	N	N	N	Y
WYOMING							
AL ***Cubin***	Y	Y	Y	N	N	Y	N

Southern states - Ala., Ark., Fla., Ga., Ky., La., Miss., N.C., Okla., S.C., Tenn., Texas, Va.

House Votes 223, 224, 225, 226, 227, 228, 229

Key

- Y Voted for (yea).
- # Paired for.
- + Announced for.
- N Voted against (nay).
- X Paired against.
- − Announced against.
- P Voted "present."
- C Voted "present" to avoid possible conflict of interest.
- ? Did not vote or otherwise make a position known.

Democrats **Republicans** *Independent*

223. HR 3150. Bankruptcy Overhaul/Democratic Substitute. Nadler, D-N.Y., substitute amendment to strike the bill's provisions regarding means-testing; requiring "adequate" income be committed to a repayment plan for unsecured creditors; and defining abuse of the bankruptcy system. Rejected 140-288: R 0-226; D 139-62 (ND 119-29, SD 20-33); I 1-0. June 10, 1998.

224. HR 3150. Bankruptcy Overhaul/Recommit. Conyers, D-Mich., motion to recommit the bill to the Judiciary Committee with instructions to report it back with an amendment to exclude child support and alimony payments from means-tests and to make accident victims priority creditors. Motion rejected 153-270: R 1-221; D 151-49 (ND 117-30, SD 34-19); I 1-0. June 10, 1998.

225. HR 3150. Bankruptcy Overhaul/Passage. Passage of the bill to overhaul the nation's bankruptcy laws by setting up a means-testing system to bar individuals with average incomes or higher from declaring bankruptcy under Chapter 7, and thus walking away from unsecured debts after the liquidation of certain assets. The bill also allows creditors, in addition to bankruptcy trustees, to challenge the validity of an individual's claim; and requires that debtors be informed of the various forms of bankruptcy relief before they file for bankruptcy. Passed 306-118: R 222-0; D 84-117 (ND 53-95, SD 31-22); I 0-1. June 10, 1998.

226. H J Res 119. Campaign Spending Constitutional Amendment/Passage. Passage of the joint resolution to propose a constitutional amendment to permit Congress and the states to go beyond court-set limits on the government's right to regulate campaign expenditures and contributions, as long as these regulations do not impair the public's right to a full and free discussion of all issues. Rejected 29-345: R 6-220; D 23-124 (ND 19-84, SD 4-40); I 0-1. June 11, 1998. A two-thirds majority vote of those present and voting (250 in this case) is required to pass a joint resolution proposing an amendment to the Constitution.

227. HR 2888. Compensation for Sales Employees/Requiring Overtime. Owens, D-N.Y., amendment to prohibit employers from requiring employees affected by the bill from working more than eight hours a day or 40 hours a week without the employee's consent. Rejected 181-246: R 1-225; D 179-21 (ND 138-11, SD 41-10); I 1-0. June 11, 1998.

228. HR 2888. Compensation for Sales Employees/Passage. Passage of the bill to provide an exemption from minimum wage and overtime laws for certain commission-earning sales employees who earn above a defined threshold per year. Passed 261-165: R 218-7; D 43-157 (ND 22-127, SD 21-30); I 0-1. June 11, 1998. A "nay" was a vote in support of the president's position.

229. HR 3494. Sexual Predator Punishment/National Hotline. Sherman, D-Calif., amendment to establish a national hotline for parents to access FBI databases and determine if an individual is registered as a convicted sexual predator. Adopted 247-175: R 124-98; D 123-76 (ND 94-53, SD 29-23); I 0-1. June 11, 1998.

	223	224	225	226	227	228	229
ALABAMA							
1 **Callahan**	N	N	Y	N	N	Y	N
2 **Everett**	N	N	Y	N	N	Y	N
3 **Riley**	N	N	Y	N	N	Y	Y
4 **Aderholt**	N	N	Y	N	N	Y	Y
5 Cramer	N	N	Y	?	N	Y	N
6 **Bachus**	N	N	Y	N	N	Y	Y
7 Hilliard	Y	Y	N	N	Y	N	–
ALASKA							
AL **Young**	N	N	Y	N	N	Y	Y
ARIZONA							
1 **Salmon**	N	N	Y	N	N	Y	Y
2 Pastor	Y	Y	Y	N	Y	N	Y
3 **Stump**	N	N	Y	N	N	Y	N
4 **Shadegg**	N	N	Y	N	N	Y	Y
5 **Kolbe**	N	N	Y	N	N	Y	Y
6 **Hayworth**	N	N	Y	N	N	Y	Y
ARKANSAS							
1 Berry	N	N	Y	N	Y	N	Y
2 Snyder	N	N	Y	N	Y	N	Y
3 **Hutchinson**	N	N	Y	N	N	Y	Y
4 **Dickey**	N	N	Y	N	N	Y	Y
CALIFORNIA							
1 **Riggs**	N	N	Y	N	N	Y	N
2 **Herger**	N	N	Y	N	N	Y	Y
3 Fazio	Y	N	Y	N	Y	N	Y
4 **Doolittle**	N	N	Y	N	N	Y	Y
5 Matsui	Y	Y	N	N	Y	N	N
6 Woolsey	Y	Y	N	P	Y	N	Y
7 Miller	Y	Y	N	P	Y	N	N
8 Pelosi	Y	Y	N	N	Y	N	N
9 Lee	Y	Y	N	N	Y	N	N
10 Tauscher	N	N	Y	P	N	Y	N
11 **Pombo**	N	N	Y	N	N	Y	N
12 Lantos	Y	Y	N	N	Y	N	N
13 Stark	Y	Y	N	N	Y	N	N
14 Eshoo	Y	Y	N	P	N	N	N
15 **Campbell**	N	N	Y	N	N	Y	N
16 Lofgren	Y	Y	N	N	Y	N	N
17 Farr	+	+	–	–	+	–	–
18 Condit	N	N	Y	N	N	Y	Y
19 **Radanovich**	N	N	Y	N	N	Y	Y
20 Dooley	N	N	Y	N	N	Y	N
21 **Thomas**	N	N	Y	N	N	Y	N
22 Capps, L.	Y	Y	N	N	Y	N	Y
23 **Gallegly**	N	N	Y	N	N	Y	Y
24 Sherman	N	N	Y	N	N	Y	Y
25 **McKeon**	N	N	Y	N	N	Y	Y
26 Berman	?	?	?	?	?	?	?
27 **Rogan**	N	N	Y	N	N	Y	Y
28 **Dreier**	N	N	Y	N	N	Y	Y
29 Waxman	Y	Y	N	P	Y	N	Y
30 Becerra	Y	Y	N	P	Y	N	?
31 Martinez	Y	Y	N	N	Y	N	Y
32 Dixon	Y	Y	N	N	Y	N	N
33 Roybal-Allard	Y	Y	N	N	Y	N	N
34 Torres	Y	Y	N	N	Y	N	Y
35 Waters	Y	Y	N	N	Y	N	Y
36 Harman	Y	N	Y	Y	Y	Y	Y
37 Millender-McD.	Y	Y	N	N	Y	N	N

	223	224	225	226	227	228	229
38 **Horn**	N	N	Y	N	N	Y	Y
39 **Royce**	N	N	Y	N	N	Y	Y
40 **Lewis**	N	N	Y	N	N	?	N
41 **Kim**	N	N	Y	N	N	Y	Y
42 Brown	Y	Y	N	N	Y	N	N
43 **Calvert**	N	N	Y	N	N	Y	Y
44 **Bono, M.**	N	N	Y	N	N	Y	Y
45 **Rohrabacher**	N	N	Y	N	N	Y	Y
46 Sanchez	Y	N	N	P	Y	N	Y
47 **Cox**	N	?	Y	N	N	Y	Y
48 **Packard**	N	N	Y	N	N	Y	Y
49 **Bilbray**	N	N	Y	N	N	Y	Y
50 Filner	Y	Y	N	N	Y	N	Y
51 **Cunningham**	N	N	Y	N	N	Y	Y
52 **Hunter**	N	N	Y	N	N	Y	N
COLORADO							
1 DeGette	Y	Y	N	N	Y	N	N
2 Skaggs	Y	Y	N	N	Y	N	N
3 **McInnis**	N	N	Y	N	N	Y	Y
4 **Schaffer**	N	N	Y	N	N	Y	Y
5 **Hefley**	N	N	Y	N	N	Y	Y
6 **Schaefer**	N	N	Y	N	N	Y	Y
CONNECTICUT							
1 Kennelly	Y	Y	Y	N	Y	N	Y
2 Gejdenson	Y	Y	N	N	Y	N	Y
3 DeLauro	Y	Y	N	P	Y	N	N
4 **Shays**	N	N	Y	N	N	Y	+
5 Maloney	N	N	Y	N	N	Y	Y
6 **Johnson**	N	N	Y	N	N	Y	Y
DELAWARE							
AL **Castle**	N	N	Y	N	N	Y	N
FLORIDA							
1 **Scarborough**	N	N	Y	N	N	Y	Y
2 Boyd	N	N	Y	–	–	+	N
3 Brown	Y	Y	N	Y	N	N	N
4 **Fowler**	N	N	Y	N	N	Y	N
5 Thurman	N	Y	N	P	Y	Y	N
6 **Stearns**	N	N	Y	N	N	Y	Y
7 **Mica**	N	N	Y	N	N	Y	Y
8 **McCollum**	N	N	Y	N	N	Y	Y
9 **Bilirakis**	N	N	Y	N	N	Y	Y
10 **Young**	N	N	Y	N	N	Y	N
11 Davis	N	N	Y	N	N	Y	Y
12 **Canady**	N	N	Y	N	N	Y	Y
13 **Miller**	N	N	Y	N	N	Y	Y
14 **Goss**	N	N	Y	N	N	Y	Y
15 **Weldon**	N	N	Y	N	N	Y	Y
16 **Foley**	N	N	Y	N	N	Y	Y
17 Meek	Y	Y	N	N	Y	N	N
18 **Ros-Lehtinen**	N	N	Y	N	N	Y	Y
19 Wexler	Y	Y	N	P	Y	N	Y
20 Deutsch	N	N	Y	P	N	Y	N
21 **Diaz-Balart**	N	N	Y	N	N	Y	Y
22 **Shaw**	N	N	Y	N	N	Y	Y
23 Hastings	Y	Y	N	N	Y	N	N
GEORGIA							
1 **Kingston**	N	N	Y	N	N	Y	N
2 Bishop	Y	Y	Y	N	Y	Y	Y
3 **Collins**	N	N	Y	N	N	Y	N
4 **McKinney**	Y	Y	N	N	Y	N	N
5 Lewis	?	?	?	?	?	?	?
6 **Gingrich**							
7 **Barr**	N	N	Y	N	N	Y	Y
8 **Chambliss**	N	N	Y	N	N	Y	Y
9 **Deal**	N	N	Y	N	N	Y	Y
10 **Norwood**	N	N	Y	N	N	Y	Y
11 **Linder**	N	N	Y	N	N	Y	N
HAWAII							
1 Abercrombie	Y	Y	N	P	Y	N	Y
2 Mink	Y	Y	N	N	Y	N	Y
IDAHO							
1 **Chenoweth**	N	N	Y	N	N	Y	Y
2 **Crapo**	N	N	Y	N	N	Y	Y
ILLINOIS							
1 Rush	Y	Y	N	N	Y	N	N
2 Jackson	Y	Y	N	N	Y	N	N
3 Lipinski	N	N	Y	N	N	Y	Y
4 Gutierrez	Y	Y	N	P	Y	N	Y
5 Blagojevich	N	N	Y	P	N	Y	N
6 **Hyde**	N	N	Y	N	N	Y	Y
7 Davis	Y	Y	N	N	Y	N	Y
8 **Crane**	N	N	Y	N	N	Y	N
9 Yates	Y	Y	N	Y	Y	N	Y
10 **Porter**	N	N	Y	N	N	Y	Y
11 **Weller**	N	N	Y	N	N	Y	Y
12 Costello	N	Y	N	N	N	Y	Y

ND Northern Democrats   SD Southern Democrats

	223	224	225	226	227	228	229
13 ***Fawell***	N	?	Y	N	N	Y	Y
14 ***Hastert***	N	?	Y	N	N	Y	N
15 ***Ewing***	N	N	Y	N	N	Y	N
16 ***Manzullo***	N	N	Y	N	N	Y	Y
17 Evans	Y	Y	N	N	Y	N	Y
18 ***LaHood***	N	N	Y	N	N	Y	N
19 Poshard	Y	Y	N	Y	Y	N	Y
20 ***Shimkus***	N	N	Y	N	N	Y	Y
INDIANA							
1 Visclosky	Y	Y	N	N	Y	N	N
2 ***McIntosh***	N	N	Y	N	N	Y	N
3 Roemer	N	N	Y	N	N	Y	Y
4 ***Souder***	N	N	Y	N	N	Y	Y
5 ***Buyer***	N	N	Y	N	N	Y	N
6 ***Burton***	N	N	Y	N	N	Y	Y
7 ***Pease***	N	N	Y	N	N	Y	Y
8 ***Hostettler***	N	N	Y	N	N	Y	Y
9 Hamilton	N	N	Y	N	N	N	N
10 Carson	Y	Y	N	N	Y	N	Y
IOWA							
1 ***Leach***	N	N	Y	Y	N	Y	Y
2 ***Nussle***	N	N	Y	N	N	Y	Y
3 Boswell	N	N	Y	N	N	Y	Y
4 ***Ganske***	N	N	Y	N	N	Y	Y
5 ***Latham***	N	N	Y	N	N	Y	Y
KANSAS							
1 ***Moran***	N	N	Y	N	N	Y	Y
2 ***Ryun***	N	N	Y	N	N	Y	Y
3 ***Snowbarger***	N	N	Y	N	N	Y	Y
4 ***Tiahrt***	N	N	Y	N	N	Y	Y
KENTUCKY							
1 ***Whitfield***	N	N	Y	N	N	Y	Y
2 ***Lewis***	N	N	Y	N	N	Y	Y
3 ***Northup***	N	N	Y	N	N	Y	N
4 ***Bunning***	N	N	Y	N	N	Y	Y
5 ***Rogers***	N	N	Y	N	N	Y	N
6 Baesler	N	N	Y	N	Y	N	Y
LOUISIANA							
1 ***Livingston***	N	N	Y	N	N	Y	N
2 Jefferson	Y	Y	Y	N	Y	N	Y
3 ***Tauzin***	N	N	Y	N	N	Y	N
4 ***McCrery***	N	N	Y	N	N	Y	N
5 ***Cooksey***	N	N	Y	N	N	Y	N
6 ***Baker***	N	N	Y	N	N	Y	N
7 John	N	N	Y	N	N	Y	Y
MAINE							
1 Allen	Y	Y	N	N	Y	N	Y
2 Baldacci	Y	Y	Y	N	Y	N	Y
MARYLAND							
1 ***Gilchrest***	N	N	Y	N	N	Y	N
2 ***Ehrlich***	N	N	Y	N	N	Y	N
3 Cardin	N	Y	Y	P	Y	N	N
4 Wynn	Y	N	Y	N	Y	N	Y
5 Hoyer	N	N	Y	P	Y	N	Y
6 ***Bartlett***	N	N	Y	N	N	Y	Y
7 Cummings	Y	Y	Y	N	Y	N	Y
8 ***Morella***	N	N	Y	N	N	Y	Y
MASSACHUSETTS							
1 Olver	Y	Y	N	N	Y	N	Y
2 Neal	Y	Y	N	P	Y	N	Y
3 McGovern	Y	Y	N	P	Y	N	Y
4 Frank	N	N	Y	P	Y	N	N
5 Meehan	Y	Y	N	P	Y	N	Y
6 Tierney	Y	Y	N	P	Y	N	Y
7 Markey	Y	Y	N	N	Y	N	Y
8 Kennedy	Y	Y	Y	N	Y	N	Y
9 Moakley	Y	Y	N	P	Y	N	?
10 Delahunt	Y	Y	N	P	Y	N	N
MICHIGAN							
1 Stupak	Y	Y	N	Y	Y	N	N
2 ***Hoekstra***	N	N	Y	N	N	Y	Y
3 ***Ehlers***	N	N	Y	N	N	Y	N
4 ***Camp***	N	N	Y	N	N	Y	N
5 Barcia	N	Y	Y	N	Y	N	Y
6 ***Upton***	N	N	Y	N	N	Y	Y
7 ***Smith***	N	N	Y	N	N	Y	Y
8 Stabenow	Y	Y	Y	P	Y	Y	N
9 Kildee	Y	Y	N	N	Y	N	Y
10 Bonior	Y	Y	N	P	Y	N	N
11 ***Knollenberg***	N	N	Y	N	N	Y	N
12 Levin	Y	Y	N	P	Y	N	Y
13 Rivers	Y	Y	Y	N	Y	Y	Y
14 Conyers	Y	Y	N	N	Y	N	N
15 Kilpatrick	Y	Y	N	N	Y	N	N
16 Dingell	Y	Y	N	Y	Y	N	N

	223	224	225	226	227	228	229
MINNESOTA							
1 ***Gutknecht***	N	N	Y	N	N	Y	N
2 Minge	Y	Y	Y	Y	Y	Y	Y
3 ***Ramstad***	N	N	Y	N	N	Y	Y
4 Vento	Y	Y	N	Y	Y	N	N
5 Sabo	Y	Y	N	N	Y	N	N
6 Luther	Y	Y	Y	Y	Y	Y	Y
7 Peterson	N	N	Y	N	Y	Y	Y
8 Oberstar	Y	Y	N	N	Y	N	Y
MISSISSIPPI							
1 ***Wicker***	N	N	Y	N	N	Y	Y
2 Thompson	Y	Y	N	N	Y	N	N
3 ***Pickering***	N	N	Y	N	N	Y	Y
4 ***Parker***	N	N	Y	N	N	Y	?
5 Taylor	N	N	Y	N	N	N	Y
MISSOURI							
1 Clay	Y	Y	N	N	Y	N	N
2 ***Talent***	N	N	Y	N	N	Y	Y
3 Gephardt	Y	Y	N	P	Y	N	Y
4 Skelton	N	N	Y	N	Y	N	Y
5 McCarthy	Y	Y	Y	P	Y	Y	Y
6 Danner	N	N	Y	N	Y	Y	Y
7 ***Blunt***	N	N	Y	N	N	Y	N
8 ***Emerson***	N	N	Y	N	N	Y	Y
9 ***Hulshof***	N	N	Y	N	N	Y	Y
MONTANA							
AL ***Hill***	N	N	Y	N	N	Y	Y
NEBRASKA							
1 ***Bereuter***	N	N	Y	Y	N	Y	Y
2 ***Christensen***	N	N	Y	N	N	Y	Y
3 ***Barrett***	N	N	Y	N	N	Y	Y
NEVADA							
1 ***Ensign***	N	Y	Y	N	N	Y	Y
2 ***Gibbons***	N	N	Y	N	N	Y	Y
NEW HAMPSHIRE							
1 ***Sununu***	N	N	Y	N	N	Y	Y
2 ***Bass***	N	N	Y	N	N	Y	N
NEW JERSEY							
1 Andrews	N	N	Y	N	N	Y	Y
2 ***LoBiondo***	N	N	Y	N	N	Y	Y
3 ***Saxton***	N	N	Y	N	N	Y	Y
4 ***Smith***	N	N	Y	N	N	Y	Y
5 ***Roukema***	N	N	Y	N	N	Y	Y
6 Pallone	Y	Y	N	P	Y	N	Y
7 ***Franks***	N	N	Y	N	N	Y	Y
8 Pascrell	Y	Y	Y	N	Y	N	Y
9 Rothman	N	N	Y	P	Y	N	Y
10 Payne	Y	Y	N	N	Y	N	Y
11 ***Frelinghuysen***	N	N	Y	N	N	Y	Y
12 ***Pappas***	N	N	Y	N	N	Y	Y
13 Menendez	N	N	Y	P	Y	N	Y
NEW MEXICO							
1 Vacant							
2 ***Skeen***	N	N	Y	N	N	Y	Y
3 ***Redmond***	N	N	+	N	N	Y	Y
NEW YORK							
1 ***Forbes***	N	N	Y	N	N	Y	Y
2 ***Lazio***	N	N	Y	N	N	Y	Y
3 ***King***	N	N	Y	N	N	Y	N
4 McCarthy	Y	Y	Y	N	N	Y	Y
5 Ackerman	Y	Y	N	N	Y	N	Y
6 Meeks	Y	Y	N	N	Y	N	N
7 Manton	Y	Y	N	N	Y	N	Y
8 Nadler	Y	Y	N	P	Y	N	Y
9 Schumer	?	?	?	?	Y	N	Y
10 Towns	Y	Y	Y	N	Y	N	Y
11 Owens	Y	Y	N	N	Y	N	N
12 Velázquez	Y	Y	Y	N	Y	N	Y
13 ***Fossella***	N	N	Y	N	N	Y	Y
14 Maloney	Y	Y	N	P	Y	N	Y
15 Rangel	Y	Y	N	N	Y	N	N
16 Serrano	Y	Y	N	N	Y	N	Y
17 Engel	Y	Y	N	Y	Y	N	Y
18 Lowey	Y	Y	N	P	Y	N	Y
19 ***Kelly***	N	N	Y	N	N	Y	Y
20 ***Gilman***	N	N	Y	N	N	N	Y
21 McNulty	Y	Y	N	N	Y	N	Y
22 ***Solomon***	N	N	Y	N	N	Y	Y
23 ***Boehlert***	N	N	Y	N	N	N	N
24 ***McHugh***	N	N	Y	Y	N	Y	Y
25 ***Walsh***	N	N	Y	N	N	Y	Y
26 Hinchey	Y	Y	N	Y	Y	N	Y
27 ***Paxon***	N	N	Y	N	N	Y	?
28 Slaughter	Y	Y	N	P	Y	N	Y
29 LaFalce	Y	Y	N	Y	Y	N	Y

	223	224	225	226	227	228	229
30 ***Quinn***	N	N	Y	N	N	Y	Y
31 ***Houghton***	N	N	Y	N	N	Y	N
NORTH CAROLINA							
1 Clayton	Y	Y	N	N	Y	N	Y
2 Etheridge	Y	Y	Y	−	+	−	Y
3 ***Jones***	N	N	Y	N	N	Y	Y
4 Price	Y	Y	Y	N	Y	Y	Y
5 ***Burr***	N	N	Y	N	N	Y	N
6 ***Coble***	N	N	Y	N	N	Y	N
7 McIntyre	N	Y	Y	N	Y	Y	Y
8 Hefner	Y	Y	N	N	Y	N	N
9 ***Myrick***	N	N	Y	N	N	Y	N
10 ***Ballenger***	N	N	Y	N	N	Y	N
11 ***Taylor***	N	N	Y	N	N	Y	Y
12 Watt	Y	Y	N	N	Y	N	N
NORTH DAKOTA							
AL Pomeroy	Y	Y	Y	P	Y	N	Y
OHIO							
1 ***Chabot***	N	N	Y	N	N	Y	Y
2 ***Portman***	N	N	Y	N	N	Y	N
3 Hall	Y	Y	N	N	Y	N	N
4 ***Oxley***	N	N	Y	N	N	Y	N
5 ***Gillmor***	N	N	Y	Y	N	Y	N
6 Strickland	Y	Y	Y	N	Y	N	Y
7 ***Hobson***	N	N	+	N	N	Y	N
8 ***Boehner***	N	N	Y	N	N	Y	N
9 Kaptur	Y	Y	N	P	Y	N	Y
10 Kucinich	Y	Y	N	P	Y	N	Y
11 Stokes	Y	Y	N	N	Y	N	N
12 ***Kasich***	N	N	Y	N	N	Y	N
13 Brown	Y	Y	N	P	Y	N	Y
14 Sawyer	Y	Y	N	P	Y	N	Y
15 ***Pryce***	N	N	Y	N	N	Y	Y
16 ***Regula***	N	N	Y	N	N	Y	N
17 Traficant	N	N	Y	N	N	Y	Y
18 ***Ney***	N	N	Y	N	N	Y	Y
19 ***LaTourette***	N	N	Y	N	N	Y	Y
OKLAHOMA							
1 ***Largent***	N	?	?	N	N	Y	Y
2 ***Coburn***	N	N	Y	N	N	Y	N
3 ***Watkins***	N	N	Y	N	N	Y	Y
4 ***Watts***	N	N	Y	N	N	Y	Y
5 ***Istook***	N	N	Y	N	N	Y	Y
6 ***Lucas***	N	N	Y	N	N	Y	Y
OREGON							
1 Furse	Y	Y	N	P	Y	N	Y
2 ***Smith***	N	N	Y	N	N	Y	N
3 Blumenauer	Y	Y	Y	N	Y	N	N
4 DeFazio	Y	Y	N	Y	Y	N	Y
5 Hooley	Y	Y	Y	N	Y	N	Y
PENNSYLVANIA							
1 Brady	Y	Y	N	P	Y	N	N
2 Fattah	Y	Y	N	P	Y	N	N
3 Borski	Y	Y	N	P	Y	N	N
4 Klink	Y	Y	N	N	Y	N	Y
5 ***Peterson***	N	N	Y	N	N	Y	Y
6 Holden	Y	Y	Y	Y	Y	Y	Y
7 ***Weldon***	N	N	Y	N	N	Y	Y
8 ***Greenwood***	N	N	Y	N	N	Y	N
9 ***Shuster***	N	N	Y	N	N	Y	N
10 ***McDade***	N	N	Y	N	N	N	N
11 Kanjorski	Y	Y	N	P	Y	N	N
12 Murtha	Y	N	N	N	Y	N	N
13 ***Fox***	N	N	Y	N	N	Y	Y
14 Coyne	Y	Y	N	P	Y	N	N
15 McHale	Y	Y	Y	N	Y	N	Y
16 ***Pitts***	N	N	Y	N	N	Y	N
17 ***Gekas***	N	N	Y	N	N	Y	N
18 Doyle	Y	Y	N	Y	Y	N	Y
19 ***Goodling***	N	N	Y	N	N	Y	Y
20 Mascara	Y	Y	N	N	Y	N	Y
21 ***English***	N	N	Y	N	N	Y	Y
RHODE ISLAND							
1 Kennedy	N	N	Y	Y	Y	N	Y
2 Weygand	N	N	Y	N	Y	N	Y
SOUTH CAROLINA							
1 ***Sanford***	N	N	Y	N	N	Y	N
2 ***Spence***	N	N	Y	N	N	Y	N
3 ***Graham***	N	N	Y	N	N	Y	Y
4 ***Inglis***	N	N	Y	N	N	Y	?
5 Spratt	N	Y	Y	N	Y	Y	Y
6 Clyburn	Y	Y	Y	N	Y	N	Y
SOUTH DAKOTA							
AL ***Thune***	N	N	Y	N	N	Y	Y

	223	224	225	226	227	228	229
TENNESSEE							
1 ***Jenkins***	N	N	Y	N	N	Y	Y
2 ***Duncan***	N	N	Y	Y	N	Y	N
3 ***Wamp***	N	N	Y	N	N	Y	Y
4 ***Hilleary***	N	N	Y	N	N	Y	Y
5 Clement	N	N	Y	N	Y	Y	N
6 Gordon	N	N	Y	P	Y	Y	Y
7 ***Bryant***	N	N	Y	N	N	Y	Y
8 Tanner	N	N	Y	N	N	Y	N
9 Ford	Y	Y	N	Y	Y	N	Y
TEXAS							
1 Sandlin	N	Y	Y	Y	Y	N	Y
2 Turner	N	N	Y	N	Y	Y	Y
3 ***Johnson, Sam***	N	N	Y	N	N	Y	N
4 Hall	N	N	Y	N	N	Y	Y
5 ***Sessions***	N	N	Y	N	N	Y	N
6 ***Barton***	N	N	Y	N	N	Y	N
7 ***Archer***	N	N	Y	N	N	Y	N
8 ***Brady***	N	N	+	N	N	Y	Y
9 Lampson	N	Y	N	N	Y	N	N
10 Doggett	N	Y	Y	N	Y	Y	Y
11 Edwards	N	Y	N	N	Y	N	N
12 ***Granger***	N	N	Y	N	N	Y	N
13 ***Thornberry***	N	N	Y	N	N	Y	N
14 ***Paul***	N	N	Y	N	N	Y	N
15 Hinojosa	Y	Y	N	N	Y	Y	Y
16 Reyes	Y	Y	N	N	Y	N	Y
17 Stenholm	N	N	Y	N	N	Y	Y
18 Jackson-Lee	N	Y	N	P	Y	N	Y
19 ***Combest***	N	N	Y	N	N	Y	N
20 Gonzalez	?	?	?	?	?	?	?
21 ***Smith***	N	N	Y	N	N	Y	N
22 ***DeLay***	N	N	Y	N	N	Y	N
23 ***Bonilla***	N	N	Y	N	N	Y	N
24 Frost	N	Y	Y	P	Y	N	Y
25 Bentsen	N	Y	Y	N	Y	Y	Y
26 ***Armey***	N	N	Y	N	N	Y	N
27 Ortiz	Y	Y	N	N	Y	N	Y
28 Rodriguez	N	Y	N	N	Y	N	Y
29 Green	N	Y	N	Y	Y	N	Y
30 Johnson, E.B.	N	Y	N	N	Y	N	N
UTAH							
1 ***Hansen***	N	N	Y	N	N	Y	Y
2 ***Cook***	N	N	Y	N	N	Y	Y
3 ***Cannon***	N	N	Y	N	N	Y	Y
VERMONT							
AL *Sanders*	Y	Y	N	N	Y	N	N
VIRGINIA							
1 ***Bateman***	N	N	Y	N	N	Y	N
2 Pickett	N	N	Y	N	N	Y	N
3 Scott	Y	Y	N	N	Y	N	N
4 Sisisky	N	N	Y	N	N	Y	N
5 Goode	N	N	Y	N	N	Y	Y
6 ***Goodlatte***	N	N	Y	N	N	Y	Y
7 ***Bliley***	N	N	Y	N	N	Y	N
8 Moran	N	Y	Y	Y	Y	Y	N
9 Boucher	N	N	Y	N	Y	N	N
10 ***Wolf***	N	N	Y	N	N	Y	N
11 ***Davis***	N	N	Y	N	N	Y	N
WASHINGTON							
1 ***White***	N	N	Y	N	N	Y	N
2 ***Metcalf***	N	N	Y	N	N	Y	Y
3 ***Smith, Linda***	N	N	Y	N	N	Y	N
4 ***Hastings***	N	N	Y	N	N	Y	N
5 ***Nethercutt***	N	N	Y	N	N	Y	N
6 Dicks	Y	?	Y	N	Y	N	N
7 McDermott	Y	Y	N	N	Y	N	N
8 ***Dunn***	N	N	Y	N	N	Y	N
9 Smith, Adam	N	N	Y	Y	Y	N	Y
WEST VIRGINIA							
1 Mollohan	N	N	Y	N	Y	N	N
2 Wise	Y	Y	Y	P	Y	N	Y
3 Rahall	Y	Y	N	N	Y	N	N
WISCONSIN							
1 ***Neumann***	N	N	Y	N	N	Y	Y
2 ***Klug***	N	N	Y	N	N	Y	N
3 Kind	N	N	Y	N	N	Y	N
4 Kleczka	N	N	Y	N	Y	N	Y
5 Barrett	N	Y	N	Y	Y	N	N
6 ***Petri***	N	N	Y	N	N	Y	Y
7 Obey	Y	Y	N	Y	Y	N	N
8 Johnson	Y	Y	Y	N	N	Y	Y
9 ***Sensenbrenner***	N	N	Y	N	N	Y	N
WYOMING							
AL ***Cubin***	N	N	Y	N	N	Y	Y

Southern states - Ala., Ark., Fla., Ga., Ky., La., Miss., N.C., Okla., S.C., Tenn., Texas, Va.

House Votes 230, 231, 232, 233, 234, 235, 236

Key

- **Y** Voted for (yea).
- **#** Paired for.
- **+** Announced for.
- **N** Voted against (nay).
- **X** Paired against.
- **−** Announced against.
- **P** Voted "present."
- **C** Voted "present" to avoid possible conflict of interest.
- **?** Did not vote or otherwise make a position known.

Democrats **Republicans** Independent

---

230. HR 3494. Sexual Predator Punishment/Passage. Passage of the bill to establish or increase penalties for Internet-based sex crimes against minors, as well as sentencing guidelines for crimes against children. Passed 416-0: R 218-0; D 197-0 (ND 145-0, SD 52-0); I 1-0. June 11, 1998.

231. James Byrd Resolution/Adoption. Adoption of the resolution to condemn the brutal killing of James Byrd Jr., in Jasper, Texas. Adopted 397-0: R 208-0; D 188-0 (ND 137-0, SD 51-0); I 1-0. June 11, 1998.

232. HR 1847. Telemarketing Fraud/Agreeing to Senate Amendment. Goodlatte, R-Va., motion to suspend the rules and agree to the Senate amendment changing specific sentencing requirements to a "substantial increase in penalties" for persons convicted of telemarketing fraud. The bill would increase penalties and require convicted persons to forfeit property used in telemarketing scams. Motion agreed to (thus clearing the bill for the president) 411-1: R 218-1; D 192-0 (ND 143-0, SD 49-0); I1-0. June 16, 1998. A two-thirds majority of those present and voting (275 in this case) is required for adoption under suspension of the rules.

233. H Res 401. Social Promotion/Adoption. Riggs, R-Calif., motion to suspend the rules and adopt the resolution to express the sense of the House that government officials, teachers and parents should encourage schools to promote students solely based on academic performance. Motion agreed to 405-1: R 217-0; D 187-1 (ND 140-1, SD 47-0); I 1-0. June 16, 1998. A two-thirds majority of those present and voting (271 in this case) is required for adoption under suspension of the rules.

234. HR 3097. Tax Code Termination/Previous Question. Hastings, R-Wash., motion to order the previous question (thus ending debate and the possibility of amendment) on the adoption of the rule (H Res 472) to provide for House floor consideration of the bill to terminate the tax code. Motion agreed to 229-194: R 220-0; D 9-193 (ND 4-146, SD 5-47); I 0-1. June 17, 1998. (Subsequently, the rule was adopted.)

235. HR 3097. Tax Code Termination/Rule. Adoption of the rule (H Res 472) to provide for House floor consideration of the bill that would terminate the tax code. Adopted 232-188: R 220-0; D 12-187 (ND 6-141, SD 6-46); I 0-1. June 17, 1998.

236. HR 2646. Education Savings Accounts Conference Report/Rule. Adoption of the rule (H Res 471) to provide for House floor consideration of the conference report to a bill that would allow individuals to set aside up to $2,000 a year in a tax-sheltered savings account that could be used to pay for educational expenses. Adopted 228-191: R 219-0; D 9-190 (ND 3-146, SD 6-44); I 0-1. June 17, 1998.

	230	231	232	233	234	235	236
ALABAMA							
1 **Callahan**	Y	?	Y	Y	Y	Y	Y
2 Everett	Y	+	Y	Y	Y	Y	Y
3 **Riley**	Y	Y	Y	Y	Y	Y	Y
4 **Aderholt**	Y	Y	Y	Y	Y	Y	Y
5 Cramer	Y	Y	Y	Y	N	Y	Y
6 **Bachus**	Y	Y	Y	Y	Y	Y	Y
7 Hilliard	+	+	?	?	?	N	N
ALASKA							
AL **Young**	Y	Y	Y	Y	Y	Y	Y
ARIZONA							
1 **Salmon**	Y	Y	Y	Y	Y	Y	Y
2 Pastor	Y	Y	Y	Y	N	N	N
3 **Stump**	Y	Y	Y	Y	Y	Y	Y
4 **Shadegg**	Y	Y	Y	Y	Y	Y	Y
5 **Kolbe**	Y	Y	Y	Y	Y	Y	Y
6 **Hayworth**	Y	Y	Y	Y	Y	Y	Y
ARKANSAS							
1 Berry	Y	Y	Y	Y	N	N	N
2 Snyder	Y	Y	Y	Y	N	N	Y
3 **Hutchinson**	?	Y	Y	Y	Y	Y	Y
4 Dickey	Y	Y	Y	Y	Y	Y	Y
CALIFORNIA							
1 **Riggs**	Y	?	Y	Y	Y	Y	Y
2 **Herger**	Y	Y	Y	?	Y	Y	Y
3 Fazio	Y	Y	Y	Y	N	N	N
4 **Doolittle**	Y	Y	Y	Y	Y	Y	Y
5 Matsui	Y	Y	Y	Y	N	?	Y
6 Woolsey	Y	Y	+	+	N	N	N
7 Miller	Y	Y	Y	Y	N	N	N
8 Pelosi	Y	Y	Y	Y	N	N	N
9 Lee	Y	Y	Y	Y	N	N	N
10 Tauscher	Y	Y	Y	Y	N	N	Y
11 **Pombo**	Y	Y	Y	Y	Y	Y	Y
12 Lantos	Y	Y	Y	Y	N	N	N
13 Stark	Y	Y	Y	Y	N	N	N
14 Eshoo	Y	Y	+	+	N	N	N
15 **Campbell**	Y	Y	Y	Y	Y	Y	Y
16 Lofgren	Y	Y	+	+	N	N	N
17 Farr	+	+	Y	Y	N	N	N
18 Condit	Y	Y	Y	Y	Y	N	N
19 **Radanovich**	Y	Y	Y	Y	Y	Y	Y
20 Dooley	Y	Y	Y	Y	N	N	N
21 **Thomas**	Y	Y	Y	Y	Y	Y	Y
22 Capps, L.	Y	Y	Y	Y	N	N	N
23 **Gallegly**	Y	Y	Y	Y	Y	Y	Y
24 Sherman	Y	Y	Y	Y	N	N	N
25 **McKeon**	Y	Y	Y	Y	Y	Y	Y
26 Berman	?	?	Y	Y	N	N	N
27 **Rogan**	Y	Y	Y	Y	Y	Y	Y
28 **Dreier**	Y	Y	Y	Y	Y	Y	Y
29 Waxman	Y	?	Y	Y	N	N	N
30 Becerra	?	?	Y	Y	N	N	N
31 Martinez	Y	Y	Y	Y	N	N	N
32 Dixon	Y	Y	Y	Y	N	N	N
33 Roybal-Allard	Y	Y	Y	Y	N	N	N
34 Torres	Y	Y	Y	Y	N	N	N
35 Waters	Y	Y	Y	?	N	?	N
36 Harman	Y	Y	Y	Y	N	N	N
37 Millender-McD.	Y	Y	Y	Y	N	N	N

	230	231	232	233	234	235	236
38 **Horn**	Y	Y	Y	Y	Y	Y	Y
39 **Royce**	Y	Y	Y	Y	Y	Y	Y
40 Lewis	Y	Y	?	?	?	?	?
41 **Kim**	Y	Y	Y	Y	Y	Y	Y
42 Brown	Y	Y	Y	?	N	N	N
43 **Calvert**	Y	Y	Y	Y	Y	Y	Y
44 **Bono, M.**	Y	Y	Y	Y	Y	Y	Y
45 **Rohrabacher**	Y	Y	Y	Y	Y	Y	Y
46 Sanchez	Y	Y	Y	Y	N	N	N
47 **Cox**	Y	Y	Y	Y	Y	Y	Y
48 **Packard**	Y	Y	Y	Y	Y	Y	Y
49 **Bilbray**	Y	Y	Y	Y	Y	Y	Y
50 Filner	Y	Y	Y	Y	N	N	N
51 **Cunningham**	Y	Y	Y	Y	Y	Y	Y
52 **Hunter**	Y	Y	Y	Y	Y	Y	Y
COLORADO							
1 DeGette	Y	Y	Y	?	N	N	N
2 Skaggs	Y	Y	Y	Y	N	N	N
3 **McInnis**	Y	Y	Y	Y	Y	Y	Y
4 **Schaffer**	Y	Y	Y	Y	Y	Y	Y
5 **Hefley**	Y	Y	Y	Y	Y	Y	Y
6 **Schaefer**	Y	Y	Y	Y	Y	Y	Y
CONNECTICUT							
1 Kennelly	Y	Y	Y	Y	N	N	N
2 Gejdenson	Y	?	Y	Y	N	N	N
3 DeLauro	Y	Y	Y	Y	N	N	N
4 **Shays**	+	+	Y	Y	Y	Y	Y
5 Maloney	Y	Y	Y	Y	N	N	N
6 **Johnson**	Y	Y	Y	Y	Y	Y	Y
DELAWARE							
AL **Castle**	Y	Y	Y	Y	Y	Y	Y
FLORIDA							
1 **Scarborough**	Y	Y	Y	Y	Y	Y	Y
2 Boyd	Y	Y	Y	Y	N	N	N
3 Brown	Y	Y	?	?	N	N	N
4 **Fowler**	Y	Y	Y	Y	Y	Y	Y
5 Thurman	Y	Y	Y	Y	N	N	N
6 **Stearns**	Y	Y	Y	Y	Y	Y	Y
7 **Mica**	Y	Y	Y	Y	Y	Y	Y
8 **McCollum**	Y	Y	Y	Y	Y	Y	Y
9 **Bilirakis**	Y	Y	Y	Y	Y	Y	Y
10 **Young**	Y	Y	Y	Y	Y	Y	Y
11 Davis	Y	Y	Y	Y	N	N	N
12 **Canady**	Y	Y	Y	Y	Y	Y	Y
13 **Miller**	Y	Y	Y	Y	Y	Y	Y
14 **Goss**	Y	Y	Y	Y	Y	Y	Y
15 **Weldon**	Y	Y	Y	Y	Y	Y	Y
16 **Foley**	Y	Y	Y	Y	Y	Y	Y
17 Meek	Y	Y	Y	Y	N	?	N
18 **Ros-Lehtinen**	Y	Y	Y	Y	Y	Y	Y
19 Wexler	Y	Y	Y	Y	N	N	N
20 Deutsch	Y	Y	Y	Y	N	N	N
21 **Diaz-Balart**	Y	Y	Y	Y	Y	Y	Y
22 **Shaw**	Y	?	Y	Y	Y	Y	Y
23 Hastings	Y	Y	?	?	?	?	?
GEORGIA							
1 **Kingston**	Y	Y	Y	Y	Y	Y	Y
2 Bishop	Y	Y	Y	Y	Y	Y	Y
3 **Collins**	Y	Y	Y	Y	Y	Y	Y
4 McKinney	Y	Y	Y	Y	N	N	Y
5 Lewis	?	?	?	?	N	N	N
6 **Gingrich**							
7 **Barr**	Y	?	Y	Y	Y	Y	Y
8 **Chambliss**	Y	Y	Y	Y	Y	Y	Y
9 **Deal**	Y	Y	Y	Y	Y	Y	Y
10 **Norwood**	Y	Y	Y	Y	Y	Y	Y
11 **Linder**	Y	Y	Y	Y	Y	Y	Y
HAWAII							
1 Abercrombie	Y	Y	Y	Y	N	?	N
2 Mink	Y	Y	Y	Y	N	N	N
IDAHO							
1 **Chenoweth**	Y	Y	Y	Y	Y	Y	Y
2 **Crapo**	Y	Y	Y	Y	Y	Y	Y
ILLINOIS							
1 Rush	Y	Y	?	?	N	N	N
2 Jackson	Y	Y	Y	Y	N	N	N
3 Lipinski	Y	Y	Y	Y	N	N	Y
4 Gutierrez	Y	?	Y	Y	N	N	N
5 Blagojevich	Y	Y	Y	Y	N	N	N
6 **Hyde**	Y	Y	Y	Y	Y	Y	Y
7 Davis	Y	Y	Y	Y	N	N	N
8 **Crane**	Y	Y	Y	Y	Y	Y	Y
9 Yates	Y	Y	Y	Y	N	N	N
10 **Porter**	Y	Y	Y	Y	Y	Y	Y
11 **Weller**	Y	Y	Y	Y	Y	Y	Y
12 Costello	Y	Y	Y	Y	N	N	N

ND Northern Democrats   SD Southern Democrats

	230	231	232	233	234	235	236
13 ***Fawell***	Y	Y	Y	Y	Y	Y	Y
14 ***Hastert***	Y	Y	Y	Y	Y	Y	Y
15 ***Ewing***	Y	Y	Y	Y	Y	Y	Y
16 ***Manzullo***	Y	Y	Y	Y	Y	Y	Y
17 Evans	Y	Y	Y	Y	N	N	N
18 ***LaHood***	Y	Y	Y	Y	Y	Y	Y
19 Poshard	Y	Y	Y	Y	N	N	N
20 ***Shimkus***	Y	Y	Y	Y	Y	Y	Y
INDIANA							
1 Visclosky	Y	Y	Y	Y	N	N	N
2 ***McIntosh***	Y	Y	Y	Y	Y	Y	Y
3 Roemer	Y	Y	Y	Y	N	N	N
4 ***Souder***	Y	Y	Y	+	Y	Y	Y
5 ***Buyer***	Y	Y	?	?	Y	Y	Y
6 ***Burton***	Y	Y	Y	Y	Y	Y	Y
7 ***Pease***	Y	Y	Y	Y	Y	Y	Y
8 ***Hostettler***	Y	Y	Y	Y	Y	Y	Y
9 Hamilton	Y	Y	Y	Y	N	N	N
10 Carson	Y	Y	Y	Y	N	N	N
IOWA							
1 ***Leach***	Y	Y	Y	Y	Y	Y	Y
2 ***Nussle***	Y	Y	Y	Y	Y	Y	Y
3 Boswell	Y	Y	Y	Y	N	N	N
4 ***Ganske***	Y	Y	Y	Y	Y	Y	Y
5 ***Latham***	Y	Y	Y	Y	Y	Y	Y
KANSAS							
1 ***Moran***	Y	Y	Y	Y	Y	Y	Y
2 ***Ryun***	Y	Y	Y	Y	Y	Y	Y
3 ***Snowbarger***	Y	Y	Y	Y	Y	Y	Y
4 ***Tiahrt***	Y	Y	+	+	Y	Y	Y
KENTUCKY							
1 ***Whitfield***	Y	Y	Y	Y	Y	Y	Y
2 ***Lewis***	Y	Y	Y	Y	Y	Y	Y
3 ***Northup***	Y	Y	Y	Y	Y	Y	Y
4 ***Bunning***	Y	Y	Y	Y	Y	Y	Y
5 ***Rogers***	Y	Y	Y	Y	Y	Y	Y
6 Baesler	Y	Y	Y	Y	N	N	N
LOUISIANA							
1 ***Livingston***	Y	Y	Y	Y	Y	Y	Y
2 Jefferson	Y	Y	Y	Y	N	N	N
3 ***Tauzin***	Y	Y	Y	Y	Y	Y	Y
4 ***McCrery***	Y	Y	Y	Y	Y	Y	Y
5 ***Cooksey***	Y	?	Y	Y	Y	Y	Y
6 ***Baker***	Y	?	Y	Y	Y	Y	Y
7 John	Y	Y	Y	Y	N	N	Y
MAINE							
1 Allen	Y	Y	Y	Y	N	N	N
2 Baldacci	Y	Y	Y	Y	N	N	N
MARYLAND							
1 ***Gilchrest***	Y	Y	Y	Y	Y	Y	?
2 ***Ehrlich***	Y	Y	Y	Y	Y	Y	Y
3 Cardin	Y	Y	Y	Y	N	N	N
4 Wynn	Y	Y	Y	Y	N	N	N
5 Hoyer	Y	Y	Y	Y	N	N	N
6 ***Bartlett***	Y	Y	Y	Y	Y	Y	Y
7 Cummings	Y	Y	Y	Y	N	N	N
8 ***Morella***	Y	Y	Y	Y	Y	Y	Y
MASSACHUSETTS							
1 Olver	Y	Y	Y	Y	N	N	N
2 Neal	Y	Y	Y	Y	N	N	N
3 McGovern	Y	Y	Y	Y	N	N	N
4 Frank	Y	Y	Y	Y	N	N	N
5 Meehan	Y	?	Y	Y	N	N	N
6 Tierney	Y	Y	Y	Y	N	N	N
7 Markey	Y	Y	Y	Y	N	N	N
8 Kennedy	Y	?	?	?	N	N	N
9 Moakley	?	?	Y	Y	N	N	N
10 Delahunt	Y	Y	Y	Y	N	N	N
MICHIGAN							
1 Stupak	Y	Y	Y	Y	N	Y	N
2 ***Hoekstra***	Y	Y	Y	Y	Y	Y	Y
3 ***Ehlers***	Y	Y	Y	Y	Y	Y	Y
4 ***Camp***	Y	Y	Y	Y	Y	Y	Y
5 Barcia	Y	Y	Y	Y	N	N	N
6 ***Upton***	Y	Y	Y	Y	Y	Y	Y
7 ***Smith***	Y	Y	Y	Y	Y	Y	Y
8 Stabenow	Y	Y	Y	Y	N	N	N
9 Kildee	Y	Y	Y	Y	N	N	N
10 Bonior	Y	Y	Y	Y	N	N	N
11 ***Knollenberg***	Y	Y	Y	Y	Y	Y	Y
12 Levin	Y	Y	Y	Y	N	N	N
13 Rivers	Y	Y	Y	N	N	N	N
14 Conyers	Y	Y	Y	Y	N	N	N
15 Kilpatrick	Y	Y	Y	Y	N	N	N
16 Dingell	Y	Y	Y	Y	N	N	N

	230	231	232	233	234	235	236
MINNESOTA							
1 ***Gutknecht***	Y	Y	Y	Y	Y	Y	Y
2 Minge	Y	Y	Y	Y	N	N	N
3 ***Ramstad***	Y	Y	Y	Y	Y	Y	Y
4 Vento	Y	Y	Y	Y	N	N	?
5 Sabo	Y	Y	Y	Y	N	N	N
6 Luther	Y	Y	Y	Y	N	N	N
7 Peterson	Y	Y	Y	Y	Y	Y	N
8 Oberstar	Y	Y	Y	Y	N	N	N
MISSISSIPPI							
1 ***Wicker***	Y	Y	Y	Y	Y	Y	Y
2 Thompson	Y	Y	Y	Y	N	N	N
3 ***Pickering***	Y	Y	Y	Y	Y	Y	Y
4 ***Parker***	?	?	Y	Y	Y	Y	Y
5 Taylor	Y	Y	Y	Y	N	N	Y
MISSOURI							
1 Clay	Y	Y	Y	Y	N	N	N
2 ***Talent***	Y	Y	Y	Y	Y	Y	Y
3 Gephardt	Y	Y	Y	Y	N	N	N
4 Skelton	Y	Y	Y	Y	N	N	N
5 McCarthy	Y	Y	Y	Y	N	N	N
6 Danner	Y	Y	Y	Y	Y	Y	N
7 ***Blunt***	Y	Y	Y	Y	Y	Y	Y
8 ***Emerson***	Y	Y	Y	Y	Y	Y	Y
9 ***Hulshof***	Y	Y	Y	Y	Y	Y	Y
MONTANA							
AL ***Hill***	Y	Y	Y	Y	Y	Y	Y
NEBRASKA							
1 ***Bereuter***	Y	Y	Y	Y	Y	Y	Y
2 ***Christensen***	Y	Y	Y	Y	Y	Y	Y
3 ***Barrett***	Y	Y	Y	Y	Y	Y	Y
NEVADA							
1 ***Ensign***	Y	Y	Y	Y	Y	Y	Y
2 ***Gibbons***	Y	Y	Y	Y	Y	Y	Y
NEW HAMPSHIRE							
1 ***Sununu***	Y	Y	Y	Y	Y	Y	Y
2 ***Bass***	Y	Y	Y	Y	Y	Y	Y
NEW JERSEY							
1 Andrews	Y	Y	Y	Y	N	N	N
2 ***LoBiondo***	Y	Y	Y	Y	Y	Y	Y
3 ***Saxton***	Y	Y	Y	Y	Y	Y	Y
4 ***Smith***	Y	Y	Y	Y	Y	Y	Y
5 ***Roukema***	Y	?	Y	Y	Y	Y	Y
6 Pallone	Y	Y	Y	Y	N	N	N
7 ***Franks***	Y	Y	Y	Y	Y	Y	Y
8 Pascrell	Y	Y	Y	Y	N	N	N
9 Rothman	Y	Y	Y	Y	N	N	N
10 Payne	Y	Y	Y	Y	N	N	N
11 ***Frelinghuysen***	Y	Y	Y	Y	Y	Y	Y
12 ***Pappas***	Y	Y	Y	Y	Y	Y	Y
13 Menendez	Y	Y	Y	Y	N	N	N
NEW MEXICO							
1 Vacant							
2 ***Skeen***	Y	Y	Y	Y	Y	Y	Y
3 ***Redmond***	Y	Y	Y	Y	Y	Y	Y
NEW YORK							
1 ***Forbes***	Y	Y	Y	Y	Y	Y	Y
2 ***Lazio***	Y	Y	Y	Y	Y	Y	Y
3 ***King***	Y	Y	Y	Y	Y	Y	Y
4 McCarthy	Y	Y	Y	Y	N	Y	N
6 Meeks	?	?	Y	Y	N	N	N
5 Ackerman	Y	Y	Y	Y	N	N	N
7 Manton	Y	Y	Y	Y	N	N	N
8 Nadler	Y	Y	Y	Y	N	N	N
9 Schumer	Y	?	?	?	N	N	N
10 Towns	Y	Y	Y	Y	N	N	N
11 Owens	Y	Y	Y	Y	N	N	N
12 Velázquez	Y	Y	Y	Y	N	N	N
13 ***Fossella***	Y	Y	Y	Y	Y	Y	Y
14 Maloney	Y	Y	Y	Y	N	N	N
15 Rangel	Y	Y	Y	Y	N	N	N
16 Serrano	Y	Y	Y	Y	N	N	N
17 Engel	Y	Y	Y	Y	N	N	N
18 Lowey	Y	Y	Y	Y	N	N	N
19 ***Kelly***	Y	Y	Y	Y	Y	Y	Y
20 ***Gilman***	Y	Y	Y	Y	Y	Y	Y
21 McNulty	Y	Y	?	?	?	?	?
22 ***Solomon***	Y	Y	Y	Y	Y	Y	Y
23 ***Boehlert***	Y	Y	Y	Y	Y	Y	Y
24 ***McHugh***	Y	Y	Y	Y	Y	Y	Y
25 ***Walsh***	Y	Y	Y	Y	Y	Y	Y
26 Hinchey	Y	Y	Y	Y	N	N	N
27 ***Paxon***	?	?	Y	Y	Y	Y	Y
28 Slaughter	Y	Y	Y	Y	N	N	N
29 LaFalce	Y	Y	Y	Y	N	N	N

	230	231	232	233	234	235	236
30 ***Quinn***	Y	Y	Y	Y	Y	Y	Y
31 ***Houghton***	Y	?	Y	Y	Y	Y	Y
NORTH CAROLINA							
1 Clayton	Y	Y	Y	?	N	N	N
2 Etheridge	Y	Y	Y	Y	N	N	N
3 ***Jones***	Y	Y	Y	Y	Y	Y	Y
4 Price	Y	Y	Y	Y	N	N	N
5 ***Burr***	Y	Y	Y	Y	Y	Y	Y
6 ***Coble***	Y	Y	Y	Y	Y	Y	Y
7 McIntyre	Y	Y	Y	Y	Y	Y	N
8 Hefner	Y	?	Y	Y	N	N	?
9 ***Myrick***	Y	Y	Y	Y	Y	Y	Y
10 ***Ballenger***	Y	Y	+	+	Y	Y	Y
11 ***Taylor***	Y	Y	Y	Y	Y	Y	Y
12 Watt	Y	Y	Y	Y	N	N	N
NORTH DAKOTA							
AL Pomeroy	Y	Y	Y	Y	N	N	N
OHIO							
1 ***Chabot***	Y	Y	Y	Y	Y	Y	Y
2 ***Portman***	Y	Y	Y	Y	Y	Y	Y
3 Hall	Y	?	Y	Y	N	N	N
4 ***Oxley***	Y	Y	Y	Y	Y	Y	Y
5 ***Gillmor***	?	?	Y	Y	Y	Y	Y
6 Strickland	Y	Y	Y	Y	N	N	N
7 ***Hobson***	Y	Y	Y	Y	Y	Y	Y
8 ***Boehner***	Y	Y	Y	Y	Y	Y	Y
9 Kaptur	Y	Y	Y	Y	N	N	N
10 Kucinich	Y	Y	Y	Y	N	N	N
11 Stokes	Y	Y	Y	Y	N	N	N
12 ***Kasich***	Y	?	Y	Y	Y	Y	Y
13 Brown	Y	Y	Y	Y	N	N	N
14 Sawyer	Y	Y	Y	Y	N	N	N
15 ***Pryce***	Y	Y	Y	Y	Y	Y	Y
16 ***Regula***	Y	Y	Y	Y	Y	Y	Y
17 Traficant	Y	Y	Y	Y	Y	Y	Y
18 ***Ney***	Y	Y	Y	Y	?	?	?
19 ***LaTourette***	Y	Y	Y	Y	Y	Y	Y
OKLAHOMA							
1 ***Largent***	Y	?	Y	Y	Y	Y	Y
2 ***Coburn***	Y	Y	Y	Y	Y	Y	Y
3 ***Watkins***	Y	Y	Y	Y	Y	Y	Y
4 ***Watts***	Y	Y	Y	Y	Y	Y	Y
5 ***Istook***	Y	Y	Y	Y	Y	Y	Y
6 ***Lucas***	Y	Y	Y	Y	Y	Y	Y
OREGON							
1 Furse	Y	Y	Y	Y	N	N	N
2 ***Smith***	Y	Y	Y	Y	Y	Y	Y
3 Blumenauer	Y	Y	Y	Y	N	N	N
4 DeFazio	Y	Y	Y	Y	N	N	N
5 Hooley	Y	Y	Y	Y	N	N	N
PENNSYLVANIA							
1 Brady	Y	Y	Y	Y	N	N	N
2 Fattah	Y	Y	Y	Y	N	N	N
3 Borski	Y	Y	Y	Y	N	N	N
4 Klink	Y	Y	Y	Y	N	N	N
5 ***Peterson***	Y	Y	Y	Y	?	?	?
6 Holden	Y	Y	Y	Y	N	N	N
7 ***Weldon***	Y	Y	Y	Y	Y	Y	Y
8 ***Greenwood***	Y	Y	Y	Y	Y	Y	Y
9 ***Shuster***	Y	Y	Y	Y	Y	Y	Y
10 ***McDade***	Y	Y	Y	Y	Y	?	Y
11 Kanjorski	Y	Y	?	Y	N	N	N
12 Murtha	Y	?	Y	Y	N	N	N
13 ***Fox***	Y	Y	Y	Y	Y	Y	Y
14 Coyne	Y	Y	Y	Y	N	N	N
15 McHale	Y	Y	Y	Y	N	N	N
16 ***Pitts***	Y	Y	Y	Y	Y	Y	Y
17 ***Gekas***	Y	Y	Y	Y	Y	Y	Y
18 Doyle	Y	Y	Y	Y	N	N	N
19 ***Goodling***	Y	Y	Y	Y	Y	Y	Y
20 Mascara	Y	Y	Y	Y	N	N	N
21 ***English***	Y	Y	Y	Y	Y	Y	Y
RHODE ISLAND							
1 Kennedy	Y	Y	Y	Y	N	N	N
2 Weygand	Y	Y	Y	Y	N	N	N
SOUTH CAROLINA							
1 ***Sanford***	Y	Y	Y	Y	Y	Y	Y
2 ***Spence***	Y	Y	Y	Y	Y	Y	Y
3 ***Graham***	Y	Y	Y	Y	Y	Y	Y
4 ***Inglis***	?	?	?	?	Y	Y	Y
5 Spratt	Y	Y	Y	Y	N	N	N
6 Clyburn	Y	Y	Y	Y	N	N	N
SOUTH DAKOTA							
AL ***Thune***	Y	Y	Y	Y	Y	Y	Y

	230	231	232	233	234	235	236
TENNESSEE							
1 ***Jenkins***	Y	Y	Y	Y	Y	Y	Y
2 ***Duncan***	Y	Y	Y	Y	Y	Y	Y
3 ***Wamp***	Y	Y	Y	Y	Y	Y	Y
4 ***Hilleary***	Y	Y	Y	Y	?	?	?
5 Clement	Y	Y	Y	Y	N	N	N
6 Gordon	Y	Y	Y	Y	N	N	N
7 ***Bryant***	Y	Y	Y	Y	Y	Y	Y
8 Tanner	Y	Y	Y	Y	N	N	N
9 Ford	Y	Y	+	+	−	N	N
TEXAS							
1 Sandlin	Y	Y	Y	Y	N	Y	N
2 Turner	Y	Y	Y	Y	N	N	N
3 ***Johnson, Sam***	?	?	Y	Y	?	?	?
4 Hall	Y	Y	Y	Y	Y	Y	Y
5 ***Sessions***	Y	Y	Y	Y	Y	Y	Y
6 ***Barton***	Y	?	Y	Y	Y	Y	Y
7 ***Archer***	Y	Y	Y	Y	Y	Y	Y
8 ***Brady***	Y	Y	Y	Y	Y	Y	Y
9 Lampson	Y	Y	Y	Y	N	N	N
10 Doggett	Y	Y	Y	Y	N	N	N
11 Edwards	Y	Y	Y	?	N	N	N
12 ***Granger***	Y	Y	Y	Y	Y	Y	Y
13 ***Thornberry***	Y	Y	Y	Y	Y	Y	Y
14 ***Paul***	P	Y	N	Y	Y	Y	Y
15 Hinojosa	Y	Y	Y	Y	N	N	N
16 Reyes	Y	Y	Y	Y	N	N	N
17 Stenholm	Y	Y	Y	Y	N	N	N
18 Jackson-Lee	Y	Y	Y	Y	N	N	N
19 ***Combest***	Y	Y	Y	Y	Y	Y	Y
20 Gonzalez	?	?	?	?	?	?	?
21 ***Smith***	Y	Y	Y	Y	Y	Y	Y
22 ***DeLay***	Y	Y	Y	Y	Y	Y	Y
23 ***Bonilla***	Y	Y	Y	Y	Y	Y	Y
24 Frost	Y	Y	Y	Y	N	N	N
25 Bentsen	Y	Y	Y	Y	N	N	N
26 ***Armey***	Y	Y	Y	Y	Y	Y	?
27 Ortiz	Y	Y	Y	Y	N	N	?
28 Rodriguez	Y	Y	Y	Y	N	N	N
29 Green	Y	Y	Y	Y	N	N	?
30 Johnson, E.B.	Y	Y	Y	Y	N	N	N
UTAH							
1 ***Hansen***	Y	Y	Y	Y	Y	Y	Y
2 ***Cook***	Y	Y	Y	Y	Y	Y	Y
3 ***Cannon***	Y	Y	Y	Y	Y	Y	Y
VERMONT							
AL *Sanders*	Y	Y	Y	Y	N	N	N
VIRGINIA							
1 ***Bateman***	Y	Y	Y	Y	Y	Y	Y
2 Pickett	Y	Y	Y	Y	N	N	N
3 Scott	Y	Y	Y	Y	N	N	N
4 Sisisky	Y	Y	Y	Y	N	N	N
5 Goode	Y	Y	Y	Y	Y	Y	N
6 ***Goodlatte***	Y	Y	Y	Y	Y	Y	Y
7 ***Bliley***	Y	Y	Y	Y	Y	Y	Y
8 Moran	Y	Y	Y	Y	N	N	N
9 Boucher	Y	Y	Y	Y	N	N	N
10 ***Wolf***	Y	Y	Y	Y	Y	Y	Y
11 ***Davis***	Y	Y	Y	Y	Y	Y	Y
WASHINGTON							
1 ***White***	Y	Y	Y	Y	Y	Y	Y
2 ***Metcalf***	Y	Y	Y	Y	Y	Y	Y
3 ***Smith, Linda***	Y	Y	?	?	?	Y	Y
4 ***Hastings***	Y	Y	Y	Y	Y	Y	Y
5 ***Nethercutt***	Y	Y	Y	Y	Y	Y	Y
6 Dicks	Y	Y	Y	Y	N	N	N
7 McDermott	Y	Y	Y	Y	N	N	N
8 ***Dunn***	Y	Y	Y	Y	Y	Y	Y
9 Smith, Adam	+	+	Y	Y	N	N	N
WEST VIRGINIA							
1 Mollohan	Y	Y	Y	Y	N	N	N
2 Wise	Y	Y	Y	Y	N	N	N
3 Rahall	Y	Y	Y	Y	N	N	N
WISCONSIN							
1 ***Neumann***	Y	Y	Y	Y	Y	Y	Y
2 ***Klug***	Y	Y	Y	Y	Y	Y	Y
3 Kind	Y	Y	Y	Y	N	N	N
4 Kleczka	Y	Y	Y	Y	N	N	N
5 Barrett	Y	Y	Y	Y	N	N	N
6 ***Petri***	Y	Y	Y	Y	Y	Y	Y
7 Obey	Y	Y	Y	Y	N	N	N
8 Johnson	Y	Y	Y	Y	N	N	N
9 ***Sensenbrenner***	Y	Y	Y	Y	Y	Y	Y
WYOMING							
AL ***Cubin***	Y	Y	?	?	Y	Y	Y

Southern states - Ala., Ark., Fla., Ga., Ky., La., Miss., N.C., Okla., S.C., Tenn., Texas, Va.

House Votes 238, 239, 241, 242, 243, 244, 245 *

237. Quorum Call. * 413 Responded. June 17, 1998.

238. HR 3097. Tax Code Termination/Recommit. Rangel, D-N.Y., motion to recommit the bill to the Ways and Means Committee with instructions to report it back with an amendment to replace the bill's language with a provision that would express the sense of Congress that tax reform should be enacted not later than April 15, 2001. Motion rejected 203-223: R 6-217; D 196-6 (ND 147-2, SD 49-4); I 1-0. June 17, 1998.

239. HR 3097. Tax Code Termination/Passage. Passage of the bill to abolish the tax code, except for the provisions that fund Social Security and Medicare, by Dec. 31, 2002. The bill would recommend that Congress enact a new tax code by July 4, 2002. Passed 219-209: R 204-20; D 15-188 (ND 6-144, SD 9-44); I 0-1. June 17, 1998. A "nay" vote was a vote in support of the president's position.

240. Quorum Call. * 392 Responded. June 17, 1998.

241. HR 2183. Campaign Finance Overhaul/White Substitute. White, R-Wash., substitute amendment to create a temporary 12-member commission to propose changes to the federal campaign finance system. Rejected 156-201: R 151-64; D 5-136 (ND 3-102, SD 2-34); I 0-1. June 17, 1998.

242. HR 2646. Education Savings Accounts/Recommit. Rangel, D-N.Y., motion to recommit the bill to the conference committee with instructions to report it back with instructions to the managers to agree to provisions regarding tax-favored financing for public school construction following the provisions of HR3320. Motion rejected 196-225: R 5-216; D 190-9 (ND 141-6, SD 49-3); I 1-0. June 18, 1998.

243. HR 2646. Education Savings Accounts/Conference Report. Adoption of the conference report on the bill to permit individuals to set aside up to $2,000 a year in a tax-sheltered savings account that could be used to pay for educational expenses. Adopted (thus sent to the Senate) 225-197: R 213-10; D 12-186 (ND 5-141, SD 7-45); I 0-1. June 18, 1998. A "nay" was a vote in support of the president's position.

244. H Res 463. Select Committee on National Security and China/Previous Question. Solomon, R-N.Y., motion to order the previous question (thus ending debate and the possibility of amendment) on adoption of the rule (H Res 476) to provide for House floor consideration of the bill to establish a Select Committee on U.S. National Security and Military/Commercial Concerns with the People's Republic of China. Motion agreed to 226-197: R 224-0; D 2-196 (ND 2-145, SD 0-51); I 0-1. June 18, 1998. (Subsequently, the rule was adopted.)

245. H Res 463. Select Committee on National Security and China/Adoption. Adoption of the resolution to establish a Select Committee on U.S. National Security and Military/Commercial Concerns with the People's Republic of China. The resolution authorizes the committee through the remainder of the 105th Congress and authorizes up to $2.5 million for committee expenses. Adopted 409-10: R 222-0; D 186-10 (ND 137-9, SD 49-1); I 1-0. June 18, 1998.

* *CQ does not include quorum calls in its vote charts.*

Key

- Y Voted for (yea).
- # Paired for.
- + Announced for.
- N Voted against (nay).
- X Paired against.
- – Announced against.
- P Voted "present."
- C Voted "present" to avoid possible conflict of interest.
- ? Did not vote or otherwise make a position known.

Democrats **Republicans** *Independent*

	238	239	241	242	243	244	245
ALABAMA							
1 Callahan	N	Y	Y	N	Y	Y	Y
2 Everett	N	Y	Y	N	Y	Y	Y
3 Riley	N	Y	Y	N	Y	Y	Y
4 Aderholt	N	Y	Y	N	Y	Y	Y
5 Cramer	N	Y	P	Y	N	N	Y
6 Bachus	N	Y	Y	N	Y	Y	Y
7 Hilliard	Y	N	P	Y	N	N	Y
ALASKA							
AL Young	N	Y	Y	N	Y	Y	Y
ARIZONA							
1 Salmon	N	Y	Y	N	Y	Y	Y
2 Pastor	Y	N	N	Y	N	N	Y
3 Stump	N	Y	Y	N	Y	Y	Y
4 Shadegg	N	Y	Y	N	Y	Y	Y
5 Kolbe	N	Y	N	Y	Y	Y	Y
6 Hayworth	N	Y	Y	N	Y	Y	Y
ARKANSAS							
1 Berry	Y	N	N	Y	N	N	Y
2 Snyder	Y	N	N	Y	N	N	Y
3 Hutchinson	N	Y	N	N	Y	Y	Y
4 Dickey	N	Y	Y	N	Y	Y	Y
CALIFORNIA							
1 Riggs	N	Y	Y	N	Y	Y	Y
2 Herger	N	Y	N	N	Y	Y	Y
3 Fazio	Y	N	N	Y	N	N	Y
4 Doolittle	N	Y	Y	N	Y	Y	Y
5 Matsui	Y	N	N	Y	N	N	Y
6 Woolsey	Y	N	P	Y	N	N	Y
7 Miller	Y	N	N	Y	N	N	Y
8 Pelosi	Y	N	N	Y	N	N	Y
9 Lee	Y	N	N	Y	N	N	Y
10 Tauscher	Y	N	P	N	Y	N	Y
11 Pombo	N	Y	Y	N	Y	Y	Y
12 Lantos	Y	N	P	Y	N	N	Y
13 Stark	Y	N	N	Y	N	N	Y
14 Eshoo	Y	N	P	N	Y	N	Y
15 Campbell	N	Y	N	N	Y	Y	Y
16 Lofgren	Y	N	P	Y	N	N	Y
17 Farr	Y	N	P	Y	N	N	Y
18 Condit	Y	Y	N	Y	N	N	Y
19 Radanovich	N	Y	–	Y	Y	Y	Y
20 Dooley	Y	N	N	Y	N	N	Y
21 Thomas	N	Y	N	N	Y	Y	Y
22 Capps, L.	Y	N	N	Y	N	N	Y
23 Gallegly	N	Y	Y	N	Y	Y	Y
24 Sherman	Y	N	?	Y	N	N	Y
25 McKeon	N	Y	Y	N	Y	Y	Y
26 Berman	Y	N	N	Y	N	N	Y
27 Rogan	N	Y	N	N	Y	Y	Y
28 Dreier	–	Y	Y	N	Y	Y	Y
29 Waxman	Y	N	N	Y	N	N	Y
30 Becerra	Y	N	P	N	N	N	Y
31 Martinez	Y	N	Y	Y	N	?	?
32 Dixon	Y	N	P	Y	N	N	Y
33 Roybal-Allard	Y	N	N	Y	N	N	Y
34 Torres	Y	N	P	?	?	?	Y
35 Waters	Y	N	Y	Y	N	N	Y
36 Harman	Y	N	P	N	Y	N	Y
37 Millender-McD.	Y	N	N	Y	N	N	Y

	238	239	241	242	243	244	245
38 Horn	N	Y	Y	N	Y	Y	Y
39 Royce	N	Y	Y	N	Y	Y	Y
40 Lewis	?	?	N	N	Y	Y	Y
41 Kim	N	Y	Y	N	Y	Y	Y
42 Brown	Y	N	N	N	N	N	Y
43 Calvert	N	Y	Y	N	Y	Y	Y
44 Bono, M.	N	Y	Y	N	Y	Y	Y
45 Rohrabacher	N	Y	Y	N	Y	Y	Y
46 Sanchez	Y	N	P	N	N	N	Y
47 Cox	N	Y	Y	N	Y	Y	Y
48 Packard	N	Y	N	N	Y	Y	Y
49 Bilbray	N	Y	P	N	Y	Y	Y
50 Filner	Y	N	N	Y	N	N	Y
51 Cunningham	N	Y	Y	?	Y	Y	Y
52 Hunter	N	Y	Y	N	Y	Y	Y
COLORADO							
1 DeGette	Y	N	P	Y	N	N	Y
2 Skaggs	Y	N	N	Y	N	N	Y
3 McInnis	N	Y	Y	N	Y	Y	Y
4 Schaffer	N	Y	N	N	Y	Y	Y
5 Hefley	N	Y	N	N	Y	Y	Y
6 Schaefer	N	Y	Y	N	Y	Y	Y
CONNECTICUT							
1 Kennelly	Y	N	N	Y	N	N	Y
2 Gejdenson	Y	N	Y	N	N	N	Y
3 DeLauro	Y	N	N	Y	N	N	Y
4 Shays	N	N	P	Y	Y	Y	Y
5 Maloney	Y	Y	P	Y	N	N	Y
6 Johnson	N	N	N	Y	N	Y	Y
DELAWARE							
AL Castle	Y	N	P	N	Y	Y	Y
FLORIDA							
1 Scarborough	N	Y	Y	N	Y	Y	Y
2 Boyd	Y	N	N	Y	N	N	Y
3 Brown	Y	N	N	Y	N	N	Y
4 Fowler	N	Y	N	N	Y	Y	Y
5 Thurman	Y	N	P	N	Y	N	Y
6 Stearns	N	Y	Y	N	Y	Y	Y
7 Mica	N	Y	Y	N	Y	Y	Y
8 McCollum	N	Y	Y	N	Y	Y	Y
9 Bilirakis	N	Y	Y	N	Y	Y	Y
10 Young	N	Y	N	N	Y	Y	Y
11 Davis	Y	N	N	N	Y	N	Y
12 Canady	N	Y	Y	N	Y	Y	Y
13 Miller	N	Y	N	N	Y	Y	Y
14 Goss	N	Y	N	N	Y	Y	Y
15 Weldon	N	Y	N	–	+	+	+
16 Foley	N	Y	Y	N	Y	Y	Y
17 Meek	Y	N	N	Y	N	N	Y
18 Ros-Lehtinen	N	Y	N	Y	Y	Y	Y
19 Wexler	Y	N	P	Y	N	N	Y
20 Deutsch	Y	N	P	N	N	N	Y
21 Diaz-Balart	N	Y	N	Y	Y	Y	Y
22 Shaw	N	N	Y	N	Y	Y	Y
23 Hastings	?	?	?	?	?	?	?
GEORGIA							
1 Kingston	N	Y	Y	N	Y	Y	Y
2 Bishop	Y	Y	P	Y	N	N	Y
3 Collins	N	Y	N	N	Y	Y	Y
4 McKinney	Y	N	N	Y	N	N	Y
5 Lewis	Y	N	N	N	N	N	N
6 Gingrich		Y		Y		Y	Y
7 Barr	N	Y	Y	N	Y	Y	Y
8 Chambliss	N	Y	N	N	Y	Y	Y
9 Deal	N	Y	Y	N	Y	Y	Y
10 Norwood	N	Y	Y	N	Y	Y	Y
11 Linder	N	Y	N	N	Y	Y	Y
HAWAII							
1 Abercrombie	Y	N	N	Y	N	N	Y
2 Mink	Y	N	N	Y	N	N	Y
IDAHO							
1 Chenoweth	N	Y	N	N	Y	Y	Y
2 Crapo	N	Y	N	N	Y	Y	Y
ILLINOIS							
1 Rush	Y	N	P	N	N	N	Y
2 Jackson	Y	N	N	Y	N	N	Y
3 Lipinski	Y	Y	N	Y	N	N	Y
4 Gutierrez	Y	N	N	Y	N	N	Y
5 Blagojevich	Y	N	N	Y	N	N	Y
6 Hyde	N	Y	Y	N	Y	Y	Y
7 Davis	Y	N	P	Y	N	N	Y
8 Crane	N	Y	Y	N	Y	Y	Y
9 Yates	Y	N	N	Y	N	N	Y
10 Porter	N	N	N	Y	Y	Y	Y
11 Weller	N	Y	Y	N	Y	Y	Y
12 Costello	Y	N	N	Y	N	N	Y

ND Northern Democrats   SD Southern Democrats

	238	239	241	242	243	244	245
13 **Fawell**	Y	N	Y	N	Y	Y	Y
14 **Hastert**	N	Y	Y	N	Y	Y	Y
15 **Ewing**	N	Y	Y	N	Y	Y	Y
16 **Manzullo**	N	Y	Y	N	Y	Y	Y
17 Evans	Y	N	N	Y	N	N	Y
18 **LaHood**	N	N	Y	N	Y	Y	Y
19 Poshard	Y	N	N	Y	N	N	Y
20 **Shimkus**	N	Y	Y	N	Y	Y	Y
INDIANA							
1 Visclosky	Y	N	N	Y	N	N	Y
2 **McIntosh**	N	+	Y	N	Y	Y	Y
3 Roemer	Y	N	N	Y	N	N	Y
4 **Souder**	N	Y	Y	N	Y	Y	Y
5 **Buyer**	N	Y	N	N	Y	Y	Y
6 **Burton**	N	Y	N	N	Y	Y	Y
7 **Pease**	N	Y	Y	N	Y	Y	Y
8 **Hostettler**	N	Y	N	N	Y	Y	Y
9 Hamilton	Y	N	N	Y	N	N	Y
10 Carson	Y	N	N	Y	N	N	Y
IOWA							
1 **Leach**	Y	N	P	+	+	Y	Y
2 **Nussle**	N	Y	Y	N	Y	Y	Y
3 Boswell	Y	N	N	Y	N	N	Y
4 **Ganske**	Y	N	N	N	Y	Y	Y
5 **Latham**	N	Y	Y	N	Y	Y	Y
KANSAS							
1 **Moran**	N	Y	N	N	Y	Y	Y
2 **Ryun**	N	Y	Y	N	Y	Y	Y
3 **Snowbarger**	N	Y	Y	N	Y	Y	Y
4 **Tiahrt**	N	Y	Y	N	Y	Y	Y
KENTUCKY							
1 **Whitfield**	N	Y	N	N	Y	Y	Y
2 **Lewis**	N	Y	N	N	Y	Y	Y
3 **Northup**	N	Y	N	N	Y	Y	Y
4 **Bunning**	N	Y	N	N	Y	Y	Y
5 **Rogers**	N	Y	N	N	Y	Y	Y
6 Baesler	Y	Y	N	Y	N	N	Y
LOUISIANA							
1 **Livingston**	N	Y	Y	N	Y	Y	Y
2 Jefferson	Y	N	N	Y	N	N	Y
3 **Tauzin**	N	Y	Y	N	Y	Y	Y
4 **McCrery**	N	Y	Y	N	Y	Y	Y
5 **Cooksey**	?	?	?	?	?	?	?
6 **Baker**	N	Y	Y	N	Y	Y	Y
7 John	Y	N	N	Y	Y	N	Y
MAINE							
1 Allen	Y	N	N	Y	N	N	Y
2 Baldacci	Y	N	N	Y	–	N	Y
MARYLAND							
1 **Gilchrest**	N	Y	N	N	Y	Y	Y
2 **Ehrlich**	N	Y	Y	N	Y	Y	Y
3 Cardin	Y	N	P	Y	N	N	Y
4 Wynn	Y	N	N	Y	N	N	Y
5 Hoyer	Y	N	N	Y	N	N	Y
6 **Bartlett**	N	Y	Y	N	Y	Y	Y
7 Cummings	Y	N	N	Y	N	N	Y
8 **Morella**	Y	N	N	Y	N	Y	Y
MASSACHUSETTS							
1 Olver	Y	N	N	Y	N	N	Y
2 Neal	Y	N	N	Y	N	N	Y
3 McGovern	Y	N	N	Y	N	N	Y
4 Frank	Y	N	N	Y	N	N	Y
5 Meehan	Y	N	N	Y	N	N	Y
6 Tierney	Y	N	N	Y	N	N	Y
7 Markey	Y	N	N	Y	N	N	Y
8 Kennedy	Y	N	N	Y	N	N	Y
9 Moakley	Y	N	N	?	?	?	?
10 Delahunt	Y	N	P	Y	N	N	Y
MICHIGAN							
1 Stupak	Y	N	P	Y	N	N	Y
2 **Hoekstra**	N	Y	Y	N	Y	Y	Y
3 **Ehlers**	N	Y	Y	N	Y	Y	Y
4 **Camp**	N	Y	Y	N	Y	Y	Y
5 Barcia	Y	N	P	Y	N	N	Y
6 **Upton**	N	N	N	N	Y	Y	Y
7 **Smith**	N	Y	Y	N	Y	Y	Y
8 Stabenow	Y	N	P	Y	N	N	Y
9 Kildee	Y	N	P	Y	N	N	Y
10 Bonior	Y	N	N	Y	N	N	Y
11 **Knollenberg**	N	Y	Y	N	Y	Y	Y
12 Levin	Y	N	N	Y	N	N	Y
13 Rivers	Y	N	P	Y	N	N	Y
14 Conyers	Y	N	N	Y	N	N	N
15 Kilpatrick	Y	N	P	Y	N	N	Y
16 Dingell	Y	N	P	Y	N	N	Y

	238	239	241	242	243	244	245
MINNESOTA							
1 **Gutknecht**	N	Y	Y	N	Y	Y	+
2 Minge	Y	N	P	N	N	N	Y
3 **Ramstad**	N	Y	N	N	Y	Y	Y
4 Vento	Y	N	N	Y	N	N	Y
5 Sabo	Y	N	N	N	N	N	Y
6 Luther	Y	N	N	Y	N	N	Y
7 Peterson	N	Y	Y	N	N	N	Y
8 Oberstar	Y	N	N	Y	N	N	N
MISSISSIPPI							
1 **Wicker**	N	Y	Y	N	Y	Y	Y
2 Thompson	Y	N	N	Y	N	N	Y
3 **Pickering**	N	Y	Y	N	Y	Y	Y
4 **Parker**	N	Y	N	N	Y	Y	Y
5 Taylor	Y	Y	N	N	Y	N	Y
MISSOURI							
1 Clay	Y	N	N	Y	N	N	Y
2 **Talent**	N	Y	Y	N	Y	Y	Y
3 Gephardt	Y	N	P	Y	N	N	Y
4 Skelton	Y	N	N	Y	N	N	Y
5 McCarthy	Y	N	N	Y	N	N	Y
6 Danner	Y	Y	N	Y	Y	N	Y
7 **Blunt**	N	Y	Y	N	Y	Y	Y
8 **Emerson**	N	Y	Y	N	Y	Y	Y
9 **Hulshof**	N	Y	N	N	Y	Y	Y
MONTANA							
AL **Hill**	N	Y	N	N	Y	Y	Y
NEBRASKA							
1 **Bereuter**	Y	N	Y	N	Y	Y	Y
2 **Christensen**	N	Y	Y	N	Y	Y	Y
3 **Barrett**	N	Y	P	N	N	Y	Y
NEVADA							
1 **Ensign**	N	Y	Y	N	Y	Y	Y
2 **Gibbons**	N	Y	Y	N	Y	Y	Y
NEW HAMPSHIRE							
1 **Sununu**	N	Y	Y	N	Y	Y	Y
2 **Bass**	N	Y	N	N	Y	Y	Y
NEW JERSEY							
1 Andrews	Y	N	P	Y	N	N	Y
2 **LoBiondo**	N	Y	P	Y	N	Y	Y
3 **Saxton**	N	Y	Y	N	Y	Y	Y
4 **Smith**	N	Y	Y	N	Y	Y	Y
5 **Roukema**	N	N	N	N	Y	Y	Y
6 Pallone	Y	N	P	Y	N	N	Y
7 **Franks**	N	Y	Y	N	Y	Y	Y
8 Pascrell	Y	N	P	Y	N	Y	Y
9 Rothman	Y	N	N	Y	N	N	Y
10 Payne	Y	N	N	Y	N	N	Y
11 **Frelinghuysen**	N	N	Y	N	Y	Y	Y
12 **Pappas**	N	Y	Y	N	Y	Y	Y
13 Menendez	Y	N	N	Y	N	N	Y
NEW MEXICO							
1 Vacant							
2 **Skeen**	N	Y	N	N	Y	Y	Y
3 **Redmond**	N	Y	Y	N	Y	Y	Y
NEW YORK							
1 **Forbes**	N	Y	N	Y	Y	Y	Y
2 **Lazio**	N	Y	N	N	Y	Y	Y
3 **King**	N	Y	N	N	Y	Y	Y
4 McCarthy	Y	N	P	Y	N	N	Y
5 Ackerman	Y	N	N	Y	N	N	Y
6 Meeks	Y	N	N	Y	N	N	Y
7 Manton	Y	N	P	Y	N	N	Y
8 Nadler	Y	N	N	Y	N	N	N
9 Schumer	Y	N	?	Y	N	N	Y
10 Towns	Y	N	N	Y	N	N	?
11 Owens	Y	N	N	Y	N	N	Y
12 Velázquez	Y	N	N	Y	N	N	Y
13 **Fossella**	N	Y	Y	N	Y	Y	Y
14 Maloney	Y	N	P	Y	N	N	Y
15 Rangel	Y	N	N	Y	N	N	Y
16 Serrano	Y	N	N	Y	N	N	Y
17 Engel	Y	N	P	Y	N	N	Y
18 Lowey	Y	N	N	Y	N	N	Y
19 **Kelly**	N	Y	N	N	Y	Y	Y
20 **Gilman**	N	Y	N	N	N	Y	Y
21 McNulty	?	?	?	?	?	?	?
22 **Solomon**	N	Y	Y	N	Y	Y	Y
23 **Boehlert**	N	N	N	N	N	Y	Y
24 **McHugh**	N	Y	N	N	Y	Y	Y
25 **Walsh**	N	N	N	N	Y	Y	Y
26 Hinchey	Y	N	N	Y	N	N	Y
27 **Paxon**	N	Y	Y	N	Y	Y	Y
28 Slaughter	Y	N	P	Y	N	N	Y
29 LaFalce	Y	N	N	Y	N	N	Y

	238	239	241	242	243	244	245
30 **Quinn**	N	Y	P	N	Y	Y	Y
31 **Houghton**	N	N	N	N	N	Y	?
NORTH CAROLINA							
1 Clayton	Y	N	N	Y	N	N	+
2 Etheridge	Y	N	P	Y	N	N	Y
3 **Jones**	N	Y	Y	N	Y	Y	Y
4 Price	Y	N	P	Y	N	N	Y
5 **Burr**	N	Y	Y	N	Y	Y	Y
6 **Coble**	N	Y	Y	N	Y	Y	Y
7 McIntyre	Y	Y	N	Y	N	N	Y
8 Hefner	Y	N	N	Y	N	N	Y
9 **Myrick**	N	Y	Y	N	Y	Y	Y
10 **Ballenger**	N	Y	Y	N	Y	Y	Y
11 **Taylor**	N	Y	Y	N	Y	Y	Y
12 Watt	Y	N	N	Y	N	N	Y
NORTH DAKOTA							
AL Pomeroy	Y	N	P	Y	N	N	Y
OHIO							
1 **Chabot**	N	Y	Y	N	Y	Y	Y
2 **Portman**	N	Y	Y	N	Y	Y	Y
3 Hall	Y	N	N	Y	Y	N	Y
4 **Oxley**	N	Y	N	N	Y	Y	Y
5 **Gillmor**	N	Y	Y	N	Y	Y	Y
6 Strickland	Y	Y	P	Y	N	N	Y
7 **Hobson**	N	Y	Y	N	Y	Y	Y
8 **Boehner**	N	Y	N	N	Y	Y	Y
9 Kaptur	Y	N	N	Y	N	N	Y
10 Kucinich	Y	N	P	Y	N	N	Y
11 Stokes	Y	N	N	Y	N	N	Y
12 **Kasich**	N	Y	?	N	Y	Y	Y
13 Brown	Y	N	P	Y	N	N	Y
14 Sawyer	Y	N	N	Y	N	N	Y
15 **Pryce**	N	Y	Y	N	Y	Y	Y
16 **Regula**	N	Y	Y	N	Y	Y	Y
17 Traficant	N	Y	Y	Y	N	Y	Y
18 **Ney**	N	Y	Y	N	Y	Y	Y
19 **LaTourette**	N	Y	Y	N	Y	Y	Y
OKLAHOMA							
1 **Largent**	N	Y	Y	N	Y	Y	Y
2 **Coburn**	N	Y	Y	N	Y	Y	Y
3 **Watkins**	N	Y	Y	N	Y	Y	Y
4 **Watts**	N	Y	Y	N	Y	Y	Y
5 **Istook**	N	Y	Y	N	Y	Y	Y
6 **Lucas**	N	Y	Y	N	Y	Y	Y
OREGON							
1 Furse	Y	N	N	Y	N	N	N
2 **Smith**	N	Y	Y	N	Y	Y	Y
3 Blumenauer	Y	N	N	Y	N	N	Y
4 DeFazio	Y	N	P	Y	N	N	Y
5 Hooley	Y	N	N	Y	N	N	Y
PENNSYLVANIA							
1 Brady	Y	N	N	Y	N	N	Y
2 Fattah	Y	N	N	Y	N	N	Y
3 Borski	Y	N	N	Y	N	N	Y
4 Klink	Y	N	N	Y	N	N	Y
5 **Peterson**	N	Y	Y	N	Y	Y	Y
6 Holden	Y	N	N	Y	N	N	Y
7 **Weldon**	N	Y	Y	N	Y	Y	Y
8 **Greenwood**	N	Y	?	N	Y	Y	Y
9 **Shuster**	N	Y	Y	N	Y	Y	Y
10 **McDade**	N	Y	Y	N	Y	Y	Y
11 Kanjorski	Y	N	N	Y	N	N	N
12 Murtha	Y	N	N	Y	N	N	N
13 **Fox**	N	Y	P	N	Y	Y	Y
14 Coyne	Y	N	N	Y	N	N	Y
15 McHale	Y	N	P	N	Y	N	Y
16 **Pitts**	N	Y	Y	N	Y	Y	Y
17 **Gekas**	N	Y	Y	N	Y	Y	Y
18 Doyle	Y	N	N	Y	N	N	Y
19 **Goodling**	N	Y	Y	N	Y	Y	Y
20 Mascara	Y	N	N	Y	N	N	Y
21 **English**	N	Y	Y	N	Y	Y	Y
RHODE ISLAND							
1 Kennedy	Y	N	N	Y	N	N	Y
2 Weygand	Y	N	N	Y	N	N	Y
SOUTH CAROLINA							
1 **Sanford**	N	Y	N	N	Y	Y	Y
2 **Spence**	N	Y	Y	N	Y	Y	Y
3 **Graham**	N	Y	Y	N	Y	Y	Y
4 **Inglis**	N	Y	Y	N	Y	Y	Y
5 Spratt	Y	N	P	Y	N	N	Y
6 Clyburn	Y	N	N	Y	N	N	Y
SOUTH DAKOTA							
AL **Thune**	N	Y	Y	N	Y	?	Y

	238	239	241	242	243	244	245
TENNESSEE							
1 **Jenkins**	N	Y	Y	N	Y	Y	Y
2 **Duncan**	N	Y	Y	N	Y	Y	Y
3 **Wamp**	N	Y	P	N	Y	Y	Y
4 **Hilleary**	N	Y	Y	N	Y	Y	Y
5 Clement	Y	N	P	Y	Y	N	?
6 Gordon	Y	N	P	Y	N	N	Y
7 **Bryant**	N	Y	Y	N	Y	Y	Y
8 Tanner	Y	N	P	Y	N	N	Y
9 Ford	Y	N	N	Y	N	N	Y
TEXAS							
1 Sandlin	N	Y	P	Y	N	N	Y
2 Turner	Y	Y	P	Y	N	N	Y
3 **Johnson, Sam**	N	Y	N	N	Y	Y	Y
4 Hall	N	Y	Y	N	Y	N	Y
5 **Sessions**	N	Y	N	N	+	Y	Y
6 **Barton**	N	Y	Y	N	Y	Y	Y
7 **Archer**	N	Y	Y	N	Y	Y	Y
8 **Brady**	N	Y	N	N	Y	Y	Y
9 Lampson	Y	N	N	Y	N	N	Y
10 Doggett	Y	N	N	Y	N	N	Y
11 Edwards	Y	N	N	Y	N	N	Y
12 **Granger**	N	Y	N	N	Y	Y	Y
13 **Thornberry**	N	Y	Y	N	Y	Y	Y
14 **Paul**	N	Y	Y	N	N	Y	Y
15 Hinojosa	Y	N	N	Y	N	N	Y
16 Reyes	Y	N	N	Y	N	N	Y
17 Stenholm	Y	N	N	Y	N	N	Y
18 Jackson-Lee	Y	N	P	Y	N	N	Y
19 **Combest**	N	Y	N	N	Y	Y	Y
20 Gonzalez	?	?	?	?	?	?	?
21 **Smith**	N	Y	N	N	Y	Y	Y
22 **DeLay**	N	Y	N	N	Y	Y	Y
23 **Bonilla**	N	Y	N	N	Y	Y	Y
24 Frost	Y	N	P	Y	N	N	Y
25 Bentsen	Y	N	N	Y	N	N	Y
26 **Armey**	N	Y	N	N	Y	Y	Y
27 Ortiz	Y	N	N	Y	N	N	Y
28 Rodriguez	Y	N	N	Y	N	N	Y
29 Green	Y	N	N	+	–	–	+
30 Johnson, E.B.	Y	N	N	Y	N	N	Y
UTAH							
1 **Hansen**	N	Y	Y	N	Y	Y	Y
2 **Cook**	N	Y	N	N	Y	Y	Y
3 **Cannon**	N	Y	N	N	Y	Y	Y
VERMONT							
AL Sanders	Y	N	N	Y	N	N	Y
VIRGINIA							
1 **Bateman**	N	N	Y	N	N	Y	Y
2 Pickett	Y	N	N	Y	N	N	Y
3 Scott	Y	N	N	Y	N	N	Y
4 Sisisky	Y	N	P	Y	N	N	Y
5 Goode	N	Y	N	N	Y	N	Y
6 **Goodlatte**	N	Y	Y	N	Y	Y	Y
7 **Bliley**	N	Y	Y	N	Y	Y	Y
8 Moran	Y	N	N	Y	Y	?	Y
9 Boucher	Y	N	Y	Y	N	N	Y
10 **Wolf**	N	N	Y	N	Y	Y	Y
11 **Davis**	N	N	Y	N	Y	Y	Y
WASHINGTON							
1 **White**	N	Y	Y	N	Y	Y	Y
2 **Metcalf**	N	Y	Y	N	Y	Y	Y
3 **Smith, Linda**	N	Y	N	N	Y	Y	Y
4 **Hastings**	N	Y	Y	N	Y	Y	Y
5 **Nethercutt**	N	Y	Y	N	Y	Y	Y
6 Dicks	Y	N	N	Y	N	N	Y
7 McDermott	Y	N	N	Y	N	N	N
8 **Dunn**	N	Y	Y	N	Y	Y	Y
9 Smith, Adam	Y	N	N	Y	N	N	Y
WEST VIRGINIA							
1 Mollohan	Y	N	N	Y	N	N	N
2 Wise	?	N	N	?	?	N	Y
3 Rahall	Y	N	P	Y	N	N	Y
WISCONSIN							
1 **Neumann**	N	Y	N	N	Y	Y	Y
2 **Klug**	N	Y	Y	N	Y	Y	Y
3 Kind	Y	N	P	Y	N	N	Y
4 Kleczka	Y	N	N	Y	N	N	Y
5 Barrett	Y	N	N	Y	N	N	Y
6 **Petri**	N	Y	Y	N	Y	Y	Y
7 Obey	Y	N	N	Y	N	N	Y
8 Johnson	Y	N	?	Y	N	N	Y
9 **Sensenbrenner**	N	Y	Y	N	Y	Y	Y
WYOMING							
AL **Cubin**	N	Y	Y	N	Y	Y	Y

Southern states - Ala., Ark., Fla., Ga., Ky., La., Miss., N.C., Okla., S.C., Tenn., Texas, Va.

House Votes 246, 247, 248, 249, 250, 251, 252

246. HR 2183. Campaign Finance Overhaul/Previous Question. Linder, R-Ga., motion to order the previous question (thus ending debate and the possibility of amendment) on adoption of the rule (H Res 458) to provide for House floor consideration of the bill to amend the Federal Election Campaign Act to overhaul campaign finance laws. The rule waives points of order on 258 non-germane, secondary amendments to the 11 substitute amendments allowed by a previously adopted rule (H Res 442). Motion agreed to 221-194: R 219-0; D 2-193 (ND 1-144, SD 1-49); I 0-1. June 18, 1998. (Subsequently, the rule was adopted.)

247. HR 2183. Campaign Finance Overhaul/Rule. Adoption of the rule to provide for House floor consideration of the bill to amend the Federal Election Campaign Act to overhaul campaign finance laws. The rule waives points of order on 258 non-germane, secondary amendments to the 11 substitute amendments allowed by a previously adopted rule (H Res 442). Adopted 221-189: R 215-0; D 6-188 (ND 2-142, SD 4-46); I 0-1. June 18, 1998.

248. HR 4059. Fiscal 1999 Military Construction Appropriations/Rule. Adoption of the rule (H Res 477) to provide for House floor consideration of the bill to provide $8.2 billion in budget authority for military construction projects in fiscal 1999. The rule also deems House approval of an overall spending ceiling (302 (a) allocation) for the Appropriations Committee that is based on last year's balanced budget agreement. Adopted 231-178: R 214-0; D 17-177 (ND 12-133, SD 5-44); I 0-1. June 19, 1998.

249. HR 2183. Campaign Finance Overhaul Shays-Meehan Substitute/Thomas Substitute. Thomas, R-Calif., substitute amendment to the Shays-Meehan substitute amendment to the bill to overhaul campaign finance laws. The amendment would specify that if any provision of the act is found unconstitutional, then the entire act shall be treated as invalid. Rejected 155-254: R 149-65; D 6-188 (ND 4-140, SD 2-48); I 0-1. June 19, 1998.

250. HR 2183. Campaign Finance Overhaul Shays-Meehan Substitute/Commission. Maloney, D-N.Y., amendment to the Shays-Meehan substitute amendment to the bill to overhaul campaign finance laws. The amendment creates a 12-member commission to recommend changes to current campaign finance laws. Adopted 325-78: R 142-69; D 182-9 (ND 133-8, SD 49-1); I 1-0. June 19, 1998.

251. HR 2183. Campaign Finance Overhaul Shays-Meehan Substitute/Voter Participation Clarification. Gillmor, R-Ohio, amendment to the Shays-Meehan substitute amendment to the bill to overhaul campaign finance laws. The amendment clarifies the rights of registered voters to participate in campaigns and elections. Adopted 395-0: R 205-0; D 189-0 (ND 141-0, SD 48-0); I 1-0. June 19, 1998.

252. HR 4060. Fiscal 1999 Energy and Water Appropriations/Nuclear Energy Research Programs. Foley, R-Fla., amendment to remove a provision that would provide $5 million in funding for nuclear energy research and development programs. Rejected 147-261: R 58-162; D 88-99 (ND 80-54, SD 8-45); I 1-0. June 22, 1998.

Key

- Y Voted for (yea).
- # Paired for.
- + Announced for.
- N Voted against (nay).
- X Paired against.
- − Announced against.
- P Voted "present."
- C Voted "present" to avoid possible conflict of interest.
- ? Did not vote or otherwise make a position known.

Democrats **Republicans** *Independent*

	246	247	248	249	250	251	252
ALABAMA							
1 **Callahan**	Y	Y	Y	Y	N	?	N
2 **Everett**	Y	Y	Y	Y	N	?	N
3 **Riley**	Y	Y	Y	Y	Y	Y	N
4 **Aderholt**	Y	Y	Y	N	Y	Y	N
5 Cramer	N	N	N	N	Y	Y	N
6 **Bachus**	Y	Y	Y	N	Y	Y	Y
7 Hilliard	N	N	N	N	Y	Y	Y
ALASKA							
AL **Young**	Y	Y	Y	Y	Y	Y	Y
ARIZONA							
1 **Salmon**	Y	Y	Y	Y	N	?	Y
2 Pastor	N	N	Y	N	Y	Y	N
3 **Stump**	Y	Y	Y	Y	N	Y	N
4 **Shadegg**	Y	Y	Y	Y	N	Y	N
5 **Kolbe**	Y	Y	Y	Y	Y	Y	N
6 **Hayworth**	Y	Y	Y	N	Y	Y	N
ARKANSAS							
1 Berry	N	N	N	N	Y	Y	N
2 Snyder	N	N	N	N	Y	Y	N
3 **Hutchinson**	Y	Y	Y	N	Y	Y	Y
4 Dickey	Y	Y	Y	Y	Y	Y	N
CALIFORNIA							
1 **Riggs**	Y	Y	Y	Y	Y	Y	N
2 **Herger**	Y	Y	Y	Y	Y	Y	N
3 Fazio	N	N	N	N	Y	Y	N
4 **Doolittle**	Y	Y	Y	Y	Y	Y	N
5 Matsui	N	N	N	N	Y	Y	N
6 Woolsey	N	N	N	N	Y	Y	N
7 Miller	N	N	N	N	Y	Y	?
8 Pelosi	N	N	N	N	Y	Y	Y
9 Lee	N	N	N	N	Y	Y	Y
10 Tauscher	N	N	N	N	Y	Y	N
11 **Pombo**	Y	Y	Y	N	Y	Y	N
12 Lantos	N	N	N	N	Y	Y	Y
13 Stark	N	N	N	N	Y	Y	Y
14 Eshoo	N	N	N	N	Y	Y	N
15 **Campbell**	Y	Y	Y	N	Y	Y	Y
16 Lofgren	N	N	N	N	Y	Y	Y
17 Farr	N	N	N	N	Y	Y	Y
18 Condit	N	N	N	N	Y	Y	N
19 **Radanovich**	Y	Y	Y	Y	N	Y	N
20 Dooley	N	N	N	N	Y	Y	N
21 **Thomas**	Y	Y	Y	Y	Y	Y	N
22 Capps, L.	N	N	N	N	Y	Y	N
23 **Gallegly**	Y	Y	Y	N	Y	Y	N
24 Sherman	N	N	N	N	Y	Y	Y
25 **McKeon**	Y	Y	Y	N	Y	Y	N
26 Berman	N	N	N	N	Y	Y	N
27 **Rogan**	Y	Y	Y	Y	Y	Y	N
28 **Dreier**	Y	Y	Y	Y	Y	Y	N
29 Waxman	N	N	N	N	Y	Y	Y
30 Becerra	?	N	N	N	Y	Y	?
31 Martinez	?	?	?	?	?	?	N
32 Dixon	N	N	N	N	Y	Y	N
33 Roybal-Allard	N	N	N	N	Y	Y	Y
34 Torres	?	?	?	?	?	?	?
35 Waters	N	N	N	N	Y	Y	N
36 Harman	N	N	N	N	Y	Y	Y
37 Millender-McD.	N	N	N	N	Y	N	N
38 **Horn**	Y	Y	Y	N	Y	Y	N
39 **Royce**	Y	Y	Y	Y	Y	Y	Y
40 **Lewis**	Y	Y	Y	Y	Y	Y	N
41 **Kim**	Y	Y	Y	Y	Y	Y	N
42 Brown	N	N	N	N	Y	Y	N
43 **Calvert**	Y	Y	Y	Y	Y	Y	N
44 **Bono, M.**	Y	Y	Y	Y	Y	Y	N
45 **Rohrabacher**	Y	Y	Y	Y	Y	Y	Y
46 Sanchez	N	N	N	N	Y	Y	Y
47 **Cox**	Y	Y	Y	Y	Y	?	Y
48 **Packard**	Y	Y	Y	Y	Y	Y	N
49 **Bilbray**	Y	Y	Y	N	Y	Y	N
50 Filner	N	N	N	N	Y	Y	N
51 **Cunningham**	Y	Y	Y	Y	Y	Y	N
52 **Hunter**	Y	Y	Y	Y	Y	Y	N
COLORADO							
1 DeGette	N	N	N	N	Y	Y	N
2 Skaggs	N	N	N	?	Y	Y	N
3 **McInnis**	Y	Y	Y	Y	Y	Y	N
4 **Schaffer**	Y	Y	Y	Y	N	Y	N
5 **Hefley**	Y	Y	Y	Y	N	Y	Y
6 **Schaefer**	Y	Y	Y	Y	N	Y	N
CONNECTICUT							
1 Kennelly	N	N	Y	N	+	Y	Y
2 Gejdenson	N	N	N	N	Y	Y	Y
3 DeLauro	N	N	N	N	Y	Y	Y
4 **Shays**	Y	Y	N	N	Y	Y	Y
5 Maloney	N	N	N	N	Y	Y	Y
6 **Johnson**	Y	Y	Y	N	Y	Y	N
DELAWARE							
AL **Castle**	Y	Y	Y	N	Y	Y	N
FLORIDA							
1 **Scarborough**	Y	Y	Y	Y	Y	Y	Y
2 Boyd	N	N	N	N	Y	Y	N
3 Brown	N	N	N	N	Y	Y	N
4 **Fowler**	Y	Y	Y	N	Y	Y	N
5 Thurman	N	N	N	N	Y	Y	N
6 **Stearns**	Y	Y	Y	Y	Y	Y	Y
7 **Mica**	Y	Y	Y	Y	Y	Y	Y
8 **McCollum**	Y	Y	Y	Y	Y	Y	N
9 **Bilirakis**	Y	Y	Y	Y	Y	Y	N
10 **Young**	Y	Y	Y	N	Y	Y	N
11 Davis	N	N	N	N	Y	Y	Y
12 **Canady**	Y	Y	Y	Y	N	Y	N
13 **Miller**	Y	Y	Y	N	Y	Y	N
14 **Goss**	Y	Y	Y	N	Y	Y	N
15 **Weldon**	+	+	+	?	+	?	+
16 **Foley**	Y	Y	Y	Y	Y	Y	Y
17 Meek	N	N	N	N	Y	Y	Y
18 **Ros-Lehtinen**	Y	Y	Y	Y	Y	Y	N
19 Wexler	N	N	N	N	Y	Y	Y
20 Deutsch	N	N	N	N	Y	Y	N
21 **Diaz-Balart**	Y	Y	Y	Y	Y	Y	N
22 **Shaw**	Y	Y	?	?	Y	Y	N
23 Hastings	?	?	?	?	?	?	Y
GEORGIA							
1 **Kingston**	Y	Y	Y	Y	Y	Y	Y
2 Bishop	N	N	N	N	Y	Y	N
3 **Collins**	Y	Y	Y	Y	N	Y	N
4 McKinney	N	N	N	N	Y	Y	Y
5 Lewis	?	?	?	?	?	?	Y
6 **Gingrich**							
7 **Barr**	Y	Y	?	?	?	?	Y
8 **Chambliss**	Y	Y	Y	Y	Y	Y	N
9 **Deal**	Y	Y	Y	Y	Y	Y	N
10 **Norwood**	Y	Y	Y	Y	Y	Y	N
11 **Linder**	Y	Y	Y	Y	N	Y	N
HAWAII							
1 Abercrombie	N	N	Y	N	Y	Y	Y
2 Mink	N	−	Y	N	Y	Y	Y
IDAHO							
1 **Chenoweth**	Y	Y	Y	Y	N	Y	N
2 **Crapo**	Y	Y	Y	Y	Y	Y	N
ILLINOIS							
1 Rush	N	N	N	N	Y	Y	?
2 Jackson	N	N	N	N	Y	Y	N
3 Lipinski	N	N	N	N	Y	Y	Y
4 Gutierrez	N	N	N	N	Y	Y	+
5 Blagojevich	N	N	N	N	Y	Y	N
6 **Hyde**	Y	Y	Y	Y	Y	Y	N
7 Davis	N	N	N	N	Y	Y	N
8 **Crane**	Y	Y	Y	N	Y	Y	N
9 Yates	N	N	N	N	Y	Y	N
10 **Porter**	Y	Y	Y	N	Y	Y	N
11 **Weller**	Y	Y	Y	Y	N	Y	N
12 Costello	N	N	N	N	Y	Y	N

ND Northern Democrats   SD Southern Democrats

	246	247	248	249	250	251	252
13 ***Fawell***	Y	Y	Y	Y	Y	Y	N
14 ***Hastert***	Y	Y	+	Y	N	Y	N
15 ***Ewing***	Y	Y	Y	Y	Y	Y	N
16 ***Manzullo***	Y	Y	Y	Y	Y	Y	N
17 Evans	N	N	N	N	Y	Y	Y
18 ***LaHood***	Y	Y	Y	Y	Y	Y	Y
19 Poshard	N	N	N	N	Y	Y	?
20 ***Shimkus***	Y	Y	Y	Y	Y	Y	N
INDIANA							
1 Visclosky	N	N	N	N	Y	Y	N
2 ***McIntosh***	Y	Y	?	#	Y	Y	Y
3 Roemer	N	N	N	N	Y	Y	N
4 ***Souder***	Y	Y	Y	N	N	Y	N
5 ***Buyer***	Y	Y	Y	Y	N	Y	N
6 ***Burton***	Y	Y	Y	Y	N	Y	N
7 ***Pease***	Y	Y	Y	Y	Y	Y	N
8 ***Hostettler***	Y	Y	Y	Y	N	Y	N
9 Hamilton	N	N	N	N	Y	Y	N
10 Carson	N	N	N	N	Y	Y	–
IOWA							
1 ***Leach***	Y	Y	Y	N	Y	P	N
2 ***Nussle***	Y	Y	Y	N	Y	Y	N
3 Boswell	N	N	N	N	Y	Y	N
4 ***Ganske***	Y	Y	Y	N	Y	Y	N
5 ***Latham***	Y	Y	Y	Y	Y	Y	N
KANSAS							
1 ***Moran***	Y	Y	Y	N	N	Y	N
2 ***Ryun***	Y	Y	Y	Y	Y	Y	N
3 ***Snowbarger***	Y	Y	Y	Y	Y	Y	Y
4 ***Tiahrt***	Y	Y	Y	Y	N	Y	N
KENTUCKY							
1 ***Whitfield***	Y	Y	Y	Y	N	Y	Y
2 ***Lewis***	Y	?	Y	Y	N	Y	N
3 ***Northup***	Y	Y	Y	Y	N	Y	N
4 ***Bunning***	Y	Y	Y	Y	N	Y	N
5 ***Rogers***	Y	Y	Y	Y	Y	Y	N
6 Baesler	N	N	N	N	Y	Y	N
LOUISIANA							
1 ***Livingston***	Y	Y	Y	Y	Y	Y	?
2 Jefferson	N	N	?	N	Y	Y	N
3 ***Tauzin***	Y	Y	Y	Y	Y	Y	N
4 ***McCrery***	Y	Y	Y	Y	N	Y	N
5 ***Cooksey***	?	?	?	?	?	?	N
6 ***Baker***	Y	Y	Y	Y	N	?	?
7 John	N	N	N	N	Y	Y	N
MAINE							
1 Allen	N	N	N	N	Y	Y	Y
2 Baldacci	N	N	N	N	Y	Y	Y
MARYLAND							
1 ***Gilchrest***	Y	Y	Y	N	Y	Y	N
2 ***Ehrlich***	Y	Y	Y	N	Y	Y	N
3 Cardin	N	N	N	N	Y	Y	N
4 Wynn	N	N	N	N	Y	Y	N
5 Hoyer	N	N	N	N	Y	Y	N
6 ***Bartlett***	Y	Y	Y	Y	Y	Y	N
7 Cummings	N	N	N	N	Y	Y	N
8 ***Morella***	Y	Y	Y	X	+	+	Y
MASSACHUSETTS							
1 Olver	N	N	N	N	Y	Y	Y
2 Neal	N	N	N	N	Y	Y	Y
3 McGovern	N	N	N	N	Y	Y	Y
4 Frank	N	N	N	N	N	Y	Y
5 Meehan	N	N	N	N	Y	Y	?
6 Tierney	N	N	N	N	Y	Y	Y
7 Markey	N	N	N	N	Y	Y	Y
8 Kennedy	N	N	N	N	?	?	Y
9 Moakley	N	N	N	N	Y	Y	Y
10 Delahunt	N	N	N	N	Y	Y	Y
MICHIGAN							
1 Stupak	N	N	N	N	Y	Y	N
2 ***Hoekstra***	Y	Y	Y	Y	Y	Y	N
3 ***Ehlers***	Y	Y	Y	Y	Y	Y	N
4 ***Camp***	Y	Y	Y	Y	Y	Y	N
5 Barcia	N	N	N	N	Y	Y	N
6 ***Upton***	Y	Y	Y	N	Y	Y	N
7 ***Smith***	Y	Y	Y	N	Y	Y	N
8 Stabenow	N	N	N	N	Y	Y	Y
9 Kildee	N	N	N	N	Y	Y	Y
10 Bonior	N	N	N	N	N	Y	Y
11 ***Knollenberg***	Y	Y	Y	Y	Y	Y	N
12 Levin	N	N	N	N	Y	Y	Y
13 Rivers	N	N	N	N	Y	Y	Y
14 Conyers	N	N	N	N	Y	?	Y
15 Kilpatrick	N	N	N	N	Y	Y	Y
16 Dingell	N	Y	N	N	Y	Y	N
MINNESOTA							
1 ***Gutknecht***	+	+	+	+	+	+	N
2 Minge	N	N	N	N	Y	Y	Y
3 ***Ramstad***	Y	Y	Y	N	Y	Y	Y
4 Vento	N	N	N	N	Y	Y	Y
5 Sabo	N	N	N	Y	N	Y	Y
6 Luther	N	N	N	N	Y	Y	Y
7 Peterson	N	N	N	Y	Y	Y	Y
8 Oberstar	N	N	N	N	N	Y	Y
MISSISSIPPI							
1 ***Wicker***	Y	Y	Y	Y	N	Y	N
2 Thompson	N	N	N	N	Y	Y	N
3 ***Pickering***	Y	Y	Y	Y	N	Y	N
4 ***Parker***	?	?	?	?	?	?	N
5 Taylor	N	Y	Y	N	Y	Y	N
MISSOURI							
1 Clay	N	N	N	N	Y	Y	Y
2 ***Talent***	Y	Y	Y	Y	Y	Y	Y
3 Gephardt	N	N	N	N	?	?	Y
4 Skelton	N	N	Y	N	Y	Y	N
5 McCarthy	N	N	N	N	Y	Y	Y
6 Danner	N	?	N	N	Y	Y	Y
7 ***Blunt***	Y	Y	?	?	?	?	N
8 ***Emerson***	Y	Y	Y	Y	Y	Y	N
9 ***Hulshof***	Y	Y	Y	Y	N	Y	Y
MONTANA							
AL ***Hill***	Y	Y	Y	N	Y	Y	N
NEBRASKA							
1 ***Bereuter***	Y	Y	Y	N	Y	Y	N
2 ***Christensen***	Y	Y	Y	Y	Y	Y	Y
3 ***Barrett***	Y	Y	Y	N	Y	Y	N
NEVADA							
1 ***Ensign***	Y	Y	Y	Y	Y	Y	Y
2 ***Gibbons***	Y	Y	Y	Y	Y	Y	Y
NEW HAMPSHIRE							
1 ***Sununu***	?	?	?	?	?	?	Y
2 ***Bass***	Y	Y	Y	N	Y	Y	Y
NEW JERSEY							
1 Andrews	N	N	N	N	Y	Y	Y
2 ***LoBiondo***	Y	Y	Y	N	Y	Y	Y
3 ***Saxton***	Y	Y	Y	Y	Y	Y	N
4 ***Smith***	Y	Y	Y	Y	Y	?	Y
5 ***Roukema***	Y	Y	Y	N	Y	Y	Y
6 Pallone	N	N	N	N	Y	Y	Y
7 ***Franks***	Y	Y	Y	N	Y	Y	Y
8 Pascrell	N	N	N	N	Y	Y	?
9 Rothman	N	N	?	?	?	?	Y
10 Payne	N	N	N	N	Y	Y	Y
11 ***Frelinghuysen***	Y	Y	Y	N	Y	Y	N
12 ***Pappas***	Y	Y	Y	N	Y	Y	Y
13 Menendez	N	N	N	N	Y	Y	Y
NEW MEXICO							
1 Vacant							
2 ***Skeen***	Y	Y	Y	Y	N	Y	N
3 ***Redmond***	Y	Y	Y	Y	Y	Y	N
NEW YORK							
1 ***Forbes***	Y	Y	Y	N	Y	Y	N
2 ***Lazio***	Y	Y	Y	N	Y	Y	N
3 ***King***	Y	Y	Y	Y	N	Y	N
4 McCarthy	N	N	N	N	Y	Y	Y
5 Ackerman	N	N	N	N	Y	Y	?
6 Meeks	N	N	?	?	?	?	Y
7 Manton	N	N	N	N	Y	Y	N
8 Nadler	N	N	N	N	Y	Y	?
9 Schumer	N	?	?	?	Y	Y	?
10 Towns	?	?	N	N	Y	Y	?
11 Owens	N	N	N	N	Y	Y	–
12 Velázquez	N	N	N	N	Y	Y	Y
13 ***Fossella***	Y	Y	Y	Y	N	Y	N
14 Maloney	N	N	N	N	Y	Y	+
15 Rangel	N	N	N	N	Y	Y	?
16 Serrano	N	N	N	N	Y	Y	Y
17 Engel	N	N	N	N	Y	Y	Y
18 Lowey	N	N	N	N	Y	Y	Y
19 ***Kelly***	Y	Y	Y	N	Y	Y	N
20 ***Gilman***	Y	Y	Y	N	Y	Y	N
21 McNulty	?	?	?	?	?	?	?
22 ***Solomon***	Y	Y	Y	Y	Y	?	N
23 ***Boehlert***	Y	Y	Y	N	Y	Y	N
24 ***McHugh***	Y	Y	Y	N	Y	Y	N
25 ***Walsh***	Y	Y	Y	N	Y	Y	N
26 Hinchey	N	N	N	N	Y	Y	Y
27 ***Paxon***	Y	Y	Y	Y	N	Y	Y
28 Slaughter	N	N	N	N	Y	Y	N
29 LaFalce	N	N	N	N	Y	Y	N
30 ***Quinn***	Y	Y	Y	N	Y	Y	N
31 ***Houghton***	Y	Y	Y	N	Y	Y	N
NORTH CAROLINA							
1 Clayton	–	–	N	N	Y	Y	N
2 Etheridge	N	N	N	N	Y	Y	N
3 ***Jones***	Y	Y	Y	Y	Y	Y	N
4 Price	N	N	N	N	Y	Y	N
5 ***Burr***	Y	Y	Y	Y	Y	Y	N
6 ***Coble***	Y	Y	Y	N	Y	Y	Y
7 McIntyre	N	N	Y	N	Y	Y	N
8 Hefner	N	N	N	N	Y	Y	N
9 ***Myrick***	Y	Y	Y	Y	Y	Y	N
10 ***Ballenger***	Y	Y	Y	Y	N	Y	N
11 ***Taylor***	Y	Y	Y	Y	Y	Y	N
12 Watt	N	N	N	N	N	Y	N
NORTH DAKOTA							
AL Pomeroy	N	N	N	N	?	Y	N
OHIO							
1 ***Chabot***	Y	Y	Y	N	Y	Y	Y
2 ***Portman***	Y	?	Y	N	Y	Y	+
3 Hall	N	N	Y	N	Y	Y	N
4 ***Oxley***	Y	Y	?	Y	N	Y	–
5 ***Gillmor***	Y	Y	Y	Y	Y	Y	N
6 Strickland	?	N	N	N	Y	Y	N
7 ***Hobson***	Y	Y	Y	Y	Y	Y	N
8 ***Boehner***	Y	Y	Y	Y	N	Y	N
9 Kaptur	N	N	N	N	Y	P	N
10 Kucinich	N	N	N	N	Y	Y	Y
11 Stokes	N	N	N	N	Y	Y	Y
12 ***Kasich***	Y	Y	Y	?	?	?	Y
13 Brown	N	N	N	N	Y	Y	Y
14 Sawyer	N	N	N	N	Y	Y	N
15 ***Pryce***	Y	Y	Y	N	Y	Y	N
16 ***Regula***	Y	?	Y	N	Y	Y	N
17 Traficant	Y	Y	Y	Y	Y	Y	N
18 ***Ney***	Y	Y	Y	Y	Y	Y	Y
19 ***LaTourette***	Y	Y	Y	N	Y	Y	N
OKLAHOMA							
1 ***Largent***	Y	Y	Y	Y	Y	Y	Y
2 ***Coburn***	Y	Y	Y	Y	?	?	Y
3 ***Watkins***	Y	Y	Y	Y	Y	Y	N
4 ***Watts***	Y	Y	Y	Y	Y	Y	N
5 ***Istook***	Y	Y	Y	Y	Y	Y	N
6 ***Lucas***	Y	Y	Y	Y	Y	Y	N
OREGON							
1 Furse	N	N	N	N	Y	Y	Y
2 ***Smith***	Y	Y	Y	Y	N	Y	N
3 Blumenauer	N	N	N	N	Y	Y	Y
4 DeFazio	N	N	N	N	Y	Y	Y
5 Hooley	N	N	N	N	Y	Y	Y
PENNSYLVANIA							
1 Brady	N	N	N	N	Y	Y	N
2 Fattah	N	N	N	N	Y	Y	N
3 Borski	N	N	N	N	Y	Y	N
4 Klink	N	N	N	N	Y	Y	N
5 ***Peterson***	Y	Y	Y	Y	Y	Y	N
6 Holden	N	N	N	N	Y	?	N
7 ***Weldon***	Y	Y	Y	Y	Y	Y	N
8 ***Greenwood***	Y	Y	Y	N	Y	Y	N
9 ***Shuster***	Y	Y	Y	Y	Y	Y	N
10 ***McDade***	Y	Y	?	?	?	?	N
11 Kanjorski	N	N	Y	N	Y	Y	N
12 Murtha	N	N	Y	N	N	Y	N
13 ***Fox***	Y	Y	Y	N	Y	Y	N
14 Coyne	N	N	N	N	Y	Y	N
15 McHale	N	N	N	N	Y	Y	N
16 ***Pitts***	Y	Y	Y	Y	N	Y	Y
17 ***Gekas***	Y	?	Y	Y	N	Y	N
18 Doyle	N	N	N	N	Y	Y	N
19 ***Goodling***	Y	Y	Y	Y	+	+	N
20 Mascara	N	N	N	N	Y	Y	Y
21 ***English***	Y	Y	Y	Y	P	Y	Y
RHODE ISLAND							
1 Kennedy	N	N	N	N	Y	Y	Y
2 Weygand	N	N	N	N	Y	Y	Y
SOUTH CAROLINA							
1 ***Sanford***	Y	Y	Y	N	Y	Y	Y
2 ***Spence***	Y	Y	Y	Y	Y	Y	N
3 ***Graham***	Y	Y	Y	N	Y	Y	N
4 ***Inglis***	Y	Y	Y	Y	Y	Y	Y
5 Spratt	N	N	N	N	Y	Y	N
6 Clyburn	N	N	N	N	Y	Y	N
SOUTH DAKOTA							
AL ***Thune***	Y	Y	Y	Y	Y	Y	Y
TENNESSEE							
1 ***Jenkins***	Y	?	Y	N	Y	Y	N
2 ***Duncan***	Y	Y	Y	N	Y	Y	Y
3 ***Wamp***	Y	Y	Y	N	Y	Y	N
4 ***Hilleary***	Y	Y	Y	N	Y	Y	N
5 Clement	N	N	N	N	Y	Y	N
6 Gordon	N	N	N	N	Y	Y	?
7 ***Bryant***	Y	Y	Y	N	Y	Y	N
8 Tanner	N	N	N	N	Y	Y	N
9 Ford	N	N	N	N	Y	Y	N
TEXAS							
1 Sandlin	N	N	N	N	Y	Y	N
2 Turner	N	N	N	N	Y	Y	N
3 ***Johnson, Sam***	Y	Y	Y	Y	?	?	N
4 Hall	Y	Y	N	Y	Y	Y	N
5 ***Sessions***	Y	Y	Y	Y	N	Y	N
6 ***Barton***	Y	Y	Y	Y	Y	Y	N
7 ***Archer***	?	Y	Y	Y	N	Y	N
8 ***Brady***	Y	Y	Y	N	N	Y	N
9 Lampson	N	N	N	N	Y	Y	Y
10 Doggett	N	N	N	N	Y	Y	Y
11 Edwards	N	N	N	N	Y	Y	N
12 ***Granger***	Y	Y	Y	Y	N	Y	N
13 ***Thornberry***	Y	Y	Y	Y	N	Y	N
14 ***Paul***	Y	Y	Y	Y	N	Y	Y
15 Hinojosa	N	N	N	N	Y	Y	N
16 Reyes	N	N	?	?	?	?	N
17 Stenholm	N	N	N	N	Y	Y	N
18 Jackson-Lee	N	N	N	N	Y	Y	N
19 ***Combest***	Y	Y	Y	Y	N	Y	N
20 Gonzalez	?	?	?	?	?	?	?
21 ***Smith***	Y	Y	Y	Y	N	Y	N
22 ***DeLay***	Y	Y	Y	Y	N	Y	N
23 ***Bonilla***	Y	Y	Y	Y	Y	Y	N
24 Frost	N	N	N	Y	Y	Y	N
25 Bentsen	N	N	N	N	Y	Y	N
26 ***Armey***	?	Y	Y	Y	N	Y	N
27 Ortiz	N	N	N	N	Y	?	N
28 Rodriguez	N	N	N	N	Y	Y	N
29 Green	–	–	–	–	+	+	N
30 Johnson, E.B.	N	N	N	N	Y	P	N
UTAH							
1 ***Hansen***	Y	Y	Y	Y	N	Y	N
2 ***Cook***	Y	Y	Y	N	Y	Y	N
3 ***Cannon***	Y	Y	Y	Y	N	Y	?
VERMONT							
AL *Sanders*	N	N	N	N	Y	Y	Y
VIRGINIA							
1 ***Bateman***	Y	Y	Y	Y	N	Y	N
2 Pickett	N	N	Y	N	Y	Y	N
3 Scott	N	N	N	N	Y	Y	N
4 Sisisky	N	N	Y	N	Y	Y	N
5 Goode	N	Y	Y	N	Y	Y	N
6 ***Goodlatte***	Y	Y	Y	Y	Y	Y	N
7 ***Bliley***	Y	Y	Y	Y	Y	Y	N
8 Moran	N	Y	N	N	Y	Y	N
9 Boucher	N	N	N	N	Y	Y	N
10 ***Wolf***	Y	Y	Y	N	Y	Y	N
11 ***Davis***	Y	Y	Y	N	Y	Y	N
WASHINGTON							
1 ***White***	Y	Y	Y	Y	Y	Y	N
2 ***Metcalf***	Y	Y	Y	N	Y	Y	Y
3 ***Smith, Linda***	Y	Y	Y	N	Y	Y	Y
4 ***Hastings***	Y	Y	Y	Y	Y	Y	N
5 ***Nethercutt***	Y	Y	Y	Y	Y	Y	N
6 Dicks	N	N	N	N	Y	Y	N
7 McDermott	N	N	N	N	N	Y	Y
8 ***Dunn***	Y	?	Y	Y	Y	Y	N
9 Smith, Adam	N	N	N	N	Y	Y	Y
WEST VIRGINIA							
1 Mollohan	N	N	Y	N	N	Y	N
2 Wise	N	N	N	N	?	Y	N
3 Rahall	N	N	Y	N	Y	Y	N
WISCONSIN							
1 ***Neumann***	Y	Y	Y	N	N	Y	Y
2 ***Klug***	Y	Y	Y	N	?	Y	Y
3 Kind	N	N	N	N	Y	Y	Y
4 Kleczka	N	N	N	N	Y	Y	Y
5 Barrett	N	N	N	N	Y	Y	Y
6 ***Petri***	Y	Y	Y	Y	Y	Y	Y
7 Obey	N	N	N	Y	N	Y	N
8 Johnson	N	N	N	N	Y	Y	N
9 ***Sensenbrenner***	Y	Y	Y	Y	Y	Y	Y
WYOMING							
AL ***Cubin***	Y	Y	Y	Y	N	Y	N

Southern states - Ala., Ark., Fla., Ga., Ky., La., Miss., N.C., Okla., S.C., Tenn., Texas, Va.

House Votes 253, 254, 255, 256, 257, 258, 259

253. HR 4060. Fiscal 1999 Energy and Water Appropriations/Passage. Passage of the bill to provide $21.1 billion in new budget authority for energy and water resources programs. The bill provides $184 million less than provided in fiscal 1998 and $648 million less than the president's request. Passed 405-4: R 217-4; D 187-0 (ND 134-0, SD 53-0); I 1-0. June 22, 1998.

254. HR 4059. Fiscal 1999 Military Construction Appropriations/Passage. Passage of the bill to provide $8.2 billion in new budget authority for military construction projects in fiscal 1999. The bill provides $450 million more than the president's request and $974 million less than the amount provided for fiscal 1998. Passed 396-10: R 216-3; D 179-7 (ND 127-6, SD 52-1); I 1-0. June 22, 1998.

255. H Con Res 288. Money Laundering/Passage. McCollum, R-Fla., motion to suspend the rules and pass the bill to express the sense of Congress that undercover law enforcement investigations are necessary to counter money-laundering schemes that involve financial institutions in the United States and other countries, including Mexico. Motion agreed to 404-3: R 217-3; D 186-0 (ND 133-0, SD 53-0); I 1-0. June 22, 1998. A two-thirds majority of those present and voting (272 in this case) is required for passage under suspension of the rules.

256. H Res 452. Postage Rate Increase/Passage. LaTourette, R-Ohio, motion to suspend the rules and pass the bill to express the sense of the House that the U.S. Postal Service's Board of Governors should reject the recommendation that postage rates be raised. Motion agreed to 393-12: R 212-6; D 180-6 (ND 127-6, SD 53-0); I 1-0. June 22, 1998. A two-thirds majority of those present and voting (270 in this case) is required for passage under suspension of the rules.

257. HR 3853. Small Business Drug-free Workplace Programs/Passage. Souder, R-Ind., motion to suspend the rules and pass the bill to authorize $10 million in fiscal 1999 to be used to stop illegal drug use by employees of small businesses. The bill would create a drug-free workplace demonstration program and authorize the Small Business Administration to make grants to nonprofit organizations to provide financial support and advice to small businesses seeking drug-free workplace programs. Motion agreed to 402-9: R 217-1; D 185-8 (ND 134-6, SD 51-2); I 0-0. June 23, 1998. A two-thirds majority of those present and voting (274 in this case) is required for passage under suspension of the rules.

258. HR 4101. Fiscal 1999 Agriculture Appropriations/Peanut Price Support Loans. Neumann, R-Wis., amendment to prohibit the use of funds in the bill to provide a peanut price-support loan greater than $550 per ton for the 1999 crop of quota peanuts. Rejected 181-244: R 101-123; D 80-120 (ND 76-73, SD 4-47); I 0-1. June 23, 1998.

259. HR 4101. Fiscal 1999 Agriculture Appropriations/Wildlife Service Livestock Protection Program. Bass, R-N.H., amendment to reduce the bill's funding by $10 million for the Agriculture Department's Wildlife Service livestock protection program, to try to reduce efforts by the agency to kill predators in Western states. Adopted 229-193: R 75-147; D 153-46 (ND 128-20, SD 25-26); I 1-0. June 23, 1998.

Key

- Y Voted for (yea).
- # Paired for.
- + Announced for.
- N Voted against (nay).
- X Paired against.
- − Announced against.
- P Voted "present."
- C Voted "present" to avoid possible conflict of interest.
- ? Did not vote or otherwise make a position known.

Democrats **Republicans** *Independent*

	253	254	255	256	257	258	259
ALABAMA							
1 Callahan	Y	Y	Y	Y	Y	N	N
2 Everett	Y	Y	Y	Y	Y	N	N
3 Riley	Y	Y	Y	Y	Y	N	N
4 Aderholt	Y	Y	Y	Y	Y	N	N
5 Cramer	Y	Y	Y	Y	Y	N	N
6 Bachus	Y	Y	Y	Y	Y	N	N
7 Hilliard	Y	Y	Y	Y	Y	?	?
ALASKA							
AL Young	Y	Y	Y	Y	Y	N	N
ARIZONA							
1 Salmon	Y	Y	Y	Y	Y	Y	N
2 Pastor	Y	Y	Y	Y	Y	N	N
3 Stump	Y	Y	Y	Y	Y	N	N
4 Shadegg	Y	Y	Y	Y	Y	Y	N
5 Kolbe	Y	Y	N	Y	Y	Y	N
6 Hayworth	Y	Y	Y	Y	Y	Y	N
ARKANSAS							
1 Berry	Y	Y	Y	Y	Y	N	N
2 Snyder	Y	Y	Y	Y	Y	N	Y
3 Hutchinson	Y	Y	Y	Y	Y	Y	N
4 Dickey	Y	Y	Y	Y	Y	Y	N
CALIFORNIA							
1 Riggs	Y	Y	Y	Y	?	Y	N
2 Herger	Y	Y	?	Y	Y	N	N
3 Fazio	Y	Y	Y	Y	Y	N	N
4 Doolittle	Y	Y	Y	Y	Y	N	N
5 Matsui	Y	Y	Y	Y	Y	N	Y
6 Woolsey	Y	Y	Y	Y	Y	N	Y
7 Miller	?	?	?	?	?	Y	Y
8 Pelosi	Y	Y	Y	Y	Y	N	Y
9 Lee	Y	Y	Y	Y	Y	Y	Y
10 Tauscher	Y	Y	Y	Y	Y	N	Y
11 Pombo	Y	Y	Y	Y	Y	N	N
12 Lantos	Y	Y	Y	Y	Y	Y	Y
13 Stark	Y	N	Y	Y	Y	Y	Y
14 Eshoo	Y	Y	Y	Y	Y	N	Y
15 Campbell	Y	Y	Y	N	Y	Y	Y
16 Lofgren	Y	N	Y	Y	Y	N	Y
17 Farr	Y	Y	Y	Y	Y	N	Y
18 Condit	Y	Y	Y	Y	Y	Y	N
19 Radanovich	Y	Y	Y	Y	Y	Y	N
20 Dooley	Y	Y	Y	Y	Y	N	N
21 Thomas	Y	Y	Y	N	Y	N	N
22 Capps, L.	Y	Y	Y	Y	Y	N	Y
23 Gallegly	Y	Y	Y	Y	Y	Y	Y
24 Sherman	Y	Y	Y	Y	Y	N	Y
25 McKeon	Y	Y	Y	Y	Y	N	N
26 Berman	Y	Y	Y	Y	Y	N	Y
27 Rogan	Y	Y	Y	Y	Y	Y	Y
28 Dreier	Y	Y	Y	Y	Y	Y	Y
29 Waxman	Y	Y	Y	Y	?	Y	Y
30 Becerra	?	?	?	?	Y	N	Y
31 Martinez	Y	Y	Y	Y	Y	N	Y
32 Dixon	Y	Y	Y	Y	Y	N	Y
33 Roybal-Allard	Y	Y	Y	Y	Y	N	Y
34 Torres	?	?	?	?	?	?	?
35 Waters	Y	Y	Y	Y	N	N	Y
36 Harman	Y	Y	Y	Y	Y	N	Y
37 Millender-McD.	Y	Y	Y	Y	Y	N	Y

	253	254	255	256	257	258	259
38 Horn	Y	Y	Y	Y	Y	Y	Y
39 Royce	Y	N	Y	Y	Y	Y	Y
40 Lewis	Y	Y	Y	Y	?	N	N
41 Kim	Y	Y	Y	Y	Y	N	N
42 Brown	Y	Y	Y	Y	Y	Y	Y
43 Calvert	Y	Y	Y	Y	Y	N	N
44 Bono, M.	Y	Y	Y	Y	Y	N	N
45 Rohrabacher	Y	Y	Y	Y	Y	N	N
46 Sanchez	Y	Y	Y	Y	N	N	Y
47 Cox	Y	Y	Y	?	Y	Y	Y
48 Packard	Y	Y	Y	Y	Y	N	N
49 Bilbray	Y	Y	Y	Y	Y	N	N
50 Filner	Y	Y	Y	Y	Y	N	Y
51 Cunningham	Y	Y	Y	Y	Y	N	N
52 Hunter	Y	Y	Y	Y	?	N	N
COLORADO							
1 DeGette	Y	Y	Y	Y	Y	Y	Y
2 Skaggs	Y	Y	Y	Y	Y	Y	Y
3 McInnis	Y	Y	Y	Y	Y	Y	N
4 Schaffer	Y	Y	Y	Y	Y	N	N
5 Hefley	Y	Y	Y	Y	Y	Y	N
6 Schaefer	Y	Y	Y	Y	?	?	?
CONNECTICUT							
1 Kennelly	Y	Y	Y	Y	Y	Y	Y
2 Gejdenson	Y	Y	Y	Y	Y	N	Y
3 DeLauro	Y	Y	Y	Y	Y	Y	Y
4 Shays	Y	Y	Y	Y	Y	Y	Y
5 Maloney	Y	Y	Y	Y	Y	Y	Y
6 Johnson	Y	Y	Y	Y	Y	Y	Y
DELAWARE							
AL Castle	Y	Y	Y	Y	Y	Y	Y
FLORIDA							
1 Scarborough	Y	Y	Y	Y	Y	Y	Y
2 Boyd	Y	Y	Y	Y	Y	N	N
3 Brown	Y	Y	Y	Y	Y	N	Y
4 Fowler	Y	Y	Y	Y	Y	N	N
5 Thurman	Y	Y	Y	Y	Y	N	N
6 Stearns	Y	Y	Y	Y	Y	N	N
7 Mica	Y	Y	Y	Y	Y	N	N
8 McCollum	Y	Y	Y	Y	Y	N	Y
9 Bilirakis	Y	Y	Y	Y	Y	N	N
10 Young	Y	Y	Y	Y	Y	N	N
11 Davis	Y	Y	Y	Y	Y	N	Y
12 Canady	Y	Y	Y	Y	Y	N	N
13 Miller	Y	Y	Y	Y	Y	Y	N
14 Goss	Y	Y	Y	Y	Y	Y	Y
15 Weldon	?	+	+	+	Y	N	N
16 Foley	Y	Y	Y	Y	Y	N	N
17 Meek	Y	Y	Y	Y	Y	N	Y
18 Ros-Lehtinen	Y	Y	Y	Y	Y	Y	Y
19 Wexler	Y	Y	Y	Y	Y	N	Y
20 Deutsch	Y	Y	Y	Y	Y	N	Y
21 Diaz-Balart	Y	Y	Y	Y	Y	N	Y
22 Shaw	Y	Y	Y	Y	Y	Y	Y
23 Hastings	Y	Y	Y	Y	Y	N	Y
GEORGIA							
1 Kingston	Y	Y	Y	Y	Y	N	N
2 Bishop	Y	Y	Y	Y	Y	N	N
3 Collins	Y	Y	Y	Y	Y	N	N
4 McKinney	Y	N	Y	Y	N	N	Y
5 Lewis	Y	Y	Y	Y	Y	N	Y
6 Gingrich							
7 Barr	Y	Y	Y	Y	Y	N	N
8 Chambliss	Y	Y	Y	Y	Y	N	N
9 Deal	Y	Y	Y	Y	Y	N	N
10 Norwood	Y	Y	Y	Y	Y	N	N
11 Linder	Y	Y	Y	Y	Y	N	N
HAWAII							
1 Abercrombie	Y	Y	Y	Y	Y	N	Y
2 Mink	Y	Y	Y	Y	Y	N	Y
IDAHO							
1 Chenoweth	Y	Y	Y	Y	Y	N	N
2 Crapo	Y	Y	Y	Y	Y	N	N
ILLINOIS							
1 Rush	?	?	?	?	Y	Y	Y
2 Jackson	Y	Y	Y	Y	Y	Y	Y
3 Lipinski	Y	Y	Y	Y	Y	Y	Y
4 Gutierrez	+	+	+	+	Y	Y	Y
5 Blagojevich	Y	Y	Y	Y	Y	Y	Y
6 Hyde	Y	Y	Y	Y	Y	N	N
7 Davis	Y	Y	Y	Y	Y	Y	Y
8 Crane	Y	Y	Y	Y	Y	N	N
9 Yates	Y	N	Y	Y	+	Y	Y
10 Porter	Y	+	Y	Y	Y	Y	Y
11 Weller	Y	Y	Y	Y	Y	N	N
12 Costello	Y	Y	Y	Y	Y	N	Y

ND Northern Democrats   SD Southern Democrats

	253	254	255	256	257	258	259
13 ***Fawell***	Y	Y	Y	Y	Y	Y	Y
14 ***Hastert***	Y	Y	Y	Y	Y	N	N
15 ***Ewing***	Y	Y	Y	Y	Y	N	N
16 ***Manzullo***	Y	Y	Y	Y	Y	Y	Y
17 Evans	Y	Y	Y	Y	Y	N	Y
18 ***LaHood***	Y	Y	Y	N	Y	N	N
19 Poshard	?	?	?	?	?	N	Y
20 ***Shimkus***	Y	Y	Y	Y	Y	N	N
INDIANA							
1 Visclosky	Y	Y	Y	Y	Y	Y	Y
2 ***McIntosh***	Y	Y	Y	Y	Y	Y	N
3 Roemer	Y	Y	Y	Y	Y	Y	Y
4 ***Souder***	Y	Y	Y	Y	Y	Y	N
5 ***Buyer***	Y	Y	Y	Y	Y	N	Y
6 ***Burton***	Y	Y	Y	Y	Y	Y	N
7 ***Pease***	Y	Y	Y	Y	Y	N	Y
8 ***Hostettler***	Y	Y	Y	Y	Y	Y	N
9 Hamilton	Y	Y	Y	Y	Y	N	Y
10 Carson	+	+	+	+	Y	N	Y
IOWA							
1 ***Leach***	Y	Y	Y	Y	Y	N	N
2 ***Nussle***	Y	Y	Y	Y	Y	N	N
3 Boswell	Y	Y	Y	Y	Y	N	N
4 ***Ganske***	Y	Y	Y	Y	Y	Y	N
5 ***Latham***	Y	Y	Y	Y	Y	N	N
KANSAS							
1 ***Moran***	Y	Y	Y	Y	Y	N	N
2 ***Ryun***	Y	Y	Y	Y	Y	Y	N
3 ***Snowbarger***	Y	Y	Y	Y	Y	Y	N
4 ***Tiahrt***	Y	Y	Y	Y	Y	Y	N
KENTUCKY							
1 ***Whitfield***	Y	Y	Y	Y	?	N	Y
2 ***Lewis***	Y	Y	Y	Y	Y	N	N
3 ***Northup***	Y	Y	Y	Y	Y	Y	Y
4 ***Bunning***	Y	Y	Y	Y	Y	N	N
5 ***Rogers***	Y	Y	Y	Y	Y	N	N
6 Baesler	Y	Y	Y	Y	Y	N	N
LOUISIANA							
1 ***Livingston***	Y	Y	Y	Y	Y	N	N
2 Jefferson	Y	Y	Y	Y	Y	N	Y
3 ***Tauzin***	Y	Y	Y	Y	Y	N	?
4 ***McCrery***	Y	Y	Y	Y	Y	N	N
5 ***Cooksey***	Y	Y	Y	Y	Y	N	N
6 ***Baker***	?	?	?	?	?	N	N
7 John	Y	Y	Y	Y	Y	N	N
MAINE							
1 Allen	Y	Y	Y	Y	Y	Y	Y
2 Baldacci	Y	Y	Y	Y	Y	N	Y
MARYLAND							
1 ***Gilchrest***	Y	Y	Y	Y	Y	N	Y
2 ***Ehrlich***	Y	Y	Y	Y	Y	Y	Y
3 Cardin	Y	Y	Y	Y	Y	Y	Y
4 Wynn	Y	Y	Y	Y	Y	N	Y
5 Hoyer	Y	Y	Y	N	Y	N	Y
6 ***Bartlett***	Y	Y	Y	Y	Y	Y	N
7 Cummings	Y	Y	Y	Y	Y	N	Y
8 ***Morella***	Y	Y	Y	Y	Y	Y	Y
MASSACHUSETTS							
1 Olver	Y	Y	Y	Y	Y	Y	Y
2 Neal	Y	Y	Y	Y	Y	Y	Y
3 McGovern	Y	Y	Y	Y	Y	Y	Y
4 Frank	Y	N	Y	Y	N	Y	Y
5 Meehan	?	?	?	?	Y	Y	Y
6 Tierney	Y	Y	Y	Y	Y	Y	Y
7 Markey	Y	Y	Y	Y	Y	Y	Y
8 Kennedy	Y	Y	Y	Y	Y	Y	Y
9 Moakley	Y	Y	Y	Y	Y	N	Y
10 Delahunt	Y	Y	Y	Y	Y	N	Y
MICHIGAN							
1 Stupak	Y	Y	Y	Y	Y	N	N
2 ***Hoekstra***	Y	Y	Y	Y	Y	Y	N
3 ***Ehlers***	Y	Y	Y	N	Y	Y	Y
4 ***Camp***	Y	Y	Y	Y	Y	N	N
5 Barcia	Y	Y	Y	Y	Y	N	Y
6 ***Upton***	Y	Y	Y	Y	Y	Y	Y
7 ***Smith***	Y	Y	Y	Y	Y	N	N
8 Stabenow	Y	Y	Y	Y	Y	N	Y
9 Kildee	Y	Y	Y	Y	Y	N	Y
10 Bonior	Y	Y	Y	Y	Y	N	Y
11 ***Knollenberg***	Y	Y	Y	Y	Y	Y	N
12 Levin	Y	Y	Y	Y	Y	Y	Y
13 Rivers	Y	Y	Y	Y	Y	Y	Y
14 Conyers	Y	N	Y	Y	N	N	Y
15 Kilpatrick	Y	Y	Y	Y	Y	N	Y
16 Dingell	Y	Y	Y	Y	Y	N	N

	253	254	255	256	257	258	259
MINNESOTA							
1 ***Gutknecht***	Y	Y	Y	Y	Y	N	N
2 Minge	Y	Y	Y	Y	Y	N	Y
3 ***Ramstad***	Y	Y	Y	Y	Y	Y	Y
4 Vento	Y	Y	Y	Y	Y	Y	Y
5 Sabo	Y	Y	Y	Y	Y	N	Y
6 Luther	Y	Y	Y	Y	Y	Y	Y
7 Peterson	Y	Y	Y	Y	Y	N	N
8 Oberstar	Y	Y	Y	Y	?	N	N
MISSISSIPPI							
1 ***Wicker***	Y	Y	Y	Y	Y	N	N
2 Thompson	Y	Y	Y	Y	?	?	?
3 ***Pickering***	Y	Y	Y	Y	Y	N	N
4 ***Parker***	Y	Y	Y	Y	Y	N	N
5 Taylor	Y	Y	Y	Y	Y	N	Y
MISSOURI							
1 Clay	Y	Y	Y	Y	N	N	Y
2 ***Talent***	Y	Y	Y	Y	Y	N	N
3 Gephardt	Y	Y	Y	Y	?	N	Y
4 Skelton	Y	Y	Y	Y	Y	N	N
5 McCarthy	Y	Y	Y	Y	Y	Y	Y
6 Danner	Y	Y	Y	Y	Y	Y	N
7 ***Blunt***	Y	Y	Y	Y	Y	N	N
8 ***Emerson***	Y	Y	Y	Y	Y	N	N
9 ***Hulshof***	Y	Y	Y	Y	Y	Y	N
MONTANA							
AL ***Hill***	Y	Y	Y	Y	Y	N	N
NEBRASKA							
1 ***Bereuter***	Y	Y	Y	Y	Y	N	Y
2 ***Christensen***	Y	Y	Y	Y	Y	Y	N
3 ***Barrett***	Y	Y	Y	Y	Y	N	N
NEVADA							
1 ***Ensign***	N	Y	Y	Y	Y	Y	N
2 ***Gibbons***	N	Y	Y	Y	Y	Y	N
NEW HAMPSHIRE							
1 ***Sununu***	Y	Y	Y	Y	Y	Y	Y
2 ***Bass***	Y	Y	Y	Y	Y	Y	Y
NEW JERSEY							
1 Andrews	Y	Y	Y	Y	Y	Y	Y
2 ***LoBiondo***	Y	Y	Y	Y	Y	Y	Y
3 ***Saxton***	Y	Y	Y	Y	Y	N	Y
4 ***Smith***	Y	Y	Y	Y	Y	Y	Y
5 ***Roukema***	Y	Y	Y	Y	Y	Y	Y
6 Pallone	Y	Y	Y	Y	Y	Y	Y
7 ***Franks***	Y	Y	Y	Y	Y	Y	Y
8 Pascrell	?	?	?	?	Y	Y	Y
9 Rothman	Y	Y	Y	Y	?	Y	Y
10 Payne	Y	Y	Y	Y	Y	?	?
11 ***Frelinghuysen***	Y	Y	Y	Y	Y	Y	Y
12 ***Pappas***	Y	Y	Y	Y	Y	Y	Y
13 Menendez	Y	Y	Y	Y	Y	Y	Y
NEW MEXICO							
1 Vacant							
2 ***Skeen***	Y	Y	Y	Y	Y	N	N
3 ***Redmond***	Y	Y	Y	Y	Y	N	N
NEW YORK							
1 ***Forbes***	Y	Y	Y	Y	Y	Y	Y
2 ***Lazio***	Y	Y	Y	Y	Y	Y	N
3 ***King***	Y	Y	Y	Y	Y	N	Y
4 McCarthy	Y	Y	Y	Y	Y	Y	Y
5 Ackerman	?	?	?	?	?	N	Y
6 Meeks	Y	Y	Y	Y	Y	N	Y
7 Manton	Y	?	?	?	Y	N	Y
8 Nadler	?	?	?	?	N	Y	Y
9 Schumer	?	?	?	?	?	?	Y
10 Towns	?	?	?	?	?	N	Y
11 Owens	+	+	+	+	Y	N	Y
12 Velázquez	Y	Y	Y	Y	Y	N	Y
13 ***Fossella***	Y	Y	Y	Y	Y	Y	Y
14 Maloney	+	+	+	+	Y	Y	Y
15 Rangel	?	?	?	?	Y	N	Y
16 Serrano	Y	Y	Y	Y	Y	N	Y
17 Engel	Y	Y	Y	Y	Y	Y	Y
18 Lowey	Y	Y	Y	Y	Y	Y	Y
19 ***Kelly***	Y	Y	Y	Y	Y	N	Y
20 ***Gilman***	Y	Y	Y	Y	Y	N	Y
21 McNulty	?	?	?	?	?	Y	Y
22 ***Solomon***	Y	Y	Y	Y	Y	N	N
23 ***Boehlert***	Y	Y	Y	Y	Y	Y	Y
24 ***McHugh***	Y	Y	Y	Y	Y	Y	N
25 ***Walsh***	Y	Y	Y	Y	Y	N	N
26 Hinchey	Y	Y	Y	Y	Y	N	Y
27 ***Paxon***	Y	Y	Y	Y	Y	N	N
28 Slaughter	Y	Y	Y	Y	Y	N	+
29 LaFalce	Y	Y	Y	Y	Y	Y	N

	253	254	255	256	257	258	259
30 ***Quinn***	Y	Y	Y	Y	Y	Y	N
31 ***Houghton***	Y	Y	Y	Y	Y	N	Y
NORTH CAROLINA							
1 Clayton	Y	Y	Y	Y	Y	N	Y
2 Etheridge	Y	Y	Y	Y	Y	N	N
3 ***Jones***	Y	Y	Y	Y	Y	N	Y
4 Price	Y	Y	Y	Y	Y	N	Y
5 ***Burr***	Y	Y	Y	Y	Y	N	N
6 ***Coble***	Y	Y	Y	Y	Y	N	N
7 McIntyre	Y	Y	Y	Y	Y	N	N
8 Hefner	Y	Y	Y	Y	Y	N	N
9 ***Myrick***	Y	Y	Y	Y	Y	N	N
10 ***Ballenger***	Y	Y	Y	Y	Y	N	N
11 ***Taylor***	Y	Y	Y	Y	Y	N	N
12 Watt	Y	Y	Y	Y	N	N	Y
NORTH DAKOTA							
AL Pomeroy	Y	Y	Y	Y	Y	N	N
OHIO							
1 ***Chabot***	Y	Y	Y	Y	Y	Y	Y
2 ***Portman***	+	+	+	+	Y	Y	N
3 Hall	Y	Y	Y	Y	Y	Y	Y
4 ***Oxley***	+	+	+	+	Y	N	N
5 ***Gillmor***	Y	Y	Y	Y	Y	Y	N
6 Strickland	Y	Y	Y	Y	Y	Y	Y
7 ***Hobson***	Y	+	Y	Y	Y	Y	N
8 ***Boehner***	Y	Y	Y	Y	Y	N	N
9 Kaptur	Y	Y	Y	Y	Y	N	N
10 Kucinich	Y	Y	Y	Y	Y	Y	Y
11 Stokes	Y	Y	Y	Y	Y	N	Y
12 ***Kasich***	Y	Y	Y	?	Y	Y	N
13 Brown	Y	Y	Y	Y	Y	Y	Y
14 Sawyer	Y	Y	Y	Y	Y	Y	Y
15 ***Pryce***	Y	Y	Y	Y	Y	Y	N
16 ***Regula***	Y	Y	Y	Y	Y	Y	N
17 Traficant	Y	Y	Y	Y	Y	N	N
18 ***Ney***	Y	Y	Y	Y	Y	Y	N
19 ***LaTourette***	Y	Y	Y	Y	Y	Y	Y
OKLAHOMA							
1 ***Largent***	Y	Y	Y	Y	Y	N	N
2 ***Coburn***	Y	Y	Y	Y	Y	N	N
3 ***Watkins***	Y	Y	Y	Y	+	N	–
4 ***Watts***	Y	Y	Y	Y	Y	N	N
5 ***Istook***	Y	Y	Y	Y	Y	N	N
6 ***Lucas***	Y	Y	Y	Y	Y	N	N
OREGON							
1 Furse	Y	N	Y	Y	Y	N	Y
2 ***Smith***	Y	Y	Y	Y	Y	N	N
3 Blumenauer	Y	Y	Y	Y	Y	Y	Y
4 DeFazio	Y	Y	Y	Y	Y	N	Y
5 Hooley	Y	Y	Y	Y	Y	Y	Y
PENNSYLVANIA							
1 Brady	Y	Y	Y	N	Y	Y	Y
2 Fattah	Y	Y	Y	Y	N	Y	Y
3 Borski	Y	Y	Y	N	Y	Y	Y
4 Klink	Y	Y	Y	N	Y	N	Y
5 ***Peterson***	Y	Y	Y	Y	Y	Y	N
6 Holden	Y	Y	Y	Y	Y	N	Y
7 ***Weldon***	Y	Y	Y	Y	Y	Y	Y
8 ***Greenwood***	Y	Y	Y	Y	Y	Y	Y
9 ***Shuster***	Y	Y	Y	?	Y	N	N
10 ***McDade***	Y	Y	Y	Y	Y	N	N
11 Kanjorski	Y	Y	Y	Y	Y	Y	Y
12 Murtha	Y	Y	Y	Y	Y	N	N
13 ***Fox***	Y	Y	Y	Y	Y	Y	Y
14 Coyne	Y	Y	Y	Y	Y	Y	Y
15 McHale	Y	Y	Y	N	Y	Y	Y
16 ***Pitts***	Y	Y	Y	Y	Y	Y	N
17 ***Gekas***	Y	Y	Y	Y	Y	Y	N
18 Doyle	Y	Y	Y	Y	Y	Y	Y
19 ***Goodling***	Y	Y	Y	Y	Y	Y	Y
20 Mascara	Y	Y	Y	Y	Y	Y	Y
21 ***English***	Y	Y	Y	Y	Y	Y	Y
RHODE ISLAND							
1 Kennedy	Y	Y	Y	Y	Y	N	Y
2 Weygand	Y	Y	Y	Y	Y	Y	Y
SOUTH CAROLINA							
1 ***Sanford***	Y	Y	N	N	Y	Y	Y
2 ***Spence***	Y	Y	Y	Y	Y	N	N
3 ***Graham***	Y	Y	Y	Y	Y	N	N
4 ***Inglis***	Y	Y	Y	Y	Y	Y	Y
5 Spratt	Y	Y	Y	Y	Y	N	N
6 Clyburn	Y	Y	Y	Y	Y	?	?
SOUTH DAKOTA							
AL ***Thune***	Y	Y	Y	Y	Y	N	N

	253	254	255	256	257	258	259
TENNESSEE							
1 ***Jenkins***	Y	Y	Y	Y	Y	N	N
2 ***Duncan***	Y	Y	Y	Y	Y	Y	Y
3 ***Wamp***	Y	Y	Y	Y	Y	Y	Y
4 ***Hilleary***	Y	Y	Y	Y	Y	N	N
5 Clement	Y	Y	Y	Y	Y	N	N
6 Gordon	?	?	?	?	Y	Y	Y
7 ***Bryant***	Y	Y	Y	Y	Y	N	N
8 Tanner	Y	Y	Y	Y	Y	N	N
9 Ford	Y	Y	Y	Y	Y	N	Y
TEXAS							
1 Sandlin	Y	Y	Y	Y	Y	N	N
2 Turner	Y	Y	Y	Y	Y	N	N
3 ***Johnson, Sam***	Y	Y	Y	Y	Y	N	Y
4 Hall	Y	Y	Y	Y	Y	N	N
5 ***Sessions***	Y	Y	Y	Y	Y	N	N
6 ***Barton***	Y	Y	Y	Y	Y	N	Y
7 ***Archer***	Y	Y	Y	Y	Y	Y	N
8 ***Brady***	Y	Y	Y	Y	Y	N	N
9 Lampson	Y	Y	Y	Y	Y	N	Y
10 Doggett	Y	Y	Y	Y	Y	Y	Y
11 Edwards	Y	Y	Y	Y	Y	N	N
12 ***Granger***	Y	Y	Y	Y	Y	N	N
13 ***Thornberry***	Y	Y	Y	Y	Y	N	N
14 ***Paul***	N	N	N	Y	N	Y	Y
15 Hinojosa	Y	Y	Y	Y	Y	N	Y
16 Reyes	Y	Y	Y	Y	Y	N	Y
17 Stenholm	Y	Y	Y	Y	Y	N	N
18 Jackson-Lee	Y	Y	Y	Y	Y	N	Y
19 ***Combest***	Y	Y	Y	Y	Y	N	N
20 Gonzalez	?	?	?	?	?	?	?
21 ***Smith***	Y	Y	Y	Y	Y	N	N
22 ***DeLay***	Y	Y	Y	Y	Y	N	N
23 ***Bonilla***	Y	Y	Y	Y	Y	N	N
24 Frost	Y	Y	Y	Y	Y	N	N
25 Bentsen	Y	Y	Y	Y	Y	N	N
26 ***Armey***	Y	Y	Y	Y	Y	Y	N
27 Ortiz	Y	Y	Y	Y	Y	N	N
28 Rodriguez	Y	Y	Y	Y	Y	N	Y
29 Green	Y	Y	Y	Y	Y	N	N
30 Johnson, E.B.	Y	Y	Y	Y	Y	N	Y
UTAH							
1 ***Hansen***	Y	Y	Y	Y	Y	N	N
2 ***Cook***	Y	Y	Y	Y	Y	Y	N
3 ***Cannon***	?	?	?	?	?	?	?
VERMONT							
AL *Sanders*	Y	Y	Y	Y	?	N	Y
VIRGINIA							
1 ***Bateman***	Y	Y	Y	Y	Y	N	N
2 Pickett	Y	Y	Y	Y	Y	N	N
3 Scott	Y	Y	Y	Y	N	N	N
4 Sisisky	Y	Y	Y	Y	Y	N	N
5 Goode	Y	Y	Y	Y	Y	N	N
6 ***Goodlatte***	Y	Y	Y	Y	Y	N	N
7 ***Bliley***	Y	Y	Y	Y	Y	N	Y
8 Moran	Y	Y	Y	Y	Y	Y	Y
9 Boucher	Y	Y	Y	Y	Y	N	N
10 ***Wolf***	Y	Y	Y	Y	Y	Y	Y
11 ***Davis***	Y	Y	Y	Y	Y	N	Y
WASHINGTON							
1 ***White***	Y	Y	Y	Y	Y	Y	N
2 ***Metcalf***	Y	Y	Y	Y	Y	N	Y
3 ***Smith, Linda***	Y	Y	Y	Y	Y	Y	N
4 ***Hastings***	Y	Y	Y	Y	Y	N	N
5 ***Nethercutt***	Y	Y	Y	Y	Y	N	N
6 Dicks	Y	Y	Y	Y	Y	N	Y
7 McDermott	Y	Y	Y	Y	Y	N	Y
8 ***Dunn***	Y	Y	Y	Y	Y	Y	N
9 Smith, Adam	Y	Y	Y	N	Y	Y	Y
WEST VIRGINIA							
1 Mollohan	Y	Y	Y	Y	Y	N	N
2 Wise	Y	Y	Y	Y	Y	N	N
3 Rahall	Y	Y	Y	Y	Y	N	N
WISCONSIN							
1 ***Neumann***	Y	Y	Y	Y	Y	Y	Y
2 ***Klug***	Y	Y	Y	Y	Y	Y	N
3 Kind	Y	Y	Y	Y	Y	Y	Y
4 Kleczka	Y	Y	Y	Y	Y	N	Y
5 Barrett	Y	Y	Y	Y	Y	Y	Y
6 ***Petri***	Y	Y	Y	Y	Y	Y	Y
7 Obey	Y	Y	Y	Y	Y	Y	Y
8 Johnson	Y	Y	Y	Y	Y	Y	Y
9 ***Sensenbrenner***	N	N	Y	Y	Y	Y	Y
WYOMING							
AL ***Cubin***	Y	Y	Y	Y	Y	N	N

Southern states - Ala., Ark., Fla., Ga., Ky., La., Miss., N.C., Okla., S.C., Tenn., Texas, Va.

House Votes 260, 261, 262, 263, 264, 265, 266

Key
- Y Voted for (yea).
- # Paired for.
- + Announced for.
- N Voted against (nay).
- X Paired against.
- − Announced against.
- P Voted "present."
- C Voted "present" to avoid possible conflict of interest.
- ? Did not vote or otherwise make a position known.

Democrats **Republicans** *Independent*

260. HR 4101. Fiscal 1999 Agriculture Appropriations/FDA Testing and Approval of Abortion Pills. Coburn, R-Okla., amendment to prohibit the Food and Drug Administration from using funds appropriated in the bill to test, develop or approve any drug for chemically induced abortions. Adopted 223-202: R 188-37; D 35-164 (ND 26-120, SD 9-44); I 0-1. June 24, 1998.

261. HR 4101. Fiscal 1999 Agriculture Appropriations/Loan Rates for Sugar Processors. Miller, R-Fla., amendment to lower the loan rates the Agriculture Department provides to sugar cane and sugar beet processors by one cent. Rejected 167-258: R 109-116; D 58-141 (ND 53-93, SD 5-48); I 0-1. June 24, 1998.

262. HR 4101. Fiscal 1999 Agriculture Appropriations/Market Access Program. Royce, R-Calif., amendment to prohibit funds appropriated by the bill from being used to pay salaries or expenses of personnel in the Market Access Program, which promotes agriculture programs abroad. Rejected 118-307: R 75-150; D 42-157 (ND 38-107, SD 4-50); I 1-0. June 24, 1998.

263. HR 4101. Fiscal 1999 Agriculture Appropriations/Wildlife Service Livestock Protection Program. Bass, R-N.H., amendment to reduce the bill's funding for the Agriculture Department's Wildlife Service livestock protection program to try to reduce efforts by the agency to kill predators in Western states. Rejected 192-232: R 60-164; D 131-68 (ND 114-32, SD 17-36); I 1-0. June 24, 1998. (The amendment was initially debated and adopted on June 23 (vote 259) but a drafting error made it necessary to vote on the amendment again. Because it failed on the second vote, neither version is included in the bill text.)

264. HR 4101. Fiscal 1999 Agriculture Appropriations/Passage. Passage of the bill to provide $55.9 billion in fiscal 1999 for agriculture programs, $42.3 billion of which is mandatory spending for programs such as food stamps. The bill provides $6.1 billion more than appropriated in fiscal 1998 and $1.9 billion less than requested by President Clinton. Passed 373-48: R 199-23; D 173-25 (ND 125-20, SD 48-5); I 1-0. June 24, 1998.

265. HR 4103. Fiscal 1999 Defense Appropriations/Rule. Adoption of the rule (H Res 484) to provide for House floor consideration of the bill to provide $250.7 billion in defense spending for fiscal 1999. The rule struck $1.6 billion in "emergency" funding for the year 2000 computer problem at the Defense Department. Adopted 221-201: R 219-2; D 2-198 (ND 2-145, SD 0-53); I 0-1. June 24, 1998.

266. HR 4103. Fiscal 1999 Defense Appropriations/Passage. Passage of the bill to provide $250.7 billion in defense spending for fiscal 1999. The bill provides $510 million less than President Clinton's request and $3 billion more than the amount appropriated for fiscal 1998. Passed 358-61: R 209-13; D 149-47 (ND 101-42, SD 48-5); I 0-1. June 24, 1998.

	260	261	262	263	264	265	266
ALABAMA							
1 *Callahan*	Y	N	Y	N	Y	Y	Y
2 *Everett*	Y	N	N	N	Y	Y	Y
3 *Riley*	Y	N	N	N	Y	Y	Y
4 *Aderholt*	Y	N	N	N	Y	Y	Y
5 Cramer	Y	N	N	N	Y	N	Y
6 *Bachus*	Y	N	Y	N	Y	Y	Y
7 Hilliard	N	N	N	Y	Y	N	Y
ALASKA							
AL *Young*	Y	N	N	N	Y	Y	Y
ARIZONA							
1 *Salmon*	Y	Y	Y	N	N	Y	Y
2 Pastor	N	N	N	Y	N	Y	Y
3 *Stump*	Y	N	N	N	N	Y	Y
4 *Shadegg*	Y	Y	Y	N	N	Y	Y
5 *Kolbe*	N	Y	N	Y	Y	Y	Y
6 *Hayworth*	Y	Y	Y	N	Y	Y	Y
ARKANSAS							
1 Berry	Y	N	N	N	N	N	N
2 Snyder	N	N	N	N	Y	N	Y
3 *Hutchinson*	Y	Y	N	Y	Y	+	Y
4 Dickey	Y	Y	N	Y	Y	Y	Y
CALIFORNIA							
1 *Riggs*	Y	Y	N	N	Y	Y	Y
2 *Herger*	Y	N	N	N	Y	Y	Y
3 Fazio	N	N	N	N	Y	N	Y
4 *Doolittle*	Y	N	N	N	Y	Y	Y
5 Matsui	N	N	N	N	Y	N	Y
6 Woolsey	N	N	N	Y	N	N	N
7 Miller	N	Y	N	Y	?	N	N
8 Pelosi	N	N	N	Y	N	N	N
9 Lee	N	N	N	Y	N	N	N
10 Tauscher	N	Y	N	Y	Y	N	Y
11 *Pombo*	Y	N	N	N	Y	Y	Y
12 Lantos	N	N	N	N	Y	N	Y
13 Stark	N	N	Y	Y	N	N	N
14 Eshoo	N	N	N	Y	Y	N	Y
15 *Campbell*	N	Y	Y	Y	N	Y	N
16 Lofgren	N	N	N	Y	N	N	N
17 Farr	N	N	N	Y	N	N	Y
18 Condit	N	N	N	N	Y	N	Y
19 *Radanovich*	Y	Y	N	Y	Y	Y	Y
20 Dooley	N	N	N	N	N	N	Y
21 *Thomas*	N	N	N	N	Y	Y	Y
22 Capps, L.	N	Y	N	Y	Y	N	Y
23 *Gallegly*	Y	N	Y	N	Y	Y	Y
24 Sherman	N	N	N	N	Y	N	Y
25 *McKeon*	Y	N	N	N	Y	Y	Y
26 Berman	N	Y	N	Y	N	N	Y
27 *Rogan*	Y	Y	Y	Y	Y	Y	Y
28 *Dreier*	Y	N	N	N	Y	Y	Y
29 Waxman	N	Y	Y	Y	N	N	Y
30 Becerra	N	N	N	N	N	N	N
31 Martinez	N	N	N	N	Y	N	Y
32 Dixon	N	N	N	N	N	N	N
33 Royal-Allard	N	N	N	N	Y	N	Y
34 Torres	N	N	?	N	Y	N	Y
35 Waters	N	N	N	N	N	N	N
36 Harman	N	N	N	N	Y	N	Y
37 Millender-McD.	N	N	N	N	Y	N	Y

	260	261	262	263	264	265	266
38 *Horn*	N	Y	Y	Y	Y	Y	Y
39 *Royce*	Y	Y	Y	Y	N	Y	N
40 *Lewis*	Y	N	N	N	Y	Y	Y
41 *Kim*	Y	Y	N	N	Y	Y	Y
42 Brown	N	N	N	Y	Y	N	N
43 *Calvert*	Y	N	N	N	Y	Y	Y
44 *Bono, M.*	Y	N	N	N	Y	Y	Y
45 *Rohrabacher*	Y	Y	N	N	Y	Y	Y
46 Sanchez	N	N	N	N	Y	N	Y
47 *Cox*	Y	Y	Y	Y	Y	Y	Y
48 *Packard*	Y	N	N	N	Y	Y	Y
49 *Bilbray*	N	N	N	Y	Y	Y	Y
50 Filner	N	N	N	Y	Y	N	N
51 *Cunningham*	Y	N	N	N	Y	Y	Y
52 *Hunter*	Y	N	N	N	Y	Y	Y
COLORADO							
1 DeGette	N	N	N	Y	Y	N	Y
2 Skaggs	N	Y	N	Y	Y	N	Y
3 *McInnis*	Y	Y	N	N	Y	Y	Y
4 *Schaffer*	Y	N	N	N	Y	Y	Y
5 *Hefley*	Y	Y	Y	N	N	Y	Y
6 *Schaefer*	Y	N	N	N	Y	Y	Y
CONNECTICUT							
1 Kennelly	N	Y	Y	Y	N	Y	Y
2 Gejdenson	N	N	Y	Y	Y	N	Y
3 DeLauro	N	N	N	Y	N	N	Y
4 *Shays*	N	Y	Y	Y	Y	N	N
5 Maloney	N	Y	Y	Y	Y	N	Y
6 *Johnson*	N	Y	Y	Y	Y	N	Y
DELAWARE							
AL *Castle*	N	Y	Y	Y	Y	Y	Y
FLORIDA							
1 *Scarborough*	Y	Y	Y	Y	N	Y	Y
2 Boyd	N	N	N	N	Y	N	Y
3 Brown	N	N	N	N	Y	N	Y
4 *Fowler*	N	N	Y	Y	Y	Y	Y
5 Thurman	N	N	N	N	Y	N	Y
6 *Stearns*	Y	N	N	N	Y	Y	Y
7 *Mica*	Y	Y	N	Y	Y	Y	Y
8 *McCollum*	Y	Y	Y	N	Y	Y	Y
9 *Bilirakis*	Y	Y	N	N	Y	Y	Y
10 *Young*	Y	Y	N	Y	Y	Y	Y
11 Davis	N	N	N	N	Y	N	Y
12 *Canady*	Y	N	N	N	Y	Y	Y
13 *Miller*	N	Y	Y	Y	Y	Y	Y
14 *Goss*	Y	Y	Y	Y	Y	Y	Y
15 *Weldon*	Y	N	N	N	Y	Y	Y
16 *Foley*	N	N	N	Y	Y	Y	Y
17 Meek	N	N	N	N	Y	N	Y
18 *Ros-Lehtinen*	Y	Y	N	N	Y	Y	Y
19 Wexler	N	N	N	Y	Y	N	Y
20 Deutsch	N	N	N	N	Y	N	N
21 *Diaz-Balart*	Y	N	N	N	Y	Y	Y
22 *Shaw*	N	Y	N	Y	Y	Y	Y
23 Hastings	N	N	N	N	Y	N	Y
GEORGIA							
1 *Kingston*	Y	Y	N	N	Y	Y	Y
2 Bishop	N	N	N	N	Y	N	Y
3 *Collins*	Y	Y	Y	N	Y	Y	Y
4 McKinney	N	Y	Y	Y	N	N	Y
5 Lewis	N	N	N	N	Y	N	Y
6 *Gingrich*							
7 *Barr*	Y	Y	Y	Y	N	Y	Y
8 *Chambliss*	Y	N	N	N	Y	Y	Y
9 *Deal*	Y	Y	Y	N	Y	Y	Y
10 *Norwood*	Y	N	N	Y	Y	Y	Y
11 *Linder*	Y	Y	Y	N	Y	Y	Y
HAWAII							
1 Abercrombie	N	N	N	N	Y	N	Y
2 Mink	N	N	N	N	Y	Y	Y
IDAHO							
1 *Chenoweth*	Y	N	N	N	N	Y	Y
2 *Crapo*	Y	N	N	N	Y	Y	Y
ILLINOIS							
1 Rush	N	Y	N	Y	Y	N	N
2 Jackson	N	Y	N	Y	Y	N	N
3 Lipinski	Y	Y	Y	Y	Y	N	?
4 Gutierrez	N	Y	N	Y	N	N	N
5 Blagojevich	N	Y	Y	Y	Y	N	Y
6 *Hyde*	Y	Y	Y	N	Y	Y	Y
7 Davis	N	Y	N	Y	N	N	Y
8 *Crane*	Y	Y	Y	N	N	Y	+
9 Yates	N	Y	Y	Y	N	N	?
10 *Porter*	N	Y	Y	Y	Y	Y	Y
11 *Weller*	Y	N	N	Y	Y	Y	Y
12 Costello	Y	N	N	N	Y	N	Y

ND Northern Democrats SD Southern Democrats

	260	261	262	263	264	265	266
13 ***Fawell***	N	Y	Y	Y	Y	?	Y
14 ***Hastert***	Y	N	Y	N	Y	Y	Y
15 ***Ewing***	Y	N	N	N	Y	Y	Y
16 ***Manzullo***	Y	Y	Y	N	Y	N	Y
17 Evans	N	N	N	Y	Y	N	Y
18 ***LaHood***	Y	N	N	N	Y	Y	Y
19 Poshard	Y	N	N	Y	Y	N	Y
20 ***Shimkus***	Y	N	N	N	Y	Y	Y
INDIANA							
1 Visclosky	N	Y	Y	N	Y	N	Y
2 ***McIntosh***	Y	Y	N	N	Y	Y	Y
3 Roemer	Y	N	N	Y	N	N	Y
4 ***Souder***	Y	Y	N	N	Y	Y	Y
5 ***Buyer***	Y	N	N	N	Y	Y	Y
6 ***Burton***	Y	N	N	N	Y	Y	Y
7 ***Pease***	Y	N	N	Y	Y	Y	Y
8 ***Hostettler***	Y	Y	Y	N	Y	Y	Y
9 Hamilton	?	?	?	?	?	?	?
10 Carson	N	N	N	Y	Y	N	Y
IOWA							
1 ***Leach***	N	N	N	N	Y	Y	Y
2 ***Nussle***	Y	N	N	N	Y	Y	Y
3 Boswell	N	N	N	N	Y	N	Y
4 ***Ganske***	N	N	N	N	Y	Y	Y
5 ***Latham***	Y	N	N	N	Y	Y	Y
KANSAS							
1 ***Moran***	Y	N	N	N	Y	Y	Y
2 ***Ryun***	Y	N	N	N	Y	Y	Y
3 ***Snowbarger***	Y	Y	N	N	Y	Y	Y
4 ***Tiahrt***	Y	N	N	N	Y	Y	Y
KENTUCKY							
1 ***Whitfield***	Y	N	N	N	Y	Y	Y
2 ***Lewis***	Y	N	N	N	Y	Y	Y
3 ***Northup***	Y	Y	N	N	+	Y	Y
4 ***Bunning***	Y	N	N	N	Y	Y	Y
5 ***Rogers***	Y	N	N	N	Y	Y	Y
6 Baesler	N	N	N	N	Y	?	?
LOUISIANA							
1 ***Livingston***	Y	N	N	N	Y	Y	Y
2 Jefferson	N	N	N	Y	Y	N	Y
3 ***Tauzin***	Y	N	N	N	Y	Y	Y
4 ***McCrery***	Y	N	N	N	Y	Y	Y
5 ***Cooksey***	N	N	N	N	Y	Y	Y
6 ***Baker***	Y	N	N	N	Y	Y	Y
7 John	Y	N	N	N	Y	N	Y
MAINE							
1 Allen	N	Y	N	Y	Y	N	Y
2 Baldacci	N	N	N	Y	Y	N	Y
MARYLAND							
1 ***Gilchrest***	N	Y	N	Y	Y	Y	Y
2 ***Ehrlich***	N	Y	Y	N	Y	Y	Y
3 Cardin	N	Y	N	Y	Y	N	Y
4 Wynn	N	N	N	Y	Y	N	Y
5 Hoyer	N	Y	N	N	Y	N	Y
6 ***Bartlett***	Y	Y	N	N	Y	Y	Y
7 Cummings	N	N	N	Y	Y	N	Y
8 ***Morella***	N	Y	Y	Y	Y	Y	N
MASSACHUSETTS							
1 Olver	N	Y	Y	Y	Y	N	N
2 Neal	N	N	Y	Y	Y	N	Y
3 McGovern	N	N	N	Y	Y	N	N
4 Frank	N	Y	Y	Y	N	N	N
5 Meehan	N	Y	Y	Y	N	N	Y
6 Tierney	N	Y	Y	Y	N	N	Y
7 Markey	?	?	?	?	?	?	?
8 Kennedy	N	Y	Y	Y	Y	N	Y
9 Moakley	N	N	N	Y	Y	N	Y
10 Delahunt	N	N	N	Y	Y	N	N
MICHIGAN							
1 Stupak	Y	N	N	N	Y	N	Y
2 ***Hoekstra***	Y	Y	Y	N	Y	Y	N
3 ***Ehlers***	Y	N	Y	Y	Y	Y	N
4 ***Camp***	Y	N	N	N	Y	Y	Y
5 Barcia	Y	N	N	N	Y	N	Y
6 ***Upton***	N	Y	N	Y	Y	Y	N
7 ***Smith***	Y	N	N	N	Y	Y	Y
8 Stabenow	N	N	N	N	Y	N	Y
9 Kildee	Y	N	N	Y	Y	N	Y
10 Bonior	N	N	N	Y	Y	N	Y
11 ***Knollenberg***	Y	N	N	N	Y	Y	Y
12 Levin	N	N	N	Y	Y	N	Y
13 Rivers	N	N	Y	Y	Y	N	Y
14 Conyers	N	N	N	Y	Y	N	N
15 Kilpatrick	N	N	N	Y	Y	N	Y
16 Dingell	?	?	?	?	?	?	?
MINNESOTA							
1 ***Gutknecht***	Y	N	N	N	Y	Y	Y
2 Minge	N	N	N	N	Y	N	N
3 ***Ramstad***	N	Y	Y	Y	N	Y	N
4 Vento	N	N	Y	Y	Y	N	N
5 Sabo	N	N	N	Y	N	N	Y
6 Luther	N	N	Y	Y	Y	N	N
7 Peterson	Y	N	N	N	Y	N	Y
8 Oberstar	Y	N	N	N	N	N	N
MISSISSIPPI							
1 ***Wicker***	Y	N	N	N	Y	Y	Y
2 Thompson	N	N	N	N	Y	N	Y
3 ***Pickering***	Y	N	N	N	Y	Y	Y
4 ***Parker***	Y	N	N	N	Y	Y	Y
5 Taylor	Y	N	Y	Y	N	N	Y
MISSOURI							
1 Clay	N	N	N	Y	Y	N	Y
2 ***Talent***	Y	N	N	N	Y	Y	Y
3 Gephardt	N	N	N	Y	Y	N	Y
4 Skelton	Y	N	N	N	Y	N	Y
5 McCarthy	N	Y	N	Y	Y	N	Y
6 Danner	N	N	N	N	Y	N	Y
7 ***Blunt***	Y	N	N	N	Y	Y	Y
8 ***Emerson***	Y	N	N	N	+	Y	Y
9 ***Hulshof***	Y	Y	N	N	Y	Y	Y
MONTANA							
AL ***Hill***	Y	N	N	N	Y	Y	Y
NEBRASKA							
1 ***Bereuter***	Y	N	N	N	Y	N	Y
2 ***Christensen***	Y	N	N	N	Y	Y	Y
3 ***Barrett***	Y	N	N	N	Y	Y	Y
NEVADA							
1 ***Ensign***	Y	Y	Y	N	N	Y	Y
2 ***Gibbons***	Y	Y	N	N	Y	Y	Y
NEW HAMPSHIRE							
1 ***Sununu***	Y	Y	Y	Y	N	Y	Y
2 ***Bass***	N	Y	Y	Y	Y	Y	Y
NEW JERSEY							
1 Andrews	N	Y	Y	Y	N	N	Y
2 ***LoBiondo***	Y	Y	Y	Y	Y	Y	Y
3 ***Saxton***	Y	N	Y	Y	Y	Y	Y
4 ***Smith***	Y	Y	N	Y	Y	Y	Y
5 ***Roukema***	N	Y	N	Y	Y	Y	Y
6 Pallone	N	Y	N	Y	Y	N	Y
7 ***Franks***	N	Y	Y	Y	N	Y	N
8 Pascrell	N	Y	Y	Y	Y	N	Y
9 Rothman	N	N	Y	Y	Y	N	Y
10 Payne	N	N	N	Y	Y	N	N
11 ***Frelinghuysen***	N	Y	N	Y	Y	Y	+
12 ***Pappas***	Y	Y	N	N	Y	Y	Y
13 Menendez	N	N	N	Y	N	N	Y
NEW MEXICO							
1 Vacant							
2 ***Skeen***	Y	N	N	N	Y	Y	Y
3 ***Redmond***	Y	N	N	N	Y	Y	Y
NEW YORK							
1 ***Forbes***	Y	Y	N	Y	Y	Y	Y
2 ***Lazio***	N	Y	N	Y	Y	Y	Y
3 ***King***	Y	N	N	N	Y	Y	Y
4 McCarthy	N	Y	Y	Y	Y	N	Y
5 Ackerman	N	N	N	Y	Y	N	Y
6 Meeks	N	N	N	Y	Y	N	N
7 Manton	Y	N	N	Y	Y	N	?
8 Nadler	N	Y	Y	Y	N	N	N
9 Schumer	N	Y	Y	Y	Y	N	Y
10 Towns	N	N	N	Y	Y	N	N
11 Owens	N	Y	N	Y	Y	N	N
12 Velázquez	N	Y	N	Y	Y	N	N
13 ***Fossella***	Y	Y	Y	N	Y	Y	Y
14 Maloney	N	Y	N	Y	Y	N	Y
15 Rangel	N	N	N	Y	Y	N	Y
16 Serrano	N	N	N	N	Y	N	Y
17 Engel	N	Y	N	Y	Y	N	Y
18 Lowey	N	Y	Y	Y	N	N	Y
19 ***Kelly***	N	Y	Y	Y	Y	Y	Y
20 ***Gilman***	N	N	N	Y	Y	Y	Y
21 McNulty	Y	Y	Y	Y	Y	N	Y
22 ***Solomon***	Y	N	N	N	Y	?	Y
23 ***Boehlert***	N	Y	Y	Y	Y	Y	Y
24 ***McHugh***	Y	Y	N	N	Y	Y	Y
25 ***Walsh***	Y	N	N	N	Y	Y	Y
26 Hinchey	N	Y	N	Y	Y	N	N
27 ***Paxon***	Y	N	N	N	Y	Y	Y
28 Slaughter	–	–	?	+	+	–	Y
29 LaFalce	Y	Y	N	N	Y	N	?
30 ***Quinn***	Y	Y	N	N	Y	Y	Y
31 ***Houghton***	N	N	N	Y	Y	Y	Y
NORTH CAROLINA							
1 Clayton	N	N	N	N	Y	N	Y
2 Etheridge	N	N	N	N	Y	N	Y
3 ***Jones***	Y	N	N	Y	Y	Y	Y
4 Price	N	N	N	Y	Y	N	Y
5 ***Burr***	Y	N	N	N	Y	Y	Y
6 ***Coble***	Y	N	N	N	Y	Y	Y
7 McIntyre	Y	N	N	N	Y	N	Y
8 Hefner	N	N	N	N	Y	N	Y
9 ***Myrick***	Y	Y	Y	N	Y	Y	Y
10 ***Ballenger***	Y	N	N	N	Y	Y	Y
11 ***Taylor***	Y	N	N	N	Y	Y	Y
12 Watt	N	N	N	Y	Y	N	N
NORTH DAKOTA							
AL Pomeroy	N	N	N	N	Y	N	Y
OHIO							
1 ***Chabot***	Y	Y	Y	Y	N	Y	Y
2 ***Portman***	Y	Y	Y	N	N	Y	Y
3 Hall	Y	Y	N	Y	Y	N	Y
4 ***Oxley***	Y	N	N	N	Y	Y	Y
5 ***Gillmor***	Y	N	Y	N	Y	Y	Y
6 Strickland	N	N	N	Y	Y	N	Y
7 ***Hobson***	Y	Y	Y	N	Y	Y	Y
8 ***Boehner***	Y	N	N	N	Y	Y	Y
9 Kaptur	N	N	N	N	Y	N	?
10 Kucinich	Y	Y	Y	Y	N	N	N
11 Stokes	N	N	N	Y	Y	N	Y
12 ***Kasich***	Y	Y	Y	N	Y	Y	Y
13 Brown	N	Y	Y	Y	Y	N	N
14 Sawyer	N	Y	N	Y	Y	N	Y
15 ***Pryce***	N	Y	Y	N	Y	Y	Y
16 ***Regula***	Y	Y	N	N	Y	Y	Y
17 Traficant	Y	N	N	N	Y	Y	Y
18 ***Ney***	Y	Y	Y	N	Y	Y	Y
19 ***LaTourette***	Y	Y	N	Y	Y	Y	Y
OKLAHOMA							
1 ***Largent***	Y	Y	Y	N	Y	Y	Y
2 ***Coburn***	Y	Y	Y	N	Y	Y	Y
3 ***Watkins***	Y	N	N	N	Y	Y	Y
4 ***Watts***	Y	N	N	N	Y	Y	Y
5 ***Istook***	Y	N	Y	N	Y	Y	Y
6 ***Lucas***	Y	N	N	N	Y	Y	Y
OREGON							
1 Furse	N	N	N	Y	Y	N	N
2 ***Smith***	Y	N	N	N	Y	Y	Y
3 Blumenauer	N	Y	N	Y	Y	N	Y
4 DeFazio	N	Y	Y	Y	Y	N	N
5 Hooley	N	N	N	N	Y	N	N
PENNSYLVANIA							
1 Brady	N	Y	Y	Y	Y	N	Y
2 Fattah	N	N	Y	Y	Y	N	N
3 Borski	Y	Y	Y	Y	Y	N	Y
4 Klink	Y	N	Y	Y	Y	N	Y
5 ***Peterson***	Y	Y	N	N	Y	Y	Y
6 Holden	Y	N	N	N	Y	N	Y
7 ***Weldon***	Y	Y	Y	Y	Y	Y	Y
8 ***Greenwood***	N	Y	N	Y	Y	Y	Y
9 ***Shuster***	Y	N	Y	N	Y	Y	Y
10 ***McDade***	Y	Y	Y	?	?	?	?
11 Kanjorski	Y	Y	N	N	Y	N	Y
12 Murtha	Y	N	N	N	Y	N	Y
13 ***Fox***	Y	Y	Y	Y	Y	Y	Y
14 Coyne	N	Y	Y	Y	Y	N	N
15 McHale	N	Y	N	Y	Y	N	Y
16 ***Pitts***	Y	Y	N	N	Y	Y	Y
17 ***Gekas***	Y	Y	N	N	Y	Y	Y
18 Doyle	+	+	+	+	+	N	Y
19 ***Goodling***	Y	Y	N	Y	Y	Y	Y
20 Mascara	Y	N	Y	N	Y	N	Y
21 ***English***	Y	Y	Y	Y	Y	Y	Y
RHODE ISLAND							
1 Kennedy	N	Y	Y	Y	Y	N	Y
2 Weygand	Y	N	N	Y	Y	N	Y
SOUTH CAROLINA							
1 ***Sanford***	Y	Y	Y	Y	N	Y	N
2 ***Spence***	Y	N	N	N	Y	Y	Y
3 ***Graham***	Y	N	N	N	Y	Y	Y
4 ***Inglis***	Y	Y	Y	Y	Y	Y	Y
5 Spratt	N	N	N	N	Y	N	Y
6 Clyburn	N	N	N	Y	Y	N	Y
SOUTH DAKOTA							
AL ***Thune***	Y	N	N	N	Y	Y	Y
TENNESSEE							
1 ***Jenkins***	Y	N	N	N	Y	Y	Y
2 ***Duncan***	Y	Y	Y	Y	Y	Y	Y
3 ***Wamp***	Y	Y	Y	Y	Y	Y	Y
4 ***Hilleary***	Y	Y	N	N	Y	Y	Y
5 Clement	N	N	N	N	Y	N	Y
6 Gordon	?	Y	N	Y	Y	N	Y
7 ***Bryant***	Y	N	N	N	Y	Y	Y
8 Tanner	N	N	N	N	Y	N	Y
9 Ford	N	N	N	Y	+	N	Y
TEXAS							
1 Sandlin	N	N	N	N	Y	N	Y
2 Turner	N	N	N	N	Y	N	Y
3 ***Johnson, Sam***	Y	N	N	N	Y	Y	Y
4 Hall	Y	N	N	N	N	N	Y
5 ***Sessions***	Y	N	N	N	Y	Y	Y
6 ***Barton***	Y	N	N	N	Y	Y	Y
7 ***Archer***	Y	Y	Y	Y	Y	Y	Y
8 ***Brady***	Y	N	N	N	Y	Y	Y
9 Lampson	N	N	N	N	Y	N	Y
10 Doggett	N	Y	Y	Y	N	N	N
11 Edwards	N	N	N	N	Y	N	Y
12 ***Granger***	N	N	N	N	Y	Y	Y
13 ***Thornberry***	Y	N	N	N	Y	Y	Y
14 ***Paul***	Y	Y	Y	Y	N	Y	N
15 Hinojosa	N	N	N	N	Y	N	Y
16 Reyes	N	N	N	N	Y	N	Y
17 Stenholm	Y	N	N	N	Y	N	Y
18 Jackson-Lee	N	N	N	+	Y	N	Y
19 ***Combest***	Y	N	N	N	Y	Y	Y
20 Gonzalez	?	?	?	?	?	?	?
21 ***Smith***	Y	N	N	N	Y	Y	Y
22 ***DeLay***	Y	Y	Y	N	Y	Y	Y
23 ***Bonilla***	Y	N	N	N	Y	Y	Y
24 Frost	N	N	N	N	Y	N	Y
25 Bentsen	N	N	N	N	Y	N	Y
26 ***Armey***	Y	Y	Y	N	Y	Y	Y
27 Ortiz	Y	N	N	N	Y	N	Y
28 Rodriguez	N	N	N	N	Y	N	Y
29 Green	N	N	N	N	Y	N	Y
30 Johnson, E.B.	N	N	N	N	Y	N	Y
UTAH							
1 ***Hansen***	Y	Y	N	N	Y	Y	Y
2 ***Cook***	Y	Y	N	N	Y	Y	Y
3 ***Cannon***	?	?	?	?	?	?	Y
VERMONT							
AL *Sanders*	N	N	Y	Y	Y	N	N
VIRGINIA							
1 ***Bateman***	Y	N	N	N	Y	Y	Y
2 Pickett	N	N	N	N	Y	N	Y
3 Scott	N	N	N	N	Y	N	Y
4 Sisisky	N	P	N	N	Y	N	Y
5 Goode	Y	N	N	N	Y	N	Y
6 ***Goodlatte***	Y	Y	N	N	Y	Y	Y
7 ***Bliley***	Y	N	N	N	Y	Y	Y
8 Moran	N	Y	Y	Y	N	N	Y
9 Boucher	N	N	N	N	Y	N	Y
10 ***Wolf***	Y	Y	N	Y	Y	Y	+
11 ***Davis***	N	Y	Y	Y	Y	Y	Y
WASHINGTON							
1 ***White***	N	Y	N	N	Y	Y	Y
2 ***Metcalf***	Y	N	N	Y	Y	Y	Y
3 ***Smith, Linda***	Y	Y	N	N	Y	Y	Y
4 ***Hastings***	Y	N	N	N	Y	Y	Y
5 ***Nethercutt***	Y	N	N	N	Y	Y	Y
6 Dicks	N	N	N	Y	Y	N	Y
7 McDermott	N	N	N	Y	N	N	N
8 ***Dunn***	Y	Y	N	N	Y	Y	Y
9 Smith, Adam	N	N	N	Y	Y	N	Y
WEST VIRGINIA							
1 Mollohan	Y	N	N	N	Y	N	Y
2 Wise	N	N	N	N	Y	N	Y
3 Rahall	Y	N	N	N	Y	N	N
WISCONSIN							
1 ***Neumann***	Y	Y	Y	Y	Y	Y	Y
2 ***Klug***	N	Y	N	N	Y	Y	Y
3 Kind	N	Y	Y	Y	N	N	N
4 Kleczka	Y	N	Y	Y	N	N	N
5 Barrett	N	Y	Y	Y	N	N	N
6 ***Petri***	Y	Y	Y	Y	N	Y	N
7 Obey	N	N	N	Y	N	N	N
8 Johnson	N	N	N	Y	N	N	N
9 ***Sensenbrenner***	Y	Y	Y	Y	N	Y	N
WYOMING							
AL ***Cubin***	Y	N	N	N	Y	Y	Y

Southern states - Ala., Ark., Fla., Ga., Ky., La., Miss., N.C., Okla., S.C., Tenn., Texas, Va.

House Votes 267, 268, 269, 270, 271, 272, 273

Key

- Y Voted for (yea).
- # Paired for.
- + Announced for.
- N Voted against (nay).
- X Paired against.
- − Announced against.
- P Voted "present."
- C Voted "present" to avoid possible conflict of interest.
- ? Did not vote or otherwise make a position known.

Democrats **Republicans**
Independent

267. Adjournment Resolution/Rule. Adoption of the rule to provide for House floor consideration of the concurrent resolution to provide for adjournment. Adopted 225-188: R 218-0; D 7-187 (ND 7-138, SD 0-49); I 0-1. June 25, 1998.

268. HR 4104. Fiscal 1999 Treasury-Postal Appropriations/Rule. Adoption of the rule (H Res 485) to provide for House floor consideration of the bill to provide $29.2 billion in fiscal 1999 for the Treasury Department, Postal Service and other general government operations. Rejected 125-291: R 65-155; D 60-135 (ND 49-97, SD 11-38); I 0-1. June 25, 1998.

269. HR 4112. Fiscal 1999 Legislative Branch Appropriations/Previous Question. Pryce, R-Ohio, motion to order the previous question (thus ending debate and the possibility of amendment) on adoption of the rule (H Res 489) to provide for House floor consideration of the bill to provide $1.8 billion in funding for the House of Representatives and other legislative branch operations. Motion agreed to 222-194: R 220-0; D 2-193 (ND 1-145, SD 1-48); I 0-1. June 25, 1998. (Subsequently, the rule was adopted.)

270. HR 4112. Fiscal 1999 Legislative Branch Appropriations/Rule. Adoption of the rule (H Res 489) to provide for House floor consideration of the bill to provide $1.8 billion in funding for the House of Representatives and other legislative branch operations. Adopted 228-188: R 219-0; D 9-187 (ND 8-139, SD 1-48); I 0-1. June 25, 1998.

271. HR 4112. Fiscal 1999 Legislative Branch Appropriations/Recommit. Obey, D-Wis., motion to recommit the bill to the Appropriations Committee with instructions to report it back with an amendment to reduce the appropriation for the "Committee Employees Standing Committees, Special and Select" by about $8.3 million. Motion rejected 192-222: R 0-219; D 191-3 (ND 144-2, SD 47-1); I 1-0. June 25, 1998.

272. HR 4112. Fiscal 1999 Legislative Branch Appropriations/Passage. Passage of the bill to provide $1.8 billion for the House of Representatives and other legislative branch operations. Passed 235-179: R 199-20; D 36-158 (ND 28-118, SD 8-40); I 0-1. June 25, 1998.

273. HR 2676. Internal Revenue Service Overhaul/Recommit. McDermott, D-Wash., motion to recommit the bill to the conference committee with instructions to the managers on the part of the House to disagree with the section relating to lower capital gains rates to apply to property held more than one year. Motion rejected 116-292: R 0-218; D 115-74 (ND 94-46, SD 21-28); I 1-0. June 25, 1998.

[1] *Heather Wilson, R-N.M., was sworn in June 25, replacing Stephen H. Schiff, R-N.M., who died March 25.*

		267	268	269	270	271	272	273
ALABAMA								
1	**Callahan**	Y	N	Y	Y	N	Y	N
2	**Everett**	Y	N	Y	Y	N	Y	N
3	**Riley**	Y	N	Y	Y	N	Y	N
4	**Aderholt**	Y	N	Y	Y	N	Y	N
5	Cramer	N	N	N	N	Y	N	N
6	**Bachus**	Y	N	Y	Y	N	Y	N
7	Hilliard	N	N	N	N	Y	N	Y
ALASKA								
AL	**Young**	Y	Y	Y	Y	N	Y	N
ARIZONA								
1	**Salmon**	Y	N	Y	Y	N	Y	N
2	Pastor	N	N	N	Y	Y	Y	N
3	**Stump**	Y	N	Y	Y	N	Y	N
4	**Shadegg**	Y	N	Y	Y	N	Y	N
5	**Kolbe**	Y	Y	Y	Y	N	Y	N
6	**Hayworth**	Y	N	Y	Y	N	Y	N
ARKANSAS								
1	Berry	N	N	N	N	Y	N	N
2	Snyder	N	N	N	N	Y	N	Y
3	**Hutchinson**	+	−	+	+	−	+	−
4	**Dickey**	Y	N	Y	Y	N	Y	N
CALIFORNIA								
1	**Riggs**	Y	N	Y	Y	N	Y	N
2	**Herger**	Y	N	Y	Y	N	Y	N
3	Fazio	N	N	N	Y	Y	Y	Y
4	**Doolittle**	Y	N	Y	Y	N	Y	N
5	Matsui	N	N	N	N	Y	N	Y
6	Woolsey	N	N	N	N	Y	N	Y
7	Miller	N	N	N	N	Y	N	Y
8	Pelosi	N	Y	N	Y	Y	N	Y
9	Lee	N	N	N	N	Y	N	Y
10	Tauscher	N	N	N	Y	N	N	N
11	**Pombo**	Y	N	Y	Y	N	Y	N
12	Lantos	N	N	N	N	Y	N	Y
13	Stark	N	N	N	N	Y	N	Y
14	Eshoo	N	Y	N	N	N	N	N
15	**Campbell**	Y	Y	Y	N	Y	Y	N
16	Lofgren	N	N	N	N	Y	N	Y
17	Farr	N	N	N	Y	Y	N	Y
18	Condit	N	N	N	N	N	N	N
19	**Radanovich**	Y	N	Y	Y	N	Y	N
20	Dooley	N	Y	N	N	Y	N	Y
21	**Thomas**	?	N	Y	Y	N	Y	N
22	Capps, L.	N	N	N	N	Y	N	Y
23	**Gallegly**	Y	N	Y	Y	N	Y	N
24	Sherman	N	N	N	N	Y	N	N
25	**McKeon**	Y	N	Y	Y	N	Y	N
26	Berman	N	Y	N	N	N	Y	?
27	**Rogan**	Y	N	Y	Y	N	Y	N
28	**Dreier**	Y	Y	Y	Y	N	Y	N
29	Waxman	N	Y	N	N	Y	?	Y
30	Becerra	N	N	N	N	Y	N	Y
31	Martinez	N	N	N	N	Y	N	N
32	Dixon	Y	Y	N	Y	Y	Y	+
33	Roybal-Allard	N	N	N	N	Y	N	Y
34	Torres	N	N	N	N	Y	N	N
35	Waters	Y	Y	N	N	Y	N	Y
36	Harman	N	Y	N	N	Y	N	N
37	Millender-McD.	−	Y	N	N	Y	N	Y

		267	268	269	270	271	272	273
38	**Horn**	Y	Y	Y	Y	N	Y	N
39	**Royce**	Y	Y	Y	Y	N	N	N
40	**Lewis**	Y	N	Y	Y	N	Y	?
41	**Kim**	Y	N	Y	Y	N	Y	N
42	Brown	?	N	N	Y	N	N	Y
43	**Calvert**	Y	N	Y	Y	N	Y	N
44	**Bono, M.**	Y	Y	Y	Y	N	Y	N
45	**Rohrabacher**	Y	N	Y	Y	N	N	N
46	Sanchez	N	Y	N	N	Y	N	N
47	**Cox**	Y	N	Y	Y	N	N	?
48	**Packard**	Y	Y	Y	Y	N	Y	−
49	**Bilbray**	Y	N	Y	Y	N	Y	N
50	Filner	N	N	N	N	Y	N	Y
51	**Cunningham**	Y	N	Y	Y	N	Y	N
52	**Hunter**	Y	N	Y	?	N	Y	N
COLORADO								
1	DeGette	N	Y	N	N	Y	N	Y
2	Skaggs	N	N	N	N	Y	Y	Y
3	**McInnis**	Y	Y	Y	Y	N	Y	N
4	**Schaffer**	Y	N	Y	Y	N	N	N
5	**Hefley**	Y	N	Y	N	N	N	N
6	**Schaefer**	Y	Y	Y	Y	N	Y	N
CONNECTICUT								
1	Kennelly	N	Y	N	N	Y	N	N
2	Gejdenson	N	Y	N	N	Y	N	Y
3	DeLauro	N	N	N	N	Y	N	Y
4	**Shays**	Y	Y	Y	Y	N	Y	N
5	Maloney	N	N	N	N	Y	N	N
6	**Johnson**	Y	Y	Y	Y	N	Y	N
DELAWARE								
AL	**Castle**	Y	Y	Y	Y	N	Y	N
FLORIDA								
1	**Scarborough**	Y	N	Y	Y	?	Y	N
2	Boyd	N	N	N	N	Y	N	N
3	Brown	N	Y	N	N	N	Y	Y
4	**Fowler**	Y	Y	Y	Y	N	Y	N
5	Thurman	N	Y	N	N	Y	N	N
6	**Stearns**	Y	N	Y	Y	N	N	N
7	**Mica**	Y	N	Y	Y	N	Y	N
8	**McCollum**	Y	N	Y	Y	N	Y	N
9	**Bilirakis**	Y	N	Y	Y	N	Y	N
10	**Young**	Y	N	Y	Y	N	Y	N
11	Davis	N	N	N	N	Y	N	N
12	**Canady**	Y	N	Y	Y	N	Y	N
13	**Miller**	Y	Y	Y	Y	N	Y	N
14	**Goss**	Y	Y	Y	Y	N	Y	N
15	**Weldon**	Y	N	Y	Y	N	Y	N
16	**Foley**	Y	Y	Y	Y	N	Y	N
17	Meek	N	N	N	N	Y	N	N
18	**Ros-Lehtinen**	Y	N	Y	Y	N	Y	N
19	Wexler	N	Y	N	N	Y	N	N
20	Deutsch	N	N	N	N	Y	N	N
21	**Diaz-Balart**	Y	Y	Y	Y	N	Y	N
22	**Shaw**	Y	Y	Y	Y	N	Y	N
23	Hastings	N	Y	N	N	Y	N	N
GEORGIA								
1	**Kingston**	Y	N	Y	Y	N	Y	N
2	Bishop	N	N	N	N	N	N	N
3	**Collins**	Y	N	Y	Y	N	Y	N
4	**McKinney**	N	Y	N	N	Y	N	N
5	Lewis	?	?	?	?	?	?	?
6	**Gingrich**							
7	**Barr**	Y	N	Y	Y	N	Y	N
8	**Chambliss**	Y	N	Y	Y	N	Y	N
9	**Deal**	Y	N	Y	Y	N	Y	N
10	**Norwood**	Y	N	Y	Y	N	Y	N
11	**Linder**	Y	Y	Y	Y	N	Y	N
HAWAII								
1	Abercrombie	N	N	N	N	Y	N	Y
2	Mink	N	N	N	N	Y	Y	Y
IDAHO								
1	**Chenoweth**	?	N	Y	Y	N	Y	N
2	**Crapo**	?	Y	Y	Y	N	Y	N
ILLINOIS								
1	Rush	N	N	N	N	Y	N	Y
2	Jackson	Y	N	N	N	Y	N	N
3	Lipinski	Y	N	N	N	Y	N	N
4	Gutierrez	N	N	N	N	Y	Y	Y
5	Blagojevich	N	Y	N	N	Y	N	N
6	**Hyde**	Y	N	Y	Y	N	Y	N
7	Davis	N	Y	N	Y	Y	N	Y
8	**Crane**	Y	N	Y	N	N	N	N
9	Yates	Y	Y	N	N	Y	N	N
10	**Porter**	Y	Y	Y	Y	N	Y	N
11	**Weller**	Y	N	Y	N	N	N	N
12	Costello	N	N	N	N	Y	N	N

ND Northern Democrats   SD Southern Democrats

	267	268	269	270	271	272	273
13 ***Fawell***	Y	Y	Y	Y	N	Y	N
14 ***Hastert***	Y	Y	Y	Y	N	Y	N
15 ***Ewing***	Y	N	Y	Y	N	Y	N
16 ***Manzullo***	Y	N	Y	Y	N	Y	N
17 Evans	N	N	N	N	Y	N	Y
18 ***LaHood***	Y	N	Y	Y	N	Y	N
19 Poshard	N	N	N	N	Y	N	Y
20 ***Shimkus***	Y	N	Y	Y	N	Y	N
INDIANA							
1 Visclosky	N	N	N	N	Y	Y	Y
2 ***McIntosh***	Y	N	Y	Y	N	?	N
3 Roemer	N	N	N	N	Y	N	N
4 ***Souder***	Y	N	Y	Y	N	Y	?
5 ***Buyer***	Y	N	Y	Y	N	Y	N
6 ***Burton***	Y	N	Y	Y	N	Y	N
7 ***Pease***	Y	N	Y	Y	N	Y	N
8 ***Hostettler***	Y	N	Y	Y	N	N	N
9 Hamilton	?	?	?	?	?	?	?
10 Carson	N	Y	N	N	Y	Y	Y
IOWA							
1 ***Leach***	Y	Y	Y	Y	N	Y	N
2 ***Nussle***	Y	N	Y	Y	N	Y	N
3 Boswell	N	N	N	N	Y	N	N
4 ***Ganske***	Y	N	Y	Y	N	Y	N
5 ***Latham***	Y	N	Y	Y	N	Y	N
KANSAS							
1 ***Moran***	Y	N	Y	Y	N	N	N
2 ***Ryun***	Y	N	Y	Y	N	Y	N
3 ***Snowbarger***	Y	N	Y	Y	N	Y	N
4 ***Tiahrt***	Y	N	Y	Y	N	Y	N
KENTUCKY							
1 ***Whitfield***	Y	N	Y	Y	N	Y	N
2 ***Lewis***	Y	N	Y	Y	N	Y	N
3 ***Northup***	Y	Y	Y	Y	N	Y	N
4 ***Bunning***	Y	N	Y	Y	N	Y	N
5 ***Rogers***	Y	N	Y	Y	N	Y	N
6 Baesler	N	N	N	N	Y	Y	N
LOUISIANA							
1 ***Livingston***	Y	Y	Y	Y	N	Y	N
2 Jefferson	N	Y	N	N	Y	Y	Y
3 ***Tauzin***	Y	N	Y	Y	N	Y	N
4 ***McCrery***	Y	N	Y	Y	N	Y	N
5 ***Cooksey***	?	?	Y	Y	N	Y	N
6 ***Baker***	Y	N	Y	Y	N	N	N
7 John	N	N	N	N	Y	Y	N
MAINE							
1 Allen	N	N	N	N	Y	N	Y
2 Baldacci	N	Y	N	N	Y	N	Y
MARYLAND							
1 ***Gilchrest***	Y	Y	Y	Y	N	Y	N
2 ***Ehrlich***	Y	Y	Y	Y	N	Y	N
3 Cardin	N	Y	N	N	Y	N	Y
4 Wynn	N	N	N	N	Y	N	N
5 Hoyer	N	N	N	N	Y	Y	Y
6 ***Bartlett***	Y	N	Y	Y	N	Y	N
7 Cummings	N	N	N	N	Y	N	Y
8 ***Morella***	Y	Y	Y	Y	N	Y	N
MASSACHUSETTS							
1 Olver	N	Y	N	N	Y	N	Y
2 Neal	N	Y	N	N	Y	N	?
3 McGovern	N	Y	N	N	Y	N	Y
4 Frank	N	N	N	N	Y	N	Y
5 Meehan	N	N	N	N	Y	N	?
6 Tierney	N	Y	N	N	Y	N	Y
7 Markey	?	?	?	?	?	?	?
8 Kennedy	N	N	N	N	Y	N	N
9 Moakley	?	?	?	?	?	?	?
10 Delahunt	N	Y	N	N	Y	N	Y
MICHIGAN							
1 Stupak	N	N	N	N	Y	N	Y
2 ***Hoekstra***	Y	N	Y	Y	N	Y	N
3 ***Ehlers***	Y	N	Y	Y	N	Y	N
4 ***Camp***	Y	N	Y	Y	N	Y	N
5 Barcia	N	N	N	N	Y	N	N
6 ***Upton***	Y	Y	Y	Y	N	Y	N
7 ***Smith***	Y	N	Y	Y	N	Y	N
8 Stabenow	N	Y	N	N	Y	N	N
9 Kildee	N	N	N	N	Y	N	Y
10 Bonior	N	?	N	N	Y	Y	Y
11 ***Knollenberg***	Y	Y	Y	Y	N	Y	N
12 Levin	N	Y	N	N	Y	N	Y
13 Rivers	N	Y	N	N	Y	N	Y
14 Conyers	N	Y	N	N	Y	N	Y
15 Kilpatrick	N	Y	N	N	Y	Y	Y
16 Dingell	?	?	?	?	?	?	?

	267	268	269	270	271	272	273
MINNESOTA							
1 ***Gutknecht***	Y	N	Y	Y	N	Y	N
2 Minge	N	Y	N	N	Y	N	Y
3 ***Ramstad***	Y	Y	Y	Y	N	Y	N
4 Vento	N	Y	N	N	Y	N	Y
5 Sabo	N	N	N	N	Y	Y	Y
6 Luther	N	Y	N	N	Y	N	Y
7 Peterson	N	N	N	N	Y	N	Y
8 Oberstar	N	N	N	N	Y	N	Y
MISSISSIPPI							
1 ***Wicker***	Y	Y	Y	Y	N	Y	N
2 Thompson	N	N	N	N	Y	N	Y
3 ***Pickering***	Y	N	Y	Y	N	Y	N
4 ***Parker***	Y	Y	Y	Y	N	Y	N
5 Taylor	N	N	N	N	Y	N	N
MISSOURI							
1 Clay	N	Y	N	N	Y	N	?
2 ***Talent***	Y	N	Y	Y	N	Y	N
3 Gephardt	N	N	N	N	Y	N	Y
4 Skelton	N	N	N	N	Y	Y	N
5 McCarthy	N	Y	N	N	Y	N	N
6 Danner	N	Y	N	Y	Y	Y	N
7 ***Blunt***	Y	N	Y	Y	N	Y	N
8 ***Emerson***	Y	N	Y	Y	N	Y	N
9 ***Hulshof***	+	−	+	+	−	−	−
MONTANA							
AL ***Hill***	Y	N	Y	Y	N	N	N
NEBRASKA							
1 ***Bereuter***	Y	N	Y	Y	N	Y	N
2 ***Christensen***	Y	N	Y	Y	N	Y	N
3 ***Barrett***	Y	N	Y	Y	N	Y	N
NEVADA							
1 ***Ensign***	Y	N	Y	Y	N	N	N
2 ***Gibbons***	Y	N	Y	Y	N	Y	N
NEW HAMPSHIRE							
1 ***Sununu***	Y	N	Y	Y	N	Y	N
2 ***Bass***	Y	Y	Y	Y	N	Y	N
NEW JERSEY							
1 Andrews	N	N	N	N	Y	N	Y
2 ***LoBiondo***	Y	N	Y	Y	N	Y	N
3 ***Saxton***	Y	N	Y	Y	N	Y	N
4 ***Smith***	Y	N	Y	Y	N	Y	N
5 ***Roukema***	Y	Y	Y	Y	N	Y	N
6 Pallone	N	N	N	N	+	N	Y
7 ***Franks***	Y	Y	Y	Y	N	Y	N
8 Pascrell	N	N	N	N	Y	Y	N
9 Rothman	N	N	N	N	Y	N	N
10 Payne	N	N	N	N	Y	N	Y
11 ***Frelinghuysen***	Y	Y	Y	Y	N	Y	N
12 ***Pappas***	Y	N	Y	Y	N	Y	N
13 Menendez	N	N	N	N	Y	N	Y
NEW MEXICO							
1 ***Wilson*** [1]							N
2 ***Skeen***	Y	N	Y	Y	N	Y	N
3 ***Redmond***	Y	N	Y	Y	N	Y	N
NEW YORK							
1 ***Forbes***	Y	N	Y	Y	N	Y	N
2 ***Lazio***	Y	Y	Y	Y	N	Y	N
3 ***King***	Y	N	Y	Y	N	Y	N
4 McCarthy	N	N	N	N	Y	N	Y
5 Ackerman	N	Y	N	N	Y	N	N
6 Meeks	N	N	N	N	Y	N	Y
7 Manton	N	N	N	N	Y	N	Y
8 Nadler	N	N	N	N	Y	N	Y
9 Schumer	N	Y	N	N	Y	N	N
10 Towns	N	N	N	N	Y	N	Y
11 Owens	N	N	N	N	Y	N	Y
12 Velázquez	N	Y	N	N	Y	N	?
13 ***Fossella***	Y	N	Y	Y	N	Y	N
14 Maloney	N	Y	N	N	Y	N	N
15 Rangel	N	N	N	N	Y	N	Y
16 Serrano	N	N	N	Y	Y	Y	?
17 Engel	N	Y	N	N	Y	N	Y
18 Lowey	N	Y	N	N	Y	N	N
19 ***Kelly***	Y	Y	Y	Y	N	Y	N
20 ***Gilman***	Y	Y	Y	Y	N	Y	N
21 McNulty	N	N	N	N	Y	N	N
22 ***Solomon***	Y	Y	Y	Y	N	Y	N
23 ***Boehlert***	Y	Y	Y	Y	N	Y	N
24 ***McHugh***	Y	N	Y	Y	N	Y	N
25 ***Walsh***	Y	N	Y	Y	N	Y	N
26 Hinchey	N	N	N	N	Y	N	Y
27 ***Paxon***	Y	Y	Y	Y	N	Y	N
28 Slaughter	N	Y	N	N	Y	N	N
29 LaFalce	N	N	N	N	Y	N	Y

	267	268	269	270	271	272	273
30 ***Quinn***	Y	N	Y	Y	N	Y	N
31 ***Houghton***	Y	Y	Y	Y	N	Y	N
NORTH CAROLINA							
1 Clayton	N	Y	N	N	Y	N	N
2 Etheridge	N	N	N	N	Y	N	Y
3 ***Jones***	Y	N	Y	Y	N	Y	N
4 Price	N	N	N	N	Y	Y	Y
5 ***Burr***	Y	N	Y	Y	N	Y	N
6 ***Coble***	Y	N	Y	Y	N	Y	N
7 McIntyre	N	N	N	N	Y	N	N
8 Hefner	N	Y	N	N	Y	N	Y
9 ***Myrick***	Y	N	Y	Y	N	Y	N
10 ***Ballenger***	Y	N	Y	Y	N	Y	N
11 ***Taylor***	Y	N	Y	Y	N	Y	N
12 Watt	N	N	N	N	Y	N	N
NORTH DAKOTA							
AL Pomeroy	N	N	N	N	Y	N	N
OHIO							
1 ***Chabot***	Y	N	Y	Y	N	Y	N
2 ***Portman***	Y	N	Y	Y	N	Y	N
3 Hall	Y	N	N	Y	Y	Y	N
4 ***Oxley***	Y	Y	Y	Y	N	Y	N
5 ***Gillmor***	Y	N	Y	Y	N	Y	N
6 Strickland	N	N	N	N	Y	N	Y
7 ***Hobson***	Y	Y	Y	Y	N	Y	N
8 ***Boehner***	Y	N	Y	Y	N	Y	N
9 Kaptur	N	N	?	N	Y	N	Y
10 Kucinich	N	N	N	N	Y	N	Y
11 Stokes	N	Y	N	N	Y	N	Y
12 ***Kasich***	Y	N	Y	Y	N	Y	N
13 Brown	N	Y	N	N	Y	N	Y
14 Sawyer	N	N	N	N	Y	N	Y
15 ***Pryce***	Y	Y	Y	Y	N	Y	N
16 ***Regula***	Y	N	Y	Y	N	Y	N
17 Traficant	Y	N	Y	Y	N	Y	N
18 ***Ney***	Y	N	Y	Y	N	Y	N
19 ***LaTourette***	Y	N	Y	Y	N	Y	N
OKLAHOMA							
1 ***Largent***	Y	N	Y	Y	N	Y	N
2 ***Coburn***	Y	Y	Y	Y	N	Y	N
3 ***Watkins***	Y	N	Y	Y	N	Y	N
4 ***Watts***	Y	N	Y	Y	N	Y	N
5 ***Istook***	Y	N	Y	Y	N	Y	N
6 ***Lucas***	Y	N	Y	Y	N	Y	N
OREGON							
1 Furse	N	Y	N	N	Y	N	Y
2 ***Smith***	Y	N	Y	Y	N	Y	N
3 Blumenauer	N	N	N	N	Y	N	Y
4 DeFazio	N	N	N	N	Y	N	Y
5 Hooley	N	Y	N	N	Y	N	N
PENNSYLVANIA							
1 Brady	N	N	N	N	Y	N	Y
2 Fattah	N	N	N	N	Y	Y	Y
3 Borski	N	N	N	N	Y	N	Y
4 Klink	N	N	N	N	Y	N	Y
5 ***Peterson***	Y	N	Y	Y	N	Y	N
6 Holden	N	N	N	N	Y	N	N
7 ***Weldon***	Y	N	Y	Y	?	?	N
8 ***Greenwood***	Y	Y	Y	Y	N	Y	N
9 ***Shuster***	Y	N	Y	Y	N	Y	N
10 ***McDade***	?	?	?	?	?	?	?
11 Kanjorski	N	N	N	N	Y	N	Y
12 Murtha	N	N	N	N	Y	Y	N
13 ***Fox***	Y	Y	Y	Y	N	Y	N
14 Coyne	N	N	N	N	Y	N	Y
15 McHale	N	N	N	N	Y	N	Y
16 ***Pitts***	Y	N	Y	Y	N	Y	N
17 ***Gekas***	Y	N	Y	Y	N	Y	N
18 Doyle	N	N	N	N	Y	N	N
19 ***Goodling***	Y	N	Y	Y	N	Y	N
20 Mascara	N	N	N	N	Y	N	N
21 ***English***	Y	N	Y	Y	N	Y	N
RHODE ISLAND							
1 Kennedy	N	N	N	N	Y	N	Y
2 Weygand	N	N	N	N	Y	N	N
SOUTH CAROLINA							
1 ***Sanford***	Y	N	Y	Y	N	N	N
2 ***Spence***	Y	N	Y	Y	N	Y	N
3 ***Graham***	Y	?	Y	Y	N	Y	N
4 ***Inglis***	Y	N	Y	Y	N	Y	N
5 Spratt	N	N	N	N	Y	N	Y
6 Clyburn	N	N	N	N	Y	N	Y
SOUTH DAKOTA							
AL ***Thune***	Y	N	Y	Y	N	Y	N

	267	268	269	270	271	272	273
TENNESSEE							
1 ***Jenkins***	Y	N	Y	Y	N	Y	N
2 ***Duncan***	Y	N	Y	Y	N	Y	N
3 ***Wamp***	Y	N	Y	Y	N	Y	N
4 ***Hilleary***	Y	N	Y	?	N	N	N
5 Clement	N	N	N	N	Y	N	N
6 Gordon	N	N	N	N	?	?	N
7 ***Bryant***	Y	N	Y	Y	N	Y	N
8 Tanner	N	N	N	N	Y	N	N
9 Ford	N	N	N	N	Y	N	Y
TEXAS							
1 Sandlin	N	N	N	N	Y	N	N
2 Turner	?	?	?	?	?	?	?
3 ***Johnson, Sam***	Y	N	Y	Y	N	Y	N
4 Hall	N	N	Y	Y	Y	Y	N
5 ***Sessions***	Y	N	Y	Y	N	Y	N
6 ***Barton***	Y	Y	Y	Y	N	Y	N
7 ***Archer***	Y	Y	Y	Y	N	Y	N
8 ***Brady***	+	−	+	+	−	+	−
9 Lampson	?	?	?	?	?	?	?
10 Doggett	N	Y	N	N	Y	N	Y
11 Edwards	N	Y	N	N	Y	N	Y
12 ***Granger***	Y	Y	Y	Y	N	Y	N
13 ***Thornberry***	Y	N	Y	Y	N	Y	N
14 ***Paul***	Y	N	Y	Y	N	N	N
15 Hinojosa	−	−	−	−	+	+	+
16 Reyes	?	?	?	?	?	?	?
17 Stenholm	N	N	N	N	Y	N	Y
18 Jackson-Lee	N	Y	N	N	Y	N	Y
19 ***Combest***	Y	N	Y	Y	N	Y	N
20 Gonzalez	?	?	?	?	?	?	?
21 ***Smith***	Y	N	Y	Y	N	Y	N
22 ***DeLay***	Y	Y	Y	Y	N	Y	N
23 ***Bonilla***	Y	Y	Y	Y	N	Y	N
24 Frost	N	N	N	N	Y	N	N
25 Bentsen	N	N	N	N	Y	N	N
26 ***Armey***	Y	Y	Y	Y	N	Y	N
27 Ortiz	N	N	N	N	Y	N	Y
28 Rodriguez	N	N	N	N	Y	N	Y
29 Green	N	N	N	N	Y	N	N
30 Johnson, E.B.	N	N	N	N	Y	N	Y
UTAH							
1 ***Hansen***	Y	N	Y	Y	N	Y	N
2 ***Cook***	Y	N	Y	Y	N	Y	N
3 ***Cannon***	Y	N	Y	Y	N	Y	N
VERMONT							
AL *Sanders*	N	N	N	N	Y	N	Y
VIRGINIA							
1 ***Bateman***	Y	N	Y	Y	N	Y	N
2 Pickett	N	N	N	N	Y	Y	N
3 Scott	N	N	N	N	Y	N	Y
4 Sisisky	N	N	N	N	Y	Y	N
5 Goode	N	N	N	N	Y	N	N
6 ***Goodlatte***	Y	N	Y	Y	N	N	N
7 ***Bliley***	Y	Y	Y	Y	N	Y	N
8 Moran	N	N	N	N	Y	N	N
9 Boucher	N	N	N	N	Y	N	N
10 ***Wolf***	Y	N	Y	Y	N	Y	N
11 ***Davis***	Y	Y	Y	Y	N	Y	N
WASHINGTON							
1 ***White***	Y	N	Y	Y	N	Y	N
2 ***Metcalf***	Y	N	Y	Y	N	Y	N
3 ***Smith, Linda***	Y	N	?	Y	N	N	N
4 ***Hastings***	Y	N	Y	Y	N	Y	N
5 ***Nethercutt***	Y	Y	Y	Y	N	Y	N
6 Dicks	N	N	N	N	Y	Y	Y
7 McDermott	N	Y	N	N	Y	N	Y
8 ***Dunn***	Y	Y	Y	Y	N	Y	N
9 Smith, Adam	N	N	N	N	Y	Y	Y
WEST VIRGINIA							
1 Mollohan	N	N	N	N	Y	Y	N
2 Wise	N	N	N	N	Y	N	Y
3 Rahall	N	N	N	N	Y	N	Y
WISCONSIN							
1 ***Neumann***	Y	N	Y	Y	N	Y	N
2 ***Klug***	Y	Y	?	?	?	?	?
3 Kind	N	N	N	N	Y	N	Y
4 Kleczka	N	N	N	N	Y	N	N
5 Barrett	N	N	N	N	Y	N	Y
6 ***Petri***	Y	N	Y	Y	N	N	N
7 Obey	N	N	N	N	Y	N	Y
8 Johnson	N	N	N	N	Y	N	N
9 ***Sensenbrenner***	Y	N	Y	Y	N	N	N
WYOMING							
AL ***Cubin***	Y	N	Y	Y	N	Y	N

Southern states - Ala., Ark., Fla., Ga., Ky., La., Miss., N.C., Okla., S.C., Tenn., Texas, Va.

House Votes 274, 275, 276, 277, 278, 279, 280

274. HR 2676. Internal Revenue Service Overhaul/Conference Report. Adoption of the conference report on the bill to restructure the management of the Internal Revenue Service by establishing an oversight board to oversee the agency's operations. Along with expanding certain taxpayer rights, the conference report also reduces from 18 months to 12 months the time a taxpayer must hold an investment before being eligible for the 20 percent tax rate on capital gains. The measure's $12.9 billion cost is offset by revenue-raising provisions, including one that permits wealthy elderly persons to convert traditional IRAs into the new Roth IRA and pay taxes on the converted money. Adopted (thus sent to the Senate) 402-8: R 220-1; D 181-7 (ND 132-7, SD 49-0); I 1-0. June 25, 1998.

275. HR 2183. Campaign Finance Overhaul/Shays-Meehan Substitute — Voter Guide Requirements. Doolittle, R-Calif., amendment to the Shays-Meehan substitute amendment to the bill to overhaul campaign finance laws. The Doolittle amendment would strike the section of the substitute that requires voter guides to list at least two candidates or federal officeholders and only include their voting record or position on certain issues, with no commentary. Rejected 201-219: R 183-40; D 18-178 (ND 11-133, SD 7-45); I 0-1. July 14, 1998.

276. HR 2183. Campaign Finance Overhaul/Shays-Meehan Substitute - Contributions. Fossella, R-N.Y., amendment to the Shays-Meehan substitute amendment to the bill to overhaul campaign finance laws. The Fossella amendment would prohibit non-citizens from making campaign contributions to federal elections. Adopted 282-126: R 200-17; D 81-109 (ND 57-84, SD 24-25); I 1-0. July 14, 1998.

277. HR 3682. Transporting Minors for an Abortion/Previous Question. Myrick, R-N.C., motion to order the previous question (thus ending debate and the possibility of amendment) on adoption of the rule (H Res 499) to provide for floor consideration of the bill to make it a federal crime for anyone other than the parent to transport a minor across state lines with the intent that she obtain an abortion. Motion agreed to 252-174: R 217-9; D 35-164 (ND 27-120, SD 8-44); I 0-1. July 15, 1998.

278. HR 3682. Transporting Minors for an Abortion/Rule. Adoption of the rule (H Res 499) to provide for House floor consideration of the bill that makes it a federal crime for anyone other than the parent to transport a minor across state lines with the intent that she obtain an abortion. The rule blocks all amendments and provides two hours of general debate. Adopted 247-173: R 209-14; D 38-158 (ND 29-117, SD 9-41); I 0-1. July 15, 1998.

279. HR 3682. Transporting Minors for an Abortion/Recommit. Scott, D-Va., motion to recommit the bill to the Judiciary Committee with instructions to report it back with an amendment to make it a federal offense only when force or a threat is used to transport a minor across state lines with the intent that she obtain an abortion. Motion rejected 158-269: R 10-216; D 147-53 (ND 110-37, SD 37-16); I 1-0. July 15, 1998.

280. HR 3682. Transporting Minors for an Abortion/Passage. Passage of the bill to make it a federal crime for anyone other than the parent to transport a minor across state lines with the intent that she obtain an abortion. Passed 276-150: R 209-14; D 67-135 (ND 43-105, SD 24-30); I 0-1. July 15, 1998. A "nay" was a vote in support of the president's position.

Key

- Y Voted for (yea).
- # Paired for.
- + Announced for.
- N Voted against (nay).
- X Paired against.
- − Announced against.
- P Voted "present."
- C Voted "present" to avoid possible conflict of interest.
- ? Did not vote or otherwise make a position known.

Democrats **Republicans** *Independent*

	274	275	276	277	278	279	280
ALABAMA							
1 *Callahan*	Y	Y	Y	Y	Y	N	Y
2 *Everett*	Y	Y	Y	Y	Y	N	Y
3 *Riley*	Y	Y	Y	Y	Y	N	Y
4 *Aderholt*	Y	Y	Y	Y	Y	?	Y
5 Cramer	Y	N	N	N	N	Y	N
6 *Bachus*	Y	Y	Y	Y	Y	N	Y
7 Hilliard	Y	N	N	N	N	Y	Y
ALASKA							
AL *Young*	Y	?	?	Y	Y	N	Y
ARIZONA							
1 *Salmon*	Y	Y	Y	Y	Y	N	Y
2 Pastor	Y	N	N	N	N	Y	N
3 *Stump*	Y	Y	Y	Y	Y	N	Y
4 *Shadegg*	Y	Y	Y	Y	Y	N	Y
5 *Kolbe*	Y	Y	Y	Y	Y	N	Y
6 *Hayworth*	Y	Y	Y	Y	Y	N	Y
ARKANSAS							
1 Berry	Y	N	Y	Y	Y	N	Y
2 Snyder	Y	N	Y	Y	Y	N	Y
3 *Hutchinson*	+	Y	Y	Y	Y	N	Y
4 *Dickey*	Y	Y	Y	Y	?	N	Y
CALIFORNIA							
1 *Riggs*	Y	Y	Y	Y	Y	N	Y
2 *Herger*	Y	Y	Y	Y	Y	N	Y
3 Fazio	N	N	N	N	N	Y	N
4 *Doolittle*	Y	Y	Y	Y	Y	N	Y
5 Matsui	N	Y	N	N	N	Y	N
6 Woolsey	Y	N	N	N	N	Y	N
7 Miller	Y	N	N	N	N	Y	N
8 Pelosi	Y	N	N	N	N	Y	N
9 Lee	Y	N	N	N	N	Y	N
10 Tauscher	Y	N	N	N	N	Y	N
11 *Pombo*	Y	Y	N	Y	Y	N	Y
12 Lantos	Y	N	N	N	N	Y	N
13 Stark	Y	?	?	N	N	Y	N
14 Eshoo	Y	N	N	N	N	Y	N
15 *Campbell*	Y	N	N	N	N	Y	N
16 Lofgren	Y	N	N	N	N	Y	N
17 Farr	Y	N	N	N	N	Y	N
18 Condit	Y	N	N	N	N	N	N
19 *Radanovich*	Y	Y	Y	Y	Y	N	Y
20 Dooley	Y	N	N	Y	N	N	N
21 *Thomas*	Y	Y	Y	Y	Y	N	Y
22 Capps, L.	Y	N	N	N	−	Y	N
23 *Gallegly*	Y	Y	Y	Y	Y	N	Y
24 Sherman	Y	Y	N	Y	N	N	N
25 *McKeon*	Y	Y	Y	Y	Y	N	Y
26 Berman	?	N	N	N	N	Y	N
27 *Rogan*	Y	Y	Y	+	+	N	Y
28 *Dreier*	Y	Y	Y	Y	Y	N	Y
29 Waxman	Y	N	N	N	N	Y	N
30 Becerra	Y	N	N	N	N	Y	N
31 Martinez	N	N	?	N	N	Y	N
32 Dixon	+	N	N	N	N	Y	N
33 Roybal-Allard	Y	N	N	N	N	+	N
34 Torres	Y	N	N	N	N	Y	N
35 Waters	Y	N	N	N	N	Y	N
36 Harman	Y	N	Y	N	N	Y	N
37 Millender-McD.	Y	N	N	N	N	Y	N

	274	275	276	277	278	279	280
38 *Horn*	Y	N	Y	N	Y	Y	N
39 *Royce*	Y	Y	Y	Y	Y	N	Y
40 *Lewis*	Y	Y	Y	Y	Y	N	Y
41 *Kim*	Y	Y	Y	Y	Y	N	Y
42 Brown	Y	N	N	N	N	Y	N
43 *Calvert*	Y	Y	Y	Y	Y	N	Y
44 *Bono, M.*	Y	Y	Y	Y	Y	N	Y
45 *Rohrabacher*	Y	Y	Y	Y	Y	N	Y
46 Sanchez	Y	N	N	Y	N	N	Y
47 *Cox*	Y	Y	Y	Y	Y	N	Y
48 *Packard*	+	Y	Y	Y	Y	N	Y
49 *Bilbray*	Y	N	Y	Y	Y	N	Y
50 Filner	Y	N	N	N	N	Y	N
51 *Cunningham*	Y	Y	Y	Y	Y	N	Y
52 *Hunter*	Y	Y	Y	Y	Y	N	Y
COLORADO							
1 DeGette	Y	N	N	N	N	Y	N
2 Skaggs	Y	N	N	N	N	Y	N
3 *McInnis*	Y	Y	Y	Y	Y	N	Y
4 *Schaffer*	Y	Y	Y	Y	Y	N	Y
5 *Hefley*	Y	Y	Y	Y	Y	N	Y
6 *Schaefer*	Y	Y	?	Y	Y	N	Y
CONNECTICUT							
1 Kennelly	Y	N	Y	N	N	Y	N
2 Gejdenson	Y	N	Y	N	N	Y	N
3 DeLauro	Y	N	Y	N	N	Y	N
4 *Shays*	Y	N	N	N	N	Y	N
5 Maloney	Y	N	N	N	N	Y	N
6 *Johnson*	Y	N	N	N	N	Y	N
DELAWARE							
AL *Castle*	Y	N	Y	N	N	N	N
FLORIDA							
1 *Scarborough*	Y	Y	Y	Y	Y	N	Y
2 Boyd	Y	N	Y	N	N	N	Y
3 Brown	Y	N	N	N	N	Y	N
4 *Fowler*	Y	?	?	Y	Y	N	Y
5 Thurman	Y	N	N	N	N	Y	N
6 *Stearns*	Y	Y	Y	Y	Y	N	Y
7 *Mica*	Y	Y	Y	Y	Y	N	Y
8 *McCollum*	Y	Y	Y	Y	Y	N	Y
9 *Bilirakis*	Y	Y	Y	Y	Y	N	Y
10 *Young*	Y	Y	Y	Y	Y	N	Y
11 Davis	Y	N	N	N	N	Y	N
12 *Canady*	Y	Y	Y	Y	Y	N	Y
13 *Miller*	Y	Y	Y	Y	Y	N	Y
14 *Goss*	Y	Y	Y	Y	Y	N	Y
15 *Weldon*	Y	Y	Y	Y	Y	N	Y
16 *Foley*	Y	N	Y	Y	Y	N	Y
17 Meek	Y	N	N	N	?	Y	N
18 *Ros-Lehtinen*	Y	N	Y	N	Y	N	Y
19 Wexler	Y	N	?	N	N	Y	N
20 Deutsch	Y	N	?	N	N	Y	N
21 *Diaz-Balart*	Y	N	Y	N	Y	N	Y
22 *Shaw*	Y	Y	Y	Y	Y	N	Y
23 Hastings	N	N	N	N	N	Y	N
GEORGIA							
1 *Kingston*	Y	Y	Y	Y	Y	N	Y
2 Bishop	Y	Y	Y	N	N	Y	Y
3 *Collins*	Y	Y	Y	Y	Y	N	Y
4 McKinney	Y	N	N	N	N	Y	N
5 Lewis	?	N	N	N	N	Y	N
6 *Gingrich*	Y	Y					
7 *Barr*	Y	Y	Y	Y	Y	N	Y
8 *Chambliss*	Y	Y	Y	Y	Y	N	Y
9 *Deal*	Y	?	?	Y	Y	N	Y
10 *Norwood*	Y	Y	Y	Y	Y	N	Y
11 *Linder*	Y	Y	Y	Y	Y	N	Y
HAWAII							
1 Abercrombie	Y	N	N	N	N	Y	N
2 Mink	Y	N	N	N	N	Y	N
IDAHO							
1 *Chenoweth*	Y	Y	Y	Y	Y	N	Y
2 *Crapo*	Y	Y	Y	Y	Y	N	Y
ILLINOIS							
1 Rush	Y	?	?	N	N	Y	N
2 Jackson	Y	N	N	N	N	Y	N
3 Lipinski	Y	N	Y	Y	Y	N	Y
4 Gutierrez	Y	N	N	N	N	Y	N
5 Blagojevich	Y	N	N	N	N	Y	N
6 *Hyde*	Y	Y	Y	Y	Y	N	Y
7 Davis	Y	N	N	N	N	Y	N
8 *Crane*	Y	Y	Y	Y	Y	N	Y
9 Yates	N	?	?	N	N	Y	N
10 *Porter*	Y	N	N	N	N	Y	−
11 *Weller*	Y	Y	Y	Y	Y	N	Y
12 Costello	Y	Y	Y	Y	Y	N	Y

ND Northern Democrats   SD Southern Democrats

	274	275	276	277	278	279	280
13 ***Fawell***	Y	N	Y	Y	Y	N	Y
14 ***Hastert***	Y	Y	Y	Y	Y	N	Y
15 ***Ewing***	Y	Y	Y	Y	Y	N	Y
16 ***Manzullo***	Y	Y	Y	Y	Y	N	Y
17 Evans	Y	N	Y	N	N	Y	N
18 ***LaHood***	Y	Y	Y	Y	Y	N	Y
19 Poshard	Y	Y	Y	Y	Y	N	Y
20 ***Shimkus***	Y	Y	Y	Y	Y	N	Y
INDIANA							
1 Visclosky	Y	N	N	N	N	Y	N
2 ***McIntosh***	Y	Y	N	Y	Y	N	Y
3 Roemer	Y	N	Y	Y	Y	N	Y
4 ***Souder***	?	Y	Y	Y	Y	N	Y
5 ***Buyer***	Y	Y	Y	Y	Y	N	Y
6 ***Burton***	Y	Y	?	Y	Y	N	Y
7 ***Pease***	Y	Y	Y	Y	Y	N	Y
8 ***Hostettler***	Y	Y	Y	Y	Y	N	Y
9 Hamilton	?	N	Y	Y	Y	N	Y
10 Carson	Y	N	N	N	N	Y	N
IOWA							
1 ***Leach***	Y	N	Y	Y	Y	N	Y
2 ***Nussle***	Y	Y	Y	Y	Y	N	Y
3 Boswell	Y	N	Y	N	N	Y	Y
4 ***Ganske***	Y	N	Y	Y	Y	N	Y
5 ***Latham***	Y	Y	Y	Y	Y	N	Y
KANSAS							
1 ***Moran***	Y	Y	Y	Y	Y	N	Y
2 ***Ryun***	Y	Y	Y	Y	Y	N	Y
3 ***Snowbarger***	Y	Y	Y	Y	Y	N	Y
4 ***Tiahrt***	Y	Y	Y	Y	Y	N	Y
KENTUCKY							
1 ***Whitfield***	Y	Y	Y	Y	Y	N	Y
2 ***Lewis***	Y	Y	Y	Y	Y	N	Y
3 ***Northup***	Y	Y	Y	Y	Y	N	Y
4 ***Bunning***	Y	Y	Y	Y	Y	N	Y
5 ***Rogers***	Y	Y	Y	Y	Y	N	Y
6 Baesler	Y	?	?	N	N	N	Y
LOUISIANA							
1 ***Livingston***	Y	Y	Y	Y	Y	N	Y
2 Jefferson	Y	N	N	N	N	Y	Y
3 ***Tauzin***	Y	Y	Y	Y	Y	N	+
4 ***McCrery***	Y	Y	Y	Y	Y	N	Y
5 ***Cooksey***	Y	Y	Y	Y	Y	N	Y
6 ***Baker***	Y	Y	Y	Y	Y	N	Y
7 John	Y	?	?	N	Y	N	Y
MAINE							
1 Allen	Y	N	N	N	N	Y	N
2 Baldacci	Y	N	Y	N	N	Y	N
MARYLAND							
1 ***Gilchrest***	Y	N	Y	Y	Y	N	N
2 ***Ehrlich***	Y	Y	Y	Y	Y	N	Y
3 Cardin	Y	N	N	N	N	Y	N
4 Wynn	Y	N	N	N	N	Y	N
5 Hoyer	Y	N	N	N	N	Y	N
6 ***Bartlett***	Y	Y	Y	Y	Y	N	Y
7 Cummings	Y	N	N	N	N	Y	N
8 ***Morella***	Y	N	N	N	N	Y	N
MASSACHUSETTS							
1 Olver	Y	?	?	N	N	Y	N
2 Neal	?	N	N	N	N	Y	N
3 McGovern	Y	N	N	N	N	Y	N
4 Frank	N	N	N	N	N	Y	N
5 Meehan	?	N	N	N	N	Y	N
6 Tierney	Y	N	N	N	N	Y	N
7 Markey	?	N	Y	N	N	Y	N
8 Kennedy	Y	N	Y	N	N	Y	N
9 Moakley	?	N	Y	?	?	N	Y
10 Delahunt	Y	N	N	N	N	Y	N
MICHIGAN							
1 Stupak	Y	Y	Y	Y	Y	N	Y
2 ***Hoekstra***	Y	Y	Y	Y	Y	N	Y
3 ***Ehlers***	Y	Y	N	Y	Y	N	Y
4 ***Camp***	Y	Y	Y	Y	Y	N	Y
5 Barcia	Y	Y	Y	Y	Y	N	Y
6 ***Upton***	Y	N	Y	Y	N	N	Y
7 ***Smith***	Y	Y	Y	Y	Y	N	Y
8 Stabenow	Y	N	Y	N	N	Y	N
9 Kildee	Y	N	Y	Y	Y	N	Y
10 Bonior	Y	N	N	N	N	N	Y
11 ***Knollenberg***	Y	Y	Y	Y	Y	N	Y
12 Levin	Y	N	Y	N	N	Y	N
13 Rivers	Y	N	Y	N	N	Y	N
14 Conyers	Y	N	N	N	N	Y	N
15 Kilpatrick	Y	N	N	N	N	Y	N
16 Dingell	?	N	N	?	?	?	?

	274	275	276	277	278	279	280
MINNESOTA							
1 ***Gutknecht***	Y	Y	Y	Y	Y	N	Y
2 Minge	Y	N	N	N	N	Y	Y
3 ***Ramstad***	Y	N	Y	Y	Y	N	Y
4 Vento	Y	N	N	N	N	Y	Y
5 Sabo	N	N	N	N	N	Y	N
6 Luther	Y	N	Y	N	N	Y	N
7 Peterson	Y	Y	Y	Y	Y	N	Y
8 Oberstar	Y	Y	N	Y	Y	N	Y
MISSISSIPPI							
1 ***Wicker***	Y	Y	Y	Y	Y	N	Y
2 Thompson	Y	N	N	N	N	Y	N
3 ***Pickering***	Y	Y	Y	Y	Y	N	Y
4 ***Parker***	Y	N	Y	Y	Y	N	Y
5 Taylor	Y	N	Y	Y	Y	N	Y
MISSOURI							
1 Clay	?	N	N	N	N	Y	N
2 ***Talent***	Y	Y	N	Y	Y	N	Y
3 Gephardt	Y	N	?	N	N	Y	N
4 Skelton	Y	N	Y	Y	Y	N	Y
5 McCarthy	Y	N	Y	N	N	Y	N
6 Danner	Y	Y	Y	N	Y	N	Y
7 ***Blunt***	Y	Y	Y	Y	Y	N	Y
8 ***Emerson***	Y	Y	Y	Y	Y	N	Y
9 ***Hulshof***	+	Y	Y	Y	Y	N	Y
MONTANA							
AL ***Hill***	Y	Y	Y	Y	Y	?	?
NEBRASKA							
1 ***Bereuter***	Y	N	Y	Y	Y	N	Y
2 ***Christensen***	Y	Y	Y	Y	Y	N	Y
3 ***Barrett***	Y	N	Y	Y	Y	N	Y
NEVADA							
1 ***Ensign***	Y	Y	Y	Y	Y	N	Y
2 ***Gibbons***	Y	Y	Y	Y	Y	N	Y
NEW HAMPSHIRE							
1 ***Sununu***	Y	Y	Y	Y	Y	N	Y
2 ***Bass***	Y	N	Y	Y	N	Y	N
NEW JERSEY							
1 Andrews	Y	N	N	N	N	Y	N
2 ***LoBiondo***	Y	N	Y	Y	Y	N	Y
3 ***Saxton***	Y	N	Y	Y	Y	N	Y
4 ***Smith***	Y	Y	Y	Y	Y	N	Y
5 ***Roukema***	Y	N	Y	Y	Y	N	Y
6 Pallone	Y	N	N	N	N	Y	N
7 ***Franks***	Y	N	Y	Y	Y	N	Y
8 Pascrell	Y	N	N	N	Y	N	Y
9 Rothman	Y	N	Y	N	N	Y	N
10 Payne	Y	?	?	?	?	?	N
11 ***Frelinghuysen***	Y	N	Y	Y	Y	N	Y
12 ***Pappas***	Y	Y	Y	Y	Y	N	Y
13 Menendez	Y	N	N	N	N	Y	N
NEW MEXICO							
1 ***Wilson***	Y	Y	Y	Y	Y	N	Y
2 ***Skeen***	Y	Y	Y	Y	Y	N	Y
3 ***Redmond***	Y	Y	Y	Y	Y	N	Y
NEW YORK							
1 ***Forbes***	Y	N	Y	Y	Y	N	Y
2 ***Lazio***	Y	N	Y	Y	Y	N	Y
3 ***King***	Y	Y	N	Y	Y	N	Y
4 McCarthy	Y	N	N	Y	Y	N	Y
5 Ackerman	Y	N	N	N	N	Y	N
6 Meeks	Y	N	N	N	N	Y	N
7 Manton	Y	N	N	Y	Y	N	Y
8 Nadler	Y	N	N	N	N	Y	N
9 Schumer	Y	N	Y	N	N	Y	N
10 Towns	Y	N	N	N	N	Y	N
11 Owens	Y	N	N	N	N	Y	N
12 Velázquez	?	N	N	N	N	Y	N
13 ***Fossella***	Y	Y	Y	Y	Y	N	Y
14 Maloney	Y	N	N	N	N	Y	N
15 Rangel	Y	N	N	N	N	Y	N
16 Serrano	?	N	N	N	N	Y	N
17 Engel	Y	?	N	N	N	Y	N
18 Lowey	Y	N	N	N	N	Y	N
19 ***Kelly***	Y	N	Y	N	N	Y	Y
20 ***Gilman***	Y	N	Y	N	N	Y	N
21 McNulty	Y	?	?	?	?	?	?
22 ***Solomon***	Y	Y	Y	Y	Y	N	Y
23 ***Boehlert***	Y	N	N	N	N	N	N
24 ***McHugh***	Y	Y	Y	Y	Y	N	Y
25 ***Walsh***	Y	N	Y	Y	Y	N	Y
26 Hinchey	Y	N	Y	N	N	Y	N
27 ***Paxon***	Y	Y	Y	Y	Y	N	Y
28 Slaughter	Y	N	N	N	N	Y	N
29 LaFalce	Y	N	Y	Y	Y	N	Y

	274	275	276	277	278	279	280
30 ***Quinn***	Y	Y	Y	Y	Y	N	Y
31 ***Houghton***	Y	N	Y	Y	N	N	N
NORTH CAROLINA							
1 Clayton	Y	N	N	N	N	Y	N
2 Etheridge	Y	N	Y	N	N	Y	Y
3 ***Jones***	Y	Y	Y	Y	Y	N	Y
4 Price	Y	N	Y	N	N	Y	N
5 ***Burr***	Y	Y	Y	Y	Y	N	Y
6 ***Coble***	Y	Y	Y	Y	Y	N	Y
7 McIntyre	Y	N	Y	Y	Y	N	Y
8 Hefner	Y	N	N	N	?	Y	N
9 ***Myrick***	Y	Y	Y	Y	Y	N	Y
10 ***Ballenger***	Y	Y	Y	Y	Y	N	Y
11 ***Taylor***	Y	Y	Y	Y	Y	N	Y
12 Watt	Y	Y	N	N	N	Y	N
NORTH DAKOTA							
AL Pomeroy	Y	N	Y	N	N	Y	Y
OHIO							
1 ***Chabot***	Y	Y	Y	Y	Y	N	Y
2 ***Portman***	Y	Y	Y	Y	Y	N	Y
3 Hall	Y	N	?	Y	Y	N	Y
4 ***Oxley***	Y	Y	Y	Y	Y	N	Y
5 ***Gillmor***	Y	N	Y	Y	Y	N	Y
6 Strickland	Y	N	Y	N	N	N	Y
7 ***Hobson***	Y	Y	Y	Y	Y	N	Y
8 ***Boehner***	Y	Y	Y	Y	Y	N	Y
9 Kaptur	Y	N	Y	N	N	Y	Y
10 Kucinich	Y	N	Y	Y	Y	N	Y
11 Stokes	Y	N	N	N	N	Y	N
12 ***Kasich***	Y	Y	Y	Y	Y	N	Y
13 Brown	Y	N	Y	N	N	Y	N
14 Sawyer	Y	N	Y	N	N	Y	N
15 ***Pryce***	Y	Y	Y	Y	Y	N	Y
16 ***Regula***	Y	Y	Y	Y	Y	N	Y
17 Traficant	Y	Y	Y	Y	Y	N	Y
18 ***Ney***	Y	Y	Y	Y	Y	N	Y
19 ***LaTourette***	Y	Y	Y	Y	Y	N	Y
OKLAHOMA							
1 ***Largent***	Y	Y	Y	Y	Y	N	Y
2 ***Coburn***	Y	Y	Y	Y	Y	N	Y
3 ***Watkins***	Y	Y	Y	Y	Y	N	Y
4 ***Watts***	Y	Y	Y	Y	Y	N	Y
5 ***Istook***	Y	Y	Y	Y	Y	N	Y
6 ***Lucas***	Y	Y	Y	Y	Y	N	Y
OREGON							
1 Furse	Y	N	N	N	N	Y	N
2 ***Smith***	Y	Y	?	Y	Y	N	Y
3 Blumenauer	Y	N	N	N	N	Y	N
4 DeFazio	Y	N	N	N	N	Y	N
5 Hooley	Y	N	Y	N	N	Y	N
PENNSYLVANIA							
1 Brady	Y	N	N	N	N	Y	N
2 Fattah	?	N	?	N	N	Y	N
3 Borski	Y	N	N	N	N	N	Y
4 Klink	Y	N	Y	Y	Y	N	Y
5 ***Peterson***	Y	Y	Y	Y	Y	N	Y
6 Holden	Y	N	Y	Y	Y	N	Y
7 ***Weldon***	Y	Y	Y	Y	Y	N	Y
8 ***Greenwood***	Y	N	Y	N	N	Y	N
9 ***Shuster***	Y	Y	?	Y	Y	N	Y
10 ***McDade***	?	?	?	Y	?	N	Y
11 Kanjorski	Y	N	N	Y	Y	N	Y
12 Murtha	Y	Y	N	Y	Y	N	Y
13 ***Fox***	Y	N	Y	Y	Y	N	Y
14 Coyne	Y	N	Y	N	N	Y	N
15 McHale	Y	N	N	N	N	N	Y
16 ***Pitts***	Y	Y	Y	Y	Y	N	Y
17 ***Gekas***	Y	Y	Y	Y	Y	N	Y
18 Doyle	Y	N	Y	Y	Y	N	Y
19 ***Goodling***	Y	Y	Y	Y	Y	N	Y
20 Mascara	Y	N	Y	Y	Y	N	Y
21 ***English***	Y	Y	Y	Y	Y	N	Y
RHODE ISLAND							
1 Kennedy	Y	N	N	N	N	Y	N
2 Weygand	Y	N	N	N	N	N	Y
SOUTH CAROLINA							
1 ***Sanford***	Y	N	N	Y	Y	N	Y
2 ***Spence***	Y	Y	Y	Y	Y	N	Y
3 ***Graham***	Y	Y	Y	Y	Y	N	Y
4 ***Inglis***	Y	Y	Y	Y	Y	N	Y
5 Spratt	Y	N	Y	N	N	Y	Y
6 Clyburn	Y	N	N	?	?	Y	N
SOUTH DAKOTA							
AL ***Thune***	Y	Y	Y	Y	Y	N	Y

	274	275	276	277	278	279	280
TENNESSEE							
1 ***Jenkins***	Y	Y	Y	Y	Y	N	Y
2 ***Duncan***	Y	N	Y	Y	Y	N	Y
3 ***Wamp***	Y	N	Y	Y	Y	N	Y
4 ***Hilleary***	Y	+	+	Y	Y	N	Y
5 Clement	Y	N	Y	N	N	N	Y
6 Gordon	Y	Y	Y	N	N	N	Y
7 ***Bryant***	Y	Y	Y	Y	Y	N	Y
8 Tanner	Y	N	N	N	N	N	Y
9 Ford	Y	N	N	N	N	Y	N
TEXAS							
1 Sandlin	Y	N	Y	N	Y	Y	Y
2 Turner	?	N	Y	Y	Y	N	Y
3 ***Johnson, Sam***	Y	Y	Y	Y	Y	N	Y
4 Hall	Y	Y	Y	Y	Y	N	Y
5 ***Sessions***	Y	Y	Y	Y	Y	N	Y
6 ***Barton***	Y	Y	Y	Y	Y	N	Y
7 ***Archer***	Y	Y	Y	Y	Y	N	Y
8 ***Brady***	+	Y	Y	Y	Y	N	Y
9 Lampson	+	N	N	N	N	Y	N
10 Doggett	Y	N	?	N	N	Y	N
11 Edwards	Y	N	Y	N	N	Y	N
12 ***Granger***	Y	Y	Y	Y	Y	N	Y
13 ***Thornberry***	Y	Y	N	Y	Y	N	Y
14 ***Paul***	Y	Y	Y	Y	Y	N	N
15 Hinojosa	+	N	N	N	N	Y	N
16 Reyes	?	N	N	N	N	Y	Y
17 Stenholm	Y	N	Y	Y	N	N	Y
18 Jackson-Lee	Y	N	N	N	N	Y	N
19 ***Combest***	Y	Y	Y	Y	Y	N	Y
20 Gonzalez	?	?	?	?	?	?	?
21 ***Smith***	Y	Y	?	Y	Y	N	Y
22 ***DeLay***	Y	Y	Y	Y	Y	N	Y
23 ***Bonilla***	Y	Y	Y	Y	Y	N	Y
24 Frost	Y	N	N	N	N	Y	N
25 Bentsen	Y	N	Y	N	N	Y	N
26 ***Armey***	Y	Y	Y	Y	Y	N	Y
27 Ortiz	Y	Y	N	Y	Y	N	Y
28 Rodriguez	Y	N	N	N	N	Y	N
29 Green	Y	N	Y	N	N	Y	N
30 Johnson, E.B.	Y	N	N	N	N	Y	N
UTAH							
1 ***Hansen***	Y	Y	Y	Y	Y	N	Y
2 ***Cook***	Y	Y	Y	Y	Y	N	Y
3 ***Cannon***	Y	Y	Y	Y	Y	N	Y
VERMONT							
AL *Sanders*	Y	N	Y	N	N	Y	N
VIRGINIA							
1 ***Bateman***	Y	Y	Y	Y	Y	N	Y
2 Pickett	Y	N	Y	N	N	Y	N
3 Scott	Y	Y	N	N	N	Y	N
4 Sisisky	Y	N	Y	N	N	Y	N
5 Goode	Y	Y	Y	?	?	?	Y
6 ***Goodlatte***	Y	Y	Y	Y	Y	N	Y
7 ***Bliley***	Y	Y	Y	Y	Y	N	Y
8 Moran	Y	N	N	N	N	Y	N
9 Boucher	Y	N	Y	N	N	Y	N
10 ***Wolf***	Y	Y	Y	Y	Y	N	Y
11 ***Davis***	Y	Y	Y	Y	Y	N	Y
WASHINGTON							
1 ***White***	Y	Y	Y	Y	Y	N	Y
2 ***Metcalf***	Y	N	Y	Y	Y	N	Y
3 ***Smith, Linda***	N	Y	Y	Y	Y	N	Y
4 ***Hastings***	Y	Y	Y	Y	Y	N	Y
5 ***Nethercutt***	Y	Y	Y	Y	Y	N	Y
6 Dicks	Y	N	N	N	N	Y	N
7 McDermott	N	N	N	N	N	Y	N
8 ***Dunn***	Y	Y	Y	Y	Y	N	Y
9 Smith, Adam	Y	N	Y	N	N	Y	N
WEST VIRGINIA							
1 Mollohan	Y	Y	N	Y	Y	N	Y
2 Wise	Y	N	Y	N	N	Y	N
3 Rahall	Y	Y	Y	Y	Y	N	Y
WISCONSIN							
1 ***Neumann***	Y	Y	Y	Y	Y	N	Y
2 ***Klug***	?	N	Y	Y	Y	N	N
3 Kind	Y	N	N	N	N	Y	N
4 Kleczka	Y	N	Y	Y	Y	N	Y
5 Barrett	Y	N	N	N	N	Y	N
6 ***Petri***	Y	Y	Y	Y	Y	N	+
7 Obey	Y	N	Y	N	N	N	Y
8 Johnson	Y	N	Y	Y	Y	Y	Y
9 ***Sensenbrenner***	Y	Y	Y	Y	Y	N	Y
WYOMING							
AL ***Cubin***	Y	Y	Y	Y	Y	N	Y

Southern states - Ala., Ark., Fla., Ga., Ky., La., Miss., N.C., Okla., S.C., Tenn., Texas, Va.

House Votes 281, 282, 283, 284, 285, 286, 287

281. HR 3267. Restore Salton Sea/Study Authorization. Miller, D-Calif., substitute amendment to authorize a study on alternatives for restoring the aquatic and environmental balance of the Salton Sea in California. The bill authorizes funds for both a study and a restoration project. Rejected 202-218: R 10-212; D 191-6 (ND 140-4, SD 51-2); I 1-0. July 15, 1998.

282. HR 3267. Restore Salton Sea/Passage. Passage of the bill to authorize a study and restoration project for the Salton Sea in Southern California and rename the area the "Sony Bono Salton Sea National Wildlife Refuge." Passed 221-200: R 195-28; D 26-171 (ND 17-127, SD 9-44); I 0-1. July 15, 1998. A "nay" was a vote in support of the president's position.

283. HR 4104. Fiscal 1999 Treasury, Postal Service Appropriations/Previous Question. Goss, R-Fla., motion to order the previous question (thus ending the possibility of amendment) on adoption of the rule (H Res 498) to provide for House floor consideration of the bill to provide $29.2 billion in fiscal 1999 for the Treasury Department, U.S. Postal Service, various offices of the Executive Office of the President and certain independent agencies. Motion agreed to 231-185: R 222-0; D 9-184 (ND 5-136, SD 4-48); I 0-1. July 15, 1998. (Subsequently, the rule was adopted.)

284. HR 4104. Fiscal 1999 Treasury, Postal Service Appropriations/Rule. Adoption of the rule (H Res 498) to provide for House floor consideration of the bill to provide $29.2 billion in fiscal 1999 for the Treasury Department, U.S. Postal Service, various offices of the Executive Office of the President and certain independent agencies. Adopted 218-201: R 198-23; D 20-177 (ND 14-130, SD 6-47); I 0-1. July 15, 1998.

285. HR 4194. Fiscal 1999 VA, HUD Appropriations/Rule. Adoption of the rule to provide for House floor consideration of the bill to provide $94.4 billion in fiscal 1999 for programs and activities of the Veterans Affairs and Housing and Urban Development departments and for independent agencies including the Environmental Protection Agency, National Science Foundation and the National Aeronautics and Space Administration. Adopted 227-195: R 222-1; D 5-193 (ND 4-141, SD 1-52); I 0-1. July 16, 1998.

286. HR 4104. Fiscal 1999 Treasury-Postal Appropriations/Funds for new Bureau of Alcohol, Tobacco and Firearms Agents. Schumer, D-N.Y., amendment to transfer to the Bureau of Alcohol, Tobacco and Firearms $2 million earmarked in the bill to compensate importers of certain assault-type weapons that were in transit when the administration extended the assault weapons ban. The amendment directs the agency to use the funds to hire additional agents. Rejected 122-301: R 3-221; D 119-79 (ND98-47, SD 21-32); I 0-1. July 16, 1998.

287. HR 4104. Fiscal 1999 Treasury-Postal Appropriations/Increase Federal Election Commission Funding. Maloney, D-N.Y., amendment to increase funding for the Federal Election Commission by $2.8 million. Adopted 214-210: R 27-196; D 186-14 (ND 139-8, SD 47-6); I 1-0. July 16, 1998.

Key

- Y Voted for (yea).
- # Paired for.
- + Announced for.
- N Voted against (nay).
- X Paired against.
- − Announced against.
- P Voted "present."
- C Voted "present" to avoid possible conflict of interest.
- ? Did not vote or otherwise make a position known.

Democrats **Republicans**
Independent

	281	282	283	284	285	286	287
ALABAMA							
1 Callahan	N	Y	Y	Y	Y	N	N
2 Everett	N	Y	Y	Y	Y	N	N
3 Riley	N	Y	Y	Y	Y	N	N
4 Aderholt	N	Y	Y	Y	Y	N	N
5 Cramer	Y	N	N	N	N	Y	Y
6 Bachus	N	Y	Y	N	Y	N	N
7 Hilliard	Y	N	N	N	N	N	Y
ALASKA							
AL Young	N	Y	Y	Y	Y	N	N
ARIZONA							
1 Salmon	N	N	Y	Y	N	N	N
2 Pastor	Y	N	N	N	N	Y	Y
3 Stump	N	N	Y	Y	Y	N	N
4 Shadegg	N	Y	Y	Y	Y	N	N
5 Kolbe	N	Y	Y	P	Y	N	N
6 Hayworth	N	Y	Y	Y	Y	N	N
ARKANSAS							
1 Berry	Y	N	N	N	N	Y	Y
2 Snyder	Y	N	N	N	N	Y	Y
3 Hutchinson	N	Y	Y	Y	Y	N	N
4 Dickey	N	Y	Y	Y	Y	N	N
CALIFORNIA							
1 Riggs	N	Y	Y	Y	Y	N	N
2 Herger	N	Y	Y	Y	Y	N	N
3 Fazio	Y	Y	N	N	N	N	Y
4 Doolittle	N	Y	Y	Y	Y	N	N
5 Matsui	Y	N	N	N	N	Y	Y
6 Woolsey	Y	N	N	N	N	Y	Y
7 Miller	Y	N	N	N	N	Y	Y
8 Pelosi	Y	N	N	N	N	Y	Y
9 Lee	Y	N	N	N	N	Y	Y
10 Tauscher	Y	N	N	N	N	Y	Y
11 Pombo	N	Y	Y	Y	Y	N	N
12 Lantos	Y	N	N	N	N	Y	Y
13 Stark	Y	N	N	N	N	Y	Y
14 Eshoo	Y	N	N	N	N	Y	Y
15 Campbell	N	N	Y	Y	Y	N	Y
16 Lofgren	Y	N	N	N	N	Y	Y
17 Farr	Y	N	N	N	N	Y	Y
18 Condit	Y	Y	N	N	N	N	Y
19 Radanovich	N	Y	Y	Y	Y	N	N
20 Dooley	Y	Y	N	N	N	N	Y
21 Thomas	N	Y	Y	Y	Y	N	N
22 Capps, L.	Y	N	N	N	N	Y	Y
23 Gallegly	N	Y	Y	Y	Y	N	N
24 Sherman	Y	N	N	N	N	Y	Y
25 McKeon	N	Y	Y	Y	Y	N	N
26 Berman	Y	N	N	N	N	Y	Y
27 Rogan	N	Y	Y	Y	Y	N	N
28 Dreier	N	Y	Y	Y	Y	N	N
29 Waxman	Y	N	N	N	N	Y	Y
30 Becerra	Y	−	N	N	N	Y	Y
31 Martinez	Y	Y	N	N	N	Y	Y
32 Dixon	Y	N	N	N	N	Y	Y
33 Roybal-Allard	+	−	−	−	−	+	+
34 Torres	Y	N	N	N	N	Y	Y
35 Waters	Y	N	N	N	N	Y	Y
36 Harman	Y	Y	N	N	N	Y	Y
37 Millender-McD.	Y	Y	N	N	N	Y	Y
38 Horn	N	Y	Y	Y	N	Y	N
39 Royce	N	Y	Y	Y	Y	N	N
40 Lewis	N	Y	Y	Y	Y	N	N
41 Kim	N	Y	Y	Y	N	N	N
42 Brown	Y	N	N	N	N	N	Y
43 Calvert	N	Y	Y	Y	Y	N	N
44 Bono, M.	N	Y	Y	Y	Y	N	N
45 Rohrabacher	N	Y	Y	Y	Y	N	N
46 Sanchez	Y	N	N	N	N	N	Y
47 Cox	N	Y	Y	Y	Y	N	N
48 Packard	N	Y	Y	Y	Y	N	N
49 Bilbray	N	Y	Y	Y	Y	N	N
50 Filner	Y	N	N	N	N	Y	Y
51 Cunningham	N	Y	Y	Y	Y	N	N
52 Hunter	N	Y	Y	Y	Y	N	N
COLORADO							
1 DeGette	Y	N	N	N	N	Y	Y
2 Skaggs	Y	N	N	N	N	Y	Y
3 McInnis	N	Y	Y	Y	Y	N	N
4 Schaffer	N	Y	Y	Y	Y	N	N
5 Hefley	N	N	Y	Y	Y	N	N
6 Schaefer	N	Y	Y	Y	Y	N	N
CONNECTICUT							
1 Kennelly	Y	N	?	?	?	?	?
2 Gejdenson	Y	N	N	N	N	Y	Y
3 DeLauro	Y	N	N	N	N	Y	Y
4 Shays	Y	N	Y	N	Y	N	Y
5 Maloney	Y	N	N	N	N	Y	Y
6 Johnson	N	Y	Y	N	Y	N	N
DELAWARE							
AL Castle	N	Y	Y	N	Y	N	Y
FLORIDA							
1 Scarborough	N	N	Y	Y	Y	N	N
2 Boyd	Y	N	N	N	N	N	Y
3 Brown	Y	N	N	N	N	Y	Y
4 Fowler	N	Y	Y	Y	Y	N	N
5 Thurman	Y	Y	N	N	N	Y	Y
6 Stearns	N	Y	Y	Y	Y	N	N
7 Mica	N	Y	Y	Y	Y	N	N
8 McCollum	N	Y	Y	Y	Y	N	N
9 Bilirakis	N	Y	Y	Y	Y	N	Y
10 Young	N	Y	Y	Y	Y	N	N
11 Davis	Y	N	N	N	N	N	Y
12 Canady	N	Y	Y	Y	Y	N	N
13 Miller	N	?	Y	Y	Y	N	N
14 Goss	N	Y	Y	Y	Y	N	N
15 Weldon	N	Y	Y	Y	Y	N	N
16 Foley	N	Y	Y	Y	Y	N	N
17 Meek	Y	N	N	N	N	Y	Y
18 Ros-Lehtinen	N	Y	Y	Y	Y	N	N
19 Wexler	Y	N	N	N	N	Y	Y
20 Deutsch	Y	N	N	N	N	Y	Y
21 Diaz-Balart	N	Y	Y	Y	N	Y	N
22 Shaw	N	Y	Y	Y	Y	N	N
23 Hastings	Y	N	N	N	N	Y	Y
GEORGIA							
1 Kingston	N	N	Y	Y	Y	N	N
2 Bishop	Y	N	N	N	N	N	Y
3 Collins	N	Y	Y	Y	N	N	N
4 McKinney	Y	N	N	N	N	Y	Y
5 Lewis	Y	N	N	N	N	Y	Y
6 Gingrich							
7 Barr	N	N	Y	Y	Y	N	N
8 Chambliss	N	Y	Y	Y	Y	N	N
9 Deal	N	Y	Y	Y	Y	N	N
10 Norwood	N	Y	Y	Y	?	N	N
11 Linder	?	?	Y	Y	Y	N	N
HAWAII							
1 Abercrombie	Y	N	N	Y	N	Y	Y
2 Mink	Y	N	N	N	N	Y	Y
IDAHO							
1 Chenoweth	N	Y	Y	Y	Y	N	N
2 Crapo	N	Y	Y	Y	?	N	N
ILLINOIS							
1 Rush	Y	N	N	N	N	Y	Y
2 Jackson	Y	N	N	N	N	Y	Y
3 Lipinski	Y	Y	N	N	N	N	Y
4 Gutierrez	Y	N	N	N	N	Y	Y
5 Blagojevich	Y	N	N	N	N	Y	Y
6 Hyde	N	Y	Y	Y	Y	N	N
7 Davis	Y	N	N	N	N	N	Y
8 Crane	N	Y	Y	Y	Y	N	N
9 Yates	?	?	?	?	?	N	Y
10 Porter	Y	N	Y	N	Y	N	Y
11 Weller	N	Y	Y	Y	Y	N	N
12 Costello	Y	N	N	N	N	N	Y

ND Northern Democrats SD Southern Democrats

	281	282	283	284	285	286	287
13 ***Fawell***	N	Y	Y	Y	Y	N	Y
14 ***Hastert***	N	Y	Y	Y	Y	N	N
15 ***Ewing***	N	Y	Y	Y	Y	N	N
16 ***Manzullo***	N	Y	Y	Y	Y	N	N
17 Evans	Y	N	N	N	N	Y	Y
18 ***LaHood***	N	Y	Y	Y	Y	N	N
19 Poshard	Y	N	N	N	N	Y	Y
20 ***Shimkus***	N	Y	Y	Y	Y	N	N
INDIANA							
1 Visclosky	Y	N	N	N	N	N	Y
2 ***McIntosh***	N	Y	Y	Y	Y	N	N
3 Roemer	Y	Y	N	N	N	N	Y
4 ***Souder***	N	Y	Y	Y	Y	N	N
5 ***Buyer***	N	Y	Y	Y	Y	N	N
6 ***Burton***	N	Y	Y	Y	Y	N	N
7 ***Pease***	N	Y	Y	Y	Y	N	N
8 ***Hostettler***	N	Y	Y	Y	Y	N	N
9 Hamilton	Y	N	N	N	N	N	Y
10 Carson	Y	N	N	N	N	Y	Y
IOWA							
1 ***Leach***	N	Y	Y	N	Y	N	Y
2 ***Nussle***	N	Y	Y	Y	Y	N	N
3 Boswell	Y	N	N	N	N	N	Y
4 ***Ganske***	N	Y	Y	N	Y	N	Y
5 ***Latham***	N	Y	Y	Y	Y	N	N
KANSAS							
1 ***Moran***	N	Y	Y	Y	Y	N	N
2 ***Ryun***	N	Y	Y	Y	Y	N	N
3 ***Snowbarger***	N	Y	Y	Y	Y	N	Y
4 ***Tiahrt***	N	Y	Y	Y	Y	N	N
KENTUCKY							
1 ***Whitfield***	N	Y	Y	?	Y	N	N
2 ***Lewis***	N	Y	Y	Y	Y	N	N
3 ***Northup***	N	Y	Y	Y	Y	N	N
4 ***Bunning***	N	Y	Y	Y	Y	N	N
5 ***Rogers***	?	Y	Y	Y	Y	N	N
6 Baesler	Y	N	N	N	N	N	Y
LOUISIANA							
1 ***Livingston***	N	Y	Y	Y	Y	N	N
2 Jefferson	Y	N	N	N	N	Y	Y
3 ***Tauzin***	N	Y	Y	Y	Y	N	N
4 ***McCrery***	N	Y	Y	Y	Y	N	N
5 ***Cooksey***	N	Y	Y	Y	Y	N	N
6 ***Baker***	N	Y	Y	Y	Y	N	N
7 John	Y	N	N	Y	N	N	N
MAINE							
1 Allen	Y	N	?	N	N	Y	Y
2 Baldacci	Y	N	N	N	N	Y	Y
MARYLAND							
1 ***Gilchrest***	N	Y	Y	N	Y	N	N
2 ***Ehrlich***	N	Y	Y	Y	Y	N	N
3 Cardin	Y	N	N	N	N	Y	Y
4 Wynn	Y	N	N	N	N	Y	N
5 Hoyer	Y	N	N	N	N	N	Y
6 ***Bartlett***	N	Y	Y	Y	Y	N	N
7 Cummings	Y	N	N	N	N	Y	Y
8 ***Morella***	N	Y	Y	N	Y	Y	Y
MASSACHUSETTS							
1 Olver	Y	N	N	N	N	Y	Y
2 Neal	Y	N	N	N	N	Y	Y
3 McGovern	Y	N	N	N	N	Y	Y
4 Frank	Y	Y	N	N	N	Y	Y
5 Meehan	Y	N	N	N	N	Y	Y
6 Tierney	Y	N	N	N	N	Y	Y
7 Markey	Y	N	N	N	N	Y	Y
8 Kennedy	N	Y	N	N	N	Y	Y
9 Moakley	Y	N	N	N	?	Y	Y
10 Delahunt	Y	N	N	N	N	Y	Y
MICHIGAN							
1 Stupak	Y	N	N	Y	N	N	Y
2 ***Hoekstra***	N	N	Y	Y	Y	N	N
3 ***Ehlers***	Y	N	Y	Y	Y	N	N
4 ***Camp***	N	N	Y	Y	Y	N	Y
5 Barcia	Y	N	Y	Y	N	N	Y
6 ***Upton***	N	N	Y	N	Y	N	Y
7 ***Smith***	N	Y	Y	Y	Y	N	Y
8 Stabenow	Y	N	N	N	N	Y	Y
9 Kildee	Y	N	Y	N	Y	Y	Y
10 Bonior	Y	N	N	N	N	Y	Y
11 ***Knollenberg***	N	Y	Y	Y	Y	N	N
12 Levin	Y	N	N	N	N	Y	Y
13 Rivers	Y	N	N	N	N	Y	Y
14 Conyers	N	N	N	N	N	Y	Y
15 Kilpatrick	Y	N	N	N	N	Y	Y
16 Dingell	?	?	?	?	N	N	Y

	281	282	283	284	285	286	287
MINNESOTA							
1 ***Gutknecht***	N	Y	Y	Y	Y	N	N
2 Minge	Y	N	N	N	N	N	Y
3 ***Ramstad***	Y	N	Y	N	Y	N	Y
4 Vento	Y	N	N	N	N	Y	Y
5 Sabo	Y	N	N	N	N	Y	Y
6 Luther	Y	N	N	N	N	Y	Y
7 Peterson	Y	N	Y	Y	N	N	Y
8 Oberstar	Y	N	N	N	N	N	N
MISSISSIPPI							
1 ***Wicker***	N	Y	Y	Y	Y	N	N
2 Thompson	Y	N	N	N	N	Y	Y
3 ***Pickering***	N	Y	Y	Y	Y	–	N
4 ***Parker***	N	Y	Y	Y	Y	N	N
5 Taylor	N	Y	N	Y	N	N	Y
MISSOURI							
1 Clay	Y	N	N	N	N	Y	Y
2 ***Talent***	N	Y	Y	Y	Y	N	N
3 Gephardt	Y	N	N	N	N	N	Y
4 Skelton	N	Y	Y	Y	N	N	Y
5 McCarthy	Y	N	N	N	N	Y	Y
6 Danner	Y	N	N	Y	N	N	Y
7 ***Blunt***	N	Y	Y	Y	?	N	N
8 ***Emerson***	N	Y	Y	Y	Y	N	N
9 ***Hulshof***	N	Y	Y	Y	Y	N	Y
MONTANA							
AL ***Hill***	?	?	?	?	?	?	?
NEBRASKA							
1 ***Bereuter***	N	Y	Y	Y	Y	N	N
2 ***Christensen***	N	Y	Y	Y	Y	N	N
3 ***Barrett***	N	Y	Y	Y	Y	N	N
NEVADA							
1 ***Ensign***	N	Y	Y	Y	Y	N	N
2 ***Gibbons***	N	Y	Y	Y	Y	N	N
NEW HAMPSHIRE							
1 ***Sununu***	?	Y	?	Y	Y	N	N
2 ***Bass***	N	Y	Y	N	Y	N	N
NEW JERSEY							
1 Andrews	Y	N	N	N	N	Y	Y
2 ***LoBiondo***	N	N	Y	Y	Y	N	Y
3 ***Saxton***	N	Y	Y	Y	Y	N	N
4 ***Smith***	N	Y	Y	Y	Y	N	N
5 ***Roukema***	N	Y	Y	N	Y	N	Y
6 Pallone	Y	N	N	N	N	Y	Y
7 ***Franks***	N	Y	Y	N	Y	N	Y
8 Pascrell	Y	N	N	N	N	Y	Y
9 Rothman	Y	N	N	N	N	Y	Y
10 Payne	Y	N	N	N	N	Y	Y
11 ***Frelinghuysen***	N	Y	Y	N	Y	N	N
12 ***Pappas***	N	Y	Y	Y	Y	N	Y
13 Menendez	Y	N	N	N	N	Y	Y
NEW MEXICO							
1 ***Wilson***	N	Y	Y	Y	Y	N	N
2 ***Skeen***	N	Y	Y	Y	Y	N	N
3 ***Redmond***	N	Y	Y	Y	Y	N	N
NEW YORK							
1 ***Forbes***	Y	N	Y	Y	Y	N	N
2 ***Lazio***	N	Y	Y	Y	Y	N	N
3 ***King***	N	Y	Y	Y	Y	N	N
4 McCarthy	Y	Y	N	N	Y	Y	Y
5 Ackerman	Y	N	N	N	N	Y	Y
6 Meeks	Y	N	?	N	N	?	Y
7 Manton	Y	N	N	N	N	Y	N
8 Nadler	Y	N	N	N	N	Y	Y
9 Schumer	?	?	?	?	N	Y	Y
10 Towns	Y	N	N	N	Y	Y	Y
11 Owens	Y	N	N	N	N	Y	Y
12 Velázquez	Y	N	N	N	N	Y	Y
13 ***Fossella***	N	Y	Y	Y	Y	N	N
14 Maloney	Y	N	N	N	N	Y	Y
15 Rangel	?	?	N	N	?	Y	Y
16 Serrano	Y	N	N	N	N	Y	Y
17 Engel	Y	N	N	N	N	Y	Y
18 Lowey	Y	N	N	N	N	Y	Y
19 ***Kelly***	N	Y	Y	N	Y	N	N
20 ***Gilman***	N	Y	Y	N	Y	N	Y
21 McNulty	?	?	?	?	?	?	?
22 ***Solomon***	N	Y	Y	Y	Y	N	N
23 ***Boehlert***	N	Y	Y	N	Y	N	Y
24 ***McHugh***	N	Y	Y	Y	Y	N	Y
25 ***Walsh***	N	Y	Y	Y	Y	N	N
26 Hinchey	Y	N	N	N	N	N	Y
27 ***Paxon***	N	Y	Y	Y	Y	N	N
28 Slaughter	Y	N	–	–	–	+	+
29 LaFalce	Y	N	N	N	N	Y	Y

	281	282	283	284	285	286	287
30 ***Quinn***	N	Y	Y	Y	Y	N	N
31 ***Houghton***	N	Y	Y	Y	Y	N	N
NORTH CAROLINA							
1 Clayton	Y	Y	N	N	N	Y	Y
2 Etheridge	Y	N	N	N	N	N	Y
3 ***Jones***	N	Y	Y	Y	Y	N	N
4 Price	Y	N	N	N	N	Y	Y
5 ***Burr***	N	Y	Y	Y	Y	N	N
6 ***Coble***	N	N	Y	Y	Y	N	N
7 McIntyre	Y	N	Y	Y	N	N	Y
8 Hefner	Y	N	N	N	N	?	Y
9 ***Myrick***	N	Y	Y	Y	Y	N	N
10 ***Ballenger***	N	Y	Y	Y	Y	N	N
11 ***Taylor***	N	Y	Y	Y	Y	N	N
12 Watt	Y	N	N	N	N	Y	Y
NORTH DAKOTA							
AL Pomeroy	Y	Y	N	N	N	N	Y
OHIO							
1 ***Chabot***	N	N	Y	Y	Y	N	N
2 ***Portman***	N	Y	Y	Y	Y	N	N
3 Hall	Y	N	N	N	N	Y	Y
4 ***Oxley***	N	?	Y	Y	Y	N	N
5 ***Gillmor***	N	Y	Y	Y	Y	N	N
6 Strickland	Y	N	N	N	N	N	Y
7 ***Hobson***	N	Y	Y	Y	Y	N	N
8 ***Boehner***	N	Y	Y	Y	Y	N	N
9 Kaptur	Y	Y	N	N	N	N	Y
10 Kucinich	Y	N	N	N	N	Y	Y
11 Stokes	Y	N	N	N	N	Y	Y
12 ***Kasich***	N	Y	Y	Y	Y	N	N
13 Brown	Y	N	N	N	N	Y	Y
14 Sawyer	Y	N	N	N	N	N	Y
15 ***Pryce***	N	Y	Y	Y	Y	N	N
16 ***Regula***	N	Y	Y	Y	Y	N	N
17 Traficant	N	Y	Y	Y	Y	N	N
18 ***Ney***	N	Y	Y	Y	Y	N	N
19 ***LaTourette***	N	Y	Y	Y	Y	Y	N
OKLAHOMA							
1 ***Largent***	N	Y	Y	Y	Y	N	N
2 ***Coburn***	N	Y	Y	Y	Y	N	N
3 ***Watkins***	N	N	Y	Y	Y	N	N
4 ***Watts***	N	Y	Y	Y	Y	N	N
5 ***Istook***	N	Y	Y	Y	Y	N	N
6 ***Lucas***	N	Y	Y	Y	Y	N	N
OREGON							
1 Furse	Y	N	N	N	N	Y	Y
2 ***Smith***	N	Y	?	?	Y	N	N
3 Blumenauer	Y	N	N	N	N	Y	Y
4 DeFazio	Y	N	N	N	N	N	N
5 Hooley	Y	N	N	N	N	Y	Y
PENNSYLVANIA							
1 Brady	Y	N	N	N	N	Y	Y
2 Fattah	Y	N	N	N	N	Y	Y
3 Borski	Y	N	N	N	N	Y	Y
4 Klink	Y	N	N	N	N	N	Y
5 ***Peterson***	N	Y	Y	Y	Y	N	N
6 Holden	Y	N	N	Y	N	N	Y
7 ***Weldon***	N	Y	Y	Y	Y	N	N
8 ***Greenwood***	N	Y	Y	N	Y	N	Y
9 ***Shuster***	N	Y	?	?	Y	N	N
10 ***McDade***	N	Y	?	?	Y	?	?
11 Kanjorski	Y	N	N	N	N	N	Y
12 Murtha	Y	N	N	N	N	N	Y
13 ***Fox***	N	Y	Y	N	Y	N	N
14 Coyne	Y	N	N	N	N	Y	Y
15 McHale	Y	N	N	N	N	Y	Y
16 ***Pitts***	N	Y	Y	Y	Y	N	N
17 ***Gekas***	N	Y	Y	Y	Y	N	N
18 Doyle	Y	N	N	N	N	N	Y
19 ***Goodling***	N	Y	Y	Y	Y	N	N
20 Mascara	Y	N	N	N	N	N	Y
21 ***English***	N	Y	Y	Y	Y	N	N
RHODE ISLAND							
1 Kennedy	Y	N	N	N	N	+	Y
2 Weygand	+	N	N	N	N	Y	Y
SOUTH CAROLINA							
1 ***Sanford***	Y	N	Y	Y	Y	N	N
2 ***Spence***	N	Y	Y	Y	Y	N	N
3 ***Graham***	N	Y	Y	Y	Y	N	N
4 ***Inglis***	N	N	Y	Y	Y	N	N
5 Spratt	Y	N	N	N	N	N	Y
6 Clyburn	Y	N	N	N	N	Y	Y
SOUTH DAKOTA							
AL ***Thune***	N	Y	Y	Y	Y	N	N

	281	282	283	284	285	286	287
TENNESSEE							
1 ***Jenkins***	N	Y	Y	Y	Y	N	?
2 ***Duncan***	Y	N	Y	Y	Y	N	N
3 ***Wamp***	Y	N	Y	Y	Y	N	N
4 ***Hilleary***	N	Y	Y	Y	Y	N	N
5 Clement	Y	N	–	–	N	N	Y
6 Gordon	Y	N	N	N	N	N	Y
7 ***Bryant***	N	Y	Y	Y	Y	N	N
8 Tanner	Y	N	N	N	N	N	Y
9 Ford	Y	N	N	N	N	N	Y
TEXAS							
1 Sandlin	Y	N	N	N	N	N	N
2 Turner	Y	N	N	N	N	N	Y
3 ***Johnson, Sam***	N	Y	Y	Y	Y	N	N
4 Hall	N	Y	Y	Y	N	N	N
5 ***Sessions***	N	Y	Y	Y	Y	N	N
6 ***Barton***	N	Y	Y	Y	Y	N	?
7 ***Archer***	N	Y	Y	Y	Y	N	N
8 ***Brady***	N	Y	Y	Y	Y	N	N
9 Lampson	Y	N	N	N	N	N	Y
10 Doggett	Y	N	N	N	N	Y	Y
11 Edwards	Y	N	N	N	N	N	Y
12 ***Granger***	N	Y	Y	Y	Y	N	N
13 ***Thornberry***	N	Y	Y	Y	Y	N	N
14 ***Paul***	Y	N	Y	Y	Y	N	N
15 Hinojosa	Y	N	N	N	N	Y	Y
16 Reyes	?	?	N	N	N	Y	Y
17 Stenholm	Y	N	Y	Y	N	N	Y
18 Jackson-Lee	Y	N	N	N	N	Y	Y
19 ***Combest***	N	Y	Y	Y	Y	N	N
20 Gonzalez	?	?	?	?	?	?	?
21 ***Smith***	N	Y	Y	Y	Y	N	N
22 ***DeLay***	N	Y	Y	Y	Y	N	N
23 ***Bonilla***	N	Y	Y	Y	Y	N	N
24 Frost	Y	Y	N	N	N	N	Y
25 Bentsen	Y	N	N	N	N	N	Y
26 ***Armey***	N	Y	Y	Y	Y	N	N
27 Ortiz	Y	Y	N	N	N	N	Y
28 Rodriguez	Y	N	N	N	–	Y	Y
29 Green	Y	Y	N	N	N	N	Y
30 Johnson, E.B.	Y	N	N	N	N	N	Y
UTAH							
1 ***Hansen***	N	Y	Y	Y	Y	N	N
2 ***Cook***	N	Y	Y	Y	Y	N	N
3 ***Cannon***	N	Y	Y	Y	Y	N	N
VERMONT							
AL *Sanders*	Y	N	N	N	N	N	Y
VIRGINIA							
1 ***Bateman***	N	Y	Y	Y	Y	N	N
2 Pickett	Y	Y	N	N	N	N	N
3 Scott	Y	N	N	N	N	Y	Y
4 Sisisky	Y	Y	N	N	N	N	?
5 Goode	Y	N	Y	Y	Y	N	N
6 ***Goodlatte***	N	N	Y	Y	Y	N	N
7 ***Bliley***	N	Y	Y	Y	Y	N	N
8 Moran	Y	N	?	N	N	Y	Y
9 Boucher	Y	N	N	N	N	N	N
10 ***Wolf***	N	Y	Y	Y	Y	N	N
11 ***Davis***	N	Y	Y	Y	Y	N	N
WASHINGTON							
1 ***White***	N	Y	Y	Y	Y	N	N
2 ***Metcalf***	N	Y	Y	Y	Y	N	N
3 ***Smith, Linda***	N	Y	Y	Y	N	N	N
4 ***Hastings***	N	Y	Y	Y	Y	N	N
5 ***Nethercutt***	N	Y	Y	Y	Y	N	N
6 Dicks	Y	N	N	N	N	N	Y
7 McDermott	Y	N	N	N	N	Y	Y
8 ***Dunn***	N	Y	Y	Y	Y	N	N
9 Smith, Adam	Y	N	N	N	N	N	Y
WEST VIRGINIA							
1 Mollohan	Y	N	N	Y	N	N	Y
2 Wise	Y	N	N	N	N	N	Y
3 Rahall	Y	N	N	Y	N	N	N
WISCONSIN							
1 ***Neumann***	N	Y	Y	Y	Y	N	N
2 ***Klug***	N	N	Y	N	Y	N	N
3 Kind	Y	N	?	N	N	N	Y
4 Kleczka	Y	N	N	N	N	N	Y
5 Barrett	Y	N	N	N	N	Y	Y
6 ***Petri***	Y	N	Y	Y	Y	N	N
7 Obey	Y	N	N	N	N	N	Y
8 Johnson	Y	N	N	N	N	N	Y
9 ***Sensenbrenner***	?	N	Y	Y	Y	N	N
WYOMING							
AL ***Cubin***	N	Y	Y	Y	Y	N	N

Southern states - Ala., Ark., Fla., Ga., Ky., La., Miss., N.C., Okla., S.C., Tenn., Texas, Va.

House Votes 288, 289, 290, 291, 292, 293, 294

Key

Y	Voted for (yea).
#	Paired for.
+	Announced for.
N	Voted against (nay).
X	Paired against.
−	Announced against.
P	Voted "present."
C	Voted "present" to avoid possible conflict of interest.
?	Did not vote or otherwise make a position known.

Democrats **Republicans** *Independent*

---

288. HR 4104. Fiscal 1999 Treasury-Postal Appropriations/Federal Employee Health Plan Abortion Coverage. DeLauro, D-Conn., amendment to eliminate provisions banning the use of funds to pay for abortions under the Federal Employees Health Benefits Program. Rejected 183-239: R 29-196; D 153-43 (ND 114-33, SD 39-10); I 1-0. July 16, 1998.

289. HR 4104. Fiscal 1999 Treasury-Postal Appropriations/Annual Congressional Cost of Living Adjustment. Hefner, D-N.C., amendment to delete the provision that blocks members of Congress from receiving an annual cost of living adjustment. Rejected 79-342: R 29-195; D 50-146 (ND 41-106, SD 9-40); I 0-1. July 16, 1998.

290. HR 4104. Fiscal 1999 Treasury-Postal Appropriations/Insurance Coverage of Contraceptives. Lowey, D-N.Y. amendment to prohibit the Office of Personnel Management from accepting a contract that provides coverage for prescription drugs unless the plan also provides equivalent coverage for prescription contraception drugs. Adopted 224-198: R 48-177; D 175-21 (ND 130-17, SD 45-4); I 1-0. July 16, 1998.

291. HR 4104. Fiscal 1999 Treasury-Postal Appropriations/Exchange Stabilization Fund Restriction. Sanders, I-Vt. amendment to prohibit the use of funds in the bill to make any loan or credit in excess of $250 million to a foreign entity or government through the Exchange Stabilization Fund without congressional approval. Rejected 195-226: R 143-82; D 51-144 (ND 41-105, SD 10-39); I 1-0. July 16, 1998.

292. HR 4104. Fiscal 1999 Treasury-Postal Appropriations/Federal Employee Health Plan Abortion Coverage Ban. Smith, R-N.J. amendment to prohibit federal employee health plans from providing insurance coverage for drugs that induce abortion. Rejected 198-222: R 172-51; D 26-170 (ND 21-126, SD 5-44); I 0-1. July 16, 1998.

293. HR 4104. Fiscal 1999 Treasury-Postal Appropriations/Passage. Passage of the bill to provide funds for the Treasury Department, U.S. Postal Service, various offices of the Executive Office of the President and certain independent agencies. Passed 218-203: R 192-33; D 26-169 (ND 14-132, SD 12-37); I 0-1. July 16, 1998.

294. HR 3731. Steve Schiff Auditorium Designation/Passage. Passage of the bill to designate an auditorium within the Sandia Technology Transfer Center in Albuquerque, N.M., as the "Steve Schiff Auditorium." Passed 409-0: R 218-0; D 190-0 (ND 141-0, SD 49-0); I 1-0. July 16, 1998.

	288	289	290	291	292	293	294
ALABAMA							
1 *Callahan*	N	N	N	Y	Y	Y	Y
2 *Everett*	N	N	N	Y	Y	Y	Y
3 *Riley*	N	N	N	Y	Y	Y	Y
4 *Aderholt*	N	N	N	Y	Y	Y	Y
5 Cramer	Y	N	N	Y	N	Y	Y
6 *Bachus*	N	N	N	Y	Y	Y	Y
7 Hilliard	Y	Y	Y	Y	N	N	Y
ALASKA							
AL *Young*	N	N	N	Y	Y	Y	Y
ARIZONA							
1 *Salmon*	N	N	N	Y	Y	Y	?
2 Pastor	Y	N	Y	N	N	Y	Y
3 *Stump*	N	N	N	N	Y	N	Y
4 *Shadegg*	N	N	N	Y	Y	Y	Y
5 *Kolbe*	Y	Y	Y	N	N	Y	Y
6 *Hayworth*	N	N	N	Y	Y	N	Y
ARKANSAS							
1 Berry	N	N	Y	N	Y	N	Y
2 Snyder	Y	N	Y	N	N	N	Y
3 *Hutchinson*	N	N	N	Y	Y	Y	Y
4 *Dickey*	N	N	N	N	Y	Y	Y
CALIFORNIA							
1 *Riggs*	N	Y	N	Y	Y	Y	Y
2 *Herger*	N	N	N	Y	N	Y	N
3 Fazio	Y	Y	Y	N	N	N	Y
4 *Doolittle*	N	Y	N	Y	N	Y	Y
5 Matsui	Y	N	Y	N	N	Y	Y
6 Woolsey	Y	N	Y	N	N	N	Y
7 Miller	Y	Y	Y	N	N	N	Y
8 Pelosi	Y	Y	Y	N	N	N	Y
9 Lee	Y	Y	Y	N	N	N	Y
10 Tauscher	Y	N	Y	N	N	Y	Y
11 *Pombo*	N	N	N	Y	Y	Y	Y
12 Lantos	Y	N	Y	N	N	N	Y
13 Stark	Y	Y	Y	N	N	N	Y
14 Eshoo	Y	N	Y	N	N	N	Y
15 *Campbell*	Y	Y	Y	N	N	N	Y
16 Lofgren	Y	N	Y	N	N	N	Y
17 Farr	Y	N	Y	N	N	N	Y
18 Condit	Y	N	Y	N	Y	N	Y
19 *Radanovich*	N	N	N	Y	Y	Y	Y
20 Dooley	Y	N	Y	N	N	Y	?
21 *Thomas*	Y	Y	Y	N	N	Y	Y
22 Capps, L.	Y	N	Y	N	N	N	Y
23 *Gallegly*	N	N	N	Y	N	N	Y
24 Sherman	Y	N	Y	N	N	N	Y
25 *McKeon*	N	Y	N	Y	Y	Y	Y
26 Berman	Y	Y	Y	N	N	N	?
27 *Rogan*	N	N	N	Y	Y	Y	Y
28 *Dreier*	N	N	N	N	Y	Y	Y
29 Waxman	Y	Y	Y	N	N	N	Y
30 Becerra	Y	N	Y	N	N	N	Y
31 Martinez	Y	Y	Y	N	N	N	?
32 Dixon	Y	N	Y	N	N	N	Y
33 Roybal-Allard	+	−	+	−	−	−	+
34 Torres	Y	N	Y	N	N	N	Y
35 Waters	Y	Y	Y	?	N	N	Y
36 Harman	Y	Y	Y	N	N	Y	?
37 Millender-McD.	Y	N	Y	N	N	N	Y

	288	289	290	291	292	293	294
38 *Horn*	Y	N	Y	N	N	Y	Y
39 *Royce*	N	N	N	Y	Y	Y	Y
40 *Lewis*	N	Y	N	Y	Y	Y	Y
41 *Kim*	N	Y	N	N	Y	N	Y
42 Brown	Y	N	Y	N	N	N	Y
43 *Calvert*	N	N	N	Y	Y	Y	Y
44 *Bono, M.*	N	N	Y	N	Y	Y	Y
45 *Rohrabacher*	N	N	N	Y	Y	Y	Y
46 Sanchez	Y	N	Y	N	N	N	Y
47 *Cox*	N	N	N	Y	Y	Y	Y
48 *Packard*	N	Y	N	N	Y	Y	Y
49 *Bilbray*	N	Y	Y	N	Y	N	Y
50 Filner	#	−	#	−	X	X	+
51 *Cunningham*	N	N	N	Y	Y	Y	Y
52 *Hunter*	N	Y	N	Y	Y	Y	Y
COLORADO							
1 DeGette	Y	N	Y	N	N	N	Y
2 Skaggs	Y	Y	Y	N	N	N	Y
3 *McInnis*	N	N	N	N	N	N	Y
4 *Schaffer*	N	N	N	Y	Y	N	Y
5 *Hefley*	N	N	N	Y	N	N	Y
6 *Schaefer*	N	Y	N	Y	Y	Y	Y
CONNECTICUT							
1 Kennelly	#	?	?	?	?	?	?
2 Gejdenson	Y	N	Y	N	N	N	Y
3 DeLauro	Y	N	Y	N	N	N	Y
4 *Shays*	Y	N	Y	N	N	N	Y
5 Maloney	Y	N	Y	N	N	N	Y
6 *Johnson*	Y	N	N	N	N	Y	?
DELAWARE							
AL *Castle*	Y	N	Y	N	N	Y	Y
FLORIDA							
1 *Scarborough*	N	N	N	Y	Y	Y	Y
2 Boyd	N	N	Y	N	N	N	Y
3 Brown	Y	N	N	N	N	N	Y
4 *Fowler*	N	Y	Y	N	Y	Y	Y
5 Thurman	Y	N	Y	N	N	N	Y
6 *Stearns*	N	N	N	N	Y	Y	Y
7 *Mica*	N	N	N	Y	Y	N	Y
8 *McCollum*	N	Y	N	Y	Y	Y	Y
9 *Bilirakis*	N	N	N	Y	Y	N	Y
10 *Young*	N	N	N	Y	Y	Y	Y
11 Davis	Y	N	Y	N	N	N	Y
12 *Canady*	N	N	N	Y	Y	Y	Y
13 *Miller*	Y	N	N	N	Y	Y	Y
14 *Goss*	N	N	N	N	Y	Y	Y
15 *Weldon*	N	Y	N	N	Y	Y	Y
16 *Foley*	Y	N	Y	N	Y	Y	Y
17 Meek	Y	Y	Y	N	N	N	Y
18 *Ros-Lehtinen*	N	Y	Y	N	Y	Y	Y
19 Wexler	Y	Y	Y	N	N	N	Y
20 Deutsch	Y	N	Y	N	N	N	Y
21 *Diaz-Balart*	N	N	N	Y	Y	Y	Y
22 *Shaw*	N	N	Y	N	N	Y	Y
23 Hastings	Y	Y	Y	N	N	N	Y
GEORGIA							
1 *Kingston*	N	N	N	Y	Y	Y	Y
2 Bishop	Y	N	Y	N	N	N	Y
3 *Collins*	N	N	N	Y	Y	Y	Y
4 *McKinney*	Y	N	Y	N	N	N	Y
5 Lewis	?	?	?	?	?	?	?
6 *Gingrich*						Y	Y
7 *Barr*	N	N	N	Y	Y	Y	Y
8 *Chambliss*	N	N	N	Y	Y	Y	Y
9 *Deal*	N	N	N	Y	Y	Y	Y
10 *Norwood*	N	N	N	Y	Y	Y	Y
11 *Linder*	N	N	N	N	Y	Y	Y
HAWAII							
1 Abercrombie	Y	N	Y	N	N	N	Y
2 Mink	Y	N	Y	Y	N	N	Y
IDAHO							
1 *Chenoweth*	N	N	N	Y	Y	Y	Y
2 *Crapo*	N	N	N	Y	Y	Y	Y
ILLINOIS							
1 Rush	Y	N	Y	Y	N	N	Y
2 Jackson	Y	Y	Y	N	N	N	Y
3 Lipinski	N	N	N	Y	N	N	Y
4 Gutierrez	Y	N	Y	Y	N	N	Y
5 Blagojevich	Y	N	Y	N	N	N	Y
6 *Hyde*	N	Y	N	N	Y	Y	Y
7 Davis	Y	N	Y	Y	N	N	Y
8 *Crane*	N	N	N	Y	N	Y	Y
9 Yates	Y	Y	Y	N	N	?	?
10 *Porter*	Y	Y	Y	N	N	Y	Y
11 *Weller*	N	N	N	Y	Y	Y	Y
12 Costello	N	N	N	Y	N	Y	Y

ND Northern Democrats   SD Southern Democrats

	288	289	290	291	292	293	294
13 ***Fawell***	Y	Y	Y	N	N	Y	Y
14 ***Hastert***	N	N	N	Y	Y	Y	Y
15 ***Ewing***	N	N	N	N	N	Y	Y
16 ***Manzullo***	N	N	N	Y	Y	Y	Y
17 Evans	Y	N	Y	Y	N	N	Y
18 ***LaHood***	N	N	N	Y	Y	Y	Y
19 Poshard	N	N	Y	Y	N	N	Y
20 ***Shimkus***	N	N	N	Y	Y	Y	Y
INDIANA							
1 Visclosky	Y	N	Y	Y	N	Y	Y
2 ***McIntosh***	N	N	N	Y	?	Y	Y
3 Roemer	N	N	Y	N	Y	N	Y
4 ***Souder***	N	N	N	Y	Y	Y	Y
5 ***Buyer***	N	N	N	N	Y	Y	Y
6 ***Burton***	N	Y	N	Y	Y	Y	Y
7 ***Pease***	N	N	N	Y	Y	Y	Y
8 ***Hostettler***	N	N	N	Y	Y	N	Y
9 Hamilton	N	N	Y	N	Y	N	Y
10 Carson	Y	N	Y	Y	N	N	Y
IOWA							
1 ***Leach***	N	N	Y	N	N	Y	Y
2 ***Nussle***	N	N	N	N	Y	Y	Y
3 Boswell	Y	N	Y	N	N	Y	Y
4 ***Ganske***	N	N	Y	Y	N	Y	Y
5 ***Latham***	N	N	N	N	Y	Y	Y
KANSAS							
1 ***Moran***	N	N	N	Y	Y	N	Y
2 ***Ryun***	N	N	N	Y	Y	Y	Y
3 ***Snowbarger***	N	N	N	Y	Y	Y	Y
4 ***Tiahrt***	N	N	N	Y	Y	N	Y
KENTUCKY							
1 ***Whitfield***	N	N	N	Y	Y	Y	Y
2 ***Lewis***	N	N	N	Y	Y	Y	Y
3 ***Northup***	N	N	N	N	Y	Y	Y
4 ***Bunning***	N	N	N	Y	Y	N	Y
5 ***Rogers***	N	N	N	Y	Y	Y	Y
6 Baesler	Y	N	Y	Y	N	Y	Y
LOUISIANA							
1 ***Livingston***	N	Y	N	Y	Y	Y	Y
2 Jefferson	Y	N	Y	N	N	N	Y
3 ***Tauzin***	N	N	N	Y	Y	Y	Y
4 ***McCrery***	N	Y	N	N	Y	Y	Y
5 ***Cooksey***	N	N	N	Y	N	Y	Y
6 ***Baker***	N	N	N	N	Y	N	Y
7 John	?	?	?	?	?	?	?
MAINE							
1 Allen	Y	N	Y	N	N	N	Y
2 Baldacci	Y	N	Y	N	N	N	Y
MARYLAND							
1 ***Gilchrest***	Y	N	Y	N	N	Y	Y
2 ***Ehrlich***	Y	N	Y	N	N	Y	Y
3 Cardin	Y	N	Y	N	N	N	Y
4 Wynn	Y	Y	Y	N	N	N	Y
5 Hoyer	Y	N	Y	N	N	Y	Y
6 ***Bartlett***	N	N	N	Y	Y	Y	Y
7 Cummings	Y	N	Y	Y	N	N	Y
8 ***Morella***	Y	N	Y	N	N	Y	Y
MASSACHUSETTS							
1 Olver	Y	N	Y	N	N	N	Y
2 Neal	N	N	Y	N	N	N	Y
3 McGovern	Y	N	Y	Y	N	N	Y
4 Frank	Y	Y	Y	N	N	N	Y
5 Meehan	Y	N	Y	N	N	N	Y
6 Tierney	Y	N	Y	N	N	N	Y
7 Markey	Y	N	Y	N	N	N	Y
8 Kennedy	Y	Y	Y	N	N	N	Y
9 Moakley	N	N	Y	N	N	N	Y
10 Delahunt	Y	Y	Y	Y	N	N	Y
MICHIGAN							
1 Stupak	N	N	N	Y	Y	N	Y
2 ***Hoekstra***	N	N	N	Y	Y	Y	Y
3 ***Ehlers***	N	N	N	N	Y	Y	Y
4 ***Camp***	N	N	N	N	Y	Y	Y
5 Barcia	N	N	N	Y	Y	N	Y
6 ***Upton***	N	N	Y	Y	N	Y	Y
7 ***Smith***	N	N	N	Y	Y	Y	Y
8 Stabenow	Y	N	Y	N	N	N	Y
9 Kildee	N	N	N	N	Y	N	Y
10 Bonior	N	N	Y	N	N	N	Y
11 ***Knollenberg***	N	Y	N	N	Y	Y	Y
12 Levin	Y	N	Y	N	N	N	Y
13 Rivers	Y	N	Y	N	N	N	Y
14 Conyers	Y	Y	Y	Y	N	N	Y
15 Kilpatrick	Y	N	Y	N	N	N	Y
16 Dingell	Y	Y	Y	N	N	N	Y
MINNESOTA							
1 ***Gutknecht***	N	N	N	Y	Y	N	Y
2 Minge	Y	N	Y	N	N	N	Y
3 ***Ramstad***	Y	N	Y	N	N	N	Y
4 Vento	Y	N	Y	N	N	N	Y
5 Sabo	Y	Y	Y	N	N	N	Y
6 Luther	Y	N	Y	N	N	N	Y
7 Peterson	N	N	N	N	Y	N	Y
8 Oberstar	N	N	Y	N	Y	N	Y
MISSISSIPPI							
1 ***Wicker***	N	N	N	N	Y	Y	Y
2 Thompson	Y	N	Y	N	N	N	Y
3 ***Pickering***	N	N	N	Y	Y	Y	Y
4 ***Parker***	?	?	?	?	?	?	?
5 Taylor	N	N	N	Y	Y	N	Y
MISSOURI							
1 Clay	Y	Y	Y	N	N	N	Y
2 ***Talent***	N	N	N	Y	Y	Y	Y
3 Gephardt	Y	N	Y	N	N	N	Y
4 Skelton	N	N	N	N	Y	N	Y
5 McCarthy	Y	N	Y	N	N	N	Y
6 Danner	N	N	Y	Y	Y	Y	Y
7 ***Blunt***	N	N	N	Y	Y	Y	Y
8 ***Emerson***	N	N	N	Y	Y	Y	Y
9 ***Hulshof***	N	N	N	Y	Y	Y	Y
MONTANA							
AL ***Hill***	X	?	?	?	?	?	?
NEBRASKA							
1 ***Bereuter***	N	N	Y	N	Y	Y	Y
2 ***Christensen***	N	N	N	Y	Y	Y	Y
3 ***Barrett***	N	N	N	N	Y	Y	Y
NEVADA							
1 ***Ensign***	N	N	Y	Y	Y	Y	Y
2 ***Gibbons***	N	N	Y	Y	N	Y	Y
NEW HAMPSHIRE							
1 ***Sununu***	N	N	N	Y	Y	Y	Y
2 ***Bass***	Y	N	Y	Y	N	Y	Y
NEW JERSEY							
1 Andrews	Y	N	Y	Y	N	N	Y
2 ***LoBiondo***	N	N	N	Y	Y	Y	Y
3 ***Saxton***	N	N	N	Y	Y	Y	Y
4 ***Smith***	N	N	N	Y	Y	N	?
5 ***Roukema***	Y	N	Y	N	N	Y	Y
6 Pallone	Y	N	Y	N	N	N	Y
7 ***Franks***	Y	N	Y	N	N	Y	Y
8 Pascrell	Y	N	Y	Y	N	N	Y
9 Rothman	Y	N	Y	N	N	N	Y
10 Payne	Y	Y	Y	N	N	N	Y
11 ***Frelinghuysen***	Y	N	Y	N	N	Y	Y
12 ***Pappas***	N	N	N	Y	Y	N	Y
13 Menendez	Y	N	Y	N	N	N	Y
NEW MEXICO							
1 ***Wilson***	N	N	Y	N	Y	Y	Y
2 ***Skeen***	N	N	N	N	Y	Y	Y
3 ***Redmond***	N	N	N	N	Y	Y	Y
NEW YORK							
1 ***Forbes***	N	N	N	Y	Y	Y	Y
2 ***Lazio***	Y	N	Y	N	N	Y	Y
3 ***King***	N	Y	N	N	Y	Y	Y
4 McCarthy	Y	N	Y	N	N	N	Y
6 Meeks	Y	Y	Y	N	N	N	Y
5 Ackerman	Y	Y	Y	N	N	N	Y
7 Manton	N	Y	Y	N	N	N	Y
8 Nadler	Y	Y	Y	Y	N	N	Y
9 Schumer	Y	N	Y	N	N	Y	Y
10 Towns	Y	Y	Y	N	N	N	Y
11 Owens	Y	Y	Y	Y	N	N	Y
12 Velázquez	Y	N	Y	Y	N	N	Y
13 ***Fossella***	N	N	N	Y	Y	Y	Y
14 Maloney	Y	N	Y	N	N	Y	Y
15 Rangel	Y	Y	Y	Y	N	N	Y
16 Serrano	Y	Y	Y	Y	N	N	Y
17 Engel	Y	Y	Y	N	N	N	Y
18 Lowey	Y	N	Y	N	N	Y	Y
19 ***Kelly***	Y	N	Y	N	N	Y	Y
20 ***Gilman***	Y	N	Y	N	N	Y	Y
21 McNulty	?	?	?	?	?	?	?
22 ***Solomon***	N	N	N	Y	Y	Y	Y
23 ***Boehlert***	Y	Y	Y	N	N	Y	Y
24 ***McHugh***	N	N	N	N	Y	Y	Y
25 ***Walsh***	N	N	N	N	Y	Y	Y
26 Hinchey	Y	N	Y	N	N	N	Y
27 ***Paxon***	N	Y	N	Y	Y	Y	Y
28 Slaughter	Y	N	Y	N	N	N	Y
29 LaFalce	N	N	N	N	Y	N	Y
30 ***Quinn***	N	N	N	Y	Y	Y	Y
31 ***Houghton***	Y	N	Y	N	N	Y	Y
NORTH CAROLINA							
1 Clayton	?	?	?	?	?	?	?
2 Etheridge	Y	N	Y	N	N	Y	Y
3 ***Jones***	N	N	N	Y	Y	N	Y
4 Price	Y	N	Y	N	N	Y	Y
5 ***Burr***	N	N	N	Y	Y	Y	Y
6 ***Coble***	N	N	N	Y	Y	Y	Y
7 McIntyre	N	N	Y	Y	N	N	Y
8 Hefner	Y	Y	Y	N	N	N	Y
9 ***Myrick***	N	–	N	Y	Y	Y	Y
10 ***Ballenger***	N	N	N	N	Y	Y	Y
11 ***Taylor***	N	N	N	N	Y	Y	Y
12 Watt	Y	Y	Y	N	N	N	Y
NORTH DAKOTA							
AL Pomeroy	Y	N	Y	N	N	N	Y
OHIO							
1 ***Chabot***	N	N	N	Y	Y	Y	Y
2 ***Portman***	N	N	N	Y	Y	Y	Y
3 Hall	N	N	N	N	Y	N	Y
4 ***Oxley***	N	N	Y	N	N	Y	Y
5 ***Gillmor***	N	N	N	Y	Y	Y	Y
6 Strickland	Y	N	Y	Y	N	N	Y
7 ***Hobson***	N	N	Y	Y	N	Y	Y
8 ***Boehner***	N	N	N	N	Y	Y	Y
9 Kaptur	N	N	Y	Y	N	N	Y
10 Kucinich	N	N	N	Y	Y	N	Y
11 Stokes	Y	Y	Y	N	N	N	Y
12 ***Kasich***	N	N	N	N	N	Y	Y
13 Brown	Y	N	Y	Y	N	N	Y
14 Sawyer	Y	N	Y	N	N	N	Y
15 ***Pryce***	Y	N	Y	N	N	Y	Y
16 ***Regula***	N	N	N	Y	N	Y	?
17 Traficant	N	N	N	Y	Y	N	Y
18 ***Ney***	N	N	N	Y	Y	N	Y
19 ***LaTourette***	N	N	N	N	Y	N	Y
OKLAHOMA							
1 ***Largent***	N	N	N	Y	Y	Y	Y
2 ***Coburn***	N	N	N	N	Y	Y	Y
3 ***Watkins***	N	N	N	Y	Y	Y	Y
4 ***Watts***	N	N	N	Y	Y	Y	Y
5 ***Istook***	N	N	N	Y	Y	Y	Y
6 ***Lucas***	N	N	N	Y	Y	Y	Y
OREGON							
1 Furse	Y	Y	Y	N	N	N	Y
2 ***Smith***	N	N	N	N	Y	Y	?
3 Blumenauer	Y	N	Y	N	N	N	Y
4 DeFazio	Y	N	Y	Y	N	N	Y
5 Hooley	Y	N	Y	N	N	Y	Y
PENNSYLVANIA							
1 Brady	Y	N	Y	N	N	N	Y
2 Fattah	Y	Y	Y	N	N	N	Y
3 Borski	N	N	Y	N	N	N	Y
4 Klink	N	N	N	Y	Y	N	?
5 ***Peterson***	N	N	N	Y	Y	Y	Y
6 Holden	N	N	N	Y	Y	N	Y
7 ***Weldon***	N	N	N	Y	Y	Y	Y
8 ***Greenwood***	Y	N	Y	N	N	Y	Y
9 ***Shuster***	N	N	N	Y	Y	Y	?
10 ***McDade***	N	Y	N	N	?	?	?
11 Kanjorski	N	Y	Y	N	N	N	Y
12 Murtha	N	Y	Y	N	N	N	Y
13 ***Fox***	N	N	Y	Y	N	Y	Y
14 Coyne	Y	N	Y	N	N	N	Y
15 McHale	N	Y	Y	N	Y	Y	Y
16 ***Pitts***	N	N	N	Y	Y	Y	Y
17 ***Gekas***	N	N	N	Y	Y	Y	Y
18 Doyle	N	N	N	Y	Y	N	Y
19 ***Goodling***	N	N	N	Y	Y	Y	Y
20 Mascara	N	N	N	Y	Y	N	Y
21 ***English***	N	N	N	Y	Y	Y	Y
RHODE ISLAND							
1 Kennedy	Y	N	Y	Y	N	N	Y
2 Weygand	N	N	Y	N	N	N	Y
SOUTH CAROLINA							
1 ***Sanford***	N	N	N	Y	Y	N	Y
2 ***Spence***	N	N	N	Y	Y	Y	Y
3 ***Graham***	N	N	N	Y	Y	Y	Y
4 ***Inglis***	N	N	N	Y	Y	N	Y
5 Spratt	Y	N	Y	N	N	N	Y
6 Clyburn	Y	N	Y	N	N	N	Y
SOUTH DAKOTA							
AL ***Thune***	N	N	N	N	Y	Y	Y
TENNESSEE							
1 ***Jenkins***	N	N	N	N	Y	Y	Y
2 ***Duncan***	N	N	N	Y	Y	N	Y
3 ***Wamp***	N	N	N	Y	Y	Y	Y
4 ***Hilleary***	N	N	N	Y	Y	N	Y
5 Clement	Y	N	Y	N	N	N	Y
6 Gordon	Y	N	Y	N	N	N	Y
7 ***Bryant***	N	N	N	Y	Y	Y	Y
8 Tanner	Y	N	Y	N	N	N	Y
9 Ford	+	–	+	–	–	–	+
TEXAS							
1 Sandlin	Y	N	Y	N	N	Y	Y
2 Turner	N	N	Y	Y	N	N	Y
3 ***Johnson, Sam***	N	Y	N	Y	Y	Y	Y
4 Hall	N	N	N	Y	Y	Y	Y
5 ***Sessions***	N	N	N	Y	Y	Y	Y
6 ***Barton***	N	N	N	N	Y	N	Y
7 ***Archer***	N	N	N	N	Y	Y	Y
8 ***Brady***	N	N	N	N	Y	Y	Y
9 Lampson	N	N	Y	N	N	Y	Y
10 Doggett	Y	N	Y	N	N	Y	Y
11 Edwards	N	N	Y	N	N	N	Y
12 ***Granger***	N	N	Y	N	N	Y	Y
13 ***Thornberry***	N	N	N	Y	Y	Y	Y
14 ***Paul***	N	N	N	Y	Y	N	Y
15 Hinojosa	Y	N	Y	N	N	N	Y
16 Reyes	Y	N	Y	N	N	N	Y
17 Stenholm	N	N	N	N	Y	N	Y
18 Jackson-Lee	Y	N	Y	N	N	N	Y
19 ***Combest***	N	N	N	N	Y	Y	Y
20 Gonzalez	?	?	?	?	?	?	?
21 ***Smith***	N	N	N	Y	Y	Y	Y
22 ***DeLay***	N	Y	N	N	Y	Y	Y
23 ***Bonilla***	Y	N	N	N	Y	Y	Y
24 Frost	Y	N	Y	N	N	N	Y
25 Bentsen	Y	N	Y	N	N	Y	Y
26 ***Armey***	N	N	N	Y	Y	Y	Y
27 Ortiz	X	–	X	–	#	#	+
28 Rodriguez	Y	N	Y	N	N	N	Y
29 Green	Y	N	Y	N	N	N	Y
30 Johnson, E.B.	Y	Y	Y	N	N	N	Y
UTAH							
1 ***Hansen***	N	N	N	N	Y	Y	Y
2 ***Cook***	N	N	Y	Y	N	Y	Y
3 ***Cannon***	N	Y	N	Y	Y	Y	Y
VERMONT							
AL *Sanders*	Y	N	Y	Y	N	N	Y
VIRGINIA							
1 ***Bateman***	N	N	N	N	Y	Y	?
2 Pickett	Y	N	Y	N	N	Y	Y
3 Scott	Y	Y	Y	N	N	N	Y
4 Sisisky	Y	N	Y	N	N	Y	Y
5 Goode	N	N	N	Y	Y	N	Y
6 ***Goodlatte***	N	N	N	Y	Y	N	Y
7 ***Bliley***	N	N	N	N	Y	Y	Y
8 Moran	Y	Y	Y	N	N	N	Y
9 Boucher	Y	N	Y	N	N	Y	Y
10 ***Wolf***	N	N	N	Y	Y	Y	Y
11 ***Davis***	Y	N	Y	N	N	Y	Y
WASHINGTON							
1 ***White***	Y	N	N	N	Y	Y	Y
2 ***Metcalf***	N	N	N	Y	Y	Y	Y
3 ***Smith, Linda***	N	N	N	Y	Y	N	Y
4 ***Hastings***	N	N	N	Y	Y	Y	Y
5 ***Nethercutt***	N	N	Y	Y	Y	Y	Y
6 Dicks	Y	N	Y	N	N	Y	Y
7 McDermott	Y	Y	Y	N	N	N	Y
8 ***Dunn***	N	N	Y	N	Y	Y	Y
9 Smith, Adam	Y	N	Y	N	N	N	Y
WEST VIRGINIA							
1 Mollohan	N	Y	N	Y	Y	N	Y
2 Wise	Y	N	Y	N	N	N	Y
3 Rahall	N	Y	N	N	Y	N	Y
WISCONSIN							
1 ***Neumann***	N	N	N	Y	Y	N	Y
2 ***Klug***	N	N	Y	Y	N	Y	Y
3 Kind	Y	N	Y	N	N	N	Y
4 Kleczka	N	N	Y	N	N	N	Y
5 Barrett	Y	N	Y	N	N	N	Y
6 ***Petri***	N	N	N	Y	Y	N	Y
7 Obey	Y	N	Y	N	N	N	Y
8 Johnson	Y	N	Y	N	N	N	Y
9 ***Sensenbrenner***	N	N	N	Y	Y	N	Y
WYOMING							
AL ***Cubin***	N	Y	N	Y	Y	Y	Y

Southern states - Ala., Ark., Fla., Ga., Ky., La., Miss., N.C., Okla., S.C., Tenn., Texas, Va.

House Votes 295, 296, 297, 298, 299, 300, 301

295. HR 4194. Fiscal 1999 VA-HUD Appropriations/Housing Vouchers Funding Increase. Stokes, D-Ohio, en bloc amendment to increase by $97 million the funds provided for new Section 8 housing vouchers for families making the transition from welfare to work. Rejected 201-215: R 14-209; D 186-6 (ND 139-5, SD 47-1); I 1-0. July 17, 1998.

296. HR 4194. Fiscal 1999 VA-HUD Appropriations/Public Housing Overhaul. Lazio, R-N.Y. amendment to overhaul public housing management and allow increased local control over rents and occupancy standards. Adopted 230-181: R 215-4; D 15-176 (ND 8-136, SD 7-40); I 0-1. July 17, 1998.

297. HR 3874. Nutrition Programs Reauthorization/Passage. Goodling, R-Pa., motion to suspend the rules and pass the bill to reauthorize through 2003 the Women, Infants and Children nutrition program and a national summer food program for children of low-income families. Motion agreed to 383-1: R 210-1; D 172-0 (ND 129-0, SD 43-0); I 1-0. July 20, 1998. A two-thirds majority of those present and voting (256 in this case) is required for passage under the suspension of the rules.

298. H Con Res 208. Affordable Housing and Home Ownership Opportunities/Passage. Leach, R-Iowa, motion to suspend the rules and pass the bill to express the sense of Congress that the nation's priorities should include providing access to safe affordable housing and expanding home ownership activities. Motion agreed to 390-0: R 214-0; D 175-0 (ND 132-0, SD 43-0); I 1-0. July 20, 1998. A two-thirds majority of those present and voting (260 in this case) is required for passage under suspension of the rules.

299. H Res 392. Japanese Economic Reform/Passage. Bereuter, R-Neb. motion to suspend the rules and pass the bill to express the sense of the House that Japan should urgently undertake several economic reforms in order to enhance cooperation with its allies. Motion agreed to 391-2: R 213-2; D 177-0 (ND 133-0, SD 44-0); I 1-0. July 20, 1998. A two-thirds majority of those present and voting (262 in this case) is required for passage under suspension of the rules.

300. H Con Res 301. Commitment to Taiwan/Passage. Gilman, R-N.Y. motion to suspend the rules and pass the bill to express the sense of Congress affirming its longstanding commitment to Taiwan in accordance with the Taiwan Relations Act. Motion agreed to 390-1: R 213-1; D 176-0 (ND 132-0, SD 44-0); I 1-0. July 20, 1998. A two-thirds majority of those present and voting (261 in this case) is required for passage under suspension of the rules.

301. HR 2183. Campaign Finance Overhaul/Shays-Meehan Substitute — White House Facilities. Wicker, R-Miss., amendment to the Shays-Meehan substitute amendment to the bill to overhaul campaign finance laws. The amendment would prohibit the use of White House facilities in exchange for campaign donations. Adopted 391-4: R 218-0; D 172-4 (ND 130-2, SD 42-2); I 1-0. July 20, 1998.

Key

- **Y** Voted for (yea).
- **#** Paired for.
- **+** Announced for.
- **N** Voted against (nay).
- **X** Paired against.
- **−** Announced against.
- **P** Voted "present."
- **C** Voted "present" to avoid possible conflict of interest.
- **?** Did not vote or otherwise make a position known.

Democrats • **Republicans** • Independent

	295	296	297	298	299	300	301
ALABAMA							
1 **Callahan**	N	?	Y	Y	Y	Y	Y
2 **Everett**	N	Y	Y	Y	Y	Y	Y
3 **Riley**	N	Y	Y	Y	Y	Y	Y
4 **Aderholt**	N	Y	Y	Y	Y	Y	Y
5 Cramer	Y	N	Y	Y	Y	Y	Y
6 **Bachus**	N	Y	Y	Y	Y	Y	Y
7 Hilliard	Y	N	?	?	?	?	?
ALASKA							
AL **Young**	N	Y	Y	Y	Y	Y	Y
ARIZONA							
1 **Salmon**	N	Y	Y	Y	Y	Y	Y
2 Pastor	Y	N	Y	Y	Y	Y	Y
3 **Stump**	N	Y	Y	Y	Y	Y	Y
4 **Shadegg**	N	Y	Y	Y	Y	Y	Y
5 **Kolbe**	N	Y	Y	Y	Y	Y	Y
6 **Hayworth**	N	Y	Y	Y	Y	Y	Y
ARKANSAS							
1 Berry	Y	N	Y	Y	Y	Y	Y
2 Snyder	?	?	Y	Y	Y	Y	Y
3 **Hutchinson**	N	Y	Y	Y	Y	Y	Y
4 **Dickey**	N	Y	Y	Y	Y	Y	Y
CALIFORNIA							
1 **Riggs**	N	Y	+	+	+	+	+
2 **Herger**	N	Y	Y	Y	Y	Y	Y
3 Fazio	Y	N	?	Y	Y	Y	Y
4 **Doolittle**	−	+	Y	Y	Y	Y	Y
5 Matsui	Y	N	Y	Y	Y	Y	Y
6 Woolsey	Y	N	Y	Y	Y	Y	Y
7 Miller	Y	N	Y	Y	Y	Y	Y
8 Pelosi	Y	N	Y	Y	Y	Y	Y
9 Lee	Y	N	Y	Y	Y	Y	Y
10 Tauscher	Y	N	Y	Y	Y	Y	Y
11 **Pombo**	N	Y	Y	Y	Y	Y	Y
12 Lantos	Y	N	Y	Y	Y	Y	Y
13 Stark	Y	N	Y	Y	Y	Y	Y
14 Eshoo	Y	N	Y	Y	Y	Y	Y
15 **Campbell**	Y	Y	Y	Y	Y	Y	Y
16 Lofgren	Y	N	Y	Y	Y	Y	Y
17 Farr	Y	N	Y	Y	Y	Y	Y
18 Condit	Y	Y	Y	Y	Y	Y	Y
19 **Radanovich**	N	Y	Y	Y	Y	Y	Y
20 Dooley	Y	Y	Y	Y	Y	Y	Y
21 **Thomas**	N	Y	Y	Y	Y	Y	Y
22 Capps, L.	Y	N	Y	Y	Y	Y	Y
23 **Gallegly**	N	Y	Y	Y	Y	Y	Y
24 Sherman	Y	N	Y	Y	Y	Y	Y
25 **McKeon**	N	Y	Y	Y	Y	Y	Y
26 Berman	Y	N	Y	Y	Y	Y	?
27 **Rogan**	N	Y	Y	Y	Y	Y	Y
28 **Dreier**	N	Y	Y	Y	Y	Y	Y
29 Waxman	Y	N	Y	Y	Y	Y	Y
30 Becerra	Y	N	Y	Y	Y	Y	Y
31 Martinez	Y	N	Y	Y	Y	Y	Y
32 Dixon	Y	N	?	?	?	?	?
33 Roybal-Allard	+	−	+	+	+	+	+
34 Torres	Y	N	?	?	?	?	?
35 Waters	Y	N	Y	Y	Y	Y	Y
36 Harman	?	?	Y	Y	Y	Y	Y
37 Millender-McD.	+	−	+	+	+	+	+

	295	296	297	298	299	300	301
38 **Horn**	N	Y	+	Y	Y	Y	Y
39 **Royce**	N	Y	Y	Y	Y	Y	Y
40 **Lewis**	N	Y	Y	Y	Y	Y	Y
41 **Kim**	N	Y	Y	Y	Y	Y	Y
42 Brown	Y	N	?	Y	Y	Y	Y
43 **Calvert**	N	Y	Y	Y	Y	Y	Y
44 **Bono, M.**	N	Y	Y	Y	Y	Y	Y
45 **Rohrabacher**	N	Y	Y	Y	Y	Y	Y
46 Sanchez	Y	N	Y	Y	Y	Y	Y
47 **Cox**	N	Y	Y	Y	Y	Y	Y
48 **Packard**	N	Y	Y	Y	Y	Y	Y
49 **Bilbray**	N	Y	Y	Y	Y	Y	Y
50 Filner	+	−	Y	Y	Y	Y	Y
51 **Cunningham**	N	Y	Y	Y	Y	Y	Y
52 **Hunter**	N	Y	Y	Y	Y	Y	Y
COLORADO							
1 DeGette	Y	N	Y	Y	Y	Y	Y
2 Skaggs	Y	N	Y	Y	Y	Y	Y
3 **McInnis**	N	Y	Y	Y	Y	Y	Y
4 **Schaffer**	N	Y	Y	Y	Y	Y	Y
5 **Hefley**	N	Y	Y	Y	N	Y	Y
6 **Schaefer**	N	Y	Y	Y	Y	Y	Y
CONNECTICUT							
1 Kennelly	?	?	Y	Y	Y	Y	Y
2 Gejdenson	Y	N	Y	Y	Y	Y	Y
3 DeLauro	Y	N	Y	Y	Y	Y	Y
4 **Shays**	N	Y	Y	Y	Y	Y	Y
5 Maloney	Y	N	+	+	+	+	Y
6 **Johnson**	N	Y	Y	Y	Y	Y	Y
DELAWARE							
AL **Castle**	N	Y	Y	Y	Y	Y	Y
FLORIDA							
1 **Scarborough**	N	Y	Y	Y	Y	Y	Y
2 Boyd	Y	N	Y	Y	Y	Y	Y
3 Brown	Y	N	Y	Y	Y	Y	Y
4 **Fowler**	N	Y	Y	Y	Y	Y	Y
5 Thurman	Y	N	Y	Y	Y	Y	Y
6 **Stearns**	N	Y	Y	Y	Y	Y	Y
7 **Mica**	N	+	Y	Y	Y	Y	Y
8 **McCollum**	N	Y	Y	Y	Y	Y	Y
9 **Bilirakis**	N	Y	?	?	?	+	+
10 **Young**	N	Y	Y	Y	Y	Y	Y
11 Davis	Y	N	Y	Y	Y	Y	Y
12 **Canady**	N	Y	Y	Y	Y	Y	Y
13 **Miller**	N	Y	Y	Y	Y	Y	Y
14 **Goss**	N	Y	Y	Y	Y	Y	Y
15 **Weldon**	N	Y	Y	Y	Y	Y	Y
16 **Foley**	N	Y	Y	Y	Y	Y	Y
17 Meek	Y	N	Y	Y	Y	Y	Y
18 **Ros-Lehtinen**	Y	Y	+	+	+	+	Y
19 Wexler	Y	N	Y	Y	Y	Y	N
20 Deutsch	Y	N	Y	Y	Y	Y	Y
21 **Diaz-Balart**	Y	Y	+	+	+	+	Y
22 **Shaw**	N	Y	Y	Y	Y	Y	Y
23 Hastings	Y	N	Y	Y	Y	Y	N
GEORGIA							
1 **Kingston**	N	Y	Y	Y	Y	Y	Y
2 Bishop	Y	N	Y	Y	Y	Y	Y
3 **Collins**	N	Y	Y	Y	Y	Y	Y
4 McKinney	Y	N	Y	Y	Y	Y	Y
5 Lewis	?	?	?	?	?	?	?
6 **Gingrich**							
7 **Barr**	N	Y	Y	Y	Y	Y	Y
8 **Chambliss**	N	Y	Y	Y	Y	Y	Y
9 **Deal**	N	Y	Y	Y	Y	Y	Y
10 **Norwood**	N	Y	?	?	?	?	Y
11 **Linder**	N	Y	Y	Y	Y	Y	Y
HAWAII							
1 Abercrombie	Y	N	Y	Y	Y	Y	Y
2 Mink	Y	N	Y	Y	Y	Y	Y
IDAHO							
1 **Chenoweth**	N	Y	Y	Y	Y	Y	Y
2 **Crapo**	N	Y	Y	Y	Y	Y	Y
ILLINOIS							
1 Rush	Y	N	Y	Y	Y	Y	Y
2 Jackson	Y	N	Y	Y	Y	Y	Y
3 Lipinski	Y	N	?	?	?	?	Y
4 Gutierrez	Y	N	?	Y	Y	Y	Y
5 Blagojevich	Y	N	?	?	?	?	Y
6 **Hyde**	N	Y	Y	Y	Y	Y	Y
7 Davis	Y	N	Y	Y	Y	Y	Y
8 **Crane**	N	Y	Y	Y	Y	Y	Y
9 Yates	Y	N	Y	Y	Y	Y	?
10 **Porter**	N	Y	Y	Y	Y	Y	Y
11 **Weller**	N	Y	Y	Y	Y	Y	Y
12 Costello	Y	N	Y	Y	Y	Y	Y

ND Northern Democrats   SD Southern Democrats

	295	296	297	298	299	300	301
13 ***Fawell***	N	Y	?	?	?	?	Y
14 ***Hastert***	N	Y	Y	Y	Y	Y	Y
15 ***Ewing***	N	Y	Y	Y	Y	Y	Y
16 ***Manzullo***	N	Y	Y	Y	Y	Y	Y
17 Evans	Y	N	Y	Y	Y	Y	Y
18 ***LaHood***	N	Y	Y	Y	Y	Y	Y
19 Poshard	Y	N	?	?	?	?	?
20 ***Shimkus***	N	Y	Y	Y	Y	Y	Y
INDIANA							
1 Visclosky	Y	N	Y	Y	Y	Y	Y
2 ***McIntosh***	N	Y	Y	Y	Y	Y	Y
3 Roemer	Y	N	Y	Y	Y	Y	Y
4 ***Souder***	N	Y	Y	Y	Y	Y	Y
5 ***Buyer***	N	Y	Y	Y	Y	Y	Y
6 ***Burton***	N	Y	Y	Y	Y	Y	Y
7 ***Pease***	N	Y	Y	Y	Y	Y	Y
8 ***Hostettler***	N	Y	Y	Y	Y	Y	Y
9 Hamilton	Y	N	Y	Y	Y	Y	Y
10 Carson	Y	N	Y	Y	Y	Y	Y
IOWA							
1 ***Leach***	N	Y	Y	Y	Y	Y	Y
2 ***Nussle***	N	Y	Y	Y	Y	Y	Y
3 Boswell	Y	N	Y	Y	Y	Y	Y
4 ***Ganske***	N	Y	Y	Y	Y	Y	Y
5 ***Latham***	N	Y	Y	Y	Y	Y	Y
KANSAS							
1 ***Moran***	N	Y	Y	Y	Y	Y	Y
2 ***Ryun***	N	Y	Y	Y	Y	Y	Y
3 ***Snowbarger***	N	Y	Y	Y	Y	Y	Y
4 ***Tiahrt***	N	Y	Y	Y	Y	Y	Y
KENTUCKY							
1 ***Whitfield***	N	Y	?	?	Y	Y	Y
2 ***Lewis***	N	Y	Y	Y	Y	Y	Y
3 ***Northup***	N	Y	Y	Y	Y	Y	Y
4 ***Bunning***	N	Y	Y	Y	Y	Y	Y
5 ***Rogers***	N	Y	Y	Y	Y	Y	Y
6 Baesler	Y	Y	Y	Y	Y	Y	Y
LOUISIANA							
1 ***Livingston***	N	?	Y	Y	Y	Y	Y
2 Jefferson	Y	?	?	?	?	?	?
3 ***Tauzin***	N	Y	Y	Y	Y	Y	Y
4 ***McCrery***	N	Y	Y	Y	Y	Y	Y
5 ***Cooksey***	N	Y	Y	Y	Y	Y	Y
6 ***Baker***	N	Y	?	?	?	?	?
7 John	?	?	?	?	?	?	?
MAINE							
1 Allen	Y	N	Y	Y	Y	Y	Y
2 Baldacci	Y	N	Y	Y	Y	Y	Y
MARYLAND							
1 ***Gilchrest***	N	Y	Y	Y	Y	Y	Y
2 ***Ehrlich***	N	Y	?	?	?	?	?
3 Cardin	Y	N	Y	Y	Y	Y	Y
4 Wynn	Y	N	Y	Y	Y	Y	Y
5 Hoyer	Y	N	Y	Y	Y	Y	Y
6 ***Bartlett***	N	Y	Y	Y	Y	Y	Y
7 Cummings	Y	N	Y	Y	Y	Y	Y
8 ***Morella***	Y	Y	Y	Y	Y	Y	Y
MASSACHUSETTS							
1 Olver	Y	N	Y	Y	Y	Y	Y
2 Neal	Y	N	Y	Y	Y	Y	Y
3 McGovern	Y	N	Y	Y	Y	Y	Y
4 Frank	Y	N	Y	Y	Y	Y	Y
5 Meehan	Y	N	Y	Y	Y	Y	Y
6 Tierney	Y	N	Y	Y	Y	Y	Y
7 Markey	Y	N	Y	Y	Y	Y	Y
8 Kennedy	Y	N	Y	Y	Y	Y	Y
9 Moakley	?	?	Y	Y	Y	Y	?
10 Delahunt	Y	N	Y	Y	Y	Y	Y
MICHIGAN							
1 Stupak	N	N	Y	Y	Y	Y	Y
2 ***Hoekstra***	N	Y	Y	Y	Y	Y	Y
3 ***Ehlers***	N	Y	Y	Y	Y	Y	Y
4 ***Camp***	N	Y	Y	Y	Y	Y	Y
5 Barcia	Y	N	Y	Y	Y	Y	Y
6 ***Upton***	N	Y	Y	Y	Y	Y	Y
7 ***Smith***	N	Y	Y	Y	Y	Y	Y
8 Stabenow	Y	N	Y	Y	Y	Y	Y
9 Kildee	Y	N	Y	Y	Y	Y	Y
10 Bonior	Y	N	Y	Y	Y	Y	Y
11 ***Knollenberg***	N	Y	Y	Y	Y	Y	Y
12 Levin	Y	N	Y	Y	Y	Y	Y
13 Rivers	Y	N	Y	Y	Y	Y	Y
14 Conyers	Y	N	Y	Y	Y	Y	Y
15 Kilpatrick	Y	N	+	+	+	+	Y
16 Dingell	Y	N	Y	Y	Y	Y	Y

	295	296	297	298	299	300	301
MINNESOTA							
1 ***Gutknecht***	N	Y	Y	Y	Y	Y	Y
2 Minge	Y	N	Y	Y	Y	Y	Y
3 ***Ramstad***	Y	Y	Y	Y	Y	Y	Y
4 Vento	Y	N	Y	Y	Y	Y	Y
5 Sabo	Y	N	Y	Y	Y	Y	Y
6 Luther	Y	Y	Y	Y	Y	Y	Y
7 Peterson	Y	N	Y	Y	Y	Y	Y
8 Oberstar	Y	N	Y	Y	Y	Y	Y
MISSISSIPPI							
1 ***Wicker***	N	Y	Y	Y	Y	Y	Y
2 Thompson	Y	N	?	?	?	?	?
3 ***Pickering***	N	Y	Y	Y	Y	Y	+
4 ***Parker***	?	?	Y	Y	Y	Y	Y
5 Taylor	Y	Y	Y	Y	Y	Y	Y
MISSOURI							
1 Clay	Y	N	Y	Y	Y	Y	Y
2 ***Talent***	N	Y	Y	Y	Y	Y	Y
3 Gephardt	Y	N	?	?	?	?	?
4 Skelton	Y	Y	Y	Y	Y	Y	Y
5 McCarthy	Y	N	Y	Y	Y	Y	Y
6 Danner	Y	Y	?	?	?	?	?
7 ***Blunt***	N	Y	Y	Y	Y	Y	Y
8 ***Emerson***	N	Y	Y	Y	Y	Y	Y
9 ***Hulshof***	N	Y	Y	Y	Y	Y	Y
MONTANA							
AL ***Hill***	?	?	Y	Y	Y	Y	Y
NEBRASKA							
1 ***Bereuter***	N	Y	Y	Y	Y	Y	Y
2 ***Christensen***	N	Y	Y	Y	Y	Y	Y
3 ***Barrett***	N	Y	Y	Y	Y	Y	Y
NEVADA							
1 ***Ensign***	Y	Y	Y	Y	Y	Y	Y
2 ***Gibbons***	N	Y	Y	Y	Y	Y	Y
NEW HAMPSHIRE							
1 ***Sununu***	N	Y	Y	Y	Y	Y	Y
2 ***Bass***	N	Y	Y	Y	Y	Y	Y
NEW JERSEY							
1 Andrews	Y	N	Y	Y	Y	Y	Y
2 ***LoBiondo***	Y	Y	Y	Y	Y	Y	Y
3 ***Saxton***	N	Y	Y	Y	Y	Y	Y
4 ***Smith***	Y	Y	Y	Y	Y	Y	Y
5 ***Roukema***	N	Y	Y	Y	Y	Y	Y
6 Pallone	Y	N	Y	Y	Y	Y	Y
7 ***Franks***	N	Y	Y	Y	Y	Y	Y
8 Pascrell	Y	N	Y	Y	Y	Y	Y
9 Rothman	Y	N	Y	Y	Y	Y	Y
10 Payne	Y	N	Y	Y	Y	Y	Y
11 ***Frelinghuysen***	N	Y	Y	Y	Y	Y	Y
12 ***Pappas***	N	Y	Y	Y	Y	Y	Y
13 Menendez	Y	N	+	Y	Y	Y	Y
NEW MEXICO							
1 ***Wilson***	N	Y	Y	Y	Y	Y	Y
2 ***Skeen***	N	Y	Y	Y	Y	Y	Y
3 ***Redmond***	N	Y	Y	Y	Y	Y	Y
NEW YORK							
1 ***Forbes***	N	Y	Y	Y	Y	Y	Y
2 ***Lazio***	N	Y	Y	Y	Y	Y	Y
3 ***King***	N	Y	Y	Y	Y	Y	Y
4 McCarthy	Y	N	Y	Y	Y	Y	Y
5 Ackerman	Y	N	?	?	?	?	?
6 Meeks	Y	N	Y	Y	Y	Y	Y
7 Manton	Y	N	Y	Y	Y	Y	Y
8 Nadler	Y	N	Y	Y	Y	Y	Y
9 Schumer	Y	N	Y	Y	Y	Y	Y
10 Towns	Y	N	?	?	?	?	?
11 Owens	Y	N	+	+	+	+	Y
12 Velázquez	Y	N	Y	Y	Y	Y	Y
13 ***Fossella***	N	Y	Y	Y	Y	Y	Y
14 Maloney	Y	N	+	+	+	+	+
15 Rangel	Y	N	Y	Y	Y	Y	Y
16 Serrano	Y	N	Y	Y	Y	Y	Y
17 Engel	Y	N	Y	Y	Y	Y	Y
18 Lowey	Y	N	Y	Y	Y	Y	Y
19 ***Kelly***	N	Y	Y	Y	Y	Y	Y
20 ***Gilman***	Y	Y	Y	Y	Y	Y	Y
21 McNulty	?	?	Y	Y	Y	Y	Y
22 ***Solomon***	N	Y	Y	Y	Y	Y	Y
23 ***Boehlert***	N	Y	Y	Y	Y	Y	Y
24 ***McHugh***	Y	N	Y	Y	Y	Y	Y
25 ***Walsh***	N	N	?	?	?	?	Y
26 Hinchey	Y	N	Y	Y	Y	Y	Y
27 ***Paxon***	N	Y	?	?	?	?	Y
28 Slaughter	Y	N	Y	Y	Y	Y	Y
29 LaFalce	Y	N	Y	Y	Y	Y	Y

	295	296	297	298	299	300	301
30 ***Quinn***	Y	Y	Y	Y	Y	Y	Y
31 ***Houghton***	N	Y	Y	Y	Y	Y	Y
NORTH CAROLINA							
1 Clayton	Y	N	Y	Y	Y	Y	Y
2 Etheridge	Y	N	Y	Y	Y	Y	Y
3 ***Jones***	N	Y	Y	Y	Y	Y	Y
4 Price	Y	N	Y	Y	Y	Y	Y
5 ***Burr***	N	Y	Y	Y	Y	Y	Y
6 ***Coble***	N	Y	+	+	+	+	+
7 McIntyre	Y	Y	Y	Y	Y	Y	Y
8 Hefner	Y	N	?	?	?	?	?
9 ***Myrick***	N	Y	Y	Y	Y	Y	Y
10 ***Ballenger***	N	Y	Y	Y	Y	Y	Y
11 ***Taylor***	N	Y	Y	Y	Y	Y	Y
12 Watt	Y	N	Y	Y	Y	Y	Y
NORTH DAKOTA							
AL Pomeroy	Y	N	?	?	Y	Y	Y
OHIO							
1 ***Chabot***	N	Y	Y	Y	Y	Y	Y
2 ***Portman***	N	Y	Y	Y	Y	Y	Y
3 Hall	Y	N	Y	Y	Y	Y	Y
4 ***Oxley***	N	Y	Y	Y	Y	Y	Y
5 ***Gillmor***	N	Y	Y	Y	Y	Y	Y
6 Strickland	Y	Y	Y	Y	Y	Y	Y
7 ***Hobson***	N	Y	Y	Y	Y	Y	Y
8 ***Boehner***	N	Y	Y	Y	Y	Y	Y
9 Kaptur	Y	N	Y	Y	Y	Y	Y
10 Kucinich	Y	N	Y	Y	Y	Y	Y
11 Stokes	Y	N	?	?	?	?	?
12 ***Kasich***	N	Y	Y	Y	Y	Y	Y
13 Brown	Y	N	Y	Y	Y	Y	Y
14 Sawyer	Y	N	Y	Y	Y	Y	Y
15 ***Pryce***	N	Y	Y	Y	Y	Y	Y
16 ***Regula***	N	Y	Y	Y	Y	Y	Y
17 Traficant	Y	Y	Y	Y	?	?	?
18 ***Ney***	N	Y	Y	Y	Y	Y	Y
19 ***LaTourette***	N	Y	Y	Y	Y	Y	Y
OKLAHOMA							
1 ***Largent***	N	Y	Y	Y	Y	Y	Y
2 ***Coburn***	N	Y	Y	Y	Y	Y	Y
3 ***Watkins***	N	Y	Y	Y	Y	Y	Y
4 ***Watts***	N	Y	Y	Y	Y	Y	Y
5 ***Istook***	N	Y	Y	Y	Y	Y	Y
6 ***Lucas***	N	Y	Y	Y	Y	Y	Y
OREGON							
1 Furse	Y	N	Y	Y	Y	Y	Y
2 ***Smith***	N	Y	Y	Y	Y	Y	Y
3 Blumenauer	Y	N	Y	Y	Y	Y	Y
4 DeFazio	Y	N	Y	Y	Y	Y	Y
5 Hooley	Y	N	Y	Y	Y	Y	Y
PENNSYLVANIA							
1 Brady	Y	N	Y	Y	Y	Y	Y
2 Fattah	Y	N	?	?	?	?	Y
3 Borski	N	Y	Y	Y	Y	Y	Y
4 Klink	N	Y	Y	Y	Y	Y	Y
5 ***Peterson***	N	Y	Y	Y	Y	Y	Y
6 Holden	N	N	Y	Y	Y	Y	Y
7 ***Weldon***	N	Y	Y	Y	Y	Y	Y
8 ***Greenwood***	N	Y	Y	Y	Y	Y	Y
9 ***Shuster***	N	Y	Y	Y	Y	Y	Y
10 ***McDade***	N	Y	?	?	?	?	?
11 Kanjorski	Y	N	Y	Y	Y	Y	N
12 Murtha	N	N	Y	Y	Y	Y	N
13 ***Fox***	Y	Y	Y	Y	Y	Y	Y
14 Coyne	Y	N	Y	Y	Y	Y	Y
15 McHale	Y	N	Y	Y	Y	Y	Y
16 ***Pitts***	N	Y	Y	Y	Y	Y	Y
17 ***Gekas***	N	Y	Y	Y	Y	Y	Y
18 Doyle	Y	N	Y	Y	Y	Y	Y
19 ***Goodling***	N	Y	Y	Y	Y	Y	Y
20 Mascara	Y	N	Y	Y	Y	Y	Y
21 ***English***	Y	Y	Y	Y	Y	Y	Y
RHODE ISLAND							
1 Kennedy	Y	N	Y	Y	Y	Y	Y
2 Weygand	Y	N	Y	Y	Y	Y	Y
SOUTH CAROLINA							
1 ***Sanford***	N	Y	Y	Y	Y	Y	Y
2 ***Spence***	N	Y	Y	Y	Y	?	Y
3 ***Graham***	N	Y	Y	Y	Y	Y	Y
4 ***Inglis***	N	Y	Y	Y	Y	Y	Y
5 Spratt	Y	N	Y	Y	Y	Y	Y
6 Clyburn	Y	N	Y	Y	Y	Y	Y
SOUTH DAKOTA							
AL ***Thune***	N	Y	Y	Y	Y	Y	Y

	295	296	297	298	299	300	301
TENNESSEE							
1 ***Jenkins***	N	Y	Y	Y	Y	Y	Y
2 ***Duncan***	N	Y	Y	Y	Y	Y	Y
3 ***Wamp***	N	Y	Y	Y	Y	Y	Y
4 ***Hilleary***	N	Y	?	Y	Y	Y	Y
5 Clement	Y	N	Y	Y	Y	Y	Y
6 Gordon	Y	N	Y	Y	Y	Y	Y
7 ***Bryant***	N	Y	Y	Y	Y	Y	Y
8 Tanner	?	?	Y	Y	Y	Y	Y
9 Ford	+	−	+	+	+	+	+
TEXAS							
1 Sandlin	Y	N	Y	Y	Y	Y	Y
2 Turner	Y	N	Y	Y	Y	Y	Y
3 ***Johnson, Sam***	N	Y	Y	Y	Y	Y	?
4 Hall	Y	Y	Y	Y	Y	Y	Y
5 ***Sessions***	N	Y	Y	Y	Y	Y	Y
6 ***Barton***	?	?	Y	Y	Y	Y	Y
7 ***Archer***	N	Y	Y	Y	Y	Y	Y
8 ***Brady***	N	Y	Y	Y	Y	Y	Y
9 Lampson	Y	N	Y	Y	Y	Y	Y
10 Doggett	Y	Y	Y	Y	Y	Y	Y
11 Edwards	Y	N	Y	Y	Y	Y	Y
12 ***Granger***	N	Y	Y	Y	Y	Y	Y
13 ***Thornberry***	N	Y	Y	Y	Y	Y	Y
14 ***Paul***	N	N	N	Y	N	N	Y
15 Hinojosa	Y	N	Y	Y	Y	Y	Y
16 Reyes	Y	N	?	?	Y	Y	Y
17 Stenholm	Y	Y	Y	Y	Y	Y	Y
18 Jackson-Lee	Y	N	Y	Y	Y	Y	Y
19 ***Combest***	N	Y	Y	Y	Y	Y	Y
20 Gonzalez	?	?	?	?	?	?	?
21 ***Smith***	N	Y	Y	Y	Y	Y	Y
22 ***DeLay***	N	Y	Y	Y	Y	Y	Y
23 ***Bonilla***	N	Y	Y	Y	Y	Y	Y
24 Frost	Y	N	?	?	?	?	?
25 Bentsen	Y	N	Y	Y	Y	Y	Y
26 ***Armey***	N	Y	Y	Y	Y	Y	Y
27 Ortiz	+	−	+	+	+	+	+
28 Rodriguez	Y	N	Y	Y	Y	Y	Y
29 Green	Y	N	Y	Y	Y	Y	Y
30 Johnson, E.B.	Y	N	Y	Y	Y	Y	+
UTAH							
1 ***Hansen***	N	Y	Y	Y	Y	Y	Y
2 ***Cook***	N	Y	+	Y	Y	Y	Y
3 ***Cannon***	N	Y	Y	Y	Y	Y	Y
VERMONT							
AL *Sanders*	Y	N	Y	Y	Y	Y	Y
VIRGINIA							
1 ***Bateman***	N	Y	Y	Y	Y	Y	Y
2 Pickett	Y	N	Y	Y	Y	Y	Y
3 Scott	Y	N	Y	Y	Y	Y	Y
4 Sisisky	Y	N	Y	Y	Y	Y	Y
5 Goode	N	Y	Y	Y	Y	Y	Y
6 ***Goodlatte***	N	Y	Y	Y	Y	Y	Y
7 ***Bliley***	N	Y	Y	Y	Y	Y	Y
8 Moran	Y	N	Y	Y	Y	Y	Y
9 Boucher	Y	N	?	?	?	?	Y
10 ***Wolf***	N	Y	Y	Y	Y	Y	Y
11 ***Davis***	Y	Y	Y	Y	Y	Y	Y
WASHINGTON							
1 ***White***	N	Y	Y	Y	Y	Y	Y
2 ***Metcalf***	N	Y	Y	Y	Y	Y	Y
3 ***Smith, Linda***	N	Y	Y	Y	Y	Y	Y
4 ***Hastings***	N	Y	Y	Y	Y	Y	Y
5 ***Nethercutt***	N	Y	Y	Y	Y	Y	Y
6 Dicks	Y	N	Y	Y	Y	Y	Y
7 McDermott	Y	N	Y	Y	Y	Y	Y
8 ***Dunn***	N	?	Y	Y	Y	Y	Y
9 Smith, Adam	Y	N	Y	Y	Y	Y	Y
WEST VIRGINIA							
1 Mollohan	Y	N	Y	Y	Y	Y	Y
2 Wise	Y	N	Y	Y	Y	Y	Y
3 Rahall	Y	N	Y	Y	Y	Y	Y
WISCONSIN							
1 ***Neumann***	N	Y	Y	Y	Y	Y	Y
2 ***Klug***	N	Y	Y	Y	Y	Y	Y
3 Kind	Y	N	Y	Y	Y	Y	Y
4 Kleczka	Y	N	Y	Y	Y	Y	+
5 Barrett	Y	N	+	+	+	+	Y
6 ***Petri***	N	Y	Y	Y	Y	Y	Y
7 Obey	Y	N	Y	Y	Y	Y	Y
8 Johnson	Y	N	Y	Y	Y	Y	Y
9 ***Sensenbrenner***	N	Y	Y	Y	Y	Y	Y
WYOMING							
AL ***Cubin***	N	Y	Y	Y	Y	Y	Y

Southern states - Ala., Ark., Fla., Ga., Ky., La., Miss., N.C., Okla., S.C., Tenn., Texas, Va.

House Votes 302, 303, 304, 305, 306, 307, 308

302. HR 2183. Campaign Finance Overhaul/Shays-Meehan Substitute — Non-Citizen Donations. Stearns, R-Fla., amendment to the Shays-Meehan substitute amendment to the bill to overhaul campaign finance laws. The amendment would prohibit donations from resident aliens and other non-citizens to state and local elections, as well as political parties. Adopted 267-131: R 195-23; D 71-108 (ND 50-84, SD 21-24); I 1-0. July 20, 1998.

303. HR 2183. Campaign Finance Overhaul/Shays-Meehan Substitute — "Willful Blindness" Defense. Pickering Jr., R-Miss., amendment to the Shays-Meehan substitute amendment to the bill to overhaul campaign finance laws. The amendment would prohibit "willful blindness" as a defense against a charge of violating the ban on accepting campaign contributions from foreign nationals. Adopted 344-56: R 203-17; D 140-39 (ND 104-30, SD 36-9); I 1-0. July 20, 1998.

304. HR 2183. Campaign Finance Overhaul/Shays-Meehan Substitute — Sense of Congress Regarding Federal Property. DeLay, R-Texas amendment to the Shays-Meehan substitute amendment to the bill to overhaul campaign finance laws. The amendment expresses the sense of Congress that federal law demonstrates that "controlling legal authority" prohibits the use of federal property to raise campaign funds. Adopted 360-36: R 219-0; D 140-36 (ND 103-28, SD 37-8); I 1-0. July 20, 1998.

305. HR 2183. Campaign Finance Overhaul/Shays-Meehan Substitute — Access in Exchange for Contributions. McInnis, R-Colo., amendment to the Shays-Meehan substitute amendment to the bill to overhaul campaign finance laws. The amendment prohibits anyone from soliciting or accepting campaign contributions in exchange for access to the White House, vice president's residence or the airplanes or helicopters on which the president or vice-president are traveling. Adopted 391-7: R 220-0; D 170-7(ND 127-5, SD 43-2); I 1-0. July 20, 1998.

306. HR 2183. Campaign Finance Overhaul/Shays-Meehan Substitute — Labor Union Reporting. Paxon, R-N.Y. amendment to the Shays-Meehan substitute amendment to the bill to overhaul campaign finance laws. The amendment would require labor unions to report all financial activities under current labor laws by category, such as political activities. Rejected 150-248: R 148-72; D 2-175 (ND 0-132, SD 2-43); I 0-1. July 20, 1998.

307. HR 2183. Campaign Finance Overhaul/Shays-Meehan Substitute — Air Force One Reimbursements. Hefley, R-Colo., amendment to the Shays-Meehan substitute amendment to the bill to overhaul campaign finance laws. The amendment would require political parties to reimburse the Air Force for the costs of using Air Force One if the president, vice president or any Cabinet secretary uses the aircraft for travel that includes a political fundraising event. Adopted 222-177: R 190-30; D 32-146 (ND 13-120, SD 19-26); I 0-1. July 20, 1998.

308. HR 2183. Campaign Finance Overhaul/Shays-Meehan Substitute — "Walking Around Money" Prohibition. Northup, R-Ky., amendment to the Shays-Meehan substitute amendment to the bill to overhaul campaign finance laws. The amendment prohibits so-called "walking around money" for candidates to be taken from campaign funds. Adopted 284-114: R 215-4; D 68-110 (ND 44-89, SD 24-21); I 1-0. July 20, 1998.

Key

- **Y** Voted for (yea).
- **#** Paired for.
- **+** Announced for.
- **N** Voted against (nay).
- **X** Paired against.
- **−** Announced against.
- **P** Voted "present."
- **C** Voted "present" to avoid possible conflict of interest.
- **?** Did not vote or otherwise make a position known.

Democrats   **Republicans**
Independent

	302	303	304	305	306	307	308
ALABAMA							
1 Callahan	Y	Y	Y	Y	Y	Y	Y
2 Everett	Y	Y	Y	Y	Y	Y	Y
3 Riley	Y	Y	Y	Y	Y	Y	Y
4 Aderholt	Y	Y	Y	Y	N	Y	Y
5 Cramer	Y	Y	Y	Y	N	Y	Y
6 Bachus	Y	Y	Y	Y	N	N	Y
7 Hilliard	?	?	?	?	?	?	?
ALASKA							
AL Young	Y	N	Y	Y	N	Y	Y
ARIZONA							
1 Salmon	N	Y	Y	Y	Y	Y	Y
2 Pastor	N	Y	Y	Y	N	N	N
3 Stump	Y	Y	Y	Y	Y	Y	Y
4 Shadegg	Y	Y	Y	Y	Y	Y	Y
5 Kolbe	Y	Y	Y	Y	Y	Y	Y
6 Hayworth	Y	Y	Y	Y	Y	Y	Y
ARKANSAS							
1 Berry	Y	Y	Y	Y	N	Y	Y
2 Snyder	Y	Y	Y	Y	N	N	N
3 Hutchinson	Y	Y	Y	Y	N	Y	Y
4 Dickey	Y	Y	Y	Y	Y	Y	Y
CALIFORNIA							
1 Riggs	+	+	+	+	+	+	+
2 Herger	Y	Y	Y	Y	Y	Y	Y
3 Fazio	N	N	N	Y	N	N	N
4 Doolittle	N	N	Y	Y	Y	N	Y
5 Matsui	N	Y	Y	Y	N	N	N
6 Woolsey	N	Y	Y	Y	N	N	N
7 Miller	N	N	N	Y	N	N	N
8 Pelosi	N	Y	Y	N	N	N	?
9 Lee	N	N	N	Y	N	N	N
10 Tauscher	Y	Y	Y	Y	N	N	Y
11 Pombo	N	N	Y	Y	Y	Y	Y
12 Lantos	Y	Y	Y	Y	N	N	Y
13 Stark	N	N	N	Y	N	N	N
14 Eshoo	N	Y	Y	Y	N	N	N
15 Campbell	N	Y	Y	Y	N	Y	Y
16 Lofgren	N	Y	Y	Y	N	N	N
17 Farr	N	N	N	N	N	N	N
18 Condit	N	Y	Y	Y	N	N	N
19 Radanovich	Y	N	Y	Y	Y	Y	Y
20 Dooley	Y	Y	Y	Y	N	N	Y
21 Thomas	Y	Y	Y	Y	N	Y	Y
22 Capps, L.	Y	Y	Y	Y	N	N	N
23 Gallegly	Y	Y	Y	Y	N	Y	Y
24 Sherman	Y	Y	Y	Y	N	N	Y
25 McKeon	Y	Y	Y	Y	Y	Y	Y
26 Berman	N	Y	Y	Y	N	N	N
27 Rogan	Y	Y	Y	Y	Y	Y	Y
28 Dreier	Y	Y	Y	Y	Y	Y	Y
29 Waxman	N	Y	N	Y	N	N	N
30 Becerra	N	N	N	Y	N	N	N
31 Martinez	?	?	?	?	?	?	?
32 Dixon	?	?	?	?	?	?	?
33 Roybal-Allard	−	+	−	+	−	−	−
34 Torres	?	?	?	?	?	?	?
35 Waters	N	N	N	N	N	N	N
36 Harman	Y	Y	Y	Y	N	N	Y
37 Millender-McD.	−	−	+	+	−	−	−
38 Horn	Y	Y	Y	Y	N	N	Y
39 Royce	Y	Y	Y	Y	Y	Y	Y
40 Lewis	N	Y	Y	Y	N	Y	Y
41 Kim	Y	Y	Y	Y	Y	Y	Y
42 Brown	N	Y	Y	Y	N	N	N
43 Calvert	Y	Y	Y	Y	Y	Y	Y
44 Bono, M.	Y	Y	Y	Y	Y	Y	Y
45 Rohrabacher	Y	Y	Y	Y	Y	Y	Y
46 Sanchez	N	N	Y	Y	N	N	N
47 Cox	Y	Y	Y	Y	Y	Y	Y
48 Packard	Y	Y	Y	Y	Y	Y	Y
49 Bilbray	N	Y	Y	Y	N	Y	Y
50 Filner	N	Y	Y	Y	N	N	N
51 Cunningham	Y	Y	Y	Y	Y	Y	Y
52 Hunter	Y	Y	Y	Y	N	Y	Y
COLORADO							
1 DeGette	N	Y	Y	Y	N	N	Y
2 Skaggs	N	N	Y	Y	N	N	N
3 McInnis	Y	Y	Y	Y	Y	Y	Y
4 Schaffer	Y	Y	Y	Y	Y	Y	Y
5 Hefley	Y	Y	Y	Y	Y	Y	Y
6 Schaefer	Y	Y	Y	Y	Y	Y	Y
CONNECTICUT							
1 Kennelly	Y	Y	Y	?	?	?	?
2 Gejdenson	Y	Y	Y	Y	N	Y	Y
3 DeLauro	Y	Y	Y	Y	N	Y	Y
4 Shays	N	Y	Y	Y	N	N	N
5 Maloney	Y	Y	Y	Y	N	N	Y
6 Johnson	N	Y	Y	Y	N	N	Y
DELAWARE							
AL Castle	Y	Y	Y	Y	N	N	Y
FLORIDA							
1 Scarborough	Y	Y	?	Y	Y	Y	Y
2 Boyd	Y	Y	Y	Y	N	Y	Y
3 Brown	N	Y	Y	Y	N	N	N
4 Fowler	Y	Y	Y	Y	Y	Y	Y
5 Thurman	Y	Y	Y	Y	N	Y	Y
6 Stearns	Y	Y	Y	Y	Y	Y	Y
7 Mica	Y	Y	Y	Y	Y	Y	Y
8 McCollum	Y	Y	Y	Y	Y	Y	Y
9 Bilirakis	+	?	+	+	?	+	+
10 Young	Y	Y	Y	Y	Y	Y	Y
11 Davis	N	Y	Y	Y	N	N	N
12 Canady	Y	Y	Y	Y	Y	Y	Y
13 Miller	Y	Y	Y	Y	Y	Y	Y
14 Goss	Y	Y	Y	Y	Y	Y	Y
15 Weldon	Y	N	Y	Y	N	Y	Y
16 Foley	Y	Y	Y	Y	Y	Y	Y
17 Meek	N	N	N	Y	N	N	N
18 Ros-Lehtinen	N	N	Y	Y	N	Y	Y
19 Wexler	N	N	N	Y	N	N	N
20 Deutsch	Y	Y	Y	Y	N	N	Y
21 Diaz-Balart	N	N	Y	Y	N	Y	Y
22 Shaw	Y	Y	Y	Y	Y	Y	Y
23 Hastings	N	N	N	Y	N	N	N
GEORGIA							
1 Kingston	Y	Y	Y	Y	Y	Y	Y
2 Bishop	N	Y	Y	Y	Y	Y	Y
3 Collins	Y	Y	Y	Y	Y	Y	Y
4 McKinney	N	Y	Y	Y	N	Y	Y
5 Lewis	?	?	?	?	?	?	?
6 Gingrich							
7 Barr	Y	Y	Y	Y	Y	Y	Y
8 Chambliss	Y	Y	Y	Y	Y	Y	Y
9 Deal	Y	Y	Y	Y	Y	Y	Y
10 Norwood	?	?	?	?	?	?	?
11 Linder	Y	Y	Y	Y	Y	Y	Y
HAWAII							
1 Abercrombie	N	Y	Y	Y	N	N	N
2 Mink	N	N	N	Y	N	N	N
IDAHO							
1 Chenoweth	N	Y	Y	Y	Y	Y	Y
2 Crapo	N	Y	Y	Y	Y	Y	Y
ILLINOIS							
1 Rush	Y	Y	Y	Y	N	N	N
2 Jackson	N	N	Y	Y	N	N	N
3 Lipinski	?	?	?	?	?	?	?
4 Gutierrez	N	N	Y	Y	N	N	N
5 Blagojevich	?	?	?	?	?	?	?
6 Hyde	Y	Y	Y	Y	Y	Y	Y
7 Davis	N	Y	Y	Y	N	N	N
8 Crane	Y	Y	Y	Y	Y	Y	Y
9 Yates	?	?	?	?	?	?	?
10 Porter	N	Y	Y	Y	N	Y	Y
11 Weller	Y	Y	Y	Y	N	Y	Y
12 Costello	Y	Y	Y	Y	N	N	Y

ND Northern Democrats   SD Southern Democrats

	302	303	304	305	306	307	308
13 ***Fawell***	Y	Y	Y	Y	Y	Y	Y
14 ***Hastert***	Y	Y	Y	Y	Y	Y	Y
15 ***Ewing***	Y	Y	Y	Y	Y	Y	Y
16 ***Manzullo***	Y	Y	Y	Y	Y	Y	Y
17 Evans	Y	Y	Y	Y	N	N	N
18 ***LaHood***	Y	Y	Y	Y	N	Y	Y
19 Poshard	?	?	?	?	?	?	?
20 ***Shimkus***	Y	Y	Y	Y	N	Y	Y
INDIANA							
1 Visclosky	N	Y	Y	Y	N	N	N
2 ***McIntosh***	Y	Y	Y	Y	Y	N	Y
3 Roemer	Y	Y	Y	Y	N	N	Y
4 ***Souder***	Y	Y	Y	Y	Y	Y	Y
5 ***Buyer***	Y	N	Y	Y	Y	Y	Y
6 ***Burton***	Y	Y	Y	Y	Y	Y	Y
7 ***Pease***	Y	Y	Y	Y	N	Y	Y
8 ***Hostettler***	Y	Y	Y	Y	Y	Y	Y
9 Hamilton	Y	Y	Y	Y	N	N	Y
10 Carson	N	N	Y	Y	N	N	N
IOWA							
1 ***Leach***	Y	Y	Y	Y	N	N	Y
2 ***Nussle***	Y	Y	Y	Y	Y	Y	Y
3 Boswell	Y	Y	Y	Y	N	N	Y
4 ***Ganske***	Y	Y	Y	Y	N	N	Y
5 ***Latham***	Y	N	Y	Y	Y	N	Y
KANSAS							
1 ***Moran***	Y	Y	Y	Y	N	Y	Y
2 ***Ryun***	Y	Y	Y	Y	Y	Y	Y
3 ***Snowbarger***	Y	Y	Y	Y	Y	Y	Y
4 ***Tiahrt***	Y	Y	Y	Y	Y	Y	Y
KENTUCKY							
1 ***Whitfield***	Y	Y	Y	Y	Y	Y	Y
2 ***Lewis***	Y	Y	Y	Y	Y	Y	Y
3 ***Northup***	Y	Y	Y	Y	Y	Y	Y
4 ***Bunning***	Y	Y	Y	Y	Y	Y	Y
5 ***Rogers***	Y	Y	Y	Y	Y	Y	Y
6 Baesler	Y	Y	Y	Y	N	N	Y
LOUISIANA							
1 ***Livingston***	Y	Y	Y	Y	Y	Y	Y
2 Jefferson	?	?	?	?	?	?	?
3 ***Tauzin***	Y	Y	Y	Y	Y	Y	Y
4 ***McCrery***	Y	Y	Y	Y	N	Y	Y
5 ***Cooksey***	Y	Y	Y	Y	Y	Y	Y
6 ***Baker***	?	?	?	?	?	?	?
7 John	?	?	?	?	?	?	?
MAINE							
1 Allen	N	Y	N	Y	N	N	N
2 Baldacci	Y	Y	Y	Y	N	N	Y
MARYLAND							
1 ***Gilchrest***	Y	Y	Y	Y	Y	Y	Y
2 ***Ehrlich***	?	?	?	?	?	?	?
3 Cardin	N	Y	Y	Y	N	N	N
4 Wynn	N	N	Y	Y	N	N	N
5 Hoyer	N	Y	Y	Y	N	N	N
6 ***Bartlett***	Y	Y	Y	Y	Y	Y	Y
7 Cummings	N	Y	Y	Y	N	N	N
8 ***Morella***	N	Y	Y	Y	N	Y	Y
MASSACHUSETTS							
1 Olver	N	Y	Y	Y	N	N	N
2 Neal	N	N	Y	Y	N	N	N
3 McGovern	N	Y	Y	Y	N	N	N
4 Frank	N	N	Y	Y	N	N	N
5 Meehan	N	Y	?	Y	N	N	N
6 Tierney	N	Y	Y	Y	N	N	N
7 Markey	Y	Y	?	?	?	?	?
8 Kennedy	Y	Y	Y	Y	N	N	N
9 Moakley	?	?	?	?	?	?	?
10 Delahunt	N	Y	Y	Y	N	N	N
MICHIGAN							
1 Stupak	Y	Y	Y	Y	N	N	Y
2 ***Hoekstra***	Y	Y	Y	Y	Y	Y	Y
3 ***Ehlers***	Y	Y	Y	Y	N	Y	Y
4 ***Camp***	Y	Y	Y	Y	Y	Y	Y
5 Barcia	Y	Y	Y	Y	N	N	Y
6 ***Upton***	Y	Y	Y	Y	Y	Y	Y
7 ***Smith***	N	Y	Y	Y	N	Y	Y
8 Stabenow	Y	Y	Y	Y	N	Y	Y
9 Kildee	Y	Y	Y	Y	N	Y	Y
10 Bonior	N	Y	Y	Y	N	N	N
11 ***Knollenberg***	Y	Y	Y	Y	Y	Y	Y
12 Levin	Y	Y	Y	Y	N	N	N
13 Rivers	N	Y	Y	Y	N	N	N
14 Conyers	N	N	N	N	N	N	N
15 Kilpatrick	N	N	Y	Y	N	N	N
16 Dingell	N	Y	Y	Y	N	N	N
MINNESOTA							
1 ***Gutknecht***	Y	Y	Y	Y	N	Y	Y
2 Minge	N	Y	Y	Y	N	N	Y
3 ***Ramstad***	Y	Y	Y	Y	N	Y	Y
4 Vento	N	Y	Y	Y	N	N	N
5 Sabo	N	N	N	Y	N	N	Y
6 Luther	Y	Y	Y	Y	N	N	Y
7 Peterson	Y	Y	Y	Y	N	N	Y
8 Oberstar	N	Y	Y	Y	N	N	N
MISSISSIPPI							
1 ***Wicker***	Y	Y	Y	Y	Y	Y	Y
2 Thompson	?	?	?	?	?	?	?
3 ***Pickering***	+	Y	Y	Y	Y	Y	Y
4 ***Parker***	Y	Y	Y	Y	Y	Y	Y
5 Taylor	Y	Y	Y	Y	Y	Y	Y
MISSOURI							
1 Clay	N	Y	N	Y	N	N	N
2 ***Talent***	N	Y	Y	Y	Y	N	Y
3 Gephardt	?	?	?	?	?	?	?
4 Skelton	Y	Y	?	Y	N	N	Y
5 McCarthy	N	Y	Y	Y	N	N	N
6 Danner	?	?	?	?	?	?	?
7 ***Blunt***	Y	N	Y	Y	N	Y	Y
8 ***Emerson***	Y	Y	Y	Y	Y	Y	Y
9 ***Hulshof***	Y	Y	Y	Y	Y	Y	Y
MONTANA							
AL ***Hill***	Y	Y	Y	Y	Y	Y	Y
NEBRASKA							
1 ***Bereuter***	Y	Y	Y	Y	N	Y	Y
2 ***Christensen***	Y	Y	Y	Y	Y	Y	Y
3 ***Barrett***	Y	Y	Y	Y	N	Y	Y
NEVADA							
1 ***Ensign***	N	N	Y	Y	N	N	Y
2 ***Gibbons***	Y	Y	Y	Y	Y	Y	Y
NEW HAMPSHIRE							
1 ***Sununu***	Y	Y	Y	Y	Y	Y	Y
2 ***Bass***	Y	Y	Y	Y	N	Y	Y
NEW JERSEY							
1 Andrews	N	Y	Y	Y	N	N	N
2 ***LoBiondo***	Y	Y	Y	Y	N	Y	Y
3 ***Saxton***	?	Y	Y	Y	N	Y	Y
4 ***Smith***	Y	Y	Y	Y	N	Y	Y
5 ***Roukema***	Y	Y	Y	Y	N	Y	Y
6 Pallone	N	Y	Y	Y	N	N	Y
7 ***Franks***	Y	Y	Y	Y	N	Y	Y
8 Pascrell	N	Y	Y	Y	N	N	Y
9 Rothman	Y	Y	Y	Y	N	Y	N
10 Payne	N	N	N	Y	N	N	N
11 ***Frelinghuysen***	Y	Y	Y	Y	N	Y	Y
12 ***Pappas***	Y	Y	Y	Y	N	Y	Y
13 Menendez	N	Y	Y	Y	N	N	N
NEW MEXICO							
1 ***Wilson***	Y	N	Y	Y	N	Y	Y
2 ***Skeen***	Y	Y	Y	Y	Y	Y	Y
3 ***Redmond***	Y	Y	Y	Y	N	Y	Y
NEW YORK							
1 ***Forbes***	Y	Y	Y	Y	N	N	Y
2 ***Lazio***	Y	N	Y	Y	N	Y	Y
3 ***King***	N	N	Y	Y	N	N	N
4 McCarthy	N	Y	Y	Y	N	N	N
5 Ackerman	?	?	?	?	?	?	?
6 Meeks	N	N	Y	Y	N	N	N
7 Manton	N	Y	Y	Y	N	N	N
8 Nadler	N	N	N	Y	N	N	N
9 Schumer	Y	Y	Y	Y	N	Y	Y
10 Towns	?	?	?	?	?	?	?
11 Owens	N	Y	Y	Y	N	N	N
12 Velázquez	N	Y	Y	Y	N	N	N
13 ***Fossella***	Y	Y	Y	Y	Y	Y	Y
14 Maloney	−	+	+	+	−	N	Y
15 Rangel	N	Y	Y	Y	N	N	N
16 Serrano	N	Y	Y	Y	N	N	N
17 Engel	N	N	N	Y	N	N	N
18 Lowey	N	Y	Y	Y	N	N	N
19 ***Kelly***	Y	Y	Y	Y	N	Y	Y
20 ***Gilman***	Y	Y	Y	Y	N	N	Y
21 McNulty	N	Y	Y	Y	N	N	N
22 ***Solomon***	Y	Y	Y	Y	Y	Y	Y
23 ***Boehlert***	N	Y	Y	Y	N	N	N
24 ***McHugh***	Y	Y	Y	Y	N	Y	Y
25 ***Walsh***	Y	Y	Y	Y	N	Y	Y
26 Hinchey	Y	Y	Y	Y	N	Y	N
27 ***Paxon***	Y	Y	Y	Y	Y	Y	Y
28 Slaughter	Y	Y	Y	Y	N	N	N
29 LaFalce	N	Y	Y	Y	N	N	N
30 ***Quinn***	Y	Y	Y	Y	N	Y	Y
31 ***Houghton***	N	Y	Y	Y	N	N	Y
NORTH CAROLINA							
1 Clayton	N	Y	Y	Y	N	N	N
2 Etheridge	Y	Y	Y	Y	N	Y	Y
3 ***Jones***	Y	Y	Y	Y	Y	Y	Y
4 Price	Y	Y	Y	Y	N	Y	Y
5 ***Burr***	Y	Y	Y	Y	Y	Y	Y
6 ***Coble***	+	+	+	+	+	+	+
7 McIntyre	Y	Y	Y	Y	N	Y	Y
8 Hefner	?	?	?	?	?	?	?
9 ***Myrick***	Y	Y	Y	Y	Y	Y	Y
10 ***Ballenger***	Y	Y	Y	Y	Y	Y	Y
11 ***Taylor***	Y	Y	Y	Y	Y	Y	Y
12 Watt	N	Y	N	Y	N	N	N
NORTH DAKOTA							
AL Pomeroy	Y	Y	Y	Y	N	N	Y
OHIO							
1 ***Chabot***	Y	Y	Y	Y	Y	Y	Y
2 ***Portman***	Y	Y	Y	Y	Y	N	Y
3 Hall	N	Y	Y	Y	N	Y	N
4 ***Oxley***	Y	Y	Y	Y	Y	Y	Y
5 ***Gillmor***	Y	Y	Y	Y	N	N	Y
6 Strickland	Y	Y	Y	Y	N	Y	Y
7 ***Hobson***	Y	Y	Y	Y	N	Y	Y
8 ***Boehner***	Y	Y	Y	Y	Y	Y	Y
9 Kaptur	Y	Y	Y	Y	N	Y	N
10 Kucinich	Y	N	N	N	N	N	N
11 Stokes	?	?	?	?	?	?	?
12 ***Kasich***	Y	Y	Y	Y	Y	Y	Y
13 Brown	Y	Y	Y	Y	N	N	N
14 Sawyer	Y	Y	Y	Y	N	N	N
15 ***Pryce***	Y	Y	Y	Y	Y	Y	Y
16 ***Regula***	Y	Y	Y	Y	N	N	Y
17 Traficant	?	?	?	?	?	?	?
18 ***Ney***	Y	Y	Y	Y	N	Y	Y
19 ***LaTourette***	Y	N	Y	Y	N	Y	Y
OKLAHOMA							
1 ***Largent***	Y	Y	Y	Y	Y	Y	Y
2 ***Coburn***	Y	Y	Y	Y	N	Y	?
3 ***Watkins***	Y	Y	Y	Y	Y	Y	Y
4 ***Watts***	Y	Y	Y	Y	Y	N	Y
5 ***Istook***	Y	Y	Y	Y	Y	Y	Y
6 ***Lucas***	Y	Y	Y	Y	Y	Y	Y
OREGON							
1 Furse	N	Y	N	Y	N	N	N
2 ***Smith***	Y	Y	Y	Y	Y	Y	Y
3 Blumenauer	N	Y	Y	Y	N	N	Y
4 DeFazio	Y	Y	Y	Y	N	N	Y
5 Hooley	Y	Y	Y	Y	N	N	Y
PENNSYLVANIA							
1 Brady	N	Y	N	Y	N	N	N
2 Fattah	N	Y	N	Y	N	N	N
3 Borski	N	Y	N	Y	N	N	N
4 Klink	Y	Y	Y	Y	N	N	N
5 ***Peterson***	Y	Y	Y	Y	Y	Y	Y
6 Holden	Y	Y	Y	Y	N	N	N
7 ***Weldon***	Y	Y	Y	Y	N	Y	Y
8 ***Greenwood***	Y	Y	Y	Y	N	Y	Y
9 ***Shuster***	Y	Y	Y	Y	Y	Y	Y
10 ***McDade***	?	?	?	?	?	?	?
11 Kanjorski	N	N	N	Y	N	N	N
12 Murtha	N	N	N	Y	N	N	N
13 ***Fox***	Y	Y	Y	Y	N	Y	Y
14 Coyne	Y	Y	Y	Y	N	Y	Y
15 McHale	N	Y	Y	Y	N	N	N
16 ***Pitts***	Y	Y	Y	Y	Y	Y	Y
17 ***Gekas***	Y	Y	Y	Y	Y	Y	Y
18 Doyle	Y	Y	Y	Y	N	N	N
19 ***Goodling***	Y	Y	Y	Y	Y	Y	Y
20 Mascara	Y	Y	Y	Y	N	Y	Y
21 ***English***	Y	Y	Y	Y	N	Y	Y
RHODE ISLAND							
1 Kennedy	N	N	Y	Y	N	N	N
2 Weygand	N	Y	Y	Y	N	N	Y
SOUTH CAROLINA							
1 ***Sanford***	Y	Y	Y	Y	N	Y	Y
2 ***Spence***	Y	Y	Y	Y	Y	Y	Y
3 ***Graham***	Y	Y	Y	Y	Y	Y	Y
4 ***Inglis***	Y	Y	Y	Y	Y	Y	Y
5 Spratt	Y	Y	Y	Y	N	N	Y
6 Clyburn	N	N	Y	N	N	N	N
SOUTH DAKOTA							
AL ***Thune***	Y	Y	Y	Y	Y	Y	Y
TENNESSEE							
1 ***Jenkins***	Y	Y	Y	Y	Y	Y	Y
2 ***Duncan***	Y	Y	Y	Y	Y	Y	Y
3 ***Wamp***	Y	Y	Y	Y	N	Y	Y
4 ***Hilleary***	Y	Y	Y	Y	Y	Y	Y
5 Clement	Y	Y	Y	Y	N	Y	N
6 Gordon	Y	Y	Y	Y	N	N	Y
7 ***Bryant***	Y	Y	Y	Y	Y	Y	Y
8 Tanner	Y	Y	N	Y	N	Y	N
9 Ford	−	+	−	+	−	−	−
TEXAS							
1 Sandlin	Y	Y	Y	Y	N	N	N
2 Turner	Y	Y	Y	Y	N	Y	Y
3 ***Johnson, Sam***	Y	Y	Y	Y	Y	N	Y
4 Hall	N	Y	Y	Y	N	Y	Y
5 ***Sessions***	Y	Y	Y	Y	Y	Y	Y
6 ***Barton***	Y	Y	Y	Y	Y	N	Y
7 ***Archer***	Y	Y	Y	Y	Y	Y	Y
8 ***Brady***	Y	Y	Y	Y	Y	Y	Y
9 Lampson	N	Y	Y	Y	N	Y	Y
10 Doggett	N	Y	Y	Y	N	N	N
11 Edwards	N	Y	Y	Y	N	N	N
12 ***Granger***	Y	Y	Y	Y	Y	N	Y
13 ***Thornberry***	N	Y	Y	Y	Y	N	Y
14 ***Paul***	N	N	Y	Y	N	Y	Y
15 Hinojosa	N	Y	Y	Y	N	N	N
16 Reyes	N	Y	Y	Y	N	N	N
17 Stenholm	N	Y	Y	Y	N	Y	Y
18 Jackson-Lee	N	N	N	Y	N	N	N
19 ***Combest***	Y	Y	Y	Y	Y	Y	Y
20 Gonzalez	?	?	?	?	?	?	?
21 ***Smith***	Y	Y	Y	Y	Y	Y	Y
22 ***DeLay***	N	Y	Y	Y	Y	Y	Y
23 ***Bonilla***	Y	Y	Y	Y	Y	N	Y
24 Frost	?	?	?	?	?	?	?
25 Bentsen	N	Y	Y	Y	N	N	N
26 ***Armey***	Y	Y	Y	Y	Y	Y	Y
27 Ortiz	+	+	+	+	−	−	+
28 Rodriguez	N	Y	Y	Y	N	N	Y
29 Green	N	Y	Y	Y	N	Y	Y
30 Johnson, E.B.	N	N	Y	Y	N	N	N
UTAH							
1 ***Hansen***	Y	Y	Y	Y	Y	Y	Y
2 ***Cook***	Y	Y	Y	Y	Y	Y	Y
3 ***Cannon***	Y	Y	Y	Y	Y	Y	Y
VERMONT							
AL *Sanders*	Y	Y	Y	Y	N	N	Y
VIRGINIA							
1 ***Bateman***	Y	Y	Y	Y	Y	Y	Y
2 Pickett	Y	Y	Y	Y	N	Y	Y
3 Scott	N	N	N	Y	N	N	N
4 Sisisky	Y	Y	Y	Y	N	Y	Y
5 Goode	Y	Y	Y	Y	Y	Y	Y
6 ***Goodlatte***	Y	Y	Y	Y	Y	Y	Y
7 ***Bliley***	Y	Y	Y	Y	Y	N	Y
8 Moran	N	N	N	Y	N	N	Y
9 Boucher	Y	Y	Y	Y	N	N	Y
10 ***Wolf***	Y	Y	Y	Y	Y	Y	Y
11 ***Davis***	Y	N	Y	Y	Y	Y	Y
WASHINGTON							
1 ***White***	Y	Y	Y	Y	N	Y	Y
2 ***Metcalf***	Y	Y	Y	Y	N	Y	N
3 ***Smith, Linda***	Y	Y	Y	Y	Y	Y	Y
4 ***Hastings***	Y	Y	Y	Y	Y	Y	Y
5 ***Nethercutt***	Y	Y	Y	Y	Y	Y	Y
6 Dicks	N	Y	Y	Y	N	N	Y
7 McDermott	N	N	N	Y	N	N	N
8 ***Dunn***	Y	Y	Y	Y	Y	Y	Y
9 Smith, Adam	Y	Y	N	Y	N	N	Y
WEST VIRGINIA							
1 Mollohan	N	N	N	Y	N	N	Y
2 Wise	Y	Y	Y	Y	N	N	Y
3 Rahall	Y	Y	N	Y	N	N	N
WISCONSIN							
1 ***Neumann***	Y	Y	Y	Y	N	Y	Y
2 ***Klug***	Y	Y	Y	Y	Y	Y	Y
3 Kind	N	Y	Y	Y	N	N	Y
4 Kleczka	Y	Y	Y	Y	N	Y	Y
5 Barrett	N	Y	Y	Y	N	N	Y
6 ***Petri***	Y	Y	Y	Y	Y	Y	Y
7 Obey	Y	Y	N	Y	N	N	Y
8 Johnson	Y	Y	Y	Y	N	N	Y
9 ***Sensenbrenner***	Y	Y	Y	Y	Y	Y	Y
WYOMING							
AL ***Cubin***	Y	Y	Y	Y	Y	Y	Y

Southern states - Ala., Ark., Fla., Ga., Ky., La., Miss., N.C., Okla., S.C., Tenn., Texas, Va.

House Votes 309, 310, 311, 312, 313, 314, 315

309. Procedural Motion/Adjourn. Yates, D-Ill. motion to adjourn. Motion rejected 7-382: R 0-207; D 7-175 (ND 7-128, SD 0-47); I 0-0. July 21, 1998.

310. HR 4193. Fiscal 1999 Interior Appropriations/Previous Question. Hastings, R-Wash., motion to order the previous question (thus ending debate and the possibility of amendment) on adoption of the rule (H Res 504) to provide for House floor consideration of the bill to provide $13.4 billion in funding for the Department of Interior and related agencies for fiscal 1999. Motion agreed to 223-196: R 220-0; D 3-195 (ND 1-147, SD 2-48); I 0-1. July 21, 1998. (Subsequently, the rule was adopted.)

311. HR 4193. Fiscal 1999 Interior Appropriations/Rule. Adoption of the rule (H Res 504) to provide for House floor consideration of the bill to provide $13.4 billion in funding for the Department of Interior and related agencies in fiscal 1999. Adopted 224-191: R 219-1; D 5-189 (ND 3-144, SD 2-45); I 0-1. July 21, 1998.

312. HR 4193. Fiscal 1999 Interior Appropriations/NEA Funding. Johnson, R-Conn., amendment to reinstate $98 million in funding for the National Endowment of the Arts in fiscal 1999, which was struck from the bill by a point of order. The amendment was made in order by the rule (H Res 405) that provided for House floor consideration of HR4193. Adopted 253-173: R 58-166; D 194-7 (ND 147-2, SD 47-5); I 1-0. July 21, 1998.

313. HR 4193. Fiscal 1999 Interior Appropriations/Energy Efficiency and Conservation Programs Funding. Skaggs, D-Colo., amendment to increase funding for certain energy efficiency and conservation programs. Rejected 212-213: R 59-166; D 152-47 (ND 117-30, SD 35-17); I 1-0. July 21, 1998.

314. HR 4193. Fiscal 1999 Interior Appropriations/Payments in Lieu of Taxes Fund Increase. Sanders, I-Vt. amendment to increase by $20 million funds in the bill earmarked for payments in lieu of taxes, which are federal payments intended to make up for taxes localities might otherwise collect if federal lands were not federally owned. Adopted 241-185: R 117-109; D 123-76 (ND 94-53, SD 29-23); I 1-0. July 21, 1998.

315. HR 4193. Fiscal 1999 Interior Appropriations/Land and Water Conservation Fund Increase. McGovern, D-Mass., amendment to increase funding by $30 million for the state-side program of the Land and Water Conservation Fund. Rejected 203-221: R 51-174; D 151-47 (ND 114-32, SD 37-15); I 1-0. July 21, 1998.

Key

- Y Voted for (yea).
- # Paired for.
- + Announced for.
- N Voted against (nay).
- X Paired against.
- – Announced against.
- P Voted "present."
- C Voted "present" to avoid possible conflict of interest.
- ? Did not vote or otherwise make a position known.

Democrats **Republicans**
Independent

	309	310	311	312	313	314	315
ALABAMA							
1 **Callahan**	N	Y	Y	N	N	N	N
2 **Everett**	N	Y	Y	N	N	N	N
3 **Riley**	N	Y	Y	N	N	N	N
4 **Aderholt**	N	Y	Y	N	N	N	N
5 Cramer	N	N	N	Y	Y	N	Y
6 **Bachus**	N	Y	Y	N	N	N	Y
7 Hilliard	N	N	?	Y	Y	Y	Y
ALASKA							
AL **Young**	?	Y	Y	N	N	Y	N
ARIZONA							
1 **Salmon**	N	Y	Y	N	Y	Y	N
2 Pastor	N	N	N	Y	Y	Y	Y
3 **Stump**	N	Y	Y	N	N	Y	N
4 **Shadegg**	N	Y	Y	N	N	Y	N
5 **Kolbe**	N	Y	Y	N	Y	N	N
6 **Hayworth**	N	Y	Y	N	Y	Y	Y
ARKANSAS							
1 Berry	N	N	N	Y	Y	Y	Y
2 Snyder	N	N	N	Y	Y	Y	Y
3 **Hutchinson**	N	Y	Y	N	N	Y	N
4 **Dickey**	N	Y	Y	N	N	N	N
CALIFORNIA							
1 **Riggs**	N	Y	Y	N	N	Y	N
2 **Herger**	N	Y	Y	N	N	N	N
3 Fazio	N	N	N	Y	Y	Y	Y
4 **Doolittle**	?	Y	Y	N	N	Y	N
5 Matsui	N	N	N	Y	Y	Y	Y
6 Woolsey	N	N	N	Y	Y	Y	Y
7 Miller	Y	N	N	Y	Y	Y	Y
8 Pelosi	?	N	N	Y	Y	N	Y
9 Lee	N	N	N	Y	Y	Y	Y
10 Tauscher	N	N	N	Y	Y	Y	Y
11 **Pombo**	N	Y	Y	N	N	Y	N
12 Lantos	N	N	N	Y	Y	N	Y
13 Stark	N	N	N	Y	Y	Y	Y
14 Eshoo	N	N	N	Y	Y	Y	Y
15 **Campbell**	N	Y	Y	Y	Y	Y	Y
16 Lofgren	N	N	N	Y	Y	Y	Y
17 Farr	N	N	N	Y	Y	Y	Y
18 Condit	N	N	N	N	N	Y	N
19 **Radanovich**	N	Y	Y	N	N	Y	–
20 Dooley	N	N	N	Y	Y	N	Y
21 **Thomas**	N	Y	Y	N	N	N	N
22 Capps, L.	N	N	N	Y	Y	Y	Y
23 **Gallegly**	N	Y	Y	N	N	Y	Y
24 Sherman	N	N	N	Y	Y	Y	Y
25 **McKeon**	N	Y	Y	N	N	N	N
26 Berman	N	N	N	Y	Y	Y	Y
27 **Rogan**	N	Y	Y	N	N	N	N
28 **Dreier**	N	Y	Y	N	N	Y	N
29 Waxman	N	N	N	Y	Y	N	Y
30 Becerra	N	N	N	Y	Y	Y	Y
31 Martinez	N	N	N	Y	Y	Y	Y
32 Dixon	?	?	?	?	?	?	?
33 Roybal-Allard	N	N	N	Y	Y	Y	Y
34 Torres	N	N	N	Y	Y	Y	Y
35 Waters	N	N	N	Y	Y	Y	Y
36 Harman	?	N	N	Y	?	?	?
37 Millender-McD.	N	N	N	Y	Y	Y	Y
38 **Horn**	N	Y	Y	N	Y	N	Y
39 **Royce**	N	Y	Y	N	N	Y	N
40 **Lewis**	N	Y	Y	N	N	Y	N
41 **Kim**	N	Y	Y	N	N	N	N
42 Brown	N	N	N	N	N	N	N
43 **Calvert**	N	Y	Y	N	N	N	N
44 **Bono, M.**	N	Y	Y	N	N	Y	N
45 **Rohrabacher**	N	Y	Y	N	N	N	N
46 Sanchez	N	N	N	N	Y	N	Y
47 **Cox**	N	Y	Y	N	N	N	N
48 **Packard**	N	Y	Y	N	N	N	N
49 **Bilbray**	N	Y	Y	N	N	Y	N
50 Filner	Y	N	N	Y	Y	Y	Y
51 **Cunningham**	N	Y	Y	N	N	N	N
52 **Hunter**	N	Y	Y	N	N	N	Y
COLORADO							
1 DeGette	N	N	N	Y	Y	Y	Y
2 Skaggs	N	N	N	Y	Y	N	N
3 **McInnis**	N	Y	Y	N	N	Y	N
4 **Schaffer**	N	Y	Y	N	N	N	N
5 **Hefley**	N	Y	Y	N	N	N	N
6 **Schaefer**	N	Y	Y	N	N	N	N
CONNECTICUT							
1 Kennelly	?	?	?	Y	N	N	Y
2 **Gejdenson**	N	N	N	Y	N	N	N
3 DeLauro	N	N	N	Y	Y	Y	Y
4 **Shays**	N	Y	Y	Y	Y	Y	Y
5 Maloney	N	N	N	Y	N	N	Y
6 **Johnson**	N	Y	Y	Y	N	N	Y
DELAWARE							
AL **Castle**	N	Y	Y	Y	Y	N	N
FLORIDA							
1 **Scarborough**	N	Y	Y	N	N	Y	N
2 Boyd	N	N	N	Y	Y	Y	Y
3 Brown	N	N	N	Y	Y	Y	Y
4 **Fowler**	N	Y	Y	N	N	N	N
5 Thurman	N	N	N	Y	Y	Y	Y
6 **Stearns**	N	Y	Y	N	N	Y	N
7 **Mica**	N	Y	Y	N	Y	N	N
8 **McCollum**	N	Y	Y	N	N	N	N
9 **Bilirakis**	?	?	?	N	Y	N	Y
10 **Young**	?	Y	Y	?	?	?	?
11 Davis	N	N	N	Y	Y	Y	Y
12 **Canady**	N	?	?	N	N	N	N
13 **Miller**	N	Y	Y	N	N	N	N
14 **Goss**	N	Y	Y	N	N	N	N
15 **Weldon**	N	Y	Y	N	N	N	N
16 **Foley**	N	Y	Y	Y	Y	Y	Y
17 Meek	N	N	N	Y	Y	Y	Y
18 **Ros-Lehtinen**	N	Y	Y	N	N	N	N
19 Wexler	N	N	N	Y	Y	Y	Y
20 Deutsch	N	N	N	Y	Y	Y	Y
21 **Diaz-Balart**	N	Y	Y	N	N	N	N
22 **Shaw**	N	Y	Y	N	N	N	N
23 Hastings	N	N	?	Y	Y	Y	Y
GEORGIA							
1 **Kingston**	N	Y	Y	N	N	N	N
2 Bishop	N	N	N	Y	Y	Y	Y
3 **Collins**	N	Y	Y	N	N	Y	N
4 McKinney	N	N	N	Y	Y	Y	Y
5 Lewis	N	N	N	Y	Y	Y	Y
6 **Gingrich**							
7 **Barr**	N	Y	Y	N	N	N	N
8 **Chambliss**	N	Y	Y	N	N	N	N
9 **Deal**	N	Y	Y	N	N	Y	N
10 **Norwood**	?	?	?	–	N	Y	N
11 **Linder**	N	Y	Y	N	N	N	N
HAWAII							
1 Abercrombie	N	N	N	Y	N	Y	Y
2 Mink	N	N	N	Y	Y	Y	Y
IDAHO							
1 **Chenoweth**	N	Y	Y	N	N	Y	N
2 **Crapo**	?	Y	Y	N	N	Y	N
ILLINOIS							
1 Rush	N	N	N	Y	Y	Y	Y
2 Jackson	N	N	N	Y	Y	Y	Y
3 Lipinski	N	N	N	Y	Y	Y	Y
4 Gutierrez	N	N	N	Y	Y	Y	Y
5 Blagojevich	N	N	N	Y	Y	Y	Y
6 **Hyde**	N	Y	Y	N	N	N	N
7 Davis	N	N	N	Y	Y	Y	Y
8 **Crane**	N	Y	Y	N	N	N	N
9 Yates	N	N	N	Y	Y	Y	Y
10 **Porter**	?	Y	Y	Y	N	N	N
11 **Weller**	N	Y	Y	N	N	N	N
12 Costello	N	N	N	N	N	Y	N

ND Northern Democrats SD Southern Democrats

	309	310	311	312	313	314	315
13 ***Fawell***	N	Y	Y	Y	Y	N	Y
14 ***Hastert***	N	Y	Y	N	Y	N	N
15 ***Ewing***	?	Y	Y	N	N	N	N
16 ***Manzullo***	N	Y	Y	N	Y	Y	N
17 Evans	?	N	N	Y	Y	Y	Y
18 ***LaHood***	N	Y	Y	Y	Y	N	N
19 Poshard	?	N	N	Y	N	N	Y
20 ***Shimkus***	N	Y	Y	N	N	N	N
INDIANA							
1 Visclosky	N	N	N	Y	N	N	N
2 ***McIntosh***	N	Y	Y	N	N	Y	N
3 Roemer	N	N	N	Y	Y	N	N
4 ***Souder***	N	Y	Y	N	N	N	N
5 ***Buyer***	N	Y	Y	N	N	Y	N
6 ***Burton***	?	Y	Y	N	N	N	Y
7 ***Pease***	N	Y	Y	N	N	Y	Y
8 ***Hostettler***	N	Y	Y	N	N	Y	N
9 Hamilton	N	N	Y	Y	N	N	N
10 Carson	N	N	N	Y	Y	Y	Y
IOWA							
1 ***Leach***	N	Y	Y	Y	Y	Y	Y
2 ***Nussle***	N	Y	Y	N	Y	Y	N
3 Boswell	N	N	N	Y	N	Y	N
4 ***Ganske***	N	Y	Y	Y	Y	Y	N
5 ***Latham***	N	Y	Y	N	N	Y	N
KANSAS							
1 ***Moran***	N	Y	Y	N	N	Y	N
2 ***Ryun***	N	Y	Y	N	N	N	N
3 ***Snowbarger***	N	Y	Y	N	N	N	Y
4 ***Tiahrt***	N	Y	Y	N	N	N	N
KENTUCKY							
1 ***Whitfield***	N	Y	Y	N	Y	Y	N
2 ***Lewis***	N	Y	Y	N	N	Y	N
3 ***Northup***	?	Y	Y	N	N	Y	N
4 ***Bunning***	N	Y	Y	N	N	Y	N
5 ***Rogers***	N	Y	Y	N	Y	Y	N
6 Baesler	N	N	N	Y	Y	Y	Y
LOUISIANA							
1 ***Livingston***	N	Y	?	N	N	N	N
2 Jefferson	N	N	N	Y	Y	Y	Y
3 ***Tauzin***	N	Y	Y	N	N	N	N
4 ***McCrery***	?	Y	Y	N	N	N	N
5 ***Cooksey***	N	Y	Y	N	N	N	N
6 ***Baker***	?	?	?	N	N	N	N
7 John	?	?	?	?	?	?	?
MAINE							
1 Allen	N	N	N	Y	Y	Y	Y
2 Baldacci	N	N	N	Y	Y	Y	Y
MARYLAND							
1 ***Gilchrest***	N	Y	Y	Y	N	N	N
2 ***Ehrlich***	N	Y	Y	N	N	Y	Y
3 Cardin	?	N	N	Y	Y	N	Y
4 Wynn	N	N	N	Y	Y	Y	Y
5 Hoyer	N	N	N	Y	Y	N	N
6 ***Bartlett***	N	Y	Y	Y	N	N	N
7 Cummings	N	N	N	Y	Y	Y	Y
8 ***Morella***	N	Y	Y	Y	Y	Y	Y
MASSACHUSETTS							
1 Olver	N	N	N	Y	Y	N	Y
2 Neal	N	N	N	Y	Y	Y	Y
3 McGovern	N	N	N	Y	Y	Y	Y
4 Frank	N	N	N	Y	Y	N	Y
5 Meehan	N	N	N	Y	Y	Y	Y
6 Tierney	N	N	N	Y	Y	N	Y
7 Markey	?	N	N	Y	Y	Y	Y
8 Kennedy	N	N	N	Y	Y	Y	Y
9 Moakley	N	N	N	Y	N	?	?
10 Delahunt	N	N	N	Y	Y	Y	Y
MICHIGAN							
1 Stupak	N	N	N	Y	Y	Y	Y
2 ***Hoekstra***	N	Y	Y	N	N	Y	N
3 ***Ehlers***	N	Y	Y	Y	Y	N	N
4 ***Camp***	N	Y	Y	N	Y	Y	Y
5 Barcia	N	N	N	Y	Y	Y	Y
6 ***Upton***	N	Y	Y	Y	Y	N	Y
7 ***Smith***	N	Y	Y	Y	N	Y	Y
8 Stabenow	N	N	N	Y	Y	Y	Y
9 Kildee	N	N	N	Y	Y	Y	Y
10 Bonior	N	N	N	Y	Y	Y	Y
11 ***Knollenberg***	N	Y	Y	N	N	N	N
12 Levin	N	N	N	Y	Y	N	Y
13 Rivers	N	N	N	Y	Y	Y	Y
14 Conyers	Y	N	N	Y	Y	Y	Y
15 Kilpatrick	N	N	N	Y	Y	Y	Y
16 Dingell	N	N	N	Y	Y	N	Y

	309	310	311	312	313	314	315
MINNESOTA							
1 ***Gutknecht***	N	Y	Y	N	N	N	N
2 Minge	N	N	N	Y	Y	Y	N
3 ***Ramstad***	N	Y	Y	Y	Y	Y	N
4 Vento	N	N	N	Y	Y	Y	Y
5 Sabo	N	N	N	Y	Y	N	N
6 Luther	N	N	N	Y	Y	Y	Y
7 Peterson	?	N	N	Y	Y	Y	N
8 Oberstar	N	N	N	Y	Y	Y	Y
MISSISSIPPI							
1 ***Wicker***	N	Y	Y	N	N	Y	N
2 Thompson	N	N	N	Y	Y	Y	Y
3 ***Pickering***	?	Y	Y	N	N	Y	N
4 ***Parker***	N	Y	Y	N	Y	Y	N
5 Taylor	N	N	N	N	N	Y	N
MISSOURI							
1 Clay	N	N	N	Y	Y	Y	N
2 ***Talent***	N	Y	Y	N	N	N	N
3 Gephardt	Y	N	N	Y	Y	N	Y
4 Skelton	N	N	N	N	Y	Y	Y
5 McCarthy	N	N	N	Y	Y	Y	Y
6 Danner	?	N	N	Y	Y	Y	Y
7 ***Blunt***	N	Y	Y	N	N	N	N
8 ***Emerson***	N	Y	Y	N	Y	Y	N
9 ***Hulshof***	N	Y	Y	N	Y	Y	Y
MONTANA							
AL ***Hill***	?	Y	Y	N	N	Y	N
NEBRASKA							
1 ***Bereuter***	N	Y	Y	Y	N	N	Y
2 ***Christensen***	N	Y	Y	N	N	N	N
3 ***Barrett***	N	Y	Y	N	N	N	N
NEVADA							
1 ***Ensign***	N	Y	Y	N	Y	Y	Y
2 ***Gibbons***	N	Y	Y	N	N	Y	N
NEW HAMPSHIRE							
1 ***Sununu***	N	Y	Y	Y	Y	Y	Y
2 ***Bass***	N	Y	Y	Y	Y	Y	Y
NEW JERSEY							
1 Andrews	N	N	N	Y	Y	Y	Y
2 ***LoBiondo***	N	Y	Y	Y	Y	Y	N
3 ***Saxton***	N	Y	Y	Y	N	N	N
4 ***Smith***	N	Y	Y	N	Y	Y	Y
5 ***Roukema***	?	Y	Y	Y	N	Y	N
6 Pallone	N	N	N	Y	Y	Y	Y
7 ***Franks***	N	Y	Y	Y	Y	Y	N
8 Pascrell	N	N	N	Y	Y	Y	Y
9 Rothman	N	N	N	Y	Y	Y	Y
10 Payne	N	N	N	Y	Y	Y	N
11 ***Frelinghuysen***	N	Y	Y	Y	N	N	N
12 ***Pappas***	N	Y	Y	N	Y	Y	Y
13 Menendez	N	N	N	Y	Y	Y	Y
NEW MEXICO							
1 ***Wilson***	N	Y	Y	N	N	N	N
2 ***Skeen***	N	Y	Y	Y	N	N	N
3 ***Redmond***	N	Y	Y	N	N	N	N
NEW YORK							
1 ***Forbes***	N	Y	Y	Y	Y	N	Y
2 ***Lazio***	N	Y	Y	Y	Y	N	Y
3 ***King***	N	Y	Y	N	Y	N	Y
4 McCarthy	N	N	N	Y	Y	Y	Y
5 Ackerman	N	N	N	Y	Y	Y	Y
6 Meeks	N	N	N	Y	Y	N	Y
7 Manton	N	N	N	Y	Y	Y	Y
8 Nadler	Y	N	N	Y	Y	Y	Y
9 Schumer	?	N	N	Y	Y	Y	Y
10 Towns	N	N	N	Y	Y	Y	Y
11 Owens	?	N	N	Y	Y	Y	Y
12 Velázquez	N	N	N	Y	Y	Y	Y
13 ***Fossella***	N	Y	Y	N	Y	N	N
14 Maloney	N	N	N	Y	Y	Y	Y
15 Rangel	N	N	N	Y	Y	N	Y
16 Serrano	N	N	N	Y	Y	Y	Y
17 Engel	?	N	N	Y	Y	N	Y
18 Lowey	N	N	N	Y	Y	N	Y
19 ***Kelly***	N	Y	Y	Y	Y	Y	Y
20 ***Gilman***	N	Y	Y	Y	Y	N	Y
21 McNulty	?	?	?	?	?	?	?
22 ***Solomon***	N	Y	Y	N	?	Y	N
23 ***Boehlert***	N	Y	Y	Y	Y	Y	Y
24 ***McHugh***	N	Y	Y	Y	Y	Y	N
25 ***Walsh***	N	Y	Y	Y	Y	N	N
26 Hinchey	N	N	?	Y	Y	Y	Y
27 ***Paxon***	N	Y	Y	N	N	N	N
28 Slaughter	N	N	N	Y	Y	Y	Y
29 LaFalce	N	N	N	Y	Y	Y	Y

	309	310	311	312	313	314	315
30 ***Quinn***	N	Y	Y	Y	Y	Y	Y
31 ***Houghton***	N	Y	Y	Y	N	Y	Y
NORTH CAROLINA							
1 Clayton	N	N	N	Y	Y	Y	Y
2 Etheridge	N	N	N	Y	Y	Y	Y
3 ***Jones***	N	Y	Y	N	N	Y	N
4 Price	N	N	N	Y	Y	N	Y
5 ***Burr***	N	Y	Y	N	N	N	N
6 ***Coble***	N	Y	Y	N	N	Y	N
7 McIntyre	N	N	N	Y	Y	Y	Y
8 Hefner	?	N	N	Y	N	Y	Y
9 ***Myrick***	N	Y	Y	N	N	Y	Y
10 ***Ballenger***	N	Y	Y	Y	N	N	N
11 ***Taylor***	N	Y	Y	N	N	Y	N
12 Watt	N	N	N	Y	Y	Y	Y
NORTH DAKOTA							
AL Pomeroy	N	N	N	Y	N	N	N
OHIO							
1 ***Chabot***	N	Y	Y	N	N	Y	N
2 ***Portman***	N	Y	Y	N	N	Y	N
3 Hall	N	N	N	Y	N	N	N
4 ***Oxley***	N	Y	Y	N	N	N	N
5 ***Gillmor***	N	Y	Y	Y	N	N	N
6 Strickland	N	N	N	Y	Y	Y	Y
7 ***Hobson***	N	Y	Y	N	N	N	N
8 ***Boehner***	N	Y	Y	N	N	N	N
9 Kaptur	?	N	N	Y	N	Y	Y
10 Kucinich	N	N	N	Y	N	N	N
11 Stokes	N	N	N	Y	?	Y	N
12 ***Kasich***	N	Y	Y	N	Y	Y	N
13 Brown	N	N	N	Y	Y	Y	Y
14 Sawyer	N	N	N	Y	Y	N	N
15 ***Pryce***	N	Y	Y	N	N	N	N
16 ***Regula***	N	Y	Y	Y	N	N	N
17 Traficant	N	Y	Y	Y	N	N	N
18 ***Ney***	N	Y	Y	N	N	N	N
19 ***LaTourette***	N	Y	Y	Y	N	Y	N
OKLAHOMA							
1 ***Largent***	N	Y	Y	N	N	N	N
2 ***Coburn***	N	Y	Y	N	N	N	N
3 ***Watkins***	N	Y	Y	N	N	N	N
4 ***Watts***	N	Y	Y	N	N	N	N
5 ***Istook***	N	Y	Y	N	N	N	N
6 ***Lucas***	N	Y	Y	N	N	N	N
OREGON							
1 Furse	N	N	N	Y	Y	Y	Y
2 ***Smith***	N	Y	Y	N	N	Y	N
3 Blumenauer	N	N	N	Y	Y	Y	Y
4 DeFazio	Y	N	N	Y	Y	Y	Y
5 Hooley	N	N	N	Y	Y	Y	Y
PENNSYLVANIA							
1 Brady	N	N	N	Y	N	N	N
2 Fattah	N	N	N	Y	N	N	N
3 Borski	N	N	N	Y	N	N	N
4 Klink	N	N	N	Y	N	N	Y
5 ***Peterson***	N	?	Y	N	N	Y	N
6 Holden	N	N	N	Y	N	N	N
7 ***Weldon***	?	Y	Y	Y	Y	N	Y
8 ***Greenwood***	N	Y	Y	Y	Y	N	Y
9 ***Shuster***	N	Y	Y	N	N	N	N
10 ***McDade***	?	?	?	?	N	N	N
11 Kanjorski	N	N	N	Y	N	N	?
12 Murtha	N	N	N	Y	N	N	N
13 ***Fox***	N	Y	Y	Y	Y	N	Y
14 Coyne	N	N	N	Y	N	N	Y
15 McHale	?	N	N	Y	Y	Y	Y
16 ***Pitts***	N	Y	Y	N	Y	N	Y
17 ***Gekas***	N	?	?	N	Y	Y	N
18 Doyle	N	N	N	Y	N	N	N
19 ***Goodling***	N	Y	Y	N	N	Y	N
20 Mascara	N	N	N	Y	N	N	N
21 ***English***	N	Y	Y	Y	Y	N	N
RHODE ISLAND							
1 Kennedy	N	N	N	Y	Y	Y	Y
2 Weygand	N	N	N	Y	Y	Y	Y
SOUTH CAROLINA							
1 ***Sanford***	N	Y	Y	N	N	N	N
2 ***Spence***	N	Y	Y	N	N	N	N
3 ***Graham***	N	Y	?	N	N	Y	Y
4 ***Inglis***	N	Y	Y	N	N	N	Y
5 Spratt	N	N	N	Y	Y	Y	Y
6 Clyburn	N	N	N	Y	Y	Y	Y
SOUTH DAKOTA							
AL ***Thune***	N	Y	Y	N	Y	Y	Y

	309	310	311	312	313	314	315
TENNESSEE							
1 ***Jenkins***	N	Y	Y	N	N	Y	N
2 ***Duncan***	N	Y	Y	N	Y	Y	N
3 ***Wamp***	N	Y	Y	N	N	N	N
4 ***Hilleary***	N	Y	Y	N	N	N	N
5 Clement	N	N	N	Y	Y	N	Y
6 Gordon	N	N	N	Y	Y	N	N
7 ***Bryant***	N	Y	Y	N	N	Y	N
8 Tanner	N	N	N	N	Y	Y	N
9 Ford	–	–	–	+	+	+	+
TEXAS							
1 Sandlin	N	N	N	Y	N	N	N
2 Turner	?	N	N	N	N	N	Y
3 ***Johnson, Sam***	N	Y	Y	N	N	N	N
4 Hall	N	Y	Y	N	N	N	N
5 ***Sessions***	N	Y	Y	N	N	N	N
6 ***Barton***	N	Y	Y	N	N	N	N
7 ***Archer***	N	Y	Y	N	N	Y	N
8 ***Brady***	N	Y	Y	N	N	N	N
9 Lampson	N	N	N	Y	N	N	Y
10 Doggett	N	N	N	Y	Y	N	Y
11 Edwards	N	N	N	Y	N	N	N
12 ***Granger***	N	Y	Y	Y	N	N	N
13 ***Thornberry***	N	Y	Y	N	N	N	N
14 ***Paul***	N	Y	Y	N	Y	Y	N
15 Hinojosa	N	–	–	Y	Y	Y	Y
16 Reyes	N	N	N	Y	N	N	Y
17 Stenholm	?	Y	Y	N	N	N	N
18 Jackson-Lee	N	N	N	Y	N	N	Y
19 ***Combest***	N	Y	Y	N	N	N	N
20 Gonzalez	?	?	?	?	?	?	?
21 ***Smith***	N	Y	Y	N	N	N	N
22 ***DeLay***	?	Y	Y	N	N	N	N
23 ***Bonilla***	N	Y	Y	N	N	N	N
24 Frost	N	N	N	Y	N	N	N
25 Bentsen	N	N	N	Y	N	N	N
26 ***Armey***	?	Y	Y	N	N	Y	N
27 Ortiz	–	–	–	Y	N	N	N
28 Rodriguez	N	N	?	Y	Y	N	Y
29 Green	N	N	N	Y	N	N	N
30 Johnson, E.B.	N	N	N	Y	Y	N	N
UTAH							
1 ***Hansen***	N	Y	Y	N	N	Y	N
2 ***Cook***	N	Y	Y	Y	N	Y	N
3 ***Cannon***	N	Y	Y	N	N	Y	N
VERMONT							
AL *Sanders*	?	N	N	Y	Y	Y	Y
VIRGINIA							
1 ***Bateman***	N	Y	Y	N	N	N	N
2 Pickett	?	N	N	Y	N	N	N
3 Scott	N	N	N	Y	Y	N	Y
4 Sisisky	N	N	N	Y	N	N	N
5 Goode	N	N	N	Y	Y	Y	Y
6 ***Goodlatte***	N	Y	Y	N	N	Y	N
7 ***Bliley***	N	Y	Y	N	N	N	N
8 Moran	N	N	N	Y	Y	N	Y
9 Boucher	N	N	N	Y	Y	Y	N
10 ***Wolf***	N	Y	Y	N	N	N	N
11 ***Davis***	N	Y	Y	Y	N	N	Y
WASHINGTON							
1 ***White***	N	Y	Y	N	N	Y	N
2 ***Metcalf***	N	Y	Y	N	Y	Y	N
3 ***Smith, Linda***	N	Y	Y	N	Y	Y	N
4 ***Hastings***	N	Y	Y	N	N	Y	N
5 ***Nethercutt***	N	Y	Y	N	N	Y	N
6 Dicks	N	N	N	Y	N	Y	Y
7 McDermott	Y	N	N	Y	Y	N	Y
8 ***Dunn***	?	Y	Y	N	Y	Y	N
9 Smith, Adam	N	N	N	Y	Y	Y	Y
WEST VIRGINIA							
1 Mollohan	N	N	N	Y	N	N	N
2 Wise	N	N	N	Y	Y	N	N
3 Rahall	N	N	N	Y	Y	Y	Y
WISCONSIN							
1 ***Neumann***	N	Y	Y	N	Y	Y	Y
2 ***Klug***	N	Y	Y	Y	Y	N	Y
3 Kind	N	N	N	Y	Y	Y	Y
4 Kleczka	N	N	N	Y	Y	Y	Y
5 Barrett	N	N	N	Y	Y	Y	Y
6 ***Petri***	N	Y	Y	N	Y	Y	Y
7 Obey	N	N	N	Y	Y	Y	Y
8 Johnson	N	N	N	Y	Y	Y	Y
9 ***Sensenbrenner***	N	Y	Y	N	N	Y	N
WYOMING							
AL ***Cubin***	N	Y	Y	N	N	Y	N

Southern states - Ala., Ark., Fla., Ga., Ky., La., Miss., N.C., Okla., S.C., Tenn., Texas, Va.

House Votes 317, 318, 319, 320, 321, 322, 323 *

316. Quorum Call.* 408 Responded. July 22, 1998.

317. H J Res 121. "Normal Trade Relations" Status for China Disapproval/Passage. Passage of the bill to deny the president's request to provide "normal trade relations" (formerly known as "most-favored-nation" or MFN trade status) for items produced in China for the period July 1998 through July 1999. Rejected 166-264: R 78-149; D 87-115 (ND 73-76, SD 14-39); I 1-0. July 22, 1998.

318. HR 1689. Securities Litigation Federal Filing Requirement/Passage. Bliley, R-Va., motion to suspend the rules and pass the bill to require class action lawsuits alleging securities fraud to be filed in federal rather than state courts. Motion agreed to 340-83: R 221-2; D 119-80 (ND 82-65, SD 37-15); I 0-1. July 22, 1998. A two-thirds majority of those present and voting (283 in this case) is required for passage under suspension of the rules.

319. HR 4193. Fiscal 1999 Interior Appropriations/Indian Health Service Support Costs Allocation. Parker, R-Miss., amendment to strike a provision in the bill that directs the Indian Health Service to allocate contract support costs funding on a pro rata basis to all tribal contractors. Rejected 135-289: R 46-178; D 89-110 (ND 67-80, SD 22-30); I 0-1. July 22, 1998.

320. HR 4193. Fiscal 1999 Interior Appropriations/Trust Fund Use Restrictions. Miller, D-Calif., amendment to prohibit the use of certain trust funds (the Knuston-Vandenberg restoration fund and the timber salvage fund) from being used for administrative overhead expenses. Adopted 236-182: R 58-163; D 177-19 (ND 137-9, SD 40-10); I 1-0. July 22, 1998.

321. HR 1122. Abortion Procedure Ban/Discharge Motion. Canady, R-Fla., motion to discharge from the Judiciary Committee and bring to the House floor the bill that would ban certain late-term abortion procedures. Motion agreed to 295-131: R 219-6; D 76-124 (ND 49-99, SD 27-25); I 0-1. July 23, 1998.

322. HR 3616. Fiscal 1999 Defense Authorization/Motion to Instruct. Skelton, D-Mo., motion to instruct the House conferees to insist upon the House bill's authorization levels for Theater Missile Defense programs and space-based lasers. Motion agreed to 424-0: R 225-0; D 198-0 (ND 147-0, SD 51-0); I 1-0. July 23, 1998.

323. HR 3616. Fiscal 1999 Defense Authorization/Closed Conference. Spence, R-S.C., motion to close portions of the conference to the public during consideration of national security issues. Motion agreed to 412-5: R 217-0; D 194-5 (ND 142-5, SD 52-0); I 1-0. July 23, 1998.

* CQ does not include quorum calls in its vote charts.

Key

- **Y** Voted for (yea).
- **#** Paired for.
- **+** Announced for.
- **N** Voted against (nay).
- **X** Paired against.
- **–** Announced against.
- **P** Voted "present."
- **C** Voted "present" to avoid possible conflict of interest.
- **?** Did not vote or otherwise make a position known.

Democrats   **Republicans**   *Independent*

	317	318	319	320	321	322	323
ALABAMA							
1 **Callahan**	N	Y	N	N	Y	Y	Y
2 **Everett**	Y	Y	N	N	Y	Y	Y
3 **Riley**	Y	Y	Y	N	Y	Y	Y
4 **Aderholt**	Y	Y	Y	N	Y	Y	Y
5 Cramer	N	Y	N	Y	Y	Y	Y
6 **Bachus**	N	Y	N	N	Y	Y	Y
7 Hilliard	N	N	Y	Y	N	Y	Y
ALASKA							
AL **Young**	Y	Y	N	N	Y	Y	Y
ARIZONA							
1 **Salmon**	N	Y	Y	Y	Y	Y	Y
2 Pastor	N	N	Y	N	N	Y	Y
3 **Stump**	N	Y	N	N	Y	Y	?
4 **Shadegg**	N	Y	N	N	Y	Y	Y
5 **Kolbe**	N	Y	N	Y	Y	Y	Y
6 **Hayworth**	N	Y	Y	N	Y	Y	Y
ARKANSAS							
1 Berry	N	Y	N	Y	Y	Y	Y
2 Snyder	N	Y	N	Y	N	Y	Y
3 **Hutchinson**	N	Y	N	Y	Y	Y	Y
4 **Dickey**	Y	Y	N	Y	Y	Y	Y
CALIFORNIA							
1 **Riggs**	N	Y	N	N	Y	Y	Y
2 **Herger**	N	?	N	N	Y	Y	Y
3 Fazio	N	Y	N	Y	N	Y	Y
4 **Doolittle**	Y	Y	N	N	Y	Y	Y
5 Matsui	N	Y	N	Y	N	Y	Y
6 Woolsey	Y	N	Y	Y	N	Y	N
7 Miller	Y	Y	N	Y	N	Y	Y
8 Pelosi	Y	N	Y	N	Y	Y	?
9 Lee	Y	N	Y	Y	N	Y	Y
10 Tauscher	N	Y	N	Y	Y	Y	Y
11 **Pombo**	Y	Y	N	Y	Y	Y	Y
12 Lantos	N	Y	N	Y	Y	Y	Y
13 Stark	Y	N	Y	N	Y	N	N
14 Eshoo	N	Y	N	Y	N	Y	Y
15 **Campbell**	N	Y	N	Y	Y	Y	Y
16 Lofgren	N	Y	N	Y	Y	Y	Y
17 Farr	N	Y	N	Y	N	Y	Y
18 Condit	Y	Y	Y	?	Y	Y	Y
19 **Radanovich**	N	Y	+	–	Y	Y	Y
20 Dooley	N	N	N	Y	Y	Y	Y
21 **Thomas**	N	Y	N	Y	Y	Y	Y
22 Capps, L.	N	Y	N	Y	N	Y	Y
23 **Gallegly**	Y	Y	N	N	Y	Y	Y
24 Sherman	N	Y	N	Y	Y	Y	Y
25 **McKeon**	N	Y	N	N	Y	Y	Y
26 Berman	N	N	N	Y	Y	Y	Y
27 **Rogan**	N	Y	N	N	Y	Y	Y
28 **Dreier**	N	Y	N	Y	Y	Y	Y
29 Waxman	Y	N	Y	Y	N	Y	Y
30 Becerra	N	N	Y	Y	N	Y	Y
31 Martinez	N	Y	N	Y	Y	Y	Y
32 Dixon	Y	Y	N	Y	Y	Y	Y
33 Royall-Allard	N	N	Y	Y	N	Y	Y
34 Torres	Y	N	N	Y	N	Y	Y
35 Waters	Y	N	Y	Y	N	Y	Y
36 Harman	N	Y	N	Y	N	Y	Y
37 Millender-McD.	N	N	Y	Y	N	Y	Y

	317	318	319	320	321	322	323
38 **Horn**	Y	Y	N	Y	N	Y	Y
39 **Royce**	Y	Y	N	N	Y	Y	Y
40 **Lewis**	N	Y	N	N	Y	Y	Y
41 **Kim**	N	Y	N	N	Y	Y	Y
42 Brown	N	N	Y	Y	N	Y	Y
43 **Calvert**	N	Y	N	N	Y	Y	Y
44 **Bono, M.**	N	Y	N	Y	Y	Y	Y
45 **Rohrabacher**	Y	Y	Y	Y	Y	Y	Y
46 Sanchez	Y	Y	N	Y	N	Y	Y
47 **Cox**	Y	Y	N	Y	Y	Y	Y
48 **Packard**	Y	Y	N	N	Y	Y	Y
49 **Bilbray**	N	Y	N	Y	Y	Y	Y
50 Filner	N	N	Y	Y	N	Y	Y
51 **Cunningham**	N	Y	N	N	Y	Y	Y
52 **Hunter**	Y	Y	?	?	Y	Y	?
COLORADO							
1 DeGette	N	N	N	Y	N	Y	Y
2 Skaggs	N	N	N	Y	N	Y	Y
3 **McInnis**	N	Y	N	N	Y	Y	Y
4 **Schaffer**	Y	Y	Y	Y	Y	Y	Y
5 **Hefley**	Y	Y	N	N	Y	Y	Y
6 **Schaefer**	Y	Y	Y	Y	Y	Y	Y
CONNECTICUT							
1 Kennelly	N	Y	Y	Y	N	Y	Y
2 Gejdenson	N	Y	N	Y	Y	Y	Y
3 DeLauro	N	Y	Y	Y	N	Y	Y
4 **Shays**	N	Y	N	Y	Y	Y	Y
5 Maloney	Y	Y	N	Y	Y	Y	Y
6 **Johnson**	N	Y	N	Y	N	Y	Y
DELAWARE							
AL **Castle**	N	Y	N	Y	Y	Y	Y
FLORIDA							
1 **Scarborough**	Y	Y	Y	Y	Y	Y	Y
2 Boyd	N	Y	N	N	Y	Y	Y
3 Brown	N	N	Y	N	N	Y	Y
4 **Fowler**	Y	Y	N	Y	Y	Y	Y
5 Thurman	N	N	Y	N	Y	Y	Y
6 **Stearns**	Y	Y	N	?	Y	Y	Y
7 **Mica**	N	Y	N	Y	Y	Y	Y
8 **McCollum**	N	Y	N	N	Y	Y	Y
9 **Bilirakis**	N	Y	N	Y	Y	Y	Y
10 **Young**	?	?	?	?	?	?	?
11 Davis	N	Y	Y	Y	Y	Y	Y
12 **Canady**	N	Y	N	N	Y	Y	Y
13 **Miller**	N	Y	N	Y	Y	Y	Y
14 **Goss**	N	Y	N	N	Y	Y	Y
15 **Weldon**	Y	Y	N	N	Y	Y	Y
16 **Foley**	N	Y	N	Y	Y	Y	Y
17 Meek	N	N	Y	N	Y	Y	Y
18 **Ros-Lehtinen**	Y	Y	N	Y	Y	Y	Y
19 Wexler	Y	Y	Y	N	Y	Y	Y
20 Deutsch	N	Y	Y	Y	N	Y	Y
21 **Diaz-Balart**	Y	Y	N	Y	Y	Y	Y
22 **Shaw**	N	Y	N	Y	Y	Y	Y
23 Hastings	Y	Y	Y	N	Y	Y	Y
GEORGIA							
1 **Kingston**	Y	Y	N	N	Y	Y	Y
2 Bishop	Y	Y	Y	Y	Y	Y	Y
3 **Collins**	Y	Y	N	N	Y	Y	Y
4 **McKinney**	Y	N	Y	N	P	Y	Y
5 Lewis	Y	N	N	?	N	Y	Y
6 **Gingrich**	N	Y					
7 **Barr**	Y	Y	N	N	Y	Y	Y
8 **Chambliss**	Y	Y	N	N	Y	Y	Y
9 **Deal**	Y	Y	N	N	Y	Y	Y
10 **Norwood**	Y	Y	N	Y	Y	Y	Y
11 **Linder**	N	Y	N	N	Y	Y	Y
HAWAII							
1 Abercrombie	Y	N	N	Y	N	?	Y
2 Mink	Y	N	N	Y	N	Y	Y
IDAHO							
1 **Chenoweth**	Y	Y	N	N	Y	Y	Y
2 **Crapo**	N	Y	N	N	Y	Y	Y
ILLINOIS							
1 Rush	N	Y	Y	N	Y	Y	Y
2 Jackson	Y	N	Y	N	N	Y	Y
3 Lipinski	Y	N	N	Y	Y	Y	Y
4 Gutierrez	N	N	Y	N	Y	Y	Y
5 Blagojevich	N	N	Y	Y	N	Y	Y
6 **Hyde**	Y	Y	N	N	Y	Y	Y
7 Davis	N	N	Y	N	Y	Y	Y
8 **Crane**	Y	Y	N	N	Y	Y	Y
9 Yates	Y	N	Y	N	Y	Y	Y
10 **Porter**	N	Y	N	Y	Y	Y	Y
11 **Weller**	N	Y	N	Y	Y	Y	Y
12 Costello	Y	N	N	Y	Y	Y	Y

ND Northern Democrats   SD Southern Democrats

	317	318	319	320	321	322	323
13 ***Fawell***	N	?	N	Y	Y	Y	?
14 ***Hastert***	N	Y	Y	N	Y	Y	Y
15 ***Ewing***	N	Y	N	N	Y	Y	Y
16 ***Manzullo***	N	Y	N	N	Y	Y	Y
17 Evans	Y	N	N	Y	N	Y	Y
18 ***LaHood***	N	Y	N	Y	Y	Y	Y
19 Poshard	N	Y	?	?	Y	Y	Y
20 ***Shimkus***	N	Y	N	N	Y	Y	Y
INDIANA							
1 Visclosky	Y	Y	N	N	Y	Y	Y
2 ***McIntosh***	N	Y	Y	N	Y	Y	Y
3 Roemer	N	Y	N	Y	Y	Y	Y
4 ***Souder***	Y	Y	N	N	Y	Y	Y
5 ***Buyer***	N	Y	N	N	Y	Y	?
6 ***Burton***	Y	Y	N	N	Y	Y	Y
7 ***Pease***	N	Y	N	N	Y	Y	Y
8 ***Hostettler***	Y	Y	N	N	Y	Y	Y
9 Hamilton	N	Y	N	Y	Y	Y	Y
10 Carson	Y	N	N	Y	N	Y	Y
IOWA							
1 ***Leach***	N	Y	N	Y	Y	?	Y
2 ***Nussle***	N	Y	Y	N	Y	Y	Y
3 Boswell	N	Y	Y	Y	Y	Y	Y
4 ***Ganske***	Y	Y	N	Y	Y	Y	Y
5 ***Latham***	N	Y	Y	N	Y	Y	Y
KANSAS							
1 ***Moran***	N	Y	Y	N	Y	Y	Y
2 ***Ryun***	N	Y	N	N	Y	Y	Y
3 ***Snowbarger***	N	Y	N	N	Y	Y	Y
4 ***Tiahrt***	Y	Y	N	N	Y	Y	Y
KENTUCKY							
1 ***Whitfield***	N	Y	N	N	Y	Y	Y
2 ***Lewis***	N	Y	N	N	Y	Y	Y
3 ***Northup***	N	Y	N	N	Y	Y	Y
4 ***Bunning***	Y	Y	N	N	Y	Y	Y
5 ***Rogers***	Y	Y	N	N	Y	Y	Y
6 Baesler	N	Y	N	Y	Y	Y	Y
LOUISIANA							
1 ***Livingston***	N	Y	N	N	Y	Y	Y
2 Jefferson	N	Y	Y	Y	Y	Y	Y
3 ***Tauzin***	N	Y	N	N	Y	Y	Y
4 ***McCrery***	N	Y	N	N	Y	Y	Y
5 ***Cooksey***	N	Y	N	N	Y	Y	?
6 ***Baker***	N	Y	N	N	Y	Y	Y
7 John	N	Y	N	+	Y	Y	Y
MAINE							
1 Allen	N	Y	N	Y	N	Y	Y
2 Baldacci	N	N	N	Y	N	Y	Y
MARYLAND							
1 ***Gilchrest***	N	Y	N	N	Y	Y	Y
2 ***Ehrlich***	Y	Y	N	N	Y	Y	Y
3 Cardin	Y	Y	Y	Y	N	Y	Y
4 Wynn	Y	Y	N	Y	N	Y	Y
5 Hoyer	Y	Y	N	N	N	Y	Y
6 ***Bartlett***	Y	Y	Y	Y	Y	Y	Y
7 Cummings	Y	N	N	Y	N	Y	Y
8 ***Morella***	N	Y	N	Y	N	Y	Y
MASSACHUSETTS							
1 Olver	Y	N	N	Y	N	Y	Y
2 Neal	N	Y	N	Y	Y	Y	Y
3 McGovern	N	Y	Y	Y	N	Y	Y
4 Frank	Y	Y	N	Y	N	Y	Y
5 Meehan	N	Y	N	Y	N	Y	Y
6 Tierney	Y	N	N	Y	N	Y	Y
7 Markey	Y	N	?	?	?	?	?
8 Kennedy	Y	Y	Y	Y	N	Y	Y
9 Moakley	N	Y	?	?	Y	Y	Y
10 Delahunt	Y	N	Y	Y	N	Y	Y
MICHIGAN							
1 Stupak	Y	N	Y	Y	Y	Y	Y
2 ***Hoekstra***	N	Y	N	N	Y	Y	Y
3 ***Ehlers***	N	Y	N	N	Y	Y	Y
4 ***Camp***	N	Y	Y	N	Y	Y	Y
5 Barcia	Y	Y	Y	Y	Y	Y	Y
6 ***Upton***	N	Y	N	Y	Y	Y	Y
7 ***Smith***	N	Y	N	N	Y	Y	Y
8 Stabenow	N	Y	Y	Y	N	Y	Y
9 Kildee	Y	Y	Y	Y	Y	Y	Y
10 Bonior	Y	N	Y	Y	Y	Y	Y
11 ***Knollenberg***	N	Y	N	N	Y	Y	Y
12 Levin	N	N	Y	Y	N	Y	Y
13 Rivers	Y	N	Y	Y	N	Y	Y
14 Conyers	N	N	N	Y	N	Y	N
15 Kilpatrick	Y	Y	Y	Y	N	Y	Y
16 Dingell	N	N	N	Y	Y	Y	Y

	317	318	319	320	321	322	323
MINNESOTA							
1 ***Gutknecht***	N	Y	N	N	Y	Y	Y
2 Minge	N	Y	Y	N	Y	Y	Y
3 ***Ramstad***	N	Y	Y	Y	Y	Y	Y
4 Vento	Y	Y	Y	Y	N	Y	Y
5 Sabo	Y	Y	Y	N	N	Y	Y
6 Luther	N	Y	N	Y	N	Y	Y
7 Peterson	N	Y	Y	N	Y	Y	Y
8 Oberstar	N	N	Y	Y	Y	Y	Y
MISSISSIPPI							
1 ***Wicker***	N	Y	Y	N	Y	Y	Y
2 Thompson	Y	N	Y	Y	N	Y	Y
3 ***Pickering***	Y	Y	Y	N	Y	Y	Y
4 ***Parker***	N	Y	Y	N	Y	Y	Y
5 Taylor	Y	N	Y	N	Y	Y	Y
MISSOURI							
1 Clay	Y	N	Y	?	N	Y	Y
2 ***Talent***	N	Y	N	N	Y	Y	Y
3 Gephardt	Y	N	N	Y	Y	Y	Y
4 Skelton	N	Y	N	Y	Y	Y	Y
5 McCarthy	N	Y	N	Y	N	Y	Y
6 Danner	Y	Y	N	Y	Y	Y	Y
7 ***Blunt***	Y	N	N	Y	Y	Y	?
8 ***Emerson***	N	Y	N	N	Y	Y	Y
9 ***Hulshof***	N	Y	Y	Y	Y	Y	Y
MONTANA							
AL ***Hill***	N	Y	N	N	Y	Y	Y
NEBRASKA							
1 ***Bereuter***	N	Y	N	N	Y	Y	Y
2 ***Christensen***	Y	Y	N	N	Y	Y	Y
3 ***Barrett***	N	Y	N	N	Y	Y	Y
NEVADA							
1 ***Ensign***	Y	Y	N	Y	Y	Y	Y
2 ***Gibbons***	Y	Y	N	Y	Y	Y	Y
NEW HAMPSHIRE							
1 ***Sununu***	Y	Y	Y	N	Y	Y	Y
2 ***Bass***	N	Y	N	N	Y	Y	Y
NEW JERSEY							
1 Andrews	N	Y	N	Y	N	Y	Y
2 ***LoBiondo***	Y	Y	Y	Y	Y	Y	Y
3 ***Saxton***	Y	Y	Y	Y	Y	Y	Y
4 ***Smith***	Y	Y	N	Y	Y	Y	Y
5 ***Roukema***	N	Y	N	Y	Y	Y	Y
6 Pallone	Y	Y	Y	Y	N	Y	Y
7 ***Franks***	N	Y	N	Y	Y	Y	Y
8 Pascrell	Y	Y	N	Y	Y	Y	Y
9 Rothman	Y	Y	Y	Y	N	Y	Y
10 Payne	Y	N	Y	Y	N	Y	Y
11 ***Frelinghuysen***	N	Y	N	N	Y	Y	Y
12 ***Pappas***	Y	Y	N	Y	Y	Y	Y
13 Menendez	Y	N	Y	Y	N	Y	Y
NEW MEXICO							
1 ***Wilson***	N	Y	N	N	Y	Y	Y
2 ***Skeen***	N	Y	N	N	Y	Y	Y
3 ***Redmond***	N	Y	Y	N	Y	Y	Y
NEW YORK							
1 ***Forbes***	Y	Y	N	Y	Y	Y	Y
2 ***Lazio***	N	Y	Y	Y	Y	Y	?
3 ***King***	Y	Y	N	Y	Y	Y	Y
4 McCarthy	Y	Y	N	Y	N	Y	Y
5 Ackerman	N	Y	N	Y	N	Y	Y
6 Meeks	N	Y	Y	Y	N	Y	Y
7 Manton	N	Y	Y	Y	Y	Y	Y
8 Nadler	Y	N	N	Y	N	Y	Y
9 Schumer	N	N	N	Y	N	Y	Y
10 Towns	N	Y	N	Y	N	Y	Y
11 Owens	Y	N	N	Y	N	Y	Y
12 Velázquez	Y	Y	N	Y	N	Y	Y
13 ***Fossella***	N	Y	Y	Y	Y	Y	Y
14 Maloney	N	Y	N	Y	N	Y	Y
15 Rangel	N	Y	Y	Y	N	Y	Y
16 Serrano	–	–	–	+	–	+	+
17 Engel	Y	N	Y	Y	N	Y	Y
18 Lowey	N	P	N	Y	N	Y	Y
19 ***Kelly***	N	Y	N	?	Y	Y	Y
20 ***Gilman***	Y	Y	N	Y	N	Y	Y
21 McNulty	?	?	Y	Y	Y	Y	Y
22 ***Solomon***	Y	Y	N	N	Y	Y	Y
23 ***Boehlert***	N	Y	N	Y	Y	Y	Y
24 ***McHugh***	N	Y	N	N	Y	Y	Y
25 ***Walsh***	N	Y	N	Y	Y	Y	Y
26 Hinchey	Y	N	N	Y	Y	Y	Y
27 ***Paxon***	N	Y	N	N	Y	Y	Y
28 Slaughter	N	Y	N	Y	N	Y	Y
29 LaFalce	N	Y	N	Y	Y	Y	Y

	317	318	319	320	321	322	323
30 ***Quinn***	N	Y	N	Y	Y	Y	Y
31 ***Houghton***	N	Y	N	Y	Y	Y	Y
NORTH CAROLINA							
1 Clayton	Y	N	N	Y	N	Y	Y
2 Etheridge	N	Y	N	Y	Y	Y	Y
3 ***Jones***	Y	Y	N	N	Y	Y	Y
4 Price	N	Y	N	Y	N	Y	Y
5 ***Burr***	Y	Y	Y	N	Y	Y	Y
6 ***Coble***	N	Y	N	N	Y	Y	Y
7 McIntyre	Y	Y	Y	Y	Y	Y	Y
8 Hefner	Y	Y	Y	Y	Y	Y	Y
9 ***Myrick***	Y	Y	N	N	Y	Y	Y
10 ***Ballenger***	N	Y	N	Y	Y	Y	Y
11 ***Taylor***	Y	Y	N	N	Y	Y	Y
12 Watt	N	N	N	Y	N	Y	Y
NORTH DAKOTA							
AL Pomeroy	N	Y	Y	Y	Y	Y	Y
OHIO							
1 ***Chabot***	N	Y	N	Y	Y	Y	Y
2 ***Portman***	N	Y	N	Y	Y	Y	Y
3 Hall	Y	N	N	Y	Y	Y	Y
4 ***Oxley***	N	Y	N	N	Y	Y	Y
5 ***Gillmor***	N	Y	N	N	Y	Y	Y
6 Strickland	Y	Y	N	Y	Y	Y	Y
7 ***Hobson***	Y	Y	N	N	Y	Y	Y
8 ***Boehner***	N	Y	Y	N	Y	Y	Y
9 Kaptur	Y	N	N	Y	Y	Y	Y
10 Kucinich	Y	N	Y	Y	Y	Y	Y
11 Stokes	Y	N	Y	Y	N	Y	Y
12 ***Kasich***	Y	Y	N	N	Y	Y	Y
13 Brown	Y	Y	N	Y	N	Y	Y
14 Sawyer	N	Y	N	Y	N	Y	Y
15 ***Pryce***	N	Y	N	N	Y	Y	Y
16 ***Regula***	N	Y	N	N	Y	Y	Y
17 Traficant	Y	Y	Y	Y	Y	Y	Y
18 ***Ney***	Y	Y	N	Y	Y	Y	Y
19 ***LaTourette***	N	Y	N	Y	Y	Y	Y
OKLAHOMA							
1 ***Largent***	N	Y	N	N	Y	Y	Y
2 ***Coburn***	Y	Y	N	N	Y	Y	Y
3 ***Watkins***	N	Y	N	N	Y	Y	Y
4 ***Watts***	N	Y	N	N	Y	Y	Y
5 ***Istook***	N	Y	N	N	Y	Y	Y
6 ***Lucas***	N	Y	N	N	Y	Y	Y
OREGON							
1 Furse	N	Y	Y	Y	N	Y	N
2 ***Smith***	N	Y	N	N	Y	Y	Y
3 Blumenauer	N	Y	N	Y	N	Y	Y
4 DeFazio	Y	N	Y	Y	N	Y	N
5 Hooley	N	+	Y	Y	N	Y	Y
PENNSYLVANIA							
1 Brady	Y	N	N	Y	N	Y	Y
2 Fattah	N	N	Y	Y	N	Y	Y
3 Borski	Y	N	N	Y	Y	Y	Y
4 Klink	Y	N	Y	N	Y	Y	Y
5 ***Peterson***	N	Y	N	N	Y	Y	Y
6 Holden	N	Y	Y	Y	Y	Y	Y
7 ***Weldon***	N	Y	N	Y	Y	Y	Y
8 ***Greenwood***	N	Y	Y	Y	N	Y	Y
9 ***Shuster***	N	Y	N	N	Y	Y	Y
10 ***McDade***	Y	Y	N	N	Y	Y	Y
11 Kanjorski	N	N	N	Y	Y	Y	Y
12 Murtha	N	Y	N	N	Y	?	?
13 ***Fox***	N	Y	N	Y	Y	Y	Y
14 Coyne	Y	N	Y	Y	N	Y	Y
15 McHale	N	Y	Y	Y	Y	Y	Y
16 ***Pitts***	N	Y	Y	N	Y	Y	Y
17 ***Gekas***	N	Y	N	N	Y	Y	Y
18 Doyle	N	Y	N	Y	Y	Y	Y
19 ***Goodling***	Y	Y	N	N	Y	Y	Y
20 Mascara	Y	Y	N	Y	Y	Y	Y
21 ***English***	N	Y	Y	Y	Y	Y	Y
RHODE ISLAND							
1 Kennedy	Y	Y	Y	Y	Y	Y	Y
2 Weygand	Y	Y	Y	Y	Y	Y	Y
SOUTH CAROLINA							
1 ***Sanford***	Y	Y	N	N	Y	Y	?
2 ***Spence***	Y	Y	N	N	Y	Y	Y
3 ***Graham***	Y	Y	N	N	Y	Y	Y
4 ***Inglis***	Y	Y	N	N	Y	Y	Y
5 Spratt	Y	Y	Y	Y	Y	Y	Y
6 Clyburn	Y	N	Y	Y	N	Y	Y
SOUTH DAKOTA							
AL ***Thune***	N	Y	N	N	Y	Y	Y

	317	318	319	320	321	322	323
TENNESSEE							
1 ***Jenkins***	Y	Y	Y	N	Y	Y	Y
2 ***Duncan***	Y	Y	N	N	Y	Y	Y
3 ***Wamp***	Y	Y	N	N	Y	Y	Y
4 ***Hilleary***	Y	Y	Y	N	Y	Y	Y
5 Clement	N	Y	N	Y	Y	Y	Y
6 Gordon	N	Y	N	Y	Y	Y	Y
7 ***Bryant***	N	Y	Y	N	Y	Y	Y
8 Tanner	N	Y	N	Y	Y	Y	Y
9 Ford	–	+	–	+	–	+	+
TEXAS							
1 Sandlin	N	Y	Y	N	Y	Y	Y
2 Turner	N	Y	Y	N	Y	Y	Y
3 ***Johnson, Sam***	N	Y	N	N	Y	Y	Y
4 Hall	N	?	Y	N	Y	Y	Y
5 ***Sessions***	N	Y	N	N	Y	Y	Y
6 ***Barton***	Y	Y	N	N	Y	Y	Y
7 ***Archer***	N	Y	N	N	Y	Y	Y
8 ***Brady***	N	Y	N	N	Y	Y	Y
9 Lampson	N	Y	Y	Y	Y	Y	Y
10 Doggett	N	N	N	Y	N	Y	Y
11 Edwards	N	Y	N	N	N	Y	Y
12 ***Granger***	N	Y	N	N	Y	Y	Y
13 ***Thornberry***	N	Y	N	N	Y	Y	Y
14 ***Paul***	N	N	N	Y	Y	Y	Y
15 Hinojosa	N	Y	N	Y	Y	Y	Y
16 Reyes	N	Y	Y	Y	Y	Y	Y
17 Stenholm	N	Y	N	N	Y	Y	Y
18 Jackson-Lee	N	Y	N	Y	N	Y	Y
19 ***Combest***	N	Y	Y	N	Y	Y	Y
20 Gonzalez	?	?	?	?	?	?	?
21 ***Smith***	N	Y	N	N	?	Y	Y
22 ***DeLay***	N	Y	Y	N	Y	Y	Y
23 ***Bonilla***	N	Y	N	N	Y	Y	Y
24 Frost	N	N	N	Y	N	Y	Y
25 Bentsen	N	Y	N	Y	N	Y	Y
26 ***Armey***	N	Y	Y	N	Y	Y	Y
27 Ortiz	N	Y	N	Y	Y	Y	Y
28 Rodriguez	N	Y	N	Y	N	Y	Y
29 Green	N	Y	–	+	–	+	?
30 Johnson, E.B.	N	N	N	Y	N	Y	Y
UTAH							
1 ***Hansen***	N	Y	N	N	Y	Y	?
2 ***Cook***	Y	Y	N	Y	Y	Y	Y
3 ***Cannon***	N	Y	N	N	Y	Y	Y
VERMONT							
AL *Sanders*	Y	N	N	Y	N	Y	Y
VIRGINIA							
1 ***Bateman***	N	Y	Y	N	Y	Y	Y
2 Pickett	N	Y	N	N	N	Y	Y
3 Scott	N	N	Y	Y	N	Y	Y
4 Sisisky	Y	Y	N	N	Y	Y	Y
5 Goode	Y	Y	N	N	Y	Y	Y
6 ***Goodlatte***	N	+	N	N	Y	Y	Y
7 ***Bliley***	N	Y	Y	N	Y	Y	Y
8 Moran	N	Y	N	N	Y	Y	Y
9 Boucher	N	Y	N	Y	N	Y	Y
10 ***Wolf***	Y	Y	N	N	Y	Y	Y
11 ***Davis***	N	Y	N	N	Y	Y	Y
WASHINGTON							
1 ***White***	N	Y	N	N	Y	Y	Y
2 ***Metcalf***	N	Y	N	Y	Y	Y	Y
3 ***Smith, Linda***	Y	Y	N	?	Y	Y	Y
4 ***Hastings***	N	Y	N	N	Y	Y	Y
5 ***Nethercutt***	N	Y	N	N	Y	Y	Y
6 Dicks	N	N	Y	N	N	Y	Y
7 McDermott	N	N	Y	Y	N	Y	Y
8 ***Dunn***	N	Y	N	N	Y	Y	Y
9 Smith, Adam	N	Y	Y	Y	N	Y	Y
WEST VIRGINIA							
1 Mollohan	Y	N	N	N	Y	Y	Y
2 Wise	N	N	N	Y	N	Y	Y
3 Rahall	N	N	N	Y	Y	Y	Y
WISCONSIN							
1 ***Neumann***	Y	Y	N	Y	Y	Y	Y
2 ***Klug***	Y	Y	N	Y	Y	Y	Y
3 Kind	N	Y	Y	Y	Y	Y	Y
4 Kleczka	N	Y	Y	Y	Y	Y	Y
5 Barrett	N	Y	Y	Y	Y	Y	Y
6 ***Petri***	N	Y	N	Y	Y	Y	Y
7 Obey	Y	N	Y	Y	Y	Y	Y
8 Johnson	N	Y	Y	Y	Y	Y	Y
9 ***Sensenbrenner***	Y	Y	N	Y	Y	Y	Y
WYOMING							
AL ***Cubin***	N	?	N	N	Y	Y	Y

Southern states - Ala., Ark., Fla., Ga., Ky., La., Miss., N.C., Okla., S.C., Tenn., Texas, Va.

House Votes 325, 326, 327, 328, 329, 330, 331 *

Key

- **Y** Voted for (yea).
- **#** Paired for.
- **+** Announced for.
- **N** Voted against (nay).
- **X** Paired against.
- **−** Announced against.
- **P** Voted "present."
- **C** Voted "present" to avoid possible conflict of interest.
- **?** Did not vote or otherwise make a position known.

Democrats   **Republicans**
Independent

324. Quorum Call.* 400 responded. July 23, 1998.

325. HR 1122. Abortion Procedure Ban/Veto Override. Passage, over President Clinton's Oct. 10, 1997 veto of the bill to ban certain late-term abortion procedures. Passed 296-132: R 219-8; D 77-123 (ND 50-98, SD 27-25); I 0-1. July 23, 1998. A two-thirds majority of those present and voting (286 in this case) of both houses is required to override a veto. A "nay" was a vote in support of the president's position.

326. HR 4193. Fiscal 1999 Interior Appropriations/National Parks Fee-Collection Programs. DeFazio, D-Ore., amendment to strike the bill's provision that extends for two years the fee-collection demonstration program in effect at various sites of the National Park Service, Forest Service, Bureau of Land Management and Fish and Wildlife Service. Rejected 81-341: R 33-190; D 47-151 (ND 40-107, SD 7-43); I 1-0. July 23, 1998.

327. HR 4193. Fiscal 1999 Interior Appropriations/Columbia River Watershed Management. McDermott, D-Wash., amendment to strike the bill's provisions that place certain limitations on the use of funds for implementation of the proposed regional strategy to manage the Columbia River watershed. Rejected 202-221: R 15-208; D 186-13 (ND 141-6, SD 45-7); I 1-0. July 23, 1998. A "yea" was a vote in support of the president's position.

328. HR 4193. Fiscal 1999 Interior Appropriations/Chugach National Forest Road Construction. Hinchey, D-N.Y., amendment to strike the bill's provisions providing for a road construction easement in the Chugach National Forest in Alaska. Rejected 176-249: R 35-191; D 140-58 (ND 118-28, SD 22-30); I 1-0. July 23, 1998.

329. HR 4193. Fiscal 1999 Interior Appropriations/Tongass National Forest Road Construction Prohibition. Miller, D-Calif., amendment to prohibit the use of funds in the bill for new road construction in the Tongass National Forest in Alaska. Rejected 186-237: R 16-206; D 169-31 (ND 135-13, SD 34-18); I 1-0. July 23, 1998.

330. HR 4193. Fiscal 1999 Interior Appropriations/National Park Service Funding Increase. Pappas, R-N.J., amendment to increase funding for National Park Service land acquisition and state assistance by $50 million. The amendment offsets the increase by reducing funding for the National Endowment for the Arts. Rejected 139-285: R 134-90; D 5-194 (ND 1-146, SD 4-48); I 0-1. July 23, 1998.

331. HR 4193. Fiscal 1999 Interior Appropriations/Passage. Passage of the bill to provide $13.4 billion in funding for the Interior Department and related agencies. The bill provides $695 million less than requested by the president. Passed 245-181: R 207-18; D 38-162 (ND 24-124, SD 14-38); I 0-1. July 23, 1998.

* CQ does not include quorum calls in its vote charts.

	325	326	327	328	329	330	331
ALABAMA							
1 *Callahan*	Y	N	N	N	N	Y	Y
2 *Everett*	Y	N	N	N	N	Y	Y
3 *Riley*	Y	N	N	N	N	Y	Y
4 *Aderholt*	Y	N	N	N	N	Y	Y
5 Cramer	Y	N	Y	N	Y	N	Y
6 *Bachus*	Y	N	N	N	N	Y	Y
7 Hilliard	N	N	Y	N	Y	N	N
ALASKA							
AL *Young*	Y	N	N	N	N	Y	Y
ARIZONA							
1 *Salmon*	Y	N	N	N	N	Y	Y
2 Pastor	N	Y	Y	Y	Y	N	N
3 *Stump*	Y	N	N	N	N	N	Y
4 *Shadegg*	Y	N	N	N	N	Y	Y
5 *Kolbe*	N	N	N	N	N	Y	Y
6 *Hayworth*	Y	N	N	N	N	Y	Y
ARKANSAS							
1 Berry	Y	N	N	N	N	Y	N
2 Snyder	N	Y	Y	Y	Y	N	N
3 *Hutchinson*	Y	N	N	N	Y	Y	Y
4 Dickey	Y	N	N	N	N	N	Y
CALIFORNIA							
1 *Riggs*	Y	N	N	N	N	Y	Y
2 *Herger*	Y	N	N	N	N	Y	Y
3 Fazio	N	N	Y	Y	Y	N	N
4 *Doolittle*	Y	N	N	N	−	Y	Y
5 Matsui	N	N	Y	Y	Y	N	N
6 Woolsey	N	N	Y	Y	Y	N	N
7 Miller	N	N	Y	Y	Y	N	N
8 Pelosi	N	N	Y	Y	Y	N	N
9 Lee	N	N	Y	Y	Y	N	N
10 Tauscher	N	N	Y	Y	Y	N	N
11 *Pombo*	Y	N	N	N	N	Y	Y
12 Lantos	N	N	Y	Y	Y	N	N
13 Stark	N	N	Y	Y	Y	N	N
14 Eshoo	N	N	Y	Y	Y	N	N
15 *Campbell*	N	N	N	N	N	Y	Y
16 Lofgren	N	N	Y	Y	Y	N	N
17 Farr	N	N	Y	Y	Y	N	N
18 Condit	Y	N	N	N	N	N	N
19 *Radanovich*	Y	N	N	N	N	N	Y
20 Dooley	N	N	Y	Y	Y	N	N
21 *Thomas*	Y	N	N	N	N	Y	Y
22 Capps, L.	N	Y	Y	Y	Y	N	N
23 *Gallegly*	Y	N	N	N	N	Y	Y
24 Sherman	N	N	Y	Y	Y	N	N
25 *McKeon*	Y	N	N	N	N	Y	Y
26 Berman	N	N	Y	Y	Y	N	N
27 *Rogan*	Y	N	N	N	N	Y	Y
28 *Dreier*	Y	N	N	N	N	Y	Y
29 Waxman	N	N	Y	Y	Y	N	N
30 Becerra	N	N	Y	Y	Y	N	N
31 Martinez	Y	N	N	N	N	N	N
32 Dixon	N	N	Y	Y	Y	N	N
33 Roybal-Allard	N	Y	Y	Y	Y	N	N
34 Torres	N	Y	Y	Y	Y	N	N
35 Waters	N	N	Y	Y	Y	N	N
36 Harman	N	Y	Y	Y	Y	N	N
37 Millender-McD.	N	N	Y	N	Y	N	N

	325	326	327	328	329	330	331
38 *Horn*	N	Y	Y	N	N	Y	Y
39 *Royce*	Y	Y	N	N	N	Y	Y
40 *Lewis*	Y	N	N	N	N	N	Y
41 *Kim*	Y	N	N	N	N	Y	Y
42 Brown	N	Y	Y	Y	Y	N	N
43 *Calvert*	Y	N	N	N	N	Y	Y
44 *Bono, M.*	Y	N	N	N	N	Y	Y
45 *Rohrabacher*	Y	N	N	N	N	Y	Y
46 Sanchez	N	Y	Y	Y	N	N	N
47 *Cox*	Y	N	N	N	N	Y	Y
48 *Packard*	Y	N	N	N	N	N	Y
49 *Bilbray*	Y	N	N	Y	N	N	N
50 Filner	N	Y	Y	Y	Y	N	N
51 *Cunningham*	Y	N	N	N	N	Y	Y
52 *Hunter*	Y	?	N	N	N	Y	N
COLORADO							
1 DeGette	N	N	Y	Y	Y	N	N
2 Skaggs	N	N	Y	Y	Y	N	N
3 *McInnis*	Y	N	N	N	N	Y	Y
4 *Schaffer*	Y	N	N	N	N	N	Y
5 *Hefley*	Y	N	N	N	N	Y	N
6 *Schaefer*	Y	N	N	N	N	Y	Y
CONNECTICUT							
1 Kennelly	N	N	Y	Y	Y	N	N
2 Gejdenson	N	N	Y	Y	Y	N	N
3 DeLauro	N	N	Y	Y	Y	N	N
4 *Shays*	Y	N	Y	Y	Y	N	N
5 Maloney	Y	N	Y	Y	Y	N	N
6 *Johnson*	N	N	N	Y	Y	N	Y
DELAWARE							
AL *Castle*	Y	N	Y	Y	Y	N	Y
FLORIDA							
1 *Scarborough*	Y	Y	?	N	N	Y	Y
2 Boyd	Y	N	N	Y	N	Y	Y
3 Brown	N	N	Y	Y	Y	N	N
4 *Fowler*	Y	N	N	N	N	N	Y
5 Thurman	N	N	Y	Y	N	N	N
6 *Stearns*	Y	Y	N	N	N	Y	Y
7 *Mica*	Y	N	N	N	N	N	Y
8 *McCollum*	Y	N	N	N	N	N	Y
9 *Bilirakis*	Y	N	N	N	N	Y	Y
10 *Young*	?	?	?	?	?	?	?
11 Davis	Y	N	Y	Y	Y	N	N
12 *Canady*	Y	N	N	N	N	Y	Y
13 *Miller*	Y	N	N	N	N	Y	Y
14 *Goss*	Y	N	N	N	N	Y	Y
15 *Weldon*	Y	N	N	N	N	Y	Y
16 *Foley*	Y	N	N	N	N	N	Y
17 Meek	N	N	Y	N	Y	N	N
18 *Ros-Lehtinen*	Y	N	N	N	N	N	Y
19 Wexler	N	Y	Y	Y	Y	N	N
20 Deutsch	N	N	Y	Y	Y	N	N
21 *Diaz-Balart*	Y	N	N	N	N	N	Y
22 *Shaw*	Y	N	N	N	N	Y	Y
23 Hastings	N	N	Y	N	Y	N	N
GEORGIA							
1 *Kingston*	Y	N	N	N	N	Y	Y
2 Bishop	Y	N	N	Y	N	Y	Y
3 *Collins*	Y	N	N	N	N	Y	Y
4 *McKinney*	N	Y	Y	Y	Y	N	N
5 Lewis	?	?	?	?	?	?	?
6 *Gingrich*	Y						
7 *Barr*	Y	N	N	N	N	Y	N
8 *Chambliss*	Y	N	N	N	N	Y	Y
9 *Deal*	Y	N	N	N	N	Y	Y
10 *Norwood*	Y	N	?	N	N	Y	Y
11 *Linder*	Y	N	N	N	N	Y	Y
HAWAII							
1 Abercrombie	N	Y	Y	N	Y	N	Y
2 Mink	N	Y	Y	Y	Y	N	N
IDAHO							
1 *Chenoweth*	Y	Y	N	N	N	Y	Y
2 *Crapo*	Y	Y	N	N	N	Y	Y
ILLINOIS							
1 Rush	N	Y	Y	N	Y	N	N
2 Jackson	N	Y	Y	Y	Y	N	N
3 Lipinski	Y	Y	Y	Y	N	Y	Y
4 Gutierrez	N	Y	Y	Y	Y	N	N
5 Blagojevich	N	Y	Y	?	Y	N	N
6 *Hyde*	Y	N	N	N	N	Y	Y
7 Davis	N	Y	Y	Y	Y	N	N
8 *Crane*	Y	N	N	N	N	N	Y
9 Yates	N	N	Y	Y	Y	N	N
10 *Porter*	Y	N	Y	Y	Y	N	N
11 *Weller*	Y	N	?	N	N	Y	Y
12 Costello	Y	N	Y	Y	N	Y	N

ND Northern Democrats   SD Southern Democrats

	325	326	327	328	329	330	331
13 **Fawell**	Y	N	N	Y	N	N	Y
14 **Hastert**	Y	N	N	N	N	N	Y
15 **Ewing**	Y	N	N	N	N	N	Y
16 **Manzullo**	Y	Y	N	N	N	Y	Y
17 Evans	N	Y	Y	Y	Y	N	N
18 **LaHood**	Y	N	N	Y	N	N	Y
19 Poshard	Y	N	Y	Y	Y	N	N
20 **Shimkus**	Y	N	N	N	N	Y	Y
INDIANA							
1 Visclosky	Y	N	Y	N	Y	N	Y
2 **McIntosh**	Y	Y	N	N	?	Y	Y
3 Roemer	Y	N	Y	Y	Y	N	N
4 **Souder**	Y	N	N	N	N	Y	Y
5 **Buyer**	Y	N	N	N	N	Y	Y
6 **Burton**	Y	N	N	N	N	Y	Y
7 **Pease**	Y	N	N	N	Y	N	Y
8 **Hostettler**	Y	Y	N	N	N	N	N
9 Hamilton	Y	N	Y	Y	Y	N	Y
10 Carson	N	Y	Y	Y	Y	N	N
IOWA							
1 **Leach**	Y	N	Y	Y	Y	N	Y
2 **Nussle**	Y	N	N	N	N	N	Y
3 Boswell	Y	Y	N	N	N	N	Y
4 **Ganske**	Y	N	N	N	N	N	Y
5 **Latham**	Y	N	N	N	N	Y	Y
KANSAS							
1 **Moran**	Y	Y	N	N	Y	Y	Y
2 **Ryun**	Y	N	N	N	N	Y	Y
3 **Snowbarger**	Y	N	N	N	N	Y	Y
4 **Tiahrt**	Y	N	N	N	N	Y	N
KENTUCKY							
1 **Whitfield**	Y	N	N	N	N	N	Y
2 **Lewis**	Y	N	N	N	N	N	Y
3 **Northup**	Y	N	N	N	N	Y	Y
4 **Bunning**	Y	N	N	N	N	N	Y
5 **Rogers**	Y	N	N	N	N	Y	Y
6 Baesler	Y	N	Y	Y	N	N	Y
LOUISIANA							
1 **Livingston**	Y	N	N	N	N	Y	Y
2 Jefferson	Y	N	Y	N	Y	N	N
3 **Tauzin**	Y	N	N	N	N	N	Y
4 **McCrery**	Y	N	N	N	N	N	Y
5 **Cooksey**	Y	N	N	N	N	Y	Y
6 **Baker**	Y	N	N	N	N	N	Y
7 John	Y	N	N	N	N	N	Y
MAINE							
1 Allen	N	N	Y	Y	Y	N	N
2 Baldacci	N	N	Y	Y	Y	N	N
MARYLAND							
1 **Gilchrest**	Y	N	N	N	N	N	Y
2 **Ehrlich**	Y	N	N	N	N	Y	Y
3 Cardin	N	N	Y	Y	Y	N	N
4 Wynn	N	N	Y	Y	Y	N	N
5 Hoyer	N	N	Y	Y	Y	N	Y
6 **Bartlett**	Y	N	N	N	N	Y	Y
7 Cummings	N	Y	Y	Y	Y	N	N
8 **Morella**	N	N	Y	Y	Y	N	Y
MASSACHUSETTS							
1 Olver	N	N	Y	Y	Y	N	N
2 Neal	Y	N	Y	Y	Y	N	N
3 McGovern	N	N	Y	Y	Y	N	N
4 Frank	N	N	Y	N	Y	N	N
5 Meehan	N	N	Y	N	Y	N	Y
6 Tierney	N	N	Y	Y	Y	N	N
7 Markey	?	?	?	?	?	?	?
8 Kennedy	N	N	Y	Y	Y	N	N
9 Moakley	Y	N	Y	Y	Y	N	N
10 Delahunt	N	N	Y	Y	Y	N	N
MICHIGAN							
1 Stupak	Y	N	Y	N	Y	N	N
2 **Hoekstra**	Y	Y	N	N	N	Y	Y
3 **Ehlers**	Y	N	N	Y	N	N	Y
4 **Camp**	Y	Y	N	N	N	Y	Y
5 Barcia	Y	Y	Y	N	N	N	N
6 **Upton**	Y	N	N	Y	N	N	Y
7 **Smith**	Y	N	N	Y	N	Y	Y
8 Stabenow	N	N	Y	Y	Y	N	N
9 Kildee	Y	N	Y	Y	Y	N	N
10 Bonior	Y	N	Y	Y	Y	N	N
11 **Knollenberg**	Y	N	N	N	N	Y	Y
12 Levin	N	N	Y	Y	Y	N	N
13 Rivers	N	N	Y	Y	Y	N	N
14 Conyers	N	Y	Y	Y	Y	–	N
15 Kilpatrick	N	N	Y	N	Y	N	N
16 Dingell	Y	N	Y	N	N	N	N
MINNESOTA							
1 **Gutknecht**	Y	N	N	N	N	Y	Y
2 Minge	Y	N	Y	Y	Y	N	N
3 **Ramstad**	Y	N	Y	Y	Y	N	Y
4 Vento	N	N	Y	Y	Y	N	N
5 Sabo	N	N	Y	Y	Y	N	N
6 Luther	N	N	Y	Y	Y	N	N
7 Peterson	Y	Y	N	N	N	N	N
8 Oberstar	Y	N	Y	N	N	N	Y
MISSISSIPPI							
1 **Wicker**	Y	N	N	N	N	Y	Y
2 Thompson	N	N	Y	N	Y	N	N
3 **Pickering**	Y	N	N	N	N	Y	Y
4 **Parker**	Y	N	N	N	?	?	Y
5 Taylor	Y	N	Y	N	N	Y	Y
MISSOURI							
1 Clay	N	N	Y	N	Y	N	N
2 **Talent**	Y	N	N	N	N	Y	Y
3 Gephardt	Y	N	Y	Y	Y	N	N
4 Skelton	Y	N	Y	N	N	Y	Y
5 McCarthy	N	N	Y	Y	Y	N	N
6 Danner	Y	N	Y	N	N	N	Y
7 **Blunt**	Y	N	N	N	N	Y	Y
8 **Emerson**	Y	Y	N	N	N	Y	Y
9 **Hulshof**	Y	Y	N	Y	N	Y	Y
MONTANA							
AL **Hill**	Y	Y	N	N	N	Y	Y
NEBRASKA							
1 **Bereuter**	Y	N	N	N	N	N	Y
2 **Christensen**	Y	N	N	N	N	Y	N
3 **Barrett**	Y	N	N	N	N	Y	Y
NEVADA							
1 **Ensign**	Y	N	N	N	N	Y	Y
2 **Gibbons**	Y	N	N	N	N	N	Y
NEW HAMPSHIRE							
1 **Sununu**	Y	Y	N	N	N	Y	Y
2 **Bass**	Y	Y	N	Y	N	N	Y
NEW JERSEY							
1 Andrews	N	N	Y	Y	Y	N	N
2 **LoBiondo**	Y	N	Y	Y	N	N	Y
3 **Saxton**	Y	N	Y	N	N	N	Y
4 **Smith**	Y	N	N	Y	N	Y	Y
5 **Roukema**	Y	N	N	Y	N	N	Y
6 Pallone	N	Y	Y	Y	Y	N	N
7 **Franks**	Y	N	N	Y	P	N	Y
8 Pascrell	Y	Y	Y	Y	Y	N	N
9 Rothman	N	Y	Y	?	Y	N	N
10 Payne	N	N	Y	N	Y	N	N
11 **Frelinghuysen**	Y	N	N	N	N	N	Y
12 **Pappas**	Y	N	Y	Y	N	Y	Y
13 Menendez	N	Y	Y	Y	Y	N	N
NEW MEXICO							
1 **Wilson**	Y	N	N	N	N	N	Y
2 **Skeen**	Y	N	N	N	N	N	Y
3 **Redmond**	Y	N	N	N	N	N	Y
NEW YORK							
1 **Forbes**	Y	N	Y	Y	Y	N	Y
2 **Lazio**	Y	N	Y	Y	N	N	Y
3 **King**	Y	N	N	N	N	Y	Y
4 McCarthy	N	N	Y	Y	Y	N	N
5 Ackerman	N	N	Y	Y	Y	N	N
6 Meeks	N	N	Y	N	Y	N	N
7 Manton	Y	N	Y	Y	Y	N	N
8 Nadler	N	Y	Y	Y	Y	N	N
9 Schumer	N	Y	Y	Y	Y	N	N
10 Towns	N	?	Y	Y	Y	N	N
11 Owens	N	Y	Y	Y	Y	N	N
12 Velázquez	N	Y	Y	Y	Y	N	N
13 **Fossella**	Y	N	N	Y	N	Y	Y
14 Maloney	N	Y	Y	Y	Y	N	N
15 Rangel	N	N	Y	Y	Y	N	N
16 Serrano	–	–	+	+	+	–	–
17 Engel	N	Y	Y	Y	Y	N	N
18 Lowey	N	N	Y	Y	Y	N	N
19 **Kelly**	Y	N	Y	Y	Y	N	Y
20 **Gilman**	N	N	N	Y	N	N	Y
21 McNulty	Y	N	Y	Y	Y	N	N
22 **Solomon**	Y	?	N	N	N	Y	Y
23 **Boehlert**	N	N	Y	Y	Y	N	Y
24 **McHugh**	Y	N	N	N	N	N	Y
25 **Walsh**	Y	N	Y	Y	Y	N	Y
26 Hinchey	N	N	Y	Y	Y	N	N
27 **Paxon**	Y	N	N	N	N	Y	Y
28 Slaughter	N	Y	Y	Y	Y	N	N
29 LaFalce	Y	N	Y	Y	Y	N	N
30 **Quinn**	Y	N	N	Y	N	N	Y
31 **Houghton**	Y	N	N	N	N	N	Y
NORTH CAROLINA							
1 Clayton	N	N	Y	Y	Y	N	N
2 Etheridge	Y	Y	Y	Y	Y	N	Y
3 **Jones**	Y	N	N	N	N	Y	Y
4 Price	N	N	Y	Y	Y	N	N
5 **Burr**	Y	N	N	N	N	Y	Y
6 **Coble**	Y	N	N	N	N	Y	Y
7 McIntyre	Y	Y	Y	N	Y	N	Y
8 Hefner	Y	Y	Y	Y	N	N	Y
9 **Myrick**	Y	N	N	N	N	Y	Y
10 **Ballenger**	Y	N	N	N	N	N	Y
11 **Taylor**	Y	N	N	N	N	?	Y
12 Watt	N	?	Y	Y	Y	N	N
NORTH DAKOTA							
AL Pomeroy	Y	N	Y	Y	Y	N	N
OHIO							
1 **Chabot**	Y	Y	N	Y	Y	Y	Y
2 **Portman**	Y	N	N	N	N	N	Y
3 Hall	Y	N	Y	Y	Y	N	N
4 **Oxley**	Y	N	N	N	N	N	Y
5 **Gillmor**	Y	N	N	N	N	N	Y
6 Strickland	Y	Y	Y	Y	Y	N	Y
7 **Hobson**	Y	N	N	Y	N	Y	Y
8 **Boehner**	Y	N	N	N	N	Y	Y
9 Kaptur	Y	N	?	Y	Y	N	Y
10 Kucinich	Y	Y	Y	Y	Y	N	N
11 Stokes	N	N	Y	N	Y	N	N
12 **Kasich**	Y	N	N	N	N	Y	Y
13 Brown	N	N	Y	Y	Y	N	N
14 Sawyer	N	N	Y	Y	Y	N	N
15 **Pryce**	Y	N	N	N	N	N	Y
16 **Regula**	Y	N	N	N	N	N	Y
17 Traficant	Y	N	N	N	N	N	Y
18 **Ney**	Y	N	N	N	N	Y	Y
19 **LaTourette**	Y	N	N	N	N	N	Y
OKLAHOMA							
1 **Largent**	Y	N	N	N	N	N	Y
2 **Coburn**	Y	N	N	N	N	Y	Y
3 **Watkins**	Y	N	N	N	N	N	Y
4 **Watts**	Y	N	N	N	N	N	Y
5 **Istook**	Y	N	N	N	N	Y	Y
6 **Lucas**	Y	N	N	N	N	N	Y
OREGON							
1 Furse	N	Y	Y	Y	Y	N	N
2 **Smith**	Y	N	N	N	N	N	Y
3 Blumenauer	N	N	Y	Y	Y	N	N
4 DeFazio	N	Y	Y	Y	Y	N	N
5 Hooley	N	Y	Y	Y	Y	N	N
PENNSYLVANIA							
1 Brady	?	?	?	?	?	?	?
2 Fattah	N	N	Y	N	Y	N	N
3 Borski	Y	N	Y	Y	Y	N	N
4 Klink	Y	N	Y	Y	Y	N	N
5 **Peterson**	Y	N	N	N	N	Y	Y
6 Holden	Y	N	Y	Y	Y	N	N
7 **Weldon**	Y	N	N	Y	N	Y	Y
8 **Greenwood**	N	N	N	N	Y	N	Y
9 **Shuster**	Y	N	N	N	N	Y	Y
10 **McDade**	Y	N	N	N	N	N	Y
11 Kanjorski	Y	N	Y	Y	Y	N	N
12 Murtha	Y	N	N	N	N	N	Y
13 **Fox**	Y	N	N	N	N	N	Y
14 Coyne	N	N	Y	Y	Y	N	N
15 McHale	Y	Y	Y	Y	Y	N	N
16 **Pitts**	Y	Y	N	N	N	Y	Y
17 **Gekas**	Y	N	N	N	N	Y	Y
18 Doyle	Y	N	Y	Y	Y	Y	N
19 **Goodling**	Y	N	N	N	N	Y	Y
20 Mascara	Y	N	Y	Y	Y	N	N
21 **English**	Y	N	N	N	N	N	Y
RHODE ISLAND							
1 Kennedy	Y	N	Y	Y	Y	N	Y
2 Weygand	Y	N	Y	Y	Y	N	N
SOUTH CAROLINA							
1 **Sanford**	Y	N	N	N	N	Y	Y
2 **Spence**	Y	N	N	N	N	Y	Y
3 **Graham**	Y	N	N	N	N	Y	Y
4 **Inglis**	Y	N	N	N	N	Y	Y
5 Spratt	Y	N	Y	Y	Y	N	N
6 Clyburn	N	N	Y	N	Y	N	N
SOUTH DAKOTA							
AL **Thune**	Y	Y	N	N	N	N	Y
TENNESSEE							
1 **Jenkins**	Y	Y	N	N	N	Y	Y
2 **Duncan**	Y	N	N	N	N	Y	Y
3 **Wamp**	Y	N	N	N	N	Y	Y
4 **Hilleary**	Y	N	N	N	N	Y	Y
5 Clement	Y	N	Y	N	Y	N	N
6 Gordon	Y	N	Y	Y	Y	N	Y
7 **Bryant**	Y	N	N	N	N	Y	Y
8 Tanner	Y	N	N	N	N	Y	N
9 Ford	–	–	+	+	–	–	–
TEXAS							
1 Sandlin	Y	N	Y	N	N	N	N
2 Turner	Y	N	N	N	N	Y	N
3 **Johnson, Sam**	Y	N	N	N	N	Y	Y
4 Hall	Y	N	N	N	N	Y	N
5 **Sessions**	Y	N	N	N	N	Y	Y
6 **Barton**	Y	N	N	N	N	Y	Y
7 **Archer**	Y	N	N	N	N	Y	Y
8 **Brady**	Y	N	N	N	N	Y	+
9 Lampson	Y	N	Y	Y	Y	N	N
10 Doggett	N	N	Y	Y	Y	N	N
11 Edwards	N	N	Y	N	N	N	N
12 **Granger**	Y	N	N	N	N	N	Y
13 **Thornberry**	Y	N	N	N	N	N	Y
14 **Paul**	Y	Y	N	N	Y	Y	N
15 Hinojosa	Y	N	Y	Y	Y	N	N
16 Reyes	Y	N	Y	N	N	N	N
17 Stenholm	Y	N	N	N	N	N	N
18 Jackson-Lee	N	N	Y	N	Y	N	N
19 **Combest**	Y	N	N	N	N	Y	Y
20 Gonzalez	?	?	?	?	?	?	?
21 **Smith**	Y	N	N	N	N	Y	Y
22 **DeLay**	Y	N	N	N	N	Y	Y
23 **Bonilla**	Y	N	N	N	N	N	Y
24 Frost	N	N	Y	Y	Y	N	N
25 Bentsen	N	N	Y	Y	Y	N	N
26 **Armey**	Y	N	N	N	N	Y	Y
27 Ortiz	Y	N	Y	N	N	N	Y
28 Rodriguez	N	N	Y	Y	Y	N	N
29 Green	N	N	Y	Y	Y	N	N
30 Johnson, E.B.	N	N	Y	N	Y	N	N
UTAH							
1 **Hansen**	Y	N	N	N	N	N	Y
2 **Cook**	Y	N	N	N	N	N	Y
3 **Cannon**	Y	N	N	N	N	Y	Y
VERMONT							
AL *Sanders*	N	Y	Y	Y	Y	N	N
VIRGINIA							
1 **Bateman**	Y	N	N	N	N	N	Y
2 Pickett	N	N	N	N	N	N	Y
3 Scott	N	N	Y	N	Y	N	N
4 Sisisky	Y	N	Y	N	N	N	Y
5 Goode	Y	N	N	N	N	N	Y
6 **Goodlatte**	Y	N	N	N	N	N	Y
7 **Bliley**	Y	N	N	N	N	Y	Y
8 Moran	Y	N	Y	N	N	N	Y
9 Boucher	N	N	Y	Y	Y	N	Y
10 **Wolf**	Y	N	N	N	N	N	Y
11 **Davis**	Y	?	N	N	N	N	Y
WASHINGTON							
1 **White**	Y	Y	N	N	N	Y	Y
2 **Metcalf**	Y	Y	N	N	Y	Y	Y
3 **Smith, Linda**	Y	Y	N	N	N	Y	N
4 **Hastings**	Y	N	N	N	N	Y	Y
5 **Nethercutt**	Y	N	N	N	N	N	Y
6 Dicks	N	N	Y	N	Y	N	Y
7 McDermott	N	N	Y	Y	Y	N	N
8 **Dunn**	Y	N	N	N	N	N	Y
9 Smith, Adam	N	N	Y	Y	Y	N	N
WEST VIRGINIA							
1 Mollohan	Y	Y	Y	N	N	N	Y
2 Wise	N	Y	Y	Y	N	N	N
3 Rahall	Y	Y	Y	Y	Y	N	Y
WISCONSIN							
1 **Neumann**	Y	N	N	Y	N	Y	Y
2 **Klug**	Y	Y	N	Y	N	N	Y
3 Kind	Y	N	Y	Y	Y	N	N
4 Kleczka	Y	N	Y	Y	Y	N	N
5 Barrett	Y	N	Y	Y	Y	N	N
6 **Petri**	Y	N	N	Y	Y	Y	N
7 Obey	Y	N	Y	Y	Y	N	N
8 Johnson	Y	N	Y	Y	Y	N	N
9 **Sensenbrenner**	Y	N	N	Y	Y	Y	N
WYOMING							
AL **Cubin**	Y	N	N	N	N	N	Y

Southern states - Ala., Ark., Fla., Ga., Ky., La., Miss., N.C., Okla., S.C., Tenn., Texas, Va.

House Votes 332, 334, 335, 336, 337, 338, 339 *

332. HR 4194. Fiscal 1999 VA-HUD Appropriations/EPA Educational Outreach Programs Clarification. Obey, D-Wis., amendment to clarify that no limitation of funds in the bill can apply to funds to be used by the Environmental Protection Agency or the Council on Environmental Quality for conducting educational outreach or informational seminars. Adopted 226-198: R 50-175; D 175-23 (ND 138-8, SD 37-15); I 1-0. July 23, 1998.

333. Quorum Call.* 352 Responded. July 23, 1998.

334. HR 4194. Fiscal 1999 VA-HUD Appropriations/EPA Fund Limitation Clarification. Waxman, D-Calif., amendment to clarify that certain bill provisions and committee report language restricting various EPA and Council on Environmental Quality actions do not apply "where such activities are authorized by law." Rejected 176-243: R 27-196; D 148-47 (ND 117-26, SD 31-21); I 1-0. July 23, 1998.

335. HR 4250. Revamp Medical Insurance Regulations/Rule. Adoption of the rule (H Res 509) to provide for House floor consideration of the bill to revamp medical insurance regulations. Adopted 279-143: R 219-3; D 60-139 (ND 42-105, SD 18-34); I 0-1. July 24, 1998.

336. HR 4250. Revamp Medical Insurance Regulations/Dingell-Ganske Substitute. Dingell, D-Mich., substitute amendment to revamp medical insurance regulations. The substitute would remove provisions allowing Medical Savings Accounts and nonprofit health organizations (HealthMarts) and would permit individuals to sue their health plans under state law for personal injury or wrongful death. Rejected 212-217: R 10-217; D 201-0 (ND 149-0, SD 52-0); I 1-0. July 24, 1998.

337. HR 4250. Revamp Medical Insurance Regulations/Motion to Table. Armey, R-Texas, motion to table (kill) the appeal of the chair's ruling that the Berry, D-Ark., motion to recommit is out of order. Motion agreed to 222-204: R 222-1; D 0-202 (ND 0-149, SD 0-53); I 0-1. July 24, 1998.

338. HR 4250. Revamp Medical Insurance Regulations/Recommit. Berry, D-Ark., motion to recommit the bill to the House Education and the Workforce Committee with instructions to report it back with an amendment to allow doctors, not health plans, to determine what can be considered medically necessary. Motion rejected 205-221: R 5-220; D 199-1 (ND 147-1, SD 52-0); I 1-0. July 24, 1998.

339. HR 4250. Revamp Medical Insurance Regulations/Passage. Passage of the bill to revise managed care and medical insurance regulations. The bill would provide a range of patient protections, create a two-step appeals process for challenging a health plan administrator's decisions and expand the availability of medical savings accounts. Passed 216-210: R 213-12; D 3-197 (ND 2-147, SD 1-50); I 0-1. July 24, 1998. A "nay" was a vote in support of the president's position.

* CQ does not include quorum calls in its vote charts.

Key

- **Y** Voted for (yea).
- **#** Paired for.
- **+** Announced for.
- **N** Voted against (nay).
- **X** Paired against.
- **−** Announced against.
- **P** Voted "present."
- **C** Voted "present" to avoid possible conflict of interest.
- **?** Did not vote or otherwise make a position known.

Democrats • **Republicans**
Independent

	332	334	335	336	337	338	339
ALABAMA							
1 **Callahan**	N	N	Y	N	Y	N	Y
2 **Everett**	N	N	Y	N	Y	N	Y
3 **Riley**	N	N	Y	N	Y	N	Y
4 **Aderholt**	N	N	Y	N	Y	N	Y
5 Cramer	N	N	Y	N	Y	N	Y
6 **Bachus**	N	N	Y	N	Y	N	Y
7 Hilliard	Y	Y	N	Y	N	Y	N
ALASKA							
AL **Young**	N	?	?	N	Y	N	Y
ARIZONA							
1 **Salmon**	N	N	Y	N	Y	N	Y
2 Pastor	Y	Y	Y	Y	N	Y	N
3 **Stump**	N	N	Y	N	Y	N	Y
4 **Shadegg**	N	N	Y	N	Y	N	Y
5 **Kolbe**	Y	N	Y	N	Y	N	Y
6 **Hayworth**	N	N	Y	N	Y	N	Y
ARKANSAS							
1 Berry	N	N	N	Y	N	Y	
2 Snyder	Y	Y	Y	Y	N	Y	N
3 **Hutchinson**	N	N	Y	N	Y	N	Y
4 Dickey	N	N	Y	N	Y	N	Y
CALIFORNIA							
1 **Riggs**	N	N	Y	N	Y	N	Y
2 **Herger**	N	N	?	N	Y	N	Y
3 Fazio	Y	Y	N	Y	N	Y	N
4 **Doolittle**	N	N	?	N	Y	N	Y
5 Matsui	Y	Y	N	Y	N	Y	N
6 Woolsey	Y	Y	N	Y	N	Y	N
7 Miller	Y	Y	N	Y	N	Y	N
8 Pelosi	Y	Y	N	Y	N	Y	N
9 Lee	Y	Y	N	Y	N	Y	N
10 Tauscher	Y	Y	N	Y	N	Y	N
11 **Pombo**	N	N	Y	N	Y	N	Y
12 Lantos	Y	Y	N	Y	N	Y	N
13 Stark	Y	?	N	Y	N	Y	N
14 Eshoo	Y	Y	N	Y	N	Y	N
15 **Campbell**	Y	Y	Y	N	Y	N	N
16 Lofgren	Y	Y	N	Y	N	Y	N
17 Farr	Y	Y	N	Y	N	Y	N
18 Condit	N	N	N	Y	N	Y	N
19 **Radanovich**	N	N	Y	N	Y	N	Y
20 Dooley	Y	N	Y	N	Y	N	Y
21 **Thomas**	N	N	Y	N	Y	N	Y
22 Capps, L.	Y	Y	N	Y	N	Y	N
23 **Gallegly**	Y	N	Y	N	Y	N	Y
24 Sherman	Y	Y	Y	Y	N	Y	N
25 **McKeon**	N	N	Y	N	Y	N	Y
26 Berman	Y	Y	N	Y	N	Y	N
27 **Rogan**	N	N	Y	N	Y	N	Y
28 **Dreier**	N	N	Y	N	Y	N	Y
29 Waxman	Y	Y	N	Y	N	Y	N
30 Becerra	Y	Y	N	Y	N	Y	N
31 Martinez	Y	N	N	Y	N	Y	N
32 Dixon	Y	Y	N	Y	N	Y	N
33 Roybal-Allard	Y	Y	N	Y	N	Y	N
34 Torres	Y	Y	?	Y	N	Y	N
35 Waters	Y	Y	N	Y	N	Y	N
36 Harman	Y	Y	N	Y	N	N	N
37 Millender-McD.	Y	Y	Y	Y	N	Y	N

	332	334	335	336	337	338	339
38 **Horn**	Y	Y	Y	Y	N	Y	N
39 **Royce**	N	N	Y	N	Y	N	Y
40 **Lewis**	Y	N	Y	N	Y	N	Y
41 **Kim**	N	N	Y	N	Y	N	Y
42 Brown	Y	Y	N	Y	N	Y	N
43 **Calvert**	N	N	Y	N	Y	N	Y
44 **Bono, M.**	N	N	Y	N	Y	N	Y
45 **Rohrabacher**	N	N	Y	N	Y	N	Y
46 Sanchez	Y	Y	N	Y	N	Y	N
47 **Cox**	N	N	Y	N	Y	N	Y
48 **Packard**	N	N	Y	N	Y	N	Y
49 **Bilbray**	Y	Y	Y	Y	Y	N	Y
50 Filner	Y	Y	N	Y	N	Y	N
51 **Cunningham**	N	N	Y	N	Y	N	Y
52 **Hunter**	N	N	Y	N	Y	N	Y
COLORADO							
1 DeGette	Y	Y	Y	Y	N	Y	N
2 Skaggs	Y	Y	N	Y	N	Y	N
3 **McInnis**	N	N	Y	N	Y	N	Y
4 **Schaffer**	N	N	Y	N	Y	N	Y
5 **Hefley**	N	N	Y	N	Y	N	Y
6 **Schaefer**	N	N	Y	N	Y	N	Y
CONNECTICUT							
1 Kennelly	Y	Y	Y	Y	N	Y	N
2 Gejdenson	Y	Y	N	Y	N	Y	N
3 DeLauro	Y	Y	N	Y	N	Y	N
4 **Shays**	Y	Y	Y	Y	N	Y	N
5 Maloney	Y	Y	N	Y	N	Y	N
6 **Johnson**	Y	Y	Y	N	?	N	Y
DELAWARE							
AL **Castle**	Y	Y	N	N	Y	N	Y
FLORIDA							
1 **Scarborough**	N	N	Y	N	Y	N	Y
2 Boyd	N	N	Y	N	Y	N	Y
3 Brown	Y	Y	N	Y	N	Y	N
4 **Fowler**	N	N	Y	N	Y	N	Y
5 Thurman	Y	Y	N	Y	N	Y	N
6 **Stearns**	N	N	Y	N	Y	N	Y
7 **Mica**	N	N	Y	N	Y	N	Y
8 **McCollum**	N	N	Y	N	Y	N	Y
9 **Bilirakis**	Y	N	Y	N	Y	N	Y
10 **Young**	?	?	?	?	?	?	?
11 Davis	Y	Y	N	Y	N	Y	N
12 **Canady**	N	N	Y	N	Y	N	Y
13 **Miller**	N	N	Y	N	Y	N	Y
14 **Goss**	Y	N	Y	N	Y	N	Y
15 **Weldon**	N	N	Y	N	Y	N	Y
16 **Foley**	N	N	Y	N	Y	N	Y
17 Meek	Y	Y	N	Y	N	Y	N
18 **Ros-Lehtinen**	Y	N	Y	N	Y	N	Y
19 Wexler	Y	Y	N	Y	N	Y	N
20 Deutsch	Y	Y	N	Y	N	Y	N
21 **Diaz-Balart**	Y	N	Y	N	Y	N	Y
22 **Shaw**	Y	N	Y	N	Y	N	Y
23 Hastings	Y	Y	N	Y	N	Y	N
GEORGIA							
1 **Kingston**	N	N	Y	N	Y	N	Y
2 Bishop	N	N	N	Y	N	Y	N
3 **Collins**	N	N	N	N	Y	N	Y
4 McKinney	Y	Y	N	Y	N	Y	N
5 Lewis	?	?	N	Y	N	Y	N
6 **Gingrich**		N		Y	N	Y	N
7 **Barr**	N	N	Y	N	Y	N	Y
8 **Chambliss**	N	N	Y	N	Y	N	Y
9 **Deal**	N	N	Y	N	Y	N	Y
10 **Norwood**	N	N	N	N	Y	N	Y
11 **Linder**	N	N	Y	N	?	?	?
HAWAII							
1 Abercrombie	Y	Y	N	Y	N	Y	N
2 Mink	Y	Y	N	Y	N	Y	N
IDAHO							
1 **Chenoweth**	N	N	?	N	Y	N	N
2 **Crapo**	N	N	Y	N	Y	N	N
ILLINOIS							
1 Rush	Y	Y	N	Y	N	Y	N
2 Jackson	Y	Y	N	Y	N	Y	N
3 Lipinski	Y	N	Y	N	Y	N	Y
4 Gutierrez	Y	N	?	Y	N	Y	N
5 Blagojevich	Y	Y	N	Y	N	Y	N
6 **Hyde**	?	N	Y	N	Y	N	Y
7 Davis	Y	Y	N	Y	N	Y	N
8 **Crane**	N	N	Y	N	Y	N	Y
9 Yates	?	?	?	?	?	?	?
10 **Porter**	Y	Y	Y	Y	N	Y	N
11 **Weller**	N	N	Y	N	Y	N	Y
12 Costello	Y	Y	N	Y	N	Y	N

ND Northern Democrats   SD Southern Democrats

	332	334	335	336	337	338	339
13 **Fawell**	N	N	Y	N	Y	N	Y
14 **Hastert**	N	N	Y	N	Y	N	Y
15 **Ewing**	Y	N	Y	N	Y	N	Y
16 **Manzullo**	N	N	Y	N	Y	N	Y
17 Evans	Y	Y	N	Y	N	Y	N
18 **LaHood**	N	N	Y	N	Y	N	Y
19 Poshard	Y	Y	N	Y	N	Y	N
20 **Shimkus**	N	N	Y	N	Y	N	Y
INDIANA							
1 Visclosky	Y	N	N	Y	N	Y	N
2 **McIntosh**	N	N	Y	N	Y	N	Y
3 Roemer	Y	N	Y	Y	N	Y	N
4 **Souder**	N	N	Y	N	Y	N	Y
5 **Buyer**	N	N	Y	N	Y	N	Y
6 **Burton**	N	N	Y	N	Y	N	Y
7 **Pease**	Y	N	Y	N	Y	N	Y
8 **Hostettler**	N	N	Y	N	Y	N	Y
9 Hamilton	Y	N	Y	Y	N	Y	N
10 Carson	Y	Y	N	Y	N	Y	N
IOWA							
1 **Leach**	Y	Y	Y	Y	Y	N	Y
2 **Nussle**	N	N	Y	N	Y	N	Y
3 Boswell	N	N	Y	Y	N	Y	N
4 **Ganske**	Y	N	Y	Y	Y	Y	N
5 **Latham**	N	N	Y	N	Y	N	Y
KANSAS							
1 **Moran**	N	N	Y	N	Y	N	Y
2 **Ryun**	N	N	Y	N	Y	N	Y
3 **Snowbarger**	N	N	Y	N	Y	N	Y
4 **Tiahrt**	N	N	Y	N	Y	N	Y
KENTUCKY							
1 **Whitfield**	N	?	Y	N	Y	N	Y
2 **Lewis**	N	N	Y	N	Y	N	Y
3 **Northup**	N	N	Y	N	Y	N	Y
4 **Bunning**	N	N	Y	N	Y	N	Y
5 **Rogers**	N	N	Y	N	Y	N	Y
6 Baesler	N	N	Y	Y	N	Y	N
LOUISIANA							
1 **Livingston**	N	N	Y	N	Y	N	Y
2 Jefferson	Y	Y	?	Y	N	Y	N
3 **Tauzin**	N	N	Y	N	Y	N	Y
4 **McCrery**	N	N	Y	N	Y	N	Y
5 **Cooksey**	N	N	Y	N	Y	N	Y
6 **Baker**	N	N	Y	N	Y	N	Y
7 John	N	N	N	Y	N	?	?
MAINE							
1 Allen	Y	Y	N	Y	N	Y	N
2 Baldacci	Y	Y	N	Y	N	Y	N
MARYLAND							
1 **Gilchrest**	Y	Y	Y	N	Y	N	Y
2 **Ehrlich**	N	N	Y	N	Y	N	Y
3 Cardin	Y	Y	N	Y	N	Y	N
4 Wynn	Y	Y	N	Y	N	Y	N
5 Hoyer	Y	Y	N	Y	N	Y	N
6 **Bartlett**	N	N	Y	N	Y	N	Y
7 Cummings	Y	Y	Y	Y	N	Y	N
8 **Morella**	Y	Y	Y	Y	Y	Y	N
MASSACHUSETTS							
1 Olver	Y	Y	N	Y	N	Y	N
2 Neal	Y	Y	N	Y	N	Y	N
3 McGovern	Y	Y	N	Y	N	Y	N
4 Frank	Y	Y	N	Y	N	Y	N
5 Meehan	Y	Y	N	Y	N	?	N
6 Tierney	Y	Y	N	Y	N	Y	N
7 Markey	?	?	?	?	?	?	?
8 Kennedy	Y	Y	Y	Y	N	Y	N
9 Moakley	Y	?	N	Y	N	Y	N
10 Delahunt	Y	Y	Y	Y	N	Y	N
MICHIGAN							
1 Stupak	Y	Y	N	Y	N	Y	N
2 **Hoekstra**	N	N	Y	N	Y	N	Y
3 **Ehlers**	Y	Y	Y	N	Y	N	Y
4 **Camp**	N	N	Y	N	Y	N	Y
5 Barcia	Y	N	N	Y	N	Y	N
6 **Upton**	Y	N	Y	N	Y	N	Y
7 **Smith**	Y	N	Y	N	Y	N	Y
8 Stabenow	Y	Y	N	Y	N	Y	N
9 Kildee	Y	Y	Y	Y	N	Y	N
10 Bonior	Y	Y	N	Y	N	Y	N
11 **Knollenberg**	N	N	Y	N	Y	N	Y
12 Levin	Y	Y	N	Y	N	Y	N
13 Rivers	Y	Y	Y	Y	N	Y	N
14 Conyers	Y	+	N	Y	N	Y	N
15 Kilpatrick	Y	Y	Y	Y	N	Y	N
16 Dingell	Y	N	Y	Y	N	Y	N
MINNESOTA							
1 **Gutknecht**	N	N	Y	N	Y	N	Y
2 Minge	Y	Y	N	Y	N	Y	N
3 **Ramstad**	Y	Y	Y	N	Y	N	Y
4 Vento	Y	Y	N	Y	N	Y	N
5 Sabo	Y	Y	N	Y	N	Y	N
6 Luther	Y	Y	N	Y	N	Y	N
7 Peterson	N	N	N	Y	N	Y	N
8 Oberstar	Y	Y	N	Y	N	Y	N
MISSISSIPPI							
1 **Wicker**	N	N	Y	N	Y	N	Y
2 Thompson	Y	Y	N	Y	N	Y	N
3 **Pickering**	N	N	Y	N	Y	N	Y
4 **Parker**	N	N	Y	N	Y	N	Y
5 Taylor	Y	N	Y	Y	N	Y	N
MISSOURI							
1 Clay	Y	Y	N	Y	N	Y	N
2 **Talent**	N	N	Y	N	Y	N	Y
3 Gephardt	Y	Y	N	Y	N	Y	N
4 Skelton	N	N	Y	Y	N	Y	N
5 McCarthy	Y	Y	Y	Y	N	Y	N
6 Danner	N	N	Y	Y	N	Y	Y
7 **Blunt**	N	N	Y	N	Y	N	Y
8 **Emerson**	N	N	Y	N	Y	N	Y
9 **Hulshof**	N	N	Y	N	Y	N	Y
MONTANA							
AL **Hill**	N	N	Y	N	Y	N	Y
NEBRASKA							
1 **Bereuter**	N	N	Y	N	Y	N	Y
2 **Christensen**	N	N	Y	N	Y	N	Y
3 **Barrett**	N	N	Y	N	Y	N	Y
NEVADA							
1 **Ensign**	N	Y	Y	N	Y	N	Y
2 **Gibbons**	N	N	Y	N	Y	N	Y
NEW HAMPSHIRE							
1 **Sununu**	N	N	Y	N	Y	N	Y
2 **Bass**	N	N	Y	N	Y	N	Y
NEW JERSEY							
1 Andrews	Y	Y	N	Y	N	Y	N
2 **LoBiondo**	N	Y	Y	N	Y	N	Y
3 **Saxton**	Y	Y	Y	N	Y	N	Y
4 **Smith**	Y	Y	Y	N	Y	N	Y
5 **Roukema**	Y	Y	Y	Y	Y	Y	N
6 Pallone	Y	Y	Y	Y	N	Y	N
7 **Franks**	Y	Y	Y	N	Y	N	Y
8 Pascrell	Y	Y	Y	Y	N	Y	N
9 Rothman	Y	Y	Y	Y	N	Y	N
10 Payne	Y	Y	N	Y	N	Y	N
11 **Frelinghuysen**	Y	N	Y	N	Y	N	Y
12 **Pappas**	N	N	Y	N	Y	N	Y
13 Menendez	Y	Y	N	Y	N	Y	N
NEW MEXICO							
1 **Wilson**	N	N	Y	N	Y	N	Y
2 **Skeen**	N	N	Y	N	Y	N	Y
3 **Redmond**	N	N	Y	N	Y	N	Y
NEW YORK							
1 **Forbes**	Y	Y	N	Y	N	Y	N
2 **Lazio**	Y	Y	Y	N	Y	N	Y
3 **King**	N	N	Y	N	Y	N	Y
4 McCarthy	Y	Y	Y	Y	N	Y	N
5 Ackerman	Y	Y	N	Y	N	Y	N
6 Meeks	Y	Y	N	Y	N	Y	N
7 Manton	Y	Y	Y	Y	N	Y	N
8 Nadler	Y	Y	N	Y	N	Y	N
9 Schumer	Y	Y	N	Y	N	Y	N
10 Towns	Y	Y	N	Y	N	Y	N
11 Owens	Y	Y	N	Y	N	Y	N
12 Velázquez	?	Y	N	Y	N	Y	N
13 **Fossella**	Y	N	Y	N	Y	N	Y
14 Maloney	Y	Y	N	Y	N	Y	N
15 Rangel	Y	Y	N	Y	N	Y	N
16 Serrano	+	+	N	Y	N	Y	N
17 Engel	Y	Y	N	Y	N	Y	N
18 Lowey	Y	Y	N	Y	N	Y	N
19 **Kelly**	Y	Y	Y	N	Y	N	Y
20 **Gilman**	Y	Y	Y	N	Y	N	Y
21 McNulty	Y	Y	N	Y	N	Y	N
22 **Solomon**	Y	N	Y	N	Y	N	Y
23 **Boehlert**	Y	Y	Y	Y	Y	N	Y
24 **McHugh**	Y	N	Y	N	Y	N	Y
25 **Walsh**	Y	N	Y	N	Y	N	Y
26 Hinchey	Y	Y	N	Y	N	Y	N
27 **Paxon**	N	N	Y	N	Y	N	Y
28 Slaughter	Y	Y	N	Y	N	Y	N
29 LaFalce	Y	Y	N	Y	N	Y	N
30 **Quinn**	Y	N	Y	N	Y	N	Y
31 **Houghton**	N	N	Y	N	Y	N	Y
NORTH CAROLINA							
1 Clayton	Y	Y	Y	Y	N	Y	N
2 Etheridge	Y	N	Y	Y	N	Y	N
3 **Jones**	N	N	Y	N	Y	N	Y
4 Price	Y	Y	N	Y	N	Y	N
5 **Burr**	N	N	Y	N	Y	N	Y
6 **Coble**	N	N	Y	N	Y	N	Y
7 McIntyre	N	N	Y	Y	N	Y	N
8 Hefner	Y	Y	Y	Y	N	Y	N
9 **Myrick**	N	N	Y	N	Y	N	Y
10 **Ballenger**	N	N	Y	N	Y	N	Y
11 **Taylor**	N	N	Y	N	Y	N	Y
12 Watt	Y	Y	N	Y	N	Y	N
NORTH DAKOTA							
AL Pomeroy	N	N	N	Y	N	Y	N
OHIO							
1 **Chabot**	N	N	Y	N	Y	N	Y
2 **Portman**	N	N	Y	N	Y	N	Y
3 Hall	Y	?	N	Y	N	Y	N
4 **Oxley**	N	N	Y	N	Y	N	Y
5 **Gillmor**	N	N	Y	N	?	N	Y
6 Strickland	Y	N	N	Y	N	Y	N
7 **Hobson**	N	N	Y	N	Y	N	Y
8 **Boehner**	N	N	Y	N	Y	N	Y
9 Kaptur	Y	Y	N	Y	N	Y	N
10 Kucinich	Y	Y	N	Y	N	Y	N
11 Stokes	Y	Y	N	Y	N	Y	N
12 **Kasich**	N	N	Y	N	Y	N	Y
13 Brown	Y	Y	N	Y	N	Y	N
14 Sawyer	Y	Y	Y	Y	N	Y	N
15 **Pryce**	N	N	Y	N	Y	N	Y
16 **Regula**	Y	N	Y	N	Y	N	Y
17 Traficant	N	N	Y	Y	N	Y	Y
18 **Ney**	N	N	Y	N	Y	N	Y
19 **LaTourette**	Y	Y	Y	Y	Y	N	Y
OKLAHOMA							
1 **Largent**	N	N	Y	N	Y	N	Y
2 **Coburn**	N	N	Y	N	Y	N	Y
3 **Watkins**	N	N	Y	N	Y	N	Y
4 **Watts**	N	N	Y	N	Y	N	Y
5 **Istook**	N	N	N	N	Y	N	Y
6 **Lucas**	N	N	Y	N	Y	N	Y
OREGON							
1 Furse	Y	Y	N	Y	N	Y	N
2 **Smith**	N	?	Y	N	Y	N	Y
3 Blumenauer	Y	Y	Y	Y	N	Y	N
4 DeFazio	Y	Y	N	Y	N	Y	N
5 Hooley	Y	Y	Y	Y	N	Y	N
PENNSYLVANIA							
1 Brady	?	?	N	Y	N	Y	N
2 Fattah	Y	Y	N	Y	N	Y	N
3 Borski	Y	Y	N	Y	N	Y	N
4 Klink	Y	N	Y	Y	N	Y	N
5 **Peterson**	N	N	Y	N	Y	N	Y
6 Holden	Y	N	Y	Y	N	Y	N
7 **Weldon**	Y	Y	Y	N	?	N	Y
8 **Greenwood**	Y	Y	Y	N	Y	N	Y
9 **Shuster**	N	?	Y	N	Y	N	Y
10 **McDade**	N	N	Y	N	Y	N	Y
11 Kanjorski	Y	N	Y	Y	N	Y	N
12 Murtha	Y	N	Y	Y	N	Y	N
13 **Fox**	Y	Y	Y	Y	Y	Y	Y
14 Coyne	Y	Y	N	Y	N	Y	N
15 McHale	Y	Y	N	Y	N	Y	N
16 **Pitts**	N	N	Y	N	Y	N	Y
17 **Gekas**	N	N	Y	N	Y	N	Y
18 Doyle	Y	N	Y	Y	N	Y	N
19 **Goodling**	N	N	Y	N	Y	N	Y
20 Mascara	Y	N	Y	Y	N	Y	N
21 **English**	N	N	Y	N	Y	N	Y
RHODE ISLAND							
1 Kennedy	Y	Y	N	Y	N	Y	N
2 Weygand	Y	Y	Y	Y	N	Y	N
SOUTH CAROLINA							
1 **Sanford**	Y	N	Y	N	Y	N	N
2 **Spence**	N	N	Y	N	Y	N	Y
3 **Graham**	N	N	Y	N	Y	N	Y
4 **Inglis**	N	N	Y	N	Y	N	Y
5 Spratt	Y	Y	N	Y	N	Y	N
6 Clyburn	Y	Y	N	Y	N	Y	N
SOUTH DAKOTA							
AL **Thune**	N	N	Y	N	Y	N	Y
TENNESSEE							
1 **Jenkins**	N	N	Y	N	Y	N	Y
2 **Duncan**	N	N	Y	N	Y	N	Y
3 **Wamp**	N	N	Y	N	Y	N	Y
4 **Hilleary**	N	N	Y	N	Y	N	Y
5 Clement	N	Y	Y	Y	N	Y	N
6 Gordon	Y	N	Y	Y	N	Y	N
7 **Bryant**	N	N	Y	N	Y	N	Y
8 Tanner	Y	N	N	Y	N	Y	N
9 Ford	+	+	−	+	−	+	−
TEXAS							
1 Sandlin	Y	N	N	Y	N	Y	N
2 Turner	Y	N	N	Y	N	Y	N
3 **Johnson, Sam**	N	N	Y	N	Y	N	Y
4 Hall	N	N	Y	Y	N	Y	N
5 **Sessions**	N	N	Y	N	Y	N	Y
6 **Barton**	N	N	Y	N	Y	N	Y
7 **Archer**	N	N	Y	N	Y	N	Y
8 **Brady**	N	N	Y	N	Y	N	N
9 Lampson	Y	Y	N	Y	N	Y	N
10 Doggett	Y	Y	N	Y	N	Y	N
11 Edwards	Y	Y	N	Y	N	Y	N
12 **Granger**	N	N	Y	N	Y	N	Y
13 **Thornberry**	N	N	Y	N	Y	N	Y
14 **Paul**	N	N	Y	N	Y	N	N
15 Hinojosa	Y	Y	N	+	N	Y	N
16 Reyes	Y	N	N	Y	N	Y	N
17 Stenholm	N	N	N	Y	N	Y	N
18 Jackson-Lee	Y	Y	Y	Y	N	Y	N
19 **Combest**	N	N	Y	N	Y	N	Y
20 Gonzalez	?	?	?	?	?	?	?
21 **Smith**	N	N	Y	N	Y	N	Y
22 **DeLay**	N	N	Y	N	Y	N	Y
23 **Bonilla**	N	N	Y	N	Y	N	N
24 Frost	Y	Y	Y	Y	N	Y	N
25 Bentsen	Y	Y	N	Y	N	Y	N
26 **Armey**	N	N	Y	N	Y	N	Y
27 Ortiz	N	N	Y	Y	N	Y	N
28 Rodriguez	N	Y	N	Y	N	Y	?
29 Green	Y	Y	N	Y	N	Y	N
30 Johnson, E.B.	Y	Y	N	Y	N	Y	N
UTAH							
1 **Hansen**	N	N	Y	N	Y	N	Y
2 **Cook**	N	N	Y	N	Y	N	Y
3 **Cannon**	N	N	Y	N	Y	N	Y
VERMONT							
AL *Sanders*	Y	Y	N	Y	N	Y	N
VIRGINIA							
1 **Bateman**	N	N	Y	N	Y	N	Y
2 Pickett	N	N	N	Y	N	Y	N
3 Scott	Y	Y	N	Y	N	Y	N
4 Sisisky	N	N	N	Y	N	Y	N
5 Goode	N	N	Y	N	Y	Y	Y
6 **Goodlatte**	N	N	Y	N	Y	N	Y
7 **Bliley**	N	N	Y	N	Y	N	Y
8 Moran	Y	Y	Y	Y	N	Y	N
9 Boucher	Y	N	N	Y	N	Y	N
10 **Wolf**	N	N	Y	N	Y	N	Y
11 **Davis**	Y	N	Y	N	Y	N	Y
WASHINGTON							
1 **White**	N	N	Y	N	Y	N	Y
2 **Metcalf**	N	N	Y	N	Y	N	Y
3 **Smith, Linda**	N	N	Y	N	Y	N	Y
4 **Hastings**	N	N	Y	N	Y	N	Y
5 **Nethercutt**	N	N	Y	N	Y	N	Y
6 Dicks	Y	Y	N	Y	N	Y	N
7 McDermott	Y	Y	N	Y	N	Y	N
8 **Dunn**	N	N	Y	N	Y	N	Y
9 Smith, Adam	Y	Y	Y	Y	N	Y	N
WEST VIRGINIA							
1 Mollohan	N	N	Y	Y	N	Y	N
2 Wise	Y	N	Y	Y	N	Y	N
3 Rahall	Y	N	Y	Y	N	Y	N
WISCONSIN							
1 **Neumann**	N	N	Y	N	Y	N	Y
2 **Klug**	Y	N	Y	N	Y	?	?
3 Kind	Y	Y	Y	Y	N	Y	N
4 Kleczka	Y	Y	N	Y	N	Y	N
5 Barrett	Y	Y	N	Y	N	Y	N
6 **Petri**	N	N	Y	N	Y	N	Y
7 Obey	Y	Y	Y	Y	N	Y	N
8 Johnson	Y	Y	N	Y	N	Y	N
9 **Sensenbrenner**	N	N	Y	N	Y	N	Y
WYOMING							
AL **Cubin**	N	N	Y	N	Y	N	Y

Southern states - Ala., Ark., Fla., Ga., Ky., La., Miss., N.C., Okla., S.C., Tenn., Texas, Va.

House Votes 340, 342, 343, 344, 345, 346, 347 *

340. H Con Res 311. Honoring the Memory of U.S. Capitol Policemen Gibson and Chestnut/Adoption. Adoption of the resolution to honor Det. John Michael Gibson and Pfc. Jacob Joseph Chestnut of the U.S. Capitol Police, who were killed in the line of duty July 24, 1998. Adopted 392-0: R 210-0; D 181-0 (ND 133-0, SD 48-0); I 1-0. July 27, 1998.

341. Quorum Call.* 378 Responded. July 28, 1998.

342. Procedural Motion/Adjourn. Gutknecht, R-Minn., motion to adjourn. Motion agreed to 392-0: R 211-0; D 180-0 (ND 133-0, SD 47-0); I 1-0. July 28, 1998.

343. HR 629. Texas, Maine and Vermont Low-Level Radioactive Waste Compact/Rule. Adoption of the rule (H Res 511) to provide for House floor consideration of the conference report on the bill that would allow Maine and Vermont to export low-level radioactive waste to a facility in Texas. Adopted 313-108: R 219-4; D 93-104 (ND 60-87, SD 33-17); I 1-0. July 29, 1998.

344. HR 629. Texas, Maine and Vermont Low-Level Radioactive Waste Compact/Conference Report. Adoption of the conference report on the bill that would allow Maine and Vermont to export low-level radioactive waste to a facility in Texas. Adopted (thus sent to the Senate) 305-117: R 197-26; D 107-91 (ND 71-77, SD 36-14); I 1-0. July 29, 1998.

345. HR 4194. Fiscal 1999 VA-HUD Appropriations/International Space Station Termination. Roemer, D-Ind., amendment to cut NASA funding by $1.6 billion and terminate the international space station. Rejected 109-323: R 47-179; D 61-144 (ND 59-92, SD 2-52); I 1-0. July 29, 1998.

346. HR 4194. Fiscal 1999 VA-HUD Appropriations/VA Health Care Network Funding Distribution. Hinchey, D-N.Y., amendment to prohibit the use of funds by the Department of Veterans Affairs to administer its Veterans Equitable Resource Allocation (VERA) System, which distributes funding for regional VA health care networks in a way that accounts for shifting populations of veterans. Rejected 146-285: R 62-164; D 83-121 (ND 82-68, SD 1-53); I 1-0. July 29, 1998.

347. HR 4194. Fiscal 1999 VA-HUD Appropriations/AIDS Patient Housing Program Funding Redistribution. Hilleary, R-Tenn. amendment to cut by $21 million the bill's appropriation for Housing Opportunities for Persons with AIDS. The amendment would redistribute the funds for VA grants to construct state extended care facilities. Adopted 231-200: R 184-42; D 47-157 (ND 21-129, SD 26-28); I 0-1. July 29, 1998.

* CQ does not include quorum calls in its vote charts.

Key

Y	Voted for (yea).
#	Paired for.
+	Announced for.
N	Voted against (nay).
X	Paired against.
−	Announced against.
P	Voted "present."
C	Voted "present" to avoid possible conflict of interest.
?	Did not vote or otherwise make a position known.

Democrats **Republicans** *Independent*

	340	342	343	344	345	346	347
ALABAMA							
1 *Callahan*	Y	Y	Y	Y	N	N	Y
2 *Everett*	Y	Y	Y	Y	N	N	Y
3 *Riley*	Y	Y	Y	Y	N	N	Y
4 *Aderholt*	Y	Y	Y	Y	N	N	Y
5 Cramer	Y	?	Y	Y	N	N	Y
6 *Bachus*	Y	Y	Y	N	N	N	Y
7 Hilliard	Y	Y	N	Y	N	N	N
ALASKA							
AL *Young*	Y	?	Y	Y	N	N	Y
ARIZONA							
1 *Salmon*	Y	Y	Y	Y	N	N	Y
2 Pastor	Y	Y	N	N	N	N	Y
3 *Stump*	Y	Y	Y	Y	N	N	Y
4 *Shadegg*	Y	Y	Y	Y	N	N	Y
5 *Kolbe*	?	Y	Y	Y	N	N	N
6 *Hayworth*	Y	Y	Y	Y	N	N	Y
ARKANSAS							
1 Berry	Y	Y	Y	Y	Y	N	Y
2 Snyder	Y	Y	Y	Y	N	N	N
3 *Hutchinson*	Y	Y	Y	N	N	N	Y
4 *Dickey*	Y	Y	Y	Y	N	N	Y
CALIFORNIA							
1 *Riggs*	?	?	Y	Y	N	N	N
2 *Herger*	Y	Y	Y	Y	Y	N	Y
3 Fazio	Y	Y	Y	Y	N	N	Y
4 *Doolittle*	Y	Y	Y	Y	N	N	Y
5 Matsui	Y	Y	N	N	N	N	N
6 Woolsey	Y	Y	N	N	N	N	N
7 Miller	Y	Y	N	N	Y	N	N
8 Pelosi	Y	Y	N	N	N	N	N
9 Lee	Y	Y	N	N	N	N	N
10 Tauscher	Y	Y	Y	Y	N	N	N
11 *Pombo*	Y	Y	Y	N	N	N	N
12 Lantos	Y	Y	N	N	N	N	N
13 Stark	?	?	N	N	N	N	N
14 Eshoo	Y	Y	N	N	N	N	N
15 *Campbell*	Y	Y	Y	Y	N	N	N
16 Lofgren	Y	Y	N	N	N	N	N
17 Farr	Y	?	Y	Y	N	N	N
18 Condit	Y	Y	Y	Y	N	N	Y
19 *Radanovich*	Y	Y	Y	Y	N	N	Y
20 Dooley	Y	Y	Y	Y	N	N	Y
21 *Thomas*	Y	Y	Y	Y	N	N	Y
22 Capps, L.	Y	Y	N	N	N	N	N
23 *Gallegly*	Y	Y	Y	Y	N	N	Y
24 Sherman	Y	Y	N	N	N	N	N
25 *McKeon*	Y	Y	Y	Y	N	N	Y
26 Berman	Y	Y	N	N	N	N	N
27 *Rogan*	Y	Y	Y	Y	N	N	Y
28 *Dreier*	Y	Y	Y	Y	N	N	N
29 Waxman	?	?	N	N	N	N	N
30 Becerra	+	Y	N	N	N	N	N
31 Martinez	Y	?	Y	Y	N	N	N
32 Dixon	Y	Y	N	N	N	N	N
33 Roybal-Allard	+	Y	N	N	N	N	N
34 Torres	?	Y	N	N	N	N	N
35 Waters	Y	Y	N	N	N	N	N
36 Harman	?	Y	Y	Y	N	N	N
37 Millender-McD.	Y	Y	N	+	N	N	N

	340	342	343	344	345	346	347
38 *Horn*	Y	Y	Y	Y	N	N	N
39 *Royce*	Y	Y	Y	Y	N	N	Y
40 *Lewis*	?	Y	Y	Y	N	N	Y
41 *Kim*	Y	Y	Y	Y	N	N	N
42 Brown	Y	Y	N	Y	N	N	N
43 *Calvert*	Y	Y	Y	Y	N	N	Y
44 *Bono, M.*	Y	Y	Y	Y	N	N	Y
45 *Rohrabacher*	Y	Y	Y	Y	N	N	Y
46 Sanchez	Y	Y	N	N	N	N	N
47 *Cox*	?	Y	Y	Y	N	N	Y
48 *Packard*	Y	Y	Y	Y	N	N	Y
49 *Bilbray*	Y	Y	Y	Y	N	N	N
50 Filner	Y	Y	N	N	N	N	N
51 *Cunningham*	Y	Y	Y	Y	N	N	Y
52 *Hunter*	Y	Y	?	Y	N	N	Y
COLORADO							
1 DeGette	Y	Y	Y	Y	N	N	N
2 Skaggs	Y	Y	Y	Y	N	N	N
3 *McInnis*	Y	Y	Y	Y	Y	N	Y
4 *Schaffer*	Y	Y	Y	Y	N	N	Y
5 *Hefley*	Y	Y	Y	Y	N	N	Y
6 *Schaefer*	?	Y	Y	Y	N	N	Y
CONNECTICUT							
1 Kennelly	Y	Y	Y	N	N	Y	N
2 Gejdenson	Y	Y	N	Y	N	Y	N
3 DeLauro	Y	Y	N	N	N	Y	N
4 *Shays*	Y	Y	Y	N	Y	Y	N
5 Maloney	Y	Y	Y	Y	N	Y	N
6 *Johnson*	Y	Y	Y	N	N	Y	N
DELAWARE							
AL *Castle*	Y	Y	Y	N	N	Y	N
FLORIDA							
1 *Scarborough*	Y	?	Y	Y	N	N	Y
2 Boyd	Y	Y	Y	Y	N	N	Y
3 Brown	Y	Y	Y	Y	N	N	N
4 *Fowler*	Y	Y	Y	Y	N	N	Y
5 Thurman	Y	Y	Y	Y	N	N	N
6 *Stearns*	Y	Y	Y	Y	N	N	Y
7 *Mica*	Y	Y	Y	Y	N	N	Y
8 *McCollum*	Y	Y	Y	Y	N	N	Y
9 *Bilirakis*	Y	Y	Y	Y	N	N	Y
10 *Young*	?	?	?	?	?	?	?
11 Davis	Y	Y	Y	Y	N	N	N
12 *Canady*	Y	Y	Y	Y	N	N	Y
13 *Miller*	Y	Y	Y	Y	N	N	Y
14 *Goss*	Y	Y	Y	Y	N	N	Y
15 *Weldon*	Y	Y	Y	Y	N	N	Y
16 *Foley*	Y	Y	Y	Y	N	N	Y
17 Meek	Y	Y	N	N	N	N	N
18 *Ros-Lehtinen*	?	Y	Y	Y	N	N	Y
19 Wexler	?	Y	N	N	N	N	N
20 Deutsch	Y	N	Y	Y	N	N	N
21 *Diaz-Balart*	Y	Y	Y	Y	N	N	Y
22 *Shaw*	Y	Y	Y	Y	N	N	Y
23 Hastings	?	?	N	N	N	N	N
GEORGIA							
1 *Kingston*	?	Y	Y	Y	Y	Y	Y
2 Bishop	Y	Y	Y	Y	N	N	N
3 *Collins*	Y	Y	Y	Y	N	N	Y
4 McKinney	Y	?	N	N	N	N	N
5 Lewis	?	Y	N	N	N	N	N
6 *Gingrich*	Y						
7 *Barr*	Y	Y	Y	Y	N	N	Y
8 *Chambliss*	Y	Y	Y	Y	N	N	Y
9 *Deal*	Y	Y	Y	N	N	N	Y
10 *Norwood*	Y	Y	Y	Y	N	N	Y
11 *Linder*	Y	?	Y	Y	N	Y	Y
HAWAII							
1 Abercrombie	Y	Y	N	N	N	N	N
2 Mink	Y	Y	N	N	Y	N	N
IDAHO							
1 *Chenoweth*	Y	Y	Y	Y	N	N	Y
2 *Crapo*	Y	Y	Y	Y	N	N	Y
ILLINOIS							
1 Rush	Y	Y	N	N	N	Y	N
2 Jackson	Y	Y	N	N	N	Y	N
3 Lipinski	?	Y	Y	N	Y	Y	Y
4 Gutierrez	Y	Y	N	Y	N	Y	N
5 Blagojevich	Y	Y	N	N	N	N	N
6 *Hyde*	Y	Y	Y	Y	N	N	Y
7 Davis	Y	Y	N	N	Y	N	N
8 *Crane*	Y	Y	Y	Y	N	Y	Y
9 Yates	?	Y	N	Y	N	Y	N
10 *Porter*	Y	Y	Y	Y	N	N	Y
11 *Weller*	Y	Y	Y	N	N	Y	Y
12 Costello	Y	Y	Y	Y	N	N	Y

ND Northern Democrats   SD Southern Democrats

	340	342	343	344	345	346	347
13 **Fawell**	Y	Y	Y	Y	N	Y	N
14 **Hastert**	Y	Y	Y	Y	N	Y	Y
15 **Ewing**	Y	Y	Y	Y	N	Y	Y
16 **Manzullo**	Y	Y	Y	Y	Y	Y	Y
17 Evans	Y	?	N	N	Y	N	N
18 **LaHood**	Y	Y	Y	Y	N	N	Y
19 Poshard	?	?	N	Y	Y	Y	N
20 **Shimkus**	Y	Y	Y	Y	N	Y	Y
INDIANA							
1 Visclosky	Y	Y	Y	N	Y	Y	N
2 **McIntosh**	Y	Y	Y	Y	N	Y	Y
3 Roemer	Y	Y	Y	Y	Y	Y	Y
4 **Souder**	Y	Y	Y	Y	N	Y	Y
5 **Buyer**	Y	?	Y	Y	N	N	N
6 **Burton**	Y	P	Y	Y	N	N	Y
7 **Pease**	Y	Y	Y	Y	N	N	Y
8 **Hostettler**	Y	Y	Y	Y	N	N	Y
9 Hamilton	Y	Y	Y	Y	Y	N	N
10 Carson	Y	Y	Y	Y	Y	N	N
IOWA							
1 **Leach**	Y	Y	Y	Y	Y	Y	N
2 **Nussle**	Y	Y	Y	Y	Y	Y	Y
3 Boswell	Y	Y	Y	Y	N	Y	Y
4 **Ganske**	Y	Y	Y	Y	Y	Y	N
5 **Latham**	Y	Y	Y	Y	Y	Y	Y
KANSAS							
1 **Moran**	Y	Y	Y	Y	N	N	Y
2 **Ryun**	Y	Y	Y	Y	N	N	Y
3 **Snowbarger**	Y	Y	Y	Y	N	N	Y
4 **Tiahrt**	+	Y	Y	Y	N	N	Y
KENTUCKY							
1 **Whitfield**	?	Y	Y	Y	N	N	Y
2 **Lewis**	Y	Y	Y	Y	N	N	Y
3 **Northup**	Y	Y	Y	Y	N	N	Y
4 **Bunning**	Y	Y	Y	Y	N	N	Y
5 **Rogers**	Y	Y	Y	Y	N	N	Y
6 Baesler	Y	Y	Y	N	N	N	Y
LOUISIANA							
1 **Livingston**	Y	Y	Y	Y	N	N	Y
2 Jefferson	Y	Y	N	N	N	N	N
3 **Tauzin**	?	Y	Y	Y	N	N	Y
4 **McCrery**	Y	Y	Y	Y	N	N	Y
5 **Cooksey**	Y	Y	Y	Y	N	N	Y
6 **Baker**	Y	Y	Y	Y	N	N	Y
7 John	Y	Y	Y	Y	N	N	N
MAINE							
1 Allen	Y	Y	Y	Y	N	Y	N
2 Baldacci	Y	Y	Y	Y	N	Y	N
MARYLAND							
1 **Gilchrest**	Y	Y	Y	Y	N	N	N
2 **Ehrlich**	Y	Y	Y	Y	N	N	Y
3 Cardin	Y	Y	N	Y	N	N	N
4 Wynn	Y	Y	N	Y	N	N	N
5 Hoyer	Y	Y	Y	Y	N	N	N
6 **Bartlett**	Y	Y	Y	Y	N	N	Y
7 Cummings	Y	Y	N	N	N	N	N
8 **Morella**	Y	Y	Y	N	N	N	N
MASSACHUSETTS							
1 Olver	Y	Y	N	Y	N	Y	N
2 Neal	Y	Y	N	Y	N	Y	N
3 McGovern	Y	Y	N	N	N	Y	N
4 Frank	Y	Y	Y	Y	Y	Y	N
5 Meehan	Y	Y	N	N	Y	Y	N
6 Tierney	Y	Y	N	N	Y	Y	N
7 Markey	?	Y	N	N	Y	Y	N
8 Kennedy	Y	Y	N	N	Y	Y	N
9 Moakley	?	?	?	?	Y	Y	N
10 Delahunt	Y	Y	N	N	Y	Y	N
MICHIGAN							
1 Stupak	Y	Y	Y	Y	Y	Y	Y
2 **Hoekstra**	Y	Y	Y	Y	Y	Y	Y
3 **Ehlers**	Y	Y	Y	Y	N	Y	Y
4 **Camp**	Y	Y	Y	Y	Y	Y	Y
5 Barcia	Y	Y	Y	Y	N	Y	Y
6 **Upton**	Y	Y	Y	Y	Y	Y	Y
7 **Smith**	Y	?	Y	Y	Y	Y	Y
8 Stabenow	Y	Y	N	N	N	Y	N
9 Kildee	Y	Y	N	Y	N	Y	N
10 Bonior	Y	Y	N	N	N	Y	N
11 **Knollenberg**	Y	Y	Y	Y	N	N	N
12 Levin	Y	Y	Y	Y	Y	Y	N
13 Rivers	Y	Y	Y	Y	Y	Y	N
14 Conyers	?	?	N	N	Y	Y	N
15 Kilpatrick	Y	Y	N	N	N	Y	N
16 Dingell	Y	Y	Y	Y	Y	N	N

	340	342	343	344	345	346	347
MINNESOTA							
1 **Gutknecht**	Y	Y	Y	Y	N	N	Y
2 Minge	Y	Y	Y	Y	Y	N	Y
3 **Ramstad**	Y	Y	Y	Y	Y	N	Y
4 Vento	Y	Y	Y	Y	Y	N	N
5 Sabo	Y	Y	Y	Y	N	N	N
6 Luther	Y	Y	N	Y	Y	N	N
7 Peterson	Y	Y	Y	Y	Y	N	Y
8 Oberstar	Y	Y	Y	Y	Y	Y	N
MISSISSIPPI							
1 **Wicker**	Y	Y	Y	Y	N	N	Y
2 Thompson	?	Y	N	N	N	N	N
3 **Pickering**	Y	Y	Y	Y	N	N	Y
4 **Parker**	Y	Y	Y	Y	N	N	Y
5 Taylor	Y	Y	Y	Y	N	N	Y
MISSOURI							
1 Clay	Y	Y	N	Y	N	N	N
2 **Talent**	Y	Y	Y	?	N	N	Y
3 Gephardt	Y	Y	Y	Y	N	N	N
4 Skelton	Y	Y	Y	Y	N	N	Y
5 McCarthy	+	Y	Y	Y	N	Y	N
6 Danner	Y	Y	Y	Y	Y	N	Y
7 **Blunt**	Y	Y	Y	Y	N	N	Y
8 **Emerson**	Y	Y	Y	Y	N	N	Y
9 **Hulshof**	Y	Y	Y	Y	N	Y	Y
MONTANA							
AL **Hill**	Y	Y	Y	Y	N	N	Y
NEBRASKA							
1 **Bereuter**	Y	Y	Y	Y	Y	Y	Y
2 **Christensen**	Y	Y	Y	Y	Y	N	Y
3 **Barrett**	Y	Y	Y	Y	N	N	Y
NEVADA							
1 **Ensign**	Y	Y	N	N	Y	N	Y
2 **Gibbons**	Y	Y	N	N	N	N	Y
NEW HAMPSHIRE							
1 **Sununu**	Y	Y	Y	Y	N	Y	N
2 **Bass**	Y	Y	Y	Y	Y	Y	Y
NEW JERSEY							
1 Andrews	Y	Y	N	N	N	Y	N
2 **LoBiondo**	Y	Y	Y	N	Y	Y	Y
3 **Saxton**	Y	Y	Y	Y	N	Y	Y
4 **Smith**	Y	Y	Y	N	N	Y	Y
5 **Roukema**	Y	Y	Y	Y	Y	Y	Y
6 Pallone	Y	Y	Y	N	Y	Y	N
7 **Franks**	Y	Y	Y	N	Y	Y	Y
8 Pascrell	Y	Y	N	N	Y	Y	N
9 Rothman	Y	Y	N	N	N	Y	N
10 Payne	Y	Y	N	N	Y	Y	N
11 **Frelinghuysen**	Y	Y	Y	Y	N	Y	N
12 **Pappas**	Y	Y	Y	N	N	Y	Y
13 Menendez	Y	Y	N	N	N	Y	N
NEW MEXICO							
1 **Wilson**	Y	Y	Y	Y	N	N	Y
2 **Skeen**	Y	Y	N	N	N	N	Y
3 **Redmond**	Y	Y	Y	Y	N	N	Y
NEW YORK							
1 **Forbes**	Y	Y	Y	N	N	Y	N
2 **Lazio**	Y	Y	Y	Y	Y	Y	N
3 **King**	Y	Y	Y	Y	N	Y	Y
4 McCarthy	Y	Y	Y	Y	N	Y	N
5 Ackerman	?	Y	N	N	N	Y	N
6 Meeks	Y	Y	N	N	N	Y	N
7 Manton	Y	?	Y	Y	N	Y	N
8 Nadler	?	?	N	N	Y	Y	N
9 Schumer	Y	?	N	N	Y	Y	N
10 Towns	Y	?	?	N	N	Y	N
11 Owens	Y	Y	N	N	N	Y	N
12 Velázquez	Y	Y	N	N	Y	?	?
13 **Fossella**	Y	Y	Y	Y	Y	Y	Y
14 Maloney	Y	Y	N	N	Y	Y	N
15 Rangel	Y	?	N	N	N	Y	N
16 Serrano	Y	Y	N	Y	N	Y	N
17 Engel	Y	Y	?	N	N	Y	N
18 Lowey	Y	Y	N	Y	Y	Y	N
19 **Kelly**	Y	Y	Y	N	Y	Y	Y
20 **Gilman**	Y	Y	Y	Y	N	Y	N
21 McNulty	Y	Y	N	N	N	Y	N
22 **Solomon**	Y	Y	Y	Y	N	Y	Y
23 **Boehlert**	Y	Y	Y	Y	N	Y	N
24 **McHugh**	Y	Y	Y	Y	Y	Y	Y
25 **Walsh**	?	Y	Y	Y	N	Y	Y
26 Hinchey	Y	Y	N	N	N	Y	N
27 **Paxon**	Y	Y	Y	Y	Y	Y	Y
28 Slaughter	Y	?	N	N	Y	Y	N
29 LaFalce	Y	Y	N	Y	Y	Y	N

	340	342	343	344	345	346	347
30 **Quinn**	Y	Y	Y	Y	N	Y	Y
31 **Houghton**	Y	Y	Y	Y	N	Y	N
NORTH CAROLINA							
1 Clayton	Y	Y	+	+	N	N	Y
2 Etheridge	Y	Y	+	+	N	N	Y
3 **Jones**	Y	Y	Y	Y	N	N	Y
4 Price	?	?	?	?	N	N	N
5 **Burr**	Y	Y	Y	Y	N	N	N
6 **Coble**	Y	Y	Y	Y	Y	N	Y
7 McIntyre	Y	?	Y	Y	N	N	Y
8 Hefner	Y	?	Y	Y	N	N	N
9 **Myrick**	Y	Y	Y	Y	N	N	Y
10 **Ballenger**	Y	Y	Y	Y	N	N	Y
11 **Taylor**	Y	Y	Y	Y	N	N	Y
12 Watt	Y	Y	N	N	N	N	N
NORTH DAKOTA							
AL Pomeroy	?	Y	Y	Y	Y	N	Y
OHIO							
1 **Chabot**	Y	Y	Y	Y	Y	N	Y
2 **Portman**	Y	Y	Y	Y	Y	N	Y
3 Hall	Y	Y	Y	Y	N	N	N
4 **Oxley**	Y	Y	Y	Y	N	N	Y
5 **Gillmor**	Y	Y	Y	Y	N	N	Y
6 Strickland	Y	Y	N	N	Y	N	N
7 **Hobson**	Y	Y	Y	Y	N	N	N
8 **Boehner**	Y	Y	Y	Y	N	N	Y
9 Kaptur	Y	Y	?	Y	Y	N	N
10 Kucinich	Y	Y	N	N	N	N	N
11 Stokes	Y	Y	N	Y	N	N	N
12 **Kasich**	Y	Y	Y	N	N	N	Y
13 Brown	Y	Y	Y	Y	Y	Y	N
14 Sawyer	Y	Y	N	Y	N	N	N
15 **Pryce**	Y	Y	Y	Y	N	N	Y
16 **Regula**	Y	Y	Y	Y	N	N	Y
17 Traficant	Y	Y	Y	Y	N	N	Y
18 **Ney**	Y	Y	Y	Y	N	N	Y
19 **LaTourette**	Y	Y	Y	Y	N	N	Y
OKLAHOMA							
1 **Largent**	?	Y	Y	Y	Y	N	Y
2 **Coburn**	Y	Y	Y	Y	Y	N	Y
3 **Watkins**	Y	?	Y	Y	N	N	Y
4 **Watts**	Y	Y	Y	Y	N	N	Y
5 **Istook**	Y	Y	Y	Y	N	N	Y
6 **Lucas**	Y	Y	Y	Y	N	N	Y
OREGON							
1 Furse	Y	?	N	N	N	N	N
2 **Smith**	Y	?	Y	Y	N	N	Y
3 Blumenauer	Y	Y	Y	Y	Y	N	N
4 DeFazio	?	Y	N	N	Y	N	N
5 Hooley	Y	Y	N	N	N	N	N
PENNSYLVANIA							
1 Brady	Y	Y	N	N	N	Y	N
2 Fattah	Y	Y	N	N	N	Y	N
3 Borski	Y	Y	N	Y	N	Y	N
4 Klink	Y	?	Y	Y	N	Y	Y
5 **Peterson**	Y	Y	Y	Y	N	Y	Y
6 Holden	Y	Y	N	N	Y	Y	Y
7 **Weldon**	Y	Y	Y	Y	N	Y	Y
8 **Greenwood**	Y	?	Y	Y	N	Y	N
9 **Shuster**	?	?	Y	Y	Y	Y	Y
10 **McDade**	?	Y	?	Y	N	Y	N
11 Kanjorski	Y	Y	N	N	Y	Y	Y
12 Murtha	?	?	Y	Y	N	Y	N
13 **Fox**	Y	Y	Y	Y	N	Y	Y
14 Coyne	Y	Y	N	Y	Y	Y	N
15 McHale	Y	Y	Y	?	N	Y	N
16 **Pitts**	Y	Y	Y	Y	N	Y	Y
17 **Gekas**	Y	Y	Y	Y	N	Y	Y
18 Doyle	Y	Y	N	N	Y	Y	Y
19 **Goodling**	Y	?	Y	Y	Y	Y	Y
20 Mascara	Y	Y	Y	Y	N	Y	Y
21 **English**	Y	Y	Y	N	N	Y	Y
RHODE ISLAND							
1 Kennedy	Y	Y	Y	N	N	Y	N
2 Weygand	Y	Y	N	N	N	Y	N
SOUTH CAROLINA							
1 **Sanford**	?	Y	Y	Y	Y	N	Y
2 **Spence**	Y	Y	Y	Y	N	N	Y
3 **Graham**	Y	Y	Y	Y	N	N	Y
4 **Inglis**	Y	Y	Y	Y	Y	N	Y
5 Spratt	Y	Y	Y	Y	N	N	Y
6 Clyburn	Y	Y	N	Y	N	N	N
SOUTH DAKOTA							
AL **Thune**	Y	Y	Y	Y	N	N	Y

	340	342	343	344	345	346	347
TENNESSEE							
1 **Jenkins**	Y	Y	Y	?	N	N	Y
2 **Duncan**	Y	Y	Y	Y	Y	N	Y
3 **Wamp**	Y	Y	Y	Y	Y	N	Y
4 **Hilleary**	Y	Y	Y	Y	Y	N	Y
5 Clement	Y	Y	Y	Y	N	N	N
6 Gordon	Y	Y	Y	Y	N	N	Y
7 **Bryant**	Y	Y	Y	Y	N	N	Y
8 Tanner	Y	Y	Y	Y	N	N	Y
9 Ford	Y	Y	N	N	N	Y	N
TEXAS							
1 Sandlin	Y	Y	Y	Y	N	N	Y
2 Turner	Y	Y	Y	Y	N	N	Y
3 **Johnson, Sam**	Y	Y	Y	Y	N	N	Y
4 Hall	Y	Y	Y	Y	N	N	Y
5 **Sessions**	Y	Y	Y	Y	N	N	Y
6 **Barton**	Y	Y	Y	Y	N	N	Y
7 **Archer**	Y	?	Y	Y	N	N	Y
8 **Brady**	Y	Y	Y	Y	N	N	Y
9 Lampson	Y	Y	Y	Y	N	N	N
10 Doggett	Y	Y	N	N	N	N	N
11 Edwards	Y	Y	Y	Y	N	N	Y
12 **Granger**	Y	?	Y	+	N	N	N
13 **Thornberry**	Y	Y	Y	Y	N	N	Y
14 **Paul**	Y	Y	Y	N	Y	N	Y
15 Hinojosa	Y	?	–	–	N	N	Y
16 Reyes	Y	Y	N	N	N	N	Y
17 Stenholm	Y	Y	Y	Y	N	N	Y
18 Jackson-Lee	Y	Y	Y	Y	N	N	N
19 **Combest**	Y	Y	Y	Y	N	N	Y
20 Gonzalez	?	?	?	?	?	?	?
21 **Smith**	Y	Y	Y	Y	N	N	Y
22 **DeLay**	Y	Y	Y	Y	N	N	Y
23 **Bonilla**	?	Y	N	N	N	N	Y
24 Frost	Y	Y	Y	Y	N	N	N
25 Bentsen	Y	Y	Y	Y	N	N	N
26 **Armey**	Y	Y	Y	Y	N	N	Y
27 Ortiz	Y	Y	N	N	N	N	Y
28 Rodriguez	Y	Y	N	N	N	N	Y
29 Green	Y	Y	Y	Y	N	N	Y
30 Johnson, E.B.	Y	Y	Y	Y	N	N	N
UTAH							
1 **Hansen**	Y	Y	Y	Y	N	N	Y
2 **Cook**	Y	Y	Y	Y	N	N	Y
3 **Cannon**	?	?	Y	Y	N	N	Y
VERMONT							
AL *Sanders*	Y	Y	Y	Y	Y	Y	N
VIRGINIA							
1 **Bateman**	Y	Y	Y	Y	Y	N	Y
2 Pickett	?	Y	Y	Y	N	N	Y
3 Scott	Y	Y	N	Y	N	N	N
4 Sisisky	Y	Y	Y	Y	N	N	Y
5 Goode	Y	Y	Y	Y	Y	N	Y
6 **Goodlatte**	Y	Y	Y	Y	Y	N	Y
7 **Bliley**	Y	Y	Y	Y	N	N	Y
8 Moran	Y	Y	Y	Y	N	N	N
9 Boucher	Y	Y	Y	Y	N	N	Y
10 **Wolf**	Y	Y	Y	Y	N	N	Y
11 **Davis**	Y	Y	Y	Y	N	N	N
WASHINGTON							
1 **White**	Y	Y	Y	Y	N	N	Y
2 **Metcalf**	Y	Y	Y	Y	N	N	Y
3 **Smith, Linda**	Y	Y	Y	Y	N	N	Y
4 **Hastings**	Y	Y	Y	Y	N	N	Y
5 **Nethercutt**	Y	Y	Y	Y	N	N	Y
6 Dicks	Y	?	Y	Y	N	N	N
7 McDermott	Y	Y	N	N	N	N	N
8 **Dunn**	Y	Y	Y	Y	N	N	Y
9 Smith, Adam	Y	Y	Y	Y	N	N	N
WEST VIRGINIA							
1 Mollohan	Y	Y	Y	Y	N	Y	N
2 Wise	Y	Y	Y	Y	N	Y	N
3 Rahall	Y	Y	Y	N	N	N	Y
WISCONSIN							
1 **Neumann**	Y	Y	Y	Y	Y	Y	Y
2 **Klug**	Y	Y	Y	Y	Y	N	Y
3 Kind	Y	Y	Y	Y	Y	Y	N
4 Kleczka	Y	Y	Y	Y	Y	Y	N
5 Barrett	Y	Y	Y	Y	Y	Y	N
6 **Petri**	Y	Y	Y	N	N	Y	Y
7 Obey	Y	Y	Y	Y	Y	Y	N
8 Johnson	Y	Y	Y	Y	N	Y	Y
9 **Sensenbrenner**	Y	Y	Y	N	N	Y	Y
WYOMING							
AL **Cubin**	Y	Y	?	Y	N	N	Y

Southern states - Ala., Ark., Fla., Ga., Ky., La., Miss., N.C., Okla., S.C., Tenn., Texas, Va.

House Votes 349, 350, 351, 352, 353, 355, 356, *

348. Quorum Call.* 414 Responded. July 29, 1998.

349. HR 4194. Fiscal 1999 VA-HUD Appropriations/San Francisco's Unmarried Domestic Partner Ordinance. Riggs, R-Calif., amendment to prohibit any funds in the bill from being used to implement the San Francisco ordinance that requires private companies and organizations contracting with or receiving grants from the city to provide health care benefits to unmarried domestic partners of their workers. Adopted 214-212: R 189-33; D 25-178 (ND 10-139, SD 15-39); I 0-1. July 29, 1998.

350. HR 4194. Fiscal 1999 VA-HUD Appropriations/VA Medical Care Funding Increase. Coburn, R-Okla., amendment to increase the bill's funding for VA medical care by $304 million. The amendment would offset the increase by cutting the funding for non-overhead administrative expenses of the Federal Housing Administration. Adopted 351-73: R 215-9; D 135-64 (ND 91-54, SD 44-10); I 1-0. July 29, 1998.

351. HR 4194. Fiscal 1999 VA-HUD Appropriations/Recommit. Obey, D-Wis., motion to recommit the bill to the Appropriations Committee with instructions to report it back with an amendment to delete provisions that prohibit funding to promulgate certain rules dealing with chemical treatment of upholstery fabrics under the Flammable Fabrics Act. Motion rejected 164-261: R 4-221; D 159-40 (ND 133-12, SD 26-28); I 1-0. July 29, 1998.

352. HR 4194. Fiscal 1999 VA-HUD Appropriations/Passage. Passage of the bill to provide $71.3 billion in discretionary spending to the Veterans Affairs and Housing and Urban Development departments and 17 independent agencies. Passed 259-164: R 205-18; D 54-145 (ND 22-124, SD 32-21); I 0-1. July 29, 1998.

353. HR 4059. Fiscal 1999 Military Construction Appropriations/Conference Report. Adoption of the conference report on the bill to provide $8.45 billion in funding for military construction projects. Adopted (thus sent to the Senate) 417-1: R 219-1; D 197-0 (ND 143-0, SD 54-0); I 1-0. July 29, 1998.

354. Quorum Call.* 403 Responded. July 29, 1998.

355. HR 4328. Fiscal 1999 Transportation Appropriations/Passage. Passage of the bill to provide $46.9 billion in funding for highways and infrastructure and other transportation related projects in fiscal 1999. Passed 391-25: R 197-23; D 193-2 (ND 140-1, SD 53-1); I 1-0. July 30, 1998.

356. H J Res 120. Disapproval of Presidential Waiver for Vietnam/Passage. Passage of the joint resolution to disapprove President Clinton's waiver that allows Vietnam to participate in certain U.S. trade support and investment promotion programs. Rejected 163-260: R 127-93; D 35-167 (ND 29-119, SD 6-48); I 1-0. July 30, 1998.

* CQ does not include quorum calls in its vote charts.

Key

- Y Voted for (yea).
- # Paired for.
- + Announced for.
- N Voted against (nay).
- X Paired against.
- – Announced against.
- P Voted "present."
- C Voted "present" to avoid possible conflict of interest.
- ? Did not vote or otherwise make a position known.

Democrats **Republicans** *Independent*

	349	350	351	352	353	355	356
ALABAMA							
1 *Callahan*	Y	Y	N	Y	Y	Y	N
2 *Everett*	Y	Y	N	Y	Y	Y	Y
3 *Riley*	Y	Y	N	Y	Y	Y	Y
4 *Aderholt*	Y	Y	N	Y	Y	Y	Y
5 Cramer	Y	Y	N	Y	Y	Y	Y
6 *Bachus*	Y	Y	N	Y	Y	Y	Y
7 Hilliard	N	Y	N	Y	Y	Y	N
ALASKA							
AL *Young*	Y	Y	N	Y	Y	Y	N
ARIZONA							
1 *Salmon*	Y	Y	N	N	Y	N	N
2 Pastor	N	Y	N	Y	Y	Y	N
3 *Stump*	Y	Y	N	Y	Y	N	Y
4 *Shadegg*	Y	Y	N	Y	Y	N	Y
5 *Kolbe*	N	N	N	Y	Y	Y	N
6 *Hayworth*	Y	Y	N	Y	Y	N	Y
ARKANSAS							
1 Berry	Y	Y	N	N	Y	Y	N
2 Snyder	N	Y	Y	N	Y	Y	N
3 *Hutchinson*	Y	Y	N	Y	Y	Y	Y
4 *Dickey*	Y	Y	N	Y	Y	Y	Y
CALIFORNIA							
1 *Riggs*	Y	Y	N	Y	Y	Y	–
2 *Herger*	Y	Y	N	N	Y	N	N
3 Fazio	N	N	Y	N	Y	?	N
4 *Doolittle*	Y	Y	N	Y	Y	Y	Y
5 Matsui	N	Y	Y	N	Y	Y	N
6 Woolsey	N	N	Y	N	Y	Y	N
7 Miller	N	N	Y	N	Y	Y	N
8 Pelosi	N	Y	Y	N	Y	Y	N
9 Lee	N	N	Y	N	Y	Y	N
10 Tauscher	N	Y	Y	N	Y	Y	N
11 *Pombo*	Y	Y	N	Y	Y	Y	N
12 Lantos	N	Y	Y	N	Y	Y	N
13 Stark	N	N	Y	N	Y	?	N
14 Eshoo	N	Y	Y	N	Y	Y	N
15 *Campbell*	N	Y	N	Y	Y	N	N
16 Lofgren	N	Y	Y	N	Y	Y	N
17 Farr	N	Y	Y	N	Y	Y	N
18 Condit	N	N	N	N	Y	Y	N
19 *Radanovich*	Y	Y	N	Y	Y	Y	Y
20 Dooley	N	N	Y	N	Y	Y	N
21 *Thomas*	Y	Y	N	Y	Y	Y	Y
22 Capps, L.	N	N	Y	N	Y	Y	N
23 *Gallegly*	Y	Y	N	Y	Y	Y	Y
24 Sherman	N	N	Y	N	Y	Y	N
25 *McKeon*	Y	Y	N	Y	Y	Y	Y
26 Berman	N	N	Y	N	Y	Y	N
27 *Rogan*	Y	Y	N	Y	Y	Y	Y
28 *Dreier*	Y	Y	N	Y	Y	Y	Y
29 Waxman	N	N	Y	N	Y	Y	N
30 Becerra	N	N	Y	N	Y	+	N
31 Martinez	N	N	N	Y	Y	Y	N
32 Dixon	N	N	Y	N	Y	Y	N
33 Roybal-Allard	N	N	Y	N	Y	Y	N
34 Torres	N	N	?	N	?	Y	Y
35 Waters	N	N	Y	N	Y	Y	N
36 Harman	N	?	?	?	?	Y	N
37 Millender-McD.	N	Y	Y	N	Y	Y	N

	349	350	351	352	353	355	356
38 *Horn*	N	Y	N	Y	Y	Y	Y
39 *Royce*	Y	Y	N	N	Y	N	Y
40 *Lewis*	N	N	N	Y	Y	Y	N
41 *Kim*	Y	N	Y	N	Y	Y	Y
42 Brown	N	N	Y	N	Y	Y	Y
43 *Calvert*	Y	Y	N	Y	Y	Y	Y
44 *Bono, M.*	Y	Y	N	Y	Y	Y	Y
45 *Rohrabacher*	Y	Y	N	Y	Y	Y	Y
46 Sanchez	N	Y	N	Y	Y	Y	Y
47 *Cox*	Y	Y	N	Y	Y	?	Y
48 *Packard*	Y	Y	N	Y	Y	Y	Y
49 *Bilbray*	N	Y	N	Y	Y	Y	Y
50 Filner	N	Y	Y	N	Y	Y	N
51 *Cunningham*	Y	Y	N	Y	Y	Y	Y
52 *Hunter*	Y	Y	N	Y	Y	Y	Y
COLORADO							
1 DeGette	N	N	Y	N	Y	Y	N
2 Skaggs	N	N	Y	N	Y	Y	N
3 *McInnis*	Y	Y	N	Y	Y	Y	Y
4 *Schaffer*	Y	Y	N	N	Y	N	Y
5 *Hefley*	Y	Y	N	Y	Y	Y	Y
6 *Schaefer*	Y	Y	N	Y	Y	Y	Y
CONNECTICUT							
1 Kennelly	N	Y	Y	N	Y	Y	N
2 Gejdenson	N	Y	Y	N	Y	Y	N
3 DeLauro	N	Y	Y	N	Y	Y	N
4 *Shays*	N	N	Y	N	Y	Y	N
5 Maloney	N	N	Y	N	Y	Y	N
6 *Johnson*	N	N	Y	N	Y	Y	N
DELAWARE							
AL *Castle*	N	Y	N	Y	Y	Y	N
FLORIDA							
1 *Scarborough*	Y	Y	N	Y	Y	Y	Y
2 Boyd	N	Y	N	Y	Y	Y	Y
3 Brown	N	Y	Y	Y	Y	Y	N
4 *Fowler*	N	Y	N	Y	Y	Y	Y
5 Thurman	N	Y	N	Y	Y	Y	N
6 *Stearns*	Y	Y	N	Y	Y	N	Y
7 *Mica*	Y	Y	N	Y	Y	Y	Y
8 *McCollum*	Y	Y	N	Y	?	Y	Y
9 *Bilirakis*	Y	Y	N	Y	Y	Y	Y
10 *Young*	?	?	?	?	?	?	?
11 Davis	N	Y	N	Y	Y	Y	N
12 *Canady*	Y	Y	N	Y	Y	Y	Y
13 *Miller*	Y	Y	N	Y	Y	Y	Y
14 *Goss*	N	Y	N	Y	Y	Y	Y
15 *Weldon*	Y	Y	N	Y	Y	Y	Y
16 *Foley*	N	Y	N	Y	Y	Y	Y
17 Meek	N	N	Y	Y	Y	Y	N
18 *Ros-Lehtinen*	Y	N	Y	Y	Y	Y	Y
19 Wexler	N	Y	Y	N	Y	Y	N
20 Deutsch	N	Y	N	Y	Y	Y	N
21 *Diaz-Balart*	Y	N	N	Y	Y	Y	N
22 *Shaw*	N	Y	N	Y	Y	Y	Y
23 Hastings	N	N	Y	N	Y	Y	N
GEORGIA							
1 *Kingston*	Y	Y	N	Y	Y	Y	Y
2 Bishop	Y	Y	N	Y	Y	Y	Y
3 *Collins*	Y	Y	N	Y	Y	Y	Y
4 *McKinney*	N	Y	Y	N	Y	Y	N
5 Lewis	N	Y	N	Y	Y	Y	N
6 *Gingrich*							
7 *Barr*	Y	Y	N	Y	Y	Y	Y
8 *Chambliss*	Y	Y	N	?	Y	Y	N
9 *Deal*	Y	Y	N	Y	Y	Y	Y
10 *Norwood*	Y	Y	N	Y	?	Y	Y
11 *Linder*	Y	Y	N	Y	?	Y	?
HAWAII							
1 Abercrombie	N	Y	Y	Y	Y	Y	N
2 Mink	N	Y	Y	N	Y	Y	N
IDAHO							
1 *Chenoweth*	Y	Y	N	N	Y	N	Y
2 *Crapo*	Y	Y	N	Y	Y	Y	Y
ILLINOIS							
1 Rush	N	N	Y	N	Y	Y	N
2 Jackson	N	N	Y	N	Y	Y	N
3 Lipinski	Y	Y	Y	Y	Y	Y	Y
4 Gutierrez	N	N	Y	N	Y	Y	N
5 Blagojevich	N	N	Y	N	Y	Y	N
6 *Hyde*	Y	Y	N	Y	Y	Y	Y
7 Davis	N	Y	Y	N	Y	Y	N
8 *Crane*	Y	Y	N	Y	Y	Y	Y
9 Yates	?	?	?	?	?	?	N
10 *Porter*	–	Y	N	Y	Y	Y	N
11 *Weller*	Y	Y	N	Y	Y	Y	Y
12 Costello	Y	Y	N	Y	Y	Y	N

ND Northern Democrats   SD Southern Democrats

	349	350	351	352	353	355	356
13 ***Fawell***	Y	N	N	Y	Y	Y	N
14 ***Hastert***	Y	Y	N	Y	Y	Y	Y
15 ***Ewing***	Y	Y	N	Y	Y	?	N
16 ***Manzullo***	Y	Y	N	Y	Y	Y	N
17 Evans	N	Y	Y	Y	Y	Y	N
18 ***LaHood***	Y	Y	N	Y	Y	Y	Y
19 Poshard	N	Y	Y	N	Y	Y	N
20 ***Shimkus***	Y	Y	N	Y	Y	Y	N

INDIANA

	349	350	351	352	353	355	356
1 Visclosky	N	Y	Y	N	Y	Y	N
2 ***McIntosh***	Y	Y	N	Y	Y	Y	N
3 Roemer	Y	Y	Y	N	Y	Y	N
4 ***Souder***	Y	Y	N	Y	Y	N	Y
5 ***Buyer***	Y	Y	N	Y	Y	Y	Y
6 ***Burton***	?	?	N	Y	Y	Y	Y
7 ***Pease***	Y	Y	N	Y	Y	Y	N
8 ***Hostettler***	Y	Y	N	N	Y	Y	Y
9 Hamilton	Y	Y	Y	N	Y	Y	N
10 Carson	N	Y	Y	N	Y	Y	N

IOWA

	349	350	351	352	353	355	356
1 ***Leach***	N	Y	N	Y	Y	Y	N
2 ***Nussle***	Y	Y	N	Y	Y	Y	N
3 Boswell	N	Y	N	Y	Y	Y	N
4 ***Ganske***	Y	Y	N	Y	Y	Y	N
5 ***Latham***	Y	Y	N	Y	Y	Y	N

KANSAS

	349	350	351	352	353	355	356
1 ***Moran***	Y	Y	N	Y	Y	N	N
2 ***Ryun***	Y	Y	N	Y	Y	Y	Y
3 ***Snowbarger***	Y	Y	N	Y	Y	Y	Y
4 ***Tiahrt***	Y	Y	N	Y	Y	Y	Y

KENTUCKY

	349	350	351	352	353	355	356
1 ***Whitfield***	Y	Y	N	Y	?	Y	Y
2 ***Lewis***	Y	Y	N	Y	Y	Y	Y
3 ***Northup***	Y	Y	N	Y	Y	Y	Y
4 ***Bunning***	Y	Y	N	Y	Y	Y	Y
5 ***Rogers***	Y	Y	N	Y	?	Y	Y
6 Baesler	Y	Y	N	Y	Y	Y	N

LOUISIANA

	349	350	351	352	353	355	356
1 ***Livingston***	Y	N	N	Y	Y	Y	N
2 Jefferson	N	Y	Y	N	Y	Y	N
3 ***Tauzin***	Y	Y	N	Y	Y	Y	Y
4 ***McCrery***	N	Y	N	Y	Y	Y	N
5 ***Cooksey***	Y	Y	N	Y	Y	Y	Y
6 ***Baker***	Y	Y	N	Y	Y	Y	Y
7 John	Y	Y	N	Y	Y	Y	N

MAINE

	349	350	351	352	353	355	356
1 Allen	N	Y	Y	N	Y	Y	N
2 Baldacci	N	Y	Y	N	Y	Y	N

MARYLAND

	349	350	351	352	353	355	356
1 ***Gilchrest***	N	N	N	Y	Y	Y	N
2 ***Ehrlich***	Y	Y	N	Y	Y	Y	Y
3 Cardin	N	Y	Y	N	Y	Y	N
4 Wynn	N	Y	Y	N	Y	Y	N
5 Hoyer	N	N	Y	N	Y	Y	N
6 ***Bartlett***	Y	Y	N	Y	Y	Y	Y
7 Cummings	N	N	Y	N	Y	Y	N
8 ***Morella***	N	Y	Y	N	Y	Y	N

MASSACHUSETTS

	349	350	351	352	353	355	356
1 Olver	N	N	Y	N	Y	Y	N
2 Neal	N	N	?	?	?	Y	?
3 McGovern	N	Y	Y	N	Y	Y	Y
4 Frank	N	N	?	?	?	?	N
5 Meehan	N	?	Y	N	Y	Y	N
6 Tierney	N	N	Y	N	Y	Y	N
7 Markey	N	N	Y	N	Y	Y	N
8 Kennedy	N	N	Y	N	Y	Y	N
9 Moakley	?	?	?	?	?	?	N
10 Delahunt	N	N	Y	N	Y	Y	N

MICHIGAN

	349	350	351	352	353	355	356
1 Stupak	N	Y	Y	N	Y	Y	Y
2 ***Hoekstra***	Y	Y	N	N	Y	N	Y
3 ***Ehlers***	Y	Y	N	Y	Y	Y	N
4 ***Camp***	Y	Y	N	Y	Y	Y	N
5 Barcia	N	Y	Y	N	Y	Y	N
6 ***Upton***	Y	Y	N	Y	Y	Y	Y
7 ***Smith***	Y	Y	N	Y	Y	Y	Y
8 Stabenow	N	Y	Y	N	Y	Y	N
9 Kildee	N	Y	Y	N	Y	Y	N
10 Bonior	N	N	Y	N	Y	Y	Y
11 ***Knollenberg***	Y	N	N	Y	Y	Y	N
12 Levin	N	Y	Y	N	Y	Y	N
13 Rivers	N	Y	Y	N	Y	Y	Y
14 Conyers	N	N	Y	N	Y	Y	N
15 Kilpatrick	N	N	Y	N	Y	Y	N
16 Dingell	N	Y	N	N	Y	?	N

MINNESOTA

	349	350	351	352	353	355	356
1 ***Gutknecht***	Y	Y	N	Y	Y	Y	Y
2 Minge	N	Y	N	N	Y	Y	N
3 ***Ramstad***	Y	Y	N	Y	Y	Y	N
4 Vento	N	N	Y	N	Y	Y	Y
5 Sabo	N	N	Y	Y	Y	Y	N
6 Luther	N	N	Y	N	Y	Y	N
7 Peterson	Y	Y	N	N	Y	Y	N
8 Oberstar	N	N	Y	N	Y	Y	N

MISSISSIPPI

	349	350	351	352	353	355	356
1 ***Wicker***	Y	Y	N	Y	Y	Y	N
2 Thompson	N	N	Y	Y	Y	Y	N
3 ***Pickering***	Y	Y	N	Y	Y	Y	N
4 ***Parker***	Y	Y	N	Y	Y	Y	N
5 Taylor	Y	Y	N	Y	Y	Y	N

MISSOURI

	349	350	351	352	353	355	356
1 Clay	N	?	Y	N	Y	Y	N
2 ***Talent***	Y	Y	N	Y	Y	Y	Y
3 Gephardt	N	Y	Y	N	Y	Y	N
4 Skelton	Y	Y	Y	N	Y	Y	N
5 McCarthy	N	Y	Y	N	Y	Y	N
6 Danner	Y	Y	N	Y	Y	Y	N
7 ***Blunt***	Y	Y	N	Y	Y	Y	Y
8 ***Emerson***	Y	Y	N	Y	Y	Y	Y
9 ***Hulshof***	Y	Y	N	Y	Y	Y	N

MONTANA

	349	350	351	352	353	355	356
AL ***Hill***	Y	Y	N	Y	Y	N	Y

NEBRASKA

	349	350	351	352	353	355	356
1 ***Bereuter***	Y	Y	N	Y	Y	Y	N
2 ***Christensen***	Y	Y	N	Y	Y	Y	Y
3 ***Barrett***	Y	Y	N	Y	Y	Y	N

NEVADA

	349	350	351	352	353	355	356
1 ***Ensign***	N	Y	N	Y	Y	Y	Y
2 ***Gibbons***	Y	Y	N	Y	Y	Y	Y

NEW HAMPSHIRE

	349	350	351	352	353	355	356
1 ***Sununu***	Y	Y	N	Y	Y	Y	N
2 ***Bass***	N	Y	N	Y	Y	Y	N

NEW JERSEY

	349	350	351	352	353	355	356
1 Andrews	N	Y	Y	N	Y	Y	Y
2 ***LoBiondo***	Y	Y	N	Y	Y	Y	Y
3 ***Saxton***	N	Y	N	Y	Y	Y	Y
4 ***Smith***	Y	Y	N	Y	Y	Y	Y
5 ***Roukema***	Y	Y	N	Y	Y	Y	N
6 Pallone	N	Y	Y	N	Y	Y	N
7 ***Franks***	N	Y	N	Y	Y	Y	N
8 Pascrell	N	Y	Y	N	Y	Y	Y
9 Rothman	N	Y	Y	N	Y	Y	N
10 Payne	N	N	Y	N	Y	Y	N
11 ***Frelinghuysen***	N	Y	N	Y	Y	Y	Y
12 ***Pappas***	Y	Y	N	Y	Y	Y	Y
13 Menendez	N	Y	Y	N	Y	Y	Y

NEW MEXICO

	349	350	351	352	353	355	356
1 ***Wilson***	Y	Y	N	Y	Y	Y	N
2 ***Skeen***	Y	Y	N	Y	Y	Y	N
3 ***Redmond***	Y	Y	N	Y	Y	Y	N

NEW YORK

	349	350	351	352	353	355	356
1 ***Forbes***	N	Y	N	Y	Y	Y	Y
2 ***Lazio***	N	N	N	Y	Y	Y	Y
3 ***King***	Y	Y	N	Y	Y	Y	Y
4 McCarthy	N	Y	Y	N	Y	Y	Y
5 Ackerman	N	Y	Y	N	Y	Y	N
6 Meeks	N	N	Y	N	Y	Y	Y
7 Manton	N	Y	Y	N	Y	Y	N
8 Nadler	N	N	Y	N	Y	Y	Y
9 Schumer	N	Y	Y	N	Y	Y	N
10 Towns	N	Y	Y	N	?	Y	?
11 Owens	N	N	Y	N	Y	Y	N
12 Velázquez	N	N	Y	N	Y	Y	N
13 ***Fossella***	Y	Y	N	Y	Y	Y	Y
14 Maloney	N	Y	Y	N	Y	Y	N
15 Rangel	N	N	Y	N	?	Y	N
16 Serrano	N	Y	Y	N	Y	Y	N
17 Engel	N	Y	Y	N	Y	Y	N
18 Lowey	N	Y	Y	N	Y	Y	N
19 ***Kelly***	N	Y	N	Y	Y	Y	Y
20 ***Gilman***	N	Y	N	Y	Y	Y	Y
21 McNulty	N	Y	Y	N	Y	Y	Y
22 ***Solomon***	Y	Y	N	Y	Y	Y	Y
23 ***Boehlert***	N	Y	N	Y	Y	Y	N
24 ***McHugh***	Y	Y	N	Y	Y	Y	N
25 ***Walsh***	Y	Y	N	Y	Y	Y	N
26 Hinchey	N	Y	Y	N	Y	Y	Y
27 ***Paxon***	Y	Y	N	Y	Y	Y	N
28 Slaughter	N	Y	Y	N	Y	Y	N
29 LaFalce	N	N	Y	N	Y	Y	N
30 ***Quinn***	Y	Y	N	Y	Y	Y	Y
31 ***Houghton***	N	Y	N	Y	Y	Y	N

NORTH CAROLINA

	349	350	351	352	353	355	356
1 Clayton	N	N	N	Y	Y	Y	N
2 Etheridge	N	Y	N	Y	Y	Y	N
3 ***Jones***	Y	Y	N	Y	Y	N	Y
4 Price	N	Y	N	Y	Y	Y	N
5 ***Burr***	Y	Y	N	Y	Y	N	–
6 ***Coble***	Y	Y	N	Y	Y	Y	Y
7 McIntyre	Y	Y	N	Y	Y	Y	Y
8 Hefner	N	Y	N	Y	Y	Y	N
9 ***Myrick***	Y	Y	N	Y	Y	Y	Y
10 ***Ballenger***	Y	Y	N	Y	Y	Y	N
11 ***Taylor***	Y	Y	N	Y	Y	Y	N
12 Watt	N	N	N	N	Y	Y	N

NORTH DAKOTA

	349	350	351	352	353	355	356
AL Pomeroy	N	Y	Y	N	Y	Y	N

OHIO

	349	350	351	352	353	355	356
1 ***Chabot***	Y	Y	N	Y	Y	N	Y
2 ***Portman***	Y	Y	N	Y	Y	Y	N
3 Hall	Y	Y	Y	Y	Y	?	N
4 ***Oxley***	Y	Y	N	Y	Y	Y	N
5 ***Gillmor***	Y	Y	N	Y	Y	Y	N
6 Strickland	N	Y	Y	N	Y	Y	Y
7 ***Hobson***	Y	Y	N	Y	Y	Y	Y
8 ***Boehner***	Y	?	N	Y	Y	Y	N
9 Kaptur	N	N	Y	Y	Y	Y	N
10 Kucinich	N	N	Y	N	Y	N	Y
11 Stokes	N	N	Y	Y	Y	Y	N
12 ***Kasich***	Y	Y	N	Y	Y	N	N
13 Brown	N	Y	Y	N	Y	Y	Y
14 Sawyer	N	Y	Y	N	Y	Y	N
15 ***Pryce***	Y	Y	N	Y	Y	Y	N
16 ***Regula***	Y	Y	N	Y	Y	Y	Y
17 Traficant	Y	Y	N	Y	Y	Y	Y
18 ***Ney***	Y	Y	N	Y	Y	Y	Y
19 ***LaTourette***	?	Y	N	Y	Y	?	N

OKLAHOMA

	349	350	351	352	353	355	356
1 ***Largent***	Y	Y	N	Y	Y	Y	N
2 ***Coburn***	Y	Y	N	Y	Y	Y	Y
3 ***Watkins***	Y	Y	N	Y	Y	Y	N
4 ***Watts***	Y	Y	N	Y	Y	Y	Y
5 ***Istook***	Y	Y	N	Y	Y	Y	?
6 ***Lucas***	Y	Y	N	Y	Y	Y	N

OREGON

	349	350	351	352	353	355	356
1 Furse	N	N	Y	N	Y	Y	N
2 ***Smith***	Y	Y	N	Y	Y	?	N
3 Blumenauer	N	N	Y	N	Y	Y	N
4 DeFazio	N	Y	Y	N	Y	Y	Y
5 Hooley	N	Y	Y	N	Y	Y	N

PENNSYLVANIA

	349	350	351	352	353	355	356
1 Brady	N	Y	Y	N	Y	Y	N
2 Fattah	N	Y	Y	N	Y	Y	N
3 Borski	N	Y	Y	N	Y	Y	N
4 Klink	N	Y	Y	N	Y	Y	N
5 ***Peterson***	Y	Y	N	Y	Y	Y	Y
6 Holden	Y	Y	Y	N	Y	Y	Y
7 ***Weldon***	Y	Y	Y	?	Y	Y	N
8 ***Greenwood***	Y	Y	N	Y	Y	Y	N
9 ***Shuster***	Y	Y	?	Y	Y	Y	Y
10 ***McDade***	?	N	N	?	Y	?	?
11 Kanjorski	N	Y	Y	N	Y	Y	N
12 Murtha	N	Y	Y	Y	Y	?	N
13 ***Fox***	Y	Y	N	Y	Y	Y	Y
14 Coyne	N	Y	Y	N	Y	Y	Y
15 McHale	N	Y	Y	N	Y	Y	N
16 ***Pitts***	Y	Y	N	Y	Y	Y	Y
17 ***Gekas***	Y	Y	N	Y	Y	Y	Y
18 Doyle	N	Y	Y	Y	Y	Y	N
19 ***Goodling***	Y	Y	N	Y	Y	Y	Y
20 Mascara	N	Y	Y	Y	Y	Y	N
21 ***English***	N	Y	N	N	Y	Y	Y

RHODE ISLAND

	349	350	351	352	353	355	356
1 Kennedy	N	N	Y	N	Y	Y	Y
2 Weygand	N	Y	Y	N	Y	Y	N

SOUTH CAROLINA

	349	350	351	352	353	355	356
1 ***Sanford***	N	Y	N	N	Y	N	N
2 ***Spence***	Y	Y	N	Y	Y	Y	Y
3 ***Graham***	Y	Y	N	Y	Y	N	Y
4 ***Inglis***	Y	Y	N	Y	Y	Y	Y
5 Spratt	N	Y	N	Y	Y	Y	N
6 Clyburn	N	Y	N	N	Y	Y	N

SOUTH DAKOTA

	349	350	351	352	353	355	356
AL ***Thune***	Y	Y	N	Y	Y	Y	Y

TENNESSEE

	349	350	351	352	353	355	356
1 ***Jenkins***	Y	Y	N	Y	Y	Y	Y
2 ***Duncan***	Y	Y	N	N	?	Y	Y
3 ***Wamp***	Y	Y	N	Y	Y	Y	Y
4 ***Hilleary***	Y	Y	N	Y	Y	Y	Y
5 Clement	N	Y	Y	Y	Y	Y	N
6 Gordon	N	Y	Y	?	Y	Y	N
7 ***Bryant***	Y	Y	N	Y	Y	Y	Y
8 Tanner	Y	Y	N	Y	Y	Y	N
9 Ford	N	Y	Y	Y	Y	Y	N

TEXAS

	349	350	351	352	353	355	356
1 Sandlin	Y	Y	N	Y	Y	Y	N
2 Turner	Y	Y	N	Y	Y	Y	Y
3 ***Johnson, Sam***	Y	Y	N	Y	Y	?	Y
4 Hall	Y	Y	N	Y	Y	Y	Y
5 ***Sessions***	Y	Y	N	Y	Y	N	Y
6 ***Barton***	Y	Y	N	Y	Y	Y	Y
7 ***Archer***	Y	Y	N	Y	Y	Y	N
8 ***Brady***	Y	Y	N	Y	Y	Y	N
9 Lampson	N	Y	Y	Y	Y	Y	N
10 Doggett	N	N	Y	N	Y	Y	N
11 Edwards	N	Y	Y	N	Y	Y	N
12 ***Granger***	Y	Y	N	Y	Y	Y	N
13 ***Thornberry***	Y	Y	N	Y	Y	Y	Y
14 ***Paul***	Y	Y	N	N	N	N	Y
15 Hinojosa	N	Y	N	Y	Y	Y	N
16 Reyes	N	Y	N	Y	Y	Y	N
17 Stenholm	Y	Y	N	Y	Y	Y	N
18 Jackson-Lee	N	Y	Y	N	Y	Y	Y
19 ***Combest***	Y	Y	N	Y	Y	Y	N
20 Gonzalez	?	?	?	?	?	?	?
21 ***Smith***	Y	Y	N	Y	Y	Y	Y
22 ***DeLay***	Y	Y	N	Y	Y	Y	Y
23 ***Bonilla***	Y	Y	N	Y	Y	Y	Y
24 Frost	N	Y	Y	N	Y	Y	N
25 Bentsen	N	N	Y	N	Y	Y	N
26 ***Armey***	Y	Y	N	Y	Y	Y	N
27 Ortiz	Y	Y	N	Y	Y	Y	N
28 Rodriguez	N	Y	Y	N	Y	Y	N
29 Green	N	N	Y	N	Y	Y	Y
30 Johnson, E.B.	N	Y	Y	N	Y	Y	N

UTAH

	349	350	351	352	353	355	356
1 ***Hansen***	Y	Y	N	Y	Y	Y	Y
2 ***Cook***	Y	Y	N	Y	Y	Y	Y
3 ***Cannon***	Y	Y	N	Y	Y	Y	N

VERMONT

	349	350	351	352	353	355	356
AL *Sanders*	N	Y	Y	N	Y	Y	Y

VIRGINIA

	349	350	351	352	353	355	356
1 ***Bateman***	Y	Y	N	Y	Y	Y	N
2 Pickett	Y	Y	N	Y	Y	Y	N
3 Scott	N	N	Y	Y	Y	Y	N
4 Sisisky	N	Y	N	N	Y	Y	N
5 Goode	Y	Y	N	Y	Y	Y	Y
6 ***Goodlatte***	Y	Y	N	Y	Y	Y	N
7 ***Bliley***	Y	Y	N	Y	Y	Y	N
8 Moran	N	N	Y	Y	Y	Y	N
9 Boucher	N	Y	N	Y	Y	Y	N
10 ***Wolf***	Y	Y	Y	Y	Y	Y	Y
11 ***Davis***	N	Y	N	Y	Y	Y	Y

WASHINGTON

	349	350	351	352	353	355	356
1 ***White***	N	Y	N	Y	Y	Y	N
2 ***Metcalf***	Y	Y	N	Y	Y	Y	Y
3 ***Smith, Linda***	Y	Y	N	N	Y	Y	?
4 ***Hastings***	Y	Y	N	Y	Y	Y	N
5 ***Nethercutt***	Y	Y	N	Y	Y	Y	N
6 Dicks	N	Y	Y	Y	Y	Y	N
7 McDermott	N	N	Y	N	Y	Y	N
8 ***Dunn***	Y	Y	N	Y	Y	Y	N
9 Smith, Adam	N	Y	Y	N	Y	Y	N

WEST VIRGINIA

	349	350	351	352	353	355	356
1 Mollohan	N	N	N	Y	Y	Y	N
2 Wise	N	Y	Y	Y	Y	Y	N
3 Rahall	N	Y	N	Y	Y	Y	?

WISCONSIN

	349	350	351	352	353	355	356
1 ***Neumann***	Y	Y	Y	Y	Y	Y	Y
2 ***Klug***	Y	Y	N	N	Y	Y	Y
3 Kind	N	Y	N	Y	Y	Y	N
4 Kleczka	N	Y	Y	N	Y	Y	N
5 Barrett	N	Y	Y	N	Y	Y	N
6 ***Petri***	Y	Y	N	N	Y	Y	N
7 Obey	N	?	Y	N	Y	Y	N
8 Johnson	N	Y	Y	N	Y	Y	N
9 ***Sensenbrenner***	Y	Y	N	N	Y	Y	N

WYOMING

	349	350	351	352	353	355	356
AL ***Cubin***	N	Y	N	Y	Y	Y	Y

Southern states - Ala., Ark., Fla., Ga., Ky., La., Miss., N.C., Okla., S.C., Tenn., Texas, Va.

House Votes 357, 358, 359, 360, 361, 362, 363

Key

- Y Voted for (yea).
- # Paired for.
- + Announced for.
- N Voted against (nay).
- X Paired against.
- − Announced against.
- P Voted "present."
- C Voted "present" to avoid possible conflict of interest.
- ? Did not vote or otherwise make a position known.

Democrats **Republicans** *Independent*

357. H Res 507. Special Investigative Authority In Teamsters Union Probe/Adoption. Adoption of the resolution to authorize the staff of the Education and the Workforce Committee to take depositions, under oath, in a closed session, as a part of the committee's investigation of the Teamsters Union. Adopted 222-200: R 219-2; D 3-197 (ND 0-146, SD 3-51); I 0-1. July 30, 1998.

358. HR 2183. Campaign Finance Overhaul/Shays-Meehan Substitute — Motor Voter Modification. Goodlatte, R-Va., amendment to the Shays-Meehan substitute amendment to the bill to overhaul campaign finance laws. The amendment would modify the "motor voter" voter registration law by requiring voters to provide proof of citizenship when registering to vote. Rejected 165-260: R 163-59; D 2-200 (ND 2-146, SD 0-54); I 0-1. July 30, 1998.

359. HR 2183. Campaign Finance Overhaul/Shays-Meehan Substitute — Photo ID requirement. Wicker, R-Miss., amendment to the Shays-Meehan substitute amendment to the bill to overhaul campaign finance laws. The amendment would allow states to require voters to produce valid photo identification at their ballot stations in order to vote. Rejected 192-231: R 185-36; D 7-194 (ND 4-143, SD 3-51); I 0-1. July 30, 1998.

360. HR 2183. Campaign Finance Overhaul/Shays-Meehan Substitute — Contributions Limitations. Calvert, R-Calif., amendment to the Shays-Meehan substitute amendment to the bill to overhaul campaign finance laws. The amendment would limit the amount of campaign contributions a candidate may accept from individuals outside his or her district to the level of contributions received from district residents. Rejected 147-278: R 137-84; D 10-193 (ND 7-142, SD 3-51); I 0-1. July 30, 1998.

361. HR 2183. Campaign Finance Overhaul/Shays-Meehan Substitute — Voter Guide Clarification. Smith, R-Wash., amendment to the Shays-Meehan substitute amendment to the bill to overhaul campaign finance laws. The amendment would clarify that only voter guides clearly advocating the election or defeat of a candidate are required to be disclosed to the Federal Election Commission. Adopted 343-84: R 152-71; D 190-13 (ND 140-9, SD 50-4); I 1-0. July 30, 1998.

362. HR 2183. Campaign Finance Overhaul/Shays-Meehan Substitute — Matching Opponent's Personal Funds. Rohrabacher, R-Calif., amendment to the Shays-Meehan substitute amendment to the bill to overhaul campaign finance laws. The amendment would allow a candidate whose opponent spends more than $1,000 in personal funds to accept contributions from any legal source up to the same amount of personal funds spent in the campaign. Rejected 155-272: R 139-84; D 16-187 (ND 12-137, SD 4-50); I 0-1. July 30, 1998.

363. HR 2183. Campaign Finance Overhaul/Shays-Meehan Substitute — Ballot Petition Signature Requirements. Paul, R-Texas, amendment to the Shays-Meehan substitute amendment to the bill to overhaul campaign finance laws. The amendment would alter certain ballot petition signature requirements to try to widen participation by third parties in national elections. Rejected 62-363: R 45-176; D 16-187 (ND 14-135, SD 2-52); I 1-0. July 30, 1998.

	357	358	359	360	361	362	363
ALABAMA							
1 *Callahan*	Y	Y	Y	Y	N	Y	N
2 *Everett*	Y	Y	Y	Y	Y	Y	N
3 *Riley*	Y	Y	Y	N	N	Y	N
4 *Aderholt*	Y	Y	N	N	Y	Y	N
5 Cramer	N	N	N	N	Y	N	N
6 *Bachus*	Y	Y	Y	Y	Y	Y	N
7 Hilliard	N	N	N	N	Y	N	N
ALASKA							
AL *Young*	Y	Y	Y	Y	Y	Y	Y
ARIZONA							
1 *Salmon*	Y	Y	Y	Y	Y	Y	N
2 Pastor	N	N	N	N	Y	N	Y
3 *Stump*	Y	Y	Y	N	Y	N	N
4 *Shadegg*	Y	Y	Y	Y	Y	Y	N
5 *Kolbe*	Y	Y	Y	Y	Y	Y	N
6 *Hayworth*	Y	Y	Y	Y	Y	Y	N
ARKANSAS							
1 Berry	N	N	N	N	Y	N	N
2 Snyder	N	N	N	N	N	N	N
3 *Hutchinson*	Y	N	N	N	N	N	N
4 *Dickey*	Y	Y	Y	Y	Y	Y	N
CALIFORNIA							
1 *Riggs*	+	+	+	+	+	−	−
2 *Herger*	Y	Y	Y	Y	N	Y	?
3 Fazio	N	N	N	N	Y	N	N
4 *Doolittle*	Y	Y	Y	N	Y	N	N
5 Matsui	N	N	N	N	Y	N	N
6 Woolsey	N	N	N	N	N	N	N
7 Miller	N	N	N	N	N	N	N
8 Pelosi	N	N	N	N	N	N	N
9 Lee	N	N	N	N	Y	N	N
10 Tauscher	N	N	N	N	N	N	N
11 *Pombo*	Y	Y	Y	N	Y	Y	Y
12 Lantos	N	N	N	N	Y	N	N
13 Stark	N	N	N	N	N	N	N
14 Eshoo	N	N	N	N	N	N	N
15 *Campbell*	Y	N	N	N	Y	N	Y
16 Lofgren	N	N	N	N	N	N	N
17 Farr	N	N	N	N	N	N	N
18 Condit	N	N	N	N	Y	N	N
19 *Radanovich*	Y	Y	Y	N	Y	N	N
20 Dooley	N	N	N	N	N	N	N
21 *Thomas*	Y	Y	Y	Y	Y	Y	N
22 Capps, L.	N	N	N	N	N	N	N
23 *Gallegly*	Y	Y	Y	Y	N	Y	N
24 Sherman	N	N	N	N	N	N	Y
25 *McKeon*	Y	Y	Y	Y	Y	Y	N
26 Berman	N	N	N	N	N	N	N
27 *Rogan*	Y	Y	Y	N	Y	Y	Y
28 *Dreier*	Y	Y	Y	N	Y	N	N
29 Waxman	N	N	N	N	N	N	N
30 Becerra	N	N	N	N	N	N	N
31 Martinez	N	N	Y	N	Y	N	N
32 Dixon	N	N	N	N	N	N	N
33 Roybal-Allard	N	N	N	N	N	N	N
34 Torres	?	N	N	N	Y	N	N
35 Waters	?	N	N	N	N	N	N
36 Harman	N	N	N	N	N	N	N
37 Millender-McD.	N	N	N	N	Y	N	N
38 *Horn*	Y	Y	Y	Y	Y	N	N

	357	358	359	360	361	362	363
39 *Royce*	Y	Y	Y	Y	N	Y	Y
40 *Lewis*	Y	Y	Y	Y	N	Y	N
41 *Kim*	Y	N	Y	Y	N	N	N
42 Brown	N	N	N	N	N	N	N
43 *Calvert*	Y	Y	Y	Y	N	Y	N
44 *Bono, M.*	Y	Y	Y	Y	N	Y	N
45 *Rohrabacher*	Y	Y	Y	N	N	Y	N
46 Sanchez	N	N	N	N	Y	N	N
47 *Cox*	?	Y	Y	N	Y	Y	N
48 *Packard*	Y	Y	Y	Y	N	Y	N
49 *Bilbray*	Y	N	N	N	Y	N	N
50 Filner	N	N	N	N	N	N	N
51 *Cunningham*	Y	Y	Y	Y	Y	Y	N
52 *Hunter*	Y	Y	Y	Y	Y	N	N
COLORADO							
1 DeGette	N	N	N	N	Y	N	N
2 Skaggs	N	N	N	N	Y	N	N
3 *McInnis*	Y	Y	Y	N	N	Y	N
4 *Schaffer*	Y	N	Y	N	Y	N	N
5 *Hefley*	Y	Y	Y	N	Y	N	N
6 *Schaefer*	Y	Y	Y	N	N	Y	Y
CONNECTICUT							
1 Kennelly	N	N	N	N	Y	N	N
2 Gejdenson	N	N	N	N	N	N	N
3 DeLauro	N	N	N	N	Y	N	N
4 *Shays*	Y	N	N	N	N	N	N
5 Maloney	N	N	N	Y	N	N	N
6 *Johnson*	Y	N	N	N	Y	N	N
DELAWARE							
AL *Castle*	Y	N	N	N	Y	N	N
FLORIDA							
1 *Scarborough*	Y	Y	?	Y	N	Y	N
2 Boyd	N	N	N	N	Y	N	N
3 Brown	N	N	N	N	N	N	N
4 *Fowler*	Y	Y	Y	N	N	Y	N
5 Thurman	N	N	N	N	Y	N	N
6 *Stearns*	Y	Y	Y	Y	N	N	N
7 *Mica*	Y	Y	Y	Y	Y	Y	Y
8 *McCollum*	Y	Y	Y	Y	N	Y	N
9 *Bilirakis*	Y	Y	Y	N	Y	Y	N
10 *Young*	?	?	?	?	?	?	?
11 Davis	N	N	N	N	N	N	N
12 *Canady*	Y	Y	Y	Y	N	Y	N
13 *Miller*	Y	Y	Y	Y	Y	Y	N
14 *Goss*	Y	Y	Y	Y	N	Y	N
15 *Weldon*	Y	Y	Y	Y	N	Y	N
16 *Foley*	Y	Y	Y	N	Y	N	N
17 Meek	N	N	N	N	N	N	N
18 *Ros-Lehtinen*	Y	N	N	N	N	N	N
19 Wexler	N	N	N	N	N	N	N
20 Deutsch	N	N	N	N	Y	N	N
21 *Diaz-Balart*	Y	N	N	N	Y	N	N
22 *Shaw*	Y	Y	Y	Y	N	Y	N
23 Hastings	N	N	N	N	N	N	N
GEORGIA							
1 *Kingston*	Y	Y	Y	Y	N	N	N
2 Bishop	N	N	N	N	Y	N	N
3 *Collins*	Y	Y	Y	Y	N	N	N
4 McKinney	N	N	N	N	N	N	N
5 Lewis	N	N	N	N	Y	N	N
6 *Gingrich*	Y						
7 *Barr*	Y	Y	Y	Y	N	N	N
8 *Chambliss*	Y	Y	Y	Y	N	N	N
9 *Deal*	Y	Y	Y	Y	N	Y	N
10 *Norwood*	Y	Y	Y	Y	Y	N	N
11 *Linder*	?	?	Y	Y	N	N	N
HAWAII							
1 Abercrombie	N	N	N	N	N	N	N
2 Mink	N	N	N	N	Y	Y	Y
IDAHO							
1 *Chenoweth*	Y	N	Y	Y	N	Y	Y
2 *Crapo*	Y	N	Y	Y	Y	Y	N
ILLINOIS							
1 Rush	N	N	N	N	Y	N	N
2 Jackson	N	N	N	N	Y	N	N
3 Lipinski	Y	N	Y	Y	Y	N	N
4 Gutierrez	N	N	N	N	N	N	N
5 Blagojevich	N	N	N	N	N	N	N
6 *Hyde*	Y	Y	Y	N	N	Y	N
7 Davis	N	N	N	N	N	N	N
8 *Crane*	Y	Y	Y	Y	Y	Y	Y
9 Yates	N	N	N	N	Y	N	N
10 *Porter*	Y	N	N	N	N	N	N
11 *Weller*	Y	Y	Y	N	N	N	Y
12 Costello	N	N	N	N	N	N	N
13 *Fawell*	Y	Y	Y	Y	N	N	N

ND Northern Democrats   SD Southern Democrats

	357	358	359	360	361	362	363
14 ***Hastert***	Y	Y	Y	Y	N	N	N
15 ***Ewing***	Y	Y	Y	Y	Y	N	N
16 ***Manzullo***	Y	N	Y	Y	N	Y	N
17 Evans	N	N	N	N	Y	N	N
18 ***LaHood***	Y	Y	Y	Y	Y	N	N
19 Poshard	N	N	N	N	Y	N	N
20 ***Shimkus***	Y	Y	Y	N	Y	Y	Y
INDIANA							
1 Visclosky	N	N	N	N	Y	N	N
2 ***McIntosh***	Y	Y	Y	N	Y	Y	Y
3 Roemer	N	N	N	N	Y	N	Y
4 ***Souder***	Y	N	Y	Y	Y	Y	N
5 ***Buyer***	Y	Y	Y	?	Y	N	N
6 ***Burton***	Y	Y	Y	Y	N	Y	N
7 ***Pease***	Y	Y	Y	Y	Y	Y	N
8 ***Hostettler***	Y	Y	Y	N	Y	Y	Y
9 Hamilton	N	N	N	N	Y	N	N
10 Carson	N	N	N	N	Y	N	N
IOWA							
1 ***Leach***	Y	N	N	N	Y	N	Y
2 ***Nussle***	Y	Y	Y	Y	Y	N	N
3 Boswell	N	N	Y	N	Y	N	Y
4 ***Ganske***	Y	N	N	Y	Y	N	N
5 ***Latham***	Y	Y	Y	N	Y	N	N
KANSAS							
1 ***Moran***	Y	Y	Y	Y	N	Y	Y
2 ***Ryun***	Y	Y	Y	N	N	Y	N
3 ***Snowbarger***	Y	Y	Y	Y	Y	Y	N
4 ***Tiahrt***	Y	Y	Y	Y	Y	Y	Y
KENTUCKY							
1 ***Whitfield***	Y	Y	Y	N	N	N	N
2 ***Lewis***	Y	Y	Y	N	Y	Y	N
3 ***Northup***	Y	N	Y	N	N	N	N
4 ***Bunning***	Y	Y	Y	N	Y	Y	N
5 ***Rogers***	Y	Y	Y	N	N	Y	N
6 Baesler	N	N	N	N	Y	N	N
LOUISIANA							
1 ***Livingston***	Y	Y	Y	Y	Y	Y	N
2 Jefferson	N	N	N	N	Y	N	N
3 ***Tauzin***	Y	Y	Y	Y	Y	N	N
4 ***McCrery***	Y	Y	Y	Y	Y	Y	N
5 ***Cooksey***	Y	Y	Y	N	Y	Y	Y
6 ***Baker***	Y	Y	Y	Y	N	Y	N
7 John	N	N	N	N	Y	N	N
MAINE							
1 Allen	N	N	N	N	Y	N	N
2 Baldacci	N	N	N	N	Y	N	N
MARYLAND							
1 ***Gilchrest***	Y	N	N	N	Y	N	N
2 ***Ehrlich***	Y	Y	Y	Y	N	Y	N
3 Cardin	N	N	N	N	Y	N	N
4 Wynn	N	N	N	N	Y	N	N
5 Hoyer	N	N	N	N	Y	N	N
6 ***Bartlett***	Y	Y	Y	Y	N	Y	Y
7 Cummings	N	N	N	N	Y	N	N
8 ***Morella***	Y	N	N	N	Y	N	N
MASSACHUSETTS							
1 Olver	N	N	N	N	Y	N	N
2 Neal	?	N	N	N	Y	N	N
3 McGovern	N	N	N	N	Y	N	N
4 Frank	N	N	N	N	Y	N	N
5 Meehan	N	N	N	N	Y	N	N
6 Tierney	N	N	N	N	Y	N	N
7 Markey	N	N	N	N	Y	N	N
8 Kennedy	N	N	?	N	Y	N	N
9 Moakley	N	?	?	?	?	?	?
10 Delahunt	N	N	N	N	Y	N	N
MICHIGAN							
1 Stupak	N	N	N	Y	Y	N	N
2 ***Hoekstra***	Y	Y	Y	Y	N	N	Y
3 ***Ehlers***	Y	Y	Y	Y	Y	N	Y
4 ***Camp***	Y	Y	Y	Y	N	N	N
5 Barcia	N	N	N	Y	Y	N	N
6 ***Upton***	Y	Y	Y	Y	Y	N	N
7 ***Smith***	Y	Y	Y	Y	N	N	N
8 Stabenow	N	N	N	N	Y	N	N
9 Kildee	N	N	N	N	Y	N	N
10 Bonior	N	N	N	N	Y	N	N
11 ***Knollenberg***	Y	Y	Y	Y	N	N	N
12 Levin	N	N	N	N	Y	N	N
13 Rivers	N	N	N	N	Y	N	N
14 Conyers	N	N	N	N	Y	Y	N
15 Kilpatrick	N	N	N	N	Y	N	N
16 Dingell	N	N	N	N	Y	N	N

	357	358	359	360	361	362	363
MINNESOTA							
1 ***Gutknecht***	Y	Y	Y	Y	Y	Y	N
2 Minge	N	N	N	N	Y	N	N
3 ***Ramstad***	Y	N	N	N	Y	N	N
4 Vento	N	N	N	N	Y	N	N
5 Sabo	N	N	N	N	Y	Y	N
6 Luther	N	N	N	Y	Y	N	N
7 Peterson	N	N	N	N	Y	N	N
8 Oberstar	N	N	N	N	Y	N	N
MISSISSIPPI							
1 ***Wicker***	Y	Y	Y	N	N	Y	N
2 Thompson	N	N	N	N	Y	N	N
3 ***Pickering***	Y	Y	Y	N	N	Y	N
4 ***Parker***	Y	N	N	N	Y	N	N
5 Taylor	Y	N	Y	Y	Y	N	N
MISSOURI							
1 Clay	N	N	N	N	Y	Y	N
2 ***Talent***	Y	Y	Y	Y	Y	Y	N
3 Gephardt	N	N	N	N	N	N	N
4 Skelton	N	N	N	N	Y	N	N
5 McCarthy	N	N	N	N	Y	N	N
6 Danner	N	N	N	N	Y	N	N
7 ***Blunt***	Y	Y	Y	Y	Y	Y	N
8 ***Emerson***	Y	Y	Y	N	Y	N	N
9 ***Hulshof***	Y	Y	Y	Y	N	N	Y
MONTANA							
AL ***Hill***	Y	N	Y	Y	Y	N	Y
NEBRASKA							
1 ***Bereuter***	Y	Y	Y	Y	Y	N	N
2 ***Christensen***	Y	Y	Y	N	Y	Y	N
3 ***Barrett***	Y	N	N	Y	Y	N	N
NEVADA							
1 ***Ensign***	Y	Y	Y	N	Y	Y	N
2 ***Gibbons***	Y	Y	Y	Y	Y	Y	N
NEW HAMPSHIRE							
1 ***Sununu***	Y	N	Y	N	N	Y	Y
2 ***Bass***	Y	N	N	N	Y	N	N
NEW JERSEY							
1 Andrews	N	N	N	N	Y	N	N
2 ***LoBiondo***	Y	N	N	N	Y	N	N
3 ***Saxton***	Y	N	Y	Y	Y	Y	N
4 ***Smith***	Y	N	Y	N	N	N	N
5 ***Roukema***	Y	N	N	N	Y	N	N
6 Pallone	N	N	N	N	Y	N	N
7 ***Franks***	Y	N	N	N	Y	N	N
8 Pascrell	N	N	N	N	Y	N	N
9 Rothman	N	N	N	N	Y	N	N
10 Payne	N	N	N	N	Y	N	N
11 ***Frelinghuysen***	Y	N	N	N	Y	N	N
12 ***Pappas***	Y	N	Y	N	N	N	N
13 Menendez	N	N	N	N	Y	N	N
NEW MEXICO							
1 ***Wilson***	Y	Y	Y	N	Y	Y	N
2 ***Skeen***	Y	Y	Y	N	N	Y	N
3 ***Redmond***	Y	Y	Y	N	Y	Y	Y
NEW YORK							
1 ***Forbes***	N	N	N	N	Y	N	N
2 ***Lazio***	Y	N	Y	N	Y	N	N
3 ***King***	Y	N	Y	N	N	Y	N
4 McCarthy	N	N	N	N	Y	N	N
5 Ackerman	N	N	N	N	Y	N	N
6 Meeks	N	N	N	N	Y	N	N
7 Manton	N	N	N	N	Y	N	N
8 Nadler	N	N	N	N	Y	N	Y
9 Schumer	N	N	N	N	Y	N	N
10 Towns	?	?	?	?	?	?	?
11 Owens	N	N	N	N	Y	N	N
12 Velázquez	N	N	N	N	Y	N	N
13 ***Fossella***	Y	Y	Y	N	Y	Y	N
14 Maloney	N	N	N	N	Y	N	N
15 Rangel	N	?	?	N	Y	N	N
16 Serrano	N	N	N	N	Y	N	N
17 Engel	N	N	N	N	Y	N	N
18 Lowey	N	N	N	N	Y	N	N
19 ***Kelly***	Y	N	N	N	Y	N	N
20 ***Gilman***	Y	N	N	N	Y	N	N
21 McNulty	N	N	N	N	Y	N	N
22 ***Solomon***	Y	Y	Y	N	N	N	N
23 ***Boehlert***	Y	N	N	N	Y	N	N
24 ***McHugh***	Y	Y	Y	Y	Y	N	N
25 ***Walsh***	Y	N	N	Y	Y	N	N
26 Hinchey	N	N	N	N	Y	N	N
27 ***Paxon***	Y	Y	Y	Y	N	Y	N
28 Slaughter	N	N	N	N	N	N	N
29 LaFalce	N	N	N	N	Y	N	N
30 ***Quinn***	Y	N	N	Y	Y	N	N

	357	358	359	360	361	362	363
31 ***Houghton***	Y	N	N	N	Y	N	N
NORTH CAROLINA							
1 Clayton	N	N	N	N	Y	N	N
2 Etheridge	N	N	N	N	Y	N	N
3 ***Jones***	Y	Y	Y	Y	N	Y	N
4 Price	N	N	N	N	Y	N	N
5 ***Burr***	+	Y	Y	Y	N	N	N
6 ***Coble***	Y	Y	Y	Y	Y	Y	Y
7 McIntyre	N	N	N	N	Y	N	N
8 Hefner	N	N	N	N	Y	N	N
9 ***Myrick***	Y	Y	Y	Y	Y	Y	N
10 ***Ballenger***	Y	Y	Y	Y	Y	Y	N
11 ***Taylor***	Y	Y	Y	Y	Y	Y	Y
12 Watt	N	N	N	N	Y	N	N
NORTH DAKOTA							
AL Pomeroy	N	N	N	N	Y	N	N
OHIO							
1 ***Chabot***	Y	N	Y	Y	Y	Y	N
2 ***Portman***	Y	N	Y	Y	Y	N	N
3 Hall	N	N	N	N	Y	N	N
4 ***Oxley***	Y	Y	Y	Y	N	N	N
5 ***Gillmor***	Y	N	Y	Y	Y	Y	N
6 Strickland	N	N	N	N	Y	N	N
7 ***Hobson***	Y	Y	Y	N	Y	Y	N
8 ***Boehner***	Y	Y	Y	Y	Y	Y	N
9 Kaptur	N	N	N	N	Y	N	N
10 Kucinich	N	N	N	N	Y	Y	N
11 Stokes	N	N	N	N	Y	N	N
12 ***Kasich***	Y	Y	Y	N	Y	Y	N
13 Brown	N	N	N	N	Y	N	N
14 Sawyer	N	N	N	N	Y	N	N
15 ***Pryce***	Y	Y	Y	Y	Y	Y	N
16 ***Regula***	Y	N	Y	Y	Y	Y	N
17 Traficant	N	Y	Y	N	Y	Y	Y
18 ***Ney***	Y	Y	Y	Y	Y	Y	N
19 ***LaTourette***	Y	N	N	Y	Y	Y	Y
OKLAHOMA							
1 ***Largent***	Y	Y	Y	N	Y	Y	Y
2 ***Coburn***	Y	Y	Y	Y	Y	Y	N
3 ***Watkins***	Y	Y	Y	Y	Y	Y	N
4 ***Watts***	Y	Y	Y	Y	Y	Y	Y
5 ***Istook***	?	?	?	?	?	?	?
6 ***Lucas***	Y	Y	Y	Y	Y	Y	N
OREGON							
1 Furse	N	N	N	N	Y	N	N
2 ***Smith***	Y	Y	Y	N	Y	N	N
3 Blumenauer	N	N	N	N	Y	N	N
4 DeFazio	N	N	N	N	Y	N	N
5 Hooley	N	N	N	N	Y	N	N
PENNSYLVANIA							
1 Brady	N	N	N	N	Y	N	N
2 Fattah	N	N	N	N	Y	N	N
3 Borski	N	N	N	N	Y	N	N
4 Klink	N	N	N	N	Y	Y	N
5 ***Peterson***	Y	Y	Y	Y	Y	Y	N
6 Holden	N	N	N	N	Y	Y	N
7 ***Weldon***	Y	Y	Y	Y	Y	Y	N
8 ***Greenwood***	Y	N	N	N	Y	N	N
9 ***Shuster***	Y	Y	Y	Y	Y	Y	N
10 ***McDade***	?	?	?	?	?	?	?
11 Kanjorski	N	N	N	N	Y	N	N
12 Murtha	N	N	N	N	N	Y	Y
13 ***Fox***	Y	N	N	–	Y	N	Y
14 Coyne	N	N	N	N	Y	N	N
15 McHale	N	N	N	N	Y	N	N
16 ***Pitts***	Y	Y	Y	N	N	N	N
17 ***Gekas***	Y	Y	Y	Y	Y	Y	N
18 Doyle	N	N	N	N	N	Y	Y
19 ***Goodling***	Y	Y	Y	Y	N	Y	Y
20 Mascara	N	N	N	N	Y	N	N
21 ***English***	Y	N	Y	Y	Y	N	N
RHODE ISLAND							
1 Kennedy	N	N	N	N	Y	N	N
2 Weygand	N	N	N	N	Y	N	N
SOUTH CAROLINA							
1 ***Sanford***	Y	N	N	N	Y	N	Y
2 ***Spence***	Y	Y	Y	Y	Y	Y	N
3 ***Graham***	Y	Y	Y	Y	Y	Y	N
4 ***Inglis***	Y	Y	Y	Y	Y	Y	N
5 Spratt	N	N	N	N	Y	N	N
6 Clyburn	N	N	N	N	Y	N	N
SOUTH DAKOTA							
AL ***Thune***	Y	Y	Y	Y	Y	Y	N

	357	358	359	360	361	362	363
TENNESSEE							
1 ***Jenkins***	Y	Y	Y	Y	Y	Y	N
2 ***Duncan***	Y	Y	Y	Y	Y	Y	N
3 ***Wamp***	Y	Y	Y	Y	Y	N	N
4 ***Hilleary***	Y	Y	Y	Y	Y	Y	Y
5 Clement	N	N	N	N	Y	N	N
6 Gordon	N	N	N	N	Y	N	N
7 ***Bryant***	Y	Y	Y	N	N	Y	N
8 Tanner	N	N	N	N	Y	N	N
9 Ford	N	N	N	N	Y	N	N
TEXAS							
1 Sandlin	N	N	N	N	Y	N	N
2 Turner	N	N	N	N	Y	N	N
3 ***Johnson, Sam***	Y	Y	Y	N	N	Y	N
4 Hall	Y	N	Y	N	Y	Y	N
5 ***Sessions***	Y	Y	Y	Y	N	Y	Y
6 ***Barton***	Y	Y	Y	Y	N	N	N
7 ***Archer***	Y	Y	Y	Y	Y	Y	N
8 ***Brady***	Y	N	Y	Y	Y	Y	N
9 Lampson	N	N	N	N	Y	N	N
10 Doggett	N	N	N	N	Y	N	Y
11 Edwards	N	N	N	N	Y	N	N
12 ***Granger***	Y	Y	Y	N	Y	Y	N
13 ***Thornberry***	Y	Y	Y	N	Y	Y	N
14 ***Paul***	N	N	Y	N	Y	Y	Y
15 Hinojosa	N	N	N	N	Y	N	N
16 Reyes	N	N	N	N	Y	N	N
17 Stenholm	N	N	N	N	Y	N	N
18 Jackson-Lee	N	N	N	N	Y	N	N
19 ***Combest***	Y	Y	Y	Y	Y	Y	N
20 Gonzalez	?	?	?	?	?	?	?
21 ***Smith***	Y	Y	Y	Y	Y	N	N
22 ***DeLay***	Y	Y	Y	Y	N	Y	N
23 ***Bonilla***	Y	Y	Y	N	Y	Y	N
24 Frost	N	N	N	N	Y	N	N
25 Bentsen	N	N	N	N	Y	N	N
26 ***Armey***	Y	Y	Y	Y	N	Y	Y
27 Ortiz	N	N	N	N	Y	N	N
28 Rodriguez	N	N	N	N	Y	N	N
29 Green	N	N	N	N	Y	N	N
30 Johnson, E.B.	N	N	N	N	Y	N	N
UTAH							
1 ***Hansen***	Y	Y	Y	Y	N	Y	N
2 ***Cook***	Y	N	N	Y	Y	N	Y
3 ***Cannon***	Y	Y	Y	Y	N	Y	N
VERMONT							
AL *Sanders*	N	N	N	N	Y	N	Y
VIRGINIA							
1 ***Bateman***	Y	Y	?	N	N	Y	?
2 Pickett	N	N	N	N	Y	N	N
3 Scott	N	N	N	N	Y	N	N
4 Sisisky	N	N	N	N	Y	N	N
5 Goode	Y	N	Y	Y	N	Y	N
6 ***Goodlatte***	Y	Y	Y	Y	Y	Y	N
7 ***Bliley***	Y	Y	Y	N	Y	Y	N
8 Moran	N	N	N	Y	Y	Y	Y
9 Boucher	N	N	N	N	Y	Y	N
10 ***Wolf***	Y	Y	Y	Y	Y	N	N
11 ***Davis***	Y	Y	Y	Y	Y	Y	N
WASHINGTON							
1 ***White***	Y	N	Y	Y	Y	Y	N
2 ***Metcalf***	Y	N	N	N	Y	N	Y
3 ***Smith, Linda***	Y	N	N	N	Y	N	Y
4 ***Hastings***	Y	Y	Y	Y	N	Y	N
5 ***Nethercutt***	Y	Y	Y	Y	Y	Y	Y
6 Dicks	N	N	N	N	Y	N	N
7 McDermott	N	N	N	N	Y	N	N
8 ***Dunn***	Y	Y	Y	Y	Y	Y	N
9 Smith, Adam	N	N	N	N	Y	N	N
WEST VIRGINIA							
1 Mollohan	N	N	N	N	N	N	N
2 Wise	N	N	N	N	Y	N	N
3 Rahall	?	N	N	N	Y	N	Y
WISCONSIN							
1 ***Neumann***	Y	Y	Y	Y	Y	N	N
2 ***Klug***	Y	N	Y	Y	Y	N	N
3 Kind	N	N	N	N	Y	N	N
4 Kleczka	N	N	N	N	Y	N	N
5 Barrett	N	N	N	N	Y	N	N
6 ***Petri***	Y	N	Y	Y	Y	Y	N
7 Obey	N	N	N	N	N	N	N
8 Johnson	N	N	N	N	Y	N	N
9 ***Sensenbrenner***	Y	Y	Y	Y	N	Y	N
WYOMING							
AL ***Cubin***	Y	Y	Y	N	Y	Y	N

Southern states - Ala., Ark., Fla., Ga., Ky., La., Miss., N.C., Okla., S.C., Tenn., Texas, Va.

House Votes 364, 365, 366, 367, 368, 369, 370

364. HR 2183. Campaign Finance Overhaul/Shays-Meehan Substitute — Open Debate Requirement. Paul, R-Texas, amendment to the Shays-Meehan substitute amendment to the bill to overhaul campaign finance laws. The amendment would require recipients of federal matching campaign funds to agree not to participate in debates to which every other candidate for that office who either qualifies for federal funds or is on the ballot in a minimum of 40 states, is not invited. Rejected 88-337: R 67-156; D 20-181 (ND 19-129, SD 1-52); I 1-0. July 30, 1998.

365. HR 2183. Campaign Finance Overhaul/Shays-Meehan Substitute — Issue Ad Restrictions. DeLay, R-Texas, amendment to the Shays-Meehan substitute amendment to the bill to overhaul campaign finance laws. The amendment would remove certain restrictions on issue ads by creating an exemption for any communication dealing with any issue that may be the subject of a vote. Rejected 185-241: R 175-48; D 10-192 (ND 7-141, SD 3-51); I 0-1. July 30, 1998.

366. HR 2183. Campaign Finance Overhaul/Shays-Meehan Substitute — Citizenship Tests. Peterson, R-Pa., amendment to the Shays-Meehan substitute amendment to the bill to overhaul campaign finance laws. The amendment would require the establishment of a voluntary pilot program to help state and local officials determine voter eligibility by testing citizenship. Rejected 165-260: R 163-59; D 2-200 (ND 1-147, SD 1-53); I 0-1. July 30, 1998.

367. HR 2183. Campaign Finance Overhaul/Shays-Meehan Substitute — Bilingual Voting Material. Barr, R-Ga., amendment to the Shays-Meehan substitute amendment to the bill to overhaul campaign finance laws. The amendment would prohibit states from providing voters with voting materials in any language other than English. Rejected 142-261: R 137-74; D 5-186 (ND 2-140, SD 3-46); I 0-1. July 31, 1998.

368. HR 2183. Campaign Finance Overhaul/Shays-Meehan Substitute — Campaign Contribution Clarification. McIntosh, R-Ind., amendment to the Shays-Meehan substitute amendment to the bill to overhaul campaign finance laws. The amendment would clarify that contact between federal office-holders and interest groups regarding pending legislation or the office-holder's position on legislation is not considered a coordinated campaign contribution. Rejected 195-218: R 184-31; D 11-186 (ND 7-139, SD 4-47); I 0-1. July 31, 1998.

369. HR 2183. Campaign Finance Overhaul/Shays-Meehan Substitute — Lower Postage Rate for Candidate Mailings. Horn, R-Calif., amendment to the Shays-Meehan Substitute amendment to the bill to overhaul campaign finance laws. The amendment would allow candidates to use the lowest available postage rate of seven cents for up to two campaign mailings per household within the district they seek to represent. Current law allows a 14 cent rate for candidates. Rejected 117-294: R 91-123; D 25-171 (ND 19-126, SD 7-44); I 1-0. July 31, 1998.

370. HR 2183. Campaign Finance Overhaul/Shays-Meehan Substitute — Contributions Raised Within State. Shaw, R-Fla., amendment to the Shays-Meehan substitute amendment to the bill to overhaul campaign finance laws. The amendment would require candidates to raise 50 percent of contributions from inside their own state. Rejected 160-253: R 152-62; D 8-190 (ND 4-143, SD 4-47); I 0-1. July 31, 1998.

Key

- Y Voted for (yea).
- # Paired for.
- + Announced for.
- N Voted against (nay).
- X Paired against.
- − Announced against.
- P Voted "present."
- C Voted "present" to avoid possible conflict of interest.
- ? Did not vote or otherwise make a position known.

Democrats   **Republicans**
Independent

	364	365	366	367	368	369	370
ALABAMA							
1 *Callahan*	N	Y	Y	Y	Y	N	Y
2 *Everett*	N	Y	Y	?	Y	N	Y
3 *Riley*	N	Y	Y	Y	Y	Y	N
4 *Aderholt*	N	Y	Y	Y	Y	Y	Y
5 Cramer	N	N	N	N	N	N	N
6 *Bachus*	N	N	N	N	Y	N	Y
7 Hilliard	N	N	N	N	N	N	N
ALASKA							
AL *Young*	Y	Y	Y	Y	Y	Y	Y
ARIZONA							
1 *Salmon*	Y	Y	Y	+	+	−	+
2 Pastor	Y	N	N	N	N	Y	N
3 *Stump*	N	Y	Y	Y	Y	Y	Y
4 *Shadegg*	Y	Y	Y	Y	Y	N	Y
5 *Kolbe*	N	Y	N	N	Y	N	Y
6 *Hayworth*	Y	Y	Y	N	Y	N	Y
ARKANSAS							
1 Berry	N	N	N	N	N	N	N
2 Snyder	N	N	N	N	N	N	N
3 *Hutchinson*	N	N	N	Y	Y	N	Y
4 Dickey	N	Y	Y	Y	Y	Y	Y
CALIFORNIA							
1 *Riggs*	−	+	+	+	+	−	+
2 *Herger*	N	Y	Y	Y	Y	N	N
3 Fazio	N	N	N	N	N	N	N
4 *Doolittle*	Y	Y	Y	Y	Y	Y	N
5 Matsui	N	N	N	N	N	N	N
6 Woolsey	N	N	N	N	N	N	N
7 Miller	N	N	N	N	N	N	N
8 Pelosi	N	N	N	N	N	N	N
9 Lee	N	N	N	N	N	N	N
10 Tauscher	N	N	N	N	N	N	N
11 *Pombo*	Y	Y	Y	Y	Y	Y	Y
12 Lantos	N	N	N	N	N	N	N
13 Stark	N	N	N	N	N	N	N
14 Eshoo	N	N	N	N	N	N	N
15 *Campbell*	Y	N	N	N	Y	N	N
16 Lofgren	N	N	N	N	N	N	N
17 Farr	N	N	N	N	N	N	N
18 Condit	N	N	N	N	N	N	N
19 *Radanovich*	N	Y	Y	Y	Y	N	Y
20 Dooley	N	N	N	N	N	N	N
21 *Thomas*	N	Y	N	Y	Y	Y	Y
22 Capps, L.	N	N	N	N	N	N	N
23 *Gallegly*	N	Y	Y	Y	Y	Y	N
24 Sherman	Y	N	N	N	N	Y	N
25 *McKeon*	N	Y	Y	Y	Y	Y	Y
26 Berman	N	N	N	N	Y	N	N
27 *Rogan*	N	Y	Y	?	?	?	?
28 *Dreier*	N	Y	Y	Y	Y	N	Y
29 Waxman	N	N	N	?	N	Y	N
30 Becerra	N	N	N	N	N	N	N
31 Martinez	N	N	N	N	N	N	N
32 Dixon	N	N	N	N	N	N	N
33 Roybal-Allard	N	N	N	N	N	N	N
34 Torres	Y	N	N	N	N	N	N
35 Waters	N	N	N	N	N	N	N
36 Harman	N	N	N	N	N	N	N
37 Millender-McD.	N	N	N	N	N	N	N
38 *Horn*	N	N	Y	N	Y	Y	N

	364	365	366	367	368	369	370
39 *Royce*	Y	Y	Y	Y	Y	N	Y
40 Lewis	N	Y	Y	Y	Y	Y	N
41 *Kim*	N	Y	N	Y	Y	Y	N
42 Brown	N	N	N	N	N	N	N
43 *Calvert*	N	Y	Y	Y	Y	Y	Y
44 *Bono, M.*	N	Y	Y	Y	Y	N	Y
45 *Rohrabacher*	N	Y	Y	Y	Y	Y	Y
46 Sanchez	N	N	N	N	N	N	N
47 *Cox*	N	Y	Y	?	Y	Y	Y
48 *Packard*	N	Y	Y	Y	Y	Y	Y
49 *Bilbray*	N	N	Y	?	N	N	Y
50 Filner	Y	N	N	N	N	N	N
51 *Cunningham*	Y	Y	Y	Y	Y	N	Y
52 *Hunter*	Y	Y	Y	Y	Y	Y	Y
COLORADO							
1 DeGette	Y	N	N	N	N	N	N
2 Skaggs	N	N	N	N	N	N	N
3 *McInnis*	N	Y	N	Y	Y	Y	N
4 *Schaffer*	N	Y	N	Y	Y	N	Y
5 *Hefley*	N	Y	N	Y	Y	N	Y
6 *Schaefer*	Y	Y	Y	N	Y	N	N
CONNECTICUT							
1 Kennelly	N	N	N	N	N	N	N
2 Gejdenson	N	N	N	N	N	N	N
3 DeLauro	N	N	N	N	N	N	N
4 *Shays*	N	N	N	N	N	N	N
5 Maloney	Y	N	N	N	N	Y	N
6 *Johnson*	N	N	N	N	Y	Y	N
DELAWARE							
AL *Castle*	N	N	N	N	N	N	N
FLORIDA							
1 *Scarborough*	Y	Y	Y	Y	Y	Y	Y
2 Boyd	N	N	N	N	N	N	N
3 Brown	N	N	N	N	N	N	N
4 *Fowler*	N	Y	Y	Y	Y	N	Y
5 Thurman	N	N	N	N	N	N	N
6 *Stearns*	N	Y	Y	Y	Y	N	Y
7 *Mica*	N	Y	Y	Y	Y	Y	Y
8 *McCollum*	N	Y	Y	Y	Y	Y	Y
9 *Bilirakis*	Y	Y	Y	Y	Y	Y	Y
10 *Young*	?	?	?	?	?	?	?
11 Davis	N	N	N	N	N	N	N
12 *Canady*	N	Y	Y	Y	Y	N	Y
13 *Miller*	N	Y	Y	Y	Y	Y	Y
14 *Goss*	N	Y	Y	Y	Y	N	Y
15 *Weldon*	N	Y	N	Y	Y	N	Y
16 *Foley*	Y	N	N	Y	Y	Y	Y
17 Meek	N	N	N	N	N	N	N
18 *Ros-Lehtinen*	N	Y	Y	Y	Y	Y	Y
19 Wexler	?	N	N	N	N	N	N
20 Deutsch	N	N	N	N	N	N	N
21 *Diaz-Balart*	Y	Y	N	Y	Y	Y	N
22 *Shaw*	N	Y	Y	Y	Y	N	Y
23 Hastings	N	N	N	N	N	N	N
GEORGIA							
1 *Kingston*	N	Y	Y	Y	Y	Y	N
2 Bishop	N	N	N	?	N	N	N
3 *Collins*	Y	Y	Y	Y	Y	Y	Y
4 McKinney	N	N	N	N	N	N	N
5 Lewis	N	N	N	N	N	N	N
6 *Gingrich*							
7 *Barr*	N	Y	Y	Y	Y	Y	N
8 *Chambliss*	Y	Y	Y	Y	Y	Y	Y
9 *Deal*	Y	Y	Y	Y	Y	Y	Y
10 *Norwood*	Y	Y	Y	Y	Y	Y	Y
11 *Linder*	N	Y	Y	Y	Y	Y	Y
HAWAII							
1 Abercrombie	Y	N	N	N	N	N	N
2 Mink	Y	N	N	N	N	N	N
IDAHO							
1 *Chenoweth*	Y	Y	N	Y	Y	N	Y
2 *Crapo*	N	Y	N	Y	Y	N	Y
ILLINOIS							
1 Rush	N	N	N	N	N	N	N
2 Jackson	N	N	N	N	N	N	N
3 Lipinski	N	N	Y	N	N	N	N
4 Gutierrez	N	N	N	N	N	N	N
5 Blagojevich	N	N	N	N	N	N	N
6 *Hyde*	N	Y	Y	Y	Y	Y	N
7 Davis	Y	N	N	N	Y	N	N
8 *Crane*	Y	Y	Y	Y	Y	Y	Y
9 Yates	?	?	?	N	N	N	N
10 *Porter*	N	N	N	N	N	N	N
11 *Weller*	Y	Y	Y	Y	Y	N	Y
12 Costello	N	Y	N	N	N	N	N
13 *Fawell*	N	Y	Y	N	Y	N	Y

ND Northern Democrats   SD Southern Democrats

	364	365	366	367	368	369	370
14 ***Hastert***	N	Y	Y	Y	Y	N	Y
15 ***Ewing***	N	Y	N	Y	N	Y	Y
16 ***Manzullo***	N	Y	Y	Y	Y	N	Y
17 Evans	N	N	N	N	N	N	N
18 ***LaHood***	N	Y	N	Y	Y	Y	Y
19 Poshard	N	N	N	N	N	N	N
20 ***Shimkus***	Y	Y	Y	Y	Y	Y	Y
INDIANA							
1 Visclosky	Y	N	N	N	N	Y	N
2 ***McIntosh***	Y	Y	Y	Y	Y	Y	Y
3 Roemer	N	N	N	N	N	N	N
4 ***Souder***	N	N	Y	Y	Y	N	Y
5 ***Buyer***	N	Y	Y	?	?	?	?
6 ***Burton***	N	Y	Y	Y	Y	Y	N
7 ***Pease***	Y	Y	Y	Y	Y	N	Y
8 ***Hostettler***	N	Y	Y	Y	Y	N	Y
9 Hamilton	N	N	N	N	N	N	N
10 Carson	N	N	N	N	N	Y	N
IOWA							
1 ***Leach***	Y	N	N	N	N	Y	N
2 ***Nussle***	N	N	N	Y	Y	Y	Y
3 Boswell	N	N	N	N	N	N	N
4 ***Ganske***	N	N	N	N	N	N	Y
5 ***Latham***	N	Y	N	Y	Y	N	Y
KANSAS							
1 ***Moran***	Y	Y	Y	N	Y	N	Y
2 ***Ryun***	N	Y	Y	Y	Y	N	N
3 ***Snowbarger***	Y	Y	Y	Y	Y	N	N
4 ***Tiahrt***	Y	Y	Y	Y	Y	N	Y
KENTUCKY							
1 ***Whitfield***	Y	Y	Y	Y	Y	N	Y
2 ***Lewis***	N	Y	N	Y	Y	N	N
3 ***Northup***	N	Y	Y	Y	Y	Y	Y
4 ***Bunning***	N	Y	N	Y	Y	N	N
5 ***Rogers***	N	Y	Y	Y	Y	N	N
6 Baesler	N	N	N	N	N	N	N
LOUISIANA							
1 ***Livingston***	N	Y	Y	Y	Y	Y	Y
2 Jefferson	N	N	N	N	N	Y	N
3 ***Tauzin***	N	Y	Y	N	Y	N	Y
4 ***McCrery***	N	Y	Y	?	?	?	?
5 ***Cooksey***	Y	Y	Y	Y	Y	N	Y
6 ***Baker***	N	Y	Y	Y	Y	N	Y
7 John	N	N	N	?	?	?	?
MAINE							
1 Allen	N	N	N	N	N	N	N
2 Baldacci	N	N	N	N	N	Y	N
MARYLAND							
1 ***Gilchrest***	N	N	N	N	N	N	N
2 ***Ehrlich***	N	Y	Y	Y	Y	Y	Y
3 Cardin	N	N	N	?	?	?	N
4 Wynn	N	N	N	–	–	+	–
5 Hoyer	N	N	N	N	N	N	N
6 ***Bartlett***	Y	Y	Y	Y	Y	Y	Y
7 Cummings	N	N	N	N	N	N	N
8 ***Morella***	N	N	N	N	N	N	N
MASSACHUSETTS							
1 Olver	N	N	N	N	N	N	N
2 Neal	N	N	N	N	N	N	N
3 McGovern	N	N	N	N	N	N	N
4 Frank	N	N	N	N	N	N	N
5 Meehan	N	N	N	N	N	N	N
6 Tierney	N	N	N	N	N	N	N
7 Markey	N	N	N	N	N	N	N
8 Kennedy	N	N	N	N	N	N	N
9 Moakley	?	?	?	?	?	?	?
10 Delahunt	N	N	N	N	N	N	N
MICHIGAN							
1 Stupak	N	N	N	N	Y	N	N
2 ***Hoekstra***	Y	Y	Y	N	Y	N	Y
3 ***Ehlers***	N	Y	Y	N	N	Y	Y
4 ***Camp***	Y	Y	Y	N	Y	Y	Y
5 Barcia	Y	Y	N	N	Y	N	N
6 ***Upton***	N	N	Y	Y	Y	N	Y
7 ***Smith***	N	N	Y	Y	Y	Y	Y
8 Stabenow	N	N	N	N	N	N	N
9 Kildee	N	N	N	N	N	N	N
10 Bonior	N	N	N	N	N	N	N
11 ***Knollenberg***	N	N	Y	Y	Y	Y	Y
12 Levin	N	N	N	N	N	N	N
13 Rivers	Y	N	N	N	N	N	N
14 Conyers	Y	N	N	?	N	N	N
15 Kilpatrick	N	N	N	N	N	N	N
16 Dingell	N	N	N	N	N	N	N

	364	365	366	367	368	369	370
MINNESOTA							
1 ***Gutknecht***	N	Y	Y	Y	Y	Y	Y
2 Minge	N	N	N	N	N	N	N
3 ***Ramstad***	N	N	N	N	N	N	N
4 Vento	N	N	N	N	N	Y	N
5 Sabo	N	N	N	N	N	Y	N
6 Luther	Y	N	N	N	N	N	Y
7 Peterson	N	Y	N	N	N	N	Y
8 Oberstar	N	N	N	N	N	N	N
MISSISSIPPI							
1 ***Wicker***	N	Y	Y	Y	Y	Y	N
2 Thompson	N	N	N	N	N	N	N
3 ***Pickering***	N	Y	Y	Y	Y	N	N
4 ***Parker***	N	N	N	?	?	?	?
5 Taylor	N	N	N	N	N	N	Y
MISSOURI							
1 Clay	N	N	N	N	N	N	N
2 ***Talent***	N	Y	Y	N	Y	N	Y
3 Gephardt	N	N	N	N	N	N	N
4 Skelton	N	N	N	N	N	N	N
5 McCarthy	Y	N	N	N	N	N	N
6 Danner	N	N	N	N	N	N	N
7 ***Blunt***	N	Y	Y	N	Y	N	Y
8 ***Emerson***	N	Y	Y	Y	Y	N	Y
9 ***Hulshof***	Y	Y	Y	Y	Y	N	Y
MONTANA							
AL ***Hill***	Y	Y	Y	Y	Y	N	Y
NEBRASKA							
1 ***Bereuter***	N	Y	Y	N	Y	N	Y
2 ***Christensen***	N	Y	Y	?	?	?	?
3 ***Barrett***	N	N	N	N	N	N	Y
NEVADA							
1 ***Ensign***	Y	Y	Y	?	Y	N	Y
2 ***Gibbons***	Y	Y	Y	Y	Y	N	Y
NEW HAMPSHIRE							
1 ***Sununu***	Y	Y	N	Y	Y	N	N
2 ***Bass***	N	N	N	N	Y	N	N
NEW JERSEY							
1 Andrews	N	N	N	N	N	N	N
2 ***LoBiondo***	N	N	N	N	N	N	N
3 ***Saxton***	N	Y	Y	N	N	Y	Y
4 ***Smith***	N	Y	N	N	Y	Y	Y
5 ***Roukema***	N	N	N	Y	N	N	N
6 Pallone	N	N	N	N	N	N	N
7 ***Franks***	N	N	N	N	N	N	N
8 Pascrell	N	N	N	N	N	N	N
9 Rothman	N	N	N	N	N	N	N
10 Payne	N	N	N	N	N	N	N
11 ***Frelinghuysen***	N	N	N	N	N	N	N
12 ***Pappas***	Y	Y	Y	Y	Y	Y	Y
13 Menendez	N	N	N	N	N	N	N
NEW MEXICO							
1 ***Wilson***	N	Y	Y	N	Y	N	N
2 ***Skeen***	N	Y	Y	N	Y	Y	N
3 ***Redmond***	Y	Y	Y	N	Y	Y	N
NEW YORK							
1 ***Forbes***	N	N	N	–	–	–	–
2 ***Lazio***	N	N	Y	N	N	N	Y
3 ***King***	N	Y	N	Y	Y	Y	N
4 McCarthy	N	N	N	N	N	N	N
5 Ackerman	N	N	N	N	N	N	N
6 Meeks	N	N	N	N	N	N	N
7 Manton	N	N	N	N	N	N	N
8 Nadler	N	N	N	N	N	Y	N
9 Schumer	N	N	N	N	N	N	N
10 Towns	?	?	?	N	N	N	N
11 Owens	N	N	N	N	N	N	N
12 Velázquez	N	N	N	?	?	?	?
13 ***Fossella***	N	Y	Y	Y	Y	Y	N
14 Maloney	N	N	N	N	N	N	N
15 Rangel	N	N	N	N	N	N	N
16 Serrano	N	N	N	N	N	N	N
17 Engel	N	N	N	–	N	N	N
18 Lowey	N	N	N	N	N	N	N
19 ***Kelly***	N	N	N	N	N	N	N
20 ***Gilman***	N	N	N	N	N	Y	N
21 McNulty	N	N	N	N	N	N	N
22 ***Solomon***	N	Y	Y	Y	Y	N	Y
23 ***Boehlert***	N	N	N	N	N	Y	N
24 ***McHugh***	Y	Y	Y	N	Y	Y	Y
25 ***Walsh***	Y	N	N	N	N	N	N
26 Hinchey	N	N	N	?	N	N	N
27 ***Paxon***	N	Y	Y	Y	Y	Y	Y
28 Slaughter	N	N	N	N	N	Y	N
29 LaFalce	N	N	N	N	N	Y	N
30 ***Quinn***	N	N	N	N	N	Y	Y

	364	365	366	367	368	369	370
31 ***Houghton***	N	N	N	N	N	N	N
NORTH CAROLINA							
1 Clayton	N	N	N	N	N	N	N
2 Etheridge	N	N	N	N	N	N	N
3 ***Jones***	N	Y	Y	Y	Y	N	Y
4 Price	N	N	N	N	N	N	N
5 ***Burr***	N	Y	Y	Y	Y	N	Y
6 ***Coble***	Y	N	Y	Y	Y	N	Y
7 McIntyre	N	N	N	N	Y	N	N
8 Hefner	N	N	N	?	?	?	?
9 ***Myrick***	N	Y	Y	Y	Y	N	N
10 ***Ballenger***	N	Y	Y	Y	Y	Y	Y
11 ***Taylor***	Y	Y	Y	Y	Y	N	Y
12 Watt	N	N	N	N	N	N	N
NORTH DAKOTA							
AL Pomeroy	N	N	N	N	N	N	N
OHIO							
1 ***Chabot***	N	Y	N	Y	Y	N	Y
2 ***Portman***	N	Y	N	N	Y	Y	Y
3 Hall	N	N	N	N	N	N	N
4 ***Oxley***	N	Y	Y	Y	Y	Y	Y
5 ***Gillmor***	N	N	Y	N	Y	N	Y
6 Strickland	N	N	N	N	N	N	N
7 ***Hobson***	Y	Y	Y	Y	Y	Y	Y
8 ***Boehner***	N	Y	Y	Y	Y	N	Y
9 Kaptur	N	N	N	N	N	N	N
10 Kucinich	N	N	N	N	N	N	N
11 Stokes	N	N	N	N	N	N	N
12 ***Kasich***	Y	Y	Y	Y	Y	N	N
13 Brown	N	N	N	?	?	?	?
14 Sawyer	N	N	N	N	N	N	N
15 ***Pryce***	Y	Y	Y	N	Y	Y	Y
16 ***Regula***	Y	Y	Y	Y	Y	Y	Y
17 Traficant	Y	Y	Y	Y	Y	Y	N
18 ***Ney***	Y	Y	Y	Y	+	–	+
19 ***LaTourette***	Y	Y	N	Y	N	Y	Y
OKLAHOMA							
1 ***Largent***	N	Y	N	Y	Y	Y	Y
2 ***Coburn***	Y	Y	Y	Y	Y	N	Y
3 ***Watkins***	Y	Y	Y	Y	Y	N	Y
4 ***Watts***	Y	Y	Y	N	Y	Y	N
5 ***Istook***	?	?	?	?	?	?	?
6 ***Lucas***	N	Y	Y	Y	Y	N	Y
OREGON							
1 Furse	N	N	N	N	N	N	N
2 ***Smith***	N	Y	N	N	Y	N	?
3 Blumenauer	N	N	N	N	N	N	N
4 DeFazio	Y	N	N	N	N	N	N
5 Hooley	Y	N	N	N	N	N	N
PENNSYLVANIA							
1 Brady	N	N	N	N	N	Y	N
2 Fattah	N	N	N	N	N	Y	N
3 Borski	N	N	N	N	N	Y	N
4 Klink	N	Y	N	N	N	N	N
5 ***Peterson***	N	Y	Y	Y	Y	Y	Y
6 Holden	N	N	N	N	N	N	N
7 ***Weldon***	N	N	N	Y	Y	N	Y
8 ***Greenwood***	N	N	N	N	N	Y	N
9 ***Shuster***	Y	Y	Y	Y	Y	Y	Y
10 ***McDade***	?	?	?	N	Y	Y	N
11 Kanjorski	N	N	N	N	N	N	N
12 Murtha	N	Y	N	N	Y	N	N
13 ***Fox***	N	N	–	N	N	N	N
14 Coyne	N	N	N	N	N	N	N
15 McHale	N	N	N	N	N	N	N
16 ***Pitts***	N	Y	Y	Y	Y	N	N
17 ***Gekas***	N	Y	Y	Y	Y	Y	Y
18 Doyle	N	N	N	N	N	Y	N
19 ***Goodling***	N	Y	Y	Y	Y	Y	Y
20 Mascara	N	N	N	N	N	N	N
21 ***English***	N	Y	Y	N	Y	Y	Y
RHODE ISLAND							
1 Kennedy	N	N	N	N	N	N	N
2 Weygand	N	N	N	N	N	N	N
SOUTH CAROLINA							
1 ***Sanford***	Y	N	N	N	Y	Y	N
2 ***Spence***	N	Y	Y	Y	Y	N	N
3 ***Graham***	N	Y	N	Y	N	N	Y
4 ***Inglis***	N	Y	N	Y	Y	N	Y
5 Spratt	N	N	N	N	N	N	?
6 Clyburn	N	N	N	N	N	Y	N
SOUTH DAKOTA							
AL ***Thune***	Y	Y	Y	Y	Y	N	Y

	364	365	366	367	368	369	370
TENNESSEE							
1 ***Jenkins***	N	Y	Y	Y	Y	N	Y
2 ***Duncan***	Y	Y	Y	Y	Y	N	Y
3 ***Wamp***	Y	N	Y	N	Y	N	Y
4 ***Hilleary***	Y	Y	Y	Y	Y	N	Y
5 Clement	N	N	N	N	N	Y	N
6 Gordon	N	N	N	N	N	Y	N
7 ***Bryant***	N	Y	Y	Y	Y	N	N
8 Tanner	N	N	N	N	N	N	N
9 Ford	N	N	N	N	N	N	N
TEXAS							
1 Sandlin	N	N	N	N	N	N	N
2 Turner	N	N	N	N	N	N	N
3 ***Johnson, Sam***	N	Y	Y	Y	Y	N	Y
4 Hall	N	Y	N	Y	Y	N	Y
5 ***Sessions***	Y	Y	Y	Y	Y	?	Y
6 ***Barton***	N	Y	Y	?	Y	N	Y
7 ***Archer***	N	Y	Y	Y	Y	Y	Y
8 ***Brady***	N	Y	Y	N	Y	Y	Y
9 Lampson	N	N	N	N	N	N	N
10 Doggett	N	N	N	N	N	Y	N
11 Edwards	N	N	N	N	N	N	N
12 ***Granger***	N	Y	Y	N	Y	N	Y
13 ***Thornberry***	N	Y	Y	N	Y	N	Y
14 ***Paul***	Y	Y	Y	N	Y	N	N
15 Hinojosa	N	N	N	N	N	N	N
16 Reyes	N	N	N	N	N	N	N
17 Stenholm	N	N	N	N	N	N	N
18 Jackson-Lee	Y	N	N	N	N	N	N
19 ***Combest***	N	Y	Y	Y	Y	Y	Y
20 Gonzalez	?	?	?	?	?	?	?
21 ***Smith***	N	Y	Y	Y	Y	Y	Y
22 ***DeLay***	N	Y	Y	?	?	?	?
23 ***Bonilla***	N	Y	Y	N	Y	N	N
24 Frost	N	N	N	N	N	N	N
25 Bentsen	N	N	N	N	N	N	N
26 ***Armey***	N	Y	N	Y	Y	Y	Y
27 Ortiz	N	N	N	N	N	N	N
28 Rodriguez	N	N	N	N	N	N	N
29 Green	N	N	N	N	N	N	N
30 Johnson, E.B.	N	N	N	?	?	?	N
UTAH							
1 ***Hansen***	N	Y	Y	Y	Y	N	Y
2 ***Cook***	Y	Y	N	Y	Y	Y	Y
3 ***Cannon***	N	Y	Y	Y	Y	Y	Y
VERMONT							
AL *Sanders*	Y	N	N	N	N	Y	N
VIRGINIA							
1 ***Bateman***	N	Y	Y	Y	Y	Y	N
2 Pickett	N	N	N	Y	N	N	N
3 Scott	N	Y	N	N	Y	Y	N
4 Sisisky	N	N	N	N	N	N	N
5 Goode	N	Y	Y	Y	Y	N	Y
6 ***Goodlatte***	N	Y	Y	Y	Y	N	Y
7 ***Bliley***	N	Y	Y	Y	Y	Y	N
8 Moran	N	N	N	?	N	N	Y
9 Boucher	N	N	N	N	N	N	N
10 ***Wolf***	N	N	Y	Y	Y	N	Y
11 ***Davis***	N	Y	Y	N	Y	N	Y
WASHINGTON							
1 ***White***	N	N	N	N	Y	N	Y
2 ***Metcalf***	Y	N	N	N	N	N	N
3 ***Smith, Linda***	Y	N	N	N	N	N	N
4 ***Hastings***	N	Y	Y	Y	Y	N	Y
5 ***Nethercutt***	Y	Y	Y	Y	Y	N	Y
6 Dicks	N	N	N	N	N	N	N
7 McDermott	N	N	N	N	N	N	N
8 ***Dunn***	N	Y	Y	Y	Y	N	Y
9 Smith, Adam	N	N	N	N	N	N	N
WEST VIRGINIA							
1 Mollohan	N	Y	N	N	N	?	N
2 Wise	N	N	N	N	N	N	N
3 Rahall	Y	N	N	N	Y	N	N
WISCONSIN							
1 ***Neumann***	Y	Y	Y	Y	Y	Y	Y
2 ***Klug***	N	N	Y	N	Y	N	Y
3 Kind	N	N	N	N	N	N	N
4 Kleczka	N	N	N	N	N	N	N
5 Barrett	N	N	N	N	N	N	N
6 ***Petri***	N	N	Y	Y	Y	Y	Y
7 Obey	N	N	N	N	N	N	N
8 Johnson	N	N	N	N	N	N	N
9 ***Sensenbrenner***	N	Y	Y	Y	Y	N	Y
WYOMING							
AL ***Cubin***	Y	Y	Y	Y	Y	N	Y

Southern states - Ala., Ark., Fla., Ga., Ky., La., Miss., N.C., Okla., S.C., Tenn., Texas, Va.

House Votes 371, 372, 373, 374, 375, 376, 377

Key

- Y Voted for (yea).
- # Paired for.
- + Announced for.
- N Voted against (nay).
- X Paired against.
- − Announced against.
- P Voted "present."
- C Voted "present" to avoid possible conflict of interest.
- ? Did not vote or otherwise make a position known.

Democrats   **Republicans**
Independent

371. HR 2183. Campaign Finance Overhaul/Shays-Meehan Substitute — FEC Clearinghouse. Kaptur, D-Ohio, amendment to the Shays-Meehan amendment to the bill to overhaul campaign finance laws. The amendment would establish a clearinghouse of political activities within the Federal Election Commission. Adopted 341-74: R 149-66; D 191-8 (ND 143-4, SD 48-4); I 1-0. July 31, 1998.

372. HR 2183. Campaign Finance Overhaul/Shays-Meehan Substitute — Political Donations From Certain Legal Residents. Stearns, R-Fla., amendment to the Shays-Meehan substitute amendment to the bill to overhaul campaign finance laws. The amendment would allow permenant legal residents who serve in the military to make political contributions. Adopted 385-29: R 190-24; D 194-5 (ND 145-2, SD 49-3); I 1-0. July 31, 1998.

373. HR 2183. Campaign Finance Overhaul/Shays-Meehan Substitute — Soft Money Solicitation. Stearns, R-Fla., amendment to the Shays-Meehan substitute amendment to the bill to overhaul campaign finance laws. The amendment would prohibit presidential and vice-presidential candidates from receiving public funding from the federal Presidential Election Campaign Fund unless the candidate certifies that they will not solicit soft money donations. Adopted 368-44: R 192-21; D 175-23 (ND 129-17, SD 46-6); I 1-0. July 31, 1998.

374. HR 2183. Campaign Finance Overhaul/Shays-Meehan Substitute — Raise Individual Contribution Limit. Whitfield, R-Ky., amendment to the Shays-Meehan substitute amendment to the bill to overhaul campaign finance laws. The amendment would raise the individual contribution limit to candidates from $1,000 to $3,000. Rejected 102-315: R 99-118; D 3-196 (ND 3-144, SD 0-52); I 0-1. July 31, 1998.

375. HR 2183. Campaign Finance Overhaul/Shays-Meehan Substitute — Express Advocacy Definition. Whitfield, R-Ky., amendment to the Shays-Meehan substitute amendment to the bill to overhaul campaign finance laws. The amendment would remove the bill's expanded version of the definition of express advocacy and maintain current law. Rejected 173-238: R 164-50; D 9-187 (ND 4-140, SD 5-47); I 0-1. July 31, 1998.

376. HR 2183. Campaign Finance Overhaul/Shays-Meehan Substitute — Contribution Bundling Ban. English, R-Pa., amendment to the Shays-Meehan Substitute amendment to the bill to overhaul campaign finance laws. The amendment would prohibit bundling of campaign contributions for distribution to candidates or political parties. Rejected 134-276: R 124-91; D 10-184 (ND 9-133, SD 1-51); I 0-1. July 31, 1998.

377. HR 3743. Withhold Contributions to Iranian Energy Program/Passage. Gilman, R-N.Y. motion to suspend the rules and pass the bill to withhold U.S. proportional voluntary contributions to the International Atomic Energy Agency (IAEA) for its programs in Iran. Motion agreed to 405-13: R 224-0; D 180-13 (ND 130-12, SD 50-1); I 1-0. Aug. 3, 1998. A two-thirds majority of those present and voting (279 in this case) is required for passage under suspension of the rules.

	371	372	373	374	375	376	377
ALABAMA							
1 *Callahan*	Y	Y	Y	Y	Y	Y	Y
2 *Everett*	Y	Y	Y	Y	Y	Y	Y
3 *Riley*	Y	Y	Y	Y	Y	N	Y
4 *Aderholt*	N	Y	Y	N	Y	N	Y
5 Cramer	Y	Y	Y	N	N	N	Y
6 *Bachus*	Y	Y	Y	N	N	N	Y
7 Hilliard	N	Y	Y	N	N	N	?
ALASKA							
AL *Young*	Y	Y	Y	Y	Y	Y	Y
ARIZONA							
1 *Salmon*	+	+	+	N	Y	Y	Y
2 Pastor	Y	Y	N	N	N	N	Y
3 *Stump*	Y	Y	Y	Y	Y	Y	Y
4 *Shadegg*	N	Y	Y	Y	Y	N	Y
5 *Kolbe*	Y	Y	Y	N	Y	N	Y
6 *Hayworth*	Y	Y	Y	N	Y	Y	Y
ARKANSAS							
1 Berry	Y	Y	Y	N	N	N	Y
2 Snyder	Y	Y	Y	N	N	N	Y
3 *Hutchinson*	N	Y	N	N	Y	N	Y
4 *Dickey*	Y	Y	Y	Y	Y	N	Y
CALIFORNIA							
1 Riggs	+	+	+	+	−	+	Y
2 *Herger*	Y	Y	Y	Y	Y	Y	Y
3 Fazio	Y	N	N	N	N	N	Y
4 *Doolittle*	N	Y	N	Y	Y	N	Y
5 Matsui	Y	Y	Y	N	N	N	Y
6 Woolsey	Y	Y	Y	N	N	N	Y
7 Miller	Y	Y	Y	N	N	N	Y
8 Pelosi	Y	Y	Y	N	N	N	Y
9 Lee	Y	Y	Y	N	N	N	Y
10 Tauscher	Y	Y	Y	N	N	N	Y
11 *Pombo*	N	Y	N	Y	Y	N	Y
12 Lantos	Y	Y	Y	N	N	N	Y
13 Stark	Y	Y	Y	N	N	N	Y
14 Eshoo	Y	Y	Y	N	N	N	Y
15 *Campbell*	Y	Y	Y	N	N	N	Y
16 Lofgren	Y	Y	Y	N	N	N	Y
17 Farr	Y	Y	N	N	N	N	Y
18 Condit	Y	Y	Y	N	N	N	Y
19 *Radanovich*	N	Y	N	Y	Y	Y	Y
20 Dooley	Y	Y	Y	N	N	N	N
21 *Thomas*	Y	Y	Y	Y	Y	Y	Y
22 Capps, L.	Y	Y	Y	N	N	N	Y
23 *Gallegly*	Y	Y	Y	N	Y	N	Y
24 Sherman	Y	Y	Y	N	N	N	Y
25 *McKeon*	N	Y	Y	N	Y	N	Y
26 Berman	Y	Y	Y	N	N	N	Y
27 *Rogan*	?	?	?	?	?	?	Y
28 *Dreier*	N	Y	Y	N	Y	N	Y
29 Waxman	Y	Y	Y	N	N	N	Y
30 Becerra	Y	Y	Y	N	N	N	Y
31 Martinez	N	Y	Y	Y	N	N	?
32 Dixon	Y	Y	Y	N	N	N	Y
33 Roybal-Allard	Y	Y	Y	N	N	N	Y
34 Torres	Y	Y	Y	N	N	N	N
35 Waters	Y	Y	?	N	N	N	Y
36 Harman	Y	Y	Y	N	N	N	Y
37 Millender-McD.	Y	Y	Y	N	N	N	Y
38 *Horn*	Y	Y	Y	N	Y	N	Y

	371	372	373	374	375	376	377
39 *Royce*	Y	Y	Y	N	Y	N	Y
40 *Lewis*	Y	N	Y	N	Y	N	Y
41 *Kim*	Y	Y	Y	N	N	N	Y
42 Brown	Y	Y	Y	N	N	N	Y
43 *Calvert*	Y	Y	Y	N	Y	N	Y
44 *Bono, M.*	Y	Y	Y	Y	Y	Y	Y
45 *Rohrabacher*	Y	Y	Y	Y	Y	N	Y
46 Sanchez	Y	Y	Y	N	N	N	Y
47 *Cox*	Y	Y	Y	Y	Y	Y	Y
48 *Packard*	N	N	Y	N	Y	N	Y
49 *Bilbray*	Y	Y	Y	N	N	N	Y
50 Filner	Y	Y	Y	N	N	N	Y
51 *Cunningham*	Y	Y	Y	Y	Y	Y	Y
52 *Hunter*	Y	Y	Y	N	Y	Y	Y
COLORADO							
1 DeGette	Y	Y	Y	N	N	N	Y
2 Skaggs	Y	Y	N	N	N	N	N
3 *McInnis*	Y	Y	N	Y	N	N	Y
4 *Schaffer*	Y	Y	Y	Y	Y	N	Y
5 *Hefley*	Y	Y	Y	Y	Y	Y	Y
6 *Schaefer*	Y	Y	Y	Y	Y	Y	Y
CONNECTICUT							
1 Kennelly	Y	Y	Y	N	N	N	Y
2 Gejdenson	Y	Y	Y	N	−	−	N
3 DeLauro	Y	Y	Y	N	N	N	Y
4 *Shays*	Y	Y	Y	N	N	N	Y
5 Maloney	Y	Y	Y	N	N	N	Y
6 *Johnson*	Y	Y	Y	N	N	N	Y
DELAWARE							
AL *Castle*	Y	Y	Y	N	N	N	Y
FLORIDA							
1 *Scarborough*	Y	Y	Y	N	N	N	Y
2 Boyd	Y	Y	Y	N	N	N	Y
3 Brown	Y	Y	Y	N	N	N	Y
4 *Fowler*	Y	Y	Y	Y	Y	Y	Y
5 Thurman	Y	Y	Y	N	N	N	Y
6 *Stearns*	Y	Y	Y	Y	Y	Y	Y
7 *Mica*	N	Y	Y	Y	Y	Y	Y
8 *McCollum*	N	N	Y	Y	Y	Y	Y
9 *Bilirakis*	N	Y	N	Y	Y	Y	Y
10 *Young*	?	?	?	?	?	?	Y
11 Davis	Y	Y	Y	N	N	N	Y
12 *Canady*	Y	Y	Y	N	N	N	Y
13 *Miller*	Y	Y	Y	N	N	N	Y
14 *Goss*	N	Y	Y	N	N	N	Y
15 *Weldon*	Y	Y	+	Y	N	N	Y
16 *Foley*	Y	Y	N	N	Y	N	Y
17 Meek	Y	Y	Y	N	N	N	Y
18 *Ros-Lehtinen*	Y	Y	Y	N	N	N	Y
19 Wexler	Y	Y	Y	N	N	N	Y
20 Deutsch	Y	Y	Y	N	N	N	Y
21 *Diaz-Balart*	Y	Y	Y	N	N	N	Y
22 *Shaw*	Y	Y	Y	Y	Y	Y	Y
23 Hastings	Y	N	Y	N	N	N	Y
GEORGIA							
1 *Kingston*	Y	Y	Y	N	Y	Y	Y
2 Bishop	Y	Y	Y	N	Y	N	Y
3 *Collins*	N	Y	Y	N	N	N	Y
4 *McKinney*	Y	Y	Y	N	N	N	Y
5 Lewis	Y	N	N	N	N	N	Y
6 *Gingrich*							
7 *Barr*	Y	Y	Y	Y	Y	N	Y
8 *Chambliss*	N	Y	Y	N	N	N	Y
9 *Deal*	N	Y	Y	N	N	N	Y
10 *Norwood*	N	N	Y	N	Y	N	Y
11 *Linder*	N	N	Y	Y	Y	Y	Y
HAWAII							
1 Abercrombie	Y	Y	Y	N	N	N	Y
2 Mink	Y	Y	Y	N	N	N	Y
IDAHO							
1 *Chenoweth*	Y	Y	Y	N	N	N	Y
2 *Crapo*	Y	Y	Y	Y	N	Y	Y
ILLINOIS							
1 Rush	Y	Y	Y	N	N	N	Y
2 Jackson	N	Y	Y	N	N	N	Y
3 Lipinski	Y	Y	Y	N	N	N	Y
4 Gutierrez	Y	Y	Y	N	N	N	Y
5 Blagojevich	Y	Y	Y	N	N	N	Y
6 *Hyde*	Y	N	N	N	N	N	Y
7 Davis	Y	Y	Y	N	N	N	Y
8 *Crane*	N	Y	Y	Y	Y	N	Y
9 Yates	Y	Y	Y	N	N	N	Y
10 *Porter*	Y	Y	Y	N	N	N	Y
11 *Weller*	Y	Y	Y	N	N	N	Y
12 Costello	Y	Y	Y	N	?	?	Y
13 *Fawell*	Y	N	Y	N	N	N	Y

ND Northern Democrats   SD Southern Democrats

	371	372	373	374	375	376	377
14 ***Hastert***	N	Y	Y	Y	Y	Y	Y
15 ***Ewing***	N	Y	Y	N	Y	Y	Y
16 ***Manzullo***	Y	Y	Y	N	Y	Y	Y
17 Evans	Y	Y	Y	N	N	N	Y
18 ***LaHood***	N	Y	Y	N	N	N	Y
19 Poshard	Y	Y	Y	N	N	N	?
20 ***Shimkus***	N	Y	Y	Y	Y	N	Y
INDIANA							
1 Visclosky	Y	Y	N	N	N	N	Y
2 ***McIntosh***	N	Y	Y	Y	Y	Y	Y
3 Roemer	Y	Y	Y	N	N	N	Y
4 ***Souder***	Y	Y	Y	N	Y	Y	Y
5 ***Buyer***	?	?	?	?	?	?	Y
6 ***Burton***	N	Y	Y	Y	Y	Y	Y
7 ***Pease***	Y	N	Y	N	Y	N	Y
8 ***Hostettler***	N	Y	Y	Y	Y	N	Y
9 Hamilton	Y	Y	Y	N	N	N	N
10 Carson	Y	Y	N	N	N	N	Y
IOWA							
1 ***Leach***	Y	Y	Y	N	N	N	Y
2 ***Nussle***	Y	Y	Y	N	N	Y	Y
3 Boswell	Y	Y	Y	N	N	N	Y
4 ***Ganske***	Y	Y	Y	N	N	N	Y
5 ***Latham***	Y	Y	Y	N	Y	Y	Y
KANSAS							
1 ***Moran***	N	N	N	N	Y	Y	Y
2 ***Ryun***	N	Y	Y	Y	Y	N	Y
3 ***Snowbarger***	Y	Y	Y	Y	Y	Y	Y
4 ***Tiahrt***	N	N	Y	Y	Y	Y	Y
KENTUCKY							
1 ***Whitfield***	Y	Y	Y	Y	Y	Y	Y
2 ***Lewis***	Y	Y	Y	Y	Y	Y	Y
3 ***Northup***	Y	Y	Y	N	Y	Y	Y
4 ***Bunning***	Y	Y	Y	N	Y	Y	Y
5 ***Rogers***	Y	Y	Y	N	Y	Y	Y
6 Baesler	Y	Y	Y	N	N	N	Y
LOUISIANA							
1 ***Livingston***	N	Y	Y	Y	Y	Y	Y
2 Jefferson	Y	Y	N	N	N	N	Y
3 ***Tauzin***	Y	Y	Y	Y	Y	Y	Y
4 ***McCrery***	?	?	?	N	Y	Y	Y
5 ***Cooksey***	N	Y	Y	Y	Y	Y	Y
6 ***Baker***	Y	Y	Y	Y	Y	Y	Y
7 John	?	?	?	?	?	?	Y
MAINE							
1 Allen	Y	Y	Y	N	N	N	Y
2 Baldacci	Y	Y	Y	N	N	N	Y
MARYLAND							
1 ***Gilchrest***	Y	?	Y	N	N	N	Y
2 ***Ehrlich***	Y	Y	Y	N	Y	Y	Y
3 Cardin	Y	Y	Y	N	N	N	Y
4 Wynn	+	+	–	–	–	–	Y
5 Hoyer	N	Y	Y	N	N	N	Y
6 ***Bartlett***	Y	Y	Y	N	Y	Y	Y
7 Cummings	Y	Y	Y	N	N	N	Y
8 ***Morella***	Y	Y	Y	N	N	N	Y
MASSACHUSETTS							
1 Olver	Y	Y	Y	N	N	N	?
2 Neal	Y	Y	Y	N	N	N	Y
3 McGovern	Y	Y	Y	N	N	N	Y
4 Frank	Y	N	Y	N	N	N	Y
5 Meehan	Y	Y	Y	N	N	N	Y
6 Tierney	Y	Y	Y	N	N	N	Y
7 Markey	Y	Y	Y	N	N	N	Y
8 Kennedy	Y	Y	Y	N	N	Y	Y
9 Moakley	?	?	?	?	?	?	Y
10 Delahunt	Y	Y	Y	N	N	?	Y
MICHIGAN							
1 Stupak	Y	Y	Y	N	N	N	Y
2 ***Hoekstra***	Y	Y	Y	N	Y	Y	Y
3 ***Ehlers***	N	Y	Y	N	Y	Y	Y
4 ***Camp***	Y	Y	Y	N	Y	Y	Y
5 Barcia	Y	Y	Y	N	N	Y	Y
6 ***Upton***	Y	Y	Y	N	N	Y	Y
7 ***Smith***	Y	Y	Y	N	N	Y	Y
8 Stabenow	Y	Y	Y	N	N	N	Y
9 Kildee	Y	Y	Y	N	N	N	Y
10 Bonior	Y	Y	N	N	N	N	Y
11 ***Knollenberg***	N	N	N	Y	Y	Y	Y
12 Levin	Y	Y	Y	N	N	N	Y
13 Rivers	Y	Y	Y	N	N	N	Y
14 Conyers	Y	Y	Y	N	N	N	?
15 Kilpatrick	Y	Y	Y	N	N	N	+
16 Dingell	Y	Y	Y	N	N	N	Y

	371	372	373	374	375	376	377
MINNESOTA							
1 ***Gutknecht***	Y	N	Y	N	Y	Y	Y
2 Minge	Y	Y	Y	N	N	N	Y
3 ***Ramstad***	N	Y	Y	N	N	N	Y
4 Vento	Y	Y	Y	N	N	N	Y
5 Sabo	Y	Y	N	N	N	N	Y
6 Luther	Y	Y	Y	N	N	Y	Y
7 Peterson	N	Y	Y	N	Y	Y	Y
8 Oberstar	Y	Y	Y	N	N	N	–
MISSISSIPPI							
1 ***Wicker***	Y	Y	Y	Y	Y	N	Y
2 Thompson	Y	Y	Y	N	N	N	Y
3 ***Pickering***	Y	Y	Y	N	Y	Y	Y
4 ***Parker***	?	?	?	?	?	?	Y
5 Taylor	Y	Y	Y	N	N	N	Y
MISSOURI							
1 Clay	Y	Y	Y	N	N	N	Y
2 ***Talent***	Y	Y	Y	N	Y	Y	Y
3 Gephardt	Y	Y	N	N	N	N	Y
4 Skelton	Y	Y	Y	N	N	N	Y
5 McCarthy	Y	Y	Y	N	N	N	Y
6 Danner	Y	Y	Y	N	N	N	Y
7 ***Blunt***	Y	Y	Y	Y	Y	N	Y
8 ***Emerson***	Y	Y	Y	N	Y	Y	Y
9 ***Hulshof***	Y	Y	Y	N	Y	Y	Y
MONTANA							
AL ***Hill***	N	Y	Y	Y	Y	Y	Y
NEBRASKA							
1 ***Bereuter***	Y	Y	N	Y	N	Y	Y
2 ***Christensen***	?	?	?	?	?	?	?
3 ***Barrett***	N	Y	Y	N	N	N	Y
NEVADA							
1 ***Ensign***	Y	Y	Y	Y	N	N	Y
2 ***Gibbons***	N	Y	Y	Y	Y	Y	Y
NEW HAMPSHIRE							
1 ***Sununu***	N	N	N	N	Y	N	Y
2 ***Bass***	Y	Y	Y	N	N	N	Y
NEW JERSEY							
1 Andrews	Y	Y	Y	N	N	N	Y
2 ***LoBiondo***	Y	Y	Y	N	N	N	Y
3 ***Saxton***	Y	Y	Y	N	Y	Y	Y
4 ***Smith***	Y	Y	Y	N	Y	Y	Y
5 ***Roukema***	Y	Y	Y	N	N	N	Y
6 Pallone	Y	Y	Y	N	N	N	Y
7 ***Franks***	Y	Y	Y	N	N	?	Y
8 Pascrell	Y	Y	Y	N	N	N	Y
9 Rothman	Y	Y	Y	N	N	N	Y
10 Payne	Y	Y	N	N	N	N	Y
11 ***Frelinghuysen***	Y	Y	Y	N	N	N	Y
12 ***Pappas***	Y	Y	Y	N	Y	Y	Y
13 Menendez	Y	Y	Y	N	N	N	Y
NEW MEXICO							
1 ***Wilson***	N	Y	Y	N	Y	N	Y
2 ***Skeen***	N	Y	Y	Y	Y	Y	Y
3 ***Redmond***	N	Y	Y	N	Y	N	Y
NEW YORK							
1 ***Forbes***	–	+	+	–	–	–	Y
2 ***Lazio***	Y	Y	Y	N	Y	N	Y
3 ***King***	Y	Y	N	Y	Y	N	Y
4 McCarthy	Y	Y	Y	N	N	N	Y
5 Ackerman	Y	Y	Y	N	N	N	Y
6 Meeks	Y	Y	Y	N	N	N	Y
7 Manton	Y	Y	Y	N	N	N	Y
8 Nadler	Y	Y	Y	N	N	N	Y
9 Schumer	Y	Y	Y	N	N	N	Y
10 Towns	Y	Y	N	N	N	N	?
11 Owens	Y	Y	N	N	N	N	Y
12 Velázquez	?	?	?	?	?	?	Y
13 ***Fossella***	N	Y	N	Y	Y	N	Y
14 Maloney	Y	Y	Y	N	N	N	Y
15 Rangel	Y	Y	Y	N	N	N	Y
16 Serrano	Y	Y	Y	N	N	N	Y
17 Engel	Y	Y	Y	N	N	N	Y
18 Lowey	Y	Y	Y	N	N	N	Y
19 ***Kelly***	N	Y	Y	N	N	N	Y
20 ***Gilman***	N	Y	Y	N	N	N	Y
21 McNulty	Y	Y	Y	N	?	?	Y
22 ***Solomon***	N	Y	N	Y	?	N	Y
23 ***Boehlert***	Y	Y	Y	N	N	N	Y
24 ***McHugh***	Y	Y	Y	N	Y	Y	Y
25 ***Walsh***	N	Y	Y	N	N	N	Y
26 Hinchey	Y	Y	Y	N	N	N	Y
27 ***Paxon***	N	Y	Y	Y	Y	Y	Y
28 Slaughter	Y	Y	Y	N	N	N	Y
29 LaFalce	Y	Y	Y	N	N	N	N
30 ***Quinn***	Y	Y	Y	N	N	N	Y

	371	372	373	374	375	376	377
31 ***Houghton***	Y	Y	Y	N	N	N	Y
NORTH CAROLINA							
1 Clayton	Y	Y	Y	N	N	N	?
2 Etheridge	Y	Y	Y	N	N	N	Y
3 ***Jones***	Y	N	Y	Y	Y	Y	Y
4 Price	Y	Y	Y	N	N	N	Y
5 ***Burr***	N	Y	N	N	Y	Y	Y
6 ***Coble***	Y	N	Y	N	N	N	Y
7 McIntyre	Y	Y	Y	N	N	N	Y
8 Hefner	?	?	?	?	?	?	Y
9 ***Myrick***	Y	Y	Y	Y	N	Y	Y
10 ***Ballenger***	N	Y	+	+	+	+	Y
11 ***Taylor***	Y	Y	Y	N	Y	Y	Y
12 Watt	Y	Y	N	N	Y	N	Y
NORTH DAKOTA							
AL Pomeroy	Y	Y	Y	N	N	N	?
OHIO							
1 ***Chabot***	Y	Y	Y	N	Y	Y	Y
2 ***Portman***	Y	Y	Y	N	Y	Y	Y
3 Hall	Y	Y	Y	N	N	N	Y
4 ***Oxley***	N	Y	Y	Y	Y	N	Y
5 ***Gillmor***	Y	Y	Y	N	N	N	Y
6 Strickland	Y	Y	Y	N	N	N	Y
7 ***Hobson***	Y	Y	Y	N	Y	Y	Y
8 ***Boehner***	Y	Y	Y	Y	Y	Y	Y
9 Kaptur	Y	Y	Y	N	N	N	Y
10 Kucinich	Y	Y	Y	N	N	N	Y
11 Stokes	Y	Y	Y	N	N	N	?
12 ***Kasich***	Y	Y	Y	Y	?	N	Y
13 Brown	?	?	?	?	?	?	Y
14 Sawyer	Y	Y	Y	N	N	N	N
15 ***Pryce***	N	Y	Y	N	Y	Y	Y
16 ***Regula***	Y	Y	Y	N	Y	Y	Y
17 Traficant	Y	Y	Y	Y	Y	Y	Y
18 ***Ney***	–	–	+	N	Y	Y	Y
19 ***LaTourette***	N	Y	Y	N	Y	Y	Y
OKLAHOMA							
1 ***Largent***	N	N	Y	N	Y	N	Y
2 ***Coburn***	N	N	Y	Y	Y	Y	Y
3 ***Watkins***	Y	Y	Y	N	Y	N	Y
4 ***Watts***	N	Y	N	N	Y	N	Y
5 ***Istook***	?	?	?	?	?	?	?
6 ***Lucas***	N	Y	Y	N	Y	Y	Y
OREGON							
1 Furse	Y	Y	Y	N	N	N	N
2 ***Smith***	N	Y	Y	Y	Y	Y	Y
3 Blumenauer	Y	Y	Y	N	N	N	Y
4 DeFazio	Y	Y	Y	N	N	N	Y
5 Hooley	Y	Y	Y	N	N	N	Y
PENNSYLVANIA							
1 Brady	Y	Y	N	N	N	N	Y
2 Fattah	Y	Y	N	N	N	N	Y
3 Borski	Y	Y	N	N	N	N	Y
4 Klink	Y	Y	N	N	N	Y	N
5 ***Peterson***	Y	Y	Y	Y	Y	Y	Y
6 Holden	Y	Y	Y	N	N	N	Y
7 ***Weldon***	Y	Y	Y	N	N	N	Y
8 ***Greenwood***	Y	Y	Y	N	N	N	Y
9 ***Shuster***	Y	Y	Y	Y	Y	Y	Y
10 ***McDade***	Y	Y	Y	Y	?	Y	?
11 Kanjorski	Y	Y	Y	N	N	N	Y
12 Murtha	Y	Y	N	Y	N	N	Y
13 ***Fox***	Y	Y	Y	N	N	N	Y
14 Coyne	Y	Y	Y	N	N	N	Y
15 McHale	Y	Y	Y	N	N	N	Y
16 ***Pitts***	N	N	Y	Y	Y	Y	Y
17 ***Gekas***	Y	Y	Y	N	Y	Y	Y
18 Doyle	Y	Y	Y	N	N	N	Y
19 ***Goodling***	Y	Y	Y	N	Y	Y	Y
20 Mascara	Y	Y	Y	N	N	N	Y
21 ***English***	Y	Y	Y	N	Y	Y	Y
RHODE ISLAND							
1 Kennedy	Y	Y	Y	N	N	N	Y
2 Weygand	Y	Y	Y	N	N	N	Y
SOUTH CAROLINA							
1 ***Sanford***	N	Y	Y	N	N	N	Y
2 ***Spence***	Y	Y	Y	N	Y	Y	Y
3 ***Graham***	Y	Y	Y	N	Y	N	Y
4 ***Inglis***	Y	Y	Y	N	Y	N	Y
5 Spratt	Y	Y	Y	N	N	N	Y
6 Clyburn	Y	Y	N	N	N	N	Y
SOUTH DAKOTA							
AL ***Thune***	Y	Y	Y	N	Y	Y	Y

	371	372	373	374	375	376	377
TENNESSEE							
1 ***Jenkins***	Y	Y	Y	Y	Y	N	Y
2 ***Duncan***	Y	Y	Y	Y	N	N	Y
3 ***Wamp***	Y	Y	Y	N	N	N	Y
4 ***Hilleary***	Y	Y	Y	N	Y	Y	Y
5 Clement	Y	Y	Y	N	N	N	Y
6 Gordon	Y	Y	Y	N	N	N	Y
7 ***Bryant***	N	N	Y	Y	Y	Y	Y
8 Tanner	Y	Y	Y	N	N	N	Y
9 Ford	Y	Y	Y	N	N	N	Y
TEXAS							
1 Sandlin	Y	Y	Y	N	N	N	Y
2 Turner	Y	Y	Y	N	N	N	Y
3 ***Johnson, Sam***	N	Y	Y	Y	Y	Y	Y
4 Hall	N	Y	Y	N	Y	N	Y
5 ***Sessions***	N	Y	Y	Y	Y	Y	Y
6 ***Barton***	Y	N	Y	Y	Y	Y	Y
7 ***Archer***	Y	Y	Y	Y	Y	Y	Y
8 ***Brady***	Y	Y	Y	Y	Y	Y	Y
9 Lampson	Y	Y	Y	N	N	N	Y
10 Doggett	Y	Y	Y	N	N	N	Y
11 Edwards	Y	Y	Y	N	N	N	Y
12 ***Granger***	Y	Y	Y	N	Y	N	Y
13 ***Thornberry***	Y	Y	N	Y	Y	N	Y
14 ***Paul***	N	Y	Y	Y	Y	N	Y
15 Hinojosa	Y	Y	Y	N	N	N	Y
16 Reyes	Y	Y	Y	N	N	N	Y
17 Stenholm	N	Y	Y	N	N	N	Y
18 Jackson-Lee	Y	Y	Y	N	N	N	Y
19 ***Combest***	Y	Y	Y	N	Y	Y	Y
20 Gonzalez	?	?	?	?	?	?	?
21 ***Smith***	Y	Y	Y	Y	Y	Y	Y
22 ***DeLay***	?	?	?	?	?	?	Y
23 ***Bonilla***	N	N	N	Y	Y	N	Y
24 Frost	Y	Y	Y	N	N	N	Y
25 Bentsen	Y	N	N	N	N	N	Y
26 ***Armey***	Y	Y	Y	Y	Y	Y	Y
27 Ortiz	Y	Y	Y	N	N	N	+
28 Rodriguez	Y	Y	Y	N	N	N	Y
29 Green	Y	Y	Y	N	N	N	Y
30 Johnson, E.B.	Y	Y	N	N	N	N	Y
UTAH							
1 ***Hansen***	N	Y	Y	Y	Y	Y	Y
2 ***Cook***	Y	Y	Y	N	Y	Y	Y
3 ***Cannon***	Y	Y	Y	Y	Y	Y	Y
VERMONT							
AL *Sanders*	Y	Y	Y	N	N	N	Y
VIRGINIA							
1 ***Bateman***	Y	Y	Y	N	Y	N	Y
2 Pickett	N	Y	Y	N	N	N	Y
3 Scott	Y	Y	Y	N	Y	N	Y
4 Sisisky	Y	Y	Y	N	N	N	Y
5 Goode	Y	N	Y	N	Y	Y	Y
6 ***Goodlatte***	Y	N	Y	N	Y	Y	Y
7 ***Bliley***	Y	Y	Y	Y	Y	Y	Y
8 Moran	Y	Y	Y	N	N	N	N
9 Boucher	Y	Y	Y	N	N	N	Y
10 ***Wolf***	Y	Y	Y	N	Y	Y	Y
11 ***Davis***	N	Y	Y	Y	Y	N	Y
WASHINGTON							
1 ***White***	Y	Y	Y	N	N	N	Y
2 ***Metcalf***	Y	Y	Y	N	N	N	Y
3 ***Smith, Linda***	Y	Y	Y	N	N	N	Y
4 ***Hastings***	Y	Y	Y	N	Y	N	Y
5 ***Nethercutt***	Y	Y	Y	N	Y	Y	Y
6 Dicks	Y	Y	Y	N	N	N	Y
7 McDermott	Y	Y	Y	N	N	N	N
8 ***Dunn***	Y	N	N	N	Y	Y	Y
9 Smith, Adam	Y	N	Y	N	N	N	Y
WEST VIRGINIA							
1 Mollohan	Y	Y	N	N	Y	?	Y
2 Wise	Y	Y	Y	N	N	N	Y
3 Rahall	Y	Y	Y	N	N	Y	N
WISCONSIN							
1 ***Neumann***	Y	Y	Y	N	Y	N	Y
2 ***Klug***	Y	Y	Y	N	N	Y	Y
3 Kind	Y	Y	Y	N	N	N	Y
4 Kleczka	Y	Y	Y	N	N	N	Y
5 Barrett	Y	Y	Y	N	N	N	Y
6 ***Petri***	Y	Y	Y	N	Y	N	Y
7 Obey	Y	Y	Y	N	N	N	N
8 Johnson	Y	Y	Y	N	N	N	Y
9 ***Sensenbrenner***	Y	N	Y	N	Y	N	Y
WYOMING							
AL ***Cubin***	Y	Y	Y	Y	Y	Y	Y

Southern states - Ala., Ark., Fla., Ga., Ky., La., Miss., N.C., Okla., S.C., Tenn., Texas, Va.

House Votes 378, 379, 380, 381, 382, 383, 384

378. S J Res 54. Condemn Iraq for Breach of International Obligations/Passage. Gilman, R-N.Y., motion to suspend the rules and pass the bill that finds the government of Iraq in an "unacceptable" breach of its international obligations because of its repeated efforts to hamper the United Nations in finding and destroying Iraq's weapons of mass destruction. Motion agreed to 407-6: R 219-1; D 187-5 (ND 137-4, SD 50-1); I 1-0. Aug. 3, 1998. A two-thirds majority of those present and voting (276 in this case) is required for passage under suspension of the rules.

379. HR 2183. Campaign Finance Overhaul/Shays-Meehan Substitute. Shays, R-Conn., substitute amendment to the bill to overhaul campaign finance laws. The amendment would ban soft money contributions for federal elections, expand regulations on advertising that advocates a candidate and tighten the definition of what constitutes coordination with a federal candidate. Adopted 237-186: R 51-175; D 185-11 (ND 138-6, SD 47-5); I 1-0. Aug. 3, 1998. Final adoption is contingent upon the outcome of votes on other substitute amendments. Whichever gets the most votes and at least a majority prevails.

380. H Con Res 213. Sense of Congress Regarding European Union Imports/Passage. Crane, R-Ill., motion to suspend the rules and pass the bill to express the sense of Congress that the European Union is unfairly restricting U.S. agricultural imports and that eliminating restrictions should be a top priority in trade negotiations. Motion agreed to 420-4: R 222-2; D 197-2 (ND 144-2, SD 53-0); I 1-0. Aug. 4, 1998. A two-thirds majority of those present and voting (283 in this case) is required for passage under suspension of the rules.

381. HR 4276. Fiscal 1999 Commerce, Justice, State Appropriations/Legal Services Corporation Funding Increase. Mollohan, D-W.Va., amendment to increase funding for Legal Services Corporation from $141 million to $250 million. Adopted 255-170: R 57-168; D 197-2 (ND 146-0, SD 51-2); I 1-0. Aug. 4, 1998.

382. HR 4276. Fiscal 1999 Commerce, Justice, State Appropriations/Eliminate TV Marti Funding. Skaggs, D-Colo., amendment to eliminate the bill's appropriation for TV Marti, a federal government television broadcast to Cuba. Rejected 172-251: R 29-195; D 142-56 (ND 109-35, SD 33-21); I 1-0. Aug. 4, 1998.

383. HR 4276. Fiscal 1999 Commerce, Justice, State Appropriations/Decrease Economic Development Administration Funding. Souder, R-Ind., amendment to decrease funding for the Economic Development Administration, and transfer the funds to "drug court" programs for juvenile drug offenders. Rejected 91-327: R 88-133; D 3-193 (ND 0-142, SD 3-51); I 0-1. Aug. 4, 1998.

384. HR 4276. Fiscal 1999 Commerce, Justice, State Appropriations/Decrease Advanced Technology Program Funding. Bass, R-N.H., amendment to decrease the bill's appropriation for the Advanced Technology Program by $43 million, in an effort to prohibit the program from awarding new grants. Rejected 155-267: R 135-88; D 20-178 (ND 12-132, SD 8-46); I 0-1. Aug. 4, 1998.

Key

- **Y** Voted for (yea).
- **#** Paired for.
- **+** Announced for.
- **N** Voted against (nay).
- **X** Paired against.
- **−** Announced against.
- **P** Voted "present."
- **C** Voted "present" to avoid possible conflict of interest.
- **?** Did not vote or otherwise make a position known.

Democrats **Republicans** Independent

	378	379	380	381	382	383	384
ALABAMA							
1 *Callahan*	Y	N	Y	N	N	N	N
2 *Everett*	Y	N	Y	N	N	N	N
3 *Riley*	Y	N	Y	N	N	N	N
4 *Aderholt*	Y	N	Y	N	N	N	N
5 Cramer	Y	Y	Y	Y	N	N	N
6 *Bachus*	Y	Y	Y	N	N	Y	Y
7 Hilliard	?	?	Y	Y	Y	N	N
ALASKA							
AL *Young*	Y	N	Y	Y	N	N	N
ARIZONA							
1 *Salmon*	Y	N	N	N	N	Y	Y
2 Pastor	Y	Y	Y	Y	N	N	Y
3 *Stump*	Y	N	N	N	Y	Y	Y
4 *Shadegg*	Y	N	N	N	Y	Y	Y
5 *Kolbe*	Y	N	Y	N	Y	Y	Y
6 *Hayworth*	Y	N	N	N	N	Y	Y
ARKANSAS							
1 Berry	Y	Y	Y	Y	Y	N	Y
2 Snyder	Y	Y	Y	Y	Y	N	N
3 *Hutchinson*	?	N	N	N	N	N	N
4 Dickey	Y	N	N	N	N	N	N
CALIFORNIA							
1 *Riggs*	Y	N	Y	N	N	Y	Y
2 *Herger*	Y	N	Y	N	N	Y	Y
3 Fazio	Y	Y	Y	Y	Y	N	N
4 *Doolittle*	Y	N	N	N	N	Y	Y
5 Matsui	Y	Y	Y	Y	Y	N	N
6 Woolsey	Y	Y	Y	Y	Y	N	N
7 Miller	Y	Y	Y	Y	Y	N	N
8 Pelosi	Y	Y	Y	Y	Y	N	N
9 Lee	N	Y	Y	Y	Y	N	N
10 Tauscher	Y	Y	Y	Y	Y	N	N
11 *Pombo*	Y	N	Y	N	N	N	Y
12 Lantos	Y	Y	Y	Y	Y	N	N
13 Stark	Y	Y	Y	Y	Y	?	N
14 Eshoo	Y	Y	Y	Y	Y	N	N
15 *Campbell*	Y	Y	Y	N	N	N	Y
16 Lofgren	Y	Y	Y	Y	Y	N	N
17 Farr	Y	Y	Y	Y	Y	N	N
18 Condit	Y	Y	Y	Y	N	N	Y
19 *Radanovich*	Y	N	N	N	N	Y	Y
20 Dooley	Y	Y	Y	Y	Y	N	N
21 *Thomas*	Y	N	Y	N	N	N	N
22 Capps, L.	Y	Y	Y	Y	Y	N	N
23 *Gallegly*	Y	N	Y	N	N	N	N
24 Sherman	Y	Y	Y	Y	Y	N	N
25 *McKeon*	Y	N	Y	N	N	Y	Y
26 Berman	Y	Y	Y	Y	Y	N	N
27 *Rogan*	Y	N	Y	N	N	Y	Y
28 *Dreier*	Y	N	N	N	N	N	N
29 Waxman	Y	Y	Y	Y	Y	N	N
30 Becerra	Y	Y	Y	Y	Y	N	N
31 Martinez	?	?	Y	Y	Y	N	N
32 Dixon	Y	Y	Y	Y	Y	N	N
33 Roybal-Allard	Y	Y	Y	Y	Y	N	N
34 Torres	Y	Y	Y	Y	Y	N	N
35 Waters	N	Y	N	Y	N	N	N
36 Harman	Y	Y	Y	Y	Y	N	N
37 Millender-McD.	Y	Y	Y	Y	Y	−	N
38 Horn	Y	Y	Y	N	N	N	N

	378	379	380	381	382	383	384
39 *Royce*	Y	N	Y	N	N	Y	Y
40 *Lewis*	Y	N	Y	Y	N	N	N
41 *Kim*	Y	N	Y	N	N	N	N
42 Brown	Y	Y	Y	Y	Y	N	N
43 *Calvert*	Y	N	Y	N	N	N	N
44 *Bono, M.*	Y	N	Y	N	N	N	N
45 *Rohrabacher*	Y	N	N	N	N	Y	Y
46 Sanchez	Y	Y	Y	Y	Y	N	N
47 *Cox*	Y	N	Y	N	N	Y	Y
48 *Packard*	Y	N	Y	N	N	N	N
49 *Bilbray*	Y	Y	Y	Y	N	N	N
50 Filner	Y	Y	Y	Y	N	N	N
51 *Cunningham*	Y	N	?	?	?	?	?
52 *Hunter*	Y	N	N	N	N	Y	Y
COLORADO							
1 DeGette	Y	Y	Y	Y	Y	N	N
2 Skaggs	Y	Y	Y	Y	Y	N	N
3 *McInnis*	Y	N	?	?	?	?	?
4 *Schaffer*	Y	N	N	N	N	Y	Y
5 *Hefley*	Y	N	N	N	Y	Y	Y
6 *Schaefer*	Y	N	N	N	N	Y	Y
CONNECTICUT							
1 Kennelly	Y	Y	Y	Y	Y	N	N
2 Gejdenson	Y	Y	Y	Y	Y	N	N
3 DeLauro	Y	Y	Y	Y	Y	N	N
4 *Shays*	Y	Y	Y	Y	Y	N	N
5 Maloney	Y	Y	Y	Y	Y	N	N
6 *Johnson*	Y	Y	Y	Y	Y	N	N
DELAWARE							
AL *Castle*	Y	Y	Y	Y	N	N	N
FLORIDA							
1 *Scarborough*	Y	N	Y	N	N	Y	Y
2 Boyd	Y	Y	Y	Y	N	N	Y
3 Brown	Y	Y	Y	Y	N	N	N
4 *Fowler*	Y	N	Y	Y	N	Y	Y
5 Thurman	Y	Y	Y	Y	Y	N	N
6 *Stearns*	Y	N	Y	N	N	N	N
7 *Mica*	Y	N	Y	N	N	N	N
8 *McCollum*	Y	N	Y	N	N	Y	Y
9 *Bilirakis*	Y	N	Y	N	N	N	Y
10 *Young*	Y	N	Y	N	N	N	N
11 Davis	Y	Y	Y	Y	Y	N	N
12 *Canady*	Y	N	Y	N	N	N	N
13 *Miller*	Y	N	Y	N	N	N	N
14 *Goss*	Y	N	Y	N	N	N	N
15 *Weldon*	Y	N	Y	N	N	Y	Y
16 *Foley*	Y	Y	Y	N	N	N	N
17 Meek	Y	Y	Y	Y	Y	N	N
18 *Ros-Lehtinen*	Y	N	Y	N	N	N	N
19 Wexler	Y	Y	Y	Y	Y	N	N
20 Deutsch	Y	Y	Y	Y	N	N	N
21 *Diaz-Balart*	Y	N	Y	N	N	N	N
22 *Shaw*	Y	N	N	N	N	N	Y
23 Hastings	Y	Y	Y	Y	N	N	N
GEORGIA							
1 *Kingston*	Y	N	Y	N	N	Y	Y
2 Bishop	Y	N	Y	N	N	N	N
3 *Collins*	Y	N	Y	N	Y	N	N
4 McKinney	N	Y	Y	Y	Y	N	N
5 Lewis	Y	Y	Y	Y	Y	N	N
6 *Gingrich*	N						
7 *Barr*	Y	N	Y	N	Y	Y	Y
8 *Chambliss*	Y	N	Y	N	N	N	N
9 *Deal*	Y	Y	Y	Y	Y	Y	Y
10 *Norwood*	Y	N	N	N	N	N	Y
11 *Linder*	Y	N	N	N	N	N	Y
HAWAII							
1 Abercrombie	Y	Y	Y	Y	Y	N	N
2 Mink	Y	Y	Y	Y	Y	N	Y
IDAHO							
1 *Chenoweth*	Y	N	N	N	N	N	N
2 *Crapo*	Y	N	Y	N	N	N	N
ILLINOIS							
1 Rush	Y	Y	Y	Y	Y	N	N
2 Jackson	N	Y	Y	Y	Y	N	N
3 Lipinski	Y	Y	Y	Y	Y	N	N
4 Gutierrez	?	Y	Y	Y	N	N	N
5 Blagojevich	Y	Y	Y	Y	Y	N	N
6 *Hyde*	Y	N	N	N	N	N	N
7 Davis	Y	Y	Y	Y	Y	N	N
8 *Crane*	Y	N	N	Y	Y	Y	Y
9 Yates	Y	Y	Y	Y	Y	?	?
10 *Porter*	Y	Y	Y	Y	N	N	N
11 *Weller*	Y	N	Y	N	N	N	N
12 Costello	Y	Y	Y	Y	N	N	N
13 *Fawell*	Y	N	Y	N	N	N	N

ND Northern Democrats   SD Southern Democrats

	378	379	380	381	382	383	384
14 ***Hastert***	Y	N	Y	N	N	Y	Y
15 ***Ewing***	Y	N	Y	N	N	N	N
16 ***Manzullo***	Y	N	Y	N	N	Y	Y
17 Evans	Y	Y	Y	Y	Y	N	N
18 ***LaHood***	Y	N	Y	Y	N	N	N
19 Poshard	?	?	?	Y	Y	N	N
20 ***Shimkus***	Y	Y	Y	N	N	N	Y
INDIANA							
1 Visclosky	Y	Y	Y	Y	Y	N	Y
2 ***McIntosh***	Y	N	Y	N	N	Y	N
3 Roemer	Y	Y	Y	Y	Y	N	N
4 ***Souder***	Y	N	Y	N	N	Y	Y
5 ***Buyer***	Y	N	Y	N	N	N	Y
6 ***Burton***	Y	N	?	N	N	Y	Y
7 ***Pease***	Y	N	Y	N	N	Y	Y
8 ***Hostettler***	Y	N	Y	N	N	Y	Y
9 Hamilton	Y	Y	Y	Y	Y	N	N
10 Carson	Y	Y	Y	Y	Y	N	Y
IOWA							
1 ***Leach***	Y	Y	Y	Y	N	Y	Y
2 ***Nussle***	Y	N	Y	N	N	N	N
3 Boswell	Y	Y	Y	Y	N	N	N
4 ***Ganske***	Y	Y	Y	Y	Y	N	Y
5 ***Latham***	Y	N	Y	N	N	N	N
KANSAS							
1 ***Moran***	Y	N	Y	N	N	N	Y
2 ***Ryun***	Y	N	Y	N	N	Y	Y
3 ***Snowbarger***	Y	N	Y	N	N	Y	Y
4 ***Tiahrt***	Y	N	Y	N	N	Y	Y
KENTUCKY							
1 ***Whitfield***	Y	N	Y	N	N	N	Y
2 ***Lewis***	Y	N	Y	N	N	N	Y
3 ***Northup***	?	N	Y	N	N	N	N
4 ***Bunning***	Y	N	Y	N	N	N	Y
5 ***Rogers***	?	N	Y	N	N	N	N
6 Baesler	Y	Y	Y	Y	Y	N	Y
LOUISIANA							
1 ***Livingston***	Y	N	Y	N	N	N	Y
2 Jefferson	Y	Y	Y	Y	Y	N	N
3 ***Tauzin***	Y	N	Y	Y	N	Y	N
4 ***McCrery***	Y	N	Y	Y	N	N	Y
5 ***Cooksey***	Y	N	Y	N	N	N	N
6 ***Baker***	Y	N	Y	N	N	N	Y
7 John	Y	N	Y	Y	N	N	N
MAINE							
1 Allen	Y	Y	Y	Y	Y	N	N
2 Baldacci	Y	Y	Y	Y	N	N	N
MARYLAND							
1 ***Gilchrest***	Y	Y	Y	Y	Y	N	N
2 ***Ehrlich***	Y	N	Y	Y	N	Y	Y
3 Cardin	Y	Y	Y	Y	N	N	N
4 Wynn	Y	Y	Y	Y	Y	N	N
5 Hoyer	Y	Y	Y	Y	Y	N	N
6 ***Bartlett***	Y	N	Y	N	N	N	N
7 Cummings	Y	Y	Y	Y	Y	N	N
8 ***Morella***	Y	Y	Y	Y	Y	N	N
MASSACHUSETTS							
1 Olver	?	Y	Y	Y	Y	N	N
2 Neal	Y	Y	Y	Y	Y	N	N
3 McGovern	Y	Y	Y	Y	Y	N	N
4 Frank	Y	Y	Y	Y	Y	N	N
5 Meehan	Y	Y	Y	Y	Y	N	N
6 Tierney	Y	Y	Y	Y	Y	N	N
7 Markey	Y	Y	Y	Y	Y	N	N
8 Kennedy	Y	Y	Y	Y	N	N	N
9 Moakley	Y	Y	Y	Y	Y	?	?
10 Delahunt	Y	Y	Y	Y	Y	N	N
MICHIGAN							
1 Stupak	Y	N	Y	Y	Y	N	N
2 ***Hoekstra***	Y	N	Y	N	Y	Y	Y
3 ***Ehlers***	Y	N	Y	Y	Y	N	N
4 ***Camp***	Y	N	Y	Y	Y	Y	Y
5 Barcia	Y	Y	Y	Y	N	N	N
6 ***Upton***	Y	Y	Y	Y	Y	Y	Y
7 ***Smith***	Y	Y	Y	N	N	Y	Y
8 Stabenow	Y	Y	Y	Y	Y	N	N
9 Kildee	Y	Y	Y	Y	Y	N	N
10 Bonior	N	Y	Y	Y	Y	N	N
11 ***Knollenberg***	Y	N	Y	N	N	N	Y
12 Levin	Y	Y	Y	Y	Y	N	N
13 Rivers	Y	Y	Y	Y	Y	N	N
14 Conyers	?	?	?	?	?	?	?
15 Kilpatrick	+	+	?	?	?	?	?
16 Dingell	Y	Y	Y	Y	Y	N	N
MINNESOTA							
1 ***Gutknecht***	Y	N	Y	N	N	Y	Y
2 Minge	Y	Y	Y	Y	Y	N	N
3 ***Ramstad***	Y	Y	Y	Y	Y	Y	Y
4 Vento	Y	Y	Y	Y	Y	N	N
5 Sabo	Y	Y	Y	Y	Y	N	N
6 Luther	Y	Y	Y	Y	Y	N	Y
7 Peterson	Y	N	Y	Y	Y	N	Y
8 Oberstar	+	+	Y	Y	Y	N	N
MISSISSIPPI							
1 ***Wicker***	Y	N	Y	N	N	N	N
2 Thompson	Y	Y	Y	Y	Y	N	N
3 ***Pickering***	Y	N	Y	N	N	–	+
4 ***Parker***	Y	Y	Y	N	Y	N	N
5 Taylor	Y	Y	Y	N	Y	N	Y
MISSOURI							
1 Clay	Y	Y	Y	Y	?	?	?
2 ***Talent***	Y	N	Y	N	N	Y	Y
3 Gephardt	Y	Y	Y	Y	N	N	N
4 Skelton	Y	Y	Y	Y	N	N	Y
5 McCarthy	Y	Y	+	+	+	–	–
6 Danner	Y	Y	Y	Y	Y	N	N
7 ***Blunt***	Y	N	Y	N	N	Y	Y
8 ***Emerson***	Y	N	Y	N	N	N	N
9 ***Hulshof***	Y	N	Y	Y	N	N	Y
MONTANA							
AL ***Hill***	Y	N	Y	N	N	N	Y
NEBRASKA							
1 ***Bereuter***	Y	Y	Y	N	N	N	N
2 ***Christensen***	?	–	Y	N	Y	Y	Y
3 ***Barrett***	Y	Y	Y	N	Y	Y	N
NEVADA							
1 ***Ensign***	Y	N	Y	N	N	N	Y
2 ***Gibbons***	Y	N	Y	N	Y	N	Y
NEW HAMPSHIRE							
1 ***Sununu***	Y	N	Y	N	Y	Y	Y
2 ***Bass***	Y	Y	Y	N	N	N	Y
NEW JERSEY							
1 Andrews	Y	Y	Y	Y	N	N	Y
2 ***LoBiondo***	Y	Y	Y	N	N	N	Y
3 ***Saxton***	Y	Y	Y	N	N	N	N
4 ***Smith***	Y	N	Y	Y	N	N	N
5 ***Roukema***	Y	Y	Y	N	Y	Y	Y
6 Pallone	Y	Y	Y	Y	N	N	N
7 ***Franks***	Y	Y	Y	Y	N	N	N
8 Pascrell	Y	Y	Y	Y	N	N	N
9 Rothman	Y	Y	Y	Y	N	N	N
10 Payne	Y	Y	Y	Y	Y	N	N
11 ***Frelinghuysen***	Y	Y	Y	Y	N	N	Y
12 ***Pappas***	Y	N	Y	N	N	N	Y
13 Menendez	Y	Y	Y	Y	N	N	N
NEW MEXICO							
1 ***Wilson***	Y	N	Y	Y	N	N	N
2 ***Skeen***	Y	N	Y	N	N	N	N
3 ***Redmond***	Y	N	Y	N	N	N	Y
NEW YORK							
1 ***Forbes***	Y	Y	Y	Y	N	N	N
2 ***Lazio***	Y	Y	Y	Y	N	N	Y
3 ***King***	Y	N	Y	N	N	N	N
4 McCarthy	?	Y	Y	Y	Y	N	N
5 Ackerman	Y	Y	Y	Y	N	N	N
6 Meeks	Y	Y	Y	Y	Y	N	N
7 Manton	Y	Y	Y	Y	N	N	N
8 Nadler	Y	Y	Y	Y	Y	N	N
9 Schumer	Y	Y	Y	?	Y	N	Y
10 Towns	?	?	?	?	?	?	?
11 Owens	Y	Y	Y	Y	Y	N	N
12 Velázquez	Y	Y	Y	Y	Y	N	N
13 ***Fossella***	Y	N	Y	N	N	N	Y
14 Maloney	Y	Y	Y	Y	Y	N	N
15 Rangel	Y	Y	Y	Y	Y	N	N
16 Serrano	Y	Y	Y	Y	Y	N	N
17 Engel	Y	Y	Y	Y	Y	N	N
18 Lowey	Y	Y	Y	Y	Y	N	N
19 ***Kelly***	Y	Y	Y	N	Y	N	N
20 ***Gilman***	Y	Y	Y	Y	N	Y	Y
21 McNulty	Y	Y	Y	Y	N	N	N
22 ***Solomon***	Y	N	Y	N	N	Y	Y
23 ***Boehlert***	Y	Y	Y	Y	Y	N	N
24 ***McHugh***	Y	N	Y	Y	N	N	Y
25 ***Walsh***	Y	Y	Y	Y	Y	N	N
26 Hinchey	Y	Y	Y	Y	Y	N	N
27 ***Paxon***	Y	N	Y	N	N	Y	Y
28 Slaughter	Y	Y	Y	Y	Y	N	N
29 LaFalce	Y	Y	Y	Y	Y	N	N
30 ***Quinn***	Y	Y	Y	Y	Y	N	N
31 ***Houghton***	Y	Y	Y	Y	Y	N	N
NORTH CAROLINA							
1 Clayton	Y	Y	Y	Y	Y	N	N
2 Etheridge	Y	Y	Y	Y	Y	N	N
3 ***Jones***	Y	N	Y	N	N	N	N
4 Price	Y	Y	Y	Y	Y	N	N
5 ***Burr***	Y	N	Y	N	N	N	N
6 ***Coble***	Y	N	Y	N	Y	Y	Y
7 McIntyre	Y	Y	Y	Y	Y	N	Y
8 Hefner	Y	Y	Y	Y	Y	N	N
9 ***Myrick***	Y	N	Y	N	N	Y	Y
10 ***Ballenger***	Y	N	Y	N	N	Y	Y
11 ***Taylor***	Y	N	Y	N	N	N	N
12 Watt	Y	Y	Y	Y	Y	N	N
NORTH DAKOTA							
AL Pomeroy	?	?	Y	Y	Y	N	N
OHIO							
1 ***Chabot***	Y	N	Y	N	N	Y	Y
2 ***Portman***	Y	N	Y	N	N	Y	Y
3 Hall	Y	Y	Y	Y	?	N	N
4 ***Oxley***	Y	N	Y	N	N	?	?
5 ***Gillmor***	Y	Y	Y	N	N	N	N
6 Strickland	Y	Y	Y	Y	Y	N	N
7 ***Hobson***	Y	N	Y	N	N	Y	Y
8 ***Boehner***	Y	N	Y	N	N	Y	Y
9 Kaptur	Y	Y	Y	Y	Y	N	N
10 Kucinich	Y	Y	Y	Y	Y	N	N
11 Stokes	Y	Y	Y	Y	Y	N	N
12 ***Kasich***	Y	N	Y	N	N	Y	Y
13 Brown	Y	Y	Y	Y	Y	N	N
14 Sawyer	Y	Y	Y	Y	Y	N	N
15 ***Pryce***	Y	N	Y	N	Y	Y	Y
16 ***Regula***	Y	Y	Y	Y	Y	N	N
17 Traficant	Y	N	Y	Y	N	N	N
18 ***Ney***	Y	N	Y	Y	N	N	Y
19 ***LaTourette***	Y	Y	Y	Y	N	N	N
OKLAHOMA							
1 ***Largent***	Y	N	Y	Y	N	Y	Y
2 ***Coburn***	Y	N	Y	N	N	Y	Y
3 ***Watkins***	Y	N	Y	N	N	N	Y
4 ***Watts***	Y	N	Y	N	N	N	Y
5 ***Istook***	?	?	Y	N	N	Y	Y
6 ***Lucas***	Y	N	Y	N	N	N	N
OREGON							
1 Furse	Y	Y	Y	Y	?	N	N
2 ***Smith***	Y	N	Y	N	N	N	N
3 Blumenauer	Y	Y	Y	Y	Y	N	N
4 DeFazio	Y	Y	N	Y	Y	N	Y
5 Hooley	Y	Y	Y	Y	Y	N	N
PENNSYLVANIA							
1 Brady	Y	Y	Y	Y	Y	N	N
2 Fattah	Y	Y	Y	Y	Y	N	N
3 Borski	Y	Y	Y	Y	Y	N	N
4 Klink	Y	Y	Y	Y	Y	N	N
5 ***Peterson***	Y	N	Y	N	N	N	N
6 Holden	Y	Y	Y	Y	Y	N	N
7 ***Weldon***	Y	Y	Y	Y	N	N	N
8 ***Greenwood***	Y	Y	Y	Y	N	N	Y
9 ***Shuster***	Y	N	Y	N	Y	N	Y
10 ***McDade***	?	Y	Y	Y	N	?	N
11 Kanjorski	Y	Y	Y	Y	Y	N	N
12 Murtha	Y	N	Y	Y	Y	N	N
13 ***Fox***	Y	Y	Y	Y	N	Y	Y
14 Coyne	Y	Y	Y	Y	N	N	N
15 McHale	Y	Y	Y	Y	Y	N	N
16 ***Pitts***	Y	N	Y	N	N	Y	Y
17 ***Gekas***	Y	N	Y	Y	N	N	N
18 Doyle	Y	Y	Y	Y	Y	N	N
19 ***Goodling***	Y	N	Y	Y	N	N	Y
20 Mascara	Y	Y	Y	Y	Y	N	N
21 ***English***	Y	N	Y	N	N	N	N
RHODE ISLAND							
1 Kennedy	Y	Y	Y	Y	N	N	N
2 Weygand	Y	Y	Y	Y	Y	N	N
SOUTH CAROLINA							
1 ***Sanford***	Y	Y	Y	N	N	Y	Y
2 ***Spence***	Y	N	Y	N	N	N	N
3 ***Graham***	Y	Y	Y	N	N	N	N
4 ***Inglis***	Y	N	Y	N	N	Y	N
5 Spratt	Y	Y	Y	Y	N	N	N
6 Clyburn	Y	Y	Y	Y	Y	N	N
SOUTH DAKOTA							
AL ***Thune***	Y	N	Y	N	N	N	Y
TENNESSEE							
1 ***Jenkins***	Y	N	Y	N	N	N	N
2 ***Duncan***	Y	Y	Y	N	N	N	Y
3 ***Wamp***	?	Y	Y	N	N	N	Y
4 ***Hilleary***	Y	N	Y	N	N	N	Y
5 Clement	Y	Y	Y	Y	Y	N	N
6 Gordon	Y	Y	Y	Y	N	N	N
7 ***Bryant***	Y	N	Y	N	N	N	Y
8 Tanner	Y	Y	Y	Y	Y	N	N
9 Ford	Y	Y	Y	Y	Y	N	N
TEXAS							
1 Sandlin	Y	Y	Y	Y	Y	N	N
2 Turner	Y	Y	Y	Y	Y	N	Y
3 ***Johnson, Sam***	Y	N	Y	N	N	Y	Y
4 Hall	Y	N	Y	N	N	Y	Y
5 ***Sessions***	Y	N	Y	N	N	Y	N
6 ***Barton***	Y	N	Y	N	N	Y	Y
7 ***Archer***	Y	N	Y	N	N	?	N
8 ***Brady***	Y	N	Y	N	N	N	N
9 Lampson	Y	Y	Y	Y	N	N	N
10 Doggett	Y	Y	Y	Y	Y	Y	N
11 Edwards	Y	Y	Y	Y	Y	N	N
12 ***Granger***	Y	N	Y	N	N	N	Y
13 ***Thornberry***	Y	N	Y	N	N	Y	Y
14 ***Paul***	N	N	N	N	Y	Y	Y
15 Hinojosa	Y	Y	Y	Y	Y	N	N
16 Reyes	Y	Y	Y	Y	N	N	N
17 Stenholm	Y	Y	Y	Y	N	N	N
18 Jackson-Lee	Y	Y	Y	Y	N	N	N
19 ***Combest***	Y	N	Y	N	N	N	N
20 Gonzalez	?	?	?	?	?	?	?
21 ***Smith***	Y	N	Y	N	N	N	N
22 ***DeLay***	Y	N	Y	N	N	Y	Y
23 ***Bonilla***	Y	N	Y	N	N	N	N
24 Frost	Y	Y	Y	Y	Y	N	N
25 Bentsen	Y	Y	Y	Y	Y	N	N
26 ***Armey***	Y	N	Y	N	N	Y	Y
27 Ortiz	+	+	Y	Y	N	N	N
28 Rodriguez	Y	Y	Y	Y	Y	N	N
29 Green	Y	Y	Y	Y	N	N	N
30 Johnson, E.B.	Y	Y	Y	Y	Y	N	N
UTAH							
1 ***Hansen***	Y	N	Y	N	N	N	Y
2 ***Cook***	Y	Y	Y	N	N	N	N
3 ***Cannon***	Y	N	Y	N	N	Y	Y
VERMONT							
AL *Sanders*	Y	Y	Y	Y	Y	N	N
VIRGINIA							
1 ***Bateman***	Y	N	Y	N	N	Y	N
2 Pickett	Y	Y	Y	Y	Y	N	N
3 Scott	Y	N	Y	Y	Y	N	N
4 Sisisky	Y	Y	Y	Y	N	N	N
5 Goode	Y	N	?	?	N	N	N
6 ***Goodlatte***	Y	N	Y	N	N	N	N
7 ***Bliley***	Y	N	Y	N	N	N	N
8 Moran	?	Y	Y	Y	Y	N	N
9 Boucher	Y	Y	Y	Y	Y	N	N
10 ***Wolf***	Y	N	Y	N	?	Y	N
11 ***Davis***	Y	N	Y	Y	N	N	N
WASHINGTON							
1 ***White***	Y	N	Y	Y	N	N	Y
2 ***Metcalf***	Y	Y	Y	N	N	N	Y
3 ***Smith, Linda***	Y	Y	Y	N	N	Y	Y
4 ***Hastings***	Y	N	Y	N	N	N	Y
5 ***Nethercutt***	Y	N	Y	Y	N	N	Y
6 Dicks	Y	Y	Y	Y	Y	N	N
7 McDermott	Y	Y	Y	Y	Y	N	N
8 ***Dunn***	Y	N	Y	N	N	N	Y
9 Smith, Adam	Y	Y	Y	Y	Y	N	N
WEST VIRGINIA							
1 Mollohan	Y	N	Y	Y	Y	N	N
2 Wise	Y	Y	Y	Y	N	N	N
3 Rahall	Y	N	Y	Y	Y	N	N
WISCONSIN							
1 ***Neumann***	Y	N	Y	N	Y	Y	Y
2 ***Klug***	Y	Y	Y	Y	N	N	N
3 Kind	Y	Y	Y	Y	Y	N	N
4 Kleczka	Y	Y	Y	Y	Y	N	N
5 Barrett	Y	Y	Y	Y	Y	N	Y
6 ***Petri***	Y	N	Y	N	N	N	Y
7 Obey	Y	Y	Y	Y	Y	N	N
8 Johnson	Y	Y	Y	Y	Y	N	N
9 ***Sensenbrenner***	Y	N	Y	N	Y	Y	Y
WYOMING							
AL ***Cubin***	Y	N	Y	N	N	Y	Y

Southern states - Ala., Ark., Fla., Ga., Ky., La., Miss., N.C., Okla., S.C., Tenn., Texas, Va.

House Votes 385, 386, 387, 388, 389, 390, 391

Key

- Y Voted for (yea).
- # Paired for.
- + Announced for.
- N Voted against (nay).
- X Paired against.
- − Announced against.
- P Voted "present."
- C Voted "present" to avoid possible conflict of interest.
- ? Did not vote or otherwise make a position known.

Democrats   **Republicans**
Independent

385. HR 4276. Fiscal 1999 Commerce, Justice, State Appropriations/Transfer Funds From "Truth-In-Sentencing" Programs to Prevention Programs. Scott, D-Va., amendment to transfer $105 million from prison "truth-in-sentencing" incentive grants to drug treatment and crime prevention programs. Rejected 149-271: R 12-210; D 136-61 (ND 102-41, SD 34-20); I 1-0. Aug. 4, 1998.

386. HR 4276. Fiscal 1999 Commerce, Justice, State Appropriations/Decrease Public Broadcasting Funding. Gutknecht, R-Minn., amendment to cut funding for public broadcasting by $6 million. Rejected 136-286: R 124-99; D 12-186 (ND 5-139, SD 7-47); I 0-1. Aug. 4, 1998.

387. HR 4276. Fiscal 1999 Commerce, Justice, State Appropriations/Fund Abortion Services for Women in Prison. DeGette, D-Ill., amendment to strike language in the bill that prohibits federal funds from being used for abortions for women in prison. Rejected 148-271: R 13-209; D 134-62 (ND 103-39, SD 31-23); I 1-0. Aug. 4, 1998.

388. HR 4276. Fiscal 1999 Commerce, Justice, State Appropriations/Allow Census Bureau to Develop Statistical Sampling. Mollohan, D-W.Va., amendment to strike the bill's restrictions on funding for the year 2000 census which would allow the Census Bureau to continue to plan, test and prepare to implement statistical sampling methods along with statistical sampling. Rejected 201-227: R 2-222; D 198-5 (ND 147-2, SD 51-3); I 1-0. Aug. 5, 1998.

389. HR 4276. Fiscal 1999 Commerce, Justice, State Appropriations/Increase Clean Water Initiative Funding. Pallone, D-N.J., amendment to fully fund the Clean Water Initiative by providing $8 million for states to develop and implement plans to control non-point course pollution. Rejected 158-267: R 44-179; D 114-87 (ND 101-47, SD 13-40); I 0-1. Aug. 5, 1998.

390. HR 4276. Fiscal 1999 Commerce, Justice, State Appropriations/Increase Public Telecommunication Facilities Program Funding. Engel, D-N.Y., amendment to provide an additional $5 million to the Public Telecommunication Facilities Planning Program. Rejected 168-259: R 26-196; D 141-63 (ND 108-42, SD 33-21); I 1-0. Aug. 5, 1998.

391. HR 4276. Fiscal 1999 Commerce, Justice, State Appropriations/Eliminate Funding for Advanced Technology Program. Royce, R-Calif., amendment to eliminate funding for the Advanced Technology Program and direct it to close out all operations. Rejected 137-291: R 127-98; D 10-192 (ND 7-141, SD 3-51); I 0-1. Aug. 5, 1998.

	385	386	387	388	389	390	391
ALABAMA							
1 *Callahan*	N	N	N	N	N	N	N
2 *Everett*	N	N	N	N	N	N	N
3 *Riley*	N	Y	N	N	N	Y	N
4 *Aderholt*	N	N	N	N	N	N	N
5 Cramer	N	N	N	Y	N	N	N
6 *Bachus*	N	Y	N	N	N	Y	N
7 Hilliard	Y	N	Y	Y	N	Y	N
ALASKA							
AL *Young*	N	N	N	N	N	N	N
ARIZONA							
1 *Salmon*	N	N	N	N	N	N	Y
2 Pastor	Y	Y	Y	Y	N	Y	N
3 *Stump*	N	Y	N	N	N	N	Y
4 *Shadegg*	N	Y	N	N	N	N	Y
5 *Kolbe*	N	N	N	N	N	N	N
6 *Hayworth*	N	Y	N	N	N	N	Y
ARKANSAS							
1 Berry	N	Y	N	Y	N	Y	Y
2 Snyder	Y	N	N	Y	Y	N	N
3 *Hutchinson*	N	N	N	N	N	N	Y
4 *Dickey*	N	N	N	N	N	N	Y
CALIFORNIA							
1 *Riggs*	N	Y	N	N	N	N	Y
2 *Herger*	N	Y	N	N	N	Y	Y
3 Fazio	Y	N	Y	Y	?	N	N
4 *Doolittle*	N	Y	N	N	N	N	Y
5 Matsui	Y	N	Y	Y	Y	Y	N
6 Woolsey	Y	N	Y	Y	Y	Y	N
7 Miller	Y	N	Y	Y	Y	Y	N
8 Pelosi	Y	N	Y	Y	Y	Y	N
9 Lee	Y	N	Y	Y	Y	Y	N
10 Tauscher	N	N	Y	Y	Y	Y	N
11 *Pombo*	N	Y	N	N	N	Y	Y
12 Lantos	Y	N	Y	Y	Y	Y	N
13 Stark	Y	N	Y	Y	Y	Y	N
14 Eshoo	Y	N	Y	Y	Y	Y	N
15 *Campbell*	Y	Y	Y	N	Y	Y	Y
16 Lofgren	Y	N	Y	Y	Y	Y	N
17 Farr	Y	N	Y	Y	Y	Y	N
18 Condit	Y	N	N	N	N	N	N
19 *Radanovich*	N	Y	N	N	N	Y	Y
20 Dooley	Y	N	Y	Y	N	Y	N
21 *Thomas*	N	N	N	N	N	N	N
22 Capps, L.	Y	N	Y	Y	Y	Y	N
23 *Gallegly*	N	Y	N	N	N	N	Y
24 Sherman	Y	N	Y	Y	Y	Y	N
25 *McKeon*	N	N	N	N	N	N	N
26 Berman	Y	N	Y	Y	Y	Y	N
27 *Rogan*	N	Y	N	N	N	N	Y
28 *Dreier*	N	N	N	N	N	N	N
29 Waxman	Y	N	Y	Y	Y	Y	N
30 Becerra	Y	N	Y	Y	Y	Y	N
31 Martinez	N	N	Y	Y	N	N	N
32 Dixon	Y	N	Y	Y	Y	Y	N
33 Roybal-Allard	Y	N	Y	Y	Y	Y	N
34 Torres	Y	N	Y	Y	Y	Y	N
35 Waters	Y	N	Y	?	Y	Y	N
36 Harman	N	N	Y	Y	Y	Y	N
37 Millender-McD.	+	N	Y	Y	Y	Y	N
38 Horn	N	N	Y	N	N	N	N

	385	386	387	388	389	390	391
39 *Royce*	N	Y	N	N	Y	N	Y
40 *Lewis*	N	N	N	N	N	N	N
41 *Kim*	N	N	N	N	N	N	N
42 Brown	Y	N	Y	N	Y	N	N
43 *Calvert*	N	N	N	N	N	N	N
44 *Bono, M.*	N	N	N	N	N	N	N
45 *Rohrabacher*	N	Y	N	N	N	N	Y
46 Sanchez	Y	N	Y	Y	Y	Y	N
47 *Cox*	N	Y	N	N	?	N	Y
48 *Packard*	N	N	N	N	N	N	N
49 *Bilbray*	N	N	N	N	N	Y	N
50 Filner	Y	N	Y	Y	Y	Y	N
51 *Cunningham*	?	?	?	?	?	?	?
52 *Hunter*	N	Y	N	N	N	N	N
COLORADO							
1 DeGette	Y	N	Y	Y	Y	Y	N
2 Skaggs	Y	N	Y	N	Y	?	N
3 *McInnis*	?	?	?	?	N	?	Y
4 *Schaffer*	N	Y	N	N	N	N	Y
5 *Hefley*	N	Y	N	N	N	Y	N
6 *Schaefer*	N	N	N	N	N	N	N
CONNECTICUT							
1 Kennelly	N	Y	Y	Y	Y	Y	N
2 Gejdenson	N	N	Y	Y	Y	Y	N
3 DeLauro	N	N	Y	Y	Y	Y	N
4 *Shays*	N	Y	Y	Y	Y	Y	N
5 Maloney	N	N	Y	Y	Y	Y	N
6 *Johnson*	N	Y	Y	N	Y	Y	N
DELAWARE							
AL *Castle*	N	N	N	N	Y	Y	N
FLORIDA							
1 *Scarborough*	N	N	N	N	N	N	N
2 Boyd	N	N	Y	N	Y	N	N
3 Brown	Y	N	Y	N	N	N	N
4 *Fowler*	N	N	N	N	N	N	N
5 Thurman	N	N	Y	Y	N	N	N
6 *Stearns*	N	Y	N	N	N	N	Y
7 *Mica*	N	N	N	N	N	N	N
8 *McCollum*	N	N	N	N	N	N	N
9 *Bilirakis*	N	N	N	N	N	N	N
10 *Young*	N	N	N	N	N	N	N
11 Davis	Y	N	Y	Y	N	N	N
12 *Canady*	N	N	N	N	N	N	N
13 *Miller*	N	Y	N	N	N	N	Y
14 *Goss*	N	Y	N	N	N	N	Y
15 *Weldon*	N	Y	N	N	N	N	Y
16 *Foley*	N	Y	N	Y	N	Y	N
17 Meek	N	N	Y	N	Y	N	N
18 *Ros-Lehtinen*	N	N	N	N	N	N	N
19 Wexler	N	N	Y	Y	N	Y	N
20 Deutsch	N	Y	Y	N	Y	Y	N
21 *Diaz-Balart*	N	N	N	N	N	N	N
22 *Shaw*	N	N	N	N	N	N	N
23 Hastings	N	N	Y	N	Y	Y	N
GEORGIA							
1 *Kingston*	N	Y	N	N	N	?	Y
2 Bishop	Y	N	Y	Y	Y	Y	N
3 *Collins*	N	N	N	N	N	N	Y
4 McKinney	Y	N	Y	Y	Y	Y	N
5 Lewis	Y	N	Y	Y	Y	Y	N
6 *Gingrich*				N			
7 *Barr*	N	Y	N	N	N	N	Y
8 *Chambliss*	N	N	N	N	N	N	N
9 *Deal*	N	Y	N	N	N	N	Y
10 *Norwood*	N	Y	N	N	N	N	Y
11 *Linder*	N	Y	N	N	N	N	Y
HAWAII							
1 Abercrombie	Y	N	Y	Y	N	Y	N
2 Mink	Y	N	Y	Y	Y	Y	N
IDAHO							
1 *Chenoweth*	N	Y	N	N	N	N	Y
2 *Crapo*	N	Y	N	N	N	N	Y
ILLINOIS							
1 Rush	Y	N	Y	Y	Y	Y	N
2 Jackson	Y	N	Y	Y	Y	N	N
3 Lipinski	N	N	N	N	N	N	N
4 Gutierrez	Y	N	Y	Y	Y	Y	N
5 Blagojevich	N	N	Y	Y	Y	Y	N
6 *Hyde*	N	N	N	N	N	N	N
7 Davis	Y	N	Y	Y	N	Y	N
8 *Crane*	N	Y	N	N	N	N	Y
9 Yates	?	?	?	Y	N	Y	N
10 *Porter*	N	N	N	N	N	N	N
11 *Weller*	N	Y	?	N	Y	N	Y
12 Costello	N	N	N	N	N	N	N
13 *Fawell*	N	N	N	Y	N	Y	N

ND Northern Democrats   SD Southern Democrats

	385	386	387	388	389	390	391
14 **Hastert**	N	Y	N	N	N	N	Y
15 **Ewing**	N	N	N	N	Y	N	N
16 **Manzullo**	N	Y	N	N	N	N	Y
17 Evans	N	N	Y	Y	N	N	N
18 **LaHood**	N	N	N	N	N	Y	N
19 Poshard	N	N	N	Y	Y	N	N
20 **Shimkus**	N	N	N	N	N	N	Y
INDIANA							
1 Visclosky	Y	N	N	Y	Y	Y	Y
2 **McIntosh**	N	Y	N	N	N	N	Y
3 Roemer	N	N	N	Y	Y	Y	N
4 **Souder**	N	Y	N	N	N	N	N
5 **Buyer**	N	Y	N	N	N	N	N
6 **Burton**	N	Y	N	N	N	N	N
7 **Pease**	Y	Y	N	N	N	Y	Y
8 **Hostettler**	N	Y	N	N	N	N	Y
9 Hamilton	Y	N	N	Y	Y	Y	N
10 Carson	Y	N	Y	Y	Y	Y	N
IOWA							
1 **Leach**	Y	N	N	N	Y	Y	Y
2 **Nussle**	N	N	N	N	N	N	Y
3 Boswell	N	N	Y	N	N	Y	N
4 **Ganske**	N	N	N	N	N	Y	Y
5 **Latham**	N	N	N	N	N	N	Y
KANSAS							
1 **Moran**	N	N	N	N	N	Y	Y
2 **Ryun**	N	Y	N	N	N	N	Y
3 **Snowbarger**	N	Y	N	N	N	Y	Y
4 **Tiahrt**	N	Y	N	N	N	Y	Y
KENTUCKY							
1 **Whitfield**	N	N	N	N	N	N	Y
2 **Lewis**	N	N	N	N	N	N	N
3 **Northup**	N	N	N	N	N	N	N
4 **Bunning**	N	N	N	N	N	N	N
5 **Rogers**	N	N	N	N	N	N	N
6 Baesler	N	N	Y	Y	N	Y	N
LOUISIANA							
1 **Livingston**	N	N	N	N	N	N	Y
2 Jefferson	Y	N	Y	Y	N	N	N
3 **Tauzin**	N	N	N	N	N	N	N
4 **McCrery**	N	N	N	N	N	N	N
5 **Cooksey**	N	N	N	N	N	N	Y
6 **Baker**	N	N	N	N	N	N	N
7 John	N	N	N	Y	N	N	N
MAINE							
1 Allen	Y	N	Y	Y	Y	N	N
2 Baldacci	Y	N	Y	Y	Y	N	N
MARYLAND							
1 **Gilchrest**	N	N	N	N	Y	N	N
2 **Ehrlich**	N	Y	N	N	N	N	Y
3 Cardin	Y	N	Y	Y	Y	Y	N
4 Wynn	Y	N	Y	Y	Y	Y	N
5 Hoyer	Y	N	Y	Y	Y	Y	N
6 **Bartlett**	N	Y	N	N	N	N	N
7 Cummings	Y	N	Y	Y	Y	Y	N
8 **Morella**	Y	N	Y	Y	Y	Y	N
MASSACHUSETTS							
1 Olver	Y	N	Y	Y	Y	Y	N
2 Neal	Y	N	N	Y	Y	N	N
3 McGovern	Y	N	Y	Y	Y	Y	N
4 Frank	Y	N	Y	Y	Y	Y	N
5 Meehan	Y	Y	Y	Y	Y	Y	N
6 Tierney	Y	N	Y	Y	Y	Y	N
7 Markey	Y	N	Y	Y	Y	Y	N
8 Kennedy	Y	N	Y	Y	Y	N	N
9 Moakley	?	?	?	Y	Y	N	N
10 Delahunt	Y	N	Y	Y	Y	N	N
MICHIGAN							
1 Stupak	N	N	N	Y	N	N	N
2 **Hoekstra**	N	Y	N	N	Y	N	Y
3 **Ehlers**	N	N	N	N	Y	N	N
4 **Camp**	N	Y	N	N	N	N	Y
5 Barcia	N	N	N	Y	Y	Y	N
6 **Upton**	N	Y	N	N	Y	N	Y
7 **Smith**	N	Y	N	N	N	N	Y
8 Stabenow	Y	N	Y	Y	Y	Y	N
9 Kildee	Y	N	N	Y	Y	Y	N
10 Bonior	Y	N	N	Y	Y	Y	N
11 **Knollenberg**	N	N	N	N	N	N	Y
12 Levin	N	N	Y	Y	N	Y	N
13 Rivers	N	N	Y	Y	Y	Y	N
14 Conyers	?	?	?	Y	N	N	N
15 Kilpatrick	?	?	?	Y	Y	Y	N
16 Dingell	N	N	N	Y	Y	Y	N

	385	386	387	388	389	390	391
MINNESOTA							
1 **Gutknecht**	N	Y	N	N	N	N	Y
2 Minge	Y	N	Y	Y	N	Y	N
3 **Ramstad**	Y	N	N	N	Y	Y	Y
4 Vento	Y	N	Y	Y	Y	Y	N
5 Sabo	Y	N	Y	Y	N	Y	N
6 Luther	Y	N	Y	Y	Y	Y	Y
7 Peterson	Y	N	N	Y	N	N	Y
8 Oberstar	Y	N	N	Y	Y	Y	N
MISSISSIPPI							
1 **Wicker**	Y	Y	N	N	N	N	N
2 Thompson	Y	N	Y	Y	N	Y	N
3 **Pickering**	–	+	–	–	–	–	–
4 **Parker**	N	N	N	N	N	N	N
5 Taylor	N	N	N	N	N	N	N
MISSOURI							
1 Clay	?	?	?	?	?	?	?
2 **Talent**	N	Y	N	N	N	N	Y
3 Gephardt	N	N	Y	Y	Y	Y	N
4 Skelton	Y	N	N	Y	N	N	N
5 McCarthy	–	–	+	Y	Y	Y	N
6 Danner	N	N	N	Y	N	Y	N
7 **Blunt**	N	Y	N	N	N	N	N
8 **Emerson**	N	Y	N	N	N	N	Y
9 **Hulshof**	N	N	N	N	Y	Y	Y
MONTANA							
AL **Hill**	N	Y	N	N	N	Y	Y
NEBRASKA							
1 **Bereuter**	N	N	N	N	N	Y	N
2 **Christensen**	N	Y	N	N	N	N	N
3 **Barrett**	N	N	N	N	N	N	N
NEVADA							
1 **Ensign**	Y	Y	N	N	Y	Y	Y
2 **Gibbons**	N	Y	N	N	N	N	Y
NEW HAMPSHIRE							
1 **Sununu**	N	Y	N	N	Y	N	Y
2 **Bass**	N	N	N	N	Y	Y	Y
NEW JERSEY							
1 Andrews	N	Y	Y	Y	Y	N	Y
2 **LoBiondo**	N	Y	N	N	Y	N	Y
3 **Saxton**	N	N	N	N	Y	N	N
4 **Smith**	N	Y	N	N	Y	N	Y
5 **Roukema**	N	N	N	N	Y	Y	N
6 Pallone	Y	N	Y	Y	Y	Y	N
7 **Franks**	N	N	N	N	Y	N	N
8 Pascrell	N	N	Y	Y	Y	Y	N
9 Rothman	N	N	Y	Y	Y	Y	N
10 Payne	Y	N	Y	Y	Y	Y	N
11 **Frelinghuysen**	N	N	Y	N	Y	N	Y
12 **Pappas**	N	Y	N	N	Y	N	Y
13 Menendez	N	N	Y	Y	Y	N	N
NEW MEXICO							
1 **Wilson**	N	N	N	N	N	N	N
2 **Skeen**	N	N	N	N	N	N	N
3 **Redmond**	N	Y	N	N	N	N	N
NEW YORK							
1 **Forbes**	N	N	N	N	Y	Y	N
2 **Lazio**	N	Y	N	N	Y	Y	N
3 **King**	N	N	N	N	N	N	N
4 McCarthy	N	N	Y	Y	Y	Y	N
5 Ackerman	Y	N	Y	Y	Y	N	N
6 Meeks	Y	Y	Y	Y	Y	Y	N
7 Manton	Y	N	N	Y	N	Y	N
8 Nadler	Y	N	Y	Y	Y	Y	N
9 Schumer	N	N	Y	Y	Y	Y	N
10 Towns	?	?	?	Y	Y	Y	N
11 Owens	Y	N	Y	Y	Y	Y	N
12 Velázquez	Y	N	Y	Y	N	Y	N
13 **Fossella**	N	Y	N	N	Y	N	Y
14 Maloney	Y	N	Y	Y	+	Y	N
15 Rangel	Y	Y	Y	Y	Y	Y	N
16 Serrano	Y	N	Y	Y	Y	Y	N
17 Engel	Y	N	Y	Y	Y	Y	N
18 Lowey	N	N	Y	Y	Y	Y	N
19 **Kelly**	N	N	N	Y	N	Y	N
20 **Gilman**	Y	Y	Y	Y	N	N	N
21 McNulty	Y	N	N	Y	Y	Y	N
22 **Solomon**	N	Y	N	N	N	N	N
23 **Boehlert**	N	N	Y	N	Y	N	N
24 **McHugh**	N	N	N	N	Y	N	N
25 **Walsh**	N	N	N	N	Y	N	N
26 Hinchey	Y	N	Y	Y	Y	Y	N
27 **Paxon**	N	Y	N	N	N	N	Y
28 Slaughter	Y	N	Y	Y	Y	Y	?
29 LaFalce	Y	N	N	Y	Y	Y	N
30 **Quinn**	N	N	N	N	N	N	N

	385	386	387	388	389	390	391
31 **Houghton**	N	N	Y	N	N	N	N
NORTH CAROLINA							
1 Clayton	Y	N	Y	Y	N	N	N
2 Etheridge	N	N	N	Y	N	Y	N
3 **Jones**	N	Y	N	N	Y	N	N
4 Price	N	N	Y	Y	N	Y	N
5 **Burr**	N	N	N	N	Y	N	N
6 **Coble**	N	Y	N	N	N	N	Y
7 McIntyre	N	N	N	Y	N	Y	Y
8 Hefner	Y	N	N	Y	N	Y	N
9 **Myrick**	N	Y	N	N	N	N	Y
10 **Ballenger**	N	Y	N	N	Y	N	Y
11 **Taylor**	N	N	N	N	N	N	N
12 Watt	Y	N	Y	Y	N	Y	N
NORTH DAKOTA							
AL Pomeroy	N	N	N	Y	N	Y	N
OHIO							
1 **Chabot**	N	Y	N	N	N	N	Y
2 **Portman**	N	Y	N	N	N	N	Y
3 Hall	Y	N	N	Y	Y	Y	N
4 **Oxley**	?	?	?	N	N	N	N
5 **Gillmor**	N	Y	N	N	N	N	N
6 Strickland	N	N	?	Y	Y	Y	Y
7 **Hobson**	N	Y	N	N	N	N	Y
8 **Boehner**	N	Y	N	N	N	N	Y
9 Kaptur	Y	N	N	Y	Y	N	N
10 Kucinich	N	N	N	Y	N	Y	N
11 Stokes	Y	N	Y	Y	Y	Y	N
12 **Kasich**	N	Y	N	N	N	N	Y
13 Brown	Y	N	Y	Y	Y	Y	N
14 Sawyer	Y	N	Y	Y	Y	Y	N
15 **Pryce**	N	Y	N	N	N	N	Y
16 **Regula**	N	N	N	N	N	N	N
17 Traficant	N	N	N	N	N	N	N
18 **Ney**	N	N	N	N	N	N	Y
19 **LaTourette**	Y	N	N	N	Y	N	N
OKLAHOMA							
1 **Largent**	N	Y	N	N	N	Y	Y
2 **Coburn**	N	Y	N	N	N	N	Y
3 **Watkins**	N	Y	N	N	N	N	Y
4 **Watts**	N	Y	N	N	N	N	Y
5 **Istook**	N	N	N	N	N	N	Y
6 **Lucas**	N	N	N	N	N	N	Y
OREGON							
1 Furse	Y	N	Y	Y	Y	Y	N
2 **Smith**	N	N	N	N	N	N	N
3 Blumenauer	Y	N	Y	Y	Y	Y	N
4 DeFazio	Y	N	Y	Y	N	Y	N
5 Hooley	N	N	Y	Y	Y	N	N
PENNSYLVANIA							
1 Brady	Y	N	Y	Y	Y	N	N
2 Fattah	Y	N	Y	Y	Y	N	N
3 Borski	N	N	N	Y	Y	N	N
4 Klink	Y	N	N	Y	Y	N	N
5 **Peterson**	N	N	N	N	N	N	N
6 Holden	N	N	N	Y	N	Y	N
7 **Weldon**	N	N	N	?	?	?	N
8 **Greenwood**	Y	Y	Y	N	N	N	Y
9 **Shuster**	N	Y	N	N	N	N	N
10 **McDade**	?	N	N	N	N	N	N
11 Kanjorski	N	N	N	Y	N	Y	N
12 Murtha	Y	N	N	Y	Y	N	N
13 **Fox**	N	Y	N	N	Y	N	Y
14 Coyne	Y	N	Y	Y	N	Y	N
15 McHale	N	N	N	Y	Y	Y	N
16 **Pitts**	N	Y	N	N	N	N	Y
17 **Gekas**	N	N	N	N	N	N	N
18 Doyle	N	N	N	Y	N	Y	N
19 **Goodling**	N	N	N	N	N	N	Y
20 Mascara	N	N	N	Y	N	Y	N
21 **English**	N	N	N	N	N	N	N
RHODE ISLAND							
1 Kennedy	Y	N	Y	Y	Y	N	N
2 Weygand	Y	N	N	Y	Y	Y	N
SOUTH CAROLINA							
1 **Sanford**	N	Y	N	N	N	N	Y
2 **Spence**	N	N	N	N	N	N	N
3 **Graham**	N	Y	N	N	Y	N	N
4 **Inglis**	N	Y	N	N	N	N	Y
5 Spratt	N	N	N	Y	N	Y	N
6 Clyburn	Y	N	Y	Y	N	Y	N
SOUTH DAKOTA							
AL **Thune**	N	Y	N	N	N	N	Y

	385	386	387	388	389	390	391
TENNESSEE							
1 **Jenkins**	N	Y	N	N	N	N	Y
2 **Duncan**	Y	Y	N	N	N	N	Y
3 **Wamp**	N	Y	N	N	N	Y	Y
4 **Hilleary**	N	N	N	N	N	N	Y
5 Clement	Y	N	N	Y	Y	Y	N
6 Gordon	N	N	N	Y	N	Y	N
7 **Bryant**	N	N	N	N	N	N	N
8 Tanner	N	Y	N	N	Y	Y	N
9 Ford	Y	N	Y	Y	?	Y	N
TEXAS							
1 Sandlin	Y	N	Y	Y	N	Y	N
2 Turner	Y	Y	N	Y	Y	N	N
3 **Johnson, Sam**	N	Y	N	N	N	N	Y
4 Hall	Y	Y	N	N	N	N	N
5 **Sessions**	N	Y	N	N	N	N	Y
6 **Barton**	N	Y	N	N	N	N	N
7 **Archer**	N	Y	N	N	N	N	Y
8 **Brady**	N	Y	N	N	N	N	N
9 Lampson	Y	N	N	Y	Y	N	N
10 Doggett	Y	N	Y	Y	Y	Y	N
11 Edwards	Y	N	N	Y	N	Y	N
12 **Granger**	N	Y	N	N	N	N	Y
13 **Thornberry**	N	Y	N	N	N	N	Y
14 **Paul**	N	Y	N	N	N	N	Y
15 Hinojosa	Y	N	Y	Y	Y	Y	N
16 Reyes	Y	N	N	Y	Y	Y	N
17 Stenholm	Y	Y	N	Y	N	N	N
18 Jackson-Lee	Y	N	Y	Y	N	Y	N
19 **Combest**	N	Y	N	N	N	N	N
20 Gonzalez	?	?	?	?	?	?	?
21 **Smith**	N	Y	N	N	N	N	N
22 **DeLay**	N	Y	N	N	N	N	Y
23 **Bonilla**	N	N	N	N	N	N	N
24 Frost	Y	N	Y	Y	N	Y	N
25 Bentsen	N	N	Y	Y	N	N	N
26 **Armey**	N	Y	N	N	N	N	Y
27 Ortiz	Y	Y	N	Y	Y	Y	N
28 Rodriguez	Y	N	Y	Y	N	Y	N
29 Green	Y	N	Y	Y	N	N	N
30 Johnson, E.B.	Y	N	Y	Y	N	Y	N
UTAH							
1 **Hansen**	N	N	N	N	N	N	Y
2 **Cook**	N	Y	N	N	N	N	N
3 **Cannon**	N	Y	N	N	N	N	Y
VERMONT							
AL *Sanders*	Y	N	Y	Y	N	Y	N
VIRGINIA							
1 **Bateman**	N	N	N	N	N	N	N
2 Pickett	Y	N	Y	Y	N	N	N
3 Scott	Y	N	Y	Y	N	N	N
4 Sisisky	Y	N	N	Y	N	N	N
5 Goode	N	N	N	N	N	N	N
6 **Goodlatte**	N	N	N	N	N	N	Y
7 **Bliley**	N	Y	N	N	N	N	N
8 Moran	Y	N	Y	Y	Y	Y	N
9 Boucher	N	N	Y	Y	N	Y	N
10 **Wolf**	N	N	N	N	N	N	N
11 **Davis**	Y	N	N	N	N	N	N
WASHINGTON							
1 **White**	N	N	N	N	Y	N	Y
2 **Metcalf**	N	N	N	N	N	N	Y
3 **Smith, Linda**	N	Y	N	N	N	N	Y
4 **Hastings**	N	Y	N	N	N	N	N
5 **Nethercutt**	N	N	N	N	N	N	Y
6 Dicks	Y	N	N	Y	N	Y	N
7 McDermott	Y	N	Y	Y	Y	N	N
8 **Dunn**	N	N	N	N	N	N	Y
9 Smith, Adam	N	N	Y	Y	Y	Y	N
WEST VIRGINIA							
1 Mollohan	Y	N	N	Y	N	Y	N
2 Wise	N	N	Y	Y	N	Y	N
3 Rahall	Y	N	N	Y	Y	Y	N
WISCONSIN							
1 **Neumann**	N	Y	N	N	N	N	Y
2 **Klug**	N	Y	N	N	N	N	Y
3 Kind	Y	N	Y	Y	N	Y	N
4 Kleczka	Y	N	Y	N	N	N	N
5 Barrett	Y	N	Y	Y	N	Y	Y
6 **Petri**	N	Y	N	N	N	N	Y
7 Obey	Y	N	?	Y	N	Y	N
8 Johnson	Y	N	N	Y	Y	N	Y
9 **Sensenbrenner**	N	Y	N	N	N	N	Y
WYOMING							
AL **Cubin**	N	Y	N	N	N	N	Y

Southern states - Ala., Ark., Fla., Ga., Ky., La., Miss., N.C., Okla., S.C., Tenn., Texas, Va.

House Votes 392, 393, 394, 395, 396, 397, 398

Key

Y Voted for (yea).
Paired for.
+ Announced for.
N Voted against (nay).
X Paired against.
− Announced against.
P Voted "present."
C Voted "present" to avoid possible conflict of interest.
? Did not vote or otherwise make a position known.

Democrats **Republicans**
Independent

392. HR 4276. Fiscal 1999 Commerce, Justice, State Appropriations/Eliminate U.N. Debt Payment Funding. Bartlett, R-Md., amendment to eliminate the $475 million allocated in the bill for debt payments to the United Nations. Rejected 151-279: R 141-84; D 10-194 (ND 6-144, SD 4-50); I 0-1. Aug. 5, 1998.

393. HR 4276. Fiscal 1999 Commerce, Justice, State Appropriations/Increase Funding for Small Business Loan Program. Talent, R-Mo., amendment to increase the Small Business Administration's business loans program account by $7.09 million to $236 million. The increase is offset by reducing funding by $7.1 million for administrative expenses. Adopted 312-114: R 219-4; D 93-109 (ND 67-83, SD 26-26); I 0-1. Aug. 5, 1998.

394. HR 4276. Fiscal 1999 Commerce, Justice, State Appropriations/Decrease U.N. Debt Payment Funding. Stearns, R-Fla., amendment to reduce appropriations for U.S. debt payments to the United Nations by $109 million. Rejected 165-261: R 155-69; D 10-191 (ND 6-141, SD 4-50); I 0-1. Aug. 5, 1998.

395. HR 4276. Fiscal 1999 Commerce, Justice, State Appropriations/Jurisdictional Parity for Fisheries Enforcement. Callahan, R-Ala., amendment to provide jurisdictional parity for fisheries enforcement in the Gulf of Mexico for the states of Alabama, Louisiana and Mississippi with the states of Florida and Texas. Rejected 141-283: R 121-101; D 20-181 (ND 8-139, SD 12-42); I 0-1. Aug. 5, 1998.

396. HR 4276. Fiscal 1999 Commerce, Justice, State Appropriations/Special Prosecutors and State Ethical Standards. Conyers Jr., D-Mich., amendment to add special prosecutors (such as an independent counsel) to the bill's list of prosecutors who would be required by the bill to follow each state's ethical standards for the states in which aspects of a case are pending. Adopted 249-182: R 48-178; D 200-4 (ND 147-3, SD 53-1); I 1-0. Aug. 5, 1998.

397. HR 4276. Fiscal 1999 Commerce, Justice, State Appropriations/Strike State Ethical Standards for Prosecutors. Hutchinson, R-Ark., amendment to strike the provision of the bill establishing a new category of punishable conduct for federal prosecutors and requiring that all federal prosecutors abide by each state's standards for the states in which aspects of a case are pending. Rejected 82-345: R 55-169; D 27-175 (ND 15-134, SD 12-41); I 0-1. Aug. 5, 1998.

398. HR 4276. Fiscal 1999 Commerce, Justice, State Appropriations/Prohibit Funding to Enforce Executive Orders. Hefley, R-Colo., amendment to prohibit funds in this bill or any other act from being used to implement or enforce two presidential executive orders. The first prohibits federal agencies from discriminating against individuals in hiring or awarding grants because of sexual orientation. The second order establishes a new set of "federalism" criteria for federal agencies to follow when formulating or implementing related policies. Rejected 176-252: R 161-63; D 15-188 (ND 3-146, SD 12-42); I 0-1. Aug. 5, 1998.

	392	393	394	395	396	397	398
ALABAMA							
1 *Callahan*	N	Y	N	Y	N	N	Y
2 *Everett*	Y	Y	Y	Y	N	N	Y
3 *Riley*	Y	Y	Y	Y	N	N	Y
4 *Aderholt*	Y	Y	Y	Y	N	N	Y
5 Cramer	N	Y	N	Y	Y	Y	Y
6 *Bachus*	Y	Y	Y	Y	N	N	Y
7 Hilliard	N	N	N	Y	Y	N	N
ALASKA							
AL *Young*	Y	Y	N	Y	N	N	Y
ARIZONA							
1 *Salmon*	Y	Y	Y	N	Y	Y	Y
2 Pastor	N	N	N	Y	Y	N	N
3 *Stump*	Y	Y	Y	Y	N	N	Y
4 *Shadegg*	Y	Y	Y	Y	N	N	Y
5 *Kolbe*	N	Y	N	N	N	N	N
6 *Hayworth*	Y	Y	Y	Y	N	N	Y
ARKANSAS							
1 Berry	N	Y	N	Y	Y	N	Y
2 Snyder	N	Y	N	Y	Y	N	N
3 *Hutchinson*	Y	Y	Y	N	Y	Y	Y
4 *Dickey*	Y	Y	Y	Y	N	N	Y
CALIFORNIA							
1 *Riggs*	N	Y	N	Y	N	Y	Y
2 *Herger*	Y	Y	Y	Y	N	N	Y
3 Fazio	N	Y	N	Y	Y	N	N
4 *Doolittle*	Y	Y	Y	Y	N	N	Y
5 Matsui	N	N	N	Y	Y	N	N
6 Woolsey	N	N	N	Y	Y	N	N
7 Miller	N	N	N	Y	Y	N	N
8 Pelosi	N	N	N	N	Y	N	N
9 Lee	N	N	N	Y	Y	N	N
10 Tauscher	N	Y	N	N	Y	N	N
11 *Pombo*	Y	Y	Y	Y	N	N	Y
12 Lantos	N	N	N	Y	Y	N	N
13 Stark	N	N	N	N	Y	N	N
14 Eshoo	N	N	N	N	Y	N	N
15 *Campbell*	N	Y	N	N	Y	N	N
16 Lofgren	N	N	N	N	Y	N	N
17 Farr	N	N	N	N	Y	N	N
18 Condit	N	Y	N	Y	Y	N	N
19 *Radanovich*	Y	Y	Y	Y	N	N	Y
20 Dooley	N	N	N	Y	Y	N	N
21 *Thomas*	N	Y	N	N	N	N	N
22 Capps, L.	N	N	N	Y	Y	N	N
23 *Gallegly*	N	Y	Y	Y	N	N	N
24 Sherman	N	N	N	N	Y	N	N
25 *McKeon*	Y	Y	Y	Y	N	N	Y
26 Berman	N	N	N	N	Y	N	N
27 *Rogan*	Y	Y	Y	N	Y	Y	Y
28 *Dreier*	N	Y	N	N	Y	N	Y
29 Waxman	N	N	N	N	Y	N	N
30 Becerra	N	N	N	N	Y	N	N
31 Martinez	N	Y	N	N	Y	N	N
32 Dixon	N	N	N	N	Y	N	N
33 Roybal-Allard	N	N	N	N	Y	N	N
34 Torres	N	Y	N	Y	Y	N	N
35 Waters	N	N	N	N	Y	N	N
36 Harman	N	N	N	N	Y	N	N
37 Millender-McD.	N	N	N	N	Y	N	N
38 *Horn*	N	Y	N	N	N	N	N

	392	393	394	395	396	397	398
39 *Royce*	Y	Y	Y	N	Y	N	Y
40 *Lewis*	N	Y	N	Y	N	N	N
41 *Kim*	N	Y	N	N	Y	N	N
42 Brown	N	N	N	N	Y	N	N
43 *Calvert*	N	Y	N	Y	N	N	Y
44 *Bono, M.*	Y	Y	Y	Y	N	N	Y
45 *Rohrabacher*	Y	Y	Y	Y	N	N	Y
46 Sanchez	N	N	N	N	Y	N	N
47 *Cox*	Y	Y	Y	Y	N	N	Y
48 *Packard*	Y	Y	Y	N	N	N	Y
49 *Bilbray*	N	Y	N	N	Y	Y	N
50 Filner	N	N	N	N	Y	N	N
51 *Cunningham*	?	?	?	?	?	?	?
52 *Hunter*	Y	Y	Y	Y	N	N	Y
COLORADO							
1 DeGette	N	N	N	Y	N	N	N
2 Skaggs	N	N	N	Y	N	N	N
3 *McInnis*	Y	Y	Y	N	N	N	Y
4 *Schaffer*	Y	Y	Y	Y	N	N	Y
5 *Hefley*	Y	Y	Y	Y	N	N	Y
6 *Schaefer*	Y	Y	Y	N	N	N	Y
CONNECTICUT							
1 Kennelly	N	Y	N	N	Y	Y	N
2 Gejdenson	N	N	N	Y	N	N	N
3 DeLauro	N	N	N	N	Y	N	N
4 *Shays*	N	Y	N	N	N	N	N
5 Maloney	N	N	N	N	Y	N	N
6 *Johnson*	N	Y	N	N	N	N	N
DELAWARE							
AL *Castle*	N	Y	N	N	N	N	N
FLORIDA							
1 *Scarborough*	Y	Y	Y	N	N	N	Y
2 Boyd	N	N	N	Y	Y	Y	N
3 Brown	N	N	N	Y	Y	N	N
4 *Fowler*	N	Y	Y	Y	N	N	Y
5 Thurman	N	N	N	Y	Y	N	N
6 *Stearns*	Y	Y	Y	Y	N	N	Y
7 *Mica*	Y	Y	Y	Y	N	N	Y
8 *McCollum*	Y	Y	Y	N	N	N	Y
9 *Bilirakis*	Y	Y	Y	Y	N	N	Y
10 *Young*	N	Y	N	Y	N	N	N
11 Davis	N	N	N	N	Y	N	N
12 *Canady*	Y	Y	Y	Y	N	N	Y
13 *Miller*	N	Y	N	N	N	N	N
14 *Goss*	N	Y	N	Y	N	N	Y
15 *Weldon*	Y	Y	Y	Y	N	N	Y
16 *Foley*	Y	Y	Y	N	N	N	Y
17 Meek	N	N	N	N	Y	N	N
18 *Ros-Lehtinen*	N	Y	N	Y	N	N	N
19 Wexler	N	Y	N	N	Y	N	N
20 Deutsch	N	N	N	N	Y	N	N
21 *Diaz-Balart*	Y	Y	Y	N	Y	N	N
22 *Shaw*	N	Y	N	N	N	N	N
23 Hastings	N	N	N	N	Y	N	N
GEORGIA							
1 *Kingston*	Y	Y	Y	Y	N	N	Y
2 Bishop	N	Y	N	Y	Y	N	N
3 *Collins*	Y	Y	Y	Y	N	N	Y
4 *McKinney*	N	Y	N	Y	Y	N	N
5 Lewis	N	?	N	N	Y	N	N
6 *Gingrich*							
7 *Barr*	Y	Y	Y	Y	N	Y	?
8 *Chambliss*	Y	Y	Y	Y	N	N	Y
9 *Deal*	Y	Y	Y	Y	N	N	Y
10 *Norwood*	Y	Y	Y	Y	N	N	Y
11 *Linder*	Y	Y	N	Y	Y	N	Y
HAWAII							
1 Abercrombie	N	N	N	Y	N	N	N
2 Mink	N	Y	N	N	Y	N	N
IDAHO							
1 *Chenoweth*	Y	Y	Y	Y	N	N	Y
2 *Crapo*	Y	?	?	Y	N	N	Y
ILLINOIS							
1 Rush	N	Y	N	N	Y	N	N
2 Jackson	N	Y	N	N	Y	N	N
3 Lipinski	N	Y	N	N	Y	N	N
4 Gutierrez	N	N	N	N	Y	N	N
5 Blagojevich	N	Y	?	N	Y	N	N
6 *Hyde*	N	Y	N	Y	N	N	N
7 Davis	N	Y	N	Y	Y	N	N
8 *Crane*	Y	Y	Y	Y	N	N	Y
9 Yates	N	N	N	N	Y	?	?
10 *Porter*	N	Y	N	Y	N	N	N
11 *Weller*	Y	Y	Y	N	N	N	N
12 Costello	N	Y	N	N	Y	N	N
13 *Fawell*	N	Y	N	N	N	N	N

ND Northern Democrats   SD Southern Democrats

H-112 — 1998 CQ ALMANAC   WWW.CQ.COM

	392	393	394	395	396	397	398
14 ***Hastert***	Y	Y	Y	N	N	N	Y
15 ***Ewing***	N	Y	Y	N	N	N	Y
16 ***Manzullo***	Y	Y	Y	N	N	N	Y
17 Evans	N	N	N	N	Y	N	N
18 ***LaHood***	N	Y	N	N	Y	N	N
19 Poshard	N	Y	N	N	Y	N	N
20 ***Shimkus***	Y	Y	Y	Y	N	N	N
INDIANA							
1 Visclosky	N	N	N	N	Y	N	N
2 ***McIntosh***	Y	Y	Y	Y	N	N	Y
3 Roemer	Y	Y	Y	N	N	N	N
4 ***Souder***	Y	Y	Y	Y	N	Y	Y
5 ***Buyer***	Y	Y	Y	?	N	N	Y
6 ***Burton***	Y	Y	Y	Y	N	N	Y
7 ***Pease***	Y	Y	Y	N	N	N	Y
8 ***Hostettler***	Y	Y	Y	Y	N	N	Y
9 Hamilton	N	Y	N	N	N	N	N
10 Carson	N	N	N	N	Y	N	N
IOWA							
1 ***Leach***	N	Y	N	N	Y	N	N
2 ***Nussle***	Y	Y	Y	N	Y	Y	Y
3 Boswell	N	Y	N	N	Y	Y	N
4 ***Ganske***	N	Y	N	N	N	N	N
5 ***Latham***	N	Y	N	N	N	Y	Y
KANSAS							
1 ***Moran***	Y	Y	Y	Y	N	N	Y
2 ***Ryun***	Y	Y	Y	Y	N	Y	Y
3 ***Snowbarger***	Y	Y	Y	Y	N	Y	Y
4 ***Tiahrt***	Y	Y	Y	Y	N	N	Y
KENTUCKY							
1 ***Whitfield***	Y	Y	Y	N	N	Y	Y
2 ***Lewis***	Y	Y	Y	Y	N	Y	Y
3 ***Northup***	N	Y	Y	Y	N	N	Y
4 ***Bunning***	Y	Y	Y	Y	N	Y	Y
5 ***Rogers***	N	Y	N	Y	N	Y	Y
6 Baesler	N	Y	N	N	Y	N	Y
LOUISIANA							
1 ***Livingston***	N	Y	N	Y	N	N	Y
2 Jefferson	N	N	N	Y	Y	Y	N
3 ***Tauzin***	Y	Y	Y	Y	N	N	Y
4 ***McCrery***	Y	Y	Y	Y	N	N	N
5 ***Cooksey***	Y	Y	Y	Y	N	Y	N
6 ***Baker***	Y	Y	Y	Y	N	Y	Y
7 John	N	Y	N	Y	Y	Y	Y
MAINE							
1 Allen	N	Y	N	N	Y	N	N
2 Baldacci	N	Y	N	N	Y	N	N
MARYLAND							
1 ***Gilchrest***	N	Y	N	N	N	N	N
2 ***Ehrlich***	Y	Y	Y	N	N	Y	N
3 Cardin	N	N	N	N	Y	N	N
4 Wynn	N	N	N	N	Y	N	N
5 Hoyer	N	N	N	N	Y	N	N
6 ***Bartlett***	Y	Y	Y	Y	N	N	Y
7 Cummings	N	N	N	N	Y	N	N
8 ***Morella***	N	Y	N	N	N	Y	N
MASSACHUSETTS							
1 Olver	N	N	N	N	Y	N	N
2 Neal	N	N	N	N	Y	N	N
3 McGovern	N	Y	N	N	Y	N	N
4 Frank	N	N	N	N	Y	N	N
5 Meehan	N	Y	N	N	Y	Y	N
6 Tierney	N	Y	N	N	Y	N	N
7 Markey	N	N	N	N	Y	N	N
8 Kennedy	N	Y	N	N	Y	N	N
9 Moakley	N	N	N	N	Y	?	?
10 Delahunt	N	N	N	N	Y	N	N
MICHIGAN							
1 Stupak	N	N	N	?	Y	N	N
2 ***Hoekstra***	Y	Y	Y	N	N	N	Y
3 ***Ehlers***	N	Y	N	N	N	N	N
4 ***Camp***	Y	Y	Y	N	N	N	Y
5 Barcia	Y	Y	Y	N	Y	N	N
6 ***Upton***	N	Y	Y	N	Y	N	N
7 ***Smith***	Y	Y	Y	N	N	Y	N
8 Stabenow	N	Y	N	N	Y	N	N
9 Kildee	N	N	N	N	Y	N	N
10 Bonior	N	Y	N	N	Y	N	N
11 ***Knollenberg***	N	Y	N	Y	N	N	N
12 Levin	N	Y	N	N	N	Y	N
13 Rivers	N	N	N	N	Y	N	N
14 Conyers	N	Y	N	N	Y	Y	N
15 Kilpatrick	N	N	N	N	Y	N	N
16 Dingell	N	N	N	Y	Y	N	N
MINNESOTA							
1 ***Gutknecht***	Y	Y	Y	Y	Y	N	Y
2 Minge	N	N	N	N	Y	N	N
3 ***Ramstad***	N	Y	N	N	Y	N	Y
4 Vento	N	N	N	N	Y	N	N
5 Sabo	N	N	N	N	Y	N	N
6 Luther	N	Y	N	N	Y	N	N
7 Peterson	N	N	Y	Y	Y	N	Y
8 Oberstar	N	N	N	N	Y	N	N
MISSISSIPPI							
1 ***Wicker***	N	Y	N	Y	Y	N	Y
2 Thompson	N	N	N	Y	Y	N	N
3 ***Pickering***	+	+	+	+	N	N	Y
4 ***Parker***	N	Y	N	Y	N	N	Y
5 Taylor	Y	Y	Y	Y	Y	N	Y
MISSOURI							
1 Clay	?	?	?	?	?	N	N
2 ***Talent***	Y	Y	Y	N	N	N	Y
3 Gephardt	N	Y	N	N	Y	N	N
4 Skelton	N	Y	N	Y	Y	N	N
5 McCarthy	N	Y	N	N	Y	N	N
6 Danner	Y	Y	Y	N	Y	N	N
7 ***Blunt***	Y	Y	Y	Y	N	N	Y
8 ***Emerson***	Y	Y	Y	Y	N	N	Y
9 ***Hulshof***	Y	Y	Y	N	N	Y	Y
MONTANA							
AL ***Hill***	Y	Y	Y	Y	Y	N	Y
NEBRASKA							
1 ***Bereuter***	N	Y	N	N	N	N	Y
2 ***Christensen***	Y	Y	Y	N	N	Y	Y
3 ***Barrett***	Y	Y	Y	Y	N	Y	Y
NEVADA							
1 ***Ensign***	Y	Y	Y	N	N	N	Y
2 ***Gibbons***	Y	Y	Y	Y	N	N	Y
NEW HAMPSHIRE							
1 ***Sununu***	N	Y	Y	N	N	Y	Y
2 ***Bass***	N	Y	N	N	N	N	Y
NEW JERSEY							
1 Andrews	N	N	N	N	Y	N	N
2 ***LoBiondo***	Y	Y	Y	N	Y	N	N
3 ***Saxton***	N	N	N	N	N	N	N
4 ***Smith***	N	Y	N	N	N	Y	Y
5 ***Roukema***	N	Y	N	N	N	N	N
6 Pallone	N	N	N	N	Y	N	N
7 ***Franks***	N	Y	N	N	Y	N	N
8 Pascrell	N	N	N	N	Y	N	N
9 Rothman	N	Y	N	N	Y	Y	N
10 Payne	N	N	N	N	Y	N	N
11 ***Frelinghuysen***	N	Y	N	N	N	N	N
12 ***Pappas***	Y	Y	Y	N	Y	N	Y
13 Menendez	N	N	N	N	Y	N	N
NEW MEXICO							
1 ***Wilson***	N	Y	Y	N	N	Y	N
2 ***Skeen***	Y	Y	Y	N	N	N	Y
3 ***Redmond***	Y	Y	Y	Y	N	Y	Y
NEW YORK							
1 ***Forbes***	N	Y	N	N	Y	N	N
2 ***Lazio***	N	Y	N	N	N	N	N
3 ***King***	N	Y	N	Y	Y	N	Y
4 McCarthy	N	Y	N	N	Y	N	N
5 Ackerman	N	Y	?	?	Y	N	N
6 Meeks	N	N	N	N	Y	N	N
7 Manton	N	Y	N	Y	Y	N	N
8 Nadler	N	N	N	N	Y	N	N
9 Schumer	N	Y	N	N	Y	N	N
10 Towns	N	N	N	N	Y	N	N
11 Owens	N	N	N	N	Y	N	N
12 Velázquez	N	Y	N	N	Y	N	N
13 ***Fossella***	Y	Y	Y	N	N	N	N
14 Maloney	N	Y	N	N	Y	Y	N
15 Rangel	Y	N	N	N	Y	N	N
16 Serrano	N	N	N	N	Y	N	N
17 Engel	N	N	N	N	Y	N	N
18 Lowey	N	N	N	N	Y	N	N
19 ***Kelly***	N	Y	N	N	Y	N	N
20 ***Gilman***	N	Y	–	N	Y	N	N
21 McNulty	N	Y	N	N	Y	N	N
22 ***Solomon***	Y	Y	Y	Y	N	N	Y
23 ***Boehlert***	N	Y	N	N	Y	N	N
24 ***McHugh***	N	Y	N	N	Y	N	Y
25 ***Walsh***	N	Y	N	N	Y	N	Y
26 Hinchey	N	N	N	N	Y	N	N
27 ***Paxon***	Y	Y	Y	Y	N	?	Y
28 Slaughter	N	N	N	N	Y	N	N
29 LaFalce	N	N	N	N	Y	Y	N
30 ***Quinn***	N	Y	N	N	N	N	Y
31 ***Houghton***	N	N	N	N	Y	N	N
NORTH CAROLINA							
1 Clayton	N	N	N	N	Y	Y	N
2 Etheridge	N	N	N	N	Y	Y	N
3 ***Jones***	Y	Y	Y	N	N	Y	Y
4 Price	N	N	N	N	Y	Y	N
5 ***Burr***	Y	Y	Y	Y	N	Y	Y
6 ***Coble***	Y	Y	Y	Y	N	N	Y
7 McIntyre	Y	Y	Y	N	Y	N	Y
8 Hefner	N	N	N	N	Y	N	N
9 ***Myrick***	Y	?	Y	Y	N	Y	Y
10 ***Ballenger***	N	Y	N	Y	N	Y	Y
11 ***Taylor***	N	Y	N	Y	N	N	Y
12 Watt	N	N	N	N	Y	Y	N
NORTH DAKOTA							
AL Pomeroy	N	Y	N	N	Y	N	N
OHIO							
1 ***Chabot***	Y	Y	Y	Y	N	Y	Y
2 ***Portman***	N	Y	Y	N	N	Y	Y
3 Hall	N	N	N	N	Y	N	Y
4 ***Oxley***	N	Y	N	Y	N	N	N
5 ***Gillmor***	N	Y	N	Y	Y	N	Y
6 Strickland	N	N	N	N	Y	N	N
7 ***Hobson***	N	Y	Y	N	N	N	N
8 ***Boehner***	N	Y	N	Y	N	N	Y
9 Kaptur	Y	Y	N	N	Y	N	N
10 Kucinich	N	N	N	N	Y	N	N
11 Stokes	N	N	N	N	Y	N	N
12 ***Kasich***	N	Y	Y	N	Y	N	Y
13 Brown	N	N	N	N	Y	N	N
14 Sawyer	N	N	N	N	Y	N	N
15 ***Pryce***	N	Y	N	N	Y	N	N
16 ***Regula***	N	Y	N	Y	N	N	N
17 Traficant	Y	Y	Y	N	Y	N	N
18 ***Ney***	Y	Y	Y	N	N	N	Y
19 ***LaTourette***	N	Y	N	N	N	N	N
OKLAHOMA							
1 ***Largent***	Y	Y	Y	N	N	N	Y
2 ***Coburn***	Y	Y	Y	?	N	Y	Y
3 ***Watkins***	Y	Y	Y	N	N	N	Y
4 ***Watts***	Y	Y	Y	Y	N	Y	Y
5 ***Istook***	Y	Y	Y	Y	N	N	Y
6 ***Lucas***	Y	Y	Y	Y	N	N	Y
OREGON							
1 Furse	N	Y	N	N	Y	N	N
2 ***Smith***	N	Y	N	Y	N	N	Y
3 Blumenauer	N	Y	N	N	Y	N	N
4 DeFazio	N	Y	N	N	Y	N	N
5 Hooley	N	Y	N	N	Y	N	N
PENNSYLVANIA							
1 Brady	N	N	N	N	Y	N	N
2 Fattah	N	N	N	N	Y	N	N
3 Borski	N	N	N	N	Y	N	N
4 Klink	N	Y	N	N	Y	N	N
5 ***Peterson***	Y	Y	Y	Y	Y	N	Y
6 Holden	N	Y	N	N	Y	N	N
7 ***Weldon***	N	Y	N	N	N	N	Y
8 ***Greenwood***	N	Y	N	N	N	N	N
9 ***Shuster***	Y	Y	Y	Y	Y	N	Y
10 ***McDade***	Y	Y	Y	?	N	N	N
11 Kanjorski	N	Y	N	N	Y	N	N
12 Murtha	N	N	N	N	Y	N	N
13 ***Fox***	N	Y	N	N	Y	N	N
14 Coyne	N	N	N	N	Y	N	N
15 McHale	N	Y	?	?	Y	N	N
16 ***Pitts***	Y	Y	Y	Y	N	N	Y
17 ***Gekas***	Y	N	N	Y	N	N	Y
18 Doyle	N	N	N	N	Y	N	N
19 ***Goodling***	Y	Y	Y	Y	N	?	?
20 Mascara	N	N	N	N	Y	N	N
21 ***English***	N	Y	N	N	Y	N	N
RHODE ISLAND							
1 Kennedy	N	N	N	N	Y	N	N
2 Weygand	N	Y	N	N	Y	N	N
SOUTH CAROLINA							
1 ***Sanford***	Y	Y	Y	N	N	N	Y
2 ***Spence***	Y	Y	Y	Y	N	N	Y
3 ***Graham***	Y	Y	Y	Y	N	N	Y
4 ***Inglis***	Y	Y	Y	N	N	Y	Y
5 Spratt	N	Y	N	N	Y	N	N
6 Clyburn	N	N	N	N	Y	N	N
SOUTH DAKOTA							
AL ***Thune***	Y	Y	Y	N	N	Y	Y
TENNESSEE							
1 ***Jenkins***	Y	Y	Y	Y	N	Y	Y
2 ***Duncan***	Y	Y	Y	Y	Y	N	Y
3 ***Wamp***	Y	Y	Y	Y	N	N	Y
4 ***Hilleary***	Y	Y	Y	Y	N	N	Y
5 Clement	N	?	N	N	Y	N	N
6 Gordon	N	Y	N	N	Y	N	N
7 ***Bryant***	Y	Y	Y	Y	N	Y	Y
8 Tanner	N	Y	N	N	Y	N	Y
9 Ford	N	N	N	N	Y	N	N
TEXAS							
1 Sandlin	N	Y	N	N	Y	Y	Y
2 Turner	N	Y	N	N	Y	N	Y
3 ***Johnson, Sam***	Y	N	Y	Y	N	N	Y
4 Hall	Y	N	Y	N	Y	N	Y
5 ***Sessions***	Y	Y	Y	Y	N	Y	Y
6 ***Barton***	Y	Y	Y	Y	N	Y	Y
7 ***Archer***	N	Y	N	N	N	N	Y
8 ***Brady***	N	Y	N	Y	N	Y	Y
9 Lampson	N	Y	N	N	Y	N	N
10 Doggett	N	Y	N	N	Y	N	N
11 Edwards	N	Y	N	N	Y	N	N
12 ***Granger***	N	Y	Y	Y	N	Y	N
13 ***Thornberry***	Y	Y	Y	Y	N	Y	Y
14 ***Paul***	Y	Y	Y	Y	Y	N	Y
15 Hinojosa	N	N	N	N	Y	N	N
16 Reyes	N	N	N	N	Y	Y	N
17 Stenholm	N	Y	N	N	Y	N	Y
18 Jackson-Lee	N	Y	N	N	Y	N	N
19 ***Combest***	Y	Y	Y	Y	N	Y	Y
20 Gonzalez	?	?	?	?	?	?	?
21 ***Smith***	N	Y	Y	Y	N	N	Y
22 ***DeLay***	Y	Y	Y	Y	N	N	Y
23 ***Bonilla***	Y	Y	Y	Y	N	N	Y
24 Frost	N	N	N	N	Y	N	N
25 Bentsen	N	Y	N	N	Y	N	N
26 ***Armey***	Y	Y	Y	Y	N	Y	Y
27 Ortiz	N	Y	N	Y	Y	N	N
28 Rodriguez	N	N	N	N	Y	N	N
29 Green	N	N	N	N	Y	N	N
30 Johnson, E.B.	N	N	N	N	Y	N	N
UTAH							
1 ***Hansen***	Y	Y	Y	Y	N	N	Y
2 ***Cook***	Y	Y	Y	Y	N	N	Y
3 ***Cannon***	Y	Y	Y	N	N	N	Y
VERMONT							
AL *Sanders*	N	N	N	N	Y	N	N
VIRGINIA							
1 ***Bateman***	N	Y	N	N	N	N	N
2 Pickett	N	N	N	Y	Y	N	N
3 Scott	N	N	N	N	Y	N	N
4 Sisisky	N	Y	N	Y	Y	N	N
5 Goode	Y	Y	Y	Y	Y	Y	Y
6 ***Goodlatte***	Y	Y	Y	Y	Y	N	Y
7 ***Bliley***	Y	Y	Y	Y	N	N	N
8 Moran	N	N	N	N	Y	?	N
9 Boucher	N	N	N	N	Y	N	N
10 ***Wolf***	N	Y	N	N	N	Y	Y
11 ***Davis***	N	Y	N	Y	N	Y	N
WASHINGTON							
1 ***White***	N	Y	N	Y	N	N	Y
2 ***Metcalf***	Y	Y	Y	Y	N	N	Y
3 ***Smith, Linda***	Y	Y	Y	Y	N	N	Y
4 ***Hastings***	Y	Y	Y	Y	N	Y	Y
5 ***Nethercutt***	Y	Y	Y	Y	N	Y	Y
6 Dicks	N	N	N	N	Y	N	N
7 McDermott	N	Y	N	N	Y	N	N
8 ***Dunn***	N	Y	Y	Y	N	Y	Y
9 Smith, Adam	N	Y	N	N	Y	N	N
WEST VIRGINIA							
1 Mollohan	N	N	N	N	Y	N	N
2 Wise	N	N	N	N	Y	N	N
3 Rahall	N	Y	N	N	Y	N	N
WISCONSIN							
1 ***Neumann***	Y	Y	Y	N	N	N	Y
2 ***Klug***	N	Y	Y	N	Y	N	N
3 Kind	N	Y	N	N	Y	Y	N
4 Kleczka	N	N	N	N	Y	Y	N
5 Barrett	N	Y	N	N	Y	Y	N
6 ***Petri***	Y	Y	Y	N	N	N	Y
7 Obey	N	Y	N	N	Y	N	N
8 Johnson	N	Y	N	N	Y	N	N
9 ***Sensenbrenner***	Y	Y	Y	N	N	N	Y
WYOMING							
AL ***Cubin***	Y	Y	Y	Y	N	Y	Y

Southern states - Ala., Ark., Fla., Ga., Ky., La., Miss., N.C., Okla., S.C., Tenn., Texas, Va.

House Votes 399, 400, 401, 402, 403, 404, 405

Key

- Y Voted for (yea).
- # Paired for.
- + Announced for.
- N Voted against (nay).
- X Paired against.
- − Announced against.
- P Voted "present."
- C Voted "present" to avoid possible conflict of interest.
- ? Did not vote or otherwise make a position known.

Democrats **Republicans** *Independent*

---

399. HR 4276. Fiscal 1999 Commerce, Justice, State Appropriations/Prohibit Funds for Enforcing Executive Order on Federalism. Kolbe, R-Ariz., amendment to prohibit any funds from the bill or any other act from being used to implement or enforce a presidential order that established new "federalism" criteria that federal agencies must follow when formulating and implementing policies that have federalism implications. Adopted 417-2: R 220-0; D 196-2 (ND 145-2, SD 51-0); I 1-0. Aug. 5, 1998.

400. HR 4276. Fiscal 1999 Commerce, Justice, State Appropriations/Funding to Implement Congressional Action Regarding International Agreement. McIntosh, R-Ind., amendment to prohibit funding for a committee to implement a 1997 agreement between the U.S., Russia, Kazakhstan, the Ukraine and Belarus on the Anti-Ballistic Missile Defense Treaty in an effort to allow congressional debate on the issue. Adopted 240-188: R 220-4; D 20-183 (ND 10-139, SD 10-44); I 0-1. Aug. 5, 1998.

401. HR 4276. Fiscal 1999 Commerce, Justice, State Appropriations/Prohibit Funds for Certain Legal Challenges. Kucinich, D-Ohio, amendment to prohibit any of the bill's funds from being used for any federal legal challenge to state, local or tribal law. Rejected 200-228: R 71-153; D 128-75 (ND 103-46, SD 25-29); I 1-0. Aug. 5, 1998.

402. HR 4276. Fiscal 1999 Commerce, Justice, State Appropriations/Passage. Passage of the bill to provide $33.5 billion in funding for the Departments of Commerce, Justice and State, related agencies and the federal judiciary in fiscal 1999. Passed 225-203: R 197-27; D 28-175 (ND 25-124, SD 3-51); I 0-1. Aug. 6, 1998. Aug. 6, 1998, in the session that began Aug. 5 and is recorded in the Aug. 5 Congressional Record.

403. HR 2183. Overhaul Campaign Finance Laws/Doolittle Substitute. Doolittle, R-Calif., substitute amendment to the bill to overhaul campaign finance laws. The amendment would eliminate all federal contribution limits and end public financing of presidential campaigns. Rejected 131-299: R 127-97; D 4-201 (ND 3-148, SD 1-53); I 0-1. Aug. 6, 1998. Aug. 6, 1998, in the session that began Aug. 5 and is recorded in the Aug. 5 Congressional Record.

404. HR 2183. Campaign Finance Overhaul/Hutchinson Substitute. Hutchinson, R-Ark., substitute amendment to the bill to overhaul campaign finance laws. The amendment would prohibit national parties from accepting soft money, double the aggregate annual limit individuals may contribute to campaigns and generally require organizations to disclose their expenditures on issue-oriented advertisements that mention congressional candidates. Rejected 147-222: R 121-102; D 26-119 (ND 13-93, SD 13-26); I 0-1. Aug. 6, 1998.

405. HR 2183. Campaign Finance Overhaul/Passage. Passage of the bill to ban soft money contributions for federal elections, expand regulations on advertising that advocates a candidate and tighten the definition of what constitutes coordination with a federal candidate. The text of the bill is the Shays-Meehan substitute adopted by the House on Aug. 3. Passed 252-179: R 61-164; D 190-15 (ND 142-9, SD 48-6); I 1-0. Aug. 6, 1998.

	399	400	401	402	403	404	405
ALABAMA							
1 Callahan	Y	Y	N	Y	Y	N	N
2 Everett	Y	Y	N	Y	Y	Y	N
3 Riley	Y	Y	Y	Y	Y	Y	N
4 Aderholt	Y	Y	Y	Y	Y	Y	N
5 Cramer	Y	Y	Y	Y	N	N	Y
6 Bachus	Y	Y	Y	Y	N	Y	Y
7 Hilliard	Y	N	N	N	N	N	Y
ALASKA							
AL Young	Y	Y	N	Y	Y	Y	N
ARIZONA							
1 Salmon	Y	Y	N	Y	Y	Y	N
2 Pastor	Y	N	Y	N	N	Y	Y
3 Stump	Y	Y	N	N	Y	N	N
4 Shadegg	Y	Y	N	Y	Y	N	N
5 Kolbe	Y	Y	N	Y	N	Y	N
6 Hayworth	Y	Y	Y	Y	Y	N	N
ARKANSAS							
1 Berry	Y	N	N	N	N	Y	Y
2 Snyder	Y	N	N	N	Y	Y	Y
3 Hutchinson	?	Y	N	N	Y	Y	N
4 Dickey	Y	Y	N	Y	Y	Y	N
CALIFORNIA							
1 Riggs	Y	N	Y	Y	Y	Y	Y
2 Herger	Y	Y	N	Y	N	N	N
3 Fazio	Y	N	N	N	N	N	Y
4 Doolittle	Y	Y	Y	Y	Y	N	N
5 Matsui	Y	N	N	N	N	N	Y
6 Woolsey	Y	N	Y	N	N	Y	Y
7 Miller	Y	N	N	N	N	N	Y
8 Pelosi	Y	N	N	N	N	N	Y
9 Lee	Y	N	Y	N	N	P	Y
10 Tauscher	Y	N	N	N	N	P	Y
11 Pombo	Y	Y	Y	Y	Y	N	N
12 Lantos	Y	N	N	N	N	N	Y
13 Stark	Y	N	N	N	N	N	Y
14 Eshoo	Y	N	N	N	N	N	Y
15 Campbell	Y	N	N	N	Y	Y	Y
16 Lofgren	Y	N	N	N	N	P	Y
17 Farr	Y	N	Y	N	Y	N	Y
18 Condit	?	Y	Y	N	Y	Y	Y
19 Radanovich	Y	Y	Y	Y	Y	N	N
20 Dooley	Y	N	N	N	N	P	Y
21 Thomas	Y	N	Y	N	Y	Y	N
22 Capps, L.	Y	N	N	N	N	P	Y
23 Gallegly	Y	Y	N	Y	Y	N	N
24 Sherman	Y	N	N	N	Y	N	Y
25 McKeon	Y	N	Y	N	Y	Y	N
26 Berman	Y	N	N	N	N	N	Y
27 Rogan	Y	Y	Y	Y	Y	N	N
28 Dreier	Y	Y	N	Y	Y	N	N
29 Waxman	Y	N	N	N	N	P	Y
30 Becerra	Y	N	N	N	N	N	Y
31 Martinez	Y	N	N	N	N	N	Y
32 Dixon	Y	N	N	N	N	N	Y
33 Roybal-Allard	Y	N	N	N	N	N	Y
34 Torres	Y	N	N	N	N	P	Y
35 Waters	Y	N	N	N	N	N	Y
36 Harman	Y	N	N	N	N	N	Y
37 Millender-McD.	Y	N	N	N	N	P	Y
38 Horn	Y	N	Y	N	Y	N	Y
39 Royce	Y	Y	N	Y	Y	N	N
40 Lewis	Y	Y	N	Y	Y	Y	N
41 Kim	Y	Y	N	Y	Y	Y	N
42 Brown	Y	N	N	N	Y	N	P	Y
43 Calvert	Y	Y	N	Y	Y	N	N
44 Bono, M.	Y	Y	Y	Y	Y	N	N
45 Rohrabacher	Y	Y	Y	Y	Y	Y	N
46 Sanchez	Y	N	N	N	N	Y	Y
47 Cox	+	Y	N	Y	Y	N	N
48 Packard	Y	Y	N	Y	Y	Y	N
49 Bilbray	Y	Y	N	Y	N	N	Y
50 Filner	Y	N	N	N	N	P	Y
51 Cunningham	?	?	?	?	?	?	?
52 Hunter	Y	Y	Y	Y	Y	Y	N
COLORADO							
1 DeGette	Y	N	Y	N	N	Y	Y
2 Skaggs	Y	N	N	N	N	P	Y
3 McInnis	Y	Y	N	Y	Y	N	N
4 Schaffer	Y	Y	Y	Y	Y	N	N
5 Hefley	Y	Y	Y	Y	Y	N	N
6 Schaefer	Y	Y	N	Y	Y	Y	N
CONNECTICUT							
1 Kennelly	Y	N	N	N	N	N	Y
2 Gejdenson	Y	N	N	N	N	N	Y
3 DeLauro	Y	N	N	N	N	P	Y
4 Shays	Y	Y	Y	N	Y	Y	Y
5 Maloney	Y	N	N	N	N	P	Y
6 Johnson	Y	Y	N	Y	N	N	Y
DELAWARE							
AL Castle	Y	Y	N	Y	−	N	Y
FLORIDA							
1 Scarborough	Y	Y	Y	Y	Y	Y	N
2 Boyd	Y	N	N	N	Y	Y	
3 Brown	Y	N	N	N	N	N	Y
4 Fowler	Y	Y	Y	Y	Y	Y	N
5 Thurman	Y	N	N	N	N	Y	Y
6 Stearns	Y	Y	Y	Y	Y	Y	N
7 Mica	Y	Y	Y	Y	Y	Y	N
8 McCollum	Y	Y	Y	Y	Y	Y	N
9 Bilirakis	Y	Y	N	Y	Y	Y	N
10 Young	Y	?	?	?	N	N	N
11 Davis	Y	N	N	N	N	N	Y
12 Canady	Y	Y	Y	Y	Y	Y	N
13 Miller	Y	Y	Y	Y	Y	Y	N
14 Goss	Y	Y	Y	Y	Y	Y	N
15 Weldon	Y	Y	N	Y	Y	N	N
16 Foley	Y	Y	N	Y	N	N	Y
17 Meek	Y	N	N	N	Y	N	Y
18 Ros-Lehtinen	Y	Y	Y	Y	Y	Y	N
19 Wexler	Y	N	N	N	N	P	Y
20 Deutsch	Y	N	N	N	N	P	Y
21 Diaz-Balart	Y	Y	Y	Y	Y	N	N
22 Shaw	Y	Y	Y	N	Y	Y	N
23 Hastings	Y	N	N	N	N	N	N
GEORGIA							
1 Kingston	Y	Y	Y	Y	Y	Y	N
2 Bishop	Y	N	N	N	N	N	N
3 Collins	Y	Y	N	Y	Y	Y	N
4 McKinney	Y	N	N	N	N	N	Y
5 Lewis	Y	N	N	N	N	P	Y
6 Gingrich	Y	N	Y				
7 Barr	Y	Y	Y	Y	Y	N	N
8 Chambliss	Y	Y	N	Y	Y	N	N
9 Deal	Y	Y	N	Y	Y	N	N
10 Norwood	Y	Y	Y	Y	Y	N	N
11 Linder	Y	Y	Y	Y	Y	Y	N
HAWAII							
1 Abercrombie	Y	N	Y	N	N	N	
2 Mink	Y	N	Y	N	N	N	N
IDAHO							
1 Chenoweth	Y	Y	Y	Y	N	N	N
2 Crapo	Y	Y	Y	Y	N	Y	N
ILLINOIS							
1 Rush	Y	N	N	N	N	N	Y
2 Jackson	Y	N	N	N	N	N	Y
3 Lipinski	Y	N	N	N	N	N	Y
4 Gutierrez	Y	N	N	N	N	P	Y
5 Blagojevich	Y	N	N	N	N	P	Y
6 Hyde	Y	Y	N	Y	N	N	Y
7 Davis	Y	N	N	N	N	N	Y
8 Crane	?	Y	N	Y	Y	N	N
9 Yates	?	?	?	?	N	Y	
10 Porter	Y	Y	N	Y	N	N	Y
11 Weller	Y	Y	N	Y	Y	N	N
12 Costello	Y	N	N	N	N	N	Y
13 Fawell	Y	Y	Y	Y	Y	Y	N

ND Northern Democrats SD Southern Democrats

	399	400	401	402	403	404	405
14 ***Hastert***	Y	Y	N	Y	Y	Y	N
15 ***Ewing***	Y	Y	N	Y	N	Y	N
16 ***Manzullo***	Y	Y	N	Y	N	N	N
17 Evans	Y	N	Y	N	N	N	Y
18 ***LaHood***	Y	Y	N	Y	N	Y	N
19 Poshard	Y	N	Y	N	N	N	Y
20 ***Shimkus***	Y	Y	N	Y	Y	Y	Y
INDIANA							
1 Visclosky	Y	Y	Y	Y	N	N	Y
2 ***McIntosh***	Y	Y	Y	Y	Y	N	N
3 Roemer	Y	N	N	N	N	N	Y
4 ***Souder***	Y	Y	N	Y	N	N	N
5 ***Buyer***	Y	Y	N	Y	Y	Y	N
6 ***Burton***	Y	Y	Y	Y	Y	N	N
7 ***Pease***	Y	Y	N	Y	Y	N	N
8 ***Hostettler***	Y	Y	N	N	Y	N	N
9 Hamilton	Y	N	N	N	N	N	Y
10 Carson	N	N	Y	N	N	P	Y
IOWA							
1 ***Leach***	Y	N	N	Y	N	N	Y
2 ***Nussle***	Y	Y	N	Y	N	Y	N
3 Boswell	Y	N	N	Y	N	Y	Y
4 ***Ganske***	Y	Y	N	Y	N	N	Y
5 ***Latham***	Y	Y	N	Y	Y	N	N
KANSAS							
1 ***Moran***	Y	Y	N	N	N	Y	N
2 ***Ryun***	Y	Y	N	Y	Y	Y	N
3 ***Snowbarger***	Y	Y	N	Y	Y	Y	N
4 ***Tiahrt***	Y	Y	N	N	Y	Y	N
KENTUCKY							
1 ***Whitfield***	Y	Y	N	Y	Y	Y	N
2 ***Lewis***	Y	Y	N	Y	Y	N	N
3 ***Northup***	Y	Y	N	Y	Y	Y	N
4 ***Bunning***	Y	Y	Y	Y	N	N	N
5 ***Rogers***	Y	Y	N	Y	Y	N	N
6 Baesler	Y	Y	Y	Y	N	N	Y
LOUISIANA							
1 ***Livingston***	Y	Y	N	Y	Y	Y	N
2 Jefferson	Y	N	N	N	N	N	Y
3 ***Tauzin***	Y	Y	N	Y	Y	Y	N
4 ***McCrery***	Y	Y	N	Y	Y	Y	N
5 ***Cooksey***	Y	Y	N	Y	Y	Y	N
6 ***Baker***	Y	Y	N	Y	Y	Y	N
7 John	Y	N	N	N	N	Y	N
MAINE							
1 Allen	Y	N	N	N	N	Y	Y
2 Baldacci	Y	N	Y	Y	N	P	Y
MARYLAND							
1 ***Gilchrest***	Y	Y	Y	Y	N	N	Y
2 ***Ehrlich***	Y	Y	N	Y	Y	N	N
3 Cardin	Y	N	N	N	N	N	Y
4 Wynn	Y	N	N	N	N	P	Y
5 Hoyer	Y	N	N	N	N	P	Y
6 ***Bartlett***	Y	Y	Y	N	Y	N	N
7 Cummings	Y	N	Y	N	N	N	Y
8 ***Morella***	Y	N	N	Y	N	N	Y
MASSACHUSETTS							
1 Olver	Y	N	N	N	N	P	Y
2 Neal	Y	N	N	N	N	N	Y
3 McGovern	Y	N	Y	N	N	P	Y
4 Frank	Y	N	Y	N	N	N	Y
5 Meehan	Y	N	Y	N	N	N	Y
6 Tierney	Y	N	Y	N	N	N	Y
7 Markey	Y	N	Y	N	N	N	Y
8 Kennedy	Y	N	Y	N	N	N	Y
9 Moakley	?	?	?	?	N	N	Y
10 Delahunt	Y	N	Y	N	N	P	Y
MICHIGAN							
1 Stupak	Y	N	Y	N	N	N	N
2 ***Hoekstra***	Y	Y	N	Y	Y	Y	N
3 ***Ehlers***	Y	Y	N	Y	Y	N	N
4 ***Camp***	Y	Y	N	Y	Y	N	N
5 Barcia	Y	N	Y	Y	N	P	Y
6 ***Upton***	Y	Y	N	Y	N	Y	Y
7 ***Smith***	Y	Y	Y	Y	N	Y	Y
8 Stabenow	Y	N	Y	Y	N	N	Y
9 Kildee	Y	N	Y	N	N	N	Y
10 Bonior	Y	N	Y	N	N	P	Y
11 ***Knollenberg***	Y	Y	N	Y	Y	N	N
12 Levin	Y	N	N	N	N	N	Y
13 Rivers	Y	N	Y	N	N	P	Y
14 Conyers	Y	N	Y	N	N	P	Y
15 Kilpatrick	Y	N	Y	N	N	P	Y
16 Dingell	Y	N	N	N	N	N	Y
MINNESOTA							
1 ***Gutknecht***	Y	Y	Y	Y	Y	N	N
2 Minge	Y	N	N	N	N	P	Y
3 ***Ramstad***	Y	Y	N	Y	N	N	Y
4 Vento	Y	N	N	N	N	N	Y
5 Sabo	Y	N	N	N	N	P	Y
6 Luther	Y	N	N	N	N	N	Y
7 Peterson	Y	Y	Y	N	N	N	N
8 Oberstar	Y	N	Y	N	N	N	Y
MISSISSIPPI							
1 ***Wicker***	Y	Y	N	Y	Y	Y	N
2 Thompson	Y	N	N	N	N	N	Y
3 ***Pickering***	Y	Y	N	N	Y	Y	N
4 ***Parker***	Y	Y	N	Y	N	N	Y
5 Taylor	Y	Y	Y	N	N	N	Y
MISSOURI							
1 Clay	?	N	Y	N	N	N	Y
2 ***Talent***	Y	Y	N	Y	N	Y	N
3 Gephardt	Y	N	Y	N	N	P	Y
4 Skelton	Y	Y	N	N	N	P	Y
5 McCarthy	Y	N	N	N	N	N	Y
6 Danner	Y	Y	Y	N	N	N	Y
7 ***Blunt***	Y	Y	N	Y	Y	Y	N
8 ***Emerson***	Y	Y	Y	Y	N	Y	N
9 ***Hulshof***	Y	Y	N	Y	N	Y	Y
MONTANA							
AL ***Hill***	Y	Y	N	Y	N	Y	Y
NEBRASKA							
1 ***Bereuter***	Y	Y	N	Y	N	N	Y
2 ***Christensen***	Y	Y	N	Y	Y	N	N
3 ***Barrett***	Y	Y	N	Y	N	N	Y
NEVADA							
1 ***Ensign***	Y	Y	Y	N	N	Y	N
2 ***Gibbons***	Y	Y	Y	N	Y	Y	N
NEW HAMPSHIRE							
1 ***Sununu***	Y	Y	N	Y	Y	Y	N
2 ***Bass***	Y	Y	N	Y	N	N	Y
NEW JERSEY							
1 Andrews	Y	Y	Y	N	N	N	Y
2 ***LoBiondo***	Y	Y	Y	Y	N	N	Y
3 ***Saxton***	Y	Y	Y	N	N	Y	Y
4 ***Smith***	Y	Y	Y	Y	N	Y	N
5 ***Roukema***	Y	Y	N	Y	N	N	Y
6 Pallone	Y	N	Y	N	N	P	Y
7 ***Franks***	Y	Y	Y	Y	N	N	Y
8 Pascrell	Y	N	Y	Y	N	N	Y
9 Rothman	Y	N	Y	N	N	N	Y
10 Payne	Y	N	Y	N	N	N	Y
11 ***Frelinghuysen***	Y	Y	N	Y	N	N	Y
12 ***Pappas***	Y	Y	Y	Y	Y	N	N
13 Menendez	Y	N	Y	N	N	P	Y
NEW MEXICO							
1 ***Wilson***	Y	Y	N	Y	Y	Y	N
2 ***Skeen***	Y	Y	N	Y	Y	N	N
3 ***Redmond***	Y	Y	N	Y	Y	N	N
NEW YORK							
1 ***Forbes***	Y	Y	Y	Y	N	N	Y
2 ***Lazio***	Y	Y	N	Y	N	N	Y
3 ***King***	Y	Y	Y	Y	Y	Y	N
4 McCarthy	Y	N	Y	N	N	N	Y
5 Ackerman	Y	N	Y	N	N	N	Y
6 Meeks	Y	N	Y	N	N	P	Y
7 Manton	Y	N	Y	N	N	N	Y
8 Nadler	Y	N	Y	N	N	N	Y
9 Schumer	Y	N	Y	N	N	N	Y
10 Towns	Y	N	Y	N	N	N	Y
11 Owens	Y	N	Y	N	N	N	Y
12 Velázquez	Y	N	Y	N	N	P	Y
13 ***Fossella***	Y	Y	N	Y	Y	N	N
14 Maloney	Y	N	Y	N	N	N	Y
15 Rangel	Y	N	Y	N	N	P	Y
16 Serrano	Y	N	Y	N	N	N	Y
17 Engel	Y	N	Y	N	N	P	Y
18 Lowey	Y	N	N	N	N	N	Y
19 ***Kelly***	Y	Y	Y	Y	N	N	Y
20 ***Gilman***	Y	Y	Y	Y	N	N	Y
21 McNulty	Y	N	Y	N	N	N	Y
22 ***Solomon***	Y	Y	N	Y	Y	Y	N
23 ***Boehlert***	Y	Y	N	Y	N	N	Y
24 ***McHugh***	Y	Y	Y	Y	N	Y	Y
25 ***Walsh***	Y	Y	Y	Y	N	N	Y
26 Hinchey	Y	N	Y	N	N	N	Y
27 ***Paxon***	Y	Y	N	Y	Y	N	N
28 Slaughter	Y	N	N	N	N	P	Y
29 LaFalce	Y	N	N	N	N	N	Y
30 ***Quinn***	Y	Y	Y	Y	N	N	Y
31 ***Houghton***	Y	Y	N	Y	N	N	Y
NORTH CAROLINA							
1 Clayton	Y	N	Y	N	N	P	Y
2 Etheridge	Y	N	N	N	N	P	Y
3 ***Jones***	Y	Y	Y	Y	Y	Y	N
4 Price	Y	N	N	N	N	P	Y
5 ***Burr***	Y	Y	N	Y	N	N	N
6 ***Coble***	Y	Y	N	Y	Y	N	N
7 McIntyre	Y	Y	Y	N	N	Y	Y
8 Hefner	Y	N	Y	N	N	N	Y
9 ***Myrick***	Y	Y	N	Y	N	Y	N
10 ***Ballenger***	Y	Y	N	Y	Y	Y	N
11 ***Taylor***	Y	Y	N	Y	Y	Y	N
12 Watt	Y	N	N	N	N	Y	Y
NORTH DAKOTA							
AL Pomeroy	Y	N	Y	N	N	P	Y
OHIO							
1 ***Chabot***	Y	Y	Y	N	N	Y	N
2 ***Portman***	Y	Y	N	Y	N	N	N
3 Hall	Y	N	N	N	N	N	Y
4 ***Oxley***	Y	Y	N	Y	Y	N	N
5 ***Gillmor***	Y	Y	Y	Y	N	Y	Y
6 Strickland	Y	N	Y	Y	N	N	Y
7 ***Hobson***	Y	Y	N	Y	Y	Y	N
8 ***Boehner***	Y	Y	N	Y	Y	N	N
9 Kaptur	Y	Y	Y	N	N	N	Y
10 Kucinich	Y	N	Y	N	N	P	Y
11 Stokes	Y	N	Y	N	N	N	Y
12 ***Kasich***	Y	Y	N	Y	Y	N	N
13 Brown	Y	N	Y	N	N	N	Y
14 Sawyer	Y	N	N	N	N	P	Y
15 ***Pryce***	Y	Y	N	Y	Y	Y	N
16 ***Regula***	Y	Y	N	Y	N	N	Y
17 Traficant	Y	Y	Y	Y	Y	N	N
18 ***Ney***	Y	Y	Y	Y	Y	N	N
19 ***LaTourette***	Y	N	Y	Y	N	P	Y
OKLAHOMA							
1 ***Largent***	Y	Y	N	N	Y	Y	N
2 ***Coburn***	?	Y	N	Y	Y	Y	N
3 ***Watkins***	Y	Y	Y	Y	N	Y	N
4 ***Watts***	Y	Y	Y	Y	N	N	N
5 ***Istook***	Y	Y	Y	Y	N	N	N
6 ***Lucas***	Y	Y	Y	Y	Y	Y	N
OREGON							
1 Furse	Y	N	Y	N	N	P	Y
2 ***Smith***	Y	?	?	?	?	Y	N
3 Blumenauer	Y	N	N	N	N	Y	Y
4 DeFazio	Y	N	Y	N	N	P	Y
5 Hooley	Y	N	N	Y	N	Y	Y
PENNSYLVANIA							
1 Brady	Y	N	Y	N	N	N	Y
2 Fattah	Y	N	Y	N	N	N	Y
3 Borski	Y	N	Y	Y	N	N	Y
4 Klink	Y	N	Y	N	N	N	Y
5 ***Peterson***	Y	Y	N	Y	Y	N	N
6 Holden	Y	N	Y	Y	N	N	Y
7 ***Weldon***	?	Y	Y	Y	N	Y	Y
8 ***Greenwood***	Y	Y	N	Y	N	N	Y
9 ***Shuster***	Y	?	?	?	Y	Y	N
10 ***McDade***	Y	Y	Y	Y	Y	?	Y
11 Kanjorski	Y	N	N	Y	N	N	Y
12 Murtha	Y	Y	Y	Y	N	N	N
13 ***Fox***	Y	Y	Y	Y	N	N	Y
14 Coyne	Y	N	Y	N	N	N	Y
15 McHale	Y	Y	N	N	N	N	Y
16 ***Pitts***	Y	Y	N	Y	N	Y	N
17 ***Gekas***	Y	Y	N	Y	Y	Y	Y
18 Doyle	Y	N	Y	Y	N	N	Y
19 ***Goodling***	?	Y	Y	Y	N	N	N
20 Mascara	Y	N	Y	Y	N	N	Y
21 ***English***	Y	Y	N	Y	N	Y	N
RHODE ISLAND							
1 Kennedy	Y	N	Y	N	N	Y	Y
2 Weygand	Y	N	N	N	N	Y	Y
SOUTH CAROLINA							
1 ***Sanford***	Y	Y	N	N	N	N	Y
2 ***Spence***	Y	Y	Y	Y	Y	Y	N
3 ***Graham***	Y	Y	Y	Y	N	Y	Y
4 ***Inglis***	Y	Y	Y	Y	?	?	?
5 Spratt	Y	N	N	N	N	N	Y
6 Clyburn	Y	N	Y	N	N	N	Y
SOUTH DAKOTA							
AL ***Thune***	Y	Y	N	Y	N	Y	Y
TENNESSEE							
1 ***Jenkins***	Y	Y	Y	Y	Y	Y	N
2 ***Duncan***	Y	Y	Y	N	N	Y	Y
3 ***Wamp***	Y	Y	Y	N	N	Y	Y
4 ***Hilleary***	Y	Y	Y	N	N	Y	N
5 Clement	Y	N	N	N	N	N	Y
6 Gordon	Y	N	Y	N	N	P	Y
7 ***Bryant***	Y	Y	N	Y	Y	Y	N
8 Tanner	Y	N	N	N	N	P	Y
9 Ford	Y	N	N	N	N	P	Y
TEXAS							
1 Sandlin	Y	N	N	N	N	P	Y
2 Turner	Y	N	N	N	N	Y	Y
3 ***Johnson, Sam***	Y	Y	N	Y	Y	N	N
4 Hall	Y	Y	Y	Y	Y	Y	N
5 ***Sessions***	Y	Y	N	Y	Y	N	N
6 ***Barton***	Y	Y	N	Y	Y	Y	N
7 ***Archer***	Y	Y	N	Y	N	Y	N
8 ***Brady***	Y	Y	N	Y	Y	Y	N
9 Lampson	?	N	N	N	N	Y	Y
10 Doggett	Y	N	Y	N	N	N	Y
11 Edwards	Y	N	N	N	N	N	Y
12 ***Granger***	Y	Y	N	Y	N	Y	N
13 ***Thornberry***	Y	Y	N	Y	Y	Y	N
14 ***Paul***	Y	Y	Y	N	Y	Y	N
15 Hinojosa	?	N	N	N	N	P	Y
16 Reyes	?	Y	N	N	N	P	Y
17 Stenholm	Y	Y	N	N	N	P	Y
18 Jackson-Lee	N	N	N	N	N	N	Y
19 ***Combest***	Y	Y	N	Y	Y	Y	N
20 Gonzalez	?	?	?	?	?	?	?
21 ***Smith***	Y	Y	N	Y	N	N	N
22 ***DeLay***	Y	Y	N	Y	Y	N	N
23 ***Bonilla***	Y	Y	N	Y	Y	N	N
24 Frost	Y	N	N	N	N	P	Y
25 Bentsen	Y	N	N	N	N	N	Y
26 ***Armey***	Y	Y	N	Y	Y	N	N
27 Ortiz	Y	N	N	N	N	N	Y
28 Rodriguez	Y	N	Y	N	N	P	Y
29 Green	Y	N	Y	N	N	N	Y
30 Johnson, E.B.	Y	N	N	N	N	N	Y
UTAH							
1 ***Hansen***	Y	Y	N	Y	Y	Y	N
2 ***Cook***	Y	Y	N	Y	N	Y	Y
3 ***Cannon***	Y	Y	N	Y	Y	N	N
VERMONT							
AL *Sanders*	Y	N	Y	N	N	N	Y
VIRGINIA							
1 ***Bateman***	Y	Y	N	Y	N	Y	N
2 Pickett	Y	Y	N	N	N	N	Y
3 Scott	Y	N	N	N	N	Y	N
4 Sisisky	Y	Y	N	N	N	Y	Y
5 Goode	Y	Y	Y	N	N	Y	Y
6 ***Goodlatte***	Y	Y	N	N	Y	Y	N
7 ***Bliley***	Y	Y	N	Y	Y	Y	N
8 Moran	Y	N	N	N	N	N	Y
9 Boucher	Y	N	Y	Y	N	N	Y
10 ***Wolf***	Y	Y	Y	Y	N	Y	N
11 ***Davis***	Y	Y	N	Y	N	Y	N
WASHINGTON							
1 ***White***	Y	Y	N	Y	Y	Y	Y
2 ***Metcalf***	Y	Y	Y	Y	N	N	Y
3 ***Smith, Linda***	Y	Y	Y	Y	N	N	Y
4 ***Hastings***	Y	Y	N	Y	Y	N	Y
5 ***Nethercutt***	Y	Y	Y	Y	Y	N	N
6 Dicks	Y	N	N	N	N	N	Y
7 McDermott	Y	N	N	N	N	P	Y
8 ***Dunn***	Y	Y	N	Y	Y	N	Y
9 Smith, Adam	Y	N	N	N	N	N	Y
WEST VIRGINIA							
1 Mollohan	Y	N	Y	Y	N	N	N
2 Wise	Y	N	Y	Y	N	N	Y
3 Rahall	Y	N	Y	Y	N	N	N
WISCONSIN							
1 ***Neumann***	Y	Y	Y	N	N	N	N
2 ***Klug***	Y	Y	N	Y	N	Y	Y
3 Kind	Y	N	N	N	N	Y	Y
4 Kleczka	Y	N	Y	N	N	N	Y
5 Barrett	Y	N	Y	N	N	N	Y
6 ***Petri***	Y	Y	N	N	N	Y	Y
7 Obey	Y	N	Y	N	N	N	Y
8 Johnson	Y	N	Y	N	N	Y	Y
9 ***Sensenbrenner***	Y	Y	N	N	N	Y	N
WYOMING							
AL ***Cubin***	Y	Y	N	Y	Y	N	N

Southern states - Ala., Ark., Fla., Ga., Ky., La., Miss., N.C., Okla., S.C., Tenn., Texas, Va.

House Votes 406, 407, 408, 409, 410, 411, 412

Key

Y	Voted for (yea).
#	Paired for.
+	Announced for.
N	Voted against (nay).
X	Paired against.
−	Announced against.
P	Voted "present."
C	Voted "present" to avoid possible conflict of interest.
?	Did not vote or otherwise make a position known.

Democrats **Republicans**
Independent

406. HR 4380. Fiscal 1999 District of Columbia Appropriations/Rule. Adoption of the rule (H Res 517) to provide for House floor consideration of the bill to appropriate $491 million in federal funds and $6.8 billion from the D.C. Treasury for government operations and activities of the District of Columbia in fiscal 1999. Adopted 220-204: R 218-3; D 2-200 (ND 1-147, SD 1-53); I 0-1. Aug. 6, 1998.

407. HR 4380. Fiscal 1999 District of Columbia Appropriations/Fund Advisory Neighborhood Commissions. Norton, D-D.C., amendment to fund the Advisory Neighborhood Commissions at the requested level of $573,000 in fiscal 1999. Rejected 187-237: R 8-215; D 178-22 (ND 139-8, SD 39-14); I 1-0. Aug. 6, 1998.

408. HR 4380. Fiscal 1999 District of Columbia Appropriations/Allow Use of Local Funds for Abortions. Norton, D-D.C. amendment to allow use of local funds for abortions. Rejected 180-243: R 27-196; D 152-47 (ND 115-31, SD 37-16); I 1-0. Aug. 6, 1998.

409. HR 4380. Fiscal 1999 District of Columbia Appropriations/Allow Use of Local Funds to Sue for Voting Rights. Norton, D-D.C., amendment to strike the prohibition against the use of local funds to sue Congress for voting rights in the House and Senate. Rejected 181-243: R 9-214; D 171-29 (ND 136-11, SD 35-18); I 1-0. Aug. 6, 1998.

410. HR 4380. Fiscal 1999 District of Columbia Appropriations/Residence Requirement for D.C. Government Employees. Norton, D-D.C., amendment to strike the provision in the bill that repeals the D.C. law requiring new D.C. government employees reside in the District of Columbia. Rejected 109-313: R 17-205; D 91-108 (ND 68-78, SD 23-30); I 1-0. Aug. 6, 1998.

411. HR 4380. Fiscal 1999 District of Columbia Appropriations/Education "Vouchers" for D.C. Students. Armey, R-Texas, amendment to establish a new program to provide education scholarships ("vouchers") to an estimated 2,000 poor D.C. public school students. Adopted 214-208: R 207-15; D 7-192 (ND 3-143, SD 4-49); I 0-1. Aug. 6, 1998.

412. HR 4380. Fiscal 1999 District of Columbia Appropriations/Needle Exchange Federal and Local Funds Prohibition. Tiahrt, R-Kan., amendment to prohibit federal and local funds from being spent on needle exchange programs in the District of Columbia. Adopted 250-169: R 205-15; D 45-153 (ND 26-120, SD 19-33); I 0-1. Aug. 7, 1998. Aug. 7, 1998, in the session that began Aug. 6 and is recorded in the Aug. 6 Congressional Record.

	406	407	408	409	410	411	412
ALABAMA							
1 *Callahan*	Y	N	N	N	N	Y	Y
2 *Everett*	Y	N	N	N	N	Y	Y
3 *Riley*	Y	N	N	N	N	Y	Y
4 *Aderholt*	Y	N	N	N	Y	Y	Y
5 Cramer	N	N	N	N	Y	N	?
6 *Bachus*	Y	N	N	N	N	Y	Y
7 Hilliard	N	Y	Y	Y	Y	N	N
ALASKA							
AL *Young*	Y	N	N	N	N	Y	Y
ARIZONA							
1 *Salmon*	Y	N	N	N	N	Y	Y
2 Pastor	N	Y	Y	Y	Y	N	N
3 *Stump*	Y	N	N	N	N	Y	Y
4 *Shadegg*	Y	N	N	N	N	Y	Y
5 *Kolbe*	Y	Y	Y	N	N	Y	N
6 *Hayworth*	Y	N	N	N	N	Y	Y
ARKANSAS							
1 Berry	N	Y	N	Y	Y	N	N
2 Snyder	N	Y	Y	Y	N	N	N
3 *Hutchinson*	Y	N	N	N	N	Y	N
4 *Dickey*	Y	N	N	N	N	Y	Y
CALIFORNIA							
1 *Riggs*	Y	N	N	N	N	Y	Y
2 *Herger*	Y	N	N	N	N	Y	Y
3 Fazio	N	Y	Y	Y	Y	N	N
4 *Doolittle*	Y	N	N	N	N	Y	Y
5 Matsui	N	Y	Y	Y	Y	N	N
6 Woolsey	N	Y	Y	Y	Y	N	N
7 Miller	N	Y	Y	Y	Y	N	N
8 Pelosi	N	Y	Y	Y	Y	N	N
9 Lee	N	Y	Y	Y	Y	N	N
10 Tauscher	N	Y	Y	Y	Y	N	N
11 *Pombo*	Y	N	N	N	N	Y	Y
12 Lantos	N	Y	Y	Y	Y	N	N
13 Stark	N	Y	Y	Y	Y	?	?
14 Eshoo	N	Y	Y	Y	Y	N	N
15 *Campbell*	Y	Y	Y	Y	Y	N	Y
16 Lofgren	N	Y	P	Y	N	N	N
17 Farr	N	Y	Y	Y	Y	N	N
18 Condit	N	Y	N	Y	N	Y	N
19 *Radanovich*	Y	N	N	N	N	Y	Y
20 Dooley	N	Y	Y	Y	N	N	N
21 *Thomas*	Y	N	N	N	N	Y	Y
22 Capps, L.	N	Y	Y	Y	Y	N	N
23 *Gallegly*	Y	N	N	N	N	Y	Y
24 Sherman	N	Y	Y	Y	Y	N	N
25 *McKeon*	Y	N	N	N	N	Y	Y
26 Berman	N	Y	Y	Y	Y	N	N
27 *Rogan*	Y	N	N	N	N	Y	Y
28 *Dreier*	Y	N	N	N	N	Y	Y
29 Waxman	N	Y	Y	Y	N	N	N
30 Becerra	N	Y	Y	Y	N	N	N
31 Martinez	N	Y	Y	Y	N	N	N
32 Dixon	N	Y	Y	Y	P	N	N
33 Roybal-Allard	N	Y	Y	Y	Y	N	N
34 Torres	N	Y	Y	Y	N	N	N
35 Waters	N	Y	Y	Y	N	N	N
36 Harman	N	?	?	?	N	N	N
37 Millender-McD.	N	Y	Y	Y	N	N	N
38 *Horn*	Y	Y	Y	Y	Y	Y	Y

	406	407	408	409	410	411	412
39 *Royce*	?	N	N	N	N	Y	Y
40 *Lewis*	Y	N	N	N	N	Y	Y
41 *Kim*	Y	Y	N	N	N	Y	Y
42 Brown	N	Y	Y	Y	Y	N	N
43 *Calvert*	Y	N	N	N	N	Y	Y
44 *Bono, M.*	Y	N	N	N	N	Y	Y
45 *Rohrabacher*	Y	N	N	N	N	Y	Y
46 Sanchez	N	Y	Y	Y	Y	N	N
47 *Cox*	Y	N	N	N	N	Y	Y
48 *Packard*	+	−	−	−	−	+	+
49 *Bilbray*	Y	N	N	N	N	Y	Y
50 Filner	N	Y	Y	Y	Y	N	N
51 *Cunningham*	?	?	?	?	?	?	?
52 *Hunter*	?	N	N	N	N	Y	Y
COLORADO							
1 DeGette	N	Y	Y	Y	Y	N	N
2 Skaggs	N	Y	Y	Y	N	N	N
3 *McInnis*	Y	N	N	N	N	Y	Y
4 *Schaffer*	Y	N	N	N	N	Y	Y
5 *Hefley*	Y	N	N	N	N	Y	Y
6 *Schaefer*	Y	N	N	N	N	Y	Y
CONNECTICUT							
1 Kennelly	N	Y	Y	Y	Y	N	N
2 Gejdenson	N	Y	Y	Y	N	N	N
3 DeLauro	N	Y	Y	Y	Y	N	N
4 *Shays*	Y	N	N	N	N	Y	N
5 Maloney	N	Y	Y	Y	N	N	N
6 *Johnson*	N	N	Y	N	N	N	N
DELAWARE							
AL *Castle*	Y	Y	Y	N	N	Y	N
FLORIDA							
1 *Scarborough*	Y	Y	N	N	N	Y	Y
2 Boyd	N	N	N	N	N	Y	Y
3 Brown	N	Y	Y	Y	Y	N	N
4 *Fowler*	Y	N	N	N	N	Y	Y
5 Thurman	N	Y	Y	Y	N	N	N
6 *Stearns*	?	N	N	N	?	Y	Y
7 *Mica*	Y	N	N	N	N	Y	Y
8 *McCollum*	Y	N	N	N	N	Y	Y
9 *Bilirakis*	Y	N	N	N	N	Y	Y
10 *Young*	Y	N	N	N	N	?	?
11 Davis	N	Y	Y	Y	N	N	N
12 *Canady*	Y	N	N	N	N	Y	Y
13 *Miller*	Y	N	N	N	N	Y	N
14 *Goss*	Y	N	N	N	N	Y	Y
15 *Weldon*	Y	N	N	N	N	Y	Y
16 *Foley*	Y	N	N	N	N	Y	N
17 Meek	N	Y	Y	Y	Y	N	N
18 *Ros-Lehtinen*	Y	N	N	N	N	Y	N
19 Wexler	N	Y	Y	Y	Y	N	N
20 Deutsch	N	Y	Y	Y	Y	N	N
21 *Diaz-Balart*	Y	N	N	N	N	Y	N
22 *Shaw*	Y	N	N	N	N	Y	Y
23 Hastings	N	Y	Y	Y	Y	N	N
GEORGIA							
1 *Kingston*	Y	N	N	N	N	Y	Y
2 Bishop	N	Y	Y	Y	N	N	N
3 *Collins*	Y	N	N	N	N	Y	Y
4 McKinney	N	Y	Y	Y	Y	N	N
5 Lewis	N	Y	Y	Y	Y	N	N
6 *Gingrich*	Y					Y	
7 *Barr*	Y	N	N	N	N	Y	Y
8 *Chambliss*	Y	N	N	N	N	Y	Y
9 *Deal*	Y	N	N	N	N	Y	Y
10 *Norwood*	Y	N	N	N	N	Y	Y
11 *Linder*	Y	N	N	N	N	Y	Y
HAWAII							
1 Abercrombie	N	Y	Y	Y	Y	N	N
2 Mink	N	Y	Y	Y	Y	N	N
IDAHO							
1 *Chenoweth*	Y	N	N	N	N	N	Y
2 *Crapo*	?	N	N	N	N	Y	Y
ILLINOIS							
1 Rush	N	Y	Y	Y	Y	N	N
2 Jackson	N	Y	Y	Y	Y	N	N
3 Lipinski	N	N	N	N	Y	Y	Y
4 Gutierrez	N	Y	Y	Y	Y	N	N
5 Blagojevich	N	Y	Y	Y	Y	N	N
6 *Hyde*	Y	N	N	N	Y	Y	Y
7 Davis	N	Y	Y	Y	Y	N	N
8 *Crane*	Y	N	N	N	N	Y	Y
9 Yates	N	?	?	?	?	?	?
10 *Porter*	Y	N	N	N	N	N	N
11 *Weller*	Y	N	N	N	N	Y	Y
12 Costello	N	N	N	N	Y	N	Y
13 *Fawell*	Y	N	N	N	N	Y	Y

ND Northern Democrats SD Southern Democrats

	406	407	408	409	410	411	412
14 ***Hastert***	Y	N	N	N	N	Y	Y
15 ***Ewing***	Y	N	N	N	N	Y	Y
16 ***Manzullo***	Y	N	N	N	N	Y	Y
17 Evans	N	Y	Y	Y	N	N	N
18 ***LaHood***	Y	N	N	N	N	Y	Y
19 Poshard	N	Y	N	Y	Y	N	Y
20 ***Shimkus***	Y	N	N	N	N	Y	Y
INDIANA							
1 Visclosky	N	Y	Y	Y	Y	N	Y
2 ***McIntosh***	Y	N	N	N	N	Y	Y
3 Roemer	N	Y	N	N	N	N	Y
4 ***Souder***	Y	N	N	N	N	Y	Y
5 ***Buyer***	Y	N	N	N	N	Y	?
6 ***Burton***	Y	N	?	N	N	Y	Y
7 ***Pease***	Y	N	N	N	N	Y	Y
8 ***Hostettler***	Y	N	N	N	N	Y	Y
9 Hamilton	N	Y	N	Y	N	N	Y
10 Carson	N	Y	Y	Y	Y	N	N
IOWA							
1 ***Leach***	Y	N	N	N	N	N	Y
2 ***Nussle***	Y	N	N	N	N	Y	Y
3 Boswell	N	Y	Y	N	N	N	Y
4 ***Ganske***	Y	N	N	N	N	Y	N
5 ***Latham***	Y	N	N	N	N	Y	Y
KANSAS							
1 ***Moran***	Y	N	N	N	N	Y	Y
2 ***Ryun***	Y	N	N	N	N	Y	Y
3 ***Snowbarger***	Y	N	N	N	N	Y	Y
4 ***Tiahrt***	Y	N	N	N	N	Y	Y
KENTUCKY							
1 ***Whitfield***	Y	N	N	N	N	Y	Y
2 ***Lewis***	Y	N	N	N	N	Y	Y
3 ***Northup***	Y	N	N	N	N	Y	Y
4 ***Bunning***	Y	N	N	N	N	Y	Y
5 ***Rogers***	Y	N	N	N	N	Y	Y
6 Baesler	N	N	N	N	N	N	Y
LOUISIANA							
1 ***Livingston***	Y	N	N	N	N	Y	Y
2 Jefferson	N	Y	Y	Y	Y	N	N
3 ***Tauzin***	Y	N	N	N	N	Y	Y
4 ***McCrery***	Y	N	N	N	N	Y	Y
5 ***Cooksey***	Y	N	N	N	N	Y	Y
6 ***Baker***	Y	N	N	N	N	Y	Y
7 John	N	N	N	N	N	N	Y
MAINE							
1 Allen	N	Y	Y	Y	N	N	N
2 Baldacci	N	Y	Y	Y	N	N	N
MARYLAND							
1 ***Gilchrest***	Y	N	Y	N	N	Y	Y
2 ***Ehrlich***	Y	N	N	N	N	Y	Y
3 Cardin	N	Y	Y	Y	N	N	N
4 Wynn	N	Y	Y	Y	N	N	N
5 Hoyer	N	Y	Y	Y	N	N	N
6 ***Bartlett***	Y	N	N	N	N	Y	Y
7 Cummings	N	Y	Y	Y	Y	N	N
8 ***Morella***	N	Y	Y	Y	N	N	N
MASSACHUSETTS							
1 Olver	N	Y	Y	Y	N	N	N
2 Neal	N	Y	N	Y	N	N	N
3 McGovern	N	Y	Y	Y	Y	N	N
4 Frank	N	Y	Y	Y	Y	N	N
5 Meehan	N	Y	Y	Y	N	N	N
6 Tierney	N	Y	Y	Y	Y	N	N
7 Markey	N	Y	Y	Y	Y	N	N
8 Kennedy	N	Y	Y	Y	Y	N	N
9 Moakley	N	?	?	?	?	?	?
10 Delahunt	N	Y	Y	Y	N	N	N
MICHIGAN							
1 Stupak	N	Y	N	Y	N	N	N
2 ***Hoekstra***	Y	N	N	N	N	Y	Y
3 ***Ehlers***	Y	N	N	N	Y	Y	Y
4 ***Camp***	Y	N	N	N	N	Y	Y
5 Barcia	N	Y	N	Y	N	N	N
6 ***Upton***	Y	N	N	N	N	Y	Y
7 ***Smith***	Y	N	N	N	Y	Y	Y
8 Stabenow	N	Y	Y	Y	N	N	N
9 Kildee	N	Y	N	Y	N	N	N
10 Bonior	N	Y	N	Y	Y	N	N
11 ***Knollenberg***	Y	N	N	N	N	Y	Y
12 Levin	N	Y	Y	Y	Y	N	N
13 Rivers	N	Y	Y	Y	Y	N	N
14 Conyers	N	Y	Y	Y	Y	?	?
15 Kilpatrick	N	Y	Y	Y	Y	N	N
16 Dingell	?	Y	Y	Y	N	N	N
MINNESOTA							
1 ***Gutknecht***	Y	N	N	N	N	Y	Y
2 Minge	N	Y	Y	Y	N	N	Y
3 ***Ramstad***	Y	N	Y	N	N	N	Y
4 Vento	N	Y	Y	Y	Y	N	N
5 Sabo	N	Y	Y	Y	N	N	N
6 Luther	N	Y	Y	Y	Y	N	Y
7 Peterson	N	N	N	Y	N	N	Y
8 Oberstar	N	Y	N	Y	N	N	N
MISSISSIPPI							
1 ***Wicker***	Y	N	N	N	N	Y	Y
2 Thompson	N	?	?	?	?	?	?
3 ***Pickering***	Y	N	N	N	N	Y	Y
4 ***Parker***	Y	N	N	N	N	Y	Y
5 Taylor	Y	N	N	N	N	Y	Y
MISSOURI							
1 Clay	?	N	Y	Y	Y	N	N
2 ***Talent***	Y	N	N	N	N	Y	Y
3 Gephardt	N	Y	Y	Y	Y	N	N
4 Skelton	N	Y	N	N	N	N	Y
5 McCarthy	N	Y	Y	Y	N	N	N
6 Danner	N	N	N	N	N	N	Y
7 ***Blunt***	Y	N	N	N	N	Y	Y
8 ***Emerson***	Y	N	N	N	N	Y	Y
9 ***Hulshof***	Y	N	N	N	N	Y	Y
MONTANA							
AL ***Hill***	Y	N	N	N	N	Y	Y
NEBRASKA							
1 ***Bereuter***	Y	N	N	Y	N	Y	Y
2 ***Christensen***	Y	N	N	N	N	Y	Y
3 ***Barrett***	Y	N	N	N	N	Y	Y
NEVADA							
1 ***Ensign***	Y	N	N	N	N	Y	N
2 ***Gibbons***	Y	N	N	N	N	Y	Y
NEW HAMPSHIRE							
1 ***Sununu***	Y	N	N	N	N	Y	Y
2 ***Bass***	Y	N	Y	N	N	Y	Y
NEW JERSEY							
1 Andrews	N	Y	Y	Y	N	N	N
2 ***LoBiondo***	Y	N	N	N	N	N	Y
3 ***Saxton***	Y	N	N	N	N	Y	Y
4 ***Smith***	Y	N	N	N	N	N	Y
5 ***Roukema***	Y	N	Y	N	N	N	Y
6 Pallone	N	Y	Y	Y	Y	N	N
7 ***Franks***	Y	N	Y	Y	N	Y	Y
8 Pascrell	N	Y	Y	Y	N	N	Y
9 Rothman	N	Y	Y	Y	Y	N	N
10 Payne	N	Y	Y	Y	Y	N	N
11 ***Frelinghuysen***	Y	N	Y	N	N	Y	N
12 ***Pappas***	Y	N	N	N	N	Y	Y
13 Menendez	N	Y	Y	Y	Y	N	N
NEW MEXICO							
1 ***Wilson***	Y	N	N	N	N	Y	Y
2 ***Skeen***	Y	N	N	N	N	Y	Y
3 ***Redmond***	Y	N	N	N	N	Y	Y
NEW YORK							
1 ***Forbes***	Y	N	N	N	N	Y	Y
2 ***Lazio***	Y	N	Y	N	Y	Y	Y
3 ***King***	Y	N	N	N	N	Y	Y
4 McCarthy	N	Y	Y	Y	N	N	N
5 Ackerman	N	Y	Y	Y	N	N	N
6 Meeks	N	Y	Y	Y	Y	N	N
7 Manton	?	?	?	?	?	?	?
8 Nadler	N	Y	Y	Y	N	N	N
9 Schumer	N	Y	Y	Y	N	N	N
10 Towns	N	Y	Y	Y	Y	N	N
11 Owens	N	Y	Y	Y	Y	N	N
12 Velázquez	N	Y	Y	Y	Y	N	N
13 ***Fossella***	Y	N	N	N	N	Y	Y
14 Maloney	N	Y	Y	Y	N	N	N
15 Rangel	N	Y	Y	Y	Y	N	N
16 Serrano	N	Y	Y	Y	Y	N	N
17 Engel	N	Y	Y	Y	N	N	N
18 Lowey	N	Y	Y	Y	N	N	N
19 ***Kelly***	Y	N	Y	N	N	Y	Y
20 ***Gilman***	Y	N	Y	Y	N	Y	Y
21 McNulty	N	Y	N	Y	N	N	N
22 ***Solomon***	Y	N	N	N	N	Y	Y
23 ***Boehlert***	Y	N	Y	N	N	N	N
24 ***McHugh***	Y	N	N	N	N	N	Y
25 ***Walsh***	Y	N	N	N	N	N	Y
26 Hinchey	N	Y	Y	Y	Y	N	N
27 ***Paxon***	Y	N	N	N	N	Y	Y
28 Slaughter	N	Y	Y	N	N	N	N
29 LaFalce	N	Y	N	Y	N	N	N
30 ***Quinn***	Y	N	N	N	N	Y	Y
31 ***Houghton***	N	N	Y	N	N	Y	N
NORTH CAROLINA							
1 Clayton	N	Y	Y	Y	Y	N	N
2 Etheridge	N	Y	N	N	N	N	Y
3 ***Jones***	Y	N	N	N	N	Y	Y
4 Price	N	Y	Y	N	N	N	N
5 ***Burr***	Y	N	N	N	N	Y	Y
6 ***Coble***	Y	N	N	N	Y	Y	Y
7 McIntyre	N	N	N	N	N	N	Y
8 Hefner	N	Y	Y	N	N	N	N
9 ***Myrick***	Y	N	N	N	N	Y	Y
10 ***Ballenger***	Y	N	N	N	N	Y	Y
11 ***Taylor***	Y	N	N	N	Y	Y	Y
12 Watt	N	Y	Y	Y	Y	N	N
NORTH DAKOTA							
AL Pomeroy	N	Y	Y	N	N	N	Y
OHIO							
1 ***Chabot***	Y	N	N	N	N	Y	Y
2 ***Portman***	Y	N	N	N	N	Y	Y
3 Hall	N	Y	N	Y	N	N	Y
4 ***Oxley***	Y	N	N	N	N	Y	Y
5 ***Gillmor***	Y	N	N	N	N	Y	Y
6 Strickland	N	Y	Y	Y	N	N	Y
7 ***Hobson***	Y	N	Y	N	Y	Y	Y
8 ***Boehner***	Y	N	N	N	N	Y	Y
9 Kaptur	N	Y	N	Y	Y	N	N
10 Kucinich	N	Y	N	Y	Y	N	N
11 Stokes	N	Y	Y	Y	Y	N	N
12 ***Kasich***	Y	N	N	N	N	Y	Y
13 Brown	N	Y	Y	Y	Y	N	N
14 Sawyer	N	Y	Y	Y	Y	N	N
15 ***Pryce***	Y	N	Y	N	N	Y	Y
16 ***Regula***	Y	N	N	N	N	Y	Y
17 Traficant	Y	Y	N	N	N	N	Y
18 ***Ney***	Y	N	N	N	N	N	Y
19 ***LaTourette***	Y	N	N	N	N	Y	Y
OKLAHOMA							
1 ***Largent***	Y	N	N	N	N	Y	Y
2 ***Coburn***	Y	N	N	N	N	Y	Y
3 ***Watkins***	Y	N	N	N	Y	Y	Y
4 ***Watts***	Y	N	N	N	N	Y	Y
5 ***Istook***	Y	N	N	N	N	Y	Y
6 ***Lucas***	Y	N	N	N	Y	Y	Y
OREGON							
1 Furse	N	Y	Y	Y	N	N	N
2 ***Smith***	Y	N	N	N	N	?	?
3 Blumenauer	N	Y	Y	Y	Y	N	N
4 DeFazio	N	Y	Y	N	N	N	N
5 Hooley	N	Y	Y	Y	Y	N	N
PENNSYLVANIA							
1 Brady	N	Y	Y	Y	Y	N	N
2 Fattah	N	Y	Y	Y	Y	N	N
3 Borski	N	Y	N	Y	Y	N	N
4 Klink	N	N	N	Y	N	N	N
5 ***Peterson***	Y	N	N	N	N	Y	Y
6 Holden	N	Y	N	Y	Y	N	Y
7 ***Weldon***	Y	N	N	N	N	Y	Y
8 ***Greenwood***	Y	N	Y	N	N	Y	N
9 ***Shuster***	Y	N	N	N	N	Y	Y
10 ***McDade***	Y	?	?	?	?	?	?
11 Kanjorski	N	Y	N	Y	N	N	N
12 Murtha	N	Y	N	Y	N	N	Y
13 ***Fox***	Y	N	N	N	N	Y	Y
14 Coyne	N	Y	Y	Y	Y	N	N
15 McHale	N	Y	Y	Y	N	N	N
16 ***Pitts***	Y	N	N	N	N	Y	Y
17 ***Gekas***	Y	N	N	?	N	Y	Y
18 Doyle	N	N	N	Y	N	N	N
19 ***Goodling***	Y	N	N	N	Y	Y	Y
20 Mascara	N	Y	N	Y	N	N	Y
21 ***English***	Y	N	N	N	N	N	Y
RHODE ISLAND							
1 Kennedy	N	Y	Y	Y	Y	N	N
2 Weygand	N	Y	N	Y	N	N	N
SOUTH CAROLINA							
1 ***Sanford***	Y	N	N	N	N	Y	Y
2 ***Spence***	Y	N	N	N	N	Y	Y
3 ***Graham***	Y	N	N	N	N	Y	Y
4 ***Inglis***	?	N	N	N	N	Y	Y
5 Spratt	N	N	Y	N	N	N	Y
6 Clyburn	N	Y	Y	Y	Y	N	N
SOUTH DAKOTA							
AL ***Thune***	Y	N	N	N	N	Y	Y
TENNESSEE							
1 ***Jenkins***	Y	N	N	N	N	Y	Y
2 ***Duncan***	Y	N	N	N	Y	Y	Y
3 ***Wamp***	Y	N	N	N	N	Y	Y
4 ***Hilleary***	Y	N	N	N	N	Y	Y
5 Clement	N	N	N	Y	Y	N	Y
6 Gordon	N	Y	Y	N	N	N	Y
7 ***Bryant***	Y	N	N	N	N	Y	Y
8 Tanner	N	Y	N	N	N	N	Y
9 Ford	N	Y	Y	Y	Y	N	N
TEXAS							
1 Sandlin	N	Y	Y	Y	Y	N	Y
2 Turner	N	Y	N	N	N	N	Y
3 ***Johnson, Sam***	Y	N	N	N	N	Y	Y
4 Hall	N	N	N	Y	N	Y	Y
5 ***Sessions***	Y	N	N	N	N	Y	Y
6 ***Barton***	Y	N	N	N	N	Y	Y
7 ***Archer***	Y	N	N	N	N	Y	Y
8 ***Brady***	Y	N	N	N	Y	Y	Y
9 Lampson	N	Y	N	Y	Y	N	N
10 Doggett	N	Y	Y	Y	Y	N	N
11 Edwards	N	Y	Y	Y	N	N	N
12 ***Granger***	Y	N	N	N	N	Y	Y
13 ***Thornberry***	Y	N	N	N	N	Y	Y
14 ***Paul***	Y	?	N	N	Y	N	Y
15 Hinojosa	N	Y	Y	N	N	N	N
16 Reyes	N	Y	Y	Y	N	N	Y
17 Stenholm	N	N	N	N	N	N	Y
18 Jackson-Lee	N	Y	Y	Y	Y	N	N
19 ***Combest***	Y	N	N	N	N	Y	Y
20 Gonzalez	?	?	?	?	?	?	?
21 ***Smith***	Y	N	N	N	N	Y	Y
22 ***DeLay***	Y	N	N	N	N	Y	Y
23 ***Bonilla***	Y	N	Y	N	N	Y	N
24 Frost	N	Y	Y	Y	N	N	N
25 Bentsen	N	Y	Y	Y	Y	N	N
26 ***Armey***	Y	N	N	N	N	Y	Y
27 Ortiz	N	Y	N	N	N	N	Y
28 Rodriguez	N	Y	Y	Y	Y	N	N
29 Green	N	Y	Y	Y	N	N	Y
30 Johnson, E.B.	N	Y	Y	Y	Y	N	N
UTAH							
1 ***Hansen***	Y	N	N	N	N	?	?
2 ***Cook***	Y	N	N	N	N	Y	Y
3 ***Cannon***	Y	N	N	N	N	Y	Y
VERMONT							
AL *Sanders*	N	Y	Y	Y	Y	N	N
VIRGINIA							
1 ***Bateman***	Y	N	N	N	N	Y	Y
2 Pickett	N	N	Y	N	N	N	Y
3 Scott	N	Y	Y	Y	Y	N	N
4 Sisisky	N	N	Y	Y	N	N	N
5 Goode	N	N	N	N	N	Y	Y
6 ***Goodlatte***	Y	N	N	N	N	Y	Y
7 ***Bliley***	Y	N	N	N	Y	Y	Y
8 Moran	N	Y	Y	Y	N	N	N
9 Boucher	N	N	N	N	N	N	N
10 ***Wolf***	Y	N	N	Y	N	Y	Y
11 ***Davis***	Y	N	N	Y	N	Y	Y
WASHINGTON							
1 ***White***	Y	N	Y	N	N	Y	Y
2 ***Metcalf***	Y	N	N	N	N	Y	Y
3 ***Smith, Linda***	Y	N	N	N	N	Y	Y
4 ***Hastings***	Y	N	N	N	N	Y	Y
5 ***Nethercutt***	Y	N	N	N	N	Y	Y
6 Dicks	N	Y	Y	Y	N	N	N
7 McDermott	N	Y	Y	Y	Y	N	N
8 ***Dunn***	Y	Y	Y	N	N	Y	Y
9 Smith, Adam	N	Y	Y	N	Y	N	N
WEST VIRGINIA							
1 Mollohan	N	Y	N	Y	N	N	Y
2 Wise	N	Y	Y	Y	N	N	Y
3 Rahall	N	Y	N	Y	N	N	N
WISCONSIN							
1 ***Neumann***	Y	N	N	N	N	Y	Y
2 ***Klug***	Y	N	Y	N	N	Y	Y
3 Kind	N	Y	Y	Y	N	N	N
4 Kleczka	N	N	Y	Y	N	N	N
5 Barrett	N	Y	Y	Y	Y	N	N
6 ***Petri***	Y	N	N	N	N	Y	Y
7 Obey	N	Y	Y	Y	Y	N	N
8 Johnson	N	Y	Y	N	Y	N	Y
9 ***Sensenbrenner***	Y	N	N	N	N	Y	Y
WYOMING							
AL ***Cubin***	Y	N	N	N	?	Y	Y

Southern states - Ala., Ark., Fla., Ga., Ky., La., Miss., N.C., Okla., S.C., Tenn., Texas, Va.

House Votes 413, 414, 415, 416, 417, 418, 419

413. HR 4380. Fiscal 1999 District of Columbia Appropriations/Needle Exchange Federal Funds Prohibition. Moran, D-Va., amendment to prohibit federal funds from being spent on needle exchange programs in the District of Columbia. Rejected 173-247: R 21-200; D 151-47 (ND 115-31, SD 36-16); I 1-0. Aug. 7, 1998. Aug. 7, 1998, in the session that began Aug. 6 and is recorded in the Aug. 6 Congressional Record.

414. HR 4380. Fiscal 1999 District of Columbia Appropriations/Prohibit Certain Joint Adoptions. Largent, R-Okla., amendment to prohibit joint adoptions in the District of Columbia by people who are not related by marriage or blood. Adopted 227-192: R 190-30; D 37-161 (ND 16-130, SD 21-31); I 0-1. Aug. 7, 1998. Aug. 7, 1998, in the session that began Aug. 6 and is recorded in the Aug. 6 Congressional Record.

415. HR 4380. Fiscal 1999 District of Columbia Appropriations/Penalty for Minors' Tobacco Possession. Bilbray, R-Calif., amendment to make it illegal for anyone under 18 years of age to possess any cigarette or tobacco product in the District of Columbia. A first violation would carry a penalty of up to $50. Adopted 283-138: R 207-14; D 76-123 (ND 48-99, SD 28-24); I 0-1. Aug. 7, 1998. Aug. 7, 1998, in the session that began Aug. 6 and is recorded in the Aug. 6 Congressional Record.

416. HR 4380. Fiscal 1999 District of Columbia Appropriations/Passage. Passage of the bill to appropriate $491 million in federal funds and $6.8 billion from the D.C. treasury for government operations and related activities in the District of Columbia in fiscal 1999. Passed 214-206: R 211-11; D 3-194 (ND 1-144, SD 2-50); I 0-1. Aug. 7, 1998. Aug. 7, 1998, in the session that began Aug. 6 and is recorded in the Aug. 6 Congressional Record. A "nay" was a vote in support of the president's position.

417. HR 678. Thomas Edison Commemorative Coin/Passage. Castle, R-Del., motion to suspend the rules and pass the bill to require the Treasury Department to issue up to 500,000 silver dollar coins that commemorate the 125th anniversary of the invention of the light bulb in 1879 by Thomas A. Edison. Motion agreed to 397-1: R 215-1; D 181-0 (ND 134-0, SD 47-0); I 1-0. Sept. 9, 1998. A two-thirds majority of those present and voting (266 in this case) is required for passage under suspension of the rules.

418. HR 1560. Lewis and Clark Expedition Commemorative Coin/Passage. Castle, R-Del., motion to suspend the rules and pass the bill to require the Treasury Department to issue silver dollar and half-dollar coins that commemorate the bicentennial of the 28-month expedition led by Meriwether Lewis and William Clark. Motion agreed to 398-2: R 214-2; D 183-0 (ND 136-0, SD 47-0); I 1-0. Sept. 9, 1998. A two-thirds majority of those present and voting (267 in this case) is required for passage under suspension of the rules.

419. H Res 459. Anniversary of U.S.-Korea Relations/Passage. Gilman, R-N.Y., motion to suspend the rules and pass the bill to express the sense of the House congratulating the Republic of Korea (South Korea) on the 50th anniversary of its founding. Motion agreed to 400-0: R 214-0; D 185-0 (ND 137-0, SD 48-0); I 1-0. Sept. 9, 1998. A two-thirds majority of those present and voting (267 in this case) is required for passage under suspension of the rules.

Key

- Y Voted for (yea).
- # Paired for.
- + Announced for.
- N Voted against (nay).
- X Paired against.
- − Announced against.
- P Voted "present."
- C Voted "present" to avoid possible conflict of interest.
- ? Did not vote or otherwise make a position known.

Democrats **Republicans** Independent

		413	414	415	416	417	418	419
ALABAMA								
1	*Callahan*	N	Y	Y	Y	Y	Y	Y
2	*Everett*	N	Y	Y	Y	Y	Y	Y
3	*Riley*	N	Y	Y	Y	Y	Y	Y
4	*Aderholt*	N	Y	Y	Y	Y	Y	Y
5	Cramer	?	?	?	?	Y	Y	Y
6	*Bachus*	N	Y	Y	Y	Y	Y	Y
7	Hilliard	Y	N	N	N	Y	Y	Y
ALASKA								
AL	*Young*	N	Y	N	Y	?	?	?
ARIZONA								
1	*Salmon*	N	Y	Y	Y	Y	Y	Y
2	Pastor	Y	N	Y	N	Y	Y	Y
3	*Stump*	N	Y	Y	Y	Y	Y	Y
4	*Shadegg*	N	Y	Y	Y	Y	Y	Y
5	*Kolbe*	N	N	Y	Y	?	?	?
6	*Hayworth*	N	Y	Y	Y	Y	Y	Y
ARKANSAS								
1	Berry	Y	Y	Y	N	Y	Y	Y
2	Snyder	Y	N	N	N	Y	Y	Y
3	*Hutchinson*	N	Y	N	Y	Y	Y	Y
4	*Dickey*	N	Y	Y	Y	Y	Y	Y
CALIFORNIA								
1	*Riggs*	N	Y	Y	Y	?	?	?
2	*Herger*	N	Y	Y	Y	Y	Y	Y
3	Fazio	Y	N	N	N	Y	Y	Y
4	*Doolittle*	N	Y	Y	Y	Y	Y	Y
5	Matsui	Y	N	N	N	Y	Y	Y
6	Woolsey	Y	N	N	N	Y	Y	Y
7	Miller	Y	N	N	N	Y	Y	Y
8	Pelosi	Y	N	N	N	Y	Y	Y
9	Lee	Y	N	N	N	Y	Y	Y
10	Tauscher	Y	N	N	N	Y	Y	Y
11	*Pombo*	N	Y	Y	Y	Y	Y	Y
12	Lantos	Y	N	N	N	Y	Y	Y
13	Stark	?	?	?	?	Y	Y	Y
14	Eshoo	Y	N	N	N	Y	Y	Y
15	*Campbell*	N	N	N	N	Y	Y	Y
16	Lofgren	Y	N	N	N	Y	Y	Y
17	Farr	Y	N	N	N	Y	Y	Y
18	Condit	Y	N	N	Y	Y	Y	Y
19	*Radanovich*	N	Y	Y	Y	Y	Y	Y
20	Dooley	Y	N	N	N	Y	Y	Y
21	*Thomas*	N	Y	Y	Y	Y	Y	Y
22	Capps, L.	Y	N	N	N	Y	Y	Y
23	*Gallegly*	Y	Y	Y	Y	Y	Y	Y
24	Sherman	N	N	N	N	Y	Y	Y
25	*McKeon*	N	Y	Y	Y	Y	Y	Y
26	Berman	Y	N	N	N	?	?	Y
27	*Rogan*	N	Y	Y	Y	Y	Y	Y
28	*Dreier*	N	Y	Y	Y	Y	Y	Y
29	Waxman	Y	N	N	N	Y	Y	Y
30	Becerra	Y	N	N	N	Y	Y	Y
31	Martinez	Y	N	N	N	Y	Y	Y
32	Dixon	Y	N	N	N	?	?	Y
33	Roybal-Allard	Y	N	N	N	Y	Y	Y
34	Torres	Y	N	N	N	Y	Y	Y
35	Waters	N	N	?	N	Y	Y	Y
36	Harman	Y	N	N	N	Y	Y	Y
37	Millender-McD.	Y	N	N	N	Y	Y	Y
38	*Horn*	Y	N	Y	Y	Y	Y	Y

		413	414	415	416	417	418	419
39	*Royce*	N	Y	Y	Y	Y	Y	Y
40	*Lewis*	N	Y	Y	Y	Y	?	Y
41	*Kim*	N	Y	Y	Y	Y	Y	Y
42	Brown	Y	N	N	N	Y	Y	Y
43	*Calvert*	N	Y	Y	Y	Y	Y	Y
44	*Bono, M.*	N	Y	Y	Y	Y	Y	Y
45	*Rohrabacher*	N	Y	Y	Y	Y	Y	Y
46	Sanchez	Y	N	N	N	Y	Y	Y
47	*Cox*	N	Y	Y	Y	Y	Y	Y
48	*Packard*	−	+	+	+	Y	Y	Y
49	*Bilbray*	N	?	Y	Y	Y	Y	Y
50	Filner	N	N	N	N	Y	Y	Y
51	*Cunningham*	?	?	?	?	Y	Y	Y
52	*Hunter*	N	Y	Y	Y	Y	Y	Y
COLORADO								
1	DeGette	N	N	N	N	Y	Y	Y
2	Skaggs	Y	N	N	N	Y	Y	Y
3	*McInnis*	N	Y	Y	Y	Y	Y	Y
4	*Schaffer*	N	Y	Y	Y	Y	Y	Y
5	*Hefley*	N	Y	Y	Y	Y	Y	Y
6	*Schaefer*	N	Y	N	Y	?	?	Y
CONNECTICUT								
1	Kennelly	Y	N	Y	N	?	?	?
2	Gejdenson	Y	N	N	N	?	?	?
3	DeLauro	Y	N	N	N	Y	Y	Y
4	*Shays*	Y	N	Y	N	Y	Y	Y
5	Maloney	Y	N	N	N	Y	Y	Y
6	*Johnson*	Y	N	Y	N	Y	Y	Y
DELAWARE								
AL	*Castle*	Y	Y	Y	N	Y	Y	Y
FLORIDA								
1	*Scarborough*	N	Y	Y	Y	Y	Y	Y
2	Boyd	Y	N	N	Y	Y	Y	Y
3	Brown	Y	N	N	N	?	?	Y
4	*Fowler*	N	Y	Y	Y	Y	Y	Y
5	Thurman	Y	N	N	Y	Y	Y	Y
6	*Stearns*	N	Y	Y	Y	Y	Y	Y
7	*Mica*	N	Y	Y	Y	Y	Y	Y
8	*McCollum*	N	Y	Y	Y	Y	Y	Y
9	*Bilirakis*	N	Y	Y	Y	Y	Y	Y
10	*Young*	?	?	?	?	Y	Y	Y
11	Davis	Y	N	N	Y	Y	Y	Y
12	*Canady*	N	Y	Y	Y	Y	Y	Y
13	*Miller*	Y	N	N	Y	Y	Y	Y
14	*Goss*	N	Y	Y	Y	Y	Y	Y
15	*Weldon*	Y	Y	Y	Y	Y	Y	Y
16	*Foley*	Y	Y	Y	Y	Y	Y	Y
17	Meek	Y	N	N	Y	?	?	Y
18	*Ros-Lehtinen*	N	Y	Y	Y	Y	Y	Y
19	Wexler	Y	N	Y	N	?	?	?
20	Deutsch	N	Y	N	Y	+	+	+
21	*Diaz-Balart*	N	Y	Y	Y	Y	Y	Y
22	*Shaw*	N	Y	Y	Y	Y	Y	Y
23	Hastings	Y	N	N	N	Y	Y	Y
GEORGIA								
1	*Kingston*	N	Y	Y	Y	Y	Y	Y
2	Bishop	Y	N	Y	Y	Y	Y	Y
3	*Collins*	N	Y	Y	Y	Y	Y	Y
4	McKinney	N	N	N	N	Y	Y	Y
5	Lewis	Y	N	N	N	Y	Y	Y
6	*Gingrich*							Y
7	*Barr*	N	Y	Y	Y	Y	Y	Y
8	*Chambliss*	N	Y	Y	Y	Y	Y	Y
9	*Deal*	N	Y	Y	Y	Y	Y	Y
10	*Norwood*	N	Y	Y	Y	Y	Y	Y
11	*Linder*	N	Y	Y	Y	Y	Y	Y
HAWAII								
1	Abercrombie	Y	N	N	N	Y	Y	Y
2	Mink	Y	N	N	N	Y	Y	Y
IDAHO								
1	*Chenoweth*	N	Y	Y	N	Y	Y	Y
2	*Crapo*	N	Y	Y	N	Y	Y	Y
ILLINOIS								
1	Rush	Y	N	N	N	?	?	?
2	Jackson	Y	N	N	N	Y	Y	Y
3	Lipinski	N	Y	Y	Y	Y	Y	Y
4	Gutierrez	Y	N	N	N	Y	Y	Y
5	Blagojevich	Y	N	N	N	Y	Y	Y
6	*Hyde*	N	Y	Y	Y	Y	Y	Y
7	Davis	Y	N	N	N	Y	Y	Y
8	*Crane*	N	Y	Y	Y	Y	Y	Y
9	Yates	?	?	?	?	Y	Y	Y
10	*Porter*	N	N	Y	Y	Y	Y	Y
11	*Weller*	N	Y	Y	Y	Y	Y	Y
12	Costello	Y	N	N	Y	Y	Y	Y
13	*Fawell*	N	N	Y	Y	Y	Y	Y

ND Northern Democrats   SD Southern Democrats

	413	414	415	416	417	418	419
14 ***Hastert***	N	Y	Y	Y	Y	Y	Y
15 ***Ewing***	N	Y	Y	Y	Y	Y	Y
16 ***Manzullo***	Y	Y	Y	Y	Y	Y	Y
17 Evans	Y	N	Y	N	Y	Y	Y
18 ***LaHood***	Y	Y	Y	Y	Y	Y	Y
19 Poshard	N	Y	Y	N	?	?	?
20 ***Shimkus***	N	Y	Y	Y	Y	Y	Y
INDIANA							
1 Visclosky	N	N	Y	N	Y	Y	Y
2 ***McIntosh***	N	Y	Y	Y	Y	Y	Y
3 Roemer	N	Y	Y	N	Y	Y	Y
4 ***Souder***	N	Y	Y	Y	Y	Y	Y
5 ***Buyer***	N	Y	Y	Y	?	?	?
6 ***Burton***	N	Y	Y	Y	Y	Y	Y
7 ***Pease***	N	Y	Y	Y	Y	Y	Y
8 ***Hostettler***	N	Y	Y	Y	Y	Y	Y
9 Hamilton	N	Y	Y	N	Y	Y	Y
10 Carson	N	N	N	N	Y	Y	Y
IOWA							
1 ***Leach***	N	N	Y	Y	Y	Y	Y
2 ***Nussle***	N	Y	Y	Y	Y	Y	Y
3 Boswell	N	N	Y	N	Y	Y	Y
4 ***Ganske***	N	Y	N	Y	Y	Y	Y
5 ***Latham***	N	Y	Y	Y	Y	Y	Y
KANSAS							
1 ***Moran***	N	Y	Y	Y	Y	Y	Y
2 ***Ryun***	N	Y	Y	Y	Y	Y	Y
3 ***Snowbarger***	N	Y	Y	Y	Y	Y	Y
4 ***Tiahrt***	N	Y	Y	Y	Y	Y	Y
KENTUCKY							
1 ***Whitfield***	N	N	Y	Y	Y	Y	Y
2 ***Lewis***	N	Y	Y	Y	Y	Y	Y
3 ***Northup***	N	Y	N	Y	Y	Y	Y
4 ***Bunning***	N	Y	Y	Y	Y	Y	Y
5 ***Rogers***	N	Y	Y	Y	Y	Y	Y
6 Baesler	N	Y	Y	N	Y	Y	Y
LOUISIANA							
1 ***Livingston***	N	Y	Y	Y	Y	Y	Y
2 Jefferson	Y	N	N	N	Y	Y	Y
3 ***Tauzin***	N	Y	Y	Y	Y	Y	Y
4 ***McCrery***	N	Y	Y	Y	Y	Y	Y
5 ***Cooksey***	N	Y	Y	Y	Y	Y	Y
6 ***Baker***	N	Y	Y	Y	Y	Y	Y
7 John	N	Y	Y	N	?	?	?
MAINE							
1 Allen	N	N	N	N	Y	Y	Y
2 Baldacci	Y	N	N	N	Y	Y	Y
MARYLAND							
1 ***Gilchrest***	Y	Y	Y	Y	Y	Y	Y
2 ***Ehrlich***	N	Y	Y	Y	?	?	?
3 Cardin	Y	N	Y	N	Y	Y	Y
4 Wynn	Y	N	N	N	Y	Y	Y
5 Hoyer	Y	N	Y	N	Y	Y	Y
6 ***Bartlett***	N	Y	Y	Y	Y	Y	Y
7 Cummings	Y	N	N	N	Y	Y	Y
8 ***Morella***	Y	N	N	N	Y	Y	Y
MASSACHUSETTS							
1 Olver	Y	N	N	N	Y	Y	Y
2 Neal	Y	N	N	N	Y	Y	Y
3 McGovern	Y	N	Y	N	Y	Y	Y
4 Frank	Y	N	N	N	Y	Y	Y
5 Meehan	Y	N	N	N	Y	Y	Y
6 Tierney	Y	N	N	N	Y	Y	Y
7 Markey	N	N	N	N	Y	Y	Y
8 Kennedy	Y	N	N	N	?	?	?
9 Moakley	?	?	?	?	?	?	?
10 Delahunt	Y	N	N	N	Y	Y	Y
MICHIGAN							
1 Stupak	Y	Y	N	N	Y	Y	Y
2 ***Hoekstra***	N	Y	Y	Y	?	?	?
3 ***Ehlers***	N	Y	Y	Y	Y	Y	Y
4 ***Camp***	N	N	Y	Y	Y	Y	Y
5 Barcia	Y	Y	Y	N	?	?	?
6 ***Upton***	Y	Y	Y	Y	Y	Y	Y
7 ***Smith***	N	Y	Y	Y	Y	Y	Y
8 Stabenow	N	N	Y	N	Y	Y	Y
9 Kildee	Y	N	N	N	Y	Y	Y
10 Bonior	N	N	N	N	Y	Y	Y
11 ***Knollenberg***	N	Y	Y	Y	Y	Y	Y
12 Levin	Y	N	Y	N	Y	Y	Y
13 Rivers	N	N	N	N	Y	Y	Y
14 Conyers	?	?	N	N	Y	Y	Y
15 Kilpatrick	Y	N	N	N	Y	Y	Y
16 Dingell	Y	N	N	N	Y	Y	Y

	413	414	415	416	417	418	419
MINNESOTA							
1 ***Gutknecht***	N	Y	Y	Y	Y	Y	Y
2 Minge	Y	Y	Y	N	Y	Y	Y
3 ***Ramstad***	N	Y	Y	N	Y	Y	Y
4 Vento	Y	N	N	N	Y	Y	Y
5 Sabo	Y	N	Y	N	Y	Y	Y
6 Luther	Y	N	Y	N	Y	Y	Y
7 Peterson	Y	Y	Y	N	Y	Y	Y
8 Oberstar	Y	N	N	N	Y	Y	Y
MISSISSIPPI							
1 ***Wicker***	N	Y	Y	Y	Y	Y	Y
2 Thompson	?	?	?	?	Y	Y	Y
3 ***Pickering***	N	Y	Y	Y	Y	Y	Y
4 ***Parker***	N	Y	Y	Y	Y	Y	Y
5 Taylor	N	Y	Y	N	Y	Y	Y
MISSOURI							
1 Clay	Y	N	N	N	Y	Y	Y
2 ***Talent***	N	Y	Y	Y	Y	Y	Y
3 Gephardt	Y	N	Y	N	Y	Y	Y
4 Skelton	N	Y	Y	N	Y	Y	Y
5 McCarthy	Y	N	N	N	Y	Y	Y
6 Danner	N	N	Y	N	Y	Y	Y
7 ***Blunt***	N	Y	Y	Y	Y	Y	Y
8 ***Emerson***	N	Y	Y	Y	Y	Y	Y
9 ***Hulshof***	N	Y	Y	Y	Y	Y	Y
MONTANA							
AL ***Hill***	N	Y	Y	Y	Y	Y	Y
NEBRASKA							
1 ***Bereuter***	N	Y	Y	Y	Y	Y	Y
2 ***Christensen***	N	Y	Y	Y	Y	Y	Y
3 ***Barrett***	N	Y	Y	Y	Y	Y	Y
NEVADA							
1 ***Ensign***	Y	Y	N	Y	Y	Y	Y
2 ***Gibbons***	N	Y	Y	Y	Y	Y	Y
NEW HAMPSHIRE							
1 ***Sununu***	N	Y	Y	Y	Y	Y	Y
2 ***Bass***	N	N	Y	Y	Y	Y	Y
NEW JERSEY							
1 Andrews	Y	N	Y	N	Y	Y	Y
2 ***LoBiondo***	N	Y	Y	N	Y	Y	Y
3 ***Saxton***	N	Y	Y	Y	Y	Y	Y
4 ***Smith***	N	Y	Y	Y	Y	Y	Y
5 ***Roukema***	N	Y	Y	Y	?	?	?
6 Pallone	Y	N	N	N	Y	Y	Y
7 ***Franks***	N	N	Y	Y	Y	Y	Y
8 Pascrell	N	N	Y	?	Y	Y	Y
9 Rothman	N	N	Y	N	Y	Y	Y
10 Payne	Y	N	N	N	Y	Y	Y
11 ***Frelinghuysen***	Y	N	Y	Y	Y	Y	Y
12 ***Pappas***	N	Y	Y	Y	Y	Y	Y
13 Menendez	Y	N	Y	N	Y	Y	Y
NEW MEXICO							
1 ***Wilson***	N	N	Y	Y	Y	Y	Y
2 ***Skeen***	N	Y	N	Y	Y	Y	Y
3 ***Redmond***	N	Y	Y	Y	Y	Y	Y
NEW YORK							
1 ***Forbes***	N	N	Y	Y	Y	Y	Y
2 ***Lazio***	N	Y	Y	Y	Y	Y	Y
3 ***King***	N	Y	Y	Y	Y	Y	Y
4 McCarthy	Y	N	Y	N	Y	Y	Y
5 Ackerman	Y	N	N	N	?	?	?
6 Meeks	Y	N	N	N	Y	Y	Y
7 Manton	?	?	?	?	Y	Y	Y
8 Nadler	Y	N	N	N	Y	Y	Y
9 Schumer	Y	N	Y	N	?	?	?
10 Towns	Y	N	N	N	?	?	?
11 Owens	Y	N	N	N	Y	Y	Y
12 Velázquez	Y	N	N	N	Y	Y	Y
13 ***Fossella***	N	Y	Y	Y	Y	Y	Y
14 Maloney	Y	N	Y	N	Y	Y	Y
15 Rangel	Y	N	N	N	Y	Y	Y
16 Serrano	N	N	N	N	Y	Y	Y
17 Engel	Y	N	N	N	Y	Y	Y
18 Lowey	Y	N	Y	N	Y	Y	Y
19 ***Kelly***	N	N	Y	Y	Y	Y	Y
20 ***Gilman***	N	N	Y	Y	Y	Y	Y
21 McNulty	Y	N	N	N	Y	Y	Y
22 ***Solomon***	N	Y	Y	Y	Y	Y	Y
23 ***Boehlert***	Y	N	Y	Y	Y	Y	Y
24 ***McHugh***	N	Y	Y	N	Y	Y	Y
25 ***Walsh***	N	Y	Y	Y	Y	Y	Y
26 Hinchey	N	N	N	N	Y	Y	Y
27 ***Paxon***	N	Y	Y	Y	Y	Y	Y
28 Slaughter	Y	N	N	N	Y	Y	Y
29 LaFalce	Y	N	N	N	Y	Y	Y
30 ***Quinn***	N	Y	Y	Y	Y	Y	Y

	413	414	415	416	417	418	419
31 ***Houghton***	N	N	Y	Y	Y	Y	Y
NORTH CAROLINA							
1 Clayton	Y	N	N	N	Y	Y	Y
2 Etheridge	N	Y	N	N	Y	Y	Y
3 ***Jones***	N	Y	Y	Y	Y	Y	Y
4 Price	Y	N	Y	N	Y	Y	Y
5 ***Burr***	N	Y	Y	Y	Y	Y	?
6 ***Coble***	N	Y	Y	Y	Y	Y	Y
7 McIntyre	N	Y	Y	Y	Y	Y	Y
8 Hefner	Y	N	N	N	Y	Y	Y
9 ***Myrick***	N	Y	Y	Y	Y	Y	Y
10 ***Ballenger***	N	Y	Y	Y	Y	Y	Y
11 ***Taylor***	N	Y	Y	Y	Y	Y	Y
12 Watt	Y	N	N	N	Y	Y	Y
NORTH DAKOTA							
AL Pomeroy	Y	Y	N	N	Y	Y	Y
OHIO							
1 ***Chabot***	N	Y	Y	Y	Y	Y	Y
2 ***Portman***	N	Y	Y	Y	Y	Y	Y
3 Hall	N	Y	Y	N	Y	Y	Y
4 ***Oxley***	N	Y	Y	Y	Y	Y	Y
5 ***Gillmor***	N	Y	Y	Y	Y	Y	Y
6 Strickland	Y	N	N	N	Y	Y	Y
7 ***Hobson***	N	N	Y	Y	Y	Y	Y
8 ***Boehner***	N	Y	Y	Y	Y	N	Y
9 Kaptur	Y	N	N	N	?	Y	Y
10 Kucinich	Y	N	Y	N	Y	Y	Y
11 Stokes	N	N	N	N	Y	Y	Y
12 ***Kasich***	N	Y	Y	Y	Y	Y	Y
13 Brown	Y	N	N	N	Y	Y	Y
14 Sawyer	Y	N	N	N	Y	Y	Y
15 ***Pryce***	N	N	Y	Y	+	+	+
16 ***Regula***	N	Y	Y	Y	Y	Y	Y
17 Traficant	N	Y	Y	Y	Y	Y	Y
18 ***Ney***	N	Y	Y	Y	Y	Y	Y
19 ***LaTourette***	N	N	Y	Y	Y	Y	Y
OKLAHOMA							
1 ***Largent***	N	Y	Y	Y	Y	Y	Y
2 ***Coburn***	N	Y	Y	Y	Y	Y	Y
3 ***Watkins***	N	Y	Y	Y	Y	Y	Y
4 ***Watts***	N	Y	Y	Y	Y	Y	Y
5 ***Istook***	N	Y	Y	Y	Y	Y	Y
6 ***Lucas***	N	Y	Y	Y	Y	Y	Y
OREGON							
1 Furse	Y	N	N	N	?	?	?
2 ***Smith***	?	?	?	?	Y	Y	Y
3 Blumenauer	N	N	N	N	?	?	Y
4 DeFazio	Y	N	N	N	Y	Y	Y
5 Hooley	Y	N	Y	N	?	?	?
PENNSYLVANIA							
1 Brady	Y	N	N	N	Y	Y	Y
2 Fattah	Y	N	N	N	Y	Y	Y
3 Borski	Y	N	N	N	?	?	?
4 Klink	Y	N	N	N	Y	Y	Y
5 ***Peterson***	N	Y	Y	Y	Y	Y	Y
6 Holden	Y	Y	Y	N	Y	Y	Y
7 ***Weldon***	N	Y	Y	Y	Y	Y	Y
8 ***Greenwood***	Y	N	N	Y	Y	Y	Y
9 ***Shuster***	N	Y	Y	Y	Y	Y	Y
10 ***McDade***	?	?	?	?	Y	Y	Y
11 Kanjorski	Y	N	N	N	Y	Y	Y
12 Murtha	Y	Y	N	N	Y	Y	Y
13 ***Fox***	N	N	Y	Y	Y	Y	Y
14 Coyne	Y	N	N	N	Y	Y	Y
15 McHale	Y	N	N	N	Y	Y	Y
16 ***Pitts***	N	Y	Y	Y	Y	Y	Y
17 ***Gekas***	N	N	Y	Y	Y	Y	Y
18 Doyle	Y	N	Y	N	Y	Y	Y
19 ***Goodling***	N	Y	Y	Y	Y	Y	Y
20 Mascara	Y	Y	Y	N	Y	Y	Y
21 ***English***	N	Y	Y	Y	Y	Y	Y
RHODE ISLAND							
1 Kennedy	N	N	N	N	Y	Y	?
2 Weygand	N	N	N	N	Y	Y	Y
SOUTH CAROLINA							
1 ***Sanford***	N	Y	Y	Y	Y	Y	Y
2 ***Spence***	N	Y	Y	Y	Y	Y	Y
3 ***Graham***	N	Y	Y	Y	Y	Y	?
4 ***Inglis***	N	Y	Y	Y	Y	Y	Y
5 Spratt	N	Y	N	N	Y	Y	Y
6 Clyburn	Y	N	N	N	Y	Y	Y
SOUTH DAKOTA							
AL ***Thune***	N	Y	Y	Y	Y	Y	Y

	413	414	415	416	417	418	419
TENNESSEE							
1 ***Jenkins***	N	Y	Y	Y	Y	Y	Y
2 ***Duncan***	N	Y	Y	N	Y	Y	Y
3 ***Wamp***	N	Y	Y	Y	Y	Y	Y
4 ***Hilleary***	N	Y	Y	Y	Y	Y	Y
5 Clement	N	Y	Y	N	Y	Y	Y
6 Gordon	N	Y	Y	N	Y	Y	Y
7 ***Bryant***	N	Y	Y	Y	Y	Y	Y
8 Tanner	Y	Y	Y	N	Y	Y	Y
9 Ford	Y	Y	N	N	+	+	+
TEXAS							
1 Sandlin	Y	Y	Y	N	Y	Y	Y
2 Turner	N	Y	Y	N	Y	Y	Y
3 ***Johnson, Sam***	N	Y	Y	Y	Y	Y	Y
4 Hall	N	Y	Y	N	Y	Y	Y
5 ***Sessions***	N	Y	Y	Y	Y	Y	Y
6 ***Barton***	N	Y	N	Y	Y	Y	Y
7 ***Archer***	N	Y	Y	Y	Y	Y	Y
8 ***Brady***	N	Y	Y	Y	Y	Y	Y
9 Lampson	Y	N	Y	N	?	?	?
10 Doggett	N	N	Y	N	Y	Y	Y
11 Edwards	Y	N	Y	N	Y	Y	Y
12 ***Granger***	N	Y	Y	Y	Y	Y	Y
13 ***Thornberry***	N	Y	Y	Y	Y	Y	Y
14 ***Paul***	N	Y	N	N	N	N	Y
15 Hinojosa	Y	N	Y	N	Y	Y	Y
16 Reyes	Y	N	Y	N	Y	Y	Y
17 Stenholm	N	Y	Y	N	Y	Y	Y
18 Jackson-Lee	Y	N	N	N	Y	Y	Y
19 ***Combest***	N	Y	Y	Y	Y	Y	Y
20 Gonzalez	?	?	?	?	?	?	?
21 ***Smith***	N	Y	Y	Y	Y	Y	Y
22 ***DeLay***	N	Y	Y	Y	Y	Y	Y
23 ***Bonilla***	Y	N	N	Y	Y	Y	Y
24 Frost	Y	N	Y	N	Y	Y	Y
25 Bentsen	Y	N	N	N	Y	Y	Y
26 ***Armey***	N	Y	Y	Y	Y	Y	Y
27 Ortiz	Y	Y	Y	N	Y	Y	Y
28 Rodriguez	Y	N	Y	N	Y	Y	Y
29 Green	N	N	Y	N	Y	Y	Y
30 Johnson, E.B.	Y	N	N	N	Y	Y	Y
UTAH							
1 ***Hansen***	?	?	?	?	Y	Y	Y
2 ***Cook***	N	Y	Y	Y	Y	Y	Y
3 ***Cannon***	N	Y	Y	Y	Y	Y	Y
VERMONT							
AL *Sanders*	Y	N	N	N	Y	Y	Y
VIRGINIA							
1 ***Bateman***	N	Y	Y	Y	Y	Y	Y
2 Pickett	N	Y	Y	N	Y	Y	Y
3 Scott	Y	N	N	N	Y	Y	Y
4 Sisisky	Y	Y	N	N	Y	Y	Y
5 Goode	N	Y	Y	Y	Y	Y	Y
6 ***Goodlatte***	N	Y	Y	Y	Y	Y	Y
7 ***Bliley***	N	Y	Y	Y	Y	Y	Y
8 Moran	Y	N	Y	N	?	Y	Y
9 Boucher	Y	N	N	N	Y	Y	Y
10 ***Wolf***	N	Y	Y	Y	Y	Y	?
11 ***Davis***	Y	Y	Y	Y	?	Y	Y
WASHINGTON							
1 ***White***	N	Y	Y	Y	Y	Y	Y
2 ***Metcalf***	N	Y	Y	Y	Y	Y	Y
3 ***Smith, Linda***	N	Y	Y	Y	?	?	?
4 ***Hastings***	N	Y	Y	Y	Y	Y	Y
5 ***Nethercutt***	N	Y	Y	Y	Y	Y	Y
6 Dicks	Y	N	Y	N	Y	Y	Y
7 McDermott	Y	N	N	N	Y	Y	Y
8 ***Dunn***	N	Y	Y	Y	Y	Y	Y
9 Smith, Adam	Y	N	Y	N	+	+	+
WEST VIRGINIA							
1 Mollohan	Y	N	N	N	Y	Y	Y
2 Wise	N	N	N	N	Y	Y	Y
3 Rahall	Y	N	N	N	Y	Y	Y
WISCONSIN							
1 ***Neumann***	N	Y	Y	Y	Y	Y	Y
2 ***Klug***	Y	Y	Y	Y	Y	Y	Y
3 Kind	Y	N	Y	N	Y	Y	Y
4 Kleczka	Y	N	Y	N	Y	Y	Y
5 Barrett	Y	N	N	N	Y	Y	Y
6 ***Petri***	N	Y	Y	Y	Y	Y	Y
7 Obey	Y	N	N	N	Y	Y	Y
8 Johnson	N	N	Y	N	Y	Y	Y
9 ***Sensenbrenner***	N	Y	Y	Y	Y	Y	Y
WYOMING							
AL ***Cubin***	N	Y	Y	Y	Y	Y	Y

Southern states - Ala., Ark., Fla., Ga., Ky., La., Miss., N.C., Okla., S.C., Tenn., Texas, Va.

House Votes 420, 421, 422, 423, 424, 425, 426

420. HR 2863. Migratory Bird Hunting Regulations/Passage. Passage of the bill to eliminate the current strict liability for hunters who shoot migratory birds over fields that have been baited to attract birds, and instead make it illegal to shoot such fowl if the hunter knew or should have known that the area had been baited. Passed 322-90: R 216-3; D 105-87 (ND 66-74, SD 39-13); I 1-0. Sept. 10, 1998.

421. HR 2538. Guadalupe-Hidalgo Treaty Land Claims/Passage. Passage of the bill to establish a presidential commission to make recommendations to resolve land claims in New Mexico by descendants of Mexican citizens when the treaty ending the Mexican-American War was signed in 1848. Passed 223-187: R 211-10; D 12-176 (ND 11-126, SD 1-50); I 0-1. Sept. 10, 1998.

422. HR 3892. Bilingual Education Block Grants/Federal Law Compliance. Martinez, D-Calif., amendment to the Riggs, R-Calif., amendmen that would allow school systems to receive subgrants only if they were not in violation of any state law or state constitutional provision regarding education of English language learners. The Martinez amendment would add, "except if necessary for the eligible entity to comply with Federal law (including a Federal court order.)" Rejected 205-208: R 14-204; D 190-4 (ND 141-1, SD 49-3); I 1-0. Sept. 10, 1998. (Subsequently, the Riggs amendment was adopted.)

423. HR 3892. Bilingual Education Block Grants/State Law Compliance. Riggs, R-Calif., amendment to allow school systems to receive subgrants only if they were not in violation of any state law or state constitutional provision regarding education of English language learners. Adopted 230-184: R 215-5; D 15-178 (ND 4-138, SD 11-40); I 0-1. Sept. 10, 1998.

424. HR 3892. Bilingual Education Block Grants/Passage. Passage of the bill to turn existing bilingual and immigrant education programs into a block grant program and provide states and local school districts with broader discretion to determine a method of teaching for students learning English as a second language. Passed 221-189: R 207-10; D 14-178 (ND 5-136, SD 9-42); I 0-1. Sept. 10, 1998. A "nay" vote was a vote in support of the president's position.

425. H Res 525. Distribution of Starr Report/Adoption. Adoption of the resolution to provide for the release and distribution of the report from Independent Counsel Kenneth W. Starr regarding allegations of criminal offenses and other misconduct by President Clinton. Under the resolution, the Judiciary Committee will review the materials to determine whether they contain grounds for impeachment. It also requires the committee to immediately release the initial 445-page report, and release other documents to the public on Sept. 28 unless the committee votes not to release certain materials. Adopted 363-63: R 224-0; D 138-63 (ND 102-46, SD 36-17); I 1-0. Sept. 11, 1998.

426. S 2206. Federal Programs Reauthorizations/Passage. Goodling, R-Pa., motion to suspend the rules and pass the bill to reauthorize several programs, including Head Start, the Community Development Block Grant and the Low Income Home Energy Assistance Program. Motion agreed to 346-20: R 185-20; D 160-0 (ND 115-0, SD 45-0); I 1-0. Sept. 14, 1998. A two-thirds majority of those present and voting (244 in this case) is required for passage under suspension of the rules.

Key

- Y Voted for (yea).
- # Paired for.
- + Announced for.
- N Voted against (nay).
- X Paired against.
- − Announced against.
- P Voted "present."
- C Voted "present" to avoid possible conflict of interest.
- ? Did not vote or otherwise make a position known.

Democrats   **Republicans**
Independent

	420	421	422	423	424	425	426
ALABAMA							
1 *Callahan*	Y	Y	N	Y	Y	Y	Y
2 *Everett*	Y	Y	N	Y	Y	Y	Y
3 *Riley*	Y	Y	N	Y	Y	Y	Y
4 *Aderholt*	Y	Y	N	Y	Y	Y	Y
5 Cramer	Y	N	Y	Y	Y	Y	Y
6 *Bachus*	Y	Y	N	Y	Y	Y	?
7 Hilliard	Y	N	Y	N	N	N	Y
ALASKA							
AL *Young*	?	#	?	?	?	?	Y
ARIZONA							
1 *Salmon*	Y	N	N	Y	Y	Y	Y
2 Pastor	Y	Y	Y	N	N	Y	Y
3 *Stump*	Y	Y	N	Y	Y	Y	N
4 *Shadegg*	?	N	N	Y	Y	Y	Y
5 *Kolbe*	Y	Y	N	Y	Y	Y	Y
6 *Hayworth*	Y	Y	N	Y	Y	Y	Y
ARKANSAS							
1 Berry	+	X	#	X	X	Y	Y
2 Snyder	Y	N	Y	N	N	Y	Y
3 *Hutchinson*	Y	Y	N	Y	Y	Y	Y
4 *Dickey*	Y	Y	N	Y	Y	Y	Y
CALIFORNIA							
1 *Riggs*	Y	Y	N	Y	Y	Y	?
2 *Herger*	Y	Y	N	Y	Y	Y	Y
3 Fazio	Y	N	Y	N	N	Y	Y
4 *Doolittle*	Y	Y	N	Y	Y	Y	N
5 Matsui	N	N	Y	N	N	Y	Y
6 Woolsey	N	N	Y	N	N	N	Y
7 Miller	N	N	Y	N	N	N	Y
8 Pelosi	N	N	Y	N	N	N	?
9 Lee	N	N	Y	N	N	N	Y
10 Tauscher	N	N	Y	N	N	Y	Y
11 *Pombo*	Y	Y	N	Y	Y	Y	N
12 Lantos	N	N	Y	N	N	Y	Y
13 Stark	N	N	Y	N	N	N	Y
14 Eshoo	N	N	Y	N	N	Y	Y
15 *Campbell*	N	Y	Y	N	N	Y	Y
16 Lofgren	N	N	Y	N	N	N	Y
17 Farr	N	N	Y	N	N	Y	Y
18 Condit	Y	Y	N	Y	Y	Y	Y
19 *Radanovich*	Y	Y	N	Y	Y	Y	N
20 Dooley	Y	?	Y	N	N	Y	Y
21 *Thomas*	Y	Y	N	Y	Y	Y	Y
22 Capps, L.	Y	N	Y	N	N	Y	Y
23 *Gallegly*	Y	Y	N	Y	Y	Y	Y
24 Sherman	N	N	Y	N	N	Y	Y
25 *McKeon*	Y	Y	N	Y	Y	Y	Y
26 Berman	N	N	Y	N	N	Y	Y
27 *Rogan*	Y	Y	N	Y	Y	Y	Y
28 *Dreier*	Y	Y	N	Y	Y	Y	?
29 Waxman	N	N	Y	N	N	Y	?
30 Becerra	N	N	Y	N	N	Y	Y
31 Martinez	N	N	Y	N	N	Y	Y
32 Dixon	Y	N	Y	N	N	Y	Y
33 Roybal-Allard	N	N	Y	N	N	Y	Y
34 Torres	N	N	Y	N	N	Y	Y
35 Waters	N	N	Y	N	N	N	Y
36 Harman	N	N	Y	N	N	Y	Y
37 Millender-McD.	N	N	Y	N	N	Y	Y
38 *Horn*	Y	Y	Y	Y	Y	Y	Y

	420	421	422	423	424	425	426
39 *Royce*	Y	N	N	Y	Y	Y	N
40 *Lewis*	Y	Y	Y	Y	Y	Y	Y
41 *Kim*	Y	Y	N	Y	Y	Y	Y
42 Brown	Y	?	Y	N	N	Y	Y
43 *Calvert*	Y	Y	N	Y	Y	Y	Y
44 *Bono, M.*	Y	Y	N	Y	Y	Y	Y
45 *Rohrabacher*	Y	Y	N	Y	Y	Y	Y
46 Sanchez	Y	N	Y	N	N	Y	Y
47 *Cox*	Y	Y	N	Y	Y	Y	Y
48 *Packard*	Y	Y	N	Y	Y	Y	Y
49 *Bilbray*	Y	Y	Y	Y	Y	Y	Y
50 Filner	N	N	Y	N	N	N	Y
51 *Cunningham*	Y	Y	N	Y	Y	Y	Y
52 *Hunter*	Y	Y	?	Y	Y	Y	Y
COLORADO							
1 DeGette	N	N	Y	N	N	Y	Y
2 Skaggs	Y	N	Y	N	N	N	Y
3 *McInnis*	Y	Y	N	Y	Y	Y	Y
4 *Schaffer*	Y	Y	N	Y	Y	Y	Y
5 *Hefley*	Y	Y	N	Y	Y	Y	Y
6 *Schaefer*	Y	Y	N	Y	Y	Y	Y
CONNECTICUT							
1 Kennelly	?	?	?	?	?	Y	?
2 Gejdenson	Y	N	Y	N	N	Y	Y
3 DeLauro	N	N	Y	N	N	Y	Y
4 *Shays*	N	Y	Y	Y	Y	Y	Y
5 Maloney	N	N	Y	N	N	Y	+
6 *Johnson*	N	Y	Y	Y	N	Y	Y
DELAWARE							
AL *Castle*	Y	Y	N	Y	Y	Y	Y
FLORIDA							
1 *Scarborough*	Y	Y	X	#	#	?	N
2 Boyd	Y	N	Y	N	Y	Y	Y
3 Brown	N	N	Y	N	N	N	?
4 *Fowler*	Y	Y	N	Y	Y	Y	Y
5 Thurman	Y	N	Y	N	N	Y	Y
6 *Stearns*	Y	Y	N	Y	Y	Y	N
7 *Mica*	Y	Y	N	Y	Y	Y	Y
8 *McCollum*	Y	Y	N	Y	Y	Y	Y
9 *Bilirakis*	Y	Y	N	Y	Y	Y	Y
10 *Young*	Y	Y	N	Y	Y	Y	?
11 Davis	Y	N	Y	N	N	Y	Y
12 *Canady*	Y	Y	N	Y	Y	Y	Y
13 *Miller*	Y	Y	N	Y	Y	Y	N
14 *Goss*	Y	Y	N	Y	Y	Y	−
15 *Weldon*	Y	Y	N	Y	Y	Y	Y
16 *Foley*	Y	Y	N	Y	Y	Y	Y
17 Meek	N	N	Y	N	N	N	Y
18 *Ros-Lehtinen*	Y	Y	Y	N	N	Y	+
19 Wexler	N	N	Y	N	N	N	Y
20 Deutsch	N	N	Y	N	N	N	Y
21 *Diaz-Balart*	Y	Y	Y	N	N	Y	Y
22 *Shaw*	Y	Y	N	Y	Y	Y	Y
23 Hastings	N	N	Y	N	N	N	?
GEORGIA							
1 *Kingston*	Y	Y	N	Y	Y	Y	Y
2 Bishop	Y	N	Y	N	N	Y	Y
3 *Collins*	Y	Y	N	Y	Y	Y	N
4 McKinney	N	N	Y	N	N	Y	Y
5 Lewis	N	N	Y	N	N	N	?
6 *Gingrich*		Y			Y		
7 *Barr*	Y	N	Y	Y	Y	Y	?
8 *Chambliss*	Y	Y	N	Y	Y	Y	Y
9 *Deal*	Y	Y	N	Y	Y	Y	N
10 *Norwood*	Y	Y	N	Y	Y	Y	Y
11 *Linder*	Y	Y	N	Y	Y	Y	Y
HAWAII							
1 Abercrombie	N	N	Y	N	N	Y	Y
2 Mink	Y	N	Y	N	N	Y	Y
IDAHO							
1 *Chenoweth*	Y	Y	N	Y	Y	Y	Y
2 *Crapo*	Y	Y	N	Y	N	Y	+
ILLINOIS							
1 Rush	?	?	Y	N	N	N	?
2 Jackson	N	N	Y	N	N	N	Y
3 Lipinski	N	N	Y	N	N	Y	Y
4 Gutierrez	N	N	Y	N	N	Y	Y
5 Blagojevich	N	N	Y	N	N	Y	Y
6 *Hyde*	Y	Y	N	Y	Y	Y	Y
7 Davis	N	N	Y	N	N	N	Y
8 *Crane*	Y	Y	N	Y	Y	Y	N
9 Yates	N	Y	Y	N	N	N	?
10 *Porter*	Y	Y	N	Y	Y	Y	Y
11 *Weller*	Y	Y	N	Y	Y	Y	Y
12 Costello	Y	N	Y	N	N	Y	Y
13 *Fawell*	Y	Y	N	Y	Y	Y	Y

ND Northern Democrats   SD Southern Democrats

	420	421	422	423	424	425	426
14 **Hastert**	Y	Y	N	Y	Y	Y	Y
15 **Ewing**	Y	Y	N	Y	Y	Y	Y
16 **Manzullo**	Y	Y	N	Y	Y	Y	?
17 Evans	N	N	Y	N	N	Y	?
18 **LaHood**	Y	?	N	Y	Y	Y	?
19 Poshard	?	?	?	?	?	?	?
20 **Shimkus**	Y	Y	N	Y	Y	Y	Y
INDIANA							
1 Visclosky	N	Y	Y	N	N	Y	Y
2 **McIntosh**	Y	Y	N	Y	Y	Y	N
3 Roemer	Y	N	Y	N	N	Y	Y
4 **Souder**	Y	Y	N	Y	Y	Y	Y
5 **Buyer**	Y	Y	N	Y	Y	Y	Y
6 **Burton**	Y	Y	N	Y	Y	Y	Y
7 **Pease**	Y	Y	N	Y	Y	Y	Y
8 **Hostettler**	Y	Y	N	Y	Y	Y	Y
9 Hamilton	Y	N	Y	N	N	Y	Y
10 Carson	Y	N	Y	N	N	N	+
IOWA							
1 **Leach**	Y	Y	Y	Y	Y	Y	Y
2 **Nussle**	Y	Y	N	Y	?	Y	Y
3 Boswell	Y	N	Y	N	N	Y	Y
4 **Ganske**	Y	N	N	Y	Y	Y	Y
5 **Latham**	Y	Y	N	Y	Y	Y	Y
KANSAS							
1 **Moran**	Y	Y	N	Y	Y	Y	Y
2 **Ryun**	Y	Y	N	Y	Y	Y	+
3 **Snowbarger**	Y	Y	N	Y	Y	Y	Y
4 **Tiahrt**	Y	Y	N	Y	Y	Y	+
KENTUCKY							
1 **Whitfield**	Y	Y	N	Y	Y	Y	Y
2 **Lewis**	Y	Y	N	Y	Y	Y	Y
3 **Northup**	Y	Y	N	Y	Y	Y	Y
4 **Bunning**	Y	Y	N	Y	Y	Y	Y
5 **Rogers**	Y	Y	N	Y	Y	Y	Y
6 Baesler	Y	N	Y	Y	Y	Y	Y
LOUISIANA							
1 **Livingston**	Y	Y	N	Y	Y	Y	Y
2 Jefferson	Y	N	Y	N	N	N	?
3 **Tauzin**	?	?	?	?	?	Y	?
4 **McCrery**	Y	Y	N	Y	?	Y	Y
5 **Cooksey**	Y	Y	N	Y	Y	Y	Y
6 **Baker**	Y	Y	N	Y	Y	Y	Y
7 John	Y	N	Y	Y	Y	Y	Y
MAINE							
1 Allen	Y	N	Y	N	N	Y	Y
2 Baldacci	Y	N	Y	N	N	Y	Y
MARYLAND							
1 **Gilchrest**	Y	Y	N	Y	Y	Y	Y
2 **Ehrlich**	Y	Y	?	?	#	Y	Y
3 Cardin	N	N	Y	N	N	Y	Y
4 Wynn	N	N	Y	N	N	Y	Y
5 Hoyer	Y	N	Y	N	N	Y	Y
6 **Bartlett**	Y	Y	N	Y	Y	Y	Y
7 Cummings	Y	N	Y	N	N	N	Y
8 **Morella**	?	Y	Y	N	N	Y	Y
MASSACHUSETTS							
1 Olver	N	N	Y	N	N	Y	Y
2 Neal	N	N	Y	N	N	N	?
3 McGovern	N	N	?	?	X	Y	Y
4 Frank	N	N	Y	N	N	N	Y
5 Meehan	N	N	Y	N	N	N	Y
6 Tierney	N	N	Y	N	N	N	Y
7 Markey	N	N	Y	N	N	N	Y
8 Kennedy	?	?	Y	N	N	N	?
9 Moakley	?	?	Y	N	N	Y	?
10 Delahunt	N	N	Y	N	N	N	Y
MICHIGAN							
1 Stupak	Y	N	Y	N	N	Y	Y
2 **Hoekstra**	Y	Y	N	Y	Y	Y	Y
3 **Ehlers**	Y	Y	N	Y	Y	Y	Y
4 **Camp**	Y	Y	N	Y	Y	Y	Y
5 Barcia	?	?	?	?	?	?	Y
6 **Upton**	Y	N	N	Y	Y	Y	Y
7 **Smith**	Y	Y	N	Y	Y	Y	Y
8 Stabenow	Y	N	Y	N	N	Y	+
9 Kildee	N	N	Y	N	N	Y	Y
10 Bonior	N	N	Y	N	N	Y	Y
11 **Knollenberg**	Y	Y	N	Y	Y	Y	Y
12 Levin	Y	N	Y	N	N	Y	Y
13 Rivers	N	N	Y	N	N	Y	Y
14 Conyers	Y	Y	Y	N	N	N	Y
15 Kilpatrick	Y	N	Y	N	N	N	+
16 Dingell	Y	?	Y	N	N	Y	?

	420	421	422	423	424	425	426
MINNESOTA							
1 **Gutknecht**	Y	Y	N	Y	Y	Y	Y
2 Minge	Y	N	Y	N	N	Y	+
3 **Ramstad**	Y	N	Y	N	Y	Y	Y
4 Vento	N	N	Y	N	N	Y	Y
5 Sabo	N	N	Y	N	N	N	Y
6 Luther	Y	N	Y	N	N	Y	Y
7 Peterson	Y	N	Y	Y	Y	Y	Y
8 Oberstar	N	N	Y	N	N	Y	+
MISSISSIPPI							
1 **Wicker**	Y	Y	N	Y	Y	Y	Y
2 Thompson	Y	N	Y	N	N	N	Y
3 **Pickering**	Y	Y	N	Y	Y	Y	+
4 **Parker**	Y	Y	N	Y	Y	Y	Y
5 Taylor	Y	N	Y	Y	Y	Y	Y
MISSOURI							
1 Clay	N	N	Y	N	N	N	Y
2 **Talent**	Y	Y	N	Y	Y	Y	Y
3 Gephardt	Y	?	?	?	?	Y	Y
4 Skelton	Y	N	Y	N	N	Y	Y
5 McCarthy	Y	N	Y	N	N	Y	+
6 Danner	Y	N	Y	Y	Y	Y	?
7 **Blunt**	Y	Y	N	Y	Y	Y	Y
8 **Emerson**	Y	Y	N	Y	Y	Y	Y
9 **Hulshof**	Y	Y	N	Y	Y	Y	Y
MONTANA							
AL **Hill**	Y	Y	N	Y	Y	Y	Y
NEBRASKA							
1 **Bereuter**	Y	Y	N	Y	Y	Y	Y
2 **Christensen**	Y	Y	N	Y	Y	Y	Y
3 **Barrett**	Y	Y	N	Y	Y	Y	Y
NEVADA							
1 **Ensign**	Y	Y	N	Y	Y	Y	Y
2 **Gibbons**	Y	Y	N	Y	Y	Y	Y
NEW HAMPSHIRE							
1 **Sununu**	Y	Y	N	Y	Y	Y	Y
2 **Bass**	Y	Y	N	Y	Y	Y	Y
NEW JERSEY							
1 Andrews	N	N	Y	N	N	Y	Y
2 **LoBiondo**	Y	Y	N	Y	Y	Y	Y
3 **Saxton**	Y	Y	N	Y	Y	Y	?
4 **Smith**	Y	Y	N	Y	Y	Y	Y
5 **Roukema**	Y	Y	N	Y	Y	Y	Y
6 Pallone	N	N	Y	N	N	Y	Y
7 **Franks**	Y	Y	N	Y	Y	Y	Y
8 Pascrell	N	N	Y	N	N	Y	Y
9 Rothman	N	N	Y	N	N	Y	?
10 Payne	N	N	Y	N	N	N	Y
11 **Frelinghuysen**	Y	Y	N	Y	Y	Y	Y
12 **Pappas**	Y	Y	N	Y	Y	Y	Y
13 Menendez	Y	N	Y	N	N	Y	Y
NEW MEXICO							
1 **Wilson**	Y	Y	N	Y	Y	Y	Y
2 **Skeen**	Y	Y	Y	Y	Y	Y	Y
3 **Redmond**	Y	Y	Y	Y	N	Y	Y
NEW YORK							
1 **Forbes**	Y	Y	N	Y	Y	Y	Y
2 **Lazio**	Y	Y	N	Y	Y	Y	Y
3 **King**	Y	Y	N	Y	Y	Y	Y
4 McCarthy	Y	N	Y	N	N	Y	Y
5 Ackerman	Y	N	Y	N	N	N	?
6 Meeks	N	N	Y	N	N	N	?
7 Manton	Y	N	Y	N	N	Y	Y
8 Nadler	N	N	Y	N	N	N	?
9 Schumer	?	?	?	?	?	Y	?
10 Towns	?	?	?	?	?	N	?
11 Owens	N	N	Y	N	N	N	?
12 Velázquez	N	N	Y	N	N	N	?
13 **Fossella**	Y	Y	N	Y	Y	Y	Y
14 Maloney	N	N	Y	N	N	Y	+
15 Rangel	Y	Y	Y	N	N	N	?
16 Serrano	N	Y	Y	N	N	N	Y
17 Engel	?	N	Y	N	N	N	?
18 Lowey	N	N	Y	N	N	Y	?
19 **Kelly**	Y	Y	N	Y	Y	Y	Y
20 **Gilman**	Y	Y	N	Y	N	Y	Y
21 McNulty	N	N	Y	N	N	Y	Y
22 **Solomon**	Y	Y	N	Y	Y	Y	Y
23 **Boehlert**	Y	Y	N	Y	Y	Y	Y
24 **McHugh**	Y	Y	N	Y	Y	Y	Y
25 **Walsh**	Y	Y	N	Y	Y	Y	Y
26 Hinchey	N	N	Y	N	N	Y	Y
27 **Paxon**	?	Y	N	Y	Y	Y	Y
28 Slaughter	N	N	Y	N	N	Y	Y
29 LaFalce	N	N	Y	N	N	Y	Y
30 **Quinn**	Y	Y	N	Y	Y	Y	Y

	420	421	422	423	424	425	426
31 **Houghton**	Y	Y	Y	Y	Y	Y	Y
NORTH CAROLINA							
1 Clayton	N	N	Y	N	N	N	?
2 Etheridge	Y	N	Y	–	–	Y	Y
3 **Jones**	Y	Y	N	Y	Y	Y	Y
4 Price	Y	N	Y	N	N	Y	Y
5 **Burr**	Y	Y	?	?	?	Y	Y
6 **Coble**	Y	Y	N	Y	Y	Y	N
7 McIntyre	Y	N	Y	Y	Y	Y	?
8 Hefner	?	?	Y	N	N	N	Y
9 **Myrick**	Y	Y	N	Y	Y	Y	Y
10 **Ballenger**	Y	Y	N	Y	Y	Y	Y
11 **Taylor**	Y	Y	N	Y	Y	Y	?
12 Watt	N	N	Y	N	N	N	?
NORTH DAKOTA							
AL Pomeroy	Y	N	Y	N	N	Y	Y
OHIO							
1 **Chabot**	Y	Y	N	Y	Y	Y	Y
2 **Portman**	Y	Y	N	Y	Y	Y	Y
3 Hall	Y	N	Y	N	N	Y	Y
4 **Oxley**	Y	Y	N	N	Y	Y	Y
5 **Gillmor**	Y	Y	N	Y	Y	Y	Y
6 Strickland	Y	N	Y	N	N	Y	Y
7 **Hobson**	Y	Y	N	Y	Y	Y	Y
8 **Boehner**	Y	Y	N	Y	Y	Y	Y
9 Kaptur	Y	N	Y	N	?	Y	Y
10 Kucinich	N	N	Y	N	N	Y	Y
11 Stokes	?	N	Y	N	N	N	Y
12 **Kasich**	Y	?	N	Y	Y	Y	Y
13 Brown	N	N	Y	N	N	Y	Y
14 Sawyer	Y	N	Y	N	N	Y	Y
15 **Pryce**	+	+	–	+	+	+	+
16 **Regula**	Y	Y	N	Y	Y	Y	Y
17 Traficant	Y	Y	Y	Y	Y	Y	Y
18 **Ney**	Y	Y	Y	N	N	Y	Y
19 **LaTourette**	Y	Y	N	Y	Y	Y	Y
OKLAHOMA							
1 **Largent**	Y	N	?	?	Y	Y	Y
2 **Coburn**	Y	Y	N	Y	Y	Y	N
3 **Watkins**	Y	Y	N	Y	Y	Y	Y
4 **Watts**	Y	Y	N	Y	Y	Y	Y
5 **Istook**	Y	Y	N	Y	Y	Y	N
6 **Lucas**	Y	Y	N	Y	Y	Y	Y
OREGON							
1 Furse	?	?	?	?	?	?	?
2 **Smith**	Y	Y	N	Y	Y	Y	Y
3 Blumenauer	N	N	Y	N	N	Y	?
4 DeFazio	Y	N	Y	N	N	Y	Y
5 Hooley	Y	N	Y	N	N	Y	?
PENNSYLVANIA							
1 Brady	N	N	Y	N	N	N	Y
2 Fattah	N	N	Y	N	N	N	Y
3 Borski	Y	N	Y	N	N	Y	Y
4 Klink	Y	N	Y	N	N	Y	?
5 **Peterson**	Y	Y	N	Y	Y	Y	Y
6 Holden	Y	N	Y	N	N	Y	Y
7 **Weldon**	Y	Y	N	Y	Y	Y	Y
8 **Greenwood**	Y	Y	N	Y	Y	Y	Y
9 **Shuster**	Y	Y	N	Y	Y	Y	Y
10 **McDade**	?	?	N	Y	Y	Y	?
11 Kanjorski	Y	N	Y	N	N	Y	Y
12 Murtha	Y	N	Y	N	N	Y	Y
13 **Fox**	Y	Y	N	Y	Y	Y	Y
14 Coyne	Y	N	Y	N	N	Y	Y
15 McHale	Y	N	Y	N	N	Y	Y
16 **Pitts**	Y	Y	N	Y	Y	Y	Y
17 **Gekas**	Y	Y	N	Y	Y	Y	Y
18 Doyle	Y	N	Y	N	N	Y	Y
19 **Goodling**	Y	Y	N	Y	Y	Y	Y
20 Mascara	Y	N	Y	N	N	Y	Y
21 **English**	Y	Y	N	Y	Y	Y	?
RHODE ISLAND							
1 Kennedy	N	N	Y	N	N	N	Y
2 Weygand	N	N	Y	N	N	Y	Y
SOUTH CAROLINA							
1 **Sanford**	Y	N	N	Y	Y	Y	N
2 **Spence**	Y	Y	N	Y	Y	Y	Y
3 **Graham**	Y	Y	N	Y	Y	Y	Y
4 **Inglis**	Y	Y	N	Y	Y	Y	Y
5 Spratt	Y	N	Y	N	N	Y	Y
6 Clyburn	N	N	Y	N	N	N	Y
SOUTH DAKOTA							
AL **Thune**	Y	Y	N	Y	Y	Y	Y

	420	421	422	423	424	425	426
TENNESSEE							
1 **Jenkins**	Y	Y	N	Y	Y	+	Y
2 **Duncan**	Y	Y	N	Y	Y	Y	N
3 **Wamp**	Y	Y	N	Y	Y	Y	Y
4 **Hilleary**	Y	Y	N	Y	Y	Y	Y
5 Clement	Y	N	Y	N	N	Y	Y
6 Gordon	Y	N	Y	N	Y	Y	Y
7 **Bryant**	Y	Y	N	Y	Y	Y	Y
8 Tanner	Y	N	Y	N	N	Y	Y
9 Ford	N	N	Y	N	N	N	Y
TEXAS							
1 Sandlin	Y	N	Y	N	N	Y	Y
2 Turner	Y	N	Y	N	N	Y	Y
3 **Johnson, Sam**	Y	Y	N	Y	Y	Y	Y
4 Hall	Y	N	N	Y	Y	Y	Y
5 **Sessions**	Y	Y	N	Y	Y	Y	?
6 **Barton**	Y	Y	N	Y	Y	Y	Y
7 **Archer**	Y	Y	?	Y	Y	Y	Y
8 **Brady**	Y	Y	N	Y	Y	Y	Y
9 Lampson	Y	N	Y	N	N	Y	Y
10 Doggett	Y	N	Y	N	N	Y	?
11 Edwards	Y	N	Y	N	N	Y	Y
12 **Granger**	Y	Y	N	Y	Y	Y	Y
13 **Thornberry**	Y	Y	N	Y	Y	Y	Y
14 **Paul**	Y	Y	N	Y	N	Y	N
15 Hinojosa	Y	N	Y	N	N	Y	Y
16 Reyes	Y	N	Y	N	N	Y	Y
17 Stenholm	Y	N	Y	Y	N	Y	Y
18 Jackson-Lee	N	N	Y	N	N	N	Y
19 **Combest**	Y	Y	N	Y	Y	Y	Y
20 Gonzalez	?	?	?	?	?	?	?
21 **Smith**	Y	Y	N	Y	?	Y	Y
22 **DeLay**	Y	Y	N	Y	Y	Y	N
23 **Bonilla**	Y	Y	N	Y	Y	Y	Y
24 Frost	Y	N	Y	N	N	Y	Y
25 Bentsen	Y	N	Y	N	N	Y	Y
26 **Armey**	Y	Y	N	Y	Y	Y	Y
27 Ortiz	Y	N	Y	N	N	Y	Y
28 Rodriguez	Y	N	Y	N	N	Y	Y
29 Green	Y	N	Y	N	N	Y	+
30 Johnson, E.B.	N	N	–	–	–	–	Y
UTAH							
1 **Hansen**	Y	Y	N	Y	Y	Y	?
2 **Cook**	Y	Y	N	Y	Y	Y	?
3 **Cannon**	Y	?	N	Y	Y	Y	Y
VERMONT							
AL *Sanders*	Y	N	Y	N	N	Y	Y
VIRGINIA							
1 **Bateman**	Y	Y	N	Y	Y	Y	Y
2 Pickett	Y	Y	N	Y	Y	Y	Y
3 Scott	Y	N	Y	N	N	N	Y
4 Sisisky	Y	?	Y	Y	N	Y	Y
5 Goode	Y	N	N	Y	Y	Y	Y
6 **Goodlatte**	Y	N	N	Y	Y	Y	Y
7 **Bliley**	Y	Y	N	Y	Y	Y	Y
8 Moran	N	N	Y	N	N	N	Y
9 Boucher	Y	N	Y	N	N	Y	Y
10 **Wolf**	Y	Y	N	Y	Y	Y	Y
11 **Davis**	Y	Y	N	Y	?	Y	Y
WASHINGTON							
1 **White**	Y	Y	N	Y	Y	Y	Y
2 **Metcalf**	Y	Y	N	Y	Y	Y	Y
3 **Smith, Linda**	Y	Y	N	Y	Y	Y	Y
4 **Hastings**	Y	Y	N	Y	Y	Y	Y
5 **Nethercutt**	Y	Y	N	Y	Y	Y	Y
6 Dicks	Y	N	Y	N	N	Y	Y
7 McDermott	Y	N	Y	N	N	N	Y
8 **Dunn**	?	Y	N	Y	Y	Y	Y
9 Smith, Adam	Y	N	Y	N	N	Y	Y
WEST VIRGINIA							
1 Mollohan	Y	N	Y	N	N	N	Y
2 Wise	Y	?	?	?	?	Y	Y
3 Rahall	Y	N	Y	N	N	Y	Y
WISCONSIN							
1 **Neumann**	Y	Y	N	Y	Y	Y	Y
2 **Klug**	Y	Y	N	Y	Y	Y	Y
3 Kind	Y	N	Y	N	N	Y	Y
4 Kleczka	Y	N	Y	N	N	Y	Y
5 Barrett	N	N	Y	N	N	Y	Y
6 **Petri**	Y	Y	N	Y	Y	Y	Y
7 Obey	Y	N	Y	N	N	Y	Y
8 Johnson	Y	N	Y	N	N	Y	Y
9 **Sensenbrenner**	Y	Y	N	Y	Y	Y	N
WYOMING							
AL **Cubin**	Y	Y	N	Y	Y	Y	Y

Southern states - Ala., Ark., Fla., Ga., Ky., La., Miss., N.C., Okla., S.C., Tenn., Texas, Va.

House Votes 427, 428, 429, 430, 431, 432, 433

427. H Con Res 304. War Crimes in Yugoslavia/Passage. Bereuter, R-Neb., motion to suspend the rules and pass the bill to express the sense of Congress that the United States should publicly declare that it considers there to be probable cause that Slobodan Milosevic, president of the Federal Republic of Yugoslavia, has committed war crimes, crimes against humanity and genocide. Motion agreed to 369-1: R 204-1; D 164-0 (ND 118-0, SD 46-0); I 1-0. Sept. 14, 1998. A two-thirds majority of those present and voting (247 in this case) is required for passage under suspension of the rules.

428. H Con Res 254. Extradition of Criminals Living in Cuba/Passage. Bereuter, R-Neb., motion to suspend the rules and pass the bill to express the sense of Congress that the government of Cuba should extradite to the United States convicted murderer Joanne Chesimard and all other individuals living in Cuba who have fled the United States to avoid prosecution or confinement for criminal offenses. Motion agreed to 371-0: R 205-0; D 165-0 (ND 119-0, SD 46-0); I 1-0. Sept. 14, 1998. A two-thirds majority of those present and voting (248 in this case) is required for passage under suspension of the rules.

429. H Con Res 185. Universal Declaration of Human Rights/Passage. Gilman, R-N.Y., motion to suspend the rules and pass the bill to express the sense of Congress, on the 50th anniversary of the signing of the Universal Declaration of Human Rights, recommitting the United States to the document's principles. Motion agreed to 370-2: R 204-2; D 165-0 (ND 119-0, SD 46-0); I 1-0. Sept. 14, 1998. A two-thirds majority of those present and voting (248 in this case) is required for passage under suspension of the rules.

430. HR 4101. Fiscal 1999 Agriculture Appropriations/Motion to Instruct/Previous Question. Coburn, R-Okla., motion to order the previous question (thus ending debate) on adoption of the Kaptur, D-Ohio, motion to instruct conferees on the fiscal 1999 Agriculture Appropriations to agree to Senate provisions providing emergency funding (with no off-setting deductions) for agricultural disaster assistance. Motion agreed to 331-66: R 154-65; D 176-1 (ND 129-0, SD 47-1); I 1-0. Sept. 15, 1998. (Subsequently, the motion to instruct was adopted by voice vote.)

431. HR 4103. Fiscal 1999 Defense Appropriations/Motion to Instruct. Obey, D-Wis., motion to instruct the House conferees to redirect funds designated for low-priority congressionally-directed projects not requested in the Defense Department budget request to high-priority military readiness projects. Motion agreed to 348-61: R 180-38; D 167-23 (ND 125-14, SD 42-9); I 1-0. Sept. 15, 1998.

432. HR 4103. Fiscal 1999 Defense Appropriations/Closed Conference. Young, R-Fla., motion to close portions of the conference to the public during consideration of national security issues. Motion agreed to 405-2: R 219-0; D 185-2 (ND 135-2, SD 50-0); I 1-0. Sept. 15, 1998.

433. HR 4328. Fiscal 1999 Transportation Appropriations/Motion to Instruct. Sabo, D-Minn., motion to instruct House conferees to disagree with a provision in the Senate bill that would allow helicopters unrestricted access to wilderness areas and national parks in Alaska. Motion agreed to 249-161: R 69-149; D 179-12 (ND 134-6, SD 45-6); I 1-0. Sept. 15, 1998.

Key

- **Y** Voted for (yea).
- **#** Paired for.
- **+** Announced for.
- **N** Voted against (nay).
- **X** Paired against.
- **−** Announced against.
- **P** Voted "present."
- **C** Voted "present" to avoid possible conflict of interest.
- **?** Did not vote or otherwise make a position known.

Democrats **Republicans**
Independent

	427	428	429	430	431	432	433
ALABAMA							
1 *Callahan*	Y	Y	Y	Y	N	Y	N
2 *Everett*	Y	Y	Y	Y	Y	Y	N
3 *Riley*	Y	Y	Y	−	Y	Y	N
4 *Aderholt*	Y	Y	Y	Y	Y	Y	N
5 Cramer	Y	Y	Y	Y	Y	Y	Y
6 *Bachus*	?	?	?	Y	N	Y	N
7 Hilliard	Y	Y	Y	Y	Y	Y	N
ALASKA							
AL *Young*	Y	Y	Y	?	N	Y	N
ARIZONA							
1 *Salmon*	Y	Y	Y	N	Y	Y	N
2 Pastor	Y	Y	Y	Y	Y	Y	Y
3 *Stump*	Y	Y	Y	N	Y	Y	N
4 *Shadegg*	Y	Y	Y	N	Y	Y	N
5 *Kolbe*	Y	Y	Y	Y	Y	Y	Y
6 *Hayworth*	Y	Y	Y	N	Y	Y	N
ARKANSAS							
1 Berry	Y	Y	Y	Y	Y	Y	Y
2 Snyder	Y	Y	Y	Y	Y	Y	Y
3 *Hutchinson*	Y	Y	Y	Y	N	Y	N
4 *Dickey*	Y	Y	Y	Y	N	Y	?
CALIFORNIA							
1 *Riggs*	?	?	?	?	?	?	?
2 *Herger*	Y	Y	Y	N	Y	Y	Y
3 Fazio	Y	Y	Y	Y	Y	Y	Y
4 *Doolittle*	Y	Y	Y	N	Y	N	N
5 Matsui	Y	Y	Y	Y	Y	Y	Y
6 Woolsey	Y	Y	Y	Y	Y	Y	Y
7 Miller	Y	Y	Y	Y	Y	Y	Y
8 Pelosi	?	?	?	Y	Y	Y	Y
9 Lee	Y	Y	Y	Y	Y	Y	Y
10 Tauscher	Y	Y	Y	Y	Y	Y	Y
11 *Pombo*	Y	Y	Y	N	Y	Y	N
12 Lantos	Y	Y	Y	Y	Y	Y	Y
13 Stark	Y	Y	Y	Y	Y	Y	Y
14 Eshoo	Y	Y	Y	?	Y	Y	Y
15 *Campbell*	Y	Y	Y	N	Y	Y	Y
16 Lofgren	Y	Y	Y	Y	Y	Y	Y
17 Farr	Y	Y	Y	Y	Y	Y	Y
18 Condit	Y	Y	Y	Y	Y	Y	Y
19 *Radanovich*	Y	Y	Y	N	N	Y	N
20 Dooley	Y	Y	Y	Y	Y	Y	Y
21 *Thomas*	Y	Y	Y	Y	Y	Y	N
22 Capps, L.	Y	Y	Y	Y	Y	Y	Y
23 *Gallegly*	Y	Y	Y	Y	Y	Y	N
24 Sherman	Y	Y	Y	Y	Y	Y	Y
25 *McKeon*	Y	Y	Y	Y	Y	Y	N
26 Berman	Y	?	Y	Y	Y	Y	Y
27 *Rogan*	Y	Y	Y	Y	Y	Y	N
28 *Dreier*	Y	Y	Y	Y	Y	Y	N
29 Waxman	?	?	?	Y	Y	Y	Y
30 Becerra	Y	Y	Y	Y	Y	Y	Y
31 Martinez	Y	Y	Y	Y	Y	Y	N
32 Dixon	Y	Y	Y	Y	Y	Y	Y
33 Roybal-Allard	Y	Y	Y	Y	Y	Y	Y
34 Torres	Y	Y	Y	?	?	?	Y
35 Waters	Y	Y	Y	Y	Y	N	Y
36 Harman	?	?	?	Y	Y	Y	?
37 Millender-McD.	Y	Y	?	?	Y	?	?
38 *Horn*	Y	Y	Y	Y	Y	Y	Y
39 *Royce*	Y	Y	Y	N	Y	Y	N
40 *Lewis*	Y	Y	Y	Y	Y	Y	Y
41 *Kim*	Y	Y	Y	Y	Y	Y	Y
42 Brown	Y	Y	Y	Y	Y	Y	Y
43 *Calvert*	Y	Y	Y	Y	Y	Y	N
44 *Bono, M.*	Y	Y	Y	Y	Y	Y	N
45 *Rohrabacher*	Y	Y	Y	?	Y	Y	N
46 Sanchez	Y	Y	Y	Y	Y	Y	Y
47 *Cox*	Y	Y	Y	N	Y	Y	N
48 *Packard*	Y	Y	Y	Y	Y	Y	N
49 *Bilbray*	Y	Y	Y	Y	Y	Y	N
50 Filner	Y	Y	Y	Y	Y	Y	Y
51 *Cunningham*	?	Y	Y	Y	Y	Y	N
52 *Hunter*	Y	Y	Y	Y	N	Y	N
COLORADO							
1 DeGette	Y	Y	Y	Y	Y	Y	Y
2 Skaggs	Y	Y	Y	Y	Y	Y	Y
3 *McInnis*	Y	Y	Y	Y	Y	Y	Y
4 *Schaffer*	Y	Y	Y	N	Y	Y	N
5 *Hefley*	Y	Y	N	Y	Y	Y	N
6 *Schaefer*	Y	Y	Y	Y	Y	Y	Y
CONNECTICUT							
1 Kennelly	?	?	?	Y	Y	Y	Y
2 Gejdenson	Y	Y	Y	Y	Y	Y	Y
3 DeLauro	Y	Y	Y	Y	Y	Y	Y
4 *Shays*	Y	Y	Y	N	Y	Y	Y
5 Maloney	+	+	+	Y	Y	Y	Y
6 *Johnson*	Y	Y	Y	Y	Y	Y	Y
DELAWARE							
AL *Castle*	Y	Y	Y	Y	Y	Y	Y
FLORIDA							
1 *Scarborough*	Y	Y	N	Y	Y	Y	N
2 Boyd	Y	Y	Y	Y	Y	Y	Y
3 Brown	?	?	?	Y	Y	Y	Y
4 *Fowler*	Y	Y	Y	Y	Y	Y	N
5 Thurman	Y	Y	Y	Y	Y	Y	Y
6 *Stearns*	Y	Y	Y	N	Y	Y	N
7 *Mica*	Y	Y	Y	Y	Y	Y	N
8 *McCollum*	Y	Y	Y	Y	Y	Y	N
9 *Bilirakis*	Y	Y	Y	Y	Y	Y	N
10 *Young*	?	?	?	Y	Y	Y	Y
11 Davis	Y	Y	Y	Y	Y	Y	Y
12 *Canady*	Y	Y	Y	Y	Y	Y	N
13 *Miller*	Y	Y	Y	Y	Y	Y	Y
14 Goss	+	+	+	+	−	+	−
15 *Weldon*	Y	Y	Y	N	N	Y	N
16 *Foley*	Y	Y	Y	Y	Y	Y	N
17 Meek	Y	Y	Y	Y	Y	Y	Y
18 *Ros-Lehtinen*	+	+	+	Y	Y	Y	N
19 Wexler	Y	Y	Y	Y	Y	Y	Y
20 Deutsch	Y	Y	Y	Y	Y	Y	Y
21 *Diaz-Balart*	Y	Y	Y	Y	Y	Y	N
22 *Shaw*	Y	Y	Y	Y	Y	Y	N
23 Hastings	?	?	?	?	Y	Y	Y
GEORGIA							
1 *Kingston*	Y	Y	Y	Y	Y	Y	N
2 Bishop	Y	Y	Y	Y	Y	Y	Y
3 *Collins*	Y	Y	Y	Y	N	Y	N
4 McKinney	Y	Y	Y	Y	Y	Y	Y
5 Lewis	?	?	?	?	?	?	?
6 *Gingrich*							
7 *Barr*	?	?	?	N	N	Y	N
8 *Chambliss*	Y	Y	Y	Y	N	Y	N
9 *Deal*	Y	Y	Y	Y	N	Y	N
10 *Norwood*	Y	Y	Y	Y	N	Y	N
11 *Linder*	Y	Y	Y	Y	Y	Y	N
HAWAII							
1 Abercrombie	Y	Y	Y	Y	N	Y	Y
2 Mink	Y	Y	Y	?	N	Y	Y
IDAHO							
1 *Chenoweth*	Y	Y	N	Y	Y	Y	N
2 *Crapo*	+	+	+	Y	Y	Y	N
ILLINOIS							
1 Rush	?	?	?	?	Y	Y	Y
2 Jackson	Y	Y	Y	Y	Y	Y	Y
3 Lipinski	Y	Y	Y	Y	Y	Y	Y
4 Gutierrez	Y	Y	Y	Y	Y	Y	Y
5 Blagojevich	Y	Y	Y	Y	Y	Y	Y
6 *Hyde*	Y	Y	Y	Y	N	Y	N
7 Davis	Y	Y	Y	Y	Y	Y	Y
8 *Crane*	Y	Y	Y	Y	Y	Y	N
9 Yates	?	?	?	Y	Y	Y	Y
10 *Porter*	Y	Y	Y	Y	Y	Y	Y
11 *Weller*	Y	Y	Y	Y	Y	Y	N
12 Costello	Y	Y	Y	Y	Y	Y	Y
13 *Fawell*	Y	Y	Y	Y	Y	Y	Y

ND Northern Democrats   SD Southern Democrats

	427	428	429	430	431	432	433
14 ***Hastert***	Y	Y	Y	Y	N	Y	N
15 ***Ewing***	Y	Y	Y	N	Y	Y	Y
16 ***Manzullo***	?	?	?	N	Y	Y	N
17 Evans	Y	Y	Y	Y	Y	Y	Y
18 ***LaHood***	?	?	?	Y	N	Y	Y
19 Poshard	?	?	?	?	?	?	?
20 ***Shimkus***	Y	Y	Y	Y	Y	Y	Y
INDIANA							
1 Visclosky	Y	Y	Y	Y	N	Y	Y
2 ***McIntosh***	Y	Y	Y	N	Y	Y	N
3 Roemer	Y	Y	Y	Y	Y	Y	Y
4 ***Souder***	Y	Y	Y	Y	Y	Y	N
5 ***Buyer***	?	Y	Y	Y	N	Y	N
6 ***Burton***	Y	Y	Y	Y	Y	Y	N
7 ***Pease***	Y	Y	Y	Y	N	Y	Y
8 ***Hostettler***	Y	Y	Y	N	N	Y	N
9 Hamilton	?	Y	Y	Y	Y	Y	Y
10 Carson	+	Y	Y	Y	Y	Y	Y
IOWA							
1 ***Leach***	Y	Y	Y	N	Y	Y	Y
2 ***Nussle***	Y	Y	Y	N	Y	Y	N
3 Boswell	Y	Y	Y	Y	Y	Y	Y
4 ***Ganske***	Y	Y	Y	Y	Y	Y	N
5 ***Latham***	Y	Y	Y	N	Y	Y	N
KANSAS							
1 ***Moran***	Y	Y	Y	Y	Y	Y	N
2 ***Ryun***	Y	Y	Y	N	N	Y	N
3 ***Snowbarger***	Y	Y	Y	N	Y	Y	N
4 ***Tiahrt***	+	+	+	N	Y	Y	N
KENTUCKY							
1 ***Whitfield***	Y	Y	Y	Y	Y	Y	Y
2 ***Lewis***	Y	Y	Y	Y	Y	Y	N
3 ***Northup***	Y	Y	Y	Y	Y	Y	Y
4 ***Bunning***	Y	Y	Y	Y	Y	Y	N
5 ***Rogers***	Y	Y	Y	Y	N	Y	N
6 Baesler	Y	Y	Y	Y	Y	Y	Y
LOUISIANA							
1 ***Livingston***	Y	Y	Y	Y	Y	Y	N
2 Jefferson	?	?	?	?	Y	Y	Y
3 ***Tauzin***	?	?	?	Y	?	?	?
4 ***McCrery***	Y	Y	Y	Y	Y	Y	N
5 ***Cooksey***	Y	Y	Y	Y	Y	Y	N
6 ***Baker***	Y	Y	Y	Y	Y	Y	N
7 John	Y	Y	Y	Y	Y	Y	Y
MAINE							
1 Allen	Y	Y	Y	Y	Y	+	Y
2 Baldacci	Y	Y	Y	Y	Y	Y	Y
MARYLAND							
1 ***Gilchrest***	Y	Y	Y	Y	Y	Y	Y
2 ***Ehrlich***	Y	Y	Y	Y	Y	Y	?
3 Cardin	Y	Y	Y	Y	Y	Y	Y
4 Wynn	Y	Y	Y	?	?	?	?
5 Hoyer	Y	Y	Y	Y	Y	Y	Y
6 ***Bartlett***	Y	Y	Y	N	N	Y	N
7 Cummings	Y	Y	Y	Y	Y	Y	Y
8 ***Morella***	Y	Y	Y	?	Y	Y	Y
MASSACHUSETTS							
1 Olver	Y	Y	Y	Y	Y	Y	Y
2 Neal	?	?	?	Y	Y	Y	Y
3 McGovern	Y	Y	Y	?	Y	Y	Y
4 Frank	Y	Y	Y	Y	Y	Y	Y
5 Meehan	Y	Y	Y	Y	Y	Y	Y
6 Tierney	Y	Y	Y	?	Y	Y	Y
7 Markey	Y	Y	Y	Y	Y	Y	Y
8 Kennedy	?	?	?	?	Y	Y	Y
9 Moakley	?	?	?	Y	Y	Y	Y
10 Delahunt	Y	Y	Y	Y	Y	Y	Y
MICHIGAN							
1 Stupak	Y	Y	Y	Y	Y	Y	Y
2 ***Hoekstra***	Y	Y	Y	N	Y	Y	Y
3 ***Ehlers***	Y	Y	Y	Y	Y	Y	Y
4 ***Camp***	Y	Y	Y	Y	Y	Y	Y
5 Barcia	Y	Y	Y	Y	Y	Y	Y
6 ***Upton***	Y	Y	Y	Y	Y	Y	Y
7 ***Smith***	Y	Y	Y	N	Y	Y	Y
8 Stabenow	+	+	+	+	Y	Y	Y
9 Kildee	Y	Y	Y	Y	Y	Y	Y
10 Bonior	Y	Y	Y	Y	Y	Y	Y
11 ***Knollenberg***	Y	Y	Y	Y	Y	Y	N
12 Levin	Y	Y	Y	Y	Y	Y	Y
13 Rivers	Y	Y	Y	Y	Y	Y	Y
14 Conyers	Y	Y	Y	Y	Y	Y	Y
15 Kilpatrick	+	+	+	Y	Y	Y	Y
16 Dingell	Y	Y	Y	Y	Y	Y	Y

	427	428	429	430	431	432	433
MINNESOTA							
1 ***Gutknecht***	Y	Y	Y	Y	Y	Y	Y
2 Minge	+	+	+	Y	Y	Y	Y
3 ***Ramstad***	Y	Y	Y	Y	Y	Y	Y
4 Vento	Y	Y	Y	Y	Y	Y	Y
5 Sabo	Y	Y	Y	Y	Y	Y	Y
6 Luther	Y	Y	Y	Y	Y	Y	Y
7 Peterson	Y	Y	Y	Y	Y	Y	N
8 Oberstar	+	+	+	+	N	Y	Y
MISSISSIPPI							
1 ***Wicker***	Y	Y	Y	Y	N	Y	N
2 Thompson	Y	Y	Y	Y	Y	Y	Y
3 ***Pickering***	+	+	+	Y	Y	?	N
4 ***Parker***	Y	Y	Y	Y	Y	Y	N
5 Taylor	Y	Y	Y	Y	N	Y	Y
MISSOURI							
1 Clay	Y	Y	Y	Y	Y	Y	Y
2 ***Talent***	Y	Y	Y	Y	Y	Y	Y
3 Gephardt	Y	Y	Y	Y	Y	Y	Y
4 Skelton	Y	Y	Y	Y	N	Y	Y
5 McCarthy	Y	Y	Y	Y	Y	Y	Y
6 Danner	Y	Y	Y	Y	Y	Y	Y
7 ***Blunt***	Y	Y	Y	Y	Y	Y	N
8 ***Emerson***	Y	Y	Y	Y	Y	Y	N
9 ***Hulshof***	Y	Y	Y	Y	Y	Y	Y
MONTANA							
AL ***Hill***	Y	Y	Y	Y	Y	Y	N
NEBRASKA							
1 ***Bereuter***	Y	Y	Y	Y	Y	Y	N
2 ***Christensen***	Y	Y	Y	N	Y	Y	N
3 ***Barrett***	Y	Y	Y	Y	Y	Y	N
NEVADA							
1 ***Ensign***	Y	Y	Y	N	Y	Y	Y
2 ***Gibbons***	Y	Y	Y	Y	N	Y	N
NEW HAMPSHIRE							
1 ***Sununu***	Y	Y	Y	N	Y	Y	N
2 ***Bass***	Y	Y	Y	Y	Y	Y	Y
NEW JERSEY							
1 Andrews	Y	Y	Y	Y	Y	Y	Y
2 ***LoBiondo***	Y	Y	Y	N	Y	Y	Y
3 ***Saxton***	Y	Y	Y	Y	Y	Y	N
4 ***Smith***	Y	Y	Y	Y	Y	Y	Y
5 ***Roukema***	Y	Y	Y	N	Y	Y	Y
6 Pallone	Y	Y	Y	Y	Y	Y	Y
7 ***Franks***	Y	Y	Y	Y	Y	Y	Y
8 Pascrell	Y	Y	Y	Y	Y	Y	Y
9 Rothman	?	?	?	Y	Y	Y	Y
10 Payne	Y	Y	Y	Y	Y	Y	Y
11 ***Frelinghuysen***	Y	Y	Y	N	Y	Y	Y
12 ***Pappas***	Y	Y	Y	N	Y	Y	Y
13 Menendez	Y	Y	Y	Y	Y	Y	Y
NEW MEXICO							
1 ***Wilson***	Y	Y	Y	Y	Y	Y	Y
2 ***Skeen***	Y	Y	Y	Y	Y	Y	N
3 ***Redmond***	Y	Y	Y	Y	Y	Y	Y
NEW YORK							
1 ***Forbes***	Y	Y	Y	Y	Y	Y	Y
2 ***Lazio***	Y	Y	?	Y	Y	Y	Y
3 ***King***	Y	Y	Y	Y	N	Y	N
4 McCarthy	Y	Y	Y	Y	Y	Y	Y
5 Ackerman	?	?	?	Y	Y	Y	Y
6 Meeks	?	?	?	?	?	?	?
7 Manton	Y	Y	Y	?	?	?	?
8 Nadler	?	?	?	?	?	?	?
9 Schumer	?	?	?	?	?	?	?
10 Towns	?	?	?	?	?	?	?
11 Owens	?	?	?	?	?	?	?
12 Velázquez	?	?	?	?	?	?	?
13 ***Fossella***	Y	Y	Y	Y	N	Y	N
14 Maloney	+	+	+	Y	Y	Y	Y
15 Rangel	?	?	?	Y	Y	Y	Y
16 Serrano	Y	Y	Y	Y	Y	Y	Y
17 Engel	?	?	?	?	?	?	?
18 Lowey	?	?	?	Y	?	Y	Y
19 ***Kelly***	Y	Y	Y	Y	Y	Y	Y
20 ***Gilman***	Y	Y	Y	Y	Y	Y	Y
21 McNulty	Y	Y	Y	Y	Y	Y	Y
22 ***Solomon***	Y	Y	Y	Y	Y	Y	N
23 ***Boehlert***	Y	Y	Y	Y	Y	Y	Y
24 ***McHugh***	Y	Y	Y	Y	N	Y	Y
25 ***Walsh***	Y	Y	Y	Y	Y	Y	Y
26 Hinchey	Y	Y	Y	Y	Y	Y	Y
27 ***Paxon***	Y	Y	Y	N	Y	Y	N
28 Slaughter	Y	Y	Y	Y	N	Y	Y
29 LaFalce	Y	Y	Y	Y	Y	Y	Y
30 ***Quinn***	Y	Y	Y	Y	Y	Y	Y

	427	428	429	430	431	432	433
31 ***Houghton***	Y	Y	Y	Y	Y	Y	N
NORTH CAROLINA							
1 Clayton	?	?	?	?	?	?	?
2 Etheridge	Y	Y	Y	Y	Y	Y	Y
3 ***Jones***	Y	Y	Y	N	Y	Y	N
4 Price	Y	Y	Y	Y	Y	Y	Y
5 ***Burr***	Y	Y	Y	N	Y	Y	N
6 ***Coble***	Y	Y	Y	N	N	Y	N
7 McIntyre	?	?	?	?	?	?	?
8 Hefner	Y	Y	Y	Y	Y	Y	Y
9 ***Myrick***	Y	Y	Y	N	Y	Y	N
10 ***Ballenger***	Y	Y	Y	Y	Y	Y	N
11 ***Taylor***	?	?	?	N	N	Y	N
12 Watt	?	?	?	Y	Y	Y	Y
NORTH DAKOTA							
AL Pomeroy	Y	Y	Y	Y	Y	Y	N
OHIO							
1 ***Chabot***	Y	Y	Y	Y	Y	Y	Y
2 ***Portman***	Y	Y	Y	Y	Y	Y	N
3 Hall	Y	Y	Y	Y	Y	Y	Y
4 ***Oxley***	Y	Y	Y	Y	Y	Y	N
5 ***Gillmor***	Y	Y	Y	Y	Y	Y	Y
6 Strickland	Y	Y	Y	Y	Y	Y	Y
7 ***Hobson***	Y	Y	Y	Y	Y	Y	Y
8 ***Boehner***	Y	?	Y	Y	Y	Y	N
9 Kaptur	Y	Y	Y	Y	Y	Y	Y
10 Kucinich	P	Y	Y	Y	Y	Y	Y
11 Stokes	Y	Y	Y	Y	Y	Y	Y
12 ***Kasich***	Y	Y	Y	Y	Y	Y	N
13 Brown	Y	Y	Y	Y	Y	Y	Y
14 Sawyer	Y	Y	Y	Y	Y	Y	Y
15 ***Pryce***	+	+	+	+	+	+	+
16 ***Regula***	Y	Y	Y	Y	Y	Y	Y
17 Traficant	Y	Y	Y	Y	Y	Y	N
18 ***Ney***	Y	Y	Y	Y	Y	Y	Y
19 ***LaTourette***	Y	Y	Y	Y	Y	Y	N
OKLAHOMA							
1 ***Largent***	Y	Y	Y	N	Y	Y	N
2 ***Coburn***	Y	Y	Y	N	Y	Y	N
3 ***Watkins***	Y	Y	Y	Y	Y	Y	N
4 ***Watts***	Y	Y	Y	Y	Y	Y	N
5 ***Istook***	Y	Y	Y	N	Y	Y	N
6 ***Lucas***	Y	Y	Y	Y	Y	Y	N
OREGON							
1 Furse	Y	Y	Y	Y	Y	Y	Y
2 ***Smith***	Y	Y	Y	N	Y	Y	N
3 Blumenauer	?	?	?	Y	Y	Y	Y
4 DeFazio	Y	Y	Y	Y	Y	N	Y
5 Hooley	?	?	?	Y	Y	Y	Y
PENNSYLVANIA							
1 Brady	Y	Y	Y	Y	N	Y	Y
2 Fattah	Y	Y	Y	?	N	Y	Y
3 Borski	Y	Y	Y	Y	N	Y	Y
4 Klink	?	?	?	Y	N	Y	Y
5 ***Peterson***	Y	Y	Y	Y	Y	Y	N
6 Holden	Y	Y	Y	Y	N	Y	Y
7 ***Weldon***	Y	Y	Y	Y	Y	Y	N
8 ***Greenwood***	Y	Y	Y	N	Y	Y	Y
9 ***Shuster***	Y	Y	Y	Y	Y	Y	N
10 ***McDade***	?	?	?	Y	?	?	?
11 Kanjorski	Y	Y	Y	Y	N	Y	N
12 Murtha	Y	Y	Y	Y	N	Y	N
13 ***Fox***	Y	Y	Y	N	Y	Y	Y
14 Coyne	Y	Y	?	Y	Y	Y	Y
15 McHale	Y	Y	Y	Y	Y	Y	Y
16 ***Pitts***	Y	Y	Y	N	Y	Y	N
17 ***Gekas***	?	Y	Y	Y	N	Y	N
18 Doyle	Y	Y	Y	Y	Y	Y	Y
19 ***Goodling***	Y	Y	Y	N	N	Y	N
20 Mascara	Y	Y	Y	Y	Y	Y	Y
21 ***English***	?	?	?	Y	Y	Y	N
RHODE ISLAND							
1 Kennedy	Y	Y	Y	Y	Y	Y	Y
2 Weygand	Y	Y	Y	?	Y	Y	Y
SOUTH CAROLINA							
1 ***Sanford***	Y	Y	Y	N	Y	Y	Y
2 ***Spence***	Y	Y	Y	Y	Y	Y	N
3 ***Graham***	Y	?	Y	?	Y	Y	N
4 ***Inglis***	Y	Y	Y	Y	Y	Y	N
5 Spratt	Y	Y	Y	Y	Y	Y	Y
6 Clyburn	Y	Y	Y	Y	Y	Y	Y
SOUTH DAKOTA							
AL ***Thune***	Y	Y	Y	Y	N	Y	N

	427	428	429	430	431	432	433
TENNESSEE							
1 ***Jenkins***	Y	Y	Y	Y	Y	Y	N
2 ***Duncan***	Y	Y	Y	N	Y	Y	N
3 ***Wamp***	Y	Y	Y	N	Y	Y	N
4 ***Hilleary***	Y	Y	Y	Y	Y	Y	N
5 Clement	Y	Y	Y	Y	N	Y	Y
6 Gordon	Y	Y	Y	Y	N	Y	Y
7 ***Bryant***	Y	Y	Y	Y	Y	Y	N
8 Tanner	Y	Y	Y	Y	Y	Y	Y
9 Ford	Y	Y	Y	Y	Y	Y	Y
TEXAS							
1 Sandlin	Y	Y	Y	Y	Y	Y	Y
2 Turner	Y	Y	Y	Y	Y	+	N
3 ***Johnson, Sam***	Y	Y	Y	N	N	Y	N
4 Hall	Y	Y	Y	Y	Y	Y	N
5 ***Sessions***	?	?	?	Y	Y	Y	N
6 ***Barton***	Y	Y	Y	Y	Y	Y	N
7 ***Archer***	Y	?	Y	N	Y	Y	N
8 ***Brady***	Y	Y	Y	N	N	Y	N
9 Lampson	Y	Y	Y	Y	Y	Y	Y
10 Doggett	Y	Y	Y	Y	Y	Y	Y
11 Edwards	Y	Y	Y	Y	Y	Y	Y
12 ***Granger***	Y	Y	?	Y	Y	Y	N
13 ***Thornberry***	Y	Y	Y	Y	N	Y	N
14 ***Paul***	N	Y	N	N	Y	Y	N
15 Hinojosa	Y	Y	Y	Y	N	Y	Y
16 Reyes	Y	Y	Y	Y	N	Y	Y
17 Stenholm	Y	Y	Y	Y	Y	Y	N
18 Jackson-Lee	Y	Y	Y	Y	Y	Y	Y
19 ***Combest***	Y	Y	Y	Y	Y	Y	N
20 Gonzalez	?	?	?	?	?	?	?
21 ***Smith***	Y	Y	Y	Y	Y	Y	Y
22 ***DeLay***	Y	Y	Y	Y	?	?	?
23 ***Bonilla***	Y	Y	Y	Y	Y	Y	N
24 Frost	Y	Y	Y	Y	N	Y	Y
25 Bentsen	Y	Y	Y	Y	Y	Y	Y
26 ***Armey***	Y	Y	Y	Y	Y	Y	N
27 Ortiz	Y	Y	Y	Y	Y	Y	Y
28 Rodriguez	Y	Y	Y	Y	N	Y	N
29 Green	+	+	+	+	Y	Y	N
30 Johnson, E.B.	Y	Y	Y	Y	Y	Y	Y
UTAH							
1 ***Hansen***	?	?	?	Y	Y	Y	N
2 ***Cook***	?	?	?	Y	Y	Y	N
3 ***Cannon***	Y	Y	Y	N	Y	Y	N
VERMONT							
AL *Sanders*	Y	Y	Y	Y	Y	Y	Y
VIRGINIA							
1 ***Bateman***	Y	Y	Y	Y	N	Y	N
2 Pickett	Y	Y	Y	Y	Y	Y	Y
3 Scott	Y	Y	Y	Y	Y	Y	Y
4 Sisisky	Y	Y	Y	Y	N	Y	Y
5 Goode	Y	Y	Y	Y	N	Y	Y
6 ***Goodlatte***	Y	Y	Y	N	Y	Y	Y
7 ***Bliley***	Y	Y	Y	Y	Y	Y	N
8 Moran	Y	Y	Y	N	Y	Y	Y
9 Boucher	Y	Y	Y	Y	Y	Y	Y
10 ***Wolf***	Y	Y	Y	Y	Y	Y	Y
11 ***Davis***	Y	Y	Y	Y	?	Y	Y
WASHINGTON							
1 ***White***	Y	Y	Y	Y	Y	Y	Y
2 ***Metcalf***	Y	Y	Y	Y	Y	Y	Y
3 ***Smith, Linda***	Y	Y	Y	?	?	?	?
4 ***Hastings***	Y	Y	Y	Y	Y	Y	N
5 ***Nethercutt***	Y	Y	Y	Y	Y	Y	N
6 Dicks	Y	Y	Y	Y	Y	Y	Y
7 McDermott	Y	Y	Y	Y	Y	Y	Y
8 ***Dunn***	Y	Y	Y	Y	Y	Y	Y
9 Smith, Adam	Y	Y	Y	Y	Y	Y	Y
WEST VIRGINIA							
1 Mollohan	Y	Y	Y	Y	N	Y	Y
2 Wise	Y	?	Y	Y	Y	Y	Y
3 Rahall	Y	Y	Y	Y	Y	Y	Y
WISCONSIN							
1 ***Neumann***	Y	Y	Y	N	Y	Y	Y
2 ***Klug***	Y	Y	Y	N	Y	Y	Y
3 Kind	Y	Y	Y	Y	Y	Y	Y
4 Kleczka	Y	Y	Y	Y	Y	Y	Y
5 Barrett	Y	Y	Y	Y	Y	Y	Y
6 ***Petri***	Y	Y	Y	N	Y	Y	Y
7 Obey	Y	Y	Y	Y	Y	Y	Y
8 Johnson	Y	Y	Y	Y	Y	Y	Y
9 ***Sensenbrenner***	Y	Y	Y	N	Y	Y	Y
WYOMING							
AL ***Cubin***	Y	Y	Y	N	N	Y	N

Southern states - Ala., Ark., Fla., Ga., Ky., La., Miss., N.C., Okla., S.C., Tenn., Texas, Va.

House Votes 434, 435, 436, 437, 438, 439, 440

434. HR 4194. Fiscal 1999 VA-HUD Appropriations/Motion to Instruct. Obey, D-Wis., motion to instruct House conferees to insist on the House position providing funds for the Department of Veterans Affairs medical care account. Motion agreed to 405-1: R 216-1; D 188-0 (ND 139-0, SD 49-0); I 1-0. Sept. 15, 1998.

435. H J Res 117. Medicinal Marijuana/Passage. McCollum, R-Fla., motion to suspend the rules and pass the joint resolution that expresses the sense of Congress to oppose efforts to circumvent existing federal processes for determining the safety of Schedule I drugs, including marijuana, for medicinal use without valid scientific evidence. Motion agreed to 310-93: R 207-6; D 103-86 (ND 67-73, SD 36-13); I 0-1. Sept. 15, 1998. A two-thirds majority of those present and voting (269 in this case) is required for passage under suspension of the rules.

436. S 2073. Juvenile Crime and Missing Children Laws Amendments/Passage. Goodling, R-Pa., motion to suspend the rules and pass the bill to authorize annual grants to the National Center for Missing and Exploited Children and to make it easier for federal authorities to prosecute and try as adults juveniles ages 14 and older who commit federal violent crimes or federal drug-trafficking offenses. Motion agreed to 280-126: R 209-6; D 71-119 (ND 42-98, SD 29-21); I 0-1. Sept. 15, 1998. A two-thirds majority of those present and voting (271 in this case) is required for passage under suspension of the rules.

437. HR 4382. Mammography Standards/Passage. Bilirakis, R-Fla., motion to suspend the rules and pass the bill to reauthorize through fiscal 2002 the Mammography Quality Standards Act, which established uniform national standards for breast cancer diagnosis tests. Motion agreed to 401-1: R 212-0; D 188-1 (ND 139-1, SD 49-0); I 1-0. Sept. 15, 1998. A two-thirds majority of those present and voting (268 in this case) is required for passage under suspension of the rules.

438. HR 4300. International Drug Interdiction and Eradication/Defense Department Counter-Drug Mission. McCollum, R-Fla., amendment to express the sense of Congress that the administrative priorities for assets of the Defense Department should be revised so that the counter-drug mission of the department be second only to its war-fighting mission. Adopted 362-61: R 215-7; D 147-53 (ND 98-48, SD 49-5); I 0-1. Sept. 16, 1998.

439. HR 4300. International Drug Interdiction and Eradication/Drug Interdiction by U.S. Armed Forces. Reyes, D-Texas amendment to the Traficant, D-Ohio amendment to ban members of the armed forces from directly patrolling U.S. borders as a part of the efforts to keep illegal drugs outside of the United States. Rejected 167-256: R 21-201; D 145-55 (ND 112-34, SD 33-21); I 1-0. Sept. 16, 1998.

440. HR 4300. International Drug Interdiction and Eradication/Drug Interdiction by U.S. Armed Forces. Traficant, D-Ohio, amendment to direct the U.S. armed forces to assist in the efforts to keep illegal drugs out of the United States. The assistance could include patrolling U.S. borders. Adopted 291-133: R 202-20; D 89-112 (ND 57-90, SD 32-22); I 0-1. Sept. 16, 1998.

Key

- **Y** Voted for (yea).
- **#** Paired for.
- **+** Announced for.
- **N** Voted against (nay).
- **X** Paired against.
- **−** Announced against.
- **P** Voted "present."
- **C** Voted "present" to avoid possible conflict of interest.
- **?** Did not vote or otherwise make a position known.

Democrats **Republicans** *Independent*

	434	435	436	437	438	439	440
ALABAMA							
1 Callahan	N	Y	Y	Y	Y	Y	N
2 Everett	N	Y	Y	Y	Y	Y	N
3 Riley	N	Y	Y	Y	Y	Y	N
4 Aderholt	N	Y	Y	Y	Y	Y	N
5 Cramer	N	Y	N	Y	Y	N	N
6 Bachus	N	Y	Y	Y	Y	Y	N
7 Hilliard	Y	Y	N	Y	Y	?	?
ALASKA							
AL Young	N	N	Y	Y	Y	Y	Y
ARIZONA							
1 Salmon	N	Y	Y	Y	Y	Y	N
2 Pastor	Y	Y	N	Y	Y	N	Y
3 Stump	N	Y	Y	Y	Y	Y	N
4 Shadegg	N	Y	Y	Y	Y	Y	N
5 Kolbe	N	Y	Y	Y	Y	N	N
6 Hayworth	N	Y	Y	Y	Y	Y	Y
ARKANSAS							
1 Berry	N	Y	N	Y	Y	N	?
2 Snyder	N	Y	N	Y	Y	N	N
3 Hutchinson	N	N	Y	Y	Y	Y	N
4 Dickey	N	Y	Y	Y	Y	Y	N
CALIFORNIA							
1 Riggs	?	?	?	?	?	?	?
2 Herger	N	Y	Y	Y	Y	Y	N
3 Fazio	Y	Y	?	?	?	N	Y
4 Doolittle	N	Y	N	Y	Y	Y	Y
5 Matsui	N	N	N	Y	Y	N	Y
6 Woolsey	Y	N	N	Y	Y	N	Y
7 Miller	Y	N	N	Y	Y	N	Y
8 Pelosi	Y	N	N	Y	Y	N	Y
9 Lee	Y	N	N	Y	Y	N	Y
10 Tauscher	N	Y	N	Y	Y	N	N
11 Pombo	N	Y	Y	Y	Y	Y	Y
12 Lantos	N	Y	?	Y	Y	N	Y
13 Stark	Y	N	N	Y	Y	N	Y
14 Eshoo	N	N	N	Y	Y	N	Y
15 Campbell	N	Y	N	Y	Y	Y	N
16 Lofgren	Y	N	N	Y	Y	N	Y
17 Farr	Y	Y	N	Y	Y	N	Y
18 Condit	N	Y	Y	Y	Y	N	Y
19 Radanovich	?	Y	Y	Y	Y	Y	Y
20 Dooley	N	Y	N	Y	Y	N	Y
21 Thomas	N	Y	Y	Y	Y	N	Y
22 Capps, L.	N	Y	Y	Y	Y	?	Y
23 Gallegly	N	Y	Y	Y	Y	Y	Y
24 Sherman	N	Y	N	Y	Y	N	Y
25 McKeon	N	Y	Y	Y	Y	Y	Y
26 Berman	N	Y	N	Y	Y	N	Y
27 Rogan	N	Y	Y	Y	Y	Y	Y
28 Dreier	N	Y	Y	Y	Y	Y	Y
29 Waxman	N	N	N	Y	Y	−	Y
30 Becerra	N	Y	N	Y	Y	−	N
31 Martinez	N	?	N	Y	Y	N	Y
32 Dixon	N	Y	N	Y	Y	N	Y
33 Roybal-Allard	Y	Y	N	Y	Y	N	Y
34 Torres	Y	N	N	Y	Y	N	Y
35 Waters	Y	Y	?	Y	Y	N	Y
36 Harman	N	?	?	Y	Y	N	Y
37 Millender-McD.	Y	Y	N	Y	Y	N	Y
38 Horn	N	?	?	Y	Y	Y	Y

	434	435	436	437	438	439	440
39 Royce	N	Y	N	Y	?	Y	Y
40 Lewis	N	Y	Y	Y	Y	Y	Y
41 Kim	N	Y	Y	Y	Y	Y	Y
42 Brown	Y	N	N	Y	Y	?	Y
43 Calvert	N	Y	Y	Y	Y	Y	N
44 Bono, M.	N	Y	Y	Y	Y	Y	Y
45 Rohrabacher	N	Y	Y	Y	Y	Y	Y
46 Sanchez	N	Y	N	Y	Y	N	+
47 Cox	N	Y	Y	Y	Y	Y	Y
48 Packard	N	Y	Y	Y	Y	Y	Y
49 Bilbray	N	Y	Y	Y	Y	Y	Y
50 Filner	Y	N	N	Y	Y	N	Y
51 Cunningham	N	Y	Y	Y	Y	?	Y
52 Hunter	N	Y	Y	Y	Y	Y	Y
COLORADO							
1 DeGette	N	Y	N	Y	Y	N	Y
2 Skaggs	N	N	N	N	Y	N	Y
3 McInnis	N	Y	Y	Y	Y	Y	N
4 Schaffer	N	Y	Y	Y	Y	Y	Y
5 Hefley	N	Y	Y	Y	Y	Y	Y
6 Schaefer	N	Y	Y	Y	Y	Y	N
CONNECTICUT							
1 Kennelly	N	Y	N	Y	Y	N	?
2 Gejdenson	N	Y	?	?	Y	N	Y
3 DeLauro	N	Y	N	Y	Y	N	Y
4 Shays	N	Y	Y	Y	Y	Y	Y
5 Maloney	N	Y	Y	Y	Y	N	N
6 Johnson	N	Y	N	Y	Y	Y	Y
DELAWARE							
AL Castle	N	Y	N	Y	Y	N	Y
FLORIDA							
1 Scarborough	N	Y	Y	Y	Y	?	N
2 Boyd	N	Y	N	Y	Y	N	Y
3 Brown	Y	N	N	Y	N	Y	Y
4 Fowler	N	Y	Y	Y	Y	Y	N
5 Thurman	N	Y	N	Y	Y	N	Y
6 Stearns	N	Y	Y	Y	Y	Y	N
7 Mica	N	Y	Y	Y	Y	Y	Y
8 McCollum	N	Y	Y	Y	Y	Y	Y
9 Bilirakis	N	Y	Y	Y	Y	Y	Y
10 Young	N	Y	Y	Y	Y	Y	Y
11 Davis	N	Y	N	Y	Y	N	N
12 Canady	N	Y	Y	Y	Y	Y	Y
13 Miller	N	Y	Y	Y	Y	Y	N
14 Goss	−	+	+	+	+	+	−
15 Weldon	N	Y	Y	Y	Y	Y	Y
16 Foley	N	Y	Y	Y	Y	Y	Y
17 Meek	Y	Y	N	Y	Y	N	?
18 Ros-Lehtinen	N	Y	Y	Y	Y	Y	Y
19 Wexler	N	Y	?	?	Y	N	N
20 Deutsch	N	Y	N	Y	Y	N	N
21 Diaz-Balart	N	Y	Y	Y	Y	Y	N
22 Shaw	N	Y	Y	Y	Y	Y	Y
23 Hastings	N	Y	N	Y	Y	N	N
GEORGIA							
1 Kingston	N	Y	Y	Y	Y	Y	N
2 Bishop	N	Y	Y	Y	Y	Y	Y
3 Collins	N	Y	N	Y	Y	Y	N
4 McKinney	Y	Y	N	Y	Y	N	Y
5 Lewis	N	N	N	Y	Y	N	?
6 Gingrich				Y			
7 Barr	N	Y	Y	Y	Y	Y	Y
8 Chambliss	N	Y	Y	Y	Y	Y	Y
9 Deal	N	Y	Y	Y	Y	Y	Y
10 Norwood	N	Y	Y	Y	Y	Y	Y
11 Linder	N	Y	N	Y	Y	Y	Y
HAWAII							
1 Abercrombie	Y	N	N	Y	Y	N	Y
2 Mink	Y	Y	N	Y	Y	?	Y
IDAHO							
1 Chenoweth	N	N	Y	Y	Y	Y	Y
2 Crapo	N	Y	N	Y	Y	Y	Y
ILLINOIS							
1 Rush	N	Y	N	Y	Y	N	?
2 Jackson	Y	N	Y	Y	Y	N	Y
3 Lipinski	N	Y	N	Y	Y	N	Y
4 Gutierrez	N	Y	N	Y	Y	?	Y
5 Blagojevich	N	Y	N	Y	Y	N	Y
6 Hyde	N	Y	Y	Y	Y	Y	Y
7 Davis	N	N	N	Y	Y	N	Y
8 Crane	N	Y	N	Y	Y	Y	Y
9 Yates	N	N	?	?	Y	N	Y
10 Porter	N	Y	Y	Y	Y	Y	Y
11 Weller	N	Y	Y	Y	Y	Y	Y
12 Costello	N	Y	N	Y	Y	N	Y
13 Fawell	N	Y	Y	Y	Y	Y	?

ND Northern Democrats   SD Southern Democrats

	434	435	436	437	438	439	440
14 ***Hastert***	N	Y	N	Y	Y	Y	N
15 ***Ewing***	N	Y	N	Y	Y	Y	N
16 ***Manzullo***	N	Y	N	Y	Y	Y	N
17 Evans	N	Y	N	Y	Y	N	Y
18 ***LaHood***	N	Y	Y	Y	Y	Y	N
19 Poshard	?	?	?	?	?	?	?
20 ***Shimkus***	N	Y	Y	Y	Y	Y	N
INDIANA							
1 Visclosky	N	N	N	Y	Y	N	Y
2 ***McIntosh***	N	Y	Y	Y	Y	Y	N
3 Roemer	N	Y	N	Y	Y	N	N
4 ***Souder***	N	Y	Y	Y	Y	Y	Y
5 ***Buyer***	N	Y	Y	?	Y	Y	N
6 ***Burton***	N	Y	Y	Y	Y	Y	N
7 ***Pease***	N	Y	Y	Y	Y	Y	N
8 ***Hostettler***	N	Y	Y	Y	Y	Y	Y
9 Hamilton	Y	N	N	Y	Y	N	N
10 Carson	Y	N	N	Y	Y	N	Y
IOWA							
1 ***Leach***	N	Y	N	Y	Y	Y	Y
2 ***Nussle***	N	Y	Y	Y	Y	Y	N
3 Boswell	N	Y	?	Y	Y	N	N
4 ***Ganske***	N	Y	N	Y	Y	Y	Y
5 ***Latham***	N	Y	Y	Y	Y	Y	N
KANSAS							
1 ***Moran***	N	Y	N	Y	Y	Y	N
2 ***Ryun***	N	Y	Y	Y	Y	Y	N
3 ***Snowbarger***	N	Y	Y	Y	Y	Y	N
4 ***Tiahrt***	N	Y	Y	Y	Y	Y	N
KENTUCKY							
1 ***Whitfield***	N	Y	N	Y	Y	?	?
2 ***Lewis***	N	Y	N	Y	Y	Y	N
3 ***Northup***	N	Y	N	Y	Y	Y	N
4 ***Bunning***	N	Y	N	Y	Y	Y	N
5 ***Rogers***	N	Y	N	Y	Y	Y	N
6 Baesler	N	Y	N	Y	Y	N	Y
LOUISIANA							
1 ***Livingston***	N	Y	N	Y	Y	Y	N
2 Jefferson	N	Y	N	Y	Y	N	N
3 ***Tauzin***	N	Y	?	?	Y	Y	N
4 ***McCrery***	N	Y	N	Y	Y	Y	N
5 ***Cooksey***	N	Y	Y	Y	Y	Y	N
6 ***Baker***	N	Y	N	Y	Y	Y	N
7 John	N	Y	?	?	?	N	N
MAINE							
1 Allen	N	Y	N	Y	Y	N	N
2 Baldacci	N	Y	N	Y	Y	N	N
MARYLAND							
1 ***Gilchrest***	N	Y	N	Y	Y	Y	Y
2 ***Ehrlich***	N	Y	N	Y	Y	Y	Y
3 Cardin	N	Y	N	Y	Y	N	Y
4 Wynn	Y	Y	N	Y	Y	N	Y
5 Hoyer	N	Y	N	Y	Y	N	Y
6 ***Bartlett***	N	Y	Y	Y	Y	Y	?
7 Cummings	N	Y	N	Y	Y	N	Y
8 ***Morella***	N	Y	N	Y	Y	N	Y
MASSACHUSETTS							
1 Olver	Y	N	N	Y	Y	N	Y
2 Neal	N	Y	N	Y	Y	N	Y
3 McGovern	N	Y	N	Y	Y	N	Y
4 Frank	N	N	N	N	Y	N	Y
5 Meehan	N	Y	N	Y	Y	N	Y
6 Tierney	Y	Y	N	Y	Y	N	Y
7 Markey	N	Y	N	Y	Y	N	Y
8 Kennedy	N	Y	N	Y	Y	N	Y
9 Moakley	Y	Y	N	Y	Y	N	Y
10 Delahunt	N	Y	N	Y	Y	N	Y
MICHIGAN							
1 Stupak	N	Y	N	Y	Y	Y	Y
2 ***Hoekstra***	N	Y	N	Y	Y	Y	Y
3 ***Ehlers***	N	Y	Y	Y	Y	Y	Y
4 ***Camp***	N	Y	Y	Y	Y	Y	Y
5 Barcia	N	Y	N	Y	Y	Y	Y
6 ***Upton***	N	Y	Y	Y	Y	Y	Y
7 ***Smith***	N	Y	Y	Y	Y	Y	Y
8 Stabenow	Y	Y	N	Y	Y	N	Y
9 Kildee	N	Y	N	Y	Y	Y	Y
10 Bonior	Y	N	N	Y	Y	N	Y
11 ***Knollenberg***	N	Y	N	Y	Y	Y	Y
12 Levin	N	Y	N	Y	Y	N	Y
13 Rivers	Y	Y	N	Y	Y	N	Y
14 Conyers	+	N	N	N	Y	N	Y
15 Kilpatrick	Y	Y	N	Y	Y	N	Y
16 Dingell	N	Y	N	N	Y	N	Y

	434	435	436	437	438	439	440
MINNESOTA							
1 ***Gutknecht***	N	Y	Y	Y	Y	Y	Y
2 Minge	Y	Y	N	Y	Y	N	N
3 ***Ramstad***	N	Y	N	Y	Y	N	Y
4 Vento	Y	N	N	Y	Y	N	Y
5 Sabo	Y	N	N	Y	Y	N	N
6 Luther	Y	Y	N	Y	Y	N	N
7 Peterson	N	Y	N	Y	Y	Y	Y
8 Oberstar	Y	N	N	Y	Y	Y	Y
MISSISSIPPI							
1 ***Wicker***	N	Y	N	Y	Y	Y	N
2 Thompson	Y	Y	N	Y	Y	N	Y
3 ***Pickering***	N	Y	Y	Y	Y	Y	N
4 ***Parker***	N	Y	Y	Y	Y	Y	N
5 Taylor	N	Y	Y	Y	Y	Y	N
MISSOURI							
1 Clay	Y	Y	?	?	Y	N	?
2 ***Talent***	N	Y	Y	Y	Y	Y	Y
3 Gephardt	Y	Y	N	Y	Y	N	?
4 Skelton	N	Y	N	Y	Y	N	N
5 McCarthy	Y	Y	N	Y	Y	N	Y
6 Danner	N	Y	?	?	Y	N	N
7 ***Blunt***	N	Y	?	+	Y	Y	N
8 ***Emerson***	N	Y	Y	Y	Y	Y	N
9 ***Hulshof***	N	Y	N	Y	Y	Y	N
MONTANA							
AL ***Hill***	N	Y	N	Y	Y	Y	N
NEBRASKA							
1 ***Bereuter***	N	Y	N	?	Y	N	N
2 ***Christensen***	N	Y	N	Y	Y	Y	Y
3 ***Barrett***	N	Y	N	Y	Y	Y	Y
NEVADA							
1 ***Ensign***	N	Y	N	Y	Y	Y	Y
2 ***Gibbons***	N	Y	Y	Y	Y	Y	N
NEW HAMPSHIRE							
1 ***Sununu***	N	Y	N	Y	Y	Y	Y
2 ***Bass***	N	Y	N	Y	Y	Y	Y
NEW JERSEY							
1 Andrews	N	Y	N	Y	Y	N	Y
2 ***LoBiondo***	N	Y	Y	Y	Y	Y	Y
3 ***Saxton***	N	Y	N	Y	Y	Y	N
4 ***Smith***	N	Y	N	Y	Y	Y	Y
5 ***Roukema***	N	Y	Y	Y	Y	N	Y
6 Pallone	N	Y	N	Y	Y	N	Y
7 ***Franks***	N	Y	Y	Y	Y	Y	Y
8 Pascrell	N	Y	N	Y	Y	N	Y
9 Rothman	N	Y	N	Y	Y	N	Y
10 Payne	Y	N	N	Y	Y	N	Y
11 ***Frelinghuysen***	N	Y	N	Y	Y	Y	Y
12 ***Pappas***	N	Y	Y	Y	Y	Y	Y
13 Menendez	N	Y	N	Y	Y	N	Y
NEW MEXICO							
1 ***Wilson***	N	Y	N	Y	Y	Y	N
2 ***Skeen***	N	Y	N	Y	Y	Y	N
3 ***Redmond***	N	Y	N	Y	Y	Y	N
NEW YORK							
1 ***Forbes***	N	Y	N	Y	?	Y	N
2 ***Lazio***	N	Y	N	Y	Y	Y	Y
3 ***King***	N	Y	N	Y	Y	Y	–
4 McCarthy	N	Y	N	Y	Y	N	Y
5 Ackerman	N	Y	N	Y	Y	N	Y
6 Meeks	?	?	?	?	Y	N	Y
7 Manton	N	Y	N	Y	Y	Y	Y
8 Nadler	Y	N	N	N	Y	N	N
9 Schumer	?	?	?	?	?	?	?
10 Towns	?	?	?	?	Y	N	Y
11 Owens	Y	N	N	Y	Y	N	Y
12 Velázquez	Y	N	N	Y	Y	N	Y
13 ***Fossella***	N	Y	Y	Y	Y	Y	Y
14 Maloney	N	Y	N	Y	Y	N	Y
15 Rangel	N	Y	N	Y	Y	N	Y
16 Serrano	N	Y	N	Y	Y	N	Y
17 Engel	N	Y	N	Y	Y	N	Y
18 Lowey	Y	Y	N	Y	Y	N	Y
19 ***Kelly***	N	Y	N	Y	Y	Y	Y
20 ***Gilman***	N	Y	N	Y	Y	Y	Y
21 McNulty	N	Y	N	Y	Y	N	Y
22 ***Solomon***	N	Y	Y	Y	Y	Y	N
23 ***Boehlert***	N	Y	N	Y	Y	Y	Y
24 ***McHugh***	?	?	Y	Y	Y	Y	Y
25 ***Walsh***	N	Y	Y	Y	Y	Y	Y
26 Hinchey	Y	Y	N	Y	Y	N	Y
27 ***Paxon***	N	Y	Y	Y	Y	Y	N
28 Slaughter	N	Y	N	Y	Y	N	Y
29 LaFalce	N	Y	N	Y	Y	N	Y
30 ***Quinn***	N	Y	Y	Y	Y	Y	N

	434	435	436	437	438	439	440
31 ***Houghton***	N	Y	N	Y	Y	Y	Y
NORTH CAROLINA							
1 Clayton	Y	Y	?	Y	Y	N	Y
2 Etheridge	N	Y	N	Y	Y	N	Y
3 ***Jones***	N	Y	Y	Y	Y	Y	Y
4 Price	N	Y	N	Y	Y	N	Y
5 ***Burr***	N	Y	Y	Y	Y	Y	Y
6 ***Coble***	N	Y	Y	Y	Y	Y	Y
7 McIntyre	N	Y	Y	Y	Y	Y	Y
8 Hefner	N	Y	?	?	?	N	Y
9 ***Myrick***	N	Y	Y	Y	Y	Y	+
10 ***Ballenger***	N	Y	Y	Y	Y	Y	N
11 ***Taylor***	N	Y	Y	Y	Y	Y	N
12 Watt	Y	N	N	Y	Y	N	Y
NORTH DAKOTA							
AL Pomeroy	N	Y	N	Y	Y	N	N
OHIO							
1 ***Chabot***	N	Y	Y	Y	Y	Y	N
2 ***Portman***	N	Y	N	Y	Y	Y	N
3 Hall	N	Y	N	Y	Y	N	Y
4 ***Oxley***	N	Y	N	Y	Y	Y	N
5 ***Gillmor***	N	Y	N	Y	Y	Y	N
6 Strickland	N	Y	N	Y	Y	N	Y
7 ***Hobson***	N	Y	N	Y	Y	Y	N
8 ***Boehner***	N	Y	N	Y	Y	Y	N
9 Kaptur	?	Y	N	Y	Y	N	N
10 Kucinich	N	Y	N	Y	Y	Y	Y
11 Stokes	Y	Y	?	?	?	N	Y
12 ***Kasich***	N	Y	N	Y	Y	Y	N
13 Brown	N	Y	N	Y	Y	N	Y
14 Sawyer	N	Y	N	Y	Y	N	Y
15 ***Pryce***	–	+	–	+	+	+	+
16 ***Regula***	N	Y	N	Y	Y	Y	N
17 Traficant	N	Y	Y	Y	Y	Y	N
18 ***Ney***	N	Y	N	Y	Y	Y	Y
19 ***LaTourette***	N	Y	N	Y	Y	Y	N
OKLAHOMA							
1 ***Largent***	N	Y	Y	Y	Y	Y	N
2 ***Coburn***	N	Y	Y	Y	Y	Y	N
3 ***Watkins***	N	Y	Y	Y	Y	Y	N
4 ***Watts***	N	Y	N	Y	Y	Y	N
5 ***Istook***	N	Y	Y	Y	Y	Y	N
6 ***Lucas***	N	Y	N	Y	Y	Y	N
OREGON							
1 Furse	Y	Y	N	Y	Y	N	Y
2 ***Smith***	N	Y	N	Y	Y	Y	N
3 Blumenauer	N	Y	N	Y	Y	N	Y
4 DeFazio	Y	N	N	Y	Y	N	Y
5 Hooley	N	Y	N	Y	Y	N	Y
PENNSYLVANIA							
1 Brady	Y	Y	N	Y	Y	N	N
2 Fattah	Y	Y	N	Y	Y	N	Y
3 Borski	N	Y	N	Y	Y	N	Y
4 Klink	N	Y	N	Y	Y	N	Y
5 ***Peterson***	N	Y	?	Y	Y	Y	N
6 Holden	N	Y	N	Y	Y	Y	Y
7 ***Weldon***	N	Y	N	Y	Y	Y	Y
8 ***Greenwood***	N	Y	N	Y	Y	Y	N
9 ***Shuster***	N	Y	N	Y	Y	Y	N
10 ***McDade***	N	Y	N	Y	Y	Y	Y
11 Kanjorski	N	Y	N	Y	Y	N	N
12 Murtha	N	Y	N	Y	Y	N	N
13 ***Fox***	N	Y	Y	Y	Y	Y	Y
14 Coyne	N	Y	N	Y	Y	N	Y
15 McHale	N	Y	N	Y	Y	N	Y
16 ***Pitts***	N	Y	N	Y	Y	Y	Y
17 ***Gekas***	N	Y	N	Y	Y	Y	N
18 Doyle	N	Y	N	Y	Y	Y	Y
19 ***Goodling***	N	Y	Y	Y	Y	Y	N
20 Mascara	N	Y	N	Y	Y	Y	Y
21 ***English***	N	Y	N	Y	Y	Y	Y
RHODE ISLAND							
1 Kennedy	N	Y	N	Y	Y	N	Y
2 Weygand	N	Y	N	Y	Y	N	Y
SOUTH CAROLINA							
1 ***Sanford***	N	N	Y	Y	Y	Y	N
2 ***Spence***	N	Y	Y	Y	Y	Y	N
3 ***Graham***	N	Y	Y	Y	Y	Y	N
4 ***Inglis***	N	Y	Y	Y	Y	Y	N
5 Spratt	N	Y	N	Y	Y	N	N
6 Clyburn	Y	Y	?	?	Y	N	Y
SOUTH DAKOTA							
AL ***Thune***	N	Y	Y	Y	Y	Y	N

	434	435	436	437	438	439	440
TENNESSEE							
1 ***Jenkins***	N	Y	Y	Y	Y	Y	N
2 ***Duncan***	N	Y	Y	Y	Y	Y	Y
3 ***Wamp***	N	Y	Y	Y	Y	Y	N
4 ***Hilleary***	N	Y	Y	Y	Y	Y	Y
5 Clement	N	Y	N	Y	Y	N	N
6 Gordon	N	Y	N	Y	Y	N	N
7 ***Bryant***	N	Y	Y	Y	Y	Y	N
8 Tanner	N	Y	N	Y	Y	N	N
9 Ford	Y	Y	N	Y	Y	N	Y
TEXAS							
1 Sandlin	N	Y	N	Y	Y	N	N
2 Turner	N	Y	Y	Y	Y	N	N
3 ***Johnson, Sam***	N	Y	N	Y	Y	Y	N
4 Hall	N	Y	Y	Y	Y	Y	Y
5 ***Sessions***	N	Y	Y	Y	Y	Y	N
6 ***Barton***	N	Y	Y	Y	Y	Y	N
7 ***Archer***	N	Y	N	Y	Y	Y	N
8 ***Brady***	N	Y	?	?	Y	+	N
9 Lampson	N	Y	N	Y	Y	N	N
10 Doggett	Y	Y	N	Y	Y	N	Y
11 Edwards	N	Y	N	Y	Y	N	N
12 ***Granger***	N	Y	Y	Y	Y	Y	N
13 ***Thornberry***	N	Y	N	Y	Y	Y	N
14 ***Paul***	Y	N	N	N	Y	?	Y
15 Hinojosa	Y	Y	N	Y	Y	N	Y
16 Reyes	N	N	N	Y	Y	N	N
17 Stenholm	N	Y	Y	Y	Y	N	N
18 Jackson-Lee	Y	N	N	Y	Y	N	N
19 ***Combest***	N	Y	Y	Y	Y	Y	N
20 Gonzalez	?	?	?	?	?	?	?
21 ***Smith***	N	Y	Y	Y	Y	Y	N
22 ***DeLay***	N	Y	N	Y	Y	Y	N
23 ***Bonilla***	N	Y	N	Y	Y	Y	N
24 Frost	N	Y	N	Y	Y	N	N
25 Bentsen	N	Y	N	Y	Y	N	N
26 ***Armey***	N	Y	N	Y	Y	Y	N
27 Ortiz	N	Y	N	Y	Y	N	N
28 Rodriguez	N	Y	N	Y	Y	N	N
29 Green	N	Y	N	Y	Y	N	N
30 Johnson, E.B.	N	Y	N	Y	Y	N	?
UTAH							
1 ***Hansen***	N	Y	Y	Y	Y	Y	N
2 ***Cook***	N	Y	Y	Y	Y	Y	Y
3 ***Cannon***	N	Y	Y	Y	Y	Y	N
VERMONT							
AL *Sanders*	Y	N	N	Y	Y	N	Y
VIRGINIA							
1 ***Bateman***	N	Y	?	?	Y	Y	N
2 Pickett	N	Y	N	Y	Y	N	N
3 Scott	Y	N	N	N	Y	N	Y
4 Sisisky	N	Y	N	Y	Y	N	Y
5 Goode	N	Y	Y	Y	Y	Y	Y
6 ***Goodlatte***	N	Y	N	Y	Y	Y	N
7 ***Bliley***	N	Y	N	Y	Y	Y	Y
8 Moran	Y	N	N	Y	Y	N	Y
9 Boucher	N	Y	N	Y	Y	N	Y
10 ***Wolf***	N	Y	N	Y	Y	Y	Y
11 ***Davis***	N	Y	N	Y	Y	Y	Y
WASHINGTON							
1 ***White***	N	Y	Y	Y	Y	Y	N
2 ***Metcalf***	N	Y	Y	Y	?	Y	N
3 ***Smith, Linda***	?	?	Y	Y	Y	Y	Y
4 ***Hastings***	N	Y	N	Y	Y	Y	N
5 ***Nethercutt***	N	Y	Y	Y	Y	Y	N
6 Dicks	N	Y	?	?	Y	N	Y
7 McDermott	Y	N	N	Y	Y	N	Y
8 ***Dunn***	N	Y	Y	Y	Y	Y	N
9 Smith, Adam	N	Y	N	Y	Y	N	Y
WEST VIRGINIA							
1 Mollohan	N	Y	N	Y	Y	Y	Y
2 Wise	N	Y	N	Y	Y	N	N
3 Rahall	N	Y	N	Y	Y	Y	Y
WISCONSIN							
1 ***Neumann***	N	Y	Y	Y	Y	Y	Y
2 ***Klug***	N	Y	N	Y	Y	N	N
3 Kind	N	Y	N	Y	Y	N	Y
4 Kleczka	Y	Y	N	Y	Y	N	Y
5 Barrett	Y	Y	N	Y	Y	N	Y
6 ***Petri***	N	Y	N	Y	Y	Y	N
7 Obey	Y	N	N	N	Y	N	Y
8 Johnson	N	Y	N	Y	Y	N	Y
9 ***Sensenbrenner***	N	Y	N	Y	Y	Y	Y
WYOMING							
AL ***Cubin***	N	Y	N	Y	Y	Y	Y

Southern states - Ala., Ark., Fla., Ga., Ky., La., Miss., N.C., Okla., S.C., Tenn., Texas, Va.

House Votes 441, 442, 443, 444, 445, 446, 447

Key

Y	Voted for (yea).
#	Paired for.
+	Announced for.
N	Voted against (nay).
X	Paired against.
–	Announced against.
P	Voted "present."
C	Voted "present" to avoid possible conflict of interest.
?	Did not vote or otherwise make a position known.

Democrats **Republicans** Independent

441. HR 4300. International Drug Interdiction and Eradication/Military Assistance. Waters, D-Calif., amendment to strike the bill's authorization for funding for direct military assistance for Colombia and Mexico. Rejected 67-354: R 1-220; D 65-134 (ND 51-94, SD 14-40); I 1-0. Sept. 16, 1998.

442. HR 4300. International Drug Interdiction and Eradication/Passage. Passage of the bill to authorize $2.3 billion through fiscal 2001 for a variety of programs to strengthen narcotics interdiction and eradication programs in Central and South America. Passed 384-39: R 219-3; D 165-35 (ND 117-29, SD 48-6); I 0-1. Sept. 16, 1998.

443. HR 4550. Drug Abuse Prevention and Treatment Programs/Drug Testing for Federal Employees. Taylor, D-Miss., amendment to require all federal employees to submit to random, unannounced drug tests. Rejected 123-281: R 113-105; D 10-175 (ND 3-133, SD 7-42); I 0-1. Sept. 16, 1998.

444. HR 4550. Drug Abuse Prevention and Treatment Programs/Passage. Passage of the bill to establish numerous new programs to help reduce the demand for illegal drugs in the United States, and to improve drug prevention and treatment programs. Passed 396-9: R 216-1; D 179-8 (ND 130-7, SD 49-1); I 1-0. Sept. 16, 1998.

445. H J Res 128. Fiscal 1999 Continuing Appropriations/Passage. Passage of the joint resolution to provide continuing appropriations through Oct. 9 for fiscal 1999 spending bills not yet enacted. The continuing resolution sets spending levels at fiscal 1998 spending levels and prohibits new initiatives and projects. Passed 421-0: R 221-0; D 199-0 (ND 147-0, SD 52-0); I 1-0. Sept. 17, 1998.

446. HR 4569. Fiscal 1999 Foreign Operations Appropriations/Rule. Adoption of the rule (H Res 542) to provide for floor consideration of the bill to provide $12.5 billion for foreign aid and export assistance. Adopted 229-188: R 211-8; D 18-179 (ND 13-131, SD 5-48); I 0-1. Sept. 17, 1998.

447. HR 4569. Fiscal 1999 Foreign Operations Appropriations/U.S. Assistance to Azerbaijan. Porter, R-Ill., amendment to eliminate a provision in the bill that repeals the Freedom Support Act, which prohibits U.S. assistance to Azerbaijan. Adopted 231-182: R 88-131; D 142-51 (ND 121-23, SD 21-28); I 1-0. Sept. 17, 1998.

		441	442	443	444	445	446	447
ALABAMA								
1	**Callahan**	N	Y	Y	Y	Y	Y	N
2	**Everett**	N	Y	Y	Y	Y	Y	N
3	**Riley**	N	Y	Y	Y	Y	Y	N
4	**Aderholt**	N	Y	Y	Y	Y	Y	N
5	Cramer	N	Y	N	Y	Y	N	N
6	**Bachus**	N	Y	Y	Y	Y	Y	N
7	Hilliard	Y	Y	N	Y	Y	?	?
ALASKA								
AL	**Young**	N	Y	N	Y	Y	Y	Y
ARIZONA								
1	**Salmon**	N	Y	Y	Y	Y	Y	N
2	Pastor	Y	Y	N	Y	Y	N	Y
3	**Stump**	N	Y	Y	Y	Y	Y	N
4	**Shadegg**	N	Y	Y	Y	Y	Y	N
5	**Kolbe**	N	Y	N	Y	Y	N	N
6	**Hayworth**	N	Y	Y	Y	Y	Y	Y
ARKANSAS								
1	Berry	N	Y	N	Y	Y	N	?
2	Snyder	N	Y	N	Y	Y	N	N
3	**Hutchinson**	N	Y	Y	Y	Y	Y	N
4	**Dickey**	N	Y	Y	Y	Y	Y	N
CALIFORNIA								
1	**Riggs**	?	?	?	?	?	?	?
2	**Herger**	N	Y	Y	Y	Y	Y	N
3	Fazio	Y	Y	?	?	?	N	Y
4	**Doolittle**	N	Y	N	Y	Y	Y	Y
5	Matsui	N	Y	N	Y	Y	N	Y
6	Woolsey	Y	N	N	Y	Y	N	Y
7	Miller	Y	N	N	Y	Y	N	Y
8	Pelosi	Y	N	N	Y	Y	N	Y
9	Lee	Y	N	N	Y	Y	N	Y
10	Tauscher	N	Y	N	Y	Y	N	N
11	**Pombo**	N	Y	N	Y	Y	Y	Y
12	Lantos	N	Y	?	?	Y	N	N
13	Stark	Y	N	N	Y	Y	N	Y
14	Eshoo	N	Y	N	Y	Y	N	Y
15	**Campbell**	N	Y	N	Y	Y	N	N
16	Lofgren	N	Y	N	Y	Y	N	Y
17	Farr	Y	Y	N	Y	Y	N	Y
18	Condit	N	Y	Y	Y	Y	N	Y
19	**Radanovich**	?	Y	Y	Y	Y	Y	Y
20	Dooley	N	Y	N	Y	Y	N	Y
21	**Thomas**	N	Y	N	Y	Y	Y	Y
22	Capps, L.	N	Y	N	Y	Y	?	Y
23	**Gallegly**	N	Y	Y	Y	Y	Y	Y
24	Sherman	N	Y	N	Y	Y	N	Y
25	**McKeon**	N	Y	N	Y	Y	Y	N
26	Berman	N	Y	N	Y	Y	N	Y
27	**Rogan**	N	Y	N	Y	Y	Y	Y
28	**Dreier**	N	Y	N	Y	Y	Y	N
29	Waxman	N	Y	N	N	Y	N	Y
30	Becerra	N	Y	N	Y	Y	–	Y
31	Martinez	N	?	N	Y	Y	N	N
32	Dixon	N	Y	N	Y	Y	N	Y
33	Roybal-Allard	Y	Y	N	Y	Y	N	Y
34	Torres	Y	N	N	Y	Y	N	Y
35	Waters	Y	Y	?	?	Y	N	Y
36	Harman	N	Y	?	?	N	Y	N
37	Millender-McD.	Y	Y	N	Y	Y	N	Y
38	**Horn**	N	?	?	Y	Y	Y	Y

		441	442	443	444	445	446	447
39	**Royce**	N	Y	N	Y	?	Y	Y
40	**Lewis**	N	Y	N	Y	Y	Y	N
41	**Kim**	N	Y	N	Y	Y	Y	N
42	Brown	Y	N	Y	Y	Y	?	Y
43	**Calvert**	N	Y	Y	Y	Y	Y	N
44	**Bono, M.**	N	Y	N	Y	Y	Y	N
45	**Rohrabacher**	N	Y	Y	Y	Y	Y	N
46	Sanchez	N	Y	N	Y	Y	N	+
47	**Cox**	N	Y	N	Y	Y	Y	N
48	**Packard**	N	Y	Y	Y	Y	Y	N
49	**Bilbray**	N	Y	Y	Y	Y	Y	Y
50	Filner	Y	N	N	Y	Y	N	Y
51	**Cunningham**	N	Y	Y	Y	Y	?	N
52	**Hunter**	N	Y	Y	Y	Y	Y	Y
COLORADO								
1	DeGette	N	Y	N	Y	Y	N	Y
2	Skaggs	N	N	N	N	Y	N	Y
3	**McInnis**	N	Y	Y	Y	Y	Y	N
4	**Schaffer**	N	Y	Y	Y	Y	Y	Y
5	**Hefley**	N	Y	Y	Y	Y	Y	N
6	**Schaefer**	N	Y	Y	Y	Y	Y	N
CONNECTICUT								
1	Kennelly	N	Y	N	Y	Y	N	?
2	Gejdenson	N	Y	?	?	Y	N	Y
3	DeLauro	N	Y	N	Y	Y	N	Y
4	**Shays**	N	Y	Y	Y	Y	Y	Y
5	Maloney	N	Y	Y	Y	Y	N	N
6	**Johnson**	N	Y	N	Y	Y	Y	Y
DELAWARE								
AL	**Castle**	N	Y	N	Y	Y	N	Y
FLORIDA								
1	**Scarborough**	N	Y	Y	Y	Y	?	N
2	Boyd	N	Y	N	Y	Y	N	N
3	Brown	Y	Y	N	Y	Y	N	Y
4	**Fowler**	N	Y	Y	Y	Y	Y	N
5	Thurman	N	Y	N	Y	Y	N	N
6	**Stearns**	N	Y	Y	Y	Y	Y	N
7	**Mica**	N	Y	Y	Y	Y	Y	Y
8	**McCollum**	N	Y	Y	Y	Y	Y	Y
9	**Bilirakis**	N	Y	Y	Y	Y	Y	Y
10	**Young**	N	Y	Y	Y	Y	Y	N
11	Davis	N	Y	N	Y	Y	N	N
12	**Canady**	N	Y	Y	Y	Y	Y	N
13	**Miller**	N	Y	Y	Y	Y	Y	Y
14	**Goss**	–	+	+	+	+	+	–
15	**Weldon**	N	Y	Y	Y	Y	Y	N
16	**Foley**	N	Y	Y	Y	Y	Y	Y
17	Meek	Y	Y	N	Y	N	Y	?
18	**Ros-Lehtinen**	N	Y	N	Y	Y	Y	Y
19	Wexler	N	Y	?	?	Y	N	N
20	Deutsch	N	Y	N	Y	Y	N	N
21	**Diaz-Balart**	N	Y	N	Y	Y	Y	Y
22	**Shaw**	N	Y	Y	Y	Y	Y	N
23	Hastings	N	Y	N	Y	N	N	N
GEORGIA								
1	**Kingston**	N	Y	Y	Y	Y	Y	N
2	Bishop	N	Y	Y	Y	Y	Y	Y
3	**Collins**	N	Y	Y	Y	Y	Y	N
4	McKinney	Y	Y	N	Y	Y	Y	Y
5	Lewis	N	N	N	Y	Y	N	?
6	**Gingrich**				Y			
7	**Barr**	N	Y	Y	Y	Y	Y	Y
8	**Chambliss**	N	Y	Y	Y	Y	Y	N
9	**Deal**	N	Y	Y	Y	Y	Y	Y
10	**Norwood**	N	Y	Y	Y	Y	Y	Y
11	**Linder**	N	Y	N	Y	Y	Y	N
HAWAII								
1	Abercrombie	Y	Y	N	Y	Y	N	Y
2	Mink	Y	Y	N	Y	Y	?	Y
IDAHO								
1	**Chenoweth**	N	N	Y	Y	Y	Y	Y
2	**Crapo**	N	Y	N	Y	Y	Y	Y
ILLINOIS								
1	Rush	N	Y	N	Y	Y	N	?
2	Jackson	Y	N	N	Y	Y	N	Y
3	Lipinski	N	Y	N	Y	Y	N	Y
4	Gutierrez	N	Y	N	Y	Y	?	Y
5	Blagojevich	N	Y	N	Y	Y	N	Y
6	**Hyde**	N	Y	N	Y	Y	Y	Y
7	Davis	N	N	N	Y	Y	N	Y
8	**Crane**	N	Y	Y	Y	Y	Y	Y
9	Yates	N	N	?	?	Y	N	Y
10	**Porter**	N	Y	N	Y	Y	Y	Y
11	**Weller**	N	Y	Y	Y	Y	Y	Y
12	Costello	N	Y	N	Y	Y	N	Y
13	**Fawell**	N	Y	Y	Y	Y	Y	?

ND Northern Democrats   SD Southern Democrats

	441	442	443	444	445	446	447
14 ***Hastert***	N	Y	N	Y	Y	Y	N
15 ***Ewing***	N	Y	N	Y	Y	Y	N
16 ***Manzullo***	N	Y	N	Y	Y	Y	N
17 Evans	N	Y	N	Y	Y	N	Y
18 ***LaHood***	N	Y	Y	Y	Y	Y	N
19 Poshard	?	?	?	?	?	?	?
20 ***Shimkus***	N	Y	Y	Y	Y	Y	N
INDIANA							
1 Visclosky	N	N	N	Y	Y	N	Y
2 ***McIntosh***	N	Y	Y	Y	Y	Y	N
3 Roemer	N	Y	N	Y	Y	N	N
4 ***Souder***	N	Y	Y	Y	Y	Y	Y
5 ***Buyer***	N	Y	Y	?	Y	Y	N
6 ***Burton***	N	Y	Y	Y	Y	Y	N
7 ***Pease***	N	Y	Y	Y	Y	Y	N
8 ***Hostettler***	N	Y	Y	Y	Y	Y	Y
9 Hamilton	Y	N	N	Y	Y	N	N
10 Carson	Y	N	N	Y	Y	N	Y
IOWA							
1 ***Leach***	N	Y	N	Y	Y	Y	Y
2 ***Nussle***	N	Y	Y	Y	Y	Y	N
3 Boswell	N	Y	?	Y	Y	N	N
4 ***Ganske***	N	Y	N	Y	Y	Y	Y
5 ***Latham***	N	Y	Y	Y	Y	Y	N
KANSAS							
1 ***Moran***	N	Y	N	Y	Y	Y	N
2 ***Ryun***	N	Y	Y	Y	Y	Y	N
3 ***Snowbarger***	N	Y	Y	Y	Y	Y	N
4 ***Tiahrt***	N	Y	Y	Y	Y	Y	N
KENTUCKY							
1 ***Whitfield***	N	Y	N	Y	Y	?	?
2 ***Lewis***	N	Y	N	Y	Y	Y	N
3 ***Northup***	N	Y	N	Y	Y	Y	N
4 ***Bunning***	N	Y	N	Y	Y	Y	N
5 ***Rogers***	N	Y	N	Y	Y	Y	N
6 Baesler	N	Y	N	Y	Y	N	Y
LOUISIANA							
1 ***Livingston***	N	Y	N	Y	Y	Y	N
2 Jefferson	N	Y	N	Y	Y	N	N
3 ***Tauzin***	N	Y	?	?	Y	Y	N
4 ***McCrery***	N	Y	N	Y	Y	Y	N
5 ***Cooksey***	N	Y	Y	Y	Y	Y	N
6 ***Baker***	N	Y	N	Y	Y	Y	N
7 John	N	Y	?	?	?	N	N
MAINE							
1 Allen	N	Y	N	Y	Y	N	N
2 Baldacci	N	Y	N	Y	Y	N	N
MARYLAND							
1 ***Gilchrest***	N	Y	N	Y	Y	Y	Y
2 ***Ehrlich***	N	Y	N	Y	Y	Y	Y
3 Cardin	N	Y	N	Y	Y	N	Y
4 Wynn	Y	Y	N	Y	Y	N	Y
5 Hoyer	N	Y	N	Y	Y	N	Y
6 ***Bartlett***	N	Y	Y	Y	Y	Y	?
7 Cummings	N	Y	N	Y	Y	N	Y
8 ***Morella***	N	Y	N	Y	Y	N	Y
MASSACHUSETTS							
1 Olver	Y	N	N	Y	Y	N	Y
2 Neal	N	Y	N	Y	Y	N	Y
3 McGovern	N	Y	N	Y	Y	N	Y
4 Frank	N	N	N	N	Y	N	Y
5 Meehan	N	Y	N	Y	Y	N	Y
6 Tierney	Y	Y	N	Y	Y	N	Y
7 Markey	N	Y	N	Y	Y	N	Y
8 Kennedy	N	Y	N	Y	Y	N	Y
9 Moakley	Y	Y	N	Y	Y	N	Y
10 Delahunt	N	Y	N	Y	Y	N	Y
MICHIGAN							
1 Stupak	N	Y	N	Y	Y	Y	Y
2 ***Hoekstra***	N	Y	N	Y	Y	Y	Y
3 ***Ehlers***	N	Y	Y	Y	Y	Y	Y
4 ***Camp***	N	Y	Y	Y	Y	Y	Y
5 Barcia	N	Y	N	Y	Y	Y	Y
6 ***Upton***	N	Y	Y	Y	Y	Y	Y
7 ***Smith***	N	Y	Y	Y	Y	Y	Y
8 Stabenow	Y	Y	N	Y	Y	N	Y
9 Kildee	N	Y	N	Y	Y	N	Y
10 Bonior	Y	N	N	Y	Y	N	Y
11 ***Knollenberg***	N	Y	N	Y	Y	Y	Y
12 Levin	N	Y	N	Y	Y	N	Y
13 Rivers	Y	Y	N	Y	Y	N	Y
14 Conyers	+	N	N	N	Y	N	Y
15 Kilpatrick	Y	Y	N	Y	Y	N	Y
16 Dingell	N	Y	N	N	Y	N	Y

	441	442	443	444	445	446	447
MINNESOTA							
1 ***Gutknecht***	N	Y	Y	Y	Y	Y	Y
2 Minge	Y	Y	N	Y	Y	N	N
3 ***Ramstad***	N	Y	N	Y	Y	N	Y
4 Vento	Y	N	N	Y	Y	N	Y
5 Sabo	Y	N	N	Y	Y	N	N
6 Luther	Y	Y	N	Y	Y	N	N
7 Peterson	N	Y	N	Y	Y	Y	Y
8 Oberstar	Y	N	N	Y	Y	Y	Y
MISSISSIPPI							
1 ***Wicker***	N	Y	N	Y	Y	Y	N
2 Thompson	Y	Y	N	Y	Y	N	Y
3 ***Pickering***	N	Y	Y	Y	Y	Y	N
4 ***Parker***	N	Y	Y	Y	Y	Y	N
5 Taylor	N	Y	Y	Y	Y	Y	N
MISSOURI							
1 Clay	Y	Y	?	?	Y	N	?
2 ***Talent***	N	Y	Y	Y	Y	Y	Y
3 Gephardt	Y	Y	N	Y	Y	N	?
4 Skelton	N	Y	N	Y	Y	N	N
5 McCarthy	Y	Y	N	Y	Y	N	Y
6 Danner	N	Y	?	?	Y	N	N
7 ***Blunt***	N	Y	?	+	Y	Y	N
8 ***Emerson***	N	Y	Y	Y	Y	Y	N
9 ***Hulshof***	N	Y	N	Y	Y	Y	N
MONTANA							
AL ***Hill***	N	Y	N	Y	Y	Y	N
NEBRASKA							
1 ***Bereuter***	N	Y	N	?	Y	N	N
2 ***Christensen***	N	Y	N	Y	Y	Y	Y
3 ***Barrett***	N	Y	N	Y	Y	Y	Y
NEVADA							
1 ***Ensign***	N	Y	N	Y	Y	Y	Y
2 ***Gibbons***	N	Y	Y	Y	Y	Y	N
NEW HAMPSHIRE							
1 ***Sununu***	N	Y	N	Y	Y	Y	Y
2 ***Bass***	N	Y	N	Y	Y	Y	Y
NEW JERSEY							
1 Andrews	N	Y	N	Y	Y	N	Y
2 ***LoBiondo***	N	Y	Y	Y	Y	Y	Y
3 ***Saxton***	N	Y	N	Y	Y	Y	N
4 ***Smith***	N	Y	N	Y	Y	Y	Y
5 ***Roukema***	N	Y	Y	Y	Y	N	Y
6 Pallone	N	Y	N	Y	Y	N	Y
7 ***Franks***	N	Y	Y	Y	Y	Y	Y
8 Pascrell	N	Y	N	Y	Y	N	Y
9 Rothman	N	Y	N	Y	Y	N	Y
10 Payne	Y	N	N	Y	Y	N	Y
11 ***Frelinghuysen***	N	Y	N	Y	Y	Y	Y
12 ***Pappas***	N	Y	Y	Y	Y	Y	Y
13 Menendez	N	Y	N	Y	Y	N	Y
NEW MEXICO							
1 ***Wilson***	N	Y	N	Y	Y	Y	N
2 ***Skeen***	N	Y	N	Y	Y	Y	N
3 ***Redmond***	N	Y	N	Y	Y	Y	N
NEW YORK							
1 ***Forbes***	N	Y	N	Y	?	Y	N
2 ***Lazio***	N	Y	N	Y	Y	Y	Y
3 ***King***	N	Y	N	Y	Y	Y	–
4 McCarthy	N	Y	N	Y	Y	N	Y
5 Ackerman	N	Y	N	Y	Y	N	Y
6 Meeks	?	?	?	?	Y	N	Y
7 Manton	N	Y	N	Y	Y	N	Y
8 Nadler	Y	N	N	N	Y	N	N
9 Schumer	?	?	?	?	?	?	?
10 Towns	?	?	?	?	Y	N	Y
11 Owens	Y	N	N	Y	Y	N	Y
12 Velázquez	Y	N	N	Y	Y	N	Y
13 ***Fossella***	N	Y	Y	Y	Y	Y	Y
14 Maloney	N	Y	N	Y	Y	N	Y
15 Rangel	N	Y	N	Y	Y	N	Y
16 Serrano	N	Y	N	Y	Y	N	Y
17 Engel	N	Y	N	Y	Y	N	Y
18 Lowey	Y	Y	N	Y	Y	N	Y
19 ***Kelly***	N	Y	N	Y	Y	Y	Y
20 ***Gilman***	N	Y	Y	Y	Y	Y	Y
21 McNulty	N	Y	N	Y	Y	N	Y
22 ***Solomon***	N	Y	Y	Y	Y	Y	N
23 ***Boehlert***	N	Y	N	Y	Y	Y	Y
24 ***McHugh***	?	?	Y	Y	Y	Y	Y
25 ***Walsh***	N	Y	Y	Y	Y	Y	Y
26 Hinchey	Y	Y	N	Y	Y	N	Y
27 ***Paxon***	N	Y	Y	Y	Y	Y	N
28 Slaughter	N	Y	N	Y	Y	N	Y
29 LaFalce	N	Y	N	Y	Y	N	Y
30 ***Quinn***	N	Y	Y	Y	Y	Y	N

	441	442	443	444	445	446	447
31 ***Houghton***	N	Y	N	Y	Y	Y	Y
NORTH CAROLINA							
1 Clayton	Y	Y	?	Y	Y	N	Y
2 Etheridge	N	Y	N	Y	Y	N	Y
3 ***Jones***	N	Y	Y	Y	Y	Y	Y
4 Price	N	Y	N	Y	Y	N	Y
5 ***Burr***	N	Y	Y	Y	Y	Y	Y
6 ***Coble***	N	Y	Y	Y	Y	Y	Y
7 McIntyre	N	Y	Y	Y	Y	Y	Y
8 Hefner	N	Y	?	?	?	N	Y
9 ***Myrick***	N	Y	Y	Y	Y	Y	+
10 ***Ballenger***	N	Y	Y	Y	Y	Y	N
11 ***Taylor***	N	Y	Y	Y	Y	Y	N
12 Watt	Y	N	N	Y	Y	N	Y
NORTH DAKOTA							
AL Pomeroy	N	Y	N	Y	Y	N	N
OHIO							
1 ***Chabot***	N	Y	Y	Y	Y	Y	N
2 ***Portman***	N	Y	N	Y	Y	Y	N
3 Hall	N	Y	N	Y	Y	N	Y
4 ***Oxley***	N	Y	N	Y	Y	Y	N
5 ***Gillmor***	N	Y	N	Y	Y	Y	N
6 Strickland	N	Y	N	Y	Y	N	Y
7 ***Hobson***	N	Y	N	Y	Y	Y	N
8 ***Boehner***	N	Y	N	Y	Y	Y	N
9 Kaptur	?	Y	N	Y	Y	N	N
10 Kucinich	N	Y	N	Y	Y	N	Y
11 Stokes	Y	Y	?	?	?	N	Y
12 ***Kasich***	N	Y	N	Y	Y	Y	N
13 Brown	N	Y	N	Y	Y	N	Y
14 Sawyer	N	Y	N	Y	Y	N	Y
15 ***Pryce***	–	+	–	+	+	+	+
16 ***Regula***	N	Y	N	Y	Y	Y	N
17 Traficant	N	Y	Y	Y	Y	Y	N
18 ***Ney***	N	Y	N	Y	Y	Y	Y
19 ***LaTourette***	N	Y	N	Y	Y	Y	N
OKLAHOMA							
1 ***Largent***	N	Y	Y	Y	Y	Y	N
2 ***Coburn***	N	Y	Y	Y	Y	Y	N
3 ***Watkins***	N	Y	Y	Y	Y	Y	N
4 ***Watts***	N	Y	N	Y	Y	Y	N
5 ***Istook***	N	Y	Y	Y	Y	Y	N
6 ***Lucas***	N	Y	N	Y	Y	Y	N
OREGON							
1 Furse	Y	Y	N	Y	Y	N	Y
2 ***Smith***	N	Y	N	Y	Y	Y	N
3 Blumenauer	N	Y	N	Y	Y	N	Y
4 DeFazio	Y	N	N	Y	Y	N	Y
5 Hooley	N	Y	N	Y	Y	N	Y
PENNSYLVANIA							
1 Brady	Y	Y	N	Y	Y	N	N
2 Fattah	Y	Y	N	Y	Y	N	Y
3 Borski	N	Y	N	Y	Y	N	Y
4 Klink	N	Y	N	Y	Y	N	Y
5 ***Peterson***	N	Y	?	Y	Y	Y	N
6 Holden	N	Y	N	Y	Y	Y	Y
7 ***Weldon***	N	Y	N	Y	Y	Y	Y
8 ***Greenwood***	N	Y	N	Y	Y	Y	N
9 ***Shuster***	N	Y	N	Y	Y	Y	N
10 ***McDade***	N	Y	N	Y	Y	Y	Y
11 Kanjorski	N	Y	N	Y	Y	N	N
12 Murtha	N	Y	N	Y	Y	N	N
13 ***Fox***	N	Y	Y	Y	Y	Y	Y
14 Coyne	N	Y	N	Y	Y	N	Y
15 McHale	N	Y	N	Y	Y	N	Y
16 ***Pitts***	N	Y	N	Y	Y	Y	Y
17 ***Gekas***	N	Y	N	Y	Y	Y	N
18 Doyle	N	Y	N	Y	Y	Y	Y
19 ***Goodling***	N	Y	Y	Y	Y	Y	N
20 Mascara	N	Y	N	Y	Y	Y	Y
21 ***English***	N	Y	N	Y	Y	Y	Y
RHODE ISLAND							
1 Kennedy	N	Y	N	Y	Y	N	Y
2 Weygand	N	Y	N	Y	Y	N	Y
SOUTH CAROLINA							
1 ***Sanford***	N	N	Y	Y	Y	Y	N
2 ***Spence***	N	Y	Y	Y	Y	Y	N
3 ***Graham***	N	Y	Y	Y	Y	Y	N
4 ***Inglis***	N	Y	Y	Y	Y	Y	N
5 Spratt	N	Y	N	Y	Y	N	N
6 Clyburn	Y	Y	?	?	Y	N	Y
SOUTH DAKOTA							
AL ***Thune***	N	Y	Y	Y	Y	Y	N

	441	442	443	444	445	446	447
TENNESSEE							
1 ***Jenkins***	N	Y	Y	Y	Y	Y	N
2 ***Duncan***	N	Y	Y	Y	Y	Y	Y
3 ***Wamp***	N	Y	Y	Y	Y	Y	N
4 ***Hilleary***	N	Y	Y	Y	Y	Y	Y
5 Clement	N	Y	N	Y	Y	N	N
6 Gordon	N	Y	N	Y	Y	N	N
7 ***Bryant***	N	Y	Y	Y	Y	Y	N
8 Tanner	N	Y	N	Y	Y	N	N
9 Ford	Y	Y	N	Y	Y	N	Y
TEXAS							
1 Sandlin	N	Y	N	Y	Y	N	N
2 Turner	N	Y	Y	Y	Y	N	N
3 ***Johnson, Sam***	N	Y	N	Y	Y	Y	N
4 Hall	N	Y	Y	Y	Y	Y	Y
5 ***Sessions***	N	Y	Y	Y	Y	Y	N
6 ***Barton***	N	Y	Y	Y	Y	Y	N
7 ***Archer***	N	Y	N	Y	Y	Y	N
8 ***Brady***	N	Y	?	?	Y	+	N
9 Lampson	N	Y	N	Y	Y	N	N
10 Doggett	Y	Y	N	Y	Y	N	Y
11 Edwards	N	Y	N	Y	Y	N	N
12 ***Granger***	N	Y	Y	Y	Y	Y	N
13 ***Thornberry***	N	Y	Y	Y	Y	Y	N
14 ***Paul***	Y	N	N	N	Y	?	Y
15 Hinojosa	Y	Y	N	Y	Y	N	Y
16 Reyes	N	N	N	Y	Y	N	N
17 Stenholm	N	Y	Y	Y	Y	N	N
18 Jackson-Lee	Y	N	N	Y	Y	N	N
19 ***Combest***	N	Y	Y	Y	Y	Y	N
20 Gonzalez	?	?	?	?	?	?	?
21 ***Smith***	N	Y	Y	Y	Y	Y	N
22 ***DeLay***	N	Y	N	Y	Y	Y	N
23 ***Bonilla***	N	Y	N	Y	Y	Y	N
24 Frost	N	Y	N	Y	Y	N	N
25 Bentsen	N	Y	N	Y	Y	N	N
26 ***Armey***	N	Y	N	Y	Y	Y	N
27 Ortiz	N	Y	N	Y	Y	N	N
28 Rodriguez	N	Y	N	Y	Y	N	N
29 Green	N	Y	N	Y	Y	N	N
30 Johnson, E.B.	N	Y	N	Y	Y	N	?
UTAH							
1 ***Hansen***	N	Y	Y	Y	Y	Y	N
2 ***Cook***	N	Y	Y	Y	Y	Y	Y
3 ***Cannon***	N	Y	Y	Y	Y	Y	N
VERMONT							
AL *Sanders*	Y	N	N	Y	Y	N	Y
VIRGINIA							
1 ***Bateman***	N	Y	?	?	Y	Y	N
2 Pickett	N	Y	N	Y	Y	N	N
3 Scott	Y	N	N	N	Y	N	Y
4 Sisisky	N	Y	N	Y	Y	N	Y
5 Goode	N	Y	Y	Y	Y	Y	Y
6 ***Goodlatte***	N	Y	N	Y	Y	Y	N
7 ***Bliley***	N	Y	N	Y	Y	Y	Y
8 Moran	Y	N	N	Y	Y	N	Y
9 Boucher	N	Y	N	Y	Y	N	Y
10 ***Wolf***	N	Y	N	Y	Y	Y	Y
11 ***Davis***	N	Y	N	Y	Y	Y	Y
WASHINGTON							
1 ***White***	N	Y	Y	Y	Y	Y	N
2 ***Metcalf***	N	Y	Y	Y	?	Y	N
3 ***Smith, Linda***	?	?	Y	Y	Y	Y	Y
4 ***Hastings***	N	Y	Y	Y	Y	Y	N
5 ***Nethercutt***	N	Y	Y	Y	Y	Y	N
6 Dicks	N	Y	?	?	Y	N	Y
7 McDermott	Y	N	N	Y	Y	N	Y
8 ***Dunn***	N	Y	Y	Y	Y	Y	N
9 Smith, Adam	N	Y	N	Y	Y	N	Y
WEST VIRGINIA							
1 Mollohan	N	Y	N	Y	Y	Y	Y
2 Wise	N	Y	N	Y	Y	Y	N
3 Rahall	N	Y	N	Y	Y	Y	Y
WISCONSIN							
1 ***Neumann***	N	Y	Y	Y	Y	Y	Y
2 ***Klug***	N	Y	N	Y	Y	N	N
3 Kind	N	Y	N	Y	Y	N	Y
4 Kleczka	Y	Y	N	Y	Y	N	Y
5 Barrett	Y	Y	N	Y	Y	N	Y
6 ***Petri***	N	Y	N	Y	Y	Y	N
7 Obey	Y	N	N	N	Y	N	Y
8 Johnson	N	Y	N	Y	Y	N	Y
9 ***Sensenbrenner***	N	Y	N	Y	Y	Y	Y
WYOMING							
AL ***Cubin***	N	Y	N	Y	Y	Y	Y

Southern states - Ala., Ark., Fla., Ga., Ky., La., Miss., N.C., Okla., S.C., Tenn., Texas, Va.

House Votes 448, 449, 450, 451, 452, 453, 454

Key

- **Y** Voted for (yea).
- **#** Paired for.
- **+** Announced for.
- **N** Voted against (nay).
- **X** Paired against.
- **−** Announced against.
- **P** Voted "present."
- **C** Voted "present" to avoid possible conflict of interest.
- **?** Did not vote or otherwise make a position known.

Democrats **Republicans** Independent

448. HR 4569. Fiscal 1999 Foreign Operations Appropriations/School of the Americas Funding. Kennedy, D-Mass., amendment to bar any funds from being made available for programs at the U.S. Army School of the Americas located at Fort Benning, Ga. Rejected 201-212: R 49-171; D 151-41 (ND 122-18, SD 29-23); I 1-0. Sept. 17, 1998.

449. HR 4569. Fiscal 1999 Foreign Operations Appropriations/Passage. Passage of the bill to provide $12.5 billion for foreign aid and export assistance. The measure also provides $3.4 billion in credits for the International Monetary Fund (IMF). Passed 255-161: R 186-34; D 69-126 (ND 49-94, SD 20-32); I 0-1. Sept. 17, 1998.

450. HR 3248. Education Block Grants/Native Hawaiian Education Act. Mink, D-Hawaii, amendment to eliminate the bill's repeal of the Native Hawaiian Education Act. Rejected 200-207: R 8-207; D 191-0 (ND 139-0, SD 52-0); I 1-0. Sept. 18, 1998.

451. HR 3248. Education Block Grants/Class Size Reduction Substitute. Martinez, D-Calif., substitute amendment to strike the bill's text and substitute provisions that establish a program intended to reduce class size in grades 1 through 3 to an average of 18 students per class. Rejected 190-215: R 5-211; D 184-4 (ND 135-0, SD 49-4); I 1-0. Sept. 18, 1998.

452. HR 3248. Education Block Grants/Passage. Passage of the bill to repeal 31 elementary and secondary education programs and establish a block grant program in their place. Programs affected would include Goals 2000, School to Work, and Eisenhower Professional Development State Grants. Passed 212-198: R 207-11; D 5-186 (ND 1-137, SD 4-49); I 0-1. Sept. 18, 1998.

453. H Res 545. Impeachment of Kenneth W. Starr/Motion to Table. LaHood, R-Ill., motion to table (kill) the Hastings, D-Fla., privileged resolution to impeach Independent Counsel Kenneth W. Starr for "high crimes and misdemeanors." Motion agreed to 340-71: R 215-0; D 125-71 (ND 92-50, SD 33-21); I 0-0. Sept. 23, 1998.

454. H Res 144. National Lewis and Clark Bicentennial Council/Passage. Chenoweth, R-Idaho, motion to suspend the rules and pass the bill to express its support of the National Lewis and Clark Bicentennial Council and the commemorative activities that it is planning for the bicentennial. Motion agreed to 416-0: R 218-0; D 198-0 (ND 144-0, SD 54-0); I 0-0. Sept. 23, 1998. A two-thirds majority of those present and voting (278 in this case) is required for passage under suspension of the rules.

	448	449	450	451	452	453	454
ALABAMA							
1 Callahan	N	Y	N	N	Y	Y	Y
2 Everett	N	Y	N	N	Y	Y	Y
3 Riley	N	Y	N	N	Y	Y	Y
4 Aderholt	N	Y	N	N	Y	Y	Y
5 Cramer	?	N	Y	N	Y	Y	Y
6 Bachus	N	Y	N	N	Y	Y	Y
7 Hilliard	Y	N	?	Y	N	N	Y
ALASKA							
AL Young	N	Y	Y	N	N	Y	Y
ARIZONA							
1 Salmon	Y	Y	N	N	Y	Y	Y
2 Pastor	Y	N	Y	Y	N	N	Y
3 Stump	N	N	N	N	Y	Y	Y
4 Shadegg	N	Y	N	N	Y	Y	Y
5 Kolbe	N	Y	N	N	Y	Y	Y
6 Hayworth	N	Y	N	N	Y	Y	Y
ARKANSAS							
1 Berry	N	N	Y	Y	N	Y	Y
2 Snyder	N	N	Y	Y	N	Y	Y
3 Hutchinson	N	Y	−	N	Y	Y	Y
4 Dickey	N	Y	N	N	Y	Y	Y
CALIFORNIA							
1 Riggs	?	?	?	?	?	?	?
2 Herger	N	N	N	N	Y	Y	Y
3 Fazio	Y	N	Y	Y	N	Y	Y
4 Doolittle	N	N	N	N	Y	Y	Y
5 Matsui	Y	N	Y	Y	N	Y	Y
6 Woolsey	Y	N	Y	Y	N	Y	Y
7 Miller	Y	N	?	?	?	Y	Y
8 Pelosi	Y	N	Y	Y	N	N	Y
9 Lee	Y	N	Y	Y	N	N	Y
10 Tauscher	+	N	Y	Y	N	Y	Y
11 Pombo	N	N	N	N	Y	Y	Y
12 Lantos	Y	Y	Y	Y	N	Y	Y
13 Stark	Y	N	Y	Y	N	N	Y
14 Eshoo	Y	N	Y	Y	N	Y	Y
15 Campbell	N	N	N	N	Y	Y	Y
16 Lofgren	Y	N	Y	N	+	+	Y
17 Farr	Y	N	Y	Y	N	N	Y
18 Condit	N	N	Y	Y	N	Y	Y
19 Radanovich	N	N	N	N	Y	Y	?
20 Dooley	Y	Y	Y	Y	N	Y	Y
21 Thomas	N	Y	N	N	Y	Y	Y
22 Capps, L.	Y	N	Y	N	N	Y	Y
23 Gallegly	N	Y	N	N	Y	Y	Y
24 Sherman	Y	Y	Y	Y	N	Y	Y
25 McKeon	N	Y	N	N	Y	Y	Y
26 Berman	Y	Y	Y	Y	N	Y	Y
27 Rogan	N	Y	N	N	Y	Y	Y
28 Dreier	N	Y	N	N	Y	Y	Y
29 Waxman	Y	Y	Y	Y	N	Y	Y
30 Becerra	Y	N	Y	?	N	Y	Y
31 Martinez	N	N	Y	Y	N	N	Y
32 Dixon	Y	Y	Y	Y	N	Y	Y
33 Roybal-Allard	Y	Y	Y	Y	N	Y	Y
34 Torres	Y	N	?	?	?	?	?
35 Waters	Y	N	Y	Y	N	N	Y
36 Harman	Y	Y	Y	Y	N	Y	Y
37 Millender-McD.	Y	N	Y	Y	N	N	?
38 Horn	N	Y	N	N	Y	Y	Y

	448	449	450	451	452	453	454
39 Royce	N	N	N	Y	Y	Y	Y
40 Lewis	N	Y	N	N	Y	Y	Y
41 Kim	N	Y	N	N	Y	Y	Y
42 Brown	Y	Y	Y	Y	?	N	Y
43 Calvert	N	Y	N	N	Y	Y	Y
44 Bono, M.	N	Y	N	N	Y	Y	Y
45 Rohrabacher	N	N	N	N	Y	Y	Y
46 Sanchez	+	−	+	+	−	?	Y
47 Cox	N	Y	?	?	Y	Y	Y
48 Packard	N	Y	N	N	Y	Y	Y
49 Bilbray	N	Y	N	N	Y	Y	Y
50 Filner	Y	N	Y	Y	N	N	Y
51 Cunningham	N	N	N	N	Y	Y	Y
52 Hunter	N	Y	N	?	Y	?	Y
COLORADO							
1 DeGette	Y	N	Y	Y	N	Y	Y
2 Skaggs	Y	N	Y	N	Y	Y	Y
3 McInnis	N	Y	N	N	Y	Y	Y
4 Schaffer	Y	Y	N	N	Y	Y	Y
5 Hefley	N	N	N	N	Y	Y	Y
6 Schaefer	N	Y	N	N	Y	Y	Y
CONNECTICUT							
1 Kennelly	?	?	?	#	X	?	?
2 Gejdenson	Y	N	Y	Y	N	Y	Y
3 DeLauro	Y	N	Y	Y	N	Y	Y
4 Shays	Y	Y	Y	Y	N	Y	Y
5 Maloney	Y	N	Y	Y	N	Y	Y
6 Johnson	Y	Y	N	N	Y	Y	Y
DELAWARE							
AL Castle	N	N	N	N	Y	Y	Y
FLORIDA							
1 Scarborough	Y	?	N	N	Y	Y	Y
2 Boyd	N	Y	Y	N	Y	Y	Y
3 Brown	Y	N	Y	Y	N	N	Y
4 Fowler	N	Y	N	N	Y	Y	Y
5 Thurman	Y	Y	Y	Y	N	Y	Y
6 Stearns	N	N	N	N	Y	Y	Y
7 Mica	N	Y	X	X	#	Y	Y
8 McCollum	N	Y	?	N	Y	Y	Y
9 Bilirakis	N	Y	N	N	Y	Y	Y
10 Young	N	N	N	N	Y	Y	Y
11 Davis	N	?	Y	Y	N	Y	Y
12 Canady	N	Y	N	N	Y	Y	Y
13 Miller	Y	Y	N	N	Y	Y	Y
14 Goss	−	+	−	−	+	+	Y
15 Weldon	Y	Y	N	N	Y	Y	Y
16 Foley	Y	Y	N	N	Y	Y	Y
17 Meek	?	?	?	?	?	N	Y
18 Ros-Lehtinen	N	Y	N	N	Y	Y	Y
19 Wexler	Y	N	Y	Y	N	N	Y
20 Deutsch	Y	N	Y	Y	N	Y	Y
21 Diaz-Balart	N	N	N	N	Y	+	+
22 Shaw	N	Y	N	N	Y	?	?
23 Hastings	N	Y	Y	Y	N	N	Y
GEORGIA							
1 Kingston	N	Y	N	N	Y	Y	Y
2 Bishop	N	Y	Y	Y	N	Y	Y
3 Collins	N	Y	N	N	Y	Y	Y
4 McKinney	Y	Y	Y	Y	N	N	Y
5 Lewis	Y	Y	Y	Y	N	N	Y
6 Gingrich					N		
7 Barr	N	N	N	N	Y	Y	Y
8 Chambliss	N	N	N	N	Y	Y	Y
9 Deal	N	Y	N	N	Y	Y	Y
10 Norwood	N	Y	N	N	Y	Y	Y
11 Linder	N	Y	N	N	Y	Y	Y
HAWAII							
1 Abercrombie	Y	Y	Y	Y	N	Y	Y
2 Mink	Y	N	Y	Y	N	N	Y
IDAHO							
1 Chenoweth	N	N	N	N	Y	Y	Y
2 Crapo	N	Y	N	N	Y	Y	Y
ILLINOIS							
1 Rush	?	?	Y	Y	N	N	Y
2 Jackson	Y	N	Y	Y	N	N	Y
3 Lipinski	Y	Y	Y	Y	N	Y	Y
4 Gutierrez	Y	Y	Y	Y	N	N	Y
5 Blagojevich	Y	N	?	?	?	Y	Y
6 Hyde	N	Y	N	N	Y	Y	Y
7 Davis	+	N	Y	Y	N	N	Y
8 Crane	N	N	N	N	Y	Y	Y
9 Yates	Y	N	Y	Y	N	Y	Y
10 Porter	Y	Y	N	N	Y	Y	Y
11 Weller	Y	Y	N	N	Y	Y	Y
12 Costello	Y	Y	Y	Y	N	Y	Y
13 Fawell	?	?	?	?	?	Y	Y

ND Northern Democrats   SD Southern Democrats

H-128 — 1998 CQ ALMANAC

WWW.CQ.COM

	448	449	450	451	452	453	454
14 **Hastert**	N	Y	N	N	Y	Y	Y
15 **Ewing**	N	Y	N	N	Y	Y	Y
16 **Manzullo**	N	Y	N	N	Y	Y	Y
17 Evans	Y	N	Y	Y	N	Y	Y
18 **LaHood**	Y	Y	N	N	Y	Y	Y
19 Poshard	?	?	?	?	?	?	?
20 **Shimkus**	N	Y	N	N	Y	Y	Y
INDIANA							
1 Visclosky	N	Y	Y	Y	N	Y	Y
2 **McIntosh**	?	Y	N	N	Y	Y	Y
3 Roemer	Y	N	Y	Y	N	Y	Y
4 **Souder**	N	Y	N	N	Y	Y	Y
5 **Buyer**	N	Y	N	N	Y	Y	Y
6 **Burton**	N	Y	–	–	+	+	+
7 **Pease**	N	Y	?	?	?	Y	Y
8 **Hostettler**	N	N	N	N	Y	Y	Y
9 Hamilton	N	N	Y	Y	N	Y	Y
10 Carson	Y	N	Y	Y	N	N	Y
IOWA							
1 **Leach**	Y	Y	N	Y	N	Y	Y
2 **Nussle**	Y	Y	N	N	Y	Y	Y
3 Boswell	N	Y	Y	Y	N	Y	Y
4 **Ganske**	N	Y	N	N	Y	Y	Y
5 **Latham**	N	Y	N	N	Y	Y	Y
KANSAS							
1 **Moran**	Y	N	N	N	Y	Y	Y
2 **Ryun**	N	Y	N	N	Y	Y	Y
3 **Snowbarger**	N	Y	N	N	Y	Y	Y
4 **Tiahrt**	N	Y	N	N	Y	Y	Y
KENTUCKY							
1 **Whitfield**	N	Y	Y	N	Y	Y	Y
2 **Lewis**	N	Y	N	N	Y	Y	Y
3 **Northup**	N	Y	N	N	Y	Y	Y
4 **Bunning**	N	Y	N	N	Y	Y	Y
5 **Rogers**	N	N	N	N	Y	Y	Y
6 Baesler	Y	Y	Y	Y	N	Y	Y
LOUISIANA							
1 **Livingston**	N	Y	N	N	Y	Y	Y
2 Jefferson	Y	N	Y	Y	N	N	Y
3 **Tauzin**	N	Y	N	N	Y	Y	Y
4 **McCrery**	N	Y	N	N	Y	Y	Y
5 **Cooksey**	N	Y	N	N	Y	Y	Y
6 **Baker**	N	Y	N	N	Y	Y	Y
7 John	N	Y	Y	Y	N	Y	Y
MAINE							
1 Allen	Y	Y	Y	Y	N	Y	Y
2 Baldacci	Y	N	Y	Y	N	Y	Y
MARYLAND							
1 **Gilchrest**	Y	Y	N	N	Y	Y	Y
2 **Ehrlich**	N	Y	N	N	Y	Y	Y
3 Cardin	Y	Y	Y	Y	N	Y	Y
4 Wynn	Y	N	Y	Y	N	N	Y
5 Hoyer	N	N	Y	?	N	Y	Y
6 **Bartlett**	N	Y	N	N	Y	Y	Y
7 Cummings	Y	N	Y	Y	N	N	Y
8 **Morella**	Y	Y	Y	Y	N	Y	Y
MASSACHUSETTS							
1 Olver	Y	N	Y	Y	N	N	Y
2 Neal	Y	N	Y	Y	N	Y	Y
3 McGovern	Y	Y	Y	Y	N	Y	Y
4 Frank	Y	N	Y	Y	N	Y	Y
5 Meehan	Y	N	Y	Y	N	Y	Y
6 Tierney	Y	Y	Y	Y	N	Y	Y
7 Markey	Y	N	Y	Y	N	Y	Y
8 Kennedy	Y	N	Y	Y	N	Y	Y
9 Moakley	Y	N	Y	Y	N	Y	Y
10 Delahunt	Y	N	Y	Y	N	Y	Y
MICHIGAN							
1 Stupak	Y	N	Y	Y	N	Y	Y
2 **Hoekstra**	N	N	N	N	Y	Y	Y
3 **Ehlers**	Y	Y	N	N	Y	Y	Y
4 **Camp**	Y	Y	N	N	Y	Y	Y
5 Barcia	Y	Y	Y	Y	N	Y	Y
6 **Upton**	Y	Y	N	N	Y	Y	Y
7 **Smith**	N	Y	N	N	Y	Y	Y
8 Stabenow	Y	Y	Y	Y	N	Y	Y
9 Kildee	Y	Y	Y	Y	N	Y	Y
10 Bonior	Y	N	Y	Y	N	N	Y
11 **Knollenberg**	N	Y	N	N	Y	Y	Y
12 Levin	Y	Y	Y	Y	N	Y	Y
13 Rivers	Y	Y	Y	Y	N	Y	Y
14 Conyers	Y	N	Y	?	N	N	Y
15 Kilpatrick	Y	N	Y	Y	N	N	Y
16 Dingell	?	N	Y	Y	N	Y	Y

	448	449	450	451	452	453	454
MINNESOTA							
1 **Gutknecht**	Y	Y	N	N	Y	Y	Y
2 Minge	Y	N	Y	Y	N	Y	Y
3 **Ramstad**	Y	Y	Y	N	N	Y	Y
4 Vento	Y	N	Y	Y	N	N	Y
5 Sabo	Y	N	Y	Y	N	N	Y
6 Luther	Y	N	Y	Y	N	Y	Y
7 Peterson	Y	Y	Y	Y	N	Y	Y
8 Oberstar	Y	N	Y	Y	N	N	Y
MISSISSIPPI							
1 **Wicker**	N	Y	N	N	Y	Y	Y
2 Thompson	Y	N	Y	Y	N	N	Y
3 **Pickering**	N	Y	N	N	Y	Y	Y
4 **Parker**	N	Y	?	?	?	Y	Y
5 Taylor	N	N	Y	Y	Y	Y	Y
MISSOURI							
1 Clay	?	?	?	?	?	N	Y
2 **Talent**	Y	Y	N	N	Y	Y	Y
3 Gephardt	?	?	Y	Y	N	N	Y
4 Skelton	N	Y	Y	Y	N	Y	Y
5 McCarthy	Y	N	Y	Y	N	Y	Y
6 Danner	Y	N	Y	Y	N	Y	Y
7 **Blunt**	N	Y	N	N	Y	Y	Y
8 **Emerson**	N	Y	N	N	Y	Y	Y
9 **Hulshof**	Y	Y	N	N	Y	Y	Y
MONTANA							
AL **Hill**	N	Y	N	N	Y	Y	Y
NEBRASKA							
1 **Bereuter**	N	Y	N	N	Y	Y	Y
2 **Christensen**	N	Y	N	N	Y	Y	Y
3 **Barrett**	N	Y	N	N	Y	Y	Y
NEVADA							
1 **Ensign**	N	Y	N	N	Y	+	+
2 **Gibbons**	N	Y	N	N	Y	Y	Y
NEW HAMPSHIRE							
1 **Sununu**	N	N	N	N	Y	Y	Y
2 **Bass**	N	Y	N	N	Y	Y	Y
NEW JERSEY							
1 Andrews	Y	Y	Y	Y	N	N	Y
2 **LoBiondo**	Y	Y	N	N	Y	Y	Y
3 **Saxton**	N	Y	N	N	Y	Y	Y
4 **Smith**	Y	Y	Y	N	Y	Y	Y
5 **Roukema**	Y	Y	N	N	Y	Y	Y
6 Pallone	Y	Y	Y	Y	N	Y	Y
7 **Franks**	Y	Y	N	N	Y	Y	Y
8 Pascrell	Y	Y	Y	Y	N	Y	Y
9 Rothman	Y	Y	Y	Y	N	Y	Y
10 Payne	Y	N	Y	Y	N	N	Y
11 **Frelinghuysen**	N	Y	N	N	Y	Y	Y
12 **Pappas**	N	Y	N	N	Y	Y	Y
13 Menendez	Y	Y	Y	Y	N	N	Y
NEW MEXICO							
1 **Wilson**	N	Y	N	N	Y	Y	Y
2 **Skeen**	N	Y	N	N	Y	Y	Y
3 **Redmond**	N	Y	N	N	Y	Y	Y
NEW YORK							
1 **Forbes**	Y	Y	N	Y	Y	Y	Y
2 **Lazio**	Y	Y	N	N	Y	Y	Y
3 **King**	–	+	N	N	Y	Y	Y
4 McCarthy	Y	Y	Y	Y	N	Y	Y
5 Ackerman	Y	N	Y	Y	N	N	Y
6 Meeks	Y	N	Y	Y	N	N	Y
7 Manton	?	?	#	?	?	Y	Y
8 Nadler	Y	Y	Y	Y	N	N	Y
9 Schumer	?	?	?	?	?	?	?
10 Towns	Y	N	Y	Y	N	?	Y
11 Owens	Y	Y	Y	Y	N	N	Y
12 Velázquez	Y	N	Y	Y	N	?	?
13 **Fossella**	N	Y	N	N	Y	Y	Y
14 Maloney	Y	Y	Y	Y	N	?	Y
15 Rangel	Y	N	Y	Y	N	N	Y
16 Serrano	Y	Y	Y	Y	N	Y	Y
17 Engel	Y	Y	Y	Y	N	N	Y
18 Lowey	Y	Y	Y	Y	N	Y	Y
19 **Kelly**	Y	Y	N	N	N	Y	Y
20 **Gilman**	N	Y	N	N	N	Y	Y
21 McNulty	Y	N	Y	Y	N	Y	Y
22 **Solomon**	N	Y	N	N	Y	Y	Y
23 **Boehlert**	Y	Y	N	N	N	Y	Y
24 **McHugh**	N	Y	N	N	Y	Y	Y
25 **Walsh**	Y	Y	N	N	Y	Y	Y
26 Hinchey	Y	Y	Y	Y	N	N	Y
27 **Paxon**	N	Y	N	N	Y	Y	Y
28 Slaughter	Y	Y	Y	Y	N	N	Y
29 LaFalce	N	N	Y	Y	N	Y	Y
30 **Quinn**	Y	Y	N	N	N	Y	Y

	448	449	450	451	452	453	454
31 **Houghton**	N	Y	N	N	Y	Y	Y
NORTH CAROLINA							
1 Clayton	Y	N	Y	Y	N	N	Y
2 Etheridge	Y	N	Y	Y	N	Y	Y
3 **Jones**	N	N	N	N	Y	Y	Y
4 Price	Y	N	Y	Y	N	Y	Y
5 **Burr**	N	Y	N	N	Y	Y	Y
6 **Coble**	Y	Y	N	N	Y	Y	Y
7 McIntyre	N	Y	Y	Y	Y	Y	Y
8 Hefner	Y	N	Y	Y	N	N	Y
9 **Myrick**	–	+	N	N	Y	Y	Y
10 **Ballenger**	N	Y	N	N	Y	Y	Y
11 **Taylor**	N	Y	N	N	Y	Y	Y
12 Watt	Y	N	Y	Y	N	N	Y
NORTH DAKOTA							
AL Pomeroy	Y	N	Y	Y	N	Y	Y
OHIO							
1 **Chabot**	N	Y	N	N	Y	Y	Y
2 **Portman**	N	Y	N	N	Y	Y	Y
3 Hall	Y	N	Y	Y	N	Y	Y
4 **Oxley**	N	Y	N	N	Y	Y	Y
5 **Gillmor**	N	Y	N	N	Y	Y	?
6 Strickland	Y	Y	Y	Y	N	Y	Y
7 **Hobson**	N	Y	N	N	Y	Y	Y
8 **Boehner**	N	Y	N	N	Y	Y	Y
9 Kaptur	N	Y	?	?	?	?	?
10 Kucinich	Y	Y	Y	Y	N	Y	Y
11 Stokes	Y	N	?	?	?	N	Y
12 **Kasich**	N	Y	N	N	Y	Y	Y
13 Brown	Y	N	Y	Y	N	N	Y
14 Sawyer	Y	N	Y	Y	N	Y	Y
15 **Pryce**	–	+	–	–	+	+	+
16 **Regula**	Y	Y	N	N	Y	Y	Y
17 Traficant	N	N	Y	Y	N	Y	Y
18 **Ney**	N	Y	N	Y	N	Y	Y
19 **LaTourette**	Y	Y	N	Y	Y	Y	Y
OKLAHOMA							
1 **Largent**	Y	Y	N	N	Y	Y	Y
2 **Coburn**	N	N	N	N	Y	?	Y
3 **Watkins**	N	N	N	N	Y	Y	Y
4 **Watts**	N	Y	?	N	Y	?	Y
5 **Istook**	N	Y	N	N	Y	Y	Y
6 **Lucas**	N	N	N	N	Y	Y	Y
OREGON							
1 Furse	Y	N	Y	Y	N	N	Y
2 **Smith**	N	Y	N	N	Y	Y	Y
3 Blumenauer	Y	Y	Y	Y	N	N	Y
4 DeFazio	Y	N	?	?	?	N	Y
5 Hooley	Y	Y	Y	Y	N	N	Y
PENNSYLVANIA							
1 Brady	N	N	Y	Y	N	N	Y
2 Fattah	Y	N	Y	Y	N	N	Y
3 Borski	Y	N	Y	Y	N	Y	Y
4 Klink	N	N	Y	Y	N	Y	Y
5 **Peterson**	N	N	N	N	Y	Y	Y
6 Holden	N	Y	Y	Y	N	Y	Y
7 **Weldon**	N	Y	N	N	Y	Y	Y
8 **Greenwood**	Y	N	N	N	Y	Y	Y
9 **Shuster**	N	Y	N	N	Y	Y	Y
10 **McDade**	N	Y	?	?	?	?	Y
11 Kanjorski	N	N	Y	Y	N	N	Y
12 Murtha	N	N	Y	Y	N	Y	Y
13 **Fox**	Y	Y	Y	N	Y	Y	Y
14 Coyne	Y	N	Y	Y	N	Y	Y
15 McHale	Y	N	Y	Y	N	Y	Y
16 **Pitts**	N	N	N	N	Y	Y	Y
17 **Gekas**	N	Y	N	N	Y	Y	Y
18 Doyle	Y	Y	Y	Y	N	Y	Y
19 **Goodling**	N	Y	N	N	Y	Y	Y
20 Mascara	N	N	Y	Y	N	Y	Y
21 **English**	Y	Y	N	N	Y	Y	Y
RHODE ISLAND							
1 Kennedy	Y	Y	Y	Y	N	N	Y
2 Weygand	Y	Y	Y	Y	N	Y	Y
SOUTH CAROLINA							
1 **Sanford**	Y	N	N	N	Y	Y	Y
2 **Spence**	N	Y	N	N	Y	Y	Y
3 **Graham**	Y	Y	N	N	Y	+	Y
4 **Inglis**	N	Y	N	N	Y	Y	Y
5 Spratt	N	N	Y	Y	N	Y	Y
6 Clyburn	N	N	Y	Y	N	N	Y
SOUTH DAKOTA							
AL **Thune**	N	Y	N	N	Y	Y	Y

	448	449	450	451	452	453	454
TENNESSEE							
1 **Jenkins**	N	Y	N	N	Y	Y	Y
2 **Duncan**	Y	N	N	N	Y	Y	Y
3 **Wamp**	Y	Y	N	N	Y	Y	Y
4 **Hilleary**	N	N	N	N	Y	Y	Y
5 Clement	Y	N	Y	Y	N	Y	Y
6 Gordon	Y	N	Y	Y	N	N	Y
7 **Bryant**	N	Y	N	N	Y	Y	Y
8 Tanner	N	N	Y	Y	N	Y	Y
9 Ford	Y	N	Y	Y	N	N	Y
TEXAS							
1 Sandlin	N	N	Y	Y	N	Y	Y
2 Turner	N	Y	Y	Y	N	Y	Y
3 **Johnson, Sam**	N	Y	N	N	Y	Y	Y
4 Hall	N	N	Y	N	Y	Y	Y
5 **Sessions**	N	Y	N	N	Y	Y	Y
6 **Barton**	N	Y	N	N	Y	Y	Y
7 **Archer**	N	Y	N	N	Y	Y	Y
8 **Brady**	N	Y	N	N	Y	Y	Y
9 Lampson	Y	Y	Y	Y	N	Y	Y
10 Doggett	Y	N	Y	Y	N	Y	Y
11 Edwards	N	N	Y	Y	N	Y	Y
12 **Granger**	N	Y	N	N	Y	Y	Y
13 **Thornberry**	N	Y	N	N	Y	Y	Y
14 **Paul**	Y	N	N	N	P	Y	Y
15 Hinojosa	Y	N	Y	Y	N	N	Y
16 Reyes	N	N	Y	Y	N	Y	Y
17 Stenholm	N	N	Y	N	N	Y	Y
18 Jackson-Lee	Y	Y	Y	Y	N	Y	Y
19 **Combest**	N	N	N	N	Y	Y	Y
20 Gonzalez	?	?	?	?	?	?	?
21 **Smith**	N	Y	N	N	Y	Y	Y
22 **DeLay**	N	Y	N	N	Y	Y	Y
23 **Bonilla**	N	Y	N	N	Y	Y	Y
24 Frost	N	Y	Y	Y	N	N	Y
25 Bentsen	Y	Y	Y	Y	N	Y	Y
26 **Armey**	N	Y	N	N	Y	Y	Y
27 Ortiz	N	Y	Y	Y	N	Y	Y
28 Rodriguez	Y	Y	Y	Y	N	Y	Y
29 Green	Y	Y	Y	Y	N	N	Y
30 Johnson, E.B.	Y	N	Y	Y	N	N	Y
UTAH							
1 **Hansen**	N	N	N	N	Y	Y	Y
2 **Cook**	N	Y	N	N	Y	Y	Y
3 **Cannon**	N	Y	Y	N	Y	Y	Y
VERMONT							
AL *Sanders*	Y	N	Y	Y	N	?	?
VIRGINIA							
1 **Bateman**	N	Y	N	N	Y	Y	Y
2 Pickett	N	Y	Y	Y	N	Y	Y
3 Scott	Y	N	Y	Y	N	N	Y
4 Sisisky	N	Y	Y	Y	N	Y	Y
5 Goode	Y	N	Y	N	Y	Y	Y
6 **Goodlatte**	N	Y	N	N	Y	Y	Y
7 **Bliley**	N	Y	N	N	Y	Y	Y
8 Moran	Y	N	Y	Y	N	Y	Y
9 Boucher	Y	N	Y	Y	N	Y	Y
10 **Wolf**	N	Y	N	N	Y	Y	Y
11 **Davis**	N	Y	Y	N	Y	Y	Y
WASHINGTON							
1 **White**	N	Y	N	N	Y	Y	Y
2 **Metcalf**	Y	Y	N	N	Y	Y	Y
3 **Smith, Linda**	N	Y	N	N	Y	Y	Y
4 **Hastings**	N	Y	N	N	Y	Y	Y
5 **Nethercutt**	N	Y	N	N	Y	Y	Y
6 Dicks	Y	Y	Y	Y	N	Y	Y
7 McDermott	Y	N	Y	Y	N	Y	Y
8 **Dunn**	N	Y	N	N	Y	Y	Y
9 Smith, Adam	Y	N	Y	Y	Y	Y	Y
WEST VIRGINIA							
1 Mollohan	N	N	Y	Y	N	Y	Y
2 Wise	N	N	Y	Y	N	Y	Y
3 Rahall	Y	N	Y	Y	N	N	Y
WISCONSIN							
1 **Neumann**	Y	Y	N	N	Y	Y	Y
2 **Klug**	Y	Y	N	N	Y	Y	Y
3 Kind	Y	N	Y	Y	N	Y	Y
4 Kleczka	Y	N	Y	Y	N	Y	Y
5 Barrett	Y	N	Y	Y	N	Y	Y
6 **Petri**	Y	N	N	N	Y	Y	Y
7 Obey	Y	N	Y	Y	N	Y	Y
8 Johnson	Y	N	Y	Y	N	Y	Y
9 **Sensenbrenner**	Y	N	N	N	Y	Y	Y
WYOMING							
AL **Cubin**	N	Y	N	N	Y	Y	Y

Southern states - Ala., Ark., Fla., Ga., Ky., La., Miss., N.C., Okla., S.C., Tenn., Texas, Va.

House Votes 455, 456, 457, 458, 459, 460, 461

455. H Res 505. Diplomatic Relations with Pacific Island Nations/Passage. Gilman, R-N.Y., motion to suspend the rules and pass the bill to encourage the United States to actively engage the governments of the South Pacific region in order to support U.S. commercial and strategic interests and promote democratic values. Motion agreed to 414-1: R 218-1; D 196-0 (ND 142-0, SD 54-0); I 0-0. Sept. 23, 1998. A two-thirds majority of those present and voting (277 in this case) is required for passage under suspension of the rules.

456. H Con Res 315. Condemn Serbian Atrocities in Kosovo/Passage. Gilman, R-N.Y., motion to suspend the rules and pass the bill to express the sense of Congress that it deeply deplores and strongly condemns the loss of life and the extensive destruction of property in Kosovo that is the consequence of the brutal actions of Serbian police and military forces against the ethnic Albanian population of the province. Motion agreed to 410-0: R 216-0; D 194-0 (ND 141-0, SD 53-0); I 0-0. Sept. 23, 1998. A two-thirds majority of those present and voting (274 in this case) is required for passage under suspension of the rules

457. HR 4112. Fiscal 1999 Legislative Branch Appropriations/Conference Report. Adoption of the conference report on the bill to provide about $2.35 billion for the House, Senate and various congressional agencies and offices, such as the Library of Congress, General Accounting Office and Congressional Budget Office. Adopted (thus sent to the Senate) 356-65: R 187-31; D 168-34 (ND 124-23, SD 44-11); I 1-0. Sept. 24, 1998.

458. HR 3616. Fiscal 1999 Defense Authorization/Conference Report. Adoption of the conference report on the bill to authorize $270.5 billion in defense spending for fiscal 1999. Adopted (thus sent to the Senate) 373-50: R 207-11; D 166-38 (ND 113-36, SD 53-2); I 0-1. Sept. 24, 1998.

459. HR 3736. High-Tech Workers Visa/Democratic Substitute. Watt, D-N.C., substitute amendment to increase the number of six-year H-1B skill and profession-based visas for foreign workers. The total increase over the next five years would be lower than the overall number allowed by the bill. The substitute amendment also would require all employers using H-1B workers attest they have tried to recruit qualified U.S. workers and have not laid off U.S. workers. Rejected 177-242: R 21-201; D 156-40 (ND 119-23, SD 37-17); I 0-1. Sept. 24, 1998.

460. HR 3736. High-Tech Worker Visas/Passage. Passage of the bill to increase the number of six-year H-1B skill and profession-based visas for foreign workers from 65,000 to 115,000 in fiscal 1999 and 2000 and 107,500 in fiscal 2001. The bill also would require some employers using H-1B workers to prove they have tried to recruit qualified U.S. workers and have not laid off U.S. workers. Passed 288-133: R 189-34; D 99-98 (ND 66-76, SD 33-22); I 0-1. Sept. 24, 1998. A "nay" was a vote in support of the president's position.

461. H Res 552. Tax Cut and Social Security Savings/Previous Question. Solomon, R-N.Y., motion to order the previous question (thus ending debate and the possibility of amendment) on adoption of the rule to provide for House floor consideration of the bills to cut taxes by $80 billion over five years (HR 4579) and to set aside 90 percent of any budget surplus in a special Treasury account until Congress enacts legislation to ensure the long-term solvency of the Social Security program (HR 4578). Motion agreed to 219-202: R 217-1; D 2-200 (ND 2-145, SD 0-55); I 0-1. Sept. 25, 1998.

Key

- Y Voted for (yea).
- # Paired for.
- + Announced for.
- N Voted against (nay).
- X Paired against.
- – Announced against.
- P Voted "present."
- C Voted "present" to avoid possible conflict of interest.
- ? Did not vote or otherwise make a position known.

Democrats **Republicans** *Independent*

		455	456	457	458	459	460	461
ALABAMA								
1	Callahan	Y	Y	Y	Y	N	Y	Y
2	Everett	Y	Y	Y	Y	N	Y	Y
3	Riley	Y	Y	Y	+	N	Y	Y
4	Aderholt	Y	Y	Y	+	N	Y	Y
5	Cramer	Y	Y	Y	Y	N	Y	N
6	Bachus	Y	Y	Y	Y	N	N	Y
7	Hilliard	Y	Y	Y	Y	Y	N	N
ALASKA								
AL	Young	Y	Y	Y	Y	N	N	Y
ARIZONA								
1	Salmon	Y	Y	N	Y	N	Y	Y
2	Pastor	Y	Y	Y	Y	Y	Y	N
3	Stump	Y	Y	N	Y	N	N	Y
4	Shadegg	Y	Y	N	Y	N	Y	Y
5	Kolbe	Y	Y	Y	Y	N	Y	Y
6	Hayworth	Y	Y	Y	Y	N	Y	Y
ARKANSAS								
1	Berry	Y	Y	Y	Y	Y	N	N
2	Snyder	Y	Y	Y	N	Y	N	N
3	Hutchinson	Y	Y	Y	Y	N	Y	Y
4	Dickey	Y	Y	Y	Y	N	Y	Y
CALIFORNIA								
1	Riggs	?	?	Y	Y	N	N	Y
2	Herger	Y	Y	N	Y	N	Y	Y
3	Fazio	Y	Y	Y	Y	Y	N	N
4	Doolittle	Y	Y	Y	Y	N	N	Y
5	Matsui	Y	Y	Y	Y	Y	Y	N
6	Woolsey	Y	Y	Y	N	Y	N	N
7	Miller	Y	Y	N	N	Y	N	N
8	Pelosi	Y	Y	Y	N	Y	N	N
9	Lee	Y	Y	N	N	Y	N	N
10	Tauscher	Y	Y	Y	Y	Y	Y	N
11	Pombo	Y	Y	Y	Y	N	Y	Y
12	Lantos	Y	Y	Y	Y	Y	Y	N
13	Stark	Y	Y	N	N	Y	N	N
14	Eshoo	Y	Y	Y	Y	Y	Y	N
15	Campbell	Y	Y	N	Y	N	Y	Y
16	Lofgren	Y	Y	N	N	Y	N	N
17	Farr	Y	Y	Y	Y	Y	N	N
18	Condit	Y	Y	N	Y	N	N	N
19	Radanovich	Y	Y	Y	Y	N	Y	Y
20	Dooley	Y	Y	Y	Y	Y	N	N
21	Thomas	Y	Y	Y	Y	N	Y	Y
22	Capps, L.	Y	Y	Y	N	Y	N	N
23	Gallegly	Y	Y	Y	Y	N	N	Y
24	Sherman	Y	Y	Y	Y	Y	N	N
25	McKeon	Y	Y	Y	Y	N	Y	Y
26	Berman	Y	Y	Y	Y	Y	Y	N
27	Rogan	Y	Y	Y	Y	N	Y	Y
28	Dreier	Y	Y	Y	Y	N	Y	Y
29	Waxman	Y	Y	Y	Y	Y	Y	N
30	Becerra	+	+	Y	Y	Y	N	N
31	Martinez	?	?	Y	Y	N	N	N
32	Dixon	Y	Y	Y	Y	Y	Y	N
33	Roybal-Allard	Y	Y	Y	Y	Y	N	N
34	Torres	?	?	Y	Y	Y	N	N
35	Waters	?	Y	N	Y	Y	?	N
36	Harman	Y	Y	Y	Y	N	Y	N
37	Millender-McD.	Y	Y	Y	Y	Y	N	N
38	Horn	Y	Y	Y	Y	N	Y	Y

		455	456	457	458	459	460	461
39	Royce	Y	Y	Y	Y	N	Y	Y
40	Lewis	Y	Y	N	Y	N	Y	Y
41	Kim	Y	Y	Y	Y	Y	Y	Y
42	Brown	Y	Y	Y	Y	Y	Y	N
43	Calvert	Y	Y	Y	Y	N	Y	Y
44	Bono, M.	Y	Y	Y	Y	N	Y	Y
45	Rohrabacher	Y	Y	N	Y	N	N	Y
46	Sanchez	+	+	Y	Y	–	+	N
47	Cox	Y	Y	N	Y	N	Y	Y
48	Packard	Y	Y	N	Y	N	Y	Y
49	Bilbray	Y	Y	Y	Y	N	Y	Y
50	Filner	Y	Y	N	N	Y	N	N
51	Cunningham	Y	Y	Y	Y	N	Y	Y
52	Hunter	Y	Y	Y	Y	N	N	Y
COLORADO								
1	DeGette	Y	Y	Y	Y	Y	N	N
2	Skaggs	Y	Y	Y	Y	Y	Y	N
3	McInnis	Y	Y	Y	Y	Y	Y	Y
4	Schaffer	Y	Y	N	Y	N	Y	Y
5	Hefley	Y	Y	N	Y	N	N	Y
6	Schaefer	Y	Y	Y	Y	?	?	Y
CONNECTICUT								
1	Kennelly	?	?	?	?	?	?	?
2	Gejdenson	Y	Y	Y	Y	Y	N	N
3	DeLauro	Y	Y	Y	Y	Y	N	N
4	Shays	Y	Y	N	N	N	Y	Y
5	Maloney	Y	Y	Y	Y	Y	Y	N
6	Johnson	Y	Y	Y	Y	N	Y	Y
DELAWARE								
AL	Castle	Y	Y	Y	Y	N	Y	Y
FLORIDA								
1	Scarborough	Y	Y	N	Y	N	Y	Y
2	Boyd	Y	Y	N	Y	N	N	N
3	Brown	Y	Y	Y	Y	N	N	N
4	Fowler	Y	Y	Y	Y	Y	Y	Y
5	Thurman	Y	Y	Y	Y	Y	N	N
6	Stearns	Y	Y	Y	Y	N	Y	Y
7	Mica	Y	Y	Y	Y	Y	Y	Y
8	McCollum	Y	Y	Y	Y	N	Y	Y
9	Bilirakis	Y	Y	Y	Y	Y	Y	Y
10	Young	Y	Y	Y	Y	N	Y	Y
11	Davis	Y	Y	Y	Y	N	Y	N
12	Canady	Y	Y	Y	Y	Y	Y	Y
13	Miller	Y	Y	Y	Y	N	Y	Y
14	Goss	+	+	+	+	–	+	+
15	Weldon	Y	Y	Y	Y	N	Y	Y
16	Foley	Y	Y	Y	Y	N	Y	Y
17	Meek	Y	Y	Y	Y	Y	N	N
18	Ros-Lehtinen	Y	Y	+	Y	Y	Y	Y
19	Wexler	Y	Y	Y	Y	?	N	N
20	Deutsch	Y	Y	N	Y	N	N	N
21	Diaz-Balart	+	+	+	+	Y	+	+
22	Shaw	?	?	?	?	N	Y	Y
23	Hastings	Y	Y	Y	Y	Y	Y	N
GEORGIA								
1	Kingston	Y	Y	Y	Y	N	Y	Y
2	Bishop	Y	Y	Y	Y	Y	N	N
3	Collins	Y	Y	Y	Y	N	N	Y
4	McKinney	Y	Y	N	N	Y	N	N
5	Lewis	Y	Y	Y	Y	N	N	N
6	Gingrich							Y
7	Barr	Y	Y	N	Y	N	N	Y
8	Chambliss	Y	Y	Y	Y	Y	Y	Y
9	Deal	Y	Y	Y	Y	Y	N	N
10	Norwood	Y	Y	Y	Y	N	N	?
11	Linder	Y	Y	?	Y	N	Y	Y
HAWAII								
1	Abercrombie	Y	Y	Y	Y	Y	N	N
2	Mink	Y	Y	Y	Y	Y	N	N
IDAHO								
1	Chenoweth	Y	Y	N	N	N	N	Y
2	Crapo	Y	Y	N	Y	N	Y	Y
ILLINOIS								
1	Rush	Y	Y	Y	N	Y	N	N
2	Jackson	Y	Y	Y	N	Y	N	N
3	Lipinski	Y	Y	Y	Y	Y	N	N
4	Gutierrez	Y	Y	N	N	Y	N	N
5	Blagojevich	Y	Y	Y	Y	N	N	N
6	Hyde	?	?	Y	Y	N	Y	Y
7	Davis	Y	Y	Y	N	Y	N	N
8	Crane	Y	Y	N	Y	N	N	Y
9	Yates	?	?	Y	N	?	N	N
10	Porter	Y	Y	Y	Y	N	Y	Y
11	Weller	Y	Y	Y	Y	N	Y	Y
12	Costello	Y	Y	Y	Y	Y	N	N
13	Fawell	Y	Y	Y	Y	N	Y	Y

ND Northern Democrats   SD Southern Democrats

	455	456	457	458	459	460	461
14 ***Hastert***	Y	Y	Y	Y	N	Y	Y
15 ***Ewing***	Y	Y	Y	Y	N	Y	Y
16 ***Manzullo***	Y	Y	Y	Y	N	Y	Y
17 Evans	Y	Y	Y	Y	Y	N	N
18 ***LaHood***	Y	Y	Y	Y	N	Y	Y
19 Poshard	?	?	?	?	?	?	N
20 ***Shimkus***	Y	Y	Y	Y	N	Y	Y
INDIANA							
1 Visclosky	Y	Y	Y	Y	Y	N	N
2 ***McIntosh***	Y	Y	Y	Y	N	Y	Y
3 Roemer	Y	Y	N	Y	Y	Y	N
4 ***Souder***	Y	?	Y	Y	N	Y	Y
5 ***Buyer***	Y	Y	Y	Y	N	Y	Y
6 ***Burton***	+	+	+	+	–	+	#
7 ***Pease***	Y	Y	Y	Y	N	Y	Y
8 ***Hostettler***	Y	Y	N	Y	N	N	Y
9 Hamilton	Y	Y	Y	Y	Y	Y	N
10 Carson	Y	Y	Y	Y	Y	N	N
IOWA							
1 ***Leach***	Y	Y	Y	Y	N	Y	Y
2 ***Nussle***	Y	Y	N	Y	N	Y	Y
3 Boswell	Y	Y	Y	Y	Y	Y	N
4 ***Ganske***	Y	Y	Y	Y	N	Y	Y
5 ***Latham***	Y	Y	Y	Y	N	Y	Y
KANSAS							
1 ***Moran***	Y	Y	N	Y	N	Y	Y
2 ***Ryun***	Y	Y	Y	Y	N	Y	Y
3 ***Snowbarger***	Y	Y	Y	Y	N	Y	Y
4 ***Tiahrt***	Y	Y	Y	Y	N	Y	Y
KENTUCKY							
1 ***Whitfield***	Y	Y	Y	Y	N	N	Y
2 ***Lewis***	Y	Y	Y	Y	N	Y	Y
3 ***Northup***	Y	Y	Y	Y	N	Y	Y
4 ***Bunning***	Y	Y	Y	Y	N	Y	Y
5 ***Rogers***	Y	Y	Y	Y	N	Y	?
6 Baesler	Y	Y	Y	Y	Y	N	N
LOUISIANA							
1 ***Livingston***	Y	Y	Y	Y	N	Y	?
2 Jefferson	Y	Y	Y	Y	Y	N	N
3 ***Tauzin***	Y	Y	Y	Y	N	Y	Y
4 ***McCrery***	Y	Y	Y	Y	N	Y	Y
5 ***Cooksey***	Y	Y	Y	Y	N	Y	Y
6 ***Baker***	Y	Y	Y	Y	N	Y	Y
7 John	Y	Y	Y	Y	N	Y	N
MAINE							
1 Allen	Y	Y	Y	Y	Y	Y	N
2 Baldacci	Y	Y	Y	Y	Y	Y	N
MARYLAND							
1 ***Gilchrest***	Y	Y	Y	Y	N	Y	Y
2 ***Ehrlich***	Y	Y	?	?	N	Y	Y
3 Cardin	Y	Y	?	Y	Y	Y	N
4 Wynn	Y	Y	Y	Y	Y	N	N
5 Hoyer	Y	Y	Y	Y	Y	Y	N
6 ***Bartlett***	Y	Y	Y	N	N	Y	Y
7 Cummings	Y	Y	Y	Y	Y	N	N
8 ***Morella***	Y	Y	Y	N	N	Y	Y
MASSACHUSETTS							
1 Olver	Y	Y	N	Y	Y	N	N
2 Neal	Y	Y	Y	Y	Y	Y	N
3 McGovern	Y	Y	N	Y	Y	Y	N
4 Frank	Y	Y	N	Y	Y	Y	N
5 Meehan	Y	Y	N	Y	Y	Y	N
6 Tierney	Y	Y	N	Y	Y	Y	N
7 Markey	Y	Y	Y	Y	Y	Y	N
8 Kennedy	Y	Y	Y	Y	Y	Y	N
9 Moakley	Y	Y	Y	Y	Y	N	X
10 Delahunt	Y	Y	Y	N	Y	Y	N
MICHIGAN							
1 Stupak	Y	Y	Y	Y	N	N	N
2 ***Hoekstra***	Y	Y	Y	N	N	Y	Y
3 ***Ehlers***	Y	Y	Y	Y	Y	Y	Y
4 ***Camp***	Y	Y	Y	Y	N	Y	Y
5 Barcia	Y	Y	Y	Y	Y	N	N
6 ***Upton***	Y	Y	Y	Y	N	Y	Y
7 ***Smith***	Y	Y	Y	Y	Y	N	Y
8 Stabenow	Y	Y	Y	Y	Y	Y	N
9 Kildee	Y	Y	Y	Y	Y	N	N
10 Bonior	Y	Y	Y	N	Y	N	N
11 ***Knollenberg***	Y	Y	Y	Y	N	Y	Y
12 Levin	Y	Y	Y	Y	Y	Y	N
13 Rivers	Y	Y	Y	N	Y	N	N
14 Conyers	Y	Y	N	N	Y	N	N
15 Kilpatrick	Y	Y	Y	Y	Y	N	N
16 Dingell	Y	Y	Y	Y	Y	N	N

	455	456	457	458	459	460	461
MINNESOTA							
1 ***Gutknecht***	Y	Y	Y	Y	N	Y	Y
2 Minge	Y	Y	N	N	Y	Y	N
3 ***Ramstad***	Y	Y	Y	Y	N	Y	Y
4 Vento	Y	Y	N	N	Y	Y	N
5 Sabo	Y	Y	Y	Y	Y	Y	N
6 Luther	Y	Y	N	N	Y	Y	N
7 Peterson	Y	Y	Y	Y	N	N	N
8 Oberstar	Y	Y	Y	N	Y	N	N
MISSISSIPPI							
1 ***Wicker***	Y	Y	Y	Y	N	Y	Y
2 Thompson	Y	Y	Y	Y	Y	N	N
3 ***Pickering***	Y	Y	Y	Y	N	Y	Y
4 ***Parker***	Y	Y	Y	Y	N	Y	Y
5 Taylor	Y	Y	N	Y	N	N	N
MISSOURI							
1 Clay	Y	Y	Y	Y	Y	N	N
2 ***Talent***	Y	Y	Y	Y	N	Y	Y
3 Gephardt	Y	Y	Y	Y	Y	Y	N
4 Skelton	Y	Y	Y	Y	?	?	N
5 McCarthy	Y	Y	Y	Y	Y	Y	N
6 Danner	Y	Y	Y	Y	Y	N	N
7 ***Blunt***	Y	Y	N	Y	N	N	Y
8 ***Emerson***	Y	Y	Y	Y	N	N	Y
9 ***Hulshof***	Y	Y	N	Y	N	Y	Y
MONTANA							
AL ***Hill***	Y	Y	Y	Y	N	Y	Y
NEBRASKA							
1 ***Bereuter***	Y	Y	Y	Y	Y	Y	Y
2 ***Christensen***	Y	Y	N	Y	N	Y	Y
3 ***Barrett***	Y	Y	Y	Y	N	Y	Y
NEVADA							
1 ***Ensign***	+	Y	N	Y	N	Y	Y
2 ***Gibbons***	Y	Y	Y	Y	N	Y	Y
NEW HAMPSHIRE							
1 ***Sununu***	Y	Y	Y	Y	N	Y	Y
2 ***Bass***	Y	Y	Y	Y	N	Y	Y
NEW JERSEY							
1 Andrews	Y	Y	Y	Y	Y	N	N
2 ***LoBiondo***	Y	Y	Y	Y	N	N	Y
3 ***Saxton***	Y	Y	Y	Y	N	Y	Y
4 ***Smith***	Y	Y	Y	Y	N	N	Y
5 ***Roukema***	Y	Y	Y	Y	N	Y	Y
6 Pallone	Y	Y	Y	Y	Y	N	N
7 ***Franks***	Y	Y	Y	N	N	N	Y
8 Pascrell	Y	Y	Y	Y	Y	Y	N
9 Rothman	Y	Y	N	Y	?	N	N
10 Payne	Y	Y	N	N	Y	N	N
11 ***Frelinghuysen***	Y	Y	Y	Y	N	Y	Y
12 ***Pappas***	Y	Y	Y	Y	N	Y	Y
13 Menendez	Y	Y	Y	Y	Y	Y	N
NEW MEXICO							
1 ***Wilson***	Y	Y	Y	Y	N	Y	Y
2 ***Skeen***	Y	Y	Y	Y	N	Y	Y
3 ***Redmond***	Y	Y	Y	Y	N	Y	Y
NEW YORK							
1 ***Forbes***	Y	Y	Y	Y	Y	Y	Y
2 ***Lazio***	Y	Y	Y	Y	N	Y	Y
3 ***King***	Y	Y	Y	Y	N	Y	Y
4 McCarthy	Y	Y	Y	Y	N	Y	Y
5 Ackerman	Y	Y	Y	Y	Y	Y	N
6 Meeks	Y	Y	Y	N	Y	N	?
7 Manton	Y	Y	Y	Y	?	?	N
8 Nadler	Y	Y	Y	N	Y	Y	N
9 Schumer	Y	Y	Y	Y	Y	Y	N
10 Towns	Y	Y	Y	Y	Y	N	N
11 Owens	Y	Y	Y	N	Y	N	N
12 Velázquez	?	?	N	N	Y	N	N
13 ***Fossella***	Y	Y	Y	Y	N	Y	Y
14 Maloney	Y	Y	Y	Y	Y	Y	N
15 Rangel	Y	Y	?	N	Y	N	N
16 Serrano	Y	Y	Y	Y	Y	N	N
17 Engel	Y	Y	Y	Y	Y	N	?
18 Lowey	Y	Y	Y	N	Y	Y	N
19 ***Kelly***	Y	Y	Y	Y	N	Y	Y
20 ***Gilman***	Y	Y	Y	Y	Y	Y	Y
21 McNulty	Y	Y	Y	Y	Y	N	N
22 ***Solomon***	Y	Y	Y	Y	N	N	Y
23 ***Boehlert***	Y	Y	Y	Y	Y	Y	Y
24 ***McHugh***	Y	Y	Y	Y	Y	Y	Y
25 ***Walsh***	Y	Y	Y	Y	N	Y	Y
26 Hinchey	Y	?	Y	Y	Y	N	N
27 ***Paxon***	Y	Y	Y	Y	N	Y	Y
28 Slaughter	Y	Y	Y	Y	Y	Y	N
29 LaFalce	Y	Y	Y	Y	Y	Y	N
30 ***Quinn***	Y	Y	Y	Y	N	Y	Y

	455	456	457	458	459	460	461
31 ***Houghton***	Y	Y	Y	Y	N	Y	Y
NORTH CAROLINA							
1 Clayton	Y	Y	Y	Y	Y	Y	N
2 Etheridge	Y	Y	Y	Y	Y	Y	N
3 ***Jones***	Y	Y	Y	Y	N	Y	Y
4 Price	Y	Y	Y	Y	Y	Y	N
5 ***Burr***	Y	Y	Y	Y	N	Y	Y
6 ***Coble***	Y	Y	Y	Y	N	Y	Y
7 McIntyre	Y	Y	Y	Y	Y	Y	N
8 Hefner	Y	Y	Y	Y	Y	Y	N
9 ***Myrick***	Y	Y	Y	Y	N	Y	Y
10 ***Ballenger***	Y	Y	Y	Y	N	Y	Y
11 ***Taylor***	Y	Y	Y	Y	N	Y	Y
12 Watt	Y	Y	Y	Y	Y	Y	N
NORTH DAKOTA							
AL Pomeroy	Y	Y	Y	Y	Y	Y	N
OHIO							
1 ***Chabot***	Y	Y	Y	Y	N	Y	Y
2 ***Portman***	Y	Y	Y	Y	N	Y	Y
3 Hall	Y	Y	Y	Y	N	Y	N
4 ***Oxley***	Y	Y	Y	Y	N	Y	Y
5 ***Gillmor***	Y	Y	Y	Y	N	Y	Y
6 Strickland	Y	Y	Y	Y	Y	N	N
7 ***Hobson***	Y	Y	Y	Y	N	Y	Y
8 ***Boehner***	Y	Y	Y	Y	N	Y	Y
9 Kaptur	Y	Y	Y	Y	Y	N	N
10 Kucinich	Y	Y	Y	N	Y	N	N
11 Stokes	Y	Y	Y	Y	Y	N	N
12 ***Kasich***	Y	Y	Y	Y	N	Y	Y
13 Brown	Y	Y	Y	Y	Y	N	N
14 Sawyer	Y	Y	Y	Y	Y	Y	N
15 ***Pryce***	+	+	+	+	–	+	+
16 ***Regula***	Y	Y	Y	Y	Y	Y	Y
17 Traficant	Y	Y	Y	Y	N	N	Y
18 ***Ney***	Y	Y	Y	Y	Y	N	Y
19 ***LaTourette***	Y	Y	Y	Y	N	Y	Y
OKLAHOMA							
1 ***Largent***	Y	Y	Y	Y	N	Y	Y
2 ***Coburn***	Y	Y	Y	Y	Y	Y	Y
3 ***Watkins***	Y	Y	Y	Y	N	Y	Y
4 ***Watts***	Y	Y	Y	Y	N	N	Y
5 ***Istook***	Y	Y	Y	Y	N	Y	Y
6 ***Lucas***	Y	Y	Y	Y	N	Y	Y
OREGON							
1 Furse	Y	Y	Y	N	Y	Y	N
2 ***Smith***	Y	Y	Y	Y	N	Y	Y
3 Blumenauer	Y	Y	Y	N	N	Y	N
4 DeFazio	Y	Y	Y	N	N	N	N
5 Hooley	Y	Y	Y	N	N	Y	N
PENNSYLVANIA							
1 Brady	Y	Y	Y	Y	Y	N	N
2 Fattah	Y	Y	Y	Y	Y	N	N
3 Borski	Y	Y	Y	Y	Y	N	N
4 Klink	Y	Y	N	Y	Y	N	N
5 ***Peterson***	Y	Y	Y	Y	N	Y	Y
6 Holden	Y	Y	Y	Y	Y	N	N
7 ***Weldon***	Y	Y	Y	Y	N	Y	Y
8 ***Greenwood***	Y	Y	Y	Y	N	Y	Y
9 ***Shuster***	Y	Y	Y	Y	N	Y	Y
10 ***McDade***	Y	Y	Y	Y	Y	Y	?
11 Kanjorski	Y	Y	Y	Y	Y	Y	N
12 Murtha	Y	Y	Y	Y	?	?	N
13 ***Fox***	Y	Y	Y	Y	N	Y	Y
14 Coyne	Y	Y	Y	Y	Y	N	N
15 McHale	Y	Y	Y	Y	Y	Y	N
16 ***Pitts***	Y	Y	Y	Y	N	Y	Y
17 ***Gekas***	Y	?	Y	Y	N	Y	Y
18 Doyle	Y	Y	Y	Y	Y	Y	N
19 ***Goodling***	Y	Y	Y	Y	N	Y	Y
20 Mascara	Y	Y	Y	Y	Y	N	N
21 ***English***	Y	Y	Y	Y	N	Y	Y
RHODE ISLAND							
1 Kennedy	Y	Y	Y	Y	Y	Y	N
2 Weygand	Y	Y	Y	Y	Y	Y	N
SOUTH CAROLINA							
1 ***Sanford***	Y	Y	N	Y	N	Y	N
2 ***Spence***	Y	Y	Y	Y	N	N	Y
3 ***Graham***	Y	Y	Y	Y	N	Y	Y
4 ***Inglis***	Y	Y	N	Y	N	Y	Y
5 Spratt	Y	Y	Y	Y	Y	Y	N
6 Clyburn	Y	Y	Y	Y	Y	N	N
SOUTH DAKOTA							
AL ***Thune***	Y	Y	Y	Y	N	Y	Y

	455	456	457	458	459	460	461
TENNESSEE							
1 ***Jenkins***	Y	Y	Y	Y	N	Y	Y
2 ***Duncan***	Y	Y	Y	Y	N	N	Y
3 ***Wamp***	Y	Y	Y	Y	N	N	Y
4 ***Hilleary***	Y	Y	N	Y	N	N	Y
5 Clement	Y	Y	Y	Y	N	Y	N
6 Gordon	Y	Y	Y	Y	Y	Y	N
7 ***Bryant***	Y	Y	Y	Y	N	Y	Y
8 Tanner	Y	Y	N	Y	N	Y	N
9 Ford	Y	Y	Y	Y	Y	Y	N
TEXAS							
1 Sandlin	Y	Y	Y	Y	N	N	N
2 Turner	Y	Y	Y	Y	N	N	N
3 ***Johnson, Sam***	Y	Y	Y	+	N	Y	Y
4 Hall	Y	Y	N	Y	N	Y	N
5 ***Sessions***	Y	Y	Y	Y	N	Y	Y
6 ***Barton***	Y	Y	Y	Y	N	Y	Y
7 ***Archer***	Y	Y	Y	Y	N	Y	Y
8 ***Brady***	Y	Y	+	+	–	+	Y
9 Lampson	Y	Y	Y	Y	Y	N	N
10 Doggett	Y	Y	N	Y	Y	Y	N
11 Edwards	Y	Y	Y	Y	N	Y	N
12 ***Granger***	Y	Y	Y	Y	N	Y	Y
13 ***Thornberry***	Y	Y	Y	Y	N	Y	Y
14 ***Paul***	N	P	N	N	N	Y	?
15 Hinojosa	Y	?	Y	Y	Y	Y	N
16 Reyes	Y	Y	Y	Y	Y	Y	N
17 Stenholm	Y	Y	N	Y	N	Y	N
18 Jackson-Lee	Y	Y	Y	Y	Y	Y	N
19 ***Combest***	Y	Y	Y	Y	N	N	Y
20 Gonzalez	?	?	Y	Y	Y	N	N
21 ***Smith***	Y	Y	Y	Y	N	Y	Y
22 ***DeLay***	Y	Y	Y	Y	N	Y	Y
23 ***Bonilla***	Y	Y	Y	Y	N	Y	Y
24 Frost	Y	Y	Y	Y	Y	Y	N
25 Bentsen	Y	Y	Y	Y	N	Y	N
26 ***Armey***	Y	Y	Y	Y	N	Y	Y
27 Ortiz	Y	Y	Y	Y	Y	Y	N
28 Rodriguez	Y	Y	Y	Y	Y	N	N
29 Green	Y	Y	N	Y	Y	N	N
30 Johnson, E.B.	Y	Y	Y	Y	Y	Y	N
UTAH							
1 ***Hansen***	Y	Y	Y	Y	N	Y	Y
2 ***Cook***	Y	Y	Y	Y	N	Y	Y
3 ***Cannon***	Y	?	Y	Y	N	Y	Y
VERMONT							
AL *Sanders*	?	?	Y	N	N	N	N
VIRGINIA							
1 ***Bateman***	Y	Y	Y	Y	N	Y	Y
2 Pickett	Y	Y	Y	Y	N	Y	N
3 Scott	Y	Y	Y	Y	Y	Y	N
4 Sisisky	Y	Y	Y	Y	Y	Y	N
5 Goode	Y	Y	N	N	N	N	N
6 ***Goodlatte***	Y	Y	N	Y	N	Y	Y
7 ***Bliley***	Y	Y	Y	Y	N	Y	Y
8 Moran	Y	Y	Y	Y	N	Y	N
9 Boucher	Y	Y	Y	Y	Y	N	N
10 ***Wolf***	Y	Y	Y	Y	N	Y	Y
11 ***Davis***	Y	Y	Y	Y	N	Y	Y
WASHINGTON							
1 ***White***	Y	Y	Y	Y	N	Y	Y
2 ***Metcalf***	Y	Y	Y	Y	N	N	Y
3 ***Smith, Linda***	Y	Y	N	Y	N	Y	Y
4 ***Hastings***	Y	Y	Y	Y	N	Y	Y
5 ***Nethercutt***	Y	Y	Y	Y	N	Y	Y
6 Dicks	Y	Y	Y	Y	Y	Y	N
7 McDermott	Y	Y	Y	N	Y	Y	N
8 ***Dunn***	Y	Y	Y	Y	N	Y	Y
9 Smith, Adam	Y	Y	Y	Y	N	Y	N
WEST VIRGINIA							
1 Mollohan	Y	Y	Y	Y	Y	N	N
2 Wise	Y	Y	Y	Y	Y	N	N
3 Rahall	Y	Y	Y	Y	Y	N	N
WISCONSIN							
1 ***Neumann***	Y	Y	N	Y	N	Y	Y
2 ***Klug***	Y	Y	Y	N	N	Y	Y
3 Kind	Y	Y	N	N	N	Y	N
4 Kleczka	Y	?	Y	Y	Y	N	N
5 Barrett	Y	Y	N	N	Y	N	N
6 ***Petri***	Y	Y	N	N	N	Y	Y
7 Obey	Y	Y	Y	N	Y	N	N
8 Johnson	Y	Y	Y	Y	Y	N	N
9 ***Sensenbrenner***	Y	Y	N	N	Y	Y	Y
WYOMING							
AL ***Cubin***	Y	Y	Y	Y	N	Y	?

Southern states - Ala., Ark., Fla., Ga., Ky., La., Miss., N.C., Okla., S.C., Tenn., Texas, Va.

House Votes 462, 463, 464, 465, 466, 467, 468

Key

- Y Voted for (yea).
- # Paired for.
- + Announced for.
- N Voted against (nay).
- X Paired against.
- − Announced against.
- P Voted "present."
- C Voted "present" to avoid possible conflict of interest.
- ? Did not vote or otherwise make a position known.

Democrats   **Republicans**   *Independent*

462. H Res 552. Tax Cut and Social Security Savings/Rule. Adoption of the rule to provide for House floor consideration of the bills to cut taxes by $80 billion over five years (HR 4579) and to set aside 90 percent of any budget surplus in a special Treasury account until Congress enacts legislation to ensure the long-term solvency of the Social Security program (HR 4578). Adopted 215-208: R 212-7; D 3-200 (ND 3-145, SD 0-55); I 0-1. Sept. 25, 1998.

463. HR 4578. Surplus to Social Security/Social Security Trust Fund. Rangel, D-N.C., substitute amendment to transfer 100 percent of any Social Security Trust Fund surpluses to the Federal Reserve Bank of New York to be held in trust for the Social Security system. Rejected 210-216: R 8-215; D 201-1 (ND 146-1, SD 55-0); I 1-0. Sept. 25, 1998.

464. HR 4578. Surplus to Social Security/Passage. Passage of the bill to set aside 90 percent of any budget surplus in a special Treasury account until Congress enacts legislation to ensure the long-term solvency of the Social Security system. Passed 240-188: R 220-5; D 20-182 (ND 12-135, SD 8-47); I 0-1. Sept. 25, 1998. A "nay" was a vote in support of the president's position.

465. HR 2621. Fast-Track Trade Authority/Previous Question. Dreier, R-Calif., motion to order the previous question (thus ending debate and the possibility of amendment) on adoption of the rule (H Res 553) to provide for House floor consideration of the bill to allow expedited negotiation and implementation of trade agreements between the executive branch and foreign countries. Motion agreed to 230-193: R 223-0; D 7-192 (ND 3-142, SD 4-50); I 0-1. Sept. 25, 1998. (Subsequently, the rule was adopted by voice vote.)

466. HR 2621. Fast-Track Trade Authority/Passage. Passage of the bill to allow expedited negotiation and implementation of trade agreements between the executive branch and foreign countries. Rejected 180-243: R 151-71; D 29-171 (ND 13-133, SD 16-38); I 0-1. Sept. 25, 1998.

467. Procedural Motion/Journal. Approval of the House Journal of Friday, Sept. 25, 1998. Approved 334-50: R 181-18; D 152-32 (ND 110-25, SD 42-7); I 1-0. Sept. 26, 1998.

468. HR 4579. Tax Cuts/Democratic Substitute. Rangel, D-N.Y., substitute amendment that includes all of the tax cuts in the underlying bill but would prohibit most from taking effect until Congress enacts legislation to ensure the long-term solvency of the Social Security system. Rejected 197-227: R 0-221; D 196-6 (ND 143-5, SD 53-1); I 1-0. Sept. 26, 1998.

	462	463	464	465	466	467	468
ALABAMA							
1 *Callahan*	Y	N	Y	Y	Y	?	X
2 *Everett*	Y	N	Y	Y	N	Y	N
3 *Riley*	Y	N	Y	Y	N	Y	N
4 *Aderholt*	Y	Y	Y	Y	N	Y	N
5 Cramer	N	Y	N	N	Y	Y	Y
6 *Bachus*	Y	N	Y	Y	Y	Y	N
7 Hilliard	N	Y	N	N	N	N	Y
ALASKA							
AL *Young*	Y	N	Y	Y	N	?	N
ARIZONA							
1 *Salmon*	Y	N	Y	Y	Y	Y	N
2 Pastor	N	Y	N	N	N	Y	Y
3 *Stump*	Y	N	Y	Y	Y	Y	N
4 *Shadegg*	Y	N	Y	Y	Y	Y	N
5 *Kolbe*	Y	N	Y	Y	Y	Y	N
6 *Hayworth*	Y	N	Y	Y	Y	Y	N
ARKANSAS							
1 Berry	N	Y	N	N	Y	Y	Y
2 Snyder	N	Y	N	N	Y	Y	Y
3 *Hutchinson*	Y	N	Y	Y	+	Y	N
4 *Dickey*	Y	N	Y	Y	Y	Y	N
CALIFORNIA							
1 *Riggs*	Y	N	Y	Y	Y	?	N
2 *Herger*	Y	N	Y	Y	Y	Y	N
3 Fazio	N	Y	N	N	N	?	Y
4 *Doolittle*	Y	N	Y	Y	Y	Y	N
5 Matsui	N	Y	N	N	N	Y	Y
6 Woolsey	N	Y	N	N	N	Y	Y
7 Miller	N	Y	N	N	N	Y	Y
8 Pelosi	N	Y	N	N	N	?	Y
9 Lee	N	Y	N	N	Y	Y	Y
10 Tauscher	N	Y	N	Y	N	Y	Y
11 *Pombo*	Y	N	Y	Y	Y	Y	N
12 Lantos	N	Y	N	N	N	Y	Y
13 Stark	N	N	N	N	N	Y	Y
14 Eshoo	N	Y	N	N	Y	Y	Y
15 *Campbell*	Y	N	Y	Y	Y	Y	N
16 Lofgren	N	Y	N	N	Y	Y	Y
17 Farr	N	Y	N	N	N	Y	Y
18 Condit	N	Y	N	N	Y	Y	Y
19 *Radanovich*	Y	N	Y	Y	Y	Y	N
20 Dooley	N	N	N	N	Y	Y	Y
21 *Thomas*	Y	N	Y	Y	Y	Y	N
22 Capps, L.	N	Y	N	N	N	Y	Y
23 *Gallegly*	Y	N	Y	Y	Y	Y	N
24 Sherman	N	Y	N	N	Y	Y	Y
25 *McKeon*	Y	N	Y	Y	Y	Y	N
26 Berman	N	Y	N	Y	N	?	#
27 *Rogan*	Y	N	Y	Y	Y	Y	N
28 *Dreier*	Y	N	Y	Y	Y	Y	N
29 Waxman	N	Y	N	N	N	?	Y
30 Becerra	N	Y	N	N	N	N	Y
31 Martinez	N	Y	N	P	?	?	Y
32 Dixon	N	Y	N	N	N	Y	Y
33 Royal-Allard	N	Y	N	N	Y	Y	Y
34 Torres	N	Y	N	N	Y	Y	Y
35 Waters	N	?	N	N	N	Y	Y
36 Harman	N	Y	N	Y	N	Y	Y
37 Millender-McD.	N	Y	N	N	Y	Y	Y
38 *Horn*	Y	N	Y	Y	Y	Y	N

	462	463	464	465	466	467	468
39 *Royce*	Y	N	Y	Y	N	Y	N
40 *Lewis*	Y	N	Y	Y	Y	Y	N
41 *Kim*	Y	N	Y	Y	Y	Y	N
42 Brown	N	Y	N	N	N	N	Y
43 *Calvert*	Y	N	Y	Y	Y	Y	N
44 *Bono, M.*	Y	N	Y	Y	Y	Y	N
45 *Rohrabacher*	Y	N	Y	Y	N	Y	N
46 Sanchez	N	Y	N	N	N	Y	Y
47 *Cox*	Y	?	Y	Y	Y	?	N
48 *Packard*	Y	N	Y	Y	Y	Y	N
49 *Bilbray*	Y	N	Y	Y	Y	?	N
50 Filner	Y	N	N	N	N	Y	N
51 *Cunningham*	Y	N	Y	Y	Y	Y	N
52 *Hunter*	Y	N	Y	Y	N	Y	N
COLORADO							
1 DeGette	N	Y	N	N	N	Y	Y
2 Skaggs	N	Y	N	N	P	Y	Y
3 *McInnis*	Y	N	Y	Y	Y	Y	N
4 *Schaffer*	Y	N	Y	Y	Y	N	N
5 *Hefley*	Y	N	Y	Y	Y	N	N
6 *Schaefer*	Y	N	Y	Y	Y	?	N
CONNECTICUT							
1 Kennelly	?	?	?	?	N	?	Y
2 Gejdenson	N	Y	N	N	Y	Y	Y
3 DeLauro	N	Y	N	N	N	Y	Y
4 *Shays*	Y	N	Y	Y	Y	Y	N
5 Maloney	N	Y	N	Y	N	N	N
6 *Johnson*	Y	N	Y	Y	Y	Y	N
DELAWARE							
AL *Castle*	Y	N	N	Y	Y	Y	N
FLORIDA							
1 *Scarborough*	Y	N	Y	Y	N	Y	N
2 Boyd	N	Y	N	N	Y	Y	Y
3 Brown	N	Y	N	N	N	?	Y
4 *Fowler*	Y	N	Y	Y	?	?	X
5 Thurman	N	Y	N	N	N	Y	Y
6 *Stearns*	Y	N	Y	Y	N	Y	N
7 *Mica*	Y	N	Y	Y	Y	Y	N
8 *McCollum*	Y	N	Y	Y	Y	Y	N
9 *Bilirakis*	Y	N	Y	Y	Y	Y	N
10 *Young*	Y	N	Y	Y	Y	?	N
11 Davis	N	Y	N	Y	Y	Y	Y
12 *Canady*	Y	N	Y	Y	Y	Y	Y
13 *Miller*	Y	N	Y	Y	Y	Y	N
14 Goss	+	−	+	+	+	+	−
15 *Weldon*	Y	N	Y	Y	Y	Y	N
16 *Foley*	Y	N	Y	Y	Y	Y	N
17 Meek	N	Y	N	N	N	Y	Y
18 *Ros-Lehtinen*	Y	N	Y	Y	N	Y	N
19 Wexler	N	Y	N	N	N	Y	Y
20 Deutsch	N	Y	N	N	Y	Y	Y
21 *Diaz-Balart*	Y	N	Y	Y	N	?	N
22 *Shaw*	Y	N	Y	Y	Y	Y	N
23 Hastings	N	Y	N	N	N	Y	Y
GEORGIA							
1 *Kingston*	Y	N	Y	Y	Y	Y	N
2 Bishop	N	Y	N	N	Y	Y	Y
3 *Collins*	Y	N	Y	N	N	Y	N
4 McKinney	N	Y	N	N	N	Y	Y
5 Lewis	N	Y	N	N	N	N	Y
6 *Gingrich*		N	Y			Y	
7 *Barr*	Y	N	Y	Y	Y	Y	N
8 *Chambliss*	Y	N	Y	Y	Y	Y	N
9 *Deal*	Y	N	Y	Y	Y	Y	N
10 *Norwood*	?	N	Y	Y	Y	Y	N
11 *Linder*	Y	?	Y	Y	Y	Y	N
HAWAII							
1 Abercrombie	N	Y	N	N	N	Y	Y
2 Mink	N	Y	N	N	N	Y	Y
IDAHO							
1 *Chenoweth*	Y	Y	Y	Y	N	Y	N
2 *Crapo*	Y	N	Y	N	N	?	N
ILLINOIS							
1 Rush	N	Y	N	?	N	Y	Y
2 Jackson	N	Y	N	N	N	Y	Y
3 Lipinski	N	N	N	N	N	N	Y
4 Gutierrez	N	Y	N	N	N	N	Y
5 Blagojevich	N	Y	N	N	Y	Y	Y
6 *Hyde*	Y	N	Y	Y	Y	Y	N
7 Davis	N	Y	N	N	N	Y	Y
8 *Crane*	Y	N	Y	Y	Y	?	N
9 Yates	N	?	?	N	N	Y	Y
10 *Porter*	Y	N	Y	Y	Y	Y	N
11 *Weller*	Y	N	Y	Y	N	N	N
12 Costello	N	Y	N	N	N	N	Y
13 *Fawell*	Y	N	Y	Y	Y	Y	N

ND Northern Democrats   SD Southern Democrats

	462	463	464	465	466	467	468
14 ***Hastert***	Y	N	Y	Y	Y	Y	N
15 ***Ewing***	Y	N	Y	Y	Y	Y	N
16 ***Manzullo***	Y	N	Y	Y	Y	Y	N
17 Evans	N	Y	N	N	N	Y	Y
18 ***LaHood***	Y	N	N	Y	Y	Y	N
19 Poshard	N	Y	N	N	N	N	Y
20 ***Shimkus***	Y	N	Y	Y	Y	Y	N
INDIANA							
1 Visclosky	N	Y	N	N	N	?	Y
2 ***McIntosh***	N	N	Y	Y	Y	Y	N
3 Roemer	Y	Y	Y	N	N	Y	N
4 ***Souder***	Y	N	Y	Y	N	Y	N
5 ***Buyer***	Y	N	Y	Y	N	Y	N
6 ***Burton***	?	X	#	?	?	?	X
7 ***Pease***	Y	N	Y	Y	Y	Y	N
8 ***Hostettler***	Y	N	Y	Y	N	Y	N
9 Hamilton	N	Y	N	Y	Y	Y	N
10 Carson	N	Y	N	N	N	Y	Y
IOWA							
1 ***Leach***	Y	N	Y	Y	Y	Y	N
2 ***Nussle***	Y	N	Y	Y	Y	Y	N
3 Boswell	N	Y	Y	Y	Y	Y	Y
4 ***Ganske***	Y	N	Y	Y	Y	Y	N
5 ***Latham***	Y	N	Y	Y	Y	Y	N
KANSAS							
1 ***Moran***	Y	N	Y	Y	Y	N	N
2 ***Ryun***	Y	N	Y	Y	Y	Y	N
3 ***Snowbarger***	Y	N	Y	Y	Y	Y	N
4 ***Tiahrt***	Y	N	Y	Y	Y	?	N
KENTUCKY							
1 ***Whitfield***	Y	N	Y	Y	N	N	N
2 ***Lewis***	Y	N	Y	Y	Y	Y	N
3 ***Northup***	Y	N	Y	Y	Y	Y	N
4 ***Bunning***	Y	N	Y	Y	Y	Y	N
5 ***Rogers***	Y	N	Y	Y	N	?	N
6 Baesler	N	Y	N	N	N	Y	Y
LOUISIANA							
1 ***Livingston***	Y	N	Y	Y	Y	Y	N
2 Jefferson	N	Y	N	?	?	Y	Y
3 ***Tauzin***	Y	N	Y	Y	Y	?	N
4 ***McCrery***	Y	N	Y	Y	Y	?	N
5 ***Cooksey***	Y	N	Y	Y	Y	Y	N
6 ***Baker***	Y	N	Y	Y	Y	Y	N
7 John	N	Y	N	N	N	Y	Y
MAINE							
1 Allen	N	Y	N	N	N	Y	Y
2 Baldacci	N	Y	N	N	N	Y	Y
MARYLAND							
1 ***Gilchrest***	Y	N	Y	Y	Y	Y	N
2 ***Ehrlich***	Y	N	Y	Y	Y	Y	N
3 Cardin	N	Y	N	N	N	Y	Y
4 Wynn	N	Y	N	N	N	Y	Y
5 Hoyer	N	Y	N	N	N	Y	Y
6 ***Bartlett***	Y	N	Y	Y	Y	N	N
7 Cummings	N	Y	N	N	N	Y	Y
8 ***Morella***	N	N	N	Y	Y	?	N
MASSACHUSETTS							
1 Olver	N	Y	N	N	N	?	#
2 Neal	N	Y	N	N	N	Y	Y
3 McGovern	N	Y	N	N	N	Y	Y
4 Frank	N	Y	N	N	N	Y	Y
5 Meehan	N	Y	N	N	N	Y	Y
6 Tierney	N	Y	N	N	N	Y	Y
7 Markey	N	Y	N	N	N	Y	Y
8 Kennedy	N	Y	N	N	N	Y	Y
9 Moakley	?	#	X	?	N	Y	Y
10 Delahunt	N	Y	N	N	N	Y	Y
MICHIGAN							
1 Stupak	N	Y	N	N	N	N	Y
2 ***Hoekstra***	Y	N	Y	Y	N	N	N
3 ***Ehlers***	Y	N	Y	Y	Y	Y	N
4 ***Camp***	Y	N	Y	Y	Y	Y	N
5 Barcia	N	Y	Y	N	N	Y	Y
6 ***Upton***	Y	N	Y	Y	Y	Y	N
7 ***Smith***	Y	Y	Y	Y	N	P	N
8 Stabenow	N	Y	N	N	N	Y	Y
9 Kildee	N	Y	N	N	N	Y	Y
10 Bonior	N	Y	N	N	N	N	Y
11 ***Knollenberg***	Y	N	Y	Y	Y	Y	N
12 Levin	N	Y	N	N	N	Y	Y
13 Rivers	N	Y	N	N	N	Y	Y
14 Conyers	N	Y	N	N	N	Y	Y
15 Kilpatrick	N	Y	N	N	N	Y	Y
16 Dingell	N	Y	N	N	N	Y	Y

	462	463	464	465	466	467	468
MINNESOTA							
1 ***Gutknecht***	N	N	Y	Y	Y	N	N
2 Minge	N	Y	N	N	Y	Y	Y
3 ***Ramstad***	Y	N	Y	Y	Y	N	N
4 Vento	N	Y	N	N	N	Y	Y
5 Sabo	N	N	N	N	N	N	N
6 Luther	N	Y	N	N	N	Y	Y
7 Peterson	N	Y	N	N	N	Y	Y
8 Oberstar	N	Y	N	N	N	N	Y
MISSISSIPPI							
1 ***Wicker***	Y	N	Y	Y	Y	N	N
2 Thompson	N	Y	N	N	N	N	Y
3 ***Pickering***	Y	N	Y	Y	Y	?	N
4 ***Parker***	Y	N	Y	Y	Y	Y	N
5 Taylor	N	Y	Y	N	N	?	#
MISSOURI							
1 Clay	N	Y	N	N	N	N	Y
2 ***Talent***	Y	N	Y	Y	Y	Y	N
3 Gephardt	N	Y	N	N	N	?	Y
4 Skelton	N	Y	N	N	Y	Y	Y
5 McCarthy	N	Y	N	N	N	Y	Y
6 Danner	N	Y	Y	N	N	Y	Y
7 ***Blunt***	Y	N	Y	Y	Y	Y	N
8 ***Emerson***	Y	Y	Y	Y	Y	Y	N
9 ***Hulshof***	Y	N	Y	Y	Y	N	N
MONTANA							
AL ***Hill***	Y	N	N	Y	N	Y	N
NEBRASKA							
1 ***Bereuter***	Y	N	Y	Y	Y	Y	N
2 ***Christensen***	Y	N	Y	Y	Y	Y	N
3 ***Barrett***	Y	N	Y	Y	Y	Y	N
NEVADA							
1 ***Ensign***	Y	N	Y	Y	N	N	N
2 ***Gibbons***	Y	N	Y	Y	N	N	N
NEW HAMPSHIRE							
1 ***Sununu***	Y	N	Y	Y	Y	Y	N
2 ***Bass***	Y	N	Y	Y	Y	Y	N
NEW JERSEY							
1 Andrews	N	Y	N	N	N	Y	Y
2 ***LoBiondo***	Y	N	Y	Y	N	N	N
3 ***Saxton***	Y	N	Y	Y	+	+	−
4 ***Smith***	Y	N	Y	Y	N	Y	N
5 ***Roukema***	Y	N	Y	Y	Y	Y	N
6 Pallone	N	Y	N	N	N	Y	Y
7 ***Franks***	Y	N	Y	Y	Y	Y	N
8 Pascrell	N	Y	N	N	N	Y	Y
9 Rothman	N	Y	N	N	N	Y	Y
10 Payne	N	Y	N	?	N	?	Y
11 ***Frelinghuysen***	Y	N	Y	Y	Y	Y	N
12 ***Pappas***	Y	N	Y	Y	Y	Y	N
13 Menendez	N	Y	N	N	N	Y	Y
NEW MEXICO							
1 ***Wilson***	Y	N	Y	Y	Y	Y	N
2 ***Skeen***	Y	N	Y	Y	Y	Y	N
3 ***Redmond***	Y	N	Y	Y	Y	Y	N
NEW YORK							
1 ***Forbes***	Y	Y	Y	Y	N	Y	N
2 ***Lazio***	Y	N	Y	Y	Y	Y	N
3 ***King***	Y	N	Y	Y	Y	Y	N
4 McCarthy	Y	Y	Y	N	N	Y	Y
5 Ackerman	N	Y	N	N	N	Y	Y
6 Meeks	?	Y	N	N	N	Y	Y
7 Manton	N	Y	N	N	N	Y	Y
8 Nadler	N	Y	N	N	N	Y	Y
9 Schumer	N	Y	N	N	N	Y	Y
10 Towns	N	Y	N	N	N	?	Y
11 Owens	N	Y	N	N	N	Y	Y
12 Velázquez	N	Y	N	N	N	N	Y
13 ***Fossella***	Y	N	Y	Y	Y	Y	N
14 Maloney	N	Y	N	N	N	Y	Y
15 Rangel	N	Y	N	N	N	Y	Y
16 Serrano	N	Y	N	N	N	Y	Y
17 Engel	N	Y	N	N	N	Y	Y
18 Lowey	N	Y	N	N	N	Y	Y
19 ***Kelly***	Y	N	Y	Y	N	Y	N
20 ***Gilman***	Y	N	Y	Y	N	Y	N
21 McNulty	N	Y	N	N	N	N	Y
22 ***Solomon***	Y	N	Y	Y	Y	Y	N
23 ***Boehlert***	Y	N	Y	Y	N	Y	N
24 ***McHugh***	Y	N	Y	Y	N	Y	N
25 ***Walsh***	Y	N	Y	Y	N	Y	N
26 Hinchey	N	Y	N	N	N	N	Y
27 ***Paxon***	Y	N	Y	Y	Y	Y	N
28 Slaughter	N	Y	N	N	N	N	Y
29 LaFalce	N	Y	N	N	N	N	Y
30 ***Quinn***	Y	N	Y	Y	N	Y	N

	462	463	464	465	466	467	468
31 ***Houghton***	Y	N	Y	Y	Y	Y	N
NORTH CAROLINA							
1 Clayton	N	Y	N	N	N	Y	Y
2 Etheridge	N	Y	N	N	Y	Y	Y
3 ***Jones***	Y	N	Y	Y	N	N	N
4 Price	N	Y	N	N	Y	Y	Y
5 ***Burr***	Y	N	Y	Y	Y	Y	N
6 ***Coble***	Y	N	Y	Y	N	Y	N
7 McIntyre	N	Y	N	N	N	Y	Y
8 Hefner	N	Y	N	N	N	Y	Y
9 ***Myrick***	Y	N	Y	Y	Y	Y	N
10 ***Ballenger***	Y	N	Y	Y	Y	Y	N
11 ***Taylor***	Y	N	Y	Y	N	Y	N
12 Watt	N	Y	N	N	N	Y	Y
NORTH DAKOTA							
AL Pomeroy	N	Y	N	N	N	Y	Y
OHIO							
1 ***Chabot***	Y	N	Y	Y	Y	Y	N
2 ***Portman***	Y	N	Y	Y	Y	Y	N
3 Hall	N	Y	N	N	N	Y	Y
4 ***Oxley***	Y	N	Y	Y	Y	Y	N
5 ***Gillmor***	Y	N	Y	Y	Y	Y	N
6 Strickland	N	Y	N	N	N	Y	Y
7 ***Hobson***	Y	N	Y	Y	Y	Y	N
8 ***Boehner***	Y	N	Y	Y	Y	Y	N
9 Kaptur	N	Y	N	N	N	?	Y
10 Kucinich	N	Y	N	N	N	N	Y
11 Stokes	N	Y	N	N	N	Y	Y
12 ***Kasich***	Y	N	Y	Y	Y	?	N
13 Brown	N	Y	?	N	N	Y	Y
14 Sawyer	N	Y	N	N	Y	Y	Y
15 ***Pryce***	+	−	+	+	+	+	−
16 ***Regula***	Y	N	Y	Y	N	Y	N
17 Traficant	Y	Y	N	N	N	Y	Y
18 ***Ney***	Y	N	Y	Y	N	Y	N
19 ***LaTourette***	Y	N	Y	Y	N	Y	N
OKLAHOMA							
1 ***Largent***	Y	N	Y	Y	Y	Y	N
2 ***Coburn***	N	N	Y	Y	N	?	?
3 ***Watkins***	Y	N	Y	Y	Y	Y	N
4 ***Watts***	Y	N	Y	Y	Y	Y	N
5 ***Istook***	Y	N	Y	Y	Y	Y	N
6 ***Lucas***	Y	N	Y	Y	Y	Y	N
OREGON							
1 Furse	N	Y	N	?	?	?	?
2 ***Smith***	Y	N	Y	Y	Y	Y	N
3 Blumenauer	N	Y	N	N	P	Y	Y
4 DeFazio	N	Y	N	N	N	N	Y
5 Hooley	N	Y	Y	N	Y	Y	Y
PENNSYLVANIA							
1 Brady	N	Y	N	N	N	N	Y
2 Fattah	N	Y	N	N	N	N	Y
3 Borski	N	Y	N	N	N	N	Y
4 Klink	N	Y	N	N	N	N	Y
5 ***Peterson***	Y	N	Y	Y	Y	Y	N
6 Holden	N	Y	N	N	N	Y	Y
7 ***Weldon***	Y	N	Y	Y	N	Y	N
8 ***Greenwood***	Y	N	Y	Y	Y	Y	N
9 ***Shuster***	Y	N	Y	Y	N	Y	N
10 ***McDade***	?	N	Y	Y	N	?	N
11 Kanjorski	N	Y	N	N	N	Y	Y
12 Murtha	N	Y	N	N	N	Y	Y
13 ***Fox***	Y	N	Y	Y	N	N	N
14 Coyne	N	Y	N	N	N	Y	Y
15 McHale	N	Y	N	N	N	Y	Y
16 ***Pitts***	Y	N	Y	Y	Y	Y	N
17 ***Gekas***	Y	N	Y	Y	Y	Y	N
18 Doyle	N	Y	N	N	N	?	Y
19 ***Goodling***	Y	N	Y	Y	N	Y	N
20 Mascara	N	Y	N	N	N	Y	Y
21 ***English***	Y	N	Y	?	N	N	N
RHODE ISLAND							
1 Kennedy	N	Y	N	N	N	Y	Y
2 Weygand	N	Y	N	N	N	Y	Y
SOUTH CAROLINA							
1 ***Sanford***	N	N	N	Y	Y	Y	N
2 ***Spence***	Y	N	Y	Y	N	Y	N
3 ***Graham***	Y	N	Y	Y	Y	Y	N
4 ***Inglis***	Y	N	Y	Y	Y	Y	N
5 Spratt	N	Y	N	N	N	Y	Y
6 Clyburn	N	Y	N	N	N	N	Y
SOUTH DAKOTA							
AL ***Thune***	Y	N	Y	Y	Y	Y	N

	462	463	464	465	466	467	468
TENNESSEE							
1 ***Jenkins***	Y	N	Y	Y	N	Y	N
2 ***Duncan***	Y	N	Y	Y	N	Y	N
3 ***Wamp***	Y	N	Y	Y	N	Y	N
4 ***Hilleary***	Y	N	Y	Y	N	Y	N
5 Clement	N	Y	N	N	Y	?	Y
6 Gordon	N	Y	Y	N	N	Y	Y
7 ***Bryant***	Y	N	Y	Y	Y	Y	N
8 Tanner	N	Y	N	Y	Y	Y	Y
9 Ford	N	Y	N	N	Y	Y	Y
TEXAS							
1 Sandlin	N	Y	Y	N	N	Y	Y
2 Turner	N	Y	Y	N	N	Y	Y
3 ***Johnson, Sam***	Y	N	Y	Y	Y	Y	N
4 Hall	N	Y	Y	Y	Y	Y	Y
5 ***Sessions***	Y	N	Y	Y	Y	Y	N
6 ***Barton***	Y	N	Y	Y	Y	?	N
7 ***Archer***	Y	N	Y	Y	Y	Y	N
8 ***Brady***	Y	N	Y	Y	Y	Y	N
9 Lampson	N	Y	N	N	N	Y	Y
10 Doggett	N	Y	N	N	N	Y	Y
11 Edwards	N	Y	N	N	Y	Y	Y
12 ***Granger***	Y	N	Y	Y	Y	Y	N
13 ***Thornberry***	?	N	Y	Y	Y	Y	N
14 ***Paul***	?	N	Y	Y	N	Y	N
15 Hinojosa	N	Y	N	N	N	Y	Y
16 Reyes	N	Y	N	N	N	P	Y
17 Stenholm	N	Y	N	Y	Y	Y	Y
18 Jackson-Lee	N	Y	N	N	N	Y	Y
19 ***Combest***	Y	N	Y	Y	Y	Y	N
20 Gonzalez	N	Y	N	N	N	?	Y
21 ***Smith***	Y	N	Y	Y	Y	Y	N
22 ***DeLay***	Y	N	Y	Y	Y	Y	N
23 ***Bonilla***	Y	N	Y	Y	Y	Y	N
24 Frost	N	Y	N	N	N	Y	Y
25 Bentsen	N	Y	N	N	Y	?	Y
26 ***Armey***	Y	N	Y	Y	Y	Y	N
27 Ortiz	N	Y	N	N	Y	Y	Y
28 Rodriguez	N	Y	N	N	N	Y	Y
29 Green	N	Y	N	N	N	N	Y
30 Johnson, E.B.	N	Y	N	N	Y	N	Y
UTAH							
1 ***Hansen***	Y	N	Y	Y	Y	Y	N
2 ***Cook***	Y	N	Y	Y	N	Y	N
3 ***Cannon***	Y	N	Y	Y	Y	Y	N
VERMONT							
AL *Sanders*	N	Y	N	N	N	Y	Y
VIRGINIA							
1 ***Bateman***	Y	N	Y	Y	Y	?	N
2 Pickett	N	Y	N	N	Y	N	Y
3 Scott	N	Y	N	N	N	Y	Y
4 Sisisky	N	Y	N	N	N	Y	Y
5 Goode	N	Y	Y	N	N	Y	Y
6 ***Goodlatte***	Y	N	Y	Y	Y	Y	N
7 ***Bliley***	Y	N	Y	Y	Y	Y	N
8 Moran	N	Y	N	N	Y	Y	Y
9 Boucher	N	Y	N	N	N	Y	Y
10 ***Wolf***	Y	N	Y	Y	N	Y	N
11 ***Davis***	Y	N	Y	Y	Y	Y	N
WASHINGTON							
1 ***White***	Y	Y	Y	Y	Y	Y	N
2 ***Metcalf***	Y	N	Y	Y	N	Y	N
3 ***Smith, Linda***	N	Y	Y	Y	N	Y	N
4 ***Hastings***	Y	N	Y	Y	Y	Y	N
5 ***Nethercutt***	Y	N	Y	Y	Y	Y	N
6 Dicks	N	Y	N	N	Y	Y	Y
7 McDermott	N	Y	N	N	Y	N	Y
8 ***Dunn***	Y	N	Y	Y	Y	Y	N
9 Smith, Adam	N	Y	N	N	N	Y	Y
WEST VIRGINIA							
1 Mollohan	N	Y	N	N	N	Y	Y
2 Wise	N	Y	N	N	N	Y	Y
3 Rahall	N	Y	N	N	N	Y	Y
WISCONSIN							
1 ***Neumann***	N	Y	Y	Y	N	Y	N
2 ***Klug***	Y	N	Y	Y	Y	Y	N
3 Kind	N	Y	N	N	N	Y	Y
4 Kleczka	N	Y	N	N	N	Y	Y
5 Barrett	N	Y	N	N	N	Y	Y
6 ***Petri***	Y	N	Y	Y	Y	Y	N
7 Obey	N	Y	N	N	N	Y	Y
8 Johnson	N	Y	N	N	N	Y	Y
9 ***Sensenbrenner***	Y	N	Y	Y	Y	Y	N
WYOMING							
AL ***Cubin***	?	N	Y	Y	Y	Y	N

Southern states - Ala., Ark., Fla., Ga., Ky., La., Miss., N.C., Okla., S.C., Tenn., Texas, Va.

House Votes 469, 470, 471, 472, 473, 474, 475

Key

- Y Voted for (yea).
- # Paired for.
- + Announced for.
- N Voted against (nay).
- X Paired against.
- – Announced against.
- P Voted "present."
- C Voted "present" to avoid possible conflict of interest.
- ? Did not vote or otherwise make a position known.

Democrats **Republicans**
Independent

469. HR 4579. Tax Cuts/Passage. Passage of the bill to cut taxes by $80.1 billion over five years, including $6.6 billion in cuts in fiscal 1999, by extending expired provisions such as the research tax credit, reducing taxes for farmers and married couples and making health insurance premiums 100 percent deductible for the self-employed. Passed 229-195: R 210-11; D 19-183 (ND 13-135, SD 6-48); I 0-1. Sept. 26, 1998. A "nay" was a vote in support of the president's position.

470. HR 3891. Product Identification Codes/Passage. Goodlatte, R-Va., motion to suspend the rules and pass the bill to establish fines and prison sentences for individuals who are convicted of tampering with or counterfeiting any product identification codes. Motion rejected 245-167: R 177-37; D 68-129 (ND 49-96, SD 19-33); I 0-1. Sept. 28, 1998. A two-thirds majority of those present and voting (275 in this case) is required for passage under suspension of the rules.

471. HR 4103. Fiscal 1999 Defense Appropriations/Conference Report. Adoption of the conference report on the bill to provide $250.5 billion in defense spending for fiscal 1999. Adopted (thus sent to the Senate) 369-43: R 204-10; D 165-32 (ND 115-30, SD 50-2); I 0-1. Sept. 28, 1998.

472. HR 4060. Fiscal 1999 Energy and Water Appropriations/Conference Report. Adoption of the conference report on the bill to provide $20.9 billion for fiscal 1999 spending on water, energy and defense-related projects. The conference report also calls for eliminating certain subsidies for the publicly funded Tennessee Valley Authority (TVA). Adopted (thus sent to the Senate) 389-25: R 199-16; D 189-9 (ND 143-3, SD 46-6); I 1-0. Sept. 28, 1998.

473. HR 3150. Consumer Bankruptcy Revisions/Motion to Instruct. Nadler, D-N.Y., motion to instruct House conferees to accept Senate provisions that would prevent credit card companies from either dropping customers who pay off all their debts each month, or charging them fees. Motion agreed to 295-119: R 100-115; D 194-4 (ND 143-3, SD 51-1); I 1-0. Sept. 28, 1998.

474. S 2073. Juvenile Crime Block Grants/Procedural Motion. Goodling, R-Pa., motion to go to conference on the bill to consolidate juvenile crime prevention funding, including boot camps, gang prevention and mentoring programs, into block grants to the states. The bill would also reauthorize programs to serve runaway and homeless youth and the National Missing Children Center. Motion agreed to 376-36: R 212-0; D 164-35 (ND 116-29, SD 48-6); I 0-1. Oct. 1, 1998.

475. HR 4104. Fiscal 1999 Treasury Postal Appropriations Conference Report/Rule. Adoption of the rule (H Res 563) to provide for House floor consideration of the conference report on the bill to provide about $27 billion in fiscal 1999 funding for the Treasury Department, U.S. Postal Service subsidies, the Executive Office of the President and several independent agencies. Rejected 106-294: R 89-117; D 17-176 (ND 13-127, SD 4-49); I 0-1. Oct. 1, 1998.

	469	470	471	472	473	474	475
ALABAMA							
1 Callahan	#	?	?	?	?	?	?
2 Everett	Y	Y	Y	Y	N	Y	Y
3 Riley	Y	Y	Y	Y	N	Y	N
4 Aderholt	N	Y	Y	N	Y	Y	Y
5 Cramer	Y	Y	Y	Y	Y	Y	N
6 Bachus	Y	N	Y	N	Y	Y	Y
7 Hilliard	N	N	Y	Y	Y	N	N
ALASKA							
AL Young	Y	Y	Y	Y	N	Y	Y
ARIZONA							
1 Salmon	Y	Y	Y	Y	Y	Y	Y
2 Pastor	N	N	Y	Y	Y	Y	N
3 Stump	Y	Y	Y	Y	N	Y	Y
4 Shadegg	Y	Y	Y	Y	Y	Y	N
5 Kolbe	Y	N	Y	Y	Y	Y	N
6 Hayworth	Y	Y	Y	Y	Y	Y	N
ARKANSAS							
1 Berry	N	N	Y	Y	Y	Y	N
2 Snyder	N	N	Y	Y	Y	Y	N
3 Hutchinson	Y	Y	Y	Y	Y	Y	N
4 Dickey	Y	N	Y	Y	N	Y	N
CALIFORNIA							
1 Riggs	Y	Y	Y	Y	N	Y	N
2 Herger	Y	Y	Y	Y	N	Y	N
3 Fazio	N	Y	Y	Y	Y	Y	N
4 Doolittle	Y	Y	Y	Y	N	Y	N
5 Matsui	N	Y	Y	Y	Y	Y	N
6 Woolsey	N	Y	Y	Y	Y	Y	N
7 Miller	N	?	?	?	?	Y	N
8 Pelosi	N	N	Y	Y	Y	N	N
9 Lee	N	N	N	Y	Y	N	N
10 Tauscher	Y	Y	Y	Y	Y	Y	N
11 Pombo	Y	Y	Y	Y	N	Y	N
12 Lantos	N	N	Y	Y	Y	Y	N
13 Stark	N	N	N	Y	Y	N	?
14 Eshoo	N	Y	Y	Y	Y	Y	N
15 Campbell	Y	N	Y	N	Y	Y	N
16 Lofgren	N	Y	N	Y	Y	N	N
17 Farr	N	Y	Y	Y	Y	N	N
18 Condit	Y	Y	Y	Y	Y	Y	N
19 Radanovich	Y	Y	Y	Y	N	Y	N
20 Dooley	N	Y	Y	N	Y	Y	N
21 Thomas	Y	Y	Y	Y	N	Y	?
22 Capps, L.	Y	Y	Y	Y	Y	Y	N
23 Gallegly	Y	Y	Y	Y	Y	Y	N
24 Sherman	Y	N	Y	Y	Y	Y	N
25 McKeon	Y	Y	Y	N	Y	Y	N
26 Berman	X	N	Y	Y	N	Y	N
27 Rogan	Y	Y	Y	Y	Y	Y	N
28 Dreier	Y	N	Y	Y	N	Y	N
29 Waxman	N	N	Y	Y	Y	Y	N
30 Becerra	N	N	Y	Y	Y	Y	N
31 Martinez	N	?	?	?	?	Y	N
32 Dixon	N	N	Y	Y	Y	Y	N
33 Roybal-Allard	N	N	Y	Y	Y	N	N
34 Torres	N	N	Y	Y	Y	Y	N
35 Waters	N	N	?	Y	Y	N	N
36 Harman	Y	Y	Y	Y	Y	Y	N
37 Millender-McD.	N	N	Y	Y	Y	Y	N
38 Horn	Y	Y	Y	Y	Y	Y	N
39 Royce	Y	Y	Y	N	Y	Y	N
40 Lewis	Y	Y	+	Y	N	Y	Y
41 Kim	Y	Y	Y	Y	N	Y	Y
42 Brown	N	Y	Y	Y	Y	Y	N
43 Calvert	Y	N	Y	Y	N	Y	N
44 Bono, M.	Y	Y	Y	Y	N	Y	N
45 Rohrabacher	Y	N	Y	N	N	Y	N
46 Sanchez	N	N	Y	Y	Y	Y	N
47 Cox	Y	N	Y	Y	Y	Y	N
48 Packard	Y	Y	Y	Y	N	+	+
49 Bilbray	Y	Y	Y	Y	Y	Y	N
50 Filner	N	N	N	Y	Y	N	N
51 Cunningham	Y	Y	Y	Y	N	?	Y
52 Hunter	Y	Y	Y	Y	N	Y	N
COLORADO							
1 DeGette	N	N	Y	Y	Y	Y	N
2 Skaggs	N	N	Y	Y	Y	Y	N
3 McInnis	Y	Y	Y	Y	N	?	Y
4 Schaffer	Y	Y	Y	Y	N	Y	N
5 Hefley	Y	Y	N	Y	N	Y	N
6 Schaefer	Y	Y	Y	Y	N	Y	N
CONNECTICUT							
1 Kennelly	Y	?	?	?	?	?	?
2 Gejdenson	N	N	Y	N	Y	Y	N
3 DeLauro	N	N	Y	Y	Y	Y	N
4 Shays	Y	N	N	Y	N	Y	Y
5 Maloney	Y	Y	Y	Y	N	Y	N
6 Johnson	Y	Y	Y	Y	N	Y	Y
DELAWARE							
AL Castle	N	Y	Y	Y	Y	Y	Y
FLORIDA							
1 Scarborough	Y	Y	Y	Y	Y	Y	Y
2 Boyd	N	Y	Y	Y	Y	Y	N
3 Brown	N	?	?	?	?	Y	Y
4 Fowler	#	?	?	?	?	?	?
5 Thurman	N	N	Y	Y	Y	Y	N
6 Stearns	Y	Y	N	N	Y	Y	N
7 Mica	Y	N	Y	Y	N	Y	Y
8 McCollum	Y	Y	Y	Y	N	Y	Y
9 Bilirakis	Y	N	Y	Y	N	Y	Y
10 Young	Y	Y	Y	Y	N	Y	?
11 Davis	N	N	Y	Y	Y	Y	N
12 Canady	Y	Y	Y	Y	Y	Y	Y
13 Miller	Y	N	Y	N	Y	Y	N
14 Goss	+	+	+	+	–	+	+
15 Weldon	Y	Y	Y	Y	Y	Y	N
16 Foley	Y	N	Y	Y	N	Y	Y
17 Meek	N	N	Y	Y	Y	Y	N
18 Ros-Lehtinen	Y	–	?	?	?	Y	Y
19 Wexler	N	N	Y	Y	Y	Y	N
20 Deutsch	N	N	Y	Y	Y	Y	N
21 Diaz-Balart	Y	N	Y	Y	Y	Y	Y
22 Shaw	Y	N	Y	Y	N	Y	N
23 Hastings	N	N	Y	Y	Y	Y	N
GEORGIA							
1 Kingston	Y	Y	Y	Y	Y	Y	Y
2 Bishop	N	Y	Y	Y	Y	Y	N
3 Collins	Y	Y	Y	Y	N	Y	Y
4 McKinney	N	N	N	Y	N	N	N
5 Lewis	N	N	Y	Y	Y	N	N
6 Gingrich	Y						
7 Barr	Y	Y	Y	Y	N	Y	Y
8 Chambliss	Y	Y	Y	Y	N	Y	Y
9 Deal	Y	Y	Y	Y	N	?	?
10 Norwood	Y	Y	Y	Y	N	Y	N
11 Linder	Y	Y	Y	Y	N	Y	Y
HAWAII							
1 Abercrombie	N	Y	Y	Y	Y	Y	N
2 Mink	N	Y	Y	Y	Y	N	N
IDAHO							
1 Chenoweth	N	Y	Y	N	N	Y	N
2 Crapo	Y	Y	Y	Y	N	Y	N
ILLINOIS							
1 Rush	N	N	Y	Y	Y	Y	N
2 Jackson	N	N	N	Y	Y	Y	N
3 Lipinski	N	Y	Y	Y	Y	Y	N
4 Gutierrez	N	N	N	Y	Y	Y	N
5 Blagojevich	N	N	Y	Y	Y	Y	N
6 Hyde	Y	Y	Y	Y	N	Y	Y
7 Davis	N	N	Y	Y	Y	Y	N
8 Crane	Y	Y	Y	N	N	?	N
9 Yates	N	N	Y	Y	Y	N	?
10 Porter	Y	Y	Y	Y	N	Y	Y
11 Weller	Y	N	Y	Y	N	Y	Y
12 Costello	N	N	Y	Y	Y	Y	N
13 Fawell	Y	Y	Y	Y	Y	?	?

ND Northern Democrats   SD Southern Democrats

	469	470	471	472	473	474	475
14 ***Hastert***	Y	N	Y	Y	Y	Y	Y
15 ***Ewing***	Y	Y	Y	Y	Y	Y	N
16 ***Manzullo***	Y	N	Y	Y	N	Y	N
17 Evans	N	Y	Y	Y	Y	Y	N
18 ***LaHood***	N	Y	Y	Y	Y	Y	N
19 Poshard	N	?	?	?	?	?	?
20 ***Shimkus***	Y	Y	Y	Y	Y	Y	N
INDIANA							
1 Visclosky	N	N	Y	Y	Y	Y	N
2 ***McIntosh***	Y	Y	Y	Y	N	Y	N
3 Roemer	Y	Y	Y	N	Y	Y	N
4 ***Souder***	Y	Y	Y	Y	Y	Y	N
5 ***Buyer***	Y	Y	Y	Y	Y	Y	N
6 ***Burton***	#	Y	Y	Y	N	Y	Y
7 ***Pease***	Y	Y	Y	Y	N	Y	N
8 ***Hostettler***	Y	Y	Y	Y	N	Y	N
9 Hamilton	N	Y	Y	Y	Y	Y	N
10 Carson	N	Y	Y	Y	Y	Y	N
IOWA							
1 ***Leach***	Y	N	Y	Y	N	Y	N
2 ***Nussle***	Y	Y	Y	Y	N	Y	N
3 Boswell	Y	Y	Y	Y	Y	Y	Y
4 ***Ganske***	Y	Y	Y	Y	Y	Y	Y
5 ***Latham***	Y	Y	Y	Y	N	Y	N
KANSAS							
1 ***Moran***	Y	Y	Y	Y	Y	Y	Y
2 ***Ryun***	Y	Y	Y	Y	N	Y	N
3 ***Snowbarger***	Y	N	Y	Y	N	Y	N
4 ***Tiahrt***	Y	Y	Y	Y	N	Y	N
KENTUCKY							
1 ***Whitfield***	Y	Y	Y	Y	Y	Y	N
2 ***Lewis***	Y	Y	Y	Y	Y	Y	N
3 ***Northup***	Y	Y	Y	Y	Y	Y	Y
4 ***Bunning***	Y	Y	Y	Y	Y	Y	N
5 ***Rogers***	Y	Y	Y	Y	Y	Y	N
6 Baesler	N	Y	Y	Y	Y	Y	N
LOUISIANA							
1 ***Livingston***	Y	N	Y	Y	Y	Y	?
2 Jefferson	N	Y	Y	Y	Y	Y	N
3 ***Tauzin***	Y	Y	Y	Y	Y	Y	?
4 ***McCrery***	Y	Y	Y	Y	N	?	Y
5 ***Cooksey***	Y	Y	Y	Y	N	Y	N
6 ***Baker***	Y	?	?	?	?	Y	N
7 John	N	?	?	?	?	Y	N
MAINE							
1 Allen	N	N	Y	Y	Y	Y	N
2 Baldacci	N	N	Y	Y	Y	Y	N
MARYLAND							
1 ***Gilchrest***	Y	Y	Y	Y	N	Y	Y
2 ***Ehrlich***	Y	Y	Y	Y	Y	Y	Y
3 Cardin	N	Y	Y	Y	Y	Y	N
4 Wynn	N	N	Y	Y	Y	N	N
5 Hoyer	N	Y	Y	Y	Y	Y	N
6 ***Bartlett***	Y	Y	Y	Y	N	Y	N
7 Cummings	N	Y	Y	Y	Y	Y	N
8 ***Morella***	N	Y	Y	Y	Y	Y	Y
MASSACHUSETTS							
1 Olver	X	N	Y	Y	Y	N	Y
2 Neal	N	?	Y	Y	Y	Y	Y
3 McGovern	N	N	Y	Y	Y	Y	Y
4 Frank	N	Y	N	Y	Y	Y	N
5 Meehan	N	N	Y	Y	Y	Y	N
6 Tierney	N	N	Y	Y	Y	Y	N
7 Markey	N	N	Y	Y	Y	Y	N
8 Kennedy	N	N	Y	Y	Y	Y	N
9 Moakley	N	N	Y	Y	Y	Y	N
10 Delahunt	N	Y	N	Y	Y	N	N
MICHIGAN							
1 Stupak	N	N	Y	Y	Y	Y	N
2 ***Hoekstra***	Y	N	N	Y	Y	Y	N
3 ***Ehlers***	Y	Y	Y	Y	Y	Y	N
4 ***Camp***	Y	Y	Y	Y	N	Y	Y
5 Barcia	Y	N	Y	Y	Y	Y	N
6 ***Upton***	Y	Y	N	Y	Y	Y	Y
7 ***Smith***	Y	N	Y	Y	Y	Y	N
8 Stabenow	N	Y	Y	Y	Y	Y	N
9 Kildee	N	N	Y	Y	Y	Y	N
10 Bonior	N	N	Y	Y	Y	N	N
11 ***Knollenberg***	Y	Y	Y	Y	N	Y	Y
12 Levin	N	N	Y	Y	Y	Y	N
13 Rivers	N	N	N	Y	Y	Y	N
14 Conyers	N	N	N	Y	Y	N	Y
15 Kilpatrick	N	N	Y	Y	Y	Y	N
16 Dingell	N	N	Y	Y	Y	Y	N

	469	470	471	472	473	474	475
MINNESOTA							
1 ***Gutknecht***	N	Y	Y	Y	Y	Y	Y
2 Minge	N	N	N	Y	Y	Y	N
3 ***Ramstad***	Y	Y	Y	Y	Y	Y	Y
4 Vento	N	N	N	Y	Y	Y	N
5 Sabo	N	N	Y	Y	Y	N	N
6 Luther	N	N	N	Y	Y	Y	N
7 Peterson	N	Y	Y	Y	Y	Y	N
8 Oberstar	N	N	N	Y	Y	N	N
MISSISSIPPI							
1 ***Wicker***	Y	Y	Y	Y	Y	Y	Y
2 Thompson	N	N	Y	Y	Y	?	N
3 ***Pickering***	Y	Y	Y	N	Y	Y	N
4 ***Parker***	Y	Y	Y	Y	N	Y	Y
5 Taylor	X	–	+	+	+	Y	N
MISSOURI							
1 Clay	N	N	Y	Y	Y	Y	?
2 ***Talent***	Y	Y	Y	Y	Y	Y	N
3 Gephardt	N	N	Y	Y	Y	Y	N
4 Skelton	N	N	Y	Y	Y	Y	N
5 McCarthy	N	N	Y	Y	Y	Y	N
6 Danner	Y	N	Y	Y	Y	Y	N
7 ***Blunt***	Y	Y	Y	N	Y	Y	Y
8 ***Emerson***	N	Y	Y	Y	Y	Y	N
9 ***Hulshof***	Y	Y	Y	Y	Y	?	Y
MONTANA							
AL ***Hill***	N	Y	Y	Y	N	Y	N
NEBRASKA							
1 ***Bereuter***	Y	Y	Y	Y	Y	Y	N
2 ***Christensen***	Y	?	?	?	?	Y	N
3 ***Barrett***	Y	Y	Y	Y	Y	Y	N
NEVADA							
1 ***Ensign***	Y	N	Y	N	Y	Y	Y
2 ***Gibbons***	Y	Y	Y	N	N	Y	Y
NEW HAMPSHIRE							
1 ***Sununu***	Y	Y	Y	Y	N	Y	N
2 ***Bass***	Y	Y	Y	Y	Y	Y	Y
NEW JERSEY							
1 Andrews	N	N	Y	Y	Y	Y	N
2 ***LoBiondo***	Y	Y	Y	Y	Y	Y	N
3 ***Saxton***	+	Y	Y	Y	Y	Y	N
4 ***Smith***	Y	Y	Y	Y	N	Y	N
5 ***Roukema***	Y	Y	Y	Y	N	Y	?
6 Pallone	N	N	Y	Y	Y	Y	N
7 ***Franks***	Y	Y	N	Y	Y	Y	N
8 Pascrell	N	N	Y	Y	Y	Y	N
9 Rothman	N	Y	Y	Y	Y	?	N
10 Payne	N	N	N	Y	Y	N	N
11 ***Frelinghuysen***	Y	Y	Y	Y	N	Y	Y
12 ***Pappas***	Y	Y	Y	Y	Y	Y	N
13 Menendez	N	Y	Y	Y	Y	Y	N
NEW MEXICO							
1 ***Wilson***	Y	Y	Y	Y	Y	Y	Y
2 ***Skeen***	Y	Y	Y	Y	N	Y	N
3 ***Redmond***	Y	Y	Y	Y	Y	Y	N
NEW YORK							
1 ***Forbes***	Y	N	Y	Y	Y	Y	Y
2 ***Lazio***	Y	N	Y	Y	Y	Y	Y
3 ***King***	Y	N	Y	Y	N	?	?
4 McCarthy	Y	N	Y	Y	Y	Y	Y
5 Ackerman	N	N	Y	Y	Y	Y	N
6 Meeks	N	N	Y	Y	Y	Y	N
7 Manton	N	N	Y	Y	Y	Y	N
8 Nadler	N	N	N	Y	Y	N	N
9 Schumer	N	?	?	?	?	Y	Y
10 Towns	N	N	Y	Y	Y	Y	?
11 Owens	N	N	N	Y	Y	N	Y
12 Velázquez	N	N	N	Y	Y	Y	N
13 ***Fossella***	Y	N	Y	Y	N	+	N
14 Maloney	N	Y	Y	Y	Y	Y	Y
15 Rangel	N	N	Y	Y	Y	Y	N
16 Serrano	N	N	Y	Y	Y	Y	N
17 Engel	N	N	Y	Y	Y	Y	Y
18 Lowey	N	N	Y	Y	Y	Y	Y
19 ***Kelly***	Y	N	Y	Y	N	Y	Y
20 ***Gilman***	Y	N	Y	Y	Y	Y	Y
21 McNulty	N	Y	Y	Y	Y	Y	N
22 ***Solomon***	Y	N	Y	Y	N	Y	Y
23 ***Boehlert***	Y	Y	Y	Y	Y	Y	Y
24 ***McHugh***	Y	Y	Y	Y	Y	Y	N
25 ***Walsh***	Y	Y	Y	Y	Y	Y	?
26 Hinchey	N	Y	Y	Y	Y	N	N
27 ***Paxon***	Y	?	?	?	?	Y	Y
28 Slaughter	N	N	Y	Y	Y	N	N
29 LaFalce	N	N	Y	Y	Y	Y	N
30 ***Quinn***	Y	Y	Y	Y	Y	?	N

	469	470	471	472	473	474	475
31 ***Houghton***	Y	Y	Y	Y	N	Y	Y
NORTH CAROLINA							
1 Clayton	N	N	Y	Y	Y	Y	N
2 Etheridge	N	Y	Y	Y	Y	Y	N
3 ***Jones***	Y	Y	Y	Y	N	Y	N
4 Price	N	N	Y	Y	Y	Y	Y
5 ***Burr***	Y	Y	Y	Y	N	Y	Y
6 ***Coble***	Y	Y	Y	Y	N	Y	Y
7 McIntyre	N	Y	Y	Y	Y	Y	N
8 Hefner	N	N	Y	Y	Y	Y	N
9 ***Myrick***	Y	Y	Y	Y	N	Y	Y
10 ***Ballenger***	Y	Y	Y	Y	N	Y	N
11 ***Taylor***	Y	Y	Y	Y	N	Y	Y
12 Watt	N	N	Y	Y	Y	Y	N
NORTH DAKOTA							
AL Pomeroy	N	N	Y	Y	Y	Y	N
OHIO							
1 ***Chabot***	Y	N	Y	Y	N	Y	N
2 ***Portman***	Y	Y	Y	Y	Y	Y	N
3 Hall	N	N	Y	Y	Y	Y	?
4 ***Oxley***	Y	Y	Y	Y	N	Y	?
5 ***Gillmor***	Y	Y	Y	Y	N	Y	Y
6 Strickland	N	Y	Y	Y	Y	Y	N
7 ***Hobson***	Y	Y	Y	Y	Y	Y	Y
8 ***Boehner***	Y	Y	Y	Y	N	Y	Y
9 Kaptur	N	Y	Y	Y	Y	Y	N
10 Kucinich	N	Y	N	Y	Y	Y	N
11 Stokes	N	N	Y	Y	Y	Y	N
12 ***Kasich***	Y	Y	Y	Y	N	Y	N
13 Brown	N	N	Y	Y	Y	Y	N
14 Sawyer	N	N	Y	Y	Y	Y	N
15 ***Pryce***	+	+	+	+	+	+	+
16 ***Regula***	Y	Y	Y	Y	Y	Y	Y
17 Traficant	N	N	Y	Y	Y	Y	N
18 ***Ney***	Y	Y	Y	Y	Y	Y	N
19 ***LaTourette***	Y	Y	Y	Y	Y	Y	Y
OKLAHOMA							
1 ***Largent***	Y	?	?	?	Y	Y	?
2 ***Coburn***	?	?	Y	Y	Y	Y	N
3 ***Watkins***	Y	Y	Y	Y	Y	Y	N
4 ***Watts***	Y	Y	Y	Y	N	Y	N
5 ***Istook***	Y	Y	Y	Y	N	Y	Y
6 ***Lucas***	Y	Y	Y	Y	N	Y	N
OREGON							
1 Furse	?	Y	N	Y	Y	N	N
2 ***Smith***	Y	Y	Y	Y	N	Y	?
3 Blumenauer	N	N	N	Y	Y	Y	N
4 DeFazio	N	N	N	Y	Y	N	?
5 Hooley	Y	Y	N	Y	Y	Y	N
PENNSYLVANIA							
1 Brady	N	Y	Y	Y	Y	Y	N
2 Fattah	N	Y	Y	Y	Y	Y	N
3 Borski	N	N	Y	Y	Y	Y	N
4 Klink	N	N	Y	Y	Y	Y	N
5 ***Peterson***	Y	Y	Y	Y	Y	Y	N
6 Holden	N	Y	Y	Y	Y	Y	N
7 ***Weldon***	Y	Y	Y	Y	Y	Y	N
8 ***Greenwood***	Y	Y	Y	Y	Y	Y	Y
9 ***Shuster***	Y	Y	Y	Y	N	Y	?
10 ***McDade***	Y	Y	Y	Y	Y	Y	?
11 Kanjorski	N	N	Y	Y	Y	Y	N
12 Murtha	N	N	Y	Y	Y	Y	?
13 ***Fox***	Y	Y	Y	Y	Y	Y	Y
14 Coyne	N	N	Y	Y	Y	Y	N
15 McHale	N	N	Y	Y	Y	Y	N
16 ***Pitts***	Y	Y	Y	Y	N	Y	N
17 ***Gekas***	Y	Y	Y	Y	N	Y	Y
18 Doyle	N	N	Y	Y	Y	Y	N
19 ***Goodling***	Y	Y	Y	Y	N	Y	N
20 Mascara	N	N	Y	Y	Y	Y	N
21 ***English***	Y	Y	Y	Y	Y	Y	Y
RHODE ISLAND							
1 Kennedy	N	Y	Y	Y	Y	N	N
2 Weygand	N	N	Y	Y	Y	Y	N
SOUTH CAROLINA							
1 ***Sanford***	N	N	N	N	N	Y	N
2 ***Spence***	Y	Y	Y	Y	N	Y	Y
3 ***Graham***	Y	Y	Y	Y	Y	Y	N
4 ***Inglis***	Y	Y	Y	Y	Y	?	N
5 Spratt	N	Y	Y	Y	Y	Y	N
6 Clyburn	N	N	Y	Y	Y	N	N
SOUTH DAKOTA							
AL ***Thune***	Y	Y	Y	Y	Y	Y	N

	469	470	471	472	473	474	475
TENNESSEE							
1 ***Jenkins***	Y	+	+	–	+	Y	Y
2 ***Duncan***	Y	Y	Y	Y	Y	Y	N
3 ***Wamp***	Y	Y	Y	Y	Y	Y	N
4 ***Hilleary***	Y	Y	Y	N	Y	Y	N
5 Clement	N	N	Y	N	Y	Y	?
6 Gordon	Y	Y	Y	N	Y	Y	N
7 ***Bryant***	Y	Y	Y	Y	N	Y	N
8 Tanner	N	Y	Y	N	Y	Y	N
9 Ford	N	N	Y	N	Y	Y	N
TEXAS							
1 Sandlin	Y	N	Y	Y	Y	Y	N
2 Turner	Y	Y	Y	Y	Y	Y	N
3 ***Johnson, Sam***	Y	Y	Y	Y	?	Y	N
4 Hall	N	Y	Y	Y	Y	Y	N
5 ***Sessions***	Y	Y	Y	Y	N	Y	N
6 ***Barton***	Y	Y	Y	Y	N	Y	N
7 ***Archer***	Y	Y	Y	Y	N	Y	Y
8 ***Brady***	Y	N	Y	Y	N	Y	N
9 Lampson	N	N	Y	Y	Y	Y	N
10 Doggett	N	N	N	Y	Y	Y	Y
11 Edwards	N	N	Y	Y	Y	Y	N
12 ***Granger***	Y	Y	Y	Y	N	Y	N
13 ***Thornberry***	Y	Y	Y	Y	N	Y	N
14 ***Paul***	Y	N	N	N	N	Y	Y
15 Hinojosa	N	N	Y	Y	Y	Y	N
16 Reyes	N	N	Y	Y	Y	Y	N
17 Stenholm	N	Y	Y	Y	Y	Y	N
18 Jackson-Lee	N	N	Y	Y	Y	N	N
19 ***Combest***	Y	?	?	?	?	Y	N
20 Gonzalez	N	Y	Y	Y	Y	Y	N
21 ***Smith***	Y	Y	Y	Y	Y	Y	N
22 ***DeLay***	Y	N	Y	Y	N	Y	Y
23 ***Bonilla***	Y	Y	Y	Y	N	Y	Y
24 Frost	N	N	Y	Y	Y	Y	N
25 Bentsen	N	N	Y	Y	Y	Y	N
26 ***Armey***	Y	?	?	?	?	Y	Y
27 Ortiz	N	Y	Y	Y	Y	Y	N
28 Rodriguez	N	N	Y	Y	Y	Y	N
29 Green	N	N	Y	Y	Y	Y	N
30 Johnson, E.B.	N	N	Y	Y	Y	Y	N
UTAH							
1 ***Hansen***	Y	Y	Y	Y	Y	Y	?
2 ***Cook***	Y	Y	Y	Y	Y	Y	N
3 ***Cannon***	Y	Y	Y	Y	N	Y	N
VERMONT							
AL *Sanders*	N	N	N	Y	Y	N	N
VIRGINIA							
1 ***Bateman***	Y	Y	Y	Y	N	Y	Y
2 Pickett	N	N	Y	Y	Y	Y	N
3 Scott	N	N	Y	Y	Y	N	N
4 Sisisky	N	N	Y	Y	Y	Y	N
5 Goode	Y	Y	Y	Y	Y	Y	N
6 ***Goodlatte***	Y	Y	Y	Y	N	Y	N
7 ***Bliley***	Y	Y	Y	Y	Y	Y	Y
8 Moran	N	Y	Y	Y	N	Y	–
9 Boucher	N	Y	Y	Y	Y	Y	N
10 ***Wolf***	Y	Y	Y	Y	Y	Y	Y
11 ***Davis***	Y	Y	Y	Y	N	Y	Y
WASHINGTON							
1 ***White***	Y	Y	Y	Y	N	Y	Y
2 ***Metcalf***	Y	Y	Y	Y	N	Y	N
3 ***Smith, Linda***	N	Y	Y	Y	N	Y	N
4 ***Hastings***	Y	Y	Y	Y	N	Y	Y
5 ***Nethercutt***	Y	Y	Y	Y	N	Y	Y
6 Dicks	N	N	Y	Y	Y	?	Y
7 McDermott	N	N	N	Y	Y	N	N
8 ***Dunn***	Y	Y	Y	Y	N	Y	Y
9 Smith, Adam	N	Y	Y	Y	Y	Y	N
WEST VIRGINIA							
1 Mollohan	N	N	Y	Y	Y	Y	N
2 Wise	N	N	Y	Y	Y	Y	N
3 Rahall	N	N	Y	Y	Y	N	N
WISCONSIN							
1 ***Neumann***	N	Y	Y	N	N	Y	N
2 ***Klug***	Y	N	Y	Y	N	Y	?
3 Kind	N	Y	Y	Y	Y	Y	N
4 Kleczka	N	Y	N	N	Y	Y	N
5 Barrett	N	Y	N	Y	Y	Y	N
6 ***Petri***	Y	Y	N	N	N	Y	N
7 Obey	N	Y	N	Y	Y	Y	N
8 Johnson	N	N	Y	Y	Y	Y	N
9 ***Sensenbrenner***	Y	Y	N	N	Y	Y	N
WYOMING							
AL ***Cubin***	Y	Y	Y	Y	Y	Y	N

Southern states - Ala., Ark., Fla., Ga., Ky., La., Miss., N.C., Okla., S.C., Tenn., Texas, Va.

House Votes 476, 477, 478, 479, 480, 481, 482

Key

Y Voted for (yea).
Paired for.
+ Announced for.
N Voted against (nay).
X Paired against.
− Announced against.
P Voted "present."
C Voted "present" to avoid possible conflict of interest.
? Did not vote or otherwise make a position known.

Democrats **Republicans** *Independent*

476. HR 4274. Fiscal 1999 Labor, Health and Human Services Appropriations/Rule. Adoption of the rule (H Res 564) to provide for House floor consideration of the bill to appropriate $290.8 billion for the Labor, Health and Human Services (HHS), and Education Departments and related agencies for fiscal 1999. Adopted 216-200: R 211-6; D 5-193 (ND 0-143, SD 5-50); I 0-1. Oct. 2, 1998.

477. Procedural Motion/Journal. Approval of the House Journal of Thursday Oct. 1, 1998. Approved 346-60: R 195-16; D 150-44 (ND 106-35, SD 44-9); I 1-0. Oct. 2, 1998.

478. HR 4101. Fiscal 1999 Agriculture Appropriations/Recommit. Pomeroy, D-N.D., motion to recommit the conference report to the conference committee with instructions to report it back with an amendment to increase emergency funding for farmers. Motion rejected 156-236: R 8-200; D 147-36 (ND 110-21, SD 37-15); I 1-0. Oct. 2, 1998.

479. HR 4101. Fiscal 1999 Agriculture Appropriations/Conference Report. Adoption of the conference report on the bill to provide about $55.9 billion in funding for agriculture spending in fiscal 1999. The conference report also provides $4.2 billion in emergency funding for aid to farmers dealing with problems including natural disasters and loss of markets. Adopted (thus sent to the Senate) 333-53: R 179-25; D 153-28 (ND 104-25, SD 49-3); I 1-0. Oct. 2, 1998. A "nay" was a vote in support of the president's position.

480. HR 4614. New Hampshire Land Transfer/Passage. Horn, R-Calif., motion to suspend the rules and pass the bill to transfer two acres of U.S. Coast Guard land to the town of New Castle, N.H. Motion rejected 230-168: R 210-0; D 20-167 (ND 10-126, SD 10-41); I 0-1. Oct. 5, 1998. A two-thirds majority of those present and voting (266 in this case) is required for passage under suspension of the rules.

481. HR 1154. Indian Tribe Federal Recognition/Passage. Young, R-Alaska, motion to suspend the rules and pass the bill to create a new process for granting federal recognition to Indian tribes. Motion rejected 190-208: R 40-171; D 149-37 (ND 109-26, SD 40-11); I 1-0. Oct. 5, 1998. A two-thirds majority of those present and voting (266 in this case) is required for passage under suspension of the rules.

482. HR 4655. Assistance for Iraqi Opposition Groups/Passage. Gilman, R-N.Y., motion to suspend the rules and pass the bill to authorize U.S. assistance to certain Iraqi opposition groups engaged in the fight against the regime of Saddam Hussein. Motion agreed to 360-38: R 202-9; D 157-29 (ND 113-22, SD 44-7); I 1-0. Oct. 5, 1998. A two-thirds majority of those present and voting (266 in this case) is required for suspension of the rules.

	476	477	478	479	480	481	482
ALABAMA							
1 *Callahan*	?	?	?	?	Y	N	Y
2 *Everett*	Y	Y	N	Y	Y	N	Y
3 *Riley*	Y	Y	N	Y	Y	N	Y
4 *Aderholt*	Y	N	N	Y	Y	N	Y
5 Cramer	N	Y	Y	Y	N	Y	Y
6 *Bachus*	Y	Y	N	Y	Y	N	Y
7 Hilliard	N	N	Y	Y	N	Y	N
ALASKA							
AL *Young*	Y	Y	N	Y	Y	Y	Y
ARIZONA							
1 *Salmon*	Y	Y	?	?	Y	Y	Y
2 Pastor	N	Y	Y	Y	N	Y	Y
3 *Stump*	Y	Y	N	Y	Y	N	Y
4 *Shadegg*	Y	Y	N	Y	Y	N	Y
5 *Kolbe*	Y	Y	N	Y	Y	N	Y
6 *Hayworth*	Y	Y	N	Y	Y	Y	Y
ARKANSAS							
1 Berry	N	Y	N	Y	N	Y	Y
2 Snyder	N	Y	N	Y	Y	N	Y
3 *Hutchinson*	Y	Y	N	Y	Y	N	Y
4 Dickey	Y	N	N	Y	Y	N	Y
CALIFORNIA							
1 *Riggs*	Y	Y	N	Y	+	−	+
2 *Herger*	Y	Y	N	Y	Y	N	Y
3 Fazio	N	N	Y	Y	N	Y	Y
4 *Doolittle*	Y	Y	N	Y	Y	N	Y
5 Matsui	N	Y	Y	Y	N	Y	Y
6 Woolsey	N	Y	Y	Y	N	Y	Y
7 Miller	N	N	Y	N	N	Y	Y
8 Pelosi	N	Y	Y	Y	?	?	Y
9 Lee	N	N	Y	N	N	Y	N
10 Tauscher	N	N	Y	N	N	Y	Y
11 *Pombo*	Y	Y	N	Y	Y	Y	Y
12 Lantos	N	Y	N	Y	N	Y	Y
13 Stark	N	Y	N	Y	N	Y	N
14 Eshoo	N	N	Y	N	N	Y	Y
15 *Campbell*	Y	Y	N	N	Y	N	Y
16 Lofgren	N	Y	N	Y	N	Y	Y
17 Farr	N	Y	N	Y	N	Y	Y
18 *Radanovich*	Y	N	Y	N	Y	N	Y
19 Dooley	N	Y	N	Y	N	Y	Y
20 *Thomas*	Y	Y	N	Y	Y	N	Y
22 Capps, L.	N	Y	N	Y	N	Y	Y
23 *Gallegly*	Y	Y	N	Y	Y	N	Y
24 Sherman	N	Y	N	Y	N	Y	Y
25 *McKeon*	Y	Y	N	Y	Y	N	Y
26 Berman	N	N	Y	N	N	Y	Y
27 *Rogan*	Y	N	N	Y	Y	Y	Y
28 *Dreier*	Y	Y	N	Y	Y	Y	Y
29 Waxman	N	?	Y	Y	N	Y	Y
30 Becerra	N	N	Y	Y	−	+	Y
31 Martinez	?	?	?	Y	N	Y	Y
32 Dixon	N	Y	Y	Y	?	?	?
33 Roybal-Allard	N	Y	Y	Y	−	+	Y
34 Torres	N	Y	?	Y	N	Y	Y
35 Waters	N	N	N	Y	N	Y	N
36 Harman	?	?	?	Y	?	?	?
37 Millender-McD.	N	Y	Y	Y	?	?	?
38 *Horn*	Y	Y	N	Y	Y	N	Y

	476	477	478	479	480	481	482
39 *Royce*	Y	Y	N	Y	Y	Y	Y
40 *Lewis*	Y	Y	N	Y	Y	Y	Y
41 *Kim*	Y	Y	N	Y	Y	Y	Y
42 Brown	N	N	Y	Y	N	Y	Y
43 *Calvert*	Y	Y	N	Y	?	?	#
44 *Bono, M.*	Y	Y	N	Y	Y	Y	Y
45 *Rohrabacher*	Y	Y	N	Y	Y	Y	Y
46 Sanchez	N	N	Y	Y	N	Y	Y
47 *Cox*	Y	Y	N	N	Y	N	Y
48 *Packard*	Y	Y	N	Y	Y	Y	Y
49 *Bilbray*	Y	Y	N	Y	Y	N	Y
50 Filner	N	N	Y	Y	N	Y	Y
51 *Cunningham*	Y	Y	?	?	Y	N	Y
52 *Hunter*	Y	Y	N	Y	Y	Y	Y
COLORADO							
1 DeGette	N	Y	Y	Y	N	Y	Y
2 Skaggs	N	Y	Y	Y	N	Y	N
3 *McInnis*	Y	Y	N	Y	Y	N	Y
4 *Schaffer*	Y	N	N	Y	Y	Y	Y
5 *Hefley*	?	?	?	?	Y	N	Y
6 *Schaefer*	Y	Y	N	Y	?	?	?
CONNECTICUT							
1 Kennelly	?	?	?	?	?	?	?
2 Gejdenson	N	Y	Y	Y	N	Y	Y
3 DeLauro	N	Y	Y	Y	N	N	Y
4 *Shays*	Y	Y	N	N	Y	N	Y
5 Maloney	N	N	Y	Y	N	Y	Y
6 *Johnson*	Y	Y	N	Y	Y	N	Y
DELAWARE							
AL *Castle*	Y	Y	N	N	Y	N	Y
FLORIDA							
1 *Scarborough*	Y	Y	N	N	?	N	Y
2 Boyd	N	Y	N	Y	N	Y	Y
3 Brown	N	Y	Y	Y	N	Y	Y
4 *Fowler*	?	?	?	?	Y	N	Y
5 Thurman	N	Y	N	Y	N	Y	Y
6 *Stearns*	Y	Y	N	N	Y	N	Y
7 *Mica*	Y	Y	N	Y	Y	N	Y
8 *McCollum*	Y	Y	N	Y	Y	N	Y
9 *Bilirakis*	Y	Y	N	Y	Y	N	Y
10 *Young*	Y	Y	N	Y	?	?	?
11 Davis	N	Y	N	Y	Y	N	Y
12 *Canady*	Y	Y	N	Y	Y	N	Y
13 *Miller*	Y	Y	N	N	Y	N	Y
14 Goss	+	+	−	−	Y	N	Y
15 *Weldon*	Y	Y	N	Y	Y	Y	Y
16 *Foley*	Y	Y	N	Y	Y	N	Y
17 Meek	N	Y	Y	?	N	N	Y
18 *Ros-Lehtinen*	Y	Y	N	Y	?	?	?
19 Wexler	N	Y	Y	Y	N	Y	Y
20 Deutsch	N	Y	?	Y	N	Y	Y
21 *Diaz-Balart*	Y	Y	N	Y	Y	N	Y
22 *Shaw*	Y	Y	N	Y	Y	N	Y
23 Hastings	N	N	Y	Y	N	Y	N
GEORGIA							
1 *Kingston*	Y	Y	N	Y	Y	N	Y
2 Bishop	N	Y	Y	Y	−	+	+
3 *Collins*	Y	Y	N	Y	Y	N	Y
4 McKinney	N	Y	N	N	N	N	N
5 Lewis	N	N	Y	N	Y	N	N
6 *Gingrich*							
7 *Barr*	Y	Y	N	N	Y	N	Y
8 *Chambliss*	Y	Y	N	N	Y	N	Y
9 *Deal*	Y	Y	N	Y	Y	N	Y
10 *Norwood*	Y	Y	N	Y	?	?	?
11 *Linder*	Y	Y	N	Y	Y	N	Y
HAWAII							
1 Abercrombie	N	Y	Y	Y	N	Y	N
2 Mink	N	Y	Y	Y	N	Y	N
IDAHO							
1 *Chenoweth*	Y	N	N	Y	N	N	N
2 *Crapo*	Y	Y	N	Y	Y	N	Y
ILLINOIS							
1 Rush	N	Y	N	Y	N	Y	N
2 Jackson	N	Y	N	Y	N	Y	N
3 Lipinski	?	?	?	?	N	N	Y
4 Gutierrez	N	Y	N	N	N	N	N
5 Blagojevich	N	Y	Y	Y	N	N	Y
6 *Hyde*	Y	Y	?	?	Y	N	Y
7 Davis	N	N	Y	Y	N	Y	N
8 *Crane*	Y	N	N	N	Y	N	Y
9 Yates	N	Y	Y	N	?	?	X
10 *Porter*	Y	Y	N	Y	Y	N	Y
11 *Weller*	N	N	Y	N	Y	N	Y
12 Costello	N	N	?	N	N	N	Y
13 *Fawell*	Y	Y	N	Y	Y	N	Y

ND Northern Democrats   SD Southern Democrats

	476	477	478	479	480	481	482
14 ***Hastert***	Y	Y	N	Y	Y	N	Y
15 ***Ewing***	Y	Y	N	Y	Y	N	N
16 ***Manzullo***	Y	Y	N	Y	Y	N	Y
17 Evans	?	Y	Y	Y	N	Y	Y
18 ***LaHood***	Y	Y	N	Y	Y	N	N
19 Poshard	?	?	?	?	?	?	?
20 ***Shimkus***	Y	Y	N	Y	Y	N	Y
INDIANA							
1 Visclosky	N	N	N	Y	N	N	Y
2 ***McIntosh***	Y	Y	N	N	Y	N	Y
3 Roemer	N	Y	Y	Y	N	N	Y
4 ***Souder***	Y	Y	N	Y	Y	N	Y
5 ***Buyer***	Y	Y	N	Y	Y	N	Y
6 ***Burton***	Y	Y	N	Y	Y	N	Y
7 ***Pease***	Y	Y	N	Y	Y	N	Y
8 ***Hostettler***	Y	Y	N	N	Y	N	N
9 Hamilton	N	Y	N	Y	N	Y	Y
10 Carson	N	P	Y	Y	N	Y	N
IOWA							
1 ***Leach***	N	Y	Y	Y	Y	N	Y
2 ***Nussle***	Y	Y	Y	Y	Y	N	Y
3 Boswell	N	Y	Y	Y	N	N	Y
4 ***Ganske***	Y	Y	N	Y	Y	N	Y
5 ***Latham***	Y	Y	N	Y	Y	N	Y
KANSAS							
1 ***Moran***	Y	N	N	Y	Y	N	Y
2 ***Ryun***	Y	Y	N	Y	Y	N	Y
3 ***Snowbarger***	Y	+	−	+	Y	N	Y
4 ***Tiahrt***	Y	Y	N	Y	Y	N	Y
KENTUCKY							
1 ***Whitfield***	Y	Y	N	?	Y	N	Y
2 ***Lewis***	Y	Y	N	Y	Y	N	Y
3 ***Northup***	Y	Y	N	Y	Y	N	Y
4 ***Bunning***	Y	Y	N	Y	Y	N	Y
5 ***Rogers***	Y	Y	N	Y	?	?	?
6 Baesler	N	Y	N	Y	Y	N	Y
LOUISIANA							
1 ***Livingston***	?	?	N	Y	Y	N	Y
2 Jefferson	N	Y	Y	Y	Y	Y	N
3 ***Tauzin***	?	?	?	?	?	?	?
4 ***McCrery***	Y	Y	N	Y	Y	N	Y
5 ***Cooksey***	Y	Y	N	Y	Y	N	Y
6 ***Baker***	Y	Y	N	Y	Y	N	Y
7 John	Y	Y	N	Y	N	Y	Y
MAINE							
1 Allen	N	Y	Y	Y	N	Y	Y
2 Baldacci	N	Y	N	Y	N	Y	Y
MARYLAND							
1 ***Gilchrest***	Y	Y	N	Y	Y	Y	Y
2 ***Ehrlich***	Y	Y	N	Y	Y	N	Y
3 Cardin	N	Y	Y	Y	N	Y	Y
4 Wynn	N	N	Y	Y	N	Y	Y
5 Hoyer	N	Y	Y	Y	N	Y	Y
6 ***Bartlett***	Y	Y	N	Y	Y	N	N
7 Cummings	N	Y	Y	Y	N	Y	Y
8 ***Morella***	N	Y	N	Y	Y	N	Y
MASSACHUSETTS							
1 Olver	N	N	Y	Y	N	Y	Y
2 Neal	N	Y	Y	Y	?	?	?
3 McGovern	N	Y	Y	Y	?	?	?
4 Frank	N	Y	Y	N	N	Y	Y
5 Meehan	N	Y	?	?	N	Y	Y
6 Tierney	N	Y	Y	Y	N	Y	Y
7 Markey	N	Y	Y	Y	N	Y	Y
8 Kennedy	N	Y	Y	Y	N	Y	Y
9 Moakley	N	Y	?	?	?	?	?
10 Delahunt	N	Y	Y	Y	Y	Y	Y
MICHIGAN							
1 Stupak	N	?	?	?	?	?	?
2 ***Hoekstra***	Y	Y	N	N	Y	N	Y
3 ***Ehlers***	Y	Y	N	Y	Y	N	Y
4 ***Camp***	Y	Y	N	Y	Y	N	Y
5 Barcia	N	Y	Y	Y	N	Y	Y
6 ***Upton***	Y	Y	N	Y	Y	N	Y
7 ***Smith***	Y	Y	N	Y	Y	N	Y
8 Stabenow	N	Y	Y	Y	N	Y	Y
9 Kildee	N	Y	Y	Y	N	Y	Y
10 Bonior	N	N	Y	Y	N	Y	Y
11 ***Knollenberg***	Y	Y	N	Y	Y	N	Y
12 Levin	N	Y	Y	Y	N	Y	Y
13 Rivers	N	Y	N	N	N	Y	N
14 Conyers	N	Y	Y	Y	N	Y	N
15 Kilpatrick	N	Y	?	?	N	Y	Y
16 Dingell	N	Y	Y	Y	N	N	Y

	476	477	478	479	480	481	482
MINNESOTA							
1 ***Gutknecht***	Y	Y	N	Y	Y	Y	Y
2 Minge	N	Y	Y	Y	Y	Y	Y
3 ***Ramstad***	Y	N	N	Y	Y	N	Y
4 Vento	N	N	Y	N	N	Y	N
5 Sabo	N	N	Y	Y	Y	Y	N
6 Luther	N	Y	Y	Y	N	Y	Y
7 Peterson	N	Y	Y	Y	Y	Y	Y
8 Oberstar	N	N	Y	N	N	Y	Y
MISSISSIPPI							
1 ***Wicker***	Y	N	N	Y	Y	N	Y
2 Thompson	N	N	Y	Y	N	Y	Y
3 ***Pickering***	Y	?	N	Y	Y	Y	Y
4 ***Parker***	?	?	?	?	Y	Y	Y
5 Taylor	Y	N	Y	N	Y	N	Y
MISSOURI							
1 Clay	?	?	?	?	N	Y	N
2 ***Talent***	Y	Y	N	Y	Y	N	Y
3 Gephardt	N	N	?	?	Y	Y	Y
4 Skelton	N	Y	N	Y	N	N	N
5 McCarthy	N	Y	N	Y	N	Y	Y
6 Danner	N	Y	Y	Y	N	Y	Y
7 ***Blunt***	Y	Y	N	Y	Y	N	Y
8 ***Emerson***	Y	Y	Y	Y	Y	Y	Y
9 ***Hulshof***	Y	N	N	Y	Y	Y	Y
MONTANA							
AL ***Hill***	Y	Y	Y	Y	Y	N	Y
NEBRASKA							
1 ***Bereuter***	Y	Y	Y	Y	Y	N	Y
2 ***Christensen***	Y	Y	N	Y	Y	N	Y
3 ***Barrett***	Y	Y	N	Y	Y	N	Y
NEVADA							
1 ***Ensign***	Y	Y	N	N	Y	N	Y
2 ***Gibbons***	Y	N	N	Y	Y	N	Y
NEW HAMPSHIRE							
1 ***Sununu***	Y	Y	?	?	Y	N	Y
2 ***Bass***	Y	Y	N	Y	Y	N	Y
NEW JERSEY							
1 Andrews	N	Y	N	N	N	N	Y
2 ***LoBiondo***	Y	N	N	Y	Y	N	Y
3 ***Saxton***	Y	N	N	Y	Y	N	Y
4 ***Smith***	Y	Y	N	Y	Y	N	Y
5 ***Roukema***	Y	Y	N	Y	Y	N	Y
6 Pallone	N	N	Y	Y	N	Y	Y
7 ***Franks***	Y	Y	N	N	Y	N	Y
8 Pascrell	N	Y	N	Y	N	Y	Y
9 Rothman	N	Y	N	N	N	Y	Y
10 Payne	N	Y	Y	N	N	Y	N
11 ***Frelinghuysen***	Y	Y	N	N	Y	N	Y
12 ***Pappas***	Y	Y	N	N	Y	N	Y
13 Menendez	N	N	?	?	N	N	Y
NEW MEXICO							
1 ***Wilson***	Y	Y	N	Y	Y	N	Y
2 ***Skeen***	Y	Y	N	Y	Y	N	Y
3 ***Redmond***	Y	Y	N	Y	Y	Y	Y
NEW YORK							
1 ***Forbes***	Y	Y	N	Y	Y	N	Y
2 ***Lazio***	Y	Y	N	Y	Y	N	Y
3 ***King***	?	?	?	?	Y	N	Y
4 McCarthy	N	Y	N	Y	N	N	Y
5 Ackerman	N	Y	Y	Y	N	Y	Y
6 Meeks	N	Y	Y	Y	N	Y	Y
7 Manton	N	Y	Y	Y	Y	Y	Y
8 Nadler	N	Y	Y	Y	Y	Y	Y
9 Schumer	N	Y	Y	Y	N	Y	Y
10 Towns	N	N	Y	Y	N	Y	N
11 Owens	N	Y	Y	?	?	?	?
12 Velázquez	N	N	Y	Y	N	Y	Y
13 ***Fossella***	Y	Y	N	Y	Y	N	Y
14 Maloney	N	Y	Y	Y	N	N	Y
15 Rangel	N	N	Y	N	Y	Y	Y
16 Serrano	N	Y	N	Y	N	Y	N
17 Engel	N	Y	Y	Y	N	Y	Y
18 Lowey	N	Y	Y	Y	N	Y	Y
19 ***Kelly***	Y	Y	N	Y	Y	N	Y
20 ***Gilman***	Y	Y	N	Y	Y	Y	Y
21 McNulty	N	N	Y	Y	N	Y	Y
22 ***Solomon***	Y	Y	N	Y	Y	N	Y
23 ***Boehlert***	Y	Y	N	Y	?	?	?
24 ***McHugh***	N	Y	N	Y	Y	N	Y
25 ***Walsh***	Y	Y	N	Y	Y	Y	N
26 Hinchey	N	N	Y	N	Y	Y	Y
27 ***Paxon***	Y	Y	N	Y	Y	N	Y
28 Slaughter	N	N	Y	Y	N	N	Y
29 LaFalce	N	N	N	Y	N	N	Y
30 ***Quinn***	Y	Y	N	Y	Y	Y	Y

	476	477	478	479	480	481	482
31 ***Houghton***	Y	Y	?	?	Y	Y	Y
NORTH CAROLINA							
1 Clayton	N	Y	Y	Y	N	Y	Y
2 Etheridge	N	Y	N	Y	N	Y	Y
3 ***Jones***	Y	Y	N	Y	Y	N	Y
4 Price	N	Y	Y	Y	N	Y	Y
5 ***Burr***	Y	Y	N	Y	Y	N	Y
6 ***Coble***	Y	Y	N	Y	Y	N	Y
7 McIntyre	N	Y	Y	Y	N	Y	Y
8 Hefner	N	N	N	Y	N	Y	Y
9 ***Myrick***	Y	Y	N	Y	Y	N	Y
10 ***Ballenger***	Y	?	N	Y	Y	N	Y
11 ***Taylor***	Y	Y	N	Y	Y	N	Y
12 Watt	N	Y	Y	Y	N	Y	Y
NORTH DAKOTA							
AL Pomeroy	N	Y	Y	N	N	N	Y
OHIO							
1 ***Chabot***	Y	Y	N	N	Y	N	Y
2 ***Portman***	Y	Y	N	Y	Y	N	Y
3 Hall	N	Y	N	Y	N	N	Y
4 ***Oxley***	Y	Y	N	Y	Y	N	Y
5 ***Gillmor***	Y	Y	N	?	Y	N	Y
6 Strickland	N	N	Y	N	Y	N	Y
7 ***Hobson***	Y	Y	N	Y	Y	N	Y
8 ***Boehner***	Y	Y	N	Y	Y	N	Y
9 Kaptur	N	Y	Y	Y	Y	Y	Y
10 Kucinich	N	N	Y	N	N	N	Y
11 Stokes	N	Y	?	?	?	?	?
12 ***Kasich***	Y	Y	N	Y	Y	N	Y
13 Brown	N	Y	Y	Y	N	Y	Y
14 Sawyer	N	Y	Y	Y	N	Y	Y
15 ***Pryce***	+	+	−	+	+	−	+
16 ***Regula***	Y	Y	N	Y	Y	N	Y
17 Traficant	N	Y	N	Y	Y	Y	Y
18 ***Ney***	N	Y	N	Y	Y	N	Y
19 ***LaTourette***	Y	Y	N	Y	Y	N	Y
OKLAHOMA							
1 ***Largent***	Y	Y	N	Y	Y	N	Y
2 ***Coburn***	Y	Y	N	Y	Y	N	Y
3 ***Watkins***	Y	Y	Y	Y	Y	N	Y
4 ***Watts***	Y	Y	N	Y	Y	N	Y
5 ***Istook***	Y	Y	N	Y	Y	N	Y
6 ***Lucas***	Y	Y	N	Y	Y	N	Y
OREGON							
1 Furse	N	Y	Y	Y	N	Y	N
2 ***Smith***	Y	Y	N	Y	Y	N	Y
3 Blumenauer	N	Y	Y	N	N	Y	Y
4 DeFazio	?	?	?	?	N	Y	Y
5 Hooley	N	Y	Y	Y	N	Y	Y
PENNSYLVANIA							
1 Brady	N	Y	?	?	N	Y	Y
2 Fattah	N	Y	?	?	N	Y	Y
3 Borski	N	N	Y	?	N	Y	Y
4 Klink	N	N	Y	Y	N	N	Y
5 ***Peterson***	Y	Y	N	Y	Y	N	Y
6 Holden	N	Y	Y	Y	N	N	Y
7 ***Weldon***	Y	Y	N	Y	Y	Y	Y
8 ***Greenwood***	Y	Y	N	Y	?	?	?
9 ***Shuster***	Y	Y	N	?	?	?	?
10 ***McDade***	Y	Y	N	Y	?	?	#
11 Kanjorski	N	Y	Y	Y	N	N	Y
12 Murtha	N	Y	N	Y	N	?	?
13 ***Fox***	N	N	N	Y	Y	N	Y
14 Coyne	N	Y	Y	Y	N	Y	Y
15 McHale	N	Y	Y	Y	N	Y	Y
16 ***Pitts***	?	?	?	?	Y	N	Y
17 ***Gekas***	Y	Y	N	Y	Y	Y	Y
18 Doyle	N	Y	Y	Y	N	N	Y
19 ***Goodling***	Y	Y	N	Y	Y	Y	Y
20 Mascara	N	Y	Y	Y	N	N	Y
21 ***English***	Y	N	N	Y	Y	N	Y
RHODE ISLAND							
1 Kennedy	N	Y	Y	Y	N	Y	Y
2 Weygand	N	Y	Y	Y	N	N	Y
SOUTH CAROLINA							
1 ***Sanford***	Y	Y	N	N	?	?	?
2 ***Spence***	Y	Y	N	Y	Y	N	Y
3 ***Graham***	Y	Y	N	Y	Y	N	Y
4 ***Inglis***	Y	Y	N	Y	Y	N	Y
5 Spratt	N	Y	Y	Y	?	?	?
6 Clyburn	N	?	Y	Y	N	Y	Y
SOUTH DAKOTA							
AL ***Thune***	Y	Y	Y	Y	Y	N	Y

	476	477	478	479	480	481	482
TENNESSEE							
1 ***Jenkins***	Y	Y	N	Y	Y	N	Y
2 ***Duncan***	Y	Y	N	Y	Y	N	Y
3 ***Wamp***	Y	Y	N	Y	Y	N	Y
4 ***Hilleary***	Y	N	N	Y	Y	N	Y
5 Clement	N	Y	Y	Y	Y	Y	Y
6 Gordon	N	Y	Y	Y	N	Y	Y
7 ***Bryant***	Y	?	N	Y	Y	N	Y
8 Tanner	N	Y	N	Y	N	Y	Y
9 Ford	N	Y	N	Y	N	Y	N
TEXAS							
1 Sandlin	N	Y	N	Y	N	Y	Y
2 Turner	N	Y	Y	Y	N	N	Y
3 ***Johnson, Sam***	Y	Y	N	N	Y	Y	Y
4 Hall	Y	Y	N	Y	Y	Y	Y
5 ***Sessions***	Y	Y	N	Y	Y	N	Y
6 ***Barton***	Y	Y	?	?	Y	N	Y
7 ***Archer***	Y	?	N	Y	Y	N	Y
8 ***Brady***	Y	Y	N	Y	Y	N	Y
9 Lampson	N	Y	Y	Y	N	Y	Y
10 Doggett	N	Y	N	N	N	Y	N
11 Edwards	N	Y	N	Y	N	Y	Y
12 ***Granger***	Y	Y	N	Y	?	?	?
13 ***Thornberry***	Y	Y	N	Y	Y	N	Y
14 ***Paul***	Y	Y	Y	N	Y	N	N
15 Hinojosa	N	Y	Y	Y	−	+	+
16 Reyes	N	Y	Y	Y	N	Y	Y
17 Stenholm	Y	N	N	Y	Y	Y	Y
18 Jackson-Lee	N	Y	Y	Y	N	Y	Y
19 ***Combest***	Y	Y	N	Y	Y	Y	Y
20 Gonzalez	N	Y	Y	Y	N	Y	Y
21 ***Smith***	Y	Y	N	Y	Y	N	Y
22 ***DeLay***	Y	?	?	?	Y	N	Y
23 ***Bonilla***	Y	Y	N	Y	Y	Y	Y
24 Frost	N	Y	Y	Y	?	?	?
25 Bentsen	N	Y	N	Y	N	N	Y
26 ***Armey***	Y	Y	?	Y	Y	Y	Y
27 Ortiz	N	Y	Y	Y	N	Y	Y
28 Rodriguez	N	Y	Y	Y	N	Y	Y
29 Green	N	N	Y	Y	N	Y	Y
30 Johnson, E.B.	N	Y	Y	Y	N	Y	Y
UTAH							
1 ***Hansen***	Y	Y	N	?	?	?	?
2 ***Cook***	Y	Y	N	Y	Y	N	Y
3 ***Cannon***	Y	Y	N	Y	Y	Y	Y
VERMONT							
AL *Sanders*	N	Y	Y	Y	N	Y	Y
VIRGINIA							
1 ***Bateman***	Y	Y	N	Y	Y	N	Y
2 Pickett	N	N	?	?	Y	N	Y
3 Scott	N	Y	Y	Y	N	Y	Y
4 Sisisky	N	Y	Y	Y	N	Y	Y
5 Goode	Y	Y	Y	Y	Y	N	Y
6 ***Goodlatte***	Y	Y	N	Y	Y	N	Y
7 ***Bliley***	Y	Y	N	Y	Y	N	Y
8 Moran	N	?	Y	Y	N	Y	Y
9 Boucher	N	Y	?	Y	N	N	Y
10 ***Wolf***	Y	Y	N	Y	Y	N	Y
11 ***Davis***	Y	Y	N	Y	Y	N	Y
WASHINGTON							
1 ***White***	Y	Y	N	Y	Y	N	Y
2 ***Metcalf***	Y	Y	N	Y	Y	N	Y
3 ***Smith, Linda***	Y	Y	N	Y	Y	N	Y
4 ***Hastings***	Y	Y	N	?	Y	N	Y
5 ***Nethercutt***	Y	Y	N	Y	Y	N	Y
6 Dicks	N	Y	Y	Y	N	Y	Y
7 McDermott	N	N	Y	N	N	Y	Y
8 ***Dunn***	Y	Y	N	Y	Y	N	Y
9 Smith, Adam	N	Y	?	?	N	Y	Y
WEST VIRGINIA							
1 Mollohan	N	Y	Y	Y	N	Y	Y
2 Wise	N	Y	?	?	N	Y	Y
3 Rahall	N	Y	Y	Y	N	Y	Y
WISCONSIN							
1 ***Neumann***	Y	Y	N	N	Y	N	Y
2 ***Klug***	Y	Y	?	?	Y	N	Y
3 Kind	N	Y	Y	N	N	Y	Y
4 Kleczka	N	Y	Y	N	N	Y	Y
5 Barrett	N	Y	Y	N	N	Y	Y
6 ***Petri***	Y	Y	N	N	Y	N	Y
7 Obey	N	N	Y	N	N	Y	Y
8 Johnson	N	N	Y	N	N	Y	Y
9 ***Sensenbrenner***	Y	Y	N	N	Y	N	Y
WYOMING							
AL ***Cubin***	Y	Y	N	Y	Y	N	Y

Southern states - Ala., Ark., Fla., Ga., Ky., La., Miss., N.C., Okla., S.C., Tenn., Texas, Va.

House Votes 483, 484, 485, 486, 487, 488, 489

483. HR 4194. Fiscal 1999 VA-HUD Appropriations/Conference Report. Adoption of the conference report on the bill to provide $93.4 billion in funding for veterans, housing, space and science programs in fiscal 1999. Adopted (thus sent to the Senate) 409-14: R 213-9; D 195-5 (ND 141-5, SD 54-0); I 1-0. Oct. 6, 1998.

484. H Res 575. Expedited Consideration of Legislative Business/Adoption. Adoption of the resolution to allow for expedited consideration of appropriations bills, appropriations conference reports and any continuing resolutions between Oct. 6 and Oct. 11, 1998. The measure, called a "martial law resolution," also allows the Speaker to schedule suspension bills on any day between Oct. 6 and Oct. 11, 1998. Adopted 218-206: R 218-3; D 0-202 (ND 0-148, SD 0-54); I 0-1. Oct. 6, 1998.

485. HR 4259. Indian Higher Education Demonstration Project/Civil Service Requirements Substitute. Cummings, D-Md., substitute amendment to require current federal civil service procedures to remain in effect for temporary alternative personnel management demonstration projects to be carried out at Haskell Indian Nations University and Southwestern Indian Polytechnic Institute. Rejected 181-244: R 0-224; D 180-20 (ND 137-9, SD 43-11); I 1-0. Oct. 6, 1998. (Subsequently, the bill was passed by voice vote.)

486. HR 3694. Fiscal 1999 Intelligence Authorization/Recommit. Barr, R-Ga., motion to recommit the bill to the conference committee with instructions to report it back with an amendment deleting the section of the bill that expands the government's power to place wiretaps on telephones. Motion rejected 148-267: R 90-127; D 57-140 (ND 44-98, SD 13-42); I 1-0. Oct. 7, 1998.

487. HR 3694. Fiscal 1999 Intelligence Authorization/Conference Report. Adoption of the conference report on the bill to authorize classified amounts in fiscal 1999 for U.S. intelligence agencies and intelligence-related activities of the U.S. government, including the Central Intelligence Agency, the National Security Agency, and the foreign intelligence activities of the Defense Department, FBI, State Department and other agencies. The total funding level is classified, but this year's authorization is reportedly slightly higher than fiscal 1998 levels. Adopted (thus sent to the Senate) 337-83: R 174-47; D 163-35 (ND 117-27, SD 46-8); I 0-1. Oct. 7, 1998.

488. HR 4570. National Parks and Public Lands Revisions/Rule. Adoption of the rule (H Res 573) to provide for House floor consideration of the bill composed of the provisions of numerous (roughly 100) independently introduced bills dealing with National Parks and other public lands. Adopted 225-198: R 222-0; D 3-197 (ND 3-142, SD 0-55); I 0-1. Oct. 7, 1998.

489. HR 4570. National Parks and Public Lands Revisions/Passage. Passage of the bill composed of the provisions of numerous (roughly 100) independently introduced bills dealing with National Parks and other public lands. Defeated 123-302: R 117-107; D 6-194 (ND 3-143, SD 3-51); I 0-1. Oct. 7, 1998. A "nay" was a vote in support of the president's position.

Key

- Y Voted for (yea).
- # Paired for.
- + Announced for.
- N Voted against (nay).
- X Paired against.
- – Announced against.
- P Voted "present."
- C Voted "present" to avoid possible conflict of interest.
- ? Did not vote or otherwise make a position known.

Democrats **Republicans** *Independent*

	483	484	485	486	487	488	489
ALABAMA							
1 Callahan	Y	Y	N	N	Y	Y	Y
2 Everett	Y	Y	N	Y	Y	Y	N
3 Riley	Y	Y	N	Y	Y	Y	Y
4 Aderholt	Y	Y	N	Y	Y	Y	Y
5 Cramer	Y	N	N	N	Y	N	N
6 Bachus	Y	Y	N	Y	N	Y	N
7 Hilliard	Y	N	Y	Y	N	N	N
ALASKA							
AL Young	Y	Y	N	N	Y	Y	Y
ARIZONA							
1 Salmon	Y	Y	N	Y	Y	Y	Y
2 Pastor	Y	N	Y	Y	N	N	N
3 Stump	Y	Y	N	N	Y	Y	Y
4 Shadegg	Y	Y	N	N	Y	Y	Y
5 Kolbe	Y	Y	N	Y	Y	Y	Y
6 Hayworth	Y	Y	N	Y	N	Y	Y
ARKANSAS							
1 Berry	Y	N	Y	N	Y	N	N
2 Snyder	Y	N	Y	N	Y	N	N
3 Hutchinson	Y	Y	N	Y	?	N	N
4 Dickey	Y	Y	N	Y	Y	Y	Y
CALIFORNIA							
1 Riggs	+	+	?	N	Y	Y	N
2 Herger	Y	Y	N	Y	Y	Y	Y
3 Fazio	Y	N	Y	N	Y	N	?
4 Doolittle	Y	Y	N	N	Y	Y	Y
5 Matsui	Y	N	?	Y	Y	N	N
6 Woolsey	Y	N	Y	N	N	N	N
7 Miller	Y	N	Y	N	N	N	N
8 Pelosi	Y	N	Y	N	Y	N	N
9 Lee	Y	N	Y	N	Y	N	N
10 Tauscher	Y	N	Y	N	Y	N	N
11 Pombo	Y	Y	N	Y	N	Y	Y
12 Lantos	Y	N	Y	N	Y	N	N
13 Stark	Y	N	?	Y	N	N	N
14 Eshoo	Y	N	Y	N	Y	N	N
15 Campbell	Y	Y	N	Y	Y	Y	N
16 Lofgren	Y	N	Y	N	Y	N	N
17 Farr	Y	N	Y	N	Y	N	N
18 Condit	Y	N	N	N	Y	N	N
19 Radanovich	Y	Y	N	Y	Y	Y	Y
20 Dooley	Y	N	Y	N	Y	N	N
21 Thomas	Y	Y	N	N	Y	Y	Y
22 Capps, L.	Y	N	Y	N	N	N	N
23 Gallegly	Y	Y	N	Y	Y	Y	Y
24 Sherman	Y	N	Y	N	Y	N	N
25 McKeon	Y	Y	N	–	+	Y	Y
26 Berman	Y	N	Y	N	N	N	N
27 Rogan	Y	Y	N	Y	Y	N	N
28 Dreier	Y	Y	N	N	Y	Y	Y
29 Waxman	Y	N	Y	N	Y	N	N
30 Becerra	Y	N	Y	N	Y	N	N
31 Martinez	Y	N	Y	?	N	N	N
32 Dixon	Y	N	Y	N	Y	N	N
33 Roybal-Allard	Y	N	Y	N	Y	N	N
34 Torres	?	N	Y	N	Y	N	N
35 Waters	Y	N	Y	Y	N	N	N
36 Harman	Y	N	Y	N	Y	N	N
37 Millender-McD.	Y	N	Y	N	Y	N	N
38 Horn	Y	Y	N	Y	N	Y	N
39 Royce	Y	Y	N	N	Y	Y	Y
40 Lewis	Y	Y	N	N	Y	Y	Y
41 Kim	Y	Y	N	N	Y	Y	Y
42 Brown	+	N	Y	N	Y	N	N
43 Calvert	Y	?	N	N	Y	Y	Y
44 Bono, M.	Y	Y	N	N	Y	Y	Y
45 Rohrabacher	Y	Y	N	N	Y	Y	Y
46 Sanchez	Y	N	Y	N	Y	N	N
47 Cox	Y	Y	N	Y	Y	Y	Y
48 Packard	Y	Y	N	Y	Y	Y	Y
49 Bilbray	Y	Y	N	N	Y	Y	N
50 Filner	Y	N	Y	N	N	N	N
51 Cunningham	Y	Y	N	Y	Y	Y	Y
52 Hunter	Y	Y	N	N	Y	Y	Y
COLORADO							
1 DeGette	Y	N	Y	N	Y	N	N
2 Skaggs	Y	N	Y	N	Y	N	N
3 McInnis	Y	Y	N	Y	Y	Y	Y
4 Schaffer	N	Y	N	Y	Y	Y	Y
5 Hefley	Y	Y	N	Y	Y	Y	Y
6 Schaefer	Y	Y	N	N	Y	Y	Y
CONNECTICUT							
1 Kennelly	?	?	?	?	?	?	?
2 Gejdenson	Y	N	Y	N	Y	N	N
3 DeLauro	Y	N	Y	N	Y	N	N
4 Shays	Y	Y	N	Y	Y	N	N
5 Maloney	Y	N	Y	Y	+	N	Y
6 Johnson	Y	Y	N	N	Y	N	N
DELAWARE							
AL Castle	Y	Y	N	N	Y	Y	N
FLORIDA							
1 Scarborough	N	Y	N	Y	N	Y	N
2 Boyd	Y	N	N	N	Y	N	N
3 Brown	Y	N	Y	N	N	N	N
4 Fowler	Y	Y	N	Y	Y	Y	Y
5 Thurman	Y	N	Y	Y	N	N	N
6 Stearns	Y	?	N	Y	N	Y	N
7 Mica	Y	Y	N	Y	Y	Y	Y
8 McCollum	Y	Y	N	Y	Y	Y	Y
9 Bilirakis	Y	Y	N	Y	Y	Y	Y
10 Young	Y	Y	N	Y	Y	Y	Y
11 Davis	Y	N	Y	N	Y	N	N
12 Canady	Y	Y	N	Y	N	Y	N
13 Miller	Y	Y	N	Y	Y	Y	Y
14 Goss	Y	Y	N	Y	Y	Y	Y
15 Weldon	Y	Y	N	N	Y	Y	Y
16 Foley	Y	Y	N	Y	Y	Y	Y
17 Meek	Y	N	Y	Y	N	N	N
18 Ros-Lehtinen	Y	Y	N	Y	Y	Y	Y
19 Wexler	Y	N	Y	N	Y	N	N
20 Deutsch	Y	N	Y	N	Y	N	N
21 Diaz-Balart	Y	Y	N	Y	Y	Y	Y
22 Shaw	Y	Y	N	Y	Y	Y	Y
23 Hastings	Y	N	Y	N	Y	N	N
GEORGIA							
1 Kingston	Y	Y	N	Y	N	Y	Y
2 Bishop	Y	N	Y	N	Y	N	N
3 Collins	Y	Y	N	Y	Y	Y	Y
4 McKinney	Y	N	Y	Y	N	N	N
5 Lewis	Y	N	Y	Y	?	N	N
6 Gingrich	Y	Y	N	Y	N	N	N
7 Barr	Y	Y	N	Y	N	Y	Y
8 Chambliss	Y	Y	N	Y	Y	Y	Y
9 Deal	Y	Y	N	Y	N	Y	Y
10 Norwood	Y	Y	N	Y	N	Y	Y
11 Linder	?	?	N	N	Y	Y	Y
HAWAII							
1 Abercrombie	Y	N	Y	Y	Y	N	N
2 Mink	Y	N	Y	Y	Y	N	N
IDAHO							
1 Chenoweth	Y	Y	N	Y	N	Y	Y
2 Crapo	Y	Y	N	Y	N	Y	N
ILLINOIS							
1 Rush	Y	N	?	N	Y	N	N
2 Jackson	Y	N	Y	Y	N	N	N
3 Lipinski	N	N	N	Y	N	N	N
4 Gutierrez	Y	N	Y	N	Y	N	N
5 Blagojevich	Y	N	Y	N	Y	N	N
6 Hyde	Y	Y	N	Y	N	Y	N
7 Davis	Y	N	Y	N	Y	N	N
8 Crane	N	Y	N	N	N	Y	Y
9 Yates	Y	N	Y	N	Y	N	N
10 Porter	Y	Y	N	N	Y	N	N
11 Weller	Y	Y	N	Y	Y	Y	Y
12 Costello	Y	N	Y	N	Y	N	N
13 Fawell	?	Y	N	Y	N	Y	N

ND Northern Democrats   SD Southern Democrats

	483	484	485	486	487	488	489
14 ***Hastert***	Y	Y	N	N	Y	Y	Y
15 ***Ewing***	Y	Y	N	N	Y	Y	N
16 ***Manzullo***	Y	Y	N	Y	N	Y	N
17 Evans	Y	N	Y	N	Y	N	N
18 ***LaHood***	Y	Y	N	N	Y	Y	N
19 Poshard	?	?	?	?	?	?	?
20 ***Shimkus***	Y	Y	N	N	Y	Y	N
INDIANA							
1 Visclosky	Y	N	Y	N	Y	N	N
2 ***McIntosh***	Y	Y	N	Y	N	Y	N
3 Roemer	N	N	Y	N	N	N	N
4 ***Souder***	Y	Y	N	?	Y	Y	Y
5 ***Buyer***	Y	Y	N	N	Y	Y	Y
6 ***Burton***	Y	Y	N	Y	N	Y	Y
7 ***Pease***	Y	Y	N	N	Y	Y	N
8 ***Hostettler***	N	Y	N	Y	N	Y	N
9 Hamilton	Y	N	N	N	Y	N	N
10 Carson	Y	N	Y	Y	Y	N	N
IOWA							
1 ***Leach***	Y	Y	N	N	Y	Y	N
2 ***Nussle***	Y	Y	N	N	Y	Y	N
3 Boswell	Y	N	Y	N	Y	N	N
4 ***Ganske***	Y	Y	N	N	Y	Y	N
5 ***Latham***	Y	Y	N	N	Y	Y	N
KANSAS							
1 ***Moran***	Y	Y	N	Y	Y	Y	N
2 ***Ryun***	Y	Y	N	Y	N	Y	N
3 ***Snowbarger***	Y	Y	N	Y	Y	Y	Y
4 ***Tiahrt***	Y	N	N	Y	N	Y	N
KENTUCKY							
1 ***Whitfield***	Y	Y	N	Y	Y	Y	N
2 ***Lewis***	Y	Y	N	Y	N	Y	Y
3 ***Northup***	Y	Y	N	N	Y	Y	N
4 ***Bunning***	Y	Y	N	N	Y	Y	Y
5 ***Rogers***	Y	Y	N	N	Y	Y	Y
6 Baesler	Y	N	N	N	Y	N	N
LOUISIANA							
1 ***Livingston***	Y	Y	N	N	Y	Y	Y
2 Jefferson	Y	N	Y	N	Y	N	N
3 ***Tauzin***	Y	Y	N	N	Y	Y	Y
4 ***McCrery***	Y	Y	N	?	?	?	?
5 ***Cooksey***	Y	Y	N	Y	Y	Y	Y
6 ***Baker***	Y	Y	N	N	Y	Y	Y
7 John	Y	N	N	N	Y	N	N
MAINE							
1 Allen	Y	N	Y	N	Y	N	N
2 Baldacci	Y	N	Y	N	Y	N	N
MARYLAND							
1 ***Gilchrest***	Y	Y	N	N	Y	Y	N
2 ***Ehrlich***	Y	Y	N	Y	Y	Y	N
3 Cardin	Y	N	Y	Y	Y	N	N
4 Wynn	Y	N	Y	N	Y	N	N
5 Hoyer	Y	N	Y	N	Y	N	N
6 ***Bartlett***	Y	Y	N	Y	Y	Y	N
7 Cummings	Y	N	Y	Y	Y	N	N
8 ***Morella***	Y	Y	N	N	Y	Y	N
MASSACHUSETTS							
1 Olver	Y	N	Y	N	Y	N	N
2 Neal	Y	N	Y	Y	Y	N	N
3 McGovern	Y	N	Y	N	Y	N	N
4 Frank	Y	N	Y	N	Y	N	N
5 Meehan	Y	N	Y	N	Y	N	N
6 Tierney	Y	N	Y	N	N	N	N
7 Markey	Y	N	Y	N	Y	N	N
8 Kennedy	Y	N	Y	?	?	?	?
9 Moakley	Y	N	Y	N	Y	N	N
10 Delahunt	Y	N	Y	Y	Y	N	N
MICHIGAN							
1 Stupak	Y	N	Y	N	Y	Y	N
2 ***Hoekstra***	Y	Y	N	N	Y	Y	N
3 ***Ehlers***	Y	Y	N	N	Y	Y	N
4 ***Camp***	Y	Y	N	Y	?	Y	N
5 Barcia	Y	N	Y	Y	Y	Y	N
6 ***Upton***	Y	Y	N	N	Y	Y	N
7 ***Smith***	Y	Y	N	Y	Y	Y	N
8 Stabenow	Y	N	Y	N	Y	N	N
9 Kildee	Y	N	Y	N	Y	N	N
10 Bonior	Y	N	Y	Y	N	N	N
11 ***Knollenberg***	Y	Y	N	N	Y	Y	Y
12 Levin	Y	N	Y	N	Y	N	N
13 Rivers	Y	N	Y	Y	Y	N	N
14 Conyers	N	N	Y	Y	N	N	N
15 Kilpatrick	Y	?	Y	Y	N	N	N
16 Dingell	Y	N	Y	N	Y	Y	Y

	483	484	485	486	487	488	489
MINNESOTA							
1 ***Gutknecht***	Y	Y	N	Y	Y	Y	N
2 Minge	Y	N	Y	N	Y	N	N
3 ***Ramstad***	Y	Y	N	N	Y	Y	N
4 Vento	Y	N	Y	N	Y	N	N
5 Sabo	Y	N	Y	N	Y	N	N
6 Luther	Y	N	Y	N	Y	N	N
7 Peterson	Y	N	N	N	Y	N	N
8 Oberstar	Y	N	Y	N	Y	N	N
MISSISSIPPI							
1 ***Wicker***	Y	Y	N	N	Y	Y	Y
2 Thompson	Y	N	Y	Y	Y	N	N
3 ***Pickering***	Y	Y	N	Y	Y	Y	Y
4 ***Parker***	Y	Y	?	Y	Y	Y	Y
5 Taylor	Y	N	N	N	Y	N	N
MISSOURI							
1 Clay	Y	N	Y	?	N	N	N
2 ***Talent***	Y	Y	N	Y	N	Y	N
3 Gephardt	Y	N	Y	N	?	N	N
4 Skelton	Y	N	N	N	Y	N	N
5 McCarthy	Y	N	Y	N	Y	N	N
6 Danner	Y	N	Y	N	Y	N	N
7 ***Blunt***	Y	Y	N	N	Y	Y	Y
8 ***Emerson***	Y	Y	N	Y	Y	Y	N
9 ***Hulshof***	Y	Y	N	N	Y	Y	N
MONTANA							
AL ***Hill***	Y	Y	N	Y	N	Y	Y
NEBRASKA							
1 ***Bereuter***	Y	Y	N	N	Y	Y	Y
2 ***Christensen***	Y	Y	N	Y	N	Y	Y
3 ***Barrett***	Y	Y	N	N	Y	Y	Y
NEVADA							
1 ***Ensign***	Y	Y	N	Y	N	Y	N
2 ***Gibbons***	Y	Y	N	N	Y	Y	Y
NEW HAMPSHIRE							
1 ***Sununu***	Y	Y	N	Y	Y	Y	N
2 ***Bass***	Y	Y	N	N	Y	Y	N
NEW JERSEY							
1 Andrews	Y	N	Y	?	Y	N	N
2 ***LoBiondo***	Y	Y	N	N	Y	Y	N
3 ***Saxton***	Y	Y	N	N	Y	Y	N
4 ***Smith***	Y	Y	N	N	Y	Y	N
5 ***Roukema***	Y	Y	N	?	Y	Y	Y
6 Pallone	Y	N	Y	N	Y	N	N
7 ***Franks***	Y	Y	N	N	Y	Y	N
8 Pascrell	Y	N	Y	N	Y	N	N
9 Rothman	Y	N	Y	N	Y	N	N
10 Payne	Y	N	Y	Y	N	N	N
11 ***Frelinghuysen***	Y	Y	N	N	Y	Y	Y
12 ***Pappas***	Y	Y	N	Y	Y	Y	N
13 Menendez	Y	N	Y	N	Y	N	N
NEW MEXICO							
1 ***Wilson***	+	Y	N	Y	Y	Y	Y
2 ***Skeen***	Y	Y	N	N	Y	Y	Y
3 ***Redmond***	Y	Y	N	Y	N	Y	Y
NEW YORK							
1 ***Forbes***	Y	Y	N	N	Y	Y	N
2 ***Lazio***	Y	Y	N	N	Y	Y	N
3 ***King***	Y	Y	N	N	Y	Y	N
4 McCarthy	Y	N	Y	N	Y	N	N
5 Ackerman	Y	N	Y	N	Y	N	N
6 Meeks	Y	N	Y	Y	N	N	N
7 Manton	Y	N	Y	N	Y	N	N
8 Nadler	Y	N	Y	N	Y	N	N
9 Schumer	Y	N	Y	N	Y	N	N
10 Towns	Y	N	Y	Y	N	N	N
11 Owens	Y	N	Y	Y	N	N	N
12 Velázquez	N	N	Y	Y	N	N	N
13 ***Fossella***	Y	Y	N	Y	Y	Y	N
14 Maloney	Y	N	Y	N	Y	N	N
15 Rangel	Y	N	Y	Y	Y	N	N
16 Serrano	Y	N	Y	Y	Y	?	N
17 Engel	Y	N	Y	N	Y	N	N
18 Lowey	Y	N	Y	N	Y	N	N
19 ***Kelly***	Y	Y	N	N	Y	Y	N
20 ***Gilman***	Y	Y	N	N	Y	?	N
21 McNulty	Y	N	Y	N	Y	N	N
22 ***Solomon***	Y	Y	N	?	Y	Y	Y
23 ***Boehlert***	Y	Y	N	N	Y	Y	N
24 ***McHugh***	Y	Y	N	N	Y	Y	Y
25 ***Walsh***	Y	Y	N	N	Y	Y	N
26 Hinchey	Y	N	Y	Y	N	N	N
27 ***Paxon***	Y	Y	N	N	Y	Y	Y
28 Slaughter	Y	N	Y	N	Y	N	N
29 LaFalce	Y	N	Y	?	?	?	?
30 ***Quinn***	Y	Y	N	N	Y	Y	N

	483	484	485	486	487	488	489
31 ***Houghton***	Y	Y	N	N	Y	Y	N
NORTH CAROLINA							
1 Clayton	Y	N	Y	Y	N	N	N
2 Etheridge	Y	N	Y	N	Y	N	N
3 ***Jones***	Y	Y	N	Y	N	Y	N
4 Price	Y	N	Y	N	Y	N	N
5 ***Burr***	Y	Y	N	N	Y	Y	N
6 ***Coble***	Y	Y	N	N	Y	Y	Y
7 McIntyre	Y	N	Y	N	Y	N	N
8 Hefner	Y	N	Y	N	Y	N	?
9 ***Myrick***	Y	Y	N	Y	N	Y	N
10 ***Ballenger***	Y	Y	N	Y	Y	Y	Y
11 ***Taylor***	Y	Y	N	N	Y	Y	Y
12 Watt	Y	N	Y	Y	N	N	N
NORTH DAKOTA							
AL Pomeroy	Y	N	Y	N	Y	N	N
OHIO							
1 ***Chabot***	Y	Y	N	Y	Y	Y	N
2 ***Portman***	Y	Y	N	N	Y	Y	N
3 Hall	Y	N	Y	N	Y	N	N
4 ***Oxley***	Y	Y	N	N	Y	Y	Y
5 ***Gillmor***	Y	Y	N	Y	Y	Y	Y
6 Strickland	Y	N	Y	N	Y	N	N
7 ***Hobson***	Y	Y	N	N	Y	Y	N
8 ***Boehner***	Y	Y	N	N	Y	Y	Y
9 Kaptur	Y	N	Y	N	Y	N	N
10 Kucinich	Y	N	Y	N	N	N	N
11 Stokes	Y	N	Y	Y	Y	N	N
12 ***Kasich***	Y	Y	N	N	Y	Y	N
13 Brown	Y	N	Y	N	N	N	N
14 Sawyer	Y	N	Y	N	Y	N	N
15 ***Pryce***	+	+	−	−	+	+	−
16 ***Regula***	Y	Y	N	N	Y	Y	Y
17 Traficant	Y	N	N	Y	Y	N	N
18 ***Ney***	Y	Y	N	Y	Y	Y	N
19 ***LaTourette***	Y	Y	N	N	Y	Y	N
OKLAHOMA							
1 ***Largent***	Y	Y	N	Y	Y	Y	N
2 ***Coburn***	Y	Y	N	Y	N	Y	N
3 ***Watkins***	Y	Y	N	Y	Y	Y	Y
4 ***Watts***	Y	Y	N	Y	N	Y	Y
5 ***Istook***	Y	N	N	Y	N	Y	Y
6 ***Lucas***	Y	Y	N	Y	N	Y	Y
OREGON							
1 Furse	Y	N	Y	Y	N	?	N
2 ***Smith***	Y	Y	N	N	Y	Y	Y
3 Blumenauer	Y	N	N	N	Y	N	N
4 DeFazio	N	N	Y	Y	N	N	N
5 Hooley	Y	N	Y	N	N	N	N
PENNSYLVANIA							
1 Brady	Y	N	Y	N	Y	N	N
2 Fattah	Y	N	Y	?	?	N	N
3 Borski	Y	N	Y	N	Y	N	N
4 Klink	Y	N	Y	Y	Y	N	N
5 ***Peterson***	Y	Y	N	?	Y	Y	N
6 Holden	Y	N	Y	N	Y	N	N
7 ***Weldon***	Y	Y	N	N	Y	?	Y
8 ***Greenwood***	Y	Y	N	N	Y	Y	N
9 ***Shuster***	Y	Y	N	N	Y	Y	Y
10 ***McDade***	Y	Y	N	Y	Y	Y	Y
11 Kanjorski	Y	N	Y	Y	Y	N	N
12 Murtha	Y	N	N	N	Y	N	N
13 ***Fox***	Y	Y	N	N	Y	Y	N
14 Coyne	Y	N	Y	Y	Y	N	N
15 McHale	?	N	Y	N	Y	N	N
16 ***Pitts***	Y	Y	N	Y	Y	Y	Y
17 ***Gekas***	Y	Y	N	N	Y	Y	+
18 Doyle	Y	N	Y	N	Y	N	N
19 ***Goodling***	Y	Y	N	?	Y	Y	Y
20 Mascara	Y	N	Y	N	Y	N	N
21 ***English***	N	Y	N	Y	Y	Y	N
RHODE ISLAND							
1 Kennedy	Y	N	Y	N	Y	N	N
2 Weygand	Y	N	Y	N	Y	N	N
SOUTH CAROLINA							
1 ***Sanford***	N	Y	N	Y	N	Y	N
2 ***Spence***	Y	Y	N	N	Y	Y	Y
3 ***Graham***	Y	Y	N	?	N	Y	N
4 ***Inglis***	Y	Y	N	Y	Y	Y	N
5 Spratt	Y	N	N	N	Y	N	N
6 Clyburn	Y	N	Y	Y	Y	N	N
SOUTH DAKOTA							
AL ***Thune***	Y	Y	N	N	Y	Y	Y

	483	484	485	486	487	488	489
TENNESSEE							
1 ***Jenkins***	Y	Y	N	Y	Y	Y	Y
2 ***Duncan***	Y	Y	N	Y	N	Y	Y
3 ***Wamp***	Y	Y	N	Y	N	Y	Y
4 ***Hilleary***	Y	Y	N	Y	N	Y	Y
5 Clement	Y	?	Y	N	Y	N	N
6 Gordon	Y	N	N	N	N	N	N
7 ***Bryant***	Y	Y	N	Y	Y	Y	Y
8 Tanner	Y	N	Y	N	Y	N	N
9 Ford	Y	N	Y	Y	Y	N	N
TEXAS							
1 Sandlin	Y	N	Y	N	Y	N	N
2 Turner	Y	N	Y	N	Y	N	N
3 ***Johnson, Sam***	Y	Y	N	N	Y	Y	Y
4 Hall	Y	N	N	N	Y	N	Y
5 ***Sessions***	Y	Y	N	N	Y	Y	Y
6 ***Barton***	Y	Y	N	N	Y	Y	Y
7 ***Archer***	Y	Y	N	N	Y	Y	Y
8 ***Brady***	Y	Y	N	N	Y	Y	Y
9 Lampson	Y	N	Y	N	Y	N	N
10 Doggett	Y	N	Y	Y	Y	N	N
11 Edwards	Y	N	Y	N	Y	N	N
12 ***Granger***	Y	Y	N	N	Y	Y	Y
13 ***Thornberry***	Y	Y	N	Y	Y	Y	Y
14 ***Paul***	N	Y	N	Y	N	Y	N
15 Hinojosa	Y	N	Y	N	Y	N	N
16 Reyes	Y	N	Y	N	Y	N	N
17 Stenholm	Y	N	N	N	Y	N	Y
18 Jackson-Lee	Y	N	Y	Y	Y	N	N
19 ***Combest***	Y	Y	N	N	Y	Y	Y
20 Gonzalez	Y	N	Y	N	Y	N	N
21 ***Smith***	Y	Y	N	N	Y	Y	Y
22 ***DeLay***	Y	Y	N	Y	Y	Y	Y
23 ***Bonilla***	Y	Y	N	Y	N	Y	Y
24 Frost	Y	N	Y	N	Y	N	N
25 Bentsen	Y	N	Y	N	Y	N	N
26 ***Armey***	Y	Y	N	N	Y	Y	Y
27 Ortiz	Y	N	Y	N	Y	N	Y
28 Rodriguez	Y	N	Y	N	Y	N	N
29 Green	Y	N	Y	N	N	N	N
30 Johnson, E.B.	Y	N	Y	N	Y	N	N
UTAH							
1 ***Hansen***	Y	Y	N	N	Y	Y	Y
2 ***Cook***	Y	Y	N	N	Y	Y	Y
3 ***Cannon***	Y	Y	N	Y	Y	Y	Y
VERMONT							
AL *Sanders*	Y	N	Y	Y	N	N	N
VIRGINIA							
1 ***Bateman***	Y	Y	N	N	Y	Y	Y
2 Pickett	Y	N	N	N	Y	N	N
3 Scott	Y	N	Y	Y	Y	N	N
4 Sisisky	Y	N	Y	N	Y	N	N
5 Goode	Y	N	N	Y	N	N	N
6 ***Goodlatte***	Y	Y	N	Y	Y	Y	N
7 ***Bliley***	Y	Y	N	N	Y	Y	Y
8 Moran	+	N	Y	N	Y	N	N
9 Boucher	Y	N	?	N	Y	N	N
10 ***Wolf***	Y	Y	N	N	Y	Y	N
11 ***Davis***	Y	?	N	N	Y	?	N
WASHINGTON							
1 ***White***	Y	Y	N	−	Y	Y	N
2 ***Metcalf***	Y	Y	N	Y	N	Y	Y
3 ***Smith, Linda***	Y	Y	N	Y	N	Y	N
4 ***Hastings***	Y	Y	N	N	Y	Y	Y
5 ***Nethercutt***	Y	Y	N	N	Y	Y	N
6 Dicks	Y	N	N	N	Y	N	N
7 McDermott	Y	N	Y	N	N	N	N
8 ***Dunn***	Y	Y	N	N	+	Y	Y
9 Smith, Adam	Y	N	Y	N	Y	N	N
WEST VIRGINIA							
1 Mollohan	Y	N	Y	Y	Y	N	N
2 Wise	Y	N	Y	N	Y	N	N
3 Rahall	Y	N	Y	N	Y	N	N
WISCONSIN							
1 ***Neumann***	Y	N	N	Y	N	Y	N
2 ***Klug***	Y	Y	N	N	Y	Y	N
3 Kind	Y	N	Y	?	Y	N	N
4 Kleczka	Y	N	Y	N	Y	N	N
5 Barrett	Y	N	Y	Y	Y	N	N
6 ***Petri***	N	Y	N	Y	N	Y	N
7 Obey	Y	N	Y	N	Y	N	N
8 Johnson	Y	N	Y	Y	Y	N	N
9 ***Sensenbrenner***	N	Y	N	Y	N	Y	N
WYOMING							
AL ***Cubin***	Y	Y	N	Y	N	Y	Y

Southern states - Ala., Ark., Fla., Ga., Ky., La., Miss., N.C., Okla., S.C., Tenn., Texas, Va.

House Votes 490, 491, 492, 493, 494, 495, 497 *

490. HR 4104. Fiscal 1999 Treasury Postal Appropriations/Rule. Adoption of the rule (H Res 579) to provide for House floor consideration of the bill to provide $13.44 billion in fiscal 1999 funding for the Treasury Department, U.S. Postal Service subsidies, the Executive Office of the President and several independent agencies. Adopted 231-194: R 217-6; D 14-187 (ND 8-139, SD 6-48); I 0-1. Oct. 7, 1998.

491. HR 4616. Corporal Harold Gomez Post Office/Passage. McHugh, R-N.Y., motion to suspend the rules and pass the bill to designate a U.S. post office in East Chicago, Indiana as the "Corporal Harold Gomez Post Office." Motion agreed to 425-0: R 222-0; D 202-0 (ND 147-0, SD 55-0); I 1-0. Oct. 7, 1998. A two-thirds majority of those present and voting (284 in this case) is required for passage under suspension of the rules.

492. HR 2348. Mervyn Dymally Post Office/Passage. McHugh, R-N.Y., motion to suspend the rules and pass the bill to designate a U.S. post office in Compton, Calif. as the "Mervyn Dymally Post Office Building." Motion agreed to 421-1: R 221-1; D 199-0 (ND 144-0, SD 55-0); I 1-0. Oct. 7, 1998. A two-thirds majority of those present and voting (282 in this case) is required for passage under suspension of the rules.

493. HR 4104. Fiscal 1999 Treasury Postal Appropriations/Recommit. Hoyer, D-Md., motion to recommit the bill to the conference committee with instructions to report it back with an amendment requiring federal health plans that cover other prescription drugs to also cover prescription contraceptives. Motion rejected 202-226: R 21-203; D 180-23 (ND 132-16, SD 48-7); I 1-0. Oct. 7, 1998.

494. HR 4104. Fiscal 1999 Treasury Postal Appropriations/Conference Report. Adoption of the conference report on the bill to provide $13.44 billion in fiscal 1999 funding for the Treasury Department, U.S. Postal Service subsidies, the Executive Office of the President and several independent agencies. Adopted (thus sent to the Senate) 290-137: R 209-15; D 81-121 (ND 51-96, SD 30-25); I 0-1. Oct. 7, 1998.

495. Procedural Motion/Journal. Approval of the House Journal of Wednesday, Oct. 7, 1998. Approved 325-72: R 190-19; D 134-53 (ND 98-40, SD 36-13); I 1-0. Oct. 8, 1998.

496. Quorum Call.* 423 Responded. Oct. 8, 1998.

497. H Res 581. Open Impeachment Inquiry/Recommit. Boucher, D-Va., motion to recommit the bill to the Judiciary Committee with instructions to report it back with an amendment that would authorize the committee to conduct an impeachment inquiry against the president after first determining whether the allegations against the president by Independent Counsel Kenneth W. Starr, if true, constituted grounds for impeachment. If the allegations did not meet this standard, then the committee could consider alternative sanctions. The committee would have to conclude its work in time for the House to consider its recommendations by Dec. 31, unless the committee requested an extension. Rejected 198-236: R 1-226; D 196-10 (ND 145-6, SD 51-4); I 1-0. Oct. 8, 1998.

CQ does not include quorum calls in its vote charts.

Key

- Y Voted for (yea).
- # Paired for.
- + Announced for.
- N Voted against (nay).
- X Paired against.
- − Announced against.
- P Voted "present."
- C Voted "present" to avoid possible conflict of interest.
- ? Did not vote or otherwise make a position known.

Democrats **Republicans**
Independent

	490	491	492	493	494	495	497
ALABAMA							
1 *Callahan*	Y	Y	Y	N	Y	Y	N
2 *Everett*	Y	Y	Y	N	Y	Y	N
3 *Riley*	Y	Y	Y	N	Y	N	N
4 *Aderholt*	Y	Y	Y	N	Y	N	N
5 Cramer	N	Y	Y	Y	Y	Y	Y
6 *Bachus*	Y	Y	Y	N	Y	N	N
7 Hilliard	N	Y	Y	Y	N	N	Y
ALASKA							
AL *Young*	Y	Y	Y	N	Y	Y	N
ARIZONA							
1 *Salmon*	Y	Y	Y	N	Y	Y	N
2 Pastor	N	Y	?	Y	Y	Y	Y
3 *Stump*	Y	Y	Y	N	N	Y	N
4 *Shadegg*	Y	Y	Y	N	Y	P	N
5 *Kolbe*	Y	Y	Y	N	Y	Y	N
6 *Hayworth*	Y	Y	Y	N	Y	Y	N
ARKANSAS							
1 Berry	N	Y	Y	N	Y	N	Y
2 Snyder	N	Y	Y	Y	Y	Y	Y
3 *Hutchinson*	Y	Y	Y	N	Y	Y	Y
4 *Dickey*	Y	Y	Y	N	Y	Y	Y
CALIFORNIA							
1 *Riggs*	Y	Y	Y	N	Y	?	N
2 *Herger*	Y	Y	Y	N	Y	Y	N
3 Fazio	N	Y	Y	Y	N	Y	Y
4 *Doolittle*	Y	Y	Y	N	N	Y	N
5 Matsui	N	Y	Y	Y	N	Y	Y
6 Woolsey	N	Y	Y	Y	N	Y	Y
7 Miller	N	?	?	Y	N	?	Y
8 Pelosi	N	Y	Y	Y	N	Y	Y
9 Lee	N	Y	Y	Y	N	N	Y
10 Tauscher	N	Y	Y	Y	Y	Y	Y
11 *Pombo*	Y	Y	Y	N	Y	Y	N
12 Lantos	N	Y	Y	Y	N	Y	Y
13 Stark	N	Y	Y	Y	N	N	Y
14 Eshoo	N	Y	Y	Y	N	Y	Y
15 *Campbell*	Y	Y	Y	N	Y	N	N
16 Lofgren	N	Y	Y	Y	N	Y	Y
17 Farr	N	Y	Y	Y	Y	Y	Y
18 Condit	N	Y	Y	Y	Y	Y	Y
19 *Radanovich*	Y	Y	Y	N	Y	Y	N
20 Dooley	N	Y	Y	Y	Y	Y	Y
21 *Thomas*	Y	Y	Y	N	Y	Y	N
22 Capps, L.	N	Y	Y	Y	N	Y	Y
23 *Gallegly*	Y	Y	Y	N	Y	Y	N
24 Sherman	N	Y	?	Y	N	Y	Y
25 *McKeon*	Y	Y	Y	N	Y	Y	N
26 Berman	N	Y	Y	Y	N	Y	Y
27 *Rogan*	Y	Y	Y	N	Y	Y	N
28 *Dreier*	Y	Y	Y	N	Y	Y	N
29 Waxman	?	Y	Y	Y	N	Y	Y
30 Becerra	N	Y	Y	Y	N	Y	Y
31 Martinez	N	Y	Y	Y	P	Y	Y
32 Dixon	N	Y	Y	Y	N	?	Y
33 Roybal-Allard	N	Y	Y	Y	N	Y	Y
34 Torres	N	Y	Y	Y	N	Y	Y
35 Waters	N	Y	Y	Y	N	N	Y
36 Harman	N	Y	Y	Y	N	Y	Y
37 Millender-McD.	N	Y	Y	Y	N	Y	Y
38 *Horn*	Y	Y	Y	Y	Y	Y	N

	490	491	492	493	494	495	497
39 *Royce*	Y	Y	Y	N	Y	Y	N
40 *Lewis*	Y	Y	Y	N	Y	Y	N
41 *Kim*	Y	Y	Y	N	Y	Y	N
42 Brown	N	Y	Y	Y	N	Y	Y
43 *Calvert*	Y	Y	Y	N	Y	Y	N
44 *Bono, M.*	Y	Y	Y	N	Y	Y	N
45 *Rohrabacher*	Y	Y	Y	N	Y	Y	N
46 Sanchez	N	Y	Y	Y	N	Y	Y
47 *Cox*	Y	Y	Y	N	Y	Y	N
48 *Packard*	Y	Y	Y	N	Y	Y	N
49 *Bilbray*	N	Y	Y	Y	Y	Y	N
50 Filner	N	Y	Y	Y	N	N	Y
51 *Cunningham*	Y	Y	Y	N	Y	P	N
52 *Hunter*	Y	Y	Y	N	Y	Y	N
COLORADO							
1 DeGette	N	Y	Y	Y	N	Y	Y
2 Skaggs	N	Y	Y	N	Y	Y	Y
3 *McInnis*	Y	Y	Y	N	Y	Y	N
4 *Schaffer*	Y	Y	Y	N	N	N	N
5 *Hefley*	Y	Y	Y	N	Y	Y	N
6 *Schaefer*	Y	Y	Y	N	Y	?	N
CONNECTICUT							
1 Kennelly	?	?	?	?	?	Y	Y
2 Gejdenson	N	Y	Y	Y	N	Y	Y
3 DeLauro	N	Y	Y	Y	N	Y	Y
4 *Shays*	N	Y	Y	Y	N	Y	Y
5 Maloney	N	Y	Y	N	?	?	Y
6 *Johnson*	Y	Y	Y	Y	Y	Y	N
DELAWARE							
AL *Castle*	Y	Y	Y	Y	Y	Y	N
FLORIDA							
1 *Scarborough*	Y	Y	Y	N	Y	?	N
2 Boyd	N	Y	Y	Y	Y	N	Y
3 Brown	N	Y	Y	Y	N	Y	Y
4 *Fowler*	Y	Y	Y	N	Y	Y	N
5 Thurman	N	Y	Y	N	Y	Y	Y
6 *Stearns*	Y	Y	Y	N	Y	Y	N
7 *Mica*	Y	Y	Y	N	Y	Y	N
8 *McCollum*	Y	Y	Y	N	Y	Y	N
9 *Bilirakis*	Y	Y	Y	N	Y	Y	N
10 *Young*	Y	Y	Y	N	Y	Y	N
11 Davis	N	Y	Y	Y	Y	?	Y
12 *Canady*	Y	Y	Y	N	Y	Y	N
13 *Miller*	Y	Y	Y	N	Y	Y	N
14 *Goss*	Y	Y	Y	N	Y	Y	N
15 *Weldon*	Y	Y	Y	N	Y	Y	N
16 *Foley*	Y	Y	Y	N	Y	Y	N
17 Meek	N	Y	Y	Y	Y	?	Y
18 *Ros-Lehtinen*	Y	Y	N	N	Y	N	N
19 Wexler	N	Y	Y	N	Y	Y	Y
20 Deutsch	N	Y	Y	Y	N	Y	Y
21 *Diaz-Balart*	N	Y	N	N	Y	N	N
22 *Shaw*	Y	Y	Y	N	Y	Y	N
23 Hastings	N	Y	Y	N	N	N	Y
GEORGIA							
1 *Kingston*	Y	Y	Y	N	Y	Y	N
2 Bishop	N	Y	Y	Y	Y	Y	Y
3 *Collins*	Y	Y	Y	N	Y	Y	N
4 *McKinney*	N	Y	Y	Y	N	Y	N
5 Lewis	N	Y	Y	Y	N	N	N
6 *Gingrich*							N
7 *Barr*	Y	Y	Y	N	Y	Y	N
8 *Chambliss*	Y	Y	Y	N	Y	Y	N
9 *Deal*	Y	Y	Y	N	Y	Y	N
10 *Norwood*	Y	Y	Y	N	Y	Y	N
11 *Linder*	Y	Y	Y	N	Y	Y	N
HAWAII							
1 Abercrombie	N	Y	Y	Y	N	Y	Y
2 Mink	N	Y	Y	Y	N	Y	Y
IDAHO							
1 *Chenoweth*	Y	Y	Y	N	N	Y	N
2 *Crapo*	Y	Y	Y	N	N	Y	N
ILLINOIS							
1 Rush	N	Y	Y	Y	N	Y	Y
2 Jackson	N	Y	Y	Y	Y	Y	Y
3 Lipinski	Y	Y	Y	N	Y	Y	N
4 Gutierrez	N	Y	Y	Y	N	N	Y
5 Blagojevich	N	Y	Y	Y	N	Y	Y
6 *Hyde*	Y	Y	Y	N	Y	?	N
7 Davis	N	Y	Y	Y	N	Y	Y
8 *Crane*	Y	Y	Y	N	N	Y	N
9 Yates	?	?	?	?	?	Y	Y
10 *Porter*	Y	Y	Y	N	Y	Y	N
11 *Weller*	?	Y	Y	N	Y	Y	N
12 Costello	N	Y	Y	Y	N	Y	Y
13 *Fawell*	Y	Y	Y	N	N	Y	N

ND Northern Democrats   SD Southern Democrats

H-140 — 1998 CQ ALMANAC

WWW.CQ.COM

	490	491	492	493	494	495	497
14 ***Hastert***	Y	Y	Y	N	Y	Y	N
15 ***Ewing***	Y	Y	Y	N	Y	Y	N
16 ***Manzullo***	Y	Y	Y	N	Y	N	N
17 Evans	N	Y	Y	Y	N	Y	N
18 ***LaHood***	Y	Y	Y	N	Y	Y	N
19 Poshard	?	?	?	?	?	N	Y
20 ***Shimkus***	Y	Y	Y	N	Y	Y	N
INDIANA							
1 Visclosky	N	Y	Y	Y	Y	N	Y
2 ***McIntosh***	Y	Y	Y	N	Y	Y	N
3 Roemer	N	Y	Y	Y	N	Y	Y
4 ***Souder***	Y	Y	Y	N	Y	Y	N
5 ***Buyer***	Y	Y	Y	N	Y	Y	N
6 ***Burton***	Y	Y	Y	N	Y	Y	N
7 ***Pease***	Y	Y	Y	N	Y	Y	N
8 ***Hostettler***	Y	Y	Y	N	Y	Y	N
9 Hamilton	N	Y	Y	Y	Y	Y	Y
10 Carson	N	Y	Y	Y	N	P	Y
IOWA							
1 ***Leach***	Y	Y	Y	Y	Y	Y	N
2 ***Nussle***	Y	Y	Y	N	Y	Y	N
3 Boswell	N	Y	Y	Y	Y	Y	Y
4 ***Ganske***	Y	Y	Y	N	Y	Y	N
5 ***Latham***	Y	Y	Y	N	Y	Y	N
KANSAS							
1 ***Moran***	Y	Y	Y	N	N	N	N
2 ***Ryun***	Y	Y	Y	N	Y	Y	N
3 ***Snowbarger***	Y	Y	Y	N	Y	Y	N
4 ***Tiahrt***	Y	Y	Y	N	Y	Y	N
KENTUCKY							
1 ***Whitfield***	Y	Y	Y	N	Y	Y	N
2 ***Lewis***	Y	Y	Y	N	Y	Y	N
3 ***Northup***	Y	Y	Y	N	Y	Y	N
4 ***Bunning***	Y	Y	Y	N	Y	Y	N
5 ***Rogers***	Y	?	Y	N	Y	Y	N
6 Baesler	N	Y	Y	Y	Y	Y	Y
LOUISIANA							
1 ***Livingston***	Y	Y	Y	N	Y	Y	N
2 Jefferson	N	Y	Y	Y	N	?	Y
3 ***Tauzin***	Y	Y	Y	N	Y	Y	N
4 ***McCrery***	?	?	?	?	?	?	N
5 ***Cooksey***	Y	?	Y	N	Y	Y	N
6 ***Baker***	Y	Y	Y	N	Y	Y	N
7 John	Y	Y	Y	N	Y	Y	Y
MAINE							
1 Allen	N	Y	Y	Y	Y	Y	Y
2 Baldacci	N	Y	Y	Y	N	Y	Y
MARYLAND							
1 ***Gilchrest***	Y	Y	Y	N	Y	Y	N
2 ***Ehrlich***	Y	Y	Y	N	Y	Y	N
3 Cardin	N	Y	Y	Y	Y	Y	Y
4 Wynn	N	Y	Y	Y	Y	N	Y
5 Hoyer	N	Y	Y	Y	Y	Y	Y
6 ***Bartlett***	Y	Y	Y	N	Y	Y	N
7 Cummings	N	Y	Y	Y	N	Y	Y
8 ***Morella***	N	Y	Y	Y	Y	Y	N
MASSACHUSETTS							
1 Olver	N	Y	Y	Y	Y	N	Y
2 Neal	Y	Y	Y	Y	Y	Y	Y
3 McGovern	N	Y	Y	Y	N	N	Y
4 Frank	N	Y	Y	Y	N	N	Y
5 Meehan	N	Y	Y	Y	N	Y	Y
6 Tierney	N	Y	Y	Y	N	Y	Y
7 Markey	N	Y	Y	Y	?	Y	Y
8 Kennedy	N	Y	Y	Y	N	Y	Y
9 Moakley	N	Y	Y	Y	Y	Y	Y
10 Delahunt	N	Y	Y	Y	N	Y	Y
MICHIGAN							
1 Stupak	N	Y	Y	N	Y	N	Y
2 ***Hoekstra***	Y	Y	Y	N	Y	Y	N
3 ***Ehlers***	Y	Y	Y	N	Y	Y	N
4 ***Camp***	Y	Y	Y	N	Y	Y	N
5 Barcia	Y	Y	Y	N	Y	Y	Y
6 ***Upton***	Y	Y	Y	Y	Y	Y	N
7 ***Smith***	Y	Y	Y	N	Y	N	N
8 Stabenow	N	Y	Y	Y	N	Y	Y
9 Kildee	Y	Y	Y	N	Y	Y	Y
10 Bonior	N	Y	Y	Y	N	N	Y
11 ***Knollenberg***	Y	Y	Y	N	Y	Y	N
12 Levin	N	Y	Y	Y	N	Y	Y
13 Rivers	N	Y	Y	Y	N	Y	Y
14 Conyers	N	Y	?	Y	N	?	Y
15 Kilpatrick	N	Y	Y	Y	N	Y	Y
16 Dingell	N	Y	Y	Y	N	Y	Y

	490	491	492	493	494	495	497
MINNESOTA							
1 ***Gutknecht***	Y	Y	Y	N	Y	N	N
2 Minge	N	Y	Y	Y	N	Y	Y
3 ***Ramstad***	Y	Y	Y	Y	Y	N	N
4 Vento	N	Y	Y	Y	Y	N	Y
5 Sabo	N	Y	Y	Y	Y	N	Y
6 Luther	N	Y	Y	Y	N	Y	Y
7 Peterson	N	Y	Y	N	N	Y	Y
8 Oberstar	N	Y	Y	Y	Y	N	Y
MISSISSIPPI							
1 ***Wicker***	Y	Y	Y	N	Y	N	N
2 Thompson	N	Y	Y	Y	N	N	Y
3 ***Pickering***	Y	Y	Y	N	Y	Y	N
4 Parker	Y	Y	Y	N	Y	Y	N
5 Taylor	Y	Y	Y	N	N	N	N
MISSOURI							
1 Clay	N	Y	Y	Y	N	N	Y
2 ***Talent***	Y	Y	Y	N	Y	Y	N
3 Gephardt	N	Y	Y	Y	N	N	Y
4 Skelton	N	Y	Y	N	Y	N	Y
5 McCarthy	N	Y	Y	Y	N	Y	Y
6 Danner	N	Y	Y	N	Y	Y	Y
7 ***Blunt***	Y	Y	Y	N	Y	Y	N
8 ***Emerson***	Y	Y	Y	N	Y	Y	N
9 ***Hulshof***	Y	Y	Y	N	Y	N	N
MONTANA							
AL ***Hill***	Y	Y	Y	N	Y	N	N
NEBRASKA							
1 ***Bereuter***	Y	Y	N	N	Y	Y	N
2 ***Christensen***	Y	Y	Y	N	Y	Y	N
3 ***Barrett***	Y	Y	Y	N	Y	Y	N
NEVADA							
1 ***Ensign***	Y	Y	Y	Y	Y	N	N
2 ***Gibbons***	Y	Y	Y	N	Y	N	N
NEW HAMPSHIRE							
1 ***Sununu***	Y	Y	Y	N	Y	Y	N
2 ***Bass***	Y	Y	Y	Y	Y	Y	N
NEW JERSEY							
1 Andrews	N	Y	Y	Y	N	Y	Y
2 ***LoBiondo***	Y	Y	Y	N	Y	N	N
3 ***Saxton***	?	Y	Y	N	Y	Y	N
4 ***Smith***	Y	Y	?	N	Y	Y	N
5 ***Roukema***	Y	Y	Y	Y	Y	Y	N
6 Pallone	N	Y	Y	Y	N	N	Y
7 ***Franks***	Y	Y	Y	N	Y	Y	N
8 Pascrell	N	Y	Y	Y	Y	Y	Y
9 Rothman	N	Y	Y	Y	N	Y	Y
10 Payne	N	Y	Y	Y	N	Y	Y
11 ***Frelinghuysen***	Y	Y	Y	Y	Y	Y	N
12 ***Pappas***	Y	Y	Y	N	Y	Y	N
13 Menendez	N	Y	Y	Y	N	N	Y
NEW MEXICO							
1 ***Wilson***	Y	Y	Y	N	Y	Y	N
2 ***Skeen***	Y	Y	Y	N	Y	?	N
3 ***Redmond***	Y	Y	Y	N	Y	Y	N
NEW YORK							
1 ***Forbes***	Y	Y	Y	N	Y	Y	N
2 ***Lazio***	Y	Y	Y	Y	Y	Y	N
3 ***King***	Y	Y	Y	N	Y	Y	N
4 McCarthy	N	Y	Y	Y	N	Y	Y
5 Ackerman	N	Y	Y	Y	N	N	Y
6 Meeks	N	Y	Y	Y	N	N	Y
7 Manton	N	Y	Y	Y	Y	P	Y
8 Nadler	N	Y	Y	Y	N	Y	Y
9 Schumer	N	Y	Y	Y	N	Y	Y
10 Towns	N	Y	Y	Y	N	N	Y
11 Owens	N	Y	Y	Y	N	N	Y
12 Velázquez	N	Y	Y	Y	N	N	Y
13 ***Fossella***	Y	Y	Y	N	Y	Y	N
14 Maloney	N	Y	Y	Y	N	Y	Y
15 Rangel	N	Y	Y	Y	N	Y	Y
16 Serrano	N	Y	Y	Y	N	Y	N
17 Engel	N	Y	Y	Y	N	?	Y
18 Lowey	N	Y	Y	Y	N	Y	Y
19 ***Kelly***	N	Y	Y	Y	Y	Y	N
20 ***Gilman***	Y	Y	Y	Y	Y	Y	N
21 McNulty	N	Y	Y	Y	N	N	Y
22 ***Solomon***	Y	Y	?	N	Y	Y	N
23 ***Boehlert***	Y	Y	Y	Y	Y	Y	N
24 ***McHugh***	Y	Y	Y	N	Y	Y	N
25 ***Walsh***	Y	Y	Y	N	Y	Y	N
26 Hinchey	N	Y	Y	Y	N	N	Y
27 ***Paxon***	Y	Y	Y	N	Y	Y	N
28 Slaughter	N	Y	Y	Y	Y	?	Y
29 LaFalce	N	Y	Y	N	Y	N	Y
30 ***Quinn***	Y	Y	Y	N	Y	Y	N

	490	491	492	493	494	495	497
31 ***Houghton***	Y	Y	Y	N	Y	?	N
NORTH CAROLINA							
1 Clayton	N	Y	Y	Y	Y	Y	Y
2 Etheridge	N	Y	Y	Y	N	Y	Y
3 ***Jones***	Y	Y	Y	N	Y	Y	N
4 Price	N	Y	Y	Y	Y	Y	Y
5 ***Burr***	Y	Y	Y	N	Y	Y	N
6 ***Coble***	Y	Y	Y	N	Y	Y	N
7 McIntyre	N	Y	Y	Y	Y	Y	Y
8 Hefner	N	Y	Y	Y	N	?	Y
9 ***Myrick***	Y	Y	Y	N	Y	Y	N
10 ***Ballenger***	Y	Y	Y	N	Y	Y	N
11 ***Taylor***	Y	Y	Y	N	Y	Y	N
12 Watt	N	Y	Y	Y	N	Y	Y
NORTH DAKOTA							
AL Pomeroy	N	Y	Y	Y	Y	Y	Y
OHIO							
1 ***Chabot***	Y	Y	Y	N	Y	Y	N
2 ***Portman***	Y	Y	Y	N	Y	Y	N
3 Hall	N	Y	Y	N	Y	Y	Y
4 ***Oxley***	Y	Y	Y	N	Y	Y	N
5 ***Gillmor***	Y	Y	Y	N	Y	Y	N
6 Strickland	N	Y	Y	Y	Y	?	Y
7 ***Hobson***	Y	Y	Y	N	Y	Y	N
8 ***Boehner***	Y	Y	Y	N	Y	Y	N
9 Kaptur	N	Y	Y	Y	Y	Y	Y
10 Kucinich	Y	Y	Y	Y	Y	N	Y
11 Stokes	N	Y	Y	Y	N	Y	Y
12 ***Kasich***	Y	Y	Y	N	Y	?	N
13 Brown	N	Y	Y	Y	N	N	Y
14 Sawyer	N	Y	Y	Y	Y	Y	Y
15 ***Pryce***	+	+	+	−	+	+	−
16 ***Regula***	Y	Y	Y	N	Y	Y	N
17 Traficant	N	Y	Y	Y	Y	Y	Y
18 ***Ney***	Y	Y	Y	N	Y	Y	N
19 ***LaTourette***	Y	Y	Y	N	Y	Y	N
OKLAHOMA							
1 ***Largent***	Y	Y	Y	N	Y	Y	N
2 ***Coburn***	Y	Y	Y	N	Y	Y	N
3 ***Watkins***	Y	Y	Y	N	Y	Y	N
4 ***Watts***	Y	Y	Y	N	Y	Y	N
5 ***Istook***	Y	Y	Y	N	Y	Y	N
6 ***Lucas***	Y	Y	Y	N	Y	Y	N
OREGON							
1 Furse	N	Y	Y	Y	N	N	Y
2 ***Smith***	Y	Y	Y	?	?	Y	N
3 Blumenauer	N	Y	Y	Y	N	Y	Y
4 DeFazio	N	Y	Y	Y	N	N	Y
5 Hooley	N	Y	Y	Y	N	Y	Y
PENNSYLVANIA							
1 Brady	N	Y	Y	Y	N	N	Y
2 Fattah	N	Y	Y	Y	N	N	Y
3 Borski	N	Y	Y	Y	Y	N	Y
4 Klink	N	Y	Y	N	Y	Y	Y
5 ***Peterson***	Y	Y	Y	N	Y	Y	N
6 Holden	N	Y	Y	N	Y	Y	Y
7 ***Weldon***	Y	Y	Y	N	Y	Y	N
8 ***Greenwood***	Y	?	Y	N	Y	Y	N
9 ***Shuster***	Y	Y	Y	N	Y	Y	N
10 ***McDade***	Y	Y	Y	N	Y	?	N
11 Kanjorski	N	Y	Y	Y	Y	Y	Y
12 Murtha	N	Y	Y	Y	Y	Y	Y
13 ***Fox***	Y	Y	Y	Y	Y	N	N
14 Coyne	N	Y	Y	Y	N	Y	Y
15 McHale	N	Y	Y	Y	Y	Y	N
16 ***Pitts***	Y	Y	Y	N	Y	Y	N
17 ***Gekas***	Y	Y	Y	N	Y	Y	N
18 Doyle	N	Y	Y	N	Y	Y	Y
19 ***Goodling***	Y	Y	Y	N	Y	Y	N
20 Mascara	N	Y	Y	N	Y	Y	Y
21 ***English***	Y	Y	Y	N	Y	N	N
RHODE ISLAND							
1 Kennedy	N	Y	Y	Y	N	N	Y
2 Weygand	N	Y	Y	Y	Y	Y	Y
SOUTH CAROLINA							
1 ***Sanford***	Y	Y	Y	N	N	P	N
2 ***Spence***	Y	Y	Y	N	Y	Y	N
3 ***Graham***	Y	Y	Y	N	Y	Y	N
4 ***Inglis***	Y	Y	Y	N	Y	Y	N
5 Spratt	N	Y	Y	Y	Y	Y	Y
6 Clyburn	N	Y	Y	Y	N	N	Y
SOUTH DAKOTA							
AL ***Thune***	Y	Y	Y	N	Y	Y	N

	490	491	492	493	494	495	497
TENNESSEE							
1 ***Jenkins***	Y	Y	Y	N	Y	Y	N
2 ***Duncan***	Y	Y	Y	N	N	Y	N
3 ***Wamp***	Y	Y	Y	N	Y	Y	N
4 ***Hilleary***	Y	Y	Y	N	Y	Y	N
5 Clement	N	Y	Y	Y	Y	Y	Y
6 Gordon	N	Y	Y	Y	N	Y	Y
7 ***Bryant***	Y	Y	Y	N	Y	Y	N
8 Tanner	N	Y	Y	Y	Y	Y	Y
9 Ford	N	Y	Y	Y	Y	Y	Y
TEXAS							
1 Sandlin	N	Y	Y	Y	N	Y	Y
2 Turner	Y	Y	Y	Y	Y	Y	Y
3 ***Johnson, Sam***	Y	Y	Y	N	Y	Y	N
4 Hall	Y	Y	Y	N	Y	Y	Y
5 ***Sessions***	Y	Y	Y	N	Y	Y	N
6 ***Barton***	Y	Y	Y	N	Y	Y	N
7 ***Archer***	Y	Y	Y	N	Y	Y	N
8 ***Brady***	Y	Y	Y	N	Y	Y	N
9 Lampson	Y	Y	Y	Y	Y	Y	Y
10 Doggett	N	Y	Y	Y	N	Y	Y
11 Edwards	N	Y	Y	Y	N	Y	Y
12 ***Granger***	Y	Y	Y	Y	Y	Y	N
13 ***Thornberry***	Y	Y	Y	N	Y	Y	N
14 ***Paul***	Y	Y	Y	N	N	Y	N
15 Hinojosa	N	Y	Y	Y	Y	+	Y
16 Reyes	N	Y	Y	Y	Y	P	Y
17 Stenholm	N	Y	Y	N	Y	N	Y
18 Jackson-Lee	N	Y	Y	Y	N	N	Y
19 ***Combest***	Y	Y	Y	N	Y	Y	N
20 Gonzalez	N	Y	Y	Y	N	Y	Y
21 ***Smith***	Y	Y	Y	N	Y	Y	N
22 ***DeLay***	Y	Y	Y	N	Y	Y	N
23 ***Bonilla***	Y	Y	Y	N	Y	Y	N
24 Frost	N	Y	Y	Y	N	Y	Y
25 Bentsen	N	Y	Y	Y	N	Y	Y
26 ***Armey***	Y	Y	Y	N	Y	Y	N
27 Ortiz	N	Y	Y	N	Y	Y	Y
28 Rodriguez	N	Y	Y	Y	Y	Y	Y
29 Green	N	Y	Y	Y	N	N	Y
30 Johnson, E.B.	N	Y	Y	Y	N	Y	Y
UTAH							
1 ***Hansen***	Y	Y	Y	N	Y	N	N
2 ***Cook***	Y	Y	Y	N	Y	Y	N
3 ***Cannon***	Y	Y	Y	N	Y	?	N
VERMONT							
AL *Sanders*	N	Y	Y	Y	N	Y	Y
VIRGINIA							
1 ***Bateman***	Y	Y	Y	N	Y	Y	N
2 Pickett	N	Y	Y	Y	Y	N	Y
3 Scott	N	Y	Y	Y	Y	N	Y
4 Sisisky	N	Y	Y	Y	Y	Y	Y
5 Goode	Y	Y	Y	N	Y	Y	N
6 ***Goodlatte***	Y	Y	Y	N	N	Y	N
7 ***Bliley***	Y	Y	Y	N	Y	Y	N
8 Moran	N	Y	Y	Y	Y	Y	Y
9 Boucher	?	Y	Y	Y	N	Y	Y
10 ***Wolf***	Y	Y	?	N	Y	Y	N
11 ***Davis***	Y	Y	Y	N	Y	Y	N
WASHINGTON							
1 ***White***	Y	Y	Y	N	Y	Y	N
2 ***Metcalf***	Y	Y	Y	N	Y	P	N
3 ***Smith, Linda***	Y	Y	Y	N	Y	Y	N
4 ***Hastings***	Y	Y	Y	N	Y	Y	N
5 ***Nethercutt***	Y	Y	Y	N	Y	Y	N
6 Dicks	N	Y	Y	Y	Y	Y	Y
7 McDermott	N	Y	Y	Y	N	Y	Y
8 ***Dunn***	Y	Y	Y	N	Y	Y	N
9 Smith, Adam	N	Y	Y	Y	N	?	Y
WEST VIRGINIA							
1 Mollohan	Y	Y	Y	N	Y	?	Y
2 Wise	N	Y	Y	Y	Y	Y	Y
3 Rahall	Y	Y	Y	N	Y	Y	Y
WISCONSIN							
1 ***Neumann***	Y	Y	Y	N	N	Y	N
2 ***Klug***	Y	Y	Y	Y	Y	Y	N
3 Kind	N	Y	Y	Y	N	Y	Y
4 Kleczka	N	Y	Y	Y	N	Y	Y
5 Barrett	N	Y	Y	Y	N	Y	Y
6 ***Petri***	Y	Y	Y	N	N	P	N
7 Obey	N	Y	Y	Y	N	?	Y
8 Johnson	N	Y	Y	Y	N	Y	Y
9 ***Sensenbrenner***	Y	Y	Y	N	N	Y	N
WYOMING							
AL ***Cubin***	Y	Y	Y	N	Y	Y	N

Southern states - Ala., Ark., Fla., Ga., Ky., La., Miss., N.C., Okla., S.C., Tenn., Texas, Va.

House Votes 498, 499, 500, 501, 502, 503, 504

Key

Y Voted for (yea).
Paired for.
+ Announced for.
N Voted against (nay).
X Paired against.
– Announced against.
P Voted "present."
C Voted "present" to avoid possible conflict of interest.
? Did not vote or otherwise make a position known.

Democrats **Republicans** *Independent*

---

498. H Res 581. Open Impeachment Inquiry/Adoption. Adoption of the resolution to authorize the Judiciary Committee to conduct an inquiry into whether sufficient grounds exist to impeach President Clinton. Adopted 258-176: R 227-0; D 31-175 (ND 17-134, SD 14-41); I 0-1. Oct. 8, 1998.

499. Procedural Motion/Adjourn. Obey, D-Wis., motion to adjourn. Motion rejected 58-349: R 0-209; D 58-139 (ND 48-96, SD 10-43); I 0-1. Oct. 8, 1998.

500. HR 4274. Fiscal 1999 Labor-HHS Appropriations/Previous Question. Dreier, R-Calif., motion to order the previous question (thus ending debate and the possibility of amendment) on adoption of the rule (H Res 584) to provide for House floor consideration of the bill to provide about $290 billion in fiscal 1999 funding for the Labor, Health and Human Services and Education departments and related agencies. Motion agreed to 224-201: R 220-0; D 4-200 (ND 4-145, SD 0-55); I 0-1. Oct. 8, 1998.

501. HR 4274. Fiscal 1999 Labor-HHS Appropriations/Procedural Motion. DeLay, R-Texas, motion to table (kill) the Furse, D-Ore., motion to reconsider the Dreier, R-Calif., motion to order the previous question. Motion agreed to 231-197: R 223-0; D 8-196 (ND 4-145, SD 4-51); I 0-1. Oct. 8, 1998.

502. HR 4274. Fiscal 1999 Labor-HHS Appropriations/Rule. Adoption of the rule (H Res 584) to provide for House floor consideration of the bill to provide about $290 billion in fiscal 1999 funding for the Labor, Health and Human Services and Education departments and related agencies. Adopted 214-209: R 201-22; D 13-186 (ND 8-136, SD 5-50); I 0-1. Oct. 8, 1998.

503. HR 4274. Fiscal 1999 Labor-HHS Appropriations/Procedural Motion. Dreier, R-Calif., motion to table (kill) the Obey, D-Wis., motion to reconsider the vote by which the House adopted the rule (H Res 584) to provide for House floor consideration of the bill to provide about $290 billion in fiscal 1999 funding for the Labor, Health and Human Services and Education departments and related agencies. Motion agreed to 230-192: R 221-0; D 9-191 (ND 5-140, SD 4-51); I 0-1. Oct. 8, 1998.

504. HR 4274. Fiscal 1999 Labor-HHS Appropriations/Parental Consent for Contraceptives Distribution. Istook, R-Okla., substitute amendment to the Greenwood, R-Pa., amendment to require parental consent or notification before minors can receive contraceptives from federally supported family planning clinics. The Greenwood amendment would have allowed clinics to dispense contraceptives to minors without parental consent or notification. Adopted 224-200: R 190-33; D 34-166 (ND 21-124, SD 13-42); I 0-1. Oct. 8, 1998. (Subsequently, the Greenwood amendment, as amended, was adopted by voice vote.)

	498	499	500	501	502	503	504
ALABAMA							
1 *Callahan*	Y	N	Y	Y	Y	Y	Y
2 *Everett*	Y	N	Y	Y	Y	Y	Y
3 *Riley*	Y	N	Y	Y	Y	Y	Y
4 *Aderholt*	Y	N	Y	Y	Y	Y	Y
5 Cramer	Y	N	N	N	N	N	Y
6 *Bachus*	Y	N	Y	Y	Y	Y	Y
7 Hilliard	N	N	N	N	N	N	N
ALASKA							
AL *Young*	Y	N	Y	Y	Y	Y	Y
ARIZONA							
1 *Salmon*	Y	N	Y	Y	Y	Y	Y
2 Pastor	N	Y	N	N	N	N	N
3 *Stump*	Y	N	Y	Y	Y	Y	Y
4 *Shadegg*	Y	N	Y	Y	Y	Y	Y
5 *Kolbe*	Y	N	Y	Y	Y	N	Y
6 *Hayworth*	Y	N	Y	Y	Y	Y	Y
ARKANSAS							
1 Berry	N	N	N	N	N	N	N
2 Snyder	N	N	N	N	N	N	N
3 *Hutchinson*	Y	?	Y	Y	Y	Y	Y
4 Dickey	Y	N	Y	Y	Y	Y	Y
CALIFORNIA							
1 *Riggs*	Y	N	Y	Y	Y	Y	Y
2 *Herger*	Y	N	Y	Y	Y	Y	Y
3 Fazio	N	N	N	N	?	?	?
4 *Doolittle*	Y	N	Y	Y	Y	Y	Y
5 Matsui	N	N	N	N	N	N	N
6 Woolsey	N	N	N	N	N	N	N
7 Miller	N	N	N	N	N	N	N
8 Pelosi	N	N	N	N	N	N	N
9 Lee	N	Y	N	N	N	N	N
10 Tauscher	Y	N	N	N	N	N	N
11 *Pombo*	Y	N	Y	Y	Y	Y	Y
12 Lantos	N	N	N	N	?	N	N
13 Stark	N	Y	N	N	N	N	N
14 Eshoo	N	N	N	N	N	N	N
15 *Campbell*	Y	N	Y	Y	Y	Y	Y
16 Lofgren	N	N	N	N	N	N	N
17 Farr	N	Y	N	N	N	N	N
18 Condit	Y	N	N	N	N	N	N
19 *Radanovich*	Y	N	Y	Y	Y	Y	Y
20 Dooley	N	N	N	N	?	?	N
21 *Thomas*	Y	N	Y	Y	Y	Y	Y
22 Capps, L.	N	N	N	N	N	N	N
23 *Gallegly*	Y	N	Y	Y	Y	Y	Y
24 Sherman	N	N	N	N	N	N	N
25 *McKeon*	Y	N	Y	Y	Y	Y	Y
26 Berman	N	N	N	N	N	N	N
27 *Rogan*	Y	N	Y	Y	Y	Y	Y
28 *Dreier*	Y	N	Y	Y	Y	Y	Y
29 Waxman	N	N	N	N	N	N	N
30 Becerra	N	Y	N	N	N	N	N
31 Martinez	N	Y	N	N	?	?	?
32 Dixon	N	N	N	N	N	N	N
33 Roybal-Allard	N	N	N	N	N	N	N
34 Torres	N	N	N	N	N	N	N
35 Waters	N	Y	N	N	N	N	N
36 Harman	N	?	N	N	N	?	N
37 Millender-McD.	N	N	N	N	N	N	N
38 *Horn*	Y	N	?	Y	N	Y	N

	498	499	500	501	502	503	504
39 *Royce*	Y	N	Y	Y	Y	Y	Y
40 *Lewis*	Y	N	Y	Y	Y	Y	Y
41 *Kim*	Y	N	Y	Y	Y	Y	Y
42 Brown	N	Y	N	N	N	N	N
43 *Calvert*	Y	N	Y	Y	Y	Y	Y
44 *Bono, M.*	Y	N	Y	Y	Y	Y	Y
45 *Rohrabacher*	Y	N	Y	Y	Y	Y	Y
46 Sanchez	N	N	N	N	N	N	N
47 *Cox*	Y	N	Y	Y	Y	?	Y
48 *Packard*	Y	N	Y	Y	Y	Y	Y
49 *Bilbray*	Y	N	Y	Y	N	Y	N
50 Filner	N	Y	N	N	N	N	N
51 *Cunningham*	Y	?	Y	Y	Y	Y	Y
52 *Hunter*	Y	N	Y	Y	Y	Y	Y
COLORADO							
1 DeGette	N	N	N	N	N	N	N
2 Skaggs	N	N	N	N	N	N	N
3 *McInnis*	Y	N	Y	Y	Y	Y	Y
4 *Schaffer*	Y	N	Y	Y	Y	Y	Y
5 *Hefley*	Y	N	Y	Y	Y	Y	Y
6 *Schaefer*	Y	N	Y	Y	Y	Y	Y
CONNECTICUT							
1 Kennelly	N	?	?	?	?	?	?
2 Gejdenson	N	N	N	N	N	N	N
3 DeLauro	N	Y	N	N	N	N	N
4 *Shays*	Y	N	Y	Y	N	Y	N
5 Maloney	Y	N	N	N	N	N	N
6 *Johnson*	Y	N	Y	Y	N	Y	N
DELAWARE							
AL *Castle*	Y	N	Y	Y	N	Y	N
FLORIDA							
1 *Scarborough*	Y	N	?	Y	Y	Y	Y
2 Boyd	N	N	N	N	N	N	N
3 Brown	N	N	N	N	N	N	N
4 *Fowler*	Y	N	Y	Y	Y	Y	Y
5 Thurman	N	N	N	N	N	N	N
6 *Stearns*	Y	N	Y	Y	Y	Y	Y
7 *Mica*	Y	N	Y	Y	Y	Y	Y
8 *McCollum*	Y	N	Y	Y	Y	Y	Y
9 *Bilirakis*	Y	N	Y	Y	Y	Y	Y
10 *Young*	Y	N	Y	Y	Y	Y	Y
11 Davis	N	N	N	N	N	N	N
12 *Canady*	Y	N	Y	Y	Y	Y	Y
13 *Miller*	Y	N	Y	Y	N	Y	Y
14 *Goss*	Y	N	Y	Y	Y	Y	Y
15 *Weldon*	Y	N	Y	Y	Y	Y	Y
16 *Foley*	Y	N	Y	Y	Y	Y	Y
17 Meek	N	Y	N	N	N	N	N
18 *Ros-Lehtinen*	Y	N	Y	Y	Y	Y	Y
19 Wexler	N	N	N	N	N	N	N
20 Deutsch	N	N	N	N	N	N	N
21 *Diaz-Balart*	Y	N	Y	Y	Y	?	Y
22 *Shaw*	Y	N	Y	Y	Y	Y	Y
23 Hastings	N	Y	N	N	N	N	N
GEORGIA							
1 *Kingston*	Y	N	Y	Y	Y	Y	Y
2 Bishop	N	N	N	N	N	N	Y
3 *Collins*	Y	N	Y	Y	Y	Y	Y
4 McKinney	N	N	N	N	N	N	N
5 Lewis	N	Y	N	N	N	N	N
6 *Gingrich*	Y					Y	
7 *Barr*	Y	?	Y	Y	Y	Y	Y
8 *Chambliss*	Y	N	Y	Y	Y	Y	Y
9 *Deal*	Y	N	Y	Y	Y	Y	Y
10 *Norwood*	Y	N	Y	Y	Y	Y	Y
11 *Linder*	Y	N	Y	Y	Y	Y	Y
HAWAII							
1 Abercrombie	N	–	N	N	N	N	N
2 Mink	N	Y	N	N	N	N	N
IDAHO							
1 *Chenoweth*	Y	N	Y	Y	Y	Y	Y
2 *Crapo*	Y	N	Y	Y	Y	Y	Y
ILLINOIS							
1 Rush	N	N	N	N	N	N	N
2 Jackson	N	N	N	N	N	N	N
3 Lipinski	Y	N	Y	Y	N	N	N
4 Gutierrez	N	N	N	N	N	N	N
5 Blagojevich	N	N	N	N	N	Y	N
6 *Hyde*	Y	N	Y	Y	Y	Y	Y
7 Davis	N	N	N	N	N	N	N
8 *Crane*	Y	N	Y	Y	Y	Y	Y
9 Yates	N	Y	N	N	?	?	?
10 *Porter*	Y	N	Y	Y	N	Y	N
11 *Weller*	Y	N	Y	Y	Y	Y	Y
12 Costello	Y	N	N	N	N	N	N
13 *Fawell*	Y	?	Y	Y	Y	?	N

ND Northern Democrats   SD Southern Democrats

	498	499	500	501	502	503	504
14 ***Hastert***	Y	N	Y	Y	Y	Y	Y
15 ***Ewing***	Y	N	Y	Y	Y	Y	Y
16 ***Manzullo***	Y	N	Y	Y	Y	Y	Y
17 Evans	Y	Y	N	N	N	N	N
18 ***LaHood***	Y	N	Y	Y	Y	Y	Y
19 Poshard	N	?	N	Y	N	N	?
20 ***Shimkus***	Y	N	Y	Y	Y	Y	Y
INDIANA							
1 Visclosky	N	N	N	N	N	N	Y
2 ***McIntosh***	Y	N	Y	Y	Y	Y	Y
3 Roemer	Y	N	N	N	N	N	Y
4 ***Souder***	Y	N	Y	Y	Y	Y	Y
5 ***Buyer***	Y	?	?	?	?	?	?
6 ***Burton***	Y	N	Y	Y	Y	Y	Y
7 ***Pease***	Y	N	Y	Y	Y	Y	Y
8 ***Hostettler***	Y	N	Y	Y	Y	Y	Y
9 Hamilton	Y	N	N	N	N	N	Y
10 Carson	N	N	N	N	N	N	N
IOWA							
1 ***Leach***	Y	N	Y	Y	N	Y	N
2 ***Nussle***	Y	N	Y	Y	Y	Y	Y
3 Boswell	Y	N	N	N	N	N	N
4 ***Ganske***	Y	N	Y	Y	N	Y	N
5 ***Latham***	Y	N	Y	Y	Y	Y	Y
KANSAS							
1 ***Moran***	Y	N	Y	Y	Y	Y	Y
2 ***Ryun***	Y	?	Y	Y	Y	Y	Y
3 ***Snowbarger***	Y	N	Y	Y	Y	Y	Y
4 ***Tiahrt***	Y	N	Y	Y	Y	Y	Y
KENTUCKY							
1 ***Whitfield***	Y	?	?	?	Y	Y	Y
2 ***Lewis***	Y	N	Y	Y	Y	Y	Y
3 ***Northup***	Y	N	Y	Y	Y	Y	Y
4 ***Bunning***	Y	N	Y	Y	Y	Y	Y
5 ***Rogers***	Y	N	Y	Y	Y	Y	Y
6 Baesler	N	?	N	N	N	N	N
LOUISIANA							
1 ***Livingston***	Y	N	Y	Y	Y	Y	Y
2 Jefferson	N	N	N	N	N	N	N
3 ***Tauzin***	Y	N	Y	Y	Y	Y	Y
4 ***McCrery***	Y	N	Y	Y	Y	Y	Y
5 ***Cooksey***	Y	N	Y	Y	Y	Y	Y
6 ***Baker***	Y	N	Y	Y	Y	Y	Y
7 John	Y	N	N	N	N	N	Y
MAINE							
1 Allen	N	Y	N	N	N	N	N
2 Baldacci	N	N	N	N	N	N	N
MARYLAND							
1 ***Gilchrest***	Y	N	Y	Y	N	Y	N
2 ***Ehrlich***	Y	N	Y	Y	N	Y	N
3 Cardin	N	N	N	N	N	N	N
4 Wynn	N	N	N	N	N	N	N
5 Hoyer	N	N	N	N	N	N	N
6 ***Bartlett***	Y	N	Y	Y	Y	Y	Y
7 Cummings	N	N	N	N	N	N	N
8 ***Morella***	Y	N	Y	Y	N	Y	N
MASSACHUSETTS							
1 Olver	N	Y	N	N	N	N	N
2 Neal	N	N	N	N	N	N	N
3 McGovern	N	Y	N	N	N	N	N
4 Frank	N	Y	N	N	N	N	N
5 Meehan	N	Y	N	N	N	N	N
6 Tierney	N	N	N	N	N	N	N
7 Markey	N	N	N	N	N	N	N
8 Kennedy	N	N	N	N	N	N	N
9 Moakley	N	Y	N	N	N	N	?
10 Delahunt	N	Y	N	N	N	N	N
MICHIGAN							
1 Stupak	N	N	N	N	N	N	Y
2 ***Hoekstra***	Y	N	Y	Y	Y	Y	Y
3 ***Ehlers***	Y	N	Y	Y	Y	Y	Y
4 ***Camp***	Y	N	Y	Y	Y	Y	Y
5 Barcia	N	N	N	Y	Y	Y	Y
6 ***Upton***	Y	N	Y	Y	N	Y	N
7 ***Smith***	Y	N	Y	Y	Y	Y	Y
8 Stabenow	N	N	N	N	N	N	N
9 Kildee	N	N	N	N	Y	Y	Y
10 Bonior	N	N	N	N	N	N	N
11 ***Knollenberg***	Y	N	Y	Y	Y	Y	Y
12 Levin	N	N	N	N	N	N	N
13 Rivers	N	N	N	N	N	N	N
14 Conyers	N	Y	N	N	N	N	N
15 Kilpatrick	N	Y	N	N	N	N	N
16 Dingell	N	N	N	N	N	N	N

	498	499	500	501	502	503	504
MINNESOTA							
1 ***Gutknecht***	Y	N	Y	Y	Y	Y	Y
2 Minge	Y	N	N	N	N	N	N
3 ***Ramstad***	Y	N	Y	Y	N	Y	N
4 Vento	N	N	N	N	N	N	N
5 Sabo	N	Y	N	N	N	N	N
6 Luther	N	N	N	N	N	N	N
7 Peterson	Y	N	N	N	Y	Y	Y
8 Oberstar	N	N	N	N	N	N	N
MISSISSIPPI							
1 ***Wicker***	Y	N	Y	Y	Y	Y	Y
2 Thompson	N	N	N	N	N	N	N
3 ***Pickering***	Y	?	?	Y	Y	Y	Y
4 ***Parker***	Y	N	Y	Y	Y	Y	Y
5 Taylor	Y	N	N	Y	Y	Y	Y
MISSOURI							
1 Clay	N	N	N	N	N	N	N
2 ***Talent***	Y	N	Y	Y	Y	Y	Y
3 Gephardt	N	Y	N	N	N	N	N
4 Skelton	Y	N	N	N	Y	N	Y
5 McCarthy	N	N	N	N	N	N	N
6 Danner	Y	N	N	N	N	N	Y
7 ***Blunt***	Y	N	Y	Y	Y	Y	Y
8 ***Emerson***	Y	N	Y	Y	Y	Y	Y
9 ***Hulshof***	Y	?	Y	Y	Y	Y	Y
MONTANA							
AL ***Hill***	Y	N	Y	Y	Y	Y	Y
NEBRASKA							
1 ***Bereuter***	Y	N	Y	Y	Y	Y	Y
2 ***Christensen***	Y	?	Y	Y	Y	Y	Y
3 ***Barrett***	Y	N	Y	Y	Y	Y	Y
NEVADA							
1 ***Ensign***	Y	?	Y	Y	Y	Y	Y
2 ***Gibbons***	Y	N	Y	Y	Y	Y	Y
NEW HAMPSHIRE							
1 ***Sununu***	Y	N	Y	Y	Y	Y	Y
2 ***Bass***	Y	N	Y	Y	N	Y	N
NEW JERSEY							
1 Andrews	N	Y	N	?	N	N	N
2 ***LoBiondo***	Y	N	Y	Y	Y	Y	Y
3 ***Saxton***	Y	N	Y	Y	Y	Y	Y
4 ***Smith***	Y	N	Y	Y	Y	Y	Y
5 ***Roukema***	Y	N	Y	Y	Y	Y	Y
6 Pallone	N	N	N	N	N	N	N
7 ***Franks***	Y	N	Y	Y	N	Y	N
8 Pascrell	N	N	N	N	N	N	N
9 Rothman	N	N	N	N	N	N	N
10 Payne	N	N	N	N	N	N	N
11 ***Frelinghuysen***	Y	N	Y	Y	Y	Y	N
12 ***Pappas***	Y	N	Y	Y	Y	Y	Y
13 Menendez	N	N	N	N	N	N	N
NEW MEXICO							
1 ***Wilson***	Y	N	Y	Y	Y	Y	Y
2 ***Skeen***	Y	N	Y	Y	Y	Y	Y
3 ***Redmond***	Y	N	Y	Y	Y	Y	Y
NEW YORK							
1 ***Forbes***	Y	N	Y	Y	Y	Y	Y
2 ***Lazio***	Y	N	Y	Y	N	Y	N
3 ***King***	Y	N	Y	Y	Y	Y	Y
4 McCarthy	Y	N	N	N	N	N	N
5 Ackerman	N	Y	N	N	N	N	N
6 Meeks	N	N	N	N	N	N	N
7 Manton	N	Y	N	N	N	N	N
8 Nadler	N	N	N	N	N	N	N
9 Schumer	N	N	N	N	N	N	N
10 Towns	N	Y	N	N	N	N	N
11 Owens	N	Y	N	N	N	N	N
†12 Velázquez	N	N	N	N	N	N	N
13 ***Fossella***	Y	?	Y	Y	Y	Y	Y
14 Maloney	N	Y	N	N	N	N	N
15 Rangel	N	N	N	N	N	N	N
16 Serrano	N	N	N	N	N	N	N
17 Engel	N	N	N	N	N	N	N
18 Lowey	N	Y	N	N	?	N	N
19 ***Kelly***	Y	N	Y	Y	Y	Y	N
20 ***Gilman***	Y	N	Y	Y	N	Y	N
21 McNulty	N	Y	N	N	N	N	N
22 ***Solomon***	Y	N	Y	Y	Y	Y	Y
23 ***Boehlert***	Y	N	Y	Y	N	Y	N
24 ***McHugh***	Y	N	Y	Y	N	Y	Y
25 ***Walsh***	Y	N	Y	Y	P	Y	Y
26 Hinchey	N	Y	N	N	N	N	N
27 ***Paxon***	Y	N	Y	Y	Y	Y	Y
28 Slaughter	N	Y	N	N	N	N	N
29 LaFalce	N	Y	N	N	N	N	Y
30 ***Quinn***	Y	N	Y	Y	Y	Y	Y

	498	499	500	501	502	503	504
31 ***Houghton***	Y	N	Y	Y	Y	Y	N
NORTH CAROLINA							
1 Clayton	N	Y	N	N	N	N	N
2 Etheridge	Y	N	N	N	N	N	N
3 ***Jones***	Y	N	Y	Y	Y	Y	Y
4 Price	N	N	N	N	N	N	N
5 ***Burr***	Y	N	Y	Y	Y	Y	Y
6 ***Coble***	Y	N	Y	Y	Y	Y	Y
7 McIntyre	Y	N	N	N	N	N	Y
8 Hefner	N	Y	N	N	N	N	N
9 ***Myrick***	Y	N	Y	Y	Y	Y	Y
10 ***Ballenger***	Y	N	Y	Y	Y	Y	Y
11 ***Taylor***	Y	N	Y	Y	Y	Y	Y
12 Watt	N	N	N	N	N	N	N
NORTH DAKOTA							
AL Pomeroy	N	N	N	N	N	N	N
OHIO							
1 ***Chabot***	Y	N	Y	Y	Y	Y	Y
2 ***Portman***	Y	N	Y	Y	Y	Y	Y
3 Hall	N	Y	N	N	Y	Y	Y
4 ***Oxley***	Y	?	Y	Y	Y	Y	Y
5 ***Gillmor***	Y	N	Y	Y	Y	Y	Y
6 Strickland	N	Y	N	N	N	N	N
7 ***Hobson***	Y	N	Y	Y	Y	Y	N
8 ***Boehner***	Y	N	Y	Y	Y	Y	Y
9 Kaptur	N	N	N	N	N	N	N
10 Kucinich	Y	N	N	N	N	N	N
11 Stokes	N	N	N	N	N	N	N
12 ***Kasich***	Y	N	Y	Y	Y	Y	Y
13 Brown	N	N	N	N	N	N	N
14 Sawyer	N	N	N	N	N	N	N
15 ***Pryce***	+	–	+	+	+	+	–
16 ***Regula***	Y	N	Y	Y	Y	Y	Y
17 Traficant	N	N	N	N	N	N	Y
18 ***Ney***	Y	?	Y	Y	N	Y	Y
19 ***LaTourette***	Y	N	Y	Y	Y	Y	N
OKLAHOMA							
1 ***Largent***	Y	N	Y	Y	Y	Y	Y
2 ***Coburn***	Y	N	Y	Y	Y	Y	Y
3 ***Watkins***	Y	N	Y	Y	Y	Y	Y
4 ***Watts***	Y	N	Y	Y	Y	Y	Y
5 ***Istook***	Y	N	Y	Y	Y	Y	Y
6 ***Lucas***	Y	N	Y	Y	Y	Y	Y
OREGON							
1 Furse	N	Y	Y	N	N	N	N
2 ***Smith***	Y	N	Y	Y	Y	Y	Y
3 Blumenauer	N	N	N	N	N	N	N
4 DeFazio	N	Y	N	N	N	N	N
5 Hooley	N	N	N	N	N	N	N
PENNSYLVANIA							
1 Brady	N	N	N	N	N	N	N
2 Fattah	N	N	?	N	N	N	N
3 Borski	N	N	N	N	N	N	N
4 Klink	N	N	N	N	N	N	N
5 ***Peterson***	Y	N	Y	Y	Y	Y	?
6 Holden	N	N	N	N	N	N	Y
7 ***Weldon***	Y	N	Y	Y	Y	Y	Y
8 ***Greenwood***	Y	?	Y	Y	Y	Y	N
9 ***Shuster***	Y	N	Y	Y	Y	Y	Y
10 ***McDade***	Y	N	?	?	?	?	?
11 Kanjorski	N	N	N	N	N	N	Y
12 Murtha	N	N	N	N	Y	N	Y
13 ***Fox***	Y	N	Y	Y	Y	Y	Y
14 Coyne	N	N	N	N	N	N	N
15 McHale	Y	N	N	N	N	N	N
16 ***Pitts***	Y	N	Y	Y	Y	Y	Y
17 ***Gekas***	Y	N	Y	Y	Y	Y	Y
18 Doyle	N	?	N	N	N	N	Y
19 ***Goodling***	Y	N	Y	Y	Y	Y	Y
20 Mascara	N	N	N	N	N	N	Y
21 ***English***	Y	N	Y	Y	Y	Y	Y
RHODE ISLAND							
1 Kennedy	N	?	N	N	N	N	N
2 Weygand	Y	N	N	N	N	N	N
SOUTH CAROLINA							
1 ***Sanford***	Y	N	Y	Y	Y	Y	Y
2 ***Spence***	Y	N	Y	Y	Y	Y	Y
3 ***Graham***	Y	N	Y	Y	Y	Y	Y
4 ***Inglis***	Y	N	Y	Y	Y	Y	Y
5 Spratt	Y	Y	N	N	N	N	N
6 Clyburn	N	N	N	N	N	N	N
SOUTH DAKOTA							
AL ***Thune***	Y	N	Y	Y	Y	Y	Y

	498	499	500	501	502	503	504
TENNESSEE							
1 ***Jenkins***	Y	N	Y	Y	Y	Y	Y
2 ***Duncan***	Y	N	Y	Y	Y	Y	Y
3 ***Wamp***	Y	?	Y	Y	Y	Y	Y
4 ***Hilleary***	Y	N	Y	Y	Y	Y	Y
5 Clement	N	N	N	N	N	N	N
6 Gordon	N	N	N	N	N	N	Y
7 ***Bryant***	Y	N	Y	Y	Y	Y	Y
8 Tanner	N	N	N	N	N	N	Y
9 Ford	N	N	N	N	N	N	N
TEXAS							
1 Sandlin	N	N	N	N	N	N	Y
2 Turner	Y	N	N	N	N	N	Y
3 ***Johnson, Sam***	Y	N	Y	Y	Y	?	Y
4 Hall	Y	N	N	Y	Y	Y	Y
5 ***Sessions***	Y	N	Y	Y	Y	Y	Y
6 ***Barton***	Y	N	Y	Y	Y	Y	Y
7 ***Archer***	Y	N	Y	Y	Y	Y	Y
8 ***Brady***	Y	N	Y	Y	Y	Y	Y
9 Lampson	Y	N	N	N	N	N	N
10 Doggett	N	N	N	N	N	N	N
11 Edwards	N	N	N	N	N	N	N
12 ***Granger***	Y	N	Y	Y	Y	Y	Y
13 ***Thornberry***	Y	N	Y	Y	Y	Y	Y
14 ***Paul***	Y	N	Y	Y	Y	Y	Y
15 Hinojosa	N	N	N	N	N	N	N
16 Reyes	N	N	N	N	N	N	N
17 Stenholm	Y	N	N	Y	Y	Y	Y
18 Jackson-Lee	N	Y	N	N	N	N	N
19 ***Combest***	Y	N	Y	Y	Y	Y	Y
20 Gonzalez	N	N	N	N	N	N	N
21 ***Smith***	Y	N	Y	Y	Y	Y	Y
22 ***DeLay***	Y	N	Y	Y	Y	Y	Y
23 ***Bonilla***	Y	N	Y	Y	Y	Y	Y
24 Frost	N	N	N	N	N	N	N
25 Bentsen	N	N	N	N	N	N	N
26 ***Armey***	Y	N	Y	Y	Y	Y	Y
27 Ortiz	N	N	N	N	Y	N	Y
28 Rodriguez	N	Y	N	N	N	N	N
29 Green	N	N	N	N	N	N	N
30 Johnson, E.B.	N	Y	N	N	N	N	N
UTAH							
1 ***Hansen***	Y	N	Y	Y	Y	Y	Y
2 ***Cook***	Y	N	Y	Y	Y	Y	N
3 ***Cannon***	Y	N	Y	Y	Y	Y	Y
VERMONT							
AL *Sanders*	N	N	N	N	N	N	N
VIRGINIA							
1 ***Bateman***	Y	N	Y	Y	Y	Y	Y
2 Pickett	Y	N	N	N	N	N	N
3 Scott	N	Y	N	N	N	N	N
4 Sisisky	Y	N	N	N	N	N	N
5 Goode	Y	N	N	Y	Y	Y	Y
6 ***Goodlatte***	Y	N	Y	Y	Y	Y	Y
7 ***Bliley***	Y	N	Y	Y	Y	Y	Y
8 Moran	Y	?	N	N	N	N	N
9 Boucher	N	N	N	N	N	N	N
10 ***Wolf***	Y	N	Y	Y	Y	Y	Y
11 ***Davis***	Y	N	Y	Y	Y	Y	N
WASHINGTON							
1 ***White***	Y	?	Y	Y	Y	Y	Y
2 ***Metcalf***	Y	N	Y	Y	Y	Y	Y
3 ***Smith, Linda***	Y	N	Y	Y	Y	Y	Y
4 ***Hastings***	Y	N	Y	Y	Y	Y	Y
5 ***Nethercutt***	Y	N	Y	Y	Y	Y	Y
6 Dicks	N	Y	N	N	N	N	N
7 McDermott	N	Y	N	N	N	N	N
8 ***Dunn***	Y	N	Y	Y	Y	Y	Y
9 Smith, Adam	N	N	N	N	N	N	N
WEST VIRGINIA							
1 Mollohan	N	N	Y	N	N	N	Y
2 Wise	N	?	N	N	N	N	N
3 Rahall	N	N	N	N	Y	N	Y
WISCONSIN							
1 ***Neumann***	Y	N	Y	Y	Y	Y	Y
2 ***Klug***	Y	N	Y	Y	N	Y	N
3 Kind	Y	N	N	N	N	N	N
4 Kleczka	N	N	N	N	N	N	N
5 Barrett	N	N	N	N	N	N	N
6 ***Petri***	Y	N	Y	Y	Y	Y	Y
7 Obey	N	Y	N	N	N	N	N
8 Johnson	N	Y	N	N	N	N	N
9 ***Sensenbrenner***	Y	N	Y	Y	Y	Y	Y
WYOMING							
AL ***Cubin***	Y	N	Y	Y	Y	Y	Y

Southern states - Ala., Ark., Fla., Ga., Ky., La., Miss., N.C., Okla., S.C., Tenn., Texas, Va.

House Votes 505, 506, 507, 508, 509, 510, 511

505. HR 3150. Consumer Bankruptcy Revisions/Recommit. Nadler, D-N.Y., motion to recommit the bill to the conference committee with instructions to report it back with an amendment to retain the status quo on rules regarding the discharge of credit card debt and to stiffen penalties for companies that force bankrupt persons into reaffirmation agreements. Motion rejected 157-266: R 3-219; D 153-47 (ND 120-26, SD 33-21); I 1-0. Oct. 9, 1998.

506. HR 3150. Consumer Bankruptcy Revisions/Conference Report. Adoption of the conference report on the bill to revise the nation's bankruptcy laws by forcing most debtors to file for Chapter 13 relief, instead of Chapter 7, if they have an above-median income and the ability to pay off at least 25 percent of their debts over five years. Adopted (thus sent to the Senate) 300-125: R 224-1; D 76-123 (ND 49-96, SD 27-27); I 0-1. Oct. 9, 1998. A "nay" was a vote in support of the president's position.

507. H Res 565. Importance of Mammograms and Biopsies/Passage. Bliley, R-Va., motion to suspend the rules and pass the resolution to express the sense of the House that mammograms and biopsies are an important part of the fight against breast cancer. Motion agreed to 424-0: R 224-0; D 199-0 (ND 145-0, SD 54-0); I 1-0. Oct. 9, 1998. A two-thirds majority of those present and voting (283 in this case) is required for passage under suspension of the rules.

508. H Con Res 331. Sewage Facilities in Tijuana, Mexico/Passage. Gilman, R-N.Y., motion to suspend the rules and pass the bill to express the sense of Congress that the sewage and infrastructure facilities in Tijuana, Mexico, are inadequate. Motion rejected 250-174: R 222-2; D 28-171 (ND 16-129, SD 12-42); I 0-1. Oct. 9, 1998. A two-thirds majority of those present and voting (283 in this case) is required for passage under suspension of the rules.

509. H Res 557. Holocaust-Era Assets/Passage. Gilman, R-N.Y. motion to suspend the rules and pass the bill to express the sense of the House in support of U.S. government efforts to identify Holocaust-era assets. Motion agreed to 427-0: R 225-0; D 201-0 (ND 147-0, SD 54-0); I 1-0. Oct. 9, 1998. A two-thirds majority of those present and voting (285 in this case) is required for passage under suspension of the rules.

510. HR 3875. Nutrition Programs Reauthorization/Conference Report. Goodling, R-Pa., motion to suspend the rules and adopt the conference report on the bill to reauthorize through 2003 the Women, Infants and Children nutrition program and a national summer food program for children of low-income families. Motion agreed to 422-1: R 225-1; D 196-0 (ND 144-0, SD 52-0); I 1-0. Oct. 9, 1998. A two-thirds majority of those present and voting (282 in this case) is required for passage under suspension of the rules.

511. Fiscal 1999 Continuing Appropriations/Passage. Passage of the joint resolution to provide continuing appropriations through Oct. 12 for fiscal 1999 spending bills not yet enacted. The continuing resolution sets spending at fiscal 1998 levels. Passed 421-0: R 223-0; D 197-0 (ND 143-0, SD 54-0); I 1-0. Oct. 9, 1998.

Key

- Y Voted for (yea).
- # Paired for.
- + Announced for.
- N Voted against (nay).
- X Paired against.
- − Announced against.
- P Voted "present."
- C Voted "present" to avoid possible conflict of interest.
- ? Did not vote or otherwise make a position known.

Democrats   **Republicans**
Independent

	505	506	507	508	509	510	511
ALABAMA							
1 **Callahan**	N	Y	Y	Y	Y	Y	Y
2 **Everett**	N	Y	Y	Y	Y	Y	Y
3 **Riley**	N	Y	Y	Y	Y	Y	Y
4 **Aderholt**	N	Y	Y	Y	Y	Y	Y
5 Cramer	N	Y	Y	Y	Y	Y	Y
6 **Bachus**	N	Y	Y	Y	Y	Y	Y
7 Hilliard	Y	N	Y	N	Y	Y	Y
ALASKA							
AL **Young**	N	Y	Y	Y	Y	Y	Y
ARIZONA							
1 **Salmon**	N	Y	Y	Y	Y	Y	Y
2 Pastor	Y	Y	Y	N	Y	Y	Y
3 **Stump**	N	Y	Y	Y	Y	Y	Y
4 **Shadegg**	N	Y	Y	Y	Y	Y	Y
5 **Kolbe**	N	Y	Y	Y	Y	Y	Y
6 **Hayworth**	N	Y	Y	Y	Y	Y	Y
ARKANSAS							
1 Berry	N	Y	Y	Y	Y	Y	Y
2 Snyder	N	Y	Y	N	Y	Y	Y
3 **Hutchinson**	N	Y	Y	Y	Y	Y	Y
4 **Dickey**	N	Y	Y	Y	Y	Y	Y
CALIFORNIA							
1 **Riggs**	N	Y	Y	Y	Y	Y	Y
2 **Herger**	N	Y	Y	Y	Y	Y	Y
3 Fazio	Y	N	Y	N	Y	Y	Y
4 **Doolittle**	N	Y	Y	Y	Y	Y	Y
5 Matsui	Y	Y	Y	N	Y	Y	Y
6 Woolsey	Y	N	Y	N	Y	Y	Y
7 Miller	Y	N	Y	N	Y	Y	Y
8 Pelosi	Y	N	Y	N	Y	Y	Y
9 Lee	Y	N	Y	N	Y	Y	Y
10 Tauscher	N	Y	Y	N	Y	Y	Y
11 **Pombo**	N	Y	Y	Y	Y	Y	Y
12 Lantos	Y	N	Y	N	Y	Y	Y
13 Stark	Y	N	Y	N	Y	Y	Y
14 Eshoo	Y	N	Y	N	Y	Y	Y
15 **Campbell**	Y	Y	Y	Y	Y	Y	Y
16 Lofgren	Y	N	Y	N	Y	Y	Y
17 Farr	Y	N	Y	N	Y	Y	Y
18 Condit	N	Y	Y	Y	Y	Y	Y
19 **Radanovich**	N	Y	Y	Y	Y	Y	Y
20 Dooley	N	Y	Y	Y	Y	Y	Y
21 **Thomas**	N	Y	Y	Y	Y	Y	Y
22 Capps, L.	Y	Y	Y	N	Y	Y	Y
23 **Gallegly**	N	Y	Y	Y	Y	Y	Y
24 Sherman	N	Y	Y	Y	Y	?	Y
25 **McKeon**	N	Y	Y	Y	Y	Y	Y
26 Berman	?	?	?	?	?	?	?
27 **Rogan**	N	Y	Y	Y	Y	Y	Y
28 **Dreier**	N	Y	Y	Y	Y	Y	Y
29 Waxman	Y	N	Y	N	Y	Y	Y
30 Becerra	Y	N	Y	N	Y	Y	Y
31 Martinez	Y	N	Y	N	Y	Y	Y
32 Dixon	Y	N	Y	N	Y	Y	Y
33 Roybal-Allard	Y	N	Y	N	Y	Y	Y
34 Torres	?	?	?	N	Y	Y	Y
35 Waters	Y	N	Y	N	Y	Y	Y
36 Harman	Y	N	Y	Y	Y	Y	Y
37 Millender-McD.	Y	N	Y	N	Y	Y	Y
38 **Horn**	N	Y	Y	Y	Y	Y	Y
39 **Royce**	N	Y	Y	Y	Y	Y	Y
40 **Lewis**	N	Y	Y	Y	Y	Y	Y
41 **Kim**	N	Y	Y	Y	Y	Y	Y
42 Brown	Y	N	Y	N	Y	Y	Y
43 **Calvert**	N	Y	Y	Y	Y	Y	Y
44 **Bono, M.**	N	Y	Y	Y	Y	Y	Y
45 **Rohrabacher**	N	Y	Y	Y	Y	Y	Y
46 Sanchez	Y	N	Y	N	Y	Y	Y
47 **Cox**	N	Y	Y	Y	Y	Y	Y
48 **Packard**	N	Y	Y	Y	Y	Y	Y
49 **Bilbray**	N	Y	Y	Y	Y	Y	Y
50 Filner	Y	N	Y	N	Y	Y	Y
51 **Cunningham**	N	Y	Y	Y	Y	Y	Y
52 **Hunter**	N	Y	Y	Y	Y	Y	Y
COLORADO							
1 DeGette	Y	N	Y	N	Y	Y	Y
2 Skaggs	Y	N	Y	N	Y	Y	Y
3 **McInnis**	N	Y	Y	Y	Y	Y	Y
4 **Schaffer**	N	Y	Y	Y	Y	Y	Y
5 **Hefley**	N	Y	Y	Y	Y	Y	Y
6 **Schaefer**	N	Y	Y	Y	Y	Y	Y
CONNECTICUT							
1 Kennelly	?	?	?	?	?	?	?
2 Gejdenson	Y	N	Y	N	Y	Y	Y
3 DeLauro	Y	N	Y	N	Y	Y	Y
4 **Shays**	N	Y	Y	Y	Y	Y	Y
5 Maloney	N	Y	Y	Y	Y	Y	Y
6 **Johnson**	N	Y	Y	Y	Y	Y	Y
DELAWARE							
AL **Castle**	N	Y	Y	Y	Y	Y	Y
FLORIDA							
1 **Scarborough**	N	Y	Y	N	Y	Y	Y
2 Boyd	N	Y	Y	N	Y	Y	Y
3 Brown	Y	N	Y	N	Y	Y	Y
4 **Fowler**	N	Y	+	+	+	Y	Y
5 Thurman	Y	N	Y	N	Y	Y	Y
6 **Stearns**	N	Y	Y	Y	Y	Y	Y
7 **Mica**	N	Y	Y	Y	Y	Y	Y
8 **McCollum**	N	Y	Y	Y	Y	Y	Y
9 **Bilirakis**	N	Y	Y	Y	Y	Y	Y
10 **Young**	N	Y	Y	Y	Y	Y	Y
11 Davis	N	Y	Y	N	Y	Y	Y
12 **Canady**	N	Y	Y	Y	Y	Y	Y
13 **Miller**	N	Y	Y	Y	Y	Y	Y
14 **Goss**	N	Y	Y	Y	Y	Y	Y
15 **Weldon**	N	Y	Y	Y	Y	Y	Y
16 **Foley**	N	Y	Y	Y	Y	Y	Y
17 Meek	Y	N	Y	N	Y	Y	Y
18 **Ros-Lehtinen**	N	Y	Y	Y	Y	Y	Y
19 Wexler	Y	N	Y	N	Y	Y	Y
20 Deutsch	Y	N	Y	N	Y	Y	Y
21 **Diaz-Balart**	N	Y	Y	Y	Y	Y	Y
22 **Shaw**	N	Y	Y	Y	Y	Y	Y
23 Hastings	Y	N	Y	N	Y	Y	Y
GEORGIA							
1 **Kingston**	N	Y	Y	Y	Y	Y	Y
2 Bishop	N	Y	Y	Y	Y	Y	Y
3 **Collins**	N	Y	Y	Y	Y	Y	Y
4 McKinney	Y	N	Y	N	Y	Y	Y
5 Lewis	Y	N	Y	N	Y	Y	Y
6 **Gingrich**							
7 **Barr**	N	Y	Y	Y	Y	Y	Y
8 **Chambliss**	N	Y	Y	Y	Y	Y	Y
9 **Deal**	N	Y	Y	Y	Y	Y	Y
10 **Norwood**	N	Y	Y	Y	Y	Y	Y
11 **Linder**	N	Y	Y	Y	Y	Y	Y
HAWAII							
1 Abercrombie	Y	N	Y	N	Y	Y	Y
2 Mink	Y	N	Y	N	Y	Y	Y
IDAHO							
1 **Chenoweth**	N	Y	Y	Y	Y	Y	Y
2 **Crapo**	N	Y	Y	Y	Y	Y	Y
ILLINOIS							
1 Rush	Y	N	Y	N	Y	Y	Y
2 Jackson	Y	N	Y	N	Y	Y	Y
3 Lipinski	Y	N	Y	N	Y	Y	Y
4 Gutierrez	Y	N	Y	N	Y	Y	Y
5 Blagojevich	Y	Y	Y	N	Y	Y	Y
6 **Hyde**	N	Y	Y	Y	Y	Y	Y
7 Davis	Y	N	Y	N	Y	Y	Y
8 **Crane**	N	Y	Y	Y	Y	Y	Y
9 Yates	Y	N	Y	N	Y	Y	?
10 **Porter**	N	Y	Y	Y	Y	Y	Y
11 **Weller**	N	Y	Y	Y	Y	Y	Y
12 Costello	Y	N	Y	N	Y	Y	Y
13 **Fawell**	N	Y	Y	Y	Y	Y	Y

ND Northern Democrats   SD Southern Democrats

	505	506	507	508	509	510	511
14 **Hastert**	N	Y	Y	Y	Y	Y	Y
15 **Ewing**	N	Y	Y	Y	Y	Y	Y
16 **Manzullo**	N	Y	Y	Y	Y	Y	Y
17 Evans	Y	N	Y	N	Y	Y	Y
18 **LaHood**	N	Y	Y	Y	Y	Y	Y
19 Poshard	?	?	?	?	?	?	?
20 **Shimkus**	N	Y	Y	Y	Y	Y	Y
INDIANA							
1 Visclosky	Y	N	Y	N	Y	Y	Y
2 **McIntosh**	N	Y	Y	Y	Y	Y	Y
3 Roemer	N	Y	Y	?	Y	Y	Y
4 **Souder**	N	Y	Y	Y	Y	Y	Y
5 **Buyer**	N	Y	Y	Y	Y	Y	Y
6 **Burton**	?	Y	Y	Y	Y	Y	Y
7 **Pease**	N	Y	Y	Y	Y	Y	Y
8 **Hostettler**	N	Y	Y	Y	Y	Y	Y
9 Hamilton	N	Y	Y	N	Y	Y	Y
10 Carson	Y	N	Y	Y	Y	Y	Y
IOWA							
1 **Leach**	N	Y	Y	Y	Y	Y	Y
2 **Nussle**	N	Y	Y	Y	Y	Y	Y
3 Boswell	N	Y	Y	Y	Y	Y	Y
4 **Ganske**	N	Y	Y	Y	Y	Y	Y
5 **Latham**	N	Y	Y	Y	Y	Y	Y
KANSAS							
1 **Moran**	N	Y	Y	Y	Y	Y	Y
2 **Ryun**	N	Y	Y	Y	Y	Y	Y
3 **Snowbarger**	N	Y	Y	Y	Y	Y	Y
4 **Tiahrt**	N	Y	Y	Y	Y	Y	Y
KENTUCKY							
1 **Whitfield**	N	Y	Y	Y	Y	Y	Y
2 **Lewis**	N	Y	Y	Y	Y	Y	Y
3 **Northup**	N	Y	Y	Y	Y	Y	Y
4 **Bunning**	N	Y	Y	Y	Y	Y	Y
5 **Rogers**	N	Y	Y	Y	Y	Y	Y
6 Baesler	N	Y	Y	Y	Y	Y	Y
LOUISIANA							
1 **Livingston**	N	Y	Y	Y	Y	Y	Y
2 Jefferson	Y	N	Y	N	Y	Y	Y
3 **Tauzin**	N	Y	Y	Y	Y	Y	Y
4 **McCrery**	N	Y	Y	Y	Y	Y	Y
5 **Cooksey**	N	Y	Y	Y	Y	Y	Y
6 **Baker**	N	Y	Y	Y	Y	Y	Y
7 John	?	?	?	?	?	?	?
MAINE							
1 Allen	Y	N	Y	N	Y	Y	Y
2 Baldacci	Y	N	Y	N	Y	Y	Y
MARYLAND							
1 **Gilchrest**	N	Y	Y	Y	Y	Y	Y
2 **Ehrlich**	N	Y	Y	Y	Y	Y	Y
3 Cardin	N	Y	Y	N	Y	Y	Y
4 Wynn	Y	Y	Y	N	Y	Y	Y
5 Hoyer	N	Y	Y	N	Y	Y	Y
6 **Bartlett**	N	Y	Y	Y	Y	Y	Y
7 Cummings	Y	N	Y	N	Y	Y	Y
8 **Morella**	N	Y	Y	Y	Y	Y	Y
MASSACHUSETTS							
1 Olver	Y	N	Y	N	Y	Y	Y
2 Neal	Y	Y	Y	N	Y	Y	Y
3 McGovern	Y	N	Y	N	Y	Y	Y
4 Frank	N	Y	Y	N	Y	Y	?
5 Meehan	Y	N	Y	N	Y	Y	Y
6 Tierney	?	?	?	?	?	?	?
7 Markey	Y	N	Y	N	Y	Y	Y
8 Kennedy	Y	N	Y	N	Y	Y	Y
9 Moakley	Y	N	Y	N	Y	Y	Y
10 Delahunt	Y	N	?	N	Y	Y	Y
MICHIGAN							
1 Stupak	Y	N	Y	N	Y	Y	Y
2 **Hoekstra**	N	Y	Y	Y	Y	Y	Y
3 **Ehlers**	N	Y	Y	Y	Y	Y	Y
4 **Camp**	N	Y	Y	Y	Y	Y	Y
5 Barcia	N	Y	Y	N	Y	Y	Y
6 **Upton**	N	Y	Y	Y	Y	Y	Y
7 **Smith**	N	Y	Y	Y	Y	Y	?
8 Stabenow	Y	N	Y	N	Y	Y	Y
9 Kildee	Y	N	Y	N	Y	Y	Y
10 Bonior	Y	N	Y	N	Y	Y	Y
11 **Knollenberg**	N	Y	Y	Y	Y	Y	Y
12 Levin	Y	N	Y	N	Y	Y	Y
13 Rivers	Y	Y	Y	N	Y	Y	Y
14 Conyers	Y	N	Y	N	Y	Y	Y
15 Kilpatrick	Y	N	Y	N	Y	Y	Y
16 Dingell	Y	N	Y	N	Y	Y	Y
MINNESOTA							
1 **Gutknecht**	N	Y	Y	Y	Y	Y	Y
2 Minge	N	Y	Y	N	Y	Y	Y
3 **Ramstad**	N	Y	Y	Y	Y	Y	Y
4 Vento	Y	N	Y	N	Y	Y	Y
5 Sabo	Y	N	Y	N	Y	Y	Y
6 Luther	Y	N	Y	N	Y	Y	Y
7 Peterson	N	Y	Y	Y	Y	Y	Y
8 Oberstar	Y	N	Y	N	Y	Y	Y
MISSISSIPPI							
1 **Wicker**	N	Y	Y	Y	Y	Y	Y
2 Thompson	Y	N	Y	N	Y	Y	Y
3 **Pickering**	N	Y	Y	Y	Y	Y	Y
4 **Parker**	N	Y	Y	Y	Y	Y	Y
5 Taylor	N	Y	Y	Y	Y	Y	Y
MISSOURI							
1 Clay	Y	N	Y	N	Y	Y	Y
2 **Talent**	N	Y	Y	Y	Y	Y	Y
3 Gephardt	Y	Y	Y	?	Y	Y	Y
4 Skelton	N	Y	Y	N	Y	Y	Y
5 McCarthy	Y	N	Y	N	Y	Y	Y
6 Danner	N	Y	Y	Y	Y	Y	Y
7 **Blunt**	N	Y	Y	Y	Y	Y	Y
8 **Emerson**	N	Y	Y	Y	Y	Y	Y
9 **Hulshof**	N	Y	Y	Y	Y	Y	Y
MONTANA							
AL **Hill**	N	Y	Y	Y	Y	Y	Y
NEBRASKA							
1 **Bereuter**	N	Y	Y	Y	Y	Y	Y
2 **Christensen**	N	Y	Y	Y	Y	Y	Y
3 **Barrett**	N	Y	Y	Y	Y	Y	Y
NEVADA							
1 **Ensign**	N	Y	Y	Y	Y	Y	Y
2 **Gibbons**	N	Y	Y	Y	Y	Y	Y
NEW HAMPSHIRE							
1 **Sununu**	N	Y	Y	Y	Y	Y	Y
2 **Bass**	N	Y	Y	Y	Y	Y	Y
NEW JERSEY							
1 Andrews	Y	Y	Y	N	Y	Y	Y
2 **LoBiondo**	N	Y	Y	Y	Y	Y	Y
3 **Saxton**	N	Y	Y	Y	Y	Y	Y
4 **Smith**	N	Y	Y	Y	Y	Y	Y
5 **Roukema**	Y	N	Y	Y	Y	Y	Y
6 Pallone	Y	N	Y	N	Y	Y	Y
7 **Franks**	N	Y	Y	Y	Y	Y	Y
8 Pascrell	Y	Y	Y	N	Y	Y	Y
9 Rothman	N	Y	Y	N	Y	Y	Y
10 Payne	Y	N	Y	N	Y	Y	Y
11 **Frelinghuysen**	N	Y	Y	Y	Y	Y	Y
12 **Pappas**	N	Y	Y	Y	Y	Y	Y
13 Menendez	Y	Y	Y	N	Y	Y	Y
NEW MEXICO							
1 **Wilson**	N	Y	Y	Y	Y	Y	Y
2 **Skeen**	N	Y	Y	Y	Y	Y	Y
3 **Redmond**	N	Y	Y	Y	Y	Y	Y
NEW YORK							
1 **Forbes**	N	Y	Y	Y	Y	Y	Y
2 **Lazio**	N	Y	Y	Y	Y	Y	Y
3 **King**	N	Y	Y	Y	Y	Y	Y
4 McCarthy	Y	Y	Y	N	Y	Y	Y
5 Ackerman	Y	N	Y	N	Y	Y	Y
6 Meeks	Y	N	Y	N	Y	Y	Y
7 Manton	Y	N	Y	N	Y	Y	?
8 Nadler	Y	N	Y	N	Y	Y	Y
9 Schumer	Y	N	Y	N	Y	Y	Y
10 Towns	Y	N	Y	N	Y	Y	Y
11 Owens	Y	N	Y	N	Y	Y	Y
12 Velázquez	Y	Y	Y	N	Y	Y	Y
13 **Fossella**	N	Y	Y	Y	Y	Y	Y
14 Maloney	Y	Y	Y	N	Y	Y	Y
15 Rangel	Y	N	Y	N	Y	Y	Y
16 Serrano	Y	N	Y	N	Y	Y	Y
17 Engel	Y	N	Y	N	Y	Y	Y
18 Lowey	Y	N	Y	N	Y	Y	Y
19 **Kelly**	N	Y	Y	Y	Y	Y	Y
20 **Gilman**	N	Y	Y	Y	Y	Y	Y
21 McNulty	Y	N	Y	N	Y	Y	Y
22 **Solomon**	N	Y	Y	Y	Y	Y	Y
23 **Boehlert**	N	Y	Y	Y	Y	Y	Y
24 **McHugh**	N	Y	Y	Y	Y	Y	Y
25 **Walsh**	N	Y	Y	Y	Y	Y	Y
26 Hinchey	Y	N	Y	N	Y	Y	Y
27 **Paxon**	N	Y	Y	Y	Y	Y	Y
28 Slaughter	Y	N	Y	N	Y	Y	Y
29 LaFalce	Y	N	Y	N	Y	Y	Y
30 **Quinn**	N	Y	Y	Y	Y	Y	Y
31 **Houghton**	N	Y	Y	Y	Y	Y	Y
NORTH CAROLINA							
1 Clayton	Y	N	Y	N	Y	Y	Y
2 Etheridge	Y	Y	Y	N	Y	Y	Y
3 **Jones**	N	Y	Y	Y	Y	Y	Y
4 Price	Y	Y	Y	N	Y	Y	Y
5 **Burr**	N	Y	Y	Y	Y	Y	Y
6 **Coble**	N	Y	Y	Y	Y	Y	Y
7 McIntyre	Y	Y	Y	Y	Y	Y	Y
8 Hefner	Y	N	Y	N	Y	Y	Y
9 **Myrick**	N	Y	Y	Y	Y	Y	Y
10 **Ballenger**	N	Y	Y	Y	Y	Y	Y
11 **Taylor**	N	Y	Y	Y	Y	Y	Y
12 Watt	Y	N	Y	N	Y	Y	Y
NORTH DAKOTA							
AL Pomeroy	Y	Y	Y	N	Y	Y	Y
OHIO							
1 **Chabot**	N	Y	Y	Y	Y	Y	Y
2 **Portman**	N	Y	Y	Y	Y	Y	Y
3 Hall	Y	N	Y	Y	Y	Y	Y
4 **Oxley**	N	Y	Y	Y	Y	Y	Y
5 **Gillmor**	N	Y	Y	Y	Y	Y	Y
6 Strickland	Y	Y	Y	N	Y	Y	Y
7 **Hobson**	N	Y	Y	Y	Y	Y	Y
8 **Boehner**	N	Y	Y	Y	Y	Y	Y
9 Kaptur	Y	N	Y	N	Y	Y	Y
10 Kucinich	Y	N	Y	Y	Y	Y	Y
11 Stokes	Y	N	Y	N	Y	Y	Y
12 **Kasich**	N	Y	Y	Y	Y	Y	Y
13 Brown	Y	N	Y	N	Y	Y	Y
14 Sawyer	Y	Y	Y	N	Y	Y	Y
15 **Pryce**	–	+	+	+	+	+	+
16 **Regula**	N	Y	Y	Y	Y	Y	Y
17 Traficant	Y	N	Y	Y	Y	Y	Y
18 **Ney**	N	Y	Y	Y	Y	Y	Y
19 **LaTourette**	N	Y	Y	Y	Y	Y	Y
OKLAHOMA							
1 **Largent**	N	Y	Y	Y	Y	Y	Y
2 **Coburn**	N	Y	Y	Y	Y	Y	Y
3 **Watkins**	N	Y	Y	Y	Y	Y	Y
4 **Watts**	N	Y	Y	Y	Y	Y	Y
5 **Istook**	N	Y	Y	Y	Y	Y	Y
6 **Lucas**	N	Y	Y	Y	Y	Y	Y
OREGON							
1 Furse	Y	N	Y	N	Y	Y	Y
2 **Smith**	N	Y	Y	Y	Y	Y	Y
3 Blumenauer	Y	Y	Y	N	Y	Y	Y
4 DeFazio	Y	N	Y	N	Y	?	Y
5 Hooley	N	Y	Y	N	Y	Y	Y
PENNSYLVANIA							
1 Brady	Y	N	Y	N	Y	Y	Y
2 Fattah	Y	?	Y	N	Y	Y	Y
3 Borski	Y	N	Y	N	Y	Y	Y
4 Klink	Y	N	Y	N	Y	Y	Y
5 **Peterson**	N	Y	Y	Y	Y	Y	Y
6 Holden	Y	Y	Y	N	Y	Y	Y
7 **Weldon**	N	Y	Y	Y	Y	Y	Y
8 **Greenwood**	N	Y	Y	Y	Y	Y	Y
9 **Shuster**	N	Y	Y	Y	Y	Y	Y
10 **McDade**	?	?	?	?	Y	Y	Y
11 Kanjorski	Y	N	Y	N	Y	Y	Y
12 Murtha	Y	N	Y	N	Y	Y	Y
13 **Fox**	Y	Y	Y	Y	Y	Y	Y
14 Coyne	Y	N	Y	N	Y	Y	Y
15 McHale	Y	Y	Y	Y	Y	Y	Y
16 **Pitts**	N	Y	Y	Y	Y	Y	Y
17 **Gekas**	N	Y	Y	Y	Y	Y	Y
18 Doyle	Y	N	Y	N	Y	Y	Y
19 **Goodling**	?	Y	Y	Y	Y	Y	Y
20 Mascara	Y	N	Y	N	Y	Y	Y
21 **English**	N	Y	Y	Y	Y	Y	Y
RHODE ISLAND							
1 Kennedy	Y	Y	Y	N	Y	Y	Y
2 Weygand	N	Y	Y	N	Y	Y	Y
SOUTH CAROLINA							
1 **Sanford**	N	Y	Y	Y	Y	Y	Y
2 **Spence**	N	Y	Y	Y	Y	Y	Y
3 **Graham**	N	Y	Y	Y	Y	Y	Y
4 **Inglis**	N	Y	Y	Y	Y	Y	?
5 Spratt	Y	Y	Y	N	Y	Y	Y
6 Clyburn	Y	N	Y	N	Y	Y	Y
SOUTH DAKOTA							
AL **Thune**	N	Y	Y	Y	Y	Y	Y
TENNESSEE							
1 **Jenkins**	N	Y	Y	Y	Y	Y	Y
2 **Duncan**	N	Y	Y	Y	Y	Y	Y
3 **Wamp**	N	Y	Y	Y	Y	Y	Y
4 **Hilleary**	N	Y	Y	Y	Y	Y	Y
5 Clement	N	Y	Y	N	Y	Y	Y
6 Gordon	N	Y	Y	N	Y	Y	Y
7 **Bryant**	N	Y	Y	Y	Y	Y	Y
8 Tanner	N	Y	Y	N	Y	Y	Y
9 Ford	Y	N	Y	N	Y	Y	Y
TEXAS							
1 Sandlin	Y	Y	Y	N	Y	Y	Y
2 Turner	Y	Y	Y	N	Y	Y	Y
3 **Johnson, Sam**	N	Y	Y	Y	Y	Y	Y
4 Hall	N	Y	Y	Y	Y	Y	Y
5 **Sessions**	N	Y	Y	Y	Y	Y	Y
6 **Barton**	N	Y	Y	Y	Y	Y	Y
7 **Archer**	N	Y	Y	Y	Y	Y	Y
8 **Brady**	N	Y	Y	N	Y	Y	Y
9 Lampson	Y	N	Y	N	Y	?	Y
10 Doggett	Y	N	Y	N	Y	?	Y
11 Edwards	Y	N	Y	N	Y	Y	Y
12 **Granger**	N	Y	Y	Y	Y	Y	Y
13 **Thornberry**	N	Y	Y	Y	Y	Y	Y
14 **Paul**	N	Y	Y	Y	Y	N	Y
15 Hinojosa	Y	N	Y	N	Y	Y	Y
16 Reyes	Y	N	Y	N	Y	Y	Y
17 Stenholm	N	Y	Y	Y	Y	Y	Y
18 Jackson-Lee	Y	N	Y	N	Y	Y	Y
19 **Combest**	N	Y	Y	Y	Y	Y	Y
20 Gonzalez	Y	N	Y	N	Y	Y	Y
21 **Smith**	N	Y	Y	Y	Y	Y	Y
22 **DeLay**	N	Y	Y	Y	Y	Y	Y
23 **Bonilla**	N	Y	Y	N	Y	Y	Y
24 Frost	N	Y	Y	N	Y	Y	Y
25 Bentsen	N	Y	Y	N	Y	Y	Y
26 **Armey**	N	Y	Y	Y	Y	Y	Y
27 Ortiz	Y	N	Y	N	Y	Y	Y
28 Rodriguez	Y	N	Y	N	Y	Y	Y
29 Green	Y	N	Y	N	Y	Y	Y
30 Johnson, E.B.	Y	N	Y	N	Y	Y	Y
UTAH							
1 **Hansen**	N	Y	Y	Y	Y	Y	Y
2 **Cook**	?	Y	Y	Y	Y	Y	Y
3 **Cannon**	N	Y	Y	Y	Y	Y	Y
VERMONT							
AL *Sanders*	Y	N	Y	N	Y	Y	Y
VIRGINIA							
1 **Bateman**	N	Y	Y	Y	Y	Y	Y
2 Pickett	N	Y	Y	Y	Y	Y	Y
3 Scott	Y	N	Y	N	Y	Y	Y
4 Sisisky	N	Y	Y	Y	Y	Y	Y
5 Goode	N	Y	Y	Y	Y	Y	Y
6 **Goodlatte**	N	Y	Y	Y	Y	Y	Y
7 **Bliley**	N	Y	Y	Y	Y	Y	Y
8 Moran	N	Y	Y	Y	Y	Y	Y
9 Boucher	N	Y	Y	N	Y	Y	Y
10 **Wolf**	N	Y	Y	Y	Y	Y	Y
11 **Davis**	N	Y	Y	Y	Y	Y	Y
WASHINGTON							
1 **White**	N	Y	Y	Y	Y	Y	Y
2 **Metcalf**	N	Y	Y	Y	Y	Y	Y
3 **Smith, Linda**	N	Y	Y	Y	Y	Y	Y
4 **Hastings**	N	Y	Y	Y	Y	Y	Y
5 **Nethercutt**	N	Y	Y	Y	Y	Y	+
6 Dicks	Y	Y	Y	N	Y	Y	Y
7 McDermott	Y	N	Y	N	Y	Y	Y
8 **Dunn**	N	Y	Y	Y	Y	Y	Y
9 Smith, Adam	N	Y	Y	N	Y	Y	Y
WEST VIRGINIA							
1 Mollohan	N	Y	Y	N	Y	Y	?
2 Wise	N	Y	Y	Y	Y	Y	Y
3 Rahall	Y	N	Y	N	Y	Y	Y
WISCONSIN							
1 **Neumann**	N	Y	Y	Y	Y	Y	Y
2 **Klug**	N	Y	Y	Y	Y	Y	Y
3 Kind	Y	Y	Y	N	Y	Y	Y
4 Kleczka	N	Y	Y	N	Y	Y	Y
5 Barrett	Y	N	Y	N	Y	Y	Y
6 **Petri**	N	Y	Y	Y	Y	Y	Y
7 Obey	Y	N	Y	N	Y	Y	Y
8 Johnson	N	Y	Y	N	Y	?	Y
9 **Sensenbrenner**	N	Y	Y	Y	Y	Y	Y
WYOMING							
AL **Cubin**	N	Y	Y	Y	Y	Y	Y

Southern states - Ala., Ark., Fla., Ga., Ky., La., Miss., N.C., Okla., S.C., Tenn., Texas, Va.

House Votes 512, 513, 514, 515, 516, 517, 518

512. Steel Anti-Dumping Laws/Privileged Resolution. Davis, R-Va., motion to table (kill) the Thomas, R-Calif., motion to appeal the ruling of the chair that the Visclosky, D-Ind., privileged resolution regarding enhanced enforcement of steel anti-dumping laws did not constitute a question of the privileges of the House. Motion agreed to 219-204: R 218-4; D 1-199 (ND 1-146, SD 0-53); I 0-1. Oct. 10, 1998.

513. Expedited Consideration of Legislative Business/Previous Question. Dreier, R-Calif., motion to order the previous question (thus ending debate and the possibility of amendment) on the resolution to allow for expedited consideration of appropriations bills, appropriations conference reports and continuing resolutions for the remainder of the 105th Congress. The measure also allows the Speaker to schedule suspension bills on any day for the rest of the session. Motion agreed to 221-201: R 221-0; D 0-200 (ND 0-147, SD 0-53); I 0-1. Oct. 10, 1998. (Subsequently, the resolution was adopted by voice vote.)

514. European Union Compliance with World Trade Organization Rules/Rule. Adoption of the rule (H Res 588) to provide for House floor consideration of the bill to require the United States Trade Representative to respond to the European Union's non-compliance with rulings of the World Trade Organization concerning bananas and beef hormones. Adopted 243-179: R 218-4; D 25-174 (ND 10-136, SD 15-38); I 0-1. Oct. 10, 1998.

515. HR 4110. Veterans Benefits Changes/Adoption. Stump, R-Ariz., motion to suspend the rules and adopt the resolution (H Res 592) to concur in Senate amendments to the bill that makes several changes to education, housing and other benefits programs within the Department of Veterans Affairs. Motion agreed to (thus clearing the bill for the president) 423-0: R 222-0; D 200-0 (ND 147-0, SD 53-0); I 1-0. Oct. 10, 1998. A two-thirds majority of those present and voting (282 in this case) is required for passage under suspension of the rules.

516. HR 4567. Medicare Reimbursement Formula/Passage. Thomas, R-Calif., motion to suspend the rules and pass the bill to create a new interim Medicare reimbursement formula for home health care agencies until a prospective payment system is ready. Motion agreed to 412-2: R 214-1; D 197-1 (ND 144-1, SD 53-0); I 1-0. Oct. 10, 1998. A two-thirds majority of those present and voting (276 in this case) is required for passage under suspension of the rules.

517. H Con Res 334. Taiwan and the World Health Organization/Passage. Solomon, R-N.Y., motion to suspend the rules and pass the bill to express the sense of Congress that Taiwan should participate in the World Health Organization in an "appropriate and meaningful" manner. Motion agreed to 418-0: R 217-0; D 200-0 (ND 147-0, SD 53-0); I 1-0. Oct. 10, 1998. A two-thirds majority of those present and voting (279 in this case) is required for passage under suspension of the rules.

518. H Con Res 320. Condemning Nazi-Soviet Pact of Non-Aggression/Passage. Gilman, R-N.Y., motion to suspend the rules and pass the bill to condemn the 1939 Nazi-Soviet Pact of Non-Aggression, under which Nazi Germany and the former Soviet Union divided Eastern Europe into spheres of influence. Motion agreed to 417-0: R 216-0; D 200-0 (ND 147-0, SD 53-0); I 1-0. Oct. 10, 1998. A two-thirds majority of those present and voting (278 in this case) is required for passage under suspension of the rules.

Key

- **Y** Voted for (yea).
- **#** Paired for.
- **+** Announced for.
- **N** Voted against (nay).
- **X** Paired against.
- **−** Announced against.
- **P** Voted "present."
- **C** Voted "present" to avoid possible conflict of interest.
- **?** Did not vote or otherwise make a position known.

Democrats   **Republicans**
Independent

	512	513	514	515	516	517	518
ALABAMA							
1 *Callahan*	Y	Y	Y	Y	Y	Y	Y
2 *Everett*	Y	Y	Y	Y	Y	Y	Y
3 *Riley*	Y	Y	Y	Y	Y	Y	Y
4 *Aderholt*	Y	Y	Y	Y	Y	Y	Y
5 Cramer	N	N	Y	Y	Y	Y	Y
6 *Bachus*	Y	Y	Y	Y	Y	Y	Y
7 Hilliard	N	N	N	Y	Y	Y	Y
ALASKA							
AL *Young*	Y	Y	Y	Y	Y	Y	Y
ARIZONA							
1 *Salmon*	Y	Y	Y	Y	Y	Y	Y
2 Pastor	N	N	Y	Y	Y	Y	Y
3 *Stump*	Y	Y	Y	Y	Y	Y	Y
4 *Shadegg*	Y	Y	Y	Y	Y	Y	Y
5 *Kolbe*	Y	Y	Y	Y	Y	Y	Y
6 *Hayworth*	Y	Y	Y	Y	Y	Y	Y
ARKANSAS							
1 Berry	N	N	Y	Y	Y	Y	Y
2 Snyder	N	N	N	Y	Y	Y	Y
3 *Hutchinson*	Y	Y	Y	Y	Y	Y	Y
4 Dickey	Y	Y	Y	Y	Y	Y	Y
CALIFORNIA							
1 *Riggs*	Y	Y	Y	Y	Y	Y	Y
2 *Herger*	Y	Y	Y	Y	Y	Y	Y
3 Fazio	N	N	N	Y	Y	Y	Y
4 *Doolittle*	Y	Y	Y	Y	Y	Y	Y
5 Matsui	N	N	N	Y	Y	Y	Y
6 Woolsey	N	N	N	Y	Y	Y	Y
7 Miller	N	N	N	Y	Y	Y	Y
8 Pelosi	N	N	N	Y	Y	Y	Y
9 Lee	N	N	N	Y	Y	Y	Y
10 Tauscher	N	N	Y	Y	Y	Y	Y
11 *Pombo*	Y	Y	Y	Y	Y	Y	Y
12 Lantos	N	N	N	Y	Y	Y	Y
13 Stark	N	N	N	Y	Y	Y	Y
14 Eshoo	N	N	N	Y	Y	Y	Y
15 *Campbell*	Y	Y	Y	Y	Y	Y	Y
16 Lofgren	N	N	N	Y	Y	Y	Y
17 Farr	N	N	N	Y	Y	Y	Y
18 Condit	N	N	Y	Y	Y	Y	Y
19 *Radanovich*	Y	Y	Y	Y	Y	Y	Y
20 Dooley	N	N	Y	Y	Y	Y	Y
21 *Thomas*	Y	Y	Y	Y	Y	Y	Y
22 Capps, L.	N	N	N	Y	Y	Y	Y
23 *Gallegly*	Y	Y	Y	Y	Y	Y	Y
24 Sherman	N	N	N	Y	Y	Y	Y
25 *McKeon*	Y	Y	Y	Y	Y	Y	Y
26 Berman	?	?	?	?	?	?	?
27 *Rogan*	Y	Y	Y	Y	Y	Y	Y
28 *Dreier*	Y	Y	Y	Y	Y	Y	Y
29 Waxman	N	N	N	Y	Y	Y	Y
30 Becerra	N	N	N	Y	Y	Y	Y
31 Martinez	N	N	N	Y	Y	Y	Y
32 Dixon	N	N	N	Y	Y	Y	Y
33 Roybal-Allard	N	N	N	Y	Y	Y	Y
34 Torres	N	N	N	Y	?	Y	Y
35 Waters	N	N	N	Y	Y	Y	Y
36 Harman	N	N	?	Y	Y	Y	Y
37 Millender-McD.	N	N	N	Y	Y	Y	Y
38 *Horn*	N	Y	Y	Y	Y	Y	Y
39 *Royce*	Y	Y	Y	Y	Y	Y	Y
40 *Lewis*	Y	Y	Y	Y	Y	Y	Y
41 *Kim*	Y	Y	Y	Y	Y	Y	Y
42 Brown	N	N	N	Y	Y	Y	Y
43 *Calvert*	Y	Y	Y	Y	Y	Y	Y
44 *Bono, M.*	Y	Y	Y	Y	Y	Y	Y
45 *Rohrabacher*	Y	Y	Y	Y	Y	Y	Y
46 Sanchez	N	N	N	Y	Y	Y	Y
47 *Cox*	Y	Y	Y	Y	Y	Y	Y
48 *Packard*	Y	Y	Y	Y	Y	Y	Y
49 *Bilbray*	Y	Y	Y	Y	+	Y	Y
50 Filner	N	N	N	Y	Y	Y	Y
51 *Cunningham*	Y	Y	Y	Y	Y	Y	Y
52 *Hunter*	Y	Y	N	Y	?	Y	Y
COLORADO							
1 DeGette	N	N	N	Y	Y	Y	Y
2 Skaggs	Y	N	N	Y	Y	Y	Y
3 *McInnis*	Y	Y	Y	Y	Y	Y	Y
4 *Schaffer*	Y	Y	Y	Y	Y	Y	Y
5 *Hefley*	Y	Y	Y	Y	Y	Y	Y
6 *Schaefer*	Y	Y	Y	Y	Y	Y	Y
CONNECTICUT							
1 Kennelly	?	?	?	?	?	?	?
2 Gejdenson	N	N	N	Y	Y	Y	Y
3 DeLauro	N	N	N	Y	Y	Y	Y
4 *Shays*	Y	Y	Y	Y	Y	Y	Y
5 Maloney	N	N	N	Y	Y	Y	Y
6 *Johnson*	Y	Y	Y	Y	Y	Y	Y
DELAWARE							
AL *Castle*	Y	Y	Y	Y	Y	Y	Y
FLORIDA							
1 *Scarborough*	Y	Y	Y	Y	Y	Y	Y
2 Boyd	N	N	Y	Y	Y	Y	Y
3 Brown	N	N	N	Y	Y	Y	Y
4 *Fowler*	Y	Y	Y	Y	Y	Y	Y
5 Thurman	N	N	Y	Y	Y	Y	Y
6 *Stearns*	Y	Y	Y	Y	Y	Y	Y
7 *Mica*	Y	Y	Y	Y	Y	Y	Y
8 *McCollum*	Y	Y	Y	Y	Y	Y	Y
9 *Bilirakis*	Y	Y	Y	Y	Y	Y	Y
10 *Young*	Y	Y	Y	Y	Y	Y	Y
11 Davis	N	N	Y	Y	Y	Y	Y
12 *Canady*	Y	Y	Y	Y	Y	Y	Y
13 *Miller*	Y	Y	Y	Y	Y	Y	Y
14 *Goss*	Y	Y	Y	Y	Y	Y	Y
15 *Weldon*	Y	Y	Y	Y	Y	Y	Y
16 *Foley*	Y	Y	Y	Y	Y	Y	Y
17 Meek	N	N	N	Y	Y	Y	Y
18 *Ros-Lehtinen*	Y	Y	Y	Y	Y	Y	Y
19 Wexler	N	N	N	Y	Y	Y	Y
20 Deutsch	N	N	N	Y	Y	Y	Y
21 *Diaz-Balart*	Y	Y	Y	Y	Y	Y	Y
22 *Shaw*	Y	Y	Y	Y	Y	Y	Y
23 Hastings	N	N	N	Y	Y	Y	Y
GEORGIA							
1 *Kingston*	Y	Y	Y	Y	Y	Y	Y
2 Bishop	N	Y	Y	Y	Y	Y	Y
3 *Collins*	?	?	?	?	?	?	?
4 McKinney	N	N	N	Y	Y	Y	Y
5 Lewis	N	N	N	Y	Y	Y	Y
6 *Gingrich*							
7 *Barr*	Y	Y	Y	Y	Y	Y	Y
8 *Chambliss*	Y	Y	Y	Y	Y	Y	Y
9 *Deal*	Y	Y	Y	Y	Y	Y	Y
10 *Norwood*	Y	Y	Y	Y	Y	?	?
11 *Linder*	Y	Y	Y	Y	Y	Y	Y
HAWAII							
1 Abercrombie	N	N	Y	Y	Y	Y	Y
2 Mink	N	N	Y	Y	Y	Y	Y
IDAHO							
1 *Chenoweth*	Y	Y	Y	Y	Y	Y	Y
2 *Crapo*	Y	Y	Y	Y	Y	Y	Y
ILLINOIS							
1 Rush	N	N	N	Y	Y	Y	Y
2 Jackson	N	N	N	Y	Y	Y	Y
3 Lipinski	N	N	Y	Y	Y	Y	Y
4 Gutierrez	N	N	N	Y	Y	Y	Y
5 Blagojevich	N	N	N	Y	Y	Y	Y
6 *Hyde*	Y	Y	Y	Y	Y	Y	Y
7 Davis	N	N	N	Y	Y	Y	Y
8 *Crane*	Y	Y	Y	Y	Y	Y	Y
9 Yates	N	N	N	Y	Y	Y	Y
10 *Porter*	Y	Y	Y	Y	Y	Y	Y
11 *Weller*	Y	Y	Y	Y	Y	Y	Y
12 Costello	N	N	N	Y	Y	Y	Y
13 *Fawell*	Y	Y	Y	Y	Y	Y	Y

ND Northern Democrats   **SD** Southern Democrats

	512	513	514	515	516	517	518
14 ***Hastert***	Y	Y	Y	Y	Y	Y	Y
15 ***Ewing***	Y	Y	Y	Y	Y	Y	Y
16 ***Manzullo***	Y	Y	Y	Y	Y	Y	Y
17 Evans	N	N	N	Y	Y	Y	Y
18 ***LaHood***	Y	Y	Y	Y	Y	Y	Y
19 Poshard	?	?	?	?	?	?	?
20 ***Shimkus***	Y	Y	Y	Y	Y	Y	Y
INDIANA							
1 Visclosky	N	N	N	Y	Y	Y	Y
2 ***McIntosh***	Y	Y	Y	Y	Y	Y	Y
3 Roemer	N	N	N	Y	Y	Y	Y
4 ***Souder***	Y	Y	Y	Y	Y	Y	Y
5 ***Buyer***	Y	Y	Y	Y	Y	Y	Y
6 ***Burton***	Y	Y	Y	Y	Y	Y	Y
7 ***Pease***	Y	Y	Y	Y	Y	Y	Y
8 ***Hostettler***	Y	Y	Y	Y	Y	Y	Y
9 Hamilton	N	N	N	Y	Y	Y	Y
10 Carson	N	N	N	Y	Y	Y	Y
IOWA							
1 ***Leach***	Y	Y	Y	Y	Y	Y	Y
2 ***Nussle***	Y	Y	Y	Y	Y	Y	Y
3 Boswell	N	N	Y	Y	Y	Y	Y
4 ***Ganske***	Y	Y	Y	Y	Y	Y	Y
5 ***Latham***	Y	Y	Y	Y	Y	Y	Y
KANSAS							
1 ***Moran***	Y	Y	Y	Y	Y	Y	Y
2 ***Ryun***	Y	Y	Y	Y	Y	Y	Y
3 ***Snowbarger***	Y	Y	Y	Y	Y	Y	Y
4 ***Tiahrt***	Y	Y	N	Y	Y	Y	Y
KENTUCKY							
1 ***Whitfield***	Y	Y	Y	Y	Y	Y	Y
2 ***Lewis***	Y	Y	Y	Y	Y	Y	Y
3 ***Northup***	Y	Y	Y	Y	Y	Y	Y
4 ***Bunning***	Y	Y	Y	Y	Y	Y	Y
5 ***Rogers***	Y	Y	Y	Y	Y	Y	Y
6 Baesler	N	N	Y	Y	Y	Y	Y
LOUISIANA							
1 ***Livingston***	Y	Y	Y	Y	Y	Y	Y
2 Jefferson	N	N	N	Y	Y	Y	Y
3 ***Tauzin***	Y	Y	Y	Y	Y	Y	Y
4 ***McCrery***	Y	Y	Y	Y	Y	Y	Y
5 ***Cooksey***	Y	Y	Y	Y	Y	Y	Y
6 ***Baker***	Y	Y	Y	Y	Y	Y	Y
7 John	N	N	Y	Y	Y	Y	Y
MAINE							
1 Allen	N	N	N	Y	Y	Y	Y
2 Baldacci	N	N	N	Y	Y	Y	Y
MARYLAND							
1 ***Gilchrest***	Y	Y	Y	Y	Y	Y	Y
2 ***Ehrlich***	Y	Y	Y	Y	Y	Y	Y
3 Cardin	N	N	N	Y	Y	Y	Y
4 Wynn	N	N	N	Y	Y	Y	Y
5 Hoyer	N	N	N	Y	?	Y	Y
6 ***Bartlett***	Y	Y	Y	Y	Y	Y	Y
7 Cummings	N	N	N	Y	Y	Y	Y
8 ***Morella***	Y	Y	Y	Y	Y	Y	Y
MASSACHUSETTS							
1 Olver	N	N	N	Y	Y	Y	Y
2 Neal	N	N	N	Y	Y	Y	Y
3 McGovern	N	N	N	Y	Y	Y	Y
4 Frank	N	N	N	Y	Y	Y	Y
5 Meehan	N	N	N	Y	Y	Y	Y
6 Tierney	N	N	N	Y	Y	Y	Y
7 Markey	N	N	N	Y	Y	Y	Y
8 Kennedy	N	N	N	Y	Y	Y	Y
9 Moakley	N	N	N	Y	Y	Y	Y
10 Delahunt	N	N	N	Y	Y	Y	Y
MICHIGAN							
1 Stupak	N	N	N	Y	Y	Y	Y
2 ***Hoekstra***	Y	Y	Y	Y	Y	Y	Y
3 ***Ehlers***	Y	Y	Y	Y	Y	Y	Y
4 ***Camp***	Y	Y	Y	Y	Y	Y	Y
5 Barcia	N	N	Y	Y	Y	Y	Y
6 ***Upton***	Y	Y	Y	Y	Y	Y	Y
7 ***Smith***	Y	Y	Y	Y	Y	Y	Y
8 Stabenow	N	N	Y	Y	Y	Y	Y
9 Kildee	N	N	N	Y	Y	Y	Y
10 Bonior	N	N	N	Y	Y	Y	Y
11 ***Knollenberg***	Y	Y	Y	Y	Y	Y	Y
12 Levin	N	N	N	Y	Y	Y	Y
13 Rivers	N	N	N	Y	Y	Y	Y
14 Conyers	N	N	N	Y	Y	Y	Y
15 Kilpatrick	N	N	N	Y	Y	Y	Y
16 Dingell	N	N	Y	Y	Y	Y	Y

	512	513	514	515	516	517	518
MINNESOTA							
1 ***Gutknecht***	Y	Y	Y	Y	Y	Y	Y
2 Minge	N	N	Y	Y	Y	Y	Y
3 ***Ramstad***	Y	Y	Y	Y	Y	Y	Y
4 Vento	N	N	N	Y	Y	Y	Y
5 Sabo	N	N	N	Y	N	Y	Y
6 Luther	N	N	N	Y	Y	Y	Y
7 Peterson	N	N	Y	Y	Y	Y	Y
8 Oberstar	N	N	N	Y	Y	Y	Y
MISSISSIPPI							
1 ***Wicker***	Y	Y	Y	Y	Y	Y	Y
2 Thompson	N	N	N	Y	Y	Y	Y
3 ***Pickering***	Y	Y	Y	Y	+	Y	Y
4 ***Parker***	?	?	?	?	?	?	?
5 Taylor	N	N	N	Y	Y	Y	Y
MISSOURI							
1 Clay	N	N	N	Y	Y	Y	Y
2 ***Talent***	Y	Y	Y	Y	Y	Y	Y
3 Gephardt	N	N	N	Y	Y	Y	Y
4 Skelton	N	N	N	Y	Y	Y	Y
5 McCarthy	N	N	N	Y	Y	Y	Y
6 Danner	N	N	N	Y	Y	Y	Y
7 ***Blunt***	Y	Y	Y	Y	Y	Y	Y
8 ***Emerson***	Y	Y	Y	Y	Y	Y	Y
9 ***Hulshof***	Y	Y	Y	Y	Y	Y	Y
MONTANA							
AL ***Hill***	Y	Y	Y	Y	Y	Y	Y
NEBRASKA							
1 ***Bereuter***	Y	Y	Y	Y	Y	Y	Y
2 ***Christensen***	Y	Y	Y	Y	Y	Y	Y
3 ***Barrett***	Y	Y	Y	Y	Y	Y	Y
NEVADA							
1 ***Ensign***	Y	Y	Y	Y	Y	?	?
2 ***Gibbons***	Y	Y	Y	Y	Y	Y	Y
NEW HAMPSHIRE							
1 ***Sununu***	Y	Y	Y	Y	Y	Y	Y
2 ***Bass***	Y	Y	Y	Y	Y	Y	Y
NEW JERSEY							
1 Andrews	N	N	N	Y	Y	Y	Y
2 ***LoBiondo***	Y	Y	Y	Y	Y	Y	Y
3 ***Saxton***	Y	Y	Y	Y	Y	Y	Y
4 ***Smith***	Y	Y	Y	Y	Y	Y	Y
5 ***Roukema***	Y	Y	Y	Y	Y	Y	Y
6 Pallone	N	N	N	Y	Y	Y	Y
7 ***Franks***	Y	Y	Y	Y	Y	Y	Y
8 Pascrell	N	N	N	Y	Y	Y	Y
9 Rothman	N	N	N	Y	Y	Y	Y
10 Payne	N	N	N	Y	Y	Y	Y
11 ***Frelinghuysen***	Y	Y	Y	Y	Y	Y	Y
12 ***Pappas***	Y	Y	Y	Y	Y	Y	Y
13 Menendez	N	N	N	Y	Y	Y	Y
NEW MEXICO							
1 ***Wilson***	Y	Y	Y	Y	Y	Y	Y
2 ***Skeen***	Y	Y	Y	Y	Y	Y	Y
3 ***Redmond***	Y	Y	Y	Y	Y	Y	Y
NEW YORK							
1 ***Forbes***	Y	Y	Y	Y	Y	Y	Y
2 ***Lazio***	?	?	?	Y	Y	Y	Y
3 ***King***	Y	Y	Y	Y	Y	Y	Y
4 McCarthy	N	N	N	Y	Y	Y	Y
5 Ackerman	N	N	N	Y	Y	Y	Y
6 Meeks	N	N	N	Y	Y	Y	Y
7 Manton	N	N	N	Y	Y	Y	Y
8 Nadler	N	N	N	Y	Y	Y	Y
9 Schumer	N	N	N	Y	Y	Y	Y
10 Towns	N	N	N	Y	Y	Y	Y
11 Owens	N	N	N	Y	Y	Y	Y
12 Velázquez	N	N	N	Y	Y	Y	Y
13 ***Fossella***	Y	Y	Y	Y	Y	Y	Y
14 Maloney	N	N	N	Y	Y	Y	Y
15 Rangel	?	?	?	?	?	?	?
16 Serrano	N	N	N	Y	Y	Y	Y
17 Engel	N	N	N	Y	Y	Y	Y
18 Lowey	N	N	N	Y	Y	Y	Y
19 ***Kelly***	Y	Y	Y	Y	Y	Y	Y
20 ***Gilman***	Y	Y	Y	Y	Y	Y	Y
21 McNulty	N	N	N	Y	Y	Y	Y
22 ***Solomon***	Y	Y	Y	Y	Y	Y	Y
23 ***Boehlert***	Y	Y	Y	Y	Y	Y	Y
24 ***McHugh***	Y	Y	Y	Y	Y	Y	Y
25 ***Walsh***	Y	Y	Y	Y	Y	?	?
26 Hinchey	N	N	N	Y	Y	Y	Y
27 ***Paxon***	Y	Y	Y	Y	Y	Y	Y
28 Slaughter	N	N	N	Y	Y	Y	Y
29 LaFalce	N	N	N	Y	Y	Y	Y
30 ***Quinn***	Y	Y	Y	Y	Y	?	?

	512	513	514	515	516	517	518
31 ***Houghton***	Y	Y	Y	Y	Y	Y	Y
NORTH CAROLINA							
1 Clayton	N	N	N	Y	Y	Y	Y
2 Etheridge	N	N	N	Y	Y	Y	Y
3 ***Jones***	Y	Y	Y	Y	Y	Y	Y
4 Price	N	N	N	Y	Y	Y	Y
5 ***Burr***	Y	Y	Y	Y	Y	Y	Y
6 ***Coble***	Y	Y	Y	Y	Y	Y	Y
7 McIntyre	N	N	N	Y	Y	Y	Y
8 Hefner	?	?	?	?	?	?	?
9 ***Myrick***	Y	Y	Y	Y	Y	Y	Y
10 ***Ballenger***	Y	Y	Y	Y	Y	Y	Y
11 ***Taylor***	Y	Y	Y	?	?	?	?
12 Watt	N	N	N	Y	Y	Y	Y
NORTH DAKOTA							
AL Pomeroy	N	N	N	Y	Y	Y	Y
OHIO							
1 ***Chabot***	Y	Y	Y	Y	Y	Y	Y
2 ***Portman***	Y	Y	Y	Y	+	Y	Y
3 Hall	N	N	N	Y	Y	Y	Y
4 ***Oxley***	Y	Y	Y	Y	Y	Y	Y
5 ***Gillmor***	Y	Y	Y	Y	Y	Y	Y
6 Strickland	N	N	N	Y	Y	Y	Y
7 ***Hobson***	Y	Y	Y	Y	Y	Y	?
8 ***Boehner***	Y	Y	Y	Y	Y	Y	Y
9 Kaptur	N	N	N	Y	Y	Y	Y
10 Kucinich	N	N	N	Y	Y	Y	Y
11 Stokes	N	N	N	Y	Y	Y	Y
12 ***Kasich***	Y	Y	Y	Y	Y	Y	Y
13 Brown	N	N	N	Y	Y	Y	Y
14 Sawyer	N	N	N	Y	Y	Y	Y
15 ***Pryce***	+	+	+	+	+	+	+
16 ***Regula***	Y	Y	Y	Y	Y	Y	Y
17 Traficant	N	N	N	Y	Y	Y	Y
18 ***Ney***	N	Y	N	Y	Y	Y	Y
19 ***LaTourette***	Y	Y	Y	Y	Y	Y	Y
OKLAHOMA							
1 ***Largent***	Y	Y	Y	Y	?	Y	Y
2 ***Coburn***	Y	Y	Y	Y	Y	Y	Y
3 ***Watkins***	Y	Y	Y	Y	Y	Y	Y
4 ***Watts***	Y	Y	Y	Y	Y	Y	Y
5 ***Istook***	Y	Y	Y	Y	Y	Y	Y
6 ***Lucas***	Y	Y	Y	Y	Y	Y	Y
OREGON							
1 Furse	N	N	N	Y	Y	Y	Y
2 ***Smith***	Y	Y	Y	Y	Y	Y	Y
3 Blumenauer	N	N	N	Y	Y	Y	Y
4 DeFazio	N	N	N	Y	Y	Y	Y
5 Hooley	N	N	N	Y	Y	Y	Y
PENNSYLVANIA							
1 Brady	N	N	N	Y	Y	Y	Y
2 Fattah	N	N	N	Y	Y	Y	Y
3 Borski	N	N	N	Y	Y	Y	Y
4 Klink	N	N	N	Y	Y	Y	Y
5 ***Peterson***	Y	Y	Y	Y	+	Y	Y
6 Holden	N	N	N	Y	Y	Y	Y
7 ***Weldon***	Y	Y	Y	Y	Y	Y	Y
8 ***Greenwood***	Y	Y	Y	Y	Y	Y	Y
9 ***Shuster***	Y	Y	Y	Y	Y	Y	Y
10 ***McDade***	Y	Y	Y	Y	Y	Y	Y
11 Kanjorski	N	N	N	Y	Y	Y	Y
12 Murtha	N	N	N	Y	Y	Y	Y
13 ***Fox***	Y	Y	Y	Y	Y	Y	Y
14 Coyne	N	N	N	Y	Y	Y	Y
15 McHale	N	N	N	Y	Y	Y	Y
16 ***Pitts***	Y	Y	Y	Y	Y	Y	Y
17 ***Gekas***	Y	Y	Y	Y	Y	Y	Y
18 Doyle	N	N	N	Y	Y	Y	Y
19 ***Goodling***	Y	Y	Y	Y	Y	Y	Y
20 Mascara	N	N	N	Y	Y	Y	Y
21 ***English***	Y	Y	Y	Y	?	Y	Y
RHODE ISLAND							
1 Kennedy	N	N	N	Y	Y	Y	Y
2 Weygand	N	N	N	Y	Y	Y	Y
SOUTH CAROLINA							
1 ***Sanford***	Y	Y	Y	Y	Y	Y	Y
2 ***Spence***	Y	Y	Y	Y	Y	Y	Y
3 ***Graham***	Y	Y	Y	Y	Y	Y	Y
4 ***Inglis***	Y	Y	Y	Y	Y	Y	Y
5 Spratt	N	N	N	Y	Y	Y	Y
6 Clyburn	N	N	N	Y	Y	Y	Y
SOUTH DAKOTA							
AL ***Thune***	Y	Y	Y	Y	Y	Y	Y

	512	513	514	515	516	517	518
TENNESSEE							
1 ***Jenkins***	Y	Y	Y	Y	Y	Y	Y
2 ***Duncan***	Y	Y	Y	Y	Y	Y	Y
3 ***Wamp***	Y	Y	Y	Y	Y	Y	Y
4 ***Hilleary***	Y	Y	Y	Y	Y	Y	Y
5 Clement	N	N	N	Y	Y	Y	Y
6 Gordon	N	N	Y	Y	Y	Y	Y
7 ***Bryant***	Y	Y	Y	Y	Y	Y	Y
8 Tanner	N	N	Y	Y	Y	Y	Y
9 Ford	N	N	N	Y	Y	Y	Y
TEXAS							
1 Sandlin	N	N	Y	Y	Y	Y	Y
2 Turner	N	N	Y	Y	Y	Y	Y
3 ***Johnson, Sam***	Y	Y	Y	Y	Y	Y	Y
4 Hall	N	N	Y	Y	Y	Y	Y
5 ***Sessions***	Y	Y	Y	Y	Y	Y	Y
6 ***Barton***	Y	Y	Y	Y	Y	Y	Y
7 ***Archer***	Y	Y	Y	Y	Y	Y	Y
8 ***Brady***	Y	Y	Y	Y	Y	Y	Y
9 Lampson	N	N	N	Y	Y	Y	Y
10 Doggett	N	N	N	Y	Y	Y	Y
11 Edwards	N	N	N	Y	Y	Y	Y
12 ***Granger***	Y	Y	Y	Y	Y	Y	Y
13 ***Thornberry***	Y	Y	Y	Y	Y	Y	Y
14 ***Paul***	Y	Y	Y	Y	N	Y	Y
15 Hinojosa	N	N	N	Y	Y	Y	Y
16 Reyes	N	N	N	Y	Y	Y	Y
17 Stenholm	N	N	Y	Y	Y	Y	Y
18 Jackson-Lee	N	N	N	Y	Y	Y	Y
19 ***Combest***	Y	Y	Y	Y	Y	Y	Y
20 Gonzalez	N	N	N	Y	Y	Y	Y
21 ***Smith***	Y	Y	Y	Y	Y	?	?
22 ***DeLay***	Y	Y	Y	Y	Y	Y	Y
23 ***Bonilla***	Y	Y	Y	Y	Y	Y	Y
24 Frost	N	N	N	Y	Y	Y	Y
25 Bentsen	N	N	N	Y	Y	Y	Y
26 ***Armey***	Y	Y	Y	Y	Y	Y	Y
27 Ortiz	N	N	Y	Y	Y	Y	Y
28 Rodriguez	N	N	Y	Y	Y	Y	Y
29 Green	N	N	N	Y	Y	Y	Y
30 Johnson, E.B.	N	N	N	Y	Y	Y	Y
UTAH							
1 ***Hansen***	Y	Y	Y	Y	Y	Y	Y
2 ***Cook***	Y	Y	Y	Y	Y	Y	Y
3 ***Cannon***	Y	Y	Y	Y	Y	Y	Y
VERMONT							
AL *Sanders*	N	N	N	Y	Y	Y	Y
VIRGINIA							
1 ***Bateman***	Y	Y	Y	Y	Y	Y	Y
2 Pickett	N	N	Y	Y	Y	Y	Y
3 Scott	N	N	N	Y	Y	Y	Y
4 Sisisky	N	N	N	Y	Y	Y	Y
5 Goode	N	N	N	Y	Y	Y	Y
6 ***Goodlatte***	Y	Y	Y	Y	Y	Y	Y
7 ***Bliley***	Y	Y	Y	Y	Y	Y	Y
8 Moran	N	N	N	Y	Y	Y	Y
9 Boucher	?	?	?	?	?	?	?
10 ***Wolf***	Y	Y	Y	Y	Y	Y	Y
11 ***Davis***	Y	Y	Y	Y	Y	Y	Y
WASHINGTON							
1 ***White***	Y	Y	Y	Y	Y	Y	Y
2 ***Metcalf***	N	?	Y	Y	Y	Y	Y
3 ***Smith, Linda***	Y	Y	Y	Y	Y	Y	Y
4 ***Hastings***	Y	Y	Y	Y	Y	Y	Y
5 ***Nethercutt***	+	+	+	+	+	+	+
6 Dicks	N	N	N	Y	Y	Y	Y
7 McDermott	N	N	N	Y	Y	Y	Y
8 ***Dunn***	Y	Y	Y	Y	Y	Y	Y
9 Smith, Adam	N	N	N	Y	Y	Y	Y
WEST VIRGINIA							
1 Mollohan	N	N	N	Y	Y	Y	Y
2 Wise	N	N	N	Y	Y	Y	Y
3 Rahall	N	N	N	Y	Y	Y	Y
WISCONSIN							
1 ***Neumann***	N	Y	N	Y	Y	Y	Y
2 ***Klug***	Y	Y	Y	Y	Y	Y	Y
3 Kind	N	N	N	Y	Y	Y	Y
4 Kleczka	N	N	N	Y	Y	Y	Y
5 Barrett	N	N	N	Y	Y	Y	Y
6 ***Petri***	Y	Y	Y	Y	Y	Y	Y
7 Obey	N	N	N	Y	Y	Y	Y
8 Johnson	N	N	N	Y	Y	Y	Y
9 ***Sensenbrenner***	Y	Y	Y	Y	Y	Y	Y
WYOMING							
AL ***Cubin***	Y	Y	Y	Y	Y	Y	Y

Southern states - Ala., Ark., Fla., Ga., Ky., La., Miss., N.C., Okla., S.C., Tenn., Texas, Va.

House Votes 519, 520, 521, 522, 523, 524, 525

519. HR 2616. Charter Schools/Passage. Riggs, R-Calif., motion to suspend the rules and concur in Senate amendments to a bill to increase the authorization for the planning, design and startup of charter schools, with the goal of building up to 2,500 new schools by the year 2000. Motion agreed to (thus clearing the bill for the president) 369-50: R 208-10; D 160-40 (ND 121-26, SD 39-14); I 1-0. Oct. 10, 1998. A two-thirds majority of those present and voting (280 in this case) is required for passage under suspension of the rules.

520. S 852. National Standard for Salvaged Car Registration/Passage. Bliley, R-Va., motion to suspend the rules and pass the bill to establish national standards for the registration of salvaged and rebuilt cars. Motion agreed to 271-133: R 205-1; D 66-131 (ND 33-111, SD 33-20); I 0-1. Oct. 10, 1998. A two-thirds majority of those present and voting (270 in this case) is required for passage under suspension of the rules.

521. HR 3494. Sexual Predator Punishment/Senate Amendments. Hutchinson, R-Ark., motion to suspend the rules and agree with Senate amendments to provide "zero tolerance" for possession of child pornography. The bill would establish or increase penalties for Internet-based sex crimes against minors, as well as sentencing guidelines for crimes against children. Motion agreed to (thus clearing the bill for the president) 400-0: R 215-0; D 184-0 (ND 136-0, SD 48-0); I 1-0. Oct. 12, 1998. A two-thirds majority of those present and voting (267 in this case) is required for passage under suspension of the rules.

522. Steel Imports/Passage. Archer, R-Texas, motion to suspend the rules and adopt the concurrent resolution to express the sense of Congress that the president should take all necessary measures under existing law to respond to the significant increase of steel imports. Motion rejected 153-249: R 153-62; D 0-186 (ND 0-136, SD 0-50); I 0-1. Oct. 12, 1998. A two-thirds majority of those present and voting (268 in this case) is required for passage under suspension of the rules. A "nay" was a vote in support of the president's position.

523. S 2095. National Fish and Wildlife Foundation/Passage. Saxton, R-N.J., motion to suspend the rules and pass the bill to reauthorize through fiscal 2003 the National Fish and Wildlife Foundation, a nonprofit organization dedicated to the conservation and restoration of natural resources. Motion rejected 153-248: R 148-66; D 5-181 (ND 1-135, SD 4-46); I 0-1. Oct. 12, 1998. A two-thirds majority of those present and voting (268 in this case) is required for passage under suspension of the rules.

524. H Res 494. Commending Citizens of Guam/Adoption. Young, R-Alaska, motion to suspend the rules and adopt the resolution to express the sense of the House recognizing 100 years of Guam's loyalty and service to the United States and urging a reaffirmation of the commitment for increased self-government in Guam. Motion agreed to 410-0: R 217-0; D 192-0 (ND 143-0, SD 49-0); I 1-0. Oct. 13, 1998. A two-thirds majority of those present and voting (274 in this case) is required for passage under suspension of the rules.

525. S 1364. Federal Reports Elimination/Passage. Horn, R-Calif., motion to suspend the rules and pass the bill to eliminate, modify or phase out certain federal reports currently required by law. Motion agreed to (thus clearing the bill for the president) 390-19: R 216-0; D 173-19 (ND 131-12, SD 42-7); I 1-0. Oct. 13, 1998. A two-thirds majority of those present and voting (273 in this case) is required for passage under suspension of the rules.

Key

- **Y** Voted for (yea).
- **#** Paired for.
- **+** Announced for.
- **N** Voted against (nay).
- **X** Paired against.
- **−** Announced against.
- **P** Voted "present."
- **C** Voted "present" to avoid possible conflict of interest.
- **?** Did not vote or otherwise make a position known.

Democrats   **Republicans**   *Independent*

	519	520	521	522	523	524	525
ALABAMA							
1 Callahan	Y	Y	Y	N	Y	Y	Y
2 Everett	Y	Y	Y	Y	Y	Y	Y
3 Riley	Y	Y	Y	Y	Y	Y	Y
4 Aderholt	Y	Y	Y	Y	Y	Y	Y
5 Cramer	Y	Y	Y	N	N	Y	Y
6 Bachus	Y	Y	Y	N	N	Y	Y
7 Hilliard	N	N	Y	N	N	Y	N
ALASKA							
AL Young	Y	Y	Y	Y	Y	Y	Y
ARIZONA							
1 Salmon	Y	Y	Y	Y	Y	Y	Y
2 Pastor	Y	Y	Y	N	Y	Y	Y
3 Stump	Y	Y	Y	Y	Y	Y	Y
4 Shadegg	Y	Y	Y	Y	Y	Y	Y
5 Kolbe	Y	Y	Y	N	Y	Y	Y
6 Hayworth	Y	Y	Y	Y	Y	Y	Y
ARKANSAS							
1 Berry	Y	Y	Y	N	Y	Y	Y
2 Snyder	Y	Y	Y	N	Y	Y	Y
3 Hutchinson	Y	Y	Y	Y	Y	Y	Y
4 Dickey	Y	Y	Y	Y	Y	Y	Y
CALIFORNIA							
1 Riggs	Y	Y	Y	Y	Y	Y	Y
2 Herger	Y	Y	Y	Y	Y	Y	Y
3 Fazio	Y	N	Y	N	N	Y	Y
4 Doolittle	Y	Y	Y	Y	Y	Y	Y
5 Matsui	Y	N	Y	N	N	Y	Y
6 Woolsey	Y	N	Y	N	N	Y	Y
7 Miller	Y	N	Y	N	N	Y	Y
8 Pelosi	Y	N	Y	N	N	Y	Y
9 Lee	N	N	Y	N	N	Y	N
10 Tauscher	Y	P	Y	N	N	Y	Y
11 Pombo	Y	Y	Y	Y	Y	Y	Y
12 Lantos	Y	N	Y	N	Y	Y	Y
13 Stark	N	N	Y	N	N	Y	Y
14 Eshoo	Y	N	Y	N	N	Y	Y
15 Campbell	Y	Y	Y	Y	Y	Y	Y
16 Lofgren	Y	N	P	N	N	Y	Y
17 Farr	Y	N	Y	N	N	Y	Y
18 Condit	Y	Y	Y	N	Y	Y	Y
19 Radanovich	Y	Y	Y	Y	Y	Y	Y
20 Dooley	Y	Y	Y	N	N	Y	Y
21 Thomas	Y	Y	Y	Y	Y	Y	Y
22 Capps, L.	Y	N	Y	N	Y	Y	Y
23 Gallegly	Y	Y	Y	Y	Y	Y	Y
24 Sherman	Y	N	Y	N	Y	Y	Y
25 McKeon	Y	Y	Y	Y	Y	Y	Y
26 Berman	?	?	?	?	?	?	?
27 Rogan	Y	Y	Y	Y	Y	Y	Y
28 Dreier	Y	Y	Y	Y	Y	Y	Y
29 Waxman	Y	N	?	?	Y	Y	Y
30 Becerra	Y	N	Y	N	?	Y	Y
31 Martinez	Y	N	Y	N	N	Y	Y
32 Dixon	Y	N	Y	N	N	Y	N
33 Roybal-Allard	Y	N	Y	N	N	Y	Y
34 Torres	Y	N	Y	N	N	Y	Y
35 Waters	N	N	Y	N	N	Y	N
36 Harman	Y	Y	Y	N	?	?	?
37 Millender-McD.	Y	N	Y	N	N	Y	N
38 Horn	Y	Y	Y	N	Y	Y	Y
39 Royce	Y	?	Y	N	Y	Y	Y
40 Lewis	Y	Y	Y	Y	Y	Y	Y
41 Kim	Y	Y	Y	Y	Y	Y	Y
42 Brown	Y	N	Y	N	N	Y	Y
43 Calvert	Y	Y	Y	Y	Y	Y	Y
44 Bono, M.	Y	Y	Y	Y	Y	Y	Y
45 Rohrabacher	Y	Y	Y	N	N	Y	Y
46 Sanchez	Y	N	Y	N	N	Y	Y
47 Cox	Y	Y	Y	Y	Y	Y	Y
48 Packard	Y	Y	Y	Y	Y	Y	Y
49 Bilbray	Y	Y	Y	N	N	Y	Y
50 Filner	N	N	Y	N	N	Y	Y
51 Cunningham	Y	Y	Y	N	Y	Y	Y
52 Hunter	Y	Y	Y	Y	Y	Y	Y
COLORADO							
1 DeGette	Y	N	Y	N	N	Y	Y
2 Skaggs	Y	N	+	−	−	Y	Y
3 McInnis	Y	?	Y	Y	Y	Y	Y
4 Schaffer	N	Y	Y	Y	Y	Y	Y
5 Hefley	Y	Y	Y	Y	Y	Y	Y
6 Schaefer	Y	Y	Y	N	Y	Y	Y
CONNECTICUT							
1 Kennelly	?	?	?	?	?	?	?
2 Gejdenson	Y	N	Y	N	N	Y	Y
3 DeLauro	Y	N	Y	N	N	Y	Y
4 Shays	Y	Y	Y	N	Y	Y	Y
5 Maloney	Y	Y	Y	N	Y	Y	Y
6 Johnson	Y	Y	Y	Y	Y	Y	Y
DELAWARE							
AL Castle	Y	Y	?	?	?	Y	Y
FLORIDA							
1 Scarborough	N	Y	?	?	?	?	?
2 Boyd	Y	N	Y	N	N	Y	Y
3 Brown	N	N	Y	N	N	Y	Y
4 Fowler	Y	Y	Y	Y	Y	Y	Y
5 Thurman	Y	N	Y	N	Y	Y	Y
6 Stearns	Y	+	Y	N	Y	Y	Y
7 Mica	Y	Y	Y	Y	Y	Y	Y
8 McCollum	Y	?	?	?	?	?	?
9 Bilirakis	Y	Y	Y	Y	Y	Y	Y
10 Young	Y	Y	Y	Y	Y	Y	Y
11 Davis	Y	Y	Y	N	Y	Y	Y
12 Canady	Y	Y	Y	Y	Y	Y	Y
13 Miller	Y	Y	Y	Y	Y	Y	Y
14 Goss	Y	Y	Y	Y	Y	Y	Y
15 Weldon	Y	Y	Y	Y	N	Y	Y
16 Foley	Y	Y	Y	Y	Y	Y	Y
17 Meek	Y	N	Y	N	N	Y	Y
18 Ros-Lehtinen	Y	Y	?	?	?	Y	Y
19 Wexler	Y	N	Y	N	N	?	?
20 Deutsch	Y	Y	+	−	−	+	+
21 Diaz-Balart	Y	Y	Y	N	Y	Y	Y
22 Shaw	Y	Y	Y	Y	Y	Y	Y
23 Hastings	N	N	Y	N	N	Y	N
GEORGIA							
1 Kingston	Y	Y	Y	Y	Y	Y	Y
2 Bishop	Y	N	Y	N	N	Y	Y
3 Collins	?	?	Y	Y	Y	Y	Y
4 McKinney	N	N	Y	N	N	Y	N
5 Lewis	N	N	Y	N	N	Y	Y
6 Gingrich							
7 Barr	Y	Y	Y	Y	Y	Y	Y
8 Chambliss	Y	?	Y	Y	Y	Y	Y
9 Deal	Y	P	Y	Y	Y	Y	Y
10 Norwood	?	?	?	?	?	Y	Y
11 Linder	Y	Y	Y	Y	Y	Y	Y
HAWAII							
1 Abercrombie	N	N	Y	N	N	Y	Y
2 Mink	N	N	Y	N	N	Y	N
IDAHO							
1 Chenoweth	N	Y	Y	N	Y	Y	Y
2 Crapo	N	Y	Y	Y	Y	Y	Y
ILLINOIS							
1 Rush	N	N	Y	N	N	Y	Y
2 Jackson	Y	N	Y	N	N	Y	Y
3 Lipinski	Y	N	Y	N	N	Y	Y
4 Gutierrez	Y	N	Y	N	N	Y	Y
5 Blagojevich	Y	N	Y	N	N	Y	Y
6 Hyde	Y	Y	Y	Y	Y	Y	Y
7 Davis	N	N	Y	N	N	Y	Y
8 Crane	Y	Y	Y	Y	Y	Y	Y
9 Yates	N	N	Y	?	?	Y	Y
10 Porter	Y	Y	Y	N	Y	Y	Y
11 Weller	Y	Y	Y	Y	Y	Y	Y
12 Costello	Y	N	Y	N	N	Y	N
13 Fawell	Y	Y	Y	N	Y	Y	Y

ND Northern Democrats   SD Southern Democrats

	519	520	521	522	523	524	525
14 **Hastert**	Y	Y	Y	Y	Y	Y	Y
15 **Ewing**	Y	Y	Y	N	N	Y	Y
16 **Manzullo**	N	Y	Y	Y	Y	Y	Y
17 Evans	N	N	Y	N	N	Y	Y
18 **LaHood**	Y	Y	Y	N	N	Y	Y
19 Poshard	?	?	?	?	?	?	?
20 **Shimkus**	Y	Y	Y	N	N	Y	Y
INDIANA							
1 Visclosky	N	N	Y	N	N	?	?
2 **McIntosh**	Y	?	Y	Y	N	Y	Y
3 Roemer	Y	N	Y	N	N	Y	Y
4 **Souder**	Y	Y	Y	Y	N	?	?
5 **Buyer**	Y	Y	Y	N	Y	Y	Y
6 **Burton**	Y	Y	Y	N	Y	Y	?
7 **Pease**	Y	Y	Y	N	N	Y	Y
8 **Hostettler**	Y	Y	Y	N	N	Y	Y
9 Hamilton	Y	N	Y	N	N	Y	Y
10 Carson	Y	N	Y	N	N	Y	Y
IOWA							
1 **Leach**	Y	Y	Y	Y	N	Y	Y
2 **Nussle**	Y	Y	Y	Y	Y	Y	Y
3 Boswell	N	N	Y	N	N	Y	Y
4 **Ganske**	Y	Y	Y	Y	N	Y	Y
5 **Latham**	Y	Y	Y	Y	N	Y	Y
KANSAS							
1 **Moran**	Y	Y	Y	Y	N	Y	Y
2 **Ryun**	Y	Y	Y	Y	Y	Y	Y
3 **Snowbarger**	Y	Y	Y	Y	Y	Y	Y
4 **Tiahrt**	Y	Y	Y	Y	Y	Y	Y
KENTUCKY							
1 **Whitfield**	Y	Y	Y	N	Y	Y	Y
2 **Lewis**	Y	Y	Y	Y	Y	Y	Y
3 **Northup**	Y	Y	Y	Y	Y	Y	Y
4 **Bunning**	Y	Y	Y	N	Y	Y	Y
5 **Rogers**	Y	Y	Y	Y	Y	Y	Y
6 Baesler	Y	Y	Y	N	N	Y	Y
LOUISIANA							
1 **Livingston**	Y	Y	Y	Y	N	Y	Y
2 Jefferson	Y	N	Y	N	N	Y	Y
3 **Tauzin**	Y	Y	Y	Y	Y	Y	Y
4 **McCrery**	Y	Y	Y	Y	Y	?	?
5 **Cooksey**	Y	Y	?	?	?	?	?
6 **Baker**	Y	Y	Y	Y	Y	Y	Y
7 John	Y	Y	?	N	N	Y	Y
MAINE							
1 Allen	Y	N	Y	N	N	Y	Y
2 Baldacci	Y	Y	Y	N	N	Y	Y
MARYLAND							
1 **Gilchrest**	Y	Y	Y	Y	N	Y	Y
2 **Ehrlich**	Y	Y	Y	Y	N	Y	Y
3 Cardin	Y	N	Y	N	N	Y	Y
4 Wynn	Y	Y	Y	N	N	Y	N
5 Hoyer	Y	N	Y	N	N	Y	Y
6 **Bartlett**	Y	Y	Y	Y	Y	Y	Y
7 Cummings	Y	Y	Y	N	N	Y	Y
8 **Morella**	Y	Y	Y	Y	N	Y	Y
MASSACHUSETTS							
1 Olver	Y	N	Y	N	N	Y	Y
2 Neal	Y	N	Y	N	N	Y	Y
3 McGovern	Y	N	Y	N	N	Y	Y
4 Frank	Y	N	Y	N	N	Y	Y
5 Meehan	Y	?	Y	N	N	Y	Y
6 Tierney	Y	N	Y	N	N	Y	Y
7 Markey	Y	N	Y	N	N	Y	Y
8 Kennedy	Y	?	Y	N	N	Y	Y
9 Moakley	Y	N	Y	N	N	Y	Y
10 Delahunt	Y	N	Y	N	N	Y	Y
MICHIGAN							
1 Stupak	N	N	Y	N	N	Y	Y
2 **Hoekstra**	Y	Y	Y	Y	Y	Y	Y
3 **Ehlers**	Y	Y	?	?	?	Y	Y
4 **Camp**	Y	Y	Y	Y	Y	Y	Y
5 Barcia	Y	N	Y	N	N	Y	Y
6 **Upton**	Y	Y	Y	Y	N	Y	Y
7 **Smith**	Y	Y	Y	N	Y	Y	Y
8 Stabenow	N	Y	Y	N	N	Y	Y
9 Kildee	Y	Y	Y	N	N	Y	Y
10 Bonior	N	N	Y	N	N	Y	Y
11 **Knollenberg**	Y	Y	Y	Y	Y	Y	Y
12 Levin	Y	N	Y	N	N	Y	Y
13 Rivers	N	N	Y	N	N	Y	Y
14 Conyers	N	N	Y	N	N	Y	N
15 Kilpatrick	N	Y	+	–	–	+	+
16 Dingell	N	N	Y	N	N	Y	Y
MINNESOTA							
1 **Gutknecht**	Y	Y	Y	Y	N	Y	Y
2 Minge	Y	Y	Y	N	N	Y	Y
3 **Ramstad**	Y	Y	Y	Y	N	Y	Y
4 Vento	Y	N	Y	N	N	Y	Y
5 Sabo	Y	N	Y	N	N	Y	Y
6 Luther	Y	N	Y	N	N	Y	Y
7 Peterson	Y	Y	Y	N	N	Y	Y
8 Oberstar	Y	N	Y	N	N	Y	Y
MISSISSIPPI							
1 **Wicker**	Y	Y	Y	Y	Y	Y	Y
2 Thompson	N	N	Y	N	N	Y	N
3 **Pickering**	Y	Y	Y	Y	Y	Y	Y
4 **Parker**	?	?	Y	Y	Y	Y	Y
5 Taylor	N	Y	?	N	N	Y	Y
MISSOURI							
1 Clay	N	N	Y	N	N	Y	N
2 **Talent**	Y	Y	Y	Y	Y	Y	Y
3 Gephardt	Y	Y	?	?	?	Y	Y
4 Skelton	Y	Y	Y	N	N	Y	Y
5 McCarthy	Y	N	+	–	–	Y	Y
6 Danner	Y	Y	Y	N	N	Y	Y
7 **Blunt**	Y	?	Y	Y	Y	Y	Y
8 **Emerson**	Y	Y	Y	N	Y	Y	Y
9 **Hulshof**	Y	Y	Y	Y	N	Y	Y
MONTANA							
AL **Hill**	Y	Y	Y	Y	Y	Y	Y
NEBRASKA							
1 **Bereuter**	Y	Y	Y	Y	N	Y	Y
2 **Christensen**	Y	Y	Y	Y	Y	Y	Y
3 **Barrett**	Y	Y	Y	Y	Y	Y	Y
NEVADA							
1 **Ensign**	?	?	Y	Y	N	Y	Y
2 **Gibbons**	Y	Y	Y	Y	Y	Y	Y
NEW HAMPSHIRE							
1 **Sununu**	Y	Y	Y	N	N	Y	Y
2 **Bass**	Y	Y	Y	Y	N	Y	Y
NEW JERSEY							
1 Andrews	Y	Y	Y	N	N	Y	Y
2 **LoBiondo**	Y	Y	Y	N	N	Y	Y
3 **Saxton**	Y	Y	Y	N	Y	Y	Y
4 **Smith**	Y	Y	Y	N	N	Y	Y
5 **Roukema**	Y	Y	Y	Y	N	Y	Y
6 Pallone	Y	N	Y	N	N	Y	Y
7 **Franks**	Y	Y	Y	Y	N	Y	Y
8 Pascrell	Y	Y	Y	N	N	Y	Y
9 Rothman	Y	N	Y	N	N	Y	Y
10 Payne	N	N	Y	N	N	Y	N
11 **Frelinghuysen**	Y	Y	Y	Y	N	Y	Y
12 **Pappas**	Y	Y	Y	N	N	Y	Y
13 Menendez	Y	N	Y	N	N	Y	Y
NEW MEXICO							
1 **Wilson**	Y	Y	Y	N	Y	Y	Y
2 **Skeen**	Y	Y	Y	N	Y	Y	Y
3 **Redmond**	Y	Y	Y	N	Y	Y	Y
NEW YORK							
1 **Forbes**	Y	?	Y	N	N	Y	Y
2 **Lazio**	Y	Y	Y	Y	N	Y	Y
3 **King**	Y	Y	Y	N	Y	Y	Y
4 McCarthy	Y	Y	Y	N	N	Y	Y
5 Ackerman	Y	N	Y	N	N	?	?
6 Meeks	Y	N	Y	N	N	Y	N
7 Manton	Y	N	Y	N	N	Y	Y
8 Nadler	Y	N	Y	?	?	Y	Y
9 Schumer	Y	N	Y	N	N	Y	Y
10 Towns	Y	N	Y	N	N	Y	N
11 Owens	Y	N	Y	N	N	Y	Y
12 Velázquez	Y	N	Y	N	N	Y	Y
13 **Fossella**	Y	Y	Y	N	N	Y	Y
14 Maloney	Y	N	Y	N	N	Y	Y
15 Rangel	?	?	Y	N	N	Y	Y
16 Serrano	Y	N	Y	N	N	Y	Y
17 Engel	Y	N	Y	N	N	Y	Y
18 Lowey	Y	N	Y	N	N	Y	Y
19 **Kelly**	Y	Y	Y	N	N	Y	Y
20 **Gilman**	Y	Y	Y	Y	N	Y	Y
21 McNulty	Y	N	Y	N	N	Y	Y
22 **Solomon**	Y	?	Y	Y	Y	Y	Y
23 **Boehlert**	Y	Y	Y	N	N	Y	Y
24 **McHugh**	Y	Y	Y	N	N	Y	Y
25 **Walsh**	?	?	Y	N	N	Y	Y
26 Hinchey	Y	N	?	?	N	Y	Y
27 **Paxon**	Y	Y	Y	Y	Y	Y	Y
28 Slaughter	Y	N	Y	N	N	Y	Y
29 LaFalce	Y	N	Y	N	N	Y	Y
30 **Quinn**	?	?	Y	N	N	Y	Y
31 **Houghton**	Y	Y	Y	N	Y	Y	Y
NORTH CAROLINA							
1 Clayton	N	N	Y	N	N	Y	Y
2 Etheridge	Y	Y	Y	N	N	Y	Y
3 **Jones**	N	Y	Y	Y	N	Y	Y
4 Price	Y	Y	Y	N	N	Y	Y
5 **Burr**	Y	Y	Y	Y	Y	Y	Y
6 **Coble**	Y	Y	Y	Y	Y	Y	Y
7 McIntyre	Y	Y	Y	N	N	Y	Y
8 Hefner	?	?	?	?	?	?	?
9 **Myrick**	Y	Y	Y	Y	Y	Y	Y
10 **Ballenger**	Y	Y	Y	Y	Y	Y	Y
11 **Taylor**	?	?	Y	Y	Y	Y	Y
12 Watt	Y	N	Y	N	N	Y	Y
NORTH DAKOTA							
AL Pomeroy	Y	Y	Y	N	Y	Y	Y
OHIO							
1 **Chabot**	Y	Y	Y	Y	N	Y	Y
2 **Portman**	Y	Y	Y	Y	N	Y	Y
3 Hall	Y	N	Y	N	N	?	?
4 **Oxley**	Y	Y	Y	Y	Y	Y	Y
5 **Gillmor**	Y	Y	Y	Y	N	Y	Y
6 Strickland	Y	Y	Y	N	N	Y	Y
7 **Hobson**	Y	Y	Y	Y	Y	Y	Y
8 **Boehner**	Y	Y	Y	N	Y	Y	Y
9 Kaptur	Y	N	Y	N	N	Y	Y
10 Kucinich	N	N	Y	N	N	Y	Y
11 Stokes	N	N	Y	N	N	Y	Y
12 **Kasich**	Y	Y	Y	Y	Y	Y	Y
13 Brown	Y	N	Y	N	N	Y	Y
14 Sawyer	Y	N	Y	N	N	Y	Y
15 **Pryce**	+	+	+	+	+	+	+
16 **Regula**	Y	Y	Y	Y	Y	Y	Y
17 Traficant	Y	Y	Y	N	N	Y	Y
18 **Ney**	Y	Y	Y	N	Y	Y	Y
19 **LaTourette**	Y	Y	Y	Y	N	Y	Y
OKLAHOMA							
1 **Largent**	Y	Y	?	?	?	?	?
2 **Coburn**	N	Y	Y	Y	N	Y	Y
3 **Watkins**	Y	Y	Y	Y	Y	Y	Y
4 **Watts**	Y	Y	Y	N	Y	Y	Y
5 **Istook**	Y	Y	Y	Y	Y	Y	Y
6 **Lucas**	Y	Y	Y	Y	Y	Y	Y
OREGON							
1 Furse	N	N	Y	N	N	Y	N
2 **Smith**	Y	Y	Y	Y	N	Y	Y
3 Blumenauer	Y	N	Y	N	N	Y	Y
4 DeFazio	N	N	Y	N	N	Y	Y
5 Hooley	Y	Y	Y	N	N	Y	Y
PENNSYLVANIA							
1 Brady	Y	N	Y	N	N	Y	Y
2 Fattah	Y	N	Y	N	N	Y	Y
3 Borski	Y	N	?	?	?	Y	Y
4 Klink	Y	N	Y	N	N	Y	Y
5 **Peterson**	Y	Y	Y	N	Y	Y	Y
6 Holden	Y	Y	Y	N	N	Y	Y
7 **Weldon**	Y	Y	Y	N	N	Y	Y
8 **Greenwood**	Y	Y	Y	Y	N	Y	Y
9 **Shuster**	Y	Y	Y	Y	Y	Y	Y
10 **McDade**	Y	Y	Y	?	?	?	?
11 Kanjorski	Y	N	Y	N	N	Y	Y
12 Murtha	Y	N	?	?	?	Y	Y
13 **Fox**	Y	Y	Y	Y	N	Y	Y
14 Coyne	Y	N	Y	N	N	Y	Y
15 McHale	Y	N	Y	N	N	Y	Y
16 **Pitts**	Y	Y	Y	Y	Y	Y	Y
17 **Gekas**	Y	Y	Y	Y	Y	Y	Y
18 Doyle	Y	Y	Y	N	N	Y	Y
19 **Goodling**	Y	Y	Y	N	Y	Y	Y
20 Mascara	Y	Y	Y	N	N	Y	Y
21 **English**	Y	Y	Y	Y	N	Y	Y
RHODE ISLAND							
1 Kennedy	Y	N	Y	N	N	Y	Y
2 Weygand	Y	Y	Y	N	N	Y	Y
SOUTH CAROLINA							
1 **Sanford**	Y	N	Y	N	N	Y	Y
2 **Spence**	Y	Y	Y	N	Y	Y	Y
3 **Graham**	Y	Y	?	?	?	?	?
4 **Inglis**	Y	?	?	?	?	?	?
5 Spratt	Y	Y	?	?	?	?	?
6 Clyburn	N	N	Y	N	N	Y	N
SOUTH DAKOTA							
AL **Thune**	Y	Y	Y	Y	Y	Y	Y
TENNESSEE							
1 **Jenkins**	Y	Y	Y	Y	Y	Y	Y
2 **Duncan**	Y	Y	Y	N	Y	Y	Y
3 **Wamp**	Y	Y	Y	Y	Y	Y	Y
4 **Hilleary**	Y	Y	Y	Y	Y	Y	Y
5 Clement	Y	Y	Y	N	N	Y	Y
6 Gordon	Y	Y	Y	N	N	Y	Y
7 **Bryant**	Y	Y	Y	Y	Y	Y	Y
8 Tanner	Y	Y	Y	N	N	Y	Y
9 Ford	Y	N	Y	N	N	Y	Y
TEXAS							
1 Sandlin	Y	Y	Y	N	N	Y	Y
2 Turner	Y	Y	Y	N	Y	Y	Y
3 **Johnson, Sam**	Y	Y	Y	Y	Y	Y	Y
4 Hall	Y	Y	Y	N	Y	Y	Y
5 **Sessions**	Y	Y	Y	Y	Y	Y	Y
6 **Barton**	Y	Y	Y	Y	Y	Y	Y
7 **Archer**	Y	Y	Y	Y	Y	Y	Y
8 **Brady**	Y	Y	Y	Y	Y	Y	Y
9 Lampson	Y	Y	?	?	?	?	?
10 Doggett	Y	Y	Y	N	N	Y	Y
11 Edwards	Y	Y	Y	N	N	Y	Y
12 **Granger**	Y	Y	Y	Y	Y	Y	Y
13 **Thornberry**	Y	Y	Y	Y	Y	Y	Y
14 **Paul**	N	?	P	N	N	Y	Y
15 Hinojosa	N	Y	Y	N	N	Y	Y
16 Reyes	Y	Y	Y	N	N	Y	Y
17 Stenholm	Y	Y	Y	N	Y	Y	Y
18 Jackson-Lee	Y	N	Y	N	N	Y	N
19 **Combest**	Y	Y	Y	Y	Y	Y	Y
20 Gonzalez	Y	N	Y	N	N	Y	Y
21 **Smith**	Y	Y	Y	Y	Y	Y	Y
22 **DeLay**	Y	Y	Y	N	Y	Y	Y
23 **Bonilla**	Y	Y	Y	Y	Y	Y	Y
24 Frost	Y	Y	Y	N	N	Y	Y
25 Bentsen	Y	Y	Y	N	N	Y	Y
26 **Armey**	Y	Y	Y	Y	Y	Y	Y
27 Ortiz	Y	Y	Y	N	N	Y	Y
28 Rodriguez	Y	Y	Y	N	N	Y	Y
29 Green	Y	Y	Y	N	N	Y	Y
30 Johnson, E.B.	Y	N	Y	N	N	Y	N
UTAH							
1 **Hansen**	Y	Y	Y	Y	Y	Y	Y
2 **Cook**	Y	Y	Y	Y	N	Y	Y
3 **Cannon**	N	Y	Y	Y	Y	Y	Y
VERMONT							
AL *Sanders*	Y	N	Y	N	N	Y	Y
VIRGINIA							
1 **Bateman**	Y	Y	Y	Y	Y	Y	Y
2 Pickett	N	Y	Y	N	Y	Y	Y
3 Scott	N	N	Y	N	N	Y	Y
4 Sisisky	Y	Y	Y	N	N	Y	Y
5 Goode	N	Y	Y	N	N	Y	Y
6 **Goodlatte**	Y	Y	Y	Y	N	Y	Y
7 **Bliley**	Y	Y	Y	Y	Y	Y	Y
8 Moran	Y	Y	Y	N	N	Y	Y
9 Boucher	?	?	?	?	?	?	?
10 **Wolf**	Y	Y	Y	Y	N	Y	Y
11 **Davis**	Y	Y	Y	N	N	Y	Y
WASHINGTON							
1 **White**	Y	Y	Y	Y	N	Y	Y
2 **Metcalf**	Y	Y	Y	N	Y	Y	Y
3 **Smith, Linda**	Y	Y	Y	Y	Y	Y	Y
4 **Hastings**	Y	Y	Y	Y	Y	Y	Y
5 **Nethercutt**	+	+	Y	Y	Y	Y	Y
6 Dicks	Y	N	Y	N	N	Y	Y
7 McDermott	N	N	Y	N	N	Y	Y
8 **Dunn**	Y	Y	Y	Y	Y	Y	Y
9 Smith, Adam	Y	Y	Y	N	N	Y	Y
WEST VIRGINIA							
1 Mollohan	Y	Y	?	?	?	Y	Y
2 Wise	Y	Y	Y	N	N	Y	Y
3 Rahall	Y	Y	?	?	?	Y	Y
WISCONSIN							
1 **Neumann**	Y	Y	Y	N	N	Y	Y
2 **Klug**	Y	Y	Y	Y	?	Y	Y
3 Kind	Y	N	Y	N	N	Y	Y
4 Kleczka	Y	Y	Y	N	N	Y	Y
5 Barrett	Y	N	Y	N	N	Y	Y
6 **Petri**	Y	Y	Y	N	N	Y	Y
7 Obey	Y	N	Y	N	N	Y	Y
8 Johnson	Y	Y	Y	N	N	Y	Y
9 **Sensenbrenner**	N	Y	Y	N	N	Y	Y
WYOMING							
AL **Cubin**	Y	Y	Y	N	Y	Y	Y

Southern states - Ala., Ark., Fla., Ga., Ky., La., Miss., N.C., Okla., S.C., Tenn., Texas, Va.

House Votes 526, 527, 528, 529, 530, 531, 532

526. HR 4756. Year 2000 Computer Problem/Passage. Morella, R-Md., motion to suspend the rules and pass the bill to increase congressional oversight of the federal government's attempts to solve the so-called Year 2000 computer problem. The measure requires all federal agencies to submit a report to Congress outlining their progress on preparing their computers for the year 2000. Motion agreed to 407-3: R 214-3; D 192-0 (ND 143-0, SD 49-0); I 1-0. Oct. 13, 1998. A two-thirds majority of those present and voting (274 in this case) is required for passage under suspension of the rules.

527. S 1754. Public Health Program Consolidation/Passage. Bliley, R-Va., motion to suspend the rules and pass the bill to consolidate 37 Public Health Service grant programs and to require that priority be given to programs for minority health workers and professionals in underserved areas. Motion agreed to 303-102: R 115-101; D 187-1 (ND 140-0, SD 47-1); I 1-0. Oct. 13, 1998. A two-thirds majority of those present and voting (270 in this case) is required for passage under suspension of the rules.

528. S 1260. Class-Action Securities Litigation/Conference Report. Bliley, R-Va., motion to suspend the rules and adopt the conference report on the bill to require that all class-action securities lawsuits involving more than 50 parties be considered in federal court, where standards established in a 1995 securities law (PL 104-67) would apply. Motion agreed to (thus clearing the conference report for the president) 319-82: R 213-1; D 106-80 (ND 74-64, SD 32-16); I 0-1. Oct. 13, 1998. A two-thirds majority of those present and voting (268 in this case) is required for passage under suspension of the rules.

529. S 1722. Women's Health Research Programs/Passage. Bilirakis, R-Fla., motion to suspend the rules and pass the bill to authorize and coordinate medical research and related programs dealing with women's health. Motion agred to (thus clearing the bill for the president) 401-1: R 212-1; D 188-0 (ND 140-0, SD 48-0); I 1-0. Oct. 13, 1998. A two-thirds majority of those present and voting (268 in this case) is required for passage under suspension of the rules.

530. HR 3963. Canyon Ferry Reservoir Cabin Sites/Passage. Hansen, R-Utah, motion to suspend the rules and pass the bill to direct the Interior Department to offer for sale 265 cabin sites near the Bureau of Reclamation's Canyon Ferry Reservoir in Montana. The bill requires the department to sell the lots to public owners at fair market value by sealed bid. Motion rejected 217-181: R 210-0; D 7-180 (ND 4-132, SD 3-48); I 0-1. Oct. 14, 1998. A two-thirds majority of those present and voting (266 inthis case) is required for passage under suspension of the rules.

531. HR 559. Service-Connected Diseases/Passage. Stump, R-Ariz., motion to suspend the rules and pass the bill to add bronchiolo-alveolar carcinoma to the list of diseases presumed to be service-connected for certain veterans exposed to atomic radiation. The veterans or their surviving dependents would then be eligible for benefits. Motion agreed to 400-0: R 213-0; D 186-0 (ND 137-0, SD 49-0); I 1-0. Oct. 14, 1998. A two-thirds majority of those present and voting (267 in this case) is required for passage under suspension of the rules.

532. H Res 598. Enforcement of Steel Imports Laws/Adoption. English, R-Pa., motion to suspend the rules and adopt the resolution expressing the sense of the House that its integrity has been impugned because the anti-dumping provisions of the Trade and Tariff Act of 1930 have not been expeditiously enforced and calling for an import ban on steel from nations found to be violating international steel accords. Motion agreed to 345-44: R 159-44; D 185-0 (ND 136-0, SD 49-0); I 1-0. Oct. 15, 1998. A two-thirds majority of those present and voting (260 in this case) is required for passage under suspension of the rules.

Key

- Y Voted for (yea).
- \# Paired for.
- \+ Announced for.
- N Voted against (nay).
- X Paired against.
- – Announced against.
- P Voted "present."
- C Voted "present" to avoid possible conflict of interest.
- ? Did not vote or otherwise make a position known.

Democrats **Republicans** Independent

	526	527	528	529	530	531	532
ALABAMA							
1 **Callahan**	Y	N	Y	Y	Y	Y	?
2 **Everett**	Y	N	Y	Y	Y	Y	Y
3 **Riley**	Y	N	Y	Y	Y	Y	Y
4 **Aderholt**	Y	N	Y	Y	Y	Y	Y
5 Cramer	Y	Y	Y	Y	N	Y	Y
6 **Bachus**	Y	Y	Y	Y	Y	Y	Y
7 Hilliard	Y	Y	N	Y	N	Y	Y
ALASKA							
AL **Young**	Y	Y	Y	Y	Y	Y	Y
ARIZONA							
1 **Salmon**	Y	N	Y	Y	Y	Y	Y
2 Pastor	Y	Y	N	Y	N	Y	Y
3 **Stump**	Y	N	Y	Y	Y	Y	N
4 **Shadegg**	Y	N	Y	Y	Y	Y	N
5 **Kolbe**	Y	N	Y	?	?	Y	N
6 **Hayworth**	Y	N	Y	Y	Y	Y	N
ARKANSAS							
1 Berry	Y	Y	Y	Y	N	Y	Y
2 Snyder	Y	Y	Y	Y	N	Y	Y
3 **Hutchinson**	Y	Y	Y	Y	Y	Y	?
4 **Dickey**	Y	Y	Y	Y	Y	Y	Y
CALIFORNIA							
1 **Riggs**	Y	N	Y	Y	Y	Y	Y
2 **Herger**	Y	N	Y	Y	Y	Y	N
3 Fazio	Y	Y	Y	Y	N	Y	Y
4 **Doolittle**	Y	N	Y	Y	Y	Y	Y
5 Matsui	Y	Y	Y	Y	N	Y	Y
6 Woolsey	Y	Y	N	Y	N	Y	Y
7 Miller	Y	Y	Y	Y	N	Y	Y
8 Pelosi	Y	Y	Y	Y	N	Y	?
9 Lee	Y	Y	N	Y	N	Y	Y
10 Tauscher	Y	Y	Y	Y	N	Y	Y
11 **Pombo**	Y	N	Y	Y	Y	Y	Y
12 Lantos	Y	Y	Y	Y	N	Y	?
13 Stark	Y	Y	Y	Y	N	Y	Y
14 Eshoo	Y	Y	Y	Y	N	Y	Y
15 **Campbell**	Y	N	Y	Y	Y	Y	N
16 Lofgren	Y	Y	Y	Y	N	Y	Y
17 Farr	Y	Y	Y	Y	N	Y	Y
18 Condit	Y	Y	Y	Y	N	Y	Y
19 **Radanovich**	Y	N	Y	Y	Y	Y	Y
20 Dooley	Y	Y	Y	Y	N	Y	Y
21 **Thomas**	Y	Y	Y	Y	N	Y	Y
22 Capps, L.	Y	Y	Y	Y	N	Y	Y
23 **Gallegly**	Y	Y	Y	Y	Y	Y	Y
24 Sherman	Y	Y	Y	Y	N	Y	Y
25 **McKeon**	Y	N	Y	Y	Y	Y	Y
26 Berman	?	?	?	?	?	?	?
27 **Rogan**	Y	N	Y	Y	Y	Y	N
28 **Dreier**	Y	N	Y	Y	Y	Y	N
29 Waxman	Y	Y	N	Y	N	Y	Y
30 Becerra	Y	Y	Y	Y	N	Y	Y
31 Martinez	Y	Y	Y	Y	N	Y	Y
32 Dixon	Y	Y	Y	Y	N	Y	Y
33 Royal-Allard	Y	Y	N	Y	N	Y	Y
34 Torres	Y	N	Y	?	?	?	?
35 Waters	Y	Y	N	Y	N	Y	?
36 Harman	?	?	?	Y	N	Y	Y
37 Millender-McD.	Y	Y	N	Y	N	Y	Y
38 **Horn**	Y	Y	Y	Y	Y	Y	Y

	526	527	528	529	530	531	532
39 **Royce**	Y	N	Y	Y	Y	Y	N
40 **Lewis**	Y	Y	Y	Y	Y	Y	Y
41 **Kim**	Y	Y	Y	Y	Y	Y	Y
42 Brown	Y	Y	N	Y	N	Y	Y
43 **Calvert**	Y	Y	Y	Y	Y	Y	Y
44 **Bono, M.**	Y	N	Y	Y	Y	Y	N
45 **Rohrabacher**	Y	N	Y	Y	Y	Y	N
46 Sanchez	Y	Y	Y	Y	N	Y	Y
47 **Cox**	Y	N	Y	Y	Y	Y	N
48 **Packard**	Y	Y	Y	Y	Y	Y	N
49 **Bilbray**	Y	Y	Y	Y	Y	Y	Y
50 Filner	Y	Y	N	Y	N	Y	Y
51 **Cunningham**	Y	Y	Y	Y	Y	Y	Y
52 **Hunter**	Y	N	Y	Y	Y	Y	Y
COLORADO							
1 DeGette	Y	Y	N	Y	N	Y	Y
2 Skaggs	Y	Y	N	Y	N	Y	Y
3 **McInnis**	Y	N	Y	Y	Y	Y	Y
4 **Schaffer**	Y	Y	Y	Y	Y	Y	Y
5 **Hefley**	Y	N	Y	Y	Y	Y	Y
6 **Schaefer**	Y	Y	Y	Y	?	?	Y
CONNECTICUT							
1 Kennelly	?	?	?	?	?	?	?
2 Gejdenson	Y	Y	Y	Y	N	Y	Y
3 DeLauro	Y	Y	Y	Y	N	Y	Y
4 **Shays**	Y	Y	Y	Y	Y	Y	Y
5 Maloney	Y	Y	Y	Y	N	Y	Y
6 **Johnson**	Y	Y	Y	Y	Y	Y	Y
DELAWARE							
AL **Castle**	Y	Y	Y	Y	Y	Y	Y
FLORIDA							
1 **Scarborough**	?	?	?	?	?	?	?
2 Boyd	Y	Y	Y	Y	N	Y	Y
3 Brown	Y	Y	N	Y	N	Y	Y
4 **Fowler**	Y	N	Y	Y	Y	Y	?
5 Thurman	Y	Y	N	Y	N	Y	Y
6 **Stearns**	Y	N	Y	Y	Y	Y	Y
7 **Mica**	Y	Y	Y	Y	Y	Y	Y
8 **McCollum**	?	?	?	?	Y	Y	N
9 **Bilirakis**	Y	Y	Y	Y	Y	Y	Y
10 **Young**	Y	Y	Y	Y	Y	Y	Y
11 Davis	Y	Y	Y	Y	N	Y	Y
12 **Canady**	Y	N	Y	Y	Y	Y	Y
13 **Miller**	Y	Y	Y	Y	Y	Y	N
14 **Goss**	Y	N	Y	Y	Y	Y	Y
15 **Weldon**	Y	Y	Y	Y	?	?	?
16 **Foley**	Y	N	Y	Y	Y	Y	Y
17 Meek	Y	Y	N	Y	N	Y	Y
18 **Ros-Lehtinen**	Y	Y	Y	Y	Y	Y	Y
19 Wexler	?	?	?	?	N	Y	Y
20 Deutsch	+	+	+	+	N	Y	Y
21 **Diaz-Balart**	Y	Y	Y	Y	Y	Y	Y
22 **Shaw**	Y	N	Y	Y	Y	Y	Y
23 Hastings	Y	Y	N	Y	N	Y	Y
GEORGIA							
1 **Kingston**	Y	Y	Y	Y	Y	Y	Y
2 Bishop	Y	Y	Y	Y	N	Y	Y
3 **Collins**	Y	N	Y	Y	Y	Y	?
4 McKinney	Y	Y	N	Y	N	Y	Y
5 Lewis	Y	Y	N	Y	N	Y	Y
6 **Gingrich**							
7 **Barr**	Y	N	Y	Y	?	?	?
8 **Chambliss**	Y	N	Y	?	Y	Y	Y
9 **Deal**	Y	Y	Y	Y	Y	Y	?
10 **Norwood**	Y	N	Y	Y	Y	Y	Y
11 **Linder**	Y	N	Y	Y	Y	Y	Y
HAWAII							
1 Abercrombie	Y	Y	N	Y	N	Y	Y
2 Mink	Y	Y	N	Y	N	Y	Y
IDAHO							
1 **Chenoweth**	N	Y	Y	Y	Y	Y	Y
2 **Crapo**	Y	Y	Y	Y	Y	Y	Y
ILLINOIS							
1 Rush	Y	Y	Y	Y	N	Y	Y
2 Jackson	Y	Y	N	Y	N	Y	Y
3 Lipinski	Y	?	?	?	?	?	Y
4 Gutierrez	Y	Y	N	Y	N	Y	Y
5 Blagojevich	Y	Y	N	Y	N	Y	Y
6 **Hyde**	Y	N	Y	Y	Y	Y	?
7 Davis	Y	+	–	+	–	+	Y
8 **Crane**	Y	N	Y	Y	Y	Y	N
9 Yates	Y	Y	N	Y	N	Y	Y
10 **Porter**	Y	Y	Y	Y	Y	Y	Y
11 **Weller**	Y	Y	Y	Y	Y	Y	Y
12 Costello	Y	Y	Y	Y	N	Y	Y
13 **Fawell**	Y	Y	Y	Y	Y	Y	N

ND Northern Democrats   SD Southern Democrats

	526	527	528	529	530	531	532
14 ***Hastert***	Y	Y	Y	Y	Y	Y	Y
15 ***Ewing***	Y	Y	Y	Y	Y	Y	Y
16 ***Manzullo***	Y	N	Y	Y	Y	Y	N
17 Evans	Y	Y	N	Y	N	Y	Y
18 ***LaHood***	Y	N	Y	Y	Y	Y	Y
19 Poshard	?	?	?	?	?	?	?
20 ***Shimkus***	Y	Y	Y	Y	Y	Y	Y
INDIANA							
1 Visclosky	?	?	?	Y	?	?	Y
2 ***McIntosh***	Y	N	Y	Y	Y	Y	?
3 Roemer	Y	Y	Y	Y	N	Y	Y
4 ***Souder***	?	?	?	?	Y	Y	Y
5 ***Buyer***	Y	N	Y	Y	Y	Y	Y
6 ***Burton***	Y	N	Y	Y	Y	Y	Y
7 ***Pease***	Y	Y	Y	Y	Y	Y	Y
8 ***Hostettler***	Y	N	Y	Y	Y	Y	Y
9 Hamilton	Y	Y	Y	Y	N	Y	Y
10 Carson	Y	Y	N	Y	–	+	Y
IOWA							
1 ***Leach***	Y	Y	Y	Y	Y	Y	Y
2 ***Nussle***	Y	Y	Y	Y	Y	Y	Y
3 Boswell	Y	Y	Y	Y	N	Y	Y
4 ***Ganske***	Y	Y	Y	Y	Y	Y	Y
5 ***Latham***	Y	Y	Y	Y	Y	Y	Y
KANSAS							
1 ***Moran***	Y	Y	Y	Y	Y	Y	Y
2 ***Ryun***	Y	N	Y	Y	Y	Y	Y
3 ***Snowbarger***	Y	N	Y	Y	Y	Y	Y
4 ***Tiahrt***	Y	N	Y	?	Y	Y	Y
KENTUCKY							
1 ***Whitfield***	Y	N	Y	Y	Y	Y	Y
2 ***Lewis***	Y	N	Y	Y	Y	Y	Y
3 ***Northup***	Y	Y	Y	Y	Y	Y	N
4 ***Bunning***	Y	Y	Y	Y	Y	Y	Y
5 ***Rogers***	Y	Y	Y	Y	Y	Y	Y
6 Baesler	Y	Y	Y	Y	N	Y	Y
LOUISIANA							
1 ***Livingston***	Y	Y	?	Y	Y	Y	N
2 Jefferson	Y	Y	Y	Y	N	Y	Y
3 ***Tauzin***	Y	Y	Y	Y	?	Y	Y
4 ***McCrery***	?	?	?	?	Y	Y	Y
5 ***Cooksey***	?	?	?	?	Y	Y	?
6 ***Baker***	Y	N	Y	Y	Y	Y	Y
7 John	Y	Y	Y	Y	Y	Y	Y
MAINE							
1 Allen	Y	Y	Y	Y	N	Y	?
2 Baldacci	Y	Y	N	Y	N	Y	Y
MARYLAND							
1 ***Gilchrest***	Y	Y	Y	Y	Y	Y	Y
2 ***Ehrlich***	Y	N	Y	Y	Y	Y	Y
3 Cardin	Y	Y	Y	Y	N	Y	Y
4 Wynn	Y	Y	Y	Y	N	Y	Y
5 Hoyer	Y	Y	Y	Y	N	Y	Y
6 ***Bartlett***	Y	N	Y	Y	Y	Y	Y
7 Cummings	Y	Y	N	Y	N	Y	Y
8 ***Morella***	Y	Y	Y	Y	Y	Y	Y
MASSACHUSETTS							
1 Olver	Y	Y	N	Y	N	Y	Y
2 Neal	Y	Y	Y	Y	?	?	Y
3 McGovern	Y	Y	Y	Y	?	?	Y
4 Frank	Y	Y	Y	Y	?	?	?
5 Meehan	Y	Y	Y	Y	N	Y	?
6 Tierney	Y	Y	N	Y	N	Y	Y
7 Markey	Y	Y	N	Y	N	Y	Y
8 Kennedy	Y	Y	Y	Y	Y	Y	Y
9 Moakley	Y	Y	Y	Y	N	Y	Y
10 Delahunt	Y	Y	N	Y	N	Y	Y
MICHIGAN							
1 Stupak	Y	Y	N	Y	N	Y	Y
2 ***Hoekstra***	Y	N	Y	Y	Y	Y	Y
3 ***Ehlers***	Y	Y	Y	Y	Y	Y	?
4 ***Camp***	Y	Y	Y	Y	Y	Y	N
5 Barcia	Y	Y	Y	Y	N	Y	Y
6 ***Upton***	Y	Y	Y	Y	Y	Y	Y
7 ***Smith***	Y	Y	Y	?	Y	Y	N
8 Stabenow	Y	Y	Y	Y	N	Y	Y
9 Kildee	Y	Y	N	Y	N	Y	Y
10 Bonior	Y	Y	N	Y	N	Y	Y
11 ***Knollenberg***	Y	Y	Y	Y	Y	Y	N
12 Levin	Y	Y	N	Y	N	Y	Y
13 Rivers	Y	Y	N	Y	N	Y	Y
14 Conyers	Y	Y	N	Y	?	?	Y
15 Kilpatrick	+	+	?	?	–	+	Y
16 Dingell	Y	Y	N	Y	N	Y	Y

	526	527	528	529	530	531	532
MINNESOTA							
1 ***Gutknecht***	Y	Y	Y	Y	Y	Y	Y
2 Minge	Y	Y	Y	Y	N	Y	Y
3 ***Ramstad***	Y	Y	Y	Y	Y	Y	N
4 Vento	Y	Y	Y	Y	N	Y	Y
5 Sabo	Y	Y	Y	Y	N	Y	Y
6 Luther	Y	Y	Y	Y	N	Y	Y
7 Peterson	Y	Y	Y	Y	N	Y	Y
8 Oberstar	Y	Y	N	Y	N	Y	Y
MISSISSIPPI							
1 ***Wicker***	Y	N	Y	Y	Y	Y	Y
2 Thompson	Y	Y	N	Y	N	Y	?
3 ***Pickering***	Y	N	Y	Y	Y	Y	Y
4 ***Parker***	Y	N	Y	Y	Y	Y	Y
5 Taylor	Y	N	N	Y	N	Y	Y
MISSOURI							
1 Clay	Y	Y	N	Y	N	Y	Y
2 ***Talent***	Y	Y	Y	Y	Y	Y	Y
3 Gephardt	Y	Y	N	Y	N	Y	Y
4 Skelton	Y	Y	Y	Y	N	Y	Y
5 McCarthy	Y	Y	Y	Y	N	Y	Y
6 Danner	Y	Y	Y	Y	Y	Y	Y
7 ***Blunt***	Y	Y	Y	Y	Y	Y	?
8 ***Emerson***	Y	Y	Y	Y	Y	Y	Y
9 ***Hulshof***	Y	Y	Y	Y	Y	Y	N
MONTANA							
AL ***Hill***	Y	N	Y	Y	Y	Y	Y
NEBRASKA							
1 ***Bereuter***	Y	N	Y	Y	Y	Y	Y
2 ***Christensen***	Y	N	Y	Y	Y	Y	Y
3 ***Barrett***	Y	N	Y	Y	Y	Y	Y
NEVADA							
1 ***Ensign***	Y	Y	Y	Y	Y	Y	Y
2 ***Gibbons***	Y	N	Y	Y	Y	Y	Y
NEW HAMPSHIRE							
1 ***Sununu***	Y	N	Y	Y	Y	Y	N
2 ***Bass***	Y	N	Y	Y	Y	Y	Y
NEW JERSEY							
1 Andrews	Y	Y	Y	Y	N	Y	Y
2 ***LoBiondo***	Y	Y	Y	Y	Y	Y	Y
3 ***Saxton***	Y	Y	Y	Y	Y	Y	Y
4 ***Smith***	Y	Y	Y	Y	Y	Y	Y
5 ***Roukema***	Y	Y	Y	Y	Y	Y	Y
6 Pallone	Y	Y	Y	Y	N	Y	Y
7 ***Franks***	Y	Y	Y	Y	Y	Y	Y
8 Pascrell	Y	Y	Y	Y	N	Y	Y
9 Rothman	Y	Y	Y	Y	?	?	Y
10 Payne	Y	Y	N	Y	N	Y	Y
11 ***Frelinghuysen***	Y	Y	Y	Y	Y	Y	Y
12 ***Pappas***	Y	Y	Y	Y	Y	Y	Y
13 Menendez	Y	Y	N	Y	N	Y	Y
NEW MEXICO							
1 ***Wilson***	Y	Y	Y	Y	+	+	+
2 ***Skeen***	Y	Y	Y	Y	Y	Y	Y
3 ***Redmond***	Y	Y	Y	Y	Y	Y	Y
NEW YORK							
1 ***Forbes***	Y	Y	Y	Y	Y	Y	Y
2 ***Lazio***	Y	Y	Y	Y	Y	Y	Y
3 ***King***	Y	N	Y	Y	Y	Y	Y
4 McCarthy	Y	Y	Y	Y	N	Y	Y
5 Ackerman	?	?	?	?	N	Y	?
6 Meeks	Y	Y	N	Y	N	Y	Y
7 Manton	Y	Y	Y	Y	N	Y	Y
8 Nadler	Y	Y	N	Y	N	Y	Y
9 Schumer	Y	Y	N	Y	N	Y	Y
10 Towns	Y	Y	Y	Y	N	Y	Y
11 Owens	Y	Y	N	Y	N	Y	Y
12 Velázquez	Y	Y	Y	Y	N	Y	Y
13 ***Fossella***	Y	N	Y	Y	Y	Y	N
14 Maloney	Y	Y	Y	Y	N	Y	Y
15 Rangel	Y	Y	N	Y	N	Y	Y
16 Serrano	Y	Y	N	Y	N	Y	Y
17 Engel	Y	Y	N	Y	N	Y	Y
18 Lowey	Y	Y	P	Y	N	Y	Y
19 ***Kelly***	Y	Y	Y	Y	Y	Y	Y
20 ***Gilman***	Y	Y	Y	Y	Y	Y	Y
21 McNulty	Y	Y	Y	Y	N	Y	Y
22 ***Solomon***	Y	N	Y	Y	Y	Y	Y
23 ***Boehlert***	Y	Y	Y	Y	Y	Y	Y
24 ***McHugh***	Y	Y	Y	Y	?	?	Y
25 ***Walsh***	Y	Y	Y	Y	Y	Y	Y
26 Hinchey	Y	Y	N	Y	N	Y	Y
27 ***Paxon***	Y	Y	Y	Y	Y	Y	Y
28 Slaughter	Y	Y	Y	Y	N	Y	Y
29 LaFalce	Y	Y	Y	Y	N	Y	Y
30 ***Quinn***	Y	Y	Y	Y	Y	Y	Y

	526	527	528	529	530	531	532
31 ***Houghton***	Y	Y	Y	Y	Y	Y	N
NORTH CAROLINA							
1 Clayton	Y	Y	N	Y	N	?	Y
2 Etheridge	Y	Y	Y	Y	N	Y	Y
3 ***Jones***	Y	N	Y	Y	Y	Y	Y
4 Price	Y	Y	Y	Y	N	Y	Y
5 ***Burr***	Y	N	Y	Y	Y	Y	N
6 ***Coble***	Y	N	Y	Y	Y	Y	N
7 McIntyre	Y	Y	Y	Y	N	Y	?
8 Hefner	?	?	?	?	?	?	?
9 ***Myrick***	Y	N	Y	Y	Y	Y	Y
10 ***Ballenger***	Y	N	Y	Y	Y	Y	N
11 ***Taylor***	Y	N	Y	Y	Y	Y	?
12 Watt	Y	Y	N	Y	?	?	Y
NORTH DAKOTA							
AL Pomeroy	Y	Y	Y	Y	Y	Y	Y
OHIO							
1 ***Chabot***	Y	N	Y	Y	Y	Y	Y
2 ***Portman***	Y	Y	Y	Y	Y	Y	Y
3 Hall	?	?	?	?	N	Y	Y
4 ***Oxley***	Y	N	Y	Y	Y	Y	Y
5 ***Gillmor***	Y	N	Y	Y	Y	Y	Y
6 Strickland	Y	Y	Y	Y	N	Y	Y
7 ***Hobson***	Y	Y	Y	Y	Y	Y	Y
8 ***Boehner***	Y	Y	Y	Y	Y	Y	Y
9 Kaptur	Y	Y	N	Y	N	Y	?
10 Kucinich	Y	Y	N	Y	N	Y	Y
11 Stokes	Y	Y	N	Y	N	Y	Y
12 ***Kasich***	Y	N	Y	Y	Y	Y	Y
13 Brown	Y	Y	Y	Y	N	Y	Y
14 Sawyer	Y	Y	Y	Y	N	Y	Y
15 ***Pryce***	+	+	+	+	+	+	+
16 ***Regula***	Y	Y	Y	Y	?	Y	Y
17 Traficant	Y	Y	Y	Y	Y	Y	Y
18 ***Ney***	Y	Y	Y	Y	Y	Y	Y
19 ***LaTourette***	Y	Y	Y	Y	Y	Y	Y
OKLAHOMA							
1 ***Largent***	?	?	?	?	?	?	?
2 ***Coburn***	Y	N	Y	Y	Y	Y	Y
3 ***Watkins***	Y	Y	Y	Y	Y	Y	Y
4 ***Watts***	Y	Y	Y	Y	Y	Y	Y
5 ***Istook***	Y	N	Y	Y	Y	Y	Y
6 ***Lucas***	Y	Y	Y	Y	Y	Y	Y
OREGON							
1 Furse	Y	Y	Y	Y	N	Y	?
2 ***Smith***	Y	?	?	?	?	?	Y
3 Blumenauer	Y	Y	Y	Y	N	Y	Y
4 DeFazio	Y	Y	N	Y	N	Y	Y
5 Hooley	Y	Y	Y	Y	N	Y	Y
PENNSYLVANIA							
1 Brady	Y	?	?	?	N	Y	Y
2 Fattah	Y	Y	N	Y	N	Y	Y
3 Borski	Y	Y	N	Y	N	Y	Y
4 Klink	Y	Y	N	Y	N	Y	Y
5 ***Peterson***	Y	Y	Y	Y	Y	Y	+
6 Holden	Y	Y	Y	Y	N	Y	Y
7 ***Weldon***	Y	Y	Y	Y	Y	Y	?
8 ***Greenwood***	Y	Y	Y	Y	?	Y	?
9 ***Shuster***	Y	N	Y	Y	?	?	Y
10 ***McDade***	?	?	?	?	Y	Y	?
11 Kanjorski	Y	Y	N	Y	N	Y	Y
12 Murtha	Y	Y	?	?	N	Y	Y
13 ***Fox***	Y	Y	Y	Y	Y	Y	Y
14 Coyne	Y	Y	N	Y	N	Y	Y
15 McHale	Y	Y	Y	Y	N	Y	Y
16 ***Pitts***	Y	N	Y	Y	Y	Y	Y
17 ***Gekas***	Y	Y	Y	Y	Y	Y	Y
18 Doyle	Y	Y	Y	Y	N	Y	Y
19 ***Goodling***	Y	Y	Y	Y	Y	Y	Y
20 Mascara	Y	Y	Y	Y	N	Y	Y
21 ***English***	Y	Y	Y	Y	Y	Y	Y
RHODE ISLAND							
1 Kennedy	Y	Y	Y	Y	N	Y	Y
2 Weygand	Y	Y	Y	Y	N	Y	Y
SOUTH CAROLINA							
1 ***Sanford***	Y	N	Y	Y	Y	Y	N
2 ***Spence***	Y	N	Y	Y	Y	Y	Y
3 ***Graham***	?	?	?	?	?	?	Y
4 ***Inglis***	?	?	?	?	?	?	?
5 Spratt	?	?	?	?	N	Y	Y
6 Clyburn	Y	Y	N	Y	N	Y	Y
SOUTH DAKOTA							
AL ***Thune***	Y	Y	Y	Y	Y	Y	Y

	526	527	528	529	530	531	532
TENNESSEE							
1 ***Jenkins***	Y	Y	Y	Y	Y	Y	Y
2 ***Duncan***	Y	Y	Y	Y	Y	Y	Y
3 ***Wamp***	Y	Y	Y	Y	Y	Y	Y
4 ***Hilleary***	Y	Y	Y	Y	Y	Y	Y
5 Clement	Y	Y	Y	Y	N	Y	Y
6 Gordon	Y	Y	Y	Y	N	Y	Y
7 ***Bryant***	Y	Y	Y	Y	Y	Y	Y
8 Tanner	Y	Y	Y	Y	N	Y	Y
9 Ford	Y	Y	Y	Y	N	Y	Y
TEXAS							
1 Sandlin	Y	Y	Y	Y	N	Y	Y
2 Turner	Y	Y	Y	Y	N	Y	Y
3 ***Johnson, Sam***	Y	N	?	Y	Y	Y	Y
4 Hall	Y	Y	Y	Y	Y	Y	Y
5 ***Sessions***	Y	N	Y	Y	Y	Y	N
6 ***Barton***	Y	N	Y	Y	Y	Y	N
7 ***Archer***	Y	N	Y	Y	?	?	N
8 ***Brady***	Y	N	Y	Y	Y	Y	N
9 Lampson	?	?	?	?	N	Y	Y
10 Doggett	Y	Y	N	Y	N	Y	Y
11 Edwards	Y	Y	Y	Y	N	?	Y
12 ***Granger***	Y	Y	Y	Y	Y	Y	Y
13 ***Thornberry***	Y	Y	Y	Y	Y	Y	Y
14 ***Paul***	N	N	N	N	Y	Y	N
15 Hinojosa	Y	Y	Y	Y	N	Y	Y
16 Reyes	Y	Y	Y	Y	?	?	Y
17 Stenholm	Y	Y	Y	Y	N	Y	Y
18 Jackson-Lee	Y	Y	Y	Y	N	Y	Y
19 ***Combest***	Y	N	Y	Y	Y	Y	Y
20 Gonzalez	Y	Y	Y	Y	N	Y	Y
21 ***Smith***	Y	N	Y	Y	Y	Y	Y
22 ***DeLay***	Y	N	Y	Y	Y	Y	N
23 ***Bonilla***	Y	Y	Y	Y	Y	Y	Y
24 Frost	Y	Y	N	Y	N	Y	?
25 Bentsen	Y	Y	Y	Y	N	Y	Y
26 ***Armey***	Y	Y	Y	Y	Y	Y	N
27 Ortiz	Y	Y	Y	Y	N	Y	Y
28 Rodriguez	Y	Y	Y	Y	N	Y	Y
29 Green	Y	Y	Y	Y	N	Y	+
30 Johnson, E.B.	Y	Y	N	Y	N	Y	+
UTAH							
1 ***Hansen***	Y	N	Y	Y	Y	Y	Y
2 ***Cook***	Y	Y	Y	Y	Y	Y	Y
3 ***Cannon***	N	N	Y	Y	Y	Y	Y
VERMONT							
AL *Sanders*	Y	Y	N	Y	N	Y	Y
VIRGINIA							
1 ***Bateman***	Y	Y	Y	Y	Y	Y	Y
2 Pickett	Y	Y	Y	Y	?	?	Y
3 Scott	Y	Y	N	Y	N	Y	Y
4 Sisisky	Y	Y	Y	Y	N	Y	Y
5 Goode	Y	?	?	?	Y	Y	Y
6 ***Goodlatte***	Y	Y	Y	Y	Y	Y	Y
7 ***Bliley***	Y	Y	Y	Y	Y	Y	N
8 Moran	Y	Y	Y	Y	N	Y	Y
9 Boucher	?	?	?	?	N	Y	Y
10 ***Wolf***	Y	Y	Y	Y	Y	Y	Y
11 ***Davis***	Y	Y	Y	Y	Y	Y	N
WASHINGTON							
1 ***White***	Y	Y	Y	Y	Y	Y	Y
2 ***Metcalf***	Y	Y	Y	Y	Y	Y	Y
3 ***Smith, Linda***	Y	N	Y	Y	Y	Y	Y
4 ***Hastings***	Y	N	Y	Y	Y	Y	?
5 ***Nethercutt***	Y	N	Y	Y	Y	Y	N
6 Dicks	Y	Y	Y	Y	N	Y	Y
7 McDermott	Y	Y	N	Y	N	Y	Y
8 ***Dunn***	Y	Y	Y	Y	Y	Y	N
9 Smith, Adam	Y	Y	Y	Y	N	Y	Y
WEST VIRGINIA							
1 Mollohan	Y	Y	N	Y	N	Y	Y
2 Wise	Y	Y	N	Y	?	Y	Y
3 Rahall	Y	Y	N	Y	N	Y	Y
WISCONSIN							
1 ***Neumann***	Y	N	Y	Y	Y	Y	Y
2 ***Klug***	Y	Y	Y	Y	Y	Y	Y
3 Kind	Y	Y	Y	Y	N	Y	Y
4 Kleczka	Y	Y	Y	Y	N	Y	Y
5 Barrett	Y	Y	Y	Y	N	Y	Y
6 ***Petri***	Y	N	Y	Y	Y	Y	Y
7 Obey	Y	Y	N	Y	N	Y	Y
8 Johnson	Y	Y	Y	Y	N	Y	Y
9 ***Sensenbrenner***	Y	N	Y	Y	Y	Y	Y
WYOMING							
AL ***Cubin***	Y	Y	Y	Y	Y	Y	Y

Southern states - Ala., Ark., Fla., Ga., Ky., La., Miss., N.C., Okla., S.C., Tenn., Texas, Va.

House Votes 533, 534, 535, 536, 537, 538

533. S 1733. Food Stamps Disbursement/Passage. Goodlatte, R-Va., motion to suspend the rules and pass the bill to direct the Social Security Administration to work with state agencies to ensure that food stamps are not issued to deceased individuals. Motion agreed to (thus clearing the bill for the president) 386-1: R 200-1; D 185-0 (ND 136-0, SD 49-0); I 1-0. Oct. 15, 1998. A two-thirds majority of those present and voting (258 in this case) is required for passage under suspension of the rules.

534. S 2133. Route 66 Designation/Passage. Hansen, R-Utah, motion to suspend the rules and pass the bill to designate Route 66 (approximately 2,200 miles of highway from Chicago to Santa Monica, Calif.) as "America's Main Street." Motion rejected 201-190: R 193-12; D 8-177 (ND 5-131, SD 3-46); I 0-1. Oct. 15, 1998. A two-thirds majority of those present and voting (261 in this case) is required for passage under suspension of the rules.

535. S 1132. Bandelier National Monument Expansion/Passage. Hansen, R-Utah, motion to suspend the rules and pass the bill to allow the National Park Service to extend the boundaries of Bandelier National Monument in New Mexico. Motion rejected 194-190: R 191-10; D 3-179 (ND 3-133, SD 0-46); I 0-1. Oct. 15, 1998. A two-thirds majority of those present and voting (256 in this case) is required for passage under suspension of the rules.

536. HR 4328. Fiscal 1999 Omnibus Appropriations/Rule. Adoption of the rule (H Res 605) to provide for House floor consideration of the conference report on the bill to provide almost $500 billion in new budget authority for those Cabinet departments and federal agencies whose fiscal 1999 appropriations bills were never enacted, and an additional $20.8 billion in "emergency" supplemental spending. Adopted 333-88: R 217-7; D 116-80 (ND 82-59, SD 34-21); I 0-1. Oct. 20, 1998.

537. H Res 604. Bandelier National Monument; S2133 Route 66 Designation/Rule. Adoption of the rule (H Res 604) to provide for House floor consideration of S1132 to allow the National Park Service to extend the boundaries of the Bandelier National Monument in New Mexico, and S2133 to designate Route 66 (approximately 2,200 miles of highway from Chicago to Santa Monica, Calif.) as "America's Main Street." Adopted 229-189: R 224-0; D 5-188 (ND 5-134, SD 0-54); I 0-1. Oct. 20, 1998.

538. HR 4328. Fiscal 1999 Omnibus Appropriations/Conference Report. Adoption of the conference report on the bill to provide almost $500 billion in new budget authority for those Cabinet departments and federal agencies whose fiscal 1999 appropriations bills were never enacted. The measure incorporates eight previously separate appropriations bills: Labor-HHS-Education, Interior, Treasury-Postal, Foreign Operations, Commerce-Justice-State, District of Columbia, Agriculture and Transportation. In addition, the bill provides $20.8 billion in "emergency" supplemental spending, including $6.8 billion for military spending ($1.9 billion of it for Bosnia operations), $5.9 billion for relief to farmers, $2.4 billion for anti-terrorism programs, $3.35 billion to address Year 2000 computer problems and $1.55 billion for disaster relief from Hurricane Georges. The measure also contains language to extend expiring tax provisions (at a cost of $9.7 billion over nine years), increase the number of H-1B visas for high-tech foreign workers, impose a three-year moratorium on new taxes on Internet access, implement the Chemical Weapons Convention and extend for six months Chapter 12 of the bankruptcy code, which is designed to help struggling farmers. Adopted 333-95: R 162-64; D 170-31 (ND 120-26, SD 50-5); I 1-0. Oct. 20, 1998. (HR 4328 was originally the fiscal 1999 Transportation Appropriations bill.) A "yea" vote was a vote in support of the president's position.

Key

- **Y** Voted for (yea).
- **#** Paired for.
- **+** Announced for.
- **N** Voted against (nay).
- **X** Paired against.
- **−** Announced against.
- **P** Voted "present."
- **C** Voted "present" to avoid possible conflict of interest.
- **?** Did not vote or otherwise make a position known.

Democrats   **Republicans**
Independent

	533	534	535	536	537	538
ALABAMA						
1 *Callahan*	?	?	?	Y	Y	Y
2 *Everett*	Y	Y	Y	Y	Y	Y
3 *Riley*	Y	Y	Y	Y	Y	Y
4 *Aderholt*	Y	Y	Y	Y	Y	Y
5 Cramer	Y	N	N	Y	N	Y
6 *Bachus*	Y	Y	Y	Y	N	Y
7 Hilliard	Y	N	N	N	N	Y
ALASKA						
AL *Young*	Y	Y	Y	Y	Y	Y
ARIZONA						
1 *Salmon*	Y	Y	Y	N	Y	N
2 Pastor	Y	N	N	Y	N	Y
3 *Stump*	Y	Y	Y	Y	Y	N
4 *Shadegg*	Y	Y	Y	Y	Y	Y
5 *Kolbe*	Y	Y	Y	Y	Y	Y
6 *Hayworth*	Y	Y	Y	Y	Y	Y
ARKANSAS						
1 Berry	Y	N	N	Y	N	Y
2 Snyder	Y	N	N	Y	N	Y
3 *Hutchinson*	?	?	?	Y	Y	Y
4 Dickey	Y	Y	Y	Y	Y	Y
CALIFORNIA						
1 *Riggs*	Y	Y	Y	Y	Y	N
2 *Herger*	Y	Y	Y	Y	Y	Y
3 Fazio	Y	N	N	?	?	?
4 *Doolittle*	Y	Y	Y	Y	Y	Y
5 Matsui	Y	N	N	Y	N	Y
6 Woolsey	Y	N	N	N	N	Y
7 Miller	Y	N	N	N	N	N
8 Pelosi	?	?	?	Y	N	Y
9 Lee	Y	N	N	N	N	N
10 Tauscher	Y	N	N	?	?	Y
11 *Pombo*	Y	Y	Y	Y	Y	Y
12 Lantos	?	?	?	Y	Y	Y
13 Stark	Y	N	N	?	?	?
14 Eshoo	Y	N	Y	N	Y	Y
15 *Campbell*	Y	N	Y	N	Y	N
16 Lofgren	Y	N	N	N	N	Y
17 Farr	Y	N	N	N	N	N
18 Condit	Y	N	N	N	N	N
19 *Radanovich*	Y	Y	Y	Y	Y	Y
20 Dooley	Y	N	N	Y	N	Y
21 *Thomas*	Y	Y	Y	Y	N	Y
22 Capps, L.	Y	N	N	N	N	Y
23 *Gallegly*	Y	Y	Y	Y	Y	Y
24 Sherman	Y	N	N	N	N	Y
25 *McKeon*	Y	Y	Y	Y	Y	Y
26 Berman	?	?	?	Y	N	Y
27 *Rogan*	Y	Y	Y	Y	Y	Y
28 *Dreier*	Y	Y	Y	Y	Y	Y
29 Waxman	Y	N	N	N	N	Y
30 Becerra	Y	N	N	?	?	Y
31 Martinez	Y	N	N	N	N	Y
32 Dixon	Y	N	N	N	N	Y
33 Roybal-Allard	Y	N	N	N	N	Y
34 Torres	?	?	?	Y	N	Y
35 Waters	?	?	?	Y	N	Y
36 Harman	Y	N	N	N	N	Y
37 Millender-McD.	Y	N	N	Y	N	Y
38 Horn	Y	Y	Y	Y	Y	Y
39 *Royce*	Y	Y	Y	Y	Y	N
40 *Lewis*	?	Y	Y	Y	Y	Y
41 *Kim*	Y	Y	Y	Y	Y	Y
42 Brown	Y	Y	N	N	N	Y
43 *Calvert*	Y	Y	Y	Y	Y	Y
44 *Bono, M.*	Y	Y	Y	Y	Y	Y
45 *Rohrabacher*	Y	Y	Y	Y	Y	Y
46 Sanchez	Y	N	N	N	N	Y
47 *Cox*	Y	Y	Y	Y	Y	Y
48 *Packard*	Y	Y	Y	Y	Y	Y
49 *Bilbray*	Y	Y	Y	Y	Y	Y
50 Filner	Y	N	N	N	N	N
51 *Cunningham*	Y	Y	Y	Y	Y	Y
52 *Hunter*	Y	Y	Y	Y	Y	Y
COLORADO						
1 DeGette	Y	N	N	N	N	N
2 Skaggs	Y	N	N	N	N	N
3 *McInnis*	?	Y	Y	Y	Y	Y
4 *Schaffer*	Y	N	N	Y	N	N
5 *Hefley*	Y	Y	Y	Y	Y	N
6 *Schaefer*	Y	Y	Y	Y	Y	Y
CONNECTICUT						
1 Kennelly	?	?	?	Y	N	Y
2 Gejdenson	Y	N	N	Y	N	Y
3 DeLauro	Y	N	N	Y	N	Y
4 *Shays*	Y	N	Y	N	Y	Y
5 Maloney	Y	N	N	N	N	Y
6 *Johnson*	Y	Y	Y	Y	Y	Y
DELAWARE						
AL *Castle*	Y	Y	Y	Y	Y	N
FLORIDA						
1 *Scarborough*	?	?	?	N	Y	N
2 Boyd	Y	N	N	Y	N	Y
3 Brown	Y	N	?	Y	N	Y
4 *Fowler*	?	?	?	Y	Y	Y
5 Thurman	Y	N	N	N	N	Y
6 *Stearns*	Y	N	Y	N	Y	N
7 *Mica*	Y	Y	Y	Y	Y	Y
8 *McCollum*	Y	Y	Y	N	Y	N
9 *Bilirakis*	Y	Y	Y	Y	Y	Y
10 *Young*	Y	Y	Y	Y	Y	Y
11 Davis	Y	N	N	N	N	Y
12 *Canady*	Y	Y	Y	Y	Y	Y
13 *Miller*	Y	N	Y	Y	Y	N
14 *Goss*	Y	Y	Y	Y	Y	Y
15 *Weldon*	?	?	?	Y	Y	N
16 *Foley*	Y	Y	Y	Y	Y	Y
17 Meek	Y	N	N	N	N	Y
18 *Ros-Lehtinen*	Y	Y	Y	Y	Y	Y
19 Wexler	Y	N	N	N	N	Y
20 Deutsch	Y	N	N	N	N	Y
21 *Diaz-Balart*	Y	Y	Y	Y	Y	Y
22 *Shaw*	Y	Y	Y	Y	Y	Y
23 Hastings	Y	N	N	N	N	Y
GEORGIA						
1 *Kingston*	Y	Y	Y	Y	Y	Y
2 Bishop	Y	N	N	Y	N	Y
3 *Collins*	?	?	?	Y	Y	N
4 McKinney	Y	N	N	N	N	Y
5 Lewis	Y	N	N	N	N	Y
6 *Gingrich*						Y
7 *Barr*	?	?	?	Y	Y	N
8 *Chambliss*	Y	Y	Y	Y	Y	Y
9 *Deal*	?	?	?	Y	Y	N
10 *Norwood*	Y	?	?	Y	Y	N
11 *Linder*	Y	Y	Y	Y	Y	Y
HAWAII						
1 Abercrombie	Y	N	N	Y	N	Y
2 Mink	Y	N	N	Y	N	Y
IDAHO						
1 *Chenoweth*	Y	Y	Y	Y	Y	Y
2 *Crapo*	Y	Y	Y	Y	Y	Y
ILLINOIS						
1 Rush	Y	N	N	N	N	Y
2 Jackson	Y	N	N	N	N	Y
3 Lipinski	?	?	?	N	N	Y
4 Gutierrez	Y	N	N	N	N	Y
5 Blagojevich	Y	N	N	N	N	Y
6 *Hyde*	?	?	?	Y	Y	N
7 Davis	Y	N	N	N	N	Y
8 *Crane*	Y	Y	Y	Y	Y	Y
9 Yates	Y	N	N	N	N	Y
10 *Porter*	Y	Y	Y	Y	Y	Y
11 *Weller*	Y	Y	Y	Y	Y	Y
12 Costello	Y	N	N	N	N	N
13 *Fawell*	?	Y	?	Y	Y	Y

ND Northern Democrats   **SD** Southern Democrats

	533	534	535	536	537	538
14 **Hastert**	Y	Y	Y	Y	Y	Y
15 **Ewing**	Y	Y	Y	Y	Y	Y
16 **Manzullo**	Y	Y	Y	Y	Y	N
17 Evans	Y	N	N	Y	N	Y
18 **LaHood**	Y	Y	Y	Y	Y	N
19 Poshard	?	?	?	?	?	?
20 **Shimkus**	Y	Y	Y	Y	Y	Y
INDIANA						
1 Visclosky	Y	N	N	Y	N	Y
2 **McIntosh**	?	?	?	Y	Y	N
3 Roemer	Y	N	N	Y	N	Y
4 **Souder**	Y	Y	Y	Y	Y	Y
5 **Buyer**	Y	Y	Y	Y	Y	Y
6 **Burton**	Y	Y	Y	Y	Y	Y
7 **Pease**	Y	Y	Y	Y	Y	Y
8 **Hostettler**	Y	Y	Y	Y	Y	N
9 Hamilton	Y	N	N	Y	N	Y
10 Carson	Y	N	N	N	N	Y
IOWA						
1 **Leach**	Y	Y	Y	Y	Y	Y
2 **Nussle**	Y	Y	Y	Y	Y	Y
3 Boswell	Y	Y	Y	Y	Y	Y
4 **Ganske**	Y	N	Y	Y	Y	Y
5 **Latham**	Y	Y	Y	Y	Y	Y
KANSAS						
1 **Moran**	Y	Y	Y	Y	Y	Y
2 **Ryun**	Y	Y	Y	Y	Y	Y
3 **Snowbarger**	Y	Y	Y	Y	Y	Y
4 **Tiahrt**	Y	Y	Y	N	Y	Y
KENTUCKY						
1 **Whitfield**	Y	Y	Y	Y	Y	Y
2 **Lewis**	Y	Y	Y	Y	Y	Y
3 **Northup**	Y	Y	+	Y	?	Y
4 **Bunning**	Y	Y	Y	Y	Y	Y
5 **Rogers**	Y	Y	Y	Y	Y	Y
6 Baesler	Y	Y	N	Y	N	Y
LOUISIANA						
1 **Livingston**	Y	Y	Y	Y	Y	Y
2 Jefferson	Y	N	N	Y	N	Y
3 **Tauzin**	Y	Y	Y	Y	Y	Y
4 **McCrery**	Y	Y	Y	Y	Y	Y
5 **Cooksey**	?	?	?	Y	Y	Y
6 **Baker**	Y	Y	Y	Y	Y	Y
7 John	Y	N	N	Y	N	Y
MAINE						
1 Allen	?	?	?	N	N	Y
2 Baldacci	Y	N	N	Y	N	Y
MARYLAND						
1 **Gilchrest**	Y	Y	Y	Y	Y	Y
2 **Ehrlich**	Y	Y	Y	Y	Y	Y
3 Cardin	Y	N	N	N	N	N
4 Wynn	Y	N	N	Y	N	Y
5 Hoyer	Y	N	N	N	N	Y
6 **Bartlett**	Y	Y	Y	Y	Y	N
7 Cummings	Y	N	N	Y	N	Y
8 **Morella**	Y	Y	Y	Y	Y	Y
MASSACHUSETTS						
1 Olver	Y	N	N	N	N	Y
2 Neal	Y	N	N	N	N	Y
3 McGovern	?	?	?	Y	N	Y
4 Frank	?	?	?	N	N	Y
5 Meehan	?	?	?	?	?	?
6 Tierney	Y	N	N	Y	N	Y
7 Markey	Y	N	N	Y	N	Y
8 Kennedy	Y	N	N	Y	N	Y
9 Moakley	Y	N	N	Y	N	Y
10 Delahunt	Y	N	N	Y	N	Y
MICHIGAN						
1 Stupak	Y	N	N	N	N	N
2 **Hoekstra**	Y	Y	Y	Y	Y	N
3 **Ehlers**	?	?	?	Y	Y	N
4 **Camp**	Y	Y	Y	Y	Y	Y
5 Barcia	Y	N	Y	Y	Y	Y
6 **Upton**	Y	Y	Y	Y	Y	N
7 **Smith**	Y	Y	Y	Y	Y	N
8 Stabenow	Y	N	N	Y	N	Y
9 Kildee	Y	N	N	N	N	Y
10 Bonior	Y	N	N	N	N	Y
11 **Knollenberg**	Y	Y	Y	Y	Y	Y
12 Levin	Y	N	N	Y	N	Y
13 Rivers	Y	N	N	N	N	N
14 Conyers	Y	N	N	N	N	Y
15 Kilpatrick	Y	N	N	Y	N	Y
16 Dingell	Y	N	N	Y	N	Y

	533	534	535	536	537	538
MINNESOTA						
1 **Gutknecht**	Y	Y	Y	Y	Y	Y
2 Minge	Y	N	N	N	N	N
3 **Ramstad**	Y	Y	Y	Y	Y	Y
4 Vento	Y	N	N	N	N	Y
5 Sabo	Y	N	N	Y	N	Y
6 Luther	Y	N	N	N	N	N
7 Peterson	Y	N	N	N	N	N
8 Oberstar	Y	N	N	?	N	Y
MISSISSIPPI						
1 **Wicker**	Y	Y	Y	Y	Y	Y
2 Thompson	?	?	?	N	N	Y
3 **Pickering**	Y	Y	Y	Y	Y	Y
4 **Parker**	Y	Y	Y	Y	Y	Y
5 Taylor	Y	N	N	N	N	N
MISSOURI						
1 Clay	Y	N	N	Y	N	Y
2 **Talent**	Y	Y	Y	Y	Y	Y
3 Gephardt	Y	N	N	Y	N	Y
4 Skelton	Y	N	N	Y	Y	Y
5 McCarthy	Y	N	N	N	N	Y
6 Danner	Y	Y	N	Y	N	Y
7 **Blunt**	?	?	?	Y	Y	Y
8 **Emerson**	Y	Y	Y	Y	Y	Y
9 **Hulshof**	Y	Y	Y	Y	Y	Y
MONTANA						
AL **Hill**	Y	Y	Y	Y	Y	Y
NEBRASKA						
1 **Bereuter**	Y	Y	Y	Y	Y	Y
2 **Christensen**	Y	Y	Y	N	Y	N
3 **Barrett**	Y	Y	Y	Y	Y	Y
NEVADA						
1 **Ensign**	Y	Y	Y	N	Y	N
2 **Gibbons**	Y	Y	Y	Y	Y	Y
NEW HAMPSHIRE						
1 **Sununu**	Y	Y	Y	Y	Y	Y
2 **Bass**	Y	Y	Y	Y	Y	Y
NEW JERSEY						
1 Andrews	Y	N	N	N	N	Y
2 **LoBiondo**	Y	Y	Y	Y	Y	Y
3 **Saxton**	Y	Y	Y	Y	Y	Y
4 **Smith**	Y	Y	Y	?	?	N
5 **Roukema**	Y	Y	Y	Y	Y	N
6 Pallone	Y	N	N	Y	N	Y
7 **Franks**	Y	N	Y	Y	Y	Y
8 Pascrell	Y	N	N	Y	N	Y
9 Rothman	Y	N	N	Y	N	Y
10 Payne	Y	N	N	N	N	Y
11 **Frelinghuysen**	Y	N	Y	Y	Y	N
12 **Pappas**	Y	Y	Y	Y	Y	N
13 Menendez	Y	N	N	N	N	Y
NEW MEXICO						
1 **Wilson**	+	Y	Y	Y	Y	Y
2 **Skeen**	Y	Y	Y	Y	Y	Y
3 **Redmond**	Y	Y	Y	Y	Y	Y
NEW YORK						
1 **Forbes**	Y	Y	Y	Y	Y	Y
2 **Lazio**	Y	Y	Y	Y	Y	Y
3 **King**	Y	Y	Y	Y	Y	N
4 McCarthy	Y	N	N	Y	N	Y
5 Ackerman	?	?	?	Y	N	Y
6 Meeks	Y	N	N	Y	N	Y
7 Manton	Y	N	N	Y	N	Y
8 Nadler	Y	N	N	N	N	Y
9 Schumer	Y	N	N	Y	N	Y
10 Towns	Y	N	N	N	N	Y
11 Owens	Y	N	N	N	N	Y
12 Velázquez	Y	N	N	Y	?	Y
13 **Fossella**	Y	Y	Y	Y	Y	Y
14 Maloney	Y	N	N	Y	N	Y
15 Rangel	Y	N	N	Y	N	Y
16 Serrano	Y	N	N	Y	N	Y
17 Engel	Y	N	N	Y	N	Y
18 Lowey	Y	N	N	Y	N	Y
19 **Kelly**	Y	Y	Y	Y	Y	Y
20 **Gilman**	Y	Y	Y	Y	Y	Y
21 McNulty	Y	N	N	Y	N	Y
22 **Solomon**	Y	Y	Y	Y	Y	Y
23 **Boehlert**	Y	Y	Y	Y	Y	Y
24 **McHugh**	Y	Y	Y	Y	Y	Y
25 **Walsh**	Y	Y	Y	Y	Y	Y
26 Hinchey	Y	N	N	Y	N	Y
27 **Paxon**	Y	Y	Y	Y	Y	Y
28 Slaughter	Y	N	N	Y	?	Y
29 LaFalce	Y	N	N	N	N	Y

	533	534	535	536	537	538
30 **Quinn**	Y	Y	Y	Y	Y	Y
31 **Houghton**	Y	Y	Y	Y	Y	Y
NORTH CAROLINA						
1 Clayton	Y	N	N	N	?	Y
2 Etheridge	Y	N	N	N	N	Y
3 **Jones**	Y	Y	N	Y	Y	N
4 Price	Y	N	N	Y	N	Y
5 **Burr**	Y	Y	Y	Y	Y	N
6 **Coble**	Y	Y	N	Y	Y	N
7 McIntyre	?	?	?	Y	N	Y
8 Hefner	?	?	?	Y	N	Y
9 **Myrick**	Y	Y	N	Y	Y	Y
10 **Ballenger**	Y	Y	Y	Y	Y	N
11 **Taylor**	?	Y	Y	Y	Y	Y
12 Watt	Y	N	N	N	N	Y
NORTH DAKOTA						
AL Pomeroy	Y	N	N	Y	N	Y
OHIO						
1 **Chabot**	Y	N	N	Y	Y	N
2 **Portman**	Y	Y	Y	Y	Y	N
3 Hall	Y	N	N	Y	N	Y
4 **Oxley**	Y	Y	Y	Y	Y	Y
5 **Gillmor**	Y	Y	Y	Y	Y	Y
6 Strickland	Y	N	N	Y	N	Y
7 **Hobson**	Y	Y	?	Y	Y	Y
8 **Boehner**	Y	Y	Y	Y	Y	Y
9 Kaptur	?	?	?	Y	N	N
10 Kucinich	Y	N	N	Y	N	Y
11 Stokes	Y	N	N	Y	N	Y
12 **Kasich**	Y	Y	Y	Y	Y	Y
13 Brown	Y	N	N	Y	?	Y
14 Sawyer	Y	N	N	Y	N	Y
15 **Pryce**	+	+	+	+	+	+
16 **Regula**	Y	Y	Y	Y	Y	Y
17 Traficant	Y	Y	Y	Y	Y	Y
18 **Ney**	Y	Y	Y	Y	Y	Y
19 **LaTourette**	Y	Y	Y	Y	Y	Y
OKLAHOMA						
1 **Largent**	?	?	?	Y	Y	N
2 **Coburn**	Y	Y	Y	Y	Y	N
3 **Watkins**	Y	Y	Y	Y	Y	Y
4 **Watts**	Y	Y	Y	Y	Y	Y
5 **Istook**	Y	Y	Y	Y	Y	N
6 **Lucas**	Y	Y	Y	Y	Y	Y
OREGON						
1 Furse	?	?	?	N	N	Y
2 **Smith**	Y	Y	Y	Y	Y	Y
3 Blumenauer	Y	N	N	Y	N	N
4 DeFazio	Y	N	N	N	N	N
5 Hooley	Y	N	N	Y	N	Y
PENNSYLVANIA						
1 Brady	Y	N	N	Y	N	Y
2 Fattah	Y	N	N	Y	N	Y
3 Borski	Y	N	N	N	N	Y
4 Klink	Y	N	N	N	N	N
5 **Peterson**	Y	Y	Y	Y	Y	Y
6 Holden	Y	N	N	N	N	N
7 **Weldon**	?	?	?	N	Y	N
8 **Greenwood**	?	?	?	Y	Y	Y
9 **Shuster**	Y	Y	Y	Y	Y	Y
10 **McDade**	?	?	Y	Y	Y	Y
11 Kanjorski	Y	N	N	N	N	N
12 Murtha	Y	N	N	N	Y	Y
13 **Fox**	Y	Y	Y	Y	Y	Y
14 Coyne	Y	N	N	N	N	Y
15 McHale	Y	N	N	N	N	Y
16 **Pitts**	Y	Y	Y	Y	Y	Y
17 **Gekas**	Y	Y	Y	Y	Y	Y
18 Doyle	Y	N	N	Y	N	Y
19 **Goodling**	Y	Y	Y	Y	Y	Y
20 Mascara	Y	N	N	N	Y	Y
21 **English**	Y	Y	Y	Y	Y	Y
RHODE ISLAND						
1 Kennedy	Y	N	N	?	?	Y
2 Weygand	Y	N	N	?	?	Y
SOUTH CAROLINA						
1 **Sanford**	Y	N	N	Y	Y	N
2 **Spence**	Y	Y	Y	Y	Y	Y
3 **Graham**	?	?	?	Y	Y	N
4 **Inglis**	?	?	?	Y	Y	N
5 Spratt	Y	N	?	Y	N	Y
6 Clyburn	Y	N	N	N	N	Y
SOUTH DAKOTA						
AL **Thune**	Y	Y	Y	Y	Y	Y

	533	534	535	536	537	538
TENNESSEE						
1 **Jenkins**	Y	Y	Y	Y	Y	Y
2 **Duncan**	Y	Y	Y	Y	Y	N
3 **Wamp**	Y	Y	Y	Y	Y	N
4 **Hilleary**	Y	Y	Y	Y	Y	Y
5 Clement	Y	N	N	Y	N	Y
6 Gordon	Y	N	N	N	N	Y
7 **Bryant**	Y	Y	Y	Y	Y	Y
8 Tanner	Y	N	N	Y	N	Y
9 Ford	Y	N	N	N	N	Y
TEXAS						
1 Sandlin	Y	N	N	Y	N	Y
2 Turner	Y	N	N	Y	N	Y
3 **Johnson, Sam**	Y	Y	Y	Y	Y	N
4 Hall	Y	Y	N	Y	N	Y
5 **Sessions**	Y	Y	Y	Y	Y	Y
6 **Barton**	Y	Y	Y	Y	Y	N
7 **Archer**	Y	Y	Y	Y	Y	Y
8 **Brady**	Y	Y	Y	Y	Y	N
9 Lampson	Y	N	N	Y	N	Y
10 Doggett	Y	N	N	N	N	N
11 Edwards	Y	N	?	N	N	Y
12 **Granger**	Y	Y	Y	Y	Y	Y
13 **Thornberry**	Y	Y	Y	Y	Y	Y
14 **Paul**	N	N	N	Y	Y	N
15 Hinojosa	Y	N	N	Y	N	Y
16 Reyes	Y	N	N	Y	N	Y
17 Stenholm	Y	N	N	Y	N	Y
18 Jackson-Lee	Y	Y	N	N	N	Y
19 **Combest**	Y	Y	Y	Y	Y	Y
20 Gonzalez	Y	N	N	Y	N	Y
21 **Smith**	Y	Y	Y	Y	Y	Y
22 **DeLay**	Y	Y	Y	Y	Y	Y
23 **Bonilla**	Y	Y	Y	Y	Y	Y
24 Frost	?	?	?	Y	N	Y
25 Bentsen	Y	N	N	N	N	Y
26 **Armey**	Y	Y	Y	Y	Y	Y
27 Ortiz	Y	N	N	Y	N	Y
28 Rodriguez	Y	N	N	Y	N	Y
29 Green	+	−	−	N	N	Y
30 Johnson, E.B.	+	+	+	N	N	Y
UTAH						
1 **Hansen**	Y	Y	Y	?	?	?
2 **Cook**	Y	Y	Y	Y	Y	Y
3 **Cannon**	Y	Y	Y	Y	Y	Y
VERMONT						
AL *Sanders*	Y	N	N	N	N	Y
VIRGINIA						
1 **Bateman**	Y	Y	Y	Y	Y	Y
2 Pickett	Y	N	N	Y	N	Y
3 Scott	Y	N	N	Y	N	Y
4 Sisisky	Y	N	N	Y	N	Y
5 Goode	Y	N	N	Y	N	N
6 **Goodlatte**	Y	Y	N	Y	Y	Y
7 **Bliley**	Y	Y	Y	Y	Y	Y
8 Moran	Y	N	N	Y	N	Y
9 Boucher	Y	N	N	Y	N	Y
10 **Wolf**	Y	Y	Y	Y	Y	N
11 **Davis**	Y	Y	Y	Y	Y	Y
WASHINGTON						
1 **White**	Y	Y	Y	Y	Y	N
2 **Metcalf**	Y	Y	Y	Y	Y	Y
3 **Smith, Linda**	Y	Y	Y	Y	Y	N
4 **Hastings**	?	?	?	Y	Y	Y
5 **Nethercutt**	Y	Y	Y	Y	Y	Y
6 Dicks	Y	N	N	Y	N	Y
7 McDermott	Y	N	N	N	N	N
8 **Dunn**	Y	Y	Y	Y	Y	Y
9 Smith, Adam	Y	N	N	Y	N	N
WEST VIRGINIA						
1 Mollohan	Y	N	N	?	?	?
2 Wise	Y	N	N	Y	N	Y
3 Rahall	Y	N	N	N	N	Y
WISCONSIN						
1 **Neumann**	Y	N	Y	Y	Y	N
2 **Klug**	Y	Y	Y	Y	Y	N
3 Kind	Y	N	N	N	N	N
4 Kleczka	Y	N	N	N	N	N
5 Barrett	Y	N	N	N	N	N
6 **Petri**	Y	Y	Y	Y	Y	N
7 Obey	Y	N	N	Y	N	Y
8 Johnson	Y	N	N	Y	N	N
9 **Sensenbrenner**	Y	N	N	Y	Y	N
WYOMING						
AL **Cubin**	Y	Y	Y	Y	Y	Y

Southern states - Ala., Ark., Fla., Ga., Ky., La., Miss., N.C., Okla., S.C., Tenn., Texas, Va.

House Votes 539, 540, 541, 542, 543, 544

Key

- **Y** Voted for (yea).
- **#** Paired for.
- **+** Announced for.
- **N** Voted against (nay).
- **X** Paired against.
- **−** Announced against.
- **P** Voted "present."
- **C** Voted "present" to avoid possible conflict of interest.
- **?** Did not vote or otherwise make a position known.

Democrats   **Republicans**
Independent

---

539. Support U.S. Troops/Adoption. Adoption of the resolution to express congressional support for the troops in and around the Persian Gulf region and to reaffirm that it should be the policy of the United States to support efforts to remove Saddam Hussein's regime from power in Iraq and promote a democratic government to replace that regime. Adopted 417-5: R 221-2; D 195-3 (ND 142-2, SD 53-1); I 1-0. Dec. 17, 1998.

540. Procedural Motion/Adjourn. Bonior, D-Mich., motion to adjourn. Motion rejected 183-225: R 0-220; D 182-5 (ND 134-2, SD 48-3); I 1-0. Dec. 18, 1998.

541. Procedural Motion/Journal. Approval of the House Journal of Friday, Dec. 18, 1998. Approved 277-125: R 202-4; D 74-121 (ND 51-90, SD 23-31); I 1-0. Dec. 19, 1998.

542. H Res 611. Impeachment of President Clinton/Censure — Appeal Ruling of Chair. Armey, R-Texas, motion to table (kill) the Gephardt, D-Mo., appeal of the ruling of the chair that the Boucher, D-Va., motion to recommit with instructions was not germane. The Boucher motion would instruct the Judiciary Committee to report the resolution back to the House with an amendment to express the sense of the House that President Clinton "fully deserves" the "censure and condemnation" of the American people and the House because of his conduct. Motion agreed to 230-204: R 226-2; D 4-201 (ND 0-150, SD 4-51); I 0-1. Dec. 19, 1998. A "nay" was a vote in support of the president's position.

543. H Res 611. Impeachment of President Clinton/Article I — Grand Jury Perjury. Adoption of Article I of the resolution, which would impeach President Clinton for "perjurious, false and misleading testimony" during his Aug. 17, 1998, federal grand jury testimony about his relationship with former White House intern Monica Lewinsky, his prior testimony in the Paula Jones sexual harassment lawsuit and his attempts to influence others' testimony in both. Adopted 228-206: R 223-5; D 5-200 (ND 1-149, SD 4-51); I 0-1. Dec. 19, 1998. A "nay" was a vote in support of the president's position.

544. H Res 611. Impeachment of President Clinton/Article II — Civil Suit Perjury. Adoption of Article II of the resolution, which would impeach President Clinton for "perjurious, false and misleading testimony" in his Dec. 23, 1997, written answers and his Jan. 17, 1998, testimony in the Paula Jones federal sexual harassment civil lawsuit about his relationship with former White House intern Monica Lewinsky. Rejected 205-229: R 200-28; D 5-200 (ND 1-149, SD 4-51); I 0-1. Dec. 19, 1998. A "nay" was a vote in support of the president's position.

	539	540	541	542	543	544
ALABAMA						
1 *Callahan*	Y	N	Y	Y	Y	Y
2 *Everett*	Y	N	Y	Y	Y	Y
3 *Riley*	Y	N	Y	Y	Y	Y
4 *Aderholt*	Y	N	Y	Y	Y	Y
5 Cramer	Y	Y	N	N	N	N
6 *Bachus*	Y	N	Y	Y	Y	Y
7 Hilliard	Y	N	N	N	N	N
ALASKA						
AL *Young*	Y	?	Y	Y	Y	Y
ARIZONA						
1 *Salmon*	Y	N	Y	Y	Y	Y
2 Pastor	Y	Y	?	N	N	N
3 *Stump*	Y	N	Y	Y	Y	Y
4 *Shadegg*	Y	N	Y	Y	Y	Y
5 *Kolbe*	Y	N	Y	Y	Y	Y
6 *Hayworth*	Y	N	Y	Y	Y	Y
ARKANSAS						
1 Berry	Y	Y	N	N	N	N
2 Snyder	Y	Y	N	N	N	N
3 *Hutchinson*	Y	N	Y	Y	Y	Y
4 Dickey	Y	N	N	Y	N	Y
CALIFORNIA						
1 *Riggs*	Y	N	?	Y	Y	Y
2 *Herger*	Y	N	Y	Y	Y	Y
3 Fazio	Y	Y	N	N	N	N
4 *Doolittle*	?	N	Y	Y	Y	Y
5 Matsui	Y	Y	N	N	N	N
6 Woolsey	Y	Y	N	N	N	N
7 Miller	?	?	?	?	?	?
8 Pelosi	Y	Y	?	N	N	N
9 Lee	N	Y	N	N	N	N
10 Tauscher	Y	Y	N	N	N	N
11 *Pombo*	Y	N	Y	Y	Y	Y
12 Lantos	Y	Y	N	N	N	N
13 Stark	Y	Y	N	N	N	N
14 Eshoo	Y	Y	N	N	N	N
15 *Campbell*	Y	N	Y	Y	N	N
16 Lofgren	Y	Y	N	N	N	N
17 Farr	Y	Y	N	N	N	N
18 Condit	Y	Y	N	N	N	N
19 *Radanovich*	Y	N	Y	Y	Y	Y
20 Dooley	Y	Y	N	N	N	N
21 *Thomas*	Y	N	Y	Y	Y	Y
22 Capps, L.	Y	Y	N	N	N	N
23 *Gallegly*	?	N	Y	Y	Y	Y
24 Sherman	Y	Y	N	N	N	N
25 *McKeon*	Y	N	Y	Y	Y	Y
26 Berman	Y	Y	N	N	N	N
27 *Rogan*	Y	N	Y	Y	Y	Y
28 *Dreier*	Y	N	Y	Y	Y	Y
29 Waxman	Y	Y	N	N	N	N
30 Becerra	Y	?	N	N	N	N
31 Martinez	Y	?	N	N	N	N
32 Dixon	Y	Y	N	N	N	N
33 Roybal-Allard	Y	?	?	N	N	N
34 Torres	Y	?	Y	N	N	N
35 Waters	Y	Y	?	N	N	N
36 Harman	Y	Y	N	N	N	N
37 Millender-McD.	Y	Y	N	N	N	N
38 *Horn*	Y	N	Y	Y	Y	Y
39 *Royce*	Y	N	Y	Y	Y	Y
40 *Lewis*	Y	N	Y	Y	Y	Y
41 *Kim*	Y	N	Y	Y	Y	N
42 Brown	Y	Y	N	N	N	N
43 *Calvert*	Y	N	Y	Y	Y	Y
44 *Bono, M.*	Y	N	Y	Y	Y	Y
45 *Rohrabacher*	Y	N	Y	Y	Y	Y
46 Sanchez	+	Y	N	N	N	N
47 *Cox*	Y	N	Y	Y	Y	Y
48 *Packard*	Y	N	Y	Y	Y	Y
49 *Bilbray*	Y	N	Y	Y	Y	Y
50 Filner	Y	Y	N	N	N	N
51 *Cunningham*	Y	N	Y	Y	Y	Y
52 *Hunter*	Y	N	Y	Y	Y	Y
COLORADO						
1 DeGette	?	Y	N	N	N	N
2 Skaggs	Y	Y	N	N	N	N
3 *McInnis*	Y	N	Y	Y	Y	Y
4 *Schaffer*	Y	N	Y	Y	Y	Y
5 *Hefley*	Y	N	Y	Y	Y	Y
6 *Schaefer*	Y	?	Y	Y	Y	Y
CONNECTICUT						
1 Kennelly	Y	Y	N	N	N	N
2 Gejdenson	Y	Y	N	N	N	N
3 DeLauro	Y	Y	N	N	N	N
4 *Shays*	Y	N	Y	Y	N	N
5 Maloney	Y	Y	N	N	N	N
6 *Johnson*	Y	N	Y	Y	Y	Y
DELAWARE						
AL *Castle*	Y	N	Y	Y	Y	N
FLORIDA						
1 *Scarborough*	?	N	Y	Y	Y	Y
2 Boyd	Y	Y	N	N	N	N
3 Brown	Y	?	N	N	N	N
4 *Fowler*	Y	N	Y	Y	Y	Y
5 Thurman	Y	Y	N	N	N	N
6 *Stearns*	Y	N	Y	Y	Y	Y
7 *Mica*	Y	N	Y	Y	Y	Y
8 *McCollum*	Y	N	Y	Y	Y	Y
9 *Bilirakis*	Y	N	Y	Y	Y	Y
10 *Young*	Y	N	?	Y	Y	Y
11 Davis	Y	Y	Y	N	N	N
12 *Canady*	Y	N	Y	Y	Y	Y
13 *Miller*	Y	N	Y	Y	Y	Y
14 *Goss*	Y	N	Y	Y	Y	Y
15 *Weldon*	Y	N	Y	Y	Y	Y
16 *Foley*	Y	N	Y	Y	Y	Y
17 Meek	Y	Y	N	N	N	N
18 *Ros-Lehtinen*	Y	N	Y	Y	Y	Y
19 Wexler	Y	Y	N	N	N	N
20 Deutsch	Y	Y	N	N	N	N
21 *Diaz-Balart*	Y	N	Y	Y	Y	Y
22 *Shaw*	Y	N	Y	Y	Y	N
23 Hastings	Y	Y	N	N	N	N
GEORGIA						
1 *Kingston*	Y	N	Y	Y	Y	Y
2 Bishop	Y	Y	N	N	N	N
3 *Collins*	Y	N	Y	Y	Y	Y
4 McKinney	N	Y	N	N	N	N
5 Lewis	Y	Y	N	N	N	N
6 *Gingrich*			Y	Y	Y	Y
7 *Barr*	Y	N	Y	Y	Y	Y
8 *Chambliss*	Y	N	Y	Y	Y	Y
9 *Deal*	Y	N	Y	Y	Y	Y
10 *Norwood*	Y	N	Y	Y	Y	Y
11 *Linder*	Y	N	Y	Y	Y	Y
HAWAII						
1 Abercrombie	Y	Y	N	N	N	N
2 Mink	Y	Y	N	N	N	N
IDAHO						
1 *Chenoweth*	Y	N	?	Y	Y	Y
2 *Crapo*	Y	N	Y	Y	Y	Y
ILLINOIS						
1 Rush	?	Y	N	N	N	N
2 Jackson	Y	Y	N	N	N	N
3 Lipinski	Y	?	Y	N	Y	N
4 Gutierrez	Y	Y	N	N	N	N
5 Blagojevich	Y	Y	N	N	N	N
6 *Hyde*	Y	N	Y	Y	Y	Y
7 Davis	Y	Y	N	N	N	N
8 *Crane*	Y	?	?	Y	Y	Y
9 Yates	Y	Y	N	N	N	N
10 *Porter*	Y	N	Y	Y	Y	Y
11 *Weller*	Y	N	Y	Y	Y	Y
12 Costello	Y	Y	N	N	N	N
13 *Fawell*	Y	N	Y	Y	Y	Y

ND Northern Democrats   SD Southern Democrats

	539	540	541	542	543	544
14 ***Hastert***	Y	N	Y	Y	Y	Y
15 ***Ewing***	Y	N	Y	Y	Y	Y
16 ***Manzullo***	Y	N	Y	Y	Y	Y
17 Evans	Y	Y	Y	N	N	N
18 ***LaHood***	Y	N	Y	Y	Y	Y
19 Poshard	Y	Y	N	N	N	N
20 ***Shimkus***	Y	N	Y	Y	Y	Y
INDIANA						
1 Visclosky	Y	Y	?	N	N	N
2 ***McIntosh***	Y	N	Y	Y	Y	Y
3 Roemer	Y	Y	Y	N	N	N
4 ***Souder***	Y	N	?	Y	N	N
5 ***Buyer***	Y	N	Y	Y	Y	Y
6 ***Burton***	Y	N	?	Y	Y	Y
7 ***Pease***	Y	N	Y	Y	Y	Y
8 ***Hostettler***	Y	N	Y	Y	Y	Y
9 Hamilton	Y	Y	Y	N	N	N
10 Carson	Y	Y	N	N	N	N
IOWA						
1 ***Leach***	Y	N	Y	Y	Y	Y
2 ***Nussle***	Y	N	Y	Y	Y	Y
3 Boswell	Y	Y	Y	N	N	N
4 ***Ganske***	Y	N	Y	Y	Y	Y
5 ***Latham***	Y	N	Y	Y	Y	Y
KANSAS						
1 ***Moran***	Y	N	Y	Y	Y	Y
2 ***Ryun***	Y	N	Y	Y	Y	Y
3 ***Snowbarger***	+	N	Y	Y	Y	Y
4 ***Tiahrt***	Y	N	Y	Y	Y	Y
KENTUCKY						
1 ***Whitfield***	Y	N	Y	Y	Y	Y
2 ***Lewis***	Y	N	Y	Y	Y	Y
3 ***Northup***	Y	N	Y	Y	Y	Y
4 ***Bunning***	Y	N	Y	Y	Y	Y
5 ***Rogers***	Y	N	Y	Y	Y	Y
6 Baesler	?	Y	N	N	N	N
LOUISIANA						
1 ***Livingston***	Y	N	Y	Y	Y	Y
2 Jefferson	Y	Y	N	N	N	N
3 ***Tauzin***	Y	N	Y	Y	Y	Y
4 ***McCrery***	Y	N	?	Y	Y	Y
5 ***Cooksey***	Y	N	Y	Y	Y	Y
6 ***Baker***	Y	N	Y	Y	Y	Y
7 John	Y	Y	Y	N	N	N
MAINE						
1 Allen	Y	?	N	N	N	N
2 Baldacci	Y	Y	N	N	N	N
MARYLAND						
1 ***Gilchrest***	Y	N	Y	Y	Y	Y
2 ***Ehrlich***	Y	N	Y	Y	Y	Y
3 Cardin	Y	Y	Y	N	N	N
4 Wynn	Y	Y	N	N	N	N
5 Hoyer	Y	Y	Y	N	N	N
6 ***Bartlett***	Y	N	Y	Y	Y	Y
7 Cummings	Y	Y	Y	N	N	N
8 ***Morella***	Y	N	Y	N	N	N
MASSACHUSETTS						
1 Olver	Y	Y	N	N	N	N
2 Neal	Y	Y	N	N	N	N
3 McGovern	Y	Y	N	N	N	N
4 Frank	Y	Y	?	N	N	N
5 Meehan	Y	Y	N	N	N	N
6 Tierney	Y	Y	N	N	N	N
7 Markey	Y	Y	N	N	N	N
8 Kennedy	Y	?	Y	N	N	N
9 Moakley	Y	Y	Y	N	N	N
10 Delahunt	Y	Y	N	N	N	N
MICHIGAN						
1 Stupak	Y	Y	N	N	N	N
2 ***Hoekstra***	Y	N	Y	Y	Y	Y
3 ***Ehlers***	Y	N	Y	Y	Y	Y
4 ***Camp***	Y	N	Y	Y	Y	Y
5 Barcia	Y	Y	Y	N	N	N
6 ***Upton***	Y	N	Y	Y	Y	Y
7 ***Smith***	Y	N	Y	Y	Y	Y
8 Stabenow	Y	Y	Y	N	N	N
9 Kildee	Y	Y	Y	N	N	N
10 Bonior	Y	Y	N	N	N	N
11 ***Knollenberg***	Y	N	?	Y	Y	Y
12 Levin	Y	Y	N	N	N	N
13 Rivers	Y	Y	Y	N	N	N
14 Conyers	N	Y	Y	N	N	N
15 Kilpatrick	Y	Y	N	N	N	N
16 Dingell	Y	Y	Y	N	N	N

	539	540	541	542	543	544
MINNESOTA						
1 ***Gutknecht***	Y	N	Y	Y	Y	Y
2 Minge	Y	Y	Y	N	N	N
3 ***Ramstad***	Y	N	Y	Y	Y	N
4 Vento	Y	Y	N	N	N	N
5 Sabo	Y	Y	N	N	N	N
6 Luther	Y	Y	N	N	N	N
7 Peterson	Y	Y	N	N	N	N
8 Oberstar	Y	?	N	N	N	N
MISSISSIPPI						
1 ***Wicker***	Y	N	Y	Y	Y	Y
2 Thompson	Y	Y	N	N	N	N
3 ***Pickering***	Y	N	?	Y	Y	Y
4 ***Parker***	Y	N	Y	Y	Y	Y
5 Taylor	Y	N	N	Y	Y	Y
MISSOURI						
1 Clay	Y	Y	N	N	N	N
2 ***Talent***	Y	N	Y	Y	Y	Y
3 Gephardt	Y	Y	N	N	N	N
4 Skelton	Y	Y	N	N	N	N
5 McCarthy	Y	Y	Y	N	N	N
6 Danner	Y	Y	Y	N	N	N
7 ***Blunt***	Y	N	Y	Y	Y	Y
8 ***Emerson***	Y	?	Y	Y	Y	Y
9 ***Hulshof***	Y	N	Y	Y	Y	Y
MONTANA						
AL ***Hill***	Y	N	Y	Y	Y	Y
NEBRASKA						
1 ***Bereuter***	Y	N	Y	Y	Y	Y
2 ***Christensen***	Y	N	Y	Y	Y	Y
3 ***Barrett***	Y	N	Y	Y	Y	Y
NEVADA						
1 ***Ensign***	Y	N	N	Y	Y	N
2 ***Gibbons***	Y	N	Y	Y	Y	N
NEW HAMPSHIRE						
1 ***Sununu***	Y	N	Y	Y	Y	Y
2 ***Bass***	Y	N	Y	Y	Y	Y
NEW JERSEY						
1 Andrews	Y	Y	Y	N	N	N
2 ***LoBiondo***	Y	N	Y	Y	Y	Y
3 ***Saxton***	Y	N	Y	Y	Y	Y
4 ***Smith***	Y	N	?	Y	Y	Y
5 ***Roukema***	Y	N	Y	Y	Y	Y
6 Pallone	Y	Y	N	N	N	N
7 ***Franks***	Y	N	Y	Y	Y	Y
8 Pascrell	Y	Y	N	N	N	N
9 Rothman	Y	Y	Y	N	N	N
10 Payne	Y	Y	N	N	N	N
11 ***Frelinghuysen***	Y	N	Y	Y	Y	Y
12 ***Pappas***	Y	N	Y	Y	Y	Y
13 Menendez	Y	Y	N	N	N	N
NEW MEXICO						
1 ***Wilson***	Y	N	Y	Y	Y	Y
2 ***Skeen***	Y	N	Y	Y	Y	Y
3 ***Redmond***	Y	N	Y	Y	Y	Y
NEW YORK						
1 ***Forbes***	Y	N	Y	Y	Y	Y
2 ***Lazio***	Y	N	Y	Y	Y	N
3 ***King***	Y	N	Y	Y	N	N
4 McCarthy	Y	Y	N	N	N	N
5 Ackerman	Y	Y	N	N	N	N
6 Meeks	Y	Y	N	N	N	N
7 Manton	?	?	N	N	N	N
8 Nadler	Y	Y	Y	N	N	N
9 Schumer	Y	Y	Y	N	N	N
10 Towns	Y	?	?	N	N	N
11 Owens	Y	?	N	N	N	N
12 Velázquez	Y	Y	N	N	N	N
13 ***Fossella***	Y	N	?	Y	Y	Y
14 Maloney	Y	Y	?	N	N	N
15 Rangel	Y	Y	?	N	N	N
16 Serrano	Y	Y	N	N	N	N
17 Engel	Y	Y	N	N	N	N
18 Lowey	Y	Y	Y	N	N	N
19 ***Kelly***	Y	N	Y	Y	Y	N
20 ***Gilman***	Y	N	Y	Y	Y	N
21 McNulty	Y	Y	N	N	N	N
22 ***Solomon***	Y	N	Y	Y	Y	Y
23 ***Boehlert***	Y	N	Y	Y	Y	Y
24 ***McHugh***	Y	N	Y	Y	Y	Y
25 ***Walsh***	Y	N	Y	Y	Y	Y
26 Hinchey	Y	?	N	N	N	N
27 ***Paxon***	Y	N	Y	Y	Y	Y
28 Slaughter	Y	Y	?	N	N	N
29 LaFalce	Y	Y	N	N	N	N
30 ***Quinn***	Y	N	Y	Y	Y	Y

	539	540	541	542	543	544
31 ***Houghton***	Y	N	Y	Y	N	N
NORTH CAROLINA						
1 Clayton	Y	Y	N	N	N	N
2 Etheridge	Y	Y	N	N	N	N
3 ***Jones***	Y	N	Y	Y	Y	Y
4 Price	Y	Y	N	N	N	N
5 ***Burr***	Y	N	Y	Y	Y	N
6 ***Coble***	Y	N	Y	Y	Y	Y
7 McIntyre	Y	Y	Y	N	N	N
8 Hefner	Y	?	N	N	N	N
9 ***Myrick***	Y	N	Y	Y	Y	Y
10 ***Ballenger***	Y	N	Y	Y	Y	Y
11 ***Taylor***	?	?	Y	Y	Y	Y
12 Watt	Y	Y	Y	N	N	N
NORTH DAKOTA						
AL Pomeroy	Y	Y	N	N	N	N
OHIO						
1 ***Chabot***	Y	N	Y	Y	Y	Y
2 ***Portman***	Y	N	Y	Y	Y	Y
3 Hall	Y	Y	N	N	N	N
4 ***Oxley***	Y	N	Y	Y	Y	Y
5 ***Gillmor***	Y	N	Y	Y	Y	Y
6 Strickland	Y	Y	N	N	N	N
7 ***Hobson***	Y	N	Y	Y	Y	N
8 ***Boehner***	Y	N	Y	Y	Y	Y
9 Kaptur	Y	?	Y	N	N	N
10 Kucinich	Y	Y	N	N	N	N
11 Stokes	Y	Y	Y	N	N	N
12 ***Kasich***	Y	N	Y	Y	Y	Y
13 Brown	Y	Y	N	N	N	N
14 Sawyer	Y	Y	N	N	N	N
15 ***Pryce***	Y	–	+	Y	Y	N
16 ***Regula***	Y	N	Y	Y	Y	Y
17 Traficant	Y	Y	Y	N	N	N
18 ***Ney***	Y	N	Y	Y	Y	N
19 ***LaTourette***	Y	N	Y	Y	Y	Y
OKLAHOMA						
1 ***Largent***	Y	N	?	Y	Y	Y
2 ***Coburn***	Y	N	Y	Y	Y	Y
3 ***Watkins***	Y	N	Y	Y	Y	Y
4 ***Watts***	Y	N	Y	Y	Y	Y
5 ***Istook***	Y	N	Y	Y	Y	Y
6 ***Lucas***	Y	N	Y	Y	Y	Y
OREGON						
1 Furse	P	Y	N	N	N	N
2 ***Smith***	Y	N	Y	Y	Y	Y
3 Blumenauer	Y	Y	Y	N	N	N
4 DeFazio	Y	Y	N	N	N	N
5 Hooley	Y	Y	N	N	N	N
PENNSYLVANIA						
1 Brady	Y	Y	N	N	N	N
2 Fattah	Y	Y	N	N	N	N
3 Borski	Y	Y	N	N	N	N
4 Klink	Y	Y	N	N	N	N
5 ***Peterson***	Y	N	Y	Y	Y	Y
6 Holden	Y	Y	N	N	N	N
7 ***Weldon***	Y	N	Y	Y	Y	Y
8 ***Greenwood***	Y	N	Y	Y	Y	N
9 ***Shuster***	Y	N	Y	Y	Y	N
10 ***McDade***	Y	?	?	Y	Y	Y
11 Kanjorski	Y	Y	N	N	N	N
12 Murtha	?	Y	Y	N	N	N
13 ***Fox***	Y	N	Y	Y	Y	Y
14 Coyne	Y	Y	N	N	N	N
15 McHale	Y	N	Y	N	Y	Y
16 ***Pitts***	Y	N	Y	Y	Y	Y
17 ***Gekas***	Y	N	Y	Y	Y	Y
18 Doyle	Y	Y	N	N	N	N
19 ***Goodling***	Y	N	Y	Y	Y	Y
20 Mascara	Y	Y	N	N	N	N
21 ***English***	Y	N	N	Y	Y	N
RHODE ISLAND						
1 Kennedy	Y	Y	N	N	N	N
2 Weygand	Y	Y	Y	N	N	N
SOUTH CAROLINA						
1 ***Sanford***	N	N	Y	Y	Y	N
2 ***Spence***	Y	N	Y	Y	Y	Y
3 ***Graham***	Y	N	Y	Y	Y	N
4 ***Inglis***	Y	N	Y	Y	Y	Y
5 Spratt	Y	Y	Y	N	N	N
6 Clyburn	Y	Y	N	N	N	N
SOUTH DAKOTA						
AL ***Thune***	Y	N	Y	Y	Y	Y

	539	540	541	542	543	544
TENNESSEE						
1 ***Jenkins***	Y	N	Y	Y	Y	Y
2 ***Duncan***	Y	N	Y	Y	Y	Y
3 ***Wamp***	Y	N	Y	Y	Y	Y
4 ***Hilleary***	Y	N	Y	Y	Y	Y
5 Clement	Y	Y	Y	N	N	N
6 Gordon	Y	?	Y	N	N	N
7 ***Bryant***	Y	N	Y	Y	Y	Y
8 Tanner	Y	Y	Y	N	N	N
9 Ford	Y	Y	N	N	N	N
TEXAS						
1 Sandlin	Y	Y	Y	N	N	N
2 Turner	Y	Y	N	N	N	N
3 ***Johnson, Sam***	Y	N	?	Y	Y	Y
4 Hall	Y	N	Y	Y	Y	Y
5 ***Sessions***	Y	N	?	Y	Y	Y
6 ***Barton***	Y	N	?	Y	Y	Y
7 ***Archer***	Y	N	Y	Y	Y	Y
8 ***Brady***	Y	N	Y	Y	Y	Y
9 Lampson	Y	Y	Y	N	N	N
10 Doggett	Y	Y	Y	N	N	N
11 Edwards	Y	Y	Y	N	N	N
12 ***Granger***	Y	N	Y	Y	Y	Y
13 ***Thornberry***	Y	N	Y	Y	Y	Y
14 ***Paul***	N	N	?	Y	Y	Y
15 Hinojosa	Y	Y	N	N	N	N
16 Reyes	Y	Y	N	N	N	N
17 Stenholm	Y	Y	Y	Y	Y	Y
18 Jackson-Lee	Y	Y	N	N	N	N
19 ***Combest***	Y	N	Y	Y	Y	Y
20 Gonzalez	Y	?	?	N	N	N
21 ***Smith***	Y	N	Y	Y	Y	Y
22 ***DeLay***	Y	N	Y	Y	Y	Y
23 ***Bonilla***	Y	N	Y	Y	Y	Y
24 Frost	Y	Y	N	N	N	N
25 Bentsen	Y	Y	Y	N	N	N
26 ***Armey***	Y	N	Y	Y	Y	Y
27 Ortiz	Y	Y	N	N	N	N
28 Rodriguez	Y	Y	N	N	N	N
29 Green	Y	Y	N	N	N	N
30 Johnson, E.B.	Y	Y	N	N	N	N
UTAH						
1 ***Hansen***	Y	N	Y	Y	Y	Y
2 ***Cook***	Y	N	Y	Y	Y	Y
3 ***Cannon***	Y	N	Y	Y	Y	Y
VERMONT						
AL *Sanders*	Y	Y	Y	N	N	N
VIRGINIA						
1 ***Bateman***	Y	N	Y	Y	Y	Y
2 Pickett	Y	Y	N	N	N	N
3 Scott	Y	Y	Y	N	N	N
4 Sisisky	Y	Y	Y	N	N	N
5 Goode	Y	N	Y	Y	Y	Y
6 ***Goodlatte***	Y	N	Y	Y	Y	Y
7 ***Bliley***	Y	N	Y	Y	Y	Y
8 Moran	Y	Y	Y	N	N	N
9 Boucher	Y	Y	Y	N	N	N
10 ***Wolf***	Y	N	Y	Y	Y	Y
11 ***Davis***	Y	N	?	Y	Y	Y
WASHINGTON						
1 ***White***	Y	N	Y	Y	Y	Y
2 ***Metcalf***	Y	N	Y	Y	Y	Y
3 ***Smith, Linda***	Y	N	?	Y	Y	Y
4 ***Hastings***	Y	N	Y	Y	Y	Y
5 ***Nethercutt***	Y	N	Y	Y	Y	Y
6 Dicks	Y	Y	N	N	N	N
7 McDermott	Y	Y	N	N	N	N
8 ***Dunn***	Y	N	Y	Y	Y	Y
9 Smith, Adam	Y	Y	Y	N	N	N
WEST VIRGINIA						
1 Mollohan	Y	Y	Y	N	N	N
2 Wise	Y	?	Y	N	N	N
3 Rahall	Y	Y	Y	N	N	N
WISCONSIN						
1 ***Neumann***	Y	N	Y	Y	Y	Y
2 ***Klug***	Y	N	?	Y	Y	N
3 Kind	Y	Y	Y	N	N	N
4 Kleczka	Y	Y	Y	N	N	N
5 Barrett	Y	N	Y	N	N	N
6 ***Petri***	Y	N	Y	Y	Y	Y
7 Obey	Y	Y	Y	N	N	N
8 Johnson	Y	?	Y	N	N	N
9 ***Sensenbrenner***	Y	N	Y	Y	Y	Y
WYOMING						
AL ***Cubin***	Y	N	Y	Y	Y	Y

Southern states - Ala., Ark., Fla., Ga., Ky., La., Miss., N.C., Okla., S.C., Tenn., Texas, Va.

House Votes 545, 546, 547

Key

- **Y** Voted for (yea).
- **#** Paired for.
- **+** Announced for.
- **N** Voted against (nay).
- **X** Paired against.
- **−** Announced against.
- **P** Voted "present."
- **C** Voted "present" to avoid possible conflict of interest.
- **?** Did not vote or otherwise make a position known.

Democrats **Republicans**
Independent

---

545. H Res 611. Impeachment of President Clinton/Article III — Obstruction of Justice. Adoption of Article III of the resolution, which would impeach President Clinton for obstruction of justice, concealing evidence and delaying proceedings in the Paula Jones federal sexual harassment civil lawsuit. Adopted 221-212: R 216-12; D 5-199 (ND 1-148, SD 4-51); I 0-1. Dec. 19, 1998. A "nay" was a vote in support of the president's position.

546. H Res 611. Impeachment of President Clinton/Article IV — Abuse of Power. Adoption of Article IV of the resolution, which would impeach President Clinton for abuse of office for refusing to respond or lying in response to 81 written questions submitted to him by the House Judiciary Committee. Rejected 148-285: R 147-81; D 1-203 (ND 0-149, SD 1-54); I 0-1. Dec. 19, 1998. A "nay" was a vote in support of the president's position.

547. Impeachment of President Clinton/Appointment of Managers. Adoption of the resolution to appoint and authorize managers, drawn from the Republican membership of the House Judiciary Committee, to conduct the impeachment trial against President Clinton in the Senate. Adopted 228-190: R 223-2; D 5-187 (ND 1-137, SD 4-50); I 0-1. Dec. 19, 1998.

		545	546	547
ALABAMA				
1	**Callahan**	Y	Y	Y
2	**Everett**	Y	Y	Y
3	**Riley**	Y	Y	Y
4	**Aderholt**	Y	Y	Y
5	Cramer	N	N	N
6	**Bachus**	Y	Y	Y
7	Hilliard	N	N	N
ALASKA				
AL	**Young**	Y	Y	Y
ARIZONA				
1	**Salmon**	Y	Y	Y
2	Pastor	N	N	N
3	**Stump**	Y	Y	Y
4	**Shadegg**	Y	N	Y
5	**Kolbe**	Y	N	Y
6	**Hayworth**	Y	Y	Y
ARKANSAS				
1	Berry	N	N	N
2	Snyder	N	N	N
3	**Hutchinson**	Y	Y	Y
4	**Dickey**	Y	N	Y
CALIFORNIA				
1	**Riggs**	Y	N	Y
2	**Herger**	Y	Y	Y
3	Fazio	N	N	N
4	**Doolittle**	Y	Y	Y
5	Matsui	N	N	N
6	Woolsey	N	N	N
7	Miller	?	?	?
8	Pelosi	N	N	N
9	Lee	N	N	N
10	Tauscher	N	N	N
11	**Pombo**	Y	Y	Y
12	Lantos	N	N	N
13	Stark	N	N	N
14	Eshoo	N	N	N
15	**Campbell**	Y	N	N
16	Lofgren	N	N	N
17	Farr	N	N	N
18	Condit	N	N	N
19	**Radanovich**	Y	Y	Y
20	Dooley	N	N	N
21	**Thomas**	Y	Y	Y
22	Capps, L.	N	N	N
23	**Gallegly**	Y	Y	Y
24	Sherman	N	N	N
25	**McKeon**	Y	Y	Y
26	Berman	N	N	N
27	**Rogan**	Y	Y	Y
28	**Dreier**	Y	Y	Y
29	Waxman	N	N	N
30	Becerra	N	N	N
31	Martinez	N	N	N
32	Dixon	N	N	N
33	Roybal-Allard	N	N	N
34	Torres	N	N	N
35	Waters	N	N	N
36	Harman	N	N	N
37	Millender-McD.	N	N	N
38	**Horn**	Y	Y	Y
39	**Royce**	Y	Y	Y
40	**Lewis**	Y	Y	Y
41	**Kim**	N	N	Y
42	Brown	N	N	N
43	**Calvert**	Y	Y	Y
44	**Bono, M.**	Y	Y	Y
45	**Rohrabacher**	Y	Y	Y
46	Sanchez	N	N	N
47	**Cox**	Y	Y	Y
48	**Packard**	Y	Y	Y
49	**Bilbray**	Y	N	Y
50	Filner	N	N	N
51	**Cunningham**	Y	Y	Y
52	**Hunter**	Y	Y	Y
COLORADO				
1	DeGette	N	N	?
2	Skaggs	N	N	N
3	**McInnis**	Y	N	Y
4	**Schaffer**	Y	Y	Y
5	**Hefley**	Y	N	Y
6	**Schaefer**	Y	Y	Y
CONNECTICUT				
1	Kennelly	N	N	?
2	Gejdenson	N	N	N
3	DeLauro	N	N	N
4	**Shays**	N	N	N
5	Maloney	N	N	N
6	**Johnson**	N	N	N
DELAWARE				
AL	**Castle**	N	N	Y
FLORIDA				
1	**Scarborough**	Y	N	Y
2	Boyd	N	N	N
3	Brown	N	N	N
4	**Fowler**	Y	Y	Y
5	Thurman	N	N	N
6	**Stearns**	Y	Y	Y
7	**Mica**	Y	Y	Y
8	**McCollum**	Y	Y	Y
9	**Bilirakis**	Y	Y	Y
10	**Young**	Y	Y	Y
11	Davis	N	N	N
12	**Canady**	Y	Y	Y
13	**Miller**	Y	Y	Y
14	**Goss**	Y	N	Y
15	**Weldon**	Y	Y	Y
16	**Foley**	Y	N	Y
17	Meek	N	N	N
18	**Ros-Lehtinen**	Y	Y	Y
19	Wexler	N	N	N
20	Deutsch	N	N	N
21	**Diaz-Balart**	Y	Y	Y
22	**Shaw**	Y	N	Y
23	Hastings	N	N	N
GEORGIA				
1	**Kingston**	Y	Y	Y
2	Bishop	N	N	N
3	**Collins**	Y	Y	Y
4	McKinney	N	N	N
5	Lewis	N	N	N
6	**Gingrich**	Y	Y	Y
7	**Barr**	Y	Y	Y
8	**Chambliss**	Y	Y	Y
9	**Deal**	Y	Y	Y
10	**Norwood**	Y	Y	Y
11	**Linder**	Y	Y	Y
HAWAII				
1	Abercrombie	N	N	N
2	Mink	N	N	N
IDAHO				
1	**Chenoweth**	Y	Y	Y
2	**Crapo**	Y	Y	Y
ILLINOIS				
1	Rush	N	N	N
2	Jackson	N	N	N
3	Lipinski	N	N	?
4	Gutierrez	N	N	N
5	Blagojevich	N	N	N
6	**Hyde**	Y	Y	Y
7	Davis	N	N	N
8	**Crane**	Y	Y	Y
9	Yates	N	N	N
10	**Porter**	Y	N	Y
11	**Weller**	Y	N	Y
12	Costello	N	N	?
13	**Fawell**	Y	N	Y

ND Northern Democrats   SD Southern Democrats

	545	546	547
14 *Hastert*	Y	Y	Y
15 *Ewing*	Y	Y	Y
16 *Manzullo*	Y	Y	Y
17 Evans	N	N	N
18 *LaHood*	Y	Y	Y
19 Poshard	N	N	?
20 *Shimkus*	Y	N	Y

INDIANA

	545	546	547
1 Visclosky	N	N	N
2 *McIntosh*	Y	N	Y
3 Roemer	N	N	N
4 *Souder*	Y	N	Y
5 *Buyer*	Y	Y	?
6 *Burton*	Y	Y	Y
7 *Pease*	Y	Y	Y
8 *Hostettler*	Y	Y	Y
9 Hamilton	N	N	N
10 Carson	N	N	N

IOWA

	545	546	547
1 *Leach*	N	N	Y
2 *Nussle*	Y	Y	Y
3 Boswell	N	N	N
4 *Ganske*	Y	N	Y
5 *Latham*	Y	N	Y

KANSAS

	545	546	547
1 *Moran*	Y	N	Y
2 *Ryun*	Y	Y	?
3 *Snowbarger*	Y	Y	Y
4 *Tiahrt*	Y	Y	Y

KENTUCKY

	545	546	547
1 *Whitfield*	Y	N	Y
2 *Lewis*	Y	Y	Y
3 *Northup*	Y	N	Y
4 *Bunning*	Y	Y	Y
5 *Rogers*	Y	N	Y
6 Baesler	N	N	N

LOUISIANA

	545	546	547
1 *Livingston*	Y	Y	Y
2 Jefferson	N	N	N
3 *Tauzin*	Y	N	Y
4 *McCrery*	Y	N	Y
5 *Cooksey*	Y	Y	Y
6 *Baker*	Y	Y	Y
7 John	N	N	N

MAINE

	545	546	547
1 Allen	?	?	?
2 Baldacci	N	N	N

MARYLAND

	545	546	547
1 *Gilchrest*	Y	N	Y
2 *Ehrlich*	Y	N	Y
3 Cardin	N	N	N
4 Wynn	N	N	N
5 Hoyer	N	N	N
6 *Bartlett*	Y	Y	Y
7 Cummings	N	N	N
8 Morella	N	N	Y

MASSACHUSETTS

	545	546	547
1 Olver	N	N	N
2 Neal	N	N	?
3 McGovern	N	N	N
4 Frank	N	N	N
5 Meehan	N	N	N
6 Tierney	N	N	N
7 Markey	N	N	N
8 Kennedy	N	N	N
9 Moakley	N	N	N
10 Delahunt	N	N	N

MICHIGAN

	545	546	547
1 Stupak	N	N	N
2 *Hoekstra*	Y	Y	Y
3 *Ehlers*	Y	Y	Y
4 *Camp*	Y	Y	Y
5 Barcia	N	N	N
6 *Upton*	Y	N	Y
7 *Smith*	Y	Y	Y
8 Stabenow	N	N	N
9 Kildee	N	N	N
10 Bonior	N	N	N
11 *Knollenberg*	Y	Y	Y
12 Levin	N	N	N
13 Rivers	N	N	N
14 Conyers	N	N	?
15 Kilpatrick	N	N	N
16 Dingell	N	N	N

MINNESOTA

	545	546	547
1 *Gutknecht*	Y	Y	Y
2 Minge	N	N	N
3 *Ramstad*	Y	Y	Y
4 Vento	N	N	N
5 Sabo	N	N	N
6 Luther	N	N	N
7 Peterson	N	N	N
8 Oberstar	N	N	N

MISSISSIPPI

	545	546	547
1 *Wicker*	Y	Y	Y
2 Thompson	N	N	N
3 *Pickering*	Y	Y	Y
4 *Parker*	Y	N	Y
5 Taylor	Y	Y	Y

MISSOURI

	545	546	547
1 Clay	N	N	N
2 *Talent*	Y	Y	Y
3 Gephardt	N	N	N
4 Skelton	N	N	N
5 McCarthy	N	N	—
6 Danner	N	N	?
7 *Blunt*	Y	Y	Y
8 *Emerson*	Y	N	Y
9 *Hulshof*	Y	N	Y

MONTANA

	545	546	547
AL *Hill*	Y	N	Y

NEBRASKA

	545	546	547
1 *Bereuter*	Y	N	Y
2 *Christensen*	Y	Y	Y
3 *Barrett*	Y	Y	Y

NEVADA

	545	546	547
1 *Ensign*	Y	N	Y
2 *Gibbons*	Y	Y	Y

NEW HAMPSHIRE

	545	546	547
1 *Sununu*	Y	Y	Y
2 *Bass*	Y	N	Y

NEW JERSEY

	545	546	547
1 Andrews	N	N	N
2 *LoBiondo*	Y	N	Y
3 *Saxton*	Y	N	Y
4 *Smith*	Y	Y	Y
5 *Roukema*	Y	Y	Y
6 Pallone	N	N	N
7 *Franks*	Y	N	Y
8 Pascrell	N	N	N
9 Rothman	N	N	N
10 Payne	N	N	N
11 *Frelinghuysen*	Y	N	Y
12 *Pappas*	Y	Y	Y
13 Menendez	N	N	N

NEW MEXICO

	545	546	547
1 *Wilson*	Y	Y	Y
2 *Skeen*	Y	Y	Y
3 *Redmond*	Y	Y	Y

NEW YORK

	545	546	547
1 *Forbes*	Y	Y	Y
2 *Lazio*	Y	N	Y
3 *King*	N	N	Y
4 McCarthy	N	N	N
5 Ackerman	N	N	N
6 Meeks	N	N	N
7 Manton	N	N	N
8 Nadler	N	N	N
9 Schumer	N	N	N
10 Towns	N	N	N
11 Owens	N	N	N
12 Velázquez	N	N	N
13 *Fossella*	Y	N	Y
14 Maloney	N	N	N
15 Rangel	N	N	N
16 Serrano	N	N	N
17 Engel	N	N	N
18 Lowey	N	N	N
19 *Kelly*	Y	N	Y
20 *Gilman*	Y	N	Y
21 McNulty	N	N	N
22 *Solomon*	Y	Y	Y
23 *Boehlert*	N	N	Y
24 *McHugh*	N	N	Y
25 *Walsh*	Y	N	Y
26 Hinchey	N	N	N
27 *Paxon*	Y	Y	Y
28 Slaughter	N	N	N
29 LaFalce	N	N	N
30 *Quinn*	Y	N	Y
31 Houghton	N	N	N

NORTH CAROLINA

	545	546	547
1 Clayton	N	N	?
2 Etheridge	N	N	N
3 *Jones*	Y	Y	Y
4 Price	N	N	N
5 *Burr*	Y	N	Y
6 *Coble*	Y	Y	Y
7 McIntyre	N	N	N
8 Hefner	N	N	N
9 *Myrick*	Y	Y	Y
10 *Ballenger*	Y	Y	Y
11 *Taylor*	Y	Y	Y
12 Watt	N	N	N

NORTH DAKOTA

	545	546	547
AL Pomeroy	N	N	N

OHIO

	545	546	547
1 *Chabot*	Y	Y	Y
2 *Portman*	Y	N	Y
3 Hall	N	N	N
4 *Oxley*	Y	Y	Y
5 *Gillmor*	Y	Y	Y
6 Strickland	N	N	N
7 *Hobson*	Y	N	Y
8 *Boehner*	Y	Y	Y
9 Kaptur	N	N	N
10 Kucinich	N	N	N
11 Stokes	N	N	N
12 *Kasich*	Y	Y	Y
13 Brown	N	N	N
14 Sawyer	N	N	N
15 *Pryce*	Y	N	Y
16 *Regula*	N	N	Y
17 Traficant	N	N	N
18 *Ney*	Y	N	Y
19 *LaTourette*	Y	N	Y

OKLAHOMA

	545	546	547
1 *Largent*	Y	N	Y
2 *Coburn*	Y	Y	Y
3 *Watkins*	Y	Y	Y
4 *Watts*	Y	Y	Y
5 *Istook*	Y	Y	Y
6 *Lucas*	Y	Y	Y

OREGON

	545	546	547
1 Furse	N	N	?
2 *Smith*	Y	Y	?
3 Blumenauer	N	N	N
4 DeFazio	N	N	N
5 Hooley	N	N	N

PENNSYLVANIA

	545	546	547
1 Brady	N	N	N
2 Fattah	N	N	N
3 Borski	N	N	N
4 Klink	N	N	N
5 *Peterson*	Y	Y	Y
6 Holden	N	N	N
7 *Weldon*	Y	N	Y
8 *Greenwood*	Y	N	Y
9 *Shuster*	Y	Y	Y
10 *McDade*	Y	Y	Y
11 Kanjorski	N	N	N
12 Murtha	N	N	?
13 *Fox*	Y	Y	Y
14 Coyne	N	N	N
15 McHale	Y	N	Y
16 *Pitts*	Y	Y	Y
17 *Gekas*	Y	Y	Y
18 Doyle	N	N	N
19 *Goodling*	Y	Y	Y
20 Mascara	N	N	N
21 *English*	N	N	Y

RHODE ISLAND

	545	546	547
1 Kennedy	N	N	N
2 Weygand	N	N	N

SOUTH CAROLINA

	545	546	547
1 *Sanford*	Y	Y	Y
2 *Spence*	Y	Y	Y
3 *Graham*	Y	Y	Y
4 *Inglis*	Y	Y	Y
5 Spratt	N	N	N
6 Clyburn	N	N	N

SOUTH DAKOTA

	545	546	547
AL *Thune*	Y	N	Y

TENNESSEE

	545	546	547
1 *Jenkins*	Y	N	Y
2 *Duncan*	Y	Y	Y
3 *Wamp*	Y	Y	Y
4 *Hilleary*	Y	Y	Y
5 Clement	N	N	N
6 Gordon	N	N	N
7 *Bryant*	Y	Y	Y
8 Tanner	N	N	N
9 Ford	N	N	N

TEXAS

	545	546	547
1 Sandlin	N	N	N
2 Turner	N	N	N
3 *Johnson, Sam*	Y	Y	Y
4 Hall	Y	N	Y
5 *Sessions*	Y	Y	Y
6 *Barton*	Y	Y	Y
7 *Archer*	Y	Y	Y
8 *Brady*	Y	Y	Y
9 Lampson	N	N	N
10 Doggett	N	N	N
11 Edwards	N	N	N
12 *Granger*	Y	N	Y
13 *Thornberry*	Y	N	Y
14 *Paul*	Y	Y	Y
15 Hinojosa	N	N	N
16 Reyes	N	N	N
17 Stenholm	Y	N	Y
18 Jackson-Lee	N	N	N
19 *Combest*	Y	Y	Y
20 Gonzalez	N	N	N
21 *Smith*	Y	Y	Y
22 *DeLay*	Y	Y	Y
23 *Bonilla*	Y	N	Y
24 Frost	N	N	N
25 Bentsen	N	N	N
26 *Armey*	Y	Y	Y
27 Ortiz	N	N	N
28 Rodriguez	N	N	N
29 Green	N	N	N
30 Johnson, E.B.	N	N	N

UTAH

	545	546	547
1 *Hansen*	Y	Y	Y
2 *Cook*	Y	Y	Y
3 *Cannon*	Y	Y	Y

VERMONT

	545	546	547
AL Sanders	N	N	N

VIRGINIA

	545	546	547
1 *Bateman*	Y	Y	Y
2 Pickett	N	N	N
3 Scott	N	N	N
4 Sisisky	N	N	N
5 Goode	Y	N	Y
6 *Goodlatte*	Y	Y	Y
7 *Bliley*	Y	Y	Y
8 Moran	N	N	N
9 Boucher	N	N	N
10 *Wolf*	Y	Y	Y
11 *Davis*	Y	N	Y

WASHINGTON

	545	546	547
1 *White*	Y	N	Y
2 *Metcalf*	Y	Y	Y
3 *Smith, Linda*	Y	Y	Y
4 *Hastings*	Y	Y	Y
5 *Nethercutt*	Y	N	Y
6 Dicks	N	N	N
7 McDermott	N	N	N
8 *Dunn*	Y	Y	Y
9 Smith, Adam	N	N	N

WEST VIRGINIA

	545	546	547
1 Mollohan	N	N	N
2 Wise	N	N	N
3 Rahall	N	N	N

WISCONSIN

	545	546	547
1 *Neumann*	Y	Y	Y
2 *Klug*	Y	N	Y
3 Kind	N	N	N
4 Kleczka	N	N	N
5 Barrett	N	N	N
6 *Petri*	Y	N	Y
7 Obey	N	N	N
8 Johnson	N	N	N
9 *Sensenbrenner*	Y	Y	Y

WYOMING

	545	546	547
AL *Cubin*	Y	Y	Y

Southern states - Ala., Ark., Fla., Ga., Ky., La., Miss., N.C., Okla., S.C., Tenn., Texas, Va.

House Votes

House Roll Call Votes By Subject

A

Abortion
  Abortion aid to minors, H-80
  Abortion-inducing drugs, H-76
  District of Columbia, H-116
  Federal employee health plan abortion coverage ban, H-84
  Overseas U.S. military hospitals, H-50
  "Partial birth" abortion, H-92, H-94
Adoption
  Joint adoption prohibition, H-118
Advanced Technology Program
  Funding, H-108, H-110
Advertising
  Issue ads, H-104
Affirmative action
  Transportation contracts, H-28
Afghanistan
  Cease fire, H-32
Agricultural price and income supports
  Peanuts, H-74
  Sugar, H-76
Agricultural trade
  Market Access Program, H-76
Agriculture and farming
  Agriculture reauthorization, H-56, H-60
  Appropriations, H-74, H-76, H-122
AIDS
  AIDS patient housing funds redistributed to veterans, H-98
  Needle exchanges, H-34
Air transportation
  Renaming National Airport for Ronald Reagan, H-4
Alaska
  Chugach National Forest, H-94
  Tongass National Forest, H-94
Anti-missile defense
  Funding to implement congressional action regarding international agreement, H-114
Appropriations
  FY 1998
    Supplementals, H-26, H-28, H-36
  FY 1999
    Agriculture, H-76, H-122, H-136
      Conference report, H-136
    Commerce, Justice, State and Judiciary, H-112, H-114, H-134
    Continuing resolutions, H-126, H-144
    Defense, H-76, H-122, H-134
    District of Columbia, H-116, H-118
    Energy and water, H-72, H-74, H-134
  Foreign operations, H-126, H-128
    Interior, H-90, H-92, H-94
    Labor, Health and Human Services, and Education, H-136, H-142
    Legislative branch, H-78
      Conference, H-130
    Military construction, H-72, H-74
      Conference report, H-100
    Omnibus appropriations, H-152
    Transportation, H-100, H-122
    Treasury, Postal Service and general government, H-78, H-82, H-84, H-134, H-140
    VA-HUD and independent agencies, H-82, H-98, H-102, H-124
      Conference report, H-138
Army (U.S.)
  School of the Americas funding, H-128
Article I - Grand jury perjury, H-154
Azerbaijan
  Foreign aid, H-126

B

Bankruptcy
  Consumer bankruptcy revisions, H-134, H-144
  Overhaul of bankruptcy law, H-64, H-66

Banks and banking
  Financial services overhaul, H-42, H-44
  Money laundering, H-74
Baseball
  International character of Little League Baseball, H-34
Bilingual education
  Block grants, H-120
Block grants
  Bilingual education, H-120
  Community Development Block Grant reauthorization, H-120
  Education, H-128
Bosnia
  Withdrawal of U.S. forces, H-18
Budget
  Budget resolution, H-60, H-62
  Budget surplus, H-132
Bureau of Alcohol, Tobacco and Firearms
  Appropriations, H-82
Burton, Dan, R-Ind. (6)
  Disapproval, H-46
Byrd, James
  Condemnation of killing, H-68

C

Cambodia
  Human rights, H-18
Campaign finance
  Access in exchange for contributions, H-88
  Air Force One reimbursement, H-88
  Ballot petition signature requirements, H-102
  Bilingual voting material, H-104
  Campaign reporting and disclosure, H-26, H-104
  Constitutional amendment, H-66
  Contribution bundling ban, H-106
  Contributions limits, H-102
  Contributions raised within state, H-104
  Express advocacy definition, H-106
  FEC clearinghouse of political activities, H-106
  Foreign campaign contributions, H-48
  Individual contribution limit, H-106
  Involuntary contributions ban, H-26
  Issue ads, H-104
  Lower postage rate for candidate mailings, H-104
  Matching opponent's personal funds, H-102
  Non-citizen donations, H-88
  Non-citizens contributions ban, H-26
  Open debate requirement, H-104
  Overhaul, H-26, H-72, H-80, H-104, H-108, H-114
  Political donations from certain legal residents, H-106
  "Soft money," H-54, H-106
  Use of federal property to raise campaign funds, H-88
  "Walking around the money" prohibition, H-88
  White House facilities, H-86
  "Willful blindness" defense, H-88
Capital punishment
  Witness protection, H-8
Capitol building
  Holocaust remembrance in Rotunda, H-14
Census
  Statistical sampling, H-110
Chestnut, Jacob
  Recognition, H-98
Child care
  Funds for parents staying home, H-6
Child support
  Computer system, H-14
  Deadbeat parents punishment, H-42

Children
  Importance of fathers, H-62
  Missing children, H-124
China
  Foreign trade, H-92
  Missile technology transfer, H-50
  Select Committee on National Security and China, H-70
  Tiananmen Square resolution, H-60
Civil rights
  Federal agency compliance, H-8
  Mandates information, H-46
Clinton, President Bill
  Alleged sexual affairs
    Censure ruling, H-154
    Distribution of Starr report, H-120
  Executive privilege, H-52
  Impeachment
    Appointment of managers, H-156
    Article I - Grand jury perjury, H-154
    Article II - Civil suit perjury, H-154
    Article III - Abuse of power, H-156
    Article IV - Obstruction of justice, H-156
  Presidential cooperation with investigation, H-52
Coast Guard (U.S.)
  New Hampshire land transfer, H-136
Commerce
  National standard for salvaged car registration, H-148
  Telemarketing fraud, H-68
Commerce, Justice, State, and the judiciary
  Appropriations, H-108, H-112
Communications and telecommunications
  Cellular telephones, H-10
  Privatization of satellite organizations, H-38
  Public telecommunications facilities program, H-110
  Wireless privacy, H-12
Community development
  Community Development Block Grant reauthorization, H-120
Computers and computer industry
  Year 2000 computer problem, H-150
Congressional affairs
  District of Columbia voting rights, H-116
  Expedited consideration of legislative business, H-138
Constitution (U.S.)
  Campaign spending, H-66
  Religious freedom, H-58
  Tax limitation constitutional amendment, H-30
Contested elections
  California, H-6
Continuing resolutions
  Oct. 9 extension, H-126
Contraceptives
  Insurance coverage, H-84
Copyright
  Copyright term extension, H-22
  Music licensing fees, H-22
Credit unions
  Membership rules, H-28
Crime and criminal justice
  Assistance for surviving families of police officers, H-30
  Extradition of criminals living in Cuba, H-122
  Gun control, H-8
  Money laundering, H-74
  Product identification code tampering, H-134
  Sexual predator punishment, H-148
  Transfer funds from "truth in sentencing" programs to prevention programs, H-110
  War crimes in Yugoslavia, H-122
  Witness protection and death penalty, H-8

Cuba
  Extradition of criminals living in Cuba, H-122
  TV Marti funding, H-108
Currency
  Lewis and Clark expedition commemorative coin, H-118
  Thomas Edison commemorative coin, H-118

D

Defense
  Appropriations, H-76, H-122, H-134
  Bosnia, H-18
  Defense authorization, H-48, H-50, H-52, H-54, H-92
    Conference report, H-130
  U.S. troop support, H-154
Disability
  Fraudulent disability claims correction, H-22
Disabled
  Vocational rehabilitation services, H-58
District of Columbia
  Abortion, H-116
  Advisory Neighborhood Commission, H-116
  Appropriations, H-116, H-118
  Joint adoption prohibition, H-118
  Needle exchange programs, H-116, H-118
  Residence requirement, H-116
  Scholarships, H-34, H-36
  School vouchers, H-116
  Teen tobacco possession, H-118
  Voting rights, H-116
Drug control
  Drug-free schools, H-38
  Drug-free workplaces, H-74
  Drug interdiction and eradication, H-48, H-124, H-126
  Drug testing for federal employees, H-126
  Drugs and children, H-40
  Medicinal marijuana, H-124
Dymally, Mervyn
  Post office designation, H-140

E

Economic Development Administration
  Funding, H-108
Education
  Block grants, H-128
  Charter schools, H-148
  Class size reduction, H-128
  College sports, H-38
  D.C. scholarships, H-34, H-36
  Drug-free schools, H-38
  Education savings accounts, H-40, H-68, H-70
  EPA educational outreach programs, H-96
  Higher education, H-36, H-38
  Indian higher education demonstration project, H-138
  National tests, H-4
  Native Hawaiian education, H-128
  School vouchers, H-116
  Social promotion, H-68
Employment and unemployment
  Fraudulent disability claims correction, H-22

Subject Index

Energy
  Energy efficiency and conservation programs funding, H-90
  Iran, H-106
  Nuclear energy research, H-72
Energy and water
  FY 1999 appropriations, H-72
Environment
  Clean water, H-110
  Columbia River Watershed management, H-94
  EPA educational outreach programs, H-96
  Global warming, H-50
  Jurisdictional parity for fisheries enforcement, H-112
  Land and Water Conservation Fund, H-90
  National Fish and Wildlife Foundation reauthorization, H-148
  Salton Sea study, H-82
  Tropical forest conservation, H-18, H-20
Environmental Protection Agency (EPA)
  EPA educational outreach programs, H-96
Ethics
  Special procurators and state ethical standards, H-112
European Union
  Agriculture markets, restrictions on U.S. imports, H-108
Executive orders
  Federalism, H-112, H-114
  Prohibit funding to enforce executive orders, H-112

F

Family and marital issues
  Child care, H-6
Family planning
  Parental consent for contraceptives distribution, H-142
FCC
  Wireless privacy, H-12
Federal Election Commission (FEC)
  Clearinghouse of political activities, H-106
Federal employees
  Drug testing, H-126
  Federal employee health plan abortion coverage ban, H-84
Federal property
  Use of federal property to raise campaign funds, H-88
Fish and fishing
  Jurisdictional parity for fisheries enforcement, H-112
Food and nutrition
  National nutrition programs, H-144
Food stamps
  Disbursements, H-152
Foreign affairs
  Condemning Nazi-Soviet Non-Aggression Pact, H-146
  Diplomatic relations with Pacific Island nations, H-130
  Exchange stabilization fund restriction, H-84
  Money laundering, H-74
Foreign aid
  Azerbaijan, H-126
Foreign operations
  Appropriations, H-126, H-128
Foreign trade
  Agricultural imports, H-108
  European compliance with World Trade Organization rules, H-146
  Fast-track trade authority, H-132
  Nuclear reactor export, H-54
  Steel imports, H-146, H-148, H-150
  Sub-Sahara Afraica development bill, H-14, H-16
Forest management
  Forest recovery and road construction, H-24

G

Gibson, John
  Recognition, H-98
Gomez, Harold
  Post Office designation, H-140
Government operations
  Federal agency compliance, H-10
  foreign entities, H-8
  Federal reports elimination, H-148
  Financial management by federal agencies, H-62
  Government performance and results, H-16
Greece
  Traveler visa waivers, H-22
Guam
  Commending U.S. citizens of Guam, H-148
Gun control
  Mandatory minimum sentences for use of firearms in a crime, H-8

H

Hawaii
  Native Hawaiian education, H-128
Head Start
  Reauthorization, H-120
Health
  Needle exchange programs, H-116, H-118
  Needle exchanges, H-34
  Parental consent for contraceptives distribution, H-142
  Public health program consolidation, H-148
  Service-connected diseases, H-150
  Women's health research programs, H-150
Health care
  Birth defects prevention, H-14
  Federal employee health plan abortion coverage ban, H-84
  Health Care Task Force sanctions, H-4
  Indian Health Service support costs allocation, H-92
  Mammograms and biopsies, H-124, H-144
  Veterans, H-98
Health insurance
  Contraceptives coverage, H-84
  Regulation, H-96
Highways and roads
  Chugach National Forest, H-94
  Route 66 designation, H-152
  Tongass National Forest, H-94
Homosexuals
  San Francisco "domestic partners" ordinance, H-100
Housing
  Affordable housing and home ownership opportunities, H-86
  Homeless housing programs consolidation, H-10
  Veterans, H-48
Human rights
  Cambodia, H-18
  China, H-18
  Universal declaration of human rights, H-122

I

Immigration
  Military support for border guards, H-52
  Skilled workers, H-130
Impeachment
  Appointment of managers, H-156
  Article I - Grand jury perjury, H-154
  Article II - Civil suit perjury, H-154
  Article III - Abuse of power, H-156
  Article IV - Obstruction of justice, H-156
  Censure ruling, H-154
Indians and Alaskan natives
  Federal recognition of Indian tribes, H-136
  Indian Health Service support costs allocation, H-92
  Indian higher education demonstration project, H-138

Intelligence
  Authorization bill, H-40, H-138
Interior
  Appropriations, H-90, H-92, H-94
International Atomic Energy Agency
  Nuclear power projects in Iran, H-106
Internet
  Pedophiles, H-68
Iran
  Sanctions, H-62
  Withhold contributions to Iranian energy program, H-106
Iraq
  Assistance for Iraqi opposition groups, H-136
  Condemnation for breach of international obligations, H-108
  U.N. weapons inspections, H-108
IRS
  Federal agency compliance, H-8
  IRS overhaul, H-56, H-78, H-80
Israel
  50th anniversary, H-34

J

Japan
  Economic reform, H-86
Judiciary
  Dispute resolution alternatives, H-30
  Jurisdiction for takings claims, H-16
  Limits on federal judges' power, H-30, H-32
  Special procurators and state ethical standards, H-112
Juvenile justice
  Block grants, H-134
  Juvenile crime and missing children laws amendments, H-124

K

Korea
  Anniversary of U.S. Korea relations, H-118
Kosovo
  Condemnation of violence, H-18
Kosovo peacekeeping
  Condemnation of Serbian atrocities, H-130

L

Labor, Health and Human Services, and Education
  Appropriations, H-142
Labor and labor unions
  Labor union organizing curbs, H-24
  Reporting requirements, H-88
  Special investigative authority in Teamsters Union probe, H-102
Law enforcement
  Bulletproof vests grants, H-42
  Honoring slain law enforcement officers, H-42
Legal issues
  Funding for legal challenges, H-114
Legal Services Corporation
  Funding, H-108
Legislation (general)
  Government performance and results, H-16
Legislative branch
  Appropriations, H-78, H-130
Line-item veto
  Military construction
    Veto override, H-6
Livestock
  Livestock protection, H-74
Low-Income Home Energy Assistance Program (LIHEAP)
  Reauthorization, H-120

M

Maine
  Nuclear waste, H-98
Medicare
  Reimbursement formula, H-146

Military construction
  Appropriations, H-74
    Conference report, H-100
  Line-item vetoes, H-6
Military personnel issues
  Military retirees, H-52
Montana
  Canyon Ferry Reservoir cabin sites, H-150
Monuments and memorials
  Bandelier National Monument expansion, H-152
  Lewis and Clark expedition commemorative coin, H-118
  National Lewis and Clark Bicentennial Council, H-128
  Steve Schiff Auditorium, H-84
  Thomas Edison commemorative coin, H-118
Morocco
  Trade, H-14
Music
  Licensing fees, H-22

N

NASA
  Space station, H-98
National Endowment for the Arts
  Funding, H-90
National Fish and Wildlife Foundation
  Reauthorization, H-148
National Park Service
  Bandelier National Monument expansion, H-150
  Fee collection, H-94
  Funding, H-94
National parks
  Omnibus parks bill, H-138
  Tongass National Forest, H-94
  Underground Railroad, H-62
National security
  Select Committee on National Security and China, H-70
New Hampshire
  Land transfer, H-136
New Mexico
  Bandelier National Monument expansion, H-152
  Guadelupe-Hidalgo treaty land claims, H-120
Northern Ireland
  Peace talks, H-18
Nuclear energy
  Nuclear energy research, H-72
  Nuclear reactor export, H-54
Nuclear waste
  Texas, Maine and Vermont low-level radioactive waste compact, H-98

O

Omnibus appropriations
  Conference report, H-152
Open impeachment inquiry, H-140, H-142

P

Pacific Island nations
  Diplomatic relations, H-130
Palestinian Authority
  Extradition of Palestinian terrorists, H-38
Pay raises
  COLAs, H-84
Pharmaceuticals
  Abortion-inducing drugs, H-76
  Medicinal marijuana, H-124
Portugal
  Traveler visa waivers, H-22
Postal Service
  Post Office designations, H-56, H-58, H-140
  Postal rate increase, H-74
Presidency
  Executive privilege, H-52
Prisons and prisoners
  Abortion services, H-110
  Prison release orders, H-48
Privacy
  Wireless privacy, H-12

House Votes

Property rights
Jurisdiction for takings claims, H-16
Public broadcasting
Funding, H-110
Public health
Mandates information, H-46
Program consolidation, H-150
Public housing
Appropriations, H-86
Public lands
Canyon Ferry Reservoir cabin sites, H-150
Omnibus parks bill, H-138
Payments in lieu of taxes fund increase, H-90
Puerto Rico
Political status, H-10, H-12

R

Reagan, former President Ronald
Renaming National Airport for Ronald Reagan, H-4
Religious freedom
Constitutional amendment, H-58
Religious persecution overseas, H-46
Retirement and pensions
Military retirees, H-52
Rivers and streams
Columbia River Watershed management, H-94

S

Sanctions
Iran, H-62
Sanders, Bernard, I-Vt. (AL)
Intelligence authorization, H-40
Schiff, Steve
Sandia Technology Transfer Center designation H-84
School of the Americas
Funding, H-128
Sex offenders
Internet, H-68
National hotline, H-66
Sexual predator punishment, H-148

Small business
Copyright term extension, H-22
Drug free workplaces, H-74
Paperwork reduction, H-22, H-24
Small business loans, H-20, H-112
Social Security
Budget surplus, H-132
National dialogue, H-34
Social Security Trust Fund, H-132
Tax cuts, H-130, H-132
"Soft money"
Campaign finance revisions, H-54
Space
Space station, H-98
Sports
College sports, H-38
International character of Little League Baseball, H-34
Starr, Kenneth W.
Distribution of Clinton investigation report, H-120
Starr impeachment, H-128
Starr impeachment, H-128
State Department
Reauthorization, H-24
Steel
Foreign trade, H-148, H-150
Stocks, bonds and securities
Class action securities lawsuits Votes, H-150
Securities litigation federal filing requirement, H-92
Supplemental appropriations
Conference report, H-36

T

Taiwan
Security, H-86
U.S. support for Taiwan, H-62
World Health Organization, H-146
Taxes and taxation
Education savings accounts, H-40
IRS overhaul, H-78, H-80
Votes, H-56
Mandates information, H-46, H-48
Payments in lieu of taxes fund increase, H-90
Tax code termination, H-68, H-70
Tax cuts, H-132, H-134

Tax cuts and social security, H-130, H-132
Tax limitation constitutional amendment, H-30
Teamsters Union
Special investigative authority in Teamsters Union probe, H-102
Telephones
Telemarketing fraud, H-68
Terrorism
Extradition of Palestinian terrorists, H-38
Texas
Nuclear waste, H-98
Tobacco
Teen tobacco possession, H-118
Transportation
Appropriations, H-100, H-122
Conference, H-56
Route 66 designation, H-152
Special projects, H-28
Surface transportation reauthorization, H-28, H-30, H-52
Welfare to work transportation, H-28
Travel
Traveler visa waivers, H-22
Treasury, Postal Service and general government
Appropriations, H-78, H-82, H-84, H-134, H-140
Treaties and international agreements
Anti-ballistic Missile Treaty, H-114
Guadelupe-Hidalgo treaty land claims, H-120

U

United Nations
Dues, H-112
Rapidly Deployable Mission Headquarters, H-50
User fees
Legislation, H-60

V

VA-HUD and independent agencies
Appropriations, H-82, H-86, H-98, H-100, H-124, H-138

Vermont
Nuclear waste, H-98
Veterans
Arlington Cemetery burials, H-20
Benefits, H-146
Health care, H-98, H-100
Housing, H-48
Service-connected diseases, H-150
Vietnam
Disapproval of presidential waiver for Vietnam, H-100
Vocational education
Vocational rehabilitation services, H-58
Voting and voter turnout
Bilingual voting material, H-104
Citizenship tests for voting eligibility, H-104
Photo ID requirement for voting, H-102
Voter eligibility verification, H-7, H-102
Voter guide clarification, H-102

W

Wages and salaries
Congressional COLA, H-84
Overtime for salespeople, H-66
Welfare and social services
Welfare to work transportation, H-28
WIC Program
Reauthorization, H-86
Wildlife and wildlife protection
Migratory bird hunting regulations, H-120
National Fish and Wildlife Foundation reauthorization, H-148
Women
Mammograms and biopsies, H-124, H-144
Women's health research programs, H-150
World Health Organization
Taiwan, H-146

Y

Youth
Teen tobacco possession, H-118
Yugoslavia
War crimes, H-122

Appendix S

SENATE ROLL CALL VOTES

Bill Number Index S-3
Individual Roll Call Votes S-4

Subject Index S-49

Senate Roll Call Votes By Bill Number

Senate Bills

S 414, S-16
S 442, S-45, S-46, S-47
S 648, S-30
S 1092, S-45
S 1173, S-6, S-7, S-8
S 1244, S-22
S 1260, S-22, S-23
S 1301, S-42, S-43, S-44
S 1415, S-24, S-25, S-26, S-27
S 1575, S-4
S 1618, S-22
S 1645, S-41, S-44
S 1663, S-5, S-6
S 1668, S-7
S 1671, S-5
S 1723, S-23, S-24
S 1768, S-9, S-10
S 1873, S-22, S-41
S 1882, S-31
S 1981, S-41
S 2037, S-23
S 2057, S-23, S-27, S-28, S-29
S 2132, S-39
S 2138, S-27
S 2159, S-32, S-33
S 2168, S-30, S-33, S-34
S 2176, S-44, S-45
S 2237, S-41, S-42
S 2260, S-34, S-35, S-36, S-37
S 2271, S-32
S 2279, S-44
S 2307, S-37
S 2312, S-38, S-39
S 2334, S-40
S 2676, S-30
S 4101, S-33

S Con Res 107, S-31
S Con Res 78, S-8
S Con Res 86, S-10, S-11, S-12, S-13, S-14, S-15

S J Res 42, S-10

S Res 187, S-8

House Bills

HR 6, S-31, S-45
HR 10, S-46
HR 629, S-40
HR 1122, S-43
HR 1150, S-22
HR 1151, S-37, S-38
HR 1270, S-25
HR 1273, S-22
HR 1385, S-20
HR 1757, S-18
HR 2400, S-24
HR 2431, S-48
HR 2631, S-5
HR 2646, S-8, S-9, S-10, S-16, S-17, S-18, S-28
HR 2676, S-21
HR 2709, S-24
HR 3150, S-44, S-48
HR 3579, S-20
HR 3616, S-45
HR 4057, S-45
HR 4059, S-40
HR 4101, S-46
HR 4103, S-39, S-45
HR 4104, S-41, S-48
HR 4112, S-34
HR 4194, S-47
HR 4250, S-48
HR 4328, S-48

Senate Votes 1, 2, 3, 4, 5, 6, 7

	1 2 3 4 5 6 7
ALABAMA	
Sessions	Y Y Y N Y N Y
Shelby	Y Y Y N Y N Y
ALASKA	
Murkowski	N Y Y N Y N Y
Stevens	Y Y Y N Y N Y
ARIZONA	
Kyl	N Y Y N Y N Y
McCain	N Y Y N Y N Y
ARKANSAS	
Hutchinson	N Y Y N Y N Y
Bumpers	Y Y Y Y N Y N
CALIFORNIA	
Boxer	Y Y Y N N N Y
Feinstein	Y Y Y N N N Y
COLORADO	
Allard	N Y Y N Y N Y
Campbell	Y Y Y N Y N Y
CONNECTICUT	
Dodd	Y Y Y N Y N Y
Lieberman	Y Y Y N Y N Y
DELAWARE	
Roth	Y Y Y N Y N Y
Biden	Y ? ? Y N N Y
FLORIDA	
Mack	Y Y Y N Y N Y
Graham	Y Y Y Y Y N Y
GEORGIA	
Coverdell	N Y Y N Y N Y
Cleland	Y Y Y Y N Y N
HAWAII	
Akaka	Y Y Y Y N Y N
Inouye	Y Y Y Y N Y N
IDAHO	
Craig	N Y Y N Y N Y
Kempthorne	Y Y Y N Y N Y
ILLINOIS	
Durbin	? Y Y N N N Y
Moseley-Braun	? Y Y Y N Y N
INDIANA	
Coats	Y ? ? ? ? ? ?
Lugar	Y Y Y N Y N Y

	1 2 3 4 5 6 7
IOWA	
Grassley	N Y Y N Y N Y
Harkin	Y Y Y Y N Y N
KANSAS	
Brownback	N Y Y N Y N Y
Roberts	N Y Y N Y N Y
KENTUCKY	
McConnell	N Y Y N Y N Y
Ford	Y Y Y Y N Y N
LOUISIANA	
Breaux	Y Y Y N Y Y Y
Landrieu	Y Y Y Y Y Y Y
MAINE	
Collins	Y Y Y N Y N Y
Snowe	N Y Y N Y N Y
MARYLAND	
Mikulski	Y Y Y Y N Y Y
Sarbanes	Y Y Y Y N Y N
MASSACHUSETTS	
Kennedy	Y Y Y N Y N Y
Kerry	Y Y Y N Y Y Y
MICHIGAN	
Abraham	N Y Y N Y N Y
Levin	Y Y Y Y N Y N
MINNESOTA	
Grams	N Y Y N Y N Y
Wellstone	Y Y Y Y Y Y Y
MISSISSIPPI	
Cochran	Y Y Y N Y N Y
Lott	N Y Y N Y N Y
MISSOURI	
Ashcroft	N Y Y N Y N Y
Bond	N Y Y N Y N Y
MONTANA	
Burns	N Y Y N Y N Y
Baucus	Y Y Y Y Y Y N
NEBRASKA	
Hagel	N Y Y N Y N Y
Kerrey	Y Y Y Y N Y Y
NEVADA	
Bryan	Y Y Y Y N Y Y
Reid	Y Y Y Y N Y Y

	1 2 3 4 5 6 7
NEW HAMPSHIRE	
Gregg	N Y Y N Y N Y
Smith	N Y Y N Y N Y
NEW JERSEY	
Lautenberg	Y Y Y Y N Y N
Torricelli	Y Y Y Y N Y N
NEW MEXICO	
Domenici	Y Y Y N Y N Y
Bingaman	Y ? ? Y N Y N
NEW YORK	
D'Amato	N Y Y N Y N Y
Moynihan	Y + + ? ? ? ?
NORTH CAROLINA	
Faircloth	– Y Y N Y N Y
Helms	N Y Y N Y N Y
NORTH DAKOTA	
Conrad	Y Y Y Y N Y N
Dorgan	Y Y Y Y N Y N
OHIO	
DeWine	Y Y Y N Y N Y
Glenn	Y Y Y Y N Y N
OKLAHOMA	
Inhofe	N Y Y N Y N Y
Nickles	N Y Y N Y N Y
OREGON	
Smith	Y Y Y N Y N Y
Wyden	Y Y Y N N N Y
PENNSYLVANIA	
Santorum	Y Y Y N Y N Y
Specter	Y Y Y N Y N Y
RHODE ISLAND	
Chafee	Y Y Y N N N Y
Reed	Y Y Y Y N Y N
SOUTH CAROLINA	
Thurmond	Y Y Y N Y N Y
Hollings	Y Y Y Y N Y N
SOUTH DAKOTA	
Daschle	Y Y Y Y Y Y N
Johnson	Y Y Y Y Y Y N
TENNESSEE	
Frist	N Y Y N Y N Y
Thompson	Y Y Y N Y N Y

Key

Y	Voted for (yea).
#	Paired for.
+	Announced for.
N	Voted against (nay).
X	Paired against.
–	Announced against.
P	Voted "present."
C	Voted "present" to avoid possible conflict of interest.
?	Did not vote or otherwise make a position known.

Democrats   **Republicans**

	1 2 3 4 5 6 7
TEXAS	
Gramm	N Y Y N Y N Y
Hutchison	N Y Y N Y N Y
UTAH	
Bennett	Y Y Y N Y N Y
Hatch	Y Y Y N Y N Y
VERMONT	
Jeffords	Y Y Y N Y N Y
Leahy	Y Y Y Y N Y Y
VIRGINIA	
Warner	N Y Y N Y Y Y
Robb	Y Y Y Y N Y N
WASHINGTON	
Gorton	Y Y Y N N N Y
Murray	Y Y Y Y N Y Y
WEST VIRGINIA	
Byrd	Y Y Y N Y N Y
Rockefeller	Y Y Y N Y N Y
WISCONSIN	
Feingold	Y Y Y Y N Y Y
Kohl	Y Y Y Y N Y Y
WYOMING	
Enzi	N Y Y N Y N Y
Thomas	Y Y Y N Y N Y

ND Northern Democrats   SD Southern Democrats

Southern states - Ala., Ark., Fla., Ga., Ky., La., Miss., N.C., Okla., S.C., Tenn., Texas, Va.

1. Aiken Nomination/Confirmation. Confirmation of President Clinton's nomination of Ann L. Aiken of Oregon to be United States District Judge for the District of Oregon. Confirmed 67-30: R 24-30; D 43-0 (ND 35-0, SD 8-0). Jan. 28, 1998. A "yea" was a vote in support of the president's position.

2. Moreno Nomination/Confirmation. Confirmation of President Clinton's nomination of Carlos R. Moreno of California to be U.S. District Judge for the central district of California. Confirmed 96-0: R 54-0; D 42-0 (ND 34-0, SD 8-0). Feb. 3, 1998. A "yea" was a vote in support of the president's position.

3. Miller Nomination/Confirmation. Confirmation of President Clinton's nomination of Christine O.C. Miller of the District of Columbia to be a judge of the U.S. Court of Federal Claims. Confirmed 96-0: R 54-0; D 42-0 (ND 34-0, SD 8-0). Feb. 3, 1998. A "yea" was a vote in support of the president's position.

4. S 1575. Renaming National Airport/Advisory Group. Robb, D-Va., amendment to establish an advisory group to review all proposals to rename federal facilities, including the proposed renaming of Washington National Airport for former President Ronald Reagan. Rejected 35-63: R 0-54; D 35-9 (ND 28-8, SD 7-1). Feb. 4, 1998.

5. S 1575. Renaming National Airport/FBI Building. Coverdell, R-Ga., motion to table (kill) the Reid, D-Nev., amendment to remove former FBI director J. Edgar Hoover's name from the FBI headquarters building in Washington, DC. Motion agreed to 62-36: R 52-2; D 10-34 (ND 8-28, SD 2-6). Feb. 4, 1998.

6. S 1575. Renaming National Airport/Local Approval. Daschle, D-S.D., amendment to require the approval of the Metropolitan Washington Airports Authority before changing the airport's name. Rejected 35-63: R 1-53; D 34-10 (ND 27-9, SD 7-1). Feb. 4, 1998.

7. S 1575. Renaming National Airport/Passage. Passage of the bill to rename Washington National Airport the "Ronald Reagan Washington National Airport" after former President Ronald Reagan. Passed 76-22: R 54-0; D 22-22 (ND 19-17, SD 3-5). Feb. 4, 1998.

Senate Votes 8, 9, 10, 11, 12, 13, 14

	8	9	10	11	12	13	14
ALABAMA							
Sessions	N	N	Y	N	Y	Y	Y
Shelby	N	N	Y	N	Y	Y	Y
ALASKA							
Murkowski	Y	N	Y	N	Y	Y	Y
Stevens	Y	Y	Y	Y	Y	Y	Y
ARIZONA							
Kyl	N	N	Y	N	Y	N	Y
McCain	Y	Y	Y	Y	Y	N	N
ARKANSAS							
Hutchinson	N	N	Y	N	Y	N	Y
Bumpers	Y	Y	N	Y	N	N	N
CALIFORNIA							
Boxer	Y	Y	N	Y	N	Y	N
Feinstein	Y	Y	N	Y	N	Y	?
COLORADO							
Allard	N	N	Y	N	Y	Y	Y
Campbell	N	N	N	Y	Y	Y	Y
CONNECTICUT							
Dodd	Y	Y	N	Y	N	N	N
Lieberman	Y	Y	N	Y	N	Y	N
DELAWARE							
Roth	Y	N	Y	N	Y	Y	N
Biden	Y	Y	N	Y	N	Y	N
FLORIDA							
Mack	Y	N	Y	N	Y	Y	Y
Graham	Y	Y	N	Y	N	Y	N
GEORGIA							
Coverdell	Y	Y	Y	N	Y	Y	Y
Cleland	Y	Y	N	Y	N	Y	N
HAWAII							
Akaka	Y	Y	N	Y	N	Y	N
Inouye	Y	Y	N	Y	N	Y	N
IDAHO							
Craig	Y	N	Y	N	Y	Y	Y
Kempthorne	N	N	Y	N	Y	Y	Y
ILLINOIS							
Durbin	Y	Y	N	Y	N	Y	N
Moseley-Braun	Y	Y	N	Y	N	Y	N
INDIANA							
Coats	N	N	Y	N	Y	N	Y
Lugar	N	N	N	Y	Y	Y	Y

	8	9	10	11	12	13	14
IOWA							
Grassley	N	N	Y	N	Y	N	Y
Harkin	Y	Y	N	Y	?	?	?
KANSAS							
Brownback	N	N	Y	N	Y	Y	Y
Roberts	N	N	Y	N	Y	Y	Y
KENTUCKY							
McConnell	N	N	Y	N	Y	Y	Y
Ford	Y	Y	N	?	N	Y	N
LOUISIANA							
Breaux	Y	Y	N	Y	N	Y	N
Landrieu	Y	Y	N	Y	N	N	N
MAINE							
Collins	Y	Y	N	Y	N	Y	N
Snowe	Y	Y	N	Y	N	Y	N
MARYLAND							
Mikulski	Y	Y	N	Y	N	Y	N
Sarbanes	Y	Y	N	Y	N	Y	N
MASSACHUSETTS							
Kennedy	Y	Y	N	Y	N	+	−
Kerry	Y	Y	N	Y	N	Y	N
MICHIGAN							
Abraham	Y	N	Y	Y	Y	N	Y
Levin	?	?	?	?	N	Y	N
MINNESOTA							
Grams	Y	N	Y	N	Y	N	Y
Wellstone	Y	Y	N	Y	N	N	N
MISSISSIPPI							
Cochran	Y	Y	Y	N	Y	N	Y
Lott	Y	N	Y	Y	Y	Y	Y
MISSOURI							
Ashcroft	N	N	Y	N	Y	Y	Y
Bond	Y	Y	Y	N	Y	Y	Y
MONTANA							
Burns	N	N	Y	N	Y	Y	Y
Baucus	Y	Y	N	Y	N	Y	N
NEBRASKA							
Hagel	Y	N	Y	N	Y	Y	Y
Kerrey	Y	Y	N	Y	N	N	N
NEVADA							
Bryan	Y	Y	−	Y	N	Y	N
Reid	Y	Y	?	?	N	Y	N

	8	9	10	11	12	13	14
NEW HAMPSHIRE							
Gregg	Y	N	Y	Y	Y	Y	Y
Smith	N	N	Y	N	Y	Y	Y
NEW JERSEY							
Lautenberg	Y	Y	N	Y	N	Y	N
Torricelli	Y	Y	N	Y	N	Y	N
NEW MEXICO							
Domenici	Y	Y	Y	Y	Y	Y	Y
Bingaman	Y	Y	N	Y	N	Y	N
NEW YORK							
D'Amato	N	N	Y	N	Y	Y	Y
Moynihan	Y	Y	N	Y	N	Y	N
NORTH CAROLINA							
Faircloth	N	N	Y	Y	Y	Y	Y
Helms	N	N	Y	N	Y	Y	Y
NORTH DAKOTA							
Conrad	Y	Y	N	Y	N	Y	N
Dorgan	Y	Y	N	Y	N	Y	N
OHIO							
DeWine	Y	Y	Y	Y	Y	Y	Y
Glenn	Y	Y	N	Y	N	Y	N
OKLAHOMA							
Inhofe	N	N	Y	N	Y	Y	Y
Nickles	Y	N	Y	N	Y	Y	Y
OREGON							
Smith	Y	N	Y	N	Y	Y	Y
Wyden	Y	Y	N	Y	N	N	N
PENNSYLVANIA							
Santorum	N	N	Y	Y	Y	Y	Y
Specter	Y	Y	N	?	N	Y	N
RHODE ISLAND							
Chafee	Y	Y	N	Y	Y	Y	Y
Reed	Y	Y	N	Y	N	Y	N
SOUTH CAROLINA							
Thurmond	Y	Y	N	Y	Y	Y	Y
Hollings	Y	Y	N	Y	N	Y	N
SOUTH DAKOTA							
Daschle	Y	Y	N	Y	N	N	N
Johnson	Y	Y	N	Y	N	N	N
TENNESSEE							
Frist	Y	Y	Y	Y	Y	Y	Y
Thompson	Y	Y	Y	N	Y	N	N

	8	9	10	11	12	13	14
TEXAS							
Gramm	N	N	Y	N	Y	N	Y
Hutchison	Y	N	Y	Y	Y	Y	Y
UTAH							
Bennett	Y	Y	N	Y	Y	Y	Y
Hatch	Y	Y	Y	Y	Y	Y	Y
VERMONT							
Jeffords	Y	Y	N	Y	N	Y	N
Leahy	Y	Y	N	Y	N	Y	N
VIRGINIA							
Warner	?	?	?	?	Y	Y	Y
Robb	Y	Y	N	Y	N	N	N
WASHINGTON							
Gorton	Y	Y	Y	Y	Y	Y	Y
Murray	Y	Y	N	Y	N	Y	N
WEST VIRGINIA							
Byrd	Y	Y	N	Y	N	Y	N
Rockefeller	Y	Y	N	Y	N	Y	N
WISCONSIN							
Feingold	Y	Y	N	Y	N	N	N
Kohl	Y	Y	N	Y	N	N	N
WYOMING							
Enzi	N	N	Y	N	Y	Y	Y
Thomas	Y	N	Y	N	Y	Y	Y

Key

- Y Voted for (yea).
- # Paired for.
- + Announced for.
- N Voted against (nay).
- X Paired against.
- − Announced against.
- P Voted "present."
- C Voted "present" to avoid possible conflict of interest.
- ? Did not vote or otherwise make a position known.

Democrats *Republicans*

ND Northern Democrats   SD Southern Democrats

Southern states - Ala., Ark., Fla., Ga., Ky., La., Miss., N.C., Okla., S.C., Tenn., Texas, Va.

8. Satcher Nomination/Cloture. Motion to invoke cloture (thus limiting debate) on the confirmation of President Clinton's nomination of Dr. David Satcher of Tennessee to be U.S. surgeon general and assistant secretary for health in the Department of Health and Human Services. Motion agreed to 75-23: R 31-23; D 44-0 (ND 36-0, SD 8-0). Feb. 10, 1998. Three-fifths of the total Senate (60) is required to invoke cloture.

9. Satcher Nomination/Confirmation. Confirmation of President Clinton's nomination of Dr. David Satcher of Tennessee to be U.S. surgeon general and assistant secretary for health in the Department of Health and Human Services. Confirmed 63-35: R 19-35; D 44-0 (ND 36-0, SD 8-0). Feb. 10, 1998. A "yea" was a vote in support of the president's position.

10. S 1601. Ban Human Cloning/Cloture. Motion to invoke cloture (thus limiting debate) on the motion to proceed to the bill banning creation of a human embryo through cloning. Motion rejected 42-54: R 42-12; D 0-42 (ND 0-34, SD 0-8). Feb. 11, 1998. Three-fifths of the total Senate (60) is required to invoke cloture.

11. Morrow Nomination/Confirmation. Confirmation of President Clinton's nomination of Margaret M. Morrow of California to be U.S. District judge for the central district of California. Confirmed 67-28: R 25-28; D 42-0 (ND 35-0, SD 7-0). Feb. 11, 1998. A "yea" was a vote in support of the president's position.

12. S 1663. Campaign Finance Revisions/Labor Union Dues. McConnell, R-Ky., motion to table (kill) the McCain, R-Ariz., substitute amendment that would revise financing of federal political campaigns. Motion rejected 48-51: R 48-7; D 0-44 (ND 0-36, SD 0-8). Feb. 24, 1998.

13. HR 2631. Military Construction Line-Item Veto Disapproval/Veto Override. Passage, over President Clinton's Nov. 13, 1997, veto, of the bill to disapprove Clinton's line-item vetoes of 38 projects, totaling $287 million, in the fiscal 1998 military construction appropriations bill (HR 2016 - PL 105-45). Passed (thus enacted into law) 78-20: R 46-9; D 32-11 (ND 27-8, SD 5-3). Feb. 25, 1998. A two-thirds majority of those present and voting (66 in this case) of both houses is required to override a veto. A "nay" was a vote in support of the president's position.

14. S 1663. Campaign Finance Revisions/Snowe Amendment. McConnell, R-Ky., motion to table (kill) the Snowe, R-Maine, amendment to the McCain, R-Ariz., substitute amendment that would replace language redefining express advocacy with language to increase certain disclosure requirements and prohibit the use of labor or corporate money to broadcast campaign ads shortly before a primary or general election. Motion rejected 47-50: R 47-8; D 0-42 (ND 0-34, SD 0-8). Feb. 25, 1998. (Subsequently, the Snowe amendment was adopted by voice vote.)

Senate Votes 15, 16, 17, 18, 19, 20, 21

	15	16	17	18	19	20	21
ALABAMA							
Sessions	Y	N	Y	Y	Y	N	N
Shelby	Y	N	Y	?	Y	Y	N
ALASKA							
Murkowski	Y	N	Y	?	Y	Y	Y
Stevens	Y	N	N	Y	Y	Y	Y
ARIZONA							
Kyl	Y	N	Y	Y	Y	N	N
McCain	N	Y	N	Y	Y	C	C
ARKANSAS							
Hutchinson	Y	N	Y	Y	Y	N	N
Bumpers	N	Y	N	Y	N	Y	Y
CALIFORNIA							
Boxer	N	Y	N	?	N	Y	Y
Feinstein	N	Y	N	Y	N	Y	Y
COLORADO							
Allard	Y	N	Y	Y	?	N	N
Campbell	Y	N	N	Y	Y	N	N
CONNECTICUT							
Dodd	N	Y	N	Y	N	Y	Y
Lieberman	N	Y	N	Y	N	Y	Y
DELAWARE							
Roth	Y	N	Y	Y	Y	Y	N
Biden	N	Y	N	?	N	Y	Y
FLORIDA							
Mack	Y	N	Y	Y	Y	N	N
Graham	N	Y	N	Y	N	N	N
GEORGIA							
Coverdell	Y	N	Y	Y	Y	Y	N
Cleland	N	Y	N	?	N	Y	Y
HAWAII							
Akaka	N	Y	N	Y	N	Y	Y
Inouye	?	Y	N	Y	?	#	Y
IDAHO							
Craig	Y	N	Y	Y	Y	N	N
Kempthorne	Y	N	Y	Y	Y	N	N
ILLINOIS							
Durbin	N	Y	N	Y	N	Y	Y
Moseley-Braun	N	Y	N	?	N	Y	Y
INDIANA							
Coats	Y	N	Y	Y	N	Y	Y
Lugar	Y	N	Y	Y	Y	Y	Y
IOWA							
Grassley	Y	N	Y	Y	Y	N	N
Harkin	?	?	?	Y	N	Y	Y
KANSAS							
Brownback	Y	N	Y	Y	Y	N	N
Roberts	Y	N	Y	Y	Y	?	N
KENTUCKY							
McConnell	Y	N	Y	Y	Y	Y	N
Ford	N	Y	N	Y	N	N	N
LOUISIANA							
Breaux	N	Y	N	Y	N	Y	N
Landrieu	N	Y	N	?	N	N	N
MAINE							
Collins	N	Y	N	Y	Y	N	N
Snowe	N	Y	N	?	Y	Y	N
MARYLAND							
Mikulski	N	Y	N	?	N	Y	Y
Sarbanes	N	Y	N	Y	N	Y	Y
MASSACHUSETTS							
Kennedy	N	Y	N	Y	N	Y	Y
Kerry	N	Y	N	?	N	Y	Y
MICHIGAN							
Abraham	Y	N	Y	Y	Y	N	N
Levin	N	Y	N	Y	N	Y	Y
MINNESOTA							
Grams	Y	N	Y	Y	Y	N	N
Wellstone	N	Y	N	Y	N	Y	Y
MISSISSIPPI							
Cochran	Y	N	Y	Y	Y	N	N
Lott	Y	N	Y	Y	Y	N	N
MISSOURI							
Ashcroft	Y	N	Y	Y	Y	N	N
Bond	Y	N	Y	Y	Y	Y	N
MONTANA							
Burns	Y	N	Y	Y	Y	N	N
Baucus	N	Y	Y	N	X	N	
NEBRASKA							
Hagel	Y	N	Y	Y	Y	N	N
Kerrey	N	Y	N	?	N	Y	Y
NEVADA							
Bryan	N	Y	N	Y	N	N	Y
Reid	N	Y	N	Y	N	N	Y
NEW HAMPSHIRE							
Gregg	Y	N	Y	Y	Y	N	N
Smith	Y	N	Y	Y	Y	N	N
NEW JERSEY							
Lautenberg	N	Y	N	Y	N	Y	Y
Torricelli	N	Y	N	Y	N	Y	Y
NEW MEXICO							
Domenici	Y	N	Y	Y	Y	Y	Y
Bingaman	N	Y	N	N	Y	Y	
NEW YORK							
D'Amato	Y	N	N	?	Y	Y	Y
Moynihan	N	Y	N	Y	N	Y	Y
NORTH CAROLINA							
Faircloth	Y	N	Y	?	Y	Y	Y
Helms	Y	N	Y	?	Y	Y	N
NORTH DAKOTA							
Conrad	N	Y	N	Y	N	Y	Y
Dorgan	N	Y	N	?	N	Y	Y
OHIO							
DeWine	Y	N	Y	Y	Y	Y	Y
Glenn	N	Y	N	Y	?	?	Y
OKLAHOMA							
Inhofe	Y	N	Y	?	Y	N	N
Nickles	Y	N	Y	?	Y	N	N
OREGON							
Smith	Y	N	Y	Y	Y	Y	Y
Wyden	N	Y	N	Y	N	Y	Y
PENNSYLVANIA							
Santorum	Y	N	Y	Y	Y	Y	Y
Specter	N	Y	Y	Y	Y	Y	Y
RHODE ISLAND							
Chafee	N	Y	N	Y	Y	Y	Y
Reed	N	Y	N	Y	N	Y	Y
SOUTH CAROLINA							
Thurmond	Y	N	Y	Y	Y	N	N
Hollings	N	Y	N	Y	N	Y	Y
SOUTH DAKOTA							
Daschle	N	Y	N	Y	N	Y	Y
Johnson	N	Y	N	Y	N	Y	Y
TENNESSEE							
Frist	Y	N	Y	Y	Y	Y	N
Thompson	N	Y	N	Y	Y	N	N
TEXAS							
Gramm	Y	N	Y	Y	Y	Y	N
Hutchison	Y	N	Y	Y	Y	Y	N
UTAH							
Bennett	Y	N	Y	?	Y	N	N
Hatch	Y	N	Y	Y	Y	Y	Y
VERMONT							
Jeffords	N	Y	N	Y	Y	?	N
Leahy	N	Y	N	Y	N	Y	N
VIRGINIA							
Warner	Y	N	Y	?	Y	Y	Y
Robb	N	Y	N	Y	N	Y	Y
WASHINGTON							
Gorton	Y	N	Y	Y	Y	Y	Y
Murray	N	Y	N	Y	N	Y	Y
WEST VIRGINIA							
Byrd	N	Y	N	Y	N	Y	Y
Rockefeller	N	Y	N	Y	N	Y	Y
WISCONSIN							
Feingold	N	Y	N	Y	N	N	N
Kohl	N	Y	N	Y	Y	Y	Y
WYOMING							
Enzi	Y	N	Y	Y	Y	N	N
Thomas	Y	N	Y	Y	Y	N	N

ND Northern Democrats   SD Southern Democrats

Southern states - Ala., Ark., Fla., Ga., Ky., La., Miss., N.C., Okla., S.C., Tenn., Texas, Va.

Key

- Y Voted for (yea).
- # Paired for.
- + Announced for.
- N Voted against (nay).
- X Paired against.
- − Announced against.
- P Voted "present."
- C Voted "present" to avoid possible conflict of interest.
- ? Did not vote or otherwise make a position known.

Democrats   Republicans

---

15. S 1663. Campaign Finance Revisions/McCain Substitute. McConnell, R-Ky., motion to table (kill) the McCain, R-Ariz., substitute amendment that would revise financing of federal political campaigns. Motion rejected 48-50: R 48-7; D 0-43 (ND 0-35, SD 0-8). Feb. 25, 1998.

16. S 1663. Campaign Finance Revisions/Cloture. Motion to invoke cloture (thus limiting debate) on the McCain, R-Ariz., substitute amendment that would revise financing of federal political campaigns. Motion rejected 51-48: R 7-48; D 44-0 (ND 36-0, SD 8-0). Feb. 26, 1998. Three-fifths of the total Senate (60) is required to invoke cloture.

17. S 1663. Campaign Finance Revisions/Cloture. Motion to invoke cloture (thus limiting debate) on the bill that would require labor organizations, banks or corporations to secure voluntary authorization from their members before using any membership dues, initiation fees or other payments to fund political activities. Motion rejected 45-54: R 45-10; D 0-44 (ND 0-36, SD 0-8). Feb. 26, 1998. Three-fifths of the total Senate (60) is required to invoke cloture.

18. Young Nomination/Confirmation. Confirmation of President Clinton's nomination of Richard L. Young of Indiana to be U.S. District judge for the Southern District of Indiana. Confirmed 81-0: R 45-0; D 36-0 (ND 30-0, SD 6-0). March 2, 1998. A "yea" was a vote in support of the president's position.

19. S 1173. Highway and Transit Reauthorization/Welfare Report. Chafee, R-R.I., motion to table (kill) the Wellstone, D-Minn., amendment to the Senate Environment and Public Works Committee substitute amendment. The Wellstone amendment would require the Health and Human Services Department to report on former welfare recipients' ability to achieve self-sufficiency. Motion Agreed to 54-43: R 53-1; D 1-42 (ND 1-34, SD 0-8). March 3, 1998.

20. S 1173. Highway and Transit Reauthorization/National Blood Alcohol Level. Lautenberg, D-N.J., amendment to the Senate Environment and Public Works Committee substitute amendment. The Lautenberg amendment would establish a national standard to prohibit driving by individuals with a blood-alcohol content of 0.08 percent or greater. Adopted 62-32: R 26-26; D 36-6 (ND 31-3, SD 5-3). March 4, 1998. A "yea" was a vote in support of the president's position.

21. S 1173. Highway and Transit Reauthorization/Open Container Ban. Dorgan, D-N.D., amendment to the Senate Environment and Public Works Committee substitute amendment that would establish a nationwide ban on having an open container of alcohol in a moving vehicle. Adopted 52-47: R 14-40; D 38-7 (ND 34-3, SD 4-4). March 5, 1998.

Senate Votes 22, 23, 24, 25, 26, 27, 28

	22	23	24	25	26	27	28
ALABAMA							
Sessions	N	N	Y	Y	?	?	Y
Shelby	N	N	Y	Y	?	?	Y
ALASKA							
Murkowski	N	Y	Y	Y	N	Y	Y
Stevens	N	Y	Y	Y	N	Y	Y
ARIZONA							
Kyl	N	N	Y	Y	Y	N	N
McCain	C	Y	Y	Y	Y	N	N
ARKANSAS							
Hutchinson	N	N	Y	Y	Y	N	Y
Bumpers	Y	Y	Y	Y	N	Y	Y
CALIFORNIA							
Boxer	Y	Y	?	Y	N	Y	Y
Feinstein	Y	Y	Y	Y	N	Y	Y
COLORADO							
Allard	N	N	Y	Y	N	Y	Y
Campbell	N	Y	Y	Y	N	Y	Y
CONNECTICUT							
Dodd	Y	Y	Y	Y	N	Y	Y
Lieberman	Y	Y	Y	Y	N	N	Y
DELAWARE							
Roth	N	Y	Y	Y	N	Y	Y
Biden	Y	Y	Y	Y	N	Y	Y
FLORIDA							
Mack	N	N	Y	Y	Y	Y	Y
Graham	N	Y	Y	Y	Y	Y	Y
GEORGIA							
Coverdell	N	N	Y	Y	Y	N	Y
Cleland	Y	Y	N	Y	N	Y	Y
HAWAII							
Akaka	Y	Y	Y	Y	N	Y	Y
Inouye	Y	Y	Y	Y	N	Y	Y
IDAHO							
Craig	N	N	Y	Y	N	Y	Y
Kempthorne	N	Y	Y	Y	N	Y	Y
ILLINOIS							
Durbin	Y	Y	?	Y	N	Y	Y
Moseley-Braun	Y	Y	Y	Y	N	Y	Y
INDIANA							
Coats	Y	?	?	Y	Y	Y	Y
Lugar	Y	N	Y	Y	Y	Y	Y

	22	23	24	25	26	27	28
IOWA							
Grassley	N	N	Y	Y	N	Y	Y
Harkin	Y	Y	Y	Y	N	Y	Y
KANSAS							
Brownback	N	N	Y	Y	Y	Y	Y
Roberts	N	N	Y	Y	N	Y	Y
KENTUCKY							
McConnell	N	N	Y	Y	Y	Y	Y
Ford	N	Y	Y	Y	N	Y	Y
LOUISIANA							
Breaux	N	Y	Y	Y	N	Y	Y
Landrieu	N	Y	Y	Y	N	Y	Y
MAINE							
Collins	N	Y	Y	Y	N	N	Y
Snowe	N	Y	Y	Y	N	N	Y
MARYLAND							
Mikulski	Y	Y	Y	Y	N	Y	Y
Sarbanes	Y	Y	Y	Y	N	Y	Y
MASSACHUSETTS							
Kennedy	Y	Y	Y	Y	N	?	?
Kerry	Y	Y	Y	Y	N	Y	Y
MICHIGAN							
Abraham	N	N	Y	Y	Y	Y	Y
Levin	Y	Y	Y	Y	Y	Y	Y
MINNESOTA							
Grams	N	N	Y	Y	Y	N	Y
Wellstone	Y	Y	Y	Y	N	Y	Y
MISSISSIPPI							
Cochran	N	N	Y	Y	N	Y	Y
Lott	N	N	Y	Y	N	Y	Y
MISSOURI							
Ashcroft	N	N	Y	Y	Y	N	Y
Bond	N	Y	Y	Y	N	Y	Y
MONTANA							
Burns	N	N	Y	Y	N	Y	Y
Baucus	N	Y	Y	Y	N	Y	Y
NEBRASKA							
Hagel	N	N	Y	Y	Y	N	Y
Kerrey	Y	Y	Y	Y	N	Y	Y
NEVADA							
Bryan	N	Y	Y	Y	N	Y	Y
Reid	N	Y	Y	Y	N	Y	Y

	22	23	24	25	26	27	28
NEW HAMPSHIRE							
Gregg	N	N	Y	N	N	N	Y
Smith	N	N	Y	N	Y	N	Y
NEW JERSEY							
Lautenberg	Y	Y	Y	Y	N	N	Y
Torricelli	Y	Y	Y	Y	N	Y	Y
NEW MEXICO							
Domenici	Y	Y	Y	Y	N	Y	Y
Bingaman	Y	Y	Y	Y	N	Y	Y
NEW YORK							
D'Amato	Y	Y	Y	Y	N	Y	Y
Moynihan	Y	Y	Y	Y	N	Y	Y
NORTH CAROLINA							
Faircloth	N	N	Y	Y	N	Y	Y
Helms	N	?	Y	N	N	Y	Y
NORTH DAKOTA							
Conrad	Y	Y	Y	Y	N	Y	Y
Dorgan	Y	Y	Y	Y	N	Y	Y
OHIO							
DeWine	Y	N	Y	Y	N	Y	Y
Glenn	Y	?	?	Y	N	Y	Y
OKLAHOMA							
Inhofe	N	N	Y	Y	Y	N	Y
Nickles	N	N	Y	N	Y	N	Y
OREGON							
Smith	Y	N	Y	Y	N	Y	Y
Wyden	Y	Y	?	Y	N	N	Y
PENNSYLVANIA							
Santorum	N	N	Y	Y	N	N	Y
Specter	Y	Y	Y	Y	N	N	N
RHODE ISLAND							
Chafee	N	Y	Y	Y	N	Y	Y
Reed	N	Y	Y	Y	N	Y	Y
SOUTH CAROLINA							
Thurmond	N	N	Y	Y	N	Y	Y
Hollings	Y	N	Y	Y	N	Y	Y
SOUTH DAKOTA							
Daschle	Y	Y	Y	Y	N	Y	Y
Johnson	Y	Y	Y	Y	N	Y	Y
TENNESSEE							
Frist	N	N	Y	Y	N	N	Y
Thompson	N	N	Y	Y	N	Y	Y

Key

Y	Voted for (yea).
#	Paired for.
+	Announced for.
N	Voted against (nay).
X	Paired against.
-	Announced against.
P	Voted "present."
C	Voted "present" to avoid possible conflict of interest.
?	Did not vote or otherwise make a position known.

Democrats   **Republicans**

	22	23	24	25	26	27	28
TEXAS							
Gramm	N	N	Y	Y	N	Y	Y
Hutchison	N	?	Y	Y	Y	N	Y
UTAH							
Bennett	N	?	Y	Y	N	Y	Y
Hatch	Y	N	Y	Y	N	Y	Y
VERMONT							
Jeffords	N	Y	Y	Y	N	Y	Y
Leahy	N	Y	?	Y	N	N	Y
VIRGINIA							
Warner	Y	Y	Y	Y	N	N	Y
Robb	Y	Y	Y	Y	N	N	Y
WASHINGTON							
Gorton	N	N	Y	N	N	N	Y
Murray	Y	Y	Y	Y	N	Y	Y
WEST VIRGINIA							
Byrd	Y	Y	Y	Y	N	N	Y
Rockefeller	Y	Y	Y	Y	N	N	Y
WISCONSIN							
Feingold	N	Y	Y	Y	N	Y	Y
Kohl	N	Y	Y	Y	N	Y	Y
WYOMING							
Enzi	N	N	Y	Y	N	N	Y
Thomas	N	N	Y	Y	N	Y	Y

ND Northern Democrats   SD Southern Democrats

Southern states - Ala., Ark., Fla., Ga., Ky., La., Miss., N.C., Okla., S.C., Tenn., Texas, Va.

22. S 1173. Highway and Transit Reauthorization/Drive-Through Liquor Sales. Bingaman, D-N.M., amendment to the Senate Environment and Public Works Committee substitute amendment that would establish a national ban on drive-through alcohol sales. Rejected 43-56: R 9-45; D 34-11 (ND 30-7, SD 4-4). March 5, 1998.

23. S 1173. Highway and Transit Reauthorization/Minority Construction Set-Asides. Chafee, R-R.I., motion to table (kill) the McConnell, R-Ky., amendment to the Senate Environment and Public Works Committee substitute amendment that would eliminate a program to reserve a portion of construction funds for disadvantaged business enterprises. Motion agreed to 58-37: R 15-36; D 43-1 (ND 36-0, SD 7-1). March 6, 1998. A "yea" was a vote in support of the president's position.

24. S 1668. Whistleblower Protection/Passage. Passage of the bill to allow government employees in the intelligence community to disclose to members of Congress evidence of possible misconduct at federal intelligence agencies. Passed 93-1: R 54-0; D 39-1 (ND 32-0, SD 7-1). March 9, 1998. A "nay" was a vote in support of the president's position.

25. S 1173. Highway and Transit Reauthorization/Mass Transit Funding. D'Amato, R-N.Y., amendment to the Senate Environment and Public Works Committee substitute amendment that would authorize $41.3 billion over fiscal 1998-2003 for mass transit programs. Adopted 96-4: R 51-4; D 45-0 (ND 37-0, SD 8-0). March 10, 1998.

26. S 1173. Highway and Transit Reauthorization/Gas Tax. Mack, R-Fla., motion to waive the Budget Act with respect to the Warner, R-Va., point of order against the Mack amendment to the Roth, R-Del., amendment to the Senate Environment and Public Works Committee substitute amendment. The Mack amendment would eliminate the 4.3-cent tax on transportation fuels. Motion rejected 18-80: R 16-37; D 2-43 (ND 1-36, SD 1-7). March 11, 1998. A three-fifths majority vote (60) of the total Senate is required to waive the Budget Act. (Subsequently, the chair upheld the point of order, and the amendment fell.)

27. S 1173. Highway and Transit Reauthorization/Ethanol Tax Break. Lott, R-Miss., motion to table (kill) the McCain, R-Ariz., amendment to the Roth, R-Del., amendment to the Senate Environment and Public Works Committee substitute amendment. The McCain amendment would remove language in the Roth amendment that would extend an ethanol tax break from 2000 to 2007. Motion agreed to 71-26: R 35-18; D 36-8 (ND 29-7, SD 7-1). March 11, 1998.

28. S 1173. Highway and Transit Reauthorization/Cloture. Motion to invoke cloture (thus limiting debate) on the Senate Environment and Public Works Committee substitute amendment which would authorize $214.3 billion over fiscal years 1998-2003 for transportation funding. Motion agreed to 96-3: R 52-3; D 44-0 (ND 36-0, SD 8-0). March 11, 1998. Three-fifths of the total Senate (60) is required to invoke cloture.

Senate Votes 29, 30, 31, 32, 33, 34, 35

	29	30	31	32	33	34	35
ALABAMA							
Sessions	Y	Y	Y	Y	Y	Y	Y
Shelby	N	Y	Y	Y	Y	Y	Y
ALASKA							
Murkowski	Y	Y	Y	Y	Y	Y	Y
Stevens	Y	Y	N	Y	Y	Y	Y
ARIZONA							
Kyl	Y	Y	Y	?	Y	Y	Y
McCain	Y	Y	Y	?	Y	Y	Y
ARKANSAS							
Hutchinson	Y	Y	Y	Y	Y	Y	Y
Bumpers	Y	Y	Y	Y	Y	Y	Y
CALIFORNIA							
Boxer	N	Y	Y	Y	Y	Y	Y
Feinstein	N	Y	Y	Y	Y	Y	Y
COLORADO							
Allard	Y	Y	Y	Y	Y	Y	Y
Campbell	N	Y	Y	Y	Y	Y	Y
CONNECTICUT							
Dodd	Y	Y	Y	Y	Y	Y	Y
Lieberman	Y	Y	Y	Y	Y	Y	Y
DELAWARE							
Roth	Y	Y	Y	Y	Y	Y	Y
Biden	Y	Y	Y	Y	Y	Y	Y
FLORIDA							
Mack	Y	Y	Y	Y	Y	Y	Y
Graham	Y	Y	Y	Y	Y	Y	Y
GEORGIA							
Coverdell	Y	Y	Y	Y	Y	Y	Y
Cleland	Y	Y	Y	Y	Y	N	Y
HAWAII							
Akaka	Y	Y	Y	Y	Y	N	Y
Inouye	Y	Y	Y	?	?	?	?
IDAHO							
Craig	Y	Y	Y	Y	Y	Y	Y
Kempthorne	Y	Y	Y	Y	Y	Y	Y
ILLINOIS							
Durbin	N	Y	Y	Y	Y	N	Y
Moseley-Braun	Y	Y	Y	?	N	Y	Y
INDIANA							
Coats	Y	Y	Y	Y	Y	Y	Y
Lugar	Y	Y	Y	Y	Y	Y	Y
IOWA							
Grassley	Y	Y	Y	Y	Y	Y	Y
Harkin	N	Y	Y	Y	Y	N	Y
KANSAS							
Brownback	Y	Y	Y	Y	Y	Y	Y
Roberts	Y	Y	Y	Y	Y	Y	Y
KENTUCKY							
McConnell	Y	Y	Y	Y	Y	Y	Y
Ford	N	Y	Y	Y	Y	N	Y
LOUISIANA							
Breaux	Y	Y	Y	Y	Y	Y	Y
Landrieu	Y	Y	Y	Y	Y	N	Y
MAINE							
Collins	Y	Y	Y	Y	Y	Y	Y
Snowe	Y	Y	Y	Y	Y	Y	Y
MARYLAND							
Mikulski	N	Y	Y	?	Y	N	Y
Sarbanes	N	Y	Y	Y	Y	N	Y
MASSACHUSETTS							
Kennedy	N	Y	Y	Y	Y	N	Y
Kerry	N	Y	Y	Y	?	Y	Y
MICHIGAN							
Abraham	Y	Y	Y	Y	Y	Y	Y
Levin	Y	Y	Y	Y	Y	N	Y
MINNESOTA							
Grams	Y	Y	N	Y	Y	Y	Y
Wellstone	N	Y	Y	Y	Y	N	Y
MISSISSIPPI							
Cochran	Y	Y	Y	Y	Y	Y	Y
Lott	Y	Y	Y	Y	Y	Y	Y
MISSOURI							
Ashcroft	Y	Y	Y	Y	Y	Y	Y
Bond	Y	Y	Y	Y	Y	Y	Y
MONTANA							
Burns	Y	Y	Y	Y	Y	Y	Y
Baucus	Y	Y	Y	Y	Y	N	Y
NEBRASKA							
Hagel	Y	Y	Y	Y	Y	Y	Y
Kerrey	Y	Y	Y	Y	Y	N	Y
NEVADA							
Bryan	N	Y	Y	Y	Y	Y	Y
Reid	N	Y	Y	Y	Y	N	Y
NEW HAMPSHIRE							
Gregg	Y	Y	Y	Y	Y	Y	Y
Smith	Y	Y	Y	Y	Y	Y	Y
NEW JERSEY							
Lautenberg	N	Y	Y	Y	Y	N	Y
Torricelli	N	Y	Y	Y	?	Y	Y
NEW MEXICO							
Domenici	Y	Y	Y	Y	Y	Y	Y
Bingaman	Y	Y	Y	Y	Y	N	Y
NEW YORK							
D'Amato	Y	Y	Y	Y	Y	Y	Y
Moynihan	Y	Y	Y	Y	Y	Y	Y
NORTH CAROLINA							
Faircloth	Y	Y	+	?	Y	Y	
Helms	Y	Y	Y	Y	Y	Y	Y
NORTH DAKOTA							
Conrad	Y	Y	Y	Y	Y	?	Y
Dorgan	Y	Y	Y	Y	Y	Y	Y
OHIO							
DeWine	Y	Y	Y	Y	Y	Y	Y
Glenn	Y	Y	N	Y	Y	N	Y
OKLAHOMA							
Inhofe	Y	Y	Y	?	?	Y	Y
Nickles	Y	Y	Y	Y	Y	Y	Y
OREGON							
Smith	Y	Y	Y	Y	?	Y	Y
Wyden	Y	Y	Y	Y	?	N	Y
PENNSYLVANIA							
Santorum	N	N	Y	Y	Y	Y	Y
Specter	N	N	Y	Y	Y	Y	Y
RHODE ISLAND							
Chafee	Y	Y	N	Y	Y	Y	Y
Reed	Y	Y	Y	Y	Y	N	Y
SOUTH CAROLINA							
Thurmond	Y	Y	N	Y	Y	Y	Y
Hollings	N	Y	Y	Y	Y	N	Y
SOUTH DAKOTA							
Daschle	Y	Y	Y	Y	Y	Y	Y
Johnson	Y	Y	Y	Y	Y	Y	Y
TENNESSEE							
Frist	Y	Y	Y	Y	Y	Y	Y
Thompson	Y	Y	Y	Y	Y	Y	Y
TEXAS							
Gramm	Y	Y	Y	Y	?	Y	Y
Hutchison	Y	Y	Y	Y	Y	Y	Y
UTAH							
Bennett	Y	Y	Y	Y	Y	Y	Y
Hatch	Y	Y	Y	Y	Y	Y	Y
VERMONT							
Jeffords	N	Y	Y	?	Y	Y	Y
Leahy	N	Y	Y	Y	Y	Y	Y
VIRGINIA							
Warner	Y	Y	Y	Y	Y	Y	Y
Robb	Y	Y	Y	Y	Y	Y	Y
WASHINGTON							
Gorton	Y	Y	Y	Y	Y	Y	Y
Murray	Y	Y	Y	Y	Y	N	Y
WEST VIRGINIA							
Byrd	N	Y	Y	Y	Y	Y	Y
Rockefeller	Y	Y	Y	Y	Y	Y	+
WISCONSIN							
Feingold	Y	N	Y	Y	Y	N	Y
Kohl	Y	N	Y	Y	Y	N	Y
WYOMING							
Enzi	Y	Y	Y	?	Y	Y	Y
Thomas	Y	Y	Y	Y	Y	Y	Y

Key

- **Y** Voted for (yea).
- **#** Paired for.
- **+** Announced for.
- **N** Voted against (nay).
- **X** Paired against.
- **−** Announced against.
- **P** Voted "present."
- **C** Voted "present" to avoid possible conflict of interest.
- **?** Did not vote or otherwise make a position known.

Democrats   **Republicans**

ND Northern Democrats   SD Southern Democrats

Southern states - Ala., Ark., Fla., Ga., Ky., La., Miss., N.C., Okla., S.C., Tenn., Texas, Va.

---

29. S 1173. Highway and Transit Reauthorization/Demonstration Projects. McCain, R-Ariz., amendment to the Senate Environment and Public Works Committee substitute amendment. The McCain amendment would require that funding for future demonstration projects be taken from a state's annual highway funding allocation, not the highway trust fund. Adopted 78-22: R 50-5; D 28-17 (ND 22-15, SD 6-2). March 12, 1998.

30. S 1173. Highway and Transit Reauthorization/Environment Committee Substitute. Senate Environment and Public Works Committee substitute amendment that would authorize $214.3 billion over fiscal years 1998-2003 for transportation programs. The amendment would authorize $41.3 billion of the six-year total for mass transit programs. Adopted 96-4: R 53-2; D 43-2 (ND 35-2, SD 8-0). March 12, 1998. (Subsequently, the Senate passed the underlying bill by voice vote. But the Senate held the bill at the desk pending receipt of the House version.)

31. S Res 187. China Human Rights/Adoption. Adoption of the resolution to urge President Clinton to push for passage of a measure criticizing China for human rights abuses when the U.N. Commission on Human Rights meets the week of March 16, in Geneva. Adopted 95-5: R 51-4; D 44-1 (ND 36-1, SD 8-0). March 12, 1998.

32. S Con Res 78. Saddam Hussein as War Criminal/Adoption. Adoption of the resolution to express the sense of Congress that the president should call for a U.N. tribunal to try Iraqi President Saddam Hussein as a war criminal. Adopted 93-0: R 49-0; D 44-0 (ND 36-0, SD 8-0). March 13, 1998.

33. Fogel Nomination/Confirmation. Confirmation of President Clinton's nomination of Jeremy D. Fogel of California to be U.S. District judge for the Northern District of California. Confirmed 90-0: R 51-0; D 39-0 (ND 31-0, SD 8-0). March 16, 1998. A "yea" was a vote in support of the president's position.

34. HR 2646. Expanding Education Savings Accounts/Cloture. Motion to invoke cloture (thus limiting debate) on the motion to proceed to the bill to allow parents, relatives or outside corporations to contribute up to a combined total of $2,000 a year of after-tax funds in tax-free savings accounts designated for educational expenses. Motion agreed to 74-24: R 55-0; D 19-24 (ND 15-20, SD 4-4). March 17, 1998. Three-fifths of the total Senate (60) is required to invoke cloture.

35. Graber Nomination/Confirmation. Confirmation of President Clinton's nomination of Susan Graber of Oregon to be judge for the 9th U.S. Circuit Court of Appeals. Confirmed 98-0: R 55-0; D 43-0 (ND 35-0, SD 8-0). March 17, 1998. A "yea" was a vote in support of the president's position.

Senate Votes 36, 37, 38, 39, 40, 41, 42

	36	37	38	39	40	41	42
ALABAMA							
Sessions	Y	Y	Y	Y	N	Y	N
Shelby	Y	Y	Y	Y	Y	Y	Y
ALASKA							
Murkowski	Y	Y	Y	Y	Y	Y	N
Stevens	Y	Y	Y	Y	Y	Y	Y
ARIZONA							
Kyl	Y	Y	Y	N	N	Y	N
McCain	Y	Y	Y	N	N	Y	N
ARKANSAS							
Hutchinson	Y	Y	Y	N	N	Y	N
Bumpers	N	Y	N	Y	Y	Y	Y
CALIFORNIA							
Boxer	N	Y	N	Y	Y	Y	Y
Feinstein	N	Y	N	N	Y	Y	Y
COLORADO							
Allard	Y	Y	Y	N	N	Y	N
Campbell	Y	Y	Y	Y	Y	Y	Y
CONNECTICUT							
Dodd	N	Y	N	Y	Y	Y	Y
Lieberman	N	Y	N	Y	Y	Y	Y
DELAWARE							
Roth	Y	Y	Y	N	Y	Y	?
Biden	N	Y	N	?	Y	Y	Y
FLORIDA							
Mack	Y	+	Y	N	Y	Y	Y
Graham	N	Y	N	N	Y	Y	Y
GEORGIA							
Coverdell	Y	Y	Y	Y	Y	Y	Y
Cleland	N	Y	N	Y	Y	Y	Y
HAWAII							
Akaka	N	Y	N	Y	Y	Y	Y
Inouye	?	?	N	Y	Y	Y	Y
IDAHO							
Craig	Y	Y	Y	Y	Y	Y	N
Kempthorne	Y	Y	Y	N	Y	Y	N
ILLINOIS							
Durbin	N	Y	N	Y	Y	Y	Y
Moseley-Braun	N	Y	–	N	Y	Y	Y
INDIANA							
Coats	Y	Y	Y	N	N	Y	N
Lugar	Y	Y	Y	N	Y	Y	Y

	36	37	38	39	40	41	42
IOWA							
Grassley	Y	Y	Y	Y	Y	N	Y
Harkin	N	Y	N	Y	Y	Y	Y
KANSAS							
Brownback	Y	Y	Y	N	N	N	N
Roberts	Y	Y	Y	Y	Y	Y	Y
KENTUCKY							
McConnell	Y	Y	Y	Y	Y	Y	Y
Ford	N	Y	N	Y	Y	Y	Y
LOUISIANA							
Breaux	N	Y	N	Y	Y	Y	Y
Landrieu	N	Y	N	?	Y	Y	Y
MAINE							
Collins	Y	Y	Y	Y	Y	Y	Y
Snowe	Y	Y	Y	Y	Y	Y	Y
MARYLAND							
Mikulski	N	Y	N	?	Y	Y	Y
Sarbanes	N	Y	N	Y	Y	Y	Y
MASSACHUSETTS							
Kennedy	N	Y	N	Y	Y	Y	Y
Kerry	N	Y	N	N	Y	Y	Y
MICHIGAN							
Abraham	Y	Y	Y	N	N	Y	N
Levin	N	Y	N	N	Y	Y	Y
MINNESOTA							
Grams	Y	Y	Y	N	N	Y	N
Wellstone	N	Y	N	Y	Y	Y	Y
MISSISSIPPI							
Cochran	Y	Y	Y	Y	Y	Y	Y
Lott	Y	Y	Y	Y	Y	Y	Y
MISSOURI							
Ashcroft	Y	Y	Y	N	N	N	N
Bond	Y	Y	Y	?	Y	Y	Y
MONTANA							
Burns	Y	Y	Y	Y	Y	Y	N
Baucus	N	Y	N	Y	Y	Y	Y
NEBRASKA							
Hagel	Y	Y	Y	Y	Y	Y	N
Kerrey	N	Y	N	–	Y	Y	Y
NEVADA							
Bryan	N	Y	N	N	Y	Y	Y
Reid	N	Y	N	Y	Y	Y	Y

	36	37	38	39	40	41	42
NEW HAMPSHIRE							
Gregg	Y	Y	Y	N	Y	Y	N
Smith	Y	Y	Y	N	N	Y	N
NEW JERSEY							
Lautenberg	N	Y	N	Y	Y	Y	Y
Torricelli	N	Y	N	Y	Y	Y	Y
NEW MEXICO							
Domenici	Y	Y	Y	Y	Y	Y	Y
Bingaman	N	Y	N	Y	Y	Y	Y
NEW YORK							
D'Amato	Y	Y	Y	?	Y	Y	Y
Moynihan	N	Y	N	Y	Y	Y	Y
NORTH CAROLINA							
Faircloth	Y	Y	Y	N	N	Y	N
Helms	Y	Y	Y	N	Y	N	N
NORTH DAKOTA							
Conrad	N	Y	N	Y	Y	Y	Y
Dorgan	N	Y	N	Y	Y	Y	Y
OHIO							
DeWine	Y	Y	Y	N	Y	Y	N
Glenn	N	Y	N	N	Y	Y	Y
OKLAHOMA							
Inhofe	Y	Y	Y	?	N	Y	N
Nickles	Y	Y	Y	N	N	N	N
OREGON							
Smith	Y	Y	Y	Y	Y	Y	Y
Wyden	N	Y	N	?	Y	Y	Y
PENNSYLVANIA							
Santorum	Y	Y	Y	N	N	Y	N
Specter	Y	Y	Y	Y	Y	Y	Y
RHODE ISLAND							
Chafee	Y	Y	Y	Y	Y	Y	Y
Reed	N	Y	N	Y	Y	Y	Y
SOUTH CAROLINA							
Thurmond	Y	Y	Y	Y	Y	Y	N
Hollings	N	Y	N	Y	Y	Y	Y
SOUTH DAKOTA							
Daschle	N	Y	N	Y	Y	Y	Y
Johnson	N	Y	N	Y	N	Y	N
TENNESSEE							
Frist	Y	Y	Y	Y	Y	Y	Y
Thompson	Y	Y	Y	N	Y	Y	N

	36	37	38	39	40	41	42
TEXAS							
Gramm	Y	Y	Y	N	N	N	N
Hutchison	Y	Y	Y	Y	N	Y	N
UTAH							
Bennett	Y	Y	Y	Y	Y	Y	Y
Hatch	Y	Y	Y	Y	Y	Y	N
VERMONT							
Jeffords	Y	Y	Y	Y	Y	Y	Y
Leahy	N	Y	N	Y	Y	Y	Y
VIRGINIA							
Warner	Y	Y	Y	Y	Y	Y	Y
Robb	N	Y	N	N	N	Y	N
WASHINGTON							
Gorton	Y	Y	Y	Y	Y	Y	Y
Murray	N	Y	N	Y	Y	Y	Y
WEST VIRGINIA							
Byrd	N	Y	N	Y	Y	Y	Y
Rockefeller	N	Y	N	Y	Y	Y	Y
WISCONSIN							
Feingold	N	Y	N	N	N	N	N
Kohl	N	Y	N	N	N	N	N
WYOMING							
Enzi	Y	Y	Y	N	Y	Y	N
Thomas	Y	Y	Y	N	Y	Y	N

Key

- **Y** Voted for (yea).
- **#** Paired for.
- **+** Announced for.
- **N** Voted against (nay).
- **X** Paired against.
- **–** Announced against.
- **P** Voted "present."
- **C** Voted "present" to avoid possible conflict of interest.
- **?** Did not vote or otherwise make a position known.

Democrats • Republicans

ND Northern Democrats   SD Southern Democrats

Southern states - Ala., Ark., Fla., Ga., Ky., La., Miss., N.C., Okla., S.C., Tenn., Texas, Va.

---

36. NATO Expansion/Motion to Proceed. Motion to proceed to the protocol (Treaty Doc. 105-36) revising the 1949 North Atlantic Treaty to admit Poland, Hungary and the Czech Republic into the North Atlantic Treaty Organization (NATO). Motion agreed to 55-44: R 55-0; D 0-44 (ND 0-36, SD 0-8). March 18, 1998.

37. Violence in Kosovo/Adoption. Adoption of the concurrent resolution to express the sense of Congress that the United States should condemn the Serbian government for human rights abuses and violence against the Albanian population in Kosovo and that the United States should demand that human rights monitors be allowed to return to Kosovo. Adopted 98-0: R 54-0; D 44-0 (ND 36-0, SD 8-0). March 18, 1998.

38. HR 2646. Expanding Education Savings Accounts/Cloture. Motion to invoke cloture (thus limiting debate) on the bill to allow parents, relatives or outside corporations to contribute up to a combined total of $2,000 a year of after-tax funds in tax-free savings accounts designated for educational expenses. Motion rejected 55-44: R 55-0; D 0-44 (ND 0-36, SD 0-8). March 19, 1998. Three-fifths of the total Senate (60) is required to invoke cloture.

39. S 1768. Fiscal 1998 Supplemental Appropriations/Spending Reductions. Stevens, R-Alaska, motion to table (kill) the McCain, R-Ariz., amendment to cut $78 million in unrequested projects from the overall amount provided by the bill. The amendment would strike $33 million by eliminating funding for levee and waterway repairs in Alabama and Mississippi. Motion agreed to 61-31: R 32-20; D 29-11 (ND 24-9, SD 5-2). March 23, 1998.

40. S 1768. Fiscal 1998 Supplemental Appropriations/Spending Offsets. Stevens, R-Alaska, motion to table (kill) the Gramm, R-Texas, amendment that would require that only that portion of spending in the bill that is obligated in fiscal 1998 be designated as emergency spending exempt from budgetary and spending caps. Motion agreed to 76-24: R 34-21; D 42-3 (ND 35-2, SD 7-1). March 24, 1998.

41. S 1768. Fiscal 1998 Supplemental Appropriations/Bosnia Spending Offsets. Stevens, R-Alaska, motion to table (kill) the Feingold, D-Wis., amendment that would remove the "emergency" designation from the provision providing about $400 million for troop deployments in Bosnia. The effect of the amendment would be to require reductions in other Pentagon programs to comply with discretionary spending caps. Motion agreed to 92-8: R 50-5; D 42-3 (ND 34-3, SD 8-0). March 25, 1998.

42. S 1768. Fiscal 1998 Supplemental Appropriations/FEMA Spending Offsets. Bond, R-Mo., motion to table (kill) the Nickles, R-Okla., amendment to the Bond amendment. The Nickles amendment would remove the "emergency" designation from all funds provided to the Federal Emergency Management Agency under the Bond amendment that are to be spent in future fiscal years. The effect would be to require reductions in other domestic programs to comply with discretionary spending caps. The Bond amendment would allocate $1.6 billion to FEMA for disaster relief programs. Motion agreed to 68-31: R 26-28; D 42-3 (ND 35-2, SD 7-1). March 25, 1998. (Subsequently, the Bond amendment was adopted by voice vote.)

Senate Votes 43, 44, 45, 46, 47, 48, 49

	43	44	45	46	47	48	49
ALABAMA							
Sessions	Y	N	Y	Y	Y	Y	Y
Shelby	Y	Y	Y	Y	Y	Y	Y
ALASKA							
Murkowski	Y	Y	Y	Y	Y	Y	Y
Stevens	Y	Y	Y	Y	Y	Y	Y
ARIZONA							
Kyl	Y	N	Y	Y	N	N	Y
McCain	Y	Y	Y	Y	N	Y	Y
ARKANSAS							
Hutchinson	Y	Y	Y	Y	Y	?	Y
Bumpers	Y	Y	N	N	N	Y	Y
CALIFORNIA							
Boxer	Y	Y	N	N	Y	Y	Y
Feinstein	N	Y	N	N	Y	Y	Y
COLORADO							
Allard	Y	N	Y	Y	Y	N	Y
Campbell	Y	N	Y	Y	N	Y	Y
CONNECTICUT							
Dodd	N	Y	N	N	N	Y	Y
Lieberman	Y	Y	N	Y	N	Y	Y
DELAWARE							
Roth	Y	Y	Y	Y	N	Y	Y
Biden	Y	Y	N	N	N	Y	Y
FLORIDA							
Mack	Y	N	Y	Y	N	Y	Y
Graham	Y	Y	N	N	N	Y	Y
GEORGIA							
Coverdell	Y	N	Y	Y	Y	Y	Y
Cleland	Y	Y	N	N	N	Y	Y
HAWAII							
Akaka	Y	Y	N	N	N	Y	Y
Inouye	Y	Y	N	N	N	Y	Y
IDAHO							
Craig	Y	Y	Y	Y	Y	Y	Y
Kempthorne	Y	Y	Y	Y	Y	Y	Y
ILLINOIS							
Durbin	Y	Y	N	N	Y	Y	Y
Moseley-Braun	Y	Y	N	N	Y	Y	Y
INDIANA							
Coats	Y	Y	Y	Y	Y	N	Y
Lugar	Y	Y	Y	Y	N	Y	Y
IOWA							
Grassley	Y	Y	Y	Y	N	N	Y
Harkin	Y	Y	N	N	Y	Y	Y
KANSAS							
Brownback	Y	Y	Y	Y	Y	Y	Y
Roberts	Y	Y	Y	Y	N	Y	Y
KENTUCKY							
McConnell	Y	Y	Y	Y	Y	N	Y
Ford	Y	Y	N	N	N	Y	Y
LOUISIANA							
Breaux	Y	Y	N	Y	N	Y	Y
Landrieu	Y	Y	N	N	N	Y	Y
MAINE							
Collins	Y	Y	Y	Y	Y	Y	Y
Snowe	Y	Y	Y	Y	Y	Y	Y
MARYLAND							
Mikulski	Y	Y	N	N	N	Y	?
Sarbanes	N	Y	N	N	N	Y	Y
MASSACHUSETTS							
Kennedy	N	Y	N	N	N	Y	Y
Kerry	N	Y	N	N	N	?	Y
MICHIGAN							
Abraham	Y	N	Y	Y	Y	N	Y
Levin	Y	Y	N	N	N	Y	Y
MINNESOTA							
Grams	Y	Y	Y	Y	Y	Y	Y
Wellstone	N	N	N	N	N	Y	Y
MISSISSIPPI							
Cochran	Y	Y	Y	Y	Y	Y	Y
Lott	Y	Y	Y	Y	N	Y	Y
MISSOURI							
Ashcroft	Y	N	Y	Y	Y	N	Y
Bond	Y	Y	N	Y	Y	Y	Y
MONTANA							
Burns	Y	Y	Y	Y	N	Y	Y
Baucus	Y	Y	N	N	N	Y	Y
NEBRASKA							
Hagel	Y	Y	Y	Y	N	Y	Y
Kerrey	Y	Y	N	N	N	Y	Y
NEVADA							
Bryan	Y	Y	N	N	N	Y	Y
Reid	Y	Y	N	N	N	Y	Y
NEW HAMPSHIRE							
Gregg	Y	Y	Y	Y	Y	Y	Y
Smith	Y	N	Y	Y	Y	N	Y
NEW JERSEY							
Lautenberg	N	Y	N	N	Y	Y	Y
Torricelli	Y	Y	N	Y	Y	Y	Y
NEW MEXICO							
Domenici	Y	Y	Y	Y	N	Y	Y
Bingaman	N	Y	N	N	N	Y	Y
NEW YORK							
D'Amato	Y	Y	N	Y	Y	Y	Y
Moynihan	Y	Y	N	N	Y	Y	Y
NORTH CAROLINA							
Faircloth	Y	N	Y	Y	Y	?	Y
Helms	Y	N	Y	Y	Y	?	Y
NORTH DAKOTA							
Conrad	Y	Y	N	N	Y	Y	Y
Dorgan	Y	Y	N	N	N	Y	Y
OHIO							
DeWine	Y	Y	Y	Y	N	N	Y
Glenn	Y	Y	N	N	N	Y	Y
OKLAHOMA							
Inhofe	Y	N	Y	Y	?	?	?
Nickles	Y	N	Y	Y	Y	N	Y
OREGON							
Smith	Y	Y	Y	Y	N	Y	Y
Wyden	Y	Y	N	N	Y	Y	Y
PENNSYLVANIA							
Santorum	Y	Y	Y	Y	Y	N	Y
Specter	Y	Y	Y	Y	Y	Y	Y
RHODE ISLAND							
Chafee	Y	Y	N	Y	N	Y	Y
Reed	Y	Y	N	N	N	Y	Y
SOUTH CAROLINA							
Thurmond	Y	Y	Y	Y	N	Y	Y
Hollings	Y	Y	N	Y	N	Y	Y
SOUTH DAKOTA							
Daschle	Y	Y	N	N	Y	Y	Y
Johnson	Y	Y	N	N	N	Y	Y
TENNESSEE							
Frist	Y	Y	Y	Y	Y	Y	Y
Thompson	Y	N	Y	Y	Y	Y	Y
TEXAS							
Gramm	Y	Y	Y	Y	Y	?	Y
Hutchison	Y	Y	Y	Y	N	Y	Y
UTAH							
Bennett	Y	Y	Y	Y	N	?	?
Hatch	Y	Y	Y	Y	N	+	+
VERMONT							
Jeffords	Y	Y	N	Y	N	Y	Y
Leahy	N	Y	N	N	Y	Y	Y
VIRGINIA							
Warner	Y	Y	Y	Y	N	N	Y
Robb	Y	Y	N	N	N	Y	Y
WASHINGTON							
Gorton	Y	Y	Y	Y	N	Y	Y
Murray	Y	Y	N	N	Y	Y	Y
WEST VIRGINIA							
Byrd	Y	Y	N	N	Y	Y	Y
Rockefeller	N	Y	N	N	N	Y	Y
WISCONSIN							
Feingold	Y	N	N	N	Y	Y	Y
Kohl	Y	Y	N	N	Y	Y	Y
WYOMING							
Enzi	Y	Y	Y	Y	Y	?	Y
Thomas	Y	Y	Y	Y	Y	Y	Y

Key
- Y Voted for (yea).
- # Paired for.
- + Announced for.
- N Voted against (nay).
- X Paired against.
- – Announced against.
- P Voted "present."
- C Voted "present" to avoid possible conflict of interest.
- ? Did not vote or otherwise make a position known.

Democrats **Republicans**

ND Northern Democrats   SD Southern Democrats

Southern states - Ala., Ark., Fla., Ga., Ky., La., Miss., N.C., Okla., S.C., Tenn., Texas, Va.

43. S 1768. Fiscal 1998 Supplemental Appropriations/U.N. Peacekeeping. Helms, R-N.C., amendment to express the sense of the Senate that the United Nations should immediately reduce the percentage of U.S. dues for U.N. peacekeeping operations from 30.4 percent to 25 percent. The amendment also would urge the president to ask the U.N. Security Council to release to all U.N. members a U.S. Defense Department report on the amount the United States has spent since Jan. 1, 1990, implementing or supporting U.N. Security Council resolutions. Adopted 90-10: R 55-0; D 35-10 (ND 27-10, SD 8-0). March 25, 1998.

44. S 1768. Fiscal 1998 Supplemental Appropriations/IMF Funding. McConnell, R-Ky., amendment to provide $17.9 billion for the International Monetary Fund, including $3.4 billion for a new program aimed at preventing global financial crises and $14.5 billion for the U.S. "quota" to the international agency. The amendment would prohibit release of the quota funds unless the IMF agrees to certain conditions, including restricting aid to nations that do not conform to international trade agreements or that provide subsidies to certain industries such as steel, textile and automobile manufacturers. Adopted 84-16: R 41-14; D 43-2 (ND 35-2, SD 8-0). March 26, 1998.

45. S 1768. Fiscal 1998 Supplemental Appropriations/Health Care Portability. Nickles, R-Okla., motion to table (kill) the Kennedy, D-Mass., amendment that would replace the language proposed to be stricken by the Nickles amendment with $8 million for the Health Care Financing Administration (HCFA) to hire more employees to enforce the 1996 health care portability law (PL 104-191). Motion agreed to 51-49: R 51-4; D 0-45 (ND 0-37, SD 0-8). March 26, 1998. (Subsequently, the Nickles amendment was adopted by voice vote and a motion to advance to third reading on the bill was agreed to by voice vote.

46. HR 2646. Expanding Education Savings Accounts/Cloture. Motion to invoke cloture (thus limiting debate) on the bill to allow parents, relatives or outside corporations to contribute up to a combined total of $2,000 a year of after-tax funds in tax-free savings accounts designated for educational expenses. Motion rejected 58-42: R 55-0; D 3-42 (ND 2-35, SD 1-7). March 26, 1998. Three-fifths of the total Senate (60) is required to invoke cloture.

47. S J Res 42. Reverse Mexico Anti-Drug Certification/Passage. Passage of the joint resolution to reverse the president's certification of Mexico as an ally in the fight against drugs. Rejected 45-54: R 30-24; D 15-30 (ND 14-23, SD 1-7). March 26, 1998. A "nay" was a vote in support of the president's position.

48. McKeown Nomination/Confirmation. Confirmation of President Clinton's nomination of M. Margaret McKeown of Washington to be a judge for the 9th U.S. Circuit Court of Appeals. Confirmed 80-11: R 36-11; D 44-0 (ND 36-0, SD 8-0). March 27, 1998. A "yea" was a vote in support of the president's position.

49. S Con Res 86. Fiscal 1999 Budget Resolution/At-Home Parents. Sessions, R-Ala., amendment to express the sense of Congress recognizing the importance of parents who forgo a second income to stay at home and raise children, and to call for tax breaks for these families. Adopted 96-0: R 52-0; D 44-0 (ND 36-0, SD 8-0). March 31, 1998.

Senate Votes 50, 51, 52, 53, 54, 55, 56

	50	51	52	53	54	55	56
ALABAMA							
Sessions	N	N	N	Y	N	Y	Y
Shelby	N	Y	N	Y	N	Y	Y
ALASKA							
Murkowski	N	N	N	Y	N	Y	Y
Stevens	N	N	N	Y	N	N	Y
ARIZONA							
Kyl	N	Y	N	Y	N	Y	Y
McCain	N	Y	N	Y	N	Y	Y
ARKANSAS							
Hutchinson	–	?	?	Y	N	Y	Y
Bumpers	Y	Y	Y	N	Y	N	N
CALIFORNIA							
Boxer	Y	Y	Y	N	Y	N	N
Feinstein	Y	Y	Y	N	Y	N	N
COLORADO							
Allard	N	Y	N	Y	N	Y	Y
Campbell	N	N	Y	Y	N	Y	Y
CONNECTICUT							
Dodd	Y	Y	Y	N	Y	N	N
Lieberman	Y	Y	Y	N	Y	N	N
DELAWARE							
Roth	N	Y	N	Y	N	Y	Y
Biden	Y	Y	Y	N	Y	N	N
FLORIDA							
Mack	N	Y	N	Y	N	N	Y
Graham	Y	Y	Y	N	Y	N	N
GEORGIA							
Coverdell	N	Y	N	Y	N	Y	Y
Cleland	Y	Y	Y	N	Y	N	N
HAWAII							
Akaka	Y	Y	Y	N	Y	N	N
Inouye	Y	Y	Y	N	Y	N	N
IDAHO							
Craig	N	Y	N	Y	N	Y	Y
Kempthorne	N	Y	N	Y	N	Y	Y
ILLINOIS							
Durbin	Y	Y	Y	N	Y	N	N
Moseley-Braun	Y	Y	Y	N	Y	N	N
INDIANA							
Coats	N	N	N	Y	N	N	N
Lugar	N	Y	N	Y	N	N	Y

	50	51	52	53	54	55	56
IOWA							
Grassley	N	Y	N	Y	N	N	Y
Harkin	Y	Y	Y	N	Y	N	N
KANSAS							
Brownback	N	Y	N	Y	N	Y	Y
Roberts	N	Y	N	Y	N	Y	Y
KENTUCKY							
McConnell	N	N	N	Y	N	Y	Y
Ford	Y	N	Y	N	N	N	N
LOUISIANA							
Breaux	Y	Y	Y	N	Y	N	Y
Landrieu	Y	Y	Y	N	Y	N	N
MAINE							
Collins	N	Y	N	N	N	N	N
Snowe	N	Y	N	N	N	N	N
MARYLAND							
Mikulski	?	?	?	N	Y	N	N
Sarbanes	Y	Y	Y	N	Y	N	N
MASSACHUSETTS							
Kennedy	Y	Y	Y	?	Y	N	N
Kerry	Y	Y	Y	?	Y	N	N
MICHIGAN							
Abraham	N	Y	N	Y	N	Y	Y
Levin	Y	Y	Y	N	Y	N	N
MINNESOTA							
Grams	N	Y	N	Y	N	Y	Y
Wellstone	Y	Y	Y	N	Y	N	N
MISSISSIPPI							
Cochran	N	N	N	Y	N	N	Y
Lott	N	N	N	Y	N	Y	Y
MISSOURI							
Ashcroft	N	Y	N	Y	N	Y	Y
Bond	N	Y	N	Y	N	N	N
MONTANA							
Burns	N	N	N	Y	N	Y	Y
Baucus	Y	Y	Y	N	Y	N	N
NEBRASKA							
Hagel	N	N	N	Y	N	N	Y
Kerrey	Y	Y	Y	N	Y	N	N
NEVADA							
Bryan	Y	Y	Y	N	Y	N	N
Reid	Y	Y	Y	N	Y	N	N

	50	51	52	53	54	55	56
NEW HAMPSHIRE							
Gregg	N	Y	N	Y	N	Y	Y
Smith	N	Y	N	Y	N	Y	Y
NEW JERSEY							
Lautenberg	Y	Y	Y	N	Y	N	N
Torricelli	Y	Y	Y	N	Y	N	N
NEW MEXICO							
Domenici	N	Y	N	Y	N	Y	Y
Bingaman	Y	Y	Y	N	Y	N	N
NEW YORK							
D'Amato	Y	Y	Y	N	N	N	N
Moynihan	Y	Y	Y	N	Y	N	N
NORTH CAROLINA							
Faircloth	Y	N	Y	Y	Y	Y	Y
Helms	N	N	N	Y	N	Y	Y
NORTH DAKOTA							
Conrad	Y	Y	Y	N	Y	N	N
Dorgan	Y	Y	Y	N	Y	N	N
OHIO							
DeWine	N	Y	N	Y	N	N	N
Glenn	Y	Y	Y	N	Y	N	N
OKLAHOMA							
Inhofe	N	N	N	Y	N	Y	Y
Nickles	N	Y	N	Y	N	Y	Y
OREGON							
Smith	N	Y	N	Y	N	Y	Y
Wyden	Y	Y	Y	N	Y	N	N
PENNSYLVANIA							
Santorum	N	Y	N	Y	N	Y	Y
Specter	N	Y	Y	N	N	N	Y
RHODE ISLAND							
Chafee	N	Y	N	Y	N	N	N
Reed	Y	Y	Y	N	Y	N	N
SOUTH CAROLINA							
Thurmond	N	Y	N	Y	N	Y	Y
Hollings	Y	N	Y	Y	Y	N	N
SOUTH DAKOTA							
Daschle	Y	Y	Y	N	Y	N	N
Johnson	Y	Y	Y	N	Y	N	N
TENNESSEE							
Frist	N	Y	N	Y	N	Y	Y
Thompson	N	Y	N	Y	N	Y	Y

	50	51	52	53	54	55	56
TEXAS							
Gramm	N	Y	N	Y	N	Y	Y
Hutchison	N	Y	N	Y	N	Y	Y
UTAH							
Bennett	N	N	N	Y	N	Y	Y
Hatch	N	N	N	Y	N	Y	Y
VERMONT							
Jeffords	N	N	Y	Y	Y	N	N
Leahy	Y	Y	Y	N	Y	N	N
VIRGINIA							
Warner	N	Y	N	Y	N	Y	Y
Robb	Y	Y	Y	N	Y	N	Y
WASHINGTON							
Gorton	N	N	N	Y	N	N	Y
Murray	Y	Y	Y	N	Y	N	N
WEST VIRGINIA							
Byrd	Y	Y	Y	N	Y	N	N
Rockefeller	Y	Y	Y	N	Y	N	N
WISCONSIN							
Feingold	Y	Y	Y	N	Y	N	N
Kohl	Y	Y	Y	N	Y	N	N
WYOMING							
Enzi	N	N	N	Y	N	Y	Y
Thomas	N	Y	N	Y	N	Y	Y

Key

- Y Voted for (yea).
- # Paired for.
- + Announced for.
- N Voted against (nay).
- X Paired against.
- − Announced against.
- P Voted "present."
- C Voted "present" to avoid possible conflict of interest.
- ? Did not vote or otherwise make a position known.

Democrats • Republicans

ND Northern Democrats   SD Southern Democrats

Southern states - Ala., Ark., Fla., Ga., Ky., La., Miss., N.C., Okla., S.C., Tenn., Texas, Va.

50. S Con Res 86. Fiscal 1999 Budget Resolution/Additional Teachers. Murray, D-Wash., motion to waive the Budget Act with respect to the Domenici, R-N.M., point of order against the Murray amendment to provide $7.3 billion over five years to hire as many as 100,000 additional school teachers. Motion rejected 46-52: R 2-52; D 44-0 (ND 36-0, SD 8-0). March 31, 1998. A three-fifths majority vote (60) of the total Senate is required to waive the Budget Act. (Subsequently, the chair upheld the point of order and the amendment fell.)

51. S Con Res 86. Fiscal 1999 Budget Resolution/Tobacco Manufacturers Immunity. Gregg, R-N.H., amendment to the Gregg amendment that would extend the list to include class-action suits. The underlying Gregg amendment would express the sense of the Senate that any tobacco settlement legislation not provide tobacco manufacturers with immunity from liability in health-related lawsuits. Adopted 79-19: R 37-17; D 42-2 (ND 36-0, SD 6-2). March 31, 1998. (Subsequently, the underlying Gregg amendment as amended was adopted by voice vote.)

52. S Con Res 86. Fiscal 1999 Budget Resolution/Child Care Funding. Dodd, D-Conn., motion to waive the Budget Act with respect to the Domenici, R-N.M., point of order against the Dodd amendment to establish a reserve fund to provide funding for child care improvements. Motion rejected 50-48: R 6-48; D 44-0 (ND 36-0, SD 8-0). March 31, 1998. A three-fifths majority vote (60) of the total Senate is required to waive the Budget Act. (Subsequently, the chair upheld the point of order and the amendment fell.)

53. S Con Res 86. Fiscal 1999 Budget Resolution/Medicare Physicians. Kyl, R-Ariz., amendment to express the sense of Congress that there should be no constraints on physicians who want to privately contract with Medicare patients for Medicare-covered services. Adopted 51-47: R 50-5; D 1-42 (ND 0-35, SD 1-7). April 1, 1998.

54. S Con Res 86. Fiscal 1999 Budget Resolution/Tobacco Settlement Revenues. Conrad, D-N.D., motion to waive the Budget Act with respect to the Domenici, R-N.M., point of order against the Conrad amendment. The Conrad amendment would permit the federal share of revenue from any tobacco settlement to be used for programs to reduce child smoking, increase health research, to provide transition assistance for tobacco farmers and help Medicare financing. Motion rejected 46-54: R 2-53; D 44-1 (ND 37-0, SD 7-1). April 1, 1998. A three-fifths majority vote (60) of the total Senate is required to waive the Budget Act. (Subsequently, the chair upheld the point of order, and the amendment fell.)

55. S Con Res 86. Fiscal 1999 Budget Resolution/Tax Cuts. McCain, R-Ariz., motion to waive the Budget Act with respect to the Lautenberg, D-N.J., point of order against the Coverdell, R-Ga., amendment. Coverdell's amendment would reduce tax revenues by $195.5 billion over five years by raising the income thresholds for the 15 percent and 28 percent tax brackets. Motion rejected 38-62: R 38-17; D 0-45 (ND 0-37, SD 0-8). April 1, 1998. A three-fifths majority vote (60) of the total Senate is required to waive the Budget Act. (Subsequently, the chair upheld the point of order, and the amendment fell.)

56. S Con Res 86. Fiscal 1999 Budget Resolution/Social Security Personal Retirement Accounts. Roth, R-Del., amendment to express the sense of the Senate that the Senate Finance Committee should in 1998 report legislation that would dedicate the federal budget surplus to the establishment of Social Security "personal retirement accounts." Adopted 51-49: R 49-6; D 2-43 (ND 0-37, SD 2-6). April 1, 1998.

Senate Votes 57, 58, 59, 60, 61, 62, 63

	57	58	59	60	61	62	63
ALABAMA							
Sessions	Y	N	Y	Y	Y	Y	N
Shelby	Y	N	Y	Y	Y	Y	N
ALASKA							
Murkowski	Y	N	Y	Y	Y	Y	N
Stevens	Y	N	Y	Y	Y	Y	N
ARIZONA							
Kyl	Y	N	Y	Y	Y	Y	N
McCain	Y	N	Y	Y	Y	Y	N
ARKANSAS							
Hutchinson	Y	N	Y	Y	Y	Y	N
Bumpers	N	Y	Y	N	Y	N	N
CALIFORNIA							
Boxer	N	Y	Y	N	Y	N	N
Feinstein	N	Y	Y	N	Y	N	N
COLORADO							
Allard	Y	N	Y	N	Y	Y	N
Campbell	Y	N	Y	N	Y	Y	N
CONNECTICUT							
Dodd	N	Y	Y	N	Y	N	N
Lieberman	N	Y	Y	N	Y	N	N
DELAWARE							
Roth	Y	N	Y	Y	Y	Y	N
Biden	N	Y	Y	N	Y	N	N
FLORIDA							
Mack	Y	N	Y	Y	Y	Y	N
Graham	N	Y	Y	N	Y	N	N
GEORGIA							
Coverdell	Y	N	Y	Y	Y	Y	N
Cleland	N	Y	Y	N	Y	N	N
HAWAII							
Akaka	N	Y	Y	N	Y	N	N
Inouye	N	Y	Y	N	Y	N	N
IDAHO							
Craig	Y	N	Y	Y	Y	Y	N
Kempthorne	Y	N	Y	Y	Y	Y	N
ILLINOIS							
Durbin	N	Y	Y	N	Y	N	N
Moseley-Braun	N	Y	Y	N	Y	N	N
INDIANA							
Coats	Y	N	Y	Y	Y	Y	N
Lugar	Y	N	Y	Y	Y	Y	N

	57	58	59	60	61	62	63
IOWA							
Grassley	Y	N	Y	Y	Y	Y	N
Harkin	N	Y	Y	N	Y	N	N
KANSAS							
Brownback	Y	N	Y	Y	Y	Y	N
Roberts	Y	N	Y	Y	Y	Y	N
KENTUCKY							
McConnell	Y	N	Y	Y	Y	Y	N
Ford	N	Y	Y	N	Y	N	N
LOUISIANA							
Breaux	N	Y	Y	N	Y	N	N
Landrieu	N	Y	Y	N	Y	N	N
MAINE							
Collins	Y	N	Y	Y	Y	Y	N
Snowe	Y	N	Y	Y	Y	Y	N
MARYLAND							
Mikulski	N	Y	Y	N	Y	N	N
Sarbanes	N	Y	Y	N	Y	N	N
MASSACHUSETTS							
Kennedy	N	Y	Y	N	Y	N	N
Kerry	N	Y	Y	N	Y	N	N
MICHIGAN							
Abraham	Y	N	Y	Y	Y	Y	N
Levin	N	Y	Y	N	Y	N	N
MINNESOTA							
Grams	Y	N	Y	Y	Y	Y	N
Wellstone	N	Y	Y	N	Y	N	N
MISSISSIPPI							
Cochran	Y	N	Y	Y	Y	Y	N
Lott	Y	N	Y	Y	Y	Y	N
MISSOURI							
Ashcroft	Y	N	Y	Y	Y	Y	N
Bond	Y	N	Y	Y	Y	Y	N
MONTANA							
Burns	Y	N	Y	Y	Y	Y	N
Baucus	N	N	Y	N	Y	N	N
NEBRASKA							
Hagel	Y	N	Y	Y	Y	Y	N
Kerrey	N	N	Y	Y	Y	N	N
NEVADA							
Bryan	N	Y	Y	N	Y	N	N
Reid	N	Y	Y	N	Y	Y	N

	57	58	59	60	61	62	63
NEW HAMPSHIRE							
Gregg	Y	N	Y	Y	Y	Y	N
Smith	Y	N	Y	Y	Y	Y	N
NEW JERSEY							
Lautenberg	N	Y	Y	N	Y	N	N
Torricelli	N	Y	Y	N	Y	N	N
NEW MEXICO							
Domenici	Y	N	Y	Y	Y	Y	N
Bingaman	N	N	Y	Y	Y	Y	N
NEW YORK							
D'Amato	N	N	Y	Y	Y	Y	N
Moynihan	N	Y	Y	N	Y	N	N
NORTH CAROLINA							
Faircloth	Y	Y	Y	Y	N	Y	N
Helms	Y	N	Y	Y	+	+	–
NORTH DAKOTA							
Conrad	N	Y	Y	N	Y	N	N
Dorgan	N	Y	Y	N	Y	N	N
OHIO							
DeWine	Y	N	Y	Y	Y	Y	N
Glenn	N	Y	Y	N	Y	N	N
OKLAHOMA							
Inhofe	Y	N	Y	Y	Y	Y	N
Nickles	Y	N	Y	Y	Y	Y	N
OREGON							
Smith	Y	N	Y	Y	Y	Y	N
Wyden	N	Y	Y	N	Y	N	N
PENNSYLVANIA							
Santorum	Y	N	Y	Y	Y	Y	N
Specter	N	N	Y	N	Y	N	N
RHODE ISLAND							
Chafee	Y	N	Y	Y	Y	Y	N
Reed	N	Y	Y	N	Y	N	N
SOUTH CAROLINA							
Thurmond	Y	N	Y	Y	Y	Y	N
Hollings	N	Y	Y	N	Y	N	N
SOUTH DAKOTA							
Daschle	N	Y	Y	N	Y	N	N
Johnson	N	Y	Y	N	Y	N	N
TENNESSEE							
Frist	Y	N	Y	Y	Y	Y	N
Thompson	Y	N	Y	Y	Y	Y	Y

Key

- Y Voted for (yea).
- # Paired for.
- + Announced for.
- N Voted against (nay).
- X Paired against.
- – Announced against.
- P Voted "present."
- C Voted "present" to avoid possible conflict of interest.
- ? Did not vote or otherwise make a position known.

Democrats **Republicans**

	57	58	59	60	61	62	63
TEXAS							
Gramm	Y	N	Y	Y	Y	Y	N
Hutchison	Y	N	Y	Y	Y	Y	N
UTAH							
Bennett	Y	N	Y	Y	Y	Y	N
Hatch	Y	N	Y	Y	Y	Y	N
VERMONT							
Jeffords	Y	N	Y	N	Y	Y	N
Leahy	N	N	Y	N	Y	N	N
VIRGINIA							
Warner	Y	N	Y	Y	Y	Y	N
Robb	N	Y	Y	Y	Y	N	N
WASHINGTON							
Gorton	Y	N	Y	Y	Y	Y	N
Murray	N	Y	Y	N	Y	N	N
WEST VIRGINIA							
Byrd	Y	Y	Y	Y	Y	Y	N
Rockefeller	N	Y	?	?	Y	N	N
WISCONSIN							
Feingold	N	Y	Y	N	Y	N	N
Kohl	N	Y	Y	N	Y	N	N
WYOMING							
Enzi	Y	N	Y	Y	Y	Y	N
Thomas	Y	N	Y	Y	Y	Y	N

ND Northern Democrats   SD Southern Democrats

Southern states - Ala., Ark., Fla., Ga., Ky., La., Miss., N.C., Okla., S.C., Tenn., Texas, Va.

57. S Con Res 86. Fiscal 1999 Budget Resolution/School Modernization Bonds. Domenici, R-N.M., motion to table (kill) the Moseley-Braun, D-Ill., amendment that would express the sense of the Senate that Congress should enact legislation to allow states and school districts to issue $21.8 billion in school modernization bonds, and that the federal government should provide income tax credits to purchasers of the bonds in lieu of interest. Motion agreed to 54-46: R 53-2; D 1-44 (ND 1-36, SD 0-8). April 1, 1998.

58. S Con Res 86. Fiscal 1999 Budget Resolution/Social Security Point of Order. Hollings, D-S.C., motion to waive the Budget Act with respect to the Domenici, R-N.M., point of order against the Hollings amendment. The Hollings amendment would revise Senate rules to require a three-fifths majority vote (60) to consider any provision that would revise budget procedures regarding Social Security. Motion rejected 42-58: R 1-54; D 41-4 (ND 33-4, SD 8-0). April 1, 1998. A three-fifths majority vote (60) of the total Senate is required to waive the Budget Act. (Subsequently, the chair upheld the point of order, and the amendment fell.)

59. S Con Res 86. Fiscal 1999 Budget Resolution/Marriage Penalty. Faircloth, R-N.C., amendment to express the sense of the Senate that Congress should begin to phase out the marriage penalty, under which some married couples pay more in income taxes than they would if filing separately, in 1998. Adopted 99-0: R 55-0; D 44-0 (ND 36-0, SD 8-0). April 1, 1998.

60. S Con Res 86. Fiscal 1999 Budget Resolution/Entitlement Spending Supermajority. Craig, R-Idaho, motion to waive the Budget Act with respect to the Lautenberg, D-N.J., point of order against the Craig amendment. The Craig amendment would revise Senate rules to require a supermajority point of order against provisions that would increase mandatory spending without offsetting the increase with reductions. Motion rejected 54-45: R 51-4; D 3-41 (ND 2-34, SD 1-7). April 1, 1998. A three-fifths majority vote (60) of the total Senate is required to waive the Budget Act. (Subsequently, the chair upheld the point of order, and the amendment fell.)

61. Murphy Nomination/Confirmation. Confirmation of President Clinton's nomination of G. Patrick Murphy of Illinois to be U.S. district judge for the Southern District of Illinois. Confirmed 98-1: R 53-1; D 45-0 (ND 37-0, SD 8-0). April 2, 1998. A "yea" was a vote in support of the president's position.

62. S Con Res 86. Fiscal 1999 Budget Resolution/Tax Code Sunset. Hutchinson, R-Ark., substitute amendment to the Dorgan, D-N.D., amendment. The Hutchinson amendment would express the sense of the Senate that the chamber should pass an IRS restructuring bill that includes taxpayer protections, expanded oversight and IRS employee accountability. It would express the sense of Congress that the federal Tax Code should sunset by the end of 2001. Adopted 59-40: R 54-0; D 5-40 (ND 5-32, SD 0-8). April 2, 1998.

63. S Con Res 86. Fiscal 1999 Budget Resolution/Federal Tax Deductions. Domenici, R-N.M., motion to table (kill) the Dorgan, D-N.D., amendment to the modified Dorgan amendment. The second-degree Dorgan amendment would express the sense of Congress that the current tax deductions for interest on home mortgages and charitable contributions should continue. Motion rejected 1-98: R 1-53; D 0-45 (ND 0-37, SD 0-8). April 2, 1998. (Subsequently, both the Dorgan amendment and the modified Dorgan amendment were adopted by voice vote.)

Senate Votes 64, 65, 66, 67, 68, 69, 70

	64	65	66	67	68	69	70
ALABAMA							
Sessions	Y	N	Y	Y	Y	N	Y
Shelby	Y	N	Y	Y	Y	N	Y
ALASKA							
Murkowski	Y	N	Y	Y	Y	N	Y
Stevens	Y	N	Y	Y	Y	N	Y
ARIZONA							
Kyl	Y	N	Y	Y	Y	N	Y
McCain	Y	N	Y	Y	Y	N	Y
ARKANSAS							
Hutchinson	Y	N	Y	Y	Y	N	Y
Bumpers	N	Y	Y	N	N	Y	N
CALIFORNIA							
Boxer	N	Y	Y	N	N	Y	N
Feinstein	N	Y	Y	N	N	Y	Y
COLORADO							
Allard	Y	N	Y	Y	Y	N	Y
Campbell	Y	N	Y	Y	Y	N	Y
CONNECTICUT							
Dodd	N	Y	Y	N	N	Y	Y
Lieberman	Y	Y	Y	Y	N	N	N
DELAWARE							
Roth	Y	N	Y	Y	Y	N	Y
Biden	N	Y	Y	N	N	Y	N
FLORIDA							
Mack	Y	N	Y	Y	Y	N	Y
Graham	N	Y	Y	N	N	Y	Y
GEORGIA							
Coverdell	Y	N	Y	Y	Y	N	Y
Cleland	N	Y	Y	Y	N	Y	Y
HAWAII							
Akaka	N	Y	Y	N	N	Y	N
Inouye	N	Y	Y	N	?	?	?
IDAHO							
Craig	Y	N	Y	Y	Y	N	Y
Kempthorne	Y	N	Y	Y	Y	N	Y
ILLINOIS							
Durbin	N	Y	Y	N	N	Y	N
Moseley-Braun	N	Y	Y	N	N	Y	N
INDIANA							
Coats	Y	N	N	N	Y	N	Y
Lugar	Y	N	Y	N	Y	N	Y

	64	65	66	67	68	69	70
IOWA							
Grassley	Y	N	Y	Y	Y	N	N
Harkin	N	Y	Y	N	N	Y	N
KANSAS							
Brownback	Y	N	Y	Y	Y	N	Y
Roberts	Y	N	Y	Y	Y	N	Y
KENTUCKY							
McConnell	Y	N	Y	Y	Y	N	Y
Ford	N	Y	Y	N	N	Y	N
LOUISIANA							
Breaux	N	Y	Y	Y	N	Y	Y
Landrieu	–	Y	Y	N	N	Y	Y
MAINE							
Collins	Y	N	Y	N	Y	N	N
Snowe	Y	N	Y	N	N	N	N
MARYLAND							
Mikulski	N	Y	Y	N	N	Y	N
Sarbanes	N	Y	Y	N	N	Y	N
MASSACHUSETTS							
Kennedy	N	Y	Y	N	N	Y	N
Kerry	N	Y	Y	N	N	Y	N
MICHIGAN							
Abraham	N	N	Y	Y	Y	N	Y
Levin	N	Y	Y	N	N	Y	N
MINNESOTA							
Grams	Y	N	Y	Y	Y	N	Y
Wellstone	N	Y	Y	N	N	Y	N
MISSISSIPPI							
Cochran	Y	N	Y	Y	Y	N	Y
Lott	Y	N	Y	Y	Y	N	Y
MISSOURI							
Ashcroft	Y	N	Y	Y	Y	N	Y
Bond	N	N	Y	Y	Y	N	Y
MONTANA							
Burns	Y	N	Y	Y	Y	N	Y
Baucus	N	Y	Y	N	Y	Y	N
NEBRASKA							
Hagel	N	N	Y	Y	Y	N	Y
Kerrey	N	Y	Y	N	N	Y	Y
NEVADA							
Bryan	N	Y	Y	Y	Y	Y	N
Reid	N	Y	Y	Y	Y	Y	Y

	64	65	66	67	68	69	70
NEW HAMPSHIRE							
Gregg	Y	N	Y	N	N	N	Y
Smith	Y	N	Y	Y	Y	N	Y
NEW JERSEY							
Lautenberg	N	Y	Y	N	N	Y	N
Torricelli	N	Y	Y	N	Y	Y	Y
NEW MEXICO							
Domenici	Y	N	Y	Y	Y	N	Y
Bingaman	N	Y	Y	N	Y	Y	Y
NEW YORK							
D'Amato	Y	Y	Y	Y	Y	N	N
Moynihan	N	Y	Y	N	N	Y	Y
NORTH CAROLINA							
Faircloth	Y	Y	Y	N	Y	N	Y
Helms	+	–	+	+	+	–	+
NORTH DAKOTA							
Conrad	N	Y	Y	Y	Y	N	Y
Dorgan	N	Y	Y	Y	N	Y	N
OHIO							
DeWine	Y	N	Y	Y	Y	N	N
Glenn	N	Y	Y	N	N	Y	N
OKLAHOMA							
Inhofe	Y	N	Y	Y	Y	?	Y
Nickles	Y	N	N	Y	Y	N	Y
OREGON							
Smith	Y	N	Y	N	Y	N	Y
Wyden	Y	Y	Y	N	Y	Y	N
PENNSYLVANIA							
Santorum	N	N	Y	Y	Y	N	N
Specter	Y	Y	Y	N	N	N	N
RHODE ISLAND							
Chafee	Y	N	Y	N	N	N	Y
Reed	N	Y	Y	N	N	Y	N
SOUTH CAROLINA							
Thurmond	Y	N	Y	Y	Y	N	Y
Hollings	N	Y	Y	N	N	N	N
SOUTH DAKOTA							
Daschle	N	Y	Y	Y	Y	Y	N
Johnson	N	Y	Y	Y	N	Y	Y
TENNESSEE							
Frist	Y	N	Y	N	Y	N	N
Thompson	Y	N	Y	Y	Y	N	Y

	64	65	66	67	68	69	70
TEXAS							
Gramm	Y	N	Y	Y	Y	N	Y
Hutchison	Y	N	Y	Y	Y	N	Y
UTAH							
Bennett	Y	N	Y	Y	Y	N	Y
Hatch	Y	N	Y	Y	Y	N	Y
VERMONT							
Jeffords	Y	N	Y	N	N	N	N
Leahy	N	Y	Y	N	N	Y	N
VIRGINIA							
Warner	Y	N	Y	Y	Y	N	Y
Robb	N	Y	Y	N	N	Y	N
WASHINGTON							
Gorton	Y	N	Y	Y	N	N	Y
Murray	N	Y	Y	N	N	Y	N
WEST VIRGINIA							
Byrd	N	N	Y	N	Y	N	Y
Rockefeller	N	Y	Y	N	N	Y	N
WISCONSIN							
Feingold	Y	Y	Y	N	N	N	N
Kohl	N	Y	Y	N	N	Y	N
WYOMING							
Enzi	Y	N	Y	Y	Y	N	Y
Thomas	Y	N	Y	Y	Y	N	Y

Key
- Y Voted for (yea).
- # Paired for.
- + Announced for.
- N Voted against (nay).
- X Paired against.
- – Announced against.
- P Voted "present."
- C Voted "present" to avoid possible conflict of interest.
- ? Did not vote or otherwise make a position known.

Democrats • Republicans

ND Northern Democrats   SD Southern Democrats

Southern states — Ala., Ark., Fla., Ga., Ky., La., Miss., N.C., Okla., S.C., Tenn., Texas, Va.

64. S Con Res 86. Fiscal 1999 Budget Resolution/Federal Debt Repayment. Domenici, R-N.M., motion to waive the Budget Act with respect to the Lautenberg, D-N.J., point of order against the Allard, R-Colo., amendment. The Allard amendment would prohibit the Senate, beginning in fiscal 2000, from considering any budget measure that would create a budget deficit or fail to reduce the federal debt enough to eliminate it by fiscal 2028. Motion rejected 53-45: R 50-4; D 3-41 (ND 3-34, SD 0-7). April 2, 1998. A three-fifths majority vote (60) of the total Senate is required to waive the Budget Act. (Subsequently, the chair upheld the point of order, and the amendment fell.)

65. S Con Res 86. Fiscal 1999 Budget Resolution/Environmental Reserve Fund. Lautenberg, D-N.J., motion to waive the Budget Act with respect to the Domenici, R-N.M., point of order against the Lautenberg amendment. The Lautenberg amendment would establish a deficit-neutral reserve fund to provide funding for the environment and natural resources. Motion rejected 47-52: R 3-51; D 44-1 (ND 36-1, SD 8-0). April 2, 1998. A three-fifths majority vote (60) of the total Senate is required to waive the Budget Act. (Subsequently, the chair upheld the point of order, and the amendment fell.)

66. S Con Res 86. Fiscal 1999 Budget Resolution/Elderly Housing. Bond, R-Mo., amendment to express the sense of the Senate that the Department of Housing and Urban Development's Section 202 Elderly Housing program should receive at least as much funding in each of the next five fiscal years as it received in fiscal 1998. Adopted 97-2: R 52-2; D 45-0 (ND 37-0, SD 8-0). April 2, 1998.

67. S Con Res 86. Fiscal 1999 Budget Resolution/Education for the Disabled. Domenici, R-N.M., motion to table (kill) the Bumpers, D-Ark., amendment to raise the aggregate revenue and spending recommendations by $311 million over five years. The amendment called for raising the revenue an additional $311 million by repealing a tax break for hard-rock mining companies and allocate it for grants to states to fund programs under the Individuals with Disabilities Education Act. Motion agreed to 55-44: R 44-10; D 11-34 (ND 9-28, SD 2-6). April 2, 1998.

68. S Con Res 86. Fiscal 1999 Budget Resolution/Discretionary Spending Cuts. Brownback, R-Kan., amendment to express the sense of the Senate that savings from the elimination of any discretionary spending program should be used for tax cuts or to revise the Social Security program. Adopted 52-46: R 48-6; D 4-40 (ND 4-32, SD 0-8). April 2, 1998.

69. S Con Res 86. Fiscal 1999 Budget Resolution/Democratic Substitute. Lautenberg, D-N.J., motion to waive the Budget Act with respect to the Domenici, R-N.M., point of order against the Lautenberg substitute amendment. The Lautenberg amendment would replace the underlying resolution with a version of President Clinton's fiscal 1999 budget. Motion rejected 42-55: R 0-53; D 42-2 (ND 35-1, SD 7-1). April 2, 1998. A three-fifths majority vote (60) of the total Senate is required to waive the Budget Act. (Subsequently, the chair upheld the point of order, and the amendment fell.)

70. S Con Res 86. Fiscal 1999 Budget Resolution/Health Research. Domenici, R-N.M., motion to table (kill) the Specter, R-Pa., amendment intended to increase fiscal 1999 funding for biomedical research by $2 billion by decreasing all discretionary spending by $2 billion through a four-tenths of 1 percent across-the-board cut. Motion agreed to 57-41: R 45-9; D 12-32 (ND 8-28, SD 4-4). April 2, 1998.

Senate Votes 71, 72, 73, 74, 75, 76, 77

	71	72	73	74	75	76	77
ALABAMA							
Sessions	Y	Y	Y	Y	Y	Y	Y
Shelby	Y	Y	Y	Y	Y	Y	Y
ALASKA							
Murkowski	Y	Y	Y	Y	Y	Y	Y
Stevens	Y	Y	Y	Y	Y	Y	Y
ARIZONA							
Kyl	Y	Y	Y	Y	Y	Y	Y
McCain	Y	Y	Y	Y	Y	Y	Y
ARKANSAS							
Hutchinson	Y	Y	Y	Y	Y	Y	Y
Bumpers	N	Y	N	N	Y	N	N
CALIFORNIA							
Boxer	N	Y	N	N	Y	N	N
Feinstein	N	Y	N	N	Y	N	N
COLORADO							
Allard	Y	Y	Y	Y	Y	Y	Y
Campbell	Y	Y	Y	Y	Y	N	Y
CONNECTICUT							
Dodd	N	Y	N	N	Y	N	N
Lieberman	N	Y	N	Y	Y	N	N
DELAWARE							
Roth	Y	Y	Y	Y	Y	Y	Y
Biden	N	Y	N	N	Y	N	N
FLORIDA							
Mack	Y	Y	Y	Y	Y	Y	Y
Graham	N	Y	N	N	Y	N	N
GEORGIA							
Coverdell	Y	Y	Y	Y	Y	N	Y
Cleland	N	Y	N	N	Y	N	Y
HAWAII							
Akaka	N	Y	N	N	Y	N	N
Inouye	?	?	?	?	?	?	?
IDAHO							
Craig	Y	Y	Y	Y	Y	Y	Y
Kempthorne	Y	Y	Y	Y	Y	Y	Y
ILLINOIS							
Durbin	N	Y	N	N	Y	N	N
Moseley-Braun	N	Y	N	N	Y	N	N
INDIANA							
Coats	Y	Y	Y	Y	Y	Y	Y
Lugar	N	Y	Y	Y	Y	Y	Y
IOWA							
Grassley	Y	Y	Y	Y	Y	Y	Y
Harkin	N	Y	N	N	Y	N	N
KANSAS							
Brownback	Y	Y	Y	Y	Y	Y	Y
Roberts	Y	Y	Y	Y	Y	Y	Y
KENTUCKY							
McConnell	Y	Y	Y	Y	Y	Y	Y
Ford	N	Y	N	Y	Y	N	N
LOUISIANA							
Breaux	N	Y	N	N	Y	Y	N
Landrieu	N	Y	N	N	Y	Y	N
MAINE							
Collins	Y	Y	Y	Y	Y	N	N
Snowe	Y	Y	Y	N	Y	N	N
MARYLAND							
Mikulski	N	Y	N	N	Y	N	N
Sarbanes	N	Y	N	N	Y	N	N
MASSACHUSETTS							
Kennedy	N	Y	N	N	Y	N	N
Kerry	N	Y	N	N	Y	N	N
MICHIGAN							
Abraham	Y	Y	Y	Y	Y	Y	Y
Levin	N	Y	N	N	Y	N	N
MINNESOTA							
Grams	Y	Y	Y	Y	Y	Y	Y
Wellstone	N	Y	N	N	Y	N	N
MISSISSIPPI							
Cochran	Y	Y	Y	Y	Y	Y	Y
Lott	Y	Y	Y	Y	Y	Y	Y
MISSOURI							
Ashcroft	Y	Y	Y	Y	Y	Y	Y
Bond	Y	Y	Y	Y	Y	N	Y
MONTANA							
Burns	Y	Y	Y	Y	Y	Y	Y
Baucus	N	Y	N	N	Y	Y	N
NEBRASKA							
Hagel	Y	Y	Y	Y	Y	Y	Y
Kerrey	N	Y	N	N	Y	Y	N
NEVADA							
Bryan	N	Y	N	N	Y	N	N
Reid	N	Y	N	N	Y	N	N
NEW HAMPSHIRE							
Gregg	Y	Y	Y	Y	Y	Y	Y
Smith	Y	Y	Y	Y	Y	Y	Y
NEW JERSEY							
Lautenberg	N	Y	N	N	Y	N	N
Torricelli	N	Y	N	N	Y	N	N
NEW MEXICO							
Domenici	Y	Y	Y	Y	Y	Y	Y
Bingaman	N	Y	N	N	Y	N	N
NEW YORK							
D'Amato	Y	Y	N	N	Y	N	Y
Moynihan	N	Y	N	N	Y	N	N
NORTH CAROLINA							
Faircloth	Y	Y	N	Y	Y	Y	Y
Helms	+	+	+	+	+	+	+
NORTH DAKOTA							
Conrad	N	Y	N	N	Y	N	N
Dorgan	N	Y	N	N	Y	N	N
OHIO							
DeWine	N	Y	N	N	Y	N	N
Glenn	N	Y	N	N	Y	N	N
OKLAHOMA							
Inhofe	Y	Y	Y	Y	Y	Y	Y
Nickles	Y	Y	Y	Y	Y	Y	Y
OREGON							
Smith	Y	Y	Y	Y	Y	Y	Y
Wyden	Y	Y	N	Y	Y	N	N
PENNSYLVANIA							
Santorum	Y	Y	Y	Y	Y	Y	Y
Specter	N	Y	N	N	Y	N	Y
RHODE ISLAND							
Chafee	N	Y	N	Y	Y	N	N
Reed	N	Y	N	N	Y	N	N
SOUTH CAROLINA							
Thurmond	Y	Y	Y	Y	Y	Y	Y
Hollings	N	Y	N	N	Y	N	N
SOUTH DAKOTA							
Daschle	N	Y	N	N	Y	N	N
Johnson	N	Y	N	N	Y	Y	N
TENNESSEE							
Frist	Y	Y	Y	Y	Y	Y	Y
Thompson	Y	Y	Y	Y	Y	Y	Y
TEXAS							
Gramm	Y	Y	Y	Y	Y	Y	Y
Hutchison	Y	Y	Y	Y	Y	Y	Y
UTAH							
Bennett	Y	Y	Y	Y	Y	Y	Y
Hatch	Y	Y	Y	Y	Y	Y	Y
VERMONT							
Jeffords	N	Y	Y	N	Y	N	N
Leahy	N	Y	N	N	Y	N	N
VIRGINIA							
Warner	Y	Y	Y	Y	Y	Y	Y
Robb	N	Y	N	N	Y	N	N
WASHINGTON							
Gorton	Y	Y	Y	Y	Y	Y	Y
Murray	N	Y	N	N	Y	N	N
WEST VIRGINIA							
Byrd	N	Y	N	N	Y	N	N
Rockefeller	N	Y	N	N	Y	N	N
WISCONSIN							
Feingold	N	Y	N	N	Y	N	N
Kohl	N	Y	N	N	Y	N	N
WYOMING							
Enzi	Y	Y	Y	Y	Y	Y	Y
Thomas	Y	Y	Y	Y	Y	Y	Y

Key
- Y Voted for (yea).
- # Paired for.
- + Announced for.
- N Voted against (nay).
- X Paired against.
- − Announced against.
- P Voted "present."
- C Voted "present" to avoid possible conflict of interest.
- ? Did not vote or otherwise make a position known.

Democrats   **Republicans**

ND Northern Democrats   SD Southern Democrats

Southern states - Ala., Ark., Fla., Ga., Ky., La., Miss., N.C., Okla., S.C., Tenn., Texas, Va.

71. S Con Res 86. Fiscal 1999 Budget Resolution/Tax Increase Supermajority. Kyl, R-Ariz., amendment to express the sense of the Senate that the Constitution should be amended to require more than a simple majority in each chamber of Congress in order to approve tax increase. Adopted 50-48: R 49-5; D 1-43 (ND 1-35, SD 0-8). April 2, 1998.

72. S Con Res 86. Fiscal 1999 Budget Resolution/Health Care Costs. Nickles, R-Okla., amendment to express the sense of the Senate that the Senate should not pass any health care legislation that would increase the costs of health care for families or divert resources away from treating patients. Adopted 98-0: R 54-0; D 44-0 (ND 36-0, SD 8-0). April 2, 1998.

73. S Con Res 86. Fiscal 1999 Budget Resolution/Patient's Bill of Rights. Nickles, R-Okla., motion to table (kill) the Kennedy, D-Mass., amendment that would express the sense of the Senate that a "patient's bill of rights" should be established for participants in health plans. The "bill of rights" would guarantee access to coverage, prohibit so-called gag clauses, and establish a procedure to provide for an independent, impartial entity to review appeals when a health plan decides to deny care. Motion agreed to 51-47: R 51-3; D 0-44 (ND 0-36, SD 0-8). April 2, 1998.

74. S Con Res 86. Fiscal 1999 Budget Resolution/Budget Surplus. Hutchison, R-Texas, amendment to express the sense of the Senate that any federal budget surplus should be dedicated to debt reduction or tax cuts. Adopted 53-45: R 49-5; D 4-40 (ND 2-34, SD 2-6). April 2, 1998.

75. S Con Res 86. Fiscal 1999 Budget Resolution/Veterans' Benefits. Rockefeller, D-W.Va., perfecting amendment to the Rockefeller amendment that would raise allocations for veterans programs by $10.5 billion in order to reinstate a Veterans' Affairs Department policy that grants compensation to veterans for smoking-related illnesses. The amendment would offset the spending by reducing highway spending by $10.5 billion. Adopted 98-0: R 54-0; D 44-0 (ND 36-0, SD 8-0). April 2, 1998.

76. S Con Res 86. Fiscal 1999 Budget Resolution/VA Smoking Benefit Study. Domenici, R-N.M., amendment to the Rockefeller, D-W.Va., amendment. The Domenici amendment would reduce veterans programs by $10.5 billion over five years by granting compensation to veterans only for smoking-related illnesses caused during a veteran's term of service. Adopted 52-46: R 47-7; D 5-39 (ND 3-33, SD 2-6). April 2, 1998. (Subsequently, the Rockefeller amendment as amended was adopted by voice vote.)

77. S Con Res 86. Fiscal 1999 Budget Resolution/Social Security Payroll Tax. Grams, R-Minn., amendment to express the sense of the Senate that any federal budget surplus should be used to reduce the Social Security payroll tax and to establish personal retirement accounts. Adopted 50-48: R 49-5; D 1-43 (ND 0-36, SD 1-7). April 2, 1998.

Senate Votes 78, 79, 80, 81, 82, 83, 84

	78	79	80	81	82	83	84
ALABAMA							
Sessions	Y	Y	Y	Y	N	N	Y
Shelby	Y	Y	Y	Y	N	N	Y
ALASKA							
Murkowski	Y	Y	Y	Y	N	N	Y
Stevens	Y	Y	Y	Y	N	N	Y
ARIZONA							
Kyl	Y	Y	Y	Y	N	N	Y
McCain	Y	Y	Y	Y	N	N	Y
ARKANSAS							
Hutchinson	Y	Y	Y	Y	N	N	Y
Bumpers	N	N	N	Y	N	N	N
CALIFORNIA							
Boxer	N	N	N	Y	N	N	N
Feinstein	N	N	N	Y	N	N	N
COLORADO							
Allard	Y	Y	Y	Y	N	N	Y
Campbell	Y	Y	Y	Y	N	N	Y
CONNECTICUT							
Dodd	N	N	N	Y	N	N	N
Lieberman	N	N	Y	N	N	N	N
DELAWARE							
Roth	Y	Y	Y	Y	N	N	Y
Biden	N	N	N	N	N	N	N
FLORIDA							
Mack	Y	Y	Y	Y	N	N	Y
Graham	Y	N	N	N	Y	Y	N
GEORGIA							
Coverdell	Y	Y	Y	Y	Y	Y	Y
Cleland	N	Y	Y	N	Y	Y	Y
HAWAII							
Akaka	N	N	N	N	Y	Y	N
Inouye	?	?	?	?	?	?	?
IDAHO							
Craig	Y	Y	Y	Y	N	N	Y
Kempthorne	Y	Y	Y	Y	N	N	Y
ILLINOIS							
Durbin	N	N	N	Y	N	N	N
Moseley-Braun	N	N	N	Y	N	N	N
INDIANA							
Coats	Y	Y	Y	Y	N	N	Y
Lugar	Y	Y	Y	Y	N	Y	Y

	78	79	80	81	82	83	84
IOWA							
Grassley	Y	Y	Y	Y	N	N	Y
Harkin	N	N	N	Y	Y	Y	N
KANSAS							
Brownback	Y	Y	Y	Y	N	N	Y
Roberts	Y	Y	Y	Y	N	N	Y
KENTUCKY							
McConnell	Y	Y	Y	Y	Y	Y	Y
Ford	N	N	N	N	Y	N	N
LOUISIANA							
Breaux	N	Y	N	Y	Y	Y	N
Landrieu	N	N	N	N	Y	Y	N
MAINE							
Collins	Y	Y	Y	Y	N	N	Y
Snowe	Y	Y	Y	Y	N	Y	Y
MARYLAND							
Mikulski	N	N	N	Y	N	N	N
Sarbanes	N	N	N	Y	N	Y	N
MASSACHUSETTS							
Kennedy	N	N	N	Y	N	Y	N
Kerry	N	N	N	Y	Y	Y	N
MICHIGAN							
Abraham	Y	Y	Y	Y	N	N	Y
Levin	N	N	N	N	Y	Y	N
MINNESOTA							
Grams	Y	Y	Y	Y	N	N	Y
Wellstone	N	N	N	N	Y	Y	N
MISSISSIPPI							
Cochran	Y	Y	Y	Y	N	N	Y
Lott	Y	Y	Y	Y	N	N	Y
MISSOURI							
Ashcroft	Y	Y	Y	Y	N	N	Y
Bond	Y	Y	Y	Y	N	N	Y
MONTANA							
Burns	Y	Y	Y	Y	N	N	Y
Baucus	N	N	N	Y	Y	Y	N
NEBRASKA							
Hagel	Y	Y	Y	Y	N	N	Y
Kerrey	N	N	N	Y	Y	Y	N
NEVADA							
Bryan	N	N	N	Y	N	N	N
Reid	N	N	N	Y	N	N	N

	78	79	80	81	82	83	84
NEW HAMPSHIRE							
Gregg	Y	N	Y	Y	N	N	Y
Smith	Y	Y	Y	Y	N	N	Y
NEW JERSEY							
Lautenberg	N	N	N	Y	Y	Y	N
Torricelli	N	N	N	Y	N	Y	N
NEW MEXICO							
Domenici	Y	Y	Y	Y	N	N	Y
Bingaman	N	Y	N	N	Y	N	N
NEW YORK							
D'Amato	Y	Y	Y	Y	N	N	Y
Moynihan	N	N	N	N	Y	Y	Y
NORTH CAROLINA							
Faircloth	Y	Y	Y	Y	N	Y	Y
Helms	+	+	?	+	–	+	–
NORTH DAKOTA							
Conrad	N	N	N	Y	Y	N	N
Dorgan	N	N	N	Y	N	N	N
OHIO							
DeWine	Y	Y	Y	Y	N	N	Y
Glenn	N	N	N	N	Y	N	N
OKLAHOMA							
Inhofe	Y	Y	Y	Y	N	N	Y
Nickles	Y	Y	Y	Y	N	N	Y
OREGON							
Smith	Y	Y	Y	Y	N	N	Y
Wyden	N	N	N	N	Y	Y	N
PENNSYLVANIA							
Santorum	Y	Y	Y	Y	N	N	Y
Specter	N	Y	Y	Y	N	Y	Y
RHODE ISLAND							
Chafee	Y	Y	Y	Y	N	N	Y
Reed	N	N	N	N	Y	N	N
SOUTH CAROLINA							
Thurmond	Y	Y	Y	Y	N	N	Y
Hollings	N	N	N	N	Y	N	N
SOUTH DAKOTA							
Daschle	N	N	N	Y	N	N	N
Johnson	N	N	N	N	Y	N	N
TENNESSEE							
Frist	Y	Y	Y	Y	N	N	Y
Thompson	Y	Y	Y	Y	N	Y	Y

Key

- Y Voted for (yea).
- # Paired for.
- + Announced for.
- N Voted against (nay).
- X Paired against.
- – Announced against.
- P Voted "present."
- C Voted "present" to avoid possible conflict of interest.
- ? Did not vote or otherwise make a position known.

Democrats   *Republicans*

	78	79	80	81	82	83	84
TEXAS							
Gramm	Y	Y	Y	Y	N	N	Y
Hutchison	Y	Y	Y	Y	N	N	Y
UTAH							
Bennett	Y	Y	Y	Y	N	N	Y
Hatch	Y	Y	Y	Y	N	N	Y
VERMONT							
Jeffords	N	Y	Y	Y	Y	N	Y
Leahy	N	N	N	N	Y	N	N
VIRGINIA							
Warner	Y	Y	Y	Y	N	Y	Y
Robb	N	N	Y	N	Y	Y	Y
WASHINGTON							
Gorton	Y	Y	Y	Y	N	N	Y
Murray	N	N	N	N	N	N	N
WEST VIRGINIA							
Byrd	Y	N	Y	N	Y	N	Y
Rockefeller	N	N	N	N	Y	Y	N
WISCONSIN							
Feingold	N	N	N	N	N	N	N
Kohl	N	N	N	N	Y	N	N
WYOMING							
Enzi	Y	Y	Y	Y	N	N	Y
Thomas	Y	Y	Y	Y	N	N	Y

ND Northern Democrats   SD Southern Democrats

Southern states - Ala., Ark., Fla., Ga., Ky., La., Miss., N.C., Okla., S.C., Tenn., Texas, Va.

78. S Con Res 86. Fiscal 1999 Budget Resolution/Education Spending. Grassley, R-Iowa, motion to table (kill) the Kennedy, D-Mass., amendment to recommend increasing spending on education programs by $1.5 billion over five years, financed by across-the-board cuts in non-defense discretionary spending. Motion agreed to 55-43: R 52-2; D 3-41 (ND 1-35, SD 2-6). April 2, 1998.

79. S Con Res 86. Fiscal 1999 Budget Resolution/Public Land Sales. Kempthorne, R-Idaho, amendment to the Reid, D-Nev., amendment. The Kempthorne amendment would express the sense of the Senate that the landowner incentive program of the Endangered Species Recovery Act may be financed from multiple funding sources, including the sale of public lands. The Reid amendment would urge that no public lands be sold to finance the program. Adopted 55-43: R 53-1; D 2-42 (ND 1-35, SD 1-7). April 2, 1998. (Subsequently, the Reid amendment as amended was adopted by voice vote.)

80. S Con Res 86. Fiscal 1999 Budget Resolution/Non-binding Amendments. Nickles, R-Okla., motion to waive the Budget Act with respect to the Lautenberg, D-N.J., point of order against the Nickles amendment. The Nickles amendment would establish a point of order under the budget act against non-binding amendments, such as those expressing the sense of Congress or the sense of the Senate, to budget resolutions during floor consideration. Motion rejected 59-39: R 54-0; D 5-39 (ND 2-34, SD 3-5). April 2, 1998. A three-fifths majority vote (60) of the total Senate is required to waive the Budget Act. (Subsequently, the chair upheld the point of order, and the amendment fell.)

81. S Con Res 86. Fiscal 1999 Budget Resolution/Education Spending. Domenici, R-N.M., motion to table (kill) the Murray, D-Wash., amendment that would recommend $5.9 billion over four years for increased education spending. Motion agreed to 55-43: R 54-0; D 1-43 (ND 1-35, SD 0-8). April 2, 1998.

82. S Con Res 86. Fiscal 1999 Budget Resolution/Disability Programs. Feingold, D-Wis., motion to waive the Budget Act with respect to the Domenici, R-N.M., point of order against the Feingold amendment. The Feingold amendment would establish a deficit-neutral reserve fund to finance programs to allow disabled individuals to function independently in society. The amendment, which would permit tax increases to finance the programs, calls for $2 billion for the fund. Motion rejected 47-51: R 4-50; D 43-1 (ND 35-1, SD 8-0). April 2, 1998. A three-fifths majority vote (60) of the total Senate is required to waive the Budget Act. (Subsequently, the chair upheld the point of order, and the amendment fell.)

83. S Con Res 86. Fiscal 1999 Budget Resolution/Tobacco Farmers. Robb, D-Va., motion to waive the Budget Act with respect to the Domenici, R-N.M., point of order against the Robb amendment. The Robb amendment would reserve federal revenue from any potential tobacco settlement for transition assistance to tobacco farmers or the Medicare hospital insurance trust fund. Motion rejected 31-67: R 7-47; D 24-20 (ND 17-19, SD 7-1). April 2, 1998. A three-fifths majority vote (60) of the total Senate is required to waive the Budget Act. (Subsequently, the chair upheld the point of order, and the amendment fell.)

84. S Con Res 86. Fiscal 1999 Budget Resolution/Adoption. Adoption of the concurrent resolution to adopt a five-year budget plan that maintains the budget surplus expected in fiscal 1998. The plan calls for any federal revenues generated from a possible tobacco settlement to be used to bolster the solvency of the Medicare program. The resolution does not provide for net tax cuts, but anticipates five-year tax cuts of $30 billion, offset by new tax revenues or reductions in mandatory spending. It also contains non-binding language calling for expiration of the tax code by Dec. 31, 2001. The resolution sets budget levels for the fiscal year ending Sept. 30, 1999: budget authority, $1,730 billion; outlays, $1,730 billion; revenues, $1,738 billion; and surplus, $8.4 billion. Adopted 57-41: R 54-0; D 3-41 (ND 1-35, SD 2-6). April 2, 1998.

Senate Votes 85, 86, 87, 88, 89, 90, 91

	85	86	87	88	89	90	91
ALABAMA							
Sessions	N	Y	Y	Y	Y	Y	Y
Shelby	Y	Y	Y	Y	Y	Y	Y
ALASKA							
Murkowski	N	Y	Y	Y	Y	Y	Y
Stevens	N	Y	Y	Y	Y	Y	Y
ARIZONA							
Kyl	N	Y	Y	Y	Y	Y	Y
McCain	N	Y	Y	Y	Y	Y	Y
ARKANSAS							
Hutchinson	N	Y	Y	Y	Y	Y	Y
Bumpers	Y	N	N	N	N	N	N
CALIFORNIA							
Boxer	Y	N	N	N	Y	N	N
Feinstein	Y	N	Y	Y	Y	N	N
COLORADO							
Allard	N	Y	Y	Y	Y	Y	Y
Campbell	Y	Y	Y	Y	Y	Y	Y
CONNECTICUT							
Dodd	Y	N	N	N	N	N	N
Lieberman	Y	Y	Y	N	Y	Y	N
DELAWARE							
Roth	Y	Y	Y	Y	Y	Y	Y
Biden	Y	Y	Y	N	Y	N	N
FLORIDA							
Mack	Y	Y	Y	Y	Y	Y	Y
Graham	Y	Y	N	N	Y	N	N
GEORGIA							
Coverdell	Y	Y	Y	Y	Y	Y	Y
Cleland	Y	N	N	N	N	N	N
HAWAII							
Akaka	Y	N	N	N	N	N	N
Inouye	?	?	N	N	N	N	N
IDAHO							
Craig	Y	Y	Y	Y	Y	Y	Y
Kempthorne	Y	Y	Y	Y	Y	Y	Y
ILLINOIS							
Durbin	Y	N	N	N	N	N	N
Moseley-Braun	Y	N	N	N	N	N	N
INDIANA							
Coats	N	Y	Y	Y	Y	Y	Y
Lugar	Y	Y	Y	Y	Y	Y	Y

	85	86	87	88	89	90	91
IOWA							
Grassley	N	Y	Y	Y	Y	Y	Y
Harkin	Y	N	N	N	N	N	N
KANSAS							
Brownback	N	Y	Y	Y	Y	Y	Y
Roberts	N	Y	Y	Y	Y	Y	Y
KENTUCKY							
McConnell	N	Y	Y	Y	Y	Y	Y
Ford	Y	N	N	N	N	N	N
LOUISIANA							
Breaux	Y	Y	Y	Y	Y	N	N
Landrieu	Y	N	N	Y	N	N	N
MAINE							
Collins	Y	Y	Y	Y	Y	Y	Y
Snowe	Y	Y	Y	Y	Y	Y	N
MARYLAND							
Mikulski	Y	N	N	N	Y	N	N
Sarbanes	Y	N	N	N	N	N	N
MASSACHUSETTS							
Kennedy	Y	N	N	N	N	N	N
Kerry	Y	N	N	N	N	N	N
MICHIGAN							
Abraham	Y	Y	Y	Y	Y	Y	Y
Levin	Y	N	N	N	N	N	N
MINNESOTA							
Grams	N	Y	Y	Y	Y	Y	Y
Wellstone	Y	N	N	N	N	N	N
MISSISSIPPI							
Cochran	Y	Y	Y	Y	Y	Y	Y
Lott	Y	Y	Y	Y	Y	Y	Y
MISSOURI							
Ashcroft	Y	Y	Y	Y	Y	Y	Y
Bond	Y	Y	Y	Y	Y	Y	Y
MONTANA							
Burns	N	Y	Y	Y	Y	Y	Y
Baucus	Y	N	N	N	N	N	N
NEBRASKA							
Hagel	Y	Y	Y	Y	Y	Y	Y
Kerrey	Y	N	N	N	N	N	N
NEVADA							
Bryan	Y	N	N	N	Y	N	N
Reid	Y	N	N	N	Y	N	N

	85	86	87	88	89	90	91
NEW HAMPSHIRE							
Gregg	Y	Y	Y	Y	Y	Y	Y
Smith	N	Y	Y	Y	Y	Y	Y
NEW JERSEY							
Lautenberg	Y	N	N	N	N	N	N
Torricelli	Y	Y	Y	Y	Y	Y	N
NEW MEXICO							
Domenici	N	Y	Y	Y	Y	Y	Y
Bingaman	Y	N	N	N	Y	N	N
NEW YORK							
D'Amato	Y	N	Y	Y	N	Y	N
Moynihan	+	–	?	?	?	?	N
NORTH CAROLINA							
Faircloth	Y	Y	Y	Y	Y	Y	Y
Helms	N	Y	Y	Y	Y	Y	?
NORTH DAKOTA							
Conrad	Y	N	N	N	Y	N	N
Dorgan	Y	N	N	N	N	N	N
OHIO							
DeWine	Y	Y	Y	Y	Y	Y	Y
Glenn	Y	N	N	N	N	N	N
OKLAHOMA							
Inhofe	Y	Y	Y	Y	Y	Y	Y
Nickles	N	Y	Y	Y	Y	Y	Y
OREGON							
Smith	N	Y	Y	Y	Y	Y	Y
Wyden	Y	N	N	N	N	N	N
PENNSYLVANIA							
Santorum	Y	Y	Y	Y	Y	Y	Y
Specter	Y	N	Y	Y	Y	N	N
RHODE ISLAND							
Chafee	Y	N	Y	Y	Y	N	N
Reed	Y	N	N	N	N	N	N
SOUTH CAROLINA							
Thurmond	Y	Y	Y	Y	Y	Y	Y
Hollings	Y	N	N	Y	N	N	N
SOUTH DAKOTA							
Daschle	Y	N	N	N	N	N	N
Johnson	Y	N	N	N	N	N	N
TENNESSEE							
Frist	Y	Y	Y	Y	Y	Y	Y
Thompson	Y	Y	Y	Y	Y	Y	Y

Key

Y Voted for (yea).
Paired for.
+ Announced for.
N Voted against (nay).
X Paired against.
– Announced against.
P Voted "present."
C Voted "present" to avoid possible conflict of interest.
? Did not vote or otherwise make a position known.

Democrats *Republicans*

	85	86	87	88	89	90	91
TEXAS							
Gramm	N	Y	Y	Y	Y	Y	Y
Hutchison	Y	Y	Y	Y	Y	Y	Y
UTAH							
Bennett	?	?	?	?	?	?	Y
Hatch	Y	Y	Y	Y	Y	Y	Y
VERMONT							
Jeffords	N	N	Y	Y	Y	Y	N
Leahy	Y	N	N	Y	N	N	N
VIRGINIA							
Warner	Y	Y	Y	Y	Y	Y	Y
Robb	Y	N	N	N	Y	N	N
WASHINGTON							
Gorton	N	Y	Y	Y	Y	Y	Y
Murray	Y	N	N	N	N	N	N
WEST VIRGINIA							
Byrd	N	Y	Y	Y	Y	Y	Y
Rockefeller	Y	N	N	N	Y	N	N
WISCONSIN							
Feingold	Y	N	N	N	N	N	N
Kohl	Y	N	N	Y	N	N	N
WYOMING							
Enzi	N	Y	Y	Y	Y	Y	Y
Thomas	N	Y	Y	Y	Y	Y	Y

ND Northern Democrats SD Southern Democrats

Southern states - Ala., Ark., Fla., Ga., Ky., La., Miss., N.C., Okla., S.C., Tenn., Texas, Va.

85. S 414. Ocean Shipping/Shipping Intermediaries. Hutchison, R-Texas, motion to table (kill) the Gorton, R-Wash., amendment to the Hutchison substitute amendment. The Gorton amendment would allow shipping intermediaries the same proprietary rights to offer service contracts to shippers as other ocean common carriers would have under the substitute amendment. The underlying substitute would eliminate requirements that ocean carriers file tariff rate increases or decreases with the Federal Maritime Commission and instead would require carriers to publish their shipping rates through a World Wide Web page or other non-governmental publication. Motion agreed to 72-25: R 30-24; D 42-1 (ND 34-1, SD 8-0). April 21, 1998. (Subsequently, the underlying substitute was adopted and the bill was passed by voice vote.)

86. HR 2646. Expanding Education Savings Accounts/Teacher Loan Forgiveness. Coverdell, R-Ga., motion to table (kill) the Kennedy, D-Mass., amendment to replace the bill's language expanding the accounts with language authorizing $7.2 million over two years to establish a federal program to forgive as much as $8,000 in unpaid student loans for each college graduate who becomes a full-time public school teacher. Motion agreed to 56-41: R 50-4; D 6-37 (ND 4-31, SD 2-6). April 21, 1998.

87. HR 2646. Expanding Education Savings Accounts/Higher Education. Gramm, R-Texas, motion to table (kill) the Glenn, D-Ohio, amendment to require that the expanded tax-free accounts may only be used for post-secondary education expenses. Motion agreed to 60-38: R 54-0; D 6-38 (ND 5-31, SD 1-7). April 21, 1998.

88. HR 2646. Expanding Education Savings Accounts/Teacher Merit Pay and Testing. Mack, R-Fla., amendment to provide incentives for states and localities to establish merit pay programs for teachers and implement teacher testing programs. Adopted 63-35: R 54-0; D 9-35 (ND 6-30, SD 3-5). April 21, 1998.

89. HR 2646. Expanding Education Savings Accounts/Same Gender Schooling. Hutchison, R-Texas, amendment to add proposals for same gender classrooms and schools to the list of "innovative assistance programs" identified under current law as eligible to receive targeted federal funding, as long as the same gender school and classroom programs offer comparable educational opportunities to students of both sexes. Adopted 69-29: R 54-0; D 15-29 (ND 11-25, SD 4-4). April 21, 1998.

90. HR 2646. Expanding Education Savings Accounts/School Construction Bonds. Coverdell, R-Ga., motion to table (kill) the Moseley-Braun, D-Ill., amendment to provide $10 billion in tax credits over ten years for purchasers of interest-free bonds to fund school construction. Motion agreed to 56-42: R 52-2; D 4-40 (ND 4-32, SD 0-8). April 21, 1998.

91. HR 2646. Expanding Education Savings Accounts/Education Block Grants. Gorton, R-Wash., amendment to require each state to decide within one year how it would like to receive its future federal education funding: administered as it is currently, sent directly to the states or sent directly to the local school districts. Adopted 50-49: R 50-4; D 0-45 (ND 0-37, SD 0-8). April 22, 1998.

Senate Votes 92, 93, 94, 95, 96, 97, 98

	92 93 94 95 96 97 98
ALABAMA	
Sessions	Y N Y Y Y N N
Shelby	Y N Y Y Y N N
ALASKA	
Murkowski	Y N Y N Y N N
Stevens	Y N Y Y Y N N
ARIZONA	
Kyl	Y N Y Y Y N N
McCain	Y N Y Y Y N N
ARKANSAS	
Hutchinson	Y N Y Y Y N N
Bumpers	Y Y N N N Y Y
CALIFORNIA	
Boxer	Y Y N N N Y Y
Feinstein	Y Y N N N N Y
COLORADO	
Allard	Y N Y Y Y N N
Campbell	Y Y Y Y Y N –
CONNECTICUT	
Dodd	Y Y N N N Y Y
Lieberman	Y Y N Y N Y Y
DELAWARE	
Roth	Y N Y N Y N N
Biden	Y Y N N N N N
FLORIDA	
Mack	Y N Y Y Y N N
Graham	Y Y N N N N Y
GEORGIA	
Coverdell	Y N Y Y Y N N
Cleland	Y Y N N Y N N
HAWAII	
Akaka	Y Y N N N Y Y
Inouye	Y Y N N N Y Y
IDAHO	
Craig	Y N Y Y Y N N
Kempthorne	Y N Y Y Y N N
ILLINOIS	
Durbin	Y Y N N N Y Y
Moseley-Braun	Y Y N N N Y Y
INDIANA	
Coats	Y N Y Y Y N N
Lugar	Y N Y Y Y N N

	92 93 94 95 96 97 98
IOWA	
Grassley	Y N Y N Y N N
Harkin	Y Y N N N Y Y
KANSAS	
Brownback	Y N Y Y Y N N
Roberts	Y N Y Y Y N N
KENTUCKY	
McConnell	Y N Y Y Y N N
Ford	Y Y N N N Y Y
LOUISIANA	
Breaux	Y Y N N N N Y
Landrieu	Y Y N N N N Y
MAINE	
Collins	Y N Y N Y N Y
Snowe	Y N Y Y Y N N
MARYLAND	
Mikulski	Y Y N N N Y Y
Sarbanes	Y Y N N N Y Y
MASSACHUSETTS	
Kennedy	Y Y N N N Y Y
Kerry	Y Y N N N Y Y
MICHIGAN	
Abraham	Y N Y Y Y N N
Levin	Y Y N N N Y Y
MINNESOTA	
Grams	Y N Y Y Y N N
Wellstone	Y Y N N N Y Y
MISSISSIPPI	
Cochran	Y N Y Y Y N N
Lott	Y N Y Y Y N N
MISSOURI	
Ashcroft	Y N Y Y Y N N
Bond	Y N Y Y Y N N
MONTANA	
Burns	Y N Y Y Y N N
Baucus	Y Y N N N N Y
NEBRASKA	
Hagel	Y N Y N Y N N
Kerrey	Y Y N N N Y Y
NEVADA	
Bryan	Y Y N N N N N
Reid	Y Y N N Y N Y

	92 93 94 95 96 97 98
NEW HAMPSHIRE	
Gregg	Y N Y Y Y N N
Smith	Y N Y Y Y N N
NEW JERSEY	
Lautenberg	Y Y N N N Y Y
Torricelli	Y Y N N N N Y
NEW MEXICO	
Domenici	Y N Y Y Y N N
Bingaman	Y Y N N N Y Y
NEW YORK	
D'Amato	Y N Y N Y N Y
Moynihan	Y Y N N N Y Y
NORTH CAROLINA	
Faircloth	Y N Y Y Y N N
Helms	? ? ? Y Y N N
NORTH DAKOTA	
Conrad	Y Y N N N Y Y
Dorgan	Y Y N N N Y Y
OHIO	
DeWine	Y N Y Y Y N N
Glenn	Y Y N N N Y Y
OKLAHOMA	
Inhofe	Y N Y Y Y N N
Nickles	Y N Y Y Y N N
OREGON	
Smith	Y N Y Y Y N N
Wyden	Y Y N N N Y Y
PENNSYLVANIA	
Santorum	Y N Y Y Y N N
Specter	Y N Y N Y N N
RHODE ISLAND	
Chafee	Y N Y Y Y N N
Reed	Y Y N N N Y Y
SOUTH CAROLINA	
Thurmond	Y N Y Y Y N N
Hollings	Y Y N N N Y Y
SOUTH DAKOTA	
Daschle	Y Y N N N Y Y
Johnson	Y Y N N N Y Y
TENNESSEE	
Frist	Y N Y Y Y N N
Thompson	Y N Y Y Y N N

	92 93 94 95 96 97 98
TEXAS	
Gramm	Y N Y Y Y N N
Hutchison	Y N Y Y Y N N
UTAH	
Bennett	Y N Y Y Y N N
Hatch	Y N Y Y Y N N
VERMONT	
Jeffords	Y Y N N Y N Y
Leahy	Y Y N N N Y Y
VIRGINIA	
Warner	Y N Y Y Y N N
Robb	Y Y N N N Y Y
WASHINGTON	
Gorton	Y N Y Y Y N N
Murray	Y Y N N N Y Y
WEST VIRGINIA	
Byrd	Y Y N N N N N
Rockefeller	Y Y N N N Y Y
WISCONSIN	
Feingold	Y Y Y N N Y Y
Kohl	Y Y N N N Y Y
WYOMING	
Enzi	Y N Y Y Y N N
Thomas	Y N Y Y Y N N

Key

Y Voted for (yea).
\# Paired for.
\+ Announced for.
N Voted against (nay).
X Paired against.
– Announced against.
P Voted "present."
C Voted "present" to avoid possible conflict of interest.
? Did not vote or otherwise make a position known.

● Democrats   **Republicans**

ND Northern Democrats   SD Southern Democrats

Southern states - Ala., Ark., Fla., Ga., Ky., La., Miss., N.C., Okla., S.C., Tenn., Texas, Va.

92. HR 2646. Expanding Education Savings Accounts/Federal Education Funding. Hutchinson, R-Ark., amendment to express the sense of Congress that 95 percent of all federal education funds should be spent for children "in their classrooms." Adopted 99-0: R 54-0; D 45-0 (ND 37-0, SD 8-0). April 22, 1998.

93. HR 2646. Expanding Education Savings Accounts/National Class Sizes. Murray, D-Wash., amendment to express the sense of Congress that Congress should support hiring 100,000 new teachers to reduce first-through third-grade class sizes to a national average of 18 students. Rejected 49-50: R 4-50; D 45-0 (ND 37-0, SD 8-0). April 22, 1998.

94. HR 2646. Expanding Education Savings Accounts/National Education Testing. Ashcroft, R-Mo., amendment to the Levin, D-Mich., amendment. The Ashcroft amendment would restore the bill's savings account expansion and would prohibit the use of any federal funds for national education testing unless Congress passes explicit authorizing legislation. The Levin amendment would replace the savings account language with a provision to increase the current 20 percent lifetime tax credit on college costs to 50 percent for elementary and secondary school teachers who return to school to receive technology training. Adopted 52-47: R 51-3; D 1-44 (ND 1-36, SD 0-8). April 22, 1998.

95. HR 2646. Expanding Education Savings Accounts/Education Tax Deductions. Coats, R-Ind., amendment to allow taxpayers to deduct from their income tax returns 110 percent of charitable contributions to groups that provide scholarships to pre-college students whose family income is below 185 percent of the poverty line. Rejected 46-54: R 45-10; D 1-44 (ND 1-36, SD 0-8). April 23, 1998.

96. HR 2646. Expanding Education Savings Accounts/High School Performance Awards. Kempthorne, R-Idaho, amendment to the Landrieu, D-La., amendment. The Kempthorne amendment would restore the bill's savings account expansion and allow states to use some of their federal education funds to provide awards to public high schools based on the schools' performance on statewide tests composed entirely by the state. Adopted 58-42: R 55-0; D 3-42 (ND 2-35, SD 1-7). April 23, 1998. (Subsequently, the Senate agreed by voice vote to consider the Kempthorne amendment as an amendment directly to the underlying bill, thus not altering the Landrieu amendment.)

97. HR 2646. Expanding Education Savings Accounts/Blue Ribbon Schools. Landrieu, D-La., amendment to replace the savings account language with language to establish a program to award $100,000 each to nationally recognized public or private "Blue Ribbon" schools. Rejected 34-66: R 0-55; D 34-11 (ND 29-8, SD 5-3). April 23, 1998.

98. HR 2646. Expanding Education Savings Accounts/IDEA Funding. Dodd, D-Conn., motion to waive the Budget Act with respect to the Coverdell, R-Ga., point of order against the Dodd amendment. The Dodd amendment would remove the bill's education savings account language and direct that any revenue generated by other provisions of the bill be used to fund special education programs under the Individuals with Disabilities Education Act. Motion rejected 46-53: R 4-50; D 42-3 (ND 35-2, SD 7-1). April 23, 1998. A three-fifths majority vote (60) of the total Senate is required to waive the Budget Act. (Subsequently, the chair upheld the point of order, and the amendment fell.)

Senate Votes 99, 100, 101, 102, 103, 104, 105

	99	100	101	102	103	104	105
ALABAMA							
Sessions	Y	N	N	Y	Y	Y	Y
Shelby	Y	N	N	Y	Y	Y	Y
ALASKA							
Murkowski	Y	N	Y	Y	Y	?	Y
Stevens	Y	N	Y	Y	Y	Y	Y
ARIZONA							
Kyl	Y	N	N	Y	Y	Y	Y
McCain	Y	N	Y	?	?	Y	Y
ARKANSAS							
Hutchinson	Y	N	N	Y	Y	Y	Y
Bumpers	N	Y	Y	N	Y	Y	N
CALIFORNIA							
Boxer	N	Y	Y	N	Y	Y	N
Feinstein	Y	Y	Y	N	Y	Y	N
COLORADO							
Allard	Y	N	N	Y	Y	Y	Y
Campbell	Y	N	Y	Y	Y	Y	Y
CONNECTICUT							
Dodd	N	Y	Y	N	Y	Y	N
Lieberman	Y	Y	Y	Y	Y	Y	Y
DELAWARE							
Roth	Y	N	Y	Y	Y	Y	N
Biden	Y	Y	Y	N	Y	Y	N
FLORIDA							
Mack	Y	N	N	Y	Y	Y	Y
Graham	N	Y	Y	Y	Y	Y	N
GEORGIA							
Coverdell	Y	N	N	Y	Y	Y	Y
Cleland	Y	Y	Y	N	Y	Y	N
HAWAII							
Akaka	N	Y	Y	N	Y	Y	N
Inouye	N	Y	Y	N	Y	?	N
IDAHO							
Craig	Y	N	Y	Y	Y	Y	Y
Kempthorne	Y	N	Y	Y	Y	Y	Y
ILLINOIS							
Durbin	N	Y	Y	N	Y	?	N
Moseley-Braun	N	Y	Y	N	Y	Y	N
INDIANA							
Coats	Y	N	N	Y	Y	Y	Y
Lugar	Y	N	N	Y	Y	Y	Y
IOWA							
Grassley	Y	N	N	Y	Y	Y	Y
Harkin	N	Y	Y	N	Y	Y	N
KANSAS							
Brownback	Y	N	N	Y	?	Y	Y
Roberts	Y	N	N	Y	Y	Y	Y
KENTUCKY							
McConnell	Y	N	Y	Y	Y	Y	Y
Ford	N	Y	Y	N	Y	Y	Y
LOUISIANA							
Breaux	Y	Y	Y	Y	Y	Y	Y
Landrieu	N	Y	Y	N	Y	Y	N
MAINE							
Collins	Y	N	Y	Y	Y	Y	Y
Snowe	Y	Y	Y	Y	Y	Y	Y
MARYLAND							
Mikulski	N	Y	Y	N	Y	Y	N
Sarbanes	N	Y	Y	N	Y	Y	N
MASSACHUSETTS							
Kennedy	N	Y	Y	N	Y	?	N
Kerry	N	Y	Y	N	Y	Y	N
MICHIGAN							
Abraham	Y	N	Y	Y	Y	Y	Y
Levin	N	Y	Y	N	Y	Y	N
MINNESOTA							
Grams	Y	N	N	Y	Y	Y	Y
Wellstone	N	Y	Y	N	Y	Y	N
MISSISSIPPI							
Cochran	Y	N	N	Y	Y	Y	Y
Lott	Y	N	N	Y	Y	Y	Y
MISSOURI							
Ashcroft	Y	N	N	Y	Y	Y	Y
Bond	Y	Y	Y	Y	Y	Y	Y
MONTANA							
Burns	Y	N	Y	Y	Y	Y	Y
Baucus	N	Y	Y	N	Y	Y	N
NEBRASKA							
Hagel	Y	N	N	Y	Y	Y	Y
Kerrey	N	Y	Y	N	Y	Y	N
NEVADA							
Bryan	N	Y	Y	N	Y	Y	N
Reid	N	Y	Y	N	Y	Y	N
NEW HAMPSHIRE							
Gregg	Y	N	N	Y	Y	?	Y
Smith	Y	N	Y	Y	Y	Y	Y
NEW JERSEY							
Lautenberg	N	Y	Y	N	Y	Y	N
Torricelli	Y	Y	Y	Y	Y	Y	N
NEW MEXICO							
Domenici	Y	N	Y	Y	Y	Y	Y
Bingaman	N	Y	N	Y	Y	Y	N
NEW YORK							
D'Amato	Y	Y	Y	Y	Y	Y	Y
Moynihan	N	Y	Y	N	Y	Y	N
NORTH CAROLINA							
Faircloth	Y	N	Y	Y	Y	?	Y
Helms	Y	N	N	Y	Y	Y	Y
NORTH DAKOTA							
Conrad	N	Y	Y	N	Y	Y	N
Dorgan	N	Y	Y	N	Y	Y	N
OHIO							
DeWine	Y	N	Y	Y	Y	Y	Y
Glenn	N	Y	Y	N	Y	Y	N
OKLAHOMA							
Inhofe	Y	N	N	Y	Y	?	Y
Nickles	Y	N	N	Y	Y	Y	Y
OREGON							
Smith	Y	N	Y	Y	Y	Y	Y
Wyden	N	Y	Y	N	Y	Y	N
PENNSYLVANIA							
Santorum	Y	N	Y	Y	Y	Y	Y
Specter	Y	Y	Y	N	Y	Y	N
RHODE ISLAND							
Chafee	Y	N	Y	Y	Y	Y	Y
Reed	N	Y	Y	N	Y	Y	N
SOUTH CAROLINA							
Thurmond	Y	N	N	Y	Y	Y	Y
Hollings	N	Y	Y	N	Y	Y	N
SOUTH DAKOTA							
Daschle	N	Y	Y	N	Y	Y	N
Johnson	N	Y	Y	N	Y	Y	N
TENNESSEE							
Frist	Y	N	N	Y	Y	Y	Y
Thompson	Y	N	Y	Y	Y	Y	Y
TEXAS							
Gramm	Y	N	Y	Y	Y	Y	Y
Hutchison	Y	N	Y	Y	Y	Y	Y
UTAH							
Bennett	Y	N	Y	Y	?	Y	Y
Hatch	Y	N	Y	Y	Y	Y	Y
VERMONT							
Jeffords	N	N	Y	N	Y	Y	N
Leahy	N	Y	Y	N	Y	Y	N
VIRGINIA							
Warner	Y	N	Y	Y	Y	Y	Y
Robb	N	Y	Y	N	Y	Y	N
WASHINGTON							
Gorton	Y	N	N	Y	Y	Y	Y
Murray	N	Y	Y	N	Y	Y	N
WEST VIRGINIA							
Byrd	Y	Y	Y	Y	Y	Y	N
Rockefeller	N	Y	Y	N	Y	Y	N
WISCONSIN							
Feingold	N	Y	N	N	Y	Y	N
Kohl	N	Y	Y	N	Y	?	N
WYOMING							
Enzi	Y	N	N	Y	Y	Y	Y
Thomas	Y	N	Y	Y	Y	Y	Y

Key

- **Y** Voted for (yea).
- **#** Paired for.
- **+** Announced for.
- **N** Voted against (nay).
- **X** Paired against.
- **−** Announced against.
- **P** Voted "present."
- **C** Voted "present" to avoid possible conflict of interest.
- **?** Did not vote or otherwise make a position known.

Democrats • Republicans

ND Northern Democrats SD Southern Democrats

Southern states – Ala., Ark., Fla., Ga., Ky., La., Miss., N.C., Okla., S.C., Tenn., Texas, Va.

99. HR 2646. Expanding Education Savings Accounts/Technology Training. Coverdell, R-Ga., motion to table (kill) the Levin, D-Mich., amendment to the modified Levin amendment. The second-degree Levin amendment would require that the expanded savings accounts could only be used for post-secondary education expenses and would increase the current 20 percent lifetime tax credit on college costs to 50 percent for elementary and secondary school teachers who return to school to receive technology training. Motion agreed to 61-39: R 54-1; D 7-38 (ND 5-32, SD 2-6). April 23, 1998. (Subsequently, the underlying Levin amendment as amended was adopted by voice vote.)

100. HR 2646. Expanding Education Savings Accounts/After-School Programs. Boxer, D-Calif., amendment to establish a $50 million annual grant program for five years to develop after-school programs. Rejected 49-51: R 4-51; D 45-0 (ND 37-0, SD 8-0). April 23, 1998.

101. HR 2646. Expanding Education Savings Accounts/School Drop-Out Prevention. Bingaman, D-N.M., amendment to establish a national grant program to help schools create dropout prevention programs. Adopted 74-26: R 30-25; D 44-1 (ND 36-1, SD 8-0). April 23, 1998.

102. HR 2646. Expanding Education Savings Accounts/Passage. Passage of the bill to allow parents, relatives or outside corporations to contribute up to a combined total of $2,000 a year of after-tax funds in tax-free savings accounts designated for educational expenses. Current law allows up to $500 for college expenses, but the bill would raise the limit to $2,000 and allow the accounts to be used for public or private elementary and secondary education expenses. The bill also would prohibit federal funding for national education testing, give states the option of receiving federal education funds through block grants directly to the state or local level and provide incentives for states and localities to establish merit pay and testing programs for teachers. Passed 56-43: R 51-3; D 5-40 (ND 3-34, SD 2-6). April 23, 1998. A "nay" was a vote in support of the president's position.

103. Northern Ireland Peace Agreement/Adoption. Adoption of the concurrent resolution to express the sense of Congress that all of the participants in the recent negotiations that led to a peace agreement concerning Northern Ireland deserve congratulations for their efforts. The resolution singles out British Prime Minister Tony Blair, Irish Taoiseach Bertie Ahern, President Clinton and former Senate Majority Leader George Mitchell, D-Maine, for particular praise. Adopted 97-0: R 52-0; D 45-0 (ND 37-0, SD 8-0). April 23, 1998.

104. Fleming Nomination/Confirmation. Confirmation of President Clinton's nomination of Scott Snyder Fleming of Virginia to be assistant secretary for legislation and congressional affairs in the Department of Education. Confirmed 92-0: R 51-0; D 41-0 (ND 33-0, SD 8-0). April 27, 1998. A "yea" was a vote in support of the president's position.

105. HR 1757. Fiscal 1998 State Department Authorization/Conference Report. Adoption of the conference report on the bill to authorize $1.75 billion in fiscal 1998 and $1.69 billion in fiscal 1999 for State Department diplomatic and consular functions, authorize $819 million over fiscal years 1998 through 2000 to pay part of the U.S. debt to the United Nations, codify restrictions on U.S. funds for international family planning and consolidate several U.S. foreign policy agencies. Adopted (thus cleared for the president) 51-49: R 49-6; D 2-43 (ND 0-37, SD 2-6). April 28, 1998. A "nay" was a vote in support of the president's position.

Senate Votes 106, 107, 108, 109, 110, 111, 112

	106	107	108	109	110	111	112
ALABAMA							
Sessions	N	Y	Y	Y	Y	N	Y
Shelby	N	Y	Y	Y	N	N	Y
ALASKA							
Murkowski	N	Y	Y	N	Y	N	N
Stevens	N	Y	Y	Y	N	N	N
ARIZONA							
Kyl	N	Y	Y	Y	N	N	N
McCain	N	Y	Y	Y	N	N	N
ARKANSAS							
Hutchinson	Y	Y	Y	Y	Y	Y	Y
Bumpers	Y	N	Y	Y	N	Y	Y
CALIFORNIA							
Boxer	N	Y	Y	N	N	N	N
Feinstein	N	Y	Y	N	N	N	N
COLORADO							
Allard	N	Y	Y	Y	N	N	N
Campbell	N	Y	Y	Y	N	N	Y
CONNECTICUT							
Dodd	N	Y	Y	N	N	N	N
Lieberman	N	Y	Y	N	N	N	N
DELAWARE							
Roth	N	Y	Y	N	N	N	N
Biden	N	Y	Y	N	N	N	N
FLORIDA							
Mack	N	Y	Y	N	N	N	N
Graham	Y	N	Y	N	N	N	N
GEORGIA							
Coverdell	N	Y	Y	N	N	N	N
Cleland	N	Y	Y	N	N	N	N
HAWAII							
Akaka	N	Y	Y	N	N	N	N
Inouye	N	Y	Y	N	N	N	N
IDAHO							
Craig	N	Y	Y	Y	Y	Y	Y
Kempthorne	Y	Y	Y	Y	Y	Y	Y
ILLINOIS							
Durbin	N	Y	Y	N	N	N	N
Moseley-Braun	Y	?	+	N	N	N	N
INDIANA							
Coats	N	Y	Y	Y	N	N	N
Lugar	N	Y	Y	N	N	N	N

	106	107	108	109	110	111	112
IOWA							
Grassley	N	Y	Y	N	Y	N	N
Harkin	Y	Y	Y	N	N	Y	Y
KANSAS							
Brownback	N	Y	Y	N	N	N	N
Roberts	N	N	Y	Y	Y	N	Y
KENTUCKY							
McConnell	N	Y	Y	N	N	N	N
Ford	N	Y	Y	N	N	N	N
LOUISIANA							
Breaux	N	Y	Y	N	N	N	N
Landrieu	N	Y	Y	N	N	N	N
MAINE							
Collins	N	Y	Y	N	N	N	N
Snowe	N	Y	Y	Y	N	N	Y
MARYLAND							
Mikulski	N	Y	Y	N	N	N	N
Sarbanes	N	N	Y	N	N	N	N
MASSACHUSETTS							
Kennedy	N	Y	Y	N	N	N	N
Kerry	N	Y	Y	N	N	N	N
MICHIGAN							
Abraham	N	Y	Y	Y	N	N	N
Levin	N	Y	Y	N	N	N	N
MINNESOTA							
Grams	N	Y	Y	N	N	N	N
Wellstone	Y	N	Y	N	N	Y	Y
MISSISSIPPI							
Cochran	N	Y	Y	N	N	N	N
Lott	N	Y	Y	N	N	N	N
MISSOURI							
Ashcroft	Y	N	Y	Y	Y	Y	Y
Bond	Y	Y	?	Y	N	N	Y
MONTANA							
Burns	N	Y	Y	Y	N	N	Y
Baucus	Y	Y	Y	N	N	N	N
NEBRASKA							
Hagel	N	Y	Y	N	N	N	N
Kerrey	N	Y	Y	N	N	N	N
NEVADA							
Bryan	N	Y	Y	N	N	N	N
Reid	N	Y	Y	N	N	N	Y

	106	107	108	109	110	111	112
NEW HAMPSHIRE							
Gregg	N	Y	Y	Y	N	N	Y
Smith	Y	N	Y	Y	Y	Y	Y
NEW JERSEY							
Lautenberg	N	Y	Y	N	N	N	N
Torricelli	Y	Y	Y	N	N	Y	Y
NEW MEXICO							
Domenici	N	Y	Y	N	N	N	N
Bingaman	N	N	Y	N	N	N	N
NEW YORK							
D'Amato	N	Y	Y	N	N	N	N
Moynihan	Y	Y	Y	N	Y	Y	Y
NORTH CAROLINA							
Faircloth	N	Y	Y	Y	N	N	Y
Helms	N	Y	Y	Y	N	N	Y
NORTH DAKOTA							
Conrad	Y	Y	Y	Y	N	N	Y
Dorgan	Y	Y	Y	Y	N	N	Y
OHIO							
DeWine	N	Y	Y	N	N	N	N
Glenn	N	Y	Y	N	N	N	N
OKLAHOMA							
Inhofe	N	Y	Y	Y	N	N	Y
Nickles	N	Y	Y	Y	Y	N	Y
OREGON							
Smith	N	Y	Y	N	N	N	N
Wyden	N	Y	Y	Y	N	Y	Y
PENNSYLVANIA							
Santorum	N	Y	Y	N	N	N	N
Specter	N	Y	Y	Y	Y	Y	Y
RHODE ISLAND							
Chafee	N	Y	Y	N	N	N	N
Reed	N	Y	Y	N	N	N	N
SOUTH CAROLINA							
Thurmond	N	Y	Y	N	N	N	N
Hollings	N	Y	Y	?	N	N	Y
SOUTH DAKOTA							
Daschle	N	Y	Y	N	N	N	N
Johnson	Y	Y	Y	N	N	N	N
TENNESSEE							
Frist	N	Y	Y	N	N	N	N
Thompson	N	Y	Y	N	N	N	N

	106	107	108	109	110	111	112
TEXAS							
Gramm	N	Y	Y	Y	Y	N	N
Hutchison	N	Y	Y	Y	Y	N	Y
UTAH							
Bennett	N	Y	Y	N	N	N	N
Hatch	N	Y	Y	Y	N	N	N
VERMONT							
Jeffords	Y	Y	Y	Y	Y	Y	Y
Leahy	Y	Y	Y	N	N	Y	Y
VIRGINIA							
Warner	Y	Y	Y	Y	Y	Y	Y
Robb	N	Y	Y	N	N	N	N
WASHINGTON							
Gorton	N	Y	Y	N	N	N	N
Murray	Y	Y	Y	N	N	Y	Y
WEST VIRGINIA							
Byrd	Y	N	Y	N	N	N	N
Rockefeller	N	Y	?	N	N	N	N
WISCONSIN							
Feingold	Y	Y	Y	N	Y	N	N
Kohl	Y	Y	Y	N	N	N	Y
WYOMING							
Enzi	N	Y	Y	Y	N	N	Y
Thomas	N	Y	Y	Y	N	N	N

Key

- Y Voted for (yea).
- # Paired for.
- + Announced for.
- N Voted against (nay).
- X Paired against.
- − Announced against.
- P Voted "present."
- C Voted "present" to avoid possible conflict of interest.
- ? Did not vote or otherwise make a position known.

• Democrats   **Republicans**

ND Northern Democrats   SD Southern Democrats

Southern states - Ala., Ark., Fla., Ga., Ky., La., Miss., N.C., Okla., S.C., Tenn., Texas, Va.

---

106. NATO Expansion/U.S. Costs. Harkin, D-Iowa, amendment to add language to the resolution of ratification that would limit U.S. support for so-called national expenses of new members to 25 percent of the total contributions made by all NATO nations. Rejected 24-76: R 7-48; D 17-28 (ND 15-22, SD 2-6). April 28, 1998. A "nay" was a vote in support of the president's position.

107. NATO Expansion/NATO Policy. Kyl, R-Ariz., amendment to add language to the resolution of ratification that would stipulate that the United States continues to support NATO policy as outlined in the 1991 Strategic Concept of NATO, which states that NATO is primarily a defensive military alliance, that strong U.S. leadership in NATO protects vital U.S. national interests and that the costs of defending Europe will be equitably shared by NATO members. Adopted 90-9: R 52-3; D 38-6 (ND 32-4, SD 6-2). April 28, 1998.

108. NATO Expansion/POW-MIAs. Smith, R-N.H., amendment to add language to the resolution of ratification that would require the president to certify to Congress before signing the treaty that the governments of Poland, Hungary and the Czech Republic are fully cooperating with U.S. efforts to recover soldiers captured or missing from past military conflicts or Cold War incidents. Adopted 97-0: R 54-0; D 43-0 (ND 35-0, SD 8-0). April 29, 1998.

109. NATO Expansion/Dispute Resolution. Hutchison, R-Texas, amendment to add language to the resolution of ratification that would direct the U.S. representative to NATO to propose a process through which NATO could resolve disputes involving one or more NATO members when military force is threatened. Rejected 37-62: R 32-23; D 5-39 (ND 4-33, SD 1-6). April 29, 1998. A "nay" was a vote in support of the president's position.

110. NATO Expansion/Troops in Bosnia. Craig, R-Idaho, amendment to add language to the resolution of ratification that would require Congress and the president to enact legislation specifically authorizing the continued deployment of U.S. troops in Bosnia before the United States ratifies the NATO expansion treaty. Rejected 20-80: R 19-36; D 1-44 (ND 1-36, SD 0-8). April 30, 1998. A "nay" was a vote in support of the president's position.

111. NATO Expansion/EU Membership. Moynihan, D-N.Y., amendment to add language to the resolution of ratification that would require Poland, Hungary and the Czech Republic to become members of the European Union before being admitted to NATO. Rejected 17-83: R 9-46; D 8-37 (ND 7-30, SD 1-7). April 30, 1998. A "nay" was a vote in support of the president's position.

112. NATO Expansion/Three Year Moratorium. Warner, R-Va., amendment to add language to the resolution of ratification that would require the president to certify to Congress that the United States will not support any further NATO expansion for three years from the date which Poland, Hungary and the Czech Republic join the alliance. Rejected 41-59: R 24-31; D 17-28 (ND 15-22, SD 2-6). April 30, 1998. A "nay" was a vote in support of the president's position.

Senate Votes 113, 114, 115, 116, 117, 118, 119

	113	114	115	116	117	118	119
ALABAMA							
Sessions	N	N	N	Y	Y	Y	Y
Shelby	N	Y	N	N	Y	Y	N
ALASKA							
Murkowski	N	Y	N	N	Y	Y	Y
Stevens	N	Y	N	N	Y	Y	Y
ARIZONA							
Kyl	N	Y	?	?	+	?	Y
McCain	N	Y	N	N	Y	Y	Y
ARKANSAS							
Hutchinson	N	N	Y	Y	N	Y	Y
Bumpers	Y	Y	Y	Y	N	N	Y
CALIFORNIA							
Boxer	N	Y	N	N	Y	Y	Y
Feinstein	N	Y	N	N	Y	Y	Y
COLORADO							
Allard	N	Y	N	N	Y	Y	N
Campbell	N	Y	N	N	Y	Y	Y
CONNECTICUT							
Dodd	N	Y	N	N	Y	Y	Y
Lieberman	N	Y	N	N	Y	Y	Y
DELAWARE							
Roth	N	Y	N	N	Y	Y	Y
Biden	N	Y	N	N	Y	Y	Y
FLORIDA							
Mack	N	Y	N	N	Y	Y	Y
Graham	N	Y	Y	N	Y	Y	Y
GEORGIA							
Coverdell	N	Y	N	N	Y	Y	Y
Cleland	N	Y	N	N	Y	Y	Y
HAWAII							
Akaka	N	Y	N	N	Y	Y	Y
Inouye	N	Y	N	N	Y	Y	Y
IDAHO							
Craig	N	N	Y	Y	N	Y	Y
Kempthorne	N	N	Y	Y	N	Y	Y
ILLINOIS							
Durbin	N	Y	N	N	Y	N	Y
Moseley-Braun	N	Y	N	N	Y	N	Y
INDIANA							
Coats	N	Y	N	N	Y	Y	Y
Lugar	N	Y	N	N	Y	Y	Y
IOWA							
Grassley	N	N	N	Y	Y	Y	Y
Harkin	Y	Y	Y	Y	N	Y	Y
KANSAS							
Brownback	N	N	N	Y	Y	Y	N
Roberts	N	N	Y	Y	Y	Y	Y
KENTUCKY							
McConnell	N	Y	N	N	Y	Y	Y
Ford	N	Y	N	N	Y	Y	Y
LOUISIANA							
Breaux	N	Y	N	N	Y	Y	Y
Landrieu	N	Y	N	N	Y	Y	Y
MAINE							
Collins	N	Y	N	N	Y	Y	Y
Snowe	N	Y	N	N	Y	Y	Y
MARYLAND							
Mikulski	N	Y	N	N	Y	Y	Y
Sarbanes	N	Y	N	N	Y	Y	Y
MASSACHUSETTS							
Kennedy	Y	Y	N	N	Y	Y	Y
Kerry	Y	Y	N	N	Y	Y	Y
MICHIGAN							
Abraham	N	Y	N	N	Y	Y	Y
Levin	N	Y	N	N	Y	Y	Y
MINNESOTA							
Grams	N	N	N	N	Y	Y	Y
Wellstone	Y	Y	Y	N	N	Y	Y
MISSISSIPPI							
Cochran	N	Y	N	N	Y	Y	Y
Lott	N	Y	N	N	Y	Y	Y
MISSOURI							
Ashcroft	N	N	Y	Y	N	N	N
Bond	N	N	N	N	Y	Y	N
MONTANA							
Burns	N	Y	N	N	Y	Y	Y
Baucus	N	Y	N	N	Y	Y	Y
NEBRASKA							
Hagel	N	Y	N	N	Y	Y	Y
Kerrey	N	Y	N	N	Y	Y	Y
NEVADA							
Bryan	Y	Y	N	N	Y	Y	Y
Reid	N	Y	N	N	N	Y	Y
NEW HAMPSHIRE							
Gregg	N	Y	N	N	Y	Y	Y
Smith	N	N	Y	N	N	N	N
NEW JERSEY							
Lautenberg	Y	Y	N	N	Y	Y	Y
Torricelli	N	Y	Y	N	Y	Y	Y
NEW MEXICO							
Domenici	N	Y	N	N	Y	Y	Y
Bingaman	Y	Y	Y	N	Y	Y	Y
NEW YORK							
D'Amato	N	Y	N	N	Y	Y	Y
Moynihan	N	Y	N	N	N	Y	Y
NORTH CAROLINA							
Faircloth	N	N	N	Y	Y	Y	?
Helms	N	N	N	N	Y	Y	?
NORTH DAKOTA							
Conrad	Y	Y	Y	Y	N	Y	Y
Dorgan	Y	Y	Y	N	N	Y	Y
OHIO							
DeWine	N	Y	N	N	Y	Y	Y
Glenn	N	Y	N	N	Y	Y	Y
OKLAHOMA							
Inhofe	N	N	Y	Y	N	N	N
Nickles	N	N	N	Y	Y	Y	Y
OREGON							
Smith	N	Y	N	N	Y	Y	Y
Wyden	Y	Y	Y	N	Y	Y	Y
PENNSYLVANIA							
Santorum	N	Y	N	N	Y	N	Y
Specter	N	Y	N	Y	N	Y	Y
RHODE ISLAND							
Chafee	N	Y	N	N	Y	Y	Y
Reed	N	Y	N	N	Y	Y	Y
SOUTH CAROLINA							
Thurmond	N	N	N	N	Y	Y	Y
Hollings	N	Y	N	N	Y	Y	Y
SOUTH DAKOTA							
Daschle	N	Y	N	N	Y	Y	Y
Johnson	Y	Y	Y	N	Y	Y	Y
TENNESSEE							
Frist	N	Y	N	N	Y	Y	Y
Thompson	N	Y	N	N	Y	Y	Y
TEXAS							
Gramm	N	Y	N	N	Y	N	Y
Hutchison	N	N	Y	Y	Y	Y	Y
UTAH							
Bennett	N	Y	N	N	Y	Y	Y
Hatch	N	Y	N	N	Y	Y	Y
VERMONT							
Jeffords	Y	Y	Y	N	N	Y	Y
Leahy	Y	Y	N	N	N	Y	Y
VIRGINIA							
Warner	N	N	Y	N	Y	Y	Y
Robb	N	Y	N	N	Y	Y	Y
WASHINGTON							
Gorton	N	Y	N	N	Y	Y	Y
Murray	Y	Y	Y	N	Y	Y	Y
WEST VIRGINIA							
Byrd	N	Y	N	N	Y	Y	Y
Rockefeller	N	Y	N	N	Y	Y	Y
WISCONSIN							
Feingold	N	Y	N	Y	N	Y	Y
Kohl	Y	Y	Y	N	Y	N	Y
WYOMING							
Enzi	N	Y	N	N	Y	Y	Y
Thomas	N	Y	N	N	Y	Y	Y

Key

- Y Voted for (yea).
- # Paired for.
- + Announced for.
- N Voted against (nay).
- X Paired against.
- − Announced against.
- P Voted "present."
- C Voted "present" to avoid possible conflict of interest.
- ? Did not vote or otherwise make a position known.

Democrats   **Republicans**

ND Northern Democrats   SD Southern Democrats

Southern states - Ala., Ark., Fla., Ga., Ky., La., Miss., N.C., Okla., S.C., Tenn., Texas, Va.

113. NATO Expansion/Nuclear Weapon Dismantlement. Conrad, D-N.D., amendment to add language to the resolution of ratification that would require the president to certify to the Senate before signing the treaty that the United States has initiated discussions with Russia on a reduction in nonstrategic nuclear weapons. Rejected 16-84: R 1-54; D 15-30 (ND 14-23, SD 1-7). April 30, 1998.

114. NATO Expansion/Defensive Alliance. Biden, D-Del., motion to table (kill) the Ashcroft, R-Mo., amendment to add language to the resolution of ratification that would require the president to certify to the Senate before signing the treaty that NATO's primary goal is to defend the territory of its member nations. Motion agreed to 82-18: R 37-18; D 45-0 (ND 37-0, SD 8-0). April 30, 1998.

115. NATO Expansion/NATO Strategic Statement. Bingaman, D-N.M., amendment to add language to the resolution of ratification that would require the president to certify to the Senate before signing the treaty that the United States will not support further expansion of NATO beyond Poland, Hungary and the Czech Republic until NATO agrees on a revised official statement of alliance strategy. Rejected 23-76: R 10-44; D 13-32 (ND 10-27, SD 3-5). April 30, 1998.

116. NATO Expansion/Bosnia Troop Deployment. Smith, R-N.H., amendment to add language to the resolution of ratification that would require both Houses of Congress to vote on legislation, prior to ratification of NATO expansion, that would authorize continued U.S. troop deployment in Bosnia. Rejected 16-83: R 15-39; D 1-44 (ND 1-36, SD 0-8). April 30, 1998.

117. NATO Expansion/Adoption. Adoption of the resolution of ratification of the protocol (Treaty Doc. 105-36) revising the 1949 North Atlantic Treaty to admit Poland, Hungary and the Czech Republic into the North Atlantic Treaty Organization. Adopted 80-19: R 45-9; D 35-10 (ND 28-9, SD 7-1). April 30, 1998. A two-thirds majority of those present and voting (66 in this case) is required for adoption of resolutions of ratification. A "yea" was a vote in support of the president's position.

118. HR 3579. Fiscal 1998 Emergency Supplemental Appropriations/Conference Report. Adoption of the conference report on the bill to appropriate $6.1 billion in supplemental spending, including $2.6 billion for disaster relief and $2.9 billion for military operations in Bosnia and the Middle East. Adopted (thus cleared for the president) 88-11: R 48-6; D 40-5 (ND 33-4, SD 7-1). April 30, 1998.

119. HR 1385. Job Training Program Consolidation/Passage. Passage of the bill to consolidate nearly 70 existing job training, vocational education and adult literacy programs into block grant programs to the states. The measure also would simplify eligibility requirements for vocational rehabilitation and job training programs; enable states to offer customized support, such as home training, for disabled individuals; and authorize random drug testing for participants in federally funded job training programs. Passed 91-7: R 46-7; D 45-0 (ND 37-0, SD 8-0). May 5, 1998. A "yea" was a vote in support of the president's position.

Senate Votes 120, 121, 122, 123, 124, 125, 126

	120	121	122	123	124	125	126
ALABAMA							
Sessions	Y	N	Y	Y	Y	N	Y
Shelby	Y	Y	Y	Y	Y	N	Y
ALASKA							
Murkowski	Y	N	Y	Y	Y	Y	Y
Stevens	Y	Y	N	N	N	Y	Y
ARIZONA							
Kyl	Y	Y	Y	Y	Y	Y	Y
McCain	Y	Y	Y	Y	Y	Y	Y
ARKANSAS							
Hutchinson	Y	Y	Y	Y	Y	Y	Y
Bumpers	N	N	N	N	N	N	Y
CALIFORNIA							
Boxer	N	N	N	N	N	N	Y
Feinstein	N	N	N	N	N	N	Y
COLORADO							
Allard	Y	N	Y	Y	Y	Y	Y
Campbell	Y	Y	N	N	Y	Y	Y
CONNECTICUT							
Dodd	N	N	N	N	N	N	Y
Lieberman	N	N	N	N	N	N	Y
DELAWARE							
Roth	Y	N	Y	Y	Y	N	Y
Biden	Y	N	N	N	N	N	Y
FLORIDA							
Mack	Y	N	Y	Y	Y	Y	Y
Graham	N	N	N	N	N	N	Y
GEORGIA							
Coverdell	Y	Y	Y	Y	Y	Y	Y
Cleland	N	N	N	N	N	N	Y
HAWAII							
Akaka	?	?	?	?	?	?	?
Inouye	N	N	N	N	N	N	Y
IDAHO							
Craig	Y	Y	Y	N	Y	Y	Y
Kempthorne	Y	Y	Y	N	Y	Y	Y
ILLINOIS							
Durbin	N	N	N	N	N	N	Y
Moseley-Braun	Y	N	N	N	N	N	Y
INDIANA							
Coats	Y	N	Y	Y	Y	Y	Y
Lugar	Y	N	Y	Y	N	Y	Y
IOWA							
Grassley	Y	N	N	Y	N	Y	Y
Harkin	N	N	N	N	N	N	Y
KANSAS							
Brownback	Y	Y	Y	Y	Y	Y	Y
Roberts	Y	N	Y	Y	Y	Y	Y
KENTUCKY							
McConnell	Y	Y	Y	Y	Y	Y	Y
Ford	N	N	N	N	N	N	Y
LOUISIANA							
Breaux	N	N	N	N	N	N	Y
Landrieu	N	N	N	N	N	N	Y
MAINE							
Collins	Y	N	N	N	N	N	Y
Snowe	Y	N	N	N	N	N	Y
MARYLAND							
Mikulski	N	N	N	N	N	N	Y
Sarbanes	N	N	N	N	N	N	Y
MASSACHUSETTS							
Kennedy	N	N	N	N	N	N	Y
Kerry	N	N	N	N	N	N	Y
MICHIGAN							
Abraham	Y	Y	Y	N	Y	Y	Y
Levin	N	N	N	N	N	N	Y
MINNESOTA							
Grams	Y	N	Y	Y	Y	Y	Y
Wellstone	N	N	N	N	N	N	Y
MISSISSIPPI							
Cochran	Y	N	Y	Y	Y	Y	Y
Lott	Y	N	Y	Y	Y	Y	Y
MISSOURI							
Ashcroft	Y	Y	Y	Y	Y	Y	Y
Bond	Y	Y	Y	Y	Y	Y	Y
MONTANA							
Burns	Y	Y	Y	N	Y	Y	Y
Baucus	N	N	N	N	N	N	Y
NEBRASKA							
Hagel	Y	N	N	N	N	N	Y
Kerrey	N	N	N	N	N	N	Y
NEVADA							
Bryan	N	N	N	N	N	N	Y
Reid	N	N	N	N	N	N	Y
NEW HAMPSHIRE							
Gregg	Y	N	Y	Y	Y	Y	Y
Smith	Y	Y	Y	Y	Y	Y	Y
NEW JERSEY							
Lautenberg	N	N	N	N	N	N	Y
Torricelli	N	N	N	N	N	N	Y
NEW MEXICO							
Domenici	Y	N	N	N	N	N	Y
Bingaman	N	N	N	N	N	N	Y
NEW YORK							
D'Amato	Y	Y	N	N	N	Y	Y
Moynihan	N	N	N	N	N	N	Y
NORTH CAROLINA							
Faircloth	Y	Y	Y	Y	Y	Y	Y
Helms	?	N	Y	Y	Y	Y	Y
NORTH DAKOTA							
Conrad	N	N	N	N	N	N	Y
Dorgan	N	N	N	N	N	N	Y
OHIO							
DeWine	Y	N	Y	Y	Y	Y	Y
Glenn	N	N	N	N	N	?	?
OKLAHOMA							
Inhofe	Y	Y	Y	Y	Y	Y	Y
Nickles	Y	Y	Y	Y	Y	N	Y
OREGON							
Smith	Y	N	Y	Y	N	N	Y
Wyden	N	N	N	N	N	N	Y
PENNSYLVANIA							
Santorum	Y	N	N	N	N	N	Y
Specter	Y	N	N	N	N	N	Y
RHODE ISLAND							
Chafee	Y	N	Y	N	N	N	Y
Reed	N	N	N	N	N	N	Y
SOUTH CAROLINA							
Thurmond	Y	Y	Y	Y	+	+	
Hollings	N	Y	N	N	N	N	Y
SOUTH DAKOTA							
Daschle	N	N	N	N	N	N	Y
Johnson	N	N	N	N	N	N	Y
TENNESSEE							
Frist	Y	Y	Y	Y	Y	Y	Y
Thompson	Y	N	Y	Y	Y	Y	Y
TEXAS							
Gramm	Y	Y	Y	Y	Y	N	Y
Hutchison	Y	N	Y	N	Y	Y	Y
UTAH							
Bennett	Y	N	Y	N	N	Y	Y
Hatch	Y	N	N	N	Y	Y	Y
VERMONT							
Jeffords	Y	N	N	N	N	N	Y
Leahy	N	N	N	N	N	N	Y
VIRGINIA							
Warner	Y	N	N	N	N	N	Y
Robb	N	N	N	N	N	N	Y
WASHINGTON							
Gorton	Y	N	Y	Y	N	N	Y
Murray	N	N	N	N	N	N	Y
WEST VIRGINIA							
Byrd	N	N	N	N	N	N	Y
Rockefeller	N	N	N	N	N	N	Y
WISCONSIN							
Feingold	N	N	N	N	N	N	Y
Kohl	N	N	N	N	N	N	Y
WYOMING							
Enzi	Y	N	Y	Y	Y	Y	Y
Thomas	Y	Y	Y	Y	Y	Y	Y

Key

- **Y** Voted for (yea).
- **#** Paired for.
- **+** Announced for.
- **N** Voted against (nay).
- **X** Paired against.
- **–** Announced against.
- **P** Voted "present."
- **C** Voted "present" to avoid possible conflict of interest.
- **?** Did not vote or otherwise make a position known.

Democrats **Republicans**

ND Northern Democrats SD Southern Democrats

Southern states - Ala., Ark., Fla., Ga., Ky., La., Miss., N.C., Okla., S.C., Tenn., Texas, Va.

120. HR 2676. Internal Revenue Service Overhaul/Roth IRAs. Roth, R-Del., amendment to allow taxpayers who are older than 70 1/2 and whose incomes are more than $100,000 to convert their traditional Individual Retirement Accounts (IRAs) to so-called Roth IRAs, which allow individuals to withdraw both contributions and investment earnings tax-free upon retirement. The amendment would raise approximately $8 billion over fiscal years 2003-2007 because the money investors withdraw from traditional IRAs to shift funds to Roth IRAs would be taxed as income. Current law prohibits taxpayers with incomes of more than $100,000 from shifting their retirement funds to Roth IRAs. Adopted 56-42: R 54-0; D 2-42 (ND 2-34, SD 0-8). May 6, 1998.

121. HR 2676. Internal Revenue Service Overhaul/IRS Oversight Board. Bond, R-Mo., amendment to replace language that would establish a nine-member part-time IRS oversight board with provisions to create a five-member full-time IRS Board of Governors. Rejected 25-74: R 24-31; D 1-43 (ND 0-36, SD 1-7). May 6, 1998.

122. HR 2676. Internal Revenue Service Overhaul/Ethics Waiver. Thompson, R-Tenn., amendment to strike language in the bill that would provide a special waiver of government ethics laws governing conflicts-of-interest for the representative of IRS employees serving on the oversight board established in the bill. Rejected 42-57: R 42-13; D 0-44 (ND 0-36, SD 0-8). May 7, 1998.

123. HR 2676. Internal Revenue Service Overhaul/Union Representation. Faircloth, R-N.C., amendment to strike language allowing a representative of IRS employees to sit on the oversight board. Rejected 35-64: R 35-20; D 0-44 (ND 0-36, SD 0-8). May 7, 1998.

124. HR 2676. Internal Revenue Service Overhaul/Treasury Secretary. Mack, R-Fla., amendment to strike language that would give the secretary of the Treasury a seat on the IRS oversight board. Rejected 40-59: R 40-15; D 0-44 (ND 0-36, SD 0-8). May 7, 1998.

125. HR 2676. Internal Revenue Service Overhaul/Random Audits. Coverdell, R-Ga., motion to waive the Budget Act with respect to the Kerrey, D-Neb., point of order against the Coverdell amendment. The Coverdell amendment would prohibit the Internal Revenue Service from initiating random taxpayer audits. Motion rejected 37-60: R 37-17; D 0-43 (ND 0-35, SD 0-8). May 7, 1998. A three-fifths majority vote (60) of the total Senate is required to waive the Budget Act. (Subsequently, the chair upheld the point of order, and the amendment fell.)

126. HR 2676. Internal Revenue Service Overhaul/Passage. Passage of the bill to restructure the management of the Internal Revenue Service by establishing an oversight board to oversee the agency's operations. The bill would expand several taxpayer rights, including shifting the burden of proof from the taxpayer to the IRS, allowing more individuals to claim "innocent spouse" relief in cases when a tax debt is determined to be the responsibility of an ex-spouse and allowing taxpayers to sue the federal government for civil damages caused by IRS employees who negligently disregard tax laws. The measure would cost approximately $18.3 billion over 10 years. Passed 97-0: R 54-0; D 43-0 (ND 35-0, SD 8-0). May 7, 1998.

Senate Votes 127, 128, 129, 130, 131, 132, 133

	127	128	129	130	131	132	133
ALABAMA							
Sessions	Y	Y	N	Y	Y	Y	Y
Shelby	Y	Y	Y	Y	Y	Y	N
ALASKA							
Murkowski	Y	N	Y	Y	Y	Y	Y
Stevens	Y	N	Y	Y	Y	Y	Y
ARIZONA							
Kyl	Y	N	N	Y	Y	Y	Y
McCain	Y	Y	Y	Y	Y	Y	P
ARKANSAS							
Hutchinson	Y	Y	Y	Y	Y	Y	Y
Bumpers	Y	N	Y	Y	N	Y	N
CALIFORNIA							
Boxer	Y	N	Y	Y	N	Y	Y
Feinstein	Y	N	Y	Y	N	Y	Y
COLORADO							
Allard	Y	Y	Y	Y	Y	Y	Y
Campbell	Y	N	Y	Y	Y	Y	Y
CONNECTICUT							
Dodd	Y	N	Y	Y	N	Y	Y
Lieberman	Y	N	Y	Y	Y	Y	Y
DELAWARE							
Roth	Y	N	Y	Y	Y	Y	Y
Biden	Y	N	Y	?	N	Y	N
FLORIDA							
Mack	Y	N	Y	Y	Y	Y	Y
Graham	Y	N	Y	Y	N	Y	N
GEORGIA							
Coverdell	Y	N	Y	Y	Y	Y	Y
Cleland	Y	N	Y	Y	N	Y	N
HAWAII							
Akaka	Y	N	Y	Y	N	Y	Y
Inouye	Y	N	Y	Y	Y	Y	N
IDAHO							
Craig	Y	N	Y	Y	Y	Y	Y
Kempthorne	Y	N	Y	Y	Y	Y	Y
ILLINOIS							
Durbin	Y	N	Y	Y	N	Y	N
Moseley-Braun	Y	N	Y	Y	N	Y	Y
INDIANA							
Coats	Y	N	Y	Y	Y	Y	Y
Lugar	Y	N	Y	Y	Y	Y	Y
IOWA							
Grassley	Y	N	Y	Y	Y	Y	Y
Harkin	Y	N	Y	Y	N	Y	Y
KANSAS							
Brownback	Y	N	Y	Y	Y	Y	Y
Roberts	Y	N	Y	Y	Y	Y	Y
KENTUCKY							
McConnell	Y	N	Y	Y	Y	Y	Y
Ford	Y	N	Y	Y	N	Y	N
LOUISIANA							
Breaux	Y	N	Y	Y	N	Y	N
Landrieu	Y	N	Y	Y	N	Y	Y
MAINE							
Collins	Y	N	Y	Y	N	Y	N
Snowe	Y	Y	Y	Y	Y	Y	N
MARYLAND							
Mikulski	Y	N	Y	Y	N	Y	Y
Sarbanes	Y	N	Y	Y	N	Y	Y
MASSACHUSETTS							
Kennedy	Y	N	Y	Y	N	Y	Y
Kerry	Y	N	Y	Y	Y	Y	Y
MICHIGAN							
Abraham	Y	Y	Y	Y	Y	Y	Y
Levin	Y	N	Y	Y	Y	Y	Y
MINNESOTA							
Grams	Y	N	Y	Y	Y	Y	Y
Wellstone	Y	N	Y	Y	N	Y	N
MISSISSIPPI							
Cochran	Y	N	Y	Y	Y	Y	Y
Lott	Y	Y	Y	Y	Y	Y	Y
MISSOURI							
Ashcroft	Y	Y	Y	Y	Y	Y	Y
Bond	Y	N	Y	Y	Y	Y	Y
MONTANA							
Burns	Y	N	Y	Y	Y	Y	Y
Baucus	Y	N	Y	Y	N	Y	Y
NEBRASKA							
Hagel	Y	N	Y	Y	Y	Y	Y
Kerrey	Y	N	Y	Y	N	Y	N
NEVADA							
Bryan	Y	N	Y	Y	N	Y	N
Reid	Y	N	Y	Y	N	Y	Y
NEW HAMPSHIRE							
Gregg	Y	Y	N	Y	Y	Y	Y
Smith	Y	Y	N	Y	Y	Y	Y
NEW JERSEY							
Lautenberg	Y	N	Y	Y	N	Y	N
Torricelli	Y	N	Y	Y	N	Y	Y
NEW MEXICO							
Domenici	Y	N	Y	Y	Y	Y	Y
Bingaman	Y	N	Y	Y	N	Y	Y
NEW YORK							
D'Amato	Y	N	Y	Y	Y	Y	Y
Moynihan	Y	N	Y	Y	N	Y	N
NORTH CAROLINA							
Faircloth	Y	Y	Y	Y	Y	Y	Y
Helms	Y	Y	N	Y	Y	Y	Y
NORTH DAKOTA							
Conrad	Y	N	Y	Y	N	Y	Y
Dorgan	Y	N	Y	Y	N	Y	N
OHIO							
DeWine	Y	N	Y	Y	Y	Y	Y
Glenn	Y	N	Y	Y	N	Y	Y
OKLAHOMA							
Inhofe	?	Y	N	Y	Y	Y	Y
Nickles	Y	Y	N	Y	Y	Y	Y
OREGON							
Smith	Y	N	Y	Y	Y	Y	Y
Wyden	Y	N	Y	Y	N	Y	Y
PENNSYLVANIA							
Santorum	Y	N	Y	Y	Y	Y	Y
Specter	Y	N	Y	Y	Y	Y	N
RHODE ISLAND							
Chafee	Y	N	Y	Y	Y	Y	Y
Reed	Y	N	Y	Y	N	Y	Y
SOUTH CAROLINA							
Thurmond	Y	Y	Y	Y	Y	Y	Y
Hollings	Y	Y	Y	Y	Y	Y	Y
SOUTH DAKOTA							
Daschle	Y	N	Y	Y	N	Y	Y
Johnson	Y	N	Y	Y	N	Y	Y
TENNESSEE							
Frist	Y	N	Y	Y	Y	Y	Y
Thompson	Y	Y	Y	Y	Y	Y	Y
TEXAS							
Gramm	Y	Y	N	Y	Y	Y	Y
Hutchison	Y	Y	Y	Y	Y	Y	Y
UTAH							
Bennett	Y	N	Y	Y	Y	Y	Y
Hatch	Y	N	Y	Y	Y	Y	Y
VERMONT							
Jeffords	Y	N	Y	Y	Y	Y	Y
Leahy	Y	N	Y	Y	N	Y	Y
VIRGINIA							
Warner	Y	N	Y	Y	Y	Y	Y
Robb	Y	N	Y	Y	N	Y	Y
WASHINGTON							
Gorton	Y	N	Y	Y	Y	Y	Y
Murray	Y	N	Y	Y	N	Y	Y
WEST VIRGINIA							
Byrd	Y	N	Y	Y	N	Y	N
Rockefeller	Y	N	Y	Y	N	Y	N
WISCONSIN							
Feingold	Y	N	Y	Y	N	Y	N
Kohl	Y	N	Y	Y	N	Y	Y
WYOMING							
Enzi	Y	Y	Y	Y	Y	Y	Y
Thomas	Y	Y	Y	Y	Y	Y	Y

Key

- Y Voted for (yea).
- # Paired for.
- + Announced for.
- N Voted against (nay).
- X Paired against.
- − Announced against.
- P Voted "present."
- C Voted "present" to avoid possible conflict of interest.
- ? Did not vote or otherwise make a position known.

Democrats **Republicans**

ND Northern Democrats   SD Southern Democrats

Southern states - Ala., Ark., Fla., Ga., Ky., La., Miss., N.C., Okla., S.C., Tenn., Texas, Va.

127. HR 1273. National Science Foundation Reauthorization/Passage. Passage of the bill to reauthorize the National Science Foundation for three years. The bill would authorize $3.5 billion in fiscal 1998, $3.8 billion in fiscal 1999 and $3.9 billion in fiscal 2000. It also would prohibit any funds for the U.S. Man and the Biosphere Program and would require the National Science Foundation director to submit an annual plan to Congress on recommended upgrades to national research facilities. Passed 99-0: R 54-0; D 45-0 (ND 37-0, SD 8-0). May 12, 1998.

128. S 1150. Agriculture Research/Motion to Recommit. Gramm, R-Texas, motion to recommit the conference report to the conference committee with instructions that Senate conferees insist that the bill's expansion of food stamp eligibility only apply to refugees and asylees who were lawfully residing in the United States on August 22, 1996. The conference report would allow future refugees and asylees to qualify for the bill's language expanding food stamp eligibility from five to seven years. Motion rejected 23-77: R 22-33; D 1-44 (ND 0-37, SD 1-7). May 12, 1998. A "nay" was a vote in support of the president's position.

129. S 1150. Agriculture Research/Conference Report. Adoption of the conference report on the bill to reauthorize federal agriculture research programs. The measure would authorize $600 million in new mandatory spending over five years for expanded food safety, genetic engineering and other technology programs, $500 million in new crop insurance under the federal crop insurance program and $100 million for rural development and research programs. The bill also would authorize $818 million over five years to restore food stamp eligibility to 250,000 legal immigrants who lost benefits under the 1996 welfare law (PL 104-193). Adopted (thus sent to the House) 92-8: R 47-8; D 45-0 (ND 37-0, SD 8-0). May 12, 1998. A "yea" was a vote in support of the president's position.

130. S 1618. Long-Distance Phone Slamming/Passage. Passage of the bill that aims to reduce incidents of "slamming," which is the unauthorized change of a customer's long-distance telephone service, by requiring telephone companies to gain oral, written or electronic verification from consumers before switching their long-distance service and by establishing criminal penalties for individuals who engage in slamming. Passed 99-0: R 55-0; D 44-0 (ND 36-0, SD 8-0). May 12, 1998. A "yea" was a vote in support of the president's position.

131. S 1873. National Missile Defense/Cloture. Motion to invoke cloture (thus limiting debate) on the motion to proceed to the bill that would make it U.S. policy to implement a national missile defense shield. The measure would not establish a specific time frame, but would declare a national policy to deploy a system to protect U.S. territory from a limited number of incoming missiles "as soon as is technologically possible." Motion rejected 59-41: R 55-0; D 4-41 (ND 3-34, SD 1-7). May 13, 1998. Three-fifths of the total Senate (60) is required to invoke cloture. A "nay" was a vote in support of the president's position.

132. S 1244. Debtor Charitable Contributions/Passage. Passage of the bill to shield contributions of up to 15 percent of an individual who files for bankruptcy's income to religious groups or charitable, nonprofit groups. The measure also would allow bankruptcy filers to include future religious donations as part of their debt repayment plan. Passed 100-0: R 55-0; D 45-0 (ND 37-0, SD 8-0). May 13, 1998.

133. S 1260. Securities Lawsuits/Statute of Limitations. D'Amato, R-N.Y., motion to table (kill) the Sarbanes, D-Md., amendment to allow plaintiffs to file lawsuits under state statutes of limitations if the bill requires them to file their class actions suits in federal court instead of state court. Motion agreed to 69-30: R 50-4; D 19-26 (ND 17-20, SD 2-6). May 13, 1998.

Senate Votes 134, 135, 136, 137, 138, 139, 140

	134	135	136	137	138	139	140
ALABAMA							
Sessions	Y	Y	N	Y	Y	Y	Y
Shelby	N	N	N	Y	Y	Y	Y
ALASKA							
Murkowski	Y	Y	Y	Y	Y	Y	Y
Stevens	Y	Y	N	Y	Y	Y	Y
ARIZONA							
Kyl	Y	Y	N	Y	Y	Y	Y
McCain	P	N	N	Y	Y	Y	Y
ARKANSAS							
Hutchinson	Y	Y	N	Y	Y	Y	N
Bumpers	N	N	N	Y	N	N	N
CALIFORNIA							
Boxer	Y	Y	N	Y	N	N	Y
Feinstein	Y	Y	N	Y	N	N	Y
COLORADO							
Allard	Y	Y	N	Y	N	N	Y
Campbell	Y	Y	N	Y	N	N	Y
CONNECTICUT							
Dodd	Y	Y	N	Y	N	N	Y
Lieberman	Y	Y	N	Y	Y	Y	Y
DELAWARE							
Roth	Y	Y	N	Y	Y	Y	Y
Biden	N	N	Y	N	N	N	N
FLORIDA							
Mack	Y	Y	N	Y	Y	Y	Y
Graham	N	Y	Y	Y	Y	Y	Y
GEORGIA							
Coverdell	Y	Y	N	Y	Y	Y	Y
Cleland	N	N	N	Y	Y	Y	N
HAWAII							
Akaka	N	N	Y	Y	N	N	Y
Inouye	N	N	Y	Y	N	N	Y
IDAHO							
Craig	Y	Y	N	Y	Y	Y	Y
Kempthorne	Y	Y	N	Y	Y	Y	Y
ILLINOIS							
Durbin	N	N	N	Y	N	N	Y
Moseley-Braun	Y	Y	N	Y	N	N	Y
INDIANA							
Coats	Y	Y	N	Y	Y	Y	Y
Lugar	Y	Y	Y	Y	Y	Y	Y
IOWA							
Grassley	Y	Y	N	Y	Y	Y	Y
Harkin	Y	Y	N	Y	N	N	N
KANSAS							
Brownback	Y	Y	N	Y	Y	Y	Y
Roberts	Y	Y	Y	Y	Y	Y	N
KENTUCKY							
McConnell	Y	Y	N	Y	Y	Y	Y
Ford	Y	Y	Y	Y	N	N	Y
LOUISIANA							
Breaux	Y	Y	N	Y	N	N	Y
Landrieu	Y	Y	N	Y	N	N	N
MAINE							
Collins	Y	Y	N	Y	Y	Y	Y
Snowe	Y	Y	N	Y	Y	Y	Y
MARYLAND							
Mikulski	Y	Y	N	N	N	N	N
Sarbanes	N	N	N	Y	N	N	N
MASSACHUSETTS							
Kennedy	N	Y	Y	Y	N	N	Y
Kerry	N	Y	N	Y	N	N	Y
MICHIGAN							
Abraham	Y	Y	N	Y	Y	Y	Y
Levin	N	N	Y	Y	–	–	–
MINNESOTA							
Grams	Y	Y	N	Y	Y	Y	Y
Wellstone	N	N	N	N	N	N	N
MISSISSIPPI							
Cochran	Y	Y	N	Y	Y	Y	Y
Lott	Y	Y	N	Y	Y	Y	Y
MISSOURI							
Ashcroft	Y	Y	N	Y	Y	Y	Y
Bond	Y	Y	N	Y	Y	Y	Y
MONTANA							
Burns	Y	Y	N	Y	Y	Y	Y
Baucus	Y	Y	Y	Y	Y	Y	N
NEBRASKA							
Hagel	Y	Y	Y	Y	Y	Y	Y
Kerrey	Y	Y	Y	Y	N	N	N
NEVADA							
Bryan	N	N	N	Y	N	N	Y
Reid	Y	Y	N	Y	N	N	Y
NEW HAMPSHIRE							
Gregg	Y	Y	N	?	Y	Y	Y
Smith	Y	Y	N	Y	Y	Y	Y
NEW JERSEY							
Lautenberg	N	N	N	Y	N	N	Y
Torricelli	N	N	N	Y	N	N	N
NEW MEXICO							
Domenici	Y	Y	N	Y	Y	Y	Y
Bingaman	Y	Y	Y	Y	Y	N	N
NEW YORK							
D'Amato	Y	Y	N	Y	Y	Y	Y
Moynihan	N	N	N	Y	N	N	N
NORTH CAROLINA							
Faircloth	Y	Y	N	Y	?	?	?
Helms	Y	Y	N	Y	Y	Y	Y
NORTH DAKOTA							
Conrad	N	N	N	Y	N	N	N
Dorgan	N	N	N	Y	N	N	Y
OHIO							
DeWine	Y	Y	N	Y	Y	Y	Y
Glenn	N	N	Y	N	N	N	N
OKLAHOMA							
Inhofe	Y	Y	N	Y	Y	Y	Y
Nickles	Y	Y	N	Y	Y	Y	Y
OREGON							
Smith	Y	Y	N	Y	Y	Y	Y
Wyden	Y	Y	N	Y	N	N	Y
PENNSYLVANIA							
Santorum	Y	Y	N	Y	Y	Y	Y
Specter	Y	Y	N	Y	Y	Y	Y
RHODE ISLAND							
Chafee	Y	Y	N	Y	Y	Y	Y
Reed	N	Y	Y	Y	N	N	N
SOUTH CAROLINA							
Thurmond	Y	Y	N	Y	Y	Y	Y
Hollings	N	Y	N	Y	N	N	N
SOUTH DAKOTA							
Daschle	Y	Y	Y	Y	N	N	Y
Johnson	N	N	Y	N	N	Y	N
TENNESSEE							
Frist	Y	Y	N	Y	Y	Y	Y
Thompson	N	Y	N	Y	Y	Y	Y
TEXAS							
Gramm	Y	Y	N	Y	Y	Y	
Hutchison	Y	Y	N	Y	Y	Y	Y
UTAH							
Bennett	Y	Y	N	Y	Y	Y	Y
Hatch	Y	Y	N	Y	Y	Y	Y
VERMONT							
Jeffords	Y	Y	N	Y	Y	Y	Y
Leahy	Y	Y	N	Y	N	N	Y
VIRGINIA							
Warner	Y	Y	N	Y	Y	Y	Y
Robb	Y	Y	Y	Y	N	N	Y
WASHINGTON							
Gorton	Y	Y	N	Y	Y	Y	Y
Murray	Y	Y	N	Y	N	N	N
WEST VIRGINIA							
Byrd	N	N	N	Y	N	N	Y
Rockefeller	N	Y	Y	N	N	N	Y
WISCONSIN							
Feingold	N	N	N	Y	N	N	N
Kohl	Y	Y	N	Y	Y	Y	Y
WYOMING							
Enzi	Y	Y	N	Y	Y	Y	Y
Thomas	Y	Y	N	Y	Y	Y	Y

Key
- Y Voted for (yea).
- # Paired for.
- + Announced for.
- N Voted against (nay).
- X Paired against.
- – Announced against.
- P Voted "present."
- C Voted "present" to avoid possible conflict of interest.
- ? Did not vote or otherwise make a position known.

Democrats *Republicans*

ND Northern Democrats   SD Southern Democrats

Southern states - Ala., Ark., Fla., Ga., Ky., La., Miss., N.C., Okla., S.C., Tenn., Texas, Va.

134. S 1260. Securities Lawsuits/Consolidation of Suits. D'Amato, R-N.Y., motion to table (kill) the Sarbanes, D-Md., amendment to remove the bill's language that would allow state judges to lump together securities lawsuits against a common defendant and ship the consolidated case to federal court if more than 50 parties are involved. Motion agreed to 72-27: R 52-2; D 20-25 (ND 16-21, SD 4-4). May 13, 1998.

135. S 1260. Securities Lawsuits/Passage. Passage of the bill to require that all class-action securities lawsuits involving more than 50 parties be filed in federal court, where standards established in a 1995 securities law (PL 104-67) would apply. Passed 79-21: R 53-2; D 26-19 (ND 20-17, SD 6-2). May 13, 1998.

136. S 2057. Fiscal 1999 Defense Authorization/Chinese Commercial Fronts. Grams, R-Minn., motion to table (kill) the Hutchinson, R-Ark., amendment that would authorize the president to monitor, seize the assets of, and ban commercial fronts operating in the United States on behalf of the Chinese army — known as the People's Liberation Army (PLA). The amendment would direct the Defense Department and several law enforcement agencies to compile and publish a list of all people or organizations in the United States that are associated with or controlled by the Chinese military. It would authorize the president to invoke the International Emergency Economic Powers Act, which allows the president to impose an array of sanctions in response to a foreign threat, against groups on the list without consulting Congress. Motion rejected 24-76: R 6-49; D 18-27 (ND 13-24, SD 5-3). May 14, 1998. (Subsequently, the Hutchinson amendment as amended was adopted by voice vote.)

137. S 2037. Digital Copyright Protection/Passage. Passage of the bill to bring the United States into compliance with two international treaties that seek to improve protection for copyrighted digital works such as computer software and movies. The bill also would provide on-line service providers with some protection against liability for infringement that takes place without their knowledge. Passed 99-0: R 54-0; D 45-0 (ND 37-0, SD 8-0). May 14, 1998.

138. S 1723. Expanding Immigration for Skilled Workers/U.S. Worker Lay-Offs. Abraham, R-Mich., motion to table (kill) the Kennedy, D-Mass., amendment that would prohibit employers from sponsoring foreign workers if they had laid off U.S. workers with similar skills in the preceding six months. Motion agreed to 60-38: R 53-1; D 7-37 (ND 5-31, SD 2-6). May 18, 1998. A "nay" was a vote in support of the president's position.

139. S 1723. Expanding Immigration for Skilled Workers/U.S. Worker Recruitment. Abraham, R-Mich., motion to table (kill) the Kennedy, D-Mass., amendment that would require employers seeking to sponsor foreign workers to attest to having first launched a significant "good faith" recruitment effort to hire a U.S. worker. Motion agreed to 59-39: R 53-1; D 6-38 (ND 4-32, SD 2-6). May 18, 1998. A "nay" was a vote in support of the president's position.

140. S 1723. Expanding Immigration for Skilled Workers/Investor Temporary Residency. Abraham, R-Mich., motion to table (kill) the Bumpers, D-Ark., amendment that would repeal the so-called EB-5 visa program, which provides up to 10,000 immigrant visas per year to foreign investors that invest enough money in a U.S. enterprise to provide jobs for at least 10 U.S. citizens. Motion agreed to 74-24: R 50-4; D 24-20 (ND 20-16, SD 4-4). May 18, 1998.

Senate Votes 141, 142, 143, 144, 145, 146, 147

	141	142	143	144	145	146	147
ALABAMA							
Sessions	Y	N	N	Y	Y	Y	Y
Shelby	Y	Y	N	Y	N	Y	Y
ALASKA							
Murkowski	Y	N	Y	Y	Y	?	?
Stevens	Y	Y	Y	Y	Y	Y	Y
ARIZONA							
Kyl	Y	N	N	Y	N	Y	N
McCain	Y	N	Y	Y	Y	?	–
ARKANSAS							
Hutchinson	N	N	N	Y	N	Y	Y
Bumpers	N	Y	Y	N	N	?	?
CALIFORNIA							
Boxer	Y	C	Y	N	C	Y	Y
Feinstein	Y	Y	Y	Y	Y	Y	Y
COLORADO							
Allard	Y	N	N	Y	N	Y	Y
Campbell	Y	N	Y	Y	N	Y	Y
CONNECTICUT							
Dodd	Y	Y	Y	N	Y	Y	Y
Lieberman	Y	Y	Y	Y	Y	Y	Y
DELAWARE							
Roth	Y	Y	Y	Y	N	Y	N
Biden	N	Y	Y	N	Y	N	Y
FLORIDA							
Mack	Y	N	Y	Y	Y	Y	Y
Graham	Y	Y	Y	N	Y	Y	Y
GEORGIA							
Coverdell	Y	N	N	Y	N	Y	Y
Cleland	Y	Y	Y	N	Y	Y	Y
HAWAII							
Akaka	N	Y	Y	N	Y	Y	Y
Inouye	Y	Y	Y	Y	Y	?	?
IDAHO							
Craig	Y	N	N	Y	N	Y	Y
Kempthorne	Y	N	N	Y	N	Y	Y
ILLINOIS							
Durbin	N	Y	Y	N	N	Y	Y
Moseley-Braun	N	Y	Y	N	Y	Y	Y
INDIANA							
Coats	Y	N	N	Y	N	Y	Y
Lugar	Y	N	Y	Y	N	N	Y

	141	142	143	144	145	146	147
IOWA							
Grassley	Y	N	Y	N	N	Y	Y
Harkin	N	Y	Y	N	Y	Y	Y
KANSAS							
Brownback	Y	N	Y	Y	N	Y	Y
Roberts	Y	N	Y	N	N	Y	Y
KENTUCKY							
McConnell	Y	N	N	Y	Y	Y	Y
Ford	Y	Y	Y	Y	Y	?	?
LOUISIANA							
Breaux	Y	Y	Y	Y	Y	Y	Y
Landrieu	Y	Y	Y	N	Y	Y	Y
MAINE							
Collins	Y	Y	Y	Y	N	Y	Y
Snowe	Y	N	Y	N	N	Y	Y
MARYLAND							
Mikulski	N	Y	Y	N	Y	Y	Y
Sarbanes	N	Y	Y	N	N	Y	Y
MASSACHUSETTS							
Kennedy	N	Y	Y	N	N	+	+
Kerry	N	Y	Y	N	Y	Y	Y
MICHIGAN							
Abraham	Y	N	N	Y	N	Y	Y
Levin	N	Y	Y	N	Y	Y	Y
MINNESOTA							
Grams	Y	N	N	Y	N	Y	Y
Wellstone	N	Y	N	N	Y	N	
MISSISSIPPI							
Cochran	Y	N	N	Y	N	Y	Y
Lott	Y	C	C	C	C	Y	Y
MISSOURI							
Ashcroft	Y	N	N	Y	N	Y	Y
Bond	Y	N	Y	N	N	Y	Y
MONTANA							
Burns	Y	N	N	Y	N	Y	Y
Baucus	Y	Y	Y	N	Y	Y	Y
NEBRASKA							
Hagel	Y	N	N	Y	N	Y	Y
Kerrey	Y	Y	Y	Y	N	Y	Y
NEVADA							
Bryan	Y	Y	Y	N	N	Y	Y
Reid	Y	Y	Y	Y	N	Y	Y

	141	142	143	144	145	146	147
NEW HAMPSHIRE							
Gregg	Y	N	Y	Y	N	Y	Y
Smith	Y	?	?	?	N	Y	Y
NEW JERSEY							
Lautenberg	Y	Y	Y	N	N	Y	Y
Torricelli	N	Y	Y	Y	N	Y	?
NEW MEXICO							
Domenici	Y	Y	N	Y	N	Y	Y
Bingaman	Y	Y	Y	N	N	Y	Y
NEW YORK							
D'Amato	?	Y	Y	N	Y	Y	Y
Moynihan	N	Y	Y	N	Y	Y	Y
NORTH CAROLINA							
Faircloth	?	N	N	Y	Y	Y	Y
Helms	Y	N	N	Y	Y	Y	Y
NORTH DAKOTA							
Conrad	Y	Y	Y	N	Y	Y	Y
Dorgan	Y	Y	Y	N	N	Y	Y
OHIO							
DeWine	Y	Y	Y	Y	Y	Y	Y
Glenn	N	Y	Y	N	Y	Y	Y
OKLAHOMA							
Inhofe	Y	N	N	Y	N	Y	Y
Nickles	Y	N	N	Y	N	Y	Y
OREGON							
Smith	Y	Y	Y	Y	N	Y	Y
Wyden	Y	Y	Y	N	Y	Y	Y
PENNSYLVANIA							
Santorum	Y	N	Y	N	N	Y	Y
Specter	Y	Y	Y	N	N	Y	N
RHODE ISLAND							
Chafee	Y	N	Y	N	Y	N	Y
Reed	Y	Y	Y	N	N	Y	Y
SOUTH CAROLINA							
Thurmond	Y	N	Y	Y	Y	Y	Y
Hollings	Y	Y	Y	Y	Y	Y	Y
SOUTH DAKOTA							
Daschle	Y	Y	Y	Y	Y	Y	Y
Johnson	Y	Y	Y	N	N	Y	Y
TENNESSEE							
Frist	Y	N	Y	Y	Y	Y	Y
Thompson	Y	Y	N	Y	N	Y	Y

Key

Y — Voted for (yea).
— Paired for.
+ — Announced for.
N — Voted against (nay).
X — Paired against.
– — Announced against.
P — Voted "present."
C — Voted "present" to avoid possible conflict of interest.
? — Did not vote or otherwise make a position known.

Democrats   **Republicans**

	141	142	143	144	145	146	147
TEXAS							
Gramm	Y	N	N	Y	N	Y	Y
Hutchison	Y	N	N	Y	Y	Y	Y
UTAH							
Bennett	Y	Y	Y	Y	Y	Y	Y
Hatch	Y	Y	Y	Y	Y	Y	Y
VERMONT							
Jeffords	Y	Y	Y	N	Y	Y	Y
Leahy	Y	Y	Y	N	N	Y	Y
VIRGINIA							
Warner	Y	N	N	Y	N	Y	Y
Robb	Y	Y	Y	Y	Y	Y	Y
WASHINGTON							
Gorton	Y	Y	Y	Y	Y	Y	N
Murray	Y	Y	Y	Y	Y	Y	Y
WEST VIRGINIA							
Byrd	N	N	Y	Y	Y	Y	Y
Rockefeller	N	Y	Y	N	Y	N	Y
WISCONSIN							
Feingold	N	Y	Y	N	Y	Y	Y
Kohl	Y	Y	Y	N	Y	Y	Y
WYOMING							
Enzi	Y	N	N	Y	N	Y	Y
Thomas	N	N	N	Y	N	Y	Y

ND Northern Democrats   SD Southern Democrats

Southern states - Ala., Ark., Fla., Ga., Ky., La., Miss., N.C., Okla., S.C., Tenn., Texas, Va.

141. S 1723. Expanding Immigration for Skilled Workers/Passage. Passage of the bill to increase the number of so-called H-1B visas, which allow highly skilled immigrants to work in the United States for six years, from the current cap of 65,000 per year to 95,000 for the remainder of fiscal 1998. The measure also would increase the cap on the visas to 105,000 for fiscal 1999 and 115,000 for the following three fiscal years, but would sunset the cap to its original level at the end of fiscal 2002. The bill also would increase the authorization for certain educational grants, authorize funding for an Internet job bank and authorize funding to provide training opportunities in information technology. Passed 78-20: R 51-2; D 27-18 (ND 20-17, SD 7-1). May 18, 1998. A "nay" was a vote in support of the president's position.

142. S 1415. Tobacco Restrictions/Cap on Attorney's Fees. Hollings, D-S.C., motion to table (kill) the Faircloth, R-N.C., amendment to the modified Senate Commerce Committee substitute amendment. The Faircloth amendment would cap at $250 per hour the amount lawyers are allowed to charge for services in relation to tobacco-related lawsuits. The amendment would not exempt suits in which states have already settled with tobacco manufacturers and it would require attorneys seeking payment to provide Congress with a detailed time accounting of related work. Motion agreed to 58-39: R 15-38; D 43-1 (ND 35-1, SD 8-0). May 19, 1998.

143. S 1415. Tobacco Restrictions/Remove Tax Provisions. Kerry, D-Mass., motion to table (kill) the Ashcroft, R-Mo., amendment to the Kennedy, D-Mass., amendment to the modified Senate Commerce Committee substitute amendment. The Ashcroft amendment would strike all provisions from the bill concerning an increase of tobacco taxes. Motion agreed to 72-26: R 27-26; D 45-0 (ND 37-0, SD 8-0). May 20, 1998.

144. S 1415. Tobacco Restrictions/Cigarette Taxes. McCain, R-Ariz., motion to table (kill) the Kennedy, D-Mass., amendment to the modified Senate Commerce Committee substitute amendment. The Kennedy amendment would replace language in the bill that would raise the federal cigarette fees by $1.10 per pack with language to raise the fees by $1.50 per pack. Motion agreed to 58-40: R 45-8; D 13-32 (ND 8-29, SD 5-3). May 20, 1998.

145. S 1415. Tobacco Restrictions/Tobacco Industry Liability. McCain, R-N.H., motion to table (kill) the Gregg, R-N.H., amendment that would eliminate the bill's $8 billion annual cap on legal damages that tobacco companies could be forced to pay. Motion rejected 37-61: R 17-37; D 20-24 (ND 14-22, SD 6-2). May 21, 1998. A "yea" was a vote in support of the president's position.

146. HR 2709. Iran Missile Sanctions/Passage. Passage of the bill to require economic sanctions against overseas companies and research institutes that have aided Iranian efforts to develop ballistic missiles that could reach Israel, U.S. forces in the Persian Gulf or Europe. The measure also contains provisions needed to implement a treaty banning chemical weapons that was approved by the Senate in 1997. Passed 90-4: R 51-2; D 39-2 (ND 33-2, SD 6-0). May 22, 1998. A "nay" was a vote in support of the president's position.

147. HR 2400. Surface Transportation Reauthorization/Conference Report. Adoption of the conference report on the bill to authorize approximately $216 billion over fiscal years 1998-2003 for federal transportation programs, including $41 billion for mass transit programs and $2 billion for highway safety. The report would offset some of the new spending by saving $15.5 billion by eliminating disability benefits for veterans with smoking-related illnesses that were not due to their military service. Adopted (thus sent to the House) 88-5: R 49-4; D 39-1 (ND 33-1, SD 6-0). May 22, 1998.

Senate Votes 148, 149, 150, 151, 152, 153, 154

	148	149	150	151	152	153	154
ALABAMA							
Sessions	Y	N	N	Y	N	N	N
Shelby	Y	N	N	Y	N	N	N
ALASKA							
Murkowski	Y	N	N	Y	N	N	N
Stevens	Y	Y	N	Y	N	N	N
ARIZONA							
Kyl	Y	Y	N	Y	N	N	N
McCain	Y	Y	N	Y	Y	N	N
ARKANSAS							
Hutchinson	Y	N	N	Y	N	N	N
Bumpers	N	Y	Y	N	Y	Y	Y
CALIFORNIA							
Boxer	?	N	Y	N	Y	Y	Y
Feinstein	N	N	Y	N	Y	Y	Y
COLORADO							
Allard	Y	Y	N	Y	N	N	N
Campbell	Y	Y	N	Y	N	N	N
CONNECTICUT							
Dodd	N	N	Y	N	Y	Y	Y
Lieberman	N	N	Y	N	Y	Y	Y
DELAWARE							
Roth	Y	Y	N	Y	N	N	N
Biden	?	?	Y	N	Y	Y	?
FLORIDA							
Mack	Y	Y	N	Y	N	N	Y
Graham	N	N	Y	N	Y	Y	Y
GEORGIA							
Coverdell	Y	N	N	Y	N	N	N
Cleland	N	N	Y	N	Y	Y	Y
HAWAII							
Akaka	N	N	Y	N	Y	Y	Y
Inouye	N	?	?	?	?	Y	Y
IDAHO							
Craig	Y	N	N	Y	N	N	N
Kempthorne	Y	N	N	Y	N	N	N
ILLINOIS							
Durbin	N	N	Y	N	Y	Y	Y
Moseley-Braun	?	N	Y	N	Y	Y	Y
INDIANA							
Coats	Y	Y	N	Y	N	N	N
Lugar	Y	Y	N	Y	N	N	N
IOWA							
Grassley	Y	N	N	Y	N	N	N
Harkin	N	N	Y	N	Y	Y	Y
KANSAS							
Brownback	Y	N	N	Y	N	N	N
Roberts	Y	N	N	Y	N	N	N
KENTUCKY							
McConnell	Y	Y	N	Y	N	N	N
Ford	N	Y	N	N	Y	N	Y
LOUISIANA							
Breaux	N	Y	Y	N	Y	Y	Y
Landrieu	N	N	Y	N	Y	Y	Y
MAINE							
Collins	Y	N	N	Y	N	N	N
Snowe	Y	N	N	Y	N	N	Y
MARYLAND							
Mikulski	N	N	Y	N	Y	Y	Y
Sarbanes	N	N	Y	N	Y	Y	Y
MASSACHUSETTS							
Kennedy	N	N	Y	N	Y	Y	Y
Kerry	N	N	Y	N	Y	Y	Y
MICHIGAN							
Abraham	Y	N	N	Y	N	N	N
Levin	Y	N	Y	N	Y	Y	Y
MINNESOTA							
Grams	Y	N	N	Y	N	N	N
Wellstone	N	N	Y	N	Y	Y	Y
MISSISSIPPI							
Cochran	Y	Y	N	Y	N	N	N
Lott	Y	C	N	Y	N	N	N
MISSOURI							
Ashcroft	Y	N	N	Y	N	N	N
Bond	Y	N	N	Y	N	N	N
MONTANA							
Burns	Y	Y	N	Y	N	N	N
Baucus	N	N	Y	N	Y	Y	Y
NEBRASKA							
Hagel	Y	Y	N	Y	N	N	N
Kerrey	N	N	Y	N	Y	Y	Y
NEVADA							
Bryan	N	N	Y	N	Y	Y	Y
Reid	N	N	Y	N	Y	Y	Y
NEW HAMPSHIRE							
Gregg	Y	N	N	Y	N	?	N
Smith	Y	Y	N	Y	N	N	N
NEW JERSEY							
Lautenberg	N	N	Y	N	Y	Y	Y
Torricelli	N	N	Y	N	Y	Y	Y
NEW MEXICO							
Domenici	Y	N	N	Y	N	N	N
Bingaman	N	N	Y	N	Y	Y	Y
NEW YORK							
D'Amato	Y	N	N	Y	N	N	N
Moynihan	N	N	Y	N	Y	Y	Y
NORTH CAROLINA							
Faircloth	Y	Y	N	Y	N	N	N
Helms	Y	Y	N	Y	N	N	N
NORTH DAKOTA							
Conrad	N	N	Y	N	Y	Y	Y
Dorgan	N	N	Y	N	Y	Y	Y
OHIO							
DeWine	Y	N	N	Y	N	N	N
Glenn	N	N	Y	N	Y	Y	Y
OKLAHOMA							
Inhofe	?	N	N	Y	N	N	N
Nickles	Y	Y	N	Y	N	N	N
OREGON							
Smith	Y	N	N	Y	N	N	N
Wyden	N	N	Y	N	Y	Y	Y
PENNSYLVANIA							
Santorum	Y	N	N	Y	N	N	N
Specter	?	?	?	?	?	?	?
RHODE ISLAND							
Chafee	Y	N	N	Y	N	N	N
Reed	N	N	Y	N	Y	Y	Y
SOUTH CAROLINA							
Thurmond	Y	Y	N	Y	N	N	N
Hollings	Y	Y	N	Y	Y	N	Y
SOUTH DAKOTA							
Daschle	N	N	Y	N	Y	Y	Y
Johnson	N	N	Y	N	Y	Y	Y
TENNESSEE							
Frist	Y	Y	N	Y	N	N	N
Thompson	Y	Y	N	Y	N	N	N
TEXAS							
Gramm	Y	N	N	Y	N	N	N
Hutchison	Y	N	N	Y	N	N	N
UTAH							
Bennett	Y	N	N	Y	N	N	N
Hatch	Y	+	N	Y	N	N	N
VERMONT							
Jeffords	Y	N	N	N	N	N	Y
Leahy	N	N	Y	N	Y	Y	Y
VIRGINIA							
Warner	Y	Y	N	Y	N	N	N
Robb	Y	Y	N	N	Y	N	Y
WASHINGTON							
Gorton	Y	Y	N	Y	N	N	N
Murray	N	N	Y	N	Y	Y	Y
WEST VIRGINIA							
Byrd	N	N	Y	N	N	N	N
Rockefeller	N	N	Y	N	Y	Y	Y
WISCONSIN							
Feingold	N	N	Y	N	Y	Y	Y
Kohl	N	N	Y	N	Y	Y	Y
WYOMING							
Enzi	Y	Y	N	Y	N	N	N
Thomas	Y	Y	N	Y	N	N	N

Key
- Y Voted for (yea).
- # Paired for.
- + Announced for.
- N Voted against (nay).
- X Paired against.
- − Announced against.
- P Voted "present."
- C Voted "present" to avoid possible conflict of interest.
- ? Did not vote or otherwise make a position known.

Democrats   Republicans

ND Northern Democrats   SD Southern Democrats

Southern states - Ala., Ark., Fla., Ga., Ky., La., Miss., N.C., Okla., S.C., Tenn., Texas, Va.

148. HR 1270. Temporary Nuclear Waste Repository/Cloture. Motion to invoke cloture (thus limiting debate) on the motion to proceed to the bill that would establish a temporary nuclear waste storage site at Yucca Mountain, Nev. Motion rejected 56-39: R 53-0; D 3-39 (ND 1-33, SD 2-6). June 2, 1998. Three-fifths of the total Senate (60) is required to invoke cloture. A "nay" was a vote in support of the president's position.

149. S 1415. Tobacco Restrictions/Look-Back Provisions. Lott, R-Miss., motion to table (kill) the Durbin, D-Ill., amendment to the Durbin amendment to the Gramm, R-Texas, motion to recommit the bill with instructions. The second-degree Durbin amendment, which is virtually identical to the underlying Durbin amendment, would toughen the bill's so-called look-back provisions, which would penalize the tobacco industry for failure to achieve targeted reductions in youth smoking. The amendment raises the underlying bill's 10-year reduction target from 60 percent to 67 percent and lifts the maximum annual penalties from $4 billion to $7 billion. Motion rejected 29-66: R 24-28; D 5-38 (ND 0-35, SD 5-3). June 4, 1998. (Subsequently, the second-degree Durbin amendment was adopted by voice vote.)

150. S 1415. Tobacco Restrictions/Cloture. Motion to invoke cloture (thus limiting debate) on the modified Senate Commerce Committee substitute amendment to the bill to increase tobacco restrictions. The substitute would require the tobacco industry to pay $516 billion over 25 years for anti-smoking, education and research programs, raise taxes on cigarettes by $1.10 per pack over five years, grant authority to the Food and Drug Administration to regulate nicotine and impose penalties on the tobacco industry if youth smoking does not decrease by 60 percent over 10 years. Motion rejected 42-56: R 0-54; D 42-2 (ND 36-0, SD 6-2). June 9, 1998.

151. S 1415. Tobacco Restrictions/Drug Prevention. Coverdell, R-Ga., amendment to the Durbin, D-Ill., amendment to the Gramm, R-Texas, motion to recommit the bill with instructions. The Coverdell amendment would authorize $16 billion over five years from the bill's tobacco revenues for drug prevention efforts. It would increase funding for border patrol, as well as anti-drug trafficking efforts of the FBI and the Drug Enforcement Administration, allow federal funds to be spent on school vouchers for public school children who have been victims of violent crimes on school property, ban federal funding for needle-exchange programs and encourage states to establish voluntary drug testing programs for all first-time individuals seeking a driver's license. Adopted 52-46: R 52-2; D 0-44 (ND 0-36, SD 0-8). June 9, 1998.

152. S 1415. Tobacco Restrictions/Democratic Drug Prevention Alternative. Daschle, D-S.D., amendment to the Durbin, D-Ill., amendment to the Gramm, R-Texas, motion to recommit the bill with instructions. The Daschle amendment would replace the text of the previously adopted Coverdell, R-Ga., amendment with a Democratic substitute. The substitute would authorize new funding for drug prevention efforts in the Coverdell amendment, but would not take revenue from the tobacco trust funds to do so. It also would not allow federal funds to be spent on school vouchers for public school children and would attach a section designed to strengthen anti-money laundering laws. Rejected 45-53: R 1-53; D 44-0 (ND 36-0, SD 8-0). June 9, 1998.

153. S 1415. Tobacco Restrictions/Cloture. Motion to invoke cloture (thus limiting debate) on the modified Senate Commerce Committee substitute amendment to the bill to increase tobacco restrictions. The substitute would require the tobacco industry to pay $516 billion over 25 years for anti-smoking, education and research programs, raise taxes on cigarettes by $1.10 per pack over five years, grant authority to the Food and Drug Administration to regulate nicotine and impose penalties on the tobacco industry if youth smoking does not decrease by 60 percent over 10 years. Motion rejected 43-55: R 0-53; D 43-2 (ND 37-0, SD 6-2). June 10, 1998.

154. S 1415. Tobacco Restrictions/Marriage Penalty. Kerry, D-Mass., motion to table (kill) the Gramm, R-Texas, amendment to the Durbin, D-Ill., amendment to the Gramm motion to recommit the bill with instructions. The Gramm amendment would allow couples with combined incomes under $50,000 a year to claim an additional $3,300 income tax deduction, thus eliminating the so-called marriage penalty for those in that income bracket, at a cost of $46 billion over 10 years. The amendment also would allow self-employed individuals to deduct the full cost of their health insurance on their income taxes. Motion rejected 48-50: R 5-49; D 43-1 (ND 36-0, SD 7-1). June 10, 1998. (Subsequently, the Gramm amendment was adopted by voice vote.)

Senate Votes 155, 156, 157, 158, 159, 160, 161

	155	156	157	158	159	160	161
ALABAMA							
Sessions	Y	N	Y	N	Y	Y	N
Shelby	Y	N	N	Y	N	N	N
ALASKA							
Murkowski	Y	N	N	N	Y	Y	N
Stevens	Y	N	Y	N	Y	Y	N
ARIZONA							
Kyl	Y	N	Y	N	Y	Y	N
McCain	Y	N	N	N	Y	Y	Y
ARKANSAS							
Hutchinson	Y	N	Y	N	Y	Y	N
Bumpers	N	Y	N	?	N	N	Y
CALIFORNIA							
Boxer	N	Y	N	C	N	C	Y
Feinstein	N	Y	N	Y	N	N	Y
COLORADO							
Allard	Y	N	Y	N	Y	Y	N
Campbell	Y	N	N	Y	Y	Y	N
CONNECTICUT							
Dodd	N	Y	N	Y	N	N	Y
Lieberman	N	Y	N	N	N	N	Y
DELAWARE							
Roth	Y	N	Y	Y	N	N	Y
Biden	?	Y	N	Y	N	N	Y
FLORIDA							
Mack	Y	N	Y	N	Y	Y	N
Graham	N	Y	N	Y	N	N	Y
GEORGIA							
Coverdell	Y	N	N	N	Y	Y	N
Cleland	N	Y	N	N	N	N	Y
HAWAII							
Akaka	N	Y	N	N	N	N	Y
Inouye	N	Y	N	Y	N	N	Y
IDAHO							
Craig	Y	N	Y	N	Y	Y	N
Kempthorne	Y	N	Y	N	Y	Y	N
ILLINOIS							
Durbin	N	Y	N	Y	–	N	Y
Moseley-Braun	N	Y	N	Y	?	N	Y
INDIANA							
Coats	Y	N	Y	N	Y	Y	N
Lugar	Y	N	Y	N	Y	Y	N

	155	156	157	158	159	160	161
IOWA							
Grassley	Y	N	N	N	Y	Y	Y
Harkin	N	Y	N	Y	N	N	Y
KANSAS							
Brownback	Y	N	Y	N	Y	Y	N
Roberts	Y	N	Y	N	Y	Y	N
KENTUCKY							
McConnell	Y	N	Y	N	Y	Y	N
Ford	N	N	N	Y	Y	N	N
LOUISIANA							
Breaux	N	Y	N	Y	N	N	Y
Landrieu	N	Y	N	Y	N	N	Y
MAINE							
Collins	Y	N	N	N	N	Y	Y
Snowe	Y	N	N	N	N	Y	Y
MARYLAND							
Mikulski	N	Y	N	Y	N	N	Y
Sarbanes	N	Y	N	Y	N	N	Y
MASSACHUSETTS							
Kennedy	N	Y	N	Y	N	N	Y
Kerry	N	Y	N	Y	N	N	Y
MICHIGAN							
Abraham	Y	N	N	N	Y	Y	Y
Levin	N	Y	N	Y	N	N	Y
MINNESOTA							
Grams	Y	N	Y	N	Y	Y	N
Wellstone	N	Y	N	Y	N	N	Y
MISSISSIPPI							
Cochran	Y	N	Y	Y	N	N	N
Lott	Y	N	Y	C	Y	C	N
MISSOURI							
Ashcroft	Y	N	Y	N	Y	Y	N
Bond	Y	N	N	N	Y	Y	N
MONTANA							
Burns	Y	N	N	N	?	Y	N
Baucus	N	Y	N	Y	N	N	Y
NEBRASKA							
Hagel	Y	N	Y	N	Y	Y	N
Kerrey	N	Y	N	Y	?	N	Y
NEVADA							
Bryan	N	Y	N	Y	N	N	Y
Reid	N	Y	N	Y	N	N	Y

	155	156	157	158	159	160	161
NEW HAMPSHIRE							
Gregg	Y	N	Y	N	Y	Y	Y
Smith	Y	N	Y	N	Y	Y	N
NEW JERSEY							
Lautenberg	N	Y	N	Y	N	N	Y
Torricelli	N	Y	N	N	N	N	Y
NEW MEXICO							
Domenici	Y	N	N	N	Y	Y	N
Bingaman	N	Y	N	?	N	N	Y
NEW YORK							
D'Amato	Y	N	N	N	Y	Y	N
Moynihan	N	Y	N	Y	Y	N	Y
NORTH CAROLINA							
Faircloth	Y	N	N	N	Y	Y	N
Helms	Y	N	Y	N	Y	Y	N
NORTH DAKOTA							
Conrad	N	Y	N	N	N	N	Y
Dorgan	N	Y	N	N	N	Y	Y
OHIO							
DeWine	Y	N	Y	N	N	Y	N
Glenn	N	Y	N	Y	N	N	Y
OKLAHOMA							
Inhofe	Y	N	Y	?	Y	N	N
Nickles	Y	N	Y	N	Y	Y	N
OREGON							
Smith	Y	N	Y	Y	Y	Y	Y
Wyden	N	Y	N	Y	N	N	Y
PENNSYLVANIA							
Santorum	Y	N	Y	N	Y	Y	N
Specter	?	?	?	?	?	?	?
RHODE ISLAND							
Chafee	Y	N	N	N	N	Y	Y
Reed	N	Y	N	Y	N	N	Y
SOUTH CAROLINA							
Thurmond	Y	N	Y	N	Y	Y	N
Hollings	N	Y	N	Y	Y	Y	Y
SOUTH DAKOTA							
Daschle	N	Y	N	N	N	N	Y
Johnson	N	Y	N	N	N	N	Y
TENNESSEE							
Frist	Y	N	Y	N	Y	Y	Y
Thompson	Y	N	Y	Y	Y	Y	N

Key

- Y Voted for (yea).
- # Paired for.
- + Announced for.
- N Voted against (nay).
- X Paired against.
- – Announced against.
- P Voted "present."
- C Voted "present" to avoid possible conflict of interest.
- ? Did not vote or otherwise make a position known.

Democrats   **Republicans**

	155	156	157	158	159	160	161
TEXAS							
Gramm	Y	N	Y	N	Y	Y	N
Hutchison	Y	N	N	N	N	Y	N
UTAH							
Bennett	Y	N	N	Y	Y	N	Y
Hatch	Y	N	N	Y	Y	N	N
VERMONT							
Jeffords	Y	N	N	N	N	N	Y
Leahy	N	Y	N	Y	N	N	Y
VIRGINIA							
Warner	Y	N	Y	N	Y	Y	N
Robb	N	N	N	Y	N	N	N
WASHINGTON							
Gorton	Y	N	Y	N	Y	Y	N
Murray	N	Y	N	Y	N	N	Y
WEST VIRGINIA							
Byrd	N	Y	N	N	N	Y	Y
Rockefeller	N	Y	N	Y	N	N	Y
WISCONSIN							
Feingold	Y	Y	N	Y	N	Y	N
Kohl	N	Y	N	Y	N	N	Y
WYOMING							
Enzi	Y	N	Y	N	Y	Y	N
Thomas	Y	N	Y	N	Y	Y	N

ND Northern Democrats   SD Southern Democrats

Southern states - Ala., Ark., Fla., Ga., Ky., La., Miss., N.C., Okla., S.C., Tenn., Texas, Va.

155. S 1415. Tobacco Restrictions/Democratic Marriage Penalty Alternative. Lott, R-Miss., motion to table (kill) the Daschle, D-S.D., amendment to the Durbin, D-Ill., amendment to the Gramm, R-Texas, motion to recommit the bill with instructions. The Daschle amendment would strike the provisions of the previously adopted Gramm amendment and replace them with language to allow couples with combined incomes under $50,000 a year to deduct 20 percent of the income of the lesser-earning spouse on their income taxes, thus eliminating the so-called marriage penalty for those in that income bracket, at a cost of $31 billion over 10 years. The amendment also would allow self-employed individuals to deduct the full cost of their health insurance on their income taxes. Motion agreed to 55-43: R 54-0; D 1-43 (ND 1-35, SD 0-8). June 10, 1998.

156. S 1415. Tobacco Restrictions/Cloture. Motion to invoke cloture (thus limiting debate) on the modified Senate Commerce Committee substitute amendment to the bill to increase tobacco restrictions. The substitute would require the tobacco industry to pay $516 billion over 25 years for anti-smoking, education and research programs, raise taxes on cigarettes by $1.10 per pack over five years, grant authority to the Food and Drug Administration to regulate nicotine and impose penalties on the tobacco industry if youth smoking does not decrease by 60 percent over 10 years. Motion rejected 43-56: R 0-54; D 43-2 (ND 37-0, SD 6-2). June 11, 1998.

157. S 1415. Tobacco Restrictions/Child Care Block Grants. McCain, R-Ariz., motion to table (kill) the Kerry, D-Mass., amendment to the Durbin, D-Ill., amendment to the Gramm, R-Texas, motion to recommit the bill with instructions. The Kerry amendment would require states to spend at least 50 percent of the restricted-use tobacco revenue, which is 50 percent of the money states would receive, on the child care and development block grant programs. Motion rejected 33-66: R 33-21; D 0-45 (ND 0-37, SD 0-8). June 11, 1998. (Subsequently, the Kerry amendment, after being modified, was adopted by voice vote.)

158. S 1415. Tobacco Restrictions/Cap on Attorney's Fees. Kerry, D-Mass., motion to table (kill) the Faircloth, R-N.C., amendment to the Durbin, D-Ill., amendment to the Gramm, R-Texas, motion to recommit the bill with instructions. The Faircloth amendment would cap at $1,000 per hour the amount lawyers are allowed to charge for services in relation to any tobacco-related lawsuits. It would not exempt suits in which states have already settled with tobacco manufacturers. Motion agreed to 50-45: R 12-41; D 38-4 (ND 31-4, SD 7-0). June 11, 1998.

159. S 1415. Tobacco Restrictions/Advertising Tax Deductions. Gorton, R-Wash., motion to table (kill) the Reed, D-R.I., amendment to the Durbin, D-Ill., amendment to the Gramm, R-Texas, motion to recommit the bill with instructions. The Reed amendment would eliminate advertising tax deductions for those tobacco companies that the Food and Drug Administration determines are directing their advertisements at children. Motion rejected 47-47: R 43-9; D 4-38 (ND 2-32, SD 2-6). June 15, 1998.

160. S 1415. Tobacco Restrictions/Cap on Attorney's Fees. Gorton, R-Wash., amendment to the Durbin, D-Ill., amendment to the Gramm, R-Texas, motion to recommit the bill with instructions. The Gorton amendment would cap at $4,000 per hour the amount lawyers for plaintiffs are allowed to charge for services in relation to any tobacco-related lawsuits filed before Dec. 31, 1994. The amendment would cap the amount at $2,000 per hour for actions filed between Dec. 31, 1994, and March 31, 1997, $1,000 per hour for actions filed between April 1, 1997, and June 15, 1998, and $500 per hour for actions filed after June 15, 1998. The cap would not apply to any attorney who received payment before June 15, 1998, or attorneys for tobacco companies. Adopted 49-48: R 45-8; D 4-40 (ND 4-32, SD 0-8). June 16, 1998.

161. S 1415. Tobacco Restrictions/Cloture. Motion to invoke cloture (thus limiting debate) on the modified Senate Commerce, Science and Transportation Committee substitute amendment to the bill to increase tobacco restrictions. The substitute would require the tobacco industry to pay $516 billion over 25 years for anti-smoking, education and research programs, raise taxes on cigarettes by $1.10 per pack over five years, grant authority to the Food and Drug Administration to regulate nicotine and impose penalties on the tobacco industry if youth smoking does not decrease by 60 percent over 10 years. Motion rejected 57-42: R 14-40; D 43-2 (ND 37-0, SD 6-2). June 17, 1998. Three-fifths of the total Senate (60) is required to invoke cloture. A "yea" was a vote in support of the president's position.

Senate Votes 162, 163, 164, 165, 166, 167, 168

	162	163	164	165	166	167	168
ALABAMA							
Sessions	N	Y	Y	Y	N	N	N
Shelby	N	Y	Y	Y	N	N	N
ALASKA							
Murkowski	N	Y	Y	Y	?	N	N
Stevens	N	Y	Y	Y	Y	Y	N
ARIZONA							
Kyl	N	Y	Y	Y	N	N	N
McCain	Y	Y	Y	Y	N	Y	N
ARKANSAS							
Hutchinson	N	Y	Y	Y	N	N	N
Bumpers	Y	Y	N	Y	Y	N	N
CALIFORNIA							
Boxer	Y	Y	N	Y	Y	N	N
Feinstein	Y	Y	N	Y	Y	N	N
COLORADO							
Allard	N	Y	Y	Y	N	N	N
Campbell	N	Y	Y	Y	N	N	N
CONNECTICUT							
Dodd	Y	Y	N	Y	Y	N	N
Lieberman	Y	Y	N	Y	Y	Y	N
DELAWARE							
Roth	Y	Y	Y	Y	Y	Y	N
Biden	Y	Y	N	Y	Y	N	N
FLORIDA							
Mack	N	Y	Y	Y	N	N	N
Graham	Y	Y	N	Y	Y	N	N
GEORGIA							
Coverdell	N	Y	Y	Y	N	N	N
Cleland	Y	Y	N	Y	Y	N	N
HAWAII							
Akaka	Y	Y	N	Y	Y	N	N
Inouye	Y	Y	N	Y	Y	N	N
IDAHO							
Craig	N	Y	Y	Y	N	N	N
Kempthorne	N	Y	Y	Y	N	N	N
ILLINOIS							
Durbin	Y	Y	N	Y	N	N	N
Moseley-Braun	Y	Y	N	?	N	N	N
INDIANA							
Coats	N	Y	Y	Y	N	N	N
Lugar	N	Y	Y	Y	Y	Y	N
IOWA							
Grassley	Y	Y	Y	Y	N	N	N
Harkin	Y	Y	N	Y	Y	N	N
KANSAS							
Brownback	N	Y	Y	Y	N	N	N
Roberts	N	Y	Y	Y	N	N	N
KENTUCKY							
McConnell	N	Y	Y	Y	N	N	N
Ford	N	Y	N	Y	Y	N	N
LOUISIANA							
Breaux	Y	N	N	Y	Y	N	N
Landrieu	Y	Y	N	Y	Y	N	N
MAINE							
Collins	Y	Y	Y	Y	Y	N	N
Snowe	Y	Y	Y	Y	Y	N	N
MARYLAND							
Mikulski	Y	Y	N	Y	Y	N	N
Sarbanes	Y	Y	N	Y	Y	N	N
MASSACHUSETTS							
Kennedy	Y	Y	N	Y	Y	N	N
Kerry	Y	Y	N	Y	Y	Y	N
MICHIGAN							
Abraham	N	Y	Y	Y	N	N	N
Levin	Y	Y	N	Y	Y	N	N
MINNESOTA							
Grams	N	Y	Y	Y	N	Y	N
Wellstone	Y	Y	N	Y	Y	N	N
MISSISSIPPI							
Cochran	N	Y	Y	Y	N	N	N
Lott	N	Y	Y	Y	N	N	N
MISSOURI							
Ashcroft	N	Y	Y	Y	N	N	N
Bond	N	N	Y	Y	N	N	N
MONTANA							
Burns	N	Y	Y	Y	N	N	N
Baucus	Y	Y	N	Y	Y	N	N
NEBRASKA							
Hagel	N	Y	Y	Y	Y	Y	N
Kerrey	Y	Y	N	Y	Y	N	N
NEVADA							
Bryan	Y	Y	N	Y	Y	N	N
Reid	Y	Y	N	Y	?	N	N
NEW HAMPSHIRE							
Gregg	N	Y	Y	Y	N	N	N
Smith	N	Y	Y	Y	N	N	N
NEW JERSEY							
Lautenberg	Y	Y	N	Y	Y	N	N
Torricelli	Y	Y	N	Y	Y	N	N
NEW MEXICO							
Domenici	N	Y	Y	Y	?	?	?
Bingaman	Y	Y	N	Y	Y	N	N
NEW YORK							
D'Amato	Y	Y	Y	Y	?	N	N
Moynihan	Y	Y	N	Y	Y	N	N
NORTH CAROLINA							
Faircloth	N	?	?	Y	N	N	N
Helms	N	Y	Y	Y	N	N	N
NORTH DAKOTA							
Conrad	Y	Y	N	Y	Y	N	N
Dorgan	Y	Y	N	Y	Y	N	N
OHIO							
DeWine	Y	Y	Y	Y	N	N	N
Glenn	Y	Y	N	Y	Y	N	N
OKLAHOMA							
Inhofe	N	Y	Y	Y	N	N	N
Nickles	N	Y	Y	Y	N	N	N
OREGON							
Smith	Y	Y	Y	Y	N	N	N
Wyden	Y	Y	N	Y	Y	N	N
PENNSYLVANIA							
Santorum	N	Y	Y	Y	N	N	N
Specter	?	?	?	?	?	?	?
RHODE ISLAND							
Chafee	Y	Y	Y	Y	?	?	N
Reed	Y	Y	N	Y	Y	N	N
SOUTH CAROLINA							
Thurmond	N	Y	Y	Y	N	N	N
Hollings	N	Y	Y	Y	N	N	N
SOUTH DAKOTA							
Daschle	Y	Y	N	Y	Y	N	N
Johnson	Y	Y	N	Y	Y	N	N
TENNESSEE							
Frist	N	Y	Y	Y	N	N	N
Thompson	N	Y	Y	Y	N	N	N
TEXAS							
Gramm	N	Y	Y	Y	N	N	N
Hutchison	N	Y	Y	Y	N	N	N
UTAH							
Bennett	Y	Y	Y	Y	?	?	?
Hatch	N	Y	Y	Y	Y	N	N
VERMONT							
Jeffords	Y	Y	Y	Y	Y	Y	N
Leahy	Y	Y	N	Y	+	N	N
VIRGINIA							
Warner	N	Y	Y	Y	N	Y	N
Robb	N	Y	N	Y	Y	Y	N
WASHINGTON							
Gorton	N	Y	Y	Y	N	N	N
Murray	Y	Y	N	Y	Y	N	N
WEST VIRGINIA							
Byrd	Y	Y	Y	Y	Y	N	N
Rockefeller	Y	Y	N	Y	Y	N	?
WISCONSIN							
Feingold	Y	Y	N	N	Y	N	N
Kohl	Y	Y	N	Y	Y	N	N
WYOMING							
Enzi	N	Y	Y	Y	N	N	N
Thomas	N	Y	Y	Y	?	Y	N

ND Northern Democrats SD Southern Democrats

Southern states - Ala., Ark., Fla., Ga., Ky., La., Miss., N.C., Okla., S.C., Tenn., Texas, Va.

Key
- Y Voted for (yea).
- # Paired for.
- + Announced for.
- N Voted against (nay).
- X Paired against.
- − Announced against.
- P Voted "present."
- C Voted "present" to avoid possible conflict of interest.
- ? Did not vote or otherwise make a position known.

Democrats • *Republicans*

---

162. S 1415. Tobacco Restrictions/Budget Act Waiver. Daschle, D-S.D., motion to waive the Budget Act with respect to the Stevens, R-Alaska, point of order against the bill to increase tobacco restrictions. The bill, as amended, would require the tobacco industry to pay $516 billion over 25 years for anti-smoking, education and research programs, raise taxes on cigarettes by $1.10 per pack over five years, grant authority to the Food and Drug Administration to regulate nicotine and impose penalties on the tobacco industry if youth smoking does not decrease by 60 percent over 10 years. Motion rejected 53-46: R 11-43; D 42-3 (ND 37-0, SD 5-3). June 17, 1998. A three-fifths majority vote (60) of the total Senate is required to waive the Budget Act. (Subsequently, the chair upheld the point of order, and the bill was returned to the Senate Commerce Committee.) A "yea" was a vote in support of the president's position.

163. Procedural Motion. Lott, R-Miss., motion to instruct the sergeant-at-arms to request the attendance of absent senators. Motion agreed to 96-2: R 52-1; D 44-1 (ND 37-0, SD 7-1). June 18, 1998.

164. S 2138. Fiscal 1999 Energy and Water Appropriations/Tobacco Restrictions. Lott, R-Miss., motion to table (kill) the Reid, D-Nev., motion to waive the Budget Act with respect to the Domenici, R-N.M., point of order against the Daschle, D-S.D., amendment. The Daschle amendment would require the tobacco industry to pay $516 billion over 25 years for anti-smoking, education and research programs, raise taxes on cigarettes by $1.10 per pack over five years, grant authority to the Food and Drug Administration to regulate nicotine and impose penalties on the tobacco industry if youth smoking does not decrease by 60 percent over 10 years. Motion agreed to 54-44: R 53-0; D 1-44 (ND 1-36, SD 0-8). June 18, 1998.

165. S 2138. Fiscal 1999 Energy and Water Development Appropriations/Passage. Passage of the bill to provide $21.4 billion in new budget authority for energy and water development programs in fiscal 1999. The bill provides $109 million more than provided in fiscal 1998 and $354 million less than requested by the Clinton administration. Passed 98-1: R 54-0; D 44-1 (ND 36-1, SD 8-0). June 18, 1998.

166. Mollway Nomination/Confirmation. Confirmation of President Clinton's nomination of Susan Oki Mollway of Hawaii to be U.S. District Judge for the District of Hawaii. Confirmed 56-34: R 14-34; D 42-0 (ND 34-0, SD 8-0). June 22, 1998. A "yea" was a vote in support of the president's position.

167. S 2057. Fiscal 1999 Defense Authorization/Chinese Forced Abortions. Warner, R-Va., motion to table (kill) the Warner-Hutchinson, R-Ark., amendment to the Warner perfecting amendment to the Warner motion to recommit the bill with instructions. The second-degree Warner-Hutchinson amendment would condemn various human rights violations of the Chinese government and would prohibit the issuing of U.S. visas to Chinese officials involved in forced abortions or forced sterilizations. Motion rejected 14-82: R 12-39; D 2-43 (ND 1-36, SD 1-7). June 23, 1998. (Subsequently, these amendments were withdrawn.)

168. S 2057. Fiscal 1999 Defense Authorization/Chinese Forced Abortions. Ashcroft, R-Mo., motion to table (kill) Division I of the Hutchinson, R-Ark., amendment to the Hutchinson amendment to the Warner, R-Va., motion to recommit the bill with instructions. Division I would prohibit U.S. visas to Chinese officials involved in forced abortions or forced sterilizations. The tabling motion was intended to test of Senate support for Division I, but opponents thwarted that intent by voting against the motion. Motion rejected 0-96: R 0-52; D 0-44 (ND 0-36, SD 0-8). June 23, 1998.

Senate Votes 169, 170, 171, 172, 173, 174, 175

	169	170	171	172	173	174	175
ALABAMA							
Sessions	Y	Y	N	N	N	Y	N
Shelby	Y	Y	Y	N	N	Y	N
ALASKA							
Murkowski	Y	Y	N	N	N	N	N
Stevens	Y	Y	Y	Y	N	N	N
ARIZONA							
Kyl	Y	Y	N	N	N	N	N
McCain	Y	Y	N	N	N	N	N
ARKANSAS							
Hutchinson	Y	Y	N	N	?	?	?
Bumpers	N	Y	Y	Y	Y	N	Y
CALIFORNIA							
Boxer	N	Y	Y	Y	Y	Y	Y
Feinstein	Y	Y	Y	Y	N	N	Y
COLORADO							
Allard	Y	Y	N	N	N	Y	N
Campbell	Y	Y	Y	N	N	Y	Y
CONNECTICUT							
Dodd	N	N	Y	N	Y	Y	Y
Lieberman	Y	N	Y	Y	N	N	N
DELAWARE							
Roth	Y	Y	Y	?	?	?	?
Biden	Y	N	Y	Y	N	N	Y
FLORIDA							
Mack	Y	Y	Y	Y	N	Y	N
Graham	N	Y	Y	Y	N	Y	N
GEORGIA							
Coverdell	Y	Y	Y	N	N	Y	N
Cleland	Y	N	Y	Y	N	Y	N
HAWAII							
Akaka	?	?	?	?	?	?	?
Inouye	N	Y	Y	Y	N	N	Y
IDAHO							
Craig	Y	Y	N	N	N	Y	N
Kempthorne	Y	Y	N	Y	N	Y	N
ILLINOIS							
Durbin	N	Y	N	Y	Y	Y	Y
Moseley-Braun	N	Y	Y	Y	Y	Y	Y
INDIANA							
Coats	Y	Y	Y	N	N	N	N
Lugar	Y	Y	Y	Y	N	N	N
IOWA							
Grassley	Y	Y	N	N	N	N	Y
Harkin	N	Y	Y	Y	N	Y	Y
KANSAS							
Brownback	Y	Y	N	N	N	N	N
Roberts	Y	Y	N	N	N	Y	N
KENTUCKY							
McConnell	Y	Y	N	N	N	Y	N
Ford	N	Y	Y	Y	Y	Y	Y
LOUISIANA							
Breaux	Y	Y	Y	Y	N	Y	Y
Landrieu	N	Y	Y	Y	N	Y	Y
MAINE							
Collins	Y	Y	Y	Y	N	Y	N
Snowe	Y	Y	N	Y	N	Y	N
MARYLAND							
Mikulski	N	Y	Y	Y	Y	Y	Y
Sarbanes	N	Y	Y	Y	N	Y	Y
MASSACHUSETTS							
Kennedy	N	Y	Y	Y	Y	N	Y
Kerry	N	Y	Y	Y	N	Y	Y
MICHIGAN							
Abraham	Y	Y	N	N	N	Y	N
Levin	N	Y	Y	Y	N	N	N
MINNESOTA							
Grams	Y	Y	N	N	N	N	N
Wellstone	N	Y	Y	Y	Y	N	Y
MISSISSIPPI							
Cochran	Y	Y	Y	N	N	Y	N
Lott	Y	Y	N	N	N	Y	N
MISSOURI							
Ashcroft	Y	Y	N	N	N	N	N
Bond	Y	Y	N	N	N	Y	N
MONTANA							
Burns	Y	Y	N	N	N	Y	N
Baucus	?	?	?	?	?	?	?
NEBRASKA							
Hagel	Y	Y	Y	N	N	Y	N
Kerrey	N	Y	Y	Y	N	N	N
NEVADA							
Bryan	N	Y	Y	Y	N	N	Y
Reid	N	Y	Y	Y	N	N	Y
NEW HAMPSHIRE							
Gregg	Y	Y	N	N	N	N	N
Smith	Y	Y	N	N	N	Y	N
NEW JERSEY							
Lautenberg	N	Y	Y	Y	Y	Y	Y
Torricelli	Y	Y	Y	Y	Y	Y	N
NEW MEXICO							
Domenici	+	?	Y	Y	N	Y	N
Bingaman	N	Y	Y	Y	N	Y	Y
NEW YORK							
D'Amato	Y	Y	Y	Y	N	Y	Y
Moynihan	N	Y	Y	Y	N	N	Y
NORTH CAROLINA							
Faircloth	Y	Y	N	N	N	Y	N
Helms	Y	Y	N	–	?	Y	N
NORTH DAKOTA							
Conrad	N	Y	Y	N	N	Y	Y
Dorgan	N	Y	Y	N	Y	Y	Y
OHIO							
DeWine	Y	Y	N	N	N	N	N
Glenn	N	Y	Y	?	?	?	?
OKLAHOMA							
Inhofe	Y	Y	N	N	N	Y	N
Nickles	Y	Y	N	N	N	N	N
OREGON							
Smith	Y	Y	N	N	N	N	N
Wyden	N	Y	Y	Y	Y	N	Y
PENNSYLVANIA							
Santorum	Y	Y	N	N	N	N	N
Specter	?	?	?	?	?	?	?
RHODE ISLAND							
Chafee	N	Y	Y	N	N	Y	N
Reed	N	Y	Y	Y	N	N	N
SOUTH CAROLINA							
Thurmond	Y	Y	Y	N	N	Y	N
Hollings	N	Y	Y	N	N	N	Y
SOUTH DAKOTA							
Daschle	N	Y	Y	Y	N	Y	Y
Johnson	N	Y	Y	Y	N	Y	Y
TENNESSEE							
Frist	Y	Y	N	N	N	N	N
Thompson	Y	Y	N	N	N	N	N
TEXAS							
Gramm	Y	Y	N	N	N	N	N
Hutchison	Y	Y	N	N	N	Y	N
UTAH							
Bennett	Y	Y	Y	Y	N	Y	N
Hatch	Y	Y	N	N	N	Y	N
VERMONT							
Jeffords	N	Y	Y	Y	Y	N	Y
Leahy	N	Y	Y	Y	N	N	Y
VIRGINIA							
Warner	Y	N	Y	N	N	N	N
Robb	N	N	Y	N	N	N	N
WASHINGTON							
Gorton	Y	Y	N	N	Y	N	N
Murray	N	Y	Y	Y	Y	Y	Y
WEST VIRGINIA							
Byrd	Y	Y	Y	N	N	N	Y
Rockefeller	?	?	?	?	?	?	?
WISCONSIN							
Feingold	N	Y	N	Y	Y	N	Y
Kohl	Y	Y	Y	Y	Y	N	Y
WYOMING							
Enzi	Y	Y	N	N	N	N	N
Thomas	Y	Y	N	Y	N	Y	N

Key

- Y Voted for (yea).
- # Paired for.
- + Announced for.
- N Voted against (nay).
- X Paired against.
- – Announced against.
- P Voted "present."
- C Voted "present" to avoid possible conflict of interest.
- ? Did not vote or otherwise make a position known.

Democrats • Republicans

ND Northern Democrats   SD Southern Democrats

Southern states - Ala., Ark., Fla., Ga., Ky., La., Miss., N.C., Okla., S.C., Tenn., Texas, Va.

169. HR 2646. Expanding Education Savings Accounts/Conference Report. Adoption of the conference report on the bill to allow individuals to contribute up to $2,000 a year of after-tax funds in tax-sheltered savings accounts that may be used to pay for educational expenses. Adopted (thus cleared for the president) 59-36: R 51-2; D 8-34 (ND 6-28, SD 2-6). June 24, 1998. A "nay" was a vote in support of the president's position.

170. S 2057. Fiscal 1999 Defense Authorization/Troops in Bosnia. Thurmond, R-S.C., amendment to express the sense of Congress that U.S. ground forces should not remain in Bosnia indefinitely and that the president should work with NATO to withdraw U.S. forces "within a reasonable period of time." Adopted 90-5: R 53-0; D 37-5 (ND 31-3, SD 6-2). June 24, 1998.

171. S 2057. Fiscal 1999 Defense Authorization/Troops in Bosnia. McCain, R-Ariz., motion to table (kill) the Smith, R-N.H., amendment that would prohibit funding for U.S. ground troop deployment in Bosnia if both houses of Congress do not vote by March 31, 1999, on legislation that would authorize continued deployment in Bosnia. Motion agreed to 65-31: R 25-29; D 40-2 (ND 32-2, SD 8-0). June 24, 1998.

172. S 2057. Fiscal 1999 Defense Authorization/Separate Gender Barracks. Snowe, R-Maine, amendment to the Brownback, R-Kan., amendment. The Snowe amendment would replace the text of the Brownback amendment with language to prohibit the Defense Department from making any changes in its gender separation policies until a commission established in the fiscal 1998 defense authorization bill issues a report early next year. Adopted 56-37: R 18-34; D 38-3 (ND 31-2, SD 7-1). June 24, 1998. (Subsequently, the Brownback amendment as amended was adopted by voice vote.)

173. S 2057. Fiscal 1999 Defense Authorization/Child Development Program. Wellstone, D-Minn., amendment to authorize an additional $270 million over five years for the Defense Department's child development program. The amendment would pay for the increase with a 0.1 percent across-the-board cut to all other programs authorized by the bill. Rejected 18-74: R 1-50; D 17-24 (ND 15-18, SD 2-6). June 25, 1998.

174. S 2057. Fiscal 1999 Defense Authorization/Base Closures and Realignments. Inhofe, R-Okla., amendment that would reduce the Defense Department's authority to close or realign military installations without congressional approval. The amendment also would express the sense of Congress that Congress should not consider further base closings until activities related to previously authorized closings are complete and that the Defense Department should report to Congress on the effect closings and realignments have on the ability to mobilize U.S. forces. Adopted 48-45: R 31-21; D 17-24 (ND 12-21, SD 5-3). June 25, 1998.

175. S 2057. Fiscal 1999 Defense Authorization/Veterans' Health Care. Harkin, D-Iowa, amendment that would transfer $329 million from defense accounts to the Veterans Affairs Department for health care programs. The amendment would order the secretary of Defense to transfer the funds from defense programs that would result in the "least significant harm" to armed forces readiness and military personnel quality of life. Rejected 38-55: R 5-47; D 33-8 (ND 28-5, SD 5-3). June 25, 1998.

Senate Votes 176, 177, 178, 179, 180, 181, 182

	176	177	178	179	180	181	182
ALABAMA							
Sessions	N	Y	N	Y	Y	Y	Y
Shelby	N	Y	N	N	Y	Y	Y
ALASKA							
Murkowski	N	Y	N	N	Y	Y	Y
Stevens	Y	Y	N	N	Y	Y	?
ARIZONA							
Kyl	N	Y	N	N	Y	Y	?
McCain	N	Y	N	N	N	Y	?
ARKANSAS							
Hutchinson	–	?	?	?	?	?	?
Bumpers	Y	N	Y	Y	Y	N	Y
CALIFORNIA							
Boxer	Y	N	Y	Y	N	Y	Y
Feinstein	Y	N	N	Y	N	Y	Y
COLORADO							
Allard	N	Y	N	N	N	Y	Y
Campbell	N	Y	N	N	Y	Y	Y
CONNECTICUT							
Dodd	Y	N	N	N	N	Y	Y
Lieberman	Y	N	N	N	N	Y	Y
DELAWARE							
Roth	?	?	?	?	?	?	?
Biden	Y	N	Y	N	N	Y	Y
FLORIDA							
Mack	N	Y	N	N	N	Y	Y
Graham	Y	N	N	N	N	Y	Y
GEORGIA							
Coverdell	N	Y	N	N	N	Y	Y
Cleland	Y	N	N	N	N	Y	Y
HAWAII							
Akaka	?	?	?	?	?	?	?
Inouye	Y	N	N	N	Y	Y	Y
IDAHO							
Craig	N	Y	N	N	Y	Y	Y
Kempthorne	N	Y	N	N	Y	Y	Y
ILLINOIS							
Durbin	Y	N	Y	Y	N	Y	Y
Moseley-Braun	Y	N	Y	Y	N	Y	Y
INDIANA							
Coats	N	Y	N	N	Y	Y	Y
Lugar	N	Y	N	N	N	Y	Y
IOWA							
Grassley	N	Y	Y	Y	Y	Y	Y
Harkin	Y	N	Y	Y	N	N	?
KANSAS							
Brownback	N	Y	N	N	Y	Y	Y
Roberts	N	Y	N	N	Y	Y	Y
KENTUCKY							
McConnell	N	Y	N	N	Y	Y	Y
Ford	N	N	N	N	Y	Y	Y
LOUISIANA							
Breaux	N	N	N	N	N	Y	Y
Landrieu	Y	N	N	N	N	Y	Y
MAINE							
Collins	Y	Y	N	N	N	Y	Y
Snowe	Y	Y	N	N	N	Y	Y
MARYLAND							
Mikulski	Y	N	Y	N	N	Y	Y
Sarbanes	Y	N	Y	N	N	Y	Y
MASSACHUSETTS							
Kennedy	Y	N	Y	Y	N	Y	Y
Kerry	Y	N	N	N	N	Y	Y
MICHIGAN							
Abraham	N	Y	N	N	Y	Y	Y
Levin	Y	N	Y	N	N	Y	Y
MINNESOTA							
Grams	N	Y	N	Y	Y	Y	Y
Wellstone	Y	N	Y	Y	N	N	+
MISSISSIPPI							
Cochran	N	Y	N	N	Y	Y	Y
Lott	N	Y	N	N	Y	Y	Y
MISSOURI							
Ashcroft	N	Y	N	N	Y	Y	Y
Bond	N	Y	N	N	N	Y	Y
MONTANA							
Burns	N	Y	N	N	Y	Y	Y
Baucus	?	?	?	?	?	?	?
NEBRASKA							
Hagel	N	Y	N	N	N	Y	Y
Kerrey	Y	N	N	N	N	Y	Y
NEVADA							
Bryan	Y	N	Y	Y	N	Y	Y
Reid	N	N	Y	N	N	Y	Y
NEW HAMPSHIRE							
Gregg	N	Y	N	N	Y	Y	Y
Smith	N	Y	N	N	Y	Y	Y
NEW JERSEY							
Lautenberg	Y	N	Y	Y	N	Y	Y
Torricelli	Y	N	N	N	Y	Y	Y
NEW MEXICO							
Domenici	N	Y	N	N	N	Y	Y
Bingaman	Y	N	N	N	N	Y	Y
NEW YORK							
D'Amato	N	Y	N	N	N	Y	Y
Moynihan	Y	N	N	N	Y	Y	Y
NORTH CAROLINA							
Faircloth	N	Y	N	N	Y	Y	Y
Helms	N	Y	N	N	Y	Y	Y
NORTH DAKOTA							
Conrad	Y	N	N	Y	Y	Y	Y
Dorgan	Y	N	N	N	N	Y	Y
OHIO							
DeWine	N	Y	N	N	Y	Y	Y
Glenn	?	?	?	?	?	?	?
OKLAHOMA							
Inhofe	N	Y	N	N	Y	Y	?
Nickles	N	Y	N	N	Y	Y	Y
OREGON							
Smith	N	N	N	N	N	Y	Y
Wyden	Y	N	+	+	–	+	+
PENNSYLVANIA							
Santorum	N	Y	N	N	Y	Y	Y
Specter	?	?	?	?	?	?	?
RHODE ISLAND							
Chafee	Y	Y	N	N	Y	Y	Y
Reed	Y	N	Y	N	N	Y	Y
SOUTH CAROLINA							
Thurmond	N	Y	N	N	Y	Y	Y
Hollings	Y	N	N	N	N	Y	Y
SOUTH DAKOTA							
Daschle	Y	N	N	Y	N	Y	Y
Johnson	Y	N	Y	Y	N	Y	Y
TENNESSEE							
Frist	N	Y	N	N	Y	Y	Y
Thompson	N	Y	N	N	N	Y	Y
TEXAS							
Gramm	N	Y	N	N	N	Y	Y
Hutchison	N	Y	N	N	N	Y	Y
UTAH							
Bennett	N	N	N	N	Y	Y	?
Hatch	N	N	N	N	Y	Y	Y
VERMONT							
Jeffords	Y	Y	N	Y	N	Y	Y
Leahy	Y	N	Y	N	Y	Y	Y
VIRGINIA							
Warner	N	Y	N	N	N	Y	Y
Robb	Y	N	N	N	N	Y	Y
WASHINGTON							
Gorton	Y	Y	N	Y	Y	Y	Y
Murray	Y	N	N	N	N	Y	Y
WEST VIRGINIA							
Byrd	Y	N	Y	Y	Y	Y	Y
Rockefeller	?	?	?	?	?	?	?
WISCONSIN							
Feingold	Y	N	Y	N	N	Y	N
Kohl	Y	N	Y	Y	N	Y	Y
WYOMING							
Enzi	N	Y	N	N	Y	Y	Y
Thomas	N	Y	N	N	N	Y	Y

Key
- Y Voted for (yea).
- # Paired for.
- + Announced for.
- N Voted against (nay).
- X Paired against.
- – Announced against.
- P Voted "present."
- C Voted "present" to avoid possible conflict of interest.
- ? Did not vote or otherwise make a position known.

Democrats *Republicans*

ND Northern Democrats   SD Southern Democrats

Southern states - Ala., Ark., Fla., Ga., Ky., La., Miss., N.C., Okla., S.C., Tenn., Texas, Va.

176. S 2057. Fiscal 1999 Defense Authorization/Overseas Military Hospital Abortions. Murray, D-Wash., amendment to repeal current law prohibiting overseas U.S. military hospitals and medical facilities from performing privately funded abortions for U.S. service members and their dependents. Rejected 44-49: R 6-46; D 38-3 (ND 32-1, SD 6-2). June 25, 1998. A "yea" was a vote in support of the president's position.

177. S 2057. Fiscal 1999 Defense Authorization/Idaho Air Force Base Expansion. Kempthorne, R-Idaho, motion to table (kill) the Reid, D-Nev., amendment that would strike language in the bill allowing the Air Force to expand training activities at the Mountain Home Air Force Base in Idaho. Motion agreed to 49-44: R 49-3; D 0-41 (ND 0-33, SD 0-8). June 25, 1998.

178. S 2057. Fiscal 1999 Defense Authorization/Navy Communications System. Feingold, D-Wis., amendment that would terminate the Navy's extremely low frequency communications system (ELF) and require that all savings from the termination be transferred to the operation and maintenance accounts of the National Guard. Rejected 20-72: R 0-52; D 20-20 (ND 19-13, SD 1-7). June 25, 1998.

179. S 2057. Fiscal 1999 Defense Authorization/F-22 Aircraft. Bumpers, D-Ark., amendment that would prohibit the Defense Department from purchasing any of the six previously ordered F-22 aircraft until 30 days after the secretary of Defense certifies that the Air Force has completed 601 hours of flight testing on the F-22. Rejected 19-73: R 3-49; D 16-24 (ND 15-17, SD 1-7). June 25, 1998.

180. S 2057. Fiscal 1999 Defense Authorization/Same-Sex Barracks and Training. Byrd, D-W.Va., amendment to the Gramm, R-Texas, amendment. The Byrd amendment would prohibit the armed forces from housing male and female recruits in the same barracks and would prohibit them from conducting gender-integrated basic training. The Gramm amendment would remove restrictions on recipients of Naval Reserve Officers' Training Corps scholarships. Rejected 39-53: R 31-21; D 8-32 (ND 5-27, SD 3-5). June 25, 1998. (Subsequently, the Gramm amendment was adopted by voice vote.) A "nay" was a vote in support of the president's position.

181. S 2057. Fiscal 1999 Defense Authorization/Passage. Passage of the bill to authorize $274 billion for defense-related activities in fiscal 1999, $462 million more than President Clinton's request. The bill also would authorize a 3.6 percent raise in military pay. Passed 88-4: R 52-0; D 36-4 (ND 29-3, SD 7-1). June 25, 1998.

182. Matz Nomination/Confirmation. Confirmation of President Clinton's nomination of A. Howard Matz of California to be U.S. district judge for the Central District of California. Confirmed 85-0: R 47-0; D 38-0 (ND 30-0, SD 8-0). June 26, 1998. A "yea" was a vote in support of the president's position.

Senate Votes 183, 184, 185, 186, 187, 188, 189

	183	184	185	186	187	188	189
ALABAMA							
Sessions	Y	Y	N	Y	Y	Y	Y
Shelby	Y	N	N	Y	Y	N	Y
ALASKA							
Murkowski	Y	Y	N	Y	Y	Y	Y
Stevens	?	Y	N	Y	Y	Y	Y
ARIZONA							
Kyl	?	Y	N	?	?	+	+
McCain	?	Y	N	Y	N	Y	Y
ARKANSAS							
Hutchinson	?	Y	Y	Y	Y	Y	Y
Bumpers	Y	Y	Y	N	N	N	Y
CALIFORNIA							
Boxer	Y	N	N	N	N	N	Y
Feinstein	Y	N	N	N	N	N	Y
COLORADO							
Allard	Y	Y	N	Y	Y	Y	Y
Campbell	Y	Y	N	Y	Y	Y	Y
CONNECTICUT							
Dodd	Y	Y	N	Y	N	N	Y
Lieberman	Y	Y	N	Y	N	N	Y
DELAWARE							
Roth	?	N	N	Y	Y	N	Y
Biden	Y	N	N	N	N	N	Y
FLORIDA							
Mack	Y	Y	N	Y	Y	Y	Y
Graham	Y	N	N	N	N	N	Y
GEORGIA							
Coverdell	Y	Y	N	Y	Y	Y	Y
Cleland	Y	N	N	N	N	N	Y
HAWAII							
Akaka	?	N	N	Y	N	N	Y
Inouye	Y	?	?	Y	N	N	Y
IDAHO							
Craig	Y	Y	N	Y	Y	Y	Y
Kempthorne	Y	Y	N	Y	Y	Y	Y
ILLINOIS							
Durbin	Y	N	N	N	N	N	Y
Moseley-Braun	Y	N	N	Y	N	N	Y
INDIANA							
Coats	Y	Y	Y	Y	Y	Y	Y
Lugar	Y	Y	Y	Y	Y	Y	Y
IOWA							
Grassley	Y	Y	N	Y	Y	Y	Y
Harkin	?	N	Y	N	N	N	Y
KANSAS							
Brownback	Y	Y	N	Y	Y	Y	Y
Roberts	Y	Y	N	Y	Y	Y	Y
KENTUCKY							
McConnell	Y	Y	N	Y	Y	Y	Y
Ford	Y	N	N	Y	N	N	Y
LOUISIANA							
Breaux	Y	N	N	Y	N	N	Y
Landrieu	Y	Y	N	Y	N	N	Y
MAINE							
Collins	Y	Y	Y	Y	N	Y	Y
Snowe	Y	Y	Y	Y	Y	Y	Y
MARYLAND							
Mikulski	Y	?	N	N	N	N	Y
Sarbanes	Y	?	N	N	N	N	Y
MASSACHUSETTS							
Kennedy	Y	N	Y	N	N	N	Y
Kerry	Y	N	N	N	N	N	Y
MICHIGAN							
Abraham	Y	Y	Y	Y	Y	Y	Y
Levin	Y	N	Y	N	N	N	Y
MINNESOTA							
Grams	Y	Y	N	Y	Y	Y	Y
Wellstone	+	N	Y	N	N	N	N
MISSISSIPPI							
Cochran	Y	Y	N	Y	Y	Y	Y
Lott	Y	Y	N	Y	Y	Y	Y
MISSOURI							
Ashcroft	Y	Y	Y	Y	Y	Y	Y
Bond	Y	Y	N	Y	N	Y	Y
MONTANA							
Burns	Y	Y	N	Y	Y	Y	Y
Baucus	?	N	Y	Y	N	Y	
NEBRASKA							
Hagel	Y	Y	N	Y	Y	Y	Y
Kerrey	Y	Y	N	Y	N	N	Y
NEVADA							
Bryan	Y	Y	N	N	N	N	Y
Reid	Y	Y	N	N	N	N	Y
NEW HAMPSHIRE							
Gregg	Y	Y	N	Y	Y	Y	Y
Smith	Y	Y	N	Y	Y	Y	Y
NEW JERSEY							
Lautenberg	Y	Y	Y	Y	N	N	Y
Torricelli	Y	N	N	Y	N	N	Y
NEW MEXICO							
Domenici	Y	Y	N	Y	Y	Y	Y
Bingaman	Y	Y	N	N	N	N	Y
NEW YORK							
D'Amato	Y	N	N	Y	N	Y	Y
Moynihan	Y	Y	Y	Y	Y	N	Y
NORTH CAROLINA							
Faircloth	Y	Y	N	Y	Y	Y	Y
Helms	Y	Y	N	Y	Y	Y	Y
NORTH DAKOTA							
Conrad	Y	N	Y	N	N	N	Y
Dorgan	Y	Y	Y	N	N	N	Y
OHIO							
DeWine	Y	Y	N	Y	Y	Y	Y
Glenn	?	Y	N	N	N	N	Y
OKLAHOMA							
Inhofe	?	Y	N	Y	Y	Y	Y
Nickles	Y	Y	N	Y	Y	Y	Y
OREGON							
Smith	Y	Y	N	Y	Y	Y	Y
Wyden	+	Y	Y	Y	N	N	Y
PENNSYLVANIA							
Santorum	Y	Y	N	Y	Y	Y	Y
Specter	?	?	Y	Y	N	Y	Y
RHODE ISLAND							
Chafee	Y	Y	Y	Y	Y	Y	Y
Reed	Y	Y	Y	N	N	N	Y
SOUTH CAROLINA							
Thurmond	Y	Y	N	Y	Y	Y	Y
Hollings	Y	N	Y	N	N	N	Y
SOUTH DAKOTA							
Daschle	Y	Y	Y	N	N	N	Y
Johnson	Y	Y	Y	N	N	N	Y
TENNESSEE							
Frist	Y	Y	N	Y	Y	Y	Y
Thompson	Y	Y	N	Y	Y	Y	Y
TEXAS							
Gramm	Y	Y	N	Y	Y	Y	Y
Hutchison	Y	?	N	?	?	?	+
UTAH							
Bennett	?	Y	N	Y	Y	Y	Y
Hatch	Y	Y	N	Y	Y	Y	Y
VERMONT							
Jeffords	Y	Y	Y	Y	Y	Y	Y
Leahy	Y	Y	Y	Y	N	N	Y
VIRGINIA							
Warner	Y	Y	Y	Y	Y	Y	Y
Robb	Y	Y	N	Y	N	N	Y
WASHINGTON							
Gorton	Y	Y	N	Y	Y	Y	Y
Murray	Y	N	N	N	N	N	Y
WEST VIRGINIA							
Byrd	Y	Y	Y	N	N	N	Y
Rockefeller	?	Y	N	N	N	N	N
WISCONSIN							
Feingold	Y	N	Y	N	N	N	Y
Kohl	Y	Y	Y	Y	N	N	Y
WYOMING							
Enzi	Y	Y	N	Y	Y	Y	Y
Thomas	Y	Y	Y	Y	Y	Y	Y

ND Northern Democrats   SD Southern Democrats

Southern states - Ala., Ark., Fla., Ga., Ky., La., Miss., N.C., Okla., S.C., Tenn., Texas, Va.

Key
Y Voted for (yea).
Paired for.
+ Announced for.
N Voted against (nay).
X Paired against.
− Announced against.
P Voted "present."
C Voted "present" to avoid possible conflict of interest.
? Did not vote or otherwise make a position known.

Democrats   **Republicans**

183. Roberts Nomination/Confirmation. Confirmation of President Clinton's nomination of Victoria A. Roberts of Michigan to be U.S. district judge for the Eastern District of Michigan. Confirmed 85-0: R 47-0; D 38-0 (ND 30-0, SD 8-0). June 26, 1998. A "yea" was a vote in support of the president's position.

184. S 648. Product Liability Overhaul/Cloture. Motion to invoke cloture (thus limiting debate) on the motion to proceed to the bill that would overhaul U.S. product liability laws. As approved by the Senate Commerce Committee, the bill would cap punitive awards against both small businesses and large companies. Motion agreed to 71-24: R 50-3; D 21-21 (ND 18-16, SD 3-5). July 7, 1998. Three-fifths of the total Senate (60) is required to invoke cloture. (Subsequently, the motion to proceed was agreed to by voice vote.)

185. S 2168. Fiscal 1999 VA-HUD Appropriations/International Space Station. Bumpers, D-Ark., amendment that would eliminate the bill's $2.3 billion appropriation for the international space station. The amendment would provide $850 million to terminate the program, $1 billion for veterans' health care programs and $450 million for low-income housing. Rejected 33-66: R 12-43; D 21-23 (ND 19-17, SD 2-6). July 7, 1998.

186. HR 2676. Internal Revenue Service Overhaul/Capital Gains Holding Period. Roth, R-Del., motion to table (kill) the Dorgan, D-N.D., appeal of the ruling of the chair rejecting the Dorgan point of order against certain provisions in the conference report. Dorgan raised a point of order that language reducing from 18 months to 12 months the time a taxpayer must hold an investment before being eligible for the 20 percent tax rate on capital gains violates Senate rules because the provisions were not in either the House-passed or Senate-passed versions of the legislation. Motion agreed to 76-22: R 53-0; D 23-22 (ND 19-18, SD 4-4). July 8, 1998.

187. HR 2676. Internal Revenue Service Overhaul/Surface Transportation Corrections. Chafee, R-R.I., motion to table (kill) the Murray, D-Wash., appeal of the ruling of the chair rejecting the Murray point of order against certain provisions in the conference report. Murray raised a point of order that provisions to make technical and other changes to the recently enacted six-year surface transportation reauthorization (PL 105-178) violate Senate rules because they were not in either the House-passed or Senate-passed versions of HR 2676. Motion agreed to 50-48: R 48-5; D 2-43 (ND 2-35, SD 0-8). July 8, 1998.

188. S 648. Product Liability Overhaul/Cloture. Motion to invoke cloture (thus limiting debate) on the Lott, R-Miss., substitute amendment to the bill that would overhaul U.S. product liability laws. The amendment would cap punitive awards against small businesses, but not large companies, at $250,000. Manufacturers of tobacco products and silicone breast implants would be exempt from the liability protections. Motion rejected 51-47: R 51-2; D 0-45 (ND 0-37, SD 0-8). July 9, 1998. Three-fifths of the total Senate (60) is required to invoke cloture.

189. HR 2676. Internal Revenue Service Overhaul/Conference Report. Adoption of the conference report on the bill to restructure the management of the Internal Revenue Service by establishing an oversight board to oversee the agency's operations. Along with expanding certain taxpayer rights, the conference report also reduces from 18 months to 12 months the time a taxpayer must hold an investment before being eligible for the 20 percent tax rate on capital gains, contains numerous technical and other changes to the recently enacted six-year surface transportation reauthorization (PL 105-178) and changes the term "most favored nation" in trade law to "normal trade relation." The measure's $12.9 billion cost over 10 years is offset by several revenue-raising provisions, including language to permit wealthy elderly individuals to convert traditional IRAs into the new Roth IRA and pay taxes on the converted money. Adopted (thus cleared for the president) 96-2: R 53-0; D 43-2 (ND 35-2, SD 8-0). July 9, 1998. A "yea" was a vote in support of the president's position.

Senate Votes 190, 191, 192, 193, 194, 195, 196

	190	191	192	193	194	195	196
ALABAMA							
Sessions	Y	N	N	N	N	Y	Y
Shelby	Y	N	N	N	N	Y	Y
ALASKA							
Murkowski	Y	N	N	N	N	Y	Y
Stevens	Y	Y	N	N	N	Y	Y
ARIZONA							
Kyl	?	?	?	?	?	?	+
McCain	Y	N	N	N	N	Y	?
ARKANSAS							
Hutchinson	Y	N	N	N	N	Y	Y
Bumpers	Y	Y	Y	Y	Y	Y	Y
CALIFORNIA							
Boxer	Y	Y	Y	Y	Y	Y	Y
Feinstein	Y	Y	Y	N	Y	Y	Y
COLORADO							
Allard	Y	Y	Y	N	N	Y	Y
Campbell	Y	N	N	N	N	Y	Y
CONNECTICUT							
Dodd	Y	Y	Y	N	Y	Y	Y
Lieberman	Y	Y	Y	N	Y	Y	Y
DELAWARE							
Roth	Y	N	N	N	N	Y	Y
Biden	Y	Y	Y	Y	Y	Y	Y
FLORIDA							
Mack	Y	N	N	N	N	Y	Y
Graham	Y	Y	Y	N	Y	Y	Y
GEORGIA							
Coverdell	Y	N	N	N	N	Y	Y
Cleland	Y	Y	Y	N	Y	Y	Y
HAWAII							
Akaka	Y	Y	Y	N	Y	Y	Y
Inouye	Y	Y	Y	N	Y	Y	Y
IDAHO							
Craig	Y	N	N	N	N	Y	Y
Kempthorne	Y	N	N	N	N	Y	Y
ILLINOIS							
Durbin	Y	Y	Y	Y	Y	Y	Y
Moseley-Braun	Y	Y	Y	Y	Y	Y	Y
INDIANA							
Coats	Y	N	N	N	N	Y	Y
Lugar	Y	N	N	Y	N	Y	Y
IOWA							
Grassley	Y	N	N	N	N	Y	Y
Harkin	Y	Y	Y	Y	Y	Y	Y
KANSAS							
Brownback	Y	N	N	N	N	Y	Y
Roberts	Y	N	N	N	N	Y	Y
KENTUCKY							
McConnell	Y	N	N	N	N	Y	Y
Ford	Y	Y	N	Y	Y	Y	Y
LOUISIANA							
Breaux	Y	Y	Y	N	Y	Y	Y
Landrieu	Y	Y	Y	N	Y	Y	Y
MAINE							
Collins	Y	Y	N	N	N	Y	Y
Snowe	Y	Y	N	N	N	Y	Y
MARYLAND							
Mikulski	Y	Y	Y	Y	N	Y	Y
Sarbanes	Y	Y	Y	N	Y	Y	Y
MASSACHUSETTS							
Kennedy	Y	Y	Y	Y	N	Y	Y
Kerry	Y	Y	Y	N	Y	Y	Y
MICHIGAN							
Abraham	Y	N	N	N	N	Y	Y
Levin	Y	Y	Y	N	Y	Y	Y
MINNESOTA							
Grams	Y	N	N	N	N	Y	Y
Wellstone	Y	Y	Y	Y	Y	Y	Y
MISSISSIPPI							
Cochran	Y	N	N	N	N	Y	Y
Lott	Y	N	N	N	N	Y	Y
MISSOURI							
Ashcroft	Y	N	N	N	N	Y	?
Bond	Y	N	N	N	N	Y	Y
MONTANA							
Burns	Y	N	N	N	N	Y	Y
Baucus	Y	Y	N	Y	Y	Y	Y
NEBRASKA							
Hagel	Y	N	N	N	N	Y	Y
Kerrey	Y	Y	N	Y	N	Y	Y
NEVADA							
Bryan	Y	Y	Y	Y	Y	Y	Y
Reid	Y	Y	Y	Y	Y	Y	Y
NEW HAMPSHIRE							
Gregg	Y	N	N	N	N	Y	Y
Smith	Y	N	N	N	N	Y	Y
NEW JERSEY							
Lautenberg	Y	Y	Y	N	Y	Y	Y
Torricelli	Y	Y	Y	Y	Y	Y	Y
NEW MEXICO							
Domenici	Y	N	N	Y	N	Y	?
Bingaman	Y	Y	Y	Y	Y	Y	?
NEW YORK							
D'Amato	Y	Y	N	N	N	Y	Y
Moynihan	Y	Y	?	?	?	?	Y
NORTH CAROLINA							
Faircloth	Y	N	N	N	N	Y	Y
Helms	Y	N	N	N	N	N	Y
NORTH DAKOTA							
Conrad	Y	Y	Y	N	N	Y	Y
Dorgan	Y	Y	Y	Y	N	Y	Y
OHIO							
DeWine	Y	N	N	N	N	Y	Y
Glenn	Y	Y	Y	Y	Y	Y	Y
OKLAHOMA							
Inhofe	Y	N	N	N	N	Y	Y
Nickles	Y	N	N	N	N	Y	?
OREGON							
Smith	Y	N	N	N	Y	Y	?
Wyden	Y	Y	Y	N	Y	Y	Y
PENNSYLVANIA							
Santorum	Y	N	N	N	N	Y	Y
Specter	Y	Y	N	N	N	Y	Y
RHODE ISLAND							
Chafee	Y	Y	N	N	N	Y	Y
Reed	Y	Y	Y	Y	Y	Y	Y
SOUTH CAROLINA							
Thurmond	Y	N	N	N	N	Y	Y
Hollings	Y	Y	Y	Y	Y	Y	Y
SOUTH DAKOTA							
Daschle	Y	Y	Y	Y	N	Y	Y
Johnson	Y	Y	Y	Y	N	Y	Y
TENNESSEE							
Frist	Y	N	N	N	N	Y	Y
Thompson	Y	N	N	N	N	Y	Y
TEXAS							
Gramm	Y	N	N	N	N	Y	Y
Hutchison	?	?	?	?	?	?	+
UTAH							
Bennett	Y	N	N	N	N	Y	Y
Hatch	Y	Y	N	N	N	Y	Y
VERMONT							
Jeffords	Y	Y	N	N	Y	Y	Y
Leahy	Y	Y	N	N	Y	Y	Y
VIRGINIA							
Warner	Y	N	N	N	N	Y	Y
Robb	Y	Y	Y	Y	Y	Y	Y
WASHINGTON							
Gorton	Y	N	N	N	N	Y	Y
Murray	Y	Y	Y	N	Y	Y	Y
WEST VIRGINIA							
Byrd	Y	Y	Y	Y	Y	Y	Y
Rockefeller	Y	Y	Y	N	Y	Y	Y
WISCONSIN							
Feingold	Y	Y	Y	N	Y	Y	Y
Kohl	Y	Y	Y	N	Y	Y	Y
WYOMING							
Enzi	Y	N	N	N	N	Y	Y
Thomas	Y	N	N	N	N	Y	Y

Key
- Y Voted for (yea).
- # Paired for.
- + Announced for.
- N Voted against (nay).
- X Paired against.
- − Announced against.
- P Voted "present."
- C Voted "present" to avoid possible conflict of interest.
- ? Did not vote or otherwise make a position known.

Democrats   *Republicans*

ND Northern Democrats   SD Southern Democrats

Southern states - Ala., Ark., Fla., Ga., Ky., La., Miss., N.C., Okla., S.C., Tenn., Texas, Va.

190. Agriculture Export Sanctions/Passage. Passage of the bill to revise the Arms Export Control Act to allow the Agriculture Department to provide credits, credit guarantees and financial assistance for the purchase of food or other agricultural commodities to previously non-nuclear nations such as India and Pakistan that the president determines have detonated a nuclear device. Under current law, the president must prohibit the department from providing credits to such nations. Passed 98-0: R 53-0; D 45-0 (ND 37-0, SD 8-0). July 9, 1998.

191. S 1882. Higher Education Act Reauthorization/Welfare Education. Wellstone, D-Minn., amendment that would allow states to count up to two years of post-secondary or vocational education toward work requirements for welfare parents under the 1996 welfare law (PL 104-193). Current law allows states to count up to one year of vocational education toward the requirement. The amendment also would prohibit states from counting teenage welfare parents' education toward the 30 percent education limitation imposed by the 1996 law. Adopted 56-42: R 11-42; D 45-0 (ND 37-0, SD 8-0). July 9, 1998.

192. S 1882. Higher Education Act Reauthorization/Market-Based Lending. Kennedy, D-Mass., amendment that would establish a pilot program to auction off the right to make student loans, thus letting the market, rather than the government, determine interest rates. Rejected 39-58: R 0-53; D 39-5 (ND 32-4, SD 7-1). July 9, 1998.

193. S 1882. Higher Education Act Reauthorization/Teacher Education. Bingaman, D-N.M., amendment that would require colleges that receive federal aid to establish, within three years of the bill's enactment, a policy that all undergraduate students preparing to be secondary school teachers complete an academic major in the academic area in which they plan to teach. Rejected 23-74: R 3-50; D 20-24 (ND 16-20, SD 4-4). July 9, 1998.

194. S 1882. Higher Education Act Reauthorization/Student Loan Fees. Harkin, D-Iowa, amendment that would reduce the federal student loan origination and insurance fee from 4 percent of the principal amount of the loan to 3 percent of the principal amount. The amendment would pay for the reduction by eliminating a subsidy to student loan insurance agencies. Rejected 41-56: R 1-52; D 40-4 (ND 32-4, SD 8-0). July 9, 1998.

195. HR 6. Higher Education Act Reauthorization/Passage. Passage of the bill to authorize $108 billion during the next five years for almost all federal higher education programs. The measure contains language that would cut interest rates on federally guaranteed student loans while providing special subsidies to banks. Passed 96-1: R 52-1; D 44-0 (ND 36-0, SD 8-0). July 9, 1998. (Before passage, the Senate struck all after the enacting clause and inserted the text of S1882 as amended.)

196. S Con Res 107. U.S. Support for Taiwan/Adoption. Adoption of the concurrent resolution to reaffirm U.S. support for Taiwan as stipulated in the Taiwan Relations Act (PL 96-8). The resolution would reaffirm that any effort to determine the future of Taiwan by other than peaceful means would be of "grave concern to the United States" and would urge President Clinton to seek a public renunciation by China of any use of force against Taiwan. Adopted 92-0: R 48-0; D 44-0 (ND 36-0, SD 8-0). July 10, 1998.

Senate Votes 197, 198, 199, 200, 201, 202, 203

	197	198	199	200	201	202	203
ALABAMA							
Sessions	Y	N	Y	Y	N	Y	Y
Shelby	Y	N	Y	Y	Y	Y	Y
ALASKA							
Murkowski	Y	N	Y	Y	N	Y	Y
Stevens	Y	N	Y	Y	Y	Y	Y
ARIZONA							
Kyl	Y	N	Y	Y	N	Y	Y
McCain	Y	N	Y	Y	Y	N	Y
ARKANSAS							
Hutchinson	Y	N	Y	Y	Y	Y	Y
Bumpers	N	Y	Y	N	N	N	N
CALIFORNIA							
Boxer	N	Y	Y	N	N	Y	N
Feinstein	N	Y	Y	N	N	Y	N
COLORADO							
Allard	Y	N	Y	Y	N	N	N
Campbell	Y	N	Y	Y	Y	Y	Y
CONNECTICUT							
Dodd	N	Y	Y	N	N	Y	N
Lieberman	N	Y	Y	N	Y	Y	Y
DELAWARE							
Roth	N	N	Y	Y	N	N	N
Biden	?	?	Y	N	N	Y	N
FLORIDA							
Mack	Y	N	Y	Y	Y	Y	Y
Graham	N	Y	Y	N	Y	Y	Y
GEORGIA							
Coverdell	Y	N	Y	Y	Y	Y	Y
Cleland	N	Y	Y	N	N	Y	N
HAWAII							
Akaka	N	Y	Y	N	Y	Y	N
Inouye	N	Y	Y	N	Y	Y	N
IDAHO							
Craig	Y	N	Y	Y	N	Y	N
Kempthorne	Y	N	Y	Y	N	Y	N
ILLINOIS							
Durbin	N	Y	Y	N	N	Y	N
Moseley-Braun	N	Y	Y	N	N	N	N
INDIANA							
Coats	Y	N	Y	Y	N	Y	N
Lugar	Y	N	Y	Y	N	Y	N
IOWA							
Grassley	Y	N	Y	Y	Y	Y	N
Harkin	N	Y	Y	N	N	Y	N
KANSAS							
Brownback	Y	N	Y	Y	N	N	N
Roberts	Y	N	Y	Y	N	Y	N
KENTUCKY							
McConnell	Y	N	Y	Y	Y	Y	Y
Ford	Y	Y	Y	N	Y	Y	Y
LOUISIANA							
Breaux	?	Y	Y	N	Y	Y	Y
Landrieu	Y	Y	Y	N	N	Y	Y
MAINE							
Collins	N	N	Y	Y	Y	Y	N
Snowe	N	N	Y	Y	Y	Y	N
MARYLAND							
Mikulski	N	Y	Y	N	Y	N	N
Sarbanes	N	Y	Y	N	Y	Y	N
MASSACHUSETTS							
Kennedy	N	Y	Y	N	Y	Y	N
Kerry	N	Y	Y	N	N	N	N
MICHIGAN							
Abraham	Y	N	Y	Y	N	N	N
Levin	N	Y	Y	N	Y	Y	Y
MINNESOTA							
Grams	Y	N	Y	Y	N	N	N
Wellstone	N	Y	Y	N	N	N	N
MISSISSIPPI							
Cochran	Y	N	Y	Y	N	Y	N
Lott	Y	N	Y	Y	Y	Y	Y
MISSOURI							
Ashcroft	Y	N	Y	Y	N	Y	N
Bond	Y	N	Y	Y	N	Y	N
MONTANA							
Burns	Y	N	Y	Y	N	Y	N
Baucus	N	Y	N	N	N	N	N
NEBRASKA							
Hagel	Y	N	Y	Y	N	Y	N
Kerrey	N	Y	Y	N	N	N	N
NEVADA							
Bryan	N	Y	Y	N	Y	N	Y
Reid	Y	Y	Y	N	Y	N	Y
NEW HAMPSHIRE							
Gregg	N	N	Y	Y	N	N	Y
Smith	Y	N	Y	Y	Y	N	Y
NEW JERSEY							
Lautenberg	N	Y	Y	N	Y	N	Y
Torricelli	?	Y	Y	N	Y	N	Y
NEW MEXICO							
Domenici	Y	N	Y	Y	N	Y	N
Bingaman	N	Y	Y	N	Y	N	?
NEW YORK							
D'Amato	?	N	Y	Y	Y	N	Y
Moynihan	N	Y	Y	N	N	N	N
NORTH CAROLINA							
Faircloth	Y	N	Y	Y	Y	Y	Y
Helms	Y	N	Y	Y	Y	Y	Y
NORTH DAKOTA							
Conrad	Y	Y	Y	N	N	N	N
Dorgan	Y	Y	Y	N	N	Y	N
OHIO							
DeWine	Y	N	Y	Y	Y	Y	N
Glenn	?	?	?	?	?	?	?
OKLAHOMA							
Inhofe	Y	N	Y	Y	Y	Y	Y
Nickles	Y	N	Y	Y	Y	Y	N
OREGON							
Smith	Y	N	Y	Y	N	Y	N
Wyden	N	Y	Y	N	Y	Y	N
PENNSYLVANIA							
Santorum	Y	N	Y	Y	N	Y	N
Specter	Y	Y	Y	Y	Y	Y	Y
RHODE ISLAND							
Chafee	N	N	Y	Y	N	Y	Y
Reed	N	Y	Y	N	N	N	N
SOUTH CAROLINA							
Thurmond	Y	N	Y	Y	Y	Y	Y
Hollings	N	Y	Y	N	Y	Y	N
SOUTH DAKOTA							
Daschle	N	Y	Y	N	N	Y	N
Johnson	N	Y	Y	N	N	Y	N
TENNESSEE							
Frist	?	N	Y	Y	N	Y	Y
Thompson	Y	N	Y	Y	N	Y	Y
TEXAS							
Gramm	Y	N	Y	Y	N	Y	Y
Hutchison	Y	N	Y	Y	N	Y	N
UTAH							
Bennett	Y	N	Y	Y	Y	Y	N
Hatch	Y	N	Y	Y	Y	Y	N
VERMONT							
Jeffords	N	N	Y	Y	N	Y	N
Leahy	N	Y	Y	N	Y	Y	N
VIRGINIA							
Warner	Y	N	Y	Y	N	Y	N
Robb	N	Y	N	N	N	N	N
WASHINGTON							
Gorton	Y	N	Y	Y	N	Y	N
Murray	N	Y	Y	N	Y	Y	N
WEST VIRGINIA							
Byrd	N	N	Y	N	N	Y	N
Rockefeller	N	Y	Y	N	N	N	N
WISCONSIN							
Feingold	N	Y	Y	Y	Y	N	N
Kohl	N	Y	Y	N	Y	Y	Y
WYOMING							
Enzi	Y	N	Y	Y	N	Y	N
Thomas	Y	N	Y	Y	N	Y	N

Key
- Y Voted for (yea).
- # Paired for.
- + Announced for.
- N Voted against (nay).
- X Paired against.
- − Announced against.
- P Voted "present."
- C Voted "present" to avoid possible conflict of interest.
- ? Did not vote or otherwise make a position known.

Democrats **Republicans**

ND Northern Democrats   SD Southern Democrats

Southern states - Ala., Ark., Fla., Ga., Ky., La., Miss., N.C., Okla., S.C., Tenn., Texas, Va.

197. S 2271. Private Property Rights/Cloture. Motion to invoke cloture (thus limiting debate) on the motion to proceed to the bill that would provide private property owners with new rights to challenge decisions of local zoning and planning boards in federal court. Motion rejected 52-42: R 47-6; D 5-36 (ND 3-31, SD 2-5). July 13, 1998. Three-fifths of the total Senate (60) is required to invoke cloture. A "nay" was a vote in support of the president's position.

198. S 2159. Fiscal 1999 Agriculture Appropriations/Tobacco Restrictions. Daschle, D-S.D., motion to waive the Budget Act with respect to the Lott, R-Miss., point of order against the Daschle amendment. The amendment would require the tobacco industry to pay $516 billion over 25 years for anti-smoking, education and research programs, raise taxes on cigarettes by $1.10 per pack over five years, codify Food and Drug Administration authority to regulate nicotine and impose penalties on the tobacco industry if youth smoking does not decrease by 60 percent over 10 years. Motion rejected 43-55: R 1-54; D 42-1 (ND 34-1, SD 8-0). July 14, 1998. A three-fifths majority vote (60) of the total Senate is required to waive the Budget Act. (Subsequently, the chair upheld the point of order, and the amendment fell.)

199. S 2159. Fiscal 1999 Agriculture Appropriations/Farming Difficulties. Daschle, D-S.D., amendment to express the sense of the Senate that Congress and the president should take immediate action to respond to the economic hardships facing agricultural producers. Adopted 99-0: R 55-0; D 44-0 (ND 36-0, SD 8-0). July 14, 1998.

200. S 2159. Fiscal 1999 Agriculture Appropriations/Agriculture Marketing Loans. Cochran, R-Miss., motion to table (kill) the Daschle, D-S.D., amendment that would lift the cap on agriculture commodity marketing loans imposed by the 1996 farm law (PL 104-127) for fiscal 1999. The new loan rate would be based on 85 percent of the average price of the product for the past five years, not including the highest and lowest years. The amendment also would extend the marketing loan term from nine months to 15 months for fiscal 1999. Motion agreed to 56-43: R 55-0; D 1-43 (ND 1-35, SD 0-8). July 15, 1998.

201. S 2159. Fiscal 1999 Agriculture Appropriations/Unilateral Economic Sanctions. Stevens, R-Alaska, motion to table (kill) the Lugar, R-Ind., amendment that would revise the process the president and Congress use to impose unilateral economic sanctions by establishing guidelines for future sanctions and setting up procedures for consideration and implementation of sanctions proposals. The amendment would prohibit the president from implementing any unilateral economic sanction without 45 days' notice, and it would express the sense of Congress that all future unilateral sanctions end within two years of their enactment unless extended by law. Motion agreed to 53-46: R 27-28; D 26-18 (ND 22-14, SD 4-4). July 15, 1998.

202. S 2159. Fiscal 1999 Agriculture Appropriations/Overseas Market Promotion. Cochran, R-Miss., motion to table (kill) the Bryan, D-Nev., amendment that would eliminate the bill's funding for subsidized overseas market promotion programs. Motion agreed to 70-29: R 43-12; D 27-17 (ND 22-14, SD 5-3). July 15, 1998.

203. S 2159. Fiscal 1999 Agriculture Appropriations/Food and Medicine Sanctions. Stevens, R-Alaska, motion to table (kill) the Dodd, D-Conn., amendment that would prohibit the president from restricting exports of food, agricultural products, medicines or medicinal equipment as part of any current or future unilateral economic sanction. Motion rejected 38-60: R 26-29; D 12-31 (ND 7-28, SD 5-3). July 15, 1998. (Subsequently, the Dodd amendment was amended by a similar Roberts amendment.)

Senate Votes 204, 205, 206, 207, 208, 209, 210

	204	205	206	207	208	209	210
ALABAMA							
Sessions	N	Y	N	N	N	Y	N
Shelby	N	Y	Y	Y	N	Y	N
ALASKA							
Murkowski	N	Y	Y	Y	N	Y	N
Stevens	N	N	Y	Y	N	Y	N
ARIZONA							
Kyl	N	Y	N	N	N	N	N
McCain	N	Y	Y	Y	Y	Y	?
ARKANSAS							
Hutchinson	N	Y	N	N	N	Y	N
Bumpers	N	N	Y	Y	Y	Y	Y
CALIFORNIA							
Boxer	N	N	Y	Y	Y	Y	Y
Feinstein	N	N	Y	Y	Y	Y	Y
COLORADO							
Allard	N	Y	N	N	N	Y	N
Campbell	N	Y	N	Y	N	Y	Y
CONNECTICUT							
Dodd	Y	N	Y	Y	Y	Y	?
Lieberman	N	N	Y	Y	Y	Y	Y
DELAWARE							
Roth	N	Y	N	Y	N	Y	N
Biden	N	N	Y	Y	Y	Y	Y
FLORIDA							
Mack	N	Y	N	Y	N	Y	N
Graham	N	Y	N	Y	Y	Y	Y
GEORGIA							
Coverdell	N	Y	N	N	Y	Y	N
Cleland	Y	N	Y	Y	Y	Y	Y
HAWAII							
Akaka	Y	N	Y	Y	Y	Y	Y
Inouye	Y	N	Y	Y	Y	Y	?
IDAHO							
Craig	N	Y	N	N	N	Y	N
Kempthorne	N	Y	Y	N	N	Y	N
ILLINOIS							
Durbin	Y	N	Y	Y	Y	Y	Y
Moseley-Braun	Y	N	Y	Y	Y	Y	Y
INDIANA							
Coats	N	Y	N	N	N	Y	N
Lugar	Y	Y	Y	Y	N	Y	N

	204	205	206	207	208	209	210
IOWA							
Grassley	N	N	Y	Y	N	Y	N
Harkin	Y	N	Y	Y	Y	Y	Y
KANSAS							
Brownback	Y	Y	Y	Y	N	Y	N
Roberts	Y	Y	Y	N	N	Y	?
KENTUCKY							
McConnell	N	Y	Y	N	N	Y	N
Ford	N	N	Y	N	N	Y	Y
LOUISIANA							
Breaux	N	Y	Y	N	N	Y	Y
Landrieu	N	N	Y	Y	Y	Y	Y
MAINE							
Collins	N	Y	Y	Y	Y	Y	Y
Snowe	N	Y	N	Y	Y	Y	Y
MARYLAND							
Mikulski	Y	N	N	Y	Y	Y	Y
Sarbanes	Y	N	N	Y	Y	Y	Y
MASSACHUSETTS							
Kennedy	Y	N	Y	Y	Y	Y	Y
Kerry	N	N	Y	Y	Y	Y	Y
MICHIGAN							
Abraham	N	Y	Y	Y	N	Y	N
Levin	N	N	N	Y	Y	Y	Y
MINNESOTA							
Grams	Y	N	Y	Y	N	Y	N
Wellstone	Y	N	N	Y	Y	Y	Y
MISSISSIPPI							
Cochran	N	Y	Y	N	Y	Y	Y
Lott	N	Y	Y	N	N	Y	N
MISSOURI							
Ashcroft	N	Y	N	N	N	Y	N
Bond	N	Y	Y	Y	Y	Y	Y
MONTANA							
Burns	N	N	Y	N	N	Y	N
Baucus	Y	Y	Y	Y	Y	Y	N
NEBRASKA							
Hagel	Y	N	Y	Y	N	Y	N
Kerrey	Y	N	Y	Y	Y	Y	Y
NEVADA							
Bryan	N	N	Y	Y	Y	Y	Y
Reid	N	N	N	Y	Y	Y	Y

	204	205	206	207	208	209	210
NEW HAMPSHIRE							
Gregg	N	Y	Y	N	N	Y	N
Smith	N	Y	N	N	N	Y	N
NEW JERSEY							
Lautenberg	N	N	N	Y	Y	Y	Y
Torricelli	N	N	N	Y	Y	Y	Y
NEW MEXICO							
Domenici	N	Y	Y	N	N	Y	N
Bingaman	?	?	Y	Y	Y	Y	Y
NEW YORK							
D'Amato	N	Y	Y	Y	Y	Y	Y
Moynihan	Y	N	Y	N	Y	Y	Y
NORTH CAROLINA							
Faircloth	N	Y	Y	N	N	Y	N
Helms	N	Y	N	N	N	Y	–
NORTH DAKOTA							
Conrad	Y	N	N	N	Y	Y	Y
Dorgan	Y	N	N	Y	Y	Y	Y
OHIO							
DeWine	N	Y	Y	Y	Y	Y	N
Glenn	?	?	?	?	?	?	?
OKLAHOMA							
Inhofe	N	Y	N	N	N	Y	N
Nickles	N	Y	N	N	N	Y	N
OREGON							
Smith	N	Y	Y	N	N	Y	N
Wyden	N	N	Y	Y	Y	Y	Y
PENNSYLVANIA							
Santorum	N	N	Y	N	N	Y	N
Specter	N	Y	Y	Y	Y	Y	Y
RHODE ISLAND							
Chafee	N	Y	Y	Y	N	Y	Y
Reed	Y	N	N	Y	Y	Y	Y
SOUTH CAROLINA							
Thurmond	N	Y	Y	N	N	Y	Y
Hollings	N	N	N	N	N	Y	Y
SOUTH DAKOTA							
Daschle	Y	N	Y	Y	Y	Y	Y
Johnson	Y	N	Y	Y	Y	Y	Y
TENNESSEE							
Frist	N	Y	Y	N	Y	Y	N
Thompson	N	Y	N	N	N	Y	N

Key

Y Voted for (yea).
Paired for.
+ Announced for.
N Voted against (nay).
X Paired against.
– Announced against.
P Voted "present."
C Voted "present" to avoid possible conflict of interest.
? Did not vote or otherwise make a position known.

Democrats   *Republicans*

	204	205	206	207	208	209	210
TEXAS							
Gramm	N	Y	Y	N	N	Y	N
Hutchison	N	Y	Y	Y	N	Y	Y
UTAH							
Bennett	N	Y	Y	N	N	Y	Y
Hatch	N	Y	Y	N	N	Y	N
VERMONT							
Jeffords	?	Y	Y	Y	N	Y	Y
Leahy	Y	N	Y	Y	Y	Y	Y
VIRGINIA							
Warner	Y	Y	Y	Y	N	Y	N
Robb	N	N	Y	Y	Y	Y	Y
WASHINGTON							
Gorton	N	Y	Y	Y	N	Y	N
Murray	N	N	Y	Y	Y	Y	Y
WEST VIRGINIA							
Byrd	Y	N	Y	Y	Y	Y	Y
Rockefeller	Y	N	Y	Y	Y	Y	Y
WISCONSIN							
Feingold	N	N	N	Y	Y	Y	Y
Kohl	N	N	Y	Y	Y	Y	Y
WYOMING							
Enzi	Y	N	N	N	N	Y	N
Thomas	Y	N	Y	N	N	Y	N

ND Northern Democrats   SD Southern Democrats

Southern states - Ala., Ark., Fla., Ga., Ky., La., Miss., N.C., Okla., S.C., Tenn., Texas, Va.

204. S 2159. Fiscal 1999 Agriculture Appropriations/Sanctions on Terrorist Nations. Dodd, D-Conn., motion to table (kill) the Torricelli, D-N.J., amendment to the Dodd amendment. The Torricelli amendment would allow the president to restrict exports of food and medicine to nations that have repeatedly provided support for acts of international terrorism. Motion rejected 30-67: R 8-46; D 22-21 (ND 21-14, SD 1-7). July 15, 1998. (Subsequently, the Torricelli amendment and the underlying Dodd amendment as amended were adopted by voice vote.)

205. S 2159. Fiscal 1999 Agriculture Appropriations/Livestock Price Reporting. Cochran, R-Miss., motion to table (kill) the Kerrey, D-Neb., amendment that would authorize a three-year pilot program to study the efficiency of requiring mandatory price reporting by livestock producers. Motion rejected 49-49: R 47-8; D 2-41 (ND 0-35, SD 2-6). July 15, 1998. (Subsequently, the Kerrey amendment was adopted by voice vote.)

206. S 2159. Fiscal 1999 Agriculture Appropriations/Relief for Farmers. Grassley, R-Iowa, amendment to express the sense of the Senate that Congress and the president should take actions to alleviate the economic effects of low commodity prices, including: reauthorizing fast-track trading authority for the president; fully funding the International Monetary Fund; overhauling the way economic sanctions are implemented; extending most-favored-nation trading status for China; revising capital gains and estate tax rates; reducing regulations on farmers; and allowing self-employed individuals to fully deduct the cost of their health insurance. Adopted 71-28: R 42-13; D 29-15 (ND 24-12, SD 5-3). July 16, 1998.

207. S 2159. Fiscal 1999 Agriculture Appropriations/Food Safety. Harkin, D-Iowa, amendment that would provide an additional $66 million for President Clinton's food safety initiative, which would increase inspections, expand research and increase consumer education programs. The amendment would offset the increased spending by reducing tobacco subsidies, Agriculture Department computer funding and Agricultural Research Service building construction funds. Adopted 65-34: R 25-30; D 40-4 (ND 35-1, SD 5-3). July 16, 1998.

208. S 2159. Fiscal 1999 Agriculture Appropriations/Teen Smoking. Harkin, D-Iowa, motion to waive the Budget Act with respect to the Domenici, R-N.M., point of order against the Harkin amendment. The Harkin amendment would increase funding for Food and Drug Administration teen anti-smoking programs by $100 million. The amendment would attempt to offset the increase in funding by imposing a fee on tobacco companies based on their share of the U.S. tobacco market. Motion rejected 49-50: R 9-46; D 40-4 (ND 35-1, SD 5-3). July 16, 1998. A three-fifths majority vote (60) of the total Senate is required to waive the Budget Act. (Subsequently, the chair upheld the point of order, and the amendment fell.)

209. HR 4101. Fiscal 1999 Agriculture Appropriations/Passage. Passage of the bill to provide $57.3 billion in new budget authority for the Agriculture Department (USDA), the Food and Drug Administration (FDA) and rural development programs in fiscal 1999. The bill provides $7.5 billion more than provided in fiscal 1998 and $500 million less than requested by President Clinton. Passed 97-2: R 53-2; D 44-0 (ND 36-0, SD 8-0). July 16, 1998. (Before passage, the Senate struck all after the enacting clause and inserted the text of S2159 as amended.)

210. S 2168. Fiscal 1999 VA-HUD Appropriations/Veterans' Tobacco-Related Illnesses. Wellstone, D-Minn., motion to waive the Budget Act with respect to the Domenici, R-N.M., point of order against the Wellstone amendment. The Wellstone amendment would repeal a provision in the six-year surface transportation reauthorization (PL 105-178) that prohibits compensation payments to veterans for tobacco-related illnesses. Motion rejected 54-40: R 13-39; D 41-1 (ND 33-1, SD 8-0). July 17, 1998. A three-fifths majority vote (60) of the total Senate is required to waive the Budget Act. (Subsequently, the chair upheld the point of order, and the amendment fell.)

Senate Votes 211, 212, 213, 214, 215, 216, 217

	211	212	213	214	215	216	217
ALABAMA							
Sessions	Y	N	N	Y	Y	Y	Y
Shelby	Y	N	Y	Y	Y	Y	Y
ALASKA							
Murkowski	Y	N	Y	Y	Y	Y	Y
Stevens	Y	Y	Y	Y	Y	Y	Y
ARIZONA							
Kyl	N	N	N	N	Y	Y	Y
McCain	?	?	N	Y	Y	Y	Y
ARKANSAS							
Hutchinson	Y	N	N	Y	Y	Y	Y
Bumpers	Y	Y	Y	Y	N	N	N
CALIFORNIA							
Boxer	Y	Y	Y	Y	N	N	N
Feinstein	Y	Y	Y	Y	N	N	N
COLORADO							
Allard	N	Y	N	N	Y	Y	Y
Campbell	Y	Y	N	Y	Y	Y	Y
CONNECTICUT							
Dodd	Y	Y	Y	Y	N	N	N
Lieberman	Y	Y	Y	Y	Y	N	N
DELAWARE							
Roth	Y	N	Y	Y	Y	Y	Y
Biden	Y	Y	Y	Y	N	N	N
FLORIDA							
Mack	N	N	Y	Y	Y	Y	Y
Graham	Y	Y	Y	Y	Y	N	N
GEORGIA							
Coverdell	Y	N	Y	Y	Y	Y	Y
Cleland	Y	Y	Y	Y	N	N	N
HAWAII							
Akaka	Y	Y	Y	Y	N	N	N
Inouye	Y	Y	Y	Y	N	N	N
IDAHO							
Craig	N	N	Y	Y	Y	Y	Y
Kempthorne	N	N	N	Y	Y	Y	Y
ILLINOIS							
Durbin	Y	Y	Y	Y	N	N	N
Moseley-Braun	Y	Y	Y	Y	N	N	N
INDIANA							
Coats	Y	Y	N	Y	Y	Y	Y
Lugar	N	N	Y	Y	Y	Y	Y
IOWA							
Grassley	Y	Y	Y	Y	Y	Y	Y
Harkin	Y	Y	Y	Y	N	N	N
KANSAS							
Brownback	N	N	N	Y	Y	Y	Y
Roberts	?	?	Y	Y	Y	Y	Y
KENTUCKY							
McConnell	N	N	Y	Y	Y	Y	Y
Ford	Y	Y	Y	Y	Y	N	N
LOUISIANA							
Breaux	Y	Y	Y	Y	Y	Y	Y
Landrieu	Y	Y	Y	Y	N	N	N
MAINE							
Collins	Y	Y	Y	Y	Y	N	N
Snowe	Y	Y	Y	Y	Y	Y	Y
MARYLAND							
Mikulski	Y	Y	Y	Y	N	N	N
Sarbanes	Y	Y	Y	Y	N	N	N
MASSACHUSETTS							
Kennedy	Y	Y	Y	Y	N	N	N
Kerry	Y	Y	Y	Y	N	N	N
MICHIGAN							
Abraham	Y	N	Y	Y	Y	Y	Y
Levin	Y	Y	Y	Y	N	N	N
MINNESOTA							
Grams	N	N	Y	Y	Y	Y	Y
Wellstone	Y	Y	N	Y	N	N	N
MISSISSIPPI							
Cochran	N	N	Y	Y	Y	Y	Y
Lott	N	N	Y	Y	Y	Y	Y
MISSOURI							
Ashcroft	N	N	N	N	Y	Y	Y
Bond	Y	Y	Y	Y	Y	Y	Y
MONTANA							
Burns	Y	N	Y	Y	Y	Y	Y
Baucus	Y	Y	Y	N	Y	Y	Y
NEBRASKA							
Hagel	N	N	Y	Y	Y	Y	Y
Kerrey	Y	Y	Y	Y	Y	N	Y
NEVADA							
Bryan	Y	Y	Y	Y	Y	Y	N
Reid	Y	?	Y	Y	Y	Y	Y
NEW HAMPSHIRE							
Gregg	N	Y	Y	Y	Y	Y	Y
Smith	N	N	N	N	Y	Y	Y
NEW JERSEY							
Lautenberg	Y	Y	Y	Y	N	N	N
Torricelli	Y	Y	Y	Y	N	N	N
NEW MEXICO							
Domenici	Y	Y	Y	Y	Y	Y	Y
Bingaman	Y	Y	Y	Y	Y	N	Y
NEW YORK							
D'Amato	Y	Y	Y	Y	Y	Y	Y
Moynihan	Y	Y	Y	Y	N	N	N
NORTH CAROLINA							
Faircloth	N	N	N	N	Y	Y	Y
Helms	?	?	N	Y	Y	Y	Y
NORTH DAKOTA							
Conrad	Y	Y	Y	Y	Y	N	N
Dorgan	Y	Y	Y	Y	Y	Y	Y
OHIO							
DeWine	N	N	N	Y	Y	N	Y
Glenn	?	?	Y	Y	N	N	N
OKLAHOMA							
Inhofe	N	N	?	?	Y	Y	Y
Nickles	N	N	Y	Y	Y	Y	Y
OREGON							
Smith	Y	N	Y	Y	Y	N	Y
Wyden	Y	Y	Y	Y	N	N	N
PENNSYLVANIA							
Santorum	Y	Y	Y	Y	N	N	N
Specter	Y	Y	Y	Y	Y	Y	Y
RHODE ISLAND							
Chafee	Y	Y	Y	Y	N	N	Y
Reed	Y	Y	Y	Y	N	N	N
SOUTH CAROLINA							
Thurmond	N	N	Y	Y	Y	Y	Y
Hollings	Y	Y	Y	Y	Y	Y	Y
SOUTH DAKOTA							
Daschle	Y	Y	Y	Y	Y	N	Y
Johnson	Y	Y	Y	Y	Y	N	Y
TENNESSEE							
Frist	Y	N	Y	Y	Y	Y	Y
Thompson	N	N	N	Y	Y	Y	Y
TEXAS							
Gramm	N	N	Y	N	Y	Y	Y
Hutchison	Y	N	Y	Y	Y	Y	Y
UTAH							
Bennett	Y	N	Y	Y	Y	Y	Y
Hatch	Y	N	Y	Y	Y	Y	Y
VERMONT							
Jeffords	Y	Y	Y	Y	Y	N	Y
Leahy	Y	Y	Y	Y	Y	Y	Y
VIRGINIA							
Warner	N	Y	Y	Y	N	Y	Y
Robb	Y	Y	Y	Y	N	Y	N
WASHINGTON							
Gorton	Y	N	Y	Y	Y	Y	Y
Murray	Y	Y	Y	Y	Y	N	Y
WEST VIRGINIA							
Byrd	Y	N	Y	Y	N	N	N
Rockefeller	Y	Y	Y	Y	N	N	Y
WISCONSIN							
Feingold	N	Y	Y	N	Y	N	Y
Kohl	N	Y	Y	Y	N	N	N
WYOMING							
Enzi	N	N	Y	Y	Y	Y	Y
Thomas	N	N	Y	Y	Y	Y	Y

ND Northern Democrats SD Southern Democrats

Southern states - Ala., Ark., Fla., Ga., Ky., La., Miss., N.C., Okla., S.C., Tenn., Texas, Va.

Key

- **Y** Voted for (yea).
- **#** Paired for.
- **+** Announced for.
- **N** Voted against (nay).
- **X** Paired against.
- **−** Announced against.
- **P** Voted "present."
- **C** Voted "present" to avoid possible conflict of interest.
- **?** Did not vote or otherwise make a position known.

Democrats   **Republicans**

---

211. S 2168. Fiscal 1999 VA-HUD Appropriations/Mortgage Lending. Bond, R-Mo., motion to table (kill) the Nickles, R-Okla., amendment that would strike language increasing from $170,362 to $197,620 the maximum value of home mortgages that the Federal Housing Administration (FHA) could insure in high-cost areas. The amendment also would increase Ginnie Mae National Mortgage Association fees from six basis points to 12. Motion agreed to 69-27: R 27-25; D 42-2 (ND 34-2, SD 8-0). July 17, 1998.

212. S 2168. Fiscal 1999 VA-HUD Appropriations/NASA Funding. Bond, R-Mo., motion to table (kill) the Sessions, R-Ala., amendment that would increase funding for NASA programs by $33 million, offset by reductions in the AmeriCorps national service program. The amendment would provide $20 million for aeronautics, space transportation and technology and $13 million for science and technology. Motion agreed to 58-37: R 16-36; D 42-1 (ND 34-1, SD 8-0). July 17, 1998. (Subsequently, the underlying $93.3 billion bill as amended was passed by voice vote.)

213. HR 4112. Fiscal 1999 Legislative Branch Appropriations/Cloture. Motion to invoke cloture (thus limiting debate) on the bill to provide $1.6 billion in new budget authority for Senate and other legislative branch operations in fiscal 1999. The bill, which excludes funds for internal House operations, would provide $51.5 million more than provided in fiscal 1998. Motion agreed to 83-16: R 39-15; D 44-1 (ND 36-1, SD 8-0). July 21, 1998. Three-fifths of the total Senate (60) is required to invoke cloture.

214. HR 4112. Fiscal 1999 Legislative Branch Appropriations/Passage. Passage of the bill to provide $1.6 billion in new budget authority for Senate and other legislative branch operations in fiscal 1999. The bill, which excludes funds for internal House operations, would provide $51.5 million more than provided in fiscal 1998 and $74.6 million less than requested by President Clinton. Passed 90-9: R 47-7; D 43-2 (ND 35-2, SD 8-0). July 21, 1998.

215. S 2260. Fiscal 1999 Commerce, Justice, State Appropriations/Gun Lock Availibility. Craig, R-Idaho, amendment that would require gun dealers to make safety devices, such as so-called trigger locks, "available" as a condition for receiving and keeping their licenses. The amendment also would establish a grant program to educate and train the public on the safe ownership, storage and use of firearms. Adopted 72-28: R 54-1; D 18-27 (ND 14-23, SD 4-4). July 21, 1998.

216. S 2260. Fiscal 1999 Commerce, Justice, State Appropriations/Gun Lock Requirement. Craig, R-Idaho, motion to table (kill) the Boxer, D-Calif., amendment that would require all gun dealers to sell so-called trigger locks with each handgun sold. The amendment would establish civil penalties for dealers that do not comply. Motion agreed to 61-39: R 52-3; D 9-36 (ND 6-31, SD 3-5). July 21, 1998.

217. S 2260. Fiscal 1999 Commerce, Justice, State Appropriations/Firearm Purchase Background Checks. Smith, R-N.H., amendment to the Smith amendment. Both amendments would prohibit the use of any taxes or fees to pay for the national instant background check required for new gun purchases under the Brady law (PL 103-159) and would require law enforcement agencies to immediately destroy any information on individuals allowed to purchase firearms after the check. Adopted 69-31: R 55-0; D 14-31 (ND 12-25, SD 2-6). July 21, 1998. (Subsequently, the underlying Smith amendment as amended was adopted by voice vote.)

Senate Votes 218, 219, 220, 221, 222, 223, 224

	218	219	220	221	222	223	224
ALABAMA							
Sessions	N	N	N	Y	N	Y	Y
Shelby	N	N	N	Y	N	Y	Y
ALASKA							
Murkowski	N	N	N	Y	N	Y	Y
Stevens	N	N	Y	N	N	Y	Y
ARIZONA							
Kyl	N	N	N	Y	N	Y	Y
McCain	N	N	Y	Y	N	Y	Y
ARKANSAS							
Hutchinson	N	N	N	Y	N	Y	Y
Bumpers	Y	Y	Y	N	Y	N	N
CALIFORNIA							
Boxer	Y	Y	Y	N	Y	Y	N
Feinstein	N	Y	Y	N	Y	N	N
COLORADO							
Allard	N	Y	N	Y	N	Y	Y
Campbell	N	N	Y	N	N	Y	Y
CONNECTICUT							
Dodd	Y	Y	Y	N	N	N	N
Lieberman	N	Y	Y	N	N	Y	Y
DELAWARE							
Roth	N	N	Y	N	N	Y	Y
Biden	N	Y	Y	N	Y	N	N
FLORIDA							
Mack	Y	Y	N	Y	N	Y	Y
Graham	Y	Y	Y	N	Y	N	N
GEORGIA							
Coverdell	N	N	N	Y	N	Y	Y
Cleland	Y	Y	Y	N	Y	Y	Y
HAWAII							
Akaka	Y	Y	Y	N	Y	N	N
Inouye	Y	Y	Y	N	Y	N	N
IDAHO							
Craig	N	N	N	Y	N	Y	Y
Kempthorne	N	N	N	Y	N	Y	Y
ILLINOIS							
Durbin	Y	Y	Y	N	Y	N	N
Moseley-Braun	Y	Y	Y	N	Y	N	Y
INDIANA							
Coats	N	N	Y	Y	N	Y	Y
Lugar	N	Y	N	Y	N	Y	Y
IOWA							
Grassley	N	Y	Y	N	N	Y	Y
Harkin	Y	Y	N	Y	N	N	N
KANSAS							
Brownback	N	Y	N	Y	N	Y	Y
Roberts	N	N	N	Y	N	Y	Y
KENTUCKY							
McConnell	N	N	N	Y	N	N	Y
Ford	Y	Y	Y	N	Y	N	Y
LOUISIANA							
Breaux	Y	Y	Y	N	Y	N	N
Landrieu	Y	Y	Y	N	Y	N	N
MAINE							
Collins	N	N	Y	N	Y	Y	Y
Snowe	N	Y	Y	Y	Y	Y	Y
MARYLAND							
Mikulski	Y	Y	Y	N	Y	N	N
Sarbanes	Y	Y	Y	N	Y	N	N
MASSACHUSETTS							
Kennedy	Y	Y	Y	N	Y	N	N
Kerry	Y	Y	Y	N	Y	N	N
MICHIGAN							
Abraham	N	N	N	Y	N	Y	Y
Levin	Y	Y	Y	N	Y	N	N
MINNESOTA							
Grams	N	Y	N	Y	N	Y	Y
Wellstone	Y	Y	Y	N	Y	N	N
MISSISSIPPI							
Cochran	N	N	N	Y	N	Y	Y
Lott	N	N	N	Y	N	N	Y
MISSOURI							
Ashcroft	N	Y	N	Y	N	Y	Y
Bond	N	N	N	Y	N	Y	Y
MONTANA							
Burns	N	N	N	Y	N	Y	Y
Baucus	Y	Y	Y	N	Y	N	Y
NEBRASKA							
Hagel	N	N	N	Y	N	Y	Y
Kerrey	Y	Y	Y	N	Y	N	Y
NEVADA							
Bryan	Y	Y	Y	N	Y	Y	Y
Reid	N	Y	Y	N	Y	Y	Y
NEW HAMPSHIRE							
Gregg	N	N	Y	Y	N	N	Y
Smith	N	N	N	Y	N	Y	Y
NEW JERSEY							
Lautenberg	Y	Y	Y	N	Y	N	N
Torricelli	Y	Y	Y	N	Y	N	N
NEW MEXICO							
Domenici	N	N	N	Y	N	N	Y
Bingaman	Y	Y	Y	N	Y	Y	Y
NEW YORK							
D'Amato	N	N	N	Y	N	N	Y
Moynihan	N	Y	Y	N	N	Y	
NORTH CAROLINA							
Faircloth	N	N	N	Y	N	N	Y
Helms	N	N	N	Y	N	N	Y
NORTH DAKOTA							
Conrad	Y	Y	Y	N	Y	N	Y
Dorgan	Y	Y	Y	N	Y	Y	Y
OHIO							
DeWine	N	Y	N	Y	N	Y	N
Glenn	Y	Y	Y	N	Y	N	N
OKLAHOMA							
Inhofe	N	Y	N	Y	N	N	Y
Nickles	N	Y	N	Y	N	N	Y
OREGON							
Smith	N	N	N	Y	N	N	Y
Wyden	Y	Y	Y	N	Y	N	N
PENNSYLVANIA							
Santorum	N	N	N	Y	N	N	Y
Specter	Y	N	Y	Y	N	Y	Y
RHODE ISLAND							
Chafee	N	N	Y	N	N	Y	N
Reed	Y	Y	Y	N	N	Y	N
SOUTH CAROLINA							
Thurmond	N	N	N	Y	N	N	Y
Hollings	Y	Y	Y	N	Y	N	Y
SOUTH DAKOTA							
Daschle	Y	Y	Y	N	Y	N	Y
Johnson	Y	Y	Y	N	Y	N	Y
TENNESSEE							
Frist	N	N	N	Y	N	Y	Y
Thompson	N	N	N	Y	N	Y	Y
TEXAS							
Gramm	N	N	N	Y	N	Y	Y
Hutchison	Y	N	Y	Y	N	N	Y
UTAH							
Bennett	N	N	Y	N	N	Y	Y
Hatch	N	Y	N	Y	N	N	Y
VERMONT							
Jeffords	N	N	Y	N	N	Y	Y
Leahy	Y	Y	Y	N	Y	N	Y
VIRGINIA							
Warner	N	N	N	Y	N	N	Y
Robb	Y	Y	Y	N	Y	N	N
WASHINGTON							
Gorton	N	N	Y	N	N	Y	Y
Murray	Y	N	Y	N	Y	Y	N
WEST VIRGINIA							
Byrd	N	Y	Y	N	Y	N	N
Rockefeller	Y	Y	Y	N	Y	N	Y
WISCONSIN							
Feingold	Y	Y	Y	N	Y	Y	Y
Kohl	N	Y	Y	N	Y	Y	N
WYOMING							
Enzi	N	N	N	Y	N	Y	Y
Thomas	N	N	N	Y	N	Y	Y

Key

- **Y** Voted for (yea).
- **#** Paired for.
- **+** Announced for.
- **N** Voted against (nay).
- **X** Paired against.
- **−** Announced against.
- **P** Voted "present."
- **C** Voted "present" to avoid possible conflict of interest.
- **?** Did not vote or otherwise make a position known.

Democrats   **Republicans**

ND Northern Democrats   SD Southern Democrats

Southern states - Ala., Ark., Fla., Ga., Ky., La., Miss., N.C., Okla., S.C., Tenn., Texas, Va.

218. S 2260. Fiscal 1999 Commerce, Justice, State Appropriations/Grand Jury Witnesses. Bumpers, D-Ark., amendment that would allow witnesses testifying before a federal grand jury to have their attorney present in the grand jury room during questioning. Rejected 41-59: R 3-52; D 38-7 (ND 30-7, SD 8-0). July 22, 1998.

219. S 2260. Fiscal 1999 Commerce, Justice, State Appropriations/Law Enforcement and Rescue Flights. Graham, D-Fla., amendment that would allow local public agencies to recover costs incurred by operating aircraft to assist other jurisdictions in law enforcement operations, search and rescue missions or when responding to an "imminent threat" to property or natural resources. Adopted 56-44: R 12-43; D 44-1 (ND 36-1, SD 8-0). July 22, 1998.

220. S 2260. Fiscal 1999 Commerce, Justice, State Appropriations/Juvenile Justice. Gregg, R-N.H., motion to table (kill) the Sessions, R-Ala., amendment that would increase funding for juvenile accountability incentive block grants, for purposes such as hiring additional juvenile judges and prosecutors, from $100 million to $150 million. To pay for the increase, the amendment would decrease funding for juvenile delinquency prevention programs from $95 million to $45 million. Motion agreed to 64-36: R 19-36; D 45-0 (ND 37-0, SD 8-0). July 22, 1998.

221. S 2260. Fiscal 1999 Commerce, Justice, State Appropriations/Social Security and Tax Cuts. Gregg, R-N.H., amendment that would express the sense of the Senate that Congress and the president should: "save Social Security first" and then return any remaining budgetary surpluses to U.S. taxpayers; work together to balance the budget without counting Social Security trust fund surpluses; and enact bipartisan legislation to ensure the financial security of the Social Security system. Adopted 55-45: R 55-0; D 0-45 (ND 0-37, SD 0-8). July 22, 1998.

222. S 2260. Fiscal 1999 Commerce, Justice, State Appropriations/Social Security. Hollings, D-S.C., amendment that would express the sense of the Senate that Congress and the president should: "save Social Security first" by reserving any fiscal 1999 budget surplus for that purpose; work together to balance the budget without counting Social Security trust fund surpluses; and enact bipartisan legislation to ensure the financial security of the Social Security system. Rejected 47-53: R 2-53; D 45-0 (ND 37-0, SD 8-0). July 22, 1998.

223. S 2260. Fiscal 1999 Commerce, Justice, State Appropriations/Patent and Trademark Office Relocation. McCain, R-Ariz., amendment that would prohibit the Patent and Trademark Office from relocating its offices until 90 days after the General Services Administration issues a report on the benefits and costs of relocating. Rejected 47-53: R 36-19; D 11-34 (ND 10-27, SD 1-7). July 22, 1998.

224. S 2260. Fiscal 1999 Commerce, Justice, State Appropriations/Gun Owner Liability. Craig, R-Idaho, motion to table (kill) the Durbin, D-Ill., amendment that would provide for penalties of up to one year in prison and a $10,000 fine for adult gun owners if a juvenile obtains access to the firearm and uses it criminally to kill, wound or exhibit the gun in a public place if the adult had not secured the gun with a trigger lock, lock box or other "safety device." Motion agreed to 69-31: R 53-2; D 16-29 (ND 12-25, SD 4-4). July 22, 1998.

Senate Votes 225, 226, 227, 228, 229, 230, 231

	225	226	227	228	229	230	231
ALABAMA							
Sessions	N	Y	Y	N	Y	Y	Y
Shelby	N	Y	Y	N	Y	Y	N
ALASKA							
Murkowski	N	Y	Y	N	Y	Y	N
Stevens	N	Y	Y	Y	N	Y	N
ARIZONA							
Kyl	N	Y	Y	N	Y	Y	N
McCain	N	Y	Y	Y	Y	Y	N
ARKANSAS							
Hutchinson	Y	N	Y	N	Y	Y	Y
Bumpers	Y	N	N	N	Y	N	N
CALIFORNIA							
Boxer	Y	N	N	Y	N	Y	N
Feinstein	Y	N	N	N	Y	N	N
COLORADO							
Allard	N	Y	Y	N	Y	Y	N
Campbell	N	Y	Y	Y	Y	Y	Y
CONNECTICUT							
Dodd	Y	N	N	N	N	N	N
Lieberman	Y	N	N	N	N	N	N
DELAWARE							
Roth	N	Y	Y	N	Y	Y	N
Biden	Y	N	N	Y	N	N	N
FLORIDA							
Mack	N	Y	P	N	Y	N	N
Graham	Y	N	N	N	Y	N	N
GEORGIA							
Coverdell	Y	Y	N	N	Y	Y	Y
Cleland	Y	N	N	N	Y	N	N
HAWAII							
Akaka	Y	N	N	N	N	N	N
Inouye	Y	N	Y	Y	N	Y	N
IDAHO							
Craig	N	Y	Y	Y	N	Y	Y
Kempthorne	N	Y	Y	Y	Y	Y	Y
ILLINOIS							
Durbin	Y	N	N	N	N	N	N
Moseley-Braun	Y	N	N	N	Y	N	Y
INDIANA							
Coats	Y	Y	Y	N	Y	N	N
Lugar	N	Y	Y	N	Y	Y	N
IOWA							
Grassley	N	Y	Y	N	Y	Y	Y
Harkin	Y	N	N	Y	N	N	N
KANSAS							
Brownback	N	Y	Y	N	Y	N	Y
Roberts	N	Y	Y	N	Y	Y	Y
KENTUCKY							
McConnell	N	Y	Y	N	Y	Y	N
Ford	Y	N	Y	N	Y	N	N
LOUISIANA							
Breaux	Y	N	Y	N	Y	N	N
Landrieu	Y	N	Y	N	Y	N	N
MAINE							
Collins	N	Y	N	Y	N	Y	N
Snowe	Y	N	Y	N	Y	Y	Y
MARYLAND							
Mikulski	Y	N	N	N	N	N	N
Sarbanes	Y	N	N	N	Y	N	N
MASSACHUSETTS							
Kennedy	Y	N	N	N	N	N	N
Kerry	Y	N	N	N	Y	N	N
MICHIGAN							
Abraham	N	Y	Y	N	Y	Y	N
Levin	Y	N	N	N	Y	N	N
MINNESOTA							
Grams	N	Y	Y	N	Y	Y	Y
Wellstone	Y	N	N	N	N	N	N
MISSISSIPPI							
Cochran	N	Y	Y	Y	Y	Y	N
Lott	N	Y	Y	N	Y	Y	Y
MISSOURI							
Ashcroft	N	Y	Y	N	Y	Y	Y
Bond	N	Y	Y	N	Y	Y	N
MONTANA							
Burns	N	Y	Y	Y	N	Y	N
Baucus	Y	N	N	N	Y	N	N
NEBRASKA							
Hagel	N	Y	Y	N	Y	Y	N
Kerrey	Y	N	Y	Y	Y	N	N
NEVADA							
Bryan	Y	N	Y	N	Y	N	N
Reid	Y	N	Y	N	Y	N	Y
NEW HAMPSHIRE							
Gregg	N	Y	Y	N	Y	Y	Y
Smith	N	Y	Y	N	Y	Y	Y
NEW JERSEY							
Lautenberg	Y	N	N	N	Y	N	N
Torricelli	Y	N	N	N	Y	N	N
NEW MEXICO							
Domenici	N	Y	Y	N	Y	N	N
Bingaman	Y	N	Y	N	Y	N	N
NEW YORK							
D'Amato	N	Y	N	Y	N	Y	N
Moynihan	N	N	Y	Y	N	N	N
NORTH CAROLINA							
Faircloth	N	Y	Y	N	Y	Y	N
Helms	N	Y	Y	N	Y	Y	Y
NORTH DAKOTA							
Conrad	Y	N	Y	N	Y	N	N
Dorgan	Y	N	N	N	Y	N	N
OHIO							
DeWine	N	Y	Y	Y	Y	N	N
Glenn	Y	N	N	N	Y	N	N
OKLAHOMA							
Inhofe	N	Y	Y	N	Y	Y	Y
Nickles	N	Y	Y	N	Y	Y	Y
OREGON							
Smith	N	Y	Y	N	Y	Y	N
Wyden	Y	N	N	N	N	N	N
PENNSYLVANIA							
Santorum	N	Y	Y	N	Y	Y	Y
Specter	N	Y	Y	N	Y	N	N
RHODE ISLAND							
Chafee	Y	N	Y	N	Y	N	N
Reed	Y	N	Y	N	Y	N	N
SOUTH CAROLINA							
Thurmond	N	Y	Y	N	Y	Y	Y
Hollings	Y	N	Y	N	Y	Y	N
SOUTH DAKOTA							
Daschle	Y	N	Y	N	N	N	N
Johnson	Y	N	N	Y	Y	N	N
TENNESSEE							
Frist	N	Y	Y	N	Y	Y	Y
Thompson	N	Y	Y	N	Y	N	N
TEXAS							
Gramm	N	Y	Y	N	Y	Y	Y
Hutchison	N	Y	Y	N	Y	Y	Y
UTAH							
Bennett	N	Y	Y	N	Y	Y	Y
Hatch	N	Y	Y	N	Y	N	Y
VERMONT							
Jeffords	Y	N	N	N	Y	Y	N
Leahy	Y	N	N	N	Y	N	N
VIRGINIA							
Warner	N	Y	Y	N	Y	Y	N
Robb	Y	N	N	N	Y	N	N
WASHINGTON							
Gorton	N	Y	Y	N	Y	Y	N
Murray	Y	N	N	N	Y	N	N
WEST VIRGINIA							
Byrd	Y	N	N	N	Y	Y	Y
Rockefeller	Y	N	N	N	Y	N	N
WISCONSIN							
Feingold	Y	N	N	N	N	N	Y
Kohl	Y	N	N	N	N	N	N
WYOMING							
Enzi	N	Y	Y	N	Y	Y	Y
Thomas	N	Y	Y	N	Y	Y	N

Key
- Y Voted for (yea).
- # Paired for.
- + Announced for.
- N Voted against (nay).
- X Paired against.
- − Announced against.
- P Voted "present."
- C Voted "present" to avoid possible conflict of interest.
- ? Did not vote or otherwise make a position known.

Democrats • Republicans

ND Northern Democrats SD Southern Democrats

Southern states - Ala., Ark., Fla., Ga., Ky., La., Miss., N.C., Okla., S.C., Tenn., Texas, Va.

225. S 2260. Fiscal 1999 Commerce, Justice, State Appropriations/Secret Phone Recordings. Bumpers, D-Ark., amendment that would prohibit the recording of any telephone conversation unless all parties agree to its recording or the conversation is being recorded as part of a criminal investigation. Rejected 50-50: R 6-49; D 44-1 (ND 36-1, SD 8-0). July 22, 1998.

226. S 2260. Fiscal 1999 Commerce, Justice, State Appropriations/Reconsider. Lott, R-Miss., motion to table (kill) the Lott motion to reconsider the vote on the Bumpers amendment. Motion agreed to 51-49: R 51-4; D 0-45 (ND 0-37, SD 0-8). July 22, 1998.

227. S 2260. Fiscal 1999 Commerce, Justice, State Appropriations/Cable Television Rates. McCain, R-Ariz., motion to table (kill) the Feingold, D-Wis., amendment that would require the Federal Communications Commission to issue a report examining whether the 1992 telecommunications law (PL 102-385) has been successful at increasing competition in the cable industry and lowering cable television rates. Motion agreed to 63-36: R 49-5; D 14-31 (ND 10-27, SD 4-4). July 22, 1998.

228. S 2260. Fiscal 1999 Commerce, Justice, State Appropriations/Indian Gaming. Craig, R-Idaho, amendment to the Kyl, R-Ariz., amendment. The Craig amendment would clarify that Indian gaming is regulated by the federal government under the Indian Gaming Regulatory Act and not the restrictions of the Kyl amendment. Rejected 18-82: R 9-46; D 9-36 (ND 9-28, SD 0-8). July 23, 1998.

229. S 2260. Fiscal 1999 Commerce, Justice, State Appropriations/Internet Gambling Ban. Kyl, R-Ariz., amendment that would ban Internet gambling by prohibiting any individual from knowingly using the Internet or any other interactive computer service to place, receive or otherwise make a bet or wager. The amendment would provide exemptions for multistate lotteries, securities trading, commodities trading and so-called fantasy rotisserie leagues. Adopted 90-10: R 52-3; D 38-7 (ND 30-7, SD 8-0). July 23, 1998.

230. S 2260. Fiscal 1999 Commerce, Justice, State Appropriations/Court-Appointed Attorney Fees. Nickles, R-Okla., amendment that would limit the amount of pay that court-appointed defense attorneys in federal death penalty cases could receive to the monthly amount allocated to U.S. attorneys in the district where the action is prosecuted. Adopted 53-47: R 45-10; D 8-37 (ND 6-31, SD 2-6). July 23, 1998.

231. S 2260. Fiscal 1999 Commerce, Justice, State Appropriations/Vietnam POW/MIAs. Gregg, R-N.H., motion to table (kill) the Kerry, D-Mass., amendment that would replace language in the bill strengthening the standard for certifying that Vietnam is cooperating with U.S. efforts to recover American POW/MIAs with language restating the current standard. Motion rejected 34-66: R 30-25; D 4-41 (ND 4-33, SD 0-8). July 23, 1998. (Subsequently, the amendment was adopted by voice vote.)

Senate Votes 232, 233, 234, 235, 236, 237, 238

	232	233	234	235	236	237	238
ALABAMA							
Sessions	Y	Y	Y	Y	N	N	N
Shelby	Y	Y	Y	Y	N	N	N
ALASKA							
Murkowski	Y	Y	Y	Y	N	Y	N
Stevens	Y	Y	Y	?	N	Y	Y
ARIZONA							
Kyl	Y	Y	Y	N	N	N	N
McCain	Y	Y	Y	?	?	N	N
ARKANSAS							
Hutchinson	Y	Y	Y	Y	N	N	N
Bumpers	Y	Y	Y	?	N	Y	Y
CALIFORNIA							
Boxer	Y	N	Y	?	Y	Y	Y
Feinstein	Y	N	Y	Y	Y	Y	Y
COLORADO							
Allard	Y	Y	Y	Y	N	N	N
Campbell	Y	Y	Y	Y	N	Y	Y
CONNECTICUT							
Dodd	Y	N	Y	Y	Y	Y	Y
Lieberman	Y	N	Y	Y	Y	Y	Y
DELAWARE							
Roth	Y	Y	Y	Y	Y	Y	Y
Biden	Y	Y	Y	Y	Y	Y	Y
FLORIDA							
Mack	Y	Y	Y	Y	N	N	N
Graham	Y	Y	Y	Y	Y	N	Y
GEORGIA							
Coverdell	Y	Y	Y	Y	N	N	N
Cleland	Y	Y	Y	Y	Y	Y	Y
HAWAII							
Akaka	Y	N	Y	Y	Y	Y	Y
Inouye	Y	N	Y	Y	Y	Y	Y
IDAHO							
Craig	Y	Y	Y	Y	N	Y	N
Kempthorne	Y	Y	Y	?	N	Y	N
ILLINOIS							
Durbin	Y	N	Y	Y	Y	Y	Y
Moseley-Braun	Y	N	Y	Y	Y	Y	Y
INDIANA							
Coats	Y	Y	Y	Y	N	N	N
Lugar	Y	Y	Y	Y	N	N	Y
IOWA							
Grassley	Y	Y	Y	Y	N	Y	N
Harkin	Y	N	Y	Y	+	+	+
KANSAS							
Brownback	Y	Y	Y	Y	N	N	N
Roberts	Y	Y	Y	Y	N	N	N
KENTUCKY							
McConnell	Y	Y	Y	Y	N	N	N
Ford	Y	N	Y	Y	Y	Y	Y
LOUISIANA							
Breaux	Y	Y	Y	Y	Y	Y	Y
Landrieu	Y	N	Y	Y	Y	Y	Y
MAINE							
Collins	Y	Y	Y	Y	N	Y	Y
Snowe	Y	Y	Y	Y	N	Y	Y
MARYLAND							
Mikulski	Y	N	Y	Y	Y	Y	Y
Sarbanes	Y	N	Y	Y	Y	Y	Y
MASSACHUSETTS							
Kennedy	Y	N	Y	Y	Y	Y	Y
Kerry	Y	N	Y	Y	Y	Y	Y
MICHIGAN							
Abraham	Y	Y	Y	Y	N	Y	N
Levin	Y	N	Y	Y	Y	Y	Y
MINNESOTA							
Grams	Y	Y	Y	Y	N	N	N
Wellstone	N	N	Y	Y	Y	Y	Y
MISSISSIPPI							
Cochran	Y	Y	Y	Y	N	N	N
Lott	Y	Y	Y	Y	N	N	N
MISSOURI							
Ashcroft	Y	Y	Y	Y	N	N	N
Bond	Y	Y	Y	Y	Y	N	Y
MONTANA							
Burns	Y	Y	Y	+	N	Y	N
Baucus	Y	Y	Y	Y	Y	Y	Y
NEBRASKA							
Hagel	Y	Y	Y	Y	N	N	N
Kerrey	N	Y	Y	Y	Y	N	Y
NEVADA							
Bryan	Y	Y	Y	Y	Y	Y	Y
Reid	Y	Y	Y	Y	Y	Y	Y
NEW HAMPSHIRE							
Gregg	Y	Y	Y	Y	N	N	N
Smith	Y	Y	Y	Y	N	N	N
NEW JERSEY							
Lautenberg	Y	N	Y	Y	Y	Y	Y
Torricelli	Y	N	Y	Y	Y	Y	Y
NEW MEXICO							
Domenici	Y	Y	Y	Y	?	?	Y
Bingaman	Y	Y	Y	Y	?	?	Y
NEW YORK							
D'Amato	Y	Y	Y	Y	N	Y	Y
Moynihan	Y	Y	Y	Y	Y	Y	Y
NORTH CAROLINA							
Faircloth	Y	Y	Y	Y	N	Y	N
Helms	Y	Y	Y	?	–	–	–
NORTH DAKOTA							
Conrad	Y	N	Y	Y	Y	Y	Y
Dorgan	Y	N	Y	Y	Y	Y	Y
OHIO							
DeWine	Y	Y	Y	Y	N	N	N
Glenn	Y	N	Y	Y	Y	Y	Y
OKLAHOMA							
Inhofe	Y	Y	Y	Y	N	N	N
Nickles	Y	Y	Y	Y	N	N	N
OREGON							
Smith	Y	Y	Y	Y	N	N	Y
Wyden	Y	Y	Y	Y	?	?	Y
PENNSYLVANIA							
Santorum	Y	Y	Y	Y	N	N	Y
Specter	Y	?	?	Y	N	Y	Y
RHODE ISLAND							
Chafee	Y	Y	Y	Y	N	N	Y
Reed	Y	N	Y	Y	Y	Y	Y
SOUTH CAROLINA							
Thurmond	Y	Y	Y	Y	N	N	N
Hollings	Y	Y	Y	Y	Y	Y	Y
SOUTH DAKOTA							
Daschle	Y	N	Y	Y	Y	N	Y
Johnson	Y	N	Y	Y	Y	Y	Y
TENNESSEE							
Frist	Y	Y	Y	Y	N	N	N
Thompson	Y	Y	Y	Y	N	N	N
TEXAS							
Gramm	Y	Y	Y	Y	N	N	N
Hutchison	Y	Y	Y	Y	N	N	N
UTAH							
Bennett	Y	Y	Y	?	N	N	N
Hatch	Y	Y	Y	Y	N	Y	N
VERMONT							
Jeffords	Y	Y	Y	Y	Y	N	Y
Leahy	Y	N	Y	Y	Y	N	Y
VIRGINIA							
Warner	Y	Y	Y	Y	N	N	Y
Robb	Y	Y	Y	Y	Y	N	Y
WASHINGTON							
Gorton	Y	Y	Y	Y	N	Y	N
Murray	Y	N	Y	Y	Y	Y	Y
WEST VIRGINIA							
Byrd	Y	N	Y	Y	Y	N	Y
Rockefeller	Y	N	Y	Y	Y	N	Y
WISCONSIN							
Feingold	Y	N	Y	Y	Y	Y	Y
Kohl	Y	N	Y	Y	Y	Y	Y
WYOMING							
Enzi	Y	Y	Y	?	N	N	N
Thomas	Y	Y	Y	Y	N	N	N

Key

Y Voted for (yea).
Paired for.
+ Announced for.
N Voted against (nay).
X Paired against.
– Announced against.
P Voted "present."
C Voted "present" to avoid possible conflict of interest.
? Did not vote or otherwise make a position known.

Democrats   *Republicans*

ND Northern Democrats   SD Southern Democrats

Southern states - Ala., Ark., Fla., Ga., Ky., La., Miss., N.C., Okla., S.C., Tenn., Texas, Va.

232. S 2260. Fiscal 1999 Commerce, Justice, State Appropriations/Japanese Financial Problems. Lieberman, D-Conn., amendment that would express the sense of the Senate that the president should inform Japan that financial and market deregulation, along with restructuring "bad bank debt," are fundamental to Japan's economic recovery, and that the first priority of Japan's new prime minister and Cabinet should be to restore growth and promote stability in international financial markets. Adopted 98-2: R 55-0; D 43-2 (ND 35-2, SD 8-0). July 23, 1998.

233. S 2260. Fiscal 1999 Commerce, Justice, State Appropriations/Temporary Farm Workers. Smith, R-Ore., amendment that would establish a registry of temporary agricultural workers to link U.S. farmworkers to agricultural jobs. If there are insufficient U.S. workers to fill the number of positions offered by a specific employer, the attorney general shall admit enough foreign workers to fill those positions. The amendment also would require that employers provide prevailing wages, housing and transportation reimbursements for the workers and would direct the attorney general to conduct a study on whether foreign workers depart the country upon completion of their authorized stay. Adopted 68-31: R 54-0; D 14-31 (ND 8-29, SD 6-2). July 23, 1998.

234. S 2260. Fiscal 1999 Commerce, Justice, State Appropriations/Passage. Passage of the bill to provide $33.2 billion in new budget authority for the departments of Commerce, Justice and State and the federal judiciary in fiscal 1999. The bill provides $1.1 billion more than in fiscal 1998 and $3.6 billion less than requested by President Clinton. Passed 99-0: R 54-0; D 45-0 (ND 37-0, SD 8-0). July 23, 1998.

235. S 2307. Fiscal 1999 Transportation Appropriations/Passage. Passage of the bill to provide $47.1 billion in new budget authority for the Department of Transportation and related agencies in fiscal 1999. The bill would provide $4.4 billion more than in fiscal 1998 and $4.1 billion more than requested by President Clinton. Passed 90-1: R 47-1; D 43-0 (ND 36-0, SD 7-0). July 24, 1998.

236. HR 1151. Credit Union Membership Rules/Low-Income Loans. Sarbanes, D-Md., motion to table (kill) the Gramm, R-Texas, amendment that would strike the bill's provisions to apply to credit unions requirements similar to the 1977 Community Reinvestment Act (PL 95-128), which requires federal regulators to consider a bank's lending record to all areas in the community it serves when deciding whether to allow a branch, merger or other endeavor. The bill's language would require the National Credit Union Administration to review credit unions to ensure that they provide affordable services to individuals of modest means within the community. Motion rejected 44-50: R 3-49; D 41-1 (ND 34-0, SD 7-1). July 27, 1998. (Subsequently, the Gramm amendment was adopted by voice vote)

237. HR 1151. Credit Union Membership Rules/Business Loans. D'Amato, R-N.Y., motion to table (kill) the Hagel, R-Neb., amendment that would reduce the cap on commercial business loans to credit union members from 12.25 percent to 7 percent of their net worth for well-capitalized credit unions. The amendment would require credit unions to count loans of up to $50,000 as business loans and would require that credit unionpersonnel who make commercial loans have at least two years of experience. Motion agreed to 53-42: R 18-35; D 35-7 (ND 29-5, SD 6-2). July 27, 1998.

238. HR 1151. Credit Union Membership Rules/Small Bank Reinvestment Exemption. D'Amato, R-N.Y., motion to table (kill) the Shelby, R-Ala., amendment that would exempt banks with assets of less than $250 million from the 1977 Community Reinvestment Act (PL 95-128). The act requires federal regulators to consider a bank's lending record to all areas in the community it serves when deciding whether to allow a branch, merger or other endeavor. Motion agreed to 59-39: R 15-39; D 44-0 (ND 36-0, SD 8-0). July 28, 1998. A "yea" was a vote in support of the president's position.

Senate Votes 239, 240, 241, 242, 243, 244, 245

	239	240	241	242	243	244	245
ALABAMA							
Sessions	Y	Y	Y	N	Y	N	N
Shelby	Y	Y	Y	N	Y	N	N
ALASKA							
Murkowski	Y	Y	Y	N	Y	N	Y
Stevens	Y	Y	N	N	Y	N	Y
ARIZONA							
Kyl	Y	Y	Y	N	Y	N	N
McCain	Y	Y	Y	N	Y	N	N
ARKANSAS							
Hutchinson	Y	Y	Y	N	Y	N	N
Bumpers	Y	N	N	Y	N	Y	N
CALIFORNIA							
Boxer	Y	N	N	Y	N	Y	N
Feinstein	Y	N	N	Y	N	Y	N
COLORADO							
Allard	Y	Y	Y	N	Y	N	N
Campbell	Y	Y	Y	N	Y	N	Y
CONNECTICUT							
Dodd	Y	N	N	Y	N	Y	N
Lieberman	Y	N	N	Y	N	Y	N
DELAWARE							
Roth	Y	Y	N	Y	Y	N	Y
Biden	Y	N	N	Y	N	Y	N
FLORIDA							
Mack	N	Y	Y	N	Y	N	Y
Graham	Y	N	N	Y	N	Y	Y
GEORGIA							
Coverdell	Y	Y	Y	N	Y	N	N
Cleland	Y	N	N	Y	N	Y	Y
HAWAII							
Akaka	Y	N	N	Y	N	Y	N
Inouye	Y	N	N	Y	N	Y	N
IDAHO							
Craig	Y	Y	Y	N	Y	N	Y
Kempthorne	Y	Y	Y	N	Y	N	N
ILLINOIS							
Durbin	Y	N	N	Y	N	Y	N
Moseley-Braun	Y	N	Y	Y	N	Y	N
INDIANA							
Coats	N	Y	Y	N	Y	N	?
Lugar	Y	N	Y	N	Y	N	Y
IOWA							
Grassley	Y	Y	N	N	Y	N	N
Harkin	+	–	–	Y	N	Y	N
KANSAS							
Brownback	Y	Y	Y	N	Y	N	N
Roberts	N	Y	N	N	Y	N	Y
KENTUCKY							
McConnell	Y	Y	Y	N	Y	N	N
Ford	Y	N	N	N	N	Y	N
LOUISIANA							
Breaux	Y	Y	N	N	Y	N	N
Landrieu	Y	N	N	Y	N	Y	N
MAINE							
Collins	Y	Y	Y	N	Y	N	N
Snowe	Y	Y	Y	Y	Y	N	N
MARYLAND							
Mikulski	Y	N	N	Y	N	Y	N
Sarbanes	Y	N	N	Y	N	Y	N
MASSACHUSETTS							
Kennedy	Y	N	N	Y	N	Y	N
Kerry	Y	N	N	Y	N	Y	N
MICHIGAN							
Abraham	Y	Y	Y	N	Y	N	N
Levin	Y	N	N	Y	N	Y	N
MINNESOTA							
Grams	Y	Y	Y	N	Y	N	N
Wellstone	Y	N	N	Y	N	Y	N
MISSISSIPPI							
Cochran	Y	Y	N	N	Y	N	Y
Lott	Y	Y	Y	N	Y	N	Y
MISSOURI							
Ashcroft	Y	Y	Y	N	Y	N	Y
Bond	Y	Y	Y	N	Y	N	N
MONTANA							
Burns	Y	Y	Y	N	Y	N	N
Baucus	Y	N	N	Y	N	Y	N
NEBRASKA							
Hagel	N	Y	N	N	Y	N	N
Kerrey	Y	N	N	Y	N	Y	N
NEVADA							
Bryan	Y	N	N	Y	N	Y	N
Reid	Y	N	Y	Y	N	Y	N
NEW HAMPSHIRE							
Gregg	Y	Y	Y	N	Y	N	Y
Smith	Y	Y	Y	N	Y	N	N
NEW JERSEY							
Lautenberg	Y	N	N	Y	N	Y	N
Torricelli	Y	N	N	Y	N	Y	N
NEW MEXICO							
Domenici	Y	Y	Y	N	Y	N	N
Bingaman	Y	Y	Y	N	Y	N	N
NEW YORK							
D'Amato	Y	N	Y	N	Y	N	N
Moynihan	Y	N	N	Y	Y	Y	Y
NORTH CAROLINA							
Faircloth	Y	Y	Y	N	Y	N	Y
Helms	–	+	+	–	+	–	?
NORTH DAKOTA							
Conrad	Y	N	N	Y	N	Y	N
Dorgan	Y	N	N	Y	N	Y	N
OHIO							
DeWine	Y	N	Y	N	Y	N	N
Glenn	Y	N	N	Y	N	Y	N
OKLAHOMA							
Inhofe	N	Y	Y	N	Y	N	N
Nickles	N	Y	Y	N	Y	N	N
OREGON							
Smith	Y	Y	Y	N	Y	N	N
Wyden	Y	N	N	Y	N	Y	N
PENNSYLVANIA							
Santorum	Y	Y	Y	N	Y	N	N
Specter	Y	Y	Y	N	Y	N	N
RHODE ISLAND							
Chafee	Y	N	N	N	Y	N	N
Reed	Y	N	N	Y	N	Y	N
SOUTH CAROLINA							
Thurmond	Y	Y	Y	N	Y	N	Y
Hollings	Y	Y	N	N	Y	N	N
SOUTH DAKOTA							
Daschle	Y	N	N	Y	N	Y	N
Johnson	Y	N	N	Y	N	Y	N
TENNESSEE							
Frist	Y	Y	Y	N	Y	N	N
Thompson	Y	Y	Y	Y	Y	N	Y
TEXAS							
Gramm	Y	Y	Y	N	Y	N	Y
Hutchison	Y	Y	Y	N	Y	N	N
UTAH							
Bennett	Y	Y	Y	N	Y	N	N
Hatch	Y	Y	Y	N	Y	N	N
VERMONT							
Jeffords	Y	N	Y	N	Y	Y	N
Leahy	Y	Y	N	Y	N	Y	N
VIRGINIA							
Warner	Y	Y	Y	N	Y	N	N
Robb	Y	N	N	Y	Y	Y	N
WASHINGTON							
Gorton	Y	Y	Y	Y	Y	N	?
Murray	Y	N	N	Y	N	Y	N
WEST VIRGINIA							
Byrd	Y	N	N	Y	Y	Y	Y
Rockefeller	Y	N	N	Y	N	Y	N
WISCONSIN							
Feingold	Y	N	N	Y	N	Y	N
Kohl	Y	N	N	Y	N	Y	N
WYOMING							
Enzi	Y	Y	Y	N	Y	N	N
Thomas	Y	Y	Y	N	Y	N	N

Key

- Y Voted for (yea).
- # Paired for.
- + Announced for.
- N Voted against (nay).
- X Paired against.
- – Announced against.
- P Voted "present."
- C Voted "present" to avoid possible conflict of interest.
- ? Did not vote or otherwise make a position known.

Democrats   **Republicans**

ND Northern Democrats   SD Southern Democrats

Southern states - Ala., Ark., Fla., Ga., Ky., La., Miss., N.C., Okla., S.C., Tenn., Texas, Va.

239. HR 1151. Credit Union Membership Rules/Passage. Passage of the bill to allow credit union members to keep their accounts and to permit credit unions to join unrelated groups as long as the groups would provide no more than 3,000 members. Passed 92-6: R 48-6; D 44-0 (ND 36-0, SD 8-0). July 28, 1998.

240. S 2312. Fiscal 1999 Treasury-Postal Service-General Government Appropriations/Large Capacity Ammunition Ban. Campbell, R-Colo., motion to table (kill) the Feinstein, D-Calif., amendment that would prohibit the importation of large capacity ammunition feeding devices. The devices are currently illegal in the United States. Motion agreed to 54-44: R 49-5; D 5-39 (ND 3-33, SD 2-6). July 28, 1998.

241. S 2312. Fiscal 1999 Treasury-Postal Service-General Government Appropriations/Tax Code Termination. Hutchinson, R-Ark., motion to waive the Budget Act with respect to the Kohl, D-Wis., point of order against the Hutchinson amendment. The Hutchinson amendment would abolish the current tax code by Dec. 31, 2002, and recommend that Congress approve a new tax code by July 4, 2002. Motion rejected 49-49: R 47-7; D 2-42 (ND 2-34, SD 0-8). July 28, 1998. A three-fifths majority vote (60) of the total Senate is required to waive the Budget Act. (Subsequently, the chair upheld the point of order, and the amendment fell.) A "nay" was a vote in support of the president's position.

242. S 2312. Fiscal 1999 Treasury-Postal Service-General Government Appropriations/Marriage Penalty. Roth, R-Del., motion to table (kill) the Brownback, R-Kan., amendment that would allow each spouse to claim one-half of the combined taxable income of both spouses as if unmarried, thus eliminating the so-called marriage penalty. Motion rejected 48-51: R 4-50; D 44-1 (ND 37-0, SD 7-1). July 29, 1998. (Subsequently, the Brownback amendment was withdrawn.)

243. S 2312. Fiscal 1999 Treasury-Postal Service-General Government Appropriations/Democratic Marriage Penalty Alternative. Campbell, R-Colo., motion to table (kill) the Daschle, D-S.D., amendment that would allow married couples with combined incomes below $50,000 a year to deduct 20 percent of the income of the lesser-earning spouse on their income taxes, thus eliminating the so-called marriage penalty for those in that income bracket. Motion agreed to 57-42: R 54-0; D 3-42 (ND 2-35, SD 1-7). July 29, 1998.

244. S 2312. Fiscal 1999 Treasury-Postal Service-General Government Appropriations/Child Labor. Harkin, D-Iowa, amendment to the Thompson, R-Tenn., amendment. The Harkin amendment would replace the text of the Thompson amendment with the bill's language regarding child labor with a few changes. That language would prohibit the government from buying products made by forced or indentured child labor and would require executive agencies to publish a list of products mined or manufactured with forced or indentured child labor. The Thompson amendment would strike all bill language concerning child labor except for a provision requiring revisions to federal acquisition regulations within 180 days of the bill's enactment. Rejected 46-53: R 1-53; D 45-0 (ND 37-0, SD 8-0). July 29, 1998. (Subsequently, the underlying Thompson amendment was adopted by voice vote.)

245. S 2312. Fiscal 1999 Treasury-Postal Service-General Government Appropriations/Post Office Closings. Cochran, R-Miss., motion to table (kill) the Baucus, D-Mont., amendment that would require the Postal Service to provide 60 days notice to the community, hold a hearing and abide by local zoning requirements before closing or relocating a post office in that community. Motion rejected 21-76: R 18-34; D 3-42 (ND 1-36, SD 2-6). July 29, 1998. (Subsequently, the Baucus amendment was adopted by voice vote.)

Senate Votes 246, 247, 248, 249, 250, 251, 252

	246	247	248	249	250	251	252
ALABAMA							
Sessions	N	Y	N	Y	Y	Y	Y
Shelby	N	Y	N	N	Y	Y	Y
ALASKA							
Murkowski	N	Y	N	Y	Y	Y	Y
Stevens	N	Y	Y	N	Y	Y	Y
ARIZONA							
Kyl	N	Y	N	Y	Y	Y	Y
McCain	N	Y	N	Y	Y	Y	Y
ARKANSAS							
Hutchinson	N	Y	N	N	Y	Y	Y
Bumpers	Y	N	Y	Y	Y	Y	Y
CALIFORNIA							
Boxer	Y	Y	N	Y	Y	N	Y
Feinstein	Y	Y	Y	Y	Y	Y	Y
COLORADO							
Allard	N	Y	N	N	Y	Y	Y
Campbell	N	Y	N	N	Y	Y	Y
CONNECTICUT							
Dodd	Y	Y	N	Y	Y	Y	Y
Lieberman	Y	Y	N	Y	Y	Y	Y
DELAWARE							
Roth	N	Y	N	Y	Y	Y	Y
Biden	Y	Y	N	Y	Y	N	Y
FLORIDA							
Mack	N	Y	N	Y	Y	Y	Y
Graham	Y	N	N	Y	Y	Y	Y
GEORGIA							
Coverdell	N	Y	N	N	Y	Y	Y
Cleland	Y	Y	Y	Y	Y	Y	Y
HAWAII							
Akaka	Y	Y	Y	Y	Y	Y	Y
Inouye	Y	Y	Y	Y	Y	Y	Y
IDAHO							
Craig	N	Y	N	N	Y	Y	Y
Kempthorne	N	Y	N	N	Y	Y	Y
ILLINOIS							
Durbin	Y	Y	N	Y	Y	N	Y
Moseley-Braun	Y	Y	N	Y	Y	N	Y
INDIANA							
Coats	N	Y	N	Y	Y	Y	Y
Lugar	N	Y	Y	Y	Y	Y	Y
IOWA							
Grassley	N	Y	N	Y	Y	Y	Y
Harkin	Y	N	N	Y	Y	N	Y
KANSAS							
Brownback	N	Y	Y	Y	Y	Y	Y
Roberts	N	Y	Y	Y	Y	Y	Y
KENTUCKY							
McConnell	N	Y	N	Y	Y	Y	Y
Ford	Y	Y	Y	Y	Y	Y	Y
LOUISIANA							
Breaux	Y	N	N	Y	Y	Y	Y
Landrieu	Y	Y	Y	Y	Y	Y	Y
MAINE							
Collins	N	Y	N	Y	Y	Y	Y
Snowe	N	Y	N	Y	Y	Y	Y
MARYLAND							
Mikulski	Y	Y	N	Y	Y	Y	Y
Sarbanes	Y	Y	N	Y	Y	N	Y
MASSACHUSETTS							
Kennedy	Y	Y	Y	Y	Y	N	Y
Kerry	Y	Y	N	Y	Y	Y	Y
MICHIGAN							
Abraham	N	Y	N	Y	Y	Y	Y
Levin	Y	Y	Y	Y	Y	Y	Y
MINNESOTA							
Grams	N	Y	N	Y	Y	Y	Y
Wellstone	Y	N	N	Y	Y	N	N
MISSISSIPPI							
Cochran	N	Y	N	Y	Y	Y	Y
Lott	N	Y	N	Y	Y	Y	Y
MISSOURI							
Ashcroft	N	Y	N	Y	Y	Y	Y
Bond	N	Y	N	Y	Y	Y	Y
MONTANA							
Burns	N	Y	N	Y	Y	Y	Y
Baucus	Y	Y	Y	Y	Y	Y	Y
NEBRASKA							
Hagel	N	Y	Y	Y	Y	Y	Y
Kerrey	Y	N	N	Y	Y	Y	Y
NEVADA							
Bryan	Y	N	N	Y	Y	Y	Y
Reid	Y	N	N	Y	Y	Y	Y
NEW HAMPSHIRE							
Gregg	N	Y	N	N	Y	Y	Y
Smith	N	Y	N	N	Y	Y	Y
NEW JERSEY							
Lautenberg	Y	N	N	Y	Y	Y	Y
Torricelli	Y	Y	N	Y	Y	Y	Y
NEW MEXICO							
Domenici	N	Y	Y	Y	Y	Y	Y
Bingaman	Y	N	Y	Y	Y	N	Y
NEW YORK							
D'Amato	N	Y	N	Y	Y	Y	Y
Moynihan	Y	Y	Y	Y	Y	Y	Y
NORTH CAROLINA							
Faircloth	N	Y	N	N	Y	Y	Y
Helms	–	+	–	–	+	+	+
NORTH DAKOTA							
Conrad	Y	N	N	Y	Y	Y	Y
Dorgan	Y	N	N	Y	Y	Y	Y
OHIO							
DeWine	N	Y	N	Y	Y	Y	Y
Glenn	Y	Y	Y	Y	Y	Y	Y
OKLAHOMA							
Inhofe	N	Y	N	N	Y	Y	Y
Nickles	N	Y	N	N	Y	Y	Y
OREGON							
Smith	N	Y	N	Y	Y	Y	Y
Wyden	Y	N	Y	Y	Y	Y	Y
PENNSYLVANIA							
Santorum	N	Y	N	Y	Y	Y	Y
Specter	N	Y	N	Y	Y	N	Y
RHODE ISLAND							
Chafee	N	Y	Y	Y	Y	Y	Y
Reed	Y	Y	Y	Y	Y	Y	Y
SOUTH CAROLINA							
Thurmond	N	Y	N	Y	Y	Y	Y
Hollings	Y	Y	Y	Y	Y	N	Y
SOUTH DAKOTA							
Daschle	Y	N	N	Y	Y	Y	Y
Johnson	Y	N	N	Y	Y	N	Y
TENNESSEE							
Frist	N	Y	N	N	Y	Y	Y
Thompson	N	Y	N	N	Y	Y	Y
TEXAS							
Gramm	N	Y	N	N	Y	Y	Y
Hutchison	N	Y	N	N	Y	N	Y
UTAH							
Bennett	N	Y	N	Y	Y	Y	Y
Hatch	N	Y	N	Y	Y	Y	Y
VERMONT							
Jeffords	N	N	Y	Y	Y	Y	Y
Leahy	Y	N	N	Y	Y	N	Y
VIRGINIA							
Warner	N	Y	N	Y	Y	Y	Y
Robb	Y	Y	Y	Y	Y	Y	Y
WASHINGTON							
Gorton	N	Y	N	N	Y	Y	Y
Murray	Y	Y	Y	Y	Y	Y	Y
WEST VIRGINIA							
Byrd	Y	Y	N	N	Y	N	Y
Rockefeller	Y	N	Y	Y	Y	Y	Y
WISCONSIN							
Feingold	Y	N	N	N	Y	N	N
Kohl	Y	N	N	Y	Y	Y	Y
WYOMING							
Enzi	N	Y	N	N	Y	Y	Y
Thomas	N	Y	Y	N	Y	Y	Y

Key

- Y Voted for (yea).
- # Paired for.
- + Announced for.
- N Voted against (nay).
- X Paired against.
- – Announced against.
- P Voted "present."
- C Voted "present" to avoid possible conflict of interest.
- ? Did not vote or otherwise make a position known.

• Democrats   • Republicans

ND Northern Democrats   SD Southern Democrats

Southern states - Ala., Ark., Fla., Ga., Ky., La., Miss., N.C., Okla., S.C., Tenn., Texas, Va.

246. S 2312. Fiscal 1999 Treasury-Postal Service-General Government Appropriations/FEC Term Limits. Glenn, D-Ohio, motion to table (kill) the McConnell, R-Ky., amendment that would impose four-year term limits on the staff director and the general counsel of the Federal Election Commission (FEC), though the officers could be elected to additional terms if four members of the six-member commission vote for reappointment. Motion rejected 45-54: R 0-54; D 45-0 (ND 37-0, SD 8-0). July 30, 1998. (Subsequently, the underlying bill, along with all pending amendments, were set aside.)

247. S 2132. Fiscal 1999 Defense Appropriations/Navy Aircraft Procurement. Stevens, R-Alaska, motion to table (kill) the Feingold, D-Wis., amendment that would reduce funding for the Navy's F/A-18 E and F aircraft procurement by $219.7 million (three planes) and redirect the funding to the operation and maintenance accounts of the National Guard. Motion agreed to 80-19: R 53-1; D 27-18 (ND 22-15, SD 5-3). July 30, 1998.

248. S 2132. Fiscal 1999 Defense Appropriations/Chinese Forced Abortions. Stevens, R-Alaska, motion to table (kill) the Hutchinson, R-Ark., amendment that would prohibit U.S. visas to Chinese officials involved in forced abortions, forced sterilizations or religious persecution. The president could waive the prohibition if he determines it is in the "national interest" to do so. Motion rejected 29-70: R 12-42; D 17-28 (ND 12-25, SD 5-3). July 30, 1998.

249. S 2132. Fiscal 1999 Defense Appropriations/Troops in Bosnia. McCain, R-Ariz., motion to table (kill) the Hutchison, R-Texas, amendment that would require the president to reduce U.S. combat forces in Bosnia to 6,500 by Feb. 2, 1999, and 5,000 by Oct. 1, 1999. Motion agreed to 68-31: R 26-28; D 42-3 (ND 34-3, SD 8-0). July 30, 1998. A "yea" was a vote in support of the president's position.

250. S 2132. Fiscal 1999 Defense Appropriations/Forced Abortions. Hutchinson, R-Ark., amendment to the Hutchinson amendment. The second-degree Hutchinson amendment would extend the underlying Hutchinson amendment to deny visas to officials of any country engaged in forced abortions, forced sterilizations or religious persecution. Adopted 99-0: R 54-0; D 45-0 (ND 37-0, SD 8-0). July 30, 1998. (Subsequently, the underlying Hutchinson amendment as amended was adopted by voice vote.)

251. S 2132. Fiscal 1999 Defense Appropriations/War Powers. Stevens, R-Alaska, motion to table (kill) the Durbin, D-Ill., amendment that would require that no funds be used to "initiate or conduct" U.S. military operations except in accordance with Article I, Section 8 of the Constitution, which vests in Congress the power to declare war and take other related actions. Motion agreed to 84-15: R 52-2; D 32-13 (ND 25-12, SD 7-1). July 30, 1998.

252. HR 4103. Fiscal 1999 Defense Appropriations/Passage. Passage of the bill to provide $252.4 billion in new budget authority for defense-related programs in fiscal 1999. The bill would provide $481 million less than requested by President Clinton and $4.7 billion more than provided in fiscal 1998. The bill would provide $48.6 billion for military procurement and $83.5 billion for Defense Department operations. Passed 97-2: R 54-0; D 43-2 (ND 35-2, SD 8-0). July 30, 1998. (Before passage, the Senate struck all after the enacting clause and inserted the text of S 2132 as amended.)

Senate Votes 253, 254, 255, 256, 257, 258, 259

	253	254	255	256	257	258	259
ALABAMA							
Sessions	Y	N	Y	N	N	Y	Y
Shelby	Y	N	Y	Y	N	Y	Y
ALASKA							
Murkowski	?	?	?	?	?	?	?
Stevens	Y	Y	Y	Y	N	Y	Y
ARIZONA							
Kyl	N	N	Y	N	N	Y	Y
McCain	N	N	Y	Y	N	Y	Y
ARKANSAS							
Hutchinson	Y	N	Y	N	N	Y	Y
Bumpers	Y	Y	Y	Y	N	Y	Y
CALIFORNIA							
Boxer	Y	Y	N	Y	N	N	Y
Feinstein	Y	Y	Y	Y	N	N	Y
COLORADO							
Allard	Y	N	Y	N	N	Y	Y
Campbell	Y	Y	Y	N	N	Y	Y
CONNECTICUT							
Dodd	Y	Y	Y	Y	N	N	Y
Lieberman	Y	Y	Y	Y	Y	N	Y
DELAWARE							
Roth	Y	N	Y	N	N	Y	Y
Biden	Y	Y	Y	Y	Y	N	Y
FLORIDA							
Mack	Y	N	N	N	N	Y	Y
Graham	Y	Y	Y	Y	N	N	Y
GEORGIA							
Coverdell	+	N	?	?	?	?	?
Cleland	Y	Y	Y	Y	Y	N	Y
HAWAII							
Akaka	Y	Y	N	Y	Y	N	Y
Inouye	?	?	?	?	?	?	?
IDAHO							
Craig	Y	N	Y	N	N	Y	Y
Kempthorne	Y	N	Y	Y	?	Y	Y
ILLINOIS							
Durbin	Y	Y	N	N	N	N	Y
Moseley-Braun	Y	Y	N	Y	N	N	Y
INDIANA							
Coats	Y	N	Y	Y	N	Y	Y
Lugar	Y	N	Y	Y	N	Y	Y

	253	254	255	256	257	258	259
IOWA							
Grassley	Y	N	Y	N	N	Y	Y
Harkin	Y	Y	N	N	N	N	Y
KANSAS							
Brownback	Y	N	Y	Y	–	Y	Y
Roberts	Y	N	Y	N	N	Y	Y
KENTUCKY							
McConnell	Y	N	Y	N	N	Y	Y
Ford	Y	Y	Y	Y	N	N	Y
LOUISIANA							
Breaux	Y	Y	Y	Y	N	N	Y
Landrieu	Y	Y	Y	Y	N	N	Y
MAINE							
Collins	Y	N	Y	Y	N	Y	Y
Snowe	Y	N	Y	Y	N	Y	Y
MARYLAND							
Mikulski	Y	Y	Y	Y	N	N	Y
Sarbanes	Y	Y	Y	Y	N	N	Y
MASSACHUSETTS							
Kennedy	Y	Y	Y	Y	N	N	Y
Kerry	Y	Y	Y	Y	N	N	Y
MICHIGAN							
Abraham	Y	N	Y	N	N	Y	Y
Levin	Y	Y	Y	Y	Y	N	Y
MINNESOTA							
Grams	Y	N	Y	N	N	Y	Y
Wellstone	Y	Y	N	Y	Y	Y	Y
MISSISSIPPI							
Cochran	Y	N	Y	N	N	Y	Y
Lott	Y	N	Y	N	Y	Y	Y
MISSOURI							
Ashcroft	Y	N	Y	N	N	Y	Y
Bond	Y	N	Y	N	N	Y	Y
MONTANA							
Burns	Y	N	Y	N	N	Y	Y
Baucus	Y	Y	Y	Y	N	N	Y
NEBRASKA							
Hagel	Y	N	Y	N	N	Y	Y
Kerrey	Y	Y	Y	Y	N	N	Y
NEVADA							
Bryan	Y	Y	N	Y	N	N	Y
Reid	Y	Y	N	Y	N	N	Y

	253	254	255	256	257	258	259
NEW HAMPSHIRE							
Gregg	Y	N	Y	Y	N	Y	Y
Smith	Y	N	Y	N	N	Y	N
NEW JERSEY							
Lautenberg	Y	Y	Y	N	N	N	Y
Torricelli	Y	Y	Y	Y	N	N	Y
NEW MEXICO							
Domenici	?	?	?	?	?	?	?
Bingaman	?	?	?	?	?	?	?
NEW YORK							
D'Amato	Y	Y	Y	Y	N	Y	Y
Moynihan	Y	Y	Y	Y	N	N	Y
NORTH CAROLINA							
Faircloth	Y	N	Y	N	N	Y	N
Helms	+	–	+	–	–	+	–
NORTH DAKOTA							
Conrad	Y	Y	Y	Y	N	N	Y
Dorgan	Y	Y	Y	Y	N	N	Y
OHIO							
DeWine	Y	N	Y	Y	N	Y	Y
Glenn	?	?	?	?	?	?	?
OKLAHOMA							
Inhofe	Y	N	Y	N	N	Y	Y
Nickles	Y	N	Y	N	N	Y	Y
OREGON							
Smith	Y	N	Y	N	N	Y	Y
Wyden	Y	Y	N	Y	N	N	Y
PENNSYLVANIA							
Santorum	Y	N	Y	N	N	Y	Y
Specter	Y	Y	Y	Y	Y	Y	Y
RHODE ISLAND							
Chafee	Y	Y	Y	Y	N	Y	Y
Reed	Y	Y	N	Y	N	N	Y
SOUTH CAROLINA							
Thurmond	Y	N	Y	N	N	Y	Y
Hollings	+	Y	Y	Y	N	N	Y
SOUTH DAKOTA							
Daschle	Y	Y	Y	Y	Y	N	Y
Johnson	Y	Y	Y	Y	N	N	Y
TENNESSEE							
Frist	Y	N	Y	N	N	Y	Y
Thompson	Y	N	Y	N	N	Y	Y

Key

Y Voted for (yea).
Paired for.
+ Announced for.
N Voted against (nay).
X Paired against.
– Announced against.
P Voted "present."
C Voted "present" to avoid possible conflict of interest.
? Did not vote or otherwise make a position known.

Democrats   **Republicans**

	253	254	255	256	257	258	259
TEXAS							
Gramm	?	?	Y	Y	N	Y	Y
Hutchison	Y	N	Y	N	N	Y	Y
UTAH							
Bennett	Y	Y	Y	Y	N	Y	Y
Hatch	Y	N	Y	N	N	Y	Y
VERMONT							
Jeffords	Y	Y	Y	Y	N	N	Y
Leahy	Y	Y	Y	Y	Y	N	Y
VIRGINIA							
Warner	?	N	Y	Y	N	Y	Y
Robb	N	Y	Y	N	N	N	Y
WASHINGTON							
Gorton	Y	N	Y	N	N	Y	Y
Murray	Y	Y	Y	Y	N	N	Y
WEST VIRGINIA							
Byrd	Y	Y	Y	N	N	N	N
Rockefeller	Y	Y	Y	Y	N	N	Y
WISCONSIN							
Feingold	Y	N	Y	N	N	N	Y
Kohl	Y	Y	Y	Y	Y	N	Y
WYOMING							
Enzi	Y	N	Y	N	N	Y	Y
Thomas	Y	N	Y	N	N	Y	Y

ND Northern Democrats   SD Southern Democrats

Southern states - Ala., Ark., Fla., Ga., Ky., La., Miss., N.C., Okla., S.C., Tenn., Texas, Va.

253. HR 4059. Fiscal 1999 Military Construction Appropriations/Conference Report. Adoption of the conference report on the bill to provide $8.45 billion in new budget authority for military construction projects in fiscal 1999. It would provide $759 million less than provided in fiscal 1998 and $666 million more than requested by President Clinton. Adopted (thus cleared for the president) 87-3: R 47-2; D 40-1 (ND 34-0, SD 6-1). Sept. 1, 1998.

254. S 2334. Fiscal 1999 Foreign Operations Appropriations/Nuclear Test Ban Funding. Specter, R-Pa., amendment that would add $28.9 million for expenses related to the Comprehensive Nuclear Test Ban Treaty Preparatory Commission. The Senate has not yet ratified the test ban treaty (Treaty Doc. 105-28). Adopted 49-44: R 7-44; D 42-0 (ND 34-0, SD 8-0). Sept. 1, 1998. A "yea" was a vote in support of the president's position.

255. HR 629. Texas, Maine and Vermont Low-Level Radioactive Waste Compact/Conference Report. Adoption of the conference report on the bill that would allow Maine and Vermont to export low-level radioactive waste to Texas. Adopted (thus cleared for the president) 78-15: R 51-0; D 27-15 (ND 19-15, SD 8-0). Sept. 2, 1998.

256. S 2334. Fiscal 1999 Foreign Operations Appropriations/IMF Lending Requirements. Hagel, R-Neb., motion to table (kill) the Kyl, R-Ariz., amendment that would replace previously passed language in the bill regarding conditions on the International Monetary Fund's use of U.S. quota resources with more restrictive language. Motion agreed to 74-19: R 33-18; D 41-1 (ND 33-1, SD 8-0). Sept. 2, 1998.

257. S 2334. Fiscal 1999 Foreign Operations Appropriations/North Korean Nuclear Development. McConnell, R-Ky., motion to table (kill) the McCain, R-Ariz., amendment that would restrict funds for the Korean Peninsula Energy Development Organization unless the president certifies that North Korea is not actively pursuing the acquisition or development of nuclear weapons. Motion rejected 11-80: R 1-48; D 10-32 (ND 9-25, SD 1-7). Sept. 2, 1998. (Subsequently, the McCain amendment as amended was adopted by voice vote.)

258. S 2334. Fiscal 1999 Foreign Operations Appropriations/Guatemala and Honduras Human Rights Records Declassification. McConnell, R-Ky., motion to table (kill) the Dodd, D-Conn., amendment that would establish a procedure for the declassification of documents related to human rights violations in Guatemala and Honduras. Motion agreed to 50-43: R 50-1; D 0-42 (ND 0-34, SD 0-8). Sept. 2, 1998.

259. S 2334. Fiscal 1999 Foreign Operations Appropriations/Passage. Passage of the bill to provide $12.6 billion in new budget authority for foreign affairs programs in fiscal 1999, plus an additional $18 billion for the International Monetary Fund and $311 million in arrears to multilateral institutions. Passed 90-3: R 49-2; D 41-1 (ND 33-1, SD 8-0). Sept. 2, 1998.

Senate Votes 260, 261, 262, 263, 264, 265, 266

	260	261	262	263	264	265	266
ALABAMA							
Sessions	Y	N	Y	Y	N	Y	Y
Shelby	Y	N	Y	N	Y	Y	Y
ALASKA							
Murkowski	?	N	Y	Y	N	Y	Y
Stevens	Y	N	Y	N	Y	Y	Y
ARIZONA							
Kyl	Y	N	Y	Y	N	Y	Y
McCain	Y	N	Y	Y	Y	Y	Y
ARKANSAS							
Hutchinson	N	N	Y	N	Y	Y	Y
Bumpers	Y	N	N	Y	Y	Y	N
CALIFORNIA							
Boxer	Y	N	N	Y	Y	Y	N
Feinstein	Y	?	N	Y	Y	Y	N
COLORADO							
Allard	Y	N	Y	Y	N	Y	Y
Campbell	Y	N	Y	N	Y	Y	N
CONNECTICUT							
Dodd	Y	?	N	Y	Y	Y	N
Lieberman	Y	N	Y	Y	Y	Y	N
DELAWARE							
Roth	Y	N	Y	N	Y	Y	Y
Biden	Y	?	N	Y	Y	Y	N
FLORIDA							
Mack	Y	N	Y	N	Y	Y	Y
Graham	Y	N	N	Y	Y	Y	N
GEORGIA							
Coverdell	Y	N	Y	N	Y	Y	Y
Cleland	Y	N	N	Y	Y	Y	N
HAWAII							
Akaka	Y	N	Y	Y	Y	Y	N
Inouye	?	N	Y	Y	Y	Y	N
IDAHO							
Craig	Y	N	Y	N	Y	Y	Y
Kempthorne	Y	?	Y	N	Y	Y	Y
ILLINOIS							
Durbin	Y	N	N	Y	Y	Y	N
Moseley-Braun	Y	?	N	Y	Y	?	?
INDIANA							
Coats	Y	N	Y	N	Y	Y	Y
Lugar	Y	N	Y	N	Y	Y	Y

	260	261	262	263	264	265	266
IOWA							
Grassley	Y	N	Y	Y	N	Y	Y
Harkin	Y	N	Y	N	Y	Y	N
KANSAS							
Brownback	N	N	Y	N	Y	Y	Y
Roberts	Y	N	Y	N	Y	Y	Y
KENTUCKY							
McConnell	Y	N	Y	N	Y	Y	Y
Ford	Y	N	N	Y	Y	Y	N
LOUISIANA							
Breaux	Y	N	Y	Y	Y	Y	N
Landrieu	Y	?	N	Y	Y	Y	Y
MAINE							
Collins	Y	N	Y	Y	Y	Y	Y
Snowe	Y	N	Y	Y	Y	Y	Y
MARYLAND							
Mikulski	Y	N	N	Y	Y	Y	?
Sarbanes	Y	N	N	Y	Y	Y	N
MASSACHUSETTS							
Kennedy	Y	?	N	Y	Y	Y	N
Kerry	Y	N	N	Y	Y	Y	N
MICHIGAN							
Abraham	Y	N	Y	Y	N	Y	Y
Levin	Y	N	N	Y	Y	Y	N
MINNESOTA							
Grams	Y	?	Y	Y	N	Y	Y
Wellstone	Y	N	N	Y	Y	Y	N
MISSISSIPPI							
Cochran	Y	N	Y	N	Y	Y	Y
Lott	Y	N	Y	N	Y	N	Y
MISSOURI							
Ashcroft	N	N	Y	N	Y	Y	Y
Bond	Y	N	Y	N	Y	N	Y
MONTANA							
Burns	Y	N	Y	Y	N	Y	Y
Baucus	Y	N	Y	Y	Y	Y	Y
NEBRASKA							
Hagel	Y	N	Y	Y	N	Y	Y
Kerrey	Y	N	N	Y	Y	?	N
NEVADA							
Bryan	Y	N	N	Y	Y	Y	N
Reid	Y	N	N	Y	Y	Y	N

	260	261	262	263	264	265	266
NEW HAMPSHIRE							
Gregg	Y	?	Y	Y	N	Y	Y
Smith	N	N	Y	Y	N	Y	Y
NEW JERSEY							
Lautenberg	Y	?	N	Y	Y	Y	N
Torricelli	Y	N	N	Y	Y	Y	?
NEW MEXICO							
Domenici	Y	N	Y	N	Y	Y	Y
Bingaman	?	N	N	Y	Y	Y	N
NEW YORK							
D'Amato	Y	N	Y	Y	N	Y	?
Moynihan	Y	N	N	Y	Y	Y	N
NORTH CAROLINA							
Faircloth	Y	N	Y	N	Y	Y	Y
Helms	+	N	Y	N	Y	Y	Y
NORTH DAKOTA							
Conrad	Y	N	N	Y	Y	Y	N
Dorgan	Y	N	N	Y	Y	Y	N
OHIO							
DeWine	Y	N	Y	N	Y	Y	Y
Glenn	Y	N	N	Y	Y	Y	N
OKLAHOMA							
Inhofe	Y	N	Y	N	Y	Y	Y
Nickles	Y	N	Y	Y	N	Y	Y
OREGON							
Smith	Y	N	Y	N	Y	Y	Y
Wyden	Y	?	N	Y	Y	Y	N
PENNSYLVANIA							
Santorum	Y	?	Y	Y	N	Y	Y
Specter	Y	N	Y	Y	Y	Y	?
RHODE ISLAND							
Chafee	Y	?	Y	Y	Y	Y	?
Reed	Y	N	N	Y	Y	Y	N
SOUTH CAROLINA							
Thurmond	Y	N	Y	N	Y	Y	Y
Hollings	Y	?	Y	Y	Y	Y	?
SOUTH DAKOTA							
Daschle	Y	N	N	Y	Y	Y	N
Johnson	Y	N	N	Y	Y	Y	N
TENNESSEE							
Frist	Y	N	Y	N	Y	Y	Y
Thompson	Y	N	Y	Y	Y	Y	Y

	260	261	262	263	264	265	266
TEXAS							
Gramm	Y	N	Y	Y	N	Y	Y
Hutchison	Y	?	Y	Y	N	Y	Y
UTAH							
Bennett	Y	N	Y	Y	N	Y	Y
Hatch	Y	N	Y	Y	N	Y	Y
VERMONT							
Jeffords	Y	N	Y	Y	Y	Y	Y
Leahy	Y	?	N	Y	Y	Y	N
VIRGINIA							
Warner	Y	N	Y	N	Y	Y	Y
Robb	Y	N	N	Y	Y	Y	N
WASHINGTON							
Gorton	Y	N	Y	N	Y	Y	Y
Murray	Y	?	N	Y	Y	Y	N
WEST VIRGINIA							
Byrd	Y	N	N	Y	Y	Y	N
Rockefeller	Y	N	N	Y	Y	?	N
WISCONSIN							
Feingold	N	N	N	Y	Y	Y	N
Kohl	Y	N	N	Y	Y	Y	N
WYOMING							
Enzi	Y	N	Y	N	Y	Y	Y
Thomas	Y	N	Y	N	Y	Y	Y

Key

Y Voted for (yea).
Paired for.
+ Announced for.
N Voted against (nay).
X Paired against.
− Announced against.
P Voted "present."
C Voted "present" to avoid possible conflict of interest.
? Did not vote or otherwise make a position known.

• Democrats   *Republicans*

ND Northern Democrats   SD Southern Democrats

Southern states - Ala., Ark., Fla., Ga., Ky., La., Miss., N.C., Okla., S.C., Tenn., Texas, Va.

260. HR 4104. Fiscal 1999 Treasury-Postal Service Appropriations/Passage. Passage of the bill to provide $29.9 billion in new budget authority for the Treasury Department, the White House, postal subsidies and civil service benefits in fiscal 1999. The bill would provide $4.6 billion more than in fiscal 1998 and $3.1 billion more than requested by President Clinton. It would provide a 3.6 percent cost of living adjustment for federal workers. Passed 91-5: R 49-4; D 42-1 (ND 34-1, SD 8-0). Sept. 3, 1998. (Before passage, the Senate struck all after the enacting clause and inserted the text of S2312 as amended.)

261. S 2237. Fiscal 1999 Interior Appropriations/Civil War Battlefield Preservation. Gorton, R-Wash., motion to table (kill) the Jeffords, R-Vt., amendment that would provide up to $10 million for matching grants to states and localities for the preservation of Civil War battlefields. Motion rejected 0-83: R 0-49; D 0-34 (ND 0-28, SD 0-6). Sept. 8, 1998.

262. S 1873. National Missile Defense/Cloture. Motion to invoke cloture (thus limiting debate) on the motion to proceed to the bill that would make it U.S. policy to implement a national missile defense shield. The measure would not establish a specific time frame, but would declare a national policy to deploy a system to protect U.S. territory from a limited number of incoming missiles "as soon as is technologically possible." Motion rejected 59-41: R 55-0; D 4-41 (ND 3-34, SD 1-7). Sept. 9, 1998. Three-fifths of the total Senate (60) is required to invoke cloture. A "nay" was a vote in support of the president's position.

263. S 1301. Consumer Bankruptcy Revisions/Cloture. Motion to invoke cloture (thus limiting debate) on the motion to proceed to the bill that would revise the nation's bankruptcy laws by allowing a bankruptcy judge to dismiss any claim for Chapter 7 relief, or convert the claim to a Chapter 13 case, if the judge determines that the debtor has sufficient income to pay at least 20 percent of his unsecured debts. The bill also would allow creditors, in addition to bankruptcy trustees and judges, to challenge the validity of an individual's claim. Motion agreed to 99-1: R 54-1; D 45-0 (ND 37-0, SD 8-0). Sept. 9, 1998. Three-fifths of the total Senate (60) is required to invoke cloture. (Subsequently, the motion to proceed was agreed to by voice vote.)

264. S 2237. Fiscal 1999 Interior Appropriations/Campaign Finance Revisions — Cloture. Motion to invoke cloture (thus limiting debate) on the McCain, R-Ariz., amendment that would overhaul laws governing the financing of federal political campaigns. Motion rejected 52-48: R 7-48; D 45-0 (ND 37-0, SD 8-0). Sept. 10, 1998. Three-fifths of the total Senate (60) is required to invoke cloture. A "yea" was a vote in support of the president's position.

265. S 1645. Transporting Minors for an Abortion/Cloture. Motion to invoke cloture (thus limiting debate) on the motion to proceed to the bill that would make it a federal crime for anyone other than the parent to transport a minor across state lines with the intent to obtain an abortion. Motion agreed to 97-0: R 55-0; D 42-0 (ND 34-0, SD 8-0). Sept. 11, 1998. Three-fifths of the total Senate (60) is required to invoke cloture.

266. S 1981. Labor Union Organizing Curbs/Cloture. Motion to invoke cloture (thus limiting debate) on the motion to proceed to the bill that would permit employers to refuse to hire, or fire, individuals who seek employment with the primary intent of organizing workers to join a labor union. Motion rejected 52-42: R 52-1; D 0-41 (ND 0-34, SD 0-7). Sept. 14, 1998. Three-fifths of the total Senate (60) is required to invoke cloture. A "nay" was a vote in support of the president's position.

Senate Votes 267, 268, 269, 270, 271, 272, 273

	267	268	269	270	271	272	273
ALABAMA							
Sessions	Y	Y	N	?	Y	Y	Y
Shelby	Y	Y	N	?	Y	Y	Y
ALASKA							
Murkowski	Y	Y	Y	Y	Y	Y	N
Stevens	Y	Y	Y	Y	Y	Y	Y
ARIZONA							
Kyl	Y	Y	N	Y	Y	Y	Y
McCain	Y	Y	N	Y	Y	Y	Y
ARKANSAS							
Hutchinson	Y	Y	N	Y	Y	Y	Y
Bumpers	N	N	Y	?	Y	N	N
CALIFORNIA							
Boxer	N	N	Y	Y	Y	N	N
Feinstein	N	N	Y	Y	Y	N	N
COLORADO							
Allard	Y	Y	N	Y	Y	Y	Y
Campbell	Y	Y	Y	Y	Y	Y	N
CONNECTICUT							
Dodd	N	N	Y	Y	Y	N	N
Lieberman	N	N	Y	Y	Y	N	N
DELAWARE							
Roth	Y	N	N	Y	Y	Y	N
Biden	N	N	Y	Y	Y	N	N
FLORIDA							
Mack	Y	Y	N	Y	Y	Y	Y
Graham	N	N	Y	Y	Y	N	N
GEORGIA							
Coverdell	Y	Y	N	Y	Y	Y	Y
Cleland	N	Y	Y	Y	Y	N	N
HAWAII							
Akaka	N	N	Y	Y	Y	N	N
Inouye	N	Y	Y	Y	Y	N	N
IDAHO							
Craig	Y	Y	Y	Y	Y	Y	Y
Kempthorne	Y	Y	Y	Y	Y	Y	Y
ILLINOIS							
Durbin	N	N	Y	Y	Y	N	N
Moseley-Braun	–	N	Y	Y	Y	N	N
INDIANA							
Coats	Y	N	N	Y	Y	Y	Y
Lugar	Y	Y	Y	Y	Y	Y	Y

	267	268	269	270	271	272	273
IOWA							
Grassley	Y	Y	Y	Y	Y	Y	Y
Harkin	N	N	Y	Y	Y	N	N
KANSAS							
Brownback	Y	Y	N	Y	Y	Y	Y
Roberts	Y	Y	Y	Y	Y	Y	Y
KENTUCKY							
McConnell	Y	Y	N	Y	Y	Y	Y
Ford	N	N	Y	Y	Y	N	N
LOUISIANA							
Breaux	N	Y	Y	N	N	N	N
Landrieu	N	N	Y	Y	Y	N	N
MAINE							
Collins	Y	N	Y	Y	Y	Y	Y
Snowe	Y	N	Y	Y	Y	Y	Y
MARYLAND							
Mikulski	?	?	?	Y	Y	N	N
Sarbanes	N	N	Y	Y	Y	N	N
MASSACHUSETTS							
Kennedy	N	N	Y	Y	Y	N	N
Kerry	N	N	Y	Y	Y	N	N
MICHIGAN							
Abraham	Y	N	Y	Y	Y	Y	Y
Levin	N	N	Y	Y	Y	N	N
MINNESOTA							
Grams	Y	Y	N	Y	Y	Y	Y
Wellstone	N	N	Y	Y	Y	N	N
MISSISSIPPI							
Cochran	Y	Y	N	Y	Y	Y	Y
Lott	Y	Y	N	Y	Y	Y	Y
MISSOURI							
Ashcroft	Y	Y	N	Y	Y	Y	Y
Bond	Y	Y	Y	Y	Y	Y	N
MONTANA							
Burns	N	Y	N	Y	Y	Y	Y
Baucus	N	Y	Y	Y	Y	N	N
NEBRASKA							
Hagel	Y	Y	N	Y	Y	Y	Y
Kerrey	N	N	Y	Y	Y	N	N
NEVADA							
Bryan	N	Y	Y	Y	Y	N	N
Reid	N	Y	Y	Y	Y	N	N

	267	268	269	270	271	272	273
NEW HAMPSHIRE							
Gregg	Y	N	Y	Y	Y	Y	Y
Smith	Y	Y	N	Y	Y	Y	Y
NEW JERSEY							
Lautenberg	N	N	Y	Y	N	N	N
Torricelli	?	N	Y	Y	N	N	N
NEW MEXICO							
Domenici	Y	Y	Y	Y	Y	Y	Y
Bingaman	N	Y	Y	Y	Y	N	N
NEW YORK							
D'Amato	?	Y	Y	Y	Y	Y	N
Moynihan	N	Y	Y	Y	Y	N	N
NORTH CAROLINA							
Faircloth	Y	Y	N	Y	Y	Y	Y
Helms	Y	Y	N	?	?	?	Y
NORTH DAKOTA							
Conrad	N	Y	Y	Y	N	N	N
Dorgan	N	Y	Y	Y	N	N	N
OHIO							
DeWine	Y	Y	N	Y	Y	Y	Y
Glenn	N	N	Y	Y	Y	N	N
OKLAHOMA							
Inhofe	Y	Y	N	Y	Y	Y	Y
Nickles	Y	Y	N	Y	Y	Y	Y
OREGON							
Smith	Y	Y	Y	Y	Y	Y	Y
Wyden	N	N	Y	Y	Y	N	N
PENNSYLVANIA							
Santorum	Y	Y	N	Y	Y	Y	Y
Specter	?	N	Y	Y	Y	Y	N
RHODE ISLAND							
Chafee	Y	N	Y	Y	Y	Y	Y
Reed	N	N	Y	Y	Y	N	N
SOUTH CAROLINA							
Thurmond	Y	Y	Y	Y	Y	Y	Y
Hollings	?	?	?	?	?	?	?
SOUTH DAKOTA							
Daschle	N	Y	Y	Y	N	N	N
Johnson	N	N	Y	Y	Y	N	N
TENNESSEE							
Frist	Y	Y	Y	Y	Y	Y	Y
Thompson	Y	Y	N	Y	Y	Y	Y

Key

- Y Voted for (yea).
- # Paired for.
- + Announced for.
- N Voted against (nay).
- X Paired against.
- – Announced against.
- P Voted "present."
- C Voted "present" to avoid possible conflict of interest.
- ? Did not vote or otherwise make a position known.

Democrats • Republicans

	267	268	269	270	271	272	273
TEXAS							
Gramm	Y	Y	N	Y	Y	Y	Y
Hutchison	Y	Y	Y	Y	Y	Y	N
UTAH							
Bennett	Y	Y	Y	Y	Y	Y	Y
Hatch	Y	Y	Y	Y	Y	Y	Y
VERMONT							
Jeffords	Y	N	Y	Y	Y	Y	N
Leahy	N	N	Y	Y	Y	N	N
VIRGINIA							
Warner	Y	N	Y	Y	Y	Y	Y
Robb	N	N	Y	Y	Y	N	N
WASHINGTON							
Gorton	Y	Y	Y	Y	Y	Y	Y
Murray	N	N	Y	Y	Y	N	N
WEST VIRGINIA							
Byrd	N	Y	Y	Y	Y	N	N
Rockefeller	N	N	Y	Y	Y	N	N
WISCONSIN							
Feingold	Y	N	Y	Y	Y	N	N
Kohl	N	N	Y	Y	Y	N	N
WYOMING							
Enzi	Y	Y	Y	Y	Y	Y	Y
Thomas	Y	Y	Y	Y	Y	Y	Y

ND Northern Democrats   SD Southern Democrats

Southern states - Ala., Ark., Fla., Ga., Ky., La., Miss., N.C., Okla., S.C., Tenn., Texas, Va.

267. S 2237. Fiscal 1999 Interior Appropriations/Agriculture Marketing Loans. Lugar, R-Ind., motion to table (kill) the Daschle, D-S.D., amendment that would lift the cap on agriculture commodity marketing loans imposed by the 1996 farm law (PL 104-127) for one year. The new loan rate would be based on 85 percent of the average price of the product for the past five years, not including the highest and lowest years. The amendment also would give the Agriculture Department authority to extend the marketing loan term from nine months to 15 months for one year. Motion agreed to 53-41: R 52-1; D 1-40 (ND 1-33, SD 0-7). Sept. 14, 1998.

268. S 2237. Fiscal 1999 Interior Appropriations/Mining Regulations. Murkowski, R-Alaska, motion to table (kill) the Bumpers, D-Ark., amendment to remove language in the bill that would prohibit the Interior Department from implementing proposed mining regulations until the National Academy of Sciences conducts a study of existing regulations governing mining on public lands. Motion agreed to 58-40: R 45-10; D 13-30 (ND 10-26, SD 3-4). Sept. 15, 1998.

269. S 2237. Fiscal 1999 Interior Appropriations/NEA Funding. Gorton, R-Wash., motion to table (kill) the Ashcroft, R-Mo., amendment that would eliminate funding for programs and activities carried out by the National Endowment for the Arts and transfer the $100 million taken from the NEA to the National Park Service. Motion agreed to 76-22: R 33-22; D 43-0 (ND 36-0, SD 7-0). Sept. 15, 1998.

270. Procedural Motion. Lott, R-Miss., motion to instruct the sergeant-at-arms to request the attendance of absent senators. Motion agreed to 94-1: R 52-0; D 42-1 (ND 37-0, SD 5-1). Sept. 16, 1998.

271. Procedural Motion. Lott, R-Miss., motion to instruct the sergeant-at-arms to request the attendance of absent senators. Motion agreed to 97-1: R 54-0; D 43-1 (ND 37-0, SD 6-1). Sept. 16, 1998.

272. Procedural Motion/Adjourn. Lott, R-Miss., motion to adjourn. Motion agreed to 55-43: R 54-0; D 1-43 (ND 1-36, SD 0-7). Sept. 16, 1998.

273. S 1301. Consumer Bankruptcy Revisions/Credit Card Finance Charges. Grassley, R-Iowa, motion to table (kill) the Reed, D-R.I., amendment that would prohibit credit card companies from terminating or refusing to renew credit to consumers who avoid finance charges by paying off their balances. The amendment also would prohibit creditors from charging such consumers a fee in lieu of finance charges. Motion rejected 47-52: R 47-8; D 0-44 (ND 0-37, SD 0-7). Sept. 17, 1998. (Subsequently, the amendment was adopted by voice vote.)

Senate Votes 274, 275, 276, 277, 278, 279, 280

	274	275	276	277	278	279	280
ALABAMA							
Sessions	Y	Y	?	Y	Y	Y	Y
Shelby	Y	Y	?	Y	Y	N	Y
ALASKA							
Murkowski	Y	Y	Y	Y	Y	Y	Y
Stevens	Y	Y	Y	Y	Y	Y	Y
ARIZONA							
Kyl	Y	Y	Y	Y	Y	Y	Y
McCain	Y	N	Y	Y	Y	Y	Y
ARKANSAS							
Hutchinson	Y	Y	Y	Y	Y	Y	Y
Bumpers	N	N	Y	N	N	N	N
CALIFORNIA							
Boxer	N	N	Y	N	N	N	N
Feinstein	N	N	Y	N	N	N	N
COLORADO							
Allard	Y	Y	Y	Y	Y	Y	Y
Campbell	Y	Y	Y	Y	Y	Y	Y
CONNECTICUT							
Dodd	N	N	Y	N	N	N	N
Lieberman	N	N	Y	N	N	N	N
DELAWARE							
Roth	Y	Y	Y	Y	Y	Y	Y
Biden	Y	Y	Y	Y	N	N	N
FLORIDA							
Mack	Y	Y	Y	Y	Y	Y	Y
Graham	N	Y	Y	N	Y	N	N
GEORGIA							
Coverdell	?	?	Y	Y	Y	Y	Y
Cleland	N	Y	Y	N	N	N	N
HAWAII							
Akaka	N	Y	Y	N	N	N	N
Inouye	N	Y	?	N	N	N	N
IDAHO							
Craig	Y	Y	Y	Y	Y	Y	Y
Kempthorne	Y	Y	Y	Y	Y	Y	Y
ILLINOIS							
Durbin	N	N	Y	N	N	N	N
Moseley-Braun	N	N	Y	N	N	N	N
INDIANA							
Coats	N	Y	?	Y	Y	Y	Y
Lugar	Y	Y	Y	Y	Y	Y	Y
IOWA							
Grassley	Y	Y	Y	Y	Y	Y	Y
Harkin	N	N	Y	N	N	N	N
KANSAS							
Brownback	Y	Y	Y	Y	Y	Y	Y
Roberts	Y	Y	Y	Y	Y	Y	Y
KENTUCKY							
McConnell	Y	Y	Y	Y	Y	Y	Y
Ford	N	Y	Y	Y	N	N	N
LOUISIANA							
Breaux	N	Y	Y	Y	N	Y	N
Landrieu	N	Y	Y	Y	N	N	N
MAINE							
Collins	Y	Y	Y	N	Y	Y	N
Snowe	Y	Y	Y	N	Y	Y	N
MARYLAND							
Mikulski	N	N	Y	N	N	N	N
Sarbanes	N	N	Y	N	N	N	N
MASSACHUSETTS							
Kennedy	N	N	?	N	N	N	N
Kerry	N	N	?	N	N	N	N
MICHIGAN							
Abraham	Y	Y	Y	Y	Y	Y	Y
Levin	N	N	?	N	N	N	N
MINNESOTA							
Grams	Y	Y	Y	Y	Y	Y	Y
Wellstone	N	N	Y	N	N	N	N
MISSISSIPPI							
Cochran	Y	Y	Y	Y	Y	Y	Y
Lott	Y	Y	Y	Y	Y	Y	Y
MISSOURI							
Ashcroft	Y	Y	Y	Y	Y	Y	Y
Bond	Y	Y	Y	Y	Y	Y	Y
MONTANA							
Burns	Y	Y	Y	Y	Y	Y	Y
Baucus	N	Y	Y	N	N	N	N
NEBRASKA							
Hagel	Y	Y	Y	Y	Y	Y	Y
Kerrey	N	Y	Y	N	N	N	N
NEVADA							
Bryan	N	N	Y	N	N	Y	N
Reid	Y	Y	Y	Y	N	Y	N
NEW HAMPSHIRE							
Gregg	Y	Y	Y	Y	Y	Y	Y
Smith	Y	Y	Y	Y	Y	Y	Y
NEW JERSEY							
Lautenberg	N	N	Y	N	N	N	N
Torricelli	N	N	Y	N	N	N	N
NEW MEXICO							
Domenici	Y	Y	Y	Y	Y	Y	N
Bingaman	N	N	Y	N	N	N	N
NEW YORK							
D'Amato	N	N	Y	Y	N	Y	N
Moynihan	N	N	+	Y	N	N	N
NORTH CAROLINA							
Faircloth	Y	Y	Y	Y	Y	Y	Y
Helms	Y	Y	?	Y	Y	Y	Y
NORTH DAKOTA							
Conrad	N	Y	Y	N	N	N	N
Dorgan	N	Y	Y	N	N	N	N
OHIO							
DeWine	Y	Y	Y	Y	Y	Y	Y
Glenn	Y	N	Y	N	?	?	?
OKLAHOMA							
Inhofe	Y	Y	Y	Y	Y	Y	Y
Nickles	Y	Y	Y	Y	Y	Y	Y
OREGON							
Smith	N	Y	Y	Y	Y	Y	N
Wyden	N	Y	Y	N	N	N	N
PENNSYLVANIA							
Santorum	Y	Y	Y	Y	Y	Y	Y
Specter	Y	Y	Y	Y	N	N	N
RHODE ISLAND							
Chafee	Y	N	Y	N	Y	Y	N
Reed	N	Y	Y	N	N	N	N
SOUTH CAROLINA							
Thurmond	Y	Y	Y	Y	Y	Y	Y
Hollings	?	?	?	Y	Y	N	N
SOUTH DAKOTA							
Daschle	N	Y	Y	Y	N	N	N
Johnson	Y	Y	Y	Y	N	N	N
TENNESSEE							
Frist	Y	Y	Y	Y	Y	Y	Y
Thompson	Y	Y	Y	Y	Y	Y	Y
TEXAS							
Gramm	Y	Y	Y	Y	Y	Y	Y
Hutchison	Y	Y	Y	Y	Y	Y	Y
UTAH							
Bennett	Y	Y	Y	Y	Y	Y	Y
Hatch	Y	Y	Y	Y	Y	Y	Y
VERMONT							
Jeffords	Y	Y	Y	N	Y	Y	N
Leahy	N	Y	Y	N	N	N	N
VIRGINIA							
Warner	Y	Y	Y	Y	Y	Y	Y
Robb	Y	Y	Y	N	N	N	N
WASHINGTON							
Gorton	Y	Y	Y	Y	Y	Y	Y
Murray	N	N	Y	N	N	N	N
WEST VIRGINIA							
Byrd	N	Y	Y	N	Y	N	Y
Rockefeller	N	Y	Y	N	N	N	N
WISCONSIN							
Feingold	Y	N	Y	N	N	N	N
Kohl	Y	N	Y	N	N	N	N
WYOMING							
Enzi	Y	Y	?	Y	Y	Y	Y
Thomas	Y	Y	Y	Y	Y	Y	Y

Key
- Y Voted for (yea).
- # Paired for.
- + Announced for.
- N Voted against (nay).
- X Paired against.
- − Announced against.
- P Voted "present."
- C Voted "present" to avoid possible conflict of interest.
- ? Did not vote or otherwise make a position known.

• Democrats **Republicans**

ND Northern Democrats   SD Southern Democrats

Southern states – Ala., Ark., Fla., Ga., Ky., La., Miss., N.C., Okla., S.C., Tenn., Texas, Va.

274. S 1301. Consumer Bankruptcy Revisions/College-Age Credit Card Consumers. Grassley, R-Iowa, motion to table (kill) the Dodd, D-Conn., amendment that would prohibit credit card issuers from issuing a card to any consumer under age 21 unless the consumer provides either parental consent or financial information indicating an independent means of repaying debt that may arise from the issuance. Motion agreed to 58-40: R 51-3; D 7-37 (ND 6-31, SD 1-6). Sept. 17, 1998.

275. S 1301. Consumer Bankruptcy Revisions/ATM Surcharges. Grassley, R-Iowa, motion to table (kill) the D'Amato, R-N.Y., amendment that would prohibit financial institutions from imposing a surcharge — a charge in addition to the interchange fee — for the use of their automated teller machines (ATMs). Motion agreed to 72-26: R 51-3; D 21-23 (ND 15-22, SD 6-1). Sept. 17, 1998.

276. S 1301. Consumer Bankruptcy Revisions/IRA Protections. Hatch, R-Utah, amendment that would provide that all funds contributed to IRS-qualified retirement plans, such as Roth IRAs, are exempt from bankruptcy proceedings. Under current law, only retirement savings held in 401(k) plans are exempt. Adopted 89-0: R 50-0; D 39-0 (ND 32-0, SD 7-0). Sept. 17, 1998.

277. HR 1122. Abortion Procedure Ban/Veto Override. Passage, over President Clinton's Oct. 10, 1997, veto, of the bill to ban a certain late-term abortion procedure, in which the physician partially delivers the fetus before completing the abortion. Anyone convicted of performing such an abortion would be subject to a fine and up to two years in prison. Rejected 64-36: R 51-4; D 13-32 (ND 9-28, SD 4-4). Sept. 18, 1998. A two-thirds majority of those present and voting (67 in this case) of both houses is required to override a veto. A "nay" was a vote in support of the president's position.

278. S 1301. Consumer Bankruptcy Revisions/Minimum Wage Increase. Lott, R-Miss., motion to table (kill) the Kennedy, D-Mass., amendment that would increase the minimum wage by 50 cents in 1999 and 50 cents in 2000, raising it from $5.15 an hour to $6.15 an hour. Motion agreed to 55-44: R 53-2; D 2-42 (ND 0-36, SD 2-6). Sept. 22, 1998. A "nay" was a vote in support of the president's position.

279. S 1301. Consumer Bankruptcy Revisions/Bankruptcy Attorneys. Grassley, R-Iowa, motion to table (kill) the Feingold, D-Wis., amendment that would replace language requiring a debtor's attorney to pay for the costs of the trustee if the attorney is found to have not been "substantially justified" in filing a Chapter 7 bankruptcy claim with language making debtors responsible for the costs of the trustee if their filing is dismissed or converted to Chapter 13. Motion agreed to 57-42: R 53-2; D 4-40 (ND 3-33, SD 1-7). Sept. 22, 1998.

280. S 1301. Consumer Bankruptcy Revisions/Filing Fee Waiver. Grassley, R-Iowa, motion to table (kill) the Feingold, D-Wis., amendment that would allow the court to waive the filing fee for an individual debtor if the court determines that the debtor is unable to pay the fee in installments. Motion rejected 47-52: R 47-8; D 0-44 (ND 0-36, SD 0-8). Sept. 22, 1998. (Subsequently, the Feingold amendment was adopted by voice vote.)

Senate Votes 281, 282, 283, 284, 285, 286, 287

	281	282	283	284	285	286	287
ALABAMA							
Sessions	Y	Y	Y	Y	Y	Y	Y
Shelby	Y	Y	Y	Y	Y	Y	Y
ALASKA							
Murkowski	Y	Y	Y	Y	Y	Y	Y
Stevens	Y	Y	Y	Y	Y	Y	Y
ARIZONA							
Kyl	Y	Y	Y	Y	Y	Y	Y
McCain	Y	Y	Y	Y	Y	N	Y
ARKANSAS							
Hutchinson	Y	Y	Y	Y	Y	Y	Y
Bumpers	N	N	N	Y	Y	N	N
CALIFORNIA							
Boxer	N	N	N	Y	Y	N	N
Feinstein	N	N	Y	Y	Y	N	N
COLORADO							
Allard	Y	Y	Y	Y	Y	Y	Y
Campbell	Y	Y	Y	Y	Y	Y	Y
CONNECTICUT							
Dodd	N	N	N	Y	Y	N	N
Lieberman	Y	N	N	Y	Y	N	N
DELAWARE							
Roth	Y	Y	Y	Y	Y	Y	Y
Biden	Y	N	Y	Y	Y	N	N
FLORIDA							
Mack	Y	Y	Y	Y	Y	N	Y
Graham	Y	N	N	Y	Y	N	Y
GEORGIA							
Coverdell	Y	Y	Y	Y	Y	Y	Y
Cleland	N	N	N	Y	Y	N	Y
HAWAII							
Akaka	N	N	N	Y	N	N	Y
Inouye	N	N	N	Y	Y	N	Y
IDAHO							
Craig	Y	Y	Y	Y	Y	Y	Y
Kempthorne	Y	Y	Y	Y	Y	Y	Y
ILLINOIS							
Durbin	N	N	N	Y	N	N	N
Moseley-Braun	N	N	Y	Y	?	?	?
INDIANA							
Coats	Y	Y	Y	Y	Y	Y	Y
Lugar	Y	Y	Y	Y	Y	Y	Y

	281	282	283	284	285	286	287
IOWA							
Grassley	Y	Y	Y	Y	Y	Y	Y
Harkin	N	N	N	Y	Y	N	Y
KANSAS							
Brownback	Y	Y	Y	Y	Y	Y	Y
Roberts	Y	Y	Y	Y	Y	Y	Y
KENTUCKY							
McConnell	Y	Y	Y	Y	Y	Y	Y
Ford	N	N	N	Y	Y	N	Y
LOUISIANA							
Breaux	Y	N	Y	Y	Y	Y	Y
Landrieu	Y	N	Y	Y	Y	N	Y
MAINE							
Collins	Y	Y	Y	Y	Y	Y	Y
Snowe	Y	Y	Y	Y	Y	Y	Y
MARYLAND							
Mikulski	N	N	N	Y	Y	N	N
Sarbanes	N	N	N	Y	Y	N	N
MASSACHUSETTS							
Kennedy	N	N	N	Y	Y	N	N
Kerry	N	N	Y	Y	Y	N	N
MICHIGAN							
Abraham	Y	Y	Y	Y	Y	Y	Y
Levin	N	N	N	Y	Y	N	N
MINNESOTA							
Grams	Y	Y	Y	Y	Y	Y	Y
Wellstone	N	N	N	N	+	–	–
MISSISSIPPI							
Cochran	Y	Y	Y	Y	Y	Y	Y
Lott	Y	Y	Y	Y	Y	Y	Y
MISSOURI							
Ashcroft	Y	Y	Y	Y	Y	Y	Y
Bond	Y	Y	Y	Y	Y	Y	Y
MONTANA							
Burns	Y	Y	Y	Y	Y	Y	Y
Baucus	N	N	N	Y	Y	N	Y
NEBRASKA							
Hagel	Y	Y	Y	Y	Y	N	Y
Kerrey	N	N	N	Y	N	N	Y
NEVADA							
Bryan	N	N	Y	Y	Y	N	Y
Reid	Y	Y	N	Y	Y	N	N

	281	282	283	284	285	286	287
NEW HAMPSHIRE							
Gregg	Y	Y	Y	Y	Y	N	Y
Smith	Y	Y	Y	Y	Y	Y	Y
NEW JERSEY							
Lautenberg	N	N	N	Y	Y	N	N
Torricelli	N	N	N	Y	Y	N	N
NEW MEXICO							
Domenici	Y	Y	Y	Y	Y	Y	N
Bingaman	N	N	Y	Y	N	Y	Y
NEW YORK							
D'Amato	Y	Y	Y	Y	Y	N	N
Moynihan	N	N	Y	Y	Y	N	N
NORTH CAROLINA							
Faircloth	Y	Y	Y	Y	Y	Y	Y
Helms	Y	Y	Y	Y	Y	Y	Y
NORTH DAKOTA							
Conrad	N	N	N	Y	Y	N	Y
Dorgan	N	N	N	Y	Y	N	Y
OHIO							
DeWine	Y	Y	Y	Y	Y	N	Y
Glenn	?	?	?	?	?	?	?
OKLAHOMA							
Inhofe	Y	Y	Y	Y	Y	Y	Y
Nickles	Y	Y	Y	Y	Y	Y	Y
OREGON							
Smith	Y	Y	Y	Y	Y	Y	Y
Wyden	N	N	Y	Y	Y	N	Y
PENNSYLVANIA							
Santorum	Y	Y	Y	Y	Y	Y	Y
Specter	Y	N	Y	Y	Y	Y	N
RHODE ISLAND							
Chafee	Y	N	Y	Y	Y	Y	Y
Reed	N	N	N	Y	Y	N	N
SOUTH CAROLINA							
Thurmond	Y	Y	Y	Y	Y	Y	Y
Hollings	N	Y	N	Y	Y	N	?
SOUTH DAKOTA							
Daschle	N	N	N	Y	Y	N	Y
Johnson	Y	N	N	Y	N	N	Y
TENNESSEE							
Frist	Y	Y	Y	Y	Y	Y	Y
Thompson	Y	Y	Y	Y	Y	N	Y

Key

- Y Voted for (yea).
- # Paired for.
- + Announced for.
- N Voted against (nay).
- X Paired against.
- – Announced against.
- P Voted "present."
- C Voted "present" to avoid possible conflict of interest.
- ? Did not vote or otherwise make a position known.

Democrats • **Republicans**

	281	282	283	284	285	286	287
TEXAS							
Gramm	Y	Y	Y	Y	Y	N	Y
Hutchison	Y	Y	Y	Y	Y	Y	N
UTAH							
Bennett	Y	Y	Y	Y	Y	Y	Y
Hatch	Y	Y	Y	Y	Y	Y	Y
VERMONT							
Jeffords	N	N	Y	Y	Y	Y	N
Leahy	N	N	Y	Y	Y	N	Y
VIRGINIA							
Warner	Y	Y	?	?	Y	Y	Y
Robb	Y	N	Y	Y	Y	N	N
WASHINGTON							
Gorton	Y	Y	N	Y	Y	N	Y
Murray	N	N	Y	Y	Y	N	N
WEST VIRGINIA							
Byrd	N	N	Y	Y	Y	N	N
Rockefeller	N	N	Y	Y	Y	N	Y
WISCONSIN							
Feingold	N	N	N	Y	Y	N	Y
Kohl	Y	N	Y	Y	Y	N	Y
WYOMING							
Enzi	Y	Y	Y	Y	Y	Y	Y
Thomas	Y	Y	Y	Y	Y	Y	Y

ND Northern Democrats   SD Southern Democrats

Southern states - Ala., Ark., Fla., Ga., Ky., La., Miss., N.C., Okla., S.C., Tenn., Texas, Va.

281. S 1301. Consumer Bankruptcy Revisions/Creditor Good Faith. Hatch, R-Utah, motion to table (kill) the Reed, D-R.I., amendment that would allow the court to consider whether a creditor who moves for dismissal or conversion of a Chapter 7 bankruptcy case has "dealt in good faith" with the debtor. Motion agreed to 63-36: R 54-1; D 9-35 (ND 5-31, SD 4-4). Sept. 22, 1998.

282. S 1645. Transporting Minors for an Abortion/Cloture. Motion to invoke cloture (thus limiting debate) on the substitute amendment to the bill that would make it a federal crime for anyone other than a parent to transport a minor across state lines with the intent to obtain an abortion. Motion rejected 54-45: R 52-3; D 2-42 (ND 1-35, SD 1-7). Sept. 22, 1998. Three-fifths of the total Senate (60) is required to invoke cloture.

283. S 1301. Consumer Bankruptcy Revisions/Federal Reserve Interest Rates. Domenici, R-N.M., motion to table (kill) the Harkin, D-Iowa, amendment that would express the sense of Congress that the Federal Reserve should decrease the Federal Funds interest rate. Motion agreed to 71-27: R 53-1; D 18-26 (ND 14-22, SD 4-4). Sept. 23, 1998.

284. HR 3150. Consumer Bankruptcy Revisions/Passage. Passage of the bill to revise the nation's bankruptcy laws by allowing a bankruptcy judge to dismiss any claim for Chapter 7 relief, or convert the claim to a Chapter 13 case, if the judge determines that the debtor has is able to pay at least 30 percent of his unsecured debt. Passed 97-1: R 54-0; D 43-1 (ND 35-1, SD 8-0). Sept. 23, 1998. A "yea" was a vote in support of the president's position. (Before passage, the Senate struck all after the enacting clause and inserted the text of S 1301.)

285. S 2176. Acting Presidential Appointments/Cloture. Motion to invoke cloture (thus limiting debate) on the motion to proceed to the bill that would clarify that all executive branch positions that are not explicitly governed by other federal statutes fall under the "Vacancies Act," which prohibits the president from appointing individuals on an "acting" basis for more than 120 days to executive branch positions that require Senate confirmation. The bill also would extend from 120 days to 150 days the length of time a department's top deputy may fill a vacancy on an "acting" basis. Motion agreed to 96-1: R 55-0; D 41-1 (ND 33-1, SD 8-0). Sept. 24, 1998. Three-fifths of the total Senate (60) is required to invoke cloture. (Subsequently, the motion to proceed was agreed to by voice vote.)

286. S 2279. Federal Aviation Administration Reauthorization/Pilot License Revocation. Inhofe, R-Okla., amendment that would allow any pilot who has had his license revoked for safety reasons by emergency action of the Federal Aviation Administration (FAA) to appeal the decision within 48 hours to the National Transportation Safety Board (NTSB). The amendment would require the NTSB to rule within five days of the appeal whether the FAA has proven the existence of an emergency that requires the immediate revocation of the license in the interest of air safety. If the NTSB rules that there is no emergency, the license is returned to the pilot while the FAA pursues its case. Rejected 46-51: R 45-10; D 1-41 (ND 0-34, SD 1-7). Sept. 24, 1998.

287. S 2279. Federal Aviation Administration Reauthorization/Noise Control. McCain, R-Ariz., motion to table (kill) the Torricelli, D-N.J., amendment that would reestablish the Environmental Protection Agency's Office of Noise Abatement and Control and would require an EPA study on airport noise. Motion agreed to 69-27: R 50-5; D 19-22 (ND 14-20, SD 5-2). Sept. 24, 1998.

Senate Votes 288, 289, 290, 291, 292, 293, 294

	288	289	290	291	292	293	294
ALABAMA							
Sessions	Y	?	?	?	?	Y	Y
Shelby	Y	Y	Y	Y	Y	Y	Y
ALASKA							
Murkowski	Y	Y	Y	Y	Y	Y	Y
Stevens	Y	Y	Y	Y	Y	Y	Y
ARIZONA							
Kyl	Y	Y	Y	Y	Y	Y	Y
McCain	Y	Y	Y	Y	Y	Y	Y
ARKANSAS							
Hutchinson	Y	Y	Y	Y	Y	Y	Y
Bumpers	Y	N	Y	Y	N	Y	N
CALIFORNIA							
Boxer	?	N	Y	Y	?	Y	N
Feinstein	Y	N	Y	Y	Y	Y	N
COLORADO							
Allard	Y	Y	Y	Y	Y	Y	Y
Campbell	Y	Y	Y	Y	Y	Y	Y
CONNECTICUT							
Dodd	Y	N	Y	Y	Y	Y	N
Lieberman	Y	N	Y	Y	Y	Y	N
DELAWARE							
Roth	Y	Y	Y	Y	Y	Y	Y
Biden	Y	N	Y	Y	Y	Y	N
FLORIDA							
Mack	Y	Y	Y	Y	Y	Y	Y
Graham	Y	N	Y	Y	N	Y	N
GEORGIA							
Coverdell	Y	Y	Y	Y	Y	Y	Y
Cleland	Y	N	Y	Y	N	Y	N
HAWAII							
Akaka	Y	N	Y	Y	Y	Y	Y
Inouye	Y	N	Y	Y	Y	Y	Y
IDAHO							
Craig	Y	Y	Y	Y	Y	Y	Y
Kempthorne	?	Y	Y	Y	Y	Y	Y
ILLINOIS							
Durbin	Y	N	Y	Y	Y	Y	N
Moseley-Braun	?	?	+	+	?	?	–
INDIANA							
Coats	Y	Y	Y	Y	Y	Y	Y
Lugar	Y	Y	Y	Y	Y	Y	Y
IOWA							
Grassley	Y	Y	Y	Y	Y	Y	Y
Harkin	Y	N	Y	Y	Y	Y	N
KANSAS							
Brownback	Y	Y	Y	Y	Y	Y	Y
Roberts	Y	Y	Y	Y	Y	Y	Y
KENTUCKY							
McConnell	Y	Y	Y	Y	Y	Y	Y
Ford	Y	N	Y	Y	Y	Y	Y
LOUISIANA							
Breaux	Y	N	Y	Y	Y	Y	Y
Landrieu	Y	N	Y	Y	Y	Y	Y
MAINE							
Collins	Y	Y	Y	Y	Y	Y	Y
Snowe	Y	Y	Y	Y	Y	Y	Y
MARYLAND							
Mikulski	Y	N	Y	Y	Y	Y	N
Sarbanes	Y	N	Y	Y	Y	Y	N
MASSACHUSETTS							
Kennedy	Y	?	Y	Y	Y	Y	N
Kerry	Y	N	Y	Y	Y	Y	N
MICHIGAN							
Abraham	Y	Y	Y	Y	Y	Y	N
Levin	Y	N	Y	Y	Y	Y	N
MINNESOTA							
Grams	Y	Y	Y	Y	Y	Y	Y
Wellstone	+	N	Y	N	Y	N	N
MISSISSIPPI							
Cochran	Y	Y	Y	Y	Y	Y	Y
Lott	Y	Y	Y	Y	Y	Y	Y
MISSOURI							
Ashcroft	?	Y	Y	Y	Y	Y	Y
Bond	Y	?	Y	Y	Y	Y	Y
MONTANA							
Burns	Y	Y	Y	Y	Y	Y	Y
Baucus	Y	N	Y	Y	Y	Y	N
NEBRASKA							
Hagel	Y	Y	?	?	?	Y	Y
Kerrey	Y	N	Y	Y	Y	Y	N
NEVADA							
Bryan	Y	N	Y	Y	Y	Y	N
Reid	Y	–	Y	Y	Y	Y	N
NEW HAMPSHIRE							
Gregg	Y	Y	Y	Y	Y	Y	?
Smith	Y	Y	Y	Y	Y	Y	Y
NEW JERSEY							
Lautenberg	Y	N	Y	Y	Y	Y	N
Torricelli	Y	?	Y	Y	Y	Y	N
NEW MEXICO							
Domenici	Y	Y	Y	Y	Y	Y	Y
Bingaman	Y	N	Y	Y	Y	Y	Y
NEW YORK							
D'Amato	Y	?	Y	Y	Y	Y	Y
Moynihan	Y	N	Y	Y	Y	Y	N
NORTH CAROLINA							
Faircloth	Y	Y	Y	Y	Y	Y	Y
Helms	Y	Y	Y	Y	Y	Y	Y
NORTH DAKOTA							
Conrad	Y	N	Y	Y	Y	Y	N
Dorgan	Y	N	Y	Y	Y	Y	N
OHIO							
DeWine	Y	Y	Y	Y	Y	Y	Y
Glenn	?	N	Y	Y	Y	?	?
OKLAHOMA							
Inhofe	Y	Y	Y	Y	Y	Y	Y
Nickles	Y	Y	Y	Y	Y	Y	Y
OREGON							
Smith	Y	Y	Y	Y	Y	Y	Y
Wyden	Y	?	Y	Y	Y	Y	N
PENNSYLVANIA							
Santorum	Y	Y	Y	Y	Y	Y	Y
Specter	Y	Y	Y	Y	Y	Y	N
RHODE ISLAND							
Chafee	Y	Y	Y	Y	Y	Y	Y
Reed	Y	N	Y	Y	Y	Y	N
SOUTH CAROLINA							
Thurmond	Y	Y	Y	Y	Y	Y	Y
Hollings	?	?	?	?	?	Y	Y
SOUTH DAKOTA							
Daschle	Y	N	Y	Y	Y	Y	N
Johnson	Y	N	Y	Y	Y	Y	N
TENNESSEE							
Frist	Y	Y	Y	Y	Y	Y	Y
Thompson	Y	Y	Y	Y	Y	Y	Y
TEXAS							
Gramm	Y	Y	Y	Y	Y	Y	Y
Hutchison	Y	Y	Y	Y	Y	Y	Y
UTAH							
Bennett	Y	Y	Y	Y	N	Y	Y
Hatch	Y	Y	Y	Y	Y	Y	Y
VERMONT							
Jeffords	Y	Y	Y	Y	Y	Y	N
Leahy	Y	N	Y	Y	Y	Y	N
VIRGINIA							
Warner	Y	Y	Y	Y	Y	Y	Y
Robb	N	N	Y	Y	Y	Y	N
WASHINGTON							
Gorton	Y	Y	Y	Y	N	Y	Y
Murray	Y	N	Y	Y	Y	Y	N
WEST VIRGINIA							
Byrd	Y	Y	Y	Y	Y	Y	Y
Rockefeller	Y	N	Y	Y	Y	Y	N
WISCONSIN							
Feingold	Y	N	Y	N	Y	N	N
Kohl	Y	N	Y	Y	Y	Y	N
WYOMING							
Enzi	Y	Y	Y	Y	N	Y	Y
Thomas	Y	Y	Y	Y	Y	Y	Y

Key

- Y Voted for (yea).
- # Paired for.
- + Announced for.
- N Voted against (nay).
- X Paired against.
- – Announced against.
- P Voted "present."
- C Voted "present" to avoid possible conflict of interest.
- ? Did not vote or otherwise make a position known.

Democrats Republicans

ND Northern Democrats   SD Southern Democrats

Southern states - Ala., Ark., Fla., Ga., Ky., La., Miss., N.C., Okla., S.C., Tenn., Texas, Va.

288. HR 4057. Federal Aviation Administration Reauthorization/Passage. Passage of the bill to reauthorize the Federal Aviation Administration for two years, including operations, facilities and equipment, as well as the Airport Improvement Program and funding for aviation safety and security improvements. The bill also would increase slot exemptions at New York's LaGuardia and John F. Kennedy airports, Chicago's O'Hare and Washington's Reagan National Airport, and would authorize exemptions to the so-called perimeter rule at Reagan National, which prohibits nonstop flights over a certain mileage. Passed 92-1: R 53-0; D 39-1 (ND 33-0, SD 6-1). Sept. 25, 1998. (Before passage, the Senate struck all after the enacting clause and inserted the text of S 2279 as amended.)

289. S 2176. Acting Presidential Appointments/Cloture. Motion to invoke cloture (thus limiting debate) on the bill that would clarify that all executive branch positions that are not explicitly governed by other federal statutes fall under the "Vacancies Act," which prohibits the president from appointing individuals on an "acting" basis for more than 120 days to executive branch positions that require Senate confirmation. The bill also would extend from 120 days to 150 days the length of time a department's top deputy may fill a vacancy on an "acting" basis. Motion rejected 53-38: R 52-0; D 1-38 (ND 1-31, SD 0-7). Sept. 28, 1998. Three-fifths of the total Senate (60) is required to invoke cloture.

290. HR 6. Higher Education Act Reauthorization/Conference Report. Adoption of the conference report on the bill to reauthorize higher education programs for five years. The measure would cut interest rates on federally guaranteed student loans while providing special subsidies to banks. Adopted (thus cleared for the president) 96-0: R 53-0; D 43-0 (ND 36-0, SD 7-0). Sept. 29, 1998. A "yea" was a vote in support of the president's position.

291. HR 4103. Fiscal 1999 Defense Appropriations/Conference Report. Adoption of the conference report on the bill to provide $250.5 billion in new budget authority for defense-related programs in fiscal 1999. The bill would provide $485 million less than requested by President Clinton and $2.8 billion more than provided in fiscal 1998. Adopted (thus cleared for the president) 94-2: R 53-0; D 41-2 (ND 34-2, SD 7-0). Sept. 29, 1998.

292. S 442. Internet Tax Moratorium/Cloture. Motion to invoke cloture (thus limiting debate) on the motion to proceed to the bill that would impose a two-year moratorium on state Internet taxation to allow state, local and federal officials and industry representatives to negotiate what type of tax treatment should be applied to Internet access and commerce. Motion agreed to 89-6: R 50-3; D 39-3 (ND 35-0, SD 4-3). Sept. 29, 1998. Three-fifths of the total Senate (60) is required to invoke cloture.

293. HR 3616. Fiscal 1999 Defense Authorization/Conference Report. Adoption of the conference report on the bill to authorize $270.5 billion in new budget authority for defense-related activities in fiscal 1999, which is $406 million less than requested by President Clinton. The bill would authorize an additional $1.86 billion, designated as emergency spending, for U.S. troop operations in Bosnia during fiscal 1999. It also would authorize a 3.6 percent raise in military pay. Adopted (thus cleared for the president) 96-2: R 55-0; D 41-2 (ND 33-2, SD 8-0). Oct. 1, 1998.

294. S 1092. King Cove Land Transfer/Passage. Passage of the bill to require the Interior Department to transfer a perpetual 100-foot-wide, 30-mile right-of-way through the Izembek National Wildlife Refuge in Alaska to the Aleutians East Borough for the purpose of constructing a gravel, one-lane public road from the remote Alaska town of King Cove to Cold Bay, which has an all-weather airport. The measure would require the King Cove Corporation, an Alaskan Native group that along with the federal government owns most of the surrounding land, to transfer 664 acres of lands south of Cold Bay to the Interior Department in exchange for the road land. Passed 59-38: R 51-3; D 8-35 (ND 4-31, SD 4-4). Oct. 01, 1998. A "nay" was a vote in support of the president's position.

Senate Votes 295, 296, 297, 298, 299, 300, 301

	295	296	297	298	299	300	301
ALABAMA							
Sessions	N	Y	Y	Y	Y	Y	N
Shelby	N	Y	Y	Y	Y	Y	N
ALASKA							
Murkowski	Y	Y	Y	Y	Y	Y	Y
Stevens	Y	Y	Y	Y	Y	Y	Y
ARIZONA							
Kyl	N	Y	Y	N	Y	Y	Y
McCain	N	Y	Y	Y	Y	Y	Y
ARKANSAS							
Hutchinson	N	Y	Y	Y	Y	Y	Y
Bumpers	Y	N	Y	N	N	N	N
CALIFORNIA							
Boxer	Y	Y	?	Y	Y	Y	Y
Feinstein	Y	Y	Y	Y	Y	Y	Y
COLORADO							
Allard	N	Y	Y	Y	Y	Y	Y
Campbell	Y	Y	Y	Y	Y	Y	Y
CONNECTICUT							
Dodd	Y	Y	Y	N	Y	Y	Y
Lieberman	Y	Y	Y	N	Y	Y	Y
DELAWARE							
Roth	Y	Y	Y	Y	Y	Y	Y
Biden	Y	Y	Y	N	Y	Y	Y
FLORIDA							
Mack	Y	Y	Y	Y	Y	Y	Y
Graham	Y	N	Y	N	N	N	Y
GEORGIA							
Coverdell	N	Y	Y	Y	Y	Y	Y
Cleland	Y	N	Y	N	N	N	Y
HAWAII							
Akaka	Y	N	Y	N	Y	Y	Y
Inouye	Y	N	Y	N	Y	N	Y
IDAHO							
Craig	N	Y	Y	Y	Y	Y	Y
Kempthorne	N	Y	Y	Y	Y	Y	Y
ILLINOIS							
Durbin	Y	Y	?	N	Y	N	Y
Moseley-Braun	?	?	Y	N	Y	Y	Y
INDIANA							
Coats	Y	Y	Y	Y	Y	Y	Y
Lugar	Y	Y	Y	Y	Y	Y	Y

	295	296	297	298	299	300	301
IOWA							
Grassley	N	Y	Y	Y	Y	Y	Y
Harkin	Y	N	Y	N	Y	N	Y
KANSAS							
Brownback	N	Y	Y	Y	Y	Y	Y
Roberts	N	N	Y	Y	Y	Y	N
KENTUCKY							
McConnell	N	Y	Y	Y	Y	Y	Y
Ford	Y	N	Y	N	N	N	Y
LOUISIANA							
Breaux	Y	N	Y	N	N	N	Y
Landrieu	Y	N	Y	N	N	N	Y
MAINE							
Collins	Y	Y	Y	Y	Y	Y	Y
Snowe	Y	Y	Y	Y	Y	Y	Y
MARYLAND							
Mikulski	Y	N	Y	N	Y	N	N
Sarbanes	Y	N	Y	N	Y	N	Y
MASSACHUSETTS							
Kennedy	Y	N	Y	N	N	N	Y
Kerry	Y	Y	Y	N	Y	Y	Y
MICHIGAN							
Abraham	N	Y	Y	Y	Y	Y	Y
Levin	Y	N	Y	N	N	N	Y
MINNESOTA							
Grams	Y	Y	Y	Y	Y	Y	Y
Wellstone	Y	N	Y	N	N	N	N
MISSISSIPPI							
Cochran	Y	N	Y	Y	Y	Y	Y
Lott	N	Y	Y	Y	Y	Y	Y
MISSOURI							
Ashcroft	N	Y	Y	Y	Y	Y	Y
Bond	?	?	Y	Y	Y	Y	Y
MONTANA							
Burns	N	Y	Y	Y	Y	Y	Y
Baucus	Y	Y	Y	N	Y	Y	Y
NEBRASKA							
Hagel	N	Y	Y	Y	Y	Y	Y
Kerrey	Y	?	Y	N	Y	Y	Y
NEVADA							
Bryan	Y	N	Y	N	Y	N	Y
Reid	Y	Y	Y	N	Y	Y	Y

	295	296	297	298	299	300	301
NEW HAMPSHIRE							
Gregg	Y	Y	Y	N	Y	Y	Y
Smith	N	Y	Y	Y	Y	Y	Y
NEW JERSEY							
Lautenberg	Y	Y	Y	N	Y	Y	Y
Torricelli	Y	Y	Y	N	Y	Y	Y
NEW MEXICO							
Domenici	Y	Y	Y	Y	Y	Y	Y
Bingaman	Y	N	Y	N	Y	Y	Y
NEW YORK							
D'Amato	Y	Y	Y	Y	Y	Y	Y
Moynihan	Y	N	+	+	?	?	Y
NORTH CAROLINA							
Faircloth	N	Y	Y	Y	Y	Y	Y
Helms	Y	Y	Y	Y	Y	Y	Y
NORTH DAKOTA							
Conrad	Y	N	Y	N	N	N	Y
Dorgan	Y	N	Y	N	N	N	N
OHIO							
DeWine	Y	Y	Y	Y	Y	Y	Y
Glenn	?	?	?	?	?	?	?
OKLAHOMA							
Inhofe	N	Y	Y	N	N	N	Y
Nickles	N	Y	Y	Y	Y	Y	Y
OREGON							
Smith	Y	Y	Y	Y	Y	Y	Y
Wyden	Y	Y	Y	N	Y	Y	Y
PENNSYLVANIA							
Santorum	Y	Y	?	N	Y	Y	Y
Specter	Y	N	Y	Y	Y	Y	Y
RHODE ISLAND							
Chafee	Y	Y	Y	Y	Y	Y	Y
Reed	Y	N	Y	N	Y	N	Y
SOUTH CAROLINA							
Thurmond	N	Y	Y	Y	Y	Y	Y
Hollings	?	?	?	N	N	N	Y
SOUTH DAKOTA							
Daschle	Y	Y	Y	N	Y	N	Y
Johnson	Y	N	Y	N	Y	N	Y
TENNESSEE							
Frist	Y	Y	Y	Y	Y	Y	Y
Thompson	N	Y	Y	Y	Y	Y	Y

	295	296	297	298	299	300	301
TEXAS							
Gramm	N	Y	Y	Y	Y	Y	N
Hutchison	N	Y	Y	Y	Y	Y	N
UTAH							
Bennett	Y	N	Y	Y	Y	N	Y
Hatch	Y	Y	?	Y	Y	Y	Y
VERMONT							
Jeffords	Y	Y	Y	Y	Y	Y	Y
Leahy	Y	Y	Y	Y	Y	Y	Y
VIRGINIA							
Warner	Y	Y	Y	Y	Y	Y	Y
Robb	Y	Y	Y	N	Y	Y	Y
WASHINGTON							
Gorton	N	N	Y	Y	N	N	N
Murray	Y	Y	Y	N	Y	Y	Y
WEST VIRGINIA							
Byrd	Y	N	Y	N	N	N	Y
Rockefeller	Y	N	Y	N	Y	N	Y
WISCONSIN							
Feingold	Y	Y	Y	N	Y	N	N
Kohl	Y	Y	Y	N	Y	Y	Y
WYOMING							
Enzi	N	N	Y	Y	Y	Y	Y
Thomas	N	Y	Y	N	Y	Y	Y

Key

Y Voted for (yea).
Paired for.
+ Announced for.
N Voted against (nay).
X Paired against.
− Announced against.
P Voted "present."
C Voted "present" to avoid possible conflict of interest.
? Did not vote or otherwise make a position known.

Democrats • Republicans

ND Northern Democrats   SD Southern Democrats

Southern states - Ala., Ark., Fla., Ga., Ky., La., Miss., N.C., Okla., S.C., Tenn., Texas, Va.

295. Sotomayor Nomination/Confirmation. Confirmation of President Clinton's nomination of Sonia Sotomayor of New York to be a judge for the 2nd U.S. Circuit Court of Appeals. Confirmed 67-29: R 25-29; D 42-0 (ND 35-0, SD 7-0). Oct. 2, 1998. A "yea" was a vote in support of the president's position.

296. S 442. Internet Tax Moratorium/Catalog Sales. McCain, R-Ariz., motion to table (kill) the Bumpers, D-Ark., amendment that would allow states to require companies selling goods through the Internet, phone or mail, such as catalog goods, to collect state or local taxes on the transaction. Motion agreed to 66-29: R 48-6; D 18-23 (ND 17-17, SD 1-6). Oct. 2, 1998.

297. HR 10. Financial Services Overhaul/Cloture. Motion to invoke cloture (thus limiting debate) on the motion to proceed to the bill that would eliminate current barriers erected by the 1933 Glass-Steagall Act and other laws that impede affiliations between banking, securities, insurance and other firms. Motion agreed to 93-0: R 53-0; D 40-0 (ND 33-0, SD 7-0). Oct. 5, 1998. Three-fifths of the total Senate (60) is required to invoke cloture.

298. HR 4101. Fiscal 1999 Agriculture Appropriations/Conference Report. Adoption of the conference report on the bill to provide $55.9 billion in new budget authority for the Agriculture Department, the Food and Drug Administration and rural development programs in fiscal 1999. The bill would provide approximately $6 billion more than provided in fiscal 1998 and $1.9 billion less than requested by President Clinton. The conference report also includes an additional $4.2 billion in emergency funding for farmers and others who have suffered financial hardship due to natural disasters or poor export markets. Adopted (thus cleared for the president) 55-43: R 50-5; D 5-38 (ND 3-32, SD 2-6). Oct. 6, 1998. A "nay" was a vote in support of the president's position.

299. S 442. Internet Tax Moratorium/Moratorium Extension. McCain, R-Ariz., motion to table (kill) the Graham, D-Fla., amendment that would require a three-fifths "supermajority" vote of each chamber of Congress in order to extend the two-year Internet tax moratorium that the bill would impose. Motion agreed to 83-15: R 53-2; D 30-13 (ND 29-6, SD 1-7). Oct. 6, 1998.

300. S 442. Internet Tax Moratorium/Sales Tax Disclosure. Gregg, R-N.H., motion to table (kill) the Bumpers, D-Ark., amendment that would require businesses selling goods over the Internet to disclose to potential customers that they may be subject to state or local sales and use taxes on their purchases depending on where they reside. Motion agreed to 71-27: R 52-3; D 19-24 (ND 18-17, SD 1-7). Oct. 6, 1998.

301. HR 10. Financial Services Overhaul/Motion to Proceed. Motion to proceed to the bill that would eliminate current barriers erected by the 1933 Glass-Steagall Act and other laws that impede affiliations between banking, securities, insurance and other firms. Motion agreed to 88-11: R 49-6; D 39-5 (ND 32-4, SD 7-1). Oct. 7, 1998.

Senate Votes 302, 303, 304, 305, 306, 307, 308

	302	303	304	305	306	307	308
ALABAMA							
Sessions	Y	Y	N	N	N	Y	Y
Shelby	Y	Y	Y	Y	Y	Y	Y
ALASKA							
Murkowski	Y	Y	N	Y	Y	Y	Y
Stevens	Y	Y	Y	Y	Y	Y	Y
ARIZONA							
Kyl	Y	Y	Y	Y	Y	N	Y
McCain	Y	Y	Y	Y	N	Y	Y
ARKANSAS							
Hutchinson	Y	Y	N	N	Y	Y	Y
Bumpers	N	Y	N	N	N	Y	N
CALIFORNIA							
Boxer	Y	Y	Y	Y	N	Y	Y
Feinstein	Y	Y	N	N	N	Y	Y
COLORADO							
Allard	Y	Y	N	N	Y	Y	Y
Campbell	Y	Y	Y	Y	Y	Y	Y
CONNECTICUT							
Dodd	Y	Y	Y	Y	N	Y	Y
Lieberman	Y	Y	Y	Y	N	Y	Y
DELAWARE							
Roth	Y	Y	N	N	Y	Y	Y
Biden	Y	Y	N	N	N	Y	Y
FLORIDA							
Mack	Y	Y	N	Y	Y	Y	Y
Graham	Y	Y	N	N	N	Y	Y
GEORGIA							
Coverdell	Y	Y	N	Y	Y	Y	Y
Cleland	Y	Y	N	N	N	Y	Y
HAWAII							
Akaka	Y	Y	N	N	N	Y	Y
Inouye	Y	Y	N	N	Y	Y	Y
IDAHO							
Craig	Y	Y	Y	Y	N	Y	Y
Kempthorne	Y	Y	N	N	Y	Y	Y
ILLINOIS							
Durbin	Y	Y	N	N	N	Y	Y
Moseley-Braun	Y	Y	Y	N	Y	N	Y
INDIANA							
Coats	Y	Y	Y	Y	N	Y	Y
Lugar	Y	Y	N	Y	N	Y	Y
IOWA							
Grassley	Y	Y	N	N	Y	Y	Y
Harkin	Y	Y	N	N	N	Y	Y
KANSAS							
Brownback	Y	Y	N	N	N	Y	Y
Roberts	Y	Y	N	N	N	Y	Y
KENTUCKY							
McConnell	Y	Y	Y	Y	Y	Y	Y
Ford	Y	Y	N	N	N	Y	Y
LOUISIANA							
Breaux	Y	Y	N	N	N	Y	Y
Landrieu	Y	Y	N	N	N	Y	Y
MAINE							
Collins	Y	Y	N	Y	N	Y	Y
Snowe	Y	Y	N	N	N	Y	Y
MARYLAND							
Mikulski	Y	Y	N	N	N	Y	Y
Sarbanes	Y	Y	N	N	N	Y	Y
MASSACHUSETTS							
Kennedy	Y	Y	N	N	N	Y	Y
Kerry	Y	Y	Y	Y	N	Y	Y
MICHIGAN							
Abraham	Y	Y	N	Y	N	Y	Y
Levin	Y	Y	N	N	N	Y	Y
MINNESOTA							
Grams	Y	Y	Y	Y	Y	Y	Y
Wellstone	Y	Y	N	N	N	Y	Y
MISSISSIPPI							
Cochran	Y	Y	N	N	Y	Y	Y
Lott	Y	Y	N	Y	Y	Y	Y
MISSOURI							
Ashcroft	Y	Y	N	N	N	Y	Y
Bond	Y	Y	N	N	N	Y	Y
MONTANA							
Burns	Y	Y	Y	Y	N	Y	Y
Baucus	Y	Y	N	N	Y	Y	Y
NEBRASKA							
Hagel	Y	Y	Y	Y	Y	Y	Y
Kerrey	Y	Y	N	N	N	Y	Y
NEVADA							
Bryan	Y	Y	N	N	N	Y	Y
Reid	Y	Y	N	N	N	Y	Y
NEW HAMPSHIRE							
Gregg	Y	Y	Y	Y	Y	Y	Y
Smith	Y	Y	Y	Y	Y	Y	Y
NEW JERSEY							
Lautenberg	Y	Y	Y	Y	N	Y	Y
Torricelli	Y	Y	Y	Y	Y	Y	Y
NEW MEXICO							
Domenici	Y	Y	N	Y	N	Y	Y
Bingaman	Y	Y	N	N	N	Y	Y
NEW YORK							
D'Amato	Y	Y	N	Y	Y	Y	Y
Moynihan	Y	Y	N	N	N	Y	Y
NORTH CAROLINA							
Faircloth	Y	Y	Y	Y	Y	Y	Y
Helms	Y	Y	N	N	Y	?	Y
NORTH DAKOTA							
Conrad	Y	Y	N	N	N	Y	Y
Dorgan	N	Y	N	N	N	Y	Y
OHIO							
DeWine	Y	Y	N	N	Y	Y	Y
Glenn	?	?	?	?	?	?	?
OKLAHOMA							
Inhofe	Y	Y	N	N	N	Y	Y
Nickles	Y	Y	N	Y	Y	Y	Y
OREGON							
Smith	Y	Y	Y	Y	N	Y	Y
Wyden	Y	Y	N	N	Y	Y	Y
PENNSYLVANIA							
Santorum	Y	Y	N	Y	Y	Y	Y
Specter	Y	Y	N	?	?	Y	Y
RHODE ISLAND							
Chafee	Y	Y	N	N	N	Y	Y
Reed	Y	Y	N	N	N	Y	Y
SOUTH CAROLINA							
Thurmond	Y	Y	N	N	N	Y	Y
Hollings	N	Y	?	?	?	?	?
SOUTH DAKOTA							
Daschle	Y	Y	N	N	N	Y	Y
Johnson	Y	Y	N	N	N	Y	Y
TENNESSEE							
Frist	Y	Y	Y	N	N	Y	Y
Thompson	Y	Y	Y	N	N	Y	Y
TEXAS							
Gramm	Y	Y	N	N	Y	Y	Y
Hutchison	Y	Y	N	N	Y	Y	Y
UTAH							
Bennett	Y	Y	N	Y	N	Y	Y
Hatch	Y	Y	N	N	Y	Y	Y
VERMONT							
Jeffords	?	Y	N	N	Y	Y	Y
Leahy	Y	N	N	N	Y	Y	Y
VIRGINIA							
Warner	Y	Y	N	Y	N	Y	Y
Robb	Y	Y	N	Y	N	Y	Y
WASHINGTON							
Gorton	N	Y	N	N	N	Y	N
Murray	Y	Y	Y	Y	N	Y	Y
WEST VIRGINIA							
Byrd	Y	Y	N	N	Y	Y	Y
Rockefeller	Y	Y	N	N	N	Y	Y
WISCONSIN							
Feingold	Y	Y	N	N	N	Y	Y
Kohl	Y	Y	Y	N	N	Y	Y
WYOMING							
Enzi	Y	Y	N	N	N	Y	Y
Thomas	Y	Y	N	N	Y	Y	Y

Key
- Y Voted for (yea).
- # Paired for.
- + Announced for.
- N Voted against (nay).
- X Paired against.
- − Announced against.
- P Voted "present."
- C Voted "present" to avoid possible conflict of interest.
- ? Did not vote or otherwise make a position known.

Democrats **Republicans**

ND Northern Democrats   SD Southern Democrats

Southern states - Ala., Ark., Fla., Ga., Ky., La., Miss., N.C., Okla., S.C., Tenn., Texas, Va.

302. S 442. Internet Tax Moratorium/Cloture. Motion to invoke cloture (thus limiting debate) on the bill that would impose a two-year moratorium on state and local Internet taxation to allow state, local and federal officials and industry representatives to negotiate what type of tax treatment should be applied to Internet commerce. Motion agreed to 94-4: R 53-1; D 41-3 (ND 35-1, SD 6-2). Oct. 7, 1998. Three-fifths of the total Senate (60) is required to invoke cloture.

303. S 442. Internet Tax Moratorium/Indecent Material. Coats, R-Ind., amendment that would exempt individuals or businesses that transfer or sell indecent sexual material over the Internet from the tax moratorium unless they restrict minors' access to the material by requiring a credit card number or other adult information for access. The amendment also would exempt Internet access providers from the moratorium unless they offer customers screening software designed to allow the customer to limit minors' access to the material. Adopted 98-1: R 55-0; D 43-1 (ND 35-1, SD 8-0). Oct. 7, 1998.

304. S 442. Internet Tax Moratorium/Interstate Taxation Review. McCain, R-Ariz., motion to table (kill) the Hutchinson, R-Ark., amendment to the McCain amendment. The Hutchinson amendment would require the commission established by the bill to examine the effect taxation on interstate sales transactions, including Internet transactions, has on retail businesses and state and local governments. The underlying McCain amendment would direct the commission to study model state legislation governing Internet taxes. Motion rejected 30-68: R 20-35; D 10-33 (ND 10-26, SD 0-7). Oct. 7, 1998. (Subsequently, the Hutchinson amendment and the underlying McCain amendment as amended were adopted by voice vote.)

305. S 442. Internet Tax Moratorium/Four-Year Moratorium. McCain, R-Ariz., amendment to the McCain amendment. The second-degree amendment would extend the moratorium from three years to four. The underlying amendment would extend the moratorium from the bill's language of two years to three years. Rejected 45-52: R 32-22; D 13-30 (ND 12-24, SD 1-6). Oct. 7, 1998.

306. S 442. Internet Tax Moratorium/Three-Year Moratorium and Current Tax Allowance. Murkowski, R-Alaska, motion to table (kill) the McCain, R-Ariz., amendment that would extend the moratorium from two years to three years and allow states that currently impose taxes on Internet access to continue doing so after the moratorium takes effect. Motion rejected 28-69: R 27-27; D 1-42 (ND 1-35, SD 0-7). Oct. 7, 1998.

307. HR 4194. Fiscal 1999 VA-HUD Appropriations/Conference Report. Adoption of the conference report on the bill to provide $93.4 billion in new budget authority for veterans, housing, space and science programs and agencies in fiscal 1999. The bill includes legislation to overhaul the nation's public housing system. Adopted (thus cleared for the president) 96-1: R 53-1; D 43-0 (ND 36-0, SD 7-0). Oct. 8, 1998.

308. S 442. Internet Tax Moratorium/Passage. Passage of the bill to impose a three-year moratorium on state and local Internet taxation to allow state, local and federal officials and industry representatives to negotiate what type of tax treatment should be applied to Internet access and commerce. The bill would allow states that currently impose taxes on Internet access to continue to do so. Passed 96-2: R 54-1; D 42-1 (ND 36-0, SD 6-1). Oct. 8, 1998.

Senate Votes 309, 310, 311, 312, 313, 314

	309	310	311	312	313	314
ALABAMA						
Sessions	N	Y	Y	Y	Y	N
Shelby	N	Y	Y	Y	Y	Y
ALASKA						
Murkowski	N	Y	Y	Y	Y	?
Stevens	Y	Y	Y	Y	Y	Y
ARIZONA						
Kyl	N	Y	Y	Y	Y	N
McCain	N	Y	Y	Y	Y	N
ARKANSAS						
Hutchinson	N	Y	Y	Y	Y	Y
Bumpers	Y	Y	N	N	Y	?
CALIFORNIA						
Boxer	Y	Y	N	N	Y	Y
Feinstein	Y	Y	N	N	Y	Y
COLORADO						
Allard	N	Y	Y	Y	Y	N
Campbell	N	Y	Y	Y	Y	Y
CONNECTICUT						
Dodd	Y	Y	N	N	Y	Y
Lieberman	Y	Y	N	N	Y	Y
DELAWARE						
Roth	Y	Y	Y	Y	Y	Y
Biden	Y	Y	N	Y	Y	Y
FLORIDA						
Mack	Y	Y	Y	Y	Y	Y
Graham	Y	Y	N	Y	Y	Y
GEORGIA						
Coverdell	N	Y	Y	Y	Y	Y
Cleland	Y	Y	N	N	Y	Y
HAWAII						
Akaka	Y	Y	N	N	Y	Y
Inouye	Y	Y	N	N	Y	?
IDAHO						
Craig	N	Y	Y	Y	Y	Y
Kempthorne	N	Y	Y	Y	Y	Y
ILLINOIS						
Durbin	Y	Y	N	N	Y	Y
Moseley-Braun	Y	Y	N	N	Y	Y
INDIANA						
Coats	N	Y	Y	Y	Y	N
Lugar	Y	Y	Y	Y	Y	N
IOWA						
Grassley	N	Y	Y	Y	Y	N
Harkin	Y	Y	N	N	N	Y
KANSAS						
Brownback	N	Y	Y	Y	Y	Y
Roberts	N	Y	Y	Y	Y	Y
KENTUCKY						
McConnell	N	Y	?	Y	Y	Y
Ford	Y	Y	N	Y	Y	Y
LOUISIANA						
Breaux	Y	Y	N	N	Y	Y
Landrieu	Y	Y	N	N	Y	Y
MAINE						
Collins	Y	Y	Y	Y	Y	N
Snowe	N	Y	Y	N	Y	N
MARYLAND						
Mikulski	Y	Y	N	N	Y	Y
Sarbanes	Y	Y	N	N	Y	Y
MASSACHUSETTS						
Kennedy	Y	Y	N	N	Y	Y
Kerry	Y	Y	N	N	Y	Y
MICHIGAN						
Abraham	N	Y	Y	Y	Y	Y
Levin	Y	Y	N	N	Y	Y
MINNESOTA						
Grams	N	Y	Y	Y	Y	N
Wellstone	Y	Y	N	–	+	N
MISSISSIPPI						
Cochran	N	Y	Y	Y	Y	N
Lott	N	Y	Y	Y	Y	Y
MISSOURI						
Ashcroft	N	Y	Y	Y	Y	N
Bond	N	Y	N	Y	?	Y
MONTANA						
Burns	N	Y	Y	Y	Y	Y
Baucus	Y	Y	N	N	Y	N
NEBRASKA						
Hagel	N	Y	Y	Y	Y	N
Kerrey	Y	Y	N	Y	Y	N
NEVADA						
Bryan	Y	Y	N	N	Y	Y
Reid	Y	Y	N	N	Y	N
NEW HAMPSHIRE						
Gregg	N	Y	Y	Y	Y	Y
Smith	N	Y	Y	Y	Y	N
NEW JERSEY						
Lautenberg	Y	Y	N	N	Y	Y
Torricelli	Y	Y	N	N	Y	Y
NEW MEXICO						
Domenici	Y	Y	Y	Y	Y	Y
Bingaman	Y	Y	N	N	Y	Y
NEW YORK						
D'Amato	Y	Y	N	Y	Y	Y
Moynihan	Y	Y	N	Y	N	N
NORTH CAROLINA						
Faircloth	N	Y	N	Y	Y	Y
Helms	N	Y	Y	Y	Y	?
NORTH DAKOTA						
Conrad	Y	Y	N	N	Y	Y
Dorgan	Y	Y	N	N	Y	Y
OHIO						
DeWine	N	Y	Y	Y	Y	Y
Glenn	?	?	?	?	?	?
OKLAHOMA						
Inhofe	N	Y	Y	Y	Y	N
Nickles	N	Y	Y	Y	Y	N
OREGON						
Smith	Y	Y	Y	Y	Y	Y
Wyden	Y	Y	N	N	Y	Y
PENNSYLVANIA						
Santorum	N	Y	Y	Y	Y	N
Specter	Y	Y	N	Y	Y	N
RHODE ISLAND						
Chafee	Y	Y	Y	Y	Y	Y
Reed	Y	Y	N	N	Y	Y
SOUTH CAROLINA						
Thurmond	N	Y	Y	Y	Y	Y
Hollings	?	?	–	?	?	?
SOUTH DAKOTA						
Daschle	Y	Y	N	N	Y	Y
Johnson	Y	Y	N	N	Y	Y
TENNESSEE						
Frist	N	Y	Y	N	Y	Y
Thompson	N	Y	Y	Y	Y	Y
TEXAS						
Gramm	N	Y	Y	Y	Y	N
Hutchison	N	Y	Y	Y	Y	Y
UTAH						
Bennett	Y	Y	Y	Y	Y	Y
Hatch	Y	Y	Y	Y	Y	Y
VERMONT						
Jeffords	Y	Y	Y	Y	Y	Y
Leahy	Y	Y	N	N	Y	Y
VIRGINIA						
Warner	N	Y	Y	Y	Y	Y
Robb	Y	Y	N	N	Y	Y
WASHINGTON						
Gorton	Y	Y	Y	Y	Y	Y
Murray	Y	Y	N	N	Y	Y
WEST VIRGINIA						
Byrd	Y	Y	N	Y	Y	N
Rockefeller	Y	Y	N	N	Y	Y
WISCONSIN						
Feingold	Y	Y	N	N	Y	N
Kohl	Y	Y	N	Y	N	N
WYOMING						
Enzi	N	Y	Y	Y	Y	N
Thomas	N	Y	Y	Y	Y	N

Key

- Y Voted for (yea).
- # Paired for.
- + Announced for.
- N Voted against (nay).
- X Paired against.
- − Announced against.
- P Voted "present."
- C Voted "present" to avoid possible conflict of interest.
- ? Did not vote or otherwise make a position known.

Democrats   *Republicans*

ND Northern Democrats   SD Southern Democrats

Southern states - Ala., Ark., Fla., Ga., Ky., La., Miss., N.C., Okla., S.C., Tenn., Texas, Va.

---

309. Fletcher Nomination/Confirmation. Confirmation of President Clinton's nomination of William A. Fletcher of California to be a judge for the 9th U.S. Circuit Court of Appeals. Confirmed 57-41: R 14-41; D 43-0 (ND 36-0, SD 7-0). Oct. 8, 1998. A "yea" was a vote in support of the president's position.

310. HR 2431. Religious Persecution Overseas/Passage. Passage of the bill to require the State Department to produce an annual report on religious persecution abroad and require the president to impose sanctions ranging from diplomatic protests to cutting off U.S. aid to nations that engage in religious persecution. Passed 98-0: R 55-0; D 43-0 (ND 36-0, SD 7-0). Oct. 9, 1998.

311. HR 4250. Revamp Medical Insurance Regulations/Motion to Proceed. Lott, R-Miss., motion to table (kill) the Daschle, D-S.D., motion to proceed to the bill that would revise managed care and medical insurance regulations. The bill would provide a range of patient protections, create a two-step appeals process for challenging a health plan administrator's decisions and expand the availability of medical savings accounts. Motion agreed to 50-47: R 50-4; D 0-43 (ND 0-36, SD 0-7). Oct. 9, 1998.

312. HR 4104. Fiscal 1999 Treasury-Postal Service Appropriations/Motion to Proceed. Motion to proceed to the conference report on the bill to provide about $27 billion in new budget authority for the Treasury Department, the White House, postal subsidies and civil service benefits in fiscal 1999. Motion agreed to 58-39: R 54-1; D 4-38 (ND 2-33, SD 2-5). Oct. 9, 1998. (Subsequently, Lott, R-Miss., pulled the bill from consideration.)

313. HR 3150. Consumer Bankruptcy Revisions/Motion to Proceed. Motion to proceed to the conference report on the bill to revise the nation's bankruptcy laws by forcing most debtors to file for relief under Chapter 13, instead of Chapter 7, if they have an above-median income and the ability to pay off at least 25 percent of their debts over five years. Motion agreed to 94-2: R 54-0; D 40-2 (ND 33-2, SD 7-0). Oct. 9, 1998. (Subsequently, the Senate moved into morning business and off consideration of the bill.)

314. HR 4328. Fiscal 1999 Omnibus Appropriations/Conference Report. Adoption of the conference report on the bill to provide almost $500 billion in new budget authority for those Cabinet departments and federal agencies whose fiscal 1999 appropriations bills were never enacted. The measure incorporates eight previously separate appropriations bills: Labor-HHS-Education, Interior, Treasury-Postal, Foreign Operations, Commerce-Justice-State, District of Columbia, Agriculture and Transportation. In addition, the bill provides $20.8 billion in "emergency" supplemental spending, including $6.8 billion for military spending ($1.9 billion of it for Bosnia operations), $5.9 billion for relief to farmers, $2.4 billion for anti-terrorism programs, $3.35 billion to address Year 2000 computer problems and $1.55 billion for disaster relief from Hurricane Georges. The measure also contains language to extend expiring tax provisions (at a cost of $9.7 billion over nine years), increase the number of H-1B visas for high-tech foreign workers, impose a three-year moratorium on new taxes on Internet access, implement the Chemical Weapons Convention and extend for six months Chapter 12 of the bankruptcy code, which is designed to help struggling farmers. Adopted (thus cleared for the president) 65-29: R 33-20; D 32-9 (ND 26-9, SD 6-0). Oct. 21, 1998. (HR 4328 was originally the fiscal 1999 Transportation appropriations bill.) A "yea" was a vote in support of the president's position.

Subject Index

Senate Roll Call Votes By Subject

A

Abortion
 Abortion aid to minors, S-41, S-44
 Forced abortions in China, S-27, S-39
 Overseas U.S. military hospitals, S-29
 "Partial birth" abortion, S-43
Agricultural trade
 India and Pakistan trade embargoes, S-31
 Overseas market promotion, S-32
Agriculture and farming
 Agriculture marketing loans, S-32, S-42
 Appropriations, S-33
 Farm relief, S-32, S-33
 Research, S-22
 Temporary farm workers, S-37
Aiken, Ann L.
 Confirmation as U.S. District Court judge, S-4
Air transportation
 Noise control, S-44
Aircraft (military)
 Navy aircraft procurement, S-39
Alaska
 King Cove land transfer, S-45
Anti-missile defense
 Cloture vote, S-22, S-41
Appropriations
 FY 1998
  Military construction
   Line-item veto disapproval, S-5
   Line-item veto disapproval veto override, S-5
  Supplementals, S-9, S-10, S-20
 FY 1999
  Agriculture
   Conference report, S-46
  Commerce, Justice, State and Judiciary, S-34, S-36, S-37
  Defense, S-39, S-45
  Energy and water, S-27
  Foreign operations, S-40
  Interior, S-41, S-42
  Legislative branch, S-34
  Military construction, S-40
  Omnibus appropriations, S-48
  Transportation, S-37
  Treasury, Postal Service and general government, S-38, S-41, S-48
  VA-HUD and independent agencies, S-34
   Conference report, S-47

B

Bankruptcy
 Bankruptcy attorneys, S-43
 Cloture vote, S-41
 Consumer bankruptcy provisions passage, S-44
 Consumer bankruptcy revisions, S-48
 Credit card finance charges, S-42
 Creditor good faith, S-44
 Debtor charitable contributions, S-22
 Federal Reserve interest rates, S-44
 Filing fee waiver, S-43
 IRA protections, S-43
Banks and banking
 ATM surcharges, S-43
 Financial services overhaul
  Cloture, S-46
 Small bank reinvestment, S-37
Block grants
 Child Care and Development Block Grant, S-26
 Education, S-16
Bosnia
 Defense authorization, S-28
 Spending offsets, S-9
 U.S. troops, S-19, S-20, S-39
Budget
 Budget deficit, S-13
 Budget resolution, S-11, S-12, S-13, S-14, S-15
 Budget surplus, S-14

C

Cable industry
 Cable rates, S-36
California
 Moreno confirmation as U.S. district judge for the central district of California, S-4
Campaign finance
 Cloture vote, S-6, S-41
 Labor union dues, S-6
 McCain substitute, S-6
 Snowe amendment, S-5
Child care
 Block grants, S-26
 Funding, S-11
 Funds for parents staying home, S-10
Children
 Child labor, S-38, S-39
 Defense Department Child Development Program, S-28
China
 Chinese commercial fronts, S-23
 Forced abortions, S-27, S-39
 Human rights, S-8
Clinton, President Bill
 Line-item veto
  Military construction disapproval/override, S-5
Commerce, Justice, State, and the judiciary
 Appropriations, S-34, S-36, S-37
Communications and telecommunications
 Telephones
  "Slamming," S-22
Computers and computer industry
 Digital copyright, S-23
Copyright
 Digital works, S-23
Credit
 College-age credit card consumers, S-43
Credit unions
 Business loans, S-37
 Low income loans, S-37
 Membership rules, S-37, S-38
Crime and criminal justice
 Law enforcement and rescue flights, S-35

D

Death penalty
 Court appointed attorney fees in death penalty cases, S-36
Defense
 Appropriations, S-39, S-45
 Base closures, S-28
 Bosnia, S-19, S-28
 Chinese commercial fronts, S-23
 Defense authorization, S-29
  Conference report, S-45
 NATO defense alliance, S-20
 Navy communications system, S-29
 War powers, S-39
Defense Department
 Child Development Program, S-28
Disabled
 Disability programs, S-15
 Education, S-13, S-17
Discretionary spending
 Spending cuts, S-13
Drug control
 Mexico anti-drug certification, S-10
Drunken driving
 Blood alcohol limit, S-6
 Drive-through liquor sales, S-7
 Open container ban, S-6

E

Education
 Additional teachers, S-11
 After-school programs, S-18
 Block grants, S-16
 Blue-ribbon schools, S-17
 Disabled, S-13, S-17
 Education savings accounts, S-8, S-9, S-10, S-16, S-17, S-18, S-28
 Education spending, S-15
 Federal funding, S-17
 High school performance awards, S-17
 Higher education, S-16
 Higher Education Act reauthorization, S-31, S-45
 Market-based lending, S-31
 National class sizes, S-17
 National tests, S-17
 Same gender schooling, S-16
 School construction bonds, S-16
 School dropout prevention, S-18
 School modernization bonds, S-12
 Tax deductions, S-17
 Teacher education, S-31
 Teacher loan forgiveness, S-16
 Teacher merit pay and testing, S-16
 Technology training, S-18
 Welfare education, S-31
Education Department
 Snyder confirmation as assistant secretary for legislation and congressional affairs in the Department of Education, S-19
Energy and water
 FY 1999 appropriations, S-27
Entitlement programs
 Entitlement spending supermajority, S-12
Environment
 Airport noise control, S-44
 Environmental reserve fund, S-13
European Union
 NATO membership, S-19
Executive branch
 Acting presidential appointments, S-44, S-45
Executive orders

F

F-22 fighter aircraft
 Authorization, S-29
FAA
 Pilot license revocation, S-44
 Reauthorization, S-45
 Term limits for staff director and general counsel, S-39
Federal Reserve
 Interest rates, S-44
FEMA
 Spending offsets, S-9
Filibusters and cloture votes
 Product liability, S-30
Fleming, Scott Snyder
 Confirmation as assistant secretary for legislation and congressional affairs in the Department of Education, S-18
Fletcher, William A.
 Confirmation as 9th Circuit Court judge, S-48
Fogel, Jeremy D.
 Confirmation as U.S. district judge for the northern district of California, S-8
Food and nutrition
 Food safety, S-33
Foreign affairs
 Forced abortions in China, S-27
 Kosovo violence, S-9
Foreign operations
 Appropriations, S-40
Foreign trade
 Ammunition device ban, S-38
 India, S-31
 Pakistan, S-31

G

Gambling
 Internet, S-36

Gasoline taxes
 Budget Act waiver, S-7
Graber, Susan
 Confirmation as judge for the 9th U.S. Circuit Court of Appeals, S-8
Guatemala
 Human rights, S-40
Gun control
 Ammunition device ban, S-38
 Firearm purchase background checks, S-34
 Gun locks, S-34
 Gun owner liability, S-35

H

Health
 Biomedical research, S-13
Health care
 Health care costs, S-14
 Patients' "bill of rights," S-14
 Veterans, S-28
Health insurance
 Portability, S-10
Highways and roads
 Construction set-asides for minority-owned businesses, S-7
 Demonstration projects, S-8
 Reauthorization, S-7, S-8
Honduras
 Human rights, S-40
Housing
 Elderly housing, S-13
Human rights
 China, S-8
 Guatemala, S-40
 Honduras, S-40

I

Immigration
 Skilled workers, S-23, S-24
 Temporary farm workers, S-37
India
 Trade sanctions, S-30
Indians and Alaskan natives
 Gambling, S-36
Individual retirement accounts
 Roth IRAs, S-21
Insurance industry
 Medical insurance regulations, S-48
Intelligence
 Whistleblower protection, S-7
Interior
 Appropriations, S-41
 Civil War Battlefield preservation, S-41
International Monetary Fund (IMF)
 Appropriations, S-10
 Lending requirements, S-40
Internet
 Gambling, S-36
 Indecent material, S-47
 Taxes, S-45, S-46, S-47
Iran
 Sanctions, S-24
Iraq
 Saddam Hussein, S-8
IRS
 Capital gains holding period, S-30
 Conference report, S-30
 Ethics waiver, S-21
 IRS oversight board, S-21
 Random audits, S-21
 Surface transportation corrections, S-30

J

Japan
 Financial problems, S-37
Job training
 Federal programs, S-20
Judiciary
 Fletcher nomination and confirmation as 9th Circuit Court judge, S-48

Senate Votes

Fogel confirmation as U.S. district judge for the northern district of California, S-4, S-8
Graber confirmation as judge for the 9th U.S. Circuit Court of Appeals, S-8
Grand jury witnesses, S-35
Judicial confirmations, S-4, S-5
Matz confirmation as district judge for the central district of California, S-29
McKeown confirmation as judge for the 9th U.S. Circuit Court of Appeals, S-10
Miller confirmation as judge of the U.S. Court of Federal Claims, S-4
Molloway confirmation as U.S. district judge for the district of Hawaii, S-27
Moreno confirmation as U.S. district judge for the central district of California, S-4
Morrow confirmation as U.S. district judge for the central district of California, S-5
Murphy confirmation as U.S. district judge for the southern district of Illinois, S-12
Roberts confirmation as U.S. district judge for the eastern district of Michigan, S-30
Sotomayor confirmation as judge for the 2nd U.S. Circuit Court of Appeals, S-46
Young confirmation as U.S. district judge for the southern district of Indiana, S-6

Juvenile justice
Block grants, S-35

K

Kosovo
Violence, S-9

L

Labor and labor unions
Labor union organizing curbs, S-41
Union dues used for campaign finance, S-6
Legislative branch
Appropriations, S-34
Livestock
Price reporting, S-33

M

Maine
Nuclear waste, S-40
Marital and family issues
At-home parents, S-10
Marriage tax penalty, S-12
Mass transit
Funding, S-7
Matz, A. Howard
Confirmation as district judge for the central district of California, S-29
McKeown, M. Margaret
Confirmation as judge for the 9th Circuit Court of Appeals, S-10
Medical ethics
Cloning, S-5
Medical research
Cloning, S-5
Funding, S-13
Medicare
Private contracting, S-11
Mexico
Anti-drug certification, S-10
Military bases
Air force base expansions, S-29
Closures and realignments, S-28
Military construction
Appropriations, S-5
FY 1999, S-40

Military personnel issues
Separate gender barracks, S-28, S-29
Miller, Christine O.C.
Confirmation as judge of the U.S. Court of Federal Claims, S-4
Mines and mining
Regulation, S-42
Minority businesses
Construction set-asides, S-7
Mollway, Susan Oki
Confirmation as U.S. district judge for the district of Hawaii, S-27
Moreno, Carlos R.
Confirmation as U.S. district judge for the central district of California, S-4
Morrow, Margaret M.
Confirmation as U.S. district judge for the central district of California, S-5
Mortgages and home loans
Mortgage lending, S-34
Murphy, G. Patrick
Confirmation as U.S. district judge for the southern district of Illinois, S-12

N

NASA
Funding, S-34
National Endowment for the Arts
Funding, S-42
National Science Foundation
Authorization, S-22
NATO
Defense alliance, S-20
European Union membership, S-19
Expansion, S-9
  Dispute resolution, S-19
  Nuclear weapons, S-20
  Policy, S-19
  POW-MIAs, S-19
  Three-year moratorium on further expansion, S-19, S-20
  Troops in Bosnia, S-19
  U.S. costs, S-19
Strategic statement, S-20
Navy (U.S.)
Communications system, S-29
Nominations and confirmations
Acting presidential appointments, S-44
Fleming as assistant secretary for legislation and congressional affairs in the Department of Education, S-18
Fletcher as 9th Circuit Court judge, S-48
Fogel as U.S. district judge for the northern district of California, S-4, S-8
Graber as judge for the 9th U.S. Circuit Court of Appeals, S-8
Judicial confirmations, S-4, S-5
Matz as district judge for the central district of California, S-29
McKeown as judge for the 9th U.S. Circuit Court of Appeals, S-10
Miller as judge of the U.S. Court of Federal Claims, S-4
Molloway as U.S. district judge for the district of Hawaii, S-27
Moreno as U.S. district judge for the central district of California, S-4
Morrow as U.S. district judge for the central district of California, S-5
Murphy as U.S. district judge for the southern district of Illinois, S-12
Roberts as U.S. district judge for the eastern district of Michigan, S-30
Satcher as surgeon general, S-5
Sotomayor as judge for the 2nd U.S. Circuit Court of Appeals, S-46
Young as U.S. district judge for the southern district of Indiana, S-6
North Korea
Energy project, S-40
Northern Ireland
Peace agreement, S-18

Nuclear waste
Nevada nuclear waste site, S-25
Waste site for three states, S-40
Nuclear weapons
Nuclear test ban funding, S-40
Nuclear weapons, S-20

P

Patents and trademarks
Office relocation, S-35
Postal Service
Post Office closings, S-38
Product liability
Cloture vote, S-30
Property rights
Cloture, S-32
Public debt
Federal debt repayment, S-13
Public lands
Sale, S-15

R

Reagan, former President Ronald
Renaming National Airport for Ronald Reagan, S-4
Religious freedom
Religious persecution overseas, S-48
Retirement and pensions
Personal retirement accounts, S-11
Roberts, Victoria A.
Confirmation as U.S. district judge for the eastern district of Michigan, S-30

S

Saddam Hussein
War crimes charges, S-8
Sanctions
Food and medicine, S-32
Iran, S-24
Terrorist nations, S-33
Unilateral economic sanctions, S-32
Satcher, David
Confirmation as surgeon general, S-5
Senior citizens
Elderly housing, S-13
Ships and shipping
Ocean shipping, S-16
Smoking
Teen smoking, S-33
Veterans' benefits, S-14, S-33
Social Security
Payroll tax, S-14
Personal retirement accounts, S-11
Tax cuts, S-35
Sotomayor, Sonia
Confirmation as judge for the 2nd U.S. Circuit Court of Appeals, S-46
Space
NASA funding, S-34
Space station, S-30
State Department
Reauthorization
  Conference, S-18
Stocks, bonds and securities
Class-action securities lawsuits, S-23
Securities lawsuits statute of limitations, S-22
Student aid
Loan fees, S-31
Teacher loan forgiveness, S-16
Supplemental appropriations
Conference report, S-20

T

Taiwan
U.S. support for Taiwan, S-31
Taxes and taxation
Capital gains holding period, S-30
Cigarette taxes, S-24

Education savings accounts, S-8, S-9, S-10, S-28
Ethanol, S-7
Federal tax deductions, S-12
Gasoline taxes, S-7
Internet taxes, S-45, S-46, S-47
IRS overhaul, S-21
  Conference report, S-30
Marriage penalty, S-12, S-25, S-26, S-38
  Votes, S-39
Random IRS audits, S-21
Tax code termination, S-12, S-38
Tax cuts, S-11, S-35
Tax deductions, S-17
Tax increase supermajority, S-14
Telephones
Secret phone recordings, S-36
"Slamming," S-22
Term limits
FEC staff, S-39
Terrorism
Sanctions on terrorist nations, S-33
Texas
Nuclear waste, S-40
Tobacco
Farmers, S-15
"Look back" penalty, S-25
Veterans' tobacco-related illnesses, S-33
Tobacco industry
Advertising, S-26
Budget Act waiver, S-27
Lawyers' fees, S-24, S-26
Liability, S-24
Restrictions, S-25, S-26, S-32
Settlement revenues, S-11
Tobacco manufacturers immunity, S-11
Transportation
Appropriations, S-37
Conference, S-28
Mass transit, S-7
Surface transportation corrections in IRS overhaul, S-30
Treasury, Postal Service and general government
Appropriations, S-39, S-41

U

United Nations
Peacekeeping, S-10

V

VA-HUD and independent agencies
Appropriations, S-34
Vermont
Nuclear waste, S-40
Veterans
Benefits, S-14
Health care, S-28
Smoking benefits, S-14, S-33
Vietnam
POWs and MIAs, S-36

W

Wages and salaries
Minimum wage, S-43
Welfare and social services
Education, S-31
Self-sufficiency of former welfare recipients, S-6

Y

Young, Richard L.
Confirmation as U.S. district judge for the southern district of Indiana, S-6
Youth
Credit cards, S-43
Teen smoking, S-33

Appendix I
GENERAL INDEX

General Index

A

Abortion. *See also* **Family planning**
  Agriculture appropriations rider, 2-5
  Federal employees' health plan coverage, 2-92, 2-93, 2-95, 2-97, 2-98
  Federal funding of, 2-64, 2-66
  Funding
    District of Columbia, 2-33, 2-36
  Medicare, 2-66, 2-74
  Parental notification, 2-64, 3-3–3-6, 17-10
  "Partial birth" abortion ban, 3-7–3-9
    key votes, C-8, C-17
  RU-486 ban, 2-9
  Separation of abortion and family planning facilities, 2-67
  State Department authorization, 16-8
Abraham, Spencer, R-Mich.
  Abortion legislation, 3-3–3-6
  Bankruptcy overhaul legislation, 5-19
  High-tech worker visas, 17-3–17-9
Abrams, Elliot
  Iran-contra hearings
    scrutiny by independent counsel Lawrence E. Walsh, 2-17
ACLU
  Internet pornography, 22-11
Action on Smoking and Health
  Tobacco legislation, 15-14
Adler, Allan (Association of American Publishers)
  Internet copyright, 22-4, 22-5
Adoption
  Unmarried couples, 2-32, 2-34, 2-35
Affirmative action
  Key votes, C-10, C-18
  Minority contract set-asides, 2-87
Afghanistan
  Sanctions, 16-14
  U.S. airstrikes, 12-9
AFL-CIO
  Campaign spending by unions, 18-11
  Fast-track trade bill, 23-6
  Managed care
    patients' bill of rights, 14-12
  Salting by labor unions, 10-6
Africa
  Foreign trade, 23-4, 23-10–23-12
    impact on U.S. jobs, 23-10
  Human rights violations, 23-10, 23-11
Agency for International Development. *See* **AID**
Agricultural price and income supports
  Maple syrup, 2-126
Agricultural trade
  Exemption of farm exports from sanctions, 2-4, 2-5
  Sanctions, 23-4
Agriculture and farming
  Agriculture spending (chart), 2-10
  Appropriations, 2-3–2-12, 4-3–4-9
  Bankruptcy, 5-15, 5-24
  Black farmers claim USDA discrimination, 2-4
  Crop insurance, 4-3–4-9
  Dairy farms, 2-6, 2-125
  Farm relief package, 2-3, 2-3–2-12
  Omnibus bill, 2-120, 23-6
  Supplemental appropriations crop insurance, 2-129
  Tax breaks, 21-18
Agriculture Committee (House)
  Fast-track trade authority, 23-3
  Members, 7-6
  Rangeland management rules, 11-8
Agriculture Committee (Senate)
  Child nutrition programs, 20-3–20-5
Agriculture Department
  Africa, 23-10
  Appropriations, 2-3–2-12
  Child nutrition program study, 20-4
  Food stamp program, 4-3
  Vietnam, 23-9
AID (Agency for International Development)
  Africa, 23-10
Aid to legal immigrants
  Food stamps, C-11, C-18

AIDS
  Funding for AIDS programs, 2-64, 2-66, 2-69, 2-72, 2-74
  Needle exchanges, 2-64, 2-66
Air Transport Association of America
  FAA guidelines, 24-34, 24-35
Air transportation
  Airline competition, 24-34–24-40
  More flights at crowded airports, 24-37, 24-39, 24-40
  Regulation, 2-116
  Smoking ban, 2-87
Aircraft (military). *See also* **Specific type of aircraft**
  Authorization, 8-4–8-6, 8-9–8-11
  Supplemental appropriations, 2-125, 8-15, 8-16
Airline Planning Group
  Airline competition, 24-39
Akaka, Daniel K, D-Hawaii
  Missile defense, 8-18, 8-20
Alaska
  Appropriations
    local construction projects, 2-114
  Chugach National Forest, 2-60
  Defense appropriations
    military construction projects, 2-81
  Izembek Road, 2-57, 2-58, 2-61, 2-63
  Military construction projects, 2-81, 2-84
  Tongass National Forest, 2-59, 2-60
Albright, Madeleine K.
  IMF funding, 2-46, 2-50, 2-51, 2-56
  Iran, 16-19, 16-22
  NATO expansion, 8-21–8-24
  Religious persecution overseas, 16-10
  State Department authorization
    international family planning, 16-4
  U.N. dues, 16-7
Alderholt, Robert B., R-Ala. (4)
  TVA, 2-44
Alexander, Donald C.
  IRS overhaul, 21-6
Allard, Wayne, R-Colo.
  Financial services overhaul, 5-13
  Juvenile crime, 17-16
Allen, Paul J. (Alliance for Competitive Electricity)
  Electricity deregulation, 15-16
Allen, Tom, D-Maine (1)
  Campaign finance overhaul, 18-10–18-13, 18-16
Alliance for Competitive Electricity
  Electricity deregulation, 15-16, 15-17
AMA
  Physician-assisted suicide, 17-19
America West
  Longer flights from D.C., 24-36
America's Community Bankers
  Financial services overhaul legislation, 5-7
American Association of Health Plans
  Managed care, 14-6, 14-9
American Association of State Highway and Transportation Officials
  Surface transportation reauthorization bill, 24-6, 24-11, 24-19, 24-25
American Automobile Association
  Highway safety, 24-7
American Bankers Association
  Financial services overhaul legislation, 5-5, 5-7, 5-8, 5-9, 5-10, 5-12
  Thrift charters, 5-7
American Bankruptcy Institute
  Bankruptcy overhaul legislation, 5-19
American Business for Legal Immigration
  High-tech worker shortage, 17-4
American Civil Liberties Union. *See* **ACLU**
American Conservative Union
  J. Dennis Hastert, R-Ill. (14) rating, 7-11
American Heart Association
  Cloning, 19-3
American Highway Users Alliance
  Gasoline tax, 24-9
American Insurance Association
  Financial services overhaul, 5-6

American League of Anglers and Boaters
  Ethanol tax credit, 24-18
American Library Association
  Digital copyright, 22-7–22-9
American Medical Association. *See* **AMA**
American Telephone & Telegraph Co. *See* **AT&T**
Americans for Computer Privacy
  Encryption export restrictions, 22-19
Americans for Democratic Action
  J. Dennis Hastert, R-Ill. (14) rating, 7-11
Americans for Tax Reform
  Renaming National Airport for Ronald Reagan, 13-8
AmeriCorps
  Funding, 2-101, 2-103, 2-105
  Supplemental appropriations, 2-125, 2-126, 2-127
Amtrak
  Funding, 2-85–2-88, 2-110, 24-10
Andrews, Robert E., D-N.J. (1)
  Labor unions, 10-6
Annan, Kofi
  United Nations dues, 16-4
Anstrom, Decker (National Cable Television Association)
  Cable rates, 22-16, 22-17
Appalachian Regional Commission
  Funding, 24-5
Appropriations
  Agriculture
    veto message, D-11
  Commerce-Justice-State
    Internet gambling, 22-7
    satellite fee increases, 22-14
  Commerce-Justice-State (chart), 2-19
  Drug control, 2-20
  FY 1998
    Supplementals, 2-121–2-131
  FY 1999
    Commerce-Justice-State, 2-12–2-20
    Defense, 2-20–2-32
    District of Columbia, 2-32–2-36
    District of Columbia (chart), 2-35
    foreign operations, 2-45–2-56
    Interior, 2-57–2-63
    Interior, 2-62
    Labor-HHS-Education, 2-64–2-74, 2-75–2-80
    Labor-HHS-Education (chart), 2-73
    legislative branch, 2-75–2-80
    legislative branch (chart), 2-79
    meat processing price reporting, 2-116
    military base closings, 2-83
    military construction, 2-80–2-84
    military construction spending (chart), 2-83
    omnibus bill, 2-112–2-114
      key votes, C-8–C-9, C-14–C-15, C-17, C-22
    supplementals, 2-117–2-120
    trucking regulation, 2-116
    VA-HUD and independent agencies, 2-101–2-111
    Labor-HHS, 12-10
    Mileposts (chart), 2-131
    TVA, 2-36–2-44
Appropriations Committee (House)
  VA-HUD appropriations, 2-102
Appropriations Committee (Senate)
  Military Construction subcommittee, 8-12
  Tobacco legislation, 15-13
Appropriations, supplemental
  Defense, 2-117
    air and sea transport, 2-32
    anti-missile defense, 2-31
    ground and air combat, 2-31, 2-32
    naval forces, 2-32
  Embassy security, 2-117
  Farm relief, 2-117
  FY 1998 (chart), 2-129
  IMF, 2-126
  War on drugs (chart), 2-119

Aquatic Resources Trust Fund
  Gasoline tax, 24-12
Archer Daniels Midland Co.
  Ethanol tax credit, 24-18, 24-21
  Thrift charters, 5-6
Archer, Bill, R-Texas (7)
  Budget, 6-8, 6-14, 6-17
  China MFN status, 16-34
  Foreign trade, 23-8
  Gasoline tax, 24-16
  IRS overhaul, 21-8, 21-9
  Managed care, 14-4
  Medicare, 14-16, 14-19
  Omnibus bill
    tax cuts, 21-15, 21-17, 21-18
  Trade Adjustment Assistance Program, 21-18
  Trade deficit, 2-79
Architect of the Capitol
  Appropriations, 2-75, 2-76
Arizona
  Defense appropriations
    military construction projects, 2-83, 2-84
Arlington National Cemetery
  Defense authorization, 8-16
Armed Services Committee (Senate)
  Export controls, 16-30
  Military base closings, 8-4–8-6
  Military spending, 8-14
  Missile defense, 8-18
  Mixed gender military training, 8-4
  Thurmond chairmanship, 8-12
  U.S. troops in Bosnia, 8-6, 8-8
Armey, Dick, R-Texas (26)
  Additional flights at crowded airports, 24-37
  Airline competition, 24-37
  Budget surplus, 2-113
  Campaign finance, 18-13, 18-14, 18-16
  China MFN status, 16-34
  D.C. school vouchers, 9-24, 9-25
  Defense appropriations
    military construction projects in home district, 2-81
  Digital copyright, 22-4
  Financial services overhaul, 5-3
  Food stamps, 4-9
  Foreign operations spending bill, 23-7
  House Impeachment inquiry, 7-9
  House Leadership challenges, 7-4, 7-6, 7-8, 7-9
  Public housing, 20-14
  Republican House leadership, 7-5
  Starr report, 12-17
  State Department authorization
    international family planning, 16-6
  Surface transportation reauthorization bill, 24-19
Arms Control and Disarmament Agency
  Satellite export application approvals, 16-30, 16-31
Army (U.S.)
  Funding issues, 5-11
  Ground combat, 8-8, 8-9
Army Corps of Engineers
  Construction projects, 2-37–2-41, 2-43, 2-44
Arts
  Funding, 2-58, 2-59, 2-60
Ashcroft, John, R-Mo.
  Africa, 23-12
  Budget, 6-6, 6-17
  Digital copyright, 22-5
  Education
    national testing, 9-28
  NATO expansion, 8-21, 8-22, 8-24
  "Partial birth" abortion ban, 3-7, 3-9
  Tax cuts, 6-13
  Tobacco, 15-5, 15-9, 15-13
Association of American Medical Colleges
  NIH funding, 2-72
Association of American Publishers
  Internet copyright, 22-4, 22-5
Association of Housing and Redevelopment Officials
  Public housing overhaul, 20-10

General Index

AT&T
　Telephone "slamming," 22-24, 22-26
Attaway, Fritz (Motion Picture Association of America)
　Internet copyright, 22-6
Automobiles and automobile industry
　Fuel economy standards, 2-85
Aviation Consumer Action Project
　Airline competition guidelines, 24-39
Aviation Trust Fund, 24-39
Azerbaijan
　Foreign aid, 2-47, 2-49, 2-56
　Sanctions, 2-45, 2-50, 2-53

B

Babbitt, Bruce
　Interior appropriations, 2-59
　Izembek Road, 2-61
Bachus, Spencer, R-Ala. (6)
　Credit unions, 5-26
　National Credit Union Administration, 22-22
Baesler, Scotty, D-Ky. (6)
　Campaign finance overhaul, 18-7
Baker, Former Sen. Nancy Kassebaum
　Mixed gender military training, 8-3, 8-4, 8-9, 8-13
Baker, Richard H., R-La. (6)
　Budget FY 1999, 2-114
　Character issues, 12-45
　Credit unions, 5-26
　Financial Services Competition Act, 5-8
　Financial services overhaul legislation, 5-11
　National Credit Union Administration, 22-22
　Republican agenda, 7-7
Ballenger, Cass, R-N.C. (10)
　Bilingual education, 9-26
　Head Start, 9-21
　Worker safety, 10-8
BancOne
　Financial services overhaul legislation, 5-7, 5-8, 5-9
Bank of America
　Financial services overhaul legislation, 5-9
Banking and Financial Services Committee (House)
　Credit unions, 5-25, 5-27–5-29
　Financial services mergers, 5-10
　Financial services overhaul, 5-4, 5-8, 5-9, 5-10, 5-12, 5-13
　IMF funding, 16-38
　Public housing, 20-14
　Y2K computer problem, 22-21
Banking, Housing and Urban Affairs Committee (Senate)
　Class-action securities suits, 5-30, 5-31
　Credit unions, 5-25, 5-27, 5-28
　Financial services overhaul, 5-3, 5-8, 5-9, 5-10–5-13
　Surface transportation reauthorization bill, 24-4
Bankruptcy
　Senate overhaul legislation (overview), 5-21
Banks and banking
　Bank Insurance Fund, 5-4
　Citicorp-Travelers Group merger, 5-8, 5-10, 5-11
　Community Reinvestment Act, 5-3, 5-8, 5-11, 5-12, 5-13–5-15, 5-25, 5-27, 5-28
　Financial Services Competition Act, 5-8
　Financial services overhaul, 5-3–5-15
　Glass Steagall Act, 5-3 (history), 5-5, 5-8, 5-9, 5-10, 5-12, 5-14 (history)
　House Banking bill (highlights), 5-4
　Key votes, C-10–C-11, C-18
　Mortgage insurance, 20-9, 20-15
　Office of Thrift Supervision, 5-4
　Reverse mortgages, 20-7
　Savings Association Insurance Fund, 5-4
　Student aid, 9-3–9-14
　Thrift charters, 5-6, 5-7
Banzhaf, John F. III (Action on Smoking and Health)
　Tobacco legislation, 15-14
Barcia, James A., D-Mich. (5)
　Superfund, 11-5
Barr, Bob, R-Ga. (7)
　Clinton impeachment
　　Judiciary Committee opening statement (excerpts), D-32
　Clinton impeachment inquiry, 12-25

Intelligence authorization
　wiretap authority, 8-26
　J. Dennis Hastert, R-Ill. (14)
　　Speakership, 7-11
　Puerto Rico, 13-6, 13-7
Barrett, Bill, R-Neb. (3)
　Clinton impeachment
　　Judiciary Committee opening statement (excerpts), D-33
　High-tech worker visas, 17-5
Barrett, Thomas M., D-Wis. (5)
　Credit unions, 5-26
Barshefsky, Charlene
　Africa trade, 23-10
Bartlett, Roscoe G., R-Md. (6)
　Mixed gender military training, 8-4, 8-13
　United Nations dues, 16-3, 16-4
Barton, Joe L. R-Texas (6)
　Agriculture appropriations, 4-8
Baseball
　Antitrust, 15-25
Bass, Gary D.
　OMB Watch
　　regulatory overhaul, 15-23
Bateman, Herbert H., R-Va. (1)
　Defense appropriations
　　military construction projects in home district, 2-81
Battalino, Barbara
　Clinton impeachment
　　perjury charges, 12-32
Baucus, Max, D-Mont.
　Interior appropriations, 2-61
　Regulatory overhaul, 15-22
　Religious persecution overseas, 16-15, 16-16
　Superfund, 11-6
Bauer, Gary (American Renewal, Inc.)
　Clinton China trip, 16-36
Bauer, Gary (Family Research Council)
　Foreign policy, 16-12
Baxter Healthcare Corp.
　Product liability, 15-19
Beasley, Gov. David, R-S.C.
　Highway Trust Fund, 24-6, 24-7
Becerra, Xavier, D-Calif. (30)
　Bilingual education, 9-27
Belew, Joe (Consumer Bankers Association)
　Student loans, 9-3
Bennett, Robert
　Clinton impeachment depositions, 12-27, 12-28, 12-30, 12-32
　Commodity Futures Trading Commission, 2-4
Bennett, Robert F., R-Utah
　Campaign finance, 18-4
　Clinton character issues, 12-4
　Credit unions, 5-26
　Legislative branch appropriations, 2-75, 2-78
　Y2K computer problem, 22-22
Bentsen, Ken, D-Texas (25)
　Toxic waste disposal, 2-23
Bereuter, Doug, R-Neb. (1)
　Africa, 23-11
　Financial services overhaul legislation, 5-11
　Religious persecution overseas, 16-12
　Taiwan, 16-37
　Technology transfers to China, 8-8
Berger, Samuel R.
　Religious persecution overseas, 16-14
　Technology transfers to China, 16-31
Berman, Howard L., D-Calif. (26)
　Clinton impeachment
　　Judiciary Committee opening statement (excerpts), D-30
　Digital copyright, 22-4
　Gingrich ethics charges, 7-3
　House Ethics committee, 7-3
　Judicial referendum, 17-12
　Missile technology transfers to China, 16-24
　Religious refugees, 16-11
　Russia technology transfers to Iran, 16-22, 16-23
Bevill, former Rep. Tom, D-Alaska (4)
　TVA, 2-39
Bevill, Don
　TVA, 2-39, 2-44
Biden, Joseph R. Jr., D-Del.
　Flag desecration, 17-11
　NATO expansion, 8-21–8-23

Offensive military action, 2-25
Religious persecution overseas, 16-14–16-16
Russia technology transfers to Iran, 16-19
State Department reauthorization, 16-4–16-9
Bilbray, Brian P., R-Calif. (49)
　Clinton impeachment
　　censure resolution, 12-53
　Clinton impeachment vote, 12-40
Bilingual education. *See under* **Education**
Bilirakis, Michael, R-Fla. (9)
　Financial services overhaul legislation, 5-11
　Managed care, 14-8
Bingaman, Jeff, D-N.M.
　Missile defense, 8-19
　NATO expansion, 8-24
　Supplemental appropriations
　　home state projects, 2-129
Binzel, William P. (MasterCard International)
　Bankruptcy overhaul legislation, 5-24
Bishop, Sanford D. Jr., D-Ga. (2)
　Religious freedom, 17-11
Bliley, Thomas J. Jr., R-Va. (7)
　Class-action securities suits, 5-32, 5-33
　Clean air standards, 24-25
　Digital copyright, 22-7
　Electricity deregulation, 15-16, 15-17
　Financial services overhaul, 5-8, 5-11, 5-13
　Internet pornography, 22-11, 22-12
　Internet taxes, 21-21
　Managed care, 14-8, 14-13, 14-14
　Telephone "slamming," 22-24, 22-25
　Tobacco, 15-3
Block grants. *See also* **Community Services Block Grant Act**
　Bilingual education, 9-25–9-28
　Education, 2-65, 2-68
　Social Services Block Grant, 2-69, 2-71, 2-74
Boehlert, Sherwood, R-N.Y. (23)
　Budget negotiations, 6-8
　Forest policy, 11-7, 11-8
　Omnibus parks bill, 11-6, 11-7
　Party unity, 7-9
　Rangeland management rules, 11-8
　Republican agenda, 7-7
　Superfund, 11-5
Boehner, John A., R-Ohio (8)
　Agriculture appropriations, 4-5
　Campaign finance, 18-12
　Farm relief, 2-11
　Fast-track trade bill, 23-6
　Financial services overhaul, 5-3, 5-5, 5-7, 5-10, 5-11
　Food stamps, 4-7
　Foreign trade, 23-7, 23-8
　Gingrich ouster attempt, 7-8
　House leadership challenge, 7-7, 7-8
　House Republican Conference chairmanship, 7-4
　Lawsuit against Jim McDermott, D-Wash. (7), for taping Gingrich call, 7-3
　Managed care legislation, 14-14
　Y2K computer problem, 22-22
Boeing
　Defense contracts, 2-23, 8-9, 8-10
　Glenn spaceflight, 19-12
Bond, Christopher S., R-Mo.
　Cloning, 19-3
　Community health centers, 2-69
　FHA, 2-102, 2-106
　Flammability standards, 2-110
　Home health care, 14-17
　IRS overhaul, 21-7
　Space station, 19-10
　Supplemental appropriations
　　Marine aircraft, 2-125
　　military projects in home state, 2-125
　Surface transportation reauthorization bill, 24-7, 24-19, 24-21
　VA-HUD appropriations, 2-102, 2-105, 2-108, 2-110
Bonilla, Henry, R-Texas (23)
　Appropriations
　　Labor-HHS-Education, 2-66
　Bilingual education, 9-27
　VA-HUD appropriations, 2-108

Bonior, David E., D-Mich. (10)
　Clinton impeachment inquiry, 12-23
　Clinton impeachment trial, 12-53
　Credit unions, 5-27, 5-28
　Minimum wage, 10-7
Bono, Mary, R-Calif. (44)
　Clinton impeachment
　　Judiciary Committee opening statement (excerpts), D-33
Bosnia
　Defense authorization, 2-80, 8-3, 8-5, 8-6, 8-7, 8-8, 8-12, 8-13
　Supplemental appropriations, 2-117
Boswell, Leonard L, D-Iowa (3)
　Farm policy, 1464
Boucher, Rick, D-Va. (9)
　Bankruptcy overhaul legislation, 5-17, 5-18, 5-20
　Cable TV advertising, 22-16
　Clinton impeachment
　　Judiciary Committee opening statement (excerpts), D-30
　Clinton investigation, 12-29–12-31, 12-33, 12-49
　Digital copyright, 22-3, 22-4, 22-6, 22-7
　Partisanship, 12-12
Bowles, Erskine
　Budget surplus, 21-5
　Lieberman's criticism of Clinton, 12-10
　Omnibus bill, 2-112
Boxer, Barbara, D-Calif.
　Criticism of Bill Clinton, 12-9
　Criticism of former Sen. Bob Packwood, 12-8
　Familial relationship to Hillary Rodham Clinton, 12-9
　Gun locks, 2-16
　Loral SpaceCom PAC contributions, 16-25
　"Partial birth" abortion ban, 3-8
Boys and Girls Clubs
　Nutrition programs, 20-3–20-5
Branson, Richard (Virgin Group Ltd.)
　Foreign ownership of domestic airlines, 24-38
Breaux, John B., D-La.
　Clinton Africa trip, 23-11
　Internet pornography, 22-11
　IRS overhaul, 21-4
　State Department authorization
　　abortion, 16-8
　Tobacco, 15-5, 15-6
Bridges, Roy D. Jr.
　Glenn spaceflight, 19-12
Brooke amendment
　Rent control, 20-9, 20-10
Brown, Corinne, D-Fla. (3)
　Ethics investigation, 7-3
Brown, George E. Jr., D-Calif. (42)
　Space station, 19-7, 19-8
Brown, Ronald H.
　Satellite technology export jurisdiction, 16-26
Brown, Sherrod, D-Ohio (13)
　Fast-track trade authority, 23-4, 23-5
Brown, Tim (Electric Power Supply Association)
　Electricity deregulation, 15-17
Brownback, Sam, R-Kan.
　Budget, 6-6, 6-17
　Campaign finance overhaul, 18-4, 18-16
　Internet pornography, 22-11
　Iran, 16-18
　Mixed gender military training, 8-12
　Regulatory overhaul, 15-22, 15-23
　Tobacco, 15-5
Bryan, Richard H., D-Nev.
　Class-action securities suits, 5-30, 5-31
　Financial services overhaul, 5-13
　Internet gambling, 2-15
　Nuclear waste, 11-3, 11-4
Bryant, Ed, R-Tenn. (7)
　Clinton impeachment
　　Judiciary Committee opening statement (excerpts), D-32
　Clinton impeachment inquiry, 12-33
Bryen, Stephen
　Export controls, 16-30
Buchanan, Pat
　1992 Presidential election
　　trade issues, 23-7
Buckman, William E.
　Africa trade, 23-4

General Index

Budget
Budget projections, 6-4
Budget reconciliation bill, 6-13
Budget resolution, 1999, 6-3–6-23
Budget Reconciliation law, 1993 college aid program, 9-3, 9-4
Budget surplus, 21-15–21-18
Continuing resolution, 2-114
Line-item veto, C-9, C-18
Medicare, 21-17
Omnibus appropriations bills, 2-112–2-114
Transportation, 6-6
Budget Committee (Senate)
Tobacco legislation, 6-4
Transportation spending offsets, 24-9, 24-17, 24-19
Bumpers, Dale, D-Ark.
Agriculture appropriations, 2-7
Electricity deregulation, 15-17
Internet taxes, 21-22, 21-23
Little Rock school designated a national historic site, 11-7
Mining regulations, 2-61
Space station, 2-102, 19-6
Bureau of Reclamation
Funding, 2-38
Burns, Conrad, R-Mont.
Appropriations
meat packing price reporting, 2-116
road projects in home state, 2-90
Hazardous materials, 2-90
Internet screening software, 2-15, 2-16
Juvenile crime, 17-16
Military construction projects, 2-80, 2-84, 8-12
School Internet policy, 22-11
Telephone "slamming," 22-24
Burton, Dan, R-Ind. (6)
China, 16-35
United Nations dues, 16-4
Bush, former President George
1998 Presidential campaign ad Willie Horton, 17-16
China MFN status, 16-36
Satellite export licensing, 16-30
Bush, Gov. George W., R-Texas
Bankruptcy overhaul, 5-20
Business Software Alliance
Piracy of copyrighted software, 22-6–22-8
Buyer, Steve, R-Ind. (5)
Bankruptcy overhaul legislation, 5-17
Clinton impeachment
Judiciary Committee opening statement (excerpts), D-31–D-32
Mixed gender military training, 8-4
Byrd, Robert C., D-W.Va.
Appropriations
projects for home state, 2-115
Clinton impeachment apology response (excerpts), D-13
Clinton impeachment trial, 12-53
Highway bill earmarks, 24-6, 24-8, 24-9, 24-11
Kyoto treaty, 2-110
Line-item veto, 2-93, 6-17, 6-20
Military construction projects in home state, 2-84
Mixed gender military training, 8-12
Supplemental appropriations
foreign steel subsidies, 2-126
Surface transportation reauthorization bill, 24-9
Transportation
Gramm-Byrd highway bill amendment, 24-5, 24-6
U.S. troops in Bosnia, 2-24, 8-6

C

Cable industry
Cable rates, 22-14–22-18
California
Defense appropriations
military construction projects, 2-81
Environmental projects, 2-40
Logging on public lands, 2-57
Proposition 227, bilingual education, 9-25
Water projects, 2-37

Callahan, Sonny, R-Ala. (1)
Africa, 23-12
IMF funding, 2-46–2-48, 2-52
Korean Peninsula Energy Development Organization, 2-47
Starr investigation of Clinton, 12-12
Calvert, Ken, R-Calif. (43)
Campaign finance, 18-15
Camp, Dave, R-Mich. (4)
Aid to legal immigrants, 20-16
Space station, 2-107, 2-108
Campaign finance
Clinton Chinese political contributions, 16-26, 16-31
Clinton-Gore political contributions, 12-28
Comparison of campaign finance bills (chart), 18-8
Issue ads, 18-4, 18-8, 18-15
Justice Department memos, 12-32
Key votes, B-43, C-3–C-4, C-13, C-16, C-20
Overhaul, 18-3–18-17
Overhaul bill (highlights), 18-15
Reserve funds used for investigations, 2-77
Soft money, 18-3, 18-7, 18-8, 18-9–18-12, 18-14, 18-15
Campbell, Ben Nighthorse, R-Colo.
Military construction projects in home state, 2-84
Salting by labor unions, 10-5, 10-6
State Department authorization abortion, 16-8
Tobacco industry campaign donations, 15-14
Campbell, Brian (Campbell-Hill Aviation Group)
Airline competition, 24-39
Campbell, Tom, R-Calif. (15)
Gingrich speakership vote, 12-12
Partisanship, 12-12
Campbell-Hill Aviation Group
Airline competition, 24-39
Canada
NATO expansion, 8-22, 8-23
Canady, Charles T., R-Fla. (12)
Abortion legislation, 3-3–3-5
Articles of Impeachment, 12-27
Clinton impeachment
Judiciary Committee opening statement (excerpts), D-31
Clinton impeachment inquiry, 12-39, 12-50, 12-51
Judicial activism, 17-12
Limiting federal prosecutors' powers, 2-17
Litigants' rights to reject judges, 17-13
Physician-assisted suicide, 17-19, 17-20
Starr report, 12-13
Cannon, Christopher B., R-Utah (3)
Articles of impeachment
perjury, 12-48
Clinton impeachment
Judiciary Committee opening statement (excerpts), D-33
High-tech worker visas, 17-6
Capitol building
Artwork in the Capitol, 2-77
Capitol shooting, 2-75, 278
Visitors' Center, 2-78
Capitol Police
Appropriations, 2-75, 2-76, 2-79
Capitol shooting, 2-75, 2-78
Salaries, 2-75
Cardin, Benjamin L., D-Md. (3)
Omnibus bill
tax cuts, 21-15
Case, Stephen H. (National Bankruptcy Conference)
Bankruptcy overhaul legislation, 5-20
Castle, Michael N., R-Del. (AL)
Budget, 6-10, 6-17
Campaign finance, 18-6
Censure resolution, 12-40
Child nutrition programs, 20-3–20-5
Clinton impeachment
censure resolution, 12-47
Clinton impeachment vote
effect on the electorate, 12-49
Highway bill earmarks, 24-12

Cato Institute
Military spending study, 8-14, 8-15
Cavanaugh, Gordon (Council of Large Public Housing Authorities)
Public housing, 20-8, 20-13, 20-14
CBO
Accuracy of forecasts, 2-76, 2-77, 2-78
Appropriations, 2-75, 2-76, 2-80
Budget projections, 6-4
Budget surplus, 6-16
Managed care legislation, 14-13
CDC (Centers for Disease Control and Prevention)
Appropriations, 2-66, 2-68, 2-69, 2-71, 2-74
Census
Methodology, 2-12, 2-13, 13-3–13-5
Census Bureau
Statistical sampling, 13-4, 13-5
Center for Democracy and Technology
Encryption export restrictions, 22-20
Center for Responsive Politics
Airline industry campaign contributions, 24-35
Alcohol industry PAC contributions, 24-15
Health care PAC contributions, 14-5
Soft money campaign contributions, 18-10, 18-11
Centers for Disease Control and Prevention. See CDC
Chabot, Steve, R-Ohio (1)
Clinton impeachment
Judiciary Committee opening statement (excerpts), D-32
Internet taxes, 21-20
Internet use by prisoners, 22-13
Television cameras in courtrooms, 17-13
Chabrow, Jay W.
Space station, 19-6, 19-7, 19-9, 19-10
Chafee, John H., R-R.I.
Abortion legislation, 3-6
Budget surplus, 6-4
Internet taxes, 21-21
Managed care, 14-13
Regulatory overhaul, 15-22
Superfund, 11-5, 11-6
Surface transportation reauthorization bill, 24-4, 24-5, 24-7–24-10, 24-16, 24-17, 24-19–24-21, 24-23, 24-24
Tobacco, 15-6
Wool tariffs, 23-6
Chemical and biological weapons
Chemical Weapons Convention, 8-20, 16-22
Treaty, 16-19
Chemical Weapons Convention, 8-20
Chenoweth, Helen, R-Idaho (1)
Timber programs, 2-60
United Nations dues, 16-4
Child support
States' computer systems, 20-6
Children
After-school programs, 2-74
Discipline for disabled children, 2-70
Head Start, 9-12–9-23
Nutrition programs, 20-3–20-5
Children's Defense Fund
Juvenile crime, 17-16, 17-17
China
Chemical weapons inspections, 8-20
Human rights, 16-37
International Covenant on Civil and Political Rights, 16-37
MFN status, 16-13, 16-26, 16-34, 16-35
MFN trade status, 23-3, 23-4
Missile technology transfers, 16-24–16-34
House action, 8-3, 8-16
Senate action, 8-7, 8-8
Satellite sanctions (history), 16-28, 16-29
Technology transfers to Pakistan, 16-30, 16-35
Tiananmen Square incident (1989), 16-26, 16-30, 16-35
Trade relations, 2-7
China Great Wall Industry Corp.
Commercial satellite launches, 16-32
Christensen, Jon, R-Neb. (2)
Budget cap, 2-115
China MFN status, 16-34

Christian Coalition
FEC investigation, 2-92
Religious freedom, 17-9, 17-11
Religious persecution overseas, 16-9, 16-11–16-15
School prayer amendment, 17-10
Christopher, Warren
Communications satellite export restrictions, 16-26
Chung, Johnny
Clinton campaign contribution controversy, 16-32
CIA
Authorization, 8-25–8-27
China technology transfer investigation, 16-31, 16-35
Cinelli, Patricia (American Bankers Association)
Financial services overhaul legislation, 5-9
Cisco Systems Inc.
Encryption export restrictions, 22-19
Citicorp Inc.
Travelers Group merger, 5-8, 5-10, 5-11, 5-12, 5-13
Citizens Against Government Waste
Transportation earmarks, 24-25
Civil Rights Act
Bilingual education, 9-26
Claiborne, Judge Harry E.
Impeachment, 12-50
Clay, William L., D-Mo. (1)
Juvenile crime, 17-18
Salting by unions, 10-5, 10-6
Youth after-school programs, 20-5
Claybrook, Joan (Public Citizen)
Campaign finance, 18-9
Cleland, Max, D-Ga.
Mixed gender military training, 8-12
Clement, Bob, D-Tenn. (5)
TVA funding, 2-44
Clinton, President Bill
Abortion legislation, 3-5–3-6
"Partial birth" abortion ban, 3-7–3-9
Africa trade, 23-10, 23-11, 23-12
Bankruptcy overhaul legislation, 5-15, 5-19, 5-24
Budget surplus, 6-16
Campaign finance abuses, 16-32, 18-11, 18-17
China MFN status, 16-36
China policy, 16-24
China visit, 8-7, 8-8
Class-action securities suits, 5-30–5-33
Clean water, 2-63
Climate initiatives, 2-63
Comp time, 10-7
Credit union legislation, 5-27, 5-29
Crime bill, 2-13
Crime proposal
"three strikes and you're out," 17-16
Defense authorization
aircraft, 8-6
anti-missile defenses, 8-17
National Guard and Reserve, 8-13, 8-16
NATO expansion, 8-22–8-24
student aid, 9-3
U.S. troops in Bosnia, 8-5, 8-6
Defense budget, 8-14
Digital copyright, 22-9
Electricity deregulation, 15-16, 15-17
Executive order
Federal cost-benefit studies, 15-22
Fast-track trade authority, 23-4, 23-5, 23-7
Financial Services Competition Act veto threat, 5-8
Financial services overhaul legislation, 5-10, 5-14
Food stamps, 4-3–4-6, 4-8, 4-9
Glenn spaceflight, 19-11
Global Positioning System standard, 19-5
Grand jury testimony (excerpts), D-23–D-29
Grazing fee schedule, 11-8
High-tech worker visas, 17-6, 17-7, 17-8, 17-9
Highway bill, 24-3, 24-14, 24-16, 24-20, 24-22, 24-23, 24-24, 24-25, 24-26
House impeachment vote, remarks, D-46–D-47

General Index

Impeachment
  abuse of power charge, 12-47
  apology, D-13
  Articles of Impeachment, 12-46,
    C-15, C-22, D-40, D-40–D-41
  censure resolution, 12-17, 12-20,
    12-30, 12-31, 12-33, 12-35, 12-36,
    12-41, 12-44, 12-47, 12-49
  criticism of Starr, 12-8
  defense, 12-36–12-39
  effect on Social Security legislation,
    12-44, 12-45
  Grand Jury testimony (excerpts),
    D-22–D-27
  Judiciary Committee opening
    statements (excerpts), D-29–D-33
  Judiciary Committee report
    (excerpts), D-42–D-45
  obstruction of justice charge, 12-18,
    12-30, 12-47
  perjury charge, 12-16, 12-18, 12-30,
    12-37, 12-44, 12-45, 12-47, 12-48,
    12-53
  points of contention (chart), 12-18
  testimony of convicted perjurers,
    12-32
  witness tampering charge, 12-37,
    12-38
Impeachment effort
  responses to Judiciary Committee
    questions, 12-47
Impeachment investigation and trial,
  12-3–12-53
  House managers' ideology, 12-11
Independent Counsel report
  White House response (excerpts),
    D-22
Independent Counsel report (excerpts),
  D-15–D-21
Internet indecency
  Starr report on the Internet, 22-11
Internet taxes, 21-21, 21-23
Iran, 16-22
Iraq, U.S. airstrikes against, 12-3, 12-6
  GOP critique of timing, 12-45, 12-49,
    12-51
IRS overhaul, 21-3, 21-6, 21-7
Judge-imposed tax increases, 17-13
Labor unions, 10-6
Lapse in judgment speech (text), D-13
  Lieberman response (excerpts), D-13–
    D-14
Line-item veto, 6-18, 6-19, 6-22, 6-23
  federal employees pension plan
    lawsuit, 2-93
Managed care, 12-6, 14-6, 14-7, 14-12,
  14-15
Medical identification number, 14-14
Military base closings, 8-4, 8-5
Military pay raises, 8-3, 8-4, 8-13, 8-14
Military recruiting and education
  benefits, 8-13, 8-14
Minimum wage, 10-7
Missile technology transfer to China,
  16-34
NASA funding, 19-8
Nevada nuclear waste site, 11-3, 11-4
Omnibus bill
  Social Security, 21-18
  State Department authorization, 16-3
  tax cuts, 21-14, 21-15, 21-17
Patients' bill of rights, 14-3, 14-4, 14-6
Product liability, 15-18
Property rights, 15-23, 15-24
Religious persecution overseas
  sanctions, 16-11, 16-16
Satellite licensing transferred from State
  Dept. to Commerce Dept., 16-30
Satellite technology transfer to China,
  16-24
Sex scandals
  effect on military ethical standards,
    8-4
  Jones sexual harassment lawsuit,
    12-3, 12-6–12-8, 12-13, 12-14,
    12-16, 12-18, 12-21, 12-26, 12-28,
    12-30, 12-37, 12-38, 12-46 (articles
    of impeachment), 12-47, 12-51
  Kathleen Willey, 12-28, 12-32
  Monica Lewinsky, 2-18, 7-5, 7-10,
    12-3–12-5, 12-6, 12-7, 12-9, 12-
    11–12-21, 12-23–12-31, 12-37,
    12-38, 12-44, 12-45, 12-46–12-50,
    16-33

release of Starr report, C-13–C-14,
  C-22
Republican response, 7-10
Social Security, 7-9
Space station, 19-5–19-9
Starr investigation, 2-17, 12-14
  chronology, 12-4, 12-5
  Whitewater, 12-26
State Department authorization
  U.N. dues, 16-3, 16-8, 16-9
State of the Union address, 12-3–12-7,
  147–149, D-3–D-8
  Republican response, D-8–D-10
  Social Security solvency, 21-14,
    21-17
Student aid, 9-3–9-4
Supplemental appropriations
  IMF funding, 2-129
  U.N. dues, 2-129
Technology transfers to China, 16-34,
  16-35
Telephone "slamming," 22-25, 22-26
Tobacco, 15-5, 15-6, 15-11
U.N. dues, D-12
U.S. airstrikes on Afghanistan and
  Sudan, 12-9
Vietnam, 23-4
Vietnam trade, 23-9
Whitewater investigation, 12-4
Y2K computer problem, 22-22
Clinton, Hillary Rodham
  Critique of right-wing extremists, 12-6
  Impeachment vote caucus, 12-49
Clinton-Gore campaign
  Campaign finance abuses, 18-9, 18-17
Cloning
  Key votes, C-3, C-16
Cloture votes. See Filibusters and
  cloture votes
Coast Guard (U.S.)
  Funding, 2-85–2-88
    drug interdiction, 2-86, 2-87
Coats, Daniel R., R-Ind.
  Bosnia mission, 2-24
  Budget surplus, 6-3
  China MFN status, 16-13
  Head Start, 9-20, 9-22, 9-23
  Internet pornography, 2-16, 22-10, 22-12
  Line-item veto, 6-23
  Low-income savings accounts, 9-22,
    9-23
  Religious persecution overseas, 16-13
  U.S. airstrikes on Afghanistan and
    Sudan, 12-9
Coble, Howard, R-N.C. (6)
  Africa, 23-11
  Clinton impeachment
    Judiciary Committee opening
      statement (excerpts), D-30
  Digital copyright, 22-3, 22-4, 22-9
  Federal judges' powers, 17-13
  Satellite retransmission licenses, 22-14
  Satellite TV fee increase, 22-15, 22-17
  Satellite TV fees, 22-14–22-17
  Textiles and clothing, 23-11
Coburn, Tom, R-Okla. (2)
  Highway projects, 24-12
  Home health care, 14-21
  Labor-HHS-Education appropriations,
    2-71
  "Partial birth" abortion ban, 3-7
  Party unity, 7-8
  RU-486 ban, 2-5, 2-9
  Veterans' medical programs, 2-108
Cochran, Thad, R-Miss.
  Anti-ballistic defense, 8-18–8-20
  Export controls, 16-27
  Farm disaster relief, 2-7
  Technology transfers to China
    investigation, 16-18
  Technology transfers to rogue states,
    16-18
Cohen, Jordan J.
  NIH funding, 2-72
Cohen, William S.
  Bosnia mission, 2-24
  MEADS system, 8-10
  Military base closings, 8-5
  Military base visits, 8-14
  Military readiness, 2-26
    subcontracting, 2-30
  Mixed gender military training, 8-4, 8-9
  NATO expansion, 8-24

COLAs (Cost of Living Adjustments)
  Members of Congress, 2-91, 2-94, 2-95
Collins, Mac, R-Ga. (3)
  Africa, 23-11
  Textiles and clothing, 23-11
Collins, Susan, R-Maine
  IRS overhaul, 21-7
  "Partial birth" abortion ban, 3-8
  State Department authorization
    international family planning, 16-7,
      16-8
    U.N. dues, 16-7, 16-8
  Telephone "slamming," 22-24, 22-26
Colorado
  Defense appropriations
    military construction projects, 2-81,
      2-84
  Military construction projects, 2-81
Colvin, Joe (Nuclear Energy Institute)
  Nevada nuclear waste site, 11-4
Commerce Committee (House)
  Class-action securities suits, 5-30, 5-32,
    5-33
  Commercial space bill, 19-5
  Digital copyright, 22-6–22-8
  Financial services overhaul legislation,
    5-4, 5-5, 5-10, 5-11
  Internet pornography, 22-11
  Internet taxation, 21-19–21-21
  Members, 7-6
  Space station audit, 19-6
  Telephone "slamming" and unsolicited
    e-mail, 22-24
  Tobacco legislation, 15-3, 15-13
Commerce Committee (Senate)
  China's ICBM program, 16-34
  Class-action securities suits, 5-31
  FAA authorization, 24-36
  Product liability, 15-18
  Satellite TV fee increases, 22-14,
    22-16–22-18
  Telephone "slamming," 22-24, 22-26
Commerce Department
  Census, 13-5
  Encryption export restrictions, 22-19
  Patent and Trademark Office relocation,
    2-92
  Satellite export application approvals,
    16-30
  Satellite export restrictions, 8-4, 8-13,
    8-16, 16-27, 16-30
  Satellite exports to China, 16-33
Commerce, Science, and Transportation
Committee (Senate)
  Internet pornography, 22-10
  Tobacco legislation, 15-3, 15-7, 15-8,
    15-11, 15-12
Commerce-Justice-State appropriations
  Census Bureau funding, 13-3
  D.C. appropriations, 2-35
  Illegal immigrant status change, 17-4
  Refugees, 17-4
  State Department authorization, 16-4
Commission on Standards of Official
Conduct (House)
  Gingrich investigation, 7-3
Commodity Credit Corporation
  Appropriations, 2-4
Common Cause
  Campaign finance, 18-7, 18-10, 18-16
Communications and
telecommunications
  Communications Decency Act, 22-10–
    22-12
  Congressional Research Service report
    on the Internet, 2-78
  Internet screening software, 2-16
  Technology transfers to China, 8-3, 8-16
    perceived effect on U.S. satellite
      companies, 8-7
  Telecommunications law, 22-15
Communications Decency Act, 22-10–
22-12
Community Development Block Grant
  Public housing, 20-15
Community Services Block Grant Act
  Appropriations, 9-23
  Bilingual and immigrant education, 9-26
  Reauthorization, 9-22, 9-23
Computers and computer industry
  Encryption export restrictions, 22-19,
    22-20
  Supplemental appropriations
    Y2K computer problem, 2-117

Y2K computer problem, 2-78, 2-79, 2-80,
  2-91–2-94, 2-97, 2-100, 22-21–22-23
Concerned Women for America
  GOP principles, 12-52
Congressional affairs
  Cost of living adjustments, 2-91, 2-94,
    2-95
  Ethics investigation of Rep. Bud
    Shuster, R-Pa. (9), 7-3
  Ethics investigation of Rep. Corinne
    Brown, D-Fla. (3), 7-3
  Ethics investigation of Rep. Jay C. Kim,
    R-Calif. (41), 7-3
  Ethics investigation of Rep. Newt
    Gingrich, R-Ga. (6), 7-3
  House leadership scandals, 7-10
  House Republican leadership votes, 7-9
  Lawsuit against Jim McDermott, D-
    Wash. (7) for taping Gingrich phone
    call, 7-3
  New House panel chairmen, 7-6
  Overview of 105th Congress, 2nd
    session, 1-3–1-6
  Second Session by the numbers, 1-6
Congressional Black Caucus
  Public release of Starr report, 12-13,
    12-17
Congressional Budget Office. See CBO
Congressional Cemetery
  Appropriations, 2-75, 2-78, 2-79, 2-80
Congressional Research Service
  Reports on the Internet, 2-78
Connelly, William F. Jr.
  Tobacco debate, 15-13
Conrad, Kent, D-N.D.
  Emergency assistance to farmers, 2-7
  Farm loans, 2-11
  Foreign trade, 23-6
  Internet taxes, 21-22
  NATO expansion, 8-24
  Tobacco, 6-5, 15-13
  Trade with Africa, 23-4
Conservation
  Land and Water Conservation Fund,
    2-57
Conservative Action Team. See House
  Conservative Action Team
Conservative Coalition
  1998 votes, B-25
  Background, B-24
  History (graph), B-9
  House votes, B-26, B-27
  Leading scorers, B-10
  Senate votes, B-28
  Vote studies, B-9–B-11
Constantine, Thomas K. (DEA)
  Physician-assisted suicide, 17-18
Constitution (U.S.)
  Takings clause, 15-24
Consumer Electronics Manufacturing
Association
  Digital copyright, 22-9
Consumer Federation of America
  Bankruptcy overhaul legislation, 5-24
Consumer Product Safety Commission.
See CPSC
Consumers Union
  Cable TV rates, 22-15
Contract With America, 7-5
  School lunch program, 20-5
Conyers, John Jr., D-Mich. (14)
  Abortion legislation, 3-4
  Bankruptcy overhaul legislation, 5-17
  Clinton impeachment hearings, 12-3,
    12-35
  House Impeachment inquiry
    opening statement (excerpts), D-29,
      D-37–D-38
  Limiting federal prosecutors' powers,
    2-17, 2-18
  Nixon Watergate investigation, 12-15
  Physician-assisted suicide, 17-19
Copyright
  Digital works, 22-3–22-9
Cost of Living Adjustments. See COLAs
Couch, Linda (National Low Income
Housing Coalition)
  Public housing vouchers, 20-15
Council of Large Public Housing
Authorities
  Public housing, 20-8
Council on Environmental Quality
  Global warming, 2-101, 2-107

General Index

Court TV
  Television cameras in courtrooms, 17-14
Coverdell, Paul, R-Ga.
  Budget resolution, 6-7
  IRS overhaul, 21-7
  Renaming National Airport for Ronald Reagan, 13-7
  School vouchers, 15-11
Cox, Archibald
  Firing, 12-21
Cox, Christopher, R-Calif. (47)
  Export controls, 16-26–16-29, 16-32
  House GOP Policy Committee leadership, 7-8, 7-10
  House speakership prospects, 7-11
  Internet taxes, 2-19–21-21
  Livingston leadership, 7-8
  Supplemental appropriations, 2-124
Coyne, Joseph R. (Federal Reserve Board)
  Citicorp-Travelers Group merger, 5-9
CPSC (Consumer Product Safety Commission)
  Flammability standards, 2-101, 2-108, 2-110
Craig, Gregory B.
  Clinton impeachment
    censure resolution, 12-31
Craig, Larry E., R-Idaho
  Budget negotiations, 6-7
  Campaign finance, 18-17
  Clinton investigation
    effect on legislative agenda, 12-9
  Drug control and Megan's law, 15-11
  Farm relief, 2-11
  Indian tribe gambling, 2-15
  Kyoto treaty, 2-102
  Labor, HHS, and Education appropriations, 2-69
  Line-item veto, 6-23
  Military construction projects, 2-82
  NATO expansion, 8-24
  Nevada nuclear waste site, 11-3, 11-4
  Nuclear power industry financing, 2-40
  Supplemental appropriations
    Forest Service, 2-126
    weapons imports, 2-130
Cramer, Robert E. "Bud," D-Ala. (5)
  Kyoto treaty, 2-104
Crane, Philip M., R-Ill. (8)
  Africa trade, 23-10
  Sudan sanctions, 16-12
Crapo, Michael D., R-Idaho (2)
  Electricity deregulation, 15-16
Crawford, Mead (National Republican Congressional Committee)
  Campaign spending by unions, 18-11
Credit Union National Association
  Credit union legislation, 5-26, 5-28, 5-29
Credit unions
  Community Reinvestment Act, 5-25, 5-27, 5-28
  Legislation, 5-7, 5-8, 5-12
  Membership issues, 5-25
Crime and criminal justice
  Identity theft, 17-16
  Law enforcement on tribal lands, 2-58
Cropper, Cabell C. (National District Attorneys Association)
  Juvenile crime bill, 17-17
Crowell, Craven
  TVA funding, 2-44
Cubin, Barbara, R-Wyo. (AL)
  National forests, 11-7
Cunningham, Randy "Duke," R-Calif. (51)
  Congressional Cemetery, 2-76
  Salting by labor unions, 10-6
  Viagra, 2-67
Cuomo, Andrew M.
  Gore 2000 campaign, 20-10
  Housing vouchers, 2-110
  Public housing, 2-103, 2-106, 2-111, 20-10, 20-11, 20-14, 20-15
Currie, Betty
  Clinton alleged witness tampering, 12-12, 12-38
Cystic Fibrosis Foundation
  Cloning, 19-3
Czech Republic
  NATO expansion, 8-21–8-23

D

D'Amato, Alfonse M., R-N.Y.
  Bankruptcy overhaul legislation, 5-20
  Breast cancer, 2-74, 2-116
  Budget, 6-15
  Campaign finance overhaul, 18-4, 18-16, 18-17
  Class-action securities suits, 5-30, 5-31
  Clinton impeachment, 12-41
  Community Reinvestment Act, 5-12
  Credit unions, 5-25, 5-27, 5-29
  Defense Production Act of 1950, 8-13
  Export controls, 16-28
  FHA, 2-103
  Financial services overhaul legislation, 5-8, 5-9, 5-10–5-14
  Flood insurance, 6-15
  Food stamps, 4-7
  Iran-Libya Sanctions Act (1996), 16-22
  Managed care, 14-3–14-6
  Minimum wage, 10-7
  Public housing, 20-10, 20-11, 20-14
  Surface transportation reauthorization bill, 24-4, 24-8, 24-9, 24-23, 24-25
  Tobacco, 15-7
Daley, William M.
  Census, 13-3, 13-5
Darbelnet, Robert L. (American Automobile Association)
  Highway safety, 24-7
Daschle, Tom, D-S.D.
  Appropriations
    meat packing price reporting, 2-116
  Chinese human rights issues, condemnation of, 8-11, 8-12
  Clinton censure, 12-20
  Clinton China trip, 16-36
  Clinton impeachment hearings in lame-duck session, 12-14
  Clinton impeachment trial duration, 12-36
  Clinton perjury charge, 12-16
  Clinton support, 12-10
  Farm relief, 2-9, 2-11, 2-114
  FEC term limits, 2-96
  High-tech worker visas, 17-6
  IMF funding, 2-45
  Managed care legislation, 2-105, 14-3, 14-7, 14-13, 14-14
  Omnibus appropriations bill
    home state projects, 2-37
  Omnibus bill
    tax cuts, 21-17
  "Partial birth" abortion ban, 3-7, 3-8
  Renaming National Airport for Ronald Reagan, 13-7, 13-8
  Russia sanctions for Iran nuclear assistance, 16-17
  State Department authorization, 16-7
  Surface transportation reauthorization bill, 24-7
    home state projects, 24-24
  Tobacco, 15-11
  Transportation legislation, 24-5
  VA-HUD appropriations
    health care rider, 2-106
Dash, Sam
  Resigns as advisor to Ken Starr, 12-27, 12-30
Davidson, Alan (Center for Democracy and Technology)
  Encryption export restrictions, 22-20
Davis, Thomas M. III, R-Va. (11)
  NRCC leadership, 7-7, 7-8, 7-10
  Renaming National Airport for Ronald Reagan, 13-9
Davis-Bacon Act
  Head Start compliance, 9-21, 9-22
DEA
  Physician-assisted suicide, 17-18, 17-19
Death on the High Seas Act (1920)
  Airline crash compensation, 24-39
DeFazio, Peter A., D-Ore. (4)
  Renaming National Airport for Ronald Reagan, 13-8, 13-9
Defense
  Appropriations, 2-20–2-32, 8-3–8-20
    active-duty forces, 8-11
    air and sea transport, 8-11
    air combat, 2-27
    AMRAAM missile defense system, 8-6
    anti-terrorism and intelligence, 2-31
    Arlington National Cemetery, 8-16
    artillery, 8-9
    Bosnia, 2-80
    cancer research, 2-27
    conference agreement (chart), 2-29
    Coast Guard Reserve, 8-11
    ground combat, 2-26
    major weapons programs, 2-22, 2-23
    military pay, 2-21, 2-22, 2-27
    military pensions, 8-15
    military personnel issues, 2-80, 2-81, 2-83
    military readiness, 2-28
    National Guard and Reserve, 8-13, 8-16
    naval forces, 2-27
    supplementals, 2-30, 2-31
    THAAD and MEADS missile defense systems, 2-20, 2-21, 2-23, 2-31, 8-3, 8-6, 8-10, 8-16, 8-17
    Y2K computer problem, 2-21–2-23
  Army and National Guard, 5-11
  Authorization amendments
    perceived effect on U.S. China relations, 8-7
  Bosnia, 2-20–2-26, 2-28, 2-29, 8-3, 8-6, 8-8, 8-12, 8-13
  Chinese acquisition of former Navy base, 8-16
  Emergency appropriations
    U.S. troops in Bosnia, 8-13
  Military ethics, 8-4
  Missile defense, 8-10, 8-15, 8-16
Defense Department
  Satellite export application approvals, 16-30
  Space launch infrastructure study, 19-9
  Y2K problem, 2-21
Defense Production Act of 1950
  Extension of, 8-13
DeGette, Diana, D-Colo. (1)
  Class-action securities suits, 5-32, 5-33
Delahunt, Bill, D-Mass. (10)
  Bankruptcy overhaul legislation, 5-19, 5-20
    homestead exemptions, 5-18
  Clinton impeachment
    Judiciary Committee opening statement (excerpts), D-32
  Clinton investigation, 12-29–12-31, 12-33
  Judge-imposed tax increases, 17-12, 17-13
DeLauro, Rosa, D-Conn. (3)
  Abortion coverage in federal employee health plans, 2-95
  Flammability standards, 2-108
  Mining regulations, 2-67–2-69
  RU-486 ban, 2-5, 2-9
DeLay, Tom, R-Texas (22)
  Bilingual education, 9-27
  Budget, 6-12
  Call for Clinton resignation, 12-34
  Campaign finance overhaul, 18-11, 18-12, 18-14, 18-16
  Censure resolution, 12-40
  Clinton impeachment, 7-8
    censure resolution, 12-17, 12-40, 12-41
    effect on legislative agenda, 12-10
    Republican party unity, 12-53
  Digital copyright, 22-9
  Disagreements with Robert L. Livingston, R-La. (1), 7-8
  Encryption export restrictions, 22-19
  Family planning, 2-67
  Fast-track trade authority, 23-4
  Gingrich ouster attempt, 7-8
  House leadership challenge, 7-4, 7-6, 7-8, 7-9
  House speakership campaign, 12-46, 12-52
  IMF funding, 2-45, 2-45–2-49, 2-52, 2-53, 2-54, 16-38
  Impeachment as penalty, 12-41
  Impeachment of judges, 12-51
  Iraq airstrikes, 12-51
  IRS overhaul, 21-6, 21-7
  J. Dennis Hastert, R-Ill. (14)
    Speakership, 7-11, 12-45
  Judicial impeachments, 17-12
  Judicial powers, 17-13
  Kyoto treaty, 2-52, 2-104
  Livingston resignation, 12-45
  Missile technology transfers to China, 16-24
  Opposition to appointment of David McCurdy to head Electronic Industries Alliance, 22-9
  Prison overcrowding, 17-12–17-14, 17-15
  Public housing, 2-103, 20-14
  Public release of Starr report, 12-12
  Religious persecution overseas, 16-12, 16-14
  Renaming National Airport for Ronald Reagan, 13-9
  Republican legislative strategy, 12-10
  Starr report, 12-9, 12-17
  State Department authorization, 16-4, 16-5, 16-8
  Supplemental appropriations, 2-123
    IMF funding, 2-128
  Surface transportation reauthorization bill, 24-3, 24-6, 24-11, 24-13
  U.S. Taiwan policy, 16-37
Dell Computers
  High-tech worker visas, 17-4
Dell, Michael (Dell Computers)
  High-tech worker visas, 17-4
Democratic Party
  "Blue Dog" coalition
    campaign finance overhaul, 18-7
    Clinton impeachment resolution, 12-24
  Campaign finance abuses, 18-9, 18-17
Denmark
  NATO expansion, 8-22, 8-23
Dershowitz, Alan
  Criticism of Hyde and the impeachment effort, 12-33
DeWine, Mike, R-Ohio
  Abortion coverage in health plans, 2-97
  Abortion legislation, 3-6
  Coast Guard drug interdiction funding, 2-87
  Drug control, 2-119
  Haiti, 2-51
  IRS overhaul, 21-7
  Job training programs, 10-3, 10-4
  Military doctor licensing, 8-13
  Property rights, 15-24
  Tobacco, 15-10
Diaz-Balart, Lincoln, R-Fla. (21)
  Religious persecution overseas, 16-13
Dickey, Jay, R-Ark. (4)
  Clinton impeachment, 12-24
  EEOC appropriations, 2-15
  NLRB funding, 2-65
Dicks, Norm, D-Wash. (6)
  Technology transfers to China, 16-32
diGenova, Joseph
  Clinton perjury charge, 12-16
Dingell, John D., D-Mich. (16)
  Automobile Heritage Area, 11-7
  Class-action securities suits, 5-32, 5-34
  Clean air standards, 24-25
  Financial services overhaul legislation, 5-5, 5-11
  Loral SpaceCom PAC contributions, 16-25
  Managed care legislation, 14-3, 14-4, 14-6, 14-14, 14-15
  Public release of Starr report, 12-12
  Telephone "slamming," 22-25
Disabled
  Discipline for disabled children, 2-70
  Education, 2-74
  Individuals with Disabilities Education Act, 2-65
Disaster aid
  Midwest flood victims, 7-8
Disney Co.
  Internet pornography, 22-12
District of Columbia
  Appropriations, 2-32–2-36, 9-24
  Commuter tax, 2-36
  Correctional facilities funding, 2-35
  School vouchers, 2-32–2-36, 9-24, 9-25
Dixon, Julian C., D-Calif. (32)
  D.C. appropriations, 2-34
Dobson, James (Focus on the Family)
  Religious freedom, 17-10, 17-11
Dodd, Christopher J., D-Conn.
  Bankruptcy overhaul legislation, 5-20
  Class-action securities suits, 5-30, 5-31
  Internet screening software, 2-15
  Product liability, 15-19

General Index

Doggett, Lloyd, D-Texas (10)
  Child care, 6-12
  Surface transportation reauthorization bill, 24-15
Dole, former Sen. Bob, R-Kan.
  Clinton impeachment
    censure resolution, 12-20,12-47, 12-53
  Gingrich ethics charges, 7-3
  NATO expansion, 8-24
  Regulatory overhaul, 15-20, 15-23
Domenici, Pete V., R-N.M.
  Appropriations
    Labor-HHS-Education, 2-68
  Army Corps of Engineers funding, 2-38, 2-40, 2-41, 2-43
  Budget, 2-116, 6-3, 6-9–6-15
  Energy Department oversight, 2-37, 2-38
  Home state appropriations, 2-41, 2-126
  IMF funding, 2-48
  IRS overhaul, 21-7
  Line-item veto, 6-17, 6-20
  Military families receiving food stamps, 2-25
  Roswell law enforcement academy, 2-120
  Russia nuclear stockpile, 2-39
  Social Security, 6-4
  Supplemental appropriations, 2-123, 2-124, 2-126
  Tobacco, 6-4, 6-5
  Transportation spending offsets, 24-6–24-9, 24-17, 24-19
  Veterans' smoking-ailment benefits, 24-8, 24-14
Doolittle, John T., R-Calif. (4)
  Campaign finance, 18-9, 18-12, 18-13, 18-15, 18-16
Dorgan, Byron L., D-N.D.
  Airline competition, 24-38
  Arms control, 8-19
  Ban on alcohol containers in cars, 24-7
  Clinton impeachment, 12-34
  Financial services overhaul legislation, 5-14
  GAO comptroller, 2-75, 2-76
  Internet taxes, 21-23
  IRS overhaul, 21-7, 21-9
  Tax policy, 6-7
  Trade deficit, 2-79
  Trade Deficit Review Commission, 2-78
Dornan, former Rep. Robert K., R-Calif. (46)
  Election challenge, 18-4, 18-5
Dow Corning Corp.
  Product liability, 15-19
Dreier, David, R-Calif. (28)
  Financial Services Competition Act, 5-8
  High-tech worker visas, 17-7
Drinan, Robert
  Constitutionality of impeachment, 12-38
Drug control
  Appropriations, 2-20
Drug Enforcement Administration. See DEA
  Supplemental appropriations, 2-119
Dukakis, Michael
  1998 Bush Presidential campaign ad
    Willie Horton, 17-16
Duke, David
  Bid for seat of Robert L. Livingston, R-La. (1), 7-12
Dunn, Jennifer, R-Wash. (8)
  House leadership challenge, 7-8, 7-9
  Internet pedophiles, 22-13
  Trade with China, 23-8
Durbin, Richard J., D-Ill.
  Abortion legislation, 3-5, 3-8–3-9
  Airline smoking ban, 2-90
  Bankruptcy overhaul, 5-15, 5-16, 5-18, 5-20, 5-22, 5-23
  Budget resolution, 6-7
  Budget surplus, 6-4
  Juvenile use of firearms, 2-16
  O'Hare airport traffic, 24-37
  Offensive military operations, 2-24, 2-25
  Tobacco, 15-10

E

Eagle Forum
  Job training, 10-3, 10-4
Echostar Communications Corp.
  Satellite TV "must carry" requirement, 22-15, 22-18
Edgar, Gov. Jim, R-Ill.
  Surface transportation reauthorization bill, 24-6
Education
  Bilingual education, 2-65, 2-127, 9-25–9-28
  Block grants, 2-65, 2-68
  Charter schools, 9-29
  Disabled, 2-74
  Education savings accounts, 9-14, 9-15, 9-16, 9-17, 9-18, C-6–C-7, C-17
  Education technology programs, 2-74
  Goals 2000 program, 2-65, 2-68, 2-69
  Head Start, 2-72, 9-19–9-23
  Head Start reauthorization, 9-23
  Higher Education Reauthorization Act, 9-3–9-14
  Individuals with Disabilities Education Act, 2-65
  Literacy programs, 2-72, 2-74
  National testing, 2-64, 2-68, 2-71
  New teachers, 2-64, 2-68, 2-70–2-72, 2-74
  Omnibus appropriations bill, 2-112
  School vouchers, 2-32–2-36, 9-24, 9-25
  Senate debate, 9-15
  Student aid, 2-129, 9-3–9-14
  Teacher training, 2-68, 2-71
Education and the Workforce Committee (House)
  Bilingual education, 9-25
  Child nutrition programs, 20-3, 20-5
  Head Start, 9-19, 9-19–9-23, 9-21, 9-22, 9-23
  Members, 7-6
  Salting by unions, 10-5, 10-6
  Student loans, 9-3, 9-4
Education Department
  Funding, 2-65
Edwards, Chet, D-Texas (11)
  Adoption, 2-34
  Clinton impeachment effort
    effect on 2000 election, 12-49
  Highway projects, 24-13
  Military construction appropriations, 2-83
  Surface transportation reauthorization bill, 24-15
Egypt
  Foreign aid, 2-45, 2-47
Ehlers, Vernon J., R-Mich. (3)
  California voter registration controversy, 18-4
Ehrlich, Robert L. Jr., R-Md. (2)
  Clinton impeachment, 12-22
  Gingrich leadership issues, 7-8
  Republican agenda, 7-7
Eisgrau, Adam (American Library Association)
  Digital copyright, 22-7–22-9
Eizenstat, Stuart E.
  State Department Office of Religious Persecution, 16-10
Electric Power Supply Association
  Electricity deregulation, 15-17
Electricity industry
  Deregulation, 15-16, 15-17
Electronic Frontier Foundation
  Internet pornography, 22-11, 22-12
Electronic Privacy Information Center
  Internet pornography, 22-12
Embassies
  State Department authorization
    proposed move of U.S. embassy from Tel Aviv to Jerusalem, 16-5, 16-6, 16-8
Employee Retirement Income Security Act. see ERISA
Employment
  College work study, 2-72
  Job training programs, 10-3, 10-4
  Summer jobs for poor youth, 2-66, 2-68
Encryption
  Export restrictions, 22-19, 22-20
  Internet, 22-3–22-9

Energy and Natural Resources Committee (Senate)
  Grazing on federal lands, 11-8
Energy and water
  FY 1999 appropriations, 2-39, 2-40, 2-42 (chart), 2-44
Energy conservation
  Appropriations, 2-57
Energy Department
  Funding, 2-36–2-38, 2-40, 2-41, 2-43, 2-44, 8-3, 8-7, 8-8, 8-12, 8-13, 8-16
  Next Generation Internet, 2-37, 2-40
  Nuclear power industry financing of, 2-40
  Nuclear stockpile stewardship, 2-41
  Nuclear waste, 11-3, 11-4
  Satellite export application approvals, 16-30
English, Phil, R-Pa. (21)
  Clinton investigation, 12-17
Ensign, John, R-Nev. (1)
  Campaign against Harry Reid, D-Nev., 11-3
  Nevada nuclear waste site, 11-3, 11-4
Environment
  Clean air standards, 24-5, 24-8
  Clean Water Action Plan, 2-57
  Climate change, 2-57, 2-63
    Kyoto treaty, 2-52, 2-59, 8-8
  Columbia Basin Ecosystem Management Plan, 2-57, 2-60
  Florida Everglades, 2-58, 2-63
  Izembek Road, 2-57, 2-58, 2-61
  Kyoto treaty, 2-101–2-102, 2-104, 2-107–2-108, 2-110
  Land and Water Conservation Fund, 2-57
  Legislative riders, 2-57, 2-60
  National forests, 2-57, 2-59
  Safe Drinking Water Law, 15-22
  Superfund, 11-5, 11-6
Environment and Public Works Committee (Senate)
  Nuclear Regulatory Commission appropriations, 2-38
  Superfund, 11-5
  Surface transportation reauthorization bill, 24-4, 24-8, 24-11, 24-20
Environmental Protection Agency. See EPA
EPA (Environmental Protection Agency)
  Appropriations (chart), 2-109
  Clean air standards, 24-5, 24-8, 24-24
  Clean water standards, 2-110, 15-22
  Global warming, 2-107
  Hazardous waste site cleanup, 11-5, 11-6
  Kyoto treaty, 2-101, 2-104, 2-110
  Oil spills, 2-105
  Superfund, 2-102, 2-104, 11-5, 11-6
Eppard, Ann
  Rep. Bud Shuster ethics investigation, 7-3
Equale, Paul A. (Independent Insurance Agents of America)
  Financial services overhaul legislation, 5-9
ERISA, 14-3–14-5, 14-12–14-15
Eshoo, Anna G., D-Calif. (14)
  Class-action securities suits, 5-33
Estonia
  NATO expansion, 8-22, 8-23
Ethics
  Federal prosecutors, 2-17
  Gingrich investigation, 7-3
Ethics Committee (House)
  Bud Shuster investigation, 7-3
  Corinne Brown investigation, 7-3
  Jay C. Kim investigation, 7-3
  Jim McDermott investigation, 7-3
  Members, 7-3
  Newt Gingrich investigation, 7-3
European Union
  Agriculture markets, restrictions on U.S. imports, 23-4
  NATO expansion
    Moynihan amendment, 8-24
Evans, Lane, D-Ill. (17)
  Land mines, 8-5
Export Control Administration Act, 16-26, 16-27
Export-Import Bank
  Vietnam, 23-9

F

F/A-18 aircraft
  Supplemental appropriations, 2-125
FAA (Federal Aviation Administration)
  Authorization, 2-85–2-88, 2-90, 24-34–24-40
  Commercial space launch vehicles, 19-5
  Private space vehicles, 19-9
Fair Labor Standards Act
  Comp time, 10-7
Faircloth, Lauch, R-N.C.
  Credit unions, 5-27
  D.C. appropriations, 2-33
  IRS overhaul, 21-7
  Military construction projects in home state, 2-84
  Mortgage insurance, 20-15
  Tobacco settlement attorneys' fees, 15-9
Family and Medical Leave Act, 10-7
Family planning. See also Abortion
  Contraceptive coverage
    key votes, C-11–C-12, C-20
  Contraceptives for minors, 2-66, 2-67, 2-71
  Separation of abortion and family planning facilities, 2-67
Farr, Sam. D-Calif. (17)
  Food stamps, 4-9
Fawell, Harris W., R-Ill. (13)
  Clinton impeachment vote, 12-39
  Managed care, 14-8
Fazio, Vic, D-Calif. (3)
  Clinton impeachment vote, 12-49
  Energy policy, 2-40
  Foreign trade, 23-8
  Kyoto treaty, 2-104
  Omnibus appropriations bill, 2-113
  Retirement, 7-7
  Tobacco, 15-13
  Tribute, 2-79
FBI (Federal Bureau of Investigation)
  Appropriations, 2-15, 2-20
  Encryption export restrictions, 22-20
  Supplemental appropriations, 2-118
FCC (Federal Communications Commission)
  Cable TV rates, 22-14–22-17
  Satellite fee increases, 22-14, 22-15, 22-18
  Supplemental appropriations, 2-126
    Internet access for schools, libraries and health care facilities, 2-127
  Telephone "slamming," 22-24–22-26
FDA (Food and Drug Administration)
  Nicotine regulation, 15-5, 15-8, 15-15
  Tobacco regulation, 15-14, 15-15
FDIC (Federal Deposit Insurance Corporation)
  Financial services overhaul, 5-6
  Y2K computer problem, 22-21
FEC (Federal Election Commission)
  Budget, 2-95, 2-97
  Campaign finance, 18-7, 18-8, 18-11, 18-15
  Term limits for staff director and general counsel, 2-91, 2-92, 2-95–2-98, 2-100
Federal Aviation Administration. See FAA
Federal Bureau of Investigation. See FBI
Federal Communications Commission. See FCC
Federal Deposit Insurance Corporation. See FDIC
Federal Election Commission. See FEC
Federal Emergency Management Agency. See FEMA
Federal employees
  Abortion coverage in health plans, 2-92, 2-93, 2-95, 2-97, 2-98
  Contraceptive coverage in health plans, 2-91, 2-94, 2-95, 2-97, 2-98, 2-100, C-11–C-12, C-20
  Pension plan lawsuit, 2-93
  Transit subsidies, 2-77
Federal Highway Administration
  Highway projects, 2-89 (chart), 2-90
  Trucking oversight, 2-88, 2-90
Federal Housing Administration. See FHA
Federal Reserve Board
  Bankruptcy overhaul legislation, 5-23

General Index

Citicorp-Travelers Group merger, 5-9, 5-10
Financial services overhaul legislation, 5-3, 5-5, 5-7, 5-8, 5-10, 5-11, 5-13, 5-14
Glass-Steagall Act revisions, 5-9
Y2K computer problem, 22-21
Federal Trade Commission. *See* FTC
Federation for American Immigration Reform
High-tech worker visas, 17-4
Federation of American Scientists
FOIA access to CIA budget figures, 8-25
Federation of Tax Administrators
Internet taxes, 21-22
Feingold, Russell D., D-Wis.
Bankruptcy overhaul legislation, 5-18, 5-19, 5-23
Campaign finance overhaul, 18-3, 18-4, 18-6, 18-7, 18-9, 18-11, 18-13, 18-15–18-17
Defense appropriations, 2-24
major weapons systems, 2-25
IRS overhaul, 21-7
Feinstein, Dianne, D-Calif.
Abortion legislation, 3-5
Bankruptcy overhaul legislation, 5-23
Clinton censure, 12-20
Clinton criticism, 12-9
Cloning, 19-3
Drug control, 2-119
Farm labor, 2-7
High-tech worker visas, 17-3, 17-4
India and Pakistan nuclear tests, condemnation of, 8-13
Indonesia, 2-51
Religious persecution overseas, 16-15, 16-16
FEMA (Federal Emergency Management Agency)
Anti-terrorism initiatives, 2-105
Supplemental appropriations, 2-125
FHA (Federal Housing Administration)
Mortgages, 2-102, 2-103, 2-106
Public housing, 2-101, 2-105, 2-110
Filibusters and cloture votes
105th Congress, Second Session (chart), 1-4
Filner, Bob, D-Calif. (50)
Domestic partner health benefits, 2-108
Finance Committee (Senate)
Africa trade, 23-10, 23-11
Internet taxes, 21-21
IRS overhaul, 21-3, 21-9
Omnibus bill, 21-15, 21-18
fast track trade authority, 23-3
Tobacco legislation, 15-7
Trade bill (summary), 23-5
Financial Services Competition Act, 5-8
Fish and fishing
Columbia Basin Ecosystem Management Plan, 2-57
Foreign vessels, 2-13
Glacier Bay National Park, 2-63
North Pacific fishing, 2-16
Flag desecration
Legislation, 17-11
Florida
Everglades, 2-58, 2-63
Tobacco settlement, 15-9
Flynt, Larry
Story on Livingston affairs, 7-11
Focus on the Family
Religious freedom, 17-10
Foley, Mark, R-Fla. (16)
Clinton impeachment vote, 12-39
State Department authorization, 16-5
Fong, Matt
Clinton impeachment effort campaign issues, 12-8
Food and Drug Administration. *See* FDA
Food Research and Action Center
Youth after-school programs, 20-5
Food stamps
Aid to legal immigrants, C-11, C-18
Appropriations, 4-3–4-9
Forbes, Steve
China, 16-36
Ford, former President Gerald R.
Clinton impeachment censure resolution, 12-47, 12-53
Fast-track trade authority, 23-3, 23-8
House role in impeachment, 12-7

Ford, Harold E. Jr., D-Tenn. (9)
Prosecution of Harold E. Ford Sr., D-Tenn. (9), 2-17
Ford, Wendell H., D-Ky.
FAA authorization, 24-36
Naming federal courthouse after Kentucky judge, 22-24, 22-26
State Department authorization abortion, 16-8
Tobacco, 2-7, 2-8, 15-6, 15-12
Tobacco farm aid, 15-5, 15-9, 15-11
Foreign affairs
Abortion, 2-45, 2-51, 2-52, 2-54, 2-56
Clinton strategy, 761
Current sanctions, 16-20, 16-21
Export Administration Act (1979), 16-27
Export controls, 16-24–16-33
NATO expansion, 8-21–8-24
Foreign aid
Armenia, 2-53
Egypt, 2-51
Greece, 2-51
Haiti, 2-51
IMF, 7-8
Indonesia, 2-51
Israel, 2-51
Russia, 2-56
Spending (chart), 2-55
Subsidies, 2-126
Tunisia, 2-51
Turkey, 2-51
Foreign Relations Authorization Act, 16-30
Foreign Relations Committee (Senate)
Africa, 23-12
NATO expansion, 8-21, 8-22
Russia technology transfers to Iran, 16-18
State Department authorization, 16-3, 16-7
Foreign trade
China MFN trade status, 16-13, 16-26, 16-34–16-36
Domestic protections, 23-11
Fast-track negotiating authority, 2-7
Fast-track trade reauthorization, 23-3–23-6, 23-8, 23-9
Generalized System of Preferences, 23-6, 23-11
International mail, 2-94
Vietnam
Jackson-Vanik trade amendments, 23-9
Most Favored Nation status, 21-8, 21-13
Omnibus trade bill (summary), 23-5
Sanctions, 23-4
Satellite technology transfers to China, 8-7, 8-8, 8-12, 8-16, 16-23–16-34
Trade deficit, 2-79
Trade Deficit Review Commission, 2-78
Transfer pricing, 21-7
U.S.-Africa Trade and Economic Cooperation Forum, 23-10
Forest Health bill, 11-8
Forest management
National forests, 11-7, 11-8
Forest Recovery and Protection Act, 11-7
Forest Service
Appropriations, 2-41, 2-57
Forest Health bill, 11-8
Fowler, Tillie, R-Fla. (4)
House leadership, 7-10
Mixed gender military training, 8-4
Fox, Jon D., R-Pa. (13)
Clinton Middle East trip, 12-40
Franc, Michael (Heritage Foundation)
Public reaction to Starr report, 12-17
Francis, Michael A.
Logging in national forests, 2-59
Frank, Barney, D-Mass. (4)
Abortion legislation, 3-4
Campaign finance overhaul, 18-12, 18-13
Clinton impeachment, 12-11
Judiciary Committee opening statement (excerpts), D-29, D-29–D-30
Republican party strategy, 12-22
witnesses, 12-25
Digital copyright, 22-3, 22-4
Fast-track trade authority, 23-7

Financial services overhaul, 5-11
House GOP impeachment strategy, 12-15
IMF funding, 23-7
Internet pornography, 22-12
Internet use by prisoners, 22-13
Judicial activism, 17-12
Judicial pay raises, 17-14
Judiciary Committee impeachment hearings
Starr testimony, 12-28
Justice Department authorization, 17-14
Medicinal marijuana, 12-11
Physician-assisted suicide, 17-19
Renaming National Airport for Ronald Reagan, 13-9
Freedom to Farm law
Loan rates, 2-3
Freeh, Louis J.
Campaign finance, 12-32, 16-32
White house leak of Hyde infidelity, 12-15
Frelinghuysen, Rodney, R-N.J. (11)
Budget, 6-17
FHA, 2-103, 2-104
TVA funding, 2-44
Frist, Bill, R-Tenn.
Cloning, 19-3
"Partial birth" abortion ban, 3-8
Space station, 19-4, 19-5
Tobacco, 15-6, 15-15
TVA funding, 2-36, 2-39, 2-43, 2-44
Frost, Martin, D-Texas (24)
Campaign finance, 18-11
FTC
Telephone "slamming," 22-25
Fund for Rural America
Agriculture appropriations, 2-3, 4-8
Furse, Elizabeth, D-Ore. (1)
Timber program, 2-60
Fuscus, David A. (Air Transport Association of America)
FAA guidelines, 24-34

G

Gallegly, Elton, R-Calif. (23)
Clinton impeachment, 12-38
Judiciary Committee opening statement (excerpts), D-31
High-tech worker visas, 17-5, 17-6
Religious refugees, 16-11
Gallo, Robert (Airline Planning Group)
Airline competition, 24-39
Ganske, Greg, R-Iowa (4)
Managed care legislation, 14-14
Medicare, 14-12
GAO (General Accounting Office)
Appropriations, 2-75, 2-80
Census, 13-4, 13-5
F-22 aircraft, 8-10
Federal regulatory agencies, 15-21
Flammability standards study, 2-101, 2-110
GAO comptroller, 2-75, 2-76
High-tech worker shortage, 17-4, 17-5
Home health care, 14-19, 14-20
Job training funding, 10-4
Satellite exports, 16-30
Space station audit, 19-6
Y2K computer problem, 2-78
Gasoline
Tax credits for ethanol, 24-18
Gates, Bill (Microsoft Corp.)
High-tech worker visas, 17-4
Gejdenson, Sam, D-Conn. (2)
Campaign finance, 18-5
Export controls, 16-27
State Department authorization
international family planning, 16-6
Gekas, George W., R-Pa. (17)
Bankruptcy overhaul legislation, 5-15–5-17, 5-19, 5-20, 5-22, 5-23
Clinton impeachment
Judiciary Committee opening statement (excerpts), D-30
Clinton perjury charges, 12-7, 12-30
Executive privilege, 12-49
Geller, Henry
Federal agency jurisdiction, 15-15
General Accounting Office. *See* GAO
General Dynamics
Defense contracts, 8-9

General Electric Co.
Thrift charters, 5-6
General Mills
WIC program, 20-4
Gentry, Richard C. (Richmond Redevelopment and Housing Authority)
Public housing, 20-8
George Washington University Medical Center
Proposed naming of emergency room for Ronald Reagan, 14-13
Georgia
Defense contracts, 2-20, 2-23, 2-25, 2-28
Gephardt, Richard A., D-Mo. (3)
Campaign finance, 18-6, 18-7, 18-12
CBO controversy, 2-76
Character issues, 12-52
China MFN status, 16-36
Clinton impeachment, 12-34
censure resolution, 12-41, 12-49
GOP partisanship, 12-20
Clinton impeachment prospects, 12-12
Clinton impeachment vote remarks (excerpts), D-46
Clinton perjury charge, 12-16
Defense appropriations, 2-23
Democratic agenda, 7-7
Fast-track trade bill, 23-5
IRS overhaul, 21-8
Line-item veto, 6-23
Livingston resignation, remarks, 7-12, 12-46, 12-47
Managed care, 14-8, 14-14
Military construction projects in home district, 2-81
"Partial birth" abortion ban, 3-7
Renaming Justice Dept. headquarters for Robert F. Kennedy, 13-8
Renaming National Airport for Ronald Reagan, 13-8
Russia technology transfers to Iran, 16-18
Starr report, 12-9
State of the Union address, 12-6
Supplemental appropriations
AmeriCorps, 2-127
Technology transfers to China, 16-28
Germany
Chemical weapons inspections, 8-20
NATO expansion, 8-23
Gibbons, Jim, R-Nev. (2)
Highway bill earmarks, 24-11
Gillespie, Ed
Budget, 6-8
Gilman, Benjamin A., R-N.Y. (20)
Embassy security, 2-118
Energy Department
nuclear technology transfers, 8-8
Food sanctions, 2-6
Religious persecution overseas, 16-10
Russia technology transfers to Iran, 16-16, 16-19, 16-22
State Department authorization, 16-4, 16-5
Supplemental appropriations, 2-118
Technology transfers to China, 8-7, 8-8
Gingrich, Newt, R-Ga. (6)
Abortion, 16-4, 16-5
Airline competition, 24-35, 24-37
Appropriations, 7-8
Budget cuts, 6-9
Budget surplus, 6-3, 6-8, 6-14, 6-15
Campaign finance overhaul, 18-5–18-7, 18-10, 18-12
Capital gains tax, 16-15
CBO controversy, 2-76
CBO forecasts, 2-77
Cellular phone eavesdropping case, 22-23
Census, 13-5
Census methodology, 2-13
Challenge to his leadership, 1997, 7-5
Clinton censure, 12-20
Clinton China policy, 16-36
Clinton China trip, 16-37
Clinton impeachment apology decorum (excerpts), D-14
Clinton impeachment inquiry, 12-23, 12-40
Credit unions, 5-27, 5-28
D.C. school vouchers, 2-34, 2-35, 9-24, 9-25

General Index

Defense authorization, 2-30, 2-31, 8-3
   CIA, 2-31
Defense contracts in home district,
   2-20, 2-23, 2-25, 2-28
Descendants of Mexicans land claims,
   9-27
Diabetes research, 2-74
Electricity deregulation, 15-16
Estate tax, 16-15
Ethanol gas tax credit, 24-18
Ethics charges, 7-3, 12-53
FAA guidelines, 24-34, 24-35
Farm agenda, 2-7
Fast-track trade authority, 23-3, 23-4,
   23-6–23-8
Financial services overhaul, 5-3, 5-5,
   5-7, 5-10, 5-11
Highway bill, 2-90, 24-3–24-5, 24-9, 24-12, 24-16, 24-17, 24-19, 24-20, 24-21
Hyde criticism, 12-33
IMF funding, 2-45, 2-47, 2-48, 16-3
International family planning, 16-3
IRAs, 6-12
Judicial activism, 17-15
Juvenile crime bill, 17-15–17-17
Lawsuit against Jim McDermott, D-Wash.
   (7) for taping cell phone call, 7-3
Marriage penalty, 16-15
Mexican descendant land claims, 9-27
Nuclear waste, 11-3, 11-4
Omnibus appropriations bill, 2-113
Omnibus bill
   covert Iraq operations, 8-27
Profile, 7-10
Promotion of J. Dennis Hastert, R-Ill.
   (14) as Speaker, 7-11
Property rights, 15-24
Public housing, 20-14
Public release of Starr report, 12-13
Puerto Rico, 13-6
Religious persecution overseas, 16-9,
   16-12
Renaming National Airport for Ronald
   Reagan, 13-8
Reserve fund, 2-77
Resignation, 7-4–7-10, 12-32, 12-34,
   12-45
Retirement accounts, 6-7
Russia technology transfers to Iran,
   16-16, 16-18, 16-22
Starr report, 12-9
State Department authorization,
   16-3–16-5
Supplemental appropriations, 2-122, 2-123
   intelligence spending, 2-117
   international family planning, 2-117
Technology transfers to China, 8-16,
   16-24, 16-28, 16-29
Tobacco, 6-4, 15-3, 15-6, 15-12, 15-14
U.S. airstrikes on Afghanistan and
   Sudan, 12-9
U.N. dues, 2-121
United Nations, 16-3–16-5
Glass-Steagall Act
Financial services overhaul legislation,
   5-3 (history), 5-5, 5-8, 5-9, 5-10, 5-12,
   5-14 (history)
Glavin, Matthew (Southeastern Legal Foundation)
Census, 13-5
Glenn, John, D-Ohio
Defense authorization
   intelligence budget, 8-6
FEC budget, 2-97
FEC term limits, 2-96
Regulatory overhaul, 15-21
Spaceflight, 19-10–19-12
Glickman, Dan
Food stamps, 4-6–4-8
Milk marketing, 2-4, 2-9
USDA discrimination against black
   farmers, 2-8
Glossary
Congressional Terms, A-3–A-13
Goldberg, Lucianne
Linda Tripp book about Lewinsky-
   Clinton affair, 12-28

Goldin, Daniel S.
NASA funding, 19-8–19-10
Space station, 19-4, 19-5, 19-8
Goldstone, Steven F.
Tobacco companies' liability, 15-6
Gonzalez, Henry B., D-Texas (20)
Financial services overhaul, 5-12
Goode, Virgil H. Jr., D-Va. (5)
Clinton impeachment vote, 12-41,
   12-48
Goodlatte, Robert W., R-Va. (6)
Campaign finance, 18-15
Church and state, 17-9, 17-10
Clinton impeachment
   Judiciary Committee opening
     statement (excerpts), D-31
Digital copyright, 22-4
Encryption export restrictions, 22-20
Food stamps, 4-4, 4-6
Forest policy, 11-8
Internet taxes, 21-20
Goodling, Bill, R-Pa. (19)
Bilingual education, 9-27
Child nutrition programs, 20-5
Education
   national testing, 9-28
Financial services overhaul legislation,
   5-11
Head Start, 9-20, 9-21, 9-23
Human service program
   reauthorization, 9-19–9-23
Job training, 10-4
Salting by labor unions, 10-5
GOPAC
Gingrich ethics charges, 7-3
Gorbunov, Sergei
Russia space station, 19-6
Gore, Vice President Al
Campaign finance abuses, 18-17
Campaign finance violations, 16-32
Drunken driving legislation, 24-21
Electricity deregulation, 15-17
Encryption export restrictions, 22-20
Interior appropriations, 2-58
House impeachment vote remarks, D-46
Property rights, 15-24
Russian technology transfers to Iran,
   16-17, 16-18, 16-22
Space station, 19-6, 19-8
Student aid, 9-3
TVA, 2-43, 2-44
Tobacco politics, 15-12
Gorton, Slade, R-Wash.
Budget negotiations, 6-8
Columbia Basin Ecosystem
   Management Plan, 2-57
Electricity deregulation, 15-17
FAA guidelines, 24-35
Farm labor, 2-16
Fishing legislation, 2-13
Interior appropriations, 2-61
Product liability, 15-18, 15-19
RU-486 ban, 2-9
Tobacco, 15-5, 15-6
Goss, Porter J., R-Fla. (14)
Intelligence authorization, 2-31, 8-25–8-26
Russia technology transfers to Iran,
   16-19
Government Printing Office
Appropriations, 2-76
Government Reform and Oversight Committee (House)
Campaign fundraising investigations,
   2-77
Clinton investigation, 12-17
Y2K computer problem, 22-22
Governmental Affairs Committee (Senate)
Regulatory overhaul, 15-20–15-23
Graham, Bob, D-Fla.
Commercial space bill, 19-5
Haitian refugees, 2-98, 17-8
Internet taxes, 21-22, 21-23, 21-24
IRS overhaul, 21-4, 21-7
Minimum wage, 10-7
Motorcycle access to federal roads,
   24-20
Tobacco, 15-7, 15-9

Graham, Fred (Court TV)
Television cameras in courtrooms,
   17-14
Graham, Lindsey, R-S.C. (3)
Clinton impeachment
   Judiciary Committee opening
     statement (excerpts), D-33
Clinton impeachment inquiry
   nature of impeachment, 12-29
   perjury charge, 12-28
Land mines, 8-5
Surface transportation reauthorization
   bill, 24-14
Gramm, Phil, R-Texas
Agriculture appropriations, 4-7
Banking, 2-25
Class-action securities suits, 5-30, 5-31
Credit unions, 5-25, 5-27–5-29
Fast-track trade bill, 23-6
Financial services overhaul, 5-3, 5-11–5-15
Food stamps, 4-6
Gas tax, 24-3–24-6
IRS overhaul, 21-4, 21-7
Managed care, 14-13
Marriage penalty, 6-14
Military personnel and voting, 2-25
Social Security, 6-4, 21-17, 21-18
Supplemental appropriations
   IMF, 2-124
Surface transportation reauthorization
   bill, 24-4, 24-7–24-9, 24-19
Tobacco, 15-8, 15-9, 15-10–15-13
Tobacco revenue, 6-4
Transportation
   Gramm-Byrd highway bill
     amendment, 24-5, 24-6
Transportation earmarks, 24-8, 24-9
Grams, Rod, R-Minn.
Budget, 6-5, 6-6
Chinese military imports, 8-6
Clinton credibility, 12-9
Defense Production Act of 1950, 8-13
Financial services overhaul, 5-14
IRS overhaul, 21-7
Sanctions for religious persecutions,
   16-14, 16-15, 16-16
U.S. China policy
   Forced sterilization and abortion, 8-12
   Satellite licensing, 8-12
   World Bank loans, 8-12
Grassley, Charles E., R-Iowa
Bankruptcy overhaul legislation, 5-15,
   5-16, 5-18–5-20, 5-22, 5-23, 5-24
   family farms, 5-15, 5-24
Home health care, 14-19, 14-22
IRS overhaul, 21-4, 21-8
Tobacco, 15-7
Greene, Sarah M.
National Head Start Association, 9-23
Greenspan, Alan
Financial services overhaul legislation,
   5-7, 5-14
IMF, 2-48, 2-53
Supplemental appropriations, 2-124
Greenwood, James C., R-Pa. (8)
Abortion legislation, 3-8
Clinton impeachment investigation,
   12-19, 12-22
EPA, 2-107
Gregg, Judd, R-N.H.
Budget resolution, 6-7
Census, 2-13, 13-4
Clinton impeachment vote
   effect on Social Security legislation,
     12-44
Internet taxes, 21-20, 21-24
Surface transportation reauthorization
   bill, 24-9
Tobacco, 15-5, 15-8
Griffin, Mary (Consumers Union)
Financial services overhaul, 5-5, 5-6
Gun control
Gun locks, 2-15
National Instant Check System, 2-12
Gun Owners of America
Juvenile crime, 17-15–17-17
Gutierrez, Luis V., D-Ill. (4)
Puerto Rico, 13-6

H

Hagel, Chuck, R-Neb.
Clinton China trip, 16-36
Credit unions, 5-27–5-29
Religious persecution overseas, 16-13,
   16-14, 16-15
Supplemental appropriations
   IMF, 2-124
Haiti
Permanent status for refugees in U.S.,
   2-91, 2-98, 2-100
Hall, Ralph M., D-Texas (4)
Clinton impeachment vote, 12-41,
   12-48
Hamilton, Lee H., D-Ind. (9)
China, 16-35
Highway bill earmarks, 24-11
Religious persecution overseas, 16-10,
   16-13, 16-14
Russia technology transfers to Iran,
   16-22, 16-23
State Department authorization, 16-5,
   16-6
Hansen, James V., R-Utah (1)
Gingrich ethics charges, 7-3
House Ethics committee, 7-3
Mortgage insurance, 20-9
Omnibus parks bill, 11-6, 11-7
Technology transfers to China, 16-29
Harkin, Tom, D-Iowa
Agriculture appropriations, 2-7, 2-11,
   4-6, 4-8
Appropriations
   Labor-HHS-Education, 2-68
Campaign finance overhaul vote, 18-3
Child nutrition programs, 20-5
Defense appropriations
   Smoking therapy, 2-25
Defense authorization, 8-12
High-tech worker visas, 17-8, 17-9
NATO expansion, 8-21, 8-23, 8-24
NIH funding, 2-72
Harman, Jane, D-Calif. (36)
Loral SpaceCom PAC contributions,
   16-25
Military abortions, 8-5
Hastert, J. Dennis, R-Ill. (14)
Character, 7-11
Drug task force, 7-11
House Speakership, 7-9, 12-45, 12-52
Managed care, 7-11, 14-6, 14-7, 14-8,
   14-13, 14-14
Slated for Speaker of the House, 7-10,
   7-11, 12-46
Hastings, Alcee L., D-Fla. (23)
Impeachment as federal judge, 12-16
Hastings, Richard "Doc", R-Wash. (4)
Columbia Basin Ecosystem
   Management Plan, 2-60
Hatch, Orrin G., R-Utah
Abortion legislation, 3-5
Bankruptcy overhaul legislation, 5-18
Baseball antitrust, 15-25
Clinton impeachment trial
   duration, 12-36
Crime, 17-16
Digital copyright, 22-4, 22-5, 22-9
DNC campaign finance violations, 16-33
Flag desecration, 17-11
Impeachable offenses, 12-7
Juvenile crime bill, 17-16, 17-17
Physician-assisted suicide, 17-19
Property rights, 15-23–15-25
Renaming FBI building, 13-8
Satellite TV programming, 22-16
Starr report, 12-13
Tobacco, 15-7, 15-9
Hawaii
Defense appropriations
   military construction projects, 2-81,
     2-84
Hawley, Air Force Gen. Richard
Military aircraft readiness, 8-10
Hayden, Marty
Interior appropriations, 2-61
HCFA (Health Care Finance Administration)
Appropriations, 2-74
Medicare, 14-16, 14-17–14-19, 14-20,
   14-21
Tobacco settlement, 2-12

General Index

Head Start
  Appropriations, 2-66, 2-69, 2-72
  Cost and quality, 9-19–9-23
  Reauthorization, 9-23
Health
  AIDS program funding, 2-64, 2-66, 2-69, 2-72, 2-74
  Needle exchange programs, 2-32, 2-33, 2-36
Health and Human Services, Department of. *See* HHS
Health Benefits Coalition
  Managed care, 14-4–14-6
Health care. *See also* Managed care
  HMO regulation, 18-16
    American Indians, 2-58
    Breast cancer, 2-74, 2-116
    Community health centers, 2-69
    Consumer Bill of Rights, 12-6
    Funding for AIDS programs, 2-64
    home health care, 2-116, 14-16–14-22
    House Republican Task Force plan, 14-7
  Managed care, 12-6
  Medicinal marijuana, 2-36
  National health care identity number, 2-69, 2-74
  Norwood-D'Amato bill, 14-3–14-6
  Patients' bill of rights, 14-3–14-6, 14-12, 14-13
Health Care Financing Administration. *See* HCFA
Health insurance
  PAC contributions, 14-6
Health Insurance Association of America. *See* HIAA
Health Security Act (1994), 14-6
Hebert, Gerald
  Census, 13-5
Hefley, Joel, R-Colo. (5)
  Affirmative action, 2-15, 2-18
  Highway projects, 24-13
  Military construction appropriations, 2-83
  Military construction projects in home district, 2-81
  Shuster ethics investigation, 7-3, 24-15
  Technology transfers to China, 8-8
Hefner, W.G. "Bill," D-N.C. (8)
  COLAs, 2-94
  Military construction projects in home district, 2-81
  Retirement, 2-94
Helms, Jesse, R-N.C.
  Comprehensive Nuclear Test Ban Treaty, 2-51
  NATO expansion, 8-21, 8-23
  Religious persecution overseas, 16-14, 16-16
  State Department authorization, 16-3, 16-3–16-5, 16-7–16-9
  Supplemental appropriations
    U.N. dues, 2-122
Heritage Foundation
  Clinton impeachment vote, 12-40
  Public reaction to Starr report, 12-17
  Starr report, 12-12
Herman, Alexis
  Salting by unions, 10-5
Hermanidad Mexicana Nacional
  California voter registration controversy, 18-4
Hewlett-Packard
  Encryption export restrictions, 22-19, 22-20
HHS (Health and Human Services)
  Medicare waste, fraud and abuse, 14-17–14-20
HIAA (Health Insurance Association of America), 14-4–14-6, 14-8
Highways and roads
  Environment
    Izembek Road, 2-57, 2-58, 2-61, 2-63
  Highway Trust Fund, 24-4, 24-6, 24-7, 24-10, 24-14, 24-16, 24-17, 24-19, 24-22, 24-23, 24-26
  National Highway System Designation Act, 24-10
  Spending increase, 6-4
Hilleary, Van, R-Tenn. (4)
  Livingston as Speaker, 7-10
  VA-HUD appropriations, 2-108
Hinchey, Maurice D., D-N.Y. (26)
  Chugach National Forest, 2-60

Hobson, David L., R-Ohio (7)
  Clinton character, 12-41
  Defense appropriations, 2-23
  J. Dennis Hastert, R-Ill. (14)
    leadership style, 7-11
Hoekstra, Peter, R-Mich. (2)
  House Republican Conference chairmanship, 7-4
Hoffman, Ann
  Union of Needletrades, Industrial and Textile Employees
    Africa trade, 23-12
Hoffman, Scott (American Business for Legal Immigration)
  High-tech worker shortage, 17-4
Hogan, Judge Thomas F.
  Line-item veto, 6-18–6-22
Hollings, Ernest F., D-S.C.
  Abortion legislation, 3-6
  Africa, 23-12
  Appropriations, 2-15
  CBO projections, 2-78
  Internet pornography, 22-11
  Minimum wage, 10-7
  Missile defense, 8-18–8-20
  Nuclear waste, 11-4
  Supplemental appropriations
    foreign subsidies, 2-126
  Textiles and clothing, 23-12
Holtzman, Elizabeth
  Constitutionality of impeachment, 12-38
Holum, John
  China missile proliferation, 16-31
Home Satellite Viewers Act, 22-16
Horn, Steve, R-Calif. (38)
  Y2K computer problem, 22-22
Hospitals
  Renovations, 2-74
Houghton, Amo, R-N.Y. (31)
  Budget, 6-10, 6-17
  Campaign finance, 18-7
  Clinton impeachment
    censure resolution, 12-47
  Clinton impeachment vote, 12-41, 12-48
  Religious persecution overseas, 16-14
House Conservative Action Team
  Budget negotiations, 6-8, 6-10, 6-13, 6-14
  Health insurance coverage, 14-12
  Strategy, 7-8
House leadership
  GOP Policy Committee, 7-8, 7-10
  House Republican Conference, 7-8
  NRCC, 7-6, 7-7, 7-8, 7-10
  Use of consultants, 2-76
House of Representatives
  Reserve fund, 2-77
House Republican Conference
  U.N. dues, 16-3
Housing
  Public housing, 2-127, 2-128
  Public housing overhaul
    key votes, C-12, C-20
Housing and Urban Development, Dept. of. *See* HUD
Howard, Jerry (National Association of Home Builders)
  Property rights, 15-25
Howard, John (U.S. Chamber of Commerce)
  Fast-track trade bill, 23-6
Hoyer, Steny H., D-Md. (5)
  Abortion legislation, 3-8
  Campaign finance, 18-5
  COLAs, 2-91
  D.C. Appropriations, 2-34
  Education block grants, 2-65, 2-68
  FEC term limits, 2-92
  Foreign trade, 23-8
  Reserve fund, 2-77
  Supplemental appropriations, 2-128
  Transit subsidies, 2-77
  Treasury-Postal Service appropriations, 2-100
  White House overtime, 2-92
Hubbell, Webster L.
  Starr report, 12-29
HUD (Housing and Urban Development Department)
  Adjustable rate mortgages, 20-11
  Appropriations, 2-101–2-111
  Manufactured housing standards, 20-11
  Section 8 housing programs, 20-7–20-11

Hudson, Paul (Aviation Consumer Action Project)
  Airline competition guidelines, 24-39
Hughes Electronics
  Chinese missile guidance systems, 16-31
Hulshof, Kenny, R-Mo. (9)
  Surface transportation reauthorization bill, 24-21
Hungary
  NATO expansion, 8-21–8-23
Hunter, Duncan, R-Calif. (52)
  Acquisition of Long Beach, CA former Navy base by a Chinese firm, 8-5
  China foreign policy, 16-24
  Technology transfers to China, 8-7, 8-8
Hussein, Saddam
  Clinton threat of airstrikes, 12-6
Hutchinson, Asa, R-Ark. (3)
  Campaign finance overhaul, 18-6, 18-7, 18-8, 18-9, 18-12, 18-13, 18-16
  Clinton impeachment
    Judiciary Committee opening statement (excerpts), D-33
  Clinton impeachment hearings
    witnesses, 12-29
  Clinton impeachment trial, 145
  Defense authorization, 16-26
  Federal prosecutors' powers, 2-17
  Internet pornography and pedophiles, 22-10
  Starr report, 12-17
Hutchinson, Tim, R-Ark.
  China MFN status, 16-35
  Chinese human rights abuses, 8-11, 8-12
  Chinese human rights issues, condemnation of, 8-11
  Chinese imports produced by slave or child labor, 8-6
  Chinese military imports, 8-6
  Defense appropriations
    technology transfers to China, 16-23, 16-24
  Forced abortions in China, 2-21
  High-tech worker visas, 17-6
  Internet taxes, 21-23
  IRS code, 2-96
  Religious persecution, 2-25
Hutchison, Kay Bailey, R-Texas
  Amtrak, 2-86
  Bosnia, 8-6
    U.S. troop reductions, 2-24, 2-25
  National health care identity number, 2-69
  NATO expansion, 8-23, 8-24
  Space station, 19-4
  Supplemental appropriations
    Oil royalties, 2-130
Hyde, Henry J., R-Ill. (6)
  Abortion legislation, 3-6
  Additional flights at crowded airports, 24-37, 24-39, 24-40
  Airline competition, 24-37
  Bankruptcy overhaul legislation, 5-17, 5-20
  Child support enforcement, 20-6
  Clinton impeachment, 12-3–12-53
    answer to Alan Dershowitz claim, 12-33
    Judiciary Committee opening statement (excerpts), D-29
    Republican strategy, 12-25
  Clinton impeachment resolution, 12-22, 12-23
  Criticism of Gingrich leadership, 12-33
  Democrats' critique of Kenneth Starr, 12-21
  Digital copyright, 22-4
  Extramarital affair, 12-15
  High-tech worker visas, 17-5
  House Impeachment inquiry, 7-9, 12-8, 12-11
    opening statement (excerpts), D-37
  House Impeachment strategy, 12-25
  House Judiciary Committee hearing on Independent Counsel's report, 12-27–12-29
  Judicial pay raises, 17-13, 17-14
  Justice Department authorization, 17-14
  Livingston resignation, remarks, 12-46
  Medicinal marijuana, 12-11
  "Partial birth" abortion ban, 3-7

Physician-assisted suicide, 17-18, 17-19
Religious freedom amendment, 17-10, 17-11
Republican House leadership, 7-5
State Department authorization
  international family planning, 16-6

I

Ickes, Harold M.
  Democratic campaign finance abuses, 18-17
Identity theft. *See under* Crime and criminal justice
IMF (International Monetary Fund)
  Appropriations, 2-45–2-56
  Funding, 2-7, 2-46, 2-50, 2-51, 2-56, 2-112, 2-122, 2-124, 2-125, 7-8, 16-3, 16-4, 16-38, 23-3, 23-4, 23-7
  History, 2-46
  Key votes, C-4, C-16
Immigration
  Border checks, 2-20
  Food stamps for legal immigrants, 4-3–4-9
  Haitian refugees, 2-51, 2-91, 2-98, 2-99, 2-100
  High-tech worker shortage, 17-4
  High-tech worker visas, 17-3–17-9
    key votes, C-5–C-6, C-14, C-16, C-22
  Omnibus bill initiatives (highlights), 17-8
  SSI benefits for legal immigrants, 17-3, 17-4
Immigration and Naturalization Service. *See* INS
Impeachment
  Andrew Johnson impeachment, 12-3, 12-8, 12-22, 12-36, 12-40, 12-45, 12-52
  Articles of Impeachment, 12-46, C-15, D-40, D-40–D-41
    abuse of power charge, 12-47
    obstruction of justice charge, 12-47
    perjury charge, 12-47
  Censure resolution, 12-30, 12-35, 12-36, 12-41, 12-44, 12-53
  Chronology, 12-4, 12-5
  Clinton defense, 12-36–12-39
  Democrats who voted for, 12-48
  Effect on 105th Congress, 1-3–1-5
  Effect on 1998 elections, 7-5, 12-25
  Effect on 2000 election, 12-44
  Effect on House leadership, 7-4
  Effect on Social Security legislation, 12-45
  House managers
    ideology (chart), 12-11
    Profiles, 145
  House Resolution, 12-24
  Perjury charge, 12-3–12-53, 12-37, 12-44, 12-45, 12-48, 12-53
    testimony of convicted perjurers, 12-32
  Points of contention (chart), 12-18
  Procedures and deadlines, 143
  Process, 12-35, 12-36
  Public opinion polls, 7-7
  Republicans who voted against, 12-48
  Starr investigation
    witnesses, 12-7
  Starr investigation (chronology), 12-4, 12-5
  Witness tampering charge, 12-37
Independent Bankers Association of America
  Financial services overhaul legislation, 5-12
Independent Counsel
  Reauthorization, 2-18
Independent Insurance Agents of America
  Financial services overhaul legislation, 5-9
India
  Nuclear detonations, 2-4, 2-12, 8-18, 8-19, 16-24
Indians and Alaskan natives
  Indian Health Service, 2-60
  Law enforcement on tribal lands, 2-58
  Nuclear waste dump on tribal land, 2-58

General Index

Individual retirement accounts. *See* IRAs
Information Technology Association of America
    Y2K computer problem, 22-22
Inglis, Bob, R-S.C. (4)
    Clinton impeachment
        Judiciary Committee opening statement (excerpts), D-30
    Clinton impeachment inquiry, 12-38
    Surface transportation reauthorization bill, 24-14
Inhofe, James M., R-Okla.
    Budget resolution, 6-6
    Clean air standards, 24-5, 24-8, 24-25
    Military base closures, 8-12
    Military construction projects in home state, 2-81
    Military doctor licensing, 8-13
    Missile defense, 8-20
    NATO expansion, 8-23
    Religious persecution overseas, 16-11
Inman, Adm. Bobby R.
    Embassy security, 2-118
Inouye, Daniel K., D-Hawaii
    Anti-missile defense, 8-18, 8-20
    Military construction projects in home state, 2-81, 2-84
    Nuclear submarines, 2-22
INS (Immigration and Naturalization Service)
    Funding, 17-8
    Omnibus bill, 2-120
    Restructuring, 2-20
Intel Corp.
    High-tech worker visas, 17-5, 17-6, 17-9
Intelligence
    Covert operations against Iraq, 8-27
    Whistleblower protection, 8-26, 8-27
Intelligence Committee (House)
    Intelligence authorization bill, 8-25–8-27
Intelligence Committee (Senate)
    Technology transfers to China investigation, 16-24
Interior Department
    Appropriations, 2-57–2-63
    Kyoto treaty, 2-104
Intermodal Surface Transportation Efficiency Act. *See* ISTEA
International Covenant on Civil and Political Rights, 16-37
International Monetary Fund. *See* IMF
International Relations Committee (House)
    Members, 7-6
    Religious persecution, 16-9–16-12
Internet
    Digital copyright, 22-3–22-9
    Encryption, 22-3–22-9
    Internet gambling, 2-15, 22-7, 22-13
    Pedophiles, 22-10–22-13
    Pornography, 2-66, 21-24, 22-10–22-13
    School policy, 22-11
    Screening software, 2-16
    Supplemental appropriations subsidies for access, 2-127
    Taxes, 21-19–21-24
    Unsolicited e-mail ("spamming"), 22-24–22-26
Iran
    18 Years of Punishment, 16-17
    Missiles, 8-17
    Sanctions, 16-16–16-23
    Shahab-3 missile, 8-17
IRAs (Individual retirement accounts)
    Bankruptcy laws, 5-16
IRS (Internal Revenue Service)
    Capital gains taxes, 21-8, 21-9
    Congressional oversight, 21-13
    Electronic filing, 21-11
    Equal employment opportunity practices, 21-7
    Innocent spouse relief, 21-11
    IRS overhaul, 21-3–21-14, 24-4
        burden of proof, 21-3, 21-5, 21-6, 21-8, 21-11
        confidentiality, 21-5
        help lines, 21-7
        House/Senate bills compared, 21-5
        interest and penalties, 21-5
        lawsuits, 21-5, 21-12
        Office of Taxpayer Advocate, 21-10
        offsets, 21-5, 21-14
        oversight board, 21-3, 21-5, 21-8

        reorganization, 21-5, 21-10, 21-11
        retaliatory audits, 21-7, 21-11
        return-free system, 21-11
        role of Congress, 21-5
        small business representative, 21-7
        taxpayer abuse, 21-3, 21-8
        taxpayer rights, 21-3, 21-5, 21-11, 21-12, 21-13
    Low-income taxpayer clinics, 21-11
    Penalty relief, 21-12
    Property seizures, 21-3, 21-8
    Reorganization, 21-10, 21-11
    Restructuring, 21-10, 21-11
    What the IRS Bill Does, 21-9–21-14
Israel
    Anti-missile defenses, 8-18
    Foreign aid, 2-45, 2-47
    Missile attack vulnerability, 8-17
    Missile intelligence, 8-17
ISTEA (Intermodal Surface Transportation Efficiency Act), 24-3, 24-6, 24-8, 24-23
    House/Senate bill comparison, 24-5
Istook, Ernest, R-Okla. (5)
    Contraceptives for minors, 2-67
    Internet pornography, 2-66
    Religious freedom, 17-9–17-11
    Supplemental appropriations, 2-123
Ivey, William J.
    NEA funding, 2-60

J

J.P. Morgan
    Financial services overhaul legislation, 5-9
Jackson, Ann
    NRC nuclear plant safety, 2-37
Jackson-Lee, Sheila, D-Texas (18)
    Abortion legislation, 3-4
    Bankruptcy overhaul legislation, 5-17, 15-18
    Clinton impeachment
        Judiciary Committee opening statement (excerpts), D-31
    Starr report, 12-15
Japan
    Chemical weapons inspections, 8-20
Jaworski, Leon
    Watergate special prosecutor report, 12-15
Jeffords, James M., R-Vt.
    Abortion legislation, 3-6
    Campaign finance, 18-4
    Energy policy, 2-40
    Job training, 10-3
    LIHEAP, 2-65
    Minimum wage, 10-7
Jenkins, Bill, R-Tenn. (1)
    Clinton impeachment
        Judiciary Committee opening statement (excerpts), D-33
Job Corps
    Funding, 10-3
Job training
    Appropriations, 2-66, 2-69
Johnson, U.S. District Judge Norma Holloway
    Campaign finance investigation, 12-32
    Starr investigation (chronology), 12-5
Johnson, Douglas (National Right to Life Committee)
    Campaign finance overhaul issue ads, 18-11
    "Partial birth" abortion ban, 3-8–3-9
Johnson, Nancy L., R-Conn. (6)
    Budget negotiations, 6-10
    Clinton impeachment vote, 12-49
    Contraceptive coverage in federal employee health plans, 2-100
    Gingrich ethics charges, 7-3
    HCFA, 14-19
    House Ethics committee, 7-3
    Medicare, 14-17
    NEA funding, 2-60
Johnson, Sam, R-Texas (3)
    Labor unions, 10-6
Johnson, Tim, D-S.D.
    Class-action securities suits, 5-30, 5-31
    Country of origin labels for food, 2-8
Johnston, former Sen. Bennett, D-La. (Alliance for Competitive Electricity)
    Electricity deregulation, 15-17

Jones, Paula Corbin
    Sexual harassment lawsuit against President Clinton, 12-3, 12-6–12-8, 12-13, 12-14, 12-16, 12-18, 12-21, 12-26, 12-28, 12-30, 12-37, 12-38, 12-46 (articles of impeachment), 12-47, 12-51
Josten, Bruce (U.S. Chamber of Commerce)
    Fast-track trade bill, 23-8, 23-9
Judge, Steve (Securities Industry Association)
    Citicorp-Travelers Group merger, 5-9, 5-10
Judiciary
    Judge-ordered tax increases, 17-12, 17-13
    Judicial activism, 17-12–17-15
    Litigants' rights to reject judges, 17-12, 17-13
    Prison overcrowding, 17-12, 17-13
    Referendum appeals, 17-12, 17-13
    Television cameras in courtrooms, 17-12, 17-13
Judiciary Committee (House)
    Articles of Impeachment, 12-5, 12-46
    Bankruptcy overhaul legislation, 5-15, 5-16, 5-22
    Cable TV competition, 22-17
    Class-action securities suits, 5-33
    Clinton impeachment inquiry, 12-5, 12-7, 12-15, 12-19, 12-33, 12-36, 12-40, 12-41, 12-53
        counsels' statements (excerpts), D-33–D-35
        members' opening statements (excerpts), D-36
        opening statements (excerpts), D-29–D-33
        Staff counsel responses (excerpts), D-33–D-35
        Starr's opening statement (excerpts), D-38, D-38–D-39
    Clinton impeachment resolution, 12-39, 12-42, 12-43
    Clinton impeachment resolution report (excerpts), D-42–D-45
    Digital copyright and Internet encryption, 22-3, 22-4, 22-6, 22-8
    High-tech worker visas, 17-3, 17-5, 17-7
    Internet gambling, 22-7
    Internet taxes, 21-20
    Judicial activism, 17-12, 17-14
    Juvenile crime, 17-16, 17-18
    Members, 12-11
    Physician-assisted suicide, 17-18–17-20
    Product liability laws, 15-18, 15-19
    Religious freedom, 17-9–17-11
    Religious persecution overseas, 16-11, 16-12, 1209
    Reserve funds used for investigations, 2-77
    Satellite retransmission license authority, 22-14
    Satellite TV fee increase, 22-18
Judiciary Committee (Senate)
    Bankruptcy overhaul legislation, 5-15, 5-18, 5-19, 5-22
    Baseball antitrust, 15-25
    Digital copyright, 22-5, 22-9
    FBI wiretapping requirements, 17-14
    Flag desecration, 17-11
    High-tech worker visas, 17-3, 17-5
    Juvenile crime bill, 17-15, 17-16
    Physician-assisted suicide, 17-19
    Property rights, 15-23–15-25
    Satellite-cable TV competition, 22-18
    Y2K computer problem, 22-23
Justice Department
    Authorization (highlights), 17-14
    Cell phone fraud, 22-23
    Citicorp-Travelers Group merger, 5-9
    Democratic fundraising investigation, 18-17
    Physician-assisted suicide, 17-19
    Public housing anti-crime initiative, 20-15
    Shuster ethics investigation, 7-3
Juvenile Diabetes Foundation
    Diabetes research, 2-74
Juvenile justice
    Juvenile crime law overhaul, 17-15–17-18

K

Kaczynski, David
    Waiver of tax on reward for turning in Theodore Kaczynski, 2-115
Kahn, Alfred
    Airline competition, 24-35, 24-38
Kamburowski, Michael (Americans for Tax Reform)
    Renaming National Airport for Ronald Reagan, 13-8
Kanjorski, Paul E., D-Pa. (11)
    Credit unions, 5-26
    Satellite technology transfers to China, 16-24
Kaptur, Marcy, D-Ohio (9)
    Artwork in the Capitol, 2-77
    Farm relief, 2-9
    FHA, 2-103
Kasich, John R., R-Ohio (12)
    Agriculture appropriations, 4-8
    Budget negotiations, 6-3–6-23
    Budget reconciliation FY 1999, 2-116
    Budget surplus, 6-4
    China MFN status, 16-36
    Defense spending, 8-8
    Gasoline tax, 24-12
    IRAs, 6-12
    Renaming National Airport for Ronald Reagan, 13-8
    Retirement accounts, 6-7
    Supplemental appropriations, 2-124
    Surface transportation reauthorization bill, 24-15, 24-26
    Tax cuts, 7-9
Katzenbach, former Attorney General Nicholas
    Impeachment, 12-38
Kelly, Sue W., R-N.Y. (19)
    Clinton impeachment vote, 12-49
    J. Dennis Hastert, R-Ill. (14) character, 7-11
    Regulatory overhaul, 15-20, 15-21
Kempthorne, Dirk, R-Idaho
    Military retirees' health care, 8-5
Kendall, David
    Judiciary Committee hearings
        Ken Starr, 12-27
    Starr report, 12-13
Kennard, William E.
    FCC
        Cable TV rate increase, 22-15, 22-16
Kennedy, Edward M., D-Mass.
    Abortion legislation, 3-5
    Bankruptcy overhaul legislation, 5-18, 5-20
    Farm labor, 2-16
    High-tech worker visas, 17-3–17-5, 17-6
    Internet taxes, 21-22
    Juvenile crime, 17-17
    Managed care legislation, 2-105, 14-3, 14-4–14-6, 14-8
    Minimum wage, 10-7
    Supplemental appropriations
        HCFA, 2-125
    Tobacco, 15-7, 15-10, 15-12
Kennedy, Joseph P. II, D-Mass. (8)
    Credit unions, 5-26, 5-29
    Military ethics, 8-4
    Public housing, 2-107, 20-9, 20-14
Kennelly, Barbara B., D-Conn. (1)
    Omnibus bill
        tax cuts, 21-15
    Retirement, 7-7
Kenya
    U.S. embassy rebuilding, 2-118
Kerrey, Bob, D-Neb.
    Clinton impeachment apology response (excerpts), D-14
    Condemnation of Clinton's behavior, 12-10
    Effect of Clinton investigation on Democratic agenda, 12-6
    Internet taxes, 21-21
    IRS overhaul, 21-3, 21-4, 21-7
    Lott's strategy on China satellite investigation, 16-32
Kerry, John, D-Mass.
    Credit unions, 5-29
    NATO expansion, 8-22
    State Department authorization
        U.N. dues, 16-8
    Tobacco, 15-5, 15-11

General Index

Kessler, David A.
  Tobacco regulation, 15-15
Key votes. *See also* under Topic of legislation
  House, C-9–C-15, C-18–C-19
  Senate, C-3–C-9, C-16–C-17
Keys, Chandler (National Cattlemen's Beef Association)
  Agriculture appropriations, 4-5
Kildee, Dale E., D-Mich. (9)
  Student aid, 9-3
Kim, Jay C., R-Calif. (41)
  Ethics investigation, 7-3
Kimmelman, Gene (Consumers Union)
  Cable TV rates, 22-15
Kind, Ron, D-Wis. (3)
  LIHEAP, 9-22
King, Peter T. R-N.Y. (3)
  Clinton impeachment effort
    effect on 1998 elections, 12-44
  Clinton impeachment vote, 12-27, 12-41, 12-48
  Starr report, 12-13
Kingston, Jack, R-Ga. (1)
  Religious freedom amendment, 17-11
  State Department authorization, 16-5
Kirkpatrick, Jeane J.
  State department authorization, 16-6
Kleczka, Gerald D., D-Wis. (4)
  Clinton impeachment vote, 12-22
Klee, Ken (National Bankruptcy Conference)
  Bankruptcy overhaul legislation, 5-17
Klink, Ron, D-Pa. (4)
  High-tech worker visas, 17-7
Klug, Scott L., R-Wis. (2)
  Digital copyright, 22-6, 22-7
Knollenberg, Joe, R-Mich. (11)
  Aid to Egypt, 2-47
  Kyoto treaty, 2-47, 2-104, 2-110
Kohl, Herb, D-Wis.
  Bankruptcy overhaul legislation, 5-16
  FHA mortgages, 2-102, 2-106
  Gun locks, 2-16
  Treasury-Postal Service appropriations, 2-95
Kolbe, Jim, R-Ariz. (5)
  Budget negotiations, 6-8
  Clinton impeachment vote, 12-40
  COLAs, 2-91
  Technology transfers to China, 16-26
  Treasury-Postal Service appropriations, 2-94, 2-100
  Y2K computer problem, 2-92
Komansky, David (Merrill Lynch & Co.)
  Financial services overhaul legislation, 5-12
Koop, C. Everett
  Tobacco regulation, 15-15
Korea, North
  Land mines, 8-5
  Missile technology transfers to Iran, 2-47
  Missiles, 8-18
  Nuclear buildup, 2-47, 2-51, 2-52, 2-56
Korean Peninsula Energy Development Organization
  Foreign aid, 2-45, 2-47, 2-50, 2-52, 2-54, 2-56
Koskinen, John
  Y2K computer problem, 22-22
Krone, David (Tele-Communications Inc.)
  Cable TV rates, 22-16
Krumholz, Sheila (Center for Responsive Politics)
  "Soft money" campaign contributions, 18-10, 18-11
Kucinich, Dennis J., D-Ohio (10)
  Bilingual education, 9-26
  Domestic partner health benefits, 2-108
Kyl, Jon, R-Ariz.
  Bankruptcy legislation, 5-18, 5-19
  Military construction appropriations, 2-84
  Missile defense, 8-19
  Mortgage insurance, 20-15, 22-7, 22-13
  NATO expansion, 8-23, 8-24
  Supplemental appropriations, 2-118
    missile defense, 2-125
  Transportation appropriations, 2-87

L

Labor and Human Resources Committee (Senate)
  Head Start, 9-20
  Minimum wage, 10-7
Labor and labor unions
  Campaign finance
    issue ads, 18-7, 18-9
    paycheck protection amendment, 18-9, 18-10
  Dues used for political campaigns, 18-5–18-7, 18-9, 18-10, 18-14
  Foreign trade, 23-8
  High-tech immigration, 17-3–17-8
  High-tech worker visas, 17-9
  Labor contract mandates, 2-86, 2-87
  Minimum wage, 10-7
  Salting, 10-5, 10-6
  Worker safety, 10-8
Labor Department
  Appropriations, 2-66, 2-69, 2-70, 2-71, 2-74
  High-tech worker visas, 17-4, 17-5
Labor-HHS-Education
  Appropriations, 2-64–2-74
LaFalce, John J., D-N.Y. (29)
  Credit unions, 5-26, 5-27, 5-29
  Financial services overhaul legislation, 5-8, 5-11
  Public housing, 2-107
LaHood, Ray, R-Ill. (18)
  Clinton impeachment inquiry, 12-24, 12-34, 12-35
  Clinton impeachment vote, 12-41, 12-49
Lake Champlain
  Supplemental appropriations
    eligibility for National Sea Grant research funds, 2-125
Land Between the Lakes National Recreation Area
  TVA funding, 2-36, 2-43
Largent, Steve, R-Okla. (1)
  1998 GOP election losses, 7-5, 12-25
  D.C. appropriations, 2-35
  Gingrich leadership issues, 7-8
  Highway projects, 24-12
  House Majority Leader prospects, 7-4, 7-6, 7-8, 7-11, 12-25
Latham, Tom, R-Iowa (5)
  Farm relief, 2-11
  Food safety, 2-5
Latvia
  NATO expansion, 8-22, 8-23
Lautenberg, Frank R., D-N.J.
  Amtrak funding, 2-88
  Campaign finance, 24-15
  Drunken driving legislation, 24-5, 24-7
  Food safety, 2-7
  Highway donor states, 24-17
  Labor contract mandates, 2-87
  Terrorism, 2-95
  Tobacco, 6-5, 15-13
  Transportation appropriations bill, 2-90
Law and Judiciary
  Attorneys' fees, 2-16
  Class-action securities suits, 5-30–5-34
  Independent Council Law: Then and now, 12-21
  Independent Counsel law, 12-21
  Independent Counsel reauthorization, 2-18
  Limiting federal prosecutors' powers, 2-17, 2-18
Law enforcement
  Foreign operations, FY 1999
    Roswell academy, 2-120
Lazio, Rick A., R-N.Y. (2)
  Clinton impeachment vote, 12-49
  Clinton Middle East trip, 12-40
  House Republican Conference chairmanship, 7-4
  Public housing, 2-103, 2-105, 2-107, 2-110–2-111, 20-7, 20-8, 20-10, 20-11, 20-14
  Republican agenda, 7-7
Leach, Jim, R-Iowa (1)
  Clinton impeachment vote, 12-40, 12-49
  Credit unions, 5-25–5-27, 5-29
  FHA, 2-103, 2-106
  Financial services overhaul legislation, 5-8, 5-9–5-11
  IMF funding, 16-38
  Sanctions, 16-12
  United Nations funding, 16-4
League of Women Voters
  Campaign finance, 18-10
Leahy, Patrick J., D-Vt.
  Abortion legislation, 3-5
  Africa, 23-12
  Baseball antitrust, 15-25
  Encryption export restrictions, 22-20
  Glenn spaceflight, 19-11
  Human rights violations, 2-25
  Juvenile crime, 17-16, 17-17
  Lake Champlain National Sea Grant eligibility, 2-125
  Land mines, 8-5, 8-13
  Physician-assisted suicide, 17-20
  Property rights, 15-24, 15-25
  Supplemental appropriations
    Home state projects, 2-125–2-126
  Y2K computer problem, 22-23
Leavitt, Gov. Michael, R-Utah
  Nuclear waste dump on tribal land, 2-58
Legal Services Corporation
  Funding, 2-13, 2-14, 2-18
Legislative branch
  Appropriations, 2-75–2-80
Legislative riders
  Environment, 2-57, 2-60, 2-61
Leitner, Peter M.
  Export controls, 16-30
Lerach, Bill
  Class-action securities suits, 5-32
Levin, Carl, D-Mich.
  Abortion legislation, 3-6
  Anti-missile defense, 8-18
    ABM treaty, 8-19
  Bosnia, 8-6
  FEC term limits, 2-98
  Military base closings, 8-5
  NATO expansion, 8-23
  Nuclear waste, 11-4
  Regulatory overhaul, 15-20, 15-21, 15-23
  Russia technology transfers to Iran, 16-19
  Social Security trust fund, 21-17
  Technology transfers to China, 16-24, 16-26
  Thompson-Levin regulatory overhaul bill, 15-20, 15-21, 15-23
    provisions, 15-22
  Treasury-Postal Service appropriations, 2-97
Levin, Sander M., D-Mich. (12)
  Campaign finance, 18-15
  Ethanol tax credit, 24-12
Lew, Jacob (OMB)
  NASA budget, 19-8, 19-9
  Russian space program, 19-8
Lewis, Jerry, R-Calif. (40)
  Domestic partner health benefits, 2-108
  FHA, 2-103
  Military base in home district, 2-31
  Public housing, 2-107
  Space station, 19-6, 19-10
  VA-HUD appropriations, 2-110
Lewis, John, D-Ga. (5)
  Africa human rights violations, 23-10
  Impeachment debate, 12-52
Lewis, Ron, R-Ky. (2)
  Lincoln Birthplace National Historic Site, 11-7
Library of Congress
  Appropriations, 2-76, 2-80
Lieberman, Joseph I., D-Conn.
  Bosnia, 2-24
  Clinton censure, 12-12
  Clinton condemnation, 12-9, 12-10
  Clinton impeachment apology response (excerpts), D-13–D-14
  Internet taxes, 21-20
  Military spending, 8-15
  Missile defense, 8-18, 8-19–8-20
  Product liability, 15-19
  Regulatory overhaul, 15-21, 15-22
  Religious persecution overseas, 16-13, 16-14, 16-16
  Russia technology transfers to Iran, 16-18, 16-19, 16-26
Lim, Wah (Loral Space and Communications)
  Technology transfers to China, 16-32

Linder, John, R-Ga. (11)
  Campaign finance, 18-11
  House leadership challenge, 7-7
  NRCC chairmanship, 7-6–7-8, 7-10
  Treasury-Postal Service appropriations, 2-94
Lindsey, Bruce R.
  Class-action securities suits, 5-30
  Clinton impeachment depositions, 12-28, 12-30, 12-32
Line-item veto
  Constitutionality of, 2-82, 2-93
    lawsuits, 6-20–6-22
    Supreme Court opinions (excerpts), 6-21
  Federal employees pension plan lawsuit, 2-93
  Judge Hogan's ruling (excerpts), 6-18
  Key votes, C-9, C-18
  Military construction projects, 2-80, 2-82
Litan, Robert E. (Brookings Institution)
  Financial services mergers, 5-9
Literacy
  Appropriations, 2-72, 2-74
Lithuania
  NATO expansion, 8-22, 8-23
Litton Industries
  Defense contracts, 2-22, 2-27, 2-32, 8-3, 8-6, 8-11
Livingston, Robert L., R-La. (1)
  Abortion rider to agriculture appropriations, 2-5
  Appropriations
    Labor-HHS-Education, 2-67
  Bilingual education, 2-65, 9-27
  Budget resolution FY 1999, 2-115
  Call for Clinton resignation, 12-45, 12-46
  CBO forecasts, 2-77
  Clinton impeachment, 7-9
  Clinton impeachment strategy, 12-35
  Clinton impeachment, censure resolution, 12-47, 12-49
  Clinton impeachment, duration of, 12-27, 12-32, 12-33
  Clinton impeachment, penalty options, 12-34
  D.C. appropriations, 2-34
  Disagreements with Dick Armey, R-Texas (26), 7-8
  Disagreements with Tom DeLay, R-Texas (22), 7-8
  Education, 2-65
  Farm relief, 2-11
  FEC budget, 2-95
  FEC term limits, 2-92, 2-97, 2-98
  FHA, 2-104
  House GOP unity, 7-8
  House Speakership, 7-4–7-12, 12-5, 12-34, 12-40
  IMF funding, 2-46–2-49, 2-52–2-54
  Infidelity admission, 12-3
  Kyoto treaty, 2-104
  Loral SpaceCom PAC contributions, 16-25
  Military construction projects in home district, 2-81
  Milk marketing, 2-4
  Missile defense, 8-18
  National Bioethics Advisory Commission, 2-92
  Puerto Rico, 13-6
  Resignation, 7-10–7-12, 12-3, 12-45, 12-50, 12-52
  Supplemental appropriations, 2-118, 2-123, 2-125, 2-126, 2-128
    defense, 2-123
    disaster relief, 2-122
    oil royalties, 2-130
    organ transplants, 2-130
  Surface transportation reauthorization bill, 24-19
  Transportation appropriations
    road projects, 2-90
  Treasury-Postal Service appropriations, 2-92
  Y2K computer problem, 2-92
Lockhart, Joe
  Bankruptcy overhaul legislation, 5-23
Lockheed Martin
  Defense contracts, 2-23, 8-5, 8-9–8-11

General Index

Lofgren, Zoe, D-Calif. (16)
Clinton impeachment
Judiciary Committee opening statement (excerpts), D-31
Encryption export restrictions, 22-20
Internet copyright, 22-4
Light-rail project, 24-13
Low-skilled worker visas, 17-6
Shuster ethics investigation, 7-3, 24-15
Loral Space and Communications
Satellite crash in China, 16-31
Technology transfers to China, 8-7, 16-23–16-26, 16-29, 16-31, 16-33, 16-35
Loral SpaceCom PAC
Campaign contributions, 16-25
Lott, Trent, R-Miss.
Abortion legislation, 3-5
Africa trade, 23-10, 23-12
Agriculture appropriations, 4-6
Amtrak funding, 2-85
Appropriations
projects in home state, 2-37, 2-38
Bankruptcy overhaul legislation, 5-20
Budget negotiations, 6-3, 6-9, 6-15
Campaign finance, 16-32, 18-3, 18-7, 18-15–18-17
China MFN status, 16-26, 16-36
Clinton China policy, 16-36
Clinton impeachment
censure resolution, 12-53
Clinton impeachment trial, 12-33, 12-36
Comprehensive Nuclear Test Ban Treaty, 2-51
Condemnation of Clinton's behavior, 12-10
Defense appropriations, 8-14
projects in home state, 2-30
Defense authorization
projects in home state, 8-11
Defense contracts in home state, 2-25, 8-11, 8-13
FAA authorization, 24-36
Fast-track trade bill, 23-7
Financial services overhaul legislation, 5-3, 5-12, 5-14
Interior appropriations, 2-57
Internet taxes, 21-21
Iran sanctions, 16-17, 16-18
Iraq airstrikes, 12-51
IRS overhaul, 2-105, 21-4, 21-6
IRS reform, 13-8
LIHEAP, 2-64
Managed care, 2-105, 14-14
Missile technology transfers to China, 16-32
NAFTA, 23-12
NATO expansion, 8-21, 8-22, 8-24
Nixon Watergate investigation, 12-15
Nuclear waste, 11-3, 11-4
Omnibus bill
tax cuts, 21-18
Product liability, 15-19
Puerto Rico, 13-6, 13-7
Regulatory overhaul, 15-20–15-23
Religious persecution overseas, 16-11, 16-14
Russia technology transfers to Iran, 16-17, 16-18
Satellite TV fee increase, 22-16
State Department authorization
abortion, 16-8
U.N. dues, 16-7
State of the Union address, 12-4
Supplemental appropriations
IMF, 2-125
international family planning, 2-125
U.N. dues, 2-122
Surface transportation reauthorization bill, 24-4, 24-6, 24-7, 24-16, 24-17, 24-19, 24-20, 24-23–24-25
home state projects, 24-24
Tax cuts, 6-13
Technology transfers to China, 8-5, 8-6, 8-14, 8-15, 8-16, 8-20, 16-24, 16-26, 16-32, 16-36
Tobacco, 2-8, 15-3, 15-5, 15-12, 15-13
Treasury-Postal Service appropriations, 2-96
VA-HUD appropriations
health care rider, 2-106
Louisiana
Defense appropriations
military construction projects, 2-81

Low-Income Home Energy Assistance Program (LIHEAP)
Funding, 2-64–2-66, 2-68, 2-70, 2-71
Reauthorization, 9-22, 9-23
Lowell, Abbe D.
Clinton impeachment
Judiciary Committee statement (excerpts), D-34, D-35–D-36
Clinton investigation, 12-32
Judiciary Committee hearings
Ken Starr testimony, 12-27–12-30
Lowenthal, TerriAnn
Census, 13-3
Lowey, Nita M., D-N.Y. (18)
Abortion legislation, 3-6, 3-8
Aid to Egypt, 2-47
Contraceptive coverage in federal employee health plans, 2-91, 2-95, 2-98, 2-100, 2-113
Drunken driving legislation, 24-12, 24-15
Food safety, 205
Military abortions, 8-8
Obstetrician-gynecologists as primary care physicians, 2-67
Lugar, Richard G., R-Ind.
Africa, 23-11
Agriculture appropriations, 4-5–4-6
child nutrition programs, 20-4, 20-5
Farm loans, 2-7
Food stamps, 4-7
Russia
Nuclear weapons disposal program, 8-11
Nuclear weapons disposal program, 2-22
Textiles and clothing, 23-11
Tobacco subsidies, 15-9, 15-11
Lungren, California Attorney General
Bilingual education, 9-26
Luntz, Frank
Republican impeachment strategy, 12-4, 12-5

M

Mack, Connie, R-Fla.
Budget, 6-3, 6-16
Cloning, 19-3
Commercial space bill, 19-5
Credit unions, 5-27
FHA mortgages, 2-106
Financial services overhaul, 5-13
Gasoline tax, 24-5, 24-9
Haitian refugees, 2-98, 17-8
IRS overhaul, 21-7
Public housing, 2-103, 2-105–2-106, 2-110–2-111, 20-7, 20-8, 20-10, 20-11, 20-14
State of the Union address, 12-6
Make-a-Wish Foundation
SSI recipients' ineligibility, 20-16
Maloney, Carolyn B., D-N.Y. (14)
FEC term limits, 2-95
Maloney, Jim, D-Conn. (5)
Financial services overhaul legislation, 5-11
Managed care
Obstetrician-gynecologists as primary care physicians, 2-67
Regulations, C-12–C-13, C-20
Side-by-side comparisons, 14-10, 14-11
Mandela, Nelson
Africa bill criticism, 23-12
Manton, Thomas J., D-N.Y. (7)
Class-action securities suits, 5-33
Manzullo, Donald, R-Ill. (16)
Judge-ordered tax increases, 17-13
Marchman, Kevin (HUD)
Public housing bill, 20-11
Markey, Edward J., D-Mass. (7)
Cable TV rates, 22-16, 22-17
Class-action securities suits, 5-32
Digital copyright, 22-6
Internet pornography, 22-11
Internet taxes, 21-20
Martinez, Matthew G., D-Calif. (31)
Bilingual education, 9-26, 9-27
Head Start, 9-21, 9-22
Human service program reauthorization, 9-21, 9-22
Massachusetts
Tobacco lawsuits, 15-9

MasterCard International
Bankruptcy overhaul legislation, 5-24
Matsui, Robert T., D-Calif. (5)
Foreign trade, 23-6–23-9, 23-12
MFN status for China, 16-26
Omnibus bill
tax cuts, 21-15
Surface transportation reauthorization bill, 24-13
May, Richard
Budget negotiations, 6-8
Mayer, Martin (Brookings Institution)
Bank mergers and competition, 5-6
McAlpin, K. C. (Federation for American Immigration Reform)
High-tech worker visas, 17-4
McBride, Ann (Common Cause)
Campaign finance, 18-10, 18-16
McCaffrey, Barry
Drug control spending, 2-119
McCain, John, R-Ariz.
Airline competition, 2-85
America West flights to D.C., 24-36
Bosnia mission, 2-24, 2-25
Campaign finance overhaul, 18-3, 18-4, 18-6, 18-7, 18-9, 18-11, 18-13, 18-15–18-17
Class-action securities suits, 5-31
Congressional Research Service reports on the Internet, 2-78
FAA authorization, 24-34, 24-36–24-40
Highway bill earmarks, 24-9–24-12, 24-24
Internet pornography, 22-11
Internet screening software, 2-15, 2-16
Internet taxes, 21-22, 21-23, 21-24
Line-item veto, 6-23
Loral SpaceCom PAC campaign contributions, 16-25
Mass transit earmarks, 2-85, 2-90
Military base closings, 8-4
Military construction appropriations, 2-84
Military construction projects, 2-82
Military construction projects in members' home states, 2-83, 2-84
National Guard, 2-84
Product liability, 15-19
Reagan National Airport perimeter rule, 24-37
Renaming National Airport for Ronald Reagan, 13-8
Satellite fee increases, 22-14
Space station, 19-4–19-10
Supplemental appropriations
free air time, 2-127
Technology transfers to China, 16-33, 16-34
Telephone "slamming," 22-24, 22-26
Tobacco bill and industry settlement, 15-4
Tobacco legislation, 15-3, 15-5–15-10, 15-12–15-15
McCollum, Bill, R-Fla. (8)
Bankruptcy overhaul legislation, 5-18
Clinton impeachment
Betty Currie, 12-38
Judiciary Committee opening statement (excerpts), D-30
Monica Lewinsky, 12-37
Republican argument, 12-32
Clinton impeachment as censure, 12-33, 12-47, 12-50
Clinton impeachment proceedings
perjury charge, 12-30
Clinton impeachment vote, 12-40, 12-41
Clinton popularity in spite of Starr report, 12-20–12-22
Credit unions, 5-26
Drug control, 2-119, 2-120
Financial Services Competition Act, 5-8
High-tech worker visas, 17-5
Intelligence authorization
Wiretap authority, 8-26
Internet pedophiles, 22-13
Juvenile crime, 17-16, 17-18
Public release of Starr report, 12-12
McConnell, Mitch, R-Ky.
Campaign finance, 18-3, 18-4, 18-11, 18-17
Clinton impeachment
effect on 1998 elections, 12-25
FEC term limits, 2-96–2-98
Minority contract set-aside programs, 2-87, 2-90, 24-5, 24-7, 24-8, 24-11

Supplemental appropriations
IMF, 2-124
Tobacco legislation, 15-13
Tobacco subsidies, 15-9, 15-11
TVA funding, 2-36, 2-39, 2-41–2-44
McConnell, William T. (American Bankers Association)
Financial services overhaul, 5-5
McCrery, Jim, R-La. (4)
Highway projects, 24-13
Medicare, 14-17
NRCC leadership, 7-7
Shuster ethics investigation, 24-15
McCurdy, former Rep. David, D-Okla. (4)
Appointment to Electronic Industries Alliance, 22-9
McCurry, Mike
Budget, 6-11
Clinton impeachment
GOP partisanship, 12-20
Clinton's China trip, 16-35
Fast-track trade authority, 23-5
Social Security solvency, 21-17
State Department authorization, 16-8
McDade, Joseph M., R-Pa. (10)
Bribery charges, 2-17
Limiting federal prosecutors' powers, 2-14, 2-17, 2-18
Supplemental appropriations
dam and levee projects, 2-39
TVA funding, 2-39, 2-40
McDermott, Jim, D-Wash. (7)
Boehner lawsuit against McDermott for taping Gingrich call, 7-3
Columbia Basin Ecosystem Management Plan, 2-60
Gingrich ethics charges, 7-3
House ethics committee, 7-3
IRS overhaul, 21-8
Managed care, 14-14
McDonnell Douglas Corp.
Supplemental appropriations
defense contracts, 2-125
McGarry, Mike (Visa USA)
Bankruptcy overhaul legislation, 5-18
McHale, Paul, D-Pa. (15)
Call for Clinton resignation, 12-23, 12-48
Call for Clinton's resignation, 12-10
Clinton condemnation and censure resolution, 12-30, 12-31
McInnis, Scott, R-Colo. (3)
Bankruptcy overhaul legislation, 5-19
Tobacco, 15-3
McIntosh, David M., R-Ind. (2)
Labor, HHS and Education appropriations, 2-71
Omnibus appropriations bill, 2-113
State Department authorization, 16-4
Supplemental appropriations, 2-113
McKeon, Howard P. "Buck," R-Calif. (25)
Student aid, 9-3, 9-4
Medicaid
D.C. initiative, 2-36
Viagra, 2-66, 2-67, 2-74
Medical devices
Liability, 15-19
Medical ethics
Cloning, 19-3, C-3, C-16
Medical research
AIDS research, 2-74
Appropriations, 2-72
Cancer research, 2-74
Cloning, 19-3, C-3, C-16
Diabetes research, 2-74
Medicare
Abortion for disabled, 2-74
Abortion services, 2-66, 2-74
Clinton plan, 12-6
Community health centers, 2-69
Disabled, 2-64
Funding, 2-65, 2-69
Home health care, 14-16–14-22
Home health care reimbursement, 2-116
Military eligibility and coverage, 8-14
Meehan, Martin T., D-Mass. (5)
Bankruptcy overhaul legislation, 5-17
Clinton impeachment
Judiciary Committee opening statement (excerpts), D-32
Meek, Carrie P., D-Fla. (17)
Cigarette labeling, 2-67
Public housing, 2-103

General Index

Menendez, Robert, D-N.J. (13)
Religious persecution overseas, 16-10
Merrill Lynch & Co.
Financial services overhaul legislation, 5-12
Mica, Daniel A. (Credit Union National Association)
Credit union legislation, 5-26
Michelman, Kate (National Abortion and Reproductive Rights Action League)
Abortion, 3-8, 3-9
Microsoft Corp.
High-tech worker visas, 17-4, 17-5, 17-6, 17-9
Mikulski, Barbara A., D-Md.
Flammability standards, 2-110
Loral SpaceCom PAC contributions, 16-25
Russia missile technology transfers to Iran, 19-7
Space station, 19-7
VA-HUD appropriations, 2-102, 2-105, 2-110
Military personnel issues
Same-sex training
key votes, C-7, C-17
Miller, Gov. Bob, D-Nev.
Nuclear waste, 11-3
Miller, Dan, R-Fla. (13)
Census, 13-4
Financial services overhaul legislation, 5-11
Miller, George, D-Calif. (7)
Chugach National Forest, 2-60
Minerals Management Service
Oil and gas royalties regulation, 2-116
Mines and mining
Mining regulations, 2-61, 2-67
Minge, David, D-Minn. (2)
Agriculture appropriations, 4-9
Surface transportation reauthorization bill, 24-16, 24-24
Minimum wage. See under **Wages and salaries**
Minnesota
Tobacco settlement, 15-9
Missiles
National missile defense, 2-30, 2-31, 2-117, 2-125, 8-3, 8-7, 8-8, 8-10, 8-15, 8-16, 8-18, 8-19, 8-20
Mississippi
Appropriations
Archusa Dam repair, 2-37
Pascagoula Harbor, 2-38
Defense contracts, 8-11
Tobacco settlement, 15-9
Missouri
Defense appropriations
military construction projects, 2-30, 2-81
Mollohan, Alan B., D-W.Va. (1)
Census, 2-13, 2-14
Kyoto treaty, 2-104
Tax cuts, 6-12
Monjan, Andrew (National Institute on Aging)
Glenn spaceflight, 19-11
Montana
Appropriations
road projects, 2-90
Moran, James P., D-Va. (8)
Bankruptcy overhaul legislation, 5-17, 5-24
Clinton criticism, 12-19, 12-23
Clinton impeachment
censure resolution, 12-41
D.C. appropriations, 2-33, 2-34
Farm aid, 2-114
Public release of Starr report, 12-13
Reagan National Airport perimeter rule, 24-37
Renaming National Airport for Ronald Reagan, 13-8, 13-9
Morella, Constance A., R-Md. (8)
Additional flights at high-traffic airports, 24-39
Clinton impeachment vote, 12-48
Clinton's videotaped testimony, 12-17
Renaming National Airport for Ronald Reagan, 13-9
Y2K computer problem, 22-22
Morley, William J. (U.S. Chamber of Commerce)
Fast-track trade authority, 23-6

Moseley-Braun, Carol, D-Ill.
Fast-track trade bill, 23-4
IRS oversight, 21-7
Minority contract set-aside programs, 2-87, 24-8
O'Hare airport traffic, 24-37
"Partial birth" abortion ban, 3-8
Mothers Against Drunk Driving (MADD)
Drunken driving legislation, 24-12
Motion Picture Association of America
Internet pornography, 22-12
Satellite fee increases, 22-14
Moynihan, Daniel Patrick, D-N.Y.
Clinton impeachment apology response (excerpts), D-13
Condemnation of Clinton's behavior, 12-10
Fast-track trade bill, 23-4, 23-6
Home health care, 14-21
IRS overhaul, 21-4, 21-8
Loral SpaceCom PAC contributions, 16-25
NATO expansion, 8-22–8-24
Murkowski, Frank H., R-Alaska
Electricity deregulation, 6-15, 15-16, 15-17
Environment
Izembek Road, 2-57, 2-63
Nevada nuclear waste site, 11-3, 11-4
Murphy, William L. (National District Attorneys Association)
Juvenile crime bill, 17-17
Murray, Patty, D-Wash.
IRS overhaul, 21-9
Military abortions, 8-12
Military construction appropriations, 2-84
Regulatory overhaul, 15-23
Murtha, John P., D-Pa. (12)
China, 16-24
Clinton impeachment vote, 12-23
Clinton's ability to govern, 12-19
Defense appropriations, 2-28
military retirement, 2-30
Kosovo, 2-23
Limiting federal prosecutors powers, 2-14
Starr report, 12-17
Supplemental appropriations, 2-127
Iraq, 2-126
Myrick, Sue, R-N.C. (9)
Highway projects, 24-12

N

Nader, Ralph
Financial institution mergers, 5-10
Nadler, Jerrold, D-N.Y. (8)
Abortion legislation, 3-3–3-4
Bankruptcy overhaul legislation, 5-16, 5-17, 5-18, 5-20, 5-24
Clinton impeachment
Judiciary Committee opening statement (excerpts), D-30–D-31
Livingston resignation, remarks, 12-46
Regulatory overhaul, 15-20, 15-21
Television cameras in courtrooms, 17-13, 17-14
NAFTA (North America Free Trade Agreement), 23-3, 23-7, 23-8, 23-12
Caribbean Basin Initiative, 23-6
NASA (National Aeronautics and Space Administration)
Authorization, 2-104, 2-109, 19-4–19-12
Glenn spaceflight, 19-10–19-12
Space station, 2-101, 2-110, 19-4–19-10
Natcher, former Rep. William, D-Ky.
Medical research, 2-72
National Abortion and Reproductive Rights Action League
"Partial birth" abortion ban, 3-8, 3-9
National Academy of Sciences
Education
National testing, 9-28
National Aeronautics and Space Administration. See **NASA**
National Air Traffic Controllers Association
Renaming National Airport for Ronald Reagan, 13-8
National Assessment Governing Board
Education
National testing, 9-28

National Association for Home Care
Home health care, 14-16, 14-17, 14-19, 14-21, 14-22
National Association of Attorneys General
Internet gambling, 22-13
National Association of Federal Credit Unions
Membership issues, 5-28, 5-29
National Association of Home Builders
Property rights, 15-24, 15-25
National Association of Manufacturers
Dual use exports, 16-27
National Bankruptcy Conference
Bankruptcy overhaul legislation, 5-17, 5-20
National Bioethics Advisory Commission, 2-92
National Cattlemen's Beef Association
Agriculture appropriations, 4-5
National Center for Missing and Exploited Children
Reauthorization, 17-15
National Corn Growers Association
Ethanol tax credit, 24-18
National Credit Union Administration
Membership issues, 5-25, 5-28, 5-29
Y2K computer problem, 22-21, 22-22
National Credit Union Share Insurance Fund, 5-26
National District Attorneys Association
Juvenile crime bill, 17-17
National Endowment for the Arts
Funding, 2-57, 2-60
National Federation of Independent Business
Regulatory overhaul, 15-21–15-23
National forests
Chugach National Forest, 2-57, 2-59, 2-60
Logging, 2-57, 2-59, 2-60
Maintenance, 2-59
Recreational fees, 2-58
Tongass National Forest, 2-57, 2-59, 2-60
National Governors Association
Drunken driving legislation, 24-12
Highway reauthorization, 24-6, 24-19
Internet taxes, 21-19–21-22
Regulatory overhaul, 15-21
National Guard
Appropriations, 2-80, 2-81
Funding issues, 5-11
National Highway System Designation Act, 24-10
National Institute on Aging
Glenn spaceflight, 19-11
National Institutes of Health. See **NIH**
National Labor Relations Board. See **NLRB**
National League of Cities
Internet taxes, 21-21
National Low Income Housing Coalition
Public housing vouchers, 20-15
National Park Service
Appropriations, 2-57, 2-58
Supplemental appropriations, 2-118
National parks
Glacier Bay Nationa Park, 2-63
Maintenance, 2-59
Recreational fees, 2-58
Zion National Park, 2-63
National Republican Congressional Committee. See **NRCC**
National Research Council
Airline competition study, 24-34
National Right to Life Committee
Abortion-related restrictions on U.S. aid, 16-3
Campaign finance overhaul
issue ads, 18-11
National School Boards Association
Teacher training, 2-71
National School Lunch Program
Reauthorization, 20-4
National Science Foundation
Appropriations, 2-101, 2-105, 2-110
National security
Omnibus bill
NSA funding, 2-120
Technology transfers to China
House action, 8-3, 8-7, 8-16
National Security Agency
Satellite crash in China, 16-31

National Security Committee (House)
Bosnia, 8-8
Defense authorization, 8-4–8-9, 8-13
F-16 and F-22 aircraft, 8-9
Land mines, 8-5
Missile defense, 8-17
Mixed gender military training, 8-4, 8-7
National Security Council. See **NSC**
NationsBank
Financial services overhaul legislation, 5-7, 5-8, 5-9
NATO (North Atlantic Treaty Organization)
Creation of, 8-22
Expansion
Czech Republic, 8-21–8-24
Estonia, 8-22, 8-23
Hungary, 8-21–8-23
Latvia, 8-22, 8-23
Lithuania, 8-22, 8-23
Pact with Russia, 8-22
Poland, 8-21–8-23
Senate approval, 8-21–8-24
Key votes, C-4–C-5, C-16
Russia, 8-22, 8-24
Spain, admittance of, 8-23
Nelson, Rick (Association of Housing and Redevelopment Officials)
Public housing overhaul, 20-10
Nesbit, Jeff
Tobacco regulation, 15-14, 15-15
Netanyahu, Benjamin
Russian technology transfers to Iran, 16-17
Nethercutt, George, R-Wash. (5)
Columbia Basin Ecosystem Management Plan, 2-60
Food sanctions, 2-5, 2-6, 1762
Neumann, Mark W., R-Wis. (1)
Defense appropriations
Y2K computer problem, 2-22
FHA, 2-103
Food sanctions, costs, 2-5
HUD mortgages, 2-110
Peanut price supports, 2-6
Supplemental appropriations, 2-124, 2-127
Tax cuts, 6-15
Viagra, 2-67
Y2K computer problem, 2-92–2-94
Nevada
Yucca Mountain nuclear waste site, 11-3, 11-4
New Mexico
Appropriations
water projects, 2-41
Grazing leases on public lands, 2-63
Ney, Bob, R-Ohio (18)
House GOP agenda, 7-10
Nickles, Don, R-Okla.
Budget, 6-6, 6-7, 6-17
FHA mortgages, 2-106
IRS overhaul, 21-4
Managed care, 14-6, 14-9, 14-12
Physician-assisted suicide, 17-18
Regulatory overhaul, 15-23
Religious persecution overseas, 16-9, 16-11–16-16
State Department authorization
abortion, 16-8
Tobacco, 6-5, 15-3, 15-6, 15-7, 15-9, 15-13
Transportation legislation, 24-5
NIH (National Institutes of Health)
Funding, 2-64, 2-65, 2-68, 2-69–2-74, 2-72
Monitoring, 2-69
Nixon, Walter L., Jr.
Impeachment as federal judge, 12-16
Nixon, former President Richard M.
Impeachment proceedings, 12-8, 12-12, 12-23, 12-40
Resignation, 12-8, 12-45
Watergate investigation, 12-12, 12-15, 12-19, 12-44, 12-50, 12-51, 12-53
NLRB (National Labor Relations Board)
Appropriations, 2-66, 2-70, 2-71
Salting by unions, 10-5, 10-6
Noble, Lawrence
FEC term limits, 2-96–2-98
North American Free Trade Agreement. See **NAFTA**

General Index

North Carolina
  Defense appropriations
    military construction projects, 2-81
North Korea
  Missiles, 8-17, 8-18
Northrup Grumman Corp.
  Defense contracts, 8-6
Northup, Anne M., R-Ky. (3)
  Campaign finance, 18-9, 18-11
  International mail, 2-94
  Mining regulations, 2-68
Norton, Eleanor Holmes, D-D.C.
  D.C. appropriations, 2-33–2-36
  D.C. school vouchers, 2-34, 2-35, 9-24
  Minority contract set-aside programs, 24-16
Norway
  NATO expansion, 8-22, 8-23
Norwood, Charlie, R-Ga. (10)
  Managed care, 14-3–14-6, 14-15
Novell
  Encryption export restrictions, 22-19, 22-20
NRC
  Funding, 2-37–2-40, 2-44
NRCC
  Chairmanship, 7-6, 7-7
NSC
  Dual-use military technology, 16-30
  Religious persecution overseas, 16-14
Nuclear Energy Institute
  Energy policy, 2-39
  Nevada nuclear waste site, 11-4
Nuclear Regulatory Commission. *See* NRC
Nuclear waste, 11-4
  Appropriations, 2-58
Nunn, former Sen. Sam, D-Ga.
  Russia
    Nuclear weapons disposal program, 2-22, 8-11
Nussle, Jim, R-Iowa (2)
  Supplemental appropriations, 2-124
  Surface transportation reauthorization bill, 24-21
  Trade bill, 23-10

O

Oberg, James
  Russian space program, 19-10
Oberstar, James L., D-Minn. (8)
  Airline competition, 24-34, 24-38
  Renaming National Airport for Ronald Reagan, 13-8
  Superfund, 11-5
  Surface transportation reauthorization bill, 24-5, 24-11, 24-12
    home state projects, 24-26
Obey, David R., D-Wis. (7)
  Agriculture appropriations, 4-5
  Appropriations, 2-113
    defense, 2-23
    Labor-HHS-Education, 2-70
    Treasury-Postal Service, 2-94
  Arts funding, 2-59
  Campaign finance, 18-12
  CBO forecasts, 2-77
  Clinton impeachment inquiry, 12-14, 12-20
  Clinton impeachment vote, 12-23
  FEC term limits, 2-98
  Global warming, 2-107
  IMF funding, 2-47, 2-56
  Milk marketing, 2-3, 2-4, 2-5, 2-6
  Nuclear waste disposal on tribal lands, 2-58
  Special investigations, 2-77
  Spending cuts, 2-65
  Starr report, 12-15
  Supplemental appropriations, 2-122, 2-125, 2-127
    defense, 2-124
  Surface transportation reauthorization bill, 24-14, 24-19, 24-25, 24-26
  Tax waiver on reward for turning in Unabomber, 2-114
  VA-HUD appropriations, 2-110
  Viagra, 2-67
OCC (Office of the Comptroller of the Currency)
  Financial regulation, 5-9

Financial services overhaul legislation, 5-4, 5-5, 5-11
Glass-Steagall Act revisions, 5-9
Y2K computer problem, 22-21
Occupational Safety and Health Administration. *See* OSHA
Office of Comptroller of the Currency. *See* OCC
Office of Management and Budget. *See* OMB
Office of Regulatory Analysis
  Federal regulations, 15-20
Office of Thrift Supervision
  Citicorp-Travelers merger, 5-9
  Financial services overhaul legislation, 5-4
  House banking bill, 5-4
  Y2K computer problem, 22-21, 22-22
Oil industry
  Regulation, 2-116
  Royalties for oil and gas leases on federal lands, 2-58, 2-63, 2-130
Oklahoma
  Defense appropriations
    military construction projects, 2-81
  Tobacco lawsuits, 15-9
Olver, John W., D-Mass. (1)
  Military construction appropriations, 2-81
OMB (Office of Management and Budget)
  Abortion legislation, 3-3, 3-5
  Budget caps, 6-8
  Budget resolution, 6-9
  Intelligence cuts, 8-26
  IRS overhaul, 21-6
  Managed care legislation, 14-14
  Regulatory overhaul, 15-22
  Space station, 19-7
  Supplemental appropriations, 2-129
  Surface transportation reauthorization bill, 24-21
OMB Watch
  Regulatory overhaul, 15-23
Omnibus bill
  Airport improvement grants, 24-34
  Appropriations, 7-5
  Bilingual education, 9-25
  Border control, 2-120
  Census funding, 2-18
  Child care tax credit, 21-18
  Customs Service
    drug control aircraft, 2-120
  Drug traffic interdiction spending, 2-118, 2-119
  Drug treatment in prisons, 2-119
  Drug treatment in the workplace, 2-119
  Health insurance deduction for self-employed, 21-18
  Immigration initiatives (highlights), 17-8
  Intelligence
    Covert operations in Iraq, 8-27
  Internet taxes, 21-24
  Middle-income tax cut, 21-15
  State Department
    drug control aircraft, 2-120
  State Department authorization, 16-3
  State Department reorganization, 16-9
  Tax credit for business research, 21-18
  Tax provisions, 21-14–21-18
    highlights, 21-16
  Trade adjustment assistance program, 21-18
  Trade agreement job losses, 21-18
  Treasury-Postal Service appropriations, 2-91
O'Neill, June E.
  CBO controversy, 2-76, 2-78
OPIC (Overseas Private Investment Corporation)
  Africa, 23-10, 23-11
  Vietnam, 23-9
Oregon
  Physician-assisted suicide, 17-18
Oregon Institute of Public Service and Constitutional Studies
  Appropriations, 2-72
Organ donation
  Distribution rules, 2-66, 2-68, 2-71
OSHA (Occupational Safety and Health Administration)
  Appropriations, 2-66, 2-69, 2-72
  House action, 10-8
  Senate action, 10-8
Overseas Private Investment

Corporation. *See* OPIC
Oversight Committee (House)
  Campaign finance overhaul, 18-4–18-6, 18-13, 18-14
  Doman/Sanchez election challenge, 18-4
Owens, Douglas Wayne
  Constitutionality of impeachment, 12-38
Oxley, Michael G., R-Ohio (4)
  Class-action securities suits, 5-31, 5-32, 5-34
  Financial services overhaul, 5-3
  Internet pornography, 22-11–22-13
  Superfund, 11-5
  Telephone "slamming," 22-25

P

Packard, Ron, R-Calif. (48)
  Bankruptcy overhaul legislation, 5-17, 15-18
  Military construction appropriations, 2-80, 2-81
  Military construction projects in home district, 2-81
Pakistan
  Nuclear arsenal, 16-30
Parker, Mike, R-Miss. (4)
  Livingston resignation, 7-12
  Surface transportation reauthorization bill, 24-14
Parsons, Pam
  Clinton impeachment
    perjury charges, 12-32
Party unity
  Background, B-19
  House votes, B-22, B-23
  Leading scorers, B-8
  Scores by chamber (graph), B-7
  Senate votes, B-21
  Vote studies, B-6–B-9
  Votes by roll call number, B-20
Pate, Carmen (Concerned Women for America)
  GOP principles, 12-52
Paul, Ron, R-Texas (14)
  Child support enforcement, 20-6
  Military construction appropriations, 2-83
Paxon, Bill, R-N.Y. (27)
  Campaign finance
    labor unions, 18-13–18-14
  House speakership campaign, 12-46
Payne, Donald M., D-N.J. (10)
  Head Start, 9-21
Pease, Ed, R-Ind. (7)
  Clinton impeachment
    Judiciary Committee opening statement (excerpts), D-33
Pelosi, Nancy, D-Calif. (8)
  China human rights practices, 16-37
  China MFN status, 16-35
  Domestic partner health benefits, 2-108
  IMF funding, 2-46, 2-47, 2-52, 2-53
Perot, Ross
  1992 Presidential election
    trade issues, 23-7
Pertschuk, Michael
  Tobacco politics, 15-15
Peterson, Ambassador Pete
  Vietnam, 23-9
Petri, Tom, R-Wis. (6)
  Surface transportation reauthorization bill, 24-15, 24-26
  Transportation, 2-88
Pharmaceuticals
  Viagra, 2-66, 2-67, 2-74
Pickett, Owen B., D-Va. (2)
  Missile defense bill, 8-18
Poland
  NATO expansion, 8-21–8-23
Policy Education Center
  Technology transfers to China, 8-7
Politics and elections
  Free air time, 2-126, 127
Pombo, Richard W., R-Calif. (11)
  Omnibus parks bill, 11-6
Pornography
  Internet, 2-66
Porter, John Edward, R-Ill. (10)
  Armey-Livingston relationship, 7-8

Clinton impeachment
  future prosecution, 12-47
Clinton impeachment vote, 7-9, 12-49
IMF funding, 2-53
Kyoto treaty, 2-104
Labor, HHS, and Education appropriations, 2-70
Medical research, 2-72
Mining regulations, 2-68
Timber programs, 2-60
Portman, Rob, R-Ohio (2)
  Campaign finance, 18-9
  Drug prevention in prisons, 2-119
  IRS overhaul, 21-3, 21-4, 21-6
Postal Service
  International mail, 2-94
  Worker safety, 10-8
Pratt, David (American Insurance Association)
  Financial services overhaul, 5-6
Presidential success
  History (graph), B-4
  Presidential position votes, B-14, B-15
Presidential support and opposition
  Background, B-13
  House votes, B-16, B-17
  Leading scorers, B-5
  Senate votes, B-18
  Vote studies, B-3–B-6
Prewitt, Kenneth
  Census Bureau nominee, 13-4
Price Waterhouse
  Class-action securities suits, 5-31
Product liability
  Legislation, 15-18, 15-19
Pryce, Deborah, R-Ohio (15)
  House leadership, 7-10
  Reserve fund, 2-77
  Tobacco, 15-3
Public Citizen
  Campaign finance, 18-9
Public housing
  Key votes, C-12, C-20
  Overhaul, 20-7–20-15
  Provisions of overhaul bill, 20-12, 20-13
  Rent control
    Brooke amendment, 20-9, 20-10
Public lands
  Appropriations, 2-59, 2-60
  Grazing, 11-8
  Logging, 2-57, 11-7, 11-8
  Omnibus parks bill, 11-6, 11-7
  Recreational fees, 2-58
  Royalties for oil and gas leases, 2-58
Public laws
  105-154 to 105-394, E-3–E-19
Public opinion polls
  China, 16-35
  Clinton approval rating, 12-3, 12-4, 12-20, 12-44
  Clinton impeachment, 12-23, 12-44, 12-48, 12-52
  Clinton job performance, 12-17, 12-45
  GOP and the impeachment, 7-7
Puerto Rico
  Mass transit projects, 24-13
  Political status, 13-6, 13-7

Q

Quincy Library Group
  National forest policy, 11-7
Quinn, Jack, R-N.Y. (30)
  Clinton impeachment vote, 12-41, 12-49

R

Radanovich, George P., R-Calif. (19)
  House Republican Conference chairmanship, 7-4
Rahall, Nick J. II, D-W.Va. (3)
  Surface transportation reauthorization bill, 24-13, 24-15
Raines, Franklin D. (OMB)
  Budget caps, 6-8
  Budget resolution, 6-9
  Regulatory overhaul, 15-22
  Space station, 19-7
  Surface transportation reauthorization bill, 24-21
Rangel, Charles B., D-N.Y. (15)
  Africa trade, 23-10, 23-11

General Index

Clinton impeachment vote, 12-23, 12-41
Foreign trade, 23-9
Medicare, 14-16
Omnibus bill
 tax cuts, 21-17
Raytheon
 Defense contracts, 8-9
Reagan, former President Ronald W.
 Renaming GWU Medical Center emergency room for Ronald Reagan, 14-13
 Renaming National Airport for Ronald Reagan, 13-8
 Satellite launch restrictions on China, 16-30
 Space shuttle payload restrictions, 16-30
Reagan, Michael
 Renaming National Airport for Ronald Reagan, 13-8
Real Estate Settlement Procedures Act (1974), 2-103
Reardon, Dr. Thomas (AMA)
 Physician-assisted suicide, 17-19
Reed, Jack, D-R.I.
 Bankruptcy overhaul, 5-20, 5-21
 Financial services overhaul, 5-13, 5-14
 NATO expansion, 8-23
Reed, John S. (Citicorp)
 Travelers Group merger, 5-9
Regula, Ralph, R-Ohio (16)
 Budget negotiations, 6-7
 Maintenance at national parks and forests, 2-59
 NEA funding, 2-57, 2-58, 2-59
Regulation
 Federal agency jurisdiction, 15-14
 Federal regulatory overhaul, 15-20–15-23
 Regulatory overhaul bill (provisions), 15-22
Rehnquist, Chief Justice William H.
 Clinton impeachment trial, 12-36, 12-39
 Juvenile crime, 17-16
Reid, Harry, D-Nev.
 Abortion legislation, 3-6
 IRS overhaul, 21-7
 Nuclear waste, 11-3, 11-4
 Renaming FBI building, 13-8
 Treasury-Postal Service appropriations, 2-95, 2-97, 2-100
Reinsch, William A.
 Hughes Electronics investigation, 16-31
Reischauer, Robert D. (Brookings Institution)
 Budget negotiations, 6-8, 6-16
Religious freedom
 Constitutional amendment, 17-10
 Sanctions on countries that persecute due to religion, 16-9–16-16
 School prayer amendment, 17-10
Religious Freedom Restoration Act, 17-10, 17-11
Religious persecution overseas, 16-10–16-12, 16-14
Rendell, Edward
 Surface transportation reauthorization bill, 24-16
Reno, Janet
 Clinton impeachment jurisdiction, 12-26
 Democratic fundraising investigation, 18-17
 Physician-assisted suicide, 17-18, 17-19
 Special counsel to investigate Chinese campaign contributions to Clinton, 12-11, 16-32
 Special counsel to investigate Clinton campaign finance violations, 12-29, 16-32, 16-33
Republican National Committee. See RNC
Republican Party
 1998 election losses, 12-34
 Internal strife, 7-7–7-12
Retirement and pensions
 IRAs, 21-4, 21-5, 21-6, 21-7, 21-14
Reyes, Silvestre, D-Texas (16)
 Border Patrol and Customs Service, 8-8
Richard, Sue (Americans for Computer Privacy)
 Encryption export restrictions, 22-19

Richmond Redevelopment and Housing Authority
 Public housing, 20-8
Riggs, Frank, R-Calif. (1)
 Bilingual education, 9-25–9-28
 Domestic partner health benefits, 2-101, 2-108, 2-110
 Head Start, 9-21, 9-22
 Highway bill earmarks, 24-12, 24-13
 Human service program reauthorization, 9-20–9-22
Riley, Bob, R-Ala. (3)
 Tuskegee Airmen National Historic Site, 11-7
Riley, Richard W.
 Bilingual education, 9-26
 D.C. school vouchers, 9-24
RJ Reynolds Tobacco Co.
 States tobacco settlement, 15-5
RNC (Republican National Committee)
 Campaign finance
 "soft money," 18-11
Robb, Charles S., D-Va.
 Military construction appropriations, 2-84
 Nuclear waste, 11-4
 Reagan National Airport traffic, 24-38
 Tobacco, 15-9, 15-12
Robert J. Dole Institute for Public Service
 Appropriations, 2-72
Roberts, Pat, R-Kan.
 Farm relief, 2-11
 Foreign policy, 16-13
 War powers, 2-21
Rockefeller, John D. IV, D-W.Va.
 Highway bill, 24-4, 24-5, 24-6, 24-14
 Product liability, 15-18, 15-19
 Tobacco, 15-5
 Veterans benefits, 6-7
Roemer, Tim, D-Ind. (3)
 Bilingual education, 9-26
 Clinton impeachment
 censure resolution, 12-41
 Clinton investigation, 12-17
 Space station, 2-107, 2-108, 19-6
Rogan, James E., R-Calif. (27)
 Clinton impeachment
 Judiciary Committee opening statement (excerpts), D-33
 Clinton impeachment inquiry, 12-19, 12-20
 perjury charge, 12-45
 High-tech worker visas, 17-5
 Internet copyright, 22-6
 Judge shopping, 17-12
 Litigants rights to reject judges, 17-13
Rogers, Harold, R-Ky. (5)
 Appropriations, 2-14
 Census funding, 2-18
 Defense appropriations
 Embassy repairs/security, 2-31
 Limiting federal prosecutors powers, 2-14
 Supplemental appropriations, 2-118
Rohrabacher, Dana, R-Calif. (45)
 Clinton China trip, 16-37
 Space station, 19-7
 Technology transfers to China, 16-35
 Vietnam, 23-9
Romero-Barceló, Carlos A.. D-P.R.
 Bilingual education, 9-26
 Puerto Rico political status, 13-6
Ros-Lehtinen, Ileana, R-Fla. (18)
 Clinton impeachment inquiry, 12-23
 Export controls, 16-26
Roselló, Gov. Pedro, D-P.R.
 Puerto Rico political status, 13-6, 13-7
Rosen, Judith
 Head Start, 9-19
Rosenker, Mark (Electronic Industries Alliance)
 Digital copyright, 22-9
Rosner, Jeremy
 NATO expansion, 8-24
Rossotti, Charles O.
 IRS overhaul, 21-7, 21-8, 21-9
Roth, William V. Jr., R-Del.
 Energy policy, 2-40
 Fast-track trade bill, 23-4–2-36
 Internet taxes, 21-22
 IRS code, 2-96, 2-97
 IRS overhaul, 21-3, 21-4, 21-7, 21-8, 21-9
 Medicare, 14-19, 14-21

NATO expansion, 8-21
Roth IRAs, 14-16, 14-21, 14-22, 21-5–21-7, 21-9
Tobacco, 15-7
Product liability, 15-18, 15-19
Retirement accounts, 6-7
Social Security, 21-18
Rothman, Steven R., D-N.J. (9)
 Bankruptcy overhaul legislation, 5-17
 Clinton impeachment
 Judiciary Committee opening statement (excerpts), D-33
Roukema, Marge, R-N.J. (5)
 Bilingual education, 9-26
 Character issues, 12-45
 Clinton impeachment
 censure resolution, 12-47
 Credit unions, 5-26
 Minority contract set-aside programs, 24-16
Rouleau, Mary (Consumer Federation of America)
 Bankruptcy overhaul legislation, 5-24
Roybal-Allard, Lucille, D-Calif. (33)
 Technology transfers to China, 16-28
Royce, Ed, R-Calif. (39)
 Market Access Program, 2-6
RU-486
 FDA approval, 2-5
Rubin, Robert E.
 Financial services overhaul legislation, 5-11, 5-14
 IMF funding, 2-48, 2-49, 2-52, 2-53
Ruff, Charles F. C.
 Clinton impeachment defense, 12-37, 12-38
 witnesses, 12-31
Rules Committee (House)
 Bankruptcy overhaul legislation, 5-20
 Clinton impeachment rules, 12-35, 12-36
 Financial services overhaul legislation, 5-7, 5-8
 Members, 7-6
 Sanctions, 16-11
 Surface transportation reauthorization bill, 24-14, 24-15
 Trade agreements, 23-7
Rumsfeld, Donald H.
 Anti-missile defense, 8-19–8-20
 Satellite surveillance of nuclear, biological and chemical weapons programs, 2-31
Russia
 IMF, 2-47–2-49, 2-54
 NATO expansion, 8-22, 8-24
 Plutonium stockpile, 2-37, 2-39
 Russian missile technology transfers to Iran, 19-7
 Space station, 19-4–19-10
 U.S. summit, 2-49
Ryan, A.F. Gen. Michael
 Air Force readiness, 8-14

S

Sabo, Martin Olaf, D-Minn. (5)
 FHA mortgages, 2-104
Salmon, Matt, R-Ariz. (1)
 Campaign finance, 18-6
 House leadership, 7-9, 7-10
 Surface transportation reauthorization bill, 24-15
Salvation Army
 Domestic partner health benefits, 2-108
Sanchez, Loretta, D-Calif. (46)
 Census, 13-4, 13-5
 Dornan election challenge, 18-4, 18-5
Sanctions
 Key votes, C-7–C-8, C-17
Sanders, Bernard, I-Vt. (AL)
 Ban on purchases from Chinese military, 2-23
 Technology transfers to China, 2-23
 Dairy policy, 2-6
 Treasury Department Exchange Stabilization Fund, 2-95
 Y2K computer problem, 2-94
Sanford, Mark, R-S.C. (1)
 Clinton impeachment vote, 12-40
Santorum, Rick, R-Pa.
 "Partial birth" abortion ban, 3-7–3-8
Sarbanes, Paul S., D-Md.
 Class-action securities suits, 5-30–5-32
 Credit unions, 5-27

FHA mortgages, 2-106
Financial services overhaul, 5-12, 5-13
Satellite Broadcasting and Communications Association
 Satellite TV rate increase, 22-15
Satellites
 Export regulation
 U.S. exports to China, 8-7, 8-16, 8-17
 TV fee increases, 22-14, 22-18
Saudi Arabia
 Missile attack vulnerability, 8-17
Saxton, H. James, R-N.J. (3)
 IMF funding, 2-45, 2-48
Scarborough, Joe, R-Fla. (1)
 Livingston leadership, 7-8
Schaefer, Dan, R-Colo. (6)
 Electricity deregulation, 15-16, 15-17
Schafer, Gov. Edward T., R-N.D.
 Surface transportation reauthorization bill, 24-7
Scheibel, John (Computer and Communications Industry Association)
 Encryption, 22-5
Schippers, David P.
 Clinton impeachment
 Judiciary committee inquiry statement (excerpts), D-34, D-34–D-35
 Clinton investigation, 12-32
Schlafly, Phyllis (Eagle Forum)
 Job training, 10-3, 10-4
Schlickeisen, Rodger
 National forests, 2-61
School prayer
 House action, 17-9–17-11
Schumer, Charles E., D-N.Y. (9)
 Breast cancer, 2-116
 Clinton impeachment
 Judiciary Committee opening statement (excerpts), D-30
 Clinton investigation, 12-32
 Transit funds, 24-8
Schwartz, Bernard
 Profile, 16-25
Schwartz, Bernard (Loral Space and Communications)
 Contributions to Clinton re-election, 16-23–16-25, 16-32, 16-33, 16-35
Schwitz, Randy (National Air Traffic Controllers Association)
 Renaming National Airport for Ronald Reagan, 13-8
Science and technology
 Biomaterials product liability, 15-19
 Global Positioning System, 19-5
 Technology transfers to China, 8-3, 8-7, 8-16
Science Committee (House)
 NASA funding, 19-8, 19-10
 Space station, 19-4, 19-6–19-8
Scott, Robert C. D-Va. (3)
 Abortion legislation, 3-3–3-5
 Church and state, 17-10
 Clinton impeachment
 Judiciary Committee opening statement (excerpts), D-31
 Judicial activism, 17-15
 Technology transfers to China, 16-28
Scott, Robert C., D-Va. (3)
 Clinton impeachment
 censure resolution, 12-49
 Impeachable offenses, 12-7
 Juvenile crime, 17-18
Scruggs, Richard F.
 Tobacco settlement by states, 15-9
SEC (Securities and Exchange Commission)
 Class-action securities suits, 5-30–5-33
 Financial services overhaul legislation, 5-4, 5-5, 5-13, 5-14
Secret Service
 Testimony in Clinton impeachment inquiry, 12-4
Securities and Exchange Commission. See SEC
Securities Industry Association
 Citicorp-Travelers Group merger, 5-9–5-10
Selig, Bud
 Baseball antitrust, 15-25
Semiconductors
 Subsidies, 2-126
Sensenbrenner, F. James Jr. R-Wis. (9)
 Clinton impeachment
 Judiciary Committee opening statement (excerpts), D-29
 perjury charge, 12-37
 Judicial pay raises, 17-13

General Index

NASA authorization, 19-5–19-10
Space station, 19-6–19-9
Serbia
  Sanctions, 2-45
Serrano, Jose E., D-N.Y. (16)
  Mariana Islands delegate request, 2-79
  Puerto Rico, 13-6
Sessions, Jeff, R-Ala.
  Bankruptcy overhaul legislation, 5-16
  IRS overhaul, 21-7
  Juvenile crime bill, 17-15–17-17
  Minority contract set-aside programs, 24-5, 24-7
  TVA, 2-43
  VA-HUD appropriations, 2-106
Shaheen, Gov. Jeanne, D-N.H.
  Highway Trust Fund, 24-6, 24-7
Shalala, Donna E.
  Head Start, 9-20, 9-21
  Managed care, 14-4
  NIH funding, 2-72
Shattuck, John
  Religious persecution overseas, 16-14
Shaw, E. Clay Jr., R-Fla. (22)
  Bankruptcy overhaul legislation, 5-20
  Child support enforcement, 20-6
  Omnibus bill
    tax cuts, 21-17
  Starr report, 12-17
  Welfare reform, 6-12
Shays, Christopher, R-Conn. (4)
  Campaign finance, 18-7
  Campaign finance overhaul, 18-3, 18-6–18-16
  Clinton impeachment
    censure resolution, 12-47
  Clinton impeachment vote, 12-48
  Supplemental appropriations
    defense, 2-124
Shelby, Richard C., R-Ala.
  Airline "peanut-free" zones, 2-90
  Airport competition, 2-86
  Amtrak funding, 2-86
  Class-action securities suits, 5-30
  Credit unions, 5-25, 5-27–5-29
  Financial services overhaul, 5-3, 5-12–5-15
  Intelligence authorization, 8-26
  Product liability, 15-18, 15-19
  Supplemental appropriations
    flood protection in home state, 2-130
  Surface transportation reauthorization bill
    home state projects, 24-25
  Transportation appropriations, 2-84
  TVA funding, 2-36, 2-39, 2-43, 2-44
Shelton, Gen. Henry H.
  Bosnia mission, 2-24
  Military readiness, 2-26, 8-14, 8-18, 8-20
Shultz, Lexi
  Interior appropriations, 2-63
Shuster, Bud, R-Pa. (9)
  Ethics investigation, 7-3, 24-10, 24-11
  FAA reauthorization, 24-34–24-37, 24-39
  Highway and transit reauthorization, 24-3–24-40
  Renaming federal buildings for Kennedy, 13-8
  Superfund, 11-5
  Surface transportation law, 2-85
  Transportation appropriations, 2-88, 2-90
Sisco, Gary (Secretary of the Senate)
  Articles of Impeachment, 12-47
Skaggs, David E., D-Colo. (2)
  Offensive military operations, 2-23
  Supplemental appropriations
    Iraq, 2-126
    TV Marti, 2-15
    War powers, 2-21
Skeen, Joe, R-N.M. (2)
  Agriculture appropriations, 2-11
  Roswell law enforcement academy, 2-120
  RU-486 ban, 2-9
Skelton, Ike, D-Mo. (4)
  Satellite exports to China, 8-7
"Slamming." See Telephones
Slater, Rodney
  Airline competition, 24-34, 24-35, 24-38
  Surface transportation reauthorization bill, 24-5, 24-7, 24-8, 24-10, 24-19, 24-23
Slaughter, Louise M., D-N.Y. (28)
  State Department authorization
    international family planning, 16-6

Smith, Bob, R-Ore. (2)
  Agriculture appropriations, 2-8, 2-11, 4-7, 4-8
  Clinton impeachment vote, 12-41
  Crop insurance, 4-9
  Fast-track trade authority, 23-3, 23-4
  National forests, 11-7
  Rangeland management, 11-8
Smith, Christopher H., R-N.J. (4)
  China human rights practices, 16-37
  Contraceptive coverage in federal employee health plans, 2-9–2-95, 2-98
  Farm agenda, 2-7
  International family planning, 2-45, 2-56, 2-131
  International family planning aid, 16-4
  Religious persecution overseas, 16-10, 16-11, 16-13
  RU-486 ban, 2-5
  State Department reorganization, 16-3
Smith, David (AFL-CIO)
  Campaign spending by unions, 18-11
  Fast-track trade bill, 23-6
Smith, Gordon H., R-Ore.
  Farm labor, 2-16
  Serbia sanctions, 2-51
  Tobacco, 15-13
Smith, Lamar, R-Texas (21)
  Clinton impeachment
    Judiciary Committee opening statement (excerpts), D-30
  Haitian refugees, 2-98, 2-99
  High-tech worker visas, 17-3, 17-5, 17-6, 17-7, 17-8
  Property rights, 15-24
  Religious persecution overseas, 16-10, 16-11
Smith, Linda, R-Wash. (3)
  Africa, 23-11
  Religious persecution overseas, 16-14
Smith, Nick, R-Mich. (7)
  Bilingual education, 9-27
Smith, Robert C., R-N.H.
  Anti-missile systems, 8-10
  Budget resolution, 6-6
  Juvenile crime, 17-16
  Superfund, 11-5
  Surface transportation reauthorization bill, 24-8
  U.S. troops in Bosnia, 8-12
Snowbarger, Vince, R-Kan. (3)
  FEC budget, 2-95
Snowe, Olympia J., R-Maine
  Campaign finance, 18-4
  Clinton impeachment investigation, 12-11
  Cloning, 19-3
  Contraceptive coverage in health plans, 2-97
  Mixed gender military training, 8-12
  "Partial birth" abortion ban, 3-8
  State Department authorization
    international family planning, 16-7, 16-8
  Telephone "slamming," 22-24
  Tobacco, 15-5, 15-10
Sobel, David (Electronic Privacy Information Center)
  Internet pornography, 22-12, 22-13
Social Security
  Budget surplus, 6-4
  Effect of impeachment effort on legislation, 12-45
  SSI benefits to legal immigrants, 4-8
  Trust fund, 21-14, 21-15, 21-17, 21-18
Social Security Administration
  SSI for legal immigrants, 20-16
Solomon, Gerald B.H., R-N.Y. (22)
  Campaign finance, 18-12
  China MFN status, 16-34
  Clinton impeachment
    censure resolution, 12-31
  Encryption export restrictions, 22-19, 22-20
  Financial services overhaul legislation, 5-11
  Food stamps, 4-8–4-9
  Iraq airstrikes, 12-51
  Puerto Rico, 13-6
  State Department authorization, 16-3
  United Nations, 16-6
Soloski, Henry (Policy Action Center)
  Export controls, 16-27, 16-31
Souder, Mark, R-Ind. (4)
  Call for Clinton resignation, 12-19
  Clinton impeachment vote, 12-48

House Republican leadership challenges, 7-4
Juvenile crime, 17-18
Low-income savings accounts, 9-22
Supplemental appropriations, 2-123
South Dakota
  Appropriations
    flood mitigation projects, 2-37
Southeastern Legal Foundation
  Census, 13-5
Southern Governors Association
  Highway Trust Fund, 24-17
Space
  Commercial space industry, 19-5
  Private space shuttles, 19-9
Spain
  NATO, 8-23
Special investigations
  Funding, 2-77
Specter, Arlen, R-Pa.
  Abortion legislation, 3-6
  Bankruptcy overhaul legislation, 5-19
  Cloning, 19-3
  Comprehensive Nuclear Test Ban Treaty, 2-51
  Flag desecration, 17-11
  Minimum wage, 10-7
  Offensive military operations, 2-25
  Religious persecution overseas, 16-9, 16-14, 16-15
  RU-486 ban, 2-9
  Surface transportation reauthorization bill, 24-9
Spence, Floyd D., R-S.C. (2)
  Export controls, 16-27, 16-28
  Missile defense, 8-17
  Technology transfers to China, 8-7–8-8
Sperling, Gene
  Class-action securities suits, 5-30
  Highway bill offsets, 24-21
Sports
  Baseball antitrust, 15-25
Spratt, John M. Jr., D-S.C. (5)
  Africa, 23-11
  Budget, 6-9
  Highway spending, 24-15
  Medicare, 14-21
  Missile defense, 8-18
  Technology transfers to China, 16-28
  Textiles and clothing, 23-11
Stabenow, Debbie, D-Mich. (8)
  Forest policy, 11-8
Standards of Official Conduct Committee (House). See Ethics Committee (House)
Stark, Pete, D-Calif. (13)
  Medicare, 14-16, 14-21
  Omnibus bill
    tax cuts, 21-15
Starr, Kenneth
  House Judiciary Committee impeachment inquiry
    impeachment vote statement (excerpts), D-38
    opening statement (excerpts), D-38, D-38–D-39
Starr, Kenneth W.
  Clinton impeachment referral, 12-32, 12-50
  House Judiciary Committee hearing on Independent Counsels report, 12-27–12-30
  Independent Counsel investigation of President Clinton, 12-3–12-53
    abuse of constitutional authority charge, 12-14
    Linda Tripp, 12-6, 12-7
    obstruction of justice charge, 12-14
    perjury charge, 12-13
    White House use of FBI files, 12-13
    Whitewater, 12-13
    witness tampering charge, 12-14
    witnesses, 12-7
  Independent Counsel law, 12-21
  Independent Counsel report on Clinton investigation (excerpts), D-15–D-21
  Release of Independent Counsel report on President Clinton, 12-5, 12-13–C-14, C-22
START
  Russian arms cuts, 8-19
State and local governments
  Extension of state water boundaries into Gulf of Mexico, 2-18
State Department
  Authorization, 2-45, 2-52, 2-54, 2-56, 2-125, 2-128, 16-3–16-9
    abortion, 16-4–16-9

    conference report highlights, 16-6
    European Security Act, 16-5
    Iraq, 16-5
    Ireland, 16-5
    NATO expansion, 16-5
    proposed move of U.S. embassy from Tel Aviv to Jerusalem, 16-5, 16-6, 16-8
  Office of Religious Persecution Monitoring, 16-10, 16-13
  Remote sensing, 19-9
  Reorganization, 16-3, 16-4, 16-8, 16-9
  Satellite export application approvals, 16-30, 16-33
  Satellite export controls, 16-27
  Satellite exports to China, 8-13, 8-16
State of the Union Address
  Republican response (text), D-8–D10
  Text, D-3–D-8
Stearns, Cliff, R-Fla. (6)
  Financial services overhaul legislation, 5-11
Steinhardt, Barry (Electronic Frontier Foundation)
  Internet pornography, 22-11, 22-12
Stenholm, Charles W., D-Texas (17)
  Agriculture appropriations, 4-5, 4-7
  Appropriations
    special projects in home district, 2-114
  Clinton apology, 12-8
  Clinton investigation, 12-17, 12-19, 12-48
  Farm loans, 2-11
  Food stamps, 4-3, 4-6, 4-8–4-9
  Forest policy, 11-7, 11-8
  Supplemental appropriations, 2-124
Stevens, Ted, R-Alaska
  Appropriations, 24-17
    Labor-HHS, 2341
    Labor-HHS-Education, 2-68, 2-69
  Bosnia, 2-21
    Floor action, 2-24
  Budget, 6-14
  Budget negotiations, 6-8
  Cancer research, 2-74
  Defense appropriations
    military construction projects in home state, 2-81, 2-84
  Environment
    Izembek Road, 2-57, 2-58, 2-61, 2-63
  Fishing legislation, 2-13
  Labor contract mandates, 2-87
  NATO expansion, 8-23, 8-24
  Nuclear submarines, 2-22
  Supplemental appropriations, 2-124, 2-126, 2-128, 2-129
    IMF, 2-125
    missile defense, 2-117
    offsets, 2-130
  Surface transportation reauthorization bill, 24-19
  Tobacco legislation, 15-13
  Transportation appropriations, 2-88
  Treasury-Postal Service appropriations, 2-94, 2-95, 2-97, 2-98
  Y2K computer problem, 2-78, 2-79
Stokes, Louis, D-Ohio (11)
  Public housing, 2-106–2-107
  VA-HUD appropriations, 2-110
Student aid
  Clinton plan, 9-3, 9-4
  Elementary and secondary students, 2-66
  Pell grants, 2-68, 2-69
  Perkins loans, 2-66
  Student loans, 9-3, 9-14
    Higher education reauthorization, 9-10, 9-11
    House action, 9-4, 9-9
    Interest rates, 9-7, 9-10–9-13
  Student loans and grants, 2-66, 2-68–2-69, 2-74
Stupak, Bart, D-Mich. (1)
  Class-action securities suits, 5-32
Sudan
  Sanctions, 16-10, 16-12
Superfund
  House action, 2-110
  Senate action, 11-5, 11-6
Supplemental appropriations
  AmeriCorps, 2-125, 2-127
  Bosnia, 2-121, 2-122, 2-125, 2-127, 2-130
  Capitol dome repairs, 2-130
  Crop insurance, 2-129
  Dairy farm relief, 2-125
  Defense, 2-122

General Index

Disaster relief, 2-121, 2-122, 2-124, 2-125, 2-127, 2-128, 2-129
Drug Enforcement Administration, 2-119
Embassy security, 2-117, 2-118
FEMA, 2-125, 2-129
Food stamps, 2-129
Guam, 2-117
IMF, 2-117, 2-122, 2-124, 2-125, 2-127, 2-128, 2-129
Intelligence, 2-117
Iraq, 2-122, 2-125, 2-127
Middle East, 2-117, 2-118, 2-122, 2-125, 2-129
Offsets, 2-128
Railroad repair, 2-125
State Department, 2-117
Supplemental bills compared (chart), 2-128
Surplus, 2-117
Terrorism, 2-117, 2-118
Treasury Department
  Secret Service training, 2-118
U.N. dues, 2-117, 2-122, 2-126, 2-128, 2-129
U.N. funding, 2-125
Y2K computer problem, 2-130
Supplemental Security Income (SSI)
Legal immigrants, 20-16
Supreme Court
Credit unions, 5-3, 5-27, 5-28
NEA funding, 2-59
Sales taxes, 21-19
School prayer, 17-10, 17-11
Supreme Court cases
Abington School District v. Schempp, 17-11
Barnett Bank of Marion County v. Nelson, 5-4
Buckley v. Valeo, 18-13
Central Bank of Denver v. First Interstate Bank of Denver, 5-32
Chevron v. Natural Resources Defense Council, 15-14
City of Boerne v. Flores, 17-11
Employment Division v. Smith, 17-11
Engel v. Vitale, 17-11
Lee v. Weisman, 17-11
Lemon v. Kurtzman, 17-11
National Credit Union Administration v. First National Bank & Trust Co., 5-29
Thornton v. Caldor, 17-11
Wallace v. Jafree, 17-11

T

Taiwan
U.S. policy, 16-37
Taiwan Relations Act (1979), 16-37
Tanner, John, D-Tenn. (8)
TVA funding, 2-41
Tanzania
U.S. embassy rebuilding, 2-118
Tauscher, Ellen O., D-Calif. (10)
Clinton impeachment
  censure resolution, 12-35, 12-41
Clinton impeachment resolution vote, 12-24
Tauzin, W.J. "Billy," R-La. (3)
Cable TV rates, 22-16
Clinton apology, 12-39
Digital copyright, 22-7
Satellite TV "must carry" requirement, 22-18
Satellite TV fee increase, 22-17
Telephone "slamming," 22-24–22-26
Tax Executives Institute
IRS overhaul, 21-6
Taxes and Taxation
Education Savings Accounts
  key votes, C-6–C-7, C-17
Taxes and taxation
Burden of proof, 21-5, 21-8
Capital gains taxes, 21-8, 21-9, 21-13
Child care, 6-12
Confidentiality, 21-5
Interest and penalties, 21-5
IRAs, 6-12
IRS overhaul, 21-3–21-14
  innocent spouse relief, 21-4, 21-5
  offsets, 21-5–21-14
  oversight board, 21-3, 21-5, 21-8
  property seizures, 21-3, 21-8
  retaliatory audits, 21-7
  role of Congress, 21-5
  taxpayer abuse, 21-3, 21-8
  taxpayer rights, 21-5
  transfer pricing, 21-7

IRS reorganization, 21-7
Lawsuits, 21-5
Marriage penalty, 2-78, 6-10, 6-14
Omnibus bill
  tax credit extension, 21-14–21-18
Tax cuts, 6-12–6-14
What the IRS Bill Does, 21-9–21-14
Taxpayer Relief Act of 1997
Highway bill spending caps, 24-3
Taylor, Charles H., R-N.C. (11)
D.C. appropriations, 2-33, 2-34
Taylor, Gene, D-Miss. (5)
Call for Clinton resignation, 12-24
Clinton impeachment vote, 12-41, 12-48
Defense authorization
  projects in home state, 8-11
Defense contracts in home district, 8-11
Renaming National Airport for Ronald Reagan, 13-8
Taylor, Peggy (AFL-CIO)
Salting by labor unions, 10-6
Taylor, Rich (Motion Picture Association of America)
Digital copyright, 22-9
Teamsters Union
Reserve funds used for investigations, 2-77
Technology Security Administration, 16-30
Tele-Communications Inc.
Cable TV rates, 22-16
Teledyne Ryan Aeronautical
Defense contracts, 8-10
Telephones
Cellular phone fraud, 22-23
Telephone "slamming," 22-24–22-26
Unauthorized switching of long-distance service ("slamming"), 22-24–22-26
Television
Cable TV rates, 22-14–22-18
Tenet, George J.
China technology transfer investigation, 16-35
Release of CIA budget figures, 8-25
Tennessee Valley Authority. *See* **TVA**
Terrorism
Prison sentences for causing train wrecks, 24-10
Supplemental appropriations, 2-117, 2-118
Texas
Defense appropriations
  military construction projects, 2-81
Tobacco settlement, 15-9
Textiles and clothing
African trade, 23-10
The Tobacco Institute
Campaign contributions, 15-12
Thomas, Bill, R-Calif. (21)
Campaign finance overhaul, 18-5, 18-6, 18-13, 18-14, 18-16
Home health care, 14-18, 14-21
Managed care legislation, 14-8, 14-12, 14-15
Medicare, 14-17, 14-19
Omnibus bill
  tax cuts, 21-17
Transit subsidies, 2-77, 24-5
Thompson, Gov. Tommy G., R-Wis.
Transportation projects, 24-26
Thompson, Fred, R-Tenn.
Abortion legislation, 3-5
Campaign finance overhaul, 18-4
IRS overhaul, 21-7
Property rights, 15-24
Regulatory overhaul, 15-20–15-23
Technology export licensing, 16-26
Technology transfers to China, 16-25, 16-26, 16-32, 16-33
Thompson-Levin regulatory overhaul bill, 15-20–15-23
  provisions, 15-22
TVA funding, 2-36, 2-39, 2-43, 2-44
Thurmond, Strom, R-S.C.
Anti-missile systems, 8-6
Armed Services Committee
  chairmanship, 8-12
Arms control, 8-13
Army National Guard, 8-13
Cloning, 19-3
Defense authorization bill, named for, 8-12
Land mines, 8-13
Military pay raise, 8-12
U.S. troops in Bosnia, 8-12
Tiahrt, Todd, R-Kan. (4)
Contraceptive coverage in federal employee health plans, 2-95

D.C. appropriations, 2-34, 2-35
Separation of abortion and family planning facilities, 2-67
Supplemental appropriations, 2-127, 2-128
Tobacco
Cigarette labeling, 2-67
Durbin-DeWine amendment, 15-10
Key votes, C-6, C-16
Legal settlement between states and tobacco industry, 2-36
Lugar-McConnell proposal, 15-9
Price supports, 15-9
Projected revenues, 2-67
S 1414 highlights, 15-8
Senate debate, 6-5
Torres, Esteban E., D-Calif. (34)
Bilingual education, 9-27
Torricelli, Robert G., D-N.J.
Airport noise, 24-39
Organ donation, 2-71
"Partial birth" abortion ban, 3-8
Regulatory overhaul, 15-22
Tobacco, 15-10, 15-12
Traficant, James A. Jr., D-Ohio (17)
Border Patrol and Customs Service, 8-8
Transportation
Appropriations, 2-84–2-90, 2-116, 21-8
  Amtrak spending, 2-85–2-88
  drunk drivers, 21-9
  FAA funding, 2-85–2-88
  mass-transit project earmarks, 2-86
  minority set-aside programs, 2-85
  safety programs, 21-9
Funding
  donor states, 24-6, 24-8, 24-9, 24-13, 24-24
Highway spending, 6-4
Highway Trust fund, 24-4, 24-6, 24-10, 24-13, 24-14, 24-16, 24-17, 24-19, 24-22, 24-23, 24-24
Key votes, C-9–C-10, C-18
Spending (chart), 2-89
Spending caps, 24-3–24-40
Surface transportation reauthorization, 24-3–24-33, 24-3–24-40
  highlights, 24-22
Transportation & Infrastructure
Legislation, 24-3–24-40
Renaming National Airport for Ronald Reagan, 13-8
Surface Transportation Act, 21-13, 24-3–24-33, 24-3–24-40
Transportation and Infrastructure Committee (House)
Airline competition, 24-34
Superfund, 11-5
Surface transportation reauthorization, 24-3, 24-9–24-20, 24-26
Transportation Department
Airline competition guidelines, 24-34, 24-36–24-39
Federal Highway Administration, 2-85, 2-88, 2-90
FY 1999 appropriations, 2-85–2-88
Surface transportation reauthorization, 24-3–24-40
Transportation Equity Act for the 21st Century
Highlights, 24-27–24-33
Travelers Group
Citicorp merger, 5-8, 5-10, 5-11, 5-12, 5-13
Treasury Department
Appropriations
  IMF, 2-125
  Credit unions, 5-28
  Financial services overhaul legislation, 5-3, 5-5, 5-8, 5-11, 5-13, 5-14
  Student loans
    Interest rate formula, 9-3–9-7
Treasury-Postal Service and general government
Spending (chart), 2-99
Treasury-Postal Service Appropriations, 2-23, 2-91–2-102
COLAs, 2-91, 2-94, 2-95
Government building construction, 2-92
Haitian refugees, 2-91, 2-98, 2-100
Y2K computer problem, 22-21
Trial lawyers
Campaign contributions to Democratic candidates, 15-13
Tripp, Linda
Starr investigation, 12-6, 12-7, 12-28
Tucker Act
Property rights, 15-24

Tuesday Group
Budget negotiations, 6-10
Turkey
Missile attack vulnerability, 8-17
TVA
Appropriations, 2-36–2-44, 2-113, 2-114
Non-power programs, 2-43
History, 2-39, 2-44

U

U.N. Population Fund
China, 2-45, 2-56
U.S. Chamber of Commerce
Fast-track trade authority, 23-6
Tobacco politics, 15-13
U.S. Judicial Conference
Judicial activism bill, 17-12
U.S. Trade Representative
International mail, 2-94
Union of Needletrades, Industrial and Textile Employees
Africa trade, 23-12
United Defense
Defense contracts, 8-9
United Nations
China, 2-45, 2-56
Dues, 2-18, 2-114, 2-117, 2-122, 2-125, 2-126, 2-128, 2-129, 16-3–16-5, 16-7–16-9
Supplemental appropriations, 2-125
United Parcel Service
International mail, 2-94
United Technologies
Defense contracts, 8-9
Upton, Fred, R-Mich. (6)
Budget negotiations, 6-10, 6-14
Clinton impeachment vote, 12-49
USDA. *See* **Agriculture Department**
Utah
Zion National Park parking lot, 2-63
Utilities
Tennessee Valley Authority, 2-38–2-41, 2-44

V

VA
Appropriations, 2-101–2-111
VA-HUD appropriations, 2-101–2-111
VA-HUD appropriations (chart), 2-109
Velázquez, Nydia M., D-N.Y. (12)
Puerto Rico, 13-6
Velleco, John (Gun Owners of America)
Juvenile crime bill, 17-17
Vento, Bruce F., D-Minn. (4)
Credit unions, 5-26
Effect of Clinton investigation on Democratic agenda, 12-6
Financial services overhaul legislation, 5-10, 5-11
Livestock producer fees, 11-8
Omnibus parks bill, 11-6
Veterans
Smoking-related ailment benefits, 6-7, 24-8, 24-14, 24-25
Veterans Affairs Department. *See* **VA**
Veterans Health Administration
Appropriations, 2-102
Vetoes, 1-5
Adoption, 2-32, 2-36
Agriculture appropriations (text), D-11
Class-action securities suits, 5-30–5-33
D.C. appropriations, 2-34, 2-35
D.C. school vouchers, 2-32, 2-36, 9-24, 9-25
Defense authorization, 8-13
Farm aid, 2-3, 2-8, 2-9
First veto
  President Washington and the Census, 13-4
IMF funding, 2-46
International family planning restrictions, 2-45
Line-item veto, 2-43, 2-80
Needle exchange program, 2-5
Omnibus spending bill, 2-3
"Partial birth" abortion ban, 3-7–3-9
RU-486 ban, 2-3, 2-5, 2-9, 2-11
Sanctions on Iran missile aid, 16-19, 16-22
State Department reauthorization, 2-45, D-12 (text)
Welfare reform, 2-12
Vietnam
Clinton policy, 23-9

General Index

Virgin Group Ltd.
　Foreign ownership of domestic airlines, 24-38
Virginia
　Defense appropriations
　　military construction projects, 2-81
Visa USA
　Bankruptcy overhaul legislation, 5-18
Visas
　Skilled-worker visas, C-5–C-6, C-14, C-16, C-22
Visclosky, Peter J., D-Ind. (1)
　Kyoto treaty, 2-104
Voinovich, Gov. George V., R-Ohio
　Head Start, 9-21
Vote studies. *See also* **under** Topic of legislation
　Guide to CQ's voting analysis, B-12
Voting and voter turnout
　Motor Voter Act, 18-14
Voting participation
　History (graph), B-11
　House votes, B-30, B-31
　Senate votes, B-29
　Vote studies, B-11, B-12

W

Waasenaar Arrangement
　Export licensing, 16-27
Wages and salaries
　Capitol Police, 2-75
　Minimum wage legislation, 10-7, 18-16
Walker, Trey (S. Carolina GOP)
　Effect of impeachment inquiry on Republican strategy, 12-8
Walsh, James T., R-N.Y. (25)
　Agriculture appropriations
　　abortion rider, 2-5
　CBO controversy, 2-76
　CBO forecasts, 2-77
　Funding for special investigations, 2-77
　Legislative branch appropriations, 2-80
　Milk marketing, 2-4
　Y2K computer problem, 2-79
Walsh, Lawrence E.
　Iran-contra probe, 12-21
Walt Disney Co. *See* Disney Co.
Wamp, Zach, R-Tenn. (3)
　Appropriations, 2-114
　Campaign finance overhaul, 18-7, 18-10, 18-16
　House leadership use of consultants, 2-76
Warner, John W., R-Va.
　Bridge projects, 24-15, 24-16
　Internet
　　Congressional Research Service report on the Internet, 2-78
　Military base closings, 8-5, 8-12
　NATO expansion, 8-21–8-23

Surface transportation reauthorization bill, 24-7, 24-9, 24-11
U.S. China policy, 8-12
Warrington, George D.
　Amtrak, 2-86
Washington
　Tobacco lawsuits, 15-9
Washington, George
　Census, 13-4
Water pollution
　Clean Water Action Plan, 2-57
Water projects
　Appropriations, 2-125
Waters, Maxine, D-Calif. (35)
　Call for Livingston resignation, 7-12, 12-46
　Clinton impeachment
　　censure resolution, 12-49
　　Judiciary Committee opening statement (excerpts), D-32
　Clinton reprimand, 12-23
　Criticism of Kenneth Starr, 2-18
　Development Fund for Africa, 23-11
Watt, Melvin, D-N.C. (12)
　Africa, 23-11
　Clinton impeachment
　　Judiciary Committee opening statement (excerpts), D-31
　High-tech worker visas, 17-6, 17-7
　Judicial powers, 17-13
　Property rights, 15-24
　Religious persecution overseas, 16-13
　Textiles and clothing, 23-11
Watts, J.C., R-Okla. (4)
　House Republican Conference Chairmanship, 7-8, 7-9
　United Nations dues, 16-4
Waxman, Henry A., D-Calif. (29)
　EPA, 2-107
Ways and Means Committee (House)
　Africa trade, 23-10
　China trade status, 16-34
　Gasoline tax credit, 24-12
　Members, 7-6
　Omnibus bill
　　tax cuts, 21-18
　Sudan, 16-11, 16-12
Weill, Sanford I. (Travelers Group)
　Citicorp merger, 5-9
Weitzner, Daniel J.
　Internet pornography, 22-10, 22-11
Weld, William F.
　Clinton impeachment
　　censure resolution, 12-53
　　perjury charge, 12-38
Weldon, Curt, R-Pa. (7)
　Missile defense, 8-17, 8-18
　Pentagon authorization, 8-18
　Satellite crash in China, 16-31
　Satellite export restrictions, 16-33
　Technology transfers to China, 16-29

Weldon, Dave, R-Fla. (15)
　Clinton's apology, 12-8
　Financial services overhaul legislation, 5-11
　Glenn spaceflight, 19-11
　Russian space program, 19-10
Welfare and social services
　Head Start coordination with welfare, 9-20
　Social Services Block Grant, 2-69, 2-71, 2-74
　Welfare to work, 2-85
Wellstone, Paul, D-Minn.
　Defense appropriations, 2-24
　Farm labor, 2-16
　Financial services overhaul, 5-13
　Minimum wage, 10-7
　NATO expansion, 8-21
　Pentagon child care system, 8-12
　Veterans' smoking-related illnesses, 2-106
West Virginia
　Appropriations
　　local projects, 2-115
　Defense appropriations
　　military construction projects, 2-84
Wetstone, Greg
　Interior appropriations, 2-63
Wexler, Robert, D-Fla. (19)
　Clinton impeachment
　　Judiciary Committee opening statement (excerpts), D-32, D-32–D-33
　Starr report, 12-29
White, Rick, R-Wash. (1)
　Campaign finance overhaul, 18-10, 18-12
　Class-action securities suits, 5-32, 5-33
　Digital copyright, 22-7
　Encryption export restrictions, 22-19
　Unsolicited e-mail ("spamming"), 22-25
WIC Program
　Reauthorization, 20-3–20-5
Wicker, Roger, R-Miss. (1)
　Flammability standards, 2-108
Willey, Kathleen
　Clinton impeachment deposition, 12-30
　Clinton impeachment inquiry, 12-32
　Starr report, 12-29
Winston, Clifford (Brookings Institution)
　Airline industry, 24-35
Wittmann, Marshall (Heritage Foundation)
　Clinton impeachment vote, 12-40
　House Republican strategy, 7-8, 7-9
　Starr report, 12-12
Wolf, Frank R., R-Va. (10)
　Coast Guard funding, 2-86, 2-87
　Religious persecution overseas, 16-9–16-13, 16-15
　Transportation earmarks, 24-11

Truck safety inspection oversight, 2-85, 2-88, 2-90
Women
　Artwork in the Capitol, 2-77
Women, Infants and Children Program. *See* WIC program
Woolsey, Lynn, D-Calif. (6)
　Head Start, 9-22
　School lunches, 20-3, 20-4
World Bank
　Funding, 2-49
World Intellectual Property Organization
　Digital copyright, 22-3–22-5
Wright, U.S. District Court judge Susan Webber
　Clinton perjury charge, 12-16
Wyden, Ron, D-Ore.
　Internet pornography, 22-11
　Internet taxes, 21-21–21-24
　Surface transportation reauthorization bill, 24-8
　Tobacco, 15-6, 15-7

Y

Yates, Sidney R., D-Ill. (9)
　Interior appropriations, 2-58
Year 2000 computer problem. *See* Computers and computer industry, Y2K computer problem
Yeltsin, Boris
　Russia space station, 19-7
Yingling, Edward (American Bankers Association)
　Banking services overhaul legislation, 5-8
　Thrift charters, 5-7
Young, C.W. Bill, R-Fla. (10)
　Appropriations Committee leadership, 7-7
　Defense appropriations
　　anti-missile defense, 2-30
　　bone marrow donation program, 2-27
　　military pay, 2-30
　Intelligence authorization, 8-25
Young, Don, R-Alaska (AL)
　Chugach National Forest, 2-59
　Motorcycle access to federal roads, 24-20
　Puerto Rico, 13-6
Youth
　Summer jobs, 2-66, 2-68
Yzaguirre, Raul (National Council of La Raza)
　Mexican descendants' land claims, 9-27

Z

Zigler, Edward
　Head Start, 9-20

STAFFORD LIBRARY
COLUMBIA COLLEGE
1001 ROGERS STREET
COLUMBIA, MO 65216